W9-BOL-022

PUBLISHING

A HISTORY OF WORLD HOCKEY

KINGS of the ICE™

AUTHORS

ANDREW PODNIEKS · ALES BREZINA · DENIS GIBBONS · DMITRI RYZKOV

IGOR RABINER · JAN BENGTSSON · JAN STARK · NIKOLAI VUKOLOV

PAVEL BARTA · SERGE CHUEV · TOM RATSCHUNAS

VLAD DIMITROV · YEVGENY BOGATYREV

YURI LUKASHIN · YURI TZYBANEV

EDITORS

SHEILA WAWANASH · WENDY THOMAS

GRAHAM MILLS · KAREN LATHE

LLOYD DAVIS · PENNY HOZY

ALAN LITTLE

NDE PUBLISHING

2002

WATERLOO PUBLIC LIBRARY

Kings of the Ice™: A History of World Hockey

Contributing Writers: Andrew Podnieks, Ales Brezina, Denis Gibbons, Dmitri Ryzkov, Igor Rabiner, Jan Bengtsson, Jan Stark, Nikolai Vukolov, Pavel Barta, Serge Chuev, Tom Ratschunas, Vlad Dimitrov, Yevgeny Bogatyrev, Yuri Lukashin, Yuri Tzybanev

Contributors: Angus Gillespie, Jefferson Davis, Paul Challen, Paul Patskou, Rob Del Mundo, Scott Colbourne, Stu McMurray

Editors: Sheila Wawanash, Wendy Thomas, Graham Mills, Karen Lathe, Lloyd Davis, Penny Hozy, Alan Little

Project Director: Vladimir Mazour
Project Coordinator: Elena Mazour
Photo Research: Vlad Dimitrov
Translators: Carl Watts, Greg Watts, Barbara Sheriff
Desktop Publishing and Typesetting: Aidyn Ismailov, Ramza Fatculova
Design: Antony Tursukoff, Aidyn Ismailov

Special thanks to ever-supportive Hockey Hall of Fame in Toronto for the permission to use photo archives, and to Craig Campbell, Tyler Wolosewich and Phil Pritchard in particular for their help.

Copyright © 2002 NDE Canada Corp.

All rights reserved. No part of this publication may be reproduced, stored in a retrieval system or transmitted in any form or by any means, electronic, mechanical, photocopying, recording or otherwise, without written permission from:
Vladimir Mazour, President and Publisher

NDE Publishing™
15-30 Wertheim Court
Richmond Hill, Ontario
Canada L4B 1B9

ISBN: 1-55321-099-9

Published in 2002 by:
NDE Publishing™
15-30 Wertheim Court
Richmond Hill, Ontario
Canada L4B 1B9
tel: (905) 731-1288
fax: (905) 731-5744
www.ndepublishing.com

NDE Publishing is a trade-mark of NDE Canada Corp.

CONTENTS

INTRODUCTION

A 20th Century Phenomenon

The 20th century saw the introduction of a multitude of phenomena that aren't easily explained. Film, radio and television are three of the more visible examples. Less tangible, however, is the never-ending quest of sportsmen and sportswomen to take the limits of physical and mental endeavor to ever higher plateaus.

Sporting games will probably always continue to rise and fall in popularity, but a select few are destined to become a medium through which human beings define themselves and indeed exceed themselves. Ice hockey, a passionate, high-octane sport with millions of faithful fans around the globe, belongs to that elite club. From its humble beginnings as a game played with sticks and stones on the frozen bogs of pioneer Canada, it has metamorphosed into a sophisticated test of mental and physical agility. It is difficult to find a sport that has lasted for more than 110 years. And its traditions live on. The annual matches between the first two teams in Kingston, Ontario—the hockey players of the Royal Military College and Queen's University—continue to this day.

Kings of the Ice: A History of World Hockey *is a tribute to the superstars of the ice who became role models for thousands of kids on both sides of the Atlantic, as well as to the unsung heroes off the ice who nurtured the game in its infancy and spread the gospel to the countries of Europe and the world. It is dedicated to the keepers of the game and its long tradition: the great men and women of the National Hockey League; the untrumpeted players of the countless leagues and associations who provide an endless supply of talent; and the amateurs of the international tournaments and the Olympics whose commitment to the game often goes unrewarded.*

Kings of the Ice *is dedicated to all these people. Those whose efforts were rewarded with fame and perhaps fortune will find their achievements among the stories told in these pages. For all the others, there is only this note of thanks.*

1843–1892

Tracking Down
the Birthplace of Hockey

In the late 1960s, a special commission was set up in Canada to determine the origins of the game of hockey. With so much of its history lost to undocumented accounts, the commission was unable to discover much of real value. Pictorial records by 17th and 18th century Dutch masters show a game involving skates and a stick, but it is generally regarded as at best a crude ancestor of the game we know now. But according to the testimony of one 83-year-old Canadian, John Nelson, his grandfather had taken part in some sort of game on ice in the New World as far back as 1837 and it was probably hockey. Similar commissions were established in subsequent years and a number of hockey histories were written. Most of the attention focused on three Canadian provinces, Nova Scotia, Ontario and Quebec. As the evidence trickled in and accumulated, however, it became apparent that because it had evolved over time, it would be difficult to credit one community or another with "inventing" the game.

Yukon, Canada.
Hockey in Dawson City.

Founded in 1788, King's College School in Windsor, Nova Scotia, is one of the oldest schools in the country and a year later King's College became the first college. Young people from London, New York, Boston, Philadelphia and Bermuda joined Canadians to study at the well-known and prestigious school, where the teaching staff included European professors from Oxford and Cambridge, Glasgow and Galway who introduced students to the games they brought with them as well as the traditional arts and sciences. Even nature itself fostered winter sports in Nova Scotia. With ice covering its bays, lakes and rivers a good part of the year, skating became a popular diversion. King's College students enjoyed ice fishing too, and oddly enough this also played a role in hockey's development.

Their professors had introduced some of the students to the Irish game of hurling, a very old game that boys played in Ireland year-round using a stick to chase flat stones over the fields. One

A HISTORY OF WORLD HOCKEY

of the students' favored fishing spots was at Chester Lake, some 15 miles from Windsor, and their route took them along the frozen sandbanks of the Avon River. Adapting the game they had learned to suit local conditions, the King's College boys chased flat stones over the ice with their sticks to pass the time during the hike. At first they played on foot, but as time passed, they began to strap skates to their boots. And at that point, hockey began to take form. Even those King's

Quebec City. One of the earliest known photos of hockey played indoors.

College students who didn't go in for ice fishing started playing hurling on skates, and soon the new game was attracting British officers and soldiers from nearby Fort Edward. Some linguists maintain that the new name for modified hurling appeared because a British officer by the name of Hockey—a common surname in 19th century England—had taken a fancy to chasing a flat wooden disk over the ice (unlike stones, the dark cherrywood disks were clearly visible). Soon disks made from the trunks of cherry trees universally replaced the flat stones in the game they were now calling "hockey."

According to some reports, the first rules of the game, called the Halifax Rules, were drawn up at about the same time. These rules were described in 1937 by Colonel B.A. Weston, who himself had played the game of hurling/hockey in Halifax in the 1860s, and were essentially as follows:

- The goals were designated by rocks.
- Lifting the wooden puck wasn't allowed, just as the stick wasn't to be raised higher than the shoulders.
- The teams changed ends after every goal scored.
- Passing forward was allowed.

Nobody knows if these rules were actually set down on paper. In fact, this very uncertainty resulted in Montrealers disputing the claim that the first hockey game took place in Nova Scotia in 1865. By their reckoning, a game only qualified as "hockey" under these conditions:

- The game was played on ice.
- Wearing skates, the players used sticks to chase the ball or puck.
- The goal was guarded by a goalkeeper (there were no goalkeepers in the game of hurling).
- There was a referee on the ice who was guided by written rules.

No matter where the first game was played, Nova Scotia retained a significant role in ice hockey's development. The first commercially made hockey skates, with wide steel blades turned up at the front and back, were produced at Dartmouth in 1861. The first indoor rink was built in Nova Scotia in 1862 and featured wooden walls and a roof for protection against wind and snow. It was meant mainly for skaters, but hockey players were granted permission to use it as well in 1883. Employing local natives from the Mi'kmaq tribe, Nova Scotia even began making its own hockey sticks—out of solid wood including the root of the hornbeam or ironwood tree—which were "exported" to Kingston, Montreal and even Boston.

Nova Scotia also took an active role in modernizing the rules. In 1880, wooden poles and a crossbar replaced the rocks that had marked the goals to that time, and fishing nets were added in 1889 (players could score from either the front or the back of the goal before the nets came into use). The referee used a bronze bell to announce the beginning and end of the game and to register goals. Until the 1890s, the goalkeeper's equipment was similar to what the other players were wearing, but in 1899 goalkeepers in Dartmouth borrowed some notions from cricket and started to protect their legs with wide pads and use a heavier stick with a wider blade.

And so it was that the Irish game of hurling on grass adapted itself to winter and ice in Nova Scotia and began its migration, first to Ontario, then to Quebec and soon after to Manitoba and Saskatchewan. By 1890, it had reached British Colombia on the west coast of Canada and it went inexorably on to become Canadian ice hockey, one of the fastest and most emotionally stirring games of the century just passed and the new one as well, and by then it had reached the whole world.

Still, the location of the first hockey game ever played hasn't and may never be established with absolute certainty. For a long time, the right to this title was claimed by Kingston, Ontario, an old army garrison and port which at one time was also the capital of Upper Canada. According to entries in the diary of a British officer, a game was played on the ice in Kingston in 1843 (it isn't known if the players wore skates), while in 1855 there were newspaper reports of soldiers from the Kingston garrison contending on the ice of Lake Ontario with skates fastened to their boots and using sticks, although there was nothing about the number of players, the score or the rules of that game. Regardless of the claims and counterclaims, in 1943 the National Hockey League and the Canadian Amateur Hockey Association selected Kingston as the site (now the International Hockey Museum) of the Hockey Hall of Fame to reward the city for doing so much to develop the sport and spread it to the eastern seaboard of the United States, first to Boston and later New York. And if Windsor, Nova Scotia, should get credit as the birthplace of hockey, then it was in Kingston, Ontario, that the game really got off the ground and in Montreal, Quebec, that it truly matured.

One of the most celebrated names from the early years of the game is that of James George Aylwin Creighton, who was born in 1850 in Halifax. He mastered hurling/hockey in his youth and later became a proficient figure skater. In 1873, he moved to Montreal as an engineer. A friend, Henry Joseph, recalled in 1936 that before Creighton arrived in the city, no one played hurling on skates. In fact, the first two dozen labeled hockey sticks made by natives in Nova Scotia were brought to Montreal by Creighton for the first official hockey game in history, which was played at the Victoria Skating Rink on March 3, 1875. The Montreal Gazette reported that instead of a lacrosse ball, the players would be using a wooden disk that couldn't be "lifted" off the ice, guaranteeing the safety of the spectators in the stands and the glass that surrounded the rink. Other reports noted that the goals were made up of two poles 6´ tall and set at a distance of 8´ from each other with no crossbar or net. Thanks again to the Montreal Gazette, we also know there were 18 players on the ice, nine on each team. A man named Torrance led one team, while Creighton himself captained the other. The game was

Ottawa Rideau Rebels, 1889. Lord Stanley's sons, Arthur (standing, second from left) and Edward (seated, left).

fast and exciting and the referee as well as the judges behind the goals had to watch very well. The Creighton team scored two "games"—the term "goal" wasn't used yet—against one for Torrance and his men. The turnout was large and spectators left the rink "quite satisfied with the thrilling evening spectacle."

After this report came to light, Montreal's role in establishing the game was confirmed. It was played by the Halifax Rules that some reports say were drawn up by James Creighton. We are certainly safe to surmise that as a staff writer for the Gazette, *he at least co-wrote the updated version, later called the McGill Rules, that appeared in that paper in 1877. More than 40 years later, former McGill student Richard F. Smith and two friends, W.L. Murray and W.R. Robertson, claimed they had authored the rules, but their memories were misty and often plain wrong. At the very least, they weren't active players and promotors, as Creighton had been and remained, and their claims are perhaps not that serious.*

The ardent French-speaking Canadians fell in love with the new game both as spectators and as participants and an ice hockey tournament became a popular feature of the Montreal Winter Carnival. It was during these competitions that a number of changes were made in the rules of the game and the format of tournaments that quickened the overall pace of development.

Ottawa, 1891.

Two teams from Montreal (the Victorias and McGill) and one from Quebec City participated in the 1883 Carnival. The students from McGill were the winners, but a major new development in the game resulted when the visiting team from Quebec arrived with seven players rather than the usual nine. The Montrealers agreed to play with seven men on each team, and by the next year seven-man teams were the rule at the Carnival tournaments. In the 1884 round, Ottawa made a name for itself as a hockey city by beating McGill by a score of 3–0. A year later, the Montreal Hockey Club won in overtime in the final game against Ottawa—and this time all the games were played indoors, at the Crystal Rink.

Hockey's popularity grew so rapidly that the one-week framework of the Carnival was soon perceived as too tight. In 1886, there was a much longer schedule and significant changes. Four participants from Montreal (Montreal Amateur Athletic Association, Victorias, McGill and Crystals) formed one division that played a round robin while two other teams, from Ottawa and Quebec City, played a home-and-home series in a second division. The best team from each then competed for the Dominion title. In what was essentially the first hockey championship in Canada, the Montreal Crystals emerged victorious on home ice in an extremely rough game that turned into a bloody battle at times. In fact, the visitors from Qubec City had to leave the ice and forfeit the game and the title when a number of players were unable to finish.

A year later, five of the six participants from that tournament formed the Amateur Hockey Association of Canada and were joined by the sixth, Quebec City, in 1888. Now the regular season stretched through the whole winter. The teams played in a round-robin pattern, but the champion was determined in a "challenge series," which meant that the club at the top of the regular-season standings could challenge any other team. In 1891, a team from Ottawa that had lost only one game in regular-season play was edged out in the challenge series by MAAA, a team that had won only one, the last game in the season. The rule was changed the following year and the team with the greatest number of wins in the round-robin tournament became the Dominion champion.

In the early 1880s, the "godfather" of hockey was making a name for himself in Ottawa. Already at the center of hockey events in the city, James Creighton popularized the new game in the press while he played on a team he'd organized, the Rideau Rebels. Made up largely of civil servants, the Rebels included a number of exalted individuals, such as three of the then Governor General's seven sons. And it may have been Creighton who suggested to these distinguished public servants the idea of inaugurating a prize: a cup for the best amateur team in the Dominion. There are accounts from those years indicating that his sons actively solicited the Governor General on that very matter. Like many English aristocrats, Fredrick Arthur, Lord Stanley of Preston and Earl of Derby as well as Governor General of Canada, was a sportsman who quick-

ly became a real fan of the Ottawa Rebels. He returned to England in 1893 just before he donated the Dominion Hockey Challenge Cup, which was awarded later that year for the first time to the MAAA as the AHAC champion and soon after adopted his name.

Having had their first taste of hockey in Canada, the Governor General's sons took the game with them when they went back home. In no time at all, they had Buckingham Palace captivated and a game was played in 1895 between a team from the palace and Lord Stanley's sons. There is no record of the game in the annals of hockey, nor was there any press coverage.

St. Luke district, Saskatchewan. River hockey.

However, we do know that Buckingham Palace scored only one goal against the brothers. We don't know how many, if any, of the brothers scored, but perhaps this was just diplomatic; after all, the palace team's goal was defended by the future George V. After the game, the man who would be King of England expressed his admiration for the way Lord Stanley's sons played, especially the one who could skillfully handle the puck while skating backwards. Five years later, the well-known Canadian player Fred "Cyclone" Taylor would amaze North American fans with the same style of stickhandling.

The NHL Stanley Cup is the legacy left at the end of the 19th century by the family of the Governor General of Canada to the game of ice hockey, a game with a remarkable history that has lasted for more than 110 years and counting. What is more, its traditions live on in the annual matches that continue to this day between the first two teams in Kingston (Royal Military College and Queen's University) and such rituals as the annual awards, trophies and regular induction of its greatest names into the Hall of Fame for fans new and old to discover and cherish.

A HISTORY OF WORLD HOCKEY

Frederick Arthur Lord Stanley of Preston

The name of Frederick Arthur, Lord Stanley of Preston, Earl of Derby, has attached itself to the oldest team trophy in North American sports competition. Since it was first awarded in 1893, the Dominion Hockey Challenge Cup has become an important athletic and cultural symbol in Canada. It is now universally known as the Stanley Cup.

The future Lord Stanley was born in London, England, in 1841. He was appointed Governor General of Canada by Queen Victoria in 1888, assumed office on June 11 of that year and served until 1893.

The first winter after his posting, Lord Stanley was invited to attend the Montreal Winter Carnival, where an ice hockey match was one of the featured attractions. This first competition that Lord Stanley witnessed turned out to be a thrilling 2–1 win by the Montreal Victorias over their crosstown rivals, the Montreal Amateur Athletic Association. The *Gazette* reported that "Lord Stanley expressed his great delight with the game of hockey and the expertise of the players." Not much later, three of his sons (Arthur, Edward and Victor) played on the Ottawa Rideau Rebels squad that toured Ontario in 1889 in a successful bid to promote the game's fortunes.

Lord Stanley came to the conclusion that the fine sport of ice hockey needed a symbol for which teams from all over Canada could compete. The idea was raised on the Governor General's behalf by Lord Kilcoursie at a dinner for the Ottawa Amateur Athletic Association on March 18, 1892. Lord Stanley was quoted in a letter he asked Kilcoursie to read:

In 1992, Lord Stanley purchased a silver cup for the sum of 10 guineas (approximately $50).

"I have for some time been thinking that it would be a good thing if there were a challenge cup which should be held from year to year by the champion hockey team in the Dominion of Canada. There doesn't appear to be any such outward sign of a championship at present, and considering the general interest which matches now elicit, and the importance of having the game played fairly and under rules generally recognized, I am willing to give a cup which shall be held from year to year by the winning team."

After much applause, the suggestion was heartily endorsed.

A short time later, Lord Stanley purchased a silver cup 7½″ high and 11½″ wide for the sum of 10 guineas (approximately $50). He immediately appointed Ottawa sheriff John Sweetland and Philip D. Ross as trustees who would administer all matters pertaining to any competition for the prize. Lord Stanley also stipulated that the Cup would remain a challenge trophy that would never become the property of any winning team regardless of how many times they won or successfully defended against a challenger.

In time, the whole Stanley family became hockey fanatics, with a number of sons and two daughters involved with the game. It was widely reported that on at least one occasion, one of the daughters, Lady Isobel Stanley, donned the blades for a Government House squad that won a game against the Rideau ladies' hockey team.

When the MAAA finished at the top of the 1893 Amateur Hockey Association of Canada standings, they were declared the first-ever winners of the Stanley Cup. During the first few years of its existence, there were only amateur clubs to compete for the Cup, but this was to change in 1910 when professional teams from the National Hockey Association began to take part in the quest for hockey's most heralded prize. With the disbanding of the Western Canada Hockey League in 1926, the Stanley Cup became the championship trophy of the National Hockey League. Lord Stanley became a charter member of the Hockey Hall of Fame in the Builders category in 1945.

1893–1916

Hockey Fever
in North America

*H*ockey has changed quite a lot in the past century or so. At the end of the 1800s, a team consisted of seven players: the customary goalkeeper, two defensemen and three forwards plus a "rover" who constantly hovered around the opposing team's goal. To prevent injuries, the goal was marked only by two poles stuck into heavy props that could slide on the ice. Often, a goalie would kick one of the props before changing ends and widen the mouth of the goal by a foot or a few extra inches. Of course, other goalies were wise to this move and it rarely gave either side an advantage.

The playing rink in those years wasn't marked off by boards but by spectators' seats and the benches for players. An official game was once played on a rink with an orchestra stand in its center. By today's standards, ticket prices were low, from 25¢ to $1. But hockey was so popular in Montreal, for example, that some games drew up to 5,000 fans. Even today that would be a high turnout in many countries in Europe.

In North America, the one powerful link between hockey then and now is the Stanley Cup. It's not the same silver cup that Lord Stanley bought for 10 guineas (about $50) in 1892. An exquisite copy mounted on a 35″ base replaced the original when it became so thin and fragile that it was thought best to preserve it in the Hockey Hall of Fame in Toronto in 1969. One of the oldest prizes in the world for professional sports, it has become a revered symbol of victory, glory and fame, and the current generation of players contends for the copy with no less fervor than the early ones who sought the original over 100 years ago.

Between 1893 and 1910, the battle for the Cup was fought by amateur hockey teams. Many of the teams and leagues that emerged in those years even included the word "amateur" in their names, right up until 1909. A number of these "amateur" teams could boast anywhere from one to four professionals in their lineups, however.

The first Stanley Cup winners, the Montreal Amateur Athletic Association, 1893.

A HISTORY OF WORLD HOCKEY

At the end of the 19th century, the main hockey league in Canada was the Amateur Hockey Association of Canada, or AHAC. Beginning in 1899, it changed quite a few times, in name more than anything else: the Canadian Amateur Hockey League, the Federal Amateur Hockey League, the Eastern Canada Amateur Hockey Association, the Eastern Canada Hockey Association and the Canadian Hockey Association. According to Lord Stanley's instructions, the AHAC champion automatically went to the finals, where they could be challenged by the strongest club from any other Canadian league or association. In the first 20 years of the Stanley Cup playoffs, teams from the AHAC and its successors won it 17 times.

The Stanley Cup—"Ticket for Montreal, please."
Railway Ticket Agent—"Return?"
The Stanley Cup—"No; I'm not coming back."

The Montreal Daily Star, 1902.

The first name to grace the silver plate on the base of the Stanley Cup was the Montreal Amateur Athletic Association. A squabble had erupted among the other leagues over who would challenge the AHAC champion. At the end of March 1893, with the season long over and the ice already melting, the Ottawa Capitals took up the challenge as champions of the Ontario Hockey Association. But the Cup trustees named by the Governor General handed down a decision that the challenge had been tabled too late, leaving MAAA as the top team in the Dominion. The trustees ruled further that the playing season within the associations and leagues, including Stanley Cup games, had to be played within a period of 15 weeks from the end of December to the beginning of March.

And who were these trustees Lord Stanley had appointed in Ottawa when he'd returned to Great Britain? The right to pass swift and final judgement was placed in the hands of two Ottawa citizens, sheriff John Sweetland and Philip D. Ross (who was from Montreal and a former player for one of the Montreal teams). These trustees were to see that Cup holders returned the trophy on time and undamaged; they had the final say in deciding who challenged the AHAC champion and who was rejected; and, finally, in disputes concerning the format of play—were the Stanley Cup finals to be decided in one game, by two out of three or, in the event of a tied series, the greatest number of goals scored—the verdict handed down by Sweetland and Ross was final and couldn't be appealed.

The first Stanley Cup game was played at Montreal's Victoria Skating Rink on March 22, 1894, and the MAAA won 3–1 against the Ottawa team that had repeated its challenge.

At the close of regular-season play in 1895, competition for the Stanley Cup took a bizarre twist. In preference to taking part in the finals against the best team from another league, the 1895 AHAC champion Montreal Victorias chose to play a post-season exhibition game in New York and offered the MAAA the opportunity to play in their stead. After protracted debate, the trustees arrived at an important decision: If the replacement team won against Queen's University (which had been selected to go up against the top AHAC team), the MAAA was to hand the Stanley Cup over to the Victorias players, who had chosen to not even play. The MAAA thrashed the Queen's players 5–1 and, sure enough, the engraving on the Stanley Cup reads: "1895. Montreal Victorias."

In February 1896, the Vics were forced to prove they could win on the ice. Since the challenging Victorias from Winnipeg were thought by Vics fans in the East to be "doomed from the outset," it was a good opportunity to win back some respect. As so often in sports, it didn't happen that way and it was the Winnipeg Vics who became the first hockey players from the West to have their names engraved on the Cup when they won the single final game 2–0. After that, the Montreal Vics did win—four years in a row to become the first dynasty in pre-NHL times—but practically every Stanley Cup playoffs that they were involved in included a confrontation of one kind or another.

After taking revenge against Winnipeg 6–5 in overtime in December 1896, the Montreal Vics beat Ottawa 14–2 in the first game of the Stanley Cup finals and refused to play the second "because it wasn't in the interests of hockey." The finals were reduced to two games and the team scoring the most goals was proclaimed the winner if the teams were equal in points (trustees Sweetland and Ross didn't lodge an objection). In 1898, the Montreal Vics had their names engraved on the Cup once again, this time without even coming out on the ice when no one dared to challenge them. A year later, a genuine scandal broke out in a two-game finals that just happened to involve the Winnipeg Vics again.

Stanley Cup champions the Winnipeg Victorias, 1901.

In the second period of the first game, the Montrealers were out in front 3–2 when their center, Bill MacDougall, used his stick like a sword to slash rover Tony Gingras across the knees. Gingras hit the ice, but referee Bill Findlay's decision sent MacDougall to the penalty box for only two minutes. The Winnipeg Vics didn't employ overly diplomatic language to tell Mr. Findlay what they thought of him and demand that MacDougall be disqualified for the rest of the game. The aggrieved referee left the ice and the Winnipeg players headed for their locker room. It appeared to be the end of the game, but 65 minutes later the referee reappeared, demanding that the game be resumed while standing by his original call with respect to MacDougall. Play didn't resume and Findlay proclaimed the Montreal Vics the winners of the game, the series and the 1899 Stanley Cup. And the trustees upheld his decision. As if to wipe out the memory, the AHAC changed its name to the Canadian Amateur Hockey League that same year.

If the Vics "dynasty" ended on a sour note, Montreal hockey's march of triumph continued with another team, though the Shamrocks were much less aggressive. In the final game for the 1900 Stanley Cup, again against the Winnipeg Vics, there wasn't a single penalty even though the struggle in the series was intense. A year later, the Winnipeggers vindicated themselves against the Montrealers 4–3 and 2–1. But the Cup was returned to Montreal in the 1902 playoffs season by the MAAA.

By that time the Silver Seven of Ottawa had already started their climb to the pinnacle. For three years in succession, from 1903 to 1905, they brought the Stanley Cup home to the capital.

In those early years, the fate of the Cup wasn't necessarily decided in three finals games. Lord Stanley had decreed that no team could hold onto the Cup as long as there was a champion from another Canadian league or association prepared to challenge them for it, and the holder of the Cup had to submit to these challenges every year. During the three years that the Stanley Cup was in Ottawa, the team was challenged twice by the Rat Portage (later Kenora, Ontario) Thistles and once by the Winnipeg Rowing Club, the Toronto Marlboros, the Brandon Wheat Kings and the Dawson City Klondikers. All of these were defeated, but feelings about the Silver Seven were mixed. Some regarded the team as the best in Canadian hockey; others referred to them as "butchers" and "bone-crackers." And both sides were right.

It has already been noted that the development of hockey in Ottawa can be credited to the sixth Governor General and his sons. Fortunately for hockey fans, Lord Stanley's replacement, the Count of Aberdeen, was also a fan of ice sports. What was more, Lady Aberdeen (Isabel Gordon, whose name graced the open-air rink in Ottawa where the first Stanley Cup games were played) didn't miss a single hockey match and was considered the real governor of the Dominion. She also became the main patroness of the Silver Seven (who acquired the moniker after their first victory in 1903, in honor of which each player received a silver nugget). After brushing off a challenge from the Rat Portage Thistles with scores of 6–2 and 6–4, the Silver Seven earned themselves the reputation of the strongest but "slowest" team in the country. One player was Lester Patrick's younger brother. After a traffic accident, Ted Patrick's leg was amputated and he ended up with a wooden replacement. Nevertheless, he was able to skate pretty well. Asked how this was possible, he remarked: "Fast skating isn't that important—the whole trick is to receive a good pass." This incredible answer wouldn't soon be forgotten.

Lady Aberdeen became the main patroness of the Ottawa Silver Seven.

In 1904, the Silver Seven, whose strength was indeed their good passing, almost lost their first game for the Stanley Cup against the fast-skating Toronto Marlboros. After the first 30 minutes of play on the hard-as-diamond and smooth-as-glass ice of the Lady Aberdeen Pavilion in Ottawa, the Torontonians were in the lead 3–1. But during the break, something very strange happened. When the teams came back out on the ice, it had somehow become soft and porous. The visitors' advantage in speed was suddenly lost and the Silver Seven slammed in five goals and took the game 6–3. The second game was a crushing defeat for Toronto in more ways than one. Ottawa trounced the visitors 11–2 and at the same time dispatched several of them to the hospital.

The High School Hockey Club, Montreal, 1899–1900. Winners of the senior championship in the Inter-School Hockey League.

The Ottawa team sported a number of colorful players. Silver Seven defenseman Harvey Pulford was a former Dominion boxing and wrestling champion who excelled in intimidating his opponents on the ice. In practically every game he played, he was loudly cheered from the stands for bodychecking an opponent right into the second row of spectators in Lady Aberdeen Pavilion, although player-coach and forward Alf Smith didn't agree with his rough style of play. But players who came up against the Silver Seven were most fascinated by rover Frank McGee, a man with blond hair and an angelic face who seemed to beat the odds every time. Not very tall, *almost blind in one eye, McGee was a natural shooter. In 12 Stanley Cup games, he scored 63 goals. And in 1905, playing against a team from Dawson City, he outdid even himself.*

A certain Colonel Joe Boyle, who had made a fortune in the Klondike gold fields, organized a hockey team in Dawson City with players from all over Canada and sent a telegram to Ottawa challenging the Silver Seven champions to a contest. They knew next to nothing about the Dawson City players, but the Stanley Cup trustees agreed. Dawson City and Ottawa are separated by a distance of 4,400 miles, and legend has it that the Klondikers started their 24-day journey by dogsled, then boarded a ship, then a train and finally reached Ottawa on January 12, 1905. The visitors showed little patience for organizational concerns and were raring to go into battle, although clearly exhausted and largely inexperienced. The only member of the Dawson City team who could be considered a veteran was Lorne Hanna from Brandon, Manitoba, while one of their players was a 17-year-old goaltender from Quebec, Albert Forrest, who remains the youngest player in history to participate in Stanley Cup games. It was no surprise when the Silver Seven crushed them 9–2 in the first game, but Colonel Boyle was an optimist and sent a telegram to Dawson City reading: "Not disappointed by defeat. Chance of winning Stanley Cup." When the text of this missive reached the general public, the Silver Seven's mood swung and the next time they thrashed their opponents 23–2.

In an interview before the second game, one of the visiting players had remarked there was "nothing special" about Frank McGee. In that game, McGee would establish records never seen again in the history of hockey. He scored 14 goals, three of them within a period of 90 seconds and another four in 140 seconds.

After their sojourn in Ottawa, the Klondikers didn't have the cash to get back and played 23 games in Quebec, Ontario and the Maritime provinces to raise it. It was late spring before the young goalkeeper made it back to Dawson City—the only one to do so—and he covered the last 350 miles on foot.

By 1906, the Silver Seven had become Ottawa idols and national heroes. They'd won the Stanley Cup three times, responding to eight separate challenges and winning 17 games out of 20. Then the Ottawa team was challenged by the Montreal Wanderers. The series consisted of two games, and in the event of an equal number of points, the winner was to be decided by the highest number of goals.

Stanley Cup champions the Montreal Shamrocks, 1899.

The Ottawa fans kept the faith. The Montreal rink where they played the first game had a seating capacity of 3,000 but was packed with 5,400. But the Wanderers, led by 22-year-old Lester Patrick, appeared to have the series in the bag when they took this game 9–1.

It still didn't look good for the hosts when they went back to Ottawa. After the first half of the second game, they were ahead 3–1 but the overall difference in goals, 10 for Montreal versus four for Ottawa, meant the Wanderers could take home the Cup even if they lost the game. During the break, the organizers repeated the trick that had turned the tide back in 1903 and sprinkled salt on the ice to make it porous and slow. The powerful but somewhat slow Harry Smith scored six goals in a row to make it 9–1 for Ottawa, and the overall points were suddenly tied at 10–10. Smith put the puck in again but the referee didn't allow it and the Silver Seven

A HISTORY OF WORLD HOCKEY

kept up their attack. After spending almost the whole game on the defensive, Montreal had a sudden rebirth. Lester Patrick exchanged words on the fly with his partners and Ottawa mounted a final assault. In the end, the Silver Seven won the game 9–3, but the Wanderers had 12 points versus Ottawa's 10 overall, so Montreal took home the Cup. As time went on, it would come to be called the greatest game in the history of hockey.

Colonel Joe Boyle and his Dawson City Klondikers, 1905.

After that, Ottawa went on a slide from which it didn't recover until 1909. They changed their "unlucky" name to the Senators and managed to acquire 23-year-old Fred "Cyclone" Taylor. In the new team's first game of the 1909–10 season, a record 7,100 spectators watched them trounce the Wanderers 12–2 in Ottawa and Cyclone Taylor was the star of the show. The Senators brought the Stanley Cup back to Ottawa in 1911 and nearly did it again in 1912. The Senators were leading 5–4 with 20 seconds left in the deciding game against the Quebec Bulldogs when Joe "Phantom" Malone tied the score. Then he slapped in the winning goal in overtime for Quebec and Ottawa's triumphant march came to an abrupt end.

A wave of changes began at the end of the 20th century's first decade. Games came to consist of three 20-minute periods. The rover was struck from the lineup, leaving six men on the ice. The dimensions of the playing rink were fixed. At the face-off, the referee used to place the puck on the ice and hold the blades of the opposing players' sticks until the whistle blew. After several refs had been injured, Fred Waghorne devised a safer way to face off that is still used today.

The Kenora (formerly Rat Portage, Ontario) Thistles, 1907. This team was from the smallest town ever to win the Stanley Cup.

Even bigger changes were in store that had no connection with the action on the ice. In January 1907, the Kenora (formerly Rat Portage, Ontario) Thistles, led by the same Art Ross who later gave his name to the trophy, challenged the Montreal Wanderers and took the Stanley Cup home. Ross, a salaried bank clerk from Brandon, was "borrowed" for the two decisive games of the season that just happened to be worth a $1,000 purse. Montreal cried foul: Ross was an "import" and a "pseudo-amateur." His mission accomplished, Art Ross left Kenora and in March of the same year the Wanderers won the Stanley Cup back in a two-game grudge match.

It wasn't this incident alone that led to amateur hockey's revamping. After 1910, the purely professional National Hockey Association and the (amateur) Ontario Hockey League began to set the standard in Canadian hockey. Quite naturally, the OHL amateurs didn't want to give up their right to compete for the Cup and the players who came out "for pleasure" condemned those who played for "victory at all costs." When the "gentlemen" of the game began losing to the professionals on a regular basis, however, it was decided to make a clean split. In 1908, Sir Montagu Allan inaugurated the Allan Cup, to be awarded, as it is to this day, to the best strictly amateur team in Canada while the Stanley Cup would still go to the strongest team in Canada regardless of its affiliation to any league or association, amateur or professional. The Stanley Cup trustees insisted on the latter part of this formula as the will of its founder, but even that ruling ran into trouble. In 1917, the "Silver Cup" for "the best team in the Dominion of Canada" was awarded to the Seattle Metropolitans from the United States of America.

Organized hockey was still young enough in 1908 that the proliferation of professional clubs differed widely in their level of play. When attendance began to go down, the owners decided to reduce the NHA until by 1912 only four teams remained (the Quebec Bulldogs, the Ottawa Senators, the Montreal Wanderers and a newcomer from Montreal, the Canadiens), though that roster of teams was short-lived. In Western Canada, Lester and Frank Patrick formed the Pacific Coast Hockey Association, and when it got on its feet, they proposed a playoff for the Stanley Cup between the strongest teams of the NHA and the PCHA. At first the trustees refused, but when the professionals from the West threatened to inaugurate a new cup in 1914, Lord Stanley's representatives were forced to concede.

The first battle between the East and the West was between the Victoria Aristocrats and the Toronto Blueshirts. At an artificial ice rink that had just been commissioned in Toronto, the hosts won in a first-three-wins format and the Stanley Cup took up temporary residence in Toronto for the first but by no means last time. A year later, the Stanley Cup finals were held west of Winnipeg for the first time when the Millionaires from Vancouver hosted the Senators from Ottawa. The superstar of those years, Cyclone Taylor (who had moved west), scored six goals in three games that drew approximately 20,000 spectators and the Cup went to Vancouver. Each of the Millionaires was paid $300 while the Senators each got $200.

The Victoria Aristocrats, Pacific Coast Hockey Association.

In the 1915–16 season, the Stanley Cup trustees had another headache to contend with. An American team from the West, the Portland Rosebuds, emerged in the finals for the most Canadian of trophies. Presuming that the prize would be theirs, the Americans acquired guardianship of the Cup from Vancouver and had their names engraved on it before even playing the finals series against the Canadiens. It was a large boost to national pride when the Montreal team captured it for the first time after taking the fifth game 2–1. The great Canadian goalkeeper Georges Vezina made his first playoffs appearance that year. But the Canadiens couldn't repeat the next year and lost the last game 9–1 and the series in four. Now another American team, the Seattle Metropolitans, walked away with the quintessentially Canadian trophy.

Fans in eastern Canada didn't take to professional hockey like those in the west. Box office returns dwindled to such an extent that clubs couldn't cover traveling expenses and they set out in "skeleton" lineups to play games on the road. It was no surprise that after the 1916–17 season, the NHA fell apart and a new organization appeared in its place in November of 1917. At the time, the National Hockey League was only four teams—the Montreal Canadiens, the Montreal Wanderers, the Ottawa Senators and the Toronto Arenas—but from humble beginnings the NHL has become the standard for world hockey with millions of fans in a hundred countries around the globe and there's no sign of stopping it.

Alf Smith

Alf was the best-known player of a skating clan—the Smith family.

The late 1890s and early 1900s were great years for hockey in the Ottawa area, in large part because of one hockey-playing family, the Smiths. The Smith family consisted of seven brothers, enough to form a full all-star team in the early days of the sport, when an extra player—the rover—patrolled the ice.

And it would have been a formidable team. Three of the brothers had successful professional careers and several others established reputations as talented amateurs. Alf Smith was the oldest and perhaps the best known of the skating clan, though younger brother Tommy had a better scoring touch and played longer in the burgeoning era of professional hockey. Both were eventually inducted into the Hockey Hall of Fame for their outstanding play.

Alf Smith is remembered as a bruising winger at one point described as the toughest, meanest player to ever call Ottawa home. He was born in Ottawa on June 3, 1873, and began playing competitive hockey in his teens, starring with the Ottawa Electrics in the city league before moving up to the Ottawa Capitals, still an amateur team, in 1892. He played his first professional hockey at the turn of the century, skating for most of one season with Pittsburgh in the International Hockey League. It was a time when many Canadian players plied their trade south of the border for part of the year, earning good money before returning home to play in the primarily amateur leagues in and around the major cities.

After taking a break from the game, Smith played with the Ottawa Hockey Club of the Canadian Amateur Hockey League and helped build the team into the powerhouse that became known as the "Silver Seven." In 1903 he captained the team to the first of three successive Stanley Cup victories. The Silver Seven played in what was considered the first professional hockey league in Canada. Smith played on a line with Frank McGee, making room for his talented teammate with his bruising style. Later his brother Harry took up a position on his line and the siblings had great success.

In 1906 Alf led a group of players in starting a second Ottawa team that played in the Federal Amateur Hockey League as the Senators. When the Senators were defeated in the 1907 playoffs by the Montreal Wanderers, Smith and teammate Harry "Rat" Westwick joined the Kenora Thistles, the team that had defeated the Silver Seven for the Stanley Cup the year before. The Thistles also lost to the eventual champion Wanderers and Smith returned to Ottawa. Continuing to play for the Senators, Smith also coached, capturing the inaugural Allan Cup with the Ottawa Cliffsides in 1908. The following year he moved south one more time and played a season for the Pittsburgh Athletic Club. He then retired as a player and turned his attention full-time to coaching.

Smith's coaching experience included the Renfrew Millionaires, a celebrated squad that featured some of the game's greatest early stars, and the Ottawa Senators in the newly formed National Hockey League. He was also the first coach of the New York Americans when the team joined the NHL in 1926.

Alf Smith stayed in hockey for most of his life, coaching and managing teams in Moncton, New Brunswick, and North Bay, Ontario. He was inducted into the Hockey Hall of Fame on June 6, 1962, nine years after his death in 1953 at the age of 80.

Harvey Pulford

A superb all-around athlete, Harvey Pulford achieved a great deal as a player with the Ottawa Hockey Club and the Ottawa Silver Seven. He later excelled as a referee in the National Hockey Association. Not a gifted skater, he concentrated on playing solid defense in his own end of the ice and used his large frame to unsettle opposing forwards.

Born in Toronto, Pulford spent nearly all his life in the Ottawa Valley. He demonstrated his exceptional athletic skills early and at the age of 13 he was declared overall sports champion at the Ottawa Model School. In 1892 he began playing defense for the Ottawa Hockey Club of the Amateur Hockey Association of Canada. Tutored by Weldy Young, Pulford remained a fixture of the club until his retirement in 1908.

In 1901 he altered his style of play from merely flipping the puck out of his own end to carrying the puck up the ice toward the opposing team's net. During the period 1902 to 1905, Pulford captained the Ottawa Hockey Club, which came to be known as the "Silver Seven." His partnership with Art Moore proved to be a formidable barrier to onrushing forwards. This team dominated the Canadian Amateur Hockey League and the Federal Amateur Hockey League while winning or defending the Stanley Cup several times between 1903 and 1905.

Harvey Pulford became famous for carrying the puck up the ice toward the opposition net.

Ottawa's first Stanley Cup came at the expense of the Montreal Victorias in a two-game series in March 1903 and the triumph was highlighted by an 8–0 rout in the decisive contest. A few days later, Pulford's crew successfully fended off the challenge of the Rat Portage (later Kenora) club of northwestern Ontario. In December the same year they overcame the Winnipeg Rowing Club in a battle that lasted three games. Not known for his scoring touch, Pulford contributed a goal in Ottawa's successful defense of the Stanley Cup against the Toronto Marlboros of the OHA in February 1904. A month later they weathered the challenge of Brandon, the Manitoba champions, in a rugged two-game set.

The 1905 season brought the Ottawa club the championship of the FAHL. In January of that year they suppressed the Cup ambitions of the Dawson City squad by an aggregate score of 32–4. Two months later, in one of Pulford's greatest performances, Ottawa survived a clash with the highly skilled Rat Portage outfit. The challengers from Ontario's northwest dominated the opening match, but Ottawa equalized two days later to set the stage for a memorable deciding game. Pulford, who was instructed to throw his weight around throughout the contest, was superb against the speedy Rat Portage forwards in a 5–4 Ottawa victory. A year later came his last two successful Cup defenses, against Queen's University and Smiths Falls.

Pulford didn't limit his accomplishments to the hockey rink. He was one of the best athletes ever produced in Canada and combined Stanley Cup success with an array of victories and awards in other sports. Rowing was one of his lifelong passions. He won numerous Canadian titles with the Ottawa Rowing Club between 1905 and 1912, and his ultimate thrill came in 1911 when his crew topped the English and Belgian teams in the prestigious Henley Royal Regatta. Pulford also achieved national success as a paddler with the Britannia Boating Club.

Other team milestones included captaining the Ottawa Rough Riders to football championships in 1898, 1899, 1900 and 1902 and captaining the Ottawa Capitals to Canadian lacrosse titles from 1897 to 1900. Individually, he was the light heavyweight and the heavyweight amateur boxing champion of eastern Canada between 1896 and 1998 and Ottawa's top squash player in 1923 and 1924. A local sports legend, Pulford was elected to the Ottawa Sports Hall of Fame in 1966. If not for Lionel Conacher, he'd likely have been the country's top male athlete of the first half of the 20th century. Pulford took his place in the Hockey Hall of Fame as a charter member in 1945.

Graham Drinkwater

Graham Drinkwater could play at the defense and forward positions.

One of the most versatile stars of the early days of the game, Graham Drinkwater was a fixture in the Montreal Victorias' lineup. He was a rare breed with an ability to function equally well at the defense and forward positions. Brilliant stickhandling, a natural scoring touch and team-permeating enthusiasm characterized Drinkwater's play. He was an integral component of the Montreal Victorias squad that became hockey's first dynasty with four Stanley Cup triumphs in the 1890s. Unfortunately, Drinkwater was one of the many early stars of the game usually overlooked by subsequent generations of fans and historians.

The Montreal native grew up playing many sports in his local neighborhood. As a teenager, he became an accomplished hockey and football player. In 1892–93, he starred with the Montreal Amateur Athletic Association junior team. This was a prestigious place to learn the ropes, given that the senior outfit won the first Stanley Cup ever presented that same season. Drinkwater also went on to play a prominent role on the McGill University junior and intermediate football teams.

Upon leaving McGill, Drinkwater signed with the Victoria Hockey Club of Montreal, where he figured to gain more playing time than with the MAAA squad. The talented Drinkwater's rookie season in 1895 was filled with achievement. He worked superbly with speedy cover point Mike Grant, Archie Hodgson and AHA leading scorer Haviland Routh. Drinkwater scored nine goals in eight contests to help the Victorias win the Amateur Hockey Association of Canada championship, and the title earned the club the distinction of being holders of the Stanley Cup.

In February 1896 the Winnipeg Victorias mounted a successful challenge, winning the Stanley Cup in Montreal. Later that year, Drinkwater scored one of the goals when the Montreal Vics gained revenge against their western namesakes, reclaiming the Cup in a thrilling 6–5 battle. A fine center, he also spent much of this period on defense, where he once again enjoyed an outstanding working relationship with Mike Grant. In addition to their multifaceted talents, the two stars were physically the biggest members of the team.

The Montreal powerhouse continued its domination of the AHAC in 1897 by winning another league crown and maintaining possession of the Stanley Cup. Along the way they humiliated the Central Canada Hockey Association champion Ottawa Capitals by a 14–2 score, leaving no doubt of their supremacy. Drinkwater, Grant, Ernest McLea and Cam Davidson dominated for the victors in one of the most lopsided encounters in Stanley Cup history.

They were even stronger the next season, when they won the AHAC title after going unde-feated in the regular season. Drinkwater registered 10 goals in eight matches that year on a team that scored an average of nearly seven times per game.

Early in the 1899 season, Winnipeg ventured east to face their archfoes from Montreal. The eastern Vics won both encounters by a single goal. Drinkwater's end-to-end goal-producing rush in the first match proved to be the most memorable point in the epic struggle. Once again he lined up on defense with Mike Grant. The twosome formed an effective and entertaining partnership that served as an integral part of the Vics' Stanley Cup triumph.

The second match was Drinkwater's swan song. It was a contest talked about for years afterwards because of a heated controversy that erupted during the game. A dispute over a penalty call caused referee J.A. Findlay to leave the arena in disgust. When he returned, the Winnipeg players refused to take to the ice. The game was awarded to Montreal, which was leading 3–2 at the point of the dispute, and the Vics retained the Cup.

A month after the battle with Winnipeg, the Shamrock club took possession of the Cup by virtue of being champions of the newly formed Canadian Amateur Hockey League. This signified the end of one of the top dynasties in the history of Stanley Cup competition.

Graham Drinkwater's smooth-skating and well-rounded game made him one of the top stars during hockey's formative period. He was always a key player on the teams for which he played. Drinkwater took his rightful place in the Hockey Hall of Fame in 1950.

Donald "Dan" Bain

Donald Henderson "Dan" Bain was an unqualified success in a number of sports, not the least of which was hockey. He first joined the Winnipeg Victorias in 1895 after reading an advertisement in a local newspaper soliciting new players. He remained in the Manitoba capital for eight seasons and played a rather large role on one of hockey's first great teams. During this time, the muscular Bain provided scoring, playmaking and a physical presence to two Stanley Cup championship squads. Along with his great skills on ice, he was blessed with natural leadership qualities.

Although he was born in Belleville, Ontario, Bain grew up in Winnipeg after his family moved there when he was a child. In 1887, at the age of 13, he attained his first of many athletic awards by winning the three-mile roller skating championship of Manitoba. He followed that up four years later by finishing at the top of the all-round category at the Winnipeg gymnastics competition. Between 1894 and 1996, Bain won three consecutive Winnipeg one-mile cycling titles. He also captured the Alberta and Manitoba pairs figure skating crown and was an accomplished lacrosse player.

Canada's outstanding athlete of the last half of the 19th century, Dan Bain.

Bain first played top-level hockey with the Victorias of the Manitoba Hockey League in 1895, quickly establishing himself as an outstanding center and valuable team leader. On February 14, 1896, the team traveled east to try to strip the Montreal Victorias of their Stanley Cup. Bain scored the winning goal in the westerners' 2–0 upset to claim the hallowed silverware. Months later, the Montreal squad reclaimed Lord Stanley's trophy from Winnipeg by a 6–5 score despite two goals from Bain.

In February 1899, the gifted center led the western Vics to another unsuccessful Stanley Cup challenge against their eastern rivals from Montreal. A year later, Bain led another Winnipeg expedition eastward to face the Shamrock club of Montreal. This time, Bain's exceptional performance in scoring four goals in three games couldn't lift the Winnipeg team past their eastern opponents, who eked out a victory by 11 goals to 10 in the total-goals series.

Winnipeg launched a successful challenge against the powerful Shamrocks in January 1901, sweeping a two-game series in Montreal. Bain proved to be the overtime hero in the second match. In the process, the skillful forward made history by registering the first-ever extra-time Cup-winning goal. That year he also caused a stir by adopting a rudimentary wooden facemask to protect his broken nose. The media labeled him the "Masked Man" for many years after his pioneering use of the equipment.

The newest Cup holders withstood a confrontation with the Toronto Wellingtons in January 1902. Two months later, they faced the Montreal Amateur Athletic Association, the winners of the first Stanley Cup in 1893 by virtue of their first-place finish in the Amateur Hockey Association of Canada. In a hard-fought three-game set, Winnipeg won the first game before succumbing in the latter two even though Bain was often the dominant forward on the ice.

After retiring as a player in 1903, the multifaceted Bain turned his attention to trapshooting. He captured the Manitoba provincial title before moving on to Toronto, where he emerged as the champion of the Dominion.

Bain's extraordinary career in sports was recognized when he was chosen Canada's outstanding athlete of the last half of the 19th century. He's a member of the Canadian Sports Hall of Fame and Manitoba Sports Hall of Fame and was one of the initial 12 players selected to the Hockey Hall of Fame when it was founded in 1945. When assessing the most versatile sports figures in Canada's history, undoubtedly Bain should be included with the legendary Lionel Conacher.

Harry Trihey

Harry Trihey was a captain and leading scorer of the Shamrock Hockey Club of Montreal.

Lieutenant-Colonel Harry Judah Trihey was an influential team player who possessed an exceptional shot. He was also blessed with superior puckhandling skills and the ability to have an emotional impact on a game. Trihey was capable of anticipating the play and staying one step ahead of the opposition.

A Christmas baby, the Montreal native involved himself with hockey, lacrosse, rugby and football while studying at St. Mary's College. Trihey graduated with a bachelor of arts, then entered law school at McGill University. While pursuing his legal studies, he led the Redmen to the Canadian university rugby championship. Soon afterward, Trihey became closely affiliated with the Shamrock Hockey Club of Montreal. It was there that he enjoyed his greatest success as an athlete, captaining a multiple Stanley Cup winner.

Trihey debuted with the Shamrock squad in a one-game appearance in 1897 before earning a regular place on the roster the following year. By the 1899 season, he was a popular star on a much-improved team. He outdistanced all scorers with 19 goals in seven games, including a remarkable 10 in one match against Quebec on February 4, 1899. This remained a regular-season record among leagues that competed for the Stanley Cup and was only eclipsed by Frank McGee's 14 in the well-known Stanley Cup challenge game in 1905.

The Shamrocks won all but one game that year and finished at the top of the Canadian Amateur Hockey League standings to automatically become holders of the Stanley Cup. When challenged by Queen's University in March, the Shamrocks encountered little trouble in winning, thanks to a three-goal outburst from Trihey.

Aided by stellar linemates Art Farrell and Fred Scanlan, Trihey continued to excel in 1900 with 17 goals. The Shamrocks repeated as CAHL champions and earned the right to defend the Stanley Cup. In February of that year, the holders again successfully fought off a challenge from Winnipeg in a thrilling series, followed by a rout of the Halifax Crescents. Trihey was responsible for 12 goals in the five games against the eager but overmatched adversaries.

Although the Shamrocks lost the Stanley Cup to the challenge of the Winnipeg Victorias in 1901, the impact of the Montreal squad on the game was firmly entrenched. As the on-ice leader of the Shamrocks, Trihey encouraged his linemates to work with him in planned strategy as opposed to improvisation. This form of offensive organization influenced other teams that previously had relied on pure skill and instinct to attain success.

Trihey also insisted that the defensemen create scoring chances by carrying the puck up the ice instead of flipping it in the air, as was the common practice. Ironically, he was known for flipping the puck up in the air and having it land behind the goalie's shoulders when he was in close. But these innovations were a crucial factor in the Shamrocks' becoming a highly successful and entertaining hockey club.

Hockey remained an important part of Trihey's life following his retirement as a player. He served as secretary-treasurer and president of the Canadian Amateur Hockey League. As an administrator, Trihey utilized the same leadership qualities he exhibited on the ice and guided the organization through the intense competition for players brought about by the establishment of the Federal Amateur Hockey League in 1903. Trihey also served as a referee and sat on the advisory board of the Montreal Wanderers Hockey Club.

An intensely proud Irish-Canadian, Lieutenant-Colonel Trihey organized the 55th Regiment Militia and 199th Battalion Irish Canadian Rangers during World War I. After the war, he founded a highly successful Montreal law firm where he continued to earn the respect of his peers. The splendid forward took his rightful place in the Hockey Hall of Fame in 1950.

Fred Waghorn

Fred Waghorn, called "Wag" and later "Old Wag" when his son adopted his nickname, was one of the game's great innovators. As a referee, he was responsible for rule changes on the ice. Off the ice, he was the guiding light of some of the best-known hockey leagues in the world. He created a network of teams and organizations across Canada that brought kids into the game who wouldn't have had a chance to play otherwise.

Waghorn was born in Tunbridge Wells, England, in 1866. He moved to Canada as a young man and brought with him a love of rugby, a sport h'd be involved in throughout his life. His interest in athletics soon broadened to include lacrosse and then hockey. He began a league in the Toronto area called the Toronto Lacrosse Hockey League, a four-team organization that fielded lacrosse teams in the summer and hockey squads during the winter months. Hockey grew in popularity and the league soon became the Toronto Hockey League. This first incarnation of major city hockey eventually disbanded, but Waghorn continued to push for better opportunities for youngsters and veterans alike to work on their skills and play in competitive, non-professional situations. He was one of four co-founders of the Beaches Hockey League in 1911. The league came to be called the Metropolitan Toronto Hockey League and today it's the largest minor hockey organization in the world. Waghorn headed up the league for many years, as did his son, Fred Waghorn Jr., or "Young Wag."

Waghorn achieved much of his lasting fame for his thousands of games as an official. With the sport still nascent and constantly developing, snap decisions during play often became the rules that have been passed down to the modern game. In the earliest days of the sport, when Waghorn was in his first of 50 seasons as a referee, the goalies weren't allowed to fall to their knees and there were no forward passes or substitutions for the seven players on each side who started the game. Indeed, it was an altogether different sport from its modern cousin seen in huge arenas around the world today.

"A few of the rinks were lighted by coal oil lamps, and the corners were dark pockets," Waghorn said of the sport's first arenas. "It was in rinks of that type that the art of puck-lifting was at its peak. The Pete Charltons of the day lofted the puck up to the rafters, beyond the goal-keeper's vision. Often the rubber seemed to drop from the roof, right in front of the surprised goalkeeper, then bounced crazily into the net. Some players could lift from end to end."

Referees used a cowbell instead of a whistle to halt proceedings, and with many of the games played outdoors or on tiny rinks with the paying public right next to the playing surface, fans who disagreed with a call could use the cover of darkness to rain down abuse and objects on the referee, who often worked the games alone. A back entrance to the rink was used by officials to avoid the milling about of upset fans following a game, and the heavy cowbell, swung back and forth in front, secured a path for the beleaguered referees. When the game was over, a long ride on the rail system, back home or to another game in a far-flung locale, awaited the poorly paid mediator. On one occasion, Waghorn was stuck for days in a town far from home because of heavy snow.

One of the changes in the game attributed to Waghorn was in the use of the cowbell. Many young men would bring bells of their own to the game to disrupt the other team or just to raise a ruckus. Waghorn was the first to use a whistle, a shrill device that wasn't as prevalent in rural Ontario as the bell. The metal version he first tried had to be scrapped because of the cold conditions in some arenas—it would stick to the referee's lips—and a plastic whistle became the norm.

Early in his career as an official, Waghorn became involved in the controversy around the status of amateur versus professional athletes. John Ross Robertson, who as president of the Ontario Hockey Association fought to keep hockey an amateur game, argued that Waghorn shouldn't be allowed to referee because he'd served as a field captain in a professional lacrosse league one summer. The proposal came up for a vote but was rejected after one member made an argument that couldn't be contradicted. "Mr. President," the member said during the debate, "if we debar Mr. Waghorn, who will referee our final games?"

During a game in Arnprior, Ontario, Waghorn made another important contribution to hockey in the form of the face-off. Previously the referee would place the puck between the centermen and then play would begin, usually with the official's ankles and shins being smacked and bruised in

One of the game's great innovators, Fred Waghorn.

the rush for the puck. Waghorn had had enough of that and informed the players that he'd drop the puck from a few feet above the ice, a move that allowed him an opportunity to jump out of the way. The change was so successful—the players liked it as well—that Waghorn reported it to the hockey associations, which later made it a regular part of the sport.

One of his stranger rulings was the result of the early use of two-piece pucks. Sometimes a forward would send a hard shot at the net and hit the post, breaking the puck into two parts, one of which went into the net. Waghorn would state quickly that there was no goal for half a puck. "The rule book says that a puck is 1″ thick," he said later of his decision. "That piece of rubber that went into the goal was only ¹/₂″ thick, so it couldn't qualify as a puck. And if it wasn't a puck, it certainly couldn't have been a goal." He also said that the scoring team would expect two goals if the puck broke and both pieces went into the net, which surely wouldn't do. Because of this unique occurrence, solid pucks were favored and it was ruled that the puck—the whole puck—must cross the goal line to constitute a goal.

Waghorn continued his contributions to hockey, lacrosse and rugby right up to his death in 1956 at the age of 90. He refereed over 2,400 hockey games and 1,500 lacrosse matches. He was inducted into the Hockey Hall of Fame in the Builders category in 1961.

Silas "Si" Griffis

Silas Seth "Si" Griffis was one of the fastest skaters in the early days of the game despite his relatively large frame. His blazing speed enabled him to dominate as a rover in the seven-man game and as a defender in the modern six-man configuration. He contributed to the Kenora Thistles' Stanley Cup triumph in 1907 and later captained the Vancouver Millionaires to hockey's ultimate prize in 1915.

A native of Onanga, Kansas, Griffis emigrated to Canada, when his family settled in St. Catharines, Ontario, when he was 18 months old. A short while later they moved permanently to the northwestern Ontario community of Rat Portage (Kenora). Griffis competed in the local minor hockey system and became involved with a number of other sports, especially rowing. He enjoyed several outstanding years as a member of the Kenora Rowing Club, including a victory at the 1905 Canadian Henley Regatta in St. Catharines.

Si Griffis was one of the fastest skaters in the early days of hockey.

Griffis joined the Rat Portage entry in the newly formed Manitoba and North West Hockey League in 1902. His play as a rover and cover point contributed significantly to the team's 1902–03 league title. The circuit was reorganized into the Manitoba Senior Hockey League in 1905 with Griffis' Rat Portage squad recognized as the most talented club. It easily won the league title to earn the right to challenge the favored Ottawa club for the Stanley Cup. The underdogs came out second best in a hotly contested three-game series in which Griffis contributed three goals and was one of the dominant players on the ice.

By 1907, the Rat Portage club had been renamed the Kenora Thistles and was even more talented than previously. They captured the Stanley Cup in a thrilling two-game series with the Montreal Wanderers in January 1907. Brilliant forward Tommy Smith scored seven of the 12 Kenora goals, while Griffis and Art Ross rushed the puck with tremendous confidence. This speedy trio was particularly difficult for the Montreal defenders to contain. In the second match, the Wanderers resorted to rough tactics in an unsavory attempt to stall and intimidate their talented adversaries. The strategy worked until late in the game, when the Thistles pulled away for an 8–6 win.

The Thistles, however, lost the subsequent challenge from the Wanderers two months later. Kenora couldn't overcome a 7–2 loss in the opening match, but in the second encounter, Griffis and defense partner Roxy Beaudro constantly jumped into the offensive rush and led their team to a 6–5 win, enabling the team to salvage some pride. The skilled Griffis was a key reason the northwestern Ontario club was firmly entrenched as one of the quality teams during the early part of the century.

The talented rover and cover point was one of the most successful American-born players ever to compete for the Stanley Cup. Soon after retiring, he considered moving to British Columbia. As soon as the word spread concerning his plans, a host of Kenorans offered to build him a new home to keep him from leaving. Griffis was touched by the gesture but opted to head for the West Coast just the same. Four years after moving, he considered restarting his hockey career.

Griffis' brief sabbatical from hockey ended officially when he joined the Vancouver Millionaires of the new Pacific Coast Hockey Association in 1912. He was rejuvenated while playing a vital role on the defense and serving as the team's captain. Griffis debuted on the West Coast in outstanding fashion by scoring twice and adding two assists in his new club's opener on January 5, 1912. His leadership was quiet, yet effective, as many of the young Vancouver players looked up to the classy veteran.

Griffis proceeded to score 38 goals for Vancouver before retiring in 1919. He was a member of the 1915 Stanley Cup-winning Millionaires. During his stay on the West Coast, Griffis formed a strong defensive partnership with Frank Patrick for four seasons before spending two years in tandem with Lloyd Cook. Griffis is a member of the Northwestern Ontario Sports Hall of Fame and was inducted into the Hockey Hall of Fame in 1950.

Frederick "Cyclone" Taylor

Frederick Wellington Taylor performed exceptionally well at several positions during his legendary career. His dynamic rushes and memorable scoring feats made him one of hockey's first superstars. He was one of the few players in the history of the game capable of skating backward as fast as many could forward.

Born in the village of Tara, Ontario, Taylor grew up in nearby Listowel, which is where he first took up hockey as well as lacrosse and soccer. Taylor exhibited promise for the first time as a member of the Listowel Mintos and Queen's Own before graduating to the city's top junior club in the OHA. He played with the Listowel juniors from 1903 to 1905 before leaving the province to broaden his horizons. Taylor jumped at the chance to play for the Portage La Prairie team of the Manitoba Senior Hockey League in 1905.

Before the end of the 1905–06 season, he was signed by the Houghton, Michigan, Portage Lakers franchise of the International Hockey League. Based in northern Michigan, this was the first professional circuit in North America. Taylor joined his new team in time for only the last six games of the season, but the Listowel Wonder wasted little time in making an impact. He took the league by storm, scoring 11 goals in the half-dozen matches and garnering a place on the IHL All-Star Team. The following year, Taylor was a major component of the Houghton club's league championship.

In 1907–08, Taylor joined the Ottawa Silver Seven of the Eastern Canada Amateur Hockey Association. It was here that he made a name for himself as an explosive rushing defenseman, scoring nine goals in 10 games. The nickname "Cyclone" was first accorded this exciting figure by local reporters after a cartoonist with the *Ottawa Journal* depicted one of his cyclonic rushes in vivid detail.

Taylor's excellent play helped Ottawa win the ECAHA championship in 1909 and the team became holders of the Stanley Cup. In a transaction that caused a stir across Canada, Taylor was signed in 1910 by the Renfrew Millionaires franchise, which was preparing to join the newly founded National Hockey Association in 1910. The salary paid to him was the highest ever for a Canadian athlete up to that time and remained so for many years. Taylor scored 22 goals in 28 games over the next two seasons before the team was disbanded.

When Taylor couldn't reach a satisfactory agreement to stay in the NHA, the Vancouver Millionaires of the Pacific Coast Hockey Association moved quickly to offer him a contract. Team manager Frank Patrick decided to switch Cyclone to the forward position, and there he thrived from 1913 to 1921.

Cyclone Taylor could skate backward as fast as many could forward.

While employed on the West Coast, Taylor averaged more than a goal per game in a formidable display of offensive prowess. His second Stanley Cup triumph came in 1915. He scored six goals in the Millionaires' three-game domination of Ottawa in the championship showdown. The sheer magnitude of Taylor's excellence in the series elevated him to the status of hero right across Canada.

Taylor led all PCHA goal scorers in 1918 and 1919 with 32 and 23 goals respectively. Even though the Toronto Arenas defeated Vancouver in the 1918 Stanley Cup championship, Taylor proved to be the most revered performer in the matchup. He finished ahead of all playoff scorers with nine goals in seven games.

Cyclone retired following the 1920–21 schedule but delighted the fans one more time by making a one-game cameo appearance for Vancouver two years later. He accumulated 194 goals in 186 regular-season games while carving out a reputation as one of hockey's surefire drawing cards. He earned the remarkable distinction of being named to the First All-Star Team everywhere he played from 1900 to 1918.

Taylor's sharp hockey mind led to his being named president of the Pacific Coast Hockey League in 1937. An active member of the Vancouver community, he helped form the British Columbia Hockey Benevolent Society, where he served as director from 1954 until his death in 1979.

A host of honors and accolades followed Taylor after he announced his retirement. On July 1, 1946, King George VI bestowed him with the Order of the British Empire in recognition of his service during World War II. On June 21, 1980, a historical plaque commemorating the area's most famous native son was unveiled in his home town of Tara. And the Vancouver Canucks of the NHL named their annual most valuable player award after Taylor.

Cyclone was voted into the Canadian Sports Hall of Fame and the British Columbia Sports Hall of Fame. He was elected as a charter member of the Hockey Hall of Fame in 1945, and he was also given the honor of turning the sod for the construction of the Hockey Hall of Fame building that opened in 1961.

Lester Patrick ▮▮▮▮▮▮

Lester Patrick played a significant role in hockey history for nearly half a century.

Beginning in 1903, Lester Patrick played a significant role in hockey history for nearly half a century. As a player, he was one of the top rushing defensemen of his day and a team leader. Patrick was also an inspirational coach and a respected team administrator. Along with his brother Frank, he pioneered the construction of artificial rinks and formed the Pacific Coast Hockey Association.

Patrick first played shinny on the frozen ponds of his native Drummondville, Quebec, before his family moved to nearby Montreal. He learned the game in the amateur leagues of Montreal but first gained fame as a star offensive blueliner with Brandon, Manitoba, of the North West Hockey League. He was a key member of the squad when it issued an unsuccessful challenge for the Stanley Cup against the Ottawa Senators in March 1904.

He returned to Montreal to play a year with the Westmount club before joining the powerful Montreal Wanderers in 1905–06. He was an instant success and helped his new club dethrone the Senators as Cup holders that same season. Patrick helped the Wanderers repeat as champions the next year. His exceptional passes benefited the likes of Ernie Russell and Cecil Blanchford.

He moved to Nelson, British Columbia, in 1907 to work in the family lumber business but continued to play on a local team. Patrick returned to the headlines with the Edmonton squad that lost a Stanley Cup challenge to the Wanderers in 1908. His brother Frank joined him at this time.

The Patrick brothers played with the Renfrew Creamery Kings during the inaugural season of the National Hockey Association in 1909–10. The following season, they returned to British Columbia and began plans for a new league of their own. Formed in 1911–12, the Pacific Coast Hockey Association attained a reputation on par with the NHA—and later the NHL—until it was renamed the Western Canada Hockey League. The Patricks lured away many top stars of the NHA to give their new loop instant legitimacy. Such icons as Cyclone Taylor and Newsy Lalonde thrived in

Patrick, Lester
D, 6´1˝, 180 lbs, b: Drummondville, Que., 12/30/1883, d: 6/1/1960

Season	Club, League	Regular Season					Playoffs				
		GP	G	A	Pts	PIM	GP	G	A	Pts	PIM
1903–04	Brandon Hockey Club, NWHL						2	0	0	0	*
1904–05	Westmount Academy, CAHL	8	4	0	4	*					
1905–06	Montreal Wanderers, ECAHA	9	17	0	17	26	2	3	0	3	3
1906–07	Montreal Wanderers, ECAHA	9	11	0	11	11	6	10	0	10	32
1907–08	Nelson Seniors, BCHL						2	1	0	1	*
1909–10	Renfrew Creamery Kings, NHA	12	23	0	23	25					
1911–12	Victoria Aristocrats, PCHA	16	10	0	10	9					
1912–13	Victoria Aristocrats, PCHA	15	14	5	19	12	3	4	0	4	*
1913–14	Victoria Aristocrats, PCHA	9	5	5	10	0	3	2	0	2	*
1914–15	Victoria Aristocrats, PCHA	17	12	5	17	15					
1915–16	Victoria Aristocrats, PCHA	18	13	11	24	27					
1916–17	Spokane Canaries, PCHA	23	10	11	21	15					
1917–18	Seattle Metropolitans, PCHA	17	2	8	10	15	2	0	1	1	0
1918–19	Victoria Cougars, PCHA	9	2	5	7	0					
1919–20	Victoria Cougars, PCHA	11	2	2	4	3					
1920–21	Victoria Cougars, PCHA	5	2	3	5	13					
1921–22	Victoria Cougars, PCHA	2	0	0	0	0					
1925–26	Victoria Cougars, WHL	23	5	8	13	20	1	0	0	0	2
1926–27	New York Rangers, NHL	1	0	0	0	2					
	NHL Totals	1	0	0	0	2					
	NHA Totals	12	23	0	23	25					
	PCHA Totals	142	72	55	127	109	8	6	1	7	0
	WHL Totals	23	5	8	13	20	1	0	0	0	2

PCHA First All-Star Team (1913, 1915, 1916, 1917)
PCHA Second All-Star Team (1918, 1920)
Won Stanley Cup (1906, 1907)

the wide-open style of the PCHA. Many considered it to be the most exhilarating pro league ever.

The brothers were also innovators. They sold the lumber company to finance the construction of the country's first artificial ice rinks in Vancouver and Victoria. As a player in the PCHA, Lester Patrick skated chiefly for the Victoria Cougars but also suited up briefly for the Seattle Metropolitans and the Spokane club.

He retired in 1922 to focus on managerial responsibilities but returned to help anchor Victoria's defense in 1925–26. Following the demise of the Western Hockey League at the end of that season, he joined the expansion New York Rangers as coach and general manager after the club's brass let Conn Smythe go because they were worried he hadn't assembled a sufficiently competitive roster.

The Rangers won the Stanley Cup in the club's second year. During the finals against the Montreal Maroons, the 44-year-old Patrick saw emergency duty in goal after Lorne Chabot was injured in the second game. The Rangers won the Cup again in 1933 and Patrick continued to guide them until 1939, when he stepped aside to focus strictly on his duties as general manager. Arguably the finest bench boss of the 1930s, he earned selection as coach of the NHL First All-Star Team six times. He was on hand when the team won its third Stanley Cup in 1940 and remained its GM until 1946.

After leaving the NHL, Patrick took over the operation of the Victoria Cougars, a minor professional outfit in the Pacific Coast/Western Hockey League. He left that post for retirement in 1954. Patrick was inducted into the Hockey Hall of Fame in 1947. Since 1966, the NHL has presented the Lester Patrick Award to honor a recipient's contribution to hockey in the United States.

The Rangers' playoff run in 1927 included the 44-year-old New York coach and general manager Lester Patrick's emergency duty in goal after Lorne Chabot was injured.

Frank McGee

One-eyed Frank McGee was the cornerstone of one of the greatest teams in hockey history. During his tenure with the Ottawa Hockey Club and Ottawa Silver Seven, the franchise won or defended the Stanley Cup over three consecutive years from 1903 to 1905. McGee's superior puckhandling skills and gifted scoring touch made him one of the most feared offensive threats of his day. At a time when the forward pass wasn't legal, McGee's remarkable talent as a stickhandler was all the more crucial to his team's success.

While growing up in his home town of Ottawa, McGee demonstrated a tremendous ability in a number of sports. In addition to dominating on the ice, he proved to be a formidable rugby player with the college and city teams. Although he lost an eye during an on-ice mishap, McGee progressed to the top level of hockey in the country and began carving a place in the folklore of the game.

McGee enjoyed a successful Canadian Amateur Hockey League debut with Ottawa on January 17, 1903, by scoring two goals in a 7–1 victory over the famous Montreal Amateur Athletic Association. This proved to be a prelude to an even greater achievement as he netted five goals against the Montreal Victorias three weeks later. A month after this, Ottawa captured the Stanley Cup at the expense of the Victorias and successfully defended a challenge from Rat Portage (later Kenora, Ontario). During the four games against these two clubs, McGee scored seven times and established a reputation for being at his best in Stanley Cup matches. A short time later, the Ottawa club became known as the "Silver Seven." The name was a tribute to the success attained by an outstanding unit of seven players that often changed—except for Frank McGee.

The 1904 and 1905 seasons witnessed an even greater period of success for McGee. On February 25, 1904, he scored a then record five goals in the second game of Ottawa's successful Stanley Cup defense against the Toronto Marlboros. He duplicated this achievement a month later while helping to defeat the Stanley Cup aspirations of Brandon, Manitoba.

The Silver Seven won the championship of the Federal Amateur Hockey League in 1905 with Frank McGee leading the way with 17 goals in only six games. In January, Ottawa successfully beat back the challenge of Dawson City. It was in this series that McGee put forth his most legendary performance by scoring a Stanley Cup record of 14 goals in the second match. During the 23–2 rout, the Ottawa star at one point recorded eight consecutive goals in less than nine minutes. A month later, he scored the winning goal in the third and deciding game versus the challengers from Rat Portage—while playing with a broken wrist.

One-eyed Frank McGee was one of the most feared offensive threats of his day.

The following year, McGee enjoyed a strong regular season with 28 goals in seven games. His last memorable showing in Stanley Cup competition took place in February and March 1906 when he scored six goals in a two-game sweep of Queen's University and then recorded nine goals during a two-game annihilation of Smiths Falls. At the end of March, the Silver Seven's three-year stranglehold on the Stanley Cup came to an end following a two-game series against the Montreal Wanderers. Ottawa fell short by a 12–10 aggregate score, but McGee played particularly well in the second match.

McGee retired prior to the commencement of the 1907 season. He was the focal point of one of hockey's early dynasties and his superior abilities enabled him to form potent forward combinations with the likes of Billy Gilmour, Hamby Shore and Alf, Tommy and Harry Smith. Frank Patrick said: "He was even better than they say he was. He'd everything—speed, stickhandling, scoring ability and was a punishing checker. He was strongly built but beautifully proportioned and he'd an almost animal rhythm."

McGee died serving his country at Courcelette, France, during World War I. One of hockey's greatest scorers, he was among the first group of players inducted into the Hockey Hall of Fame in 1945.

Art ROSS

In addition to an exemplary career as a defenseman, Art Ross contributed to the development of hockey through his off-ice endeavors. Ross recorded 58 goals in 131 regular-season games and provided stability and savvy in the defensive zone. He won the Stanley Cup twice as a player and later added another in his 18 years behind the bench. Ross also improved the construction of goal nets and the design of the puck.

Ross was born in northern Ontario, the son of a Hudson's Bay trading post manager. He learned to skate on Whitefish Bay using rudimentary equipment. After leaving home, his formative years in sports were spent in Montreal, Quebec, and Brandon, Manitoba. While in Montreal, he carved out a reputation as a local sports legend by excelling at hockey, football, baseball, boxing, soccer and trapshooting. In 1905 Ross made his first appearance for a major hockey organization by scoring 10 goals in eight games for the Westmount franchise in the Canadian Amateur Hockey League. He rapidly earned the distinction of being one of the top rushing defensemen in the game.

The following year he skated for Brandon of the Manitoba Hockey League. Ross's play attracted the attention of the Kenora Thistles, who worked out a loan agreement with Brandon in time for their Stanley Cup challenge against the Montreal Wanderers in January 1907. During the two-game set, he received numerous ovations from the Montreal crowd. Although he didn't score, Ross made a number of quality offensive rushes that contributed to Kenora's Stanley Cup win.

Art Ross was excellent at hockey, football, baseball, boxing, soccer and trapshooting.

A year later, Ross's services were purchased by the Wanderers in a move that strengthened an already formidable outfit. Ross was a key reason the Red Bands finished at the top of the Eastern Canada Amateur Hockey Association standings and then beat back the Stanley Cup challenges from Winnipeg, Toronto and Edmonton.

Ross next spent a few months with the All-Montreal squad in the short-lived Canadian Hockey Association. By January 1910, the National Hockey Association was the preeminent league in the country and Ross was signed by the Haileybury franchise. After a season in Ontario's mining country, Ross returned to the Wanderers, where he played another four years. During the 1911 players' uprising against the owners, he was a strong and eloquent voice in the quest to attain a fair share of revenues for the athletes. He followed with two years in Ottawa, where he introduced the "kitty bar the door" defensive alignment that baffled teams preferring a freewheeling offensive game. He then returned to Montreal to close out his playing career with the Wanderers.

After retiring as a player, Ross took a turn as an on-ice official before moving into coaching and management. He landed his first coaching position with the Hamilton Tigers' senior club, where he demonstrated that not all of his ability was left behind on the ice. When Charles F. Adams secured an NHL franchise for the Boston area, he jumped at the chance to offer Ross the coach's job.

Between 1924 and 1954, Ross served as either coach or manager of the Boston Bruins. Over this period the club finished at the top of the league standings 10 times and captured the Stanley Cup on three occasions. He was the driving force behind the Bruins' ability to acquire such future stars as Eddie Shore and Milt Schmidt. It was while serving in his administrative capacities that Ross argued successfully for

Ross, Art
D, 5′11″, 190 lbs, b: Naughton, Ont., 1/13/1886, d: 8/5/1964

Season	Club, League	Regular Season					Playoffs				
		GP	G	A	Pts	PIM	GP	G	A	Pts	PIM
1904–05	Montreal Merchants, CAHL	8	10	0	10	*					
1905–06	Brandon Kings, MHL Sr.	7	6	0	6	*					
1906–07	Brandon Kings, MHL Sr.	9	5	0	5	*	2	1	0	1	0
	Kenora Thistles, MHL Sr.						2	0	0	0	0
1907–08	Montreal Wanderers, ECAHA	10	8	0	8	27	5	3	0	3	23
	Pembroke Lumber Kings, Ott-Sr.	1	5	0	5	*					
1908–09	Montreal Wanderers, ECHA	9	2	0	2	30	2	0	0	0	13
	Montreal Wanderers, NYSHL	2	2	0	2	3					
	Cobalt Silver Kings, TPHL						2	1	0	1	0
1909–10	Haileybury Silver Kings, NHA	12	6	0	6	25					
	All-Montreal, CHA	4	4	0	4	3					
1910–11	Montreal Wanderers, NHA	11	4	0	4	24					
1911–12	Montreal Wanderers, NHA	18	16	0	16	35					
1912–13	Montreal Wanderers, NHA	19	11	0	11	58					
1913–14	Montreal Wanderers, NHA	18	4	5	9	74					
1914–15	Ottawa Senators, NHA	16	3	1	4	55	5	2	0	2	0
1915–16	Ottawa Senators, NHA	21	8	8	16	69					
1916–17	Montreal Wanderers, NHA	16	6	2	8	66					
1917–18	Montreal Wanderers, NHL	3	1	0	1	12					
	NHL Totals	3	1	0	1	12					
	NHA Totals	131	58	17	75	403	5	2	0	2	0

Won Lester Patrick Trophy (1984)
Won Stanley Cup (1907, 1908)

the adoption of synthetic as opposed to natural rubber pucks. He also brought about the replacement of the league's square goal nets with a rounded-back version, complete with superior mesh.

Ross was a multidimensional influence in hockey. As a tribute to him, the NHL introduced the trophy bearing his name in 1947–48 to be awarded annually to the league's top scorer. The B-shaped net he brought into being lasted until the 1980s, while his synthetic bevel-edged puck was still in use in the late 1990s. In 1945 Ross was part of the first group of players elected to the newly founded Hockey Hall of Fame.

Frank Patrick

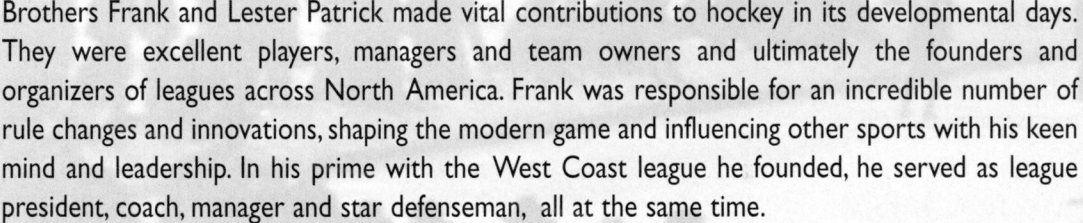

Frank Patrick was responsible for an incredible number of rule changes and innovations.

Brothers Frank and Lester Patrick made vital contributions to hockey in its developmental days. They were excellent players, managers and team owners and ultimately the founders and organizers of leagues across North America. Frank was responsible for an incredible number of rule changes and innovations, shaping the modern game and influencing other sports with his keen mind and leadership. In his prime with the West Coast league he founded, he served as league president, coach, manager and star defenseman, all at the same time.

Frank Patrick was born on December 21, 1885, two years after Lester, and grew up in Montreal. He attended McGill University and earned varsity letters in hockey, track and football before his graduation with a bachelor of arts degree. During his university days, he was also prominent as a referee, officiating in the Montreal Senior Hockey League. He refereed his first Stanley Cup game at the age of 20. As a player, Frank was revolutionary, much like Lester, who was then a star with the Montreal Wanderers. In the years prior to the Patricks' rise, the position of defense was used strictly to protect a team's own goal. Together, they were the first defensemen to rush with the puck and play an offensive role. The family moved to Nelson, British Columbia, where the brothers continued to win converts to their rushing style.

Lester's amateur career was cut short when he received three telegrams at his home in British Columbia. All three were invitations to turn pro, with Ottawa, Montreal and the Renfrew Millionaires. He responded to the Renfrew offer by asking for $3,000, an unheard-of sum, because he didn't really want to play in such a small place. He also wanted a guarantee that Frank could play as well, for $2,000. Renfrew acquiesced. When Frank was introduced as a Millionaire, he was called the best defenseman in the world. Still only 24, he was very likely just that. He was a tricky stickhandler and lightning fast moving out of his own zone. He scored goals like a skilled forward and had the speed to retreat and defend if necessary. Frank teamed with Cyclone Taylor in Renfrew, playing the defensive positions known then as point and cover point.

Following their first year in Renfrew, Lester and Frank met with their father shortly after the elder Patrick sold the family lumber company. Frank advocated beginning a league on the West Coast, using the proceeds from the sale of the business to build artificial rinks in a part of the country where the sport was little known and rarely played. Lester at first disagreed, afraid the idea wasn't financially feasible, but their father backed Frank's idea. They spent $350,000 on a 10,000-seat arena in Vancouver, creating what was at the time the largest building in Canada, and another $125,000 on a rink in Victoria that accommodated 4,200.

The league was called the Pacific Coast Hockey Association and it began play in 1911–12. Frank was in charge of the Vancouver Millionaires as well as being the league president. In the league's second year, Frank convinced his former defense partner, Cyclone Taylor, to join his team, giving the young league a boost of star power. That season, Patrick scored six goals in one game, establishing a record that has never been surpassed by NHL defenders. Frank was the leader, on the ice and in the boardroom, of a Vancouver team that won the Stanley Cup.

The innovations Frank brought to hockey during the formation and development of the PCHA are key components of the modern game. He introduced the blue line, the forward pass and the playoff system, a change adopted by other leagues and sports around the world. Together with Lester, he began using numbers on players' sweaters and in programs to help fans identify the skaters. They allowed the puck to be kicked (everywhere but into the net) and allowed goaltenders to fall to the ice to make a save, if need be, instead of forcing them to remain standing. They were responsible for crediting assists when a goal was scored and they invented the penalty shot. In all, Frank was credited with 22 changes that remain in the NHL rulebook to this day. It's no wonder he was called "the brains of modern hockey."

The PCHA, however, as Lester had foreseen, had a difficult time financially. Frank played fewer and fewer games as he took care of the business side of the league. With only two teams remaining in 1924, Vancouver and Victoria joined the Western Canada Hockey League. Two years later, with professional hockey all but dead in the west, Frank arranged the sale of the six teams' players to the NHL for the substantial sum of $250,000. Frank stayed out west even though offers to join the new NHL teams were numerous. Lester accepted one of the offers and began a long and successful tenure as coach and then manager of the New York Rangers. Frank did move east in 1933 to act as managing director of the NHL. He then coached the Boston Bruins for two seasons from 1934 to 1936, and after a brief move back to British Columbia, he took over the business operations of the Montreal Canadiens in 1939. He left the team after a heart seizure in 1941.

Frank was inducted into the Hall of Fame in 1958 in the Builders category. On June 1, 1960, Lester passed away after a battle with cancer. Less than a month later, on June 29, Frank was gone as well, the victim of a heart attack. He was 74. With the sport popular around the world, it's hard to imagine hockey without the entertaining and practical innovations introduced by Frank Patrick.

With the West Coast league Frank Patrick founded, he was a league president, a coach, a manager and a star defenseman, all at the same time.

Edouard "Newsy" *Lalonde*

A remarkable scorer who could also play a rough style of hockey, Edouard "Newsy" Lalonde was one of the premier forwards in the early days of the NHL. His tenacity on the ice became as legendary as his natural affinity for putting the puck in the net. Throughout his hockey career, Lalonde was also the nation's best lacrosse player. In fact, had he not been allowed to play both, Lalonde's hockey exploits might never have happened, since lacrosse paid much better. But during his hockey-playing days, he earned a reputation as one of the game's bad boys because he knew how to take care of himself. Dick Beddoes wrote that "Lalonde was a survivor of a truly permissive age when hockey was genuinely a mug's racket, mottled with roughnecks who preferred to drink an opponent's blood at body temperature, or near there."

Newsy Lalonde was a remarkable scorer who could also play a rough style of hockey.

The native of Cornwall, Ontario, earned his nickname by working in a local newsprint plant as a youth. He excelled at his two chosen sports and made his debut in organized hockey with Cornwall in 1905. This squad was known as the "Sweepers" because the players cleared the ice in lieu of renting it. Lalonde next moved to Woodstock, in southwestern Ontario, where his outstanding play at center caught the attention of several scouts.

Unexpected to Newsy, an offer came from the Sault Ste. Marie franchise in the International Hockey League, the first professional circuit in North America. More important to Lalonde was that his first pro game was almost his last. He arrived by train just in time for the game and was slammed into the fence on one of his first shifts. He was slumped on the bench when a boxer named Jack Hammond handed him a bottle and told him to have a swig. It burned Lalonde's mouth and throat but he returned to play just the same. It turned out that Hammond intended to give him a drink of whiskey but passed him ammonia instead. Lalonde was barely able to eat the week after the accident.

The team across the river in Sault Ste. Marie, Michigan, tried to obtain his services, but the Canadian Soo matched the American offer and kept the young star in town. In 1907 Lalonde joined the Toronto club of the newly formed Ontario Professional Hockey League. This was where he first gained wide attention by winning the scoring race with 32 goals in only nine matches. The Toronto squad captured the inaugural OPHL crown that year but lost out to the Montreal Wanderers in the Stanley Cup challenge.

Lalonde played a second year in Toronto before moving closer to his roots to suit up for the newly formed Montreal Canadiens National Hockey Association franchise in 1910. Partway through the season he was traded to the Renfrew Millionaires, but this only enhanced his performance. On March 11, 1910, he scored nine goals in one game, an NHA record that was never beaten and only equaled by Tommy Smith. He also won the league's inaugural scoring title.

In 1911–12, Lalonde headed west to play with the Vancouver Millionaires of the Pacific Coast Hockey Association, where he led the league with 27 goals. The next year he returned to the Canadiens and won another NHA scoring championship. His offensive gifts were a significant factor behind the franchise's first Stanley Cup title in 1915–16.

Lalonde remained with the Canadiens when the club joined the NHL in 1917–18. His scoring continued and he led all NHL scorers in 1918–19 and 1920–21. On January 19, 1920, he

Lalonde, Edouard "Newsy"
C, 5´9″, 168 lbs, b: Cornwall, Ont., 10/31/1888, d: 11/21/1971

Season	Club, League	Regular Season					Playoffs				
		GP	G	A	Pts	PIM	GP	G	A	Pts	PIM
1906–07	Canadian Soo, IHL	18	29	4	33	27					
1907–08	Portage la Prairie, MHL Sr.	1	0	0	0	0					
	Toronto Professionals, OPHL	9	32	0	32	37	1	2	0	2	*
	Haileybury Silver Kings, TPHL						1	3	0	3	0
1908–09	Toronto Professionals, OPHL	11	29	0	29	79					
1909–10	Montreal Canadiens, NHA	6	16	0	16	40					
	Renfrew Creamery Kings, NHA	5	22	0	22	16					
1910–11	Montreal Canadiens, NHA	16	19	0	19	63					
1911–12	Vancouver Millionaires, PCHA	15	27	0	27	51					
1912–13	Montreal Canadiens, NHA	18	25	0	25	61					
1913–14	Montreal Canadiens, NHA	14	22	5	27	23	2	0	0	0	2
1914–15	Montreal Canadiens, NHA	7	4	3	7	17					
1915–16	Montreal Canadiens, NHA	24	28	6	34	78	4	3	0	3	41
1916–17	Montreal Canadiens, NHA	18	28	7	35	61	5	2	0	2	47
1917–18	Montreal Canadiens, NHL	14	23	7	30	51	2	4	2	6	17
1918–19	Montreal Canadiens, NHL	17	22	10	32	40	5	11	2	13	6
1919–20	Montreal Canadiens, NHL	23	37	9	46	34					
1920–21	Montreal Canadiens, NHL	24	33	10	43	36					
1921–22	Montreal Canadiens, NHL	20	9	5	14	20					
1922–23	Saskatoon Sheiks, WCHL	29	30	4	34	44					
1923–24	Saskatoon Crescents, WCHL	21	10	10	20	24					
1924–25	Saskatoon Crescents, WCHL	22	8	6	14	42	2	0	0	0	4
1925–26	Saskatoon Crescents, WHL	3	0	0	0	2	2	0	0	0	2
1926–27	New York Americans, NHL	1	0	0	0	2					
1927–28	Quebec Castors, Can-Am	1	0	0	0	0					
	NHL Totals	99	124	41	165	183	7	15	4	19	23
	NHA Totals	108	163	19	182	351	12	5	0	5	56
	PCHA Totals	15	27	0	27	51					
	WCHL/WHL Totals	75	48	20	68	112	4	0	0	0	6

PCHA First All-Star Team (1912)
WCHL First All-Star Team (1924)
NHL Scoring Leader (1919, 1921)
Won Stanley Cup (1916)

scored six goals in one game. Ten days later he embarrassed himself by scoring on his own net. During a game against the Quebec Bulldogs, Lalonde thought he heard a whistle and playfully deked the puck past teammate Georges Vezina. Unfortunately, the play hadn't been blown dead. Later in the period, Lalonde made up for his miscue by firing the winning goal.

After a falling out with Canadiens owner Leo Dandurand, he was traded to the Saskatoon Sheiks for Aurel Joliat in a move that benefited both parties. In his first year in Saskatchewan, player-coach Lalonde added the Western Canada Hockey League scoring title to his list of accomplishments. Lester Patrick once said, "The only way to stop him from scoring was to have three or four players—more if you could spare them—skate him to the side and picket him."

Newsy Lalonde was inducted into the Hockey Hall of Fame in 1950.

Lalonde returned to the NHL as coach of the New York Americans in 1927. He also coached the Ottawa Senators and Montreal Canadiens before leaving the game for good in 1935. He was inducted into the Hockey Hall of Fame in 1950. That same year he was chosen Canada's top lacrosse player of the first half of the century. In November 1971 he suffered a hip injury and later that month passed away in a Montreal convalescent home.

Hobart "Hobey" Baker

Hobart Amery Hare "Hobey" Baker was arguably the first hockey legend born in the United States. His standard of achievement both on and off the ice elevated him to unique status in that country's hockey world. Baker's most passionate conviction was that the game should be played with the utmost sportsmanship in addition to skill to preserve its integrity.

John Davis wrote the following in *The Legend of Hobey Baker*: "Like his contemporaries Jim Thorpe, Ty Cobb, and Jack Johnson, Hobey Baker was a fabulous athlete; like them he'd a great physique, fantastic reflexes, instant coordination of hand and eye, iron discipline, blazing courage. But to these rare abilities he added another dimension all his own…during his career at Princeton and St. Nick's, he was a college athlete supreme: the gentleman sportsman, the amateur in the pure sense of playing the game 'pour le sport,' who never fouled, despised publicity, and refused professional offers."

Born in Wisahicton, Pennsylvania, in 1892, Baker spent two years at St. Paul's School in Concord, New Hampshire, from 1908 to 1910. It was here that he first crafted the reputation of being a tremendous and versatile athlete as well as a gentleman in competition. Baker vowed to take his skating and puckhandling ability to the highest level in order to compensate for his lack of size.

By the time he entered Princeton University in 1910, Baker was an extremely well-rounded sportsman. As a freshman, however, he was too busy displaying his proficiency in football, swimming,

Hobey Baker was the first hockey legend born in the United States.

track, gymnastics and golf to devote any time to hockey. The next year he skated a bit more and made the varsity hockey team, where he exhibited the blazing speed and stickhandling wizardry for which he later became famous.

The budding star led the Tigers through an undefeated season in 1911–12 that culminated in an intercollegiate championship. As a rover, he was given the freedom to improvise and display his immense ability all over the ice. Baker became well known for his end-to-end rushes and an unheard-of level of stamina that enabled him to dominate an entire game. He was such a one-man show at times that the Princeton squad came to be known as "Baker and Six Other Players."

His high-quality performance was augmented by his sincere concern if any fouls took place in a game, even if he wasn't directly involved. He also made a habit of venturing into the opposition's dressing room after the game to congratulate them on a fine effort.

Baker left college on a high note by captaining the Tigers to another collegiate title in his senior year of 1913–14. He also served as captain of the school's varsity football team, where he received accolades equal to those he earned while starring on the ice. Throughout his entire college program, he matched his athletic achievements with exemplary scholastic results, becoming a role model for students whether or not they were involved in sports.

Hobey Baker was awarded the Croix de Guerre for his superior conduct under fire.

Following his graduation, Baker suited up for the St. Nicholas amateur team in New York City, where each player was required to pay his own way to participate. Although he caught the attention of professional clubs, Baker's intention was always to play hockey for the sheer enjoyment of it. He left the game during World War I and distinguished himself as a pilot. He was awarded the Croix de Guerre for his superior conduct under fire. Tragically, Baker lost his life as a result of a post-war flying accident in Toul, France.

The various symbols of achievement affiliated with his name provide testimony to Baker's remarkable legacy. The Hobey Baker Memorial Award is presented annually to the outstanding collegiate hockey player in the United States. Each year the Hobey Baker Stick is awarded at his old prep school in Concord, while the Princeton Tigers named their hockey arena after their most famous player. Baker is a member of the United States Hockey Hall of Fame and the Pro Football Hall of Fame. In 1945 he was part of the initial group of players inducted into the Hockey Hall of Fame.

"HOBEY" BAKER MEETS DEATH IN FRANCE

Killed in Airplane Crash Near Toul, France

FORMER PRINCETON STAR

Captain Hobart A. H. Baker, the famous Princeton athlete, known in his college days as "Hobey" Baker, an aviator in the American army in France, has been killed in the fall of his plane. News of his death was received yesterday by his friend, Percy Pyne.

Mr. Pyne received a cable message from Paris signed "Inglehart," a member of Baker's air squadron, which said that Captain Baker had been killed in an airplane acident, and requested that his family be notified. No details were given.

Captain Baker was 27 years old. He began his athletic career at St. Paul's school, Concord, Mass., where he learned to play hockey, a sport in which he later excelled; in fact, he was considered one of the best, if not the best, hockey player in the United States.

Joe "Phantom" Malone

One of the most gifted and prolific goal scorers ever to play the game, Joe Malone became an enduring legend for decades after his retirement. While known for his unique upright skating style and revered for his excellent conduct on the ice, what set "Phantom" Joe Malone apart from the rest was an ability to find openings and weave his way through the defensive alignments of the opposition. Deceptively quick, Malone was the fastest player in the pros and possessed a lethal instinct around the net.

A native of Sillery, a suburb of Quebec City, Malone grew up on the shores of the St. Lawrence River. He was a well-rounded athlete, playing hockey, lacrosse and baseball as a boy. At 17, he played with the Quebec City Crescents in his first organized hockey game. In 1909 Malone graduated to the Quebec Bulldogs of the Eastern Canada Amateur Hockey Association, where he offered a preview of his future brilliance by accounting for eight goals in 12 games. The following year Malone played two games in Quebec, but the team ceased operations when it refused to join the newly formed National Hockey Association. He finished up the 1909–10 season with Waterloo of the Ontario Professional Hockey League.

Quebec reacquired Malone when they joined the NHA in 1911 and immediately installed him as captain. The Phantom enjoyed an outstanding seven-year career with the Bulldogs, during which the club won the Stanley Cup twice and Malone led the league in scoring for three years. The team emerged as Stanley Cup winners after taking the regular-season title in 1912. In March of that year, the Bulldogs crushed the challengers from Moncton, New Brunswick, with Malone and linemate Jack McDonald accumulating 14 of the team's 17 goals.

The 1912–13 season witnessed a powerful offensive display by Malone as he won the scoring race with 43 goals in 20 games. He centered a dominant forward line with Tommy Smith and Jack Marks. His Quebec team romped to a first-place finish in the regular season and went on to humiliate Sydney, Nova Scotia, in the Stanley Cup finals, with Malone scoring a stunning nine goals in the first match on March 8, 1913. And he continued to score at an unprecedented pace over the next four seasons, earning another scoring title in 1917.

The Bulldogs didn't join the NHL when it was formed in December 1917 and Malone soon found himself playing left wing in a Montreal Canadiens uniform. He scored a personal-best 44 goals in 20 games as part of an outstanding line with Newsy Lalonde and Didier Pitre.

Malone remained with the Canadiens for one more season before returning to Quebec

Joe Malone was one of the most prolific goal scorers ever to play the game.

Malone, Joe "Phantom"
C/LW, 5'10", 150 lbs, b: Quebec City, Que., 2/28/1890, d: 5/15/1969

Season	Club, League	Regular Season					Playoffs				
		GP	G	A	Pts	PIM	GP	G	A	Pts	PIM
1908–09	Quebec Bulldogs, ECHA	12	8	0	8	17					
1909–10	Quebec Bulldogs, ECHA	2	5	0	5	3					
	Waterloo Professionals, OPHL	11	9	0	9	10					
1910–11	Quebec Bulldogs, NHA	13	9	0	9	3					
1911–12	Quebec Bulldogs, NHA	18	21	0	21	0	2	5	0	5	0
1912–13	Quebec Bulldogs, NHA	20	43	0	43	34	4	9	0	9	0
1913–14	Quebec Bulldogs, NHA	17	24	4	28	20					
1914–15	Quebec Bulldogs, NHA	12	16	5	21	21					
1915–16	Quebec Bulldogs, NHA	24	25	10	35	21					
1916–17	Quebec Bulldogs, NHA	19	41	8	49	15					
1917–18	Montreal Canadiens, NHL	20	44	4	48	30	2	1	0	1	3
1918–19	Montreal Canadiens, NHL	8	7	2	9	3	5	5	0	5	0
1919–20	Quebec Bulldogs, NHL	24	39	10	49	12					
1920–21	Hamilton Tigers, NHL	20	28	9	37	6					
1921–22	Hamilton Tigers, NHL	24	24	7	31	4					
1922–23	Montreal Canadiens, NHL	20	1	0	1	2	2	0	0	0	0
1923–24	Montreal Canadiens, NHL	10	0	0	0	0					
	NHL Totals	126	143	32	175	57	9	5	1	6	3
	NHA Totals	123	179	26	205	111	6	14	0	14	0

NHL Scoring Leader (1918, 1920)
Won Stanley Cup (1912, 1913, 1924)

for the 1919–20 schedule. It was during his last game for his hometown club against Toronto that Malone scored seven goals to establish an NHL record never matched, even by the likes of Richard, Hull, Esposito, Gretzky or Lemieux.

Malone spent the 1920–21 and 1921–22 seasons with the Hamilton Tigers, where he assumed the dual responsibilities of player and coach. He demonstrated that his offensive skill was still intact by recording 52 goals in 44 games over the two seasons. After refusing to attend the Tigers' training camp in 1922, Malone was sent back to Montreal and spent his last two years as a substitute with the Montreal Canadiens. The team won the Stanley Cup during his final NHL season in 1923–24.

One of hockey's most naturally gifted scorers, Malone totaled 344 goals in 274 regular-season contests between 1909 and 1924. He scored five or more goals in a single game 10 times in his career. Malone is a member of the Canadian Sports Hall of Fame and was inducted into the Hockey Hall of Fame in 1950.

Harry "Hap" Holmes

One of the preeminent netminders of his era, Hap Holmes excelled in all five of the top pro leagues from 1912 to 1928. He made an impact in the National Hockey Association, Pacific Coast Hockey Association, Western Canada Hockey League, Western Hockey League and National Hockey League. A sterling playoff performer, Holmes backstopped two Stanley Cup wins in Toronto and one each in Seattle and Victoria. He was the leading goalie six times in the Pacific Coast Hockey Association/Western Canada Hockey League when such rivals as Hugh Lehman and George Hainsworth were still on the ice. In Stanley Cup play, he out-dueled such legends as Georges Vezina and Clint Benedict. Holmes was also one of the top lacrosse goalies of his day and often played semipro in the summer. Ultimately he decided to focus more on hockey. It was said that he was a serious competitor who never smiled and consequently was labeled "nerveless."

Harry Holmes was a goaltender who never smiled and was labeled "nerveless."

Before turning pro, the native of Aurora, Ontario, played with the Toronto-based Canoe Club, Parkdale Canoe Club and Tecumsehs. He debuted in the NHA with the Toronto Blueshirts in 1912–13 and enjoyed an outstanding sophomore year by leading the league in wins and helping the club become the first Toronto team to win the Stanley Cup.

Early in the 1915–16 season, he joined the Seattle Metropolitans with former Toronto mates Jack Walker and Frank Foyston. Once again Holmes was a part of history when he backstopped the Metropolitans to the first Stanley Cup won by a U.S.-based outfit. Holmes continued his knack of being in the right place at the right time when he was loaned to the Toronto Arenas in January 1918; he helped the club win the Stanley Cup in the inaugural NHL season.

Holmes returned to Seattle for the 1918–19 season and remained for more than five years. In his first year back, he was present during the tragic final series against the Canadiens that was called off due to the global influenza epidemic. The fourth game of the series was arguably his finest performance. Following a scoreless 60 minutes of regulation time and 20 minutes of overtime, referee Mickey Ion declared the game a draw.

Holmes ventured east again with Seattle in 1920 to challenge Ottawa for the Stanley Cup. Despite his brilliance, the westerners lost a close series to the powerhouse Senators. He led the PCHA in shutouts four times and in wins on two occasions. He enjoyed two successful years with the Victoria Cougars from 1924 to 1926, leading the WCHL/WHL in his goals-against average.

In 1924–25, his brilliance led Victoria past the Saskatoon Sheiks in the WCHL playoffs. In the Stanley Cup championship match with the Montreal Canadiens, Holmes starred along with Jack Walker and Frank Frederickson as Victoria became the last non-NHL team to win the Stanley Cup. The heroic netminder became the first goalie to win the Cup with four different franchises. That year he also attained his own personal triumph over Habs netminder Georges Vezina, against whom he'd waged the memorable but undecided battle in the 1919 championship series.

Following the disbanding of the WHL in 1926, players headed to the enlarged NHL. The expansion Detroit Cougars were the benefactors of Holmes' last two years as an active player. He recorded 17 shutouts in two seasons and proved to be a veteran workhorse who helped give the young NHL side some confidence.

Holmes passed away while vacationing in Florida in 1940. A few months later, the Harry Holmes Memorial Trophy was inaugurated to honor the top goalie in the American Hockey League. He was posthumously inducted into the Hockey Hall of Fame in 1972.

Holmes, Harry "Hap"
G, 5′10″, 170 lbs, b: Aurora, Ont., 2/21/1892, d: 6/27/1941

Season	Club, League	Regular Season				Playoffs			
		GP	Mins	GA	Avg	GP	Mins	GA	Avg
1909–10	Toronto Canoe Club, OHA Sr.	4	240	26	6.50				
1910–11	Toronto Parkdale Canoe Club, OHA Sr.	4	240	12	3.00	2	120	9	4.50
1911–12	Toronto Tecumsehs, Sr.	1	60	3	3.00				
1912–13	Toronto Blueshirts, NHA	15	779	58	4.47				
1913–14	Toronto Blueshirts, NHA	20	1204	65	3.24	5	315	10	1.90
1914–15	Toronto Blueshirts, NHA	20	1218	84	4.18				
1915–16	Toronto Blueshirts, NHA	1	60	6	6.00				
	Seattle Metropolitans, PCHA	18	1080	66	3.67				
1916–17	Seattle Metropolitans, PCHA	24	1465	80	3.28	4	140	11	2.75
1917–18	Toronto Arenas, NHL	16	965	76	4.73	2	120	7	3.50
1918–19	Toronto Arenas, NHL	2	120	9	4.50				
	Seattle Metropolitans, PCHA	20	1225	46	2.25	2	120	5	2.50
1919–20	Seattle Metropolitans, PCHA	22	1340	55	2.46	2	120	3	1.50
1920–21	Seattle Metropolitans, PCHA	24	1551	68	2.63	2	120	13	6.50
1921–22	Seattle Metropolitans, PCHA	24	1479	64	2.60	2	120	2	1.00
1922–23	Seattle Metropolitans, PCHA	30	1844	106	3.45				
1923–24	Seattle Metropolitans, PCHA	30	1824	99	3.26	2	134	4	1.79
1924–25	Victoria Cougars, WCHL	28	1683	63	2.25	4	240	5	1.25
1925–26	Victoria Cougars, WHL	30	1894	53	1.68	4	249	6	1.45
1926–27	Detroit Cougars, NHL	41	2685	100	2.23				
1927–28	Detroit Cougars, NHL	44	2740	79	1.73				
	NHL Totals	103	6510	264	2.43	7	420	28	4.00
	NHA Totals	56	3261	213	3.92	5	3.15	10	1.90
	PCHA Totals	192	11808	584	2.96	24	1390	63	2.72
	WCHL/WHL Totals	58	3577	116	1.94	12	728	19	1.56

WCHL All-Star Team (1925)
PCHA Second All-Star Team (1916, 1917, 1919, 1920, 1921, 1922, 1923)
Won Stanley Cup (1914, 1917, 1918, 1925)

Sir Montagu Allan

Sir Montagu Allan—a native of Montreal, Quebec, and former president of the Montreal Jockey Club whose horses had won the prestigious Queen's Plate on numerous occasions—is synonymous with outstanding amateur hockey competition in Canada. His donation of a cup bearing his name in 1908 ensured that there would be a symbol to which many of the top amateur clubs in the nation could aspire each year.

When the Stanley Cup was restricted to professional clubs, a tremendous void suddenly opened up for amateur teams, who had no crown to fight for. The lack of a suitable amateur trophy was addressed by William Northey, a strong voice in the amateur hockey circles of Montreal. Northey successfully persuaded his friend, Sir Montagu Allan, to donate a trophy that would represent the highest level of achievement for amateur teams across Canada.

The Ottawa Cliffsides were the first holders of the Allan Cup, but they soon lost it after a series against Queen's University. At the time, all challenges for the Allan Cup had to be approved by a board of trustees. When the Canadian Amateur Hockey Association was formed in 1914, the Allan Cup was officially adopted by the new body as the preeminent senior amateur trophy in the country. Competition for the cup initially conformed to existing regulations, but 14 years later the Allan Cup was donated outright to the CAHA.

Sir Montagu Allan's contribution to hockey fostered one of Canada's oldest competitive traditions, involving communities from every corner of the country. On a number of occasions, the Allan Cup winners represented the nation at the World Hockey Championships or Olympic Games. The Winnipeg Falcons, Toronto Granites, Toronto Varsity Grads, Kimberley Dynamiters, Trail Smoke Eaters, Penticton Vees, Whitby Dunlops and Belleville McFarlands all followed up Allan Cup triumphs with Olympic or World Championship gold medal performances.

The name of Sir Montagu Allan is synonymous with amateur hockey competition in Canada.

After the formation of the Canadian national team program for international play in 1964, the Allan Cup became strictly a national senior competition. Although dreams of gold medal glory were dashed, local passion to bring the prize home to such places as Petrolia, Ontario, and Stephenville, Newfoundland, remained a powerful motivator for hockey players in senior leagues.

By the 1990s, the proliferation of minor professional leagues, particularly in the United States, diminished the number of players available for Canadian senior hockey. Nonetheless, the competition carried on until the Stony Plain Eagles became the last Allan Cup winners of the 20th century.

Sir Allan's significant contribution to the game was recognized in 1945 when he was elected as a charter member of the Hockey Hall of Fame in the Builders category. He passed away in September 1951, but as the new century dawned, the annual competition bearing his name continued to bring people together and his name will forever live on in amateur hockey lore, as Lord Stanley's does in the NHL's.

Jack Darragh

Jack Darragh was one of those old-time players who grew up, played and died in the same city—his home town of Ottawa, Ontario. Although he'd been skating since childhood, he didn't begin to play at a competitive level until he was a teenager and joined the Stewartons, a team that competed in one of the many local church leagues in Ottawa. From there he went to the Cliffsides of the city league, where he made such a great impression that he was offered a professional contract by the Senators, Ottawa's entry in the National Hockey Association, the precursor to the NHL.

Darragh was a rarity in that he played right wing but was a left-hand shot. While not an unusual strategy today, in the early days of the century, playing on the "wrong wing" was pioneering. He was a superb skater, a very clever stickhandler and had a good backhand shot. As a result, Darragh was a prolific scorer. In 1919–20, he scored 22 goals in 23 games, and over his 13-year pro career he averaged better than a goal every two games. Baz Bastien wrote of him: "Jack Darragh was a great speeder. Underway, Darragh could match strides with anybody. His famous rushes from the defense and backhanded shots are still fresh in my memory." In an era of fierce and often violent hockey, Darragh also had a reputation for being a pacifist.

Darragh won four Stanley Cup championships, all with the Ottawa Senators. His first victory came in 1911 during two challenges. On March 13 the Sens defeated Galt, which had won the Ontario Professional Hockey League title. The 7–4 score was generous to Galt and Darragh was acknowledged to have been one of the best players on the ice. Three days later the Sens had to defend their championship against the Port Arthur Bearcats after the Bearcats had beaten Prince Albert to earn the right to challenge. This time the Senators swamped Port Arthur 14–4, with Marty Walsh scoring 10 goals and Darragh anchoring the defense once again.

Darragh's Senators made only one other foray for the Cup during the years of the NHA. In March 1915 the Senators and the Canadiens were tied for top spot in the league. The two teams played a two-game, total-goals series that Ottawa won 4–1. But in the best-of-five finals against the Pacific Coast champions, the Vancouver Millionaires, the Sens were no match and lost in three lop-sided games.

While player movement in the early days of hockey was frequent—many players swapped teams between the NHA and PCHA—Darragh remained constant to Ottawa, a decision that reaped tremendous rewards once the NHA folded in 1917 and gave way to the NHL. In the spring of 1920, the Sens were champions of the new NHL and played the Seattle Metropolitans for the Stanley Cup. Although the best-of-five series was supposed to have been played entirely in Ottawa, mild weather forced the final two games to be shifted to the artificial ice of Toronto's Mutual Street Arena. In game one of the series, Darragh scored the game-winning goal in a 3–2 win, and in the fifth and deciding game for the Cup, he scored a hat-trick in a 6–1 clobbering of the Mets.

But as coach Tommy Gorman relates, Darragh's participation in the final game wasn't assured: "Jack Darragh was one of the most temperamental players that ever figured in the National Hockey League. Jack had a strange disposition and at times it was almost impossible to humor him. In fact, it was just through luck and good judgement that we attracted him back to Toronto for the final game of the memorable series of 1920. Following Ottawa's defeat in the first match at Toronto, Darragh threw down his skates and announced that he was going home to Ottawa. He dashed out of

Jack Darragh was one of the most temperamental players who ever figured in the NHL.

Darragh, Jack
RW, 5´10˝, 168 lbs, b: Ottawa, Ont., 12/4/1890, d: 6/25/1924

Season	Club, League	Regular Season					Playoffs				
		GP	G	A	Pts	PIM	GP	G	A	Pts	PIM
1909–10	Ottawa Cliffsides, City Sr.						3	4	0	4	0
1910–11	Ottawa Senators, NHA	16	18	0	18	36	2	0	0	0	6
1911–12	Ottawa Senators, NHA	17	15	0	15	10					
1912–13	Ottawa Senators, NHA	20	15	0	15	16					
1913–14	Ottawa Senators, NHA	20	23	5	28	69					
1914–15	Ottawa Senators, NHA	18	11	2	13	32	5	4	0	4	9
1915–16	Ottawa Senators, NHA	21	16	5	21	41					
1916–17	Ottawa Senators, NHA	20	24	4	28	28	2	2	0	2	3
1917–18	Ottawa Senators, NHL	18	14	5	19	26					
1918–19	Ottawa Senators, NHL	14	11	30	14	33	5	2	0	2	3
1919–20	Ottawa Senators, NHL	23	22	14	36	22					
1920–21	Ottawa Senators, NHL	24	11	15	26	20	27	0	0	0	2
1922–23	Ottawa Senators, NHL	24	6	9	15	10	2	1	0	1	2
1923–24	Ottawa Senators, NHL	18	2	0	2	2	2	0	0	0	2
	NHA Totals	132	122	16	138	221	9	6	0	6	9
	NHL Totals	121	66	46	112	113	11	3	0	3	9

Won Stanley Cup (1911, 1920, 1923)

the arena, jumped into a taxi and made his train connections before we could persuade him to return. 'I've had enough hockey for this winter,' Darragh shouted. 'You will have to get along without me in the final game.'

"Some of the club owners and players were in favor of letting Darragh remain in Ottawa, but we thought the matter over and finally sent him a rush message as follows: 'Nighbor and Gerard have taken sick. Don't throw us down. We need you for the game tomorrow and the world championship is at stake.' So the midnight express out of Ottawa brought Darragh up to Toronto again."

The next season the Sens again won the Cup, and again Darragh was the hero. The best-of-five series was played in Vancouver that year and once more the Cup was decided in the fifth game. Darragh scored both Ottawa goals in a 2–1 win and the Senators became the first NHL team to win consecutive Cups. In all, Darragh had seven goals in seven playoff games in 1921.

Darragh took the entire 1921–22 season off, but when he returned to the Senators the next year, it was as though nothing had changed. The Sens beat first the Millionaires and then the Edmonton Eskimos to win their third Stanley Cup in four years. Darragh played one more full season in the NHL, but in the summer of 1924 he succumbed to peritonitis.

Georges Vezina

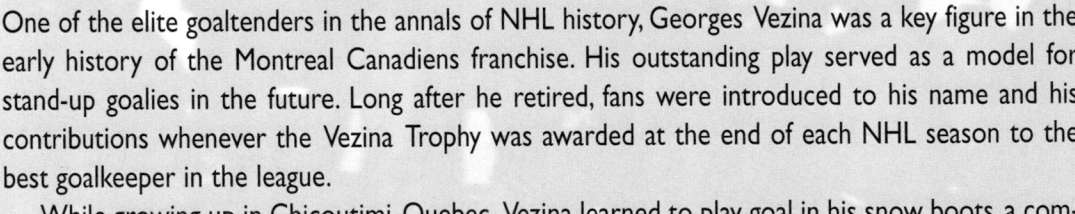

Georges Vezina's outstanding play served as a model for stand-up goalies in the future.

One of the elite goaltenders in the annals of NHL history, Georges Vezina was a key figure in the early history of the Montreal Canadiens franchise. His outstanding play served as a model for stand-up goalies in the future. Long after he retired, fans were introduced to his name and his contributions whenever the Vezina Trophy was awarded at the end of each NHL season to the best goalkeeper in the league.

While growing up in Chicoutimi, Quebec, Vezina learned to play goal in his snow boots, a common practice at the time. He didn't learn to skate until he was 18 years old but quickly made up for lost time. He was a local hero when the Montreal Nationals arrived in Chicoutimi for an exhibition match in 1910. Vezina frustrated the Nationals' shooters in leading his hometown club to a 2–0 upset win. His puck-stopping talents were brought to the attention of entrepreneur George Kennedy, who was granted a new franchise in the National Hockey Association known as the Canadiens.

Vezina stood out in the Canadiens' net even though he played in a league that was very offensive-minded and on a team that initially struggled. In addition, goalies were forbidden to fall to the ice to make a save, so Vezina managed to perfect an early version of the stand-up style of goaltending. A quiet, clean-living man who operated a tannery business in his home town during the off-season, his calm and cool demeanor resulted in his being labeled the "Chicoutimi Cucumber."

During his rookie year, 1910–11, Vezina led the NHA in his goals-against average, a feat he duplicated in his sophomore campaign. In 1914 he led the Canadiens to a first-place finish in the NHA standings, though they lost the league championship series that year to the Stanley Cup-winning Toronto Blueshirts. Two years later, his superior netminding skills enabled Montreal to win another NHA regular-season crown and the first Stanley Cup triumph in the club's history. The Canadiens emerged victorious from a memorable five-game set against the PCHA champion

Portland Rosebuds in a series that represented the first of many appearances in the Stanley Cup finals for the Canadiens and the inaugural one by an American team.

Despite Vezina's heroics, Montreal lost the sacred silverware to the powerful Seattle Metropolitans the following year and the Washington State team became the first Stanley Cup winner from south of the border. Two years later, in the fateful rematch that was eventually canceled by the influenza epidemic, the normally quiescent Vezina was described as being high-strung. It was a portent of the goaltending showdown that was about to take place between the Habs star and the legendary Harry "Hap" Holmes of Seattle. The Canadiens entered the inaugural NHL schedule in 1917–18 with Vezina as one of their pillars. He topped all NHL goalkeepers in his goals-against average that year and again in 1924 and 1925.

Vezina's heroics were a vital component of the Canadiens' second Stanley Cup championship in 1924. He stymied the Ottawa Senators in the NHL playoffs before helping Montreal overcome the challenges of Vancouver and Calgary of the PCHA and the Western Canada Hockey League respectively. In the regular season, he led all NHL netminders in his goals-against average, ending a five-year dominance by the great Clint Benedict.

While sweating through training camp workouts prior to the 1925–26 season, Vezina was obviously not in good health. Despite a high fever, he was performing admirably in the Canadiens' season opener versus the Pittsburgh Pirates, but when he was forced to retire from the game, Vezina was diagnosed with advanced tuberculosis. Sadly, his condition only worsened until he passed away on March 27, 1926, but his family history was full of tragedy, as only two of his 24 children lived to adulthood.

The esteem Canadian fans had for Vezina could be measured by the immense volume of mail he received in the months before his passing.

Vezina's impact on the game was felt for many years. His combined NHA and NHL regular-season totals added up to 328 games played, 15 career shutouts and a goals-against average of 3.49. Prior to the start of the 1926–27 season, Canadiens owners Leo Dandurand, Leo Letourneau and Joseph Cattaranich immortalized Vezina's name by establishing a trophy to be presented annually to the top netminder in the NHL. New York Rangers star Frank Boucher noted: "Vezina was a pale, narrow-featured fellow, almost frail-looking, yet remarkably good with his stick. He'd pick off more shots with it than he did with his glove."

Fittingly, the first recipient of the trophy was George Hainsworth, the brilliant young goalie who was presented with the task of replacing the legendary Vezina in Montreal. Another trophy was created in Vezina's name as a means of acknowledging the top goalkeeper in the Quebec senior league. Vezina was among the first 12 individuals inducted into the Hockey Hall of Fame when it was founded in 1945.

Vezina, Georges
G, 5'6", 185 lbs, b: Chicoutimi, Que., 1/21/1887, d: 3/27/1926

Season	Club, League	Regular Season				Playoffs			
		GP	Mins	GA	Avg	GP	Mins	GA	Avg
1910–11	Montreal Canadiens, NHA	16	980	62	3.80				
1911–12	Montreal Canadiens, NHA	18	1109	66	3.57				
1912–13	Montreal Canadiens, NHA	20	1217	81	3.99				
1913–14	Montreal Canadiens, NHA	20	1222	64	3.14	2	120	6	3.00
1914–15	Montreal Canadiens, NHA	20	1257	81	3.86				
1915–16	Montreal Canadiens, NHA	24	1482	76	3.08	5	300	13	2.60
1916–17	Montreal Canadiens, NHA	20	1217	80	3.94	6	240	29	4.80
1917–18	Montreal Canadiens, NHL	21	1282	84	3.93	2	120	10	5.00
1918–19	Montreal Canadiens, NHL	18	1117	78	4.19	10	636	37	3.49
1919–20	Montreal Canadiens, NHL	24	1456	113	4.66				
1920–21	Montreal Canadiens, NHL	24	1436	99	4.14				
1921–22	Montreal Canadiens, NHL	24	1468	94	3.84				
1922–23	Montreal Canadiens, NHL	24	1488	61	2.46	2	120	3	1.50
1923–24	Montreal Canadiens, NHL	24	1459	48	1.97	6	360	6	1.00
1924–25	Montreal Canadiens, NHL	30	1860	56	1.81	6	360	18	3.00
1925–26	Montreal Canadiens, NHL	1	20	0	0.00				
	NHL Totals	190	11586	633	3.28	26	1596	74	2.78
	NHA Totals	138	8484	510	3.61	13	660	48	4.36

Won Stanley Cup (1916, 1924)

Frank Foyston

Frank Foyston was capable of dominating a game from center, rover or either of the wing positions.

An exceptional scorer and playmaker, Frank C. Foyston was capable of dominating a game from center, rover or either of the wing positions. He was a supreme natural talent who earned accolades and fame wherever he played. While playing in the top leagues on the continent, Foyston was one of the first players to score over 200 career goals.

The native of Minesing, Ontario, played his early organized hockey in Barrie, just north of Toronto. The gifted forward starred with the Barrie Dyment Colts in 1908–09 before moving up to the local intermediate squad. He next landed a job in Toronto with the T. Eaton Company in 1911 and played with the firm's hockey team. They won the 1912 OHA senior crown, with Foyston's superb play proving to be the deciding factor.

Foyston made his professional debut with the Toronto Blueshirts of the National Hockey Association in 1912–13. He soon formed a potent forward line with the talented Scotty Davidson and Jack Walker. That productive trio was key to the Toronto club's NHA title in 1913–14 and their subsequent Stanley Cup championship win over the Victoria Cougars of the Pacific Coast Hockey Association. Foyston scored the decisive goal in the 2–1 Cup-clinching triumph.

The Seattle Metropolitans of the PCHA were able to lure "Frank the Flash" to the American West Coast at the beginning of the 1915–16 schedule. He stayed there for nine seasons, topping the league in goal-scoring twice and contributing to a Stanley Cup championship. Foyston helped the Metropolitans claim hockey's ultimate prize in 1916–17 in an exhilarating four-game series against the Montreal Canadiens—the first time a U.S. team won the Cup.

Years later, the *Seattle Post-Intelligencer* wrote: "You missed one of the all-time greats if you never saw Frank Foyston perform with a hockey stick. He wielded it like Fritz Kreisler his bow, Willie Mays his bat and Arnold Palmer his two-iron."

During the 1917 title series against Montreal, Foyston scored six goals and was a constant menace around the Canadiens' goal. At season's end, he was voted the right wing position on the PCHA First All-Star Team. Two years later, he led Seattle into a Stanley Cup rematch with the Canadiens. The crafty forward scored an incredible eight goals in the first four matches of the series, one of which was abandoned because of the influenza epidemic. It proved to be the only year in which the Stanley Cup wasn't awarded.

Foyston, Frank
C/RW, 5′9″, 158 lbs, b: Minesing, Ont., 2/2/1891, d: 1/19/1966

| Season | Club, League | Regular Season | | | | | Playoffs | | | |
		GP	G	A	Pts	PIM	GP	G	A	Pts	PIM
1911–12	Toronto Eaton's, OHA Sr.	6	15	0	15	*	4	5	0	5	9
1912–13	Toronto Blueshirts, NHA	16	8	0	8	8					
1913–14	Toronto Blueshirts, NHA	19	16	2	18	8	5	4	0	4	0
1914–15	Toronto Blueshirts, NHA	20	13	9	22	11					
1915–16	Toronto Blueshirts, NHA	1	0	0	0	0					
	Seattle Metropolitans, PCHA	18	9	4	13	6					
1916–17	Seattle Metropolitans, PCHA	24	36	12	48	51	4	7	3	10	3
1917–18	Seattle Metropolitans, PCHA	13	9	5	14	9	2	0	0	0	3
1918–19	Seattle Metropolitans, PCHA	18	15	4	19	0	2	3	0	3	0
1919–20	Seattle Metropolitans, PCHA	22	26	3	29	3	2	3	0	3	0
1920–21	Seattle Metropolitans, PCHA	23	26	4	30	10	2	1	0	1	0
1921–22	Seattle Metropolitans, PCHA	24	16	7	23	25	2	0	0	0	3
1922–23	Seattle Metropolitans, PCHA	30	20	8	28	21					
1923–24	Seattle Metropolitans, PCHA	30	17	6	23	8	2	1	0	1	0
1924–25	Victoria Cougars, WCHL	27	6	5	11	6	4	1	1	2	2
1925–26	Victoria Cougars, WHL	12	6	3	9	8	3	2	0	2	4
1926–27	Detroit Cougars, NHL	41	10	5	15	16					
1927–28	Detroit Cougars, NHL	23	7	2	9	16					
	Detroit Olympics, Can-Pro	19	3	2	5	14					
1928–29	Detroit Olympics, Can-Pro	42	18	6	24	20	7	0	0	0	9
1929–30	Detroit Olympics, IAHL	31	2	1	3	6	3	0	0	0	0
	NHA Totals	56	37	11	48	27	5	4	0	4	0
	PCHA Totals	202	174	53	227	135	16	15	3	18	9
	WCHL/WHL Totals	39	12	8	20	14	7	3	1	4	6
	NHL Totals	64	17	7	24	32					

PCHA First All-Star Team (1917, 1918, 1920, 1921, 1923, 1924)
PCHA Second All-Star Team (1919, 1922)
PCHA MVP (1917)
Won Stanley Cup (1914, 1917, 1925)

During the last two seasons of the PCHA, Foyston played admirably back in Victoria. He helped the Cougars become the last non-NHL club to get its hands on the Stanley Cup with a victory in 1925 over the dreaded Canadiens. Foyston's versatility was proven by his selection in various years to the PCHA First All-Star Team at three positions—left wing, center and rover.

With the sale of the Victoria players to the new Detroit Cougars franchise of the National Hockey League, Foyston ventured east to close out his professional career. He scored 17 goals in just under two NHL seasons before joining the Detroit Olympics of the Canadian Professional Hockey League as a player-coach. His contribution in Motown was aptly described in an Olympics game program: "His play from the very first was of the highest type, and his headwork was responsible for many brilliant attacks and sallies on the opponent's goal, resulting with great frequency in scores for his team."

Following the 1928–29 Can-Pro season, he retired permanently as a player. He continued to manage the Olympics the following year before journeying to Syracuse to guide the Stars in 1930–31. Foyston also coached the Bronx Tigers of the Can-Am league in 1931–32 and the Seattle Seahawks of the North West Hockey League in 1934 and 1935. He also served as a scout with the Detroit Red Wings in 1943–44 before leaving the game for good.

During a big-league career that spanned 16 years, Foyston accumulated 240 regular-season goals and 39 more in the playoffs. He was considered an offensive magician and star attraction wherever he played. One of the greatest talents of his time, Foyston was inducted into the Hockey Hall of Fame in 1958.

1917–1941

The Early Years
of the NHL

F. NIGHBOR

WELCOME HOME
WORLDS CHAMPIONS

*T*he National Hockey League played its first season in the winter of 1917–18. Three of the original four teams finished the regular season, but the Wanderers were left out of the finals when a fire destroyed their home base, the Montreal Arena. First place in the round-robin tournament went to the Toronto Arenas, who beat the Canadiens 10–7 in a two-game series to become the first NHL champions.

According to standard practice at the time, the top team in the Pacific Coast Hockey Association was permitted to challenge the new NHL champion for the Stanley Cup. As it turned out, the Vancouver Millionaires were to face off against the Toronto Arenas in a best-of-five series to be played in Toronto, but the format of play did present a few problems peculiar to that stage of development. In the East, the role of rover had already been struck from the lineup and games were played with six men on each team. In the West, the seven-man lineup was still the rule, and the press there took great pains to demonstrate that the six-and-six format made for less exciting hockey and left coaches with fewer strategic options. To keep everyone happy, a compromise was struck. The first and third games of the finals would be played with six men on each side, the second and fourth with seven, and the fifth would revert to six since the finals were being played in the East. In the end, each team won the games in the format they were accustomed to using and Toronto took the decisive final game by a score of 2–1. In the games played with seven, however, the Millionaires outscored the Arenas 14–5.

In 1919, the Stanley Cup playoffs moved to the Pacific Coast and preserved the compromise format, with results that were similar to the previous year's. The Seattle Metropolitans of the PCHA won the first and third games with scores of 7–0 and 7–2, the Montreal Canadiens took the second with a score of 4–2 and tied the fourth 0–0 (a tied score was possible because only

The Toronto Maple Leafs' training camp. McIntyre Arena, Timmins, Ontario.

A HISTORY OF WORLD HOCKEY

one overtime period was played to determine the winner in those years). But this time, in the fifth (seven-man) game, the visiting Canadiens bounced back. Montreal's Newsy Lalonde had scored all four goals in the second game and played the rover position in the fifth, where he added another two goals to give the visitors a 4–3 victory. The final and deciding match slated for April 1 never happened. The Spanish flu brought down five hockey players (Canadiens defenseman Joe Hall died in hospital) and the 1919 Stanley Cup holder was left undetermined.

Thus, even after the league had been founded, the Stanley Cup's fate was decided between the top teams from the PCHA in the West and the NHL in the East. But between 1918 and 1926, western clubs won the Stanley Cup only once (the Victoria Cougars in 1925) whereas the Ottawa Senators alone won it three times.

Even in the days before agents and megabucks contracts, a number of conditions had to be met if a community wanted to field a professional hockey club. Besides having a lineup of top-notch players, the game had to be popular in the community and it needed a rink that could handle the crowds.

In Ottawa, there was no need to make hockey more popular; it had won enough hearts when the Silver Seven had been at their peak. Built in 1923, the Auditorium could seat 11,000, and the Senators had a number of top-rated players. Hockey fans packed the stands to see Clint Benedict—who with 16 playoff shutouts was one of the best goalkeepers in Canada in those years—and illustrious defenseman Eddie Gerard. Center Frank Nighbor became the first player in the NHL to be awarded the Hart Trophy as the most valuable player, while the Art Ross Trophy for the top scoring performance went to Harry "Punch" Broadbent, who made 46 points in the 24 games of the 1921–22 season and scored at least one goal in 16 games in succession. A subsequent Art Ross winner from Ottawa, Cy Denneny, racked up 22 goals and an assist in 21 games in the 1923–24 season. All in all, the Senators dominated the Stanley Cup playoffs from 1920 to 1923 and brought the prize home to Ottawa in three out of those four seasons.

Toronto Maple Leafs–New York Americans. Maple Leaf Gardens.

In the early days of the NHL, before rules and traditions were firmly established, there was no shortage of curious episodes. When the Metropolitans arrived in Ottawa from Seattle for the finals in 1920, it was discovered that their uniforms were the same color as the ones the Senators wore. To avoid a conflict, the hosting team donned white suits, which would later become the Senators' standard. Both teams had to adapt after the third game of the finals, however. The Senators were leading 2–1 when Ottawa suddenly had a spell of warm weather and the ice in the outdoor arena was starting to melt. The organizers had to move the series to Toronto's Mutual Street Arena and its artificial ice. In the first game in Toronto, the fourth of the series, the Metropolitans managed to tie up the score in the series, but in the fifth and decisive game, Jack Darragh scored three goals for the Senators to clinch both the game and the finals.

Darragh was also the hero of the Stanley Cup finals a year later. In Vancouver, 51,000 people bought tickets to the playoffs, though perhaps not to see Darragh score two goals in the final game to give the Senators a 2–1 win over the Millionaires.

Ottawa finally lost its grip on the league in the 1921–22 season. After leading the NHL for the third time in five years, they couldn't pull off a win in two playoff games against the Toronto St. Patricks (formerly the Arenas). They dropped the first game 5–4 and managed a 0–0 tie in the second. The best-of-five finals saw the St. Pats pitted against the Vancouver Millionaires. Toronto racked up an overall total of 16 goals to beat Vancouver, and nine of them, including two game-winners, were credited to Cecil Dye.

New York Americans–Toronto Maple Leafs. Madison Square Garden.

Before the 1923 Stanley Cup finals, the West finally switched over to six-man hockey and the format of the final series was changed. At first the Senators met the Vancouver ex-Millionaires, renamed the Maroons, for the 1923 Stanley Cup. Thanks to five goals from Punch Broadbent in the deciding game, the team from the East beat the one from the West, but three days later—and still in Vancouver—the Senators took up a challenge from the Edmonton Eskimos, champions of the Western Canada Hockey League. This time Ottawa goalie Clint Benedict had shutouts in two games while forward Punch Broadbent again clinched a victory in the deciding game with a score of 1–0. Over the course of 16 days, the Senators had won the Stanley Cup and defended it too.

One of the few Canadians who wasn't too thrilled with the Senators' victory was the first NHL president, Frank Calder. And it wasn't for personal reasons. In the 1920s, Ottawa played very defensive hockey. The two defensemen as well as one of the forwards stayed behind in their own zone even when the Senators were attacking. With this style of play, the Senators racked up one success after another and their following grew ever larger. But it wasn't a high-scoring style and the game was beginning to seem less attractive; the league couldn't allow it. In 1924, Calder added a rule in the NHL charter that allowed no more than two field players in their own zone if the puck wasn't in that zone—the first of many changes in the rules in the interests of spectators over the course of NHL history. And there was an immediate victim as well. It took the Ottawa team almost three seasons to change its style of play.

In the 1924 Stanley Cup finals, the Canadiens went up against the Vancouver Maroons of the PCHA and then the Calgary Tigers of the WCHL. Both teams went down to defeat against Montreal, which isn't surprising since many of those Canadiens can be found in the most storied annals of hockey and loom large among the early inductions to its Hall of Fame.

Canadiens manager Leo Dandurand had a knack for spotting talented rookies. It was he who picked Howie Morenz from among the best amateur forwards. Already 21, Morenz made his debut in the league in the 1923–24 season and lived up to Dandurand's expectations right away. In the first game of the Stanley Cup finals against Calgary, Morenz scored two goals and added another in the second, while his forward line partner, Billy Boucher, also turned in a dazzling performance in that series.

If speed was the hallmark of these Montreal forwards, the main defensive duo of Sprague Cleghorn and Billy Coutu was the roughest and toughest in the NHL. And Georges Vezina was without equal both as a goalie and as a person. Georges didn't miss a single game in 16 years with the Canadiens. In the game that opened the 1924–25 season, for example, he came out on the ice even though he was running a temperature of more than 102 and played the first period before asking to be replaced. He died of tuberculosis on March 27, 1926, and hockey's loss was

Boston Bruins. 1929.

duly noted when the Vezina Trophy was named after him. And with Vezina gone, the Canadiens wound up in the cellar of the NHL in the 1925–26 season, the year after the only time the West managed to wrest the Stanley Cup from the NHL (the faster Victoria Cougars had outplayed the Canadiens in four games in 1925).

In those days, the NHL was struggling to survive financially. Realizing that professional clubs could survive fairly easily in big cities, where the demand for hockey was high, league president Calder bet on three of them: Montreal, Ottawa and Toronto. He also managed to increase the number of games in the regular season as well as in the Stanley Cup playoffs.

In the 1925–26 season, the NHL battled the strongest clubs in the West for the Stanley Cup for the last time. This time it was the Montreal Maroons against the Victoria Cougars in the Montreal Forum, and Victoria didn't stand a chance. They went down to defeat 3–0 in the first game, 3–0 in the second, pulled off a 3–2 win in the third and lost the fourth 2–0. The heroes of the playoffs were Nels Stewart, a rookie forward who scored six of Montreal's 10 goals, and goalkeeper Clint Benedict, who chalked up three shutouts (Benedict brought 12 seasons of experience with the Senators, including three Stanley Cups, when he joined the Maroons).

Beginning with the 1926–27 season, the National Hockey League monopolized North American hockey. It was split into two divisions: Canadian (the Ottawa Senators, the Montreal Canadiens and Montreal Maroons, the Toronto St. Patricks and the New York Americans) and American (clubs from Boston and Pittsburgh and three newcomers, Chicago, Detroit and the New York Rangers).

As the trailblazers in the league in the U.S., the New York Americans recruited players in eastern Canada, particularly in the Hamilton area. In the late 1920s, players also went to American teams from the bankrupt PCHA and the WCHL. On the whole, Canadian players were eager to move south. At home they earned at best up to $4,000 whereas in the States they were paid not less than $10,000. The Boston Bruins acquired Eddie Shore and the Rangers Frank Boucher and coach Lester Patrick, the architect of the former PCHA; nearly all the players from Portland migrated to Chicago; the Victoria Cougars moved to Detroit, to a club that was at first called the Cougars, then the Falcons and became the Red Wings at last in 1933.

The Americans got their money's worth from the more than 30 "immigrants" they took on. All 10 of the top scorers on American teams in the 1926–27 season were later inducted into the Hockey Hall of Fame in Toronto. There were also first-class defensemen, headed by Eddie Shore, as well as goalkeepers of the likes of George Hainsworth, whose performance in the 1929–30 season (a goals-against average of 0.92 per game and 22 shutouts in 44 games) is remarkable even today. In fact, the high caliber of the players from Canada only encouraged the American teams to recruit north of the border rather than locally, and there were more than enough available Canadians to supply all the teams.

The first regular season of the revamped NHL differed from those of the past only in the number of games at 44 per team. The Ottawa Senators topped the Canadian Division and beat the Canadiens for the division title to go on to the Stanley Cup playoffs. In the second division, the Rangers proved to be the strongest of the American clubs, but it was the Bruins who confounded all expectations and went to the Stanley Cup finals.

As a relatively new team, the Boston Bruins didn't have the Senators' experience in playoffs. The Bruins had attacking defenseman Eddie Shore, but the Senators had defenseman Frank Clancy (who had already earned the moniker "King"). And Bruins general manager and

The Toronto Maple Leafs at training camp.

coach Art Ross had only begun to select promising forwards and didn't yet have a lot to put up against the experienced line of Jack Adams, Cy Denneny and Frank Nighbor. Ottawa won two games with identical 3–1 scores and tied two, 0–0 and 1–1. The rules at the time didn't have a proviso for sudden-death play, and after a single 20-minute overtime period, NHL president Calder awarded the Stanley Cup to the Senators.

Hockey changed in major ways in the 1930s. At the beginning of the 20th century, the success of a club often depended on one or two stars. By the end of the 1920s and in the early 1930s, rugged individualism was on its way out and team play was emerging as the standard. One team that initiated this new style of play was the New York Rangers. Conn Smythe had built the team, but when Lester Patrick replaced him as manager and coach, Patrick crafted a star forward line. Brothers Bill and Bun Cook were matched up with elegant playmaker Frank Boucher (who would go on to win the Lady Byng Trophy for gentlemanly play seven times in eight seasons). The distribution of roles in that forward line, with Boucher as the playmaker, Bun Cook as the "soldier" and Bill Cook as the "triggerman," became a classic for a number of years. For a decade, Bill Cook was regularly among the top five scorers in the NHL and the line brought the Rangers the Stanley Cup in 1928 and 1933.

Luck also played a small role in the Rangers' win in 1928. In the second game of the best-of-five finals between the Rangers and the Maroons, New York was left without a goalie in the 24th minute when Lorne Chabot was taken to hospital with a serious eye injury. Since he didn't have a backup goalkeeper, Patrick rushed to find a replacement and came up with Ottawa goalie Alex Connell, who just happened to be in the stands. Maroons manager Eddie Gerard stubbornly insisted that only a player who had a contract with the New York team could stand in for the injured Chabot. After a good deal of debate, the 44-year-old manager and coach took it upon himself to tend the Rangers' net. Over the course of 43 minutes, including seven minutes of over-time, the elegant, grey-haired Lester Patrick deflected 18 shots on goal and missed only one and the Rangers won 2–1 and tied the series 1–1.

In the fifth and deciding match, Boucher scored both his team's goals in a 2–1 win that gave the Rangers the Stanley Cup. But some of the credit has to go to goaltender Joe Miller, borrowed from the New York Americans, who allowed only three goals in the last three games of the series. His face was slashed with a hockey stick during the first period and he too ended up in the hospital, but he finished the game and played brilliantly right to the end. Miller never appeared in Stanley Cup playoffs again, but at least he was king for a day.

Major Conn Smythe training the troops during World War II.

The first dynasty in the NHL was born in Toronto in the latter half of the 1940s, and there isn't the slightest shadow of a doubt that its "father" was Conn Smythe, who became owner and manager of the Maple Leafs in 1927. In the NHL, a prize is awarded to the most valuable player in the playoffs. It takes into account the number of points for goals and assists, but also a player's ability to lead by example, to spur teammates to stand and deliver. It's highly appropriate that the prize is called the Conn Smythe Trophy, since Conn Smythe was an MVP for the Leafs for a very long stretch.

Smythe's talents were diverse. He was able to determine what a junior would be capable of in the future with almost 100% accuracy. When he invited the 1928 junior champions of Canada (Joe Primeau, Charlie Conacher and Reginald Horner) to his club in 1931, Smythe was displaying some of the incredible foresight that would later bring fame to his team. Together with Harvey Jackson, Primeau and Conacher would form the team's crack line in their very first season, while defenseman Horner—soon nicknamed "Red"—would form the backbone of the club's defense along with Clarence "Hap" Day and would have the honor of replacing King Clancy, who joined the Leafs defense line in the 1931–32 season.

Even then, Clancy was becoming a living legend. The only thing that had so far been lacking to get him for Toronto was money. Ottawa had pinned a price tag of $35,000 on Clancy: an unheard-of sum at a time when the Great Depression had brought North America almost to its knees. But Conn Smythe applied his talents as a businessman and found sponsors and the con-tract with Clancy was signed—for the full price and a couple of players. At the same time, goal-keeper Lorne Chabot was purchased from the Rangers. And so it was that even the Depression had a limited effect on Conn Smythe's Maple Leafs and in 1932, after a series against the Rangers that ended in three games, the Stanley Cup came to Toronto.

In 1933, a rule was introduced that eliminated ties in Stanley Cup playoff games. Teams were to play overtime periods until one of them scored on a sudden-death basis, which resulted in another of those curious episodes that marked the early days of the league.

The Leafs and the Bruins met in the 1933 Stanley Cup semifinals and there was still no score in the game at the end of regulation play on April 3. After five overtime periods and 100 minutes of playing time, the result was the same. The team managers, Conn Smythe of Toronto and Art Ross of Boston, asked league president Calder to carry the game over to the next evening. He refused. Ross suggested flipping a coin. The Toronto players agreed. Calder hesitated. And when the referees started heading for center ice to determine the best team by the toss of a coin, the 14,539 Toronto fans who had stayed in the stands until almost 2 in the morning anticipating a victory let loose such an uproar the game was continued. After 164 minutes and 46 seconds of overtime, Ken Doraty finally put a goal in the Boston net.

But the victory was short-lived for Toronto. In the first-three-wins finals, they bowed out to the Rangers in four games, winning only the third one 3–2 and losing the others 5–3, 3–1 and 1–0. The lone goal of the fourth game that determined the 1933 Cup winner was scored in overtime by Bill Cook, the triggerman on New York's top line. At the time, they had two extra players on the ice—an event never to be repeated in Stanley Cup playoffs.

By the 1939–40 season, the only Rangers left from the glory days were manager Lester Patrick and former forward Frank Boucher, who had by then become coach. Still, New York managed to make it to the Stanley Cup finals and crossed sticks again with the Leafs, who had also been totally revamped at that point. In a final series to be determined by the first four wins—the current format—Toronto was regarded as the favorite. Yet again, with two overtime victories (2–1 in the second game and 3–2 in the seventh), the Rangers repeated their win.

Frank Calder

Frank Calder guided the NHL through its crucial first quarter-century.

One of hockey's greatest visionaries, Frank Calder guided the National Hockey League through its first half-century. He addressed all issues affecting the league decisively and logically and his steadfast dedication to its betterment garnered him the permanent respect of his peers.

Born in Bristol, England, in 1877, Calder emigrated to Canada very early in the 1900s to teach at a private school in Montreal. After a few years in the classroom, he switched careers to become a sportswriter with the *Montreal Witness* and later became sports editor of the *Montreal Herald*.

As a young man, Calder was involved in soccer, rugby, golf, handball and cricket. He became one of the founders of the Montreal school rugby league and served as secretary of the Montreal and district football league. Calder possessed a knowledge of sports and a direct and insightful way of speaking. Former Montreal Canadiens owner George Kennedy was so impressed with Calder's forthright style that he helped facilitate his election to the position of secretary of the National Hockey Association, forerunner to the NHL. When the NHA folded and the National Hockey League was formed in 1917, Calder was the overwhelming choice for the new league's first president. Over the next 25 years, his vision and initiative were vital components in the success of the league.

Almost immediately after assuming his new position, Calder was ratifying the sale of the Quebec franchise to the Toronto Arenas. He later scrutinized a number of franchise applications and transfers, enabling such traditional clubs as the Boston Bruins, New York Rangers, Detroit Red Wings and Chicago Black Hawks to be formed.

The NHL's first president attended as many games as possible to monitor the state of the league on the ice and in the community.

Calder helped ensure the survival of the NHL during the two world wars and the Great Depression. The two global conflicts depleted the numbers of available players, while the worldwide economic downturn caused several franchises to cease operations or relocate to other cities. A big reason why the league was able to weather these storms was the proactive involvement of Calder as president. He made a point of attending as many games as possible to monitor the state of the league on the ice and in the community. If he felt the actions or policies of the various team governors weren't in the best interests of the NHL, he didn't hesitate to confront them. Calder was the driving force behind the Ace Bailey and Howie Morenz charity games, demonstrating his sincere concern for the players in the league and their families.

By 1943, Calder's dedication to the job had caused his health to deteriorate. He was honored during the NHL's 25th anniversary celebrations, but Calder was overwrought from trying to maintain the survival of the league in the face of World War II. The strain of trying to balance the demands of the game with the needs of the military caused him to collapse at a league meeting. A plan was made to grant Calder a much-deserved rest and have Mervyn "Red" Dutton temporarily assume his responsibilities. Unfortunately, Calder passed away the day after the motion was passed. He literally gave his life in the service of the National Hockey League. One league executive said, "I could never get along with Calder at all—but I don't know how I will get along without him."

Since 1933, Calder had shown his support for hockey with a trophy he purchased and awarded annually to the NHL's top rookie. Following his death in 1943, it was established as a permanent award and renamed the Calder Memorial Trophy. Another trophy, the Calder Cup, is presented annually to the American Hockey League championship team. Calder was inducted into the Hockey Hall of Fame in the Builders category in 1947.

Harry "Punch" Broadbent

A multidimensional star, Harry "Punch" Broadbent was as talented as he was tough. He was an artist with the puck, at times scoring at will, but he also gained a notorious reputation for using his elbows to make a point. He could dance around or skate over an opponent as the situation demanded. Many considered Broadbent to be one of the first true power forwards of the game. And his fame would likely have been far greater had he not lost three years in the prime of his career to military service during World War I.

A star in the Ottawa city league with the Cliffsides and the New Edinburghs, Broadbent became a local hero at an early age. In 1912 he joined the Ottawa Senators on a part-time basis when they played in the National Hockey Association. Broadbent described the arrangement as "They gave me $600 to use me when and wherever they needed me, and in between I'd go back and play amateur hockey."

Harry "Punch" Broadbent was one of the first true power forwards.

Broadbent scored an incredible 24 goals in only 20 matches in 1914–15. That year he was part of an Ottawa expedition that traveled to Vancouver for an unsuccessful Stanley Cup challenge against the Millionaires. Other famous names found on the Ottawa roster at this time included Clint Benedict, Jack Darragh, Art Ross and Hamby Shore.

In 1915 Broadbent left hockey to serve Canada in World War I. He was awarded the Military Medal for his heroic conduct overseas. When he returned to the Senators in 1918–19, they were playing in the newly formed National Hockey League.

Broadbent scored 19 goals in 21 games during the 1919–20 season but enjoyed his greatest success two years later. In 1921–22, he scored 32 goals in the 24-game schedule. Included in this run of good fortune was an NHL record of 16 consecutive games with at least one goal, eclipsing Joe Malone's previous record of 14. The streak began during a 10–0 rout of the Montreal Canadiens on Christmas Eve and lasted through to a 6–6 tie with the same team seven weeks later on February 15. In addition to goal-scoring skills and toughness, Broadbent possessed superior backchecking. This last quality helped the Senators play smothering defensive hockey when protecting a lead.

His offensive wizardry and robust style of play contributed significantly to the Senators' three Stanley Cup wins in 1920, 1921 and 1923. He was the right winger on one of hockey's top forward lines with Frank Nighbor and Cy Denneny. In the 1923 series versus the Edmonton Eskimos, Ottawa needed to find a way to stop the explosive Duke Keats. Everyone figured this responsibility would rest with defensive stalwart Frank Nighbor. Early in the contest, Keats skated close to Broadbent and took one of the latter's famous elbows in the midsection. The star of the western side failed to make much of an impression the rest of that evening.

Prior to the 1924–25 season, Broadbent and future Hall of Fame goalie Clint Benedict were traded to the expansion Montreal Maroons in a blockbuster deal. Those who felt that Broadbent was past his prime were silenced by his five-goal performance on January 7, 1925, during a 6–2 win over the Hamilton Tigers. In reality, Broadbent and Benedict had been sent to the new club to make the league appear as balanced as possible.

The Montrealers won the Stanley Cup in 1925–26 with Broadbent at his roughest. He scored two goals in eight post-season matches but also accumulated 36 minutes in penalties. "Old Elbows" was a force throughout the series that serves as a microcosm of his impact throughout his career.

Broadbent returned to his roots with the Senators in 1927–28. The reunion lasted only one year, as he was sold to the New York Americans in the summer. The 1928–29 season with New York proved to be his last in the NHL. He retired during the great stock market crash of 1929 and rejoined the air force. Broadbent was inducted into the Hockey Hall of Fame in 1962.

Broadbent, Harry "Punch"
RW, 5'7", 183 lbs, b: Ottawa, Ont., 7/13/1892, d: 3/6/1971

Season	Club, League	Regular Season					Playoffs				
		GP	G	A	Pts	PIM	GP	G	A	Pts	PIM
1909–10	Ottawa Cliffsides, City Sr.						3	1	0	1	6
1910–11	Ottawa Cliffsides, City Sr.	6	14	0	14	*	1	1	0	1	0
1911–12	Ottawa New Edinburghs, City Sr.	*	*	*	*	*	*	*	*	*	*
1912–13	Ottawa Senators, NHA	20	20	0	20	15					
1913–14	Ottawa Senators, NHA	17	6	7	13	61					
1914–15	Ottawa Senators, NHA	20	24	3	27	115	5	3	0	3	*
1918–19	Ottawa Senators, NHL	8	4	3	7	12	5	2	3	5	42
1919–20	Ottawa Senators, NHL	21	19	6	25	40	4	0	0	0	3
1920–21	Ottawa Senators, NHL	9	4	1	5	10	7	2	2	4	4
1921–22	Ottawa Senators, NHL	24	32	14	46	28	2	0	1	1	8
1922–23	Ottawa Senators, NHL	24	14	0	14	32	8	6	1	7	12
1923–24	Ottawa Senators, NHL	22	9	4	13	44	2	0	0	0	4
1924–25	Montreal Maroons, NHL	30	15	4	17	75					
1925–26	Montreal Maroons, NHL	36	12	5	17	112	8	2	0	2	36
1926–27	Montreal Maroons, NHL	42	9	5	14	88	2	0	0	0	0
1927–28	Ottawa Senators, NHL	43	3	2	5	62	2	0	0	0	0
1928–29	New York Americans, NHL	44	1	4	5	59	2	0	0	0	2
	NHL Totals	303	122	48	170	562	42	12	7	19	111

NHL Scoring Leader (1922)
Won Stanley Cup (1920,1921,1923,1926)

Sprague Cleghorn

A remarkably talented and fierce competitor, Sprague Cleghorn was admired, despised and feared during his playing days. Wherever he skated, Cleghorn served as the anchor of his team's defense or occasionally posed an offensive threat as a forward. His on-ice accomplishments and physical style of play made him a virtual archetype of the hard-nosed star of hockey's early days.

The Montreal native attended Westmount Academy as a young man. Here, at the age of 15, he first crafted his reputation as an extremely tough competitor. Between 1906 and 1909, he played with several amateur teams in the city before spending a year with the New York Wanderers in the United States Amateur Hockey Association.

The original "Big Train" made his professional debut with the Renfrew Millionaires of the National Hockey Association in 1910–11. He began that season as a forward but was quickly moved back to defense, where he was such an intimidating presence. At this time, Cleghorn was heavily influenced by his teammate Fred "Cyclone" Taylor. Cleghorn rushed forward with the puck in much the same fashion as the illustrious defender and was one of the earliest incarnations of an offensive defenseman.

The 1911–12 season brought Cleghorn back to his home town to suit up for the mighty Wanderers. His end-to-end rushes and cantankerous defensive play rapidly endeared him to the

Sprague Cleghorn also tried his hand at coaching in a number of leagues.

Montreal fans. The bruising star came to be known simply as "Peg" by his adoring public. On December 27, 1913, he scored five goals in one game against the Toronto Ontarios. Cleghorn recorded a personal best of 21 goals in 19 games during the 1914–15 schedule. Another facet of his game was to protect his brother and teammate Odie. Many times Sprague lost his temper and violently punished individuals who took liberties with his sibling, such as star forward Newsy Lalonde, who once checked Odie hard and was made to pay for his action. Cleghorn stayed with the Wanderers until the franchise's arena burned down, whereupon he was signed by the Toronto Arenas and later transferred to the Ottawa Senators.

Cleghorn was a major factor in Ottawa's Stanley Cup triumphs in 1920 and 1921. During the 1920 championship series against the Seattle Metropolitans, he formed an effective backline tandem with fellow star Eddie Gerard. Although Cleghorn spent most of the 1920–21 regular season with the Toronto St. Patricks, he rejoined Ottawa in time to be a part of the squad's Stanley Cup triumph over Vancouver in a hotly contested and often violent championship series.

Following the 1921 Cup triumph with Ottawa, Cleghorn returned to Montreal to suit up for the Canadiens. Teamed with Billy Coutu, the Canadiens had what was arguably the most feared defensive tandem in hockey at that time. After he attacked Ottawa defenseman Lionel Hitchman in the 1923 playoffs, Cleghorn was suspended by team owner Leo Dandurand, who described his player's actions as "befitting an animal."

Cleghorn claimed his third Stanley Cup win in 1923–24 when his playing helped Montreal eliminate Vancouver and Calgary from the Pacific league in the playoffs. Cleghorn served as team captain from 1921 to 1925. The hard-nosed rearguard concluded his NHL career playing with the Boston Bruins until 1928.

After retiring, Cleghorn tried his hand at coaching in a number of leagues. He began with the Newark and Providence franchises of the Can-Am league. In 1931–32, he guided the Montreal Maroons to the Stanley Cup semifinals in his only year at the helm of an NHL team. He later coached Pittsburgh of the International-American Hockey League in 1935–36 and the Cornwall Cougars of the Quebec provincial circuit in 1947–48.

Over his 17-year career in the NHA and the NHL, Cleghorn accumulated 169 goals, mostly from the defense position. At the time of his retirement he trailed only Harry Cameron among defenders on the all-time scoring list in the pro leagues. His goal contribution and competitive nature were key components to the success of every team he played on.

As well known as he was for his speculative rushes on offense, Cleghorn was lauded for his play even when he didn't have the puck. Many

Sprague Cleghorn was well known for his end-to-end rushes and cantankerous defense.

Cleghorn, Sprague
D, 5´10˝, 190 lbs, b: Montreal, Que., 3/11/1890, d: 7/11/1956

Season	Club, League	Regular Season					Playoffs				
		GP	G	A	Pts	PIM	GP	G	A	Pts	PIM
1909–10	New York Wanderers, USAHA	8	7	0	7	*					
1910–11	Renfrew Millionaires, NHA	12	5	0	5	27					
1911–12	Montreal Wanderers, NHA	18	9	0	9	40					
1912–13	Montreal Wanderers, NHA	19	12	0	12	46					
1913–14	Montreal Wanderers, NHA	20	12	8	20	17					
1914–15	Montreal Wanderers, NHA	19	21	12	33	51	2	0	0	0	17
1915–16	Montreal Wanderers, NHA	8	9	4	13	22					
1916–17	Montreal Wanderers, NHA	19	16	3	19	53					
1918–19	Ottawa Senators, NHL	18	7	9	16	27	5	2	2	4	12
1919–20	Ottawa Senators, NHL	21	16	5	21	85	5	0	1	1	4
1920–21	Ottawa Senators, NHL	3	2	3	5	9					
	Toronto St. Pats, NHL	13	3	5	8	31	1	0	0	0	0
	Ottawa Senators, NHL						5	1	2	3	36
1921–22	Montreal Canadiens, NHL	24	17	9	26	80					
1922–23	Montreal Canadiens, NHL	24	9	4	13	34	1	0	0	0	0
1923–24	Montreal Canadiens, NHL	23	8	3	11	39	6	2	1	3	2
1924–25	Montreal Canadiens, NHL	27	8	1	9	82	6	1	2	3	4
1925–26	Boston Bruins, NHL	28	6	5	11	49					
1926–27	Boston Bruins, NHL	44	7	1	8	84	8	1	0	1	8
1927–28	Boston Bruins, NHL	37	2	2	4	14	2	0	0	0	0
1928–29	Newark Bulldogs, Can-Am	3	0	0	0	0					
	NHL Totals	262	85	47	132	534	39	7	8	15	66
	NHA Totals	115	84	27	111	256	2	0	0	0	17

Won Stanley Cup (1920, 1921, 1924)

of the game's top forwards were less inclined to venture near a net guarded by a tough defender. But Cleghorn wasn't a mere bully; he was respected for exceptional defensive play that was considered to be at the same level as such stars as Eddie Gerard and George Boucher. Cleghorn was inducted into the Hockey Hall of Fame in 1958.

Clint Benedict

Nearly 30 years before Jacques Plante's innovative mask, Clint Benedict used a protective cover over his nose.

One of hockey's first superstar netminders, Clint Benedict often dominated the headlines in the era of Georges Vezina and George Hainsworth. His strategy of "accidentally" falling to the ice to make a save or smother loose pucks led the NHL to change the rule that had required goalies to remain standing throughout the game. Toronto fans referred to him as "Praying Benny" since he spent so much time on his knees. Benedict was a stellar workhorse for the Ottawa Senators and Montreal Maroons during 13 NHL seasons split almost equally between the two. A tough competitor, Benedict often played when injured and wasn't afraid to mix it up with the more aggressive forwards on the opposition.

The Ottawa native starred as an amateur with the local New Edinburghs before joining the Senators for five seasons in the NHA. He enjoyed a solid beginning to his pro career and gained valuable experience by guiding Ottawa to a 1915 Stanley Cup challenge that was lost to the Vancouver Millionaires. When not starring on the ice in Ottawa, Benedict was an accomplished lacrosse player in the off-season.

Benedict truly blossomed when the franchise became one of the founding members of the NHL in 1917–18. On February 25, 1918, he recorded the second shutout in NHL history when the Senators blanked the Canadiens 8–0. The losing goaltender that night was Georges Vezina, who had registered the NHL's first blank sheet a week earlier. For six of the seven years he spent in Ottawa, Benedict led the NHL in wins. He was part of one of the game's early dynasties when he helped the team win three Stanley Cups in four seasons between 1920 and 1923. His most impressive season was arguably 1919–20, when his 2.66 goals-against mark was 2.13 goals better than the league average, a mark that was never equaled.

In October 1924 he and fellow star Punch Broadbent were shipped to the Montreal Maroons. In 1925 he was presented with the Mappin Trophy as top player on the team. Benedict starred with four shutouts and a 1.00

Benedict, Clint
G, b: Ottawa, Ont., 9/26/1892, d: 11/12/1976

Season	Club, League	Regular Season				Playoffs			
		GP	Mins	GA	Avg	GP	Mins	GA	Avg
1910–11	Ottawa New Edinburghs, City Sr.	5	300	14	2.80	3	180	13	4.25
1912–13	Ottawa Senators, NHA	10	275	16	3.49				
1913–14	Ottawa Senators, NHA	9	474	29	3.67				
1914–15	Ottawa Senators, NHA	20	1243	65	3.14	2	120	2	0.50
1915–16	Ottawa Senators, NHA	24	1447	72	2.99				
1916–17	Ottawa Senators, NHA	18	1103	50	2.72	2	120	7	3.50
1917–18	Ottawa Senators, NHL	22	1337	114	5.12				
1918–19	Ottawa Senators, NHL	18	1152	53	2.86	5	300	26	5.20
1919–20	Ottawa Senators, NHL	24	1443	64	2.66	5	300	11	2.20
1920–21	Ottawa Senators, NHL	24	1457	75	3.09	7	420	12	1.71
1921–22	Ottawa Senators, NHL	24	1508	84	3.34	2	120	5	2.50
1922–23	Ottawa Senators, NHL	24	1486	54	2.18	8	480	10	1.25
1923–24	Ottawa Senators, NHL	22	1356	45	1.99	2	120	5	2.50
1924–25	Montreal Maroons, NHL	30	1843	65	2.12				
1925–26	Montreal Maroons, NHL	36	2288	73	1.91	8	480	8	1.00
1926–27	Montreal Maroons, NHL	43	2748	65	1.42	2	132	2	0.91
1927–28	Montreal Maroons, NHL	44	2690	76	1.70	9	555	8	0.86
1928–29	Montreal Maroons, NHL	37	2300	57	1.49				
1929–30	Montreal Maroons, NHL	14	752	33	2.63				
1930–31	Windsor Bulldogs, IAHL	40	2478	92	2.23				
	NHL Totals	362	22360	858	2.30	48	2907	87	1.80
	NHA Totals	81	4542	232	3.06	4	240	9	2.25

Won Stanley Cup (1920, 1921, 1923, 1926)

goals-against average when Montreal won the Stanley Cup in 1926. This last triumph gave Benedict the distinction of being the first netminder to backstop two different NHL teams to the Stanley Cup. He was virtually impenetrable in the four-game championship set against Victoria with a 0.75 goals-against mark.

His tactic of pretending to fall on the puck was copied by rival goalies. It was common practice for goalies to observe and adopt each other's tricks. As Benedict said: "You had to do something. Quite a few of the players could put a curving drop on a shot, and the equipment wasn't exactly the greatest in those days."

Things sailed along for Benedict until the 1929–30 season, when he was hit in the nose by a shot from Canadiens superstar Howie Morenz. On the play he was screened by his own defenseman, Jim Ward. Nearly 30 years before Jacques Plante's innovative goalie mask, Benedict returned to action a few weeks later with a protective cover over his nose. Unfortunately it obscured his vision on low shots and he was forced to abandon the NHL's first facemask. Later in the season he was hit in the throat by another Morenz blast which effectively ended his NHL tenure. Benedict played the 1930–31 season with the Maroons' farm club, the Windsor Bulldogs of the International-American Hockey League, and led the team to the league championship in what proved to be his career finale.

Benedict retired at the end of the season with 191 NHL wins and 58 shutouts to his credit. Throughout his career he remained loyal to his original thin, cricket-style pads even when the larger leather pads were popularized in the 1930s. He moved to Atlantic Canada and coached the Saint John Beavers of the Maritime Senior Big 4. Later he moved to England to work as a hockey manager with the Wembley Lions in the rejuvenated British league. After four years in the U.K., he returned to Ottawa and worked for the municipal government until his retirement. In the early 1960s, he faced another battle when a serious hip injury forced him to undergo months of intensive physiotherapy. He was inducted into the Hockey Hall of Fame in 1965. One of the game's greatest netminders passed away in an Ottawa hospital in 1976.

Clint Benedict forced the NHL to change the rule that had required goalies to remain standing throughout the game.

Eddie Gerard

Rarely in hockey history has a defenseman exhibited as high a level of play and gentlemanly conduct as Eddie Gerard. While playing a position that constantly required physical confrontation, he performed with superior efficiency but in sportsmanlike fashion. Gerard was a fine skater with superior puckhandling capabilities who was a fair match for any adversary at either end of the ice, while his leadership skills made him the ideal captain for the Stanley Cup-winning Ottawa Senators and a fine coach with the Cup champion Montreal Maroons in 1926.

The Ottawa native excelled in a variety of sports before making his mark in hockey. At the age of 15, he contributed to the Ottawa-Edinburgh Canoe Club's Dominion paddling championship. In 1909 Gerard turned his energy to football and consequently landed a position in the backfield of the Ottawa Rough Riders of the Canadian Football League, where he remained until 1913.

Eddie Gerard captained the Senators to three Stanley Cup wins between 1920 and 1923.

Gerard first signed with hockey's Ottawa Senators in 1913–14, a transaction that reaped many benefits for the club. He began as a forward, playing on a line with Jack Darragh and Skene Ronan, and didn't switch to defense for another three years. Following this positional shift, Gerard established himself as a tower of strength on his squad's defense while serving as the team's inspirational heart. He formed an outstanding defensive partnership with George Boucher and was the natural choice for team captain.

Gerard captained the version of the Senators that was dubbed the "Super Six" as a tribute to their winning three Stanley Cups in four years between 1920 and 1923. During the 1920 Stanley Cup series against the Seattle Metropolitans, Gerard formed an impenetrable defensive wall with Sprague Cleghorn in his own zone and scored on a dramatic end-to-end rush in the deciding game. The Senators retained the Cup the following year in an emotionally charged series versus the PCHA champion Vancouver Millionaires. In one of the most keenly watched Stanley Cup encounters of the 1920s, Ottawa triumphed in the fifth and deciding game with a 2–1 score.

The Senators didn't fare as well during the 1921–22 schedule, finishing first overall but then falling to Toronto for the NHL championship. Oddly enough, Gerard also found himself competing for the Stanley Cup on behalf of the Toronto St. Patricks. The St. Pats were riddled with injuries during their Cup encounter with the Vancouver Millionaires, so Vancouver manager Lester Patrick agreed to allow the Toronto club to call on any defense player in eastern Canada for the remainder of the series. Gerard was quickly summoned and played a crucial part in the St. Pats' victory in the fourth game of the matchup. In fact, he was so impressive that Patrick balked at allowing Gerard to participate in the fifth and deciding contest. It mattered little, as Toronto won the final match 5–1, with much of the credit for the shift in momentum resting with Gerard's involvement in the previous game.

The 1922–23 season found Gerard on his fourth straight Stanley Cup-winning side. The Ottawa club defeated Vancouver three games to one, then vanquished Edmonton in two straight matches to claim hockey's ultimate prize. The final match against Edmonton on March 31, 1923, proved to be Gerard's swan song in pro hockey.

On retiring as a player, Gerard turned his attention to coaching. He became bench boss with the Montreal Maroons at the start of the 1925–26 schedule and promptly led that franchise to its first Stanley Cup championship. In 1930 he moved on to manage the New York Americans before returning to the Maroons two years later. Gerard ventured on to St. Louis to handle the Eagles in 1934–35 but was forced to step down due to his failing health. His career was one filled with a great deal of success both on and off the ice. A member of the Canadian Sports Hall of Fame, Gerard was among the first 12 inductees when the Hockey Hall of Fame was founded in 1945.

Gerard, Eddie
LW/D, 5'9", 168 lbs, b: Ottawa, Ont., 2/22/1890, d: 12/7/1937

Season	Club, League	Regular Season					Playoffs				
		GP	G	A	Pts	PIM	GP	G	A	Pts	PIM
1910–11	Ottawa New Edinburghs, City Sr.	6	8	0	8	*					
1913–14	Ottawa Senators, NHA	11	6	7	13	34					
1914–15	Ottawa Senators, NHA	20	9	10	19	39	5	1	0	1	6
1915–16	Ottawa Senators, NHA	24	13	5	18	57					
1916–17	Ottawa Senators, NHA	19	17	9	26	37	2	1	0	1	3
1917–18	Ottawa Senators, NHL	20	13	7	20	26					
1918–19	Ottawa Senators, NHL	18	4	10	14	17	5	3	0	3	3
1919–20	Ottawa Senators, NHL	22	9	7	16	19	5	2	1	3	3
1920–21	Ottawa Senators, NHL	24	11	4	15	18	7	1	0	1	53
1921–22	Ottawa Senators, NHL	21	7	11	18	16	2	0	0	0	8
	Toronto St. Pats, NHL						1	0	0	0	0
1922–23	Ottawa Senators, NHL	23	6	8	14	24	7	1	0	1	4
	NHL Totals	128	50	47	97	120	27	7	1	8	71
	NHA Totals	74	45	31	76	167	7	2	0	2	9

Won Stanley Cup (1920, 1921, 1923)

Frank Nighbor

An outstanding two-way center throughout his career, Frank Nighbor played a vital part on some of Canada's mightiest professional teams and his exemplary conduct on the ice earned him the respect of fans and players across the country. Nighbor was considered the master of the "poke-check," which he used to full advantage against the game's most dangerous scorers. A smooth skater, he worked superbly with his wingers as a crafty and unselfish playmaker.

Growing up in Pembroke, Ontario, Nighbor quickly developed into an advanced skater. When he was 16, he suited up for a local squad known as the Debaters. The following year he competed on behalf of the Pembroke Seniors of the Upper Ottawa Valley Hockey League. At this point in his career, he seemed to hit a barrier as his lack of size started to become a hindrance.

In 1911 Nighbor's friend Harry Cameron was invited to play for the Port Arthur senior club. Cameron refused to go without Nighbor and, although the club agreed to bring him along, they left the youngster on the bench. Nighbor was pressed into service only as a result of an injury bug that hit the team. He made the most of this opportunity by registering six goals in his first dramatic appearance. The "Pembroke Peach" quickly became an indispensable component of his new club.

After being signed by the Toronto Blueshirts of the NHA in 1912, Nighbor again wasted little time in making a good impression. As a 19-year-old rookie, he scored 25 goals in 19 games, including six against the famous Montreal Wanderers on February 15, 1913, in a 10–3 Toronto romp. In a startling move, the Vancouver Millionaires of the PCHA were able to lure Nighbor away from Toronto the next season. He accounted for 33 goals in 28 matches on the West Coast and was a vital member of the squad during its 1915 Stanley Cup win. His work with linemates Cyclone Taylor and Mickey MacKay tormented the opposition and delighted the Vancouver fans. Nighbor recorded five goals in Vancouver's three-game domination of the Ottawa Senators in the Stanley Cup challenge. It was during his sojourn on the West Coast that he perfected his famous "poke-check" while becoming a top-flight defensive forward.

Nighbor returned east in 1915–16 to play with the Ottawa Senators of the NHA. The "Flying Dutchman" enjoyed the finest chapter of his career in the nation's capital. Throughout the 1916–17 season, he waged a memorable goal-scoring battle with Joe Malone of the Quebec Bulldogs that resulted in the two men both finishing with a league high of 41 goals in only 19 games.

Between 1920 and 1923, the Senators won the Stanley Cup three times. Nighbor was brilliant in the 1920 Cup challenge versus the Seattle Metropolitans, when he registered six goals in a hotly contested five-game set. The following season, his checking was crucial to Ottawa's successful Stanley Cup repeat in a low-scoring five-game series against the Vancouver Millionaires. At the conclusion of the 1922–23 schedule, the Senators faced Vancouver and Edmonton in consecutive Cup challenges.

In the matchup against Vancouver, Nighbor scored the winning goal in the critical fourth game to tie the series at two games apiece. Ottawa seized the momentum and captured the deciding game 5–1. In Ottawa's triumph over the Edmonton Eskimos in the next challenge, Nighbor emerged as the victor in the highly anticipated matchup with Duke Keats. This victory was also

In 1924, Frank Nighbor was the first winner of the Hart Trophy as the most valuable player in the NHL.

attributed to the intimidating play of his linemate, Punch Broadbent. Nighbor won his fourth Stanley Cup with Ottawa in 1926–27 after a final series victory over the Boston Bruins.

Nighbor, Frank "the Pembroke Peach"
C, 5′9″, 160 lbs, b: Pembroke, Ont., 1/26/1893, d: 4/13/1966

Season	Club, League	Regular Season					Playoffs				
		GP	G	A	Pts	PIM	GP	G	A	Pts	PIM
1912–13	Toronto Blueshirts, NHA	19	25	0	25	9					
1913–14	Vancouver Millionaires, PCHA	11	10	5	15	6					
1914–15	Vancouver Millionaires, PCHA	17	23	7	30	12	3	4	6	10	6
1915–16	Ottawa Senators, NHA	23	19	5	24	26					
1916–17	Ottawa Senators, NHA	19	41	2	43	18	2	1	0	1	6
1917–18	Ottawa Senators, NHL	10	11	8	19	6					
1918–19	Ottawa Senators, NHL	18	18	9	27	30	2	0	2	2	3
1919–20	Ottawa Senators, NHL	23	26	15	41	18	5	6	1	7	2
1920–21	Ottawa Senators, NHL	24	19	10	29	10	7	1	4	5	2
1921–22	Ottawa Senators, NHL	20	8	10	18	4	2	2	1	3	4
1922–23	Ottawa Senators, NHL	22	11	7	18	16	8	1	2	3	10
1923–24	Ottawa Senators, NHL	20	10	3	13	14	2	0	1	1	2
1924–25	Ottawa Senators, NHL	26	5	2	7	18					
1925–26	Ottawa Senators, NHL	35	12	13	25	40	2	0	0	0	2
1926–27	Ottawa Senators, NHL	38	6	6	12	26	6	1	1	2	0
1927–28	Ottawa Senators, NHL	42	8	5	13	46	2	0	0	0	2
1928–29	Ottawa Senators, NHL	30	1	4	5	22					
1929–30	Ottawa Senators, NHL	19	0	0	0	0					
	Toronto Maple Leafs, NHL	22	2	0	2	2					
1930–31	Buffalo Bisons, IAHL	1	0	0	0	0					
	NHL Totals	349	137	92	229	252	36	11	12	23	27
	NHA Totals	61	85	7	92	53	2	1	0	1	6
	PCHA Totals	28	33	12	45	18	3	4	6	1	6

PCHA First All-Star Team (1915)
Won Hart Trophy (1924)
Won Lady Byng Trophy (1925, 1926)
Won Stanley Cup (1915, 1920, 1921, 1923, 1927)

Although he was a consummate team player, Nighbor received a number of significant individual accolades during his career in Ottawa. Following the 1922–23 season, he became the first-ever winner of the Hart Trophy as the most valuable player in the NHL. Two years later he was invited to Rideau Hall by avid fan Lady Byng, the wife of Canada's Governor General. Nighbor didn't know it, but she'd had a new trophy made to be given to the most gentlemanly player in the league. He was even more surprised to find that it was Lady Byng's intention to inaugurate the new trophy by presenting it to him, based on his performance in the 1924–25 season. Nighbor repeated as the Lady Byng winner in 1925–26.

Nighbor retired as a player in 1930 after splitting his last NHL season between the Senators and the Toronto Maple Leafs. He scored 255 regular-season goals in over 18 years spent in four different top-level pro leagues. Nighbor turned his attention to coaching in the 1930s with the Buffalo Bisons and the London Tecumsehs of the old International-American Hockey League and the New York Rovers of the Eastern Hockey League.

"Peerless Frank" enjoyed success in both offensive and defensive roles during his career. Fans and players alike admired him for his sportsmanlike behavior on the ice that never hindered his will to compete. Nighbor was inducted into the Canadian Sports Hall of Fame and Ottawa Sports Hall Fame and took his place in the Hockey Hall of Fame in 1947.

Dick Irvin

James Dickenson Irvin was one of the most significant hockey figures of the 20th century. He initially made a name for himself as one of the game's top centers in the 1920s. Irvin was lauded for his exceptional stickhandling ability, a hard, accurate shot and a cool temperament that kept him out of the penalty box. His on-ice accomplishments earned him selection to the Hockey Hall of Fame in 1958. Following his playing days, Irvin became one of the finest coaches of his generation.

Born in Hamilton, Ontario, Irvin moved to Winnipeg, Manitoba, as a youngster. There he learned the game and became a star, first in the local church league and then in the junior ranks with the Strathconas. This was followed by a valuable tenure with the senior Winnipeg Monarchs, with whom he won the Allan Cup in 1915.

Irvin turned pro with the Portland Rosebuds of the PCHA in 1916–17 and made an immediate impact. His 35 goals placed the rookie fourth among the league's snipers. Irvin's professional ambitions were put on hold when he enlisted in the Canadian Army, but since he wasn't sent overseas, Irvin was able to play senior hockey as a soldier. He spent the last year of World War I with the Winnipeg Ypres team and then three seasons with the Regina Vics of the Saskatchewan Senior Hockey League.

The Regina Capitals were the benefactors of Irvin's return to the pro ranks in 1921–22. He helped the club win the WCHL title that year, but their Stanley Cup aspirations collapsed when they lost to the Vancouver Millionaires. In 1925–26, the team was transferred to Portland, where it was recreated as the Rosebuds. Irvin starred with 31 goals in 30 matches to tie Bill Cook of Saskatoon for the league lead. When the league disbanded at the end of the year, Irvin was one of several players purchased by the expansion Chicago Black Hawks of the NHL.

Although his finest work as a player was behind him, Irvin still had an impact on the NHL. He was named the Hawks' first captain in 1926–27 and scored an impressive 36 points in 43 contests. That total put him second only to scoring champion Bill Cook of the New York Rangers. Early the next season, Irvin suffered a fractured skull. Even though he returned to play 39 games in 1928–29, he wasn't as effective and decided to retire as a player.

Irvin next became a coach in what proved to be an equally rewarding chapter in his life. It began in 1930–31 with his old NHL club in Chicago, where he helped the team win 24 games in the 44-game schedule. Early in the 1931–32 season, he was lured to Toronto by persuasive owner Conn Smythe. A few months later, Irvin guided the franchise to its first Stanley Cup as the Maple Leafs. Despite not winning the Cup again, he led the squad to the finals six more times before resigning in 1940.

In 1940–41, Irvin was hired to revive a Montreal Canadiens franchise that was floundering on the ice and at the box office, and became one of the key reasons behind the club's return to prominence. In fact, it has often been said that his leadership and vision helped him to save the team from bankruptcy by turning its fortunes around in short order. Irvin was demanding but fair as a bench boss. He quite enjoyed seeing the players practise with vigor and take their frustrations out on one another. The bottom line was that his

Dick Irvin was named the Chicago Black Hawks' first captain in 1926–1927.

Irvin, Dick
C, 5'9", 162 lbs, b: Hamilton, Ont., 7/19/1892, d: 3/16/1957

Season	Club, League	Regular Season					Playoffs				
		GP	G	A	Pts	PIM	GP	G	A	Pts	PIM
1912–13	Winnipeg Strathconas, MHL Sr.	7	32	0	32	12	1	0	0	0	0
	Winnipeg Monarchs, MHL Sr.	2	5	0	5	*					
1913–14	Winnipeg Strathconas, MHL Sr.	3	11	0	11	*					
	Winnipeg Monarchs, MHL Sr.	7	23	1	24	*					
1914–15	Winnipeg Monarchs, MHL Sr.	6	23	3	26	30	8	27	0	27	16
1915–16	Winnipeg Monarchs, MHL Sr.	8	17	4	21	38	2	7	1	8	2
1916–17	Portland Rosebuds, PCHA	23	35	10	45	24					
1917–18	Winnipeg Ypres, MHL Sr.	9	29	8	37	26					
1919–20	Regina Vics, SSHL	12	32	4	36	22	2	1	0	1	4
1920–21	Regina Vics, SSHL	11	19	5	24	12	4	8	0	8	4
1921–22	Regina Capitals, WCHL	20	21	7	28	17	4	3	0	3	2
1922–23	Regina Capitals, WCHL	25	9	4	13	12	2	1	0	1	0
1923–24	Regina Capitals, WCHL	29	15	8	23	33	2	0	2	2	4
1924–25	Regina Capitals, WCHL	28	13	5	18	38					
1925–26	Portland Rosebuds, WHL	30	31	5	36	29					
1926–27	Chicago Black Hawks, NHL	43	18	18	36	34	2	2	0	2	4
1927–28	Chicago Black Hawks, NHL	12	5	4	9	14					
1928–29	Chicago Black Hawks, NHL	39	6	1	7	30					
	NHL Totals	94	29	23	52	78	2	2	0	2	4
	PCHA Totals	23	35	10	45	24					
	WCHL/WHL Totals	132	89	29	118	129	8	4	2	6	6

WCHL First All-Star Team (1924)
PCHA Second All-Star Team (1917)
WCHL Second All-Star Team (1922)

Persuasive Maple Leafs owner Conn Smythe and coach Dick Irvin (right) in the Leafs' dressing room, 1930s.

teams skated with passion. Soon after he took over as coach, Maurice Richard emerged, displaying the level of conviction on the ice that Irvin was looking for.

The Habs attained mediocre results during the first two years under Irvin but became a .500 team in 1942–43. The next year they posted a remarkable 38–5–7 record and won their first Stanley Cup since 1930–31. In the 1944–45 season, they posted 38–8–4 but lost to the Toronto Maple Leafs in the semifinals. Irvin led the Habs to Stanley Cup glory again in 1946 and 1953, and when he stepped aside for the incoming Toe Blake in 1955, the team was on the cusp of winning five straight championships.

Irvin returned to the Black Hawks for the 1955–56 season before retiring with 693 regular-season wins. This impressive total stood at the top of the NHL coaching record list until it was surpassed by Al Arbour and Scotty Bowman in the 1980s. Unfortunately Irvin died in 1957, a year before he took his rightful place in the Hockey Hall of Fame.

George Hainsworth

George Hainsworth was one of hockey's dominant goaltenders of the 1920s and 1930s and his netminding heroics became a legacy that lasted many years after he retired. He appeared relaxed while performing between the pipes, as though giving a minimum of effort. His laid-back approach and exceptional puck-stopping ability continually frustrated opposing players.

Two dominant goalies of the 1920s and 1930s, George Hainsworth (left) and Roy Worters.

The Toronto native enjoyed a strong amateur career in Berlin (later Kitchener), Ontario. It began with a solid season with the Berlin Union Jacks junior outfit in 1911–12, leading the league in victories. This was followed by four years with the city's senior club. In the second year he backstopped the team to the OHA championship. In all four seasons, Hainsworth led the OHA in wins while developing a reputation as one of the top amateur goaltending prospects in Canada.

The emerging star spent the 1916–17 season with the Kew Beach team, based in the east end of Toronto. Hainsworth next moved on to play six seasons with the Kitchener Greenshirts senior OHA team and he added another honor to his portfolio with an Allan Cup triumph in 1918.

Western Canada benefited from Hainsworth's professional debut. He spent three years with the Saskatoon Crescents of the WCHL/WHL before becoming a legend in the NHL. In 1924–25, he led the club to a second-place finish in the regular-season standings. This strong team also featured the likes of Corb Denneny as well as Bill and Bun Cook. Hainsworth's goals-against mark of 2.70 was bettered only by Harry "Hap" Holmes of the Victoria Cougars. The Crescents met the favored Cougars in the playoffs. Hainsworth was strong,

*George Hainsworth with
the Berlin City Seniors.*

George Hainsworth (right) won the Vezina Trophy for the first three years it was presented, from 1927 to 1929.

but the Saskatoon club lost a tough series by a 6–4 aggregate score. In each of the three years he spent out west, he led the league in games played.

Hainsworth signed with the Montreal Canadiens on August 23, 1926, after Newsy Lalonde commended him to owner Leo Dandurand. This proved to be an accurate appraisal and the newcomer became an instant hit. He won the Vezina Trophy each of the first three years it was presented, from 1927 to 1929. In 1928–29, he enjoyed his greatest season by allowing only 43 goals in 44 games and registering 22 shutouts.

A veritable workhorse, Hainsworth led all NHL goalkeepers in games played for nine years out of 10 from 1926 to 1936. He hit double figures in shutouts in his first three years in the league while posting a goals-against mark of less than 1.50.

Following his record-breaking season, the NHL's forward passing rules were modernized, making it virtually impossible for Hainsworth to post such remarkable numbers again. Still, he backstopped the Habs to the Stanley Cup in 1930 and 1931.

In 1933 he was traded to the Toronto Maple Leafs for Lorne Chabot. This transaction made the two netminders the first goalies to play for both storied franchises. Hainsworth helped Toronto win two Canadian Division titles and make appearances in the Stanley Cup finals. On February 14, 1934, he was the Toronto goaltender in the historic Ace Bailey Benefit Game.

As a member of the Maple Leafs, Hainsworth twice led the NHL in wins, but in

Hainsworth, George
G, 5′6″, 150 lbs, b: Toronto, Ont., 6/26/1895, d: 10/9/1950

Season	Club, League	Regular Season				Playoffs			
		GP	Mins	GA	Avg	GP	Mins	GA	Avg
1911–12	Berlin Union Jacks	4	240	13	3.25	6	360	30	5.00
1912–13	Berlin City Seniors, OHA Sr.	4	240	12	3.00	8	480	35	4.38
1913–14	Berlin City Seniors, OHA Sr.	7	420	11	1.57	9	590	31	3.15
1914–15	Berlin City Seniors, OHA Sr.	5	300	9	1.80	4	240	19	4.75
1915–16	Berlin City Seniors, OHA Sr.	8	480	18	2.85	4	280	18	3.86
1917–18	Kitchener Greenshirts, OHA Sr.	9	540	31	3.44	5	298	10	2.01
1918–19	Kitchener Greenshirts, OHA Sr.	9	570	28	2.95				
1919–20	Kitchener Greenshirts, OHA Sr.	8	480	16	2.00	2	150	6	2.40
1920–21	Kitchener Greenshirts, OHA Sr.	10	600	22	2.20	1	60	6	6.00
1921–22	Kitchener Greenshirts, OHA Sr.	10	600	38	3.80				
1922–23	Kitchener Greenshirts, OHA Sr.	12	720	32	2.67				
1923–24	Saskatoon Crescents, WCHL	30	1871	73	2.34				
1924–25	Saskatoon Crescents, WCHL	28	1698	75	2.65	2	120	6	3.00
1925–26	Saskatoon Crescents, WHL	30	1821	64	2.11	2	129	4	1.86
1926–27	Montreal Canadiens, NHL	44	2732	67	1.47	4	252	6	1.43
1927–28	Montreal Canadiens, NHL	44	2730	48	1.05	2	128	3	1.41
1928–29	Montreal Canadiens, NHL	44	2800	43	0.92	3	180	5	1.67
1929–30	Montreal Canadiens, NHL	42	3008	108	2.15	6	481	6	0.75
1930–31	Montreal Canadiens, NHL	44	2740	89	1.95	10	722	21	1.75
1931–32	Montreal Canadiens, NHL	48	2998	110	2.20	4	300	13	2.60
1932–33	Montreal Canadiens, NHL	48	2980	115	2.32	2	120	8	4.00
1933–34	Toronto Maple Leafs, NHL	48	3010	119	2.37	5	302	11	2.19
1934–35	Toronto Maple Leafs, NHL	48	2957	111	2.25	7	460	12	1.57
1935–36	Toronto Maple Leafs, NHL	48	3000	106	2.12	9	541	27	2.99
1936–37	Toronto Maple Leafs, NHL	3	190	9	2.84				
	Montreal Canadiens, NHL	4	270	12	2.67				
	NHL Totals	465	29415	937	1.91	52	3486	112	1.93

Won Vezina Trophy (1927, 1928, 1929)
Won Stanley Cup (1930, 1931)

1936–37, the club decided to go with young star Turk Broda on a full-time basis. Consequently Hainsworth was allowed to sign as a free agent with the Canadiens, where he played his last four big-league games.

"Little George" retired in 1937 with a 1.91 career goals-against mark, the lowest in NHL history along with Alex Connell. His 94 career shutouts were an NHL record until Terry Sawchuk surpassed him in 1963–64. His professional total would include 10 shutouts in the WHL, giving him 104—one more than the NHL's all-time leader. His miniscule 1.91 goals-against mark reflected the low scoring climate that existed during all but two of his seasons. Although the rule changes saw his average climb only late in his career, Hainsworth was one of the top backstoppers of his time.

Hainsworth was an efficient and cool competitor no matter how heated the action on the ice became. To some observers, he was even a tad boring. Hainsworth once said: "I can't look excited because I'm not. I can't shout at other players because that's not my style. I can't dive on easy shots and make them look hard. I guess all I do is stop pucks." Hainsworth was inducted into the Hockey Hall of Fame in 1961, the first year at a year-round location on the grounds of the Canadian National Exhibition in Toronto.

Alf "Dutch" Skinner

Alf "Dutch" Skinner played competitive hockey at the highest levels for almost two decades. The fiery right wing played in eight different leagues, from the early days of loosely organized amateur hockey until the game evolved into a professional sport, and his greatest success came when he was a surprise scoring star in the 1918 playoffs for the Stanley Cup.

Born and raised in Toronto, Alfred Skinner was only 16 when he entered the ranks of the Ontario Hockey Association in 1912 with the Parkdale Canoe Club. The next season, still splitting his time between summer months on the water and winter on the ice, he graduated to the senior circuit of the OHA with the Toronto Rowing Club. He joined the National Hockey Association in 1914 and spent three seasons honing his skills. He played on two Toronto teams, the Shamrocks and the Blueshirts, and made the trip east one season to play for the Montreal Wanderers for one season.

Alf Skinner played at high levels in eight different leagues for two decades.

When the NHA gave way to the National Hockey League in 1917, Skinner was a natural choice for his hometown team, the Toronto Arenas. The Toronto entry in the new league easily won the regular-season title. Skinner had a good year, scoring 13 goals, but he was overshadowed on the championship team by such standouts as Reg Noble and Corb Denneny. All that changed when the Arenas met the Vancouver Millionaires, the champions of the Pacific Coast Hockey League, for the 1918 Stanley Cup. Cyclone Taylor had joined the Patrick brothers in Vancouver and as a superstar was expected to dominate for the Millionaires in the finals. But instead it was Skinner who exploded, scoring seven goals in the first three games of the five-game series. He scored again in the final game to help Toronto win the title and gain the newly formed NHL the instant recognition that comes with a Stanley Cup.

Skinner played one more season in Toronto and was then enticed to join the Vancouver team he'd helped defeat the previous year. He played in Vancouver for five years, three with the

Skinner, Alf "Dutch"
RW, 5'10", 180 lbs, b: Toronto, Ont., 1/26/1896, d: 4/11/1961

Season	Club, League	Regular Season					Playoffs				
		GP	G	A	Pts	PIM	GP	G	A	Pts	PIM
1913–14	Toronto Rowing Club, OHA Sr.	6	4	0	4	0					
1914–15	Toronto Shamrocks, NHA	16	5	2	7	68					
1915–16	Toronto Blueshirts, NHA	23	7	4	11	66					
1916–17	Toronto Blueshirts, NHA	14	5	2	7	49					
	Montreal Wanderers, NHA	6	5	1	6	26					
1917–18	Toronto Arenas, NHL	20	13	5	18	34	7	8	3	11	27
1918–19	Toronto Arenas, NHL	16	12	5	17	26					
1919–20	Vancouver Millionaires, PCHA	22	15	2	17	28	2	1	0	1	0
1920–21	Vancouver Millionaires, PCHA	24	20	4	24	22	5	7	1	8	18
1921–22	Vancouver Millionaires, PCHA	24	11	2	13	21	9	1	0	1	13
1922–23	Vancouver Maroons, PCHA	23	13	2	15	28	6	1	1	2	6
1923–24	Vancouver Maroons, PCHA	29	5	2	7	38	7	0	0	0	2
1924–25	Boston Bruins, NHL	9	0	0	0	6					
	Montreal Maroons, NHL	18	1	1	2	22					
1925–26	Pittsburgh Pirates, NHL	7	0	0	0	2					
1926–27	Duluth Hornets, AHA	23	2	3	5	40					
1927–28	Kitchener Millionaires, Can-Pro	18	4	0	4	42					
1928–29	Kitchener Dutchmen, Can-Pro	39	14	5	19	63	3	0	0	0	10
	NHL Totals	70	26	11	37	90	7	8	3	11	27
	NHA Totals	59	22	9	31	209					
	PCHA Totals	122	64	12	76	137	29	10	2	12	39

PCHA Second All-Star Team (1920, 1921, 1922, 1923)
Won Stanley Cup (1918)

Millionaires and two with the Maroons. His team went almost all the way, reaching four Stanley Cup finals, but he never repeated the success of his first games in the west.

When the PCHA was swallowed up by the Western Canada Hockey League, Skinner once again joined the NHL. He played for two expansion teams, the Boston Bruins and the Montreal Maroons, in 1924–25 and then joined another new entry, the Pittsburgh Pirates, the next season. He played only seven games for the Pirates and then spent three years in the minors, finishing his career in hockey as coach of the Guelph Maple Leafs in 1929–30.

After his retirement from the game, Skinner took a job with the city of Toronto and became politically active, at one time serving as president of the Men's Progressive Conservative Association. He passed away on April 11, 1961, at the age of 65.

Reg Noble

Reg Noble was a winner at both the amateur and professional levels throughout his career. His consistent scoring and natural skill granted him status as one of the game's top left wings. He was also one of hockey's most independent thinkers, and he often got himself into trouble by ignoring training schedules and team curfews. Despite his free spirit, he was a brilliant stickhandler who played hard and earned the favor of fans everywhere.

His hockey skills were refined with the Collingwood Business College squad, the town's OHA junior outfit at the time. In 1914–15, Noble helped the Collingwood juniors win their league before they lost out to Berlin (later Kitchener) in the provincial semifinals. The next season he played a major role in the Toronto Riversides' OHA senior championship by leading all scorers with six goals in four games. That spring he was also called in to aid the St. Michael's Majors' drive to the junior title. Noble was the top player on the squad with nine goals in six games.

Noble joined the professional ranks with the NHA's Toronto Blueshirts in 1916–17. He was enjoying a solid year with nine goals in 14 games when the team folded and he was picked up by the Montreal Canadiens. As a member of the Canadiens, he contributed four goals in six matches but was deemed too late an addition to be eligible for Montreal's quest for the Stanley Cup. He missed out on the club's trip to Seattle, where the Metropolitans made history as the first American team to win the Cup.

Noble's rights weren't retained when the NHA disbanded and the Canadiens prepared to enter the newly formed NHL. Instead, he was signed a week later by the Toronto Arenas. The new signee scored 30 goals in 20 games during the inaugural NHL season to finish third in the scoring race. More importantly, the Toronto club became the new league's first Stanley Cup winners.

Noble remained a stalwart with the franchise when it was renamed the St. Patricks in 1919–20. During this period, he formed one of hockey's great early lines with right winger Cecil "Babe" Dye and center Corb Denneny. Noble was a crowd favorite at the old Mutual Street Arena and one loyal fan used to wind up a siren whenever Noble stole the puck from an opposing attacker, sending the rest of the crowd into a frenzy. Noble's poke-check to thwart the enemy became nearly as famous as his goal-scoring exploits.

In their third year as the St. Pats, the club finished in second place and faced the powerful Ottawa Senators in the playoffs. They won the first match at home and the second game was played amid large pools of water on the natural surface of the Day Arena in the nation's capital. This proved to be the last time an NHL game was played on natural ice. The St. Pats held the home side to a scoreless draw to earn the right to play the PCHA champion Vancouver Maroons for the Stanley Cup and the eastern squad triumphed three games to two. Dye scored nine of his club's 16 goals in the final series. Noble's wily play in the Cup-clinching match was described by sportswriter Lou Marsh: "The work of Capt. Reg Noble at center was by far his best effort of the season and bulked big in the St. Pats' success. He showed plenty of hockey north of his shoulder blades. He swung his stick as long as a bass rod and he broke up play after play in the goulash area in mid-ice."

In December 1924 Noble was traded to the Montreal Maroons and was part of a third Cup triumph in 1925–26. Beginning in 1927, he spent over five seasons as a defenseman with the Detroit Cougars/Falcons when Jack Adams refused to believe the rumors that Noble was washed up as a player. Noble still managed to add 23 goals to his career total while functioning in a defensive role. He went on to serve as the second captain in franchise history from 1927 to 1930.

Noble played his last 20 NHL games for the Maroons in the second half of the 1932–33 season. His career totals of 167 goals and 97 assists reflect the fact that assists were credited infrequently during this era. The following year he skated as a pro for the final time with the Cleveland Indians of the IAHL.

After retiring as a player, Noble returned to the NHL for two seasons as a referee. During World War II, he was persuaded to step onto the ice again with the Married Men of Alliston recreational team. Reg Noble died of a massive coronary at his home in Alliston, Ontario, on January 19, 1962, at the age of 65. He was elected to the Red Wings Hall of Fame in 1944 and the Hockey Hall of Fame in 1962.

Reg Noble's consistent scoring made him one of the game's top left wings.

Noble, Reg
C/D, 5'8", 180 lbs, b: Collingwood, Ont., 6/23/1896, d: 1/19/1962

Season	Club, League	Regular Season					Playoffs				
		GP	G	A	Pts	Plm	GP	G	A	Pts	Plm
1915–16	Toronto Riversides, OHA Sr.	10	14	0	14	*	4	6	0	6	*
1916–17	Toronto Blueshirts, NHA	14	9	3	12	51					
	Montreal Canadiens, NHA	6	4	0	4	15	2	0	0	0	3
1917–18	Toronto Arenas, NHL	20	30	10	40	35	7	3	2	5	22
1918–19	Toronto Arenas, NHL	17	10	4	14	43					
1919–20	Toronto St. Pats, NHL	24	24	9	33	51					
1920–21	Toronto St. Pats, NHL	24	19	8	27	54	2	0	0	0	0
1921–22	Toronto St. Pats, NHL	24	17	11	28	19	9	0	1	1	21
1922–23	Toronto St. Pats, NHL	24	12	10	22	41					
1923–24	Toronto St. Pats, NHL	23	12	3	15	23					
1924–25	Toronto St. Pats, NHL	3	1	0	1	4					
	Montreal Maroons, NHL	27	7	6	13	58					
1925–26	Montreal Maroons, NHL	33	9	9	18	96	8	1	1	2	12
1926–27	Montreal Maroons, NHL	43	3	3	6	112	2	0	0	0	2
1927–28	Detroit Cougars, NHL	44	6	8	14	63					
1928–29	Detroit Cougars, NHL	43	6	4	10	52	2	0	0	0	2
1929–30	Detroit Cougars, NHL	43	6	4	10	72					
1930–31	Detroit Falcons, NHL	44	2	5	7	42					
1931–32	Detroit Falcons, NHL	48	3	3	6	72	2	0	0	0	0
1932–33	Detroit Falcons, NHL	5	0	0	0	6					
	Montreal Maroons, NHL	20	0	0	0	16	2	0	0	0	2
1933–34	Cleveland Indians, IAHL	40	2	3	5	43					
	NHA Totals	20	13	3	16	66	2	0	0	0	3
	NHL Totals	509	167	97	264	859	34	4	4	8	61

Won Stanley Cup (1918, 1922, 1926)

Duncan "Mickey" MacKay

Mickey MacKay was blessed with instinct and timing on the ice.

A marvelous skater and goal scorer, Duncan McMillan "Mickey" MacKay was blessed with instinct and timing on the ice that was matched by few contemporaries. A star rover and center in a number of leagues during his career, he was particularly successful in the Pacific Coast Hockey Association, where his offensive heroics made him one of the Vancouver Millionaires' most popular stars.

Born in Chesley, Ontario, MacKay learned to skate as a boy on the frozen ponds in his community as well as on the nearby Saugeen River. He later joined the Chesley Colts junior club of the northern Ontario league, where he first gained local fame. MacKay's reputation grew to the point where he was lured to western Canada to play for the Edmonton senior club and later the Grand Forks outfit in the Kootenay league.

In 1914 McKay was signed by the Vancouver Millionaires of the PCHA and he quickly embarked on the most fruitful period of his hockey career. MacKay dazzled the West Coast fans with a three-goal effort in his first league game on December 8, 1914, playing on a line with Frank Nighbor and Ken Mallen. His 33 goals in 17 games as a rookie exceeded all other rivals. During the Stanley Cup victory over Ottawa, MacKay continued to impress with four goals in the three-game series that his team dominated.

The scoring exploits of MacKay didn't abate during the coming years. He was sensational during Vancouver's heartbreaking loss to the Toronto Arenas in the 1918 Stanley Cup series, scoring five goals in as many games playing as a rover and right wing.

"The Wee Scot" spent the 1919–20 schedule with the Calgary Columbus of the Alberta Big 4 Hockey League before returning to Vancouver the next year. He topped the PCHA in goals scored during its last year of operation in 1923–24. That same year his Vancouver squad lost to the Montreal Canadiens in the last Stanley Cup championship series involving a PCHA team.

The Vancouver franchise joined the Western Canada Hockey League in 1924–25 and MacKay led the way on the strength of a league high of 27 goals in 28 games. The loop was renamed the Western Hockey League prior to the 1925–26 schedule. When the league folded a few months later, MacKay was among the stars coveted and purchased by NHL teams. Consequently he joined the Chicago Black Hawks for their inaugural season in 1926–27.

MacKay, Duncan "Mickey"
C, 5´9˝, 162 lbs, b: Chesley, Ont., 5/25/1894, d: 5/21/1940

Season	Club, League	Regular Season					Playoffs				
		GP	G	A	Pts	PIM	GP	G	A	Pts	PIM
1914–15	Vancouver Millionaires, PCHA	17	33	11	44	9	3	4	2	6	9
1915–16	Vancouver Millionaires, PCHA	14	12	7	19	32					
1916–17	Vancouver Millionaires, PCHA	23	22	11	33	37					
1917–18	Vancouver Millionaires, PCHA	18	10	8	18	31	7	7	5	12	15
1918–19	Vancouver Millionaires, PCHA	17	9	9	18	9					
1919–20	Calgary Columbus Club, Big 4	11	4	6	10	14					
1920–21	Vancouver Millionaires, PCHA	21	10	8	18	15	7	0	4	4	0
1921–22	Vancouver Millionaires, PCHA	24	14	12	26	20	9	1	0	1	6
1922–23	Vancouver Maroons, PCHA	30	28	12	40	38	6	3	0	3	16
1923–24	Vancouver Maroons, PCHA	28	21	4	25	2	7	3	0	3	2
1924–25	Vancouver Maroons, WCHL	28	27	6	33	17					
1925–26	Vancouver Maroons, WHL	27	12	4	16	24					
1926–27	Chicago Black Hawks, NHL	34	14	8	22	23	2	0	0	0	0
1927–28	Chicago Black Hawks, NHL	36	17	4	21	23					
1928–29	Pittsburgh Pirates, NHL	10	1	0	1	2					
	Boston Bruins, NHL	30	8	2	10	18	3	0	0	0	2
1929–30	Boston Bruins, NHL	37	4	5	9	13	6	0	0	0	4
	NHL Totals	147	44	19	63	79	11	0	0	0	6
	PCHA/WCHL/WHL Totals	247	198	92	290	234	39	18	11	29	48

PCHA First All-Star Team (1915, 1917, 1919, 1922, 1923)
WCHL First All-Star Team (1925)
WHL First All-Star Team (1926)
PCHA Second All-Star Team (1916, 1918, 1921)
Won Stanley Cup (1915, 1929)

MacKay spent two years in the Windy City, recording 31 goals playing on a line with Dick Irvin.

Acquired by the Pittsburgh Pirates in the off-season, MacKay was traded again, this time to the Boston Bruins, on December 21, 1928. He scored eight goals while helping the Bruins finish at the top of the American Division standings. In the Stanley Cup finals, MacKay helped the Beantowners quell the New York Rangers in two straight games and got his name on the Cup for the second time in his career. He retired as a player partway through the next season to assume the task of business manager with the Bruins.

Mickey MacKay was inducted into the Hockey Hall of Fame in 1952.

MacKay settled in Grand Forks, British Columbia, after leaving Boston. He was maintaining his interest in the game as coach of several local minor hockey teams when he was tragically killed in an automobile accident at the age of 46. MacKay scored 260 regular-season and playoff goals in three top-flight leagues between 1914 and 1929. He was inducted into the British Columbia Sports Hall of Fame and earned a place in the Hockey Hall of Fame in 1952.

Cy Denneny

One of the top-scoring left wings of his era, Cy Denneny topped the 20-goal mark eight times in his stellar career. Although he wasn't the swiftest skater, Denneny used his shot to deadly effect. Much to the chagrin of opposing netminders, he also became one of the first players to experiment with a curved stick. Denneny was the top goal-getter in the history of the Ottawa Senators franchise, and when he retired, he trailed only Newsy Lalonde and Joe Malone among players of his era.

Denneny was born in Farrow's Point, Ontario, a small community near Cornwall which was eventually flooded by the St. Lawrence Seaway. He starred as an amateur in the local county league between 1910 and 1912 before moving out of his home area. After spending the 1912–13 season with the Russell team of the Lower Ottawa Valley league, Denneny moved on to the O'Brien Mine team of the Cobalt Mining League. His play was a big reason the club won the CML championship that year.

Cy Denneny was one of the first players to experiment with a curved stick.

In 1914–15, the talented forward stepped into a larger spotlight with the Toronto Shamrocks of the NHA, where he starred, scoring six goals in eight games. That year the Toronto club also received the benefit of his gifted brother Corb. The next year, Cy stayed in Toronto with the Blueshirts, where he became a bright star with 24 goals in as many games. The Denneny brothers were centered by Duke Keats on the top-scoring line in the NHA. "The Cornwall Colt" then moved to Ottawa for the prime of his career.

While with the Senators, Denneny saw the franchise become one of the founding members of the NHL in 1917 and win the Stanley Cup four times in the 1920s. He was a productive scorer despite the fact that he was often in charge of protecting his good-natured linemates Jack Darragh and Frank Nighbor. Later he teamed with rugged Punch Broadbent. The two were so adept at keeping the toughest foes at bay that they became known as "the Gold Dust Twins."

Denneny became the all-time leading Ottawa goal scorer, leading the league in 1923–24. On six other occasions he finished as the runner-up in the scoring derby. This included the 1917–18 season, when he finished with a career high of 36 goals in 20 matches but still trailed the Canadiens' 44-goal scorer, Joe Malone. On March 7, 1921, Denneny scored five goals in one game against the Hamilton Tigers. In so doing, he became the sixth player in NHL history to accomplish this feat. The fifth had been his brother Corb, who five weeks earlier had potted five of his own against the Tigers.

Denneny, Cy
LW, 5′7″, 168 lbs, b: Farrow's Point, Ont., 12/23/1891, d: 10/12/1970

Season	Club, League	Regular Season					Playoffs				
		GP	G	A	Pts	PIM	GP	G	A	Pts	PIM
1914–15	Ontarios — Shamrocks, NHA	8	6	0	6	43					
1915–16	Toronto Blueshirts, NHA	24	24	4	28	57					
1916–17	Ottawa Senators, NHL	10	3	1	4	25	2	1	0	1	8
1917–18	Ottawa Senators, NHL	20	36	10	46	80					
1918–19	Ottawa Senators, NHL	18	18	6	24	55	7	5	3	8	9
1919–20	Ottawa Senators, NHL	24	16	6	22	31	5	0	2	2	3
1920–21	Ottawa Senators, NHL	24	34	5	39	10	7	4	2	6	15
1921–22	Ottawa Senators, NHL	22	27	12	39	20	2	2	0	2	4
1922–23	Ottawa Senators, NHL	24	21	10	31	20	8	3	1	4	6
1923–24	Ottawa Senators, NHL	21	22	1	23	10	2	2	0	2	10
1924–25	Ottawa Senators, NHL	28	27	15	42	16					
1925–26	Ottawa Senators, NHL	36	24	12	36	18	2	0	0	0	4
1926–27	Ottawa Senators, NHL	42	17	6	23	16	6	5	0	5	0
1927–28	Ottawa Senators, NHL	44	3	0	3	12	2	0	0	0	0
1928–29	Boston Bruins, NHL	23	1	2	3	2	2	0	0	0	0
	NHA Totals	42	33	5	38	125	2	1	0	1	8
	NHL Totals	326	246	85	331	290	43	21	8	29	51

NHL Scoring Leader (1924)
Won Stanley Cup (1920, 1921, 1923, 1927, 1929)

One of the most dangerous shooters in league history, Denneny actually stood number one as the NHL's all-time leading goal scorer at the end of the 1919–20 season, although he was passed by Joe Malone the following year. In 1922–23, he regained the lead in career goals scored and remained the all-time league leader when he retired. His lofty position lasted until Howie Morenz set a new NHL standard in 1933–34.

Denneny also left the game as the top point scorer in league history with 331 points to his credit. Morenz passed him when he earned his 332nd point in 1931–32. The combined total of 475 regular-season points made Cy and Corb Denneny one of the most famous sibling pairs in the NHL and certainly one of the more productive prewar brother combinations.

After bringing his rewarding career with the Senators to a close, Denneny joined the Boston Bruins as player, coach and assistant manager in 1928–29. He contributed valuable leadership and savvy while helping the Beantowners win their first Stanley Cup in franchise history by defeating New York Rangers in 1929.

Denneny tried his hand at refereeing from 1929 to 1931. In 1931–32, he spent a busy year in the coaching ranks at various levels in the Ottawa city league as well as both the Upper and Lower Ottawa Valley leagues. This was followed by a year as coach and manager of the financially crippled Ottawa Senators in 1932–33. Cy Denneny was inducted into the Hockey Hall of Fame in 1959.

George "Buck" Boucher

A member of one of hockey's best-known families, George "Buck" Boucher was a stellar defenseman during a professional career that spanned two decades. Although he wasn't blessed with lightning speed, his proficient stickhandling and competitive zeal assured his status among the NHL's best.

Boucher came by his hockey prowess honestly. His younger brother Frank enjoyed an exceptional career that led to his election to the Hockey Hall of Fame in 1958. Billy and Bob Boucher also performed solidly in the pros. Before his tenure in hockey, George Boucher displayed superior all-round athletic ability. He was a proficient halfback for the Ottawa Rough Riders of the Canadian Football League and excelled at baseball as a catcher, although he never played professionally.

Boucher gained valuable training in the Ottawa city league with the Aberdeens and the New Edinburghs before embarking on a pro career in 1915 with the hometown Senators of the National Hockey Association. Boucher remained with the franchise when it became one of the founding members of the National Hockey League in 1917. In the nation's capital he was partnered with King Clancy to form one of the toughest, most effective duos in the league. In fact, Boucher helped nurture the young Clancy from his first days with Ottawa. The King himself said: "They teamed me with him on defense and it was a lucky break for me. I made a million mistakes, but he'd cover up for me. He was a great competitor and there never was a better team player. He could do everything and had hockey brains besides." This talented duo's puckhandling savvy and will to compete contributed significantly to the Senators' four Stanley Cup triumphs in 1920, 1921, 1923 and 1927.

George Boucher was a stellar defenseman during a career that spanned two decades.

During the latter stages of the 1928–29 schedule, the Senators were in the midst of a struggle to hold on to a playoff spot. Boucher felt the harsh criticism of impatient fans at this time. His effectiveness as a player had decreased somewhat, but his desire and sense of pride were still strong. Ottawa owner Frank Ahearn, a players' owner if there ever was one, couldn't bear to see one of his most dedicated soldiers suffer this way. Reluctantly, he approached other teams concerning possible interest in Boucher and Eddie Gerard of the Montreal Maroons jumped at the opportunity to acquire a wily veteran who would stabilize his defense corps.

Boucher completed his NHL career with the Chicago Black Hawks in 1931–32 after they picked him up on waivers early in the season. His total of 120 goals in 449 regular-season games was a notable achievement in this era. Boucher's last professional work consisted of nine games with the Boston Cubs of the Can-Am league the following season.

The realm of coaching was the next step for Boucher. He earned his stripes as bench boss with the 1930–31 Montreal Maroons. The team finished two games over .500 and a respectable third in the Canadian Division but failed to qualify for the post-season. In 1932–33, he led the Boston Bruins' farm team, the Bruins Cubs, to the Can-Am league championship in his only year as the team's coach.

Boucher returned to NHL coaching with the Ottawa Senators in 1933–34, but the Great Depression took its toll on the once proud franchise, which finished in last place and was relocated to St. Louis as the Eagles. Boucher stayed on as coach for one last season, but the team's fortunes didn't improve in the American Midwest and it folded in 1935. Between 1935 and 1938, Boucher guided the Springfield Indians of the Can-Am circuit. This was followed by one-year placements with Noranda of the Gold Belt league and the Quebec Beavers of the Quebec Senior Hockey League before Boucher took a five-year sabbatical from the game.

Tommy Gorman had been the manager of the great Ottawa clubs that won four Stanley Cups in the 1920s. After the Senators folded, he oversaw the new Senators franchise in the Quebec Senior Hockey League. Prior to the 1946–47 season, Gorman persuaded Boucher to come out of retirement and coach his club. In 1949 they vanquished the Regina Capitals to claim the Allan Cup as Canadian senior champions—Boucher's first championship in 16 years of professional hockey.

Boucher, George "Buck"
D, 5′9″, 169 lbs, b: Ottawa, Ont., 8/19/1896, d: 10/17/1960

Season	Club, League	Regular Season					Playoffs				
		GP	G	A	Pts	Plm	GP	G	A	Pts	Plm
1913–14	Ottawa New Edinburghs, City Sr.	5	1	0	1	*					
1914–15	Ottawa New Edinburghs, City Sr.	15	12	0	12	*					
1915–16	Ottawa Senators, NHA	19	9	1	10	62					
1916–17	Ottawa Senators, NHA	18	10	3	13	27	2	1	0	1	3
1917–18	Ottawa Senators, NHL	21	9	8	17	46					
1918–19	Ottawa Senators, NHL	17	4	2	6	32	7	3	0	3	12
1919–20	Ottawa Senators, NHL	23	9	8	17	55	5	2	0	2	3
1920–21	Ottawa Senators, NHL	23	11	8	19	53	5	2	0	2	9
1921–22	Ottawa Senators, NHL	23	13	12	25	12	2	0	0	0	4
1922–23	Ottawa Senators, NHL	23	15	9	24	44	8	2	1	3	8
1923–24	Ottawa Senators, NHL	21	14	5	19	28	2	0	1	1	4
1924–25	Ottawa Senators, NHL	28	15	4	19	80					
1925–26	Ottawa Senators, NHL	36	8	4	12	64	2	0	0	0	10
1926–27	Ottawa Senators, NHL	40	8	3	11	115	6	0	0	0	43
1927–28	Ottawa Senators, NHL	43	7	5	12	78	2	0	0	0	4
1928–29	Ottawa Senators, NHL	29	3	1	4	60					
	Montreal Maroons, NHL	12	1	1	2	10					
1929–30	Montreal Maroons, NHL	37	2	6	8	50	3	0	0	0	2
1930–31	Montreal Maroons, NHL	30	0	0	0	25					
1931–32	Chicago Black Hawks, NHL	43	1	5	6	50	2	0	1	1	0
1932–33	Boston Cubs, Can-Am	9	0	0	0	8					
	NHA Totals	37	19	4	23	89	2	1	0	1	3
	NHL Totals	449	120	81	201	802	44	9	3	12	99

Won Stanley Cup (1920, 1921, 1923, 1927)

Boucher was called in to assist with the player selection and training for the 1948 Winter Olympics in St. Moritz, Switzerland. The Canadian representatives were the Ottawa RCAF Flyers. The team went on to post a 7–0–1 record while capturing the gold medal.

Following his Olympic involvement, Boucher was named head coach of the Boston Bruins in 1949 after Dit Clapper's unexpected retirement. His year behind the Bruins' bench was extremely trying. The club was short on talent and finished in fifth place in the six-team NHL standings. Their 15 wins over the 70-game schedule were largely attributable to the hard-working spirit of the often overmatched side. This work ethic was clearly instilled in the team by their coach. When the season was over, it became apparent that Boucher, though he didn't yet know it, was about to be dropped by the Bruins management.

In 1950–51, Boucher coached the Ottawa RCAF Flyers of the Quebec Senior Hockey League, then took another break before returning for one last assignment behind the bench of the Quebec Hockey League's Ottawa Senators. Boucher was inducted into the Hockey Hall of Fame in 1960 while he was battling throat cancer. In a moving ceremony, he was presented his Hall of Fame insignia at his hospital bed. Three weeks later, after a courageous six-year battle, Boucher succumbed to his illness on October 17, 1960.

Frank "Raffles" Boucher

A description of Frank Boucher must include both his brilliant playmaking as a center and his reputation as one of the most gentlemanly figures ever associated with the NHL. Teamed with Bill and Bun Cook, he formed the dangerous Bread Line of the New York Rangers and dominated the annual voting for the Lady Byng Trophy between 1928 and 1935.

A native of Ottawa, Boucher began playing hockey on the Rideau Canal at the age of eight. He was on his public school team with Aurel Joliat before he joined the intermediate and senior levels of competition. He spent most of the 1919–20 season with the Ottawa New Edinburghs squad before joining the Lethbridge, Alberta, detachment of the Royal North West Mounted Police. In 1920 he was sent to Regina, Saskatchewan, for training and made a name for himself as a standout member of the 1920–21 Redcoats. It was at this point that Boucher attracted the attention of the Ottawa Senators, who eventually purchased his discharge and placed him in the lineup in time for the 1921–22 NHL schedule.

Raffles Boucher spent one year in the nation's capital before he was sold to the Vancouver Maroons of the PCHA, where he became one of the stars of the West Coast, scoring 58 goals in 113 games over four seasons. Although he accumulated respectable offensive totals, Boucher's popularity derived from his exceptional passing. Beginning in 1922–23, he was chosen as either a starter or a substitute on the PCHA All-Star Team for three straight years. When the league disbanded in 1926, Boucher was claimed by the Boston Bruins. However, before playing a single game in Boston, he was purchased by the New York Rangers at the insistence of his old western rivals, Bill and Bun Cook, who had experienced Boucher's skills firsthand.

True gentleman Frank Boucher dominated the annual voting for the Lady Byng Trophy between 1928 and 1935.

"Gentleman Frank" was inserted between the Cook brothers during the Rangers' inaugural NHL season in 1926–27. The unit jelled and exhibited an advanced level of play that surpassed all expectations. The Bread Line developed into one of the most formidable combinations in NHL history. They were such a perfect fit that New York coach Lester Patrick allowed them to devise plays at one end of the rink while the remainder of the team practised down at the other.

During the decade they played together, Boucher and the Cooks accumulated over 1,100 points. They led the Rangers to their first Stanley Cup in the team's second year of existence in the spring of 1928. Boucher dominated the post-season scoring with seven goals and 10 points, including both of New York's goals in the Cup-clinching 2–1 triumph over the Montreal Maroons in the final game of the best-of-five series. Five seasons later, he contributed four points to the Blueshirts' second Cup victory at the expense of the Toronto Maple Leafs.

Boucher retired partway through the 1937–38 season, but he returned for 15 games in 1943–44 when players enlisted in the army and the Rangers' roster was depleted. He scored 14 points in 15 games during this brief comeback appearance to bring his career totals to 160 goals and 423 points in 14 regular seasons.

Coaching became Boucher's passion as soon as he retired as a player. He guided the New York Rovers to the championship of the Eastern Hockey League in 1938–39 before rejoining the Rangers the following year. Boucher made a triumphant return to the Blueshirts by coaching them to victory over the Toronto Maple Leafs in the 1940 Stanley Cup finals. That same regular season he pulled goaltender Dave Kerr with two minutes left in the game in an attempt to tie the score, initiating a trend that would become exceedingly popular in the coming years.

Boucher remained New York's bench boss for the next 10 winters, adding the portfolio of general manager to his responsibilities in 1946–47. He remained coach and general manager until 1948–49, when he co-coached the

Boucher, Frank "Raffles"
C, 5'9", 185 lbs, b: Ottawa, Ont., 10/7/1901, d: 12/12/1977

Season	Club, League	Regular Season					Playoffs				
		GP	G	A	Pts	PIM	GP	G	A	Pts	PIM
1917–18	Ottawa Munitions, City Sr.	1	0	0	0	0	1	0	0	0	0
1918–19	Ottawa New Edinburghs, City Sr.	7	1	2	3	5					
1920–21	Lethbridge Vets, ASHL	*	*	*	*	*	*	*	*	*	*
1921–22	Ottawa Senators, NHL	24	8	2	10	4	1	0	0	0	0
1922–23	Vancouver Maroons, PCHA	29	11	9	20	2	6	2	1	3	4
1923–24	Vancouver Maroons, PCHA	28	15	5	20	10	7	3	1	4	2
1924–25	Vancouver Maroons, WCHL	27	16	12	28	6					
1925–26	Vancouver Maroons, WCHL	29	15	7	22	14					
1926–27	New York Rangers, NHL	44	13	15	28	17	2	0	0	0	4
1927–28	New York Rangers, NHL	44	23	12	35	15	9	7	1	8	2
1928–29	New York Rangers, NHL	44	10	16	26	8	6	1	0	1	0
1929–30	New York Rangers, NHL	42	26	36	62	16	3	1	1	2	0
1930–31	New York Rangers, NHL	44	12	27	39	20	4	0	2	2	0
1931–32	New York Rangers, NHL	48	12	23	35	18	7	3	6	9	0
1932–33	New York Rangers, NHL	46	7	28	35	4	8	2	2	4	6
1933–34	New York Rangers, NHL	48	14	30	44	4	2	0	0	0	0
1934–35	New York Rangers, NHL	48	13	32	45	2	4	0	3	3	0
1935–36	New York Rangers, NHL	48	11	18	29	2					
1936–37	New York Rangers, NHL	44	7	13	20	5	9	2	3	5	0
1937–38	New York Rangers, NHL	18	0	1	1	2					
1943–44	New York Rangers, NHL	15	4	10	14	2					
	NHL Totals	557	160	263	423	119	55	16	18	34	12

NHL First All-Star Team (1933, 1934, 1935)
NHL Second All-Star Team (1931)
Won Lady Byng Trophy (1928, 1929, 1930, 1931, 1933, 1934, 1935)
Won Lester Patrick Trophy (1993)
Won Stanley Cup (1928, 1933)

team with Lynn Patrick before stepping aside to focus strictly on the responsibilities of GM. He stayed on in that capacity until 1954–55, although he helped Murray Patrick coach the club in 1953–54.

While still affiliated with the Rangers, Boucher functioned as chairman of the NHL rules committee for 15 years. He worked in tandem with Cecil Duncan of the Canadian Amateur Hockey Association to bring about the introduction of the center red line in 1943–44. This innovation allowed teams to pass the puck out of their own zone and consequently produced a more exciting brand of hockey throughout the league. After leaving the NHL permanently, Boucher returned to amateur hockey to use his administrative expertise. Between 1959 and 1967 he served as commissioner of the Saskatchewan Junior Hockey League. During the 1966–67 season he performed the same duties for the Canadian junior league as well.

Frank Boucher (center) was teamed with Bill (left) and Bun Cook (right) to form the dangerous Bread Line for the New York Rangers.

Frank Boucher was one of the finest all-round players of his time, while his gentlemanly conduct on the ice served as a benchmark for many who followed him. On February 9, 1962, Boucher was presented the Sportsmanship Brotherhood's annual award in New York. He was honored posthumously with the Lester Patrick Trophy in 1993 for his immense contribution to the game in the United States. A member of the Canadian Sports Hall of Fame and the Ottawa Sports Hall of Fame, Boucher was inducted into the Hockey Hall of Fame in 1958.

Jack "Jolly" Adams

Although he was inducted into the Hockey Hall of Fame as a player, "Jolly" Jack Adams spent the greater part of his life as coach and general manager of the Detroit Red Wings. He's the only man to have his name on the Stanley Cup as a player, general manager and coach. "Maybe I was wrong," he said later in life as if to apologize, "but I wanted to win, and if that's wrong, then I made a mistake."

As a skater, his fame was established during the war when he played in Peterborough with the 247th Battalion team. In each of 12 games, Adams routinely scored five or six goals. Both fans and scouts saw his immense talents emerge, as this account confirms: "Adams, the Petes' right winger, looks good enough to catch a place with any team. He's a husky gent with plenty of speed and packs a healthy shot." He then joined the old Toronto Arenas during the 1917–18 inaugural NHL season and won his first Stanley Cup. After one more season with Toronto, he moved to Vancouver and played in the PCHA for the Millionaires for three years.

Jack Adams is the only man to have his name on the Stanley Cup as a player, general manager and coach.

In Vancouver, Adams did something which hadn't happened hadn't before or since. In the last game of the 1920–21 season, against the Victorias, he accidentally scored a goal on his own net. On this occasion the referee awarded Adams with having scored the goal and he became the only player ever to be credited with a goal on his own net. The next year he won the scoring title in the PCHA.

Adams returned east for the 1922–23 season, joining the Toronto St. Pats for four years before finishing his skating days with Ottawa in 1926–27, where he ended as he'd begun, winning a Stanley Cup. His teammates that year included a veritable who's who of the Hockey Hall of Fame—King Clancy, Frank Nighbor, Cy Denneny, Frank Finnigan, Alex Connell and George Boucher.

Although his playing days were over, Adams' life in hockey was still in its infancy. NHL president Frank Calder suggested that he coach the Detroit Falcons, a second-year team that had lost money and struggled badly in its first year in the NHL. "I think you're just the man they need in Detroit," Calder remarked, and he couldn't have been more correct.

Jack Adams (top row, second from the right) wasn't always the smallest on the team.

When Adams first joined the Detroit Falcons, the team played its home games in Windsor, Ontario. Whenever the team won, they were booed, because the locals had come to see the Yanks get killed by a Canadian team. The next year the team moved into its own building, the Olympia in Detroit, and its on-ice success improved slightly. James Norris became owner and said to Adams, "I'll give you a year, on probation." That was his best offer of continued employment.

The team quickly improved and in 1934 the Red Wings, as Norris decided to call them, made it to the finals before losing to Chicago. Two years later they won their first Stanley Cup and they repeated as champions in 1937. Adams wasn't only Detroit's on-ice authority but also its business manager, traveling secretary and publicist. He was loud and pugnacious, first as a player and then as an executive. Adams would storm the officials' room at the Olympia to berate the referee for calls he objected to. But in the off-season he fought tooth and nail at the governors' meetings for pay raises for the officials. That was his style—tough and fair.

After the two Cups in the 1930s, the Red Wings had a tough time keeping pace with Toronto, Boston and Montreal. They made it to the finals in 1941, when they lost to the Bruins. The following year came the famous series when Adams and his Wings blew a 3–0 lead in games and lost the Stanley Cup to Toronto after the Leafs won the last four games. The next year they again lost the finals to Boston. Then in 1945 Detroit fought Toronto back from 3–0 down in games to force a seventh game. But unlike the Wings in 1942, the Leafs didn't lose a fourth game in a row.

Adams, Jack "Jolly"
C, 5´9˝, 175 lbs, b: Fort William, Ont., 6/14/1895, d: 5/1/1968

Season	Club, League	Regular Season					Playoffs				
		GP	G	A	Pts	PIM	GP	G	A	Pts	PIM
1917–18	Sarnia Sailors, OHA Sr.	6	15	0	15	*					
	Toronto Arenas, NHL	8	0	0	0	31	2	1	0	1	6
1918–19	Toronto Arenas, NHL	18	3	3	6	47					
1919–20	Vancouver Millionaires, PCHA	22	9	6	15	18	2	0	0	0	0
1920–21	Vancouver Millionaires, PCHA	24	17	12	29	60	7	5	0	6	8
1921–22	Vancouver Millionaires, PCHA	24	26	4	30	24	9	7	0	7	25
1922–23	Toronto St. Pats, NHL	23	19	9	28	42					
1923–24	Toronto St. Pats, NHL	22	13	3	16	49					
1924–25	Toronto St. Pats, NHL	27	21	8	29	66	2	1	0	1	7
1925–26	Toronto St. Pats, NHL	36	21	5	26	52					
1926–27	Ottawa Senators, NHL	40	5	1	6	66	6	0	0	0	2
	NHL Totals	174	82	29	111	353	10	2	0	2	15
	PCHA Totals	70	52	22	74	102	18	12	1	13	33

PCHA First All-Star Team (1921, 1922)
Won Stanley Cup (1918, 1927)
PCHA Champion (1921, 1922)

In the 1920–21 season, Jack Adams (right) accidentally scored a goal on his own net and became the only player ever to be credited with an own goal.

Jack Adams (right) wasn't only Detroit's on-ice authority but also its business manager, traveling secretary and publicist.

The highlight of Jolly Jack's career came right after the war when the Wings finished in first place for seven successive years, from 1948 to 1955, during which time he also won four of his seven Stanley Cups. By this time he'd retired as a coach to concentrate on being general manager, developing a superior farm system and ensuring new talent would be challenged at every training camp. "Our 1951–52 champions that won the playoffs in eight games was the greatest hockey club ever assembled," he boasted years later. His pride and joy was Gordie Howe, the man he found, signed, developed and helped mature into the greatest player of all time. "Picking him out of a bunch of kids at training camp and watching him develop has been my greatest thrill," he happily admitted. "He's a living memorial to my career." His other great players included Ted Lindsay, Terry Sawchuk, Alex Delvecchio, Red Kelly and many other stars who had tremendous careers with the Winged Wheel.

Because of his success and longevity, the NHL created the coach of the year award in his honor, and to this day the Jack Adams Award represents a coach's finest praise. Adams brought great pride to Detroit and will forever be remembered in that city for his lifelong contribution to the game and to the Red Wings' success.

Adams, Jack "Jolly"
Head Coach, b: Fort William, Ont., 6/14/1895, d: 5/1/1968

Season	Club, League	Regular Season					Playoffs				
		GC	W	L	T	W%	GC	W	L	T	W%
1922–23	Toronto St. Patricks, NHL	18	10	7	1	0.583					
1927–28	Detroit Cougars, NHL	44	19	19	6	0.500					
1928–29	Detroit Cougars, NHL	44	19	16	9	0.534	2	0	2	0	0.000
1929–30	Detroit Cougars, NHL	44	14	24	6	0.386					
1930–31	Detroit Falcons, NHL	44	16	21	7	0.443					
1931–32	Detroit Falcons, NHL	48	18	20	10	0.479	2	0	1	1	0.250
1932–33	Detroit Red Wings, NHL	48	25	15	8	0.604	4	2	2	0	0.500
1933–34	Detroit Red Wings, NHL	48	24	14	10	0.604	9	4	5	0	0.444
1934–35	Detroit Red Wings, NHL	48	19	22	7	0.469					
1935–36	Detroit Red Wings, NHL	48	24	16	8	0.583	7	6	1	0	0.857
1936–37	Detroit Red Wings, NHL	48	25	14	9	0.615	10	6	4	0	0.600
1937–38	Detroit Red Wings, NHL	48	12	25	11	0.365					
1938–39	Detroit Red Wings, NHL	48	18	24	6	0.438	6	3	3	0	0.500
1939–40	Detroit Red Wings, NHL	48	16	26	6	0.396	5	2	3	0	0.400
1940–41	Detroit Red Wings, NHL	48	21	16	11	0.552	9	4	5	0	0.444
1941–42	Detroit Red Wings, NHL	48	19	25	4	0.438	12	7	5	0	0.583
1942–43	Detroit Red Wings, NHL	50	25	14	11	0.610	10	8	2	0	0.800
1943–44	Detroit Red Wings, NHL	50	26	18	6	0.580	4	1	4	0	0.200
1944–45	Detroit Red Wings, NHL	50	31	14	5	0.670	14	7	7	0	0.500
1945–46	Detroit Red Wings, NHL	50	20	20	10	0.500	5	1	4	0	0.200
1946–47	Detroit Red Wings, NHL	60	22	27	11	0.458	5	1	4	0	0.200
	NHL Totals	982	423	397	162	0.513	105	52	52	1	0.500

NHL First All-Star Team (1937, 1943)
NHL Second All-Star (1945)
Won Lester Patrick Trophy (1966)
Won Stanley Cup (1936, 1937, 1943)

Francis Michael "King" *Clancy*

Few players in any era matched Francis Michael "King" Clancy's competitive spirit and charisma. He won legions of fans as star defenseman for the Ottawa Senators and Toronto Maple Leafs from 1921 to 1936, and right up to his death in 1986, Clancy remained one of the game's top ambassadors and most colorful figures.

Clancy developed his game in the amateur system of his home town of Ottawa. While skating with the local St. Brigid's Athletic Club of the Ottawa city league, he came to terms with the fact that he was below average size in a rough sport. Clancy was taught to use his stick as a means of defending himself, and with it the Irishman managed to annoy short-tempered foes throughout his career.

King Clancy was sold to the Maple Leafs for the shocking sum of $35,000 and two players at the start of the 1930–31 season.

In describing his first pro camp, Clancy noted: "My first time out they tried to knock me around quite a bit. Every rookie has to go through this. They knew all the tricks and could make it rough on a kid coming in trying to catch a place on the club. Especially if the kid was only 5'7" and weighed about as much as a sack of potatoes." He gained valuable experience during his first two years in the big leagues when he fit in well on the Ottawa blue line. Clancy also earned the respect of his teammates and peers, standing up to the challenges of the league's toughest forwards despite being only 5'7" and 155 lbs. He learned how to compete well in the most heated battles when he helped Ottawa win the Stanley Cup in 1923.

Following the retirement of Eddie Gerard in 1923, Clancy moved alongside George Boucher on the blue line. They quickly developed into one of the top defensive tandems in the business and helped the Senators win the Stanley Cup in 1927, their fourth Cup of the decade.

Clancy's spirited play, stickhandling and relentless backchecking continually endeared him to the fans in the capital. He was unquestionably one of the quickest players in the league because of his unrivaled acceleration.

Their on-ice success couldn't save the small-market Ottawa Senators from the ravages of the Great Depression. In a transaction that sent shock waves throughout the NHL, Clancy was sold to the Toronto Maple Leafs for $35,000 and two players at the start of the 1930–31 season. In only his second season in Toronto, his presence helped the franchise win its first Stanley Cup as the Maple Leafs in

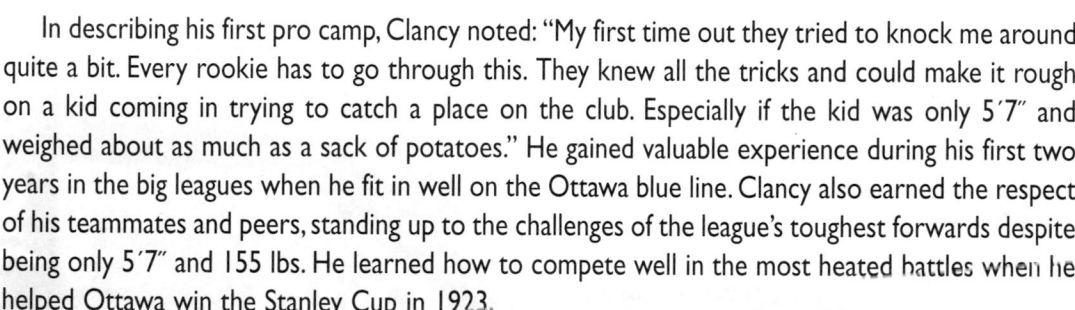

Clancy, Francis Michael "King"
D, 5'7", 155 lbs, b: Ottawa, Ont., 2/25/1903, d: 11/8/1986

Season	Club, League	Regular Season					Playoffs				
		GP	G	A	Pts	PIM	GP	G	A	Pts	PIM
1918–19	Ottawa St. Brigid's, City Sr.	8	0	1	1	3	1	0	0	0	6
1919–20	Ottawa St. Brigid's, City Sr.	8	1	0	1	*					
1920–21	Ottawa St. Brigid's, City Sr.	11	6	0	6	*	6	5	1	6	12
1921–22	Ottawa Senators, NHL	24	4	6	10	21	2	0	0	0	2
1922–23	Ottawa Senators, NHL	24	3	1	4	20	8	1	0	1	2
1923–24	Ottawa Senators, NHL	24	9	8	17	18	2	0	0	0	4
1924–25	Ottawa Senators, NHL	29	14	5	19	61					
1925–26	Ottawa Senators, NHL	35	8	4	12	80	2	1	0	1	8
1926–27	Ottawa Senators, NHL	43	9	10	19	78	6	1	1	2	14
1927–28	Ottawa Senators, NHL	39	8	7	15	73	2	0	0	0	6
1928–29	Ottawa Senators, NHL	44	13	2	15	89					
1929–30	Ottawa Senators, NHL	44	17	23	40	83	2	0	1	1	2
1930–31	Toronto Maple Leafs, NHL	44	7	14	21	63	2	1	0	1	0
1931–32	Toronto Maple Leafs, NHL	48	10	9	19	61	7	2	1	3	14
1932–33	Toronto Maple Leafs, NHL	48	13	12	25	79	9	0	3	3	14
1933–34	Toronto Maple Leafs, NHL	46	11	17	28	62	3	0	0	0	8
1934–35	Toronto Maple Leafs, NHL	47	5	16	21	53	7	1	0	1	8
1935–36	Toronto Maple Leafs, NHL	47	5	10	15	61	9	2	2	4	10
1936–37	Toronto Maple Leafs, NHL	6	1	0	1	4					
	NHL Totals	592	137	144	281	906	61	9	8	17	92

NHL First All-Star Team (1931, 1934)
NHL Second All-Star Team (1932, 1933)
Won Stanley Cup (1923, 1927, 1932)

1931–32. Hap Day was the captain of the team, but Clancy was the acknowledged heart and soul of the club. After winning the Cup, the team captured three more Canadian Division titles before Clancy retired partway through the 1936–37 season.

Clancy went on to try other roles in hockey after his playing days concluded. He served as the coach of the Montreal Maroons for the first half of the 1937–38 season, but he resigned as rumors spread concerning the team's inevitable financial demise. Clancy next moved into officiating, where he proved to be just as colorful as in his playing days. Many of the most vivid photographs of heated discussions taking place on the ice in the 1940s involved referee Clancy and irate players. But he was among the most respected officials during the decade he wore the striped jersey.

Many of the most vivid photographs of heated discussions taking place on the ice in the 1940s involved irate players and King Clancy (center) in his days as a referee.

Clancy returned to the Maple Leafs to coach the team from 1953 to 1956 and then served as assistant general manager to Punch Imlach. Twice he moved in to guide the team from behind the bench when the head coach fell ill. The first time occurred in 1966–67 when he replaced Imlach for 10 games and helped spark Toronto to a late-season surge that qualified them for the post-season and led to a Stanley Cup.

He was also assisting on the bench in the famous 1971 playoff incident when the Rangers' Vic Hadfield threw Bernie Parent's mask into the crowd. The fiery King had to be restrained as he jumped up into the stands to retrieve the face protection himself. In 1972 he stepped into the coaching position on a temporary basis as a replacement for John McClellan, who was suffering from serious ulcer problems.

Over the last 15 years of his life, Clancy remained visible in hockey circles as the constant companion to bombastic Toronto owner Harold Ballard. As abrasive and annoying as Ballard was, Clancy charmed fans and the media with his anecdotes and wit. In a dark period for the Maple Leafs both on and off the ice, he was one of the lone bright spots. His passing on November 8, 1986, brought an atmosphere of sadness to Maple Leaf Gardens for many days. Ballard donated the King Clancy Trophy in 1988 as an annual trophy for the player most dedicated to charitable work. Clancy was inducted into the Hockey Hall of Fame in 1958.

Cecil "Babe" Dye

Cecil Dye, a fine all-round athlete during his school days in Toronto, was nicknamed "Babe" because of his baseball abilities, but he became the most prolific goal scorer during the early years of the NHL. He was born in Hamilton, Ontario, but after his father died when Babe was just a year old, his mother moved the family to Toronto. Dye played on school teams, including the one at De La Salle College, a private school where from 1917 he played on one of the finest kids' hockey teams of all time. It featured defensemen Jess Spring and Dutch Cain, Red Green on left wing, Duke McCurry on right and Dye in the middle. His most famous opponents of the day included Lionel Conacher and Nels Stewart. Incredibly, all went on to play in the NHL.

Dye was a halfback for the Toronto Argonauts and such a good baseball player that Connie Mack offered him the extraordinary salary of $25,000 to join his Philadelphia Athletics team in 1921. But Dye limited his baseball to playing outfield with Baltimore, Buffalo and Toronto in the International League, winning a championship with Toronto in 1926. His real career was in professional hockey. For his natural athletic ability, he credited his mother. "She knew more about hockey than I ever did, and she could throw a baseball right out of the park," he recollected.

Dye joined the Toronto St. Pats in 1918, when the team was still a senior OHA operation, and led them to the championship. The coach of that team was the same man who coached the De La Salle team, Eddie Powers Sr., and Dye cited this man's influence as a major factor in his development as a player. Dye went on to play with the NHL St. Pats in 1919–20 on a line with Reg Noble and Jack Adams. Later, when Adams left Toronto to play in the Pacific league with Vancouver, Corb Denneny played on the line in his place. Dye was short at 5′8″ and slight at just 150 pounds, and his strengths and weaknesses as a player were quickly exposed. On the downside, his skating ability was behind other NHLers, but because of his brilliant stickhandling and hard shot he made an impressive contribution to the team, scoring 11 goals in just twice as many games during his first season. He was a bit of an anomaly in that he did everything left-handed except shoot a puck. He threw a baseball and batted left, kicked left and wrote left, but shot a puck from the right side.

In normal life, Babe Dye did everything left-handed except shoot a puck.

Dye's goal-scoring ability was based on a quick release, near-perfect accuracy and sheer force of speed. One day, while practising at the Mutual Street Arena, Dye delighted a crowd of children by standing at center ice and firing pucks at the arena's clock at one end of the building. His first shot smashed the clock to bits, and in a torrid series of shots he missed the tattered timepiece only twice. "Babe had the most deadly shot in the NHL," King Clancy said. "He wasn't a really good skater, but he could blast that puck like dynamite and he was a terrific competitor. When I was with Ottawa, coach Tommy Gorman would say to me, 'King, if you check Dye tonight and he fails to score, there'll be an extra fifty bucks in your paycheck.' That's all I needed to hear. I'd check Babe like a hawk." The great Aurel Joliat concurred. "I remember once in Ottawa he scored from center ice against Clint Benedict. The puck was going so fast that Clint couldn't move fast enough to get it."

Three times—1921, 1923 and 1925—Dye led the league in goal scoring. He twice scored goals in 11 consecutive games and in the 1924–25 season he counted 38, a Toronto record that stood for 35 years, until Frank Mahovlich entered the NHL. In his first six seasons, Dye scored a remarkable 175 goals in just 172 games, a pace that wasn't equaled until Wayne Gretzky came along in the 1980s and rewrote the NHL record book. Because of his weak skating combined with his high scoring, Dye always had an unbalanced goals-to-assists ratio. During his career, he scored 201 goals but made only 41 assists.

Dye's name is also in the record book on account of the 1922 Stanley Cup playoffs. The St. Pats played the champions of the Western Canada Hockey League, the Vancouver Millionaires, in a best-of-five finals. Dye scored two game-winning goals, including four in the fifth and final game, a 5–1 Toronto rout. In all, he scored nine of the team's 16 goals, and those nine are still a Stanley Cup finals record. This was to be Dye's only taste of Cup victory.

Ironically, Dye's departure from Toronto to Chicago contributed to Conn Smythe, who was then general manager of the New York Rangers, becoming owner of the Toronto franchise and later renaming the team the Maple Leafs. At the start of the 1926–27 season, the St. Pats sold Dye to Chicago. When Rangers owner Colonel Hammond discovered that Smythe hadn't expressed an interest in Dye, Hammond fired him. "I didn't sign Dye," Smythe explained curtly, "because I figured he was nearing the end of the trail and he wouldn't help us too much. The Colonel didn't think so."

Dye, Cecil "Babe"
RW, 5′8″, 150 lbs, b: Hamilton, Ont., 5/3/1898, d: 1/2/1962

Season	Club, League	Regular Season					Playoffs				
		GP	G	A	Pts	PIM	GP	G	A	Pts	PIM
1918–19	Toronto St. Pats, OHA Sr.	9	13	1	14	*	2	3	0	3	0
1919–20	Toronto St. Pats, NHL	23	11	3	14	10					
1920–21	Hamilton Tigers, NHL	1	2	0	2	0					
	Toronto St. Pats, NHL	23	33	5	38	32	2	0	0	0	7
1921–22	Toronto St. Pats, NHL	24	31	7	38.	39	2	2	0	2	2
1922–23	Toronto St. Pats, NHL	22	26	11	37	19					
1923–24	Toronto St. Pats, NHL	19	16	3	19	23					
1924–25	Toronto St. Pats, NHL	29	38	8	46	41	2	0	0	0	0
1925–26	Toronto St. Pats, NHL	31	18	5	23	26					
1926–27	Chicago Black Hawks, NHL	41	25	5	30	14	2	0	0	0	2
1927–28	Chicago Black Hawks, NHL	10	0	0	0	0					
1928–29	New York Americans, NHL	42	1	0	1	17	2	0	0	0	0
1929–30	New Haven Eagles, Can-Am	34	11	4	15.	16					
1930–31	Toronto Maple Leafs, NHL	6	0	0	0	0					
	NHL Totals	271	201	47	248	221	10	2	0	2	11

NHL Scoring Leader (1923, 1925)
Won Stanley Cup (1922)

Dye played one season with the Hawks on a line with George Hay and Dick Irvin. But at training camp in Winnipeg for his second year, Dye suffered a broken leg that caused him to miss most of the 1927–28 season and in effect end his career. He was sold to the Americans the next year but scored only one goal, and the year after that he played with New Haven in the minors. After a few games with Smythe's Maple Leafs in 1930–31, he retired for good with the best goals-to-games ratio in the history of the game.

But Dye's life in hockey was by no means over. He coached Port Colborne in OHA senior, the Chicago Shamrocks of the American Hockey Association and the St. Louis Eagles during their only NHL season. He then returned to the NHL as a referee from 1935 to 1940. When Black Hawks forward Doug Bentley approached 200 career goals in 1950, Dye got a call from NHL president Clarence Campbell asking him to make a special presentation to Bentley after he reached the historic milestone. Dye gladly accepted. He was inducted into the Hockey Hall of Fame in 1970.

Aurel Joliat

Aurel Joliat was a prolific scorer and relentless backchecker during 16 rewarding seasons with the Montreal Canadiens. He never allowed his comparatively small frame to impede his progress in the NHL. Joliat often teamed with his good friend Howie Morenz to form one of the most potent offensive duos in league history. His blazing forays down the port side made him one of hockey's most exciting left wingers of all time, and his combination of speed and small size made him one of the trickiest skaters to bodycheck. Although many tagged him as one of the best French-Canadians in the game, Joliat was actually the son of a Swiss Protestant immigrant.

The Ottawa native played football and baseball before moving on to hockey. In fact he starred as a kicker and fullback with the Ottawa Rough Riders and Regina Wascana Boat Club before switching sports. Joliat first established himself as a budding hockey star with the Ottawa New Edinburghs club and the Iroquois Falls club in northern Ontario. The latter was the farm team of the Saskatoon Sheiks of the Western Canada Hockey League, but before he'd had the opportunity to play in a Sheiks uniform, Joliat was acquired by the Montreal Canadiens when he was traded for the legendary Newsy Lalonde.

In his rookie campaign year, the Mighty Atom impressed fans with his speed and puckhandling abilities. He was also a feisty adversary who frustrated his larger opponents. Joliat scored 13 goals in 24 games from his left wing position that year. The following season he was placed on a line with Howie Morenz in one of the more successful moves in the history of the Canadiens hockey club.

By the time the 1923–24 post-season began, the line made up of Joliat and Morenz and Billy Boucher was operating at peak efficiency. This formidable trio led the Montrealers to victory over the Ottawa Senators in the NHL playoffs and followed with successful matchups against Vancouver and Calgary to claim the Stanley Cup. Many labeled Morenz as the key member of this explosive unit, but Joliat was unquestionably of equal value as a catalyst. Morenz himself said, "If it wasn't for Joliat, you wouldn't be writing about me so much."

The Little Giant topped all NHL goal scorers in 1924–25 with 30 goals to his credit. He continued to be among the league leaders in this category over the next dozen seasons. Joliat played on his second Stanley Cup champion team in 1929–30 when he contributed to the Habs' upset victory over the heavily favored Boston Bruins in a two-game sweep in the best-of-three finals. The following year the Canadiens repeated as Cup winners in a tough five-game series with the Chicago Black Hawks.

At the conclusion of the 1930–31 season, Joliat was chosen as the left wing on the inaugural NHL First All-Star Team. Subsequently he was selected to the Second Team in 1932, 1934 and 1935. In 1933–34, he registered his third 20-goal season and was the recipient of the Hart Trophy. A frustrated Babe Dye of the Toronto St. Pats once shouted at the Montreal bench and the team's owner, Leo Dandurand, "Move him to center, Leo, hold a mirror to each side of him, and you'll have the fastest line in hockey."

When he retired in 1938, Joliat's regular-season output read 270 goals and 460 points. His ability to break up plays defensively and quickly lead the counterattack provided the Canadiens with a feared transitional game. Over time, he earned the respect of many of the toughest players in the NHL because of his fearless refusal to back down in on-ice confrontations. The small black cap Joliat wore during games throughout his career reminded fans and players of his willingness to retaliate. Taunting him by knocking his hat to the ice always brought a swift reaction and consequently it didn't happen often.

After his close friend Morenz died in 1937, Joliat was never the same on ice. His passion and trademark speed were no longer evident and he retired in 1938. After ending his playing

Tagged as one of the best French-Canadians in the game, Aurel Joliat was actually the son of a Swiss Protestant immigrant.

Joliat, Aurel
LW, 5'7", 136 lbs, b: Ottawa, Ont., 8/29/1901, d: 6/2/1986

Season	Club, League	Regular Season					Playoffs				
		GP	G	A	Pts	PIM	GP	G	A	Pts	PIM
1918–19	Ottawa New Edinburghs, City Sr.	8	5	3	8	9					
1919–20	Ottawa New Edinburghs, City Sr.	7	12	0	12	*					
1920–21	Iroquois Falls Flyers, NOHA	*	*	*	*	*	*	*	*	*	*
1921–22	Iroquois Falls Flyers, NOHA	*	*	*	*	*	*	*	*	*	*
1922–23	Montreal Canadiens, NHL	24	12	9	21	37	2	1	0	1	11
1923–24	Montreal Canadiens, NHL	24	15	5	20	27	2	1	1	2	0
1924–25	Montreal Canadiens, NHL	25	30	11	41	85	1	0	0	0	5
1925–26	Montreal Canadiens, NHL	35	17	9	26	52					
1926–27	Montreal Canadiens, NHL	43	14	4	18	79	4	1	0	1	10
1927–28	Montreal Canadiens, NHL	44	28	11	39	105	2	0	0	0	4
1928–29	Montreal Canadiens, NHL	44	12	5	17	59	3	1	1	2	10
1929–30	Montreal Canadiens, NHL	42	19	12	31	40	6	0	2	2	6
1930–31	Montreal Canadiens, NHL	43	13	22	35	73	10	0	4	4	12
1931–32	Montreal Canadiens, NHL	48	15	24	39	46	4	2	0	2	4
1932–33	Montreal Canadiens, NHL	48	18	21	39	53	2	2	1	3	2
1933–34	Montreal Canadiens, NHL	48	22	15	37	27	3	0	1	1	0
1934–35	Montreal Canadiens, NHL	48	17	12	29	18	2	1	0	1	0
1935–36	Montreal Canadiens, NHL	48	15	8	23	16					
1936–37	Montreal Canadiens, NHL	47	17	15	32	30	5	0	3	3	2
1937–38	Montreal Canadiens, NHL	44	6	7	13	24					
	NHL Totals	655	270	190	460	771	46	9	13	22	66

NHL First All-Star Team (1931)
NHL Second All-Star Team (1932, 1934, 1935)
Won Hart Trophy (1934)
Won Stanley Cup (1924, 1930, 1931)

days, he coached Quebec senior hockey in Verdun and Valleyfield. He also tried his hand at being a linesman but was forced to hang up his skates permanently after being diagnosed with arthritis. He stayed in Montreal and ran his own grocery store and worked for the provincial liquor board. Joliat then returned to Ottawa as an employee of the Canadian National Railway, where he was employed until his death in 1986.

Joliat was voted into the Canadian Sports Hall of Fame and the Ottawa Sports Hall of Fame. The Montreal Canadiens paid tribute to his glorious career by placing the Mighty Atom on their 75th anniversary dream team in 1984. In addition, his number 4 was co-retired with Jean Beliveau. Joliat was inducted into the Hockey Hall of Fame in 1945.

Herb Gardiner

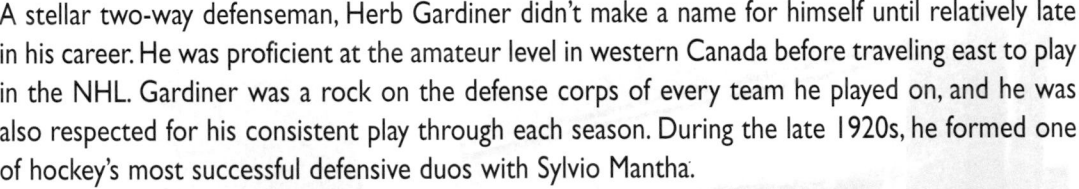

A stellar two-way defenseman, Herb Gardiner didn't make a name for himself until relatively late in his career. He was proficient at the amateur level in western Canada before traveling east to play in the NHL. Gardiner was a rock on the defense corps of every team he played on, and he was also respected for his consistent play through each season. During the late 1920s, he formed one of hockey's most successful defensive duos with Sylvio Mantha.

The native of Winnipeg, Manitoba, played many sports at the city's Alexandria High School and the University of Manitoba. Gardiner made his hockey debut with the Winnipeg Victorias of the city's senior hockey league in 1908. The next year he played with the Northern Crown Bank squad that secured the championship of the Winnipeg Bankers League. This success was followed by a four-year hiatus from the game during which Gardiner worked as a surveyor with the Canadian Pacific Railway and then served with the Canadian Army during World War I.

Herb Gardiner was a rock on the defense corps of every team he played on.

Following the Great War, Gardiner returned to Canada and set up residence in Calgary, Alberta. He continued working for the railway in the summer while rekindling his hockey aspirations with the Calgary Rotarians over the winter months. Gardiner turned professional in 1921–22 with the Calgary Tigers of the newly created Western Canada Hockey League, where he spent five long but rewarding seasons.

He enjoyed his greatest success partnered with future NHLer and league president Red Dutton on defense. In 1924 Gardiner helped the Tigers gain the WCHL crown in a tough series versus Regina. He and Dutton provided stellar work in their own end against the likes of superstars George Hay, Dick Irvin and Barney Stanley. Gardiner scored a key goal in the first match at Regina, which ended in a 2–2 deadlock. The Tigers clinched the total-goals series with a 2–0 win on home ice.

Following this achievement, the Tigers ventured east with the Pacific Coast Hockey Association champion Vancouver Maroons to confront the Montreal Canadiens. Calgary and Montreal disposed of Vancouver, setting up a final in which the Canadiens proved to be too strong. Matched against the speed of Howie Morenz and Aurel Joliat, the Tigers lost 6–1. Despite the Tigers' setback, Gardiner made a strong impression on the Montreal management. The most notable feature of the contest from a Calgary perspective was that defensemen Dutton and Gardiner gave no ground to Sprague Cleghorn and Billy Coutu on the winning side.

The following year Calgary succumbed in the Western championships to the Victoria squad that went on to defeat the Canadiens and become the last non-NHL team to win the Stanley Cup. Gardiner was solid once again for the Tigers, but the Cougars were led by superb performances by Frank Frederickson, Jack Walker and netminder Harry "Hap" Holmes.

Recalling his excellent play two years earlier, the Canadiens invited Gardiner to training camp in 1926. The experienced defender represented a vital addition to the Montreal defensive brigade when he joined the team that year. His play was so impressive with the rebuilding Montreal franchise that he was awarded the Hart Trophy as league MVP—no small achievement, as he beat out New York Rangers superstar Bill Cook to cop the award. During this time, he formed one of the NHL's most proficient duos on defense with Sylvio Mantha.

Gardiner was loaned to the Chicago Black Hawks in 1928–29 but was recalled by the Canadiens near the end of the regular season. The following year he was sold to the Boston Bruins, who moved him to the Philadelphia Arrows of the Canadian-American Hockey League as player-coach.

Gardiner adapted well to the additional responsibilities coaching entailed. He remained with the Arrows until 1935–36 before joining

Gardiner, Herb
D, 5′10″, 190 lbs, b: Winnipeg, Man., 5/8/1891, d: 1/11/1972

Season	Club, League	Regular Season					Playoffs				
		GP	G	A	Pts	PIM	GP	G	A	Pts	PIM
1919–20	Calgary Wanderers, Big 4	12	8	9	17	6	2	0	0	0	2
1920–21	Calgary Wanderers, Big 4	13	3	7	10	6					
1921–22	Calgary Tigers, WCHL	24	4	1	5	6	2	0	0	0	0
1922–23	Calgary Tigers, WCHL	29	9	3	12	9					
1923–24	Calgary Tigers, WCHL	22	5	5	10	4	2	1	0	1	0
1924–25	Calgary Tigers, WCHL	28	12	8	20	18	2	0	0	0	0
1925–26	Calgary Tigers, WHL	27	3	1	4	10					
1926–27	Montreal Canadiens, NHL	44	6	6	12	26	4	0	0	0	10
1927–28	Montreal Canadiens, NHL	44	4	3	7	26	2	0	1	1	4
1928–29	Chicago Black Hawks, NHL	13	0	0	0	0					
	Montreal Canadiens, NHL	7	0	0	0	0	3	0	0	0	2
1929–30	Philadelphia Arrows, Can-Am	1	0	0	0	0					
1931–32	Philadelphia Arrows, Can-Am	1	0	0	0	0					
1934–36	Philadelphia Arrows, Can-Am	12	0	0	0	0					
	NHL Totals	108	10	9	19	52	9	0	1	1	14
	WCHL/WHL Totals	130	33	18	51	47	6	1	0	1	0

WCHL First All-Star Team (1923, 1925)
Won Hart Trophy (1927)

Philadelphia's American Hockey League franchise, the Ramblers. Gardiner coached this team to the Calder Cup finals in 1937 and 1939. He concluded his coaching endeavors with the Philadelphia Falcons of the Eastern Hockey League from 1944 to 1946. In 1947 he was named general manager of the Philadelphia Maroons, a proposed NHL franchise that was never realized. As both a defenseman and coach, Gardiner always put his keen understanding of the game to excellent use. He was inducted into the Hockey Hall of Fame in 1958.

Bill Cook

William Osser Cook was considered by many to be the greatest right winger ever to play the game. He was a remarkably gifted and rugged competitor who served as the catalyst on the New York Rangers' famous Bread Line with his brother Bun and Frank Boucher. Cook's input was crucial to the Rangers' first two Stanley Cup triumphs in 1928 and 1933.

Born in Brantford, Ontario, Cook grew up farther east, in the Kingston area. He learned to skate on the nearby Rideau Canal and made his junior hockey debut with the Kingston Frontenacs in 1916. His play impressed the local fans, who compared him with the legendary Scotty Davidson. But Cook had to leave hockey for three years to serve in France and Russia during World War I.

as a member of the Canadian Field Artillery, where he earned the Military Medal for distinguished service.

Bill Cook was the first player officially signed by the New York Rangers and became the team's first captain.

Following the Great War, Cook returned to Kingston and suited up with the Frontenacs' intermediate outfit. His inspired play helped the team reach the OHA finals that year. The next season he led the Sault Ste. Marie Greyhounds to the championship of the Northern Ontario Hockey Association.

Cook ventured away from the east to make his professional debut in 1921–22 with the Saskatoon Sheiks of the Western Canada Hockey League. During his five years in Saskatoon, the team's name changed to the Crescents and he attained monumental status by winning the league's scoring championship twice. This included a personal high of 31 goals in 30 games during the last year of the Western Hockey League in 1925–26.

In preparing for their initial NHL season in 1926, the New York Rangers signed Cook from the defunct WHL. In addition to being the first skater signed officially by the club, he became the team's first captain and the foundation on which the club was built. Fittingly, he scored the first goal in franchise history on November 16, 1926, when the Broadway Blueshirts shut down the Montreal Maroons 1–0 to begin their NHL life in style.

In these early days of the franchise, Cook was joined by his younger brother Bun and center Frank Boucher to form one of hockey's most successful forward combinations. This trio dominated opposing defenses for several years with their precision passing and relentless effort. The elder Cook led all scorers in 1926–27 with 37 points and was runner-up in the Hart Trophy voting.

The Bread Line led the Rangers to their first Stanley Cup triumph in 1928 by accounting for every one of the team's goals in a thrilling five-game final series with the Montreal Maroons. New York reached the finals again the following season, but they came up short against the Boston Bruins, who won their inaugural championship in a two-game sweep in the best-of-three finals.

Cook and his linemates played well despite their loss to the Toronto Maple Leafs in the 1932 Stanley Cup finals. They were in top form the next year, with Cook leading the way with his second scoring title. Once again he finished runner-up in the Hart Trophy selection, this time to Bruins star rearguard Eddie Shore. And the Rangers exacted their revenge on the

Cook, Bill
RW, 5'10", 170 lbs, b: Brantford, Ont., 10/9/1896, d: 4/6/1986

Season	Club, League	Regular Season					Playoffs				
		GP	G	A	Pts	PIM	GP	G	A	Pts	PIM
1919–20	Kingston Frontenacs, OHA Sr.	*	*	*	*	*	*	*	*	*	*
1920–21	Soo Greyhounds, City Sr.	12	12	4	18	*					
	Soo Greyhounds, NOHA	9	12	7	19	48	5	5	1	6	*
1921–22	Soo Greyhounds, City Sr.	12	20	8	28	*					
	Soo Greyhounds, NOHA	8	7	5	12	38	2	1	1	2	2
1922–23	Saskatoon Sheiks, WCHL	30	9	16	25	19					
1923–24	Saskatoon Crescents, WCHL	30	26	14	40	20					
1924–25	Saskatoon Crescents, WCHL	27	22	10	32	79	2	0	0	0	4
1925–26	Saskatoon Crescents, WHL	30	31	13	44	26	2	2	0	2	26
1926–27	New York Rangers, NHL	44	33	4	37	58	2	1	0	1	6
1927–28	New York Rangers, NHL	43	18	6	24	42	9	2	3	5	26
1928–29	New York Rangers, NHL	43	15	8	23	41	6	0	0	0	6
1929–30	New York Rangers, NHL	44	29	30	59	56	4	0	1	1	11
1930–31	New York Rangers, NHL	43	30	12	42	39	4	3	0	3	4
1931–32	New York Rangers, NHL	48	34	14	48	33	7	3	3	6	2
1932–33	New York Rangers, NHL	48	28	22	50	51	8	3	2	5	4
1933–34	New York Rangers, NHL	48	13	13	26	21	2	0	0	0	2
1934–35	New York Rangers, NHL	48	21	15	36	23	4	1	2	3	7
1935–36	New York Rangers, NHL	44	7	10	17	16					
1936–37	New York Rangers, NHL	21	1	4	5	6					
1937–38	Cleveland Barons, AHL	5	0	0	0	5	1	0	0	0	0
	NHL Totals	474	229	138	367	386	46	13	11	24	68

NHL First All-Star Team (1931, 1932, 1933)
NHL Second All-Star Team (1934)
NHL Scoring Leader (1927, 1933)
Won Stanley Cup (1928, 1933)

Maple Leafs by capturing their second Stanley Cup by 3–1 in the best-of-five finals. To cap an extraordinary year, Cook scored the dramatic first-ever NHL Stanley Cup-winning overtime goal.

"The Original Ranger" continued to register impressive numbers for New York until his retirement in 1936–37. On top of his two scoring championships, Cook was selected as the right wing on the NHL First All-Star Team three times and the Second Team once. His 229 regular-season goals accounted for nearly one-fifth of the Rangers' total during the club's first decade of play.

A successful tenure as coach awaited Cook after he retired as a player. He guided the AHL's Cleveland Barons to the 1939 and 1941 Calder Cup championships during his six years at the helm that began in 1937–38. In 1950 he coached the Minneapolis Millers to the Paul W. Loudon Trophy in the United States Hockey League. He also coached the Denver Falcons of the same league the following season before returning to Saskatoon.

He was coaching the Saskatoon Quakers of the Pacific Coast Hockey League in 1951–52 when the New York Rangers turned to him to help revitalize their sagging fortunes. Cook couldn't refuse, since the appeal came from the general manager of the Blueshirts, his old linemate Frank Boucher. Cook spent just under two seasons coaching his old club before permanently retiring from the game at the conclusion of the 1952–53 season.

His immense contribution to the New York franchise didn't go unnoticed. On January 10, 1986, just three months before he passed away, the New York Rangers presented him with their alumni association award before a cheering crowd at Madison Square Garden. Cook is a member of the Canadian Sports Hall of Fame and was inducted into the Hockey Hall of Fame in 1952.

Ivan "Ching" Johnson

Defenseman Ching Johnson matched his rugged defensive play with an ability to contribute inside the opposition's blue line. He was a valuable team leader and fan favorite throughout his 12-year NHL career.

During his playing days, Johnson was considered one of the hardest bodycheckers ever to play the game. More significantly, he perfected the technique of nullifying the opposition by clutching and grabbing them as discreetly as possible—a pragmatic defensive strategy for the wily but slow-footed rearguard.

As a young boy, the native of Winnipeg, Manitoba, played lacrosse and football. He served Canada in World War I, then embarked on a hockey career, beginning with the Winnipeg Monarchs seniors in 1919. He gained valuable playing experience when the Monarchs went on a post-season exhibition tour of the United States.

Soon afterward, Johnson moved to Eveleth, Minnesota, where he spent three years on the blue line of the city's team in the United States Amateur Hockey Association. In 1923 Johnson moved on to the semiprofessional Minneapolis Millers, where he was paired on defense with Clarence "Taffy" Abel.

New York Rangers manager Conn Smythe purchased the services of both rearguards for the team's NHL debut in 1926–27. The burly Johnson spent 11 productive years with the Blueshirts and was part of the team's first two Stanley Cup triumphs in 1928 and 1933. Johnson and Abel's

Ching Johnson had a reputation as a hard bodychecker in his playing days.

blanket defensive coverage was particularly evident during the 1928 finals against the Montreal Maroons, a low-scoring series in which the teams combined to score only 11 goals in five games.

At first glance, Johnson seemed the most genial of players, but author Damon Runyon described his expression as "a true castor oil smile," meaning that his outward appearance didn't match his tough approach toward the opposition.

Johnson, Wilfred Ivan "Ching"
D, 5′11″, 210 lbs, b: Winnipeg, Man., 12/7/1898, d: 6/17/1979

Season	Club, League	Regular Season					Playoffs				
		GP	G	A	Pts	PIM	GP	G	A	Pts	PIM
1919–20	Winnipeg Monarchs, MHL Sr.	7	6	3	9	10					
1920–21	Eveleth Rangers, USAHA	*	*	*	*	*	*	*	*	*	*
1921–22	Eveleth Rangers, USAHA	*	*	*	*	*	*	*	*	*	*
1922–23	Eveleth Rangers, USAHA	20	4	0	4	*					
1923–24	Minneapolis Millers, USAHA	20	9	3	12	*					
1924–25	Minneapolis Rockets, USAHA	40	8	0	8	*					
1925–26	Minneapolis Millers, USAHA	38	14	5	19	92	3	2	0	2	6
1926–27	New York Rangers, NHL	27	3	2	5	66	2	0	0	0	8
1927–28	New York Rangers, NHL	42	10	6	16	146	9	1	1	2	46
1928–29	New York Rangers, NHL	8	0	0	0	14	6	0	0	0	26
1929–30	New York Rangers, NHL	30	3	3	6	82	4	0	0	0	14
1930–31	New York Rangers, NHL	44	2	6	8	77	4	1	0	1	17
1931–32	New York Rangers, NHL	47	3	10	13	106	7	2	0	2	24
1932–33	New York Rangers, NHL	48	8	9	17	127	8	1	0	1	14
1933–34	New York Rangers, NHL	48	2	6	8	86	2	0	0	0	4
1934–35	New York Rangers, NHL	29	2	3	5	34	4	0	0	0	2
1935–36	New York Rangers, NHL	47	5	3	8	58					
1936–37	New York Rangers, NHL	35	0	0	0	2	9	0	1	1	4
1937–38	New York Americans, NHL	31	0	0	0	10	6	0	0	0	2
1938–39	Minneapolis Millers, AHA	47	2	9	11	60	4	0	2	2	0
1939–40	Minneapolis Millers, AHA	48	0	4	4	26	3	0	0	0	2
	NHL Totals	436	38	48	86	808	61	5	2	7	161

NHL First All-Star Team (1932, 1933)
NHL Second All-Star Team (1931, 1934)
Won Stanley Cup (1928, 1933)

Following the 1931–32 season, Johnson was runner-up to Canadiens superstar Howie Morenz in the voting for the Hart Trophy. The next year he and defense partner Earl Seibert aided the Rangers in their Stanley Cup victory over the Toronto Maple Leafs. Johnson played his hard-hitting game to perfection during the playoffs and scored the key first goal in the Blueshirts' 2–0 win over Detroit in game one of the semifinals. The Rangers sagged somewhat in the second match but held on for a 4–3 win. Johnson's supreme defensive work was considered to be the key factor in the club's not having to play a third and deciding contest. In the finals, the Rangers' speed was too much for the Maple Leafs. When Toronto did venture into New York territory, Johnson and Seibert controlled the play. Johnson would knock the Maple Leafs forwards off the puck, then send it over to his swifter partner to launch the next counterattack.

Ching Johnson was selected to the NHL First All-Star Team in 1932 and 1933 and he made the Second Team in 1931 and 1934. On February 14, 1934, Johnson took part in the landmark Ace Bailey Benefit Game to aid the former Maple Leaf star whose career was ended prematurely by a vicious Eddie Shore hit.

When the Rangers released Johnson after the 1936–37 season, the New York Americans jumped at the chance to offer him a contract. Amerks manager Red Dutton didn't share the Rangers' view that the veteran was too old and slow to be effective. Johnson accepted the new challenge and spent one year with his new team as a player and interim coach before retiring after 12 years and more than 400 NHL games.

His playing days weren't over, though. The rugged defender next skated for two years with the Minneapolis Millers of the American Hockey Association in the dual role of player-coach for two years. Johnson's last season in pro hockey was as coach of the Washington Lions of the Eastern amateur league in 1940–41. He also tried his hand at officiating in Washington over the next two years.

Johnson accumulated 86 points in his 12 NHL seasons. But it was his physical play and his charismatic leadership that made him one of the most valuable rearguards of his time. Ching Johnson was inducted into the Hockey Hall of Fame in 1958.

Nels "Old Poison" Stewart

Between 1940 and 1952, Nels Stewart was the NHL's all-time goal-scoring leader. One of the most lethal offensive players of his day, he earned the nickname "Old Poison" because of his deadly accurate shot. Stewart also had a dark side, and he was more than willing to use his stick or mix it up with members of the opposition whenever the mood struck him.

Stewart was born in Montreal but he grew up in Toronto, which is where he first learned the game. At the same time he became proficient in a number of other sports, prompting sportswriter Ted Reeve to observe: "Nels was the best natural all-round athlete that I have ever seen in Canada and, naturally, over the years that takes in a lot of territory and much consideration, for when he was a kid all the boys of a neighborhood played sports, hard and rough and tumble as was the style of the rather parochial Hogtown [Toronto] of those times."

After excelling in hockey with the Parkdale Canoe Club in 1919–20, Stewart embarked on a successful five-year tenure with the Cleveland Indians of the USAHA. He led the league in goals scored in four of those seasons before he and Babe Siebert were signed by the Montreal Maroons in 1925.

The fiery center burst onto the NHL scene in 1925–26, scoring a league-high 34 goals in his first season. He also won the regular-season scoring title with 42 points and was awarded the Hart Trophy as the league's most valuable player. Stewart's infusion of skill and production helped the Maroons win the Stanley Cup in their sophomore NHL season.

In 1929–30, Stewart was teamed with Siebert and Hooley Smith to form the dreaded S Line. This formidable trio fused talent and physical play at a level rarely seen in NHL history. Stewart responded to this new assignment with a personal-best 39 goals in only 44 games. He was presented with his second Hart Trophy and his reputation as one of the most effective pivots in league history was solidified.

On January 3, 1931, Stewart set an NHL record by scoring two goals in four seconds against the Boston Bruins. This feat was unmatched until December 1995, when Deron Quint of the Winnipeg Jets produced two quick goals. The S Line was broken up when Stewart was traded to Boston prior to the 1932–33 season. In 1934 Stewart was selected to be one of the NHL All-Stars who faced off against the Toronto Maple Leafs in the historic Ace Bailey Benefit Game.

Nels Stewart was the NHL's all-time leader in scoring until 1952.

Stewart, Nels "Old Poison"
C, 6'1", 195 lbs, b. Montreal, Que., 12/29/1902, d: 8/21/1957

Season	Club, League	Regular Season					Playoffs				
		GP	G	A	Pts	PIM	GP	G	A	Pts	PIM
1919–20	Parkdale Canoe Club, OHA Sr.	8	18	2	20	*	1	1	0	1	*
1920–21	Cleveland Indians, USAHA	10	23	0	23	*	8	6	0	6	*
1921–22	Cleveland Indians, USAHA	12	13	0	13	*					
1922–23	Cleveland Indians, USAHA	20	22	0	22	*					
1923–24	Cleveland Indians, USAHA	20	21	8	29	*	8	5	2	7	*
1924–25	Cleveland Indians, USAHA	40	21	0	21	*	8	6	3	9	24
1925–26	Montreal Maroons, NHL	36	34	8	42	119	4	0	2	2	10
1926–27	Montreal Maroons, NHL	43	17	4	21	133	2	0	0	0	4
1927–28	Montreal Maroons, NHL	41	27	7	34	104	9	2	2	4	13
1928–29	Montreal Maroons, NHL	44	21	8	29	74					
1929–30	Montreal Maroons, NHL	44	39	16	55	81	4	1	1	2	2
1930–31	Montreal Maroons, NHL	42	25	14	39	75	2	1	0	1	6
1931–32	Montreal Maroons, NHL	38	22	11	33	61	4	0	1	1	2
1932–33	Boston Bruins, NHL	47	18	18	36	62	5	2	0	2	4
1933–34	Boston Bruins, NHL	48	22	17	39	68					
1934–35	Boston Bruins, NHL	47	21	18	39	45	4	0	1	1	0
1935–36	New York Americans, NHL	48	14	15	29	16	5	1	2	3	4
1936–37	Boston Bruins, NHL	11	3	2	5	6					
	New York Americans, NHL	32	20	10	30	31					
1937–38	New York Americans, NHL	48	19	17	36	29	6	2	3	5	2
1938–39	New York Americans, NHL	46	16	19	35	43	2	0	0	0	0
1939–40	New York Americans, NHL	35	6	7	13	6	3	0	0	0	0
	NHL Totals	650	324	191	515	953	50	9	12	21	47

Won Hart Trophy (1926, 1930)
NHL Scoring Leader (1926)
Won Stanley Cup (1926)

Fiery center Nels Stewart burst onto the NHL scene in 1925–26 with a league high of 34 goals in his first season.

Stewart reached the 20-goal mark twice in Beantown before a trade sent him to the New York Americans in 1936–37. The trip to the Big Apple agreed with Old Poison, as he scored 20 goals in his last 32 games of the season and won the regular-season goal-scoring title for the first time since his rookie year in the NHL.

Ted Reeve summed up one of the game's brightest stars with appropriate accuracy: "Stew, with his big, rangy frame and wonderful eye and tomcat quickness, had that nature-given extra, extra step. Reflexes, coordination…whatever you label it. If he'd grown up in California, he'd have been Davis Cup material."

Stewart retired in 1940 with an NHL record 324 goals to his credit and his total stood as the league standard until Maurice Richard eclipsed it on November 8, 1952. The hard-driven star took his rightful place in the Hockey Hall of Fame in 1962.

Roy "Shrimp" Worters

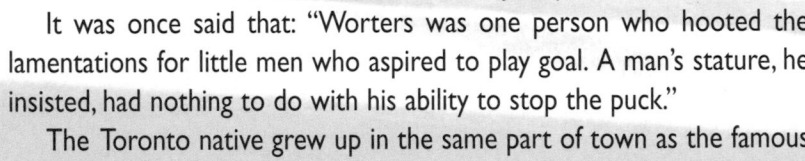

Despite his 5′3″ frame, the aptly named "Shrimp" Worters seemed like a giant to opposing shooters. He became one of the NHL's all-time great goalkeepers, chalking up a phenomenal 66 shutouts in only 12 seasons. But because his tenure was chiefly with the Pittsburgh Pirates and New York Americans, Worters never felt the exhilaration of a Stanley Cup win.

Despite his 5′3″ frame, the aptly named "Shrimp" Worters could seem like a giant to shooters.

It was once said that: "Worters was one person who hooted the lamentations for little men who aspired to play goal. A man's stature, he insisted, had nothing to do with his ability to stop the puck."

The Toronto native grew up in the same part of town as the famous Conacher brothers, Charlie and Lionel. As an amateur he first gained prominence with the Aura Lee squad, the Parkdale Canoe Club and the Toronto Canoe Club Paddlers. Leaving town for a year in 1920–21, he turned in a strong performance in northern Ontario with the Porcupine Miners. Worters was also an accomplished second baseman on the local baseball circuit.

A suspension prevented Worters from competing in 1921–22, but he returned the next year as a member of the Argonauts in the Toronto city senior league. The next autumn saw the 23-year-old venturing south of the border to stop pucks for the Pittsburgh Yellow Jackets of the United States Amateur Hockey Association. Over the next two years, Worters led all netminders in a host of categories and became a fan favorite. In 1924–25, he led the team to 25 wins and registered 17 shutouts in 39 games. He was a key reason that the Yellow Jackets won consecutive championships in the USAHA.

In 1925–26, Worters made his first foray into the NHL with the expansion Pittsburgh Pirates. The new club boasted essentially the same lineup as the Yellow Jackets' championship team of

1924–25, but Worters would have topped the new team's wish list in any event. The man they called "Shrimp" played three seasons with the Pirates, playing in all the team's games in their second and third years. The Pirates were weak defensively, but Worters routinely kept them competitive. One night in their first year, Worters stopped 70 of 73 shots in a 3–1 loss to the New York Americans.

Prior to the 1928–29 season, Worters rejected the Pirates' contract offer, prompting NHL president Frank Calder to suspend the diminutive netminder. A trade to the New York Americans resolved the issue, and Worters would spend the rest of his pro career—except for two games—in the Big Apple. Over a nine-year span, the Americans qualified for the post-season only twice. One of those playoff appearances came in Worters' first year, after he registered a 1.15 goals-against average to elevate the play of a team that had finished in last place the year before. His heroics made Worters the first goalie to win the Hart Trophy as the league's most valuable player.

Shrimp soldiered on, solidifying his place as one of the game's elite goalies. In 1930–31, he led all NHL netminders with a 1.61 goals-against mark and captured the Vezina Trophy. During the ensuing contract negotiations with the Amerks, his legend grew when he demanded—and received—$8,500 per season, an enormous sum for a goalie at that time. What made this coup all the more remarkable was that he'd outbargained Americans owner Bill Dwyer, a notorious bootlegger who continually defied the U.S. Prohibition laws.

Even though the Americans remained weak, Worters continued to rack up shutouts and keep his goals-against mark respectable. He was placed on the NHL Second All-Star Team in 1932 and 1934.

One of the toughest competitors in league history, Worters was once hit in the windpipe by a Charlie Conacher shot. Rather than drop to the ice, he clung stubbornly to the crossbar

Worters, Roy "Shrimp"
G, 5'3", 135 lbs, b: Toronto, Ont., 10/19/1900, d: 11/7/1957

Season	Club, League	Regular Season				Playoffs			
		GP	Mins	GA	Avg	GP	Mins	GA	Avg
1920–21	Porcupine Miners, NOHA	10	630	27	2.57	2	120	10	5.00
1922–23	Toronto Argonauts, City Sr.	10	558	37	3.98				
1923–24	Pittsburgh Yellow Jackets, USAHA	20	1225	25	1.23	13	840	12	0.86
1924–25	Pittsburgh Yellow Jackets, USAHA	39	1895	34	0.81	8	400	8	1.20
1925–26	Pittsburgh Pirates, NHL	35	2145	68	1.90	2	120	6	3.00
1926–27	Pittsburgh Pirates, NHL	44	2711	108	2.39				
1927–28	Pittsburgh Pirates, NHL	44	2740	76	1.66	2	120	6	3.00
1928–29	New York Americans, NHL	38	2390	46	1.15	2	150	1	0.40
1929–30	New York Americans, NHL	36	2270	135	3.57				
	Montreal Canadiens, NHL	1	60	2	2.00				
1930–31	New York Americans, NHL	44	2760	74	1.61				
1931–32	New York Americans, NHL	40	2459	110	2.68				
1932–33	New York Americans, NHL	47	2970	116	2.34				
	Quebek Castors, Can-Am	1	60	3	3.00				
1933–34	New York Americans, NHL	36	2240	75	2.01				
1934–35	New York Americans, NHL	48	3000	142	2.84				
1935–36	New York Americans, NHL	48	3000	122	2.44	5	300	11	2.20
1936–37	New York Americans, NHL	23	1430	69	2.90				
	NHL Totals	484	30175	1143	2.27	11	690	24	2.09

NHL Second All-Star Team (1932, 1934)
Won Hart Trophy (1929)
Won Vezina Trophy (1931)

and insisted on playing the rest of the game. His throat became so swollen that he was unable to eat solid food for two weeks. Over the years, he accumulated more than 200 stitches and a host of other ailments that he refused to let interfere with his work. "A cut around the head—unless it's right in the eye, so that the sight is blurred—shouldn't bother anybody," he once reflected. "The injuries that stop you are on the arms or legs, so that you can't move around."

He retired after the 1936–37 season. Gritty to the end, he refused to take himself out of the lineup in his final days even though he was suffering from a painful hernia. He never played on any powerhouses, which made his 66 shutouts, 171 wins and his durability all the more impressive. Shrimp was also known as the first goalie to consistently use the back of his hands to divert a puck to the corner and was renowned for giving up very few rebounds.

An enduring story about Worters' diminutive stature started on a train as the New York club dealt with Canada Customs. An officer sent aboard to count the players couldn't locate the star netminder, so he approached Lionel Conacher. The burly defender told the officer to check Worters' berth in the sleeping car. When he responded that he'd already done so, Conacher told him to check again, since Worters was bound to be "in there somewhere."

After he retired, Worters stayed in touch with hockey by involving himself with the NHL Oldtimers' Hockey Association. He also devoted a great deal of his time to helping handicapped children. A successful businessman, he ran a hotel business in Toronto, which he sold for a profit before he was 50 years old. He died in Toronto on November 7, 1957, after a battle with throat cancer. Worters was inducted into the Hockey Hall of Fame in 1969.

Lorne Chabot

One of the top netminders of the 1920s and 1930s, Lorne Chabot attained great success as both an amateur and a professional. He played on Allan Cup and Stanley Cup winners and took part in some of the most memorable games in NHL history—including the two longest overtime contests of all time.

Lorne Chabot played in the two longest overtime contests of all time.

The Montreal native learned the game in his home town before venturing west to serve as an instructor at the RCMP college in Regina, Saskatchewan. He was an accomplished soccer player on the Mounties' squad and became friends with an employee at the local Canadian Pacific Railway hotel. He was soon put in touch with the manager of the CPR's establishment in Brandon, Manitoba, who offered to buy Chabot's way out of the RCMP so that he could play goal for the local team. As a result, Chabot apprenticed for two seasons with the Brandon Wheat Kings of the Manitoba senior league between 1920 and 1922. He then moved farther east to play for the Port Arthur Ports and Bearcats.

It was in that northwestern Ontario community that Chabot first gained widespread fame. His relatively large 6′1″ frame and quick reflexes made him hard to beat. His stellar play contributed to Port Arthur's consecutive Allan Cup triumphs in 1925 and 1926. After the second of these, Conn Smythe signed Chabot to play for the New York Rangers.

As a rookie, Sad Eyes won 22 games, recorded 10 shutouts and took the starting netminder's job away from Hal Winkler. In 1927–28, he played all 44 regular-season matches and helped New York reach the Stanley Cup finals. In the second game of the championship series against the Montreal Maroons, an injury to Chabot precipitated one of the most famous maneuvers in Stanley Cup playoff history. Teams didn't carry a backup goalie, so Rangers manager Lester Patrick was forced to make an emergency appearance between the pipes. The Silver Fox backstopped the Blueshirts to an overtime win that shifted the momentum of the series and helped New York win its first Stanley Cup.

Chabot owned a sharp wit and he once said, "I always shave before each game because I stitch better when my skin is smooth."

Prior to the 1928–29 schedule, Chabot was sent to Toronto, where he posted a career-best 1.61 goals-against average and 12 shutouts. In 1931–32, he helped the franchise win its first Stanley Cup under the Maple Leafs banner. In the fifth game of the 1933 semifinals against Boston, the teams played 164 minutes and 46 seconds of scoreless hockey before the Leafs' Ken Doraty scored in the sixth overtime period. Chabot earned the shutout in what was the longest game in NHL history to that date. But in the finals the Rangers prevented the Leafs from repeating as champions.

In the fall of 1933, Chabot was traded to the Montreal Canadiens for George Hainsworth. The trade made the two men the first goalies ever to play for both storied teams. Following the death of the legendary Charlie Gardiner in 1934, the Chicago Black Hawks acquired Chabot in a trade that also involved Hall of Famers Howie Morenz and Lionel Conacher. Chabot showed no ill effects at having to replace the popular Gardiner as he went on to lead the NHL with a 1.80 goals-against mark. The NHL acknowledged his excellence by placing him on the First All-Star Team and presenting him with the Vezina Trophy.

Old Bulwarks played 16 regular-season games for the Montreal Maroons in 1935–36, and during the playoffs, on March 24, 1936, he played in the longest game in NHL history. Despite his heroic efforts in that game—the first of the semifinals—the Montrealers suc-

Chabot, Lorne
G, 6'1", 185 lbs, b: Montreal, Que., 10/5/1900, d: 10/10/1946

Season	Club, League		Regular Season				Playoffs		
		GP	Mins	GA	Avg	GP	Mins	GA	Avg
1920–21	Brandon Wheat Kings, MHL Sr.	1	60	3	3.00				
1922–23	Port Arthur Ports, MHL Sr.	16	960	57	3.56	2	120	3	1.50
1923–24	Port Arthur Ports, MHL Sr.	15	900	37	2.46	2	120	6	3.00
1924–25	Port Arthur Bearcats, MHL Sr.	20	1200	51	2.55	2	120	4	2.00
1925–26	Port Arthur Bearcats, TBSHL	20	1200	42	2.10	3	180	4	1.33
1926–27	New York Rangers, NHL	36	2307	56	1.46	2	120	3	1.50
	Springfield Indians, Can-Am	1	60	2	2.00				
1927–28	New York Rangers, NHL	44	2730	79	1.74	6	321	8	1.50
1928–29	Toronto Maple Leafs, NHL	43	2458	66	1.61	4	242	5	1.24
1929–30	Toronto Maple Leafs, NHL	42	2620	113	2.59				
1930–31	Toronto Maple Leafs, NHL	37	2300	80	2.09	2	139	4	1.73
1931–32	Toronto Maple Leafs, NHL	44	2698	106	2.36	7	438	15	2.05
1932–33	Toronto Maple Leafs, NHL	40	2946	111	2.26	9	686	18	1.57
1933–34	Montreal Canadiens, NHL	47	2928	101	2.07	2	131	4	1.83
1934–35	Chicago Black Hawks, NHL	48	2940	88	1.80	2	124	1	0.48
1935–36	Montreal Maroons, NHL	16	1010	35	2.08	3	297	0	1.21
1936–37	New York Americans, NHL	6	370	25	4.05				
	NHL Totals	411	25307	860	2.04	37	2498	58	1.39

NHL First All-Star Team (1935)
Won Vezina Trophy (1935)
Won Stanley Cup (1928, 1932)

cumbed to the Detroit Red Wings when Mud Bruneteau scored the game's only goal after 116 minutes and 30 seconds of overtime. Chabot played six games with the New York Americans in 1936–37 before retiring with 201 wins and 73 shutouts.

Lionel "Big Train" Conacher

Named Canada's top male athlete of the half-century in 1950, Lionel Conacher excelled in virtually every sport he took part in. Aptly named "the Big Train," the 6'2", 195-pound Conacher was a proficient NHL skater. He normally played left defense and was best known for his imposing physical presence, leadership skills and rock-solid play in his own zone. One of his signature moves was to drop to one knee and use a sliding motion to break up passes or block shots. This technique also brought Conacher the label "the Traveling Netminder."

He always considered hockey his weakest sport, but he was lured to the NHL by the money he could make donning the blades. The Toronto native didn't start skating until he was 16 years old, but he made up for lost time, refining his game with the Toronto Century Rovers and the Aura

"The Big Train" (Lionel Conacher) was elected to the Ontario Legislature in 1937 and the federal House of Commons in 1949.

Lee Athletic Club before joining the Toronto Canoe Club juniors in 1919–20. The Paddlers captured both the OHA junior crown and the Memorial Cup later that season. Following this junior success, Conacher returned to the Aura Lees to play for their senior team for two years. In 1920 he also hit the game-winning home run to give his team the Toronto semipro baseball crown, then promptly took a taxi across the city and scored four goals for his lacrosse team, which was losing 3–0 when he arrived. In 1921 he scored two touchdowns to lead the Toronto Argonauts to victory in the Grey Cup game.

In 1922–23, Conacher played hockey for the North Toronto Seniors and he was on hand when they played Midland on February 8, 1923, in the first match ever broadcast on radio. At this stage, Conacher was so highly regarded that the Toronto St. Pats and Montreal Canadiens both invited him to play in the NHL. Although he declined to sign with either of these teams, it was to be only a matter of time before he made his big-league debut.

He maintained his amateur status long enough to accept an athletic scholarship offered from Bellefonte Academy in Pittsburgh, Pennsylvania. Conacher then captained the Pittsburgh Yellow Jackets in 1924 and 1925 as they won consecutive United States Amateur Hockey Association titles.

In 1925–26, the Big Train finally made his professional hockey debut. He was instrumental in keeping most of the Yellow Jackets together when the team renamed itself the Pirates and was admitted to the NHL as an expansion squad. The burly rearguard captained the team and scored the first goal in franchise history, against the Boston Bruins on November 26, 1925. A year later he was traded to the New York Americans, where he played four seasons and helped Leo Reise and Bill Brydge anchor the club's defense corps.

Conacher functioned as the Amerks' player-coach in 1929–30, then joined the Montreal Maroons the next season. He enjoyed three excellent years there, including a career-best 28 points in 1932–33. The Chicago Black Hawks obtained his services in time for the 1933–34 schedule, and Conacher was a key figure in the club's first-ever Stanley Cup victory that season. His impact was such that he finished second to the Canadiens' Aurel Joliat in the voting for the Hart Trophy and earned a spot on the NHL First All-Star Team.

Conacher, Lionel "the Big Train"
D, 6′2″, 195 lbs, b: Toronto, Ont., 5/24/1901, d: 5/26/1954

Season	Club, League	Regular Season					Playoffs				
		GP	G	A	Pts	PIM	GP	G	A	Pts	PIM
1920–21	Toronto Aura Lee, OHA Sr.	10	3	2	5	*					
1921–22	Toronto Aura Lee, OHA Sr.	20	7	2	9	*	2	2	0	2	0
1922–23	North Toronto Seniors, OHA Sr.						6	12	4	16	*
1923–24	Pittsburgh Yellow Jackets, USAHA	20	12	4	16	*	13	6	3	9	*
1924–25	Pittsburgh Yellow Jackets, USAHA	40	14	0	14	*	8	5	0	5	*
1925–26	Pittsburgh Pirates, NHL	33	9	4	13	64	2	0	0	0	0
1926–27	Pittsburgh Pirates, NHL	9	0	0	0	12					
	New York Americans, NHL	30	8	9	17	81					
1927–28	New York Americans, NHL	35	11	6	17	82					
1928–29	New York Americans, NHL	44	5	2	7	132	2	0	0	0	10
1929–30	New York Americans, NHL	40	4	6	10	73					
1930–31	Montreal Maroons, NHL	36	4	3	7	57	2	0	0	0	2
1931–32	Montreal Maroons, NHL	45	7	9	16	60	4	0	0	0	2
1932–33	Montreal Maroons, NHL	47	7	21	28	61	2	0	1	1	0
1933–34	Chicago Black Hawks, NHL	48	10	13	23	87	8	2	0	2	4
1934–35	Montreal Maroons, NHL	38	2	6	8	44	7	0	0	0	14
1935–36	Montreal Maroons, NHL	46	7	7	14	65	3	0	0	0	0
1936–37	Montreal Maroons, NHL	47	6	19	25	64	5	0	1	1	2
	NHL Totals	498	80	105	185	882	35	2	2	4	34

NHL First All-Star Team (1934)
NHL Second All-Star Team (1933, 1937)
Won Stanley Cup (1934, 1935)

After one year in Chicago, Conacher returned to the Maroons, where he'd spend his last three NHL seasons and take part in a second Cup triumph in 1935. He brought his distinguished career to a close after the Maroons were eliminated from the playoffs by the New York Rangers on April 23, 1937. Rather than risk becoming a fading star, he went out on a high note: He was runner-up to Babe Siebert in the 1937 Hart Trophy voting and was placed on the NHL Second All-Star Team.

Conacher's significance as an NHL player was only one facet of his immense athletic portfolio. A Canadian football star and Grey Cup hero, he was selected the country's top gridiron player of the first half-century. Conacher was also a legendary figure in the sport of lacrosse. The Canadian Press paid homage to him by attaching his name to the annual award it presents to the nation's top male athlete.

The Big Train was elected to the Ontario Legislature in 1937 and to Parliament 12 years later. He served as an MP until his death on May 26, 1954. Fittingly, he was playing in a charity softball match and collapsed while running the bases after a hit. Conacher was a charter member of the Canadian Sports Hall of Fame in 1955, the Canadian Football Hall of Fame and Museum in 1963 and the Canadian Lacrosse Hall of Fame and Museum in 1966. In 1994 he was inducted into the Hockey Hall of Fame.

Named Canada's top male athlete of the first half of the century, Lionel Conacher excelled in every sport he attempted.

Howie Morenz

Howie Morenz has often been referred to as hockey's first bona fide superstar. He electrified fans and confounded the opposition in a way that ensured his exalted status in hockey history. Remarkably, Morenz's total of 284 regular-season and playoff goals in 14 NHL seasons represents only one aspect of the enormous impression he left on the sport.

The native of southwestern Ontario was dubbed "the Mitchell Meteor" in honor of both his home town and his natural speed. He demonstrated advanced playing skills from a very young age, but more often than not he found himself tending goal. Morenz started in net during his first game with the Mitchell Juveniles in 1916–17, but it quickly became apparent that he was more suited to an offensive role. Morenz was clearly the fastest player in the league, a quality that contributed significantly to Mitchell's western Ontario juvenile championship that same year.

The Morenz family moved to nearby Stratford in May 1917, and Howie's unique talent gained him a place on the Stratford Midgets in time for the 1917–18 season. He and linemate Frank Carson were so impressive that they were enlisted by the city's senior team for the occasional match. During one senior exhibition contest against Preston in 1919–20, the 17-year-old Morenz was the dominant performer on the ice. In another game, against Kitchener, he faced future teammate George Hainsworth in a match that brought out the best in both future stars.

Howie Morenz's blinding speed and puckhandling were key factors behind the Canadiens' consecutive Stanley Cup wins in 1930 and 1931.

Morenz was in such demand in 1920–21 that he appeared with the Stratford midget and intermediate teams as well as the Grand Trunk Railroad apprentice club. He led all three outfits to their respective championships and he suited up for the Midgets in the Memorial Cup finals against the Winnipeg Falcons.

When Morenz's amateur career ended in 1923, he was courted by a host of professional teams. After declining offers from Toronto, Victoria and Saskatoon, the Morenz family agreed to a contract with the Montreal Canadiens. The Stratford Streak enjoyed an outstanding decade with the Habs, accumulating nearly 250 regular-season goals.

Morenz's first year as a Canadien culminated in a Stanley Cup win. Playing on an exciting line with Aurel Joliat and Billy Boucher, Morenz accounted for three of his team's five goals in the two-game NHL playoff series against the Ottawa Senators. A week later, Montreal embarked on wins over both the Vancouver Maroons, champions of the Pacific Coast Hockey Association, and the Calgary Tigers, who were the Western Canada Hockey League's best.

Morenz also contributed to the Canadiens' consecutive Stanley Cup wins in 1930 and 1931. His blinding speed and puckhandling wizardry were key factors in Montreal's upset win over Boston in the 1930 finals. The Bruins had finished the regular season with an astonishing 38–5–1 record, and they were prohibitive favorites to win the Cup, but the Habs swept the best-of-three series. In 1931 Montreal defeated Chicago in a hard-fought struggle that lasted five games. In the deciding match, a 2–0 Canadiens win, Morenz scored the insurance goal despite playing with a badly injured shoulder.

Morenz was one of the dominant offensive forces in the league in the late 1920s. He scored a league-high 51 points in 1927–28 and was presented with the Hart Trophy. Two years later he registered an incredible 40 goals in 44 games. In 1930–31, he won his second Hart Trophy and scoring title with another 51-point season. Morenz was also selected to the NHL's inaugural First All-Star Team in 1931. The following year he scored 49 points in 48 games and was awarded his third Hart Trophy in five seasons as well as another spot on the First All-Star Team.

By the mid-1930s, the tenacious and often violent attention of the opposition's defenders had taken its toll on Morenz's trademark speed. He was sent to the Chicago Black Hawks in 1934 and spent parts of two seasons there before joining the New York Rangers for the last 19 games of 1935–36. Canadiens head coach Cecil Hart spearheaded Morenz's return to Montreal for the 1936–37 season. Playing with a renewed sense of purpose, the Canadien Comet teamed with Johnny Gagnon and Aurel Joliat to help Montreal to a first-place lead in the regular-season standings.

Morenz's rejuvenation was cut short when he suffered a broken leg in a home game against the Black Hawks on January 28, 1937. It was generally agreed that the injury would end his career. A few weeks later, on March 8, the hockey world was stunned by the news of Morenz's death, brought on by complications related to his injury. Three days later the Canadiens turned the Forum into a shrine in

Howie Morenz demonstrated advanced playing skills from a very young age but more often found himself tending goal.

Season	Club, League	Regular Season					Playoffs				
		GP	G	A	Pts	PIM	GP	G	A	Pts	PIM
1921–22	Stratford Indians, OHA Sr.	4	10	3	13	2	8	15	8	23	21
1922–23	Stratford Indians, OHA Sr.	10	15	13	28	19	10	28	7	35	36
1923–24	Montreal Canadiens, NHL	24	13	3	16	20	2	3	1	4	6
1924–25	Montreal Canadiens, NHL	30	28	11	39	46	2	3	0	3	4
1925–26	Montreal Canadiens, NHL	31	23	3	26	39					
1926–27	Montreal Canadiens, NHL	44	25	7	32	49	4	1	0	1	4
1927–28	Montreal Canadiens, NHL	43	33	18	51	66	2	0	0	0	12
1928–29	Montreal Canadiens, NHL	42	17	10	27	47	3	0	0	0	6
1929–30	Montreal Canadiens, NHL	44	40	10	50	72	6	3	0	3	10
1930–31	Montreal Canadiens, NHL	39	28	23	51	49	10	1	4	5	10
1931–32	Montreal Canadiens, NHL	48	24	25	49	46	4	1	0	1	4
1932–33	Montreal Canadiens, NHL	46	14	21	35	32	2	0	3	3	2
1933–34	Montreal Canadiens, NHL	39	8	13	21	21	2	1	1	2	0
1934–35	Chicago Black Hawks, NHL	48	8	26	34	21	2	0	0	0	0
1935–36	Chicago Black Hawks, NHL	23	4	11	15	20					
	New York Rangers, NHL	19	2	4	6	6					
1936–37	Montreal Canadiens, NHL	30	4	16	20	12					
	NHL Totals	550	271	201	472	546	39	13	9	22	58

Morenz, Howie
C, 5′9″, 165 lbs, b: Mitchell, Ont., 6/21/1902, d: 3/8/1937

NHL First All-Star Team (1931, 1932)
NHL Second All-Star Team (1933)
Won Hart Trophy (1928, 1931, 1932)
NHL Scoring Leader (1928, 1931)
Won Stanley Cup (1924, 1930, 1931)

honor of their fallen star. Thousands of fans lined the streets and crowded the arena in a tremendous outpouring of emotion and respect for one of hockey's immortals. Inducted into the Canadian Sports Hall of Fame, Morenz was one of the first to be inducted into the Hockey Hall of Fame when it was established in 1945.

Bun Cook

Bun Cook was a popular left wing who compiled 302 points during an 11-year NHL career spent chiefly with the New York Rangers. He and brother Bill lined up on either side of center Frank Boucher to form the Bread Line, one of the most revered forward units in NHL history. Recognized as an innovator, Bun Cook has been credited with introducing and perfecting the drop pass.

Bun Cook was an innovator of the drop pass.

A native of Kingston, Ontario, Cook first acquired a passion for the game between 1917 and 1920 when he played on the St. Marys, Regiopolis and Kingston junior clubs, followed by a stint with the Guelph Agricultural Club. In 1922–23, he joined the Sault Ste. Marie Greyhounds of the northern Ontario league, where he contributed to an Allan Cup championship the following season. Cook made his professional debut in 1924–25 with the Saskatoon Crescents of the Western Canada Hockey League.

In 1926 the Cook brothers were an integral part of the eastward move of talented players to the expansion New York Rangers. In 1927–28, teamed with Boucher, the Cooks were a key factor in the Rangers' first Stanley Cup championship.

Bun was less dangerous around the net than Bill, but he was no less determined, and his work ethic and ability to carve out a niche of his own despite being the brother of a hockey legend earned him respect throughout the league. He was a fan favorite at Madison Square Garden because of his dedication, and he did manage to finish among the league's top 10 scorers on three occasions.

Cook registered a personal high of 24 goals in 1929–30 and was selected to the NHL Second All-Star Team the next season. The 1932–33 campaign brought the Rangers their second Stanley Cup as the irrepressible Bread Line led the way. During the mid-1930s, the Cook brothers, along with fellow veterans Frank Boucher, Murray Murdoch and Ching Johnson, served as Lester Patrick's players' committee—the accepted team leaders who quelled a brewing controversy that had arisen in the dressing room when Patrick played his son Lynn on a regular basis. The dissent proved unjustified, as the junior Patrick was a useful young player on a team laden with veterans.

In 1935–36, Cook was forced to the sidelines as a result of an arthritic condition. Prior to the 1936–37 season, he was acquired by the Boston Bruins, with whom he played his final year. During his 11 years of NHL service, Cook was responsible for 158 goals and 302 points. During the post-season, he accumulated an additional 15 goals and 18 points for the Blueshirts.

Cook, Bun
LW, 5´11˝, 180 lbs, b: Kingston, Ont., 9/18/1903, d: 3/19/1988

Season	Club, League	Regular Season					Playoffs				
		GP	G	A	Pts	PIM	GP	G	A	Pts	PIM
1921–22	Soo Greyhounds, NOHA	3	2	1	3	2					
1922–23	Soo Greyhounds, NOHA	8	2	3	5	10	5	0	2	2	0
1923–24	Soo Greyhounds, NOHA	8	3	3	6	10	7	1	0	1	8
1924–25	Saskatoon Crescents, WCHL	28	17	4	21	44	2	0	1	1	0
1925–26	Saskatoon Crescents, WHL	30	8	4	12	22	2	0	0	0	0
1926–27	New York Rangers, NHL	44	14	9	23	42	2	0	0	0	6
1927–28	New York Rangers, NHL	44	14	14	28	45	9	2	1	3	10
1928–29	New York Rangers, NHL	43	13	5	18	70	6	1	0	1	12
1929–30	New York Rangers, NHL	43	24	18	42	55	4	2	0	2	2
1930–31	New York Rangers, NHL	44	18	17	35	72	4	0	0	0	2
1931–32	New York Rangers, NHL	45	14	20	34	43	7	6	2	8	12
1932–33	New York Rangers, NHL	48	22	15	37	35	8	2	0	2	4
1933–34	New York Rangers, NHL	48	18	15	33	36	2	0	0	0	2
1934–35	New York Rangers, NHL	48	13	21	34	26	4	2	0	2	0
1935–36	New York Rangers, NHL	26	4	5	9	12					
1936–37	Boston Bruins, NHL	40	4	5	9	8					
1937–38	Providence Reds, AHL	19	0	1	1	4	4	0	0	0	2
1938–39	Providence Reds, AHL	11	1	3	4	4					
1939–40	Providence Reds, AHL	1	0	0	0	0	2	0	0	0	0
1940–41	Providence Reds, AHL	1	0	0	0	0					
1941–42	Providence Reds, AHL	2	0	1	1	0					
1942–43	Providence Reds, AHL	3	1	1	2	4					
	NHL Totals	473	158	144	302	444	46	15	3	18	50
	WCHL Totals	28	17	4	21	44	2	0	1	1	0
	WHL Totals	30	8	4	12	22	2	0	0	0	0

NHL Second All-Star Team (1931)
Won Stanley Cup (1928, 1933)

After his playing career, Cook turned to coaching. As a rookie bench boss in 1937–38, he led the Providence Reds to the American Hockey League's Calder Cup championship, a feat he duplicated in 1939–40. In 1943–44, Cook moved behind the bench of the Cleveland Barons of the same league and guided that team to an incredible five Calder Cup triumphs before he retired from minor pro hockey in 1956. Cook went down in history as one of the most popular and successful coaches in AHL history.

Cook spent the 1956–57 schedule as coach of the Sault Ste. Marie Greyhounds of the Northern Ontario Hockey Association. The following three seasons he steered the Kingston Frontenacs of the Eastern Professional Hockey League. Cook's outstanding hockey career came to a close in 1961, when he stepped down as coach of the Kingston Frontenacs.

Seven years after his death in 1988, he was inducted into the Hockey Hall of Fame.

Clarence "Hap" Day

Clarence Day's perpetually cheery demeanor earned him the nickname "Happy," which was later shortened to "Hap." Day was born in Owen Sound, Ontario, and he played his minor hockey there. He routinely walked five miles—carrying his equipment—to games in the closest big town, Port McNicholl, and later in life he maintained his penchant for walking. During his teens he ended up in Hamilton, where he played senior hockey with the Tigers. He also enrolled at the University of Toronto, where he majored in pharmacy and played for the Varsity team. By this time he was considered one of the finest amateurs in the country and one of the best skaters outside the NHL.

Charlie Querrie, owner of the St. Pats—the NHL's Toronto entry—and Bert Corbeau, the team's star player, saw Day play one night and knew immediately that he could contribute at the game's highest level. But Day was reluctant to turn pro, and he agreed only after the St. Pats offered him an eye-popping $5,000 salary along with a promise that he wouldn't miss too many classes at U of T. Day would be associated with the club for more than 30 years.

On December 10, 1924, Day made his NHL debut as a left wing, and his linemates were none other than future Hall of Famers Jack Adams and Babe Dye. After his rookie year, he shifted to defense, where he spent the rest of his career.

During his playing days, Day also ran a drugstore in Maple Leaf Gardens. Eventually he gave up this business and Dick Dowling's Grill took its place.

For much of his career he was known as "Clarence the Clutch" because of his reputation for grabbing opponents' sticks. Although he was rarely penalized for such holding infractions, players occasionally made him look bad by letting go of their own sticks so the referee could see plainly that Day was holding two. "One night," Day related, "I was told to make sure I stopped Bill Cook. He came down and I bumped him and grabbed his stick with my hand. I looked around to follow the play, and when I looked back I was holding nothing but his stick—in plain view of everybody. Bill had skated off and left me holding it!"

Day sustained numerous minor injuries during his career, but the most serious was a torn Achilles heel he suffered on February 2, 1928, when another player stepped on the back of his leg. He tried to return to action, but the injury triggered an onslaught of further maladies that cost him the rest of the season. Over time, the heel recovered fully and he'd miss very few games over the next decade. The injury also led Leafs' trainer Tommy Naylor to devise an ankle guard to prevent such horrific accidents in the future.

Day was a born leader, and when the Leafs captaincy became available, there was no doubt as to who would lead the team. He was team captain from 1926 until 1936. Starting in 1931, he was paired on defense with King Clancy; together they formed one of the best twosomes in the league.

In the spring of 1932, the Leafs christened their new home, Maple Leaf Gardens, with the team's first Stanley Cup championship under Conn Smythe's management and Day scored a key goal. In a two-game, total-goals semifinal against the Montreal Maroons, the teams tied the first leg 1–1. In the second game, Day made a spectacular rush—something defense players rarely did then—to tie the score and send the game into overtime. Bob Gracie got the winner for the Leafs and they moved on to the finals against the New York Rangers. Day scored three goals in the first two games and the Leafs won the famous "tennis series" by scores of 6–4, 6–2 and 6–4. "That was my eighth season in pro hockey and I was beginning to think I'd never play for a Stanley Cup winner," Day said later. In fact, it was the only Cup Day would win as a player.

Throughout their careers, Day and Clancy were notorious for their practical jokes. On road trips, they'd tie the bedsheets in every player's room in knots; they once cut Charlie Conacher's new fedora to ribbons; and, on a $20 bet from all his teammates, Day dove into a swimming pool dressed as if he'd just come off the train. Everything—his suit and hat, his suitcase full of clothes, his shoes—was soaked. Clancy and Conacher couldn't believe he took the dare and Day was delighted to collect his prize.

Clarence Day on his wedding day.

Day, Clarence "Hap"
D, 5'11", 175 lbs, b: Owen Sound, Ont., 6/14/1901, d: 2/17/1990

Season	Club, League	Regular Season					Playoffs				
		GP	G	A	Pts	PIM	GP	G	A	Pts	PIM
1922–23	Hamilton Tigers, OHA Sr.	11	4	11	15	4	2	0	0	0	0
1923–24	Hamilton Tigers, OHA Sr.	10	6	11	17	*	2	1	1	2	*
1924–25	Toronto St. Pats, NHL	26	10	12	22	33	2	0	0	0	0
1925–26	Toronto St. Pats, NHL	36	14	2	16	26					
1926–27	Toronto Maple Leafs, NHL	44	11	5	16	50					
1927–28	Toronto Maple Leafs, NHL	22	9	8	17	48					
1928–29	Toronto Maple Leafs, NHL	44	6	6	12	84	4	1	0	1	4
1929–30	Toronto Maple Leafs, NHL	43	7	14	21	77					
1930–31	Toronto Maple Leafs, NHL	44	1	13	14	56	2	0	3	3	7
1931–32	Toronto Maple Leafs, NHL	47	7	8	15	33	7	3	3	6	6
1932–33	Toronto Maple Leafs, NHL	47	6	14	20	46	9	0	1	1	21
1933–34	Toronto Maple Leafs, NHL	48	9	10	19	35	5	0	0	0	6
1934–35	Toronto Maple Leafs, NHL	45	2	4	6	38	7	0	0	0	4
1935–36	Toronto Maple Leafs, NHL	44	1	13	14	41	9	0	0	0	8
1936–37	Toronto Maple Leafs, NHL	48	3	4	7	20	2	0	0	0	0
1937–38	New York Americans, NHL	43	0	3	3	14	6	0	0	0	0
	NHL Totals	581	86	116	202	601	53	4	7	11	56

Won Stanley Cup (1932)

Day played his final season with the New York Americans in 1937–38, then acted as a referee for two years while coaching in the Toronto area. He won the coveted Memorial Cup with the West Toronto juniors in 1936, and the next season he coached the Toronto Dominions to the OHA senior title before losing to the eventual Allan Cup winners, the Sudbury Tigers, in the provincial championships.

During his playing days in Toronto, Clarence Day (second from the left) also ran a drug store in Maple Leaf Gardens.

Fortune smiled on Day in 1940 when Leafs coach Dick Irvin packed up and moved to Montreal to coach the Canadiens. Leafs owner Conn Smythe immediately hired Day as Irvin's replacement, and over the next 10 years he was the most successful coach in the NHL. In his first year the Leafs made it to the semifinals before losing to Boston in seven games. But in 1942 he coached the team to the greatest Stanley Cup comeback of all time. The Leafs lost the first three games of the finals to Detroit and seemed destined to finish the season as losers of the Cup.

"You didn't have to be a genius to figure something had to be done when you were down 3–0," Day said of his team's predicament. So he benched two of his veteran players, Gord Drillon and Bucko McDonald, and played the relatively inexperienced Bob Goldham and Gaye Stewart. The Leafs won game four in Detroit by a score of 4–3 and stormed back to win the Cup, the only time in the history of the contest that a team has overcome a 3–0 disadvantage in the finals. After the game, while all the players swilled champagne from the bowl of the Cup, Day dipped a finger into the bubbly and sucked it dry—the only drinking binge of his life.

Day was a taskmaster who demanded the most from his men. While he preached conditioning to his players, he also skated and ran alongside them as proof that he could keep up with them. A nonsmoker and teetotaler, he strongly discouraged drinking on road trips. Much to the dismay of some on-ice officials, he knew the rule book inside out and could quote it verbatim. In all, he won five Cup championships as coach of the Leafs: in 1942 and 1945, then three in a row from 1947 to 1949—the first time in NHL history that a Stanley Cup hat-trick was accomplished.

After he gave up coaching in 1950, the Leafs immediately appointed Day assistant to general manager Conn Smythe, although Day in fact had the responsibility of running the team until 1957. He picked up another Stanley Cup with coach Joe Primeau in 1951, and was appointed general manager for 1957–58. Day was inducted into the Hockey Hall of Fame in 1977.

Sylvio Mantha

One of the best two-way defensemen of his era, Sylvio Mantha enjoyed plenty of individual and team success in 14 NHL seasons. He spent most of his big-league tenure with the Montreal Canadiens, with whom he was an important component of three Stanley Cup teams. His offensive rushes aided the club's transitional play, while his disciplined checking in the defensive zone rounded out his game.

Born and bred in the St. Henri district of Montreal, Mantha first made a name for himself as a right wing with the Notre Dame de Grace juniors in 1918–19. That was followed by apprenticeships with Verdun in the Intermediate Mount Royal Hockey League, Montreal Imperial Tobacco and Montreal Northern Electric in the city's industrial league and a short stint with the Montreal Nationales of the Quebec senior amateur league. Well-known coach Arthur Therrien made an indelible impression on Mantha while coaching him at Verdun.

Mantha's four goals in nine games with the Nationales impressed the Montreal Canadiens enough to sign him in December 1923. Although he broke into the Canadiens lineup as a forward, he was soon moved back to fill a void on the right side of the team's blue line. Montreal was also trying to add youth to their defense corps, as veterans Sprague Cleghorn and Billy Coutu were on the downside of their careers.

Later that season, Mantha gained his first exposure to Stanley Cup glory when he helped Montreal vanquish the Vancouver Maroons and the Calgary Tigers. Then Cleghorn was traded prior to the 1925–26 season, paving the way for Mantha to take a more prominent role on the team. Mantha became a fixture on the Habs defense, pairing with Western Canada Hockey League veteran Herb Gardiner. On November 20, 1928, Mantha scored the first-ever goal in Boston Garden in a 1–0 Canadiens triumph over the Bruins.

Arguably, Mantha's two most rewarding seasons were 1929–30 and 1930–31. He contributed to consecutive Stanley Cup triumphs and was named to the NHL Second All-Star Team both years. By this time, Mantha was entrenched as one of the most revered defensive defensemen in the game. Further satisfaction came from sharing this success with his younger brother Georges, who was a defenseman and left wing for the Canadiens from 1928 to 1941.

In 1935–36, Mantha took on a greater challenge by serving as the Canadiens' player-coach. Unfortunately, the club didn't fare well and missed out on post-season play for the first time in a decade. Late in the 1936–37 season, he was signed by the Boston Bruins, for whom he played his last four regular-season games as defensive insurance.

After retiring, Mantha tried his hand as a linesman and referee in the American Hockey League and the NHL. However, the grueling travel schedule of an on-ice official proved to be too much. Mantha decided to stay in Montreal and ply his trade as an amateur coach. He guided the Montreal Concordias until 1943, when he switched to the junior ranks. Mantha passed his wealth of experience on to young players on the Laval Nationales from 1943 to 1945, the Verdun Maple Leafs from 1945 to 1947 and the St. Jerome Eagles from 1947 to 1948.

By the end of the 1940s, Mantha was ready to make a clean break from the game. In 1960 he was inducted into the Hockey Hall of Fame and he died in August 1974 in Montreal, scene of many of his fondest memories, on or off the ice.

Sylvio Mantha was one of the best two-way defensemen of his era.

Mantha, Sylvio
D, 5´10˝, 178 lbs, b: Montreal, Que., 4/14/1902, d: 8/7/1974

Season	Club, League	Regular Season					Playoffs				
		GP	G	A	Pts	PIM	GP	G	A	Pts	PIM
1922–23	Montreal Nationales, City Sr.	9	4	0	4	*					
1923–24	Montreal Canadiens, NHL	24	1	3	4	11	2	0	0	0	0
1924–25	Montreal Canadiens, NHL	30	2	3	5	18	2	0	1	1	0
1925–26	Montreal Canadiens, NHL	34	2	1	3	66					
1926–27	Montreal Canadiens, NHL	43	10	5	15	77	4	1	0	1	0
1927–28	Montreal Canadiens, NHL	43	4	11	15	61	2	0	0	0	6
1928–29	Montreal Canadiens, NHL	44	9	4	13	56	3	0	0	0	0
1929–30	Montreal Canadiens, NHL	44	13	11	24	108	6	2	1	3	18
1930–31	Montreal Canadiens, NHL	44	4	7	11	75	10	2	1	3	26
1931–32	Montreal Canadiens, NHL	47	5	5	10	62	4	0	1	1	8
1932–33	Montreal Canadiens, NHL	48	4	7	11	50	2	0	1	1	2
1933–34	Montreal Canadiens, NHL	48	4	6	10	24	2	0	0	0	2
1934–35	Montreal Canadiens, NHL	47	3	11	14	36	2	0	0	0	2
1935–36	Montreal Canadiens, NHL	42	2	4	6	25					
1936–37	Boston Bruins, NHL	4	0	0	0	2					
	NHL Totals	542	63	78	141	671	39	5	5	10	64

NHL Second All-Star Team (1931, 1932)
Won Stanley Cup (1924, 1930, 1931)

Babe Siebert

Babe Seibert grew up in Zurich, Ontario, where he played hockey every day as a child.

Although born in Plattsville, Ontario, Babe Siebert grew up in nearby Zurich, where he played hockey virtually every day of his childhood. In the winter he'd skate outside and on rainy days he'd play with friends in the school gym. He moved slowly upward through the various leagues, eventually playing junior with Kitchener. Frank Selke first saw the potential of this great star when Kitchener played the Toronto St. Marys in a playoff game in 1924. "Every time we threatened to score," Selke said of his Toronto team, "Babe Siebert somehow retrieved the puck, carrying us right back to our own end of the arena. I can't recall any other player dominating his team's defensive stand as did Siebert on this occasion. It was something to remember for a lifetime."

Siebert entered the NHL with the Montreal Maroons in 1925–26 and almost immediately became part of the famous S Line that also featured Hooley Smith and Nels Stewart. In that first year the team finished second to Ottawa in the standings but beat the Senators in the playoffs and then finished off Victoria, the PCHL champs, to win the Stanley Cup.

The S Line was the most feared line in hockey until 1932, when Siebert was traded to the Rangers. Although the line won no more Cup championships after that first year together, the three were consistently near the top of the league in scoring. Stewart was the natural scorer on the line, and Smith was the passer, but Siebert was equally well known for his rushing, his sheer physical strength and his relentless backchecking to get the team possession of the puck.

In New York, Siebert won his second Stanley Cup in 1933 when the Blueshirts defeated Toronto three games to one in the best-of-five finals. He was traded to Boston midway through the following season, but in 1936 Cecil Hart became coach of the Canadiens and insisted the club reacquire Howie Morenz and pick up Siebert. And so, in the twilight of his career, Babe returned to Montreal. His speed was gone, so Hart wisely put him back on defense, where he was just as effective as ever. In his first year with the Canadiens, he won the Hart Trophy.

By this time, Siebert was as popular off the ice as on. His wife had been paralyzed from the waist down after complications during the birth of their second child, and Babe was ever-faithful to her. NHL president Frank Calder recalled: "The same bruising Siebert—who relentlessly dealt out one of hockey's hardest bodychecks—carried his ailing wife each hockey night into the Forum at Montreal to a rinkside seat. After the game, he carried her tenderly out to his car."

Elmer Ferguson of the *Montreal Gazette* described this most moving of images: "Babe would stride along the promenade until he reached the chair where his wife was waiting,

Siebert, Babe
LW/D, 5'10", 182 lbs, b: Plattsville, Ont., 1/14/1904, d: 8/25/1939

Season	Club, League	Regular Season					Playoffs				
		GP	G	A	Pts	PIM	GP	G	A	Pts	PIM
1923–24	Kitchener Twin City, OHA Sr.	10	9	4	13	*					
1924–25	Niagara Falls Cataracts, OHA Sr.	20	9	2	11	26	3	2	0	2	3
1925–26	Montreal Maroons, NHL	35	16	8	24	108	4	1	0	1	4
1926–27	Montreal Maroons, NHL	42	5	3	8	116	2	1	0	1	2
1927–28	Montreal Maroons, NHL	39	8	9	17	109	9	2	0	2	26
1928–29	Montreal Maroons, NHL	40	3	5	8	52					
1929–30	Montreal Maroons, NHL	39	14	19	33	94	3	0	0	0	0
1930–31	Montreal Maroons, NHL	43	16	12	28	76	2	0	0	0	6
1931–32	Montreal Maroons, NHL	48	21	18	39	64	4	0	1	1	4
1932–33	New York Rangers, NHL	43	9	10	19	38	8	1	0	1	12
1933–34	New York Rangers, NHL	13	0	1	1	18					
	Boston Bruins, NHL	32	5	6	11	31					
1934–35	Boston Bruins, NHL	48	6	18	24	80	4	0	0	0	6
1935–36	Boston Bruins, NHL	45	12	9	21	66	2	0	1	1	0
1936–37	Montreal Canadiens, NHL	44	8	20	28	38	5	1	2	3	2
1937–38	Montreal Canadiens, NHL	37	8	11	19	56	3	1	1	2	0
1938–39	Montreal Canadiens, NHL	44	9	7	16	36	3	0	0	0	0
	NHL Totals	592	140	156	296	982	49	7	5	12	62

NHL First All-Star Team (1936, 1937, 1938)
Won Hart Trophy (1937)
Won Stanley Cup (1926, 1933)

and reaching down he'd kiss her, then he'd gather her up into his great muscular arms…and stride on out of the rink."

Most of Siebert's income and savings went to nursing his wife, but he neither complained nor solicited help. After the 1938–39 season, he retired, and just a few weeks later he was named the new coach of the Canadiens. Tragedy struck, however, on August 25, 1939, when he drowned at the family resort while swimming out to get an inflatable tire that his children had been playing with. As the tire drifted away from shore, Siebert apparently grew fatigued and simply disappeared from sight. "It was really a double tragedy," former teammate Wilf Cude said, "because he meant so much to his wife." Indeed the hockey world was shocked by the loss of Siebert, and the NHL arranged a memorial game at the Forum, with the proceeds going to his wife. It was the third such game in league history—the first, in 1934, had been for Ace Bailey after his career was ended by an Eddie Shore hit; the second, for the family of Howie Morenz, was held in 1937—and these were the forerunners to the All-Star Game which became an annual fixture starting in 1947. The Siebert game raised more than $15,000 for his family even though attendance was surprisingly weak at just 6,000. Siebert was posthumously inducted into the Hockey Hall of Fame in 1964.

Irvine "Ace" Bailey

Ace Bailey was born in Bracebridge, Ontario, but he grew up in Toronto, where he played minor hockey in the Toronto hockey association. Although he was a fine player, he'd no intention of turning pro, and when he was 18 he enrolled at the University of Toronto. But he also played the 1924–25 and 1925–26 seasons for the Peterborough Seniors and caught the attention of the Toronto St. Pats, who convinced him to try out. He made the team—as well as an immediate impression—with both his speed and his shooting ability. During his brief career, he was once the league's leading goal scorer and in 1928–29 he won the scoring title with 22 goals and 10 assists in 44 games.

Bailey was one of the most popular players ever to skate for the Leafs during his few years in the NHL, but he will forever be linked to one of the worst on-ice accidents in the history of the game. On December 12, 1933, during the second period of a Leafs' visit to Boston Garden, Eddie Shore was checked hard by Leafs defenseman Red Horner while Shore was rushing the puck into the Leafs' end.

Ace Bailey will be linked forever to one of worst on-ice accidents in the history of hockey.

As play moved back into Boston territory, Shore, dazed by the hit and full of vengeance, skated wildly toward Bailey, thinking that he was charging Red Horner. Shore used his stick to trip Bailey heavily from behind and Ace fell to the ice with a sickening thud. He lost consciousness and began bleeding from the head. Red Horner skated over to the stricken Bailey and, seeing his teammate seriously injured, asked Shore in no uncertain terms just what he'd been thinking. Shore just smiled, prompting a furious Horner to deck him with one punch, knocking him unconscious to the ice.

As Leafs players gathered around Bailey, Bruin trainers looked after Shore, and both men had to be carried off the ice by worried teammates. Shore suffered a three-inch gash to his head, but Bailey's injury was far more serious. He lay in the Bruins dressing room, where Shore, upon regaining consciousness, came over to apologize. "It's all part of the game," Bailey said in forgiveness before convulsing and falling unconscious again.

Bailey was rushed to Audubon Hospital with what seemed to be a fractured skull. But by the following morning, Bailey's condition was grave and the prospect of his death was almost certain. Overnight, he'd suffered cerebral hemorrhaging, and at noon Dr. Donald Munro, a brain specialist, consulted with Ace's wife, Mabel, about a very necessary but dangerous operation. At the same time, Boston homicide detectives were interviewing Shore and other players about the incident and it became known that, in the event of Bailey's death, Shore would be charged with manslaughter.

Bailey was transferred to City Hospital, where Dr. Munro performed two operations to relieve the pressure on his brain. After the second operation, on December 18, Dr. Munro said simply, "His chances of living are very slim," and a priest was called to read Bailey's last rites. His pulse was 160, his temperature almost 106° Fahrenheit, and the doctors were reluctant even to measure his life expectancy in minutes. By the very next morning, however, Bailey had miraculously fought off death, and in the ensuing days he grew stronger and stronger. By Christmas, his life was no longer hanging in the balance and Ace was on the road to recovery.

When Ace Bailey's father heard of the incident, he flew into a rage. He bolted from his Toronto home and boarded the first train to Boston, carrying a loaded gun and telling anyone who would listen that he was going to kill Eddie Shore. Conn Smythe, who was in Boston to keep an eye on his star player, got wind of the news and phoned Frank Selke back in Toronto for help. Selke knew of only one solution. He phoned a friend in Boston, Bob Huddy, who was a member of the Boston police force. Selke explained the dire situation to Huddy, who went straight to the bar of the hotel where Bailey senior was staying. Sure enough, Ace's father was ranting to one and all about what he'd do to that so-and-so Shore when they met face to face. Huddy calmed him down, got him to hand over the revolver and put him on the next train back to Toronto with instructions to the conductor not to let him off before the train reached its destination.

Blame and accusations followed the Shore-Bailey incident. League president Frank Calder absolved the two referees—Odie Cleghorn and Eusebe Daignault—of any breach of responsibility in their handling of the game. But Red Horner blamed Shore for the attack, while Shore protested that he wasn't conscious of what he was doing after being dazed by Horner's check. Meanwhile, Leafs owner Conn Smythe blamed the Boston writers for generating malicious hype leading up to the game and inciting the Boston players to violence.

Calder suspended Horner until January 1, 1934, and barred Shore indefinitely. Shore wasn't permitted to visit Bailey in hospital, but when Boston manager Art Ross managed to gain access to his room, Ace again absolved Shore of any willful wrongdoing. Shore, exhausted and near collapse from both his own injury and his worry over Bailey's condition, went to Bermuda for three weeks to convalesce.

Bailey, Irvine "Ace"
RW, 5'10", 160 lbs, b: Bracebridge, Ont., 7/3/1903, d: 4/7/1992

Season	Club, League	Regular Season					Playoffs				
		GP	G	A	Pts	PIM	GP	G	A	Pts	PIM
1922–23	Toronto St. Mary's, OHA	4	2	1	3	*	4	2	1	3	*
1923–24	Toronto St. Mary's, OHA Sr.	8	10	0	10	*					
1924–25	Peterborough Seniors, OHA Sr.	8	5	0	5	*	2	3	0	3	2
1925–26	Peterborough Seniors, OHA Sr.	9	9	2	11	2	2	2	1	3	*
1926–27	Toronto Maple Leafs, NHL	42	15	13	28	82					
1927–28	Toronto Maple Leafs, NHL	43	9	3	12	72					
1928–29	Toronto Maple Leafs, NHL	44	22	10	32	78	4	1	2	3	4
1929–30	Toronto Maple Leafs, NHL	43	22	21	43	69					
1930–31	Toronto Maple Leafs, NHL	40	23	19	42	46	2	1	1	2	0
1931–32	Toronto Maple Leafs, NHL	41	8	5	13	62	7	1	0	1	4
1932–33	Toronto Maple Leafs, NHL	47	10	8	18	52	8	0	1	1	4
1933–34	Toronto Maple Leafs, NHL	13	2	3	5	11					
	NHL Totals	313	111	82	193	472	21	3	4	7	12

NHL Scoring Leader (1929)
Won Stanley Cup (1932)

Once it was clear that Bailey would live but would never play again, president Calder announced that Shore would be allowed back to the NHL as of January 28, after an absence of 16 games. Shore's presence in the Boston lineup was vital to the franchise's success. When he played, Boston Garden was routinely sold out. During his suspension, attendance had plummeted to about 6,000 per game.

By mid-January, when it was clear that Bailey would recover, Shore tried again to visit him in the hospital, but Dr. Munro continued to bar Shore from seeing him. "I am afraid the excitement of the meeting would be too much at this time," he explained. On January 18, 1934, Bailey was transferred to Toronto with explicit instructions that he do no exercise at all. He was alive, he was home, but his health was still fragile—and he'd never play hockey again.

On January 24, 1934, the NHL's board of governors decided that a special benefit game featuring the Leafs against the best of the rest of the league would be staged in Toronto and the proceeds would go to Bailey and his family. The idea had originally been proposed by Walter Gilhooley, sports editor of the *Journal* in Montreal, in the form of an open letter to the league. The Leafs' opposition, an "All-Star" team, would be selected by a committee consisting of Frank Calder, Frank Patrick and league director Thomas Arnold.

Prior to the game, held on Valentine's Day 1934, the All-Star players skated onto the ice in their regular team sweaters and had their picture taken as a group. They were then presented with their All-Star uniforms by president Calder, Lester Patrick and Leaf club officials, including Ace Bailey himself. The first in line was goalie Charlie Gardiner, who received his number 1 jersey, and he was followed immediately by number 2, Eddie Shore. An apprehensive silence fell over the Gardens as Shore skated to center ice. But as Bailey extended his hand to the Bruin, the crowd went wild. Bailey's extraordinarily sportsmanlike gesture made clear his forgiveness of Shore.

The ceremonies culminated in a historic presentation. Conn Smythe handed Ace his number 6 Leafs sweater with the words: "Allow me to present this sweater that you have worn so long and nobly for the Maple Leafs. No other player will ever use this number on the Maple Leaf hockey team."

Before the opening face-off, Ace gave president Calder a special trophy in Bailey's own name. It had been commissioned by the Maple Leafs in the hope that it would be the prize of an annual All-Star Game that would be staged to set up a fund for injured players. The paid attendance at the Gardens that night raised $20,909.40 for Bailey and his family.

Bailey later coached both the Toronto Marlies and the University of Toronto Blues, and he worked as an off-ice official at Maple Leaf Gardens almost to the day he died, on April 7, 1992. He was inducted into the Hockey Hall of Fame in 1975.

Eddie Shore

An imposing blend of raw talent and intimidation, defenseman Eddie Shore was one of the greatest ever to play his position in any era and his end-to-end rushes became every bit as famous as his crushing bodychecks and nasty disposition. When Shore retired as a player, he became a team owner and manager and continued to be a demanding and successful hockey figure.

Eddie Shore's end-to-end rushes became as famous as his crushing bodychecks and angry disposition.

Shore grew up on a horse ranch at Cupar, a small community in southern Saskatchewan near the North Dakota border, where his years of breaking in ponies, herding stock and hauling grain prepared him for the physical grind of pro hockey. While studying with his brother at the Manitoba Agricultural College in Winnipeg, Eddie took exception to his sibling's charge that he'd never be a good player. A determined Shore played briefly with the college team, but he gained more valuable experience in 1923–24 with the Melville Millionaires, a well-known amateur team.

Shore's abrasive style soon earned him a job in the pro ranks with the Western Canada Hockey League's Regina Caps in 1924–25 and the Edmonton Eskimos the next season. He skated as a forward with Regina but shifted back to his natural defense position with the Eskimos. By 1926, his dynamic rushes had earned him the nickname "the Edmonton Express."

When the western league folded at the conclusion of 1925–26, Boston Bruins owner Charles Adams stocked his newly formed NHL team with seven WCHL/WHL players and Shore was one of them. Old Blood and Guts was an instant star in Boston, and his fearless style of play and passion for the game helped ensure the success of big-league hockey in Beantown. During his first NHL season, Shore established a new record with 130 penalty minutes while also scoring 12 goals. His goal total exceeded that of all but three Boston forwards and it became apparent that he was capable of fully controlling a game when he was on the ice.

During the 1928–29 season, Shore led the Bruins to first place in the American Division. They went through the playoffs without losing a game and won the first Stanley Cup in team history. Shore was at his hard-hitting and playmaking best as Boston eliminated the Montreal Canadiens in the semifinals prior to a two-game sweep of the New York Rangers.

Following the 1930–31 season, Shore finished second in the voting for the Hart Trophy and was placed on the NHL First All-Star Team. He won the Hart Trophy in 1933, 1935, 1936 and 1938, becoming the only defenseman ever to be so honored four times. Over the next several years, Shore was selected to the NHL First All-Star Team six more times and the Second Team once. He originally formed an outstanding defensive tandem with Lionel Hitchman but eventually teamed with the likes of Dit Clapper and Flash Hollett. Shore recorded 105 goals and 284 points in 14 seasons.

In December 1933 Shore was involved in an unfortunate on-ice collision that ended the career of Toronto forward Ace Bailey. As a result of the tragedy, the first large-scale benefit game in NHL history was held at Maple Leaf Gardens on February 14, 1934. One of the

Shore, Eddie
D, 5'11", 190 lbs, b: Fort Qu'Appelle, Sask., 11/25/1902, d: 3/16/1985

Season	Club, League	Regular Season					Playoffs				
		GP	G	A	Pts	PIM	GP	G	A	Pts	PIM
1923–24	Melville Millionaires, SSHL						11	10	8	18	0
1924–25	Regina Caps, WCHL	24	6	0	6	75					
1925–26	Edmonton Eskimos, WHL	30	12	2	14	86	2	0	0	0	8
1926–27	Boston Bruins, NHL	40	12	6	18	130	8	1	1	2	40
1927–28	Boston Bruins, NHL	43	11	6	17	165	2	0	0	0	8
1928–29	Boston Bruins, NHL	39	12	7	19	96	5	1	1	2	28
1929–30	Boston Bruins, NHL	42	12	19	31	105	6	1	0	1	26
1930–31	Boston Bruins, NHL	44	15	16	31	105	5	2	1	3	24
1931–32	Boston Bruins, NHL	45	9	13	22	80					
1932–33	Boston Bruins, NHL	48	8	27	35	102	5	0	1	1	14
1933–34	Boston Bruins, NHL	30	2	10	12	57					
1934–35	Boston Bruins, NHL	48	7	26	33	32	4	0	1	1	2
1935–36	Boston Bruins, NHL	45	3	16	19	61	2	1	1	2	12
1936–37	Boston Bruins, NHL	20	3	1	4	12					
1937–38	Boston Bruins, NHL	48	3	14	17	42	3	0	1	1	6
1938–39	Boston Bruins, NHL	44	4	14	18	47	12	0	4	4	19
1939–40	Boston Bruins, NHL	4	2	1	3	4					
	New York Americans, NHL	10	2	3	5	9	3	0	2	2	2
	Springfield Indians, AHL	15	1	14	15	18	2	0	1	1	0
1940–41	Springfield Indians, AHL	56	4	13	17	66	3	0	0	0	2
1941–42	Springfield Indians, AHL	35	5	12	17	61	5	0	3	3	6
1943–44	Buffalo Bisons, AHL	1	0	0	0	0					
	NHL Totals	550	105	179	284	1047	55	6	13	19	181

NHL First All-Star Team (1931, 1932, 1933, 1935, 1936, 1938, 1939)
NHL Second All-Star Team (1934)
Won Hart Trophy (1933, 1935, 1936, 1938)
Won Lester Patrick Trophy (1970)
Won Stanley Cup (1929, 1939)

most unforgettable scenes in hockey history occurred prior to the opening face-off when Shore and Bailey shook hands.

In 1939, 10 years after leading the Bruins to their first Stanley Cup, Shore contributed to their second. Shore's leadership and endurance were pivotal factors behind Boston's success in a hard-fought, seven-game struggle against the New York Rangers and Toronto Maple Leafs.

Early in the 1939–40 season, Shore sensed that his NHL days were numbered. He seized the opportunity to purchase the Springfield Indians of the American Hockey League, where he became player-owner. A few weeks into the season, the Bruins were floundering and Boston manager Art Ross approached Shore about a possible comeback. A short-term arrangement was made whereby Shore would play strictly in home games.

In his first NHL season, Eddie Shore (left) scored 12 goals and set a record with 130 minutes in penalties.

Before the season was out, Ross traded the burly rearguard to the New York Americans for Eddie Wiseman and cash. Shore's strong play contributed to the Americans' reaching the post-season, where they lost a tough quarterfinals to the Detroit Red Wings. At one point in March, Shore appeared in six playoff encounters in as many nights—three with New York and three with Springfield.

Shore retired from the NHL at the conclusion of that topsy-turvy year to devote his full attention to his minor-league investment. When the U.S. Army took over the Springfield Coliseum during World War II, Shore moved to Buffalo and coached the Bisons to two AHL Calder Cup championships. The Indians franchise was reactivated in 1946–47 and Shore remained part of the team until he sold it in 1976. As an AHL owner and coach, Shore gained a reputation as a demanding yet innovative teacher of the game. Many players were upset by his extreme methods, but others would claim they learned valuable hockey lessons they wouldn't have received anywhere else.

One of the many honors conferred upon Shore came his way when the Bruins retired his sweater in front of a cheering Boston Garden crowd. The AHL created the Eddie Shore Plaque, which is presented annually to the league's outstanding defenseman. Shore was inducted into the Hockey Hall of Fame in 1945, and he's also a member of the IIHF Hockey Hall of Fame.

Charles "Chuck" Gardiner

Chuck Gardiner was one of the game's preeminent goaltenders during the 1920s and 1930s. He attained NHL stardom with the Chicago Black Hawks, where he guarded the cage from 1927 to 1934. Prior to his untimely death in June 1934, Gardiner led the Black Hawks to their first Stanley Cup and recorded 42 shutouts and a goals-against average of 2.02 over only seven years of NHL service.

Gardiner was one of the few European-born players to make it to the NHL during his era. The native of Edinburgh, Scotland, emigrated to Canada with his family when he was seven years old. They made their new home in Winnipeg, Manitoba, one the country's major hotbeds of hockey.

When he first tried to learn the game, Gardiner struggled with his skating and never felt completely at ease until he took a turn as netminder. He continued to play goal with his school team before joining the Assiniboines and Tigers clubs in the Winnipeg amateur hockey system.

Charlie Gardiner was born in Scotland and became one of the few non-North American players to make it to the NHL during the early years of the league.

Gardiner cracked the lineup of the Selkirk Fishermen senior hockey club in the fall of 1924. His play was inspirational and he recorded two shutouts to go with a sparkling 1.83 goals-against mark. Gardiner moved up to the Winnipeg Maroons the next year and became a workhorse, appearing in 74 regular-season games and eight playoff matches over two years. Once again he'd met the challenge successfully, posting six shutouts each year and goals-against averages of 2.16 and 2.14. Most significantly, he demonstrated that he was a bona fide NHL prospect who didn't wilt over the course of a long season.

The Chicago Black Hawks had kept a close eye on Gardiner's development and decided to give him a chance to play in the big league during their sophomore NHL season in 1927–28. On joining the Hawks, he was initially slotted to be the understudy to incumbent Hugh Lehman, but Gardiner quickly won the confidence of coach Barney Stanley and played the bulk of the games. A major influence on Gardiner at this time was former scoring star Duke Keats, who helped him learn to outguess opposing forwards. As a result, he became one of the toughest netminders to face one-on-one.

Lehman ended up retiring and taking over the coaching duties when Stanley retired in mid-season. Gardiner's rookie term was a personal success as he registered three shutouts and a respectable 2.83 goals-against average on a team that was overwhelmed most evenings. He transcended the Black Hawks' woeful showing in 1928–29 by establishing himself as one of the NHL's outstanding netminders with five shutouts and a solid 1.85 goals-against record.

Gardiner's hands and feet were lightning quick, as was his mind. Rarely was he caught unaware on the ice by an opposing shooter. He was also a fierce competitor who periodically left his net to thwart an attack or dove into a pile of players to seize the puck.

Beginning in 1929–30, Gardiner would play a key role in Chicago's vast improvement. In 1930–31, he recorded a league-high 12 shutouts and a stellar goals-against mark of 1.73. He also earned his first of three selections to the NHL First All-Star Team. The following year his netminding heroics brought him the Vezina Trophy. Gardiner's exceptional play was augmented by his ability to direct his teammates on the ice, a factor that led to his being chosen to serve as team captain in 1933–34.

That 1933–34 season was both triumphant and tragic for Chuck Gardiner. During the regular season, he led the NHL with 10 shutouts en route to his second Vezina Trophy. In the playoffs, his goalkeeping was the backbone of Chicago's first-ever Stanley Cup championship, over the Red Wings. For the third time in his career, Gardiner topped all playoff goalies in shutouts. Tommy Gorman observed, "Never before in the history of hockey had a better

Gardiner, Charles "Chuck"
G, 176 lbs, b: Edinburgh, Scotland, 12/31/1904, d: 6/13/1934

Season	Club, League	Regular Season				Playoffs			
		GP	Mins	GA	Avg	GP	Mins	GA	Avg
1924–25	Selkirk Fishermen, Wpg-Sr.	18	1080	33	1.83	2	120	6	3.00
1925–26	Winnipeg Maroons, USAHA	38	2280	82	2.16	5	300	10	2.00
1926–27	Winnipeg Maroons, AHA	36	2203	77	2.14	3	180	8	2.67
1927–28	Chicago Black Hawks, NHL	40	2420	114	2.83				
1928–29	Chicago Black Hawks, NHL	44	2758	85	1.85				
1929–30	Chicago Black Hawks, NHL	44	2750	111	2.42	2	172	3	1.05
1930–31	Chicago Black Hawks, NHL	44	2710	78	1.73	9	638	14	1.32
1931–32	Chicago Black Hawks, NHL	48	2989	92	1.85	2	120	6	3.00
1932–33	Chicago Black Hawks, NHL	48	3010	101	2.01				
1933–34	Chicago Black Hawks, NHL	48	3050	83	1.63	8	542	12	1.33
	NHL Totals	316	19687	664	2.02	21	1472	35	1.43

NHL First All-Star Team (1931, 1932, 1934)
NHL Second All-Star Team (1933)
Won Vezina Trophy (1932, 1934)
Won Stanley Cup (1934)

exhibition of goalkeeping been given than that which Gardiner put up against Detroit in that championship final." A gifted and durable performer, Gardiner led all NHL goalkeepers by playing every minute in six consecutive seasons from 1928–29 to 1933–34.

Unfortunately, Gardiner passed away on June 13, 1934, as a result of a brain hemorrhage. His death, just a few weeks after winning the Stanley Cup, was one of the most poignant stories of the NHL's early days. The Wee Scot was considered by his peers to be among the elite netminders of his time. Many in fact referred to him as the finest ever at his craft. A member of the Canadian Sports Hall of Fame, Gardiner was inducted into the Hockey Hall of Fame as a charter member in 1945.

Ralph "Cooney" Weiland

One of the slickest players of his era, center Cooney Weiland tormented opposing defenses with his trickery. A magician with the puck, he helped the Boston Bruins win the Stanley Cup in 1929 as a member of the famous Dynamite Line with Dit Clapper and Dutch Gainor. And his offensive totals might have been even greater than they were had Weiland not also been such an adept penalty killer.

Weiland grew up near Seaforth, Ontario, where he was proficient in a number of sports including running, swimming, soccer, baseball and hockey. As an amateur he starred with the Owen Sound Greys when they captured the Memorial Cup in 1924. In time he moved on to the Minneapolis Rockets of the USAHA and stayed in the Minnesota city to turn pro with the Millers the following season. In 1927–28, he led the AHA with 21 goals in 40 games.

Cooney Weiland registered 43 goals in 44 games as the Bruins dominated the NHL in 1929–30.

While learning the ropes as an NHL rookie with the Bruins in 1928–29, Weiland scored a respectable 11 goals in the regular season and contributed to the first Stanley Cup win in franchise history. The next year the league relaxed its forward-passing rules, and the changes were tailor-made for the Dynamite trio. Weiland registered an astounding 43 goals in 44 games, while linemate Dit Clapper scored 41 more. Not only did Weiland lead the league in goal-scoring, he also won the points title with 73, shattering Howie Morenz's single-season record of 51 points.

The Bruins dominated the NHL with a record of 38–5–1, including a streak of 14 consecutive regular-season victories that wasn't bettered until the New York Islanders strung together 15 wins in 1982. But their bid to repeat as Cup champs was blocked by the surprising Montreal Canadiens, who swept the best-of-three finals. During this time, many of Weiland's off-ice duties went unpublicized. He was, for instance, Art Ross's traveling secretary on road trips.

The Dynamite Line was broken up in 1932 when Weiland was traded to the Ottawa Senators because of conflicts with Ross. He led Ottawa in scoring, but the once proud franchise was decimated by the Great Depression and owner Frank Ahearn was forced to sell Weiland to the Detroit Red Wings. There he worked with talented wingers Larry Aurie and Herbie Lewis and put up the best numbers of his career since his glory days in Boston.

Their differences apparently resolved, Ross reacquired Weiland in June 1935. He played his last four NHL seasons with the Bruins and was often teamed with Dit Clapper and Charlie Sands. After the Kraut Line rose to prominence in Beantown, Weiland became a utility forward who often played with Ray Getliffe and Mel Hill.

Weiland retired in 1939 after contributing to a second Stanley Cup championship and immediately took over the team's coaching reins. He guided the club to another Cup in 1941 before heading to the AHL, where he coached the Hershey Bears for four seasons and put in a year behind the bench of the New Haven Ramblers.

Weiland, Ralph "Cooney"
C, 5′7″, 150 lbs, b: Seaforth (Edmondville), Ont., 11/5/1904, d: 7/3/1985

Season	Club, League	Regular Season					Playoffs				
		GP	G	A	Pts	PIM	GP	G	A	Pts	PIM
1924–25	Minneapolis Rockets, USAHA	35	8	0	8	*					
1925–26	Minneapolis Millers, CHL	26	10	4	14	20	3	1	1	2	0
1926–27	Minneapolis Millers, AHA	36	21	2	23	30	6	4	1	5	0
1927–28	Minneapolis Millers, AHA	40	21	5	26	34	8	2	2	4	0
1928–29	Boston Bruins, NHL	42	11	7	18	16	5	2	0	2	2
1929–30	Boston Bruins, NHL	44	43	30	73	27	6	1	5	6	2
1930–31	Boston Bruins, NHL	44	25	13	38	14	5	6	3	9	2
1931–32	Boston Bruins, NHL	46	14	12	26	20					
1932–33	Ottawa Senators, NHL	48	16	11	27	4					
1933–34	Ottawa Senators, NHL	9	2	0	2	4					
	Detroit Red Wings, NHL	39	11	19	30	6	9	2	2	4	4
1934–35	Detroit Red Wings, NHL	48	13	25	38	10					
1935–36	Boston Bruins, NHL	48	14	13	27	15	2	1	0	1	2
1936–37	Boston Bruins, NHL	48	6	9	15	6	3	0	0	0	0
1937–38	Boston Bruins, NHL	48	11	12	23	16	3	0	0	0	0
1938–39	Boston Bruins, NHL	45	7	9	16	9	12	0	0	0	0
	NHL Totals	509	173	160	333	147	45	12	10	22	12

NHL Second All-Star Team (1935)
Won Lester Patrick Trophy (1972)
NHL Scoring Leader (1930)
Won Stanley Cup (1929, 1939)

Weiland took over as head coach of Harvard's varsity team in 1950 and stayed there for mor than two decades. He was the eighth coach in the team's history, but only the first non-Harvard man. He became Harvard's winningest coach with 315 victories to his credit as well as eight Ivy League crowns, two East Coast Athletic Conference championships and five appearances in the NCAA final four. In 1955 and 1971 he won the Spencer T. Penrose Memorial Trophy as coach of the year as selected by the American Hockey Coaches Association. His teaching style was aptly described by J. Concannon of the *Boston Globe*: "Cooney Weiland stands at one end of the Harvard hockey team bench in Watson Rink, watching in studied silence the game that has been his life."

Weiland was inducted into the Hockey Hall of Fame in 1971 and his contribution to hockey in the United States was recognized the following year when he was awarded the Lester Patrick Trophy. Harvard established a scholarship fund in his name, to be awarded to outstanding candidates in need of financial assistance.

Cecil "Tiny" Thompson

Star netminder Cecil "Tiny" Thompson stood a substantial 5′10″; his nickname referred to his minuscule goals-against average. The brother of New York Rangers and Chicago Black Hawks forward Paul Thompson, Tiny spent most of his career with the Boston Bruins. His spectacular play was exceeded only by his endurance. During his 12-year NHL career, Thompson led all goalies in games played nine times, while his four Vezina Trophy wins stood as the NHL standard until 1949, when Montreal's Bill Durnan won his fifth.

After gaining experience with the Calgary Monarchs, Pacific Grain Seniors and Bellevue Bulldogs of the Alberta Senior Hockey League, Thompson left the nest to further his development. He spent a year with the Duluth Hornets of the United States Amateur Hockey Association before moving on to the Minneapolis Millers. It was in Duluth that Thompson purchased the leg pads he used throughout his pro career. In 1927–28, in the renamed American Hockey Association, he recorded a league-leading 28 wins in 40 matches for the Minnesota squad. The next year, joined by Minneapolis teammate Ralph "Cooney" Weiland, he embarked on a stellar NHL career with the Bruins.

Few players have made a bigger impact in their rookie season. After Boston coach Cy Denneny opted to start him in the season opener ahead of incumbent Hal Winkler, Thompson's glorious career was launched. He posted a stingy 1.15 goals-against mark and led Boston to 26 wins while appearing in all 44 games. In the playoffs, he helped the Bruins win the first Stanley Cup in franchise history. In the finals against the Rangers, he faced his brother Paul in the only sibling confrontation in the playoffs until the Esposito brothers some 40 years later.

Tiny Thompson gave up his passion for reading on the grounds that "After all, the only thing a goaltender has is his eyes."

During his sophomore season, Thompson was forced to adjust to a more wide-open style of play as the NHL revised its forward-passing rules. His goals-against average grew to 2.19, but it stood as the league's best—the first of four times Tiny would lead this category. Thompson also decided at this time to give up his passion for reading in his spare time. His reasoning: "After all, the only thing a goaltender has is his eyes."

The 1929–30 version of the Beantowners dominated the regular-season standings, and Thompson's 38–5–1 record was one of the most impressive in league history, but Boston was stunned by the Montreal Canadiens in the finals. With Thompson guarding the cage, Boston finished atop the NHL's American Division six times, but he'd never again lead them to a Cup victory.

In 1930–31, the nervous netminder's anxiety got the better of him for a short stretch of the season and Percy Jackson had to be pressed into action. Fortunately Thompson's health improved and in 1931–32 he led the NHL with a career-high 11 shutouts.

On April 3, 1933, Thompson made history as the losing goaltender in the longest playoff game to that date, a match that was dubbed "the Ken Doraty Derby." In the fifth and deciding game of the Bruins' semifinal series with Toronto, both teams were held scoreless throughout regulation time as Tiny and his opposite number, Lorne Chabot, played superbly. The deadlock held through 104 minutes and 46 seconds of overtime before the Leafs' Doraty beat an exhausted Thompson.

During the 1935–36 season, Thompson

Thompson, Cecil "Tiny"
G, 5'10", 160 lbs, b: Sandon, Alta., 5/31/1905, d: 2/11/1981

Season	Club, League	Regular Season				Playoffs			
		GP	Mins	GA	Avg	GP	Mins	GA	Avg
1924–25	Duluth Hornets, USAHA	40	1920	59	1.38				
1925–26	Minneapolis Millers, USAHA	36	2160	59	1.64	3	180	1	0.33
1926–27	Minneapolis Millers, AHA	38	2253	51	1.42	6	361	8	1.33
1927–28	Minneapolis Millers, AHA	40	2475	51	1.23	8	520	3	0.38
1928–29	Boston Bruins, NHL	44	2710	52	1.15	5	300	3	0.60
1929–30	Boston Bruins, NHL	44	2680	98	2.19	6	432	12	1.67
1930–31	Boston Bruins, NHL	44	2730	90	1.98	5	343	13	2.27
1931–32	Boston Bruins, NHL	43	2698	103	2.29				
1932–33	Boston Bruins, NHL	48	3000	88	1.76	5	438	9	1.23
1933–34	Boston Bruins, NHL	48	2980	130	2.62				
1934–35	Boston Bruins, NHL	48	2970	112	2.26	4	273	7	1.54
1935–36	Boston Bruins, NHL	48	2930	82	1.68	2	120	8	4.00
1936–37	Boston Bruins, NHL	48	2970	110	2.22	3	180	8	2.67
1937–38	Boston Bruins, NHL	48	2970	89	1.80	3	212	6	1.70
1938–39	Boston Bruins, NHL	5	310	8	1.55				
	Detroit Red Wings, NHL	39	2397	101	2.53	6	374	15	2.41
1939–40	Detroit Red Wings, NHL	46	2830	120	2.54	5	300	12	2.40
1940–41	Buffalo Bisons, AHL	1	40	1	1.50				
1942–43	Calgary RCAF Mustangs, ASHL	*	*	*	*	4	*	11	3.00
	NHL Totals	553	34175	1183	2.08	44	2972	93	1.88

NHL First All-Star Team (1936, 1938)
NHL Second All-Star Team (1931, 1935)
Won Vezina Trophy (1930, 1933, 1936, 1938)
Won Stanley Cup (1929)

entered the record book when he fed a pass to defenseman Babe Siebert, who went on to score. Thompson became the first goalie ever to earn an assist in the NHL. In 1938 he and brother Paul, then in Chicago, were both named to the First All-Star Team—only the second such brother act after Lionel and Charlie Conacher.

Thompson sat out two games at the start of the 1938–39 season because his eyes were bothering him. A young American by the name of Frank Brimsek stepped in and played so well that Bruins chief Art Ross decided he represented the club's goalkeeping future. On November 16, 1938, a Bruins era ended when Thompson was traded to Detroit for fellow netminder Norman Smith and $15,000. Thompson played 39 games that year for the Red Wings and a full season the next. After trying in vain to help Detroit upset the Toronto Maple Leafs in the 1940 semifinals, Thompson left the NHL. He later played one game with the Buffalo Bisons of the American league in 1940–41 and a handful of contests for the Calgary RCAF Mustangs during World War II. He was inducted into the Hockey Hall of Fame in 1959.

Soon after retiring, Thompson took the job of chief scout for the Chicago Black Hawks. He eventually shifted to scouting western Canada for the Hawks so he could be closer to his Calgary home. He was the scout who brought Cliff Koroll and Keith Magnuson, among others, to the Windy City. As the years passed, he observed many changes in the attitude of young players compared with those in his playing days. He was often heard to say: "I just don't understand that young man. All he's to do is work an hour a day at practice, two and a half hours during games and he could live the greatest life in the world."

Marvin "Cy" Wentworth

Cy Wentworth was named Chicago's captain while still in his early 20s.

Cy Wentworth was known as a steady-going defender and a consistent, solid and clean checker who took care of business in his own end before worrying about taking the play toward the opposing goal. Later in his career, which lasted for a 13 full seasons, he grew confident enough in his ability to command the defensive zone to allow himself the odd rush carrying the puck. In time he became an effective two-way threat and one season he even led the league in playoff scoring. He was the nucleus of the Montreal Maroons team in the 1930s and led the squad to a Stanley Cup after failing to bring the trophy home in his first visit to the finals with the other team he's often identified with, the Chicago Black Hawks.

Wentworth was born in 1905 in Grimsby, Ontario. He played his junior hockey in the Windsor area and worked his way up to the Windsor Hornets in the Ontario Hockey Association as a 20-year-old. He played for half a season before he was sold to the Chicago Cardinals of the American Hockey Association. The Black Hawks saw enough of him in 34 games with the Cardinals to know he was a solid professional. He played his first NHL game in 1927 and was an instant leader. He took a penalty only if it seemed a goal was about to be scored and combined his gentlemanly ways with a quick wit and a flair for the practical joke.

At the end of the 1928–29 season, the Black Hawks made a deal to bring the tough Clarence "Taffy" Abel to the team. Abel was 6′1″ and 225 pounds, and his partnership with the smaller but quicker Wentworth—who was three inches shorter and over 50 pounds lighter—was the most formidable in the league. Abel would use his size and strength to clear the front of the net, while Wentworth's skill and positional play let him steal the puck from opposing forwards along the boards.

While Abel and Wentworth solidified the Chicago defense, team scoring improved by leaps and bounds, from a pitiful 33 goals in 1928–29 to 117 the next season. The Hawks leapt to second place in the American Division, a ranking they would hold in five of six seasons between 1929–30 and 1934–35. In 1930–31, Wentworth played all 44 games and served only 12 minutes in penalties even though he saw more ice time than any other Hawk except the goaltender. That year Chicago made the Stanley Cup finals for the first time, eliminating the Toronto Maple Leafs and New York Rangers before losing to the Montreal Canadiens. Game two of the finals, played at Chicago Stadium, drew a crowd of 18,000, one of the largest in NHL history.

In 1931–32, Wentworth, who had become the picture of defensive efficiency, was named the team's captain. The move paid dividends for Chicago coach Dick Irvin; in Wentworth he'd a player with such poise that it was as if an assistant coach was patrolling the blue line. Near the beginning of the 1932–33 season, the rearguard was traded to the Montreal Maroons, again for cash. In Montreal, Wentworth became the leader of a fine defense corps that included Lionel Conacher and Baldy Northcott and he won his first and only Stanley Cup when his Maroons defeated Toronto in the 1935 finals after eliminating his old teammates from Chicago. Wentworth was Montreal's leading point-getter in those playoffs with three goals and two assists in seven games.

Wentworth, Marvin "Cy"											
D, 5'10", 170 lbs, b: Grimsby, Ont., 1/24/1905, d: 10/14/1982											
Season	Club, League		Regular Season					Playoffs			
		GP	G	A	Pts	PIM	GP	G	A	Pts	PIM
1925–26	Windsor Hornets, OHA Sr.	20	6	5	11	9					
1926–27	Chicago Cardinals, AHA	34	8	4	12	40					
1927–28	Chicago Black Hawks, NHL	43	5	5	10	31					
1928–29	Chicago Black Hawks, NHL	44	2	1	3	44					
1929–30	Chicago Black Hawks, NHL	37	3	4	7	28					
1930–31	Chicago Black Hawks, NHL	44	4	4	8	12	9	1	1	2	14
1931–32	Chicago Black Hawks, NHL	48	3	10	13	30	2	0	0	0	0
1932–33	Montreal Maroons, NHL	47	4	10	14	48	2	0	1	1	0
1933–34	Montreal Maroons, NHL	48	2	5	7	31	4	0	2	2	2
1934–35	Montreal Maroons, NHL	48	4	9	13	28	7	3	2	5	0
1935–36	Montreal Maroons, NHL	48	4	5	9	24	3	0	0	0	0
1936–37	Montreal Maroons, NIIL	43	3	4	7	29	5	1	0	1	0
1937–38	Montreal Maroons, NHL	48	4	5	9	32					
1938–39	Montreal Canadiens, NHL	45	0	3	3	12	3	0	0	0	4
1939–40	Montreal Canadiens, NHL	32	1	3	4	6					
	NHL Totals	575	39	68	107	355	35	5	6	11	20

NHL Second All-Star Team (1935)
Won Stanley Cup (1935)

The Maroons finished first in the Canadian Division the following year and their semifinal opponents were the American Division-leading Detroit Red Wings. Game one of that series lives on in the history books as the longest NHL game ever played. Wentworth and his defensive colleagues repelled all Red Wing attacks, but the going was just as tight in the Detroit end and the game was scoreless at the end of regulation time. The overtime periods mounted, one after another, until Detroit's Mud Bruneteau finally broke the deadlock after 116 minutes and 30 seconds of extra play. Later in his career, Wentworth's pride would cause him to dispute claims that he was on the ice when the winning goal was finally scored.

Wentworth was traded, again for cash, just before the Maroons folded in 1938. He didn't have to move far to continue his career, however, as he was traded to the Montreal Canadiens. He played two seasons with the Habs before retiring in 1940, after which he moved to Toronto and became involved in a variety of business interests.

On October 14, 1982, Cy Wentworth passed away at Toronto Western Hospital. He was 77.

Marty **Barry**

Between 1929 and 1939, Marty Barry missed only two NHL regular-season games.

Wherever he played, Marty Barry was a productive center whose work ethic was lauded by teammates and opponents alike. His stamina and dedication made him one of the most consistent and durable performers of his era. Between 1929 and 1939, he missed only two NHL regular-season games. Bob Murphy of the *Detroit News* commented: "As in hockey, so it's in life with Marty Barry. He moves along the even tenor of his way. He looks for the good in people and strives quickly to forget the bad. Truly, here is a man in this warring cycle of sports who seems definitely at peace with the world."

Although he was born in Shannon, just north of Quebec City, Barry grew up and learned to play hockey in Montreal. He played in the Mount Royal intermediate league with the Gurney Foundry team in 1922–23, with St. Michael's the following year and then with St. Anthony for two seasons after that. A proficient scorer, he was known by the local sportswriters as "Goal-a-Game" Barry.

After a strong season with the Montreal Bell Telephone team, he was signed by New York Americans manager Newsy Lalonde in 1927, but he played only nine games with the Amerks before they sent him down to the Philadelphia Arrows of the Can-Am league for conditioning. The next season, with the New Haven Eagles, he led that league with 19 goals and 29 points.

Barry got a major break when the Boston Bruins claimed him from the Americans in the Intra-League Draft in May 1929. He joined a powerhouse team that was entering the 1929–30 season as the defending Stanley Cup champions. That year the Dynamite Line of Cooney Weiland, Dutch Gainor and Dit Clapper, along with defensemen Eddie Shore and Lionel Hitchman, led the Bruins to a remarkable 38–5–1 record. Barry was one of the team's best players with three goals in a semifinal victory over the Montreal Maroons. The team seemed certain to repeat as title-holders, but the Montreal Canadiens mounted a stunning upset in the finals.

Barry gradually assumed a more prominent role with the Bruins, racking up five consecutive 20-goal seasons from 1930 to 1935. Barry made his first appearance among the NHL's top 10 scorers in 1933–34, when his 27 goals were second only to Toronto star Charlie Conacher's total of 32.

On June 30, 1935, Barry was involved in a blockbuster trade that sent him to Detroit while ex-Bruin Cooney Weiland came back to Boston. With the Red Wings, Barry formed one of the NHL's top forward units with Herbie Lewis and Larry Aurie. According to long-time Detroit coach Jack Adams, "Marty

Barry, Marty
C, 5′11″, 175 lbs, b: Quebec City, Que., 12/8/1905, d: 8/20/1969

Season	Club, League	Regular Season					Playoffs				
		GP	G	A	Pts	PIM	GP	G	A	Pts	PIM
1925–26	Montreal St. Anthony, City Sr.	*	*	*	*	*	*	*	*	*	*
1926–27	Montreal St. Anthony, City Sr.	*	*	*	*	*	*	*	*	*	*
1927–28	New York Americans, NHL	9	1	0	1	2					
	Philadelphia Arrows, Can-Am	33	11	3	14	70					
1928–29	New Haven Eagles, Can-Am	35	19	10	29	54	2	0	1	1	2
1929–30	Boston Bruins, NHL	44	18	15	33	34	6	3	3	6	14
1930–31	Boston Bruins, NHL	44	20	11	31	26	5	1	1	2	4
1931–32	Boston Bruins, NHL	48	21	17	38	22					
1932–33	Boston Bruins, NHL	47	24	13	37	40	5	2	2	4	6
1933–34	Boston Bruins, NHL	48	27	12	39	12					
1934–35	Boston Bruins, NHL	48	20	20	40	33	4	0	0	0	2
1935–36	Detroit Red Wings, NHL	48	21	19	40	16	7	2	4	6	6
1936–37	Detroit Red Wings, NHL	47	17	27	44	6	10	4	7	11	2
1937–38	Detroit Red Wings, NHL	48	9	20	29	34					
1938–39	Detroit Red Wings, NHL	48	13	28	41	4	6	3	1	4	0
1939–40	Montreal Canadiens, NHL	30	4	10	14	2					
	Pittsburgh Hornets, AHL	6	2	0	2	0	7	2	1	3	4
1940–41	Minneapolis Millers, AHA	32	10	10	20	8	3	1	0	1	0
	NHL Totals	509	195	192	387	231	43	15	18	33	34

NHL First All-Star Team (1937)
Won Lady Byng Trophy (1937)
Won Stanley Cup (1936, 1937)

Barry was an artist with the puck and his dexterity and determination made a forward line that ranks with the all-time great units in National Hockey League history." His 40-point total in the 48-game schedule in 1935–36 placed him second in the league scoring race to Sweeney Schriner. The following season he recorded a career-high 44 points, was selected to the NHL First All-Star Team and was the first Red Wing to win the Lady Byng Trophy for gentlemanly conduct.

Barry's play was crucial to the Detroit franchise's enormous success during this period. The team finished at the top of the NHL regular-season standings and won the Stanley Cup in both 1936 and 1937, making the Wings the first U.S.-based team to capture back-to-back championships.

In November 1939 Barry signed with the Montreal Canadiens, for whom he played his last NHL season. He left the league with the reputation of being a consistent offensive producer as well an "iron man" who almost never missed a game. In 1940–41, he performed for the Minneapolis Millers of the AHA, then retired as a player.

In the 1940s, Barry embarked on a rewarding coaching career with the Halifax St. Mary's juniors. Under his tutelage the team reached the eastern Canada finals, one step short of the Memorial Cup, in 1947. Barry entered the business world after leaving hockey, and he eventually ran a grocery business in Dartmouth, Nova Scotia. He gained a place in the Red Wings Hall of Fame in 1944 and the Hockey Hall of Fame in 1965. Barry died of a heart attack in Halifax, Nova Scotia, at the age of 64.

Joe "Gentleman Joe" Primeau

Primeau played all nine of his NHL seasons with the Toronto Maple Leafs and his clean but still hard-nosed play earned him the nickname "Gentleman Joe." Although he was born in Lindsay, Ontario, and raised in Victoria, British Columbia, he moved to Toronto at an early age, where he played with St. Michael's College in a four-team prep school league that included Upper Canada College, University of Toronto Schools and St. Andrew's.

In 1924 he moved on to the Toronto St. Mary's team and his play impressed Frank Selke—who was running the Toronto Ravinas of the Can-Pro league—who arranged for him to play with the senior Marlboros in 1926–27. From there he was assigned to play for the Ravinas and his exploits—a league-leading 26 goals in 41 games—earned him a two-game tryout with the Maple Leafs. Primeau spent most of 1928–29 with the Can-Pro league's London Panthers, but he was recalled by the Leafs for the last six games of the season.

Joe Primeau was a key figure in the Kid Line.

During the 1929–30 season, Primeau's pro career finally took flight when Leafs coach Conn Smythe put the 23-year-old center on a line with a pair of 18-year-old rookies, Charlie Conacher and Harvey "Busher" Jackson. The Kid Line was born.

The three young players—all superstars, Stanley Cup winners and Hall of Famers in the making—complemented each other's style perfectly. "Conacher was a student of the game," Primeau said. "He studied the game so thoroughly he could recall every play from start to finish.

All through his playing days, Joe Primeau was also involved in a business originally called Joe Primeau Block, which soon expanded to include five plants across the country.

And, boy, could he shoot…. Jackson did everything with speed and grace." And in the middle was Primeau, the setup man who led the league in assists in three of the six years the line was together. "I never knew Joe to make a bad pass," King Clancy once said of his teammate. "You know that players like to take passes in different ways. Conacher used to stand up pretty straight and had to take a pass close in to his body, and Jackson liked his farther out. I always used a very flat stick and liked a pass way ahead of me. All Joe would have to do was take a short peek and zingo! There was the puck right on the end of your stick."

A testament to Primeau's playmaking ability was the fact that Jackson won a scoring title while Conacher twice led the league. But as Primeau revealed, it was chemistry as much as talent that made the line work. "Timing is of the essence," he said of their game. "You can have a simple play, but when you time the pass right and your teammates time their speed right, the result is usually a goal."

In 1931 the Leafs moved into a new rink, leaving the Mutual Street Arena for the palatial Maple Leaf Gardens. That first season, the team won the Stanley Cup, led by the incomparable Kid Line.

Throughout his playing days, Primeau was also involved in business, and his early retirement from the game in 1936, when he was just 30 years old, was directly attributable to Conn Smythe. "I turned professional in 1927," Primeau related, "and Conn Smythe sent me down to work for Larkin Malone in the construction supply business. I met up with an old Dutchman who had been making concrete blocks in his backyard. He and I formed a company, and by 1936 I was so involved in this block business that I felt I must quit hockey." The business was first called Joe Primeau Block but soon amalgamated to form Primeau-Argo Block and expanded to include five plants across the country.

Once he'd established the business, his interest in returning to the rink grew and grew. During his playing days, in 1932, Primeau had coached the West Toronto Juniors, and he continued to work behind the bench for local teams right through the war—most notably a six-year stint with the Upper Canada College team. In 1944–45, he returned to St. Mike's as coach and won the coveted Memorial Cup in his first season. He then coached the RCAF team stationed in Toronto, and after he was discharged he hooked up with the Marlboro seniors, whom he led to the Allan Cup championship in 1949. In 1950–51, he became coach of the Maple Leafs and won a Stanley Cup in his first year. Thus he became—and remains—the only man to coach teams to the Allan, Memorial and Stanley cups.

Primeau, Joe "Gentleman Joe"
C, 5´11˝, 153 lbs, b: Lindsay, Ont., 1/29/1906, d: 5/14/1989

Season	Club, League	Regular Season					Playoffs				
		GP	G	A	Pts	PIM	GP	G	A	Pts	PIM
1926–27	Toronto Marlboros, OHA Sr.	10	11	3	14	4					
1927–28	Toronto Maple Leafs, NHL	2	0	0	0	0					
	Toronto Ravinas, Can-Pro	41	26	13	39	36	2	1	0	1	0
1928–29	Toronto Maple Leafs, NHL	6	0	1	1	2					
	London Panthers, Can-Pro	35	12	10	22	16					
1929–30	Toronto Maple Leafs, NHL	43	5	21	26	22					
1930–31	Toronto Maple Leafs, NHL	38	9	32	41	18	2	0	0	0	0
1931–32	Toronto Maple Leafs, NHL	46	13	37	50	25	7	0	6	6	2
1932–33	Toronto Maple Leafs, NHL	48	11	21	32	4	8	0	1	1	4
1933–34	Toronto Maple Leafs, NHL	45	14	32	46	8	5	2	4	6	6
1934–35	Toronto Maple Leafs, NHL	37	10	20	30	16	7	0	3	3	0
1935–36	Toronto Maple Leafs, NHL	45	4	13	17	10	9	3	4	7	0
	NHL Totals	310	66	177	243	105	38	5	18	23	12

NHL Second All-Star Team (1934)
Won Lady Byng Trophy (1932)
Won Stanley Cup (1932)

During these years, Primeau also taught a course at the University of Toronto that focused on preparing men to coach physical fitness. Later, NHL president Clarence Campbell asked him to go to western Canada to conduct schools for amateur coaches.

Aubrey Victor "Dit" *Clapper*

While demonstrating a high level of skill both as a defenseman and as a forward, Dit Clapper became one of the league's most versatile performers. In a career that lasted two decades, he forged a reputation as a tenacious yet honest competitor. He rarely looked for trouble on the ice, but if the game turned rough, he was one of the league's more accomplished pugilists. Throughout his pro tenure, Clapper was a respected leader on the ice and in the dressing room. This quality was an asset after he retired and become a coach in the NHL and the American Hockey League.

Born in Newmarket, Ontario, Clapper started playing hockey on the Aurora Grammar School team. While he was still a youngster, his family moved to Hastings, a small community near Oshawa. It was at this point that Clapper first became heavily involved in athletics. He was particularly adept at lacrosse and also furthered his hockey apprenticeship by playing with the Hastings and Oshawa juniors. Toronto minor hockey coach Fred Hogarth, who owned a cottage near the Clapper family's, took notice of Dit's overall athleticism and later attended one of Clapper's matches. He was intrigued by Clapper's blend of natural talent and competitive spirit and eventually brought the young phenomenon to the big city to play for the Toronto Parkdale Canoe Club.

Clapper had trouble cracking the Parkdale lineup because coach Harry Watson didn't approve of his aggressive play in the team's practices. Eventually this matter was resolved and Clapper helped his team reach the 1925–26 OHA finals, where they succumbed to Kingston. At this time the defenseman attracted the attention of Eddie Powers, coach of the Boston Tigers of the Canadian-American league, the minor-pro affiliate of the NHL's Boston Bruins. When Powers signed Clapper, it represented one of the most noteworthy acquisitions in the Bruins' young history.

After a year of seasoning with the Tigers, Clapper was sold to the parent club in October 1927, and he'd remain in the Bruins' lineup for the next 20 years—becoming the first 20-year man in NHL history. As an experiment, Boston coach Art Ross used Clapper as a right wing, and Clapper adjusted well to his new position. He scored a key goal in the Bruins' first-ever Stanley Cup win in 1928–29, which came at the expense of the New York Rangers in a best-of-three finals.

Eventually Clapper formed the ever-dangerous Dynamite Line with Cooney Weiland and Dutch Gainor. This unit reached its zenith during the 1929–30 season when it led Boston to an unprecedented 38–5–1 regular-season mark. Clapper scored 41 goals in 44 games, second only to Weiland's 43. In 1931 and 1935 Clapper was chosen as the right wing on the NHL Second All-Star Team.

By the 1937–38 season, the Boston defense corps was in need of an overhaul. Meanwhile, the Kraut Line of Milt Schmidt, Woody Dumart and Bobby Bauer had taken on the lion's share of the scoring chores. Clapper was therefore moved back to his original position on defense, and the

Dit Clapper was a respected leader on the ice and in the dressing room.

The ever-dangerous Dynamite Line of Dit Clapper (left)–Cooney Weiland (center)–Dutch Gainor (right) led Boston to an unprecedented 38–5–1 mark in the 1929–1930 season

reassignment inspired him to play some of the best hockey of his career. The work of Clapper and Eddie Shore was crucial to Boston's win over the Toronto Maple Leafs in the 1939 Stanley Cup finals, and between 1939 and 1941 he was named to the NHL First All-Star Team three consecutive times.

Clapper demonstrated his well-known sportsmanship when he scored his 200th career goal at Maple Leaf Gardens on January 8, 1941. After the game, he presented the stick he used to reach this milestone to Maple Leafs assistant general manager Frank Selke as a token of his admiration. Later that year, Clapper contributed five playoff assists as the Bruins won their third Stanley Cup by sweeping Detroit in four straight games.

During the 1941–42 season, Clapper suffered a severed tendon and it was believed that the injury would end his career. Typically, Clapper's resilience and determination inspired him to return the following year with his customary effective play. After the 1943–44 schedule, Clapper was chosen to the NHL Second All-Star Team. In 1945–46, he assumed the role of player-coach and guided the Bruins to a Stanley Cup finals against the eventual champions, the Montreal Canadiens. The following year, unhappy with his diminishing ability, the 41-year-old retired as a player six games into the season.

In an emotional ceremony at the Boston Garden on February 12, 1947, Clapper was honored for his multitude of accomplishments and the Bruins retired his number 5 sweater. In all, Clapper was responsible for 228 goals and 474 points in the regular season as well as 13 playoff goals. He was Boston captain from 1932 to 1938 and again from 1939 until his retirement in 1947. He also served as the Bruins' coach for four seasons and led the team to 78 regular-season wins.

A member of the Canadian Sports Hall of Fame, Clapper was inducted into the Hockey Hall of Fame in 1947 when the customary waiting period was waived in recognition of his obvious greatness.

Clapper, Aubrey Victor "Dit"
RW/D, 6′2″, 195 lbs, b: Newmarket, Ont., 2/9/1907, d: 1/21/1978

Season	Club, League	Regular Season					Playoffs				
		GP	G	A	Pts	PIM	GP	G	A	Pts	PIM
1926–27	Boston Tigers, Can-Am	29	6	1	7	57					
1927–28	Boston Bruins, NHL	40	4	1	5	20	2	0	0	0	2
1928–29	Boston Bruins, NHL	40	9	2	11	48	5	1	0	1	0
1929–30	Boston Bruins, NHL	44	41	20	61	48	6	4	0	4	4
1930–31	Boston Bruins, NHL	43	22	8	30	50	5	2	4	6	4
1931–32	Boston Bruins, NHL	48	17	22	39	21					
1932–33	Boston Bruins, NHL	48	14	14	28	42	5	1	1	2	2
1933–34	Boston Bruins, NHL	48	10	12	22	6					
1934–35	Boston Bruins, NHL	48	21	16	37	21	3	1	0	1	0
1935–36	Boston Bruins, NHL	44	12	13	25	14	2	0	1	1	0
1936–37	Boston Bruins, NHL	48	17	8	25	25	3	2	0	2	5
1937–38	Boston Bruins, NHL	46	6	9	15	24	3	0	0	0	12
1938–39	Boston Bruins, NHL	42	13	13	26	22	12	0	1	1	6
1939–40	Boston Bruins, NHL	44	10	18	28	25	5	0	2	2	2
1940–41	Boston Bruins, NHL	48	8	18	26	24	11	0	5	5	4
1941–42	Boston Bruins, NHL	32	3	12	15	31					
1942–43	Boston Bruins, NHL	38	5	18	23	12	9	2	3	5	9
1943–44	Boston Bruins, NHL	50	6	25	31	13					
1944–45	Boston Bruins, NHL	46	8	14	22	16	7	0	0	0	0
1945–46	Boston Bruins, NHL	30	2	3	5	0	4	0	0	0	0
1946–47	Boston Bruins, NHL	6	0	0	0	0					
	NHL Totals	833	228	246	474	462	82	13	17	30	50

NHL First All-Star Team (1939, 1940, 1941)
NHL Second All-Star Team (1931, 1935, 1944)
Won Stanley Cup (1929, 1939, 1941)

Charlie Conacher

In his time, Charlie "the Big Bomber" Conacher had the hardest shot in hockey, a notorious blast that eluded goaltenders and dented rink boards. As a member of one of the most dangerous lines in hockey history, the Toronto Maple Leafs' Kid Line of the 1930s, right wing Conacher and left wing Harvey "Busher" Jackson were the beneficiaries of center Joe Primeau's slick passes as the threesome found itself near the top of the scoring lists for the better part of a decade.

Charlie Conacher came from a family of 10 siblings, many of whom were also gifted athletes. Few would dispute that Charlie was the best hockey-playing Conacher, although older brother Lionel and younger brother Roy are also Hall of Famers. Nicknamed "the Big Train," Lionel was nine years Charlie's senior. A standout in football, baseball and lacrosse, among other sports, he was named Canada's athlete of the half-century in 1950. When he became a respected defenseman in the NHL, his success motivated young Charlie to start taking the sport seriously. But Charlie had another incentive to succeed: Professional hockey represented a way to turn a hobby into a steady, paying job for a young man eager to escape the poverty and unemployment that provided the backdrop to much of his upbringing. "It represented money," Charlie said of hockey in those early years. "We didn't have a pretzel. We didn't have enough money to buy toothpaste."

The Big Bomber (Charlie Conacher) had the hardest shot in hockey in his time.

Charlie began playing hockey on downtown Toronto streets, without skates, and he worked long hours on his shot and his stickhandling. When he did take to the ice, his skating was so poor he was forced to play goal. (Lionel didn't take up the game until he was 16 and he too had struggled with the finer points of skating.) Charlie made up his mind he wasn't meant for netminding duties, so he put in long hours to develop his skating, working "until I thought my legs would drop off," as he put it later in life. The next year he played center on the neighborhood rink and continued to improve in leaps and bounds. He'd never be the swiftest or most graceful of men on the ice, but his strength and dexterity made him a constant scoring threat.

Conacher played a year of junior hockey with North Toronto before joining the Toronto Marlboros in 1927. He and Busher Jackson were members of the Marlies' Memorial Cup-winning team in 1929, and together they made the jump to the Maple Leafs in 1929–30. There they were teamed with Joe Primeau, who had been a Leafs farmhand to that point, and because of their youth and inexperience, the three were called "the Kid Line."

With his linemates' help, Conacher became the best right wing in the game over the next half-decade. He was a daring and explosive scorer who used his size—6'1" and 195 pounds in his heyday—to his advantage. He could beat goalies equally well with his booming shot or with a deft move from close range. Once he got moving, he was famous for bowling over anyone between him and the net—and then often the net itself as he crossed the goal line just a few seconds after the puck.

Dick Irvin Sr. coached the Kid Line when it was at the height of its powers. "King Clancy and Syl Apps were great because they could rally a team," he said. "But Charlie Conacher was the guy who could score the big goal for you, and he could score in a lot of different ways."

Five times between 1930 and 1936, Conacher either led or tied for the league lead in goal-scoring. He was a Second Team All-Star in his second and third years in the league and a First Team selection for three consecutive seasons beginning in 1933–34. He also helped the Leafs win the Stanley Cup in 1932.

Conacher's style of play—which featured all-out attacks—didn't lend itself to a long career and injuries began to wear the big man down. After nine years with Toronto, he was sold to the Detroit Red Wings, where he played for one year before moving to the New York Americans for two seasons. He retired from play in 1941 but stayed in the game as a coach, guiding the Oshawa Generals to a Memorial Cup championship in 1944 before tutoring younger brother Roy and the rest of the Chicago Black Hawks for three years in the late 1940s.

Conacher, Charlie
RW, 6'1", 195 lbs, b: Toronto, Ont., 12/20/1909, d: 12/30/1967

Season	Club, League	Regular Season					Playoffs				
		GP	G	A	Pts	PIM	GP	G	A	Pts	PIM
1926–27	Noth Toronto Seniors, OHA Sr.	2	1	0	1	2					
1927–28	Toronto Marlboros, OHA Sr.	1	2	0	2	0					
1928–29	Toronto Marlboros, OHA Sr.	8	18	3	21	*	2	7	0	7	*
1929–30	Toronto Maple Leafs, NHL	38	20	9	29	48					
1930–31	Toronto Maple Leafs, NHL	37	31	12	43	78	2	0	1	1	0
1931–32	Toronto Maple Leafs, NHL	44	34	14	48	66	7	6	2	8	6
1932–33	Toronto Maple Leafs, NHL	40	14	19	33	64	9	1	1	2	10
1933–34	Toronto Maple Leafs, NHL	42	32	20	52	38	5	3	2	5	0
1934–35	Toronto Maple Leafs, NHL	47	36	21	57	24	7	1	4	5	6
1935–36	Toronto Maple Leafs, NHL	44	23	15	38	74	9	3	2	5	12
1936–37	Toronto Maple Leafs, NHL	15	3	5	8	13	2	0	0	0	5
1937–38	Toronto Maple Leafs, NHL	19	7	9	16	6					
1938–39	Detroit Red Wings, NHL	40	8	15	23	39	5	2	5	7	2
1939–40	New York Americans, NHL	47	10	18	28	41	3	1	1	2	8
1940–41	New York Americans, NHL	46	7	16	23	32					
	NHL Totals	459	225	173	398	523	49	17	18	35	49

NHL First All-Star Team (1934, 1935, 1936)
NHL Second All-Star Team (1932, 1933)
NHL Scoring Leader (1934, 1935)
Won Stanley Cup (1932)

Aside from his bullet-like shot, Conacher was also known for his practical jokes and his sometimes dark sense of humor. He once held teammate Baldy Cotton out a seventh-floor window to prove a point. Cotton, deathly afraid of heights, quickly conceded the argument to Charlie. Conacher later teamed up with Cotton to play a famous prank on King Clancy hours before a game in Boston. The two men used hotel linens to tie Clancy to his bed, gagged his mouth with a towel, then left for the rink to prepare for that evening's game. Coach Irvin found Clancy after he heard moans coming from the room. Angry at first—had Irvin not stumbled on him, King would have missed the game—the coach softened after his Leafs won the match.

Charlie Conacher inspired a generation of Leaf players with his hard work and determination. The one battle he couldn't win was with cancer. He died in 1967 after a year-long fight with throat cancer, but in typical Conacher fashion, his legacy has helped in the search for a cure to the disease that claimed him. The Charlie Conacher Research Fund has raised millions for cancer research. Each year the Charlie Conacher Memorial Trophy is awarded to an NHL player for outstanding humanitarian and public service contributions.

Earl Seibert

Even as a child, Earl Seibert was groomed by his father to be a hockey player. It just happened that his dad, Oliver, had been a star in lacrosse and hockey, where he started out as a goalie before making his name as a forward. The elder Seibert was also one of the great inventors of hockey's early days, coming up with a skate design for CCM in which the toe of the boot didn't curl right over the front of the blade. It was said that Oliver could skate as fast backward as forward and he became a legend when he raced a horse for a mile along the frozen Grand River—and won. He also once played on a team made up entirely of Seibert family members.

Earl played his junior hockey in his home town, Kitchener, and turned pro in 1929 with the Springfield Indians of the Can-Am league. During his two-year term in Springfield, he suffered a serious concussion and for the rest of his career wore a helmet, making him the first player to wear headgear on a regular basis. In 1931 Seibert joined the New York Rangers, beginning a 15-year NHL career during which he'd become one of the league's premier players.

Near the beginning of Earl's second season, he received a special gift from his father, the result of a bet made some nine years before. When he was 12, Earl and his friends had built a shack behind the Seibert house and the boys talked and played there throughout the summer of 1922. But one day Earl's father came home early and discovered the boys were smoking. Oliver issued this challenge: If Earl promised not to smoke until he was 21, he'd get a gold watch from his dad as a special present. Seibert never smoked again.

Earl's demeanor was always serious. On the ice, this manifested itself in mature play and tremendous leadership. Off-ice, it meant he was a tough negotiator in contract talks. During his second season, Seibert enlisted his father as his agent in some acrimonious negotiations with the Rangers, but any ill feelings were forgotten by the time New York won the Stanley Cup that spring, beating the Leafs 3–1 in a best-of-five final series. Eventually, though, the Rangers brass tired of Seibert's tenacious haggling and he was traded to Chicago for Art Coulter.

It was in the Windy City that Seibert established himself as one of the best defensemen of his era. He was named to the First or Second All-Star Team each year between 1935 and 1944, a feat surpassed only by Gordie Howe, Maurice Richard, Bobby Hull and Doug Harvey. Seibert was generally regarded as second only to Eddie Shore in terms of skill and rugged play, and Shore once confessed that Seibert was the only man he was afraid to fight. Defensively, Seibert was one of the best shot-blockers in the game, and he could move the puck just as quickly as anyone.

A writer for the *Springfield Daily News*, Sam Pompei, once commented, "I've heard a lot of people say Earl was the best player of his era, but Eddie Shore stole the spotlight with his color." Hall of Famer Clint Smith elaborated: "The only thing about Earl was that he decided when he wanted to play and when he didn't. His attitude was his worst enemy. He decided if they were only going to pay him $7,500, that's all they were going to get out of him. If he'd played like Eddie Shore—100% every night—he could have been one of the greats."

Although his career was full of great accomplishments, it was compromised by one of the worst accidents in the history of the game. On January 28, 1937, in a game against the Montreal Canadiens, Seibert and Howie Morenz chased after a puck behind the Chicago net.

Even as a child, Earl Seibert was groomed by his father to be a player.

Seibert, Earl
D, 6'2", 198 lbs, b: Berlin, Ont., 12/7/1911, d: 5/12/1990

Season	Club, League	Regular Season					Playoffs				
		GP	G	A	Pts	PIM	GP	G	A	Pts	PIM
1927–28	Kitchener Greenshirts, OHA Sr.	1	0	0	0	2					
1929–30	Springfield Indians, Can-Am	40	4	1	5	84					
1930–31	Springfield Indians, Can-Am	38	16	11	27	96	4	2	0	2	16
1931–32	New York Rangers, NHL	46	4	6	10	88	7	1	2	3	14
1932–33	New York Rangers, NHL	45	2	3	5	92	8	1	0	1	14
1933–34	New York Rangers, NHL	48	13	10	23	66	2	0	0	0	4
1934–35	New York Rangers, NHL	48	6	19	25	86	4	0	0	0	6
1935–36	New York Rangers, NHL	17	2	3	5	6					
	Chicago Black Hawks, NHL	15	3	6	9	19	2	2	0	2	0
1936–37	Chicago Black Hawks, NHL	43	9	6	15	46					
1937–38	Chicago Black Hawks, NHL	48	8	13	21	38	10	5	2	7	12
1938–39	Chicago Black Hawks, NHL	48	4	11	15	57					
1939–40	Chicago Black Hawks, NHL	36	3	7	10	35	2	0	1	1	8
1940–41	Chicago Black Hawks, NHL	46	3	17	20	52	5	0	0	0	12
1941–42	Chicago Black Hawks, NHL	46	7	14	21	52	3	0	0	0	0
1942–43	Chicago Black Hawks, NHL	44	5	27	32	48					
1943–44	Chicago Black Hawks, NHL	50	8	25	33	20	9	0	2	2	2
1944–45	Chicago Black Hawks, NHL	22	7	8	15	13					
	Detroit Red Wings, NHL	25	5	9	14	10	14	2	1	3	4
1945–46	Detroit Red Wings, NHL	18	0	3	3	18					
	Indianapolis Capitals, AHL	24	2	9	11	19	5	0	0	0	0
	NHL Totals	645	89	187	276	746	66	11	8	19	76

NHL First All-Star Team (1935, 1942, 1943, 1944)
NHL Second All-Star Team (1936, 1937, 1938, 1939, 1940, 1941)
Won Stanley Cup (1933, 1938)

Seibert tied up his man on the play, but Morenz fell awkwardly into the boards, shattering his leg. Just six weeks later, Morenz died in hospital, having never recovered emotionally from the devastation of the career-ending injury. Seibert never really got over the trauma; whenever he was asked if he'd ever played against Morenz, he'd reply bitterly, "Yeah. I killed him."

In 1938 he led the Black Hawks to the Stanley Cup, defeating the Toronto Maple Leafs in five games. "The biggest reason we won," coach Bill Stewart asserted, "was that we had Earl Seibert on our defense. The big guy played about 55 minutes a game." He was such a favorite with the team's owner, Major Frederic McLaughlin, that he was given part ownership of the team. However, when McLaughlin died, manager Bill Tobin refused to acknowledge this gesture and instead traded Seibert to the Detroit Red Wings. He played just 43 games over a season and a half in the Motor City before he retired.

When Eddie Shore asked Seibert to coach his Springfield Indians, the team he'd begun his career with, Earl accepted. The relationship, however, was perpetually strained, and Seibert left after only one season, bitter for the experience and wanting to have nothing more to do with hockey. In 1963 he was inducted into the Hockey Hall of Fame and, along with his father, who was elected in 1961, became the first father-son combination ever elected as players.

Art Coulter

In the 1939–40 season, Art Coulter had just one goal and a career high of 68 penalty minutes, but he was named to the Second All-Star Team.

Born in Winnipeg in 1909, Art Coulter began playing hockey as so many kids did in Canada's west—in sub-zero temperatures on the outdoor rinks and frozen ponds near his home. He'd skate for hours and hours at a time. He first played organized hockey on defense for the St. John's Cathedral team. While he learned the fundamentals of the game, St. John's won three consecutive city championships, and when he was 17 Art moved on to play for the Winnipeg Pilgrims juvenile team. There he helped win the city championships for 1926–27, and played two more seasons.

In the summer of 1929, his family moved to Pittsburgh and Coulter had no idea where he was going to play next. He requested a tryout with a local team in Pittsburgh, and during the workout he was spotted by a scout for the Philadelphia Arrows of the Can-Am league. He was invited to Philadelphia for another audition and just a few days later signed his first pro contract with the team. Coulter played nearly three years with the Arrows, and during the 1931–32 season, he was acquired by the Chicago Black Hawks. Coulter was stunned by the move, and within days he was playing in the NHL with a team that had competed in the Stanley Cup finals just the year before.

In his first year with Chicago, 1931–32, the team was eliminated in the first round of the playoffs by Toronto, but Coulter was one of the best players on the ice. He demonstrated incredible stamina and physical strength that were to be his trademarks throughout his career. He was the consummate defensive defenseman.

Although the Hawks failed to qualify for the playoffs the next year, they won the Stanley Cup in the spring of 1934, allowing just seven goals as they beat the Detroit Red Wings three games to one. Coulter was now the anchor of a strong blue line squad that included Lionel Conacher, Taffy Abel and Roger Jenkins.

Midway through the 1935–36 season, he was traded for the only time in his NHL career, to the New York Rangers for Earl Seibert. The deal helped both teams: Seibert's steady defensive play helped Chicago, while Coulter's willingness to put the team ahead of himself was music to the ears of New York boss Lester Patrick, who'd clashed with Seibert repeatedly at contract time. It came as no surprise when Patrick named Art captain of the Rangers in 1937 after Bill Cook retired.

The Rangers lost the 1937 Stanley Cup finals to Detroit after taking a 2–1 lead in the best-of-five series. But three years later the Blueshirts claimed the prize. They eliminated the first-place Boston Bruins in the semifinals, then confronted the Toronto Maple Leafs in a series Coulter described as the strangest he'd ever played. Madison Square Garden's owners rented out the building to the circus in Aprl in those days, so when the Rangers made it to the 1940 finals, they had to play most of their "home" games in their opponent's building. So despite being entitled to the home-ice advantage, the Rangers played only two games in New York and four in Toronto. Still, the New Yorkers overcame the apparent obstacle to win the series—the only time Coulter would have his name engraved on the Cup.

Coulter's career was altered irrevocably by the war. He enlisted in 1942, and when he was discharged two years later, the 35-year-old discovered that the league had no place for him. He'd played most of the time from 1942 to 1944 with the Coast Guard Cutters, but after the war he went into insurance. Such was his tremendous reputation, though, that he was inducted into the Hockey Hall of Fame in 1970.

Art Boucher died on October 14, 2000, in a retirement home in Mobile, Alabama.

Coulter, Art
D, 5′11″, 185 lbs, b: Winnipeg, Man., 5/31/1909, d.10/14/2000

Season	Club, League	Regular Season					Playoffs				
		GP	G	A	Pts	PIM	GP	G	A	Pts	PIM
1929–30	Philadelphia Arrows, Can-Am	35	2	2	4	40	2	0	0	0	2
1930–31	Philadelphia Arrows, Can-Am	40	4	8	12	109					
1931–32	Philadelphia Arrows, Can-Am	26	9	4	13	42					
	Chicago Black Hawks, NHL	13	0	1	1	23	2	1	0	1	0
1932–33	Chicago Black Hawks, NHL	46	3	2	5	53					
1933–34	Chicago Black Hawks, NHL	46	5	2	7	39	8	1	0	1	10
1934–35	Chicago Black Hawks, NHL	48	4	8	12	68	2	0	0	0	5
1935–36	Chicago Black Hawks, NHL	25	0	2	2	18					
	New York Rangers, NHL	23	1	5	6	26					
1936–37	New York Rangers, NHL	47	1	5	6	27	9	0	3	3	15
1937–38	New York Rangers, NHL	43	5	10	15	90					
1938–39	New York Rangers, NHL	44	4	8	12	58	7	1	1	2	6
1939–40	New York Rangers, NHL	48	1	9	10	68	12	1	0	1	21
1940–41	New York Rangers, NHL	35	5	14	19	42	3	0	0	0	0
1941–42	New York Rangers, NHL	47	1	16	17	31	6	0	1	1	4
1942–43	Coast Guard Cutters, EHL	37	13	20	33	32	10	4	1	5	8
1943–44	Coast Guard Cutters, EHL	26	10	13	23	10	12	6	8	14	8
	NHL Totals	465	30	82	112	543	49	4	5	9	61

NHL Second All-Star Team (1935, 1938, 1939, 1940)
Won Stanley Cup (1934, 1940)

Harvey "Busher" Jackson

Busher Jackson was an enormously talented player, a gifted rink rat who could—and did—score as well as the best of all time; in 1932 he became the youngest player to date to win an NHL scoring title.

Jackson was a flashy member of the Kid Line, the Toronto Maple Leafs trio that dominated the National Hockey League in the 1930s. Along with big Charlie Conacher and the slick-passing Joe Primeau, Jackson established himself as a star on the left wing with his flair and wicked backhand.

Born in 1911, he first learned to skate on a little rink in Toronto's West End that was known as "Poverty Pond." He wore girls' skates, the only kind at hand, until he could afford a more suitable pair. When he wasn't in school, he was on the ice. He even arranged with an employee at the

Ravina Gardens to let him clear the ice with a shovel in exchange for being allowed to skate and shoot when the rink was unoccupied. At 15, when he was approached about playing in the T&Y league, Jackson asked for a shirt and shoes to make up for the money he'd lose when he stopped scraping the ice.

One day, after one of his practices, Frank Selke brought a team of juniors onto the ice to practise. None of the older players could catch Jackson or take the puck from him. Selke, then a scout for the Toronto Maple Leafs organization, called him over and asked him if had been signed by any team. "Haven't signed and don't want to," young Harvey replied. Selke refused to let him continue skating until he signed, so he did, reluctantly. Jackson played for two seasons with the Toronto Marlboros of the Ontario Hockey Association, a team Selke coached and one that won the Memorial Cup in 1929. Jackson led those playoffs in scoring with seven goals in the three games.

Jackson signed with the Maple Leafs in 1929, joining his Marlboro teammate Charlie Conacher, who'd turned pro just a few games before him. At 18, Jackson was the youngest player in the league, but he was brash and confident. In his first game—against the Montreal Canadiens at the Mutual Street Arena—he knocked down his idol, Howie Morenz. From the ice, Morenz offered his opinion of the awestruck newcomer: "You'll do."

A handsome kid with a quick smile, Busher got his nickname when he was injured and the team's trainer, Tim Daly, asked him to carry sticks, as was the tradition. "I'm not here to carry sticks. I'm here to play hockey," replied Jackson. "You ain't nothing but a fresh busher!" Daly retorted. The name, which could be mistaken to mean he was from the bush leagues or the backwoods, stuck for the rest of Jackson's life.

The Kid Line wasn't formed right away. It was only in the middle of the 1929–30 season that Joe Primeau, whose NHL career was off to an unremarkable start, was placed between the hard-shooting Conacher and the speedy Jackson. The line caught fire almost immediately, however, and the three players were consistently among the league's scoring leaders over the next five years.

Jackson was a great rusher, with good size and a pure ability to score goals. He was famous for his backhand shot, which was lethal as he darted across the ice from the left side. His shiftiness and deft moves were equally notable. Red Dutton, then a bruising defenseman with the New York Americans, later tried to describe "Jackson's shift," which left many defenders feeling the brush of his sweater as he maneuvered past them: "He comes at you taking a stroke on his left skate, and then, instead of taking the next stroke with his right foot, he seems to take another with his left."

With his physique and natural talent, Jackson avoided serious injuries even though he'd a driving, entertaining style of play. In 1932, at the tender age of 21, he registered 28 goals and 53 points to lead the league in scoring. The Kid Line was at its peak and the Maple Leafs won their first Stanley Cup since their name change from the St. Patricks. Jackson was named to the league's First All-Star Team, one of three such selections he'd earn.

Off the ice, Jackson was also larger than life. He drove expensive cars and was photographed at social events across the country. A frustrated Smythe tried to get his young star to put some money aside for after his playing days, offering to match his savings, but Jackson was in love with the high life. His notoriety increased in 1931, when he entered a blazing cottage in Wasaga Beach, Ontario, and carried two men to safety.

After Primeau retired in 1936, Busher played on a line with his brother Art for one season before joining Syl Apps and Gord Drillon on yet another high-scoring Leafs unit. When Busher's

Busher Jackson became the youngest player to lead the league in scoring.

output sagged in 1938–39, Smythe traded his controversial charge to the New York Americans for Sweeney Schriner. He played two years with the Americans and then three more with Boston—even spending some time on the Bruins blue line—before retiring in 1944.

But Busher found it hard to make the transition to life after hockey. He went through several failed marriages and he was unlucky in business. He struggled with alcohol, and at one point he could be found selling hockey sticks outside Maple Leaf Gardens to support himself. In 1958 he suffered a broken neck in a fall down a flight of stairs and he battled constantly with health problems, most notably a failing liver. His story, one of the sadder tales in the sport's history, was a motivating factor in the creation of the NHL Players' Association.

He died in 1966 at the age of 55 without living to see himself enshrined in the Hockey Hall of Fame, an honor he'd wanted to share with his young son. His old Toronto boss, Conn Smythe, was adamant that Jackson didn't deserve a place in the Hall because of his conduct off the ice—and Smythe chaired the selection committee. In 1971 the committee decided it was time to recognize Busher's outstanding play and Smythe resigned from it in protest. At the induction ceremony, Jackson's son, Kim, accepted the honor on his father's behalf and the NHL gave him a scholarship to the university of his choice. It was a fitting tribute for a man Frank Selke called "the classiest player I have ever seen."

Jackson, Harvey "Busher"
LW, 5'11", 195 lbs, b: Toronto, Ont., 1/19/1911, d: 6/25/1966

Season	Club, League	Regular Season					Playoffs				
		GP	G	A	Pts	PIM	GP	G	A	Pts	PIM
1929–30	Toronto Maple Leafs, NHL	31	12	6	18	29					
1930–31	Toronto Maple Leafs, NHL	43	18	13	31	81	2	0	0	0	0
1931–32	Toronto Maple Leafs, NHL	48	28	25	53	63	7	5	2	7	13
1932–33	Toronto Maple Leafs, NHL	48	27	17	44	43	9	3	1	4	2
1933–34	Toronto Maple Leafs, NHL	38	20	18	38	38	5	1	0	1	8
1934–35	Toronto Maple Leafs, NHL	42	22	22	44	27	7	3	2	5	2
1935–36	Toronto Maple Leafs, NHL	47	11	11	22	19	9	3	2	5	4
1936–37	Toronto Maple Leafs, NHL	46	21	19	40	12	2	1	0	1	2
1937–38	Toronto Maple Leafs, NHL	48	17	17	34	18	6	1	0	1	8
1938–39	Toronto Maple Leafs, NHL	41	10	17	27	12	7	0	1	1	2
1939–40	New York Americans, NHL	43	12	8	20	10	3	0	1	1	2
1940–41	New York Americans, NHL	46	8	18	26	4					
1941–42	Boston Bruins, NHL	26	5	7	12	18	5	0	1	1	0
1942–43	Boston Bruins, NHL	44	19	15	34	38	9	1	2	3	10
1943–44	Boston Bruins, NHL	42	11	21	32	25					
	NHL Totals	633	241	234	475	437	71	18	12	30	53

NHL First All-Star Team (1932, 1934, 1935, 1937)
NHL Second All-Star Team (1033)
NHL Scoring Leader (1932)
Won Stanley Cup (1932)

Ebenezer "Ebbie" Goodfellow

Ebbie Goodfellow played amateur hockey in his native Ottawa before being discovered by Detroit general manager and coach Jack Adams. Although Goodfellow was originally the property of the New York Americans, Adams bought him and sent him to the Detroit Olympics, a minor-league affiliate, for the 1928–29 season. Goodfellow led the Can-Pro league in scoring, and the very next year he was in the starting lineup for the NHL's Detroit Cougars, who were soon to be named the Falcons.

Goodfellow began his career as a center and because of his skating ability played on Detroit's top line with Herbie Lewis and Larry Aurie. Almost instantly he gained a reputation as a clever stickhandler with a long reach—he was 6' tall. His shot was accurate and hard, his style of play determined but sportsmanlike and he was one of the first players to take physical conditioning seriously seven days a week. He was also an excellent backchecker as well as a physical presence on the ice. He was, in short, one of the emerging superstars in the league.

Ebbie Goodfellow was one of the first players to take physical conditioning seriously— seven days a week.

Ebbie Goodfellow was crucial in bringing the Stanley Cup to Detroit for the first time in 1936.

In 1930–31, Goodfellow finished second in the league scoring race behind only the great Howie Morenz. Over time, however, coach Jack Adams sensed that he was losing a bit of his blazing speed and reassigned him to the blue line. Ebbie responded by becoming one of the best defensemen in the league, earning a spot on the First All-Star Team twice and the Second Team once between 1935 and 1940. Starting in 1935, Ebbie took on more of a leadership role on the team, acting as coach Adams' assistant—helping run practices, guiding young players and acting as a role model for his teammates.

Goodfellow was integral in bringing the Stanley Cup to Detroit for the first time in 1936. On March 24–25 he played in game one of the semifinals, which ended at 2:25 a.m., nearly six hours after the opening face-off. The game was the longest ever played in the NHL and the Red Wings beat the Montreal Maroons 1–0 in the sixth overtime period. Detroit went on to defeat the Toronto Maple Leafs three games to one in the finals.

The following year the Red Wings played the Rangers for the Cup, and since Madison Square Garden had already been rented out for a circus, four of the five games in the series were played at Detroit's Olympia. With a 3–0 win in the deciding game, Detroit became the first American-based team to win back-to-back championships.

In the 1940s the Wings went to the finals in three successive years, losing in 1941 and 1942 before winning their third Cup in 1943 in a decisive 4–0 sweep of Boston. But injuries prevented Goodfellow from playing much in those last two seasons and he didn't play at all in the playoffs in either year.

In all, Ebbie played 557 games in the NHL over 14 seasons, all of them with Detroit, and his greatest personal accomplishment came in 1940 when he was named winner of the Hart Trophy as the league's most valuable player—a rare distinction for a defenseman.

After the 1942–43 season, the 36-year-old Goodfellow joined the army for two years. When he was discharged, he knew his playing days were behind him and he took a job coaching the American league's St. Louis Flyers, who were affiliated with the Chicago Black Hawks. Chicago owner Bill Tobin gave Ebbie a simple assignment: He'd two years in which to make the last-place team competitive. In 1948–49, his second year in St. Louis, Goodfellow made his team division champions, and in 1950 Tobin hired him to replace Charlie Conacher as head coach of the Hawks.

"Ebbie was a fighting player during his career," Tobin said when he announced the hiring. "He never went out of his way to make trouble, yet he never backed away from any-

Goodfellow Ebenezer "Ebbie"
C/D, 6´, 175 lbs, b: Ottawa, Ont., 4/9/1907, d: 9/10/1965

Season	Club, League	Regular Season					Playoffs				
		GP	G	A	Pts	PIM	GP	G	A	Pts	PIM
1927–28	Ottawa Montagnards, City Sr.	15	7	2	9	*	6	4	1	5	*
1928–29	Detroit Olympics, Can-Pro	42	26	8	34	45	7	3	2	5	8
1929–30	Detroit Cougars, NHL	44	17	17	34	54					
1930–31	Detroit Falcons, NHL	44	25	23	48	32					
1931–32	Detroit Falcons, NHL	48	14	16	30	56	2	0	0	0	0
1932–33	Detroit Red Wings, NHL	41	12	8	20	47	4	1	0	1	11
1933–34	Detroit Red Wings, NHL	48	13	13	26	45	9	4	3	7	12
1934–35	Detroit Red Wings, NHL	48	12	24	36	44					
1935–36	Detroit Red Wings, NHL	48	5	18	23	69	7	1	0	1	4
1936–37	Detroit Red Wings, NHL	48	9	16	25	43	9	2	2	4	12
1937–38	Detroit Red Wings, NHL	30	0	7	7	13					
1938–39	Detroit Red Wings, NHL	48	8	8	16	36	6	0	0	0	8
1939–40	Detroit Red Wings, NHL	43	11	17	28	31	5	0	2	2	9
1940–41	Detroit Red Wings, NHL	47	5	17	22	35	3	0	1	1	9
1941–42	Detroit Red Wings, NHL	9	2	2	4	2					
1942–43	Detroit Red Wings, NHL	11	1	4	5	4					
	NHL Totals	557	134	190	324	511	45	8	8	16	65

NHL First All-Star Team (1937, 1940)
NHL Second All-Star Team (1936)
Won Hart Trophy (1940)
Won Stanley Cup (1936, 1937, 1943)

body and always gave as good as or better than he received. He stresses that fighting spirit in his players and always looks for aggressiveness in picking new players."

Goodfellow's NHL coaching career lasted only two dismal seasons during which his team's record was 30–91–19 before he slipped into retirement. He was inducted into the Hockey Hall of Fame in 1963.

Dave "Sweeney" Schriner

Sweeney Schriner was a skilled and speedy left wing who led the league in scoring early in his career despite playing for a terrible team, the New York Americans. Schriner was a smooth player, athletic and entertaining, who found both an appreciative audience and the thrill of winning after a 1939 blockbuster trade sent him to Toronto, where he established himself as one of the best ever to play his position.

Although almost every document from the National Hockey League lists his birthplace as Calgary, Alberta, Schriner was actually born in Saratov, Russia, in 1911. When he was still an infant, his parents heard from a relative about prospects in Canada, specifically in the developing new western province of Alberta. They moved to Calgary, where young David first learned to skate on an outdoor pond near their first home. His parents were worried he was playing too much and they tried to prevent him from leaving the house with his skates. Schriner's response was to throw the skates out the second-floor window of his bedroom into the snow, then walk out the front door to retrieve them after telling his mother he was going out for a walk.

Sweeney Schriner was the first Russian-born NHL star.

Soon he was playing in a rink, though it was still outdoors, and was a star at an early age on teams that represented Calgary in competitions across the country. He was also a talented football and soccer player in the summer months, and he became a big fan of a local semipro baseball player named Bill Sweeney. When Schriner began to play baseball, he emulated the older player and soon earned the nickname "Li'l Sweeney," which was eventually shortened to Sweeney. Aside from his family, and a few official documents, he was never again called by his given name—in fact Sweeney was the only name to which Schriner would usually respond.

At the age of 19, Schriner played two games with the Calgary Canadians of the Alberta Junior Hockey League, then spent the next two years with the senior Calgary Bronks. He led his league in scoring in each of those two seasons—in both the regular season and playoffs—earning him the attention of the New York Americans. In 1933 he was invited to the Amerks' training camp in Oshawa, Ontario, and although he didn't make the final cut, his speed down the wing impressed the coaching staff enough to assign him to the Syracuse Stars of the International-American Hockey League. It was around this time that the confusion regarding his birthplace began.

"I was a month old when my parents migrated to Canada," Schriner said. "When I turned pro with Syracuse in 1933, that Russian birthplace meant a hassle at every border crossing. I quickly discovered it was much simpler to tell them I was from Calgary. It stuck."

Schriner was soon crossing that border with the New York Americans and wearing their red, white and blue uniforms. In his first NHL season, 1934–35, he placed ninth in the league in scoring with 18 goals and 40 points in 48 games. He made such a splash that 26 of 27 voters for the Calder Trophy made him their choice as rookie of the year.

The lowly Amerks desperately needed the youngster's firepower. Even Schriner wasn't convinced the team had a chance—he later said the team had "more playboys than players." He followed his debut with a pair of scoring titles in 1935–36 and 1936–37. In 1936 he was a First Team All-Star and he made the Second Team in 1937. He was cool and polished on the ice and had an uncanny ability to elude checking opponents. He was rarely touched, let alone injured, and in five years with the Amerks he never missed a game.

On May 15, 1939, in one of the decade's biggest trades, Schriner was sent to the Toronto Maple Leafs for five players—including Busher Jackson, a future Hall of Famer who had patrolled the Leafs' left wing with the legendary Kid Line. Schriner was now a star on a contending team. He was selected to the league's First All-Star Team again in 1941, but he earned his lasting fame during the Maple Leafs' amazing run against Detroit in the 1942 finals.

During game one of the series, the Red Wings pushed the Leafs around, and Conn Smythe, the opinionated Toronto owner, was incensed. He ordered coach Hap Day to adopt a tougher style of play. That only made things worse and the Leafs dropped the next two games. Down 3–0, the Stanley Cup seemed all but lost. "We had no doubt we were out of it," Schriner said later. "All the players felt it was a mistake switching our system after the first game. We couldn't knock over a row of peas; for us to switch to a hitting game just wasn't our style."

With nothing to lose in game four, the Leafs benched Gordie Drillon, their best scorer, and defenseman Bucko McDonald in favor of the younger legs of Don Metz and Bob Goldham. More important, at Schriner's urging, they returned to their high-tempo style and stormed back to win the next three games to tie the series. In the seventh game, Schriner put the icing on Toronto's miraculous comeback with two goals in Toronto's 3–1 win. It remains the only time in Stanley Cup history that a team has recovered from a 3–0 deficit in the finals.

Schriner sat out the 1943–44 season because of a salary dispute with the Leafs. He returned to play two more seasons in Toronto, winning his second Stanley Cup with the team in 1945, before taking coaching positions with the Lethbridge Maple Leafs and then the Regina Capitals. He had his amateur status reinstated and played for one more season with Regina before retiring in 1949 to devote more time to his interests in the oil and gas industry in Calgary.

He was inducted into the Hockey Hall of Fame in 1962. In 1977, Maple Leaf fans were

---

Schriner, Dave "Sweeney"
LW, 6´, 185 lbs, b: Saratov, Russia, 11/30/1911, d: 7/4/1990

Season	Club, League	Regular Season					Playoffs				
		GP	G	A	Pts	PIM	GP	G	A	Pts	PIM
1931–32	Calgary Bronks, ASHL	18	19	3	22	32	3	1	2	3	0
1932–33	Calgary Bronks, ASHL	15	22	4	26	8	5	3	1	4	6
1933–34	Syracuse Stars, IAHL	44	17	11	28	28	4	0	0	0	0
1934–35	New York Americans, NHL	48	18	22	40	6					
1935–36	New York Americans, NHL	48	19	26	45	8	5	3	1	4	2
1936–37	New York Americans, NHL	48	21	25	46	17					
1937–38	New York Americans, NHL	48	21	17	38	22	6	1	0	1	0
1938–39	New York Americans, NHL	48	13	31	44	20	2	0	0	0	30
1939–40	Toronto Maple Leafs, NHL	39	11	15	26	10	9	1	3	4	4
1940–41	Toronto Maple Leafs, NHL	48	24	14	38	6	7	2	1	3	4
1941–42	Toronto Maple Leafs, NHL	47	20	16	36	21	13	6	3	9	10
1942–43	Toronto Maple Leafs, NHL	37	19	17	36	13	4	2	2	4	0
1943–44	Calgary Combines, WCSHL	10	9	9	18	14	3	3	2	5	4
	Vancouver St. Regis, PCHL						3	6	3	9	0
1944–45	Toronto Maple Leafs, NHL	26	22	15	37	10	13	3	1	4	4
1945–46	Toronto Maple Leafs, NHL	47	13	6	19	15					
1948–49	Regina Capitals, WCSHL	36	26	27	53	30	8	10	2	12	0
	NHL Totals	484	201	204	405	148	59	18	11	29	54

NHL First All-Star Team (1936, 1941)
NHL Second All-Star Team (1937)
NHL Rookie of the Year (1935)
NHL Scoring Leader (1936, 1937)
Won Stanley Cup (1942, 1945)

asked to elect an "all-time team" and were given three choices at each position. Schriner was one choice for the left wing spot, as was the man he replaced, Busher Jackson. Frank Mahovlich took the honors, perhaps because he was fresher in the fans' memories.

Schriner remained close to hockey, at one point acting as president of the Calgary Oldtimers' Hockey Association, and was an active member of the Calgary community until his death in 1990 at the age of 78 after a long battle with illness.

Clint "Snuffy" Smith

A diminutive and gentlemanly player, Snuffy Smith was at one time the most prolific point scorer in professional hockey. He played in five professional leagues, including 11 high-scoring seasons in the National Hockey League. In 483 NHL games, he accumulated only 24 minutes in penalties, a remarkable total that—along with his impressive record of 397 points—accounts for his two Lady Byng Trophy wins as the league's most sportsmanlike player. He was also runner-up for the award on three other occasions.

Clint Smith became the first player to win the Lady Byng Trophy with two different teams.

Over his long career, he set records and accomplished firsts with startling regularity, though these distinctions seemed never to stay in the books for long nor to earn him lasting fame. Smith's reputation as a clean and talented player merited the centerman a late but much-deserved spot in the Hockey Hall of Fame 40 years after he hung up his skates.

He was born in small-town Saskatchewan, in Assiniboia, on December 12, 1913. He moved to Saskatoon in 1929 and played with the Wesley juveniles and juniors. In 1931–32, he was promoted to the senior ranks, where he led the Saskatoon Crescents in goal-scoring before helping the juniors to the Memorial Cup semifinals, where they lost to the Winnipeg Monarchs. In October 1932 the New York Rangers convinced the 18-year-old to turn pro and he was given a spot on the Springfield Indians in the Can-Am league. At the time, he was considered the second-youngest man ever to turn pro—Dede Klein had joined the Saskatoon Sheiks at 17.

After four years of bouncing around the minors, from Springfield to Saskatoon, Vancouver and Philadelphia, Smith made his debut with the Rangers in 1936–37, earning a full-time roster spot the following season. In 1938–39, he was awarded the Lady Byng Trophy on the strength of 41 points and only two minutes in penalties in 48 games. In 1940, when the Rangers won the Stanley Cup, Snuffy was one of their star centers. "We had three strong lines, two good sets of defense and a great goalie in Davey Kerr," Smith recalled of his one championship team. "We had a string on the puck and we never gave it back."

In 1943–44, the Chicago Black Hawks signed Smith as a free agent and he led the league with 49 assists—then an NHL record—and finished sixth among scorers with 72 points in 50 games. The line of Smith, Bill Mosienko and Doug Bentley was the most productive trio the league had ever seen, their 219 points easily outdistancing a 14-year-old record of 183 set by Boston's Dit Clapper, Cooney Weiland and Norm Gainor. Smith capped his amazing year with his second Lady Byng Trophy, becoming the first player to win the award with two different teams.

One of Smith's goals, on November 11, 1943, against the Bruins, was yet another first. With Boston trailing 5–4 late in the game, Bruin coach Art Ross pulled goalie Bert Gardiner for an extra

On November 11, 1943, Clint Smith scored the first empty-net goal in hockey history.

attacker. Smith corralled a loose puck and sent it into the empty net—the first empty-net goal in history. Rules had always allowed a team to pull its goalie, but this had been viewed as a last-ditch tactic and it wasn't widely used until the mid-1950s.

Smith's name was erased from the record books the very next season. Elmer Lach of the Montreal Canadiens collected 54 assists, while the Canadiens' famous Punch Line of Lach, Rocket Richard and Toe Blake tallied 221 points. Smith exacted some revenge on March 4, 1945, in a game against Hall of Fame goalie Bill Durnan and the Montreal powerhouse. The Hawks were down 2–1 entering the third period, but Smith scored four goals in the final frame as Chicago stormed back to win 6–4. "They were checking Bentley and Mosienko closely, so those two just started throwing the puck back into the middle for me," Smith said of the four goals in a period. The feat has been matched nine times—including once by Wayne Gretzky—but on only two other occasions during the six-team era.

Smith stood 5'8" inches and weighed just over 165 pounds for most of his playing career. The model of gentlemanly play, Smith was assessed only one minor penalty in 42 career playoff games—and he avoided the sin bin completely in three full seasons. "I never got into much trouble because I wasn't big enough," he'd say later.

Smith left the NHL in 1947 to become a player-coach with the Tulsa Oilers of the United States Hockey League. In his first year, the Oilers reached the semifinals and Smith, with 71 points in 64 games, was named the league's most valuable player. He played and coached for four more years in professional hockey, with St. Paul in the USHL and the Cincinnati Mohawks in the American league. In 1952 Smith retired to Vancouver, British Columbia, where he stayed close to the sport by serving for six years as president of the British Columbia Benevolent Hockey Association, an organization that helped former players and their families.

Smith's record for most points in professional hockey was broken the year he retired and he was somewhat forgotten by the hockey establishment until 1991, when he was inducted into the Hockey Hall of Fame.

Smith, Clint "Snuffy"
C, 5'8", 165 lbs, b: Assiniboia, Sask., 12/12/1913

Season	Club, League	Regular Season					Playoffs				
		GP	G	A	Pts	PIM	GP	G	A	Pts	PIM
1931–32	Saskatoon Crescents, SSHL	18	19	3	22	0	4	6	0	6	4
1932–33	Springfield Indians, Can-Am	12	0	0	0	0					
	Saskatoon Quakers, NWHL	27	7	6	13	8					
1933–34	Vancouver Lions, NWHL	34	25	14	39	8	7	5	4	9	2
1934–35	Vancouver Lions, NWHL	32	22	22	44	2	8	3	5	8	4
1935–36	Vancouver Lions, NWHL	40	21	32	53	10	7	2	4	6	2
1936–37	New York Rangers, NHL	2	1	0	1	0					
	Philadelphia Ramblers, AHL	47	25	29	54	15	6	4	3	7	0
1937–38	New York Rangers, NHL	48	14	23	37	0	3	2	0	2	0
1938–39	New York Rangers, NHL	48	21	20	41	2	7	1	2	3	0
1939–40	New York Rangers, NHL	41	8	16	24	0	11	1	3	4	2
1940–41	New York Rangers, NHL	48	14	11	25	0	3	0	0	0	0
1941–42	New York Rangers, NHL	47	10	24	34	4	5	0	0	0	0
1942–43	New York Rangers, NHL	47	12	21	33	4					
1943–44	Chicago Black Hawks, NHL	50	23	49	72	4	9	4	8	12	0
1944–45	Chicago Black Hawks, NHL	50	23	31	54	0					
1945–46	Chicago Black Hawks, NHL	50	26	24	50	2	4	2	1	3	0
1946–47	Chicago Black Hawks, NHL	52	9	17	26	6					
1947–48	Tulsa Oilers, USHL	64	38	33	71	10	2	0	1	1	0
1948–49	St. Paul Saints, USHL	2	2	0	2	2					
1949–50	St. Paul Saints, USHL	21	7	15	22	2	2	0	0	0	2
1950–51	St. Paul Saints, USHL	23	3	9	12	0					
1951–52	Cincinnati Mohawks, AHL	2	0	0	0	2					
	NHL Totals	483	161	236	397	24	42	10	14	24	2

Won Lady Byng Trophy (1939, 1944)
Won Stanley Cup (1940)

Bill "Cowboy" Cowley

Bill Cowley was one of the top playmaking forwards in NHL history—three times in his 13-year career he led the NHL in assists—who always seemed to know where his linemates were positioned. An unselfish player who always aimed to set a colleague up for a goal before taking a shot himself, he rarely jeopardized his team's fortunes by taking a penalty. Because of his ability to see the whole ice, he was arguably the Wayne Gretzky of his era.

William Mailes Cowley was born in Bristol, Quebec, a small town 45 minutes northwest along the Ottawa River from the nation's capital. He played goal before moving out to the forward line, first with the Cambridge Public School team and later at Ottawa's Glebe Collegiate. The main reason for the shift out of the nets was that Cowley didn't get hold of the puck often enough to suit him.

He first drew attention to himself with his exemplary play with the Primrose and Shamrocks clubs in the Ottawa City Junior League from 1930 to 1932. He graduated to the Shamrocks' senior team full-time in 1932–33, and he proved he could handle the tougher competition. Cowley first put up big numbers with the Halifax Wolverines of the Maritime Senior Hockey League in 1933–34, dominating the scoring race with 25 goals and 50 points in 38 games.

In 1934–35, he embarked on an NHL career with the St. Louis Eagles, who had just relocated from Ottawa. Cowley is the only Hall of Fame player to have begun his career with this club. When the team folded prior to the next season, Cowley was claimed by the Boston Bruins in a dispersal draft. The Bruins, a team stacked with experienced forwards, originally used him as a left wing, but his swift skating and precise passes forced them to move him to center.

Cowley broke through in 1937–38 with 39 points and selection to the NHL First All-Star Team. The following season he recorded a league-high 34 assists. His passing and puck-handling wizardry helped the powerful Bruins squad win the second Stanley Cup in franchise history that year. He formed a lethal combination with Mel "Sudden Death" Hill, who scored an NHL record three overtime game-winners in the semifinals against the Rangers. Each tally was the result of Cowley's playmaking artistry. Two years later, in 1940–41, Cowley won the NHL scoring championship and helped the Bruins win their second Cup in three years.

For a short time he formed the revered Three Gun Line with Roy Conacher and Eddie Wiseman. Cowboy Cowley again topped the

Because of his ability to see the whole ice, Bill Cowley was arguably the Wayne Gretzky of his era.

Cowley, Bill "Cowboy"
C, 5´10˝, 165 lbs, b: Bristol, Que., 6/12/1912, d: 12/31/1993

Season	Club, League	Regular Season					Playoffs				
		GP	G	A	Pts	PIM	GP	G	A	Pts	PIM
1931–32	Ottawa Jr. Shamrocks, City Jr.	2	2	1	3	2	3	4	4	8	2
1931–32	Ottawa Shamrocks, City Sr.						1	0	0	0	0
1932–33	Ottawa Shamrocks, City Sr.	14	7	6	13	24	4	1	0	1	4
1933–34	Halifax Wolverines, MSHL	38	25	25	50	42	6	2	2	4	2
1934–35	St. Louis Eagles, NHL	41	5	7	12	10					
	Tulsa Oilers, AHA	1	0	0	0	5					
1935–36	Boston Bruins, NHL	48	11	10	21	17	2	2	1	3	2
1936–37	Boston Bruins, NHL	46	13	22	35	4	3	0	3	3	0
1937–38	Boston Bruins, NHL	43	17	22	39	8	3	2	0	2	0
1938–39	Boston Bruins, NHL	34	8	34	42	2	12	3	11	14	2
1939–40	Boston Bruins, NHL	48	13	27	40	24	6	0	1	1	7
1940–41	Boston Bruins, NHL	46	17	45	62	16	2	0	0	0	0
1941–42	Boston Bruins, NHL	28	4	23	27	6	5	0	3	3	5
1942–43	Boston Bruins, NHL	48	27	45	72	10	9	1	7	8	4
1943–44	Boston Bruins, NHL	36	30	41	71	12					
1944–45	Boston Bruins, NHL	49	25	40	65	12	7	3	3	6	0
1945–46	Boston Bruins, NHL	26	12	12	24	6	10	1	3	4	2
1946–47	Boston Bruins, NHL	51	13	25	38	16	5	0	2	2	0
1947–48	Ottawa Army, OHA Sr.	*	*	*	*	*	*	*	*	*	*
1948–49	Vancouver Canucks, PCHL	*	*	*	*	*	*	*	*	*	*
	NHL Totals	549	195	353	548	143	64	12	34	46	22

NHL First All-Star Team (1938, 1941, 1943, 1944)
NHL Second All-Star Team (1945)
Won Hart Trophy (1941, 1943)
NHL Scoring Leader (1941)
Won Stanley Cup (1939, 1941)

In the 1940–41 season, Bill Cowley (left) won the NHL scoring championship and helped the Bruins win their second Cup in three years.

NHL in assists in 1940–41 and 1942–43, registering 45 in each year. His 1941 output, recorded during a 48-game schedule, represented a new league standard. After both of these seasons, Cowley was awarded the Hart Trophy and placed on the NHL First All-Star Team. He earned another First Team selection—the fourth of his career—in 1944 after scoring a career-high 30 goals, despite missing 12 games with an injury. Before the injury, Cowley held a comfortable lead in the points race, and although he ended up in seventh place—Herbie Cain won the title with 82 points—his total of 71 points in 36 games hints strongly at what might have been.

Cowley played with the Bruins until the end of the 1946–47 season, and on February 12 of that season he surpassed Syd Howe as the NHL's career point leader. This mark stood for five years until Elmer Lach overtook him. Along the way, Cowley recorded at least 30 assists on five occasions. Clem Kealey of the *Ottawa Journal* saluted his unselfish playmaking, saying, "Cowley has made better and more wings than Boeing." In 549 regular-season matches, he accumulated 548 points and was one of the game's most reliable producers.

After leaving hockey, Cowley worked for a year with the Ontario Department of Lands and Forests before returning to coach hockey in Renfrew, Ontario, and in Vancouver with the Canucks of the old western league. He later opened a successful hotel in Smiths Falls, south of the nation's capital, and ran Ottawa's well-known Elmdale Tavern. He also became a part owner of the Ottawa 67s junior hockey franchise. Cowley was inducted into the Hockey Hall of Fame in 1968. He died of a heart attack in Ottawa on New Year's Eve, 1993.

Gordie Drillon

When he first got to Toronto, they called Gordie Drillon "the gorgeous right winger" and "the boy from the Maritimes." One of the few New Brunswickers to make it to the NHL, "Lefty"—or "Drill," as he was often called—began his career playing in his home town, Moncton, before moving to Toronto in 1933 to play for the Young Rangers. Leafs owner Conn Smythe immediately took a shine to him and offered Drillon a wad of 1,000 $1 bills, wrapped tightly with an elastic band, and a contract. Drillon signed instantly, then ran down the street to deposit the money in the bank, terrified that he might be robbed at any second.

Drillon's NHL career began under the most serendipitous of circumstances. Early in the 1936–37 season, the Leafs decided to give Charlie Conacher, their aging superstar, a brief respite from the schedule and called Drillon up from the American Hockey League's Syracuse Stars. Drillon debuted at right wing on the top line with Syl Apps and Buzz Boll. On his first shift, he split the Montreal defense and set up Boll for a goal. It was an auspicious beginning to a great career. When Boll was injured later in the year, Busher Jackson took the left side and the result was one of the best lines in the league. Although only a rookie, Drillon finished ninth in the league in scoring and was runner-up for both the Lady Byng and Calder trophies.

In his second season, the 23-year-old Drillon got even better. He played on the Leafs' famous DAD Line with Apps and Bob Davidson and his 26 goals and 52 points were both tops in the league.

Although the Leafs lost the Stanley Cup finals to Chicago, Drillon scored a league-high seven goals and eight points in the playoffs. He was also elected to the First All-Star Team, and this year he won the Lady Byng, having incurred only four minutes in penalties over the full 48-game season.

Drillon was consistently the Leafs' most talented scorer, as captain Syl Apps proudly confirmed: "Of all the players with whom I have played and against whom I have played in the National league, none was better around the net than Gordie." Linemate Bob Davidson concurred: "Gordie had a real touch around the net. I've never seen anyone who took better advantage of the chances he got than Gordie. He'd just hang around in front of the net, and before you knew it, the puck was in."

There was one notable exception to this rule. In the spring of 1942 the Leafs made it to the finals to play Detroit for the Cup. But after losing the first three games, Toronto coach Hap Day made some drastic changes to the lineup, one of them being to scratch Drillon in favor of the younger Don Metz. "The Red Wings had forechecked us to death in the first three games," linemate Davidson remembered. "Gordie was a great goal scorer, but he wasn't too strong at digging the puck out of the corners. So Hap moved Don Metz onto our line, and he became one of the stars of the series."

Coach Day was as upset over the benching as Drillon. "I hated to sit out Drillon, but we had to do something," he said. And true enough, the strategy worked. The Leafs made a miraculous come-back to win the Stanley Cup in seven games. Drillon never quite got over the slight, however, and the Leafs sold him to the Montreal Canadiens that summer. In his first season as a Canadien, Drillon played on a line with Buddy O'Connor and Ray Getliffe and scored a career-high 28 goals. At the peak of his career, at age 29, Drillon joined the army and served his country for two years. By the time he was discharged, there was no longer a place for him in the NHL and he moved back to New Brunswick to play senior hockey. All these years later, he's still the last Maple Leaf to lead the NHL in point-scoring.

Although he was out of the glare of the NHL spotlight after the war, he was immensely popular in the Maritimes his whole life. He was considered the finest softball pitcher in New Brunswick's history. He also played competitive tennis, curling and golf, but his legacy will always be at the hockey rink. He was inducted into the Hockey Hall of Fame in 1970.

In his second season in the NHL, Gordie Drillon (right) won the scoring championship with 52 points.

Drillon, Gordie
RW, 6′2″, 178 lbs, b: Moncton, N.B., 10/23/1914, d: 10/22/1986

Season	Club, League	Regular Season					Playoffs				
		GP	G	A	Pts	PIM	GP	G	A	Pts	PIM
1932–33	Moncton Hawks, MSHL	4	13	3	16	0	2	2	1	3	4
	Moncton Swift's, City Sr.	7	11	3	14	*	6	13	4	17	*
1934–35	Toronto Dominions, OHA Sr.	11	12	6	18	2	3	2	1	3	4
1935–36	Pittsburgh Yellow Jackets, EHL	40	22	12	34	4	8	3	2	5	0
1936–37	Toronto Maple Leafs, NHL	41	16	17	33	2	2	0	0	0	0
	Syracuse Stars, AHL	5	2	3	5	0					
1937–38	Toronto Maple Leafs, NHL	48	26	26	52	4	7	7	1	8	2
1938–39	Toronto Maple Leafs, NHL	40	18	16	34	15	10	7	6	13	4
1939–40	Toronto Maple Leafs, NHL	43	21	19	40	13	10	3	1	4	0
1940–41	Toronto Maple Leafs, NHL	42	23	21	44	2	7	3	2	5	2
1941–42	Toronto Maple Leafs, NHL	48	23	18	41	6	9	2	3	5	2
1942–43	Montreal Canadiens, NHL	49	28	22	50	14	5	4	2	6	0
1944–45	Dartmouth RCAF, City Sr.	1	0	1	1	0					
	Walleyfield Braves, QPHL	8	11	4	15	0	14	8	6	14	2
1945–46	Halifax RCAF, City Sr.	3	7	8	15	4					
1946–47	Charlottetown Legionnaires, PEI Sr.	4	10	8	18	16	11	41	12	53	4
1947–48	North Sydney Victorias, CBSHL	2	0	1	1	0					
1949–50	Saint John Beavers, NBSHL	49	48	24	72	40	11	1	4	5	12
	NHL Totals	311	155	139	294	56	50	26	15	41	10

NHL First All-Star Team (1938, 1939)
NHL Second All-Star Team (1942)
Won Lady Byng Trophy (1938)
NHL Scoring Leader (1938)
Won Stanley Cup (1942)

Lynn Patrick

Lynn Patrick is a member of one of hockey's most famous families.

Lynn Patrick is a member of one of hockey's most famous families. His father, Lester, and uncle Frank both had long playing careers that spanned the sport's early decades. The two men went on to own and operate teams, and even whole leagues, establishing a legacy of involvement and innovation.

Lynn didn't take up the game competitively until he was in his 20s, but quickly showed he'd inherited the talent necessary to become one of the National Hockey League's high-scoring forwards. His career was interrupted by World War II, but he'd again follow in the footsteps of his father, becoming a highly respected coach and executive after his playing days.

Lynn Patrick was born in Victoria, British Columbia, in 1912, three years before brother Murray, or "Muzz," as he was universally known. The brothers didn't get a chance to play much hockey in their home town as youngsters because the Victoria Arena burned down while they were in high school. They played other sports instead and established themselves as two of the most gifted athletes in Canadian history. Together they led the Victoria Blue Ribbons to a Canadian basketball championship; Muzz won Canada's amateur heavyweight boxing championship; Lynn became a star on the track and on the rugby pitch, playing wing on a Canadian All-Star team that toured the United States and Japan. Lynn also played pro football for the Winnipeg Blue Bombers and Montreal Winged Wheelers, and at one time he held the record for the longest touchdown pass.

Lester Patrick insisted that his sons further their hockey careers, so they moved east to get more ice time. The boys had lost four or five years of skating because of the fire in Victoria and their other athletic interests, but Lynn was a smooth skater and strong puck carrier and the more refined player of the two. In 1933–34, he joined the Montreal Royals and Lester, as manager of the New York Rangers, monitored his progress. The elder Patrick felt that Lynn could contribute at the NHL level but was reluctant to sign him for fear of being accused of favoritism. After a game between the Rangers and his Maple Leafs, Toronto owner Conn Smythe met Lester in a hotel lobby and warned that if the Rangers didn't place Lynn and Muzz on their negotiation list, the Leafs would snap them up. Lester was forced to act, and and so Lynn made his Ranger debut in 1934–35 while Muzz, a defenseman, joined the eastern league's New York Crescents that same year.

Many observers still felt Lynn's rapid ascent to the NHL was a case of nepotism, pointing out that he hadn't even been on skates until the age of 16, but the left wing soon silenced all doubters. He was a solid and workmanlike player in his first five years in the league. Muzz joined the team in 1938 and together they helped the Rangers win the Stanley Cup in 1940.

Patrick, Lynn
C/LW, 6´1˝, 192 lbs, b: Victoria, B.C., 2/3/1912, d: 1/26/1980

Season	Club, League	Regular Season					Playoffs				
		GP	G	A	Pts	PIM	GP	G	A	Pts	PIM
1933–34	Montreal Royals, City Sr.	15	5	3	8	4	2	0	0	0	0
1934–35	New York Rangers, NHL	48	9	13	22	17	4	2	2	4	0
1935–36	New York Rangers, NHL	48	11	14	25	29					
1936–37	New York Rangers, NHL	45	8	16	24	23	9	3	0	3	2
1937–38	New York Rangers, NHL	48	15	19	34	24	3	0	1	1	2
1938–39	New York Rangers, NHL	35	8	21	29	25	7	1	1	2	0
1939–40	New York Rangers, NHL	48	12	16	28	34	12	2	2	4	4
1940–41	New York Rangers, NHL	48	20	24	44	12	3	1	0	1	14
1941–42	New York Rangers, NHL	47	32	22	54	18	6	1	0	1	0
1942–43	New York Rangers, NHL	50	22	39	61	28					
1945–46	New York Rangers, NHL	38	8	6	14	30					
1946–47	New Haven Ramblers, AHL	16	2	6	8	16	3	1	0	1	2
	NHL Totals	455	145	190	335	240	44	10	6	16	22

NHL First All-Star Team (1942)
NHL Second All-Star Team (1943)
Won Lester Patrick Trophy (1989)
Won Stanley Cup (1940)

Over the next three seasons, Lynn became one of the game's superstars, substantially increasing his point production each year. He led the league in goals in 1941–42 with 32, often playing on a line with Bryan Hextall and Phil Watson. He was second in the league in total points, two behind Hextall's total of 56, and Patrick was selected to the league's First All-Star Team. The next year he increased his point total to 61 in 50 games, good for fourth overall in the NHL and a spot on the Second All-Star Team.

Patrick was involved in one of the era's more humorous incidents against the Toronto Maple Leafs during the 1942–43 season. Ranger goalie Steve Buzinski, in one of his few NHL games, was seemingly knocked unconscious in a goalmouth scramble. Behind the net, Patrick complained strenuously to the referee that Leaf winger Bob Davidson had high-sticked the netminder. When Davidson skated over to assert his innocence, saying it was the puck that had done the damage, Buzinski suddenly sat bolt upright and said, "That's a damn lie!" before falling back to the ice and closing his eyes. Patrick was laughing so hard he could barely skate to the bench.

Lynn Patrick hadn't even been on skates until the age of 16, but he became one of the game's outstanding scorers and playmakers.

Just as he was coming into his own after such a late start, becoming one of the game's outstanding scorers and playmakers, Patrick left the NHL to spend two years in the Canadian military during World War II. He returned to play one season with the Rangers, but he was no longer the player he'd been. He spent part of the 1946–47 season with the New Haven Ramblers before returning to New York in the middle of 1948–49 to take the Blueshirts' coaching reins.

In 1949–50, Patrick's Rangers made it to the Stanley Cup finals—a hard-fought series the Detroit Red Wings won in the second overtime period of game seven. Lynn also helped his father run the Victoria Cougars, a Pacific Coast league team they co-owned. In 1950–51, Patrick took the job as head coach of the Boston Bruins and the team made the playoffs in each of his four full seasons, advancing to the finals in 1952 and 1953. During the 1954–55 season, he moved into the GM's office in Boston, where he stayed until 1966. He accepted the St. Louis Blues' invitation to be the team's first coach and general manager when they entered the league in 1967, but after 16 games he handed the coaching duties to Scotty Bowman. The St. Louis squad that Patrick assembled made the Stanley Cup finals in each of its first three years in the NHL.

In the 1970s, a third generation of Patricks entered the NHL in the form of Lynn's sons Craig and Glenn. Craig has had a long NHL career as a player, coach and general manager and has earned a spot in the U.S. Hockey Hall of Fame. Lynn remained in the Blues front office until 1977, when the team was sold and he, along with most of the front office staff, was replaced. He also took over behind the bench briefly in 1975–76, following the dismissal of coach Garry Young.

On January 26, 1980, Lynn Patrick suffered a heart attack after a game between the Blues and the Colorado Rockies. He died soon afterward at the age of 68. Sadly, he didn't live to see the fruits of Craig's first foray into management as assistant coach and assistant general manager of the 1980 U.S. Olympic squad that pulled off the Miracle on Ice and won the gold medal. In June of that year, Lynn Patrick was inducted posthumously into the Hockey Hall of Fame.

Bryan Hextall Sr.

Bryan Hextall Sr. was the first of a long line of his family to play in the NHL.

During his decade in the NHL, right winger Bryan Hextall was a proficient scorer whose exemplary conduct on and off the ice earned him much admiration. He scored 187 goals and contributed valuable leadership in a career spent entirely with the New York Rangers. He was the first of a long line of family members who played in the NHL—his son Bryan, his nephew Dennis and his grandson Ron have all had careers in the NHL.

Born in Grenfell, Saskatchewan, Bryan Sr. grew up in Poplar Point, Manitoba, where he contributed to a provincial juvenile championship in 1929–30. This was followed by a short stint with the Winnipeg Monarchs. After leading the Portage Terriers in scoring in 1932–33, he turned pro with the Vancouver Lions of the North West Hockey League. In his second full season as a Lion, 1935–36, he dominated the competition with 27 goals in 40 games and helped the club to the league title. His coach on the West Coast was Guy Patrick, brother of the more famous Lester and Frank.

Hextall's next stop was the Philadelphia Ramblers, where he led the American Hockey League with 29 goals in 18 games. It was obvious to the Rangers that he was ready for the NHL, and his emergence as a star helped fill the void that had been left by the disbanding of the popular Bread Line (Bill and Bun Cook and Frank Boucher) in the fall of 1936.

During his first full season, 1937–38, Hextall scored 17 times and showed all the poise of a veteran. By 1939–40, he was among the top young stars in the game. He scored a league-high 24 goals in the regular season before experiencing his most memorable playoffs. The Rangers faced the Toronto Maple Leafs in the 1940 finals and Hextall fired three goals past Turk Broda in game two to lead his club to a 6–2 win and 2–0 series lead. New York was leading the series three games to two and the score in game six was tied when Phil Watson scored off a Hextall rebound and appeared to have given the Blueshirts the championship. Unfortunately, referee Mickey Ion spotted Hextall in the goal crease and nullified the goal.

In overtime, Hex wasted little time making amends, scoring the Cup-winning goal with help from linemates Phil Watson and Dutch Hiller to bring the Rangers their third title. It was the first time in NHL history that the Stanley Cup had been won in overtime. It's also worthy of note that the Rangers had finished eight points ahead of the Leafs in the standings, but because the circus had squeezed them out of Madison Square Garden, games three

Hextall, Bryan Sr.
RW, 5′10″, 180 lbs, b: Grenfell, Sask., 7/31/1913, d: 7/25/1984

Season	Club, League	Regular Season					Playoffs				
		GP	G	A	Pts	PIM	GP	G	A	Pts	PIM
1933–34	Vancouver Lions, NWHL	5	2	0	2	0					
1934–35	Vancouver Lions, NWHL	32	14	10	24	27	8	0	0	0	10
1935–36	Vancouver Lions, NWHL	40	27	9	36	65	7	1	2	3	15
1936–37	Philadelphia Ramblers, AHL	18	29	23	52	34	6	2	4	6	6
	New York Rangers, NHL	3	0	1	1	0					
1937–38	New York Rangers, NHL	48	17	4	21	6	3	2	0	2	0
1938–39	New York Rangers, NHL	48	20	15	35	18	7	0	1	1	4
1939–40	New York Rangers, NHL	48	24	15	39	52	12	4	3	7	11
1940–41	New York Rangers, NHL	48	26	18	44	16	3	0	1	1	0
1941–42	New York Rangers, NHL	48	24	32	56	30	6	1	1	2	4
1942–43	New York Rangers, NHL	50	27	32	59	28					
1943–44	New York Rangers, NHL	50	21	33	54	41					
1944–45	St. Catharines Saints, OHA Sr.	1	0	1	1	0					
1945–46	New York Rangers, NHL	3	0	1	1	0					
1946–47	New York Rangers, NHL	60	20	10	30	18					
1947–48	New York Rangers, NHL	43	8	14	22	18	6	1	3	4	0
1948–49	Cleveland — Washington, AHL	57	18	23	41	16					
	NHL Totals	449	187	175	362	227	37	8	9	17	19

NHL First All-Star Team (1940, 1941, 1942)
NHL Second All-Star Team (1943)
NHL Scoring Leader (1942)
Won Stanley Cup (1940)

through six had to be played at Maple Leaf Gardens. Hextall described the resulting euphoria: "There are Rangers swarming all over me. They give me a worse beating in about 10 seconds than the Leafs have given me in the whole series."

Hextall again led all NHL snipers in 1940–41 with 26 goals. A year later he won his first scoring title with 56 points in 48 games. Hextall bettered that total by three after the introduction of the center red line in 1942–43 but slipped to sixth in the scoring race. In all, he reached the 20-goal mark for six straight years from 1938 to 1944. His uncanny ability to stickhandle in close quarters and place himself in a position to score made Hextall one of the league's toughest forwards to check. The gifted winger was selected to the NHL First All-Star Team for three straight years from 1940 to 1942 and made the Second Team in 1943.

Bryan Hextall Sr. (left) scored the first overtime Cup-clincher in the history of the NHL.

The 1947–48 season was Hextall's last in the NHL. He split the next season between Cleveland and Washington of the AHL before hanging up his skates for good. He continued to oversee the two Saskatchewan wheat farms he'd purchased early in his career. He settled into his retirement in Poplar Point, where he operated a lumber yard, and remained attached to the game as a coach and official in the local minor hockey system.

On July 25, 1984, Hextall died at his home of a massive heart attack. He'd been inducted into the Hockey Hall of Fame in 1969, and at the time of this writing, his 1942 scoring title was the last to be won by a member of the New York Rangers.

Neil "Frosty" Colville

Known for his consistently high standard of play, Neil Colville excelled as both a forward and defenseman during a decade-long NHL career. He was also a fine leader who served as the captain of the New York Rangers for six seasons and helped the club win the Stanley Cup in 1940.

Between 1929 and 1934, Colville starred on various junior teams in his native Edmonton, Alberta. He led his league in scoring during the 1933–34 season—his last as a junior—and led the Edmonton Athletic Club to the Memorial Cup finals against Toronto's St. Michael's. The following year he graduated to the New York Crescents of the Eastern Hockey League, where he tore up the league with 24 goals in 21 matches and helped the team win the league championship.

Neil Colville centered his brother Mac and Alex Shibicky in the second incarnation of the Bread Line.

The New York Rangers signed Colville as a free agent in October 1935 and gave him a one-game trial. He spent his first professional season with the Philadelphia Ramblers of the Can-Am league, where he easily made the adjustment to superior competition. In fact he was leading the team in scoring with six weeks to go in the regular season when an injury ended his year.

Colville joined the Broadway Blueshirts on a full-time basis in 1936–37 and was placed on a line with his brother Mac and Alex Shibicky. The trio clicked and remained intact for six years during which the three men were hailed for their nifty passing and accurate shooting. Neil was the backbone of the line, for it was his deceptive body motion that baffled defenders and created openings

Neil Colville (number 6) was the backbone of the Bread Line since it was his deceptive moves that baffled defenders and created openings for the others.

for the others. The line was called "the Bread Line" because it was formed at the height of the Great Depression—it was also the name of an earlier Ranger unit comprising Bill and Bun Cook and Frank Boucher.

Colville broke into the top 10 in scoring for the first time in 1937–38, then again the following year when he gained a place on the NHL Second All-Star Team. The Bread Line was a huge factor in New York's Stanley Cup win in 1940 and a regular-season crown in 1941–42. In 1942 Colville and his two linemates all joined the Canadian Armed Forces and were stationed in Ottawa. While completing his assignment, Neil captained the Ottawa Commandos to the 1943 Allan Cup as Canadian senior champions. This was followed by a two-year term as a navigator for the Royal Canadian Air Force.

Following his discharge at the end of World War II, Colville returned to the NHL and shifted to the Rangers' defense. Unfortunately, his release from the Air Force came several days after a ruling that hockey players with no overseas service who weren't on NHL active lists before January 10, 1945, couldn't obtain cross-border privileges. For a short time, therefore, he could only play for New York in matches that took place in Canada.

Once Frosty joined the team for all its games in 1945–46, the Rangers named him captain, a position he held for four years. According to Gene Ward of the *New York Daily News*, "With Neil as captain of the Rangers, it was like having a second coach out there on the ice." In 1948 he was named to the NHL Second All-Star Team as a defenseman.

Colville played his last 14 NHL games in 1948–49 before he was sent to the New Haven Ramblers of the AHL. There he took over the coaching reins from Lynn Patrick, who'd become the new bench boss of the Rangers. He played one more season in Connecticut before retiring in 1950. A chronic groin injury prevented him from continuing. In 1950–51, he was again called upon to replace Patrick, this time at the major-league level. The 36-year-old was the youngest coach in the NHL at the time, but he was forced to step down 23 games into the 1951–52 season because of recurring ulcers.

Colville, Neil "Frosty"
C/D, 5′11″, 175 lbs, b: Edmonton, Alta., 8/4/1914, d: 12/26/1987

Season	Club, League	Regular Season					Playoffs				
		GP	G	A	Pts	PIM	GP	G	A	Pts	PIM
1934–35	New York Crescents, EHL	21	24	11	35	16	8	8	4	12	2
1935–36	New York Rangers, NHL	1	0	0	0	0					
	Philadelphia Ramblers, Can-Am	35	15	16	31	8	4	0	2	2	0
1936–37	New York Rangers, NHL	45	10	18	28	33	9	3	3	6	0
1937–38	New York Rangers, NHL	45	17	19	36	11	3	0	1	1	0
1938–39	New York Rangers, NHL	47	18	19	37	12	7	0	2	2	2
1939–40	New York Rangers, NHL	48	19	19	38	22	12	2	7	9	18
1940–41	New York Rangers, NHL	48	14	28	42	28	3	1	1	2	0
1941–42	New York Rangers, NHL	48	8	25	33	37	6	0	5	5	6
1942–43	Ottawa Commandos, QSHL	22	12	30	42	32	12	14	14	28	17
	Ottawa Army, City Sr.	12	11	12	23	4					
1944–45	New York Rangers, NHL	4	0	1	1	2					
	Winnipeg RCAF, City Sr.	6	5	4	9	4					
	Ottawa — Quebec, QSHL	5	1	2	3	0	7	2	5	7	4
1945–46	New York Rangers, NHL	49	5	4	9	25					
1946–47	New York Rangers, NHL	60	4	16	20	16					
1947–48	New York Rangers, NHL	55	4	12	16	25	6	1	0	1	6
1948–49	New York Rangers, NHL	14	0	5	5	2					
	New Haven Ramblers, AHL	11	0	3	3	8					
1949–50	New Haven Ramblers, AHL	17	3	4	7	13					
	NHL Totals	464	99	166	265	213	46	7	19	26	32

NHL Second All-Star Team (1939, 1940, 1948)
Won Stanley Cup (1940)

Colville later ran a trucking company, then headed north to Yukon to manage a closed-circuit television station. He eventually settled in Vancouver and was inducted into the Hockey Hall of Fame in 1967. Colville was later honored with a place on the Hall of Fame selection committee, which he held until his health failed. In 1984 he lost a leg to cancer but regained some mobility thanks to an artificial limb. A popular figure in the Vancouver area, Colville always gave up time in support of minor hockey in the area and joined the city's Benevolent Hockey Association.

Frank "Mr. Zero" Brimsek

Netminder Frank Brimsek was one of the greatest players ever to hail from the United States. In a decade of NHL service, the accurately nicknamed "Mr. Zero" registered 80 shutouts and won 252 regular-season games. He led all netminders in shutouts, goals-against average and wins twice each and backstopped Boston to Stanley Cup wins in 1939 and 1941. Known as somewhat of an eccentric, Brimsek was often observed during a game checking his pad straps with obsessive regularity. He also detested posing for photos because he feared the flash bulbs would damage his eyesight.

The Minnesota native starred with his hometown Eveleth Rangers in 1934–35, then joined the formidable Pittsburgh Yellow Jackets of the USAHA later that same year. Steeltown agreed with Brimsek, as he recorded 14 wins in 16 matches. The next season he, and the entire team, switched to the pro ranks in the Eastern Hockey League. The promising youngster registered a league-high 20 wins and eight shutouts during the 1935–36 schedule. At the conclusion of the season, he was placed on the EHL First All-Star Team and presented the George L. Davis Jr. Trophy for allowing the fewest goals.

Next it was off to the Providence Reds, where he led the AHL with 48 games played and a 1.75 goals-against mark. His unlimited potential convinced the Boston Bruins to sign him to replace their aging incumbent, Tiny Thompson. During his rookie season, Brimsek showed no sign of buckling under the pressure of replacing an NHL legend. In one of the greatest first-year performances ever, he was in goal

Frank Brimsek, nicknamed "Mr. Zero," registered 80 shutouts and won 252 regular-season games.

Brimsek, Frank "Mr. Zero"
G, 5'9", 170 lbs, b: Eveleth, MN, 9/26/1915, d: 11/12/1998

Season	Club, League	Regular Season				Playoffs			
		GP	Mins	GA	Avg	GP	Mins	GA	Avg
1934–35	Pittsburgh Yellow Jackets, USAHA	16	960	39	2.44				
1935–36	Pittsburgh Yellow Jackets, EHL	38	2280	74	1.95	8	480	19	2.36
1936–37	Pittsburgh Yellow Jackets, EHL	47	2820	142	3.02				
1937–38	Providence Reds, AHL	48	2950	86	1.75	7	515	16	1.86
	New Haven Eagles, AHL					1	93	3	1.94
1938–39	Boston Bruins, NHL	43	2610	68	1.56	12	863	18	1.25
	Providence Red, AHL	9	570	18	1.89				
1939–40	Boston Bruins, NHL	48	2950	98	1.99	6	360	15	2.50
1940–41	Boston Bruins, NHL	48	3040	102	2.01	11	678	23	2.04
1941–42	Boston Bruins, NHL	47	2930	115	2.35	5	307	16	3.13
1942–43	Boston Bruins, NHL	50	3000	176	3.52	9	560	33	3.54
1945–46	Boston Bruins, NHL	34	2040	111	3.26	10	651	29	2.67
1946–47	Boston Bruins, NHL	60	3600	175	2.92	5	343	16	2.80
1947–48	Boston Bruins, NHL	60	3600	168	2.80	5	317	20	3.79
1948–49	Boston Bruins, NHL	54	3240	147	2.72	5	316	16	3.04
1949–50	Chicago Black Hawks, NHL	70	4200	244	3.49				
	NHL Totals	514	31210	1404	2.70	68	4395	186	2.54

NHL First All-Star Team (1939, 1942)
NHL Second All-Star Team (1940, 1941, 1943, 1946, 1947, 1948)
Won Vezina Trophy (1939, 1942)
Won Calder Trophy (1939)
Won Stanley Cup (1939, 1941)

for 33 Boston wins and topped the league with 10 shutouts and a 1.56 goals-against mark. In addition, he posted two shutout streaks of more than 200 minutes each. During the playoffs, he recorded eight wins in 12 games as Boston won its second Stanley Cup. Brimsek's heroics between the pipes were confirmed when he was awarded the Calder Trophy.

Frank Brimsek detested having his photo taken as he feared the flash would damage his eyes.

Brimsek was a classic stand-up goalie whose confidence on the ice threw off many a shooter. On breakaways and penalty shots, he'd often lean back calmly against his net as the foe approached. But he wasn't a passive figure while guarding his cage—Brimsek used his custom-made heavy stick to knock the puck off opposition sticks or to take the feet out from under someone who took too many liberties around his goal.

In 1941 his stellar goalkeeping contributed to the Bruins' second Stanley Cup in three years. That year he won his first of two Vezina awards and was selected to the NHL First All-Star Team. The 1941–42 season arguably spoke the loudest for Brimsek's importance to the Bruins. After the famous Kraut Line of Milt Schmidt, Bobby Bauer and Woody Dumart enlisted in the Canadian Armed Forces, Mr. Zero almost single-handedly guided his club to a spot in the playoffs. In 1943 World War II interrupted Brimsek's career and he spent a year each with the Coast Guard Cutters team and in the military.

Brimsek returned to the Bruins in 1945–46, and considering the layoff, he did well to earn selection to the NHL Second All-Star Team. He played three more years with Boston, but the team wasn't as strong as it had been before the war. Brimsek's netminding heroics kept the Bruins in many games during this period, and in 1948 he finished second to the Rangers' Buddy O'Connor in the Hart Trophy voting.

In September 1949 the Bruins sold Brimsek to the Chicago Black Hawks. He played all 70 games in the expanded NHL schedule behind a weak squad. He finally retired after the team failed to qualify for the post-season. Although he didn't go out on a high note, his superb record over the years wasn't forgotten. Brimsek registered nine 20-win seasons and logged over 31,000 minutes of ice time.

After he retired, Brimsek worked as a freight train engineer for 25 years. In 1966 he was inducted into the Hockey Hall of Fame and, fittingly, Mr. Zero was also one of the first players elected to the United States Hockey Hall of Fame, located in his home town of Eveleth, Minnesota. The netminding legend ended up settling in Virginia, Minnesota, a few miles down the road. He died unexpectedly at his home on November 11, 1998, at the age of 83.

Bobby Bauer

Robert Theodore Bauer successfully fused skillful play and sportsmanship during his 10 years with the Boston Bruins, earning much acclaim as the right wing on the famed Kraut Line with Milt Schmidt and Woody Dumart. Bauer amassed 260 points in 327 regular-season games in a career that was interrupted by his service with the Royal Canadian Air Force during World War II.

A native of Waterloo, Ontario, Bauer played city league hockey before moving to Toronto. Once there, he split the 1932–33 season between the British Consols and the National Sea Fleas of the Toronto Mercantile League. Bauer helped the latter outfit win the city championship that year. This was followed by a rewarding stint with the St. Michael's College juniors in 1933–34, and Bauer's stellar play was an integral factor in the club's Memorial Cup triumph that season. He spent the 1934–35 season near his home town with the Kitchener Greenshirts, where he contributed to an OHA title.

The Boston Bruins became aware of Bauer's talent and acted quickly to sign him. He was assigned to play for the Boston Cubs of the Can-Am league, where the parent club could closely monitor his development. Bauer didn't look out of place in his first pro season in 1935–36, recording 15 goals and 28 points in 48 games. The next year, with the American Hockey League's Providence Reds, he scored 14 times and was teamed for the first time with Milt Schmidt and Woody Dumart to form a potent trio. During that season he also scored a goal in his only appearance with the Bruins.

In 1942, Bobby Bauer and linemates Wilt Schmidt and Woody Dumart became the first big-league players to join the RCAF.

In 1937–38, Bauer enjoyed a promising rookie season, becoming an integral part of the Boston lineup and scoring 20 goals. That same year the Kraut Line made its big-league debut and played a key role in Boston's finishing in first place in the NHL's American Division. During each of the following three seasons, Boston finished first in the NHL standings, winning the Stanley Cup in 1939 and 1941 while Bauer won consecutive Lady Byng awards in 1940 and 1941.

Toward the end of the 1941–42 season, Bauer—along with linemates Schmidt and Dumart—became the first big-league players to join the Royal Canadian Air Force. Initially they were based in Ottawa and continued to play hockey for the Ottawa Commandos, who were affiliated with the Quebec Senior Hockey League. That spring they led the club to the Allan Cup championship. The following year the Kraut Line was stationed in Halifax, where they helped that team capture the city championship. The next season this squad continued to function independently and play exhibition matches. Bauer and his linemates spent 1943 to 1945 engaged in combat on behalf of their country.

Bauer returned to Boston for two more seasons, from 1945 to 1947. In his first year back, his post-season play was particularly strong as he aided the Bruins' drive to the Stanley Cup finals, where they came up short against the Montreal Canadiens. In 1946–47, he enjoyed a personal best 30-goal season and won his third Lady Byng Trophy.

Retiring in 1947, Bauer moved closer to home to coach the Guelph Biltmore juniors. Later that year, he regained his amateur status and embarked on a successful career with the senior Kitchener-Waterloo Dutchmen. Bauer's guiding influence took the squad to the OHA

Bauer, Bobby
RW, 5′6″, 150 lbs, b: Waterloo, Ont., 2/16/1915, d: 9/16/1964

Season	Club, League	Regular Season					Playoffs				
		GP	G	A	Pts	PIM	GP	G	A	Pts	PIM
1935–36	Boston Cubs, Can-Am	48	15	13	28	8					
1936–37	Boston Bruins, NHL	1	1	0	1	0	1	0	0	0	0
	Providence Reds, AHL	41	14	4	18	2	2	0	1	1	0
1937–38	Boston Bruins, NHL	48	20	14	34	9	3	0	0	0	2
1938–39	Boston Bruins, NHL	48	13	18	31	4	12	3	2	5	0
1939–40	Boston Bruins, NHL	48	17	26	43	2	6	1	0	1	2
1940–41	Boston Bruins, NHL	48	17	22	39	2	11	2	2	4	0
1941–42	Boston Bruins, NHL	36	13	22	35	11					
	Ottawa RCAF, City Sr.						6	7	6	13	4
1942–43	Halifax RCAF, City Sr.	7	12	8	20	0	5	7	5	12	0
1945–46	Boston Bruins, NHL	39	11	10	21	4	10	4	3	7	2
1946–47	Boston Bruins, NHL	58	30	24	54	4	5	1	1	2	0
1947–48	Kitchener Dutchmen, OHA Sr.	8	8	7	15	22	10	5	4	9	6
1948–49	Kitchener Dutchmen, OHA Sr.	31	17	21	38	13	12	4	4	8	0
1949–50	Kitchener Dutchmen, OHA Sr.	23	10	14	24	9	9	1	2	3	2
1951–52	Boston Bruins, NHL	1	1	1	2	0					
	Kitchener Dutchmen, OHA Sr.	37	8	10	18	14	1	0	1	1	0
	NHL Totals	327	123	137	260	36	48	11	8	19	6

NHL Second All-Star Team (1939, 1940, 1941, 1947)
Won Lady Byng Trophy (1940, 1941, 1947)
Won Stanley Cup (1939,1941)

senior finals in three straight years between 1948 and 1950. He retired as a player after the 1949–50 season but returned for one game with Boston in 1951–52. On March 18, 1952, Bauer scored a goal and an assist as the Kraut Line reunited for one night to lead the Bruins to victory over Chicago.

Bauer's talent for communicating with players was evident throughout his career, so it was a natural progression for him to step into a coaching position after his playing days were over. Beginning in 1952, he went on to serve as general manager, coach and president of the Kitchener-Waterloo Dutchmen. Under his tutelage the club won two OHA championships and two Allan Cup championships. The second triumph resulted in the Dutchmen being chosen to represent Canada at the 1956 Winter Olympics in Cortina, Italy, where they earned the bronze medal. When he returned to Canada, Bauer gave up coaching, but four years later he was talked into guiding the Dutchmen at the 1960 Games in Squaw Valley, California, where they won silver.

After the 1960 Olympics, Bauer passed along his experience during countless sessions with his younger brother, Father David Bauer. Prior to his death on September 16, 1964, Bobby Bauer helped put together Canada's national team program. He was inducted into the Hockey Hall of Fame in 1996.

1885–1939

Europe Catches
the Hockey Bug

*G*iven the links explored in earlier chapters between hockey and Lord Stanley's sons, we have already seen that Great Britain was the first country in Europe to adopt and promote the new game far and wide. Students at Oxford and Cambridge played the first game in the Old World in 1885 (10 years before the one at Buckingham Palace involving Lord Stanley's sons and the future George V), and by 1895 there were five teams in England and Scotland. The first artificial ice rink in Europe was built in London in 1903 and an English team, the London Canadians, won the first European Championship. So it seems only logical that Great Britain would be one of the four founding members of the International Ice Hockey Federation.

In the 1910s and 1920s, hockey came from the Canadian rivers and lakes to the mountains of Europe.

Some time in 1908, a contributing editor to the Prague papers Illustrated Courier *and* Vox Populi, *Emil Prochazka, met a French journalist (and speed-skating champion of France who was one of the first advocates of ice sports in that country) named Louis Magnus. Prochazka described Magnus as obsessed with the idea of popularizing Canadian ice hockey in Europe. Magnus told Prochazka that an organization for international hockey was soon to be founded, and Prochazka immediately sent a message to Paris requesting that the Czech Hockey Union be accepted as one of the founders of the IIHF (though oddly enough there was no Czech hockey let alone a league at the time). In all likelihood, the ambitious Prochazka, an ardent fan of the Prague bandy club Slavia, was positioning himself to become the head of a yet to be founded hockey union to ensure Slavia certain privileges in the new sporting event. And Prochazka was partly successful; the Czechs were recognized as "co-founders" of the IIHF. But he never did make it to the president's chair.*

The IIHF Constituent Congress was held in Paris in May 1908 and Great Britain, France, Switzerland and Belgium were represented. Louis Magnus was elected its first president and

Czechoslovakia duly joined the four founders. Russia was officially a member from 1911 to 1917, but that was the extent of its participation in Europe's hockey life.

A typical team from the early years of European hockey.

Representatives of the Czech clubs met in a pub by the name of Charles IV four times in the winter of 1908, and men with more influence than Prochazka took over the leadership of the Czech Hockey Union when it was finally established on December 11, 1908. Among them was Josef Gruss, a professor at Charles University and the first to translate the game's rules into Czech, who also became the first goaltender of the first team in the country's history—a team that attended the first international tournament in Europe in Chamonix, France, in 1909 even though its players had to pay their own way and borrow sweaters from the Slavia team.

Teams from Great Britain, France, Germany, Belgium and Switzerland as well as Czechoslovakia participated in that first tournament, which was in essence a trial European championship. Josef Gruss would later remember it thus:

"We set out for France without any kind of preparation, having taken along with us only bandy equipment. I considered it a stroke of luck when I was able to get hold of a goalie stick in Chamonix. The victory in Chamonix went to the London Princes Club, while we, having lost all of our games, ended up in last place. However, after the tournament, Louis Magnus wrote, 'The Czech players, when they get accustomed to Canadian hockey sticks and learn how to shoot on goal, will become serious competitors.'"

The first true European Championship was played in Switzerland in 1910. Four teams participated and the players from Great Britain won, as expected. The London Princes Club beat the runners-up from Germany 1–0, the last-place Swiss 5–1 and tied the third-place Belgians 1–1.

The first European Championship was organized in Switzerland in 1910.

But the words of IIHF president Magnus proved prophetic. The Czechs debuted as an actual hockey team in the second European Championship, held for the first time on an indoor rink in Berlin in 1911, and managed to become the new champions even though they were plagued with a wide range of problems.

The Czech players arrived in Berlin early on the day of the tournament. Disembarking from a third-class coach with wooden seats, they learned they had to be on the ice against the Swiss in six hours. Worse, they were to play Germany at 10 o'clock that same night. Nevertheless the Czechs won both games with scores of 13–0 and 4–1, respectively, and the next day they won the deciding game against the Belgians 3–0.

For the next three years, the Czechs were rated number one on the continent. Confident that they were still the best in the Old World, the English players didn't even bother to participate in those early tournaments on the mainland. Correspondingly, the Czechs won the next two

European Championships—though the results of one were subsequently annulled and they let the Belgians squeak by them in 1913 on goals scored.

Competitive European hockey was interrupted by World War I and it was 1920 before Europeans once again took up the game at the Olympic Summer Games at Antwerp. They were about to cross sticks with the pioneers of the game for the first time ever, and the question on everybody's mind was to what extent the hockey players of the Old World had mastered the North American game.

Statistically and by all other accounts the results were decisive. The Canadians (in the shape of the Winnipeg Falcons) walloped the national team of Czechoslovakia 15–0 and the Swedish team 12–1 while the U.S. team pounded the Swiss 29–0, the Swedes 7–0 and the Czechs 16–0. The final result was 79–1 in favor of the North Americans and the Europeans had good reason to be glum. The Canadians edged out the Americans 2–0 to become the first world and Olympic champions, but the second title was unofficial since the Olympics in Antwerp were technically Summer Games and the first official Olympic ice hockey tournament was played at the 1924 Winter Olympics in Chamonix.

In the four years that passed between those Olympic events, the balance of forces in world hockey remained the same. At the 1924 Winter Olympics, the Canadians (this time in the shape of the Toronto Granites) outscored the national teams of Sweden, Czechoslovakia, Switzerland and Great Britain 104–2 overall while the American team went 72–0 against Great Britain, France, Belgium and Sweden. And the Canadians once again beat their North American neighbors 6–1 to become the first official Olympic champions. But beginning in the 1920s, the ranks of European hockey began to shift radically and teams that had dominated the game since it was first played there were slowly ousted by newcomers.

In the beginning of the century, Canada didn't select national All-Star teams made up of the top talent from around the country but sent the top amateur club to wear the national colors at international games.

Sweden's love affair with hockey is due to a string of unusual circumstances. In 1919, a prosperous movie mogul arrived in Stockholm with the intention of building a network of picture palaces in the country. Raoul La Mat's project was so successful that the American businessman decided he'd also introduce a new sport after he attended some bandy games in the Swedish championship. Bandy had been popular in the country since 1896, and La Mat soon decided that players who could cope with the stick and the ball it employed would adapt readily enough to a puck.

And La Mat was persistent. He managed to convince the Swedish Olympic Committee to send a hockey team to the Olympic Summer Games in Antwerp, but that was only half the battle. As always, financing was the other. In the end, the players were given third-class coach seats on the train to Antwerp, with porridge and boiled eggs for breakfast.

The American mogul was new to organizing the game, so the Swedes sought a homegrown specialist. One of their own who had conducted business in Germany was soon found for the role. Nils Molander had played for the Berliner Schlittschuh-Club hockey club and was thus more familiar with the game than La Mat. And so it was that Molander set out for Antwerp to participate in an exhibition tournament that was subsequently recognized as the first World Championship with the 10 best Swedish bandy players from Stockholm, Uppsala and Gavle.

The Swedes had beginner's luck in Antwerp. The Americans made a gift of hockey sticks to the team managed by their compatriot, and even if the gifts didn't help much against the team from Canada (which beat them 12–1) and the one from the States (ditto 7–0), they came quite close to taking third place. The Czechs were already three-time European champions, but they barely triumphed over the Swedes by a score of 1–0. And in regular tournament play, the Swedes whipped Belgium 8–0, France 4–0 and Switzerland by the same score.

As a reward for this plucky debut, the first official postwar championship on the continent was held in Stockholm in the winter of 1921. A unique championship, it included a mere two participants, none of the familiar faces, and a single game decided the outcome. When the Swedes took it from the Czech national team by a score of 6–4, it marked the beginning of a long and highly successful era for the Swedish national team, Tre Kronor, that continues to this day.

Team Canada at the opening ceremony of the 1928 Winter Olympics in St. Moritz, Switzerland.

The new sport took hold in Sweden with the establishment of seven boot leagues. A Swedish Ice Hockey Union was created as early as 1922, and it immediately kicked off a national championship. For a long time, hockey was dominated by seven Stockholm clubs while the rest of the country remained loyal to bandy. But after the Stockholm players became European champions in 1923 (and runners-up in 1922 and 1924 to a newly minted Tre Kronor), hockey began to usurp bandy and establish a foothold even in the most remote regions.

As previously noted, not all of the IIHF founding countries participated in the prewar European Championships, including France, which had been the first on the continent to master hockey after Canadian pro George Meagher helped popularize the game there in 1894. The first official game was played in 1903 between teams from Paris and Lyons, les Patineurs de Paris became the first officially registered hockey club in Europe, and in 1904 France became the second European country (after Great Britain) to hold a national championship.

For 20 years after that, France largely ignored the European Championships. When they finally took an interest, however, they sparkled. In 1923 they ranked second in Europe after the Swedes and a year later they took first place by beating Tre Kronor 2–1 in the final game. And that was both the beginning and the end of the heady days of French hockey. In the 75 years since then, the French haven't once made the list of top 10 in the world.

A similar fate was in store for another IIHF founder, Switzerland. Swiss players also began by showing potential. The Swiss were the first to hold "open" championships with foreign teams, starting with the Germans; the first to build rinks with artificial ice; and in 1926 they became European champions. And unlike the French, the Swiss played against the top teams at the World and European Championships right up until the 1950s. Since then, there has been a more than 40-year slump.

The Canadians showed up in Europe again in February 1928 when the Allan Cup holders arrived in St. Moritz, Switzerland. The framework was again the Winter Olympics, to be followed by the World Championship, and only the Allan Cup winners had retained amateur status and thus the right to travel to Europe for the competition. It was the Canadians' first opportunity since the Olympics in Chamonix four years before to see whether the Europeans had made any progress.

Having learned from bitter experience in 1920 and 1924, the European organizers of the tournament placed the three best European national squads in three separate subgroups and left the Canadians out till the finals. And it was a good thing the Americans didn't show up. In the end, the Europeans didn't do any better than on previous occasions and weren't in the least vindicated. University of Toronto students on the Toronto Varsity Grads trounced the three European champions with an overall 38–0 shutout made up of scores against Sweden of 11–0, the Swiss 13–0 and the English 14–0.

The 1930 World Championship was conducted in three countries: France (Chamonix), Germany (Berlin) and Austria (Vienna). Still seeking to retain some of the glory for European players and fans, the organizers limited the participation of the Canadians (represented by the Port Arthur Bearcats) to one game. Of course, in the final game against the national team from Germany, the Canadians won with a "modest" score of 6–1.

Both the Canadians (represented by the Manitoba Grads rather than the Allan Cup-winning Montreal Amateur Athletic Association) and the Americans participated in

Hockey in Davos, Switzerland.

the World Championship in Poland in 1931. As expected, the deadly North American duo held the Europeans to third place, and a similar scenario was played out at the 1932 Winter Olympics in Lake Placid (in fact, in the two subsequent World Championships, all of the national teams of Europe managed to score but a single goal in eight games against the Canadians).

In the 1932 Olympic tournament at Lake Placid, which was also the sixth World Championship, the Winnipeg Hockey Club represented Canada and traditionally and without difficulty outplayed the Germans (4–1 and 5–0) and the Poles (9–0 and 10–0). In the final struggle for first place against the Americans, the pioneers of hockey didn't have it so easy, winning the first game 2–1 and barely eking out a 2–2 tie in the second. But it was enough.

At the World Championship in Prague in 1933, the teams from Canada and the United States were as usual only allowed into the semifinal groups, and as usual the overseas teams made short shrift of the Europeans. In the final game, however, the Massachusetts Rangers managed to edge out a Canadian team assembled from the Toronto National Sea Fleas—which had never won the Allan Cup before and wouldn't do it again—by a score of 2–1.

Before the tournament at the 1936 Winter Olympics in Garmisch-Partenkirchen, Germany, the Canadian Amateur Hockey Association ran into problems. The CAHA was planning to send the Allen Cup-winning Halifax Wolverines, but at the start of the season this team found it was short of several key players. To guarantee a win at the upcoming Olympics, the CAHA created a hybrid team in which seven players from Port Arthur joined the Halifax club. In Canada's first experience with forming a "national" team, it was expected that everything would turn out as usual, and indeed the Canadians made it to the semifinals without losing a game. They were slated to play against the other Group A teams from Great Britain, Germany and Hungary, but the outcome was even more sensational than the one that saw the Americans fall to the Italians 2–1 earlier in the contest. The Canadians bowed to Great Britain 2–1 and four teams (Great Britain, Canada, the U.S. and Czechoslovakia) faced off in the finals. There was still a chance the Americans could inadvertently help, but they too were unable to outplay the English and the game ended in a 0–0 tie. After beating the Czechs 5–0, the British team mounted the pedestal to claim the gold medals and the Canadians and Americans occupied second and third place, respectively. The Europeans had finally had their revenge.

At the 1936 Winter Games in Garmisch-Partenkirchen, Germany, Great Britain shocked the world with its improbable gold medal victory over Canada.

But were they in fact Europeans? Of all the players on the championship team (which was coached by future IIHF president John "Bunny" Ahearne), only Carl Erhardt was a British subject. All the rest were of British origin but had been raised and trained—where else?—in the Dominion of Canada, as were the players who formed the core of the French team.

And this had been known before the tournament started. The Canadians had even lodged a protest and demanded that the teams from Great Britain and France be disqualified, though they later rescinded the one against Britain for the sake of honor and also because they didn't regard the "British-Canadians"—or "Canadian-British"—as serious contenders.

In the next three tournaments, the Canadians again took the World Championship but not as easily as they had before. On two occasions, the British were runners-up in the absence of the Americans (who didn't participate in 1937 and 1938). At the 1939 World Championship, the Americans took back second place. After that, there were no significant fluctuations in the hockey standings in Europe: The game was still dominated by teams from the United Kingdom, Czechoslovakia and Switzerland while the Swedes had drifted into the background and the German national team made some serious gains to take the bronze medal in the European Championships three times before World War II was declared.

Herb Drury

Born in Midland, Ontario, in 1895, Herb Drury is best known among hockey historians as a member of the U.S. Olympic team that competed in the first Winter Games in Chamonix, France, in 1924.

Drury's U.S. squad won its preliminary group, defeating Belgium 19–0, France 22–0, and Great Britain 11–0. In the medal round, they blanked Sweden 20–0 before losing 6–1 to Canada and capturing the silver medal. Drury scored an amazing 22 goals and chipped in three assists for 25 points in the five games. In the gold medal game, Drury notched the Americans' lone marker.

Prior to joining the U.S. team, Drury had begun his hockey career with the Midland Seniors of the OHA senior league in 1914–15, then joined Port Colborne of the same league a year later. In 1916–17, he joined Pittsburgh of the USAHA, where he stayed through 1924. During Drury's time in Pittsburgh, the team changed its name from the Pittsburgh Athletic Association to the Stars, then to the Yellow Jackets. His career in Pittsburgh was interrupted in 1918–19 by military service.

Herb Drury scored 22 goals for Team USA in five games at the first Winter Olympics.

When the Olympics ended, Drury returned to Pittsburgh, signing with the Pirates of the NHL in September 1925. He played for the Pirates for five years until 1929–30. His best year in Pittsburgh was 1927–28, when he recorded six goals and four assists for 10 points in 44 games. In October 1930 Drury followed the Pittsburgh franchise to Philadelphia, where they became the Quakers. He played 24 games for the Quakers that year, recording only two assists.

In all, Drury played 213 games in the NHL. But he will best be remembered for his high-scoring performance in the first Olympic hockey tournament in 1924.

Drury, Herb
D/RW, 5′7″, 165 lbs, b: Midland, Ont., 3/2/1895, d: 08/24/1963

Season	Club, League	Regular Season					Playoffs				
		GP	G	A	Pts	PIM	GP	G	A	Pts	PIM
1914–15	Midland Seniors, OHA Sr.	1	2	0	2	*					
1915–16	Port Colborne Seniors, OHA Sr.	1	0	0	0	0					
1916–17	Pittsburgh AA, USAHA	6	1	0	1	*					
1917–18	Pittsburgh AA, USAHA	12	10	0	10	*					
WC–20	USA	5	23	0	23	*					
1920–21	Pittsburgh AA, USAHA	*	*	*	*	*	*	*	*	*	*
1921–22	Pittsburgh Stars, USAHA	*	*	*	*	*	*	*	*	*	*
1922–23	Pittsburgh Yellow Jackets, USAHA	20	5	0	5	*					
1923–24	Pittsburgh Yellow Jackets, USAHA	2	2	0	2	*	13	5	0	5	*
OWG–24	USA	5	22	3	25	*					
1924–25	Pittsburgh Yellowjackets, USAHA	33	7	0	7	*	8	4	0	4	*
1925–26	Pittsburgh Pirates, NHL	33	6	2	8	40	2	1	0	1	0
1926–27	Pittsburgh Pirates, NHL	42	5	1	6	48					
1927–28	Pittsburgh Pirates, NHL	44	6	4	10	44	2	0	1	1	0
1928–29	Pittsburgh Pirates, NHL	43	5	4	9	49					
1929–30	Pittsburgh Pirates, NHL	27	2	0	2	12					
1930–31	Philadelphia Quakers, NHL	24	0	2	2	10					
	OWG/WC Totals	10	45	3	48	*					
	NHL Totals	213	24	13	37	203	4	1	1	2	0

Reginald "Hooley" Smith

Forward Hooley Smith excelled at several facets of the game during his 17 years in the NHL. A prolific scorer, he retired in 1941 as one of the few skaters to reach the 200-goal mark. Smith was also considered a dogged checker and one of the most physically imposing combatants in the league.

Hooley Smith recorded 33 points to help Canada win the gold medal at the 1924 Olympics.

The Toronto native came from a large family of athletes. Five of his older brothers were skilled paddlers and football players whose careers were curtailed by enlistment in World War I. Before committing full-time to hockey, Smith was a star paddler for the Balmy Beach Club. He also won a national junior football title with St. Aidens and excelled at lacrosse with the Aura Lee team. He even played baseball, often competing in his bare feet.

Smith spent the 1920–21 hockey season with the OHA's Parkdale Canoe Club before graduating to the city's prestigious Granites squad of the senior league. His most fulfilling year came in 1923–24, when he led all players with 14 assists in the regular season and added 16 more helpers in the club's drive to the Allan Cup title. Smith was a standout when the Granites represented Canada at the 1924 Olympics. He recorded 17 goals and a tournament-high 16 assists while helping Canada annihilate the opposition en route to winning the gold medal.

He debuted as a professional with the Ottawa Senators in 1924 and remained in the nation's capital for three seasons. Early in his NHL career he perfected a sweeping hook-check that stymied many opponents' offensive surges. When he was teamed with Frank Nighbor and Cy Denneny, his hook-check combined neatly with Nighbor's poke-check to give the Ottawa team an unrivaled defensive forward line. Smith didn't lose any of his scoring abilities, however, and so he developed into one of the game's most complete performers.

Smith was a talented and confident figure whose brashness on the ice got him into many hostile situations. He let his temper get the better of him while the Senators vanquished Boston in the 1926–27 Stanley Cup finals. Incensed with Bruins forward Harry Oliver, Smith attacked his opponent and laid on a beating so severe that NHL president Frank Calder leveled a one-month suspension effective at the start of the next season.

Ottawa chose this time to add desperately needed cash to their bank account by selling the hard-nosed forward to the Montreal Maroons for $22,500, a record fee at the time. This turned out to be a beneficial move for the 5′10″ winger. In 1927–28, he played on a line with Nels Stewart and Jimmy Ward and helped the Maroons reach the Cup finals.

It was with the Maroons' "M" on his jersey that he gained the greatest acclaim in his career. When Babe Siebert took Ward's place, the dreaded S Line was born. It was a combination that terrorized the NHL for several years. Each member of the S Line was skilled, and just as willing to skate over an opponent as

Smith, Reginald "Hooley"
C/RW, 5′10″, 155 lbs, b: Toronto, Ont., 1/7/1903, d: 8/24/1963

Season	Club, League	Regular Season					Playoffs				
		GP	G	A	Pts	PIM	GP	G	A	Pts	PIM
1921–22	Toronto Granites, OHA Sr.	5	1	0	1	*	1	0	0	0	*
1922–23	Toronto Granites, OHA Sr.	8	3	3	6	*	2	1	0	1	2
1923–24	Toronto Granites, OHA Sr.	15	10	14	24	*					
OWG-24	Canada	5	17	16	33	4					
1924–25	Ottawa Senators, NHL	30	10	13	23	81					
1925–26	Ottawa Senators, NHL	28	16	9	25	53	2	0	0	0	14
1926–27	Ottawa Senators, NHL	43	9	6	15	125	6	1	0	1	16
1927–28	Montreal Maroons, NHL	34	14	5	19	72	9	2	1	3	23
1928–29	Montreal Maroons, NHL	41	10	9	19	120					
1929–30	Montreal Maroons, NHL	42	21	9	30	83	4	1	1	2	14
1930–31	Montreal Maroons, NHL	39	12	14	26	68					
1931–32	Montreal Maroons, NHL	43	11	33	44	49	4	2	1	3	2
1932–33	Montreal Maroons, NHL	48	20	21	41	66	2	2	0	2	2
1933–34	Montreal Maroons, NHL	47	18	19	37	58	4	0	1	1	6
1934–35	Montreal Maroons, NHL	46	5	22	27	41	6	0	0	0	14
1935–36	Montreal Maroons, NHL	47	19	19	38	75	3	0	0	0	2
1936–37	Boston Bruins, NHL	44	8	10	18	36	3	0	0	0	0
1937–38	New York Americans, NHL	47	10	10	20	23	6	0	3	3	0
1938–39	New York Americans, NHL	48	8	11	19	18	2	0	0	0	14
1939–40	New York Americans, NHL	47	7	8	15	41	3	3	1	4	2
1940–41	New York Americans, NHL	41	2	7	9	4					
	NHL Totals	715	200	225	425	1013	54	11	8	19	109
	OWG Totals	5	17	16	33	4					

NHL First All-Star Team (1936)
NHL Second All-Star Team (1932)
Won OWG (1924)
Won Stanley Cup (1927, 1935)

around them. They were usually near the top of the league in both scoring and penalty minutes. Smith waged a year-long battle with Toronto's rugged defenseman Red Horner that was followed closely by fans and media throughout the league.

Smith was placed on the NHL Second All-Star Team in 1932 after scoring 44 points. Remarkably for the time, 33 of his points were assists. After Stewart's departure, Smith formed a successful unit with Ward and Baldy Northcott.

Smith captained the Maroons to their second and last Stanley Cup win in 1934–35. The following year he scored 19 goals and added the same number of assists to earn selection to the NHL First All-Star Team. On March 24–25, 1936, Smith's Maroons lost the longest game in NHL history, a match against the Detroit Red Wings that went to a sixth overtime period. Hooley could take some consolation from the fact that the game didn't end in the fourth extra period when he drew a minor penalty at the nine-second mark.

In December 1936 Hooley was traded to the Boston Bruins, but he struggled without his old linemates and earned only 18 points. Smith's last four NHL seasons were spent with the New York Americans, where his offensive production dropped because he spent part of his time on defense.

At first, retirement was difficult for Smith to accept. He wanted to try refereeing but refused to go to the minor leagues to learn the craft. Later he opened his own business in Montreal, manufacturing soaps and other cleaning products. He died of a heart attack in a Montreal hospital on August 24, 1963. One of hockey's early power forwards, Smith was inducted into the Hockey Hall of Fame in 1972.

Bobby Benson

At only 5′6″ and 135 pounds, diminutive defenseman Bobby Benson played only one season in the NHL with the Boston Bruins, in 1924–25, recording one assist in eight games. But for Benson the NHL experience wasn't the highlight of his successful hockey career. He was in fact a part of Canada's hockey history before he ever turned pro.

Born in Winnipeg in 1894, Benson played four seasons with the Winnipeg Falcons of the Manitoba Hockey League, from 1913 to 1917. He spent the next two years in the military, during which time he played, along with the entire Falcons squad, for the Winnipeg 223rd Scandinavian Battalion team.

In 1920 Benson competed in a hockey tournament that would prove to be the true highlight of his career when he was a member of the 1920 Canadian Olympic team that traveled to Antwerp, Belgium, for the first and only time that ice hockey was played in the Summer Olympics.

In those days, Canada didn't select a national team composed of the top talent from around the country; instead, the nation's top amateur club earned the right to wear the national colors. Benson's Winnipeg Falcons, led by coach Frank Rankin and general manager and secretary William Hewitt, had a strong nucleus made up mostly of players of Icelandic descent, including team captain and center Frank Fredrickson, forward Chris Fridfinnson and winger Slim Halderson. They defeated the University of Toronto seniors in a two-game Allan Cup final series in March 1920 and were invited to represent Canada at the Olympics.

Olympic hockey was played at those Games using seven-man teams, the six positions we know today plus a "rover." Canada's competition consisted of teams from Belgium, the host nation, Czechoslovakia, France, Sweden, Switzerland and the U.S. In the opening round, Canada defeated the Czechs 15–0 on seven goals from Halderson, while Benson performed yeoman's duty on defense in helping goalie Wally Byron preserve the shutout. Things were a lot closer in the next semifinal round, as the Canadians squeaked past the U.S. 2–0. Benson was again a standout on defense, thwarting rush after rush.

In the final game on April 26, Team Canada exploded, this time with a 12–1 hammering of the Swedes—who were used to playing a style of hockey very closely related to the sport of bandy, with short sticks and a ball—to win the gold. After Canada went up 3–0 in the first half, Sweden scored for the first and only time, spoiling the Canucks' perfect goals-against record for the tournament. But then Canada scored nine unanswered goals, including one by Benson, to win. The Winnipeg Falcons were Olympic champions.

After the Games, Benson had a whirlwind career as a pro. He signed as a free agent with the Saskatoon Crescents of the Western Canada Hockey League, where he played two seasons before being traded to the Calgary Tigers of the same league. After three more seasons he was traded again, this time to the Montreal Maroons, on January 6, 1925. But that same day he was traded to the Bruins for Alf Skinner. After his brief stint with Boston he returned to Saskatoon but was traded to Edmonton of the Western Hockey League a few months later. Then came seasons with the Moose Jaw Maroons, Minneapolis Miners, Seattle Eskimos and Hollywood Stars, all in various professional and semipro leagues in the western part of Canada and the U.S. This nomadic pro career may obscure the fact that Bobby Benson was a key defensive skater in Canada's early Olympic hockey history.

Benson, Bobby
D, 5'6", 135 lbs, b: Winnipeg, Man., 5/18/1894, d: 9/7/1965

Season	Club, League	Regular Season					Playoffs				
		GP	G	A	Pts	PIM	GP	G	A	Pts	PIM
1912–13	Winnipeg Strathconas, City Sr.	8	3	0	3	*	2	0	0	0	0
1913–14	Winnipeg Falcons, City Sr.	12	2	0	2	*					
1914–15	Winnipeg Falcons, MHL Sr.	8	3	0	3	*	2	0	0	0	6
1915–16	Winnipeg Falcons, MHL Sr.	7	2	0	2	12					
1916–17	Winnipeg 223rd Battalion, MHL Sr.	8	3	1	4	4					
1919–20	Winnipeg Falcons, MHL Sr.	9	2	1	3	26	6	0	5	5	13
WC–20	Canada	3	0	1	1	*					
1920–21	Saskatoon Crescents, SSHL	16	12	1	13	39	4	2	1	3	12
1921–22	Saskatoon Crescents, WCHL	23	9	4	13	21					
1922–23	Calgary Tigers, WCHL	27	7	1	8	22					
1923–24	Calgary Tigers, WCHL	26	5	5	10	24	7	0	1	1	2
1924–25	Calgary Tigers, WCHL	9	0	1	1	4					
	Boston Bruins, NHL	8	0	1	1	4					
1925–26	Saskatoon Crescents, WHL	12	0	0	0	0					
	Edmonton Eskimos, WHL	12	0	0	0	0	2	0	0	0	2
1926–27	Moose Jaw Maroons, PHL	32	6	4	10	65					
1927–28	Winnipeg — Minneapolis, AHA	23	2	0	2	36	8	0	1	1	31
1928–29	Minneapolis Millers, AHA	40	3	4	7	92	4	0	0	0	2
1929–30	Seattle Eskimos, PCHL	36	2	3	5	82					
1930–31	Seattle Eskimos, PCHL	33	2	2	4	76	4	0	0	0	8
1931–32	Hollywood Stars, Cal-Pro	*	1	1	2	*					
	NHL Totals	8	0	1	1	4					
	WC Totals	3	0	1	1	*					

Won WC (1920)

Frank Fredrickson

A dynamic offensive center, Frank Fredrickson followed up a brilliant amateur career with an impressive tenure as a professional. Along the way, the Winnipeg native won an Olympic gold medal and a Stanley Cup and played his way into the Hockey Hall of Fame.

The talented youngster debuted in senior hockey in 1913–14 with the Winnipeg Falcons and quickly carved out a reputation as one of the top amateur players in Canada. Fredrickson and most

In 1920 the Winnipeg Falcons traveled to Antwerp to represent Canada for the first and only time hockey was played at the Summer Olympics. Harold Halderson (fourth from the left), Frank Fredrickson (fifth from the left), Bobby Benson (third from the right).

of his teammates were of Icelandic descent and were forced to deal with a fair degree of prejudice while competing in the Manitoba capital. That the team won almost every game it played made the Falcons an even more visible target.

Fredrickson led the Falcons to the league title during his second year with the team in 1914–15. The next season he captained the squad while performing the same role for the University of Manitoba's hockey team. With World War I raging, Fredrickson enlisted in the army with the 196th Western Universities Battalion but was soon reassigned with his fellow Nordic-Canadians to the 223rd Scandinavian Battalion. He was joined there by many of his Falcons teammates. Fredrickson helped form a military hockey team in 1916–17 before the troop was shipped overseas to see action. The respected Icelander played a prominent role off the ice as a pilot and flight instructor before returning to Winnipeg after the war.

One of the first tasks Fredrickson undertook was to reorganize the Falcons in time for the 1919–20 schedule. The team picked up where it left off and won the league title before representing western Canada in the Allan Cup finals, where the Winnipeg outfit vanquished the University of Toronto to become amateur champions of the country. And this status earned them the honor of representing their country when ice hockey was admitted as a demonstration event at the 1920 Antwerp Summer Olympics.

The journey overseas was more of a struggle than the competition itself. The cost of the voyage was estimated at $10,000, an enormous sum that was raised by combining Allan Cup receipts with generous donations from the Manitoba government and the city of Winnipeg. On the ship to Europe, the only incident of note took place when Fredrickson was shaken up after falling out of his bunk. On the ice, the Canadians won gold after manhandling Czechoslovakia and Sweden and turning back the United States 2–0. During the 12–1 rout of the Swedes, Fredrickson was virtually unstoppable, registering seven goals.

The crafty forward debuted as a professional with the Victoria Cougars of the PCHA in 1920–21. The league's wide-open style suited Fredrickson's offensive gifts and he continued to score at will. In 1922–23, he led the league with 39 goals and set a new record with 55 points. When the Cougars joined the WCHL two years later, Fredrickson led the club to the league title and a Stanley Cup triumph over the Montreal Canadiens. Overall he was placed on the PCHA First All-Star Team in four straight years from 1921 to 1924 and he made the WCHL First All-Star squad in 1926.

Fredrickson, Frank
C, 5′11″, 180 lbs, b: Winnipeg, Man., 6/11/1895, d: 4/28/1979

Season	Club, League	Regular Season					Playoffs				
		GP	G	A	Pts	PIM	GP	G	A	Pts	PIM
1913–14	Winnipeg Falcons, MIHL	11	13	7	20	*					
1914–15	Winnipeg Falcons, MIHL	8	10	5	13	*	1	1	0	1	2
1915–16	Winnipeg Falcons, MHL Sr.	6	13	3	16	14					
1916–17	Winnipeg Falcons, MHL Sr.	8	17	3	20	40					
1919–20	Winnipeg Falcons, MHL Sr.	10	23	5	28	12	6	22	5	27	6
WC–20	Canada	3	10	1	11	*					
1920–21	Victoria Cougars, PCHA	21	20	12	32	3					
1921–22	Victoria Cougars, PCHA	24	15	10	25	26					
1922–23	Victoria Cougars, PCHA	30	39	16	55	26	2	2	0	2	4
1923–24	Victoria Cougars, PCHA	30	19	8	27	28					
1924–25	Victoria Cougars, WCHL	28	22	8	30	43	4	3	1	4	2
1925–26	Victoria Cougars, WHL	30	16	8	24	89	4	2	0	2	6
1926–27	Detroit Cougars, NHL	16	4	6	10	12					
	Boston Bruins, NHL	28	14	7	21	33	8	2	4	6	22
1927–28	Boston Bruins, NHL	41	10	4	14	83	2	0	1	1	4
1928–29	Boston Bruins, NHL	12	1	3	4	24					
	Pittsburgh Pirates, NHL	31	3	7	10	28					
1929–30	Pittsburgh Pirates, NHL	9	4	7	11	20					
1930–31	Detroit Falcons, NHL	24	1	2	3	6					
	Detroit Olympics, IAHL	6	0	1	1	2					
	WC Totals	3	10	1	11	*					
	PCHA Totals	105	93	46	139	83	2	2	0	2	4
	WCHL/WHL Totals	58	38	16	54	132	16	8	6	14	24
	NHL Totals	161	39	34	73	206	10	2	3	5	24

PCHA First All-Star Team (1921, 1922, 1923, 1924)
WHL First All-Star Team (1926)
Won WC (1920)
Won Stanley Cup (1925)

Fans of the NHL had a chance to enjoy Fredrickson's talents after the Detroit Cougars purchased Victoria's players in 1926. Partway through his first NHL season he was traded to Boston, where he excelled with 14 goals in 28 matches. Fredrickson later played with the Pittsburgh Pirates and Detroit Falcons before bringing his NHL career to a close in 1931. During the 1929–30 season, Fredrickson served as player-coach of the Pittsburgh franchise. He played his last six games as a pro with the Detroit Olympics of the old International-American Hockey League toward the end of the 1930–31 schedule.

After his playing career ended, Fredrickson turned his attention to coaching on a full-time basis and worked behind the benches in Winnipeg, Princeton University, the Royal Canadian Air Force and the University of British Columbia. One of the greatest amateur stars in Canadian history and an excellent pro, Fredrickson was inducted into the Hockey Hall of Fame in 1958.

Harold "Slim" Halderson

Harold Halderson was known as "Slim" throughout his long career. He was a strapping 6′3″ in an era when most players were much smaller, but his 200-pound frame was lean and gangly. He had a loose-limbed skating style that looked awkward at first, but his rushes down the wing, combined with his defensive savvy, allowed him to play for 20 years in leagues across North America. He achieved lasting recognition in Canada for his play at the 1920 Summer Olympics in Antwerp, Belgium.

Halderson was born on January 6, 1900, in Winnipeg, Manitoba. He played amateur hockey in his home town for several teams, including the Winnipeg Ypres in 1917–18, the Monarchs in 1918–19 and finally the Falcons in 1919–20. Halderson was one of the younger players when the Falcons began training for the 1919–20 season. During an early practice, coach Fred "Steamer"

Maxwell was trying hard to keep the players from straying from their positions. One of the worst offenders was Halderson, a good puck carrier who would get up a head of steam going down his right wing and then continue across center when he entered the offensive zone.

Halderson bumped heads with another player during a drill designed to keep him on his part of the ice. A few minutes later, he again carried the puck across his imaginary line and the coach smacked the winger across the seat with his stick to stop him. Halderson apologized, saying, "It must have been the bump on the head."

The practices paid off for both Halderson and the team. He played with Frank Fredrickson on left wing and the speedy Mike Goodman, North America's fastest speed skater, at center. These were the days of seven-man hockey, the six modern positions plus a rover, and as in soccer, the players who started the contest would often play the entire game. With their fast, skilled forward line, the Falcons became one of the powerhouses of Canadian amateur hockey. Halderson scored 10 goals and added 11 assists in the 10-game regular season and the Falcons went on to win the Manitoba Hockey League title.

The Falcons earned a trip to Toronto and the Allan Cup finals after beating Fort William easily in a two-game series to become the best team in the West. The Varsity team, representing the University of Toronto, was heavily favored going into the two-game final but was surprised 8–3 in the first game. Winnipeg closed out the series with a 3–2 win. In addition to the Allan Cup, the Falcons won the privilege of representing Canada at the Olympics in Antwerp, Belgium, where ice hockey was a last-minute addition as a demonstration sport.

Halderson, Harold "Slim"
D, 6′3″, 200 lbs, b: Winnipeg, Man., 1/6/1900, d: 8/1/1965

Season	Club, League	Regular Season					Playoffs				
		GP	G	A	Pts	PIM	GP	G	A	Pts	PIM
1917–18	Winnipeg Ypres, MHL Sr.	7	5	6	11	4	4	4	3	7	4
1918–19	Winnipeg Monarchs, MHL Sr.	9	3	5	8	4					
1919–20	Winnipeg Falcons, MHL Sr.	9	10	11	21	10	6	4	5	9	6
WC–20	Canada	3	9	2	11	*					
1920–21	Saskatoon Crescents, SSHL	16	12	3	15	38	4	8	0	8	9
1921–22	Victoria Cougars, PCHA	23	7	3	10	13					
1922–23	Victoria Cougars, PCHA	29	10	5	15	26	2	0	0	0	0
1923–24	Victoria Cougars, PCHA	30	6	2	8	50					
1924–25	Victoria Cougars, WCHL	28	3	6	9	71	4	1	0	1	12
1925–26	Victoria Cougars, WHL	23	3	1	4	51	3	1	0	1	6
1926–27	Detroit Cougars, NHL	19	2	0	2	29					
	Toronto Maple Leafs, NHL	25	1	2	3	36					
1927–28	Quebec Castors, Can-Am	40	13	5	18	71	6	1	1	2	14
1928–29	Newark Bulldogs, Can-Am	40	6	3	9	107					
1929–30	Kansas City Pla-Mors, AHA	48	8	7	15	76	5	0	0	0	8
1930–31	Kansas City Pla-Mors, AHA	47	5	7	12	77	8	1	1	2	10
1931–32	Kansas City Pla-Mors, AHA	46	9	3	12	69	4	2	0	2	0
1932–33	Kansas City Greyhounds, AHA	26	1	4	5	30					
	Wichita Blue Jays, AHA	24	7	2	9	40					
1933–34	Tulsa Oilers, AHA	48	9	12	21	66	4	0	2	2	4
	Wichita Vikings, AHA	2	0	0	0	0					
1934–35	Tulsa Oilers, AHA	48	6	13	19	65	5	1	2	3	2
1935–36	Tulsa Oilers, AHA	48	6	14	20	25	3	0	0	0	4
1936–37	Wichita Skyhawks, AHA	48	5	4	9	30					
	NHL Totals	44	3	2	5	65					
	PCHA Totals	82	23	10	33	89	2	0	0	0	0
	WCHL/WHL Totals	51	6	7	13	122	15	5	1	6	38
	WC Totals	3	9	2	11	*					

PCHA First All-Star Team (1923)
PCHA Second All-Star Team (1922)
Won WC(1920)
Won Stanley Cup (1925)

Without even returning home after their Allan Cup win, Halderson and the Falcons continued east to Saint John, New Brunswick, to board the ship that would take them to Europe. After the week-long voyage, during which the ship's carpenter had made 24 hockey sticks from wood the team brought with them, they arrived ready to see what the rest of the world had to offer. Besides the American team, which had no fewer than seven Canadians on its roster, the competition was far behind. Many of the European teams arrived with no padding and wearing clothes usually found in other sports.

After watching the Canadian team practise and seeing the speed with which players such as Halderson could shoot the puck, Sweden's goaltender hurriedly found some cotton padding to wrap around himself. Meanwhile, the Czech players, Canada's first opponents, ran on their skates like track athletes and relied solely on individual rushes. In their first-round game, Halderson scored against the Czechs with ease, finishing with seven goals to lead the Canadians to a 15–0 victory. The next round was much tougher as Canada squeaked by the Americans with a 2–0 score to make the finals.

The Swedish team, which had learned a great deal by watching the Canadians, had advanced to the gold medal round with wins over France and Belgium. They weren't guaranteed the silver, however, because of a unique setup that featured playdowns for each medal. The Swedes were easily overcome by Canada. Halderson scored the first-ever goal in an Olympic final just over a minute into the game. He added another goal in the third period as Canada won 12–1 to capture the tournament. The United States took the silver and the Czechs won the bronze.

After the tournament, the Canadians went on a long tour of Europe, then headed back through Canada, where they were given banquets in each city they passed through. Finally, there was a large get-together in Winnipeg to celebrate their championship and to close out months of traveling and playing.

Halderson stayed in competitive hockey for another 17 years, playing in seven leagues with 12 different teams. After a five-year stint with the Victoria Cougars, who were purchased by the new Detroit entry in the National Hockey League to stock their roster, Halderson entered the NHL as a 26-year-old "rookie" in 1926–27. He was traded halfway through the year to Toronto for Pete Bellefeuille and played 25 games with the Maple Leafs. The next season he was in the Canadian-American League with Quebec before moving throughout the United States with various teams in the American Hockey Association. He finished his career in 1937 with the Wichita Skyhawks. After a brief illness, Slim Halderson died in 1965.

Bert "Mac" McCaffery

Winger/defenseman Bert "Mac" McCaffery played his seven NHL seasons during the 1920s and 1930s for the Toronto St. Pats, the Toronto Maple Leafs, the Pittsburgh Pirates and the Montreal Canadiens. Born in Chesley, Ontario, he entered the NHL in 1924–25 after four years with the Ontario Hockey Association's Toronto Granites. In his rookie campaign with the St. Pats, he scored nine goals and six assists. The next season was his best from an individual standpoint, 14 goals and seven assists for 21 points in 36 games.

St. Pats management traded him to Pittsburgh during the early part of the 1927–28 season as part of a three-team deal that brought Ed Rodden to Toronto from Chicago and sent Ty Arbour to the Windy City. McCaffery was traded again in 1929, this time to Montreal for Gord Fraser. After just over a year with the Canadiens, Mac went to the Providence Reds of the old Can-Am league, and then to the Philadelphia Arrows of the same league, where he rounded out his playing career in 1933.

Perhaps the greatest highlight of McCaffery's career came during his final year as an amateur with the OHA's Granites, when he competed in the 1924 Winter Olympic Games in Chamonix, France. In those days, Canada would send its top amateur club to wear the national colors, and with McCaffery at right wing, the Granites, a team founded by ex-servicemen after World War I, were dominant, winning the Allan Cup in 1922 and 1923. Supplemented by a couple of players from other teams who replaced those Granites players who couldn't make the trip, the nine-player, two-coach team traveled to France to represent Canada.

McCaffery, along with teammates Harry Watson on left wing and Hooley Smith at center, formed an effective scoring trio for coach Frank Rankin. The Granites opened the seven-game tournament with a 30–0 pasting of Czechoslovakia, followed by a 22–0 crushing of Sweden and a 33–0 drubbing of Switzerland. McCaffery had hat-tricks in the first two games, then exploded for an incredible eight goals, including three in a row, in the contest against Switzerland.

After these preliminary games, Canada steamrollered through the medal round with equal ease. Although they allowed their first two goals of the tournament in the semifinal match against Great Britain, it hardly mattered, as Canada scored 19 goals for the win, and McCaffery supplied five of them.

In the finals, Canada took on the United States on the outdoor ice of Chamonix for the gold medal. Watson, who had been hired by the *Toronto Telegram* to write a first-person, behind-the-scenes account of the team's trip to France, boasted that Canada would beat the Americans 10 or 12 to nothing, a prediction that didn't seem all that unlikely, considering some of the scores during qualifying. His forecast earned Watson a stick in the face from an unappreciative American during the early minutes of the game. But as things settled down, Canada took control and won the gold medal by a score of 6–1. McCaffery scored once in the final and finished the tournament with 20 goals in five games, second to Watson's 36 (assists weren't recorded).

After the medals were handed out, McCaffery joined his teammates on a tour of France and England. Their two-month Olympic trip ended with a huge parade in Toronto. A few months later, McCaffrey turned pro with the NHL's St. Pats.

Bert McCaffery passed away in April 1955. In addition to his successful career as a pro, he will long be remembered by Canadian hockey fans as one of the country's great early Olympic hockey players because of his heroics in Chamonix in 1924.

Bert McCaffery finished second in scoring on Team Canada with 20 goals in five games at the 1924 Olympics.

McCaffrey, Bert "Mac"
RW/D, 5'10", 180 lbs, b: Chesley, Ont., 1896, d: 4/15/1955

Season	Club, League	Regular Season					Playoffs				
		GP	G	A	Pts	PIM	GP	G	A	Pts	PIM
1916–17	Toronto Riversides, OHA Sr.	8	9	0	9	*	2	1	0	1	4
1917–18	Toronto Crescents, OHA Sr.	9	23	0	23	*					
1918–19	Toronto Dentals, OHA Sr.	6	7	1	8	*	2	0	0	0	*
1919–20	Parkdale Canoe Club, OHA Sr.	6	6	3	9	*	1	1	1	2	*
1920–21	Toronto Granites, OHA Sr.	10	1	3	4	*	2	0	2	2	*
1921–22	Toronto Granites, OHA Sr.	10	5	8	13	*	8	8	4	12	*
1922–23	Toronto Granites, OHA Sr.	12	10	4	14	*	2	3	2	5	8
1923–24	Toronto Granites, OHA Sr.	14	18	10	28	*					
OWG–24	Canada	5	19	15	34	*					
1924–25	Toronto St. Pats, NHL	30	10	6	16	12	2	1	0	1	4
1925–26	Toronto St. Pats, NHL	36	14	7	21	42					
1926–27	Toronto Maple Leafs, NHL	43	5	5	10	43					
1927–28	Toronto Maple Leafs, NHL	9	1	1	2	9					
	Pittsburgh Pirates, NHL	35	6	3	9	14					
1928–29	Pittsburgh Pirates, NHL	42	1	0	1	34					
1929–30	Pittsburgh Pirates, NHL	15	3	4	7	12					
	Montreal Canadiens, NHL	28	1	3	4	26	6	1	1	2	6
1930–31	Montreal Canadiens, NHL	22	2	1	3	10					
	Providence Reds, Can-Am	20	6	2	8	24	2	2	1	3	2
1931–32	Philadelphia Arrows, Can-Am	35	7	9	16	26					
1932–33	Philadelphia Arrows, Can-Am	7	1	0	1	2					
	NHL Totals	260	42	30	72	202	8	2	1	3	10
	OWG Totals	5	19	15	34	*					

Won OWG (1924)
Won Stanley Cup (1930)

Clarence "Taffy" *Abel*

Taffy Abel was the first American-born player to earn a regular spot in the NHL.

"Taffy" Abel was the first U.S.-born player to earn a regular spot in the National Hockey League. He was one of his era's biggest skaters, standing 6′1″ and weighing over 225 pounds. At a time when forward passing wasn't allowed in the offensive zone, he was a bruising defensive force to be reckoned with.

Abel was born in 1900 in Sault Ste. Marie, Michigan, but incredibly he didn't play his first organized hockey game until he was 18 years old. He spent four seasons learning the game with the Michigan Soo Nationals of the state senior league, and in 1922 he joined the St. Paul Athletic Club, a Minnesota team that played in the United States Amateur Hockey Association. His solid play and size earned him a berth on the U.S. Olympic team that traveled to the 1924 Winter Games in Chamonix, France.

Though he was far from an offensive standout over his long career—he scored only 18 goals in 333 NHL games—Abel counted 15 goals in five games at Chamonix. In the final game against Canada, the eventual champions, he was held scoreless, though he did lead the way in penalties. He was involved in three altercations in a match very much lacking in Olympic spirit and gentlemanly conduct.

His reputation buoyed by his silver medal performance, Abel joined the Minneapolis Millers of the competitive Central Hockey League for the 1925–26 season. When the New York Rangers were formed in 1926, Abel was signed to strengthen the nascent club's blue line. He played that role for only three seasons in the Big Apple, often teaming with another hockey giant, Ivan "Ching" Johnson, to make for a formidable combination. Together the defensive partners weighed in at over 428 pounds.

In the 1928 Stanley Cup playoffs, defense became especially important to the Rangers when their goalie, Lorne Chabot, was injured in the second game of the finals against the Montreal Maroons. New York's 44-year-old manager and coach, Lester Patrick, put on the pads and filled in for Chabot despite never having played goal in the NHL before. With Abel and Johnson clearing the zone and protecting their inexperienced netminder, the Rangers won the game and eventually the Stanley Cup.

On April 15, 1929, Abel was sold to the Chicago Black Hawks for $15,000. He became a fan favorite in Chicago and was a defensive stalwart for the Hawks for five seasons. In 1934 Abel helped the Hawks win their first Stanley Cup. His big body bruised and his legs sore from years of abuse, Abel decided to hang up his skates on a high note and he retired following the Cup victory.

Abel, Clarence "Taffy"
D, 6′1″, 225 lbs, b: Sault Ste. Marie, MI., 5/28/1900, d: 8/1/1964

Season	Club, League	Regular Season					Playoffs				
		GP	G	A	Pts	PIM	GP	G	A	Pts	PIM
1918–19	Michigan Soo Nationals, TBSHL	*	*	*	*	*	*	*	*	*	*
1919–20	Michigan Soo Nationals, TBSHL	8	3	1	4	26	*	*	*	*	*
1920–21	Michigan Soo Nationals, TBSHL	*	*	*	*	*	*	*	*	*	*
1921–22	Michigan Soo Nationals, TBSHL	*	*	*	*	*	*	*	*	*	*
1922–23	St. Paul Athletic Club, USAHA	18	3	0	3	*	4	0	0	0	*
1923–24	St. Paul Athletic Club, USAHA	3	1	0	1	*	8	0	0	0	*
OWG–24	United States	5	15	0	15	*					
1924–25	St. Paul Athletic Club, USAHA	39	8	0	8	*	*	*	*	*	*
1925–26	Minneapolis Millers, CHL	35	12	9	21	56	3	0	1	1	6
1926–27	New York Rangers, NHL	44	8	4	12	78	2	0	1	1	8
1927–28	New York Rangers, NHL	23	0	1	1	28	9	1	0	1	14
1928–29	New York Rangers, NHL	44	3	1	4	41	6	0	0	0	8
1929–30	Chicago Black Hawks, NHL	38	3	3	6	42	2	0	0	0	10
1930–31	Chicago Black Hawks, NHL	43	0	1	1	45	9	0	0	0	8
1931–32	Chicago Black Hawks, NHL	48	3	3	6	34	2	0	0	0	2
1932–33	Chicago Black Hawks, NHL	47	0	4	4	63					
1933–34	Chicago Black Hawks, NHL	46	2	1	3	28	8	0	0	0	8
	OWG Totals	5	15	0	15	*					
	NHL Totals	333	19	18	37	359	38	1	1	2	58

Won Stanley Cup (1928, 1934)

Abel owned and operated a tourist resort called Taffy's Lodge in his home town of Sault Ste. Marie following his retirement from the game. He died there on August 1, 1964. When the United States Hockey Hall of Fame opened in 1973, Taffy Abel was one of its charter members.

Beattie Ramsay

Defenseman Beattie Ramsay was born in Lumsden, Saskatchewan, in 1895, and went on to enjoy tremendous success in all levels of the game—junior, collegiate, international and the pros.

He was a member of the University of Toronto junior team, captained by Conn Smythe, that won the OHA junior title in 1915, the first time in 23 years U of T had captured the crown. Later that year the entire team enlisted for service in World War I and Ramsay served in Italy with the Royal Flying Corps.

From 1919 until 1922, Ramsay was a member of the powerhouse U of T senior team that went to the Allan Cup finals in 1920 and won the trophy in 1921 after an undefeated season. The team also won the senior intercollegiate championship three years in a row. In 1922–23, Ramsay was made an honorary coach of U of T's senior and intermediate teams and both of them won their respective intercollegiate championships. That same year he joined the Toronto Granites squad that captured the OHA senior title and the Allan Cup.

In 1924 Ramsay went with the Granites to Chamonix, France, to compete in the Olympic Games. The Canadian squad, coached by Frank Rankin and featuring stars such as Cyril "Sig" Slater, Reginald "Hooley" Smith, Harry Watson and Dunc Munro, won the gold medal. The team blasted Czechoslovakia 30–0, Sweden 22–0 and Switzerland 33–0 in the preliminary round before defeating Great Britain 19–2 and the U.S. 6–1 in the finals. Ramsay contributed to the deluge of goals with a hat-trick against the Czechs, five goals against Sweden and a pair against the Swiss. Ramsay also had the honor of refereeing contests between France and Great Britain and France and the U.S.

After the Games, Ramsay coached for two seasons at Princeton University, the Ivy League juggernaut, then joined the Toronto Maple Leafs in 1927–28 for their first full NHL campaign. There he played alongside two other legendary Leaf defenders, Hap Day and Ace Bailey.

After playing in his only NHL season, Ramsay coached the Yorkton Terriers of the Saskatchewan league, then continued his coaching career with the Prince Albert Mintos from 1932 to 1934 and the Regina Aces from 1934 to 1936.

From 1945 to 1952, he was president of the Regina Pats junior hockey club. He'd earned a considerable income outside of hockey through his road contracting business, and in those years he often funded the team out of his own pocket. Murray Armstrong, the team's coach, once called Ramsay "the finest man and the finest sportsman that it has been my privilege to be associated with."

Ramsay, Beattie
D, 5'7", 143 lbs, b: Lumsden, Sask., 12/12/1895, d: 9/30/52

Season	Club, League	Regular Season					Playoffs				
		GP	G	A	Pts	PIM	GP	G	A	Pts	PIM
1919–20	University of Toronto, OHA Sr.	6	3	2	5	*	6	4	4	8	*
1920–21	University of Toronto, OHA Sr.	10	5	4	9	*	3	0	1	1	*
1921–22	University of Toronto, OHA Sr.	10	11	4	15	*					
1922–23	Toronto Granites, OHA Sr.						2	0	0	0	0
1923–24	Toronto Granites, OHA Sr.	12	7	7	14	*					
OWG–24	Canada	5	9	6	15	*					
1927–28	Toronto Maple Leafs, NHL	43	0	2	2	10					
	NHL Totals	43	0	2	2	10					
	OWG Totals	5	9	6	15	*					

Won OWG (1924)

Dunc Munro

Dunc Munro captained Canada's gold medal-winning team at the first Winter Olympic Games, in 1924 at Chamonix, France. A few years later, the defenseman and sometime left winger starred with the Montreal Maroons in the young National Hockey League. His leadership and rink savvy eventually earned him the job of player-coach and manager of the Maroons.

Munro was born in Moray, Scotland, in 1901. He first started playing hockey as a youngster when his family moved to Toronto. The best senior team in the country at the time was the Toronto Granites, a club made up of ex-servicemen from the First World War. Munro joined the team in 1920, when the squad was virtually unbeatable. The Granites won the John Ross Robertson Cup in 1922 and 1923. Winning the Allan Cup in both of those years earned Munro and his teammates, including a few replacements from other Canadian amateur teams, an invitation to Chamonix to represent their country.

At the 1924 Olympics in France, the Canadians had little trouble defeating their opponents and won all their games by wide margins. Beattie Ramsay (top row, fourth from the right), Dunc Munro (bottom row, second from the right).

In France, the Canadians had little trouble against their poorly skilled opponents, winning all of their opening-round games by incredibly lopsided scores. They captured the gold medal after a somewhat harder-fought final against the United States, a very physical 6–1 win. With Munro, Harry Watson and Hooley Smith leading the way, Canada outscored its opponents 110–3 in Chamonix. Munro, named the team's captain prior to the Games, played defense for much of the tournament but still finished with 18 goals in five games. He also served as a referee when he wasn't playing, officiating the Belgium–United States game.

When he returned to Canada, Munro was signed by the expansion Montreal Maroons, who were playing their first season in the NHL. It was a difficult year, as Montreal stayed out of last place only because of the poor performance of another new league entry, the Boston Bruins. In 1925–26, the Maroons improved dramatically. After finishing second in the regular season and winning twice as many games as they did in their inaugural year, the Maroons marched to the NHL championship, winning the final series over the favored Ottawa Senators. The Maroons then captured the Stanley Cup by defeating the Victoria Cougars. It was the last time that a team from outside of the NHL challenged for the Cup.

Munro and the Maroons were back in the Stanley Cup finals in 1928, but this time they were outclassed by the New York Rangers. The Broadway Blueshirts were aided by an emergency net-minding performance from the team's coach and manager, Lester Patrick, after goalie Lorne Chabot was injured in the second game of the finals.

Later that year, after playing only one game of the 1928–29 season, Munro suffered a minor heart attack and was forced to sit out the whole season to convalesce. When he returned in 1929, he was named the team's coach and manager while still taking a regular shift on the ice. Although Montreal was well above .500 during his tenure, Munro was playing less and less and was unable to deliver a successful playoff drive in 1931.

He left the Maroons after the 1930–31 season, but just before the beginning of the next season, he was signed by the rival Montreal Canadiens, for whom he played one full year before retiring from the game in 1932.

Dunc Munro, his heart weakened by several attacks over the years, died in 1958, two weeks before his 57th birthday.

Munro, Dunc
D, 5′8″, 190 lbs, b: Moray, Scotland, 1/19/1901, d: 1/3/1958

Season	Club, League	Regular Season					Playoffs				
		GP	G	A	Pts	PIM	GP	G	A	Pts	PIM
1920–21	Toronto Granites, OHA Sr.	8	4	5	9	*	2	1	0	1	*
1921–22	Toronto Granites, OHA Sr.	10	4	6	10	*	2	2	1	3	*
1922–23	Toronto Granites, OHA Sr.	12	7	7	14	*	2	2	0	2	4
1923–24	Toronto Granites, OHA Sr.	15	9	5	14	*					
OWG –24	Canada	5	18	4	22	2					
1924–25	Montreal Maroons, NHL	27	5	1	6	16					
1925–26	Montreal Maroons, NHL	33	4	6	10	55	2	0	0	0	0
1926–27	Montreal Maroons, NHL	43	6	5	11	42	2	0	0	0	4
1927–28	Montreal Maroons, NHL	43	5	2	7	35	9	0	2	2	8
1928–29	Montreal Maroons, NHL	1	0	0	0	0					
1929–30	Montreal Maroons, NHL	40	7	2	9	10	4	2	0	2	8
1930–31	Montreal Maroons, NHL	4	0	1	1	0					
1931–32	Montreal Canadiens, NHL	48	1	1	2	14	4	0	0	0	2
	NHL Totals	239	28	18	46	172	21	2	2	4	18
	OWG Totals	5	18	4	22	2					

Won OWG (1924)
Won Stanley Cup (1926)

Hugh Plaxton

Compact winger Hugh Plaxton—he was 5′10″ inches and 184 pounds—was born in Barrie, Ontario, in 1904. His career was marked by successes at the collegiate and international levels, although commitments outside the game slowed him down in the pros.

Plaxton started his career in 1921 with the University of Toronto Varsity Blues of the OHA senior league, but his first year with the team was somewhat less than stellar: He played only three games and recorded not a single point. Plaxton picked up his scoring pace the next year, though, as he notched 11 goals and three assists in only six games. His performance improved even more in 1923–24. Still with the U of T squad, he registered 18 goals and three assists in just eight games.

When he was finished with the Varsity Blues, Plaxton joined the Toronto Grads in 1925. He sat out the 1925–26 season before recording a career-best campaign with the Grads in 1926–27, scoring an impressive 31 goals and seven assists in nine games. In 1928 Plaxton was a member of

Plaxton, Hugh
LW, 5´10˝, 184 lbs, b: Barrie, Ont., 5/16/1904, deceased.

Season	Club, League	Regular Season					Playoffs				
		GP	G	A	Pts	PIM	GP	G	A	Pts	PIM
1921–22	University of Toronto, OHA Sr.	3	0	0	0	*					
1922–23	University of Toronto, OHA Sr.	6	11	3	14	*	1	0	0	0	0
1923–24	University of Toronto, OHA Sr.	8	18	3	21	10	5	1	2	3	8
1924–25	University of Toronto, OHA Sr.	8	4	2	6	*	6	5	2	7	*
1926–27	Toronto Varsity Grads, OHA Sr.	9	31	7	38	11	13	21	5	26	26
1927–28	Toronto Varsity Grads, OHA Sr.	12	20	10	30	*					
OWG –28	Canada	3	12	2	14	*					
1932–33	Montreal Maroons, NHL	15	1	2	3	4					
	Windsor Bulldogs, IAHL	10	1	1	2	4					
	Vancouver Maroons, WCHL	8	0	0	0	0					
	NHL Totals	15	1	2	3	4					
	OWG Totals	3	12	2	14	*					

Won OWG (1928)

the Canadian Olympic team that traveled to St. Moritz, Switzerland. He recorded 12 goals and two assists in Canada's three-game gold medal-winning run in the Games.

After the 1928 Games, Plaxton sat out five seasons while pursuing a career as a lawyer in Ontario. In January 1929 the Boston Bruins, who held his professional rights, traded them to Toronto. But in 1932–33, when Plaxton returned to the game as a pro, it was with the Montreal Maroons. After scoring only one goal in 15 games with Montreal, he completed the season with the Windsor Bulldogs of the International-American league and the Vancouver Maroons of the Western Canada Hockey League before retiring.

Dave Trottier

Sturdy winger Dave Trottier was born in Pembroke, Ontario, in 1906. He spent his junior career with the St. Michael's Majors of the OHA from 1923–1925 before joining the Toronto Varsity Grads in the OHA senior league from 1925 to 1928. His best season with the Majors was in 1923–24, when he scored 13 goals and added two assists in six games. As a Grad, his best year was 1927–28: 33 goals and 10 assists for a total of 43 points in just 12 games.

The speedy Trottier also represented Canada as a member of the Grads in 1928 at the Olympic Games in St. Moritz, Switzerland, where he helped the Canadian squad win the gold medal by scoring 12 goals and setting up three others in the short three-game tournament.

Such was his reputation that in September 1928 Trottier's pro rights were acquired by the Montreal Maroons for an incredible $10,000. Trottier began his NHL career with the Maroons in 1928–29, playing 37 games in his first season but recording only two goals and four assists. He also spent time with the Montreal Victorias in the city senior league but was better suited to the faster pace of the NHL.

Trottier's performance in the pro ranks improved quickly, and in 1931–32 he scored 26

Trottier, Dave
LW, 5´10˝, 170 lbs, b: Pembroke, Ont., 6/25/1906, d: 1956

Season	Club, League	Regular Season					Playoffs				
		GP	G	A	Pts	PIM	GP	G	A	Pts	PIM
1925–26	Toronto Varsity Grads, OHA Sr.	*	*	*	*	*	*	*	*	*	*
1926–27	Toronto Varsity Grads, OHA Sr.	11	23	8	31	7	14	10	7	17	34
1927–28	Toronto Varsity Grads, OHA Sr.	12	33	10	43	*					
OWG –28	Canada	3	12	3	15	*					
1928–29	Montreal Maroons, NHL	37	2	4	6	69					
	Montreal Victorias, City Sr.	2	0	0	0	0					
1929–30	Montreal Maroons, NHL	41	17	10	27	73	4	0	2	2	8
1930–31	Montreal Maroons, NHL	43	9	8	17	58	2	0	0	0	6
1931–32	Montreal Maroons, NHL	48	26	18	44	94	4	1	0	1	0
1932–33	Montreal Maroons, NHL	48	16	15	31	38	2	0	0	0	6
1933–34	Montreal Maroons, NHL	48	9	17	26	47	4	0	0	0	6
1934–35	Montreal Maroons, NHL	34	10	9	19	22	7	2	1	3	4
1935–36	Montreal Maroons, NHL	46	10	10	20	25	3	0	0	0	4
1936–37	Montreal Maroons, NHL	43	12	11	23	33	5	1	0	1	5
1937–38	Montreal Maroons, NHL	47	9	10	19	42					
1938–39	Detroit Red Wings, NHL	11	1	1	2	16					
	Pittsburgh Hornets, AHL	10	5	3	8	6					
	NHL Totals	446	121	113	234	517	31	4	3	7	39
	OWG Totals	3	12	3	15	*					

Won OWG (1928)
Won Stanley Cup (1935)

Hugh Plaxton (bottom row, third from the right) and Dave Trottier (bottom row, second from the right) played on the first-place Canadian team at the Olympics in St. Moritz, Switzerland, in 1928.

goals and recorded 18 assists for 44 points in 48 games. But his game featured more than scoring—Trottier was also earning a reputation as one of the pro game's best checking forwards. In 1934–35, he was an important part of the Maroons' drive to the Stanley Cup, a playoffs that climaxed in a three-game sweep of the Leafs in the best-of-five finals. His consistent play with Montreal earned him a spot in the Howie Morenz Memorial Game in 1937, a precursor to the All-Star Game.

In December 1938 Trottier was traded to the Detroit Red Wings for cash. Trottier played only 11 games for the Wings in 1938–39, recording a single goal and a single assist. He finished that year with a 10-game stay in the minors, with the Pittsburgh Hornets of the American Hockey League, before hanging up his skates.

Although Trottier scored 121 goals and earned 113 assists in 446 NHL games, he'll be best remembered by fans and hockey historians as one of the key members of the 1928 gold medal-winning team in Switzerland. Trottier passed away in 1956 at the age of 50.

John Francis "Bunny" Ahearne

Although he never played the game, Bunny Ahearne played a major role in international hockey. A cheerful Irishman who lived most of his life in England, Ahearne was a travel agent whose efficiency and organizational skills guided him up through the ranks of the British Ice Hockey Association.

He was appointed secretary of the BIHA in 1933, a position he held for 40 years. He also served as Britain's delegate to the International Ice Hockey Federation from 1934 until the start of World War II in 1939. But among Olympic hockey fans, he's best known for managing the British national team to an improbable gold medal victory over Canada at the 1936 Winter Games in Garmisch-Partenkirchen, Germany.

In 1947, with the war safely over, Ahearne traveled to Canada and the United States as a member of the IIHF delegation that successfully negotiated the return of both countries to active membership in the organization. On the strength of his ambassadorial skills, IIHF officials elected him vice-president in 1955, and he became president two years later. He continued to serve in both capacities until he retired 20 years later. During his tenure, he was also active in transforming the World Championships from an underappreciated competition into a major sporting event.

Often the central figure in international hockey disputes, Ahearne always said that he was "Canada's best friend" when it came to negotiating with the Europeans on matters of hockey protocol. And friend and foe alike knew that Ahearne rarely walked away from a good argument.

In 1969 Ahearne was at the center of an international hockey controversy that would have important implications for world hockey for years to come. That year the IIHF approved the use of nine professional players by any team in a world hockey tournament, provided they hadn't played in the National Hockey League that same season. But Ahearne wanted to make it clear that no other country besides Canada could use this rule to its advantage. In response to Russian claims that Canada would "find loopholes for professionals" in the 1970 World Championships—to be held in Montreal and Winnipeg—Ahearne said that he'd never allow this to happen. "Canada must fill its roster with 11 amateur players who have never been professional," he declared. "This is the agreement I made with the Canadians and that is the way it's going to be."

The International Olympic Committee refused to back Ahearne's plan, and Canada withdrew from the World Championships. The Canadians would refuse to field a team in the tournament until 1977.

Ahearne was an early advocate of the involvement of television in sports. He played a major role in securing profitable broadcasting rights to international games, while also popularizing the idea of selling advertising space on the boards in arenas. Much of the revenue produced by these promotional avenues helped finance the growth of international hockey as a whole.

In 1977 Bunny Ahearne was inducted into the Hockey Hall of Fame in the Builders category.

Bunny Ahearne managed the British national team to an improbable gold medal victory over Canada at the 1936 Olympics.

Joe **Benoit**

Joe Benoit recorded nine points in six games and helped Canada win gold at the World Championship in 1939.

An entertaining right winger, Joe Benoit was a member of the Montreal Canadiens, providing the team with spectacular scoring during the early 1940s.

Between 1940 and 1943, Benoit was one of the team's leading point-getters. He made his presence felt in his first season with 16 goals and 16 assists in only 45 games. The following year he recorded 20 goals and 16 assists, then improved to an impressive 30 goals and 27 helpers in 49 games.

Military service prevented him from playing in the NHL during the 1943–44 season. The following year he joined the Calgary Army team in that city's senior league. In 1945–46, Benoit was back with the Canadiens, with whom he played for two more seasons before being sent to the Springfield Indians of the American Hockey League during the 1946–47 season. He didn't play the following year and in 1948–49 played one game for the Montreal Royals of the Quebec Senior Hockey League before being appointed to a coaching position with the Spokane Flyers in the Kootenay league.

International hockey fans are most familiar with Benoit as a member of the Trail (British Columbia) Smoke Eaters squad that represented Canada in the World Championships at the end of the 1938–39 season. In seven games during the World tournament, he recorded six goals and three assists for nine points, helping Canada win the gold medal. In the summer of 1940, the Toronto Maple Leafs, who held his professional rights, traded him to the Montreal Canadiens for Frankie Eddolls, who in turn was later traded to Montreal for one of the greatest Leafs of all time, Ted Kennedy.

Prior to joining the Trail club, Benoit, who was born in St. Albert, Alberta, had played junior hockey with the Edmonton Athletics in the city's junior league. He passed away in 1981.

Benoit, Joe
RW, 5´10″, 160 lbs, b: St. Albert, Alta., 2/27/1916, d: 10/19/1981

Season	Club, League	Regular Season					Playoffs				
		GP	G	A	Pts	PIM	GP	G	A	Pts	PIM
1936–37	Trail Canadians, Kootenay	13	13	7	20	18					
1937–38	Trail Smoke Eaters, Kootenay	20	26	6	32	21	5	5	3	8	8
1938–39	Trail Smoke Eaters, Kootenay	*	*	*	*	*	*	*	*	*	*
WEC–39	Canada	7	6	3	9	*					
1939–40	Trail Smoke Eaters, Kootenay	24	26	17	43	49	7	2	4	6	10
1940–41	Montreal Canadiens, NHL	45	16	16	32	32	3	4	0	4	2
1941–42	Montreal Canadiens, NHL	46	20	16	36	27	3	1	0	1	5
1942–43	Montreal Canadiens, NHL	49	30	27	57	23	5	1	3	4	4
1944–45	Calgary Army, City Sr.	13	7	3	10	8	2	1	0	1	2
1945–46	Montreal Canadiens, NHL	39	9	10	19	8					
1946–47	Montreal Canadiens, NHL	6	0	0	0	4					
	Springfield Indians, AHL	34	9	10	19	4	2	0	0	0	0
1948–49	Montreal Royals, QSHL	1	0	0	0	0					
	WEC Totals	7	6	3	9	*					
	NHL Totals	185	75	69	144	94	11	6	3	9	11

Won WEC (1939)

Josef Malecek

When hockey experts in the Czech Republic set about choosing the best players of the last century, Josef Malecek was the only one from the prewar era to make the top 10.

After the communist takeover in 1948, Malecek left Czechoslovakia. A few years later he became a sports commentator with Radio Free Europe and subsequently with Voice of America. His forbidden radio commentaries, broadcast from foreign stations that the Czech communists tried to jam, were listened to secretly by thousands of people, many of whom would have been the same fans who had cheered him on the ice.

Josef Malecek was born in Prague on June 18, 1903. He grew up on the vast Letenska plain in the Moldau region, near a point where it overlooks the river. He got his first skates even before he went to school. In the winters, it was possible to skate on the river.

Malecek inherited his versatility from his father, who was probably the top athlete in prewar Czechoslovakia. In 1926 AC Sparta named Malecek's father an honorary member. Fifty-seven years later, in 1983, Josef and his brothers were among the founders of AC Kralovske Vinohrady, which only a few months later took on the Sparta name.

Josef was an excellent tennis player and represented his country in the Davis Cup. He also excelled in soccer, field hockey (for a long time he was the best player on the national team), water polo, golf, table tennis, chess, billiards, cycling and athletics. For a time he even held the Czech record in the 400-meter hurdles. But it was hockey that enchanted him the most.

In 1922 Malecek went to the European Championships for the first time, as a replacement for another player. Ten years would pass before he missed a tournament, and then only due to injury. Before the Second World War, he played in three Winter Olympics and attended every world or continental championship. Five times he and his team became European champions. He scored 114 goals in 107 games for the national team. As one of Czechoslovakia's brightest stars, he was often compared in the mid 1930s to the best forwards from the National Hockey League. In Europe, only the brilliant Swiss player Bibi Torriani could compare with him.

He played at center for AC Sparta until 1927, and then until 1943 for LTC Prague, where he was a defenseman. Later he put in an excellent performance as a player-coach for OAP Bratislava, the 1944 champions, where he stayed until his exile. He had his whims, but he could also respect real authority. Like Vladimir Zabrodsky after him, Malecek gained recognition as a true leader while with LTC Prague.

Josef Malecek (top row, third from the left)

In the late 1930s, Malecek crossed paths with a Canadian hockey emissary by the name of Mike Buckna, who was a brilliant player and an old-fashioned tough guy. As a player-coach, Buckna wouldn't let anything or anybody get in his way. One day he got the feeling that Malecek wasn't taking his instructions seriously and he slapped him in front of the entire team. The great Malecek just hung his head and went out on the ice. As he passed Buckna, he said in a low voice, "Sorry, Mike."

Malecek was a strong-willed man who made a living out of sports. He and some teammates from LTC opened a sports equipment shop. As a member of the social elite, he rubbed shoulders with actors and business people and acted in television commercials. Not a week went by that he wasn't interviewed by the media. One author—well known at the time but since forgotten—wrote a fairy tale about him, and half of Prague showed up for his wedding.

After the end of the war and the Nazi occupation, he was charged with collaboration. Although his enemies were unable to prove their allegations, he went into exile and coached the Swiss HC Davos club from 1948 to 1952. During the Spengler Cup in 1948, he was involved in efforts to persuade the full lineup of LTC Prague to create a team of Czech exiles. For a long time afterwards, his voice was heard over the airwaves of Radio Free Europe, which he'd helped found, and later on the Voice of America. Josef Malecek died in Bar Port, on New York's Long Island, on September 26, 1982.

A story from the prewar era tells how Malecek's friends prepared a surprise tribute to him before an important international hockey match. They hired a bugler to play his favorite piece of music from the roof of the bandstand. As soon as he heard the first notes, he folded his arms in his usual manner, leaned on his stick and listened closely. When the game began, he took the puck, skated past three players and scored. Maybe it isn't all true, but legends and famous people go together quite nicely.

1942–1967

The Original Six:
Facts and Fables

*I*n 1926, the National Hockey League brought together four Canadian and six American clubs to become the only professional hockey league in North America. With the onset of the Great Depression and the subsequent burden of World War II, however, the Ottawa and Pittsburgh teams were no longer financially viable, and eventually the Montreal Maroons went under as well. They had few playing achievements to boast of, but the New York Americans stayed afloat a bit longer. When even New York proved too small for two NHL clubs, they too left the league in 1942. Thus began the 25-year reign of the Original Six: the Toronto Maple Leafs, Montreal Canadiens, Detroit Red Wings, Chicago Black Hawks, Boston Bruins and New York Rangers.

The year 1942 marked the beginning of the era of the Original Six, which lasted 25 seasons.

The Detroit Red Wings brought a reputation as one of the most inconsistent clubs of the six. No sooner had sportscasters begun referring to the birth of a Red Wings dynasty in the mid-1930s than Detroit virtually crashed. In the 1937–38 season, they were last in the regular season in their division with the second-worst set of statistics in the league. But three years after that they were back in contention and crowned their rise with first place in the regular season and a four-game sweep of the Bruins in the 1943 Stanley Cup finals in the Original Six's first season.

After an interval of more than 10 years, the Montreal Canadiens had a rebirth of their own in the 1943–44 season, but their victory in the Stanley Cup finals is remembered today primarily because it marked the debut of a new NHL star—Maurice "the Rocket" Richard.

That year had seen the astonishing rise of the trio of Richard, Elmer Lach and Toe Blake that came to be known as the Punch Line. In post-season play, the Leafs were the first to feel the wrath of the Rocket in the semifinals. In game two, Richard scored all five Canadiens goals in a 5–1 win over Toronto. In game two of the finals, Richard scored all three in a 3–1 win over Chicago. In the third period of game four, the Black Hawks were expecting a victory. Five minutes before the end of regulation time, with the score at 4–2, Richard whipped in two quick ones to tie it and Blake fired in the decisive goal in overtime to win the game and the series.

A HISTORY OF WORLD HOCKEY

The 1944 playoffs also marked the beginning of a star-studded (though short-lived) career for another Canadien. At 27, Bill Durnan was making his debut in the NHL with the Montreal squad. He hung up his skates in a scant seven seasons, but after six of those he was awarded the Vezina Trophy as the best goalkeeper in the NHL and no goalie in the league's history matched his goals-against numbers until Ken Dryden retired with a regular-season goals-against average of 2.24.

The following season wasn't as successful for the Canadiens. After leading the league at the end of the regular season, they bowed out to Toronto in the semifinals. Richard managed to scale one more height by becoming the first NHL player to score 50 goals in a regular season. And the 50th came in the last of 50 games (against Boston).

In April 1945, Toronto and Detroit repeated the first six games of the 1942 finals with the same results in reverse. This time the Maple Leafs won the first three games with rookie goal-keeper Frank McCool living up to owner-manager Conn Smythe's expectations by turning in three straight shutouts (playing a total of 188 minutes and 35 seconds without a goal scored against him). And the Red Wings learned from bitter experience not to throw in the towel in the face of a 3–0 deficit. They nearly accomplished the impossible by winning the next three, but the Leafs eked out game seven 2–1. Even while he was being congratulated, however, Conn Smythe noted a lack of star talent on his forward lines.

In the 1946 finals against Boston, the Punch Line again turned in brilliant individual performances, racking up 19 goals in five games, and the Canadiens marked another new milestone by winning the Stanley Cup for the second time in three years. Montreal fans

In 1949 the Toronto Maple Leafs won the Stanley Cup for the third year in a row and became the first dynasty in the history of the NHL.

were disappointed that their team didn't take the Cup for three years in succession to become an official dynasty, but the first of those would have to wait for the Maple Leafs of the late 1940s.

The end of the war solved the problem Smythe cited above. Syl Apps and a number of other experienced forwards came back from military service and center Ted Kennedy brought his confidence to the second-string line. After a year of restructuring, the Maple Leafs re-emerged in the Stanley Cup finals in 1947 to face the Montreal Canadiens led by Maurice Richard. The Rocket couldn't be quenched by youth or experience, by rookie defensemen Gus Mortson or Jim Thomson or goalie Turk Broda (who was also just back from the war), and topped the list of play-off scorers with six goals and five assists for a total of 11 points (and also led the dubious black-list with 44 penalty minutes). Even so, the Leafs took the lead in the series after losing game one at the Forum 6–0.

As the games went on, Montreal's job of neutralizing the Leafs' three forward lines proved no less difficult than Toronto's of stopping Richard. When Toronto scored four unanswered goals during power-plays in game two, the united front of Conn Smythe and coach Hap Day demonstrated the superiority of team play and well-organized hockey. Toronto won in six games.

In a trade with Chicago the following season, the Maple Leafs acquired a third top-notch center, Max Bentley, the top NHL scorer in the spring of 1947. Bentley was only fifth on the team on the list of high scorers the year he came to Toronto, but he'd had the good fortune to join a Stanley Cup winner. In the finals, the Leafs swept their traditional rivals from Detroit in four games and Detroit's already famous Production Line of Sid Abel, Ted Lindsay and Gordie Howe picked up only one point.

After the second Stanley Cup victory in a row, Toronto fans started talking about a dynasty in the making. There was some concern after Syl Apps retired, but Smythe found a replacement when he acquired Cal Gardner from the Rangers. During the regular 1948–49 season, however, the team just didn't click and the Leafs wound up fourth. The Red Wings eclipsed them by 18 points to take the regular-season title, while the Production Line churned out a total of 66 goals. But Toronto and Detroit met again in the finals, where the Leafs shut the Production Line down in four games (and again held the line to one goal). Toronto had won the Stanley Cup for the third year in a row and become the first dynasty in NHL history.

But they didn't stop there. In the spring of 1951, they captured the Stanley Cup for the fifth time in seven seasons, this time from the Canadiens. The game tally of 4–1 in the finals appeared to confirm the superiority of the Leafs. In reality, though, all five games ended in overtime for the first time in league history. Overtime goals were scored by Sid Smith, Ted Kennedy and Harry Watson, each for the only time in his career. And with 32 seconds to go in the third period of the last game, Montreal was leading 2–1. Toronto's new coach, Joe Primeau, pulled his goalie and tied up the score. Just into the overtime period, defenseman Bill Barilko received a slick pass from Howie Meeker (future Leafs coach and manager and all-around hockey guy) and put in the winning goal. With that glorious finish, the first dynasty for the Leafs withered away and fans had to wait a little over 10 years for its rebirth in 1961–62.

Beginning with the 1948–49 season, the Red Wings led the standings for seven straight seasons and won the Cup in 1950, 1952, 1954 and 1955 but failed to win the title of dynasty. At the beginning of the 1950s, the scoring talent on the Red Wings was concentrated in only one forward line—the Production Line— while defense had Red Kelly, Marcel Pronovost and Bob Goldham (who was known for his powerful shots on goal). When Terry Sawchuk appeared in the lineup in the 1949–50 season, the team's goaltending problems were also—and masterfully—solved.

The New York Rangers managed to surface in the finals that season for the first time in 10 years. After five games, coach and general manager Tommy Ivan's Wings were losing 3–2. New York was hungry for victory, and 16 minutes before the final whistle in game six they were leading 4–3 when the Lindsay–Abel tandem saved the day for the Wings and they pulled out a 5–4 win. And at last, in the second overtime period of the final game, with the score tied 3–3, Pete Babando—one of the few Americans playing in the NHL at the time—scored the winning goal. After a seven-year drought, a new generation of Red Wings took a sip from the Cup.

In 1952 perhaps the main event occurred in the semifinals between the Canadiens and the Bruins. After slamming into defenseman Bill Quackenbush in the second period of game seven, Maurice Richard was rushed to the Forum's clinic with a deep gash in his forehead. When it was stitched shut and a bandage applied, he demanded to be taken back to the bench, where he reappeared in the third period with the scoreboard reading 1–1.

Beginning with the 1948–49 season, the Detroit Red Wings led the standings for seven straight seasons and won the Cup in 1950, 1952, 1954 and 1955. With the appearance of Terry Sawchuk (front) in the lineup in the 1949–50 season, the team's goaltending problems were solved.

Four minutes before the final whistle, Richard told coach Irvin he was ready to go out on the ice. And as soon as he did, he got hold of the puck behind his own net and picked up speed, out-maneuvering the three Boston forwards and two defensemen on his way down the ice. Goalkeeper Sugar Jim Henry rushed out to meet him and tried to stop Richard with his stick. The Rocket hopped over it and poked the puck into the net as he fell. The fate of the series was sealed, but Richard was covered with blood and unable to get to his feet.

Detroit and Montreal met again in the finals. Having barely beaten the Bruins, the Canadiens were a pretty tired team as they came out against the Red Wings. And Richard was injured. Sawchuk was practically impenetrable (wholly so on home ice) and the Red Wings swept it in four.

Just as the Red Wings seemed ready to assume the mantle of dynasty, they were stopped in their tracks in the 1953 semifinals by the Bruins, led by the indomitable Milt Schmidt and Woody Dumart, who were both playing their 17th season. Before the series started, coach Lynn Patrick gave Dumart the job of neutralizing Gordie Howe, which he managed quite well. In six games, Howe scored only two goals and Detroit dropped the series 4–2. But the next two Cup finals saw Detroit and Montreal face off again.

The 1954 playoffs came down to a showdown between a revamped Production Line—Sid Abel had retired and Alex Delvecchio replaced him—and Maurice Richard and Bert Olmstead. Neither team had a clear advantage and after six games the series was tied. So was game seven until Tony Leswick scored a fluke goal for the Red Wings in overtime. Better known for checking than scoring, Leswick fired the puck at a sharp angle into the opposition's zone in the fifth minute of overtime. All-Star defenseman Doug Harvey tried to stop the puck but it ricocheted off his glove over goalkeeper Gerry McNeil's shoulder and ended up in the net. Stunned by the turn of events, the Canadiens refused to participate in the ceremony to award the Cup.

If the 1954 Stanley Cup finals ended in a scandal, the 1955 playoffs were preceded by one. In a game against Boston on March 13, at the end of the regular season, the notoriously feisty Maurice Richard whacked Hal Laycoe on the back with his stick and then took a punch at linesman Cliff Thompson. The response from NHL president Clarence Campbell was swift: Richard was suspended for the rest of the season including the playoffs. The result was a riot directed at first against Campbell himself.

When Campbell arrived at the Forum on March 17, a fan who had managed to squirm through the police cordon stretched out his hand as if to shake the league president's hand. Campbell reciprocated—and was hit in the face. At that point, the Forum and adjacent St. Catherine Street turned into a pitched battle between fans and police. The game was halted and forfeited to Detroit. Only a radio plea from Richard the next day restored peace in Montreal while Detroit won the regular season.

After a prologue like that, it's not difficult to imagine the atmosphere that dominated the 1955 Stanley Cup finals between the Red Wings and the Canadiens. Detroit won the first two games at home due to the efforts of the latest Production Line (Lindsay scored five goals while Howe and Delvecchio chalked up one apiece). Back in the Forum, the Canadiens repaid the Red Wings in kind, with every Canadien playing not only for himself but also for the absent Richard. Away for game five, Montreal suffered a 5–1 loss to Gordie Howe's hat-trick. Back at the Forum, it was Howe's turn to be shut down; along with a young Jean Beliveau, Boom Boom Geoffrion led the Canadiens to a 6–3 win. The deciding match was played at Detroit's Olympia, where the home team hadn't lost a game in almost four months. And the record would hold. With two goals by Delvecchio and one by Howe, Detroit clinched the series and the Cup while Gordie Howe set an NHL record with nine goals and 11 assists for a total of 20 points in the playoffs.

The Canadiens won the 1955–56 regular season for the first time since 1947; Jean Beliveau won the Art Ross Trophy over Gordie Howe; the list of top 10 scorers now included Maurice Richard, Bert Olmstead and Bernie Geoffrion; and goalkeeper Jacques Plante received the first of the six Vezina Trophies he'd eventually win. And Montreal continued its triumphant march forward in the Stanley Cup finals that season. Detroit managed to neutralize Maurice Richard to some extent, but his role as top scorer in the playoffs was already being performed by Jean Beliveau, who racked up 12 goals. The Canadiens lost one game to the Red Wings, took the series in five, then went on to win three of the four subsequent finals in fewer than seven (in the 1958 finals, for example, Boston bowed out to the Canadiens after six). Their 20 victories in 25 games of Stanley Cup finals gave Montreal five straight Stanley Cups—a feat that has never been matched.

Fans at Maple Leaf Gardens.

With a defense line headed by seven-time Norris Trophy winner Doug Harvey and a net tended by Jacques Plante (consistently selected the league's top goaltender), Montreal didn't allow many goals in those five seasons. Coach Toe Blake had two top forward lines, which only Detroit could hope to match in the Original Six. In the critical moments of those five final series, however, and especially in overtime, it was Maurice Richard who caused his team's opponents most grief.

The dynasty reigned for five years and no team has ever repeated, but the Canadiens were conspicuously absent from the Stanley Cup finals for the four years after that as they rejuvenated their lineup. Quite unexpectedly, it was the Chicago Black Hawks who took up the slack.

The Black Hawks had won the Stanley Cup twice before but didn't even get to the playoffs in 11 of the first 12 years of the reign of the Original Six. One reason was that the club's scouting system worked far less efficiently than that of the Canadiens or the Leafs. Hawks lineups were built mainly on trades. Only when James D. Norris Jr. took over as owner and vowed to buy players until the scouting started to work was the situation resolved—which is how Bobby Hull and Stan Mikita made their way from the Ontario junior leagues to the Black Hawks' camp in the latter half of the 1950s and "rebels" Tod Sloan and Jim Thomson from Toronto and "disturbers of the peace" Ted Lindsay and Glenn Hall from Detroit arrived in Chicago around the same time.

In those days, players became a club's property when they signed a contract. Since they could barely make a move (or even retire) without getting permission, it shouldn't have come as a great surprise when a few stars tried to organize a union for NHL players in 1946–47. Nothing came of it then, but at least the league was compelled to adopt a pension plan for the players. Another attempt to establish a union in the second half of the 1950s led to the emergence of "rebels" and "disturbers of the peace" the owners of the Leafs and the Red Wings didn't mind getting rid of.

Tommy Ivan had moved to Chicago, and after weighing all the pros and cons, he decided to take on the experienced troublemakers and began to reap the rewards in the 1960–61 season. Goalkeeper Glenn Hall lived up to all expectations, and for the first time in 17 years the Black Hawks made it to the finals against the Red Wings (who had edged out the Leafs in five games). In game five, both teams demonstrated a superior attack that resulted in 80 shots on goal. But things didn't click in those finals for Detroit's leading attacker, Gordie Howe. In the sixth and deciding game, the Black Hawks tore the Detroit defense lines apart and won with a convincing score of 5–1.

After that, the Hawks suffered a relapse in spite of record individual successes for its players. During the next six years, the club climbed higher and higher in the standings and even captured first place in the 1966–67 season; Bobby Hull and Stan Mikita took turns winning the Art Ross Trophy for four years in succession; and Glenn Hall won the Vezina Trophy twice. Critics suggest that Chicago lost out because they were unwilling to take chances—the kind of chances taken the following year by new Maple Leafs coach and general manager George "Punch" Imlach.

Almost 10 years had passed since the first Maple Leafs dynasty drifted out of the limelight, and when Imlach came to Toronto in the 1958–59 season, he had to start from scratch. Not wanting to waste five years building a new base, he relied on veterans to form the core of the team (including quite a few from the rest of the Original Six) while a second half was made up of talented young players from Toronto's own farm clubs. Ten years later, the names of many of those young players would be familiar even in Europe.

Some critics scoffed at Imlach for imagining that a team of "bearded veterans and greenhorns" could win the Stanley Cup, but the theory was soon put to the test. The Maple Leafs met the Black Hawks in the 1962 finals for the first time since 1938 and the veterans attacked it knowing it could well be their last chance to win. Even when they lost their main goalie, Johnny Bower ("the China Wall"), in game five because of an injury, Toronto refused to go on the defensive and won by a convincing margin of 8–4. Then they finished the job 2–1 in game six with a winning goal scored by Dick Duff on a pass from 32-year-old Tim Horton, who set a new record for a defenseman in playoff games with 12 assists.

In the 1963 finals, Gordie Howe scored three goals and earned three assists but the Leafs had five players who could score at least two goals a game. In game one, it was Dick Duff (who set a record by whipping in two goals within 68 seconds of the opening face-off). Now with Toronto, defenseman Red Kelly scored twice in game four, while another was scored in that game by a young but fast-rising Dave Keon. In the fifth and last game, Keon set a new NHL playoffs record by scoring twice while his team was a man short. And that clinched the Cup.

Toronto took another run at becoming a dynasty in the spring of 1964. This time Detroit took it to seven for the first time since 1943 but went down to defeat in spite of a stellar performance by Gordie Howe, who at times seemed to be fighting Toronto single-handedly, just as he had in the previous year. The Toronto goals were scored by half a dozen different forwards headed by Andy Bathgate (acquired before the end of the regular season from the Rangers), Frank Mahovlich and Keon again, but the hero of the game was Bob Baun.

Shortly before the end of regulation time in game six, with the score at 3–3, Baun's ankle was fractured by a flying puck and he had to be helped off the ice. The ankle was taped and Baun came back on the ice after the first minute of overtime. Bob Pulford won the face-off in the

Detroit zone and flipped the puck back to Baun. Baun took a shot and the puck did a series of ricochets but then made it past Sawchuk into the net. The emotional upsurge on the Toronto team was so great that in game seven they shut down the Red Wings 4–0. And that third Stanley Cup in a row was a fitting reward for Punch Imlach and the team he had whipped into shape even though their average age was the oldest in the NHL.

Now headed by Jean Beliveau and Henri Richard, Montreal didn't have more than half a dozen players left from their first dynasty of the late 1950s. The Canadiens also lost their star goalie, the very determined Jacques Plante, when Sam Pollock traded him to New York for Lorne "Gump" Worsley. It turned out to be a good trade. In his first season with Montreal, Worsley reached the Stanley Cup finals for the first time in 12 years in the league and provided the strongest link in the Canadiens' chain of defense. Another newcomer, Yvan Cournoyer, scored his first goal in the playoffs, and defenseman Jean-Claude Tremblay excelled in the assists department. But the main figure in the Montreal lineup was again Jean Beliveau, who became the first player to be awarded the newly inaugurated Conn Smythe Trophy as his team's MVP in the Stanley Cup playoffs with three winning goals and one winning assist. And the Canadiens won their 12th Stanley Cup.

In the spring of 1966, Chicago's leading attacker, Bobby Hull, ended the regular season as the first NHL player to surpass Richard's record of 50 goals in a season and established a new league points record with 54 goals and 34 assists for a total of 97. Teammate Stan Mikita was runner-up with 30 goals and 48 assists for 78. Still, the Black Hawks failed to hurdle the barrier of the semifinals and it was the Canadiens who faced the Red Wings in the finals.

Meanwhile, Detroit had decided to try Punch Imlach's strategy and added the newly acquired Andy Bathgate and 37-year-old defenseman Bill Gadsby to a veteran lineup that included Howe and Delvecchio. They also hired forward Paul Henderson (who had just turned 20) and goalkeeper Roger Crozier. And it seemed to be working. After the first two games of the finals, Detroit was ahead 2–0. Then they dropped the next four and their only reward was when Roger Crozier became the first goalie to be named MVP.

In the 1961–62 season, the Cup-winning goal was scored by Dick Duff on a pass from 32-year-old veteran Tim Horton (right), who set a new record for a defenseman in the playoffs with 12 assists.

In 1967, all of Canada was hoping to see two Canadian clubs in the Stanley Cup finals to mark the country's Centennial. At the time, 95% of NHL players were Canadian, and that season marked the last and the largest struggle among the Original Six.

On May 2nd, with Toronto leading the series against Montreal 3–2, play returned to Maple Leaf Gardens. Gump Worsley replaced Vachon in the net and didn't let in a goal in the first period. Toronto took the lead 2–0, but one minute before the end of the third period, the Canadiens pulled Worsley and scored. Imlach called Allan Stanley over and told him, "You gotta win the face-off from Beliveau." As Stanley would later recall, he hadn't won a face-off in the past five or six years, but the force of Punch Imlach's words was so great he obeyed "the order." Stanley won the puck and flipped it to Armstrong, who scored into the empty net for a 3–1 result and the Maple Leafs' ninth Stanley Cup. Imlach himself summed it up: "Everybody wrote us off as being just a bunch of old guys. They were old, but they were also winners." And that was the last time Toronto would take the Cup home to the date of this writing.

Hector "Toe" Blake

Toe Blake became known as "the Old Lamplighter" because of his ability to put the puck in the net.

Long before he became a coaching legend, left wing Hector "Toe" Blake was a talented scorer and NHL star. He totalled 235 career goals, including six 20-goal seasons and became known as "the Old Lamplighter" in honor of his skill for putting the puck in the net. During the 1940s he formed one of the league's most dangerous lines, the Punch Line, with Maurice Richard and Elmer Lach.

Blake fine-tuned his game while playing junior and senior hockey in the Sudbury area from 1929 to 1932. Teams on which he played included the Cochrane Dunlops and the 1932 Memorial Cup champion Sudbury Cub Wolves under coach Max Silverman. Blake next excelled with the Hamilton Tigers at the Ontario Hockey Association senior level while also playing baseball. In his first year the Tigers lost the Ontario crown to Niagara Falls, but the next year they triumphed in Ontario before losing to Moncton's all-star import team in the Allan Cup semifinals. After an outstanding year in 1934–35, the sensational young star was offered a contract by Tommy Gorman of the Montreal Maroons.

Although his name was synonymous with the great Canadiens teams of the 1940s, Blake made his NHL debut with their crosstown rivals, the Maroons, just before the 1935 playoffs. They won the Stanley Cup that year, but because of Blake's inexperience he was relegated to watching from the bench. He started the 1935–36 season in Providence under coach Bert "Battleship" Leduc. In February 1936 the Canadiens acquired him when he was enjoying a solid year with the Reds of the Can-Am league. Blake played 11 games for the Canadiens that year and earned a full-time spot on the roster in 1936–37.

Blake's first two full NHL seasons were solid, but he took his game to a higher level with a league-leading 47 points in 1938–39. His effort was rewarded with the Hart Trophy and placement on the NHL First All-Star Team. He was teamed up with Elmer Lach and Maurice Richard in 1943 and the Punch Line led Montreal to the Stanley Cup later that season. It was the Old Lamplighter's goal at 9:12 of overtime in game four that gave Montreal a 5–4 win over Chicago and possession of hockey's ultimate prize. That year he led all post-season scorers with seven goals and 18 points. His record for that playoffs of two points per game went untouched until Wayne Gretzky took over the NHL record book in the 1980s.

Blake, Hector "Toe"
LW, 5'10", 165 lbs, b: Victoria Mines, Ont., 8/21/1912, d: 5/17/1995

Season	Club, League		Regular Season					Playoffs			
		GP	G	A	Pts	PIM	GP	G	A	Pts	PIM
1929–30	Cochrane Dunlops, City Sr.	7	3	0	3	4					
1930–31	Sudbury Cub Wolves, NOHA	6	3	1	4	12	2	0	0	0	6
	Sudbury Industries, City Sr.	8	7	1	8	10	3	1	1	2	4
1931–32	Sudbury Cub Wolves, NOHA	3	5	0	5	4					
	Falconbridge Falcons, City Sr.	10	8	1	9	18	2	1	0	1	2
1932–33	Hamilton Tigers, OHA Sr.	22	9	4	13	26	2	0	0	0	2
1933–34	Hamilton Tigers, OHA Sr.	23	19	14	33	28	4	3	4	7	4
1934–35	Montreal Maroons, NHL	8	0	0	0	0	1	0	0	0	0
	Hamilton Tigers, OHA Sr.	18	15	11	26	48					
1935–36	Providence Reds Can-Am	33	12	11	23	65	7	2	3	5	2
	Montreal Canadiens, NHL	11	1	2	3	28					
1936–37	Montreal Canadiens, NHL	43	10	12	22	12	5	1	0	1	0
1937–38	Montreal Canadiens, NHL	43	17	16	33	33	3	3	1	4	2
1938–39	Montreal Canadiens, NHL	48	24	23	47	10	3	1	1	2	2
1939–40	Montreal Canadiens, NHL	48	17	19	36	48					
1940–41	Montreal Canadiens, NHL	48	12	20	32	49	3	0	3	3	5
1941–42	Montreal Canadiens, NHL	48	17	28	45	19	3	0	3	3	2
1942–43	Montreal Canadiens, NHL	48	23	36	59	26	5	4	3	7	0
1943–44	Montreal Canadiens, NHL	41	26	33	59	10	9	7	11	18	2
1944–45	Montreal Canadiens, NHL	49	29	38	67	25	6	0	2	2	5
1945–46	Montreal Canadiens, NHL	50	29	21	50	2	9	7	6	13	5
1946–47	Montreal Canadiens, NHL	60	21	29	50	6	11	2	7	9	0
1947–48	Montreal Canadiens, NHL	32	9	15	24	4					
1948–49	Buffalo Bisons, AHL	18	1	3	4	0					
1949–50	Valleyfield Braves, QSHL	43	12	15	27	15	3	0	1	1	0
	NHL Totals	577	235	292	527	272	58	25	37	62	23

NHL First All-Star Team (1939, 1940, 1945)
NHL Second All-Star Team (1938, 1946)
Won Hart Trophy (1939)
Won Lady Byng Trophy (1946)
NHL Scoring Leader (1939)
Won Stanley Cup (1944, 1946)

In 1944–45, Blake notched a personal-best 67 points while helping linemate Richard become the first 50-goal shooter in NHL history. The next year Blake led all playoff scorers with seven goals in nine games to help bring the team its second championship in three years. That year the veteran winger was also presented the Lady Byng Trophy for his sportsmanlike play.

Blake retired at the conclusion of the 1947–48 season with 235 regular-season goals and 25 playoff markers to his credit. He immediately accepted a coaching position with the Houston Huskies of the United States Hockey League. After stops in Buffalo and Valleyfield, Blake rejoined the Canadiens as bench boss in 1955–56 as successor to the legendary Dick Irvin. One of the main reasons he was hired was to help control the explosive temper of his former linemate, Maurice Richard.

One of the main reasons Toe Blake (center) was hired as a Montreal coach was to help control the explosive temper of his former linemate, Maurice Richard.

Blake's performance behind the Montreal bench between 1955 and 1968 was unparalleled. He won an incredible eight Stanley Cup titles in just 13 seasons, including five in a row in his first five years of coaching. In all, his playoff record was 82–37, a wins-to-losses ratio rarely matched in the NHL. His Habs teams never had a losing record and they never failed to make the playoffs.

The famous Hab also ran a popular men-only tavern down the street from the Forum. In 1966, after coaching the Habs to the Stanley Cup, he was inducted into the Hockey Hall of Fame in the Players category. In 1982 Blake was presented the Order of Canada.

Bill Durnan

Bill Durnan entered the professional game late and didn't stay for long, but he packed an entire career's worth of awards and recognition into his seven National Hockey League seasons with the Montreal Canadiens. He was a talented athlete with a unique gift that separated him from any other NHL goalie—he was ambidextrous and could use either hand to catch the puck or hold his stick. He won the Vezina Trophy as the league's top netminder an amazing six times, missing out on the award only once when Toronto's Turk Broda borrowed it in 1948.

Durnan was born in Toronto in 1916 and was raised by his father after the death of his mother when he was five. At an early age, he began to take advantage of his ambidextrous skills.

"It was a tremendous asset and I owe that gift to Steve Faulkner, one of my coaches in a church league in Toronto when I was a youngster," Durnan said of the two-handed style he credited with his success. "Steve showed me how to switch the stick from one hand to the other. It wasn't easy at first because I was so young and the stick seemed so heavy. But Steve kept after me and gradually the stick became lighter and I could switch it automatically."

Durnan had a very successful amateur career, playing goal in the winter and starring as a softball pitcher in the summer months. He first gained attention as a goalie with Sudbury in the Ontario Hockey Association when he took the team to the league finals. After playing with a variety of teams in the Toronto area, he was signed to a Maple Leafs contract, but not long after, he injured his knee while wrestling with a friend on a beach. The ligament damage forced him to sit out a year and Toronto lost patience, cutting the young player when the knee continued to give him problems. In 1936 Durnan returned to hockey to play in the northern Ontario league with the Kirkland Lake Blue Devils. He spent four seasons with the Devils, backstopping the team to the Allan Cup in 1940. Friends in Montreal convinced him to take a job with the Royals in that city following his success with Kirkland Lake. After three years in the Quebec senior league he finally caught the attention of a National Hockey League team when the Montreal Canadiens began noticing the goalie star in their own backyard.

Up to that point, Durnan had earned at most $15 per week between playing hockey, softball and doing a variety of odd jobs. Canadiens manager Tommy Gorman, was known to drive a hard bargain when it came to negotiating contracts with his players. At the Habs' training camp in 1943, he settled on Durnan as his goalie, but the amateur didn't make it easy on the general manager.

Durnan proved to be a tough negotiator, saying he was happy as an amateur and happy with less money if it meant avoiding the stress of the professional game. On opening night, the goalie still wasn't signed. A mere 10 minutes before the first face-off, he spoke with Gorman and the Montreal skipper finally mumbled the figures Durnan was waiting to hear. He signed his name to the contract and ran down the hall to dress for the game. The ink was hardly dry on the signature when he finished his debut, a 2–2 draw with the Boston Bruins. Incredibly, the rookie netminder was a few months shy of his 29th birthday.

That first season the Canadiens had the offensive services of the Punch Line—Elmer Lach, Rocket Richard and Toe Blake—but it was the often spectacular play of Durnan that took Montreal back to the Stanley Cup after 13 years of frustration. He led the league in games played, wins and goals-against average in the regular season and in the playoffs, when he allowed only 1.53 goals per game as the Canadiens skated to the title. Durnan was awarded the Vezina Trophy, the first rookie to win the award, and was selected to the league's First All-Star Team.

It's hard to imagine a better four-year introduction to the NHL than Durnan's. He won the Vezina Trophy for four consecutive seasons and cemented himself on the First All-Star Team. Montreal won the Stanley Cup again in 1946 and finished first in the league after the regular season each year. Durnan suffered his only losing season in 1947–48. For the first and only time, he didn't lead the league in goals-against average and Montreal missed the playoffs. Broda, with the powerhouse Maple Leafs, took Durnan's spot on the First All-Star Team and had his name engraved on the Vezina Trophy as well as the Stanley Cup. Durnan returned to his winning ways

Durnan, Bill
G, 6´, 190 lbs, b: Toronto, Ont., 1/22/1916, d: 10/31/1972

Season	Club, League	Regular Season				Playoffs			
		GP	Mins	GA	Avg	GP	Mins	GA	Avg
1932–33	Sudbury Wolves, NOHA	6	360	6	1.00	2	120	4	2.00
1934–35	Toronto All-Stars, City Sr.	2	120	9	4.50				
	Toronto McColl, City Sr.	15	900	62	4.13				
1935–36	Toronto Dominions, City Sr.	1	60	6	6.00				
1936–37	Kirkland Lake Blue Devils, NOHA	4	240	5	1.25	4	240	8	2.00
1937–38	Kirkland Lake Blue Devils, NOHA	11	610	27	2.66	2	120	2	1.00
1938–39	Kirkland Lake Blue Devils, NOHA	7	420	7	1.00	2	120	3	1.50
1939–40	Kirkland Lake Blue Devils, NOHA	6	360	12	2.00				
1940–41	Montreal Royals, QSHL	34	2000	100	3.00	8	480	24	3.00
1941–42	Montreal Royals, QSHL	39	2340	143	3.67				
1942–43	Montreal Royals, QSHL	31	1860	130	4.19	4	240	11	2.75
1943–44	Montreal Canadiens, NHL	50	3000	109	2.18	9	549	14	1.53
1944–45	Montreal Canadiens, NHL	50	3000	121	2.42	6	373	15	2.41
1945–46	Montreal Canadiens, NHL	40	2400	104	2.60	9	581	20	2.07
1946–47	Montreal Canadiens, NHL	60	3600	138	2.30	11	720	23	1.92
1947–48	Montreal Canadiens, NHL	59	3505	162	2.77				
1948-49	Montreal Canadiens, NHL	60	3600	126	2.10	7	468	17	2.18
1949–50	Montreal Canadiens, NHL	64	3840	141	2.20	3	180	10	3.33
	NHL Totals	383	22945	901	2.36	45	2871	99	2.07

NHL First All-Star Team (1944, 1945, 1946, 1947, 1949, 1950)
Won Vezina Trophy (1944, 1945, 1946, 1947, 1949, 1950)
Won Stanley Cup (1944, 1946)

in 1948–49, setting a modern league record with a shutout streak that lasted over 309 minutes and four games. In the next two seasons he was once again the best goalie in the league.

Durnan was an easygoing man, friendly and calm, but over time the stress of playing—and the mental and physical toll of so many minutes and games between the posts—began to wear him down. In 1950 he abruptly retired from the game at the age of 35, while still in his prime. "It got so bad that I couldn't sleep on the night before a game. I couldn't even keep my meals down," he said of his reasons for hanging up the pads. "I felt that nothing was worth that kind of agony."

Although Durnan was loath to let his backup play during his time in Montreal—he didn't want to lose the job it had taken him so long to earn—he was one of the first goaltending stars to suggest that NHL teams carry two goalies, especially as the season stretched longer and longer into the spring, to prevent the shortening of careers.

After he retired, he coached in several junior leagues and then took the reins of the Kitchener-Waterloo Dutchmen, a celebrated senior team in the Ontario Hockey Association. He left the team because of an internal squabble just before the Dutchies were due to represent Canada at the 1960 Olympics.

Durnan was inducted into the Hockey Hall of Fame in 1964. He battled illness for several years and was admitted to North York General Hospital in Toronto on October 24, 1972. A week later he passed away at the age of 57. His old rival, Turk Broda, the man who prevented Durnan from hoisting the Vezina Trophy seven consecutive times, had died after a heart attack only two weeks earlier.

Bill Durnan was a talented goalie with a unique gift: He could use either hand to stop the puck or hold his stick.

Babe Pratt

Babe Pratt was a funny and outgoing man off the ice, keen on jokes and always good for a laugh, but he was considerably tougher with his hockey equipment on. Over a long career in leagues across North America, he proved consistently that the best defense is often a good offense. He was a defenseman who kept the puck deep in the other team's zone, sometimes deep in their net, and goalies on his squads could be sure their goals-against averages would drop when he was at his best. His leadership and ability are backed up by his remarkable winning record, from the National Hockey League to junior, as his teams won 15 championships over his 26 years in the game.

Walter Pratt was born in Stony Mountain, Manitoba, in 1916. He played minor hockey in Winnipeg, much of it with the Atlantic Avenue Rink. He won the Winnipeg Playground Championship in the under-12 division with the club as a 10-year-old. Pratt's love after hockey was baseball and he was a promising young player. He was nicknamed "Babe," after Babe Ruth, for his ability to hit the ball long, and the moniker remained with him for the rest of his life. Beginning in 1931–32, Pratt had an incredible streak of winning and scoring. He took his Elmwood Maple Leaf team to the midget championship, leading the league in scoring. The next season he won the

Babe Pratt was a defensemen who kept the puck deep in the other team's zone, and sometimes deep in their net.

Manitoba juvenile title with Elmwood and led the league again in scoring. In 1933 he played for five teams in his area—high school, church league, juvenile, a senior league squad and the commercial league. Amazingly, every team won a championship. Later that year he made the move to the Kenora Thistles as a 17-year-old to play junior. Again he led the league in scoring, and the team easily won the Manitoba junior title. In his second year in junior he had 46 points in 20 games, tops in the league, and brought the Thistles to within a game of the final of the Memorial Cup, when they lost to the Winnipeg Monarchs.

He turned professional in 1935, having been signed by the New York Rangers. Ranger scout Al Ritchie called Pratt the best prospect he'd ever seen. Pratt justified Ritchie's confidence with his play for the Rangers' farm team, the Philadelphia Ramblers, and midway through his first season with the Ramblers he was called up by the Rangers. In his rookie year, he had some veteran defenders to watch and play with, including Ching Johnson, Art Coulter and Ott Heller. In 1939–40, Pratt teamed with Heller to form the league's best defense pairing. In 48 games, they allowed only 17 goals and their play was instrumental in the Rangers' Stanley Cup win that season. Pratt had 28 points in 1941–42 as the Rangers won the regular-season championship.

Midway through the 1942–43 season, Pratt was traded to the Toronto Maple Leafs for Hank Goldup and Red Garrett. Pratt had his best seasons with the Maple Leafs. In 1943–44, he led all defensemen with 57 points in 50 games—the best total ever by a defender and a mark that would stay in the books for 21 seasons. When Pierre Pilote broke the record with 59 points, he'd played in 20 more games than Pratt. In 1944 Pratt was awarded the Hart Trophy as the league's most valuable player, an award rarely given to defensemen, and was placed on the league's First All-Star Team. He was a Second Team All-Star the next season, when the Maple Leafs won the Stanley Cup and he scored the winning goal.

Some of Pratt's outgoing nature off the ice got him into trouble during the 1945–46 season. It was alleged that he'd bet on hockey, though it was more an act of misguided bravado than a dishonest attempt to win money. Still, the incident raised a great deal of controversy and he was suspended by NHL president Red Dutton. Pratt appealed the ruling, admitting he'd made a mistake, and was reinstated after missing nine games. Conn Smythe, the Leafs' tough owner, traded Pratt after the season to the Boston Bruins for Eric Pogue and cash. Although Smythe was quick to trade Pratt following his problems with the league, he later said that the defenseman was one of the best to ever wear the blue and white when he was asked to select his all-time great Toronto team.

Pratt, Babe (Walter)
D, 6´3˝, 212 lbs, b: Stony Mountain, Man., 1/7/1916, d: 12/16/1988

Season	Club, League	Regular Season					Playoffs				
		GP	G	A	Pts	PIM	GP	G	A	Pts	PIM
1933–34	Kenora Thistles, NOHA	16	14	7	21	33	9	6	2	8	18
1934–35	Kenora Thistles, NOHA	18	19	23	42	18	2	0	4	4	2
	Brandon Wheat Kings, Wpg-Sr.	1	0	0	0	0					
1935–36	New York Rangers, NHL	17	1	1	2	16					
	Philadelphia Ramblers, Can-Am	28	7	8	15	48	4	0	0	0	2
1936–37	New York Rangers, NHL	47	8	7	15	23	9	3	1	4	11
1937–38	New York Rangers, NHL	47	5	14	19	56	2	0	0	0	2
1938–39	New York Rangers, NHL	48	2	19	21	20	7	1	2	3	9
1939–40	New York Rangers, NHL	48	4	13	17	61	12	3	1	4	18
1940–41	New York Rangers, NHL	47	3	17	20	52	3	1	1	2	6
1941–42	New York Rangers, NHL	47	4	24	28	55	6	1	3	4	24
1942–43	New York Rangers, NHL	4	0	2	2	6					
	Toronto Maple Leafs, NHL	40	12	25	37	44	6	1	2	3	8
1943–44	Toronto Maple Leafs, NHL	50	17	40	57	30	5	0	3	3	4
1944–45	Toronto Maple Leafs, NHL	50	18	23	41	39	13	2	4	6	8
1945–46	Toronto Maple Leafs, NHL	41	5	20	25	36					
1946–47	Boston Bruins, NHL	31	4	4	8	25					
	Hershey Bears, AHL	21	5	10	15	23	11	3	5	8	19
1947–48	Hershey — Cleveland, AHL	52	3	18	21	47	2	0	0	0	0
1948–49	New Westminster Royals, PCHL	63	18	48	66	64	12	1	8	9	10
1949–50	New Westminster Royals, PCHL	59	8	29	37	56	18	2	6	8	22
1950–51	New Westminster Royals, PCHL	65	8	15	23	54	7	0	0	0	4
1951–52	Tacoma Rockets, PCHL	63	7	31	38	20	5	0	1	1	0
	NHL Totals	517	83	209	292	463	63	12	17	29	90

NHL First All-Star Team (1944)
NHL Second All-Star Team (1945)
Won Hart Trophy (1944)
Won Stanley Cup (1940, 1945)

Midway through the next season, Pratt struggled in a game against the Toronto Maple Leafs, the team he'd been a star with at the peak of his career. With many younger players returning to the game after World War II, Boston general manager Art Ross decided to send Pratt to the Bruins' farm team in Hershey. Don "Count" Grosso made the trip with Pratt, and as it turned out, neither player made his way back to the big league again.

Pratt continued to play hockey for six more years, many of them in the Pacific Coast Hockey League. Twice he was the league's most valuable player. He was a high-scoring defender with the two-time league champion New Westminster Royals, a team in his adopted province of British Columbia, and he later coached the club when he retired from play in 1952.

Babe Pratt (center) was a funny and outgoing man off the ice, keen on jokes and always good for a laugh, but he was considerably tougher when he donned his gear.

Pratt later worked in the forestry industry before joining the Vancouver Canucks in public relations and as an assistant to the vice-president. He toured the country making speeches full of humorous recollections of his playing days and promoting the game to youngsters on a television show before games broadcast on CBS in the northwestern United States. He was inducted into the Hockey Hall of Fame in 1966, the year before his son, Tracy, entered the National Hockey League for his first of 10 seasons in the league. On December 16, 1988, at the age of 72, Babe Pratt died in Vancouver.

Walter "Turk" Broda

Like many a child who is smaller than his friends, Walter Broda was forced to play goal rather than the defense position he wanted when he was out on a pond or the street with his friends. The freckled youngster's neck also tended to turn red whenever he became angry, and one day someone remarked, "Look at the turkey!" The nickname, shortened to "Turk" along the way, stuck for the rest of his life.

Broda grew up in Manitoba and was developed as a player in the Detroit minor system, playing with the Olympics in 1935–36. He was discovered by Leafs owner Conn Smythe, who was in Detroit to check out another goalie, Earl Robertson. But when Smythe saw Broda at the other end, he immediately contacted Jack Adams of the Red Wings about acquiring Broda, which he did for just $7,500 cash. Broda joined the Leafs that fall and remained the crease guardian in Toronto for most of the next 15 years.

"Broda hasn't a nerve in his body," said Jack Adams. "He could tend goal in a tornado and never blink an eye."

Turk was renowned for his casual and friendly personality, and not surprisingly he's considered by many to be the finest "money goalie," or playoff goalie, of all time. "He hasn't a nerve in his body," Jack Adams said. "He could tend goal in a tornado and never blink an eye." Broda himself acknowledged his greatest asset with equal aplomb. "I just love the pressure situation of the playoffs. I have always thought of myself as an easygoing guy, and the pressure never seemed to bother me the way it did some guys. Instead, it brought out the best in me."

Turk Broda (right) won the Stanley Cup four times with the Maple Leafs in the 1940s and once more in 1951, when all five games went into overtime against Montreal.

Turk's outgoing style made him hugely popular with Leafs fans and loved by his teammates. "The Leafs pay me for my work in practices," he joked, "and I throw in the games for free." His first stint with the Leafs lasted until 1943 and included the historic Cup of 1942, when the Leafs rebounded from a 3–0 series deficit to beat Detroit in seven games. But in 1943 Broda joined the army and went off to England for two years, primarily to play hockey. He never saw action, but during one army game in Amsterdam he was hit in the mouth by a puck and lost five teeth. Incredibly, it was the first time he'd been hit in the mouth, and the hit was so devastating that he wired the Leafs from England to say he was retiring from pro hockey. "Can you imagine getting it from some joker after catching the best from the best of them?" he asked, despondent over the accident.

With a little time, though, he reconsidered his decision, and when he was discharged in 1945, he went straight to the Gardens and resumed practising with the team. He was back in the nets, and there he stayed for four more Stanley Cup finals, three in a row from 1947 to 1949 and one more in 1951 in which all five games went into overtime against Montreal. "I couldn't beat him. Toe Blake couldn't. None of the Canadiens could," Maurice Richard said after that series. Broda played the entire season in goal in eight of his 11 seasons, and part of two others, leading the league in shutouts twice. But for all his fame and glory, he's also remembered for his weight problems, which Conn Smythe used as a kind of playful publicity stunt.

Smythe ended Broda's run of more than 200 starts in a row when he ordered Broda out of the goal until he got his weight down to 189 pounds. "An overweight netminder can't stop goals!" Smythe barked. "I'm taking Broda out of the nets, and he's not coming back until he loses seven pounds."

For days afterward, newspaper articles showed the smiling goalie sitting on a scale eating steak or drinking juice for dinner in an effort to lose the poundage. Broda joined a fitness club and took up handball to stay lean, and his wife, Betty, became famous for being the one person who could help him lose weight and save the city's team. Although everyone else called him "Turk," his teammates razzed him with the more blatant moniker "Fat Boy." His children too were expected to help (they, like their mother, all had "B" names—Barbara, Bonny and Betty).

Broda in practice was also famous. When the players had to skate laps around the ice, coach Day would skate directly behind Broda, who was in full equipment, hollering at him to keep up and join the race. When in goal, Broda would face wave after wave of shots, then Day would take the goalie's stick away and force him to stop another series of pucks using only his arms and legs.

Broda, Walter "Turk"
G, 5'9", 180 lbs, b: Brandon, Man., 5/15/1914, d: 10/17/1972

Season	Club, League	Regular Season				Playoffs			
		GP	Mins	GA	Avg	GP	Mins	GA	Avg
1933–34	Winnipeg Monarchs, MSHL	1	60	6	6.00				
1934–35	Detroit Farm Crest, Sr.	2	120	4	2.00				
1935–36	Detroit Olympics, IAHL	47	2890	101	2.14	6	360	8	1.32
1936–37	Toronto Maple Leafs, NHL	45	2770	106	2.30	2	133	5	2.26
1937–38	Toronto Maple Leafs, NHL	48	2980	127	2.56	7	452	13	1.73
1938–39	Toronto Maple Leafs, NHL	48	2990	107	2.15	10	617	20	1.94
1939–40	Toronto Maple Leafs, NHL	47	2900	108	2.23	10	657	19	1.74
1940–41	Toronto Maple Leafs, NHL	48	2970	99	2.00	7	438	15	2.05
1941–42	Toronto Maple Leafs, NHL	48	2960	136	2.76	13	780	31	2.38
1942–43	Toronto Maple Leafs, NHL	50	3000	159	3.18	6	439	20	2.73
1945–46	Toronto Maple Leafs, NHL	15	900	53	3.53				
1946–47	Toronto Maple Leafs, NHL	60	3600	172	2.87	11	680	27	2.38
1947–48	Toronto Maple Leafs, NHL	60	3600	143	2.38	9	557	20	2.15
1948–49	Toronto Maple Leafs, NHL	60	3600	161	2.68	9	574	15	1.57
1949–50	Toronto Maple Leafs, NHL	68	4040	167	2.48	7	450	10	1.33
1950–51	Toronto Maple Leafs, NHL	31	1827	68	2.23	8	492	9	1.10
1951–52	Toronto Maple Leafs, NHL	1	30	3	6.00	2	120	7	3.50
	NHL Totals	629	38167	1609	2.53	101	6389	211	1.98

NHL First All-Star Team (1941, 1948)
NHL Second All-Star Team (1942)
Won Vezina Trophy (1941, 1948)
Won Stanley Cup (1942, 1947, 1948, 1949, 1951)

Although he played well under pressure, it was only with remarkable determination. "I always get butterflies in my stomach before a game. The heebie-jeebies run right up and down my spine. Once on the ice, the knots loosen up and I can face pucks without tension. If the butterflies come back in tense moments," he added with humor, "I find it helps to yell at the defensemen."

He retired after playing only one game in the 1951–52 season. Broda was accorded a special night at the Gardens by Conn Smythe, one of the rarest honors bestowed upon a Leaf. That night came on December 22, 1951, and players and executives from Toronto, the opposing Bruins and every other NHL team gathered to pay respects to one of the greatest goalies of all time. He was inducted into the Hockey Hall of Fame in 1967.

Syl Apps Sr.

Perhaps never has a finer man played in the NHL than Syl Apps. A remarkably skilled hockey player, he was big and strong and possessed one of the best shots in the league. He never drank or smoked, never swore and was as loyal to his boss, Conn Smythe, as to his team, the Toronto Maple Leafs.

Smythe was alerted to Apps when a friend told the Leafs' owner of a great football player at McMaster University who was studying economics. When he heard the young man's name was Sylvanus Apps, Smythe laughed and said, "Nobody with a name like that could possibly become a pro hockey player." Still, he traveled to Hamilton to watch Apps play football. Smythe was so impressed that he offered Apps a hockey contract right then and there, but Apps declined, saying he still had to compete in the pole vault at the 1936 Olympics in Berlin. Apps had previously won the British Empire championship with a jump of 12´6˝. And those were the days when poles were made of bamboo and players landed on their feet in a sand pit.

In his first season with Toronto, Syl Apps was the first Leaf to be honored with the Calder Trophy.

Apps was only too glad to clear up the origins of his name for Smythe: "My mother's people came from England—their name was Wrigley, like the chewing gum—and there was a Sylvanus Wrigley. I was named after him." But Smythe wasn't the only one who had trouble with his name. While traveling by ship to attend the Olympics, Apps had been given a placement with a girl when the person doing the partnering thought Sylvanus was a female name.

Upon finishing sixth at Berlin and winning a point for Canada in the standings, Apps demurred and joined the Maple Leafs. He had learned his hockey in Paris, Ontario, playing on a frozen front-yard rink his father had made and practising his shot by trying to hit the lid of a garbage can nailed to his garage door. In his first NHL season with the Leafs, he won the Calder Trophy, the first Leaf so honored, and his career continued to flourish. During that first year, many players thought he was too nice and not tough at all. Flash Hollett discovered this belief was mistaken one night when he high-sticked Apps, knocking out two teeth. Apps dropped his gloves and pummelled Hollett, but he got into only two other skirmishes in his whole career. In 1941–42, he went the whole season without getting a single penalty and was awarded the Lady Byng Trophy for his gentlemanly play. At the end of that season, he led the Leafs to the most improbable Stanley Cup win in NHL history, a series against Detroit that he calls his career highlight. The Leafs lost the first three games of the finals to the Red Wings but somehow won the next four in a row to win the Cup, the only time this has happened.

Syl Apps (right) never drank, never smoked, never swore and was always loyal to his boss, Conn Smythe, and his team, the Toronto Maple Leafs.

Apps quickly became known for his abilities inside the opposition blue line. He moved so quickly, made perfect passes at top speed and got open so frequently that most observers felt these moves were all set plays. "Most plays were spur-of-the-moment things," he explained, "reflex actions when something opened up." He was able to pierce the defense or go around to the outside, whatever the occasion called for, and his quickness around the net ensured his ability to score consistently. He played on a line with Gord Drillon and Bob Davidson, and this unit quickly became the team's best line. He teamed with Harry Watson and Bill Ezinicki after the war, once again forming a powerful offensive unit. Watson and Ezinicki were ideal linemates for Apps because they could score goals and take advantage of Apps' ability to draw players to him before passing the puck.

Off the ice, his conduct was exemplary. He'd build neighborhood rinks for friends, speak at the YMCA or other group halls, read the lesson at church on Sunday morning or help underprivileged kids get through life a little happier. He also coached children in Toronto for many years, even while he was still playing for the Leafs. Apps once crashed into the goal post during the 1942–43 season, breaking his leg. He missed almost half the season, and one day during his time off for his injury he went into owner Conn Smythe's office with a check for $1,000. "He was getting $6,000 for the season," Smythe recollected, "and he came to me and said, 'Conn, I'm making more than I deserve. I want to give you this check.' Well, I almost died of heart failure. Of course, I refused his check. I felt that anyone who thought in such terms was bound to square off what he thought was a debt the following season." At the end of that season, while in the prime of his career, he left the team to join the Canadian Army. There he stayed for two years until the war was over. When he resumed his career, he put the captain's "C" back on his sweater and promptly picked up where he'd left off.

In 1947 he was appointed the athletic commissioner for sport in Ontario by Premier George Drew, who introduced him with the most complimentary of remarks: "I feel sure that it will be generally agreed that there is no finer or cleaner sportsman in the whole of Ontario. He will bring to this very important work wide experience in different branches of sport." The next year, Apps was voted father of the year by the Canadian Father's Day Council for his work with young children. Later he became a Conservative member of the Legislature, representing Kingston. Apps was chairman of the select committee on youth until appointed Correctional Services minister in

Apps, Syl
C, 6´, 185 lbs, b: Paris, Ont., 1/18/1915, d: 12/24/98

Season	Club, League	Regular Season					Playoffs				
		GP	G	A	Pts	PIM	GP	G	A	Pts	PIM
1935–36	Toronto Dominions, OHA Sr.	1	0	1	1	0					
1936–37	Toronto Maple Leafs, NHL	48	16	29	45	10	2	0	1	1	0
1937–38	Toronto Maple Leafs, NHL	47	21	29	50	9	7	1	4	5	0
1938–39	Toronto Maple Leafs, NHL	44	15	25	40	4	10	2	6	80	2
1939–40	Toronto Maple Leafs, NHL	27	13	17	30	5	10	5	2	7	2
1940–41	Toronto Maple Leafs, NHL	41	20	24	44	6	7	3	2	5	2
1941–42	Toronto Maple Leafs, NHL	38	18	23	41	0	13	5	9	14	2
1942–43	Toronto Maple Leafs, NHL	29	23	17	40	2					
1945–46	Toronto Maple Leafs, NHL	40	24	16	40	2					
1946–47	Toronto Maple Leafs, NHL	54	25	24	49	6	11	5	1	6	0
1947–48	Toronto Maple Leafs, NHL	55	26	27	53	12	9	4	4	8	0
	NHL Totals	423	201	231	432	56	69	25	29	54	8

NHL First All-Star Team (1939, 1942)
NHL Second All-Star Team (1938, 1941, 1943)
Won Calder Trophy (1937)
Won Lady Byng Trophy (1942)
Won Stanley Cup (1942, 1947, 1948)

1971. He is the only member of all three Hockey Halls of Fame, the Canadian Sports Hall of Fame and the Canadian Amateur Athletics Hall of Fame, and in 1993 his number was honored at Maple Leaf Gardens, one of only six so designated in franchise history.

Doug Bentley

Doug Bentley's life in hockey stretched over some 30 years, beginning with the Delisle Tigers in his home town in Saskatchewan and finishing as a coach in the Western Hockey League. He played most of his minor hockey with the Moose Jaw Millers and joined the Chicago Black Hawks for the 1939–40 season, and the following year his brother Max joined the team. In 1946 they played with Bill Mosienko on a line that became known as the Pony Line because of the public relations efforts of Chicago's PR man, J.C. Farrell, who was determined to make this threesome famous.

Doug Bentley weighed a scant 145 pounds during his heyday, but he was a natural goal scorer.

After seeing a tremendous exhibition of hockey by the line, Farrell was reading a newspaper story about a "gazelle boy" in India who could run 50 miles an hour. He exclaimed, "The Gazelle Line!" because he thought the nickname conveyed the tremendous speed of the three players. Eventually he replaced "gazelle" with "pony" and the name became popular.

Doug played left wing and was known as a "complete" player. Although he weighed only 145 pounds during his heyday, he had tremendous speed and was a natural goal scorer. Six times he had 20 or more goals in a season, and in 1942–43 he led the NHL in points even though the team finished in fifth place and out of the playoffs. It was during that season that the Bentleys made history. Their youngest brother, Reggie, was called up from the minors and played 11 games with Doug and Max, the first time three brothers played as a complete forward line. Doug was also exciting to watch and frequently had more ice time than anyone else in the game. Because of his speed, he was one of the great backcheckers of his era as well. "He was one of the marvels of the game," coach Johnny Gottselig said. "He was the smallest of any of the great players, smaller than Howie Morenz. He was a crowd pleaser, always in the thick of things, driving down the middle. I would put him in the class of Morenz."

For the first few years of their hockey careers, the Bentley brothers played with a variety of linemates, but as a twosome they

Bentley, Doug
LW, 5´8˝, 145 lbs, b: Delisle, Sask., 9/3/1916, d: 11/24/1972

Season	Club, League	Regular Season					Playoffs				
		GP	G	A	Pts	PIM	GP	G	A	Pts	PIM
1934–35	Regina Vics, SSHL	19	10	4	14	21	6	0	0	0	13
1935–36	Moose Jaw Millers, SSHL	20	3	3	6	30					
1936–37	Moose Jaw Millers, SSHL	24	18	19	37	49	3	3	0	3	4
1937–38	Drumheller Miners, SSHL	21	25	18	43	20	6	6	8	14	6
1938–39	Drumheller Miners, SSHL	32	24	29	53	31	6	7	0	7	6
1939–40	Chicago Black Hawks, NHL	39	12	7	19	12	2	0	0	0	0
1940–41	Chicago Black Hawks, NHL	47	8	20	28	12	5	1	1	2	4
1941–42	Chicago Black Hawks, NHL	38	12	14	26	11	3	0	1	1	4
1942–43	Chicago Black Hawks, NHL	50	33	40	73	18					
1943–44	Chicago Black Hawks, NHL	50	38	39	77	22	9	8	4	12	4
1944–45	Laura Beavers, SSHL	*	*	*	*	*	*	*	*	*	*
1945–46	Chicago Black Hawks, NHL	36	19	21	40	16	4	0	2	2	0
1946–47	Chicago Black Hawks, NHL	52	21	34	55	18					
1947–48	Chicago Black Hawks, NHL	60	20	37	57	16					
1948–49	Chicago Black Hawks, NHL	58	23	43	66	38					
1949–50	Chicago Black Hawks, NHL	64	20	33	53	28					
1950–51	Chicago Black Hawks, NHL	44	9	23	32	20					
1951–52	Chicago Black Hawks, NHL	8	2	3	5	4					
	Saskatoon Quakers, PCHL	35	11	14	25	12	13	6	6	12	4
1952–53	Saskatoon Quakers, WHL	70	22	23	45	37	13	6	3	9	14
1953–54	New York Rangers, NHL	20	2	10	12	2					
	Saskatoon Quakers, WHL	42	8	13	21	18					
1954–55	Saskatoon Quakers, WHL	61	14	23	37	52					
1955–56	Saskatoon — Brandon, WHL	60	7	26	33	21					
1957–58	Saskatoon — St. Paul, WHL	19	11	16	27	0					
1961–62	Los Angeles Blades, WHL	8	0	2	2	2					
	NHL Totals	566	219	324	543	217	23	9	8	17	8

NHL First All-Star Team (1943, 1944, 1947)
NHL Second All-Star Team (1949)
NHL Scoring Leader (1943)

In the 1941–42 season, the Bentleys made history. Their youngest brother, Reggie, was called up from the minors and played 11 games with Doug (left) and Max, the first time three brothers played as a complete forward line.

were always dangerous. The night of December 4, 1941, was one spectacular evening—just three days before the Japanese attack on Pearl Harbor—when the Hawks clobbered Montreal 9–2. Doug had a hat-trick in the game and Max assisted on all three goals.

On January 28, 1943, they and Bill Thoms had one of the best nights a line has ever had in the NHL. The Hawks beat the Rangers 10–1 and the three combined for 17 scoring points including six goals. Doug had two goals and six points; Max four and three; and Thoms five assists.

Doug's career and life took an unexpected turn during the war. At the start of the 1944–45 season, the Hawks traveled to Canada to play an exhibition game. When it came time to cross the border to return to Chicago, Doug was denied permission to leave his homeland. As a result, he spent the entire year playing senior hockey for the Laura Beavers, out of the NHL.

Although he had much personal success, Doug's Hawks rarely excelled. He played 566 regular-season games but only 23 playoff games, a clear reflection of the team's poor performance in the standings. Much of the blame for the team's failings rested on the shoulders of owner Bill Tobin, who took over as manager after the sudden death of Major McLaughlin on December 17, 1944. "Tobin is so cheap," Leafs owner Conn Smythe said, "that he wouldn't pay 10 cents to see the Statue of Liberty take a swan dive into New York Harbor." In 1950 Doug Bentley was voted by the *Herald American* as the top hockey player in Chicago for the first half of the century.

Woody Dumart

An outstanding defensive left winger with an above-average scoring touch, Woodrow Wilson Clarence Dumart played nearly 800 regular-season games for the Boston Bruins between 1935 and 1954. He was best known for his achievements with Milt Schmidt and Bobby Bauer on the feared Kraut Line. His leadership and high standard of play made Dumart a fan favorite and helped the Bruins win the Stanley Cup twice.

The native of Kitchener, Ontario, learned the game in his home town before joining the local Empires for the 1933–34 season. He scored eight goals in 12 games and was promoted by the parent Boston Bruins to the famous Kitchener Greenshirts squad for the following season. Dumart experienced little difficulty making the jump to advanced competition. He led the OHA with 28 points in 17 matches and appeared ready to try his hand at the pros.

Dumart gained valuable experience with the Boston Cubs of the Can-Am league in 1935–36 and earned a one-game call-up to the NHL. The next year he appeared in 17 games for the Bruins, but his development wasn't rushed. Dumart played two-thirds of the year with the Providence Reds of the AHL in an effort to polish his game. It was here that he was first paired with Schmidt and Bauer on an effective forward unit. Providence coach Albert "Battleship" Leduc originally labeled them "the Sauerkraut Line" in reference to their German ancestry.

The young winger made an impression during his first full season in the NHL in 1937–38 when he was paired with his old friend Schmidt and Dit Clapper. He proved to be a determined competitor who relished the chance to perform a checking role. Dumart also chipped in with a respectable 27 points in 48 games that year. Dumart's excellence was summed up best by Milt Schmidt: "I have known few men who exceeded Woody in his talent, both ways. The only comparison that comes readily to mind is Bob Davidson. Opponents hated to play against him because he was so strong and checked them so closely. But they never resented him because he played it cleanly."

Opponents hated to play against him because Woody Dumart was so strong and checked them so closely.

By the 1938–39 season, the Kraut Line was working wonders in the NHL. Their offensive proficiency and competitive spirit were crucial to the Bruins' second Stanley Cup win in franchise history in 1939. Dumart continued to check the top right wingers in the game and also recorded his first 20-goal season in 1939–40. The following season he helped Boston win its second Stanley Cup title in three years. Dumart's stellar contribution didn't go unnoticed. Following both the 1939–40 and 1940–41 seasons he was voted to the NHL's Second All-Star Team.

Late in the 1941–42 season, Dumart and his linemates joined the Canadian effort in World War II. That spring they played on the Ottawa RCAF and helped the unit win the Allan Cup, the top senior amateur title in Canada at that time. In 1944 and 1945 Dumart served overseas. After the war, he returned to the league and enjoyed some of his finest seasons, statistically. He recorded four 20-goal seasons between 1946 and 1951 and took part in the first two annual NHL All-Star games in 1947 and 1948. The veteran was placed on the Second All-Star Team for the third time in his career after the 1946–47 season.

Dumart left the Bruins after their elimination at the hands of the Montreal Canadiens in the 1954 semifinals. In the following year, he played 15 games for the Providence Reds of the AHL before retiring. Over the years, he accumulated 211 goals and 429 points while becoming one of the most respected and popular Bruins of his era. The classy veteran was inducted into the Hockey Hall of Fame in 1992.

Dumart, Woody
LW, 6´, 190 lbs, b: Kitchener, Ont., 12/23/1916

Season	Club, League	Regular Season					Playoffs				
		GP	G	A	Pts	PIM	GP	G	A	Pts	PIM
1935–36	Boston Bruins, NHL	1	0	0	0	0					
	Boston Cubs, Can-Am	46	11	10	21	15					
1936–37	Boston Bruins, NHL	17	4	4	8	2	3	0	0	0	0
	Providence Reds, AHL	32	4	7	11	10					
1937–38	Boston Bruins, NHL	48	13	14	27	6	3	0	0	0	0
1938–39	Boston Bruins, NHL	46	14	15	29	2	12	1	3	4	6
1939–40	Boston Bruins, NHL	48	22	21	43	16	6	1	0	1	0
1940–41	Boston Bruins, NHL	40	18	15	33	2	11	1	3	4	9
1941–42	Boston Bruins, NHL	35	14	15	29	8					
	Ottawa RCAF, City Sr.						6	7	5	12	7
1942–43	Ottawa RCAF, OHA Sr.	6	6	5	11	*					
1945–46	Boston Bruins, NHL	50	22	12	34	2	10	4	3	7	0
1946–47	Boston Bruins, NHL	60	24	28	52	12	5	1	1	2	8
1947–48	Boston Bruins, NHL	59	21	16	37	14	5	0	0	0	0
1948–49	Boston Bruins, NHL	59	11	12	23	6	5	3	0	3	0
1949–50	Boston Bruins, NHL	69	14	25	39	14					
1950–51	Boston Bruins, NHL	70	20	21	41	7	6	1	2	3	0
1951–52	Boston Bruins, NHL	39	5	8	13	0	7	0	1	1	0
1952–53	Boston Bruins, NHL	62	5	9	14	2	11	0	2	2	0
1953–54	Boston Bruins, NHL	69	4	3	7	6	4	0	0	0	0
1954–55	Providence Reds, AHL	15	2	2	4	0					
	NHL Totals	772	211	218	429	99	88	12	15	27	23

NHL Second All-Star Team (1940, 1941, 1947)
Won Stanley Cup (1939, 1941)

Elmer Lach

One of the top playmaking centers ever to compete in the NHL, Elmer Lach spent his entire 14-year career with the Montreal Canadiens. He helped "les glorieux" win the Stanley Cup three times and gained much acclaim as the center on the club's dreaded Punch Line with Toe Blake and Maurice Richard. Lach also received accolades for his determination on the ice and his resilience in battling a host of serious injuries.

A tireless and fearless style of play endeared Elmer Lach (left) to the Montreal fans but also contributed to a career-long battle with injuries. He could complete only five of his 14 seasons with the Canadiens.

The Nokomis, Saskatchewan, native learned the fundamentals of the game in and around the nearby town of Weyburn. He played briefly with the Regina Abbots of the Saskatchewan junior league but was quickly deemed sufficiently talented to try his hand at the senior level of competition. Lach excelled for the Saskatchewan Senior Hockey League's Weyburn Beavers for two years beginning in 1936. This was followed by an even more successful two-year placement with the Moose Jaw Millers of the SSHL. In 1938–39, he led the league in assists and was firmly established as the loop's top star. Most observers were particularly impressed with his blinding speed and devotion to defensive play.

Lach debuted with a respectable 21 points in 43 games as an NHL rookie in 1940–41. He was brash and confident but quickly earned the respect of the coaching staff and his peers through his dogged work ethic, which was evident on every shift. It quickly became apparent that Lach was prepared to do whatever was necessary to stay in the big leagues. As a result, he accepted checking assignments with the same enthusiasm as a chance on a power-play. It didn't take long for him to develop a reputation as one of the NHL's fiercest and most determined checkers.

A tireless and fearless style of play also became characteristic of the Nokomis Flash. This endeared him to the Montreal fans but also contributed to a career-long battle with injuries. Only five times was he able to play a complete season. Few competitors in NHL history have matched Lach's resolve to return to action after suffering a major injury. Additionally, he earned acclaim by never complaining about his health. In one game against Toronto in February 1947, a Maple Leafs blueliner checked Lach so hard that he fell head-first to the ice and suffered a skull fracture. It was widely felt that his career was over, but Lach persevered and enjoyed a stellar year in 1947–48.

In the last game of the 1948–49 season against Detroit, an opponent's elbow broke Lach's jaw. Lach first tried to downplay the injury because he desperately wanted to be ready for the upcoming semifinal series with the Red Wings in the playoffs. The fact that he could barely open his mouth to speak was an obvious sign of the severity of his injury, but that didn't stop him from trying to get a plastic helmet/mask device approved by NHL president Clarence Campbell. His bid failed, but his reputation as one of the game's toughest competitors was intact.

An experiment in practice by head coach Dick Irvin in 1943–44 yielded a bountiful return when Lach combined beautifully with Maurice Richard and Toe Blake to form a forward line. The trio became known as the Punch Line and served as one of the most potent units in league history. Led by this combination, the Habs became a force in the mid-1940s. Lach's wizardry and spirit were crucial to the team's good fortunes. Many in the league felt his touch with the puck and ability to flip it to teammates were unrivaled. Irvin summed up his star center's play as follows: "Elmer goes forwards backwards, and crossways—both ways."

His first experience of Stanley Cup glory came in 1943–44 when the Habs beat Toronto in a five-game semi-final and swept Chicago in four straight in the finals. Lach was placed on the NHL Second All-Star Team. The following year he reached the pinnacle of individual accomplishments. He won the NHL scoring title with 80 points and led all playmakers with 54 assists. He was one of the key reasons behind linemate Richard's becoming the NHL's first 50-goal shooter. Lach was also presented with the Hart Trophy and voted to the NHL First All-Star Team. In addition, the Punch Line accumulated a startling 220 points as a trio, an NHL record that lasted until the late 1960s.

One of the top playing centers ever to compete in the NHL, Elmer Lach (right) spent his entire 14-year career with the Montreal Canadiens.

The 1945–46 season brought Lach his second Stanley Cup ring. Once again he led all NHL skaters with 34 assists and earned a place on the NHL Second All-Star squad. In 1948 he was the inaugural winner of the Art Ross Trophy after leading the NHL in scoring for the second time in his career.

Lach topped the league in assists for the third time with 50 to his credit in 1951–52. This helped garner him a slot on the NHL First All-Star Team. Lach saved the biggest goal of his career for his penultimate season as a pro. He scored the Cup-clinching goal against the Boston Bruins at 1:22 of the first overtime period in the 1953 playoffs, his last taste of hockey's ultimate triumph. Later, Lach quipped, "I took the hardest check of my life when the Rocket jumped on top of me when the puck went in." On February 23, 1952, he recorded his 549th point to pass Bill Cowley as the NHL's all-time leader in scoring.

Lach retired after the 1953–54 season to coach the Montreal Junior Canadiens. He also guided the Montreal Royals for two seasons before focusing full-time on personal business interests. A tribute to Lach's impact on the club was that it experienced a difficult transition replacing him, even though youngsters Henri Richard and Jean Beliveau were embarking on their own Hall of Fame careers. After leaving the NHL, the personable Lach began a successful career in public relations with a transport firm. He was inducted into the Hockey Hall of Fame in 1966.

Lach, Elmer
C, 5'10", 165 lbs, b: Nokomis, Sask., 1/22/1918

Season	Club, League	Regular Season					Playoffs				
		GP	G	A	Pts	PIM	GP	G	A	Pts	PIM
1936–37	Weyburn Beavers, SSHL	23	16	6	22	27	3	0	1	1	4
1937–38	Weyburn Beavers, SSHL	22	12	12	24	44	3	2	1	3	0
1938–39	Moose Jaw Millers, SSHL	29	17	20	37	23	10	6	4	10	8
1939–40	Moose Jaw Millers, SSHL	30	15	29	44	20	8	5	9	14	12
1940–41	Montreal Canadiens, NHL	43	7	14	21	16	3	1	0	1	0
1941–42	Montreal Canadiens, NHL	1	0	1	1	0					
1942–43	Montreal Canadiens, NHL	45	18	40	58	14	5	2	4	6	6
1943–44	Montreal Canadiens, NHL	48	24	48	72	23	9	2	11	13	4
1944–45	Montreal Canadiens, NHL	50	26	54	80	37	6	4	4	8	2
1945–46	Montreal Canadiens, NHL	50	13	34	47	34	9	5	12	17	4
1946–47	Montreal Canadiens, NHL	31	14	16	30	22					
1947–48	Montreal Canadiens, NHL	60	30	31	61	72					
1948–49	Montreal Canadiens, NHL	36	11	18	29	59	1	0	0	0	4
1949–50	Montreal Canadiens, NHL	64	15	33	48	33	5	1	2	3	4
1950–51	Montreal Canadiens, NHL	65	21	24	45	48	11	2	2	4	2
1951–52	Montreal Canadiens, NHL	70	15	50	65	36	11	1	2	3	4
1952–53	Montreal Canadiens, NHL	53	16	25	41	56	12	1	6	7	6
1953–54	Montreal Canadiens, NHL	48	5	20	25	28	4	0	2	2	0
	NHL Totals	664	215	408	623	478	76	19	45	64	36

NHL First All-Star Team (1945, 1948, 1952)
NHL Second All-Star Team (1944, 1946)
Won Hart Trophy (1945)
Won Art Ross Trophy (1948)
NHL Scoring Leader (1945)
Won Stanley Cup (1944, 1946, 1953)

Milt **Schmidt**

Milton Schmidt was frequently called "Uncle Milty" when referred to in the singular, but early in his career he became known as something even more famous—a member of Boston's remarkable Kraut Line.

Milt Schmidt was called the fastest playmaker of all time.

Like the other members of the line, Woody Dumart and Bobby Bauer, Schmidt was a Kitchener native and by rights should have been a Toronto Maple Leaf his whole life. The Leafs had already signed Bauer and sent him to Syracuse, and assistant general manager Frank Selke suggested to Conn Smythe that they sign Bauer's teammates, Dumart and Schmidt, the latter of whom was playing junior at age 14. Smythe wasn't convinced, and when Bauer attended Boston's training camp in Quebec City in the fall of 1935, he brought his friends with him. They never left the Bruins.

Ironically, it was Bauer who was the last to join the team. The trio had played together for the Providence Reds, and it was there that coach Albert Leduc referred to them as "the Krauts" because of their common German heritage. In 1936–37, Schmidt and Dumart were recalled by the Bruins. It wasn't until the last day of that season, however, that Bauer was brought up, and they combined to score their first goal as a line just minutes into the game. "I think the thing that made us click was something off the ice, not on it," Schmidt explained. "When the Bruins sent us to Providence in the 1936–37 season, there was nothing to indicate we would combine to be the line we were. It was a year later, when we were living together in Boston, that our first inkling came. Living together as we did, we solved our hockey problems by discussion. We clicked first as personalities, then as hockey players."

Schmidt, Milt
C/D, 6´, 185 lbs, b: Kitchener, Ont., 3/5/1918

Season	Club, League	Regular Season					Playoffs				
		GP	G	A	Pts	PIM	GP	G	A	Pts	PIM
1936–37	Boston Bruins, NHL	26	2	8	10	15	3	0	0	0	0
	Providence Reds, AHL	23	8	1	9	12					
1937–38	Boston Bruins, NHL	44	13	14	27	15	3	0	0	0	0
1938–39	Boston Bruins, NHL	41	15	17	32	13	12	3	3	6	2
1939–40	Boston Bruins, NHL	48	22	30	52	37	6	0	0	0	0
1940–41	Boston Bruins, NHL	45	13	25	38	23	11	5	6	11	9
1941–42	Boston Bruins, NHL	36	14	21	35	34					
	Ottawa RCAF, City Sr.						6	4	7	11	10
1945–46	Boston Bruins, NHL	48	13	18	31	21	10	3	5	8	2
1946–47	Boston Bruins, NHL	59	27	35	62	40	5	3	1	4	4
1947–48	Boston Bruins, NHL	33	9	17	26	28	5	2	5	7	2
1948–49	Boston Bruins, NHL	44	10	22	32	25	4	0	2	2	8
1949–50	Boston Bruins, NHL	68	19	22	41	41					
1950–51	Boston Bruins, NHL	62	22	39	61	33	6	0	1	1	7
1951–52	Boston Bruins, NHL	69	21	29	50	57	7	2	1	3	0
1952–53	Boston Bruins, NHL	68	11	23	34	30	10	5	1	6	6
1953–54	Boston Bruins, NHL	62	14	18	32	28	4	1	0	1	20
1954–55	Boston Bruins, NHL	23	4	8	12	26					
	NHL Totals	776	229	346	575	466	86	24	25	49	60

NHL First All-Star Team (1940, 1947, 1951)
NHL Second All-Star Team (1952)
Won Hart Trophy (1951)
Won Lester Patrick Trophy (1996)
NHL Scoring Leader (1940)
Won Stanley Cup (1939, 1941)

Schmidt was by far the most aggressive and physically imposing of the three. During his career he suffered so many ailments it was hard to keep track: a broken jaw courtesy of Mac Colville; torn cartilage in his ribs; and ligament damage to both knees courtesy, most notably, of Bill Barilko. All were the result of his style of play. Teammate Johnny Crawford explained: "Milt always rushes along the boards. He goes down the side and around back of the net. He always has boards on one side of him, so that when he's hit, he crashes into them. If he stayed out in the center, some of the terrific bangs he takes would be just another check as he'd have space to fall or recover his balance."

Coach Art Ross felt powerless to tone down Schmidt's play. "He told me," Ross said of Schmidt, "I've just got to play hard or not at all. I just have to give all I have, even though I get hurt." Instead, Ross smartly played Schmidt on defense in his later years, hoping that he'd be less physical and last longer because he'd be carrying the puck less frequently. Schmidt was called the fastest playmaker of all time, and referee Red Storey described his abilities in this way: "I'd take five Milt Schmidts, put my grandmother in the net, and we'd beat any team."

Although he played 16 years in the NHL, Schmidt missed much time during the height of his career when he left the team to join the air force, a stint that lasted three and a half seasons. He always maintained that the night of January 10, 1942, was his biggest thrill in hockey. "That was the last game Bobby Bauer, Pork Dumart and I played before going into the service," he explained. "It was against the Canadiens, and we beat them badly. I don't think I'll ever forget what happened after the game. The players on both teams lifted the three of us on their shoulders and carried us off the ice and the crowd gave us an ovation. A man couldn't ever forget a thing like that."

Milt Schmidt (number 19) explained to coach Art Ross: "I've just got to play hard or not at all. I just have to give all I have, even though I get hurt."

The only night that could come close for memory's sake was March 18, 1952, when the Kraut Line reformed for one special night toward the end of the 1951–52 season. Bobby Bauer had retired in 1947 to manage his father-in-law's skate business, but when he heard his friends Dumart and Schmidt were being honored, he agreed to take part in the festivities somehow. In pre-game ceremonies, NHL president Clarence Campbell presented the three with gold watches, silver services and assorted other gifts of thanks. During the game, Schmidt scored his 200th career goal, making the evening all the more precious to the Krauts.

Prior to his departure for the war, Schmidt was key to the Bruins' winning the Stanley Cup twice, once in 1939 in five games over Toronto, and again in 1941 against Detroit. That year the Bruins became the first team to win the Cup in the fewest games possible—eight. They were Schmidt's only Cup triumphs, even though he played another 10 years after the war. Perhaps his other great prewar highlight came as the 1939–40 season ended and for the first time in league history an entire forward line finished 1–2–3 in the NHL's scoring race, with Schmidt leading the way with 52 points.

Midway through the 1954–55 season, Schmidt retired as a player and took over the head coaching job for the Bruins, a position he held until 1966 with the exception of one season, 1960–61. His coaching record never matched his playing success, however, and when Washington entered the NHL in 1974, he became that franchise's general manager and coach during the team's leanest years. He was inducted into the Hockey Hall of Fame in 1961.

Jack "Black Jack" Stewart

Jack Stewart was the complete package on defense during his dozen years in the NHL. One of the most punishing bodycheckers of his day, Black Jack was able to rush with the puck when the need arose. His rock-solid play contributed to Detroit's Stanley Cup wins in 1943 and 1950, and his willingness to resort to a rough style of play when necessary gave him a reputation as one of the game's bad boys. Stewart wasn't an unpleasant player, however, and off the ice he was a quiet and likable person. He also had sartorial style and was one of the best-dressed players in the league, a habit that was recognized by *Sport* magazine one year.

Born and raised in the farm country of Manitoba, Stewart learned early the value of working hard to get ahead. He began skating on the outdoor rinks in his home area and developed a passion for the game. In the amateur hockey ranks, he excelled with the Portage Terriers in his native Manitoba. Stewart received his break when Winnipeg businessman Gene Houghton recommended him to his friend, Detroit owner James Norris Sr. The Red Wings sent Stewart to the Pittsburgh Hornets of the AHL for a year of seasoning. Halfway through the 1938–39 schedule, he joined the parent club and began stepping into opposing forwards with the confidence of a veteran. Regarding his nickname, Stewart himself said, "I got the nickname when a player reportedly woke up in the dressing room and said, 'Who hit me with the blackjack?'"

Black Jack Stewart was one of the most punishing bodycheckers of his day.

Stewart helped the Wings capture the regular-season title and the Stanley Cup in 1943 while earning his initial selection to the NHL First All-Star Team. A devastating hitter, Stewart was at his best in the hardest-fought games. "When the going became rugged," Jim Coleman wrote, "he wore a strange smile on his handsome face. Rivals learned to be wary of that smile. They'd say to themselves: 'Look out! Old Blackjack is loading up to knock me out of my jockstrap.'" He was a tough foe but not a dirty competitor. In fact, he led the NHL only once in penalty minutes. Stewart was also admired for his defensive poise. He rarely miscued in his own zone or neglected his position to take a run at an opposing player.

A solid work ethic and excellent stamina were also major features of the rugged defender's game. He was a wiry 190 pounds but extremely powerful. Stewart spent his younger days and off-seasons as a pro on the family wheat farm in Pilot Mound, Manitoba. During World War II, he spent a year with the Montreal RCAF and afterward with the Winnipeg detachment. After the war he returned to Detroit and was teamed successfully with Bill Quackenbush on defense. As a unit the two made life difficult for the opposition, but in different ways. Stewart used brute force and strength to nullify opposing forwards while his partner used positioning and subtle clutching and grabbing to defend the goal.

Stewart was placed on the NHL First All-Star Team in both 1948 and 1949. During this period, he waged a legendary battle with Boston forward Milt Schmidt. The two would often exchange devastating but clean open-ice hits against one another that at times gained more attention than the score of the game.

The Wings won the Cup again in 1950, then Stewart was traded to the Chicago Black Hawks. He played his last two seasons in the Windy City before leaving the NHL. During his

Stewart, Jack "Black Jack"
D, 5´10˝, 190 lbs, b: Pilot Mound, Man., 5/6/1917, d: 5/25/1983

Season	Club, League	Regular Season					Playoffs				
		GP	G	A	Pts	PIM	GP	G	A	Pts	PIM
1937–38	Pittsburgh Hornets, AHL	48	0	1	1	16	2	0	0	0	0
1938–39	Pittsburgh Hornets, AHL	21	0	0	0	20					
	Detroit Red Wings, NHL	32	0	1	1	18					
1939–40	Detroit Red Wings, NHL	48	1	0	1	40	5	0	0	0	4
1940–41	Detroit Red Wings, NHL	47	2	6	8	56	9	1	2	3	8
1941–42	Detroit Red Wings, NHL	44	4	7	11	93	12	0	1	1	12
1942–43	Detroit Red Wings, NHL	44	2	9	11	68	10	1	2	3	35
1943–44	Montreal RCAF, QSHL	7	3	5	8	18					
1944–45	Winnipeg RCAF, City Sr.	2	0	1	1	2					
1945–46	Detroit Red Wings, NHL	47	4	11	15	73	5	0	0	0	14
1946–47	Detroit Red Wings, NHL	55	5	9	14	83	5	0	1	1	12
1947–48	Detroit Red Wings, NHL	60	5	14	19	91	9	1	3	4	6
1948–49	Detroit Red Wings, NHL	60	4	11	15	96	11	1	1	2	32
1949–50	Detroit Red Wings, NHL	65	3	11	14	86	14	1	4	5	20
1950–51	Chicago Black Hawks, NHL	26	0	2	2	49					
1951–52	Chicago Black Hawks, NHL	37	1	3	4	12					
1952–53	Chatham Maroons, OHA Sr.	45	2	27	29	134					
1953–54	Chatham Maroons, OHA Sr.	21	0	8	8	35	6	0	0	0	8
	NHL Totals	565	31	84	115	765	80	5	14	19	143

NHL First All-Star Team (1943, 1948, 1949)
NHL Second All-Star Team (1946, 1947)
Won Stanley Cup (1943, 1950)

first year in Chicago, in 1950–51, he made a lasting impression on the club's younger rearguards. Stewart's presence also inspired the forwards to backcheck responsibly.

The team's defensive record was improving before Stewart was injured in late November. Lacking their blue line leader, the Hawks immediately went into a tailspin that saw them win only one of the first nine games after Stewart was out of the lineup. The defense seemed lost and the forwards stopped taking pride in their checking duties. Unfortunately, there were allegations from several corners that Detroit boss Jack Adams traded Stewart with the knowledge that the disc problem in his back was career-threatening.

Stewart's chronic back pain became too great to withstand the rigors of the pro game. Following a routine hit against a Toronto opponent, X-rays revealed a slipped spinal disc. On January 8, 1951, he formally announced his retirement. A clean break from the game was too much for the fierce competitor to bear, however. He skated two years with the OHA senior Chatham Maroons before hanging up his equipment for good. Many historians felt that he was one of the last of a dying breed of fierce hitters. After Stewart left the NHL, Leo Boivin was the only player able to earn the same accolades while playing a regular shift.

Solid defensive play by Jack Stewart (left) contributed to Detroit's Stanley Cup wins in 1943 and 1950, but he could rush with the puck when the need arose.

Following his retirement, Stewart served as a harness racing judge and an amateur and minor pro coach. The teams he guided included the AHL's Pittsburgh Hornets, the Kitchener Juniors and the Chatham Maroons of the OHA senior loop. He was inducted into the Hockey Hall of Fame in 1964. He moved to Florida in the latter stages of his life before returning to Michigan for treatment of cancer. On May 23, 1983, he passed away at the age of 66 after a long battle with the disease.

Max Bentley

Known as the "Dipsy-Doodle-Dandy from Delisle" because of his fancy skating and superb stick-handling, Max was the youngest of the three NHL Bentleys (the other two were Doug and Reggie). Max grew up on a farm, one of 13 children, six of whom were boys. All of the kids played sports, and at one time five of the boys played on the same hockey team, the Drumheller Miners.

Max originally had a tryout with Boston as a 16-year-old, but he looked so small the Bruins sent him packing. On his way home, he stopped off in Montreal to try out with the Habs, and there the Canadiens' manager said Max looked so sick he should see a doctor. Incredibly, the doctor told Max he had a heart condition. If he didn't go home and forget about hockey, the doctor said, Max wouldn't live a year. Similarly, when Bill Tobin traveled to Saskatchewan one time to watch the brothers play, he said of Max—and apparently it could also have been said of his brother Doug—"He's the first walking ghost I've ever seen."

The prognosis wasn't without accuracy. Max always looked gaunt and pale, and throughout his career he was plagued by minor injuries, pains, aches, dry throat, burning eyes, upset stomach, ulcers, diabetes and kidney trouble. He was often called "a walking drug store" because of his pharmacological tendencies, and for 155 pounds he was also quite resilient.

Max Bentley was often called "a walking drug store" because of his pharmacological tendencies.

Although the Hawks liked Max, they wanted him to develop in Kansas City, the team's farm club. At first, Max balked at reporting and decided to retire at 18 years of age. But Johnny Gottselig, a former great Max admired who was the current coach in K.C., promised to look after him and make sure he got to the NHL. Max reported the next day. Just a week later, injuries forced Chicago to call a forward up from the farm and Gottselig pointed to Max. He never saw the minors again.

In his first year, Max played on a line with brother Doug and Mush March, but the following season the coach put Bill Thoms on the line as a policeman for the two high scorers. That was the turning point of the season, as Max finished third in the NHL's scoring race—Doug was first—and won the Lady Byng Trophy.

Max became famous for his drive to the net, his aggressive play to score and the fact that he was constantly in motion. He never stopped skating and had as many moves in his day, contemporaries would later say, as Wayne Gretzky did during his era.

Bill Mosienko, his Pony Line mate, observed the art of Max's play. "Max could certainly handle the puck," he said. "He was deceptive. He had a very fast shot; he was able to release the puck extremely fast. And he was the one that always worked hard." His health was also a constant source of joking. "There were times when he'd say he wasn't feeling too well," Mosienko laughed. "But when he was complaining, he'd go out and have a tremendous game."

Max won the 1946–47 scoring championship on the last day of the season—his second consecutive scoring title. Going into the game against New York, he was one point ahead of Rocket Richard, whose Canadiens were playing Boston. The game itself didn't matter for the Hawks, who were so far down in last place they couldn't see up at all. Max was getting reports about the Montreal game, and in the first two periods Richard had two points and moved ahead. But in the third period, Max had an early assist to tie Richard. Then, midway through the period, he took a Mosienko pass at center and returned the favor at the blue line and cut to the net. Mosienko fed a perfect pass to the slot and Max's quick shot to the corner slid past the sprawling glove hand of Charlie Rayner. The Rocket was held off the score sheet and Max won the scoring title by one point. One of his idols, Milt Schmidt, flattered Max when he commented, "Max is one of the very few players who can make a fantastic play while still going at high speed."

While his years with his brother in Chicago were rewarding, the turning point of his career

Bentley, Max
C, 5′10″, 155 lbs, b: Delisle, Sask., 3/1/1920, d: 1/19/1984

| Season | Club, League | Regular Season | | | | | Playoffs | | | | |
		GP	G	A	Pts	PIM	GP	G	A	Pts	PIM
1937–38	Drumheller Miners, SSHL	26	28	15	43	10	5	7	1	8	2
1938–39	Drumheller Miners, SSHL	32	29	24	53	16	6	5	3	8	6
1939–40	Saskatoon Quakers, ASHL	31	37	14	51	4	4	1	1	2	2
1940–41	Providence Reds, AHL	9	4	2	6	0					
	Kansas City Americas, AHA	5	5	5	10	0					
	Chicago Black Hawks, NHL	36	7	10	17	6	4	1	3	4	2
1941–42	Chicago Black Hawks, NHL	39	13	17	30	2	3	2	0	2	0
1942–43	Chicago Black Hawks, NHL	47	26	44	70	2					
1943–44	Calgary Currie Army, City Sr.	15	18	13	31	26	2	3	4	7	0
1944–45	Calgary Currie Army, City Sr.	12	14	14	28	24	3	3	2	5	0
1945–46	Chicago Black Hawks, NHL	47	31	30	61	6	4	1	0	1	4
1946–47	Chicago Black Hawks, NHL	60	29	43	72	12					
1947–48	Chicago Black Hawks, NHL	6	3	3	6	4					
	Toronto Maple Leafs, NHL	53	23	25	48	10	9	4	7	11	0
1948–49	Toronto Maple Leafs, NHL	60	19	22	41	18	9	4	3	7	2
1949–50	Toronto Maple Leafs, NHL	69	23	18	41	14	7	3	3	6	0
1950–51	Toronto Maple Leafs, NHL	67	21	41	62	34	11	2	11	13	4
1951–52	Toronto Maple Leafs, NHL	69	24	17	41	40	4	1	0	1	2
1952–53	Toronto Maple Leafs, NHL	36	12	11	23	16					
1953–54	New York Rangers, NHL	57	14	18	32	15					
1954–55	Saskatoon Quakers, WHL	40	24	17	41	23					
1955–56	Saskatoon Quakers, WHL	10	2	2	4	20					
1958–59	Saskatoon Quakers, WHL	26	6	12	18	2					
	NHL Totals	646	245	299	544	179	51	18	27	45	14

NHL First All-Star Team (1946)
NHL Second All-Star Team (1947)
Won Hart Trophy (1946)
Won Lady Byng Trophy (1943)
Won Scoring Leader (1946, 1947)
Won Stanley Cup (1948, 1949, 1951)

came on November 2, 1947, when he and Cy Thomas were traded to Toronto for an unprecedented five players—Bud Poile, Bob Goldham, Gaye Stewart, Gus Bodnar and Ernie Dickens. While many thought Conn Smythe was crazy to make the trade, the Leafs won the Stanley Cup three times in the next four years with Max. He assisted on the game-tying goal in game five of the 1951 finals that saw Bill Barilko score the Cup winner in overtime.

Although many fans in Chicago were horrified to lose Max, coach Johnny Gottselig made one good point. "Max Bentley is a great player, but the fact is, the Black Hawks couldn't win with him no matter what he did. We were too weak as a team. We needed depth." A full all-star line and defensive tandem helped, but Chicago still didn't qualify for the playoffs until 1953. Bentley himself was at first saddened by the trade and the loss of playing with his brother. But he immediately became a star on a star team and helped the Leafs to victory, and his popularity in Chicago was never as great as it was almost instantly in Toronto. One night at the Gardens, the Leafs needed a goal. Charlie Hempstead, a racehorse owner and season ticket subscriber who sat right by the Leafs bench, petitioned Max. "Score a goal and I'll give you a horse," he proposed. Max did and Charlie obliged.

Max Bentley (center) became famous for his drive, his aggressive play and the fact that he was constantly in motion.

Conn Smythe loved Max dearly. "He is the greatest pivot man on a power-play that the game has ever seen," he opined. But Smythe was also aware of Max's hypochondria. One time, Max came to see Smythe and complained that he had cancer of the testicles and needed time off. Smythe didn't miss a beat and said that he'd just read about a cure for such a cancer in Scotland that involved cutting off the sick region. Max left the office and never again complained to Smythe about his cancer.

During the 1952–53 season, Max was hampered by a genuine back injury and played only 36 games before retiring. The Leafs sold his rights to the Rangers, and he was reunited briefly with brother Doug for part of the 1953–54 season in New York. When he retired, he'd scored 245 goals and was second among active players only to Maurice Richard.

Sid "Boot Nose" *Abel*

Sid Abel excelled in a number of capacities during his extended hockey career. On the ice, he was an accomplished playmaking center and team leader who contributed to three Stanley Cup championships in Detroit. Abel also fared well as an NHL head coach and television commentator. His life in hockey, centered mostly in Detroit, made him one of the most recognizable figures on that city's sporting scene.

The Red Wings' western Canada scout, Goldie Smith, signed Abel to his first contract, but just as he was about to mail the documents to Jack Adams, Smith passed away. Abel was performing well at his first pro camp when Adams informed him that they didn't have his contract. The affable forward joked, "By this time, I was hoping they wouldn't find the original because I figured I could sign again for more money." The executors soon found the original piece of paper, however, and Abel's NHL journey was once again underway.

On the ice, Sid Abel was an accomplished playmaking center and team leader who contributed to three Stanley Cup championships in Detroit.

After spending a year each with the Saskatoon Wesleys and Flin Flon Bombers in Canada's western junior system, Abel played 15 games with Detroit in 1938–39. He didn't look out of place but was sent to Pittsburgh of the AHL to work on his overall game. After splitting the next season between the Motor City and Indianapolis of the AHL, Abel plied his trade in the big league on a permanent basis beginning in 1940–41.

In only his second full NHL season, he averaged more than a point per game playing on the Liniment Line with Don Grosso and Eddie Wares and was selected to the NHL Second All-Star Team. Abel's excellence contributed to the Wings' Stanley Cup championship run in the 1943 playoffs. That year he also served as the team's captain at the age of 24.

He missed two full seasons due to military service during World War II but returned for seven games toward the end of the 1945–46 season. While in the service, he was based in Montreal and skated with the RCAF and the city's Car team. He also spent part of the year in Britain, where he managed to get on the ice with the Wembley Lions.

In 1946–47, he was teamed with wingers Gordie Howe and Ted Lindsay for the first time. The line clicked and began to dominate opposing defenses. In 1948–49, they were dubbed the "Production Line." Abel led all Detroit scorers and was the recipient of the Hart Trophy—only the second Detroit player so honored after Ebbie Goodfellow in 1940. The next year Abel set career highs with 34 goals and 69 points. That same year, Lindsay, Abel and Howe finished 1–2–3 in the NHL scoring parade and the Red Wings won the Stanley Cup.

Along the way, Abel picked up the nickname "Boot Nose" after he taunted Maurice Richard and paid for his insult with a punch that broke his nose. Abel topped the 60-point mark for the second time in his career in 1950–51, then earned his third Stanley Cup ring with Detroit in the 1952 post-season. In a heart-wrenching move, the Wings traded him to Chicago on July 22, 1952, bringing an important era to a close. It was a difficult yet prudent decision for general manager Jack Adams since Abel's best years were behind him.

During his two years in the Windy City, Abel tried his hand as a player-coach. He scored only nine points but, more importantly, realized that he truly enjoyed instructing the players. Abel was encouraged by the role he played in getting Chicago into the playoffs for the first time in nine years. He retired as a player early in 1953–54, then took some time off before planning his next move.

He tried his hand in the mid-1950s as a commentator on the Detroit television broadcasts for a few games but decided he wasn't quite ready for this type of work. Partway through the 1957–58 season, he took over the

Abel, Sid "Boot Nose"
C, 5'11", 170 lbs, b: Melville, Sask., 2/22/1918, d: 2/27/2000

Season	Club, League		Regular Season				Playoffs				
		GP	G	A	Pts	PIM	GP	G	A	Pts	PIM
1937–38	Flin Flon Bombers, City Sr.	23	12	16	28	13	8	4	4	8	17
1938–39	Detroit Red Wings, NHL	15	1	1	2	0	6	1	1	2	2
	Pittsburgh Hornets, AHL	41	22	24	46	27					
1939–40	Detroit Red Wings, NHL	24	1	5	6	4	5	0	3	3	21
	Indianapolis Capitals, AHL	21	7	11	18	10					
1940–41	Detroit Red Wings, NHL	47	11	22	33	29	9	2	2	4	2
1941–42	Detroit Red Wings, NHL	48	18	31	49	45	12	4	2	6	8
1942–43	Detroit Red Wings, NHL	49	18	24	42	33	10	5	8	13	4
1943–44	Montreal RCAF, QSHL	7	5	4	9	12					
	Montreal Canada Car, City Sr.	2	1	0	1	4					
1944–45	Montreal RCAF, City Sr.	4	6	8	14	4					
	Lachine Rapides, QPHL	2	2	2	4	0					
1945–46	Detroit Red Wings, NHL	7	0	2	2	0	3	0	0	0	0
1946–47	Detroit Red Wings, NHL	60	19	29	48	29	3	1	1	2	2
1947–48	Detroit Red Wings, NHL	60	14	30	44	69	10	0	3	3	16
1948–49	Detroit Red Wings, NHL	60	28	26	54	49	11	3	3	6	6
1949–50	Detroit Red Wings, NHL	69	34	35	69	46	14	6	2	8	6
1950–51	Detroit Red Wings, NHL	69	23	38	61	30	6	4	3	7	0
1951–52	Detroit Red Wings, NHL	62	17	36	53	32	7	2	2	4	12
1952–53	Chicago Black Hawks, NHL	39	5	4	9	6	1	0	0	0	0
1953–54	Chicago Black Hawks, NHL	3	0	0	0	4					
	NHL Totals	612	189	283	472	376	97	28	30	58	79

NHL First All-Star Team (1949, 1950)
NHL Second All-Star Team (1942, 1951)
Won Hart Trophy (1949)
Won Stanley Cup (1943, 1950, 1952)

Red Wings' coaching position when Jimmy Skinner was forced to resign due to an illness. The coaching assignment ended up lasting a decade, nearly as long as his playing career. Under Abel's guidance, the Red Wings reached the Stanley Cup finals four times—1961, 1963, 1964 and 1966. They captured the regular-season championship in 1964–65 but were upset by Chicago in the semifinals. Known as a player's coach, Abel described one of his basic coaching principles: "When you're forced to put on a uniform every day of the week, it gets to be a chore. In my last few years, I practised only when I felt I needed it. I believe if you treat players right you get more out of them. I'd rather have a happy hockey player than one who hates my guts."

Abel added the responsibilities of general manager to his portfolio in 1962–63, a post he held until 1970–71. One of the major transactions he oversaw was the blockbuster trade that brought Frank Mahovlich to Detroit and sent Norm Ullman to Toronto in March 1968. While still holding the position of Detroit general manager, Abel was inducted into the Hockey Hall of Fame in 1969.

In the 1949–50 season, linemates Ted Lindsay, Sid Abel (left) and Gordie Howe finished 1–2–3 in the NHL in scoring and the Red Wings won the Stanley Cup.

In 1971 Abel accepted a post as scout and player consultant with the expansion Los Angeles Kings. A few weeks later he couldn't resist the chance to become the general manager of the St. Louis Blues, where he remained until 1974. At one point in 1971–72 he stepped behind the bench on an emergency basis for 10 games. Abel followed this up by taking on the same responsibilities with the expansion Kansas City Scouts in 1974–75. Although they finished with only 41 points that first season, Abel's Scouts accumulated nearly double the number of points that their expansion cousins, the Washington Capitals, did. In his second year the team regressed in the standings and he was replaced at the end of the schedule.

After leaving the game for good, Abel managed a restaurant and worked in a sales position for a heating business. He also provided commentary on the Red Wings' radio and television broadcasts, where he earned a reputation for speaking his mind. On April 12, 1995, his number 12 was retired in an emotional ceremony at Joe Louis Arena. In 1997 word came out concerning his struggle with both cancer and a broken hip. Abel's spirits were lifted when he watched on television from his bed in suburban Detroit as the hometown Wings won the Stanley Cup for the first time since 1955 and repeated the victory the next season.

Maurice "The Rocket" Richard

An argument for right winger Maurice "Rocket" Richard as the greatest pure goal scorer in NHL history would certainly have merit. If anything, this assessment would rank as an oversimplification. Richard's offensive talent was unquestionable, but it was also generated by outstanding puckhandling and skating skills and a competitive nature that was unmatched. In fact, Richard was first referred to as "the Rocket" by sportswriter Baz O'Meara, who was commenting on his remarkable speed. Richard was also respected and feared because he was every bit as vicious as he was talented.

Maurice Richard (left) was a hero to hockey fans across Canada, but he attained godlike status in his native Quebec.

Richard grew up in the tough Bordeaux section of Montreal and learned the game in the city's amateur system, where he skated with teams such as Parc Lafontaine and the Verdun Maple Leafs. He also competed with the Montreal Royals before joining the Canadiens for the 1942–43 season.

His potential was obvious to coach Dick Irvin, and his talent helped reawaken a franchise that had been struggling for a few years. Richard scored his first NHL goal on November 8, 1942, against the New York Rangers. Irvin teamed him for the most part with Gord Drillon and Buddy O'Connor. He was enjoying a fine start to his career with five goals in 16 games when his debut was cut short by a broken ankle.

Richard scored 32 goals in 46 games during his first full season, then contributed 12 scores in nine contests to lead Montreal to the Stanley Cup over Chicago in 1944. This included the first of his three career record hat-tricks in the finals. Teamed with Elmer Lach and Toe Blake on the dreaded Punch Line, Richard became the NHL's first 50-goal shooter in 1944–45. This feat was accomplished in 50 games, a performance that wouldn't be equaled until Mike Bossy did it in 1980–81. On December 28, 1944, Richard became the first player in NHL history to score eight points in one game. This remained the league standard until Darryl Sittler's 10-point night in 1976.

The Rocket went on to top the NHL in goal-scoring four more times in his career. He also gained a place on the NHL All-Star Team 14 consecutive times from 1944 to 1957, and eight of these selections were for the First All-Star Team.

During the 1952 semifinals against Boston, Richard was knocked unconscious by a check courtesy of Leo Labine. He was revived but remained in a semiconscious state when he scored the dramatic winning goal on Sugar Jim Henry. This became one of the moments that defined Richard's image in the minds of hockey fans across the league. On November 8, 1952, he scored his 326th regular-season goal against Chicago to surpass Nels Stewart as the NHL's all-time leader.

The fiery temper that often inspired Richard to greatness caused him to spend a fair bit of time in the penalty box. This trait also caused one of the most notorious incidents in league history. On March 13, 1955, Richard was

Richard, Maurice "the Rocket"
RW, 5′10″, 170 lbs, b: Montreal, Que., 8/4/1921, d: 5/27/2000

Season	Club, League	Regular Season					Playoffs				
		GP	G	A	Pts	PIM	GP	G	A	Pts	PIM
1939–40	Verdun Sr. Maple Leafs, Mtl Sr.	1	0	0	0	0					
1940–41	Montreal Royals, QSHL	1	0	1	1	0					
1941–42	Montreal Royals, QSHL	31	8	9	17	27	6	2	1	3	6
1942–43	Montreal Canadiens, NHL	16	5	6	11	4					
1943–44	Montreal Canadiens, NHL	46	32	22	54	45	9	12	5	17	10
1944–45	Montreal Canadiens, NHL	50	50	23	73	46	6	6	2	8	10
1945–46	Montreal Canadiens, NHL	50	27	21	48	50	9	7	4	11	15
1946–47	Montreal Canadiens, NHL	60	45	26	71	69	10	6	5	11	44
1947–48	Montreal Canadiens, NHL	53	28	25	53	89					
1948–49	Montreal Canadiens, NHL	59	20	18	38	110	7	2	1	3	14
1949–50	Montreal Canadiens, NHL	70	43	22	65	114	5	1	1	2	6
1950–51	Montreal Canadiens, NHL	65	42	24	66	97	11	9	4	13	13
1951–52	Montreal Canadiens, NHL	48	27	17	44	44	11	4	2	6	6
1952–53	Montreal Canadiens, NHL	70	28	33	61	112	12	7	1	8	2
1953–54	Montreal Canadiens, NHL	70	37	30	67	112	11	3	0	3	22
1954–55	Montreal Canadiens, NHL	67	38	36	74	125					
1955–56	Montreal Canadiens, NHL	70	38	33	71	89	10	5	9	14	24
1956–57	Montreal Canadiens, NHL	63	33	29	62	74	10	8	3	11	8
1957–58	Montreal Canadiens, NHL	28	15	19	34	28	10	11	4	15	10
1958–59	Montreal Canadiens, NHL	42	17	21	38	27	4	0	0	0	2
1959–60	Montreal Canadiens, NHL	51	19	16	35	50	8	1	3	4	2
	NHL Totals	978	544	421	965	1285	133	82	44	126	188

NHL First All-Star Team (1945, 1946, 1947, 1948, 1949, 1950, 1955, 1956)
NHL Second All-Star Team (1944, 1951, 1952, 1953, 1954, 1957)
Won Hart Trophy (1947)
Won Stanley Cup (1944, 1946, 1953, 1956, 1957, 1958, 1959, 1960)

Maurice Richard

Teamed with Elmer Lach and Toe Blake on the dreaded Punch Line, Maurice Richard (left) became the NHL's first 50-goal shooter in 1944–45.

given a match penalty for deliberately injuring Hal Laycoe and punching linesman Cliff Thompson. A formal inquiry took place after which NHL president Clarence Campbell suspended Richard for the remainder of the season. This decision came when the Rocket was leading the NHL in scoring and the Habs were battling for first place in the standings. Needless to say, Montreal supporters were outraged. A memorable scene saw Campbell being pelted with eggs when he tried to take his seat at the Forum for a game against Detroit the following St. Patrick's Day. The crowd became so unruly that the game was forfeited to the Red Wings and the building evacuated. A riot ensued outside, causing $500,000 in damage and leaving some deep wounds, particularly among the francophone community. Despite all the ill feeling that surrounded this event, Campbell summed up Richard by saying: "We all have a lesson to learn from this man… what he's accomplished through complete and utter dedication to his work. Never have I met a man with such a singleness of purpose and so completely devoted to his profession."

On October 19, 1957, Richard beat Glenn Hall of Chicago to become the first NHL player to score 500 regular-season goals. The historic tally was assisted by future Hall of Famers Dickie Moore and Jean Beliveau. Richard was often at his best in the most important games. His six career overtime goals set an NHL record. In all, he played on eight Stanley Cup-winning teams in Montreal. Even when injuries slowed him down just before the end of his career, Richard's presence in the lineup inspired his teammates and helped them win their fourth and fifth consecutive championships in 1959 and 1960. During the late 1950s, he gained much satisfaction playing occasionally on the same line as his brother Henri. On March 20, 1960, he beat Al Rollins of the New York Rangers to score his 544th and last regular-season NHL goal. He scored his last playoff goal on April 12, 1960, to help Montreal take a three-games-to-none lead over Toronto on their way to a four-game sweep in the finals.

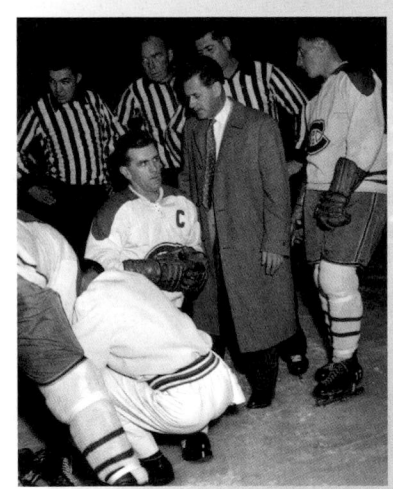

Maurice Richard (center) was respected and feared because he was every bit as aggressive as he was talented.

The Rocket retired after this last triumph and was inducted into the Hockey Hall of Fame in 1961 when the customary three-year waiting period was waived. Years later, Chicago goalie Glenn Hall described what it was like to face the Rocket: "When he was coming down on you, the puck glued to the end of the stick, his eyes were flashing and gleaming like the lights of a pinball machine. It was frightening."

Richard remained visible in the Montreal area throughout his retirement. He served as the first coach of the WHA's Quebec Nordiques in 1972 but stepped down after two weeks because he didn't like the pressure and the fact that he was away from his family. Richard officially rejoined the Canadiens in 1980 when he agreed to represent the team at various public events. He craved a job in hockey but was never given the opportunity even after his recommendation to draft Mike Bossy in 1977 made him look a great deal smarter than many people might have given him credit for. Richard also worked as a representative for Molson Breweries and S. Albert Oil Limited.

Richard was a hero to hockey fans across Canada, but he attained godlike status in his native Quebec. In 1983, when the Montreal daily *La Presse* conducted a survey of the top men of the

20th century, Richard trailed only folksinging legend Felix Leclerc. On June 25, 1998, the NHL board of governors voted to honor Richard with a trophy in his name to be presented annually to the league's top goal scorer. The Rocket was on hand at the 1999 NHL Awards to present the trophy to its inaugural winner, Teemu Selanne. As the century came to a close, Richard battled cancer with the same determination that brought him so many admirers as a player, but he succumbed to his illness on May 27, 2000. He was given a state funeral that was broadcast across the country—the first time such an honor was accorded an athlete.

Maurice Richard remained visible in the Montreal area throughout his retirement.

Edgar Laprade

A tremendous playmaking center and smooth skater, Edgar Laprade was one of the NHL's best forwards during the late 1940s. Blessed with exceptional lateral mobility and an effortless skating style, he was a brilliant penalty killer and determined checker. Laprade could also score and was one of the league's most dangerous skaters on the counterattack. Unfortunately, many of his exploits took place when he played for a New York Rangers franchise that was in decline.

Laprade grew up in Port Arthur (now part of Thunder Bay), Ontario, on the northwest shore of Lake Superior. He starred in the local minor hockey system, winning championships with the Cougar Hockey Club in 1932–33 and the McDonald-Cartier Midgets the next season. Between 1936 and 1938 he developed with the Port Arthur Juniors in the Thunder Bay junior league. In 1939 he moved up to the senior Bearcats and stood out among the older players. He helped the team win the Allan Cup later that year, but their hopes of playing for Canada at the 1940 Olympics were dashed with the outbreak of World War II and the cancellation of those Games.

During the war years, Laprade remained with the Bearcats and led the Thunder Bay senior league in scoring in 1941 and 1942. In 1939 and 1941 the popular star was presented with the Gerry Trophy as the league's top performer. In 1941 the city of Port Arthur held a special night in honor of Laprade and his brother Burt, who was also a popular local sports figure. Following the Bearcats' season in 1943, Laprade joined the Canadian Forces and suited up for the Montreal RCAF team. After a transfer to Winnipeg in 1944, he played for the army club in that city's services hockey league.

An accomplished playmaker and smooth skater, Edgar Laprade was one of the NHL's outstanding centers in the late 1940s.

Laprade, Edgar
C, 5´8˝, 160 lbs, b: Port Arthur, Ont., 10/10/1919

Season	Club, League	Regular Season					Playoffs				
		GP	G	A	Pts	PIM	GP	G	A	Pts	PIM
1938–39	Port Arthur Seniors, TBSHL	10	11	9	20	7	19	25	7	32	10
1939–40	Port Arthur Bearcats, TBSHL	22	20	15	35	8	3	5	1	6	2
1940–41	Port Arthur Bearcats, TBSHL	20	26	21	47	7	12	13	10	23	60
1941–42	Port Arthur Bearcats, TBSHL	15	18	23	41	4	17	12	21	33	6
1942–43	Port Arthur Bearcats, TBSHL	8	7	10	17	0	3	7	4	11	4
1943–44	Winnipeg Army, City Sr.	6	10	3	13	0					
1944–45	Barriefield Bears, City Sr.	*	19	28	47	2	4	5	8	13	0
1945–46	New York Rangers, NHL	49	15	19	34	0					
1946–47	New York Rangers, NHL	58	15	25	40	9					
1947–48	New York Rangers, NHL	59	13	34	47	7	6	1	4	5	0
1948–49	New York Rangers, NHL	56	18	12	30	12					
1949–50	New York Rangers, NHL	60	22	22	44	2	12	3	5	8	4
1950–51	New York Rangers, NHL	42	10	13	23	0					
1951–52	New York Rangers, NHL	70	9	29	38	8					
1952–53	New York Rangers, NHL	11	2	1	3	2					
1953–54	New York Rangers, NHL	35	1	6	7	2					
1954–55	New York Rangers, NHL	61	3	11	14	0					
	NHL Totals	501	108	172	280	42	18	4	9	13	4

Won Calder Trophy (1946)
Won Lady Byng Trophy (1950)

Emile "Butch" Bouchard

The Montreal Canadiens relied heavily on defenseman Butch Bouchard for 15 seasons.

The Montreal Canadiens relied heavily on defenseman Butch Bouchard for 15 seasons. His robust play contributed to the Habs' defense while his alert passing was an integral component of the team's exemplary transitional game. Bouchard was a tall and strong competitor who used his physical attributes to advantage although he was never known as a bully by his peers.

The Montreal native gained valuable amateur experience with the Verdun Maple Leafs and Montreal Junior Canadiens. Late in the 1940–41 season, the Habs sent him to the Providence Reds of the AHL for a 12-game trial. Bouchard exhibited tremendous poise and impressed coaches by registering three goals in his relatively short minor pro stint.

The young rearguard made his biggest impression at the Canadiens' training camp prior to the 1941–42 season. Unlike some of the veterans, and rare for the day, he was in top physical condition from the outset of the pre-season. He upset some of his teammates with his tough physical approach to practices. Angry veteran left winger Murph Chamberlain offered the following advice to new coach Dick Irvin: "If I were you, I would order this young elephant to calm down and show less aggressiveness, because if he keeps on the way he's going a few more days, you will find yourself without a player to open the season." This outburst was music to Irvin's ears. The Canadiens hadn't fared well in recent years and, if anything, they required an injection of youthful passion to help ignite the team again. This may have been one of Bouchard's most important contributions to the organization.

He developed into a tough stay-at-home defenseman whose physical game was a superb complement to defense partner Doug Harvey, one of the game's all-time great rushing blueliners. And it shouldn't be overlooked that Bouchard's exceptional hockey sense and accurate passing often started the offensive rushes for which the Canadiens became famous in the 1940s and 1950s.

Physically, Bouchard was remarkably strong and often broke up fights on the ice by grabbing hold of each combatant with his enormous hands. To his credit, he never abused his powerful attributes and most opponents wisely avoided provoking him. In turn, he rarely fought.

On retiring, Bouchard turned his interests to amateur hockey in the Montreal area. While serving as one of the veterans of the Habs' blue line in the early 1950s, he'd derived a great deal of satisfaction from tutoring younger defensemen and Canadiens management considered him briefly to replace Dick Irvin as coach before settling on Toe Blake. Instead, he began working as a coach and president of junior teams in the province, which proved to be a logical and rewarding move for the recently retired star.

Bouchard, Emile "Butch"
D, 6'2", 205 lbs, b: Montreal, Que., 9/11/1920

Season	Club, League	Regular Season					Playoffs				
		GP	G	A	Pts	PIM	GP	G	A	Pts	PIM
1940–41	Providence Reds, AHL	12	3	1	4	8	3	0	1	1	8
1941–42	Montreal Canadiens, NHL	44	0	6	6	38	3	1	1	2	0
1942–43	Montreal Canadiens, NHL	45	2	16	18	47	5	0	1	1	4
1943–44	Montreal Canadiens, NHL	39	5	14	19	52	9	1	3	4	4
1944–45	Montreal Canadiens, NHL	50	11	23	34	34	6	3	4	7	4
1945–46	Montreal Canadiens, NHL	45	7	10	17	52	9	2	1	3	17
1946–47	Montreal Canadiens, NHL	60	5	7	12	60	11	0	3	3	21
1947–48	Montreal Canadiens, NHL	60	4	6	10	78					
1948–49	Montreal Canadiens, NHL	27	3	3	6	42	7	0	0	0	6
1949–50	Montreal Canadiens, NHL	69	1	7	8	88	5	0	2	2	2
1950–51	Montreal Canadiens, NHL	52	3	10	13	80	11	1	1	2	2
1951–52	Montreal Canadiens, NHL	60	3	9	12	45	11	0	2	2	14
1952–53	Montreal Canadiens, NHL	58	2	8	10	55	12	1	1	2	6
1953–54	Montreal Canadiens, NHL	70	1	10	11	89	11	2	1	3	4
1954–55	Montreal Canadiens, NHL	70	2	15	7	81	12	0	1	1	37
1955–56	Montreal Canadiens, NHL	36	0	0	0	22	1	0	0	0	0
	NHL Totals	785	49	144	193	863	113	11	21	32	121

NHL First All-Star Team (1945, 1946, 1947)
NHL Second All-Star Team (1944)
Won Stanley Cup (1944, 1946, 1953, 1956)

The high opinion in which Bouchard was held within the community contributed to his election as alderman (councillor) for the Montreal suburb of Longueuil in the early 1960s. His lifelong love of all sports made him a champion of community interests relating to recreation and sporting activities. Bouchard founded a local junior baseball club and lent his name and financial support to several regional sports endeavors. For several years he served as president of the Montreal Royals baseball club in the International League and remained active with his first love, hockey, by suiting up with the Quebec oldtimers.

Prior to the 1968–69 season, he was named president of the Metropolitan Junior A Hockey League. One of Bouchard's first ideas was the organization of an all-star game between his metro league and the Quebec provincial junior circuit. The proceeds from such a contest would be placed in an "emergency fund" to be spent on players who were crippled or permanently hurt playing the game.

Bouchard also dabbled in the restaurant business, which proved a perfect undertaking for someone so admired by the public. He later ran a beef cattle farm near Montreal with his son Pierre, a hockey player with the Canadiens who won four Cup titles during his time with them in the 1970s. Butch Bouchard took his rightful place in the Hockey Hall of Fame in 1966.

Butch Bouchard's (front) exceptional hockey sense and accurate passing often started the offensive rushes for which the Canadiens became famous in the 1940s and 1950s.

Ken Reardon

Ken Reardon was a fearless, frightening player. His headlong rushes and all-out physical game left enemies in his wake and himself often injured, though he showed extraordinary toughness in playing while he was in pain. He had a short career in the NHL, spending several years overseas in combat during World War II. He was awarded a rare medal for his heroism on the battlefields of France, a feat that wouldn't have surprised fans who watched him throw himself around on rinks across North America. Though never mistaken for a gifted skater or dangerous offensive force, Reardon earned a berth in the Hockey Hall of Fame for his toughness and consistent placement on the league's All-Star teams.

Ken Reardon was born in Winnipeg, Manitoba, on April Fool's Day in 1921. He began playing hockey in the Clifton community league and quickly claimed the position of defense. At first he was no star. He improved slowly and couldn't showcase his flair for the physical game until he grew and was able to play in leagues that allowed contact. By 1937 he'd matured into an intimidating presence with the Winnipeg Monarchs juvenile team. A year later his life changed completely when he lost his parents in a tragic accident. In 1938 he was sent to live with an uncle in British Columbia who was to act as his guardian. The uncle suggested that Kenny try a junior team, the Edmonton Athletic Club Juniors, which he knew needed tough defensemen. That first year in Edmonton he was used sparingly and listed as an extra defenseman when the team made its way through the playoffs to the Memorial Cup finals in Toronto. Edmonton was playing a powerhouse

"He is a disorganizing influence," said Leafs coach Hap Day of Ken Reardon. "He can make a whole team forget to play hockey."

recorded eight assists in his rookie year with the Brooklyn club before the Americans disbanded just two years later. The next season he went to the Detroit Red Wings, where he was an instant hit. In his first year there, his 13 goals helped the Red Wings finish first overall in the regular season. In the playoffs he was dominant as the Wings beat Boston in four straight games to win Stanley Cup.

Like many players of the day, Watson spent two years in the Canadian Armed Forces during his time with Detroit. He was stationed in Montreal, Winnipeg and Saskatoon with the RCAF during the 1943–44 and 1944–45 seasons. Watson kept his skates sharp during his service years, and in 1944 he helped the Saskatoon RCAF win the Western Command Senior Hockey Championships. Watson rejoined the Red Wings for the 1945–46 season, but the next year Conn Smythe acquired him for the Toronto Maple Leafs—a trade Watson later said was one of the highlights of his career. No wonder. In Toronto, he quickly teamed up with center Syl Apps and tough guy Bill Ezinicki to form a scoring trio feared around the league. This troika helped the Leafs win the Stanley Cup four times during Watson's nine seasons at Maple Leaf Gardens, giving him a total of five Cup wins in his career.

Fans remember Harry Watson as the player who assisted on Bill Barilko's legendary overtime Cup-winning goal in 1951.

As an individual, Watson's best year was with the Leafs in 1948–49. He led the club in scoring with 26 goals and, unbelievably, didn't record a single penalty minute throughout the season. He also scored the eventual Stanley Cup-winning goal that year en route to a 4–0 swamp of his old team, the Red Wings. Leafs fans also remember Watson as the one who assisted on Bill Barilko's legendary overtime Cup-winning goal in 1951 against goalie Gerry McNeil of Montreal. His time in Toronto didn't last forever, though. After the first eight games of the 1954–55 season, Conn Smythe sold him to Chicago for cash. He played three seasons with the Black Hawks before finishing his NHL career, but Watson's involvement with hockey wasn't over—not by a long shot.

In 1957–58, he became player-coach of the Buffalo Bisons in the American Hockey League. When he gave up playing for good at the end of that season, he and Ken Mosdell held the distinction of being the last active members of the old New York Americans.

Overall, Watson played in 809 regular-season games in the NHL, scoring 236 career goals to go with 207 assists for 443 career points. In addition to his five Stanley Cup wins, Watson's teams succeeded in making the playoffs in nine of the 14 years he played. He also played in seven All-Star games, usually as a member of the Cup-winning team. Following his retirement from the Bisons, Watson jumped full-time into coaching with the St. Catharines TeePees—a farm team for the Black Hawks—in the Ontario Hockey Association Junior A league. He coached several other minor teams as well, and even led the Windsor Bulldogs to the OHA Senior A league's Allan Cup in 1963.

In addition to coaching, Watson played NHL oldtimers hockey for another 20 years after retiring. He was also extremely active in the promotion of the sport. Watson was general manager of one of the biggest hockey schools in North America and treasurer of the Professional Hockey Players Golf Tournament, which raised money for several charities. In addition to all this hockey activity, Watson also operated a sales agency in Markham, Ontario, well into his 70s.

Bill Quackenbush

Defenseman Bill Quackenbush excelled at both offensive and defensive aspects of the game. During 14 seasons, he was among the NHL's elite rushing blueliners. More significantly, he was a superior defender in his own end who relied on positioning and discipline rather than physical intimidation for his success. Consequently, his penalty minute totals were remarkably low considering his role on the ice.

While growing up in Toronto, Quackenbush developed into one of the top high school athletes in Canada. In addition to hockey, he was particularly adept at soccer and football. In fact, Quackenbush turned down a chance to play football professionally in order to pursue his dream of making it to the NHL. His given names were Hubert George, but he was nicknamed "Bill" by an aunt who disliked his less masculine given names.

Quackenbush began gaining local attention with the OHA's Toronto Native Sons in 1940–41 when he registered 13 points in as many games. Detroit Red Wings scout Carson Cooper noticed him the following year while he was playing with the Brantford Juniors under coach Tommy Ivan, who himself later became head coach of the Red Wings.

The young rearguard wasn't looking out of place during a 10-game call-up with Detroit in 1942–43 until he broke his wrist. After recovering from his injury, the parent club decided it was preferable that he spend the remainder of his first pro year with the Indianapolis Capitals of the AHL. He joined the Red Wings' defense corps permanently the following season.

By the late 1940s, he'd evolved into one of hockey's top blueliners. Three times, Quackenbush was placed on the NHL's First All-Star Team and twice he was selected to the Second Team. At the conclusion of the 1948–49 season, he became the first defenseman to win the Lady Byng Trophy. It was at this time that Quackenbush was in the midst of one of the NHL's more astounding individual achievements. He managed to go 131 consecutive games without drawing a penalty. The streak began with the final five regular-season games and 10 playoff games in 1947–48, 60 regular-season and 11 post-season matches the next year and the first 45 games in 1949–50. During this penalty-free period, Quackenbush's regular defense partner was the equally mild-mannered Red Kelly, who later became the second rearguard to win the Lady Byng. Quackenbush reflected on his ability to stay out of the sin bin: "We played far more in the neutral zone. Now the whole game is played in the offensive and defensive zones. With all the forechecking in the game, you'll never see a defenseman go without a penalty today."

Bill Quackenbush was a superior defender who relied on positioning and discipline rather than physical intimidation.

Quackenbush, Bill
D, 5´11˝, 190 lbs, b: Toronto, Ont., 3/2/1922, d: 9/12/1999

Season	Club, League	Regular Season					Playoffs				
		GP	G	A	Pts	PIM	GP	G	A	Pts	PIM
1942–43	Detroit Red Wings, NHL	10	1	1	2	4					
	Indianapolis Capitals, AHL	37	6	13	19	0	7	0	1	1	6
1943–44	Detroit Red Wings, NHL	43	4	14	18	6	2	1	0	1	0
	Indianapolis Capitals, AHL	1	1	0	1	0					
1944–45	Detroit Red Wings, NHL	50	7	14	21	10	14	0	2	2	2
1945–46	Detroit Red Wings, NHL	48	11	10	21	6	5	0	1	1	0
1946–47	Detroit Red Wings, NHL	44	5	17	22	6	5	0	0	0	2
1947–48	Detroit Red Wings, NHL	58	6	16	22	17	10	0	2	2	0
1948–49	Detroit Red Wings, NHL	60	6	17	23	0	11	1	1	2	0
1949–50	Boston Bruins, NHL	70	8	17	25	4					
1950–51	Boston Bruins, NHL	70	5	24	29	12	6	0	1	1	0
1951–52	Boston Bruins, NHL	69	2	17	19	6	7	0	3	3	0
1952–53	Boston Bruins, NHL	69	2	16	18	6	11	0	4	4	4
1953–54	Boston Bruins, NHL	45	0	17	17	6	4	0	0	0	0
1954–55	Boston Bruins, NHL	68	2	20	22	8	5	0	5	5	0
1955–56	Boston Bruins, NHL	70	3	22	25	4					
	NHL Totals	774	62	222	284	95	80	2	19	21	8

NHL First All-Star Team (1948, 1949, 1951)
NHL Second All-Star Team (1947, 1953)
Won Lady Byng Trophy (1949)

Amazingly, he incurred only one major penalty in his entire career, and that was a dubious call based on a quick wrestling match he had with Gaye Stewart. To many observers, he was the prototype of efficiency and finesse in defensive zone coverage. Quackenbush was also considered a master at diffusing any forward's attempt to generate offense from behind his opponent's net.

A month before training camp in 1949, Quackenbush and Pete Horeck were traded to the Bruins for several players, including future Stanley Cup hero Pete Babando. Quack's rushes with the puck helped endear him to the Beantown supporters, who hadn't seen this type of daring play from the blue line since the days of Eddie Shore.

Between 1948 and 1950, Bill Quackenbush (second from the right) managed to go 131 consecutive games without a penalty and in 1948–49 became the first defenseman to win the Lady Byng Trophy.

In 1950–51, the elder Quackenbush had the opportunity to play with his younger brother Max, a lanky defenseman who was 3″ taller. Later that season, the Bruins' blue line brigade was decimated by injury, leaving Quackenbush as the only experienced player. He was forced to play 55 minutes in one contest, a test of his stamina and experience.

One of Quackenbush's most significant challenges occurred late in his career following the 1953–54 season. In the off-season, he underwent surgery to remove a bone fragment in his wrist caused by a fracture back in his days with the Red Wings. Originally, Quackenbush had planned to have the surgery at the conclusion of his career, but the discomfort and lack of full range of motion began to hamper his stickhandling and passing. The operation was a success, but a few days later, while visiting her husband in hospital, Mrs. Quackenbush noticed he was turning blue and struggling to breathe. It turned out that he'd suffered a rare reaction to the anesthesia and this caused a massive buildup of mucus in the throat.

When Quackenbush retired, he embraced the chance to further his education and create business opportunities. He worked as a manufacturer's representative for an engineering company while studying at college. In 1962 he received his degree in civil engineering from Northeastern University. Never far from his first love of sports, Quackenbush took over the head coaching position of the men's team at Princeton University in 1967. He later coached the school's women's hockey team from 1978 to 1985 and guided them to three consecutive Ivy League championships from 1982 to 1984.

An avid golfer, Quackenbush led the varsity team from 1971 to 1985, including eight Ivy League crowns. His passion for athletics extended to the grassroots level as he became involved in youth hockey in his local community of Lawrenceville, New Jersey, including its annual youth hockey tournament. Quackenbush also served as an instructor at several hockey camps in New York, New Jersey, Massachusetts and Connecticut. He retired from Princeton in 1985 and moved to sunny Orlando, Florida, for several years before returning to New Jersey in 1997. He passed away two years later at the age of 77.

Doug Harvey

Doug Harvey was unquestionably the top defenseman of his era. Along with Eddie Shore and Bobby Orr, he probably had the greatest impact of any player at that position. His dramatic rushes and superior defensive work allowed him to dominate the game. In a franchise deep in heroes, Harvey gained an immortal place in the storied history of the Montreal Canadiens. His role in the Habs' record-setting five straight Cup wins from 1956 to 1960 was paramount.

Along with Eddie Shore and Bobby Orr, Doug Harvey (left) was one of the game's greatest defensemen.

Harvey was born in the anglophone enclave of Notre Dame de Grace on the west side of Montreal, Quebec. A well-rounded athlete, Harvey excelled at football, hockey and particularly baseball, which brought him some attention from the Boston Braves. Harvey also caught the eye of the CFL's Alouettes, but he settled on hockey and starred with several Montreal amateur teams in the 1940s. Harvey contributed to his first major hockey title in 1947 when he helped the senior Royals win the Allan Cup.

In 1947–48, he debuted with the Montreal Canadiens, embarking on a stellar pro career. His talent on the ice was matched by unqualified loyalty to the team. Howard Riopelle, a teammate who also roomed with Harvey with the Montreal Royals, said: "He was a real team guy. He was well-liked by everybody. That's where the humility comes in."

Harvey proved to be an exceptionally talented and versatile player for the Habs. He quarterbacked the power-play, set the tempo for the transitional game and the counterattack, defended tenaciously, blocked shots and intimidated the opposition by merely stepping on the ice. As much as any skater before or since, he was the complete player who meant everything to his team.

Years later, he was looked upon as the precursor to Bobby Orr. Howie Meeker noted: "He was an early Bobby Orr, except he did it in semi-slow motion. You always knew what was coming—you could see it happening—but you couldn't do anything about it." Harvey wasn't a rough player, but few people challenged him on the ice. Most opponents were cognizant of the fact that he'd been the heavyweight boxing champion of the Canadian Navy during World War II.

Doug Harvey (second from the left) wasn't a rough player, but few people challenged him on the ice. Most opponents knew he'd been heavyweight boxing champion of the Canadian Navy during World War II.

Beginning in 1951–52, he was selected to the NHL All-Star Team 11 consecutive years, 10 of them on the First Team. He also had a stranglehold on the Norris Trophy, winning it seven times in eight years from 1955 to 1962. His play was a vital component of Montreal's Stanley Cup win in 1953 and the NHL record of five straight from 1956 to 1960.

Following the retirement of Maurice Richard in 1960, Harvey took over as the Canadiens' captain.

Unfortunately for Harvey, he was one of the individuals blacklisted by the league because of his involvement with the first attempt to form a players' association. In fact, his number wasn't retired by the Canadiens until 1985.

In 1960–61, he joined the New York Rangers as player-coach. He guided the Blueshirts to their first post-season appearance in four years and was presented with his seventh Norris Trophy that summer. After trying both jobs for one year, he went back to being strictly a player for two seasons before retiring from the NHL. He continued to play, chiefly in the AHL, and then made a two-game return with Detroit in 1966–67.

Harvey began the 1967–68 schedule with the Kansas City Blues of the Central Hockey League before rejoining the NHL with expansion St. Louis for the playoffs. He aided the squad's drive to the Stanley Cup finals, where they were swept by his old team from Montreal. The following year he played all 70 regular-season games with the Blues before retiring for good. The legendary blueliner remained in hockey for one more season as the coach of the Laval Saints of the Quebec junior league.

In 1973, as an assistant coach and scout with the WHA's Houston Aeros, Harvey played a key role in luring the Howe family to Texas.

Harvey was unanimously inducted into the Hockey Hall of Fame in 1973. He became the first player to refuse his election because he felt he should have been inducted sooner. On the day of the ceremonies of his induction, Harvey wasn't there. He was upset that the NHL passed judgement on him concerning his lifestyle. He compared his situation to former Toronto Maple Leafs great Harvey "Busher" Jackson, who had experienced similar troubles.

Harvey's battle with alcohol was widely known. His inability to hold a steady job was the main reason he never found a place in hockey after retiring. The Canadiens tried to help by giving him a part-time job as a scout in the Ottawa area the last few years of his life. This reconciliation with his past encouraged Harvey to participate in a few oldtimers' hockey games and golf tournaments each year. Wherever he reappeared, the former great still made a positive impact on people. Harvey was always well-liked off the ice and in the dressing room. His compassion for fellow teammates was a trait often overshadowed by his undisputed talent. In the late 1980s, Harvey handled security at the Connaught Racetrack in the nation's capital. In December 1989 he succumbed to cirrhosis of the liver in a Montreal hospital, one week after he turned 65.

Harvey, Doug
D, 5'11", 187 lbs, b: Montreal, Que., 12/19/1924, d: 12/26/1989

Season	Club, League	Regular Season					Playoffs				
		GP	G	A	Pts	PIM	GP	G	A	Pts	PIM
1942–43	Montreal Navy, City Sr.	4	0	0	0	0					
	Montreal Roayls, QSHL	1	0	0	0	0					
1943–44	Montreal Roayls, QSHL	1	1	1	2	2					
	Montreal Navy, City Sr.	15	4	1	5	24	5	3	1	4	15
1944–45	Montreal Navy, City Sr.	3	0	2	2	2	6	3	1	4	6
1945–46	Montreal Roayls, QSHL	34	2	6	8	90	11	1	6	7	37
1946–47	Montreal Roayls, QSHL	40	2	26	28	171	11	2	4	6	62
1947–48	Montreal Canadiens, NHL	35	4	4	8	32					
	Buffalo Bisons, AHL	24	1	7	8	38					
1948–49	Montreal Canadiens, NHL	55	3	13	16	87	7	0	1	1	10
1949–50	Montreal Canadiens, NHL	70	4	20	24	76	5	0	2	2	10
1950–51	Montreal Canadiens, NHL	70	5	24	29	93	11	0	5	5	12
1951–52	Montreal Canadiens, NHL	68	6	23	29	82	11	0	3	3	8
1952–53	Montreal Canadiens, NHL	69	4	30	34	67	12	0	5	5	8
1953–54	Montreal Canadiens, NHL	68	8	29	37	110	10	0	2	2	12
1954–55	Montreal Canadiens, NHL	70	6	43	49	58	12	0	8	8	6
1955–56	Montreal Canadiens, NHL	62	5	39	44	60	10	2	5	7	10
1956–57	Montreal Canadiens, NHL	70	6	44	50	92	10	0	7	7	10
1957–58	Montreal Canadiens, NHL	68	9	32	41	131	10	2	9	11	16
1958–59	Montreal Canadiens, NHL	61	4	16	20	61	11	1	11	12	22
1959–60	Montreal Canadiens, NHL	66	6	21	27	45	8	3	0	3	6
1960–61	Montreal Canadiens, NHL	58	6	33	39	48	6	0	1	1	8
1961–62	New York Rangers, NHL	69	6	24	30	42	6	0	1	1	2
1962–63	New York Rangers, NHL	68	4	35	39	92					
1963–64	New York Rangers, NHL	14	0	2	2	10					
	St. Paul Rangers, CHL	5	2	2	4	6					
	Quebec Aces, AHL	52	6	36	42	30	9	0	4	4	10
1964–65	Quebec Aces, AHL	64	1	36	37	72	4	1	1	2	9
1965–66	Baltimore Clippers, AHL	67	7	32	39	80					
1966–67	Baltimore — Pittsburgh, AHL	52	2	18	20	32	9	0	0	0	2
	Detroit Red Wings, NHL	2	0	0	0	0					
1967–68	Kansas City Blues, CHL	59	4	16	20	12	7	0	6	6	6
	St. Louis Blues, NHL						8	0	4	4	12
1968–69	St. Louis Blues, NHL	70	2	20	22	30					
	NHL Totals	1113	88	452	540	1216	137	8	64	72	152

NHL First All-Star Team (1952, 1953, 1954, 1955, 1956, 1957, 1958, 1960, 1961, 1962)
NHL Second All-Star Team (1959)
Won James Norris Trophy (1955, 1956, 1957, 1958, 1960, 1961, 1962)
Won Stanley Cup (1953, 1956, 1957, 1958, 1959, 1960)

Ted "Teeder" Kennedy

Never the fastest or smoothest of skaters, Teeder Kennedy became a remarkable leader with an infectious combination of determination and confidence. Known as one of the game's great face-off men and an antagonistic forechecker, Kennedy had the ability to score the important goal, to make the right check at the right time—to do all the little things that win big games and championships, which his Toronto Maple Leafs did on a regular basis.

In 1941 Kennedy attended the Montreal Canadiens' training camp as a 16-year-old, but he was so homesick that he left early. A year later, the Toronto Maple Leafs' Frank Selke, the interim manager of the team during owner Conn Smythe's service in the Second World War, acquired Kennedy's rights from Montreal in a trade for Frank Eddolls. When Smythe returned, he was furious that the deal had been made without his having been consulted, and this disagreement between Smythe and Selke was one of the factors in Selke's decision to move to Montreal in 1946. Smythe, however, would later call Kennedy one of his favorite players, praising him as the "greatest competitor in hockey."

Kennedy joined the Leafs on a full-time basis in 1943–44. The next season he was the team's top point-getter and the overall goal- scoring leader in the playoffs as the Leafs surprised the Montreal Canadiens by winning the Stanley Cup. Beginning in 1946, Kennedy was placed on a line with Howie Meeker and Vic Lynn. Known as the Kid Line II, after the famous Toronto line of the 1930s, and later as the KLM Line, they paced the Leafs to three consecutive Stanley Cup championships in 1947 to 1949. For the last in the string, in 1948–1949, Kennedy was the captain, having succeeded Syl Apps the previous fall.

In the 1949–50 semifinals, the Leafs met the Detroit Red Wings, a team they had beaten easily in the two previous playoffs. Toronto was leading 3–0 in the first game when the Wings' developing superstar, Gordie Howe, sustained a serious head injury attempting to check Kennedy. Howe was rushed to the hospital for emergency surgery to reduce the pressure on his brain. He recovered but didn't play again that season. Jack Adams, the Detroit general manager, claimed Kennedy had intentionally injured Howe on the play.

"I was carrying the puck and Howe came after me, to put me into the boards," Kennedy said. "I pulled up and he tripped, or fell, into the

Teeder Kennedy (right) had the ability to score the important goal, to make the right check at the right time—to do all the little things that win big games and championships.

Kennedy, Ted "Teeder"										

C, 5′11″, 175 lbs, b: Humberstone, Ont., 12/12/1925

Season	Club, League	Regular Season					Playoffs				
		GP	G	A	Pts	PIM	GP	G	A	Pts	PIM
1942–43	Port Colborne Sailors, OHA Sr.	23	23	29	52	15					
	Toronto Maple Leafs, NHL	2	0	1	1	0					
1943–44	Toronto Maple Leafs, NHL	49	26	23	49	2	5	1	1	2	4
1944–45	Toronto Maple Leafs, NHL	49	29	25	54	14	13	7	2	9	2
1945–46	Toronto Maple Leafs, NHL	21	3	2	5	4					
1946–47	Toronto Maple Leafs, NHL	60	28	32	60	27	11	4	5	9	4
1947–48	Toronto Maple Leafs, NHL	60	25	21	46	32	9	8	6	14	0
1948–49	Toronto Maple Leafs, NHL	59	18	21	39	25	9	2	6	8	2
1949–50	Toronto Maple Leafs, NHL	53	20	24	44	34	7	1	2	3	8
1950–51	Toronto Maple Leafs, NHL	63	18	43	61	32	11	4	5	9	6
1951–52	Toronto Maple Leafs, NHL	70	19	33	52	33	4	0	0	0	4
1952–53	Toronto Maple Leafs, NHL	43	14	23	37	42					
1953–54	Toronto Maple Leafs, NHL	67	15	23	38	78	5	1	1	2	2
1954–55	Toronto Maple Leafs, NHL	70	10	42	52	74	4	1	3	4	0
1956–57	Toronto Maple Leafs, NHL	30	6	16	22	35					
	NHL Totals	696	231	329	560	432	78	29	31	60	32

NHL Second All-Star Team (1950, 1951, 1954)
Won Hart Trophy (1955)
Won Stanley Cup (1945, 1947, 1948, 1949, 1951)

dasher. They said I butt-ended him, but there was no way. I was carrying the puck and, in the position I was in, it was impossible to butt-end anybody."

Toronto did win the game, but Detroit was an angry team in the next game of the series. They vented their anger on Kennedy and the Leafs in a fight-filled win. Detroit went on to capture the series in seven games and then the Stanley Cup over the New York Rangers. Kennedy maintained that the controversy around Howe's injury inspired the Wings and cost his team a chance at five consecutive Stanley Cup wins. The Leafs came back the next year to win the championship, making it four titles in five years.

In 1953 Conn Smythe created an award expressly for Teeder Kennedy (right). The J.P. Bickell Trophy was given to the most valuable Leaf.

Individual honors for the Leafs' captain were few and far between. Three times he was selected to the NHL's Second All-Star Team, but Toronto fans and management believed he deserved more recognition in the year-end major awards. In 1953 Conn Smythe created an award expressly for Kennedy, the J.P. Bickell Trophy, which was given to the most valuable Maple Leaf.

Ironically, Kennedy would also win the Bickell in the one year he didn't need to, 1955, when he was finally given the Hart Trophy as the league's most valuable player. Kennedy retired after that season, saying he still loved the game but his legs were through with it. He did return briefly in January of 1956, playing for 30 games when the Leafs were short-manned due to injuries.

Kennedy's legacy, aside from his leadership and winning ways, was his amazing success in the face-off circle, where he became virtually unbeatable. "I always went all-out on face-offs, especially those in our own end. A face-off is the only time when play is at a standstill and you can set up a system, predetermining what happens next," Kennedy said. "Everything was decided by signals. I would gesture with my hand or nod my head. It didn't always work out, but when it did, they were where they were supposed to be."

In close games or behind a goal or two, Toronto fans knew their team had a chance if Kennedy could engineer a comeback with a timely goal or face-off win. One fan in particular, John Arnott, attempted to lift Kennedy and the team with a call from the rafters that became part of the club's history. A quiet man until he entered the usually staid Maple Leaf Gardens, Arnott would cup his hands together and shout, "Come o-n-n-n-n Teeder!" from his seat high above the ice. It was a rallying cry that would ring out even after Kennedy retired from the game, though it grew sadder as the realization sank in that Teeder wouldn't be returning to save the home team.

Harry "Apple Cheeks" Lumley

Known as "Apple Cheeks" for his ruddy complexion when he blushed, Harry Lumley first started people talking about his goaltending skills when he was a 17-year-old rookie in the National Hockey League. Many goalies were thrust into the spotlight during the war years, replacements for stars serving overseas, but most sank back into obscurity when the league had its full complement of players in the late 1940s. But Lumley's career was just getting underway and he went on to become one of the league's top netminders over a 16-year professional career that included stays with five of the Original Six teams.

Lumley was born in Owen Sound, Ontario, on November 11, 1926. He was an easygoing young man, as he would be throughout his playing days. The only time he didn't have a smile on his face was immediately after a puck slid behind him for a goal. His expressive features, a favorite with photographers, registered such grief and pain that it seemed as though he'd never recover after being scored upon. Early in his career, as a junior with the Barrie Colts in the Ontario Hockey Association, he didn't let many pucks escape him, and consequently he was signed by the Detroit Red Wings at the tender age of 15.

Lumley didn't look as though he was professional material in his first two games in the NHL during the 1943–44 season after being called up from the Indianapolis Capitols of the American Hockey League. He gave up 13 goals in the Detroit losses, though most people excused the 17-year-old, who at the time wasn't old enough to vote or cross the border without permission. Later that season, he was loaned to the New York Rangers after their goalie was injured. Lumley was sent back to Indianapolis for half of the next season before earning a starting job with the Wings. He was especially effective in the playoffs, backstopping Detroit to within one game of the 1945 Stanley Cup. Detroit met the Toronto Maple Leafs in the finals. The Leafs' goalie, Frank McCool, was also a rookie and got off to a fast start, winning the first three games of the series by shutouts to set an NHL record. Lumley rebounded in games five and six to post two shutouts of his own to force a seventh and deciding game, a 2–1 thriller won by Toronto.

Over the next five years, Lumley and the Red Wings established themselves among the league's best in a very competitive era. Twice he led the league in wins and games played and he had the most shutouts during the regular season in 1947–48. In the 1950 Stanley Cup playoffs, Detroit overcame the loss of Gordie Howe to a serious injury in the semifinal series against Toronto. The Leafs were the three-time defending champions and the team that had swept the Wings in the two previous finals. The Wings defeated the New York Rangers after playing two games of the final series in hated Toronto because of the circus using the arena in New York, and Lumley won his first and only Stanley Cup. He had three shutouts in the playoffs and a minuscule 1.85 goals-against average.

Harry Lumley's 13 shutouts in 1947–48 set a modern record that would stand until Tony Esposito registered 15 in 1969–70.

Lumley, Harry "Apple Cheeks"
G, 6´, 195 lbs, b: Owen Sound, Ont., 11/11/1926, d: 9/6/1998

Season	Club, League	Regular Season				Playoffs			
		GP	Mins	GA	Avg	GP	Mins	GA	Avg
1943–44	Indianapolis Capitals, AHL	52	3120	147	2.84	5	300	18	3.60
	Detroit Red Wings, NHL	2	120	13	6.50				
	New York Rangers, NHL	1	20	0	0.00				
1944–45	Indianapolis Capitals, AHL	21	1260	46	2.14				
	Detroit Red Wings, NHL	37	2220	119	3.22	14	871	31	2.14
1945–46	Detroit Red Wings, NHL	50	3000	159	3.18	5	310	16	3.10
1946–47	Detroit Red Wings, NHL	52	3120	159	3.06				
1947–48	Detroit Red Wings, NHL	60	3592	147	2.46	10	600	30	3.00
1948–49	Detroit Red Wings, NHL	60	3600	145	2.42	11	726	26	2.15
1949–50	Detroit Red Wings, NHL	63	3780	148	2.35	14	910	28	1.85
1950–51	Chicago Black Hawks, NHL	64	3785	246	3.90				
1951–52	Chicago Black Hawks, NHL	70	4180	241	3.46				
1952–53	Toronto Maple Leafs, NHL	70	4200	167	2.39				
1953–54	Toronto Maple Leafs, NHL	69	4140	128	1.86	5	321	15	2.80
1954–55	Toronto Maple Leafs, NHL	69	4140	134	1.94	4	240	14	3.50
1955–56	Toronto Maple Leafs, NHL	59	3527	157	2.67	5	304	13	2.51
1956–57	Buffalo Bisons, AHL	63	3780	264	4.19				
1957–58	Buffalo Bisons, AHL	17	1029	63	3.67				
	Boston Bruins, NHL	24	1440	70	2.42	1	60	5	5.00
1958–59	Providence Reds, AHL	58	3480	208	3.59				
	Boston Bruins, NHL	11	660	27	2.45	7	436	20	2.75
1959–60	Boston Bruins, NHL	42	2520	146	3.48				
1960–61	Kingston Frontenacs, EPHL	2	120	7	3.50				
	Winnipeg Warriors, WHL	61	3660	213	3.49				
	NHL Totals	803	48044	2206	2.75	76	4778	198	2.40

NHL First All-Star Team (1954, 1955)
Won Vezina Trophy (1954)
Won Stanley Cup (1950)

During the tail end of the 1949–49 season, Lumley was injured and young Terry Sawchuk was called up to man the Detroit net for seven games. Sawchuk impressed Red Wings manager Jack Adams, and only a week after hoisting the Cup, Lumley was traded to the Chicago Black Hawks, the league's worst team, in a nine-player deal. Lumley spent two seasons with the hapless Hawks before being traded to another struggling franchise, the faded Leafs, in 1952.

Harry Lumley (left) twice led the league in wins and games played and had the most shutouts during the regular season in 1947–48.

Lumley had his best individual seasons in Toronto. At the time, the Vezina Trophy was decided by goals-against average and Lumley had a seemingly insurmountable lead over the man who took his job in Detroit, Sawchuk, with two games left in the regular season in 1953–54. The New York Rangers made it a closer race when they bombarded Lumley with five goals in Toronto's penultimate game, setting up a head-to-head matchup between the Maple Leafs and the Red Wings—and the teams' goalies. Sawchuk was within six goals of Lumley and, amazingly, Detroit scored six goals against the Leafs' netminder that night. The only thing that saved the trophy for Lumley was an improbable goal from an even more improbable source. Jim Thompson, who'd scored two goals in 206 games, sent an 80-foot shot wobbling toward Sawchuk. The puck hit the ice and bounced oddly before eluding the Red Wing goalie. Some scribes jokingly suggested that Lumley had altered the rubber content in the puck, but the final result, a 6–1 loss, earned Lumley his only Vezina with a 1.86 average. His 13 shutouts also set a modern record that would stand until Tony Esposito registered 15 in 1970. Lumley was selected to the league's First All-Star Team, a distinction he'd earn again the next season.

During the summer of 1956, Lumley was reading a newspaper when he came upon a story in which Maple Leafs owner Conn Smythe was quoted as saying, "You'll never see Lumley play another game as a Leaf." A few days later, Lumley was sold along with Eric Nesterenko back to Chicago. Lumley wanted no part of the struggling Black Hawks and refused to sign. He played instead with the Buffalo Bisons of the American Hockey League for most of the next two seasons. He was brought back to the NHL by the Boston Bruins in 1957 when the team was having injury problems. He stayed with the Bruins, playing sporadically, until he retired in 1960.

Lumley returned to Owen Sound at the end of his playing days and had several successful businesses, including a car dealership and a standardbred horse stable that had its share of winning harness racers. Lumley occasionally raced his stable's horses himself. He was inducted into the Hockey Hall of Fame in 1980, and the local arena was renamed after him soon afterward. On September 6, 1998, while at home in Owen Sound, Lumley suffered a heart attack. He was taken to Victoria Hospital in London, where he died one week later at the age of 71. At the time of his death, he was called his small home town's top athlete of the century.

Allan "Snowshoes" Stanley

Allan Stanley wasn't the type of player to make an end-to-end rush to win an important game. His nickname, after all, was "Snowshoes." His was a game of prevention, of turning up with a strong hit or a subtle poke-check when the opposition seemed sure to score. He was a positional defenseman with size and grit, a leader who showed remarkable staying power and consistency. He was reluctant to enter the professional game, and though he threatened more than once to retire during his late 30s—and more often in his early 40s—he was a stalwart on National Hockey League blue lines for 21 seasons.

Stanley was born in Timmins, Ontario, in 1926. He wasn't convinced he wanted to pursue hockey as a career while showing a strong presence with minor teams in Timmins. In 1943 the Timmins juvenile club won the All-Ontario finals, a showcase for professional teams looking for young talent. Sixteen-year-old Stanley was one of several members of the team invited to NHL training camps and made a trip to Boston, though he had no strong interest in leaving home and school to devote himself to hockey as far away as Beantown. During the camp he received an invitation to play for the Oshawa Generals, but when he told Boston's general manager Art Ross and coach Dit Clapper of the plan, they strenuously objected to his playing in the backyard of the rival Toronto Maple Leafs. The Canadian Hockey Association became involved and young Stanley was convinced to stay with the Bruins for an extended training camp. He was assigned to the Boston Olympics, a senior team in the Quebec Senior Hockey League.

He spent the better part of three years in Boston and was slowly rounding into a solid defensive presence. In 1946, after an earlier trade, Ross owed the Providence Reds a player and the decision came down to Bill Shill or Stanley. On the night Ross had to make his choice, he went to the Olympics game. "I guess I had a bad night the game Art Ross took in to decide between Shill and myself," Stanley said. "I had been in bed for a week with the flu and just couldn't get going." Shill's career would turn out to be a short one, and Stanley's was just beginning.

He played two seasons in Providence and his steady play came to the attention of Frank Boucher, general manager of the New York Rangers. Boucher gave the Reds $70,000 for the rights to Stanley, a large amount for an

Allan Stanley was a positional defenseman with size and grit and a leader who showed remarkable staying power and consistency.

Stanley, Allan "Snowshoes"
D, 0′1″, 170 lbs, b: Timmins, Ont., 3/1/1926

Season	Club, League	Regular Season					Playoffs				
		GP	G	A	Pts	PIM	GP	G	A	Pts	PIM
1943–44	Boston Olympics, EHL	40	10	32	42	10					
1944–45	Porcupine Combines, NOHA	*	5	4	9	7					
1945–46	Boston Olympics, EHL	30	8	15	23	35					
1946–47	Providence Reds, AHL	54	8	13	21	32					
1947–48	Boston Olympics, QSHL	1	0	0	0	0					
	Providence Reds, AHL	68	9	32	41	81	5	0	0	0	4
1948–49	New York Rangers, NHL	40	2	8	10	22					
	Providence Reds, AHL	23	7	16	23	24					
1949–50	New York Rangers, NHL	55	4	4	8	58	12	2	5	7	10
1950–51	New York Rangers, NHL	70	7	14	21	75					
1951–52	New York Rangers, NHL	50	5	14	19	52					
1952–53	New York Rangers, NHL	70	5	12	17	52					
1953–54	New York Rangers, NHL	10	0	2	2	11					
	Vancouver Canucks, WHL	47	6	30	36	43	13	2	5	7	10
1954–55	New York Rangers, NHL	12	0	1	1	2					
	Chicago Black Hawks, NHL	52	10	15	25	22					
1955–56	Chicago Black Hawks, NHL	59	4	14	18	70					
1956–57	Boston Bruins, NHL	60	6	25	31	45					
1957–58	Boston Bruins, NHL	69	6	25	31	37	12	1	3	4	6
1958–59	Toronto Maple Leafs, NHL	70	1	22	23	47	12	0	3	3	2
1959–60	Toronto Maple Leafs, NHL	64	10	23	33	22	10	2	3	5	2
1960–61	Toronto Maple Leafs, NHL	68	9	25	34	42	5	0	3	3	0
1961–62	Toronto Maple Leafs, NHL	60	9	26	35	24	12	0	3	3	6
1962–63	Toronto Maple Leafs, NHL	61	4	15	19	22	10	1	6	7	8
1963–64	Toronto Maple Leafs, NHL	70	6	21	27	60	14	1	6	7	20
1964–65	Toronto Maple Leafs, NHL	64	2	15	17	30	6	0	1	1	12
1965–66	Toronto Maple Leafs, NHL	59	4	14	18	35	1	0	0	0	0
1966–67	Toronto Maple Leafs, NHL	53	1	12	13	20	12	0	2	2	10
1967–68	Toronto Maple Leafs, NHL	64	1	13	14	16					
1968–69	Philadelphia Flyers, NHL	64	4	13	17	28	3	0	1	1	4
	NHL Totals	1244	100	333	433	792	109	7	36	43	80

NHL Second All-Star Team (1960, 1961, 1966)
Won Stanley Cup (1962, 1963, 1964, 1967)

Allan Stanley (second from the right) was reluctant to enter the professional game—and threatened more than once to retire—but remainded a stalwart on NHL blue lines for 21 seasons.

untried player, and there was a great deal of hype surrounding the handsome young defenseman when he arrived in New York. Expectations were high, but for his part, Stanley was still contemplating a different life for himself, right up to the moment he played his first game for the Rangers in 1948. "While I was playing with Boston Olympics, I was happy and unconcerned. The same when I played for Providence. I still had no burning desire to make hockey my career," Stanley said. "But this desire changes once you are up here in the NHL. Suddenly you acquire a burning desire to stay."

He did stay, and played a strong positional game, guiding opposing forwards away from scoring opportunities and keeping the front of his net clear. The Ranger fans, however, had expected a thumping hitter, an exciting rusher who threw his big body around. Stanley made the game look easy, never taking a stride if he didn't need to. The fans in New York wanted him to be boisterous and entertaining and, mistaking Stanley's easy-going proficiency for laziness, nicknamed the hard-working defender "Sonia Henie," after the figure skating star. In 1953–54, after five full seasons with the Rangers, he was sent to the minors. Boucher, who acknowledged it was the fans' ire that led to the demotion and not his play, paid Stanley a full NHL salary while he was with the Vancouver Canucks of the western league. Stanley returned to the Rangers the next season and played 12 games before being traded to the Chicago Black Hawks with Nick Mickoski and Richard Lamoureaux for Pete Conacher and Bill Gadsby, who would later please the Ranger faithful when he developed into one of the game's tougher stars.

Stanley played one full season with Chicago before he was sold to a familiar organization, the Boston Bruins. Lynn Patrick, Boston's manager, had coached the Rangers in 1950 to a Stanley Cup final and knew Stanley's value to a team. Stanley was one of the best defensemen on the team in his first year, 1956–57. With six games left in the season, however, he landed awkwardly after a check from the Toronto Maple Leafs' Gerry James and damaged his knee, ending his season and forcing him to miss Boston's run to the finals. Bruins coach Milt Schmidt said losing Stanley was the main reason his team fell to the Montreal Canadiens in the finals. The next season Stanley was voted the team's most valuable player when Boston returned to the

Allan Stanley (left) ended up playing 10 seasons in Toronto and finally lived up to his name when the Maple Leafs won the Cup in 1962, the first of four he'd win with the team.

championship series against the Canadiens, though once again the Montreal squad took the Stanley Cup. Before the 1958–59 season began, Stanley was once again on the move, this time to the Toronto Maple Leafs for Jim Morrison. The Bruins felt Stanley's legs were gone and his time in the league was limited.

Stanley would prove yet another franchise wrong when he became a fixture on the Leafs' championship teams in the 1960s. He was often teamed with Tim Horton, another big veteran who knew a bit about positional play, and was a large part of the league's best defensive unit with Carl Brewer, Bobby Baun and Marcel Pronovost. Stanley also used his veteran savvy in the offensive zone and was placed on the Leafs' power-play because of his accurate passes. Beginning in

1960, rumors began to circulate about his retirement. That season, Stanley was voted to the league's Second All-Star Team. The next season there were more rumors and once again Stanley was an alternate All-Star. He ended up playing 10 seasons in Toronto, finally living up to his last name when the Maple Leafs won the Cup in 1962, the first of his four Cup wins with the team. His final title came in 1967, and after one more season with Toronto, he moved to the Philadelphia Flyers in 1968. He finally retired in 1969 at the age of 43.

Stanley was one of the first players to open hockey camps in Ontario and had several on the go before entering the family resort business. He was inducted into the Hockey Hall of Fame in 1981 along with John Bucyk, another survivor of many NHL campaigns, and Stanley's former team-mate in Toronto, Frank Mahovlich.

Fernie Flaman

Basing his game on discipline and a strong physical presence, Ferdinand Charles Flaman was one of the game's top stay-at-home defensemen in the 1950s. Although he contributed to his team's transitional game when needed, it was as an open-ice bodychecker and for his ability to clear opponents from around his goal that Flaman acquired his reputation.

The native of Dysart, Saskatchewan, moved to Regina with his family when he was a child. In his youth, Flaman was a star running back on the local football team and a promising second baseman on the diamond. While playing peewee hockey for the Regina Rangers, Flaman idolized Babe Pratt of the New York Rangers. Pratt, who also had baseball blood in him, was one of the biggest, finest defensemen in the game. After a solid amateur career, Flaman jumped to the pros with the Boston Olympics and Brooklyn Crescents of the EHL. He later split time between the minors and the parent Boston Bruins before earning a full-time place in the Boston lineup in 1947–48.

Basing his game on discipline and a strong physical presence, Fernie Flaman was one of the game's top stay-at-home defensemen in the 1950s.

Like many other NHLers of the time, Flaman's development was rushed because of the player shortage caused by World War II. He may have been as young as 16 when he was called up to scrimmage with the Bruins for the first time. After only part of a season with the Hershey Bears, he was summoned to Boston for regular NHL duty at the age of 20.

He helped anchor the Bruins defense for over three seasons before he was involved in a multi-player transaction with the Toronto Maple Leafs. In order to acquire Flaman, the Leafs had to part with Bill Ezinicki, Vic Lynn and Leo Boivin, one of the hardest hitters in the history of the NHL. Despite the load of players they acquired in exchange for Flaman, many Bruins observers panned the deal as a detriment to their club. Flaman fitted in with his new club and became renowned for his hitting. Later that spring, he played an integral role on the blue line when Toronto won the Stanley Cup on Bill Barilko's dramatic overtime goal against Montreal. A naturalized U.S. citizen, he followed Doc Romnes and Roger Jenkins as only the third American player to play for the Blue and White.

Like many other NHLers of the time, Fernie Flaman (second from the right) was rushed into developing fast because of the shortage of players during World War II.

Flaman's solid play on the blue line became even more significant for Toronto following the tragic loss of Barilko in a plane crash a few weeks after the 1951 Stanley Cup celebrations. Following the 1953–54 season, the Maple Leafs felt comfortable with their blue line corps and traded Flaman back to Boston, where he went on to play the best hockey of his career. During his second stint in Beantown, he took on a greater leadership role than previously. Flaman captained the squad for four years and was one of the founders of the first players' association to be recognized by the NHL, a crude precursor to the union that was formalized in 1967.

His solid play on Boston's blue line contributed to the team's run to the Stanley Cup finals in 1957 and 1958. His performances didn't go unnoticed, as he was placed on the NHL Second All-Star Team in 1955, 1957 and 1958. He retired in 1961 after playing more than 900 NHL games.

After leaving the NHL, Flaman found plenty of hockey challenges elsewhere. He joined the Rhode Island Reds of the AHL in 1961 and remained with the organization until 1965. In 1963–64, he functioned as player, coach and general manager. Most significantly, Flaman discovered a passion for coaching. An immensely popular figure with the Reds, he was elected to the Rhode Island Hockey Hall of Fame in 1965.

Flaman, Fernie
D, 5′10″, 190 lbs, b: Dysart, Sask., 1/25/1927

Season	Club, League	Regular Season					Playoffs				
		GP	G	A	Pts	PIM	GP	G	A	Pts	PIM
1943–44	Boston Olympics, EHL	32	12	7	19	31	12	2	6	8	14
	Brooklyn Crescents, EHL	11	5	9	14	12					
1944–45	Boston Bruins, NHL	1	0	0	0	0					
	Boston Olympics, EHL	46	16	27	43	75	10	3	5	8	13
1945–46	Boston Bruins, NHL	1	0	0	0	0					
	Boston Olympics, EHL	45	11	23	34	80	12	2	7	9	11
1946–47	Boston Bruins, NHL	23	1	4	5	41	5	0	0	0	8
	Hershey Bears, AHL	38	4	8	12	64					
1947–48	Boston Bruins, NHL	56	4	6	10	69	5	0	0	0	12
1948–49	Boston Bruins, NHL	60	4	12	16	62	5	0	1	1	8
1949–50	Boston Bruins, NHL	69	2	5	7	122					
1950–51	Boston Bruins, NHL	14	1	1	2	37					
	Toronto Maple Leafs, NHL	39	2	6	8	64	9	1	0	1	8
	Pittsburgh Hornets, AHL	11	1	6	7	24					
1951–52	Toronto Maple Leafs, NHL	61	0	7	7	110	4	0	2	2	18
1952–53	Toronto Maple Leafs, NHL	66	2	6	8	110					
1953–54	Toronto Maple Leafs, NHL	62	0	8	8	84	2	0	0	0	0
1954–55	Boston Bruins, NHL	70	4	14	18	150	4	1	0	1	2
1955–56	Boston Bruins, NHL	62	4	17	21	70					
1956–57	Boston Bruins, NHL	68	6	25	31	108	10	0	3	3	19
1957–58	Boston Bruins, NHL	66	0	15	15	71	12	2	2	4	10
1958–59	Boston Bruins, NHL	70	0	21	21	101	7	0	0	0	8
1959–60	Boston Bruins, NHL	60	2	18	20	112					
1960–61	Boston Bruins, NHL	62	2	9	11	59					
1961–62	Providence Reds, AHL	65	3	33	36	95	3	0	1	1	6
1962–63	Providence Reds, AHL	68	4	17	21	65	6	0	2	2	0
1963–64	Providence Reds, AHL	22	1	5	6	21	3	0	1	1	4
	NHL Totals	910	34	174	208	1370	63	4	8	12	93

NHL Second All-Star Team (1955, 1957, 1958)

Next Flaman moved on to become coach and general manager of the Fort Worth Red Wings of the Central Hockey League. Flaman returned to the NHL as a scout for Boston in 1969–70. His chief responsibility was assessing college prospects in the north-eastern U.S. This experience led to his longest job placement ever when Northeastern University hired him as head coach in 1970. Among his high points as a college coach was the ECAC and NCAA coach of the year award in 1982, one ECAC title and an appearance in the NCAA Final Four. He was inducted into the Hockey Hall of Fame in 1990 as a veteran player.

Fernie Flaman captained the Bruins for four years and was known for his hard and clean bodychecks.

Ted "Terrible Ted" Lindsay

Nicknames sometimes say a great deal about the person they are attached to. Ted Lindsay's moniker—"Terrible Ted"—tells only half of his story. Lindsay was indeed a rough, often mean competitor who spent more time in the penalty box than any player in his time. He was only 5′8″ and 160 pounds but could hold his own in fights and in the corners with much larger opponents. But Lindsay was also a gifted offensive player, a natural goal scorer who set records for a left wing and made up one third of Detroit's famous Production Line in the 1940s and 1950s. Nine times he was an All-Star, eight of those selections to the First Team. Such a combination, in such a small, powerful package, hadn't been seen in the National Hockey League before the arrival of Terrible Ted Lindsay, and it hasn't been seen since.

Ted Lindsay spent more time in the penalty box than any other player of his time.

Ted Lindsay was born in 1925 in Renfrew, Ontario, a small town that once boasted one of the great teams of early professional hockey, the Renfrew Millionaires. Ted's father, Bert, starred with the Millionaires, among other teams, as a goaltender. Ted was a standout in minor hockey in Kirkland Lake before moving to the St. Michael's College junior team in Toronto. St. Michael's was defeated in the Ontario junior championship by the Oshawa Generals in 1943–44, but teams at the time were allowed to take four players from other clubs as wartime replacements. The Generals coach, Toronto Maple Leafs great Charlie Conacher, chose four from St. Michael's including Lindsay and Gus Mortson, and Oshawa, bolstered by the imports, went on to win the Memorial Cup. Lindsay was so impressive that he was invited to the Detroit Red Wings' training camp. He was offered a two-year deal by Detroit that included a no-minor-league clause guaranteeing he'd play in the NHL, and Lindsay decided to turn professional for the 1944–45 season.

Lindsay spent two quite ordinary seasons in Detroit until 1946–47, when he was put on a line with veteran center Sid Abel and rookie right wing Gordie Howe. In 1948 the threesome was dubbed "the Production Line," partly because they plied their trade in Detroit, the automotive manufacturing center of the U.S., and partly, of course, because they produced goals, assists and wins. At the end of the 1947–48 season, Lindsay was in the top 10 in scoring for the first time. In 1949–50, the line placed 1–2–3 in the league scoring race with Lindsay leading the way and the Red Wings won the Stanley Cup, as they did in 1952, 1954 and 1955, the latter two with Lindsay replacing Abel as team captain.

In 1957 Lindsay had what could arguably be called his best individual season, leading the league in assists and finishing with a career-high 85 points. With the help of other high-profile players including Montreal's Doug Harvey, Chicago's Gus Mortson, New York's Bill Gadsby and Jim Thomson of Toronto, Lindsay organized the NHL Players' Association. They were intent on ensuring that the league dealt fairly with the players on such issues as the pension fund, covering expenses after trades and instituting a minimum salary for first-year players. Lindsay and Jack Adams, Detroit's general manager, hadn't spoken for three years prior to 1957 even though the rugged winger was captain of the Wings. Lindsay's role in the NHLPA certainly didn't help their relationship. Before the 1957–58 season, Adams traded Lindsay, at the time the league's third all-time goal scorer, and goalie Glenn Hall to the lowly Chicago Black Hawks in a move that was more a punishment than a sound hockey move. In 1991

Ted Lindsay (second from the right) was a natural scorer who set records for a left winger and made up a third of Detroit's famous Production Line in the 1940s and 1950s.

the story of Lindsay and the union's genesis was recounted in a best selling book, *Net Worth*. Four years later, a highly successful film of the same name was shown on Canadian television, featuring the Lindsay character as its fiery hero.

Lindsay spent three seasons in Chicago, helping the Black Hawks return to respectability after almost a decade of poor results. He retired following the 1959–60 season, having played 999 games in the NHL. He devoted himself to his business interests in the automotive industry but continued to play hockey and stay in shape, often practising with the Red Wings. In 1964 Sid Abel, the Detroit bench boss and general manager, offered Lindsay a chance to make a comeback. The feisty winger agreed, though reaction to the news was mixed, to say the least.

"This is the blackest day in hockey history when a 39-year-old man can make a comeback in the world's fastest sport," league president Clarence Campbell said at the beginning of the season. A few months later, however, Lindsay had won Campbell and the other critics over with his astonishing play. "This is one of the most amazing feats in professional sports," Campbell said. "I didn't think it could be done. He's to be rated a truly amazing athlete."

It was an amazing year for Lindsay and the Red Wings team, which finished first in the league for the first time since Lindsay's initial departure. At the end of the year, Lindsay left the playing grind behind for good. In 1966 he was inducted to the Hockey Hall of Fame. Lindsay politely declined to attend the ceremonial banquet since it was an all-male affair and

Lindsay, Ted "Terrible Ted"
LW, 5′8″, 163 lbs, b: Renfrew, Ont., 7/29/1925

Season	Club, League	Regular Season					Playoffs				
		GP	G	A	Pts	PIM	GP	G	A	Pts	PIM
1944–45	Detroit Red Wings, NHL	45	17	6	23	43	14	2	0	2	6
1945–46	Detroit Red Wings, NHL	47	7	10	17	14	5	0	1	1	0
1946–47	Detroit Red Wings, NHL	59	27	15	42	57	5	2	2	4	10
1947–48	Detroit Red Wings, NHL	60	33	19	52	95	10	3	1	4	6
1948–49	Detroit Red Wings, NHL	50	26	28	54	97	11	2	6	8	31
1949–50	Detroit Red Wings, NHL	69	23	55	78	141	13	4	4	8	16
1950–51	Detroit Red Wings, NHL	67	24	35	59	110	6	0	1	1	8
1951–52	Detroit Red Wings, NHL	70	30	39	69	123	8	5	2	7	8
1952–53	Detroit Red Wings, NHL	70	32	39	71	111	6	4	4	8	6
1953–54	Detroit Red Wings, NHL	70	26	36	62	110	12	4	4	8	14
1954–55	Detroit Red Wings, NHL	49	19	19	38	85	11	7	12	19	12
1955–56	Detroit Red Wings, NHL	67	27	23	50	161	10	6	3	9	22
1956–57	Detroit Red Wings, NHL	70	30	55	85	103	5	2	4	6	8
1957–58	Chicago Black Hawks, NHL	68	15	24	39	110					
1958–59	Chicago Black Hawks, NHL	70	22	36	58	184	6	2	4	6	13
1959–60	Chicago Black Hawks, NHL	68	7	19	26	91	4	1	1	2	0
1964–65	Detroit Red Wings, NHL	69	14	14	28	173	7	3	0	3	34
	NHL Totals	1068	379	472	851	1808	133	47	49	96	194

NHL First All-Star Team (1948, 1950, 1951, 1952, 1953, 1954, 1956, 1957)
NHL Second All-Star Team (1949)
Won Art Ross Trophy (1950)
Won Stanley Cup (1950, 1952, 1954, 1955)

he felt he owed a debt to his family for its support over his long career. Not coincidentally, the next year the banquet was opened up to include both sexes.

Lindsay returned to the league and to the Red Wings as a general manager in 1977 and later as an interim head coach. As a GM, he was also a tough man to get along with, battling with Alan Eagleson of the players' association and making roster moves involving 41 players in his first year. As in his playing days, his toughness had winning results, as the Wings rebounded as a franchise and Lindsay was awarded several executive of the year honors.

Sid Smith

Sid Smith was known early in his career as a gifted offensive player and a gentlemanly sportsman, but also as a player who seemed lost in his own zone. There was no doubting his great hands—many of his goals were subtle deflections and tip-ins—and he'd a marksman's patience in waiting for goalies to commit themselves, but only with time and hard work did he mini-mize his defensive liabilities. Then timely goals and leadership became vital ingre-dients to powerhouse Toronto Maple Leafs teams for 10 years in the 1940s and 1950s. Though his accomplishments warrant his inclusion, and many have peti-tioned in his favor, Sid Smith has yet to be inducted into the Hockey Hall of Fame.

For much of his time with the team, Sid Smith (left) was the only Maple Leaf born in Toronto.

Smith was born in Toronto in 1925. He played minor hockey in the Toronto league and joined the Oshawa Generals in the Ontario Hockey League as a 19-year-old. His coach with the Generals was another man known for his opportunist goal-scoring, Toronto Maple Leaf great Charlie Conacher. Smith moved to the sen-ior league in 1945 with the Toronto Staffords and led the team in playoff scoring that year with 13 points in 10 games. The next season he played with three teams in three leagues, including the National Hockey League with his hometown Maple Leafs for 14 games.

He spent half of the next season with the Leafs, but almost had his career ended during a game in March of 1948. He injured his knee in a game in Maple Leaf Gardens and was being treated by the team physician when Conn Smythe, the outspoken owner of the Leafs, asked for a word with the doctor. Smith overheard Smythe and Dr. Galloway arguing about whether to ice the knee, which Smythe advocated because he wanted the left winger back in the game. Dr. Galloway resis-ted, fearing additional damage, and only reluctantly agreed after a long discussion. Smith did rein-jure the knee shortly after returning to the ice and his season was over. Toronto management felt his career may have been over as well, but Smith worked hard in the summer, undergoing therapy twice a day. Dr. Galloway resigned from the team because of the incident.

Smith was placed in the Pittsburgh Hornets' lineup in 1948–49 to rehabilitate the knee and work on his game. The off-season conditioning paid off as he led the American Hockey League in scoring with 112 points in 68 games. His total of 55 goals, matched that year by Carl Liscombe, stayed on the record books in the AHL for 34 years. At the end of his year with the Hornets, he was promoted to the Leafs to bolster the team as it attempted to hoist the Stanley Cup for the third consecutive season. Smith had an immediate impact, scoring two goals and assisting on another in the first game of the semifinal series against the Boston Bruins. In the second game of the Stanley Cup finals against Gordie Howe and the Detroit Red Wings, Smith scored all three goals, each of them on the power-play, in a 3–1 Toronto win. At the end of the game, Howe asked reporters, "Who's Sid Smith?"

"Up to that point in my career, I had spent only parts of three seasons with the Leafs and hadn't yet become a regular," Smith said. "But after scoring those three goals against the Red Wings, that solidified my standing with the club. It was just my way of letting the Leafs and the rest of NHL know that I wanted to play and stay in the NHL."

Toronto swept the Red Wings and won the record-setting third consecutive Cup, winning its ninth consecutive game in the final series. Smith had a regular spot with the Leafs the next season, playing on a line alongside Toronto captain Ted Kennedy and Bill Ezinicki, the trio that had been so productive in the playoffs.

Some of Smith's many goals were momentous, including an overtime goal in the 1951 Stanley Cup finals against Montreal, a series that featured extra-time thrillers in each of the five games it took for Toronto to win its fifth Cup in six years. He also scored the winning goal in the first televised Maple Leafs game, against the Boston Bruins on November 1, 1952.

A model of consistency, Smith recorded six consecutive seasons with 20 or more goals, achieving that distinction in 1954–55 along with Gordie Howe. Only four others had been so reliable—Cy Denneny, Brian Hextall, Maurice Richard and Ted Lindsay—and Smith led the Leafs in scoring categories for eight seasons, four times for goals and four times for total points. Twice Smith was awarded the Lady Byng Trophy as the league's most gentlemanly player, in 1951, when he cracked the top 10 in league scoring with 51 points, and again in 1955, when he recorded a career-high 33 goals. Three times he was a league All-Star, earning First Team honors in 1955. He played in the All-Star Game in seven of his eight full

Smith, Sid
LW, 5′10″, 173 lbs, b: Toronto, Ont., 7/11/1925

Season	Club, League	Regular Season					Playoffs				
		GP	G	A	Pts	PIM	GP	G	A	Pts	PIM
1945–46	Toronto Staffords, OHA Sr.	13	9	12	21	2	10	6	7	13	0
1946–47	Toronto Maple Leafs, NHL	14	2	1	3	0					
	Quebec Aces, QSHL	15	12	5	17	6					
	Pittsburgh Hornets, AHL	23	12	5	17	4					
1947–48	Toronto Maple Leafs, NHL	31	7	10	17	10	2	0	0	0	0
	Pittsburgh Hornets, AHL	30	23	17	40	11					
1948–49	Toronto Maple Leafs, NHL	1	0	0	0	0	6	5	2	7	0
	Pittsburgh Hornets, AHL	68	55	57	112	4					
1949–50	Toronto Maple Leafs, NHL	68	22	23	45	6	7	0	3	3	2
1950–51	Toronto Maple Leafs, NHL	70	30	21	51	10	11	7	3	10	0
1951–52	Toronto Maple Leafs, NHL	70	27	30	57	6	4	0	0	0	0
1952–53	Toronto Maple Leafs, NHL	70	20	19	39	6					
1953–54	Toronto Maple Leafs, NHL	70	22	16	38	28	5	1	1	2	0
1954–55	Toronto Maple Leafs, NHL	70	33	21	54	14	4	3	1	4	0
1955–56	Toronto Maple Leafs, NHL	55	4	17	21	8	5	1	0	1	0
1956–57	Toronto Maple Leafs, NHL	70	17	24	41	4					
1957–58	Toronto Maple Leafs, NHL	12	2	1	3	2					
	Whitby Dunlops, OHA Sr.	28	24	19	43	4					
WEC–58	Canada	7	9	5	14	2					
1958–59	Whitby Dunlops, OHA Sr.	51	35	35	70	20	10	7	4	11	2
	NHL Totals	601	186	183	369	94	44	17	10	27	2
	WEC Totals	7	9	5	14	2					

NHL First All-Star Team (1955)
NHL Second All-Star Team (1951, 1952)
Won Lady Byng Trophy (1952, 1955)
Won WEC (1958)
Won Stanley Cup (1948, 1949, 1951)

seasons in the NHL. When Teeder Kennedy retired at the beginning of the 1955–56 season, Smith was elected the team captain, a role he filled with his quiet brand of leadership for one season before Kennedy returned to put the "C" back on his sweater in late 1956.

Twelve games into the 1957–58 season, Smith decided to retire from the Maple Leafs. At the time of his retirement, only three active players—Howe, Richard and Lindsay—had scored more goals. He was the Leafs' top goal scorer of the decade and was involved in 25% of the team's scoring plays during his highly productive stay.

Smith became a player-coach with the Whitby Dunlops, a senior team in the Ontario Hockey Association, in 1957. The Dunlops were Allan Cup champions, and Smith prepared the team to represent Canada at the 1958 World Championships in Hungary. The Canadian entry had lost the year before and the pressure was on to regain the country's expected glory. Much of the tournament was played outdoors, a novelty for the

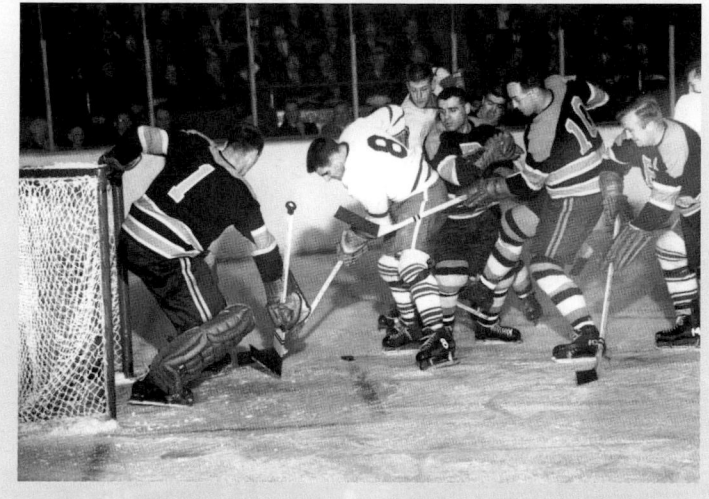

Sid Smith (second from the left) scored the winning goal in the first televised Maple Leafs game, against the Boston Bruins on November 1, 1952.

North Americans after years of playing in rinks, and the Dunlops overcame a shaky start to defeat the Soviet Union 4–2 in the final. Smith, showing he still had his goal-scoring touch, had nine goals and 14 points in seven games. After one more season with Whitby in the OHA, leading the league in goal-scoring in the regular season and the playoffs, Smith left the game. He worked for a paper company for 21 years as a salesman and then in the photography industry before retiring in Toronto.

Bert Olmstead

A western boy, Murray Bert Olmstead began his career as a junior with Moose Jaw in the Saskatchewan league. He played for two years and then turned pro. The Montreal Canadiens assigned him to Kansas City of the United States Hockey League, but his rights were traded to Chicago and in 1948–49 he made his NHL debut with the Hawks, playing on a line with Metro Prystai and Bep Guidolin. The next year, his first full season in the league, he scored 20 goals and established himself as a bona fide NHLer. The 1950–51 year was both confusing and important to Olmstead in establishing himself in the NHL. On December 10, 1950, he was traded to Detroit, but just nine days later the Red Wings sent him back to Montreal. It was there that he stayed for the next eight years, winning the Stanley Cup three times in succession with the Habs.

Bert Olmstead was known for his leadership qualities, for getting the most out of his teammates and for inspiring those around him to excel.

For much of his time in Montreal, he played on the number one line. Initially this meant playing with Elmer Lach and Maurice Richard, succeeding the retired Toe Blake on the famed scoring line. Later he was on the left wing with Jean Beliveau and Boom Boom Geoffrion, and, surprisingly, it was his more famous linemates who claimed Bert was the key to the combination. "I always felt he got the best out of me," Beliveau said of Olmstead. "He made me do smarter things than I'd have done myself. He was older than we were and I guess he was tougher, too, and he didn't stand for any nonsense from us. If he met me in the left corner, he'd growl at me, 'Get the hell out of here!' He didn't want me in there, getting in his way when he was going after the puck. I did what he said because Bert was about the best wing I ever saw when it came to fighting for possession of the puck. And if I was where he wanted me, parked in front of the net, his pass would be perfect."

Although he wasn't known as a scorer or point-getter, Olmstead did set an NHL record for most assists in a season with 56 in 1955–1956, a record that wasn't broken until Jean Beliveau collected 61 five years later. He also scored eight points in a game, tying a league record, but most of all he was known for his leadership qualities, for getting the most out of his teammates and inspiring those around him to play better. As Punch Imlach later said, he coached himself.

Olmstead's departure from Montreal wasn't pleasant. After the 1957–58 season, the Montreal doctors told him he'd no strength left in his knees and the Habs left him unprotected in the Intra-League Draft. Toronto coach Billy Reay pounced at the chance to claim him, and just like that Olmstead went from the Canadiens to the dreaded enemy, the Maple Leafs.

In Toronto, his career was rejuvenated and his experience proved a catalyst to the team's improved fortunes as the 1950s became the 1960s. Early in the 1958–59 season, assistant general manager Punch Imlach fired coach Reay and installed himself as coach, immediately naming Olmstead his player-assistant. In day-to-day life, this meant that Imlach would handle the club and coach games and Olmstead would run the practices. The Leafs, who began the year as though they'd never win another game, played increasingly better and in the last two weeks made one of the greatest playoff qualifying comebacks of all time. On the last day of the season, a win over Detroit would have put the Leafs in the playoffs, one point ahead of the Rangers, who had lost earlier in the day. But after two periods, the Leafs were trailing. Larry Regan was in the dressing room during that game. "Before the third period," he recounted, "Bert worked everybody over. He said: 'Baun, you call yourself a hockey player? You haven't scored one bloody goal all season.' Well, Boomer was so fired up he went out and got one of the goals we had to have."

The Leafs were in the playoffs. That was Olmstead. "The finest period of hockey I ever saw Frank Mahovlich play," Regan continued, "followed a tongue-lashing Bert gave him in the dressing room. It's lucky the coach opened the door or Big Frank would have gone right through it."

After three months as player-assistant, Olmstead resigned as assistant and kept to his on-ice responsibilities with his linemates Bob Pulford and Ron Stewart. The team made it to the finals in 1960 and two years later won the Stanley Cup, in large measure because of Olmstead's role on the team and despite his having missed two months of the season with a badly broken shoulder.

That summer, Olmstead was shocked to learn he'd been claimed by the New York Rangers in

Olmstead, Bert
LW, 6′1″, 180 lbs, b: Scepter, Sask., 9/4/1926

Season	Club, League	Regular Season					Playoffs				
		GP	G	A	Pts	PIM	GP	G	A	Pts	PIM
1946–47	Kansas City Pla-Mors, USHL	60	27	15	42	34	12	2	3	5	4
1947–48	Kansas City Pla-Mors, USHL	66	26	26	52	42	7	1	4	5	0
1948–49	Chicago Black Hawks, NHL	9	0	2	2	4					
	Kansas City Pla-Mors, USHL	52	33	44	77	54	2	0	1	1	0
1949–50	Chicago Black Hawks, NHL	70	20	29	49	40					
1950–51	Chicago Black Hawks, NHL	15	2	1	3	0					
	Milwaukee Seagulls, USHL	12	8	7	15	11					
	Montreal Canadiens, NHL	39	16	22	38	50	11	2	4	6	9
1951–52	Montreal Canadiens, NHL	69	7	28	35	49	11	0	1	1	4
1952–53	Montreal Canadiens, NHL	69	17	28	45	83	12	2	2	4	4
1953–54	Montreal Canadiens, NHL	70	15	37	52	85	11	0	1	1	19
1954–55	Montreal Canadiens, NHL	70	10	48	58	103	12	0	4	4	21
1955–56	Montreal Canadiens, NHL	70	14	56	70	94	10	4	10	14	8
1956–57	Montreal Canadiens, NHL	64	15	33	48	74	10	0	9	9	13
1957–58	Montreal Canadiens, NHL	57	9	28	37	71	9	0	3	3	0
1958–59	Toronto Maple Leafs, NHL	70	10	31	41	74	12	4	2	6	13
1959–60	Toronto Maple Leafs, NHL	53	15	21	36	63	10	3	4	7	0
1960–61	Toronto Maple Leafs, NHL	67	18	34	52	84	3	1	2	3	10
1961–62	Toronto Maple Leafs, NHL	56	13	23	36	10	4	0	1	1	0
	NHL Totals	848	181	421	602	884	115	16	43	59	101

NHL First All-Star Team (1953, 1956)
Won Stanley Cup (1953, 1956, 1957, 1958, 1962)

the Intra-League Draft, exposed by Toronto just as Montreal had exposed him a few years earlier. "I wanted to keep him," Imlach said, "but I had to take the chance. I lost." Olmstead wasn't so casual. "I was healthier in 1962 than I was when I got to Toronto in '58." He refused to report to New York, and then the Canadiens phoned him and promised that if he reported, they'd make a trade within a month. He demanded the trade be made right away or not at all and the deal never materialized. Olmstead's career was over in a flash.

He later became coach of the hapless Oakland Seals during that team's first year of operation, but after a dismal season he never returned behind the bench, although he was at one time rumored to be John McLellan's replacement in Toronto in the early 1970s. He was finally inducted into the Hall of Fame in 1985, much too late for his liking. "I knew a few people on the selection committee had to die before I'd get in," was all he ever said of the late honor.

Bill Gadsby

Bill Gadsby's character was formed when he was a small boy. At the age of 12, he went to England with his mother to visit family in Lancashire. This was 1939, and with the outbreak of the war, returning home to Canada was almost impossible. The Gadsbys had to wait a month for passage aboard the *Athenia*, which turned out to be the last vessel to cross the ocean in peacetime. Shortly after leaving port, however, the ship was hit by a torpedo and Gadsby and his mother clung to a lifeboat in the darkness of the Irish Sea, waiting for help.

In his first NHL game, Bill Gadsby was cut for 12 stitches.

"My mother rushed me up to our lifeboat station," he remembered. "She was as calm as could be, though terribly frightened. I'll never forget the sights I saw. Men and women going crazy with panic. The horror, the panic, the tragedy is something I never want to see again. No matter how rough or nasty a hockey game is, it will never bother me after that gruesome experience." It was many hours before they were saved by another ship and taken back to England and another few weeks before they could board the *Mauritania* for safe passage to Canada.

When Gadbsy was a child back home in cozy Alberta, he'd routinely stay out late at night, playing hockey with his friends until he was exhausted or in so much trouble with his parents he knew it was time to go. He'd creep into the house under cover of night and try to get his equipment dry enough for the next day's skating. It was against this background that his father asked him one day whether he wanted to continue his schooling or pursue a career in hockey. Gadsby said hockey, and his father supported the decision from that day forward.

Gadsby left Calgary to play junior in nearby Edmonton with the Canadians, and while there he gained the admiration of Chicago scout Bill Tobin. Gadsby, a lifelong Hawks fan, was delighted to sign with Tobin for the astronomical sum of $7,500 plus a $3,000 bonus. He joined the team's minor-league affiliate in Kansas City under coach Doc Romnes. Such was the speed of his development that after only 12 games in the minors, the 19–year-old was promoted to the parent team in the Windy City. In his first game, he was cut for 12 stitches, a portentous NHL debut in light of his future penchant for damaging his body in the line of defensive duty. Late in the season, he scored a game-winning goal against Harry Lumley in the Detroit net with one second to go in the game. It was one of the biggest thrills of his life.

While Bill Gadsby was always a star in the league and was chosen to the First All-Star Team three times and the Second Team four times, he never won a Stanley Cup.

Gadsby remained a Black Hawk for the better part of nine years, during which time he had to overcome another tragedy that might have beaten a lesser man. Now Chicago's captain, he was diagnosed with 58% polio in his body in 1952. A reading of 65% would have meant paralysis, but Gadsby fought off the disease and resumed his career with a minimum of fuss. "There were a lot of people who had polio in the area I was living in when I had it," he recalls. "The team had just gone to training camp in North Bay when I began to come down with some of polio's symptoms.... I'd have my legs and arms going all day, exercising, moving, doing anything I could to stay active. I got a lot of medication, a lot of needles, and after 10 or 11 days the symptoms went away. I really lucked out."

After six seasons with the Rangers, Gadsby was involved in a trade that was to have sent him to the Red Wings. He and Eddie Shack were going to Motown for Billy McNeill and Red Kelly. But two days later, Kelly couldn't be convinced to report to New York and the deal was nullified. However, a year and a half later, the Rangers successfully sent Gadsby packing to Detroit. This time he remained a Red Wing until the day he retired at the end of the 1965–66 season after 20 years in the NHL.

While Gadsby was always a star in the league—a First Team All-Star choice three times, a Second Team All-Star four times—he never won the Stanley Cup. In fact, although he played some 1,248 regular-season games, he played only 67 playoff games, making it to the finals three times. In 1963 and 1964 his Red Wings lost to the Leafs and in 1966 Detroit lost in six games to Montreal.

As the years passed, he became as famous for his cuts as his play. He reputedly received more than 600 stitches to his face, a statistic he laughs about because he was one of only a few players to take out insurance on cuts, which paid him $5 for every stitch he received. His nose also suffered numerous breaks and he was heir to a host of other injuries, both great and small, during his lengthy career. All of these were due entirely to his physical play and reckless abandon. His style changed after 1950–51, however, when he suffered a serious shoulder separation and then a broken leg.

Although he played in an era of defensive hockey, Gadsby set a record for assists by defensemen with 46 in 1958–59. For his offensive talents, he credits coach Charlie Conacher. "He straightened me out," he said. "He told me

Gadsby, Bill
D, 6´, 180 lbs, b: Calgary, Alta., 8/8/1927

Season	Club, League	Regular Season					Playoffs				
		GP	G	A	Pts	PIM	GP	G	A	Pts	PIM
1946–47	Chicago Black Hawks, NHL	48	8	10	18	31					
	Kansas City Pla-Mors, USHL	12	2	3	5	8					
1947–48	Chicago Black Hawks, NHL	60	6	10	16	66					
1948–49	Chicago Black Hawks, NHL	50	3	10	13	85					
1949–50	Chicago Black Hawks, NHL	70	10	25	35	138					
1950–51	Chicago Black Hawks, NHL	25	3	7	10	32					
1951–52	Chicago Black Hawks, NHL	59	7	15	22	87					
1952–53	Chicago Black Hawks, NHL	68	2	20	22	84	7	0	1	1	4
1953–54	Chicago Black Hawks, NHL	70	12	29	41	108					
1954–55	Chicago Black Hawks, NHL	18	3	5	8	17					
	New York Rangers, NHL	52	8	8	16	44					
1955–56	New York Rangers, NHL	70	9	42	51	84	5	1	3	4	4
1956–57	New York Rangers, NHL	70	4	37	41	72	5	1	2	3	2
1957–58	New York Rangers, NHL	65	14	32	46	48	6	0	3	3	4
1958–59	New York Rangers, NHL	70	5	46	51	56					
1959–60	New York Rangers, NHL	65	9	22	31	60					
1960–61	New York Rangers, NHL	65	9	26	35	49					
1961–62	Detroit Red Wings, NHL	70	7	30	37	88					
1962–63	Detroit Red Wings, NHL	70	4	24	28	116	11	1	4	5	36
1963–64	Detroit Red Wings, NHL	64	2	16	18	80	14	0	4	4	22
1964–65	Detroit Red Wings, NHL	61	0	12	12	122	7	0	3	3	8
1965–66	Detroit Red Wings, NHL	58	5	12	17	72	12	1	3	4	12
	NHL Totals	1248	130	438	568	1539	67	4	23	27	92

NHL First All-Star Team (1956, 1958, 1959)
NHL Second All-Star Team (1953, 1954, 1957, 1965)

I could carry the puck well, that I was better on the ice than in the penalty box." Gadsby became particularly dangerous anchoring the point on the power-play because of his low shot and stick-handling abilities, and he was never afraid to try to generate offense.

Gadsby's last five years in the league were with the Wings and shortly after retiring he became the team's head coach. He was behind the bench for all of 1968–69, but the team missed the playoffs and he was replaced just two games into the following season.

Terry Sawchuk

Called "the Uke" or "Ukey" because of his Ukrainian heritage, Terry Sawchuk played more games and recorded more shutouts than any goalie in the history of the NHL. He began like Turk Broda, born of a not particularly well-off western family, playing for the love of the game. He was coached by his older brother Mike, who died of a heart murmur when Terry was only 10. His other brother, Roger, also died in his youth of pneumonia. These tragedies had a great impact on Terry and also prophesied his own premature death.

When he was 12, Sawchuk hurt his arm badly playing a friendly game of rugby. He kept the injury to himself and two years later doctors discovered the arm had been broken badly and subsequently healed poorly; it was 2″ shorter than his left arm. Terry, however, was an outstanding athlete as a youth. He played baseball well enough to be offered a tryout with the St. Louis Cardinals, which he turned down, and the Cleveland Indians, which he accepted. He was to have been assigned to the minors in the Indians system, but Terry demurred and continued to pursue a hockey life.

Although he was originally Boston property, he was traded to Detroit before he played in the NHL. His big break came toward the end of the 1949–50 season when Red Wings incumbent Harry Lumley was injured and Sawchuk had to play seven games toward the end of the season. He allowed just 16 goals in those games and along the way earned his first shutout. He made a huge impression. "There are three big-league goalies in hockey, and one of them is in the minors," Rangers coach Lynn Patrick said at the time in referring to Sawchuk.

Detroit general manager Jack Adams showed enormous confidence in Sawchuk based on those seven games he'd played. The Wings won the Cup that spring of 1950 with Lumley back in goal, but over the summer Adams was so sure of Sawchuk that he traded Lumley to Chicago. The next season, 1950–51, Sawchuk played every game for the Red Wings and led the league in wins and shutouts, winning the Calder Trophy in the process. Sawchuk's first years as a pro were remarkable in that he was the first player ever to be named rookie of the year in three different leagues: with Omaha in the USHL, with Indianapolis in the American Hockey League and in his first full year with Detroit in the NHL.

Sportswriter Trent Frayne described Sawchuk's style in this way: "He was the most acrobatic goaltender of his time. He didn't move so much as he exploded into a desperate release of energy—down the glove, up the arm, over the stick, up the leg pad. He sometimes seemed a human pinwheel. He played the whole game in pent-up tension, shouting at his teammates, crouching, straightening, diving, scrambling, his pale face drawn and tense."

Terry Sawchuk played more games and recorded more shutouts than any goalie in the history of the NHL.

The pressure of playing in the NHL deeply affected him and Terry Sawchuk (right) battled injuries for most of his career.

Indeed Sawchuk wasn't a relaxed goalie. The pressure of playing in the NHL got to him and affected his health and he was battling some sort of injury for most of his career. He had bone chips removed from his elbow after the 1952 Stanley Cup, he suffered chest injuries from a car accident and his back was perpetually in knots because of his style of play. And he won more games than any other goalie in the history of the game.

During his 1956–57 season with Boston, Sawchuk retired from the game at the age of 27, citing extreme emotional strain. "My nerves are shot," he explained. "I can't eat or sleep. I'm getting out of the game." But by the next season he was back with Detroit, although circumstances had changed greatly. Montreal was now the dominant team and the Wings were only decent. Bobby Hull and his slapshot were all the rage in Chicago, and Ukey felt the full wrath of the changing times when Hull hit him flush in the face one night in 1963. Sawchuk started to wear a mask, but then Bob Pulford of Toronto skated over his hand and Sawchuk needed surgery to sew up the deep, long wound. "The doctor didn't remember how many stitches," Sawchuk said, "but I counted 79."

In the summer of 1964, Detroit left the aging goalie exposed in the Intra-League Draft and Punch Imlach of the Leafs claimed him. For three years, Sawchuk paired with Johnny Bower to form the most successful duo in the league. Sawchuk was 37 years old and Bower was 42 when they won a historic Stanley Cup in 1967. After three final seasons with successive teams—Los Angeles, Detroit and New York—tragedy befell Sawchuk at a bar near his beach home in New York.

On April 29, 1970, he was having a few drinks with his close friend and teammate Ron Stewart. All the details will never be known, but they began to horse around and after some playful wrestling Sawchuk wound up landing awkwardly on Stewart's knee. He had to be rushed to hospital, where his gall bladder was removed, and just a month later he died from internal injuries, some of which, like the broken arm, he'd probably had for some time without even knowing or bothering to have checked

Sawchuk, Terry
G, 5′11″, 195 lbs, b: Winnipeg, Man., 12/28/1929, d: 5/31/1970

Season	Club, League	Regular Season				Playoffs			
		GP	Mins	GA	Avg	GP	Mins	GA	Avg
1946–47	Galt Red Wings, OHA	30	1800	94	3.13	2	125	9	4.32
1947–48	Windsor Spitfires, OHA	4	240	11	2.75				
	Windsor Hettche Spitfires, IHL	3	180	5	1.67				
	Ohama Knights, USHL	54	3248	174	3.21	3	180	9	3.00
1948–49	Indianapolis Capitals, AHL	67	4020	205	3.06	2	120	9	4.50
1949–50	Indianapolis Capitals, AHL	61	3660	188	3.08	8	480	12	1.50
	Detroit Red Wings, NHL	7	420	16	2.29				
1950–51	Detroit Red Wings, NHL	70	4200	139	1.99	6	463	13	1.68
1951–52	Detroit Red Wings, NHL	70	4200	133	1.90	8	480	5	0.63
1952–53	Detroit Red Wings, NHL	63	3780	120	1.90	6	372	21	3.39
1953–54	Detroit Red Wings, NHL	67	4004	129	1.93	12	751	20	1.60
1954–55	Detroit Red Wings, NHL	68	4080	132	1.94	11	660	26	2.36
1955–56	Boston Bruins, NHL	68	4080	181	2.66				
1956–57	Boston Bruins, NHL	34	2040	81	2.38				
1957–58	Detroit Red Wings, NHL	70	4200	207	2.96	4	252	19	4.52
1958–59	Detroit Red Wings, NHL	67	4020	209	3.12				
1959–60	Detroit Red Wings, NHL	58	3480	156	2.69	6	405	20	2.96
1960–61	Detroit Red Wings, NHL	37	2150	113	3.17	8	465	18	2.32
1961–62	Detroit Red Wings, NHL	43	2580	143	3.33				
1962–63	Detroit Red Wings, NHL	48	2775	119	2.57	11	660	36	3.27
1963–64	Detroit Red Wings, NHL	53	3140	138	2.64	13	677	31	2.75
1964–65	Toronto Maple Leafs, NHL	36	2160	92	2.56	1	60	3	3.00
1965–66	Toronto Maple Leafs, NHL	27	1521	80	3.16	2	120	6	3.00
1966–67	Toronto Maple Leafs, NHL	28	1409	66	2.81	10	565	25	2.65
1967–68	Los Angeles Kings, NHL	36	1936	99	3.07	5	280	18	3.86
1968–69	Detroit Red Wings, NHL	13	641	28	2.62				
1969–70	New York Rangers, NHL	8	412	20	2.91	3	80	6	4.50
	NHL Totals	971	57228	2401	2.52	106	6290	267	2.55

NHL First All-Star Team (1951, 1952, 1953)
NHL Second All-Star Team (1954, 1955, 1959, 1963)
Won Calder Trophy (1951)
Won Vezina Trophy (1952, 1953, 1955, 1965)
Won Lester Patrick Trophy (1971)
Won Stanley Cup (1952, 1954, 1955, 1967)

*Terry
Sawchuk*

out. "He fell on me," Stewart said, horrified at the recollection. "But through his career, Terry took much worse falls on the ice and he always bounced back. It doesn't make sense."

The usual five-year waiting period was waived for Sawchuk's induction into the Hockey Hall of Fame. Dead at 41 years of age, he finished with an incredible 447 wins and 103 shutouts in 971 games played.

Red Kelly

Red Kelly was an integral part of Detroit's winning formula in the 1950s.

Red Kelly was a unique player—versatile and talented enough to be one of the National Hockey League's best defensemen early in his career and a high-scoring center at the end. The red-haired gentleman was cool and calculating on the ice and never swore, but there was no doubt about his ability to take care of himself. He'd been a championship boxer at Toronto's St. Michael's College, skills the four-time winner of the Lady Byng Trophy wouldn't display often during his 20-year NHL career.

Born in Simcoe, Ontario, in 1927, Kelly was 20 years old when the Detroit Red Wings brought him up to the big league directly from St. Michael's. A solid but mobile and skilled defenseman, he quickly found a home on the team playing with such superstars as Gordie Howe, Ted Lindsay and Sid Abel. Kelly was an effective checker, at home on the blue line or on the left wing, where he was sometimes used due either to injuries or to add a little muscle on the offense. One of his first roommates was Bill Quackenbush, another man who didn't like to waste words. An article in a Detroit program from Kelly's early years with the Wings noted that if more than three words were spoken in a day by either man, the other would complain to the coach, "There is too much conversation going on."

Red Kelly may not have been a standout in his early years with the Wings, but his attributes weren't lost on his coach, Tommy Ivan. "Kelly is the greatest all-round player in hockey and also the most underrated," Ivan said in 1949. "We've used Kelly at every job except goalie and he's been outstanding wherever we put him. He may not get the All-Star votes, but I only wish we had 10 like him."

Kelly would get those All-Star votes in 1950, enough to earn a spot on the NHL's Second Team and the chance to play in the All-Star Game. The Red Wings, well on their way to being the league's dominant team, won the Stanley Cup that year, as they would in three of the next five seasons. And Kelly was an integral part of Detroit's winning formula. His puck-carrying ability allowed the Wings to move from their own zone quickly and provided them with a quick transition game. Frank Boucher, the great New York Ranger center and Hall of Famer, would pick Kelly over Howe to build a team. "The redhead attacks like a great forward and defends like an even greater defenseman," Boucher said of Kelly. "There's nobody like him for taking the pressure off his own team and, in a few seconds, applying it on the other guys."

Kelly was an All-Star for eight consecutive seasons with the Red Wings, six times on the First Team, and won the Lady Byng Trophy three times. In 1954 he was chosen as the first recipient of the James Norris Memorial Trophy as the outstanding defenseman in the league. In 1956 he was named team captain, a job he held until the end of 1957–58 season.

In 1960 the relationship between Kelly and Detroit management began to sour when complaints about his play became public. Kelly had been playing with a broken bone in his foot, a fact only the top executives of the club knew. The Wings announced a trade, sending Kelly to the New York Rangers for Eddie Shack on February 4, 1960. Kelly, upset with his treatment, refused to report to New York and announced his retirement the next day. Toronto coach Punch Imlach attempted to talk him out of it and managed to acquire his rights from Detroit for Marc Reaume. NHL president Clarence Campbell gave Kelly a week to rescind his retirement. Red had been a Toronto fan all his life but soured on the team after a few visits to Maple Leaf Gardens as a junior player. He didn't like the building and was further put off when his team lost some important games there. His alienation was a throwback to his early playing days, when a Toronto scout proclaimed that Red would never play more than 20 games in the NHL and went so far as to bet a hat on his prognostication. Despite all this, Kelly decided to take Imlach up on his offer and join the Maple Leafs, though not as a defenseman. Imlach moved him up to the center position and, days after retiring, he began what could be called a second career as a successful full-time forward. Any of Kelly's bad memories were quickly forgotten when the Toronto fans gave him a rousing welcome in his first game with the Leafs.

Frank Mahovlich played on the left wing in Kelly's first full season with the Leafs and set a team record with 48 goals, many of them due to the veteran's playmaking skills. In addition to his talent, Kelly brought his winning ways to the Leafs. In his eight years with the team, Toronto won the Stanley Cup four times. He won even when he entered the world of politics in 1962: He was elected to the Canadian Parliament, where he served for three years until retiring in 1965 to concentrate on hockey again. In 1967, after winning his last Stanley Cup—and the Maple Leafs' last championship as well—Kelly was traded to the expansion Los Angeles Kings, where he was named head coach. As a coach, he'd prove a winner yet again, guiding the Kings into two consecutive playoffs. After a

Red Kelly (second from the left) was a unique player. Whatever position he played, his teams won.

Kelly, Red
D/C, 5′11″, 180 lbs, b: Simcoe, Ont., 7/9/1927

Season	Club, League	Regular Season					Playoffs				
		GP	G	A	Pts	PIM	GP	G	A	Pts	PIM
1947–48	Detroit Red Wings, NHL	60	6	14	20	13	10	3	2	5	2
1948–49	Detroit Red Wings, NHL	59	5	11	16	10	11	1	1	2	10
1949–50	Detroit Red Wings, NHL	70	15	25	40	9	14	1	3	4	2
1950–51	Detroit Red Wings, NHL	70	17	37	54	24	6	0	1	1	0
1951–52	Detroit Red Wings, NHL	67	16	31	47	16	5	1	0	1	0
1952–53	Detroit Red Wings, NHL	70	19	27	46	8	6	0	4	4	0
1953–54	Detroit Red Wings, NHL	62	16	33	49	18	12	5	1	6	0
1954–55	Detroit Red Wings, NHL	70	15	30	45	28	11	2	4	6	17
1955–56	Detroit Red Wings, NHL	70	16	34	50	39	10	2	4	6	2
1956–57	Detroit Red Wings, NHL	70	10	25	35	18	5	1	0	1	0
1957–58	Detroit Red Wings, NHL	61	13	18	31	26	4	0	1	1	2
1958–59	Detroit Red Wings, NHL	67	8	13	21	34					
1959–60	Detroit Red Wings, NHL	50	6	12	18	10					
	Toronto Maple Leafs, NHL	18	6	5	11	8	10	3	8	11	2
1960–61	Toronto Maple Leafs, NHL	64	20	50	70	12	2	1	0	1	0
1961–62	Toronto Maple Leafs, NHL	58	22	27	49	6	12	4	6	10	0
1962–63	Toronto Maple Leafs, NHL	66	20	40	60	8	10	2	6	8	6
1963–64	Toronto Maple Leafs, NHL	70	11	34	45	16	14	4	9	13	4
1964–65	Toronto Maple Leafs, NHL	70	18	28	46	8	6	3	2	5	2
1965–66	Toronto Maple Leafs, NHL	63	8	24	32	12	4	0	2	2	0
1966–67	Toronto Maple Leafs, NHL	61	14	24	38	4	12	0	5	5	2
	NHL Totals	1316	281	542	823	327	164	33	59	92	51

NHL First All-Star Team (1951, 1952, 1953, 1954, 1955, 1957)
NHL Second All-Star Team (1950, 1956)
Won James Norris Trophy (1954)
Won Lady Byng Trophy (1951, 1953, 1954, 1961)
Won Stanley Cup (1950, 1952, 1954, 1955, 1962, 1963, 1964, 1967)

three-year stint with the Pittsburgh Penguins, he returned to Toronto and took the Leafs to four straight quarterfinal appearances.

Red Kelly was indeed a unique player in the National Hockey League. Whatever position he played, his teams won. In 20 playing years, the always composed Kelly missed the playoffs only once.

"He was one of the premier defensemen in the NHL during the first half of his career," said Hall of Famer Dave Keon, who played with Kelly in Toronto. "In the second half of his career, he moved to center and became an All-Star at that position. That will never be done again."

Tom Johnson

An accomplished skater and puckhandler, defenseman Tom Johnson played a valuable role on the powerful Montreal Canadiens teams of the 1950s. He contributed to the Habs' rapid transitional game and would have scored more points had the team not already been blessed with Doug Harvey to quarterback the power-play. One of his key traits was an ability to recover almost immediately after making a mistake on the ice.

The Icelandic-Canadian was born in the hamlet of Baldur, Manitoba, and grew up playing strictly on outdoor rinks. In his first year of junior with the Winnipeg Monarchs in 1946–47, Johnson was deemed to have too many rough edges to be worthy of a spot on the Toronto Maple Leafs' list of 18 sponsored players. Following a match in which he scored the tying and winning goal on end-to-end rushes, a Montreal Canadiens scout worked out a cash settlement with the Leafs and placed him on their negotiation list.

One of Tom Johnson's key traits was an ability to recover almost immediately after he made a mistake on the ice.

The first year Johnson came to Montreal, general manager Frank Selke was unable to gain a transfer from the Canadian Amateur Hockey Association. The young blueliner spent a year playing informal hockey, taking a few classes at McGill University and spending valuable time around the Habs' winning environment at the Forum. Beginning the next year, he made two brief appearances with the big club but spent the majority of his first three pro seasons refining his game with the Montreal Royals of the Quebec senior league and then the Buffalo Bisons of the AHL. In the minors he impressed coaches both with his enthusiasm from the bench and his work ethic on the ice. He also improved his skating, which had always been his one major drawback.

Johnson stepped into a starting role with the Habs in 1950–1951 and impressed them with his eagerness and durability in playing all 70 regular-season games. He was, however, vulnerable to common rookie mistakes such as hasty decision-making and taking unwise penalties. Johnson soon became a stalwart on the penalty-killing unit, where the team utilized his speed and his ability to win the majority of the battles in the corners. One of Johnson's patented moves was to steal the puck from an attacking forward without bodily contact. This allowed him to feed a pass to one of his teammates while the opposition was still heading toward the Montreal net.

Although Johnson rarely saw power-play duty, coach Dick Irvin often switched him to center if the Habs needed a goal late in the game. Johnson won his first Stanley Cup ring in 1953 when the Habs defeated Boston. He later played a vital role on the Canadiens squad that won the Stanley Cup an unprecedented five consecutive times from 1956 to 1960.

By the time the team began dominating the NHL, Johnson was beginning to receive his due credit. In 1956 he was selected to the NHL Second All-Star Team. Three years later, he won the Norris Trophy and earned a spot on the First All-Star lineup. That year he was arguably the most valuable player on the team as he stepped into the void created when Doug Harvey was injured. Johnson didn't have Harvey's speed, but he was a superb stickhandler and a consistent, accurate passer who rarely erred in his own end of the rink.

Johnson remained a key veteran following the glory years. Johnson's fortunes took a turn for the worse in 1962–63 when he suffered a horrific facial injury that damaged his eye muscles to the point that his career was in jeopardy. In a difficult business decision, the Canadiens left him unprotected in the Waiver Draft since it was unclear whether he could fully recover his vision. Boston took a chance and claimed him, a decision that would quickly help improve their fortunes, which had sagged in recent years.

A patented Tom Johnson (left) move was to steal the puck from an attacking forward without bodily contact.

The burly Johnson played 121 games in Beantown before a skate severed the nerves in his leg and forced him to the sidelines permanently. His 51 goals, 264 points and six Stanley Cup rings spoke loudest for his contribution to the game. Many observers claimed that Johnson rode on the back of Doug Harvey. This analysis proved to be unfair, as he more than held his own on the Habs' back line and often stayed back to cover possible counterattacks when Harvey rushed with the puck. Virtually every defenseman in NHL history would have benefited from a pairing with the legendary number 2.

After retiring, Johnson accepted a position in the Boston front office as assistant to the president and general manager, where he helped Harry Sinden build a team that would eventually win the Stanley Cup in 1970 and 1972. Johnson coached the first of these championship squads and was the assistant general manager of the second. He was inducted into the Hockey Hall of Fame in 1970.

Johnson, Tom
D, 6´, 180 lbs, b: Baldur, Man., 2/18/1928

Season	Club, League	Regular Season					Playoffs				
		GP	G	A	Pts	PIM	GP	G	A	Pts	PIM
1947–48	Montreal Canadiens, NHL	1	0	0	0	0					
	Montreal Royals, QSHL	16	0	4	4	10					
1948–49	Buffalo Bisons, AHL	68	4	18	22	70					
1949–50	Buffalo Bisons, AHL	58	7	19	26	52	5	0	0	0	20
	Montreal Canadiens, NHL						1	0	0	0	0
1950–51	Montreal Canadiens, NHL	70	2	8	10	128	11	0	0	0	6
1951–52	Montreal Canadiens, NHL	67	0	7	7	76	11	1	0	1	2
1952–53	Montreal Canadiens, NHL	70	3	8	11	63	12	2	3	5	8
1953–54	Montreal Canadiens, NHL	70	7	11	18	85	11	1	2	3	30
1954–55	Montreal Canadiens, NHL	70	6	19	25	74	12	2	0	2	22
1955–56	Montreal Canadiens, NHL	64	3	10	13	75	10	0	2	2	8
1956–57	Montreal Canadiens, NHL	70	4	11	15	59	10	0	2	2	13
1957–58	Montreal Canadiens, NHL	66	3	18	21	75	2	0	0	0	0
1958–59	Montreal Canadiens, NHL	70	10	29	39	76	11	2	3	5	8
1959–60	Montreal Canadiens, NHL	64	4	25	29	59	8	0	1	1	4
1960–61	Montreal Canadiens, NHL	70	1	15	16	54	6	0	1	1	8
1961–62	Montreal Canadiens, NHL	62	1	17	18	45	6	0	1	1	0
1962–63	Montreal Canadiens, NHL	43	3	5	8	28					
1963–64	Boston Bruins, NHL	70	4	21	25	33					
1964–65	Boston Bruins, NHL	51	0	9	9	30					
	NHL Totals	978	51	213	264	960	111	8	15	23	109

NHL First All-Star Team (1959)
NHL Second All-Star Team (1956)
Won James Norris Trophy (1959)
Won Stanley Cup (1953, 1956, 1957, 1958, 1959, 1960)

Marcel **Pronovost**

Marcel Pronovost was a strong, hard-working defenseman, a solid performer in his own end and a dangerous threat in the offensive zone. His effective bodychecks and rushing style—holding on to the puck and threading his way through checks and hits—took its toll as he endured many injuries over his long career. He survived for 20 National Hockey League seasons, paced his teams to five Stanley Cup wins and earned himself a plaque in the Hockey Hall of Fame for his leadership and consummate professionalism and skill.

Pronovost was born in 1930 in Lac la Tortue, Quebec, one of 12 children including nine brothers; pretty well a hockey team in itself as younger members donned their older siblings' used garb to continue the family tradition on the ice. After a move with the brood to Shawinigan Falls, Marcel was a standout with Shawinigan Tech, his high school team, but he wasn't snapped up by the Montreal Canadiens like so many other Quebec youngsters. The crosstown rival Shawinigan High

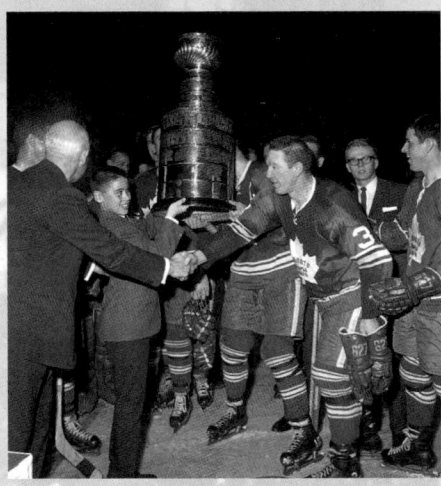

Marcel Pronovost (number 3) won the Stanley Cup five times and was on four consecutive All-Star Teams including the First Team in 1960 and 1961.

team was the area's powerhouse squad, led by brothers Larry and John Wilson, both highly praised junior players who received most of the attention in the city. The Wilson boys were in a tournament in Quebec City when Larry was signed by the Detroit Red Wings, while Marcel was stolen out from under the eyes of the Canadiens when Detroit scout Marcel Cote heeded Larry's advice and went to see Pronovost, who was then a high-scoring center. He was sent to the Windsor Spitfires, where he was moved back to defense, and then spent two years with the Wings' International Hockey League team before turning pro in 1949 with Detroit's farm team in Omaha.

In 1950 the Red Wings were in a tough semifinal series with the Toronto Maple Leafs when Gordie Howe was seriously injured. Red Kelly, a defender, was thrust into duty as a forward and Pronovost was called up from Omaha to take Kelly's place on the blue line. His name was engraved on the Stanley Cup when the Red Wings recovered from Howe's loss to defeat the Leafs and then the Rangers to win the championship. Pronovost was in the minors for part of the next season but won a permanent job with Detroit in 1951–52. He'd win the Cup three more times with the Wings, garner seven regular-season titles and be on four consecutive league All-Star teams including the First Team in 1960 and 1961.

Pronovost worked hard to become fluent in English. He was the team representative and was known to read three books a week during the season. He was popular across the league, even in Montreal, not usually a hotbed of positive feelings for Red Wings players, and he was given his own night, including a car from admiring fans, when Detroit visited the Forum in 1960.

A player like Pronovost, who delivered hits and took even more on his rushes, could expect to receive a daunting array of injuries. Many of them were accidental, results of his determination to score or prevent a goal, and not signs of malice from stick-wielding opponents. While Pronovost was learning his trade in the minors, an insurance company came up with a novel way to attract the business of professional players. They undertook to pay $5 per stitch to players cut during games. Pronovost was once called "the most embroidered man in hockey," sporting the scars of hundreds of stitches. He was upset that he missed out on the money when the scheme was quickly discontinued, although he was equally concerned because "I sort of felt the insurance should be saved for something really important. I was getting stitches all the time," he said. "If I kept collecting for them, the company might have got fed up if I broke an arm or a collarbone."

In one three-game stretch with the Red Wings, his face was struck by seemingly every conceivable hard surface in a rink—the puck, when his own goalie attempted to clear it; an opponent's stick, though not on purpose; and, on a memorable dive through two defenders, the ice, the net and then the boards. He had four long cuts requiring stitches and a broken nose from the week's work. He estimated at the end of his career that he'd broken his nose 14 times, and the list of his many aches and pains reads like a medical exam for trauma care.

In 1965–66, Pronovost was sent to the Toronto Maple Leafs in an eight-player deal that involved Andy Bathgate's going to Detroit. Pronovost joined a solid core of defenders in Toronto and was an integral part of the Over-the-Hill Gang that won Toronto's last Stanley Cup in 1967 under coach Punch Imlach.

Pronovost retired after playing seven games in 1969–70, feeling he no longer had the legs to compete in the league. He played with the Tulsa Oilers in the Central Hockey League for a season and a half until he decided to hang up the blades at the age of 41. He coached in Tulsa before accepting a job behind the bench in Buffalo, where his former boss with the Maple Leafs, Imlach, was the general manager. He steered the Sabres to a 105-point season in 1977–78 but was shown the door midway through the next season, following Imlach out of the organization when the team struggled. After a brief stint with the Ontario Hockey Association's Windsor Spitfires in 1982–83, he became a scout with the NHL's Central Scouting Service and later with the New Jersey Devils. Three brothers followed him into the NHL, including Jean, who played almost 1,000 games in the league, primarily with the Pittsburgh Penguins. Marcel was inducted into the Hall of Fame in 1978.

Marcel Pronovost (number 3) estimated at the end of his career that he'd broken his nose 14 times, while the list of his aches and pains is even longer.

Pronovost, Marcel
D, 6′, 190 lbs, b: Lac la Tortue, Que., 6/15/1930

Season	Club, League	Regular Season					Playoffs				
		GP	G	A	Pts	PIM	GP	G	A	Pts	PIM
1947–48	Detroit Auto Club, IHL	19	5	3	8	53					
1948–49	Detroit Auto Club, IHL	9	4	4	8	24	6	3	1	4	15
1949–50	Omaha Knights, USHL	69	13	39	52	100	7	4	9	13	9
	Detroit Red Wings, NHL						9	0	1	1	10
1950–51	Detroit Red Wings, NHL	37	1	6	7	20	6	0	0	0	0
	Indianapolis Capitals, AHL	34	9	23	32	44					
1951–52	Detroit Red Wings, NHL	69	7	11	18	50	8	0	1	1	10
1952–53	Detroit Red Wings, NHL	68	8	19	27	72	6	0	0	0	6
1953–54	Detroit Red Wings, NHL	57	6	12	18	50	12	2	3	5	12
1954–55	Detroit Red Wings, NHL	70	9	25	34	90	11	1	2	3	6
1955–56	Detroit Red Wings, NHL	68	4	13	17	46	10	0	2	2	8
1956–57	Detroit Red Wings, NHL	70	7	9	16	38	5	0	0	0	6
1957–58	Detroit Red Wings, NHL	62	2	18	20	52	4	0	1	1	4
1958–59	Detroit Red Wings, NHL	69	11	21	32	44					
1959–60	Detroit Red Wings, NHL	69	7	17	24	38	6	1	1	2	2
1960–61	Detroit Red Wings, NHL	70	6	11	17	44	9	2	3	5	0
1961–62	Detroit Red Wings, NHL	70	4	14	18	38					
1962–63	Detroit Red Wings, NHL	69	4	9	13	48	11	1	4	5	8
1963–64	Detroit Red Wings, NHL	67	3	17	20	42	14	0	2	2	14
1964–65	Detroit Red Wings, NHL	68	1	15	16	45	7	0	3	3	4
1965–66	Toronto Maple Leafs, NHL	54	2	8	10	34	4	0	0	0	6
1966–67	Toronto Maple Leafs, NHL	58	2	12	14	28	12	1	0	1	8
1967–68	Toronto Maple Leafs, NHL	70	3	17	20	48					
1968–69	Toronto Maple Leafs, NHL	34	1	2	3	20					
1969–70	Toronto Maple Leafs, NHL	7	0	1	1	4					
	Tulsa Oilers, CHL	53	1	16	17	24	2	0	0	0	0
1970–71	Tulsa Oilers, CHL	17	0	0	0	4					
	NHL Totals	1206	88	257	345	851	134	8	23	31	104

NHL First All-Star Team (1960, 1961)
NHL Second All-Star Team (1958, 1959)
Won Stanley Cup (1950, 1952, 1954, 1955, 1967)

Tommy *Ivan*

Tommy Ivan's dreams of playing in the NHL ended early in his career. While playing senior hockey in Brantford before the war, he suffered a serious cheekbone fracture and gave up the sport, turning at first to refereeing and later coaching as a means of staying in the game. He joined the army and was made sergeant, acting as an instructor in chemical warfare. After the war he was hired by the Detroit Red Wings to coach their minor pro affiliates, first in Omaha and later in Indianapolis, and it was there he first encountered a 17-year-old named Gordie Howe. "I was no genius at spotting talent," he said later, "but I knew he was a National Hockey League prospect."

In 1947 circumstances were such with the parent club that Ivan was named coach of the Wings—the only one of the Original Six coaches of the day who'd never played in the NHL. His timing couldn't have been better, for Howe was now in Detroit as a rising star, as was young goalie Terry Sawchuk. Ivan led the team to first place in the standings for six years in a row and to three Stanley Cup wins during the early 1950s; the first, in 1950, was decided in double overtime of game seven with a Pete Babando goal.

Tommy Ivan (right) suffered a career-ending cheekbone fracture playing senior hockey, turning at first to refereeing and later coaching to stay in the game.

The 1952 Cup win was particularly impressive for Ivan because Detroit swept both series against their greatest rivals, Toronto and Montreal, and won the Cup in the bare minimum eight games. That team also had an incredible eight future members of the Hockey Hall of Fame: Sawchuk, Howe, Ted Lindsay, Alex Delvecchio, Sid Abel, Red Kelly, Marcel Pronovost and Bob Goldham. After the third of these Stanley Cup wins, in the spring of 1955, Ivan left Detroit to assume general manager duties in Chicago. "It was the challenge more than anything," he said of the controversial job change.

His time in the Windy City was remarkably successful, not just for the short term but for the long-term benefit of the organization. "We put a lot of money into player development," he noted. "We built up the farm systems and sponsored clubs. And eventually the players developed—Bobby and Dennis Hull, Pierre Pilote, Elmer Vasko, Chico Maki, Stan Mikita." Ivan ended up coaching for a year and a half because of the illness of coach Dick Irvin. He brought the team up from last place to consistent respectability, and as a result he increased attendance from pitiful crowds of 3,000 or 4,000 a game to near sellouts every night.

In 1960–61, Ivan won the Stanley Cup with Chicago, one of the biggest thrills in his career as general manager and the result of years of hard work and the aforementioned planning. A few years later, however, he was to be pilloried for making one of the worst trades in league history, sending Phil Esposito, Ken Hodge and Fred Stanfield to Boston for Gilles Marotte, Pit Martin and Jack Norris. Ivan was quick to point out that he soon traded Norris and Bill White to Montreal for Tony Esposito, one of the greatest goalies of the modern era, and sent Marotte to Los Angeles for Gerry Desjardins. So, he reasoned, the Phil Esposito deal wasn't that bad!

Throughout his career with Detroit and Chicago, Ivan never had a contract, such was the strength and value of his relationships with the owners, first the Norris family, then the Wirtz family. "Their word was their bond," he said.

Because he consistently took the Wings to the finals, he also was named All-Star Game coach on a regular basis, and to this day his 3–0–1 record is the best in league history for the annual game. But perhaps his most famous association with the game came in 1961 when Toronto hosted the All-Stars as Cup champs and he was Chicago's general manager. He accompanied Jim Norris to the Royal York Hotel in Toronto to a meeting with Stafford Smythe and Harold Ballard of the Leafs and was holding in his pocket a check for $1,000,000 that Norris was willing to hand over for the sale of Frank Mahovlich. It was the most sensational offer of the era, and although rejected the next morning by the Leafs, Norris' offer upstaged the All-Star Game itself for sheer magnitude of publicity.

Ivan, Tommy
Head Coach, b: Toronto, Ont., 1/31/1911, d: 6/24/1999

Season	Club, League	Regular Season					Playoffs				
		GC	W	L	T	W%	GC	W	L	T	W%
1947–48	Detroit Red Wings, NHL	60	30	18	12	0.600	10	4	6	0	0.400
1948–49	Detroit Red Wings, NHL	60	34	19	7	0.625	11	4	7	0	0.364
1949–50	Detroit Red Wings, NHL	70	37	19	14	0.629	14	8	6	0	0.571
1950–51	Detroit Red Wings, NHL	70	44	13	13	0.721	6	2	4	0	0.333
1951–52	Detroit Red Wings, NHL	70	44	14	12	0.714	8	8	0	0	1.000
1952–53	Detroit Red Wings, NHL	70	36	16	18	0.643	6	2	4	0	0.333
1953–54	Detroit Red Wings, NHL	70	37	19	14	0.629	12	8	4	0	0.667
1956–57	Chicago Black Hawks, NHL	70	16	39	15	0.336					
1957–58	Chicago Black Hawks, NHL	33	10	17	6	0.394					
	NHL Totals	573	288	174	111	0.599	67	36	31	0	0.537

Won Lester Patrick Trophy (1975)
Won Stanley Cup (1950, 1952, 1954)

Ivan was also known as the best dresser among his bench-bossing brethren. "Even if I didn't have a dollar, I'd wear a good suit of clothes," he said with pride. He was inducted into the Hall of Fame in 1974 and died in Chicago on June 24, 1999.

Tim Horton

Though it would be impossible to prove, the case could be made that Tim Horton was the strongest man ever to lace up skates in the National Hockey League. His bodychecks, most often cleanly delivered, were legendary for being bone-crunching. He combined this strength with a smooth skating style and the ability to carry the puck. He patrolled the blue line for 18 years for the Toronto Maple Leafs, anchoring their four Stanley Cup teams of the 1960s, and played in the NHL for 24 seasons.

Like another league strongman, Gordie Howe, Horton had a reputation as a man not to be riled. Worse than his punch was a move that came to be called "the Horton Bear Hug," a rib-cracking maneuver that settled fights before they were started. But for all his power, Horton wasn't a mean or nasty player. "There were defensemen you had to fear more because they were vicious and would slam you into the boards from behind," Bobby Hull said. "But you respected Horton because he didn't need that type of intimidation. He used his tremendous strength and talent to keep you in check."

As a junior player with the St. Michael's College team in the Ontario Hockey League, Horton had NHL scouts and executives claiming he'd be the league's all-time great defenseman. But Horton's career, for all of its early promise, got off to a slow start. Though his attributes were obvious, he took a while to mature as a defensive player and spent several years moving back and forth between Toronto and its minor-league team in Pittsburgh. When he did find a regular job with the Maple Leafs during the 1952–53 season, respect was hard to come by, mostly because

Tim Horton was arguably the strongest man ever to lace up skates in the NHL.

the expectations had been so high during his junior days. For several years, his profile in the Leafs' program had the title "Is This Tim's Year?"

In 1954, having just turned 24, Horton was selected to the league's Second All-Star Team and his career took off from there. With a few weeks left in the 1954–55 season, however, Horton broke his leg and jaw in a thunderous collision with the New York Rangers' Bill Gadsby. Toronto won the game that night, but Horton, even though he missed the third period, was selected as the game's third star for his standout play. Gadsby later said it was the hardest hit he ever delivered. Horton, in traction and fed intravenously for days afterwards in the hospital, certainly agreed. When he returned to the ice after missing almost half of the 1955–56 season, he was slow to regain his form. Hap Day, the Leafs' tough general manager, didn't show a great deal of patience with his defenseman. "It took me a little while to get back into shape, but it didn't take Hap Day very long to fine me. In fact, after three games he slapped a $100 fine on me for indifferent play," Horton recalled in 1971. "When Day fined you, you'd get a receipt from a charitable organization thanking you for your contribution."

In 1958–59, Horton was paired on the blue line with Allan Stanley. Stanley's solid play allowed Horton to take a few more chances carrying the puck, knowing he had the speed to recover should he lose possession and that Stanley would be there to back him up. With Bobby Baun and Carl Brewer also starring on defense, the Leafs had a core of skilled, rugged and reliable defensemen. And the defense was the foundation of a Toronto team that won the Stanley Cup in 1962, 1963 and 1964, with Horton earning a spot on the Second All-Star Team in 1963 and First Team honors in 1964. The team went through a minor slump in 1965 and for part of the season coach Punch Imlach moved Horton to the right wing, another defenseman turned forward. Horton scored 12 goals, many of them with his huge slapshot from close range.

After the Leafs' last Stanley Cup win in 1967—after which Horton was once again selected to the league's Second All-Star Team—the Maple Leafs went into decline. Many of the stars of the championship teams moved on or retired. Though he remained and was a First Team All-Star the following two seasons, Horton was tempted to retire in 1969 because of the success of his business off the ice, a chain of donut shops bearing his name, and of Punch Imlach's dismissal as coach of the club. Horton claimed he wanted double his salary to even consider returning, though later he said he never seriously thought the Leafs

Horton, Tim
D, 5'10", 180 lbs, b: Cochrane, Ont., 1/12/1930, d: 2/14/1974

Season	Club, League	Regular Season					Playoffs				
		GP	G	A	Pts	PIM	GP	G	A	Pts	PIM
1949–50	Toronto Maple Leafs, NHL	1	0	0	0	2	1	0	0	0	2
	Pittsburgh Hornets, AHL	60	5	18	23	83					
1950–51	Pittsburgh Hornets, AHL	68	8	26	34	129	13	0	9	9	16
1951–52	Toronto Maple Leafs, NHL	4	0	0	0	8					
	Pittsburgh Hornets, AHL	64	12	19	31	146	11	1	3	4	16
1952–53	Toronto Maple Leafs, NHL	70	2	14	16	85					
1953–54	Toronto Maple Leafs, NHL	70	7	24	31	94	5	1	1	2	4
1954–55	Toronto Maple Leafs, NHL	67	5	9	14	84					
1955–56	Toronto Maple Leafs, NHL	35	0	5	5	36	2	0	0	0	4
1956–57	Toronto Maple Leafs, NHL	66	6	19	25	72					
1957–58	Toronto Maple Leafs, NHL	53	6	20	26	39					
1958–59	Toronto Maple Leafs, NHL	70	5	21	26	76	12	0	3	3	16
1959–60	Toronto Maple Leafs, NHL	70	3	29	32	69	10	0	1	1	6
1960–61	Toronto Maple Leafs, NHL	57	6	15	21	75	5	0	0	0	0
1961–62	Toronto Maple Leafs, NHL	70	10	28	38	88	12	3	13	16	16
1962–63	Toronto Maple Leafs, NHL	70	6	19	25	69	10	1	3	4	10
1963–64	Toronto Maple Leafs, NHL	70	9	20	29	71	14	0	4	4	20
1964–65	Toronto Maple Leafs, NHL	70	12	16	28	95	6	0	2	2	13
1965–66	Toronto Maple Leafs, NHL	70	6	22	28	76	4	1	0	1	12
1966–67	Toronto Maple Leafs, NHL	70	8	17	25	70	12	3	5	8	25
1967–68	Toronto Maple Leafs, NHL	69	4	23	27	82					
1968–69	Toronto Maple Leafs, NHL	74	11	29	40	107	4	0	0	0	7
1969–70	Toronto Maple Leafs, NHL	59	3	19	22	91					
	New York Rangers, NHL	15	1	5	6	16	6	1	1	2	28
1970–71	New York Rangers, NHL	78	2	18	20	57	13	1	4	5	14
1971–72	Pittsburgh Penguins, NHL	44	2	9	11	40	4	0	1	1	2
1972–73	Buffalo Sabres, NHL	69	1	16	17	56	6	0	1	1	4
1973–74	Buffalo Sabres, NHL	55	0	6	6	53					
	NHL Totals	1446	115	403	518	1611	126	11	39	50	183

NHL First All-Star Team (1964, 1968, 1969)
NHL Second All-Star Team (1954, 1963, 1967)
Won Stanley Cup (1962, 1963, 1964, 1967)

would come up with such a lofty sum that he'd "just pulled… out of a hat." Lacking any veteran leadership on its blue line, Toronto surprised Horton by giving him over $80,000, roughly double his salary of the year before. The team, so young that Horton was the oldest defender by 16 years, was dead last in the league in the spring of 1970. Horton's large salary was impractical for a team with little promise and he was traded to the New York Rangers. He spent a full season in New York in 1970–71, but was then selected in the next two intra-league expansion drafts, moving first to Pittsburgh for an injury-plagued season in 1971–72 and then to Punch Imlach's Buffalo Sabres.

Early in the morning of February 14, 1974, Tim Horton was killed in a single-car crash while driving home to Buffalo after a game in Toronto against his old team. Police who chased the sports car reported that it was traveling over 100 miles per hour before it crashed just outside of St. Catharines, Ontario. He left behind a wife and four daughters. He was inducted into the Hockey Hall of Fame in 1977. And today there are Tim Horton donut shops all across Canada.

On February 14, 1974, Tim Horton (left) was killed in a single-car crash while he was driving home to Buffalo after a game in Maple Leaf Gardens against his old team.

Jacques Plante

If not the best goalie of all time, Jacques Plante was certainly the most important—the man who introduced the art of modern goaltending to the NHL and whose influence is seen every night a game is played. Jake the Snake was born in Shawinigan Falls, Quebec, and from the time he started playing, his destiny was to play for the Montreal Canadiens.

After a usual four-year apprenticeship with the Montreal Royals in Quebec senior hockey and two years with the Buffalo Bisons, Plante quickly emerged as Montreal's goalie of the future. He played a few games for the Habs in 1952–53 and 1953–54, and in his first full season began an incredible run of five consecutive Stanley Cup wins and five consecutive Vezina Trophy wins, records that have yet to be equaled.

Plante began wearing a mask in practices as early as 1956. Coach Toe Blake endorsed the move cautiously because it kept his goalie healthy and happy, but he warned Plante that a mask wasn't permitted during games. However, during a Montreal versus New York game the night of November 2, 1959, Plante was hit in the face by a shot. He went off to the dressing room for stitches and when he returned he was wearing a mask. Blake was livid, but he'd no other goalie to call upon and Plante refused to return to the goal unless he kept the mask. Blake agreed on condition that Plante discard the mask when the cut had healed. In the ensuing days, Plante refused, and as the team continued to win, Blake became less obstinate. The Montreal record stretched into an 18-game unbeaten streak with Plante protected and the mask was in the NHL for good.

In his first full season with the Canadiens, Jacques Plante began an incredible run of five consecutive Stanley Cup wins and Vezina trophies.

By the early 1970s, after Jacques Plante's (right) retirement, virtually every goalie at every level in every league was wearing a mask.

Jacques Plante (number 1) was certainly the most important if not the best goalie of all time and introduced the art of modern goaltending to the NHL.

Plante, Jacques
G, 6´, 175 lbs, b: Shawinigan Falls, Que., 1/17/1929, d: 2/26/1986

Season	Club, League	Regular Season				Playoffs			
		GP	Mins	GA	Avg	GP	Mins	GA	Avg
1949–50	Montreal Royals, QSHL	58	3480	180	3.10	6	360	20	3.33
1950–51	Montreal Royals, QSHL	60	3670	201	3.29	7	420	26	3.71
1951–52	Montreal Royals, QSHL	60	3560	201	3.39	7	420	21	3.00
1952–53	Montreal Royals, QSHL	29	1760	61	2.08				
	Montreal Canadiens, NHL	3	180	4	1.33	4	240	7	1.75
	Buffalo Bisons, AHL	33	2000	114	3.42				
1953–54	Buffalo Bisons, AHL	55	3370	148	2.64				
	Montreal Canadiens, NHL	17	1020	27	1.59	8	480	15	1.88
1954–55	Montreal Canadiens, NHL	52	3080	110	2.14	12	640	30	2.81
1955–56	Montreal Canadiens, NHL	64	3840	119	1.86	10	600	18	1.80
1956–57	Montreal Canadiens, NHL	61	3660	123	2.02	10	616	18	1.75
1957–58	Montreal Canadiens, NHL	57	3386	119	2.11	10	618	20	1.94
1958–59	Montreal Canadiens, NHL	67	4000	144	2.16	11	670	28	2.51
1959–60	Montreal Canadiens, NHL	69	4140	175	2.54	8	489	11	1.35
1960–61	Montreal Royals, EPHL	8	480	24	3.00				
	Montreal Canadiens, NHL	40	2400	112	2.80	6	412	16	2.33
1961–62	Montreal Canadiens, NHL	70	4200	166	2.37	6	360	19	3.17
1962–63	Montreal Canadiens, NHL	56	3320	138	2.49	5	300	14	2.80
1963–64	New York Rangers, NHL	65	3900	220	3.38				
1964–65	New York Rangers, NHL	33	1938	109	3.37				
	Baltimore Clippers, AHL	17	1018	51	3.01	5	315	14	2.67
1968–69	St. Louis Blues, NHL	37	2139	70	1.96	10	589	14	1.43
1969–70	St. Louis Blues, NHL	32	1839	67	2.19	6	324	8	1.48
1970–71	Toronto Maple Leafs, NHL	40	2329	73	1.88	3	134	7	3.13
1971–72	Toronto Maple Leafs, NHL	34	1965	86	2.63	1	60	5	5.00
1972–73	Toronto Maple Leafs, NHL	32	1717	87	3.04				
	Boston Bruins, NHL	8	480	16	2.00	2	120	10	5.00
1974–75	Edmonton Oilers, WHA	31	1592	88	3.32				
	NHL Totals	837	49533	1965	2.38	112	6652	240	2.16
	WHA Totals	31	1592	88	3.32				

NHL First All-Star Team (1956, 1959, 1962)
NHL Second All-Star Team (1957, 1958, 1960, 1971)
Won Hart Trophy (1962)
Won Vezina Trophy (1956, 1957, 1958, 1959, 1960, 1962, 1969)
Won Stanley Cup (1953, 1956, 1957, 1958, 1959, 1960)

The sight of the green mask at first scared many fans, so Plante painted it various colors to make it more visually friendly. He finally settled on a skin-tone, but still many fans were upset that he was wearing one at all. He also altered its design radically over the next decade, trying to increase its safety every step of the way as the slapshot became ever more popular among ever-stronger players. After about five different styles, he settled on one that covered the entire face and had small holes so his skin could breathe. By the early 1970s, after Plante's retirement, virtually every goalie in every league at every level was wearing a mask.

Plante was a pioneer of the style of play for goaltenders as well. While there had been other goalies before him who periodically came out of their crease to play the puck, he was the first to skate in behind the net to stop the puck for his defensemen. He also was the first to raise his arm on an icing call to let his defensemen know what was happening on the ice, and he perfected a stand-up style of goaltending that emphasized positional play, cutting down the angles and staying square to the shooter. His book, *The Art of Goaltending*, was the first of its kind and solidified his place in the game as not just a great stopper but a man who truly understood hockey and wanted to have an influence on how the game would be played in the future.

Plante retired in 1965 after playing two seasons with the Rangers, but he was lured out of retirement by the St. Louis Blues and the prospects of sharing the goaltending with the great Glenn Hall for the expansion team. Together they took the Blues to two Stanley Cup finals, and in 1969 Plante shared the Vezina Trophy with Hall at the ripe old age of 40. He also played with Toronto and Boston and played for one final season with the Edmonton Oilers in the WHA before becoming a scout and goalie coach in St. Louis. In 1962 he was the last goalie to win the Hart Trophy before Dominik Hasek in 1997, and he ranks among the leaders in games played and shutouts. He was inducted into the Hockey Hall of Fame in 1978 and died of stomach cancer in Switzerland in 1986.

Bernie "Boom Boom" Geoffrion

Bernie Geoffrion, nicknamed "Boom Boom," gained NHL fame for his hard shot and feisty temperament. Born and raised in Montreal, he played right wing for the Montreal Canadiens' dynasty teams in the 1950s and 1960s alongside Maurice "Rocket" Richard and Jean Beliveau. The powerful combination with these two superstar teammates brought the Stanley Cup home to Montreal an amazing six times during Geoffrion's time there, and he also won the league scoring title twice and the Hart Trophy in 1961.

Many claim Geoffrion invented and perfected the slapshot—not bad for a kid who was once told by the assistant coach of a junior hockey team that he'd never make it in big-time hockey. "That made me mad," he remembered many years later. "I was only a kid and then somebody tells me I can't make the NHL. I thought that maybe I'd show him something." He certainly did. Geoffrion played his junior hockey with the Montreal (and Laval) Nationales, and from the moment he joined the NHL, he proved to be a talented and determined star. It was no surprise when the league voted him for the Calder Trophy in 1952.

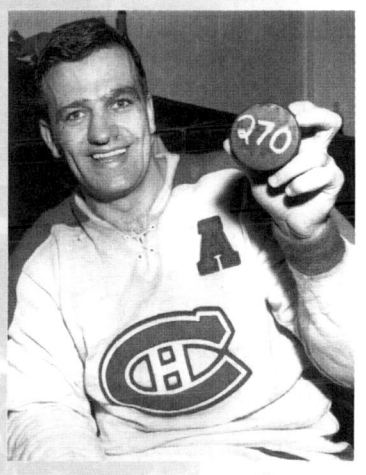

Bernie Geoffrion, nicknamed "Boom Boom," gained NHL fame for his hard shot and feisty temperament.

Although he and the Rocket were teammates, they were also rivals. In 1955 Richard seemed to have the league scoring title clinched, but he was suspended by NHL president Clarence Campbell for hitting a referee. Fans begged Geoffrion to cut down his scoring so Richard could win the title, but Boom Boom ignored them. And when he beat the Rocket for the title by a single point on the final day of the year, the crowd in the Montreal Forum booed him. But by 1961 it seemed Montreal fans had forgiven him—they gave him a 10-minute standing ovation at the Forum when he scored his 50th goal of the season. Geoffrion became only the second NHL player to hit the 50-goal mark after his teammate Rocket Richard.

Geoffrion broke his nose nine times and had 400 stitches during his 16-year career in the NHL. He also had numerous stomach problems and operations, but they never seemed to slow him down. He once remarked, "I can't have ulcers—I don't have enough stomach left to have them in." One scary moment occurred during a routine practice in 1958 when Geoffrion collided with a teammate. He skated another few seconds and then collapsed. When the team doctor couldn't feel his pulse for 15 seconds, the doctor desperately turned Geoffrion upside down so blood could rush to his head. It worked, and Geoffrion was rushed to the hospital for emergency surgery for a ruptured bowel. He was even given last rites, but in the end Boom Boom pulled through.

Stubbornly, and against the advice of his doctors, Geoffrion returned to the Canadiens lineup to skate in the playoff series against Boston. Remarkably, he scored the first goal in his first game back, assisted on the second and banged home the winner as Montreal beat Boston 3–2 and roared to yet another Stanley Cup.

Boom Boom retired from the Canadiens in 1964. For a brief time he coached the Quebec Aces in the AHL, hoping to one day to coach the Canadiens, but he wasn't asked to do so. This stirred up some bitterness toward the Canadiens. "Not one of their older players—not Maurice Richard, not Butch Bouchard, or me—are in their organization," he said. "I don't know why. I suppose this is life." Little did he know that one day that dream would be realized.

Geoffrion came back from his retirement in 1966 and played two more seasons with the New York Rangers. "I don't intend to go out as a bum. If I can keep on scoring, don't worry," he said. "I'll know when it's time to quit." He played well but wasn't the Boom Boom of old: "My timing was off and it was hard work to skate," he recalled. "I would like to have been like I was, but I soon realized that this was impossible." Despite the fact that he wasn't the powerhouse of his younger days, Geoffrion still led the Rangers in scoring for the first few weeks of his first season back.

In 1972 he moved to Atlanta to coach the Flames for two and a half years and went on to become the team's vice-president. When he first arrived, Geoffrion said in typically outgoing fashion: "I don't know what kind of team we are going to have. But I think we are going to have some fun." He coached the Flames to the Stanley Cup playoffs in only his second season with the team. Geoffrion really took to the city, even though he said it felt a little strange to have hockey in the South. Of course, he was a big hit with the fans, and even remained in Georgia over the summers. Geoffrion once summed up his coaching philosophy in Atlanta: "You have to make the guys like you. So what if I scored 400 goals? That doesn't mean anything to these guys. That's gone, and you have to go along with them."

In the NHL, Geoffrion was known as much for his amazing scoring ability as he was for his hot temper. He once made a popular beer commercial where he told fans, "If you played hockey the way I do, you would have a lot of enemies too." Geoffrion was involved in many nasty incidents on the ice. In 1963 he was suspended for throwing a stick, spear-style, at a referee. In 1953 he was fined for checking another referee into the boards. And he once hit New York Ranger Ron Murphy over the head with his stick, baseball-style. Later he said he regretted that particular incident but never

Geoffrion, Bernie "Boom Boom"
RW, 5´9˝, 166 lbs, b: Montreal, Que., 2/14/1931

Season	Club, League	Regular Season					Playoffs				
		GP	G	A	Pts	PIM	GP	G	A	Pts	PIM
1949–50	Montreal Royals, QSHL	1	0	0	0	0					
1950–51	Montreal Canadiens, NHL	18	8	6	14	9	11	1	1	2	6
1951–52	Montreal Canadiens, NHL	67	30	24	54	66	11	3	1	4	6
1952–53	Montreal Canadiens, NHL	65	22	17	39	37	12	6	4	10	12
1953–54	Montreal Canadiens, NHL	54	29	25	54	87	11	6	5	11	18
1954–55	Montreal Canadiens, NHL	70	38	37	75	57	12	8	5	13	8
1955–56	Montreal Canadiens, NHL	59	29	33	62	66	10	5	9	14	6
1956–57	Montreal Canadiens, NHL	41	19	21	40	18	10	11	7	18	2
1957–58	Montreal Canadiens, NHL	42	27	23	50	51	10	6	5	11	2
1958–59	Montreal Canadiens, NHL	59	22	44	66	30	11	5	8	13	10
1959–60	Montreal Canadiens, NHL	59	30	41	71	36	8	2	10	12	4
1960–61	Montreal Canadiens, NHL	64	50	45	95	29	4	2	1	3	0
1961–62	Montreal Canadiens, NHL	62	23	36	59	36	5	0	1	1	6
1962–63	Montreal Canadiens, NHL	51	23	18	41	73	5	0	1	1	4
1963–64	Montreal Canadiens, NHL	55	21	18	39	41	7	1	1	2	4
1966–67	New York Rangers, NHL	58	17	25	42	42	4	2	0	2	0
1967–68	New York Rangers, NHL	59	5	16	21	11	1	0	1	1	0
	NHL Totals	883	393	429	822	689	132	58	60	118	88

NHL First All-Star Team (1961)
NHL Second All-Star Team (1955, 1960)
Won Hart Trophy (1961)
Won Art Ross Trophy (1955, 1961)
Won Calder Trophy (1952)
Won Stanley Cup (1953, 1956, 1957, 1958, 1959, 1960)

regretted his physical play. "I think most of this talk about violence in hockey is unfair," said Geoffrion a decade after his retirement. "A good bodycheck is never going to hurt a person. Believe me, the game was tougher in my day than today."

In 1979 Geoffrion realized his dream of coaching the Canadiens. Sadly, he lasted only 30 games due to stomach problems. "I would have liked to stay with the Canadiens, but I couldn't take it any more," he said. "I have to think of my family." Geoffrion's wife, Marlene, the daughter of former Canadiens great Howie Morenz, was the 1950 Canadian junior figure skating champion.

Many claimed Boom Boom Geoffrion (left) invented and perfected the slapshot.

When he resigned, Geoffrion took the opportunity to voice his displeasure with what he considered the lax attitude of the modern athlete. "I'm sick and tired of them. They aren't acting like professional athletes," he said of his Montreal players. "Why should I get sick over a bunch of guys who won't listen to me?" He'd had enough of coaching, and when his team had its slowest start to the season in seven years, he said, "I'm not going to stick around and let everyone blame me for what's happening, because it's not my fault."

But while Geoffrion found it frustrating to coach players who, unlike him, weren't always giving 100% on the ice, the same could never be said of him. As one of the most determined players in the history of the game, his place in hockey history was secure and he was inducted into the Hall of Fame in 1972.

Jean "le Gros Bil" Beliveau

Jean Beliveau was one of the all-time classiest players in the NHL, both on the ice and off. He made his career as a strong skater and was hard if not impossible to slow down. He was nicknamed after a popular French song of the day by the same name, "le Gros Bil," and in all he played on an incredible 10 Stanley Cup-winning teams as a member of the Montreal Canadiens.

Born in Trois Rivieres, Quebec, in 1931, Beliveau first played organized hockey in Victoriaville, Quebec. He played junior hockey as a member of the Quebec City Citadelles and senior hockey for the Quebec Aces. The Canadiens wanted the young Beliveau in their lineup, but he wasn't all that eager to play for them. "It was a very personal decision to stay in Quebec [City] when the Canadiens first asked me to come to Montreal," he explained. "They'd given me a car, a place to use my talents. I'm a very loyal person and I wanted to pay back my public and Punch Imlach, my coach in Quebec." Years later, when he was coach of the Leafs, Imlach returned the loyalty. "Jean Beliveau is the best thing that ever came down the pike," Imlach said. "He could play for me anywhere, any time, in this world or the next."

Jean Beliveau played on 10 Stanley Cup-winning teams as a member of the Montreal Canadiens.

But the Canadiens owned the rights to Beliveau, so he couldn't play for another pro team unless Montreal traded him. Since the Aces were an amateur team, there was no conflict with his staying there. Finally, Montreal purchased the entire Quebec Senior Hockey League, turned it pro

wear street shoes inside to make them fit. He practised more than he played, shooting and honing moves in the winter and juggling a tennis ball with his stick in the summer. In organized games he was often made to play goal, though the stagnant parts of the game that he spent watching the action at the other end of the ice finally drove him out of the net after he helped his team capture the city championship when he was 12. That summer he worked as a ditch digger, hard labor that helped develop the arm and shoulder strength that would serve him so well over his NHL years. His team won the city championship again the next year with the bulked-up Gordie on defense.

Howe grew and matured quickly, and when he was 15 he made a bid to play with the New York Rangers, attending the team's training camp in Winnipeg. He was homesick, however, and before the end of the camp he returned to Saskatchewan. He made a better impression with the Detroit

Red Wings the next year, joining a group of Red Wing veterans and untried youngsters to work out in front of Detroit boss Jack Adams. The ambidextrous Howe drew Adams' attention from the start with a sizzling rush down the left wing and a sharp shot. The next minute he escaped down the right wing, switched his stick to the other side and, still with a forehand, zipped another shot at the goal. "In hockey, switch-hitters are as rare as snowflakes in July," Adams said. "Gordie Howe was the best prospect I ever saw."

Howe made his professional debut when he was 18, taking up the right wing for Detroit at the beginning of the 1946–47 season. He was 6′ tall and just over 200 pounds,

Gordie Howe could stand at his own goal line and send a wrist shot over the glass at the other end of the rink. The puck was still rising when it landed at last in the stands.

making him one of the heavier players in the league. He scored in his first game but wasn't at all confident that he'd stay in the league for long. He kept a scrapbook of his first year, proof for future generations that he'd in fact played in the NHL. But Howe need not have worried about his hockey future. Though he only scored seven goals in his rookie season, he created a buzz among fans and opponents alike. He threw his weight around and he never backed away from a fight. Another tough star, Maurice "Rocket" Richard, challenged the rookie with a shove and a few angry words in Howe's first game in Montreal. Howe knocked Richard out cold with one punch.

Howe was put on a line with Sid Abel and Ted Lindsay and over the next three years the troika and the Detroit team became the league's best. Howe more than doubled his scoring in his third year and played in his first All-Star Game in 1948. True to his nature in his early years, he spent five minutes of the All-Star showcase in the penalty box for fighting. The Howe–Lindsay–Abel line was named "the Production Line" for its scoring proficiency in 1948–49, when Lindsay and Abel placed third and fourth in league scoring. Lindsay was the truculent and tough left winger who also had the skills to make and finish plays. Abel, the center, was a smooth skater and an accurate passer, and at seven years their senior the veteran of the line. Howe could do it all, and his scoring improved as he spent less time in the penalty box.

The three linemates finished the 1949–50 season 1–2–3 in the year-end scoring race, with Abel winning the Hart Trophy for his league-leading total and young Howe almost doubling his scoring total to place third. In the playoffs, in the first game of an acrimonious series against the Toronto

Gordie "Mr. Hockey" Howe

Maple Leafs, the club that had dispatched the Red Wings in the teams' previous 11 playoff games, Howe was involved in an on-ice accident that almost ended his career and his life. The Leafs' Ted "Teeder" Kennedy was moving with the puck toward the Detroit goal, skating down the left wing about six feet from the boards. He had just passed the center line when Howe attempted to body-check him. Kennedy stopped abruptly and Howe went crashing into the boards head first. He lay unconscious on the ice, blood covering his face, until emergency staff removed him on a stretcher. For the next few hours, many thought the worst. His mother was called in case his condition worsened and an operation was performed to relieve the pressure on his brain. Howe had fractured his skull and was out for the rest of the playoffs, but he did make a remarkable recovery. The Wings, stirred by Howe's injury, defeated the Leafs in overtime of the seventh game, ending Toronto's three-year reign as Stanley Cup champions. When Detroit won the Cup with a victory over the New York Rangers, again in overtime of the seventh game, Howe was cheered when he gingerly walked onto the Olympia ice to touch the trophy.

The seeds of Gordie Howe's long career were sown in his first five seasons in the league. He established himself as man who wouldn't back down—a man who would in fact repay any infraction with equal or greater measure. Not averse to using his stick or his sizeable fists as weapons, Howe also met challengers with those sharp elbows at the ready. "We had very poor equipment and I have very sloping shoulders," Howe said. "It was almost a necessity to get my elbow out." Opposing players, though many wouldn't admit it, began to give the right winger a little more room than they'd ordinarily allow. Over his many seasons, Howe was hit hard and often, but self-preservation was foremost in the minds of the defenders taking him on. Howe, with a few notable exceptions such as the Kennedy incident, escaped the kind of injuries that gradually wear down a marked man in the NHL.

Apart from his forbidding temperament, Howe's athletic and savvy playing style also contributed to his longevity. He never wasted energy if he didn't need to, especially after he cut down on the number of fights he'd take part in early in his career. He was economical with his movements, anticipating when and

Howe, Gordie "Mr. Hockey"
RW, 6´, 205 lbs, b: Floral, Sask., 3/31/1928

Season	Club, League	Regular Season					Playoffs				
		GP	G	A	Pts	PIM	GP	G	A	Pts	PIM
1946–47	Detroit Red Wings, NHL	58	7	15	22	52	5	0	0	0	18
1947–48	Detroit Red Wings, NHL	60	16	28	44	63	10	1	1	2	11
1948–49	Detroit Red Wings, NHL	40	12	25	37	57	11	8	3	11	19
1949–50	Detroit Red Wings, NHL	70	35	33	68	69	1	0	0	0	7
1950–51	Detroit Red Wings, NHL	70	43	43	86	74	6	4	3	7	4
1951–52	Detroit Red Wings, NHL	70	47	39	86	78	8	2	5	7	2
1952–53	Detroit Red Wings, NHL	70	49	46	95	57	6	2	5	7	2
1953–54	Detroit Red Wings, NHL	70	33	48	81	109	12	4	5	9	31
1954–55	Detroit Red Wings, NHL	64	29	33	62	68	11	9	11	20	24
1955–56	Detroit Red Wings, NHL	70	38	41	79	100	10	3	9	12	8
1956–57	Detroit Red Wings, NHL	70	44	45	89	72	5	2	5	7	6
1957–58	Detroit Red Wings, NHL	64	33	44	77	40	4	1	1	2	0
1958–59	Detroit Red Wings, NHL	70	32	46	78	57					
1959–60	Detroit Red Wings, NHL	70	28	45	73	46	6	1	5	6	4
1960–61	Detroit Red Wings, NHL	64	23	49	72	30	11	4	11	15	10
1961–62	Detroit Red Wings, NHL	70	33	44	77	54					
1962–63	Detroit Red Wings, NHL	70	38	48	86	100	11	7	9	16	22
1963–64	Detroit Red Wings, NHL	69	26	47	73	70	14	9	10	19	16
1964–65	Detroit Red Wings, NHL	70	29	47	76	104	7	4	2	6	20
1965–66	Detroit Red Wings, NHL	70	29	46	75	83	12	4	6	10	12
1966–67	Detroit Red Wings, NHL	69	25	40	65	53					
1967–68	Detroit Red Wings, NHL	74	39	43	82	53					
1968–69	Detroit Red Wings, NHL	76	44	59	103	58					
1969–70	Detroit Red Wings, NHL	76	31	40	71	58	4	2	0	2	2
1970–71	Detroit Red Wings, NHL	63	23	29	52	38					
1973–74	Houston Aeros, WHA	70	31	69	100	46	13	3	14	17	34
1974–75	Houston Aeros, WHA	75	34	65	99	84	13	8	12	20	20
1975–76	Houston Aeros, WHA	78	32	70	102	76	17	4	8	12	31
1976–77	Houston Aeros, WHA	62	24	44	68	57	11	5	3	8	11
1977–78	New England Whalers, WHA	76	34	62	96	85	14	5	5	10	15
1978–79	New England Whalers, WHA	58	19	24	43	51	10	3	1	4	4
1979–80	Hartford Whalers, NHL	80	15	26	41	42	3	1	1	2	2
1997–98	Detroit Wipers, IHL	1	0	0	0	0					
	NHL Totals	1767	801	1049	1850	1685	157	68	92	160	220
	WHA Totals	419	174	334	508	399	78	28	43	71	115

NHL First All-Star Team (1951, 1952, 1953, 1954, 1957, 1958, 1960, 1963, 1966, 1968, 1969, 1970)
WHA First All-Star Team (1974, 1975)
NHL Second All-Star Team (1949, 1950, 1956, 1959, 1961, 1962, 1964, 1965, 1967)
Won Hart Trophy (1952, 1953, 1957, 1958, 1960, 1963)
Won Art Ross Trophy (1951, 1952, 1953, 1954, 1957, 1963)
Won Gary Davidson Trophy — WHA MVP (1974)
Won Lester Patrick Trophy (1967)
Won Stanley Cup (1950, 1952, 1954, 1955)
Won Avco Cup (1974, 1975)

where the play would intersect with his effortless progress around the ice. He often played 45 minutes of a game when the average total was 25. Observers noticed that when his exhausted line returned to the bench, Howe was the first to recover and raise his head, ready for another shift.

In all, Howe was selected to 21 NHL All-Star squads, 12 times to the First Team. Six times he led the NHL in scoring to capture the Art Ross Trophy and six times he won the Hart as the league's most valuable player. His Detroit teams won the Stanley Cup four times. "There are four strong teams in this league and two weak ones," Dave Keon of the Maple Leafs said in 1963, following his Toronto team's victory over the Red Wings in the Cup final. "The weak ones are Boston and New York and the strong ones are Toronto, Chicago, Montreal and Gordie Howe."

Howe had been in his prime during a defensive era, the 1940s and 1950s, when scoring was difficult and checking was tight. When he was 40, in 1967, the league expanded from six to 12 teams and the number of offensive opportunities grew with it. Howe played the 1968–69 season on a line with Alex Delvecchio and Frank Mahovlich, the mercurial but talented star who had moved to Detroit from Toronto. Mahovlich was big, fast and skilled and Delvecchio was a gifted playmaker. The three were dubbed "the Production Line 2" and Howe's scoring returned to the levels of his youth and then beyond. He topped 100 points for the first time, scoring 44 goals and adding a career-high 59 assists.

Howe was among the top 10 scorers for the 21st consecutive year in 1969–70, but arthritis in his left wrist finally forced him to the sidelines following the 1970–71 season, his 25th in the league. For years, stories circulated about Howe leaving the game, but with each new campaign he proved the prognosticators wrong. This time it appeared to be the end. "Say retired, not quit," Howe said. "I don't like the word 'quit.'" He took a job in the Red Wings organization and was immediately inducted into the Hockey Hall of Fame, joining two other greats honored that year—Jean Beliveau and Bernie "Boom Boom" Geoffrion.

"There are four strong teams in this league and two weak ones," said Dave Keon in 1963. "The weak ones are Boston and New York and the strong ones are Toronto, Chicago, Montreal and Gordie Howe [center]."

But Howe's retirement was short-lived. In 1973 he was given a unique opportunity, one he couldn't refuse. Two of his sons, Mark and Marty, were promising young players in junior hockey. The Houston Aeros of the World Hockey Association offered Gordie a chance to play with his boys on the same team, even on the same line. Gordie had an operation to improve his wrist and came out from behind his desk to play again. He did his best to make hockey fly in Houston, going to unusual lengths to promote the game. During his first season, while driving up to the hotel parking lot, he witnessed a thief snatch a woman's purse, jump into a waiting car and speed away. Howe chased him for several blocks until the criminal pulled over and dumped the stolen booty out the window. When Howe returned the purse to its rightful owner, the woman's friend asked what they could do to repay him. "Well, I'm a player with the Houston Aeros," Howe said. "How about attending some of our games?" The couple promised to become regular fans. The Aeros did win consecutive championships in the Howes' first two seasons and Gordie was selected as the WHA's most valuable player in 1974 for his 100-point revival.

Gordie moved with Mark and Marty to the New England Whalers in 1977 when the Aeros struggled. When the WHA merged with the NHL in 1979, Howe, age 51, played one final season, competing in all 80 games of the schedule with the Hartford Whalers. The elder Howe was appointed to the roster for the 1980 NHL All-Star Game by coach Scotty Bowman. He and Phil Esposito and Jean Ratelle, stars of the game at the end of their careers, skated out onto the ice at Joe Louis Arena in Detroit alongside the youngest to ever play in the game, 19-year-old Wayne Gretzky. Gretzky had idolized Gordie and wore number 99 in homage to his boyhood hero. Having played in All-Star games spanning five decades, Howe was given a tremendous standing ovation by the Detroit fans. It lasted so long that he finally had to skate to the bench in an attempt to stop the cheering. When he collected an assist on an insurance goal in his side's 6–3 win, the ovation was once again long and heartfelt.

Gretzky would later break many of Howe's records, and the two all-time greats became close friends when Howe traveled with Gretzky as each Howe benchmark was matched and then eclipsed by the Great One. One record Gretzky—or probably anyone else—will never reach was further stretched when Howe played professional hockey in a sixth decade in 1997. He was signed to a one-game contract by the Detroit Vipers of the International Hockey League and, almost 70 years old, made a stirring return to the ice for one shift. The event had its share of controversy but ultimately failed to tarnish a career renowned for its longevity and distinction.

Alex "Fats" Delvecchio

Alex Delvecchio was a superior playmaker and team leader and one of the game's true gentlemen.

One of the most talented and classiest stars ever to play in the NHL, Alex Delvecchio spent more than two decades with the Detroit Red Wings. He was a superior playmaker and team leader and one of the game's true gentlemen. When he retired in 1973, he trailed only long-time teammate Gordie Howe in games played, assists and total points in a career that extended from Detroit's glory years of the early 1950s to their dismal 1970s.

As an amateur, Delvecchio starred in his home town of Fort William in northwestern Ontario before heading south to play for the Oshawa Generals under the tutelage of former Red Wings great Larry Aurie. In 1950–51, he led the OHA with 72 assists and had a one-game trial with Detroit. After starting the 1951–52 schedule with the Indianapolis Capitals of the AHL, he joined the Red Wings for good and began by playing on the third line with Metro Prystai and Johnny Wilson.

Delvecchio impressed as a rookie by helping Detroit win the Stanley Cup in 1952. The youngster's patience on the ice impressed many people, including Paul Chandler of the *Detroit News*: "He's a playmaker, a hockey 'planner' rather than the hot-skating, raw forward who provides the typical picture of a rookie." In 1952–53, he replaced Sid Abel on the Production Line between Gordie Howe and Ted Lindsay and was named to the NHL Second All-Star Team.

The powerhouse Wings won the Stanley Cup in 1954 and 1955. In the second of these two triumphs, Delvecchio starred with seven goals and eight assists. A serious ankle injury forced him to sit out 22 games in 1956–57, but over the balance of his career, he missed only 21 contests in becoming one of the most durable stars in hockey history. He was also a versatile forward, earning

All-Star selection at both center and left wing, and followed Dit Clapper and Sid Abel as only the third player in NHL history to be so honored at two positions.

In 1959 he won his first of three Lady Byng trophies. Throughout the 1960s, he was a consistent 20-goal scorer and solid playoff performer. A popular player in the dressing room, Delvecchio was given the affectionate nickname "Fats" as a tribute to his round face. More important, the esteem in which his peers held him led to his choice as team captain in 1962, a position he held until he retired. In 1966 he helped the Red Wings reach the finals with a playoff-leading 11 assists. Delvecchio was presented the Lady Byng Trophy again in 1966 and 1969.

Following the acquisition of Frank Mahovlich from Toronto on March 3, 1968, Delvecchio enjoyed a short period where he formed a lethal forward line with the Big M and Gordie Howe. In 1968–69, the trio scored 118 goals to break the NHL standard set by the Habs' Punch Line of Toe Blake, Elmer Lach and Maurice Richard in the 1940s. Their success didn't last long, however, as Mahovlich was traded to Montreal in January 1971.

In the latter stages of his career, Delvecchio shared a host of milestones with long-time colleague Gordie Howe. On October 30, 1970, Fats stole the puck from Bruins phenomenon Bobby Orr to score his 400th goal. Later in the same game, Howe registered his 1,000th assist on Delvecchio's second goal of the night. Delvecchio also set up Mr. Hockey's 700th goal, while another Howe goal marked Delvecchio's 1,000th NHL point.

By the early 1970s, the Red Wings were in decline and Delvecchio was among the oldest players in the league. He remained one of the clubs few bright spots courtesy of his fluid skating style and quickness while handling or shooting the puck. In June 1970, Delvecchio's renamed home town of Thunder Bay held a day in his honor that attracted 30,000 admirers.

Early in the 1973–74 season, Delvecchio retired after spending parts of 24 seasons in the NHL. His career totals of 456 goals and 1,281 points carved him a permanent place in hockey history. Later that year, his service to one of the oldest U.S.-based franchises was acknowledged when he was awarded the Lester Patrick Trophy. Following teammate Gordie Howe, Delvecchio was only the second player in league history to play more than 20 seasons with the same team. His old linemate tried to convince him to jump to Houston of the WHA, but Delvecchio decided to stay in the NHL.

Delvecchio, Alex "Fats"
C, 6′, 195 lbs, b: Fort William, Ont., 12/4/1932

Season	Club, League	Regular Season					Playoffs				
		GP	G	A	Pts	PIM	GP	G	A	Pts	PIM
1950–51	Detroit Red Wings, NHL	1	0	0	0	0					
1951–52	Detroit Red Wings, NHL	65	15	22	37	22	8	0	3	3	4
	Indianapolis Capitals, AHL	6	3	6	9	4					
1952–53	Detroit Red Wings, NHL	70	16	43	59	28	6	2	4	6	2
1953–54	Detroit Red Wings, NHL	69	11	18	29	34	12	2	7	9	7
1954–55	Detroit Red Wings, NHL	69	17	31	48	37	11	7	8	15	2
1955–56	Detroit Red Wings, NHL	70	25	26	51	24	10	7	3	10	2
1956–57	Detroit Red Wings, NHL	48	16	25	41	8	5	3	2	5	2
1957–58	Detroit Red Wings, NHL	70	21	38	59	22	4	0	1	1	0
1958–59	Detroit Red Wings, NHL	70	19	35	54	6					
1959–60	Detroit Red Wings, NHL	70	19	28	47	8	6	2	6	8	0
1960–61	Detroit Red Wings, NHL	70	27	35	62	26	11	4	5	9	0
1961–62	Detroit Red Wings, NHL	70	26	43	69	18					
1962–63	Detroit Red Wings, NHL	70	20	44	64	8	11	3	6	9	2
1963–64	Detroit Red Wings, NHL	70	23	30	53	11	14	3	8	11	0
1964–65	Detroit Red Wings, NHL	68	25	42	67	16	7	2	3	5	4
1965–66	Detroit Red Wings, NHL	70	31	38	69	16	12	0	11	11	4
1966–67	Detroit Red Wings, NHL	70	17	38	55	10					
1967–68	Detroit Red Wings, NHL	74	22	48	70	14					
1968–69	Detroit Red Wings, NHL	72	25	58	83	8					
1969–70	Detroit Red Wings, NHL	73	21	47	68	24	4	0	2	2	0
1970–71	Detroit Red Wings, NHL	77	21	34	55	6					
1971–72	Detroit Red Wings, NHL	75	20	45	65	22					
1972–73	Detroit Red Wings, NHL	77	18	53	71	13					
1973–74	Detroit Red Wings, NHL	11	1	4	5	2					
	NHL Totals	1549	456	825	1281	383	121	35	69	104	29

NHL Second All-Star Team (1953, 1959)
Won Lady Byng Trophy (1959, 1966, 1969)
Won Lester Patrick Trophy (1974)
Won Stanley Cup (1952, 1954, 1955)

Alex Delvecchio (center) followed Dit Clapper and Sid Abel as the third player in NHL history to earn All-Star selection at two positions, center and left wing.

On retiring, Delvecchio remained in the Red Wings fold as head coach, a posting that took in parts of four seasons from 1973 to 1977. When he replaced harsh disciplinarian Ted Garvin in November 1973, Fats used the same savvy that served him as a player to win over his team. They started winning and thinking about the opposition instead of dreading their coach. "There's a cool, controlled elegance of movement and manner that spells leadership and demands respect," writer Earl McRae suggested. "It's an elusive quality, a gift possessed by few." Delvecchio made his point with players he felt weren't contributing while still infusing the dressing room with a positive outlook.

Delvecchio handled the coaching duties for the entire 1974–75 campaign before stepping down in favor of Doug Barkley so he could focus on his duties as general manager. Barkley lasted only until November 1975, when Delvecchio stepped in on an interim basis before hiring Billy Dea on New Year's Eve. He moved back behind the bench on December 17, 1976, in yet another effort to improve the sad plight of the club.

Alas, several years of poor drafting and questionable personnel moves put the Wings in such a hole that not even Delvecchio's experience and charm could improve the fortunes of the franchise or mollify the fans. The sting from his firing in 1976–77 subsided when he was inducted into the Hockey Hall of Fame later that year.

The classy Delvecchio also proved to be a success in the business world. He founded his own company, which manufactured and engraved signs for plaques and nameplates all over the United States. On November 10, 1991, the Red Wings paid tribute to one of their icons by raising his number 10 to the rafters of Joe Louis Arena.

Glenn "Mr. Goalie" Hall

Gordie Howe was known as "Mr. Hockey," but that name didn't take into account the netminding duties so important to the game. For that there was Glenn Hall, nicknamed "Mr. Goalie" for his consistent and long-lasting success in the National Hockey League. Year after year, Hall was a familiar and intimidating sight in nets across the continent. He hardly missed a game or an award in his 18 NHL seasons and only four times did he finish a season with a losing record. His 84 career shutouts, third of all time, guaranteed his place in the Hockey Hall of Fame as one of the sport's best goaltenders.

Hall was born in Humboldt, Saskatchewan, in 1931. He could skate soon after he could walk and enjoyed playing as a forward as well as in goal. He evaluated his own talent when he was 10 years old and set his sights on playing in the NHL, specifically in one of the six goaltending jobs in the league at that time. He played his junior hockey with the Windsor Spitfires in the Ontario Hockey Association and was signed by the Detroit Red Wings in 1951. He played in their farm system for two seasons, in Edmonton with the Flyers and Indianapolis with the Capitols. In 1952–53, he made his first appearance in the NHL with Detroit, playing in six games and allowing only 1.67 goals against. He spent much of the next two years with Edmonton, making just two more appearances with the Wings in 1955.

In his time in the minors, Hall perfected his style of goaltending, a rather awkward but effective combination of flopping and standing his ground. Purists who liked their goalkeepers to remain upright hated the way Hall would throw himself to the ice to block the lower corners of the net. Hall had the ability to splay his pads along the ice with his knees practically together in what is referred to today as "the butterfly style." If the puck appeared to be heading for the upper reaches of the net, he'd dig his blades into the ice to pop back up to an almost standing position. He was a determined goalie who often sacrificed his body in his scrambles to keep the puck out.

Glenn Hall hardly missed a game or an award in his 18 NHL seasons.

Detroit had the great Terry Sawchuk in goal in the early 1950s and it seemed as though Hall would have to wait his turn to get a chance at full-time play in the league. Red Wings manager Jack Adams, however, had brought Sawchuk up as a youngster even though Harry Lumley, the Detroit keeper at the time, was still effective and in his prime. Adams decided to do the same with Hall and traded Sawchuk to the Boston Bruins in 1955. Hall took his place between the posts for the Wings at the beginning of the 1955–56 season and rewarded Adams for the confidence the manager had shown in him with an incredible rookie year, coming within one shutout of Lumley's modern record of 13 set two seasons previously. He allowed only 2.11 goals against as he played in each and every game and won the Calder Trophy as the NHL's top rookie. He played one more full season with Detroit, again not missing a game, before he too was shown the door by Adams. He was sent to the Chicago Black Hawks in the infamous Ted Lindsay trade motivated by Adams' anger at Lindsay's attempts to form a players' union.

Hall merely continued his streak of consecutive complete games during his time with the Hawks. Though he suffered many injuries, he played for 502 straight regular-season games and another 50 in the playoffs. The endurance record finally came to an end on November 8, 1963, when he injured his back. Ironically, he pulled a muscle not in a game but while getting dressed when he bent over to adjust a strap. Hall spent 10 seasons in Chicago and was placed on the All-Star Team eight times, five of those on the First Team. In 1961 he backstopped the Hawks to their first Stanley Cup championship since 1938.

Hall, Glenn "Mr. Goalie"
G, 5′11″, 180 lbs, b: Humboldt, Sask., 10/3/1931

| Season | Club, League | | Regular Season | | | | Playoffs | | |
		GP	Mins	GA	Avg	GP	Mins	GA	Avg
1951–52	Indianapolis Capitals, AHL	68	4190	272	3.89				
1952–53	Edmonton Flyers, WHL	63	3780	207	3.29	15	905	53	3.51
	Detroit Red Wings, NHL	6	360	10	1.67				
1953–54	Edmonton Flyers, WHL	70	4200	259	3.70	13	783	44	3.37
1954–55	Edmonton Flyers, WHL	66	3960	187	2.83	16	1000	43	2.58
	Detroit Red Wings, NHL	2	120	2	1.00				
1955–56	Detroit Red Wings, NHL	70	4200	148	2.11	10	604	28	2.78
1956–57	Detroit Red Wings, NHL	70	4200	157	2.24	5	300	15	3.00
1957–58	Chicago Black Hawks, NHL	70	4200	202	2.89				
1958–59	Chicago Black Hawks, NHL	70	4200	208	2.97	6	360	21	3.50
1959–60	Chicago Black Hawks, NHL	70	4200	180	2.57	4	249	14	3.37
1960–61	Chicago Black Hawks, NHL	70	4200	180	2.57	12	772	27	2.10
1961–62	Chicago Black Hawks, NHL	70	4200	186	2.66	12	720	31	2.58
1962–63	Chicago Black Hawks, NHL	66	3910	166	2.55	6	360	25	4.17
1963–64	Chicago Black Hawks, NHL	65	3860	148	2.30	7	408	22	3.24
1964–65	Chicago Black Hawks, NHL	41	2440	99	2.43	13	760	28	2.21
1965–66	Chicago Black Hawks, NHL	64	3747	164	2.63	6	347	22	3.80
1966–67	Chicago Black Hawks, NHL	32	1664	66	2.38	3	176	8	2.73
1967–68	St. Louis Blues, NHL	49	2858	118	2.48	18	1111	45	2.43
1968–69	St. Louis Blues, NHL	41	2354	85	2.17	3	131	5	2.29
1969–70	St. Louis Blues, NHL	18	1010	49	2.91	7	421	21	2.99
1970–71	St. Louis Blues, NHL	32	1761	71	2.42	3	180	9	3.00
	NHL Totals	906	53484	2239	2.51	115	6899	321	2.79

NHL First All-Star Team (1957, 1958, 1960, 1963, 1964, 1966, 1969)
NHL Second All-Star Team (1956, 1961, 1962, 1967)
Won Vezina Trophy (1963, 1967, 1969)
Won Conn Smythe Trophy (1968)
Won Calder Trophy (1956)
Won Stanley Cup (1961)

Hall shared the Vezina Trophy with Denis Dejordy in 1967. At the end of that season, at the age of 36, he was left unprotected in the Expansion Draft and was chosen by the St. Louis Blues. Due in large part to Hall's improbable heroics, the Blues marched all the way to the Stanley Cup final in their first year in the league. Though they would eventually lose to the Montreal Canadiens in four games, Hall was awarded the Conn Smythe Trophy as the league's top playoff performer. In 1968–69, Jacques Plante joined the team and the two veterans shared the goaltending duties. For the first time, Hall—who estimated at the end of his career that he'd had 300 stitches, many of them around his mouth—finally wore a mask during games. Plante and Hall, playing determined hockey to prove they still belonged in the league despite their combined age of over 77, split the Vezina Trophy in 1969.

Glenn Hall (left) suffered numerous injuries but still played 502 straight games in the regular season and another 50 in playoffs.

Hall was a unique character, a farmer who didn't seem to relish the idea of returning to the league following comfortable rural summers. He had a farm in Stony Plains, Alberta, and often missed training camps because he refused to report until the barn was dry following his annual fall painting. The idea of stopping all those speeding pucks, or worse, allowing an important goal, made him nervous and agitated. Throughout his career, Hall would get nauseous before each game. He was often sick to his stomach in the minutes leading up to taking the ice. One teammate even suggested his bucket should have been placed in the Hall of Fame. He retired several times, once with Chicago in 1966 and again with St. Louis in 1969. Each time, though, he was talked into returning, usually with a promise of more money, but he didn't profess to enjoy his livelihood, saying often that he'd meant to retire since he was 15.

"The truth is, I don't like to play hockey anymore," Hall said in 1968 while attending the All-Star Game in Toronto. "I don't like it, but it's a marvelous sport. I like the people, the talk, even the dinners. I love everything about hockey except the games."

Hall retired for good in 1971. He stayed in hockey, usually part-time while he tended to his farm, and worked with the Blues and the Calgary Flames as a consultant and goaltending coach. He was inducted into the Hall of Fame in 1975. Toe Blake, trying to put his finger on what makes a great goalie, dismissed speed and eyesight and flexibility. "With great ones, like Hall, it's something else," Blake said. "You get four goals off them, or five, but the goal you've got to have to win, somehow the great ones don't let you get it."

Pierre "Pete" *Pilote*

His teammates and friends called him "Pete," and although he was a small man, he was one of the most feared defensemen of Original Six hockey in the NHL. Pierre Pilote was born in Kenogami, Quebec, but his family moved to Fort Erie, Ontario, when he was young. He learned to skate as a child, but between the ages of 14 and 17 he never played at all because the local rink burned down and he had nowhere to go. As a result, Pilote didn't play his first game of organized hockey until he was 17, and even then he almost had to quit because of bad luck.

He had saved all his money to buy a new pair of skates, but once he got on the ice he found they were much too big for him. Once he acquired a proper-fitting pair, his skating improved dramatically and he was discovered by Rudy Pilous of Chicago, who invited him to try out for the Hawks' OHL team, the St. Catharines Teepees. Pilote wasn't all that talented, but he worked hard and developed skills with each game. By the midway point of his second year in St. Catharines, he was called up to the Buffalo Bisons to play minor pro for two games, and it was there that he began to assert himself physically.

He called it "the Barilko treatment" in honor of Bill Barilko, and he patented the hipcheck so that every forward coming down his side of the ice feared it. He also upset many a skater because of his physical play and had to develop fighting abilities to survive. "I had that animal instinct in me as a kid," he said, "and I still do. That's what drives me. Without it, I'd be dead." Indeed, his ability to survive was one of his greatest attributes, along with his tremendous determination. He played parts of five seasons with "the Herd," as the Bisons were sometimes called, but during 1955–56 he was called up to the Black Hawks to try the NHL game. On his first shift, Tod Sloan of the Leafs walked around him for a great scoring chance, but his play improved steadily and by the next fall he was part of the team full-time.

Pilote also became renowned as a tough guy who should be avoided, a reputation enhanced when he knocked both Henri and Maurice Richard out cold during the same mixup. "Henri was a rookie," he explained, "trying to prove he belonged in the NHL. One thing I have to do every year is teach rookies to respect me.... Maurice was playing big brother, trying to defend him." The result was a double kayo that affirmed his toughness in spades.

Pilote played the next 376 games in a row with Chicago, including five seasons without missing a game. His "iron man" streak finally ended when he dislocated a shoulder during the 1961–62 season. Pilote was a superb defenseman at both ends of the ice. In his own zone he blocked shots fearlessly, but he also wasn't afraid to join the rush and he was a first-rate passer. He teamed with Elmer "Moose" Vasko on the blue line, and together they formed the best duo in the league in the late 1950s and throughout the 1960s.

Pierre Pilote (number 3) learned to skate as a child, but between the ages of 14 and 17 he didn't play at all when the local rink burned down and he had nowhere to go.

Pilote, Pierre "Pete"
D, 5′10″, 178 lbs, b: Kenogami, Que., 12/11/1931

Season	Club, League	Regular Season					Playoffs				
		GP	G	A	Pts	PIM	GP	G	A	Pts	PIM
1951–52	Buffalo Bisons, AHL	2	0	1	1	4					
1952–53	Buffalo Bisons, AHL	61	2	14	16	85					
1953–54	Buffalo Bisons, AHL	67	2	28	30	108	3	0	0	0	6
1954–55	Buffalo Bisons, AHL	63	10	28	38	120	10	0	4	4	18
1955–56	Chicago Black Hawks, NHL	20	3	5	8	34					
	Buffalo Bisons, AHL	43	0	11	11	118	5	0	2	2	4
1956–57	Chicago Black Hawks, NHL	70	3	14	17	117					
1957–58	Chicago Black Hawks, NHL	70	6	24	30	91					
1958–59	Chicago Black Hawks, NHL	70	7	30	37	79	6	0	2	2	10
1959–60	Chicago Black Hawks, NHL	70	7	38	45	100	4	0	1	1	8
1960–61	Chicago Black Hawks, NHL	70	6	29	35	165	12	3	12	15	8
1961–62	Chicago Black Hawks, NHL	59	7	35	42	97	12	0	7	7	8
1962–63	Chicago Black Hawks, NHL	59	8	18	26	57	6	0	8	8	8
1963–64	Chicago Black Hawks, NHL	70	7	46	53	84	7	2	6	8	6
1964–65	Chicago Black Hawks, NHL	68	14	45	59	162	12	0	7	7	22
1965–66	Chicago Black Hawks, NHL	51	2	34	36	60	6	0	2	2	10
1966–67	Chicago Black Hawks, NHL	70	6	46	52	90	6	2	4	6	6
1967–68	Chicago Black Hawks, NHL	74	1	36	37	69	11	1	3	4	12
1968–69	Toronto Maple Leafs, NHL	69	3	18	21	46	4	0	1	1	4
	NHL Totals	890	80	418	498	1251	86	8	53	61	102

NHL First All-Star Team (1963, 1964, 1965, 1966, 1967)
NHL Second All-Star Team (1960, 1961, 1962)
Won James Norris Trophy (1963, 1964, 1965)
Won Stanley Cup (1961)

Pierre Pilote (center) became renowned as a tough guy who should be avoided, a reputation that was only enhanced when he knocked both Maurice and Henri Richard out cold during the same mixup.

Pilote was made captain in 1960 after the Hawks traded Ed Litzenberger to Detroit. His first year as team leader was his best, as the Hawks went on to win the Stanley Cup in the spring of 1961. On a team that also featured Bobby Hull, Stan Mikita and Glenn Hall, Pilote was the quiet superstar, but he was much valued around the league for his skills. "He's our best man in both directions," admitted coach Pilous. "And he's a good captain, for he understands the players' side of the game and knows their problems."

He was named to the First or Second All-Star Team every year from 1960 to 1967 and played in eight consecutive All-Star games during that time. He won the Norris Trophy for three successive years, 1963 to 1965, and finished as one of Chicago's leading scorers from the blue line. In 1968 the Hawks traded their aging hero to Toronto for Jim Pappin, but Pilote played just one season with the Leafs before retiring. When he left the game, he made no apologies, shed no tears and didn't look back for a second. "First you worry about making it," he explained, "and then you worry about getting out of it." He was inducted into the Hockey Hall of Fame in 1975.

Dickie "Digging Dickie" Moore

Dickie Moore was one of hockey's most productive and exciting forwards during the 1950s. The talented left winger scored at least 20 goals six times, played on six Stanley Cup championship teams and is remembered as part of a potent forward line with Maurice and Henri Richard. Moore was among the NHL's best shooters and puckhandlers and could also skate better than most—an aggressive player whose robust style of play earned him the nickname "Digging Dickie."

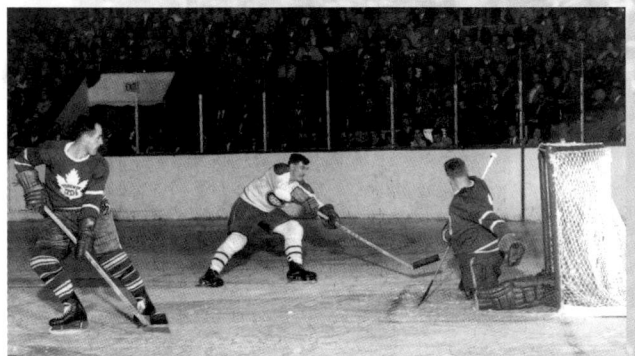

Dickie Moore (center) scored at least 20 goals six times and played on six Stanley Cup championship teams.

Born in the anglophone Park Extension area of north Montreal, Moore foreshadowed his hockey career by breaking his leg twice as a baby. He learned the game on the city's outdoor rinks playing with his older brother Jimmy, a minor pro player. He started on his own team at the age of 13, getting secondhand equipment from the Montreal Forum. An amateur star with the Montreal Junior Royals and Junior Canadiens, Moore won a Memorial Cup with the Royals in 1949 and the Junior Canadiens in 1950—the first two Quebec teams to capture the top prize in Canadian junior hockey. While with the Royals, his rambunctious play upset coach Tag Miller to the point that he approached Frank Selke about finding another place for him to play.

Through his amateur days, Moore worked for the Canadian Pacific Railway. This steady employment gave him some leverage when Selke tried to get his name on a contract in Montreal. Part of his first contract was a guarantee that, if he started the season in the minors, he'd be with the Canadiens by Christmas.

After a promising beginning with 33 points in as many games for the Habs in 1951–52, Moore struggled to keep a regular place on the roster until 1954–55, but once he solidified his position in Montreal, he became a major offensive contributor on the franchise's Stanley Cup dynasty from 1956 to 1960. In 1957–58, he led all NHL snipers with 36 goals. He also won the scoring title with 84 points despite playing the final three months of the season with a cast on his broken wrist. His resolve to carry on regardless of the hardships incurred was an integral part of his personality. As Red Fisher wrote: "Moore always has been a stubborn man. He was argumentative. He hatched an idea or spawned a view and he fought to preserve them. Maybe that's what made him a great hockey player. He played all-out and with heart in everything he did on and off the ice."

The pinnacle of Moore's career came in 1958–59 when he got the Art Ross Trophy for an astonishing 96-point performance. He also led all playoff scorers with 17 points in 11 games. The 96-point effort broke Gordie Howe's league record and ended up as the second-highest single-season total of the pre-expansion era. Moore was selected to the NHL First All-Star Team both years he won the scoring championship and was placed on the Second Team in 1961. Despite many injuries that caused him to miss a host of regular-season games, Moore was always ready to compete in the post-season. Stan Fischler summed up his important role in the Habs' success: "Moore is the architect of Richard's goals. He does the body- and backchecking for Geoffrion. He does the fighting for Beliveau. Somewhere in between, he finds the time to do plenty of scoring on his own."

By the end of the 1962–63 season, injuries had taken their toll on the skillful winger. He retired immediately after the season but was convinced by the Canadiens brass to attend training camp, after which he stuck to his original plan to step away from the game. Over the years, Moore had prepared for his life after hockey by launching a dairy bar and investing in a golf club and contractors' equipment business.

Moore did return for 38 games with Toronto in 1964–65 and 27 matches with St. Louis in 1967–68. The comeback in St. Louis was initiated by scout Cliff Fletcher, who happened to attend one of Moore's oldtimers' games. Moore rediscovered his scoring touch in the playoffs with 14 points in 18 games when the team reached the Stanley Cup finals, only to lose out to Montreal. A popular and gifted NHL star, Moore was inducted into the Hockey Hall of Fame in 1974. After retiring, he founded his own construction equipment sales and rental business in Montreal. Always close to his family, Moore and his wife were forced to deal with the tragic loss of their son Richard in a car accident in 1974.

Moore, Dickie "Digging Dickie"
LW, 5′10″, 168 lbs, b: Montreal, Que., 1/6/1931

Season	Club, League	Regular Season					Playoffs				
		GP	G	A	Pts	PIM	GP	G	A	Pts	PIM
1951–52	Montreal Canadiens, NHL	33	18	15	33	44	11	1	1	2	12
	Montreal Royals, QSHL	26	15	20	35	32					
1952–53	Montreal Canadiens, NHL	18	2	6	8	19	12	3	2	5	13
	Buffalo Bisons, AHL	6	2	3	5	10					
1953–54	Montreal Canadiens, NHL	13	1	4	5	12	11	5	8	13	8
	Montreal Royals, QHL	2	0	1	1	4					
1954–55	Montreal Canadiens, NHL	67	16	20	36	32	12	1	5	6	22
1955–56	Montreal Canadiens, NHL	70	11	39	50	55	10	3	6	9	12
1956–57	Montreal Canadiens, NHL	70	29	29	58	56	10	3	7	10	4
1957–58	Montreal Canadiens, NHL	70	36	48	84	65	10	4	7	11	4
1958–59	Montreal Canadiens, NHL	70	41	55	96	61	11	5	12	17	8
1959–60	Montreal Canadiens, NHL	62	22	42	64	54	8	6	4	10	4
1960–61	Montreal Canadiens, NHL	57	35	34	69	62	6	3	1	4	4
1961–62	Montreal Canadiens, NHL	57	19	22	41	54	6	4	2	6	8
1962–63	Montreal Canadiens, NHL	67	24	26	50	61	5	0	1	1	2
1964–65	Toronto Maple Leafs, NHL	38	2	4	6	68	5	1	1	2	6
1967–68	St. Louis Blues, NHL	27	5	3	8	9	18	7	7	14	15
	NHL Totals	719	261	347	608	652	135	46	64	110	122

NHL First All-Star Team (1958, 1959)
NHL Second All-Star Team (1961)
Won Art Ross Trophy (1958, 1959)
Won Stanley Cup (1953, 1956, 1957, 1958, 1959, 1960)

Andy **Bathgate**

Andy Bathgate was a hockey stylist—an athletic, graceful skater who handled the puck with skill and flash. Known for his blazing, accurate shot, he was one of the first men to use the slapshot to overpower goaltenders. Bathgate was a creative playmaker on the ice and often did the unexpected, throwing off opposing defenders with imaginative feints and passes. He accomplished all of this wearing heavy knee braces, the result of a serious injury during his first shift as a junior player in Guelph, Ontario. That injury required a steel plate to be inserted in his left knee to repair the damage. "Andy's got a plate in one knee and a prayer in the other," Rangers goaltender Gump Worsley once remarked. "It's a wonder he can skate at all."

Unfortunately, the New York team that Bathgate spent the best years of his career with had one of its worst runs, and his great play was often forgotten once the playoffs began, usually without his Rangers.

Born in Winnipeg in 1932, Bathgate spent the beginning and end of his career shuttling between the pro leagues and the minors. He played on the Memorial Cup-winning team in Guelph in 1952 and then first cracked the Rangers during the 1952–53 season. He finally made it as a regular in 1954–55 and had an immediate impact, scoring 20 goals and collecting 20 assists. For the next eight years, he led the Rangers in points and established himself as one of the most gifted offensive players in the league. He had arguably his best year in 1958–59, leading the NHL in scoring and performing well enough to win the Hart Trophy as the league's most valuable player even though the Rangers finished a point behind the fourth-place Toronto Maple Leafs and missed the playoffs. Bathgate was also voted to the league's First All-Star Team that year, beating out the great Gordie Howe for right wing honors.

Like Howe, Bathgate could play the physical game and was known as a fierce fighter when the occasion warranted it, perhaps an attribute from his youth in a tough Winnipeg neighborhood known for its boxers. Bathgate made the First All-Star Team again in 1961–62 and was voted to the Second Team the next year. Though truly an individualist on the ice and off, he always placed the team above his own accomplishments and was disappointed with the Rangers' consistently poor performances. In February 1964 he was traded to the Toronto Maple Leafs, a team preparing itself for

Andy Bathgate is closely associated with two innovations in hockey equipment—the goalie mask and the banana blade.

Bathgate, Andy
C, 5´8˝, 140 lbs, b: Winnipeg, Man., 8/28/1932

Season	Club, League	Regular Season					Playoffs				
		GP	G	A	Pts	PIM	GP	G	A	Pts	PIM
1952–53	New York Rangers, NHL	18	0	1	1	6					
	Vancouver Canucks, WHL	37	13	13	26	29	9	11	4	15	2
1953–54	New York Rangers, NHL	20	2	2	4	18					
	Vancouver Canucks, WHL	17	12	10	22	6					
	Cleveland Barons, AHL	36	13	19	32	44	9	3	5	8	8
1954–55	New York Rangers, NHL	70	20	20	40	37					
1955–56	New York Rangers, NHL	70	19	47	66	59	5	1	2	3	2
1956–57	New York Rangers, NHL	70	27	50	77	60	5	2	0	2	27
1957–58	New York Rangers, NHL	65	30	48	78	42	6	5	3	8	6
1958–59	New York Rangers, NHL	70	40	48	88	48					
1959–60	New York Rangers, NHL	70	26	48	74	28					
1960–61	New York Rangers, NHL	70	29	48	77	22					
1961–62	New York Rangers, NHL	70	28	56	84	44	6	1	2	3	4
1962–63	New York Rangers, NHL	70	35	46	81	54					
1963–64	New York Rangers, NHL	56	16	43	59	26					
	Toronto Maple Leafs, NHL	15	3	15	18	8	14	5	4	9	25
1964–65	Toronto Maple Leafs, NHL	55	16	29	45	34	6	1	0	1	6
1965–66	Detroit Red Wings, NHL	70	15	32	47	25	12	6	3	9	6
1966–67	Detroit Red Wings, NHL	60	8	23	31	24					
	Pittsburgh Hornets, AHL	6	4	6	10	7					
1967–68	Pittsburgh Penguins, NHL	74	20	39	59	55					
1968–69	Vancouver Canucks, WHL	71	37	36	73	44	8	3	5	8	5
1969–70	Vancouver Canucks, WHL	72	40	68	108	66	16	7	5	12	8
1970–71	Pittsburgh Penguins, NHL	76	15	29	44	34					
1974–75	Vancouver Blazers, WHA	11	1	6	7	2					
	NHL Totals	1069	349	624	973	624	54	21	14	35	76
	WHA Totals	11	1	6	7	2					

NHL First All-Star Team (1959, 1962)
NHL Second All-Star Team (1958, 1963)
Won Hart Trophy (1959)
Won Stanley Cup (1964)

a run at the Stanley Cup. Bathgate would realize his greatest thrill in hockey when the Leafs, helped by his timely goals in the playoffs, won the championship that year.

The next year, however, Bathgate publicly criticized coach Punch Imlach. "There is a limit to a player's endurance," he said, "and Imlach pushed a few of the players beyond that limit—physically and mentally. We played some of our best games in practice." Imlach, a strict disciplinarian, wouldn't tolerate such dissension and Bathgate, who missed a number of games in the 1964–65 season with his continuing knee problems, was sent to the Detroit Red Wings. He helped the Wings during their surprising run to the Stanley Cup finals in 1965–66. In 1967 he was picked by the Pittsburgh Penguins in the Expansion Draft. He spent a year with the Penguins and then two with the Western Hockey League's Vancouver team, earning the MVP award in that league in 1969–70. Bathgate was a rare veteran in that he didn't mind playing in the minors late in his career. He said he'd rather play a regular shift in a lesser league than sit on the bench in the NHL. He did return to the NHL for one last season, again with the Penguins, and then ended his career as a player-coach in division A in Switzerland. He made one last late comeback, playing 11 games with the World Hockey Association's Vancouver Blazers, a team he'd coached the previous season, in 1974–75.

Andy Bathgate (number 9) was a hockey stylist—a graceful but athletic skater who handled the puck with skill and flash.

Andy Bathgate is closely associated with two innovations related to hockey equipment, though his connection to the second is still a matter of some debate. The first originated on November 1, 1959. Bathgate sent a shot toward goalie Jacques Plante of the Montreal Canadiens. The puck struck the All-Star goalie in the face and opened a gash that required stitches. When Plante returned to the ice, he was wearing a mask, a piece of equipment now universally used. Bathgate also claims he was the first to use the curved stick, an invention widely credited to Stan Mikita. Bathgate said he began using a curved stick several years ahead of Mikita and Bobby Hull and Mikita snatched one of his sticks to model his own version. Mikita, in a good-natured way, denied Bathgate's assertion: "Maybe he's thinking about his nine-iron," Mikita said, referring to Bathgate's other passion of golf. Bathgate was a top amateur golfer and tried the professional tour several times. He owned a golf course following his hockey career.

A smooth player and class act, Andy Bathgate was elected to the Hall of Fame in 1978 along with Marcel Provonost, the player he was traded for when he went to Detroit from Toronto, and, ironically, Jacques Plante.

Bobby "the Golden Jet" Hull

Few of the game's superstars could match the physical talents of Bobby Hull. The Golden Jet combined speed, a feared slapshot and a powerful physique to rise to the elite of the NHL in the 1960s. Depending on the source, his shot was timed at approximately 120 miles per hour. His powerful legs never stopped moving and his muscular upper body enabled him to handle the rough side of the game. Hull was a legend in Chicago and later enjoyed success in the World Hockey Association and on the international stage while representing Canada.

Hull grew up on a farm near Belleville, Ontario, two hours east of Toronto. From a young age it was apparent that his raw talent was exceptional. He moved rapidly through the minor hockey system and was signed by the Chicago Black Hawks organization. As a 15-year-old, he played a handful of games with the Galt Black Hawks of the OHA and didn't look out of place.

The Hawks next moved Hull up to the main junior affiliate, the OHA's St. Catharines Teepees. During his second year, in 1956–57, Hull scored 16 points in 13 playoff matches for the Garden City team. A few months later, he put two pucks past New York Rangers goalie Gump Worsley

in a pre-season game to launch one of the greatest of NHL careers. Former Chicago defenseman Pierre Pilote remembered: "The first time I saw him was in training camp in St. Catharines. He practised with us and then he played a game against New York, I think it was, and he got two goals. Tommy Ivan said, 'Why, you're comin' home with us. You're not gonna play junior hockey anymore.'"

Hull's highly anticipated regular-season debut came in 1957–58. He didn't disappoint the Hawks' fans and brass and turned in a fine 47-point effort that year to finish runner-up to Toronto's Frank Mahovlich in the Calder Trophy voting at the end of the season. Hull improved by three points in his sophomore year before breaking out in 1959–60 with a league-high 39 goals and 81 points. Teamed with Bill Hay and Murray Balfour on the Million Dollar Line, Hull won the Art Ross Trophy and earned a place on the NHL First All-Star Team.

Bobby Hull combined speed, a feared slapshot and a powerful physique to rise to the elite of the NHL in the 1960s and the WHA in the 1970s.

More important, the young star helped resurrect the fortunes of a struggling franchise. Prior to his arrival, Chicago had missed the playoffs 11 out of the previous 12 seasons. The atmosphere around the organization was dismal and the once proud fans stayed away in droves. Hull's arrival along with Stan Mikita helped rekindle the spark within the franchise and raised the team's profile among the sports fans of the Windy City.

According to historian Paul Greenland, the gifted left winger's shots "were known to send goalies backwards into the net, numb their legs through their pads and tear their gloves from their hands." Former Chicago goalie Glenn Hall looked back on what it was like facing this weapon in practice: "Well, I didn't really enjoy it much. The one thing Bobby enjoyed was shooting the puck. He didn't care who he was shooting at or where he was shooting, he just enjoyed shooting it." Together with teammate Mikita, Hull developed the curved hockey stick, which gave the shooter more velocity and caused the puck to move differently at times. And what goalies throughout the league didn't need was the most feared shot in the NHL behaving like a curve ball.

The 1960–61 regular season was somewhat of a letdown for Hull individually, but in the post-season he scored 14 points in 12 games as Chicago won the Stanley Cup for the first time since 1938. The next year he became the third player in league history to score 50 goals in a season.

Hull's ability to play while in pain and his refusal to abide the advice of doctors was becoming legendary. During the 1963 playoffs, Gary Ronberg wrote: "Hull played with a nose so smashed that the fracture extended into the skull. With the Hawks one game from elimination, Hull ignored the orders of his doctors, checked out of a Chicago hospital and flew by himself to Detroit. That night, with both his eyes blackened, his nose enclosed in tape, and blood draining into his throat, he played against the Red Wings." The Hawks won the game but not the series.

In 1964–65, despite missing nine games due to injury, the Golden Jet scored 39 goals and helped Chicago reach the Stanley Cup finals, where they lost out to Montreal. At season's end he was awarded the Hart and Lady Byng trophies. The following season he set an NHL record with 54 goals and repeated as the Hart Trophy winner. Former Habs great Jacques Plante once said: "His shot is like a piece of lead. You have to see it coming toward you to believe it."

In 1966–67, Hull's 52 goals helped Chicago win its first regular-season championship since coach Pete Muldoon cursed the team after he was fired in 1938. Their march to the Stanley Cup was cut short in the semifinals by the Toronto Maple Leafs under Punch Imlach.

Hull scored 44 goals during the first expansion season, then followed up with a record-breaking performance in 1968–69. His 58 goals set a single-season record that fans thought would last many years. As it turned out, Boston's Phil Esposito hit the back of the net 76 times two years later. In January 1970, Hull was named by the Associated Press as the top NHL player of the 1960s.

As the decade closed, Hull was forced to adjust to the more disciplined style of play preached by new coach Billy Reay. Initially things didn't go well, as Hull admitted: "I can't get the feel of the game if all I'm going to do is check my man. What's the difference if we win 7–6 or 2–1?"

While Esposito was leading the Bruins through a magical regular season in 1970–71, the Hawks were led by Hull's 44 goals and captured the West Division crown. On February 14, 1971, he scored twice against the Vancouver Canucks to surpass Maurice Richard for second place on the NHL's all-time goal-scoring list. Hull then embarked on the most productive post-season of his career with 11 goals and 25 points in 18 games as Chicago came within one period of winning the Stanley Cup. Leading 2–1 late in the second period of game seven, the Hawks couldn't hold the lead and lost 3–2 in front of a disappointed home crowd. One of the indelible images of this final game was the Habs' lanky netminder, Ken Dryden, using his long reach to foil a sure goal by Hull.

The great Jacques Plante once said of Bobby Hull (center): "His shot is like a piece of lead. You have to see it coming toward you to believe it."

In 1971–72, Hull hit the 50-goal mark for the fifth time in his career, playing with Pit Martin and Chico Maki. When asked about his chances of catching Gordie Howe in the all-time scoring race, Hull responded: "If I play long enough, maybe. It depends on how I feel and whether I get hurt or not. That's an awful lot of goals he has. No matter what, he will always be the king to me." At this stage of his career, many observers noted that he was playing his most well-rounded hockey ever. Boston Bruins general manager Milt Schmidt commented: "Hull is a changed player from the old one-man show which was the Bobby Hull of the early '60s. He backchecks even when the Hawks aren't a man short and he paces himself a bit more." Ironically, this complete version of Bobby Hull was the last NHL fans would see of him for several years.

In February 1972, an ominous event in the form of the World Hockey Association General Player Draft took place. The Winnipeg Jets selected Hull and a few months later shocked the hockey world by signing him to the first $1-million contract in hockey history. Hull summed up the situation with Chicago: "I made their side of it easier when I said publicly at the start of all this that I wanted to stay in Chicago and I didn't expect them to come close to matching the Winnipeg offer. They didn't need me as much as the new league did and I knew that. But they never took any serious steps to offer me a contract, not even to sit down and talk and start negotiating. I guess there was pride involved on both sides. They felt I should come to them and I felt they should come to me."

This turn of events was the major coup needed by the WHA to legitimize itself. The NHL was bitter and exacted revenge on the Golden Jet by blocking his participation on behalf of Canada in the 1972 Summit Series versus the Soviets. When Hull left the NHL, his 604 goals ranked him second in league history to Gordie Howe. Toronto forward Ron Ellis noted: "Now I'll have a chance to do something when we play the Black Hawks. Up to now I've spent all my time watching Hull."

Overall, Hull's play in the Manitoba capital helped the Jets become a major success in the new league, but the adjustment took its toll, as he developed ulcers in response to the stress of playing several games on consecutive nights under conditions that were quite poor compared to the NHL. Hull elaborated: "In New Jersey, it was hilarious. We'd put on our equipment in the Holiday Inn, then bus over to the arena in our street shoes and go into a little dressing room in shifts to put our skates on. The room was so tiny we couldn't all go in at once. And the rink was tilted! By the end of the period, with the snow built up on the ice, you really had to be able to shoot the puck just to ice it."

Hull soon formed one of the top forward lines anywhere in the world with Swedes Anders Hedberg and Ulf Nilsson. Hull later reflected: "Without those kids, I probably would have retired three years ago. I've said it many times before, but I'm feeling younger with them around." The Golden Jet was particularly impressed with his center, Nilsson: "I've played with Billy Hay and Phil Esposito and they were great centers, but Ulf has complemented me as much and more than any centerman I've ever played with. He's unselfish and gets the daylights knocked out of him while he's doing it. And he comes back for more."

The 1974–75 season was particularly special, as he finally had a chance to compete against the Soviets in the second Canada–USSR series at the start of the year. He also went on to score 77 goals for Winnipeg in the regular season to establish a new record for a professional league.

Hull, Bobby "the Golden Jet"
LW, 5´10˝, 195 lbs, b: Point Anne, Ont., 1/3/1939

Season	Club, League	Regular Season					Playoffs				
		GP	G	A	Pts	PIM	GP	G	A	Pts	PIM
1957–58	Chicago Black Hawks, NHL	70	13	34	47	62					
1958–59	Chicago Black Hawks, NHL	70	18	32	50	50	6	1	1	2	2
1959–60	Chicago Black Hawks, NHL	70	39	42	81	68	3	1	0	1	2
1960–61	Chicago Black Hawks, NHL	67	31	25	56	43	12	4	10	14	4
1961–62	Chicago Black Hawks, NHL	70	50	34	84	35	12	8	6	14	12
1962–63	Chicago Black Hawks, NHL	65	31	31	62	27	5	8	2	10	4
1963–64	Chicago Black Hawks, NHL	70	43	44	87	50	7	2	5	7	2
1964–65	Chicago Black Hawks, NHL	61	39	32	71	32	14	10	7	17	27
1965–66	Chicago Black Hawks, NHL	65	54	43	97	70	6	2	2	4	10
1966–67	Chicago Black Hawks, NHL	66	52	28	80	52	6	4	2	6	0
1967–68	Chicago Black Hawks, NHL	71	44	31	75	39	11	4	6	10	15
1968–69	Chicago Black Hawks, NHL	74	58	49	107	48					
1969–70	Chicago Black Hawks, NHL	61	38	29	67	8	8	3	8	11	2
1970–71	Chicago Black Hawks, NHL	78	44	52	96	32	18	11	14	25	16
1971–72	Chicago Black Hawks, NHL	78	50	43	93	24	8	4	4	8	6
1972–73	Winnipeg Jets, WHA	63	51	52	103	37	14	9	16	25	16
1973–74	Winnipeg Jets, WHA	75	53	42	95	38	4	1	1	2	4
1974–75	Winnipeg Jets, WHA	78	77	65	142	41					
1975–76	Winnipeg Jets, WHA	80	53	70	123	30	13	12	8	20	4
CCup-76	Canada	7	5	3	8	2					
1976–77	Winnipeg Jets, WHA	34	21	32	53	14	20	13	19	22	2
1977–78	Winnipeg Jets, WHA	77	46	71	117	23	9	8	3	11	12
1978–79	Winnipeg Jets, WHA	4	2	3	5	0					
1979–80	Winnipeg Jets, WHA	18	4	6	10	0					
	Hartford Whalers, NHL	9	2	5	7	0	3	0	0	0	0
	NHL Totals	1063	610	560	1170	640	119	62	67	129	102
	WHA Totals	411	303	335	638	183	60	43	37	80	38
	CCup Totals	7	5	3	8	2					

NHL First All-Star Team (1960, 1962, 1964, 1965, 1966, 1967, 1968, 1969, 1970, 1972)
WHA First All-Star Team (1973, 1974, 1975)
NHL Second All-Star Team (1963, 1971)
WHA Second All-Star Team (1976, 1978)
Won Hart Trophy (1965, 1966)
Won Gary Davidson Trophy — WHA MVP (1973, 1975)
Won Art Ross Trophy (1960, 1962, 1966)
Won Lady Byng Trophy (1965)
Won Lester Patrick Trophy (1969)
Won Stanley Cup (1961)
Won Avco Cup (1976, 1978, 1979)
Won CCup (1976)

*Bobby "the Golden Jet"
Hull*

Frank Selke Sr.

Frank Selke Sr. became manager of the Iroquois Bantams in Berlin (now Kitchener), Ontario, at the tender age of 14.

Frank Selke Sr. began his life as a hockey executive while still in his teens. At just 14, he became manager of the Iroquois Bantams in Berlin (now Kitchener), Ontario, and later he met Conn Smythe during a tournament in which both men had teams competing. In 1919 Selke coached the University of Toronto Schools to a Memorial Cup championship in its first year of competition and shortly after began the Toronto Ravinas hockey team, a semipro outfit that soon provided players to the NHL. When Smythe purchased the Toronto St. Pats franchise and changed the team's name to Maple Leafs, he recruited Selke to be his assistant general manager. So began a 20-year relationship as strong as any in sports.

Selke wasn't only Smythe's right-hand man, he brought enormous energy, determination and success to the team. As coach of the Maple Leafs' junior club, the Toronto Marlboros, he won another Memorial Cup in 1929 and helped Smythe raise the necessary finances to build Maple Leaf Gardens and move the team from the dingy Arena Gardens (also known as Mutual Street Arena). He was also extremely valuable as an advisor to Smythe, someone whose sense of player evaluation was consistently astute and who could find talent where others might have dismissed a player's promise.

With this superb front office tandem, the Leafs won the Stanley Cup in 1931–32, the team's first year in the impressive new building. Although they didn't win a second Cup for a decade, they were the elite of the league and appeared in seven finals series from 1932 to 1940. In the spring of 1942, the Leafs became the first and still only team to rally from 3–0 down in the finals to win the Cup. Early in the 1942–43 season, fresh on the heels of that historic win, Smythe left the team and country to fight for Canada in France. He left the handling of all the Maple Leafs' operations in Selke's hands, knowing he could trust his friend, associate and hockey equal.

The Smythe–Selke relationship was scarred at this time however, when Selke traded an unknown player in the Toronto system—Frank Eddolls—to Montreal for Ted Kennedy, a 17-year-old prospect Selke had preferred over Smythe's liking for Eddolls. Smythe was furious that, even though he was overseas, he wasn't consulted about the deal, which Selke knew he'd have nixed had he had the chance. Smythe never forgave him, and matters were made worse when Kennedy turned out to be one of the finest players ever to skate for the Leafs and Eddolls's career never took flight—thus, in essence, proving Selke right and Smythe wrong in this one instance. Further problems occurred because Selke opened up the Gardens to other entertainment and rental opportunities that weren't hockey related, which Smythe also objected to. These events, however, generated large sums of money, and when Smythe returned to Toronto in 1945, he was greeted by a team board of directors that wanted Selke to remain the boss, something Smythe obviously couldn't endure.

Smythe fought tooth and nail to regain control of the team and building, but his victory cost him a friend and partner. In the summer of 1946, Selke resigned from the Leafs and became general manager of the nemesis Montreal Canadiens. Under Selke, the Habs became the league's dominant team within a few years, but only, ironically, after the Leafs enjoyed their period of greatest success. Smythe's team won the Cup four times in five years (1947 to 1949 and 1951) but the 1950s belonged to Montreal, which won in 1953 and then put together a record streak of five consecutive Cup wins (1956 to 1960).

Selke was inducted into the Hockey Hall of Fame in 1960 for his lifelong dedication and contribution to the game, which included his efforts to help build the Hall in Toronto. Four years later he retired, just as the Leafs were entering another golden age and the Habs were on the verge of one more of their own. The league later introduced a trophy bearing his name, awarded annually to the best defensive forward in the game. Selke died on July 3, 1985.

Selke's son, Frank Jr., followed in his footsteps, starting a career with the Leafs as editor of the team's program and moving his way up the executive ladder. In 1967 Frank Jr. joined the Oakland Seals as the team's president, just before their entry into the NHL. The second Selke proved to be an excellent judge of the way teams come together. The following season the Seals improved drastically, capturing second place in the NHL West Division. Many fans of the team credited Selke Jr. with the improvement, due in large part to some canny trades he'd managed to orchestrate, including acquiring the dynamic young duo of Carol Vadnais and Norm Ferguson. In 1970 the Seals made the playoffs again, finishing fourth in their division.

Under Frank Selke Sr. (right), the Habs became the league's dominant team and put together a record streak of five consecutive Cup wins between 1956 and 1960.

But despite the successes the team was enjoying on the ice, the Seals were undergoing some serious problems in their front office, which led ultimately to the franchise being sold five times in only three years. The ownership flip-flops were hurting the team's ability to sign good players and Selke was upset that he couldn't do more on the open market, saddled as he and Glover were with a limited checkbook and unstable backing.

Finally, in 1970, Selke couldn't take the difficulties any more and resigned just after Charles O. Finley bought the club in the summer of that year. After leaving the Seals, he became executive vice-president of the Canadian Sports Network and worked for Ohlmeyer Communications and Molstar Communications, all in Toronto, from 1971 to 1989. Starting in 1984, he was also president of a company called Redskin Holdings, a consulting and promotional company that worked with broadcasters, particularly in hockey. From 1989 to 1990, he was president of the P. Lawson Travel company's branch at the SkyDome in Toronto.

The junior Selke was very active in charitable causes, acting as president and director of the Ontario Special Olympics. He was also a member of the Hockey Hall of Fame selection committee.

1947–1962

Postwar Passions Run High

With World War II raging from 1939 to 1945, a period of eight years separated the 13th World Championship in 1939 and the 14th in 1947. Even so, occupied Czechoslovakia was the site of two "international" games in that time.

In 1940, Germany announced that the German Imperial Hockey Union and a team from the Protectorate of Bohemia and Moravia would play two hockey games at Prague's Winter Stadium, which was then in the territory of the Third Reich. The German players were to give the Czechs a lesson in the superiority of the Aryan spirit on the ice for propaganda purposes, and the games would be covered live on the radio since the Germans had absolutely no doubts about how they'd turn out. The few hundred Prague citizens who were allowed into the stands—as well as tens of thousands of people listening to the radio at home all over Czechoslovakia—expected a different result. For players in an occupied country, these two games came to mean more than a struggle to win the World Championship and the Czechs won them both. The Imperial Germans left the ice after losses of 5–1 and 3–0, disappointing the bulk of those who had seats at the games, who were mostly officers and soldiers of the German Wehrmacht.

The first USSR championship, Dynamo–CSKA, 1946.

After the end of war, international sports ties were slowly revived and hockey players were among the first to hold a World Championship. And again Prague was the host, under very different circumstances, in February 1947. Canada didn't attend, and in their absence Czechoslovakia and Sweden were considered the favorites. When Tre Kronor managed to edge Czechoslovkia out on the second-last day of the tournament by a score of 2–1, King Gustav V sent a telegram congratulating his subjects. From the King's point of view, the Swedes simply couldn't lose the last game.

The game between Sweden and Austria happened to coincide with an afternoon production of The Barber of Seville *at Prague's National Theater. In the opera's last act, Bartholo suddenly turned to his audience, and instead of addressing the libretto's words to his servant, he sang, "Hurry to Don Bazilio and tell him that the Austrians beat the Swedes 2–1!" And the crowd went wild. That evening, all of Prague and Czechoslovakia celebrated their players (who were mostly from the LTC Prague club). After thrashing a weak American team 6–1, they had edged out the Swedes and become world champions for the first time.*

USSR–Czechoslovakia, 1948.

A year later, the Czechs came close to becoming Olympic champions at St. Moritz, too, but Canada took home the medals on the basis of goals differential (69–5 versus 80–18) after a scoreless final game between Canada and Czechoslovakia.

Team Czechoslovakia remained at the pinnacle of hockey for one more season. Even after the air disaster that killed five of their players over the English Channel on November 8, 1948, they were still favored for the 1949 World Championship in Stockholm—where they lost to the Americans 2–0 but for the first time beat the Canadians with a score of 3–2 to repeat as world champions. Goalkeeper Bohumil Modry was superlative, as he had been in 1947, while Vladimir Zabrodsky set the pace for the forwards and Josef Trousilek led the defense. All three were repeating the championship title, as was forward Gustav Bubnik, who went on to win greater fame as a coach. An exciting future appeared to be in store for the Czech team.

Then the communists took over in 1948, and a state that had been one of the most democratic in prewar Central Europe endured the swift and ruthless establishment of a new order. Emigration was forbidden, which is why a few leading Czech players— Oldrich Zabrodsky (Vladimir's brother), Jaroslav Drobny and Josef Malecek—defected when they got a chance, such as during a Spengler Cup tournament in Davos, Switzerland, at the end of 1948. In 1950, a number of players from the national team and the LTC club were arrested on suspicion of trying to emigrate, among them the idol of Czech hockey fans, goalkeeper Bohumil Modry. The unfairly accused were released years later, but for many—including Modry—their careers were effectively over by then.

USSR–Czechoslovakia. 1948.

As a result of all these events, a very different Team Czechoslovakia entered the 1950s and would fail to place among the top three at World Championships until 1955 (they didn't even attend in 1950 and 1951, and in 1953 they were recalled after the death of president Klement Gottwald). It wasn't until the 1961 World Championship in Switzerland that the Czech team came to the fore once again when they beat the Soviets 6–4 and tied Canada 1–1, though Canada took gold again on the goals differential and the Czechs settled for silver.

In early postwar Europe, Czechoslovakia's main competition came from Sweden while other prewar favorites from Austria, Germany and Great Britain plunged in the standings, mostly because of failing economies. Sweden and Switzerland had maintained neutrality and were practically the only countries in Europe that hadn't been devastated by the war, with the result that the Swedes were active in international competition and could also afford to host the World Championships.

Even so, the Swedes only placed fourth in 1949 and third in 1954, allowing not only Canada but even the USSR national team—which was making its debut in the latter competition—to outplay them. From 1947 to 1962, the Swedes captured the gold medals three times on the road, however, even if one was a less than spectacular triumph. The teams from Canada and the U.S. didn't participate in the 1953 World Championship, and the Czech players were recalled after two games, so there were only three teams (Sweden, West Germany and Switzerland) in the finals. But there was a full slate of European teams in the 1957 World Championship in Moscow when the Swedes took the gold. And Tre Kronor took the title at Colorado Springs five years later in a championship that was just the reverse of the 1957 tournament—Canada and the United States were there, but the USSR and Czechoslovakia were absent.

Swedish defensemen like Lars Bjorn and Roland Stoltz were tall, sturdy and effective at shooting, but they weren't quick or mobile enough against the best skaters. Indeed most of the Team Sweden players were rated highly for their technique—but only when the game was played at a moderate pace. Sven Johansson, Nils Nilsson, Ronald Pettersson and Ulf Sterner were all very good players. Sven Johansson wasn't yet 20 when he made his debut with Tre Kronor in an exhibition game against Team USA in preparation for the 1951 World Championship, but he scored five goals. At the Olympic Games in Oslo a year later, Johansson became the top scorer on the Swedish team, helping them win the Olympic bronze medals and a nickname for himself ("Tumba"). Years later, Johansson, who was

Medal ceremony at 1948 Olympics, St. Moritz, Switzerland.

then at the end of his playing career, and Sterner, who was just starting his, helped Tre Kronor beat the team from Canada (the Galt Terriers) by a score of 5–3 to take gold at the 1962 World Championship in Colorado Springs.

NHL managers had been watching the Swedish players and their finely honed technique as far back as the era of the Original Six, even though practically no European player could have made it into an NHL lineup in those days. The New York Rangers invited Sven Johansson to come for a tryout at the end of the 1950s and Ulf Sterner tried playing in the NHL a bit later. Both met with a lack of success. In four games with the Rangers, Sterner couldn't cope with the tough style of play and returned to Sweden.

As previously noted, Team USSR made its debut at the 21st World Championship that took place in Stockholm from February 26 to March 7, 1954. The newcomers kicked off with a 7–1 win against the Finns and followed up with a 7–0 rout over Norway, a 6–2 win over West Germany, a 5–2 victory over Czechoslovakia and a 4–2 win over Switzerland. In the second round, the Soviets finally lost a point in the game against Tre Kronor.

A HISTORY OF WORLD HOCKEY

The game was played on an outdoor rink in Stockholm's Royal Stadium in such a heavy snowstorm that just a few minutes after the face-off the ice was invisible. The Swedes managed to score the first goal in the last of four 15-minute periods, but shortly before the final siren, Viktor Shuvalov put in the equalizer. In fact, the puck slid into the Tre Kronor net under the snow. The Swedish goalie didn't see it, but the referees did, and the game ended 1–1, a result that created enough excitement that tickets for a game between the USSR and Sweden were being sold from the morning of the day the final game between the USSR and Canada would be played. In the event of a Canadian victory over the Soviets, this additional game between Sweden and the USSR would be necessary to determine the European champion—and that Canada would win was something that no one except the players of Team USSR even thought to have doubts about.

In those days, the majority of Europe's national teams played against the Canadians by huddling in front of their own net in hopes of getting out with an honorable defeat. Team Canada had become accustomed to the style of play and went overboard on offense without giving much thought to defense. The Soviet coaches and players had pondered all this and the forward lines of Babich–Shuvalov–Bobrov and Bychkov–Guryshev–Khlystov were ready.

The final game of the 1957 World Championship between the USSR and Sweden generated such tremendous interest that it was transferred to an outdoor rink in Luzhniki, where some 50,000 spectators crammed into the stands.

Just five minutes into the game, Alexei Guryshev picked up a long, quick pass from his defenseman and zeroed in on goalie Don Lockhart to open the scoring. Viktor Shuvalov got the second goal in the 11th minute, and not long after, Vsevolod Bobrov outsmarted the Canadian defense, fooled the goalie and lobbed the puck into an empty net. And it went on from there. The 16,000 spectators at the Royal Stadium witnessed the World Championship rookies trounce the pioneers of the game 7–2.

Canada sent the Penticton Vees, spearheaded by the Warwick brothers—Bill, Grant and Dick—to the 1955 World Championship in West Germany. After the East York Lyndhursts' bitter experience the year before, the Canadians played a very technical game against Team USSR and won 5–0 to re-establish their reputation. But the Soviets became the top team in Europe.

The 1956 Winter Olympics were held at Cortina d'Ampezzo in the Italian Alps and, as usual in those days, three titles were up for grabs in the hockey tournament: Olympic, World and European. Before the last round, Team USA came up with a surprise 4–1 win over Team Canada (represented by the Kitchener-Waterloo Dutchmen) in a game where Canada's edge was blunted by American goalie Willard Ikola, who proved to be all but impenetrable. As a result, Canada needed a high-scoring victory in the last game of the tournament, while the Soviet team—which had defeated the Americans 4–0—could make do with a tie.

The pitch was understandably feverish in the deciding game. The Canadians stormed the Soviet net in wave after wave from the outset, but every attack was repelled by goalie Nikolai Puchkov and the hockey world was shocked by another Canadian loss.

After that competition, the prize for the best goalkeeper was awarded to Willard Ikola, who asked to be photographed receiving it with Nikolai Puchkov. Later he presented the photo to the

Soviet goalie with the inscription, "You deserve it no less than I do." Ikola's sentiment was confirmed when Puchkov was named the best goalie at the 1959 World Championship. Incredibly enough, Puchkov hadn't even known how to skate just 10 years before the 1956 Olympics. A self-taught goalie, he devised any number of tactics and practised them for hours on end. In the 1956 Olympic finals, the Soviet goalkeeper had only one goal scored against him per game—and not even one in the deciding game against the Kitchener-Waterloo Dutchmen—while the Soviets scored two against Dennis Brodeur.

The Soviets went into the 1957 World Championship in Moscow the favorites, but both the Swedish and the Czech teams proved to be top contenders. The Soviets ended up one point shy in the final game against Sweden as a result of a 2–2 tie with Czechoslovakia while the Swedes had swept all six of their games. Up to this point, the games had been played in a new stadium specially built for the purpose, the Luzhniki Sports Palace in Moscow, but the final game between the USSR and Sweden generated so much enthusiasm that it had to be transferred to an outdoor rink in the nearby Grand Sports Arena. On March 5, 1957, some 50,000 spectators crammed into the stands.

Hockey fans at the 1956 Olympics at Cortina d'Ampezzo.

At the end of the first period, the Swedes were up 2–0 and stayed there until the middle of the second period, when Team USSR turned up the heat and went into the second intermission with a 4–2 advantage. And the sudden reversal of fortunes would have been more extreme had it not been for Swedish goalkeeper Tord Flodqvist. The Soviets now appeared certain to win the game and the tournament until an incredible effort by Tumba Johansson turned the tide and the Swedes emerged as champions with a 4–4 tie. After the awards ceremony, Moscow fans poured onto the ice and hoisted and tossed Johansson around as the man of the hour.

If the Canadians had looked down on European hockey before this, their attitude changed after Stockholm and Cortina d'Ampezzo. Not long before, they had claimed it was silly to invite European teams to Canada because no one would come out to watch. An exception was made for Team USSR in 1957, which was the first North American tour for Soviet players. Wanting to test players with very different styles of playing against Canadian amateur teams, the new senior coach of Team USSR, Anatoli Tarasov, took along an experimental lineup.

By his second year as head coach, in 1962, Arne Stromberg (left) enjoyed well-deserved fame as a man who made Sweden world champions.

The Soviets lost their first game 7–2 against the Whitby Dunlops, the 1957 Allan Cup winners, while the next two games resulted in a 5–5 tie in Windsor and 4–2 loss in Kitchener. Then the visitors adjusted to their new surroundings and won five. But Tarasov's long-term strategy could wait to bear fruit.

A HISTORY OF WORLD HOCKEY

At the 1958 World Championship in Oslo, Team USSR was squeezed out by the Whitby Dunlops, and not only did the Canadians get revenge 4–2 in games, they were so powerful in their attacks that in seven games they scored twice as often as the Soviets. The outcome of the 1959 World Championship in Prague was the same. The Canadians, represented this time by the Belleville McFarlands, were again the world champions and Team USSR came in second. But a year later, at the Winter Olympics in Squaw Valley, the Americans proved to be top contenders and threatened to break up the Canada–USSR rivalry.

Public opinion in the United States didn't rate Team USA's participation in World Championships highly. The Olympics were another thing altogether and the team trained conscientiously, which had already been demonstrated in the 1956 games in Cortina d'Ampezzo. At home in Squaw Valley in 1960, the Americans turned in a brilliant performance and won all of their games, even when they played against Canada. Among the outstanding new champions were goalie Jack McCartan, former forward turned defenseman John Mayasich, the Cleary brothers—forwards Bill and Bob—and another brotherly duo, Bill and Roger Christian. The Canadians were runners-up, while the Soviets had to settle for third.

After the Olympics, Arkady Chernyshev took Tarasov's place as head coach of Team USSR. It changed nothing. At the 1961 World Championship in Switzerland, the Soviet team was still in third place, this time behind the Canadians and Czechs.

Ladislav Trojak

On an early November evening in 1948, eight members of the hockey team representing Czechoslovakia had taken to the ice at Wembley in London, England. Fog swirled around the city while, on the other side of the English Channel, in Paris, five stranded Czech players waited for another flight to take them across the Channel.

Ladislav Trojak was the first native of Slovakia to represent Czechoslovakia in hockey.

As the teams went into the second period, the English, with their sense of fair play, also used only eight players for the rest of the game. The guests from Czechoslovakia won 5–3, but by this time the results weren't important. Their concern was for their five comrades. The rest of the team never did arrive in London. They had disappeared without a trace in the nasty weather over the English Channel.

Among them was Ladislav Trojak, the oldest of the group and the most experienced in tournament play. When he first came to Prague from his native Kosice, his fans called him "Trojacek." His fellow players called him "Patrik" or "Skot" (Scotsman) for his frugality, but mostly because he was tough and unyielding.

In 1934 the hockey team Slavia Prague had won the Tatra Cup in Poprad. News of the incredibly fast right winger from the CsSK team of Kosice—the easternmost city in Czechoslovakia—spread quickly.

Representatives from the famous LTC club went to see the miracle youngster up close. Although Trojak had already signed a transfer to the HC Tatra of Poprad, LTC simply ignored it and took him to Prague and virtually detained him until they got the deal they wanted. When one of the Tatra hockey officials came in person to take him back, the LTC people didn't even let him talk to Trojak.

It wasn't exactly a fair hiring process, but the rewards were worth it. The player known as "the Slovak Scorer" quickly matured on the LTC team, which at the time was a top team even by international standards. Soon Trojak appeared on the national team and in 1936 he played in his first big tournament—the Winter Olympics in Garmisch-Partenkirchen. He was the first native Slovak to represent the joint Czech and Slovak state in hockey.

With his speed, he had the prerequisites to become a first-rate star, but he chose to put his exceptional skating skills to use in the service of other players. He skated tirelessly from net to net, fighting for every puck. His style of playing the whole rink and his versatility put him decades ahead of the way the game was played at the time.

He worked his way up to be a forward with LTC; on the national team, he lined up on the right wing on the side of Oldrich Kucera and the renowned center Josef Malecek. Later he played next to Stanislav Konopasek and Vladimir Zabrodsky. His role was to create opportunities for the greatest goal scorers. He would often win the puck deep in the defensive zone, then put on a burst of speed toward the opponent's net and leave the rest up to the scorer. He had no regrets when the successful scorer was cheered by the spectators and by the press the next day.

Trojak, Ladislav
RW, 5'11", 185 lbs, b: Kosice, Austria, 6/15/1914, d: 11/8/1948

Season	Club, League	Regular Season				
		GP	G	A	Pts	PIM
1933–34	CsSK Kosice, Czechoslovakia	*	*	*	*	*
1934–36	LTC Prague, Czechoslovakia	*	*	*	*	*
OWG–36	Czechoslovakia	8	0	*	*	*
1936–37	LTC Prague, Czechoslovakia	*	*	*	*	*
WEC–37	Czechoslovakia	8	3	*	*	*
1937–38	LTC Prague, Czechoslovakia	*	*	*	*	*
WEC–38	Czechoslovakia	6	3	*	*	*
WEC–39	Czechoslovakia	9	6	*	*	*
1945–47	LTC Prague, Czechoslovakia	*	*	*	*	*
WEC–47	Czechoslovakia	7	5	*	*	*
1947–48	LTC Prague, Czechoslovakia	*	*	*	*	*
OWG –48	Czechoslovakia	8	7	*	*	*
	Czechoslovakia Totals	*	*	*	*	*
	OWG/WEC Totals	46	24	*	*	*

Won WEC (1947)
Czechoslovakia Champion (1937, 1938, 1946, 1947, 1948)

He was a hard worker, a self-sacrificing teammate and, 10 years older than most of his team-mates, a patron of the team's rookies. Had it not been for World War II, he could have played in four Olympics and would probably have taken part in more World Championships. He was the oldest player in the 1947 World Championship, the last one he played in. Despite his age, in the 1948–49 season he was indispensable to the national team.

The plane carrying the five Czech hockey stars never landed. The world went dark for five Prague families, and the Czech national team lost five brilliant players. The Kosice stadium would later bear Trojak's name. In people's memories, Patrik—aka the Scotsman—will always represent great passing and hard work on the ice.

Bohumil Modry

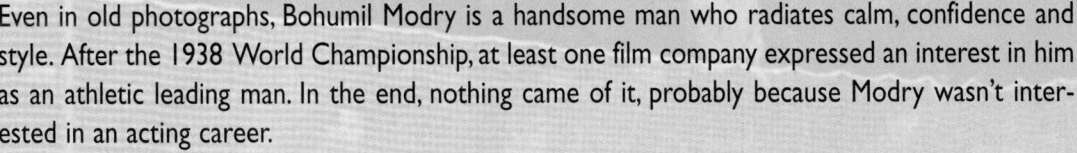

Goaltender Bohumil Modry helped Team Czechoslovakia to its first scoreless tie with Canada.

Even in old photographs, Bohumil Modry is a handsome man who radiates calm, confidence and style. After the 1938 World Championship, at least one film company expressed an interest in him as an athletic leading man. In the end, nothing came of it, probably because Modry wasn't interested in an acting career.

By that time, Bohumil Modry was already an internationally known goaltender. Exceptionally bright (he spoke German, English and Russian), pensive and honest, he was a versatile sports talent. After trying his hand at a number of sports, he settled on hockey and handball, but his fame would come from his role on the ice as a goaltender.

"Hockey, LTC Prague, the national team, all that meant success and glory, but there was another side to the coin. People used servility to cover up envy, people I didn't even know got chummy but were gone when I was going through tough times," he said in later years.

Born in Prague on September 24, 1916, Bohumil Modry was invited to join LTC Prague, the most famous Czech hockey club of the 1930s and 1940s, and in 1937 he went to his first World Championship. He fell easily into a leadership role on the team and played an important part in the team's winning Czechoslovakia's first World Championship titles in 1947 and 1949. He would instruct or advise his potential successors and even rivals with enthusiasm. One such occasion was LTC Prague's trip to Moscow in 1948, when Czech stars taught hockey to a new generation of Soviet players. But as busy as Modry was playing sports, he also found the time to study. Soon after graduating with a diploma in technology, Modry worked briefly as a designer.

After the 1948 Winter Olympics in St. Moritz, Switzerland, where as the goalie he helped his team to its first-ever scoreless tie with Canada, the country that invented hockey expressed an interest in him. At the time, he was considered number one in Europe. Although other goaltenders probably had his keen powers of observation, lightning reflexes and courage, none went to such lengths preparing for the game. And none penetrated the philosophy of the game as deeply as Modry; he even published his observations in Czech magazines, indirectly contributing to the eventual establishment of a strong Czech goaltending contingent.

In 1950, at the age of 33, he had 12 seasons under his belt and 71 matches as a member of the national squad, including six World Championships. Having decided it was time to quit, he wasn't nominated to play in the World Championship in London and didn't even take part in the organizational meetings. In the end, the team didn't go to London to defend the previous year's gold medal. The players learned at the very last minute, just before their flight on March 13, that their participation in the World Championship was canceled. For the previous two years the country had been under the rule of the communists, and the following years were marked by harsh reprisals against a great number of people who were sentenced for disagreeing with communist ideology, for belonging to a different social class or origin, or for no reason at all. A list of charges against hockey representatives was fabricated, partly to intimidate the general population. These actions managed to retard the development of Czech hockey by several years. The cancellation of the trip to London was allegedly to protest Britain's refusal to grant visas to two radio journalists, an action that was later proven to have never happened. Meanwhile, Modry and his wife and two daughters were vacationing in the mountains and were unaware of what was happening. He received a phone call to tell him that the team hadn't gone and that 10 of the 17 players had been arrested in a Prague restaurant, supposedly for disturbing the peace. Although he hadn't been there for the disturbance, the secret police came to get him shortly afterward. He was sentenced to 15 years' imprisonment.

By the time Modry was released at the age of 39, his playing days were over. After his retirement, a whole new crop of excellent goaltenders who could look to Modry's skills for inspiration were raised in the Czech Republic.

Modry, Bohumil
G, 6´3˝, 195 lbs, b: Prague, Czechoslovakia, 9/24/1916, d: 7/21/1963

Season	Club, League	Regular Season		
		GP	GA	Avg
1936–37	LTC Prague, Czechoslovakia	*	*	*
WEC–37	Czechoslovakia	4	5	1.25
1937–38	LTC Prague, Czechoslovakia	*	*	*
WEC–38	Czechoslovakia	4	3	0.75
1938–39	LTC Prague, Czechoslovakia	*	*	*
WEC–39	Czechoslovakia	8	8	1.00
1945–47	LTC Prague, Czechoslovakia	*	*	*
WEC–47	Czechoslovakia	6	5	0.83
1947–48	LTC Prague, Czechoslovakia	*	*	*
OWG–48	Czechoslovakia	6	11	1.83
1948–49	LTC Prague, Czechoslovakia	*	*	*
WEC–49	Czechoslovakia	6	10	1.66
1949–50	Stadion Prague, Czechoslovakia	*	*	*
	Czechoslovakia Totals	*	*	*
	OWG/WEC Totals	38	42	1.11

Won WEC (1947, 1949)
Czechoslovakia Champion (1937, 1938, 1946, 1947, 1948, 1949)

Jaroslav Drobny

It is said that the team that won Czechoslovakia its first World Championship title in 1947 could have made hockey waves much sooner had it not been for World War II. That may be true, but it couldn't have been accomplished without the considerable talent of forward Jaroslav Drobny.

Drobny was born in Prague on October 12, 1921. His father, originally a carpenter by trade, worked as a caretaker at the facilities of a sports club on the Prague island of Stvanice. From early childhood, Drobny played tennis, and even competed at Wimbledon before World War II. He was just as serious about hockey, and in 1939, at the age of 17, he went to his first World Championship.

Had it not been for the war and the German occupation, he might have devoted himself to tennis. But in the isolation that enveloped his country afterward, he had a hard time finding players to challenge on the courts. Knowing there was no competition worthy of him in his homeland, he turned his attention to hockey, joining the CLTK club.

Many saw Drobny as a successor to Josef Malecek, the best Czech hockey player of the 1930s. An excellent skater with great technique, he had an ability to play not only for himself but to create a good game as well. Drobny would draw attention to himself with his individual style, but he was also skillful at getting the puck to his other teammates. In the late 1930s, the rival LTC Prague tried to acquire him. During the war years, when he had no competition among forwards, opposing clubs intensified their efforts to recruit him, but he continued to resist. Not only was he attached to his club in a way that is difficult to comprehend today, but he also respected his father's livelihood and didn't want to jeopardize it.

Later he was often compared to Vladimir Zabrodsky. Although they had much in common, they also differed in many ways. Each played forward for one of the two best clubs in the country. Both were excellent tennis players. Both studied business. However, many of their contemporaries claim that, even when Drobny was dividing his time fairly equally between hockey and tennis, he was the better hockey player of the two.

Drobny was without a doubt fiercer and more assertive. Zabrodsky sometimes seemed to lack a fighting spirit and was too careful when the sparks flew. He was also more selfish on the ice but could think more strategically, whereas Drobny was more impulsive and hardheaded. They each played best when playing alongside each other. But this happened only during the heady moments of international matches, where glory was harder to come by against the stiffer competition.

In 1946 Drobny was chosen as the nation's top athlete in the first extensive opinion poll. But Drobny wasn't around for the acclaim—he had left for a tennis tour of India that was scheduled to last several months. However, because of a sore elbow, he was back in Prague by mid-February of 1947 when the World Championship was starting in that city. Despite the sore elbow, and ignoring appeals to let it heal, Drobny was determined to play in the championship. He entered the lineup and played an important role in Czechoslovakia's first-ever victory in the tournament.

At the St. Moritz Winter Olympics in Switzerland a year later, he jumped in again at the last minute and proved just as valuable as his team came in second to Canada. Next season, he returned from abroad at Christmas and played a few games wearing his old club's sweater. The national team needed him as never before—the team had been seriously reduced by an airline tragedy over the English Channel in which five top Czech hockey players were killed. Another two went into exile after the communists rose to power in February of 1948.

But Drobny was never again to belong to a World Championship hockey team; he failed as well to take advantage of offers to join the NHL as the first European ever. In 1949 the Boston Bruins put him on their reserve list. He said: "The offer stated $20,000, but I refused. Amateur hockey, which we played, was quite different from professional hockey. Furthermore, by going to the NHL, I would have lost the chance to play in international tennis tournaments."

Drobny had reached a crossroads in his life. He couldn't take advantage of all the options open to him and keep his place among the world's best players as long as he lived under the communist regime. So went abroad. In 1954, as an Egyptian citizen, he was the first—and for a long time afterward the only—native Czech ever to win the famous Wimbledon tennis tournament. Every year between 1949 and 1952 he made it to the finals, and until 1955 he numbered among the world's top 10 players. Later he settled in England and visited the new Czech Republic only after the fall of the Iron Curtain. In 1997 he was inducted into the International Ice Hockey Federation's Hall of Fame.

Jaroslav Drobny is still the only hockey player to win at Wimbledon too.

Drobny, Jaroslav
C, 6", 185 lbs, b: Prague, Czechoslovakia, 10/12/1921

Season	Club, League	Regular Season				
		GP	G	A	Pts	PIM
1937–39	CLTK Prague, Czechoslovakia	*	*	*	*	*
WEC–39	Czechoslovakia	9	6	*	*	*
1945–47	CLTK Prague, Czechoslovakia	*	*	*	*	*
WEC–47	Czechoslovakia	7	15	*	*	*
1947–48	CLTK Prague, Czechoslovakia	*	*	*	*	*
OWG–48	Czechoslovakia	8	9	*	*	*
1948–49	CLTK Prague, Czechoslovakia	*	*	*	*	*
	Czechoslovakia Totals	*	*	*	*	*
	OWG/WEC Totals	24	30	*	*	*

Won WEC (1947)

Grant Warwick

An unselfish decision turned out to be the best one Grant Warwick ever made in his hockey career.

With Canada's Penticton Vees senior club set to face the Soviet Union in the game that would decide the gold medal at the 1955 World Championship, the 33-year-old player-coach announced to his players that he wouldn't play. Warwick was so intent on winning the world title that he wanted to concentrate on his duties behind the bench, although he'd been effective earlier in the tournament on a line with his brothers, Bill and Dick.

Before the game in Krefeld, West Germany, Warwick warned his players that if they lost, they'd better not go home, they might as well go to China. The year before, in Stockholm, the Soviets, competing in their first world tournament, had dealt a huge blow to Canadian hockey pride by trouncing the Toronto East York Lyndhursts 7–2 to win the gold medal. Penticton played almost a perfect game, shutting out the defending champions 5–0, and the Warwick brothers, who grew up in Regina, Saskatchewan, became the toast not only of Penticton, British Columbia, but of all Canada.

An unselfish decision turned out to be the best one Grant Warwick made in his hockey career.

In the 1952–53 season, volunteers from the Penticton fan club had raised $1,300 by passing the hat at a game to help pay for Warwick's release from the Buffalo Bisons of the American Hockey League. After joining the Vees in British Columbia's Okanagan Senior Hockey League in December, Warwick scored 19 goals in 31 games as the Penticton club won the Western Canada senior championship and traveled east to face the Kitchener-Waterloo Dutchmen in the Allan Cup finals. The Vees lost the series but made no mistake the following year when they played host to the Sudbury Wolves and won the Allan Cup in seven games despite trailing early in the series. Warwick scored two key goals in the fifth game to tie the score twice and keep Penticton alive. As a result of their championship, the Vees were selected by the Canadian Amateur Hockey Association to represent their country at the 1955 World Championship and Warwick was named player-coach for the 1954–55 season.

Grant "Knobby" Warwick had been the NHL's rookie of the year in the 1941–42 season with the New York Rangers and had spent eight seasons and part of a ninth in the league, also playing briefly with Boston and Montreal. He scored 20 or more goals three times and finished his NHL career with 147 goals in 395 games.

Warwick, Grant
RW, 5'6", 155 lbs, b: Regina, Sask., 10/11/1921

Season	Club, League	Regular Season					Playoffs				
		GP	G	A	Pts	PIM	GP	G	A	Pts	PIM
1940–41	Regina Rangers, RCHL	31	14	18	32	16	8	5	1	6	2
1941–42	New York Rangers, NHL	44	16	17	33	36	6	0	1	1	2
1942–43	New York Rangers, NHL	50	17	18	35	31					
1943–44	New York Rangers, NHL	18	8	9	17	14					
1944–45	New York Rangers, NHL	42	20	22	42	25					
1945–46	New York Rangers, NHL	45	19	18	37	19					
1946–47	New York Rangers, NHL	54	20	20	40	24					
1947–48	New York Rangers, NHL	40	17	12	29	30					
	Boston Bruins, NHL	18	6	5	11	8	5	0	3	3	4
1948–49	Boston Bruins, NHL	58	22	15	37	14	5	2	0	2	0
1949–50	Montreal Canadiens, NHL	26	2	6	8	19					
	Buffalo Bisons, AHL	37	19	28	47	33	3	2	0	2	0
1950–51	Buffalo Bisons, AHL	65	34	65	99	43	4	2	1	3	2
1951–52	Buffalo Bisons, AHL	55	24	41	65	35	3	0	0	0	2
	Halifax St. Mary's, MMHL						5	1	0	1	2
1952–53	Penticton Vees, OSHL	31	19	27	46	49	11	7	8	15	15
1953–54	Penticton Vees, OSHL	54	36	43	79	79	10	11	7	18	8
1954–55	Penticton Vees, OSHL	38	22	34	56	62					
WEC–55	Canada	8	6	11	17	5					
1955–56	Penticton Vees, OSHL	54	54	59	113	44	7	5	3	8	16
1956–57	Trail Smoke Eaters, WHL	43	18	30	48	70	8	5	5	10	8
1957–58	Kamloops Chiefs, OSHL	49	9	31	40	45	15	1	13	14	14
	NHL Totals	395	147	142	289	220	16	2	4	6	6
	WEC Totals	8	6	11	17	5					

Won Calder Trophy (1942)
Won WEC (1955)

Warwick was selected to play in the first NHL All-Star Game at Maple Leaf Gardens in 1947 along with some of hockey's greatest stars, such as Maurice Richard and Gordie Howe.

When he was only 17 years old, he'd been invited to the Bruins' training camp in Hershey, Pennsylvania, and learned a lot from the famous Kraut Line of Milt Schmidt, Bobby Bauer and Woody Dumart. Warwick once said he used to fall asleep under the radio listening to broadcasts of Syl Apps playing, never thinking that one day he would be playing against him. He was only 5´6″ and 155 pounds, and because he was so small, he was often injured in the NHL. Playing against the Detroit Red Wings on Christmas Eve in the 1943–44 season, he suffered a fractured skull and wound up going home to Regina to recuperate. But the next season he bounced back to average a point a game in 42 games.

Often in the doghouse in Boston for taking too many penalties, Warwick was welcomed with open arms in Montreal, where he played on a line with Bill Reay. But early in the 1949–50 season with Montreal, he broke his nose and eventually ended up with the AHL Bisons.

He was traded to Boston in February of 1948 for three players, then sold to the Canadiens in October of 1949. He has been inducted into the Saskatchewan Sports Hall of Fame.

Bill Warwick

In a very real sense, Bill Warwick was just what the doctor ordered to help restore the pride of Canadian hockey.

Bill Warwick was named the best forward at the 1955 World Championship.

Humiliated by the 7–2 loss the Toronto East York Lyndhursts suffered at the hands of the Soviet Union at the 1954 World Championship in Stockholm, the Canadian Amateur Hockey Association was banking heavily on Warwick and his teammates when it selected the 1954 Allan Cup champion Penticton Vees to represent Canada at the 1955 World Championship in West Germany.

A hard-nosed product of the playgrounds of Regina, Saskatchewan, Warwick had been a star in senior hockey and played well in the minor professional ranks, even though he couldn't hold down a job in the NHL. When he arrived in Penticton in 1952, he brought with him not only an excellent array of skills but also a mean streak that would eventually put the fear of God into the best players in Europe.

Warwick scored 50 goals in 58 games with the Penticton club in British Columbia's Okanagan Senior Hockey League in the 1953–54 season and led that league in penalty minutes twice, although he stood only 5´7″ and weighed just 155 pounds. At a team practice in Berlin prior to the 1955 world tournament, he shocked onlookers by getting into a fight with teammate George McAvoy. Crowds in Germany started calling him "Der Wilder Bill" because of his rough play. As a result of a head injury he'd suffered in an auto accident, Warwick wore a helmet and was easy to pick out on the ice in an era when few North American players used headgear.

When the tournament opened, Warwick was a leader for the Canadian team, which was determined to bring home the gold medal. He scored six goals in a 12–1 romp over the United States.

In an all-important match with Czechoslovakia, he brought the Canadian team from behind twice with tying goals in a 5–3 victory. And playing on a line with his brothers, Grant and Dick, he sparked the Vees to a 5–0 victory over the Soviets in the game that decided the gold medal while millions of Canadians listening to Foster Hewitt's radio broadcast of the game rejoiced at home.

A heavy smoker, Warwick hadn't had a cigarette since the team left Canada one month before. But on this joyous day in Krefeld, he celebrated by lighting one up as soon as he got to the dressing room. For his efforts on the ice, Warwick was named winner of the award for the best forward of the tournament.

The World Championship cup was very dirty and was separated from its base, so on his own initiative, Warwick later had a replica made. But he kept the original in his restaurant in Penticton. The battered cup eventually wound up in The Penalty Box bar in Edmonton, which he managed.

While playing with the Ottawa Senators of the Quebec Senior Hockey League in the 1951–52 season, Warwick had opened the Budget Market, a shop that specialized in horsemeat. Ottawa had previously legalized the sale of horsemeat and the government-inspected meat came from the Canadian Co-operative Processors abattoir in Swift Current, Saskatchewan. Six Senators players — Tommy Gorman, Fritz Fraser, Larry Regan, Bob Robertson, Bill Johnson and Gordie Hudson—were there for the official opening.

Following their careers as players in North America, the Warwick brothers were invited to visit Poland and the three traveled there to coach and play exhibition games with the Gornik team in Katowice. Bill was surprised to see that the European players were learning fast. He renewed acquaintances with Stanislav Bacilek, who had played with the Polish national team at the 1955 championship. The enterprising Bacilek was using a stick Warwick had given him at that tournament as a model for a new line of sticks he was producing in Poland.

Earlier in Bill's career, when he joined brother Grant as a member of the New York Rangers in the 1942–43 season, the Warwicks became the fourth brothers combination in the history of the club. Brother duos Bill and Bun Cook, Neil and Mac Colville and Lynn and Muzz Patrick had previously played in New York.

But Bill played only one game for the Rangers that season before joining the New York Rovers of the Eastern Hockey League and 13 more for the Broadway Blueshirts in the 1943–44 campaign. He had a long career in the minor pros with stops in Hershey, Providence, Philadelphia, Springfield, Fort Worth, Minneapolis, Cleveland and Denver.

Warwick, Bill
LW, 5′7″, 155 lbs, b: Regina, Sask., 11/17/1924

Season	Club, League	Regular Season					Playoffs				
		GP	G	A	Pts	PIM	GP	G	A	Pts	PIM
1942–43	New York Rangers, NHL	1	0	1	1	4					
	New York Rovers, EHL	43	26	29	55	47	10	9	4	13	6
1943–44	New York Rangers, NHL	13	3	2	5	12					
	Brooklyn Crescents, EHL	2	0	1	1	0					
	New York Rovers, EHL	27	14	14	28	34	11	7	9	16	12
1944–45	Hershey Bears, AHL	40	10	7	17	26	6	0	0	0	0
	New York Rovers, EHL	1	2	1	3	2					
1945–46	Providence Reds, AHL	42	14	13	27	34	2	0	0	0	2
1946–47	Providence — Philadelphia, AHL	64	25	27	52	42					
1947–48	Springfield Indians, AHL	3	0	0	0	2					
	Fort Worth Rangers, USHL	46	23	15	38	41	4	1	1	2	2
1948–49	Springfield Indians, AHL	14	3	4	7	10					
	Fort Worth Rangers, USHL	52	32	27	59	30	2	1	0	1	15
1949–50	Minneapolis Millers, USHL	70	35	46	81	47	7	3	0	3	4
	Cleveland Barons, AHL						2	0	3	3	2
1950–51	Denver Falcons, USHL	40	13	23	36	20					
1951–52	Ottawa Senators, QSHL	28	0	3	3	30					
	Halifax St. Mary's, MMHL	39	17	24	41	18	9	3	2	5	20
1952–53	Penticton Vees, OSHL	38	21	34	55	82	11	3	11	14	35
1953–54	Penticton Vees, OSHL	58	50	45	95	127	10	8	6	14	28
1954–55	Penticton Vees, OSHL	54	36	37	73	168					
WEC–55	Canada	8	14	8	22	12					
1955–56	Penticton Vees, OSHL	49	32	44	76	210					
1956–57	Trail Smoke Eaters, WHL	45	27	34	61	166	9	2	5	7	44
1957–58	Kamloops Chiefs, OSHL	47	17	28	45	148	8	2	5	7	10
	NHL Totals	14	3	3	6	16					
	WEC Totals	8	14	8	22	12					

Named Best Forward at WEC (1955)
Won WEC (1955)

Al **Dewsbury**

Winning friends and influencing people wasn't Al Dewsbury's primary goal when he played for Canada at the 1959 World Championship.

Winning friends and influencing people wasn't Al Dewsbury's goal when he signed with the Belleville McFarlands for the 1958–59 season. The defending Allan Cup champions had been selected to represent Canada at the 1959 World Championship in Czechoslovakia. In an exhibition game against the Finnish national team in February, the 6´2˝, 202-pound rearguard punched a referee and was thrown out of the game.

He was also fingered in Czech newspapers, including the Communist Party publication *Pravda*, as a player brought to Europe by the Canadian team specifically to intimidate the opposition. Fans whistled and booed every time he appeared on the ice. Reporting from Bratislava, *Toronto Star* sports columnist Milt Dunnell said Dewsbury "seems determined to make Europeans forget about Blue Beard, the Hunchback of Notre Dame and other fearsome figures of the past. He's practically a lifer in the sneezer over here."

But Dewsbury was on his best behavior, steering clear of penalties entirely in the game that mattered most as the Canadian team defeated the powerful Soviet Union 3–1. Teammates claimed he had been the target of referees earlier in the tournament simply because he was big. In spite of a 5–3 loss to host Czechoslovakia, the Canadian team won the gold medal.

A native of Goderich, Ontario, Dewsbury was raised in Toronto, learned to skate in Riverdale Park and won a city junior school championship with Winchester Street school. He played junior hockey with the Toronto Young Rangers before turning pro in the Detroit Red Wings organization. He made his pro debut with the Omaha Knights of the United States Hockey League in 1945–46, the same year that Gordie Howe was a rookie there, and picked up tips from his defense partner, the veteran Jake Forbes. His first coach in Omaha was Mud Bruneteau, the player who had scored in overtime to end the longest game in NHL history with the Detroit Red Wings in 1936. Dewsbury won a Calder Cup championship with the Indianapolis Capitols of the AHL in the 1949–50 season, being named to the league's Second All-Star Team in the process. In the 1950 Stanley Cup playoffs, he was promoted by Detroit and contributed three important assists in four playoff games as the Red Wings won the Stanley Cup in seven games on Pete Babando's overtime goal. Dewsbury said Red Wing coach Tommy Ivan was the man who taught him the most about hockey.

He was in the woods near Bala, Ontario, when he was traded to Chicago and didn't find out about it until he got home two weeks later. The nine-player blockbuster deal sent

Dewsbury, Al
D, 6´2˝, 202 lbs, b: Goderich, Ont., 4/12/1926

Season	Club, League	Regular Season					Playoffs				
		GP	G	A	Pts	PIM	GP	G	A	Pts	PIM
1945–46	Omaha Knights, USHL	41	6	6	12	28	7	1	2	3	0
1946–47	Detroit Red Wings, NHL	23	2	1	3	12	2	0	0	0	4
	Indianapolis Capitals, AHL	34	6	4	10	80					
1947–48	Indianapolis Capitals, AHL	10	0	4	4	34					
	Omaha Knights, USHL	32	11	7	18	57	3	0	2	2	9
	Detroit Red Wings, NHL						1	0	0	0	0
1948–49	Indianapolis Capitals, AHL	65	8	24	32	103	2	0	2	2	0
1949–50	Detroit Red Wings, NHL	11	2	2	4	2	4	0	3	3	8
	Indianapolis Capitals, AHL	30	15	22	37	75	8	2	5	7	16
1950–51	Chicago Black Hawks, NHL	67	5	14	19	79					
1951–52	Chicago Black Hawks, NHL	69	7	17	24	99					
1952–53	Chicago Black Hawks, NHL	69	5	16	21	97	7	1	2	3	4
1953–54	Chicago Black Hawks, NHL	69	6	15	21	44					
1954–55	Chicago Black Hawks, NHL	2	0	1	1	10					
	Montreal Royals, QHL	41	7	9	16	80	14	3	2	5	34
1955–56	Chicago Black Hawks, NHL	37	3	12	15	22					
	Buffalo Bisons, AHL	31	8	18	26	48	5	0	3	3	4
1956–57	Buffalo — Hershey, AHL	59	6	31	37	101	5	0	0	0	2
1957–58	Hershey Bears, AHL	60	7	31	38	114	1	0	0	0	0
1958–59	Belleville McFarlands, EOHL	40	7	31	38	114					
WEC–59	Canada	8	3	2	5	8					
	NHL Totals	347	30	78	108	365	14	1	5	6	16
	WEC Totals	8	3	2	5	8					

Won WEC (1959)
Won Stanley Cup (1950)

Dewsbury to the Black Hawks with Harry Lumley, Jack Stewart, Don Morrison and Pete Babando for Sugar Jim Henry, Bob Goldham, Gaye Stewart and Metro Prystai. Lumley and Stewart both made the Hockey Hall of Fame. When the format for the NHL All-Star Game was changed in 1951 to have the First All-Star Team playing the Second All-Star Team, Dewsbury was named to play for the First All-Star Team in the dream game at Maple Leaf Gardens.

With no hope of post-season play, Chicago loaned him to the Montreal Canadiens for the remainder of the 1954–55 season, but he wound up with the Habs' Quebec league farm club, the Montreal Royals, and led the league in penalty minutes during the playoffs. Dewsbury had a second tour of duty on defense with the Black Hawks under coach Dick Irvin in the 1955–56 season. He was 32 when he moved to Belleville, Ontario, to play with the McFarlands for the 1958–59 season after obtaining his release from the Hershey Bears of the American Hockey League.

Bill Shill

A rangy 6´1˝ and 175-pound right winger from Toronto, Bill Shill entered the NHL with the Boston Bruins in 1942–43 but spent only part of the season there, the other portion being spent with the Toronto Navy team in the Ontario Hockey Association Senior division.

He spent the 1943–44 season away from hockey and in the military, and the following year his hockey playing was limited to a stint with the Cornwallis Navy team in the Nova Scotia Senior Hockey League. By 1945–46, Shill was back in the big leagues, recording his best NHL season that year with 15 goals and 12 assists. He spent one more partial year with the Bruins before being sent to the Hershey and Buffalo teams in the American Hockey League.

In 1947 Shill joined the Dallas Texans of the United States Hockey League before becoming a member of the Vancouver Canucks in the Pacific Coast Hockey League from 1948 to 1952. It was during the 1949–50 season that he had his best scoring year as a pro, recording 34 goals and 42 assists for 76 points in 69 games. That beat his record of the previous year, when he registered 43 goals and 69 points. In 1951 he was named to the PCHL First All-Star Team.

After his four years in Vancouver, Shill made a brief stop in Ottawa to play with the Senators of the Quebec Senior Hockey League and then moved to Brantford, Ontario, to join the Redmen of the Ontario Hockey Association Senior division. In 1952–53, he had another excellent scoring year with 36 goals and 27 assists. The following season he landed a job with the Toronto Lyndhursts of the city's senior league as a coach, not competing anywhere as a player.

However, Shill did represent Canada in the World Championship in 1954 as a member of the East York

Bill Shill represented Canada at the World Championship in 1954 and scored six goals and three assists in seven games.

Shill, Bill											
RW, 6´1˝, 175 lbs, b: Toronto, Ont., 3/6/1923											
Season	Club, League	Regular Season					Playoffs				
		GP	G	A	Pts	PIM	GP	G	A	Pts	PIM
1942–43	Boston Bruins, NHL	7	4	1	5	4					
	Toronto Navy, OHA Sr.	6	6	6	12	11	7	3	3	6	2
1944–45	Cornwallis Navy, NSSHL	13	7	6	13	2	3	4	1	5	0
1945–46	Boston Bruins, NHL	45	15	12	27	12	7	1	2	3	2
1946–47	Boston Bruins, NHL	27	2	0	2	2					
	Hershey — Buffalo, AHL	20	1	3	4	2					
1947–48	Dallas Texans, USHL	66	16	21	37	30					
1948–49	Seattle — Vancouver, PCHL	63	43	26	69	38	3	0	2	2	0
1949–50	Vancouver Canucks, PCHL	69	34	42	76	20	12	7	6	13	2
1950–51	Vancouver Canucks, PCHL	70	36	21	57	33					
1951–52	Vancouver Canucks, PCHL	17	5	3	8	9					
	Ottawa Senators, QSHL	3	0	1	1	0					
	Brantford Redmen, OHA Sr.	31	25	25	50	16	7	2	5	7	6
1952–53	Brantford Redmen, OHA Sr.	46	36	27	63	44	5	2	3	5	4
WEC–54	Canada	7	6	3	9	2					
	NHL Totals	79	21	13	34	18	7	1	2	3	2
	WEC Totals	7	6	3	9	2					

Lyndhursts and scored six goals and three assists for nine points in only seven tournament games. For that effort he was named to the first All-Star team for the tournament, though Canada eventually lost to the Soviets and had to settle for the silver medal.

Jean-Paul Lamirande

In 1958, Jean-Paul Lamirande represented Canada at the World Championship and brought home the gold medal.

Born in Shawinigan Falls, Quebec, Jean-Paul Lamirande began his professional hockey career with the Montreal Army team in the city's senior league, spending two years on the military team from 1943 to 1945 before joining the Montreal Royals for the 1945–46 season.

His six goals and eight assists for the Royals attracted the attention of the NHL's New York Rangers, who called him up for the 1946–47 season. But Lamirande managed only one goal and one assist with the Broadway Blueshirts before being sent to the New Haven Ramblers of the American Hockey League and the Saint Paul Saints of the United States Hockey League for the rest of the year.

In 1947–48, however, Lamirande was recalled by the Rangers for 18 games. His time in the NHL was short-lived and he spent the rest of that season and the whole of the next season in New Haven. Then again in 1949–50 he was summoned by the Rangers for another partial season, followed by yet another trip to New Haven to complete the year. But Lamirande wasn't quite finished playing in the NHL. He spent the next season with the Saint Louis Flyers of the AHL before signing with the Chicoutimi Sagueneens for three seasons from 1951 to 1954. He recorded 69 assists for Chicoutimi, attracting the attention of the Montreal Canadiens, who acquired him for cash from the Rangers and used him for a single game in the 1954–55 season.

Lamirande then made various stops in the Quebec Hockey League playing Senior A hockey, ending up with the Quebec Aces in 1957–58 and representing Canada at the World Championship as an addition to the Whitby Dunlops. The Dunnies brought home gold for Canada. The next season, Lamirande joined the Belleville McFarlands and represented Canada at the 1959 World Championship, in which he was named the best defenseman and won a second consecutive gold medal. He completed his career with a series of minor-league teams, notably the Windsor Bulldogs, Kingston Frontenacs and Clinton Comets.

Lamirande, Jean-Paul
LW/D, 5′8″, 170 lbs, b: Shawinigan Falls, Que., 8/21/1924, d: 1/30/76

Season	Club, League	Regular Season					Playoffs				
		GP	G	A	Pts	PIM	GP	G	A	Pts	PIM
1943–44	Montreal Army, City Sr.	2	0	0	0	0	2	0	0	0	2
1944–45	Montreal Army, City Sr.	14	3	5	8	10	3	0	0	0	2
1945–46	Montreal Royals, QSHL	36	6	8	14	60	9	2	2	4	22
1946–47	New York Rangers, NHL	14	1	1	2	14					
	New Haven Ramblers, AHL	4	0	1	1	6					
	St. Paul Saints, USHL	26	0	4	4	18					
1947–48	New York Rangers, NHL	18	0	1	1	6	6	0	0	0	4
	New Haven Ramblers, AHL	46	7	20	27	22					
1948–49	New Haven Ramblers, AHL	30	3	7	10	18					
1949–50	New York Rangers, NHL	16	4	3	7	6	2	0	0	0	0
	New Haven Ramblers, AHL	52	26	31	57	16					
1950–51	St. Louis Flyers, AHL	64	13	36	49	6					
1951–52	Chicoutimi Sagueneens, QSHL	58	11	28	39	32	18	2	7	9	4
1952–53	Chicoutimi Sagueneens, QSHL	56	4	19	23	36	20	2	6	8	17
1953–54	Chicoutimi Sagueneens, QSHL	68	5	22	27	65	7	0	0	0	4
1954–55	Montreal Canadiens, NHL	1	0	0	0	0					
	Shawinigan Cataracts, QHL	60	3	29	32	59	11	2	4	6	8
1955–56	Trois – Rivieres – Shawinigan, QHL	58	6	16	22	44	11	1	2	3	10
1956–57	Quebec Aces, QHL	67	4	14	18	52	10	0	5	5	6
1957–58	Quebec Aces, QHL	45	3	16	19	24	13	1	2	3	6
WEC–58	Canada	7	1	4	5	0					
1958–59	Belleville McFarlands, EOHL	20	5	8	13	10					
WEC–59	Canada	8	1	0	1	0					
1959–60	Windsor Bulldogs, OHA Sr.	49	6	16	22	50	14	0	4	4	2
1960–61	Kingston Frontenacs, EPHL	2	0	1	1	2					
	Clinton Comets, EHL	52	6	27	33	22	4	0	1	1	7
	NHL Totals	49	5	5	10	26	8	0	0	0	4
	WEC Totals	15	2	4	6	0					

Named Best Defenseman at WEC (1959)
Won WEC (1958, 1959)

Vladimir Zabrodsky

With his fancy loops and accurate shots, Vladimir Zabrodsky had the ability to make players who opposed him on the ice lose their confidence. He was reputed to have the same flair for living. "A scoundrel, but a hockey genius," commented another legendary Czech hockey player, Jaroslav Drobny, decades later.

Zabrodsky, a very tall man, was playful. He liked to outsmart other people and often won money at cards. A hockey legend in the early postwar years, he treated the game not only as a sport but as an art.

When Josef Malecek, the greatest Czech hockey star of the 1930s, ended his career, Zabrodsky became number one, whether in the LTC Prague club (where his father, Oldrich, had raised a whole generation of brilliant players), on the national team or with Spartak, which he joined in 1950.

A coach's life with Zabrodsky wasn't always easy. After LTC returned from a successful tour in England and Scotland at the end of the first postwar hockey season, Jiri Tozicka gave up his post of coach due to a conflict with Zabrodsky. Two years later, the national team returned from a successful performance at the St. Moritz Olympics and Canadian Mike Buckna resigned as coach with the club and the national team—again after a conflict with Zabrodsky.

Vladimir Zabrodsky treated the game not only as a sport but as an art and became a legend in the postwar years of hockey.

Tozicka and Buckna argued that they bore the responsibility for the team's output and thus had to have the final word: The coach should always be right. But Zabrodsky sometimes schemed his way around that unwritten rule. At other times, he simply stretched the truth in a charming, humorous way. Even after Buckna left, not much changed. Antonin Vodicka became the official coach of the LTC and of the Czech national team, but in reality these teams were directed from the ice and from the players' bench by the forward and captain, Zabrodsky, who was also known as "the Boss."

Zabrodsky had been with LTC since the juniors. He brought the Czech team the World Championship title between 1947 and 1949. For the national team he played 93 games and scored 158 goals. In total he took part in six World Championships and Olympics between 1948 and 1956. At the first Olympics in St. Moritz, the team didn't lose a game and defended its historic first win, even against Canada. However, with the Czech team's lower goals differential, the gold medal went to the Canadians.

"Back then we probably had our best team ever," Zabrodsky remembered years later. "Too bad about the tie with Canada. We should have beaten them, but we were a bit cowardly. This was the point of contention between Buckna and myself. But each generation always lasts four, six or eight years. Later there was a plane accident which took the lives of five players. Other players emigrated, but we were able to deal with it quite well."

In 1950, however, the development of Czech hockey was interrupted by a fabricated political trial involving 12 hockey players who were given sentences of eight months to 15 years for alleged espionage and high treason. For some reason, Zabrodsky wasn't among those who were arrested and later sentenced. Even at the end of 1948, during the Spengler Cup tournament in Davos, Zabrodsky had been negotiating the emigration of the complete LTC team and the creation of a national team in exile. According to some observers, he collaborated with the secret police, but according to him, the regime of the day deliberately left him alone because he was so visible.

To this day, none of the allegations have been either corroborated or disproven. Zabrodsky played in the Czech league until 1960, when he was suspended for three years after a scandal concerning the selling of results and betting. To the four titles earned with LTC between 1946 and 1949, he added another in 1953 and again in 1954 while wearing a Spartak Prague jersey. He was the best league scorer five times in all, and in 230 matches he scored 306 goals. Between 1963 and 1965, he ended his career with the Bohemians Prague. Then he decided to go abroad.

He settled in Sweden, where he coached the Leksand and Rogle teams. He was also an excellent tennis player. In the 1950s he played for Czechoslovakia at the Davis Cup. In Stockholm he became a member of the Royal Tennis Club and together with his two sons, Vladimir and Jan, he opened a tennis school. "Hockey training took place in the evenings. During the day I played tennis. My wife complained that I was hardly ever at home, so I left hockey. Maybe I would have stayed longer, but the Czechoslovak authorities blacklisted me. Until the fall of communism, I couldn't travel to the East and this is where hockey was being played at the time. Furthermore, as one gets older, one becomes more of an individualist who wants everything his way. For that reason too I chose tennis."

After the velvet revolution in November 1989, he returned to Bohemia only three times. The last time was during the meeting of the first world champions 50 years later, in 1997. "It is too far to travel from Sweden. Besides, I have grown a bit resentful. Many lies have surfaced in connection with myself and the 1950 trial. People who knew me well were unable to stand behind me. I was here in Sweden and couldn't object, much less defend myself." He was inducted into the International Ice Hockey Federation Hall of Fame in 1997.

Zabrodsky, Vladimir
C, 5'11", 180 lbs, b: Prague, Czechoslovakia, 3/7/1923

Season	Club, League	Regular Season				
		GP	G	A	Pts	PIM
1945–46	LTC Prague, Czechoslovakia	*	*	*	*	*
1946–47	LTC Prague, Czechoslovakia	*	17	*	*	*
WEC–47	Czechoslovakia	7	29	*	*	*
1947–48	LTC Prague, Czechoslovakia	*	*	*	*	*
OWG–48	Czechoslovakia	8	21	*	*	*
1948–49	LTC Prague, Czechoslovakia	*	19	*	*	*
WEC–49	Czechoslovakia	7	10	*	*	*
1950–53	Spartak Prague Sokolovo, Czechoslovakia	*	*	*	*	*
1953–54	Spartak Prague Sokolovo, Czechoslovakia	*	30	*	*	*
WEC–54	Czechoslovakia	7	4	*	*	*
1954–55	Spartak Prague Sokolovo, Czechoslovakia	*	*	*	*	*
WEC–55	Czechoslovakia	8	13	*	*	*
1955–56	Spartak Prague Sokolovo, Czechoslovakia	*	*	*	*	*
OWG–56	Czechoslovakia	7	2	*	*	*
1956–57	Spartak Prague Sokolovo, Czechoslovakia	*	33	*	*	*
1957–58	Spartak Prague Sokolovo, Czechoslovakia	*	*	*	*	*
1958–60	Spartak Prague Sokolovo, Czechoslovakia	*	23	*	*	*
1963–65	Bohemians Prague, Czechoslovakia	*	*	*	*	*
	Czechoslovakia Totals	230	306	*	*	*
	OWG/WEC Totals	44	79	*	*	*

Won WEC (1947, 1949)
Czechoslovakia Champion (1946, 1947, 1948, 1949, 1953, 1954)

Stanislav Konopasek

Stanislav Konopasek wouldn't have traded the number 5 on his jersey for anything in the world, having worn it ever since he played peewee. "I love players with number 5" was often scribbled on the walls of houses in Prague. As a young man, Konopasek was a good-looking, sporty type who looked as if he had it all together. He could be equally elegant on ice.

But besides natural ability, it was luck more than charm that landed Konopasek in the big leagues of hockey. He was born on April 18, 1923, in Horovice, not far from Prague. When his parents moved to the capital, Stanislav chose to stay close to home near Stvanice Island, the mecca of Czech hockey at the time, and it may have been that decision that sealed his fate as a hockey player.

He didn't have an especially large build. As he approached 10 years old, he looked more like seven and, to make matters worse, he had a habit of squinting. Vladimir Zabrodsky, who was the same age, was taller by a head. But from the moment that Zabrodsky's father brought them together at the age of 11, the two boys paired extremely well on the ice. Although they weren't great buddies, they played great hockey together and even came to depend on each other.

Together they made it all the way to LTC Prague's A team. In 1939, when they were only 17, they went with the B team to play in Vienna. But the war put an end to international hockey. In the newly established German protectorate, only teams from Bohemia and Moravia played against one another.

Many teammates took turns playing alongside them on right wing—Frantisek Pergl, Josef Kus and the experienced Ladislav Trojak. Neither Konopasek nor Zabrodsky cared much for fighting, and they didn't much like defending either. Czech defenseman Trojak, an honest, hard-working player, would often take a beating, win the puck, pass it to one of the boys and then secure them from his defensive position. He worked well with them.

Stanislav Konopasek scored the last goal in the 1947 World Championship in Prague to lead Czechoslovakia to a 6–1 win over the United States. He racked up a total of 14 goals during the tournament and shared second place in team rankings with Jaroslav Drobny. With as many goals to his credit as the two second-place players put together, Vladimir Zabrodsky scored 29 goals on opposition nets. But that was the job he was assigned, and when it came to choosing the best forward of the tournament, Konopasek still managed to come out on top. At the time, there was no better left winger in all of Europe.

Over the next three years, not much changed. At the Winter Olympics in St. Moritz, Switzerland, Zabrodsky once again led the team in scoring, but Konopasek finally pulled ahead at the next World Championship in Stockholm in 1949. During the elimination round with Sweden and Finland, he scored five goals, and in the finals he racked up seven, including the winning goal in Czechoslovakia's memorable first-ever win, by a score of 3–2, against Canada.

By then Konopasek was 26 and at the threshold of hockey maturity. He didn't make it to the World Championship in 1950, ending up in jail instead. In a conflict with the communist government of his country, who fabricated charges against him, he was sentenced to 12 years; other players were given sentences of varying lengths.

In 1955 he was among the last of those players to be set free. He went to work at the Tatra Smichov auto plant in Prague. His former teammates from LTC Prague also ended up there, as the communist administration effectively shut the team down. Konopasek was allowed to play only in intercity championships. The following year, however, he got to play for Sparta Prague, later known as Motorlet. But he was no longer the brilliant number 5 with the amazing talent and a knack for creating memorable endings to great tournaments.

Konopasek ended his hockey career in 1963. He went on to become coach of the Motorlet in Prague, of the Katowice team in Poland and finally of Sparta. In spite of adversity, Konopasek stayed in his native country. In 1968 he was rehabilitated by the political establishment, but they couldn't give him back the lost years.

Stanislav Konopasek wouldn't have traded the number 5 on his jersey for anything.

Konopasek, Stanislav
LW, 5'10", 175 lbs, b: Horovice, Czechoslovakia, 4/18/1923

Season	Club, League	Regular Season				
		GP	G	A	Pts	PIM
1945–47	LTC Prague, Czechoslovakia	*	*	*	*	*
WEC–47	Czechoslovakia	7	14	*	*	*
1947–48	LTC Prague, Czechoslovakia	*	*	*	*	*
OWG–48	Czechoslovakia	8	10	*	*	*
1948–49	LTC Prague, Czechoslovakia	*	*	*	*	*
WEC–49	Czechoslovakia	7	12	*	*	*
1949–50	LTC Prague, Czechoslovakia	*	*	*	*	*
1955–56	Tatra Smichov, Czechoslovakia	*	*	*	*	*
1956–62	Spartak Prague, Czechoslovakia	*	*	*	*	*
1962–63	Motorlet Prague, Czechoslovakia	*	*	*	*	*
	Czechoslovakia Totals	130	92	*	*	*
	OWG/WEC Totals	22	36	*	*	*

Won WEC (1947, 1949)
Czechoslovakia Champion (1946, 1947, 1948, 1949)

Yevgeny **Babich**

Yevgeny Babich was a real spark plug in the Army and Air Force teams during the postwar years.

Yevgeny Babich was a real spark plug in the Army and Air Force teams during the postwar years. He was national champion many times and holder of the USSR Ice Hockey Cup as well as champion of the World, European and Olympic Games. He was a player who could ignite his partners; he constantly revved up the pace of the game by rushing forward and raising the intensity of every play.

Babich hung up his skates more than 40 years ago, but fans still remember his irrepressible streaks down the boards, his ability to stop on a dime, to twist out of the way of an oncoming bodycheck and to pass the puck neatly to his partner. It is for his style rather than his scoring ability that Babich is best remembered. He never focused attention on himself or made himself stand out from the rest of his teammates. Battering through defense lines, he would come out one-on-one before the goalie, but at the very last second, after getting the goalie out of position, he'd flick the puck to his partner, who would slam it into an undefended corner of the net. He derived great pleasure from the game itself, from a well-executed feint or a goal-scoring situation that he had created himself.

In spite of his average height and being a bit on the thin side, Babich's natural agility, speed and excellent coordination made him a threat to any defense line. It wasn't easy to stop him or to get the puck away from him. His opponents tried every imaginable strategy—hooking, tripping and tackling—but even then he managed to pass the puck to his partner. His technique was superb. He could outplay the defense at high speed, and in close combat he demonstrated rare intuition and feline dexterity.

And of course he had great courage. Head-on clashes meant nothing to him, and he spared neither himself nor his rivals in order to slam the puck into the net. At times, when he was pasted to the boards, it seemed as if Babich couldn't possibly get up and continue the game. But he'd do just that. At other times he'd just manage to get out of the way of a flying bodycheck and then, to the joy of the fans, the defenseman who'd been trying to stop Babich would ram into the boards himself.

There were two reasons that Yevgeny Babich was able to develop his talent so quickly and excel at the game of hockey. First, he was already an experienced master at bandy, a form of hockey similar to ice hockey, and second, Babich's regular partner was the great Vsevolod Bobrov. Bandy gave Babich a strong foundation—top-notch physical training and superb skating ability. In the huge bandy rinks, he honed his skating and high-speed technique. Players skated from goal to goal at whirlwind speeds, punctuated by sudden changes in pace and unexpected swerves.

Babich met Vsevolod Bobrov in 1944. Both were young officers just out of military school, and both were in love with bandy. But like many others at the time, Babich was unwilling to

Babich, Yevgeny
RW, 5'7", 160 lbs, b: Moscow, USSR, 1/7/1921, d: 6/11/1972

Season	Club, League	Regular Season				
		GP	G	A	Pts	PIM
1946–47	CDKA, USSR	7	4	*	*	*
1947–48	CDKA, USSR	18	22	*	*	*
1948–49	CDKA, USSR	18	14	*	*	*
1949–50	CDKA, USSR	10	12	*	*	*
	VVS MVO, USSR	*	8	*	*	*
1950–51	VVS MVO, USSR	*	14	*	*	*
1951–52	VVS MVO, USSR	*	15	*	*	*
1952–53	VVS MVO, USSR	*	7	*	*	*
1953–54	CDSA, USSR	14	14	*	*	*
WEC–54	USSR	6	1	*	*	*
1954–55	CSK MO, USSR	14	14	*	*	*
WEC–55	USSR	7	2	*	*	*
1955–56	CSK MO, USSR	20	9	*	*	*
OWG–56	USSR	7	2	*	*	*
1956–57	CSK MO, USSR	20	11	*	*	*
WEC–57	USSR	6	1	*	*	*
	USSR Totals	130	144	*	*	*
	OWG/WEC Totals	26	6	*	*	*

Won OWG (1956)
Won WEC (1954)
USSR Champion (1948, 1949, 1950, 1951, 1952, 1953, 1955, 1956)

accept the new game of ice hockey. It was only due to the persistence of Bobrov, who by that time had become a role model for Babich, that he felt compelled to try mastering the new game.

The Bobrov–Babich duo was a rare and fortunate alliance—a coach's dream. Both were distinguished by their creative approach to the game. Both appreciated the value of unexpected moves and ingenious decisions. They constantly analyzed their game, looking for ways to improve it. One of their successful innovations was a combination play in which the attacking player would leave the puck behind him for his partner. According to Bobrov, it was Babich who devised the tactic.

Natural agility, speed and excellent coordination made Yevgeny Babich (center) a threat to any defense team.

Babich and Bobrov demonstrated this play at the 1956 Olympic ice hockey tournament in Cortina d'Ampezzo. The USSR's 4–0 victory over the United States was one of the highlights of the tournament. After the game, U.S. coach John Mariucci remarked, "That was the best game I've ever seen."

The second goal was especially spectacular. Babich broke out toward the American goal. Goalie Willard Ikola came out to meet him in order to narrow the shooting angle. Babich continued to approach the goalie, but all of a sudden swerved sharply to the right while passing the puck to the left. Ikola had been outwitted by Babich's maneuver, and it was too late to react to Bobrov, who was zeroing in on goal and fired the puck into the top corner of the net.

Babich said later: "I felt that Bobrov would be there. I've known him for many years. He has a remarkable feel for the game, and he is always in the right spot at the right time. I let go of the puck by intuition—and I wasn't mistaken!"

Yevgeny Babich's life ended tragically when, not yet 60, he took his own life. What caused him to take such a terrible step remains a mystery to his family and friends.

Vlastimil Bubnik

Throughout the history of Czech hockey, an abundance of players have made it to the top in two or more sports. The most common combination has been hockey and tennis. One reason is that both sports were seasonal. Hockey was played in the winter and tennis in the summer. Many hockey players were also great soccer players. Vlastimil Bubnik was one of these sportsmen.

Bubnik was born on March 18, 1931, in the village of Kelci, near the Moravian town of Hranice. Three years later, his family moved to Brno. He began playing top-level sports at age 13 and managed to divide his time and energy equally between the two most popular sports in the country.

"I didn't differentiate between soccer and hockey. In the spring I would always look forward to the end of the winter season and to running on the grass. By September my palms were itching to pick up the hockey stick. Switching to another sport always changed my way of life for half a year. I had no time to get in a rut. Besides, I was able to avoid the demanding summer meets and

Vlastimil Bubnik (right) scored 121 goals in 127 games for the Czech national team and was named the best forward at the 1961 World Championship.

unpleasant training off the ice. However, running and skating are completely different moves. I must admit that I found it easier to transfer from soccer to hockey than vice versa."

On the ice, he usually played right wing, and in his day he was the best in Europe. In 127 games for the national team, he scored 121 goals. He played in five World Championships and four Olympics. Bubnik was in excellent physical condition and was an elegant skater and first-class stickhandler. He could get maximum return from minimal input. In the European Championship in 1961, he was named best forward, but he never enjoyed gold in Olympic or World Championship play.

In soccer, Bubnik was a typical if somewhat restrained center. He had great passing, a sense for putting plays together and an ability to score quickly and well. He played in the Czech soccer league for 10 years, compared with 16 in top-flight hockey competition, but he managed 11 games on the national team. In 1960 he brought home a bronze medal from the European Championship in France. Two years later, he declined to participate in the World Championship in Chile and the Czechs ended up in second place. By the age of 30, Bubnik had decided to concentrate on soccer. The hockey seasons were getting longer and staying at the top in two very demanding sports was no longer possible.

Vlastimil Bubnik began his hockey career with the SK Kralovo Pole club, but after 1953 he joined the Ruda Hvezda Brno team—later known as ZKL Brno—and was nicknamed "Kometa" (the Comet); the team enjoyed a long winning streak with him on it. Bubnik usually played offense alongside Bronislav Danda and Slavomir Barton and contributed to the team's winning 11 titles between 1955 and 1958 and 1960 and 1966.

He premiered on the national team in 1947 at the age of 17, shortly after the team returned from Stockholm as world champions. The next season he was nominated to play in the World Championship, but Czechoslovakia opted not to participate, in the end. The team was then dissolved, with many players—not including Bubnik—being sent to jail on charges trumped up by the communist administration. At the age of 20, Bubnik was suddenly one of the most experienced players on what remained of the team. "The continuity was broken. We were

Bubnik, Vlastimil
RW, 6´, 185 lbs, b: Kelci, Czechoslovakia, 3/18/1931

Season	Club, League	Regular Season				
		GP	G	A	Pts	PIM
1947–52	SK Kralovo Pole Brno, Czechoslovakia	*	*	*	*	*
OWG–52	Czechoslovakia	9	9	*	*	*
1952–53	SK Kralovo Pole Brno, Czechoslovakia	*	*	*	*	*
WEC–53	Czechoslovakia	4	4	*	*	*
1953–54	Ruda Hvezda Brno, Czechoslovakia	*	*	*	*	*
WEC–54	Czechoslovakia	7	11	*	*	*
1954–55	Ruda Hvezda Brno, Czechoslovakia	*	*	*	*	*
WEC–55	Czechoslovakia	8	17	*	*	*
1955–56	Ruda Hvezda Brno, Czechoslovakia	*	*	*	*	*
OWG–56	Czechoslovakia	7	3	*	*	*
1956–60	Ruda Hvezda Brno, Czechoslovakia	*	*	*	*	*
OWG–60	Czechoslovakia	7	5	*	*	*
1960–61	Ruda Hvezda Brno, Czechoslovakia	*	*	*	*	*
WEC–61	Czechoslovakia	7	4	*	*	*
1961–62	Ruda Hvezda Brno, Czechoslovakia	*	*	*	*	*
1962–63	ZKL Brno, Czechoslovakia	*	*	*	*	*
WEC–63	Czechoslovakia	7	1	*	*	*
1963–64	ZKL Brno, Czechoslovakia	*	*	*	*	*
OWG–64	Czechoslovakia	6	3	*	*	*
1964–66	ZKL Brno, Czechoslovakia	*	*	*	*	*
1966–68	Vitkovice, Czechoslovakia	*	*	*	*	*
1968–71	Feldkirch, Austria	*	*	*	*	*
	Czechoslovakia Totals	320	300	*	*	*
	OWG/WEC Totals	62	57	*	*	*

Best Forward at WEC (1961)
Czechoslovakia Champion (1955, 1956, 1957, 1958, 1960, 1961, 1962, 1963, 1964, 1965, 1966)

starting from zero. There was no one to guide me. Another thing which we didn't have in order to bring home gold from the World Championship was luck. All it took in 1961 was for Canada to beat the Soviets 3–0 in the finals. Canada won 5–1 and we were second."

His greatest disappointment came at the 1956 Olympics in Cortina d'Ampezzo. The team didn't fare badly during preliminary play, and many saw the Czechs as potential winners. However, they were quite exhausted after a tour of Switzerland just before the peak of the season, and many changes to the lineup were suddenly introduced. The Czech team came in fifth, a result that led to nasty accusations and personal attacks. Bubnik quit the national team. "Danda and I decided that it was just too much. All the blame was piled on us guys from RH Brno. They left most of the others, including Karel Gut and Vladimir Zabrodsky, alone. During a match of the league in Bratislava, someone threw a knife at us. In Chomutov, mice came flying onto the ice."

Bubnik returned once more in 1960 and six years later quit the national team for good. He spent two years with the TJ Vitkovice club and ended his career with EV Feldkirch in Austria. Later he coached his former team in Brno as well as HC Jesenice in Slovenia but lasted only six years in that job.

Commenting on that time, he said: "The hockey player and the coach have completely different points of view. In the old days, all it took was to nod your head, jump onto the ice and try to score a goal. The coach, however, cannot do anything by himself. He is dependent on the players and on what they can do. I couldn't deal with that. I understood quickly enough that this type of work wasn't for me." He was inducted into the International Ice Hockey Federation's Hall of Fame in 1997.

Arkady Chernyshev

The most prestigious titles in world hockey are Olympic champion; world champion; holder of the Canada Cup, the World Cup and the Stanley Cup. The man who tops the list of those who have won the most honors among both Russian players and coaches is Arkady Chernyshev. Altogether, Chernyshev holds 15 titles as a coach. But the time the first Canada Cup tournament was played, he was no longer coaching the Soviet national team, and he never had the opportunity of working in the NHL.

Arkady Chernyshev tops the list of Russian coaches with 15 titles.

With such an impressive career as a coach, Chernyshev's days as a player seem to fade in comparison, but he was a notable hockey player. He scored the first-ever goal in the first national championship and coached the first champion team of the USSR. Like all players of his generation, Chernyshev played bandy before he learned to play Canadian-style hockey. He was a remarkable bandy player and won the USSR Cup five times.

Chernyshev was a mentor to two famous hockey players of the USSR national squad— Alexander Maltsev and Valeri Vasiliev. Maltsev was a gifted hockey player, but it was thanks to Chernyshev that he achieved his fame. The same can be said for defenseman Vasiliev. Many others who encountered Chernyshev when they joined the national team also considered him their champion. "When I came to the national squad, it was sometimes difficult for us newcomers to

Chernyshev, Arkady
C, 6´, 185 lbs, b: Moscow, USSR, 3/16/1919, d: 1992

Season	Club, League	Regular Season				
		GP	G	A	Pts	PIM
1946–47	Dynamo Moscow, USSR	5	4	*	*	*
1947–48	Dynamo Moscow, USSR	7	0	*	*	*
1948–49	Dynamo Moscow, USSR	4	0	*	*	*
	USSR Totals	16	4	*	*	*

USSR Champion (1947)

Chernyshev, Arkady
Head Coach, b: Moscow, 3/16/1914, d.1992

Season	Club, League	Regular Season				
		GC	W	L	T	W%
1946–47	Dynamo Moscow, USSR	7	5	2	0	0.714
1947–48	Dynamo Moscow, USSR	18	11	3	4	0.722
1948–49	Dynamo Moscow, USSR	18	11	4	3	0.694
1949–50	Dynamo Moscow, USSR	22	16	3	3	0.795
1950–51	Dynamo Moscow, USSR	15	12	3	0	0.800
1951–52	Dynamo Moscow, USSR	16	10	5	1	0.656
1952–53	Dynamo Moscow, USSR	21	16	4	1	0.785
1953–54	Dynamo Moscow, USSR	16	15	1	0	0.937
WEC–54	USSR	7	6	0	1	0.928
1954–55	Dynamo Moscow, USSR	18	14	2	2	0.833
WEC–55	USSR	8	7	1	0	0.875
1955–56	Dynamo Moscow, USSR	28	23	5	0	0.821
OWG–56	USSR	7	7	0	0	1.000
1956–57	Dynamo Moscow, USSR	30	25	3	2	0.866
WEC–57	USSR	7	5	0	2	0.857
1957–58	Dynamo Moscow, USSR	33	20	11	2	0.636
1958–59	Dynamo Moscow, USSR	27	18	5	4	0.740
1959–60	Dynamo Moscow, USSR	36	19	15	2	0.555
1960–61	Dynamo Moscow, USSR	33	23	5	5	0.772
WEC–61	USSR	7	5	2	0	0.714
1961–62	Dynamo Moscow, USSR	38	31	5	2	0.842
1962–63	Dynamo Moscow, USSR	37	26	8	3	0.743
WEC–63	USSR	7	6	1	0	0.857
1963–64	Dynamo Moscow, USSR	36	25	10	1	0.708
OWG–64	USSR	8	8	0	0	1.000
1964–65	Dynamo Moscow, USSR	36	18	11	7	0.597
WEC–65	USSR	7	7	0	0	1.000
1965–66	Dynamo Moscow, USSR	36	20	13	3	0.597
WEC–66	USSR	7	6	0	1	0.928
1966–67	Dynamo Moscow, USSR	44	26	14	4	0.613
WEC–67	USSR	7	7	0	0	1.000
1967–68	Dynamo Moscow, USSR	44	28	12	4	0.681
OWG–68	USSR	7	6	1	0	0.857
1968–69	Dynamo Moscow, USSR	42	21	15	6	0.715
WEC–69	USSR	10	8	2	0	0.800
1969–70	Dynamo Moscow, USSR	44	22	17	5	0.556
WEC–70	USSR	10	9	1	0	0.900
1970–71	Dynamo Moscow, USSR	40	27	9	4	0.725
WEC–71	USSR	10	8	1	1	0.850
1971–72	Dynamo Moscow, USSR	32	20	8	4	0.625
OWG–72	USSR	5	4	0	1	0.900
1972–73	Dynamo Moscow, USSR	32	19	12	1	0.609
1973–74	Dynamo Moscow, USSR	32	16	12	4	0.562
1974–75	Dynamo Moscow, USSR	12	2	6	4	0.333
	USSR Totals	843	539	223	81	0.687
	OWG/WEC Totals	114	99	9	6	0.894

Won OWG (1956, 1964, 1968, 1972)
Won WEC (1954, 1963, 1965, 1966, 1967, 1969, 1970, 1971)
USSR Champion (1947, 1954)

find acceptance on the team," Boris Mikhailov admits. "We always went to Chernyshev, knowing that he would help us and never allow anyone to mistreat us."

In the legendary Chernyshev–Tarasov tandem, Anatoli Tarasov was frequently the center of attention, but the last word always went to the head coach and that was Chernyshev. Calm, reserved and intelligent, Chernyshev held great sway with the players and was an authority figure for them. An incomparable strategist and tactician, Chernyshev smoothly controlled the game. He had an uncanny sixth sense and was able to assess a situation quickly and make a decision that in the end would benefit the team.

In the hockey encyclopedia that was published in the USSR a couple of decades ago, Chernyshev's qualities are described very briefly: "An outstanding hockey specialist who molded scores of hockey masters. A brilliant game strategist and tactician. One of the first to elaborate the principles of an attack by two forwards along one flank and to introduce active defense at the blue line; distinguished by an unexcelled ability to spot and develop a player's potential. Besides his superb coaching capabilities, he is known as a teacher possessing rare tact and an ability to approach a wide range of people."

Chernyshev's work as head coach of Dynamo Moscow deserves special mention. In the 28 years he headed the team, they failed to finish in the top three in the national championship only four times. His team twice won the gold medal and the USSR Cup. At the club level, it was difficult for Dynamo to compete with the Central Red Army club because that team had first choice in selecting players. Nevertheless, the veteran Chernyshev created both the Yuri Krylov–Alexander Uvarov–Valentin Kuzin and the Stanislav Petukhov–Vladimir Yurzinov–Yuri Volkov forward lines for Dynamo and the national squad.

In the first USSR championship tournament, the gold medal was won by Dynamo Moscow with Arkady Chernyshev as captain. In 1954 the national team of the rapidly growing and popular sport made its debut at the World Championship and exceeded all expectations. The Soviet team was coached by Chernyshev, who also coached the team at its first Olympic hockey tournament two years later when it again won the gold medal.

The period from 1963 to 1972 marked a golden era for Soviet hockey. The Soviets won top awards during these years at nine World Championships and three Olympic hockey tournaments. During those years, Arkady Chernyshev was at the helm of the Soviet nationals while his assistant, Anatoli Tarasov, was the coach of the best Soviet Army club.

After their triumph at the 1972 Olympics, Chernyshev and Tarasov left the national squad. A number of versions of the story attempt to explain the reasons for their departure. Most agree that the two coaches had become too independent and difficult to control in the eyes of the country's sports leaders, so they were "persuaded" to resign. Chernyshev was inducted into the International Ice Hockey Federation's Hall of Fame in 1999.

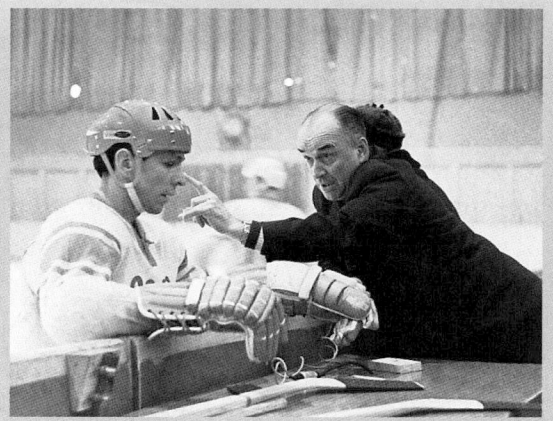

Arkady Chernyshev (right) scored the first goal in the first national championship and coached the first champion team of the USSR.

Alexei Guryshev

To this day, the name Alexei Guryshev remains synonymous in the minds of Soviet hockey fans with the Krylja Sovetov team (Soviet Wings). For 15 years, Guryshev spearheaded the Wings' forward line and was the top scorer four times during his career.

Tall, well built and resilient, Guryshev's superb stickhandling and skating technique resulted in a style that was both elegant and strategic. A player of exceptional control, Guryshev never resorted to battering-ram-style charges or frenzied scuffles for the puck. His specialty was cutting through the confusion with split-second timing and sending the puck into the net.

An uncanny instinct for goal-scoring and a superb finishing shot were his trump cards, but Guryshev may best be remembered for his unusual slapshot—matched only by fellow players Zdenek Zikmund and Viktor Shuvalov. With no windup, it was a short, quick slap causing the puck to sail straight through midair like a bullet. Guryshev's control of the stick, holding it with a short grip in an almost horizontal position, enabled him to slap the puck on the fly with amazing speed. Guryshev was top scorer four times in the Soviet national championships between 1949 and 1958. With a total of 379 goals, he still holds the record as the third-highest scorer in Soviet hockey following Boris Mikhailov and Vyacheslav Starshinov.

Alexei Guryshev was the top scorer in Soviet national championships four times between 1949 and 1958.

Guryshev's strength as a forward and leading goal scorer depended on wingers Pyotr Kotov and Sergei Mitin, who drew opposition defensemen away from Guryshev while feeding passes to him as he positioned himself near the net. Kotov and Mitin were later replaced by Nikolai Khlystov and Mikhail Bychkov. Wings coach Vladimir Yegorov consciously built the game around Guryshev's exceptional scoring ability, freeing him from defense duties and limiting his zone of action to the red line and the opposition net.

The opposition's greatest challenge was to neutralize Guryshev. The strongest and most experienced defensemen were always assigned the job, but they were rarely successful. Even compared to the famous Bobrov line, considered the best forward line in Soviet hockey, Guryshev's troika chalked up impressive scores during the 1955 and 1957 World Championships. During the 1954 World Championship game against the Canadians, it was Guryshev who scored the significant first goal.

Guryshev, Alexei
C, 6′, 185 lbs, b: Moscow, USSR, 3/14/1925, d: 1983

Season	Club, League	Regular Season				
		GP	G	A	Pts	PIM
1947–48	Krylja Sovetov, USSR	*	*	*	*	*
1948–49	Krylja Sovetov, USSR	*	29	*	*	*
1949–50	Krylja Sovetov, USSR	*	27	*	*	*
1950–51	Krylja Sovetov, USSR	*	*	*	*	*
1951–52	Krylja Sovetov, USSR	*	21	*	*	*
1952–53	Krylja Sovetov, USSR	*	26	*	*	*
1953–54	Krylja Sovetov, USSR	*	30	*	*	*
WEC–54	USSR	7	5	*	*	*
1954–55	Krylja Sovetov, USSR	*	41	*	*	*
WEC–55	USSR	8	7	*	*	*
1955–56	Krylja Sovetov, USSR	*	30	*	*	*
OWG–56	USSR	7	7	*	*	*
1956–57	Krylja Sovetov, USSR	*	32	*	*	*
WEC–57	USSR	7	8	*	*	*
1957–58	Krylja Sovetov, USSR	*	40	*	*	*
WEC–58	USSR	6	3	0	3	2
1958–59	Krylja Sovetov, USSR	*	15	*	*	*
WEC–59	USSR	6	5	*	*	*
1959–61	Krylja Sovetov, USSR	*	*	*	*	*
	USSR Totals	300	379	*	*	*
	OWG/WEC Totals	41	35	*	*	*

Won OWG (1956)
Won WEC (1954)
USSR Champion (1957)

Guryshev always remained in control of his game, never losing his cool despite constant attempts to neutralize him. His skill lay in being able to size up the goalie's position and stance, the possibility of the enemy's defense line blocking his shot and the position of his teammates on the ice with instant precision. Then, with split-second accuracy, Guryshev would take advantage of his opponents' confusion to fire the puck into the net.

Even after his former partners, Kotov, Mitin, Bychkov and Khlystov, had hung up their skates, Guryshev continued to play and score goals. At the age of 30, he scored 41 goals; in the next three seasons, he chalked up 36, 32 and 40 goals. Even at 36, Guryshev scored an impressive 19 goals during the 1960–61 season.

When he retired from playing hockey, Alexei Guryshev became a referee and in the world of hockey occupied a place of respect earned through an understanding of the subtleties of the game and an exceptional playing career.

Ike Hildebrand

Ike Hildebrand scored the winning goal in the sensational 3–1 victory over the USSR that won Canada the gold medal at the 1959 World Championship.

It was excellence in lacrosse, Canada's national sport, that earned Ike Hildebrand his induction into Canadian Sports Hall of Fame. But his most rewarding moment in sports came in hockey. It was Hildebrand who scored the winning goal in the thrilling 3–1 victory over the Soviet Union to bring Canada, represented by the Belleville (Ontario) McFarlands, the gold medal at the 1959 World Championship in Czechoslovakia.

Belleville had rallied from a three-games-to-one deficit to defeat the Kelowna Packers in seven games in the 1958 Allan Cup finals, in which all seven games were played in British Columbia. That earned the club an invitation from the Canadian Amateur Hockey Association to go to the world tournament the next season. Canada and the Soviets finished with identical records, but the McFarlands had beaten the Soviets in the only match between the two teams and also had an advantage in the goals-for-and-against differential. "There's a little tarnish on the cup, but we won it," said Hildebrand, puffing on a cigar at the victory celebration. He was referring to a 5–3 setback Canada had suffered at the hands of the host Czechs.

When Bep Guidolin had left the Belleville club to play for the Windsor Bulldogs two years earlier, McFarlands manager Drury Denyes had made Hildebrand player-coach. Gordon "Red" Berenson, who had scored 46 goals in 51 games for the Regina Pats juniors the previous season, was probably the best player on the team, and there were others who surpassed Hildebrand in talent, but in naming him player-coach, Denyes was banking on his NHL experience.

Likewise, in making the final cuts to the roster prior to the World Championship, Hildebrand hung on to NHL vets like Al Dewsbury and Pete Conacher. "When the chips are down, give me the old pros," he said. As player-coach, Hildebrand was responsible for keeping track of all the line changes as well as taking a regular shift. Conditions in Czechoslovakia were quite a bit below what the former pros had been used to. While playing the preliminary round of the tournament in Bratislava, the McFarlands had to put their hockey uniforms on at the hotel, then take the bus to the arena.

Hildebrand, who packed plenty of fight into his 5′7″, 147-pound frame, won the Mike Kelly Award as MVP in the Mann Cup Canadian senior lacrosse championship when he was only 17. A prolific goal scorer, he twice won the scoring championship while playing on the West Coast for the New Westminster Salmonbellies and then twice again after moving east to join the Peterborough Trailermen. In 1955, in one Mann Cup game against Victoria, he scored seven goals.

A native of Winnipeg, Hildebrand played junior hockey with the Oshawa Generals in 1945–46 and 1947–48 and with the senior Toronto Marlboros in 1947–48. At Oshawa, he led all playoff scorers in the 1945–46 season with 21 goals and 32 points in only 12 games. He won a Calder Cup championship with the Cleveland Barons of the American Hockey League in the 1952–53 season and earned a

| Hildebrand, Ike |||||||||||
| RW, 5′7″, 147 lbs, b: Winnipeg, Man., 5/27/1927 |||||||||||

Season	Club, League	Regular Season					Playoffs				
		GP	G	A	Pts	PIM	GP	G	A	Pts	PIM
1947-48	Toronto Marlboros, OHA Sr.	35	29	37	66	29	5	2	0	2	6
1948-49	Los Angeles Monarchs, PCHL	45	17	19	36	32	7	1	5	6	17
1949-50	Los Angeles Monarchs, PCHL	63	24	36	60	28	17	6	8	14	20
1950-51	Kansas City Royals, USHL	63	42	49	91	67					
1951-52	Cleveland Barons, AHL	48	31	16	47	19	5	1	3	4	7
1952-53	Cleveland Barons, AHL	64	38	34	72	40	11	1	1	2	11
1953-54	New York Rangers, NHL	31	6	7	13	12					
	Vancouver Canucks, WHL	8	0	0	0	2					
	Chicago Black Hawks, NHL	7	1	4	5	4					
1954-55	Chicago Black Hawks, NHL	3	0	0	0	0					
	Montreal Royals, QHL	53	17	25	42	27	14	1	6	7	14
1955-56	Cleveland Barons, AHL	54	9	19	28	43	8	1	1	2	10
1956-57	Pembroke Lumber Kings, EOHL	23	6	12	18	44					
	Belleville McFarlands, EOHL	25	19	36	55	73	10	2	5	7	10
1957-58	Belleville McFarlands, EOHL	51	15	39	54	55	13	5	19	24	2
1958-59	Belleville McFarlands, EOHL	46	30	36	66	31					
WEC-59	Canada	8	6	6	12	4					
1959-60	Belleville McFarlands, OHA Sr.	45	23	22	45	20	12	3	11	14	4
	NHL Totals	41	7	11	18	16					
	WEC Totals	8	6	6	12	4					

Won WEC (1959)

berth at right wing on the league's First All-Star Team. He led all goal scorers with 38, although he had only one goal and one assist in 11 playoff games. Hildebrand played a total of 41 NHL games with the New York Rangers and Chicago Black Hawks, recording seven goals and 11 assists for 18 points. In his very first game with Chicago in the 1953–54 season, he scored a goal and assisted on another as the last-place Black Hawks embarrassed the defending Stanley Cup champion Montreal Canadiens 8–3 in front of a small crowd of close to 8,000 at Chicago Stadium.

He coached hockey in Ontario—in Pembroke, Belleville and Orillia—and was active in the NHL oldtimers' games in Toronto.

Augustin Bubnik

Bubnik is a famous name in Czech hockey. There were three Bubniks in total, and they all made their mark on hockey history. All had ancestors in southern Bohemia and were distant cousins. The oldest, Vaclav, was a robust defenseman with a good aim. The youngest, Vlastimil, became famous as a great shooter.

The middle one, Augustin Bubnik, was the most versatile and stayed with hockey the longest. For many years he played center and left wing but finished his career as a defenseman. After retiring from playing, he was a coach for over 30 years. But everything might have been different. He belonged to the "lost generation" whose talent was stifled by the oppressive communist regime.

Bubnik was born on November 21, 1928, in Prague and began playing hockey with SK Davice. During his childhood, every boy dreamed of making it to the famous LTC Prague. They chose him when he was just nine. When he was picked for the national team, he wasn't even 20. He brought a silver medal home from the 1948 St. Moritz Olympics although he played in only two matches. Bubnik had originally gone to the competition as a substitute, but appendicitis kept him from taking part in other games.

When he was only 22, Augustin Bubnik was sentenced to 14 years in prison for high treason on charges fabricated by the state.

In November of the same year a match against England was planned. The trip involved a stopover in Paris, where the departure was marred by complications. Five representatives had to wait for the next connecting flight a day later than the rest of the team. Gusta Bubnik wanted to see Paris and tried to persuade a teammate, Miloslav Pokorny, to trade places. Fortunately for him, he had to forfeit his plans to tour the city and travel on the first plane. The second plane never made it to London.

At the 1949 World Championship in Stockholm, he was lined up as a winger for the level-headed Vladimir Bouzek. The offense was often rounded out by Cenek Picha. In spite of the tragedy that befell the team that November, Czechoslovakia won gold for the second time. Following this, Bubnik had to do his military service, during which time he played with ATK Prague. With 26 goals, he became the top goal scorer in the league. His team won the national title, but more importantly, they were the first to end the many years of dominance by LTC Prague.

His participation in the next championship in London was inevitable. However, the national team didn't get to go to Great Britain after all. The pretext for the team's cancellation was that the host country had refused to make the necessary arrangements for some members of the entourage. The truth was that the whole affair was orchestrated by the communist secret police. Then, when he was only 22, Bubnik was sentenced to 14 years for high treason on charges fabricated by the state. Five years later he was pardoned.

After he returned from the labor camp, he spent one year with Zbrojovka in Brno. After he was once again banned by the regime from top-level competition, he played in the second league for Moravia Olomouc from 1956 until 1958. Then he appeared in the league with Motorlet Prague and finally Slovan Bratislava.

Like the other victims of the political trials, he wasn't allowed to represent his country, his name couldn't appear in print and his photos couldn't be published. Only later was he officially rehabilitated through the courts. To this day he hasn't learned the real story behind the events which robbed him of a good part of his life.

League records probably would have credited him with 10 seasons, some 180 games and 73 goals in spite of the forced break. But his hockey career was cut short by a serious back injury

Bubnik Avgustin (Gustav)
C/LW/D, b: Prague, Czechoslovakia, 11/21/1928

Season	Club, League	Regular Season				
		GP	G	A	Pts	PIM
1947–48	LTC Prague, Czechoslovakia	*	*	*	*	*
OWG–48	Czechoslovakia	8	2	*	*	*
1948–49	LTC Prague, Czechoslovakia	*	*	*	*	*
WEC–49	Czechoslovakia	7	2	*	*	*
1949–50	ATK Prague, Czechoslovakia	*	26	*	*	*
1955–56	Spartak Brno, Czechoslovakia	*	*	*	*	*
1956–58	Motorlet Prague, Czechoslovakia	*	*	*	*	*
1958–62	Slovan Bratislava, Czechoslovakia	*	*	*	*	*
	Czechoslovakia Totals	180	73	*	*	*
	OWG/WEC Totals	15	4	*	*	*

Won WEC (1949)
Czechoslovakia Champion (1948, 1949)

during a Pilsen–Slovan game in the 1961–62 season. He spent a year in treatment and tried to come back, but doctors forbade him to play, so he dedicated himself to Slovan, working with juniors. And another chapter in the career of Augustin Bubnik—this time as a coach—opened up. From 1962 until 1965, he led Litvinov and after that Motorlet.

Then for three years he was responsible for the Finnish national team, and in 1967, during the championship in Vienna, he was in the background as the team gained its historic first victory over Czechoslovakia. Later he coached a variety of other teams: Skoda Pilsen, CSA Karvina, Zetor Brno, AS Mlada Boleslav, Slavia Prague and ATSE Graz of Austria. In addition, he worked with the junior nationals of Czechoslovakia from 1974 until 1976. After a contract in the 1981–82 season with the national team of the Netherlands, which at the time played in the A group of the World Championships, he became the coach of Litvinov after responding to a job ad. His final resting place in the league—for the third time in his career—was Brno.

He built a reputation as a hard-working but impulsive and sometimes argumentative coach. Whenever he wasn't busy with a team, he was a public speaker, like his father had been. Twice he even ran for the post of chairman of the Czech Federation. But he could never go very long without hockey, and even after he was elected to parliament in 1998 for the Civic Democratic Party (ODS), whenever possible he still helped out the Finnish teams when they toured the Czech Republic.

Viktor Shuvalov

When hockey fans think of the famous Bobrov forward line, they usually first remember Bobrov and Babich, and then recall the equally outstanding Viktor Shuvalov. Bobrov and Babich had made a name for themselves in hockey well before Shuvalov came along. But it was when Shuvalov joined the Bobrov line that it achieved the status it holds to this day. Shuvalov became the driving force behind Vsevolod Bobrov's troika.

Bobrov and Shuvalov joined the Air Force team at about the same time—Bobrov from the Central Red Army club and Shuvalov from the Traktor Chelyabinsk team. They played shoulder to shoulder in soccer as well as hockey. Both were leaders; both had a strong character. Bobrov always demanded that the game be focused on him. But Shuvalov also knew how to score, which he did often. Their relationship wasn't always smooth and there were many instances of friction between them. But in time, expediency took over. Once Shuvalov understood that it was Bobrov who always drew at least two opposing players to the center line, he reconciled himself to the fact that Bobrov was the dominant member of the line.

Viktor Shuvalov was the real driving force behind Vsevolod Bobrov's troika.

Shuvalov's style of play changed correspondingly. At the beginning of an attack, Shuvalov would get Bobrov and Babich to the opposing team's goal with a series of strategic passes. If the attack folded up, Shuvalov could be counted on to back up his partners, and he frequently functioned as an offensive defenseman. He had quickly become a skillful and versatile player. Shuvalov also varied his game in front of the opposition's goal. He would position himself not right in front of the goal itself but somewhat farther back, giving himself the opportunity to attack and if need be fall back and take up a defense position.

Viktor Shuvalov (shooting) developed a number of original techniques, among them his famous slapshot where the puck would zoom toward the goal about four to six inches above the ice.

The fact that opposing teams beefed up their efforts to guard Babich and Bobrov meant Shuvalov was often left unguarded, and he lost no time taking advantage of the situation. He would fire at the net on the fly, without bothering to set up the puck. His stability on ice was a great boon to him. With his bowed legs spread wide in a low crouching stance, he could avoid sudden body-checks.

A hockey master is remembered by fans because of his unique abilities and individuality. This can take many forms—superb stickhandling, shots on goal, speed and superior strategy. Viktor Shuvalov had a number of original techniques, among them his famous slapshot on goal when the puck would zoom toward the goal at about four to six inches above the ice. But Shuvalov was modest about this particular ability. "What slapshot?" he'd ask. "More often I fired wrist shots, which are pretty tough for a goalie to catch." And with a smile he would add, "Executing slapshots with the hockey sticks we had then usually ended with picking up a mass of splinters."

Despite Bobrov's dominance, Shuvalov was a very valuable member of the famous forward line. His often dazzling and original playing style was backed up by high-scoring performances. In 150 national championship games, Shuvalov scored 220 goals. He was the top scoring forward in the 1949–50 and 1952–53 seasons. Add to this the fact that when Shuvalov played alongside Bobrov at World Championships, their scoring performances were virtually equal.

Viktor Shuvalov was a man with a highly developed sense of personal dignity, with his own views on the game and on the training process. Such players often insist on maintaining very high standards, and perhaps that was why Shuvalov quit playing hockey prematurely to take up coaching. Whatever the reason, his record is uncommonly impressive—he was a member of teams that were four times USSR national champions, two times silver medalists, four times holders of the USSR Cup, two times world and European champions and one time Olympic champions.

Shuvalov stayed faithful to his own high standards when he became a coach. He wasn't willing to accept athleticism just for the sake of athleticism. "It is necessary to mold players, not strongmen," he used to say. He demanded originality in playing the game, initiative during workouts and inventiveness in tactical patterns. The way European hockey is played today wasn't to his liking—not enough creativity, too much dirty playing and lacking true competition with open and clean bodychecking. "The game is beginning to look like Canadian hockey," Shuvalov noted. "Our traditional playing style, with its high speeds, maneuvering, techniques, ingenuity and agility is gradually fading out."

Shuvalov, Viktor
C, 6´, 190 lbs, b: Ruzajevka, USSR, 12/15/1923

| Season | Club, League | Regular Season | | | | |
		GP	G	A	Pts	PIM
1948–49	Dzerzhinets Chelyabinsk, USSR	18	16	*	*	*
1949–50	VVS MVO, USSR	14	31	*	*	*
1950–51	VVS MVO, USSR	15	26	*	*	*
1951–52	VVS MVO, USSR	16	31	*	*	*
1952–53	VVS MVO, USSR	21	44	*	*	*
1953–54	CDKA, USSR	15	20	*	*	*
WEC–54	USSR	7	7	*	*	*
1954–55	CSK MO, USSR	*	13	*	*	*
WEC–55	USSR	8	6	*	*	*
1955–56	CSK MO, USSR	*	21	*	*	*
OWG–56	USSR	7	5	*	*	*
1956–57	CSK MO, USSR	*	7	*	*	*
1957–58	SKVO Kalinin, USSR	*	13	*	*	*
	USSR Totals	150	222	*	*	*
	OWG/WEC Totals	22	18	*	*	*

Won OWG (1956)
Won WEC (1954)
USSR Champion (1951, 1952, 1953, 1955, 1956)

Dmitri Ukolov

Asked to list the greatest defensemen in Soviet hockey during the 1950s, many fans will first name Nikolai Sologubov, Alfred Kuchevsky and Ivan Tregubov. The name Dmitri Ukolov may not be at the top of many lists, but as a member of teams that were national champions, Olympic champions, world champions twice and European champions five times, Ukolov deserves a place in the lineup. He may not have been as outstanding as Sologubov when it came to good, hard bodychecking, but Ukolov's unique playing style and skill as a positional player have earned him a place among hockey's greatest defensemen.

Dmitri Ukolov's (front) unique playing style and skill as a positional player have earned him a place among hockey's greatest defensemen.

Ukolov wasn't an attack defenseman and hardly ever made a daring breakaway at the opposing team's goal. His principal strategy was to maintain total control of the zone around his goal and to back up his partners in the defense line by instantly stepping into the breach. In a positional game, it is very important for a player to anticipate events on the ice and to choose his position with unerring accuracy. Ukolov's deft choices are testimony to his sophisticated understanding of the complexities of hockey.

But Ukolov's actions on the ice weren't limited to the area around his own goal. When the opposing team was locked in its own zone, Ukolov joined his teammates in firing shots on goal. Taking up his position on the blue line, he would wait until the goalie was blocked out by his own and the other team's players before letting go with a sizzling slapshot.

Playing for the national team, Ukolov scored eight goals—an exceptional accomplishment for a defenseman playing a positional style of game. Many of Ukolov's assists were crucial game-clinchers. When it came to stiff bodychecking, Ukolov's excellent physical condition secured his reputation as a tough opponent, even against the formidable Canadians.

Dmitri Ukolov played 11 years in Soviet major-league hockey—from 1949 to 1960. In five of those seasons, he played for the USSR national team. And in all of those years, both with his home team and in the national lineup, he was considered one of the most reliable players. Ukolov never vied for a leading role but did the work that had to be done on the ice honestly and skillfully, never taking the easy way out. It was these qualities that assured him a permanent place in the lineup despite stiff competition from his fellow players on both his home team and the national squad.

Ukolov, Dmitri
D, 5'9", 190 lbs, b: Moscow, USSR, 10/23/1929, d: 1993

Season	Club, League	Regular Season				
		GP	G	A	Pts	PIM
1948–49	Spartak Moscow, USSR	*	3	*	*	*
1949–50	CDKA, USSR	*	3	*	*	*
1950–51	CDKA, USSR	*	5	*	*	*
1951–52	CSK MO, USSR	*	8	*	*	*
1952–53	CSK MO, USSR	*	4	*	*	*
1953–54	CSK MO, USSR	11	3	*	*	*
WEC–54	USSR	7	3	*	*	*
1954–55	CSK MO, USSR	*	1	*	*	*
WEC–55	USSR	8	2	*	*	*
1955–56	CSK MO, USSR	*	2	*	*	*
OWG–56	USSR	5	1	*	*	*
1956–57	CSK MO, USSR	*	5	*	*	*
1957–58	CSK MO, USSR	*	4	*	*	*
WEC–58	USSR	7	2	1	3	4
1958–59	CSK MO, USSR	*	4	*	*	*
WEC–59	USSR	5	0	*	*	*
1959–60	CSK MO, USSR	*	6	*	*	*
1960–61	CSKA, USSR	*	0	*	*	*
	USSR Totals	250	48	*	*	*
	OWG/WEC Totals	32	8	*	*	*

Won OWG (1956)
Won WEC (1954)
USSR Champion (1950, 1955, 1956, 1958, 1959, 1960, 1961)

Alexander Uvarov

Uvarov was a team player of the highest caliber, always placing the team's interests above his own.

Alexander Uvarov came to Canadian-style hockey from the bandy rink, so he was well qualified to make fast progress in the new type of hockey played with a puck instead of a ball. He had speed, a smooth skating style and stamina. It didn't take him long to master the technique of stickhandling the puck, and within two years of switching to hockey, Uvarov had become an exceptional player.

Uvarov had all the requirements—speed, technique, powerful shots on goal and an ability to help out in defense, never using his body to block shots. He had an outstanding ability to think on the ice. He controlled the game and orchestrated play by speeding up or slowing down the pace of the game when needed. In short, he was the pace-setter.

He had excellent peripheral vision of the entire rink, quickly assessed the situation and, knowing the capabilities of his partners, fed them the puck at the right moment for a breakaway. When Valentin Kuzin or Yuri Krylov scored brilliant goals on passes from Uvarov, he often seemed to remain in the background, only occasionally sending the puck into the net himself. In fact, Uvarov had a knack for being in the right place at the right time and anticipating goal-scoring positions.

Better than anyone else, Uvarov was able to conceal his intentions on the ice, frequently baffling his opponents. He would stop in the middle of the rink as if looking for someone to pass the puck to. Just when it looked as if he'd missed the chance for an attack by holding on to the puck too long and the opposition was about to grab the puck, Uvarov would flip it over to a teammate, who would score the goal.

Another of Uvarov's special talents was his versatility, a characteristic shared by his fellow forwards on the Dynamo line of Krylov–Uvarov–Kuzin. These three players usually set the pace of the game by attacking aggressively and scoring the most goals. But on the national team, the Uvarov line was frequently given another assignment. At the time, the Czechs, Swedes and to a lesser extent the Canadians had strike lines that were especially powerful. To contain these lines or neutralize them was a real challenge for their opponents. The Dynamo line on Team USSR specialized in defusing the opposition without sacrificing their own goal-scoring record.

Their principal strategy was to keep the puck away from the opposition using a series of short, swift passes. After luring their opponents to the middle zone, the Dynamo line would then instigate several unexpected and swift counterattack maneuvers, creating a crisis situation at the opposing team's goal. A classic example was the final game between the USSR and Canada for the gold medal at the 1956 Olympic hockey tournament. The game was virtually won by the Dynamo forward line, with two goals scored by Krylov and Kuzin that were set up by high-precision passes from Uvarov. Having distracted the Canadians with a protracted series of whirlwind passes, the Dynamo players then capitalized on opportunities to mount their own attacks on goal.

Uvarov, Alexander
C, 5′7″, 160 lbs, b: Moscow, USSR, 3/7/1922, d: 1998

| Season | Club, League | Regular Season | | | | |
		GP	G	A	Pts	PIM
1948–49	Dynamo Moscow, USSR	17	16	*	*	*
1949–50	Dynamo Moscow, USSR	22	20	*	*	*
1950–51	Dynamo Moscow, USSR	15	21	*	*	*
1951–52	Dynamo Moscow, USSR	16	15	*	*	*
1952–53	Dynamo Moscow, USSR	18	19	*	*	*
1953–54	Dynamo Moscow, USSR	16	24	*	*	*
WEC–54	USSR	7	2	*	*	*
1954–55	Dynamo Moscow, USSR	18	28	*	*	*
WEC–55	USSR	8	3	*	*	*
1955–56	Dynamo Moscow, USSR	23	15	*	*	*
OWG–56	USSR	7	3	*	*	*
1956–57	Dynamo Moscow, USSR	20	16	*	*	*
WEC–57	USSR	5	0	*	*	*
1957–58	Dynamo Moscow, USSR	33	11	*	*	*
1958–59	Dynamo Moscow, USSR	25	6	*	*	*
1959–60	Dynamo Moscow, USSR	36	11	*	*	*
	USSR Totals	259	202	*	*	*
	OWG/WEC Totals	27	8	*	*	*

Won OWG (1956)
Won WEC (1954)
USSR Champion (1954)

But these counterattacks were only one of the techniques employed by the Dynamo line. Another utilized high-speed attacks down the wings. This maneuver relied on the precise coordination of all three members of the line. Unlike the Central Army and Soviet Wings lines, the Dynamo line didn't distinguish between scoring and assisting players. Each one worked for the other, and the right to finish off an attack was given to the player in the most expedient position. Changing positions was commonplace, and many times center Uvarov would pass the puck from the flanks or from behind the goal to wingers closest to the goal crease.

Alexander Uvarov (wearing a hat) could take in the whole rink with his excellent peripheral vision, quickly assess the situation and feed his partners the puck at the right time because he knew what they could do.

Uvarov was a team player of the highest caliber, always placing the team's interests above his own. It is no wonder that Alexander Uvarov wore his team captain armband for 11 seasons in a row. He continued to play hockey until he was 38 years old.

Sven "Tumba" Johansson

Sven "Tumba" Johansson made his debut in Swedish national hockey in the early 1950s, a period during which the game experienced a resurgence in popularity and a new generation of players took to the ice and became world-class stars. At the age of 20, the long-legged youth from the Stockholm suburb of Tumba joined the national team roster without ever having played junior-league hockey—a rare occurrence.

It was during the 1950s, with the rookie Johansson playing for Sweden's Tre Kronor team, that the Swedes twice took the World Championship. On December 12, 1951, at Stockholm's Olympic Stadium, Johansson scored a total of five goals, beating the United States 10–1.

Always closely watched by his opponents, Sven "Tumba" Johansson (right) met with plenty of tough bodychecks during his career but never resorted to a combative style himself.

Johansson played for Tre Kronor until the 1966 World Championship in Ljubljana, Yugoslavia. In the 245 games he played for the national squad, he scored a total of 259 goals.

While Tumba was playing for Stockholm's Djurgarden, the team won the Swedish championship eight times; he was on Swedish teams that won the European championship four times; three times he was on teams that won the World Championship—and he held that record for 36 years, until 1998 in Switzerland, when Jonas Bergqvist and Mats Sundin joined him as record holders.

Sven Johansson (right) was world champion with Sweden three times, a record he held for 36 years until he was joined by Jonas Bergqvist and Mats Sundin.

Johansson easily baffled his opponent's defense line with his fantastic starting speed, excellent technique and hockey savvy. At the 1957 World Championship in Moscow, Soviet coaches, fearful of Johansson's reputation, assigned one of their players the sole task of guarding Tumba and keeping him out of play. Johansson quickly figured out the Soviet ploy and turned the tables on his opponents by dogging one of the Soviet players, with the result that two members of the USSR squad were effectively taken out of active play. That strategy left the Swedes free to take on what was left of the Soviet team. Tre Kronor's win over the heavily favored Soviet home team created a sensation in Moscow. The Swedish forward line of Eilert Maatta, Tumba Johansson and Erling Lindstrom dominated the game.

Always closely watched by his opponents, Johansson met with plenty of tough bodychecks during his career but never resorted to that combative style of play himself. For Johansson, the best revenge was always scoring brilliant goals. Johansson was a natural forward and a true sportsman. He once said, "Anyone trying to kill individual play kills the game of hockey itself."

In 1962 Johansson was plagued by injuries and the Tre Kronor coaches seriously considered not sending him to the World Championship in Colorado Springs. But Johansson wasn't easily beaten. Throughout his career, he had proven he was extremely resilient and had the capacity to recuperate quickly. Known for his rigorous training schedule, Johansson would jog or skate every morning to increase his strength and stamina. At the last minute, Tumba was included as the 17th and final player on the roster. True to form, he made an amazing recovery and played his usual brilliant game in Colorado; the Swedish team captured the title.

Johansson, Sven "Tumba"
C, 6′2″, 181 lbs, b: Stockholm, Sweden, 8/27/1931

Season	Club, League	Regular Season				
		GP	G	A	Pts	PIM
1948–52	Djurgarden, Sweden	*	*	*	*	*
OWG–52	Sweden	8	7	*	*	*
1952–53	Djurgarden, Sweden	*	*	*	*	*
WEC–53	Sweden	5	5	*	*	*
1953–54	Djurgarden, Sweden	*	*	*	*	*
WEC–54	Sweden	7	7	*	*	*
1954–55	Djurgarden, Sweden	*	*	*	*	*
WEC–55	Sweden	8	9	*	*	*
1955–56	Djurgarden, Sweden	*	*	*	*	*
OWG–56	Sweden	7	3	*	*	*
1956–57	Djurgarden, Sweden	*	*	*	*	*
WEC–57	Sweden	7	6	*	*	*
1957–58	Djurgarden, Sweden	*	*	*	*	*
WEC–58	Sweden	7	7	7	14	2
1958–60	Djurgarden, Sweden	*	*	*	*	*
OWG–60	Sweden	6	5	*	*	*
1960–61	Djurgarden, Sweden	*	*	*	*	*
WEC–61	Sweden	7	2	*	*	*
1961–62	Djurgarden, Sweden	*	*	*	*	*
WEC–62	Sweden	7	7	6	13	2
1962–63	Djurgarden, Sweden	*	*	*	*	*
WEC–63	Sweden	7	6	6	12	0
OWG–64	Djurgarden, Sweden	*	*	*	*	*
WEC–64	Sweden	7	8	3	11	0
1964–65	Djurgarden, Sweden	*	*	*	*	*
WEC–65	Sweden	7	4	0	4	6
1965–66	Djurgarden, Sweden	*	*	*	*	*
WEC–66	Sweden	7	3	*	*	*
	Sweden Totals	*	*	*	*	*
	OWG/WEC Totals	97	79	84	163	*

Named Best Forward at WEC (1957, 1962)
Won WEC (1953, 1957, 1962)
Sweden Champion (1954, 1955, 1958, 1959, 1960, 1961, 1962, 1963)

Johansson's enthusiasm for the game of hockey never left him. He was a frequent guest on radio programs, promoted his favorite brand of hockey stick and even appeared at a water-skiing school with Sweden's Princess Birgitta. He taught the Swedish monarch how to ice skate, wrote a weekly hockey commentary for a popular newspaper and published two books in Sweden, *Tumba Speaks Frankly* and *Tumba's Hockey School*.

Johansson went into private business after hanging up his skates for good in 1966 and opened a number of golf clubs. Always a generous benefactor where his former hockey comrades were concerned, Johansson once arranged for a former Soviet opponent, Viktor Yakushev, to have thigh surgery in Stockholm—a gesture very much in character. He was inducted into the International Ice Hockey Federation's Hall of Fame in 1997.

Yuri Pantyukhov

For Yuri Pantyukhov, there was never one specific role or single partner during his career on the ice. He was a first-class forward who could take on any assignment. He was referred to as a "clutch" player because he always came to the rescue when the going got tough, and he did it in a very matter-of-fact way, without ever trying to steal the limelight.

Pantyukhov's strong points were his high speed, excellent maneuvering, sharp and wide peripheral vision and his ability to keep cool even in the most challenging situations. His coach, Anatoli Tarasov, claimed that Pantyukhov's starting speed wasn't always up to par, but Pantyukhov more than made up for this one shortcoming with his many other exceptional skills.

Another of Pantyukhov's great talents was the ease with which he was able to get along with all his partners, no mean feat since great hockey stars aren't always easygoing and even-tempered.

Yuri Pantyukhov began playing bandy with the Dynamo Moscow club and then played Canadian-style hockey with the Krylja Sovetov (Soviet Wings) lineup from 1949 to 1951. He was then sent to the Air Force team and from 1953 to 1961 wore the uniform of the Central Red Army club. This constant moving around was because Pantyukhov was regarded as a valuable player and desirable teammate. He was a courageous player who didn't shun tough bodychecking, even when up against a brawny adversary.

In the 13 years that Pantyukhov played top-level hockey, his team won the national championship eight times and the USSR Cup six times. He was also on World and Olympic

Yuri Pantyukhov never had a specific role or single partner throughout his career on the ice.

Pantyukhov, Yuri
RW, 5'9", 166 lbs, b: Moscow, USSR, 3/15/1931, d: 1981

Season	Club, League	Regular Season				
		GP	G	A	Pts	PIM
1949–50	Krylja Sovetov, USSR	*	0	*	*	*
1950–51	Krylja Sovetov, USSR	*	1	*	*	*
1951–52	VVS MVO, USSR	*	10	*	*	*
1952–53	VVS MVO, USSR	*	11	*	*	*
1953–54	CDSA, USSR	11	5	*	*	*
1954–55	CSK MO, USSR	*	19	*	*	*
1955–56	CSK MO, USSR	*	25	*	*	*
OWG–56	USSR	7	2	*	*	*
1956–57	CSK MO, USSR	*	16	*	*	*
WEC–57	USSR	6	7	*	*	*
1957–58	CSK MO, USSR	*	20	*	*	*
WEC–58	USSR	7	2	2	4	*
1958–59	CSK MO, USSR	*	7	*	*	*
WEC–59	USSR	8	2	*	*	*
1959–60	CSKA, USSR	*	6	*	*	*
1960–61	CSKA, USSR	*	1	*	*	*
	USSR Totals	230	121	*	*	*
	OWG/WEC Totals	28	13	*	*	*

Won OWG (1956)
USSR Champion (1952, 1953, 1955, 1956, 1958, 1959, 1960, 1961)

A HISTORY OF WORLD HOCKEY

Yuri Pantyukhov (front) never shunned bodychecking even a brawny opponent and never shied away from confrontation.

championship teams and three times on European championship teams.

Pantyukhov scored 121 goals in 230 games in national championship play. If this seems less than spectacular, it may be because Pantyukhov was frequently given a multitude of tasks to perform on the ice. At the 1957 World Championship in Moscow, Pantyukhov replaced Mikhail Bychkov on the right wing of Alexei Guryshev's line. In that tournament, the Pantyukhov–Guryshev–Khlystov line scored 18 goals—eight by Guryshev and seven by Pantyukhov. Guryshev's line was focused on maximizing the scoring capabilities of the forward, so to score almost as many goals as Guryshev did was a notable accomplishment.

During Team USSR's first trip to Canada for a series of exhibition games in 1957, Pantyukhov put his best foot forward and showed that he was a powerful competitor.

Karel Gut

The players Karel Gut (right) coached called him "Vraska" (Wrinkle) because of his worried expression, which faded only when he managed a slight smile.

The first player Czech hockey experts ever described as a "defensive forward," Karel Gut loved to make daring moves that weren't very popular with coaches. But with 35 goals in 114 international matches to his credit, he hasn't yet been outperformed by any other defenseman.

Part of the reason for his versatility may be that he started out as a forward and was retrained as a defenseman when he transferred from a small, unknown club to big-league hockey. Born on September 16, 1927, Gut comes from the community of Uhrineves, which was countryside when he was young but has now been engulfed by the city of Prague. He played soccer as a boy and was also skilled at field hockey. During World War II, he played on a team with some of the stars of the day, including Josef Malecek and Jaroslav Drobny.

His first break came in 1949 when he attended "boot camp" with ATK Prague. "Two seasons with this club influenced my whole life. I shared changing rooms with such greats as Vladimir Kobranov or Premysl Hainy. Across the hall was the famous LTC Prague, with Stanislav Konopasek, Vaclav Rozinak, Bohumil Modry and Josef Trousilek. I had respect, but I also had the desire and patience to assert myself."

It took him some time to get into that lineup, but an opportunity finally presented itself. In one of his first matches in the league, he had scored three goals. After playing a few more games, his confidence increased so much that he could comfortably do his job alongside some of the best players in the game. He got his next chance on the Czech national team. Then, after two years of military service, he accepted an offer from Tatra Smichov even though LTC, and then Spartak Prague, had also shown an interest.

Two years later, however, he appeared with Spartak after all. He spent 11 seasons with that team, playing beside some of the greatest names in Czech hockey and at one point forming a defensive duo with Frantisek Tikal. "When I went on the attack, he covered my back. Of course, we both made mistakes, but we treated one another with patience. That's why our partnership lasted so long."

Between 1952 and 1960, he took part in nine World Championships and in 1955 he was named best defenseman. However, as a player, Gut was never on a gold medal team. That came much later when, together with Jan Starsi, he led the Czech national team from the bench.

Gut played for Spartak till 1964 and immediately transferred to coaching. Among other achievements, he developed a new summer training program with harder and more frequent workouts. He was already well on his way to success coaching Spartak and the German club EV Landshut. While he was with EV Landshut, they won championship titles in 1970 and 1983. He alternated between the two clubs until 1973, when, after a contract with the juniors and the Czech B team, he became a coach of the national team, a position he held for 10 years.

The players he coached called him "Vraska" (Wrinkle) because of his worried expression, which faded when he managed a slight smile. It was a fairly accurate nickname, for Gut always radiated calm and showed little emotion. "I was basing everything on hard work in the preparation. At the same time, I preferred the psychology of dealing with people. A coach has to be demanding, consistent and precise. However, the player must feel that he is the coach's partner, with different rights and obligations, not his subordinate."

Gut, Karel
D, 5′10″, 190 lbs, b: Uhrineves, Czechoslovakia, 9/16/1927

Season	Club, League	Regular Season				
		GP	G	A	Pts	PIM
1949–51	ATK Prague, Czechoslovakia	*	*	*	*	*
1951–52	Tatra Smichov, Czechoslovakia	*	*	*	*	*
OWG–52	Czechoslovakia	8	2	*	*	*
1952–53	Tatra Smichov, Czechoslovakia	*	*	*	*	*
WEC–53	Czechoslovakia	4	2	*	*	*
1953–54	Spartak Prague Sokolovo, Czechoslovakia	*	*	*	*	*
WEC–54	Czechoslovakia	7	1	*	*	*
1954–55	Spartak Prague Sokolovo, Czechoslovakia	*	*	*	*	*
WEC–55	Czechoslovakia	8	2	*	*	*
1955–56	Spartak Prague Sokolovo, Czechoslovakia	*	*	*	*	*
OWG–56	Czechoslovakia	7	4	*	*	*
1956–57	Spartak Prague Sokolovo, Czechoslovakia	*	*	*	*	*
WEC–57	Czechoslovakia	7	4	*	*	*
1957–58	Spartak Prague Sokolovo, Czechoslovakia.	*	*	*	*	*
WEC–58	Czechoslovakia	7	1	*	*	*
1958–59	Spartak Prague Sokolovo, Czechoslovakia	*	*	*	*	*
WEC–59	Czechoslovakia	7	2	*	*	*
1959–60	Spartak Prague Sokolovo, Czechoslovakia	*	*	*	*	*
OWG–60	Czechoslovakia	7	1	*	*	*
1960–64	Spartak Prague Sokolovo, Czechoslovakia	*	*	*	*	*
	Czechoslovakia Totals	300	86	*	*	*
	OWG/WEC Totals	62	19	*	*	*

Named Best Defenseman at WEC (1955)
Czechoslovakia Champion (1954)

His approach led to success on international ice. Under his coaching, Czechoslovakia won the World Championship two years in a row—1976 and 1977. A year later, Czechoslovakia ended up one goal away from a third gold medal. Instead, the Soviet players had cause to rejoice.

Karel Gut and his wife, Irena, were married on New Year's Eve 1949. They chose this special date because they wanted a church wedding, which would be disallowed under new regulations imposed by the communist government starting in the new year. Their union has lasted to this day.

Gut's marriage with hockey has lasted even longer. He left the national team after the Lake Placid Olympics in 1980, which was followed by another contract with Landshut. In 1983 he became head of the Czech Hockey Union. He started mapping hockey history in great detail and published many books on the subject that were also firsts. He heads the union to this day. "I try to do this job as honestly as all others before that. We have had results. Therefore, one day when I am replaced by someone younger, I will leave with the satisfaction that I haven't hindered Czech hockey in any way." He was inducted into the International Ice Hockey Federation's Hall of Fame in 1998.

Valentin Kuzin

After winning 2–0 against the Canadians on February 4, 1956, in Cortina d'Ampezzo, Italy, Team USSR, first-time participants in the Olympic hockey tournament, won the gold medal. Both goals were scored by players from Dynamo's forward line—Yuri Krylov and Valentin Kuzin, who had played for many years alongside teammate Alexander Uvarov.

That was a glorious moment for the famous forward line that is rightfully considered one of the best in Soviet hockey.

No one in Russian hockey players could skate like Valentin Kuzin (center)—not even Bobrov or Kharlamov.

Terrific speed and sudden, unpredictable moves were the hallmarks of the style of play that Valentin Kuzin (center) perfected.

Kuzin, Valentin
LW, 5′9″, 175 lbs, b: Novosibirsk, USSR, 9/23/1926, d: 1998

Season	Club, League	Regular Season				
		GP	G	A	Pts	PIM
1948–50	Dynamo Novosibirsk, USSR	*	*	*	*	*
1950–51	Dynamo Moscow, USSR	15	12	*	*	*
1951–52	Dynamo Moscow, USSR	16	14	*	*	*
1952–53	Dynamo Moscow, USSR	20	16	*	*	*
1953–54	Dynamo Moscow, USSR	14	15	*	*	*
WEC–54	USSR	6	2	*	*	*
1954–55	Dynamo Novosibirsk, USSR	18	12	*	*	*
WEC–55	USSR	8	4	*	*	*
1955–56	Dynamo Novosibirsk, USSR	22	10	*	*	*
OWG–56	USSR	7	4	*	*	*
1956–57	Dynamo Novosibirsk, USSR	25	14	*	*	*
1957–58	Dynamo Novosibirsk, USSR	33	21	*	*	*
1958–59	Dynamo Novosibirsk, USSR	27	15	*	*	*
1959–60	Dynamo Novosibirsk, USSR	36	17	*	*	*
1960–61	Dynamo Novosibirsk, USSR	7	1	*	*	*
	USSR Totals	233	147	*	*	*
	OWG/WEC Totals	21	10	*	*	*

Won OWG (1956)
Won WEC (1954)
USSR Champion (1954)

Those who saw the outstanding Valentin Kuzin in action still regard him as one of the best forwards in Russian hockey. He could play either left wing or center, and his terrific speed was probably a result of his years of playing bandy. He was a bold and stubborn player who had mastered the art of stickhandling and had a powerful shot that he could execute on the fly.

He began playing in Novosibirsk and by the age of 17 was playing for the city's leading team. Kuzin's remarkable skills were honed on the frozen expanses of Siberian ice. In fact, that level of proficiency was typical of all the early players of Canadian-style hockey in the USSR. But probably one of the most distinguishing features of those pioneers was their superb and effortless way of skating. Kuzin seemed to fly over the ice and was able to swerve in any direction without losing his pace. Whenever he received a pass, he would raise his head and never look down at the puck again. Terrific speed and sudden, unpredictable moves with head held high were the hallmarks of this forward's style of play.

Lars "Lasse" Bjorn

It has become one of the legends of Swedish hockey, but what happened in Moscow in 1957 when Lars "Lasse" Bjorn was asked to lead the Tre Kronor national team in singing the Swedish national anthem is a true story. At the crucial moment, Bjorn, as acting captain of the victorious Swedish team, couldn't remember the words to anything but a well-known and very popular Swedish drinking song, "Heland Ger" (Let's Drink It All).

"I've been asked about this many times," Lars Bjorn says. "And yes, it really happened. You know, standing there in front of so many people made me nervous, and when I looked back at the guys behind me, I realized that the only song I could remember was this drinking song. So that's why..."

Bjorn was amazed to find himself on the podium at the Lenin Stadium in Moscow at all. It was only because a late goal by Eilert Maatta ended the game in a 4–4 draw against the heavily favored Soviet team that the gold medal was awarded to Tre Kronor. And Bjorn, in that glorious moment for Swedish and world hockey, gave 55,000 spectators a rousing rendition of the popular Swedish drinking anthem.

Lars Bjorn was a giant of a man and a giant among hockey players. Born on December 16, 1931, Bjorn was on two World Championship teams and an Olympic bronze-winning team and had nine Swedish titles in his career with the Djurgarden team of Stockholm.

It is appropriate that the word "bjorn" means bear in Swedish. When the Djurgarden boys came out to play, Bjorn was the player everyone was afraid to challenge. At the international level, he was one of the first Swedes to show the world that the Canadians were just hockey players, not the supermen everyone believed them to be. "There's one good way of getting around in hockey," Lars Bjorn said. "It's to fear nothing. If someone hits me, I'm gonna hit him back and see to it that he never tries it with me again."

Bjorn's career began with the suburban Traneberg team, just across the bridge from Stockholm. He started playing for Djurgarden in 1947 for a less than spectacular sum of money compared to the millions of dollars that move around in the hockey world today. "They gave me a new pair of skates, and I really appreciated that," he remembers.

Bjorn made his debut with the national Tre Kronor team in 1951 and played 217 games for them, making him one of the all-time greats in Swedish hockey. He was paired with Djurgarden teammate Roland Stoltz to form a hulking defense duo known for their tough hockey playing but also loved by all for their easygoing charm outside the rink. The well-built Djurgarden duo often sandwiched attacking opponents between them.

Lars Bjorn (center) was referred to as "Lasse" (the Menace)—the player everyone was afraid to challenge.

Bjorn, Lars "Lasse"
D, 6'2", 191 lbs, b: Stockholm, Sweden, 12/16/1931

Season	Club, League	Regular Season				
		GP	G	A	Pts	PIM
1949–52	Djurgarden, Sweden	*	*	*	*	*
OWG–52	Sweden	7	0	*	*	*
1952–53	Djurgarden, Sweden	*	*	*	*	*
WEC–53	Sweden	5	0	*	*	*
1953–54	Djurgarden, Sweden	*	*	*	*	*
WEC–54	Sweden	7	1	*	*	*
1954–55	Djurgarden, Sweden	*	*	*	*	*
WEC–55	Sweden	8	1	*	*	*
1955–56	Djurgarden, Sweden	*	*	*	*	*
OWG–56	Sweden	7	3	*	*	*
1956–57	Djurgarden, Sweden	*	*	*	*	*
WEC–57	Sweden	7	3	*	*	*
1957–58	Djurgarden, Sweden	*	*	*	*	*
WEC–58	Sweden	7	1	1	2	8
1958–59	Djurgarden, Sweden	*	*	*	*	*
WEC–59	Sweden	8	0	*	*	*
1959–60	Djurgarden, Sweden	*	*	*	*	*
OWG–60	Sweden	1	0	*	*	*
1960–61	Djurgarden, Sweden	*	*	*	*	*
WEC–61	Sweden	7	1	*	*	*
1961–67	Djurgarden, Sweden	*	*	*	*	*
	Sweden Totals	*	*	*	*	*
	OWG/WEC Totals	64	10	*	*	*

Named Best Defenseman at WEC (1954)
Won WEC (1953, 1957)
Sweden Champion (1950, 1954, 1955, 1958, 1959, 1960, 1961, 1962, 1963)

Another often-quoted story claims that once, when Stoltz followed teammate Sven "Tumba" Johansson across the blue line, losing the puck to an opposing forward, he yelled back to defenseman Bjorn, "Nail him, Lasse, nail him." And Lasse nailed him. This so-called legend also happens to be true.

Bjorn was inducted into the International Ice Hockey Federation's Hall of Fame in 1998.

Nikolai **Puchkov**

Fans came to games especially to watch Nikolai Puchkov play.

The Central Red Army hockey club was once playing at the USSR national championships in Siberia. It was bitterly cold, the mercury hovering around -40° Celsius. The Moscow goalie was frozen stiff and allowed a couple of easy goals, one from the center of the rink. "You have to toughen yourself," coach Anatoli Tarasov told him after the game.

A couple of weeks later, coach Tarasov went out for some fresh air at the team's training camp outside Moscow. It wasn't as cold as in Siberia—only about 20 below. Tarasov encountered the goalie, Nikolai Puchkov, who was also taking a stroll. As they stood there chatting, the coach suddenly noticed that the goalie was barefoot. "I'm toughening myself," Puchkov explained.

He was a sportsman to the core. Puchkov could have made a career as a soccer goalkeeper—he once blocked two penalty shots in a single game. Instead, he chose to explore the unfamiliar game of Canadian hockey to achieve his dream. From morning until night he devoted himself to the art of defending the goal. After a regular team workout, with only a quilted jacket to protect him, he would ask his forwards to pepper him with shots as fast and hard as they could. "I'm doing this for the team," Puchkov would explain.

Puchkov aimed for perfection and became one of the most skillful Soviet hockey players of his generation. Fans came to games especially to watch him. The supple athleticism of this massive and powerful man was indeed impressive. He made it look easy to nab a sizzling puck in his glove while doing the splits. Puchkov tended goal for the Soviet nationals during their first two championship seasons in 1954 and 1956. The team's 2–0 Olympic victory against the Canadians in 1956 was won largely thanks to the inspired moves of the goalkeeper.

But after only a year and a half, Puchkov was in trouble with the national coaches. The Soviet team was invited for the first time to play a series of games in Canada. And the slot in front of the net was often occupied by another goalie, Yevgeny Yorkin, even though Puchkov was a better goaltender on practically all counts. Puchkov, then 27 and in his prime, was controlling his game brilliantly. The coaches had only one, very significant, complaint: Puchkov believed Canadian hockey was superior to Soviet hockey.

Puchkov had decided to examine the very essence of hockey in his own way. He was the only one among the Soviet players to

Puchkov, Nikolai
G, 5´10˝, 180 lbs, b: Moscow, USSR, 1/30/1930

Season	Club, League	Regular Season		
		GP	GA	Avg
1949–53	VVS MVO, USSR	*	*	*
1953–54	CDSA, USSR	*	*	*
WEC–54	USSR	5	5	1.00
1954–55	CSKA MO, USSR	*	*	*
WEC–55	USSR	5	8	1.60
1955–56	CSKA MO, USSR	*	*	*
OWG–56	USSR	7	7	1.00
1956–57	CSKA MO, USSR	*	*	*
WEC–57	USSR	5	8	1.60
1957–58	CSKA MO, USSR	*	*	*
WEC–58	USSR	5	7	1.40
1958–59	CSKA MO, USSR	*	*	*
WEC–59	USSR	6	13	2.17
1959–60	CSKA, USSR	*	*	*
OWG–60	USSR	5	19	3.80
1960–62	CSKA, USSR	*	*	*
1962–63	SKA Leningrad, USSR	*	*	*
	USSR Totals	220	*	*
	OWG/WEC Totals	38	67	1.76

Named Best Goaltender at WEC (1959)
Won OWG (1956)
Won WEC (1954)
USSR Champion (1951, 1952, 1953, 1955, 1956, 1958, 1959, 1960, 1961)

quickly learn the English language and he filled his room with Canadian books about hockey. Tarasov recalls in his memoirs that Puchkov became much too cautious with respect to the Canadians. "Our talented players are out of their league," Puchkov decided, "and that is why we must now play defensively against the pioneers of hockey; otherwise, they will tear us apart."

As a result, Puchkov wasn't invited to the 1961 World Championship. When the new goalies on the USSR national squad performed poorly, Puchkov told the coaches to their faces, "You're making a terrible mistake—I'm the best goalie." Before the 1963 championship, the problem of selecting the goalie for the national squad became crucial. Coaches Arkady Chernyshov and Anatoli Tarasov decided to give Puchkov one last chance. By that time, Puchkov had already left Tarasov's Central Army club and was playing for Leningrad. With Puchkov in the net against the U.S. team, the Soviets won 12–3. In the game in which Puchkov's competitors stood in the net, the Soviets won 12–0. The coaches decided against using him on the team.

Nikolai Puchkov (right) was the only Soviet player of his era to believe Canadian hockey was superior.

He was a man of unusual courage and stubbornness. At workouts, if he missed a terrific shot on goal and the puck slammed him in the forehead, he would say (after coming to), "Let's keep going; we haven't finished yet." Puchkov was the first player who dared to show his dissatisfaction with Tarasov as a coach when the latter failed to bring a special training manual for goalies to the workout.

In 1963 Puchkov became a coach and for almost 15 years he was head coach of the Leningrad Army club. Under his guidance, the Leningrad team took third place in the 1971 national championship for the first time. Puchkov remained true to his beliefs while coaching. His team played "from the goalkeeper," relying on a dependable defense and sending out dagger-like counterattacks. Under Puchkov's coaching, this strategy had been honed to perfection and was wonderful to watch. But Tarasov, now Puchkov's competitor, remarked indignantly, "That team is playing Stone Age hockey."

For Puchkov, the game of hockey meant more than anything. He traveled the road he believed in and did things in his own way.

Nikolai Sologubov

On December 22, 1946, the first national ice hockey (or Canadian hockey, as it was called then) tournament was held in the USSR. Fifty years later, in 1996, the date was commemorated by the selection of an imaginary All-Star team from among the all-time greats of Soviet hockey. Among the defensemen, the two names most frequently mentioned were Sologubov and Fetisov. Fetisov was acclaimed beyond the borders of present-day Russia, but Sologubov had just as formidable a reputation inside the country.

Almost every North American hockey fan knows Slava Fetisov, yet Nikolai Sologubov, who retired from the game in the early 1960s, is practically a stranger in Canada. Veterans of the Whitby Dunlops, the Belleville McFarlands and the Kitchener-Waterloo Dutchmen who met with Sologubov at World Championships and during the Soviet tour of Canada in the late 1950s and early 1960s would remember this Russian defenseman, however.

Nikolai Sologubov was born in Moscow in 1924. The Sologubov family lived on the outskirts of the city, near a meat-processing plant that sponsored a soccer and hockey club. From his early teens, Nikolai played on its junior team. He was considered by some to be a ruthless, daredevilish boy who belonged on an outdoor rink playing bandy, a Russian version of hockey.

After the Nazi invasion of the USSR in the summer of 1941, Sologubov's life changed drastically. He was drafted into the Red Army and joined the marines. Then he switched to military intelligence and during his service in that department was wounded three times, the third time receiving considerable shrapnel in his legs.

After the Nazi invasion of the USSR in 1941, Nikolai Sologubov joined the marines and was wounded three times.

After 15 months of treatment for his injuries, Sologubov was released from hospital with a warning to forget about playing hockey. But with blind persistence and dedication, Sologubov managed to overcome his ailments and return to the ice. At first he had to put in long hours of training just to build up his strength. Then he began playing on the Russian Red Army hockey team in Khabarovsk and was voted the best defenseman. When the Red Army command was instructed by government authorities to develop the game of hockey, Nikolai Sologubov, now a 25-year-old officer, was summoned to Moscow and appointed to the CSKA (Central Red Army club). At 32, Sologubov made his debut on the Soviet national team at the 1956 World and European Championships. After the 1956 Olympics, which were won by the Soviets, Bob Bauer, coach of Canada's Kitchener-Waterloo Dutchmen, said that the new Russian defenseman Sologubov was talented enough to play on any NHL team.

Legendary Russian forward Vsevolod Bobrov once played alongside Sologubov with the CSKA. Later he joined the Air Force hockey club, and a showdown between Sologubov and Bobrov followed. Their duel attracted up to 25,000 spectators to Dynamo Moscow's outdoor rink.

Bobrov later recalled: "He was the fastest and most powerful defenseman of his time. Even if I was in a better position at any playing moment, I could never allow myself to relax, since Sologubov would never stop fighting—he would overtake me and prevent me from shooting the puck and often slide the puck off my blade. Yet I didn't have problems with many defensemen, including Canadians, whereas playing against Nikolai, I could be happy if I scored just a single goal in a game."

His stickhandling and his mobility on the ice were superb. Even coach Anatoli Tarasov, who taught that a defenseman ought never to take chances when playing against an opponent

Sologubov, Nikolai
D, 5′10″, 185 lbs, b: Moscow, USSR, 3/8/1924, d: 1988

Season	Club, League	Regular Season				
		GP	G	A	Pts	PIM
1949–50	CDKA, USSR	*	7	*	*	*
1950–51	CDKA, USSR	*	5	*	*	*
1951–52	CDSA, USSR	*	15	*	*	*
1952–53	CDSA, USSR	*	13	*	*	*
1953–54	CDSA, USSR	16	12	*	*	*
1954–55	CSK MO, USSR	*	6	*	*	*
WEC–55	USSR	7	1	*	*	*
1955–56	CSK MO, USSR	*	5	*	*	*
OWG–56	USSR	6	1	*	*	*
1956–57	CSK MO, USSR	*	10	*	*	*
WEC–57	USSR	7	9	*	*	*
1957–58	CSK MO, USSR	*	12	*	*	*
WEC–58	USSR	6	0	1	1	2
1958–59	CSK MO, USSR	*	7	*	*	*
WEC–59	USSR	8	1	*	*	*
1959–60	CSKA, USSR	*	11	*	*	*
OWG–60	USSR	5	1	8	9	2
1960–61	CSKA, USSR	*	6	*	*	*
WEC–61	USSR	6	0	0	0	0
1961–62	CSKA, USSR	*	12	*	*	*
1962–63	CSKA, USSR	*	5	*	*	*
WEC–63	USSR	1	1	0	1	0
1963–64	CSKA, USSR	*	3	*	*	*
1964–65	SKA Kalinin, USSR	2	4	*	*	*
	USSR Totals	350	128	*	*	*
	OWG/WEC Totals	46	14	*	*	*

Named Best Defenseman at OWG/WEC (1956, 1957, 1960)
Won OWG (1956)
Won WEC (1963)
USSR Champion (1950, 1955, 1956, 1958, 1959, 1960, 1961, 1963, 1964)

in his own zone, made an exception for Sologubov. He would rush into the opposition zone, outfox his opponents and either score a goal himself or make a very good pass to his teammate, allowing the teammate to score.

Nikolai Sologubov's career was short-lived. He didn't play an official game of hockey until the age of 25. Yet at 32, he was already a European superstar and voted the best defenseman at international contests in 1956, 1957 and 1960. In 1963 Sologubov, almost 40 years old, won a second and final world title with the Soviet national team. The following year, Sologubov left the Central Red Army club forever.

Nikolai Sologubov (front) didn't play an official game of hockey until he was 25, but at 32 he was a European superstar and was three times voted the best defenseman at international tournaments.

Robert John "Jackie" McLeod

Robert John "Jackie" McLeod was born in Regina, Saskatchewan, in 1930. His career in hockey began at the age of 15 with the Notre Dame Hounds of the Saskatchewan Junior Hockey League. A right winger, McLeod played with the Hounds for two seasons before moving on to join the Moose Jaw Canucks, which won the provincial championships in 1949. A multi-sport athlete, McLeod spent his off-seasons playing lacrosse, football and baseball to stay in shape for hockey.

At the age of 19, McLeod became a professional. He joined the New York Rangers and stayed with them for five seasons, although except for 1950–51 he played more frequently for the Saskatoon Quakers than he did for the Rangers. At the end of the fifth season, he moved over to the Western Hockey League to join the Quakers. During that time, he was a regular member of the WHL All-Star Team.

McLeod was traded to Vancouver by the New York Rangers for Bill Ezinicki and cash in 1955. He was claimed by the Rangers after a stint with the Vancouver Canucks, then of the WHL, in an Intra-League Draft in 1958, and then traded again to Victoria by Calgary (again in the WHL) for cash in 1960.

With 10 goals and four assists, Jackie McLeod was the leading scorer on the Canadian team that won the World Championship in 1961.

In 1961 he was a key member of the Trail (British Columbia) Smoke Eaters—a team that played one exhibition season in 1960–61 but won the World Championship, the last Canadians to do so for more than 35 years. With 10 goals and four assists, McLeod was the team's leading scorer and was named to the tournament All-Star team.

The following year, McLeod again competed in the Worlds, this time as a member of the Moose Jaw (Saskatchewan) Canucks. He scored five goals and registered seven assists in that tournament, and in the next edition of the World Championship, playing with the Saskatoon Quakers, McLeod registered five goals and eight assists in only seven games.

McLeod, Robert John "Jackie"
RW, 5´9˝, 150 lbs, b: Regina, Sask., 4/30/1930

Season	Club, League	Regular Season					Playoffs				
		GP	G	A	Pts	PIM	GP	G	A	Pts	PIM
1949–50	New York Rangers, NHL	38	6	9	15	2	7	0	0	0	0
1950–51	New York Rangers, NHL	41	5	10	15	2					
1951–52	New York Rangers, NHL	13	2	3	5	2					
	Cincinnati Mohawks, AHL	49	14	18	32	38	2	0	1	1	2
1952–53	New York Rangers, NHL	3	0	0	0	2					
	Saskatoon Quakers, WHL	55	30	47	77	28	13	8	11	19	19
1953–54	Saskatoon Quakers, WHL	69	33	38	71	46	6	4	1	5	4
1954–55	New York Rangers, NHL	11	1	1	2	4					
	Saskatoon — Vancouver, WHL	51	20	31	51	44	5	2	1	3	14
1955–56	Saskatoon Quakers, WHL	70	34	49	83	97	3	1	1	2	14
1956–57	Vancouver Canucks, WHL	41	30	19	49	30					
1957–58	Vancouver Canucks, WHL	68	44	27	71	45	9	14	4	18	8
1958–59	Saskatoon Quakers, WHL	63	27	26	53	44					
1959–60	Calgary Stampeders, WHL	62	28	28	56	50					
1960–61	Moose Jaw Canucks, SSHL	12	6	6	12	6					
	Trail Smoke Eaters, WHL	17	14	13	27	21					
WEC–61	Canada	7	10	4	14	6					
1961–62	Moose Jaw Canucks, SSHL	29	27	25	52	36					
WEC–62	Canada	7	5	7	12	6					
1962–63	Saskatoon Quakers, SSHL	31	37	51	88	22	1	0	0	0	2
WEC–63	Canada	7	5	8	13	6					
1963–64	Saskatoon Quakers, SSHL	40	52	52	104	22	11	7	8	15	6
1964–65	Moose Jaw Canucks, SSHL	2	3	4	7	12	10	12	12	24	10
WEC–66	Canada	7	4	0	4	4					
	NHL Totals	106	14	23	37	12	7	0	0	0	0
	WEC Totals	28	30	20	50	26					

Won WEC (1961)

A few years later, McLeod turned his skills to coaching. In 1965 he became general manager and coach of Canada's national team, the team introduced by Father David Bauer to train players during the full hockey season both on the ice and in the classroom. Under McLeod's guidance, the Canadian Olympic team won the bronze medal in the 1968 Winter Games.

In the early 1970s, McLeod was named coach and general manager of the Saskatoon Blades in the Western Hockey League, a position he held for a decade. More than just a behind-the-bench coach, McLeod was well known for giving much of his time to counseling young athletes and preparing them for life after hockey.

McLeod retired from the Western Hockey League in 1980 and was inducted into the Saskatchewan Sports Hall of Fame on June 6, 1984. In 1999 he was inducted into the International Ice Hockey Federation's Hall of Fame.

Alfred Kuchevsky

Even stars like Vsevolod Bobrov respected Alfred Kuchevsky's expert passing ability.

Alfred Kuchevsky, defenseman for the Krylja Sovetov Moscow (Soviet Wings), is rightfully regarded as a star after 12 years with his home team and six years in the national lineup. For both teams, he was the linchpin of the defense line. During his entire playing career, Kuchevsky was the only member of the Soviet Wings to play in the national lineup.

Kuchevsky was tall, well built, handsome and refined, and on the ice he was level-headed and restrained. This didn't prevent him from taking chances, but his moves never involved harmful intent, rough play or excessive risk. He could accurately size up the situation on the ice, and when things looked complicated, he preferred not to take chances. When necessary, he could hold the puck to slow down the pace of the game, and when there was an opening, he could stickhandle his way past his opponent and flip the puck over to an attacking forward.

When it came to precision passing, Kuchevsky was in a class by himself, although sometimes he was accused of holding the puck too long. But his skillful passing would usually bring the game within close range of the other team's goal. Even stars like Vsevolod Bobrov respected Kuchevsky's expert passing ability.

Bobrov and Kuchevsky played side by side on the national squad and enjoyed being teammates, but locally they played for rival clubs. The coach always gave Kuchevsky, his most experienced and reliable defenseman, the job of checking powerful and aggressive forwards. And the most powerful of all, by Kuchevsky's own admission, was Bobrov. From Bobrov's perspective, there was no defenseman he couldn't outwit.

Kuchevsky wasn't always the ideal defenseman. Sometimes he got carried away with the game or monopolized the puck to the detriment of team play. Yet he had one very valuable asset—when it was critical, he could focus his energy and play to the limit of his ability.

Hockey fans often ask whether a star player of the 1950s would be able to hold his own on the ice today. We can compare hockey players of different eras only on the basis of natural talent, because everything else—physical condition and technical and tactical skills—can be acquired and improved with time and training. If we measure Alfred Kuchevsky by that yardstick, he would be one of the best players on the ice today.

Kuchevsky, Alfred
D, 5'11", 175 lbs, b: Moscow, USSR, 5/17/1931

Season	Club, League	Regular Season				
		GP	G	A	Pts	PIM
1949–54	Krylja Sovetov, USSR	*	*	*	*	*
WEC–54	USSR	7	3	*	*	*
1954–55	Krylja Sovetov, USSR	*	*	*	*	*
WEC–55	USSR	8	0	*	*	*
1955–56	Krylja Sovetov, USSR	*	*	*	*	*
OWG–56	USSR	4	0	*	*	*
1956–58	Krylja Sovetov, USSR	*	*	*	*	*
WEC–58	USSR	2	0	0	0	0
1958–60	Krylja Sovetov, USSR	*	*	*	*	*
OWG–60	USSR	7	0	3	3	8
1960–61	Krylja Sovetov, USSR	*	*	*	*	*
	USSR Totals	240	37	*	*	*
	OWG/WEC Totals	28	3	*	*	*

Won OWG (1956)
Won WEC (1954)
USSR Champion (1957)

Connell "Connie" Broden

A native of Montreal, Quebec, Connell "Connie" Broden spent his entire professional hockey life with his hometown team, the Canadiens, in only three NHL seasons from 1955 to 1958. His entire NHL totals are similarly unimpressive at first glance—six games, two goals and one assist.

But Broden is in the pro hockey record books because in 1957–58 he packed into a single season two achievements that most players spend an entire career trying to accomplish. That year, Broden played with the Whitby (Ontario) Dunlops, the OHA senior league team that won the World Championship for Canada in Norway, and the Canadiens squad that captured the Stanley Cup.

That season, Broden, who had graduated from Loyola University in Montreal, initially decided not to report to the Canadiens' farm team in Springfield, Massachusetts, in the American Hockey League. He thought he'd retire instead. "Whitby was looking for players and they approached Sam Pollock, the manager of the Canadiens," recalled Broden. "They really wanted Ralph Backstrom, who was then playing junior, but they wound up with me." Pollock gave Broden permission to play for the Dunlops and he ended up being an important part of the gold medal team.

In the 1957–58 season, Connie Broden won the World Championship with the Canadian team and also captured the Stanley Cup with the Montreal Canadiens.

Broden, Connel "Connie"
C, 5'8", 160 lbs, b: Montreal, Que., 4/6/1932

Season	Club, League	Regular Season					Playoffs				
		GP	G	A	Pts	PIM	GP	G	A	Pts	PIM
1950–51	Montreal Royals, QSHL	1	0	0	0	0					
1952–53	Cincinnati Mohawks, IHL	57	29	38	67	39	9	4	3	7	8
1953–54	Cincinnati Mohawks, IHL	59	32	37	69	34	11	3	2	5	14
1954–55	Shawinigan Cataracts, QHL	62	27	35	62	25	13	5	7	12	15
1955–56	Montreal Canadiens, NHL	3	0	0	0	2					
	Shawinigan Cataracts, QHL	61	17	40	57	45	11	2	8	10	8
1956–57	Shawinigan Cataracts, QHL	68	20	29	49	32					
	Montreal Canadiens, NHL						6	0	1	1	0
1957–58	Whitby Dunlops, OHA Sr.	7	5	9	14	0					
WEC–58	Canada	7	12	7	19	6					
1957–58	Montreal Canadiens, NHL	3	2	1	3	0	1	0	0	0	0
1958–59	Hull-Ottawa Canadiens, EOHL	26	11	12	23	40	7	0	4	4	20
	NHL Totals	6	2	1	3	2	7	0	1	1	0
	WEC Totals	7	12	7	19	6					

Won WEC (1958)
Won Stanley Cup (1957, 1958)

Broden scored at least one goal in every game of the 1958 World Championship in Oslo, Norway, and finished the tournament as the top scorer for Canada. The Dunlops steamrollered through the round-robin competition, hammering Poland 14–1, Norway 12–0, Finland 24–0 (including a 10-goal third period), Sweden 10–2, Czechoslovakia 6–0 and the U.S. 12–1. In the final game, against the USSR, the score was tied 1–1 in the final period when Broden scored to put the Canucks in front. But the USSR scored once more to tie before Canada scored two late ones to win it by a score of 4–2. In all, Canada outscored the competition 82–6 and Broden recorded 11 goals and seven assists.

When the World Championship was over, Broden returned home, this time to play professionally for Montreal in the NHL, where he helped the Habs to a Cup win that year over the Boston Bruins. To date, there is only one other player who has won a world title and a Stanley Cup in the same year—Ken Morrow, who was a member of the 1980 U.S. Olympic squad that won the gold at Lake Placid and a defenseman on the Islanders' championship team the same spring.

After he retired from pro hockey, Broden stayed in the city of his birth and went to work for Molson Breweries, attaining the position of vice-president and director of production services for the company.

Nikolai Khlystov

Though he played in Alexei Guryshev's shadow, Nikolai Khlystov always maintained his own style.

Nikolai Khlystov, left winger for the Krylja Sovetov Moscow (Soviet Wings) and Team USSR, occupies a special place in the history of Soviet hockey. Even though he wasn't of the same caliber as players like Bobrov, Babich or Guryshev, his contribution to the sport was significant.

Khlystov was the one player in Soviet hockey who possessed all the capabilities required of a forward—instantaneous start and superb speed, stickhandling and maneuverability. In a matter of seconds, Khlystov could streak down the ice from one goal to the other in spite of the opposition's attempts to stop him. He had an uncanny ability to slip between the boards and a rival player and appear behind the opponent's net in the blink of an eye. Besides his innate gift of speed, he had a unique skating technique that was natural and effortless. His stickhandling was characterized not by the typical wide, sweeping movements but rather by short, almost combat-style maneuvers. But Khlystov was really in his element when playing in the opposing team's zone, avoiding body contact with defensemen with his deft moves.

At 18 years old, Khlystov joined the Wings when the team already had a star goal scorer in Alexei Guryshev. When the coaches placed Khlystov on the left wing in Guryshev's line, he accepted the position without question. During his entire career, he played left wing to Guryshev, never aspiring to anything greater. Khlystov always supported Guryshev and made no attempt to change his status. Some might have viewed this as a lack of ambition, but for Khlystov, that wasn't important. While seeming to play in Guryshev's shadow, Khlystov always maintained his individuality and style.

One of Khlystov's most remarkable talents was his passing ability; for this alone he deserves recognition. His passes were always dead accurate, well timed and expedient, no matter where they came from. He had an uncanny ability to sense Guryshev's every move, knowing all the secrets of his game and doing everything possible to maximize them.

It is regrettable for Khlystov that the system of points for goals plus assists hadn't yet been introduced in Soviet hockey. This would have made it possible to view such players of the past as Babich, Viktor Yakushev and Khlystov in a different light. Guryshev scored most of his goals on assists from Khlystov. When Khlystov left hockey and Guryshev continued with new partners, the role Khlystov had played in the Guryshev line became all the more apparent. Guryshev's game was never the same without Khlystov feeding him the puck, proving that the line is only as good as the individuals in it.

Khlystov, Nikolai
LW, 5'5", 142 lbs, b: Moscow, USSR, 11/10/1932, d: 1999

Season	Club, League	Regular Season				
		GP	G	A	Pts	PIM
1950–52	Krylja Sovetov, USSR	*	*	*	*	*
1952–53	Krylja Sovetov, USSR	*	22	*	*	*
1953–54	Krylja Sovetov, USSR	*	*	*	*	*
WEC–54	USSR	6	0	*	*	*
1954–55	Krylja Sovetov, USSR	*	20	*	*	*
WEC–55	USSR	8	2	*	*	*
1955–56	Krylja Sovetov, USSR	*	22	*	*	*
OWG–56	USSR	7	1	*	*	*
1956–57	Krylja Sovetov, USSR	*	*	*	*	*
WEC–57	USSR	7	3	*	*	*
1957–58	Krylja Sovetov, USSR	*	*	*	*	*
WEC–58	USSR	7	0	*	*	*
1958–61	Krylja Sovetov, USSR	*	*	*	*	*
	USSR Totals	250	150	*	*	*
	OWG/WEC Totals	35	6	*	*	*

Won OWG (1956)
Won WEC (1954)
USSR Champion (1957)

Genrikh Sidorenkov

Some hockey players are considered ahead of their time, anticipating the future and introducing new elements to the game that then get picked up by other players. These innovators, such as Nikolai Sologubov, rely on their teammates' abilities and dependable playing style to back them up. When Sologubov played defense for the Central Red Army club and the national squad, his defense partner was Genrikh Sidorenkov, a skilled and reliable player.

Sidorenkov wasn't an innovator like Sologubov, nor was he considered a dazzling player. Nonetheless, he had mastered all the techniques and skills required of a good defenseman and could be depended on by his team's attacking forwards whenever they were

Genrikh Sidorenkov's common-sense style was evident in practically everything he did on the ice.

Sidorenkov, Genrikh
D, 5´10″, 185 lbs, b: Moscow, USSR, 8/11/1931, d: 1992

Season	Club, League	Regular Season				
		GP	G	A	Pts	PIM
1949–50	Krylja Sovetov, USSR	*	1	*	*	*
1950–51	Krylja Sovetov, USSR	*	4	*	*	*
1951–52	CDSA, USSR	*	0	*	*	*
1952–53	CDSA, USSR	*	1	*	*	*
1953–54	CDSA, USSR	16	1	*	*	*
WEC–54	USSR	3	0	*	*	*
1954–55	CSK MO, USSR	*	2	*	*	*
1955–56	CSK MO, USSR	*	7	*	*	*
OWG–56	USSR	6	0	*	*	*
1956–57	CSK MO, USSR	*	2	*	*	*
WEC–57	USSR	7	2	*	*	*
1957–58	CSK MO, USSR	*	3	*	*	*
WEC–58	USSR	6	1	2	3	0
1958–59	CSK MO, USSR	*	5	*	*	*
WEC–59	USSR	7	0	*	*	*
1959–60	CSK MO, USSR	*	6	*	*	*
OWG–60	USSR	7	1	2	3	8
1960–61	CSKA, USSR	*	1	*	*	*
WEC–61	USSR	7	3	4	7	2
1961–62	CSKA, USSR	*	3	*	*	*
1962–63	SKA Leningrad, USSR	32	4	*	*	*
1963–64	SKA Leningrad, USSR	30	2	*	*	*
1964–66	SKA MVO (2), USSR	*	*	*	*	*
	USSR Totals	310	42	*	*	*
	OWG/WEC Totals	43	7	*	*	*

Won OWG (1956)
Won WEC (1954)
USSR Champion (1955, 1956, 1958, 1959, 1960, 1961)

in the opposition zone. With his low-key playing style, Sidorenkov preferred hard wrist shots that the goalie couldn't see coming rather than slapshots that telegraphed themselves.

In the 1950s, when Sidorenkov was playing, it wasn't yet a standing rule that defensemen join a forward attack on the opponent's goal. Yet in the eight years he played for the national squad, he scored a dozen goals in 100 games.

Sidorenkov's common-sense style was evident in practically everything he did on the ice. He was a pragmatic and cautious player, exerting the minimum effort required in bodychecking while maximizing his excellent physical attributes of height and weight. Sidorenkov was respected for his well-organized game and nearly flawless performance.

For any hockey player in the international arena, playing against Canadian teams has been considered an important test of both his professional and competitive qualities. Sidorenkov played against the Canadians a number of times and passed this test with honors. Never tense in the face of adversity, he always played with a relaxed confidence that set him apart from the other players and garnered him the respect he deserved.

Lars-Erik Lundvall

When Tre Kronor won a silver medal at the 1964 Olympics, Lars-Erik Lundvall was awarded the Golden Skate as Sweden's best player.

Swedish forward Lars-Erik Lundvall is always remembered along with two other great forwards, Ronald Pettersson and Nils Nilsson. It was the coach of the national team, Volke Jansson, who brought them together, and they became one of the best lineups in the history of Swedish hockey, making their debut at the Cortina d'Ampezzo Olympics in 1956. Unfortunately, the team, Tre Kronor, didn't excel that year in the Italian resort town. But the next year, in Moscow, Sweden caused a sensation when they captured the world gold by tying the decisive game with the USSR 4–4.

In Moscow, the rookie threesome scored 24 out of Sweden's 64 goals, and they continued playing together long after they were no longer rookies. Lundvall, a skillful skater, had an excellent wrist shot and was a good tactician, adapting well to Nilsson's irregular style.

Lundvall was born on April 3, 1934, in Karlskoga and at nine years of age played for the local Bofors. At 15, he played on the adolescent, junior and adult teams of this club.

He first appeared on the national team in a game against Norway on November 12, 1954, and on November 24, playing against Norway again, he scored his first goal. That same day, Ronald Pettersson made his debut with Tre Kronor. Lundvall's most memorable goal is the one he scored against the USSR at the 1963 World Championship in Stockholm when Sweden beat the Soviets 2–1.

The glory of Gothenburg's hockey is tied to Lundvall, Pettersson and Ulf Sterner. Playing for Vastra Frolunda in the second division, Lundvall and Pettersson, together with center Ove Sterner, brother of the famed Ulf Sterner, scored 95 goals—six to eight per game. Both scorers remained on the national team even though they were now playing in the second division.

When Vastra Frolunda made it to the senior league, Ulf Sterner was added to the lineup. They made a perfect threesome. One of their unforgettable moments came on November 8, 1962, when Lundvall scored two goals against Stockholm's Djurgarden—national champion at the time—at the Nea Ullevi arena, packed with 23,000 excited fans. Vastra Frolunda won the game 3–2.

Unfortunately, Lundvall was plagued by injuries, two of which could have ended his career. In 1961 he didn't go to Switzerland to play in the world tournament because he'd been badly hurt in a friendly game against Canada and carried off on a stretcher. A knee ligament was torn, but despite grim prospects, Lundvall returned to the ice in a big way. In 1962, in Colorado Springs, he helped his team capture the World Championship.

After the 1964 Olympics in Innsbruck, where Tre Kronor achieved second place, Lundvall was awarded the Golden Skate as Sweden's best player. He continued to play for the national team until 1965, but was seriously injured again in a friendly game against the U.S. before the World Championship in Tampere, Finland. This time he was forced to quit. In all, he appeared in 207 games playing for Tre Kronor.

He left the ice but not hockey, choosing instead to become a coach. He had coached from 1960 to 1963 while playing for Gothenburg's Vastra Frolunda and returned to coaching in 1964 to 1966 and 1973 to 1975.

When he finally said goodbye to hockey, Lundvall settled in Gothenburg and bought a gas station, later selling it because of a disagreement over the municipal ecology policies. He and his wife have no children and are now retired. From time to time, Lars-Erik Lundvall participates in veteran games and still loves to watch the sport to which he devoted the best years of his life.

Lundvall, Lars-Erik
LW, 5´11˝, 176 lbs, b: Karlskoga, Sweden, 4/3/1934

Season	Club, League	Regular Season				
		GP	G	A	Pts	PIM
1950–55	Bofors, Sweden	*	*	*	*	*
WEC–55	Sweden	7	1	*	*	*
1955–56	Sodertalje, Sweden	*	*	*	*	*
OWG–56	Sweden	7	3	*	*	*
1956–57	Sodertalje, Sweden	*	*	*	*	*
WEC–57	Sweden	7	5	*	*	*
1957–58	Sodertalje, Sweden	*	*	*	*	*
WEC–58	Sweden	7	3	*	*	*
1958–59	Sodertalje, Sweden	*	*	*	*	*
WEC–59	Sweden	8	4	*	*	*
1959–60	Sodertalje, Sweden	*	*	*	*	*
OWG–60	Sweden	7	9	*	*	*
1960–62	Vastra Frolunda, Sweden	*	*	*	*	*
WEC–62	Sweden	6	7	3	10	2
1962–63	Vastra Frolunda, Sweden	*	*	*	*	*
WEC–63	Sweden	5	3	0	3	6
1963–64	Vastra Frolunda, Sweden	*	*	*	*	*
OWG–64	Sweden	7	2	3	5	0
1964–68	Vastra Frolunda, Sweden	*	*	*	*	*
	Sweden Totals	*	*	*	*	*
	OWG/WEC Totals	61	37	*	*	*

Won WEC (1957, 1962)
Sweden Champion (1956, 1965)

Pete Conacher

In possession of one of the most famous surnames in hockey, left winger Pete Conacher, who was born in 1932 in Toronto, played professionally for the Chicago Black Hawks, the New York Rangers and his hometown Leafs. His NHL career spanned the years 1951 to 1958, and he went on to play in the AHL with the Buffalo Bisons and the Hershey Bears until 1966.

Pete Conacher wasn't a star like his father or uncle, but he won a gold medal for Canada in 1959.

His father, Charlie, began as a goalie in minor hockey before setting out on an NHL Hall of Fame career as a right winger. Young Pete played junior hockey for the Galt (Ontario) Black Hawks and at 19 was signed by the big-league Chicago team of the same name in 1951. In fact, on the very day that Pete was called up by Chicago—November 16—his uncle Roy, who was the league scoring champion back in 1948–49, decided to hang up his skates. "The papers all had the story that I was replacing my uncle, but they were just bringing me up for a three-day trial," Pete remembered later.

In a further family connection, Pete's uncle Lionel Conacher was a Hall of Fame defenseman who played for the Pittsburgh Pirates, New York Americans, Montreal Maroons and Chicago Black Hawks of the old NHL in the 1920s and 1930s.

Pete was aware that comparisons were going to be made between him and the famous relatives who had preceded him in the pro ranks. "I was certainly conscious of the comparisons that writers made between me and my father and uncle," he said. "It never bothered me…because they accepted me for what I was, but it bothered the fans because I was never going to be as good." In his three-team pro career, Pete Conacher scored 47 goals and 39 assists in 229 total games.

Not just a one-sport athlete, Pete played sandlot baseball five nights a week when he returned to Toronto in the off-seasons. In the last six years of his career, he had no regrets about staying in the AHL. "I was really a much more complete hockey player by then," he says. "But I have no regrets that I didn't go up again. I think that I had my chances. You only get so many. In those days, there were a lot of great players in the AHL."

When he retired, he played for the NHL old-timers' team for 15 years and then took a job as a floor trader on the Toronto Stock Exchange, a job that he had first held during his summers off from pro hockey.

Conacher, Pete
LW, 5′10″, 165 lbs, b: Toronto, Ont., 7/29/1932

Season	Club, League	Regular Season					Playoffs				
		GP	G	A	Pts	PIM	GP	G	A	Pts	PIM
1951–52	Chicago Black Hawks, NHL	2	0	1	1	0					
1952–53	Chicago Black Hawks, NHL	41	5	6	11	7	2	0	0	0	0
	St. Louis Flyers, AHL	29	12	16	28	6					
1953–54	Chicago Black Hawks, NHL	70	19	9	28	23					
1954–55	Chicago Black Hawks, NHL	18	2	4	6	2					
	New York Rangers, NHL	52	10	7	17	10					
1955–56	New York Rangers, NHL	41	11	11	22	10	5	0	0	0	0
	Buffalo Bisons, AHL	18	17	15	32	6					
1956–57	Buffalo Bisons, AHL	60	26	29	55	16					
1957–58	Toronto Maple Leafs, NHL	5	0	1	1	5					
	Buffalo Bisons, AHL	48	12	32	44	2					
1958–59	Belleville McFarlands, EOHL	1	0	0	0	0					
WEC–59	Canada	8	7	3	10	2					
1959–60	Buffalo Bisons, AHL	56	5	10	15	16					
1960–61	Hershey Bears, AHL	69	11	24	35	4	8	1	2	3	4
1961–62	Hershey Bears, AHL	70	27	29	56	16	7	2	0	2	5
1962–63	Hershey Bears, AHL	70	29	24	53	6	15	5	4	9	0
1963–64	Hershey Bears, AHL	72	34	26	60	12	6	0	3	3	2
1964–65	Hershey Bears, AHL	63	34	24	58	10	15	8	2	10	4
1965–66	Hershey Bears, AHL	60	14	20	34	4					
	NHL Totals	229	47	39	86	57	7	0	0	0	0
	WEC Totals	8	7	3	10	2					

Won WEC (1959)

John **Mayasich**

When John Mayasich was added to a lineup composed mainly of college players on the American Olympic hockey team in 1960, he was considered one of the best amateur hockey players in the United States. Team officials were glad he accepted their invitation, because his tenacity and physical style played a major role in the Americans' unexpected gold medal.

Mayasich grew up as a promising young star in Eveleth, Minnesota. His high school hockey team won 79 consecutive games and four state championships between the 1947–48 and 1950–51 seasons. He continued his stalwart play with the University of Minnesota Gophers as well, being named an all-American in 1952–53, 1953–54 and 1954–55. Mayasich was named to the NCAA All-Tournament Team in 1954 after he orchestrated the Gophers' trip to the collegiate finals that year. He also led the Western Collegiate Hockey Association in scoring with 78 points in 1953–54 and 80 points the following year.

The 1960 Olympics in Squaw Valley, California. In front of the home crowd, Bill Cleary (front row, third from the left) scored the first goal against the USSR, and the U.S. held on to win the final game 3–2. The tenacity and physical style of John Mayasich (back row, first from the left) also played a major role in the Americans' unexpected gold medal.

Mayasich started off internationally in 1956 as a part of the United States Olympic team that won the silver medal. In addition to the victorious 1960 Olympic team, he represented the U.S. at the World Championships on five more occasions, in 1958, 1961, 1962, 1966 and 1969. Mayasich was highly sought after by professional teams but stayed with the amateur Green Bay Bobcats after his collegiate years and during his international heyday. He was a jack of all trades on the Bobcats— player, coach, general manager and even sales manager.

Off the ice, Mayasich was a high school teacher, an encyclopedia salesman and an employee at a radio station, where he became as respected in the field of communications as he was in hockey. "Hopefully, players of today and tomorrow can be so lucky," said Mayasich of his post-hockey career. One local sportswriter said of the retired Mayasich that he "always recognized the pressure—for his teams to win, to do well himself, to get to college, to graduate, and pressure with his current job. It is a story of living with what one perceives as pressure and succeeding."

For his part, Mayasich was always aware of his position as a role model for children and of his obligation to maximize his talents. "In my era, and for a lot of us who played hockey up on the Iron Range, hockey opened doors to opportunity," he said. "A hockey player with academic prowess had opportunities others didn't enjoy. And when a college scholarship was offered to you, it was

A HISTORY OF WORLD HOCKEY

assumed by everyone you would accept. It was never a question, 'Is this what I want?'" he added. "But, again, it was an opportunity I couldn't afford to turn down."

Mayasich developed the ability to cope with pressure early in his life. His father had worked in the mines for 45 years, and the expectations that his son would succeed in college were extremely high. "Everyone expected me to score a couple of goals every game and do well academically," he said, "but it was a welcome challenge to the alternative, a life in those very mines."

Dave Peterson, the 1988 Olympic hockey coach for the United States, once said that Mayasich "was probably one of the best American hockey players I have ever seen. But he played during an era that didn't include Americans in the pro game." Mayasich was inducted into the United States Hockey Hall of Fame in 1976 and the International Ice Hockey Federation's Hall of Fame in 1997.

Bill Cleary

Long associated with the prestigious hockey program at Harvard University, Bill Cleary provided the offensive firepower for the American national team in two of its best Olympic showings. He was a prolific scorer in the college ranks, setting records with Harvard as a player in the 1950s, and led the U.S. to a silver medal at the 1956 Games and then a gold at the Olympics in 1960. He later became the head coach at Harvard and guided the team to consistently good results for 19 years, including a national college championship in 1989.

Cleary attended Belmont Hill, a prep school known for its hockey prospects, in his home town of Cambridge, Massachusetts. He and his family were surrounded by hockey and the world of academia in equal measure, watching and playing for the teams at nearby Harvard. Cleary had one of the greatest seasons in U.S. college history in 1954–55. He set records that still stand today at Harvard, including 42 goals and 89 points in only 21 games. He tied a school record with six goals in one game and set a new mark with eight goals in another. Cleary was selected as an all-Ivy League player, all-East and finally all-American. His team won the Beantop Tournament, a Boston-area competition, then took the Ivy League title before finishing third at the national NCAA tournament.

Cleary first joined the U.S. national team prior to the 1956 Olympic Games at Cortina d'Ampezzo, Italy. The Americans were surprisingly strong and finished just behind the Soviet Union, edging out Canada for the silver medal. Cleary was back on the team in 1959 at the World Championship, though the Americans struggled and finished fourth. Just before the 1960 Olympics in Squaw Valley, California, Cleary's younger brother, Bob, also an outstanding player for Harvard, was added to the U.S. squad. The Cleary brothers were put on a line with Bob McVey. It was a potent combination. The Americans were undefeated in the preliminary round and scored a close-fought 2–1 victory over the Canadians in the medal round to set up a championship game with the Soviet Union. In front of the home crowd, with millions watching on television, Bill Cleary scored the first goal against the USSR and the U.S. held on to win the game 3–2. Cleary was his team's top scorer with seven goals and seven assists, averaging two points per game, and finished third in total points in the tournament.

Cleary hung up his skates soon after the U.S. victory and started a successful insurance business. He maintained a close relationship with Harvard hockey and was the freshman coach at the school starting in 1968. He was an assistant to the legendary Cooney Weiland in 1970 and took over the head coaching job after it was vacated by Weiland in 1971. He was behind the bench until his retirement in 1990, compiling a 324–201–22 record. Harvard won 11 Ivy League titles under his guidance and reached the final four in the NCAA tournament seven times. He won his first national title in his third trip to the championship game. Cleary was selected to the United States Hockey Hall of Fame in 1976 and was inducted into the International Ice Hockey Federation's Hall of Fame in 1997.

Ivan Tregubov

In the winter of 1952, a uniformed soldier appeared in a tiny reception room at the CSKA (Central Red Army club) training camp. "Private Tregubov is here, upon your order!" the soldier said. Private Tregubov was being summoned to the Central Red Army sports club on the advice of Nikolai Sologubov, who served with him and played on the same team with him in Khabarovsk in Russia's Far East. When Tregubov saw a puck lying on the table, he asked what it was doing there. "It is the puck, son, and you have to learn to handle it as soon as possible."

The Army hockey team was stationed on the outskirts of Moscow and conducted its training exercises there. On an undersized rink, which the players themselves watered down, Tregubov received his basic training in the game of hockey, spending six to eight hours a day learning all the tricks of the game: forward and backward skating, stickhandling, passing, checking and shooting.

Ivan Tregubov saw the puck for the first time when he was 22 years old.

By the end of his first week, Tregubov had played a couple of practice games and on the eighth day he was included on the team roster for a game against the CSKA's toughest opponent at the time, Dynamo Moscow. On coach Anatoli Tarasov's advice, the 22-year-old Tregubov was to share a room with Nikolai Sologubov. The two men from Khabarovsk were surprisingly alike in their preferences and their idiosyncrasies, and they spent a lot of free time together. The camaraderie between the two defensemen contributed significantly to their excellent coordination on the ice when they were playing on the same line.

Some of the mental aspects of Tregubov's game were a mirror reflection of Sologubov's style. In strength and stamina, Tregubov was superior to

Tregubov, Ivan
D, 5′1″, 183 lbs, b: Komsomolsk-Na-Amure, USSR, 1/19/1930, d: 1992

Season	Club, League	Regular Season				
		GP	G	A	Pts	PIM
1951–52	CDSA, USSR	*	2	*	*	*
1952–53	CDSA, USSR	*	4	*	*	*
1953–54	CDSA, USSR	15	6	*	*	*
1954–55	CSK MO, USSR	*	4	*	*	*
WEC–55	USSR	8	1	*	*	*
1955–56	CSK MO, USSR	*	8	*	*	*
OWG–56	USSR	7	2	*	*	*
1956–57	CSK MO, USSR	*	7	*	*	*
WEC–57	USSR	7	4	*	*	*
1957–58	CSK MO, USSR	*	8	*	*	*
WEC–58	USSR	7	2	6	8	6
1958–59	CSK MO, USSR	*	5	*	*	*
WEC–59	USSR	8	1	*	*	*
1959–60	CSK MO, USSR	*	5	*	*	*
1960–61	CSKA, USSR	*	6	*	*	*
WEC–61	USSR	7	4	2	6	2
1961–62	CSKA, USSR	*	2	*	*	*
1962–63	SKA Kujbyshev, USSR	*	0	*	*	*
1963–64	SKA Kujbyshev (2), USSR	*	0	*	*	*
1964–65	Khimik Voskresensk, USSR	*	0	*	*	*
	USSR Totals	221	57	*	*	*
	OWG/WEC Totals	44	14	*	*	*

Named Best Defenseman at WEC (1958, 1961)
Won OWG (1956)
USSR Champion (1955, 1956, 1958, 1959, 1960, 1961)

When Ivan Tregubov took a wrist shot in a game in Siberia when it was 20 degrees below zero, the puck hit the goal post and broke into pieces.

his older partner, but they had the same dedication and ruthlessness and the same loathing for defeat. Yet the younger man didn't copy his superior; rather they supplemented each other and that made them perfect partners on the ice.

Ivan Tregubov was more inclined to be a defensive defenseman, and while he would join his teammates on the attack, he never skated too deep into the opposition zone. He preferred to shoot at the net from the blue line, but his long, powerful slapshot put fear in the hearts of opposition goalies. Once, during a game in Siberia at about 20 degrees below zero, when Tregubov took a wrist shot, the puck hit the goal post and broke into pieces.

In one regard, however, the two defensemen's tastes were polar opposites. Sologubov was tough—he would tackle his opponents like enemies on a battlefield. Tregubov was also inclined to strike back when under attack, but he never got rough with opponents who preferred gentlemanly play. His brilliant skating and excellent stickhandling allowed him to gain an advantage over opponents even without heavy contact. Due to his fair play, Tregubov was voted the best defenseman at the 1958 and 1961 World Championships.

Ivan Tregubov was part of that first generation of Soviet hockey players who got their initial lessons in the game as mature men. In Russia today, children are taught the science of ice hockey from the age of six, but Tregubov learned the basics of the game in only a week and measured against today's highly trained players would still be considered a leading defenseman.

Yuri Krylov

Yuri Krylov played without shoulder pads because he felt less constrained.

Yuri Krylov immediately caught the attention of Soviet hockey fans when he stepped onto the ice in the Dynamo lineup and showed off his explosive starting speed and extraordinary stability on the ice. Although he wasn't very tall, he was strong and had broad shoulders. Skating on his slightly bowed legs, it was a rare bodycheck that could knock him off his feet.

In addition, he had terrific maneuverability and could stop on a dime. It was common to see him streaking away from his pursuer and then all of a sudden put on the brakes. As a shower of sparkling ice flew out from under his skates, his unprepared pursuer would zip past him. This was how Krylov would gain a couple of precious seconds to pass the puck to his partner or fire a shot on goal.

Krylov was a formidable forward, even though he wasn't a natural goal scorer. The full force of his game was focused on the opponent's goal, and he had a powerful—and quite often unexpected—shot.

He didn't shun tough body contact and in fact often seemed to seek it out. Tossing caution to the wind, and without sparing himself, Krylov would think nothing of crashing into tough defensemen who were barring his way to the net. For a long time he played without shoulder pads because he felt less constrained.

In Soviet hockey in the 1950s, there was still a clear-cut division of roles: Forwards and wingers attacked; defensemen defended their zone and their own goal. Krylov was one of the few forwards who worked as hard at defense as on the attacking line. And he was just as good as any defenseman. Meeting his opponents at the blue line, he was ingenious at taking away the puck, and when necessary he blocked shots with his body. Such versatility enabled him to prolong his playing career. When he lost some of his speed due to age, he switched over to the defense line. But even in his new position, Krylov's performance was exceptional.

Krylov was a never-say-die player. There were times when his Dynamo team was losing by what seemed a hopeless score and some of the players were merely going through the motions to finish the game. But not Krylov. He maintained a professional approach to the game. He came out on the ice to work and he never allowed himself to take it easy. Krylov simply gave his all right to the end of every game, never holding back or settling for second best.

Yuri Krylov (front) was one of the few forwards in the Soviet hockey of the 1950s who worked as hard at defense as on putting the puck in the net.

Krylov, Yuri
RW/D, 5'7", 172 lbs, b: Moscow, USSR, 3/11/1930, d: 1979

Season	Club, League	Regular Season				
		GP	G	A	Pts	PIM
1951–52	Dynamo Moscow, USSR	8	1	*	*	*
1952–53	Dynamo Moscow, USSR	20	15	*	*	*
1953–54	Dynamo Moscow, USSR	16	14	*	*	*
WEC–54	USSR	7	3	*	*	*
1954–55	Dynamo Moscow, USSR	18	19	*	*	*
WEC–55	USSR	8	4	*	*	*
1955–56	Dynamo Moscow, USSR	25	21	*	*	*
OWG–56	USSR	7	3	*	*	*
1956–57	Dynamo Moscow, USSR	21	10	*	*	*
1957–58	Dynamo Moscow, USSR	33	13	*	*	*
WEC–58	USSR	7	3	1	4	2
1958–59	Dynamo Moscow, USSR	25	8	*	*	*
WEC–59	USSR	8	2	*	*	*
1959–60	Dynamo Moscow, USSR	36	8	*	*	*
1960–61	Dynamo Moscow, USSR	18	7	4	11	30
1961–62	Dynamo Moscow, USSR	38	6	2	8	26
1962–63	Dynamo Moscow, USSR	36	8	0	8	28
1963–64	Dynamo Moscow, USSR	34	7	*	*	*
1964–65	Dynamo Moscow, USSR	5	0	0	0	6
	USSR Totals	344	140	*	*	*
	OWG/WEC Totals	37	15	*	*	*

Won OWG (1956)
Won WEC (1954)
USSR Champion (1954)

Roland Stoltz

There is a story about the Swedish player Roland Stoltz that many claim to be true. During one of Tre Kronor's international games, Stoltz apparently skated right up to the popular Swedish radio sportscaster Lennart Hulland, who was sitting by the boards, and said to him, "Could you please go a little more slowly, because we can't keep up with you?"

Defenseman Stoltz played the best years of his hockey career alongside Lars Bjorn, and this famous defense duo was regarded as one of the best in the history of Swedish and European hockey. Born on August 1, 1931, Roland Stoltz was a pretty good soccer player before he started playing hockey. He began his hockey career playing for the Atlas Diesel IF team while working as a mechanic for Atlas Kopco, a well-known mining machinery manufacturer in Sweden. After the Atlas team fell apart, Stoltz joined the Stockholm Djurgarden team in 1955, but only because

The defense duo of Roland Stoltz and Lars Bjorn was regarded as one of the best in the history of Swedish hockey.

Roland Stoltz (with the captain's armband) made an impressive debut in the Tre Kronor lineup on November 13, 1955, and scored a goal though he still hadn't learned how to lift the puck.

another Stockholm hockey club, Hammarby, rejected him as a defenseman, thinking he was too slow. The Hammarby coaches no doubt regretted their decision when they saw how this "slowpoke" made short work of opponents with his neat bodychecks.

Stoltz began playing Swedish hockey during his formative years and he matured as he gained experience on the ice. Stoltz made an impressive debut in the Tre Kronor lineup on November 13, 1955, in a game against Norway's national team in Oslo. The game ended 7–1 in favor of the Swedes, with one of those goals scored by the rookie Stoltz, who still hadn't learned how to lift the puck.

There are probably not many who know that Lars Bjorn and Roland Stoltz feel indebted to this day to Canadian coach Ed Reigle, who worked in Swedish hockey at the end of the 1950s. It was Reigle who showed them how to bodycheck; it was Reigle who taught them the art of wrist shots and slapshots. As a former defenseman who had gone through the tough NHL school, Reigle was able to teach them a great deal about the tactics and techniques of playing hockey.

With Stoltz on the team, Djurgarden won the Swedish national championship title six times in a row. In the lineup for the Swedish national squad, Stoltz played in 199 official games without interruption from the fall of 1956 until the 1968 Olympic hockey tournament in Grenoble. In Colorado Springs, in 1962, he scored the winning goal against the U.S. nationals in a crucial game for Tre Kronor on the road to the gold medal.

Stoltz twice became world champion—in 1957 and again in 1962—but the highlight of his career was the 1963 World Championship in Stockholm, when he was voted best defenseman. He once admitted that his toughest opponent was Soviet forward Veniamin Alexandrov. Most memorable for Stoltz were the games against the USSR nationals in Moscow in 1957 and the Canadian team in Colorado Springs in 1962 and the Olympic hockey tournament at Innsbruck in 1964.

Adjusting to wearing a helmet during play was difficult for Stoltz, and even after they became obligatory, he refused to wear one. His defiance earned him the reputation of being an uncompromising and courageous hockey player and Swedish fans loved him even more for his fearless disdain for the perils of hockey. Stoltz stands as number 52 on the list of Swedish "Hockey Greats." He is recognized as a staunch and selfless player, qualities that epitomize the Swedish style of hockey playing. He was inducted into the International Ice Hockey Federation's Hall of Fame in 1999.

Stoltz, Roland
D, 6´2˝, 189 lbs, b: Stockholm, Sweden, 8/1/1931

Season	Club, League	Regular Season				
		GP	G	A	Pts	PIM
1955–57	Djurgarden, Sweden	*	*	*	*	*
WEC–57	Sweden	7	0	*	*	*
1957–58	Djurgarden, Sweden	*	*	*	*	*
WEC–58	Sweden	7	2	1	3	6
1958–59	Djurgarden, Sweden	*	*	*	*	*
WEC–59	Sweden	8	2	*	*	*
1959–60	Djurgarden, Sweden	*	*	*	*	*
OWG–60	Sweden	7	0	*	*	*
1960–61	Djurgarden, Sweden	*	*	*	*	*
WEC–61	Sweden	7	1	*	*	*
1961–62	Djurgarden, Sweden	*	*	*	*	*
WEC–62	Sweden	6	1	5	6	4
1962–63	Djurgarden, Sweden	*	*	*	*	*
WEC–63	Sweden	7	1	3	4	2
1963–64	Djurgarden, Sweden	*	*	*	*	*
OWG–64	Sweden	7	2	4	6	6
1964–65	Djurgarden, Sweden	*	*	*	*	*
WEC–65	Sweden	7	1	1	2	6
1965–66	Djurgarden, Sweden	*	*	*	*	*
WEC–66	Sweden	7	3	*	*	*
1966–67	Djurgarden, Sweden	*	*	*	*	*
WEC–67	Sweden	7	1	2	3	10
1967–68	Djurgarden, Sweden	*	*	*	*	*
OWG–68	Sweden	3	1	*	*	*
1968–70	Djurgarden, Sweden	*	*	*	*	*
	Sweden Totals					
	OWG/WEC Totals	80	15	*	*	*

Named Best Defenseman at WEC (1963)
Won WEC (1957, 1962)
Sweden Champion (1958, 1959, 1960, 1961, 1962, 1963)

Charlie Burns

While playing junior hockey with the Toronto Marlboros, Charlie Burns suffered a fractured skull that almost ended his career. But he underwent surgery to have a metal plate inserted in his head and made a courageous comeback, wearing a heavily padded helmet in all games and practices during his professional hockey career until he was 38.

Wren Blair, who coached the Whitby Dunlops to the gold medal at the 1958 World Championship in Oslo, Norway, said Burns worked his butt off along with defensemen Harry Sinden and Ted O'Connor to kill off penalties after the Soviet Union had taken a 1–0 lead early in the first period with the gold medal on the line. "They had a very powerful team and our guys were so uptight," he said. "If we had gone down 2–0, we would have been dead in the water." The Soviets were still smarting from having finished second to Sweden at the 1957 world tournament in Moscow, but the Dunlops scored two late goals to beat them 4–2 while millions of Canadians tuned in on radio at home.

Burns finished the tournament with three goals and seven points in seven games and was selected the outstanding forward. The Dunlops won all seven of their games, outscoring the opposition by a total of 82–6. Concerned about the possibility of legal action down the road, Blair had asked Burns's parents to sign a waiver establishing that Charlie didn't suffer the head injury while playing with Whitby.

The next season, Burns was signed by the Detroit Red Wings and he played in the Motor City for one season before being claimed by the Boston Bruins in the 1959 Intra-League Draft. He became an outstanding utility man with the Bruins. Bruins coach Phil Watson used him to shadow the league's greatest stars—Gordie Howe, Bobby Hull and Frank Mahovlich. Watson said Burns was a good man for the job because he was an excellent skater and didn't let anything get under his skin. But in a departure from his usual exemplary behavior, he once spent the better part of a weekend in the penalty box. After going the first three weeks of the 1959–60 season without a penalty, Burns picked up 27 minutes in two games during a home-and-home series with the Toronto Maple Leafs. He was charged with high-sticking, cross-checking and fighting and fined $50. Carl Brewer and Bob Baun, two former teammates with the 1956 Toronto Marlboros Memorial Cup championship team, were among his adversaries.

Charlie Burns finished the 1958 World Championship with seven points in seven games and was selected the outstanding forward of the tournament.

Burns, Charlie
C, 5'11", 170 lbs, b: Detroit, MI, 2/14/1936

Season	Club, League	Regular Season					Playoffs				
		GP	G	A	Pts	PIM	GP	G	A	Pts	PIM
1956–57	Whitby Dunlops, EOHL	40	16	25	41	29	5	4	6	10	2
1957–58	Whitby Dunlops, EOHL	31	24	28	52	32					
WEC-58	Canada	7	3	4	7	0					
1958–59	Detroit Red Wings, NHL	70	9	11	20	32					
1959–60	Boston Bruins, NHL	62	10	17	27	46					
1960–61	Boston Bruins, NHL	62	15	26	41	16					
	Kingston Frontenacs, EPHL	8	3	6	9	4					
1961–62	Boston Bruins, NHL	70	11	17	28	43					
1962–63	Boston Bruins, NHL	68	12	10	22	13					
1963–64	San Francisco Seals, WHL	68	33	36	69	27	11	1	3	4	2
1964–65	San Francisco Seals, WHL	51	27	36	63	19					
1965–66	San Francisco Seals, WHL	40	10	35	45	26	7	1	5	6	0
1966–67	California Seals, WHL	71	22	38	60	29	6	0	0	0	9
1967–68	Oakland Seals, NHL	73	9	26	35	20					
1968–69	Pittsburgh Penguins, NHL	76	13	38	51	22					
1969–70	Minnesota North Stars, NHL	50	3	13	16	10	6	1	0	1	2
1970–71	Minnesota North Stars, NHL	76	9	19	28	13	12	3	3	6	2
1971–72	Minnesota North Stars, NHL	77	11	14	25	24	7	1	1	2	2
1972–73	Minnesota North Stars, NHL	65	4	7	11	13	6	0	0	0	0
1973–74	New Haven Nighthawks, AHL	64	10	19	29	73	10	1	3	4	16
	WEC Totals	7	3	4	7	0					
	NHL Totals	749	106	198	304	252	31	5	4	9	6

Named Best Forward at WEC (1958)

Toronto coach Punch Imlach said that from that point on the Leafs were going to treat Burns the same as any other player. The intimation was that Toronto players had been taking it easy on him because of the head injury he'd suffered. In the same season, Burns was caught with his head down by Chicago defenseman Pierre Pilote and wound up in the hospital with a mild concussion suffered when his head struck the ice. But Milt Schmidt, the Boston coach at that time, conceded after the game that it was a clean hit.

When the NHL expanded from six to 12 teams for the 1967–68 season, Burns was playing with the San Francisco Seals of the Western Hockey League and his NHL rights were transferred to the Oakland Seals after the San Francisco owners were granted an NHL franchise. He later played with the Pittsburgh Penguins and the Minnesota North Stars. Always known more for his excellent defensive skills, he collected 13 goals and 51 points in his best NHL season, for Pittsburgh, in 1968–69.

If he had played longer in the post-expansion era, Burns certainly would have been a candidate for nomination as the NHL's best defensive forward. But the Frank J. Selke Trophy wasn't awarded for the first time until 1978, five years after he'd played his last NHL game.

Jack McCartan

The day before the penultimate game of the 1980 Olympics in Lake Placid, New York, between the Soviet Union and Team USA, sports reporters went looking for the one man who was best qualified to predict the game's outcome. They found him at a Dairy Queen restaurant in Minneapolis, Minnesota.

With Jack McCartan's stellar netminding, the American Olympic squad won gold over highly favored teams from Canada, the Soviet Union and Czechoslovakia in 1960.

The man was Jack McCartan, who'd been the goaltender on the last U.S. team to have won the gold, back in 1960 in Squaw Valley, California. Retired and working part-time as the owner of an ice cream parlor, McCartan was more than ready to offer his pronouncements on the game. "I'd love to say that they could beat the Russians, but I can't say that I think they will," he offered. "But then again, we [the 1960 team] weren't expected to do anything either."

Luckily for both the 1960 and the 1980 U.S. Olympic squads, McCartan was a much better goaltender than sports forecaster. The more recent edition of Team USA went on to defeat the Russians 4–3 and capture the Miracle on Ice gold medal with a win over Finland in their last game. And the 1960 version, with McCartan's stellar netminding, won the gold over much more highly favored teams from Canada, the Soviet Union and Czechoslovakia.

McCartan remembered that the American team he belonged to was a very close-knit hockey family. "We really played well as a unit. Overall, we proved what a lot of teamwork could do," he said. "The turning point in the whole series came when we beat Canada. After we beat them, I felt we had something going and that maybe we could win the gold medal."

Prior to joining that magical collection of U.S. players for the 1960 Olympics, McCartan had been a college standout at the University of Minnesota (in his home state). After he graduated with a degree in education, McCartan joined the army. While a member of the armed forces, he represented the U.S. in the World Championship in Prague, an event that provided the Americans with invaluable experience leading up to the Olympics in Squaw Valley.

After the Olympics, McCartan was called up to the NHL, appearing in four games near the end of the 1959–60 season with the New York Rangers, the team that signed him after his impressive play in Squaw Valley. "There was a lot of pressure on me after the Olympics," he recalled. "I'll never forget my first game against the Detroit Red Wings. The highlight came when I stopped Gordie Howe on a breakaway. The puck somehow landed under me and I fell on it. That save took a lot of pressure off me. Had Howe beaten me, it might have been a different story."

The save on Howe was about as good as it got for goalie McCartan in the NHL. After allowing a whopping 35 goals in only seven and a half games in 1960–61, he was sent to the minors by the Rangers and never returned to the big leagues, although he did play for the Minnesota Fighting Saints of the WHA for three seasons. He stayed in hockey as a scout for the Vancouver Canucks after his playing days were over.

Although his NHL career was far from spectacular, Jack McCartan will long be remembered by Olympic hockey fans as the man between the pipes during the amazing upset victory registered by the U.S. in 1960, and it was on the strength of that performance that he was inducted into the United States Hockey Hall of Fame in 1983.

McCartan, Jack
G, 6′1″, 195 lbs, b: St. Paul, MN, 8/5/1935

Season	Club, League	Regular Season				Playoffs			
		GP	Mins	GA	Avg	GP	Mins	GA	Avg
1955–56	University of Minnesota, WIHL	24	1440	67	2.79				
1956–57	University of Minnesota, WCHA	15	900	43	2.87				
1957–58	University of Minnesota, WCHA	28	1680	89	3.18				
1959–60	Minneapolis Rangers, CMHL	5	300	17	3.40				
OWG–60	USA	5	300	11	2.20				
	New York Rangers, NHL	4	240	7	1.75				
1960–61	New York Rangers, NHL	8	440	35	4.72				
	Kitchener-Waterloo Beavers, EPHL	52	3120	145	2.79	7	421	20	2.85
1961–62	Kitchener-Waterloo Beavers, EPHL	70	4200	217	3.10	7	451	20	2.66
1962–63	Los Angeles Blades, WHL	60	3600	187	3.12	3	181	9	2.98
1963–64	St. Louis Braves, CHL	67	4020	262	3.91	6	361	27	4.49
1964–65	St. Louis Braves, CHL	5	300	27	5.40				
	Los Angeles Blades, WHL	32	1948	122	3.76				
1965–66	San Francisco Seals, WHL	53	3229	183	3.40				
1966–67	California Seals, WHL	61	3784	200	3.17	5	300	13	2.60
1967–68	Omaha Knights, CHL	43	2380	148	3.77				
1968–69	San Diego Gulls, WHL	43	2380	134	3.38	1	20	2	6.00
1969–70	San Diego Gulls, WHL	52	3025	162	3.21	4	199	19	5.73
1970–71	San Diego Gulls, WHL	55	3239	161	2.98	6	379	24	3.80
1971–72	San Diego Gulls, WHL	36	1955	112	3.44	2	118	6	3.05
1972–73	Minnesota Fighting Saints, WHA	38	2160	129	3.58	4	213	14	3.94
1973–74	Minnesota Fighting Saints, WHA	2	42	5	7.14				
	Suncoast Suns, SHL	6	323	26	4.83				
1974–75	Minnesota Fighting Saints, WHA	2	61	5	4.92				
	NHL Totals	12	680	42	3.71				
	WHA Totals	42	2263	139	3.69	4	213	14	3.94
	OWG Totals	5	300	11	2.20				

Named Best Goaltender at OWG (1960)
Won OWG (1960)

Darryl Sly

Always a fierce competitor, Darryl Sly would go through a brick wall to win a hockey game. Coaches and general managers admired his fighting spirit and versatility so much that he was often recruited to strengthen clubs competing for international honors.

While playing for the Senior A Galt Terriers in the 1960–61 season, Sly was invited to join the Trail (British Columbia) Smoke Eaters, who had been chosen to represent Canada in the 1961

Always a fierce competitor, Darryl Sly would have gone through a brick wall to win a hockey game.

World Championship in Switzerland, and he jumped at the opportunity. In an exhibition game in Sweden, Sly, who didn't wear shoulder pads, nailed Tre Kronor star Nils Nilsson and broke his jaw. Then he had a rematch of the fisticuffs he'd engaged in with Swedish legend Sven "Tumba" Johansson at the 1960 Winter Olympics in Squaw Valley, California. A policeman reached over the boards and grabbed Sly, and the next day the Swedish press showed photos of Nilsson in a hospital bed. The headline read, "Canada sabotages Sweden's national team."

Sly, defense partner Don Fletcher and goalie Seth Martin were particularly outstanding in stymying the powerful attack of the Soviet Union in the game that decided the gold medal in Geneva. The Smokies won 5–1 and were the last amateur team to beat the Soviets in a world tournament. Sly scored four goals in seven tournament games and was named to the All-Star team on defense.

Desperately trying to atone for their disappointing third-place finish at the 1956 Olympics in Italy, Bobby Bauer's Kitchener-Waterloo Dutchmen, with Sly in uniform, were foiled in an attempt to strike gold in Squaw Valley by the spectacular goaltending of American Jack McCartan. Despite outplaying the U.S. by a wide margin, the Canadian team lost 2–0. Surprisingly, the Yanks also beat both Russia and Czechoslovakia and the Dutchmen had to settle for the silver medal.

A native of the shipbuilding town of Collingwood, Ontario, on the shores of Georgian Bay, Sly became the property of the Toronto Marlboros junior club after leading the town's juvenile team to a provincial championship in 1955–56. But because he was interested in getting an education, he asked to be transferred to the St. Michael's College Majors. Both teams were affiliates of the Toronto Maple Leafs, and Leafs owner Conn Smythe approved the request. As a rookie with St. Mike's in the 1956–57 season, Sly played on a team with Frank Mahovlich as its star, and although he'd been a center with the Collingwood juveniles, he was made a defenseman by coach Bob Goldham, one of the best shot-blockers in NHL history.

Sly graduated from St. Michael's College high school in 1958 and attended teacher's college in his final season, 1958–59, when he captained the team, which lost to Peterborough in the OHA Junior A finals. The Leafs offered him $3,500 a year and a $1,500 signing bonus to turn pro, but Father David Bauer, then the Majors' coach, advised him against it, suggesting he go and play for the priest's brother Bobby with the Kitchener-Waterloo Dutchmen of the OHA Senior A League.

Sly, Darryl
D, 5′11″, 185 lbs, b: Collingwood, Ont., 4/3/1939

Season	Club, League	Regular Season					Playoffs				
		GP	G	A	Pts	PIM	GP	G	A	Pts	PIM
1958–59	Kitchener-Waterloo Dutchmen, OHA Sr.	1	0	0	0	0					
1959–60	Kitchener-Waterloo Dutchmen, OHA Sr.	47	4	8	12	63	8	1	1	2	14
OWG–60	Canada	7	1	1	2	9					
1960–61	Galt Terriers, OHA Sr.	12	4	6	10	22	15	7	8	15	24
	Trail Smoke Eaters, WHL	13	7	12	19	*					
WEC–61	Canada	7	4	2	6	6					
1960–61	Rochester Americans, AHL	2	0	0	0	0					
1961–62	Rochester Americans, AHL	70	8	16	24	50	2	0	0	0	0
1962–63	Rochester Americans, AHL	70	4	14	18	52	2	0	0	0	7
1963–64	Rochester Americans, AHL	72	16	16	32	41	2	0	0	0	0
1964–65	Rochester Americans, AHL	72	3	18	21	56	10	1	2	3	8
1965–66	Rochester Americans, AHL	67	5	15	20	49	12	2	2	4	12
	Toronto Maple Leafs, NHL	2	0	0	0	0					
1966–67	Rochester Americans, AHL	72	8	25	33	56	13	1	0	1	14
1967–68	Toronto Maple Leafs, NHL	17	0	0	0	4					
	Rochester Americans, AHL	52	3	22	25	36	11	1	6	7	12
1968–69	Vancouver Canucks, WHL	74	6	16	22	45	8	0	1	1	8
1969–70	Minnesota North Stars, NHL	29	1	0	1	6					
	Iowa Stars, CHL	10	0	8	8	2	11	1	8	9	8
1970–71	Vancouver Canucks, NHL	31	0	2	2	10					
	Rochester Americans, AHL	37	3	4	7	28					
971–72	Barrie Flyers, OHA Sr.	33	7	17	24	32					
1972–73	Barrie Flyers, OHA Sr.	41	3	19	22	42					
	Rochester Americans, AHL	1	1	2	3	0					
1973–74	Barrie Flyers, OHA Sr.	31	3	12	15	15					
	Rochester Americans, AHL	1	0	0	0	2					
1974–75	Barrie Flyers, OHA Sr.	40	4	10	14	28					
1975–76	Barrie Flyers, OHA Sr.	44	4	16	20	24					
1976–77	Barrie Flyers, OHA Sr.	34	1	10	11	26					
1977–78	Barrie Flyers, OHA Sr.	38	0	5	5	16					
	NHL Totals	79	1	2	3	20					
	OWG/WEC Totals	14	5	3	8	15					

Won WEC (1961)

"Father Bauer was a great man," said Sly. "He was my mentor. I just did whatever he told me to do and he didn't steer me the wrong way. Kitchener got me a job teaching school in Elmira and I made $2,900 teaching and $125 a week to play senior hockey."

The Leafs sent coach Punch Imlach and chief scout Bob Davidson to see the final game of the 1961 Allan Cup final between Galt and the Winnipeg Maroons, and Sly scored two goals. In the summer of 1961, he finally signed a pro contract and was assigned to play for the Rochester Americans of the American Hockey League the following season. Under three successive coaches—Johnny Crawford, Rudy Migay and Joe Crozier—he started the season on defense but was later moved up to play right wing.

The Rochester club was overstocked with good defense-man with Al Arbour, Larry Hillman, Arnie Brown and Don

At the 1961 World Championship, Darryl Sly scored four goals in seven games and was named to the All-Star team on defense.

Cherry in the lineup. Sly played only 19 games with the Leafs and split 60 more between the Minnesota North Stars and Vancouver Canucks. He scored his only NHL goal with the North Stars in the 1969–70 season. But the Americans were so good that even in the days of the Original Six teams, they were considered very close to NHL caliber and won the Calder Cup as champions of the AHL three times between 1965 and 1968.

Following his professional career, Sly went back to senior hockey with the Barrie Flyers. He was player-coach of the Flyers when they won the Allan Cup in 1975. Sly retired from hockey at the age of 40 and is now the owner of the Blue Mountain Chrysler dealership in Collingwood.

1963–1972

The Russians March West

The day before the World Championship opened at Stockholm's Johanneshof in 1963, Team USA left the ice after a one-hour workout during which they chased the puck and limbered up the goalie but didn't even work up a sweat. The Canadians and Swedes did pretty much the same thing, and high-profile Swedish coach Arne Stromberg told the press why he didn't work his players too hard: "If I allowed myself to do this, half of my players wouldn't show up for the next training session." By contrast, the Soviet players trained as if they were in a real game and worked two or three times as hard as their counterparts from the West. For players who were well known, it was even more dangerous to make a half-hearted effort because there were even such penalties as performing a few rounds of somersaults around the rink's perimeter.

Of the first generation of Soviet players who had been on winning World Championship and Olympic teams, only captain and defenseman Nikolai Sologubov went to Stockholm that year. There were eight players who had gained valuable experience at the 1961 World Championship and whose names would appear in the world's hockey press for years to come: goalkeeper Viktor Konovalenko, defensemen Alexander Ragulin and Vladimir Brezhnev and forwards Alexander Almetov, Boris and Yevgeny Mayorov, Vyacheslav Starshinov and Vladimir Yurzinov. The rest of the team was all new, and by 1963, so was the team's style of play.

In their first game, the USSR nationals crossed sticks with Tre Kronor and the Soviets were defeated 2–1. The USSR then whipped the Czech team 3–1 and Canada lost to Sweden 4–1. Tre Kronor was still at the top of the standings with a good shot at gold even after they lost to the Czechs 3–2. In the final game between the USSR and Canada, the outcome depended not only on who won but also the score. To become world champions for the first time since 1956, the Soviets needed either a 1–0 win or a minimum of a two-goal margin if they let in a goal (with any other result, the Swedes would get gold). In the first minute, Canadian goalie Seth Martin gave up the first goal to Almetov, and by the middle of the game the USSR was ahead 4–0. But the Canadians fought to the end and mounted a furious attack that scored in the last minute of play. Two Soviet

In the final game between the USSR and Canada at the 1963 World Championship, everything depended not only on who won but also by what score.

A HISTORY OF WORLD HOCKEY

hockey players were sent to the penalty box, the Canadians pulled their goalie and scored once again and the score was 4–2 with only 12 seconds remaining. One more goal for the Canadians and the Swedes would have been the world champions, but as it was, a second generation of Soviet players won their first World Championship title.

At the 1964 Winter Olympics in Innsbruck, four national squads were considered the favorites: the USSR, Czechoslovakia, Sweden and Canada. By then, Canada was represented by a full-fledged national team instead of a particular club, and coach David Bauer (also a practising priest known as Father Bauer) brought some good players with him. After the tournament, three of them—goalie Seth Martin, defenseman Rod Seiling and forward Roger Bourbonnais—were picked as All-Stars. But good players don't always make a good team and the Canadians found themselves in fourth place again even though they racked up as many points (10) as the teams from Sweden and Czechoslovakia that won silver and bronze.

The Soviets won for the second year in succession at Innsbruck when they took all their games, just as the preceding generation had in 1956 in the Italian Alps. The USSR–Czechoslovakia game was into its fifth minute when the daring Alexander Almetov suddenly put on a burst of speed. In

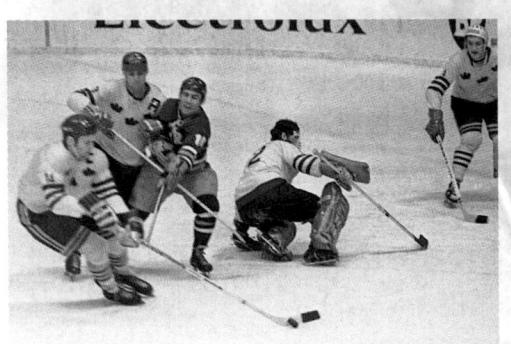

Before the 1968 World Championship, a proposal by the North Americans to allow bodychecking the entire length of the rink as in the NHL was adopted after heated debate.

front of him was a defensive wall. He flicked a quick pass to Konstantin Loktev—and almost got nailed to the boards by Czech defenseman Frantisek Tikal—but by then Veniamin Alexandrov had the puck. He seemed to appear out of nowhere right in front of Vladimir Dzurilla's goal and put the Soviets ahead 1–0. In the end, the Czech team lost 7–5 to the Soviets, as did the Swedes 4–2 and the Canadians 3–2. And that was just the beginning of a triumphant era for the Almetov line.

At the 1965 World Championship at Tampere, Finland, and again in 1966 at Ljubljana, Yugoslavia, the fate of the gold medal again depended in large measure on the outcome of the USSR–Czechoslovakia game. The Czechs hadn't yet lost a match and went in with an edge, while the Soviet players were short a point after playing the Swedes to a tie.

From the opening face-off, there was a flurry of activity around the Czech goal. Vyacheslav Starshinov started the scoring race almost immediately and Central Red Army forward Konstantin Loktev made it 2–0, then Starshinov whipped in a third—all in four minutes and two seconds. After that, the outcome was pretty much settled. Unlike the Canadians, European players tended to throw in the towel and the Czechs were trounced 7–1. Meanwhile, Father Bauer's Canadians lost to the Soviet champions 3–0 and the Czech runners-up 2–1 but worked their way up to bronze.

The Soviet style in Ljubljana made such an impression that they were the only team besides Canada to be represented among the MVPs as well as in the All-Star selection. The IIHF selected Seth Martin as the best goalie, Alexander Ragulin as the best defenseman and Konstantin Loktev as the best forward, while the journalists who picked six more players added defenseman Gary Begg and forwards Fran Huck and Veniamin Alexandrov.

A year, later at the 1967 World Championship in Vienna, the Soviet team sported several new rookie forwards (one of who, Alexander Yakushev, was to become the hero of the 1972 Summit Series), but that didn't slow them down any and they again stole the championship, this time by five points, from the Swedes, who won silver. But that outcome was partly due to the game between the USSR and Canada.

This time, Father Bauer had brought along two professional defensemen who had recently played in the NHL, Carl Brewer and Jack Bownass. Together with goalkeeper Martin, these two provided a strong defense line for a team that also had plenty of young, fast and spirited forwards. In the first period of the game against the Soviet squad, the Canadians went all out and scored. Anatoli Tarasov later recalled:

"Our forwards could do nothing with goalie Seth Martin. In one of the episodes, Firsov got so carried away in a tussle that he hung his head and skated to the boards, expecting to hear a reprimand for bad discipline. But quite unexpectedly, the puck slid up to him, and Anatoli, without even looking, lobbed it into the air in the direction of the Canadian goal. Defenseman Bownass tried to knock down the puck with his glove, but he did it so awkwardly that at first the puck went upwards, flew over Martin's head and slid down his back into the net: 1–1."

In the last period, Starshinov blasted in the winning goal to give the Soviet team a 2–1 edge and that pushed the Canadians into third place (any other result would have given them silver). In the post-game press conference, journalists asked Anatoli Firsov how he had managed to score against the veteran Seth Martin from a distance of over 100 feet. Without batting an eye, Firsov replied: "Well, I saw that Martin had let his guard down...that the upper corner was open...and that's where I dispatched the puck."

At the end of the 1960s, a new wave of players appeared on the Czech national team. The style of hockey they played was different from that of the Soviets as well as the Swedes and came from coach Vladimir Kostka, who was assisted at first by Vladimir Bouzek and later by Jaroslav Pitner. Neither Kostka nor Pitner had been outstanding players, but after he retired, Kostka would become one of the leading theoreticians not only of Czech but world hockey while Pitner ably applied Kostka's theories to real-life situations.

From the 1963 World Championship in Stockholm till the 1972 Olympics in Sapporo, the Soviet Union team won every major international tournament.

During those years, the Czech team would allow and at times even lure an opponent into their zone, leaning heavily on their goalkeepers and defense lines to stop goals, the point being to create an opportunity to grab the puck and mount a surprise counterattack. It was a dangerous game to play and it often got them in trouble. At Ljubljana in 1966, for example, Soviet forwards fired off three shots and couldn't penetrate goalie Jiri Holcek's defenses, but then he let in three goals and the Czechs came to a very bad end.

At the 1968 Olympic Games in Grenoble, Czechoslovakia managed to win a game (5–4) against the Soviet team for the first time in years. To win Olympic gold and the World and European Championships, the Czechs only had to overcome the Swedes, which didn't seem an impossible mission. The Swedes would remain in fourth no matter what happened, however, which permitted the Tre Kronor players to wait calmly in their own zone, depriving the Czechs of their customary counterattack and compelling them to build positional attacks, which wasn't one of their strengths. The 2–2 final score left the Soviet team in first place.

The atmosphere at the 1969 World Championship in Stockholm was strongly influenced by an event unrelated to hockey. The armed forces of the Warsaw Pact had entered Czechoslovakia in August of 1968. Soviet tanks rumbled through Prague to quell anti-communist uprisings, thousands of refugees fled, and many of them emigrated to Sweden. During the games between the USSR and Czechoslovakia, quite a few of these former Czechs raised placards bearing inscriptions in Russian, "Your tanks, our goals." The Czech players came out on the ice with a do or die atti-tude, as if it were an actual battlefield, and won two games with scores of 2–0 and 4–3. Now the Czechs only needed a tie with Tre Kronor to become the world champions.

Josef Golonka and the Holik brothers, Jiri and Jaroslav, had no shortage of chances to score, but all their efforts were wasted against Swedish goalie Leif Holmqvist (who was later voted the best goalkeeper of the championship). But one of the rare Swedish attacks was successful and the final score was 1–0. Three teams earned 16 points each, but the goal differential gave the USSR the gold, Sweden the silver and Czechoslovakia the bronze.

In 1970, Canada was to host the World Championship for the first time in history. Games were scheduled for Winnipeg and Montreal, but it still wasn't clear which group of players would rep-resent Canada. The job of putting together a team had been entrusted to Hockey Canada, an organization set up specifically for that purpose in 1968. After studying the disappointing experi-ence of Canadian teams at World Championships through the 1960s, Hockey Canada executives announced that the hosts of the coming championship could put on a worthy performance only if pros from the NHL were allowed to participate.

The question of allowing professionals to play in World Championships was brought up in 1969 at the IIHF Congress in Stockholm in March and again at the summer congress in Switzerland, but the Europeans were still wary of NHL players, and their representatives, espe-cially from the socialist countries, were in no hurry to agree. A proposal by the North Americans to allow the NHL style of bodychecking the entire length of the rink was adopted after heated debate, but it was decided not to allow NHL players to compete in World Championships. As an experiment, the Canadians would be allowed to use nine professionals from more junior leagues for the 1970 contest.

Two months before the championship was scheduled to open in Canada, even this measure was countermanded by IIHF president Bunny Ahearne, whose antipathy toward Canadian—and sym-pathy for Soviet—hockey was an open secret. The president of the International Olympic Committee, Avery Brundage, championed "genuine amateur sports" and supported Ahearne, declaring that amateur sportsmen who competed with professionals in official tournaments wouldn't be allowed to participate in Olympic Games. In response, the Canadians refused to host the World Championship or take part in future tournaments. They would remain conspicuous by their absence at World Championships until 1977.

To save the 1970 tournament, the Swedes took it over in Stockholm, and once again the edge that a revamped USSR squad had over its competitors was impressive. The Swedish hosts came in second again, three points behind the leader, while Alexander Maltsev, who had just turned 20, ended up way out in front in the scoring race (with 15 goals to his credit, he even eclipsed the record set by Vsevolod Bobrov). A year later, in Switzerland, the Czech team racked up three points against the Soviets with 3–3 and 5–2 wins, but the Soviets won all the rest of their games while the Czechs lost to the Swedes and Americans.

It was a new generation of Soviet hockey players who won the gold medals at the Sapporo Olympics in 1972. Of all their competitors, only the Swedes were able to keep the Soviets to a tie of 3–3. The Americans were whipped 7–2 to take silver, while the Czechs were trounced 5–2. In short, the performance of the USSR national squad in Sapporo was a triumph.

Anatoli Tarasov

Rumor has it that Anatoli Tarasov penalized one of the players of his Central Red Army club for a misdemeanor by ordering him to do 50 laps around the rink with heavy weights attached to his belt. It was getting quite late and the training session was long over. Tarasov had left for the night and, with the rink deserted, the player began to carry out his punishment all alone. And there are hundreds of such stories about Tarasov.

Anatoli Tarasov made hockey a phenomenon in the Soviet Union.

At the end of the 1940s, the Central Red Army was spearheaded by the Yvgeny Babich–Anatoli Tarasov–Vsevolod Bobrov forward line. In the early days of hockey in the Soviet Union, Bobrov was considered the king of the ice. He scored equally well against any team and paid little heed to warnings and advice from coaches. In those years, a coach wasn't considered all that important and Bobrov's coach at the time pretty much left him to his own devices. Babich, a very skillful player in his own right, devoted his entire game to Bobrov, feeding him passes at the slightest hint. Tarasov was also a very adept player, but his talent couldn't compare with that of Bobrov, who played his own style of the game. In fact, Bobrov quite often raised objections about the way Tarasov conducted himself on the ice.

At the beginning of the 1950s, Bobrov went to play for the top-rated Air Force hockey club. Tarasov's Army was the only team that could put up any real resistance to the Air Force stars headed by Bobrov, and even those small successes came only when the Air Force team was in a slump. But in 1953 the Air Force team was disbanded and Bobrov returned to the Army club. In that same year, Tarasov's self-esteem received another, albeit indirect, blow from Bobrov. The Soviet national team was slated to make its debut in the World Championship, but because the almighty forward Bobrov was injured, the debut was postponed. Tarasov, who attended the championship, expressed his indignation when he returned: "We should have gone. We would have won even without Bobrov."

A year later, Bobrov found himself in another confrontation with Tarasov after the USSR won its first World Championship title. The leading forward accused Tarasov, as coach and observer, of suggesting that the Soviet team not play at full throttle against the Canadian team—since they would lose anyway—in order to save their strength to play against the Swedes.

The duel between Bobrov and Tarasov lit a fire under Soviet hockey. Bobrov's best years as a player were receding. Meanwhile, as coach, Tarasov went on analyzing games and leaned heavily on his rich imagination to come up with the perfect training process. In those years, no one in the USSR really knew what was involved in training hockey players.

In 1958, Tarasov took the reins of the USSR nationals for the first time, and his team gave up the gold at two World Championships and the 1960 Olympics. The veterans of the Central Red Army temporarily ousted him and once again Arkady Chernyshev came to the helm of the national squad. He didn't win either. But before the 1963 World Championship, Chernyshev and Tarasov appeared as a duo to lead the national squad. They went on to sweep every championship for the next 10 years, topping that winning streak off with the 1972 Olympic title.

Chernyshev's position with the USSR national squad was more important than that of Tarasov. In the beginning, they were each attentive to and respectful of the other. They shared the duties and argued long and often about the right way to play hockey. Chernyshev looked after the defense, while Tarasov focused on the forwards.

A HISTORY OF WORLD HOCKEY

Tarasov, Anatoli
C, 5'9'', 180 lbs, b: Moscow, USSR, 12/10/1918, d: 1996

Season	Club, League	Regular Season				
		GP	G	A	Pts	PIM
1946–47	VVS MVO, USSR	6	14	*	*	*
1947–48	CDKA, USSR	18	23	*	*	*
1948–49	CDKA, USSR	18	16	*	*	*
1949–50	CDKA, USSR	22	27	*	*	*
1950–51	CDKA, USSR	10	5	*	*	*
1951–52	CDKA, USSR	16	13	*	*	*
1952–53	CDKA, USSR	9	6	*	*	*
	USSR Totals	99	104	*	*	*

USSR Champion (1948, 1949, 1950)

Tarasov, Anatoli
Head Coach, b: Moscow, USSR, 12/10/1918, d: 1996

Season	Club, League	Regular Season				
		GC	W	L	T	W%
1947–48	CDKA, USSR	18	16	1	1	0.916
1948–49	CDKA, USSR	18	15	1	2	0.888
1949–50	CDKA, USSR	22	19	2	1	0.886
1950–51	CDKA, USSR	15	9	5	1	0.633
1951–52	CDSA, USSR	17	13	3	1	0.794
1952–53	CDSA, USSR	20	16	2	2	0.850
1953–54	CDSA, USSR	16	13	2	1	0.843
1954–55	CSK MO, USSR	18	17	1	0	0.944
1955–56	CSK MO, USSR	28	28	0	0	1.000
1956–57	CSK MO, USSR	30	28	1	1	0.950
1957–58	CSK MO, USSR	34	30	2	2	0.911
WEC–58	USSR	7	5	1	1	0.785
1958–59	CSK MO, USSR	27	19	4	4	0.777
WEC–59	USSR	8	7	1	0	0.875
1959–60	CSKA, USSR	36	28	6	2	0.805
OWG–60	USSR	7	4	2	1	0.643
1962–63	CSKA, USSR	37	32	4	1	0.878
WEC–63	USSR	7	6	1	0	0.857
1963–64	CSKA, USSR	36	32	3	1	0.902
OWG–64	USSR	8	8	0	0	1.000
1964–65	CSKA, USSR	36	33	1	2	0.944
WEC–65	USSR	7	7	0	0	1.000
1965–66	CSKA, USSR	36	32	2	2	0.916
WEC–66	USSR	7	6	0	1	0.928
1966–67	CSKA, USSR	44	35	5	4	0.841
WEC–67	USSR	7	7	0	0	1.000
1967–68	CSKA, USSR	44	38	2	4	0.909
OWG–68	USSR	7	6	1	0	0.857
1968–69	CSKA, USSR	42	32	8	2	0.785
WEC–69	USSR	10	8	2	0	0.800
1969–70	CSKA, USSR	44	38	5	1	0.875
WEC–70	USSR	10	9	1	0	0.900
1970–71	CSKA, USSR	40	32	7	1	0.815
WEC–71	USSR	10	8	1	1	0.850
1971–72	CSKA, USSR	32	27	2	3	0.890
OWG–72	USSR	5	4	0	1	0.900
1972–73	CSKA, USSR	32	26	4	2	0.843
1973–74	CSKA, USSR	32	18	10	4	0.625
	USSR Totals	754	626	83	45	0.860
	OWG/WEC Totals	100	85	10	5	0.875

Won OWG (1964, 1968, 1972)
Won WEC (1963, 1965, 1966, 1967, 1969, 1970, 1971)
USSR Champion (1948, 1949, 1950, 1955, 1956, 1958, 1959, 1960, 1963,
       1964, 1965, 1966, 1968, 1970, 1971, 1972, 1973)

However, the difference in their temperaments and their approach to hockey eventually got the upper hand and Tarasov became the new hockey god. As the official leader and head coach of the team, Chernyshev acknowledged his helplessness before Tarasov, who won support with his common-sense approach. Chernyshev reported to the leadership of his Dynamo team: "All promising players wind up, first of all, in the Central Army under Tarasov's wing. And that is why Dynamo cannot take first place away from the Central Army in the national championship. I can't do anything about this. If you don't like all this, remove me from my post."

Tarasov was very ambitious, perhaps even too ambitious for a model Soviet citizen. Hockey, previously a curiosity from overseas, offered him the chance to express himself 100%. With no precedent to follow for the development of the game in the Soviet Union, hockey in Tarasov's hands became the clay out of which he molded whatever came to mind. He rigorously copied the methods of the best coaches in soccer and other sports and, some would say, even drew upon some of the lesser qualities of politicians. Tarasov could act and he could charm people—whoever and whenever necessary. He also knew how to leave a person speechless, and how to compel a person to think profoundly.

Much later, when he was already advanced in age and had trouble walking, he remarked, "In old age, I want to sell myself for the highest price possible." Even at the peak of his career, that was what preoccupied him most. But with this attitude, he generated an incredible amount of publicity for the game of hockey, even though people in the Soviet Union in the 1960s had only a very vague understanding of the concept of publicity. It was Tarasov who turned hockey into a phenomenon in the Soviet Union. He knocked on all the doors of officialdom to arrange highly cherished foreign hockey tours for his players. He regularly appeared on TV programs shamelessly promoting his players. "Our glorious boys…our great Firsovs, Kharlamovs, Tretiaks…"

Others saw him as a devil in disguise. Having gotten himself the position of coach after a struggle with Bobrov that was sometimes out in the open and at other times behind the scenes, Tarasov had an uncanny knack for sensing when his players were beginning to feel their omnipotence and posed a threat to his power as a coach. There wasn't a single player who suited Tarasov completely.

Tarasov's classic dictum was:, "The game is spontaneity, while training is a purposeful process." The rigorous training that Soviet players underwent was Tarasov's exclusive creation. Anyone who happened to drop in on a workout by the Central Army might think that he'd entered a circus arena. There were players riding on each other's shoulders. Others juggled metal weightlifting disks. Some were busy performing somersaults and other acrobatics. And directing it all was Tarasov.

He squeezed every ounce of energy and performance out of his players. Even the slightest hint of self-importance was dealt with immediately. According to Tarasov, egoism on the ice was the gravest of all sins. In the end, Tarasov must be given credit for his work in creating a phenomenon in Soviet hockey unparalleled elsewhere—superstar forward lines. The members of those lines interacted with one another apparently without the slightest effort, as if they had no need to see each other and could function purely on instinct.

Hockey offered Anatoli Tarasov the chance to express himself fully.

In 1969, during an intermission of the World Championship final against Sweden, Tarasov was said to be singing the "Internationale"—the anthem of the proletariat—in the locker room of Stockholm's Johanneshof Palace.

By the end of the 1960s, many of the Soviet leaders had had their fill of Tarasov, complaining that he'd built a state within a state and crowned himself king in an autocratic USSR. To make matters worse, he led his Central Red Army team off the ice in 1969 during a decisive game against Spartak—and in the presence of leading statesmen. For 40 minutes, they tried to talk Tarasov into sending his players back out on the ice, but he objected to the referee's disallowing a goal scored by his team. He did lead the team back onto the ice but lost the game, and Tarasov was subsequently stripped of his Merited Coach title. He handed the reins of the Central Red Army over to second coach Boris Kulagin, who quickly established himself as the main coach and began rejuvenating the lineup.

In subsequent games, however, Tarasov began sitting closer and closer to the Army bench. And in the final match to determine the Soviet entry at the European Championship, with the Central Army losing 5–3 to Spartak and the whole country watching at home, Tarasov could no longer contain himself. He went over to the bench and in a fit of temper began running the show. The Central Red Army suddenly came back to life and whipped Spartak 8–5. To add insult to injury, Tarasov gave Kulagin a public tongue-lashing for "bringing such a glorious team to ruin by senselessly reshuffling the lineup."

Much of what is said about Tarasov is only half true, for he didn't even know the whole truth himself. He was a complex and often contradictory individual. According to reports, Tarasov criticized the NHL greats as lazy and selfish, yet he was afraid of a direct encounter with them on the ice. And according to other reports, the opposite is true. Apparently Tarasov, with the help of the world's first cosmonaut, Yuri Gagarin, tried to convince the top Soviet leaders to hold matches with the NHL at the national level.

"The game is spontaneity, while training is a purposeful process," was Anatoli Tarasov's (second from the left) classic dictum.

Tarasov and Chernyshev left the national team in the winter of 1972, half a year before the Summit Series. Tarasov worked with the Central Army club for another two years, but after losing the championship in 1974, he stepped aside to make way for Konstantin Loktev. He ended his career behind the bench before exhausting a coach's best years. After that, he conducted hockey competitions for young amateurs throughout the country. He did some teaching and became a hockey observer for the leading newspapers.

"I attend all of Tarasov's seminars," declared Valeri Belousov, the coach of Metallurg Magnitogorsk—one of the strongest teams in Russia today. "He compels me to wiggle my brains." The legendary coach of the Philadelphia Flyers, Fred Shero, said he read Tarasov's books over and over again. The great Scotty Bowman said: "I remember the time when Tarasov watched my workouts with the Montreal Canadiens. And he approved them. I was extremely pleased to hear that."

Tarasov left a lasting impression on people he dealt with on a personal level. However, most of those people shunned the very work in which he immersed himself. Tarasov's daughter Tatyana became a well-known figure skating coach. Talented figure skaters often expressed a desire to be tutored by her sooner or later, and those who did usually became champions. Tarasov's daughter has the same hard, concentrated look in her eyes and the same slightly hooked nose. And just like her father, Tatyana is unbelievably tough and ambitious. She worships her father and his genius.

Johnny Bower

Although Johnny Bower's nickname was "the China Wall," it might better have been "Perseverance," for although he had a Hall of Fame career in the NHL, it certainly didn't adhere to the traditional notion of what a life in pro hockey should be about.

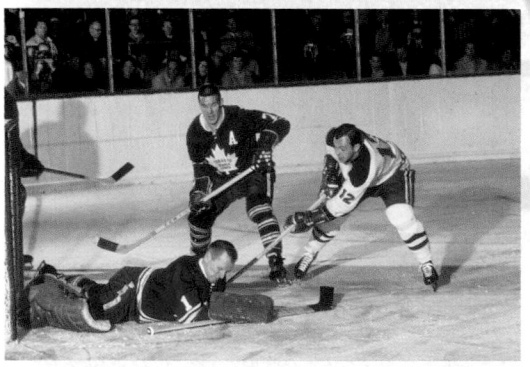

Even without a mask, Johnny Bower (in goal) never shied away from an attacking player and in fact patented the most dangerous move a goalie can make—the poke-check.

Bower grew up in rural Saskatchewan, the only boy in a family of nine children. He was dirt poor and never had the proper equipment. He made his goalie pads from an old mattress; he made pucks, "cow pies," from horse manure; his dad would look for suitably crooked tree branches to shave into sticks; a friend gave him his first pair of skates because his father couldn't afford to buy him a pair; and still he refined his game to become one of the best goalies of all time. In 1940, when he was 15 years old, Bower lied about his age for the first time, though not the last, in order to enlist in the army. He was sent to a training camp in British Columbia and was eventually called up by the Queen's Own Cameron Highlanders and shipped to England. Four years later, he became sick during his service and was discharged in 1944, at which time he resumed his junior career with Prince Albert. He laughed at the contradiction: "I was a four-year war veteran and still eligible for junior."

From there he began a career in the American Hockey League, which is where most goalies start out. The difference was that Bower played for Providence and Cleveland for an incredible eight full seasons before playing a single NHL game. In 1953–54, he played the entire season for the Rangers, but then spent most of the next four seasons right back in the minors, having lost the starting job in New York to Gump Worsley. During his 14 years in the minors, he won the Les Cunningham Award as the AHL's best player three times and the Hap Holmes Award for top goaltender another three times.

Bower's big break came in the summer of 1958 when the Leafs claimed him from Cleveland at the Intra-League Draft. Bower was at first reluctant to join the Leafs, even though they had finished in last place the previous season, telling them he could be of no help to the team. It was only after being threatened with suspension that he showed up for training camp that fall, and within days he'd established himself as the team's number one goalie at age 34. He was to play a total of 12 years with the Leafs.

Bower instantly brought to the team not only great goaltending but also a superior attitude. "He was always an inspiration to us," captain George Armstrong said. "He shamed us into hard work, always putting out full effort in workouts. He gave everything he could, and we weren't about to let that old guy show us up, so we worked harder too." Bower had a more desperate take on his approach to the game. "The club kept bringing in goalies that wanted my job—Gerry Cheevers, Suitcase Smith, Bruce Gamble, Al Smith—but I didn't like the prospect of being number two. When the competition got stiffer, I worked three times as hard. Competition drove me."

Bower, like his other five Original Six brethren, became famous for his fearless play. Maskless, he never shied away from an attacking player and in fact patented the most dangerous move a goalie can make—the poke-check. Diving head-first into the skates of an attacking player at full speed, Bower would routinely flick the puck off that player's stick and out of harm's way. One time he got a skate in his cheek, knocking a tooth out through his cheek. He suffered innumerable cuts to his mouth and lips and lost virtually every tooth in his mouth from sticks and pucks, but almost to his last game, he never wore a mask. And under the confident eye of coach Punch Imlach, Bower got better and better. He led the Leafs into the playoffs his first season with a miracle comeback ending to the schedule, and then lost two finals in a row before winning three consecutive Stanley Cup championships—1962 to 1964.

At this time, Bower's career seemed precarious. Imlach noticed that Bower was having trouble with long shots and ordered his keeper to undergo an eye exam. Sure enough, he was short-sighted. But Bower refused to retire and kept right on going, teaming with Terry Sawchuk

Johnny Bower (left) suffered countless cuts to his mouth and lips and lost virtually every tooth in his mouth to sticks and pucks, but almost to his last game, he never wore a mask.

Bower, Johnny "the China Wall"
G, 5'11", 189 lbs, b: Prince Albert, Sask., 11/8/1924

Season	Club, League	Regular Season				Playoffs			
		GP	Mins	GA	Avg	GP	Mins	GA	Avg
1945–46	Cleveland Barons, AHL	41	2460	160	3.90				
	Providence Reds, AHL	1	48	4	5.00				
1946–47	Cleveland Barons, AHL	40	2400	124	3.10				
1947–48	Cleveland Barons, AHL	31	1880	83	2.65				
1948–49	Cleveland Barons, AHL	37	2200	127	3.43	5	329	23	4.19
1949–50	Cleveland Barons, AHL	61	3660	201	3.30	9	548	27	2.96
1950–51	Cleveland Barons, AHL	70	4280	213	2.99	11	703	32	2.73
1951–52	Cleveland Barons, AHL	68	4110	165	2.41	5	300	17	3.40
1952–53	Cleveland Barons, AHL	61	3680	155	2.53	11	745	21	1.69
1953–54	New York Rangers, NHL	70	4200	182	2.60				
1954–55	Vancouver Canucks, NHL	63	3780	171	2.71	5	300	16	3.20
	New York Rangers, NHL	5	300	13	2.60				
1955–56	Providence Reds, AHL	61	3710	174	2.81	9	540	23	2.56
1956–57	Providence Reds, AHL	57	3501	138	2.37	5	300	15	3.00
	New York Rangers, NHL	2	120	7	3.50				
1957–58	Cleveland Barons, AHL	64	3870	140	2.17				
1958–59	Toronto Maple Leafs, NHL	39	2340	106	2.72	12	746	38	3.06
1959–60	Toronto Maple Leafs, NHL	66	3960	177	2.68	10	645	31	2.88
1960–61	Toronto Maple Leafs, NHL	58	3480	145	2.50	3	180	8	2.67
1961–62	Toronto Maple Leafs, NHL	59	3540	151	2.56	10	579	20	2.07
1962–63	Toronto Maple Leafs, NHL	42	2520	108	2.60	10	600	16	1.60
1963–64	Toronto Maple Leafs, NHL	51	3009	106	2.11	14	850	30	2.12
1964–65	Toronto Maple Leafs, NHL	34	2040	81	2.38	5	321	13	2.43
1965–66	Toronto Maple Leafs, NHL	35	1998	75	2.25	2	120	8	4.00
1966–67	Toronto Maple Leafs, NHL	27	1431	63	2.64	4	183	5	1.64
1967–68	Toronto Maple Leafs, NHL	43	2239	84	2.25				
1968–69	Toronto Maple Leafs, NHL	20	779	37	2.85	4	154	11	4.29
1969–70	Toronto Maple Leafs, NHL	1	60	5	5.00				
	NHL Totals	552	32016	1340	2.51	74	4378	180	2.47

NHL First All-Star Team (1961)
Won Vezina Trophy (1961, 1965)
Won Stanley Cup (1962, 1963, 1964, 1967)

to win the memorable 1967 Cup with Toronto's Over-the-Hill Gang of players, led by the 42-year-old Bower himself. Imlach never forgot Bower's dedication to and love of the game. "Bower is the most remarkable hockey player I've ever seen. I keep telling him: 'I don't care how old you are. As long as you can stop the puck, you have a job.' And he keeps telling me, 'I've got two more years left.' He's been telling everyone that for 10 years."

After he retired in 1970 as the oldest goalie ever to play in the NHL, Bower remained with the Leafs for many years as a scout and then goalie coach, putting the pads on and helping Leaf goalies in practice. At one injury-riddled time during the 1979–1980 season, he came within a whisker, at age 56, of dressing as the team's backup. A member of the Hockey Hall of Fame, Bower is one of only a select few to have his number honored by the Leafs.

Gump Worsley

Hall of Famer "Gump" Worsley got his nickname courtesy of New York Rangers teammate Phil Watson, who thought Lorne looked like the comic book character of the same name. Watson also said that the Gumper had a beer belly, a jibe that aggravated Worsley to no end and usually produced the heated response: "I don't drink beer! I drink only whiskey!"

Although Worsley played 21 years in the NHL, his career didn't begin until he was 24 years old. Prior to his 1952–53 rookie season with the Rangers, he played in five different leagues, winning honors and trophies at virtually every stop along the way. He was named the top rookie and best goalie in the USHL with the St. Paul Saints in 1950–51, was named the league's MVP in the western league during his year with the Vancouver Canucks in 1953–54 and was placed on All-Star teams just about everywhere he went.

Gump Worsley played 21 years in the NHL but didn't begin his career until he was 24 years old.

He won the Calder Trophy his first year in the NHL despite a record of 13–29–8, testament to his tremendous play on an otherwise weak team. But the next season the Rangers sent him to Vancouver, the only time a Calder winner never played a single NHL game the year after being so honored. The following year he made the Broadway Blueshirts and stayed in the pro crease for the next decade.

Glenn Hall once commented that the only thing that ever bothered Gump was flying. Worsley agreed and told a story about the first time he was in a plane. "It all started in 1949 when I was with the New York Rovers. We were coming into Pittsburgh and one of the engines caught fire and we had to make an emergency landing. I never was too wild about planes after that." But he was indeed unflappable in the crease, and his happy-go-lucky style went a long way toward giving him the skills needed to be a goalie in the days before masks protected the face. In fact, he was one of the very last men of the crease to wear facial protection.

Worsley's years with the Rangers were impressive but not particularly successful. They made the playoffs only four of the 10 seasons, and although he was spectacular as the last line of defense, the team wasn't very good. But in 1963 the general managers' meetings were in Montreal and Worsley was traded from New York to the Habs during the course of the June weekend. His hockey perspective changed in a flash. "There was a big difference between playing for the Montreal Canadiens and the New York Rangers," he confessed. "In New York, you wanted to win;

in Montreal, you had to win. Two losses in succession were a disaster. People would stop you on the street. In New York, you could hide."

The additional pressure from this Montreal expectation of winning seemed to have nothing but a positive impact on Worsley's game. In his first season, however, he hurt his knee and played most of the year in the minors with the Quebec Aces to get in shape. He started the next season with the Aces but was called up to the Forum in mid-season and played heroically the rest of the way in leading the Habs to the 1965 Stanley Cup. He would never play in the minors again. In his seven seasons with Montreal, he was on four Cup-winning teams, but his career with the *bleu, blanc et rouge* ended on November 28, 1969, in Chicago when his fear of flying got the better of him during an NHL schedule that demanded almost constant air travel. "I just can't take it any more," he protested at O'Hare Airport. "Los Angeles one day and Boston the next. The trip to Chicago only took two hours and 15 minutes, but we were strapped in there for two hours of the time." He took the train home, vowing never to return. "I tried to reason with Gump and ask him to play home games, but he wouldn't listen," Montreal general manager Sam Pollock said. "We had no choice but to bring up another goalie."

Later in that 1969–70 season, Worsley was convinced by Minnesota general manager Lou Nanne to return to the expansion North Stars for the last few games of the season. Minnesota didn't have too many plane trips in its schedule, and Nanne was also willing to pay Gump an additional $500 for a win, $250 for a tie and $100 for a shutout, over and above his salary. Worsley accepted and spent four more years in the NHL. He didn't retire until he was 44 years old, and it was only in the final six games of that final 1973–74 season that he wore a mask.

Gump Worsley (right) was unflappable in the crease and his happy-go-lucky style took him a long way toward acquiring the skills a goalie needed in the days before goalie masks.

Worsley, Lorne, John "Gump"
G, 5′7″, 180 lbs, b: Montreal, Que., 5/14/1929

Season	Club, League	Regular Season				Playoffs			
		GP	Mins	GA	Avg	GP	Mins	GA	Avg
1948–49	New York Rovers, QSHL	2	120	5	2.50				
1949–50	New York Rovers, EHL	47	2830	133	2.86	12	720	27	2.25
	New Haven Ramblers, AHL	2	120	4	2.00				
1950–51	St. Paul Saints, USHL	64	3920	184	2.82	4	247	9	2.19
1951–52	Saskatoon Quakers, PCHL	66	3960	206	3.07	13	818	31	2.27
1952–53	Saskatoon Quakers, WHL	13	780	50	3.84				
	Edmonton Flyers, WHL	1	60	2	2.00				
	New York Rangers, NHL	50	3000	153	3.06				
1953–54	Vancouver Canucks, WHL	70	4200	168	2.40	12	709	29	2.45
1954–55	New York Rangers, NHL	65	3900	197	3.03				
1955–56	New York Rangers, NHL	70	4200	203	2.90	3	180	15	5.00
1956–57	New York Rangers, NHL	68	4080	220	3.24	5	316	22	4.18
1957–58	New York Rangers, NHL	37	2220	86	2.32	6	365	28	4.60
	Providence Reds, AHL	25	1528	83	3.26				
1958–59	New York Rangers, NHL	67	4001	205	3.07				
1959–60	New York Rangers, NHL	39	2301	137	3.57				
	Springfield Indians, AHL	15	900	33	2.20				
1960–61	New York Rangers, NHL	59	3473	193	3.33				
1961–62	New York Rangers, NHL	60	3531	174	2.96	6	384	22	3.44
1962–63	New York Rangers, NHL	67	3980	219	3.30				
1963–64	Montreal Canadiens, NHL	8	444	22	2.97				
	Quebec Aces, AHL	47	2820	128	2.72	9	543	29	3.20
1964–65	Quebec Aces, AHL	37	2247	101	2.70				
	Montreal Canadiens, NHL	19	1020	50	2.94	8	501	14	1.68
1965–66	Montreal Canadiens, NHL	51	2899	114	2.36	10	602	20	1.99
1966–67	Montreal Canadiens, NHL	18	888	47	3.18	2	80	2	1.50
1967–68	Montreal Canadiens, NHL	40	2213	73	1.98	12	669	21	1.88
1968–69	Montreal Canadiens, NHL	30	1703	64	2.25	7	370	14	2.27
1969–70	Montreal Canadiens, NHL	6	360	14	2.33				
	Minnesota North Stars, NHL	8	453	20	2.65	3	180	14	4.67
1970–71	Minnesota North Stars, NHL	24	1369	57	2.50	4	240	13	3.25
1971–72	Minnesota North Stars, NHL	34	1923	68	2.12	4	194	7	2.16
1972–73	Minnesota North Stars, NHL	12	624	30	2.88				
1973–74	Minnesota North Stars, NHL	29	1601	86	3.22				
	NHL Totals	861	50183	2432	2.91	70	4081	192	2.82

NHL First All-Star Team (1968)
NHL Second All-Star Team (1966)
Won Vezina Trophy (1966, 1968)
Won Calder Trophy (1953)
Won Stanley Cup (1965, 1966, 1968, 1969)

A HISTORY OF WORLD HOCKEY

Ken **Wharram**

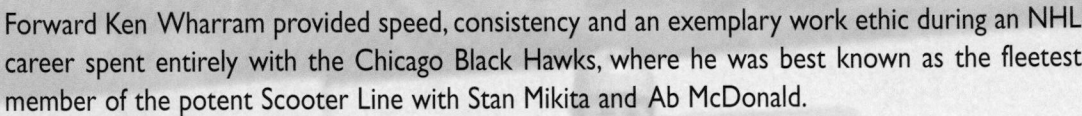

Forward Ken Wharram provided speed, consistency and an exemplary work ethic during an NHL career spent entirely with the Chicago Black Hawks, where he was best known as the fleetest member of the potent Scooter Line with Stan Mikita and Ab McDonald.

Ken Wharram was best known as the fleetest member of the potent Scooter Line with Stan Mikita and Ab McDonald.

Wharram first honed his on-ice skills in the North Bay minor hockey system. He actually began as a goalie with his public school in the North Bay suburb of Ferris. In 1949–50, he made a brief appearance with the North Bay Black Hawks of the Eastern Ontario Senior Hockey League. Wharram caught the attention of the Chicago Black Hawks, who signed him to be developed on their OHA junior affiliate in Galt. He totaled 261 points in three junior seasons and played respectably in a 29-game call-up to the parent club in 1953–54.

Initially, Wharram struggled to gain a place in the Chicago lineup. After playing briefly with the Quebec Aces of the QHL, he was traded by the Hawks to the AHL's Buffalo Bisons, where he completed four productive years and was heavily influenced by coach Harry Watson. He was reacquired by Chicago in May 1958. Beginning in 1958–59, he earned a permanent roster position that lasted 11 seasons. He started out trying to forge an identity on the fourth line with the likes of Danny Lewicki and Lorne Ferguson.

Wharram soon proved to be the perfect complement to the Hawks' gifted young center Stan Mikita. Often known as "Whip," he was lightning-quick and a master of timing his move at the opposition blue line so that he seldom caused an offside. Once a Mikita pass found him, his puck control was among the best in the business. The two became fast friends off the ice and roomed together on road trips, often discussing strategy.

The first edition of the Scooter Line featured Wharram and Mikita with Ted Lindsay. When the latter moved on after one year, Ab McDonald was brought in to play left wing. When McDonald went to the Bruins, Doug Mohns was added in his place because of his ability to dig out the puck, score and play solid defensive hockey. They often had different ways of yelling each other's names to adjust a play during game action. Wharram once explained: "If you shout once, it means you think you have a little time to get a shot away. If you're in tight with some guy bearing down on you, you yell twice, 'Kita! Kita!' Then Stan knows he's got to rush you the puck."

Mohns summed up Wharram: "Kenny is the ideal right winger for Mikita. Stan needs a man who can break fast from a standing start and is able to time his move across the blue line, pick up the puck and move without breaking stride into the payoff zone."

Wharram, Ken
RW/C, 5′9″, 160 lbs, b: North Bay, Ont., 7/2/1933

Season	Club, League	Regular Season					Playoffs				
		GP	G	A	Pts	PIM	GP	G	A	Pts	PIM
1951–52	Chicago Black Hawks, NHL	1	0	0	0	0					
1953–54	Chicago Black Hawks, NHL	29	1	7	8	8					
	Quebec Aces, QHL	29	7	10	17	8					
1954–55	Buffalo Bisons, AHL	63	33	49	82	15	10	9	7	16	4
1955–56	Chicago Black Hawks, NHL	3	0	0	0	0					
	Buffalo Bisons, AHL	59	27	63	90	27	5	4	2	6	2
1956–57	Buffalo Bisons, AHL	64	28	49	77	18					
1957–58	Buffalo Bisons, AHL	58	31	26	57	14					
1958–59	Chicago Black Hawks, NHL	66	10	9	19	14	6	0	2	2	2
1959–60	Chicago Black Hawks, NHL	59	14	11	25	16	4	1	1	2	0
1960–61	Chicago Black Hawks, NHL	64	16	29	45	12	12	3	5	8	12
1961–62	Chicago Black Hawks, NHL	62	14	23	37	24	12	3	4	7	8
1962–63	Chicago Black Hawks, NHL	55	20	18	38	17	6	1	5	6	0
1963–64	Chicago Black Hawks, NHL	70	39	32	71	18	7	2	2	4	6
1964–65	Chicago Black Hawks, NHL	68	24	20	44	27	12	2	3	5	4
1965–66	Chicago Black Hawks, NHL	69	26	17	43	28	6	1	0	1	4
1966–67	Chicago Black Hawks, NHL	70	31	34	65	21	6	2	2	4	2
1967–68	Chicago Black Hawks, NHL	74	27	42	69	18	9	1	3	4	0
1968–69	Chicago Black Hawks, NHL	76	30	39	69	19					
	NHL Totals	766	252	281	533	222	80	16	27	43	38

NHL First All-Star Team (1964, 1967)
Won Lady Byng Trophy (1964)
Won Stanley Cup (1961)

Since Wharram weighed only 160 pounds, his speed, agility and on-ice smarts proved to be his ticket to survival in the rough and tumble NHL. As Keith L. Jackson wrote, "Kenny has survived, though, because of his great speed and agility, as defensemen with mayhem in their hearts have tried, on many occasions, to annihilate this speeding Scooter, only to miss their target and end up with only the hard boards to absorb the shock."

In September 1969 Wharram was coming off his seventh straight 20-goal season. One day, after a morning workout, he experienced severe chest pains when he tried to remove his skates. He soon found himself in the intensive care unit diagnosed with myocarditis, a virus that attacks the muscles of the heart with symptoms similar to a coronary. His condition worsened to the point that he had to start from scratch building up the ability to stay awake through a normal day. This whole process took several weeks, and in the end there was no question that he was finished as a hockey player. His heart recovered to the point where he could lead a normal life but not put his body through the sudden exertion that takes place in hockey. He made his retirement official prior to the opening of the Hawks' training camp in September 1970.

He had an offer to work for the Northland Sticks in Minneapolis, Minnesota, but turned it down even though they offered to pay his commuting expenses in full. After recovering from his condition, Wharram decided to remain in North Bay on a full-time basis to be with his family regardless of what job offers were forthcoming. After recovering in full, Wharram turned to his other love, carpentry, until he retired.

Since Ken Wharram (left) weighed only 160 pounds, his speed, agility and on-ice smarts proved to be his ticket to survival in the rough and tumble NHL.

Ronald *Pettersson*

Many believe that forward Ronald Pettersson of Sweden was born ahead of his time. He was so adept at the subtleties of the game—what was going to happen, what his partners were planning to do, where to pass and how to receive a pass—that he would have made any team in the NHL today.

He was born on April 16, 1935, and came up from the juniors to play in the pro league. His mature hockey years coincided with the greatest period in Swedish hockey. Pettersson began as a defenseman with Sodertalje and made his debut with the junior team of Sweden on February 14, 1954, the same year that Team Sweden beat Team Norway by a score of 10–0 on November 26. In that game, his partner on the defense line was Bertz Zetterberg of Stockholm's Djurgarden.

However, Ronald Pettersson really made a name for himself as a forward and member of a threesome that has gone down in the annals of Swedish hockey as a line that could do anything on the ice. Up until the beginning of the 1960s, it was the only line that remained intact on Team Sweden.

That lineup was created in the autumn of 1955 in two friendly games against Stockholm Hammarby and the Paris Paisley Pirates. The official debut of the Ronald Pettersson, Nils Nilsson and Lars-Eric Lundvall line on Team Sweden was January 27, 1956, against the USSR at the Olympic Games in Cortina D'Ampezzo. The Soviets won that game 5–1, and Nils Nilsson, one of the best European forwards of those years, scored the only Swedish goal.

The three players fit very well together. Their forward line was the best on the team in the course of six seasons and could have remained so for many more years were it not for an injury sustained by Lundvall. The still junior lineup was prominent at the 1957 World Championship in Moscow, where Team Sweden won the gold by tying the final game against the Soviets 4–4. The tie put Sweden ahead of the USSR. The most goals scored in that tournament for Team Sweden were by Nils Nilsson with 10, Ronald Pettersson with nine and Laris-Eric Lundvall with five—a truly remarkable performance.

Many believe that forward Ronald Pettersson was born ahead of his time.

Ronald Pettersson played 14 seasons for Team Sweden, was world champion in 1957 and 1962 and won the silver at the 1964 Olympic Games in Innsbruck. He was Swedish champion in 1956, playing for Sodertalje, as well as in 1959, when he played for Gothenburg's Vastra Frolunda.

In the 1962–63 season, he scored 26 goals in 20 games. Fans recall the game on November 8, 1962, in Gothenburg between Vastra Frolunda and Stockholm's Djurgarden—one of the best teams at that time, boasting an amazing 57-game winning streak in the local championship. Stockholm was leading 2–0 at one point but lost the game 3–2. The culmination of the game was a breakaway by Pettersson from his own zone, sending a perfect pass to Lundwall, who completed the goal. That play was shown on television scores of times and Vastra Frolunda became the most popular club in Sweden.

It is worth noting that Ronald Pettersson also played 13 games for Gothenburg in the Swedish soccer championship.

The brilliant career of this fine athlete ended unexpectedly and tragically. In a game in Vastraros on December 14, 1967, Pettersson lost has balance and fell on the ice. It was impossible to determine whether it was because of a crack in the ice or because someone had thrown a coin onto the ice, but a broken leg put an end to his distinguished playing career. However, Pettersson didn't leave hockey altogether. He coached the Swedish junior team for a number of years—a team that won the gold at the 1972 European Championship. He also coached Team Sweden from 1974 to 1976.

For many years, Ronald Pettersson headed the list of most games played for Team Sweden at 252. Later that record was eclipsed by Thomas Rundqvist with 267 games, and then in 1998 by Jonas Bergqvist with 272 games. Pettersson retains his third-place standing as confirmation of his outstanding contribution to Swedish hockey.

Pettersson, Ronald
RW, 6´, 183 lbs, b: Surahammar, Sweden, 4/16/1935

Season	Club, League	Regular Season				
		GP	G	A	Pts	PIM
1951–55	Surahammar, Sweden	*	*	*	*	*
WEC–55	Sweden	1	0	*	*	*
1955–56	Sodertalje, Sweden	*	*	*	*	*
OWG–56	Sweden	7	1	*	*	*
1956–57	Sodertalje, Sweden	*	*	*	*	*
WEC–57	Sweden	7	9	7	16	*
1957–58	Sodertalje, Sweden	*	*	*	*	*
WEC–58	Sweden	7	5	5	10	0
1958–59	Sodertalje, Sweden	*	*	*	*	*
WEC–59	Sweden	8	5	*	*	*
1959–60	Sodertalje, Sweden	*	*	*	*	*
OWG–60	Sweden	7	5	*	*	*
1960–61	Vastra Frolunda, Sweden	*	*	*	*	*
WEC–61	Sweden	7	6	*	*	*
1961–62	Vastra Frolunda, Sweden	*	*	*	*	*
WEC–62	Sweden	7	2	2	4	0
1962–63	Vastra Frolunda, Sweden	*	*	*	*	*
WEC–63	Sweden	7	3	1	4	0
1963–64	Vastra Frolunda, Sweden	*	*	*	*	*
OWG–64	Sweden	7	3	3	6	2
1964–65	Vastra Frolunda, Sweden	*	*	*	*	*
WEC–65	Sweden	7	5	3	8	2
1965–66	Vastra Frolunda, Sweden	*	*	*	*	*
WEC–66	Sweden	7	3	*	*	*
1966–67	Vastra Frolunda, Sweden	*	*	*	*	*
WEC–67	Sweden	3	1	0	1	0
	Sweden Totals	*	*	*	*	*
	OWG/WEC Totals	82	48	*	*	*

Won WEC (1957, 1962)
Sweden Champion (1956, 1965)

Harry Howell

Henry Vernon Howell, known by everybody as Harry, had played more games than any defenseman in major-league hockey history by the time he retired. Howell played in a total of 1,581 contests, 1,411 in the NHL and 170 in the World Hockey Association. Born in Hamilton, Ontario, in 1932, Howell was known as a dedicated, dependable player on the ice and a classy guy off it.

Howell started playing junior hockey for the Guelph Biltmores and his professional career began in 1952 with the New York Rangers. He quickly gained a reputation as a durable, dependable "iron man" and, amazingly, missed only 17 games in his first 16 seasons as a Ranger. Howell's best season was in 1966–67, when he won the Norris Trophy as the NHL's top defenseman.

In 1969 Howell was sold to the Oakland Seals, giving the team a "needed shot of vitamin D—for defense," said team official Bob Bestor. Howell had recently had a spinal fusion operation prior to moving over to join the Seals. He admitted: "It will be a little while yet before I'm in top-notch condition. But these things will come after I've played several games." Surgery didn't seem to dampen the response to Howell on the West Coast. Both the team and its fans were thrilled to have him on board. And on the ice, the Seals were happy to have an experienced player like Howell to guide their young defense. "His experience and intelligence helps anyone he's playing with," said Seals coach Fred Glover, "and his ability to handle the puck makes him a valuable asset to the power play." The Oakland crowd welcomed Howell with a huge standing ovation at his first game.

Howell was traded to the Los Angeles Kings in February of 1971 and played there until the end of the 1973 season. He then moved over to the WHA to play for the San Diego, New Jersey and Calgary franchises and in 1975 he retired from hockey after playing a final 31 games.

After his retirement, Howell moved to a front office position as assistant general manager with the Cleveland Barons in 1976. "Harry is one of the finest hockey men in the nation," said general manager Bill McCreary, "and the Barons are fortunate to acquire his services." He later moved up to become a full-fledged general manager with Cleveland until they merged with the Minnesota North Stars in 1978. Howell continued to coach the Stars in 1978–79 for 17 games and he later became the team's chief scout.

Looking back over his 1,581 games in hockey, Howell was asked about his biggest

Harry Howell had played more games than any major-league defenseman by the time he retired.

Howell, Harry
D, 6´1˝, 195 lbs, b: Hamilton, Ont., 12/28/1932

Season	Club, League	Regular Season					Playoffs				
		GP	G	A	Pts	PIM	GP	G	A	Pts	PIM
1951–52	Cincinnati Mohawks, AHL	1	0	0	0	0					
1952–53	New York Rangers, NHL	67	3	8	11	46					
1953–54	New York Rangers, NHL	67	7	9	16	58					
1954–55	New York Rangers, NHL	70	2	14	16	87					
1955–56	New York Rangers, NHL	70	3	15	18	77	5	0	1	1	4
1956–57	New York Rangers, NHL	65	2	10	12	70	5	1	0	1	6
1957–58	New York Rangers, NHL	70	4	7	11	62	6	1	0	1	8
1958–59	New York Rangers, NHL	70	4	10	14	101					
1959–60	New York Rangers, NHL	67	7	6	13	58					
1960–61	New York Rangers, NHL	70	7	10	17	62					
1961–62	New York Rangers, NHL	66	6	15	21	89	6	0	1	1	8
1962–63	New York Rangers, NHL	70	5	20	25	55					
1963–64	New York Rangers, NHL	70	5	31	36	75					
1964–65	New York Rangers, NHL	68	2	20	22	63					
1965–66	New York Rangers, NHL	70	4	29	33	92					
1966–67	New York Rangers, NHL	70	12	28	40	54	4	0	0	0	4
1967–68	New York Rangers, NHL	74	5	24	29	62	6	1	0	1	0
1968–69	New York Rangers, NHL	56	4	7	11	36	2	0	0	0	0
1969–70	Oakland Seals, NHL	55	4	16	20	52	4	0	1	1	2
1970–71	California Golden Seals, NHL	28	0	9	9	14					
	Los Angeles Kings, NHL	18	3	8	11	4					
1971–72	Los Angeles Kings, NHL	77	1	17	18	53					
1972–73	Los Angeles Kings, NHL	73	4	11	15	28					
1973–74	New York–New Jersey, WHA	65	3	23	26	24					
1974–75	San Diego Mariners, WHA	74	4	10	14	28	5	1	0	1	10
1975–76	Calgary Cowboys, WHA	31	0	3	3	6	2	0	0	0	2
	NHL Totals	1411	94	324	418	1298	38	3	3	6	32
	WHA Totals	170	7	36	43	58	7	1	0	1	12

NHL First All-Star Team (1967)
Won James Norris Trophy (1967)

Harry Howell's (number 3) best season was in 1966–67, when he won the Norris Trophy as the NHL's top defenseman.

thrill and regret. The regret, of course, was that he never won a Stanley Cup. "A couple of times I thought we had good chances," he said, "but we ran up against a powerhouse team in Chicago the year they won the Cup. We played the Canadiens three times in a row in the playoffs. I think it's been unfortunate for the Rangers in that every time they seem to get it right, there is always a team that is a little bit better."

And Howell's biggest thrill? "That would have to be the Harry Howell Night celebrations," held in Madison Square Garden on January 25, 1967. On that night, fans and businesses in New York and in Howell's home town showered him with gifts, including engraved watches, a new car, trips to resorts, a gas barbecue, a box of cigars, a seven-foot artificial Christmas tree and a year's supply of cheese. "We won the game against Boston and they had so many people in, gifts given, interviews," remembered Howell. "It was a tremendous night. And, of course, that same year I won the Norris Trophy, and that is something they can't take away from me."

Howell was inducted into the Hockey Hall of Fame in 1979.

Charlie Hodge

He was only 5′6″, but goalie Charlie Hodge reached impressive heights with three different NHL clubs.

Although he stood only 5′6″, goalie Charlie Hodge reached impressive heights with three different NHL clubs. His experience ranged from the awe-inspiring tradition of the Montreal Canadiens to the exuberant youth of expansion teams in Oakland and Vancouver. Along the way, he fought tenaciously to earn a place in the big leagues and forge an identity among his peers and fans.

The native of Lachine, Quebec, caught the attention of the Montreal Canadiens' scouts as a youth. Once committed to *le bleu, blanc et rouge*, Hodge began his apprenticeship with the Junior Canadiens in 1949–50. As a Quebec junior league rookie, he helped the club defeat the Regina Pats to win the Memorial Cup. Famous teammates in this wide-open victory over the western club included Dickie Moore and Don Marshall. In his sophomore season, Hodge posted a league-best 2.59 goals-against mark while justifying the faith the parent organization had placed in him.

In 1951–52, he became the undisputed starter on the junior Habs and turned in another league-low goals-against average, this time a minuscule 2.22 mark. The following season, Hodge won 35 of his 44 starts and led the Quebec junior league with five shutouts. His next move was to the professional ranks in 1953–54 with the Cincinnati Mohawks of the International Hockey League. Hodge's lone season in southern Ohio proved spectacular, with a league-high 10 shutouts and a 2.34 goals-against average. His goaltending was an integral part of the team's regular-season and Turner Cup championship performance.

The young netminder earned his first NHL action in 1954–55 with a Montreal club that was on the verge of embarking on the greatest Stanley Cup run in league history. Hodge demonstrated skill and noteworthy poise while registering a 7–3–4 record in 14 appearances. Through the remainder of the decade, he played behind Jacques Plante on the Canadiens' depth chart. Consequently, he played in only 15 more NHL matches between 1957 and 1960. Hodge later noted: "I didn't really consider it such a bad situation being the backup to Plante. As far as I was concerned, Jacques was the best goaltender I ever saw, and that includes ranking him above Glenn Hall, Terry Sawchuk, Ken Dryden and Bernie Parent."

While waiting patiently for a chance to play in the NHL on a full-time basis, Hodge's minor pro tour took him through the Quebec senior league, the Western Hockey League, the American Hockey League and the Eastern Professional Hockey League. He proved to be a workhorse and a success wherever he strapped on his pads. Four times he was placed on either the First or Second All-Star teams of the league in which he played. Hodge thought he caught his first major break with a 19-win and four-shutout performance in 30 appearances for the Habs in 1960–61, but it wasn't to be.

Hodge's morale hit an all-time low when the Canadiens left him unprotected in the annual Waiver Draft of players after the NHL meetings in 1961. When no teams put in a claim, he approached Habs boss Frank Selke to announce his intention to retire. Hodge was tired of moving his family around the country, but nevertheless he agreed to stay with Montreal when Selke posted him in Quebec City and quipped, "Jacques Plante can't go on forever."

Early in 1963–64, he was starting his third consecutive season with the AHL's Quebec Aces when the tide finally turned in his favor. Hodge was called in to replace injured Gump Worsley as the Canadiens' first-string netminder. He stepped in admirably by registering 33 wins and an NHL-best eight shutouts. His stellar work was recognized at the conclusion of the season when he was named the winner of the Vezina Trophy and selected to the NHL Second All-Star Team.

During this period, the two-goalie system was developing, which provided Hodge with a bit more job security but not more happiness. He later said that, "The NHL increased the number of games a team played during the regular season, the shots were getting harder and the position as a whole was becoming more of a strain to play."

Hodge, Charlie
G, 5′6″, 150 lbs, b: Lachine, Que., 7/28/1933

Season	Club, League	Regular Season				Playoffs			
		GP	Mins	GA	Avg	GP	Mins	GA	Avg
1951–52	Montreal Royals, QSHL	1	40	3	4.50				
1952–53	Montreal Royals, QSHL	1	60	4	4.00				
1953–54	Cincinnati Mohawks, IHL	62	3720	145	2.34	11	660	19	1.73
	Buffalo Bisons, AHL	3	180	10	3.33				
1954–55	Providence Reds, AHL	5	300	18	3.60				
	Montreal Canadiens, NHL	14	840	31	2.21	4	83	6	4.34
	Montreal Royals, QHL	35	2100	113	3.23				
1955–56	Seattle Americans, WHL	70	4245	239	3.38				
1956–57	Rochester Americans, AHL	41	2460	132	3.22				
	Shawinigan Cataracts, QHL	14	859	39	2.72				
1957–58	Montreal Canadiens, NHL	12	720	31	2.58				
	Montreal Royals, QHL	48	2880	153	3.19	7	380	25	3.95
1958–59	Montreal Royals, QHL	24	1440	67	2.79	2	120	4	2.00
	Rochester Americans, AHL	4	240	12	3.00				
	Montreal Canadiens, NHL	2	120	6	3.00				
1959–60	Montreal Royals, EPHL	33	1980	96	2.91				
	Hull–Ottawa Canadiens, EPHL	26	1560	74	2.85	7	430	24	3.35
	Montreal Canadiens, NHL	1	60	3	3.00				
1960–61	Montreal Royals, EPHL	22	1320	74	3.36				
	Montreal Canadiens, NHL	30	1800	76	2.53				
1961–62	Quebec Aces, AHL	65	3900	185	2.85				
1962–63	Quebec Aces, AHL	67	4020	190	2.84				
1963–64	Quebec Aces, AHL	10	600	32	3.20				
	Montreal Canadiens, NHL	62	3720	140	2.26	7	420	16	2.29
1964–65	Montreal Canadiens, NHL	53	3180	135	2.55	5	300	10	2.00
1965–66	Montreal Canadiens, NHL	26	1301	56	2.58				
1966–67	Montreal Canadiens, NHL	37	2055	88	2.57				
1967–68	Oakland Seals, NHL	58	3311	158	2.86				
1968–69	Oakland Seals, NHL	14	781	48	3.69				
	Vancouver Canucks, WHL	13	779	32	2.54	8	497	12	1.45
1969–70	Oakland Seals, NHL	14	738	43	3.50				
1970–71	Vancouver Canucks, NHL	35	1967	112	3.42				
	NHL Totals	358	20593	927	2.70	16	803	32	2.39

NHL Second All-Star Team (1964, 1965)
Won Vezina Trophy (1964, 1966)
Won Stanley Cup (1959, 1960, 1965, 1966)

Charlie Hodge's (left) NHL resume listed a number of individual and team accomplishments along with 24 career shutouts and four Stanley Cups.

Despite being a part-time veteran of the NHL, many wondered if Hodge's success in 1963–64 was a fluke. These reservations proved inaccurate as the plucky netminder put up a 26–16–10 mark in 1964–65. His fine work contributed to the Habs' first Stanley Cup win since 1959–60.

Hodge and Worsley worked superbly together in 1965–66. The shining duo led Montreal to a repeat Stanley Cup performance and shared the Vezina Trophy after recording the stingiest goals-against mark in the NHL. But the very next year, things began to unravel for Hodge. He appeared in 37 regular-season games but was the odd man out after young phenomenon Rogie Vachon was called up late in the schedule and played superbly.

Left unprotected by Montreal, Hodge was claimed by the Oakland Seals in the 1967 Expansion Draft. In a matter of months, the veteran backstopper went from an elite defensive club to an inexperienced outfit that guaranteed his exposure to an enormous number of shots. Hodge fought on bravely in 1967–68 with three shutouts and 13 wins in 58 games while sharing the goaltending chores with youngster Gary Smith.

His playing time diminished in 1968–69 and he was demoted to the Vancouver Canucks of the WHL. Hodge played a handful of games the following season before he was claimed by the Vancouver Canucks in the NHL's 1970 Expansion Draft. It seemed that the black cloud of disappointment surrounding his demotion to the WHL two years earlier had a silver lining. Hodge, Dunc Wilson and George Gardner provided the NHL's newest club with solid goaltending, a factor contributing to a respectable 56-point showing for the team.

Hodge retired after his only season in Vancouver. His NHL resume listed a number of individual and team accomplishments along with 24 career shutouts and 151 regular-season victories. The former netminder settled in Langley, British Columbia, and embarked on a fruitful career in real estate.

Konstantin Loktev

He had the potential to become one of the greats in Soviet hockey, both as a player and as a coach. At his first World Championship in Moscow in 1957, he chalked up the highest number of points. He was voted the best forward after his last World Championship in Ljubljana in 1966. In his first season as coach of the Central Red Army club, he regained the national championship title that Anatoli Tarasov had lost. After that, together with his club, he played a game with the Montreal Canadiens that was called the match of the century. But only three years after he started, he suddenly ended his coaching career with the national champions and Viktor Tikhonov was put in his place at the Central Red Army club. Konstantin Loktev put in a short stint abroad but didn't want to coach any team but the Central Red Army.

As a young right winger, Loktev was a frisky player who seemed to have a chip on his shoulder. He began playing with Spartak Moscow, but then he was called up to the army. They put him on the team in Leningrad, and from there he was invited to play with the Central Red Army. Shortly afterward, two of the most powerful teams in the Soviet Union—the Central Red Army and the Air Force—merged, throwing all the stars together in one lineup.

Loktev was advised to switch to bandy, where the competition wasn't so stiff, but the great Vsevolod Bobrov talked him out of it. Not long afterward, Loktev became Bobrov's partner.

At the World Championship in 1957, Loktev made an impressive debut with the national squad, scoring 11 goals in seven games, but it wasn't enough to prevent the USSR team from losing to the Swedes. Loktev had a tendency to play a risky game, at top speed, and he wasn't at all afraid of being slammed into the boards. In fact, he even provoked his opponents at times by holding his stick at arm's length and challenging them to take the puck away from him. But at the very last second, Loktev would veer off in the other direction and zero in on the net.

There were two brilliant partners—Veniamin Alexandrov and Alexander Almetov—with whom he was even willing to engage in team play. "As soon as I saw Almetov in action with the junior team, I immediately sensed that he was a partner," Loktev recalls. He went on to say that a forward line clicked when he was planning the next five moves and his partner was right in sync with him. For Loktev, Alexandrov and Almetov were such partners.

Konstantin Loktev replaced Anatoli Tarasov as coach of the Central Red Army club.

Loktev was the oldest player on the forward line—a full seven years older than Almetov—but on the ice he looked the youngest and the most venturesome. He eagerly took on the dirty work. Alexandrov and Almetov played a different style. They followed the more Soviet style team approach. Of all Loktev's technical skills, Tarasov most valued his ability to score a goal from the trickiest positions. But Loktev himself was most fond of drilling the puck from the flank of the opponent's blue line. The puck would zip along just above the ice and hook the far lower corner of the net. It was a difficult shot for the goalie to see coming and could even look like a pass.

The Loktev–Almetov–Alexandrov trio was probably the first forward line in Soviet hockey in which all the players had equal ability and where each supplemented the other. After receiving a pass from his defense, Loktev would skate a little with the puck and then get it to Almetov, who was already racing up the left flank. Alexandrov, in the center slot, would then switch places with Almetov. The whole play took only a couple of seconds.

The Almetov line was Tarasov's first encounter with such a close-knit forward line. A powerful line like that could even challenge a coach's absolute power, so Tarasov decided to make life miserable for them. "He would tell me, 'Pretend you're heading towards the boards, but skate to the center,'" recalled Loktev. "I began doing that, but then they started dumping me on the ice. 'You're pretty weak, Konstantin,' Tarasov said then, 'I can't trust you with a place in the forward line.'"

Loktev, Konstantin
RW, 5'7", 165 lbs, b: Moscow, USSR, 4/16/1933, d: 1998

Season	Club, League	Regular Season				
		GP	G	A	Pts	PIM
1952–53	Spartak Moscow, USSR	*	0	*	*	*
1953–54	ODO Leningrad, USSR	6	4	*	*	*
1954–55	CSK MO, USSR	*	5	*	*	*
1955–56	CSK MO, USSR	*	17	*	*	*
1956–57	CSK MO, USSR	*	13	*	*	*
WEC–57	USSR	7	11	7	18	*
1957–58	CSK MO, USSR	*	28	*	*	*
WEC–58	USSR	7	7	4	11	4
1958–59	CSK MO, USSR	*	20	*	*	*
WEC–59	USSR	8	3	*	*	*
1959–60	CSKA, USSR	*	14	*	*	*
OWG–60	USSR	6	6	2	8	8
1960–61	CSKA, USSR	*	18	*	*	*
WEC–61	USSR	7	5	4	9	6
1961–62	CSKA, USSR	*	10	*	*	*
1962–63	CSKA, USSR	*	8	*	*	*
1963–64	CSKA, USSR	*	24	*	*	*
OWG–64	USSR	8	6	10	16	8
1964–65	CSKA, USSR	*	25	*	*	*
WEC–65	USSR	7	7	4	11	6
1965–66	CSKA, USSR	*	16	*	*	*
WEC–66	USSR	7	5	5	10	4
1966–67	CSKA, USSR	*	2	*	*	*
	USSR Totals	340	213	*	*	*
	OWG/WEC Totals	57	50	*	*	*

Named Best Forward at WEC (1966)
Won OWG (1964)
Won WEC (1965, 1966)
USSR Champion (1955, 1956, 1958, 1959, 1960, 1961, 1963, 1964, 1965, 1966)

At the 1957 World Championship, Konstantin Loktev (second from the right) made an impressive debut with the Soviet national squad, scoring 11 goals in seven games.

But it wasn't easy for Tarasov to order Loktev around. Loktev was still playing when Tarasov admitted that his player was almost ready to be a coach, and a good one at that. He possessed an uncanny ability to analyze a game. As a matter of fact, it was Loktev who advised the coaches to shift Alexandrov from the center slot to the wing.

And it was Loktev who replaced Tarasov in the coach's saddle of the Central Red Army club. With his mimicry and his expressive behavior—the sly look in his squinty eyes, the playful smile and the typical shrugging of his shoulders—coach Loktev even resembled Tarasov. But he didn't want to become a second Tarasov as a matter of principle. His approach to work was sensible. He even talked to the players as equals, as if to say, "Let practice decide which of us is right." And more often than not, his method worked.

Many former players who become coaches hardly seem like the same people they used to be—but not Loktev. He remained true to himself after switching jobs. In his work as coach, he did his best to preserve all the values he'd acquired on the ice. For him, there was nothing more sacred than the camaraderie between a coach and his players.

In their first series of games against NHL clubs in December 1975 and January 1976, he marched the Central Red Army club back to their locker room in protest against the rough play by Philadelphia and the biased refereeing. He didn't want to see his players crippled. That game—his team played it to the end after receiving guarantees of safety—was the only loss that Loktev's team sustained in that series.

As Boris Kulagin's assistant, Loktev only had an indirect bearing on the two successive losses of the Soviet national squad in 1976 and 1977. Nonetheless, he was dismissed from his posts with both the national team and the Central Red Army.

Had Loktev been more persistent and inclined toward intrigue, he might have put up a fight. But he vowed that outside the Red Army, his life in hockey would be meaningless. At the age of 44—when coaches are in their prime—Loktev ended his promising career.

Nils Nilsson

One of the memorable moments in hockey belongs to the famous Swedish forward Nils Nilsson.

A vivid hockey personality distinguished for skating speed and natural-born stickhandling, he was fond of outwitting the opposing defense lines, to the tremendous glee of the spectators.

Nilsson started with the Forshaga club in 1952 and moved to Leksand, where he finished his career, crowning it with gold in the Swedish national championship in the 1968–69 season. Together with Ronald Pettersson and Lars-Eric Lundvall, he made up one of the most famous and highest-scoring forward lines in the history of Swedish hockey. He played 205 official games with the Swedish national squad, was twice a world champion and holds two European Championship titles, while at the 1964 Winter Olympics in Innsbruck, he won a silver medal.

But for Nils Nilsson, the 1962 World Championship game between the national teams of Canada and Sweden in Colorado Springs, USA, was the high point of his career, and Swedish fans remember it even today. There was a tremendous amount of nervous tension. The Swedes were leading 4–0 after the first period and it looked like a certain win. But against the Canadians, you played 100% percent from the opening face-off to the final siren or you lost. The Swedes knew that, but they forgot it and that was a mistake.

The Canadians roared back into the game, quickly gaining the upper hand and reducing the gap to one goal. With only 38 seconds left in the third period, Canada pulled their goalie and came out with six attackers. The Canadians were all over the ice. The atmosphere was electric. But then came the goal.

Lars-Eric Lundvall won the face-off in his own zone and the puck bounced over to Nilsson on the boards. Nilsson let the puck fly at the Canadian net, and suddenly the game was over. The Swedes beat the Canadians by a score of 5–3, and Nilsson set a tournament record of 12 goals and six assists. Tre Kroner won the World Championship for the third time in its history.

In Sweden, when they talk about romantics and knights in hockey, Nils Nilsson comes to mind first. He earned this acclaim through loyalty to the game and mastery of a style that triggered standing ovations among hockey fans everywhere.

For Nils Nilsson (front), the game between Canada and Sweden at the 1962 World Championship was the high point of his career.

Nilsson, Nils
C, 5′11″, 175 lbs, b: Forshaga, Sweden, 3/8/1936

Season	Club, League	Regular Season				
		GP	G	A	Pts	PIM
1952–56	Forshaga, Sweden	*	*	*	*	*
OWG–56	Sweden	7	0	*	*	*
1956–57	Forshaga, Sweden	*	*	*	*	*
WEC–57	Sweden	7	10	6	16	*
1957–58	Forshaga, Sweden	*	*	*	*	*
WEC–58	Sweden	7	7	4	11	2
1958–60	Forshaga, Sweden	*	*	*	*	*
OWG–60	Sweden	7	4	*	*	*
1960–62	Forshaga, Sweden	*	*	*	*	*
WEC–62	Sweden	7	12	6	18	0
1962–63	Leksand, Sweden	*	*	*	*	*
WEC–63	Sweden	6	6	1	7	0
1963–64	Leksand, Sweden	*	*	*	*	*
OWG–64	Sweden	6	5	0	5	2
1964–65	Leksand, Sweden	*	*	*	*	*
WEC–65	Sweden	7	5	3	8	0
1965–66	Leksand, Sweden	*	*	*	*	*
WEC–66	Sweden	7	5	*	*	*
1966–67	Leksand, Sweden	*	*	*	*	*
WEC–67	Sweden	7	2	3	5	2
1967–69	Leksand, Sweden	*	*	*	*	*
	Sweden Totals	*	*	*	*	*
	OWG/WEC Totals	68	56	*	*	*

Named Best Forward at OWG (1960)
Won WEC (1957, 1962)
Sweden Champion (1969)

Bob Baun

With the exception of 1972 Team Canada hero Paul Henderson, there is perhaps no other professional hockey player who has become as well known for his exploits in just a single game as Robert Neil "Bob" Baun.

Baun's career-making night was the sixth game of the 1964 Stanley Cup final, with Baun playing for the Toronto Maple Leafs against Detroit. Baun describes what happened halfway through the

Like Summit Series hero Paul Henderson, Bob Baun has become famous for his achievements in a single game.

third period with the score tied 3–3 at the Detroit Olympia: "I got hit in the foot by a shot by Gordie Howe, so they took me to the Olympia infirmary. The guys who looked at it didn't think I could hurt it any more than I already had, so they froze it and I went back to play the game," recalls Baun, who had had to be taken from the ice on a stretcher. "I knew it was broken; I didn't need any X-rays to tell me that. But I didn't want to miss the overtime. I told the trainer he had to do everything possible to get me out there. He gave me a shot of painkiller, which numbed the ankle, and taped it tight. Then I laced up my skate and went back to the bench."

His foot did turn out to be broken—Baun later jokingly called it "the best break I ever had"—but that didn't stop him. And for the Leafs, it was a good thing the stalwart defenseman decided to rejoin the action in game six. Just two minutes into the overtime, Baun made himself a hockey legend. He took a pass near the blue line. His shot deflected off the skate of Detroit's Bill Gadsby, past Terry Sawchuk and into the net.

Two nights later, the Leafs won game seven, and with it the Stanley Cup. The irrepressible Baun played a regular shift in the deciding game. "People talk about me scoring the goal in great pain. That wasn't bad," said Baun. "The really tough part of it was playing in the seventh game. Now that just plain hurt!"

The upshot of Baun's painful goal-scoring heroics was that he was never much of a marksman during his 17-year NHL career, recording just 37 goals and 187 assists in 964 career games. From the standpoint of personal stats, his best season was one goal and 20 assists in 1970–71. Instead of wowing the fans with impressive offense, though, Baun was known as a hard-checking pure defender, and he was a mainstay of the "Big Four" of Leafs defenders in the 1960s.

Born in Lanigan, Saskatchewan, in 1936, Baun started off in the junior ranks with the Toronto Marlboros and then was assigned to the American Hockey League's Rochester Americans. He was brought up to the Leafs for the 1956–57 season and soon after joined young future stars Tim Horton and Carl Brewer on defense. After 11 seasons with the Leafs, in which he played on Stanley Cup-winning teams from 1962 to 1964 and in 1967, Baun was picked by the Oakland Seals in the 1967 Expansion Draft. After only one season in California, he asked to be traded back to one of the Original Six teams and the Seals complied, dealing him to Detroit, where he played for three years. Finally, he came back to the Leafs in 1970–71 and played there until 1972–73.

Baun, Bob
D, 5′9″, 175 lbs, b: Lanigan, Sask., 9/9/1936

Season	Club, League	Regular Season					Playoffs				
		GP	G	A	Pts	PIM	GP	G	A	Pts	PIM
1956–57	Toronto Maple Leafs, NHL	20	0	5	5	37					
	Rochester Americans, AHL	46	2	13	15	117					
1957–58	Toronto Maple Leafs, NHL	67	1	9	10	91					
1958–59	Toronto Maple Leafs, NHL	51	1	8	9	87	12	0	0	0	24
1959–60	Toronto Maple Leafs, NHL	61	8	9	17	59	10	1	0	1	17
1960–61	Toronto Maple Leafs, NHL	70	1	14	15	70	3	0	0	0	8
1961–62	Toronto Maple Leafs, NHL	65	4	11	15	94	12	0	3	3	19
1962–63	Toronto Maple Leafs, NHL	48	4	8	12	65	10	0	3	3	6
1963–64	Toronto Maple Leafs, NHL	52	4	14	18	113	14	2	3	5	42
1964–65	Toronto Maple Leafs, NHL	70	0	18	18	160	6	0	1	1	14
1965–66	Toronto Maple Leafs, NHL	44	0	6	6	68	4	0	1	1	8
1966–67	Toronto Maple Leafs, NHL	54	2	8	10	83	10	0	0	0	4
1967–68	Oakland Seals, NHL	67	3	10	13	81					
1968–69	Detroit Red Wings, NHL	76	4	16	20	121					
1969–70	Detroit Red Wings, NHL	71	1	18	19	112	4	0	0	0	6
1970–71	Detroit Red Wings, NHL	11	0	3	3	24					
	Toronto Maple Leafs, NHL	58	1	17	18	123	6	0	1	1	19
1971–72	Toronto Maple Leafs, NHL	74	2	12	14	101	5	0	0	0	4
1972–73	Toronto Maple Leafs, NHL	5	1	1	2	4					
	NHL Totals	964	37	187	224	1493	96	3	12	15	171

Won Stanley Cup (1962, 1963, 1964, 1967)

Baun is best known as—and has his fondest memories of being—a member of the classic Leafs teams of the 1960s. "We were known as the milkshake team," he remembers. "I never had a beer till I was 24. And I finally did only because my teammate Allan Stanley told me I'd never last 10 years in the league if I didn't." His clean living translated to the ice, as well. Known as "the Honest Defenseman," he was candid about how he developed his tough style of play and what he thought it took to make it as an NHL defenseman. "I know what has to come from inside," he said. "You can be a good, developed player, but more has to come up than just that 100%."

For all the licks he gave out, though, Baun's career ended because of a hit he took during the 1972–73 season at the hands of the Red Wings' Mickey Redmond. Baun describes what happened: "Mike Pelyk had the puck and I had lost my stick. I shouted at him to ice the puck, but he probably didn't hear me because he threw it behind the net," Baun recalls. "I tried to kick at it with Mickey Redmond closing in. I had hit Mickey pretty hard in the first period, and when my feet went from under me while trying to kick the puck, Mickey helped me along towards the ice. I realized immediately that I would land on my head unless I went into a tuck position. I knew something about that because I used to do some trampoline work and diving. Because of the tuck, I landed on my neck and not my head. I knew right away something had happened to my neck."

At first, Baun thought it was a recurrence of an old neck injury, one he had suffered while playing for the Seals, but it turned out to be something new and more serious, what doctors told him was some nerve damage to his spinal column. "The doctors said if I got hurt again, there was a 95% chance I could wind up in a wheelchair, and I didn't like the odds and decided to retire," Baun said. He immediately went into full-time cattle farming on his land outside of Toronto.

Baun's close friend and teammate Tim Horton died shortly after Baun's retirement from the game, and for a while Baun operated a Tim Horton's donut franchise and was involved with Tim Horton Memorial Fund kids' camps. He also set up an operation called the Professional Hockey Alumni. "Our main thrust is helping the youth of Canada," Baun explained right after his retirement. "We're trying to set up bursaries and have patterned ourselves after the alumni association of the National Football League."

But Baun didn't remain out of the game for very long. He went on to coach the Toronto Toros of the WHA in 1975–76. "I still have a maple leaf stamped on my ass, but now I have a bull, too," he joked upon being named the team's coach, adding his unique take on how he planned to counsel his new players: "I don't know how to motivate people unless I understand what their thinking is, their background, how they were brought up.… I don't think a player is like a tap. He can't be turned on and off. If the preparation isn't there, he just can't do the job."

Baun once fined every member of the Toros $500 after a game against Cleveland when the team botched an 8–2 lead and lost 10–9. He later refunded the money but was replaced as coach in 1976. Baun continued to farm and also had a sideline selling insurance in his retirement.

"I never had a beer till I was 24," Bob Baun (number 21) recalls. "And I finally did only because my teammate Allan Stanley told me I'd never last 10 years in the league if I didn't."

Norm **Ullman**

Norm Ulman recorded 20-goal seasons 16 times, including 12 in a row from 1957 to 1969.

One of hockey's all-time great centers, Norm Ullman excelled at many things, including avoiding the limelight. Had he been a media darling, he would have gained a more prominent position in hockey lore. Ullman was a consistent scorer and playmaker and one of the more tenacious forecheckers ever to play. His longevity was also something for the record books. It was often said that he did things in such efficient yet unspectacular fashion that only true students of the game could appreciate him.

While a junior star with the Maple Leaf Athletic Club and later the Edmonton Oil Kings of the WCJHL, Ullman caught the eye of Detroit scout Clarence Mohr. There followed an impressive developmental year with the Edmonton Flyers of the WHL, where he received valuable tutoring from coach Norman "Bud" Poile. In 1955–56, he played his first of 13 seasons for the Detroit Red Wings. Ullman arrived just a little late for the team's glory days, but they remained a formidable squad, with the likes of Howe, Delvecchio and Kelly to help show him the ropes. The youngster fit in well and developed into a superior two-way center. He also received some playing time between legends Ted Lindsay and Gordie Howe.

Ullman went on to record 16 20-goal seasons, including 12 in a row from 1957 to 1969. His consistent production was matched by his durability, as he missed only 21 games in a 10-year span.

One of his patented moves was to skate across the other team's blue line, delay, pass the puck to his wings and move down the slot for a return pass or rebound. His powerful arm strength and quick anticipation made him one of the game's toughest forecheckers and face-off men. More often than not, Ullman would go into the corners or along the boards and emerge with the puck. Paul Dulmage wrote, "His checking style reminds you of one of those old movies where the hero is trying to free his girl's foot from the railroad tracks as the train bears down on them."

Ullman's skating style symbolized his career. He wasn't the flashiest to watch, but he always ended up where he wanted to be when he wanted to be there. Diligence and deception were his hallmark qualities, as he seemed to be everywhere without giving himself away. Toe Blake remarked: "He isn't all that fast and sometimes I don't even know he is there. I sure don't expect him to be. And then the loud-speaker announces 'goal by Ullman' or 'assist by Ullman' and I know he was there all the

Ullman, Norm
C, 5′10″,175 lbs, b: Provost, Alta., 12/26/1935

Season	Club, League	Regular Season					Playoffs				
		GP	G	A	Pts	PIM	GP	G	A	Pts	PIM
1953–54	Edmonton Flyers, WHL	1	1	0	1	0					
1954–55	Edmonton Flyers, WHL	60	25	34	59	23	9	3	1	4	6
1955–56	Detroit Red Wings, NHL	66	9	9	18	26	10	1	3	4	13
1956–57	Detroit Red Wings, NHL	64	16	36	52	47	5	1	1	2	6
1957–58	Detroit Red Wings, NHL	69	23	28	51	38	4	0	2	2	4
1958–59	Detroit Red Wings, NHL	69	22	36	58	42					
1959–60	Detroit Red Wings, NHL	70	24	34	58	46	6	2	2	4	0
1960–61	Detroit Red Wings, NHL	70	28	42	70	34	11	0	4	4	4
1961–62	Detroit Red Wings, NHL	70	26	38	64	54					
1962–63	Detroit Red Wings, NHL	70	26	30	56	53	11	4	12	16	14
1963–64	Detroit Red Wings, NHL	61	21	30	51	55	14	7	10	17	6
1964–65	Detroit Red Wings, NHL	70	42	41	83	70	7	6	4	10	2
1965–66	Detroit Red Wings, NHL	70	31	41	72	35	12	6	9	15	12
1966–67	Detroit Red Wings, NHL	68	26	44	70	26					
1967–68	Detroit Red Wings, NHL	58	30	25	55	26					
	Toronto Maple Leafs, NHL	13	5	12	17	2					
1968–69	Toronto Maple Leafs, NHL	75	35	42	77	41	4	1	0	1	0
1969–70	Toronto Maple Leafs, NHL	74	18	42	60	37					
1970–71	Toronto Maple Leafs, NHL	73	34	51	85	24	6	0	2	2	2
1971–72	Toronto Maple Leafs, NHL	77	23	50	73	26	5	1	3	4	2
1972–73	Toronto Maple Leafs, NHL	65	20	35	55	10					
1973–74	Toronto Maple Leafs, NHL	78	22	47	69	12	4	1	1	2	0
1974–75	Toronto Maple Leafs, NHL	80	9	26	35	8	7	0	0	0	2
1975–76	Edmonton Oilers, WHA	77	31	56	87	12	4	1	3	4	2
1976–77	Edmonton Oilers, WHA	67	16	27	43	28	5	0	3	3	0
	NHL Totals	1410	490	739	1229	712	106	30	53	83	67
	WHA Totals	144	47	83	130	40	9	1	6	7	2

NHL First All-Star Team (1965)
NHL Second All-Star Team (1967)

time. I don't know how he does it. If I knew, I'd stop him." His tireless effort could be partially attributed to his affection for running in the summer and on non-game days. When interviewed, he was reticent and thoughtful when responding, but typically he focused on the team rather than himself. He earned the apt title "the Quiet Man," but few who tried to keep the puck away from him would say his presence wasn't felt. Jack Adams's sarcastic wit brought about the nickname "Noisy," but this was more of an inside joke.

Ullman led all playoff scorers with 16 points in 1962–63 even though they lost out to Toronto. In 1964–65, he led the league with 42 goals and was selected to the NHL First All-Star Team. For a time, he enjoyed playing on a potent line with Gordie Howe and Alex Delvecchio. He also played with Bruce MacGregor and Paul Henderson on the energetic Hummer Line. On April 11, 1965, during the semifinals, Ullman beat Chicago's Glenn Hall twice in five seconds to establish a new NHL record for the fastest two playoff goals. The following season, he helped the Wings reach the finals, where they lost to Montreal. For the second time in his career, Ullman finished at the head of the post-season scoring list. At one point, coach Sid Abel claimed that Ullman was his most valuable performer.

The team needed a shakeup by the late 1960s. Trading Gordie Howe would have started a riot, but management wasn't thrilled when Ullman was elected president of the NHL Players' Association in January 1968. When Frank Mahovlich became available in March, Ullman was the centerpiece of the package sent to the Maple Leafs. The next year, he played chiefly with Paul Henderson and Floyd Smith. He eventually formed a solid forward line with Henderson and Ron Ellis, which became the team's most consistent unit for a number of years. The self-effacing Ullman once scored a hat-trick to reach the 350-goal mark for his career, but he had to be reminded of the feat by linemate Henderson, who made him retrieve the puck. Ullman was also largely responsible for making the players' association acceptable in the Toronto dressing room.

Norm Ullman (number 7) was a consistent scorer and playmaker and one of the most tenacious forecheckers ever.

The 1969–70 season proved to be very trying as Ullman experienced the worst slump of his career. His linemates also struggled and the Maple Leafs fared poorly in the standings. He regained his form in the early 1970s, but the Ballard era was difficult for the Maple Leafs players. In 1970–71, Ullman did register a personal-best 85 points, but this still placed him 67 points behind scoring champion Phil Esposito. As the decade wore on, the average age of a player decreased, making it difficult for someone like Ullman, in his late 30s, to make an impact. In June 1975, Ullman cleared waivers.

The Edmonton Oilers of the WHA refused to believe that Ullman was washed up and offered him a chance to finish his playing career back home. They had originally selected him in the 1972 General Player Draft and waited patiently for his services. He rewarded their faith with 130 points over two seasons, along with the classy leadership people came to expect. He retired in 1977 after being arguably the most anonymous 490-goal scorer in NHL history. Ullman gained a place in the Hockey Hall of Fame in 1982 and stayed in touch with the game by playing on the Labatt's Original Six Hockey Heroes tour.

John Paul Bucyk

John Bucyk (left) had a marathon career of 23 years, almost all with the Boston Bruins.

John Paul Bucyk had a marathon career of 23 years, almost all of which was spent with the Boston Bruins. He was nicknamed "the Chief" after a Boston sports cartoonist mistook him for a native Canadian because of his dark features. Bucyk loved the nickname and it stuck.

He grew up in Edmonton, Alberta, and played Junior A hockey on the Edmonton Oil Kings with his older brother Bill, who later played in the Western Hockey League but never made it to the NHL. For the next three seasons, Bucyk shifted back and forth between the Detroit Red Wings and the Oil Kings. Finally, in 1954, he was "discovered" in an Oil Kings game by Boston general manager Lynn Patrick, but it would still be three more years before he actually put on a Bruins jersey. In 1957 Boston obtained Bucyk from Detroit in a trade for Terry Sawchuk. "In those days, Sawchuk was one of the top-notch goaltenders," recalled Bucyk, "so being traded for him made me feel pretty good."

Bucyk, John Paul "Chief"
LW, 6´, 215 lbs, b: Edmonton, Alta., 5/12/1935

Season	Club, League	Regular Season					Playoffs				
		GP	G	A	Pts	PIM	GP	G	A	Pts	PIM
1953–54	Edmonton Flyers, WHL	2	2	0	2	2					
1954–55	Edmonton Flyers, WHL	70	30	58	88	57	9	1	6	7	7
1955–56	Detroit Red Wings, NHL	38	1	8	9	20	10	1	1	2	8
	Edmonton Flyers, WHL	6	0	0	0	9					
1956–57	Detroit Red Wings, NHL	66	10	11	21	41	5	0	1	1	0
1957–58	Boston Bruins, NHL	68	21	31	52	57	12	0	4	4	16
1958–59	Boston Bruins, NHL	69	24	36	60	36	7	2	4	6	6
1959–60	Boston Bruins, NHL	56	16	36	52	26					
1960–61	Boston Bruins, NHL	70	19	20	39	48					
1961–62	Boston Bruins, NHL	67	20	40	60	32					
1962–63	Boston Bruins, NHL	69	27	39	66	36					
1963–64	Boston Bruins, NHL	62	18	36	54	36					
1964–65	Boston Bruins, NHL	68	26	29	55	24					
1965–66	Boston Bruins, NHL	63	27	30	57	12					
1966–67	Boston Bruins, NHL	59	18	30	48	12					
1967–68	Boston Bruins, NHL	72	30	39	69	8	3	0	2	2	0
1968–69	Boston Bruins, NHL	70	24	42	66	18	10	5	6	11	0
1969–70	Boston Bruins, NHL	76	31	38	69	13	14	11	8	19	2
1970–71	Boston Bruins, NHL	78	51	65	116	8	7	2	5	7	0
1971–72	Boston Bruins, NHL	78	32	51	83	4	15	9	11	20	6
1972–73	Boston Bruins, NHL	78	40	53	93	12	5	0	3	3	0
1973–74	Boston Bruins, NHL	76	31	44	75	8	16	8	10	18	4
1974–75	Boston Bruins, NHL	78	29	52	81	10	3	1	0	1	0
1975–76	Boston Bruins, NHL	77	36	47	83	20	12	2	7	9	0
1976–77	Boston Bruins, NHL	49	20	23	43	12	5	0	0	0	0
1977–78	Boston Bruins, NHL	53	5	13	18	4					
	NHL Totals	1540	556	813	1369	497	124	41	62	103	42

NHL First All-Star Team (1971)
NHL Second All-Star Team (1968)
Won Lady Byng Trophy (1971, 1974)
Won Lester Patrick Trophy (1977)
Won Stanley Cup (1970, 1972)

A member of the so-called Uke Line in Boston with fellow Ukrainian-Canadians Bronco Horvath and Vic Stasiuk, Bucyk set an astounding number of Bruins records (some of which have now been surpassed by Ray Bourque)—for the most seasons (21), the most games (1,436), the most goals (545), the most assists (794) and the most points (1,339). "I've hit more posts than nets," said the always modest Chief, "but the numbers are nice. I'm thrilled to think of it. It's an honor to be up with those guys. I've thought of myself as a spear-carrier, not a star really. I'm not a glamor guy and I've just gone along getting what I could out of every game, and it's added up."

The modesty is probably how Bucyk got the reputation as being one of the game's classic nice guys—and a hard worker to boot. That, and the fact that he and his brother bought a new home for their parents with the first whack of money they earned in pro hockey.

Bucyk's seasonal scoring totals got better as he got older. Again, the modest Bucyk said it was all because he played on better teams. "Don't forget the quality of the team we had, with Orr and Esposito and the rest," he liked to remind people. But his fans argued that it was only because Bucyk picked up his game a notch when paired with those other high-quality players that the Bruins rose to win two Stanley Cup victories, in 1970 and 1972. "The first Cup was the sweetest thing I ever won," said Bucyk. "I accepted the Cup as captain and it felt terrific."

Unfortunately, Bucyk's career almost ended when he was in his mid-30s because of a back injury. From then on he had to wear a harness, but he continued to play left wing well into his 40s. It wasn't the only extra bit of equipment he wore, either. Bucyk also sported a special medallion for good luck that four of his teammates gave him after his 500th goal.

In 1976, as he neared the end of his playing career, Bucyk was aware that his age was showing. But it didn't seem to be affecting his game as he continued his streak of 10 straight seasons of more than 20 goals. "It's hard to believe. I just keep going. I guess it helps that I am a positional player," he explained. "I skate up and down my wing, doing the most I can with the least amount

A member of the Uke Line with fellow Ukranian-Canadians Bronco Horvath and Vic Stasiuk, John Bucyk (front) set an astounding number of Bruins records.

of effort. I get tired at times and it's tough to go on at times, especially by the end of a season. But by the start of a new season, after a summer of rest, I'm ready to go again. I can still go—I've got the good legs." He added with a laugh, "I'm old enough to be a father to some of these kids, but if they call me 'Pop,' I'll lay one on them!"

"I take the cuts and bruises in stride by now," he continued. "But I've been lucky. It takes longer to recover from injuries than it used to. But if you're going to get goals, you've got to get in where the action is."

And go there he did. Bucyk ended his career with the Bruins as the fourth-leading scorer in NHL history at the time.

He and his wife, Anne, had three kids, and during his career he liked to spend the off-season in British Columbia as a partner in a swimming pool and auto repair business. Bucyk was figuring that those businesses would be his future when he retired from the game, but he was wrong. It seemed he just couldn't break away from the Bruins. He did some assistant coaching in his last years under Bruins coach Don Cherry and after that continued to work with the team in its public relations department in addition to doing color commentary on games on the radio.

In 1978, during a game against Detroit, the Bruins retired the number 9 sweater that Bucyk wore throughout his career with the team. In 1981 Bucyk was inducted into the Hockey Hall of Fame.

Veniamin Alexandrov

Veniamin Alexandrov was an outstanding forward for the Central Red Army and USSR national teams and one of those players whose career takes on a kind of legendary status.

In 1955, Alexandrov replaced injured left winger Vsevolod Bobrov and made his first appearance in the main lineup of the Central Army team alongside Viktor Shuvalov and Yevgeny Babich. With his mature technique and elegant style that closely resembled that of the player he had

Veniamin Alexandrov was one of those rare players whose career becomes legendary.

replaced—Bobrov—the 18-year-old rookie immediately caught the eye of hockey experts. When Bobrov returned to the lineup, Alexandrov changed partners several times before taking the center position in a trio with Konstantin Loktev and Alexander Cherepanov. The young Army trio performed well from the start. At the 1957 World Championship, Alexandrov's line was the top scorer with 25 goals to its credit.

For Alexandrov, hockey was a refined pursuit reserved for the elite. He handled the puck as if it were a precious gem—deftly and carefully. The stick was like a magic wand in his hand and the puck at its tip wove an intricate pattern. He skated with his body at a slight incline and his head held high. Playing alongside Bobrov, Alexandrov had learned to copy his most complicated technique—the ability to suddenly switch his tempo at top speed.

In hockey, Alexandrov was a true aesthete. He loathed everything connected with on-ice fighting, including the use of brute force and punches. He was one of the top Soviet scorers. There were only four players who scored more goals than Alexandrov in USSR national championship play: Boris Mikhailov, Vyacheslav Starshinov, Alexander Guryshev and Vladimir Petrov. At the World Championships, Alexandrov consistently scored the most crucial game-tying and winning goals.

When Alexander Almetov replaced Cherepanov in the lineup, the famous Loktev–Almetov–Alexandrov troika was formed and dominated the ice for six years. But Loktev hung up his skates in 1966 and a year later Almetov followed suit. They had been an extremely close-knit threesome, and after the departure of his partners, Alexandrov became known as "the Lone Ranger." Although he excelled as a soloist, Alexandrov had always derived his greatest satisfaction from masterminding tricky combinations with his partners. At the 1968 Olympics, he played in a line with Boris Mayorov and Vyacheslav Starshinov, who had been his chief rivals from Spartak in the national championship and long-standing competitors for supremacy in the USSR national lineup.

Boris Mayorov said of Alexandrov: "I first saw him when he was already popular and I was nobody. He held himself as befits a famous personality—he didn't notice anyone around him. Alexandrov the hockey player and Alexandrov off the ice were two quite different people. On the hockey rink, Alexandrov was a blinding explosion of fireworks. Outside the rink, he was unusually reticent when it came to emotions and words. It seemed as if he was carrying within himself the art of playing hockey and was afraid it might spill out."

Vyacheslav Starshinov said: "He is a remarkable partner! Refined, cunning, unconventional and superb at passing. As I see it, the very idea of a forward line as a unified, single entity realized its full potential for the first time when the game was played by the Almetov forward line."

Alexandrov, Veniamin
LW/C, 5´11˝, 178 lbs, b: Moscow, USSR, 4/18/1937, d: 11/12/91

Season	Club, League	Regular Season				
		GP	G	A	Pts	PIM
1955–56	CSK MO, USSR	*	18	*	*	*
1956–57	CSK MO, USSR	*	18	*	*	*
WEC–57	USSR	7	8	*	*	*
1957–58	CSK MO, USSR	*	32	*	*	*
WEC–58	USSR	7	9	3	12	2
1958–59	CSK MO, USSR	*	14	*	*	*
WEC–59	USSR	8	4	*	*	*
1959–60	CSKA, USSR	*	19	*	*	*
OWG–60	USSR	7	7	6	13	16
1960–61	CSKA, USSR	*	19	*	*	*
WEC–61	USSR	7	6	2	8	4
1961–62	CSKA, USSR	*	21	*	*	*
1962–63	CSKA, USSR	*	53	*	*	*
WEC–63	USSR	7	4	6	10	2
1963–64	CSKA, USSR	*	39	*	*	*
OWG–64	USSR	8	7	4	11	7
1964–65	CSKA, USSR	*	25	*	*	*
WEC–65	USSR	7	4	5	9	8
1965–66	CSKA, USSR	*	31	*	*	*
WEC–66	USSR	7	9	8	17	4
1966–67	CSKA, USSR	*	27	*	*	*
WEC–67	USSR	7	7	7	14	4
1967–68	CSKA, USSR	*	23	*	*	*
OWG–68	USSR	4	3	3	6	0
1968–69	CSKA, USSR	*	12	*	*	*
	USSR Totals	400	351	*	*	*
	OWG/WEC Totals	76	68	*	*	*

Won OWG (1964, 1968)
Won WEC (1963, 1965, 1966, 1967)
USSR Champion (1956, 1958, 1959, 1960, 1961, 1963, 1964, 1965, 1966, 1968)

But Alexandrov was already becoming disillusioned with hockey. Even while still partnered with Almetov, he was often at loggerheads with new young players on the Central Red Army team. After Almetov's departure, Alexandrov had to try to fit himself in with the younger lineup of Boris Mikhailov and Vladimir Petrov. Both Mikhailov and Petrov would tear around the rink scrambling for the puck no matter where it was. Alexandrov despised that kind of hockey and would frequently make sarcastic remarks about them. He explained his reaction to coach Tarasov by saying: "They can't even make a decent pass. They don't understand me."

On ice, Veniamin Alexandrov (center) was a blinding explosion of fireworks. Off the ice, he was unusually reticent when it came to words and emotions.

Alexandrov constantly vied with Mikhailov and Petrov to determine which of them was the most important in the forward line. At some level, they were really arguing about the essence of hockey. The younger players didn't know how to accommodate Alexandrov, the hockey master. With their unbridled energy and drive, they wanted to set the pace themselves. Alexandrov, for his part, yearned for the unique and genuine partnership he had shared with Loktev and Almetov.

Stanislav Petukhov

When Stanislav Petukhov first appeared in the Dynamo Moscow lineup, he was noticed right away. He was tall, well built and at the same time graceful and agile. He made his hockey debut just as one generation of players was being replaced by another. The big stars of the 1940s and 1950s had already retired or were about to do so, but the rookies hadn't yet shown their capability. Unless you were another Vsevolod Bobrov, it wasn't easy to make a brilliant impression on the ice in your first game. Hockey is a team sport, and even for a gifted player, it isn't easy to play outstanding hockey without good partners.

Stanislav Petukhov became a star because he had a number of exceptional abilities, including an excellent skating style, great speed and a powerful shot. This winger's physical strength and consummate technical skill enabled him to play a good game in front of the opponent's net, where he always felt comfortable. As well, he had an exceptional ability to slap the puck into the net after it was deflected by the goaltender.

Stanislav Petukhov played only 17 games for Team USSR but scored 12 goals.

He had his own particular way of playing in the crease, as well as a feel for polished, diversified and well-set-up plays. He never tried to take advantage of his huge frame. Always keeping his eye on the puck, he ignored attempts to push him out of the crease. Whenever he could, he would take a shot on goal without hesitation.

If Petukhov appeared to lack passion and drive in his game, it may have been because Dynamo Moscow traditionally adhered to a strict playing discipline and positional play based on gaining the puck. Dynamo players, especially the forwards, weren't noted for their aggressive style.

Petukhov's skill at the boards and in the corners of the rink—something most forwards lacked—also distinguished his style of play. This wasn't only because of his physical strength. His game near the boards wasn't a spontaneous reaction to what was happening there but a conscious strategy aimed at further developing plays. His tactical maturity was evident in the mutual understanding he developed with partners who had a different style of play.

Petukhov, Stanislav
RW, 6´1˝, 200 lbs, b: Moscow, USSR, 8/19/1937

Season	Club, League	Regular Season				
		GP	G	A	Pts	PIM
1955–56	Dynamo Moscow, USSR	9	1	*	*	*
1956–57	Dynamo Moscow, USSR	23	14	*	*	*
1957–58	Dynamo Moscow, USSR	33	20	*	*	*
1958–59	Dynamo Moscow, USSR	26	18	*	*	*
1959–60	Dynamo Moscow, USSR	33	23	*	*	*
OWG–60	USSR	6	4	4	8	4
1960–61	Dynamo Moscow, USSR	23	17	*	*	*
1961–62	Dynamo Moscow, USSR	29	25	4	29	24
1962–63	Dynamo Moscow, USSR	24	10	0	10	18
WEC–63	USSR	7	4	4	8	4
1963–64	Dynamo Moscow, USSR	36	21	*	*	*
OWG–64	USSR	5	4	1	5	2
1964–65	Dynamo Moscow, USSR	35	7	1	8	22
1965–66	Dynamo Moscow, USSR	36	5	1	6	18
1966–67	Dynamo Moscow, USSR	42	6	6	12	24
1967–68	Dynamo Moscow, USSR	39	6	2	8	14
	USSR Totals	388	173	*	*	*
	OWG/WEC Totals	18	12	9	21	10

Won OWG (1964)
Won WEC (1963)

Petukhov played major-league hockey for 13 years, all of them with Dynamo Moscow. He was lucky to avoid any serious injury, loss of capability and conflicts with coaches. Petukhov began playing as a forward and ended his career on the defense line. This wasn't by choice but due to changes in team tactics. To his credit, Petukhov immediately accepted the coach's decision, putting aside his personal ambitions.

There are obvious differences between playing defense and being on the forward line, and Petukhov quickly mastered the new skills. His previous experience as a forward made his game in defense more polished and streamlined. But whenever he charged from one end of the rink to the other, you could feel that he was essentially a forward. Yet when he returned to his own zone, he would meet oncoming opponents with a stiff bodycheck in order to get hold of the puck or paste them to the boards like a true defenseman.

Petukhov played 17 games with Team USSR at World Championship and Olympic hockey tournaments and scored a total of 12 goals. He spent the better part of his career on the ice as a forward and is best remembered for his achievements as a forward rather than as a defenseman.

Boris Mayorov

Boris Mayorov played his first World Championship in March 1961. He was then the top scorer and was selected to the first-ever All-Star team. In June of the same year, Mayorov received his engineering degree.

A year later, the forward line consisting of the Mayorov brothers—Boris and Yevgeny—and Vyacheslav Starshinov led Spartak to its first gold medal in the USSR Championship. Soon after, Boris was elected captain of the Soviet national squad.

The Starshinov line was distinguished by its synchronous actions and total reciprocal awareness. Boris played left wing and the center slot was filled by the left-handed Starshinov. It would be a mistake, however, to say that the Mayorov brothers always got along well. At times, they fought like kids in the backyard. At their debut in the World Championship, the Soviet team was winning quite handily over the East German team, but the Starshinov forward line didn't seem to be clicking. The quarreling between the Mayorov brothers reached the point where Boris whacked his brother with his stick and Yevgeny paid him back in kind. Coach Arkady Chernyshev sent them both off to the locker room.

Boris Mayorov was a natural leader, prime mover and innovator.

The first to come to his senses, Boris, said, "Let's go apologize and ask to be let out on the ice again." But Yevgeny was stubborn. "I've got nothing to apologize for," he replied. It usually took him longer to cool off than his brother. In the end, coach Anatoli Tarasov (who operated in tandem with Chernyshev) told 26-year-old Yevgeny to pack his bags. When he was coaching the national team, Army coach Tarasov didn't have much use for a forward line from the opposition Spartak, much less a forward line that was independent and bothersome.

Boris was able to end his career with the national team with more dignity than his brother. Before the 1969 World Championship, he was straightforward at a meeting with his teammates, telling them honestly that due to injuries he would be unable to play at his best in all the games.

Boris Mayorov was a natural-born leader, and Starshinov cited him as a prime mover and innovator. When his playing career ended, Mayorov coached Spartak twice during a six-year period.

Boris Mayorov was unique for having played all the possible roles in hockey. He was a player, team captain, coach, director of the Soviet hockey federation, coach of the championship team of Finland, manager of Team USSR and, finally, TV sportscaster. He made his television debut at the age of 60, and here too he excelled. A year later he added president of Spartak Moscow to his long list of titles.

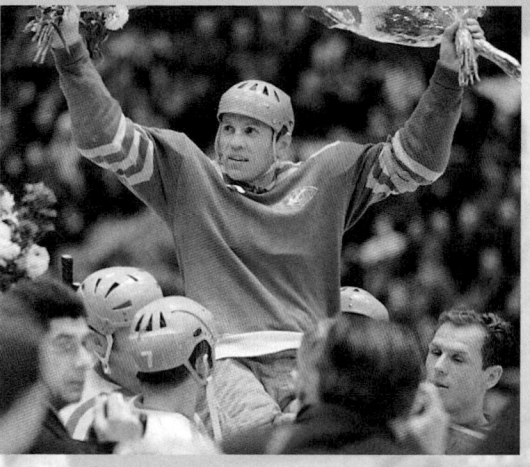

Boris Mayorov (top) was a player, team captain, coach, manager, TV sportscaster, president of Spartak Moscow and director of the Soviet Hockey Federation.

Mayorov, Boris
LW, 5′9″, 158 lbs, b: Moscow, USSR, 2/11/1938

Season	Club, League	GP	G	A	Pts	PIM
1955–56	Spartak Moscow, USSR	*	1	*	*	*
1956–57	Spartak Moscow, USSR	*	3	*	*	*
1957–58	Spartak Moscow, USSR	*	8	*	*	*
1958–59	Spartak Moscow, USSR	*	18	*	*	*
1959–60	Spartak Moscow, USSR	*	10	*	*	*
1960–61	Spartak Moscow, USSR	*	20	*	*	*
WEC–61	USSR	7	7	10	17	0
1961–62	Spartak Moscow, USSR	*	30	*	*	*
1962–63	Spartak Moscow, USSR	*	27	*	*	*
WEC–63	USSR	7	3	6	9	0
1963–64	Spartak Moscow, USSR	*	18	*	*	*
OWG–64	USSR	8	7	4	11	0
1964–65	Spartak Moscow, USSR	*	25	*	*	*
WEC–65	USSR	7	5	3	8	6
1965–66	Spartak Moscow, USSR	*	22	*	*	*
WEC–66	USSR	7	3	3	6	2
1966–67	Spartak Moscow, USSR	*	27	*	*	*
WEC–67	USSR	7	2	3	5	9
1967–68	Spartak Moscow, USSR	*	29	*	*	*
OWG–68	USSR	7	3	3	6	2
1968–69	Spartak Moscow, USSR	38	16	*	*	*
	USSR Totals	400	255	*	*	*
	OWG/WEC Totals	50	30	32	62	19

Won OWG (1964, 1968)
Won WEC (1963, 1965, 1966, 1967)
USSR Champion (1962, 1967, 1969)

Josef Golonka

Josef Golonka could never remember how many goals he scored. In fact, he didn't want to play hockey in the first place, preferring tennis and thinking he had the talent necessary to succeed in that sport. But he never made it to Wimbledon and came to resent the sport. For hockey fans in the former Czechoslovakia, it was a good thing.

Fans cheered Josef Golonka even when he was given a penalty.

With the exception of two seasons spent during military service with the Dukla Jihlava club, Golonka played out his career in Bratislava, where he was born on January 6, 1938. From 1955 to 1957 and from 1959 to 1969, he devoted himself to Slovan. Here he grew to be one of the best centers of his day. While he was impulsive, temperamental and hard to tame, he was also a very good stickhandler and was very productive. He was the favorite of hockey fans whenever he was playing on their side.

Whenever Golonka scored, the fans almost brought the roof of Bratislava hall down. They even cheered him when he had to go to the penalty box for one of his many offenses. To some he was known as "Jozo" or the more endearing "Jozinko." For others he was "Ziletka" (Razor Blade), a player who didn't curry favor with anyone—in fact an all-around holy terror for his opponents, the referees and even some coaches he often angered by ignoring their instructions and doing things his own way. But hockey was in his blood, and he played with enormous enthusiasm. Golonka could be the heart and soul of the team, captivating players and fans alike and seldom disappointing them.

Golonka was often sought out by journalists, who enjoyed interviewing him for his clever remarks. He spoke plainly, calling a spade a spade, and he was intelligent. Besides playing hockey, he studied economics. "It bugged me that athletes are thought to be idiots. Naturally, there are stupid and clever people among them," Golonka once complained, though he seldom let his darker moods show. "I am as flushed as a two-hump camel," he used to say after a match.

Although he grew up in an orderly environment, Golonka liked to refer to himself as a street kid. He did work for everything he got in life, but he was hardly abandoned. His sister was a promising figure skater at one time. In the 1960s, Golonka became the most significant and most popular hockey player in the country. He knew how to give that little bit extra and put on a show for the fans. "I play hockey—I don't play-act. If I were to play it in a movie, I would never be able to do it. When I feel pain, I really feel it. When I feel joy, it is real joy. When I am angry, I show it."

A unique shot of him standing with his arms broadly outstretched celebrating a goal became the material for a statue by artist Zdenek Nemecek which to this day stands in front of the Sports Hall in Prague. Its miniature version is awarded annually to the country's best player. From 1969, it was awarded to the best player in Czechoslovakia, and since the country split up, it goes to the best player in the Czech Republic—equivalent to the European Golden Hockey Stick trophy.

Golonka never got to share in a victory at the international level. He was already retiring from the national team during the 1969 World Championship. Originally the tournament was to take place in Prague, but after the 1968 invasion of Czechoslovakia by the Warsaw Pact armies, it was transferred to Stockholm. Golonka didn't play very well; His meniscus injury was bothering him. The team didn't win a medal, even though they beat the Soviets 2–0 and 4–3. Still, those two victories in such difficult times for his country warmed Golonka's heart more than a gold medal around his neck would have.

Golonka, Josef
C, 5´8″, 169 lbs, b: Bratislava, Czechoslovakia, 1/6/1938

Season	Club, League	Regular Season				
		GP	G	A	Pts	PIM
1955–57	Slovan, Czechoslovakia	*	*	*	*	*
1957–59	Dukla Jihlava, Czechoslovakia	*	*	*	*	*
WEC–59	Czechoslovakia	8	7	4	11	*
1959–60	Slovan, Czechoslovakia	*	*	*	*	*
OWG–60	Czechoslovakia	7	6	*	*	*
1960–61	Slovan, Czechoslovakia	*	35	*	*	*
1961–64	Slovan, Czechoslovakia	*	*	*	*	*
OWG–64	Czechoslovakia	7	5	2	7	10
1964–65	Slovan, Czechoslovakia	*	*	*	*	*
WEC–65	Czechoslovakia	7	6	8	14	2
1965–66	Slovan, Czechoslovakia	*	*	*	*	*
WEC–66	Czechoslovakia	7	2	4	6	4
1966–67	Slovan, Czechoslovakia	*	*	*	*	*
WEC–67	Czechoslovakia	7	5	7	12	6
1967–68	Slovan, Czechoslovakia	*	*	*	*	*
OWG–68	Czechoslovakia	10	4	6	10	8
1968–69	Slovan, Czechoslovakia	*	*	*	*	*
WEC–69	Czechoslovakia	10	2	1	3	8
1969–72	Riessersee, FRG	*	*	*	*	*
	Czechoslovakia Totals	330	298	*	*	*
	OWG/WEC Totals	63	37	*	*	*

He wanted to leave the game at the height of his glory. At 31, after 14 seasons in the league, he headed to Garmisch-Partenkirchen to play for the German club SC Riessersee. Supposedly the town took up a collection to be able to acquire him, as Slovan exacted a high price for the release of its best player. He finished his hockey career in 1975 in Zvolen, where he was pampered like royalty.

Later he coached, and not for a minute did he think he should have been doing something different. "I have devoted my life to hockey and now I should work in an office? Not on your life!"

He led SC Riessersee for a total of four seasons. In 1978 they won the league title. Later he worked with Kolner EC, with whom he won the league title six years later. Then he moved on to Zetor Brno and Slovan Bratislava. From 1979 to 1981, he worked with the junior national team and the following season with Czechoslovakia's B team. During the 1997 World Championship, he coached the independent Slovak national team. Then he tried to retire but couldn't stand it for long. During the 1999–2000 season, he once again worked with SC Riessersee, which dropped into a lower level of competition. "I cannot stay inactive. The minute old friends called, I knew I wouldn't stay at home."

Eduard Ivanov

Eduard Ivanov began his career in Soviet major-league hockey with great promise and then seemed to disappear. In fact, Ivanov continued to play hockey until the age of 32, a notable achievement. But he spent his last three seasons playing for an average minor-league Army team in the town of Kalinin in the USSR.

How did a four-time world champion end up back in the minor leagues?

Eduard Ivanov began playing hockey at the Young Pioneers Stadium in Moscow. At the age of 17, he was invited to join Khimik, where he played for two seasons. He was a favorite of Khimik coach Nikolai Epshtein, who recognized Ivanov's talent and allowed him to move up from the number 10 team to the number one team in the country at that time, the Krylja Sovetov (Soviet Wings). However, during the five years he played for the Wings, Ivanov never became national champion.

The team had begun a slow downward slide by the time Ivanov moved on to play for the Central Red Army. With Central Army, Ivanov started winning gold medals and for four years in a row he was national champion. He had become firmly entrenched on the national squad. There is no doubt that the years he played for Army were the best years of his career. But Ivanov's time in the majors wasn't as long as it could have or should have been.

Less than a year before Ivanov's second Olympic hockey tournament, he was already dreaming of bringing home the gold medal a second time. But a disagreement with coach Anatoli Tarasov led to Tarasov's decision to get rid of him. If the conflict had occurred today, it wouldn't have had such drastic results. Ivanov would have been sent to another team and the case would have been closed. But things were different then. Ivanov not only played for the main Army club, he was also serving in the Army. The Central Red Army club wasn't interested in building up any other teams, such as Spartak. So the Army commanders decided to send defenseman Ivanov, who was in his

Eduard Ivanov was a versatile, all-round player—equally powerful and effective on both defense and offense.

At the 1964 Olympics, the prize for the best forward was awarded to a defenseman, Eduard Ivanov (front).

prime, to serve in a farm club in Kalinin. It was a form of banishment. Finding himself in the farm club lineup, a player could forget about getting onto the national team.

No one could have predicted there would be tension between Tarasov and Ivanov. Tarasov was proud of his successful experiment with the team. Instead of the conventional two defensemen and three forwards, Tarasov changed the configuration to one defenseman (Alexander Ragulin), two forwards (Vladimir Vikulov and Anatoli Firsov) and two "semi-defensemen" (Ivanov and Viktor Polupanov). It was a revolutionary undertaking but it produced excellent results. The line, which Tarasov called "the System," went to the World Championship in Vienna as a third-stringer but ended up making a significant contribution to the USSR's resounding victory. Of the top scorers, Firsov was first, Polupanov second and Vikulov fifth. And it was all achieved thanks to the efforts of Ivanov.

Ivanov was a versatile, all-round player—equally powerful and effective on both defense and offense. Physically well built, bold, swift and an excellent checker, Ivanov also had a knack for organizing attacks with strong and accurate passes, as well as a powerful slapshot from the blue line.

The 1964 Olympics was Ivanov's most successful. He scored six goals and proved to be as formidable an opponent as any of the forwards on the line. It is significant that the organizing committee that traditionally selects the best players on each line awarded special prizes to Canadian goalie Seth Martin and Czech defenseman Frantisek Tikal but gave the prize for the best forward to Soviet team captain Boris Mayorov so the coaches and players themselves could decide which individual was most deserving. They awarded the prize to Ivanov. Ironically, the prize for best forward was awarded to a defenseman.

Ivanov, Eduard
D, 5´10˝, 185 lbs, b: Moscow, USSR, 4/25/1938

Season	Club, League	Regular Season				
		GP	G	A	Pts	PIM
1955–56	Khimik Moscow, USSR	*	*	*	*	*
1956–57	Khimik Voskresensk, USSR	*	*	*	*	*
1957–62	Krylja Sovetov, USSR	*	*	*	*	*
1962–63	CSKA, USSR	*	4	*	*	*
WEC–63	USSR	7	4	0	4	6
1963–64	CSKA, USSR	*	2	*	*	*
OWG–64	USSR	8	6	1	7	6
1964–65	CSKA, USSR	*	1	*	*	*
WEC–65	USSR	7	2	3	5	6
1965–66	CSKA, USSR	*	5	*	*	*
1966–67	CSKA, USSR	*	11	*	*	*
WEC–67	USSR	7	0	3	3	16
1967–70	SKA MVO (2), USSR	*	*	*	*	*
	USSR Totals	300	40	*	*	*
	OWG/WEC Totals	29	12	7	19	34

Named Best Forward at OWG (1964)
Won OWG (1964)
Won WEC (1963, 1965, 1967)
USSR Champion (1963, 1964, 1965, 1966)

Viktor Yakushev

Viktor Yakushev was a unique hockey player not only in the Soviet Union but internationally. The circumstances of his career are even more remarkable than the many peculiarities of his game. He played for only one team, Lokomotiv Moscow, which in 1961 was among the top three in the USSR national championship tournament. He played until the age of 42, by which time Lokomotiv had been reduced to a minor-league team that folded entirely after Yakushev ended his playing career.

At the World Championships, he played for the USSR nationals eight times in six different line-ups. It is worth noting the character of that time, the lineups and the morals that prevailed then. Anatoli Tarasov, the virtual ruler of the nationals, had whipped into shape a whole detachment of candidates from his own local CSKA club for the national lineup, capitalizing on the competitive pride of each candidate. Tarasov virtually ignored the forwards from Arkady Chernyshev's club, even though as Dynamo coach he was the senior coach of the nationals. Dynamo's best forward, Vladimir Yurzinov, only made it to the World Championships twice. Tarasov also seemed to enjoy breaking up the talented forward lines of Spartak Moscow in order to weaken his competitors in the domestic championships.

Viktor Yakushev played for a single team, Lokomotiv Moscow, until the age of 42.

Tarasov used Viktor Yakushev as a pawn in his own political game because he wasn't a threat to his CSKA club. Yet Tarasov valued the Lokomotiv forward because Yakushev played a key role for the nationals, not just by handling problems and performing well. In 1963, when the Canadians managed to bring the score from 4–0 to 4–2 in the final game against the USSR, the Soviets faced losing the World Championship title if they let in one more goal. Yakushev fought for the gold right to the final seconds of the game. A year later, at the Olympics in Innsbruck, where the USSR nationals were returning as reigning champions, the extremely loyal and conscientious Yakushev was assigned the job of guarding the eminent Swedish forward Sven "Tumba" Johansson. Yakushev scored nine goals and became the top scorer for the team.

One of Yakushev's cohorts, Boris Mayorov, said of his partnership with Yakushev at the 1966 World Championship: "Yakushev was an outstanding player who simply had to be in the nationals lineup. It is with a special feeling of pleasure that I recall the seven games played shoulder to shoulder with Yakushev in Ljubljana." At that championship, Yakushev made 11 assists, proving he was an invaluable partner on the ice.

What did Yakushev have that the national squad couldn't do without? What was it that made Yakushev feel at home on any forward line? If Yakushev had been playing for a team like Lokomotiv in the media frenzy of today, there is little doubt that he would have been heralded as the best player ever. There is no denying that Yakushev was an outstanding player with an exceptional ability to collaborate with other players. Flexibility, adaptability and compatibility were Viktor Yakushev's strengths. "Compatibility established right at our very first training workouts," he once said, "no matter with whom. After that, I did my best to work out the particulars of real teamwork."

On the ice, Viktor Yakushev played common-sense hockey. When he celebrated his 40th birthday, veteran coach Nikolai Epshtein, who at the time was at the helm of Novosibirsk, noted: "If I could accomplish the impossible and somehow tempt, win over or purchase Yakushev, I would bring him over here to Siberia and say to him, 'You can play for me as long as you want in any game. If you want to play more, go ahead. Less? Go ahead. If you want, you can play till you're 60. In short, do

Yakushev, Viktor
C, 5'9", 180 lbs, b: Moscow, USSR, 11/16/1937

Season	Club, League	Regular Season				
		GP	G	A	Pts	PIM
1955–58	Lokomotiv Moscow, USSR	*	*	*	*	*
1958–59	Lokomotiv Moscow, USSR	*	21	*	*	*
WEC–59	USSR	8	6	*	*	*
1959–60	Lokomotiv Moscow, USSR	*	*	*	*	*
OWG–60	USSR	7	1	4	5	0
1960–61	Lokomotiv Moscow, USSR	*	*	*	*	*
WEC–61	USSR	6	2	1	3	10
1961–63	Lokomotiv Moscow, USSR	*	*	*	*	*
WEC–63	USSR	7	4	1	5	0
1963–64	Lokomotiv Moscow, USSR	*	*	*	*	*
OWG–64	USSR	8	9	4	13	0
1964–65	Lokomotiv Moscow, USSR	*	*	*	*	*
WEC–65	USSR	7	4	4	8	2
1965–66	Lokomotiv Moscow, USSR	*	*	*	*	*
WEC–66	USSR	7	2	11	13	0
1966–67	Lokomotiv Moscow, USSR	*	*	*	*	*
WEC–67	USSR	7	2	5	7	0
1967–70	Lokomotiv Moscow, USSR	*	*	*	*	*
1970–71	Lokomotiv Moscow (2), USSR	*	*	*	*	*
1971–72	Lokomotiv Moscow, USSR	27	2	*	*	*
1972–77	Lokomotiv Moscow (2), USSR	*	*	*	*	*
	USSR Totals	400	161	*	*	*
	OWG/WEC Totals	57	30	*	*	*

Won OWG (1964)
Won WEC (1963, 1965, 1966, 1967)

what you feel is necessary. Every minute you are on the ice, every minute of your caliber of hockey is worth more than a dozen training sessions and 30 sermons.'"

But Yakushev remained loyal to Lokomotiv. In those days, that kind of dedication and loyalty to family, home and team was genuine and widely shared.

Yakushev appeared on the ice at most of the major hockey competitions in the world. At the end of his career, he played in a minor league in the remote Uzbek capital of Tashkent. Words such as "popularity," "image" and "ambition" weren't in Yakushev's vocabulary. What he loved most was playing hockey for Lokomotiv—nothing else mattered as much. Yakushev played the game longer than any other Soviet hockey player. When he continued to play in the minor leagues, he ignored the many comments about his age. Throughout his more than 20 years as a hockey player, Viktor Yakushev missed only three training workouts.

Viktor Konovalenko

Viktor Konovalenko was considered the coolest player under pressure on the Soviet Union's national team.

In the 1960s, thousands of boys wanted to be Viktor Konovalenko, the best goaltender in the Soviet Union. One of those boys was Vladislav Tretiak. It was his cherished dream to become a goalie like Konovalenko and to wear Konovalenko's number 20 on his jersey. At the age of 16, the future goaltender got the opportunity to train with his idol. Konovalenko looked at the young Tretiak, shook his hand and said, "Don't be afraid." Later, when they were both goalies with the national squad, Konovalenko, knowing Tretiak's long-time dream, offered him the coveted number.

Konovalenko was considered the coolest player on the Soviet Union's national team. When he was first invited to play for the nationals, Anatoli Tarasov decided to test the newcomer. "How are you feeling?" he asked Konovalenko. "Fine," was the reply. "And if we decide to put you in the net against the Canadians tomorrow?" "Fine," said Konovalenko. After which the new goalie ate a hearty meal and immediately fell asleep. Tarasov was surprised to hear Konovalenko snoring in the next room.

It is possible that his easygoing attitude caused Konovalenko to make mistakes at various stages of his career and may even have led to his becoming a goalie in the first place. In his home town of Gorky, he failed to gain acceptance as a forward or a defenseman and he realized that guarding the net was his only chance, as there were few contenders for the job. Not everyone wants to have pucks fired at them; it requires a particular kind of courage as well as patience. And Konovalenko knew how to tolerate pain; he tested himself often. His first experience as a goalie was wearing Russian felt boots stuffed with old books that acted as pads.

Konovalenko went to his first World Championship in 1961 as a first-string goalie but ended up playing as a sub. For the occasion, Konovalenko had equipped himself with a new glove, a gift from American hockey player and coach John Mariucci, whom he had met while in America with the national junior team. But in a trial game against the Swiss, Konovalenko missed six pucks with his new glove.

At the next World Championship, in 1963, Konovalenko made a serious mistake in a game against Sweden for which he would never forgive himself. He had been studying the tactics of forwards coming at him in one-on-one confrontations and had decided to become the aggressor because he knew that the goalie usually ended up the loser. With the score at 1–1, Konovalenko skated out to the blue line to meet the oncoming Nils Nilsson, who outplayed him and scored the winning goal for his team. "If only I had stayed in the net," he kept saying over and over.

Konovalenko liked to compete against the Canadians, especially when they peppered him with powerful shots. He became friends with Canadian goalkeeper Seth Martin. As a token of respect, Martin made a special goalie's mask for Konovalenko in 1963. It was Konovalenko's first mask, for at the time masks weren't yet prevalent among Soviet goalies. He kept the mask for several years, until it was stolen.

In the 1960s, thousands of boys wanted to be Viktor Konovalenko (left), the best goalkeeper in the Soviet Union.

In 1969, before leaving for the tournament, the players were given a day off and each player made his own plans. Konovalenko was the only player who wasn't from Moscow. It was March 8, Women's Day, and his wife and young daughter were alone in Gorky. Konovalenko set out for his home town, where he was warmly received by his family. Unfortunately, he fell asleep and missed the train back to Moscow. He turned up very late and was subsequently sacked from the national squad.

In the first game of the 1970 World Championship tournament against the Swedes, Konovalenko was badly injured. The medics came out on the ice with stretchers, but when the goalie came to and saw his so-called rescuers, he escaped as fast as his legs would carry him. The next day he felt fine and was ready for his training workout. In the next game, against the Finns, he received a hard whack on the bridge of his nose. Under the mask his face was covered with blood, but no one knew about it until the end of the game. The journalists focused on his playing skills, not his courage, and for Konovalenko, it was his best championship.

Most hockey players were confounded by Konovalenko's behavior on the ice. He often stood as still as a statue, making not a movement or a gesture and prompting the players to take bets as to when he would snap out of it. Suddenly he would come to life and tune in to the action on the ice. During an attack on his goal, Konovalenko moved like a boxer, using swift and polished movements. Mentally agile and resourceful, he would spring between goal posts as easily and smoothly as a cat.

Viktor Konovalenko died in relative obscurity, never complaining, even though he suffered from heart trouble. It was never his practice to complain. All of Gorky came to his funeral and the city's Sports Palace was later named in his honor.

Konovalenko, Viktor
G, 5'8", 167 lbs, b: Gorky, USSR, 3/11/1938, d: 2/20/1996

Season	Club, League	Regular Season		
		GP	GA	Avg
1956–61	Torpedo Gorky, USSR	*	*	*
WEC–61	USSR	3	4	1.33
1961–63	Torpedo Gorky, USSR	*	*	*
WEC–63	USSR	7	8	1.14
1963–64	Torpedo Gorky, USSR	*	*	*
OWG–64	USSR	7	10	1.43
1964–65	Torpedo Gorky, USSR	*	*	*
WEC–65	USSR	5	10	2.00
1965–66	Torpedo Gorky, USSR	*	*	*
WEC–66	USSR	6	7	1.17
1966–67	Torpedo Gorky, USSR	*	*	*
WEC–67	USSR	6	8	1.33
1967–68	Torpedo Gorky, USSR	*	*	*
OWG–68	USSR	5	9	1.80
1968–70	Torpedo Gorky, USSR	*	*	*
WEC–70	USSR	8	7	0.87
1970–71	Torpedo Gorky, USSR	*	*	*
WEC–71	USSR	7	18	2.57
1971–72	Torpedo Gorky, USSR	*	*	*
	USSR Totals	450	*	*
	OWG/WEC Totals	54	81	1.50

Won OWG (1964, 1968)
Won WEC (1963, 1965, 1966, 1967, 1970, 1971)

Ulf Sterner

In the era of the Original Six, Ulf Sterner was the first European-trained player to join the NHL.

In November 1997 a jubilee game to commemorate the 75th anniversary of Sweden's hockey union was played at Stockholm's Globe Arena. Tre Kronor met a European All-Star team consisting of Europeans playing for Swedish clubs. A souvenir booklet accompanying the game featured many of Sweden's hockey celebrities, including Ulf Sterner, who was labeled "the greatest talent."

Ulf Sterner made his debut with Tre Kronor when he was only 17 years and nine months old—the national team's youngest rookie of all times. He was born February 11, 1941, in a small town called Deje, lost among the lakes and woods in the region of Varmland. Sterner recalled, "I got my first skates as soon as I learned to stand up and played for a junior team my father coached." And it was a good team that won most of its tournaments. At 15, Sterner was accepted onto a second-division club and soon local fans were spreading the word about a speedy young virtuoso who could sneak through a bunch of men and score a goal.

He first appeared with Tre Kronor in a friendly game against Czechoslovakia at Johanneshof on November 12, 1959. The Swedish team won the game 11–3. The young Sterner scored his first goal—the first of what would be many more. "Overall, I played 2,161 games," Sterner recalled. "I scored 842 goals and made 1,002 passes. For the national team I appeared in 209 games, scored 108 goals and made 188 assists." However, Sterner was left off the Swedish hockey union's "200 List" for a long time before finally being included.

What is remembered is that in the late 1950s and early 1960s, Ulf Sterner, along with Sven "Tumba" Johansson, Nils Nilsson and Ronald Pettersson, was one of Sweden's most popular hockey players and an international star. It was Sterner who invented the famous fake "stick-skate-stick" maneuver.

In Sterner's opinion, he scored his most memorable goal against Canada at the 1962 World Championship in Colorado Springs, bringing the score to 3–0. "After somebody struck me with a stick, I was carried off on a stretcher. But I returned to the ice, got the

Sterner, Ulf
LW, 6′2″, 187 lbs, b: Deje, Sweden, 2/11/1941

Season	Club, League	Regular Season					Playoffs				
		GP	G	A	Pts	PIM	GP	G	A	Pts	PIM
1956–57	Forshaga, Sweden	7	3	0	3	*					
1957–58	Forshaga, Sweden	14	2	0	2	*					
1958–59	Forshaga, Sweden	11	7	8	15	*					
1959–60	Forshaga, Sweden	14	17	6	23	14					
OWG–60	Sweden	5	0	1	1	0					
1960–61	Forshaga, Sweden	13	14	8	22	2					
WEC–61	Sweden	7	5	0	5	2					
1961–62	Vastra Frolunda, Sweden	13	12	9	21	26	7	6	4	10	5
WEC–62	Sweden	7	9	7	16	2					
1962–63	Vastra Frolunda, Sweden	14	14	6	20	6	7	7	4	11	0
WEC–63	Sweden	7	7	2	9	2					
1963–64	Vastra Frolunda, Sweden	12	10	2	12	6	7	1	4	5	10
OWG–64	Sweden	7	6	5	11	0					
1964–65	New York Rangers, NHL	4	0	0	0	0					
	St. Paul Rangers, CHL	16	12	9	21	2					
	Baltimore Clippers, AHL	52	18	26	44	12	5	1	0	1	2
1965–66	Rogle, Sweden	15	32	11	43	*	6	12	3	15	*
WEC–66	Sweden	7	4	1	5	0					
1966–67	Rogle, Sweden	19	4	11	15	11					
WEC–67	Sweden	7	2	3	5	7					
1967–68	Farjestad, Sweden	21	16	8	24	19					
1968–69	Vastra Frolunda, Sweden	19	19	20	39	10	7	5	7	12	2
WEC–69	Sweden	10	5	9	14	8					
1969–70	Farjestad, Sweden	17	14	22	36	*	5	3	4	7	2
WEC–70	Sweden	10	1	7	8	7					
1970–71	Farjestad, Sweden	6	4	7	11	13	14	10	3	13	14
WEC–71	Sweden	10	2	2	4	2					
1971–72	Farjestad, Sweden	14	10	15	25	28	14	5	6	11	24
1972–73	Farjestad, Sweden	14	7	15	22	23	14	10	2	12	29
WEC–73	Sweden	9	5	2	7	6					
	Sweden Totals	223	185	148	333	*	81	59	37	96	*
	OWG/WEC Totals	86	46	39	85	36					
	NHL Totals	4	0	0	0	0					

Named Best Forward at WEC (1969)
Won WEC (1962)

puck, moved around the Canadians and shot it behind the back of goalie Seth Martin. It was my second goal in that game—a memorable game because it was Sweden's first win over Canada. We won the game 5–3 and captured the Worlds gold."

When asked who he loved to play with most of all, Sterner answered, "It was the so-called powerful three, Carl-Goran Eberg–Ulf Sterner–Hans Mild, the strongest lineup at the 1963 World Championship in Stockholm." Back then, in Stockholm, Tre Kronor was very successful thanks to greats like Sven Johansson, Roland Stoltz and Bert-Ola Nordlander. Ulf Sterner was a major force on the ice.

On March 15, 1963, Sweden defeated Canada 4–1 with Sterner getting a hat-trick. The crowd was elated and Sweden's aged King Gustav VI jumped up and applauded like a schoolboy. After the game, Sterner and Tumba Johansson went into the stands to meet the monarch and receive his royal congratulations. The Swedes appeared to have the world title sewn up, but they still had to get one more point in the last game against the Czechs. The last day of the tournament was the tensest and most exciting, but the Swedes lost and the gold medal went to the Soviet team.

Sterner was a great athlete and didn't look for excuses to explain the failure. He believed that the Soviets' hockey playing had been exemplary. "For me," he said, "Soviet hockey is always number one. Its style embodies velocity, power, techniques, team spirit and discipline." According to Sterner, the world's best forward line was Mikhailov–Petrov–Kharlamov. When asked which goalie was the most difficult, he answered, surprisingly, "Jacques Plante of the New York Rangers in 1965 when I was in the NHL."

Ulf Sterner was Europe's first player to join the NHL at a time when the league consisted of six great clubs—the Montreal Canadiens, the Boston Bruins, the Toronto Maple Leafs, the Chicago Black Hawks, the Detroit Red Wings and the New York Rangers. "Back then, the very fact that a European was playing in the NHL was a big deal," Sterner recalls. "And since there were only six teams, the competition was heavy. I think I did fine, but my coach insisted that I should play tougher and shoot on goal more often. Finally they sent me to the St. Paul Rangers in the Central Hockey League, where the famed Fred Shero was coach. I was the team's best scorer. Then I appeared in 52 games with the AHL's Baltimore Clippers and was voted the most valuable player. But I was dissatisfied with the training methods and the management. Also, they lacked discipline, and team morale was low. At this, we Europeans were better."

In the late 1950s and early 1960s, Ulf Sterner (right) was one of Sweden's more popular players and an international star.

Unfortunately, according to Sterner, there are no more enthusiastic and romantic coaches committed to hockey the way Arne Stromberg and Anatoli Tarasov were. With their enthusiasm, knowledge and experience, they helped hockey develop. "And now we have to keep an eye on what is going on in European hockey. We have to make a greater effort to train the juniors who will eventually become superior players."

Sterner's wife, Pia, is a hockey coach, too. This hockey family lives on a small farm near Carlstad, where Sterner has four horses that have regular names as well as nicknames for Sterner's former teammates and friends. One of the horses once smashed Sterner's nose and was nicknamed "Alexander Ragulin" because it was as strong as the famed Russian defenseman. Sterner's connection to his hockey past remains as powerful as ever.

Vladimir Yurzinov

Even though Vladimir Yurzinov (left) was the star forward of Dynamo Moscow in the 1960s, he was on the Soviet national team only twice.

Vladimir Yurzinov's facial expressions can range from a beaming smile to a nasty scowl. Viktor Tikhonov once said of his long-standing coaching assistant, "He is one of the most intelligent coaches, but his team is a gang of renegades."

Even though he was the star center of Dynamo Moscow in the 1960s, Yurzinov wasn't destined to become a full-fledged member of the nine-time World Championship-winning team. He was in the World Championship lineup only twice. Ironically, if the future goals-plus-assists system had been in place in 1963, Yurzinov would have been top scorer on the USSR nationals.

Unlike most of his colleagues, Yurzinov didn't go into hockey for the love of the game. He was one of the very few hockey players who succeeded in getting a university education. His classmates in the journalism department at Moscow State University recall that when he was at hockey training camps, Yurzinov was better able to study for his exams because there was nothing else to do after workouts.

However, Yurzinov was effectively demoted from Dynamo Moscow and banished to Riga and the tryouts in Finland for saying things like: "So what if we didn't score? I was thinking of switching to journalism anyway." And he was proud of his reputation as an oddball.

So why did an apparently easygoing person like Yurzinov decide to go into such a punishing profession as coaching? Perhaps it was because, by Soviet standards, coaching wasn't even considered a real profession. Yurzinov, in his own peculiar way, was determined to prove everyone wrong, both about coaching and about his ability to do it well.

Yurzinov's aggressive desire to get back at his critics was apparent from his earliest days as a coach. He liked to draw attention to his singular position in the hockey world. His two main targets on the national team during the 1960s were the not-so-charming Anatoli Tarasov and the not-so-gentle Arkady Chernyshev. Even the media took special note of Yurzinov's neat suit and snow-white shirt at training sessions. While coaching Dynamo and the national team, he distinguished himself from his colleagues by being the first to keep a notebook and pen at hand. He subsequently filled more than a hundred of these notebooks.

Sometimes Yurzinov would retaliate with words. When "Tarasov the Terrible" dressed down the junior coaches in a newspaper article, Yurzinov was heard to say, "Does he think he's the only great coach?" But the hard-working coaching alliance of Tikhonov and Yurzinov was considered dull and

Yurzinov, Vladimir
C, 5′11″, 200 lbs, b: Moscow, USSR, 2/20/1940

Season	Club, League	Regular Season				
		GP	G	A	Pts	PIM
1957–58	Dynamo Moscow, USSR	26	4	*	*	*
1958–59	Dynamo Moscow, USSR	27	11	*	*	*
1959–60	Dynamo Moscow, USSR	36	18	*	*	*
1960–61	Dynamo Moscow, USSR	8	6	*	*	*
WEC–61	USSR	3	0	2	2	0
1961–62	Dynamo Moscow, USSR	31	27	4	31	24
1962–63	Dynamo Moscow, USSR	27	16	7	23	6
WEC–63	USSR	7	5	7	12	0
1963–64	Dynamo Moscow, USSR	24	10	*	*	*
1964–65	Dynamo Moscow, USSR	32	10	6	16	4
1965–66	Dynamo Moscow, USSR	29	15	2	17	10
1966–67	Dynamo Moscow, USSR	39	25	5	30	26
1967–68	Dynamo Moscow, USSR	44	23	8	31	20
1968–69	Dynamo Moscow, USSR	40	25	*	*	*
WEC–69	USSR	2	3	1	4	0
1969–70	Dynamo Moscow, USSR	42	19	*	*	*
1970–71	Dynamo Moscow, USSR	39	16	7	23	8
1971–72	Dynamo Moscow, USSR	28	6	6	12	12
	USSR Totals	472	231	*	*	*
	WEC Totals	12	8	10	18	0

Won WEC (1963, 1969)

uninspired by spirited hockey fans, who felt the pair lacked a sense of sportsmanship and competition.

Yurzinov would go out of his way to emphasize his role as assistant trainer, obligingly giving way to Tikhonov at the local team level. Even though he tried his best, Yurzinov's limited coaching ability in those early years failed to inspire the team. Players at the time sarcastically remarked that Yurzinov, as assistant coach of the nationals, did his best to correct the gait of each and every one of them whenever they went out for a walk.

Yurzinov was still a servant of the existing system, and his relationship with Tikhonov grew out of this. If he hadn't eventually outdone Tikhonov by winning the silver medal in the national championship when he was banished to Riga (which Tikhonov had been unable to do when he was coaching there), he might have remained just a coach with a notepad.

Viktor Tikhonov once said of Vladimir Yurzinov (left), "He is one of the most intelligent coaches, but his team is a gang of renegades."

But in his later years as a coach, Yurzinov went from being a servant of the system to being the creator of a system. He got his revenge by being the only Russian hockey coach to win national championships in his own country and in another country, Finland, with TPS. But that wasn't all. Yurzinov left his own distinct mark as a coach.

He'd been coaching Dynamo Moscow for nearly seven years, and the team's style of play clearly showed his handiwork. Finnish stars now playing in the NHL, including Saku Koivu, are the first to acknowledge Yurzinov's guidance. The Latvian national hockey team, remembering him when he coached Dynamo Riga, owe a debt to Yurzinov every time they play at a World Championship. And many Russian-born stars in the NHL trained in Turku under Yurzinov's watchful eye, the most notable being Alexei Yashin.

Today Yurzinov creates hockey strategy and hockey plays with the help of a computer. He uses both logic and cunning to achieve his ends. He often repeats the claim that, "My hockey players are the best," and by doing so maintains the loyalty and devotion of those Russian-born NHL stars who wanted him as their coach at the Nagano Olympics.

Ralph Backstrom

Ralph Backstrom was a swift skater with a deft scoring touch whose defensive and team-oriented play earned him accolades throughout his career. The most significant years of his pro tenure were spent with the Montreal Canadiens, with whom he won the Stanley Cup six times between 1959 and 1969.

Backstrom spent two seasons with the Montreal Junior Canadiens before graduating to the Ottawa-Hull Canadiens, the Habs' top minor affiliate in eastern Canada. He captained the team to the Memorial Cup in 1958, when he was arguably the top junior skater in the country. The Canadiens planned to send Backstrom to the Rochester Americans of the AHL for a year of minor pro seasoning, but his performance at training camp was so impressive that the Habs brain trust decided to give him a shot at the big league right away.

The most significant years of Ralph Backstrom's tenure in the pros were spent with the Montreal Canadiens, where he won six Stanley Cups.

Backstrom rewarded Montreal by scoring 40 points and earning the Calder Trophy. His freshman season was so laudable that he received more than double the votes of runner-up Carl Brewer of Toronto. The following year he impressed coach Toe Blake by approaching his sophomore training camp with increased dedication and enthusiasm. His production dropped to 28 points, but he solidified his place as a key defensive forward on the club.

Although he was overshadowed by Montreal's top two centers, Jean Beliveau and Henri Richard, Backstrom became an important two-way forward on six Stanley Cup-winning teams. He and teammate Claude Provost garnered reputations as two of the most dogged forwards in the game. Even though he often drew checking assignments, Backstrom produced five 20-goal seasons, including a personal high of 27 in 1961–62. Years later, Backstrom reflected on this period: "There were times in my career that I felt I could have played better statistically if I would have played on another team besides the Canadiens. But there was nothing like the team successes that the Canadiens had during the time I played with them."

By the end of the 1960s, Backstrom sensed that he had accomplished all that he could in a Canadiens uniform. Two prolonged scoring slumps underscored his frustration. One in fact lasted 20 games in 1968–69. A high point occurred on April 10, 1969, when he scored the first overtime winner of his career in the opening game of the semifinals against Boston.

During the 1970 off-season, it became apparent that Backstrom wanted a change of scenery, preferably on the West Coast. The thought of returning to Montreal as a role player was so discouraging to him that he notified the team that he'd likely retire. Backstrom had a change of heart and reported for training camp, but his uncertainty remained and came to a head when he left the Canadiens on the eve of their 1970–71 season opener. He eventually returned to the team but was used sparingly.

Backstrom received his requested move when he was involved in a notorious transaction between Montreal and Los Angeles. In May 1970 shrewd Habs general manager Sam Pollock acquired the Oakland Seals' first-round pick with the hope that they'd finish last overall and give him a chance to draft junior star Guy Lafleur. Halfway through the 1970–71 season, it was clear that the L.A. Kings were having a sufficiently bad season to challenge for the first pick in the draft. Consequently, Backstrom was sent west in a move that gave him a new lease on life and boosted the Kings in the NHL standings.

In February 1973 he was acquired by the Chicago Black Hawks, for whom he scored the last six of his 278 regular-season NHL goals. That year

Backstrom, Ralph
C, 5′10″, 165 lbs, b: Kirkland Lake, Ont., 9/18/1937

Season	Club, League	Regular Season					Playoffs				
		GP	G	A	Pts	PIM	GP	G	A	Pts	PIM
1956–57	Montreal Canadiens, NHL	3	0	0	0	0					
1957–58	Montreal Royals, QHL	1	0	1	1	0					
	Rochester Americans, AHL	2	0	0	0	0					
	Montreal Canadiens, NHL	2	0	1	1	0					
1958–59	Montreal Canadiens, NHL	64	18	22	40	19	11	3	5	8	12
1959–60	Montreal Canadiens, NHL	64	13	15	28	24	7	0	3	3	2
1960–61	Montreal Canadiens, NHL	69	12	20	32	44	5	0	0	0	4
1961–62	Montreal Canadiens, NHL	66	27	38	65	29	5	0	1	1	6
1962–63	Montreal Canadiens, NHL	70	23	12	35	51	5	0	0	0	2
1963–64	Montreal Canadiens, NHL	70	8	21	29	41	7	2	1	3	8
1964–65	Montreal Canadiens, NHL	70	25	30	55	41	13	2	3	5	10
1965–66	Montreal Canadiens, NHL	67	22	20	42	10	10	3	4	7	4
1966–67	Montreal Canadiens, NHL	69	14	27	41	39	10	5	2	7	6
1967–68	Montreal Canadiens, NHL	70	20	25	45	14	13	4	3	7	4
1968–69	Montreal Canadiens, NHL	72	13	28	41	16	14	3	4	7	10
1969–70	Montreal Canadiens, NHL	72	19	24	43	20					
1970–71	Montreal Canadiens, NHL	16	1	4	5	0					
	Los Angeles Kings, NHL	33	14	13	27	8					
1971–72	Los Angeles Kings, NHL	76	23	29	52	22					
1972–73	Los Angeles Kings, NHL	63	20	29	49	6					
	Chicago Black Hawks, NHL	16	6	3	9	2	16	5	6	11	0
1973–74	Chicago Cougars, WHA	78	33	50	83	26	18	5	14	19	4
1974–75	Chicago Cougars, WHA	70	15	24	39	28					
1975–76	Denver–Ottawa, WHA	41	21	29	50	14					
	New England Whalers, WHA	38	14	19	33	6	17	5	4	9	8
1976–77	New England Whalers, WHA	77	17	31	48	30	3	0	0	0	0
	NHL Totals	1032	278	361	639	386	116	27	32	59	68
	WHA Totals	304	100	153	253	104	38	10	18	28	12

* Won Calder Trophy (1959)
Won Paul Deneau Trophy — WHA (1974)
Won Stanley Cup (1959, 1960, 1965, 1966, 1968, 1969)

also represented the seventh time in his career that Backstrom reached the 20-goal mark.

Prior to the 1973–74 season, Backstrom signed with the crosstown rival Cougars of the World Hockey Association. That first year he scored 83 points and won the Paul Deneau Trophy as the WHA's most gentlemanly player. A few weeks later, he was invited to join the WHA All-Star Team that was being assembled to represent Canada in the 1974 series against the USSR. Skating on a line with Gordie and Mark Howe, Backstrom performed superbly and was one of the top forwards in the competition with eight points in as many games. Backstrom registered a disappointing 39 points for the Cougars in 1974–75 and was left exposed in the off-season WHA Expansion Draft. He was claimed by the Denver Spurs but spent only half the season there before a trade brought him to the New England Whalers. Backstrom's last pro season was a 48-point effort for the Whalers in 1976–77.

Following his retirement, Backstrom turned immediately to coaching. Beginning in 1977, he joined the University of Denver as its assistant coach, a position he held for three years. Following this apprenticeship, he assumed the head coaching responsibilities until 1989–90. Backstrom's first opportunity to coach a professional team came with the Phoenix Roadrunners of the International Hockey League in 1990–91.

Ralph Backstrom (number 6) and his teammate Claude Pronovost garnered a reputation as two of most dogged forwards in the game.

Jaroslav *Jirik*

"We are like comedians. We travel from town to town, entertaining people," Jaroslav Jirik once said about his mission as a hockey player. For him, playing the game was more than just a job. His fame stemmed mainly from his talent as a scorer, even though he couldn't shoot from a distance and didn't have a very hard slapshot. Most of the goals he put in the net while playing in the Czech league and on the national team were scored practically from the crease area. He would literally push and shove at the puck or try to poke it in behind the goalie.

Jirik was famous for the way he parked himself in front of the net and assumed a pose like a tripod, with his stick out in front of him. It was nearly impossible to get him away from the net, to push him off balance or lift his stick. He provoked almost everybody he encountered—pushing

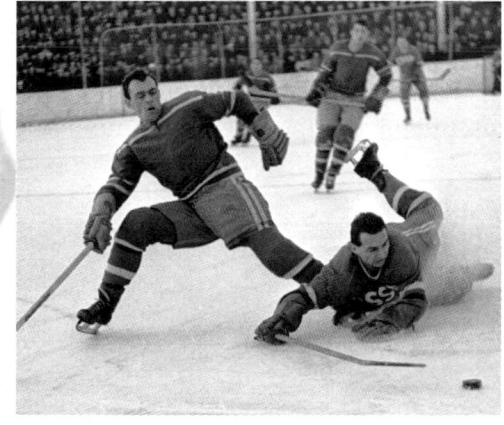

"We are like comedians. We travel from town to town, entertaining people," Jaroslav Jirik (right) once said of his mission as a hockey player.

and jabbing at the defensemen and the scorers and sometimes flying into a rage. They were afraid of him. He was the terror of all defensemen. He also had a weakness for referees and constantly irritated them with his aggressive style of play. In his day, the game wasn't as rough, so he stood out. And his aggression was just as verbal as it was physical.

For as long as anyone can remember, Jirik's nickname has been "Brambor" (Potato). His teammates in Kladno gave it to him when he was very young. It isn't certain whether they were hockey teammates, for Jaroslav Jirik also used to be an excellent soccer goalkeeper.

Jirik had a tendency to get deeply absorbed in the game and very passionate about its outcome. He hated losing and couldn't stand for pessimism, no matter who the opponent was. To him, losing was a disgrace. Even during training, when there was nothing at stake, he would often say or do whatever it took to win. And if he didn't come out a winner, he would get very frustrated.

Jaroslav Jirik grew up in Kladno after his family was expelled from the Czech border regions during the German occupation. He was born on December 10, 1939, in the village of Vojnuv Mestec, some 120 miles as the crow flies from the town where he learned to play hockey.

In 1961 he returned to Moravia to play for the famous RH Brno hockey club and practically became a permanent resident on the team. For a long time, local patriots on the team teased him because his native village lay exactly between Bohemia and Moravia, but Jirik was never offended. He had a thick skin and was never offended by jokes, even if they were personal.

In 1958 he had won the national title while with Kladno, only to follow it up in Brno with five more between 1962 and 1966. Jirik became the darling of the fans. On the national team he played forward, usually with his Brno teammate Frantisek Sevcik and Slovak Josef Golonka. He took part in 10 international tournaments, three of which were Olympics. At the time, the World Championship and the Winter Olympic hockey tournaments were rolled into one and only took place every four years.

Jaroslav Jirik liked to think of himself as invincible and he had a need to push himself to the limit. He played in one tournament from start to finish with a broken arm. During his career, Jirik scored 83 goals for the national team, and he also scored 300 goals in the Czech league over 17 seasons. Nevertheless, he had a variety of other interests. He learned to fly an airplane and had an interest in the theater. In Brno he got to know writer Milan Kundera before he became world-renowned.

In the summer of 1969, after topping the league in scoring, Jirik went to the NHL. He was the second European after Swede Ulf Sterner and the first Czech to play in the NHL. At the time, the St. Louis Blues were also interested in the strapping defenseman Josef Horesovsky and another forward, Jan Havel, who were both playing for Sparta. But in the end they signed Jirik.

While Sterner played only four matches for the New York Rangers in the 1964–65 season, Jirik appeared in a total of three. The rest of the time was spent on a farm team in Kansas City. A European hockey player was pretty hot property in the NHL at the time. There were only 12 teams in the league and the competition was stiff. But Jirik didn't return the next year. He thought they wouldn't be interested in him and his heart wasn't really in it. He'd gotten married and his wife was expecting a baby. Over time, he regretted his decision. "But you cannot bring back time. I had a different mindset at the time," he remembered years later.

Jirik, Jaroslav
RW, 5´11˝, 170 lbs, b: Vojnuv Mestec, Czechoslovakia, 12/10/1939

Season	Club, League	Regular Season				
		GP	G	A	Pts	PIM
1957–58	Kladno, Czechoslovakia	*	*	*	*	*
WEC–58	Czechoslovakia	*	*	*	*	*
1958–59	Kladno, Czechoslovakia	*	*	*	*	*
WEC–59	Czechoslovakia	8	6	*	*	*
1959–60	Kladno, Czechoslovakia	*	*	*	*	*
OWG–60	Czechoslovakia	*	*	*	*	*
1960–61	Kladno, Czechoslovakia	*	*	*	*	*
1961–63	Brno, Czechoslovakia	*	*	*	*	*
WEC–63	Czechoslovakia	7	4	3	7	9
1963–64	Brno, Czechoslovakia	*	*	*	*	*
OWG–64	Czechoslovakia	7	3	1	4	6
1964–65	Brno, Czechoslovakia	*	*	*	*	*
WEC–65	Czechoslovakia	7	8	4	12	5
1965–66	Brno, Czechoslovakia	*	*	*	*	*
WEC–66	Czechoslovakia	7	4	1	5	2
1966–67	Brno, Czechoslovakia	*	*	*	*	*
WEC–67	Czechoslovakia	6	5	3	8	2
1967–68	Brno, Czechoslovakia	*	*	*	*	*
OWG–68	Czechoslovakia	4	3	3	6	0
1968–69	Brno, Czechoslovakia	*	*	*	*	*
WEC–69	Czechoslovakia	5	2	3	5	0
1969–70	St. Louis Blues, NHL	3	0	0	0	0
	Kansas City Blues, AHL	53	19	16	35	11
1970–75	Brno, Czechoslovakia	*	*	*	*	*
	Czechoslovakia Totals	450	300	*	*	*
	NHL Totals	3	0	0	0	0
	OWG/WEC Totals	61	37	21	58	26

Czechoslovakia Champion (1959, 1962, 1963, 1964, 1965, 1966)

Jirik ended his playing career in 1975. Several times he returned to the players' bench as the coach of Zetor and later Kometa Brno. From 1977 to 1980, he coached the Swiss national team. He also worked with the Slovak team Plastika Nitra and with Skoda Plzen. He has seen his share of good times and bad, and not only in sports. Once he even survived crashing his plane. After finally retiring from the life of a professional athlete, he started working as an agent for players. But he will always be remembered as the hockey player on the tripod.

Vitali **Davydov**

On March 21, 1971, when the USSR played Finland during the final World Championship of his career, defenseman Vitali Davydov scored in the last minute. For Davydov, who played in every Olympic hockey tournament from 1964 to 1972, it was the last time he would score in world competition.

Vitali Davydov—timid forward, powerful defenseman.

Davydov began his hockey career as a forward in the Dynamo lineup. But he formally ended his career as a forward when he stepped into the defense line. As a forward, Davydov was fast but timid. He was unsuited to the position and unable to display his real talent. At that time, forwards didn't go in for bodychecking. Arkady Chernyshev, coach of the Dynamo and Team USSR, reasoned that if small but agile players were used as guards in basketball, why not try the same thing in hockey?

At first, Anatoli Tarasov, the second coach of the nationals, disagreed with the decision. But coaches in those days had clear lines of authority. Tarasov was in charge of the forward lines, Chernyshev the defense lines. In the end, Chernyshev's decision prevailed and Tarasov gave in.

The change was remarkable. Once a timid forward, Davydov turned into a powerful defenseman. His natural speed and agility enabled him to effectively check oncoming forwards who were considerably heavier. In the defense line, Davydov played in tandem with Viktor Kuzkin, also a former forward. Whereas Kuzkin sometimes played the role of fourth forward, Davydov always stayed back to hold the defense line.

A highly principled and conscientious defenseman, Davydov never landed in the penalty box more than twice during a tournament, even at World Championships.

Davydov remained loyal to the Dynamo, becoming coach and vice-president of the team. He also coached the USSR juniors to their World Championship title when future great Viacheslav Fetisov was at the beginning of his career.

Davydov, Vitali
D, 5´8˝, 158 lbs, b: Moscow, USSR, 4/1/1939

Season	Club, League	Regular Season				
		GP	G	A	Pts	PIM
1957–58	Dynamo Moscow, USSR	17	1	*	*	*
1958–59	Dynamo Moscow, USSR	27	1	*	*	*
1959–60	Dynamo Moscow, USSR	33	3	*	*	*
1960–61	Dynamo Moscow, USSR	29	3	*	*	*
1961–62	Dynamo Moscow, USSR	29	3	3	6	10
1962–63	Dynamo Moscow, USSR	28	2	1	3	12
WEC–63	USSR	6	0	2	2	4
1963–64	Dynamo Moscow, USSR	35	7	*	*	*
OWG–64	USSR	7	1	1	2	4
1964–65	Dynamo Moscow, USSR	23	1	2	3	4
WEC–65	USSR	6	0	1	1	0
1965–66	Dynamo Moscow, USSR	35	1	2	3	20
WEC–66	USSR	7	0	0	0	2
1966–67	Dynamo Moscow, USSR	41	3	1	4	18
WEC–67	USSR	7	0	0	0	2
1967–68	Dynamo Moscow, USSR	41	5	3	8	14
OWG–68	USSR	7	0	4	4	4
1968–69	Dynamo Moscow, USSR	42	2	*	*	*
WEC–69	USSR	9	0	1	1	2
1969–70	Dynamo Moscow, USSR	38	3	*	*	*
WEC–70	USSR	10	0	1	1	2
1970–71	Dynamo Moscow, USSR	40	1	6	7	6
WEC–71	USSR	9	1	1	2	2
1971–72	Dynamo Moscow, USSR	30	0	0	0	0
OWG–72	USSR	4	0	1	1	4
1972–73	Dynamo Moscow, USSR	31	3	0	3	8
	USSR Totals	519	39	*	*	*
	OWG/WEC Totals	72	2	12	14	26

Named Best Defenseman at WEC (1967)
Won OWG (1964, 1968, 1972)
Won WEC (1963, 1965, 1966, 1967, 1969, 1970, 1971)

Josef Cerny

Between 1964 and 1970, Josef Cerny was the highest scorer in Czech pro level competition.

The Cerny family from Rozmital pod Tremesinem, a small town in central Bohemia, raised nine children. Eight were girls. On October 18, 1930, a boy was born and they named him Josef. His father made him his first pair of skates with his own hands and Josef had to go no farther than the pond behind their house to use them. Winters used to be harsh then. You could skate on the pond from November until March.

At the young age of 14, Josef Cerny played for the local Spartak team. In the 1958–59 season, he made his debut in the Czech league wearing the Pilsen club's jersey. His career only took off, however, with his arrival on the Ruda Hvezda team. As a forward alongside Frantisek Vanek in the center and the hard worker Rudolf Scheuer on the right wing, he immediately began to demonstrate his ability. From his very first games, he started to assert himself as a scorer. He picked up Vanek's passes, which were remarkably accurate, and took full advantage of those opportunities as a very fast skater.

"Who is that player wearing number 15, with the small build and crooked legs?" they asked his center, who was a respected hockey great. "Josef Cerny. I took him in to play next to me because soon he will perform well for the national team," replied Vanek. He was right. From 1959, Cerny had a regular place on the national team. Later he even became captain.

Cerny stayed on the Czech team until 1972. He lined up in nine World Championships and took part in the Olympic Games four times. For this accomplishment, Cerny, Vlastimil Bubnik and Jiri Holik share a Czech record. He played an incredible 21 seasons in the league, and with his 686 matches, he stayed at the top of the overall games list for a long time. Only in the 1998–99 season was his record surpassed by forward Tomas Jelinek. Between 1964 and 1970, Cerny was the best scorer in pro-level competition.

From 1960 to 1966, he won the Czech league title seven times in a row with Ruda Hvezda and ZKL. He was there in 1961 when Czechoslovakia won the European Championship, a highly coveted award at that time. Quite unexpectedly, however, he gave up representing his country after the 1972 Sapporo Olympics, allegedly to make room for the younger generation. Throughout his career, he grabbed every opportunity that came along to compete at a higher level, yet he missed the most glorious moment of his own free will. During the World Championship held in Prague in the spring, the Czech national team won its first gold medal in 23 years. Josef Cerny was only watching from the stands.

"In Sapporo we ended up with the bronze. At the time it wasn't enough. There was sharp criticism of our play. I feared

Cerny, Josef
LW, 5'8", 168 lbs, b: Rozmital, Czechoslovakia, 10/18/1930

Season	Club, League	Regular Season				
		GP	G	A	Pts	PIM
1957–58	Skoda, Czechoslovakia	*	*	*	*	*
1958–59	Ruda Hvezda, Czechoslovakia	*	*	*	*	*
WEC–59	Czechoslovakia	7	2	*	*	*
1959–60	Ruda Hvezda, Czechoslovakia	*	*	*	*	*
OWG–60	Czechoslovakia	7	4	*	*	*
1960–61	Ruda Hvezda, Czechoslovakia	*	*	*	*	*
WEC–61	Czechoslovakia	7	3	1	4	12
1961–62	Ruda Hvezda, Czechoslovakia	*	*	*	*	*
1962–63	ZKL, Czechoslovakia	*	*	*	*	*
WEC–63	Czechoslovakia	7	4	1	5	2
1963–64	ZKL, Czechoslovakia	*	43	*	*	*
OWG–64	Czechoslovakia	7	6	5	11	2
1964–65	ZKL, Czechoslovakia	*	*	*	*	*
WEC–65	Czechoslovakia	7	4	4	8	2
1965–66	ZKL, Czechoslovakia	*	*	*	*	*
WEC–66	Czechoslovakia	2	0	2	2	2
1966–67	ZKL, Czechoslovakia	*	*	*	*	*
WEC–67	Czechoslovakia	6	1	2	3	2
1967–68	ZKL, Czechoslovakia	*	*	*	*	*
OWG–68	Czechoslovakia	7	0	6	6	0
1968–69	ZKL, Czechoslovakia.	*	*	*	*	*
WEC–69	Czechoslovakia	10	3	2	5	6
1969–70	ZKL, Czechoslovakia	*	31	*	*	*
WEC–70	Czechoslovakia	2	0	1	1	0
1970–71	ZKL, Czechoslovakia	*	*	*	*	*
WEC–71	Czechoslovakia	10	5	3	8	2
1971–72	ZKL, Czechoslovakia	*	*	*	*	*
OWG–72	Czechoslovakia	6	2	2	4	0
1972–76	ZKL, Czechoslovakia	*	*	*	*	*
1976–78	Zetor, Czechoslovakia	*	*	*	*	*
	Czechoslovakia Totals	686	403	*	*	*
	OWG/WEC Totals	85	34	*	*	*

Czechoslovakia Champion (1960, 1961, 1962, 1963, 1964, 1965, 1966)

other failures and told myself that it would be good to leave at the right time. Maybe it was a mistake, but at the time I couldn't act differently. However, even today, I don't feel that I made a mistake. Of course I continued rooting for the team. I even had the feeling I still belonged. I wanted the guys to get the gold. After all, it was mine too in a way."

He met his wife in Brno and built himself a house in the suburbs. His dad, proud of his famous son, helped him. All the women in the family had to wait on him hand and foot. Although he had traveled the world, or at least wherever hockey was played, Josef Cerny remained a country boy to the end. While playing hockey, he also completed his studies in the field of education.

Josef Cerny (right) played in nine World Championships and four Olympics.

On the national team, he started out playing alongside Ludek Bukac and Frantisek Vanek and finished next to Jiri Holik and Vaclav Nedomansky. After he retired from the league, he spent the 1978–79 season with the Austrian club ATSE Graz. He then coached WAT Stadlau in Vienna and the teams in Zilina and Prostejov, Ingstav Brno and Ytong Brno. He gradually ended up in the teaching profession.

Cerny needed the soil under his feet as much as he did the ice. He was an avid gardener. After he was released from the players' bench in Brno after the 1982–83 season, he told people that he lived off his savings and whatever crops he could grow behind his house.

He liked to return to his native town, claiming that in no other woods was there such an abundance of mushrooms. And he had another passion—pigeons. Once he even smuggled a pair of the feathered creatures to Holland. To this day, they haven't returned.

Carl Brewer

Nobody ever knew what Carl Brewer was going to do next. On the ice, he was a tough but agile defenseman who could stickhandle with a deceptive creativity. He had the ability to cross the opposing blue line and then pause, using dekes to ward off checkers, waiting for a teammate to get into the open for one of his feathery passes. In the defensive zone, he was adept at getting in an opponent's way, using clean tactics and not-so-clean tactics, such as cutting the palm out of his gloves to facilitate a sneaky kind of holding. Off the ice, he was a scholar and a freethinker who retired several times from hockey, only to turn up later playing on different teams or in different countries.

Brewer played his junior hockey with the Toronto Marlboros and earned his first pro experience as a 19-year-old, playing two games for the Toronto Maple Leafs in the 1957–58 season. The next year he became a regular with the Leafs. Brewer's speed and agility were well known, but his tendency to end up in the penalty box was a problem, especially early in his career. Twice he led the NHL in penalty minutes, in 1959–60 sitting out the equivalent of two and a half games. He had a trigger temper and often took penalties by retaliating after hits and jibes from other players.

Brewer claimed publicly that his goal was to become the league's best defenseman and set about curbing his temper and reducing his penalty minutes. "I'm doing my best to avoid those chippy penalties," he said in 1961. "It's tough to hold your temper when somebody pulls something sneaky on you, but you have to realize they're trying to sucker you into a cheap penalty. The trick is to await your chance and pay them back later in the game."

His reformation was a success and his overall game improved as his temper calmed. In 1962 he went seven games without a penalty, a long stretch for a man who had averaged more than two minutes per game earlier in his career, and he was selected to the league's Second All-Star Team.

The Leafs' savvy defensive standouts—Brewer, Allan Stanley, Bob Baun and Tim Horton—were the foundation of the Toronto team that captured the Stanley Cup for three consecutive seasons beginning in 1961–62. Brewer was selected to the First All-Star Team following Toronto's championship run in 1962–63. Even with the success—or perhaps because of it—Brewer found the pressure of playing professional hockey in a city like Toronto overwhelming. He was a tense man during his time with the Leafs. He disliked media attention and the added pressure of playing in front of hockey-mad fans didn't sit well with a player who already pushed himself to be the best at his position. He also had conflicts with management, especially coach Punch Imlach. Brewer first retired following the 1960 season, upset about $100 he felt he was owed by the team to cover medical expenses. He announced he was going to play football at McMaster University in Hamilton, Ontario, where he had been taking courses toward his bachelor of arts degree. The Leafs eventually convinced him to return and gave him $200. Brewer admitted later his reasons for playing again had little to do with the money in question. "It was really prompted by learning that I needed a third playing year to qualify for the NHL pension fund," he said.

During training camp in 1965, Brewer had an on-ice disagreement with teammate Johnny Bower that continued into the dressing room. Imlach sent the defenseman home for a few days "to think about it." Brewer did think about it, and decided to retire from professional hockey. He would stay out of the NHL for four years.

He decided he wanted to play for Canada's national team in 1966 but had to struggle, again with Imlach, to regain his amateur standing. Imlach, who could hardly stand in the way of a man who wanted to play for his country, finally allowed Brewer to play for the national team, which he did for one year. He then spent a season as a player-coach with the Muskegon, Michigan, team in the International Hockey League, earning a share of the gate because of his star status. His next stop was in Finland— again as a player-coach—with the Finnish national team while he took courses at the University of Helsinki. After his team suffered

Nobody ever knew what Carl Brewer was going to do next.

Brewer, Carl
D, 5′9″, 180 lbs, b: Toronto, Ont., 10/21/1938

Season	Club, League	Regular Season					Playoffs				
		GP	G	A	Pts	PIM	GP	G	A	Pts	PIM
1957–58	Toronto Maple Leafs, NHL	2	0	0	0	0					
1958–59	Toronto Maple Leafs, NHL	69	3	21	24	125	12	0	6	6	40
	Rochester Americans, AHL	1	0	1	1	2					
1959–60	Toronto Maple Leafs, NHL	67	4	19	23	150	10	2	3	5	16
1960–61	Toronto Maple Leafs, NHL	51	1	14	15	92	5	0	0	0	4
1961–62	Toronto Maple Leafs, NHL	67	1	22	23	89	8	0	2	2	22
1962–63	Toronto Maple Leafs, NHL	70	2	23	25	168	10	0	1	1	12
1963–64	Toronto Maple Leafs, NHL	57	4	9	13	114	12	0	1	1	30
1964–65	Toronto Maple Leafs, NHL	70	4	23	27	177	6	1	2	3	12
WEC–67	Canada	7	1	6	7	10					
1967–68	Muskegon Mohawks, IHL	63	13	55	68	82	9	3	9	12	4
1969–70	Detroit Red Wings, NHL	70	2	37	39	51	4	0	0	0	2
1970–71	St. Louis Blues, NHL	19	2	9	11	29	5	0	2	2	8
1971–72	St. Louis Blues, NHL	42	2	16	18	40					
1973–74	Toronto Toros, WHA	77	2	23	25	42	12	0	4	4	11
1979–80	New Brunswick Hawks, AHL	3	0	0	0	0					
	Toronto Maple Leafs, NHL	20	0	5	5	2					
	NHL Totals	604	25	198	223	1037	72	3	17	20	146
	WEC Totals	7	1	6	7	10					
	WHA Totals	77	2	23	25	42	12	0	4	4	11

NHL First All-Star Team (1963)
NHL Second All-Star Team (1962, 1965, 1970)
Won Stanley Cup (1962, 1963, 1964)

an exhibition loss to Anatoli Tarasov's Central Red Army club, Brewer arranged for a famous meeting with the Soviet coach. It resulted in Brewer's practising with the Central Red Army team and a long debate about the merits of the North American game versus the European one. Tarasov is said to have pronounced that Brewer wouldn't make the cut with his Soviet national team, though in an article he wrote after the meeting he was much more generous in his praise of Brewer's courage and skill.

While Brewer was away, his professional rights were traded by the Leafs to the Detroit Red Wings, along with Frank Mahovlich, Pete Stemkowski and Garry Unger, for Norm Ullman, Paul Henderson and Floyd Smith. It took Detroit manager Sid Abel more than a year to sign Brewer, which he did just before those rights would have reverted to the Maple Leafs. Brewer was partially convinced by Mahovlich and Bob Baun, former teammates in Toronto whose careers were rejuvenated with the Red Wings. Mahovlich, who had wilted under Imlach's intense pressure in Toronto as well, called Brewer in Finland several times to encourage his return to the NHL. Brewer had an incredible season in 1969–70 with the Red Wings, earning a place on the league's Second All-Star Team. In the summer of 1970, he sent a two-paragraph letter to Abel setting out his retirement, an announcement that shocked his teammates and management. He did return the next year, but this time to Scotty Bowman's St. Louis Blues, where he played for two years before retiring again. He joined the Toronto Toros of the World Hockey Association in 1973–74 and played for one year. In 1979–80, after almost six years out of the game, he made a comeback with the Maple Leafs. "I guess I've always had it on my mind," the 41-year-old said, "to die a Maple Leaf." He played for 20 games before quitting for good.

His speed and agility were well known, but Carl Brewer (number 2) also had a tendency to take bad penalties, especially in his early career.

Player agent and union leader Alan Eagleson had been instrumental in Brewer's reinstatement as an amateur in 1966. After his career finally ended, however, Brewer began to investigate some of Eagleson's business dealings. Brewer's findings led to Eagleson's eventual conviction on a number of fraud-related charges. The former head of the players' association was jailed in 1998, thanks in large measure to Brewer's efforts on behalf of the alumni association.

Alexander Almetov

Alexander Almetov's whole life was hockey. As the youngest in the forward line that included Konstantin Loktev and Veniamin Alexandrov, Almetov appeared to have the smoothest ride. Konstantin Loktev's climb to hockey fame had been much more difficult. Veniamin Alexandrov's rise, on the other hand, had been meteoric. Almetov's entry into the world of hockey was comparatively easy.

Coach Anatoli Tarasov singled out Almetov, a student at the Central Red Army hockey school, when he wasn't yet 15. Tarasov later remarked that even as a youth, Almetov displayed talent as

Alexander Almetov (left), was always nominated as second best and considered next in line because he was young and still had time to mature.

a hockey player. With his uninhibited stance, his head held high, smooth and effortless stickhandling and a sharp wrist shot, the young Almetov showed great promise from the beginning. He was also open and sincere and able to communicate easily with anyone.

Almetov could focus 100% on the game and play whatever role was necessary. In defense, he could be cool and strategic. Although not as powerful as many of his opponents, he more than made up for this by his ability to think fast on the ice. Coaches always used him when they were one or two players short because he could hold the puck better than anyone. He could literally confuse the opposition into losing the advantage. When mounting an attack, he was swift, logical and very focused on his teammates. And he could finish off an attack with remarkable speed.

Vyacheslav Starshinov, Almetov's chief competitor for the title of number one center in those years, said, "In my opinion, he played practically flawless hockey all the time." On the ice, Almetov was like a machine. He was never temperamental. He had no lofty notions or pretentions. Flexibility and grace were his trademarks. He seemed to glide effortlessly across the ice and almost never wound up before firing the puck at the goal. Yet he managed to score repeatedly from his favorite spot near the blue line.

Almetov didn't like to talk about the game. He had a feel for the game that was beyond words. The captain of the USSR nationals in those years, Boris Mayorov, an acknowledged leader who was known for his ability to spearhead an attack by his team, admitted that he depended on Almetov for his confidence. "What are you worrying about?" Almetov would tell the captain. "Of course we'll win." Almetov always believed things would turn out all right.

After their 2–1 defeat by the Swedes in 1963, the Soviet nationals didn't lose a single game at the World Championships and the Olympics in five years until they were beaten by the Czech nationals in 1968. By that time, Almetov was no longer in the Soviet lineup.

The Almetov troika was an organic entity with a life of its own. As the years went by, Konstantin Loktev, a happy-go-lucky prankster, mellowed both professionally and personally without losing his boyish sense of fun. Veniamin Alexandrov represented breeding and class in the line. Alexander Almetov was always easygoing and carefree. The three were very good friends.

Almetov was the least responsible of the three personally, but the bond he felt with his partners was the most important thing in his life. When Loktev hung up his skates at the age of 33, having reached the age ceiling that was strictly observed in Soviet sport in those days, Almetov ended his hockey career

Almetov, Alexander
C, 5′10″, 185 lbs, b: Moscow, USSR, 1/18/1940, d: 1992

Season	Club, League	Regular Season				
		GP	G	A	Pts	PIM
1958–59	CSK MO, USSR	*	8	*	*	*
1959–60	CSKA, USSR	*	16	*	*	*
OWG–60	USSR	7	2	3	5	2
1960–61	CSKA, USSR	*	21	*	*	*
WEC–61	USSR	7	4	3	7	6
1961–62	CSKA, USSR	*	29	*	*	*
1962–63	CSKA, USSR	*	23	*	*	*
WEC–63	USSR	7	6	5	11	8
1963–64	CSKA, USSR	*	40	*	*	*
OWG–64	USSR	8	5	4	9	0
1964–65	CSKA, USSR	*	26	*	*	*
WEC–65	USSR	7	7	5	12	0
1965–66	CSKA, USSR	*	24	*	*	*
WEC–66	USSR	7	5	8	13	0
1966–67	CSKA, USSR	*	1	*	*	*
WEC–67	USSR	7	8	7	15	0
	USSR Totals	220	212	*	*	*
	OWG/WEC Totals	50	37	35	72	16

Won OWG (1964)
Won WEC (1963, 1965, 1966, 1967)
USSR Champion (1959, 1960, 1961, 1963, 1964, 1965, 1966)

the following year. He was only 27, and many wondered why he'd come to such a decision without any plans for the future and no other professional aspirations outside of hockey. It was unheard-of for a hockey star to end his playing career so early.

But Almetov had already made up his mind to stop playing hockey when Loktev left the ice, believing the game wouldn't be the same for him. Almetov was never recognized as best forward at any of the seven World Championships he played in. He was always nominated second best and considered next in line because he was young and still had time to acquire the title. But he never did.

In no other sport is there an entity like the threesome that makes up the forward line in hockey. In Soviet hockey, great forward lines in which all three players are equal and play together on the ice for a long time are few in number. There was the Starshinov line, the Petrov line and the Larionov line. The line that included Konstantin Loktev, Veniamin Alexandrov and Alexander Almetov is at the top of the list. Today, no one from that forward line is left. Almetov, the center, lived a very unsettled life after he hung up his skates, and his death was as untimely as his departure from hockey.

Anatoli Firsov

National team coach Anatoli Tarasov once said of his favorite player, Anatoli Firsov, "He's a star who never fell prey to the egoism of stardom." Tarasov always admired Firsov, and together they were a fortunate combination. They both valued hockey above anything else in their lives. For them, hockey was where you could be creative and invent new strategies every day.

For Tarasov, Firsov's total dedication to hockey was backed by a unique combination of abilities. Firsov's style of play was based on his speed in several aspects of the game. The first was his ability to think fast. Firsov's game was a continuous flow of actions. In tough situations, he got his bearings instantly and came up with the most unexpected solutions. He also displayed uncanny speed in executing any technical maneuver in handling or passing the puck. And finally there was his terrific skating speed. Each of these abilities compounded the others. During a play, his thoughts and actions were synchronous and usually resulted in a complete and correct solution.

Anatoli Firsov often played with a smile on his face because he was happiest when playing.

Firsov's game on the ice consisted of a blend of his own peculiar manner of back and forth skating, stickhandling and sudden and covert passes topped off with a variety of shots on goal. He moved all the time without knowing it, even when taking a shot on goal. He was especially good at the trick of "losing" the puck by letting it slide towards his foot. Naturally the opposing defenseman would make a grab for it, but Firsov would pass the puck with his skate up to the blade of his stick, all the time picking up speed.

No one was as selflessly dedicated to hockey as Firsov or as hard on himself and fanatical in workouts. He even augmented the tough drills designed by Tarasov. Coming down the ice with the puck, he would perform a variety of hops, skips and jumps at the same time.

Firsov came to the Central Red Army and coach Tarasov as a scrawny kid—his bones protruded from under the thin layer of muscle. But at training sessions, he strengthened his body by choosing the roughest, toughest defensemen as his opponents—Alexander Ragulin and Viktor Kuzkin.

Coach Anatoli Tarasov once said of his favorite player, Anatoli Firsov (left), "He's a star who never fell prey to the egoism of stardom."

Only a person who had a tough time making it in hockey could be so intensely dedicated to the game. "I really had it pretty hard," Firsov wrote in his autobiography. "There were three kids in the family. My father was killed in the war when I was just a month old. My mother worked as a stoker at the kindergarten, and we didn't have any extra money. I learned how to make my own hockey stick, but with skates it was a much more difficult problem. That's why the leaders of our backyard team put me on the defense line. At that time, defensemen were considered to be second-rate players. So kids without skates or a stick, and smaller kids, were put in that position."

Firsov often played with a smile on his face because he was happiest when playing. At the age of 25, already an Olympic and two-time world champion, he was given two new partners on the line—greenhorns Vladimir Vikulov and Viktor Polupanov. In their company, Firsov literally made a second debut in hockey. At the 1967 World Championship and the 1968 Olympics, he chalked up the highest number of goals and assists.

When the International Ice Hockey Federation named Firsov best forward at the 1971 World Championship, Tarasov told him: "You've exhausted yourself as a left winger. You can no longer take the hard bodychecks and clashes on the ice. I don't see your smile anymore, and you linger on the ice too long. I can't trust you as a forward anymore, but I can give you the position of 'halfback.'" Tarasov offered him the role of playmaker and gave him a day to think it over.

The following day, Firsov agreed to the deal. At the 1972 Olympic Games, the new forward line scored the most goals. Kharlamov and Vikulov were in top form, and Firsov did an excellent job in his new role.

That was the last major tournament for both Tarasov and Firsov. Vsevolod Bobrov, the new coach, dropped Firsov from the national team. He reasoned that Firsov had been Tarasov's man throughout his career. There was no guarantee, in Bobrov's mind, that under new management, his participation or presence would continue to benefit the team.

Firsov's greatest dream had always been to play against the North American professionals. He missed the 1972 Summit Series with the national team by just six months, although he continued to play for Central Red Army for another two years.

Firsov, Anatoli
LW/C, 5´9″, 154 lbs, b: Moscow, USSR, 2/1/1941, d: 7/24/2000

Season	Club, League	Regular Season				
		GP	G	A	Pts	PIM
1958–61	Spartak Moscow, USSR	*	*	*	*	*
1961–62	Spartak Moscow, USSR	*	0	*	*	*
	CSKA, USSR	*	17	*	*	*
1962–63	CSKA, USSR	*	20	*	*	*
1963–64	CSKA, USSR	*	34	*	*	*
OWG–64	USSR	8	6	3	9	2
1964–65	CSKA, USSR	*	21	*	*	*
WEC–65	USSR	6	5	4	9	8
1965–66	CSKA, USSR	*	40	*	*	*
WEC–66	USSR	6	3	2	5	4
1966–67	CSKA, USSR	*	41	*	*	*
WEC–67	USSR	7	11	11	22	2
1967–68	CSKA, USSR	43	33	*	*	*
OWG–68	USSR	7	12	4	16	4
1968–69	CSKA, USSR	38	28	*	*	*
WEC–69	USSR	10	10	4	14	6
1969–70	CSKA, USSR	38	33	*	*	*
WEC–70	USSR	8	6	10	16	2
1970–71	CSKA, USSR	33	17	*	*	*
WEC–71	USSR	10	11	8	19	4
1971–72	CSKA, USSR	29	18	10	28	*
OWG–72	USSR	5	2	5	7	0
1972–73	CSKA, USSR	32	25	8	33	*
1973–74	CSKA, USSR	4	1	1	2	*
	USSR Totals	474	344	*	*	*
	OWG/WEC Totals	67	66	51	117	32

Named Best Forward at OWG/ WEC (1967, 1968, 1971)
Won OWG (1964, 1968, 1972)
Won WEC (1965, 1966, 1967, 1969, 1970, 1971)
USSR Champion (1963, 1964, 1965, 1966, 1968, 1970, 1971, 1972, 1973)

Bobby **Rousseau**

Speedy right wing Bobby Rousseau brought a number of useful qualities to the NHL. He was blessed with a devastating slapshot, quick feet that made him difficult to catch on open ice and fast hands that made him an excellent stickhandler as well as a threat with his quick wrist shot. Although well known as a member of the Montreal Canadiens in the 1960s, Rousseau played over three years on a strong New York Rangers outfit in the early 1970s.

The Montreal native was signed by the local Canadiens as a teenager. One of 12 children, Rousseau was under a great deal of pressure from his family to make the pros after two of his older brothers failed in their attempts to reach the NHL. Rousseau noted: "I was worried that I would let them down. My brothers were pretty good hockey players, too, and they couldn't stay in the NHL."

In 1955–56, Rousseau led the Quebec junior league when he scored 53 goals in 44 games for the St. Jean Braves. The next two years he split between the Hull-Ottawa franchises in the OHA junior circuit and the minor Eastern Professional Hockey League.

While in junior, Rousseau contributed to the Hull-Ottawa Canadiens' Memorial Cup championship in 1958. In one of the most competitive finals in the history of the fabled Cup, Rousseau played with and against many future NHL teammates. The Canadiens and the Regina Pats were both stocked with players destined to play for *le bleu, blanc et rouge*. The Western Pats featured such future NHL stars as Terry Harper, Bill Hicke and Red Berenson while Rousseau's Hull-Ottawa mates included Jean-Claude Tremblay, captain Ralph Backstrom and Gilles Tremblay.

The explosive winger acquired valuable international experience while helping Canada win the silver medal at the 1960 Squaw Valley Olympics. He was able to do so because the Habs loaned him to the Canadian representatives that year, the Kitchener-Waterloo Dutchmen. The Dutchies were short on players after losing the likes of Bill Kennedy and George Gosselin to the pros, but the addition of people like Rousseau, Harry Sinden and Bob Attersley buoyed their spirits. Rousseau put in four goals in a 19–1 rout of Japan and later scored a key marker in a crucial 6–5 win over Sweden. The youngster finished with nine points in seven games and came back to Canada with greater confidence and a better-rounded game.

In 1960–61, Rousseau earned his first chance with the Habs and played steadily in a 15-game debut. He gained a full-time place on the roster the next year and scored 21 goals—fine first season that brought him the Calder Trophy ahead of runner-up Cliff Pennington of

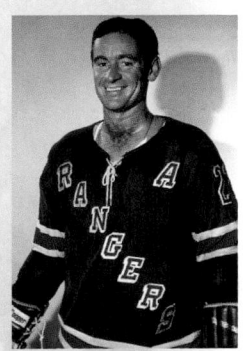

Well-known as a Montreal Canadien in the 1960s, Bobby Rousseau played more than three years for the Rangers in the early 1970s.

Rousseau, Bobby
RW, 5′10″, 178 lbs, b: Montreal, Que., 7/26/1940

Season	Club, League	Regular Season					Playoffs				
		GP	G	A	Pts	PIM	GP	G	A	Pts	PIM
1958–59	Rochester Americans, AHL	2	0	0	0	0					
1959–60	Hull-Ottawa Canadiens, EPHL	4	4	2	6	4					
OWG–60	Canada	7	5	4	9	2					
1960–61	Montreal Canadiens, NHL	15	1	2	3	4					
	Hull-Ottawa Canadiens, EPHL	38	34	26	60	18	14	12	7	19	10
1961–62	Montreal Canadiens, NHL	70	21	24	45	26	6	0	2	2	0
1962–63	Montreal Canadiens, NHL	62	19	18	37	15	5	0	1	1	2
1963–64	Montreal Canadiens, NHL	70	25	31	56	32	7	1	1	2	2
1964–65	Montreal Canadiens, NHL	66	12	35	47	26	13	5	8	13	24
1965–66	Montreal Canadiens, NHL	70	30	48	78	20	10	4	4	8	6
1966–67	Montreal Canadiens, NHL	68	19	44	63	58	10	1	7	8	4
1967–68	Montreal Canadiens, NHL	74	19	46	65	47	13	2	4	6	8
1968–69	Montreal Canadiens, NHL	76	30	40	70	59	14	3	2	5	8
1969–70	Montreal Canadiens, NHL	72	24	34	58	30					
1970–71	Minnesota North Stars, NHL	63	4	20	24	12	12	2	6	8	0
1971–72	New York Rangers, NHL	78	21	36	57	12	16	6	11	17	7
1972–73	New York Rangers, NHL	78	8	37	45	14	10	2	3	5	4
1973–74	New York Rangers, NHL	72	10	41	51	4	12	1	8	9	4
1974–75	New York Rangers, NHL	8	2	2	4	0					
	NHL Totals	942	245	458	703	359	128	27	57	84	69
	OWG Totals	7	5	4	9	2					

NHL Second All-Star Team (1966)
Won Calder Trophy (1962)
Won Stanley Cup (1965, 1966, 1968, 1969)

the Boston Bruins. More important, he developed into a versatile forward whose exemplary two-way play caused coach Toe Blake to deploy him on both the power-play and penalty-killing units.

A fine shooter, Rousseau kept himself limber each summer by playing golf, and his proficiency on the links was such that he was invited to take part in the 1962 Canadian Open. He quipped: "Only the grip is different between a golf swing and my slapshot. The motion is the same."

In 1963–64, he scored 25 goals, five of which came in one game versus the Detroit Red Wings on February 1, 1964. By contributing to the Habs' 9–3 win over the Wings, Rousseau became only the seventh member of the Canadiens to record a five-goal game. The next year his 13 points in as many playoff games were an integral part of the Habs' first Stanley Cup win since the last year of the 1950s dynasty.

Bobby Rousseau (number 15) scored five goals against the Red Wings on February 1, 1964, and became only the seventh member of the Canadiens to record a five-goal game.

Matters improved even more for Rousseau the next season when he led the team in scoring with 30 goals and 78 points. His 48 assists tied for the league lead with teammate Jean Beliveau and Chicago star Stan Mikita. Rousseau was an important factor when the Habs came back from a two-games-to-none deficit against Detroit in the finals to defend their Stanley Cup title. His excellence didn't go unnoticed and he was selected to the NHL Second All-Star Team at the end of the 1965–66 season.

Adept at jumping out of the way of bodychecks, Rousseau was accused at times of not being sufficiently rugged for the NHL. He defended his approach in this way: "I'm not scared when I do that. It's just that I'm trying to avoid getting hit with a solid check. Early in the game, a stiff check will slow you down, and I rely on my speed. Late in the game, when you're tired, you are most likely to get hurt."

Rousseau helped Montreal reach the Stanley Cup finals again in 1966–67, when the Canadiens lost to the Maple Leafs in Canada's Centennial year. Montreal was back on top in 1967–68 and 1968–69 with the skillful winger playing a prominent role once again. Following a 24-goal performance in 1969–70, Rousseau was deemed expendable as the Habs began to introduce a few younger players into the lineup. He was traded to Minnesota, where he spent the 1970–71 season. After the deal was announced, Rousseau reflected: "You know, it might be wonderful. In Montreal, the pressure was always on. Everybody knew you, everybody was a coach and a critic."

In June 1971 Rousseau was sent to the Rangers, where his career was rejuvenated. Playing with Bruce MacGregor and Ted Irvine, he scored 21 goals and helped the Rangers reach the Stanley Cup finals. They lost to the powerful Boston Bruins, but it was Rousseau's third-period goal that stunned the Boston Garden crowd and forced a sixth game in Madison Square Garden. Rousseau retired from the NHL in 1974–75 with 245 career goals, four Stanley Cup rings and an Olympic silver medal to his credit.

Leif Holmqvist

Leif Holmqvist was idolized by Swedish hockey fans and became the nation's favorite goaltender during his career. Holmqvist never wore a goaltender's mask while playing and is remembered by the hockey world wearing an ordinary blue helmet while standing in the net. Whether it was bravado or contempt for danger, or just a more comfortable way for him to catch the puck, Holmqvist captivated the whole world with his daring and bold style of play and his phenomenal split-second reaction time. Later in life, Holmqvist admitted that he had been wrong for being so careless about his appearance. His face is marked by some 200 scars received playing hockey.

It was sheer accident that originally put Holmqvist in the net. As an 11-year-old, he was put in the goal of the kids' team in his home town of Stromsbro against his will when the main goalkeeper fell ill. After that fateful incident, he remained a goalkeeper all his life. Many believe that Sweden never had a better goalkeeper than "Honken," as he was nicknamed by fans.

At the age of 16, he made his debut in the Swedish league, and in 1965 he was invited to play for AIK Stockholm, triggering a scandal in Swedish hockey. The Stromsbro club lodged a complaint with the Swedish hockey union, as a result of which AIK had to pay the provincial club 17,000 krona—an astronomical sum in those years.

Holmqvist reached his peak with AIK. He had made his debut with Tre Kronor in 1962 in an exhibition game against Switzerland that the Swedes won 7–3. In that game, it became clear that Swedish hockey had a goaltender who would continue the tradition of great Swedish goalkeepers that included Lennart Haggroth and Kjell Svensson. During Sweden's tour of Canada in December 1964, Honken caught the eye of a young Scotty Bowman, who was training the Montreal Canadiens' juniors. "An extremely artful goalie—his place is among the pros," noted the future NHL coach after Tre Kronor beat the Canadiens by a score of 3–2.

The years 1969 and 1970 are considered the best of Honken's sports career. Holmqvist himself admitted that his best games were played against the USSR nationals at the 1964 Olympics in Innsbruck and against Czechoslovakia at the 1969 World Championship in Stockholm.

In the eyes of many, Sweden has never had a better goalkeeper than Leif Holmqvist.

Holmqvist, Leif "Honken"
G, 5'9", 175 lbs, b: Stromsbro, Sweden, 11/22/1942

Season	Club, League	Regular Season		
		GP	GA	Avg
1958–64	Stromsbro, Sweden	*	*	*
1964–65	AIK, Sweden	*	*	*
WEC–65	Sweden	2	0	0.00
1965–66	AIK, Sweden	*	*	*
WEC–66	Sweden	*	*	*
1966–67	AIK, Sweden	*	*	*
WEC–67	Sweden	4	15	3.75
1967–68	AIK, Sweden	*	*	*
OWG–68	Sweden	*	*	*
1968–69	AIK, Sweden	*	*	*
WEC–69	Sweden	8	17	2.13
1969–70	AIK, Sweden	*	*	*
WEC–70	Sweden	8	13	1.63
1970–72	AIK, Sweden	*	*	*
OWG–72	Sweden	3	6	2.00
WEC–72	Sweden	7	20	2.86
1972–73	AIK, Sweden	*	*	*
1973–74	London Lions, England	*	*	*
1974–75	AIK, Sweden	*	*	*
WEC–75	Sweden	7	22	3.14
1975–76	Indianapolis Racers, WHA	19	58	3.00
	Sweden Totals	*	*	*
	OWG/WEC Totals	*	*	*

Named Best Goaltender at WEC (1969)

That was an especially memorable championship since it was held against the backdrop of the tense political atmosphere surrounding recent events in Czechoslovakia. Stockholm was selected as the venue for the World Championship out of turn when it became apparent that the tournament couldn't be held in Prague. In Stockholm, Czechoslovakia managed to outplay the Soviets in two games in a very tense struggle. When it seemed that the coveted prize was within reach of the Czech players—they only had to win the second game against the Swedes—Tre Kroner beat them 1–0, depriving the Czech players of the gold.

Leif Holmqvist (right) never adopted a mask and the hockey world remembers him standing in the net wearing an ordinary blue helmet.

After the game, the Swedish players picked up their goalie and tossed him into the air to celebrate his brilliant performance. Holmqvist's popularity soared and his photograph was on the front page of all the newspapers. He was asked to award prizes at beauty contests and participate in the traditional cycling race around Lake Vatter. Swedes loved him especially because fame didn't seem to spoil him; he shouldered the burden of fame with ease and shared it with his adoring countrymen.

Holmqvist played in 237 national team games for Sweden and completed his career with the professional London Lions and Indianapolis clubs in the 1975–76 season.

Ironically, the outstanding goalkeeper, who was known around the world, never won a single major tournament. He was never world champion because in the years when he played the USSR national team ruled the world of hockey and only Czechoslovakia was considered a serious contender. Nor did Holmqvist become champion of Sweden, since Swedish hockey was dominated by Brynas from Gavle at the time. In spite of this, no one doubted Holmqvist's greatness. He distinguished himself by playing the game brilliantly for nearly a decade, and his name ranks 66th on Sweden's "Great Men" list. He was elected to the IIHF Hockey Hall of Fame in 1999.

He stopped playing hockey while with the XB–71 Club when it was in the first division of the Swedish championship tournament. Then he coached with Tranos and Stavanger in Norway. Upon his return to Linchoping, where he lives now, he earned a professional diploma and successfully sold cars for a while.

Today, the popular goalie still eagerly participates in veterans' games playing for AIK and Sweden. He also works in the Sweden Hockey Pool, which is active in sponsoring World Championships and assisting Sweden's participation in them.

Holmqvist is also very highly regarded by the new generation of Swedish hockey fans. The talented 21-year-old goalkeeper of Brynas, Johan Holmqvist, who became champion of Sweden in the 1998–99 season and was selected to play for Sweden, has been nicknamed "Honken" by hockey fans.

^{Ed} Giacomin

Ed Giacomin was one of the most successful and popular players ever to wear the uniform of the New York Rangers. He played over 500 of his 610 regular-season games with the Blueshirts and helped the team reach the Stanley Cup final in 1972. He was placed on the NHL First All-Star

Team twice and the Second Team three times. His fiery nature and wandering style on the ice endeared him to the demanding Madison Square Garden supporters.

He grew up in Gatchell, a small town on the outskirts of Sudbury, Ontario. A relatively late bloomer, Giacomin failed to attract the attention of junior clubs while fine-tuning his game in the Sudbury minor hockey system, but his love for hockey was such that he turned down an athletic scholarship in football and baseball from a school in California.

Tragedy struck Giacomin as a teenager when a kitchen stove blew up in his face and caused second- and third-degree burns on his legs and feet. He underwent skin grafts and his legs were bandaged for a year. Doctors told him to forget about hockey, but Giacomin was more determined than ever. He found a job and played goal in the industrial men's league that played at midnight. Giacomin had to pay to play and helped scrape the ice, but at least he could get back to hockey.

In 1958 he attended the Detroit Red Wings' training camp but, sensing an opportunity, he moved on to Washington of the Eastern Hockey League as a replacement for his brother. The team's fortunes went sour and it decided to give the youngster a chance on a regular basis. He sparked a six-game winning streak and caught the attention of Providence Reds owner Lou Pieri.

Giacomin's next break came when the New York Rangers acquired him from Providence in May 1965. He appeared in 36 games as a rookie, splitting the goaltending chores with Cesare Maniago. He endured a rocky beginning when his shaky play earned him a two-week reprimand in the minors. On the positive side, Giacomin's time in Baltimore gave him a chance to play with the legendary Doug Harvey. When he returned, starting goalie Cesare Maniago annoyed coach Emile Francis when he pulled himself out of a game because of an injury. Giacomin was sent in and immediately things fell into place as his play improved and he landed in the good books of the Rangers brass.

The Rangers missed the playoffs, but the following season Giacomin backstopped them to their first post-season appearance in five years. He also led the NHL with nine shutouts and was placed on the league's First All-Star Team. This started a run of nine straight years of playoff qualification. Giacomin also gained fame by taking Jacques Plante's wandering style an extra step further by trying to skate up ice and hit a teammate with a pass.

Early in the 1975–76 season, New York put its all-time shutout leader on waivers and Detroit claimed Ed Giacomin.

Giacomin, Ed
G, 5´11˝, 180 lbs, b: Sudbury, Ont., 6/6/1939

Season	Club, League	Regular Season				Playoffs			
		GP	Mins	GA	Avg	GP	Mins	GA	Avg
1958–59	Washington–Clinton, EHL	4	240	13	3.25				
1959–60	Clinton–NY Rovers, EHL	51	3060	206	4.04				
	Providence Reds, AHL	1	60	4	4.00				
1960–61	Providence Reds, AHL	43	2510	183	4.37				
1961–62	Providence Reds, AHL	40	2400	144	3.60				
	New York Rovers, EHL	12	720	54	4.50				
1962–63	Providence Reds, AHL	39	2340	102	2.62	6	359	31	5.18
1963–64	Providence Reds, AHL	69	4140	232	3.37	3	120	12	4.00
1964–65	Providence Reds, AHL	59	3527	226	3.84				
1965–66	New York Rangers, NHL	36	2096	128	3.66				
	Baltimore Clippers, AHL	7	420	21	3.00				
1966–67	New York Rangers, NHL	68	3981	173	2.61	4	246	14	3.41
1967–68	New York Rangers, NHL	66	3940	160	2.44	6	360	18	3.00
1968–69	New York Rangers, NHL	70	4114	175	2.55	3	180	10	3.33
1969–70	New York Rangers, NHL	70	4148	163	2.36	5	280	19	4.07
1970–71	New York Rangers, NHL	45	2641	95	2.16	12	759	28	2.21
1971–72	New York Rangers, NHL	44	2551	115	2.70	10	600	27	2.70
1972–73	New York Rangers, NHL	43	2580	125	2.91	10	539	23	2.56
1973–74	New York Rangers, NHL	56	3286	168	3.07	13	788	37	2.82
1974–75	New York Rangers, NHL	37	2069	120	3.48	2	86	4	2.79
1975–76	New York Rangers, NHL	4	240	19	4.75				
	Detroit Red Wings, NHL	29	1740	100	3.45				
1976–77	Detroit Red Wings, NHL	33	1791	107	3.58				
1977–78	Detroit Red Wings, NHL	9	516	27	3.14				
	NHL Totals	610	35693	1675	2.82	65	3838	180	2.81

NHL First All-Star Team (1967, 1971)
NHL Second All-Star Team (1968, 1969, 1970)
Won Vezina Trophy (1971)

The solidification of the goaltending picture helped the Rangers become one of the most competitive teams in the league during the late 1960s and early 1970s. In 1970–71, Giacomin helped the club set a franchise record with 109 points. He and Gilles Villemure were the top netminding duo in the league that year and shared the Vezina Trophy, and it was the second time in his career that he earned a spot on the NHL First All-Star Team.

Ed Giacomin (left) was one of the most successful and popular players ever to don Rangers gear.

In 1971–72, the club matched its 109 points of the previous year but enjoyed a solid playoff run. In succession they eliminated the defending Stanley Cup champion Montreal Canadiens and the previous year's finalist, the Chicago Black Hawks, to make the club's first appearance in the finals since 1949–50. They put up a strong fight but in the end couldn't quite match the powerful Boston Bruins.

Giacomin helped the Rangers reach the semifinals in both 1973 and 1974, but they never did break through for a championship season. Early in the 1975–76 season, New York put its all-time shutout leader and several other veterans on waivers. Detroit claimed Giacomin and was amazed to find that he wasn't recalled by Emile Francis. Giacomin described the toughest day in his pro career: "I remember having such an empty feeling. I had given 10 years of my life to that team and the worst part about it was there was nobody around. My teammates were on their way to Montreal. And here I am in this empty parking lot walking to my car, and I had visions of walking straight into the bay."

His first game with his new teammates came in an emotionally charged match at Madison Square Garden against his former club. In one of the most memorable scenes in the history of that storied arena, the New York faithful continually chanted "Eddie! Eddie!" They drowned out the national anthem, forcing the emotional netminder to raise his stick twice in a plea for silence. Detroit won the game, and when his former comrades scored on him, they apologized.

The Red Wings decided to go with Jimmy Rutherford and Ron Low in goal after training camp ended in 1977 and the veteran Giacomin retired with 54 shutouts and nearly 300 wins on his playing resume. Ironically, he was inducted into the Hockey Hall of Fame in 1987, when the ceremony was held for the first time in Detroit.

After leaving the game, Giacomin operated a popular sports bar in the Motor City. He experienced disappointment in 1978 when the Rangers coaching position he felt he'd been promised went instead to Fred Shero. Giacomin moved on to work as an assistant with the Islanders and the Red Wings. In 1986 he returned to the organization as goaltending coach and special assignment scout and was honored at a ceremonial face-off at the home opener in 1985–86.

Jean-Claude Tremblay

A veritable wizard with the puck, J.C. Tremblay suited the flashy offensive character of the Montreal Canadiens to a tee. He was part of five Stanley Cup teams with the Habs and earned a reputation for being one of the most naturally skilled players at his position.

A talented left winger for most of his amateur days, Tremblay made the pragmatic switch to defense when he was notified of the shortage of blue line prospects in the Canadiens system. In his first full pro season with the Hull-Ottawa Canadiens of the Eastern Professional Hockey League in 1959–60, he accumulated 25 goals and 56 points in 55 games and his effort garnered him the league's most valuable player honors. He played 11 games for Montreal that season and the following season he was called up to the parent club for 29 games. He quickly began to establish himself as a regular in the lineup.

Throughout the 1960s, Tremblay developed into one of the NHL's top playmaking rearguards. His patented move consisted of a quick shift one way, forcing his opponent to commit, then a sharp move in the opposite direction. This basic move was so effective because of Tremblay's deft stick-handling and effortless skating style.

He experienced his first Stanley Cup triumph in 1965 when he led all post-season skaters with nine assists in Montreal's victory over Chicago. This was particularly significant for the club since it lost key defender Jacques Laperriere to an injury. Tremblay gained prominence in the eyes of demanding Canadiens supporters for the first time. He was equally brilliant the following season, when he scored 11 points in 10 playoff games to help the Habs repeat as champions against Detroit. Following the series, Tremblay narrowly lost out to Red Wings goalie Roger Crozier in the voting for the Conn Smythe Trophy.

Tremblay continued to produce offensively and helped Montreal to consecutive Stanley Cup wins in 1968 and 1969. Following the 1967–68 season, he finished runner-up in the James Norris Trophy voting to Boston superstar Bobby Orr. Nevertheless, the team was feeling the ire of the Forum crowd as their defensive play wasn't as stellar as in the past and they tended to struggle against the perceived "weak" expansion clubs.

Prior to the 1970–71 season, the Habs were deciding which of their veteran defensemen to unload as part of a rebuilding program. Tremblay's desire to play for the club was under scrutiny for the first time. A proud competitor, he voiced his desire to stay with the Canadiens. That year Tremblay broke Doug Harvey's team record for single-season points by a defenseman. He totaled a personal high of 63 points, then went on to register 17 points in 20 playoff matches to help the Canadiens win the Stanley Cup. After the playoffs, he was named to the NHL First All-Star Team for

A veritable wizard with the puck, Jean-Claude Tremblay suited the Canadiens' style of flashy offense to a tee.

Tremblay, Jean-Claude
D, 5´11˝, 170 lbs, b: Bagotville, Que., 1/22/1939, d: 12/7/1994

Season	Club, League	Regular Season					Playoffs				
		GP	G	A	Pts	PIM	GP	G	A	Pts	PIM
1958–59	Rochester Americans, AHL	3	0	0	0	0					
1959–60	Montreal Canadiens, NHL	11	0	1	1	0					
	Hull–Ottawa Canadiens, EPHL	55	25	31	56	55	7	1	4	5	2
1960–61	Montreal Canadiens, NHL	29	1	3	4	18	5	0	0	0	2
	Hull–Ottawa Canadiens, EPHL	37	7	33	40	28					
1961–62	Montreal Canadiens, NHL	70	3	17	20	18	6	0	2	2	2
1962–63	Montreal Canadiens, NHL	69	1	17	18	10	5	0	0	0	0
1963–64	Montreal Canadiens, NHL	70	5	16	21	24	7	2	1	3	0
1964–65	Montreal Canadiens, NHL	68	3	17	20	22	13	1	9	10	18
1965–66	Montreal Canadiens, NHL	59	6	29	35	8	10	2	9	11	2
1966–67	Montreal Canadiens, NHL	60	8	26	34	14	10	2	4	6	2
1967–68	Montreal Canadiens, NHL	73	4	26	30	18	13	3	6	9	2
1968–69	Montreal Canadiens, NHL	75	7	32	39	18	13	1	4	5	6
1969–70	Montreal Canadiens, NHL	58	2	19	21	7					
1970–71	Montreal Canadiens, NHL	76	11	52	63	23	20	3	14	17	15
1971–72	Montreal Canadiens, NHL	76	6	51	57	24	6	0	2	2	0
1972–73	Quebec Nordiques, WHA	75	14	75	89	32					
1973–74	Quebec Nordiques, WHA	68	9	44	53	100					
1974–75	Quebec Nordiques, WHA	68	16	56	72	18	11	0	10	10	2
1975–76	Quebec Nordiques, WHA	80	12	77	89	16	5	0	3	3	0
1976–77	Quebec Nordiques, WHA	53	4	31	35	16	17	2	9	11	2
1977–78	Quebec Nordiques, WHA	54	5	37	42	26	1	0	1	1	0
1978–79	Quebec Nordiques, WHA	56	6	38	44	8					
	NHL Totals	794	57	306	363	204	108	14	51	65	49
	WHA Totals	454	66	358	424	216	34	2	23	25	4

NHL First All-Star Team (1971)
WHA First All-Star Team (1973, 1975, 1976)
NHL Second All-Star Team (1968)
WHA Second All-Star Team (1974)
Won Dennis A. Murphy Trophy — WHA Top Defenseman (1973, 1975)
Won Stanley Cup (1965, 1966, 1968, 1969, 1971)
Won Avco Cup (1977)

In the 1970–71 season, Jean-Claude Tremblay (right) tallied a personal high of 63 points and went on to register 17 points in 20 playoff matches to help the Canadiens win the Stanley Cup.

the only time in his career. Another factor that helped Tremblay was when he relinquished the distracting task of being the team's representative in the NHL Players' Association.

In 1971–72, Tremblay posted strong numbers once again with 57 points, but the defending champions were defeated by the New York Rangers in the quarterfinals. While negotiating a new contract with team president Sam Pollock, Tremblay was offered a deal by the WHA's Quebec Nordiques that he couldn't refuse.

During the league's seven-year existence, Tremblay was one of the biggest stars. He led the league in assists on two occasions and helped the Nordiques win the Avco Cup in 1976. Twice he was the recipient of the Dennis A. Murphy Trophy as the top defenseman in the WHA.

Tremblay was a key member of the WHA All-Star squad that represented Canada during the 1974 series against the Soviet Union. His partnership with 1972 Summit Series veteran Pat Stapleton proved to be one of the strengths of the team, and it was this set of games that finally established Tremblay as an internationally recognized star. Following the series, some of the Soviet coaches commented that Tremblay was the most accomplished Canadian player they had seen. Never one to downplay his talent, Tremblay took a shot at the local media: "I was surprised, yes, because the Canadian newspapermen who were covering the series didn't name me the most valuable player in even one game."

Tremblay retired after the announced merger of the WHA and the NHL in 1979. An interesting sidelight was that his number 3 was retired by the Nordiques for his WHA exploits. Thus, he and John McKenzie became the only two players to enjoy retired-number status with NHL clubs even though they never played with those teams when they were in the league. After bringing his playing career to a close, Tremblay accepted the position of European scout for the Montreal Canadiens, based in Geneva, Switzerland.

Punch **Imlach**

Like most coaches in the NHL, Punch Imlach played hockey as a boy and dreamed one day of winning the Stanley Cup. Punch was never quite good enough or determined enough to make the grade as a player, but he did go on to become one of the most successful bench bosses of all time.

An only child, Imlach played for the Young Rangers as a teenager before moving up to the Marlboros and then the Goodyears, all Toronto-area teams in the 1930s. During the war, he enlisted in the army, where he continued to play and where he coached for the first time in Cornwall, Ontario. After being discharged, he was invited to the Detroit Red Wings training camp but declined the offer because he felt he'd put on too much weight during his military service. Instead, he went to work in the accounting department of Anglo-Canadian Pulp and Paper, a business operating in Quebec City. It was there that he started first to play and then coach the company-owned team known as the Quebec Aces.

Imlach remained with the Aces for 11 years, eventually becoming general manager and part owner of a successful team that for years featured Jean Beliveau, who Imlach always regarded as the greatest player he coached. "If there was a higher league than the NHL," he said, "Beliveau would have been its star." Imlach moved on to coach the Springfield Americans of the American Hockey League in 1957–58. The very next year he was hired as an assistant general manager for the Toronto Maple Leafs, a nebulous position at best because there was no single general manager, but a committee. It was at this point that his life took a remarkable turn for the better. Just a month into the 1958–59 season, the last-place Leafs showed no signs of improvement under head coach Billy Reay. Imlach fired Reay and took over, promising one and all that this sixth-place team would be in the playoffs by the end of the regular season. Most people laughed at his prediction.

A month into the 1958–59 season, Punch Imlach fired coach Billy Reay and took over, promising that the last-place Leafs would be in the playoffs. Most people laughed at his prediction.

With three games to go in the regular season, the Leafs still trailed the Rangers by five points, but in one of the most incredible finishes of all time, Toronto won all its games and the Rangers lost all theirs. Imlach's prediction had come true, and he was credited with being a genius. The Leafs lost in the semifinals or finals the next three years in a row, but in 1962 the team won its first of three successive Stanley Cup championships under Imlach's direction. They won again in 1967, but after being hammered by Boston in four embarrassing games in the 1969 playoffs, Leaf GM Stafford Smythe fired Imlach and his reign was over after 11 prosperous years and four Stanley Cup triumphs.

Imlach was as notorious as he was famous. He refused to negotiate players' contracts until training camp, feeling that the strategy got the players to work harder because they felt less secure about their positions. He routinely scheduled 15 to 20 exhibition games for the team because players never got paid for them but the Leafs got remuneration. But perhaps most notable of all was his running feud with superstar Frank Mahovlich. The Big M, a quiet, reserved man, was for years harassed and bullied by Imlach to the point where twice he had to leave the team because he was on the verge of a nervous breakdown. Yet Imlach got the most out of Mahovlich and won the Stanley Cup four times, a record that was always difficult to argue with.

Imlach's relationship with the other Leafs players depended entirely upon how they adapted to his philosophy. He was an anti-union man through and through and vilified those Leafs who joined the NHL Players' Association when it was first formed in 1967. His ongoing belligerence also cost him the services of defenseman Carl Brewer, who quit the team after a dressing room fight with Imlach. Brewer didn't return to the league for four years, such was his obstinacy. Perhaps Imlach's greatest handling of a player was when

Imlach, George "Punch"
Head Coach, b: Toronto, Ont., 3/15/1918, d: 12/1/1987

Season	Club, League	Regular Season					Playoffs				
		GC	W	L	T	W%	GC	W	L	T	W%
1958–59	Toronto Maple Leafs, NHL	50	22	20	8	0.520	12	5	7	0	0.417
1959–60	Toronto Maple Leafs, NHL	70	35	26	9	0.564	10	4	6	0	0.400
1960–61	Toronto Maple Leafs, NHL	70	39	19	12	0.643	5	1	4	0	0.200
1961–62	Toronto Maple Leafs, NHL	70	37	22	11	0.607	12	8	4	0	0.667
1962–63	Toronto Maple Leafs, NHL	70	35	23	12	0.586	14	8	6	0	0.571
1963–64	Toronto Maple Leafs, NHL	70	33	25	12	0.557	10	8	2	0	0.800
1964–65	Toronto Maple Leafs, NHL	70	30	26	14	0.529	6	2	4	0	0.333
1965–66	Toronto Maple Leafs, NHL	70	34	25	11	0.564	4	0	4	0	0.000
1966–67	Toronto Maple Leafs, NHL	70	32	27	11	0.536	12	8	4	0	0.667
1967–68	Toronto Maple Leafs, NHL	74	33	31	10	0.514					
1968–69	Toronto Maple Leafs, NHL	76	35	26	15	0.559	4	0	4	0	0.000
1970–71	Buffalo Sabres, NHL	78	24	39	15	0.404					
1971–72	Buffalo Sabres, NHL	41	8	23	10	0.317					
1979–80	Toronto Maple Leafs, NHL	10	5	5	0	0.500	3	0	3	0	0.000
	NHL Totals	889	402	337	150	0.537	92	44	48	0	0.478

Won Stanley Cup (1962, 1963, 1964, 1967)

he acquired Red Kelly from Detroit and then converted him from a defenseman to a center. Four Cup wins later, Imlach again looked like a genius.

Imlach himself was forced to leave the team during the 1966–67 season because of severe exhaustion, yet managed to return 10 games later to lead the team to the Stanley Cup in Canada's Centennial year. It was his greatest accomplishment because it was done with the Over-the-Hill

Gang of Leafs, the core of the team being players in their late 30s and early 40s who every other team had given up on. "The old players are the best," he rationalized. "Each one of them has tremendous desire. That's what keeps them in there…the ones who last a long time are the guys who work hardest—the ones who really give out in practice."

Most important of all to Imlach was loyalty, and he stayed close by those players who were loyal and equally felt no such compunction to those who were not. After the terrible loss in the 1969 playoffs, a number of players, led by Tim Horton and Johnny Bower, announced they would immediately retire from the game because Punch was no longer their coach.

But Imlach wasn't unemployed for very long. The Buffalo Sabres hired him to fill the dual roles of general manager and coach, a task he relished because it gave him the opportunity to beat the Leafs. His first selection at that year's Amateur Draft was Gil Perreault, and Imlach never looked back. He got the team into the finals in just five years, but along the way a greater toll was taken on his health. He suffered a heart attack during the 1971–72 season and had to give up coaching, and by 1979 he was fired by the Sabres after the team failed to maintain a high level of play after a 1975 run to the finals.

Like most coaches in the NHL, Punch Imlach played hockey as a boy and dreamed of winning the Stanley Cup.

In 1979 Leafs owner Harold Ballard hired Imlach to try to resuscitate the dying team. Hailed as the Second Coming in Toronto, Imlach's brief two years was the most controversial time in the history of Maple Leaf Gardens. "I'll try to make as many trades as I can," he promised during the press conference to welcome him back. And he didn't disappoint people. He got rid of a number of popular players, including Lanny McDonald, which caused an enormous rift in the Leafs dressing room and failed to improve the club's on-ice performance. He suffered another heart attack in 1981 and was forced to leave the Leafs entirely. In 1984 he was inducted into the Hockey Hall of Fame. A third heart attack in 1985 further weakened him, and he died two years later from a fourth.

Vladimir Dzurilla

Vladimir Dzurilla was a big, stocky fellow who always had a smile on his face. Sometimes he liked to reminisce about the highlights of his career—the three World Championship titles and especially the first year of the Canada Cup in 1976.

Such is the life of a goaltender that one minute he's a hero and the next he's being cursed.

"Things were going so well for me as never before. When we defeated Canada 1–0 in the group, the audience went silent but then started applauding. The host team lost, but the people knew they had given all they had. Quite simply, they had encountered a strong opponent. When coach Karel Gut told me that I would be in the net, I felt like a soldier in the front line about to approach bayonets."

The Canadians won the 1976 Canada Cup only after Darryl Sittler scored a goal in overtime. At that point, Dzurilla went over to Rogie Vachon, gave him a friendly hug and traded jerseys with him. It used to be more of a soccer ritual, but Dzurilla made history by introducing the custom to hockey.

Dzurilla was one of those goalies who don't roam, but instead station themselves between the posts and rely on their fast reflexes, strong skating and position play. An active goaltender for almost 30 years, until 1982, the native of Bratislava earned a reputation for longevity. He participated in eight World Championships. The first was in 1963 and the last in Vienna 14 years later to mark the end of his colorful career. He also took part in three Olympics. In the Czech league, he was goaltender in an impressive 571 matches over 19 seasons. While with Slovan Bratislava, he created a splendid tandem with Marcel Sakac. In the final days of his career, he guarded the nets of Zetor Brno and the German teams of Augsburg and Riessersee.

"I loved hockey. I just loved it. When you do something for so many years, it is hard to suddenly let go and do something else. Goaltenders have the advantage that with the right diet and proper training, they generally last longer than players on the ice do. I only left the net at 40 when my contract with Riessersee ended. I felt I could go on for longer but over time I came to the conclusion that it was right. What I regret the most is that I made many mistakes in my life. I regret wrong attitudes and words that I sometimes uttered more than those pucks that I didn't catch. I also regret not having won Olympic gold and a domestic title. In Slovan, we always thought that things would finally work out. However, Brno usually triumphed. When I went there, different teams reigned."

The only domestic title that he ever won was in 1957, but that was in field hockey and not on the ice. Later he entered the coaching profession in Brno and Germany, as well as for the Slovan club, to which he had close ties.

Dzurilla once confessed that if he returned to the game, he would never allow himself to get so emotionally attached to one club. He loved Slovan almost more than the game itself. He tended goal for them for 13 years. Yet when he lined up for the Bratislava team in his last match, no one thought of thanking

Vladimir Dzurilla (right) was a big, burly man who was always smiling.

Dzurilla, Vladimir
G, 5'10", 205 lbs, b: Bratislava, Czechoslovakia, 8/2/1942, d: 7/7/1995

Season	Club, League	Regular Season		
		GP	GA	Avg
1959–63	Slovan, Czechoslovakia	*	*	*
WEC–63	Czechoslovakia	4	8	2.00
1963–64	Slovan, Czechoslovakia	*	*	*
OWG–64	Czechoslovakia	2	4	2.00
1964–65	Slovan, Czechoslovakia	*	*	*
WEC–65	Czechoslovakia	5	6	1.20
1965–66	Slovan, Czechoslovakia	*	*	*
WEC–66	Czechoslovakia	6	10	1.67
1966–68	Slovan, Czechoslovakia	*	*	*
OWG–68	Czechoslovakia	7	16	2.29
1968–69	Slovan, Czechoslovakia	*	*	*
WEC–69	Czechoslovakia	9	16	1.78
1969–70	Slovan, Czechoslovakia	*	*	*
WEC–70	Czechoslovakia	10	25	2.50
1970–72	Slovan, Czechoslovakia	*	*	*
OWG–72	Czechoslovakia	5	7	1.40
WEC–72	Czechoslovakia	4	6	1.50
1972–73	Slovan, Czechoslovakia	*	*	*
1973–76	Zetor, Czechoslovakia	*	*	*
WEC–76	Czechoslovakia	2	1	0.50
CCup–76	Czechoslovakia	5	9	1.80
1976–77	Zetor, Czechoslovakia	*	*	*
WEC–77	Czechoslovakia	7	19	2.71
1977–78	Zetor, Czechoslovakia	*	*	*
1978–79	Augsburg, FRG	*	*	*
1979–82	Riessersee, FRG	*	*	*
	Czechoslovakia Totals	571	*	*
	OWG/WEC/CCup Totals	66	127	1.92

Named Best Goaltender at WEC (1965)
Won WEC (1972, 1976, 1977)
FRG Champion (1981)

Vladimir Dzurilla (right) was one of those goalies who stations himself between the posts and relies on his fast reflexes, strong skating and position playing.

him publicly. "I continued having good relations with the club, but I never heard a word of thanks. Later I may have, but never at the right time."

His best friends were Josef Golonka and Vaclav Nedomansky. But he also got along well with Ivan Hlinka, Frantisek Pospisil and Oldrich Machac. Back when the country was still united, those fellow Czechs were his teammates on the national team. "We had the same goal. There may have been some rivalry between Jiri Holecek and myself, but that stemmed from the nature of the goaltenders' art. Not many goaltenders want to be number two."

There aren't many activities in which the former Czechoslovakia ranked among the best in the world, but hockey was one of them. The generation that in 1972, 1976 and 1977 won gold medals in the World Championships started a tradition and inspired many up-and-coming young players. Even after the country split up, players from the golden era met on a regular basis.

Vlado Dzurilla tended goal in 1995 during a match in Stockholm for oldtimers. Another Slovak native, Stan Mikita, was there as well. Dzurilla was friendly with everyone and offered plenty of advice. "For a long time I was refusing such offers, but I let them convince me this time. I always feel good with pleasant people," he used to say. Three months later, he died in Dusseldorf, Germany. "Terrible. He was 53. Not so long ago, we were flying back and forth on the ice and now he is gone," commented Ivan Hlinka. Dzurilla was inducted into the IIHF Hockey Hall of Fame in 1998.

Dave Keon

Dave Keon had one the best backhands in the game.

Dave Keon was an exceptional two-way forward, adept at using his speed and craftiness to score goals and to prevent them with equal success. He used angles to forecheck and rarely took penalties, making up for his small size by thinking one step ahead of his often larger and stronger opponents.

Keon could be a dazzling offensive player, utilizing bursts of speed and deft moves around the net. He also had what is widely considered to be one of the best backhands in the game, a deceptive, often powerful shot that flummoxed opposing goaltenders. Yet Keon always put defense first. He was a true believer in the maxim that a goal scored is nothing compared to a goal given up. He was a tenacious defensive player and, though he was arguably the best forechecker in the game, hardly ever missed getting back on defense. Many of his goals came as a result of forcing the other team to make mistakes; he then had the talent and ability to take advantage.

All-time great goaltender Jacques Plante played with Keon and against him. "He's a superb checker. Everyone knows that. It's his offensive game that impresses me," Plante said of Keon in 1971, the first year the veteran goalie joined Keon's Leafs. "There are few players with more moves going in on a goalie. He can beat you on the backhand or on the forehand. He's proof that it's not the size of the body but the size of the heart that counts in this game."

Keon was 5'9" and around 165 pounds in his playing days. He used his agility to avoid opponents' hits and remained injury-free for much of his career. He also used his speed and maneuverability as a pesky penalty killer, covering a large portion of the ice and turning shorthanded situations into scoring chances for his own team. He set a league record for most goals while killing penalties with eight in the 1970–71 season, a remarkable total since the most any Toronto team had managed up to that year had been 14.

Had it not been for his mother, Toronto fans would never have had the chance to make Keon one of their all-time favorites. As a teenager in Noranda, Quebec, Keon was heavily courted by the Detroit Red Wings. His mother, however, objected to his moving so far away. He stayed in Noranda for another winter and was soon noticed by the Maple Leafs. The next year he went to St. Michael's College, as so many Leaf prospects did, and began to improve remarkably quickly. The Leafs informed him that he would be given a chance in the pro league in 1960, when he'd be 19. He was told by Bob Goldham and Father David Bauer, the St. Michael's coaches, that he could either learn how to play the defensive game—the game without the puck—in the summer or he could spend the next year in the minors working on it. He put in the extra time and effort and made the Leafs that fall.

Keon won the Calder Trophy as the top rookie that year and was a Second Team All-Star the next. Along with Red Kelly and Bob Pulford, Keon provided the Maple Leafs with a solid stable of centers, a nucleus of talent that would play a large role in the Leafs' four Stanley Cup triumphs in the 1960s. Keon was the playoff MVP in 1967, the last year the Maple Leafs won the Stanley Cup. Also in that span, he won the Lady Byng Trophy twice, in 1962 and 1963, as the NHL's most gentlemanly player. He had only two minutes in penalties each season, a remarkable total for such an effective forechecker and defensive player. At one time, Keon was the Maple Leafs' all-time leading scorer, overtaking Frank Mahovlich and George Armstrong, who had shared the record with 296 goals apiece. His record has since been bettered by Darryl Sittler, but his offensive totals are startling when Keon's attitude to the game are considered. "I have no major scoring targets. I set a mark of 20 before each season and hope to better it," he said late in his career. He was much more concerned with the team game than with his own accomplishments.

Keon seemed to be always at odds with Toronto management when it came to contract

Keon, Dave
C, 5'9", 165 lbs, b: Noranda, Que., 3/22/40

Season	Club, League	Regular Season					Playoffs				
		GP	G	A	Pts	PIM	GP	G	A	Pts	PIM
1959–60	Kitchener-Waterloo Dutchmen, OHA	1	1	0	1	0					
	Sudbury Wolves, EPHL						4	2	2	4	2
1960–61	Toronto Maple Leafs, NHL	70	20	25	45	6	5	1	1	2	0
1961–62	Toronto Maple Leafs, NHL	64	26	35	61	2	12	5	3	8	0
1962–63	Toronto Maple Leafs, NHL	68	28	28	56	2	10	7	5	12	0
1963–64	Toronto Maple Leafs, NHL	70	23	37	60	6	14	7	2	9	2
1964–65	Toronto Maple Leafs, NHL	65	21	29	50	10	6	2	2	4	2
1965–66	Toronto Maple Leafs, NHL	69	24	30	54	4	4	0	2	2	0
1966–67	Toronto Maple Leafs, NHL	66	19	33	52	2	12	3	5	8	0
1967–68	Toronto Maple Leafs, NHL	67	11	37	48	4					
1968–69	Toronto Maple Leafs, NHL	75	27	34	61	12	4	1	3	4	2
1969–70	Toronto Maple Leafs, NHL	72	32	30	62	6					
1970–71	Toronto Maple Leafs, NHL	76	38	38	76	4	6	3	2	5	0
1971–72	Toronto Maple Leafs, NHL	72	18	30	48	4	5	2	3	5	0
1972–73	Toronto Maple Leafs, NHL	76	37	36	73	2					
1973–74	Toronto Maple Leafs, NHL	74	25	28	53	7	4	1	2	3	0
1974–75	Toronto Maple Leafs, NHL	78	16	43	59	4	7	0	5	5	0
1975–76	Minnesota Fighting Saints, WHA	57	26	38	64	4					
	Indianapolis Racers, WHA	12	3	7	10	2	7	2	2	4	2
1976–77	Minnesota Fighting Saints, WHA	42	13	38	51	2					
	New England Whalers, WHA	34	14	25	39	8	5	3	1	4	0
1977–78	New England Whalers, WHA	77	24	38	62	2	14	5	11	16	4
1978–79	New England Whalers, WHA	79	22	43	65	2	10	3	9	12	2
1979–80	Hartford Whalers, NHL	76	10	52	62	10	3	0	1	1	0
1980–81	Hartford Whalers, NHL	80	13	34	47	26					
1981–82	Hartford Whalers, NHL	78	8	11	19	6					
	NHL Totals	1296	396	590	986	117	92	32	36	68	6
	WHA Totals	301	102	189	291	20	36	13	23	36	8

NHL Second All-Star Team (1962, 1971)
Won Conn Smythe Trophy (1967)
Won Calder Trophy (1961)
Won Lady Byng Trophy (1962, 1963)
Won Paul Deneau Trophy — WHA (1977, 1978)
Won Stanley Cup (1962, 1963, 1964, 1967)

negotiations but was able to smooth over differences before they interfered with his play. In 1972 the Ottawa Nationals of the World Hockey Association announced that they were going to do everything in their power to sign the productive center. Keon was trying out at the time for Team Canada, hoping for an opportunity to play against the Soviets in the Summit Series. He was kept off that team because of the possibility that he might leave the NHL. He was later convinced to remain with the Leafs by vice-president King Clancy and signed the richest contract the team had ever offered, but he did regret not playing in the 1972 series with teammates Paul Henderson and Ron Ellis.

Although Dave Keon (left) was much more concerned with the team game than his own accomplishments, at one time he was the Maple Leafs' all-time leading scorer.

Keon's leadership and productivity over his 15 years with the Leafs were all forgotten in the summer of 1975, at least by Harold Ballard, the cantankerous and headstrong owner of the team. He began to complain publicly about the lack of leadership Keon had shown to his younger teammates. Since Ballard was determined to rebuild the team with youth, Keon, the Leaf captain at the time, wasn't re-signed. It was insult on top of injury and Keon, though a classy individual on the ice and off, has refused for years to have much to do with the team he was—and is—so strongly identified with.

He signed as a free agent with the Minnesota Fighting Saints and spent four years in the WHA with the Fighting Saints, Indianapolis Racers and New England Whalers. In 1979–80, he returned to the NHL with the Hartford Whalers. Very quietly, in the summer of 1982, Keon ended his 22-year professional career. There was no fanfare. Keon, at the time the NHL's oldest player at 42, informed Hartford director of hockey operations Larry Pleau of his decision and then declined to have a press conference, saying he'd like to end his career without formality.

Though his name remains high on scoring lists, it is for his play without the puck that Keon is most often remembered. Defense was a subject he loved, above goal-scoring or individual records, and if there was a textbook on clean, effective checking, Dave Keon would be its author. He was inducted into the Hockey Hall of Fame in 1986.

"I maneuver my body so that the opposing player is forced to commit himself. Then he's in trouble," Keon explained in 1971. "Here's what you do: Skate at the puck carrier. Look him in the eye. Fade away and come back and worry him. Use your body to force him. Be persistent. Discourage him. The beauty of it all is you can play this way without taking penalties. I play aggressively. I do lots of hitting. But I feel you can accomplish anything at all in hockey without taking penalties."

Jaroslav Holik

A complex man, Jaroslav Holik's life has had a lot of ups and downs. But he has been one of the most talked about people in the world of hockey, whether as a player or as a coach.

Holik played a hard, highly focused game of hockey. He had very high expectations of himself and of others—his opponents on the ice, his disciples he later trained and the players on the bench and in the locker room. He had no tolerance for insincerity or hypocrisy. "My dad instilled in me a strong will, or maybe it was the land around us where we were growing up. I got my harsh, straightforward nature from my father. My younger brother Jiri was more cautious, a diplomat. He took after my mother."

In the town of Havlickuv Brod, in a hilly region between Bohemia and Moravia, winters were harsh. He was born there on August 3, 1942. When he was four, he got his first pair of skates for Christmas. He took some of his first steps on local ponds with names like Cihlar and Kotlasa. One year the town built a winter stadium, and after that even his father couldn't get him off the ice. "I guess he wanted us to be skiers. He was a good ski jumper. But when he saw the enthusiasm we had for hockey, he didn't stop us. On the contrary, he pushed us. He wanted to raise us to be achievers."

In 1961 he left Havlickuv Brod to play for Jihlava. For the next few years, he stayed in his home town and commuted by bicycle. Every day he would pedal 25 kilometers through the hills to get there and another 25 to get back, even in rain or sleet. On top of that, he'd go jogging in the woods in the evenings.

Jaroslav Holik (right) has been one of the most talked about people in hockey for years, as a player and later as a coach.

He was only 19 when he was offered a spot on an elite team to play against Canada. It didn't take long before he was considered one of the greatest talents of his time. But then a serious injury hindered his further development. During a trip with Dukla Jihlava to Moscow in September 1962, he was struck with a puck just above his right ankle and came down with a bone marrow infection. Soon after recovering, he was beset with misfortune again. During a match against Djurgarden in Stockholm, a puck hit him in the same place, breaking his leg.

He went to his first World Championship in 1965 at the age of 23. It was the first of seven he would attend, but he was never assured of a place on the team until the last minute. Before a match against the USSR during the 1969 championship in Stockholm, he pasted over the five-point star on the old Czech state emblem to protest the Soviet occupation of his country in August 1968. He was only suspended from the team in 1971 when the communist regime adopted a more hard-line policy. Had many players not been injured just before the 1972 Olympics in Sapporo, he might not have been invited to play. And he might not have had the good fortune to celebrate a World Championship win in the spring of that year.

The forward line he formed while with the Jihlava club, which included Jan Klapac and his brother, was considered at the time among the best in the league and on the national team. Klapac was a scorer, a right wing sharpshooter. Holik was mostly a defenseman, a tireless worker who inspired the other players because he never considered a match to be lost. "Every time I went on the ice I was convinced that we had to win. I knew no other option. From the first face-off I was in a different world. I didn't differentiate between whether we were winning or losing. I always fought with equal passion. Once you let up, it is over." He had the same hard-nosed determination to win whether in the league or on the national team. "The very thought that you are playing for your country must give you a double dose of strength."

Holik, Jaroslav
C, 5′11″, 182 lbs, b: Havlickuv Brod, Czechoslovakia, 8/3/1942

Season	Club, League	Regular Season				
		GP	G	A	Pts	PIM
1961–65	Dukla Jihlava, Czechoslovakia	*	*	*	*	*
WEC–65	Czechoslovakia	6	0	3	3	2
1965–66	Dukla Jihlava, Czechoslovakia	*	*	*	*	*
WEC–66	Czechoslovakia	5	0	0	0	6
1966–67	Dukla Jihlava, Czechoslovakia	*	*	*	*	*
WEC–67	Czechoslovakia	7	3	5	8	8
1967–69	Dukla Jihlava, Czechoslovakia	*	*	*	*	*
WEC–69	Czechoslovakia	10	4	10	14	18
1969–70	Dukla Jihlava, Czechoslovakia	*	*	*	*	*
WEC–70	Czechoslovakia	10	2	3	5	10
1970–72	Dukla Jihlava, Czechoslovakia	*	*	*	*	*
OWG–72	Czechoslovakia	4	2	1	3	0
WEC–72	Czechoslovakia	10	8	7	15	8
1972–73	Dukla Jihlava, Czechoslovakia	*	*	*	*	*
WEC–73	Czechoslovakia	8	5	2	7	10
1973–79	Dukla Jihlava, Czechoslovakia	*	*	*	*	*
	Czechoslovakia Totals	602	267	*	*	*
	OWG/WEC Totals	60	24	31	55	62

Won WEC (1972)
Czechoslovakia Champion (1967, 1968, 1969, 1970, 1971, 1972, 1974)

He won the Czech hockey title seven times with Jihlava and spent 18 seasons—until 1979, when he was 37—competing at the highest level. Holik really lived the games he played, never dodging blows or avoiding skirmishes. "Sometimes I had the feeling that I am being much too hard on the opponent. But I realized all that only after the siren sounded. Even though I was an old, seasoned player who had seen a lot of the world, I found it difficult to fall asleep after a match. I would take two sleeping pills, which didn't work. It was all coming back to me."

Though many other clubs showed an interest in Holik over the years, he stayed loyal to his home territory. After he retired from active sports, he continued as a trainer with Dukla Jihlava, first as an assistant and later as head coach. He also made professional athletes of his own children. His daughter, Andrea, wife of defenseman Frantisek Musil, was an excellent tennis player and his son, Robert—Bob to most people—plays in the NHL.

Staying in his homeland, Holik never had the opportunities his children did, but he readily admitted the idea of living in North America didn't intrigue him. With the Jihlava club he won a total of five titles, the last in 1991. Except for a brief stop in Pardubice, he remained with the team. He coached Havlickuv Brod for a while, but in his absence, Jihlava went into a slump and he decided to come to the rescue once again.

When the Czech junior team under Holik's leadership set out for the World Championship at the end of 1999, they didn't inspire much confidence in their countrymen. But Holik pulled off a coup and led the team to its first world title. As he always said, a game's never lost until the final siren.

Lennart Svedberg

In his childhood he played the accordion, and perhaps it was this gift for music that helped Lennart Svedberg develop the sense of rhythm that, combined with his remarkable skating, would turn him into a real hockey artist. He trained less than many of his colleagues, but everything he did on the ice appeared so easy and elegant that it amazed hockey experts in Sweden and around the world.

Lennart Svedberg was named the best defenseman at the 1970 World Championship.

His best years are connected with Brynas in Gavle, but he made his debut with Vifsta Ostrand in the town of Timra at the age of 15. After just turning 17, he made his first appearance with Tre Kronor, where he played right wing on a forward line with Ulf Sterner and

Svedberg, Lennart
F/D, 5′11″, 180 lbs, b: Timra, Sweden, 2/29/1944, d: 7/29/1972

Season	Club, League	Regular Season				
		GP	G	A	Pts	PIM
1960–62	Vifsta Ostrand, Sweden	*	*	*	*	*
1962–63	Grums, Sweden	*	*	*	*	*
1963–65	Brynas, Sweden	*	*	*	*	*
WEC–65	Sweden	7	1	3	4	4
1965–66	Brynas, Sweden	*	*	*	*	*
WEC–66	Sweden	7	2	*	*	*
1966–67	Brynas, Sweden	*	*	*	*	*
1967–68	Mora, Sweden	*	*	*	*	*
OWG–68	Sweden	7	2	*	*	*
1968–69	Mora, Sweden	*	*	*	*	*
WEC–69	Sweden	10	1	0	1	8
1969–70	Timra, Sweden	*	*	*	*	*
WEC–70	Sweden	10	1	3	4	4
1970–71	Timra, Sweden	*	*	*	*	*
WEC–71	Sweden	10	1	1	2	2
1971–72	Timra, Sweden	*	*	*	*	*
	Sweden Totals	*	*	*	*	*
	OWG/WEC Totals	51	8	*	*	*

Named Best Defenseman at WEC (1970)
Sweden Champion (1964)

Uno Erlund. That was on December 8, 1961, in Stockholm in a game against the Czechoslovak national team—a game that Tre Kronor won 4–3, with Svedberg scoring a goal.

Even after he became a defenseman, Svedberg continued to score goals as he sliced through opposition lines at high speed like a hot knife through butter. It was Brynas defenseman Lennart Johansson—known for spotting talent—who recommended that Svedberg change his specialty. It turned out to be a prophetic decision, for it was as a defenseman that Lennart Svedberg became known to the entire hockey world. On the ice, he performed like a true master. When he was at his best, he reigned supreme in all three zones, always just a little ahead of his opponent.

On the international level, Svedberg was named best defenseman at the 1970 World Championship and selected three times to All-Star teams: at the 1968 Olympics and at the 1969 and 1970 World Championships. In the Swedish national lineup, the gifted defenseman played in 138 games (117 official games) and ranked number 71 in the list of "Great Men."

But no one could have foreseen how brief his hockey career would be. On a summer morning in 1972, Svedberg perished in a car accident at the age of 28. In the memories of those who know and love hockey, Lennart Svedberg will remain a virtuoso defenseman who was always a gentleman on the ice and in everyday life, where he captivated everyone with his smile.

At his best, Lennart Svedberg (number 4) reigned supreme in all three zones and was always just ahead of his opponent.

Arne Stromberg

Arne Stromberg will always be remembered as a devoted enthusiast who made a major contribution to the growth of contemporary hockey in Sweden. He was obsessed and captivated by hockey his whole life.

His many colleagues around the world admired his commitment to hockey and considered him a friend. Among them were Soviet coaches Arkady Chernyshev and Anatoli Tarasov, who were often stymied by the experienced Stromberg's tactics in the well-remembered games of the 1960s.

Stromberg was born in Stockholm on July 30, 1920, and as a teenager played hockey for the provincial IF Skuru. In the late 1940s, he joined the big league's Mattias Pojkarna but didn't make it to the national team as a player. However, he enjoyed well-deserved fame as the Tre Kronor coach who made Sweden a world champion and he became an internationally acknowledged hockey expert. When he was head coach of Stockholm's Djurgarden, Stromberg led the popular club to eight national championship wins, a record that remains unbroken.

A man of diverse knowledge and skills, Arne Stromberg's comments were frequently quoted and many became part of hockey legend. "God save me from the big scorers," he muttered after Hans Lindberg (who later became Tre Kronor's head coach) performed less than brilliantly at the 1967 Vienna World Championship. The phrase was often repeated, although few remembered its ending—"when they play like this." No hockey authority has been quoted—and misquoted—as often as Stromberg. He frequently tried to disavow his tape-recorded words.

Hockey was a life-long obsession for Arne Stromberg.

Arne Stromberg (top) enjoyed well-deserved fame as the Tre Kronor coach who made Sweden a world champion.

In 1959, with Canadian Ed Reigle, Stromberg started working with the Swedish national team and in 1961, at the World Championship in Switzerland, he was appointed head coach, a position he held for 10 years.

When the time came, he resigned with characteristic conviction. At the 1971 World Championship, Tre Kronor lost to West Germany 2–1. Many at the time believed it was the bitterest defeat in Sweden's hockey history, and the infuriated Helge Berglund, president of the Swedish hockey union, called Stromberg and the team's scouts "unscrupulous creatures" during the competition. The ensuing controversy resulted in Stromberg's resignation. His high standards would allow nothing less.

Stromberg left the national team but he didn't quit hockey. He coached for Gothenburg's Vastra Frolunda, then for Ostersund and then Mora. After that he went to Switzerland to coach for SC Langnau, but he didn't stay there long because he felt they didn't take hockey seriously enough. He didn't like working with amateurs.

Back home, he returned to Vastra Frolunda and supervised the team during its first years in the senior league. In his later years he went to Stockholm to work with juniors in a small club outside the Swedish capital. Even as a retiree, he was the same energetic, expressive person who always took the time to explain and instruct. He died in 1988 at the age of 67.

Arne Stromberg was a major force behind Sweden's becoming a hockey superpower. During the many years he headed the national team, they failed to win a medal only three times. Stromberg's Tre Kronor won the World Championship in 1962, two World Championship bronzes and five silvers and Olympic silver in Innsbruck in 1964. He was inducted into the IIHF Hockey Hall of Fame in 1998.

Stromberg, Arne
Head Coach, b: Stockholm, Sweden, 7/30/1920, d: 1988

Season	Club, League	Regular Season				
		GC	W	L	T	W%
WEC–61	Sweden	7	4	3	0	0.571
WEC–62	Sweden	7	7	0	0	0.100
WEC–63	Sweden	7	6	1	0	0.857
OWG–64	Sweden	8	6	2	0	0.750
WEC–65	Sweden	7	4	2	1	0.643
WEC–66	Sweden	7	3	3	1	0.500
WEC–67	Sweden	7	4	2	1	0.643
OWG–68	Sweden	7	4	2	1	0.643
WEC–69	Sweden	10	8	2	0	0.800
WEC–70	Sweden	10	7	2	1	0.750
WEC–71	Sweden	10	5	4	1	0.550
	OWG/WEC Totals	87	57	23	6	0.701

Won WEC (1962)

Vaclav Nedomansky

Vaclav Nedomansky was a man of action but could keep his cool under any circumstances. Commenting on his own personality, he once said: "Skating over to your partner and hitting him with a stick or a fist, that is the last resort. On ice, one should play hockey." A low-key fellow who avoided the fanfare of the professional game, he preferred things done calmly and quietly with no fuss and no long explanations. With his relaxed demeanor, he could appear either very well adjusted or introverted to the point of being cold-blooded. More likely than not, he simply had his emotions under tight rein.

He was born on March 14, 1944, in Hodonin, but throughout his entire Czech career he was in some way tied to Slovan Bratislava, a team where he spent 12 seasons. Had he not decided to go for hockey, he would have made a good soccer player. He even played one match for Slovan in the Czech league. But in the end, hockey won out and Nedomansky went on to become practically indispensable to the Czech national team.

A bit of a loner on and off the ice, he sometimes created the impression that he was playing for himself or losing interest in the game or the team. It didn't help that on the Czech national team, there was high turnover among his teammates. And even as a young man he was used to carrying a great deal of responsibility. When the going got tough and it was down to the deciding moments of a game, he would set an example for the others by giving the order to attack.

A tall, well-built center, he had very strong skating skills. Deception was a major element in his game. He would fake passes and catch the eye of an opponent just to mislead him. With his hard, accurate slapshot, he was a goaltender's nightmare. Only his weak defense was sometimes criticized. "You know how our system of a defending left wing was born?" joked the legendary coach and former player Vladimir Bouzek. "It is Vaclav's fault. As center he refused to return. They had to think of something new." Nedomansky himself didn't save the team from many goals. But he more than made up for it with the goals that he scored.

Four times he was number one in the league in goals scored. Including his time on the national team, he put 559 shots into the net altogether and led the historic ranking of the Czech Club of League Scorers, which rates players by total goals scored on the professional level. Only Milan Novy and, in the 1998–99 season, Vladimir Ruzicka have been able to beat him. Nedomansky played in two Olympics and on nine World Championship teams, including the one that won the title in 1972. During his career, his name has been linked to most of the successes as well as the failures in Czech hockey. But then one day it all came to an end.

"Political reasons weren't what led me to my decision to leave. It was purely professional and human. I wanted to continue shaping as a player and as a human being, in order to continue my career on the highest possible level and lead life according to my ideas." With these words he explained the reasons that led him to defect in the summer of 1974.

Vaclav Nedomansky's self-imposed exile to the NHL influenced many other Czech players.

Nedomansky, Vaclav "Big Ned"
RW, 6′2″, 205 lbs, b: Hodonin, Czechoslovakia, 3/14/1944

Season	Club, League	Regular Season					Playoffs				
		GP	G	A	Pts	PIM	GP	G	A	Pts	PIM
1962–65	Slovan, Czechoslovakia	*	*	*	*	*	*	*	*	*	*
WEC–65	Czechoslovakia	7	4	2	6	2					
1965–66	Slovan, Czechoslovakia	*	*	*	*	*	*	*	*	*	*
WEC–66	Czechoslovakia	7	5	2	7	8					
1966–67	Slovan, Czechoslovakia	*	*	*	*	*	*	*	*	*	*
WEC–67	Czechoslovakia	7	1	2	3	14					
1967–68	Slovan, Czechoslovakia	*	*	*	*	*	*	*	*	*	*
OWG–68	Czechoslovakia	7	5	2	7	4					
1968–69	Slovan, Czechoslovakia	*	*	*	*	*	*	*	*	*	*
WEC–69	Czechoslovakia	10	9	2	11	10					
1969–70	Slovan, Czechoslovakia	*	*	*	*	*	*	*	*	*	*
WEC–70	Czechoslovakia	10	10	7	17	11					
1970–71	Slovan, Czechoslovakia	*	*	*	*	*	*	*	*	*	*
WEC–71	Czechoslovakia	10	8	0	8	0					
1971–72	Slovan, Czechoslovakia	*	*	*	*	*	*	*	*	*	*
OWG–72	Czechoslovakia	6	8	3	11	0					
WEC–72	Czechoslovakia	9	9	6	15	0					
1972–73	Slovan, Czechoslovakia	*	*	*	*	*					
WEC–73	Czechoslovakia	10	9	3	12	2					
1973–74	Slovan, Czechoslovakia	*	*	*	*	*	*	*	*	*	*
WEC–74	Czechoslovakia	10	10	3	13	4					
1974–75	Toronto Toros, WHA	78	41	40	81	19	6	3	1	4	9
1975–76	Toronto Toros, WHA	81	56	42	98	8					
1976–77	Birmingham Bulls, WHA	81	36	33	69	10					
1977–78	Birmingham Bulls, WHA	12	2	3	5	6					
	Detroit Red Wings, NHL	63	11	17	28	2	7	3	5	8	0
1978–79	Detroit Red Wings, NHL	80	38	35	73	19					
1979–80	Detroit Red Wings, NHL	79	35	39	74	13					
1980–81	Detroit Red Wings, NHL	74	12	20	32	30					
1981–82	Detroit Red Wings, NHL	68	12	28	40	22					
1982–83	St. Louis Blues, NHL	22	2	9	11	2					
	New York Rangers, NHL	35	12	8	20	0					
	Czechoslovakia Totals	419	349	*	*	*	*	*	*	*	*
	WHA Totals	252	135	118	253	43	6	3	1	4	9
	NHL Totals	421	122	156	278	88	7	3	5	8	0
	OWG/WEC Totals	93	78	32	110	55					

Named Best Forward at WEC (1974)
Won Paul Deneau Trophy — WHA (1976)
Won WEC (1972)

It all began when he and a fellow player on the national team, Richard Farda, applied for permission to accept a foreign contract. They were 30 years old at the time and had a collection of medals around their necks to prove that they had contributed their fair share to Czech hockey. It didn't help and they were denied permission, so they left on their own.

Vaclav Nedomansky (left) played in nine World Championships and two Olympics, and in 1972 he became a world champion.

They made it to Toronto via Switzerland and for three years they played for the local Toros and later for the Birmingham Bulls of the WHA. They wanted to move up, but if they were to suit up in another league, they could be suspended from play for 18 months for breach of contract. Farda later returned to Switzerland. Nedomansky, also known as "Big Ned," got the Paul Deneau Trophy in 1976 for most gentlemanly player and followed it up with another career move. He transferred to the NHL, playing for Detroit, the New York Rangers and St. Louis, then called it quits at the age of 39.

Other Czech players were sought after too, but not many of them had the strength or determination to take such a big leap. "I lost contact with family and friends and realized that I might never go back home," Nedomansky admitted years later.

The self-imposed exile of Nedomansky and Farda influenced many other players, however. Among others, it inspired Peter Stastny and his brothers Anton and Marian to leave their homeland. At the same time, it led to a certain amount of relaxation of the rules for players who wanted to go abroad through official channels. But it continued to be restricted to players at a more advanced age who had already served for many years on the national team.

From 1987 to 1989, Nedomansky coached the German club Schwenningen and for one season the Innsbruck hockey club in Austria. He also wrote regular columns for the Swiss magazine *Sport*. Only after the fall of the Iron Curtain was he able to return to his homeland. By that time, he was working as a European talent scout for the Los Angeles Kings.

"I have heard a lot about you," the 18-year-old Jaromir Jagr told him in 1990, even though Jagr had only been two when Nedomansky left for Canada. His own son, Vaclav Jr., saw him play only overseas. In the 1993–94 season, he himself played in the Czech league for Litvinov. "I have read much about my dad in books and newspapers. But only here in the Czech Republic do I understood what a great player he used to be. I hear words of respect at every step."

Jacques Laperriere

A tall and mobile defenseman, Jacques Laperriere was a key component of the Montreal Canadiens' success during the late 1960s and early 1970s. Standing 6´2″ and possessing an enormous reach, the lanky defender was a consistent impediment to opposing forwards. His poise and ability to move the puck forward after breaking up the play was crucial to the Habs' outstanding transition game. Many opposing skaters became annoyed with Laperriere's persistence, but he was rarely coaxed into taking a bad penalty and was never intimidated.

The Montreal Canadiens scouted the tall teenager while he was playing in the system of his home town of Rouyn, Quebec, in the heart of the province's mining country. He spent a year of Junior B with the Brockville Canadians, which proved to be a test for the young francophone. Following this season, he was developed in the Habs' junior and minor pro franchises in Ottawa-Hull and Montreal before joining the NHL on a full-time basis in 1963–64.

Montreal fans were treated to an impressive rookie season on the part of the young defenseman. Laperriere scored 30 points, made few defensive errors and calmly influenced the pace of the game night in, night out. His solid debut was acknowledged when he was awarded the Calder Trophy and the accolades of the demanding Montreal fans and media. He also garnered selection to the NHL Second All-Star Team. NHL president Clarence Campbell was so impressed that he said, "Never in my years in professional hockey have I seen a young man take over and lead a team as Laperriere has done."

Through the remainder of his career, Laperriere's style was constant, as were his numbers. He never scored more than seven goals and registered between 30 and 40 points five times between 1963–64 and 1969–70. His poise and reliability were key components in Stanley Cup triumphs in 1965, 1966, 1968 and 1969. Following the 1965–66 season, he was presented the James Norris Trophy and was an NHL First Team All-Star after both the 1964–65 and 1965–66 seasons and a Second Team selection at the end of the 1969–70 schedule.

Laperriere later reflected on his conservative approach to his position: "It's a simple thing. You cover the area you're responsible for. You don't get caught out of position. You gain control of the puck. You pass it to somebody else or else you carry it over the blue line and then pass it to somebody else. You don't take chances—that's for the forwards to do. Stay away from offense unless it's absolutely safe."

As Montreal entered the 1970s, the Orr- and Esposito-led Boston Bruins were the talk of the NHL. They seemed a sure bet to win the Stanley Cup after a record-breaking season in 1970–71. But in the quarterfinals, Laperriere and the Habs were ready for them and upset the mighty Beantowners in seven games. They later bested the favored Black Hawks to earn a surprise Stanley Cup triumph. This may have been Laperriere's greatest post-season, as he accounted for four goals and 13 points while dictating the pace of the game whenever he was on the ice. Fittingly, he was sent out by coach Al MacNeil to defend the 3–2 lead in game seven against Chicago and was the first player to hug young goalie phenomenon Ken Dryden when the final buzzer sounded.

Two years later the rock-steady defender was on hand again when Montreal won its second Stanley Cup in three years. Laperriere recorded the top plus-minus rating in the NHL while utilizing his mobility and reach to full extent. Once again the Habs vanquished the frustrated Hawks, this time in six games.

Jacques Laperriere's style was constant throughout his career, and so were his numbers.

Laperriere, Jacques
D, 6'2", 180 lbs, b: Rouyn, Que., 11/22/1941

Season	Club, League	Regular Season					Playoffs				
		GP	G	A	Pts	PIM	GP	G	A	Pts	PIM
1963–64	Montreal Canadiens, NHL	65	2	28	30	102	7	1	1	2	8
1964–65	Montreal Canadiens, NHL	67	5	22	27	92	6	1	1	2	16
1965–66	Montreal Canadiens, NHL	57	6	25	31	85					
1966–67	Montreal Canadiens, NHL	61	0	20	20	48	9	0	1	1	9
1967–68	Montreal Canadiens, NHL	72	4	21	25	84	13	1	3	4	20
1968–69	Montreal Canadiens, NHL	69	5	26	31	45	14	1	3	4	28
1969–70	Montreal Canadiens, NHL	73	6	31	37	98					
1970–71	Montreal Canadiens, NHL	49	0	16	16	20	20	4	9	13	12
1971–72	Montreal Canadiens, NHL	73	3	25	28	50	4	0	0	0	2
1972–73	Montreal Canadiens, NHL	57	7	16	23	34	10	1	3	4	2
1973–74	Montreal Canadiens, NHL	42	2	10	12	14					
	NHL Totals	691	40	242	282	674	88	9	22	31	101

NHL First All-Star Team (1965, 1966)
NHL Second All-Star Team (1964, 1970)
Won James Norris Trophy (1966)
Won Calder Trophy (1964)
Won Stanley Cup (1965, 1966, 1968, 1969, 1971, 1973)

A tall and mobile defenseman, Jacques Laperriere (second from the left) was a key component of the Montreal Canadiens' success during the late 1960s and early 1970s.

Laperriere's return from an injury early in the finals was crucial to the Habs' championship. Coach Scotty Bowman noted: "We were so disorganized in our own zone. There was no way we could have won if that had continued. The return of Jacques Laperriere changed all that."

Unfortunately, a serious knee injury cut his season down to 42 games in 1973–74 and he was forced to retire with six Stanley Cup rings and nearly 300 career points. Laperriere's excellence received the ultimate validation in 1987 when he was inducted into the Hockey Hall of Fame.

After retiring as a player, Laperriere took on the position of coach of the Montreal Junior Canadiens prior to the 1975–76 season. Partway through the following year he resigned, as the pressure and violence at the amateur level caused him to sour on his new profession. In 1980–81, he returned to the Habs as a part-time assistant to head coach Claude Ruel. The following year he began a 16-year tenure as an assistant coach with the club. He served under six different head coaches, including Stanley Cup wins with Jean Perron in 1986 and Jacques Demers in 1993.

Under Pat Burns from 1988 to 1992, Laperriere kept the Habs' defense corps near the top of the NHL. Burns noted: "I was hired in 1988, and since then, we've replaced some top defensemen—Larry Robinson, Rick Green, Craig Ludwig and Chris Chelios. And we're leading the league by a wide margin. That says it all, right?" Prior to the 1997–98 season, Laperriere was reunited with his old boss in Boston, where he continued to function as one of the top assistant coaches in the game.

Jiri Holecek

Jiri Holecek was one of the first Europeans to use the spread kneeling position.

When it comes to the school of European goaltending, the names that most often come to mind are Dominik Hasek and Vladislav Tretiak. In his time, Jiri Holecek was just as good as the former and better and at least as famous as the latter.

In his homeland they called him "Fakir," not for his acrobatic catching style but for his tall, skinny build. "I was the thinnest of all. I think it was Jaroslav Holik on the national team who started it. I reminded him of an Indian fakir, lying on a bed of nails and blowing the pipe to boot."

After watching Canadian goaltender Seth Martin during World Championships in the 1960s, he became one of the first Europeans to use the spread kneeling position. Holecek perfected the move and encountered no competition. "I have looser joints and thus greater reach. That's why I was good at the spread kneeling position."

Holecek was born in Prague on March 18, 1944. As a boy, he started out in hockey by playing on a pond in the city quarter of Zizkov. Later he played with the local club as a forward. After failing to make it onto the elite Bohemians Prague team when he was 13, he left Tatra Smichov for Slavia and retrained as a goaltender.

He stayed with this club until 1963, when he decided to play for Dukla, later VSZ Kosice, in the easternmost part of the country. He stayed for 10 years. In 1973 he returned to the capital and tended goal for Sparta Prague. "Kosice had an average team. We were always in the middle of the charts. Sparta was in a crisis when I got there. It was only three places away from ending up in the lower competition ranking. Then we ended up second. We missed the title twice after that, too. But I have no regrets. I made up for that with other successes."

But his greatest disappointment was yet to come. His debut in the World Championship was in 1966, but it was in the next World Championship in Vienna the following year that personal defeat marred an otherwise successful career. "For the first time in history, we lost against Finland and ended up fourth. Playing for us in this match was rookie Vladimir Nadrchal. The score was 2–0 [for Finland] when they sent me out there in the 10th minute of the game. I managed to let only one goal get by. We lost 3–1, so for 50 minutes I was chasing 1–1. Still I was blamed for the defeat and expelled from the national team for three years."

He only returned again in 1971.

At the World Championships, he was usually paired with Vladimir Dzurilla. They were equally ambitious, so there was a certain rivalry between them. "In every team there should be a goaltender who knows he is number one. When we went to the tournament, they said, 'You are lined up as number one; you keep in mind that you are a replacement.' It isn't a nice feeling to be in second place. But usually I didn't get stuck with that."

Holecek played in a total of 10 World Championships. In 1972, 1976 and 1977 he was part of a gold medal win, and five times he was named the tournament's best goaltender. At the time, he preferred to face technical teams like the Soviets. They always put together tricky plays to work their way to an empty net. Holecek was very mobile; he could move quickly from place to place with the passes. He could also predict who would have the completing move. "I always looked forward to playing with the Russians. They were terribly afraid of us because failure to defeat us was equivalent to suicide. They had to win; we had nothing to lose. I would tell them, 'Don't be crazy, it's only hockey.'"

Holecek never considered Vladislav Tretiak a top goaltender.

"Average—in our league he would be in fifth place. But he had excellent defensemen in front of him. In those days, when

In his homeland, they called Jiri Holecek (left) "Fakir."

			Regular Season		
Holecek, Jiri					
G, 5´11˝, 165 lbs, b: Prague, Czechoslovakia, 3/18/1944					
Season	Club, League		GP	GA	Avg
1963–66	Dukla Kosice, Czechoslovakia		*	*	*
WEC–66	Czechoslovakia		2	5	2.50
1966–67	Dukla Kosice, Czechoslovakia		*	*	*
WEC–67	Czechoslovakia		4	10	2.50
1967–71	VSZ Kosice, Czechoslovakia		*	*	*
WEC–71	Czechoslovakia		8	12	1.50
1971–72	VSZ Kosice, Czechoslovakia.		*	*	*
OWG–72	Czechoslovakia		3	8	2.67
WEC–72	Czechoslovakia		6	10	1.67
1972–73	VSZ Kosice, Czechoslovakia		*	*	*
WEC–73	Czechoslovakia		8	17	2.13
1973–74	Sparta Prague, Czechoslovakia		*	*	*
WEC–74	Czechoslovakia		6	14	2.33
1974–75	Sparta Prague, Czechoslovakia		*	*	*
WEC–75	Czechoslovakia		9	14	1.56
1975–76	Sparta Prague, Czechoslovakia		*	*	*
OWG–76	Czechoslovakia		5	9	1.80
WEC–76	Czechoslovakia		8	13	1.62
CCup–76	Czechoslovakia		5	9	1.80
1976–77	Sparta Prague, Czechoslovakia		*	*	*
WEC–77	Czechoslovakia		4	13	3.25
1977–78	Sparta Prague, Czechoslovakia		*	*	*
WEC–78	Czechoslovakia		9	19	2.11
1978–80	Munich, FRG		*	*	*
1980–81	Essen, FRG		*	*	*
	Czechoslovakia Totals		488	*	*
	OWG/WEC/CCup Totals		77	153	1.99

Named Best Goaltender at WEC (1971, 1973, 1975, 1976, 1978)
Won WEC (1972, 1976, 1977)

we beat the Russians, we might have dumped as many as nine goals into his net. He wasn't used to being aimed at too often. Four or five aims per period, and from the blue line at that. In the series against the best in the NHL in 1972, he made a name for himself. No one believed that the Russians could have such a goaltender. But the thing was that the Canadians couldn't pass to each other as well as our team's Vladimir Martinec or Bohuslav Stastny could, for instance. They were shooting from all directions. Tretiak would even skate out of the net and they would shoot the puck directly at him. When playing against us, he hardly caught a thing. Still, he was the best goaltender the Russians had had in 20 years."

Holecek's last great tournament was the 1979 World Championship in Prague. After his career in his homeland ended, he worked in Germany with the EHC Munich club for two years and one season with EHC Essen. From 1981 he worked as a trainer for goaltenders, led a national junior team, coached in Sapporo, Japan, and with Slavia Prague. Then he almost disappeared from hockey, helping out only now and then as a color commentator for TV coverage. He also devoted time to his job in an advertising agency.

"My only regret isn't winning Olympic gold and not having a chance to try the NHL. Nothing else. But on the other hand, I should consider myself lucky that I survived the net in good health."

Jan Suchy

Jan Suchy (number 17) was the only player on the Czech national team to be granted the privilege of smoking.

If the current political climate in Czechoslovakia had existed in the 1960s and 1970s, one name would surely have appeared in the international hockey annals. In his day, Jan Suchy was the best defenseman in Europe. He was the Czechs' answer to Bobby Orr or Doug Harvey.

Suchy was an excellent skater and made sacrifices as a defenseman to set his teammates up with a play. He was the first in Europe to use his body to stop goals in front of his net, and he could let go a mean shot at the other end of the rink as well. But as much as he wanted to, he couldn't freely leave for the NHL, for the communists refused him permission. He ran into trouble with the regime numerous times and it prevented him from joining the world champions in 1972. Even so, his career was quite remarkable. "Souska," as he was nicknamed, had few equals in more ways than one.

He was one of the few defensemen who could make spectators get up out of their seats. At a time when every move of the players on the national team was being watched even off the ice, Suchy, a heavy smoker, was the only privileged one on the national team officially allowed to smoke. "The coaches weren't pleased, but they didn't forbid me anything. They forbade others. Some of them used to smoke in my room and then we said it was me." But his unhealthy habit didn't appear to affect his physical condition. He was a terrific player right up until the age of 40.

Born in Havlickuv Brod on October 10, 1944, Jan Suchy started paying hockey on natural ice, on a frozen pond called Cihlar. Growing up with him were other future legends of Czech hockey—brothers Jaroslav and Jiri Holik and Josef Augusta, among others. All were known for their toughness, fighting spirit and harsh personalities. "It is the land around here. There is nothing else but rocks and potatoes. People here must work hard; they get nothing for free. But then again, maybe the environment has nothing to do with my personality. I have always been hard on myself."

Suchy also played three matches for the national junior soccer team. Even the famous Dukla Prague wanted him. But he chose to stick with hockey in the end. From 1963 he played for Dukla Jihlava, which at the time reigned supreme in Czech hockey and was referred to as the hockey university. During his 16 years in the league, he scored 162 goals in 562 matches to become the best scoring defenseman in the history of hockey competition. Seven times he won championship titles, and in 1969 and 1970 he won the Golden Stick Award as most valuable player.

Jan Suchy (number 17) was the Czech version of Bobby Orr or Doug Harvey.

He suited up for the Czech national squad in 160 matches and scored 44 goals. He took part in seven World Championships and the 1968 Olympics. In 1969 and 1971 he was named the best defenseman of the tournament. Many people were of the opinion that he should have received the award in 1970 as well. That year, Swedish player Lennart Svedberg got it, but after accepting the trophy, he skated over to Suchy and patted him on the back appreciatively. "I don't know if he understood what I was saying, but I wanted to let him know how much I respected him. Never in my life had I seen a better defenseman," stated Svedberg.

In 1971 Suchy was in a serious car accident during which two fellow passengers almost died. Tests revealed alcohol in the blood. He spent 18 months in detention and, after intervention by someone in authority, he was expelled from the national team for several years. When Czechoslovakia won the World Championship for the first time in 23 years in 1972, Suchy wasn't among the players on the team. "I even made the training camp. But as a man who got into trouble, I didn't deserve to play on the national team, according to some influential people of the time. They gave me money for the train and I went home just before the tournament. That's life. If I do something wrong, I have to be prepared to accept punishment. I served my time, but they didn't have to prevent me from playing in the World Championships."

He returned to the national team in 1974. Until the 1978–79 season, he worked in Jihlava, although he was still being lured by Sparta Prague and Brno. "My wife comes from Havlickuv Brod and didn't want to move. Besides, both of us had parents there and Jihlava was closer." The Boston Bruins of the NHL set their sights on him, and Suchy became the first European to be placed on the protected list. "I had offers from

Suchy, Jan
D, 5'8", 161 lbs, b: Havlickuv Brod, Czechoslovakia, 10/10/1944

Season	Club, League	Regular Season				
		GP	G	A	Pts	PIM
1963–65	Dukla Jihlava, Czechoslovakia	*	*	*	*	*
WEC–65	Czechoslovakia	6	1	1	2	2
1965–66	Dukla Jihlava, Czechoslovakia	*	*	*	*	*
WEC–66	Czechoslovakia	7	0	0	0	4
1966–67	Dukla Jihlava, Czechoslovakia	*	*	*	*	*
WEC–67	Czechoslovakia	7	1	2	3	4
1967–68	Dukla Jihlava, Czechoslovakia	*	*	*	*	*
OWG–68	Czechoslovakia	7	2	4	6	8
1968–69	Dukla Jihlava, Czechoslovakia	*	*	*	*	*
WEC–69	Czechoslovakia	8	5	4	9	12
1969–70	Dukla Jihlava, Czechoslovakia	*	*	*	*	*
WEC–70	Czechoslovakia	10	8	7	15	13
1970–71	Dukla Jihlava, Czechoslovakia	*	*	*	*	*
WEC–71	Czechoslovakia	10	2	3	5	2
1971–74	Dukla Jihlava, Czechoslovakia	*	*	*	*	*
WEC–74	Czechoslovakia	10	2	4	6	2
1974–79	Dukla Jihlava, Czechoslovakia	*	*	*	*	*
1979–81	Stadlau, Austria	*	*	*	*	*
1981–82	Kaufbeuren, FRG	*	*	*	*	*
1982–83	Landsberg, FRG	*	*	*	*	*
1983–84	Modling, Austria	*	*	*	*	*
	Czechoslovakia Totals	562	162	*	*	*
	OWG/WEC Totals	65	21	25	46	47

Named Best Defenseman at WEC (1969, 1971)
Czechoslovakia Champion (1967, 1968, 1969, 1970, 1971, 1972, 1974)

other teams, including some in Sweden. They wanted Jiri Holik and me. However, the Czech government of the time wasn't in favor of people going abroad. I would have had to go into exile and I don't think I would have been able to do that."

At 35, he was allowed to go abroad. He played for the Austrian club WAT Stadlau and for ESV Kaufbeuren in Germany. He spent the 1983–84 season in Modling, Austria. Later he played in a regional competition in Trest. He finally gave up hockey in his native Havlickuv Brod. "I had enough strength for this competition. But whenever we advanced higher, I just wasn't up to it. Sometimes they shouted at me, telling me to stop. Originally I planned that I would play until 50, but I quit at 45."

Jiri Holik

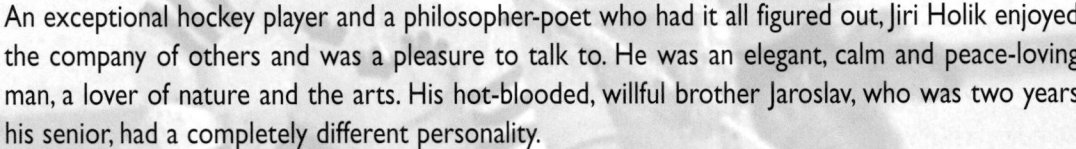

Jiri Holik was such a reliable left winger that no one could imagine Team Czechoslovakia without him.

An exceptional hockey player and a philosopher-poet who had it all figured out, Jiri Holik enjoyed the company of others and was a pleasure to talk to. He was an elegant, calm and peace-loving man, a lover of nature and the arts. His hot-blooded, willful brother Jaroslav, who was two years his senior, had a completely different personality.

As a person, Holik had all the bases covered, and as an excellent skater, he had the entire rink covered. He was such a reliable left winger that for 14 years no one could imagine the Czechoslovakian national team without him. Yet, surprisingly, he never won the Golden Stick Award as the best player in his country. Twice he came in second and once he was third.

For a long time he held a record on the national team for the greatest number of starts—at 319. Only in the 1980s did German defenseman Udo Kiessling make a point of exceeding his total by one match. Holik was once again bumped into second place. "I don't desire any records. They only stemmed out of the fact that I had been with hockey for so long. I don't even know if that was good," was his response.

Born in Havlickuv Brod on July 9, 1944, Holik played hockey on a frozen pond from the age of four. The Holiks didn't have a television set or a car. To go to Prague, some 60 miles away, was almost like traveling abroad. The first star to come out of this town—which had only natural ice and therefore only outdoor hockey—and make it in the big leagues was a player by the name of Vaclav Chytracek. Suddenly the Holik boys had before their very eyes a player who made it to Czechoslovakia's B team. "We were growing up in a somewhat closed environment and suddenly a terrific hockey player appeared. He had excellent skating skills and technique. For us, Chytracek was a tremendous role model."

It wasn't very long before his fans, the Holiks, surpassed Chytracek. In nearby Jihlava, local boys who played on the pond were growing up to be world-class hockey players. At first, Jiri Holik thought he would go to Sparta. "But my brother took ill. He had an inflammation of the bone marrow. Then he broke his leg in the same spot and it looked as if he might give up hockey. Father said I had to go help Jihlava. I obeyed and was lucky. At 19, I was already playing for the national team."

With the Dukla Jihlava club he spent 15 seasons, and seven times he won the national title. Over this same period, he participated in 12 World Championships, in three of which he won the gold—in 1972, 1976 and 1977. Four times he took part in the Winter Olympics and he also played in the 1976 Canada Cup.

In the 1974 World Championship, he captained the national team. But he didn't stay very long in that role. "The constant meets were getting to me. I was married with children. During nice weather, I had to struggle somewhere near the ice. In April we finished, but come May, there was the practice camp. The federation president at the time, Zdenek Andrst, would say, 'Guys, finish playing and then you will go on that well-deserved vacation.' When I got my invitation, I replied that I was enjoying my well-deserved vacation. I quit as captain, but at the time I wasn't a leader type anyway."

He could have left Jihlava several times for bigger and better things—he and Jan Suchy once got an offer from Detroit. "At that time I thought communism would never come to an end. I didn't have the courage to emigrate like Vaclav Nedomansky, who did so at 30. It took a certain personality." After winning the World Championship title in 1972, Holik and his brother wanted to go to a different club. But because they were playing for a military team, again they weren't allowed to change jerseys.

After they won the championship, a photo of him and his brother in an embrace made it around the world. It was a very rare picture, for the two were like fire and water. It might well have been the first time in their lives that they hugged like that. "We fought when we were little. Jaroslav was older and didn't want to take me into his gang. Even later, when we shared a bedroom, we didn't talk to one another much. We may not even have said 'Good night.' Outside hockey, we didn't do much together. He had his friends, I had mine. Maybe this was good, because we played together ever since we were small and lived next to one another for 40 years."

In 1978 he left for Rosenheim, Germany. After two seasons, he spent a year in Stadlau, Austria, and in the 1984–85 season he was a player-coach for EV Vienna. Then he disappeared from professional hockey for a while. Later he managed the Dukla Jihlava team and also returned to Havlickuv Brod for a while. In the 1999–2000 season, he coached the Weiden club in Germany.

Jiri Holik (left) could have left Dukla Jihlava for better clubs a number of times, but because he was playing for a military team, he wasn't allowed to change jerseys.

Holik, Jiri
LW, 5′10″, 183 lbs, b: Havlickov Brod, Czechoslovakia, 7/9/1944

Season	Club, League	Regular Season				
		GP	G	A	Pts	PIM
1963–64	Dukla Jihlava, Czechoslovakia	*	*	*	*	*
OWG–64	Czechoslovakia	7	3	3	6	0
1964–65	Dukla Jihlava, Czechoslovakia	*	*	*	*	*
WEC–65	Czechoslovakia	7	1	1	2	4
1965–66	Dukla Jihlava, Czechoslovakia	*	*	*	*	*
WEC–66	Czechoslovakia	7	4	1	5	2
1966–67	Dukla Jihlava, Czechoslovakia	*	*	*	*	*
WEC–67	Czechoslovakia	7	2	2	4	4
1967–68	Dukla Jihlava, Czechoslovakia	*	*	*	*	*
OWG–68	Czechoslovakia	7	1	1	2	4
1968–69	Dukla Jihlava, Czechoslovakia	*	*	*	*	*
WEC–69	Czechoslovakia	9	4	4	8	4
1969–70	Dukla Jihlava, Czechoslovakia	*	*	*	*	*
WEC–70	Czechoslovakia	9	4	3	7	4
1970–71	Dukla Jihlava, Czechoslovakia	*	*	*	*	*
WEC–71	Czechoslovakia	10	3	5	8	4
1971–72	Dukla Jihlava, Czechoslovakia	*	*	*	*	*
OWG–72	Czechoslovakia	6	1	4	5	2
WEC–72	Czechoslovakia	10	8	1	9	26
1972–73	Dukla Jihlava, Czechoslovakia	*	*	*	*	*
WEC–73	Czechoslovakia	10	5	10	15	23
1973–74	Dukla Jihlava, Czechoslovakia	*	*	*	*	*
WEC–74	Czechoslovakia	10	5	5	10	6
1974–75	Dukla Jihlava, Czechoslovakia	*	*	*	*	*
WEC–75	Czechoslovakia	10	4	2	6	6
1975–76	Dukla Jihlava, Czechoslovakia	*	*	*	*	*
OWG–76	Czechoslovakia	5	3	2	5	4
WEC–76	Czechoslovakia	10	7	5	12	2
CCup–76	Czechoslovakia	7	0	3	3	0
1976–77	Dukla Jihlava, Czechoslovakia	*	*	*	*	*
WEC–77	Czechoslovakia	10	4	3	7	2
1977–78	Dukla Jihlava, Czechoslovakia	*	*	*	*	*
1978–80	Rosenheim, FRG	*	*	*	*	*
1980–81	Stadlau, Austria	*	*	*	*	*
1984–85	EV Vien, Austria	*	*	*	*	*
	Czechoslovakia Totals	553	283	*	*	*
	OWG/WEC/CCup Totals	141	59	55	114	97

Won WEC (1972, 1976, 1977)
Czechoslovakia Champion (1967, 1968, 1969, 1970, 1971, 1972, 1974)

In 1991 he ran for president of the Czech Ice Hockey Federation. "Today, I am grateful for not being elected. Such a post takes much time and is good for doing oneself in. I have no ambition of running Czech hockey; the post wouldn't sit well with me. I wanted to be with my family, and I got a bit lazy. I like my comfort, I like to sit at home on the terrace and look at the forest, go for walks. I wouldn't want nerve-racking and stressful work."

Ken Hodge

In the 1968–69 season, Ken Hodge (center) scored 45 times, but the more he scored, the more Boston fans booed him.

Ken Hodge began his career in the Chicago Black Hawks system, playing junior with St. Catharines, Chicago's junior team in Ontario, before moving up to the NHL at the end of the 1964–65 season for one game. Because most of the team was small and Hodge was 6´2″ and 210 pounds, he was expected to be the team's policeman for the next two years. "It was my job and I did it, but it cost me offensively," he said. "I wound up in my fair share of fights. But it's not really my nature. I don't like playing the bully, and it hindered my development as a player. I didn't take a regular shift, and when I was on the ice, I had other responsibilities."

His most glaring weakness at this time was his skating, but he worked tirelessly on it over the summer months to improve. However, during the summer of 1967, Hodge was involved in one of the most lopsided trades of all time. Chicago sent him, Phil Esposito and Fred Stanfield to Boston for Gilles Marotte, Pit Martin and Jack Norris, virtually assuring Boston of two Stanley Cup wins in the coming years. Ironically, Hodge had been in the Boston system when he played for a Lakeshore team in Toronto as a 15-year-old, but Chicago beat the Bruins to the punch when they signed him to the standard C-Form on his 16th birthday.

Over time, Hodge came to play on the Bruins' number one line with Esposito and Wayne Cashman and his confidence exploded. He started to use his strength to hold onto the puck and create scoring chances instead of fighting, and he became one of the best scorers in the league because of his excellent shot. In 1968–69, he scored 45 times, one of the best seasons in league history. But his productivity had a curious effect on the Boston fans. The more he scored, the more they booed him.

"Sometimes, I feel like telling them all to go to hell," he admitted. "But I figure the boos come from people who just don't understand...."

Hodge, Ken
RW, 6´2″, 210 lbs, b: Birmingham, England, 6/25/1944

Season	Club, League	Regular Season					Playoffs				
		GP	G	A	Pts	PIM	GP	G	A	Pts	PIM
1964–65	Chicago Black Hawks, NHL	1	0	0	0	2					
	Buffalo Bisons, AHL	2	0	2	2	0	4	0	0	0	4
1965–66	Chicago Black Hawks, NHL	63	6	17	23	47	5	0	0	0	8
1966–67	Chicago Black Hawks, NHL	69	10	25	35	59	6	0	0	0	4
1967–68	Boston Bruins, NHL	74	25	31	56	31	4	3	0	3	2
1968–69	Boston Bruins, NHL	75	45	45	90	75	10	5	7	12	4
1969–70	Boston Bruins, NHL	72	25	29	54	87	14	3	10	13	7
1970–71	Boston Bruins, NHL	78	43	62	105	113	7	2	5	7	6
1971–72	Boston Bruins, NHL	60	16	40	56	81	15	9	8	17	62
1972–73	Boston Bruins, NHL	73	37	44	81	58	5	1	0	1	7
1973–74	Boston Bruins, NHL	76	50	55	105	43	16	6	10	16	16
1974–75	Boston Bruins, NHL	72	23	43	66	90	3	1	1	2	0
1975–76	Boston Bruins, NHL	72	25	36	61	42	12	4	6	10	4
1976–77	New York Rangers, NHL	78	21	41	62	43					
1977–78	New York Rangers, NHL	18	2	4	6	8					
	New Haven Nighthawks, AHL	52	17	29	46	13	15	3	4	7	20
1979–80	Binghamton Dusters, AHL	37	10	20	30	24					
	NHL Totals	881	328	472	800	779	97	34	47	81	120

NHL First All-Star Team (1971, 1974)
Won Stanley Cup (1970, 1972)

I gather that the people feel I'm not aggressive enough. But I don't think you have to run around crashing into people to qualify as a hockey player."

One disgusted fan even hung a number 8 sweater in effigy from the Garden's rafters, but Hodge came to deal with the local criticism as part of playing the game. He simply wasn't as physical in the corners as John McKenzie was, and his penalty totals were never a part of the Big Bad Bruins reputation.

Hodge helped the team win the Stanley Cup in 1970 and 1972 and he was with the team for nine seasons. His scoring began in earnest when coach Harry Sinden stepped down after the 1970 Cup win and Tom Johnson took over, giving Hodge more power-play and ice time. "It's no secret that I didn't get along too well with coach Sinden," he confessed. "We didn't see eye to eye on a lot of things. Tom Johnson is quite a guy. I'd do anything for him."

Hodge also changed sticks for the first time in his pro career. Previously, he used one of the

Ken Hodge (right) used one of the biggest hooks in the NHL, but in the fall of 1970 he switched to an almost straight blade when the league started regulating the size of curves.

biggest hooks in the league, but in the fall of 1970 he switched to an almost straight blade at a time the league was regulating the size of curves. This, he felt, gave him another shot in his arsenal— the backhand. "I think it's only a matter of time before the straight stick will be the only kind we're allowed to use," he said, explaining his decision to change.

Hodge twice scored 100 points in a season, and in 1973–74 he scored 50 goals for the first and only time in his career. But in the summer of 1976 he was traded in a rather acrimonious manner. After being sent to the Rangers, Hodge was verbally attacked by current Boston coach Don Cherry, who was instrumental in getting rid of him. "The biggest problem with Ken Hodge is that he's a country clubber. He doesn't want to pay the price. He simply isn't a team player. If we won and he felt he hadn't played enough, he'd skate directly to the dressing room. He's the type of guy who would be happy if he scored three goals and we lost 4–3." Hodge retired after the 1977–78 season, although he played a few games with Binghamton of the AHL two years later. Despite playing in three All-Star games, which were his proudest accomplishments other than the Stanley Cup wins, he never won an individual trophy in the NHL.

Rogie Vachon

Goaltender Rogie Vachon attained much success during his 16-year NHL tenure. Known for an aggressive style and a quick glove hand, Vachon recorded 51 shutouts and was one of just a handful of NHL goalies to record more than 350 regular-season victories. His most original contribution as a pro was playing a disciplined stand-up style of goal despite his small body. Vachon's technique influenced many young goalies who lacked size and previously felt that reflexes and acrobatics were the only tools at their disposal.

A native of Palmarolle, Quebec, less than an hour north of the mining center of Rouyn-Noranda, Vachon grew up on the family's dairy farm. He learned to play hockey locally, then ventured south to Montreal to play for the Notre Dame de Grace Junior B club in 1963–64. His main ambition at this time was to tend goal for the Junior A Canadiens. It was with the Houston Apollos of the CHL in 1965–66 that he received his first break as a pro when he was given the opportunity to play 34 matches after starter Gerry Desjardins hurt his knee.

Vachon joined the Montreal Canadiens in 1966–67 to back up Gump Worsley and ended up playing the majority of their playoff games when they reached the Stanley Cup finals. The fact that Vachon's formative years as an amateur were spent at the Junior B level wasn't lost on Toronto coach Punch Imlach, who belittled the Habs' backstopper at the outset of the series. "We're not going to lose to a Junior B goalie," he boasted. Sure enough, Toronto won the Cup, but the diminutive Vachon earned a permanent place in the big league with his excellent play.

In 1967–68, Vachon excelled in 39 regular-season contests and shared the Vezina Trophy with teammate Gump Worsley. Their goals-against mark of 2.26 was the league's best since 1958–59. His play contributed significantly to Montreal's consecutive Stanley Cup championships in 1968 and 1969. After Worsley's fear of flying led him to move out of Montreal, Vachon inherited the starting job in the Montreal net. He played well in 1969–70 but was blamed by many when the defending champions failed to make the playoffs. The next year his play was inconsistent and he was eventually relegated to the bench while rookie Ken Dryden led the Habs to the Stanley Cup.

In 1971–72, Vachon requested a trade after he allowed four goals in his only period of action. He was given a new lease on life when the Los Angeles Kings acquired his services in November 1971. He went on to enjoy some of his finest seasons and helped the Kings become a competitive hockey club. He recorded 32 of his 51 career shutouts in Los Angeles and was a two-time selection to the NHL Second All-Star Team. Vachon became the most popular figure in franchise history and was selected the team's most valuable player four times in five years between 1973 and 1977.

The steady Gary Edwards served as Vachon's backup during these years and gave the Kings one of the rosiest goaltending pictures in the NHL. In 1974–75, the Kings set a franchise record with 105 points and a fourth-place finish in the NHL's overall standings. That season, Vachon's 1.41 goals-against mark in the first 17 games represented the best start in the league since Jacques Plante's fine beginning in 1957–58. Unfortunately, the team was eliminated in the first round by a Toronto team that underachieved in the regular season. The Kings never did excel in the post-season despite

Rogie Vachon's most original contribution as a pro was a disciplined, stand-up style of goaltending despite his small size.

Vachon, Rogie
G, 5'7", 170 lbs, b: Palmarolle, Que., 9/8/1945

Season	Club, League	Regular Season				Playoffs			
		GP	Mins	GA	Avg	GP	Mins	GA	Avg
1965–66	Quebec Aces, AHL	10	601	30	3.00				
1966–67	Houston Apollos, CHL	34	2020	99	2.91				
	Montreal Canadiens, NHL	19	1137	47	2.48	9	555	22	2.38
1967–68	Montreal Canadiens, NHL	39	2227	92	2.48	2	113	4	2.12
1968–69	Montreal Canadiens, NHL	36	2051	98	2.87	8	507	12	1.42
1969–70	Montreal Canadiens, NHL	64	3697	162	2.63				
1970–71	Montreal Canadiens, NHL	47	2676	118	2.65				
1971–72	Montreal Canadiens, NHL	1	20	4	12.00				
	Los Angeles Kings, NHL	28	1586	107	4.05				
1972–73	Los Angeles Kings, NHL	53	3120	148	2.85				
1973–74	Los Angeles Kings, NHL	65	3751	175	2.80	4	240	7	1.75
1974–75	Los Angeles Kings, NHL	54	3239	121	2.24	3	199	7	2.11
1975–76	Los Angeles Kings, NHL	51	3060	160	3.14	7	438	17	2.33
CCup–76	Canada	7	432	10	1.39				
1976–77	Los Angeles Kings, NHL	68	4059	184	2.72	9	520	36	4.15
1977–78	Los Angeles Kings, NHL	70	4107	196	2.86	2	120	11	5.50
1978–79	Detroit Red Wings, NHL	50	2908	189	3.90				
1979–80	Detroit Red Wings, NHL	59	3474	209	3.61				
1980–81	Boston Bruins, NHL	53	3021	168	3.34	3	164	16	5.85
1981–82	Boston Bruins, NHL	38	2165	132	3.66	1	20	1	3.00
	NHL Totals	795	46298	2310	2.99	48	2876	133	2.77
	CCup Totals	7	432	10	1.39				

NHL Second All-Star Team (1975, 1977)
Won Vezina Trophy (1968)
Won Stanley Cup (1968, 1969, 1971)
Won CCup (1976)

Vachon's brilliance between the pipes. Following that glorious regular season, Bobby Clarke edged out Vachon in the voting for the Hart Trophy.

What Vachon attained anonymously on the West Coast was a chance to forge his own identity on the ice and thrive in an environment that was very different from hockey-crazy Montreal. As hockey historian Doug Hunter wrote, "His physical and emotional character was tailor-made for a warm California reception."

Vachon's finest hour came as Team Canada's goalie in the inaugural Canada Cup tournament in 1976. Since Ken Dryden and Bernie Parent were unavailable, Vachon, Gerry Cheevers and Glenn Resch were invited to compete for the job. Vachon emerged with the hot hand and played every one of his team's games. His spectacular play helped Canada to the championship and resulted in his selection as the team's most valuable player. Many observers felt he deserved the tournament MVP award, but that honor went to sentimental choice Bobby Orr. Vachon was open about his disappointment: "I have to be honest. I thought I deserved the big award. Everyone said I would get it and I was disappointed when I did not."

Rogie Vachon (left) recorded 32 of his 51 career shutouts in Los Angeles and was a two-time selection to the NHL Second All-Star Team.

Vachon went on to close out his career with two seasons each in Detroit and Boston. The experience with the Red Wings was difficult. Lured by a lucrative five-year contract, Vachon startled the hockey world by leaving Los Angeles and signing with the Red Wings as a free agent. In the ensuing tangle, an arbitrator ordered the Wings to send Dale McCourt to the Kings as a form of compensation. The young forward refused to comply and instead obtained a restraining order to ensure he didn't have to move. The Detroit fans soured on McCourt and were displeased with Vachon's sub-par performance in goal. The Wings ended up placing Vachon on waivers, attracting the attention of the Boston Bruins. Rogie played better in Beantown, but his skills had deteriorated to the point that Vachon felt he was no longer able to contribute sufficiently.

He retired following the 1981–82 season with a career goals-against mark of 2.99. Vachon returned to Los Angeles in 1983–84, where he went on to serve as coach, general manager and chief hockey operating officer. The Kings honored their popular puck stopper by retiring his number in January 1985. He retired as general manager in 1991 but returned to the Kings a short time later as assistant to the club president.

Bobby Orr

Truly special athletes, the ones that fathers talk about to their sons and daughters, change the game they play. Arguments emerged late in the 20th century about who most deserved to be called the greatest hockey player of all time. Perhaps it was the retirement of Wayne Gretzky in 1999, surely a contender as hockey player of the century, or perhaps it was a desire to sum up 100 years of a sport that had come into its own and grown exponentially around the world that led to these discussions.

A HISTORY OF WORLD HOCKEY

In whichever country the debate raged, one name had to be placed at or near the top precisely because he fundamentally changed the sport he dominated. Bobby Orr was a defenseman who could score like a superstar forward, pass like a playmaking center and defend with the savvy of a defensive specialist. He had different gears of skating speed, a sense of balance and grace that allowed him to move from fast to slow to fastest, dashing between gaps when they opened or delaying with a few deft moves until they did. Only injuries could stop Orr, which they did, in the form of two bad knees, after less than a decade at the top level of the game. What he accomplished in those years, aided by imagining what he could have done without all the injuries, given his awe-inspiring gift, turned Orr into a hockey legend and earned him steady support as the greatest player of all time.

Bobby Orr (right) was a defenseman who could score like a superstar forward, pass like a playmaking center and defend with the savvy of a stay-at-home blueliner.

Hockey fans in Parry Sound, Ontario, in the late 1950s saw a lot of this hockey genius in its infancy. Doug Orr, Bobby's dad, had been a speedy player and gifted scorer in his own right. He wanted his son, still small for his age but also enormously talented, to play forward in order to take advantage of his speed and puckhandling abilities. Bucko McDonald, a former NHLer who played defense in the 1930s and 1940s and coached Bobby when the youngster was 11 and 12, believed his charge had all the makings of an outstanding defenseman. He taught Bobby the ins and outs of the position and encouraged him to use his offensive skills as well. "It wasn't hard," McDonald later said of teaching Orr, "because even at that age, you could see Bobby was special."

Professional teams agreed. The Boston Bruins went to unusual lengths to land the small prospect. When Orr was 14, Boston made arrangements for him to play with the Oshawa Generals in the metro Junior A league. He continued to live at home and commute to each game. Though he didn't attend a single practice with the team, Orr was selected to the league's Second All-Star Team. All the speedy youngster required was size to make him a bona fide star. He was 5′6″ and 135 pounds at 14. The next year, when he moved to an Oshawa high school and played in the Ontario junior league, he was 5′9″ and 25 pounds heavier. By the time his junior career was over—when he was all of 17 and a man playing with boys—he was a sturdy 6′ and almost 200 pounds. The phenomenon Boston fans had been reading about since he was a freckle-faced kid with a brushcut was ready to enter the professional game.

In his first National Hockey League game, against the Detroit Red Wings and Gordie Howe, 18-year-old Orr impressed the home crowd and the many reporters with his defensive abilities. He blocked shots, made checks and moved opposing players away from the net. He also recorded his first point—an assist. "He'll do, for sure," Howe said after the game. "The kid's all right. He anticipates well, he makes good passes, and I guess he does just about what you'd expect of a good defenseman."

Orr was better than good in his first season. He won the Calder Trophy as the best rookie and also made the NHL's Second All-Star Team. He was second in the league in scoring by defensemen and was a plus-30. Not only did he score and pass, he fought when needed, defeating his

Bobby Orr (front).

opponent more often than not, and could play a physical game. But some observers felt he was too daring, that he left himself open to hits with his all-out rushes and that his body had yet to develop to sustain him over the regular-season grind. Orr did suffer an injury in his rookie season, hurting his left knee on a daring rush. It was the beginning of a long battle with his knees that eventually ended his career.

Orr won his first Stanley Cup in 1970 and it was with a flourish only he could manage. His Bruins, a team that hadn't won the Cup in 29 years, were attempting to sweep the St. Louis Blues in the finals. Game four went into overtime. Derek Sanderson, Orr's flamboyant teammate, recalled the events that led to one of the most famous pictures in the sport's history.

"Did you see the way he gambled to start that play?" Sanderson asked reporters after the game. "No other defenseman would have risked so much in an overtime game. But for Orr, with his natural talent and great anticipation, it was no gamble. Their man played it right, tried to dump the puck past Orr for a breakaway. Orr trapped the puck, fed it to me, I moved around the backboards until he floated into position and then fed it to him.

"I knew it was over when the puck left his stick. You can't stop a laser beam."

Orr had taken Sanderson's pass from the corner and flashed in front of the net to bury it behind Blues goalie Glenn Hall. As Orr streaked past the net, he was upended by defenseman Noel Picard. Orr jumped, or flew, as he saw the puck beat Hall and the arena erupted. The resulting picture, with Orr's arms raised and his body floating three feet above the ice, was in newspapers and magazines around the world. Orr was awarded the Conn Smythe Trophy as the playoffs' most valuable player, an award he would win when Boston again won the title in 1972, again with the Cup-winning goal coming off Orr's stick.

Orr revolutionized the sport with his scoring ability and playmaking from the blue line. Other defenders, beginning as early as Lester Patrick in the nascent days of the game, had been offensive threats, but Orr dominated. He won two scoring titles, the only defender to accomplish that feat, and had career season highs of 46 goals and 102 assists. More than just statistics, Orr had the ability to control the game, to take over. He had the speed to float away from defenders and also to recover should he lose possession or get caught on a rush. Often, odd-man rushes in the other team's favor were reversed by his effortless strides. Some argued that he wasn't defensively sound, but hockey people rejected these claims. "A few people knocked Orr and Gretzky and Guy Lafleur as being ineffective defensively, which made me just shake my head," legendary coach Scotty Bowman said.

Orr, Bobby
D, 6´, 197 lbs, b: Parry Sound, Ont., 3/20/1948

Season	Club, League	Regular Season					Playoffs				
		GP	G	A	Pts	PIM	GP	G	A	Pts	PIM
1966–67	Boston Bruins, NHL	61	13	28	41	102					
1967–68	Boston Bruins, NHL	46	11	20	31	63	4	0	2	2	2
1968–69	Boston Bruins, NHL	67	21	43	64	133	10	1	7	8	10
1969–70	Boston Bruins, NHL	76	33	87	120	125	14	9	11	20	14
1970–71	Boston Bruins, NHL	78	37	102	139	91	7	5	7	12	25
1971–72	Boston Bruins, NHL	76	37	80	117	106	15	5	19	24	19
1972–73	Boston Bruins, NHL	63	29	72	101	99	5	1	1	2	7
1973–74	Boston Bruins, NHL	74	32	90	122	82	16	4	14	18	28
1974–75	Boston Bruins, NHL	80	46	89	135	101	3	1	5	6	2
1975–76	Boston Bruins, NHL	10	5	13	18	22					
CCup–76	Canada	7	2	7	9	8					
1976–77	Chicago Black Hawks, NHL	20	4	19	23	25					
1978–79	Chicago Black Hawks, NHL	6	2	2	4	4					
	NHL Totals	657	270	645	915	953	74	26	66	92	107
	CCup Totals	7	2	7	9	8					

NHL First All-Star Team (1968, 1969, 1970, 1971, 1972, 1973, 1974, 1975)
NHL Second All-Star Team (1967)
Won Hart Trophy (1970, 1971, 1972)
Won James Norris Trophy (1968, 1969, 1970, 1971, 1972, 1973, 1974, 1975)
Won Conn Smythe Trophy (1970, 1972)
Won Art Ross Trophy (1970, 1975)
Won Calder Trophy (1967)
Won Lester Patrick Trophy (1979)
Won Lester B. Pearson Award (1975)
NHL Plus-Minus Leader (1969, 1970, 1971, 1972, 1974, 1975)
Named CCup MVP (1976)
Won Stanley Cup (1970, 1972)
Won CCup (1976)

"When my teams played against Orr and Gretzky—and Lafleur was on my side—much of the time they were on the ice, they had the puck. It's difficult for the opposition to score in that situation and that seems like rather good defense to me.

"And if they didn't have the puck," he added, "they were the best at stripping it from the opposition."

For eight consecutive seasons, Orr won the Norris Trophy as the best defenseman and three times he was the league's most valuable player to collect the Hart Trophy. Orr's plus-minus rating when he was at his best was untouchable at plus-124 in 1970–71, when he scored 139 points.

At the beginning of the 1971–72 season, Orr signed a contract that guaranteed him $200,000 per season over five years. It was the first $1-million deal in hockey and Orr's agent, Alan Eagleson, predicted at the time that Orr would someday own part of the team if he continued to star for Boston. As it turned out, when it came time to negotiate a new contract prior to the 1976–77 season, the Bruins did offer Orr a piece of the ownership, but the star player said his agent never informed him of the proposed deal. Orr, who had struggled with his left knee and played only 10 games in 1975–76, felt as though Boston no longer wanted him and signed instead with the Chicago Black Hawks. Once considered the savior and then the hero of the rejuvenated Bruins, Orr left the team that had been a part of his career since he was a teen in Parry Sound.

What Bobby Orr (left) accomplished, aided by imagining what he could have done without injuries, given his awe-inspiring talent, turned him into a legend.

Orr took advantage of a chance to play in a major international competition—the 1976 Canada Cup—when Chicago management gave him permission to play. Having missed all of the Summit Series, the Canada Cup proved to be Orr's only major appearance in a competition against the best the world had to offer. He was outstanding in the Canadian team's run to the championship. He was co-leader of the team in scoring, finishing the seven games tied with another great defender, the New York Islanders' Denis Potvin, with nine points. Orr was selected to the tournament All-Star team and capped the experience with the most valuable player award.

Orr's performance at the Canada Cup had the Chicago faithful energized for his first appearance in colors other than Bruins black and gold. But Orr's left knee would once again impede his career. He played 20 games of his first season in Chicago weakened by his sixth operation on the knee in April 1976. He spent the entire 1977–78 season recuperating, trying to revive his battered knee, which doctors described as nothing but bone rubbing bone after so many operations and injuries.

He made a valiant attempt to return, playing six games at the start of the 1978–79 season. Though Orr didn't feel incredible amounts of pain, he was limited in his movements and unable to practise much with the team. In one game against the Detroit Red Wings, he was on the ice for four Detroit goals and described his play as "terrible." At the age of 30, he decided he was only

A HISTORY OF WORLD HOCKEY

hindering his Chicago squad. Howard Cosell, the legendary sportscaster, announced in October 1978 that Orr had retired, though it later turned out he had mistaken Orr for Bobby Hull, who was also contemplating leaving the game. A few days later, Orr called Cosell and told him he was indeed retiring and asked him to attend the press conference. Cosell refused, jokingly saying that he didn't "cover old news."

On November 8, 1978, Orr made it official. "I will not make another comeback attempt," he said. "I'm happy I attempted this one, but the leg just can't handle playing. I know now…I am no longer able to play." He summed up his career by saying he had been "rewarded unbelievably for what I consider having fun."

Fans of hockey all over the world were moved by his inability to continue. "It is with sadness that we receive Bobby's retirement," NHL president John Ziegler said. "Bobby's skill, competitiveness and determination are already legendary. The discipline and dedication that it took for Bobby to come back and play this year are probably unequaled in professional sport."

Because of his continuing problems, Orr had never collected a paycheck from the Black Hawks. He said he was paid to play hockey, and after his retirement he accepted a reduced salary to become an assistant coach, a position he had filled while sitting out the year before.

Orr was inducted into the Hockey Hall of Fame in 1979. He worked frequently with charities in the coming years and maintained close links with the game. He later became an agent, helping young players benefit by sharing his difficult early experiences through the business side of the sport.

1972

The '72 Summit Series

Of all the great competitions in the later part of the 20th century, the 1972 Summit Series between Canada and the USSR stands in a class by itself. Indeed, it marked the beginning of a new era in hockey. Tournaments had previously been clearly divided into professional and amateur. After September 1972, that line started to fade and by the 1990s it had disappeared altogether.

The Summit Series was unique for other reasons as well. For one thing, even by current standards, it was hockey of the highest caliber. Each of the eight games drew approximately 100 million viewers in the USSR, some 25 million more in Canada and the United States and a few million more in Europe. And the outcome was still in the balance until 34 seconds before the siren signaled the end of the eighth and last game.

September of 1972 marked the beginning of a new era in hockey.

By the early 1970s, the Soviets had come to dominate international competition and had won World and European Championships and Olympic tournaments year in and year out for a decade. The Canadians had ruled the World Championships from 1920 until their 19th win in Switzerland in 1961 but now had to settle for bronze—at best. Then, when the International Ice Hockey Federation vetoed Canada's use of professional and ex-professional players in a World Championship series that had been scheduled for Canada for 1970, the game's founders boycotted the annual tournament from that year until 1977. Meanwhile, the Canadian pros wanted a showdown with the best from the USSR, who in February of 1972 won the gold medals at the Winter Olympics in Sapporo for their third consecutive Olympic title as well as gold in nine previous World Championships.

In Canada, forming a select team of professionals was a novelty and generated heated disputes over who should be invited to play. The Soviets had agreed that only professionals from the NHL were to make up Team Canada. However, the whole country—including Canadian Prime Minister Pierre Trudeau—demanded that Bobby Hull be included even though he had recently signed with the newly formed World Hockey Association. In the end, Hull and three other players who had switched to the WHA (goalie Gerry Cheevers, defenseman J.C. Tremblay and center Derek Sanderson) were scratched from the list. But it was August 13—almost a month and a half later than the USSR national team—before the NHL players gathered in Toronto to begin training.

Soon after that, scouts appeared in both Toronto and Moscow to observe and make progress reports (John McLellan and Bob Davidson from the Toronto Maple Leafs went to Moscow while Arkady Chernyshev and Boris Kulagin came to Canada). The Canadian scouts filed a scathing report; the passing, the shooting, the style of attack and young goalie Vladislav Tretiak's performance were all heavily criticized. After feedback like that, Canadian fans expected their idols to win all eight games. But the hasty underestimation of the Soviets' skills was deadly for the Canadian players.

Team USSR.

Meanwhile, back at the Soviet training camp in Moscow, the lineup was pretty much finalized. The only surprise was that it didn't include Anatoli Firsov, one of the finest forwards in the USSR in the early days of the national squad. The reason still isn't clear. According to some, Firsov refused to play as a token of protest because Anatoli Tarasov wasn't among the team's coaches. According to others, the famous forward was scratched for "subversive activity" against coaches Vsevolod Bobrov and Boris Kulagin.

In North America, Harry Sinden and John Ferguson got all the players they wanted except Bobby Orr, who was in camp but injured and not expected to play, and the four who had gone to the WHA. However, of the 20 forwards selected, only Jean Ratelle, Vic Hadfield and Rod Gilbert from the New York Rangers formed a ready-made forward line, albeit one of the best in the NHL at the time. In mid-August, any other combinations were still in the planning stage, paper tigers, so to speak.

By 7 p.m. on September 2, the Montreal Forum was packed to the rafters. Prime Minister Trudeau was in attendance to drop the puck to open the series—and to see his team win—and it certainly got off to a rip-roaring start. Just 30 seconds after the official face-off, Phil Esposito picked up a rebound and opened the scoring to an unbelievable roar of support from the stands. Six minutes later, Bobby Clarke won the face-off and flicked the puck over to Paul Henderson, who fired such a blistering shot Tretiak didn't have time to react. The score was 2–0 Canada.

The USSR squad appeared nervous at the beginning of the game, but they soon realized they had nothing to lose and settled into their own high-speed, technical style. In the 12th minute, on the receiving end of a pass from Vladimir Shadrin, Alexander Yakushev found himself in a good position for a shot. Canadian goaltender Ken Dryden was expecting it, but Yakushev suddenly flipped the puck to Yevgeny Zimin, who was open at the far goal post, and he slapped the puck into the net before Dryden could move over.

In the 18th minute, Alexander Ragulin was sent to the penalty box. The Canadian forwards took up positions in front of Tretiak's net and their defensemen lobbed the puck back and forth across the rink at the blue line. Boris Mikhailov intercepted it and broke away with Vladimir Petrov. Dryden managed to deflect Mikhailov's shot, but Petrov picked up the rebound and finished off the attack to tie the score at 2–2.

By the start of the second period, there wasn't much talk of the Canadians having the edge.

Frank Mahovlich and Rod Gilbert had scoring chances, but Tretiak fought them off comfortably. Less than three minutes into the period, Valeri Kharlamov scooped a pass from Alexander Maltsev and swept past Gilbert, faked his way past the sluggish Don Awrey and fired at the net. Dryden wasn't prepared and the puck slipped between his skates. Less than eight minutes later, the red lamp lit up again with another goal by Kharlamov on another assist from Maltsev. Now the Russians were leading 4–2.

In the third period, the Canadians found themselves with nothing to lose but out of steam as well, with the exception of a line that had formed around Bobby Clarke in the training camp. Ron Ellis and Paul Henderson helped Clarke reduce the gap to 4–3. Then Mikhailov, Zimin and Yakushev all scored in the last seven minutes and dealt the Canadians a devastating 7–3 loss.

The game in Montreal began at 4 in the morning Moscow time. No live transmission to the USSR had been organized, but a videotape was to be shown at prime time on September 3. The entire leadership of the country—including General Secretary of the Communist Party Leonid Brezhnev—was among those rooting for the USSR, and the media had strict instructions not to announce the score until the end of the video. Zealous fans deluged editorial offices and TV stations with calls early that morning, however, while others tuned in to the Voice of America, and celebrations started at noon, hours before the scheduled telecast. Still, the overwhelming majority of Soviet fans experienced the euphoria of the victory in Montreal late the next day, when Canada was already in mourning and the stars and coaches of Team Canada were still wondering what had gone wrong.

Team Canada.

Canadian journalists predictably ranted and raved about the humiliation of the best North America had to offer. The Toronto Star published words to the effect that, while making their debut in world-caliber hockey, the pampered Canadian professionals acted as if they had just met. But even 35 top players couldn't become a team overnight. For that, you need time, a commodity Harry Sinden was short of. Making matters worse was the bravado that reigned prior to the Montreal game, which had been fueled by the press itself.

Physically, the Canadians, and especially their defense lines, were no match for the Soviets. Vladislav Tretiak made Ken Dryden look like an amateur. In the face of fast, one-touch passes by the Soviet forwards, defensemen Don Awrey and Rod Seiling didn't know which way to skate. The forwards headed by Phil Esposito would have been outstanding in an All-Star Game, but the brilliant solo efforts that had been honed for years and especially prepared for this series didn't prevail against a fit and highly organized team. Ratelle and his Rangers teammates weren't in condition for fast team play and their slower attacks were ineffective against the Soviets. The only parallel to the Soviet style was the line of Ellis–Clarke–Henderson. The Toronto wingers picked up on the smallest signals from their linemates and Clarke fit right in at center. For the second game, in Toronto, Harry Sinden sent the entire Rangers forward line to the press gallery, where they were joined by five other players from game one, including Ken Dryden.

The Canadians began the game at Maple Leaf Gardens cautiously. The defense stuck to their positions. None of them recklessly joined an attack and there were no rink-wide passes that the Soviet forwards could intercept as they had at the Forum. The forwards didn't linger at center ice but quickly dumped the puck into the Soviet zone and chased after it. Outwardly, their game appeared quite rational and included plenty of bodychecking. Wayne Cashman and Jean-Paul Parise repeatedly won the tussles in the corners and fed the puck to Esposito, who planted himself in front of Tretiak's net. The new strategy even brought the team some success. In the middle of the second period, Esposito picked up a pass from Cashman and fired a shot on the Soviet net from his favorite spot about 20 feet out. That opened the scoring and the period ended that way.

At the beginning of the third period, Cournoyer capitalized on an early power-play and made it 2–0. On a Soviet power-play at 5:13, Yakushev reduced the gap less than a minute later. Then Pete Mahovlich stole the show. The Canadians had been playing a man short for about 30 seconds and had no intention of mounting an attack when Esposito intercepted the puck and Mahovlich put on a burst of speed and raced down center ice. Esposito fed him the puck and he got through the Soviet defense. After a series of feints in front of Tretiak's net, he appeared to casually lob the puck in. The fans were highly impressed, especially when Pete's big brother Frank scored another one two minutes later.

It was thought in North America that the Soviets had come to Canada to learn how to play hockey.

Coaches don't generally tamper with the lineup of a winning team and neither did Sinden. The only change saw Ratelle return before game three in Winnipeg to replace Bill Goldsworthy. The Soviet lineup was changed a lot more.

At first the game at the Winnipeg Arena seemed to be going just like the one in Toronto. Once again the Soviets had their hands full when the Cashman–Esposito–Parise line was on the ice. Parise opened the scoring and after the teams exchanged goals Esposito brought the score to 3–1 on passes from Parise and Cashman in the second. Midway through the game the Soviets were a man short after Yuri Lebedev was penalized for tripping. For almost two minutes, the Canadians bombarded Tretiak's net to no avail. Kharlamov then picked up a long, accurate pass from defenseman Gennady Tsygankov and scored a shorthand goal. Less than a minute later, Henderson put one in the net while falling to the ice. Late in the second period, a young trio from Krylja Sovetov (Soviet Wings) put on a burst of speed and went on the attack. Lebedev and then Alexander Bodunov evened the score to 4–4. But it was a goalkeeper's game in the third period. Tony Esposito saved a blistering shot by Alexander Maltsev 13 seconds before the siren and Tretiak, who had already faced 37 shots on goal, managed to stop a shot Henderson fired from about 10 feet away.

Eight minutes into the fourth game, in Vancouver, the USSR was already up 2–0 after two power-play goals by Mikhailov. A solo effort by Gilbert Perreault early in the second period reduced the gap to one, but less than a minute later, Vladimir Petrov's line clicked once more and Yuri Blinov beat Dryden to make it 3–1. Shortly after that, Maltsev and Kharlamov set Vladimir Vikulov up for a goal to bring it to 4–1. In the last period, Vladimir Shadrin lit the red lamp when the center finished off an attack started by defensemen Valeri Vasiliev and Yakushev. A few minutes earlier, Phil Esposito set Goldsworthy up for a goal and Dennis Hull managed to slip in a last one for the Canadians with 22 seconds remaining, but the final score was 5–3 in favor of the USSR. Tretiak again played a superior game and only Phil Esposito and his wingers were able to offer at least some opposition to the three attacking Soviet lines.

A full two weeks separated the games in Canada and the ones in Moscow. The Soviet players returned home to train while Team Canada flew to Stockholm to accustom themselves to European hockey rinks at the Johanneshof arena. The Canadians played two exhibition games with the Swedes and came out with scores of 4–1 and 4–4.

Team Canada finally arrived in Moscow on September 20 and faced another crisis when Jocelyn Guevremont, Vic Hadfield and Rick Martin deserted the team and flew home. On September 21, the diminished number had a light workout to get acquainted with the Sports Palace in Luzhniki. They were surprised to see wire mesh instead of Plexiglas above the boards behind the goals, and during this practice they tried to determine which way the puck would bounce. The conclusion was that it was unpredictable.

On September 22, the Luzhniki Sports Palace was as completely packed as the Canadian rinks had been. Sitting in the government box was General Secretary Brezhnev, an avid fan, and his closest associates. Indeed, many if not most of the seats were occupied by officials and other VIPs, since not to attend such a match was tantamount to admitting that the Soviet team was inferior. It was only the cheers of 3,200 Canadian fans that to some extent lightened the stiff atmosphere in the minutes heading up to the opening face-off.

Pete Mahovlich (left) stole the show in game two.

The Canadians appeared to have learned their lessons from the previous four games. The defensemen stopped taking risks and played a strictly positional game. Even when they lost the puck in the Soviet zone, the forwards didn't skate back out but thrashed it out. As a result, the Soviets were often thwarted in their efforts to set up attacks with that seminal first pass. Rod Gilbert, who had sat out half the Canadian leg of the series, was especially active in this respect. In the 16th minute, he snagged a loose puck and fed it to the already speeding Perreault, who sidestepped Ragulin and passed to Parise on a dime. The Canadians took the lead 1–0.

The second period unfolded in a similar fashion. Clarke and Henderson put both the Soviet defense and Tretiak off balance. Minutes into the period, Henderson zipped the puck to Clarke, who had managed to shake off his check. Instead of firing off the shot Tretiak was expecting, Clarke zeroed in on the goalie and poked the puck between his legs. In the middle of the period, Clarke mounted an attack and Henderson managed to slap in the rebound for a 3–0 lead.

In the end, the Canadians simply didn't have the stamina to play three highly aggressive periods. The efficiency of their forechecking dropped sharply by the third period and the Soviet defense went to work as opportunities to join the attack suddenly opened. The first to take advantage was veteran defenseman Viktor Kuzkin, who launched an attack that was finished off by Blinov to bring the score to 3–1. Henderson and Clarke teamed up for Canada's fourth goal, at 4:56 of the third, but from the middle of the period the Canadians were mired deep in their defensive zone. The end of the first game in Moscow was much like it had been in Montreal. The Canadians couldn't find a way out against the powerful compositional play of the Soviet squad and in the last 11 minutes four shots went past Tony Esposito.

Before the second game in Moscow, the atmosphere in both camps resembled the feelings in Montreal before the series began—but reversed. Now the Soviet fans had begun to look down on the North American pros and demanded that their idols win all the games in Luzhniki, while the

Canadians were backed into a corner and had to win all three that were left. Then Buffalo center Gilbert Perreault decided that he'd had enough and flew home after being used in only two of six games.

The pressure in the last three games of the 1972 Summit Series easily matched a Stanley Cup playoff. And most of Canada's players had at least a dozen Stanley Cup games to their credit, while the Soviet players—like other Europeans of the time—had no idea what to expect.

In the second game in Moscow, Sinden made better use of his defensive options, especially since Serge Savard was now off the injured list and three pairs of reliable players were available to shore up the defense. Throughout the entire first period of game six, the Soviets attacked almost non-stop. Moreover, in the second period, West German referees Josef Kompalla and Franz Baader left Team Canada undermanned for almost six minutes. But Ken Dryden put on a remarkable performance. In the 22nd minute, a shot by Yuri Lyapkin ricocheted into the Canadian net, but Team Canada answered right back, scoring three goals in just 83 seconds (the first was executed by Hull, the second by Cournoyer and the third by Paul Henderson). Canada was in the lead 3–1.

Valeri Kharlamov (right) was the most dangerous player for the Soviet squad in the first four games, in Canada.

After Henderson's goal, Team Canada had been given 29 minutes and the USSR two minutes in penalties in the second period. Led by Yakushev, the Soviets capitalized on one of these situations and headed to the dressing room down a single goal at 3–2. In the last period, the Canadians were a man short only once for two minutes. Playing a strictly positional game, they managed to hang on to win.

During the Canada leg of the series, American officials Len Gagnon and Gordie Lee, Steve Dowling and Frank Larsen penalized Team Canada for 40 minutes and the USSR 33. In Moscow, Rudolf Bata (Czechoslovakia) and Uve Dahlberg (Sweden), Josef Kompalla and Franz Baader (West Germany) penalized the Soviets 51 minutes and the Canadians 107. Of course, referees everywhere can and do make mistakes—but some are more apparent than others. Of all the referees who officiated at the Summit Series, Josef Kompalla was the most incredibly generous to the Moscow hosts.

The first period of game seven belonged to Phil Esposito. Whenever he was on the ice, he would take a position near the goal crease in front of Tretiak. According to the Soviet plan, it was Yevgeny Mishakov's job to guard Esposito, but Mishakov couldn't stop a player who was a head taller and as solid as a rock on the ice. Four minutes into the game, Esposito whipped in a goal from his favorite spot to open the scoring. Later in the period, the outstanding Soviet forward in that game, Alexander Yakushev, outwitted Brad Park and caught Tony Esposito off guard, then Petrov put the USSR out in front 2–1 during a power-play, but shortly afterward Savard again spotted Phil Esposito parked in front of the net. In a moment of despair, Mishakov hooked him in the neck with the blade of his stick, but Esposito brushed it off and tied the game 2–2.

No goals were scored in the second period, but there was also no shortage of penalties. The Bata–Dahlberg tandem dispatched Canadian players to the box five times and the Soviets three times, most often for roughing. At the beginning of the third period, Rod Gilbert forced Tretiak to make a mistake. The Canadian came out from behind the net and rammed the puck between the goalie's legs, but then Yakushev tied it 3–3.

At 17:54 of the third period, just when a tie appeared certain, a long pass from Serge Savard hit Paul Henderson at center, and while being knocked to the ice, Henderson managed to unleash a shot that went between Tretiak's arm and body to give Canada a 4–3 win to tie the series 3–3.

Before the final and deciding game of the series, the Soviet nationals questioned whether Valeri Kharlamov would be able to play after he'd been injured in game six. The Canadians were sure to shadow him, which would free up his teammates, so naturally Valeri said yes.

There was one other question. The original agreement called for the final game in the series to be refereed by the Josef Kompalla–Franz Baader team from West Germany. But after game six, the Canadians demanded that the German refs be replaced by Uve Dahlberg of Sweden and Rudy Bata of Czechoslovakia or they wouldn't come out on the ice. The diplomatic tussle was resolved by the head of the IIHF refereeing committee, Andrei Starovoytov, who sacrificed Baader but preserved Kompalla and threatened Dahlberg with disqualification from international refereeing if he didn't say he was ill. He was replaced by Bata, who was less qualified than the Swede—and less particular.

The game was only in its third minute when Bata sent Bill White to the penalty box for two minutes; 36 seconds later, Kompalla sent Pete Mahovlich off to keep his teammate company. It took the Soviets 33 seconds to capitalize on their two-man advantage. Yakushev slapped the puck in the net after Dryden deflected a long shot by Maltsev and the score was 1–0. Ten seconds later, the game was interrupted for about 15 minutes.

Phil Esposito (left) starred for Team Canada as the leading individual scorer—with seven goals and six assists—and inspirational leader of the team.

A dispute erupted when Kompalla penalized Jean-Paul Parise for a questionable check on a player who didn't have the puck. Parise didn't choose his words carefully in addressing the issue, for which he received 10 minutes from Bata on top of his two minutes from Kompalla. Furious, the Canadian player brought his stick up to swing at the German's head. Although he had second thoughts at the last minute and smashed it against the boards, he was given a game misconduct.

The time it took Sports Palace attendants to clear the ice of towels, gloves, broken sticks and even chairs that had been thrown from Team Canada's bench was enough to allow tempers to cool, but the incident appeared to have some effect on Bata. Up to that point, he had ignored numerous infractions by Soviet players. Now he suddenly sent Tsygankov to the box. Surrounded in front of the goal by the entire Soviet defense, Esposito tied the score 17 seconds into the penalty. In the 13th minute, another Canadian was sent to the box (this time it was Cournoyer). Almost immediately, Kharlamov mounted an attack that Vladimir Lutchenko finished off with a long shot. Screened by players from both teams, Dryden didn't see the puck coming. Less than four minutes later, Brad Park and Rangers teammate Jean Ratelle came in on Tretiak's goal from the center line with precision passing. The brilliant rushing defenseman Park sent the puck sizzling over Tretiak's shoulder to make it 2–2. Team Canada clearly had no intention of playing a defensive game here.

In their first practice at the rink in Luzhniki, the Canadians had tried to figure out where the puck would go when it hit the wire mesh above the boards in back of the goal and came away with the conclusion that it was unpredictable. Their theory was proved wrong 21 seconds into the second period. From a fair distance back, Yakushev flipped the puck in the air toward the

During the Moscow games, the Sports Palace attendants had to clear the ice of towels, gloves, broken sticks and even chairs that had been thrown from the Canadian bench.

Canadian goal and the mesh deflected it practically in front of the crease, where Shadrin slapped it into the net for a 3–2 result. The USSR was in the lead for the third time in the game. But once again a Canadian defenseman tied the score. Rod Gilbert had skated into the Soviet zone to the right and come to a stop near the boards. While the defenders were trying to figure out what he was up to, Bill White slipped down the left side behind them toward Tretiak.

In the 31st minute, the Canadians' persistence was tested again. As Phil Esposito and his linemates rushed forward to take a pass, it ricocheted to Yakushev, who was lingering in the Canadian zone. Dryden didn't stand a chance against a pinpoint shot into the corner of the net and the Soviets took a 4–3 lead. Five minutes later, Soviet defenseman Valeri Vasiliev spearheaded a power-play attack to give the team a 5–3 lead. The teams were into the final minutes of the second period and the score looked devastating for the Canadians.

In the third period, Phil Esposito played with a variety of wingers and hardly came off the ice, while the Soviets had eased up a bit and found that they just couldn't stop him. Three minutes into the period, Esposito took a pass from Pete Mahovlich right in front of Tretiak. Esposito stopped the puck with his glove and brought it down right on the tip of his stick and proceeded to reduce the gap to 5–4. After that, the entire team played a desperate game and Dryden became a spectator with nothing to do but watch the volleys of pucks fired on Vladislav Tretiak.

Near the 13-minute mark, Brad Park dumped the puck into the Soviet zone from the blue line. Esposito deflected it and it ended up on Cournoyer's stick after a series of ricochets. Cournoyer sent it into the net at 12:56, but the red light didn't come on and the referees didn't signed a goal. Alan Eagleson ran around the rink to face off against the official behind the net. At that moment, the aisles in the stands of the Sports Palace began filling with grey-blue greatcoats. A number of soldiers serving as arena security got hold of Eagleson and tried to lead him away. Canadian players dashed across the rink, wrestled him away and escorted him straight across the ice to their bench. Then the silent and menacing columns of soldiers positioned themselves in the passageways. Had the Soviet coaches or players publicly attempted to contest the goal, the game may have had a far different outcome. Fortunately, the Soviets acted in the spirit of sportsmanship and the scoreboard in the Sports Palace registered a 5–5 tie.

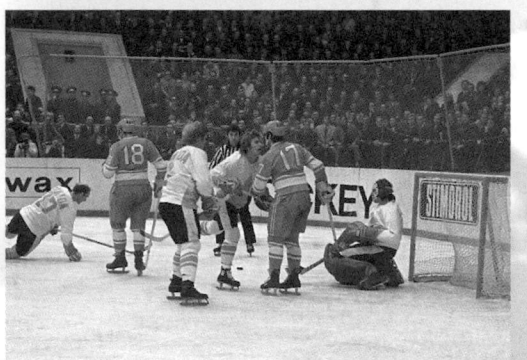

After the first game at Luzhniki stadium, the situation was critical for the Canadians. It was do or die. Bobby Clarke (third from the right) was more displeased than anyone with the way the games had gone.

In the eyes of the Soviets a tie score would have meant victory based on goals differential, 32–30. The tie stood till the very last minute as the Soviet players fought off furious attacks by the Canadians. At one point, the puck bounced off the boards and Esposito and Cournoyer rushed to get it. Meanwhile, a heavily guarded Henderson had taken a position near Tretiak's goal. All of a sudden the puck flew to the left of the face-off circle and landed on the tip of Henderson's stick. Henderson fired a shot, but Tretiak stopped it. Henderson got the rebound and fired again, and this time it went into the net. Canada was leading 6–5. In the remaining 34 seconds, the Canadians defended like mad dogs, refusing to grant the Soviets a decent shot on goal, and the period ended with a score of 6–5. Canada had won the game and the series—and defended its national pride.

Frank Mahovlich

Frank Mahovlich was a talented and classy winger, a large man with the skills and hands of a pure scorer. Known as "the Big M," Mahovlich was touted as a superstar while still a teenager. He went on to have a marvelous career, patrolling the left wing for 22 professional seasons in both the NHL and WHA. Many of those years were filled with glory as he earned individual awards and the Stanley Cup, but Mahovlich struggled through most of his hockey life with the stress that comes from great expectations.

He played in three of the most intense NHL cities—Montreal, Toronto and Detroit—and his style of play frustrated as many fans and observers as it entertained. He was graceful and powerful, but perhaps because of that grace and power and his long skating stride, he appeared lackadaisical and disinterested at times. His reputation for being lazy was misplaced. Often the result of his floating opportunism was a burst of easy speed and a goal.

High expectations weighed most heavily on Mahovlich during his years in Toronto with the Maple Leafs. Born in Timmins, a small town in northern Ontario, he was a prodigy with the St. Michael's team that represented Toronto in the Ontario Hockey Association. When he was 18, he scored 24 goals and scouts and fans alike began to fill the arenas where he played to get a look at the big kid everybody was talking about. The next season he fired 52 goals in 49 games, won the Red Tilson Trophy as the league's most valuable player and made his first three appearances with the Leafs. Those who saw him play in junior talked about his potential to dominate, even at the professional level.

Frank Mahovlich was a talented and classy winger, a large man with the skills and hands of a pure scorer.

In his first full season in the NHL, 1957–58, he was solid and at times spectacular and his 20 goals and 36 points were enough to earn him the Calder Trophy as top rookie. He beat out Bobby Hull, who also entered the league that year as a much talked about youngster. At 19, Mahovlich seemed on the cusp of not just a great but a record-shattering career.

His next two seasons were erratic on the ice but consistent on the score sheet. He hovered around 20 goals, good totals for a young player, but many Toronto fans wanted a superstar performance each night, on every shift, and 20 goals wasn't good enough. In 1960–61, he began to play the way everyone had always expected. Still only 23 years old, he had an exceptional start to the season and led the league for much of the year in goals. With 14 games remaining, he had 48 goals, two less than Maurice Richard's record of 50. He seemed destined to seize the position of the game's top scorer. Those final two goals never came, however. Bernie Geoffrion overtook him late in the year, tying the Rocket's record in the process. People began talking not about how much talent Mahovlich had, how he'd scored 48 goals at such a young age, but what was missing in him that prevented him from achieving more.

"A superstar has to have a mean streak in him. Gordie Howe sure does and so does Bobby Hull," Toronto executive Harold Ballard said at the time. "But Frank doesn't, and that's what he lacks."

King Clancy, another long-time employee of the Leafs, agreed with his boss. "Frank's as nice a man as I've ever known. Perhaps that's his trouble. He has the talent to be the greatest hockey player that ever lived if only he were a little meaner. But he isn't, and there is nothing anyone can do about it."

With such friends, Mahovlich hardly needed enemies. Although the Leafs won the Stanley Cup for three consecutive seasons beginning in 1962, and even though Mahovlich averaged over 30 goals a year, he was the focus of much criticism and constant boos when he played in front of the home crowd. When he failed to score a goal in the 1963 playoffs, he was booed during and after the game in which the Leafs clinched the title. Even the next day the heckling continued at a reception in downtown Toronto for the Cup winners.

Mahovlich was quiet in the dressing room. Bob Baun, a defenseman with Toronto and Mahovlich's teammate for 13 seasons, later said they didn't share more than "22 words" in all those years—and he had an ongoing quiet but disruptive feud with Toronto manager and coach Punch Imlach. The tough bench boss insisted that Mahovlich wasn't trying hard enough. "He can do everything that Hull can do and some things Hull can't," said Imlach, comparing Mahovlich to the Chicago winger, as many did. Hull went on to break the record he shared with Richard and Geoffrion in 1966. "Frank doesn't give his best effort all the time. If he would push himself, he could score 60 goals, 80 goals, even 100 goals," his coach claimed.

Mahovlich responded to Imlach's berating by not reacting to it. He admitted later that the two men didn't speak for five years. "I liked Punch when I first came up with the team," Mahovlich said. "We got along fine. But after that we didn't get along. And things have become considerably worse. My doctor told me to put an imaginary curtain around myself whenever Punch was around." Though the team and the doctors didn't admit it for several years, Mahovlich was hospitalized in 1964, suffering from acute tension and depression. He returned to the team but struggled on the ice, his goal production dropping to 18 in 1966–67, the year of his final Cup victory with Toronto.

The Leafs played the Montreal Canadiens on November 1, 1967—an important game between long-time foes. Mahovlich played a wonderful game, scoring a goal and adding two assists in Toronto's 5–0 win. He was named one of the three stars of the game and took his bow in front of the remaining fans, as was the custom at the end of the evening. Many in the crowd cheered the big winger, but there were also boos, even on that night. The next day, with the Leafs leaving on a trip to Detroit, Mahovlich got up from his seat on the train, told a teammate he was going home and left. He was soon under the care of the Toronto General Hospital psychiatric staff. He was in a deep depression and, according to many reports, had suffered a nervous breakdown.

Mahovlich, Frank
LW, 6′, 205 lbs, b: Timmins, Ont., 1/10/1938

Season	Club, League	Regular Season					Playoffs				
		GP	G	A	Pts	PIM	GP	G	A	Pts	PIM
1956–57	Toronto Maple Leafs, NHL	3	1	0	1	2					
1957–58	Toronto Maple Leafs, NHL	67	20	16	36	67					
1958–59	Toronto Maple Leafs, NHL	63	22	27	49	94	12	6	5	11	18
1959–60	Toronto Maple Leafs, NHL	70	18	21	39	61	10	3	1	4	27
1960–61	Toronto Maple Leafs, NHL	70	48	36	84	131	5	1	1	2	6
1961–62	Toronto Maple Leafs, NHL	70	33	38	71	87	12	6	6	12	29
1962–63	Toronto Maple Leafs, NHL	67	36	37	73	56	9	0	2	2	8
1963–64	Toronto Maple Leafs, NHL	70	26	29	55	66	14	4	11	15	20
1964–65	Toronto Maple Leafs, NHL	59	23	28	51	76	6	0	3	3	9
1965–66	Toronto Maple Leafs, NHL	68	32	24	56	68	4	1	0	1	10
1966–67	Toronto Maple Leafs, NHL	63	18	28	46	44	12	3	7	10	8
1967–68	Toronto Maple Leafs, NHL	50	19	17	36	30					
	Detroit Red Wings, NHL	13	7	9	16	2					
1968–69	Detroit Red Wings, NHL	76	49	29	78	38					
1969–70	Detroit Red Wings, NHL	74	38	32	70	59	4	0	0	0	2
1970–71	Detroit Red Wings, NHL	35	14	18	32	30					
	Montreal Canadiens, NHL	38	17	24	41	11	20	14	13	27	18
1971–72	Montreal Canadiens, NHL	76	43	53	96	36	6	3	2	5	2
SS–72	Canada	6	1	1	2	0					
1972–73	Montreal Canadiens, NHL	78	38	55	93	51	17	9	14	23	6
1973–74	Montreal Canadiens, NHL	71	31	49	80	47	6	1	2	3	0
1974–75	Toronto Toros, WHA	73	38	44	82	27	6	3	0	3	2
1975–76	Toronto Toros, WHA	75	34	55	89	14					
1976–77	Birmingham Bulls, WHA	17	3	20	23	12					
1977–78	Birmingham Bulls, WHA	72	14	24	38	22	3	1	1	2	0
	NHL Totals	1181	533	570	1103	1056	137	51	67	118	163
	WHA Totals	237	89	143	232	75	9	4	1	5	2
	SS Totals	6	1	1	2	0					

NHL First All-Star Team (1961, 1963, 1973)
NHL Second All-Star Team (1962, 1964, 1965, 1966, 1969, 1970)
Won Calder Trophy (1958)
Won Stanley Cup (1962, 1963, 1964, 1967, 1971, 1973)

Mahovlich stayed away from the rink to deal with his nervous condition. After a month, during which he missed 11 games, he made his return at home in a game against the Canadiens. When Mahovlich stepped on the ice, he was on a line with Mike Walton and the Leafs captain, George Armstrong. Mahovlich gathered the puck at center and sailed down the right wing into the Montreal zone, pulling a defenseman wide with him to open up the middle. With one perfectly placed pass, Mahovlich found Walton, who fired it into the net. In all it took 18 seconds of his first shift for the Big M to announce his return, and now the fans were united in their applause.

Near the end of the season, the Leafs decided to part ways with their big winger. In the biggest trade of the year, he was sent to the Detroit Red Wings with Pete Stemkowski, Garry Unger and the rights to another Leaf enigma, Carl Brewer, for Paul Henderson, Norm Ullman and Floyd Smith. Freed in Detroit from all the pressure and conflict in Toronto, Mahovlich experienced a rebirth. He also joined his younger brother, Pete, known as "the Little M" even though he had five inches on Frank. The elder Mahovlich became more outgoing, joking with teammates and fans. He was put on a line with Gordie Howe and Alex Delvecchio and had his best goal-scoring year in his first full season with the team, 49 goals in 1968–69.

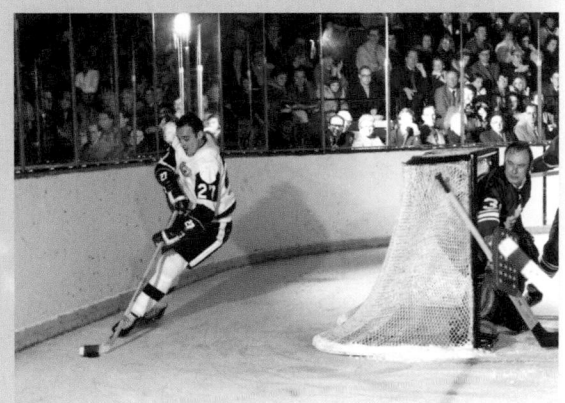

In Detroit, Frank Mahovlich (left) was put on a line with Gordie Howe and Alex Delvecchio and had his best year of scoring with 49 goals in the 1968–69 season.

"Howe and Delvecchio do a lot of things that ordinary players wouldn't do," Mahovlich said in 1969. "For one thing, they hold on to the puck longer…. They wait until you're in the clear. If you're not clear, they won't throw it in. I was going offside a lot earlier in the season, until I got used to it."

Howe, 40 years old at the time, also took some time to get used to his new linemate. "I play him the way Ted Lindsay used to play me," Howe said shortly after Mahovlich joined the Wings. "When Frank is skating full out, I know he's going to shoot. When he's going, I head for the corner, the way Lindsay did with me, and if he misses, I have a chance to get it coming around the boards. When he's going to pass, he slows up."

In Detroit, Mahovlich played more minutes than ever on the first line on the power-play and sometimes even killed penalties. When Howe became the third player to break the 100-point plateau in 1968–69, Mahovlich was cited as a significant factor.

After three years in Detroit, Mahovlich was on the move again, the victim of a Detroit team that was struggling and dumping high-priced players to rebuild. The Montreal Canadiens were preparing for a run to the Cup and acquired the big left winger for three players in January 1971. Once again, Mahovlich was teamed with his brother, Pete, who had joined the Canadiens the year before. Mahovlich had a spectacular playoffs with a Montreal team that won the Stanley Cup that year due in large part to his league-leading 14 goals and 27 post-season points. Mahovlich was truly happy in Montreal. He had his best overall season in 1971–72, collecting 96 points, and earned a place on the Canadian team that battled the Soviets in the 1972 Summit Series.

In 1973 Mahovlich was selected to the NHL's First All-Star Team, one of only three times he achieved that honor. And once again he was outstanding in the playoffs, capturing his sixth and final Stanley Cup. Mahovlich and Montreal were a natural fit and only his aging legs and a move toward younger athletes in the Canadiens organization prevented him from continuing to put up big numbers late into his career.

Though Toronto fans still strongly supported him, Mahovlich was sent to Detroit in 1968, the biggest trade of the year.

Instead of finishing his career in Montreal, Mahovlich signed a lucrative contract with the World Hockey Association. The Houston team selected him in the 1972 Entry Draft and then traded him to the Toronto Toros, who attempted to sign both Mahovlich brothers. They were thrilled when Frank, at age 36, signed a four-year deal. He was one of the league's top scorers and headlined the team in its attempt to compete with the Leafs. The Toros team moved after two seasons to Birmingham, deep in the southern U.S., and became the Bulls. Though Mahovlich still had a great desire to play, the Bulls didn't capture the imagination of the fans. At the end of his four-year contract, having just turned 40, Mahovlich parted ways with Birmingham, which was replacing its expensive veterans with unproven juniors in an attempt to stay afloat. Mahovlich's NHL rights were still controlled by the Canadiens, and many teams who were interested in the winger's experience were loath to compensate Montreal for signing a 40-year-old player, even if his name was Mahovlich. The Pittsburgh Penguins came the closest to signing him but backed out at the last minute. Though he contacted other teams and waited by the phone several weeks into the 1978–79 season, Mahovlich finally conceded his career was over. A year later, when a final come-back with Detroit was aborted, his retirement was a quiet and private affair, though his honours were just beginning.

Frank Mahovlich was inducted into the Hockey Hall of Fame in 1981 and the Canadian Sports Hall of Fame in 1990. Four years later he was named to The Order of Canada, and in 1998, in recognition of his years of class on the ice and off, he was appointed to the Canadian Senate by Prime Minister Jean Chretien.

Alexander Ragulin

Alexander Ragulin was world champion 11 times.

Alexander Ragulin was a legend in Soviet hockey. Probably no other hockey player in the 1960s had more apocryphal stories told about him.

Legend has it that as boys, Alexander and his two brothers, Anatoli and Mikhail, played together as a musical trio to earn pin money. Alexander, because he was the biggest, played the biggest instrument—the bass fiddle. The brothers also once swiped hockey sticks from a team's locker room. They were caught red-handed. The team was Khimik, and the coach, Nikolai Epshtein, said to them: "You want to play hockey? Then come on over to our team."

The tall, well-built and handsome Ragulin was very attractive to women. Another story claims that in 1966, at the zenith of his career, when Ragulin was voted best defenseman at the World Championship, he was besieged by a millionairess who had a crush on him. It was rumored that she was ready to buy out the farewell banquet at the championship in Ljubljana, in Slovenia, just to spend one evening with Ragulin. The best defenseman knew the team was planning a big bash and said: "I can't. My buddies are waiting for me."

Ragulin could be both demanding and magnanimous on the ice. Physical strength was his trump card and he was comfortable using his size to crush an opponent. But Ragulin was usually a congenial hockey player. He was very careful and judicious when it came to bodychecking. The puck interested him more than the sound of cracking bones. For his size, Ragulin handled the puck with surprising ease and used his bulk to block shots fired at the goal. At four World Championships between 1963 and 1967 and at the 1964 Olympics, he was picked to join the All-Star team.

Building defense tandems based on the good guy–bad guy principle was standard in Soviet hockey during those years. One such pairing was Nikolai Sologubov as the bad guy and Ivan Tregubov as the good guy. They were eventually replaced by Eduard Ivanov and Alexander Ragulin. It was an ideal partnership. The fearless Ivanov, whose motto was "Win at any cost!" was unforgiving on the ice and liked a crisis to motivate him. The steady and composed Ragulin, on the other hand, was always kindhearted and heroic. Even when in the heat of the game an opponent smashed Ragulin's face at the 1968 Olympics, the Soviet defenseman held him in a tight bear hug until he cooled off.

Ivanov and Ragulin usually shared the same hotel room while on tour. From the hall, one could hear the frequent changing of television channels and quarreling voices. "Those crazy shootouts are enough to deafen anyone," Ragulin might have grumbled to Ivanov, who loved watching cowboy movies. "And your stupid dances drive me nutty," Ivanov would probably respond to Ragulin, who was a great jazz fan.

Everyone respected Ragulin, including his coach, Anatoli Tarasov. The coach respected his player's reasonable use of strength and lack of malice. There is no doubt that Ragulin was one of the most popular players in the Central Red Army club and on the national team.

It was for Ragulin's sake that Tarasov eventually resorted to a new tactic in order to keep his best defenseman. The already hefty Ragulin had gained some additional weight. Even in his best years, he had never been the fastest defenseman. Now, at 30, he wasn't at the top of his game. So Tarasov decided to beef up his best forward line of Valeri Kharlamov, Anatoli Firsov and Vladimir Vikulov with a youthful and energetic player named Gennady Tsygankov. Ragulin's new partner turned out to be a carbon copy of Ivanov. The only difference was that Tsygankov skated twice as fast. So Ragulin now had an excellent opportunity to play the role of cleanup man and concentrate on defending the immediate attacks on goal.

According to Tarasov, the five-man Firsov line didn't participate in a single losing match in the entire 1971–72 season, whether playing for the Red Army club or the national team. As the last line of defense, Ragulin played a brilliant game, flawlessly and with ease, just as he had in his best years. At the end of the season, he was rewarded with an invitation to join the Soviet All-Star team.

Well-built and good-looking, Alexander Ragulin was always a favorite among the opposite sex.

Ragulin, Alexander
D, 6´, 220 lbs, b: Moscow, USSR, 5/5/1941

Season	Club, League	Regular Season				
		GP	G	A	Pts	PIM
1957–61	Khimik Voskresensk, USSR	*	*	*	*	*
WEC–61	USSR	7	1	1	2	4
1961–62	Khimik Voskresensk, USSR	*	*	*	*	*
1962–63	CSKA, USSR	*	2	*	*	*
WEC–63	USSR	7	2	1	3	2
1963–64	CSKA, USSR	*	9	*	*	*
OWG–64	USSR	8	3	6	9	0
1964–65	CSKA, USSR	*	4	*	*	*
WEC–65	USSR	7	0	2	2	8
1965–66	CSKA, USSR	*	6	*	*	*
WEC–66	USSR	7	4	2	6	4
1966–67	CSKA, USSR	*	8	*	*	*
WEC–67	USSR	7	2	5	7	6
1967–68	CSKA, USSR	40	5	*	*	*
OWG–68	USSR	7	0	2	2	2
1968–69	CSKA, USSR	40	6	*	*	*
WEC–69	USSR	10	1	1	2	6
1969–70	CSKA, USSR	41	3	*	*	*
WEC–70	USSR	10	0	0	0	2
1970–71	CSKA, USSR	36	4	*	*	*
WEC–71	USSR	10	1	2	3	4
1971–72	CSKA, USSR	28	0	*	*	*
OWG–72	USSR	5	0	3	3	0
WEC–72	USSR	10	0	0	0	8
SS–72	USSR	6	0	1	1	4
1972–73	CSKA, USSR	28	0	*	*	*
WEC–73	USSR	7	0	1	1	6
	USSR Totals	427	53	*	*	*
	OWG/WEC/SS Totals	108	14	27	41	56

Named Best Defenseman at WEC (1966)
Won OWG (1964, 1968, 1972)
Won WEC (1963, 1965, 1966, 1967, 1969, 1970, 1971, 1973)
USSR Champion (1963, 1964, 1965, 1966, 1968, 1970, 1971, 1972, 1973)

At his last World Championship in 1973, Ragulin didn't appear on the ice very often. But the new coach of the nationals, Vsevolod Bobrov, knew how important it was to the legendary hockey player to become a 10-time world champion—until 1972, Olympic tournaments incorporated the World Championships—and he gave Ragulin the chance. He was the only player still in the lineup that had taken part in the team's unbeaten championship run 10 years earlier.

Gary Bergman

Gary Bergman played an important role on defense for Team Canada in the 1972 Summit Series.

Gary Bergman was a solid all-around defenseman in his 12-year NHL tenure. A fine skater with a knack for making smart decisions on offense, he also took a physical approach to the game when guarding his end of the ice. Known primarily for his decade-long service in Detroit, Bergman also impressed as a member of Team Canada during the 1972 Summit Series.

A native of northwestern Ontario, Bergman enjoyed a fine amateur career in neighboring Manitoba. After two seasons with the Winnipeg Braves of the Manitoba junior league, he joined that city's pro franchise in the Western Hockey League. Bergman gained experience and solidified his status as an intriguing prospect while skating with four different AHL squads from 1960 to 1964.

He joined the Detroit Red Wings in 1964–65 and looked very comfortable as a freshman. In 58 games, Bergman held back his offensive instincts while focusing on his defensive work. Gradually he gained confidence and seniority on the team. He played solidly when the Wings reached the 1966 Stanley Cup finals and lost to Montreal in six games. Little did he know that he'd only see action in one more playoff series in his career.

His well-rounded play made him useful on both the power-play and penalty-killing units for the Wings. Although he incurred his share of penalties, Bergman wasn't considered a surly opponent on the ice. He rarely looked for trouble but also never backed down from an onrushing opponent, whether he was a fancy scorer or a power forward.

A huge compliment came Bergman's way when Harry Sinden and John Ferguson invited him to play with Team Canada in the 1972 Summit Series. He played an important defensive role in all eight games and chipped in with three assists. Bergman recounted the day he was asked to play for his country: "Harry called me Sunday morning. Janie and the kids and I were just going out the door to church, and I had to stop. Janie was saying, 'Would you get off the damn phone, we have to get to church.' It was Harry Sinden on the phone asking me if I'd be part of the team."

Bergman, Gary
D, 5′11″, 188 lbs, b: Kenora, Ont., 10/7/1938, d: 8/12/2000

Season	Club, League	Regular Season					Playoffs				
		GP	G	A	Pts	PIM	GP	G	A	Pts	PIM
1957–58	Winnipeg Warriors, WHL	2	0	0	0	0					
1959–60	Winnipeg Warriors, WHL	58	1	9	10	147					
1960–61	Buffalo Bisons, AHL	67	5	14	19	104	4	0	0	0	12
1961–62	Cleveland Barons, AHL	68	10	30	40	164	6	1	2	3	14
1962–63	Quebec – Cleveland, AHL	55	5	21	26	141	7	1	5	6	10
1963–64	Springfield Indians, AHL	60	13	24	37	106					
1964–65	Detroit Red Wings, NHL	58	4	7	11	85	5	0	1	1	4
1965–66	Detroit Red Wings, NHL	61	3	16	19	96	12	0	3	3	14
	Memphis Wings, CHL	5	2	3	5	4					
1966–67	Detroit Red Wings, NHL	70	5	30	35	129					
1967–68	Detroit Red Wings, NHL	74	13	28	41	109					
1968–69	Detroit Red Wings, NHL	76	7	30	37	80					
1969–70	Detroit Red Wings, NHL	69	6	17	23	122	4	0	1	1	2
1970–71	Detroit Red Wings, NHL	68	8	25	33	149					
1971–72	Detroit Red Wings, NHL	75	6	31	37	138					
SS–72	Canada	8	0	3	3	13					
1972–73	Detroit Red Wings, NHL	68	3	28	31	71					
1973–74	Detroit Red Wings, NHL	11	0	6	6	18					
	Minnesota North Stars, NHL	57	3	23	26	66					
1974–75	Detroit Red Wings, NHL	76	5	25	30	104					
1975–76	Kansas City Scouts, NHL	75	5	33	38	82					
	NHL Totals	838	68	299	367	1249	21	0	5	5	20
	SS Totals	8	0	3	3	13					

Bergman's consistent play often went unnoticed in the early 1970s. All eyes were on young superstars like Bobby Orr and Brad Park. In addition, the Red Wings were a mediocre team that received less attention each year, especially with the retirement of Gordie Howe and the trading of Frank Mahovlich to Montreal. During this period, Bergman derived much satisfaction from his work in his community and was particularly involved with helping disabled children and adults. He was one of the most-liked NHLers off the ice. In 1973 he was named co-winner of the Charlie Conacher Humanitarian Award.

One of the most accomplished all-round defenseman in the 1960s, Gary Bergman (right) played only 21 post-season games in 12 seasons.

After more than 600 games in a Detroit uniform, Bergman was traded to the Minnesota North Stars for fellow veteran blueliner Ted Harris. He was presented a plane ticket out of town because, as a veteran on the team, he felt obligated to speak out when he disagreed with the decisions of coach Ned Harkness. In the off-season, he was reacquired by the Wings and posted a respectable 30 points. Another trade sent Bergman to Kansas City, where he played his final year with the second-year Scouts.

Bergman retired with 367 points in 838 regular-season games. In nearly a decade and a half of NHL service, he had the chance to play in only 21 post-season games, 12 of them in 1966. Randy Schultz described Bergman as a working-class player "because, like his counterpart in the working world, he goes out, does his job day in and day out and never gets the recognition he deserves."

A personable figure, Bergman went into sales after retiring from the NHL and also started his own building company in Detroit. He continued to work with various charities and programs that benefited children. One of his activities was serving as coach of the Michigan floor hockey team in the Special Olympics held annually at Maple Leaf Gardens in Toronto. Bergman remained close to the Red Wings organization and served a term in the late 1990s as president of the team's alumni association.

Gary Bergman died on December 8, 2000, after an eight-month battle with cancer. He was 62.

Viktor Kuzkin

Viktor Kuzkin's outstanding career as a hockey player ended on a high note. In his second-to-last season, in 1974–75, he became the first player ever to win 13 USSR national championships. By the time Viacheslav Fetisov matched this achievement, Kuzkin had become the holder of 24 national championship victories as both player and coach. It is hard to imagine that anyone will ever beat that record. In addition, Kuzkin is one of only six hockey players in the world to hold three Olympic gold medals.

Viktor Kuzkin was the first to win 13 USSR national championships.

As a captain, Kuzkin led the Central Red Army to victory in four national and two USSR Cup tournaments, as well as three European Championships. Again as captain, Kuzkin led Team USSR to gold medal wins at the 1966 World Championship and the 1972 Olympics. Last but not least, Kuzkin was Team USSR captain at the 1972 Summit Series.

Viktor Kuzkin (right) is one of only six hockey players to win three Olympic gold medals.

Kuzkin is considered one of the best defensemen in Soviet hockey. For nearly 20 years, he was among the most talented players on the defense line. He was distinguished by his agility, speed and capacity to quickly size up the situation on the ice. He was also a superlative stickhandler. He began his career as a center and later switched to defense, still maintaining his ability to finish off an attack on goal.

"When he moved to the defense line from his forward position with Red Army, Kuzkin put his previous experience to use in his new role," Anatoli Tarasov, coach of the Army and national teams, recalls. "Viktor never lost his cool in tough situations and had a knack for rallying the team. It's no coincidence that he captained the Army and national squads for many years. An exemplary sportsman, and very courageous on the ice, Kuzkin was generous and unassuming in everyday life. He was never belligerent or antagonistic to anyone because it would have been completely out of character for him."

Viktor Kuzkin's achievements as a coach are only slightly less distinguished than his record as a player. He was never a head coach, but the 11 gold medals that Red Army won while he was an assistant on the coaching team speak for themselves. Viktor Tikhonov chose Kuzkin to be his assistant, knowing the importance of the role and recognizing Kuzkin's experience and coaching abilities. In the pantheon of head and assistant coaches, only Tarasov and Tikhonov, who led the Army to 12 national victories, surpass Kuzkin's record.

The 50th anniversary of Russian hockey was observed in December 1996 with veteran players and leading sportswriters selecting the all-time dream team of the USSR and Russia. Viktor Kuzkin was one of those chosen.

Kuzkin, Viktor
D, 5´10˝, 185 lbs, b: Moscow, USSR, 7/6/1940

Season	Club, League	Regular Season				
		GP	G	A	Pts	PIM
1958–59	CSKA, USSR	*	0	*	*	*
1959–60	CSKA, USSR	*	3	*	*	*
1960–61	CSKA, USSR	*	3	*	*	*
1961–62	CSKA, USSR	*	9	*	*	*
1962–63	CSKA, USSR	*	6	*	*	*
WEC–63	USSR	7	1	0	1	8
1963–64	CSKA, USSR	*	5	*	*	*
OWG–64	USSR	8	2	3	5	6
1964–65	CSKA, USSR	*	4	*	*	*
WEC–65	USSR	7	2	1	3	4
1965–66	CSKA, USSR	*	9	*	*	*
WEC–66	USSR	7	1	1	2	4
1966–67	CSKA, USSR	*	5	*	*	*
WEC–67	USSR	7	2	0	2	9
1967–68	CSKA, USSR	40	3	*	*	*
OWG–68	USSR	7	1	1	2	0
1968–69	CSKA, USSR	39	7	*	*	*
WEC–69	USSR	3	0	1	1	2
1969–70	CSKA, USSR	32	3	*	*	*
1970–71	CSKA, USSR	40	3	*	*	*
WEC–71	USSR	10	2	2	4	4
1971–72	CSKA, USSR	31	4	*	*	*
OWG–72	USSR	5	1	0	1	0
WEC–72	USSR	9	0	2	2	4
SS–72	USSR	7	0	1	1	8
1972–73	CSKA, USSR	29	3	*	*	*
1973–74	CSKA, USSR	30	0	3	3	*
1974–75	CSKA, USSR	28	1	1	2	2
1975–76	CSKA, USSR	36	2	2	4	2
	USSR Totals	530	70	*	*	*
	OWG/WEC/SS Totals	77	12	12	24	49

Won OWG (1964, 1968, 1972)
Won WEC (1963, 1965, 1966, 1967, 1969, 1971)
USSR Champion (1959, 1960, 1961, 1963, 1964, 1965, 1966, 1968, 1970, 1971, 1972, 1973, 1975)

Vyacheslav Starshinov

In the golden era of the 1960s, Vyacheslav Starshinov was the linchpin of Team USSR's game. He was an unusually powerful center who had mastered Canadian-style hockey. As a result, he quickly gained recognition for his exceptional performance in the highly technical game of Soviet hockey.

As a boy, Starshinov played both soccer and bandy for Spartak. In 1958 Spartak coach Alexander Igumnov put the 18-year-old Starshinov on the forward line with the Mayorov brothers, Boris and Yevgeny. Spartak's first game with this lineup was against the Central Red Army and they lost 13–1. And that marked the inauspicious beginning of a forward line that would lead the Soviet national squad to several Olympics and World Championships. At the national level, the line would bring a formerly lackluster team to the level of first-class competitor against Red Army and remain virtually undefeated for the next 10 years.

The line began to come into its own at the end of the 1958–59 season, when they were included in the junior lineup that was set to play against senior players from the United States. The team won two games, and eight out of the 10 goals scored were attributed to the Starshinov line.

The Mayorov brothers had learned how to work with their new partner by the end of their first season together. They realized that what their fast but uneven line had lacked was the power of an aggressive, straight-ahead player like Starshinov. "I was never really interested in using evasive tactics on the ice," Starshinov recalls. "I always believed that a player's technique should be pragmatic. The simpler, the better. The main thing was to head to the opposing team's net as fast as possible. I was never afraid of head-on clashes with opposing defensemen. The important thing was to use an effective bodycheck to prevent the opponent from getting hold of the puck."

Starshinov and the Mayorov brothers were united by a sense of pride and a belief that victory belonged to the strongest. The brothers were spirited players and often had difficulty controlling their volatility in showdowns. Heated exchanges frequently sent them to the penalty box.

The forward line worked from the start to build itself up. At first Spartak lost practically every game it played. However, their moment of glory came in 1962 in a historic game against Red Army. Starshinov was on the ice for the last five minutes of the game. He and his partners successfully defended the goal against five Army players. A year later, the coaches of the national team gave Starshinov the same job in the decisive game against Team Canada at the World Championship.

In 1967 Spartak took the national championship for the second time, winning hands down against the Army club.

Vyacheslav Starshinov—a Soviet star who mastered Canadian-style hockey.

Starshinov, Vyacheslav
C, 5'9", 183 lbs, b: Moscow, USSR, 5/6/1940

Season	Club, League	Regular Season				
		GP	G	A	Pts	PIM
1957–58	Spartak Moscow, USSR	*	0	*	*	*
1958–59	Spartak Moscow, USSR	*	12	*	*	*
1959–60	Spartak Moscow, USSR	*	16	*	*	*
1960–61	Spartak Moscow, USSR	*	16	*	*	*
WEC–61	USSR	7	6	3	9	11
1961–62	Spartak Moscow, USSR	38	29	*	*	*
1962–63	Spartak Moscow, USSR	37	23	*	*	*
WEC–63	USSR	7	8	3	11	10
1963–64	Spartak Moscow, USSR	*	34	*	*	*
OWG–64	USSR	8	8	4	12	6
1964–65	Spartak Moscow, USSR	*	25	*	*	*
WEC–65	USSR	7	6	2	8	12
1965–66	Spartak Moscow, USSR	*	22	*	*	*
WEC–66	USSR	7	11	1	12	8
1966–67	Spartak Moscow, USSR	*	47	*	*	*
WEC–67	USSR	7	4	2	6	2
1967–68	Spartak Moscow, USSR	*	46	*	*	*
OWG–68	USSR	7	6	6	12	2
1968–69	Spartak Moscow, USSR	41	40	*	*	*
WEC–69	USSR	10	6	1	7	6
1969–70	Spartak Moscow, USSR	39	34	*	*	*
WEC–70	USSR	9	5	5	10	6
1970–71	Spartak Moscow, USSR	39	22	*	*	*
WEC–71	USSR	9	4	5	9	6
1971–72	Spartak Moscow, USSR	25	15	*	*	*
SS–72	USSR	1	0	0	0	0
1974–75	Spartak Moscow, USSR	27	13	8	21	*
1975–76	Oji Seishi, Tamakomai, Japan	15	20	12	32	*
1976–77	Oji Seishi, Tamakomai, Japan	18	22	17	39	*
1977–78	Oji Seishi, Tamakomai, Japan	15	13	11	24	*
1978–79	Spartak Moscow, USSR	37	11	7	18	30
	USSR Totals	540	405	*	*	*
	OWG/WEC/SS Totals	79	64	32	96	69

Named Best Forward at WEC (1965)
Won OWG (1964, 1968)
Won WEC (1963, 1965, 1966, 1967, 1969, 1970, 1971)
USSR Champion (1962, 1967, 1969)
Japan Champion (1976, 1977)

Vyacheslav Starshinov is still the second-highest scorer in Russian hockey.

Starshinov (center) played alongside the Mayorov brothers with Spartak for nearly 10 years and lost count of the goals he scored on passes from Boris Mayorov.

Starshinov played alongside the Mayorov brothers for nearly 10 years, losing count of the goals he scored on passes from Boris Mayorov. These passes, according to Starshinov, were extremely opportune and proved totally unexpected for the opposition. His opponents were familiar with Mayorov's style of play, but somehow he always managed to fool them and alert Starshinov through a shared sixth sense when a pass was coming.

Boris Mayorov ended his playing career in 1969, but Starshinov continued to play for the national team. He played his last World Championship in 1971, accepting the championship trophy as team captain.

For the 1972 Summit Series, coach Vsevolod Boborov included Starshinov in the lineup. He knew he needed aggressive players with strength and stamina to beat the professional players they would be up against. When his playing career ended, Starshinov, like the Mayorov brothers, coached for Spartak. He returned to the ice to play in Japan and played for Spartak two more times, the last in 1977–78 when he was 38 years old.

Red Berenson

A solid all-around performer, Gordon "Red" Berenson enjoyed 17 productive years in the NHL. He was a fine sportsman who could check or score equally well depending on the situation. Along the way he registered seven 20-goal seasons and played on one Stanley Cup championship team in Montreal.

Berenson was a gifted scorer with his hometown Regina Pats of the SJHL from 1956 to 1958. His speed and skill with the puck impressed the officials of the Belleville McFarlands as they prepared to compete in the World Championships, and Canada captured the gold medal thanks in part to Berenson's nine goals.

Following this rewarding experience overseas, Berenson spent three years with the University of Michigan against the advice of the Montreal Canadiens, who held his rights. Berenson continued to draw praise when he scored 79 career goals and was a two-time CCHA First Team All-Star.

He also earned a place on the 1962 NCAA champion all-tournament team. After the college season ended, he joined the Habs and became the first Canadian to make the jump from the U.S. collegiate system to the big leagues. He continued to study in the off-season and earned a master's degree in business administration.

Berenson split the 1962–63 season between the Habs and their EPHL farm team in Hull-Ottawa. He played the entire 1963–64 season with the Habs but split the next two between Montreal and the American Hockey League—a reflection of the depth Montreal enjoyed at center during this period. Berenson looked up to the likes of Jean Beliveau, Henri Richard and Ralph Backstrom and knew he was never going to beat those men out of a job.

The Habs traded Berenson to the New York Rangers, where he played parts of two seasons. Late in the first year of expansion, he was traded to St. Louis, where he blossomed. The Blues felt Berenson was worth the cost of parting with top scorer Ron Stewart. Red scored 51 points in the last 55 games of the 1967–68 season and then helped the Blues reach the Stanley Cup finals against his old team, Montreal. Coach Scotty Bowman turned him into a true workhorse, playing him 35 to 40 minutes a game, including plenty of time with both specialty teams. He was also known throughout the league for using one of the longest sticks among NHL skaters, which helped him win more than his share of face-offs and to forecheck effectively.

Red Berenson could check or score equally well, depending on the situation.

During his first full season in Missouri, "the Red Baron" scored a personal high of 82 points. A significant chunk of his production came during an 8–0 thrashing of the Philadelphia Flyers at the Spectrum. That night Berenson became the first player since Syd Howe in 1944 to score six goals in a single game, a feat that entered the record books on its own since it represented the only six-goal performance by a player on the road. In fact, he could have notched a seventh had one of the 10 shots he sent toward Doug Favell not struck the crossbar. And none of them was scored on power-plays or deflections. In the dressing room after the second period, the Blues were ahead 5–0, with all goals courtesy of Berenson. Veteran Doug Harvey is supposed to have said, "You know, this would be a great game if you weren't playing."

The Blues reached the finals for three straight years, only to be swept each time. Late in 1970–71, they jumped at the chance to acquire Garry Unger from the Red Wings even though it meant giving up one of their most popular players when they traded Berenson. The Detroit team was below average, but

Berenson, Gordon "Red"
C, 6´, 185 lbs, b: Regina, Sask., 12/8/1939

Season	Club, League	Regular Season					Playoffs				
		GP	G	A	Pts	PIM	GP	G	A	Pts	PIM
1958–59	Belleville McFarlands, EOHL	1	2	1	3	2					
WEC–59	Canada	8	9	4	13	*					
1959–60	University of Michigan, CCHA	*	12	7	19	12					
1960–61	University of Michigan, CCHA	*	24	25	49	*					
1961–62	University of Michigan, CCHA	*	43	29	72	40					
	Montreal Canadiens, NHL	4	1	2	3	4	5	2	0	2	0
1962–63	Montreal Canadiens, NHL	37	2	6	8	15	5	0	0	0	0
	Hull-Ottawa Canadiens, EPHL	30	23	25	48	28					
1963–64	Montreal Canadiens, NHL	69	7	9	16	12	7	0	0	0	4
1964–65	Montreal Canadiens, NHL	3	1	2	3	0	9	0	1	1	2
	Quebec Aces, AHL	65	22	34	56	16	5	1	2	3	8
1965–66	Montreal Canadiens, NHL	23	3	4	7	12					
	Quebec Aces, AHL	34	17	36	53	14	6	1	5	6	2
1966–67	New York Rangers, NHL	30	0	5	5	2	4	0	1	1	2
1967–68	New York Rangers, NHL	19	2	1	3	2					
	St. Louis Blues, NHL	55	22	29	51	22	18	5	2	7	9
1968–69	St. Louis Blues, NHL	76	35	47	82	43	12	7	3	10	20
1969–70	St. Louis Blues, NHL	67	33	39	72	38	16	7	5	12	8
1970–71	St. Louis Blues, NHL	45	16	26	42	12					
	Detroit Red Wings, NHL	24	5	12	17	4					
1971–72	Detroit Red Wings, NHL	78	28	41	69	16					
SS–72	Canada	2	0	1	1	0					
1972–73	Detroit Red Wings, NHL	78	13	30	43	8					
1973–74	Detroit Red Wings, NHL	76	24	42	66	28					
1974–75	Detroit Red Wings, NHL	27	3	3	6	8					
	St. Louis Blues, NHL	44	12	19	31	12	2	1	0	1	0
1975–76	St. Louis Blues, NHL	72	20	27	47	47	3	1	2	3	0
1976–77	St. Louis Blues, NHL	80	21	28	49	8	4	0	0	0	4
1977–78	St. Louis Blues, NHL	80	13	25	38	12					
	WEC/SS Totals	10	9	5	14	*					
	NHL Totals	987	261	397	658	305	85	23	14	37	49

Won WEC (1959)
Won Stanley Cup (1965)

Berenson enjoyed a solid career and played two games for Canada during the 1972 Summit Series against the Soviet Union. Four years after trading him, St. Louis reacquired Berenson to anchor their checking line. He filled that role well and recorded two 20-goal seasons. He retired in 1978 with 658 career points.

Following his playing career, Berenson became a coach. He served as assistant for the St. Louis Blues for 18 months and was then named head bench boss on December 8, 1979. The high point in his NHL coaching tenure was a team record of 107 points in 1980–81, which garnered him the Jack Adams Award. His selection was the first unanimous vote in the history of the award as the Blues finished second only to the New York Islanders in the NHL's overall standings. Unfortunately, the Blues were upset in the quarterfinals by the New York Rangers in a tough six-game series. They were never able to build on the promise of that great season. Berenson paid the price when he was fired in 1982 after the club accumulated 27 fewer points and was bounced in the opening round of the playoffs. A few months later, he joined the Buffalo Sabres as an assistant under his old St. Louis coach, Scotty Bowman. This arrangement worked well until Berenson received an irresistible opportunity to coach at his alma mater in Michigan.

After leaving the NHL, Berenson became one of the NCAA's most successful bench bosses. The eighth coach in the history of the Wolverines led the school to the national championship in 1996, its first since 1964. He helped develop such notable NHL skaters as Brendan Morrison and Bill Muckalt. Over the years, Berenson has been in demand on the public speaking circuit and has operated a traveling hockey school across North America. Among his accolades was placement in the University of Michigan Hall of Honor and the Michigan Sports Hall of Fame.

Stan Mikita

One of the cleverest and most successful forwards in league history, right winger Stan "Stosh" Mikita won awards in numbers not seen again until Wayne Gretzky arrived in the NHL. A slick playmaker with a gifted scoring touch, Mikita had a career that spanned four decades, from the late 1950s until 1980. His longevity and consistency were nearly as impressive as his raw talent and left him near the top of a number of NHL categories when he retired after 22 seasons.

Although he didn't possess blinding speed, Mikita was adept at finding holes or weaknesses in opposition defense. His perseverance on the ice helped him outplay his talented foes on a regular basis. Former teammate Glenn Hall noted how he was able to change his plan in mid-stride or partway through a shot to confound the opposition.

Born Stanislaus Guoth in Sokolce, Czechoslovakia, Mikita emigrated to Canada in 1948 as an eight-year-old with his aunt and uncle and took their family name of Mikita. They settled in St. Catharines, south of Toronto on Lake Ontario. Adjusting to his new surroundings was a difficult experience. "I didn't know the language. When you don't understand something, you always think that people are talking about you. I thought they might have been making fun of me, which at times they might have been." Despite the rough start in his adopted home, Mikita looked back on the fact that it was quite unlike his place of birth. "I liked the idea of being able to do whatever you wanted without somebody looking over your shoulder, because of the way it was with the communist rule."

He learned to play hockey in the Niagara Peninsula and quickly became known locally as a note-worthy talent. "The way it all started was that some kids were playing road hockey in front of the house. That's how I got into the game. I'd just look at them from inside the house through the curtains, then from the porch for a couple of days, and finally from the sidewalk. Eventually they said, 'Why don't you come and join us?' and that probably took a good week."

The Chicago Black Hawks moved quickly to sign the promising youngster and put him on their top junior affiliate, the St. Catharines Teepees, in 1956–57. He responded with 47 points as an OHA rookie. During his last season as an amateur, he led the OHA with 59 assists and 97 points.

Mikita earned a three-game tryout with an NHL club in 1958–59. Former Hawks coach Billy Reay recalled: "We were playing the Canadiens, and about two minutes before the end of the second period I told him, 'You look after yourself there,' and I sent him out to face off against Beliveau. Beliveau was more mesmerized, 'Who in the hell's this kid!' They dropped the puck and he grabbed it and damn near scored. So that was his first effort in the National Hockey League."

The youngster competed well in his first full NHL season in 1959–60, scoring 26 points. Along with Bobby Hull, Mikita provided the impetus for the on-ice improvement of a Hawks franchise that had been dismal for many years and lost a host of supporters. During his sophomore season in 1960–61, he more than doubled his point total to 53. In the post-season, he led all goal scorers with six and was a key reason behind the franchise's first Stanley Cup win since 1938.

Mikita was as tough as he was instinctive on the ice. Hall of Fame defenseman Bill Gadsby recalled: "I'd hit him some nights and he'd have to crawl to the bench. But he'd always be back for the next shift. He had a lot of guts."

A slick playmaker with a gift for scoring, Stan Mikita played in four decades.

By 1961–62, Mikita was in the upper echelon of NHL skaters and was teamed by coach Rudy Pilous with Ken Wharram and Ab McDonald on the original Scooter Line. That year he scored 77 points and was voted onto the NHL First All-Star Team. Although the Hawks failed to repeat as Cup champs when Toronto beat them in the finals, Mikita enjoyed an outstanding post-season with 21 points in 12 games. In 1963–64, he won his first Art Ross Trophy with 89 points and duplicated the feat the next year with 87 points. By this time, Doug Mohns had replaced McDonald on the Scooter Line and helped the unit attain even greater heights. In 1964–65, the team also reached its third Stanley Cup finals of the decade but lost to the Montreal Canadiens.

The scoring exploits of Stosh reached new heights in 1966–67, when he won the Art Ross Trophy after scoring a personal best of 97 points. In addition, he was presented the Hart and Lady Byng trophies. The latter of these two awards is of interest since it was the culmination of a dramatic change in Mikita's style of play.

During his first seven NHL seasons, he was considered a "chippy" player. Mikita's habit of winding up in the penalty box frustrated his coaches, who preferred to see his immense talent remain on the ice. He recorded more than 100 penalty minutes four times and seemed far from ever winning the Lady Byng Trophy. But after his daughter questioned his style of play, Mikita vowed to clean up his act and did just that by registering only six minor penalties in 1966–67. Consequently, he became the first player in NHL history to win the Art Ross, Hart and Lady Byng trophies in the same season. As Mikita himself said, "If a two-year-old can see there's something wrong about it, why can't a 26-year-old find out why he has to be in that box all the time?" He also quipped, "Bobby Hull got more endorsements with his golden smile than I did with nastiness, so I tried it the other way."

Mikita enjoyed another stellar year in 1967–68 and repeated his unprecedented trophy haul. During the late 1960s, he continued to work well with Mohns and with Wharram before Wharram suffered a career-ending heart attack prior to the 1969–70 season. A serious back injury midway through the 1968–69 season hampered Mikita's play to varying extents through the remainder of his career. In 1970–71, he scored 18 points in as many games while helping the Hawks reach the finals for the first time in six years. There they lost in a tough seven-game series to the Montreal Canadiens.

Another strength of Mikita's game was the positive effect he had on less talented or experienced linemates. Following the untimely loss of winger Ken Wharram in 1969, Stosh helped young Cliff Koroll step into the Hawks lineup straight out of college. "With Mikita's help, I believe I have developed into a pretty fair winger," Koroll said. "I don't believe I would have adjusted those first two years except for Mikita."

Mikita's exploits in the NHL didn't go unnoticed in his country of birth. He played a solid role on Team Canada when they defeated the Soviets in the unforgettable Summit Series in September 1972. The day after the dramatic win in Moscow, the Canadians arrived in Prague to fulfill a commitment to play the Czech national team. While most of the Canadians were exhausted after a long series and the post-victory celebrations, this exhibition game marked an emotional homecoming for Mikita. The tied score was immaterial when compared to the welcome given the Canadian hero during the player introductions and on the streets of the Czech capital city.

The Hawks and Mikita enjoyed a fine season in 1972–73. He scored 83 points despite missing a quarter of the season through injury and the team reached the Stanley Cup finals, where they lost again to the Habs. After this season, the team remained competitive but was never again a Stanley Cup threat.

After suffering a concussion, Mikita designed a helmet according to his own specifications to protect his head. This turned into a lucrative business, as the "Stan Mikita style" of helmet became increasingly popular in the amateur and pro ranks during the 1970s.

Mikita remained an excellent playmaker, penalty killer and team leader through the remainder of the decade. He played alongside the likes of John Marks, Dennis Hull and Jean-Paul Bordeleau, but the team gradually declined. Aging stars such as Mikita, Tony Esposito, Dennis Hull and Pit Martin weren't replaced, not to mention the loss of Bobby Hull to the WHA. Mikita summed up the latter half

Mikita, Stan (Stanislaus Guoth)
RW, 5′9″, 169 lbs, b: Sokolce, Czechoslovakia, 5/20/1940

Season	Club, League	Regular Season					Playoffs				
		GP	G	A	Pts	PIM	GP	G	A	Pts	PIM
1958–59	Chicago Black Hawks, NHL	3	0	1	1	4					
1959–60	Chicago Black Hawks, NHL	67	8	18	26	119	3	0	1	1	2
1960–61	Chicago Black Hawks, NHL	66	19	34	53	100	12	6	5	11	21
1961–62	Chicago Black Hawks, NHL	70	25	52	77	97	12	6	15	21	19
1962–63	Chicago Black Hawks, NHL	65	31	45	76	69	6	3	2	5	2
1963–64	Chicago Black Hawks, NHL	70	29	50	89	146	7	3	6	9	8
1964–65	Chicago Black Hawks, NHL	70	28	59	87	154	14	3	7	10	53
1965–66	Chicago Black Hawks, NHL	68	30	48	78	58	6	1	2	3	2
1966–67	Chicago Black Hawks, NHL	70	35	62	97	12	6	2	2	4	2
1967–68	Chicago Black Hawks, NHL	72	40	47	87	14	11	5	7	12	6
1968–69	Chicago Black Hawks, NHL	74	30	67	97	52					
1969–70	Chicago Black Hawks, NHL	76	39	47	86	50	8	4	6	10	2
1970–71	Chicago Black Hawks, NHL	74	24	48	72	85	18	5	13	18	16
1971–72	Chicago Black Hawks, NHL	74	26	39	65	46	8	3	1	4	4
SS–72	Canada	2	0	1	1	0					
1972–73	Chicago Black Hawks, NHL	57	27	56	83	32	15	7	13	20	8
1973–74	Chicago Black Hawks, NHL	76	30	50	80	46	11	5	6	11	8
1974–75	Chicago Black Hawks, NHL	79	36	50	86	48	8	3	4	7	12
1975–76	Chicago Black Hawks, NHL	48	16	41	57	37	4	0	0	0	4
1976–77	Chicago Black Hawks, NHL	57	19	30	49	20	2	0	1	1	0
1977–78	Chicago Black Hawks, NHL	76	18	41	59	35	4	3	0	3	0
1978–79	Chicago Black Hawks, NHL	65	19	36	55	34					
1979–80	Chicago Black Hawks, NHL	17	2	5	7	12					
	NHL Totals	1394	531	926	1467	1270	155	59	91	150	169
	SS Totals	2	0	1	1	0					

NHL First All-Star Team (1962, 1963, 1964, 1966, 1967, 1968)
NHL Second All-Star Team (1965, 1970)
Won Hart Trophy (1967, 1968)
Won Art Ross Trophy (1964, 1965, 1967, 1968)
Won Lady Byng Trophy (1967, 1968)
Won Lester Patrick Trophy (1976)
Won Stanley Cup (1961)

of the 1970s: "For the last five years, I haven't been as productive goal-wise and there are times that I wonder if I'm still useful. Sure, my confidence goes a little, and instead of letting it happen naturally, I'll think about it and wind up messing up a shot."

Mikita's contribution to the Hawks and the betterment of hockey in the United States was recognized when he received the Lester Patrick Trophy in 1976. Mikita continued to work hard on behalf of the Hawks and served as interim captain twice before retiring in 1979–80. Veteran NHL coach Tom McVie remembered: "In my three years at Washington, he was the guy who killed us the most. More than Guy Lafleur, more than Bryan Trottier, more than any other player. It just seemed like he never lost a face-off. And he constantly was setting up people."

The skillful forward left the NHL as one of most popular stars and all-time leading scorers with 541 goals and nearly 1,500 points. Former Chicago coach Billy Reay once said, "He does more with everything he's got than any player I've ever seen." Further evidence of his consistency was the 14 consecutive 20-goal seasons between 1961 and 1975.

Mikita was inducted into the Hockey Hall of Fame in 1983 along with former teammate Bobby Hull. Mikita was stunned and said: "It took me completely by surprise. I thought you had to wait five years, and I've only been retired three years. Our old teammate Billy Hay is on the selection committee. He called me early this morning and told me I was going to be voted in. But Billy kids a lot. I didn't know if I should take him seriously until I asked, 'Who else got in?' and he said, 'Bobby, and Ken Dryden.' Then I knew he wasn't kidding."

After retiring as a player, Mikita embarked on a fruitful business career based in the Chicago area. He worked a number of years in the golf business before joining forces with former teammate Glen Skov as a sales representative for manufacturers in the plastics industry. Mikita also continued to make public appearances on behalf of the Hockey Hall of Fame, where he was consistently one of the most popular figures. The former star also founded a hockey school for the deaf in Northbrook, Illinois, which attracted kids from all over the United States. Among the instructors hired by Mikita was NHL defenseman Jim Kyte, who made it into the NHL despite a hearing disability. Mikita was also an active member in the Chicago Black Hawks Alumni Association.

In 1966–67, Stan Mikita (number 21) became the first player in NHL history to win the Ross, Hart and Lady Byng trophies in the same season.

Yevgeny **Mishakov**

"The playing fury and fighting spirit of this normally reserved person are really astounding," the great goalkeeper Vladislav Tretiak once said about Yevgeny Mishakov. "In workouts he's possessed and in games he can, if need be, spend five and even 10 shifts on the ice without substitutions. And when he is replaced by another player, he'll sit on the bench as if nothing has happened, wink at one guy, nudge another in the ribs as though he has just had a good rest."

On the hockey rink, Mishakov was a natural. He delighted in his role on the ice like an actor on stage, always anxious to escape the humdrum of Soviet life. Mishakov was one of those players marked by an unbridled spirit.

Yevgeny Mishakov was always in a good mood and excellent shape.

A compact, somewhat clumsy fellow with rugged features, Mishakov fitted well in the kind of hockey favored by Anatoli Tarasov. Teammates Veniamin Alexandrov, Anatoli Firsov, Valeri Kharlamov, Vladimir Vikulov, Alexander Maltsev and Alexander Yakushev sometimes felt out of place on the ice next to this hockey "grunt." It was very rare that Tarasov gave his best players a chance to play together with Mishakov.

The expression "checking line" has long been included in the NHL vocabulary. In the 1960s, when the refined skills of European forwards were in greater demand than sheer energy and athletic power, Tarasov introduced a special division to the Central Red Army. He called this unit "the System." This line of forwards included Yuri Moiseyev and Anatoli Ionov as well as Mishakov. Compared to their teammates in Army and on the national team, they were average players. They had to skate three times as fast and maneuver more to score a goal than the forwards in Firsov's line, for example. Scoring, for them, was the culmination of a lot of hard work. They were often given the job of checking the top players on the opposing team, and they performed this task rigorously. The only thing they didn't do was follow them into their locker room.

Mishakov appeared only once at the 1968 Olympics as part of the System. Later on, more skilled players were added to the line. Mishakov could always be depended on to be ready and raring to go, and this suited Tarasov perfectly. He remained on the national team roster for another five years after the 1968 tournament, often playing as a substitute for someone from the Army line or on a special assignment to wake up the "lazy" Spartak line.

Vyacheslav Starshinov once said, "I don't know where and why he is running all the time." At times Mishakov seemed to be from another planet. But compared to many first-class players, he was always in excellent shape and in a good mood. Nothing ever bothered him on the ice.

In his time, Mishakov was never considered a hero by sportswriters, and Tarasov usually favored other players as models of excellence in hockey. Mishakov seemed to exemplify perpetual motion and tireless effort. When some of the younger players couldn't stand up to the rigorous training standards and protested, Tarasov would point to Mishakov as an example of energy and perseverance, leaving the rookies without a reply.

After the 1972 Olympic hockey tournament, it was learned that coaches Arkady Chernyshev and Tarasov had received instructions from high up to tie the last game with the Czechs so that they'd take second place ahead of Team USA. The Soviet team, led by their coaches, ignored these instructions and won the game 5–2. The fourth and fifth goals were scored by one of Tarasov's most loyal players, Yevgeny Mishakov.

Mishakov, Yevgeny
C, 5'8", 180 lbs, b: Moscow, USSR, 2/22/1941

Season	Club, League	Regular Season				
		GP	G	A	Pts	PIM
1959–62	Lokomotiv Moscow, USSR	*	*	*	*	*
1962–63	SKA MVO, USSR	*	*	*	*	*
1963–68	CSKA, USSR	*	*	*	*	*
OWG–68	USSR	7	4	1	5	2
1968–69	CSKA, USSR	*	*	*	*	*
WEC–69	USSR	9	4	3	7	4
1969–70	CSKA, USSR	*	*	*	*	*
WEC–70	USSR	7	6	2	8	4
1970–71	CSKA, USSR	*	*	*	*	*
WEC–71	USSR	6	6	1	7	2
1971–72	CSKA, USSR	*	*	*	*	*
OWG–72	USSR	4	2	1	3	2
WEC–72	USSR	2	1	1	2	0
SS–72	USSR	6	0	0	0	11
1972–73	CSKA, USSR	*	13	*	*	*
1973–74	CSKA, USSR	30	4	1	5	14
	USSR Totals	400	181	*	*	*
	OWG/WEC/SS Totals	41	23	9	32	25

Won OWG (1968, 1972)
Won WEC (1969, 1970, 1971)
USSR Champion (1964, 1965, 1966, 1968, 1970, 1971, 1972, 1973)

As a result, this Olympic tournament turned out to be Tarasov's last. The coach had given Mishakov, who was over 30, a long life in hockey. Mishakov could no longer make the main lineup with Red Army and never went to another Olympics. The new coach of the Soviet team, Vsevolod Bobrov, didn't neglect Mishakov, however, and included him on the roster for the next

Yevgeny Mishakov (center) was a key figure in Anatoli Tarasov's "System," the Soviet version of the checking line.

World Championship in 1972 and the Summit Series with Team Canada, putting his most energetic player on the ice whenever he was shorthanded.

Bill White

A relatively late bloomer, Bill White developed into one of the game's steadiest defensemen. Although he didn't play in the NHL until he was 28 years old, he enjoyed an exemplary 11-year career. While playing with the Chicago Black Hawks, he formed one of the top blue line tandems in the league with Pat Stapleton. He was an effective positional rearguard who didn't have to play rough to achieve his goals. An editorial in *Hockey News* said, "He isn't a heavy hitter, but he locks up attackers in his long arms, reaches out and lifts the puck from them and clears it by skating out with strong, sure strokes or by laying a perfect pass on a teammate's stick."

Bill White didn't play in the NHL until he was 28 years old.

A solid performer with the junior Toronto Marlboros from 1956 to 1960, White was a respected leader who served as team captain for part of his OHA tenure. He then went on to spend most of his first eight years as a pro in the AHL. He was developing in Rochester in preparation for a chance to play with the Maple Leafs when a trade sent him to "Eddie Shore's graveyard" in Springfield. Chicago tried to acquire the lanky defender but, as was his style, Shore demanded too much in return. In the meantime, White's mental toughness and defensive game were strengthened as he played under one of the strictest coaches in the history of the game. In May 1967 White finally caught a break when his rights were acquired by the expansion Los Angeles Kings. White went on to demonstrate the benefit of increased roster space for NHL-caliber players.

White scored 38 points in 74 games as a "rookie" in 1967–68 and helped solidify the club's blue line. Many felt he outplayed Calder Trophy winner Derek Sanderson, but the fact that he was 28 years old may have played a role in his not winning the top rookie honors. He played one more full season on the West Coast and led all West Division backliners with 28 assists. Then his career changed forever when he was involved in a multi-player trade with Chicago in February 1970. The Hawks were in the midst of jumping from last to first in the standings in one season and were assembling a top-flight defensive unit to play Billy Reay's style of hockey.

Bill White helped the Chicago Black Hawks reach the Stanley Cup finals in 1971 and 1973.

It was in the Windy City with defense partner Pat Stapleton that White found his niche as a pro. Playing superb defense and making smart offensive plays when called upon, White helped the Black Hawks reach the Stanley Cup finals in 1971 and 1973 and was placed on the NHL Second All-Star Team for three straight years from 1972 to 1974.

A high point in his career came when he played seven of the eight games for Canada in the 1972 Summit Series versus the USSR. White's only goal of the series was a crucial one that tied the score 3–3 in the second period of the eighth and deciding match. It was his textbook defense and ability to thwart opposition attacks without ending up in the penalty box that made White such an important member of the blue line corps. After the series, one of the Soviet coaches praised the effort of "that bald fellow" on defense. White's strong play didn't go undetected, as he won honors as co-player of the game for Canada following the seventh game of the series.

White remained a pillar on the Chicago defense after his long-time partner Stapleton joined the WHA in 1973. He often teamed effectively with Dick Redmond, who said playing with White was "like going to school for defensemen."

White's career was ended by an injury he suffered during the 1976 quarterfinals versus the Montreal Canadiens. While chasing a puck in the corner, Habs forwards Doug Jarvis and Bob Gainey converged on him, causing White to fall awkwardly into the boards. He was diagnosed with an injury to the cervical nerves route and wasn't able to gain full use of his right arm for months.

White stepped in to coach the Hawks during the last four months of the 1976–77 schedule after Billy Reay was fired. He spent the 1977–78 season relaxing and sorting out what the next step in his life would be. In 1978–79, he was hired to succeed George Armstrong as coach and Frank Bonello as general manager of the Toronto Marlboros of the OHA. A likable teammate in his playing days, the steady backliner proved to be a tough disciplinarian who quickly alienated many of his junior players. White once held a 3 a.m. practice after a dismal loss on the road. He was fired after one disappointing season behind the bench, but he remained in Toronto and embarked on a successful career in sales.

White, Bill
D, 6′2″, 195 lbs, b: Toronto, Ont., 8/26/1939

Season	Club, League	Regular Season					Playoffs				
		GP	G	A	Pts	PIM	GP	G	A	Pts	PIM
1959–60	Rochester Americans, AHL	1	0	0	0	0					
1960–61	Sudbury Wolves, EPHL	21	1	2	3	20					
	Rochester Americans, AHL	47	1	9	10	37					
1961–62	Rochester Americans, AHL	67	5	21	26	58	2	0	1	1	2
1962–63	Springfield Indians, AHL	69	8	38	46	38					
1963–64	Springfield Indians, AHL	72	7	31	38	76					
1964–65	Springfield Indians, AHL	71	7	31	38	66					
1965–66	Springfield Indians, AHL	68	5	14	19	42	6	0	2	2	6
1966–67	Springfield Indians, AHL	69	5	29	34	68					
1967–68	Los Angeles Kings, NHL	74	11	27	38	100	7	2	2	4	4
1968–69	Los Angeles Kings, NHL	75	5	28	33	38	11	1	4	5	8
1969–70	Los Angeles Kings, NHL	40	4	11	15	21					
	Chicago Black Hawks, NHL	21	0	5	5	18	8	1	2	3	8
1970–71	Chicago Black Hawks, NHL	67	4	21	25	64	18	1	4	5	20
1971–72	Chicago Black Hawks, NHL	76	7	22	29	58	8	0	3	3	6
SS–72	Canada	7	1	1	2	8					
1972–73	Chicago Black Hawks, NHL	72	9	38	47	80	16	1	6	7	10
1973–74	Chicago Black Hawks, NHL	69	5	31	36	52	11	1	7	8	14
1974–75	Chicago Black Hawks, NHL	51	4	23	27	20	8	0	3	3	4
1975–76	Chicago Black Hawks, NHL	59	1	9	10	44	4	0	1	1	2
	NHL Totals	604	50	215	265	495	91	7	32	39	76
	SS Totals	7	1	1	2	8					

NHL Second All-Star Team (1972, 1973, 1974)

Pat Stapleton

Pat "Whitey" Stapleton was a smart playmaking defenseman who could also take care of matters in his own end of the ice. He spent a decade in the NHL and five years in the WHA. A respected veteran, he appeared in both the 1972 and 1974 series against the USSR.

The Sarnia native played with the Sarnia Legionnaires Junior B club before spending two seasons with the Chicago-sponsored St. Catharines Teepees of the OHA. As a junior, he was often the smallest player on the ice. As writer Brian McFarlane quipped, "It was a fact of life that most big-league clubs were simply not interested in defensemen who might be confused with the team stick boy." After a solid year with the Sault Ste. Marie Thunderbirds of the Eastern Professional Hockey League, Stapleton was claimed by Boston in the Intra-League Draft in June 1961. The Bruins were a weak outfit at this time and were able to give Stapleton a fair 18-month trial before sending him to the minors.

Pat Stapleton appeared in both of the Canada–USSR series, in 1972 and 1974.

Stapleton played 90 games for the Bruins and then spent nearly three years in the minors. He excelled with the Portland Buckaroos of the WHL from 1963 to 1965, where he often played center. He scored 29 goals in 1963–64 from his pivot spot. In 1964–65, he returned to his normal position and won the Hal Laycoe Cup as top defenseman in the league. In addition, he was placed on the league's First All-Star Team. Stapleton credited Portland coach Hal Laycoe with instilling confidence in him and turning his career in a positive direction.

A successful 55-game showing for Chicago in 1965–66 earned him a permanent place in the league, but it only came about because of an injury to regular Elmer "Moose" Vasko forced Chicago to call Stapleton up from the minors. Stapleton was voted to the NHL Second All-Star Team in 1966 and duplicated this honor in 1971 and 1972. He played with the Hawks until the end of the 1972–73 season and helped the squad reach the Stanley Cup finals in 1971 and 1973. His quick hands and lightning reflexes, combined with a hard, accurate shot, made him one of the more effective point men in the NHL. Defensively, he was a master of the poke-check and was able to consistently steer opponents away from the goal.

Stapleton and defense partner Bill White developed into one of the NHL's elite tandems. They were the key to the Hawks winning four straight West Division crowns, and in the 1972 Summit Series against the USSR they were teamed in seven of the eight games. Stapleton

Stapleton, Pat
D, 5´8˝, 180 lbs, b: Sarnia, Ont., 7/4/1940

Season	Club, League	Regular Season					Playoffs				
		GP	G	A	Pts	PIM	GP	G	A	Pts	PIM
1959–60	Buffalo Bisons, AHL	1	0	0	0	2					
1960–61	Sault Ste. Marie Thunderbirds, EPHL	59	5	43	48	22	12	1	8	9	2
1961–62	Boston Bruins, NHL	69	2	5	7	42					
1962–63	Boston Bruins, NHL	21	0	3	3	8					
	Kingston Frontenacs, EPHL	49	10	26	36	92	5	4	2	6	12
1963–64	Portland Buckaroos, WHL	70	5	44	49	80	5	1	6	7	0
1964–65	Portland Buckaroos, WHL	70	29	57	86	61	10	3	4	7	16
1965–66	Chicago Black Hawks, NHL	55	4	30	34	52	6	2	3	5	4
	St. Louis Braves, CHL	14	2	4	6	6					
1966–67	Chicago Black Hawks, NHL	70	3	31	34	54	6	1	1	2	12
1967–68	Chicago Black Hawks, NHL	67	4	34	38	34	11	0	4	4	4
1968–69	Chicago Black Hawks, NHL	75	6	50	56	44					
1969–70	Chicago Black Hawks, NHL	49	4	38	42	28					
1970–71	Chicago Black Hawks, NHL	76	7	44	51	30	18	3	14	17	4
1971–72	Chicago Black Hawks, NHL	78	3	38	41	47	8	2	2	4	4
SS–72	Canada	7	0	0	0	6					
1972–73	Chicago Black Hawks, NHL	75	10	21	31	14	16	2	15	17	10
1973–74	Chicago Cougars, WHA	78	6	52	58	44	12	0	13	13	36
1974–75	Chicago Cougars, WHA	68	4	30	34	38					
1975–76	Indianapolis Racers, WHA	80	4	40	44	48	7	0	2	2	2
1976–77	Indianapolis Racers, WHA	81	8	45	53	29	9	2	6	8	0
1977–78	Cincinnati Stingers, WHA	65	4	45	49	28					
	NHL Totals	635	43	294	337	353	65	10	39	49	38
	WHA Totals	372	26	212	238	187	28	2	21	23	38
	SS Totals	7	0	0	0	6					

WHA First All-Star Team (1974)
NHL Second All-Star Team (1966, 1971, 1972)
WHA Second All-Star Team (1976)
Won Dennis A. Murphy Trophy — WHA Top Defenseman (1974)

was on the ice when Paul Henderson scored the dramatic series-winning goal with 34 seconds left in the third period. Amid all the celebrations, he grabbed the historic puck, a treasure he preserves at home to this day. Stapleton and White were also known for their pranks that helped keep the Chicago and Canada teams loose.

Pat Stapleton (secont from the left) and his defense partner, Bill White, developed into one of the NHL's elite tandems and were teamed in seven of the eight games in the Summit Series.

In December 1972 Chicago coach Billy Reay split up his All-Star defense tandem. Citing increased depth on the blue line, he decided that Stapleton's offensive creativity could be used on the third forward unit. He was placed at center for the first time since minor pro with such wingers as Chico Maki, Jerry Korab and J.P. Bordeleau.

Prior to the 1973–74 season, Stapleton signed with the Chicago Cougars of the WHA as player-coach. In his first year he scored 58 points in 78 games and won the Dennis A. Murphy Trophy as the league's top defenseman. He was also named to the WHA First All-Star Team. In a unique twist, he and teammates Dave Dryden, Ralph Backstrom and Rod Zaine bought the team to keep it going for the duration of the season. The club lasted one more year before folding, whereupon Stapleton joined the Indianapolis Racers.

His last pro season in 1975–76 proved very rewarding. In only its second year of operation, the Racers won the East Division championship of the WHA and came within one game of reaching the Avco Cup finals. The team started poorly but improved dramatically as Stapleton's influence on the younger players began to have an affect.

Before the start of the next season, he played in the 1974 series which pitted the USSR against the top Canadian players from the WHA. Before retiring from the game, Stapleton moved on to the Indianapolis Racers and the Cincinnati Stingers.

Whitey Stapleton left hockey in 1978 after scoring 337 points in the NHL and 238 in the WHA. He turned to working full-time on his farm in Strathroy, a small town in southwestern Ontario. Stapleton also stayed close to hockey by serving as an executive member of the Strathroy Rockets Junior B team. Under his management, the club won its first-ever junior B league championship in 1996–97. He also formed a company called Fundamentals In Action, which was designed to teach youngsters and adults to improve their everyday skills through the lessons they learned in hockey.

Rod *Gilbert*

Rod Gilbert was a consistent scorer during an excellent NHL career with the New York Rangers that lasted 18 seasons. He blossomed as the right winger on the famous G-A-G Line (Goal-A-Game) with Jean Ratelle and Vic Hadfield, and although he never played on a Cup champion, he was often at his best in the post-season.

The Montreal native excelled in a number of sports in his youth. He was brilliant on the ice but also gifted on the baseball diamond. His baseball potential brought an invitation from the Milwaukee

Braves to attend spring training, but he opted to pursue his ice hockey dream instead. An amateur scoring star with the OHA's Guelph Biltmore Mad Hatters, Gilbert came close to winning the scor-

ing title but lost the scoring crown to Chico Maki on the last day of the 1959–60 schedule. He won the title in 1960-61 with 103 points. Gilbert had just received word that he was an emergency call-up to the Rangers when disaster struck. In the last junior game of the year, he skated over some debris thrown on the ice that caused him to fall awkwardly into the boards. The impact resulted in a broken fifth vertebra in his back. To repair the damage, doctors removed bone from his left leg and used it to bind the fourth, fifth and sixth vertebrae together. Frightening complications arose in the aftermath of the procedure. Blood clots developed in the leg, which stunted the healing process in the original wound. Gilbert's condition deteriorated to the point that amputation became a possibility. Two weeks later, however, the leg began to heal and Gilbert was able to get his life back on course.

Rod Gilbert (center) was a deceptively fast skater who could elude the league's wiliest checkers.

On November 27, 1960, he made the most of a one-game call-up to the big leagues by assisting on Dean Prentice's third-period goal that gave New York a 3–3 tie with Chicago. Gilbert gained some professional seasoning with the Kitchener-Waterloo Beavers of the EPHL in 1961-62. Following an injury to Ken Schinkel, Gilbert was an emergency recall during the 1962 semifinal series against Toronto. He didn't look out of place and contributed five points in the four games he played with linemates Dave Balon and Johnny Wilson.

Gilbert finally made the team outright at training camp in 1962. He scored 31 points as a rookie, then registered his first of 12 20-goal seasons in his sophomore year. Gilbert was a deceptively fast skater with an ability to elude many of the league's wiliest checkers. He was blessed with a hard shot that often dipped and he didn't shy away from battling hard in the corners or in front of the opposition net.

Meanwhile, the surgery Gilbert underwent wasn't totally successful. The bone graft loosened over time and eventually disintegrated as a result of the bodily contact so common in hockey. Prior to his third season, it was discovered that the surgically repaired vertebrae were damaged and required further attention.

He tried to play the 1965–66 schedule by wearing a special custom-fitted brace, but the extra equipment affected his breathing and, to some extent, his stamina. In January 1966 he was forced to abandon the season and undergo an operation to save his career. Gilbert came through the surgery and rehabilitation well and scored 28 goals the next year when he led the Rangers into the playoffs for the first time in four years. He was inspired by new teammate Bernie Geoffrion, who came out of retirement in time for the start of the 1966–67 schedule. Gilbert commented on Boom Boom: "He was older than anybody in camp, but he never loafed, never relaxed. I said to myself, 'If he can put out that way at his age, I can give a little extra too.'" In 1967–68, the Rangers finished second in the East Division standings and Gilbert recorded the fifth-highest point total in the NHL.

In the 1971–72 season, Rod Gilbert (number 7) set personal records with 43 goals and 97 points and helped the New York Rangers reach the Stanley Cup finals.

It was in 1970–71 that he began playing with Ratelle and Hadfield. The line clicked and helped the Rangers set a franchise record of 109 points. The following season Gilbert set personal bests of 43 goals and 97 points and helped the team reach the Stanley Cup finals. The line made history by becoming the first on which all three members reached the 40-goal mark. Additionally, all three finished in the top five of the NHL's scoring race. Flying down the ice with elan and purpose, Gilbert caught the imagination of Manhattan's sporting public. His movie-star looks and love of the nightlife made Gilbert a natural fit in the Big Apple.

During the fall of 1972, Gilbert represented Canada in the Summit Series against the USSR. His desire to play for Canada was so great that he ignored the many overtures that were sent his way by teams in the newly founded World Hockey Association. Between 1972 and 1977, he scored at least 75 points six straight years, but the Rangers never made it past the semifinals. On March 24, 1974, his goal against Dave Dryden of the Buffalo Sabres made him the first 300-goal scorer in the history of the New York Rangers. In 1976 Gilbert was presented the Bill Masterton Memorial Trophy as a tribute to his dedication on and off the ice.

On December 12, 1976, he celebrated his 1,000th game by setting up three New York goals in a 5–2 home-ice win over the Stanley Cup champion Canadiens. Gilbert was also on hand when professionals were allowed to take part in the 1977 World Championship. He and linemates Walt McKechnie and Guy Charron helped Canada finish fourth in the historic competition. Before the start of the 1977–78 season, Gilbert was engaged in difficult contract negotiations with Rangers general manager John Ferguson. Following a 15-day holdout, Gilbert never really got going and only lasted 19 games before retiring. His output totaled 406 goals and 1,021 points along with a host of New York scoring records.

After retiring, Gilbert remained visible to fans by working for two years in the Rangers front office. Later he tried his hand at being a television commentator on Rangers broadcasts. Gilbert's Manhattan restaurant, Cafe de Sports, became a popular spot for hockey fans. And he came back to the Rangers as the community relations representative and director of special projects. The classy winger was inducted into the Hockey Hall of Fame in 1982.

Gilbert, Rod
RW, 5′9″, 180 lbs, b: Montreal, Que., 7/1/1941

Season	Club, League	Regular Season					Playoffs				
		GP	G	A	Pts	PIM	GP	G	A	Pts	PIM
1959–60	Trois Rivieres Lions, EPHL	3	4	6	10	0	5	2	2	4	2
1960–61	New York Rangers, NHL	1	0	1	1	2					
1961–62	New York Rangers, NHL	1	0	0	0	0	4	2	3	5	4
	Kitchener-Waterloo Beavers, EPHL	21	12	11	23	22	4	0	0	0	4
1962–63	New York Rangers, NHL	70	11	20	31	20					
1963–64	New York Rangers, NHL	70	24	40	64	62					
1964–65	New York Rangers, NHL	70	25	36	61	52					
1965–66	New York Rangers, NHL	34	10	15	25	20					
1966–67	New York Rangers, NHL	64	28	18	46	12	4	2	2	4	6
1967–68	New York Rangers, NHL	73	29	48	77	12	6	5	0	5	4
1968–69	New York Rangers, NHL	66	28	49	77	22	4	1	0	1	2
1969–70	New York Rangers, NHL	72	16	37	53	22	6	4	5	9	0
1970–71	New York Rangers, NHL	78	30	31	61	65	13	4	6	10	8
1971–72	New York Rangers, NHL	73	43	54	97	64	16	7	8	15	11
SS–72	Canada	6	1	3	4	9					
1972–73	New York Rangers, NHL	76	25	59	84	25	10	5	1	6	2
1973–74	New York Rangers, NHL	75	36	41	77	20	13	3	5	8	4
1974–75	New York Rangers, NHL	76	36	61	97	22	3	1	3	4	2
1975–76	New York Rangers, NHL	70	36	50	86	32					
1976–77	New York Rangers, NHL	77	27	48	75	50					
WEC–77	Canada	9	2	2	4	12					
1977–78	New York Rangers, NHL	19	2	7	9	6					
	NHL Totals	1065	406	615	1021	508	79	34	33	67	43
	WEC/SS Totals	15	3	5	8	21					

NHL First All-Star Team (1972)
NHL Second All-Star Team (1968)
Won Bill Masterton Trophy (1976)
Won Lester Patrick Trophy (1991)

Jean Ratelle

A talented center who exhibited class and style throughout his career, Jean Ratelle spent two decades in the NHL with the New York Rangers and the Boston Bruins. He was one of the most gifted and respected players of his era but had the misfortune of never playing in a Stanley Cup championship. His superior wrist shot and effective deke made him one of the most dangerous forwards in the NHL. A soft-spoken family man, Ratelle made many friends and no enemies during his stellar pro career.

Ratelle hailed from Lac Ste. Jean, a small town in Quebec more than 300 miles north of Montreal. He starred with the Guelph Biltmore juniors, where he accumulated 139 points in three seasons. Toward the end of the 1959–60 season, he played his first three pro games with the Trois-Rivieres Lions of the Eastern Professional Hockey League and racked up eight points. The promising forward was sent back to Guelph for another year of junior. Ratelle was the top player on the renamed Royals and led the OHA with 61 assists.

Ratelle split the 1961–62 schedule between the Kitchener-Waterloo Beavers of the EPHL and the New York Rangers. He was forced to work on his game while spending much of the next two seasons with the American Hockey League's Baltimore Clippers. In 1963–64, a serious back injury resulted in a spinal fusion operation and the subsequent rehabilitation was painful and time-consuming. Ironically, it was his old friend and future linemate Rod Gilbert who also dealt with a serious back injury early in his career.

Ratelle gained a regular place in the New York lineup in 1964–65. The next year another back injury slowed his progress even though the team's fortunes were on the upswing. Initially Ratelle was placed on the third line but at the insistence of Rod Gilbert was reunited with his junior colleague with great success. By 1967–68, he was a star in the league and recorded his first of eight 30-goal seasons. He gained much fame as the pivot on the famous G-A-G (Goal-A-Game) Line with Gilbert and Vic Hadfield in the early 1970s.

A model performer along the lines of Jean Beliveau, Ratelle was awarded the Bill Masterton Memorial Trophy in 1971. The 1971–72 season represented the high point of Ratelle's career. He established his personal high of 46

Jean Ratelle scored at least 70 points a season 12 times in his career.

Ratelle, Jean
C, 6´1˝, 180 lbs, b: Lac Ste. Jean, Que., 10/3/1940

Season	Club, League	Regular Season					Playoffs				
		GP	G	A	Pts	PIM	GP	G	A	Pts	PIM
1959–60	Trois-Rivieres Lions, EPHL	3	3	5	8	0	4	0	3	3	0
1960–61	New York Rangers, NHL	3	2	1	3	0					
1961–62	New York Rangers, NHL	31	4	8	12	4					
	Kitchener-Waterloo Beavers, EPHL	32	10	29	39	8	7	2	6	8	2
1962–63	New York Rangers, NHL	48	11	9	20	8					
	Baltimore Clippers, AHL	20	11	8	19	0	3	0	0	0	0
1963–64	New York Rangers, NHL	15	0	7	7	6					
	Baltimore Clippers, AHL	57	20	26	46	2					
1964–65	New York Rangers, NHL	54	14	21	35	14					
	Baltimore Clippers, AHL	8	9	4	13	6					
1965–66	New York Rangers, NHL	67	21	30	51	10					
1966–67	New York Rangers, NHL	41	6	5	11	4	4	0	0	0	2
1967–68	New York Rangers, NHL	74	32	46	78	18	6	0	4	4	2
1968–69	New York Rangers, NHL	75	32	46	78	26	4	1	0	1	0
1969–70	New York Rangers, NHL	75	32	42	74	28	6	1	3	4	0
1970–71	New York Rangers, NHL	78	26	46	72	14	13	2	9	11	8
1971–72	New York Rangers, NHL	63	46	63	109	4	6	0	1	1	0
SS–72	Canada	6	1	3	4	0					
1972–73	New York Rangers, NHL	78	41	53	94	12	10	2	7	9	0
1973–74	New York Rangers, NHL	68	28	39	67	16	13	2	4	6	0
1974–75	New York Rangers, NHL	79	36	55	91	26	3	1	5	6	2
1975–76	New York Rangers, NHL	13	5	10	15	2					
	Boston Bruins, NHL	67	31	59	90	16	12	8	8	16	4
1976–77	Boston Bruins, NHL	78	33	61	94	22	14	5	12	17	4
1977–78	Boston Bruins, NHL	80	25	59	84	10	15	3	7	10	0
1978–79	Boston Bruins, NHL	80	27	45	72	12	11	7	6	13	2
1979–80	Boston Bruins, NHL	67	28	45	73	8	3	0	0	0	0
1980–81	Boston Bruins, NHL	47	11	26	37	16	3	0	0	0	0
	NHL Totals	1281	491	776	1267	276	123	32	66	98	24
	SS Totals	6	1	3	4	0					

NHL Second All-Star Team (1972)
Won Bill Masterton Trophy (1971)
Won Lady Byng Trophy (1972, 1976)
Won Lester B. Pearson Award (1972)

goals and 109 points and was the recipient of the Lady Byng Trophy and the Lester B. Pearson Award as the top player in the NHL as chosen by his peers.

Each member of the potent trio finished in the top five of the league's regular-season scoring list, though a broken ankle suffered in March cost Ratelle a chance at the scoring title and limited his effectiveness in the playoffs. Even though the Rangers made it all the way to the finals, they might have fared better against Boston with a healthy Ratelle.

Jean Ratelle's (center) superior wrist shot made him one of the most dangerous forwards in the NHL.

Later that year, the classy forward was an important component of Team Canada when it defeated the USSR in the 1972 Summit Series. He scored four points in six matches while playing chiefly a defensive role, and his overall skill and calm temperament impressed the Soviet players and coaching staff.

During the 1975–76 season, Ratelle was involved in arguably the biggest trade of the decade when he was packaged to Boston along with defenseman Brad Park and defenseman Joe Zanuzzi in return for Phil Esposito and Carol Vadnais. Ratelle performed admirably with Bruins coach Don Cherry's Lunch Bucket Crew as he topped the 70-point mark five straight years. In 1976 he was presented the Lady Byng Trophy for the second time.

The running joke was that Ratelle was forced to apologize to coach Don Cherry after receiving this honor. The coach couldn't have been more pleased with his superb two-way play and on-ice leadership. In fact, Ratelle thrived following the trade from Manhattan with 90 points in 67 games as a Bruin and his continuing excellence helped Boston reach consecutive Stanley Cup finals in 1977 and 1978. He was often joined by Rick Middleton and Stan Jonathan on one of hockey's hardest-working lines.

On March 21, 1977, Ratelle played his 1,000th regular-season game against the Montreal Canadiens in front of an appreciative Boston Garden crowd. Twelve times in his career the classy veteran scored at least 70 points in a season. He retired in 1980–81 with 491 goals and 1,267 points, an output that placed him sixth on the NHL's all-time points list at the time. He was inducted into the Hockey Hall of Fame in 1985.

Phil Esposito

He was the centerman who held the greatest scoring record of them all before Wayne Gretzky came along and broke it—76 goals in a single season in 1970–71. Espo won the Art Ross Trophy five times, the Hart Trophy twice, the Lester B. Pearson Award twice and the Lester Patrick Trophy for service to hockey in the United States. What's more, he was a 10-time All-Star and represented Canada in the 1972 Summit Series, the 1976 Canada Cup and the 1977 World Championship.

While a member of the Boston Bruins, he scored 40 or more goals in seven straight seasons and 50 or more in five straight seasons. In his 76-goal season, he also recorded an amazing 76 assists for a league record at the time of 152 points.

Phil Esposito grew up in Sault Ste. Marie, Ontario, and must have had plenty of target practice against his younger brother Tony, who went on to become one of the game's great goalies. Unbelievably, Phil had a hard time at first even breaking into the NHL. He played for the St. Louis Braves in the Central Hockey League and EPHL from 1962 until 1964. In his first year with the Braves, he scored 90 points in just 71 games and waited expectantly to be called up by the Chicago Black Hawks, the team that owned his rights. But the Hawks kept him waiting and he responded by recording another 80 points in just 43 games in his second year with the Braves before finally getting the call to the Hawks.

"Happy Worrier"
Phil Esposito.

"There were times when I almost quit," Esposito said of the period he spent waiting for the summons to the NHL. "I went home and drove a truck for my dad. But that didn't work. Believe me, playing hockey beats driving a truck any day!" Once he was in the NHL, Espo "decided to give it everything I had." He scored 23, 27 and 21 goals in his first three full seasons in the Windy City, and fans of the team noted he was often in on key scoring situations with linemate Bobby Hull.

But Esposito never felt that Hawks coach Billy Reay had very much confidence in him. Sure enough, he was shipped to the Boston Bruins for the 1967–68 season—a move that set in motion one of the strangest television trade announcements in hockey history. Viewers of CJIC-TV in Sault Ste. Marie were amazed to see Phil on the screen announcing: "Hi, sports fans. Yours truly has just been traded to Boston with Ken Hodge and Fred Stanfield for Gilles Marotte, Pit Martin and Jack Norris. This is no hoax!"

Esposito laughed when he remembered the incident, but he was a lot more somber about how he learned about the trade and what he thought it was going to mean for his hockey future. "I got a call from my wife. She told me the Black Hawks press guy had phoned and told her I was traded to Boston. It wasn't the coach or the general manager, just the press guy. When I got off the phone, I was white," recalled Phil. "I remember thinking at the time, 'Jeez, there goes all that playoff money down the drain.' There were two teams I didn't want to play for—Boston and New York. I didn't like the idea of New York because of my wife and kids, and I didn't like Boston because they were always in last place. It just shows you how wrong a guy can be."

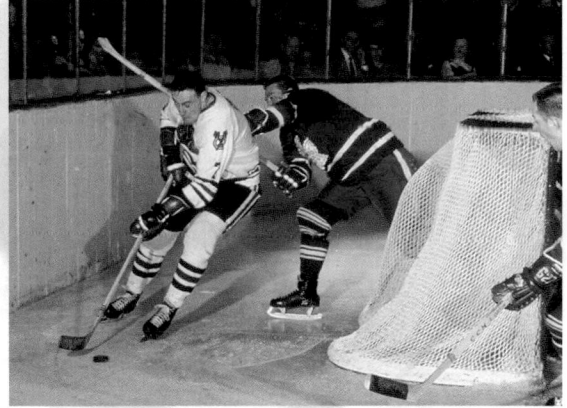

"There were two teams I didn't want to play for," Phil Esposito (left) once declared, "Boston and New York."

Esposito's fortune-telling abilities were, as he suggested, way off when it came to the Bruins' future. The Black Hawks thought they were unloading an unproven talent to the Boston club, but in fact the trade only went in favor of the Bruins. Over his career in Beantown, he joined up with greats Bobby Orr, Wayne Cashman, Ken Hodge and Gerry Cheevers on a powerhouse team that won two Stanley Cups in three years.

Critics said he was ungainly and only scored because of his size, but Esposito didn't care—scoring was scoring to him. His take on what the critics were saying? "I don't care any more how they describe my goals," he said. "I just want lots of them. I'm tall, I've got enough size that I can reach over a guy and still get off a shot. Size is number one. I haven't got a fast shot or a hard shot, but

Phil Esposito

I can put it where I want it, even when a defenseman is leaning on me and giving me the stick. I slap it, but not very often. I don't think I get too many goals with slapshots."

But not everyone thought that Esposito was a one-dimensional scoring machine. Bruins coach Tom Johnson was one of the advocates of the Phil-as-complete-player school of thought. "We've known all along—he's one of the better all-time centers I've ever seen," said Johnson. "Espie is a very strong skater. The reason he may not seem to be going so fast is his size." But Phil revealed that foot speed was something he had been forced to work on, especially under the tutelage of Hawks coach Billy Reay. "He had a special drill for Hodgie [Ken Hodge] and me, chasing Bobby Hull around the rink. That's bound to do something for your skating!"

While Espo was gaining a reputation among NHL coaches and fans as a goal scorer, his fellow players were also beginning to recognize that they were dealing with a real character and a practical joker in the dressing room and on road trips. He liked to smoke cigars, and one reporter, noting his constantly furrowed brow and droopy expression, started calling him "the Happy Worrier."

Besides these traits, teammates noticed that he was a player who stuck steadfastly to ritual. One night, when a sore throat caused him to put on a black turtleneck, he played especially well. From then on, the turtleneck became a regular part of his game-time garb. This was just one example of the quirky Esposito's adherence to game-day habits. "I never knew a guy to be so superstitious," revealed Derek Sanderson, who occupied a regular spot next to Phil in the Bruins dressing room. "He only wants me to be the guy who adjusts his pads and pulls down his sweater for him. And it has got to be done just right. When we were on a winning streak this winter, he wouldn't let me change the cotton in my shin pads as long as the streak lasted. By the time we finally lost a game, those pads wouldn't stop anything. But it seems to work for him."

On the international front, Phil starred for Team Canada in the classic Summit Series as the leading individual scorer—with seven goals and six assists—and inspirational leader of the team that defeated the Soviets in the best eight-game series ever played. He joined brother Tony, who was teaming with Ken Dryden as the Canadian netminder on the legendary team.

After the glory years in Boston, Esposito was traded to the New York Rangers early in the 1975–76 season and found life a lot different in the world's media capital. He had slowed down a step, and the critics were descending

Esposito, Phil
C, 6′1″, 205 lbs, b: Sault Ste.Marie, Ont., 2/20/1942

Season	Club, League	Regular Season					Playoffs				
		GP	G	A	Pts	PIM	GP	G	A	Pts	PIM
1961–62	Sault Ste. Marie Thunderbirds, EPHL	6	0	3	3	2					
1962–63	St. Louis Braves, EPHL	71	36	54	90	51					
1963–64	Chicago Black Hawks, NHL	27	3	2	5	2	4	0	0	0	0
	St. Louis Braves, CHL	43	26	54	80	65					
1964–65	Chicago Black Hawks, NHL	70	23	32	55	44	13	3	3	6	15
1965–66	Chicago Black Hawks, NHL	69	27	26	53	49	6	1	1	2	2
1966–67	Chicago Black Hawks, NHL	69	21	40	61	40	6	0	0	0	7
1967–68	Boston Bruins, NHL	74	35	49	84	21	4	0	3	3	0
1968–69	Boston Bruins, NHL	74	49	77	126	79	10	8	10	18	8
1969–70	Boston Bruins, NHL	76	43	56	99	50	14	13	14	27	16
1970–71	Boston Bruins, NHL	78	76	76	152	71	7	3	7	10	6
1971–72	Boston Bruins, NHL	76	66	67	133	76	15	9	15	24	24
SS–72	Canada	8	7	6	13	15					
1972–73	Boston Bruins, NHL	78	55	75	130	87	2	0	1	1	2
1973–74	Boston Bruins, NHL	78	68	77	145	58	16	9	5	14	25
1974–75	Boston Bruins, NHL	79	61	66	127	62	3	4	1	5	0
1975–76	Boston Bruins, NHL	12	6	10	16	8					
	New York Rangers, NHL	62	29	38	67	28					
CCup–76	Canada	7	4	3	7	0					
1976–77	New York Rangers, NHL	80	34	46	80	52					
WEC–77	Canada	10	7	3	10	14					
1977–78	New York Rangers, NHL	79	38	43	81	53	3	0	1	1	5
1978–79	New York Rangers, NHL	80	42	36	78	37	18	8	12	20	20
1979–80	New York Rangers, NHL	80	34	44	78	73	9	3	3	6	8
1980–81	New York Rangers, NHL	41	7	13	20	20					
	NHL Totals	1282	717	873	1590	910	130	61	76	137	138
	WEC/SS/CCup Totals	25	18	12	30	29					

NHL First All-Star Team (1969, 1970, 1971, 1972, 1973, 1974)
NHL Second All-Star Team (1968, 1975)
Won Hart Trophy (1969,1974)
Won Art Ross Trophy (1969, 1971, 1972, 1973, 1974)
Won Lester B. Pearson Award (1971, 1974)
Won Lester Patrick Trophy (1978)
Won Stanley Cup (1970, 1972)
Won CCup (1976)

Phil Esposito (center) starred in the classic Summit Series as Team Canada's inspirational leader and top scorer.

on him, perhaps because he had been such a brash character in his prime. "My life is different here than in Boston," he said. "I have a longer, harder drive to games. The games aren't as much fun. My legs aren't as strong. I get tired faster. I try to get by on my wits more. I'm tired of the travel. But I can still play the game and I like to play. I'm more of a loner. I'm not with old buddies here." There was always some lingering resentment in his mind that he'd been let go from the Bruins without a fair shake for all he'd given the club. "I gave them eight seasons of class and they don't have any," he complained. "At first I thought of not reporting to the Rangers, but then I decided, hell, I'll show them they made a mistake."

In 1981 Espo decided to hang up his skates after 6 seasons in New York. In an emotional night at Madison Square Garden, the Rangers retired his sweater and brought in a host of great players from the past and present to honor him. But perhaps the best tribute of all came from a Rangers rookie named Dave Silk. "I feel like I'm losing part of my family," he said. "He was my idol when I was growing up in Boston. I could probably describe more of his goals than he could." For his part, Espo felt he had given the game all he could. "I couldn't handle the pressure any more," he said. "It really affected me—I gave it all I had, but I had nothing more to give."

After retiring from the Rangers, Esposito became one of the team's assistant coaches and then moved on to a position as a TV analyst for the Madison Square Garden network. In 1986 he was named vice-president and general manager of the Rangers, a position he later accepted with the expansion Tampa Bay Lightning when that team entered the league.

Yvan **Cournoyer**

Scouts were all but unanimous in thinking Yvan Cournoyer was too small for the tough world of the NHL.

There are players who seem destined for greatness from early childhood, players with so much talent and promise that the only questions concern when they will play at the top level and how many records they'll break. Yvan Cournoyer represents the other kind of player, the juniors who are pegged as lacking one or more of the supposed ingredients for greatness. In Cournoyer's case, just about every coach and scout deemed that he was too small at 5'7" and 165 pounds, and it was assumed he would wilt in the tough world of the National Hockey League.

Cournoyer proved his detractors wrong with his electrifying speed, puckhandling savvy and quick shot. Nicknamed "the Roadrunner," he won 10 Stanley Cups with the Montreal Canadiens and was team captain from 1975 to 1978. By the time he retired, he was among the all-time leaders in scoring for the storied franchise and he and his team had proven many doubters wrong about his adaptability and perseverance.

Cournoyer was born in Drummondville, Quebec, in 1943. Like so many other Quebec youngsters, he idolized the Canadiens and dreamed about playing for Montreal. He set about making his dream a reality by working on his game year-round, even if he wasn't on the ice. "When I played other sports like baseball, football, track and basketball, it was because I wanted to stay in shape for hockey," he said. "When I delivered beer for Labatt for three summers, I knew it would make me strong for hockey. And as a child, I knew that by scraping the ice and pushing the snow it would give me strong legs."

By the time he was an 18-year-old star with the Montreal Junior Canadiens, Cournoyer's legs were so muscular that his pants had to be specially tailored to fit his legs. He constantly practised his shot using a lead puck that weighed more than four pounds and was soon known for his quick and heavy wrist shot. He totaled 111 points, leading the league with 63 goals in his final year with the Junior Canadiens. He made his debut with the big-time Canadiens during the 1963–64 season and earned a full-time spot on the roster the next season after only seven games with the Quebec Aces in the American Hockey League.

Though he had shown enough skill and speed to be used on the power-play, the Montreal coach, Toe Blake, deemed Cournoyer too much of a defensive liability to give him a regular shift. It would be that way for most of his first four seasons in the league, though Cournoyer was compensated with the Stanley Cup three times. When Blake left following the 1968 championship, Cournoyer became a better all-around player. With Claude Ruel behind the bench and Cournoyer

Yvan Cournoyer (right) had a career-high 47 goals in 1971–72 and added three more for Team Canada in the Summit Series.

taking a regular shift, the speedy winger blossomed, scoring 43 goals in 1968–69. He worked hard at both ends of the rink and earned a berth on the NHL's Second All-Star Team that season, as he would in three consecutive years beginning in 1971. Shortly after Scotty Bowman took over as coach in 1971, Cournoyer was placed on a line with Guy Lafleur at center and Steve Shutt on left wing. The Roadrunner had a career high of 47 goals in 1971–72 and was at the top of his game, stickhandling and skating around his much bigger opponents with surprising consistency.

Cournoyer played for Canada in the 1972 Summit Series, scoring three goals, and returned to North America to have his best post-season. He collected 12 points, six of them goals, in the final series against the Chicago Black Hawks and was awarded the Conn Smythe Trophy as the most valuable playoff performer.

Cournoyer, Yvan
RW, 5'7", 178 lbs, b: Drummondville, Que., 11/22/1943

Season	Club, League	Regular Season					Playoffs				
		GP	G	A	Pts	PIM	GP	G	A	Pts	PIM
1963–64	Montreal Canadiens, NHL	5	4	0	4	0					
1964–65	Montreal Canadiens, NHL	55	7	10	17	10	12	3	1	4	0
	Quebec Aces, AHL	7	2	1	3	0					
1965–66	Montreal Canadiens, NHL	65	18	11	29	8	10	2	3	5	2
1966–67	Montreal Canadiens, NHL	69	25	15	40	14	10	2	3	5	6
1967–68	Montreal Canadiens, NHL	64	28	32	60	23	13	6	8	14	4
1968–69	Montreal Canadiens, NHL	76	43	44	87	31	14	4	7	11	5
1969–70	Montreal Canadiens, NHL	72	27	36	63	23					
1970–71	Montreal Canadiens, NHL	65	37	36	73	21	20	10	12	22	6
1971–72	Montreal Canadiens, NHL	73	47	36	83	15	6	2	1	3	2
SS–72	Canada	8	3	2	5	2					
1972–73	Montreal Canadiens, NHL	67	40	39	79	18	17	15	10	25	2
1973–74	Montreal Canadiens, NHL	67	40	33	73	18	6	5	2	7	2
1974–75	Montreal Canadiens, NHL	76	29	45	74	32	11	5	6	11	4
1975–76	Montreal Canadiens, NHL	71	32	36	68	20	13	3	6	9	4
1976–77	Montreal Canadiens, NHL	60	25	28	53	8					
1977–78	Montreal Canadiens, NHL	68	24	29	53	12	15	7	4	11	10
1978–79	Montreal Canadiens, NHL	15	2	5	7	2					
	NHL Totals	968	428	435	863	255	147	64	63	127	47
	SS Totals	8	3	2	5	2					

NHL Second All-Star Team (1969, 1971, 1972, 1973)
Won Conn Smythe Trophy (1973)
Won Stanley Cup (1965, 1966, 1968, 1969, 1971, 1973, 1976, 1977, 1978, 1979)

In 1975 Henri Richard, the team's captain, retired and the leadership focus shifted to Cournoyer. He was made the Canadiens' captain and he responded by playing with even greater determination, spurred by his desire to show the way for the whole team. It wasn't long, however, before the tough Montreal fans and media began to question whether Cournoyer could keep his fast pace as he got older. He slowed down a step in the 1976–77 season, but it had little to do with his age. A disc in his back was pressing a nerve and causing him pain in his right leg if he stayed on his feet for more than a few minutes at a time. Surgery was required, though Cournoyer stayed quiet about his pain in an effort to continue playing.

Like many young Quebecers, Yvan Cournoyer (left) idolized the Canadiens and dreamed of playing for Montreal.

But in one game against the New York Rangers in February 1977, Cournoyer put on a display at Madison Square Garden that had even the home fans cheering for the speedy Canadiens star. He picked up the puck just outside the blue line and darted into the Rangers' zone. He circled the net once, then again, making two full circles around the bewildered defenders, who had given up chasing him. "Not bad for an old man, eh?" Cournoyer said after the game, easily won by Montreal 8–1. "They stood there, and their heads were turning and turning and their eyes were big. It was funny. I laughed too."

Just two weeks after he skated circles around the Rangers, Cournoyer announced he was done for the season. The surgery couldn't wait and the Canadiens captain was forced to miss the post-season and the team's second consecutive run to the championship. Because of new rules regarding which names could be engraved on the Stanley Cup, Montreal coach Scotty Bowman was happy to announce that Cournoyer, who had played in 60 regular-season games, would be included. Previously, not being in the playoffs would have meant not getting his name on the Cup.

Cournoyer returned to the Canadiens lineup in 1977–78 and scored 24 goals in the regular season, though it was obvious, even if he refused to complain, that his back continued to give him problems. In the playoffs he added seven goals as Montreal won the Stanley Cup again, making it nine titles for the captain. He made an effort to continue in training camp the next season and played 15 games before being forced to the sidelines again. Cournoyer was adamant that he'd play again and bristled when Jean Beliveau, then a vice-president of the organization, suggested it would be better if he retired. At 35, after playing 15 outstanding seasons in a tough league, Cournoyer was reluctant to let go of his hockey life. But after another back operation in 1978, he was forced to concede defeat. At the end of his career, he trailed only Guy Lafleur, Maurice Richard and Jean Beliveau on the Canadiens' all-time goal-scoring list.

The Roadrunner opened a successful *brasserie* (bar) in Montreal and a chain of hamburger restaurants called Burger 12. In 1982 he was inducted into the Hockey Hall of Fame. His tender back ruled out playing oldtimers' hockey for much of the next 20 years. In 2000, during the All-Star Game festivities in Toronto, he returned to thrill fans at the Legends game, showing flashes of the speed that made him a constant threat to defenders and goalies and a hero in Montreal.

Paul Henderson

A skilled right winger, Paul Henderson used his speed and a willingness to gamble on offense to great effect during his pro tenure. He scored at least 20 goals seven times in the NHL and was a top performer in the World Hockey Association. Despite an exemplary career as a professional, Henderson carved his permanent place in hockey history with his scoring heroics for Team Canada in the 1972 Summit Series against the Soviets.

Born in Kincardine, Ontario, Henderson was signed as a teenager by the Detroit Red Wings organization. He was a standout with the parent club's top junior affiliate, the Hamilton Red Wings, where he scored an OHA best of 49 goals in 48 games during the 1962–63 season. That impressive year also featured a two-game call-up to the Wings. The next year he split his playing time between the Motor City and the Pittsburgh Hornets of the American Hockey League.

Henderson developed into a consistent, full-time NHL winger in 1964–65, playing on a line with Pit Martin and Larry Jeffrey. The following year he recorded his first 20-goal season and helped Detroit reach the Stanley Cup finals, where they succumbed to the Montreal Canadiens in six games. Henderson lost 24 games to injury in 1966–67 but still managed to score 21 goals.

Early in his playing days, he was also known as one of the few NHL regulars who put safety first and insisted on wearing a helmet. He explained that after a serious head injury earlier in his career, he would take no chances. "A helmet is simply a part of my uniform. I put it on as naturally as I would a pair of shin pads."

Paul Henderson scored at least 20 goals a season seven times.

Late in the 1967–68 season, Henderson was involved in a multi-player deal that brought him to the defending Stanley Cup champion Toronto Maple Leafs. Norm Ullman was the key player joining Henderson in Hogtown, while the Wings' prize catch was Frank Mahovlich.

Henderson scored 27 goals during his first full year in Toronto in 1968–69. He formed an effective partnership with former Red Wings teammate Norm Ullman and emerging star Ron Ellis. Between this season and 1971–72, the Ullman–Henderson–Ellis line established a host of Maple Leafs single-season scoring records for a forward line. In 1970–71, Henderson scored a career high of 60 points, then registered a personal best of 38 goals the following season.

What was lacking from this period of individual success for Henderson was any sort of post-season achievement by Toronto. After being in 33 playoff games in three seasons from 1963 to 1966 with Detroit, Henderson took part in only 19 post-season matches in seven seasons with the Maple Leafs.

The triumph that stands out in Henderson's career is from the early 1970s. Coming off his 38-goal performance in 1971–72, the speedy winger was deemed a potential asset on the Canadian squad that was being assembled for the upcoming Summit Series against the Soviets. Team Canada coaches Harry Sinden and John Ferguson believed that Henderson would add depth and stability to their squad, but nobody on either team could have anticipated what would transpire during the series.

During Canada's disappointing 1–2–1 showing in the first four games of the series in Montreal, Toronto, Winnipeg and Vancouver, Henderson performed admirably on what was essentially a checking line. He and linemates Ron Ellis and Bobby Clarke were the most cohesive unit from the first day of training camp and they were arguably three of the most consistent players among the Canadian contingent in the first half of the series.

Paul Henderson (right).

After a heartbreaking loss in the first game in Moscow—game five of eight—Canada stormed back to win the last three games, each by a goal. Remarkably, Henderson scored the winner in each of these one-goal decisions. The most spectacular was the winner with two minutes to go in game seven, which gave Canada a 4–3 win.

Late in the eighth game, with the score tied 5–5, Henderson called for Pete Mahovlich to come off the ice. He immediately headed for the net and narrowly missed his first chance before jumping on the rebound of a Phil Esposito shot. Henderson took two swipes at the puck before slipping the series winner past Vladislav Tretiak with 34 seconds left in the game. This historic moment earned Henderson a special place in Canadian history. Nearly every Canadian who's old enough is able to recall where they were when "the goal" was scored. After the game, the Canadian winger told the Soviet press to tell Tretiak that he played well. Henderson was told, "He says you were lucky to score that goal," to which he responded, "Tell him to go to hell."

Nearly all Canadians alive at the time can recall where they were when "the goal" was scored.

Exhausted and distracted, in 1972–73, Henderson managed to play only 40 games for Toronto. The team was seriously weakened by defections to the World Hockey Association and finished well back of playoff contention. Improvements came the following season and Henderson scored 24 goals in 69 games. During this period, Maple Leafs owner Harold Ballard feuded with many of his players. After experiencing the euphoria of the Summit Series, Henderson felt the environment around the Toronto team seemed stale, and this contributed to the famous winger's yearning for a change of scenery.

Henderson stayed in Toronto but joined the Toros franchise of the World Hockey Association prior to the 1974–75 season. He noted, "All I'll say is that I'm not making one million, but money was a secondary issue." Before suiting up for his new club, he took part in the 1974 series that matched most of the Soviets from the previous series against a Team Canada squad made up of the top stars from the WHA. Skating with the likes of Gordie Howe, Bobby Hull and '72 series veteran Frank Mahovlich, Henderson was expected to come up with some pretty good offense and leadership. He played well, but the Soviets were out for revenge and posted a 4–1–3 series win.

Henderson, Paul
RW, 5'11", 180 lbs, b: Kincardine, Ont., 1/28/1943

Season	Club, League	Regular Season					Playoffs				
		GP	G	A	Pts	PIM	GP	G	A	Pts	PIM
1962–63	Detroit Red Wings, NHL	2	0	0	0	9					
1963–64	Detroit Red Wings, NHL	32	3	3	6	14	14	2	3	5	6
	Pittsburgh Hornets, AHL	38	10	14	24	18					
1964–65	Detroit Red Wings, NHL	70	8	13	21	30	7	0	2	2	0
1965–66	Detroit Red Wings, NHL	69	22	24	46	34	12	3	3	6	10
1966–67	Detroit Red Wings, NHL	46	21	19	40	10					
1967–68	Detroit Red Wings, NHL	50	13	20	33	35					
	Toronto Maple Leafs, NHL	13	5	6	11	8					
1968–69	Toronto Maple Leafs, NHL	74	27	32	59	16	4	0	1	1	0
1969–70	Toronto Maple Leafs, NHL	67	20	22	42	18					
1970–71	Toronto Maple Leafs, NHL	72	30	30	60	34	6	5	1	6	4
1971–72	Toronto Maple Leafs, NHL	73	38	19	57	32	5	1	2	3	6
SS–72	Canada	8	7	3	10	4					
1972–73	Toronto Maple Leafs, NHL	40	18	16	34	18					
1973–74	Toronto Maple Leafs, NHL	69	24	31	55	40	4	0	2	2	2
1974–75	Toronto Toros, WHA	58	30	33	63	18					
1975–76	Toronto Toros, WHA	65	26	29	55	22					
1976–77	Birmingham Bulls, WHA	81	23	25	48	30					
1977–78	Birmingham Bulls, WHA	80	37	29	66	22	5	1	1	2	0
1978–79	Birmingham Bulls, WHA	76	24	27	51	20					
1979–80	Atlanta Flames, NHL	30	7	6	13	6	4	0	0	0	0
	Birmingham Bulls, CHL	47	17	18	35	10					
1980–81	Birmingham Bulls, CHL	35	6	11	17	38					
	NHL Totals	707	236	241	477	304	56	11	14	25	28
	WHA Totals	360	140	143	283	112	5	1	1	2	0
	SS Totals	8	7	3	10	4					

In five seasons with the Toronto Toros/Birmingham Bulls franchise, Henderson scored 140 goals but took part in only five playoff games. On September 17, 1979, he was signed by the Atlanta Flames and split the season between that NHL team and the Birmingham Bulls of the Central Hockey League. Henderson scored his last 13 NHL points in Dixie before retiring from the league. One night in March, he gained a measure of revenge against Ballard by scoring two goals in a 5–1 Atlanta win at Maple Leaf Gardens, which earned him selection as the game's first star.

Henderson played his last pro season in 1980–81 and then retired. His NHL total is 236 goals, but it was his unforgettable moments on the ice at the Luzhniki Sports Palace in Moscow that ensured his immortality in hockey history.

Vladimir Vikulov

Vladimir Vikulov was one of the outstanding puckhandlers in Soviet hockey.

Only one forward playing in the NHL today can be compared with Vladimir Vikulov in handling the puck, and that's Teemu Selanne. Some may consider this an unfair comparison because they played in different eras and have never been together on the ice. But Vikulov's playing career wasn't that long ago; he played in the first Canada Cup tournament in 1976 against such greats as Bobby Orr, Larry Robinson, Guy Lafleur, Bobby Hull, Marcel Dionne and Bob Gainey.

In 1976 the USSR team was playing without their leading Petrov and Shadrin lines. The lineup consisted of a number of players who had never donned the national team jersey before. Vikulov was sidelined on the bench until the third game against Finland, when one of the Soviet forwards was injured. Vikulov came out on the ice and scored three goals against Finland, one goal and three assists against the U.S. team and the only Soviet goal against Canada.

As a child, Vikulov had been gentle and good-natured and as a player he was never hostile or overbearing. By the time he was 30, younger, more aggressive players were being let out on the ice and Vikulov was no longer playing in major competitions. He told his coaches he wasn't interested in playing in the Canada Cup as a substitute. "I'm used to being a forward with my line," he said, "and I don't want to just fill in."

Vikulov always played with the best forward lines—with Viktor Polupanov and Anatoli Firsov, with Firsov and Valeri Kharlamov and with Kharlamov and Alexander Maltsev. His place was firmly among the elite of Soviet hockey.

Nothing, not even coach Anatoli Tarasov, contributed to Vikulov's technique more than his boyhood experiences on the ice. "I had a favorite pastime when we played in our backyard or on the rink. I would choose someone my own age as a partner and we would play against six or eight younger boys. Some of those kids had skates and some didn't, some had hockey sticks, others just an ordinary stick; some didn't have anything. They would hang on to you from all sides, dive under your skates, grab you by the leg and push. Trying to keep control of the puck in such a free-for-all and not lose sight of your partner was much harder than in a real game trying to outplay two skilled defensemen. I retained my affection for this kind of game for many years, and during my free time I played backyard hockey, even when I was already playing in the majors," Vikulov recalls.

Vikulov was one of the last of a select number of players who didn't seem to exert any effort when playing. For him, playing was almost like resting, something good for his soul. Vikulov went head-on against opponents protecting their net using wide and smooth stickhandling, but as he got closer to the net, his movements would become tighter and then he would change his rhythm and switch into high gear. Vikulov always excelled at attacking on the fly when he played for both the national team and Central Red Army club.

Vikulov stood 5′9″ inches and weighed 176 pounds, but he wasn't afraid of any defenseman. As he skated closer to the action, he had the ability to see all of his partners and guess what his opponents were going to do. Exceptional coordination, combined with a permanent poker face, could drive his opponents into a frenzy that usually landed them in the penalty box. Tarasov wrote: "One time, the coaches didn't want to take Vikulov to a World Championship. In order to convince them that they were wrong, I had to remind them that in the definitive games, Vikulov could gain from four to six minutes for the team by putting opponents in the penalty box, and that this would decide the fate of the team."

The beginning of Vikulov's hockey career was similar to that of Boris Mikhailov. But while the latter smashed down the door and stormed into hockey without much experience, Vladimir Vikulov came through a door that was already open for him.

"There are many possibilities to make a name for yourself in hockey so that even the most inattentive fan will notice you right away. But is this necessary? Sometimes the young fans like the way a player breaks through. The forward picks up speed along the ice, not outplaying but merely bypassing the opponent. But while he's passing the players, his partners are bored waiting for him to remember them. It's much more interesting when you play the game with a definite strategy in mind—a game in which, even if you don't see him, you feel and guess what your partner is going to do. Hockey isn't only speed, lightning, thunder and sparring. The fate of a game, like the fate of a coup, is decided behind the scenes. Movement, the right movement even without the puck, is the basis of success. To hide from your opponent and anticipate, then jump out in the most unexpected place—this is what appeals to me most in hockey."

Exceptional coordination, combined with a permanent poker face, could drive opponents of Vladimir Vikulov (number 18) into a frenzy that put them in the penalty box.

Vikulov, Vladimir
RW, 5′9″, 176 lbs, b: Moscow, USSR, 7/20/1946

Season	Club, League	Regular Season				
		GP	G	A	Pts	PIM
1963–64	CSKA, USSR	*	2	*	*	*
1964–65	CSKA, USSR	*	1	*	*	*
1965–66	CSKA, USSR	*	12	*	*	*
WEC–66	USSR	7	4	2	6	2
1966–67	CSKA, USSR	*	27	*	*	*
WEC–67	USSR	7	6	6	12	8
1967–68	CSKA, USSR	43	29	*	*	*
OWG–68	USSR	7	2	10	12	2
1968–69	CSKA, USSR	40	13	*	*	*
WEC–69	USSR	9	2	4	6	0
1969–70	CSKA, USSR	43	25	*	*	*
WEC–70	USSR	10	9	5	14	0
1970–71	CSKA, USSR	39	19	*	*	*
WEC–71	USSR	10	6	5	11	0
1971–72	CSKA, USSR	31	34	8	42	*
OWG–72	USSR	5	5	3	8	0
WEC–72	USSR	10	12	4	16	0
SS–72	USSR	6	2	1	3	0
1972–73	CSKA, USSR	32	21	19	40	*
1973–74	CSKA, USSR	32	14	19	33	18
1974–75	CSKA, USSR	36	17	23	40	26
WEC–75	USSR	6	6	2	8	2
1975–76	CSKA, USSR	35	19	17	36	18
CCup–76	USSR	4	4	3	7	0
1976–77	CSKA, USSR	35	22	18	40	12
1977–78	CSKA, USSR	34	12	22	34	12
1978–79	CSKA, USSR	33	12	10	22	14
	SKA Leningrad, USSR	8	3	4	7	2
	USSR Totals	520	283	*	*	*
	OWG/WEC/SS/CCup Totals	81	58	45	103	14

Won OWG (1968, 1972)
Won WEC (1966, 1967, 1968, 1969, 1970, 1971, 1972, 1975)
USSR Champion (1964, 1965, 1966, 1968, 1970, 1971, 1972, 1973, 1975, 1977, 1978, 1979)

Ron Ellis

Ron Ellis played a strong checking role in the 1972 series.

Many factors worked in Ron Ellis's favor as he tried to become a successful NHL player. His blazing speed and quick release were natural skills and he worked to perfect them over the course of his career. The same perfection that brought him over 300 goals made him one of the top defensive forwards of his time. Ellis's commitment to disciplining himself when he didn't have the puck earned him respect throughout the league and in international circles.

Born in Lindsay, Ontario, an hour northeast of Toronto, the swift right winger gained his amateur training with the fabled Toronto Marlboros. He was a prolific scorer in junior and starred when the Marlies won the Memorial Cup in 1963–64.

The young winger impressed coaches and fans in his first NHL season by scoring 23 goals and narrowly losing the Calder Trophy race to Detroit netminder Roger Crozier. He was immediately a vital two-way performer playing on a line with stalwarts Dave Keon and Bob Pulford. The veterans were impressed with the fact that the youngster's zeal was as strong while checking as it was when racing in on the opposition's goal.

Ellis summed up his own play: "I worked as a two-way player. I hope that's how people will remember me. 'Yes, he could score goals, but he could also be counted on to check a big line or to play in the last few minutes of a close game.' Certainly in Toronto I wasn't known as a flashy player. In some cases people thought I played a robot style of hockey, but the people that were paying my salary and the coach and general manager as well as my opponents appreciated and respected my style."

In 1966–67, he was one of the youthful troops that supported such legendary oldtimers as Red Kelly, Johnny Bower, Terry Sawchuk and George Armstrong. This gritty squad overcame a mediocre regular season to win the Stanley Cup. Ellis provided the crucial first goal in the sixth game of the finals versus Montreal, which the team won 3–1 to take the series in six games.

Following the trade of Frank Mahovlich to Detroit, Ellis played on his most cohesive forward unit with Paul Henderson and Norm Ullman. This trio was adept at forechecking and opportunistic scoring. Ellis's role was crucial since he usually stayed back to guard against the counterattack while his linemates pushed forward.

Prior to the 1968–69 schedule, former Maple Leafs great Irvine "Ace" Bailey insisted that Ellis wear his retired number 6 because he admired his high-caliber yet clean style of play. One of the young forward's greatest accomplishments wasn not resorting to rough or

Ellis, Ron
RW, 5´9˝, 195 lbs, b: Lindsay, Ont., 1/8/1945

Season	Club, League	Regular Season					Playoffs				
		GP	G	A	Pts	PIM	GP	G	A	Pts	PIM
1963–64	Toronto Maple Leafs, NHL	1	0	0	0	0					
1964–65	Toronto Maple Leafs, NHL	62	23	16	39	14	6	3	0	3	2
1965–66	Toronto Maple Leafs, NHL	70	19	23	42	24	4	0	0	0	2
1966–67	Toronto Maple Leafs, NHL	67	22	23	45	14	12	2	1	3	4
1967–68	Toronto Maple Leafs, NHL	74	28	20	48	8					
1968–69	Toronto Maple Leafs, NHL	72	25	21	46	12	4	2	1	3	2
1969–70	Toronto Maple Leafs, NHL	76	35	19	54	14					
1970–71	Toronto Maple Leafs, NHL	78	24	29	53	10	6	1	1	2	2
1971–72	Toronto Maple Leafs, NHL	78	23	24	47	17	5	1	1	2	4
SS–72	Canada	8	0	3	3	8					
1972–73	Toronto Maple Leafs, NHL	78	22	29	51	22					
1973–74	Toronto Maple Leafs, NHL	70	23	25	48	12	4	2	1	3	0
1974–75	Toronto Maple Leafs, NHL	79	32	29	61	25	7	3	0	3	2
WEC–77	Canada	10	5	4	9	2					
1977–78	Toronto Maple Leafs, NHL	80	26	24	50	17	13	3	2	5	0
1978–79	Toronto Maple Leafs, NHL	63	16	12	28	10	6	1	1	2	2
1979–80	Toronto Maple Leafs, NHL	59	12	11	23	6	3	0	0	0	0
1980–81	Toronto Maple Leafs, NHL	27	2	3	5	2					
	NHL Totals	1034	332	308	640	207	70	18	8	26	20
	WEC/SS Totals	18	5	7	12	10					

Won Stanley Cup (1967)

dirty tactics while doggedly checking such stars as Bobby Hull and former teammate Frank Mahovlich.

Boston Bruins general manager Harry Sinden was another Ellis admirer. He was the impetus behind the Toronto winger's invitation to training camp when Team Canada 1972 was being assembled prior to the Summit Series against the Soviets. Despite a serious neck injury suffered in the opening game, Ellis played a strong checking role in all eight games of the series. The classy winger had this to say as he looked back on the matchup:

Between 1966 and 1975, Ron Ellis (left) recorded nine straight 20-goal seasons.

"I think the '72 series showed that Canada wasn't the only hockey power in the world. A lot of people believed that if you're a Canadian, you should be a better player than someone from another country. Consider a country like the USSR. With their population and the number of players at their dis-posal, they're going to have a few superstars of their own. I think it made Canadians realize, 'Hey, our players are good, but they're up against top competition.' Winning the Stanley Cup was a great highlight of my career, but playing for my country in the '72 series is even more memorable."

Between 1966 and 1975, Ellis recorded nine straight 20-goal seasons, but the stress of the NHL grind became too great for him to bear and he retired after scoring 32 goals in 1974–75. During his two-year sabbatical, Ellis pursued a business career that enabled him to gain valuable experi-ence away from the hockey rink. He also focused on the Christian faith, which had become an important part of his life.

When Ellis first heard the news that Canadian professionals were eligible for the World Championship in 1977, he volunteered his services as a consultant. It turned out that he was asked to try out for the team, which he did successfully. Canada finished fourth, but many observers noted that Ellis played some of his best hockey in years.

Feeling spiritually recharged, Ellis agreed to come to the Toronto Maple Leafs' training camp in 1977 under new coach and fellow Christian Roger Neilson. He reached the 20-goal mark for the team record of 10 straight years and helped the team reach the Stanley Cup semifinals for the first time since winning it all in 1967.

The following year he lost 17 games to injury and the team began to disintegrate because of the destructive antics of owner Harold Ballard. One of the most distasteful incidents in the mis-management of the Toronto team during this period occurred when Ellis arrived at Maple Leaf Gardens to find that his equipment was locked away and that his services were no longer needed.

Following his retirement, Ellis continued to work in the business world and eventually returned to the game under the auspices of the Hockey Hall of Fame in 1992. His ability in public relations and involvement with the Hall's educational outreach programs have proven invaluable.

Alexander Yakushev

As a player, Yakushev almost always wore the same pensive, concentrated expression on his face. Unlike other Russian coaches who are quite dramatic behind the bench, he has retained this expression even today as head coach of Team Russia.

The NHL stars of the 1970s have the clearest picture of him, and they gave him high marks in interviews. Bobby Hull said that no one compared with him. "I consider Yakushev to be the best left winger of all times." Phil Esposito liked to imagine having him as a partner. "With a wing like Yakushev, we could tear apart any defense." In a recent interview 25 years later, he repeated: "During all these years, I haven't found any new Russian player who I could place on the same level with Yakushev. To me, he is undoubtedly player number one across the ocean."

In 1972 Alexander Yakushev was chosen as MVP of the Soviet team in all four games played in Moscow during the Summit Series. That was quite a compliment, considering that the Soviets had the cream of the crop on their squad. After the series, Yakushev's stick was sent to the Hockey Hall of Fame in Toronto—one of the very few from overseas. Yakushev commented with a smile: "You know, I've never had a chance to visit that museum. I think my stick was sent there by accident. It's a very short stick, the shortest in my club, Spartak. I've got long arms."

At 6′3″, Alexander Yakushev was one of the tallest players in Soviet hockey.

He is just about the same age as Russian hockey. He was born in 1947, a year after ice hockey appeared in the Soviet Union. At 6′3″ and 198 pounds, Yakushev was one of the tallest players in Soviet hockey. When he was setting out in his career, he was at a disadvantage; they weren't looking for such burly forwards in the Soviet Union. They valued swifter, more agile and craftier players for close contact. Instead of size, players had an incredible amount of training.

The huge workload that was heaped on Yakushev—he began his tenure on the USSR national team under the coaching of Anatoli Tarasov and ended under Viktor Tikhonov—didn't change his style of play at all. Tarasov said, "Training is the foundation of a hockey life." By contrast, Vsevolod Bobrov argued, "The god of hockey is the player." Yakushev the forward quietly chose to go the way of Bobrov. To those who followed him in action, he was always full of surprises, a symbol of innate talent that was still revealing itself at the end of his career.

"I'm pretty tall, no matter how you look at it, especially in hockey," Yakushev said. "A huge stride and long arms—all that is well and good. But there are also minus points. My center of gravity is much higher, and as a result my stability was less than that of other players with whom I came into contact. And with the years, when my maneuverability began to wane, my height didn't help me all the time."

But even in his best years, and especially on the national team coached by Tarasov, Yakushev had spells when he seemed to be hemmed in on the ice and his stride appeared to be too long for the rink. While playing with many outstanding coaches, trainers, officials and players, he quietly resisted any attempt on their part to constrict his style of play, even if it meant resorting to one of his favorite tricks—switching the stick to his other hand.

Canadians generally give a higher assessment of the most gifted players than do the Soviet coaches. During the Summit Series in 1972 and the one in 1974, the Canadians were quite outspoken about Yakushev's talents: his ability to break through defense lines and his wrist shots and slapshots—tried and true methods for which there was no need to set up a play.

Yakushev is quite unabashed in recalling those games. "Many consider the goal scored against Tony Esposito from the blue line in 1972 as outstanding. I wouldn't even remember it as one of my greats. I picked up the puck in our own end and quickly moved in on Esposito. Behind me, just to the side, was a defenseman, and I felt if I continue to go ahead, he'll either catch me or dump me. I decided on a long slapshot. It turned out to be right on dead center and the puck slipped between his pads into the net. I understand such a goal made an impression on the Canadians

Alexander Yakushev

because all the talk up to that time was that the Soviets don't know how to shoot and they can't even lift the puck."

One would expect that crossing sticks with the best Canadian hockey professionals was a high point in the career of Alexander Yakushev. Two giants of the game who were seeing each other for the first time and had no experience playing against each other went out on the ice and clashed. That's how it would have looked from the sidelines.

But Yakushev himself insists on downplaying the significance of his achievements. "That's their accepted way of commenting upon my successes. I think they intentionally exaggerated things and tried to play it up as something sensational. I believe that you can draw a conclusion about this or that player only after seeing him in action for a number of years and not on the basis of a few good games. This didn't touch me in the least. They say something about you, and this gets you thinking…"

Yakushev claims that his most important goals were scored against Czechoslovakia at the World Championships in 1974 and 1975 and at the Olympic Games in 1976. In the USSR in those years, the World Championships and the Olympic Games were regarded as the most important competitions.

As a player and coach in the Soviet Union (subsequently Russia), Yakushev belonged to only one team—Spartak Moscow, a unique team in the world of hockey. It was a team quite opposite in style to the leaders of that period, the Central Red Army club and Dynamo. Spartak was the embodiment of freedom of personality on the ice. They preferred attack to defense, a strong opponent to a weak one. Winding up his career in 1980, in his last game against "the most bitter enemy," the CSKA hockey club, Yakushev scored four goals against Tikhonov's squad. And to the very end he played by his own rules.

During the late 1980s and early 1990s, with Yakushev at the helm of Spartak, his team put the boots to Tikhonov's Central Red Army club. But in 1992 Spartak crossed sticks with the powerful and well-honed Dynamo in the quarterfinals. The Dynamo found themselves facing a team that had a very shallow offensive unit. With only two and a half forward lines, Spartak stood their ground for two games but finally caved in. Dynamo had Alexei Yashin, Alexei Kovalyov and Alexei Zhamnov whereas Spartak didn't have any players of that caliber on their roster.

Then one day, despite Yakushev's ongoing troubles in the Russian hockey world that went unnoticed by the NHL clubs, the opportunity arose for Yakushev to coach the Russian national squad. In two games at the 1999 World Championship against the eventual champions and the runner-up—the Czech Republic and Finland—the play was more exciting than at the 1998 Winter Olympics.

Yakushev, Alexander
LW, 6´3˝, 198 lbs, b: Moscow, USSR, 1/2/1947

Season	Club, League	Regular Season				
		GP	G	A	Pts	PIM
1963–64	Spartak Moscow, USSR	*	1	*	*	*
1964–65	Spartak Moscow, USSR	*	5	*	*	*
1965–66	Spartak Moscow, USSR	*	7	*	*	*
1966–67	Spartak Moscow, USSR	44	34	*	*	*
WEC–67	USSR	2	1	0	1	0
1967–68	Spartak Moscow, USSR	44	17	*	*	*
1968–69	Spartak Moscow, USSR	42	50	*	*	*
WEC–69	USSR	6	1	1	2	2
1969–70	Spartak Moscow, USSR	43	33	*	*	*
WEC–70	USSR	6	3	3	6	8
1970–71	Spartak Moscow, USSR	40	13	*	*	*
1971–72	Spartak Moscow, USSR	32	17	*	*	*
OWG–72	USSR	5	0	3	3	4
WEC–72	USSR	10	11	4	15	0
SS–72	USSR	8	7	4	11	4
1972–73	Spartak Moscow, USSR	29	26	10	36	*
WEC–73	USSR	10	9	6	15	2
1973–74	Spartak Moscow, USSR	32	26	11	37	12
WEC–74	USSR	10	7	7	14	2
1974–75	Spartak Moscow, USSR	35	16	18	34	34
WEC–75	USSR	9	11	5	16	2
1975–76	Spartak Moscow, USSR	36	31	20	51	15
OWG–76	USSR	6	4	9	13	2
WEC–76	USSR	10	6	1	7	0
1976–77	Spartak Moscow, USSR	31	17	11	28	24
WEC–77	USSR	10	7	4	11	0
1977–78	Spartak Moscow, USSR	32	10	9	19	12
1978–79	Spartak Moscow, USSR	44	19	20	39	44
WEC–79	USSR	8	4	2	6	8
1979–80	Spartak Moscow, USSR	43	17	12	29	20
1980–81	SV Kapfenberg, Austria	34	46	44	90	61
1981–82	SV Kapfenberg, Austria	37	29	43	72	*
1982–83	SV Kapfenberg, Austria	38	33	58	91	*
	USSR Totals	568	339	*	*	*
	OWG/WEC/SS Totals	100	71	49	120	34

Named Best Forward at WEC (1975)
Won OWG (1972, 1976)
Won WEC (1967, 1969, 1970, 1972, 1973, 1974, 1975, 1976, 1979)
USSR Champion (1967, 1969, 1976)

Yakushev not only made history during his career in hockey, he did so while going his own way. To some small extent, luck was on his side. Yakushev had a long partnership with center Vladimir Shadrin, who took upon himself all the dirty work so that Yakushev's talent could reign much more freely. They never parted ways during a game.

In future, Yakushev intends to boost the image of the many shining examples of Soviet hockey who have long been forgotten, even in Russia. In the chaos of modern Russia, nobody is clamoring for the old "people's Spartak." The team is halfway to the bottom of the Russian rating table. We've seen some of the high points in Yakushev's career and we've seen some of the low points. But the votes aren't all in, so the significance of Alexander Yakushev's role in the history of Russian hockey is yet to be determined.

Alexander Yakushev was chosen the Soviet team's MVP in all four of the Moscow games of the Summit Series.

Yevgeny Zimin

When he wasn't yet 20, Lokomotiv Moscow forward Yevgeny Zimin received an invitation from coach Vsevolod Bobrov to play for Spartak. Almost immediately, Zimin became a USSR champion on his new team's lineup. After playing right wing on Yevgeny Mayorov's number one Spartak forward line, Zimin was given the leading role playing alongside Vyacheslav Starshinov and Boris Mayorov. By the age of 20, he'd become an Olympic champion in Grenoble. At 21 he held two USSR national and two World Championship titles.

In 1972 Bobrov, head coach of the Soviet team, put Zimin on the ice in the Summit Series with Vladimir Shadrin and Alexander Yakushev. Zimin would score two goals but play in only one more game. And this pattern would persist throughout his entire hockey career—a strong bid for stardom followed by a weak follow-through, and then nothing.

In all fairness, Zimin should have been able to play hockey as hard and as long as he wanted. His family was welloff—his father held a high government post and his mother was a doctor. However, as most of his Soviet teammates knew, his childhood was difficult and unsettled. Zimin's career makes one wonder if hockey would have had such a glorious image had life in the Soviet Union been better and living conditions more favorable. Hockey offered many players a unique opportunity to rise above their circumstances and achieve some form of success.

Yevgeny Zimin scored two goals in the Summit Series game opener.

Zimin always went on the ice to have a good time. The puck seemed to be glued to his stick and, being small and agile, he could zip around the ice for the sheer fun of it. But playing alongside such formidable masters as Mayorov and Starshinov forced him, at least in the beginning, to play to a higher standard. However, when the protracted leapfrogging of Spartak coaches began, Zimin began to backslide more than the other players.

Bobrov, the predominant coach in Zimin's life, was more exasperated by him than most. "Many, myself included, were captivated by Zimin's dazzling and unique style of play. But every time we put together a national team, the same question would come up: Should we or shouldn't we enlist

The puck seemed to be glued to Yevgeny Zimin's stick and the small, agile player could zip around the ice for sheer joy.

Zimin? More often than not, the answer was negative. And the reasons were always the same: He's not ready; he's not in shape; he can't cope with the high speeds and heavy bodychecking. But Valeri Kharlamov, who was very much like Zimin in terms of strength and physique, was always ready. I could see how hard Kharlamov, Petrov, Yakushev, Shadrin and Mikhailov would sweat during workouts. But I could also see how carefully Zimin looked after himself, how moody he was, how often he said he was unwell, and I understood why there was such a great difference in the destinies of hockey players."

And Zimin, a young man who thought very highly of himself and led an unconventional lifestyle, wasn't the least bit bothered by Bobrov's assessment. He merely shrugged it off, as if to say, "I went into hockey not to be a workhorse, not to sacrifice myself, but to skate circles around my opponents and have a good time."

Zimin, Yevgeny RW, 5'8", 160 lbs, b: Moscow, USSR, 8/6/1947						
Season	Club, League	Regular Season				
		GP	G	A	Pts	PIM
1964–65	Lokomotiv Moscow, USSR	*	*	*	*	*
1965–68	Spartak Moscow, USSR	*	*	*	*	*
OWG–68	USSR	4	3	2	5	8
1968–69	Spartak Moscow, USSR	*	*	*	*	*
WEC–69	USSR	10	1	2	3	4
1969–71	Spartak Moscow, USSR	*	*	*	*	*
WEC–71	USSR	4	2	1	3	0
1971–72	Spartak Moscow, USSR	*	*	*	*	*
OWG–72	USSR	1	1	0	1	0
SS–72	USSR	2	2	1	3	0
1972–74	Spartak Moscow, USSR	*	*	*	*	*
1974–76	SKA MVO, USSR	*	*	*	*	*
1976–77	Krylja Sovetov, USSR	*	*	*	*	*
	USSR Totals	315	184	*	*	*
	OWG/WEC/SS Totals	21	9	6	15	12

Won OWG (1968, 1972)
USSR Champion (1967, 1969)

But life in hockey was tough in those days and Zimin got swept up just like everyone else. He hadn't yet reached his hockey prime when he was recruited by Spartak. But the team soon gave up on Zimin, considering him a bad bet. He had a chance to make a comeback with Red Army, but because he couldn't apply himself to a training regimen, he lost out again. For two years he marked time with an Army team in the remote town of Lipetsk. When Spartak refused to take him back, Krylja Sovetov (Soviet Wings) accepted him.

There are some who feel confined by professional pressures. Yevgeny Zimin didn't like to take orders and in his post-playing years tried out the roles of coach, TV commentator and scout. The public remembers him best as the coach of the Russian NHL Stars who played at the annual Spartak Cup tournament in Moscow. It was the one tournament where the Stars could take it easy and play exclusively for their own pleasure. Zimin said he was always happiest coaching that team.

Yuri Lyapkin

Yuri Lyapkin had a country-boy image that gave him an aura of gentle submissiveness. But this so-called farmer played for the USSR in the Summit Series and again in 1974 and was part of an Olympic legend. In 1976, playing against the Czechs, Lyapkin was one of three who broke away from five opposing players when the Soviets were losing 2–0.

Lyapkin was included only once on Anatoli Tarasov's national team—in 1971 for the World Championship, where he sat out most of the game. Tarasov had included him "just in case." Lyapkin was already 25 by then, the age when players were considered past their prime, according to the wisdom of the day.

However, the inclusion of Lyapkin on the national team at all was a sign that hockey was opening up. It meant that even an outsider had a chance to show what he was worth. It is doubtful that someone like Lyapkin could have entered hockey from a national school, no matter if he'd been Canadian, Czech or Swedish. Even leading Russian teams like the Central Red Army and Dynamo Moscow, who had a fast and tough style, would have given Lyapkin a cool reception. He was considered unusual, someone who would appeal only to a very open-minded coach and suitable only for a renegade team.

Such a coach did exist in the Soviet Union, however, and he was Nikolai Epshtein. The team was Khimik from Voskresensk. Compared to Red Army, Khimik was like a guerrilla unit creeping out of the jungle to attack a well-trained force.

Yuri Lyapkin always played more like a forward than a defenseman.

Lyapkin entered hockey relatively late, but Epshtein molded him from a forward into a defenseman because he saw that the "country boy" played a good game. In the following season, during the Summit Series, Lyapkin played for Spartak Moscow and emerged as a leading player.

Lyapkin was still more of a forward than a defenseman, even when playing on the defense line. Turning up the heat, he could scatter his opponents and zero in on the opposition net for a one-on-one with the goalie. He was frequently the subject of criticism because of both his character and his style of play. His style was based on superb technique and strategic vision, and he was in top form at all times. But if his energy began to wane, it was extremely difficult for him to bring himself back. He was often blamed when things went wrong—no longer seen as a defenseman but the object of censure for his lack of speed or energy.

Spartak's best seasons were in the 1970s, when they seemed to play with abandon. Lyapkin appeared rejuvenated and Alexander Yakushev, another Spartak star, was energized and conducted his attacks with vigor. Spartak had always been considered somewhat weak in defense, often leaving forwards stranded halfway between ends. The first thing that Lyapkin did was reinforce the attack. The wing of the leading forward line, Vladimir Shadrin, at times had a new partner in Lyapkin, who was able to improvise endlessly. Shadrin played like Larionov, someone who paid a lot of attention to detail.

Coach Nikolai Karpov, who led Spartak to the gold in the 1976 national championship, said: "It seems to me that Lyapkin was born to be on this line. He and the forward line perform such miracles on the ice that later, when we show them the tape of the game, they don't believe their eyes. Lyapkin never was a fast and hard-hitting player, but his best qualities—technique and tactical vision—improved with age."

Alexander Yakushev, whose game was uneven, didn't need much coddling from his teammates. The main thing was that

Lyapkin, Yuri
D, 6´, 180 lbs, b: Balashikha, USSR, 1/21/1945

Season	Club, League	Regular Season				
		GP	G	A	Pts	PIM
1964–71	Khimik, USSR	*	*	*	*	*
WEC–71	USSR	2	0	0	0	2
1971–72	Khimik, USSR	*	*	*	*	*
SS–72	USSR	6	1	5	6	0
1972–73	Spartak Moscow, USSR	*	*	*	*	*
WEC–73	USSR	8	0	10	10	6
1973–74	Spartak Moscow, USSR	*	*	*	*	*
WEC–74	USSR	10	1	1	2	2
1974–75	Spartak Moscow, USSR	*	*	*	*	*
WEC–75	USSR	9	1	5	6	10
1975–76	Spartak Moscow, USSR	*	*	*	*	*
OWG–76	USSR	6	1	3	4	2
WEC–76	USSR	10	4	3	7	8
1976–78	Khimik, USSR	*	*	*	*	*
1978–79	Spartak Moscow, USSR	*	*	*	*	*
	USSR Totals	437	126	*	*	*
	OWG/WEC/SS Totals	51	8	27	35	30

Won OWG (1976)
Won WEC (1971, 1973, 1974, 1975)
USSR Champion (1976)

Turning up the heat, Yuri Lyapkin (second from the right) could scatter his opponents and zero in on the net for a one-on-one chance against the goalie.

the player who was going to pass him the puck should do it at the moment when Yakushev switched into high gear. Lyapkin did this with a kind of sixth sense. When Lyapkin returned to Khimik in 1976, Yakushev seemed to lose his touch.

Lyapkin was lucky with coaches, including Vsevolod Bobrov and Boris Kulagin on the national team and Karpov with Spartak. All of them had an open mind about the game when compared to Tarasov and Viktor Tikhonov. Lyapkin once said of his trainers: "Karpov's most important trait was that he was able to find a kind word for every player. I felt Kulagin was essentially an amiable person although he could be very strict."

Tony Esposito

As one half of perhaps the most colorful brother act in NHL history, Tony O revolutionized goaltending in the NHL with his legs-open "butterfly" style and his spectacular flop-on-the-ice saves during the 16 years he spent in the league, all except one with the Chicago Black Hawks.

Tony Esposito gained a reputation as the quickest glove in the game, and though his style was unorthodox it was extremely effective.

As the younger brother of scoring star Phil, Tony had something to prove when he entered the league in 1968. After a collegiate career with the Michigan Tech Huskies and the Vancouver Canucks of the Western Hockey League, he spent time with Houston of the Central Hockey League. His first partial year with Montreal was unspectacular—the Canadiens had Gump Worsley and Rogie Vachon ahead of him—but after being traded to Chicago, he was impressive in his first full season, recording a Calder and Vezina Trophy-winning year in 1969–70 with a 2.17 goals-against average and a modern-era record of 15 shutouts.

Fans of the game were quick to point out that the Hawks, under coach Billy Reay, were a defensive-minded squad and that at 5´11˝ and 185 pounds, Esposito was a stocky, very mature 26-year-old rookie. But more important, he was fast gaining a reputation as having the quickest glove hand in the game and an unorthodox style that was confounding but nevertheless extremely effective. The Vezina win in his first year made him the first rookie to win the trophy since Frank Brimsek in 1939.

For the Black Hawks, the return to defensive hockey paid huge dividends, as the team went from sixth to first place in the East Division. The team's GM Tommy Ivan summed up Tony O's contribution: "You might say that we solved all of our goaltending problems in one season." "He's very alert," coach Reay said in agreement. "A few goalies are a split second behind the play, but Tony's that little bit ahead of things. He may be awkward, but he is rarely out of position. It's a bit funny that people have knocked him for his lack of great style. He keeps the puck out of the net."

CBS broadcaster Dan Kelly once shared a similar sentiment: "How he ever stops the puck with that style is more than most hockey men can understand—but he does the job."

One of the NHLers who was puzzled by Tony's style was the Maple Leafs' Mike Walton. "I don't see how he is as good as he is," complained Walton. "He allows rebounds to come out in front, and he doesn't clear the puck into the corner like he should, but somehow he beats you!" For his part, though, Esposito said that there was considerable method to the seeming madness of his style. "I probably watched Glenn Hall, the former Hawk goalie, more than any other netminder. He is just sort of an expedient type of goalie and I think that's my style. I just try to stop the puck."

The Black Hawks never failed to make the playoffs while Tony Esposito (right) played for them.

Tony's brother Phil wasn't the only important family connection he had to hockey. In 1962 his father, Patrick, combined with four friends to invest in the Junior A Sault Ste. Marie Greyhounds and entered them in the Northern Ontario Hockey League. Still, the young Tony wasn't a real hockey fanatic. While an outstanding young player, he preferred football in his teen years and only agreed, Phil remembers, to join the Greyhounds "because they didn't have anyone else to play goal."

Even so, Tony was good enough between the pipes to win a scholarship to Michigan Tech, graduating in three years with a business degree and attaining all-American status each year. As a pro, he quickly gained a reputation as an emotional, vocal goalie who would yell regularly at his defensemen and stay well back in his crease except when he came out to poke-check skaters. He added to his rookie Vezina win by sharing the trophy with Gary Smith in 1972 and tying Bernie Parent in 1974. In his career, he totaled 76 regular-season shutouts.

Although he was one of the coolest and most relaxed goalies when he was in the net, Esposito had a terrible time with the pre-game jitters. "I get very nervous before a game," he admitted. "I have trouble with my emotions and my nerves. I keep my food down okay because I eat about seven hours before game-time. But I always worry about making a mistake. If I make a bad play, the puck is in, and everybody sees it. That feeling is what makes me sick."

Esposito usually shunned the spotlight, preferring to give most of the credit to his defenders. "In case you aren't familiar with the

Esposito, Tony
G, 5´11˝, 185 lbs, b: Sault Ste. Marie, Ont., 4/23/1943

Season	Club, League		Regular Season				Playoffs		
		GP	Mins	GA	Avg	GP	Mins	GA	Avg
1964–65	Michigan Tech Huskies, WCHA	17	1020	40	2.35				
1965–66	Michigan Tech Huskies, WCHA	19	1140	51	2.68				
1966–67	Michigan Tech Huskies, WCHA	15	900	39	2.60				
1967–68	Vancouver Canucks, WHL	63	3734	199	3.20				
1968–69	Montreal Canadiens, NHL	13	746	34	2.73				
	Houston Apollos, CHL	19	1139	46	2.42	1	59	3	3.05
1969–70	Chicago Black Hawks, NHL	63	3763	136	2.17	8	480	27	3.38
1970–71	Chicago Black Hawks, NHL	57	3325	126	2.27	18	1151	42	2.19
1971–72	Chicago Black Hawks, NHL	48	2780	82	1.77	5	300	16	3.20
SS–72	Canada	4	240	13	3.25				
1972–73	Chicago Black Hawks, NHL	56	3340	140	2.51	15	895	46	3.08
1973–74	Chicago Black Hawks, NHL	70	4143	141	2.04	10	584	28	2.88
1974–75	Chicago Black Hawks, NHL	71	4219	193	2.74	8	472	34	4.32
1975–76	Chicago Black Hawks, NHL	68	4003	198	2.97	4	240	13	3.25
1976–77	Chicago Black Hawks, NHL	69	4067	234	3.45	2	120	6	3.00
WEC–77	Canada	9	510	27	3.17				
1977–78	Chicago Black Hawks, NHL	64	3840	168	2.63	4	252	19	4.52
1978–79	Chicago Black Hawks, NHL	63	3780	206	3.27	4	243	14	3.46
ChCup–79	NHL All-Stars	0	0	0	0.00	0	0	0	0.00
1979–80	Chicago Black Hawks, NHL	69	4140	205	2.97	6	373	14	2.25
1980–81	Chicago Black Hawks, NHL	66	3935	246	3.75	3	215	15	4.19
CCup–81	USA	5	300	20	4.00				
1981–82	Chicago Black Hawks, NHL	52	3069	231	4.52	7	381	16	2.52
1982–83	Chicago Black Hawks, NHL	39	2340	135	3.46	5	311	18	3.47
1983–84	Chicago Black Hawks, NHL	18	1095	88	4.82				
	NHL Totals	886	52585	2563	2.92	99	6017	308	3.07
	WEC/SS/ChalCup/CCup Totals	18	1050	60	3.43				

NHL First All-Star Team (1970, 1972, 1980)
NHL Second All-Star Team (1973, 1974)
Won Vezina Trophy (1970, 1972, 1974)
Won Calder Memorial Trophy (1970)
Won Stanley Cup (1969)

Esposito personality," wrote hockey reporter Bob Verdi, "he isn't one to praise himself. If the Black Hawks win with him in goal, the guys played great in front of him. If the Hawks lose when he is playing, then it was his fault. Every, but every, goal is his fault. Folks who cover the team are waiting for someone to score an empty-net goal on the Hawks to see if Tony O will take the blame for that one, too."

Incredibly, the Black Hawks never failed to make the playoffs while Esposito was on the team. Internationally, he was a standout as well. In 1972 he shared the goaltending role with Ken Dryden on Team Canada in the Summit Series. And in 1981 he tended goal during the Canada Cup, but not for Team Canada. "I was born a Canadian, and I will always be a Canadian," said Tony. "Except

when he is playing goal—then he's a U.S. citizen," countered reporter Neil Campbell in the *Globe and Mail*. Campbell went on to explain that Esposito had been able to get his U.S. citizenship only during training camp for the cup series and had then had to wait as United States officials persuaded cup rulemakers to bend the regulation that said that once a player had competed for one country, he could never play for another.

Later in his career, Esposito began to gain a reputation as one of the grand old men of the NHL. But it wasn't always easy. By the early 1980s, he'd become dissatisfied with the way his teammates were performing in Chicago. "We had absolutely no desire to win," he said. "The only desire was to survive, to get your paycheck. There were people who didn't care about anything else. The attitude was terrible, and I made up my mind that if it didn't change I wouldn't

Tony Esposito revolutionized goaltending in the NHL with his open-legged "butterfly" style and flopping saves.

be back. I couldn't be associated with it any more." For his part, Tony O's goals-against average had ballooned to over four per game, almost double what it was for most of his career.

But by 1982, with Tony's help, the Hawks turned their game around again. As the oldest player in the league, Tony started to play like he was a decade younger in the 1982 playoffs, with a goals-against average under 2.00. "When you see desire after so long, it comes as a welcome relief," he said. "When guys go back to block shots and come back up to pick up their checks, that's what you want to see. I don't want to be on any damned 17th- or 18th- or 19th-place team—and I won't be!"

By 1983–84, Tony was the oldest player in the league and the only one over 40 years of age. Observers started to notice that while he was once the type of player who insisted on playing every minute of every game, he wisely realized that, at his age, he had to pick his spots and he happily shared the goalie's duties with backup Murray Bannerman. "I have always had a pretty heavy workload and I liked it that way," said Tony. "But the two-goalie system is how the team wants it, and so far it has worked out well. I do find it a bit tough when I play in a game on, say, a Sunday and then don't play again until the next Saturday. But I am satisfied with my play." So was coach Orval Tessier. "No coach could ask for anything more than Tony has been for this team," he said. "From the first day of camp, he worked his butt off and has been nothing but a very positive influence on this team."

But it was eventually time for Tony O to hang up the big pads and he was released by the Hawks in 1984. He wasn't long out of the pro game, though, before the Pittsburgh Penguins made him director of hockey operations. "I'm a hockey man," said Espo when he was asked about his lack of experience in the front office. "I know the business."

Other managers around the league weren't surprised by the Penguins' decision. "It didn't surprise me at all," said Minnesota's Lou Nanne. And former teammate Cliff Koroll remembered that Esposito "was always evaluating the guys he played with, talking about areas where we needed to improve. There's no doubt in my mind he will succeed."

After his time in Pittsburgh, Tony joined brother Phil in the front office of the expansion Tampa Bay Lightning. He was inducted into the Hockey Hall of Fame in 1988. But he will be best remembered as one of the true pioneers among netminders in the NHL.

Serge Savard

Rangy defenseman Serge Savard played 17 seasons in the NHL, 15 (his first season consisted of two games) with his hometown team, the Montreal Canadiens, and two with the Winnipeg Jets, who lured him out of retirement after he'd left Montreal following the 1980–81 season.

A member of the Canadiens "Big Three" defensive stars along with Guy Lapointe and Larry Robinson, Savard was known as "the Senator" by his teammates for his involvement in activities—mostly in politics—outside the game. In the mid-1980s, he served as general manager of the Habs, and later as an organizer for the Union Nationale party in Quebec and for the Liberals in federal politics.

Serge Savard was known as "the Senator" for his involvement in politics.

But hockey had been the first thing on Savard's mind since his boyhood in Montreal. When he was 15, a scout noticed him playing a school league game and put him on the team's list of promising reserves. Savard progressed quickly and within a few seasons was captain of the Junior Canadiens. Unlike many prospects of the day, Savard wanted to complete high school. But the Habs signed him to a contract and sent him to Houston to play for the Apollos of the Central Hockey League in 1966. He won the rookie of the year award that season with Houston and the following year was called up by the Habs. By the 1968–69 season, only his second full one in the NHL, he won the Conn Smythe Trophy as the Habs won the Cup in a four-game sweep over the Blues in the finals.

Fans and coaches alike began to appreciate the defensive ability and all-around play that Savard brought to the team, a style that complemented the Habs' flashier players. "His versatility is one of his strong points," said Montreal assistant general manager Floyd Curry. "Just look at the length of his arms and you'll see the reason why he can poke out his stick and break up so many plays. He has everything that is necessary to become a great star. In only two seasons he picked up one trophy, and goodness knows how many more he is going to earn." Although Savard was overshadowed by his better-known teammates, he did win another significant award during his years as a player. In 1979 the NHL presented him with the Bill Masterton Memorial Trophy, awarded annually to "the player who best exemplifies the qualities of perseverance, sportsmanship and dedication to hockey."

Savard almost didn't make it much further in NHL play, however. In a game during the 1970–71 season against the Rangers, he skated after New York's Rod Gilbert, trying to stop a breakaway. Savard dove for the puck and felt his left leg crumble underneath him. The result was five separate

Serge Savard (front) played five games in the Summit Series. Team Canada won four of them and tied the other.

fractures and three operations that took him out of the game for three months. Many Canadiens fans thought that, at age 24, Serge Savard had played his last game.

The Senator, however, had a different agenda. "It didn't upset me," he said. "When you're young and healthy, your morale is good, you feel you can cope with whatever happens." Still, he continued to have problems with the leg and further injuries. In the 1971–72 season, he suffered a new fracture to the same leg after being hit. In 1973 he injured his ankle severely as he tried to help firefighters break down a door during a fire at the Canadiens' hotel in St. Louis.

But the injuries failed to stop Savard. Upon his return to the game, he started to blend his patient, hard-working style with the hard-charging, rushing play of Lapointe and Robinson, the skillful scoring of Guy Lafleur and the outstanding play in the net of Ken Dryden. The result was another Cup for the Habs in 1976, when they swept the defending champion Philadelphia Flyers in four straight games, a victory that many relieved fans hailed as a triumph of skilled play over the fight-filled game of the Broad Street Bullies. "This isn't only a victory for the Canadiens, it is a victory for hockey," said Savard in the dressing room after the Habs had clinched the Cup. "I hope that this era of intimidation and violence that is hurting our national sport is coming to an end. Young people have seen that a team can play electrifying, fascinating hockey and win while still behaving like gentlemen."

Montreal coach Scotty Bowman was a little less philosophical regarding Savard's contributions to the team. "There are few superior players in the league, and there are few who contribute more to this team," said Bowman. "And there are few who have shown more courage." Internationally, Savard's attitude was rewarded by his being named to the Canadian team for the 1972 Summit Series. He appeared in five of the eight games, and—as Savard liked to remind people—Canada won four of those games and tied the other.

By 1981, Savard had had enough of being knocked around in the NHL. He had, after all, played on eight Stanley Cup-winning teams with Montreal and had seen more doctors and surgeons than he cared to remember. His retirement didn't last long, though. He was lured out of inactivity by the Winnipeg Jets, who wanted him for his experience on a young but improving team. "I don't see my role here as any sort of coach," said Savard. "I came here first as a player. This is a good spot for me because I won't have to carry the puck much. I'll just give it to the fast kids to carry."

Savard, Serge
D, 6´3´´, 210 lbs, b: Montreal, Que., 1/22/1946

Season	Club, League	Regular Season					Playoffs				
		GP	G	A	Pts	PIM	GP	G	A	Pts	PIM
1964–65	Omaha Knights, CHL	2	0	0	0	0	4	0	1	1	4
1966–67	Montreal Canadiens, NHL	2	0	0	0	0					
	Houston Apollos, CHL	68	7	25	32	155	5	1	3	4	17
	Quebec Aces, AHL						1	0	0	0	2
1967–68	Montreal Canadiens, NHL	67	2	13	15	34	6	2	0	2	0
1968–69	Montreal Canadiens, NHL	74	8	23	31	73	14	4	6	10	24
1969–70	Montreal Canadiens, NHL	64	12	19	31	38					
1970–71	Montreal Canadiens, NHL	37	5	10	15	30					
1971–72	Montreal Canadiens, NHL	23	1	8	9	16	6	0	0	0	10
SS–72	Canada	5	0	2	2	0					
1972–73	Montreal Canadiens, NHL	74	7	32	39	58	17	3	8	11	22
1973–74	Montreal Canadiens, NHL	67	4	14	18	49	6	1	1	2	4
1974–75	Montreal Canadiens, NHL	80	20	40	60	64	11	1	7	8	2
1975–76	Montreal Canadiens, NHL	71	8	39	47	38	13	3	6	9	6
CCup–76	Canada	7	0	3	3	0					
1976–77	Montreal Canadiens, NHL	78	9	33	42	35	14	2	7	9	2
1977–78	Montreal Canadiens, NHL	77	8	34	42	24	15	1	7	8	8
1978–79	Montreal Canadiens, NHL	80	7	26	33	30	16	2	7	9	6
ChCup–79	NHL All-Stars	3	0	0	0	0					
1979–80	Montreal Canadiens, NHL	46	5	8	13	18	2	0	0	0	0
1980–81	Montreal Canadiens, NHL	77	4	13	17	30	3	0	0	0	0
1981–82	Winnipeg Jets, NHL	47	2	5	7	26	4	0	0	0	2
1982–83	Winnipeg Jets, NHL	76	4	16	20	29	3	0	0	0	2
	NHL Totals	1040	106	333	439	592	130	19	49	68	88
	SS/CCup/ChalCup Totals	15	0	5	5	0					

NHL Second All-Star Team (1979)
Won Conn Smythe Trophy (1969)
Won Bill Masterton Trophy (1979)
Won Stanley Cup (1968, 1969, 1973, 1976, 1978, 1979)
Won CCup (1976)

Savard lasted two seasons in his comeback with Winnipeg before the Canadiens came calling again. They bought him out of the final year of his contract with the Jets so he could return to Montreal as the team's managing director. Savard, who had been active in the business world during his last days as a player and during his retirement, inspired the confidence of the Habs players and management. "I know everybody will try to win for him," said goalie Richard Sevigny.

Although Sevigny was talking about Savard the front office man, it was a fitting comment about a man who was inducted into the Hockey Hall of Fame in 1986 and who always tried to win on the ice, too.

Wayne Cashman

For 14 seasons, Wayne Cashman made a living in the corners of rinks around the National Hockey League, always wearing the black and yellow of the Boston Bruins. He was a courageous battler, big and tough and also rather nasty, the kind of player who is loved by teammates and fans but hated by his opponents. Though he was considered a threat with his fists, he was more than an enforcer. He had eight seasons with more than 20 goals and was a vital part of one of hockey's most productive lines when he was teamed with Phil Esposito and Ken Hodge.

Wayne Cashman was a courageous battler, big and tough and a bit nasty, too.

"Cash is a player. He is the kind of player every coach wants. He is a worker, a hitter and absolutely unselfish," Boston coach Don Cherry said of his rugged charge in 1975. "He sacrifices himself for his teammates and his team. He plays hurt when he has to. He suffers serious injuries and battles back. He is an amazing man."

Born in Kingston, Ontario, in 1945, Cashman began his professional career in 1964–65, playing one game with the Bruins. In 1968–69, after three seasons moving up and down between the Bruins, Blazers and Hershey Bears of the American Hockey League, Cashman finally earned a regular spot in the Boston lineup. Over the next few years, the Bruins would become one of the dominant teams in the league with such stars as Bobby Orr, Phil Esposito, John Bucyk and Gerry Cheevers in goal. They were known as the Big Bad Bruins and their physical play was matched by their offensive explosiveness.

The Cashman–Esposito–Hodge line was the highest-scoring threesome in the league for five consecutive seasons and was an integral part of Boston's two Stanley Cup victories in 1970 and 1972, but it was a line put together by accident. Harry Sinden, Boston coach at the time, needed a replacement for Ron Murphy, the veteran left winger, who was injured. Sinden decided to move Cashman from his post on the right wing to fill the gap, an experiment that worked immediately. While Cashman used his physical prowess to dig out the puck in the corners, Esposito staved off defenders in front of the net, ready to snap any pass past the goalie. Hodge was a burly winger with speed and a blasting shot from the right wing who also had good hands around the net. "When Cashman went into the corner, nine times out of 10 he came out of it with the puck," Esposito said. "We worked on it a lot. I'd know by the position he took when he went into the corner where he would get the puck to me."

With Cashman's help, Esposito set a record for scoring in 1970–71 with 76 goals—a number that topped the league until Wayne Gretzky came along—and also had three other seasons with

For 17 seasons, Wayne Cashman (right) made his living in the corners of NHL rinks, always wearing the black and yellow of the Boston Bruins.

more than 60 goals. Though the line had a simple formula for success, it wasn't always easy. One night in Buffalo, Esposito was waiting in front of the net as Cashman battled with two Sabres in the corner. Espo thought he saw the puck pop loose and went in to find it. "Cash did come up with the puck and got it out to the slot," Esposito said, "but I wasn't there. Buffalo picked it up and went down the ice to score. When we got back to the bench, I apologized to him for not being where I was supposed to be." Cashman told Esposito, his friend and roommate of seven years, that he'd beat him up if he found him in a corner again!

Cashman was a surprise selection to the Canadian roster in the Summit Series against the Soviet Union in 1972. The manager-coach of that team, the Bruins' Harry Sinden, knew Cashman well and said after the series that it was Cashman's play when he was inserted into the series' second game that turned things around for Canada. "We want people who can do great things with the puck," Sinden said, "but we also need guys like Cashman and J.P. Parise who'll get it for them." Though instrumental in the early games, Cashman was forced to miss the Moscow half of the matchup after receiving a serious injury against a Swedish team in an exhibition game in Stockholm.

For a man who played such a physical game, who sustained such a beating night after night, Cashman's career lasted a remarkably long time. By the time he retired in 1983, he and Carol Vadnais were the last members of the Bruins dynasty of the early 1970s still playing in Boston. In fact, he was the last survivor of the Original Six still in the NHL. Cashman was a fit player with stamina, but he also had the ability to play hurt. Early in his career he'd had a devastating pain in his back. When doctors operated, they found and removed a bone chip that had been embedded in a nerve. "But before they operated, he was coming to the dressing room on his hands and knees, literally, and somehow getting in the whirlpool and getting loosened up enough to play," Sinden recalled. "He played three or four games that way."

Wayne Cashman was a tough man and, according to Cheevers, the best to ever play his position. In 1986 he joined the New York Rangers as a scout and then as an assistant coach. He was later an assistant in Tampa Bay and San Jose and was on the staff of Canada's 1997 World Championship team. After Canada's victory, Cashman was briefly made the head coach in Philadelphia, stepping aside midway through his first season when the Flyers hired Roger Neilson.

Cashman, Wayne
LW, 6′1″, 208 lbs, b: Kingston, Ont., 6/24/1945

Season	Club, League	Regular Season					Playoffs				
		GP	G	A	Pts	PIM	GP	G	A	Pts	PIM
1964–65	Boston Bruins, NHL	1	0	0	0	0					
1966–67	Oklahoma City Blazers, CPHL	70	20	36	56	98	11	3	4	7	4
1967–68	Oklahoma City Blazers, CPHL	42	21	30	51	66					
	Boston Bruins, NHL	12	0	4	4	2	1	0	0	0	0
1968–69	Boston Bruins, NHL	51	8	23	31	49	6	0	1	1	0
	Hershey Bears, AHL	21	6	9	15	30					
1969–70	Boston Bruins, NHL	70	9	26	35	79	14	5	4	9	50
1970–71	Boston Bruins, NHL	77	21	58	79	100	7	3	2	5	15
1971–72	Boston Bruins, NHL	74	23	29	52	103	15	4	7	11	42
SS–72	Canada	2	0	2	2	14					
1972–73	Boston Bruins, NHL	76	29	39	68	100	5	1	1	2	4
1973–74	Boston Bruins, NHL	78	30	59	89	111	16	5	9	14	46
1974–75	Boston Bruins, NHL	42	11	22	33	24	1	0	2	2	0
1975–76	Boston Bruins, NHL	80	28	43	71	87	11	1	5	6	16
1976–77	Boston Bruins, NHL	65	15	37	52	76	14	1	8	9	18
1977–78	Boston Bruins, NHL	76	24	38	62	69	15	4	6	10	13
1978–79	Boston Bruins, NHL	75	27	40	67	63	10	4	5	9	8
1979–80	Boston Bruins, NHL	44	11	21	32	19	10	3	3	6	32
1980–81	Boston Bruins, NHL	77	25	35	60	80	3	0	1	1	0
1981–82	Boston Bruins, NHL	64	12	31	43	59	9	0	2	2	6
1982–83	Boston Bruins, NHL	65	4	11	15	20	8	0	1	1	0
	NHL Totals	1027	277	516	793	1041	145	31	57	88	250
	SS Totals	2	0	2	2	14					

NHL Second All-Star Team (1974)
Won Stanley Cup (1970, 1972)

Alexander Gusev

Until Alexander Gusev stepped onto the ice, no Soviet hockey player allowed himself to play exactly as he wanted without taking into account the interests of the team. On the defense line, Gusev acted like a force of nature rather than a member of the team at a time when responsibility and reliability were the two most highly valued qualities among defensemen.

Anatoli Tarasov put Gusev in the Central Red Army lineup but never allowed him to play in the USSR national team's most important games. Gusev only played in top-level games when Vsevolod Bobrov became coach. Gusev's entire career with the national team spanned the period from 1972 to 1977, during the so-called "coaching thaw" or open period in Soviet hockey.

When comparing Gusev, two other players come to mind—Bobby Orr and Viacheslav Fetisov. Gusev, who preceded Fetisov in Soviet hockey, had the same energetic moves during attacks on goal and determination on the ice. There was only one difference—Fetisov was a team player through and through; he was prepared to place his life on the line for his team. Gusev, on the other hand, played his own game, for himself, heeding only his own impulses. Fetisov's solutions to problems on the ice and his techniques stemmed from his ambitious style of play and from his energy. But when Gusev played, each of his feints, passes and shots was honed into a separate entity, and in this way he resembled Orr.

Alexander Gusev was the first player in Soviet hockey who permitted himself to play exactly as he wanted.

Gusev had an interesting pattern of play, not only in the attack zone but also in his own zone. If he found himself to be the last man in the line of defense, the coach would begin to worry because Gusev always took risks. He liked to provoke his opponent in a way that said, "Come and get me, because I'm in a tough spot with no backup." But at the very last second, Gusev would use his superb technique and maneuverability to execute a totally unexpected feint and clear the way to launch a forceful attack.

From his position in the net, Vladislav Tretiak was accustomed to watching his teammates somewhat objectively, and he had this to say about the unpredictable defenseman Gusev: "He has tremendous potential—powerful, precise and unexpected shots; smooth, natural stickhandling; broad tactical range; flawless passes from any distance. But he's moody, so it's not surprising when he suddenly comes apart for some trivial reason. When he loses heart, he can come to a total halt on the ice until he brings himself around."

At the 1973 World Championship, the USSR won the gold medal for the first time under coach Vsevolod Bobrov. Bobrov, unlike Tarasov, valued a gifted player over loyalty to the common cause. At that tournament, Gusev had a field day, scoring seven goals and chalking up seven assists. The team was captained for the first time by Boris Mikhailov, who recalled: "Understandably, he sometimes made mistakes. But no one said anything to him about these mistakes and treated him as if he

Gusev, Alexander
D, 6´1˝, 180 lbs, b: Moscow, USSR, 1/21/1947

Season	Club, League	Regular Season				
		GP	G	A	Pts	PIM
1965–67	SKA MVO (2), USSR	*	*	*	*	*
1967–68	CSKA, USSR	4	4	*	*	*
1968–69	CSKA, USSR	22	1	*	*	*
1969–70	CSKA, USSR	42	9	*	*	*
1970–71	CSKA, USSR	35	7	*	*	*
1971–72	CSKA, USSR	25	5	*	*	*
WEC–72	USSR	9	1	2	3	6
SS–72	USSR	6	1	0	1	2
1972–73	CSKA, USSR	23	7	*	*	*
WEC–73	USSR	10	7	7	14	4
1973–74	CSKA, USSR	23	5	1	6	*
WEC–74	USSR	10	3	3	6	8
1974–75	CSKA, USSR	32	9	14	23	42
1975–76	CSKA, USSR	36	10	12	22	36
OWG–76	USSR	6	1	2	3	6
CCup–76	USSR	5	0	5	5	0
1976–77	CSKA, USSR	23	2	2	4	10
WEC–77	USSR	7	0	3	3	0
1977–78	CSKA, USSR	12	4	0	4	0
1978–79	SKA Leningrad, USSR	29	1	8	9	28
	USSR Totals	306	64	*	*	*
	OWG/WEC/SS/CCup Totals	53	13	22	35	26

Won OWG (1976)
Won WEC (1973, 1974, 1975)
USSR Champion (1970, 1971, 1972, 1973, 1975, 1977)

At the 1973 World Championship, Alexander Gusev (right) scored seven goals and added seven assists.

always did everything right. You only had to give him a dressing down and he would become so offended, so nervous, that he would immediately lose it."

No one ever managed to penetrate the depths of Gusev's character. He played with an indifferent and disagreeable expression on his face that made it difficult to guess what he was thinking. If Gusev had played out his career at a time when there were rewards and incentives for goals and assists, perhaps he would have worn a different expression.

In the 1974 series against the WHA's best, the Soviet team was losing one of their home games 5–2. The gap was eventually reduced to 5–4. "Well, who's going to score the clincher?" coach Boris Kulagin asked as he walked up and down in front of the team bench. "He'll be a hero for sure."

The goal was scored by a very motivated Gusev with a terrific slapshot from the blue line.

Vladimir Shadrin

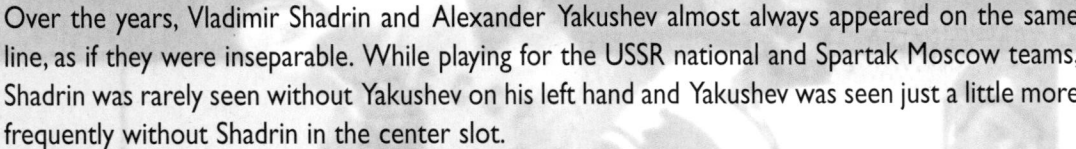

Over the years, Vladimir Shadrin and Alexander Yakushev almost always appeared on the same line, as if they were inseparable. While playing for the USSR national and Spartak Moscow teams, Shadrin was rarely seen without Yakushev on his left hand and Yakushev was seen just a little more frequently without Shadrin in the center slot.

Beginning with Boris and Yevgeny Mayorov playing alongside Vyacheslav Starshinov—the famous founders of the special Spartak style of hockey—there were quite a few illustrious forwards on that team. All were fastidious players, although as artists on ice, each put his personal stamp on the team and brought his own idiosyncrasies. In this respect, Shadrin was an exception in that he didn't see any hockey talent in himself. He had a lack of self-confidence and doubted whether he even had the right to be in big-league hockey. In an unusual start for a hockey player, he graduated from a special mathematics school with honors and then enrolled in an institute specializing in the petrochemical and gas industry.

Vladimir Shadrin (front) was a statistician who brought some measure of regularity to his team.

While with Spartak in the 1970s, Shadrin chose a role for himself that no one else vied for—the team workhorse. In contrast to the new forwards, who fluttered about the rink waiting for just the right moment to "put on a show," Shadrin was notable for his low-key role in the plays that garnered the most attention from the fans. It wasn't until 1975, when he was already 26, that his confidence finally matched his importance on the ice and he began to look like a hockey personality in his own right. To a lesser extent, the same held true for his teammates, thanks to their coach Nikolai Karpov. "He was a cunning man, but cunning in the good sense of the word," Shadrin recalled. "Those who followed him were sure to have his kindness, benevolence and trust. We could always feel that there was someone who looked after our interests, someone who would stick up for us. It was only under Karpov's leadership that I felt totally unshackled, that I could breathe freely. But in the national lineup, under other coaches, this feeling of constraint returned."

Under the tutelage of Anatoli Tarasov, Shadrin was one of the most unremarkable players on the national team. Tarasov didn't get to see his speed, his technique or the complex plays that outwitted opponents. Shadrin emerged in key positions on the USSR national team beginning with the 1972 Summit Series when Vsevolod Bobrov was the coach. And it was Tarasov himself who responded most enthusiastically to Shadrin's new playing status. "When I first met Shadrin, he seemed a little bit of a sissy to me. And because of that, I was afraid that he wouldn't be able to hold his own against the Canadians, who were known to be aggressive and tough. But when it came to crossing sticks with the Canadians, Shadrin's performance was beyond all praise. They roughed him up, but he showed that he could take it. He reliably controlled the puck and at the right moment would pass it to his partner. It wasn't that he simply carried out the coach's instructions, but he did so in an exemplary way and with pride. A player with such qualities helps a coach to plan victories."

Vladimir Shadrin (left) emerged in a key position on the USSR national team in the Summit Series.

Shadrin's job with Spartak and the national squad was specific. Whereas the Spartak wingers played an individualistic and undisciplined style of hockey, Shadrin was the mathematician who brought some measure of regularity to the team. As one of the best forward lines for the team in the mid-1970s, the Shalimov–Shadrin–Yakushev line was a firm runner-up in the Soviet squad to the Petrov line. But there was no comparison in the style of play between the two lines. The Spartak line specialized in fancy footwork and stickhandling. Shalimov and Yakushev held onto the puck for long spells at a time—something that Mikhailov and Kharlamov would never do. Shalimov and Yakushev would mount an attack, but without the fury and energy so typical of the Petrov line. And Shadrin had his own special role. He would suddenly appear in possession of the puck when it seemed irretrievable. Or he would show up just in time to help the wingers mount another dash at the opposing goal. He had a knack for making a play happen completely unnoticed and with the smallest of movements, often setting himself up as a bridge or shortcut to the net and making way for one of his linemates to score.

The Spartak line played a much too refined and fanciful style, and much of their work would have come to nothing had it not been for Shadrin. Hard work and cool calculation constituted Shadrin's motto in hockey. At the Olympic tournament in 1976, the season when he openly admitted for the first time that he had taken a real liking to hockey and had gotten the hang of it, Shadrin scored more goals than all the other forwards for the only time in his career.

In 1977 Vladimir Shadrin was only 28. At the helm of the national squad was Viktor Tikhonov, while Spartak was being coached by Robert Cherenkov. Shadrin quietly and prematurely ended his playing career. He tried coaching for a while but was unable to make an impact.

Shadrin, Vladimir
C, 5′11″, 190 lbs, b: Moscow, USSR, 6/6/1948

Season	Club, League	Regular Season				
		GP	G	A	Pts	PIM
1965–67	Spartak Moscow, USSR	*	*	*	*	*
1967–68	Spartak Moscow, USSR	*	10	*	*	*
1968–69	Spartak Moscow, USSR	42	12	*	*	*
1969–70	Spartak Moscow, USSR	31	28	*	*	*
WEC–70	USSR	1	1	4	5	0
1970–71	Spartak Moscow, USSR	37	22	*	*	*
WEC–71	USSR	5	6	2	8	0
1971–72	Spartak Moscow, USSR	31	14	*	*	*
OWG–72	USSR	3	1	0	1	2
WEC–72	USSR	9	5	5	10	6
SS–72	USSR	8	3	5	8	0
1972–73	Spartak Moscow, USSR	31	24	15	39	16
WEC–73	USSR	9	3	7	10	4
1973–74	Spartak Moscow, USSR	32	18	11	29	14
WEC–74	USSR	10	6	5	11	20
1974–75	Spartak Moscow, USSR	35	14	14	28	14
WEC–75	USSR	9	8	7	15	4
1975–76	Spartak Moscow, USSR	35	17	18	35	20
OWG–76	USSR	6	10	4	14	2
WEC–76	USSR	9	2	3	5	6
1976–77	Spartak Moscow, USSR	29	14	17	31	14
WEC–77	USSR	10	3	6	9	2
1977–78	Spartak Moscow, USSR	20	7	14	21	12
1978–79	Spartak Moscow, USSR	22	9	8	17	6
1979–80	Oji Seishi Tomakomai, Japan	15	17	14	31	-
1980–81	Oji Seishi Tomakomai, Japan	20	16	23	39	-
1981–82	Oji Seishi Tomakomai, Japan	30	25	54	79	-
1982–83	Oji Seishi Tomakomai, Japan	30	20	49	69	-
	USSR Totals	445	213	*	*	*
	OWG/WEC/SS Totals	79	48	48	96	46

Won OWG (1972, 1976)
Won WEC (1970, 1971, 1973, 1974, 1975)
USSR Champion (1967, 1969, 1976)

Vladimir **Petrov**

Vladimir Petrov was at first rejected by the Dynamo hockey school for a perceived lack of talent.

Democracy was unknown to Soviet hockey players until the end of the 1980s. Up to that point, the coach was always right. Vladimir Petrov, a man of unique character, never let that stop him. He behaved as if democracy had always existed to the fullest extent in hockey. His coach, Anatoli Tarasov, who could hurt a person more with words than with his fist, reserved his most humiliating epithets for the headstrong Petrov. Referring to a disgruntled Viktor Tikhonov, Petrov once said, "When I hung up my skates, he didn't even allow me to coach the Army hockey school for kids."

But in fact Tarasov needed Petrov. He needed this actively aggressive, brazen, down-to-earth player from the Moscow region because he was exactly right for Tarasov's new tactic of putting on the pressure and checking all the way down the entire length of the ice. Tarasov dreamed of a confrontation at the highest level—with the Canadians—and he was in dire need of players who could beat the Canadians at their own game.

Petrov was the only possible player to assist and anchor a lineup with the superb skater Valeri Kharlamov and the master of brilliant on-the-spot decisions, Boris Mikhailov. Petrov, a center with plenty of power, pulled these two polar opposites together.

Petrov came into top-level hockey very early. At first he was rejected by the Dynamo hockey school for lack of talent. Having made it to the CSKA (Central Red Army) in a roundabout way through the Krylja Sovetov (Soviet Wings—a mediocre team at that time), he demonstrated many qualities similar to the legendary pros. He loved to start a commotion out of nothing during a game, over how his opponent held his stick during a face-off, for example. Behind the simple and even good-natured appearance of this Russian giant, there was a cunning mind and a passionate heart. He knew how to turn up the heat on an opponent in one-on-one combat. He knew how to play to win, and what to do in that crucial moment when he needed to break his opponent. He could appear impassive while forcing stronger opponents to give up. Petrov played according to his own rules.

Through sheer driving force and the amount of time spent on the ice, he became the kind of center that was unique to Soviet hockey. Add to this an insatiable ambition and there was no one who could compare to Petrov back then or even years later.

He began playing on a forward line with Veniamin Alexandrov, a second-generation player, and ended playing in the 1981 World Championship in a trio that included Sergei Makarov

Petrov, Vladimir
C, 6′, 198 lbs, b: Moscow, USSR, 6/30/1947

Season	Club, League	Regular Season				
		GP	G	A	Pts	PIM
1965–66	Krylja Sovetov, USSR	23	1	8	9	*
1966–67	Krylja Sovetov, USSR	44	15	9	24	*
1967–68	CSKA, USSR	38	21	19	40	*
1968–69	CSKA, USSR	39	27	18	45	*
WEC–69	USSR	10	6	2	8	16
1969–70	CSKA, USSR	43	51	21	72	*
WEC–70	USSR	10	5	3	8	8
1970–71	CSKA, USSR	37	16	16	32	*
WEC–71	USSR	9	8	3	11	2
1971–72	CSKA, USSR	32	21	16	37	*
OWG–72	USSR	4	0	2	2	0
WEC–72	USSR	10	6	6	12	6
SS–72	USSR	8	3	4	7	10
1972–73	CSKA, USSR	30	27	22	49	*
WEC–73	USSR	10	18	16	34	12
1973–74	CSKA, USSR	28	14	14	28	34
WEC–74	USSR	8	4	7	11	0
1974–75	CSKA, USSR	34	27	26	53	58
WEC–75	USSR	10	6	12	18	2
1975–76	CSKA, USSR	34	22	22	44	46
OWG–76	USSR	6	6	3	9	8
1976–77	CSKA, USSR	35	26	36	62	57
WEC–77	USSR	10	7	14	21	8
1977–78	CSKA, USSR	31	28	28	56	41
WEC–78	USSR	8	3	1	4	14
1978–79	CSKA, USSR	43	26	37	63	54
WEC–79	USSR	8	7	8	15	10
1979–80	CSKA, USSR	32	21	20	41	28
OWG–80	USSR	7	4	2	6	6
1980–81	CSKA, USSR	40	19	24	43	42
WEC–81	USSR	8	4	6	10	6
1981–82	SKA Leningrad, USSR	20	4	3	7	24
1982–83	SKA Leningrad, USSR	12	4	4	8	18
	USSR Totals	595	370	343	713	*
	OWG/WEC/SS Totals	126	87	89	176	108

Won OWG (1972, 1976)
Won WEC (1969, 1970, 1971, 1973, 1974, 1975, 1978, 1979, 1981)
USSR Champion (1968, 1970, 1971, 1972, 1973, 1975, 1978, 1979, 1981)

and Vladimir Krutov. He also played with the young Andrei Khomutov in the national championship. For Petrov, for whom it had been difficult to make it in hockey—he nearly became a professional dancer—it was extremely important to maintain a youthful outlook. The aim, for Petrov, justified the means.

Boris Mikhailov never considered himself as gifted a player as Valeri Kharlamov. Petrov did. And this wasn't arrogance. Petrov believed he was energized by hockey. The only difference was that Kharlamov was able to find a more effective way of transforming his energy on the ice.

Vladimir Petrov (right) knew how to turn up the heat in one-on-one combat.

Pete Mahovlich

At 6´5˝, Pete Mahovlich was five inches taller than his older brother but was still called "the Little M."

Pete Mahovlich was an accurate passer and skilled with the puck, making up for a lack of speed with craftiness and size (for years he was the National Hockey League's biggest player). A humorous character and part of a famous hockey family along with big brother Frank, Pete is perhaps best known for coming off the ice at a crucial moment in the 1972 Summit Series against the Soviet Union.

Frank, called "the Big M," was already an established star with the Toronto Maple Leafs when Pete began his career in the Detroit Red Wings organization in 1963. After three lackluster junior seasons with the Hamilton Red Wings in the Ontario Hockey Association, he was brought up to the NHL and played for three games before being sent down again. This up and down movement lasted four seasons, and despite the brief happiness of playing with his brother, who joined the Wings in 1968, Mahovlich came close to quitting the game because of his frustration with finding a permanent hockey home. Over those four years with Detroit, he scored only nine goals in 82 games, but his play and his size impressed the Montreal Canadiens and general manager Sam Pollock.

"Mahovlich's problem in Detroit was that he was brought up when he still had a year or two of junior eligibility left," Pollack said. "And he was brought up to a team and sent down to others which weren't very good."

In June 1969, at the age of 23, he was acquired by the Canadiens in a trade for Garry Monahan and Doug Piper. He spent the next season again splitting time between the American Hockey League and the NHL, scoring nine goals in 36 games with Montreal. At 6´5˝ and 210 pounds, he was 5˝ taller than his brother and was jokingly called "the Little M." Mahovlich should have been a force to be reckoned with, but many people felt that the big center was simply too easygoing to throw his weight around and be aggressive. He was a prankster and a little bit odd off the ice, setting fire to newspapers while people were reading them and growing plants in his locker stall. He said he kept things light off the ice to minimize the pressure.

Pete Mahovlich (right) scored a key goal in the second game of the 1972 Summit Series, skating around three Soviets to score shorthanded and secure the win.

"Everybody who has played this game likes this game and I guess I've liked it so much that I've been a little too pleasant," Mahovlich said in 1970. "But I can't be that way anymore. The Canadiens want me to hit, so that's the attitude I have to take. That's the attitude I want to take on the ice. Off the ice—well, I wouldn't want to change anything."

He began to wear knee braces, reducing the number of games he missed with injuries, and, when he joined the Habs, toughened his approach to the game. In 1970–71, Mahovlich had a regular spot on the Canadiens roster, often playing with Henri Richard, and halfway through the season he was reunited with his brother when Frank was acquired from the Red Wings. Pete vastly improved his scoring ways and his tough play, finishing the regular season with 35 goals and 181 penalty minutes. In the playoffs he added 10 goals and 16 points in 20 games as Montreal marched to the Stanley Cup.

He scored 35 goals again the next season and was chosen to play with Team Canada against the Soviet Union in 1972. He scored a key goal in the second game, skating around three Soviets to score shorthanded and secure the only win in Canada for the home team. In the final game in Moscow, he ventured into a crowd of Red Army soldiers to rescue Alan Eagleson, the hockey executive who was causing trouble in the stands. With Canada needing a goal in the dying seconds of the game, Paul Henderson called Mahovlich off the ice. After Henderson's heroic goal won the series for the Canadiens, neither man could explain why they'd made the change. Henderson "felt" something and Mahovlich, still easy-going when it came to his teammates, simply obliged.

Mahovlich won three more Stanley Cups with Montreal in the 1970s and was a key part of the league's top scoring line with Guy Lafleur and Steve Shutt for two seasons. In 1974–75, he was fifth in the league with 117 points, including 82 assists, and topped 100 points again the next season. Mahovlich was as outgoing as his brother was quiet and acquired the nickname "Good Time Pete" for his partying ways—not attributes loved by Montreal coach Scotty Bowman. The player-coach relationship soured further in 1976–77. Mahovlich wasn't happy with his playing time and argued constantly with Bowman, something he came to regret later in his career. "I was trying to tell him how to run the team and I shouldn't have been," Mahovlich said. "I was young and a little foolish."

Mahovlich, Pete
C, 6′5″, 210 lbs, b: Timmins, Ont., 10/10/1946

Season	Club, League	Regular Season					Playoffs				
		GP	G	A	Pts	PIM	GP	G	A	Pts	PIM
1965–66	Detroit Red Wings, NHL	3	0	1	1	0					
1966–67	Detroit Red Wings, NHL	34	1	3	4	16					
	Pittsburgh Hornets, AHL	18	4	7	11	37	9	0	0	0	2
1967–68	Detroit Red Wings, NHL	15	6	4	10	13					
	Fort Worth Wings, CHL	42	20	14	34	103					
1968–69	Detroit Red Wings, NHL	30	2	2	4	21					
	Fort Worth Wings, CHL	34	19	17	36	54					
1969–70	Montreal Canadiens, NHL	36	9	8	17	51					
	Montreal Voyageurs, AHL	31	21	19	40	77					
1970–71	Montreal Canadiens, NHL	78	35	26	61	181	20	10	6	16	43
1971–72	Montreal Canadiens, NHL	75	35	32	67	103	6	0	2	2	12
SS–72	Canada	7	1	1	2	4					
1972–73	Montreal Canadiens, NHL	61	21	38	59	49	17	4	9	13	22
1973–74	Montreal Canadiens, NHL	78	36	37	73	122	6	2	1	3	4
1974–75	Montreal Canadiens, NHL	80	35	82	117	64	11	6	10	16	10
1975–76	Montreal Canadiens, NHL	80	34	71	105	76	13	4	8	12	24
1976–77	Montreal Canadiens, NHL	76	15	47	62	45	13	4	5	9	19
1977–78	Montreal Canadiens, NHL	17	3	5	8	4					
	Pittsburgh Penguins, NHL	57	25	36	61	37					
1978–79	Pittsburgh Penguins, NHL	60	14	39	53	39	2	0	1	1	0
1979–80	Detroit Red Wings, NHL	80	16	50	66	69					
1980–81	Detroit Red Wings, NHL	24	1	4	5	26					
	Adirondack Red Wings, AHL	37	18	18	36	49	18	1	18	19	23
1981–82	Adirondack Red Wings, AHL	80	22	45	67	71	4	2	1	3	2
1985–86	Toledo Goaldiggers, IHL	23	4	10	14	50					
	NHL Totals	884	288	485	773	916	88	30	42	72	134
	SS Totals	7	1	1	2	4					

Won Stanley Cup (1971, 1973, 1976, 1977)

In December 1977 Mahovlich was sent with Peter Lee to the Pittsburgh Penguins for Pierre Larouche. After one injury-shortened season with the Penguins, he was once again on the move, traded to the Detroit Red Wings for Nick Libett in 1979. He was signed to a $1-million, five-year contract by Detroit general manager Ted Lindsay—a tough man just about everywhere except the negotiating room. Mahovlich was now 32 and had obviously slowed a step. In his first season with the Wings he had 65 points in 80 games. The next year he broke his wrist early in the season, and when he returned, Lindsay was gone from behind the bench and the organization. Mahovlich never got along with Lindsay's coaching replacement, Wayne Maxner, and was soon sent down to Detroit's American Hockey League farm team in Adirondack.

Both Mahovlich brothers struggled with depression. Frank required two leaves of absence from the Toronto Maple Leafs to deal with his, and Pete, who failed to live up to expectations and his high salary in Detroit, had problems after his demotion and the death of his father. He did help the Adirondack team win the Calder Cup—he had also won it 14 seasons before during one of his stays with the Pittsburgh Hornets—and played one full season in the AHL, still receiving his sizeable NHL paycheck from the Red Wings before deciding to retire in 1982. He returned briefly to the game in 1985–86, playing with the Toledo Goaldiggers in the International Hockey League for 23 games.

Boris Mikhailov

The best sniper in Soviet ice hockey history was Boris Mikhailov. In 572 games, he scored 452 goals and had an unknown number of assists, since those statistics weren't so thoroughly kept in the old USSR. He began his career as a checker and was good at it. Tough, ruthless and fast, he could cover a lot of ice in the run of a game. While playing for the minor-league Energy Saratov team, he gave the game everything he had, and he did the same for Lokomotiv Moscow later on. In 1967 Mikhailov's partner, Yevgeny Mishakov, who had switched to the CSKA, persuaded coach Tarasov to try the young forward.

Boris Mikhailov was the best sniper in the history of Soviet hockey.

Later, Tarasov recalled that he was quite skeptical of Mishakov's advice. The 24-year-old Mikhailov, who lacked a proper hockey education and disappointed the highly experienced coach with his clumsy technique, didn't look like a future star. But Tarasov firmly believed that the potential of a player showed in the seriousness with which he trained. Seeing how stubbornly and persistently the young forward worked out, the coach began to believe in him.

The Army club's 24-year-old rookie would never become a classy forward. It is much easier to acquire the necessary skills in early childhood than to attempt to retrain at a later age. Mikhailov never learned to score as elegantly and gracefully as, say, Jean Beliveau. However, Mikhailov played only half the games in the Soviet national league that Beliveau did in the NHL. All the same, the

Boris Mikhailov (number 13) was especially dangerous right in front of the net.

Soviet forward was just a little behind the Canadian player's record as a goal scorer (452 goals versus Beliveau's 507).

Soviet players claimed that the traffic generated by Canadian defensemen in front of their net was so heavy that it would be easier to cross Broadway at rush hour. Even the young forwards of today prefer to avoid that traffic. Mikhailov, by contrast, got particular satisfaction out of clashing with the opposition defensemen on their own territory. He would take them on in their zone, hitting and getting hit and preventing the goalie from following the puck. Once he got hold of the puck, the odds were pretty high that it would end up as a goal. Mikhailov was considered especially dangerous right in front of the net, and though he was never credited for elegance, he was good at what counted in the game of hockey.

By the mid-1970s, Boris Mikhailov was already more than just a checker. His career took a highly positive turn when coach Tarasov put him with two famous forwards, Valeri Kharlamov and Vladimir Petrov, to form a trio that soon became the best in the world. The Mikhailov–Petrov–Kharlamov line was very different from the classic Canadian pattern of playmaker–triggerman–soldier. Any of that Soviet line's three players could function in any of the three roles. If the remarkably talented Valeri Kharlamov defined the mystery and unpredictability of the trio's game, Boris Mikhailov added his ruthlessness, his hunger to score and his desire for victory, regardless of the finer details of the play.

After Valeri Kharlamov's death in a car crash, the magnificent trio was broken up. Boris Mikhailov didn't retire, however. In the early 1980s, he was coach of the Army club in Leningrad, and then he returned to the CSKA and assisted chief coach Viktor Tikhonov. Afterward, he spent time coaching in Switzerland but with little of the success he enjoyed as a player. In 1993, as head of the Russian national team, coach Boris Mikhailov, despite widespread skepticism, led his team to victory at the World Championship in Germany. But at the 1996 World Cup, even Boris Mikhailov was unable to inspire what he considered the money-hungry Russian NHLers to dazzle their audience.

Mikhailov, Boris
RW, 5'9", 169 lbs, b: Moscow, USSR, 10/6/1944

Season	Club, League	Regular Season				
		GP	G	A	Pts	PIM
1965–66	Lokomotiv Moscow, USSR	28	18	8	26	8
1966–67	Lokomotiv Moscow, USSR	44	20	7	27	16
1967–68	CSKA, USSR	43	29	16	45	16
1968–69	CSKA, USSR	42	36	14	50	14
WEC–69	USSR	9	9	5	14	6
1969–70	CSKA, USSR	44	40	15	55	22
WEC–70	USSR	10	7	3	10	2
1970–71	CSKA, USSR	40	32	15	47	16
WEC–71	USSR	9	7	3	10	2
1971–72	CSKA, USSR	31	20	13	33	18
OWG–72	USSR	3	2	0	2	0
WEC–72	USSR	10	11	2	13	6
SS–72	USSR	8	3	2	5	9
1972–73	CSKA, USSR	30	24	13	37	20
WEC–73	USSR	10	16	13	29	4
1973–74	CSKA, USSR	31	18	9	27	12
WEC–74	USSR	10	8	8	16	16
1974–75	CSKA, USSR	35	40	11	51	30
WEC–75	USSR	9	7	8	15	2
1975–76	CSKA, USSR	36	31	7	38	43
OWG–76	USSR	5	3	1	4	2
WEC–76	USSR	10	7	6	13	8
1976–77	CSKA, USSR	34	28	23	51	10
WEC–77	USSR	10	12	7	19	4
1977–78	CSKA, USSR	35	32	20	52	18
WEC–78	USSR	10	9	3	12	6
1978–79	CSKA, USSR	43	30	24	54	23
WEC–79	USSR	8	4	8	12	0
1979–80	CSKA, USSR	41	27	23	50	19
OWG–80	USSR	7	6	5	11	2
1980–81	CSKA, USSR	15	4	5	9	4
	USSR Totals	572	429	223	652	289
	OWG/WEC/SS Totals	128	111	74	185	69

Named Best Forward at WEC (1973, 1979)
Won OWG (1972, 1976)
Won WEC (1969, 1970, 1971, 1973, 1974, 1975, 1978, 1979)
USSR Champion (1968, 1970, 1971, 1972, 1973, 1975, 1977, 1978, 1979, 1980, 1981)

Ken Dryden

Ken Dryden won the Stanley Cup six times in just eight NHL seasons.

When Ken Dryden's name is mentioned, nobody imagines a frustrated goalie slashing at the puck as it comes dangerously close to the net, but rather a quiet man standing in front of the net with his arms crossed, leaning on his stick. With his great height, people tended to take notice of him when he was calm and poised, watching the action unfold at the other end of the rink. He wore a look of deep concentration and complete self-confidence. Those were the two aspects of the Montreal Canadiens' number 29.

In the late 1960s and early 1970s, the Montreal Canadiens had no room for underperformers on their team. On the famous club's roster, there were enough talented and highly experienced players to put together several teams. Like all top teams, the old guard gradually retired and the team had to be reinforced with young players. But rookies spent as much time in the press box as on the ice. When in the spring of 1971 Dryden was called up from a farm club, he thought of it as a reward. If you showed good results on a farm team, you would get to suit up for more pro matches. Dryden appeared in six games and surprised everybody by putting on a superb performance, but also by helping the team to win six straight games.

But nobody expected to see the young goaltender in the playoff series. In the first round, the Montreal Canadiens were scheduled to go up against the Boston Bruins, who had set several NHL records that season. Boston had Phil Esposito, Bobby Orr, Wayne Cashman, Ken Hodge and Johnny Bucyk. And they had another advantage—playing on home ice. In such a situation, coaches usually prefer to rely on experienced players, yet Al MacNeil took a chance on his novice. And Ken defeated the Bruins almost single-handedly. The series lasted for seven games, and Dryden rescued his team after quite a few sloppy plays and from goals that should have been scored. The Boston players were frustrated time and again by the goalie who shouldn't have been in the playoffs. Phil Esposito, who had scored 76 goals in 78 regular-season games, couldn't believe that "the giraffe" had allowed him to score only three goals in the entire series.

After accomplishing the near impossible in the first round, the Montreal Canadiens eventually took the six-game series from the Minnesota North Stars and the next series of seven games from the Chicago Black Hawks to capture the Stanley Cup. Dryden's contribution was a major one, and his goals-against average was almost unparalleled in the league for a rookie. It came as no surprise when he was awarded the Conn Smythe Trophy as the playoffs' most outstanding performer.

In Dryden's third game with the Canadiens, with Montreal hosting the Buffalo Sabres and the Forum filled to capacity, a unique event took place. The fans were anxious to see the Dryden brothers, who were goalies on the opposing teams, in action. When the lineups were announced, the audience had to swallow their disappointment. The coaches were more interested in the outcome of the game and the two brothers remained on the benches. But then the Canadiens' regular goaltender, Rogie Vachon, was injured in the second period and Dryden was sent out to replace him. On seeing this, Sabres coach Punch Imlach immediately substituted his goaltender as well, sending Dave Dryden out on the ice. For the first time in NHL history, two brothers faced each other from opposite ends of the rink. Both were visibly nervous, but Ken was luckier. After the game, Imlach explained that he pulled the switch to give his team some fighting spirit, even though what happened was quite the contrary. The first shot on Dave Dryden's net went in. The Montreal

Canadiens won 5–2. After the siren, the Drydens met in the center ice area and shook hands. The audience gave them a standing ovation and a new chapter was written in NHL chronicles.

During his short first season in the NHL, Ken Dryden demonstrated brilliant technique as a goalie and an ability to win even in unfavorable situations—qualities acquired with experience. The Canadiens management was convinced and Dryden was made the team's main goaltender. During the 1971–72 season, he displayed ever more self-assurance and played 64 games with a goals-against average of 2.24. He was elected rookie of the year and later became the first goalie in the NHL to get the Conn Smythe Trophy and then the Calder Trophy. The next year, Dryden was firmly established as the Montreal Canadiens' top goaltender and at the end of the season was awarded another prize, the Vezina Trophy, as the league's best goalie.

But after winning three individual prizes and two Stanley Cups in three incomplete seasons in the NHL, Dryden suddenly declared that his career was over at age 26. He joined the law offices of Osler, Hoskin and Harcourt in Toronto as an articling student with an annual salary of $7,500. Dryden never hid the fact that his life wasn't limited to hockey, and he told reporters about his dream of becoming a lawyer. Still, it is difficult to understand his dropping hockey at the moment of his primacy and his greatest success. A simple explanation was that Ken's salary with the Montreal Canadiens was too modest and he thought he deserved a much more generous reward. His negotiations with the Canadiens bosses resulted in nothing. The club didn't want to pay him more, so Dryden quit.

The next season, the Montreal Canadiens' three remaining goalies took turns in the net and their performance left much to be desired. The season was over for the Montreal Canadiens when they were knocked out by the New York Rangers in the first round of the playoffs. Meanwhile, Dryden was working in a law office hundreds of miles from Montreal, playing off and on with an amateur team as a defenseman. Ken's boycott ended in victory. Between seasons, the two parties came to a financial compromise and Dryden returned to the Montreal Canadiens. After a year in self-imposed exile, he was still sharp, but he wasn't the brilliant goaltender he used to be.

From the 1975–76 season up until the end of his career in 1979, Dryden once again performed superbly. The proof is in his remarkable individual stats. He never exceeded the goals-against mark of 2.30 per game and his team won the Stanley Cup four times in a row. Dryden was awarded the Vezina Trophy four more times. Five times he was included on the First All-Star Team and once on the Second All-Star Team. In his career, he had 46 shutouts and his overall average was an impressive 2.24. The 1976–77 season was his best ever—56 games, 10 shutouts and a goals-against average

Dryden, Ken
G, 6´4˝, 205 lbs, b: Hamilton, Ont., 8/8/1947

Season	Club, League	Regular Season				Playoffs			
		GP	Mins	GA	Avg	GP	Mins	GA	Avg
1966–67	Cornell University, ECAC	27	1646	40	1.46				
1967–68	Cornell University, ECAC	29	1620	41	1.52				
1968–69	Cornell University, ECAC	27	1578	47	1.79				
WEC–69	Canada	2	120	4	2.00				
1970–71	Montreal Voyageurs, AHL	33	1899	84	2.68				
	Montreal Canadiens, NHL	6	327	9	1.65	20	1221	61	3.00
1971–72	Montreal Canadiens, NHL	64	3800	142	2.24	6	360	17	2.83
SS–72	Canada	4	240	19	4.75				
1972–73	Montreal Canadiens, NHL	54	3165	119	2.26	17	1039	50	2.89
1974–75	Montreal Canadiens, NHL	56	3320	149	2.69	11	688	29	2.53
1975–76	Montreal Canadiens, NHL	62	3580	121	2.03	13	780	25	1.92
1976–77	Montreal Canadiens, NHL	56	3275	117	2.14	14	849	22	1.55
1977–78	Montreal Canadiens, NHL	52	3071	105	2.05	15	919	29	1.89
1978–79	Montreal Canadiens, NHL	47	2814	108	2.30	16	990	41	2.48
ChCup–79	NHL All-Stars	2	120	7	3.50				
	NHL Totals	397	23352	870	2.24	112	6846	274	2.40
	WEC/SS/ChalCup Totals	8	480	30	3.75				

NHL First All-Star Team (1973, 1976, 1977, 1978, 1979)
NHL Second All-Star Team (1972)
Won Vezina Trophy (1973, 1976, 1977, 1978, 1979)
Won Conn Smythe Trophy (1971)
Won Calder Trophy (1972)
Won Stanley Cup (1971, 1973, 1976, 1977, 1978, 1979)

Ken Dryden

of 2.14 in regular-season play and 14 games, four shutouts and an incredible 1.56 in playoff games. Those were the days when the Canadiens forwards were on a scoring streak. Ken gained a reputation for his exceptionally quick reflexes and his brilliant work with the goalie stick. He even got 23 assists during his career. But the most important statistic of all is the six Stanley Cup wins in eight seasons.

In his years with the Montreal Canadiens, Dryden gained a reputation for being an extremely frugal financier. Montreal fans would joke that Ken became a goalie just so he could pick up coins the audience threw onto the ice during a game. The field players, busy racing around the rink, wouldn't have had time for that. Dryden even agreed with the fans. But his willingness to pick up a coin added a much-needed human dimension to him. As the Montreal Canadiens' unquestionable IQ leader, Ken was the best educated, most erudite and most cultured man on the team, but for those very traits he was also an outsider at first.

Ken Dryden (right) demonstrated brilliant technique and an ability to win even in bad situations.

In his debut with the Montreal Canadiens, Dryden found himself living in a somewhat closed world. Characters here were diverse. There were loners who resorted to self-analysis (Bill Nyrop and Doug Jarvis), pranksters (Serge Savard and Guy Lapointe) and true comedians (Larry Robinson and Pete Mahovlich). Dryden's thrift became the subject of much teasing and joking, but in the end he was accepted as an equal. After a while, Ken became the team's favorite son and its official spokesman. Whatever the outcome of a game, he would go out and deal with the questions from the press.

Dryden analyzed himself the way he explored hockey in all its intricate detail. Once, while giving an interview, he started on his usual introspective monologue and the reporter interrupted him to say, "I'm a journalist, not an analyst!" But Dryden took himself and his work seriously.

Ken Dryden was born on August 8, 1947, in Hamilton, west of Toronto. Dryden made his debut in Maple Leaf Gardens at the age of seven when he played for the Humber Valley Hornets. Ken and his older brother Dave played roller hockey together on a junior team. In each of the three seasons from 1966 to 1969 that Dryden played for Cornell University, he allowed fewer than 2.00 goals per game and was picked for the league's All-Star Team.

It was after his appearance on the national team in the 1969 World Championship that Dryden signed a contract with the Montreal Canadiens. He was a participant in the historic first series between Canada and the USSR. While Ken was the Canadiens' goalie, the team won 258 games, tied 74 and lost 57. In 1983 he was inducted into the Hockey Hall of Fame. Even while playing for the Montreal Canadiens, Dryden studied law at McGill University and later earned his doctorate degree from the University of Windsor.

At the 1980, 1984 and 1988 Olympics, Dryden was a TV hockey commentator. He has taught at the University of Toronto and worked in the Ministry of Education. Dryden participated in a criminal investigation at the University of Moncton, where student players beat up the referee on the ice. Over a period of 18 years, he has written a number of books that were bestsellers: *The Game* and *Home Game* on the subject of hockey and *In School* on the subject of education. He also played an active part in the creation of a TV series on the origin of hockey in Canada.

Dryden has a lot of admiration for the game that Canadians are proud to call their invention. He regards it as a cultural heritage, cherishes its traditions and believes that hockey made a contribution to the formation of the national character. Dryden is perhaps one of the brightest lights in the modern world of hockey, and that is why in 1997 he was invited by the Toronto Maple Leafs to help rebuild the team. In a few short years, the new president has managed to transform a mediocre franchise into the league's most aggressive and highest-scoring team.

Gennady Tsygankov

His story reads like a Hollywood script from the past. By the age of 13, when some boys have already played for junior teams and traveled around the world, Gennady Tsygankov hadn't only never played hockey, he had never even seen the game.

Born in the port of Vanino, in the Far East of the former USSR, Tsygankov was a defenseman with the Central Red Army in Khabarovsk when he was brought to Moscow at age 22 to be assessed by Anatoli Tarasov. A year later, in 1971, USSR national team coach Tarasov would ignore his own strict training standards and announce that at his first World Championship, Tsygankov was the second-best defenseman after Czech Jan Suchy. He was weak in handling the puck and outplaying his opponents and his bearing on the ice left much to be desired. However, the authoritarian but acclaimed Tarasov had been captivated by the rookie's most valuable quality—his fiery, intense eyes. Tarasov was full of praise for Tsygankov, saying he was totally committed, fast to react and move and a well-built athlete. And most important, Tsygankov liked the intense training.

Tarasov found what he admired in Tsygankov, and Tsygankov got his big chance with Tarasov. "If I ever achieved anything in hockey," he said, "it was thanks to Tarasov. At 22, I couldn't do anything that 16-year-olds could do. For example, I didn't learn how to score many goals, although I had a pretty good shot, but there were technical problems with my shooting."

In his second major tournament, the 1972 Olympic Games, Tsygankov played in the number one lineup with Alexander Ragulin, Anatoli Firsov, Valeri Kharlamov and Vladimir Vikulov. Tarasov had a special reason for placing his favorite new defenseman in such good company. He considered this line to be "the Future Five." As in soccer, Tsygankov and the virtuoso Firsov were the "halfbacks," Ragulin was the "terminator," while Kharlamov and Vikulov were the "flying forwards."

By the age of 13, Gennady Tsygankov had never even seen a hockey game.

Tsygankov, Gennady
D, 5´11˝, 209 lbs, b: Vanino, USSR, 8/16/1947

Season	Club, League	Regular Season				
		GP	G	A	Pts	PIM
1966–68	SKA Khabarovsk, USSR	*	*	*	*	*
1968–69	CSKA, USSR	6	0	*	*	*
1969–70	CSKA, USSR	37	5	*	*	*
1970–71	CSKA, USSR	40	4	*	*	*
WEC–71	USSR	10	0	3	3	8
1971–72	CSKA, USSR	32	7	*	*	*
OWG–72	USSR	5	3	2	5	4
WEC–72	USSR	7	2	3	5	4
SS–72	USSR	8	0	2	2	6
1972–73	CSKA, USSR	29	4	*	*	*
WEC–73	USSR	10	0	2	2	4
1973–74	CSKA, USSR	28	2	3	5	32
WEC–74	USSR	10	1	2	3	9
1974–75	CSKA, USSR	29	3	4	7	20
WEC–75	USSR	10	0	5	5	2
1975–76	CSKA, USSR	33	3	3	6	10
OWG–76	USSR	6	1	2	3	2
WEC–76	USSR	10	0	0	0	2
1976–77	CSKA, USSR	33	8	8	16	12
WEC–77	USSR	10	2	1	3	4
1977–78	CSKA, USSR	34	7	9	16	42
WEC–78	USSR	6	0	2	2	6
1978–79	CSKA, USSR	41	7	10	17	29
WEC–79	USSR	7	1	1	2	6
1979–80	CSKA, USSR	10	1	2	3	8
	SKA Leningrad, USSR	9	1	0	1	60
	SKA Leningrad, USSR-Q	6	0	0	0	2
	USSR Totals	362	52	*	*	*
	OWG/WEC/SS Totals	99	10	25	35	57

Won OWG (1972, 1976)
Won WEC (1971, 1973, 1974, 1975, 1978, 1979)
USSR Champion (1970, 1971, 1972, 1973, 1975, 1977, 1978, 1979)

One of most gifted athletes on the USSR national team, Gennady Tsygankov (number 7) lacked aggression but relied on technique.

Firsov, nearest in style to Tsygankov, said about the so-called hick from the Far East: "I've been playing hockey for over 10 years and have never seen such a gifted athlete as Gennady. He's a person of unbelievable strength. During one shift on the ice, it seems as if he's been in every corner of the rink. In the third period, he's as fresh as he was in the first period. However, paradoxical as it may seem, when fighting for the puck, Tsygankov lacks aggressiveness and relies mostly on his technique. He has a powerful shot, but quite often it isn't very accurate. He wants to overcome his shortcomings so much that it is hard to get him off the ice after our training workouts."

Tsygankov played in all the major tournaments from 1971 to 1979. Viktor Tikhonov, whose demands as a coach differed substantially from those of his predecessors, called on him for two more World Championships when he was past 30. He was called up at the last minute to the World Championship in 1979 and played in tandem with Vladimir Lutchenko from beginning to end.

A latecomer to hockey, Tsygankov was always excited by fighting for the puck, but he never felt special or thought of himself as a star. He was a rare combination of principal and subordinate player.

The harshest assessment of Tsygankov's game came from the usually amiable Vladislav Tretiak, who, like Firsov, was Tsygankov's partner on the ice. "Modern hockey isn't just muscles, fast skating and courage," he said. "It also, and most importantly, demands the ability to think continuously while on the ice and to solve the endless number of tactical problems."

Valeri Kharlamov

Valeri Kharlamov was one of the all-time superstars of the game.

Speeding down the ice with the puck, he dodged the first Canadian player, using his classic feint. He turned his head to one side and the Canadian player chased after him in that direction while Kharlamov actually went the other way. The second Canadian was about to check him, but Kharlamov jammed on the brakes and twisted his body. His opponent missed him and flew right by. As he approached the third man, he pretended to lose control of the puck. The Canadian player got his stick on the puck, but before he could regain his balance and make off with it, Kharlamov gave him a shoulder check, dumping him onto the ice. With the puck once again in his possession, he suddenly found himself one-on-one with the goalkeeper, Gerry Cheevers.

With a grin on his face, he approached the great Canadian goalkeeper, raised his stick and swerved to the left with the intention of shooting at the upper right corner of the net. Kharlamov's feint—the position of his body, his eyes and even the smile—was so natural that the goalie, anticipating his intentions, shifted to the right. But Kharlamov once again went the other way. In a blur of motion, he fired the puck into the top left-hand corner of the net, and the goalie couldn't believe his eyes.

That was one of the "super-goals" scored by Kharlamov in 1974 against the WHA as described in the story "Three Speeds of Valeri Kharlamov" by Anatoli Tarasov. Was it a fluke? In a television interview during intermission of the first game of the 1981 Canada Cup, some famous Canadians had lots to say about Kharlamov.

Scotty Bowman: "Any coach, having Kharlamov on his team, would simply be obliged to create a first-class forward line. He was a great all-round hockey personality."

Larry Robinson: "Defense players usually pick up a lot of useful things by studying the style of this or that forward. This wouldn't work against Kharlamov. He wasn't subordinate to the usual manner of playing. In hockey, he was exclusively free and enterprising."

Bob Gainey: "If I could do half of what Kharlamov did, my name would be heard everywhere—morning, day and night."

One time the Canadians decided to invite a guest from among Soviet hockey players. And in a mark of their sincere admiration for a great hockey personality, they unanimously chose Kharlamov, the man who had scored such beautiful goals against them. Kharlamov was a world-class player both to Russians and Canadians.

The best Russian forwards of the game at the end of the 1960s were noted for their inventive play and their virtuosity in handling the puck. Anatoli Firsov, Vladimir Vikulov, Alexander Yakushev, Alexander Maltsev and Yevgeny Zimin: Each of these players put his stamp on the game and each brought more and more fans into the stands. When forwards were allowed to check the full length of the rink in 1968, they suddenly had to pit their skills against the defense.

The only way to shut Valeri Kharlamov (center) down was to hit him, over and over again, as the Canadians did in the 1972 Summit Series.

Yakushev was pinned to the boards from both sides. Maltsev was no longer able to play the kingpin role in games against his most powerful opponents—the Canadians. People began to ask, "Is Zimin not a fighter?" or "What happened to Vikulov?" The Boris Mikhailov–Vladimir Petrov–Valeri Kharlamov forward line was born at about this time. After years of brilliant playing, Mikhailov and Petrov had already proven that major challenges could only be overcome with unwavering perseverance or by taking unbelievable chances.

Kharlamov was a wizard at managing the new style of play. His mark of greatness lay not in scoring fantastic goals like that famous one against the Canadians. In fact, his claim to fame had nothing to do with scoring goals. Kharlamov was at his best when the opposing defenseman got him up against the boards. The defenseman would bear down on the forward at full speed in an attempt, if not to hurt him, then at least to slow him down for two or three seconds. He would prepare to throw a hard bodycheck, but it usually didn't happen. Kharlamov would skate away without even flinching. "You simply have to feel the beginning of the attack," he explains. Kharlamov's technique was studied and adopted by such future greats of hockey as Wayne Gretzky and Igor Larionov. Chess theoreticians might call Kharlamov's move "the Kharlamov Defense."

Kharlamov had his own particular style of handling the puck and defending against an attack. Rather than resorting to the fencing motions or wide, smooth sweeps with the stick that were typical before the introduction of checking by forwards, he chose quick feints and deviations of his body to hang on to the puck or take it from an opponent. Bypassing defensemen, he would guide the puck just barely, the way an experienced jockey controls his horse with movements invisible to the eye. When he was racing down the ice, his entire body was in motion, weaving and jerking, trying to puzzle his opponent.

A typical and rather amusing example of Kharlamov's style of play was the goal he scored against the WHA on Canadian ice. Two defensemen saw him coming. Throwing him a quick glance, Pat Stapleton guessed Kharlamov was going to pass him on the outside. J.C. Tremblay expected the oncoming forward to pass on his outside. But Kharlamov skated right down the middle between the two and scored!

In the Soviet Union, it was Vladimir Petrov's forward line that was the first to use the new heavy-hitting style while at the same time playing the technical game to which they were accustomed. As expected, Kharlamov adopted the mixed style as readily as his partners did, making sure never to use more force than was necessary or allowed. He didn't get carried away. And he never lost interest in the puck even for a moment.

For Kharlamov, there was no such thing as a teammate not worth using on a play. He took advantage of every player and opportunity and played full out in every game. Whether he came out wearing the uniform of the Soviet national team against Canada, Czechoslovakia or Sweden or in the colors of the CSKA team playing against Spartak, he poured everything he had into it. The only way to shut him down was to nail him, over and over again, as the Canadians did in the 1972 Summit Series.

But it was difficult to nail him. At the same time, it hardly seemed fair, for he'd had his fair share of bad luck, and the worst was yet to come. Valeri Kharlamov had been born on the road when his mother couldn't make it to the hospital in time. In 1948, when he was a kid, he had a heart problem and almost couldn't play hockey. And in 1976, at the age of 28, he was in a car accident and suffered a double fracture of the right shin, two broken ribs and a concussion. It seemed that fate was giving him a warning.

With a mix of Russian and Spanish blood—his mother fled to the USSR from the regime of General Franco—Kharlamov brought something to hockey from some higher place, from another world. He played the game with abandon and lived a happy and full life through the sport he loved. Living his life on the ice was a bold challenge, and he poured this powerful creative energy into the smallest and simplest moves. It gives fans great pleasure to observe a player of that caliber at work.

There are players who skate as easily as we can walk, who handle the puck as if they were born with a stick in their hand. He wasn't actually one of them. There were plenty of players who skated better than Kharlamov, and there were better stickhandlers who were more dangerous when shooting at the net. In fact, he never set any scoring records. Yet he was quite simply an extraordinarily gifted hockey player, one of the all-time superstars of the game.

Kharlamov, Valeri
LW, 5'8", 165 lbs, b: Moscow, USSR, 1/14/1948, d: 1981

Season	Club, League	Regular Season				
		GP	G	A	Pts	PIM
1967–68	CSKA, USSR	15	2	3	5	6
1968–69	CSKA, USSR	42	37	12	49	24
WEC–69	USSR	10	6	7	13	4
1969–70	CSKA, USSR	33	33	10	43	16
WEC–70	USSR	9	7	3	10	4
1970–71	CSKA, USSR	34	40	12	52	18
WEC–71	USSR	10	5	12	17	2
1971–72	CSKA, USSR	31	26	16	42	22
OWG–72	USSR	5	9	7	16	2
WEC–72	USSR	9	8	6	14	10
SS–72	USSR	7	3	4	7	16
1972–73	CSKA, USSR	27	19	13	32	22
WEC–73	USSR	10	9	14	23	31
1973–74	CSKA, USSR	26	20	10	30	28
WEC–74	USSR	10	5	5	10	8
1974–75	CSKA, USSR	31	15	24	39	35
WEC–75	USSR	9	10	6	16	4
1975–76	CSKA, USSR	34	18	18	36	6
OWG–76	USSR	6	3	6	9	6
WEC–76	USSR	10	4	10	14	4
1976–77	CSKA, USSR	21	18	8	26	16
WEC–77	USSR	10	9	7	16	4
1977–78	CSKA, USSR	29	18	24	42	35
WEC–78	USSR	10	4	5	9	4
1978–79	CSKA, USSR	41	22	26	48	36
WEC–79	USSR	8	7	7	14	4
1979–80	CSKA, USSR	42	16	22	38	40
OWG–80	USSR	7	3	8	11	2
1980–81	CSKA, USSR	30	9	16	25	14
	USSR Totals	436	293	214	507	318
	OWG/WEC/SS Totals	130	92	107	199	105

Named Best Forward at WEC (1976)
Won OWG (1972, 1976)
Won WEC (1969, 1970, 1971, 1973, 1974, 1975, 1978, 1979)
USSR Champion (1968, 1970, 1971, 1972, 1973, 1975, 1977, 1978, 1979, 1980, 1981)

Valeri Kharlamov (right).

Then in 1981 he was killed in a car accident. On the eve of the big Canada Cup tournament in Winnipeg, TV screens everywhere suddenly flashed the grim faces of Soviet hockey players bent over his obituary in the newspaper. There was real sorrow on the faces of men not known for their compassion. At the press center, an elderly Canadian, Mr. K. Morrison, publisher of the *Gladstone Age Press*, commented, "As you pass people in the stores and in the streets, all you hear is Kharlamov...Kharlamov..." Mr. Morrison didn't even know the correct name for Kharlamov's country—whether to call it the Soviet Union or Russia. But he captured in those few words the sentiment of hockey fans the world over. Suddenly, the Canadian bit his lower lip, as if to ease the pain. "What happened? Kharlamov.... When we received the news that he perished in a car crash, all the cares and worries of the people of Gladstone were put aside."

Coach Viktor Tikhonov hadn't taken Kharlamov to the Canada Cup tournament. Some even went so far as to blame Tikhonov for Kharlamov's death. But Tikhonov, the toughest and most fanatical coach in Soviet hockey, made it quite clear: Sport is only a means to an end, not a style of life.

Alexander Maltsev

With 211 career goals, Alexander Maltsev was the highest scorer on the USSR national team.

Harry Sinden, coach of the Canadian stars in the 1972 Summit Series, recalled years later that many of the Russian players had made quite an impression on him. But there was one player, Alexander Maltsev, whose superb style of play made him stand out from the others.

Maltsev was a natural-born hockey player who from an early age had a habit of focusing on the game to the exclusion of everything else around him. Maltsev came from a town by the name of Kirovo-Chepetsk with a population of 60,000. In the 19th century, it was a place of exile for political prisoners, and that is perhaps the only remarkable thing about his home town.

"The kids in Kirovo-Chepetsk had a huge ice-covered pond and three backyard rinks at their disposal," Alexander explains. "In essence, that is where we lived. We spent all of our time at the skating rink. Every time we went there, the place was packed. We would weave through the people, maneuvering, making split-second decisions, putting on the speed or the brakes. At that time, we used to skate pretty good and fast."

As a youth, no one taught Maltsev the rules of the game or badgered him into playing one position or another. Both on and off the ice, he did whatever he wanted. Throughout his hockey career, he refused to work out with barbells, preferring instead to jog on a daily basis. When news of Maltsev eventually filtered through to Moscow—at first through TV appearances while playing for local teams—people began to ask questions, and Maltsev realized he needed a plan. He set his sights on playing for Dynamo Moscow, or more precisely on playing for Arkady Chernyshev, feeling that this coach, with his serious disposition, wouldn't force him to change his freewheeling ways.

The appearance of Maltsev in major-league hockey coincided with the introduction by the IIHF of forechecking down the full length of the rink. He looked very unfavorably on that development in the game, afraid that the new close bodychecking style of play would constrict his own style. Surprisingly, Maltsev retained a certain degree of clumsiness and a lack of synchronization throughout his career.

But the new rule led to surprising results for Maltsev. Maneuvers that forwards used to take two or three seconds to complete, he executed in a fraction of a second. He claimed that he could "feel the situation on the ice," anticipating the movements of his own players and the opponents with a sixth sense. And he did all this much faster and more accurately than forwards who had practised the same moves for years. Most of his moves were nearly impossible to predict, and his handling of the puck and even his shots on goal were hard to follow from the stands.

Hockey is a team sport where every player has his own position. Maltsev played for nearly a quarter of a century with 45 different partners on the forward line with the USSR national team. There were 68 different combinations or plays when he came out on the ice with other players. Statistics like these are normal in the NHL, where coaches combine players any way they choose. But in Soviet hockey, a well-oiled forward combination was considered the greatest threat to the opposition and players were rarely shuffled around.

With 211 goals, Maltsev was the highest scorer on the national team, yet he was very generous about passing the puck to other players. Practically every player who came onto the ice with him had some kind words for him. In turn, Maltsev had fond recollections of his teammates. When he hung up his skates at the end of his career, he said: "I'm thankful to everyone I have played with. Maybe it's because I had so many partners that I was happy in hockey."

Maltsev was in his natural element on the ice. He enjoyed inventing his own plays, fooling around with the other players and otherwise making mischief. If he'd always followed the rules of the game and the obligations associated with it with more or less constant partners, he would have lost some of the pleasure he found in hockey. But despite his outward confidence, to the end he harbored a tendency toward self-doubt.

"I never played second fiddle to anyone. Never. Because if I did, I'd lose the thread of my game. I played my own game, but it required constant attention to my partners. It would be different if they let them play with me for two or three years instead of half a season. I wouldn't lose face and would make some concessions of my own to perestroika. In other words, I'd give a little."

It is hard to imagine Maltsev making concessions to his coaches. He had no reason to. His teammates on Dynamo

Maltsev, Alexander
C, 5'9", 174 lbs, b: Kirovo-Chepetsk, USSR, 4/20/1949

Season	Club, League	Regular Season				
		GP	G	A	Pts	PIM
1967–68	Dynamo Moscow, USSR	23	9	2	11	4
1968–69	Dynamo Moscow, USSR	42	26	*	*	*
WEC–69	USSR	10	5	6	11	0
1969–70	Dynamo Moscow, USSR	42	32	*	*	*
WEC–70	USSR	10	15	6	21	8
1970–71	Dynamo Moscow, USSR	37	36	20	56	8
WEC–71	USSR	10	10	6	16	2
1971–72	Dynamo Moscow, USSR	26	20	11	31	14
OWG–72	USSR	5	4	3	7	0
WEC–72	USSR	10	10	12	22	0
SS 72	USSR	8	0	5	5	0
1972–73	Dynamo Moscow, USSR	27	20	16	36	30
WEC–73	USSR	9	7	6	13	12
1973–74	Dynamo Moscow, USSR	32	25	22	47	14
WEC–74	USSR	10	6	4	10	2
1974–75	Dynamo Moscow, USSR	32	18	16	34	28
WEC–75	USSR	10	8	6	14	2
1975–76	Dynamo Moscow, USSR	29	28	19	47	0
OWG–76	USSR	6	7	7	14	0
WEC–76	USSR	5	3	3	6	0
CCup–76	USSR	5	3	4	7	2
1976–77	Dynamo Moscow, USSR	33	31	27	58	4
WEC–77	USSR	8	1	9	10	2
1977–78	Dynamo Moscow, USSR	24	17	12	29	22
WEC–78	USSR	10	5	8	13	0
1978–79	Dynamo Moscow, USSR	8	2	3	5	0
1979–80	Dynamo Moscow, USSR	36	11	28	39	10
OWG–80	USSR	7	6	4	10	0
1980–81	Dynamo Moscow, USSR	38	14	28	42	8
WEC–81	USSR	8	6	7	13	2
CCup–81	USSR	4	1	1	2	0
1981–82	Dynamo Moscow, USSR	37	19	22	41	6
1982–83	Dynamo Moscow, USSR	32	14	15	29	0
WEC–83	USSR	8	1	3	4	0
1983–84	Dynamo Moscow, USSR	32	7	15	22	6
	USSR Totals	530	329	*	*	*
	OWG/WEC/SS/CCup Totals	143	98	100	198	32

Named Best Forward at WEC (1970, 1972, 1981)
Won OWG (1972, 1976)
Won WEC (1969, 1970, 1971, 1973, 1974, 1975, 1978, 1981, 1983)
Won CCup (1981)

Alexander Maltsev's shots on goal were hard to follow from the stands and most of his moves were nearly impossible to predict.

Moscow included a number of very good hockey players, but they were still a class below him in talent and ability. Concessions to these players might cost the team in goals. His motto was, "Do as I do."

"Once we were fooling around during a training session. Suddenly I took the puck and circled around an imaginary opponent 360 degrees. I liked that. I used to do that only very rarely, but pretty well. I remember just before Lake Placid, I practised that gimmick and ended up putting the puck into the American net. I never saw anyone trying to do an exact copy of what I did. It's strange—why not? Maybe it's because you lose your bearings for a split second."

Valeri Kharlamov, though a great hockey player in his own right, always dreamt of scoring a Maltsev-style goal—standing behind the net, flipping the puck over it, skating out in front and batting it in on the fly. Maltsev did that once in a game against Dynamo Berlin. The fans there didn't even know what had happened. Coach Chernyshov called him over to the bench and said with a smile, "That's all for today, go take a shower."

Maltsev was uneasy whenever he went abroad and only felt at home when he was on ice. It upset him that after he hung up his skates, his fame was relatively short-lived. His name was slowly forgotten. Though he never actually says it, he seems to expect a city to be named after him or a monument to be erected in the public square in his honor. There can be no doubt that he was one of the great stars of hockey. But though there are still towns like Kirovo-Chepetsk in Russia, and the people there live just as they did during Maltsev's childhood, values have changed greatly. And so has hockey. Fans are quick to respond to talent but just as quick to forget.

Vladimir Lutchenko

Vladimir Lutchenko was one of the fastest and most mobile defensemen on the USSR national team.

Vladimir Lutchenko was born January 2, 1949, in the small town of Ramenskoye, 30 miles from Moscow. Like every boy in Russia, he played soccer in summer and hockey in winter. In the postwar period in Russia, the game of hockey was little known, having first appeared only three years before Lutchenko was born. Since Moscow was so close, the "Canadian hockey" phenomenon rapidly reached Ramenskoye. Vladimir was so overwhelmed by the new game that he decided to dedicate his life to it. As a young man, he chose to acquire his skills with the famous CSKA (Central Red Army club).

Coaches liked a novice who was willing to undergo the rigorous training conducted by the junior Army team. Besides, Lutchenko was well built and had very good skating technique. When they found out, however, that the boy lived in Ramenskoye, they admitted him on one condition—that he not miss a single exercise session.

Several times a week for several years, weighed down by a huge duffle bag filled with hockey equipment, he would rush off at 6 in the morning to the railroad station in order to be at the CSKA rink three hours later. After the workout, Lutchenko made the return trip home. He could have earned himself a place in the Guinness Book of World Records for the miles he logged.

During his training and development, Vladimir Lutchenko didn't set any records or win any awards while on the CSKA kids' team, the adolescent team or the junior team. Yet Lutchenko graduated from the juniors with laurels and in 1966 he was among the few graduates who were invited to play for the regular Central Red Army team.

Lutchenko began playing alongside aces like Alexander Ragulin and Viktor Kuzkin. Coach Anatoli Tarasov, who never made allowances for players just because they were young, appointed the 19-year-old defenseman to the first lineup. Soon Vladimir was considered one of the fastest and most mobile defensemen. With his heavy hitting style, opposing forwards were loath to clash with him in front of either the CSKA's or the Soviet national team's net. The young defenseman had only one serious shortcoming: He didn't score often.

After a North American tour by the Central Red Army, coach Konstantin Loktev, while speaking about Bobby Orr at a press conference, said: "Bobby Orr of course is a great player. And I, as a coach, would be happy to have but one player like Orr. But only one. Plus five obscure—in the eyes of journalists—defensemen. Those who can toil like Vladimir Lutchenko or," remembering the 1972 Summit Series, "like Canadians Gary Bergman, Bill White or Pat Stapleton. These three scored just one goal in the series, but they helped Team Canada to win three games in Moscow and the whole Summit Series."

But Loktev's tribute to defensive defensemen was largely ignored. And Vladimir Lutchenko, after 15 seasons playing for the CSKA and the national team, retired from hockey without ever being properly accredited by the media or by international hockey authorities, who never once declared him the best defenseman of any international contest.

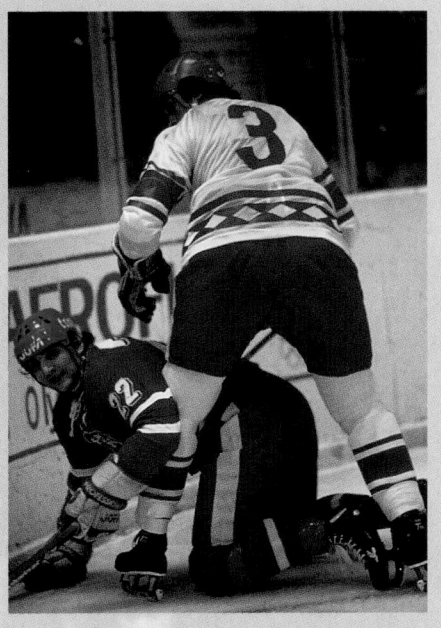

Opposing forwards were loath to clash with Vladimir Lutchenko (number 3) and his heavy hitting style in front of the net.

Lutchenko, Vladimir
D, 6´, 205 lbs, b: Ramenskoye, USSR, 1/2/1949

Season	Club, League	Regular Season				
		GP	G	A	Pts	PIM
1966–67	CSKA, USSR	2	0	*	*	*
1967–68	CSKA, USSR	38	5	*	*	*
1968–69	CSKA, USSR	34	1	*	*	*
WEC–69	USSR	9	0	1	1	8
1969–70	CSKA, USSR	39	2	*	*	*
WEC–70	USSR	10	0	0	0	4
1970–71	CSKA, USSR	40	4	*	*	*
WEC–71	USSR	10	3	1	4	6
1971–72	CSKA, USSR	26	1	*	*	*
OWG–72	USSR	5	0	1	1	2
WEC–72	USSR	10	0	4	4	8
SS–72	USSR	8	1	3	4	0
1972–73	CSKA, USSR	32	5	*	*	*
WEC–73	USSR	9	1	2	3	12
1973–74	CSKA, USSR	32	10	5	15	20
WEC–74	USSR	7	2	2	4	6
1974–75	CSKA, USSR	33	10	5	15	32
WEC–75	USSR	10	1	2	3	6
1975–76	CSKA, USSR	33	4	7	11	16
OWG–76	USSR	6	0	2	2	4
WEC–76	USSR	10	1	1	2	0
CCup–76	USSR	3	0	1	1	2
1976–77	CSKA, USSR	35	6	4	10	22
WEC–77	USSR	10	2	3	5	2
1977–78	CSKA, USSR	34	5	3	8	22
WEC–78	USSR	10	1	2	3	2
1978–79	CSKA, USSR	36	2	4	6	20
WEC–79	USSR	8	0	2	2	4
1979–80	CSKA, USSR	38	3	9	12	22
1980–81	CSKA, USSR	9	0	0	0	2
	USSR Totals	459	58	*	*	*
	OWG/WEC/SS/CCup Totals	125	12	27	39	66

Won OWG (1972, 1976)
Won WEC (1969, 1970, 1971, 1973, 1974, 1975, 1978, 1979)
USSR Champion (1968, 1970, 1971, 1972, 1973, 1975, 1977, 1978, 1979, 1980)

A HISTORY OF WORLD HOCKEY

Valeri **Vasiliev**

It is difficult to recall anyone ever knocking Valeri Vasiliev off his feet.

In the 1972 Summit Series, there were moments when it appeared to fans of the Soviet national team that the NHL squad possessed total physical superiority. It even looked for a while as if the Soviet hockey players would be literally smashed to pieces. But there was always some relief when Valeri Vasiliev stepped onto the ice. While his teammates were afraid to take their adversaries on in a physical contest, let alone get into fights, Vasiliev had no such qualms.

If in such skirmishes he didn't take off the gloves and go all the way, it was only out of self-restraint and in obedience to the coach's instructions. Nevertheless, with a poke here and a jab there he let it be known among the NHL players that he wasn't to be messed with. And it was enough to give him the satisfaction of knowing that he was doing what had to be done when facing off against the NHL. He was playing big-time hockey, where you never bowed down before an opponent. The entire bearing of his body while on the ice revealed his attitude—shoulders spread, head high and a penetrating look.

A trait peculiar to Vasiliev yet unnoticed by most fans was once pointed out by Anatoli Tarasov. While skating, he had an unusual way of propelling himself down the ice. He could really turn on the speed without lifting his skates, and it was this that gave him his remarkable stability on ice. It is hard to remember anyone ever knocking Vasiliev off his feet.

It is said that if Vasiliev hadn't entered the world of hockey, where the roles of each participant are clearly defined, he might have been quite comfortable as a boxer or a bouncer, since he had all the makings. From everything he'd heard about the first legendary Russian defensemen, Ivan Tregubov and Nikolai Sologubov, Vasiliev chose to remember only that Sologubov was unusually spiteful. He never forgave anyone even the slightest offense and relished making his opponents quiver.

"At first," Vasiliev recalled, "it took practically nothing to knock me off kilter. If anyone clipped me sneakily, I had only one thing on my mind—how to get even with that guy. He was the only one I saw on the ice, and I would rush to nail him, putting all I had into a bodycheck. But at that same moment I found out that he had passed the puck away long ago and that I myself was a long distance away from the main events that were unfolding in front of our goal. That happened time and again, until I finally realized that a defenseman was obliged to keep his cool. Gradually I learned how to control myself and useless passions very rarely got out of my control."

Vasiliev joined Dynamo Moscow, a team known for its highly restrained tempers. In the very beginning, he looked like an overambitious and somewhat obnoxious loner. Besides his "measures of physical persuasion," as he liked to call them, Vasiliev was quite fond of demonstrating his speed-skating prowess. "I was even very much attracted by the possibility of wreaking havoc on the enemy's rear. I could see how the opposing team panicked when I joined an assault on their goal." But in the Dynamo club, the tough but foolhardy Vasiliev was reined in by his partner, Vitali Davydov, one of the big names of the preceding generation. Davydov put a lot of effort into changing Vasiliev's way of thinking and taught him the ABCs of Dynamo's science of playing hockey. "So, what did you achieve? So, you skated like a whirlwind from one goal to the other, dumping some players along the way, but it ended with me alone facing three of their forwards."

Strongman Vasiliev eventually transformed into a refined tactician. He was able to determine quite well when to get physical with his adversary and when to concentrate more on the puck, when to forecheck aggressively and perhaps even con his rival into skating alongside him for a while until the right time came to smash him into the boards and when to recognize an opportunity to steal the puck using nothing but his stick. Still, Vasiliev truly enjoyed making his opponents feel like rabbits facing down a boa constrictor. It was a tactic at which he was especially adept when a superior number of opponents raided his team's rear.

Vasiliev learned to switch off his anger and even his temper to such an extent that during a game he was able to strike up the most unexpected conversations with his opponents or with the referee. During the years when the Canadians didn't participate in World Championships, the formidable defenseman with aggressive reflexes lapsed into an almost lethargic slumber. Tarasov openly admitted that Vasiliev was "a great defenseman." He also admitted that in the Central Red Army club's games against Dynamo, he'd worked out special strategies so that the most skillful forwards—Valeri Kharlamov and Anatoli Firsov—wouldn't encounter Vasiliev face to face. However, if any of the young forwards was able to hold his own in a tussle with Vasiliev, it meant that the youngster was obviously a promising player.

In 1976, halfway through his hockey career, the former scrapper Vasiliev spoke about the game of his colleagues on NHL defense lines: "We play a more diversified game, we play a cleaner and I think more elegant game. Is it permissible for a defenseman to carry his stick eye-high? After all, we aren't enemies of one another. For example, Brad Park's tough game has its limits, and he resorts to it only when there is no other way out. His main weapon lies in his technique of regaining control of the puck, stickhandling and passing. And besides that, he's a smart player."

Vasiliev was the only captain of the USSR national squad ever to hold the Canada Cup in his hands. That was in 1981. Not one to be despondent, he nevertheless appeared just a little disappointed when, in the bus shuttling the Soviet team to the games, he leafed through a booklet dedicated to the tournament and pointed out to the journalist sitting next to him: "Just take a look—practically all the Canadians who played in 1972 have already hung their skates on the nail. Yeah, even on our side, Tretiak, along with Maltsev and myself, are the only ones remaining."

Valeri Vasiliev displays the 1981 Canada Cup to Soviet fans.

Vasiliev, Valeri
D, 5'11", 187 lbs, b: Volkovo, USSR, 8/3/1949

Season	Club, League	Regular Season				
		GP	G	A	Pts	PIM
1967–68	Dynamo Moscow, USSR	41	2	1	3	28
1968–69	Dynamo Moscow, USSR	35	2	1	3	34
1969–70	Dynamo Moscow, USSR	43	5	2	7	37
WEC–70	USSR	6	0	0	0	2
1970–71	Dynamo Moscow, USSR	40	2	4	6	36
1971–72	Dynamo Moscow, USSR	31	4	0	4	35
OWG–72	USSR	2	0	0	0	2
WEC–72	USSR	9	2	2	4	2
SS–72	USSR	5	1	2	3	6
1972–73	Dynamo Moscow, USSR	29	3	1	4	59
WEC–73	USSR	10	0	7	7	6
1973–74	Dynamo Moscow, USSR	31	4	11	15	42
WEC–74	USSR	10	0	6	6	16
1974–75	Dynamo Moscow, USSR	34	7	5	12	34
WEC–75	USSR	10	2	4	6	0
1975–76	Dynamo Moscow, USSR	28	6	15	21	13
OWG–76	USSR	6	1	2	3	2
WEC–76	USSR	10	5	2	7	8
CCup–76	USSR	5	0	3	3	6
1976–77	Dynamo Moscow, USSR	34	3	12	15	21
WEC–77	USSR	10	1	2	3	8
1977–78	Dynamo Moscow, USSR	33	2	6	8	30
WEC–78	USSR	10	3	3	6	6
1978–79	Dynamo Moscow, USSR	42	6	14	20	26
WEC–79	USSR	8	1	3	4	0
1979–80	Dynamo Moscow, USSR	41	8	10	18	26
OWG–80	USSR	7	2	1	3	2
1980–81	Dynamo Moscow, USSR	43	6	7	13	16
WEC–81	USSR	8	0	0	0	2
CCup–81	USSR	6	0	1	1	4
1981–82	Dynamo Moscow, USSR	36	3	12	15	18
WEC–82	USSR	10	1	2	3	0
1982–83	Dynamo Moscow, USSR	32	5	7	12	16
1983–84	Dynamo Moscow, USSR	44	3	7	10	14
	USSR Totals	617	71	115	186	485
	OWG/WEC/SS/CCup Totals	132	19	40	59	72

Named Best Defenseman at WEC (1973, 1977, 1979)
Won OWG (1972, 1976)
Won WEC (1970, 1973, 1974, 1975, 1978, 1979, 1981, 1982)
Won CCup (1981)

Brad Park

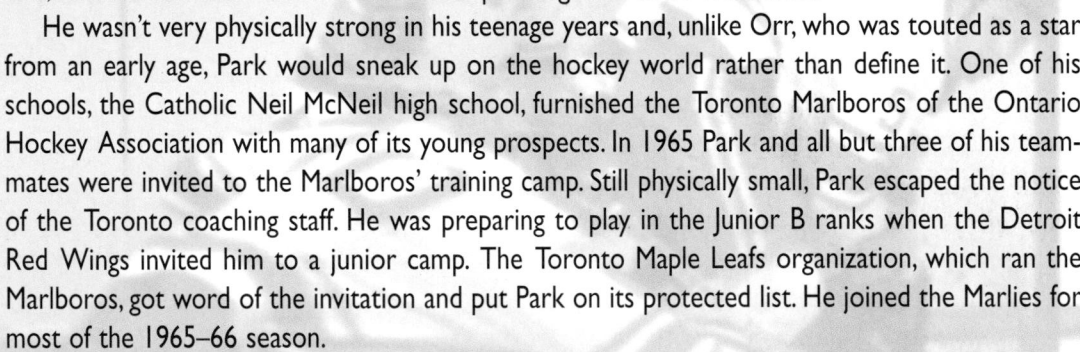

In just about any other era, Brad Park would have been considered the best defenseman of his generation. He had size and played aggressively, taking care of business in his own zone. Offensively, he was a pinpoint passer and a deceptive stickhandler, abilities which made him a natural and potent

power-play threat. He had the skating speed and the instincts to join the rush, providing his team with a fourth attacker. But Park played at the same time as Bobby Orr, the greatest blueliner of any era, and later in his career his stellar achievements were second to Denis Potvin's dominating play with the powerhouse New York Islanders. Park was the runner-up six times for the Norris Trophy as the NHL's best defender and earned a berth on the league's All-Star Team seven times. He was an easy choice for induction into the Hockey Hall of Fame in 1988.

Park was born in Toronto, Ontario, in 1948, the same year as Orr. He began playing hockey at age five and played for teams coached by his father from atom through to midget. The Park family would sit at the kitchen table and diagram plays and possible situations using the salt and pepper shakers, and Brad, always a quick study, picked up a solid understanding of the game through such simple tabletop strategy. He practised his shot against the house, sending pucks at doors, shingles and the front steps in the process. "By the time we decided to move to another home," his mother, Betty,

Brad Park was the runner-up for the Norris Trophy as the NHL's best defender six times.

said, "there were more dents in the wood paneling than there were nails."

He wasn't very physically strong in his teenage years and, unlike Orr, who was touted as a star from an early age, Park would sneak up on the hockey world rather than define it. One of his schools, the Catholic Neil McNeil high school, furnished the Toronto Marlboros of the Ontario Hockey Association with many of its young prospects. In 1965 Park and all but three of his teammates were invited to the Marlboros' training camp. Still physically small, Park escaped the notice of the Toronto coaching staff. He was preparing to play in the Junior B ranks when the Detroit Red Wings invited him to a junior camp. The Toronto Maple Leafs organization, which ran the Marlboros, got word of the invitation and put Park on its protected list. He joined the Marlies for most of the 1965–66 season.

Park gained weight, putting just under 200 pounds on his 6′ frame, and his skating and puck-handling developed to the point that in the summer of 1966, just before the NHL Amateur Draft, he was considered a sure bet for the professional leagues. Park and his family were more modest and he expressed hopes of ending up with the Maple Leafs. Instead, he was chosen second overall by the New York Rangers. Park and his parents were shocked but came to terms with the implications soon after hearing of his high selection at midnight the night of the draft. "When you think about it, New York needs a defenseman, and you couldn't have come along at a better time," Betty said after letting the news sink in.

Park stayed with the Marlies for two more seasons, becoming an outstanding defenseman and making the league's All-Star Team in 1968. At his first training camp with New York, he was shy and reluctant to mix openly with the more experienced Rangers. He was assigned to the Buffalo Bisons of the American Hockey League, where he played 17 games before returning to the NHL to stay. He scored his first goal in a game against the Boston Bruins, though it meant little as New

York was already leading 8–0. Park, with his characteristic dry humor, called his first goal the game's "clincher."

After a solid rookie season, Park established himself as one of the top defensemen in the league in his second year. He earned the respect of his teammates and the fans in New York, and soon the whole league was talking about his savvy and poised play. Park was named to the NHL's First All-Star Team alongside Orr and placed second to the Bruins star in voting for the Norris Trophy. He was the youngest Ranger ever to earn a place on the league's first team. "I call him Mr. Park—with respect," Rangers general manager Emile Francis said of the 22-year-old Park in 1970. "This is a tremendous hockey player. Mr. Park is so cool with the puck and deliberate in his passes. But what I like about him best is his toughness. Nobody goes into a corner with him without getting hit."

Park's offensive numbers improved in each of his first four years with the Rangers. He was chosen to play for Canada in the Summit Series in 1972 and was impressive on the blue line for the embattled Canadians, finishing with five points in eight games. For the next several seasons, Park, whose Rangers had redeveloped into one of the league's better teams, was regularly compared to Orr, who was struggling with knee problems but still revolutionizing the position with his outstanding play. And Park didn't always lose in these comparisons. "Park is a tremendous defenseman. He moves the puck well, he rushes it and he's sound defensively," Detroit Red Wings general manager Ned Harkness said. "He's a great one. By comparison, Orr is more offensive-minded. But Brad, defensively, is sounder than Orr. Park turns well and is good around the net."

Park was an expert at taking forwards out of the play and away from the middle of the rink. Opponents would feel as though they'd beaten the defender to open ice, only to find they no longer had a good view of the net. Though Park had knee problems of his own, many hockey people predicted his career would stretch further than Orr's. "Park is tough and aggressive," said Hal Laycoe, the head coach of the Vancouver Canucks in 1971. "I'd say he's likely to have a longer and therefore more productive career than Orr's."

That prediction would come true. Due to his poor knees, Orr played only 10 games in the 1975–76 season. He would play only a few

Brad Park (number 2) scored his first career goal against Boston. New York was already leading 8–0, but he called his goal the game's "clincher."

Park, Brad
D, 6′, 200 lbs, b: Toronto, Ont., 7/6/1948

Season	Club, League	Regular Season					Playoffs				
		GP	G	A	Pts	PIM	GP	G	A	Pts	PIM
1967–68	Toronto Marlboros, OHA Sr.	1	0	0	0	0					
1968–69	New York Rangers, NHL	54	3	23	26	70	4	0	2	2	7
	Buffalo Bisons, AHL	17	2	12	14	49					
1969–70	New York Rangers, NHL	60	11	26	37	98	5	1	2	3	11
1970–71	New York Rangers, NHL	68	7	37	44	114	13	0	4	4	42
1971–72	New York Rangers, NHL	75	24	49	73	130	16	4	7	11	21
SS–72	Canada	8	1	4	5	2					
1972–73	New York Rangers, NHL	52	10	43	53	51	10	2	5	7	8
1973–74	New York Rangers, NHL	78	25	57	82	148	13	4	8	12	38
1974–75	New York Rangers, NHL	65	13	44	57	104	3	1	4	5	2
1975–76	New York Rangers, NHL	13	2	4	6	23					
	Boston Bruins, NHL	43	16	37	53	95	11	3	8	11	14
1976–77	Boston Bruins, NHL	77	12	55	67	67	14	2	10	12	4
1977–78	Boston Bruins, NHL	80	22	57	79	79	15	9	11	20	14
1978–79	Boston Bruins, NHL	40	7	32	39	10	11	1	4	5	8
1979–80	Boston Bruins, NHL	32	5	16	21	27	10	3	6	9	4
1980–81	Boston Bruins, NHL	78	14	52	66	111	3	1	3	4	11
1981–82	Boston Bruins, NHL	75	14	42	56	82	11	1	4	5	4
1982–83	Boston Bruins, NHL	76	10	26	36	82	16	3	9	12	18
1983–84	Detroit Red Wings, NHL	80	5	53	58	85	3	0	3	3	0
1984–85	Detroit Red Wings, NHL	67	13	30	43	53	3	0	0	0	11
	NHL Totals	1113	213	683	896	1429	161	35	90	125	217
	SS Totals	8	1	4	5	2					

NHL First All-Star Team (1970, 1972, 1974, 1976, 1978)
NHL Second All-Star Team (1971, 1973)
Won Bill Masterton Trophy (1984)

more over the next three years before leaving the game. The man the Bruins brought in to replace him was Park, the result of one of the biggest trades in NHL history. On November 7, 1975, Phil Esposito and Carol Vadnais were sent to the Rangers for Joe Zanussi, Jean Ratelle and Park, who left New York as the team's all-time leading scorer for defensemen. In Boston, Park was a natural fit, his offensive skills meshing perfectly with the team's style of play. He enjoyed some his finest individual seasons with the Bruins and brought the club to the Stanley Cup finals in two consecutive seasons, 1977 and 1978, though the team failed to capture the title either time. Twice Park was second in the voting for the Norris Trophy while he played in Boston, beaten out both times by the emerging Denis Potvin of the Islanders.

In 1983 Park signed as a free agent with the Detroit Red Wings. He spent two seasons with the Wings, and though he had slowed a step, he proved he still had a unique sense of the game and the passing skills to take advantage of the openings he saw—he collected 53 assists in 1983–84. He retired from play following the 1984–85 season and coached the lowly Wings for half of the next season, winning only nine of 45 games before stepping aside.

Vladislav Tretiak

In the minds of hockey fans around the world, Vladislav Tretiak's name is closely linked with goaltending excellence.

In the minds of hockey fans around the world, the name Vladislav Tretiak is so closely linked with goaltending excellence that it's hard to imagine that before 1972, the Soviet superstar was almost completely unknown to the North American sporting public. But that's pretty much the way it happened. Canadian hockey scouts had dismissed him as a weak link in the Soviet defense prior to the Canada–USSR series in 1972, calling him inconsistent, with a weak glove hand that could be exploited almost at will. And so coaches and fans hardly paid any attention to him in the pre-series buildup. By the time the Summit Series was over, though, Tretiak was no longer a mystery to NHL fans, who saw him turn away Canada's top goal-scoring stars time and again for eight frustrating, nail-biting games.

Tretiak's stellar performance in the 1972 showdown—as a mere 20-year-old—was only the beginning of his amazing international play. Behind his unprecedented 1.78 goals-against average in 98 international games, the Soviets won Olympic gold medals in 1972, 1976 and 1984. They also captured 10 World Championships and nine European titles and remained virtually undefeated for the better part of a decade in IIHF tournament play.

In addition to shining in international championship play, Tretiak also habitually inspired himself to play his very best during exhibition games against NHL teams. In a game against the Montreal Canadiens on New Year's Eve, 1975—one that many hockey fans still consider the greatest goaltending performance of all time—Tretiak held the Habs to a 3–3 tie despite being widely outshot, 38–13. He was the MVP of the 1981 Canada Cup, leading the vaunted USSR to their first victory, and the following year turned in another standout series of games on the Soviet All-Stars tour of North America, the highlight of which was his 5–0 shutout of those same Canadiens in the Forum.

In the midst of all of the Canada versus USSR hockey rivalry, a testament to Tretiak's excellence was that he was the one player on Team USSR who managed to circumvent all the Cold

War rivalry that went on when the two nations met. No less a player than Wayne Gretzky, writing in the foreword to the 1987 book *Tretiak: The Legend*, summed up this characteristic of the Soviet netminder: "On a truly global scale, Vladislav Tretiak has given more back to his sport than he has gained from it. He has always shown the diplomacy, charisma and warmth of an international ambassador. Which is exactly what Vladislav happens to be. He has caused borders to be forgotten, political beliefs to be withheld, and cultures to be exchanged, while always standing tall in his representation of his team and country."

From 1971 to 1984, Vladislav Tretiak (right) was the Soviet league's First All-Star Team goalie—14 consecutive seasons as the number one man in the Soviet cage.

Tretiak was born in Moscow in April 25, 1952. As a child, he first wanted to become a pilot like his father. But as it turned out, it was his mother, a gymnastics teacher, who soon encouraged him to move into another area in which lightning-quick reflexes would come in handy and he developed an interest in becoming a hockey goalie. Beginning at age 11, young Vladislav played for the hockey school of the Central Red Army club. Falling under the early influence of the Russian coach Anatoli Tarasov, Tretiak started on a detailed program that Tarasov told him would one day turn him into one of the world's best netminders. Before long, Tretiak was practising with the Central Red Army team and made it onto the club's roster at the preposterously young age of 17. As a junior international, he played on Team USSR in three European championships from 1969 to 1971 and was named outstanding goaltender in the 1971 tournament.

As expected, Tretiak matured and developed with each game he played, and the more responsibility he was given, the better he played. Every level he moved up, he was able to match that level of competition. From 1971 to 1984, he was the Soviet league's First Team All-Star goalie, spending 14 consecutive seasons as the number one man in the Soviet cage. During this amazing string with the Central Red Army squad, Tretiak won 13 league titles, captured the MVP honors in the Soviet league five times, was awarded the Order of Lenin for his service to the USSR in 1978 and won the coveted Golden Hockey Stick as the outstanding player in all of Europe in 1981, 1982 and 1983. In the 1981 Canada Cup, he was the tournament MVP and the First All-Star Team goalie, posting an amazing 1.33 goal-against average over six games against the world's best teams.

With the Central Red Army squad, Vladislav Tretiak (in goal) won 13 league titles, Soviet league MVP honors five times and was awarded the Order of Lenin in 1978 for his service to the USSR.

Other than the game eight disappointment in 1972, which can hardly be called a disaster for Tretiak, coming as it did at the tail end of the series that really launched him onto the world hockey scene, there was only one dark spot on his entire stellar career in the international arena. It appeared in the 1980 Olympics in Lake Placid, New York, a competition won by the squad from the U.S. In the second-to-last game, Tretiak was the victim of a fluke goal by Mark Johnson in the first period and was pulled in favor of Vladimir Myshkin. "If I had played the full three periods of that game, we would have won," Tretiak said later. "It was the first time I ever was taken out of a game. It wasn't my idea. The coach decided. In that situation, you don't ask; you don't argue."

Tretiak retired from active play on a high note in 1984, after shutting out Czechoslovakia 2–0 to win the Olympic gold in Sarajevo. The actual close of his career, which saw him take part in 287 games overall with the national squad, came at the end of the Izvestia tournament in December 1984. He and fellow Soviet standouts Valeri Vasiliev and Alexander Maltsev took part in a special All-Star game between the USSR and European players who had taken part in the Izvestia games. The contest ended with a huge ovation for the tearful Tretiak as he said his goodbyes, never to compete for his nation again at the highest level.

Tretiak always wanted to play for an NHL team—the Canadiens were always his favorite choice—but never got the chance. Originally drafted by Montreal in 1983, he was a victim of Soviet restrictions on foreign travel abroad which kept him out of the North American pro game. With the influx of ex-Soviets into the NHL in the 1990s, Tretiak admitted that he was "a little jealous" of them. "I was ready to come here for so long and I think I would have done well. I've dedicated my whole life to hockey and I would have given playing in the NHL 150%." Although Tretiak never made it into an NHL lineup, he was nevertheless inducted into the Hockey Hall of Fame in 1989, making him the first European player to receive such an honor. He earned it through his international play, including play against the finest Canada had to offer through the years.

Nonetheless, Tretiak got his chance to participate in the NHL wars in another way. Just before the start of the 1990–91 season, Chicago Blackhawks coach Mike Keenan announced that he would be signing Tretiak as a member of his coaching staff, in particular to work with the squad's young goaltending corps that included Ed Belfour. Under Tretiak's guidance, Belfour would win the Calder and Vezina trophies in his early career, and to this day, Belfour, now a member of the Dallas Stars, still sports a number 20 sweater in honor of his Russian mentor. "I think we can all agree that Vladislav, during the course of his career, was one of the finest goaltenders in the world," Keenan told reporters in announcing his decision to bring Tretiak onto his coaching staff. "Throughout his competitive life in the Soviet Union, his record speaks for itself. But I think, more importantly, his knowledge of the game is second to none as far as the position of goaltending."

His intellectual knowledge and understanding of the position is equaled perhaps only by Jacques Plante, who wrote the first book on being a goalie and detailed everything from strategy to conditioning. Coaching had always been part of Tretiak's post-playing plans. He started a series of hockey schools as part of a life-long love of teaching kids about the sport. "Youngsters with dreams of becoming hockey players

Tretiak, Vladislav
G, 6´1´´, 202 lbs, b: Moscow, USSR, 4/25/1952

Season	Club, League	Regular Season		
		GP	GA	Avg
1968–69	CSKA, USSR	3	2	*
1969–70	CSKA, USSR	34	76	*
WEC–70	USSR	6	4	0.67
1970–71	CSKA, USSR	40	81	*
WEC–71	USSR	5	6	1.20
1971–72	CSKA, USSR	30	78	*
OWG–72	USSR	4	10	2.50
WEC–72	USSR	8	15	1.88
SS–72	USSR	8	31	3.87
1972–73	CSKA, USSR	30	80	2.67
WEC–73	USSR	7	14	2.00
1973–74	CSKA, USSR	27	94	3.48
WEC–74	USSR	8	12	1.50
1974–75	CSKA, USSR	35	104	2.97
WEC–75	USSR	8	18	2.25
1975–76	CSKA, USSR	33	100	3.03
OWG–76	USSR	4	10	2.50
WEC–76	USSR	10	19	1.90
CCup–76	USSR	5	14	2.80
1976–77	CSKA, USSR	35	98	2.80
WEC–77	USSR	9	17	1.89
1977–78	CSKA, USSR	29	72	2.48
WEC–78	USSR	8	21	2.63
1978–79	CSKA, USSR	40	111	2.78
WEC–79	USSR	7	12	1.71
1979–80	CSKA, USSR	36	85	2.36
OWG–80	USSR	5	9	1.80
1980–81	CSKA, USSR	18	32	1.78
WEC–81	USSR	7	13	1.86
CCup–81	USSR	6	8	1.33
1981–82	CSKA, USSR	41	65	1.70
WEC–82	USSR	8	19	2.38
1982–83	CSKA, USSR	29	40	1.46
WEC–83	USSR	7	4	0.57
1983–84	CSKA, USSR	22	40	1.89
OWG–84	USSR	6	4	0.67
	USSR Totals	482	1158	2.40
	OWG/WEC/SS/CCup Totals	136	260	1.91

Named Best Goaltender at WEC (1974, 1979, 1981, 1983)
Won OWG (1972, 1976, 1984)
Won WEC (1970, 1971, 1973, 1974, 1975, 1978, 1979, 1981, 1982, 1983)
Won CCup (1981)
USSR Champion (1970, 1971, 1972, 1973, 1975, 1977, 1978, 1979, 1980, 1981, 1982, 1983, 1984)

Vladislav Tretiak (number 20).

Vladislav Tretiak (center) started a series of hockey schools in his life-long dedication to teaching the game to a new generation.

ask me how to master the mysteries of the sport," he wrote in his own book, *The Hockey I Love*. "They ask me how to develop courage, quick reactions and endurance. They ask me how to play hockey, what subjects I studied in school, how I became a goaltender for the national team. How many years must you train to be chosen as goalie for a good team?" Kids could have found no better person to ask. As a superb goalie, sports ambassador and teacher of both pros and children, Vladislav Tretiak defined all three roles in his long career in hockey. The Hockey Hall of Fame is richer for his inclusion in its hallowed rooms.

Guy Lapointe

Born in Montreal on March 18, 1948, Guy Lapointe set new standards for NHL defensemen during his 16-year NHL career. Although he played for the St. Louis Blues and the Boston Bruins, he spent most of his time in the league with the Montreal Canadiens, and it was with the Habs that he established himself as a member of the team's "Big Three" defensive specialists. Along with Larry Robinson and Serge Savard, he played a major role in the Canadiens' winning the Stanley Cups six times during his time with the team.

Lapointe had originally dreamed of a completely different career. "I was accepted to try the examinations for the police force," he recalled. "But my father was a fireman and he told me to give professional hockey a try first. I could still join the police force until I was 25. But I never expected to make it as a pro."

He played his junior hockey with Maisonneuve, Verdun and the Montreal Junior Canadiens. He then became a professional in 1968–69, signing on as player with the Houston Apollos of the Central Hockey League before moving on to the Montreal Voyageurs of the AHL the following year. He joined the Canadiens in 1970–71, and although Habs management loved his obvious potential, they were a little unsure of his steadiness in the pro game. "I can certainly say he lacks experience, and that covers a lot," said Montreal assistant coach Al MacNeil when Lapointe was in the early stages of his career there. "He's a little too anxious and has a tendency to get over-enthusiastic."

But Lapointe overcame this youthful inconsistency and quickly established himself as one of the game's all-time great defensemen. He was a solid checker and opposing goalies feared his slapshot, which was particularly effective on the Habs' lethal power-play. Being a solid two-way player was something he worked hard on throughout his career. It was a source of pride for Lapointe. "The scorer attracts the attention, but it's the all-around play that means the most," he said. "I think consistency counts as much as anything. When the team wins as we have been winning, there is more than enough money and glory and satisfaction to go around."

Lapointe wasn't the only one in the Montreal dressing room who placed emphasis on his value as an all-around player. "He does a lot of things," said coach Scotty Bowman. "He's really a mobile type, and has a great shot from the point. We use him on the power-play and to kill penalties, too." Still, with all this emphasis on complete play, Lapointe's offensive abilities shone through and coaches and general managers around the league quickly recognized him as one of the game's outstanding offensive defensemen.

Near the start of his NHL career, Lapointe was chosen to play in the historic 1972 Summit Series against the USSR. He also competed internationally for Canada in the 1976 Canada Cup and the 1979 Challenge Cup against the Soviets, which replaced that year's All-Star Game.

Among his teammates with the Habs and on Team Canada, Lapointe was a well-known practical joker. Aware of international teammate Phil Esposito's superstition about wearing the same pair of sandals for every shower, Lapointe once taped Espo's sandals together with several yards of tape, which in turn took an hour to unravel before the sandals were ready for the shower. Once, as a junior on a team where everyone had to wear coats, ties and hats, Lapointe sneaked into the dressing room and cut holes in the tops of everyone's hat—including his own, eliminating himself as a suspect. He then watched, withholding his chuckles, as the team confronted the one bewildered player with a hole-less hat. "When we finish practice, we rush back to the dressing room," his Canadiens teammate Pierre Bouchard related. "And nobody leaves the room to go on the ice until they make sure Guy has gone already."

In 1982 Montreal traded Lapointe to St. Louis. He had been unhappy because of dwindling ice time with the Canadiens but realized that the Habs had a group of up-and-coming defensemen. "I think Montreal traded me not

Guy Lapointe had originally dreamed of a career as a police officer.

Lapointe, Guy
D, 6′, 205 lbs, b: Montreal, Que., 3/18/1948

Season	Club, League		Regular Season					Playoffs			
		GP	G	A	Pts	PIM	GP	G	A	Pts	PIM
1968–69	Montreal Canadiens, NHL	1	0	0	0	2					
	Houston Apollos, CHL	65	3	15	18	120	3	1	0	1	6
1969–70	Montreal Canadiens, NHL	5	0	0	0	4					
	Montreal Voyageurs, AHL	57	8	30	38	92	8	3	5	8	6
1970–71	Montreal Canadiens, NHL	78	15	29	44	107	20	4	5	9	34
1971–72	Montreal Canadiens, NHL	69	11	38	49	58	6	0	1	1	0
SS–72	Canada	7	0	1	1	6					
1972–73	Montreal Canadiens, NHL	76	19	35	54	117	17	6	7	13	20
1973–74	Montreal Canadiens, NHL	71	13	40	53	63	6	0	2	2	4
1974–75	Montreal Canadiens, NHL	80	28	47	75	88	11	6	4	10	4
1975–76	Montreal Canadiens, NHL	77	21	47	68	78	13	3	3	6	12
CCup–76	Canada	7	0	4	4	2					
1976–77	Montreal Canadiens, NHL	77	25	51	76	53	12	3	9	12	4
1977–78	Montreal Canadiens, NHL	49	13	29	42	19	14	1	6	7	16
1978–79	Montreal Canadiens, NHL	69	13	42	55	43	10	2	6	8	10
ChCup–79	NHL All-Stars	1	0	0	0	0					
1979–80	Montreal Canadiens, NHL	45	6	20	26	29	2	0	0	0	0
1980–81	Montreal Canadiens, NHL	33	1	9	10	79	1	0	0	0	17
1981–82	Montreal Canadiens, NHL	47	1	19	20	72					
	St. Louis Blues, NHL	8	0	6	6	4	7	1	0	1	8
1982–83	St. Louis Blues, NHL	54	3	23	26	43	4	0	1	1	9
1983–84	Boston Bruins, NHL	45	2	16	18	34					
	NHL Totals	884	171	451	622	893	123	26	44	70	138
	SS/CCup/ChalCup Totals	15	0	5	5	8					

NHL First All-Star Team (1973)
NHL Second All-Star Team (1975, 1976, 1977)
Won Stanley Cup (1971, 1973, 1976, 1977, 1978, 1979)
Won CCup (1976)

Guy Lapointe (right) quickly established himself as one of the game's all-time greatest defensemen.

because Guy Lapointe asked for it, but for the good of the team," he said. "We've got six good defensemen who can do the job and one more in the minors. So I think it is a good time for me to leave. And I think that Montreal is going to have good memories of Guy Lapointe because I was playing good hockey. It's better to leave now than wait until I'm in my decline and people start to boo me," he said, in reference to the Montreal fans' treatment of his co-defensive stalwart Serge Savard in his final, lesser years with the team. Lapointe had also suffered a serious eye injury that many observers felt had slowed him down.

In his first year with the Blues, Lapointe broke his cheekbone and played only 50 games. The next season he signed with Boston as the Bruins tried to replace their star defenseman, Brad Park. For his part, Lapointe was anxious to show fans that the eye and face injuries of previous years wouldn't slow him down. "People wonder if I can still play," he said. "But the injuries have been to my face, not my legs."

Lapointe went on to become general manager of the Longueuil Chevaliers of the Quebec Major Junior Hockey League, then an assistant coach with the Quebec Nordiques and later a scout with the Calgary Flames. In 1993 he was inducted into the Hockey Hall of Fame.

Outside of the game, Lapointe's prized possession was a 1938 Chevrolet. But he confessed that his mind was never far from the game. "In the off-season," he once said, "I take all the time I can with my family. I listen to music, spend time with them—and think about hockey."

Bobby *Clarke*

Bobby Clarke was famous for his toothless smile.

In 1913 five geologists under the leadership of Tom Creighton left Winnipeg, Manitoba, and headed north. During their journey overland, Creighton came across a book that was still in fairly good condition despite having lain in the woods for a long time. It was a paperback novel called *The Sunless City*, written by English author J.E. Preston-Muddock. The hero of the adventure story, Professor Josiah Flintabbatey Flonatin, discovered a city of gold while exploring the depths of a bottomless lake in his submarine.

Two years later, the geologists crossed a lake and afterwards lit a bonfire inside a cave to dry out their clothing. Suddenly, a vein of rich ore appeared under the melted ice. Creighton didn't find a city of gold but instead discovered rich deposits of copper, zinc and silver. And that's where he founded a city. It was given the name Flin Flon after the hero of that well-thumbed book the geologists had read during the expedition.

Flin Flon is built on solid masses of rock. Supplies have to be transported in from far away. It is 300 miles from Winnipeg, the nearest major city. The town has a museum with a copy of the science fiction novel whose character it was named after. Many of the town's 10,000 inhabitants work in mines whose shafts go down 5,000 feet and stretch out for 50 miles at 70 different levels. You can come across many nationalities in Flin Flon, but there hasn't been a crime committed there as long as anyone can remember.

This is the town where Robert Earle Clarke, better known in the hockey world as Bobby Clarke, was born on August 13, 1949. His parents say that Bobby began to play hockey when they sat him in a highchair and gave him a toy hockey stick and puck. When Bobby was learning to skate, he spent from morning until night on an outdoor rink near his home.

His father once took him to Winnipeg, the capital of Manitoba. Clarke Senior wanted his son to see the lights of the big city. But Bobby laid his eyes on a rink and made his father stay there the whole evening so he could watch the kids playing with a puck.

Bobby began to play for his home team, the Flin Flon Bombers, when he was eight. In the beginning, he was nothing special as far as his friends were concerned. Hockey in Flin Flon was the only pastime. The Flin Flon Bombers' arena seated 2,000 and was always packed. The Bombers were practically impossible to beat on their home ice. It took 10 hours to get to Flin Flon by bus from Winnipeg. It was such an ordeal to get there that opposing teams were too exhausted to turn in a good performance.

Playing for the Bombers in the 1967–68 season, Clarke racked up 168 points (51 goals plus 117 assists). That was the best performance in the league. By all accounts, Bobby should have been first in the draft, but there were rumors in the NHL that Clarke was a diabetic and most probably wouldn't be able to play in the top league because of that. Pat Ginnell, head coach of the Bombers, didn't waste any time. He made arrangements with the Mayo Clinic, one of the best hospitals in North America, and took Bobby to Minnesota.

The doctors concluded that Clarke could play professional hockey if he looked after his health. The coach asked the doctors to put their statement in writing and returned home satisfied. When the following season began and NHL scouts began to visit Flin Flon, Ginnell showed them the verdict from the Mayo Clinic. On ice, Clarke hardly looked like a man with a serious affliction. He totaled 137 points with 51 goals and 86 assists and was again at the top of the league. Clarke also demonstrated superior leadership skills, which are highly valued in the NHL.

His behavior on the ice was so far from heroic that Bobby Clarke (left) was dubbed "Mr. Fair Play" with a heavy-handed irony.

The 1969 draft was ample evidence that there were those in the league who believed in Clarke. Bobby was selected 17th by the Philadelphia Flyers in the second round. Sam Pollock, manager of the Montreal Canadiens, who were 1969 Stanley Cup winners, immediately offered a deal that the Flyers management could hardly refuse. But Philadelphia turned it down. Next in line was Detroit Red Wings chief scout Jimmy Skinner, who offered two veterans for the 20-year-old diabetic. But the Flyers made it clear that Clarke wasn't up for sale.

For Clarke, the start of his professional career was rough. During training camp, he had two serious diabetic seizures. One of the Philadelphia coaches, Frank Lewis, conducted his own investigation and learned that in both instances Clarke had had only a light breakfast before the workout. Lewis drew up a complete dietary plan, which Bobby strictly followed for years to come. Before a game, Clarke would drink a bottle of Coca-Cola with three spoonfuls of dissolved sugar. Between periods he downed half a glass of orange juice with sugar added, and after the game a whole glass. Lewis always stashed several chocolate bars and a tube of 100% glucose in his bag, just in case.

The personal diet plan developed by his coach went without a hitch and Bobby Clarke didn't miss a single game in his first NHL season. At the same time, Clarke didn't put on any spectacular performances either, with 15 goals and 31 assists for a total of 46 points.

The following season, the Flyers were playing on home ice against the Stanley Cup winners, the Boston Bruins. In order to give his players some additional incentive to win, Flyers owner Ed Snider came into the locker room before the game and promised each player two new suits if they whipped the Bruins. The Flyers gave it their best shot. Clarke scored two goals and seemed to be on the ice all 60 minutes of the game, but Boston came out on top. After the siren sounded to end the game, Bobby left for the locker room with his head down so that no one would see the tears streaming down his face.

Clarke's 27 goals and 36 assists helped Philadelphia to capture the number three slot in their division, but in the first round of the playoffs the Phillies were KO'd by the Chicago Black Hawks 4–0. Bobby himself felt that he'd made improvements in all the elements of his game during the second season. There was plenty of praise for the young center, but the question remained: How long could a diabetic keep on playing at the professional level?

Diabetics were susceptible to infectious diseases and even a slight scratch could be dangerous. And Clarke played a very physical game and did his share of bleeding. The blood's sugar content was a major source of danger. If the concentration was low, the player could lose his physical coordination. If it was high, his legs would feel as heavy as lead. Gradually Bobby proved to all the skeptics that he was able to deal with his ailment. There were plenty of players out there with injuries that hadn't fully healed. Some with back injuries were compelled to wear a corset under their uniform. Others with knee injuries had to wear tight knee bandages before coming out on the ice. Clarke had diabetes and fought his illness by consuming sugar-laced juices.

By the third season, everyone had forgotten about Clarke's diabetes. Not only did Clarke chalk up the highest number of points in the club's history—35 goals plus 46 assists for a total of 81 points—he became the uncontested leader of the team, and that at the age of 22. At the end of the season, he was awarded the Bill Masterton Memorial Trophy for perseverance and dedication—a first for the Philadelphia team.

It was no surprise when in the summer of 1972 the head coach of Team Canada, Harry Sinden, named Bobby Clarke as one of the first candidates for the Summit Series against the USSR. Clarke had two wingers from the Toronto Maple Leafs, Ron Ellis and Paul Henderson, and this threesome made a strong impression on observers during exhibition play. In the first game, which ended in a fiasco for the Canadians, Clarke more than anyone else was dissatisfied with the way things had gone.

Clarke, Bobby
C, 5'10", 185 lbs, b: Flin Flon, Man., 8/13/1949

Season	Club, League	Regular Season					Playoffs				
		GP	G	A	Pts	PIM	GP	G	A	Pts	PIM
1969–70	Philadelphia Flyers, NHL	76	15	31	46	68					
1970–71	Philadelphia Flyers, NHL	77	27	36	63	78	4	0	0	0	2
1971–72	Philadelphia Flyers, NHL	78	35	46	81	87					
SS–72	Canada	8	2	4	6	18					
1972–73	Philadelphia Flyers, NHL	78	37	67	104	80	11	2	6	8	6
1973–74	Philadelphia Flyers, NHL	77	35	52	87	113	17	5	11	16	42
1974–75	Philadelphia Flyers, NHL	80	27	89	116	125	17	4	12	16	16
1975–76	Philadelphia Flyers, NHL	76	30	89	119	136	16	2	14	16	28
CCup–76	Canada	6	1	2	3	0					
1976–77	Philadelphia Flyers, NHL	80	27	63	90	71	10	5	5	10	8
1977–78	Philadelphia Flyers, NHL	71	21	68	89	83	12	4	7	11	8
1978–79	Philadelphia Flyers, NHL	80	16	57	73	68	8	2	4	6	8
ChCup–79	NHL All-Stars	3	0	1	1	0					
1979–80	Philadelphia Flyers, NHL	76	12	57	69	65	19	8	12	20	16
1980–81	Philadelphia Flyers, NHL	80	19	46	65	140	12	3	3	6	6
1981–82	Philadelphia Flyers, NHL	62	17	46	63	154	4	4	2	6	4
WEC–82	Canada	9	0	1	1	6					
1982–83	Philadelphia Flyers, NHL	80	23	62	85	115	3	1	0	1	2
1983–84	Philadelphia Flyers, NHL	73	17	43	60	70	3	2	1	3	6
	NHL Totals	1144	358	852	1210	1453	136	42	77	119	152
	WEC/SS/CCup/ChalCupTotals	26	3	8	11	24					

NHL First All-Star Team (1975, 1976)
NHL Second All-Star Team (1973, 1974)
Won Hart Trophy (1973, 1975, 1976)
Won Frank J. Selke Trophy (1983)
Won Bill Masterton Trophy (1972)
Won Lester B. Pearson Award (1973)
Won Lester Patrick Trophy (1980)
NHL Plus-Minus Leader (1976)
Won Stanley Cup (1974, 1975)
Won CCup (1976)

Bobby was named best player among the Canadians, but his efforts weren't enough. Before game two, Clarke reminded his team of the irony of the situation.

It was thought that the Russians had come to Canada to learn how to play hockey. The lesson the Canadians learned from the game in Montreal was that you had to be in good shape for a series where the pride of a nation was at stake and passions ran high. Judging by how they skated, the Russians knew this better than the Canadian team did. "We'll see what they can do after two or three games," said Bobby Clarke. But Team USSR adopted none of the techniques of the supposedly superior pros from the NHL and continued to play their own style of hockey. Before game four in Vancouver, the fans booed their own Canadian players. Bobby was furious. It was one thing if you were jeered by the fans of your club, but this was the national team of Canada!

The series was looking more and more like an embarrassment for Team Canada. The Canadians arrived in Moscow one game down on their opponents. After the first game at the Luzhniki Sports Palace, the gap doubled. A mistake by Clarke in the final minutes of the game cost the Canadians a tie. He was trying to control the puck near the boards and shot a pass to his partner, Rod Seiling. But Valeri Kharlamov intercepted the pass and flipped the puck to Vladimir Vikulov, who beat Tony Esposito at the net. The situation was critical. One more loss and the Canadians, whose considerable prestige was at stake, would blow the series. It was do or die.

At this point, Clarke took a more active role on his team and did his best to inspire the other players. At first he'd felt somewhat uncomfortable in the company of such stars as Phil Esposito and Brad Park. But facing the threat of an impending disaster, all players on the team became equal. The Canadians had to lay out everything they had to win game six, which they did with a score of 3–2. The battle would be uphill all the way, for the Soviets had home ice advantage and still led the series, but a slim chance had opened up for the Canadian team to win the series.

And suddenly Canadians demonstrated support for their players like never before. The team received over 50,000 telegrams. There were even messages from the town of Flin Flon. Bobby, smiling, said that he knew he wouldn't be forgotten. In the end, the Clarke trio was instrumental to the overall win of Team Canada. They won game seven by a score of 4–3. And Bobby's partner, Paul Henderson, scored the winning goal in the dying seconds of the final game to win it 6–5. Canada won the series.

In his third season in the NHL, Bobby Clarke (center) chalked up the highest number of points in Flyers history and became the team's undisputed leader.

Bobby Clarke could have become a national hero. The merits he accumulated during his career were impressive. As a player, the former Philadelphia captain led his club to Stanley Cup championships in 1974 and 1975. He also captured numerous individual awards, including the Hart Trophy as the league's most valuable player in 1973, 1975 and 1976, and made the All-Star Team four times. But Clarke's behavior on ice was far from heroic. Under the captaincy of Clarke, Philadelphia played a very aggressive game of hockey.

Dirty play, endless clashes and fisticuffs resulted in hours and hours of penalties. In the 1972–73 season, Philadelphia players spent 1,754 minutes in the penalty box. That was nearly 30 full games playing shorthanded. The Philadelphia fans liked the aggressive play of their idols and considered Clarke to be their own hero. In other cities, the Flyers were despised. Bobby Clarke, in all irony, was nicknamed "Mr. Fair Play." The Philly forward blamed all the hullabaloo around him on journalists who had nothing else to write about.

The bloody fights instigated by the Flyers on the ice didn't go unnoticed by the league management. Clarence Campbell, the NHL president, warned that if the Philadelphia players continued to intimidate the referees and their opponents, he would resort to special measures. Keith Allen, the Flyers' manager, immediately retorted, "We're not going to change our playing style." Bobby Clarke supported him all the way.

He had a famous, captivating smile—with about a dozen missing teeth. That is how Bobby Clarke will be remembered by those who saw him on ice. One of the best checkers in the entire history of the league, he was also a ruffian and a warrior. And a victor. The hockey player who gave the northern town of Flin Flon worldwide renown is now the president and general manager of the Flyers.

Vsevolod Bobrov

As a coach, Vsevolod Bobrov had a different view of hockey and the relationship between players than Anatoli Tarasov.

In the second round of playoffs in the first USSR championship, the two main rivals, CDKA (Red Army) and VVS MVO (Air Force), vied for the privilege of going to the finals. The Air Force was heavily favored since their forward line, spearheaded by Anatoli Tarasov, had turned in exceptional performances during training games. The Red Army lineup included Vsevolod Bobrov, one of the best bandy players around, but he was hampered by an injury. He came out on the ice anyway and scored three out of five goals, allowing Red Army to beat Air Force by a score of 5–3. He didn't play again that winter but still ended up the second-best scorer for his team, ensuring them a place in the finals.

The individual scoring record still belongs to Vsevolod Bobrov. In the 1947–48 USSR championship, he had established the all-time goal-scoring record by slamming in an average of 2.8 goals per game for a total of 52 goals in 18 games. During the second round of the national championship in 1948–49 between Red Army and Spartak Moscow, he scored eight consecutive goals. During the USSR championship in the 1950–51 season, Bobrov, who was then playing for the Air Force team against Dynamo Leningrad, scored a total of 10 goals.

Bobrov's athletic talent was first spotted when he was a youngster in the town of Sestroretsk, near Leningrad, where his family had settled in 1925. His

Bobrov, Vsevolod
LW, 5'11", 176 lbs, b: Sestroretsk, USSR, 12/1/1922, d: 7/1/1979

Season	Club, League	Regular Season				
		GP	G	A	Pts	PIM
1946–47	CDKA, USSR	1	3	*	*	*
1947–48	CDKA, USSR	18	52	*	*	*
1948–49	CDKA, USSR	*	27	*	*	*
1949–50	CDKA, USSR	*	0	*	*	*
	VVS MVO, USSR	13	29	*	*	*
1950–51	VVS MVO, USSR	15	43	*	*	*
1951–52	VVS MVO, USSR	16	37	*	*	*
1952–53	VVS MVO, USSR	*	7	*	*	*
1953–54	CDSA, USSR	7	15	*	*	*
WEC–54	USSR	7	8	*	*	*
1954–55	CSK MO, USSR	*	25	*	*	*
WEC–55	USSR	6	4	*	*	*
1955–56	CSK MO, USSR	0	0	*	*	*
OWG–56	USSR	7	9	*	*	*
1956–57	CSK MO, USSR	*	17	*	*	*
WEC–57	USSR	5	13	*	*	*
	USSR Totals	130	254	*	*	*
	OWG/WEC Totals	25	34	*	*	*

Named Best Forward at WEC (1954)
Won OWG (1956)
Won WEC (1954)
USSR Champion (1948, 1949, 1951, 1952, 1953, 1955, 1956)

first instructor was his elder brother Vladimir, who was considered to have a brilliant sports career ahead of him. However, because of a serious leg wound he received during World War II, this didn't happen.

By the time he appeared on the Red Army roster in the late fall of 1944, Bobrov was already a star in both bandy and soccer. Red Army soccer coach Boris Arkadiev had first seen Bobrov when he was playing bandy and immediately recognized him to be a sports prodigy. Bobrov went on to win acclaim on the soccer field playing for Arkadiev. During the 1945 soccer season, Bobrov became top scorer, won second place in playoff competition and USSR Cup tournaments and was loaned to Dynamo Moscow for a tour of Great Britain, where he won top honors.

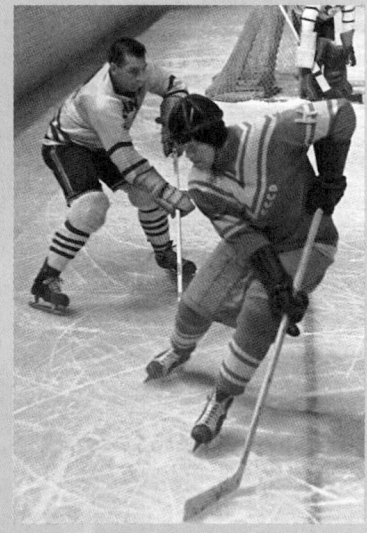

In the 1947–48 USSR championship, Vsevolod Bobrov (front) established an all-time record by averaging 2.8 goals per game.

In London, the Dynamo Moscow soccer players saw Canadian-style hockey being played by Canadian professionals competing in Great Britain. The Russian athletes were given skates and sticks and challenged to a game. Their talent was immediately apparent to the British and the Canadians. This was Vsevolod Bobrov's introduction to the puck version of ice hockey, a year before the game gained a foothold in the Soviet Union.

In his first hockey season, Vsevolod Bobrov played only one game. In the second season, having recovered from a soccer injury, he began playing at the top of his form and made a decisive contribution to Red Army's first championship title. In the 18 games that Bobrov played that season, he racked up 52 goals. In subsequent years, he was consistently among the top scorers. In 1954 Bobrov became the first captain of the USSR national hockey team.

When Bobrov played his first game with the USSR nationals (it was also the team's first-ever game), he was already 31. From 1954 to 1957, he managed to play in the national team lineup 57 times and scored 91 goals. Of those 57 games, the team won 50 and lost only three. In 1954 Bobrov was named best forward at the World Championship.

Bobrov created a number of unusual plays during his career. For example, while stickhandling past a player, Bobrov would switch the stick from his left hand to his right hand and outplay his opponent by going through at a much wider radius on the opposite side. Bobrov honed this play to perfection.

His unique talent allowed him to score a great many goals, but he could be contentious and was often the cause of discord among his teammates. His understanding of the game was much more profound than theirs. He could evaluate his options at decisive moments in the game with great agility and would get angry when he didn't receive a pass on time. He complained about his partners, Babich and Shuvalov, and while playing for Red Army he complained about coach Anatoli Tarasov as well. He usually cooled off quickly, but the hard feelings remained on both sides.

Bobrov, Vsevolod
Head Coach, b: Morshansk, USSR, 12/1/1922, d: 7/1/1979

Season	Club, League	Regular Season				
		GC	W	L	T	W%
1950–51	VVS MVO, USSR	15	13	0	2	0.933
1951–52	VVS MVO, USSR	17	16	1	0	0.941
1963–64	Spartak, USSR	36	24	10	2	0.694
1964–65	Spartak, USSR	36	24	7	5	0.736
1965–66	Spartak, USSR	36	24	8	4	0.722
1966–67	Spartak, USSR	44	38	3	3	0.898
WEC–72	USSR	10	7	1	2	0.800
SS-72	USSR	8	3	4	1	0.438
WEC–73	USSR	10	10	0	0	1.000
WEC–74	USSR	10	9	1	0	0.900
	USSR Totals	184	139	29	16	0.798
	WEC/SS Totals	38	29	6	3	0.803

Won WEC (1973, 1974)
USSR Champion (1951, 1952, 1967)

In 1954 Vsevolod Bobrov became the first captain of the USSR national team.

Tarasov, a powerful personality in Soviet hockey and a playing coach for Red Army, had an authoritarian style. He tried to put all the players on an equal footing by compelling everyone, including Bobrov, to train the same way. But it didn't work. The clash of personalities became a major conflict that forced Bobrov to leave Red Army at the end of 1949 and to quit hockey altogether in 1957 when he could have continued playing.

Bobrov also had an outstanding career as a hockey coach. His first full season after leaving Red Army and joining the Air Force team was the winter of 1950–51. Formally, the team was then managed by a coaching council consisting of the leading players of the club, but Bobrov, as player-coach, was the chairman of the council. The following season, Air Force became the champion, nosing out Red Army, where Tarasov was the player-coach.

As a coach, Bobrov's views on hockey and on the relationship between players were different from Tarasov's. Bobrov didn't try to squeeze his players into a rigid structure as the Army coach was known to do. Boborov's criticism of his players' performance was always constructive and it motivated them to train harder and achieve greater heights.

Vsevolod Bobrov lived a remarkable life in sports. He was the only person in the world who became captain of both the national hockey and soccer teams in the Olympics. He also twice coached the hockey team that became world champion. His fame was international. He was rewarded many times for his ability and is remembered by sports fans to this day.

Gilbert Perreault

On April 3, 1982, Gilbert Perreault became the 16th player in the NHL to register 1,000 points.

One of the most naturally gifted forwards in NHL history, Gilbert Perreault dazzled fans and the opposition defenses with his end-to-end rushes. He was the first building block in place when Punch Imlach began assembling the Buffalo Sabres in 1970. Throughout a nearly 17-year career that was spent entirely with Buffalo, Perreault was consistently one of the game's most entertaining figures. His laid-back and shy personality kept him from gaining the fame of some of the other stars of his era.

Perreault was a junior phenomenon when he led the Montreal Junior Canadiens to consecutive Memorial Cup wins in 1969 and 1970. After leading the club to their repeat national championship, Perreault was named the most valuable player in the OHA.

The Buffalo Sabres acquired the first pick in the 1970 Amateur Draft when coach and general manager Imlach won a spin of the wheel over expansion cousin Vancouver. Perreault was the obvious choice, and he lived up to his advance billing by establishing rookie scoring records of 38 goals and 72 points in 1970–71. He easily outdistanced runner-up Jude Drouin of the Minnesota North Stars in the Calder Trophy voting. In his sophomore year, he scored 26 goals and 74 points while being chosen to play for Canada in the 1972 Summit Series against the USSR.

The fortunes of the Buffalo franchise were enhanced by the placement of wingers Richard Martin and Rene Robert with Perreault. The French Connection became the most exciting trio in the league and was a major reason the Sabres qualified for the playoffs in only their third year of existence. A gentleman on the ice, Perreault was the recipient of the Lady Byng Trophy in 1973.

The team didn't fare as well in 1973–74 and missed the playoffs. A major factor in their regression was a broken leg suffered by Perreault that limited him to 55 games. The French Connection and the team rebounded in dramatic fashion the next year. They recorded a franchise record of 113 points and reached the Stanley Cup finals, where they lost to

Many observers in the NHL considered Gilbert Perreault (right) the most naturally gifted skater in the league in the 1970s.

defending champion Philadelphia in a competitive six-game series. Each member of Buffalo's top forward unit finished in the top 10 of the NHL scoring parade during the regular season.

The Sabres never attained the playoff success of 1975 again, but Perreault did record a personal high of 113 points in 1975–76. Later that year, he helped his country win the inaugural Canada Cup. He continued to excel through the rest of the decade and enjoyed his finest post-season in 1980 with 21 points in 14 games as Buffalo reached the Stanley Cup semifinals.

Although he was in his prime at the same time as Guy Lafleur, Marcel Dionne, Bobby Orr and Darryl Sittler, Perreault still managed to turn heads with his own style of play. Every time he grabbed the puck and headed up ice on one of his patented solo dashes, there was a sense of antic-

ipation. Perreault was able to stickhandle and use his lethal head fake to confound All-Star caliber opponents throughout the league. Twice he was placed on the NHL Second All-Star Team, but this only served as a token acknowledgment. Many observers in the NHL considered him the most naturally gifted forward in the league for much of the 1970s.

Although he was in the latter stages of his career in the 1980s, Perreault turned in four straight 30-goal seasons between 1981 and 1985. He starred as Wayne Gretzky's linemate at the 1981 Canada Cup, and he was playing some of the best hockey of his career with nine points in four games when he was forced out of the tournament with a broken ankle.

Following the trade of Danny Gare to Detroit on December 2, 1981, Perreault was named Buffalo's team captain, a position he held until his retirement in 1986–87. On April 3, 1982, he became the 16th player to register 1,000 points. Perreault scored his 500th goal

Perreault, Gilbert
C, 6´1˝, 180 lbs, b: Victoriaville, Que., 11/13/1950

Season	Club, League	Regular Season					Playoffs				
		GP	G	A	Pts	PIM	GP	G	A	Pts	PIM
1970–71	Buffalo Sabres, NHL	78	38	34	72	19					
1971–72	Buffalo Sabres, NHL	76	26	48	74	24					
SS–72	Canada	2	1	1	2	0					
1972–73	Buffalo Sabres, NHL	78	28	60	88	10	6	3	7	10	2
1973–74	Buffalo Sabres, NHL	55	18	33	51	10					
1974–75	Buffalo Sabres, NHL	68	39	57	96	36	17	6	9	15	10
1975–76	Buffalo Sabres, NHL	80	44	69	113	36	9	4	4	8	4
CCup–76	Canada	7	4	4	8	2					
1976–77	Buffalo Sabres, NHL	80	39	56	95	30	6	1	8	9	4
1977–78	Buffalo Sabres, NHL	79	41	48	89	20	8	3	2	5	0
1978–79	Buffalo Sabres, NHL	79	27	58	85	20	3	1	0	1	2
ChCup–79	NHL All-Stars	3	1	1	2	2					
1979–80	Buffalo Sabres, NHL	80	40	66	106	57	14	10	11	21	8
1980–81	Buffalo Sabres, NHL	56	20	39	59	56	8	2	10	12	2
CCup–81	Canada	4	3	6	9	2					
1981–82	Buffalo Sabres, NHL	62	31	42	73	40	4	0	7	7	0
1982–83	Buffalo Sabres, NHL	77	30	46	76	34	10	0	7	7	8
1983–84	Buffalo Sabres, NHL	73	31	59	90	32					
1984–85	Buffalo Sabres, NHL	78	30	53	83	42	5	3	5	8	4
1985–86	Buffalo Sabres, NHL	72	21	39	60	28					
1986–87	Buffalo Sabres, NHL	20	9	7	16	6					
	NHL Totals	1191	512	814	1326	500	90	33	70	103	44
	SS/CCup/ChalCup Totals	16	9	12	21	6					

NHL Second All-Star Team (1976, 1977)
Won Calder Trophy (1971)
Won Lady Byng Trophy (1973)
Won CCup (1976)

against Alain Chevrier on March 9, 1986. After playing 20 games the following season, he retired with 512 goals and 1,326 points to his credit. Perreault was inducted into the Hockey Hall of Fame in 1990.

Harry Sinden

When Harry Sinden accepted the job of coaching Team Canada in the 1972 Summit Series with the Soviet Union, he had no idea he was about to become part of the biggest hockey story of the century.

Sinden rode a roller coaster of emotions during those 28 days, until his powerful collection of NHL stars staged a dramatic comeback on Moscow ice to win the series four games to three with one game tied. Paul Henderson scored the winning goal with 34 seconds left in the final game as millions of Canadians watching at home on TV jumped for joy.

Sinden had been the target of critics earlier in the series when the Soviets took a 3–1–1 lead in games. He also faced the difficult task of keeping a large squad of more than 30 stars happy with their playing time. Selected as coach on the basis of his international experience as a player, Sinden was available because he had gone into the home-building business in Rochester, New York, after the Boston Bruins rejected his request for more money.

When Harry Sinden accepted the job of coaching Team Canada in the 1972 Summit Series, he had no idea he was about to become part of the biggest hockey event of the century.

In the 1969–70 season, with Bobby Orr and Phil Esposito playing starring roles, Sinden coached the Boston Bruins to their first Stanley Cup since 1940–41. Later he succeeded Milt Schmidt as general manager of the club in 1972–73. Over the years, Sinden gained a reputation as a penny pincher in negotiating contracts with players. But he always managed to put a respectable team on the ice in Boston.

In the summer of 1999, he made history by becoming the first GM to turn his back on a salary arbitration award, letting Dmitri Khristich, a 29-goal scorer, walk away from the team with no compensation. Sinden had been highly critical of Khristich's performance in the playoffs and was highly incensed when an arbitrator awarded him a salary of $2.8 million. Khristich became a free agent and signed with the Toronto Maple Leafs for the 1999–2000 season. In the 1996–97 season, Sinden was fined $5,000 by the National Hockey League for a verbal assault on a video replay judge in Ottawa. During a January 22 game between the Bruins and Senators, Sinden jumped all over Ian Sandercock after he'd disallowed a goal in the second period of Boston's 4–1 win.

Although he was an outstanding amateur hockey player, Sinden never played in the National Hockey League. Born in Collins Bay, Ontario, near Kingston, he captained the Whitby Dunlops to the Allan Cup Canadian senior championship in 1957, then to the World Championship title, representing Canada in Oslo, Norway, in 1958.

Sinden, Harry
Head Coach, b: Collins Bay, Ont., 9/14/1932

Season	Club, League	Regular Season					Playoffs				
		GC	W	L	T	W%	GC	W	L	T	W%
1966–67	Boston, NHL	70	17	43	10	0.314					
1967–68	Boston, NHL	74	37	27	10	0.568	4	0	4	0	0.000
1968–69	Boston, NHL	76	42	18	16	0.658	10	6	4	0	0.600
1969–70	Boston, NHL	76	40	17	19	0.651	14	12	2	0	0.857
SS–72	Canada	8	4	3	1	0.563					
1979–80	Boston, NHL	7	6	1	0	0.857	10	4	6	0	0.400
1984–85	Boston, NHL	24	11	10	3	0.521	5	2	3	0	0.400
	NHL Totals	327	153	116	58	0.557	43	24	19	0	0.558
	SS Totals	8	4	3	1	0.563					

Won Lester Patrick Trophy (1999)

After the Dunlops scored two quick goals late in the game to defeat the Soviet Union 4–2, the Canadian anthem was played and Sinden stood on the top pedestal of the medals stand, leaning over to give the captain Nickolai Sologubov a hug. The Dunlops won all seven games, outscoring the opposition by a whopping margin of 82–6.

Sinden was also recruited by the Kitchener-Waterloo Dutchmen to play in the 1960 Olympic Winter Games in Squaw Valley, California, winning a silver medal. He went on to become a player-coach with the Kingston Frontenacs of the Eastern Professional Hockey League. In the 1961–62 season, he shared the award for best defenseman in the league with Jean Gauthier of the Hull-Ottawa Canadiens.

Although Harry Sinden was an outstanding amateur hockey player, he never played in the NHL.

In 1965–66, as player-coach of the Oklahoma City Blazers of the Central Professional Hockey League, Sinden won the Jack Adams Award when he guided the team to second place in regular-season play, then to eight straight playoffs wins to become CPHL champions.

USA Hockey honored Sinden in 1999 by granting him and the U.S. women's hockey team the Lester Patrick Trophy for outstanding hockey service in the United States. The U.S. team had defeated Canada to win their first women's Olympic gold medal in hockey at Nagano, Japan, in February of 1998.

Sinden was inducted into the Hockey Hall of Fame in Toronto in 1983.

1972–1990

*New Dynasties
Smash Old Records*

Two professional leagues kicked off the 1972–73 season: the venerable National Hockey League and the brand-new World Hockey Association organized in February 1972. At first the NHL didn't take the upstart league very seriously. And if anything like it had happened in the era of the Original Six, when the supply of young players easily outstripped demand, the older league would have laughed. But expansion had changed the dynamics and the possibility of players being siphoned off to the WHA was a real danger—especially when Bobby Hull went from Chicago to the Winnipeg Jets on a 10-year, $2.75-million contract. The greatest NHL stars couldn't even imagine a contract like that, and soon such ace veterans as Frank Mahovlich and talented newcomers like goalkeeper Bernie Parent also started heading for WHA clubs. What was more, almost half of the new league's 12 clubs were in cities considered the old league's domains: Boston, Chicago, New York, Philadelphia, Toronto.

In an effort to enhance its international prestige, the WHA clubs played a number of games against Soviet teams. Vladislav Tretiak (left) and Bobby Hull (right).

In the end, there wasn't a mass exodus. A 45-year-old Gordie Howe and his sons Mark and Marty went over, but the majority of NHL stars preferred to wait and see if the WHA would prove to be viable. So the new league turned to Europe.

In those days, European players weren't given any favors in the NHL. Ace Swedish forwards Sven "Tumba" Johansson and Ulf Sterner had been the first to be invited over from the Old World, in the 1960s. When they failed, the verdict was unanimous and categorical: The Europeans couldn't take it and were physically weak.

Even such a strong presupposition meant nothing to the WHA clubs, whose vital signs depended on acquiring high-class players wherever they could. And when two forwards from Sweden joined the Winnipeg lineup in 1974, they immediately demonstrated that they weren't afraid of tough hockey. The international line of Anders Hedberg, Ulf Nilsson and Bobby Hull soon became one of the best in North America, such that by the WHA's third season, Hull and his overseas partners were achieving phenomenal statistical results: Hull's total goals reached the 181 mark and he repeated Maurice Richard's achievement of 50 goals in 50 games. After that,

A HISTORY OF WORLD HOCKEY

the ranks of "the foreign legion" in the WHA swelled to include Finnish forwards Matti Hagman and Veli-Pekka Ketola and one of the best forwards in Europe, the Czech player Vaclav Nedomansky.

In an effort to enhance its international prestige, the WHA played a series of eight games against the USSR in the fall of 1974. The organizers tried to make it a carbon copy of the 1972 Summit Series—beginning with calling it Canada–USSR—but it didn't turn out to be up to its predecessor's standard, first of all because the WHA still had only one dazzling star. Bobby Hull scored seven goals in eight games, supported by 46-year-old Gordie Howe (three goals) as far as his strength and age would allow; 37-year-old ex-Canadien Ralph Backstrom (four goals), who even in his best years hadn't won any individual trophies except for the Calder back in 1959; 36-year-old Frank Mahovlich (one goal); and Paul Henderson (two goals), who simply couldn't repeat his hour of glory in Summit '72 without Phil Esposito and Yvan Cournoyer.

Even so, Team Canada managed to turn in a better performance in the Canadian leg of Series '74 than the 1972 NHL team. The first game ended in a 3–3 tie, but Canada won the next one 4–1 at Maple Leaf Gardens, lost only the game played in Winnipeg (8–5) and tied the one in Vancouver 5–5. After that, the Soviet defense line and goalie Vladislav Tretiak managed to keep Bobby Hull on a starvation diet and he scored only once in Moscow. As a result, the Canadians were outplayed at the Sports Palace in Luzhniki by scores of 3–2, 5–2, 4–4 and 3–2.

Beginning with 1974, the World Championships boiled down more and more to a duel between the USSR and Czechoslovakia for the highest titles.

The WHA's third season in 1974–75 was the turning point. The WHA clubs based in cities considered the NHL's domain just couldn't stand up to the stiff competition. For example, the Philadelphia Blazers migrated at first to Vancouver and then Calgary, losing Bernie Parent along the way (he finally returned to the Flyers). The Toronto Toros hung out their shingle twice and ended up the Birmingham Bulls. By the 1977–78 season, only eight of the 12 founding clubs remained, mainly because WHA hockey was dominated by aging veterans, still didn't have many stars and thus remained considerably inferior to NHL hockey as a spectacle. The league staggered along until 1979 and then faded away after seven seasons, after which the NHL took four of the more successful and well-to-do WHA clubs under its wing: the Edmonton Oilers, Winnipeg Jets, Quebec Nordiques and Hartford Whalers.

In Europe, the Soviet dynasty reigned from 1963 to 1972, during which time it won every World Championship and Olympic tournament. The first hitch occurred at the 1972 World Championship in Prague. Having earned only one point in two games against Czechoslovakia (a 3–3 tie and a 3–2 loss), the Soviet team at long last stepped aside.

The finals between Montreal and Chicago in the 1972–73 season were expected to turn into a duel between goalies Ken Dryden and Tony Esposito, but Dryden allowed slightly less than four goals against per game while Esposito did even worse with a five-goals-against average. In game four, Dryden finally took on the role and it ended 4–0. The next game was again marked by an avalanche of attacks and 12 goals were scored in the first 40 minutes. The Black Hawks won that game 8–7 and were leading 2–0 in game six, but Henri Richard reduced the gap before the end of the period and right after the break Frank Mahovlich tied it 2–2. Cournoyer scored the game-winning goal and Montreal took it in six.

The Soviet national squad once again had no equals at the 1973 World Championship in Moscow. In 10 games, the team racked up a nearly perfect performance, scoring 100 goals while allowing only 18 against Vladislav Tretiak.

After Philadelphia's tremendous surge in the 1973–74 regular season, the Flyers didn't let their fans down in the playoffs and took out Atlanta (4–0) and the Rangers (4–3) on the way to the finals. But the Bruins were waiting.

The Bruins hadn't lost a single game against an expansion team in playoffs since 1968 and they were the favorites in this one as well. The first game affirmed the forecast and Boston won it 3–2. In game two, Boston again took the lead (2–0), but the Flyers tied it eight minutes before the end of the third period and Bobby Clarke scored the clincher in overtime. At home in the Spectrum, Philly compelled the Bruins to capitulate twice (4–1 and 4–2) when Bobby Orr couldn't score against Bernie Parent. Game five had more than its fair share of fisticuffs, and with both teams playing four against four more than once, Orr managed two goals. The Bruins won that one 5–1 and narrowed the gap in the series to 3–2. But Bernie Parent was at the top of his form in game six and an expansion team won the Stanley Cup for the first time.

Team USSR dominated on the international level between 1978 and 1983.

In the 1974–75 season, clubs from Kansas City and Washington joined the NHL and the 18-club league was reorganized into four divisions and two conferences named after some of the game's builders. The Norris and Adams divisions made up the Prince of Wales Conference, while the Clarence Campbell Conference included the Patrick and Smythe divisions. The formula for the Stanley Cup playoffs was also changed. The top three teams in each division qualified and the four first-place winners went straight to the quarterfinals while the others battled through a preliminary round. And for the first time in history, none of the pre-expansion teams participated in the Stanley Cup finals when Philadelphia and Buffalo—which featured the great French Connection Line of Rick Martin, Gilbert Perreault and Rene Robert—made their way there in 1975.

Though the Flyers failed to gain territorial supremacy in the first two games at home in the Spectrum, they made maximum use of even minimal possibilities and won both. Then Buffalo won the next two at home and the series was tied 2–2. In game five, the Flyers displayed phenomenal discipline and had a player in the penalty box only four times, thereby depriving the Sabres of a trump card: scoring in power-plays. And this time Philadelphia derived the maximum out of their minimal possibilities in the form of five goals and it ended 5–1. Then they finished it in game six in Buffalo. In the first two periods, Bernie Parent blocked all 26 of the Sabres' shots on goal, while in the third period precise shots by Bob "Hound Dog" Kelly and Bill Clement brought the Flyers their second Stanley Cup in a row.

Beginning in 1974, the World Championships became almost exclusively a duel between the USSR and Czechoslovakia. Sweden had seen a mass exodus of its best players to the NHL and couldn't put up much competition, and Canada was boycotting the tournament. In 1974 and 1975 the Soviets won two more championship titles, as if to prove to their Czechoslovakian rivals that they could count on being eternal runners-up.

Team USA. The author of a Miracle on Ice at the 1980 Olympics in Lake Placid.

The paths of Soviet and NHL hockey crossed again in December 1975, this time at club level, when CSKA (Central Red Army) and Krylja Sovetov (Soviet Wings) played four games each with the leading NHL teams. To this day, the game that was played in Montreal on December 31, 1975, is considered one of the most spectacular in the history of hockey. The Canadiens dominated in the first half of the game and were leading 2–0 and 3–1 in the course of the match. But then Vladislav Tretiak shut down the scoring and Valeri Kharlamov and Boris Alexandrov made it 3–3 in swift counterattacks.

After that, Christmas tours by Soviet clubs became standard practice and teams from the USSR met NHL clubs on about a hundred occasions until interest started to wane in the 1980s and such tours became senseless in the 1990s. With the USSR's disintegration, Russian hockey declined so that it was in no way comparable to the level of play in the NHL.

The 1975–76 finals were the shortest in the decade; four games sufficed for the Canadiens to win the Cup. As a rule, the Flyers caved in during the third period. In game one, for example, Jacques Lemaire tied the score 3–3 in the last period and defenseman Guy Lapointe slapped in the winning goal 62 seconds before the final siren. Guy Lafleur and Lemaire brought Montreal one more victory (2–1) in the Forum, Pierre Bouchard scored in the third period to win game three 3–2, and in game four the third period began with a score of 3–3, but breakaways by Lafleur and Pete Mahovlich in the 54th and 59th minutes compelled goalkeeper Wayne Stephenson to capitulate 5–3.

The USSR and Czechoslovakia met once again in the decisive game at the 1976 Olympics in Innsbruck. The Czech players were leading 2–0 and had a two-man advantage for almost two minutes. By the third period, the game was tied, and in the end Valeri Kharlamov and Alexander Yakushev scored a goal apiece for a 4–3 victory. At the World Championship in Poland two months later, the Czech players had their revenge and pushed the Soviet team into second. But the main event of that year was the first Canada Cup. Soviet coaches took an "experimental" team to North America—and ended up in third place—while Team Czechoslovakia reaffirmed its reputation by reaching the finals, where it lost in two games to the hosts of the tournament.

The Canadiens lost only eight games in the 1976–77 regular season and emerged all but effortlessly in the Stanley Cup finals. Under new coach Don Cherry, the Bruins overcame the Flyers in four games in the semifinals, but they had nothing to put up against the Canadiens in the finals.

Montreal won the first two games at home easily (7–3 and 3–0), then gave the Bruins a lesson in power-plays at the Boston Garden. A scant six shots on goal during three Boston penalties turned into three goals in Gerry Cheevers' net and Lafleur put in a finishing touch to make it 4–2. Only when they were backed into a corner in game four did the Bruins demonstrate their best game; they were leading 1–0 until Lemaire tied the score. The Bruins continued to attack, but the same Lemaire received a perfect pass from Lafleur and dashed their hopes 2–1 in overtime.

At the 1978 World Championship, Erich Kuhnhackl (right) from Germany led all scorers with eight goals and 16 points in 10 games, finishing ahead of marquee players like Ivan Hlinka of Czechoslovakia, Alexander Maltsev and Boris Mikhailov of the USSR and Canada's Marcel Dionne.

Team Canada arrived in Vienna for the World Championship in the spring of 1977 after an eight-year absence. And this time the Canadiens brought stars of the first magnitude: Phil and Tony Esposito and Rod Gilbert. After the preliminary rounds, the teams from Sweden, the USSR, Czechoslovakia and Canada emerged in the Finals of Four—which became one of the most unpredictable in the history of World Championships.

Led by Phil Esposito, the Canadiens routed the Swedes 7–0 while the Soviets were unable to overcome the Czechs and lost 4–3. In the second round, the USSR easily outplayed Canada 8–1 while Sweden dropped another game 2–1. On the final day of the championship, tireless Phil outplayed the 1976 world champion Czech team 8–2 and gave the USSR one more shot at the gold. But the Swedes did the impossible. Playing deep in defense, they allowed their opponents into Goran Hogosta's net only once. In the third period, Roland Eriksson lit the red lamp twice to bring the score to 3–1 in favor of Tre Kronor, giving the Czech players a wonderful gift: back-to-back world titles for the first time in history.

The Stanley Cup finalists in the 1977–78 season were again the Canadiens and the Bruins, but this time Boston coach Don Cherry had learned his lesson. Since Boston had virtually no chance in high-speed play, something had to slow Montreal down. But what? In the first game, Cherry decided to bet on defense. However, tough play can earn penalties and two power-play goals clinched a Canadiens victory (4–1). In the next game, Gerry Cheevers turned in an exceptional performance for Boston and the Canadiens eked out a 3–2 win only when Lafleur scored the tie-breaker in overtime.

A HISTORY OF WORLD HOCKEY

The Boston Garden's home ice was the smallest in the league, and now it helped the hosts put a damper on speed. They held the puck on the boards and won the next two games at home (4–0 and 4–3 in overtime). To penetrate Boston's tough defense, Montreal coach Scotty Bowman started to use unexpected raids by his defensemen—Larry Robinson, Serge Savard and Guy Lapointe—and the Canadiens won the next two games 4–1. Indeed, Larry Robinson chalked up a total of 21 points in the playoffs to become the third defenseman to win the Conn Smythe Trophy after Serge Savard and Bobby Orr. And with their third Stanley Cup in a row, Bowman's players had earned the right to be called the second Canadiens dynasty.

The 1978 World Championship in Prague was again decided in the game between Czechoslovakia and the USSR. The hosts could afford to lose, but not by more than one goal, and they lost by two (3–1). This time Canada won the bronze medals.

Dennis Potvin led the New York Islanders to four consecutive Stanley Cups from 1979 to 1983.

At the end of the regular 1978–79 season, the Canadiens were squeezed out of first place by newcomers from New York, the Islanders. But Montreal passed the test of the playoffs while the Islanders bowed out to their crosstown rivals, the Rangers. Phil Esposito and Anders Hedberg were the heroes of the first game (which New York won 4–1), but Ken Dryden was so nervous Bowman had to replace him with Michel Larocque at the beginning of the third period. Dryden was still shaky for the second game and began by allowing two goals on two shots, though the Canadiens recovered and won it 6–2. By game three, Dryden had rehabilitated himself and helped his team win 4–1. In the next game, the Rangers played their best game in the finals but lost 4–3 in overtime. Back at the Forum for what turned out to be the last game, the hosts restricted the Rangers to 15 shots on Dryden and all of the Montreal forward lines played with the same confidence. The New Yorkers never did figure out who could be left unguarded and all the goals in a 4–1 game were scored by different Canadiens.

After the failure in Vienna in 1977, the Soviets undertook a series of reforms. Viktor Tikhonov was chosen as coach of the national team and sports functionaries made a unique decision to pool all the strongest players in the country in one club, CSKA (Central Red Army). And it was the smooth style of all their forward lines that brought the team a victory in February 1979 at the Challenge Cup tournament when the NHL All-Star Team met the USSR in a series at Madison Square Garden that replaced the All-Star Game that season. The hosts won the first game 4–2, but the Soviets won the next two 5–4 and 6–0.

At the 1979 World Championship in Moscow, Czechoslovakia only made it to second. The ex-champions lost to the Soviet team 11–1 and 6–1, lagging the winners by six points and surpassing the bronze-winning Swedes by five.

The 1979–80 finals between the Islanders and the Flyers turned into a thriller. Denis Potvin's clincher won game one 4–3 for the Islanders. In the next game, new spark plug Paul Holmgren recorded a hat-trick and the Flyers took it 8–3. Game three turned into a demonstration on the art of the power-play delivered by the Islanders to the visitors in Nassau Coliseum. The Isles scored five goals in power-plays and another when they were a man short. In game four, the Flyers naturally tried to avoid penalties, but the Islanders' attacking machine clicked again even when both teams were playing at full strength and they won 5–2. The Flyers won 6–3 at home in the Spectrum thanks to the efforts of Bobby Clarke and Rick MacLeish, but the finals didn't go to game seven. In New York, Philly—who were losing 2–0 after sizzling shots by Bryan Trottier—did the maximum possible and tied the score by the middle of the third period and in the last 10 minutes outshot the Islanders 11–5. But Billy Smith was impenetrable and Bob Nystrom, on the receiving end of a pinpoint pass from John Tonelli, registered a win of 5–4 in overtime for the Islanders' first Stanley Cup in their first finals.

In 1980 the 12 teams in the Olympic tournament at Lake Placid were divided into two groups and the Finns and Americans became the troubleshooters who didn't allow such strong national squads as Canada and Czechoslovakia to go to the finals. And the Americans achieved much more than that. With an average age of 22, the American team consisted mainly of students, but what coach Herb Brooks' players did in the game against the obvious favorite from the USSR was aptly called a Miracle on Ice. Several seconds before the end of the first period, it was 2–1 in favor of the Soviet team when Vladislav Tretiak sloppily parried a shot from the blue line by Dave Christian. Center Mark Johnson was the first to get to the deflected

In the 1990s, new franchises began to rule the NHL.

puck and immediately dispatched it into the net. According to the scoreboard, there was only one second left in the period. After that goal, coach Viktor Tikhonov yanked Tretiak out of the net and put Vladimir Myshkin in his stead—a fatal mistake. The Americans believed they could win and decided it in the last period. Once again, Johnson gave his team a one-goal lead, and in the 51st minute, Team USA captain Mike Eruzione whipped in another one. Still, to become Olympic champions for the second time in history, the Americans had to beat the Finns. So that's what they did, 4–2.

The New York Islanders easily won the first two games of the 1981 Stanley Cup finals against the Minnesota North Stars (both ended 6–3) and Butch Goring dominated game three for the Isles. A tireless checker, Goring surpassed himself in this game to record three goals, including the game-winner (7–5). It was only in the next game that the North Stars had their first—and last— taste of victory (4–2), thanks to the practically faultless game of goalie Don Beaupre. Within 10 minutes of the face-off in the last game, the Islanders had five goals to their credit with the opener again scored by Goring, who was awarded the Conn Smythe Trophy at the end of the game.

The results at Lake Placid had consolidated the need to restructure and renew the USSR's national team. Accordingly, Viktor Tickhonov brought a new team with four forward lines to the 1981 World Championship in Sweden—a strategy that proved effective when the Soviets trounced the home team 13–1 before the final round and thus ensured the title well ahead of schedule. The Canadians placed fourth behind Czechoslovakia and the Swedes came in second in Stockholm.

The 1981 Canada Cup permitted pros, so Canada mustered a team of stars who were counting on winning and looked very strong in the preliminaries when they knocked out the Soviets 7–3. The two teams met again in the final match at Montreal's Forum, and right from the start, Vladislav Tretiak was hit by a storm of attacks. Even the combined forces of Wayne Gretzky, Mike Bossy, Bryan Trottier, Guy Lafleur and Marcel Dionne couldn't do much with the steadfast Soviet goalie, however, while Sergei Shepelev and the KLM Line ensured the Soviets an 8–1 victory with a hat-trick and four goals respectively.

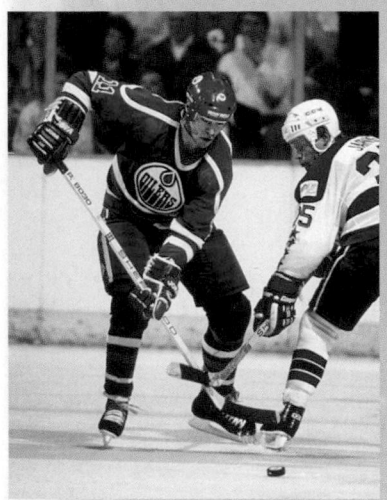

The Edmonton Oilers became the first NHL club to score more than 400 goals when they made it 417 in the 1981–82 regular season. And the pundits had almost no doubts that the Islanders' defense—even though it was the best in the league—wouldn't be able to stand up to Gretzky and Co. Alas, the Islanders and the Oilers weren't destined to meet in the finals that year. The Los Angeles Kings knocked Edmonton out in the first round in a best-of-five series and the Vancouver Canucks went to the finals from the Clarence Campbell Conference—a club that had 34 fewer points in the regular season and was 11th overall in the league. The Islanders swept the Canucks 6–5, 6–4, 3–0 and 3–1 and the first game was the only one where the New Yorkers had to come from behind. In the 57th minute of regular play, Mike Bossy tied it 5–5, and just two seconds before the end of the first overtime, he also slammed in the game-winner. Bossy scored 17 goals in those playoffs and earned the Conn Smythe Trophy.

When the Edmonton Oilers won the first of their four Stanley Cups in five years in 1984, Mark Messier (center) was on a team with such stars as Wayne Gretzky, Paul Coffey and Grant Fuhr, but was still MVP in the playoffs.

After officially becoming a dynasty in the 1982 playoffs, the Islanders had slipped to sixth place by the end of the next regular season. Then they lived up to their reputation by beating the Boston Bruins in six games in the Prince of Wales Conference finals. The other finalist in the 1983 Stanley Cup series was the Oilers—a team that had lost only one game in all of the preceding rounds of the playoffs.

The series kicked off at Edmonton's Northlands Coliseum. In spite of being constantly checked, the Oilers fired 35 shots at Billy Smith—most from a distance and they didn't go in—whereas Duane Sutter scored one against Andy Moog in the first period and Ken Morrow added an empty-net goal to make it 2–0. And when Mike Bossy returned to the lineup after missing the first game with tonsillitis, the Islanders switched their scoring into high gear. In the course of five minutes in the first period in game two, they scored three against Moog, while another two in a 38-second interval in the second period clinched the 6–3 outcome for good.

In the course of the first 40 minutes of the next game, at Nassau Coliseum, it seemed the puck was only fired at one goal and it was the Isles'. But Billy Smith erred only once and the teams came out on the ice in the third period with the score tied 1–1. When the game was over, the scoreboard showed 5–1 in favor of the Islanders.

In game four, the hosts didn't permit the Oilers a moment of joy. In the first period, leading Islanders Trottier and Bossy—and Tonelli, who joined them—whipped in three goals in a matter of 90 seconds, while at the end of the game Morrow, an infrequent scorer, put another one into an empty net to make it 4–2. The New Yorkers again took it in four, for their fourth Stanley Cup in a row.

After those finals, Edmonton coach and general manager Glenn Sather didn't make the usual references to the refereeing and admitted that the Islanders had played a practically impeccable game in defense. But he ended by saying the Oilers would have their revenge in a year.

The Oilers and Islanders indeed met again in the 1984 Stanley Cup finals, and the first game demonstrated that the Oilers had learned their lesson. The Edmonton players replied to the Islanders' checking with checks of their own (Mark Messier was especially brilliant in this) while their defense was solidly anchored by goalkeeper Grant Fuhr. As a result, the game ended 1–0 for the Oilers. Then the Islanders restored the status quo 6–1 in game two with the help of a Clark Gillies hat-trick.

The New Yorkers continued to feel quite comfortable in the first 39 minutes of the first game in Northlands Coliseum with a score of 2–2, but the last minute in the second period became a nightmare for them. In 17 seconds, Glenn Anderson and Paul Coffey put two past Billy Smith and he couldn't get over the shock in the last period. He was benched and his team lost 7–2. The next game finished with the same score and two goals to Gretzky's credit. But Gretzky didn't stop there. At the beginning of game five, Gretzky received pinpoint passes from Jari Kurri to put Edmonton in the lead 2–0, after which a disgruntled Billy Smith again left the ice. When the game ended 5–2, the Oilers took their first sip of champagne from the Cup.

Mario Lemieux (second from the left) scored a series-winning goal against the Soviet Union in the final game of the Rendez-Vous series in 1987.

The USSR dominated the 1982 and 1983 World Championships and the 1984 Olympics, partly because the Soviet national team wasn't affected by the problem of their best players departing for the NHL, a problem that plagued virtually every other leading hockey country. The Canadians put together a last-minute national team of players from clubs that were knocked out of the first round of the playoffs, but it didn't provide stiff competition. Even when Wayne Gretzky, Darryl Sittler, Bobby Clarke and Bill Barber all arrived to play in the 1982 World Championship, the tournament was half over before they started to click.

In the 1984–85 regular season, Mike Keenan made his coaching debut in the NHL and took the Philadelphia Flyers to first place. A new generation of Philly stars including Swedish goalie Pelle Lindberg and hard-hitting forwards Brian Propp and Tim Kerr led the Flyers into the finals with the Oilers.

Philadelphia won the opener convincingly enough (4–1), but in the second game the fast-skating Edmonton players replied with their own power and won it 3–1. In their first home game, the Oilers started out with endless attacks, three of which Wayne Gretzky finished off with goals in the first period. The Flyers subsequently closed the gap but lost 4–3. Soon after the start of the next game, Philly was already out in front 3–1. However, the Oilers only had to switch their usual combination plays into high gear and the powerful but not very nimble Flyers began

A HISTORY OF WORLD HOCKEY

traveling to the penalty box one after another. Four power-play goals—two by Gretzky—brought the Oilers another victory (5–3). And the coup de grace *in game five (which ended 8–3) was administered by Gretzky and Coffey, who together racked up 10 goals in the finals.*

And before the next season, the Black Hawks officially became the Blackhawks—as they'd been off and on through reported history—when team president and part owner (and long-time chairman of the NHL board of directors) Bill Wirtz made a final decision.

There was every reason to believe that the Edmonton Oilers would become the next hockey dynasty by winning the Stanley Cup for the third time in a row in the 1985–86 season. Wayne Gretzky set all-time records for assists (163) and points (215), defenseman Paul Coffey looked more like Bobby Orr in his prime and the team seemed unstoppable. As it happened, Edmonton was weak in one area: luck. In the deciding seventh game of the second round against Calgary, the Flames took a 2–0 lead. The Oilers rallied to tie it 2–2 as the third period began, but then young Edmonton defenseman Steve Smith fired the puck from behind the net, through the crease, and the puck caromed off Grant Fuhr's leg into the net. The score was 3–2. For the Flames.

In the finals, the Canadiens lost the opening game to the Flames before storming back with four straight victories. Two Montreal rookies were a big part of this success: Patrick Roy had a 1.92 goals-against average, while Claude Lemieux scored 10 goals in the playoffs.

In the 1986–87 season, Edmonton was once again the number one team in the league and again met Philadelphia in the finals. The first two games in Edmonton put Glenn Anderson, Jari Kurri and Paul Coffey in the limelight and went to the Oilers 4–2 and 3–2. In the Spectrum, the Flyers were trailing 3–0 when they bounced back with five unanswered goals to win the third game 5–3. However, in game four, the goals by Kevin Lowe (with a man short) and Randy Gregg (on a power-play) ensured Edmonton a 4–1 victory that instilled hope the Edmonton fans would see the Stanley Cup presented to the Oilers at their next hometown game.

And it seemed to be heading that way. Right off the bat, the hosts took the lead 2–0 and 3–1. After that came the unimaginable. First, rookie goalkeeper Ron Hextall—who would later be awarded the Conn Smythe Trophy—stopped the Edmonton forwards, after which Brian Propp slipped three ingenious assists to his partners to make it 4–3 for the Flyers. The presentation of the award was postponed.

Back at the Spectrum, the home team worked more magic. They were losing 2–0 when Lindsay Carson, Propp and J.J. Daigneault all lit the red lamp for a score of 3–2 on the game and 3–3 in the series.

In game seven, the Flyers opened the scoring, but Mark Messier and Jari Kurri put the Oilers in the lead 2–1. In the third period, the Oilers were wiser from their bitter experience in previous games and allowed only two goal-scoring situations but slammed in one more themselves to make it 3–1. And at last the Cup was presented at home to the Oilers.

The new formula introduced at the 1983 World Championship gave the USSR's opponents a chance by not taking into account the points that were picked up before the round-robin Finals of Four. The Soviets were so heavily favored all through the 1980s that rivals had structured their game on defense and dreamed of finishing off rare attacks with a goal. Eventually, such tactics demonstrated a degree of merit. At the 1985 World Championship in Prague, the Soviets bowed to the Czechs 2–1 and the Canadians 3–1 (and Mario Lemieux made his debut) and the USSR had to make do with bronze medals. A year later, the Soviet squad took revenge by winning its 20th World Championship in Moscow. But the Prague story was repeated at Vienna in 1987. Having spent practically the whole game at their opponent's net, the Soviet players were unable to capitalize on their advantages. As a result, they wrenched a victory from the Czechs with great difficulty (2–1) and tied the games with Sweden and Canada. This time the Swedes became champions on their goals-scored and goals-against numbers.

The finals between Edmonton and Boston crowned the 1987–88 season. The opener was played with great caution; both teams had a total of 36 shots on goal and only three of them lit the red lamp (2–1 in favor of Edmonton). The fate of the next game was sealed by the "Big Four"—Messier, Gretzky, Anderson and Kurri—who each scored a goal for a score of 4–2. In game three, brilliant performances were turned in by Esa Tikkanen (three goals) and Wayne Gretzky (four assists) for a score of 6–3. But for only the second time in NHL history, game four wasn't played to the end.

Although Al MacInnis won the Conn Smythe Trophy, it was Mike Vernon (right) that paved the way for the Calgary Flames' success by winning 16 games and recording three shutouts to lead all post-season goalies in 1989.

On May 24, Boston was enduring a heat wave. The cooling units in the old Garden overheated and the game had to be interrupted several times because of the mist that enveloped the rink. With the score at 3–3, the electric transformer couldn't cope with the overload and the Garden was plunged into darkness. The repairmen who arrived on the scene couldn't guarantee that the breakdown would be rectified soon, so it was decided to play game five in Edmonton and return to game four if there was a need after that.

But there was no need. The Oilers won on home ice 6–3. Wayne Gretzky chalked up 13 points in four (official) games, which became one more NHL record the Great One rewrote. And it earned him the Conn Smythe Trophy as playoffs MVP.

A few months before the 1988 Olympics in Calgary, it was decided for the first time to allow pros to play. However, the NHL didn't want to make a break in the regular championship so its best players could participate in the Olympics and the hosting Canadians only secured seven NHLers. And only goalie Andy Moog (who was available because he was involved in a contract dispute) had star status. The Canadians lost to both the Soviets and the Finns and came in fourth, while Olympic gold went once again to the USSR, which had four players—Vladimir Krutov, Igor Larionov, Viacheslav Fetisov and Sergei Makarov—in the list of the six highest scorers at the games.

For years, the Edmonton Oilers were referred to as the Great One's team—and not without grounds—so Edmonton fans were dumbfounded by Gretzky's departure to the Los Angeles Kings in the summer of 1988. Wayne parted from his team with tears in his eyes. But he left.

Naturally enough, the 1988–89 season wasn't a huge success for the Oilers. Los Angeles and Calgary got ahead of them in the Smythe Division and in the playoffs the Oilers bowed out to Gretzky's new team even though they had been leading the series 3–1. And the 1989 Stanley Cup was won for the first and last time by the Calgary Flames, who to some extent copied Edmonton's style. In the finals, the Flames beat the Canadiens 4–2.

Team Canada coach Dave King brought a strong squad consisting of a number of top-notch forwards to the 1989 World Championship in Sweden, but while Mark Messier, Steve Yzerman, Glenn Anderson and Brian Bellows were racking up goals, the Canadian defensemen were making so many mistakes that even goalies of the likes of Grant Fuhr and Sean Burke were unable to help. It was precisely this weakness in the Canadian team's defense line that was taken advantage of by the KLM Line when it scored four goals in the decisive game of the tournament, which ended 5–3 for the Soviets. Still, the Canadians won silver for the first time since 1962.

In the 1989–90 regular-season, the Oilers finished fifth and their road to the finals was hard. In the course of the playoffs, Edmonton trailed both Winnipeg (3–1) and Chicago (2–1). Then they met the Bruins, who had surpassed everyone in the regular season.

Game one turned into one of the tensest in the series. Adam Graves and Glenn Anderson didn't bring the Oilers to the lead by 2–0 until the third period, but almost immediately Boston defenseman Ray Bourque made it even again. And it took another 55 minutes of overtime for Petr Klima (who hadn't played at all in the 60 minutes of regulation time) to score the winning goal against ex-Oiler Andy Moog.

In the next game, the Oilers trounced the Bruins 7–2, but a day later Andy Moog avenged himself and brought Boston a 2–1 victory in Edmonton. And then Boston was done. Anderson clinched game four 5–1 by scoring two goals and adding a couple of assists to his partners. In the last game, four different players—Glenn Anderson, Craig Simpson, Steve Smith and Joe Murphy—scored the goals that contributed to Edmonton's victory, while the Bruins got one past playoff MVP Bill Ranford to make it 4–1 shortly before the final siren.

At the World Championship in Switzerland in 1990, the team from the USSR included two NHLers. Viacheslav Fetisov and Sergei Makarov turned in their best performances in the decisive games of the tournament and helped their team win gold medals. Furthermore, in the final round, coach Viktor Tikhonov's team swept all three games with an aggregate score of 15–1.

Tord Lundstrom

Whenever the talk turns to Tord Lundstrom, Swedish hockey fans remember the indomitable spirit of the forward whose name is permanently linked to Brynas and the city of Gavle. No matter how difficult a game might be for Brynas or for the Swedish national squad, for which Lundstrom played 200 official games, he would always stubbornly clench his teeth and infect his teammates with his sheer dynamism, inspiring them to play the game with the same fierce intensity.

Born on March 4, 1945, in Kiruna, a town above the Arctic Circle that has given Swedish hockey a whole host of leading hockey stars, Lundstrom began playing with the local Kiruna AIF, where the talented player caught the eye of Brynas scouts. Other teams offered Lundstrom more attractive contracts, but he gave his word to Brynas. On June 1, 1963, the day when the rules allowed all players to sign contracts, Lundstrom kept his word and got off the train at the station in Gavle.

This marked the beginning of a remarkable career in Swedish hockey. Lundstrom's achievements include nine gold medals, four silver medals and one bronze medal from the Swedish national championships, in which Lundstrom played 428 games and scored 307 goals.

Swept along by the wave that carried many of the best Swedish players to the NHL, Lundstrom joined the Detroit Red Wings for the start of the 1973–74 season. But the North American hockey scene wasn't for everyone and Lundstrom, like many other excellent Swedish hockey players, returned home in 1973 and rejoined his native Brynas.

In 1981 Lundstrom coached Brynas for a single season. In 1986 he was persuaded to work with the team once more, but the first-class forward didn't shine as a coach. "As a coach, you're at work all the time, and questions that trouble you are always in your head. As a player, you do your job on the ice with nothing else except your own performance to worry you," was how Lundstrom expressed his views on the difference between being a coach and a hockey player.

Tord Lundstrom is the holder of the unique title of Brynas' Best Player of All Time. He was awarded the title after an opinion poll was conducted among the fans of the popular club, which in the 1998–99 season won the championship title of Sweden for the 12th time, second in the number of championship wins in

Swept along by the wave that carried many of the top Swedish players to the NHL, Tord Lundstrom joined the Detroit Red Wings in 1973.

Lundstrom, Tord
LW, 5´11˝, 176 lbs, b: Kiruna, Sweden, 3/4/1945

Season	Club, League	Regular Season					Playoffs				
		GP	G	A	Pts	PIM	GP	G	A	Pts	PIM
1963–64	Brynas, Sweden	14	10	6	16	8	7	7	7	14	11
1964–65	Brynas, Sweden	14	14	10	24	4	14	17	12	29	4
WEC–65	Sweden	7	6	3	9	4					
1965–66	Brynas, Sweden	14	10	9	19	4	7	7	5	12	6
WEC–66	Sweden	7	0	1	1	4					
1966–67	Brynas, Sweden	14	18	6	24	12	6	5	6	11	0
1967–68	Brynas, Sweden	14	15	14	29	4	7	6	7	13	2
OWG–68	Sweden	7	2	3	5	6					
1968–69	Brynas, Sweden	14	7	8	15	2	7	6	6	12	6
WEC–69	Sweden	10	5	2	7	12					
1969–70	Brynas, Sweden	14	17	10	27	8	14	10	6	16	6
WEC–70	Sweden	10	5	5	10	0					
1970–71	Brynas, Sweden	14	17	13	30	2	14	9	16	25	14
WEC–71	Sweden	10	6	4	10	4					
1971–72	Brynas, Sweden	14	8	6	14	4	14	9	10	19	4
OWG–72	Sweden	6	3	2	5	2					
WEC–72	Sweden	10	4	5	9	8					
1972–73	Brynas, Sweden	14	16	11	27	4	14	10	4	14	6
WEC–73	Sweden	10	3	2	5	0					
1973–74	Detroit Red Wings, NHL	11	1	1	2	0					
	London Lions, Great Britain	45	38	31	69	24					
1974–75	Brynas, Sweden	21	15	17	32	32	6	0	3	3	2
WEC–75	Sweden	10	11	4	15	2					
1975–76	Brynas, Sweden	35	21	27	48	16	7	4	1	5	0
CCup–76	Sweden	5	1	3	4	6					
1976–77	Brynas, Sweden	36	16	19	35	37	4	1	7	8	0
1977–78	Brynas, Sweden	36	20	15	35	28	3	0	1	1	0
1978–79	Brynas, Sweden	36	12	13	25	29					
	Sweden Totals	304	216	184	400	194	124	91	91	182	61
	OWG/WEC/CCup Totals	92	46	34	80	48					
	NHL Totals	11	1	1	2	0					

Sweden Champion (1964, 1966, 1967, 1968, 1970, 1971, 1972, 1976, 1977)

Tord Lundstrom (left) is the holder of the unique title of Brynas' Best Player of All Time. The legendary Borje Salming was runner-up.

Swedish hockey. The results of the poll, conducted by the newspaper *Arbetarbladet*, put Lundstrom in first place with 1,237 points. To underscore the significance of this achievement, it's worth noting that the runner-up was the legendary defenseman Borje Salming with 1,235 points.

Lundstrom remains a recognized name in Swedish hockey, standing 77th on the list of "Great Men." When they talk about Lundstrom, Swedish fans still recall his resolute spirit. In recognition of his contribution to the team, the hockey jersey bearing number 6 that Lundstrom wore while playing for Brynas now hangs forever in the Gavlerinken hockey stadium.

Gerry Cheevers

In the 1968–69 season, Gerry Cheevers (left) began to paint stitches on his mask to show where he'd been hit by a puck.

One of the first aggressive, straying goalies, "Cheesy" was the backbone of the offensively talented Boston Bruins that won the Stanley Cup in 1970 and 1972. It was an improbable peak to a career that began inauspiciously during the Original Six years, when there were exactly six goalies in the National Hockey League—and he wasn't one of them.

Born in St. Catharines, Ontario, Cheevers was raised in Toronto and the Leafs were interested in him from the time he was a youngster. They sent him to the St. Michael's Majors in the Ontario junior league to develop, and that is exactly what happened. Although he played a few games at left wing for the Majors, he was a goalie for most of his five years there. But the Leafs had Johnny Bower in goal and Cheevers wasn't going to displace the China Wall from the Leaf cage.

Cheevers was sent to the farm team in Pittsburgh and played two games with Toronto without making much of an impression. And he didn't join Boston until 1965-66 after being claimed by the Bruins in the summer Intra-League Draft when Punch Imlach left him open for the taking. "Cheevers could be a flop or he could become a terrific goaltender. It was a chance I had to take," he reasoned.

By 1968 he was the number one man in Boston, the savior on a team that had the incomparable Bobby Orr and, soon, Phil Esposito and the other great scoring stars. While all the others were in the offensive zone putting the puck in the net, Cheevers was frequently left to his own devices to prevent goals. The only criticism, one that stuck with him his whole career, was that he roamed too much, sometimes with negative consequences.

But his stickhandling, which he learned from playing lacrosse in the summer, meant he was like a third defenseman for Boston. "I've made a fool out of myself more than once," he admitted of his style, which was a gamble. "I can especially recall one game against the Red Wings.... The puck was shot into our zone and Gordie Howe was the closest man to it as it skidded into the corner to my right. So I said to myself, 'You can get to that puck before the old man, Gerry,' and out I went. Next thing I knew I was sprawled in the corner and the old man had walked around me and put it in the net. Boy, I could've crawled under the ice, I was so embarrassed."

During practice in the 1968-69 season, he began what was to be his most famous trademark—painting stitches on his mask to indicate where a puck had hit him. "I was trying to get out of practice one day," he explained, "when this shot that couldn't have broken an egg hit me in the mask. I faked a serious injury and went into the dressing room. I was sitting there having a Coke when Harry Sinden came in and told me to get back out onto the ice. All the guys were laughing, so I knew I had to do something. I told the trainer to paint a 30-stitch gash on the mask. Then I went out and told Harry, 'See how bad it is!'" In ensuing years, he periodically added more scars and his mask became a symbol of the first generation of mask-wearing goalies demonstrating the safety of face protection.

In the summer of 1972, fresh from a Stanley Cup, Cheevers was one of a number of superstars to leave the NHL and join the upstart World Hockey Association. He signed an incredible seven-year, $1.4-million contract with the Cleveland Crusaders, which he thought would be the last contract of his career. But after less than four years he asked to be bought out and returned to the Bruins and the NHL for most of the next four seasons.

Cheevers was considered the finest playoff goalie of his day thanks in part to his team attitude. He didn't care how many goals he let in as long as his Bruins scored one more. Shutouts and trophies meant nothing. Only the Stanley Cup counted. "Pride," he said. "I get it out of winning. I've got pride in this league for what we're trying to do." His career playoff record was 53-34, one of the best ratios in league history.

Cheevers' alter ego spent every free minute at the racetrack. Ever since 1968 he'd owned horses and his love of the animal and his own fierce competitive spirit inspired him, as in hockey, to be as successful as possible. This culminated in 1976 with the development of Royal Ski, who earned more money as a two-year-old than any other horse on the continent. Other

Gerry Cheevers (center) performed like a third defenseman for Boston because he played lacrosse in the summer and learned stickhandling skills.

Cheevers, Gerry "Cheesy"
G, 5'11", 185 lbs, b: St. Catharines, Ont., 12/7/1940

Season	Club, League	Regular Season				Playoffs			
		GP	Mins	GA	Avg	GP	Mins	GA	Avg
1961–62	Pittsburgh Hornets, AHL	5	300	21	4.20				
	Rochester Americans, AHL	19	1140	69	3.63	2	120	8	4.00
	Sault Ste. Marie Thunderbirds, EPHL	29	1740	103	3.55				
	Toronto Maple Leafs, NHL	2	120	6	3.00				
1962–63	Rochester Americans, AHL	19	1140	75	3.95				
	Sudbury Wolves, EPHL	51	3060	212	4.15	8	485	29	3.59
1963–64	Rochester Americans, AHL	66	3960	187	2.84	2	120	8	4.00
1964–65	Rochester Americans, AHL	72	4359	195	2.68	10	615	24	2.34
1965–66	Boston Bruins, NHL	7	340	34	6.00				
	Oklahoma City Blazers, CHL	30	1760	73	2.49	9	540	19	2.11
1966–67	Boston Bruins, NHL	22	1298	72	3.33				
	Oklahoma City Blazers, CHL	26	1520	71	2.80	11	677	29	2.57
1967–68	Boston Bruins, NHL	47	2646	125	2.83	4	240	15	3.75
1968–69	Boston Bruins, NHL	52	3112	145	2.80	9	572	16	1.68
1969–70	Boston Bruins, NHL	41	2384	108	2.72	13	781	29	2.23
1970–71	Boston Bruins, NHL	40	2400	109	2.73	6	360	21	3.50
1971–72	Boston Bruins, NHL	41	2420	101	2.50	8	483	21	2.61
1972–73	Cleveland Crusaders, WHA	52	3144	149	2.84	9	548	22	2.41
1973–74	Cleveland Crusaders, WHA	59	3562	180	3.03	5	303	18	3.56
1974–75	Cleveland Crusaders, WHA	52	3076	167	3.26	5	300	23	4.60
1975–76	Cleveland Crusaders, WHA	28	1570	95	3.63				
	Boston Bruins, NHL	15	900	41	2.73	6	392	14	2.14
CCup–76	Canada	0	0	0	0.00	0	0	0	0.00
1976–77	Boston Bruins, NHL	45	2700	137	3.04	14	858	44	3.08
1977–78	Boston Bruins, NHL	21	1086	48	2.65	12	731	35	2.87
1978–79	Boston Bruins, NHL	43	2509	132	3.16	6	360	15	2.50
ChCup–79	NHL All-Stars	1	60	6	6.00				
1979–80	Boston Bruins, NHL	42	2479	116	2.81	10	619	32	3.10
	NHL Totals	418	24394	1174	2.89	88	5396	242	2.69
	WHA Totals	191	11352	591	3.12	19	1151	63	3.28
	CCup/ChalCup Totals	1	60	6	6.00				

WHA First All-Star Team (1973)
WHA Second All-Star Team (1974, 1975)
Won Ben Hatskin Trophy — WHA Best Goaltender (1973)
Won Stanley Cup (1970, 1972)
Won CCup (1976)

horses were named after his teammates or were hockey-related, including Wing to Wing, Two On One, In the Net, Around the Boards and Number Four (for his silent partner in the business, Bobby Orr). After he retired, his racetrack reputation and acumen were so well respected that he became director of the Rockingham Park track in Salem, New Hampshire. In 1985 Cheevers was inducted into the Hockey Hall of Fame.

Frantisek Pospisil

Frantisek Pospisil (center) played in three World Championships—1972, 1976 and 1977—where Czechoslovakia won gold medals.

Frantisek Pospisil played for the Czech national team for 11 years, leaving just after the 1978 World Championship in Prague. His life followed very closely the ups and downs of the team and few people could imagine its defense without him. At 33, he wasn't yet so old that he couldn't have intended his international career if he chose, but he'd made his decision and it was final.

Many people would ask themselves why he left voluntarily. "These debates are useless." Pospisil said at the time. "One has to know the right time to quit. I want to make room for the younger generation. I hope that people won't interpret my step as a sign that I feel that I no longer have what it takes and that I am a bad player."

One of the leading personalities in Czech hockey in the 1970s, Pospisil quietly controlled the action on the ice from inside his own zone. In defending against an opponent, he leaned heavily on solid positional play. He could set a teammate loose on the opposing net with an accurate and well-timed pass. "I never was a great skater. I never had the right speed. Therefore I tried to think quickly. I adhered to the principle that a pass is quicker than a player."

While in Kladno, Frantisek Kaberle and he were inseparable and on the national team he played for a long time in tandem with Oldrich Machac from Brno. They complemented each other splendidly. The stocky Machac had a wicked slapshot, played a good physical game and had strong offensive skills. Pospisil was more level-headed.

They played together in three World Championships—1972, 1976 and 1977—when Czechoslovakia won gold medals. "When the coaches put us together for the championship in 1967, they took a big risk. But ultimately we spent great moments together. Some were exceptionally successful. I never looked at hockey through the eyes of a coach. I was a player. I didn't like to go on the ice with the feeling that no mistake may happen. Hockey is built on mistakes, and by not allowing for any such feelings I was less restricted. I could play in a relaxed manner, with a broader view and sort of above things, able to think in peace."

Not only did Pospisil play a great game of hockey, he also formulated plenty of opinions about the game, which he readily shared with the press. But in interviews he never talked only about hockey. As captain, he often expressed views about the world around him as well. He was a true role model for young people—in the proud way he carried himself, in how he behaved and in the words he spoke.

Born on April 2, 1944, in Unhost, near Prague, Pospisil's career was closely intertwined with the Poldi SONP hockey club. In the Czech league, he played 622 matches in 17 seasons for Kladno. At his peak, he was in third place on the historic Czech chart of all-time greats after Josef Cerny and Jaroslav Vins. In the 1970s he won the title four times while with Kladno. In 1971 and 1972 he won the Golden Stick Award as Czechoslovakia's most valuable player.

"I was lucky that even as a junior I was surrounded by many individualists who wanted to assert themselves. This shaped me. This environment forced me not to underestimate anything, even during practice, and do my best work on every pass. Hockey is a play of pairs, trios and complete quintets. Even then I had collective thinking and that has stayed with me. To make a good pass was the best thing that I could do for my team."

He always tried to keep both feet on the ground, to be rooted in reality. "Neither in the clouds, nor in the basement," he used to say. "I never succumbed to the feeling that I of all people was the best and that others were out to get me when things weren't exactly going my way." Pospisil felt compelled to continue playing until they carried him off the ice, but the game of hockey charmed him enough that he stuck with it all his life.

In the 1978-79 season, he played for EV Landshut in Germany. Then he quit and threw himself into coaching. First he led Kladno for four seasons. From 1983 to 1985, it was Litvinov. At the same time, he was responsible for the national junior team. That team missed out on the gold at the 1985 World Junior Championship in Finland when they went down to defeat at the hands of the Canadians. Beginning in the 1985–86 season, Pospisil managed the national team along with Jan Starsi.

At the 1986 World Championship, his team lost to Poland and ended up in fifth place. A year, later in Vienna, they were within reach of the World Championship title, but after failing to tie with the Soviets, they wound up third. The 1988 Calgary Olympics were another heartbreaker. "I had seen a lot, rises and falls. But one always likes to remember the nice moments. The most beautiful one for me will be the defeat of the Russians in Prague in 1972, when we became world champions after 23 years. That endless joy must be lived, it cannot be described. I wish for everyone to have a chance to savor this feeling at least once."

Pospisil was selected to the International Ice Hockey Federation's Hall of Fame in 1999.

One of the leading personalities in Czech hockey in the 1970s, Frantisek Pospisil (left) had a quiet way of controlling the action from his own zone.

Pospisil, Frantisek
D, 6´, 190 lbs, b: Unhost, Czechoslovakia, 4/2/1944

Season	Club, League	Regular Season				
		GP	G	A	Pts	PIM
1961–67	SONP Kladno, Czechoslovakia	*	*	*	*	*
WEC–67	Czechoslovakia	7	1	2	3	4
1967-68	SONP Kladno, Czechoslovakia	*	*	*	*	*
OWG–68	Czechoslovakia	5	0	1	1	6
1968–69	SONP Kladno, Czechoslovakia	*	*	*	*	*
WEC–69	Czechoslovakia	10	1	1	2	6
1969–70	SONP Kladno, Czechoslovakia	*	*	*	*	*
WEC–70	Czechoslovakia	10	2	3	5	6
1970–71	SONP Kladno, Czechoslovakia	*	*	*	*	*
WEC–71	Czechoslovakia	10	1	3	4	4
1971–72	SONP Kladno, Czechoslovakia	*	*	*	*	*
OWG–72	Czechoslovakia	6	2	2	4	8
WEC–72	Czechoslovakia	10	1	6	7	0
1972–73	SONP Kladno, Czechoslovakia	*	*	*	*	*
WEC–73	Czechoslovakia	10	1	7	8	4
1973–74	SONP Kladno, Czechoslovakia	*	*	*	*	*
WEC–74	Czechoslovakia	10	0	2	2	4
1974–75	SONP Kladno, Czechoslovakia	*	*	*	*	*
WEC–75	Czechoslovakia	10	1	2	3	4
1975–76	SONP Kladno, Czechoslovakia	*	*	*	*	*
OWG–76	Czechoslovakia	5	2	4	6	6
WEC–76	Czechoslovakia	10	0	4	4	2
CCup–76	Czechoslovakia	7	1	1	2	0
1976–77	Poldi SONP Kladno, Czechoslovakia	*	*	*	*	*
WEC–77	Czechoslovakia	10	0	6	6	2
1977–78	Poldi SONP Kladno, Czechoslovakia	*	*	*	*	*
1978–79	Landshut, FRG	*	*	*	*	*
	Czechoslovakia Totals	622	134	*	*	*
	OWG/WEC/CCup Totals	120	13	44	57	56

Named Best Defenseman at WEC (1972, 1976)
Won WEC (1972, 1976, 1977)
Czechoslovakia Champion (1975, 1976, 1977, 1978)

Lars-Erik *Sjoberg*

He may have been under 5′8″, but Lars-Erik Sjoberg became the Swedish national team's leading defenseman in the early 1970s.

In 1972, when the team of NHL All-Stars went overseas to Moscow as part of the historic Summit Series with the USSR, they stopped in Stockholm and played two exhibition games against Tre Kronor.

The exhibition games proved to be tough, as the Swedes vigorously battled the Canadians. Among the Swedish defensemen, a short, robust man displayed his abilities. He refused to surrender to the big, powerful players from Canada and he frequently used his favorite maneuver, the hipcheck. In one instance, the mighty Swede bodychecked Vic Hadfield of the New York Rangers, sending the latter flying into the air. The upset Hadfield hit the defenseman in the face and broke his nose. Since then, Lars-Erik Sjoberg's nose has protruded somewhat more noticeably.

At under 5′8″, the compact player managed to become the Swedish national team's leading defenseman in the late 1960s and early 1970s because of his excellent skating skills and persistent training. His talent for choosing the right position, combined with effective bodychecking, made him a virtually impenetrable force to opposing forwards. At the same time, he managed to avoid foul play and behaved with the dignity befitting a true athlete.

Born May 4, 1944, near Falun in the small village of Tallberg in central Sweden, he began his career with one of the local junior teams. His friend, future chief coach of the Swedish national team Bengt Ulsson, also played for one of those teams. Lars-Erik Sjoberg won his first national gold medal in 1969 playing for Leksand, a city not far from his home town.

During his career, Sjoberg played for the provincial Leksand, Stockholm's Djurgarden and Gothenburg's Vastra Frolunda. At the 1974 World Championship in Finland, he was voted the best defenseman. That same year he turned professional, joining the WHA's Winnipeg Jets, where he spent six seasons. He was highly regarded in Canada and was the first Swedish hockey player to be elected a captain. In Winnipeg, they referred to him affectionately as "Professor" or "Little General." He was the captain of the Swedish team in the 1976 Canada Cup and was 75th on the "Great Men" list, playing 134 official games for Tre Kronor.

After he left hockey, Sjoberg became a successful businessman. In 1980 he returned to Sweden and settled in the old university town of Uppsala. Acting as the New York Rangers'

Sjoberg, Lars-Erik
D, 5′8″, 179 lbs, b: Tallberg, Sweden, 4/5/1944, d: 1987

Season	Club, League	Regular Season					Playoffs				
		GP	G	A	Pts	PIM	GP	G	A	Pts	PIM
1963–67	Djurgarden, Sweden	*	*	*	*	*					
1967–68	Leksand, Sweden	*	*	*	*	*					
OWG–68	Sweden	7	0	0	0	4					
1968–69	Leksand, Sweden	*	*	*	*	*					
WEC–69	Sweden	9	3	2	5	2					
1969–70	Vastra Frolunda, Sweden	14	2	1	3	10					
WEC–70	Sweden	10	1	1	2	0					
1970–71	Vastra Frolunda, Sweden	13	8	4	12	6					
1971–72	Vastra Frolunda, Sweden	27	4	11	15	4					
OWG–72	Sweden	6	1	1	2	2					
WEC–72	Sweden	10	1	1	2	0					
1972–73	Vastra Frolunda, Sweden	14	1	6	7	0					
WEC–73	Sweden	10	1	2	3	2					
1973–74	Vastra Frolunda, Sweden	41	4	35	39	21					
WEC–74	Sweden	9	1	0	1	2					
1974–75	Winnipeg Jets, WHA	75	7	53	60	30					
1975–76	Winnipeg Jets, WHA	81	5	36	41	12	13	0	5	5	12
CCup–76	Sweden	5	0	3	3	6					
1976–77	Winnipeg Jets, WHA	52	2	38	40	31	20	0	6	6	22
1977–78	Winnipeg Jets, WHA	78	11	39	50	72	9	0	9	9	4
1978–79	Winnipeg Jets, WHA	9	0	3	3	2	10	1	2	3	4
1979–80	Winnipeg Jets, NHL	79	7	27	34	48					
	Sweden Totals	*	*	*	*	*					
	OWG/WEC/CCup Totals	66	8	10	18	18					
	NHL Totals	79	7	27	34	48					
	WHA Totals	295	25	169	194	147					

WHA First All-Star Team (1978)
Named Best Defenseman at WEC (1974)
Won Dennis A. Murphy Trophy — WHA Top Defenseman (1978)
Won Avco Cup (1976, 1978, 1979)
Sweden Champion (1969)

overseas scout, Sjoberg recognized a future hockey star in a young, tall and awkward Kjell Samuelsson and promoted him in Canada despite the doubts of skeptics. Samuelsson went on to become one of the NHL's most enduring leading defensemen.

When Sjoberg died in 1987 at just 43, eulogies arrived in Uppsala from all over the world.

Highly regarded in Canada, Lars-Erik Sjoberg was the first Swedish player to be elected a captain (of the Winnipeg Jets).

Bernie Parent

"Sixty minutes of hell." That is what Bernie Parent once called playing goal in the NHL. But something about the fire and brimstone must have appealed to him. "I like playing in that place," he said. "I always have."

In the early part of his career, Parent tended goal with the Boston Bruins and the Toronto Maple Leafs, but he was best known for being netminder on the Philadelphia Flyers' championship teams of the mid 1970s, the first expansion franchise to win the Stanley Cup. Bobby Clarke, the Flyers' captain, once described Parent's ability to guard the net: "Bernie makes you feel like you can walk on water." But Parent saw himself in a different light. "You don't have to be crazy to be a goalie," he said, " but it helps."

Bernie Parent once called playing goal in the NHL "60 minutes of hell."

Parent was a stand-up goalie, a technique he learned from his boyhood hero, Jacques Plante. Many years later, when the slumping Parent talked about retiring, Plante talked him out of it. In addition, Plante coached Parent on some fundamental points that Bernie had been missing in his game. Plante watched him practise in Philly for two days and didn't say anything. Then he told Parent exactly what he was doing wrong—sitting back on his heels, backing into his crease and losing concentration. "As Jacques kept talking to me, I came to the conclusion that I had drifted away from my game," said Parent. "At first I was confused by what he was telling me, but then it dawned on me. Then it was up to me to convince myself I'd get it back. It may take time, but I'll get back on the right track." He added, "I think all NHL teams should have a coach for goalies, because a goalie can't see his own mistakes."

Parent was a master at moving out to cut down a shooter's angle. "When he's doing it right, Bernie won't have to move his glove or his foot an inch either way to make a save," said Fred Shero, his coach on the Flyers. Shero well knew the goalie's value to his team. "When Parent is out there, we know we can win games we have no business winning."

Parent admitted he had considerable fear of playing goaltender in the NHL, and that fear helped him play better. "It comes and goes. When I'm tired, I might start thinking about getting injured and about my family. Thank God it doesn't happen all the time, because it affects your play. I ask God to protect me and help the team, but I never ask Him to win." On game nights, Parent never appeared without his mask on, even going to and from the dressing room.

He also had a strict pre-game ritual. He sat alone under a miniature Stanley Cup and thought about the opposing players he would face, then slept for eight hours, had a steak for lunch and then slept again.

Parent grew up in Montreal in the early 1950s and played pickup games on the street with a tennis ball. Somewhat of a loner as a kid, he liked playing goal. "I stopped the first shot, and that was it," he recalled. "The challenge to make a save was always there."

Remarkably, Parent didn't learn to skate until he was 11. In his first game as a kid, he sheepishly admitted, he let in 20 goals, not a great start for someone aiming for the pros. But he had the dedication. Many years later, when he was an established pro, his brother remembered: "All he ever wanted to be was a professional hockey player. He didn't study, he didn't go with girls. He played hockey."

By 1965 Parent had moved his way up to the Bruins' farm system. Boston brought him up to the NHL, where he played badly in his first two seasons, letting in an average of 3.67 goals per game. In 1967 Parent was claimed by the Flyers in the Intra-League Draft. It was there that he started to establish his reputation as a top goalie. But in 1971 Parent was traded to Toronto in a very controversial deal. The Flyers had another young goalie, Doug Favell, and thought that Bernie would be better trade bait. In the end, the trade was good for Parent because it was in Toronto that he became a teammate of his hero, Jacques Plante.

Parent left the Leafs with great acrimony in 1972 when he became the first Leaf to defect from the NHL ranks to the World Hockey Association. He signed with the Miami Screaming Eagles for $750,000 over five years. "Anyone would be stupid if he'd get an offer like this and turned it down," Parent explained. "At my present salary, it would take me 10 to 15 years to make the kind of money I'm going to make with Miami. Even if this new league doesn't get started, I'm going to get my money, and that's all I care about."

Miami's team didn't even have a rink when Parent signed and he ended up with the Philadelphia Blazers in the WHA for $600,000 instead. Parent quit the team during the 1973 playoffs in a pay dispute and forced the Leafs to trade him back to the Flyers.

Returning to the Flyers, Parent became a sports hero in the City of Brotherly Love. One local bumper sticker read, "Only the Lord saves more than Bernie Parent." Now part of the Flyers' Broad Street Bullies, Parent and his teammates won the Stanley Cup twice in a row, in 1974 and 1975. In both seasons, Parent won the Vezina Trophy as best goalie and the Conn Smythe Trophy as playoff MVP.

Bobby Taylor, who was backup to Parent in the two years the Flyers won the Cup, remembered Bernie's wizardry between the pipes.

Parent, Bernie
G, 5′10″, 180 lbs, b: Montreal, Que., 4/3/1945

Season	Club, League	Regular Season				Playoffs			
		GP	Mins	GA	Avg	GP	Mins	GA	Avg
1965–66	Oklahoma City Blazers, CHL	3	180	11	3.67				
	Boston Bruins, NHL	39	2083	128	3.69				
1966–67	Boston Bruins, NHL	18	1022	62	3.64				
	Oklahoma City Blazers, CHL	14	820	37	2.70				
1967–68	Philadelphia Flyers, NHL	38	2248	93	2.48	5	355	8	1.35
1968–69	Philadelphia Flyers, NHL	58	3365	151	2.69	3	180	12	4.00
1969–70	Philadelphia Flyers, NHL	62	3680	171	2.79				
1970–71	Philadelphia Flyers, NHL	30	1586	73	2.76				
	Toronto Maple Leafs, NHL	18	1040	46	2.65	4	235	9	2.30
1971–72	Toronto Maple Leafs, NHL	47	2715	116	2.56	4	243	13	3.21
1972–73	Philadelphia Blazers, WHA	63	3653	220	3.61	1	70	3	2.57
1973–74	Philadelphia Flyers, NHL	73	4314	136	1.89	17	1042	35	2.02
1974–75	Philadelphia Flyers, NHL	68	4041	137	2.03	15	922	29	1.89
1975–76	Philadelphia Flyers, NHL	11	615	24	2.34	8	480	27	3.38
1976–77	Philadelphia Flyers, NHL	61	3525	159	2.71	3	123	8	3.90
1977–78	Philadelphia Flyers, NHL	49	2923	108	2.22	12	722	33	2.74
1978–79	Philadelphia Flyers, NHL	36	1979	89	2.70				
	NHL Totals	608	35136	1493	2.55	71	4302	174	2.43
	WHA Totals	63	3653	220	3.61	1	70	3	2.57

NHL First All-Star Team (1974, 1975)
WHA Second All-Star Team (1973)
Won Vezina Trophy (1974, 1975)
Won Conn Smythe Trophy (1974, 1975)
Won Stanley Cup (1974, 1975)

"He was by far the best I ever saw. Bernie played 65 games a year, and there would only be a handful of bad performances," said Taylor. "The rest weren't just good but great. He was always there, like the sun, rising in the east and setting in the west. Later there were maybe two handfuls of bad ones. He wasn't quite as consistent, but he still played the game better than anyone, played the rebounds better than anyone did. Technically, he was the soundest of any goalie who ever played the game."

Sadly, Parent's remarkable career was short-lived. In a freak accident, a stick hit him in his right eye when he was 34, causing permanent damage to his depth perception and his ability to focus. Parent was forced to retire from hockey in 1979. He was then signed by the Flyers as "special assignments" coach in 1979, notably to advise goalies, just as Plante had once helped him.

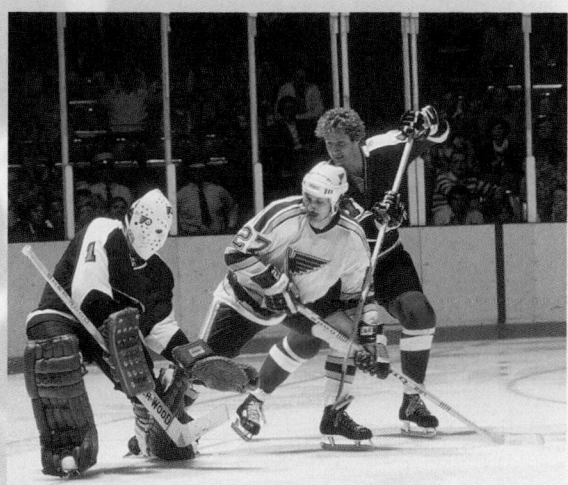

A Philadelphia bumper sticker read, "Only the Lord saves more than Bernie Parent" (left).

Parent had a tough time adjusting to life outside hockey and became a heavy drinker. He openly admitted he badly missed the sports spotlight. "I figured I had five or six years left [before the injury], but suddenly I didn't have a damn thing to do," he said. "I was all set financially. I had plenty of money, but that wasn't enough. There was no challenge. Life was boring. I was so self-oriented, life was hell for my family." He joined AA to get his problems under control. "I'm a lot more grateful for things. When you play, it's easy to forget. You live in a fantasy world," he said.

Certainly in the bright lights of the NHL Parent had created his own fantasy, a tale of one of the world's greatest goalies, with him as the star. Fans of great goaltending will never forget him.

Veli-Pekka Ketola

Veli-Pekka Ketola was one of the pioneering players from Finland to cross the Atlantic. As a 20-year-old, he was invited to the Detroit Red Wings' training camp together with legendary Swedish defenseman Lennart Svedberg. Summing up his experiences while at the training camp, Ketola said, "It was pointed out to me that over there [in the NHL], it is a really tough game for really tough men, not boys, and we Finns aren't ready for this."

Ten years later, the situation had changed dramatically. A Finn had played at the side of Wayne Gretzky in winning the Stanley Cup and Finns had participated in All-Star games. The scouts had begun to expand their recruitment drive to take in Europeans.

In the 1974 World Championship, Ketola showed that he was a leader on the international level and offers of a professional career started to come in. The only surprise came when he signed a contract not with the Detroit Red Wings, who held his NHL rights, but with the Winnipeg Jets of the WHA.

Veli-Pekka Ketola was one of the pioneering players from Finland.

In Finland, Ketola's number 13 was already legendary, but in North America he wasn't allowed to use it. In Winnipeg, he became number 12. Playing for Winnipeg, he had the good fortune to be part of a winning franchise led by hockey's first $1-million man, Bobby Hull. At the time, Hull was being ably assisted by a pair of Swedes, center Ulf Nilsson and right wing Anders Hedberg.

Nilsson's predominant role with the team left centerman Ketola without much ice time. Nevertheless, he managed to end his WHA career with a respectable 183 points in 235 games. The highlight of his years in the World Hockey Association was his second season, when the Jets won the Avco Cup. He'd signed a three-year pact with Winnipeg, but during his final year, 1976–77, he was traded to the Calgary Cowboys.

Ketola then returned to Finland to play, but in 1981 he returned for a second stint in North America, this time with the Colorado Rockies of the NHL. He lasted one season and 44 games. Ketola had the size necessary for an NHL player, but the powers that be felt that he didn't use his gifts to full advantage. Ketola, who was brought up in the European mold and taught that technique came before physique, didn't like that attitude.

Veli-Pekka Ketola's number 13 was already legendary in Finland, but he wasn't allowed to use it in North America.

On the international level, Finland didn't have much success during his era. Making matters worse was the doping scandal in 1974 involving the unfortunate goalie Stig Wetzell. Finland was on the brink of winning its first medal, only to have a key 5–0 victory over Czechoslovakia reversed when Wetzell tested positive. Wetzell has never admitted to any wrongdoing and there is even reason to believe that he was unfairly targeted by members of his own national team. The net result was that first Wetzell and then Ketola refused to play on the national team again.

The goalie never went back on his promise, but Ketola rescinded his boycott to participate in three more World Championship tournaments. Even though he lost some key years in his international career, he still makes the all-time top 10 list with the national team with 105 points in 186 games. The latter mark ranks sixth in team history, as do his 60 goals.

In Finland, Ketola helped his home town of Pori win three national titles. The first one came in 1965 with the club nicknamed Karhut (the Bears). Two years later, the two hockey clubs in Pori joined forces and became known as Assat (the Aces). In the 1970s, Assat won two national championships, both times with Ketola as the team's top scorer.

The Finnish league has immortalized Ketola for his prowess. A trophy presented to the Finnish league's top points scorer is named after him. In addition to winning the scoring crown himself, his most notable awards are the two player of the year trophies he picked up in 1974 and 1978. He is one of only 18 players to

Ketola, Veli-Pekka
C, 6′3″, 220 lbs, b: Pori, Finland, 3/28/1948

Season	Club, League	Regular Season					Playoffs				
		GP	G	A	Pts	PIM	GP	G	A	Pts	PIM
1963–65	Karhut Pori, Finland	*	*	*	*	*					
1965–66	Karhut Pori, Finland	19	8	3	11	12					
1966–67	Karhut Pori, Finland	22	15	10	25	30					
1967–68	Assat Pori, Finland	20	12	13	25	16					
OWG–68	Finland	7	2	1	3	10					
1968–69	Assat Pori, Finland	20	15	9	24	22					
WEC–69	Finland	8	0	2	2	2					
1969–70	Jokerit Helsinki, Finland	22	25	12	37	26					
WEC–70	Finland	10	4	3	7	32					
1970–71	Assat Pori, Finland	31	25	17	42	31					
WEC–71	Finland	6	5	1	6	4					
1971–72	Assat Pori, Finland	32	16	14	30	25					
OWG–72	Finland	6	1	3	4	7					
WEC–72	Finland	9	4	3	7	4					
1972–73	Assat Pori, Finland	36	25	16	41	74	10	2	2	4	12
WEC–73	Finland	10	2	2	4	12					
1973–74	Assat Pori, Finland	35	23	21	44	44	10	7	3	10	4
WEC–74	Finland	10	7	3	10	4					
1974–75	Winnipeg Jets, WHA	74	23	28	51	25					
1975–76	Winnipeg Jets, WHA	80	32	36	68	32	13	7	5	12	2
CCup–76	Finland	5	0	0	0	0					
1976–77	Calgary Cowboys, WHA	17	4	6	10	2					
	Winnipeg Jets, WHA	64	25	29	54	59					
1977–78	Assat Pori, Finland	36	27	29	54	59	9	10	10	20	22
1978–79	Assat Pori, Finland	36	23	49	72	66					
1979–80	Assat Pori, Finland	36	22	38	60	61	7	3	7	10	40
1980–81	Assat Pori, Finland	36	23	39	62	61	2	0	0	0	2
CCup–81	Finland	5	0	0	0	0					
1981–82	Colorado Rockies, NHL	44	9	5	14	4					
1982–83	KalPa Kuopio, Finland	6	4	8	12	0					
	Finland Totals	387	263	278	541	527	38	22	22	44	80
	OWG/WEC/CCup Totals	76	25	18	43	75					
	WHA Totals	235	84	99	183	118	13	7	5	12	2
	NHL Totals	44	9	5	14	4					

Won Avco Cup (1976)
Finland Champion (1965, 1971, 1978)

have racked up more than 500 points in the national league. And all that is on top of the four seasons he played in the prime of his career in North America.

After hanging up his skates, he turned to coaching. Then came a promotion to general manager of Assat, which ended in the spring of 2000 as the club, full of ambition at the start of the season, failed to make the playoffs. In Pori, however, he will still be known as "Mr. Hockey" for years to come.

Vladimir Martinec

A contradiction of sorts, Vladimir Martinec had all the romantic, crowd-pleasing qualities yet never lost sight of the technical skills necessary for the fast-paced game. The creative Martinec had an excellent gift for improvisation. With his ingenious evasive measures and clever passes, he drove his opponents crazy and got the spectators up out of their seats.

"Of course, I was born with some of this. But in my time, technique could be polished in various ways. I was an active soccer player for a long time—till the age of 15. I tried table tennis and other sports. That versatility came in handy later."

He wasn't particularly tall at 5′9″ and he weighed only 178 pounds. But he had the skills and the wits to outsmart the opposition. He also had a disarming smile, which he wore frequently, even when he was cross-checked or when he was pulling a fast one on the opposing team and putting the puck in the net.

Vladimir Martinec won the Golden Stick Award as Czech player of the year four times.

Martinec was born on December 22, 1949, in Lomnice nad Popelkou, and like most of his contemporaries, he grew up on the local pond. "We spent days there. As soon as we returned from school, we grabbed the skates and hockey sticks and stayed on the ice till dark." That is where Horymir Sekera, the legendary coach from Pardubice, discovered him some time in 1965. With the exception of a six-month break during the 1978-79 season when he played for the army team, Dukla Jihlava, Martinec spent the rest of his career in that city.

In Pardubice, the right wing, together with Jiri Novak and Bohuslav Stastny, created one of the most dangerous formations of the time. As early as 1966 they won the junior title together. In the 1967-68 season, coach Bohumil Rejda sent them out on the ice for the first time as seniors.

The three played so well together that they were a joy to watch. At times they outsmarted the goalie so completely that they were scoring into an empty net. As a trio they scored over 800 goals and in 1973 brought Pardubice a Czech league championship. With a lot of hard work, they managed to keep the team near the top of the league.

"Marcello," as Martinec was nicknamed by his teammates, was the first to appear for the national team, in 1970. Eleven years later, he was the last to leave it.

In 1972 the Brno player Richard Farda lined up between Martinec and Stastny to help bring Czechoslovakia its first World Championship title in 23 years. Jiri Novak appeared only a year later in Moscow, but in the next championship both wings played again, either with Farda or Jiri Kochta. The gold medals won in Katowice in 1976 and in Vienna in 1977 were joint efforts by the players from Pardubice. "I have fond memories of the tournament in Katowice. Our generation had made it to the top in the world of hockey. Furthermore, I was named the best forward and turned out

A contradiction of sorts, Vladimir Martinec (right) had all the qualities that please crowds yet never lost sight of technical necessities in the fast pace of the game.

to be the best scorer. I was in an excellent shape back then," said Martinec.

At the Innsbruck Olympics, even before the World Championship, Czechoslovakia's team was striving for gold but the team was struck by the flu. The team posted a 7-1 win over Poland but was immediately quarantined because Frantisek Pospisil tested positive for codeine in a doping check, but it turned out that the drug had been prescribed by a doctor against the flu.

In the fall of that year, the famous Canada Cup event took place. "We had already played with the best Canadians in the NHL in 1972 and had measured our strength against the elite of the WHA in 1974. But this was something else. It has become routine to fly overseas, but a quarter of a century ago, it was an exceptional event. This had been a very hard season. But we were doing well and were in great shape psychologically. Everything was working out by itself, we didn't feel any problems or fatigue."

Martinec, whose boyhood idol was Vlastimil Bubnik, a star from the 1950s and 1960s, once said that the best player he was ever lined up against was Phil Esposito. He himself never got to play in the NHL, although in 1981 he could have gone to Vancouver with Ivan Hlinka and Jiri Bubla. "Even in the 1970s it was hinted to me several times that I should stay in Canada. But I had a wife and children back home. I couldn't imagine what would happen if I were to stay in exile. When the opportunity arose to emigrate in a normal fashion, I was 32. I no longer felt like being in the NHL."

Martinec played for Pardubice until 1981. During 14 seasons, he scored 343 goals in 539 matches. In 1979 he was the top scorer. Four times he won the Golden Stick Award as most valuable player. Only Dominik Hasek broke his record by winning it for the fifth time in 1998. From 1981 to 1985, Martinec worked for the Kaufbeuren club in Germany, then he returned to coach Pardubice, winning the Czech title in 1989. Afterward he returned to Kaufbeuren. In 1995 he worked with the Czech juniors and in the 1996-97 season he assisted the national seniors. With them he won the Olympic gold in 1998 and in 1999 his fourth World Championship title.

Martinec was an assistant coach for the Czech national team—the overall sixth he'd been with—that won three successive World Championships beginning in 1999 and assumed the same post under head coach Josef Augusta at the 2002 Olympics, where Russia knocked the defending gold medalists out of medal contention in the playoff round.

"I never had the feeling that hockey took something away

Martinec, Vladimir
RW, 5´9˝, 168 lbs, b: Lomnici nad Popelkou, Czechoslovakia, 12/22/1949

Season	Club, League	Regular Season				
		GP	G	A	Pts	PIM
1965–70	Tesla Pardubice, Czechoslovakia	*	*	*	*	*
WEC–70	Czechoslovakia	9	3	0	3	6
1970–71	Tesla Pardubice, Czechoslovakia	*	*	*	*	*
WEC–71	Czechoslovakia	10	2	2	4	0
1971–72	Tesla Pardubice, Czechoslovakia	*	*	*	*	*
OWG–72	Czechoslovakia	6	4	2	6	0
WEC–72	Czechoslovakia	10	4	7	11	6
1972–73	Tesla Pardubice, Czechoslovakia	*	*	*	*	*
WEC–73	Czechoslovakia	8	1	5	6	8
1973–74	Tesla Pardubice, Czechoslovakia	*	*	*	*	*
WEC–74	Czechoslovakia	10	9	6	15	12
1974–75	Tesla Pardubice, Czechoslovakia	*	*	*	*	*
WEC–75	Czechoslovakia	9	7	4	11	4
1975–76	Tesla Pardubice, Czechoslovakia	*	*	*	*	*
OWG–76	Czechoslovakia	5	5	3	8	2
WEC–76	Czechoslovakia	10	9	11	20	2
CCup–76	Czechoslovakia	7	3	4	7	2
1976–77	Tesla Pardubice, Czechoslovakia	*	*	*	*	*
WEC–77	Czechoslovakia	10	6	9	15	4
1977–78	Tesla Pardubice, Czechoslovakia	*	*	*	*	*
WEC–78	Czechoslovakia	10	4	4	8	0
1978–79	Dukla Jihlava, Czechoslovakia	*	42	*	*	*
WEC–79	Czechoslovakia	7	5	3	8	2
1979–80	Tesla Pardubice, Czechoslovakia	*	*	*	*	*
OWG–80	Czechoslovakia	2	1	1	4	0
1980–81	Tesla Pardubice, Czechoslovakia	*	*	*	*	*
WEC–81	Czechoslovakia	8	3	5	8	0
1981–85	Kaufbeuren, FRG	*	*	*	*	*
	Czechoslovakia Totals	539	343	*	*	*
	OWG/WEC/CCup Totals	121	66	66	134	48

Named Best Forward at WEC (1976)
Won WEC (1972, 1976, 1977)
Czechoslovakia Champion (1973)

from me," he once said. "We lacked the opportunities which today's young men have. In our prime, we were prevented from going abroad. But I have no regrets. If I were starting at the beginning, I would decide for hockey all over again."

Mats Ahlberg

There are players who may not be distinguished among their peers by height, dexterity or strength but who are natural-born scorers, accumulating goal after goal. Swedish forward Mats Ahlberg of Leksand was one of those players. Many believe he was Sweden's best forward during the 1970s. What is remarkable is that Ahlberg never played in the NHL at a time when the league attracted many of Sweden's best hockey players. Ahlberg was invited to join the Minnesota North Stars, the Detroit Red Wings, the Hartford Whalers and the Atlanta Flames, but he turned them all down.

He later explained: "There are many reasons. One of the main ones was that a life of constant motion filled with training and games almost every day didn't appeal to me." As well, Ahlberg had long before decided he wanted to get a good education. And he did, confirming the opinion of many that an educated player with intelligence and a wide range of interests is able to achieve more than his teammates.

Ahlberg also tried his hand at soccer and bandy but chose ice hockey in the end, playing with Leksand his entire career and becoming, according to many, the successor of the great Nils Nilsson. In 1969 he won his first Swedish championship. He played 15 seasons for Leksand, contributing much, along with his teammates, to the club's famed rise in the mid-1970s.

Back then, the four-time national champions had a brilliant roster of players, including forwards Roland Eriksson, Dan Labraaten, Bengt Lundholm and Per-Olov Brasar, twins Crister (goalie) and Thommy (defenseman) Abrahamsson, defenseman Hans Jax and goalie Goran Hogosta. They were Leksand's foundation and they all played for Tre Kronor as well. Ahlberg made his debut on the national team in 1971 against the Finns in a game Sweden won 3–1. He played with Inge Hammarstrom and Lars-Goran Nilsson, and each of the three scored a goal.

Overall, he played 164 games for the national team. His most frequent partner was Dan Soderstrom of Leksand, who is currently the director of the city's ice palace. At the 1977 World Championship in Vienna, Ahlberg was elected captain and the Swedish team achieved the impossible, winning two games against the unbeatable USSR. As captain, Ahlberg worked wonders on the ice, getting a hat-trick in a game against the U.S. and leading Tre Kronor to the silver.

Ahlberg tried several times to retire from hockey. The first time was after the 1978 World Championship in Prague, where Tre Kronor didn't even win bronze. So he decided to wait until

Mats Ahlberg was invited to join the pros in Minnesota, Detroit, Hartford and Atlanta, but he turned them all down.

Ahlberg, Mats
C, 5'11", 180 lbs, b: Leksand, Sweden, 5/16/1947

Season	Club, League	GP	G	A	Pts	PLM
1966–72	Leksand, Sweden	*	*	*	*	*
OWG–72	Sweden	1	0	*	*	*
1972–73	Leksand, Sweden	*	*	*	*	*
WEC–73	Sweden	10	7	8	15	6
1973–74	Leksand, Sweden	*	*	*	*	*
WEC–74	Sweden	10	3	6	9	10
1974–75	Leksand, Sweden	*	*	*	*	*
WEC–75	Sweden	10	5	12	17	10
1975–76	Leksand, Sweden	*	*	*	*	*
WEC–76	Sweden	10	4	3	7	12
CC–76	Sweden	4	1	1	2	0
1976–77	Leksand, Sweden	*	39	25	64	*
WEC–77	Sweden	10	7	2	9	4
1977–78	Leksand, Sweden	*	*	*	*	*
WEC–78	Sweden	10	4	*	*	*
1978–80	Leksand, Sweden	*	*	*	*	*
OWG–80	Sweden	7	6	4	10	13
1980–81	Leksand, Sweden	*	*	*	*	*
	Sweden Totals	371	247	*	*	*
	OWG/WEC/CC Totals	72	37	*	*	*

Sweden Champion (1969, 1973, 1974, 1975)

after the Lake Placid Olympics to quit. After the Olympics, however, Leksand was in a slump, so he put on the jersey again to help them out.

After leaving hockey, Ahlberg went into the auditing business. His family, golf and tennis became his favorite preoccupations. Pro hockey was finally behind him.

His record of 39 goals and 25 assists in the 1976–77 season is still legendary in Leksand. It was an impressive achievement in a time when players used to play 36 games per season in the Elite Series. Ahlberg holds 88th place on Sweden's "Great Men" list.

Rene Robert

The right winger on the Buffalo Sabres' French Connection Line, Rene Robert, reached the 20-goal mark for eight straight years.

During an NHL career that extended to a dozen seasons, Rene Robert was an important offensive weapon. The right wing on the French Connection Line with Gilbert Perreault and Rick Martin, Robert reached the 20-goal mark eight straight years between 1972 and 1980. Possessing blinding speed and a lethal shot, Robert was a fine complement to the slick playmaking of Gilbert Perreault.

The native of Trois-Rivieres, Quebec, was originally the property of the Toronto Maple Leafs. After playing junior with the hometown Leafs of the Quebec junior league, Robert was signed by Toronto and then spent most of his first three professional seasons in the minors. In an odd turn of events, he was first claimed by the Buffalo Sabres at the June 1971 Intra-League Draft, then left unprotected and picked up by the Pittsburgh Penguins. He received his first extensive NHL action in Steeltown. Forty-nine games into the season, he was traded to Buffalo for popular forward Eddie Shack. Knowing he was replacing a solid NHL veteran, Robert became energized with his new club. His nine points in the last 12 games of the regular season served as a precursor of what was to follow.

In 1972–73, Robert and his linemates helped the Sabres reach the post-season in only their third NHL year. The flashy right wing scored 40 goals and became one of the team's most recognizable stars. Two years later he reached the 40-goal mark again and recorded a career-best 100 points. Robert established himself as one of the league's most accomplished point men on the power-play and often excelled on the second-line penalty-killing unit.

In 1975 the high-flying right wing contributed 13 points in 16 playoff games as the Sabres drove all the way to a Stanley Cup showdown with the defending champion Philadelphia Flyers. Robert provided the overtime heroics in the pivotal fifth game of the

Robert, Rene
RW, 5´10˝, 184 lbs, b: Trois-Rivieres, Que., 12/31/1948

Season	Club, League	Regular Season					Playoffs				
		GP	G	A	Pts	PIM	GP	G	A	Pts	PIM
1967–68	Tulsa Oilers, CHL	3	0	2	2	0	2	0	4	4	14
1968–69	Tulsa Oilers, CHL	59	21	30	51	57	7	4	3	7	2
1969–70	Vancouver Canucks, WHL	5	0	0	0	2					
	Rochester Americans, AHL	49	23	40	63	57					
1970–71	Toronto Maple Leafs, NHL	5	0	0	0	0					
	Tulsa Oilers, CHL	58	26	36	62	85					
	Phoenix Roadrunners, WHL	7	4	3	7	6	10	5	3	8	7
1971–72	Pittsburgh Penguins, NHL	49	7	11	18	42					
	Buffalo Sabres, NHL	12	6	3	9	2					
1972–73	Buffalo Sabres, NHL	75	40	43	83	83	6	5	3	8	2
1973–74	Buffalo Sabres, NHL	76	21	44	65	71					
1974–75	Buffalo Sabres, NHL	74	40	60	100	75	16	5	8	13	16
1975–76	Buffalo Sabres, NHL	72	35	52	87	53	9	3	2	5	6
1976–77	Buffalo Sabres, NHL	80	33	40	73	46	6	5	2	7	20
1977–78	Buffalo Sabres, NHL	67	25	48	73	25	7	2	0	2	23
1978–79	Buffalo Sabres, NHL	68	22	40	62	46	3	2	2	4	4
1979–80	Colorado Rockies, NHL	69	28	35	63	79					
1980–81	Colorado Rockies, NHL	28	8	11	19	30					
	Toronto Maple Leafs, NHL	14	6	7	13	8	3	0	2	2	2
1981–82	Toronto Maple Leafs, NHL	55	13	24	37	37					
	NHL Totals	744	284	418	702	597	50	22	19	41	73

NHL Second All-Star Team (1975)

semifinals against the Montreal Canadiens. The Habs never recovered and dropped the sixth game on home ice. In the third game of the finals, Robert scored one of the most famous overtime goals in history. On the winning play, he blew a shot past All-Star netminder Bernie Parent, who was unable to judge the movement of the puck because Buffalo's Memorial Auditorium ice was shrouded in a thick layer of fog. The Sabres lost the series after six hard-fought games. Following the season, Robert was voted to the NHL's Second All-Star Team.

Robert played another four years in Buffalo before he was traded to the lowly Colorado Rockies for offensive defenseman John Van Boxmeer. When informed of the trade, Robert was stunned and pondered retirement. Coach Don Cherry convinced him that he would bring in a few players and instill a winning attitude on the club. He looked to Robert to be one of the pillars in the rebuilding process.

In the third game of the 1975 finals against Philadelphia, Rene Robert (number 14) scored one of the most famous overtime goals in NHL history.

When Cherry was fired halfway through the 1980-81 season, Robert was one of the most vocal dissenters. He noted in 1986, "I'm convinced if they had kept Don there as coach, they would still have hockey in Denver." His candor at the time of the coaching change led to his trade to Toronto, the organization that had originally held his rights. By the next season, Robert was more comfortable with his new surroundings. He contributed checking and offense and was genuinely surprised when he was released after 55 games. The Maple Leafs may have been the worst place for Robert to rejuvenate his career, as they were at the lowest point of the Harold Ballard years.

The veteran winger retired after his release by Toronto. The knock against Robert had always been that he was moody and difficult to handle at times. Some even suggested he rode on the coattails of Perreault and Martin. Robert's quick adjustment to new teams and situations during his career dispelled this opinion.

In fact, Robert was somewhat under-appreciated when he was in the midst of his finest years with the French Connection. As Neil Campbell wrote: "Linemates Gil Perreault and Richard Martin were flashier, perhaps more skilled than Robert, but he may have been the most complete player of the three. He was the foot soldier, the winger who checked and went into the corners." His consistent production was evident in his career totals of 284 goals and 702 points in 744 regular-season matches. He eventually moved to Toronto and worked as a sales coordinator in eastern Ontario for Molson Breweries.

Ivan Hlinka

"Whenever you do something, you should set goals to achieve gradually. When a player is in the peewees, he doesn't say, 'I want to play in the NHL.' First he must push through to the juniors and seniors and assert himself there. Few manage to skip one of these stepping stones and still be successful."

Ivan Hlinka (right) enjoyed a stellar career both as a player and as a coach.

That is the philosophy of Ivan Hlinka, a man who enjoyed a stellar career both as a player and as a coach. In the 1970s, he won three world titles with Czechoslovakia's national team. Later, while managing the national team of the Czech Republic, he achieved something that eluded him as a player—Olympic gold. After the hockey tournament in Nagano in 1998, there was a lot of talk of the superhuman performance of Dominik Hasek. But Hlinka and co-coach Slavomir Lener deserve much of the credit for putting together a bunch of players that functioned exceptionally well as a team. They were the brains behind the triumph. One year later, Hlinka led the team to the World Championship title.

Litvinov is a small town in northern Bohemia—so small that it doesn't even have a maternity ward in the local hospital. But even though its population is only 30,000, it has become famous as a hatchery of some of the best hockey players ever to come out of Czechoslovakia. Most players who went on to the NHL came from there, including Hlinka, who was born on January 26, 1950, in nearby Most and stayed loyal to Litvinov for most of his life. As a small boy, Vladimir Ruzicka used to go and watch the strapping center play hockey. Other players from a later generation who grew up as fans of Hlinka include Robert Reichel, Jiri Slegr and Martin Rucinsky. In fact, he coached many young stars himself, and they were there with him to celebrate the Olympic gold medal win—the greatest triumph in the history of Czech hockey.

On the ice, Hlinka's excellent physique and great stickhandling often led him to generate his own plays, but he could also work well with his teammates to create opportunities. A natural leader, he gave the play purpose. He was an infallible scorer with his wrist shot and a master of both long and short passes.

With the exception of a six-month contract he signed with Dukla Trencin in 1978 that lasted until the 1980-81 season, Hlinka played almost exclusively for Litvinov from the age of nine on. Even at the end of 1986-87, when the team sank to near the bottom of the standings, he briefly returned to the ice. He took part in

Hlinka, Ivan
C, 6'2", 220 lbs, b: Most, Czechoslovakia, 1/26/1950

Season	Club, League	Regular Season					Playoffs				
		GP	G	A	Pts	PIM	GP	G	A	Pts	PIM
1967–70	Litvinov, Czechoslovakia	*	*	*	*	*					
WEC–70	Czechoslovakia	4	0	0	0	2					
1970–71	Litvinov, Czechoslovakia	*	*	*	*	*					
WEC–71	Czechoslovakia	10	4	2	6	2					
1971–72	Litvinov, Czechoslovakia	*	*	*	*	*					
OWG–72	Czechoslovakia	6	5	3	8	2					
WEC–72	Czechoslovakia	5	2	3	5	0					
1972–73	Litvinov, Czechoslovakia	*	*	*	*	*					
WEC–73	Czechoslovakia	8	2	1	3	0					
1973–74	Litvinov, Czechoslovakia	*	*	*	*	*					
WEC–74	Czechoslovakia	10	9	4	13	2					
1974–75	Litvinov, Czechoslovakia	*	36	42	78	*					
WEC–75	Czechoslovakia	6	2	4	6	2					
1975–76	Litvinov, Czechoslovakia	*	*	*	*	*					
OWG–76	Czechoslovakia	5	3	3	6	7					
WEC–76	Czechoslovakia	10	7	8	15	4					
CCup–76	Czechoslovakia	7	2	2	4	12					
1976–77	Litvinov, Czechoslovakia	*	*	*	*	*					
WEC–77	Czechoslovakia	10	9	3	12	5					
1977–78	Litvinov, Czechoslovakia	*	*	*	*	*					
WEC–78	Czechoslovakia	10	4	10	14	4					
1978–79	Dukla Trencin/Litvinov,										
	Czechoslovakia	*	17	20	37	*	13	4	8	12	*
WEC–79	Czechoslovakia	8	3	5	8	6					
1979–80	Litvinov, Czechoslovakia	*	*	*	*	*	*	*	*	*	*
1980–81	Litvinov, Czechoslovakia	40	21	31	52	*	28	5	15	20	*
WEC–81	Czechoslovakia	8	0	3	3	0					
1981–82	Vancouver Canucks, NHL	72	23	37	60	16	12	2	6	8	4
1982–83	Vancouver Canucks, NHL	65	19	44	63	12	4	1	4	5	4
1983–85	Zug, Switzerland	*	*	*	*	*	*	*	*	*	*
	Czechoslovakia Totals	544	347	*	*	*	*	*	*	*	*
	NHL Totals	137	42	81	123	28	16	3	10	13	8
	OWG/WEC/CCup Totals	107	52	51	103	48					

Won WEC (1972, 1976, 1977)

11 World Championships, two Olympics and the 1976 Canada Cup with the national team. In 1978 he won the Golden Stick Award as the country's most valuable player.

He spent his best years in the former Czechoslovakia because in his time hockey players couldn't live abroad legally. But in 1981 he and defenseman Jiri Bubla became the first Czech hockey players in a very long time to get the blessing of the communist regime to play in the NHL. "I was 31. Furthermore, I had a badly worn out knee after two operations. Still, I am glad that we took the chance," he said much later.

In 1981 Ivan Hlinka (right) and Jiri Bubla became the first Czech players in a very long time to be granted the communist regime's permission to play in the NHL.

The 1981–82 season had become the most successful in the history of the Vancouver Canucks. For the first time, they made it to the Stanley Cup finals. Hlinka, who according to rules of the time was still considered a rookie, drew attention by earning 23 goals and 60 points, a rookie record for the club. While Bubla spent a total of four years with the Canucks, Hlinka returned to Europe after two seasons and spent an equal length of time with the Swiss EV Zug hockey club. After that, he decided it was time to move on.

"I am not of the opinion that the coach should be a buddy to the players. Camaraderie should manifest itself in unfavorable situations, but it doesn't mean avoiding conflict. The rules of the game must be clearly set in advance because neither the coach without players nor players without a coach stand a chance of succeeding." There he was again philosophizing on the game. Hlinka had an excellent career as a hockey player and afterwards as a coach. His players respected him and he returned it.

With the exception of the 1989–90 season when he coached the Freiburg club in Germany, he devoted his days to the Litvinov team. Later he transferred to the post of general manager. At the same time he worked as vice-president of the Czech hockey federation. He led the national team from 1991 to 1994. He got two bronze medals in World Championship play and one at the Olympics in 1992. He has had to live with failures at the 1994 Lillehammer Olympics and the World Championship in Italy the same year. But with a comeback in March 1997, he was no longer the king of bronze.

Hlinka always liked to remind people how fine the line was between success and failure. He came very close to that line in the Olympic quarterfinals against the USA in 1998—the Czechs went on to win the gold medal—and again leading up to their World Championship in 1999. But by nature he remained a player and never let the hunger for success control him. He kept a sober outlook even in February 2000, when he left for Pittsburgh to become assistant coach.

At the start of the 2001–02 season, Hlinka returned to the Czech Republic to help the country's team prepare for the Salt Lake Olympics. Fired as head coach of the Penguins amid reports that he wasn't getting along with the principle executives in the organization, he was general manager of the Czech team when the defending Olympic champions returned home empty-handed after losing the right to advance to the semifinals to Russia.

Reggie Leach

Reggie Leach's natural goal-scoring gift was augmented by a shot that was clocked at 115 miles an hour.

One of the most-feared goal scorers of the 1970s, right wing Reggie Leach overcame poverty and personal struggles as a youth to make a life for himself through hockey. He played on four NHL clubs but was best remembered as a sharpshooting member of the Philadelphia Flyers. His natural goal-scoring gift was augmented by a shot that was measured at 115 miles per hour, just a shade slower than Bobby Hull's.

An aboriginal Canadian who grew up in Riverton, Manitoba, Leach was raised by his paternal grandparents. After struggling as a youngster, he began to gain discipline and self-esteem through his gift on the ice. "The Riverton Rifle" was blessed with pure speed and the ability to shoot the puck hard and accurately along the ice while in full flight. This unique talent tormented goalies in the amateur and pro ranks for years.

Growing up, Leach's only ambition was to play hockey, as he had no interest in any subjects at school. He was good enough to make an industrial league team in Edmonton at the age of 13, and it was here he was noticed by a Detroit Red Wings scout and immediately signed up to play with the organization's junior club in Flin Flon, Manitoba.

One of the greatest scorers in the history of the Western Canada Junior Hockey League, Leach found the back of the net 188 times in three seasons with the Flin Flon Bombers. He led the WCJHL/WHL in goal-scoring twice, including a remarkable total of 87 goals in 1967–68. Leach was a junior teammate of Bobby Clarke, a factor that later changed the course of his NHL career. Following each of his junior seasons, he was placed on the WCJHL/WHL First All-Star Team.

After graduating from junior, Leach was the third player claimed in the 1970 Amateur Draft when the Boston Bruins called his name. The Beantowners were in the midst of winning the Stanley Cup twice in three years and were too deep in talent to give the youngster a fair shot at the pros.

On February 23, 1972, Leach was part of the package sent by Boston to California to acquire Carol Vadnais. The Golden Seals were blatantly overmatched most nights, but Leach's talent began to shine through the depression of losing. In 1972–73 and 1973–74, he recorded consecutive 20-goal seasons. In the second of these years, he formed the team's top line with Walt McKechnie and Joey Johnston.

A few days after winning their first-ever Stanley Cup, the Philadelphia Flyers took a giant step toward repeating the triumph when they fleeced the Seals in a deal for Leach. Former junior teammate Clarke was a factor in the

Leach, Reggie
RW, 6´, 180 lbs, b: Riverton, Man., 4/23/1950

Season	Club, League		Regular Season					Playoffs			
		GP	G	A	Pts	PIM	GP	G	A	Pts	PIM
1968–69	Flin Flon Bombers, WHL	22	36	10	46	49	18	13	8	21	0
1969–70	Flin Flon Bombers, WHL	57	65	46	111	168	17	16	11	27	50
1970–71	Boston Bruins, NHL	23	2	4	6	0	3	0	0	0	0
	Oklahoma City Blazers, CHL	41	24	18	42	32					
1971–72	Boston Bruins, NHL	56	7	13	20	12					
	California Golden Seals, NHL	17	6	7	13	7					
1972–73	California Golden Seals, NHL	76	23	12	35	45					
1973–74	California Golden Seals, NHL	78	22	24	46	34					
1974–75	Philadelphia Flyers, NHL	80	45	33	78	63	17	8	2	10	6
1975–76	Philadelphia Flyers, NHL	80	61	30	91	41	16	19	5	24	8
CCup–76	Canada	6	1	1	2	4					
1976–77	Philadelphia Flyers, NHL	77	32	14	46	23	10	4	5	9	0
1977–78	Philadelphia Flyers, NHL	72	24	28	52	24	12	2	2	4	0
1978–79	Philadelphia Flyers, NHL	76	34	20	54	20	8	5	1	6	0
1979–80	Philadelphia Flyers, NHL	76	50	26	76	28	19	9	7	16	6
1980–81	Philadelphia Flyers, NHL	79	34	36	70	59	9	0	0	0	2
1981–82	Philadelphia Flyers, NHL	66	26	21	47	18					
1982–83	Detroit Red Wings, NHL	78	15	17	32	13					
1983–84	Montana Magic, CHL	76	21	29	50	34					
	NHL Totals	934	381	285	666	387	94	47	22	69	22
	CCup Totals	6	1	1	2	4					

NHL Second All-Star Team (1976)
Won Conn Smythe Trophy (1976)
Won Stanley Cup (1975)
Won CCup (1976)

astute maneuver on the part of Philly. After the trade was made official, the Flyers captain beamed, "Even in an ordinary year, he'll get 40 goals for us."

In 1974–75, Leach teamed with Clarke and Bill Barber to score 45 goals and earn the respect of the tough fans in the City of Brotherly Love. While helping the Flyers repeat as Cup winners, Leach scored eight goals in 17 post-season games. The winger noted: "It's easy to play here. There's a definite system to everything—not like a lot of clubs I've played for—and all you have to do is follow it. And we've got a hell of a leader in Bobby. If you've got a problem, he's the guy to see."

During the 1975–76 season, Reggie Leach (front) scored 61 regular-season goals and added 19 more in 16 playoff games, which earned him the Conn Smythe Trophy.

It was in the Flyers' failed attempt at a third triumph in the playoffs that Leach's star shone the brightest. During the 1975–76 season, he scored 61 regular-season goals but saved his best for the post-season. Leach's 19-goal effort in 16 games earned him the Conn Smythe Trophy even though his team was swept by the Montreal Canadiens in the Stanley Cup finals. Of further significance was the fact that the Riverton Rifle scored 80 combined goals (regular-season and playoffs) to break Phil Esposito's standard set in 1970–71. Playing on a potent line with his old friend Clarke, Leach noted, "Clarke makes the bombs and I drop them."

Leach earned placement on the NHL Second All-Star Team at the end of the season. A few months later, he was selected to play for his country in the inaugural Canada Cup tournament. He enjoyed three decent but unspectacular years between 1976 and 1979 as the Flyers mini-dynasty vanished. He took the criticism that his skills were fading in stride for a while, but when trade rumors and doubt began to follow him, he complained: "You know, I wish that 80-goal season had never happened to me. It was a fluke thing anyway—I'm really just a 30- or 40-goal scorer—but you do it one year and they expect it every year."

Incredibly, in 1979–80 the wily veteran scored 50 times and helped the Flyers set an NHL record by going undefeated in 35 consecutive games from October 14 to January 6. More important, Leach took on defensive responsibilities and killed penalties for the first time in his career. He also scored 16 points while helping Philly reach the Stanley Cup finals, where they lost to the New York Islanders in six games.

Somewhat of an individualist, Leach wasn't the easiest player to motivate. Coaches Fred Shero, Bob McCammon and Pat Quinn took turns trying to light a consistent fire under him. In the end, they always relied on Clarke's input, which turned out to be the best solution for everyone.

The fleet winger registered 60 goals during his last two seasons in Philadelphia before joining the Detroit Red Wings as a free agent prior to the 1982–83 season. Leach scored his last 15 NHL goals wearing the famous winged wheel. In 1983–84, he skated for the Montana Magic of the Central Hockey League before bringing his pro career to a close. Leach finished with 381 goals in 934 regular-season games while earning a reputation as one of the top snipers of his day.

After retiring, Leach successfully battled a drinking problem that had plagued him for years. He built up his own lawn care business and proved to be every bit as much a success off the ice as he was on it.

Glenn Resch

Glenn Resch was a key ingredient in the New York Islanders' ascent to the upper echelons of the NHL in the 1970s.

A successful puck stopper and one of the most well-liked players of his time, Glenn "Chico" Resch spent more than 13 years in the NHL. He supplied acrobatic saves and a positive influence in the dressing room wherever he played. Resch was a key ingredient in the ascension of the New York Islanders to the upper reaches of the NHL in the 1970s. He later served as a tutor and stabilizing influence with Colorado/New Jersey and Philadelphia.

Resch was one of the last players to go through the old sponsorship system when he signed to be a part of the Montreal Canadiens organization as a 12-year-old. As it turned out, rather than taking the traditional route of Canadian junior hockey, Resch honed his skills and received an education in the United States. He was quoted as saying: "I went to college because I didn't think I had a future in hockey. I went to the only college that would give me a hockey scholarship, the University of Minnesota at Duluth." Following his senior year in 1970–71, he was selected to the WCHA Second All-Star Team.

After failing to crack the Montreal Canadiens' roster at training camp in 1971, he was traded to the expansion New York Islanders in June 1972. Ironically, it was Ken Dryden, a goalie he'd faced in college, who was the undisputed incumbent at Resch's first pro camp. But the Montreal experience wasn't a waste for Resch. As an amateur, he patterned himself after Glenn Hall, whose size and reflexes allowed him to go down often to make a save. Resch struggled at times in junior and college because his style didn't suit his relatively small frame. While at the Habs' training camp, he watched equally diminutive netminder Rogie Vachon utilize a stand-up style while still playing the angles well. Resch altered his style accordingly and went on to enjoy an exemplary career.

His first year as a pro was a success, with a league-leading four shutouts for the Muskegon Mohawks of the IHL. His efforts earned him the James Norris Memorial Trophy for having the league's lowest goals-against mark and a place on the First All-Star squad. He next played with the New Haven Nighthawks of the AHL in 1972–73. Apart from a two-game stint on Long Island, Resch played 55 games for the CHL's Fort Worth Wings the following season.

Beginning in 1974–75, Resch began to play more regularly with the Islanders and became a fan favorite at Nassau Coliseum. That spring he won eight of 12 playoff games as the upstart

Resch, Glenn
G, 5'9", 165 lbs, b: Moose Jaw, Sask., 7/10/1948

Season	Club, League	Regular Season				Playoffs			
		GP	Mins	GA	Avg	GP	Mins	GA	Avg
1968–69	Univ. of Minnesota-Duluth, WCHA	24	1424	117	4.93				
1969–70	Univ. of Minnesota-Duluth, WCHA	25	1500	97	3.88				
1970–71	Univ. of Minnesota-Duluth, WCHA	26	1518	107	4.23				
1971–72	Muskegon Mohawks, IHL	59	3488	180	3.09	11	617	29	2.82
1972–73	New Haven Nighthawks, AHL	43	2408	166	4.13				
1973–74	New York Islanders, NHL	2	120	6	3.00				
	Fort Worth Wings, CHL	55	3300	175	3.18	5	300	21	3.60
1974–75	New York Islanders, NHL	25	1432	59	2.47	12	692	25	2.17
1975–76	New York Islanders, NHL	44	2546	88	2.07	7	357	18	3.03
CCup–76	Canada	0	0	0	0.00	0	0	0	0.00
1976–77	New York Islanders, NHL	46	2711	103	2.28	3	144	5	2.08
1977–78	New York Islanders, NHL	45	2637	112	2.55	7	388	15	2.32
1978–79	New York Islanders, NHL	43	2539	106	2.50	5	300	11	2.20
1979–80	New York Islanders, NHL	45	2606	132	3.04	4	120	9	4.50
1980–81	New York Islanders, NHL	32	1817	93	3.07				
	Colorado Rockies, NHL	8	449	28	3.74				
1981–82	Colorado Rockies, NHL	61	3424	230	4.03				
WEC–82	USA	4	239	21	5.27				
1982–83	New Jersey Devils, NHL	65	3650	242	3.98				
1983–84	New Jersey Devils, NHL	51	2641	184	4.18				
CCup–84	USA	2	108	9	5.00				
1984–85	New Jersey Devils, NHL	51	2884	200	4.16				
1985–86	New Jersey Devils, NHL	31	1769	126	4.27				
	Philadelphia Flyers, NHL	5	187	10	3.21	1	7	1	8.57
1986–87	Philadelphia Flyers, NHL	17	867	42	2.91	2	36	1	1.67
	NHL Totals	571	32279	1761	3.27	41	2044	85	2.50
	CCup/WEC Totals	6	347	30	5.19				

NHL Second All-Star Team (1976, 1979)
Won Bill Masterton Trophy (1982)
Won Stanley Cup (1980)
Won CCup (1976)

Islanders came from three games down to beat Pittsburgh 4–3 in the best-of-seven quarterfinal series. Resch played in the last four games of his club's stirring comeback.

In 1976 he served as a spare for Team Canada at the inaugural Canada Cup tournament. Over the next three seasons, he and Billy Smith became one of the most respected goaltending tandems in the NHL. By the time the club won its first Stanley Cup in 1979–80, Smith was the undisputed first-stringer. Initially Resch went through a difficult time sitting on the bench during the Islanders' playoff run. That same spring he embraced Christianity and became a person more at peace with himself and his role on the team.

Midway through the 1980–81 schedule, Resch faced a new challenge when he was traded to the inexperienced Colorado Rockies. His upbeat nature injected a breath of fresh air into a downcast franchise. In addition, Resch's netminding skill brought the Rockies a few undeserved points. He remained with the franchise until early in the 1985–86 season, when it was known as the New Jersey Devils. His dual citizenship gave him the chance to play for the United States at the 1982 World Championships and the 1984 Canada Cup. During the latter stages of his career, Resch refused to sign a multi-year contract. He insisted on reaffirming his commitment to the game and earning playing time on an annual basis.

Glenn Resch supplied acrobatic saves and a positive influence in the dressing room wherever he played.

Resch's veteran savvy appealed to the Philadelphia Flyers. In 1986–87, he backed up sensational rookie Ron Hextall when the team reached the Stanley Cup finals. Resch inadvertently started a famous pre-game brawl with Montreal in the semifinals, when he and teammate Ed Hospodar prevented Claude Lemieux from scoring on their empty net, as was his ritual.

Resch retired after the club lost to the champion Edmonton Oilers. Resch's impressive totals read 231 wins and 26 shutouts. A respected professional, he was presented the Bill Masterton Trophy in 1982.

After retiring, he was able to spend more time with his other love, collecting hockey memorabilia. He also coached the Tri-Cities junior franchise in the Western Canada Major Junior Hockey League and served as a goaltending coach and consultant with the Minnesota North Stars and the Ottawa Senators.

Erich **Kuhnhackl**

To truly understand how great a player Erich Kuhnhackl was, one must consider that at age 25 he was making so much money in West Germany that he couldn't afford to sign with the NHL's New York Rangers. John Ferguson, who was general manager of the Rangers at that time, said the club offered the prolific scorer a deal worth somewhere between $80,000 and $100,000 after he led his country to a bronze medal at the 1976 Olympics in Innsbruck, Austria. Kuhnhackl, who finished in a four-way tie for top spot in scoring with three stars of the gold medalist Soviet team—Vladimir Shadrin, Alexander Maltsev and Viktor Shalimov—rejected the offer.

At 6'6", Erich Kuhnhackl (right) was the tallest player of his time anywhere in the world.

Kuhnhackl was known as "Der Schlaksig," (The Lanky One) because he stood 6'6" and was an imposing figure on the ice. At the time, the two tallest players in the NHL were center Peter Mahovlich of Montreal and Vancouver defenseman Bob Dailey, and both were an inch shorter than Kuhnhackl.

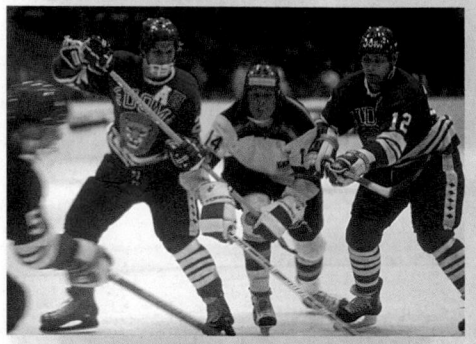

At age 25, Erich Kuhnhackl (center) was making so much money in West Germany he couldn't afford to sign with the New York Rangers.

The German giant scored 131 goals in 211 matches with the West German national team and an incredible 708 goals in 743 games in the German federal league. In a poll conducted by the *German Eishockey News*, he was named the best German player of all time. At the 1978 World Championship in Prague, he led all scorers with eight goals and 16 points in 10 games, finishing ahead of marquee players like Ivan Hlinka of Czechoslovakia, Alexander Maltsev and Boris Mikhailov of the Soviet Union and Canada's Marcel Dionne. Still, he wasn't selected to either the First or Second All-Star teams. The spots went to Hlinka and Dionne. He also led all scorers at the 1984 Olympics in Sarajevo with eight goals and 14 points in six games as West Germany narrowly missed qualifying for the playoffs.

Despite his impressive statistics, Kuhnhackl didn't get the credit he deserved. Only once—in 1983–84, following his superb performance at the Olympics—was he among the top 10 vote-getters in polling for the Golden Hockey Stick, which is presented annually to the best player in Europe. He placed ninth in the voting, which was topped by Soviet defenseman Viacheslav Fetisov. Critics claimed the German league was inferior to those in the other established European hockey nations and noted that Kuhnhackl picked up many of his scoring points at World Championship and Olympic tournaments in the regulation pool against weak nations.

Kuhnhackl was born in Citice, Czechoslovakia, very close to the German border, and played minor hockey in nearby Sokolov. But both of his parents were German and the family moved to West Germany in 1968. It was Kuhnhackl's leadership that led to a breakthrough by the West German team in the early 1980s. First the West Germans sent shock waves through Europe by upsetting Czechoslovakia 4–2 at the 1982 World Championship in Finland. Then they tied the Czechs 3–3 and upset Finland 4–3 while hosting the 1983 world tournament.

In fact, the West Germans played so well they earned a berth in the 1984 Canada Cup. Only the top four European nations—the Soviet Union, Czechoslovakia, Sweden and Finland—had been invited to the first two Canada Cup competitions in 1976 and 1981, but tournament organizer Alan Eagleson had made a deal with the International Ice Hockey Federation for the top four European finishers

Kuhnhackl, Erich
C, 6´6´´, 220 lbs, b: Citice, Czechoslovakia, 10/17/1950

Season	Club, League	Regular Season					Playoffs				
		GP	G	A	Pts	PIM	GP	G	A	Pts	PIM
1968–69	Landshut, FRG	14	6	2	8	2					
1969–70	Landshut, FRG	35	21	14	35	14					
1970–71	Landshut, FRG	35	16	12	28	18					
1971–72	Landshut, FRG	32	24	19	43	36					
OWG–72	FRG	6	2	4	6	*					
1972–73	Landshut, FRG	40	38	30	68	43					
WEC–73	FRG	10	6	*	*	*					
1973–74	Landshut, FRG	36	50	26	76	40					
WEC–74 (2)	FRG	7	9	5	14	*					
1974–75	Landshut, FRG	35	47	20	67	90					
WEC–75 (2)	FRG	7	6	4	10	*					
1975–76	Landshut, FRG	35	29	17	46	73					
OWG–76	FRG	6	6	5	11	10					
WEC–76	FRG	10	7	*	*	*					
1976–77	Kolner, Cologne, FRG	40	47	26	73	79					
WEC–77	FRG	10	5	*	*	*					
1977–78	Kolner, Cologne, FRG	46	52	43	95	43					
WEC–78	FRG	10	8	8	16	*					
1978–79	Kolner, Cologne, FRG	52	59	58	117	99					
1979–80	Landshut, FRG	48	83	72	155	67					
1980–81	Landshut, FRG	44	40	46	86	74	5	4	2	6	4
WEC–81	FRG	8	3	*	*	*					
1981–82	Landshut, FRG	38	41	61	102	34	8	6	9	15	*
WEC–82	FRG	7	3	*	*	*					
1982–83	Landshut, FRG	36	32	48	80	70	10	7	7	14	10
WEC–83	FRG	10	5	*	*	*					
1983–84	Landshut, FRG	42	35	52	87	75	10	4	11	15	18
OWG–84	FRG	6	8	*	*	*					
1984–85	Landshut, FRG	36	30	39	69	59					
WEC–85	FRG	10	3	*	*	*					
1985–86	EHC Olten, Switzerland	35	22	23	45	88					
1986–87	EHC Olten, Switzerland	11	6	16	22	*					
1987–88	Landshut, Germany	35	20	29	49	47					
1988–89	Landshut, Germany	36	21	38	59	67					
	Germany Totals	715	691	652	1343	1030	33	21	29	50	*
	OWG/WEC Totals	107	71	*	*	*					

FRG Champion (1970, 1977, 1979, 1983)

in the 1983 World Championship to take part. West Germany placed fifth and Finland seventh. However, North American fans didn't get a chance to see Kuhnhackl in action. He suffered a broken leg in April of 1984 and wasn't fully recovered in time to play in the Canada Cup, where the West Germans managed only a tie in five matches.

Kuhnhackl won two West German championships with Cologne and two with Landshut before winding up his career with Olten of the Swiss league. Later he worked as coach with Landshut, then as an assistant to head coach Xavier Unsinn with the national team. He was also head coach of the German team at the 1990 World Championship in Bern.

Kuhnhackl was inducted into the International Ice Hockey Hall of Fame in 1997.

Marc Tardif

Marc Tardif began his professional hockey career in the standard way. He was drafted second overall by Montreal in 1969, the last year the Canadiens could draft the first two French-Canadians available, and then he played for the Junior Canadiens in the OHL. He played most of his first four pro years with the Montreal Canadiens from 1969 to 1973, developing into a true goal scorer Habs fans were starting to admire.

Marc Tardif was drafted second overall by Montreal in 1969, the last year the Canadiens could draft the first two French-Canadians available.

But in June 1973 he stunned the team by signing a three-year, $350,000 contract with the Los Angeles Sharks of the two-year-old World Hockey Association. This represented an enormous increase over the $40,000 he had made with Montreal the previous season, and Tardif was quick to admit as much. "My first consideration was for a no-trade contract, and my second consideration was money. The money here is better than what I was offered in Montreal, so I felt I had better come here."

It was in the WHA that he played the prime six years of his life, joining the Quebec Nordiques midway through the following season and becoming a provincial hero for all French-Canadians in Quebec. In 1975–76, he signed an unprecedented 10-year contract with the Nordiques, then went out and led the league in goals, assists and points. But in the playoffs he suffered a horrific injury in a game against the Calgary Cowboys. He was charged from behind by Rick Jodzio, who hammered Tardif in the chest and head area with his stick. Tardif fell to the ice unconscious, but Jodzio jumped on top of him and continued to punch him violently.

Tardif suffered extensive damage to his mouth and teeth, but he also suffered a brain contusion that at first threatened his very

Tardif, Marc
LW, 6´, 195 lbs, b: Granby, Que., 6/12/1949

Season	Club, League	Regular Season					Playoffs				
		GP	G	A	Pts	PIM	GP	G	A	Pts	PIM
1969–70	Montreal Canadiens, NHL	18	3	2	5	27					
	Montreal Voyageurs, AHL	45	27	31	58	70	8	3	6	9	29
1970–71	Montreal Canadiens, NHL	76	19	30	49	133	20	3	1	4	40
1971–72	Montreal Canadiens, NHL	75	31	22	53	81	6	2	3	5	9
1972–73	Montreal Canadiens, NHL	76	25	25	50	48	14	6	6	12	6
1973–74	Los Angeles Sharks, WHA	75	40	30	70	47					
1974–75	Michigan Stags, WHA	23	12	5	17	9					
	Quebec Nordiques, WHA	53	38	34	72	70	15	10	11	21	10
1975–76	Quebec Nordiques, WHA	81	71	77	148	79	2	1	0	1	2
1976–77	Quebec Nordiques, WHA	62	49	60	109	65	12	4	10	14	8
1977–78	Quebec Nordiques, WHA	78	65	89	154	50	11	6	9	15	11
1978–79	Quebec Nordiques, WHA	74	41	55	96	98	4	6	2	8	4
1979–80	Quebec Nordiques, NHL	58	33	35	68	30					
1980–81	Quebec Nordiques, NHL	63	23	31	54	35	5	1	3	4	2
1981–82	Quebec Nordiques, NHL	75	39	31	70	55	13	1	2	3	16
1982–83	Quebec Nordiques, NHL	76	21	31	52	34	4	0	0	0	2
	NHL Totals	517	194	207	401	443	62	13	15	28	75
	WHA Totals	446	316	350	666	418	44	27	32	59	35

WHA First All-Star Team (1976, 1977, 1978)
WHA Second All-Star Team (1975)
Won Stanley Cup (1971, 1973)
Won Avco Cup (1977)

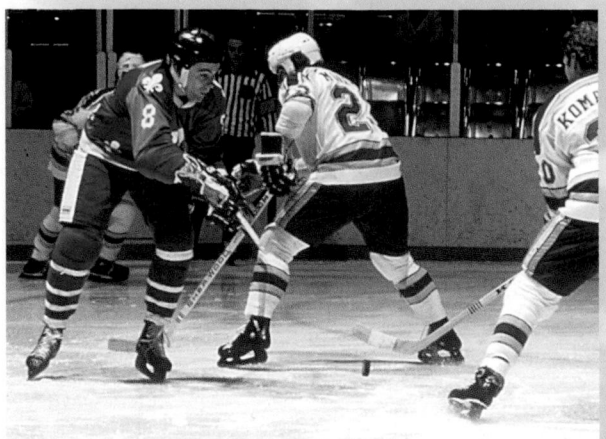

Marc Tardif's number 8 was retired by the Quebec Nordiques near the start of the 1983- 84 season.

well-being. "I can't guarantee anything for the next six months," was all the hope his doctor would give. Tardif was unconscious for 30 minutes after the assault, and still doesn't know what triggered the attack. "I didn't see it happen," he said. "I didn't see him. I didn't even know he was coming at me." Jodzio was charged with assault causing bodily harm with intent to injure.

For weeks afterward, Tardif wasn't allowed to leave his house because the exertion of just walking was too much for him. Once fears had been lifted about possible paralysis and brain damage, Tardif was able to move slowly. By the end of the summer, he was in good enough shape to exercise, but he had to decline an invitation to Team Canada's training camp for the Canada Cup.

The following March he filed a $150,000 lawsuit against Jodzio, claiming a loss of $20,000 from Canada Cup participation and a further $130,000 for pain, permanent disability and disruption of normal life during his convalescence. Remarkably, he continued to play and score, and in 1979, when the Nordiques joined the NHL, Tardif was still playing, though relations with the club weren't always smooth.

At training camp in 1979, he was criticized by the media for holding out on his contract. He argued that the one he signed was valid for playing in the WHA, but now that the team was in the NHL, he deserved more than the $180,000 he was making. His tactic worked, and within days he signed a new five-year deal at $240,000 a season.

After four more years back in the NHL, Tardif retired a hero in Quebec and was given a proud sendoff. His number 8 was retired by the Nordiques near the start of the 1983–84 season, and Maurice Filion was quick to praise him. "It was of great importance for the Nordiques that this athlete, who has done so much for hockey in Quebec, could retire from active competition with his head high, happy and proud." The ceremony was all the grander for the appearance of Jean Beliveau, J.C. Tremblay and Tardif's friends and family.

Ulf Nilsson was on the NHL All-Star Team that met the USSR at the Challenge Cup tournament in 1979.

Ulf Nilsson

During the sports gala of January 2000 at Stockholm's Globe Arena where Sweden's best athletes of the last century were honored, five masked men wearing Tre Kronor hockey jerseys stepped into the limelight and performed a jig. When they took off their masks, they revealed themselves to the spectators as defenseman Borje Salming and forwards Mats Naslund, Kent Nilsson, Anders Hedberg and Ulf Nilsson.

Ulf Nilsson was born May 11, 1950, in Nynashamn, nearly 50 miles to the south of Stockholm. There, at the age of eight, he began playing for Nynashamn IF and later, as a junior, switched to the capital city's AIK.

Nilsson was one of the players who introduced Swedish hockey to Canada when in 1974 he made his debut with the WHA's Winnipeg Jets, where his partner in offense was another great

Swedish forward, Anders Hedberg. Both were often among the league's best scorers and, thanks to the Swedish duo's excellent performance, the Winnipeg Jets twice won the Avco Cup.

The legendary Bobby Hull, partnered with Hedberg and Nilsson, was able once again to demonstrate his extraordinary ability and set his amazing scoring record of 1,000 goals. The very fact that such a unique international trio existed deserves mention in any hockey encyclopedia.

Nilsson made his debut with the Swedish national team at the 1972 Izvestia Cup Tournament in Moscow. The next year, again in Moscow, he took part in his first World Championship along with Swedish aces Ulf Sterner and Stig-Goran Johansson.

At the 1976 Canada Cup, he played exceptionally well for Tre Kronor and in a game against the USSR scored the decisive goal against Vladislav Tretiak. Nilsson was also included on the NHL All-Star Team pitted against the USSR at the 1979 Challenge Cup tournament.

The most memorable game for Nilsson was the one between the Winnipeg Jets and the USSR in 1978 in Winnipeg, which the Canadian team won 5–3. In that game, Hull scored three goals, Nilsson scored two, and the Nilsson–Hull–Hedberg trio won their own game against one of the world's best lineups, the Mikhailov–Petrov–Kharlamov trio.

Unfortunately, Nilsson was plagued with injuries that prevented him from reaching his full potential. During four seasons with the NHL's New York Rangers, his scoring results fell short of his WHA record.

Among his trophies are a silver medal won at the 1973 World Championship and a bronze medal from the 1974 World Championship. He also played for Sweden in the 1981 Canada Cup tournament. Considering the many high points of his career and the fact that he was one of Europe's pioneers in Canadian hockey, it is clear why Ulf Nilsson is so popular in Sweden.

At present, Nilsson works for Bredbandbulaget, a company specializing in information technology. He has retired from hockey and now prefers to play golf.

Ulf Nilsson was one of the players who introduced Swedish hockey to Canada when he made his debut with the WHA's Winnipeg Jets in 1974.

Nilsson, Ulf
C, 5′11″, 175 lbs, b: Nynashamn, Sweden, 5/11/1950

Season	Club, League	Regular Season					Playoffs				
		GP	G	A	Pts	PIM	GP	G	A	Pts	PIM
1969–70	AIK, Sweden	14	6	6	12	10	14	5	3	8	2
1970–71	AIK, Sweden	14	10	3	13	6	14	2	4	6	8
1971–72	AIK, Sweden	14	5	6	11	2	8	5	1	6	2
1972–73	AIK, Sweden	14	11	7	18	4	14	10	8	18	23
WEC–73	Sweden	10	5	3	8	4					
1973–74	AIK, Sweden	*	*	*	*	*	*	*	*	*	*
WEC–74	Sweden	2	0	0	0	0					
1974–75	Winnipeg Jets, WHA	78	26	94	120	79					
1975–76	Winnipeg Jets, WHA	78	38	76	114	84	13	7	19	26	6
CCup–76	Sweden	5	1	1	2	6					
1976–77	Winnipeg Jets, WHA	71	39	85	124	89	20	6	21	27	33
1977–78	Winnipeg Jets, WHA	73	37	89	126	89	9	1	13	14	12
1978–79	New York Rangers, NHL	59	27	39	66	21	2	0	0	0	2
ChCup–79	NHL All-Stars	2	0	0	0	0					
1979–80	New York Rangers, NHL	50	14	44	58	20	9	0	6	6	2
1980–81	New York Rangers, NHL	51	14	25	39	42	14	8	8	16	23
CCup–81	Sweden	4	1	2	3	2					
1981–82	Springfield Indians, AHL	2	0	0	0	0					
1982–83	New York Rangers, NHL	10	2	4	6	2					
	Tulsa Oilers, CHL	3	2	1	3	4					
	Sweden Totals	56	32	22	54	22	50	22	16	38	35
	WEC/CCup/ChalCup Totals	23	7	6	13	12					
	WHA Totals	300	140	344	484	341	42	14	53	67	51
	NHL Totals	170	57	112	169	85	25	8	14	22	27

WHA First All-Star Team (1976, 1978)
WHA Second All-Star Team (1977)
Won WHA Playoff MVP Trophy (1976)
Won Avco Cup (1976, 1978)

Anders Hedberg

Four seasons with the Winnipeg Jets were the happiest in Anders Hedberg's career.

Anders Hedberg was one of the best Swedish forwards of the 1970s. As a teenager, he was a gifted player with a great future ahead of him. Swedish hockey fans remember October 22, 1967, as the day when 16-year-old Hedberg made his extraordinary debut in the Swedish Premier Division.

That morning Hedberg played in the final game of the popular junior *TV-Pukken* tournament for the regional Ongermanland team against Norbotten. The entire game was shown on TV and viewers witnessed a virtual one-man show. Hedberg scored five goals and one assist, leading his team to a 6–0 win. Hedberg then caught a cab to the airport in time to make the flight to Ernsholdsviq, where his team, MoDo, was playing that night against Stockholm AIK with goalie Leif "Honken" Holmqvist in the net. Although MoDo lost 5-3, Hedberg managed to score one goal against the great Honken.

In 1969 the head coach of the Swedish national team invited the 17-year-old forward to join the national team, but his studies prevented him from accepting. Hedberg made his first appearance in the national lineup the following year and immediately proved he was a player with great talent. He was even nicknamed "the New Tumba" after 1950s Swedish hockey star Sven "Tumba" Johansson. Hedberg played 100 official games for Sweden.

One of Hedberg's most memorable goals was the third one he scored against Vladislav Tretiak in the 1976 Canada Cup tournament. On a perfect pass from defenseman Borje Salming, Hedberg went one-on-one with the Soviet goalkeeper and tied the score 3–3.

By this time, he had already left Stockholm's Djurgarden and joined the Winnipeg Jets in the newly formed World Hockey Association. In what was perhaps the happiest time in his sports career, Hedberg played with teammate Ulf Nilsson on the same line as the legendary Canadian hockey player Bobby Hull—a line that was then considered the best in the WHA. Hull often stated that he'd never had partners who had mastered the fine points of hockey as well as the two Swedes, Hedberg and Nilsson. Bobby Hull scored his 1,000th career goal while playing in the lineup with the two Scandinavians.

After the demise of the WHA, Hedberg played seven seasons with the New York Rangers for a total of 465 games in which he scored 172 goals.

Hedberg, Anders
RW, 5′11″, 175 lbs, b: Ornskoldsvik, Sweden, 2/25/1951

Season	Club, League	Regular Season					Playoffs				
		GP	G	A	Pts	PIM	GP	G	A	Pts	PIM
1969–70	MoDo, Sweden	14	9	14	23	2					
WEC–70	Sweden	9	2	3	5	0					
1970–71	MoDo, Sweden	14	7	6	13	0					
1971–72	MoDo, Sweden	2	1	0	1	0					
WEC–72	Sweden	10	6	5	11	4					
1972–73	Djurgarden, Sweden	12	6	3	9	2	14	6	7	13	4
WEC–73	Sweden	10	2	5	7	0					
1973–74	Djurgarden, Sweden	*	*	*	*	*	*	*	*	*	*
WEC–74	Sweden	10	7	3	10	2					
1974–75	Winnipeg Jets, WHA	65	53	47	100	45					
1975–76	Winnipeg Jets, WHA	76	50	55	105	48	13	13	6	19	15
CCup–76	Sweden	5	3	2	5	4					
1976–77	Winnipeg Jets, WHA	68	70	61	131	48	20	13	16	29	13
1977–78	Winnipeg Jets, WHA	77	63	59	122	60	9	9	6	15	2
1978–79	New York Rangers, NHL	80	33	45	78	33	18	4	5	9	12
ChCup–79	NHL All-Stars	2	0	0	0	0					
1979–80	New York Rangers, NHL	80	32	39	71	21	9	3	2	5	7
1980–81	New York Rangers, NHL	80	30	40	70	52	14	8	8	16	6
CCup–81	Sweden	5	4	2	6	0					
1981–82	New York Rangers, NHL	4	0	1	1	0					
1982–83	New York Rangers, NHL	78	25	34	59	12	9	4	8	12	4
1983–84	New York Rangers, NHL	79	32	35	67	16	5	1	0	1	0
1984–85	New York Rangers, NHL	64	20	31	51	10	3	2	1	3	2
	Sweden Totals	*	*	*	*	*	*	*	*	*	*
	WEC/CCup/ChalCup Totals	51	24	20	44	10					
	WHA Totals	286	236	222	458	201	42	35	28	63	30
	NHL Totals	465	172	225	397	144	58	22	24	46	31

WHA First All-Star Team (1976, 1977, 1978)
WHA Second All-Star Team (1975, 1978)
Won Bill Masterton Trophy (1985)
Won Lou Kaplan Trophy – WHA Rookie of the Year (1975)
Won AVCO Cup (1976, 1978)

In a ceremony during the 1997 World Championship in Finland, Anders Hedberg and Tumba Johansson were among those inducted into the European Hockey Hall of Fame.

After completing his hockey career, Hedberg spent several years scouting for talented players in Europe for the Toronto Maple Leafs and was appointed assistant general manager of the team. In August 1999 Swedish newspapers reported that Hedberg had turned down an offer to continue as Toronto's scout. Back in Sweden, he now serves as general manager for the Swedish national team. During the round-robin portion of the Salt Lake City Olympics, the Swedes appeared to be the odds-on favorites to take gold and looked particularly strong in a 5–2 thrashing of Canada. However, the Swedes returned home without a medal after a shocking loss to Belarus in the medal round—a game that some say is the biggest upset in Olympic hockey history.

After the demise of the WHA, Anders Hedberg played seven seasons with the New York Rangers.

Viktor Shalimov

It was in the winter of 1975–76 that hockey teams from the USSR—Central Red Army and Krylja Sovetov (Soviet Wings)—first played a series of games against NHL teams in North America. After one of the goals scored by the Wings in their last game against the New York Islanders, all the players on the Soviet bench burst out laughing. It was scored by Viktor Shalimov, who was playing on a forward line together with Vladimir Shadrin and Alexander Yakushev, and the goal actually was kind of funny.

"We were doing our best to defend our net because we were one man short," Shalimov recalls. "One of our players lobbed the puck into the Islanders' zone. I rushed into their zone just in case, although I realized that the American goalie would be the first to reach the puck. And then the unexpected happened. The goalie's stick split in half. Shadrin yells to me, 'Shoot!' A defenseman took up the goalie's position in the net. Then I zipped behind the net, and the defenseman followed me. I managed to sweep around the net, but he didn't, and by that time the puck had already crossed the goal crease…"

In that series, Shalimov scored a goal in every game—into the nets of Pittsburgh, Buffalo, Chicago and the New York Islanders. Together with Valeri Kharlamov and Sergei Kapustin, Shalimov chalked up the greatest number of points among the Soviet players.

Whenever Shalimov played in games at the highest level, he almost always played well or even brilliantly. But he sometimes missed out on the most crucial games. In the 1974 series against the best of the WHA, the coach of the Soviet team, Boris Kulagin, kept the Spartak right wing in reserve for seven games and let him out on the ice only in the last game. And Shalimov scored two goals. The following spring, at the age of 24, Shalimov made his debut in the World Championships. And right off the bat he racked up the highest number of points, in games against Germany. The Spartak forward line proved to be the best in the Soviet lineup. A year later,

When the Soviet Wings played a series of games against NHL clubs in the winter of 1975–76, Viktor Shalimov scored a goal in every game.

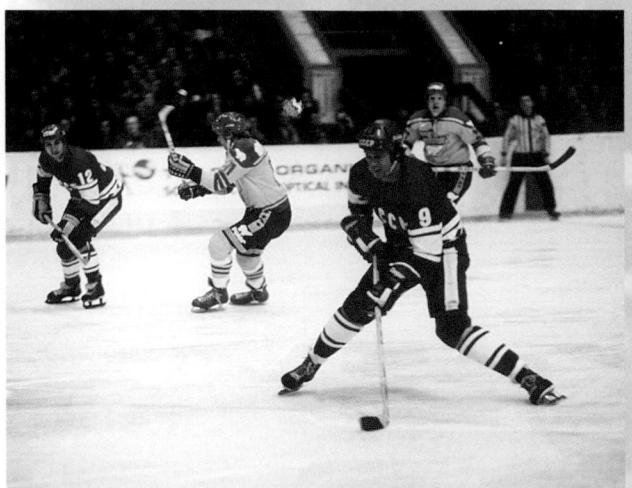

Viktor Shalimov (front) always played well and was frequently brilliant in high-level games.

Shalimov made his Olympic debut. Once again, Shadrin's line was tops in the Soviet squad, while Shalimov was among the highest scorers.

In 1976 Spartak won the championship title. It appeared that Shalimov had a long and productive career ahead of him. But Spartak was a capricious and uneven team. Coaches came and went. Shalimov was matched up with faster partners and earmarked as the playmaker. Not only that, his line was often given the job of neutralizing the leading players of the strongest opposing teams.

Shalimov, who had joined the world of hockey to score goals, win victories and experience thrills, was starting to get bored. He spent time wasting away in secondary roles until he was placed on Spartak's main forward line together with Shadrin and Yakushev. At that time, the line thrived on Yakushev's scoring talents. His partners merely fed passes to him. But with the arrival of Shalimov, the forward line experienced rejuvenation. Things started to click. The scoring ability of all three players evened out and Yakushev got his second wind. Their game began to really sparkle.

Shalimov was always thought of as an optimist, and he glowed when everything was running smoothly for the team. When a game was well played, he couldn't contain his enthusiasm and had to share it with others. But in the second half of the 1970s, he began to wilt. He went through a long drought during which the coaches of the national team seemed to have forgotten his name.

Having slept through some of the best years of his hockey life, he tuned back into the game in 1980 on the eve of this 30th birthday. Boris Kulagin, the new coach of Spartak, shook up the lines in an attempt to bring the team out of its slump. The virtually unknown Sergei Shepelev and the famous Sergei Kapustin were paired off with Shalimov, and once again an excellent forward line began to produce results on the ice.

More than anyone else, Shalimov was thrilled with the realignment. He got a chance to relive the glory days of the mid-1970s. He once again gave his game everything he had, stickhandling his way around the ice at top speed in the best tradition of Soviet hockey.

The Shepelev line outperformed the others during the 1981 World Championship. In the final match against Sweden, the USSR nationals routed the hosts by a remarkable score of 13–1. Leading up to the second Canada Cup tournament, nobody doubted that Shalimov, Shepelev and Kapustin would be picked for the Soviet national squad. In

Shalimov, Viktor
RW, 5'11", 170 lbs, b: Moscow, USSR, 4/20/1951

Season	Club, League	Regular Season				
		GP	G	A	Pts	PIM
1969–70	Spartak Moscow, USSR	2	1	*	*	*
1970–71	Spartak Moscow, USSR	15	6	*	*	*
1971–72	Spartak Moscow, USSR	32	13	*	*	*
1972–73	Spartak Moscow, USSR	30	16	*	*	*
1973–74	Spartak Moscow, USSR	32	17	10	27	18
1974–75	Spartak Moscow, USSR	36	20	11	31	6
WEC–75	USSR	10	11	8	19	2
1975–76	Spartak Moscow, USSR	36	28	25	53	8
OWG–76	USSR	6	7	7	14	2
WEC–76	USSR	10	3	5	8	2
CCup–76	USSR	1	0	1	1	0
1976–77	Spartak Moscow, USSR	36	18	17	35	10
WEC–77	USSR	6	4	0	4	0
1977–78	Spartak Moscow, USSR	36	26	11	37	10
1978–79	Spartak Moscow, USSR	42	12	17	29	18
1979–80	Spartak Moscow, USSR	44	34	19	53	12
1980–81	Spartak Moscow, USSR	47	21	32	53	12
WEC–81	USSR	8	3	4	7	2
CCup–81	USSR	7	2	2	4	2
1981–82	Spartak Moscow, USSR	47	27	32	59	34
WEC–82	USSR	10	8	5	13	8
1982–83	Spartak Moscow, USSR	44	14	16	30	18
1983–84	Spartak Moscow, USSR	44	24	21	45	4
1984–85	Spartak Moscow, USSR	49	16	22	38	30
	USSR Totals	572	293	*	*	*
	OWG/WEC/CCup Totals	58	38	32	70	18

Named Best Forward at WEC (1982)
Won OWG (1976)
Won WEC (1975, 1981, 1982)
Won CCup (1981)
USSR Champion (1976)

that tournament, the Shepelev forward line put in an incredible performance. In the most important games—the semifinal game against Czechoslovakia and the final against Canada—Shalimov and Shepelev cooked up some real magic, dazzling the spectators with their feints and lightning passes. In tough contests on rinks narrower than Shalimov was accustomed to, he proved that he didn't have to have free, open spaces for his style of play to work. He was in such good shape that, against all resistance, he was able to create his own free ice.

The magic lasted through one more World Championship. Shalimov was older than his partners and called it quits before the others. In spite of his quiet years, he was a truly remarkable hockey player. He had a refined feel for the game and displayed a high degree of coordination, maneuverability and self-composure. He was almost an ideal hockey player, but right to the end, he never felt he was the master of his own fate.

Butch Goring

Robert "Butch" Goring's 16-year career included time with Los Angeles and Boston, but he will best be remembered for helping the New York Islanders win the Stanley Cup four times in the early 1980s.

Drafted by Los Angeles in 1969, Goring was promoted from Springfield to the Kings during his first pro season. He was supposed to stay in Los Angeles the next year, but a serious case of mononucleosis forced him to miss much of the season and he spent the rest of the year in Springfield getting his health and his timing back. After that he became a steady but unspectacular regular with the Kings for nine years, averaging 30 goals a season though not getting much credit because he played on the remote West Coast.

Butch Goring was famous for a helmet he was given when he was 12 years old and continued to wear for his whole career as a pro.

In Los Angeles, he developed into one of the most complete players in the league. An excellent penalty killer, he could also score goals with the best of them. He was good on face-offs and was a team leader in the dressing room. His passing was first-rate and he had a reputation for being one of the best shooters on breakaways. He also had an "iron man" streak, going 379 games without missing one to injury.

A long-time racehorse owner, Goring was famous for a helmet that he was given when he was 12 years old and continued to wear his entire professional career. He was also known for being one of the poorer dressers in the league, a fact confirmed by a robber. On a road trip with the Kings, a burglar sneaked into his hotel room and took everything that belonged to his roommate but left all of Goring's clothes hanging in the closet untouched.

After the 1977–78 season, he was offered a huge five-year, $1-million contract by the Edmonton Oilers, then still in the WHA. Although he turned that incredible offer down, he realized he wasn't under-appreciated around the league, a fact verified at the trading deadline during the 1979–80 season. Just before midnight, Islanders general manager Bill Torrey acquired Goring for Billy Harris and Dave Lewis. "We decided we had to have a second grade A center to take the

His passing was first-rate and Butch Goring (front) was rated one of the best shooters on breakaways.

pressure off Bryan Trottier if we were going to get anywhere," Torrey explained. "It's no secret our first choice was Darryl Sittler. When I realized Sittler was going to at least finish the year in Toronto, I figured Goring was the next best of those centers who might be available."

The trade was sheer genius and had exactly the desired effect for the New Yorkers. That same spring, Goring helped the Islanders win their first Stanley Cup, and the next year he was awarded the Conn Smythe Trophy for being the outstanding player of those playoffs. In all, he won four championships in a row with the Islanders and filled just about every role imaginable on the team. "I've always taken pride in the fact that I can play better when I don't have the puck than most guys," he said. "It takes a lot of self-discipline. Probably some people don't even notice you're out there, but it's a role I like."

After winning the Conn Smythe, Goring was named the team's player-assistant coach, a role that in practical terms meant running the penalty-killing during practice. But this experience gave him his first taste of coaching responsibilities, and he savored every moment. After being traded to Boston during the 1984–85 season, he knew he was near the end of his career, but he was determined to be a coach one day. That opportunity came in 1985 when the Bruins hired him to replace Harry Sinden, who was filling in temporarily behind the bench after firing Gerry Cheevers. His dream job lasted only a year and a half. After being fired by Boston, he reported with full equipment to the Halifax Oilers, the AHL affiliate of the Edmonton Oilers, in the hope of reviving his playing career. After just 10 uneventful games with Halifax, he retired from play for good and went on to coach the New York Islanders for the 1999–2000 season.

Prior to the 2001-02 season, Goring accepted the head coaching job with the Frankfurt Lions, but still has aspirations of returning to the NHL coaching ranks.

Goring, Butch
C, 5′9″, 170 lbs, b: St. Boniface, Man., 10/22/1949

Season	Club, League	Regular Season					Playoffs				
		GP	G	A	Pts	PIM	GP	G	A	Pts	PIM
1969–70	Los Angeles Kings, NHL	59	13	23	36	8					
	Springfield Kings, AHL	19	13	7	20	0					
1970–71	Los Angeles Kings, NHL	19	2	5	7	2					
	Springfield Kings, AHL	40	23	32	55	4	12	11	14	25	0
1971–72	Los Angeles Kings, NHL	74	21	29	50	2					
1972–73	Los Angeles Kings, NHL	67	28	31	59	2					
1973–74	Los Angeles Kings, NHL	70	28	33	61	2	5	0	1	1	0
1974–75	Los Angeles Kings, NHL	60	27	33	60	6	3	0	0	0	0
1975–76	Los Angeles Kings, NHL	80	33	40	73	8	9	2	3	5	4
1976–77	Los Angeles Kings, NHL	78	30	55	85	6	9	7	5	12	0
1977–78	Los Angeles Kings, NHL	80	37	36	73	2	2	0	0	0	2
1978–79	Los Angeles Kings, NHL	80	36	51	87	16	2	0	0	0	0
1979–80	Los Angeles Kings, NHL	69	20	48	68	12					
	New York Islanders, NHL	12	6	5	11	2	21	7	12	19	2
1980–81	New York Islanders, NHL	78	23	37	60	0	18	10	10	20	2
CCup–81	Canada	7	3	2	5	4					
1981–82	New York Islanders, NHL	67	15	17	32	10	19	6	5	11	12
1982–83	New York Islanders, NHL	75	19	20	39	8	20	4	8	12	4
1983–84	New York Islanders, NHL	71	22	24	46	8	21	1	5	6	2
1984–85	New York Islanders, NHL	29	2	5	7	2					
	Boston Bruins, NHL	39	13	21	34	6	5	1	1	2	0
1986–87	Nova Scotia Oilers, AHL	10	3	5	8	2					
	NHL Totals	1107	375	513	888	102	134	38	50	88	28
	CCup Totals	7	3	2	5	4					

Won Conn Smythe Trophy (1981)
Won Lady Byng Trophy (1978)
Won Bill Masterton Trophy (1978)
Won Stanley Cup (1980, 1981, 1982, 1983)

Darryl Sittler

During much of his long stay with the Toronto Maple Leafs, Darryl Sittler was the team's best and most popular player. He had a choppy skating style, but his great hands and work ethic, combined with the size and toughness needed to survive as a marked man in a tough era of hockey, enabled him to become the career points leader in Toronto's rich history. Unfortunately for Sittler, the stories surrounding the Leafs organization during his playing days were mostly negative, especially in his conflict-ridden final years with the team.

During much of his long stay with the Maple Leafs, Darryl Sittler (front) was the team's best and most popular player.

Born in 1950 in Kitchener, Ontario, one of eight children in the Sittler family, Darryl first played his way to prominence with the London Knights of the Ontario Hockey Association. Sittler played a determined game and the Leafs made him the eighth pick overall in the 1970 Entry Draft. He saw limited action in his first pro season in 1970–71 and had an unremarkable sophomore year. In 1972–73, he began to establish himself as an offensive star, finishing with 77 points—a total he would better in all but three of his subsequent 12 seasons in the NHL. The Leafs were in a rebuilding phase early in his career and many veterans either retired or were traded. When Dave Keon moved to the World Hockey Association, the 24-year-old Sittler took over the captain's duties, becoming the second-youngest captain in Leafs history after Teeder Kennedy.

Sittler had an incredible year in 1975–76. On February 7, 1976, he produced the greatest offensive game in the history of the National Hockey League, guaranteeing his place in the record books even after such potent forces as Wayne Gretzky and Mario Lemieux had come and gone. Toronto was hosting the Boston Bruins, a team on a seven-game winning streak. The Bruins had recently reacquired Gerry Cheevers, but coach Don Cherry wanted to give the goalie a rest before his upcoming Boston homecoming and started rookie net-minder Dave Reece instead. The Leafs beat up the Bruins 11–4, but Sittler was the big story. He had two assists in the first period, three goals and two assists in the second and another hat-trick in the third. The total of six goals and four assists set a league record for points in one game that had previously been held by Maurice "Rocket" Richard with eight.

"Look at my face [in video highlights] on the 10th point, when I tried to pass in front and it hit Brad Park's skate and went in," Sittler said

Sittler, Darryl
C, 6´, 190 lbs, b: Kitchener, Ont., 9/18/1950

Season	Club, League	Regular Season					Playoffs				
		GP	G	A	Pts	PIM	GP	G	A	Pts	PIM
1970–71	Toronto Maple Leafs, NHL	49	10	8	18	37	6	2	1	3	31
1971–72	Toronto Maple Leafs, NHL	74	15	17	32	44	3	0	0	0	2
1972–73	Toronto Maple Leafs, NHL	78	29	48	77	69					
1973–74	Toronto Maple Leafs, NHL	78	38	46	84	55	4	2	1	3	6
1974–75	Toronto Maple Leafs, NHL	72	36	44	80	47	7	2	1	3	15
1975–76	Toronto Maple Leafs, NHL	79	41	59	100	90	10	5	7	12	19
CCup–76	Canada	7	4	2	6	4					
1976–77	Toronto Maple Leafs, NHL	73	38	52	90	89	9	5	16	21	4
1977–78	Toronto Maple Leafs, NHL	80	45	72	117	100	13	3	8	11	12
1978–79	Toronto Maple Leafs, NHL	70	36	51	87	69	6	5	4	9	17
ChCup–79	NHL All-Stars	3	0	1	1	0					
1979–80	Toronto Maple Leafs, NHL	73	40	57	97	62	3	1	2	3	10
1980–81	Toronto Maple Leafs, NHL	80	43	53	96	77	3	0	0	0	4
1981–82	Toronto Maple Leafs, NHL	38	18	20	38	24					
	Philadelphia Flyers, NHL	35	14	18	32	50	4	3	1	4	6
WEC–82	Canada	10	4	3	7	2					
1982–83	Philadelphia Flyers, NHL	80	43	40	83	60	3	1	0	1	4
WEC–83	Canada	10	3	1	4	12					
1983–84	Philadelphia Flyers, NHL	76	27	36	63	38	3	0	2	2	7
1984–85	Detroit Red Wings, NHL	61	11	16	27	37	2	0	2	2	0
	NHL Totals	1096	484	637	1121	948	76	29	45	74	137
	WEC/CCup/ChalCup Totals	30	11	7	18	18					

NHL Second All-Star Team (1978)
Won CCup (1976)

On February 7, 1976, Darryl Sittler (right) produced the greatest offensive game in NHL history with six goals and four assists.

in 1994. "That smile and shrug say it all. As much as people fault Reece, it was just a night when everything I shot and passed somehow found the way to the right place." Reece's career lasted only 14 games and Sittler never spoke in person with the goalie. He did, however, receive some news in 1996 while visiting Lake Placid, New York. "His niece recognized me in the crowd and said, 'I think you know my uncle,'" Sittler recalled. "Apparently he's teaching school in Rhode Island or somewhere in New England. I hope he's doing well for himself."

The big night helped Sittler become the first Leaf to reach the 100 mark in scoring in a season, collecting 41 goals and 59 assists. But he wasn't finished. During the playoffs in April against the Philadelphia Flyers, Sittler scored five goals in one game, tying the playoff record. In September, during the Canada Cup in Montreal, Sittler would make headlines again with his scoring ways. This time it wasn't the quantity but the quality and the timeliness that made the impression. In overtime of the second game of the best-of-three finals versus Czechoslovakia, Sittler held onto the puck on a partial breakaway until Czech goalie Vladimir Dzurilla committed himself and an opening presented itself. The goal secured the championship and made Sittler an overnight hero in Canada.

In 1977–78, Sittler registered 117 points and was selected to league's Second All-Star Team. The Leafs had their best playoff showing in years, making it to the semifinals. But things began to fall apart, for the franchise and for its captain, in 1979–80 when cantankerous owner Harold Ballard replaced much of his management, bringing in Punch Imlach to run the team. Sittler was represented by Alan Eagleson, a lawyer and agent who never saw eye to eye with Ballard or Imlach. Relations were strained to the point that Sittler took a pair of scissors to the "C" on his sweater before a game in late 1979 to protest, among other things, the trade of Lanny McDonald to the Colorado Rockies. Ballard then threatened to lock Sittler out before the beginning of the next season. The two men resolved some of their differences and Sittler returned as captain, but it was a tenuous reconciliation. Midway through the 1981–82 season, Sittler went AWOL and demanded a trade. He was depressed and worn out from his battles with management in Toronto. In January he was sent to the Philadelphia Flyers, a one-time nemesis but a team that nonetheless had a great deal of respect for Sittler.

After recovering from the nasty divorce with the Leafs, Sittler had a great season in 1982-83, netting 83 points and a spot in the All-Star Game. He was shocked when Philadelphia traded him to the Detroit Red Wings before the 1984–85 season. Unsure if he wanted to continue and move his family to yet another city, Sittler refused to report for five days. He did end up playing one year with Detroit, though at times he struggled to find a place in the lineup. He retired after the season.

Darryl Sittler was inducted into the Hockey Hall of Fame in 1989, but returned to the Leafs two years later, this time in management, in marketing and public relations. Under the leadership of new president and general manager Cliff Fletcher, Sittler was given a greater role in the organization and remains with the Leafs as community representative, working in marketing, promotions and public relations. On October 6, 2001, Sittler lost his 53-year-old wife, Wendy, to cancer.

Sergei Kapustin

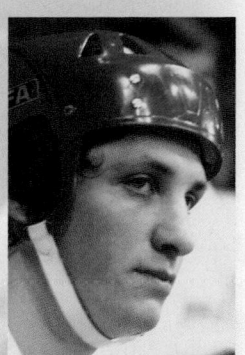

During the early 1980s, a computer analysis was done to find out who the ideal hockey player was, the one most capable of success on the ice. The computer searched a database for the best physical characteristics and playing style of a star and came up with Sergei Kapustin. More recently, a scout who was assessing hockey players across the board stated that, "Among the '70s generation of Russian players, the most talented ones were Kharlamov and Kapustin."

A powerful skater equipped with a smashing wrist shot, Kapustin had what it took to become an NHL star forward such as Bobby Hull or Brett Hull if he'd wanted it, but it never happened.

Had he lived—he died before turning 40—Kapustin would probably smile inwardly if he heard this assessment. He was essentially a lone wolf, finding and hanging on to his place in the pack but never leading it.

He entered pro hockey right at a time when a new, tougher kind of play was being introduced in Europe. Kapustin was in the right place at the right time. He disliked nursing the puck like the great wingers before him. When faced with a decision, he never hesitated to make a pass via the boards.

Kapustin was never formally taught to play hockey in his small northern home town of Ukhta. Up in the land of white silence, they never needed artificial ice, for the natural ice lasted from October through May. "I remember when I was a kid," Kapustin would recall, "they would announce over the radio that because of severe frost, classes in school were suspended, and we would play with the puck from dawn till dusk."

The young forward left his home town when invited by Boris Kulagin to join Krylja Sovetov (Soviet Wings). Of the many goals he scored during his career, Kapustin admitted that only two or three dozen were memorable. He scored his very first goal playing against a powerful opponent—CSKA. "I just ended an intricate offensive play," was how he modestly described it. "Nothing important."

Here is his verbatim recollection of another memorable goal, scored at the 1978 World Championship against Canada: "I sped up to their zone and emerged to the right of the goal. A defenseman cornered me, and I pretended to stop. He took the bait, and I then charged ahead and pretended to shoot. The goalie moved to the far corner while I turned 180 degrees, like a screwdriver, and shot at the opposite corner."

He could score a goal out of nowhere, as in the second, decisive game of the 1979 Challenge Cup tournament, where his goal doomed the Canadians. He had a 50% accuracy rate—one out of every two shots on the opponent's net would score.

A powerful skater with a smashing wrist shot, Sergei Kapustin had all it takes to become an NHL star.

Kapustin, Sergei
LW, 5′11″, 194 lbs, b: Ukhta, USSR, 2/13/1953, d: 1988

Season	Club, League	Regular Season				
		GP	G	A	Pts	PIM
1970–71	Neftianik Ukhta (2), USSR	*	*	*	*	*
1971–72	Krylja Sovetov, USSR	30	12	*	*	*
1972–73	Krylja Sovetov, USSR	32	14	7	21	26
1973–74	Krylja Sovetov, USSR	32	12	8	20	26
WEC–74	USSR	10	10	1	11	6
1974–75	Krylja Sovetov, USSR	32	23	9	32	20
WEC–75	USSR	10	10	3	13	2
1975–76	Krylja Sovetov, USSR	36	25	13	38	34
OWG–76	USSR	6	6	1	7	8
WEC–76	USSR	5	3	1	4	0
CCup–76	USSR	5	3	3	6	0
1976–77	Krylja Sovetov, USSR	23	15	4	19	29
WEC–77	USSR	10	9	7	16	7
1977–78	CSKA, USSR	33	9	11	20	16
WEC–78	USSR	10	6	5	11	10
1978–79	CSKA, USSR	42	21	15	36	28
WEC–79	USSR	8	6	1	7	12
1979–80	CSKA, USSR	30	18	14	32	12
1980–81	Spartak Moscow, USSR	45	36	25	61	30
WEC–81	USSR	8	4	4	8	2
CCup–81	USSR	6	2	2	4	6
1981–82	Spartak Moscow, USSR	38	30	22	52	32
WEC–82	USSR	10	3	9	12	8
1982–83	Spartak Moscow, USSR	44	12	8	20	38
WEC–83	USSR	10	4	3	7	6
1983–84	Spartak Moscow, USSR	41	22	21	45	46
1984–85	Spartak Moscow, USSR	19	5	1	6	10
1985–86	Spartak Moscow, USSR	38	23	13	36	50
	USSR Totals	519	277	*	*	*
	OWG/WEC/CCup Totals	98	66	40	106	67

Won OWG (1976)
Won WEC (1974, 1975, 1978, 1979, 1981, 1982, 1983)
Won CCup (1981)
USSR Champion (1974, 1978, 1979, 1980)

Sergei Kapustin was never formally taught to play hockey in his small northern home town of Ukhta.

"Your business is to score and you have to do anything to make it happen," his first and favorite coach, Boris Kulagin, would tell him. And he scored whenever he wanted to. The catch was, he didn't always seem to want to.

He played on internationally acclaimed forward lines. First he was teamed with Helmut Balderis and Viktor Zhluktov on the Soviet national team. Kapustin and Balderis were then sent to CSKA. The wingers were ideal partners who developed a good friendship on and off the ice.

Coach Kulagin then created a forward line for Spartak that consisted of Viktor Shalimov, Sergei Shepelev and Kapustin. National team coach Viktor Tikhonov took them to the 1981 Canada Cup, where the Spartak teammates skated circles around the dismayed Canadians. Their greatest triumph was the final game, where they trounced Canada 8–1. Shalimov was the solo star then, with Kapustin assisting.

He was always put on the national team, whether he played for the Wings, CSKA or Spartak. He played and won consistently, but it didn't matter to him whether he was included on the All-Star teams or not.

Kapustin never knew what he wanted to achieve in hockey or in life. Alexander Mogilny, another player who came to Moscow from the hinterland, resembled Kapustin a great deal in his playing style. Unlike Kapustin, however, Mogilny burned the whole time he played in Russia with ambition to play in the NHL. When his dream came true, he was set for life. Kapustin never had that kind of ambition and in the end lived a short and confused life.

Billy **Smith**

Goalie Billy Smith battled just about everyone and everything during his long and glorious NHL career.

Goalie Billy Smith battled just about everything and everyone during his long and glorious National Hockey League career. He fought opposing players, using his stick like a scythe to rid his crease of encroaching forwards; he fought the media with his bold tirades; and he occasionally took on his own teammates and coaches, challenging them to raise their performance to match his own. Most of all, though, Battling Billy fought the puck he hated and attempted to keep away, especially when the Stanley Cup was on the line. Combative and competitive, Smith was one of the best of his era, winning the Stanley Cup four consecutive times with the New York Islanders at the beginning of the 1980s.

He was born in Perth, Ontario, in 1950 and learned the hard knocks of the netminding trade in junior hockey in Smiths Falls and with the Cornwall Royals in the Quebec junior league. Smith was drafted by the Los Angeles Kings, the team's sixth selection and 59th overall, in the 1970 Amateur Draft. He played the next two seasons with the Springfield Kings in the American Hockey League and led the squad to the Calder Cup in 1971. He played five games with Los Angeles before he was claimed by the Islanders in the 1972 Expansion Draft, a move that changed his life.

In his first season on Long Island, he earned a record number of penalty minutes for a goalie and actually fought some of the league's tougher forwards. In one game against the Buffalo Sabres, Smith broke three of his sticks on the ankles of opposing players in one period. "A goaltender has to protect his crease," Smith said. "If they're going to come that close, I have to use any means to get them out of there. If I have to use my stick, I'll use my stick." And he did. Soon he was called "Hatchet Man."

After several difficult early years with the expansion Islanders, Smith was left as the number one goalie in 1974–75 when veteran incumbent Gerry Desjardins bolted to the World Hockey Association. Smith would play 58 games that year and his winning record led New York into the playoffs for the first time. In those playoffs, however, Glenn "Chico" Resch, a rookie, grabbed the spotlight in a few important games as the Islanders went further into the post-season than expected.

For the next few seasons, coach Al Arbour made both men his "number one goaltender." Still, Resch stole most of the attention because of his outgoing personality. The two goalies were friends and even played tennis together—a sport Smith credited with improving his footwork—and supported one another on the ice, but Resch loved to talk to the reporters and fans. Smith stayed quiet or gave terse replies when he was interviewed. But the two opposites were solid on the ice and helped make the Islanders into a powerhouse in the late 1970s.

When the 1980 Stanley Cup playoffs began, Smith was the Islanders' main netminder. He played all but one of the Islanders' 21 games while on their way to the team's first Stanley Cup. Midway through the 1980–81 season, Resch was traded to the Colorado Rockies. The Islanders, with Smith dominating in the playoffs, went on to win their second consecutive Cup. Smith was a hero in New York, but his aggressive style and his petulance enraged fans throughout the league.

"I know I'm not a well-liked hockey player," he said in the middle of the 1982 season. "You go into any city in the league and they'll be more than willing to tell you that. But if I were traded to any other hockey team, I'd probably be welcomed by just about everybody—even though they hate my guts now."

Only once, in 1982, did Smith lead the league in goals against to take the Vezina Trophy. But five times, from 1980 to 1984, he led the NHL in playoff victories. With his clutch play and the increased number of games in the expanded post-season format—from three rounds to four, from best-of-five to best-of-seven—Smith quickly surpassed all other goalies in playoff wins. He passed Ken Dryden on April 28, 1984, in a win over the Montreal Canadiens, his 81st victory. Smith, as usual, was less than impressed with the individual honor.

"I know I got the record," Smith said following the game. "So what? The only thing that's important is winning. You can get all the records you want, but if we don't win the Stanley Cup, it means nothing."

Aside from his reputation as a clutch performer, Billy Smith (left) is also remembered for scoring the first goal by a netminder.

Smith, Billy
G, 5´10˝, 185 lbs, b: Perth, Ont., 12/12/1950

Season	Club, League	Regular Season				Playoffs			
		GP	Mins	GA	Avg	GP	Mins	GA	Avg
1970–71	Springfield Kings, AHL	49	2728	160	3.51	11	682	29	2.56
1971–72	Los Angeles Kings, NHL	5	300	23	4.60				
	Springfield Kings, AHL	28	1649	77	2.80	4	192	13	4.06
1972–73	New York Islanders, NHL	37	2122	147	4.16				
1973–74	New York Islanders, NHL	46	2615	134	3.07				
1974–75	New York Islanders, NHL	58	3368	156	2.78	6	333	23	4.14
1975–76	New York Islanders, NHL	39	2254	98	2.61	8	437	21	2.88
1976–77	New York Islanders, NHL	36	2089	87	2.50	10	580	27	2.79
1977–78	New York Islanders, NHL	38	2154	95	2.65	1	47	1	1.28
1978–79	New York Islanders, NHL	40	2261	108	2.87	5	315	10	1.90
1979–80	New York Islanders, NHL	38	2114	104	2.95	20	1198	56	2.80
1980–81	New York Islanders, NHL	41	2363	129	3.28	17	994	42	2.54
CCup–81	Canada	0	0	0	0.00	0	0	0	0.00
1981–82	New York Islanders, NHL	46	2685	133	2.97	18	1120	47	2.52
1982–83	New York Islanders, NHL	41	2340	112	2.87	17	962	43	2.68
1983–84	New York Islanders, NHL	42	2279	130	3.42	21	1190	54	2.72
1984–85	New York Islanders, NHL	37	2090	133	3.82	6	342	19	3.33
1985–86	New York Islanders, NHL	41	2308	143	3.72	1	60	4	4.00
1986–87	New York Islanders, NHL	40	2252	132	3.52	2	67	1	0.90
1987–88	New York Islanders, NHL	38	2107	113	3.22				
1988–89	New York Islanders, NHL	17	730	54	4.44				
	NHL Totals	680	38431	2031	3.17	132	7645	348	2.73
	CCup Totals	0	0	0	0.00	0	0	0	0.00

NHL First All-Star Team (1982)
Won Vezina Trophy (1982)
Won Conn Smythe Trophy (1983)
Won William M. Jennings Trophy (1983)
Won Stanley Cup (1980, 1981, 1982, 1983)

Aside from his reputation as a clutch performer, Smith is also remembered for scoring the first goal by a netminder, though he had little to do with actually putting the puck in the opponent's net. The Islanders were playing in Denver against the Colorado Rockies on November 28, 1979. In the early minutes of the third period, the referee signaled a delayed penalty against the Islanders. Colorado coach Don Cherry pulled his goalie for the extra attacker. The puck was sent into the New York zone and bounced off Smith's chest into the corner. Rockies defenseman Rob Ramage moved in from the point to collect it but then made a blind pass to the position he'd just vacated. The puck floated 190 feet down the ice into the Rockies' unprotected net. The goal was at first given to Islander defenseman Dave Lewis, but after the game the official scorer viewed the tapes and Smith, as the last Islander to touch the puck, was given credit for the goal. It didn't help New York, as the Islanders lost the game 7–4, but it was a historic use of the chest protector!

Billy Smith retired from the game after the 1988–89 season, still an Islander. He finished his career with 305 wins and 88 more in the playoffs. He stayed with the Islanders for several years as a goaltending coach before joining the Florida Panthers organization in the same capacity. In 1993 this unique winner, who danced to the beat of his own drum throughout his hockey life, was inducted into the Hockey Hall of Fame.

Borje **Salming**

It could be argued that every Swedish player collecting a salary in the NHL today owes a share to Borje Salming.

It could be argued that every Swedish player collecting a salary in the NHL today owes a share to Borje Salming. Way back in 1973, he opened the doors to North American professional hockey for his fellow countrymen. At that time, after the first Summit Series, Canadians and Americans had come to respect the disciples of the Soviet hockey school, but the Scandinavian players were nicknamed "Swedish chickens." The joke was based on Sweden's national colors, but no doubt it had a double meaning. Borje Salming helped eradicate that stereotype. Six years after he retired in North America, the name of the "King"—his nickname in Toronto—was immortalized in the Hockey Hall of Fame. Salming was the first Swede to be so honored.

Salming ended up in Canada quite by accident. In 1973 the Toronto Maple Leafs were interested in a different Swede, the winger Inge Hammarstrom. Leafs scout Gerry McNamara, who happened to be in Sweden at the time, saw Salming in action and immediately called his boss in Canada to tell him about another Scandinavian genius. Salming remembered it as follows: "For me, hockey then was rather a hobby than a job. Leaving for Canada, I was thinking, 'Well, I'll try, and if I fail on the Toronto Maple Leafs, I'll play a little in minor leagues and then go back home.' It so happened, though, that I spent 17 seasons in the NHL, and if you're working for so long in the major leagues, you can achieve something."

Salming was too modest. In his first game with the team, Toronto defeated Buffalo 7–4 and he was voted the best player. At the end of his first season, the Swedish rookie had 39 points—an excellent result for a defenseman. But he had more trouble than it might have appeared adapting to the North American game. "Early in the morning, before my first appearance with the Maple Leafs, Tommy Bergman, Sweden's coach, called me. We talked about the nasty morals in the NHL, how awful it was that players were prone to fistfighting, and all that. Back then, if players took off their gloves during a regular-season game in Sweden, they were immediately given a two-minute penalty and disqualified for a number of subsequent games. I didn't have an opportunity to use my fists in my first game, but during my second, I clashed with Philadelphia's captain, Dave Schultz. I wasn't bad in my first fight. I didn't permit him to drop me to the ice—that's important, and I clutched Schultz so fiercely as if my life was at stake. Partners told me after that, 'Atta boy, Borje!' It was the toughest guy in the NHL—Sledgehammer Schultz! I was just sighing to myself, 'My God, where am I?'"

The Vancouver Canucks former coach Harry Neale once confessed that he urged his players to provoke Salming to get into fights. "That sounds stupid today, but at that time there was a common belief that a European couldn't take that pressure. Yet Borje never complained, never avoided those clashes, and he was able to defend himself, so after a while he was left alone."

Having passed the "durability test," the King focused on the game itself and succeeded in it. In 16 seasons with Toronto, Salming made 620 assists (a club record) and scored 148 goals for 768 points. He was included on the First All-Star Team once and fives times on the Second All-Star Team, again a Toronto record. In 1980 he came up a few votes short for the Norris Trophy as the season's best defenseman. In the history of the Toronto Maple Leafs, only two players appeared in more games than Salming—George Armstrong and Tim Horton. The King appeared in 1,099 games. He added two goals and 17 assists to his personal scorecard after a season with the Detroit Red Wings as a free agent. Afterward, the 39-year-old veteran returned home and played for three seasons with AIK of Solna. The owner of a brewery and a garment factory, Salming has since abandoned hockey for business.

Salming is remembered for his slalom rushes across the rink and his powerful wrist shots in the style of Bobby Orr, as well as for his tricky but accurate passes so typical of the European game. Al Arbour, the great coach who in the early 1980s led the New York Islanders four times to the Stanley Cup, once commented on Salming when he was at the peak of his career. He called him a great athlete with an ability to perform excellently on both defense and offense. Yet, for a hockey player capable of gaining points on the offensive, his eagerness to be a human shield and stop a slapshot was quite incredible. And he did it without much hesitation. Arbour saw him for the first time in Moscow in 1973 and was highly impressed with his performance back then. But when his own team went up against Toronto, he lamented all those same qualities that made Salming a great player.

Salming, Borje
D, 6'1", 193 lbs, b: Kiruna, Sweden, 4/17/1951

Season	Club, League	Regular Season					Playoffs				
		GP	G	A	Pts	PIM	GP	G	A	Pts	PIM
1970–71	Brynas, Sweden	14	0	5	5	6	13	2	1	3	16
1971–72	Brynas, Sweden	14	1	1	2	20	14	0	4	4	30
WEC–72	Sweden	4	0	0	0	6					
1972–73	Brynas, Sweden	14	2	3	5	10	12	3	1	4	24
WEC–73	Sweden	10	4	6	10	8					
1973–74	Toronto Maple Leafs, NHL	76	5	34	39	48	4	0	1	1	4
1974–75	Toronto Maple Leafs, NHL	60	12	25	37	34	7	0	4	4	6
1975–76	Toronto Maple Leafs, NHL	78	16	41	57	70	10	3	4	7	9
CCup–76	Sweden	5	4	3	7	2					
1976–77	Toronto Maple Leafs, NHL	76	12	66	78	46	9	3	6	9	6
1977–78	Toronto Maple Leafs, NHL	80	16	60	76	70	6	2	2	4	6
1978–79	Toronto Maple Leafs, NHL	78	17	56	73	76	6	0	1	1	8
ChCup–79	NHL All-Stars	3	0	0	0	2					
1979–80	Toronto Maple Leafs, NHL	74	19	52	71	94	3	1	1	2	2
1980–81	Toronto Maple Leafs, NHL	72	5	61	66	154	3	0	2	2	4
CCup–81	Sweden	5	0	2	2	10					
1981–82	Toronto Maple Leafs, NHL	69	12	44	56	170					
1982–83	Toronto Maple Leafs, NHL	69	7	38	45	104	4	1	4	5	10
1983–84	Toronto Maple Leafs, NHL	68	5	38	43	92					
1984–85	Toronto Maple Leafs, NHL	73	6	33	39	76					
1985–86	Toronto Maple Leafs, NHL	41	7	15	22	48	10	1	6	7	14
1986–87	Toronto Maple Leafs, NHL	56	4	16	20	42	13	0	3	3	14
1987–88	Toronto Maple Leafs, NHL	66	2	24	26	82	6	1	3	4	8
1988–89	Toronto Maple Leafs, NHL	63	3	17	20	86					
WEC–89	Sweden	8	1	1	2	8					
1989–90	Detroit Red Wings, NHL	49	2	17	19	52					
1990–91	AIK, Sweden	36	4	9	13	46					
CCup–91	Sweden	6	0	0	0	10					
1991–92	AIK, Sweden	38	6	14	20	98	3	0	2	2	6
OWG–92	Sweden	8	4	3	7	4					
1992–93	AIK, Sweden	6	1	0	1	10					
	Sweden Totals	122	14	32	46	190	42	5	8	13	76
	OWG/WEC/CCup/ChalCup Totals	49	13	15	28	50					
	NHL Totals	1148	150	637	787	1344	81	12	37	49	91

NHL First All-Star Team (1977)
NHL Second All-Star Team (1975, 1976, 1978, 1979, 1980)
Sweden Champion (1971, 1972)

A HISTORY OF WORLD HOCKEY

Borje Salming

KINGS OF THE ICE

Former Leafs general manager Gord Stellick remembered: "If you saw how he was doing his exercises, you would know how much Borje was fond of hockey. I have always said Borje was born with hockey skates on his feet. I think he would have achieved more if he had played side by side with other great defensemen like Larry Robinson and Denis Potvin. At least the players who captured the Norris Trophy in subsequent years, Doug Wilson and Randy Carlyle, weren't as prominent in the league as Borje was in his time."

Borje Salming (left) is remembered for his slalom-style rushes, his powerful wrist shots in the style of Bobby Orr and the tricky but accurate passes typical of the European game.

Another of Salming's strengths was his phenomenal stamina. There are plenty of legends about him. According to one, he was born and brought up in Kiruna, a small coal-mining town near the Arctic Circle. He lived with a grandfather who bred reindeer. Once, the young Borje went hunting on skis and got lost. He knew he had to keep moving so he wouldn't freeze. The town doctor was surprised when, after several hours, a rescue team found him; an ordinary man would have collapsed from cold and exhaustion.

Even at 38, while Salming was playing out his last season in Toronto, he would spend 30 to 40 minutes on the ice per game. In 1986, in a game against the Detroit Red Wings, he was badly injured when his face was cut with a skate. In photos taken at the time, Salming looked like a character out of a horror movie. But three days later he was back on the ice.

In 1986, during an interview, Salming confessed that he took cocaine on occasion but had no addiction to it. He was immediately disqualified for eight games. Appreciating his honesty, Toronto fans stood behind their man and continued to cheer him on. "That was indeed a critical moment in my career, and I am happy the fans were kind to me. Speaking of utter triumph, I would say it was the game against the USSR at the 1976 Canada Cup. I feared they would condemn me for wearing Sweden's national jersey, but they gave me a standing ovation instead."

In 1996, before a game against Montreal, the audience at Maple Leaf Gardens gave him another standing ovation when Salming appeared as part of the ceremony dedicated to his induction into the Hockey Hall of Fame.

If Salming is so loved in Canada, what does he mean to Swedes? Mats Sundin, the Toronto Maple Leafs captain who began his hockey career in Salming's school, says: "Every Swede respects Borje and pays him tribute for what he has done. For us—Swedish hockey players—he is the man who showed us the right way; he is a trailblazer."

Rick Martin

Rick Martin was best known as the sniper on the Buffalo Sabres' French Connection Line.

Rick Martin was one of the NHL's elite marksmen in the 1970s. His mix of speed with a blistering shot was respected throughout the league, where he was best known as the sniper on the Buffalo Sabres' French Connection Line with Gilbert Perreault and Rene Robert.

After scoring 38 goals in 40 games for the Thetford Canadiens of the Quebec junior league in 1967–68, Martin joined the powerhouse Montreal Junior Canadiens of the OHA the next year. He and future NHL linemate Gilbert Perreault helped the squad win a Memorial Cup in 1969 and the two became close friends when Perreault boarded with Martin and his family in junior.

After a 71-goal season in 1970–71, Buffalo made Martin the fifth player chosen in the 1971

Nobody but those in attendance witnessed the historic 39th goal Rick Martin (left) scored as a rookie because the technicians at the CBC were on strike at the time.

Amateur Draft. Along the way, he spent a year at Sir George Williams University in Montreal before deciding that he couldn't pass up the financial potential of a pro hockey career.

The Sabres' interim coach, Joe Crozier, reunited Martin with his junior teammate Perreault. Martin proceeded to better Perrault's NHL rookie scoring records with 44 goals and 74 points. As Red Burnett wrote, "The young left winger has those important ingredients that go to make up a goal scorer: split-second timing and thinking, potent slap and wrist shots, which he gets off with surprising suddenness—ask any goaltender—classic moves in close either with the forehand or backhand." Martin also demonstrated a willingness to battle for the puck in the corners regardless of the foe.

His historic 39th goal as a rookie came in Maple Leaf Gardens against legendary goalie Jacques Plante. Unfortunately, nobody but those in attendance witnessed the feat since the CBC technicians were on strike at the time. Later that year Martin was selected to represent Canada in the 1972 Summit Series against the USSR. Discouraged by his lack of playing time, Martin left the team before the series concluded. Another concern for the young winger during his days with Team Canada was that he needed to prepare adequately for the coming season and would thus be better served at Buffalo's training camp.

Martin recorded consecutive 52-goal seasons in 1973–74 and 1974–75 and was selected to the NHL First All-Star Team both times. During the Sabres' drive to the Stanley Cup finals in 1975, he scored seven goals and made 15 points in 17 playoff matches. Martin finally got his chance to face the USSR on January 4, 1976, when he scored four goals in a 12–6 Buffalo rout over the touring Wings of the Soviet team. Later in the year he was picked to play for his country in the inaugural Canada Cup and registered four points in five contests for the victorious Canadians.

Although Martin's production slowed somewhat in the late 1970s, he did rebound with a 45-goal showing in 1979–80, playing chiefly with his old friend Perreault and Ric Seiling. The next year he was traded to the Los Angeles Kings but played only four games with his new club due to serious knee and back problems. Doctors warned Martin that he'd be crippled by the time he was 40 if he continued to play. He retired in 1981–82 after scoring nearly 400 goals and accumulating over 700 points but left the NHL with a bitter taste in his mouth. Martin felt the Sabres forced him to play hurt during his last year with the team.

After coming to terms with the end of his playing days, Martin opened his own restaurant in Niagara Falls, New York. He also operated an automotive shop in Buffalo, worked with a financial company and operated his own trucking firm. Martin even tried investing in a gold-mining project in West Africa that proved fairly successful and he later purchased a 120-acre farm in New York State.

Martin, Rick
LW, 5'11", 179 lbs, b: Verdun, Que., 7/26/1951

Season	Club, League	Regular Season					Playoffs				
		GP	G	A	Pts	PIM	GP	G	A	Pts	PIM
1971–72	Buffalo Sabres, NHL	73	44	30	74	36					
1972–73	Buffalo Sabres, NHL	75	37	36	73	79	6	3	2	5	12
1973–74	Buffalo Sabres, NHL	78	52	34	86	38					
1974–75	Buffalo Sabres, NHL	68	52	43	95	72	17	7	8	15	20
1975–76	Buffalo Sabres, NHL	80	49	37	86	67	9	4	7	11	12
CCup–76	Canada	4	3	2	5	0					
1976–77	Buffalo Sabres, NHL	66	36	29	65	58	6	2	1	3	9
1977–78	Buffalo Sabres, NHL	65	28	35	63	16	7	2	4	6	13
1978–79	Buffalo Sabres, NHL	73	32	21	53	35	3	0	3	3	0
1979–80	Buffalo Sabres, NHL	80	45	34	79	54	14	6	4	10	8
1980–81	Buffalo Sabres, NHL	23	7	14	21	20					
	Los Angeles Kings, NHL	1	1	1	2	0	1	0	0	0	0
1981–82	Los Angeles Kings, NHL	3	1	3	4	2					
	NHL Totals	685	384	317	701	477	63	24	29	53	74
	CCup Totals	4	3	2	5	0					

NHL First All-Star Team (1974, 1975)
NHL Second All-Star Team (1976, 1977)
Won CCup (1976)

Al Arbour

A place among the greatest head coaches in NHL history will always be held by Alger Joseph Arbour. His career totals of 1,606 games behind the bench and 781 victories trail only the legendary Scotty Bowman in the record ledger. Arbour's guidance contributed significantly to the New York Islanders' rapid ascent to competitive status in the 1970s and the club's subsequent run of four consecutive Stanley Cup wins from 1980 to 1983.

Al Arbour's career total of 1,606 games and 781 victories behind the bench trail only the legendary Scotty Bowman's.

The Sudbury, Ontario, native played defense on the junior Windsor Spitfires of the OHA. After distinguishing himself as an amateur, he was signed by the Detroit Red Wings and joined the pro ranks with the Edmonton Flyers of the Western Hockey League in 1952–53. He split the next four years between Alberta, the Motor City and Sherbrooke in the Quebec senior loop.

In 1957–58, Arbour played his first full NHL season in the red and white of the Wings. Following that season, he was claimed by the Chicago Black Hawks, where he toiled for three years including 1961, the year of the franchise's Stanley Cup triumph. Arbour next played five seasons with the Toronto Maple Leafs and earned his second Stanley Cup ring in 1962. After spending the 1966–67 season in the AHL, he returned to contribute experience and stability to the defense corps of the expansion St. Louis Blues in 1967–68. Early in 1970–71, he retired as a player after 600 games over 14 years. Arbour was also one of the few players in league history to wear glasses while playing.

Upon retiring, Arbour was immediately hired to stand in as coach of the Blues for the remainder of the 1970–71 schedule. During the last 50 games of the season, the team responded well by posting a 21–15–14 mark before falling to the Minnesota North Stars in the quarterfinals of the playoffs.

Arbour guided St. Louis on an interim basis over the next two seasons but jumped at the greatest challenge of his young coaching career in 1973. Prior to the 1973–74 schedule, the New York Islanders were coming off a difficult expansion season in which they'd accumulated a mere 30 points. The organization felt it had some promise and required a young, ambitious

Arbour, Al
D, 6´, 180 lbs, b: Sudbury, Ont., 11/1/1932

Season	Club, League	Regular Season					Playoffs				
		GP	G	A	Pts	PIM	GP	G	A	Pts	PIM
1952–53	Washington Lions, EHL	4	0	2	2	0					
	Edmonton Flyers, WHL	8	0	1	1	2	15	0	5	5	10
1953–54	Detroit Red Wings, NHL	36	0	1	1	18					
	Sherbrooke Saints, QHL	19	1	3	4	24	2	0	0	0	2
1954–55	Edmonton Flyers, WHL	41	3	9	12	39					
	Quebec Aces, QHL	20	4	5	9	55	4	0	0	0	2
1955–56	Edmonton Flyers, WHL	70	5	14	19	109	3	0	0	0	4
	Detroit Red Wings, NHL						4	0	1	1	0
1956–57	Detroit Red Wings, NHL	44	1	6	7	38	5	0	0	0	6
	Edmonton Flyers, WHL	24	2	3	5	24					
1957–58	Detroit Red Wings, NHL	69	1	6	7	104	4	0	1	1	4
1958–59	Chicago Black Hawks, NHL	70	2	10	12	86	6	1	2	3	26
1959–60	Chicago Black Hawks, NHL	57	1	5	6	66	4	0	0	0	4
1960–61	Chicago Black Hawks, NHL	53	3	2	5	40	7	0	0	0	2
1961–62	Toronto Maple Leafs, NHL	52	1	5	6	68	8	0	0	0	6
1962–63	Toronto Maple Leafs, NHL	4	1	0	1	4					
	Rochester Americans, AHL	63	6	21	27	97	2	0	2	2	2
1963–64	Toronto Maple Leafs, NHL	6	0	1	1	0	1	0	0	0	0
	Rochester Americans, AHL	60	3	19	22	62	2	1	0	1	0
1964–65	Rochester Americans, AHL	71	1	16	17	88	10	0	1	1	16
	Toronto Maple Leafs, NHL						1	0	0	0	2
1965–66	Toronto Maple Leafs, NHL	4	0	1	1	2					
	Rochester Americans, AHL	59	2	11	13	86	12	0	2	2	8
1966–67	Rochester Americans, AHL	71	3	19	22	48	13	0	1	1	16
1967–68	St. Louis Blues, NHL	74	1	10	11	50	14	0	3	3	10
1968–69	St. Louis Blues, NHL	67	1	6	7	50	12	0	0	0	10
1969–70	St. Louis Blues, NHL	68	0	3	3	85	14	0	1	1	16
1970–71	St. Louis Blues, NHL	22	0	2	2	6	6	0	0	0	6
	NHL Totals	626	12	58	70	617	86	1	8	9	92

Won Stanley Cup (1961, 1962, 1964)

Al Arbour was one of the few players in the NHL to wear glasses while playing.

figure to steer the team in the right direction. Arbour's positive impact on the team was immediate. The squad improved its total to 56 points and began building around talented defenseman Denis Potvin.

The 1974–75 season saw the arrival of Arbour's Islanders as a competitive NHL franchise. They won 33 regular-season matches before enjoying a memorable playoff run. They defeated Pittsburgh in a seven-game quarterfinals after losing the first three games. In the semifinals, they fell one game short of doing the same thing to the defending champion Philadelphia Flyers.

During each of the next four seasons, the Islanders finished with more than 100 points. This didn't translate into a Stanley Cup triumph, but the team did gain valuable experience. Following the 1978–79 campaign, Arbour was presented the Jack Adams Award as the NHL's top coach. In 1979–80, the Islanders attained their ultimate goal by defeating the Philadelphia Flyers in six games to win the Stanley Cup in their eighth season. They repeated this accomplishment in each of the next three years to become only the second NHL club to win four straight titles (Montreal did it twice). Their drive for five consecutive championships fell short when they lost to the Edmonton Oilers in the 1984 finals.

Afterward, Arbour marshaled the Islanders to solid if unspectacular results before stepping down following the 1985–86 season. He served as the organization's vice-president of player development before returning as the team's bench boss partway through the 1988–89 season. Arbour's contribution to the development of hockey in the United States was acknowledged in 1992 when his name was engraved on the Lester Patrick Trophy.

The pinnacle of his second instalment behind the New York bench occurred in 1992–93 when the Islanders upset the defending Stanley Cup champion Pittsburgh Penguins to reach the semifinals. Arbour retired in 1994 as the second-winningest coach of all time, with 781 regular-season victories and 123 post-season triumphs to his credit. One of the major foundations in the history of the New York Islanders, Arbour was an obvious choice to enter the Hockey Hall of Fame Builders category in 1996.

Arbour, Al
Head Coach, b: Sudbury, Ont., 11/1/1932

Season	Club, League	Regular Season					Playoffs				
		GC	W	L	T	W%	GC	W	L	T	W%
1970-71	St. Louis, NHL	50	21	15	14	0.560					
1971-72	St. Louis, NHL	44	19	19	6	0.500	11	4	7	0	0.364
1972-73	St. Louis, NHL	13	2	6	5	0.346					
1973-74	NY Islanders, NHL	78	19	41	18	0.359					
1974-75	NY Islanders, NHL	80	33	25	22	0.550	17	9	8	0	0.529
1975-76	NY Islanders, NHL	80	42	21	17	0.631	13	7	6	0	0.538
1976-77	NY Islanders, NHL	80	47	21	12	0.633	12	8	4	0	0.667
1977-78	NY Islanders, NHL	80	48	17	15	0.694	7	3	4	0	0.429
1978-79	NY Islanders, NHL	80	51	15	14	0.725	10	6	4	0	0.600
1979-80	NY Islanders, NHL	80	39	28	13	0.569	21	15	6	0	0.714
1980-81	NY Islanders, NHL	80	48	18	14	0.688	18	15	3	0	0.833
1981-82	NY Islanders, NHL	80	54	16	10	0.738	19	15	4	0	0.789
1982-83	NY Islanders, NHL	80	42	26	12	0.600	20	15	5	0	0.750
1983-84	NY Islanders, NHL	80	50	26	4	0.650	21	12	9	0	0.571
1984-85	NY Islanders, NHL	80	40	34	6	0.538	10	4	6	0	0.400
1985-86	NY Islanders, NHL	80	39	29	12	0.563	3	0	3	0	0.000
1988-89	NY Islanders, NHL	53	21	29	3	0.425					
1989-90	NY Islanders, NHL	80	31	38	11	0.456	5	1	4	0	0.200
1990-91	NY Islanders, NHL	80	25	45	10	0.375					
1991-92	NY Islanders, NHL	80	34	35	11	0.494					
1992-93	NY Islanders, NHL	84	40	37	7	0.518	18	9	9	0	0.500
1993-94	NY Islanders, NHL	84	36	36	12	0.500	4	0	4	0	0.000
	NHL Totals	1606	781	577	248	0.564	209	123	86	0	0.589

Won Jack Adams Award (1979)
Won Lester Patrick Trophy (1992)
Won Stanley Cup (1980, 1981, 1982, 1983)

Marcel Dionne

A naturally gifted goal scorer and playmaker, center Marcel Dionne was one of the most productive offensive performers in NHL history. His consistency at such a high level earned him respect and accolades throughout the league. And Dionne's accomplishments would have been more widely recognized had he not spent the bulk of his career in the relative hockey obscurity of Los Angeles. Hockey was never a top sport in that city, and his yearly excellence was rarely seen on television in the larger markets of the east.

The native of Drummondville, Quebec, was a junior superstar with the St. Catharines Black Hawks of the OHA. He accumulated 375 points in three junior seasons and helped his team reach the Memorial Cup Eastern finals in 1971. Dionne led the OHA in scoring in 1970 and was selected to the league's Second All-Star Team. He defended his scoring title in 1971 and was elevated to the First All-Star roster.

Despite his brilliance as an amateur, Dionne was overshadowed by Quebec Remparts phenomenon Guy Lafleur. In most years, Dionne would have been the top choice in the NHL Amateur Draft, but not in 1971. After Montreal snagged Lafleur first overall, the Detroit Red Wings happily selected Dionne second.

The young Detroit rookie shone with 77 points in 1971–72 and earned an invitation to Team Canada for the 1972 Summit Series versus the USSR. His 49 assists that year had set a new NHL standard for first-year players that was broken by Bryan Trottier in 1975–76. In all, Dionne enjoyed four productive years in Detroit, especially 1974–75, when he recorded 121 points. That year he also set an NHL record with 10 shorthanded goals, a mark that stood until Wayne Gretzky established a new standard in 1983–84. According to Detroit general manager Ned Harkness, Dionne gave the fans some excitement to compensate for the loss of Gordie Howe.

A contract squabble with the Wings brought about Dionne's trade to the Los Angeles Kings prior to the 1975–76 season and he went on to play the prime of his career on the West Coast. Over nearly a dozen full seasons with the Kings, the Little Beaver topped the 100-point mark seven times, was a two-time winner of the Lady Byng Trophy and the

Center Marcel Dionne was one of the most productive offensive performers in NHL history.

Dionne, Marcel
C, 5′9″, 190 lbs, b: Drummondville, Que., 8/3/1951

Season	Club, League	Regular Season					Playoffs				
		GP	G	A	Pts	PIM	GP	G	A	Pts	PIM
1971–72	Detroit Red Wings, NHL	78	28	49	77	14					
1972–73	Detroit Red Wings, NHL	77	40	50	90	21					
1973–74	Detroit Red Wings, NHL	74	24	54	78	10					
1974–75	Detroit Red Wings, NHL	80	47	74	121	14					
1975–76	Los Angeles Kings, NHL	80	40	54	94	38	9	6	1	7	0
CCup–76	Canada	7	1	5	6	4					
1976–77	Los Angeles Kings, NHL	80	53	69	122	12	9	5	9	14	2
1977–78	Los Angeles Kings, NHL	70	36	43	79	37	2	0	0	0	0
WEC–78	Canada	10	9	3	12	2					
1978–79	Los Angeles Kings, NHL	80	59	71	130	30	2	0	1	1	0
ChCup–79	NHL All-Stars	2	0	1	1	0					
WEC–79	Canada	7	2	1	3	4					
1979–80	Los Angeles Kings, NHL	80	53	84	137	32	4	0	3	3	4
1980–81	Los Angeles Kings, NHL	80	58	77	135	70	4	1	3	4	7
CCup–81	Canada	6	4	1	5	4					
1981–82	Los Angeles Kings, NHL	78	50	67	117	50	10	7	4	11	0
1982–83	Los Angeles Kings, NHL	80	56	51	107	22					
WEC–83	Canada	10	6	3	9	2					
1983–84	Los Angeles Kings, NHL	66	39	53	92	28					
1984–85	Los Angeles Kings, NHL	80	46	80	126	46	3	1	2	3	2
1985–86	Los Angeles Kings, NHL	80	36	58	94	46					
WEC–86	Canada	10	4	4	8	8					
1986–87	Los Angeles Kings, NHL	67	24	50	74	54					
	New York Rangers, NHL	14	4	6	10	6	6	1	1	2	2
1987–88	New York Rangers, NHL	67	31	34	65	54					
1988–89	New York Rangers, NHL	37	7	16	23	20					
	Denver Rangers, IHL	9	0	13	13	6					
	NHL Totals	1348	731	1040	1771	600	49	21	24	45	17
	WEC/CCup/ChalCup Totals	52	26	18	44	24					

Named Best Forward at WEC (1978)
NHL First All-Star Team (1977, 1980)
NHL Second All-Star Team (1979, 1981)
Won Art Ross Trophy (1980)
Won Lady Byng Trophy (1975, 1977)
Won Lester B. Pearson Award (1979, 1980)
Won CCup (1976)

In the 1974–75 season, Marcel Dionne (right) set an NHL record with 10 shorthanded goals.

Lester B. Pearson Award and was selected to the NHL First and Second All-Star Teams twice each. In 1979–80, he was declared the winner of the Art Ross Trophy after he tied young superstar Wayne Gretzky with 137 points but edged him in goals scored. Between 1975 and 1983, he was the top point-getter on the Kings every year.

Beginning in the 1979–80 season, Dionne formed the lethal Triple Crown Line with Charlie Simmer and Dave Taylor. They became one of the highest-scoring trios in league history before a serious injury to Simmer split the line up for a lengthy period. The trio was machine-like in its efficiency. The crafty pivot, Dionne, feathered passes to his linemates, who worked the corners and the slot to perfection.

The only element lacking in Dionne's career was playoff success. His best post-season came in 1981–82, when he scored 11 points in 10 games to help the Kings stun the record-setting Edmonton Oilers in the first round before losing to Vancouver.

During the early 1980s, Dionne began establishing a number of personal milestones. On January 7, 1981, he recorded his 1,000th point in his 740th game. This represented the fastest trip to that scoring plateau in NHL history until Guy Lafleur set a new record a short time later. On December 14, 1982, Dionne scored his 500th NHL goal when he beat Al Jensen of the Washington Capitals.

Dionne joined the playoffs-bound New York Rangers just prior to the March trading deadline in 1987, but the Blueshirts didn't fare any better in the post-season and were eliminated in the first round. During his first full year in New York, Dionne recorded the 14th 30-goal season of his career. On October 31, 1987, he registered his 700th goal when he beat Kelly Hrudey of the New York Islanders. Later that season, on February 14, 1988, he passed Phil Esposito to become the second-highest goal scorer in NHL history.

He retired after 37 games in 1988–89 with 731 goals and 1,771 points. At the time of his retirement, those totals placed him third on the NHL all-time scoring list behind only Gretzky and Howe. The popular and gregarious Dionne was inducted into the Hockey Hall of Fame in 1992.

Guy Lafleur

Guy Damien Lafleur, the Flower, had a 17-year NHL career spanning two decades, from 1971 until 1991. He spent the first 14 years with the Montreal Canadiens, followed by a three-year retirement, and then he came back to skate with the New York Rangers for one season and the Quebec Nordiques for two.

Known as one of the greatest right wingers ever to play the game and one of the most exciting offensive players of all time, Lafleur was also known as "le Demon Blond" (the Blond Demon) for his long hair, wild rushes down the ice and booming shot.

Although he is best known for his glory years with Montreal, he only ended up with the Habs because they had arranged a complicated series of deals with the California Golden Seals to get the Seals' first draft pick in 1971—and used it to pick Lafleur from the Quebec Remparts of the Quebec junior league. Scouts had been watching Lafleur as he led the Remparts to the Memorial

Cup in 1971, and Montreal GM Sam Pollock was keen on ensuring Lafleur wound up in a Montreal sweater.

When Lafleur came to the Canadiens, Jean Beliveau, who'd retired that very spring, offered to give him his number 4 sweater. It was the same number Guy had worn while dominating the Quebec junior league. But daunted by the expectations that wearing that number would bring, Guy politely declined and took the number 10 shirt instead.

As a child, Lafleur was so in love with hockey that he used to sneak into the arena in his home town of Thurso, Quebec, early on Sundays and weekday mornings to get extra ice time when no one else was around. He also slept in his hockey equipment to make his trip to the arena in the morning easier. "When I was a kid, all we saw on TV was the Canadiens, and all I wanted to be was Beliveau. We had one *bleu, blanc et rouge* Canadiens sweater and I fought the others for the right to wear it. I dreaded to be drafted by any other team but the Canadiens, and when they took me I was so happy. If any other team had taken me, I would have signed with the Quebec team in the other league [the Nordiques, who were then in the WHA]. But the Canadiens had the greatest tradition in hockey and it was my dream to play for them."

Lafleur joined the Montreal Canadiens the very fall he was drafted and became the first player

Guy Lafleur was one of the greatest right wingers of all time.

in NHL history to score at least 50 goals and 100 points in six consecutive seasons. When asked about developing his talent from a young age up to that of a consistent 50-goal scorer, Lafleur said: "I think it was always there and it was maybe a matter of bringing it out. It was harder than I thought it would be and I had to try harder. I had to regain my confidence, maybe the most important thing. I have learned a lot to relax. I know what I can do now, and I do it."

Lafleur was a First Team All-Star in all six of those consecutive 50-goal seasons and won the scoring title three times, the Hart Trophy twice and the Conn Smythe Trophy once. He has the highest career point and assist totals in Montreal history, as well as the second-highest goal total behind Rocket Richard. And when Lafleur reached the 1,000-point mark, he did it in just 720 games, the shortest time taken to hit that milestone in NHL history. After that, he concluded: "I'm not going to say that now that I have 1,000 points I can sit down and relax. I've got five or six years to go and I can shoot for more."

Lafleur, Guy
RW, 6′, 185 lbs, b: Thurso, Que., 9/20/1951

Season	Club, League	Regular Season					Playoffs				
		GP	G	A	Pts	PIM	GP	G	A	Pts	PIM
1971–72	Montreal Canadiens, NHL	73	29	35	64	48	6	1	4	5	2
1972–73	Montreal Canadiens, NHL	69	28	27	55	51	17	3	5	8	9
1973–74	Montreal Canadiens, NHL	73	21	35	56	29	6	0	1	1	4
1974–75	Montreal Canadiens, NHL	70	53	66	119	37	11	12	7	19	15
1975–76	Montreal Canadiens, NHL	80	56	69	125	36	13	7	10	17	2
CCup–76	Canada	7	1	5	6	12					
1976–77	Montreal Canadiens, NHL	80	56	80	136	20	14	9	17	26	6
1977–78	Montreal Canadiens, NHL	78	60	72	132	26	15	10	11	21	16
1978–79	Montreal Canadiens, NHL	80	52	77	129	28	16	10	13	23	0
ChCup–79	NHL All-Stars	3	1	2	3	0					
1979–80	Montreal Canadiens, NHL	74	50	75	125	12	3	3	1	4	0
1980–81	Montreal Canadiens, NHL	51	27	43	70	29	3	0	1	1	2
WEC–81	Canada	7	1	0	1	2					
CCup–81	Canada	7	2	9	11	0					
1981–82	Montreal Canadiens, NHL	66	27	57	84	24	5	2	1	3	4
1982–83	Montreal Canadiens, NHL	68	27	49	76	12	3	0	2	2	2
1983–84	Montreal Canadiens, NHL	80	30	40	70	19	12	0	3	3	5
1984–85	Montreal Canadiens, NHL	19	2	3	5	10					
1988–89	New York Rangers, NHL	67	18	27	45	12	4	1	0	1	0
1989–90	Quebec Nordiques, NHL	39	12	22	34	4					
1990–91	Quebec Nordiques, NHL	59	12	16	28	2					
	NHL Totals	1126	560	793	1353	399	128	58	76	134	67
	WEC/CCup/ChalCup Totals	24	5	16	21	14					

NHL First All-Star Team (1975, 1976, 1977, 1978, 1979, 1980)
Won Hart Trophy (1977, 1978)
Won Art Ross Trophy (1976, 1977, 1978)
Won Conn Smythe Trophy (1977)
Won Lester B. Pearson Award (1976, 1977, 1978)
NHL Plus-Minus Leader (1978)
Won Stanley Cup (1973, 1976, 1977, 1978, 1979)
Won CCup (1976)

Sportswriter Bill Libby said that Lafleur "typifies what is best about this sport. He is an artist on skates, creating scoring plays the way a painter puts a vivid scene on a canvas with a brush. His start is explosively quick and his stride is swifter than the others. He sees where his opponents and teammates are and anticipates where they will be. He is a spectacular athlete in a spectacular sport and it is wonderful watching him work."

During his 14 years with the Canadiens, Lafleur and his teammates won the Stanley Cup five times. After Montreal won the Stanley Cup in 1978, he borrowed it for the weekend—without telling anyone—to show his friends back home in Thurso. Lafleur boldly displayed it on his front lawn for all his neighbors to see!

In the late 1970s, Lafleur became a television star in Canada, doing commercials for a wide range of products including Yoplait yogurt, Shasta pop, Koho hockey sticks, Bauer skates, cars and a line of school supplies. For many fans, this was a bit odd, for the chain-smoking Lafleur had always been very shy of the media during interviews. "Guy has charisma for the English and in Quebec," explained his agent, Jerry Petrie. "He's almost a Beliveau." It was also rumored that in 1976 Lafleur's game in the playoffs was affected by hearsay that there was a plot to kidnap him for ransom.

Then came a turning point in Lafleur's life. After a night of partying with teammates in 1981, he was involved in a serious car accident and later admitted it changed his life. "I decided to slow down after that," said Lafleur. "I realized that my family was more important to me than downtown night life. The crowd doesn't give a crap as long as you bring the money in. When trouble comes, it's your family that supports you."

As a child, Guy Lafleur was so enamoured of hockey that he slept in his equipment to simplify his early-morning trip to the arena.

To sum up what Lafleur meant to hockey, teammate Serge Savard said: "Guy Lafleur is the best. He was made for this game." Another Canadien, Steve Shutt, saw Lafleur in a different light. "He was strange. I mean, any guy who would be in his hockey uniform, skates tied tight, sweater on and a stick beside him at 4 o'clock for an 8 o'clock game has to be a little strange. But on the ice he played 100% on instinct and emotion."

Lafleur played 19 games at the start of the 1984–85 season but had only two goals in those games. It was then he decided to retire. In front of 18,000 fans at the Montreal Forum, he took one last skate around the ice and the crowd gave him a five-minute standing ovation. "After 13 years, I couldn't accept to be number two. I'm proud of what I did in the past and I'm proud I played for the Canadiens, especially on five Stanley Cup winners. I was in a slump and I wasn't scoring much at the time. I was frustrated."

But even when Lafleur wasn't in top form, he could still command respect from opponents and admiration from his fans. "Even when Guy wasn't at his best, when he got the puck and got into full flight," explained teammate Larry Robinson, "the fans were out of their seats when he went flying down the wing."

Brian O'Neill, NHL executive vice-president, said: "I don't believe any other player has come down in the past 12 years who could lift fans out of their seats like Rocket Richard. Guy Lafleur did that. He was a great one, and to us in the NHL, he symbolized how the game should be played. We are certainly going to miss him." Lafleur was joined in the on-ice ceremony by his parents, his wife, Lise, one of his two sons and Iva Baribeau—his landlady when he played with the Quebec Remparts.

Lafleur became the sixth Canadien to have his sweater number retired after Jacques Plante, Doug Harvey, Jean Beliveau, Howie Morenz and Maurice and Henri Richard. He was in tears as team president Ronald Corey presented him with the number 10. Journalist Red Fisher commented: "Everybody knew that he represented something special as a maker of excellence on the ice. What not enough people are aware of is his decency off the ice. In all the years I've covered the Canadiens, I don't think any one of the teams had more rapport with or respect from fans in the other cities. The respect and reaction of out-of-town fans was almost surprising—as if they felt that Guy belonged not only to the Canadiens but in large part to them as well."

Retiring as a player at age 33, Lafleur went into a front office position with the Canadiens. "I'm leaving the ice, but I want everybody to know that I'll never leave the sport." But his time with the Canadiens front office was short. Lafleur called the $75,000 they were offering him "clerk's pay."

But he was right about not leaving the game. In 1988 he was inducted into the Hockey Hall of Fame, but he believed he could still play and his love for the game hadn't diminished. He signed with the New York Rangers and played one year there, scoring 18 goals and getting 27 assists in 67 games, thus becoming only the second player after Gordie Howe to play in the NHL after being inducted into the Hall of Fame. He helped the Rangers move into first place in the Patrick Division until an injury knocked him out of the lineup at mid-season. Then in 1989 Lafleur followed his good friend and coach Michel Bergeron from the Rangers to the Quebec Nordiques, reportedly turning down a $1-million offer from the L.A. Kings. "It was a very pleasant year in exile in New York," remarked Lafleur, "but now I would like to end my career in Quebec, where it began."

Guy Lafleur was the first player in NHL history to score at least 50 goals and 100 points in six consecutive seasons.

When it was suggested he be named co-captain of the Quebec Nordiques, Lafleur laughed. "The day you hear someone call me captain will be the day I buy a boat. Anyway, I've never been captain in 16 years in the NHL. But that didn't stop me being a leader in my own way." Two years later he retired from the ice once again and took another front office job in Montreal. Lafleur's sage advice in his farewell speech after retiring for good with Quebec was this: "Play every game as if it is your last one."

Larry Robinson

Veteran sportswriter Frank Orr once summed up the career of Larry Robinson: "He has represented large amounts of the good things the game of hockey offers. He's a man of style, dignity and humility, an imposing presence."

Known as "Big Bird," Robinson often dwarfed opposing players with his 6´4″, 225-pound frame. Despite his imposing size, he was passed over three times by the Canadiens in the 1971 Amateur Draft. When they finally did take him as their fourth pick, he was only the 20th player selected overall. Ironically, two decades later, there were only two players from that draft active in the league—Robinson and Guy Lafleur—both Canadiens and both Hall of Famers.

A HISTORY OF WORLD HOCKEY

Larry Robinson had the physique, but he wasn't a fighter.

Although he was physically imposing, Robinson wasn't a fighter. Overall in his career, he averaged less than two penalty minutes per game. Though he wasn't often in the penalty box, Robinson admitted he did like to play physically. "Hockey isn't ballet, where everybody dances around in tutus," he once said. "Hockey is a contact sport. It's like telling a football player to block the line but don't touch anybody; it's just impossible."

Robinson was born and raised on a dairy farm in eastern Ontario. He played junior hockey for the Brockville Braves of the Ontario Junior Hockey League and the Kitchener Rangers of the Ontario Hockey Association. His junior coach in Brockville, Dan Dexter, described the young Robinson: "The quality that stood out both on and off the ice was his unselfishness. He commuted from his home just outside Ottawa to Brockville three times a week for practice and he never missed."

Robinson first turned professional with the Nova Scotia Voyageurs of the American Hockey League and helped them win the 1971–72 Calder Cup, the first Canadian-based team to do so. Later that year, Robinson joined the Canadiens, winning his first Stanley Cup in his rookie year. He went on to help his team win the Cup many more times, including four in a row from 1976 to 1979 and one more in 1986. This last one was a surprise win for Montreal, and commentators remarked that Robinson seemed to come alive in the finals against the Boston Bruins after being elbowed by Bruin Louis Sleigher. "The stupidest thing in the world when you play Montreal," remarked Don Cherry, "is to wake up Larry Robinson!"

Although four straight Cup wins in Montreal in the 1970s was satisfying, the win in 1986 was perhaps the sweetest for Robinson. "I'm not exactly at the peak of my career now and I would have to say that makes this one a little more special than the others. It might be the ideal time to call it quits. My children [a 16-year-old son and a nine-year-old daughter] are getting older. Before you know it, they'll be grown up and I'll wonder where they went because I haven't spent much time with them."

His teammate Serge Savard applauded Robinson for the 1986 Cup win. "Over the

Robinson, Larry
D, 6'4", 225 lbs, b: Winchester, Ont., 6/2/1951

Season	Club, League	Regular Season					Playoffs				
		GP	G	A	Pts	PIM	GP	G	A	Pts	PIM
1971–72	Nova Scotia Voyageurs, AHL	74	10	14	24	54	15	2	10	12	31
1972–73	Nova Scotia Voyageurs, AHL	38	6	33	39	33					
	Montreal Canadiens, NHL	36	2	4	6	20	11	1	4	5	9
1973–74	Montreal Canadiens, NHL	78	6	20	26	66	6	0	1	1	26
1974–75	Montreal Canadiens, NHL	80	14	47	61	76	11	0	4	4	27
1975–76	Montreal Canadiens, NHL	80	10	30	40	59	13	3	3	6	10
CCup–76	Canada	7	0	0	0	0					
1976–77	Montreal Canadiens, NHL	77	19	66	85	45	14	2	10	12	12
1977–78	Montreal Canadiens, NHL	80	13	52	65	39	15	4	17	21	6
1978–79	Montreal Canadiens, NHL	67	16	45	61	33	16	6	9	15	8
ChCup–79	NHL All-Stars	3	1	0	1	0					
1979–80	Montreal Canadiens, NHL	72	14	61	75	39	10	0	4	4	2
1980–81	Montreal Canadiens, NHL	65	12	38	50	37	3	0	1	1	2
WEC–81	Canada	6	1	1	2	2					
CCup–81	Canada	7	0	1	1	2					
1981–82	Montreal Canadiens, NHL	71	12	47	59	41	5	0	1	1	8
1982–83	Montreal Canadiens, NHL	71	14	49	63	33	3	0	0	0	2
1983–84	Montreal Canadiens, NHL	74	9	34	43	39	15	0	5	5	22
CCup–84	Canada	8	1	2	3	2					
1984–85	Montreal Canadiens, NHL	76	14	33	47	44	12	3	8	11	8
1985–86	Montreal Canadiens, NHL	78	19	63	82	39	20	0	13	13	22
1986–87	Montreal Canadiens, NHL	70	13	37	50	44	17	3	17	20	6
1987–88	Montreal Canadiens, NHL	53	6	34	40	30	11	1	4	5	4
1988–89	Montreal Canadiens, NHL	74	4	26	30	22	21	2	8	10	12
1989–90	Los Angeles Kings, NHL	64	7	32	39	34	10	2	3	5	10
1990–91	Los Angeles Kings, NHL	62	1	22	23	16	12	1	4	5	15
1991–92	Los Angeles Kings, NHL	56	3	10	13	37	2	0	0	0	0
	NHL Totals	1384	208	750	958	793	227	28	116	144	211
	CCup/ChalCup/WEC Totals	31	3	4	7	6					

NHL First All-Star Team (1977, 1979, 1980)
NHL Second All-Star Team (1978, 1981, 1986)
Named Best Defenseman at WEC (1981)
Won James Norris Trophy (1977, 1980)
Won Conn Smythe Trophy (1978)
NHL Plus-Minus Leader (1977)
Won Stanley Cup (1973, 1976, 1977, 1978, 1979, 1986)
Won CCup (1976, 1984)

entire season, he kept our team shooting at the top in a very rough division. If the big guy was named the most valuable player in the league, it wouldn't be an injustice."

But Robinson didn't retire after the 1985–86 season. "I need the money," he explained jokingly about his decision to keep playing into his 15th season. At the time, one of Robinson's main interests outside the rink was breeding polo horses, and he noted, "Polo ponies are very hungry animals."

Canadiens coach Scotty Bowman once said: "Larry was always ready to take on whatever share of the job necessary to get it done, no matter how big it was. He had a very straightforward approach to everything. Even when he was an All-Star, he never wanted any extra edge or anything, to be anything but one of the guys."

Robinson played 17 seasons for the Canadiens and then three more for the L.A. Kings, from 1989 to 1992. He won the Norris Trophy twice as the league's best defenseman, in the 1976–77 and 1979–80 seasons, and the Conn Smythe Trophy in 1977–78. Not only was Robinson a great defensive player, he was also very good with the puck. He held the NHL record for most playoff games at 227 until surpassed by Mark Messier, and the most consecutive years in the playoffs with 20. He also became a veritable regular in All-Star games, playing in 10 of them. His final NHL totals were impressive: 208 goals, 750 assists and 958 regular-season points, as well as 144 points in 227 playoff games.

In 1981 Larry Robinson (center) represented Canada at the World Championship and was named to the tournament All-Star team.

What was Robinson's secret? "I haven't changed since day one," Robinson declared. "The only thing that has changed is my age. A lot of people say I haven't matured. One of the things that has helped me stay in the game is that I've kept a fun attitude."

Internationally, Robinson represented Team Canada in the 1976, 1981 and 1984 Canada Cup tournaments. All three were Canadian victories. In 1981 he represented Canada in the World Championship and was named to the tournament All-Star team.

It was the 1984 Canada Cup that convinced Robinson he still had a lot of hockey left in him. He had reached the point in his career when he was beginning to wonder if he should retire. "The Canada Cup changed everything around for me and I say thanks to Glen Sather for picking me. It truly was a big surprise when I was selected," Robinson said. "I figured I was from another era of hockey and didn't belong with the new platoon of top defensemen, guys like Ray Bourque, Paul Coffey and Doug Wilson. When I made the team, had a good tournament and Team Canada won it, I was a new man. I had wondered if I was capable of playing the game at the very top level, and when I did, it I got my confidence back."

Robinson was eager to participate in charity events and always granted interviews to the media. He supported Canadian Guide Dogs for the Blind, multiple sclerosis and juvenile diabetes charities and the heart fund. "It's never been any big obligation for me to do what I can to help people," he said unabashedly. "It's just something I like to do."

In 1993 Robinson was appointed assistant coach with the New Jersey Devils. Two years later, in 1995, the team won the Stanley Cup. Later that same year, Robinson was named head coach of the L.A. Kings, his former team. Kings chairman Joe Cohen boasted: "This is a landmark event for the Kings franchise—truly a new beginning. Larry Robinson is a winner." After leaving Los Angeles at the end of the 1998–99 season, Robinson signed as assistant in New Jersey. Midway through 1999–2000, head coach Robbie Ftorek was fired and Robinson came in and not only assumed coaching duties but took his team to a Stanley Cup victory—his first as head coach. The next year, his Devils went to game seven of the finals before losing to Colorado.

The 2001–02 season started off badly for the Devils and Robinson, with the team under-achieving so badly that a berth in the playoffs was by no means guaranteed midway through the year. As the pressure built, general manager Lou Lamoriello took the drastic step of firing Robinson and replacing him with Kevin Constantine. After sitting at home pondering his future, Robinson surprisingly accepted the Devils' offer to return as an assistant coach.

Bill **Barber**

Wayne Gretzky may have had the most significant backyard rink any kid ever had, but Bill Barber likely had the biggest.

Perhaps Wayne Gretzky had the most important backyard rink when he was a kid, but Bill Barber likely had the biggest. "Just to make sure we had everything going for us, dad built us a rink that was almost regulation size, had hydro poles put up and lights strung out," he rec-ollected. Barber was a native of Callander, Ontario, and his homemade outdoor rink did have one drawback. "It snows a lot up there, and you'd just get through ploughing a foot of it off the rink and it'd start again and you had to clear off another foot. I think all that ploughing was the thing that made my arms as strong as they are."

Indeed his strength was one of his most important attributes. In junior, he centered a line with Jerry Byers and Al Blanchard in Kitchener and this trio was among the top scoring lines. All three were drafted high in the 1972 Amateur Draft. Barber was selected seventh overall by Philadelphia and was the only one of the three who went on to make a significant impact in the NHL.

Initially he was assigned to Richmond of the AHL by the Flyers, but after just 11 games he was recalled when Bill Flett sprained his knee. In a matter of days, Barber had proved himself indispen-sable to the team. "He played so well for us," coach Fred Shero said, "we couldn't send him back to Richmond." Instead, Barber was among the top rookies all year, finishing the season with 30 goals and placing second in voting for the Calder Trophy to Steve Vickers of the Rangers. "I think Barber is and will continue to be a better all-around hockey player," Shero observed. "New York could have done very well without Vickers. We couldn't do without Barber."

Part of his immediate success was in coach Shero's decision to play Barber as a left wing to Bobby Clarke on the first line rather than keep him at his natural center position on a fourth line. Clarke quickly realized Barber had an excellent shot and good hands and endeavored to get the puck to the port side whenever possible. "Bobby Clarke sacrificed everything for me," Barber acknowledged. "Every time I looked up, I saw the puck. He just kept feeding me and feeding me." And Barber just kept on converting those passes. He scored 34 goals in each of the next two years, then exploded for a career year in 1975–76 by scoring 50 and getting 112 total points. Along the way, and not coincidentally, the Flyers were winning the Stanley Cup. They became the first expansion team to win in 1974 and took home the sacred silverware again the next year. But the wins were controversial and weren't as admired as previous Cup wins had been.

The Broad Street Bullies emphasized goon hockey—fighting and intimidation—to win. And Barber, though not a true fighter, had his own specialty in diving, a reputation he didn't play down or feel embarrassed about. "Sure I go down when I know somebody has a good hold on me and the referee is looking," he admitted. "I think it makes sense." Opponents disagreed with these unsportsmanlike tactics, especially since diving was the antithesis of what the Flyers preached—tough hockey. But this was Flyers hockey, and for two years it was almost impossible to beat.

In 1975–76, Bill Barber (front) exploded to a career high with 50 goals and 112 total points—and it wasn't a coincidence that the Flyers were also in the process of winning the Cup.

Barber had four more 40-goal seasons during his career, but the continuing deterioration of his left knee forced him to retire and he was unable to finish the 1983–84 season. He first injured the knee crashing into the boards while backchecking in December 1982 in Pittsburgh. He recovered after missing a few games, but the same knee gave out on him again later in the season. By the spring he required surgery, and once the knee was opened, doctors discovered massive damage to the joints and cartilage that had been masked for years by strong muscle mass around the bone. It was completely reconstructed and he missed the entire 1984–85 season trying to recover. After the year was over, he knew he would never be strong enough to endure the physical demands of the NHL.

He finished his career with 420 goals and was inducted into the Hockey Hall of Fame in 1990, one of only three players from those Flyers teams—Bernie Parent and Bobby Clarke were the others—so honored.

Barber got into coaching immediately after his retirement, taking over the reins of the AHL's Hershey Bears, who were at the time the minor-league affiliate of the Flyers. After several jobs within the Flyers' organization he took over as head coach of the Philadelphia Phantoms of the AHL, the Flyers' current minor-league affiliate, starting in 1996. He coached them for four years, leading the Phantoms to a Calder Cup championship in 1998. Barber then became an assistant coach with the Flyers on July 5, 2000, and took over as the team's 14th head coach on December 10, 2000.

Barber, Bill
LW, 6', 195 lbs, b: Callander, Ont., 7/11/1952

Season	Club, League	Regular Season					Playoffs				
		GP	G	A	Pts	PIM	GP	G	A	Pts	PIM
1972–73	Philadelphia Flyers, NHL	69	30	34	64	46	11	3	2	5	22
	Richmond Robins, AHL	11	9	5	14	4					
1973–74	Philadelphia Flyers, NHL	75	34	35	69	54	17	3	6	9	18
1974–75	Philadelphia Flyers, NHL	79	34	37	71	66	17	6	9	15	8
1975–76	Philadelphia Flyers, NHL	80	50	62	112	104	16	6	7	13	18
CCup–76	Canada	7	2	0	2	4					
1976–77	Philadelphia Flyers, NHL	73	20	35	55	62	10	1	4	5	2
1977–78	Philadelphia Flyers, NHL	80	41	31	72	34	12	6	3	9	2
1978–79	Philadelphia Flyers, NHL	79	34	46	80	22	8	3	4	7	10
ChCup–79	NHL All-Stars	3	0	1	1	0					
1979–80	Philadelphia Flyers, NHL	79	40	32	72	17	19	12	9	21	23
1980–81	Philadelphia Flyers, NHL	80	43	42	85	69	12	11	5	16	0
1981–82	Philadelphia Flyers, NHL	80	45	44	89	85	4	1	5	6	4
WEC–82	Canada	10	8	1	9	10					
1982–83	Philadelphia Flyers, NHL	66	27	33	60	28	3	1	1	2	2
1983–84	Philadelphia Flyers, NHL	63	22	32	54	36					
	NHL Totals	903	420	463	883	623	129	53	55	108	109
	WEC/CCup/ChalCup Totals	20	10	2	12	14					

NHL First All-Star Team (1976)
NHL Second All-Star Team (1979, 1981)
Won Stanley Cup (1974, 1975)
Won CCup (1976)

Viktor Zhluktov

Viktor Zhluktov didn't come to Moscow to play hockey but to study at the Aviation Institute.

Hockey was one of many pastimes for Viktor Zhluktov. He also played basketball and volleyball, the clarinet and the accordion. Most of all, he was fascinated by airplanes and launched gliders in his free time.

Zhluktov got his first taste of hockey at the national level when at the age of 13 he played for Inta, his hometown club, in a tournament for youth teams. On that occasion he didn't catch the eye of the talent spotters, including Anatoli Tarasov, who were in attendance. But it didn't matter to him. He set out for Moscow not to play ice hockey but to study at the Aviation Institute.

One day he dropped in on a workout of the Central Red Army junior team to see a hometown buddy. The second time he visited, he was invited to join the other players on the ice. He took up their offer to step out on the ice and that's where he stayed, with no regrets. At first the tremendous workloads in the training sessions were a bit scary for Zhluktov. At that time, he still valued more than anything his status as an aviation student. But he was quite happy to give hockey a chance. He decided that if it grew on him enough, he'd let go of his other distractions, including airplanes.

Coach Tarasov ordered his assistant and future successor in the Red Army club, Konstantin Loktev, to keep an eye on the center. The great Anatoli Firsov was already winding up his hockey career and there was a problem with his replacement. For some reason, Loktev took a liking to Zhluktov and the die was cast. Zhluktov had to give up his studies at the institute.

Zhluktov made his first appearance in the 1974 World Junior Championship in Leningrad. A hefty and determined player, in the eyes of the fans he looked a bit like Alexander Yakushev, with one important difference. Playing for the liberal Spartak team, Yakushev set out on his hockey career with his mind set on dazzling the fans with his scoring ability, and that is how he played until the very end. Zhluktov stepped out on the ice with a different goal in mind—to become a player who never let his team down. Moreover, the functions of a center compelled him to concentrate more on defense.

In the Red Army club and on the national junior team, the Viktor Zhluktov–Boris Alexandrov tandem gained quite a reputation. Zhluktov was the lanky center and Alexandrov the small, sleek right wing. The conscientious Zhluktov and the scrappy Alexandrov skated shoulder to shoulder against the most eminent North American professionals. In his first tournament with the team, in 1975–76, Alexandrov scored the tying goal in the "game of the century" between Central Red Army and the Montreal Canadiens. In the 1976 Canada Cup tournament, the same forward line, together with Vladimir Vikulov, scored four out of the five goals against the U.S. national team and the only goal against the Canadiens. But

Zhluktov, Viktor
C, 6'2", 200 lbs, b: Inta, USSR, 1/29/1954

Season	Club, League	Regular Season				
		GP	G	A	Pts	PIM
1972–73	CSKA, USSR	5	2	*	*	*
1973–74	CSKA, USSR	28	8	3	11	*
1974–75	CSKA, USSR	35	19	11	30	20
1975–76	CSKA, USSR	36	22	14	36	25
OWG–76	USSR	6	2	9	11	2
WEC–76	USSR	9	4	6	10	0
CCup–76	USSR	5	5	4	9	0
1976–77	CSKA, USSR	36	17	20	37	2
WEC–77	USSR	10	5	5	10	2
1977–78	CSKA, USSR	24	11	6	17	8
WEC–78	USSR	9	3	5	8	6
1978–79	CSKA, USSR	44	20	24	44	12
WEC–79	USSR	8	4	3	7	2
1979–80	CSKA, USSR	36	17	13	30	8
OWG–80	USSR	7	3	8	11	0
1980–81	CSKA, USSR	49	30	26	56	18
WEC–81	USSR	8	2	3	5	8
CCup–81	USSR	7	2	0	2	4
1981–82	CSKA, USSR	47	20	24	44	16
WEC–82	USSR	10	3	0	3	2
1982–83	CSKA, USSR	39	12	7	19	16
WEC–83	USSR	10	3	5	8	2
1983–84	CSKA, USSR	42	12	11	23	8
1984–85	CSKA, USSR	34	9	10	19	8
	USSR Totals	455	199	*	*	*
	OWG/WEC/CCup Totals	89	36	48	84	28

Won OWG (1976)
Won WEC (1978, 1979, 1981, 1982, 1983)
Won CCup (1981)
USSR Champion (1975, 1977, 1978, 1979, 1980, 1981, 1982, 1983, 1984, 1985)

Alexandrov, with his aggressive manner, never appeared in the USSR national lineup again. Neither did Vikulov. Zhluktov, whose more visible talents were considered a notch above those of his partners, was nevertheless in great demand.

Zhluktov made his debut in the national lineup in the 1976 Winter Olympics hockey tournament in Innsbruck. Again he was on a forward line with two illustrious soloists, Alexander Maltsev and Sergei Kapustin. The USSR was down 2–0 in the decisive match against Czechoslovakia when the referee sent Zhluktov and Sergei Babinov off to the penalty box for two minutes. The three remaining Soviets managed to kill off the penalty—and that is possibly what saved the newcomer Zhluktov's hockey career. "The fact that you were cooling off for two minutes," his partners joked, "turned the tide in the game." The USSR team managed a comeback and went on to win the gold medal.

On the ice, Viktor Zhluktov (right) was a real workhorse.

On the ice, Zhluktov was a workhorse. A conscientious player, he knew he was being sent out onto the ice to play hockey for all he was worth and that is exactly what he did. In those years, his starry-eyed partners were looking to get something different out of the game. They wanted to score as many goals as possible for their own pleasure and for the glory that went with it. In the 1977 World Championship, the third man rounding out the forward line of Kapustin and Zhluktov was Helmut Balderis, the Latvian "prince" who played as if he was his own master. But that new forward line caught the fancy of hockey fans. The jet-propelled wings were suddenly thrown together with a reliable center who could also play defense when needed. And the trio knew how to score goals.

The next season, an order was issued from above for the transfer of Kapustin and Balderis to the Central Red Army team so they could play alongside Zhluktov. The idea was to foster a lasting friendship among the three and as a result build another forward line on a par with the leading Petrov line. Coach Viktor Tikhonov was also transferred to the Red Army club to keep an eye on the budding trio.

But Balderis and Kapustin played with less and less enthusiasm and as a result Zhluktov became sullen. He remembered the generous support he had had from Vikulov before he was unceremoniously dumped from the team and he recalled the close bond between Petrov, Mikhailov and Kharlamov as they went on to become stars. They were smart enough to realize that none of them would make it alone. But Zhluktov's new partners made no effort to build a powerful forward line. They played as individuals and took every opportunity that came along to score and otherwise bask in the glow of an adoring public.

Zhluktov came to realize that the role of supporting actor, the job of backup man, was to be his forever and resorted less and less frequently to his remarkable slapshot. And it became more and more difficult for him to influence the work of his wingers.

Two years later, Kapustin and Balderis left Central Red Army. Understandably, Zhluktov remained with his "native" club. Tikhonov ordered Zhluktov to center a new forward line with Sergei Makarov and Vladimir Krutov. But then Tikhonov surreptitiously invited Igor Larionov from the Voskresensk team and in doing so effectively demoted Zhluktov to a secondary role. Zhluktov played on the fourth-string forward line of the national team until 1983.

A HISTORY OF WORLD HOCKEY

But Zhluktov wasn't destined to become an Olympic champion a second time. Bothered by a strained back and the effects of recent surgery in the United States, he left the ranks of the national squad just before the 1984 Olympic hockey tournament in Sarajevo.

Steve Shutt

Steve Shutt developed into one of the game's elite left wingers and recorded numerous key goals for Montreal in the 1970s.

One of the most naturally talented goal scorers of his generation, Steve Shutt played to his strengths effectively during 13 NHL seasons. He developed into one of the game's elite left wings and scored many key goals for the Montreal Canadiens when they dominated the NHL in the 1970s. His skating style appeared awkward and his helmet never looked like it fit him, but this was immaterial when the puck was dropped. Shutt beat many players in races for the puck and could shoot like few before or since.

The native of Toronto, Ontario, first gained attention as a scoring star with the North York Rangers of the tough Metropolitan Toronto Hockey League, but the powerful Toronto Marlboros weren't about to miss out on a local phenomenon like Shutt. He was quickly recruited and eventually formed one of the most potent lines in OHA history with Dave Gardner and Billy Harris. In three junior seasons, Shutt scored 144 goals and was one of the top prospects available in the 1972 Amateur Draft.

Habs general manager Sam Pollock used the same shrewd maneuvering that landed Guy Lafleur in 1971 to acquire the fourth choice in the 1972 draft. As luck would have it, Harris, Jacques Richard and Don Lever were claimed with the first three choices, leaving Shutt available to Montreal.

During his rookie season in 1972–73, Shutt played well on a deep club that went on to win the Stanley Cup. He continued to progress the following year before breaking out with 30 goals in 1974–75 while playing on a line with Pete Mahovlich and Guy Lafleur. The big center Mahovlich was deceptively quick, and Lafleur's natural speed and style tormented the opposition. This gave Shutt sufficient room to fly up and down his wing and release his patented shots. He was also used effectively as the point man on the power-play since he was able to

Shutt, Steve
LW, 5'11", 185 lbs, b: Toronto, Ont., 7/1/1952

Season	Club, League	Regular Season					Playoffs				
		GP	G	A	Pts	PIM	GP	G	A	Pts	PIM
1972–73	Montreal Canadiens, NHL	50	8	8	16	24	1	0	0	0	0
	Nova Scotia Voyageurs, AHL	6	4	1	5	2					
1973–74	Montreal Canadiens, NHL	70	15	20	35	17	6	5	3	8	9
1974–75	Montreal Canadiens, NHL	77	30	35	65	40	9	1	6	7	4
1975–76	Montreal Canadiens, NHL	80	45	34	79	47	13	7	8	15	2
CCup–76	Canada	6	1	2	3	8					
1976–77	Montreal Canadiens, NHL	80	60	45	105	28	14	8	10	18	2
1977–78	Montreal Canadiens, NHL	80	49	37	86	24	15	9	8	17	20
1978–79	Montreal Canadiens, NHL	72	37	40	77	31	11	4	7	11	6
ChCup–79	NHL All-Stars	2	0	1	1	0					
1979–80	Montreal Canadiens, NHL	77	47	42	89	34	10	6	3	9	6
1980–81	Montreal Canadiens, NHL	77	35	38	73	51	3	2	1	3	4
1981–82	Montreal Canadiens, NHL	57	31	24	55	40					
1982–83	Montreal Canadiens, NHL	78	35	22	57	26	3	1	0	1	0
1983–84	Montreal Canadiens, NHL	63	14	23	37	29	11	7	2	9	8
1984–85	Montreal Canadiens, NHL	10	2	0	2	9					
	Los Angeles Kings, NHL	59	16	25	41	10	3	0	0	0	4
	NHL Totals	930	424	393	817	410	99	50	48	98	65
	CCup/ChalCup Totals	8	1	3	4	8					

NHL First All-Star Team (1977)
NHL Second All-Star Team (1978, 1980)
Won Stanley Cup (1973, 1976, 1977, 1978, 1979)
Won CCup (1976)

direct the puck along the ice at high speeds. The trio was so successful that Mahovlich set a Canadiens single-season record for a center with 117 points in 1974–75.

The sharpshooting Shutt reflected on his success with humility. "I'm not individually a good player," he said. "I can't stickhandle through a team like Pete Mahovlich or skate circles around people like Guy Lafleur, but what I can do and what I do well is adapt to whoever I play with, their style, their timing. A lot of people don't notice me out there. I know that. But at the end of a game, just look at me and I'll have a goal and two assists. I'm usually in the right place at the right time. It's not being in front of the net that's important, anyone can get in front of the net. It's knowing when to be in front of the net, when to pounce."

In 1976–77, Steve Shutt was partnered with Jacques Lemaire and Guy Lafleur to form the top line in the NHL.

Shutt improved to 45 goals in 1975–76 and the Habs began a four-year Stanley Cup run. A few months later he helped his country win the inaugural Canada Cup. His ability to utilize his wrist shot and slapshot, tip shots from the point with his cat-like reflexes and pounce on rebounds were of tremendous value to the team.

In 1976–77, the fleet scorer was partnered with Jacques Lemaire and Guy Lafleur to form the top line in the NHL. Their offensive dominance helped Montreal post the greatest regular season in league history with an astonishing 60–8–12 record. That year Shutt led the NHL with 60 goals and in the process set a new league and team record for left wingers that remained the NHL standard until Luc Robitaille's 63-goal performance in 1992–93. Following the season, he was placed on the NHL's First All-Star Team.

The next year he helped Montreal win its third consecutive Cup by registering a personal best of nine goals and 17 points in the playoffs. Coach Scotty Bowman quipped: "Superstar is a much abused term. There are only three or four genuine ones in the league. To me, it's someone who can do everything well. Score, check, pass and set up plays. Superstars draw the crowds. Their greatness gives them an aura. I think Steve's heading in the right direction."

Once the Habs dynasty ended, the veteran Shutt continued to score. The team remained successful in the regular season and he was paired with the likes of Mark Napier, Doug Wickenheiser, John Chabot and Perry Turnbull. Early in the 1984–85 season, Shutt was traded to the Los Angeles Kings. He recorded 41 points in 59 games, but after 930 regular-season games, he'd had enough of the rigors of the NHL. Shutt retired with 424 goals and in 1993 was inducted into the Hockey Hall of Fame. As he pointed out: "I'm retiring. I don't want to fight anymore for a job with the Canadiens and I don't want to play in another city. Now I want to get out."

Following his playing career, the effervescent Shutt worked as a television commentator. In 1993–94, he returned to Montreal as an assistant coach and worked there until the end of the 1996–97 season. The club made clear why Shutt was hired—the team's offense was in need of some sort of direction. The new assistant said, "I'm a firm believer that you can teach people how to score—not actually how to put the puck in the net, but simply being in the right place at the right time."

Matti Hagman

Matti Hagman became the first Finn in the NHL.

"Mr. HIFK" was the first title ever acquired on the Finnish hockey scene by Matti Hagman, a nickname he earned for being the top playmaking center on the HIFK Helsinki team every year he played for the team. The second title, one that nobody can ever challenge, is for being the first Finn in the NHL when at age 21 he joined the Boston Bruins for the 1976–77 season.

His illustrious career with HIFK Helsinki started when he was only 17 years old. An injury to the top center gave him an opening to play on a line with two legends of the game, Esa Peltonen and Juhani Tamminen. During the 1976 Canada Cup, Hagman was selected the most valuable player on the Finnish national squad and came to the attention of NHL scouts. Drafted by Boston, in his rookie season he saw action in 75 games and earned a total of 28 points.

The following year he started with the Bruins again but became involved in a unique intra-league trade when Boston shipped him to the Quebec Nordiques of the WHA. For the Nordiques, he played backup center to their regular number one, Chris Bordeleau.

Hagman was the third Finn drafted into the NHL when the Bruins signed him in 1975. The first two—Tommi Salmelainen, who was co-opted by St. Louis and also played for HIFK Helsinki in 1969, and Martti Jarkko, who was signed by the New York Islanders in 1974—never played in the league.

In the absence of the French-Canadian Bordeleau, Hagman scored more than a point per game in 53 outings. When Bordeleau returned, he was released altogether, making for a dramatic start to Hagman's NHL career. He next saw action that spring on the Finnish national team at the World Championship in Prague. Returning to Finland for two seasons, he led HIFK Helsinki to the championship in 1980. He then spent two years with the Edmonton Oilers.

In Edmonton, he didn't frustrate team management with his earlier youthful excess. Rather, he was the one who was frustrated. In the role of center behind Wayne Gretzky, who to Hagman was seemingly playing non-stop, he got very little ice time. Despite two commendable seasons of 50-plus points, he decided to go home. Returning to HIFK again, he led the team to the championship in 1983.

Hagman's second stint in North America produced a remarkable though unexpected

Hagman, Matti
C, 6´1˝, 184 lbs, b: Helsinki, Finland, 9/21/1955

Season	Club, League	Regular Season					Playoffs				
		GP	G	A	Pts	PIM	GP	G	A	Pts	PIM
1972–73	HIFK, Finland	13	11	5	16	7					
1973–74	HIFK, Finland	35	30	9	39	20					
1974–75	HIFK, Finland	35	30	16	46	27					
WEC–75	Finland	9	2	3	5	4					
1975–76	HIFK, Finland	36	24	34	58	39	4	1	1	2	5
OWG–76	Finland	6	1	4	5	2					
WEC–76	Finland	10	4	7	11	14					
CCup–76	Finland	5	2	4	6	6					
1976–77	Boston Bruins, NHL	75	11	17	28	0	8	0	1	1	0
1977–78	Boston Bruins, NHL	15	4	1	5	2					
	Quebec Nordiques, WHA	53	25	31	56	16					
WEC–78	Finland	5	1	2	3	8					
1978–79	HIFK, Finland	36	20	37	57	53	6	1	6	7	4
1979–80	HIFK, Finland	36	37	50	87	26	7	3	10	13	6
1980–81	Edmonton Oilers, NHL	75	20	33	53	16	9	4	1	5	6
CCup–81	Finland	5	1	2	3	4					
1981–82	Edmonton Oilers, NHL	72	21	38	59	18	3	1	0	1	0
1982–83	HIFK, Finland	36	23	41	64	50	9	9	8	17	11
WEC–83	Finland	10	2	5	7	4					
1983–84	HIFK, Finland	37	22	47	69	33	2	1	1	2	2
1984–85	HIFK, Finland	34	23	44	67	24					
1985–86	Landshut, Germany	36	23	41	64	24					
1986–87	HIFK, Finland	44	17	51	68	37	3	0	1	1	10
CCup–87	Finland	5	1	0	1	0					
1987–88	HIFK, Finland	44	17	43	60	37	6	4	5	9	6
1988–89	HIFK, Finland	44	11	30	41	23	2	0	1	1	0
1989–90	Hockey-Reipas, Finland	44	18	47	65	4	4	2	3	5	0
1990–91	Hockey-Reipas, Finland	41	11	30	41	23					
1991–92	HIFK, Finland	42	8	20	28	20					
	NHL Totals	237	56	89	145	36	20	5	2	7	6
	WHA Totals	53	25	31	56	16					
	Finland Totals	557	302	504	806	423	43	21	36	57	44
	OWG/WEC/CCup Totals	55	14	27	41	42					

Finland Champion (1974, 1980, 1983)

result when it saw the introduction of Jari Kurri, Finland's greatest ever NHL star. Hagman recollects: "We were on the lawn in front of the Haga fire station, where I was working at the time—Jari Kurri, Edmonton scout Matti Vaisanen and myself. Kurri had been offered a deal by Edmonton but was reluctant to set out on this adventure. When Jari found out that I was going, he changed his mind, and thus started a career from which he has never looked back."

Hagman mildly regrets having made the decision to leave. The 1983–84 season, only two years away, would have made him a Stanley Cup winner, but he'd chosen to return to Helsinki, where he enjoyed his role as the undisputed king on his team. He nevertheless became the first player in Finland to produce a 100-point season between the regular season and the playoffs in the title-winning 1979–80 season. Since then, it has only been surpassed once, during 1986–87, when Karpat center Kari Jalonen bettered the mark by three points.

In the all-time scoring race, Matti Hagman ended up in the number two slot. In his 14 years of play, he scored 288 goals and ran up a total of 750 points. The overall leader, with 43 points more during an 18-year career, is Pori ace Arto Javanainen. But while Javanainen is the undisputed master in the goal-scoring department, Hagman is the all-time assists leader with 462 to his name, and a four-time point-scoring leader, weighted heavily each time in favor of assists.

As a center who alternated with Wayne Gretzky in Edmonton, Matti Hagman didn't see a lot of ice time.

Denis Potvin

The New York Islanders drafted Denis Potvin first overall in 1973 to serve as the foundation of their developing expansion team. He surpassed all expectations and became the first NHL defenseman to score 1,000 career points, all while functioning as the cornerstone of the franchise's four consecutive Stanley Cup championships from 1980 to 1983. Potvin's wealth of natural talent allowed him to jump into the offensive rush while serving as a tough physical presence in his own end of the rink. He was one of the most complete blueliners to ever step onto the ice. A less discussed facet of Potvin's game was his mean streak. Opposing forwards learned quickly that they were better served avoiding confrontations with one of the NHL's lesser-known tough guys.

The native of Ottawa, Ontario, excelled at football and hockey as a youngster. Having opted to pursue the latter, he made the Ottawa 67s of the Ontario Hockey Association in 1968–69. Potvin enjoyed an outstanding junior career, registering 329 points in five seasons. He was often paired with the offensively gifted Ian Turnbull to form one of the most lethal blue line partnerships ever seen in junior hockey circles. During Potvin's last year in Ottawa, he established an OHA single-season record for defensemen with 123 points.

Denis Potvin distinguished himself on the international stage by participating in Canada's 1976 and 1981 Canada Cup teams.

As the highly touted first pick in the 1973 Amateur Draft, Potvin quickly made his presence felt in the NHL. He amassed 54 points in 1973–74 while displaying the confidence of a 10-year veteran. Potvin was the obvious choice in the Calder Trophy voting at the conclusion of the season. That year he also lived out a dream by playing with his brother Jean, who remained with the club for nearly five years.

Denis Potvin (left) became the first NHL defenseman to score 1,000 career points, all as the cornerstone of the New York Islanders' four consecutive Stanley Cup championships.

Potvin emerged as one of the leaders of a rapidly improving Islanders squad that reached the Stanley Cup semifinals in only its third season. That year he played a key role on the ice and in the dressing room of a club that showed tremendous resolve. During the quarterfinals against Pittsburgh, the Islanders trailed three games to none but fought back to claim the series 4–3. They faced the same situation versus the defending Stanley Cup champions from Philadelphia in the next round. Once again, the Islanders fought back to force a seventh game but fell short in the deciding encounter.

Following the 1975–76 campaign, Potvin was awarded the Norris Trophy, an honor he also received in 1978 and 1979. He experienced his most productive offensive output in the last of those years with 101 points. Between 1980 and 1983, he captained New York when they became only the second team in NHL history to win the Stanley Cup four times in succession (Montreal did it twice). His overtime goal in the 1980 finals against Philadelphia gave his team the momentum and confidence it needed to win its first title. Potvin's top post-season output occurred in 1980–81, when he recorded 25 points in 18 games.

Potvin, Denis
D, 6´, 205 lbs, b: Ottawa, Ont., 10/29/1953

Season	Club, League	Regular Season					Playoffs				
		GP	G	A	Pts	PIM	GP	G	A	Pts	PIM
1973–74	New York Islanders, NHL	77	17	37	54	175					
1974–75	New York Islanders, NHL	79	21	55	76	105	17	5	9	14	30
1975–76	New York Islanders, NHL	78	31	67	98	100	13	5	14	19	32
CCup–76	Canada	7	1	8	9	16					
1976–77	New York Islanders, NHL	80	25	55	80	103	12	6	4	10	20
1977–78	New York Islanders, NHL	80	30	64	94	81	7	2	2	4	6
1978–79	New York Islanders, NHL	73	31	70	101	58	10	4	7	11	8
ChCup–79	NHL All-Stars	2	0	0	0	0					
1979–80	New York Islanders, NHL	31	8	33	41	44	21	6	13	19	24
1980–81	New York Islanders, NHL	74	20	56	76	104	18	8	17	25	16
CCup–81	Canada	7	2	5	7	12					
1981–82	New York Islanders, NHL	60	24	37	61	83	19	5	16	21	30
1982–83	New York Islanders, NHL	69	12	54	66	60	20	8	12	20	22
1983–84	New York Islanders, NHL	78	22	63	85	87	20	1	5	6	28
1984–85	New York Islanders, NHL	77	17	51	68	96	10	3	2	5	10
1985–86	New York Islanders, NHL	74	21	38	59	78	3	0	1	1	0
WEC–86	Canada	7	1	4	5	6					
1986–87	New York Islanders, NHL	58	12	30	42	70	10	2	2	4	21
1987–88	New York Islanders, NHL	72	19	32	51	112	5	1	4	5	6
	NHL Totals	1060	310	742	1052	1356	185	56	108	164	253
	WEC/CCup/ChalCup Totals	23	4	17	21	34					

NHL First All-Star Team (1975, 1976, 1978, 1979, 1981)
NHL Second All-Star Team (1977, 1984)
Won James Norris Trophy (1976, 1978, 1979)
Won Calder Trophy (1974)
Won Stanley Cup (1980–1983)
Won CCup (1976)

The talented defenseman distinguished himself on the international stage through his play on Canada's 1976 and 1981 Canada Cup teams. He retired at the conclusion of the 1987–88 season with regular-season totals of 310 goals and 1,052 points. Potvin also registered 56 goals and 164 points in the playoffs. In addition to his four major trophies, Potvin was selected to the NHL First All-Star Team five times and the Second All-Star Team twice.

The leadership qualities demonstrated by Potvin, along with his exceptional talent at both ends of the ice, placed him in a category reserved for only a handful of NHL defensemen. The Ottawa 67s hosted a special gala in his honor and raised his number to the rafters of the Ottawa Civic Center. Following a game on March 31, 1988, a cheering Nassau Coliseum audience paid homage to his career when his number 5 sweater was retired. Potvin was inducted into the Hockey Hall of Fame in 1991 and the ceremony was held in his home town of Ottawa for the first time.

Zinatula **Bilyaletdinov**

Few Russians could pronounce the name of Dynamo Moscow and Soviet national defenseman Zinatula Bilyaletdinov, so they nicknamed him "Bil." In the U.S. and Canada, most knew him as the first Russian coach to work for an NHL team on a permanent basis.

During his Soviet playing years, he got little attention. Even the sports pages of the major newspapers dismissed him and fellow Dynamo defenseman Vasili Pervukhin as merely second best on the national team. But the two were in fact as reliable as the leading Fetisov–Kasatonov line.

Bilyadletdinov and Pervukhin never followed the traditional rule of play where one defenseman rushes forward and the second defenseman stays back. Pervukhin seldom rushed forward and Bilyaletdinov never did. Pervukhin consistently scored more and Bilyaletdinov got more penalty minutes—five times more than his partner. Bilyaletdinov was indispensable for other reasons.

He was assigned all the dirty work in the defensive zone, and he did it with the commitment of a kamikaze pilot. He was a model defenseman, playing an aggressive, heavy-hitting North American style of hockey.

After working with coach Vladimir Yurzinov, Bilyaletdinov went to Winnipeg for a while. When he returned to his native Dynamo team as head coach, it wasn't long before his team started manifesting some of the North American tricks he had learned. His Dynamo players have acquired a North American kind of energy apparent in their intrinsic impulse to rush. At the boards they take off like demons and don't lose any face-to-face contests with opposition forwards. During the last minutes of a game, they can charge into the opposition's defensive zone and battle until the puck is in the net.

The stubbornest coaches in Russia are former defensemen who can endure any hardship and stay the course. Bilyaletdinov is cut from the same cloth as the stalwart Viktor Tikhonov, and that says it all.

Zinatula Bilyaletdinov (front) was assigned all the dirty work in the defensive zone, and he did it with the commitment of a kamikaze pilot.

Bilyaletdinov, Zinatula
D, 6´, 190 lbs, b: Moscow, USSR, 3/13/1955

Season	Club, League	Regular Season				
		GP	G	A	Pts	PIM
1973–74	Dynamo Moscow, USSR	23	0	1	1	2
1974–75	Dynamo Moscow, USSR	36	2	1	3	6
1975–76	Dynamo Moscow, USSR	33	1	2	3	13
CCup–76	USSR	5	0	1	1	4
1976–77	Dynamo Moscow, USSR	33	1	4	5	18
1977–78	Dynamo Moscow, USSR	35	2	3	5	27
WEC–78	USSR	10	0	1	1	17
1978–79	Dynamo Moscow, USSR	43	6	4	10	55
WEC–79	USSR	8	3	4	7	2
1979–80	Dynamo Moscow, USSR	43	14	9	23	44
OWG–80	USSR	7	1	3	4	2
1980–81	Dynamo Moscow, USSR	49	6	5	11	54
WEC–81	USSR	8	1	2	3	4
CCup–81	USSR	7	0	1	1	8
1981–82	Dynamo Moscow, USSR	47	6	11	17	28
WEC–82	USSR	9	2	1	3	14
1982–83	Dynamo Moscow, USSR	42	1	8	9	20
WEC–83	USSR	7	0	3	3	10
1983–84	Dynamo Moscow, USSR	42	2	6	8	36
OWG–84	USSR	7	1	1	2	0
CCup–84	USSR	6	0	0	0	12
1984–85	Dynamo Moscow, USSR	36	4	7	11	24
WEC–85	USSR	10	0	0	0	14
1985–86	Dynamo Moscow, USSR	40	10	14	24	38
WEC–86	USSR	8	0	1	1	14
1986–87	Dynamo Moscow, USSR	40	6	5	11	12
WEC–87	USSR	3	0	2	2	4
1987–88	Dynamo Moscow, USSR	46	1	10	11	20
	USSR Totals	588	62	90	152	397
	OWG/WEC/CCup Totals	95	8	20	28	105

Won OWG (1984)
Won WEC (1978, 1979, 1981, 1982, 1983, 1986)
Won CCup (1981)

A HISTORY OF WORLD HOCKEY

Rick **Middleton**

Bruins general manager Harry Sinden once said "Rick Middleton (left) can spice up a dull game."

Rick Middleton began his professional hockey career as the first-round draft pick for the New York Rangers in 1973. He finished off the season with a flourish as rookie of the year in the American Hockey League, then played left wing with the Rangers for two years before he was traded to the Boston Bruins in 1976 for Ken Hodge. After a few years, sportswriters began calling it one of the most lop-sided deals in recent hockey history—in favor of the Bruins. Things were looking pretty bright right from the start of Middleton's arrival in Boston, as he scored a hat-trick in his first-ever game as a Bruin.

Middleton was born in Toronto. He played his junior hockey for the Oshawa Generals and led the Ontario Hockey Association in goals in his last season as an amateur. When Middleton arrived in Boston in 1976, he came with a reputation as a playboy and a fellow who wasn't going to let the fact that he made his living as a pro athlete get in the way of his active social life. At Middleton's first Bruins training camp, Don Cherry, the team's coach, told him, "You look a little pudgy to me," and waited for an apology. "Yeah, I had a good summer," laughed Rick. Right then and there, Cherry decided he'd found a new "project" for the season.

Despite his sense of humor, Middleton was respected as a tough but very clean player. "Rick Middleton is probably the best all-around forward in the league," Bruins GM Harry Sinden once said. "He can spice up a dull game." Others were equally unstinting in their praise. "Defensively, he is going to pick your pockets," said his teammate Brad Park. "And offensively, he is going to turn you inside out. He's just the total player, offensively and defensively. His moves offensively make him such a threat because of his goal production. Defensively, he positions himself so well, he's going to knock the puck away." By 1985, Middleton had earned his place as captain of the Bruins.

Middleton credits much of his success in hockey to Cherry, who very early in his career encouraged him to work on his defense. "Don once told me that if you aren't doing well offensively, work on your defense and the offense will take care of itself. I've never forgotten what Grapes said." He added, "I play a complete game and I owe it to Don. I respect the man and I'm glad he made me work on my game."

Without a doubt, Middleton was one of very few players in the NHL who was strong on both the power-play and as a penalty killer. "Middleton draws the people in Boston," said Sinden. "We play a lousy game here and Ricky

Middleton, Rick
RW, 5′11″, 170 lbs, b: Toronto, Ont., 12/4/1953

Season	Club, League	Regular Season					Playoffs				
		GP	G	A	Pts	PIM	GP	G	A	Pts	PIM
1973–74	Providence Reds, AHL	63	36	48	84	14	15	9	6	15	2
1974–75	New York Rangers, NHL	47	22	18	40	19	3	0	0	0	2
1975–76	New York Rangers, NHL	77	24	26	50	14					
1976–77	Boston Bruins, NHL	72	20	22	42	2	13	5	4	9	0
1977–78	Boston Bruins, NHL	79	25	35	60	8	15	5	2	7	0
1978–79	Boston Bruins, NHL	71	38	48	86	7	11	4	8	12	0
1979–80	Boston Bruins, NHL	80	40	52	92	24	10	4	2	6	5
1980–81	Boston Bruins, NHL	80	44	59	103	16	3	0	1	1	2
CCup–81	Canada	7	1	2	3	0					
1981–82	Boston Bruins, NHL	75	51	43	94	12	11	6	9	15	0
1982–83	Boston Bruins, NHL	80	49	47	96	8	17	11	22	33	6
1983–84	Boston Bruins, NHL	80	47	58	105	14	3	0	0	0	0
CCup–84	Canada	7	4	4	8	0					
1984–85	Boston Bruins, NHL	80	30	46	76	6	5	3	0	3	0
1985–86	Boston Bruins, NHL	49	14	30	44	10					
1986–87	Boston Bruins, NHL	76	31	37	68	6	4	2	2	4	0
1987–88	Boston Bruins, NHL	59	13	19	32	11	19	5	5	10	4
	NHL Totals	1005	448	540	988	157	114	45	55	100	19
	CCup Totals	14	5	6	11	0					

NHL Second All-Star Team (1982)
Won Lady Byng Trophy (1982)
Won CCup (1984)

will put on a move or score a goal that's almost worth the price of admission."

Middleton also gave credit to his wife and family for nurturing and maturing him, especially after he suffered a serious injury in mid-career after getting hit in the head with a puck in the days when not many NHL players wore helmets. "I used to lose my concentration a lot," he once admitted in reference to his maturing as a player. "And that became a big problem for me. Now I'm into the game more and I bear down harder."

Rick Middleton (center) was one of very few players in the NHL who was equally strong on the power-play and as a penalty killer.

In 1981 and 1984 Middleton was a member of the Canadian team in the Canada Cup. But his biggest success in international hockey, he claimed, happened in 1984 while he was a member of coach Scotty Bowman's team. Middleton played on a line with Wayne Gretzky and Gilbert Perreault. Gretzky himself was amazed at Middleton's abilities on ice and remarked, "He delivers the puck fast and right where he wants it to be, but it just seems to jump off his stick on its own!"

Udo Kiessling

He played only one game in the NHL, but Udo Kiessling will go down in history as one of the best players Germany ever produced. Kiessling, a rugged defenseman with talent, set a new record in 1992 in Meribel, France, by appearing in his fifth consecutive Olympic tournament. In a poll of readers of the German *Eishockey News*, he was chosen the best German defenseman of all time, receiving 4,921 votes to 3,871 for second-place Uwe Krupp, who scored the winning goal in overtime to give the Colorado Avalanche the Stanley Cup in 1996. Center Erich Kuhnhackl was the only other player to poll more votes than Kiessling, who was named player of the year in German hockey in 1977, 1984 and 1986 and also appeared in 13 World Championships between 1976 and 1991. "Since I have been on the national team, Udo has been the heart and Gerd Truntschka the soul," goalie Helmut De Raaf once said.

Udo Kiessling played his first game on the West German national team at the age of 17, with his father as coach.

Lou Nanne, the former Minnesota North Stars rearguard, was coach of the U.S. team at the 1977 World Championship in Vienna and saw Kiessling play when he was just 21. Nanne tried to get him to come to North America in 1979, but he declined. But when Kiessling's Dusseldorf team made an early exit from the playoffs in 1982, Nanne called again. This time Kiessling, who was on a try-out, saw action in one game. The North Stars wanted him to sign a contract, but he wanted to play in the World Championship in Finland and decided to go back home.

Udo Kiessling (right) played only one game in the NHL, but he will go down in history as one of the best players Germany ever produced.

Kiessling was born in Crimmitschau, East Germany, in 1955. His father, Gerhard Kiessling, was the East German national team coach and was the first of the family to sneak into the West. He was followed by Udo's sister and mother and then a few hours later by Udo and his grandmother. All had different official excuses for going to the West. The Kiesslings first went to West Berlin but eventually settled in Frankfurt. Gerhard coached the West German national team from 1966 to 1973, including appearances at the 1968 and 1972 Olympics.

Gerhard bought Udo's first skates in Canada and had him on the ice at age two. Udo played his first game on the West German national team at age 17, with his father as coach.

He made his first appearance in the Olympics at Innsbruck in 1976 at the age of 20, and with both Canada and Sweden not participating, the West Germans surprisingly defeated the United States 4–1 to win the bronze medal. Ernst Koepf scored the winning goal in that game, and 15 years later, at the 1991 World Championship in Finland, Kiessling played with Koepf's 23-year-old son, Ernst Jr. "I saw Koepf on the back of his jersey and I tried to make myself play like I was 21 again, but I couldn't," Kiessling joked.

At the 1987 World Championship in Vienna, Kiessling was named to the First All-Star team on defense along with Viacheslav Fetisov of the Soviet Union, perhaps the greatest European star in history. Dominik Hasek of Czechoslovakia was the goalie. At the 1988 Olympics in Calgary, Kiessling was a member of the underdog West German team that again beat the U.S. 4–1 to put an outstanding collection of collegiate stars, coached by Dave Peterson, out of medal contention.

Although West German fans viewed him as an ambassador of the sport, some Canadians playing in the Bundesliga called him the dirtiest player in the league and charged that the referees protected him because of his stature.

Kiessling played most of his career with the Cologne and Dusseldorf clubs in Germany. He retired as an active player with the Landshut team at the end of the 1995–96 season, shortly before his 41st birthday.

Kiessling, Udo
D, 5'10", 180 lbs, b: Crimmitschau, GDR, 5/21/1955

Season	Club, League	Regular Season					Playoffs				
		GP	G	A	Pts	PIM	GP	G	A	Pts	PIM
1972–73	Riessersee, FRG	40	8	6	14	44					
WEC–73	FRG	10	0	0	0	6					
1973–74	Augsburg, FRG	36	16	6	22	52					
1974–75	Rosenheim, FRG	34	20	18	38	73					
1975–76	Rosenheim, FRG	34	30	22	52	72					
OWG–76	FRG	6	0	1	1	8					
WEC–76	FRG	10	0	1	1	8					
1976–77	Kolner, Cologne, FRG	46	13	21	34	143					
WEC–77	FRG	10	1	2	3	6					
1977–78	Kolner, Cologne, FRG	39	16	18	34	48					
WEC–78	FRG	10	0	5	5	10					
1978–79	Kolner, Cologne, FRG	40	28	32	60	78					
WEC–79	FRG	8	2	4	6	14					
1979–80	Dusseldorf, FRG	48	39	44	83	84	7	2	2	4	10
OWG–80	FRG	5	2	2	4	6					
1980–81	Dusseldorf, FRG	39	14	29	43	93	11	8	4	12	22
1981–82	Dusseldorf, FRG	38	15	22	37	54	2	0	0	0	7
	Minnesota North Stars, NHL	1	0	0	0	2					
WEC–82	FRG	7	1	3	4	12					
1982–83	Fussen, FRG	21	12	13	25	52					
	Kolner, Cologne, FRG	9	4	0	4	2	9	3	7	10	18
WEC–83	FRG	4	0	1	1	10					
1983–84	Kolner, Cologne, FRG	45	9	19	28	74					
OWG–84	FRG	6	3	1	4	4					
CCup–84	FRG	4	0	1	1	4					
1984–85	Kolner, Cologne, FRG	36	14	26	40	38	9	4	10	14	22
WEC–85	FRG	10	0	3	3	16					
1985–86	Kolner, Cologne, FRG	37	18	27	45	41					
WEC–86	FRG	10	4	2	6	22					
1986–87	Kolner, Cologne, FRG	42	10	34	44	70	9	4	11	15	10
WEC–87	FRG	10	5	3	8	18					
1987–88	Kolner, Cologne, FRG	46	12	27	39	76					
OWG–88	FRG	8	1	5	6	20					
1988–89	Kolner, Cologne, FRG	31	11	24	35	38	9	6	4	10	8
WEC–89	FRG	10	2	0	2	12					
1989–90	Kolner, Cologne, FRG	35	7	15	22	45					
WEC–90	FRG	10	2	1	3	10					
1990–91	Kolner, Cologne, FRG	35	7	13	20	36	12	2	4	6	18
WEC–91	FRG	10	0	1	1	6					
1991–92	Kolner, Cologne, Germany	42	11	23	34	38	4	2	0	2	2
OWG–92	Germany	8	0	0	0	6					
1992–93	Landshut, Germany	44	9	19	28	50					
1993–94	Landshut, Germany	44	3	16	19	74					
1994–95	Landshut, Germany	41	7	15	22	40	18	3	7	10	22
1995–96	Landshut, Germany	50	3	19	22	44	7	0	2	2	4
	FRG/Germany Totals	952	336	508	844	1459	97	34	51	85	143
	NHL Totals	1	0	0	0	2					
	OWG/WEC/CCup Totals	156	23	36	59	198					

FRG/Germany Champion (1977, 1979, 1984, 1986, 1987, 1988)

Bob Gainey

Termed the world's best all-around player by Soviet national team coach Viktor Tikhonov, Bob Gainey brought many elements to the Montreal Canadiens during his 16-year NHL career. The burly left winger was a tenacious competitor, relentless checker, respected team leader and capable contributor on the offense. His presence on the Habs' roster helped the team win the Stanley Cup five times in the decade between 1976 and 1986.

The native of Peterborough, Ontario, started playing organized hockey at the age of seven. Originally a defenseman, Gainey was switched to left wing by church league coach Red Wasson. Under Roger Neilson, he starred with the hometown Petes of the Ontario Hockey Association. Gainey was blessed with immense speed, but his numerous scoring chances often went for naught, as he lacked the hands to be a sniper. His ability to shut down the best players on the opposition impressed many scouts. Montreal Canadiens general manager Sam Pollock knew a surefire NHLer when he saw one. He made sure the Habs chose Gainey in the first round of the NHL Amateur Draft in 1973.

As a rookie, Gainey demonstrated his commitment to defensive hockey and his clean but feared bodychecking. He showed even more poise as a sophomore in 1974–75, when he played on the team's second line with Jacques Lemaire and Yvan Cournoyer. Following his third NHL season, Gainey was picked to represent his country in the inaugural Canada Cup in 1976 and his combination of speed, tenacity and physical play enabled him to fill an important role on the victorious Canadian contingent. While helping Montreal win four consecutive Stanley Cup titles from 1976 to 1979, Gainey became a star despite never being a flashy scorer. His name appeared in the game summary far less frequently than most of his teammates, but without him the Habs quite possibly wouldn't have won.

Gainey exploded for 16 points when the Habs won the Cup for the fourth straight time in 1979. In the finals, the Rangers won the first match and started strongly in the second. Gainey's winning goal in game two shifted the

Left winger Bob Gainey became a star even though he was never a flashy scorer.

Gainey, Bob
LW, 6′2″, 200 lbs, b: Peterborough, Ont., 12/13/1953

Season	Club, League	Regular Season					Playoffs				
		GP	G	A	Pts	PIM	GP	G	A	Pts	PIM
1973-74	Montreal Canadiens, NHL	66	3	7	10	34	6	0	0	0	6
	Nova Scotia Voyageurs, AHL	6	2	5	7	4					
1974-75	Montreal Canadiens, NHL	80	17	20	37	49	11	2	4	6	4
1975-76	Montreal Canadiens, NHL	78	15	13	28	57	13	1	3	4	20
CCup-76	Canada	5	2	0	2	2					
1976-77	Montreal Canadiens, NHL	80	14	19	33	41	14	4	1	5	25
1977-78	Montreal Canadiens, NHL	66	15	16	31	57	15	2	7	9	14
1978-79	Montreal Canadiens, NHL	79	20	18	38	44	16	6	10	16	10
1979-80	Montreal Canadiens, NHL	64	14	19	33	32	10	1	1	2	4
1980-81	Montreal Canadiens, NHL	78	23	24	47	36	3	0	0	0	2
CCup-81	Canada	7	1	3	4	2					
1981-82	Montreal Canadiens, NHL	79	21	24	45	24	5	0	1	1	8
WEC-82	Canada	10	2	1	3	0					
1982-83	Montreal Canadiens, NHL	80	12	18	30	43	3	0	0	0	4
WEC-83	Canada	10	0	6	6	2					
1983-84	Montreal Canadiens, NHL	77	17	22	39	41	15	1	5	6	9
1984-85	Montreal Canadiens, NHL	79	19	13	32	40	12	1	3	4	13
1985-86	Montreal Canadiens, NHL	80	20	23	43	20	20	5	5	10	12
1986-87	Montreal Canadiens, NHL	47	8	8	16	19	17	1	3	4	6
1987-88	Montreal Canadiens, NHL	78	11	11	22	14	6	0	1	1	6
1988-89	Montreal Canadiens, NHL	49	10	7	17	34	16	1	4	5	8
	NHL Totals	1160	239	262	501	585	182	25	48	73	151
	WEC/CCup Totals	32	5	10	15	6					

Won Frank J. Selke Trophy (1978, 1979, 1980, 1981)
Won Conn Smythe Trophy (1979)
Won Stanley Cup (1976, 1977, 1978, 1979, 1986)
Won CCup (1976)

momentum in Montreal's favor and sent the Habs on their way to the Cup. For his immense contribution, he was awarded the Conn Smythe Trophy. As writer and columnist Rick Salutin noted, "Lafleur fulfils our every stereotype of French-Canadian finesse, while Gainey does the same for our notions of the earnest, achieving English Canadian."

Gainey's style of play and ability to check and skate with the NHL's top forwards inspired the league to create a new post-season award. Beginning in 1978, the NHL presented the Frank J. Selke Trophy to the top defensive forward in the game. Fittingly, Gainey was the recipient in each of the first four years it was awarded.

Bob Gainey (number 23) had a style of play and an ability to check and skate with the NHL's top forwards that inspired the league to create a new post-season award, the Frank J. Selke Trophy.

Prior to the 1981–82 season, Gainey was named Serge Savard's successor as captain of the Canadiens. As one of the few remaining links to the glorious 1970s, he was expected to oversee the passing along of the organization's winning tradition to the younger players. The team remained a top-flight outfit in the regular season but experienced three straight first-round playoff losses from 1981 to 1983. In a reversal of the pattern, the team attained a disappointing 75 points in 1983–84 before embarking on a surprising run to the semifinals. Gainey and linemates Guy Carbonneau and Chris Nilan played a key role in shutting down the top guns on the heavily favored Bruins and Nordiques before giving the defending champion Islanders all they could handle in the semis.

The veteran captain hoisted the Stanley Cup for the fifth time in his career in 1986. Playing with the energy of a rookie, Gainey scored five goals and 10 points while patrolling his wing with customary efficiency. His poise and leadership helped the team register consecutive 100-point seasons in 1987–88 and 1988–89. In the latter of those, the Habs reached the finals, then succumbed to the Calgary Flames in six games. Following the series, Gainey announced his retirement.

After leaving the NHL, Gainey signed on for a year as player-coach of the Epinal franchise in French hockey's first division. He made a triumphant return to North America and was appointed general manager of the Minnesota North Stars in January 1992. In his first year behind the bench, he guided the team to the second Stanley Cup finals, appearance in franchise history and he remained with the organization when it relocated to Dallas in 1993. In Texas, Gainey helped build the team into a league powerhouse. Unfortunately, this period in his life was marred by the tragic passing of his wife, Cathy, after a valiant battle with cancer.

Gainey stepped down as coach in 1995 to focus solely on the duties of general manager. He masterminded the acquisition of key performers such as Joe Nieuwendyk, Pat Verbeek, Brett Hull and Ed Belfour, who augmented homegrown U.S. talent like Derian Hatcher and Jamie Langenbrunner. The Stars won the Presidents' Trophy for having the most points in the NHL in 1998 and 1999 and the first Stanley Cup in the history of the franchise in the second of these seasons. When the Stars slumped badly in 2001–02, Gainey made the drastic move of firing head coach Ken Hitchcock and replacing him with Rick Wilson on an interim basis while at the same time removing himself as general manager. He remains with the organization, however, and has lived in Dallas with his children since his wife's death at 39 in 1995. An unqualified success since entering the NHL, Gainey was inducted into the Hockey Hall of Fame in 1992.

Lanny **McDonald**

A blazing shot and an uninhibited enthusiasm for the game were two of the multitude of positive qualities associated with Lanny McDonald. He could skate, shoot, win the battles in the corners and lead by example on the ice or in the dressing room. McDonald was a consummate professional whose quick release helped him score 500 career goals.

The native of Hanna, Alberta, in the heart of the province's cattle country, first made a name for himself with the Lethbridge Sugar Kings of the Alberta Junior Hockey League. He became known to scouts all over North America when he graduated to the Western Canada Junior Hockey League, briefly with the Calgary Centennials but most significantly in the uniform of the Medicine Hat Tigers. The high-scoring right winger scored 50 and 62 goals in his two seasons with the Tigers. He and linemate Tom Lysiak terrorized the league and helped their club reach the 1972–73 Memorial Cup tournament.

On the international stage, Lanny McDonald (left) helped win the Canada Cup in 1976 and captained Team Canada at the 1981 World Championship.

Prior to the 1973 Amateur Draft, the Toronto Maple Leafs were trying to decide between Dennis Vervegaert of the London Knights and McDonald. As it turned out, the Vancouver Canucks did them a favor by choosing the London star third overall, one spot ahead of Toronto, leaving the Leafs to choose McDonald.

The 1973–74 season was an exciting year of rebuilding in Toronto as McDonald was joined by rookies Ian Turnbull, Borje Salming and Inge Hammarstrom. McDonald scored 14 and 17 goals in his first two years and caused a few concerns among doubters who believed these totals were unacceptably low. The 1975–76 season with linemates Darryl Sittler and Errol Thompson proved to be his breakthrough. McDonald scored 93 points and helped Sittler score an NHL-record 10 points in one game against Boston on February 7, 1976.

Three straight 40-goal seasons followed, and many felt McDonald might break Frank Mahovlich's team record for one year. However, he fell just short, with his highest output being 47 in 1977–78. That same year the Maple Leafs enjoyed their best season since the mid-1960s with 92 points. The pinnacle of their year came courtesy of McDonald's game seven overtime winner against the New York Islanders, which propelled the team into the semifinals for the first time since their Stanley Cup triumph in 1967.

On the international stage, McDonald excelled in a defensive role for his country when the Canadian team won the inaugural Canada Cup tournament in September 1976. In fact, although he was a prolific scorer, the upbeat winger relished the chance to shut down the top line on the opposition when required. His quick release and wrist strength remained the traits that caused goalies the most headaches. McDonald summed up his offensive success: "Outside of Gretzky, there aren't any scorers in this league who don't need plenty of help. I'm the type of shooter who comes down the wing and needs a clear alley to the net, and that's not something you can create yourself."

Although he scored 43 times in 1978–79, the team struggled, and renegade owner Harold Ballard exacerbated the situation by ridiculing the team and coach Roger Neilson in the media.

A blazing shot and an uninhibited enthusiasm for the game were two of the many positive qualities associated with Lanny McDonald (right).

The following season, under the out-of-touch direction of general manager Punch Imlach and coach Floyd Smith, the team sank to the level of mediocrity. McDonald was caught in a war between Ballard and Sittler that saw him banished to the Colorado Rockies in one of the most unpopular trades in team history.

McDonald was named captain of the Rockies, and he was fairly productive on a bad team. He scored 66 goals in 142 games in Denver and played for Canada in the 1981 World Championship. However, his passion had been damaged by his mistreatment in Toronto and it appeared that his best days might be behind him.

Early in the 1981–82 season, the spark was put back in McDonald's skates when a trade sent him home to play for the Calgary Flames. He scored 34 times in 55 games and seemed rejuvenated on a team that was trying to build a contender but remained in the shadow of the mighty Edmonton Oilers. Flames general manager Cliff Fletcher enthused: "Lanny McDonald is probably the most popular Alberta-born athlete today. When you have a Gretzky just 180 miles up the road, you'd better have some credibility yourself. That's about all the grounds you would need for the deal we made."

In 1982–83, the sharpshooter recorded a career-best 66 goals and 98 points but the team was crushed by the Oilers in the post-season. McDonald's tremendous year and competitive spirit were acknowledged when he was presented the Bill Masterton Trophy. Calgary coach Bob Johnson noted, "When he gets that shot where he wants it to go, the light goes on."

Through the remainder of the decade, McDonald provided unselfish play and superb checking on one of the league's most powerful teams. An invaluable leader, he served as co-captain at various times with Doug Risebrough, Jim Peplinski and Tim Hunter. While McDonald evolved into a valuable role player in the latter stages of his career, the Flames emerged as a league powerhouse.

In 1985–86, the Flames stunned Edmonton in the Smythe Division finals, then defeated St. Louis to reach the Stanley Cup finals for the first time in franchise history. Although they lost to Montreal in five games in the finals, the team was learning to win in the post-season. In 1987–88, Calgary won the Presidents' Trophy

McDonald, Lanny
RW, 6´, 185 lbs, b: Hanna, Alta., 2/16/1953

Season	Club, League	Regular Season					Playoffs				
		GP	G	A	Pts	PIM	GP	G	A	Pts	PIM
1973-74	Toronto Maple Leafs, NHL	70	14	16	30	43					
1974-75	Toronto Maple Leafs, NHL	64	17	27	44	86	7	0	0	0	2
1975-76	Toronto Maple Leafs, NHL	75	37	56	93	70	10	4	4	8	4
CCup-76	Canada	5	0	2	2	0					
1976-77	Toronto Maple Leafs, NHL	80	46	44	90	77	9	10	7	17	6
1977-78	Toronto Maple Leafs, NHL	74	47	40	87	54	13	3	4	7	10
1978-79	Toronto Maple Leafs, NHL	79	43	42	85	32	6	3	2	5	0
ChalCup-79	NHL All-Stars	3	0	0	0	2					
1979-80	Toronto Maple Leafs, NHL	35	15	15	30	10					
	Colorado Rockies, NHL	46	25	20	45	43					
1980-81	Colorado Rockies, NHL	80	35	46	81	56					
WEC-81	Canada	8	3	0	3	4					
1981-82	Colorado Rockies, NHL	16	6	9	15	20					
	Calgary Flames, NHL	55	34	33	67	37	3	0	1	1	6
1982-83	Calgary Flames, NHL	80	66	32	98	90	7	3	4	7	19
1983-84	Calgary Flames, NHL	65	33	33	66	64	11	6	7	13	6
1984-85	Calgary Flames, NHL	43	19	18	37	36	1	0	0	0	0
1985-86	Calgary Flames, NHL	80	28	43	71	44	22	11	7	18	30
1986-87	Calgary Flames, NHL	58	14	12	26	54	5	0	0	0	2
1987-88	Calgary Flames, NHL	60	10	13	23	57	9	3	1	4	6
1988-89	Calgary Flames, NHL	51	11	7	18	26	14	1	3	4	29
	NHL Totals	1111	500	506	1006	899	117	44	40	84	120
	WEC/CCup/ChalCup Totals	16	3	2	5	6					

NHL Second All-Star Team (1977, 1983)
Won Bill Masterton Trophy (1983)
Won King Clancy Trophy (1988)
Won Bud Man of the Year Award (1989)
Won Stanley Cup (1989)
Won CCup (1976)

after leading the NHL with 105 points, but lost an emotional playoff series to the archrival Oilers.

The following season McDonald reached the 500-goal and 1,000-point marks and the team racked up 117 points in the regular season. In the playoffs they relied on their depth and the previous three years' experience to win the Stanley Cup for the first time. Fittingly, the veteran McDonald scored a goal in the Cup-clinching win over the Montreal Canadiens. This represented the first time an opposing team had captured the Stanley Cup at the fabled Montreal Forum.

McDonald retired in 1989 on a high note with a Stanley Cup ring and the 500-goal and 1,000-point milestones on his record. Three years later he was inducted into the Hockey Hall of Fame, where he joined former teammate and long-time friend Darryl Sittler. The first player to have his number retired by the Flames, he moved into the Calgary front office after his playing career and was a perfect fit in the community relations department. In August 2000 he announced he was retiring to spend more time with his family, but shortly thereafter assumed duties as general manager for Canada's entry in the 2001 World Championship.

Mark Howe

Blessed with natural offensive ability, Mark Howe succeeded as a forward and defenseman in his 22 years of pro hockey. Following in the footsteps of his legendary father, Gordie, Mark forged his own identity as a skillful player who used finesse and raw talent to great effect.

Howe played minor hockey in his home town of Detroit with the Tier II Junior Red Wings. In 1970–71, at the age of 15, he scored 107 points for the Wings to lead the entire Western Ontario Junior A circuit. A knee injury knocked him out for the first three months of the next season. When he regained his health, Howe decided to play with the U.S. national team, and in 1972 he helped the U.S. Olympic team win the silver medal at the Sapporo games. As a youngster, Howe was allowed to watch his father practise and to attend training camp. When he was older, Mark was allowed to suit up for the occasional team scrimmage at the Olympia.

Mark Howe's mobility and experience were key ingredients in the Flyers' run to the semifinals in 1985 and 1987.

After a deal was worked out with the London Knights, Howe and his brother Marty joined the Toronto Marlboros of the OHA in 1972–73. In his only year of major junior hockey, he scored 104 points and then contributed four goals and four assists in three games to lead the Marlies to the Memorial Cup championship. For his yeoman's service, Mark was the recipient of the Stafford Smythe Memorial Trophy as the tournament's outstanding player.

The Howe family made hockey history with the Houston Aeros of the WHA in 1973–74 when Gordie came out of retirement to play with his two sons on the same forward line. Mark scored his first professional goal 27 years to the day after his father tallied for the first time in a Detroit uniform. After a 38-goal output, Mark was presented the Lou Kaplan Trophy as the league's top rookie and placed on the Second All-Star Team. A few months later, he scored six points in seven

The Howe family made history with the Houston Aeros of the WHA in 1973–74 when Gordie (center) came out of retirement to play on the same forward line with sons Mark (right) and Marty.

games for the WHA's Canadian stars in the 1974 series versus the USSR.

In 1975 Mark led all playoff scorers with 10 goals and 22 points in 13 games while leading Houston to the Avco Cup. Because he was an extremely versatile player, coach Bill Dineen made good use of him on both forward and defense. One season, Howe made the WHA mid-season All-Star squad at left wing. He played defense the second half of the year and excelled to the point that he ended up as one of the rearguards on the All-Star squad at the end of the season. In 1977–78, he joined the New England franchise and remained with it when it joined the NHL as the Hartford Whalers in 1979. Howe made the transition to the NHL with ease, scoring 80 points that season. Coach Don Blackburn moved him back to the blue line to improve the team's transition game and quarterback the power-play. Later he was moved back to forward to add offensive punch and check the opposition's top scoring line.

After he recorded five assists in Hartford's 8–2 romp over Boston, Bruins general manager Harry Sinden commented: "The first time I saw Mark Howe play, I got goosebumps. Only five or six players have I felt that way about, and he's one of them." In 1981 he was a key member of Team USA at the Canada Cup tournament.

Among all his good fortune, Howe did experience one major setback that influenced the rest of his career. On December 27, 1980, he was seriously injured by one of the older-style nets. During the game, Howe lost his balance when chasing a loose puck in his own zone and went feet first into the goal. His skates raised the goal posts off the ice, causing the elevated point at the center back to pierce him in the buttock, just missing the spinal column. This accident forced the NHL to install safer nets without sharp points and with magnetic fasteners that would allow the goal to become dislodged more easily. This injury hit him in the prime of his career, and when he didn't bounce back as quickly as hoped, the Whalers became a little anxious.

Howe, Mark
LW/D, 5´11˝, 185 lbs, b: Detroit, MI., 5/28/1955

Season	Club, League	Regular Season					Playoffs				
		GP	G	A	Pts	PIM	GP	G	A	Pts	PIM
OWG–72	USA	6	0	0	0	0					
1973–74	Houston Aeros, WHA	76	38	41	79	20	14	9	10	19	4
1974–75	Houston Aeros, WHA	74	36	40	76	30	13	10	12	22	0
1975–76	Houston Aeros, WHA	72	39	37	76	38	17	6	10	16	18
1976–77	Houston Aeros, WHA	57	23	52	75	46	10	4	10	14	2
1977–78	New England Whalers, WHA	70	30	61	91	32	14	8	7	15	18
1978–79	New England Whalers, WHA	77	42	65	107	32	6	4	2	6	6
1979–80	Hartford Whalers, NHL	74	24	56	80	20	3	1	2	3	2
1980–81	Hartford Whalers, NHL	63	19	46	65	54					
CCup–81	USA	6	0	4	4	2					
1981–82	Hartford Whalers, NHL	76	8	45	53	18					
1982–83	Philadelphia Flyers, NHL	76	20	47	67	18	3	0	2	2	4
1983–84	Philadelphia Flyers, NHL	71	19	34	53	44	3	0	0	0	2
1984–85	Philadelphia Flyers, NHL	73	18	39	57	31	19	3	8	11	6
1985–86	Philadelphia Flyers, NHL	77	24	58	82	36	5	0	4	4	0
1986–87	Philadelphia Flyers, NHL	69	15	43	58	37	26	2	10	12	4
1987–88	Philadelphia Flyers, NHL	75	19	43	62	62	7	3	6	9	4
1988–89	Philadelphia Flyers, NHL	52	9	29	38	45	19	0	15	15	10
1989–90	Philadelphia Flyers, NHL	40	7	21	28	24					
1990–91	Philadelphia Flyers, NHL	19	0	10	10	8					
1991–92	Philadelphia Flyers, NHL	42	7	18	25	18					
1992–93	Detroit Red Wings, NHL	60	3	31	34	22	7	1	3	4	2
1993–94	Detroit Red Wings, NHL	44	4	20	24	8	6	0	1	1	0
1994–95	Detroit Red Wings, NHL	18	1	5	6	10	3	0	0	0	0
	WHA Totals	426	208	296	504	198	74	41	51	92	48
	NHL Totals	929	197	545	742	455	101	10	51	61	34
	OWG/CCup Totals	12	0	4	4	2					

NHL First All-Star Team (1983, 1986, 1987)
WHA First All-Star Team (1979)
WHA Second All-Star Team (1974)
Won Lou Kaplan Trophy—WHA Rookie of the Year (1974)
NHL Plus-Minus Leader (1986)
Won Avco Cup (1974, 1975)

Howe was involved in a multi-player transaction in August 1982 that saw him end up in Philadelphia, where he became a fixture on one of the NHL's top clubs and twice recorded 20-goal seasons. The accident in Hartford curtailed his offensive capabilities to an extent, but nonetheless he remained a top player. His mobility and experience were key ingredients in the team's run to the finals against the triumphant Edmonton Oilers in 1985 and 1987. Howe was selected to the NHL First All-Star Team in 1983, 1986 and 1987.

Despite having to live up to being the son of one of the icons of 20th century sports, Howe never felt pressured. "I've always been serious. I'm not into the showman part of the game. I'm not flashy. I play my game. There are things I try to avoid. I know what Dad did. I know what I can do. I'm extremely proud to be Colleen and Gordie Howe's son. But I am my own person."

In 1992 Howe lived out a childhood fantasy by signing as a free agent with his father's old team, the Detroit Red Wings. This also represented a chance for him to play on a potential Stanley Cup winner at this late stage in his career. He played parts of three seasons in Motown before retiring in 1995 due to recurring back problems. The difficult decision to retire was made easier when Howe wasn't used in the finals against New Jersey. The next year he accepted an administrative position with the Wings and soon began scouting and working with the young defensemen in the minors while making occasional publicity appearances on behalf of the club.

Viktor Tikhonov

Many regarded Viktor Tikhonov as a slave driver who endeavored to squeeze the most out of his subordinates for the sake of victory. Yet Tikhonov maintained the same standard for himself. Many will doubtlessly be surprised to learn that the septuagenarian coach is still working hard at the helm of the CSKA hockey club, which at the beginning of the 21st century is at the bottom of the Russian hockey standings.

The following words describing Tikhonov the player can be found in a hockey manual:

No other coach has ever acquired Viktor Tikhonov's national prominence.

"Possessed a high level of positional play on the rink, excellent bodychecks. Played with utmost attention and responsibility."

In Moscow in 1958, the Dynamo club crossed sticks with the Kelowna Packers from Canada. Playing opposite Tikhonov was Russ Kowalchuk, a very hefty player. Early in the game, Kowalchuk pasted Tikhonov against the boards. When Tikhonov returned to the ice, he had his head bandaged. And right to the very end of the game, the slightly built Tikhonov kept Kowalchuk in check no matter where he was on the ice.

Tikhonov, Viktor
D, 5′11″, 190 lbs, b: Moscow, USSR, 6/4/1930

Season	Club, League	Regular Season				
		GP	G	A	Pts	PIM
1949–50	VVS MVO, USSR	16	1	*	*	*
1950–51	VVS MVO, USSR	15	0	*	*	*
1951–52	VVS MVO, USSR	16	2	*	*	*
1952–53	VVS MVO, USSR	21	3	*	*	*
1953–54	Dynamo Moscow, USSR	15	6	*	*	*
1954–55	Dynamo Moscow, USSR	18	4	*	*	*
1955–56	Dynamo Moscow, USSR	21	0	*	*	*
1956–57	Dynamo Moscow, USSR	24	5	*	*	*
1957–58	Dynamo Moscow, USSR	33	1	*	*	*
1958–59	Dynamo Moscow, USSR	27	2	*	*	*
1959–60	Dynamo Moscow, USSR	34	2	*	*	*
1960–61	Dynamo Moscow, USSR	18	1	4	5	6
1961–62	Dynamo Moscow, USSR	38	5	3	8	24
	USSR Totals	296	32	*	*	*

USSR Champion (1951, 1952, 1953, 1954)

The courageous and defiant hockey player who in 1958 fought the brawny Kowalchuk for every inch of ice expected the same dogged determination from the players he coached. Tikhonov places heavy emphasis on the ability of a player to work hard and to persevere and on a player's will to succeed. Preference is given to physical conditioning during workouts, even more than tactical and technical maneuvers. He considers it pointless to spend long hours reviewing video recordings of plays. "I once asked a colleague how many defense systems he knew," Tikhonov recalls. "He replied, 'Two.' But I know more, and a whole lot of variants."

Over the life of his coaching career, he's seen very few changes. In the first half of the 1970s, he was extremely popular in the Soviet Union. At that time he coached the provincial Riga team and was able to drag it out of the cellar of the league all the way to fourth place. The state then gave him its blessing to take total control of the CSKA club and the USSR national team.

Tikhonov can't be compared with any of the coaches who worked during the same era. No other coach, whether in the Soviet Union, Canada, Czechoslovakia or Sweden, acquired such national prominence. No one else was given such a clean slate to rebuild a team from the ground up. Tikhonov could only be compared with Anatoli Tarasov—the previous "monarch," who in essence wielded the same power and enjoyed the same rights.

Viktor Tikhonov is still plying his trade, turning down all other offers. "I'm a practical coach," he persists. And today it is with a sense of pleasure that he recalls how he managed to outstrip his competitors by about a decade back in those "golden years." He points out that NHL club scouts prefer to drop in to see his weaker CSKA hockey club than the provincial teams that are high up in the standings in Russia. "The scouts are interested in whether I have thought up something new. Yes, I have—you can be sure of that!"

Tikhonov once admitted that he was unable to watch hockey as a spectator, that he was unable to derive pleasure from a game as a

Tikhonov, Viktor
Head Coach, b: Moscow, USSR, 6/4/1930

Season	Club, League	Regular Season					Playoffs				
		GC	W	L	T	W%	GC	W	L	T	W%
1973–74	Dynamo Riga, USSR	32	13	17	2	0.437					
1974–75	Dynamo Riga, USSR	36	15	12	9	0.541					
1975–76	Dynamo Riga, USSR	36	16	15	5	0.514					
CCup–76	USSR	5	2	2	1	0.500					
1976–77	Dynamo Riga, USSR	36	17	12	7	0.569					
1977–78	CSKA, USSR	36	28	5	3	0.819					
WEC–78	USSR	10	9	1	0	0.900					
1978–79	CSKA, USSR	44	35	7	2	0.818					
WEC–79	USSR	8	8	0	0	1.000					
1979–80	CSKA, USSR	44	39	3	2	0.909					
OWG–80	USSR	8	7	1	0	0.875					
1980–81	CSKA, USSR	49	40	3	6	0.877					
WEC–81	USSR	8	6	0	2	0.875					
CCup–81	USSR	7	5	1	1	0.785					
1981–82	CSKA, USSR	47	40	4	3	0.883					
WEC–82	USSR	10	9	0	1	0.905					
1982–83	CSKA, USSR	44	40	3	1	0.920					
WEC–83	USSR	10	9	0	1	0.905					
1983–84	CSKA, USSR	44	43	1	0	0.977					
OWG–84	USSR	7	7	0	0	1.000					
CCup–84	USSR	6	5	1	0	0.833					
1984–85	CSKA, USSR	40	31	3	6	0.850					
WEC–85	USSR	10	8	2	0	0.800					
1985–86	CSKA, USSR	40	32	3	5	0.865					
WEC–86	USSR	10	10	0	0	1.000					
1986–87	CSKA, USSR	40	36	2	2	0.925					
WEC–87	USSR	10	8	0	2	0.900					
CCup–87	USSR	9	5	3	1	0.611					
1987–88	CSKA, USSR	44	32	5	7	0.807					
OWG–88	USSR	8	7	1	0	0.875					
1988–89	CSKA, USSR	44	30	8	6	0.750					
WEC–89	USSR	10	10	0	0	1.000					
1989–90	CSKA, USSR	48	33	9	6	0.750					
WEC–90	USSR	10	8	1	1	0.850					
1990–91	CSKA, USSR	46	24	9	13	0.844					
WEC–91	USSR	10	7	1	2	0.800					
CCup–91	USSR	5	2	3	0	0.400					
1991–92	CSKA, Russia	44	30	12	2	0.704					
OWG–92	Russia	8	7	1	0	0.875					
WEC–92	Russia	6	4	2	0	0.667					
1992–93	CSKA, Russia	42	7	28	7	0.250					
1993–94	CSKA, Russia	46	20	21	5	0.498					
OWG–94	Russia	7	4	3	0	0.571					
1994–95	CSKA, Russia	52	25	20	7	0.548	2	0	2		00.000
1995–96	CSKA, Russia	26	8	13	5	0.404					
1996–97	HK CSKA, Russia	44	17	16	11	0.511	2	0	2		00.000
1997–98	HK CSKA, Russia	26	6	17	3	0.288					
	USSR/Russia Totals	1030	657	248	125	0.698	4	0	4		00.000
	OWG/WEC/CCup Totals	182	147	23	12	0.840					

Won OWG (1984, 1988, 1992)
Won WEC (1978, 1979, 1981, 1982, 1983, 1986, 1989, 1990)
Won CCup (1981)
USSR Champion (1978, 1979, 1980, 1981, 1982, 1983, 1984, 1985, 1986, 1987, 1988, 1989)

spectacle. He valued the game—not only hockey, but soccer and basketball as well—as a case study, borrowing strategies and techniques to apply in his own club. It may be that Tikhonov has doubts whether hockey is interesting for the spectators. After all, he's a man who believes that in order to know a game, you have to play it yourself.

He was inducted into the International Ice Hockey Federation's Hall of Fame in 1998.

As a player, Viktor Tikhonov (left) was an excellent bodychecker and high-level positional player.

Helmut Balderis

Helmut Balderis was an extraordinary stickhandler and a unique forward. He belonged neither to the Soviet school of hockey nor to his native Latvian, but rather was the result of a singular upbringing.

When Balderis was a child in Latvia's capital city of Riga, boys were accepted on junior hockey teams at age 11, but figure skating schools accepted them at four. So from the age of four to 11, Balderis never even knew what a hockey stick was, but he could do a perfect figure eight on the ice. The first time he held a stick in his hand, however, he knew he had found his calling.

In Latvia, then a part of the USSR, ice hockey was the number one sport. Riga's Dynamo, under Viktor Tikhonov, rocketed into the big league and competed with Moscow teams as an equal. With just a few Latvians on a roster dominated by Russians, there were inevitable political conflicts. Riga's ice hockey arena was always packed to capacity, and hard bodychecking was Riga's calling card. Balderis didn't like to play rough, but he did have a rather un-Baltic fiery temperament.

The great goaltender Vladislav Tretiak had to call for help from his defensemen whenever Balderis rushed his net. Balderis could score three or four goals in a game, an unheard-of number by any player, Soviet or foreign, against Tretiak.

Helmut Balderis was the only Soviet player of his generation to play in the NHL, with the Minnesota North Stars.

In 1977 Balderis and Tikhonov were transferred to CSKA "in the interests of the national team." The Latvian players were insulted and annoyed by the heavy-handed treatment, but Balderis was clever. He performed the role he was forced into in a way that Latvians found amusing. He would fool around on the ice with such finesse that even the tough taskmaster Tikhonov couldn't reprimand him.

"Well," Balderis would say, "I can get away with it on CSKA. If I don't score, Mikhailov, Petrov or Kharlamov will." It

Helmut Balderis (front) could fool around on the ice with such finesse that even a tough taskmaster like Viktor Tikhonov couldn't reprimand him.

A HISTORY OF WORLD HOCKEY

was his way of saying to the authorities, "You forced me to be here, so you get what you deserve." CSKA's veteran players weren't happy with the situation, always having to fight hard for their due while the prankster Balderis was Tikhonov's favorite no matter what he did.

"Tikhonov and I played a kind of cops-and-robbers game. He was the coach and I was the player. Either he would get me or I would get him. It was a great time." No other player who played for the tyrannical Tikhonov would dare say such a thing—even today.

The fun-loving Balderis, a natural and self-assured player, was allowed to play for three years with CSKA, then was let go. "Of course the individual games mattered. But when I was on the ice challenging the goalie face to face, nothing mattered except my desire to fake him out. Later I would watch the tape and relive the moment, considering all the nuances of the game."

Among his predecessors, he thought highly of Anatoli Firsov, but he wasn't particularly impressed by fame. "Before I started playing for CSKA, I noticed that Tretiak missed the puck more often when it was shot from a good distance, so instead of trying to fake him out, I shot from a long or middle distance."

Balderis was the only player of his generation to play in the NHL, with the Minnesota North Stars. Trained by the most demanding and toughest of coaches—Tikhonov and Vladimir Yurzinov—he managed to stay on their good side and yet remain true to himself. For Balderis, that was always the greatest satisfaction. He was inducted into the International Ice Hockey Federation's Hall of Fame in 1998.

Balderis, Helmut
RW, 5´11˝, 190 lbs, b: Riga, USSR, 6/30/1952

Season	Club, League	Regular Season					Playoffs				
		GP	G	A	Pts	PIM	GP	G	A	Pts	PIM
1973–74	Dynamo Riga, USSR	24	9	6	15	13					
1974–75	Dynamo Riga, USSR	36	34	14	48	20					
1975–76	Dynamo Riga, USSR	36	31	14	45	18					
WEC–76	USSR	10	3	7	10	6					
CCup–76	USSR	5	2	3	5	6					
1976–77	Dynamo Riga, USSR	35	40	23	63	57					
WEC–77	USSR	9	8	7	15	4					
1977–78	CSKA, USSR	36	17	17	34	30					
WEC–78	USSR	10	9	2	11	8					
1978–79	CSKA, USSR	41	24	24	48	53					
ChCup–79	USSR	3	1	1	2	0					
WEC–79	USSR	8	4	5	9	9					
1979–80	CSKA, USSR	42	26	35	61	21					
OWG–80	USSR	7	5	4	9	5					
1980–81	Dynamo Riga, USSR	44	26	24	50	28					
1981–82	Dynamo Riga, USSR	41	24	19	43	48	9	15	5	20	2
1982–83	Dynamo Riga, USSR	40	32	31	63	39					
WEC–83	USSR	10	4	5	9	22					
1983–84	Dynamo Riga, USSR	39	24	15	39	18					
1984–85	Dynamo Riga, USSR	39	31	20	51	52					
1989–90	Minnesota North Stars, NHL	26	3	6	9	2					
	USSR Totals	453	318	237	555	397	9	15	5	20	2
	NHL Totals	26	3	6	9	2					
	OWG/WEC/CCup/ChalCup Totals	62	36	34	70	60					

Named Best Forward at WEC (1977)
Won WEC (1978, 1979, 1983)
Won ChalCup (1979)
USSR Champion (1978, 1979, 1980)

Roland Eriksson ■ Goran Hogosta ■

Any star player cherishes the most memorable moments of his career. For forward Roland Eriksson and goalie Goran Hogosta, those moments were during the 1977 World Championship in Vienna.

Sweden's Tre Kronor twice defeated the skilled Soviet team in Vienna. However, this would be the Swedes' first and last double victory against the Soviets, who rarely lost twice to one team during a tournament. Sweden won the first game 5–1 on May 2, adding greatly to the competition's suspense. Both the spectators and the press could hardly wait to watch the second-round game between the contenders. Few doubted that the Russians would smash the Swedes, yet some still hoped that Sweden would defy predictions.

The second game on May 8 was a sensation, with Sweden winning 3–1 and capturing the silver medal while the Czechs took the gold. During that second game, the two players who stood out were Roland Eriksson and Goran Hogosta. They were regarded as the heroes who had beaten the unbeatable Russians and their pictures appeared in every Swedish newspaper.

Roland Eriksson (front) spent one season with the Minnesota North Stars, where he chalked up 25 goals and 69 points in 80 games.

Roland Eriksson, who scored all three goals, said after the game it was "absolutely the greatest moment in my entire sports life." Not many players in the world could boast that they'd scored three goals against Tretiak in one game. The 23-year-old Eriksson came to Vienna from the Minnesota North Stars, and thanks to these two games against USSR, the Vienna World Championship was the zenith of the young player's career.

The three goals were exceptional, but Eriksson prized the first one most, when he cheated a Soviet defenseman and then took Tretiak by surprise. In fact, the entire 1976–77 season was a lucky one for the young Swedish forward. He appeared on the national team in the Canada Cup of 1976, was voted rookie of the year and was invited to join the NHL. His second game against the USSR was his 110th of the season—a record.

Goran Hogosta's unparalleled performance in the Vienna championship game intimidated the husky Soviet forwards. In the first period, the Soviets made 20 shots on Hogosta's goal, while the Swedes managed only three shots. Vladimir Shadrin scored a single goal at the beginning of the game, and it looked like Sweden would suffer inevitable defeat. But it was Hogosta, standing like a stone wall, who denied the Russians their victory. "He demoralized the Russian forwards," the Swedish newspaper *Dagens Nyheter* wrote.

The Swede performed impossible skate and stick saves and even somersaults; he fearlessly moved forward as far as possible to kick off the powerful long shots; he dove to prevent the fast-skating Soviets from making it too close to the net. He withstood nine waves of attacks. By preventing the Soviets from scoring, he enabled his team to achieve victory.

At the time of the Vienna tournament, Hogosta's career was going remarkably well. Both Eriksson and Hogosta had begun their careers as kids playing for Tunabro in Burleng, where they attended the same school. Later

Eriksson, Roland
C, 6′3″, 190 lbs, b: Storatuna, Sweden, 3/1/1954

Season	Club, League	Regular Season					Playoffs				
		GP	G	A	Pts	PIM	GP	G	A	Pts	PIM
1974–75	Leksand, Sweden	28	11	16	27	14	5	3	1	4	0
1975–76	Leksand, Sweden	36	21	14	35	16	10	8	7	15	0
WEC–76	Sweden	10	8	7	15	0					
CCup–76	Sweden	5	2	2	4	2					
1976–77	Minnesota North Stars, NHL	80	25	44	69	10	2	1	0	1	0
WEC–77	Sweden	10	7	6	13	0					
1977–78	Minnesota North Stars, NHL	78	21	39	60	12					
WEC–78	Sweden	10	1	2	3	2					
1978–79	Vancouver Canucks, NHL	35	2	12	14	4					
	Winnipeg Jets, WHA	33	5	10	15	2	10	1	4	5	0
1979–80	Leksand, Sweden	35	18	21	39	12	2	3	1	4	0
1980–81	Dusseldorfer, FRG	40	31	55	86	24	11	6	15	21	0
WEC–81	Sweden	8	2	1	3	2					
1981–82	Dusseldorfer, FRG	37	30	38	68	14					
1982–83	Leksand, Sweden	36	20	27	47	16					
WEC–83	Sweden	10	2	2	4	2					
1983–84	Leksand, Sweden	36	20	20	40	20					
1984–85	HV–71(2), Sweden	*	*	*	*	*	*	*	*	*	*
1985–86	HV–71, Sweden	35	11	15	26	10	2	0	0	0	2
	Sweden Totals	206	101	113	214	88	19	14	9	23	2
	WHA Totals	33	5	10	15	2	10	1	4	5	0
	NHL Totals	193	48	95	143	26	2	1	0	1	0
	WEC/CCup Totals	53	22	20	42	8					

Won Avco Cup (1979)
Sweden Champion (1975)

Goran Hogosta played only 22 games in two seasons in the NHL, but he was in the net for the NHL's Future Stars Team in Moscow in 1978.

they moved to Leksand, one of Sweden's top teams in the 1970s.

In 1977 Hogosta was voted the Vienna championship's best goalie, thanks to his outstanding performance in the game against the USSR. It was his greatest triumph. Hogosta would never again display such excellence, although he played for the New York Islanders and the Quebec Nordiques and was invited to play for the Swedish national team.

Before the Vienna World Championship, Roland Eriksson had spent one season with the Minnesota North Stars, where he chalked up 25 goals and 69 points in 80 games. But he didn't stay long in the NHL or the WHA, where he played for the Vancouver Canucks. Canadian coaches had expected the tall, powerful forward (6´3˝, 190 pounds) to perform boldly, but he continued to play a more characteristic European-style game of subtlety and finesse.

He soon returned to Europe, where he played for the West German Dusseldorfer EG, then settled down in his home country. He was always welcomed by Tre Kronor and played in World Championship matches until 1983, when he turned 30.

After the Vienna World Championship, Hogosta signed a contract with the New York Islanders, but he couldn't compete with the team's brilliant goaltenders, Glenn Resch and Bill Smith. He appeared for only nine minutes in one game with the Islanders. And he wasn't first goalie for the Quebec Nordiques when they made their debut in the NHL two years later, nor did he shine on the NHL's Future Stars Team in Moscow in 1978. Later he played in the minor leagues for the Fort Worth Texans and the Hershey Bears. When asked about his best games, he doesn't hesitate: "The two games against the USSR in Vienna."

In his last four seasons, Hogosta played at home for Vastra Frolunda and quit playing at 30. After leaving pro hockey, Hogosta coached young players for Leksand and then turned to the beer business. Eriksson worked for a long time in the administration end of the Vasteras club and since 1999 has been the team's assistant coach.

The two went their separate ways, but every time local fans talk about Tre Kronor's heroes, they recall the Vienna World Championship and the names Roland Eriksson and Goran Hogosta.

Hogosta, Goran
G, 6´1˝, 179 lbs, b: Appelbo, Sweden, 4/15/1954

Season	Club, League	Regular Season				Playoffs			
		GP	Mins	GA	Avg	GP	Mins	GA	Avg
1974–75	Leksand, Sweden	30	1800	80	2.67	5	304	15	2.96
WEC–75	Sweden	4	220	12	3.27				
1975–76	Leksand, Sweden	27	1620	118	4.37				
WEC–76	Sweden	6	360	20	3.33				
CCup–76	Sweden	1	60	1	1.00				
1976–77	Leksand, Sweden	33	1921	126	3.94	4	245	16	3.92
WEC–77	Sweden	7	412	9	1.31				
1977–78	New York Islanders, NHL	1	9	0	0.00				
	Fort Worth Texans, CHL	5	297	19	3.84				
	Hershey Bears, AHL	23	1254	82	3.92				
WEC–78	Sweden	7	392	22	3.37				
1978–79	Fort Worth Texans, CHL	61	3332	195	3.51	3	167	9	3.23
1979–80	Quebec Nordiques, NHL	21	1199	83	4.15				
	Syracuse Firebirds, AHL	17	1037	69	3.99				
1980–81	Vastra Frolunda, Sweden	18	1078	76	4.23	1	60	6	6.00
1981–82	Vastra Frolunda, Sweden	28	1582	89	3.38				
1982–83	Vastra Frolunda, Sweden	34	1980	140	4.24				
1983–84	Vastra Frolunda, Sweden	36	1093	151	8.29				
	NHL Totals	22	1208	83	4.12				
	WEC/CCup Totals	25	1444	64	2.66				

Named Best Goaltender at WEC (1977)
Sweden Champion (1975)

Stefan Persson

At the World Junior Championship held in December 1999 and January 2000 in Umeo and Skelleftea, Sweden, a smiling, middle-aged man could often be seen in the Swedish camp. The Junior Tre Kronor general manager, Stefan Persson, was trying to give back to hockey what hockey had given to him. A brilliant defenseman during the 1980s, Persson had indeed been given much.

Persson was with the NHL's New York Islanders for four Stanley Cup wins. Few Canadians or Americans can boast of this kind of success.

But Persson's record is also remarkable because those wins were in four successive years: 1980, 1981, 1982 and 1983. He also set another record with the Islanders—playing more games than any other Swedish player. Persson has his own explanation for the Islanders' preeminence in the early 1980s: "The team was a perfect mix. It had players of all types—shooters, leaders and fighters. It was a very well-balanced team."

During nine seasons with the Islanders, including playoffs, Persson played in 724 games, scored 59 goals and made 367 scoring passes. He sent the four diamond rings he received for the four Stanley Cup wins to his father, Gosta, in the northern city of Pitea, where he'd begun his hockey career.

Persson was born on December 22, 1954, and made his debut as a defenseman with Pitea IF. In 1973 he joined Brynas. While with Brynas, he received his first national championship silver medal and two national championship gold medals, in 1976 and 1977. Then he went overseas to play in the NHL. Back home after his NHL career ended, Persson joined Sweden's big-league Boras HS and was later given an administrative position with the team. After that he was asked to become the national junior team's general manager.

The former defenseman lives in Boras with his family and is co-owner of a candy factory.

Stefan Persson is the only Swedish player who has won the Stanley Cup four times.

Persson, Stefan
D, 6'1", 189 lbs, b: Umea, Sweden, 12/22/1954

Season	Club, League	Regular Season					Playoffs				
		GP	G	A	Pts	Plm	GP	G	A	Pts	Plm
1974–75	Brynas, Sweden	30	5	7	12	34	6	1	0	1	2
1975–76	Brynas, Sweden	34	8	9	17	51	4	0	2	2	10
1976–77	Brynas, Sweden	31	5	11	16	70	4	1	0	1	2
WEC–77	Sweden	10	2	0	2	20					
1977–78	New York Islanders, NHL	66	6	50	56	54	7	0	2	2	6
1978–79	New York Islanders, NHL	78	10	56	66	57	10	0	4	4	8
1979–80	New York Islanders, NHL	73	4	35	39	76	21	5	10	15	16
1980–81	New York Islanders, NHL	80	9	52	61	82	7	0	5	5	6
CCup–81	Sweden	5	0	0	0	2					
1981–82	New York Islanders, NHL	70	6	37	43	99	13	1	14	15	9
1982–83	New York Islanders, NHL	70	4	25	29	71	18	1	5	6	18
1983–84	New York Islanders, NHL	75	9	24	33	65	16	0	6	6	2
1984–85	New York Islanders, NHL	54	3	19	22	30	10	0	4	4	4
1985–86	New York Islanders, NHL	56	1	19	20	40					
	Sweden Totals	95	18	27	45	155	14	2	2	4	14
	NHL Totals	622	52	317	369	574	102	7	50	57	69
	WEC/CCup Totals	15	2	0	2	22					

Won Stanley Cup (1980, 1981, 1982, 1983)
Sweden Champion (1976, 1977)

Danny Gare

A feisty winger with a gifted scoring touch, Danny Gare was an immensely popular member of the exciting Buffalo Sabres teams of the 1970s. He topped the 30-goal mark five times while refusing to yield any ground wherever he played on the ice. The latter part of his 13-year career would have been productive if not for a chronic back condition that hampered his play.

As a member of the Calgary Centennials of the Western Canada Junior Hockey League, the native of British Columbia amassed 242 points in his three junior seasons. Following a 68-goal and

Danny Gare topped the 30-goal mark five times while refusing to yield an inch wherever he played on the ice.

127-point season in 1973–74, he was placed on the league's First All-Star Team. In junior, Gare played with such future NHLers as John Davidson, Bob Nystrom and Mike Rogers, but the team lost out to the powerful Regina Pats in 1974. The Buffalo Sabres chose him 29th overall in that summer's Amateur Draft.

The rookie spark plug wasted little time making an impact when he fought Philadelphia enforcer Dave Schultz 40 seconds into his first exhibition game, and 18 seconds into his first NHL regular-season shift he scored. This fell three seconds short of the NHL record held by Gus Bodnar. Gare tallied 31 times that year and showed poise by scoring 13 points while helping the Buffalo Sabres reach the Stanley Cup finals. He formed what could have been the best two-way line in hockey that year with Don Luce and Craig Ramsay.

Rather than experience the sophomore jinx, he hit the 50-goal mark in 1975–76. Later that year he played for his country in the inaugural Canada Cup. Unfortunately, a hit he absorbed from Bob Gainey during pre-tournament scrimmages damaged his spine. This condition hampered his effectiveness the rest of his career, but before his back flared up partway through the tournament, Gare had the opportunity to play on a line with Marcel Dionne and Bobby Hull.

The Sabres remained near the top of the NHL regular-season standings the rest of the decade but never duplicated their playoff success of 1975. In 1979–80, Gare set a personal high by tying for the NHL goal-scoring lead with 56. His 50th goal of the season on March 27 was arguably the most satisfying of his career, as it signified a return to form after battling his back condition for three years. He scored 11 points in 14 playoff games as the Sabres had their longest post-season run in five years. After the season, Gare was selected to the NHL Second All-Star Team.

The feisty winger also served as the Buffalo captain from 1977 until his trade to Detroit in December 1981.

The 1981–82 season proved to be very strenuous. After scoring six points in the 1981 Canada Cup, he played 22 games in Buffalo before an emotional trade sent him to Detroit. The shock of leaving his only previous NHL team was difficult. More painful was the death of his father, Ernie, just a short time before the transaction.

Gare reached the 20-goal mark twice for the Wings and emerged as a veteran leader in the dressing room. In a bizarre incident in March 1983, he received a death threat prior to a game in Toronto. Initially shaken, Gare went out and scored two late third-period goals to lift Detroit to a 4–3 win.

Gare, Danny
RW, 5′9″, 175, lbs, b: Nelson, B.C., 5/14/1954

Season	Club, League	Regular Season					Playoffs				
		GP	G	A	Pts	PIM	GP	G	A	Pts	PIM
1974–75	Buffalo Sabres, NHL	78	31	31	62	75	17	7	6	13	19
1975–76	Buffalo Sabres, NHL	79	50	23	73	129	9	5	2	7	21
CCup–76	Canada	1	0	0	0	0					
1976–77	Buffalo Sabres, NHL	35	11	15	26	73	4	0	0	0	18
1977–78	Buffalo Sabres, NHL	69	39	38	77	95	8	4	6	10	37
1978–79	Buffalo Sabres, NHL	71	27	40	67	90	3	0	0	0	9
1979–80	Buffalo Sabres, NHL	76	56	33	89	90	14	4	7	11	35
1980–81	Buffalo Sabres, NHL	73	46	39	85	109	3	3	0	3	8
CCup–81	Canada	7	1	5	6	2					
1981–82	Buffalo Sabres, NHL	22	7	14	21	25					
	Detroit Red Wings, NHL	36	13	9	22	74					
1982–83	Detroit Red Wings, NHL	79	26	35	61	107					
1983–84	Detroit Red Wings, NHL	63	13	13	26	147	4	2	0	2	38
1984–85	Detroit Red Wings, NHL	71	27	29	56	163	2	0	0	0	10
1985–86	Detroit Red Wings, NHL	57	7	9	16	102					
1986–87	Edmonton Oilers, NHL	18	1	3	4	6					
	NHL Totals	827	354	331	685	1285	64	25	21	46	195
	CCup Totals	8	1	5	6	2					

NHL Second All-Star Team (1980)
Won CCup (1976)

He served four years as the team captain in Motown, where he helped the club reach the playoffs in 1984 for the first time since 1977–78. One of his most pleasant tasks was tutoring young linemates Steve Yzerman and Gerard Gallant. Later he formed an effective checking unit with Dwight Foster and converted defenseman Bob Manno. Gare joined the Edmonton Oilers for his last 18 NHL games in 1986–87.

As a rookie, Danny Gare (center) wasted little time making an impact. He fought Flyers enforcer Dave Shultz 40 seconds into his first exhibition game and scored 18 seconds into his first regular-season shift.

In 1980 Gare published *The Coach's Drill Manual* with his father. This book sold very well across North America and was well received in coaching circles. He also spent six years as a broadcaster in Canada with CTV, the Bufflalo Sabres and the expansion Tampa Bay Lightning. He was hired as an assistant coach with the Lightning in July 1993 and worked there for two years. He has since returned to Buffalo to work as a radio announcer for Sabres games.

Milan Novy

"Life goal? I have no such thing. Every goal scored was equally important to me," said the greatest Czech gunner, Milan Novy. On a domestic or even a world scale, there has probably never been a better center. His brilliant play determined the outcome of many matches, and he holds his place in history among the rankings of all Czechs and Slovaks who ever played hockey. He also put in solid performances in the NHL, in Switzerland, in Austria and in lower-level competition. At least one goal of his career made history. It was scored in the 1976 Canada Cup in a game against the home team. Czechoslovakia won 1–0 and for the first time ever beat the pick of the NHL in the country that gave birth to the game of hockey.

Milan Novy (right) scored a historic winning goal in the 1976 Canada Cup. Czechoslovakia won 1–0 and beat the pick of the NHL for the first time ever.

Milan Novy wasn't the kind of hockey player whose personal style captured the imagination of fans. At first glance, he wasn't too tall—rather inconspicuous, in fact—but he was a very tough forward and remarkably efficient. Always in the right place at the right time and very quick to take a shot, he could reap the maximum benefit from almost every opportunity.

The essence of his efficiency on the ice was his sense of a timely approach for a pass, for a hard, accurate flick of the wrist, a short swing, and a determination to follow through on a play. "It takes a little bit of everything," he explained many years later. "Talent, honest preparation, being lucky with teammates. But the most important are the prerequisites. Having a good feel for goals constitutes up to 70% of success. If someone isn't naturally gifted, all the hard training—

Milan Novy (right) won the Golden Stick Award as the best player in the Czech league three times and set a record by not missing a single game for eight seasons in a row.

weeks, months and years—will not help. I learned to skate on a pond, and when I came to Kladno for my first practice, I had no hockey gear and knew no one. But I started firing those goals in right away, even though no one taught me how to do it before. I guess it was in me."

But Novy never took any shortcuts in training. It was often reported that in addition to regular workouts with the team, he took private lessons. He would go for long jogs with weights on his chest. During summer training, he would shoot at the net with steel pucks to strengthen his arms. "If you want to make it to higher levels, you must do something for it. I, too, had moments when I just couldn't score. That's when I intensified my training. When you work hard, you overcome crises better and get back into shape faster."

Over the years, he got stuck with the nickname "Balik," which means "country bumpkin." He also goes by another nickname with a much more illustrious origin. Novy was born on September 23, 1951, in a village by the name of Kamenne Zehrovice. Long ago, his ancestors brought stone from his village to be used in the building of the Charles Bridge in Prague. When Novy first came to the Kladno team, they called him "Balvan" (boulder), until eventually Balvan became Balik.

In Kladno, he played hockey from the age of 12, but he first attracted attention while on the army team of Dukla Jihlava from 1972 to 1974. In his first season, he became the best scorer in the league. He managed to do this three more times. One such time was in 1976–77, when he led many a splendid attack with Eduard Novak and Lubomir Bauer on his wings and the defensive duo Frantisek Pospisil and Frantisek Kaberle at his back and managed to rack up a record 59 goals in 44 games. Six times he was named the team's most productive player, and three times he won the Golden Stick Award for being the best player in the league. With Kladno, he won the national title five times. And in 1976 and 1977 he became a world champion.

"I may not have manifested it so much at first. I lined up with seasoned jocks such as Josef Vimmer and Jindrich Lidicky who could put me in my place. I think it did me a world of good. Three young guys next to one another usually do not get along. I remember that at the end of my career, coaches put Jaromir Jagr in as forward. He was 16 and I was almost 38. We were like father and son. But we worked very well on the ice together."

Novy, Milan
C, 5´10˝, 196 lbs, b: Kamenne Zehrovice, Czechoslovakia, 9/23/1951

Season	Club, League	Regular Season					Playoffs				
		GP	G	A	Pts	PIM	GP	G	A	Pts	PIM
1974–75	SONP Kladno, Czechoslovakia	40	46	22	68	*					
WEC–75	Czechoslovakia	10	4	4	8	4					
1975–76	SONP Kladno, Czechoslovakia	32	32	25	57	14	*	*	*	*	*
OWG–76	Czechoslovakia	5	5	0	5	0					
WEC–76	Czechoslovakia	10	9	6	15	4					
CCup–76	Czechoslovakia	7	5	3	8	2					
1976–77	Poldi SONP Kladno, Czechoslovakia	44	59	31	90	*					
WEC–77	Czechoslovakia	10	7	9	16	2					
1977–78	Poldi SONP Kladno, Czechoslovakia	44	40	35	75	64					
WEC–78	Czechoslovakia	9	4	1	5	2					
1978–79	Poldi SONP Kladno,, Czechoslovakia	22	24	15	39	4					
WEC–79	Czechoslovakia	5	0	2	2	4					
1979–80	Poldi SONP Kladno, Czechoslovakia	44	36	30	66	*					
OWG–80	Czechoslovakia	6	7	8	15	0					
1980–81	Poldi SONP Kladno, Czechoslovakia	16	19	42	61	*					
WEC–81	Czechoslovakia	5	6	2	8	2					
CCup–81	Czechoslovakia	6	1	2	3	7					
1981–82	Poldi SONP Kladno, Czechoslovakia	44	29	38	67	40					
WEC–82	Czechoslovakia	10	3	1	4	6					
1982–83	Washington Capitals, NHL	73	18	30	48	16	2	0	0	0	0
1984–85	Zurich, Switzerland B	40	40	44	84	*	4	1	3	4	*
1985–86	EV Vienna, Austria	40	31	50	81	16					
1987–88	Poldi SONP Kladno, Czechoslovakia	47	24	29	53	10					
	NHL Totals	73	18	30	48	16	2	0	0	0	0
	Czechoslovakia Totals	333	309	267	576	*					
	OWG/WEC/CCup Totals	83	51	38	89	33					

Won WEC (1976, 1977)
Czechoslovakia Champion (1975, 1976, 1977, 1978, 1980)

Stamina was Milan Novy's other great strength. He earned another record by not missing a single game in the league eight seasons in a row.

Before the 1981–82 season, he left for the NHL, where he played for the Washington Capitals. The number 6 he usually wore on his jersey was already taken. At first he wore number 26 and then 66, later made famous by Mario Lemieux. "Originally, I wanted it right away. But at the time only true stars could afford to have their way. In the first match, however, I scored and got two assists. Before the next match I came to the cabin and was surprised. Apparently the club management wanted to show their appreciation of my efforts."

A year later he played for the Swiss team SC Zurich and spent one season with EV Vienna in Austria. At the age of 35, he returned to Kladno. Originally it was only to help out for a year because the club was trying to advance to the top level of competition. He ended up staying three seasons. When it came time to retire from playing, he worked as the Kladno team secretary. For the last nine years, in a complete departure from sports, he has been in the cosmetics business. "I had no idea what I would be doing. It was basically an accident. I started with nothing, but hockey taught me that you get nothing for free. I cannot complain."

Clark Gillies

Although he never won a major trophy and appeared in only one All-Star Game, in 1978, Clark Gillies was one of the most important members of the New York Islanders team that won the Stanley Cup four times in succession from 1980 to 1983.

Clark Gillies was renowned for his ability to raise the level of his game when he got mad, and the word around the league was, "Don't wake him up!"

After playing three years with the Regina Pats, Gillies was drafted fourth overall by the Islanders in 1974 and joined the team that fall, never having played a game in the minors. At 6′3″ and 215 pounds, and looking even larger and more ferocious with a full beard, he was an intimidating presence on the ice throughout his career. He became renowned for his ability to raise the level of his game when he became angry, and around the league the word was, "Don't wake him up." When riled, Gillies became unstoppable.

"I have to get into a game either by hitting someone or else having someone hit me just to get my dander up," he readily admitted. His coach, Al Arbour, likened this characteristic to another star of his own era. "Gordie Howe was the same way. 'Don't get him mad,' we'd say, 'just keep him happy out there. Check him, but don't do anything to him. When you get him mad, we're in a helluva lot of trouble.'" Early in his rookie year, Gillies beat up Dave "the Hammer" Schultz of the Flyers in a legendary fight, and getting respect for himself and his teammates became immeasurably easier after that. "I fight when I have to," he said, "but I don't like to. I think I help my team more when I play clean, hard hockey and stay out of the penalty box."

Like teammate Bob Bourne, he was also a fine baseball player and played in the Houston Astros system. He played in the Appalachian League for Covington from 1970 to 1972 as a first baseman and outfielder before finally choosing hockey over ball. Thanks to some experimenting during the exhibition season by coach Arbour, Gillies almost instantly became linemates with Bryan Trottier

After early exits from the playoffs in 1978 and 1979, Clark Gillies (left) resigned as captain because he "suffered tension headaches from trying to play and lead at the same time."

and Mike Bossy as the number one line in the game, and they were nicknamed "the Trio Grande" for their offensive abilities. The line played as a unit later in the 1981 Canada Cup for Team Canada. Not a gifted scorer nor a natural passer, he nonetheless seized the moment when he had chances. "I'm not very nifty," he admitted. "My game is guts hockey." Still, Gillies scored 30 or more goals six times in his career.

Midway through the 1976–77 season, captain Ed Westfall removed the "C" from his sweater, and in a secret dressing room vote, the 22-year-old Gillies was chosen as his replacement. The honor inspired him and as a result contributed to his finest personal accomplishments. He scored three consecutive game-winning goals in the 1977 playoffs against Buffalo to tie an NHL record. However, after consecutive early exits in the playoffs to Toronto in 1978 and to the Rangers in 1979, Gillies too resigned as captain because he "suffered tension headaches from trying to play and lead at the same time." It was a move both in his own and the team's best interests, he felt.

The resignation seemed to have a positive impact, for the Islanders won the Stanley Cup in 1980 by beating the Flyers in six games with Denis Potvin as captain. Then they repeated Montreal's tremendous feat of four in a row before losing to the Edmonton Oilers in five games in 1984. Gillies remained with the team through 1986 but was left exposed in the Waiver Draft that summer and was claimed by Buffalo. After two uninspiring years with the Sabres, he retired. On December 7, 1996, his number 9 was retired by the Islanders to hang in the rafters of the Nassau Coliseum in perpetuity, a constant reminder of his contribution to one of hockey's greatest teams.

Gillies, Clark
LW, 6'3", 215 lbs, b: Moose Jaw, Sask., 4/7/1954

Season	Club, League	Regular Season					Playoffs				
		GP	G	A	Pts	PIM	GP	G	A	Pts	PIM
1974–75	New York Islanders, NHL	80	25	22	47	66	17	4	2	6	36
1975–76	New York Islanders, NHL	80	34	27	61	96	13	2	4	6	16
1976–77	New York Islanders, NHL	70	33	22	55	93	12	4	4	8	15
1977–78	New York Islanders, NHL	80	35	50	85	76	7	2	0	2	15
1978–79	New York Islanders, NHL	75	35	56	91	68	10	1	2	3	11
ChCup–79	NHL All-Stars	3	1	2	3	2					
1979–80	New York Islanders, NHL	73	19	35	54	49	21	6	10	16	63
1980–81	New York Islanders, NHL	80	33	45	78	99	18	6	9	15	28
CCup–81	Canada	7	2	5	7	8					15
1981–82	New York Islanders, NHL	79	38	39	77	75	19	8	6	14	34
1982–83	New York Islanders, NHL	70	21	20	41	76	8	0	2	2	10
1983–84	New York Islanders, NHL	76	12	16	28	65	21	12	7	19	3
1984–85	New York Islanders, NHL	54	15	17	32	73	10	1	0	1	9
1985–86	New York Islanders, NHL	55	4	10	14	55	3	1	0	1	6
1986–87	Buffalo Sabres, NHL	61	10	17	27	81					
1987–88	Buffalo Sabres, NHL	25	5	2	7	51	5	0	1	1	25
	NHL Totals	958	319	378	697	1023	164	47	47	94	271
	ChalCup/CCup Totals	10	3	7	10	10					

NHL First All-Star Team (1978, 1979)
Won Stanley Cup (1980, 1981, 1982, 1983)

Bob Bourne

Bob Bourne was one of the anomalies in the history of the NHL Amateur Draft. After an excellent junior career with Saskatoon in the western league, he was selected 38th overall by the expansion Kansas City Scouts in the 1974 draft. But before he ever played a game with the Scouts or their affiliates, he was traded to the New York Islanders for Bart Crashley and Larry Hornung. That his career lasted 964 games ranks him beside Doug Jarvis as one of the two most successful players to be traded (Toronto to Montreal) and drafted in the same summer.

Bob Bourne's career of 964 games exactly matches that of Doug Jarvis, making them the two most successful players to be drafted and traded in the same summer.

While he was playing junior hockey in the winter, he was playing baseball in the summer, and playing so well that the Houston Astros signed him to a one-year contract. Bourne played a year in the minors but decided he was more interested in hockey and signed with the Islanders.

The man who made the trade for Bourne was Islanders general manager Bill Torrey, the genius who was quickly shaping the team into a Stanley Cup dynasty. Although Bourne spent his entire rookie season with the Islanders, he spent most of his sophomore season in the minors with Fort Worth before making the grade for good in 1976–77. He had excellent speed and offensive skills, but perhaps his greatest weakness was low self-confidence. Playing with the likes of Bryan Trottier and Mike Bossy, he didn't think he had the capability to score 30 or 40 goals, though Torrey, coach Al Arbour and his teammates disagreed. "For him never to score 40 goals in a season is the biggest joke of all," teammate and long-time friend Clark Gillies said, knowing full well that Bourne was too skilled around the net not to score consistently. Bourne himself agreed. "I still don't know how good I can be."

An important quality Bourne brought to the team was focused determination, a characteristic that he acquired naturally from private life. His son Jeffrey suffered from spina bifida and required constant care and attention, and Bourne appreciated perhaps more than most NHL players how lucky he was to have the gifts that allowed him to play in the NHL. During his prime years, the Islanders won the Cup four consecutive times, from 1980 to 1983, and Bourne's leadership was a key ingredient in all of those wins.

During the peak of that dynasty, Bourne was invited to Team Canada's training camp for the 1981 Canada Cup, but after a few days at camp, he left. He was a free agent, and he feared an injury would jeopardize both his career and his ability to support his family, upon whom so much of his life relied. His free-agent status at this time came during the era of equal compensation in the NHL, so although he was voted the fourth-best left winger in the game, there were no offers for his services because other teams were afraid to risk losing their own star players of equal value to the Islanders. He re-signed with Long Island and remained there another six seasons. "I regret that decision to this very day," he said of leaving Team Canada. "I always look back and ask myself why I made that decision, but maybe if I'd been injured playing for Team Canada, I wouldn't be saying that." In 1984

Bourne, Bob
C, 6´3˝, 200 lbs, b: Kindersley, Sask., 6/21/1954

Season	Club, League	Regular Season					Playoffs				
		GP	G	A	Pts	Plm	GP	G	A	Pts	Plm
1974–75	New York Islanders, NHL	77	16	23	39	12	9	1	2	3	4
1975–76	New York Islanders, NHL	14	2	3	5	13					
	Fort Worth Texans, CNL	62	29	44	73	80					
1976–77	New York Islanders, NHL	75	16	19	35	30	8	2	0	2	4
1977–78	New York Islanders, NHL	80	30	33	63	31	7	2	3	5	2
1978–79	New York Islanders, NHL	80	30	31	61	48	10	1	3	4	6
1979–80	New York Islanders, NHL	73	15	25	40	52	21	10	10	20	10
1980–81	New York Islanders, NHL	78	35	41	76	62	14	4	6	10	19
1981–82	New York Islanders, NHL	78	27	26	53	77	19	9	7	16	36
1982–83	New York Islanders, NHL	77	20	42	62	55	20	8	20	28	14
1983–84	New York Islanders, NHL	78	22	34	56	75	8	1	1	2	7
CCup–84	Canada	8	0	3	3	0					
1984–85	New York Islanders, NHL	44	8	12	20	51	10	0	2	2	6
1985–86	New York Islanders, NHL	62	17	15	32	36	3	0	0	0	0
1986–87	Los Angeles Kings, NHL	78	13	9	22	35	5	2	1	3	0
1987–88	Los Angeles Kings, NHL	72	7	11	18	28	5	0	1	1	0
	NHL Totals	966	258	324	582	605	139	40	56	96	108
	CCup Totals	8	0	3	3	0					

Won Bill Masterton Trophy (1988)
Won Stanley Cup (1981, 1982, 1983, 1984)
Won CCup (1984)

Although Bob Bourne had 258 career goals, it took him 699 games to score his first hat-trick in the NHL.

he realized his dream regardless and played for Canada's winning team in the 1984 Canada Cup.

Although Bourne had three 30-goal seasons and 258 career goals, it wasn't until his 699th career game that he scored his first hat-trick, in a 5–1 win over New Jersey. He scored each goal under different circumstances: one at even strength, one on a power-play and one short-handed. And he did it using the borrowed stick of teammate Stefan Persson, using white tape instead of black for the first time in his career—serendipitous decisions that all contributed to a career highlight night.

Charlie Simmer

A sub-par skater, Charlie Simmer (right) used his exceptional hands and hockey smarts to become a devastating scorer.

As the left winger on the Los Angeles Kings' famed Triple Crown Line with Marcel Dionne and Dave Taylor, Charlie Simmer became one of hockey's top goal scorers. A classy performer, he rarely took an ill-advised or retaliatory penalty even though he was subject to a great deal of physical abuse when parking himself near the opposition's net. A below-average skater, Simmer used his exceptional hands and hockey smarts to become a devastating scorer. Had he not battled serious injuries in the prime of his career, Simmer's offensive accomplishments would have been even more impressive.

Simmer grew up in Terrace Bay, a northern Ontario town served only by the Trans-Canada Highway and the Canadian Pacific Railway. The community was a hockey hotbed and a major feeder for the Junior B leagues. Consequently, Simmer got a late start on Tier II Junior with the Kenora Muskies. He scored 156 points in two seasons with this squad, based in northwestern Ontario but affiliated with the junior league in the neighboring province of Manitoba.

By chance, a scout from the Sault Ste. Marie Greyhounds of the Ontario Hockey Association caught one of Simmer's games and recommended the club draft him. After a strong 45-goal performance as a 19-year-old with the Soo, Simmer was selected 39th overall by the California Golden Seals at the 1974 Amateur Draft. He split his first three pro seasons between the parent club and the Salt Lake Golden Eagles of the Central Hockey League and remained with the franchise when it relocated to Cleveland and was renamed the Barons in 1976.

In August 1977 Simmer attempted to gain a new lease on life when he signed as a free agent with the Los Angeles Kings. Matters seemed to regress in 1977–78 as the big left winger played three games with L.A. and spent the rest of the year with the AHL's Springfield Indians. The following year he was called up to the NHL halfway through the season and began turning heads for the first time as a pro. He registered 21 goals in 38 games and played solidly in the Kings' first-round playoff loss to the New York Rangers.

Both Simmer and the Kings were in an optimistic frame of mind at the dawn of the 1979–80 season. That year he exceeded all expectations by scoring 56 goals and making 101 points. Suddenly he was a well-known sports figure throughout North America, and the newly formed Triple Crown Line, made up of Simmer, Dionne and Taylor, was respected by every NHL opponent. Simmer also scored at least one goal in each of 13 straight games to become the first player to threaten Punch Broadbent's record of 16 that dated back over five decades. After the season, he was named to the NHL's First All-Star Team.

The next year he duplicated his 56-goal output but suffered a devastating compound fracture of his leg toward the end of the season during a game at Maple Leaf Gardens. His regular-season excellence still garnered him a spot on the NHL First All-Star Team for the second year running. The Kings finished fourth in the overall standings, but in the absence of their star left winger were upset by the New York Rangers in the first round of the playoffs.

Simmer spent the off-season and the early stages of the 1981–82 schedule recuperating from his injury. He tried to return in November, but the dampness in the eastern cities aggravated the joints in his ankle and leg and he was forced to take off more time. He suited up for 50 contests, but his 15 goals were a disappointment compared to his past performances. Steve Bozek took his place alongside Dionne and Taylor and the Kings were forced to give Simmer only spot duty. He took an additional two weeks off before returning to play with his original linemates, but his year was salvaged in the playoffs when he recorded 11 points in 10 games as the Kings shocked the mighty Edmonton Oilers in the first round before losing to Vancouver.

In an odd turn of events in 1982–83, Simmer recorded nearly twice as many assists (51) as goals (29). More important, he stayed healthy and played in all 80 regular-season games for Los Angeles. The team missed the playoffs, but Simmer's season continued with Team Canada at that year's World Championship.

The Triple Crown Line enjoyed one more year of greatness in 1983–84. Simmer himself rebounded with 44 goals and 92 points. Five games into the 1984–85 schedule, he was traded to the Boston Bruins, where he scored 33 goals and averaged a point per game on a team that was more defensively oriented than the Kings and played home games on a smaller surface than the L.A. Forum. Simmer quickly found a home on a spirited line with Ken Linseman and Keith Crowder.

Despite experiencing injury troubles in 1985–86, Simmer scored 36 goals in only 55 games, and his remarkable comeback was acknowledged when he was presented the Bill Masterton Trophy after the season. The following year he suited up for all 80 contests but his production was beginning to subside. On January 12, 1987, his power-play goal against the New York Rangers represented the

Charlie Simmer (right) rarely took a retaliatory penalty even though he was subject to a lot of abuse when he parked himself near the opposition net.

Simmer, Charlie
LW, 6'3", 210 lbs, b: Terrace Bay, Ont., 3/20/1954

Season	Club, League	Regular Season					Playoffs				
		GP	G	A	Pts	PIM	GP	G	A	Pts	PIM
1974–75	California Golden Seals, NHL	35	8	13	21	26					
	Salt Lake Golden Eagles, CHL	47	12	29	41	86					
1975–76	California Golden Seals, NHL	21	1	1	2	22					
	Salt Lake Golden Eagles, CHL	42	23	16	39	96					
1976–77	Cleveland Barons, NHL	24	2	0	2	16					
	Salt Lake Golden Eagles, CHL	51	32	30	62	37					
1977–78	Los Angeles Kings, NHL	3	0	0	0	2					
	Springfield Indians, AHL	75	42	41	83	100	4	0	1	1	5
1978–79	Los Angeles Kings, NHL	38	21	27	48	16	2	1	0	1	2
	Springfield Indians, AHL	39	13	23	36	33					
1979–80	Los Angeles Kings, NHL	64	56	45	101	65	3	2	0	2	0
1980–81	Los Angeles Kings, NHL	65	56	49	105	62					
1981–82	Los Angeles Kings, NHL	50	15	24	39	42	10	4	7	11	22
1982–83	Los Angeles Kings, NHL	80	29	51	80	51					
WEC–83	Canada	10	2	3	5	8					
1983–84	Los Angeles Kings, NHL	79	44	48	92	78					
1984–85	Los Angeles Kings, NHL	5	1	0	1	4					
	Boston Bruins, NHL	63	33	30	63	35	5	2	2	4	2
1985–86	Boston Bruins, NHL	55	36	24	60	42	3	0	0	0	4
1986–87	Boston Bruins, NHL	80	29	40	69	59	1	0	0	0	2
1987–88	Pittsburgh Penguins, NHL	50	11	17	28	24					
1988–89	Frankfurt, Germany	36	19	32	51	68	4	1	2	3	13
1990–91	San Diego Gulls, IHL	43	16	7	23	63					
1991–92	San Diego Gulls, IHL	1	0	0	0	0					
	NHL Totals	712	342	369	711	544	24	9	9	18	32
	WEC Totals	10	2	3	5	8					

NHL First All-Star Team (1980, 1981)
Won Bill Masterton Trophy (1986)

13,000th regular-season goal in Boston Bruins history. During his last NHL season, with the Pittsburgh Penguins in 1987–88, he spent some time on a line with Mario Lemieux and Craig Simpson but had a difficult year adjusting since he was bounced from one line to the next. He played one last year as a pro with the Eintracht Frankfurt franchise in the West German Bundesliga.

Simmer took a year away from hockey but found he was still missing the game. He provided some offense and experience to the San Diego Gulls of the International Hockey League in 1990–91. After playing one game for the squad in 1991–92, Simmer hung up his skates for good. A resilient and talented sniper, Charlie Simmer scored 342 times in 712 regular-season games.

Dave Taylor

Dave Taylor was one of the NHL's luckiest players.

A tenacious competitor who could score and check, Dave Taylor was always one of the NHL's luckiest players. The fact that he made it into the NHL was a miracle in itself, since he was barely noticed by the various clubs until the L.A. Kings took a chance by choosing him late in the 1975 draft. Taylor played his entire career with Los Angeles and was well known as the right winger on the productive Triple Crown Line with Marcel Dionne and Charlie Simmer.

The Ontario native attended Clarkson College in Potsdam, New York. Following his first year, he was selected 210th overall by the Kings in the 1975 Amateur Draft. During his last year of eligibility in 1976–77, his goals, assists and point totals of 41–67–108 led the Eastern Collegiate Athletic Conference. It appeared that the Kings had been quite astute two years earlier. The hard-working winger was named an NCAA all-American and the ECAC player of the year.

Taylor burst onto the NHL scene with a 22-goal performance in 1977–78. He even went as far as enrolling in a speech therapy class to conquer his nervous stuttering. The young winger was convinced that this would enable him to represent himself and his NHL employers more effectively in the community.

The next year he exploded with 43 goals, and the following season he was teamed with Marcel Dionne and Charlie Simmer on the Triple Crown Line. This unit was among the best in the league and Taylor was arguably the best two-way player of the three. In addition to being the line's defensive conscience, he was the grinder who fended off the toughest checkers on the opposing team.

In 1980–81, the competitive right winger registered career highs of 47 goals and 112 points. Following the season, he was placed on the NHL Second All-Star Team. His 106 points the following season were a credit to himself and Dionne since they had to do without Simmer for much of the year as the result of a badly broken leg he had suffered late in the previous season.

Between 1983 and 1986, Taylor represented Canada at three World Championships. His best performance was seven points in 10 matches in 1986; the low point was a shattered wrist suffered in 1983, an injury that affected him for nearly a year. By the mid-1980s, Taylor was a respected veteran on the team and the natural choice to succeed Terry Ruskowski as captain in 1985–86.

Taylor's accomplishments were less heralded because he played in Los Angeles. He observed: "Not a lot of people were following the Kings. There just wasn't a lot of interest in hockey." One critic wrote: "It didn't help the franchise that any year which seemed promising was all but inevitably followed by a season of disappointment, or by a collapse in the playoffs." Taylor continued: "We had one year of 99 points and people were interested and we sold a few more season's seats. But the next year we dropped down to under .500. Then the people went away again."

Although his scoring totals dropped during the latter stages of his career, he remained a 20-goal threat and a respected defensive player. Prior to the 1988–89 season, he enthusiastically turned over his captaincy to incoming superstar Wayne Gretzky. The Great One drew attention to the Kings franchise and some of its notable stars—like Dave Taylor.

On February 5, 1991, he registered his 1,000th point at the Philadelphia Spectrum. Following the season, the soft-spoken winger's involvement in the community was also lauded and in 1990–91 he was presented with both the Bill Masterton and the King Clancy awards.

In his 16th NHL season, in 1992–93, Taylor finally reached the Stanley Cup finals, where the Kings lost to the Montreal Canadiens. He played 33 games in 1993–94, then retired after the Kings failed to make the playoffs.

Many remember Taylor best because he was drafted so late and was such a tenacious competitor. He was also a legitimate star who appeared in five NHL All-Star games and finished in the top 10 of the NHL's scoring race three times. His tireless work for the Kings as community/player relations director and with charities such as the Juvenile Diabetes Foundation made him one of the most respected figures in the NHL.

When Taylor left the game, he stood second on L.A.'s all-time goals and points rankings behind his old linemate Marcel Dionne. In 1995 he followed Dionne and Rogie Vachon as the third member of the Kings to have his number retired by the team. He eventually took a position in the Kings' administration and was named the club's vice-president and general manager on April 22, 1997.

Dave Taylor (center) registered career highs of 47 goals and 112 points in the 1980–81 season.

Taylor, Dave
RW, 6′, 190 lbs, b: Levack, Ont., 12/4/1955

Season	Club, League	Regular Season					Playoffs				
		GP	G	A	Pts	PIM	GP	G	A	Pts	PIM
1974–75	Clarkson College, ECAC	32	20	34	54	*					
1975–76	Clarkson College, ECAC	31	26	33	59	*					
1976–77	Clarkson College, ECAC	34	41	67	108	*					
	Fort Worth Texans, CHL	7	2	4	6	6					
1977–78	Los Angeles Kings, NHL	64	22	21	43	47	2	0	0	0	5
1978–79	Los Angeles Kings, NHL	78	43	48	91	124	2	0	0	0	2
1979–80	Los Angeles Kings, NHL	61	37	53	90	72	4	2	1	3	4
1980–81	Los Angeles Kings, NHL	72	47	65	112	130	4	2	2	4	10
1981–82	Los Angeles Kings, NHL	78	39	67	106	130	10	4	6	10	20
1982–83	Los Angeles Kings, NHL	46	21	37	58	76					
WEC–83	Canada	10	1	4	5	4					
1983–84	Los Angeles Kings, NHL	63	20	49	69	91					
1984–85	Los Angeles Kings, NHL	79	41	51	92	132	3	2	2	4	8
WEC–85	Canada	10	3	2	5	4					
1985–86	Los Angeles Kings, NHL	76	33	38	71	110					
WEC–86	Canada	10	3	4	7	12					
1986–87	Los Angeles Kings, NHL	67	18	44	62	84	5	2	3	5	6
1987–88	Los Angeles Kings, NHL	68	26	41	67	129	5	3	3	6	6
1988–89	Los Angeles Kings, NHL	70	26	37	63	80	11	1	5	6	19
1989–90	Los Angeles Kings, NHL	58	15	26	41	96	6	4	4	8	2
1990–91	Los Angeles Kings, NHL	73	23	30	53	148	12	2	1	3	12
1991–92	Los Angeles Kings, NHL	77	10	19	29	63	6	1	1	2	20
1992–93	Los Angeles Kings, NHL	48	6	9	15	49	22	3	5	8	31
1993–94	Los Angeles Kings, NHL	33	4	3	7	28					
	NHL Totals	1111	431	638	1069	1589	92	26	33	59	145
	WEC Totals	30	7	10	17	20					

NHL Second All-Star Team (1981)
Won Bill Masterton Trophy (1991)
Won King Clancy Trophy (1991)

A HISTORY OF WORLD HOCKEY

Kent Nilsson

The "Nilsson Feint" was named after the great Swedish player Kent Nilsson.

The famous "Nilsson Feint" was named after forward Kent Nilsson, who earned his place among Sweden's hockey greats. He first showed the move in 1989 at the Stockholm World Championship in a game against the U.S. He sped up to confront the opponent's goalie, John Vanbiesbrouck, moved left to provoke the goalie to mimic his movement, and then switched the stick from his left hand to his right hand and sent the puck into the right corner. Peter Forsberg used the same maneuver in an overtime shootout in the 1994 Olympic final game against Canada in Lillehammer.

As a kid, Nilsson would shoot the puck at his father's garage until he was exhausted. He cherished a dream to become a great hockey forward. He began his career with Stockholm's Djurgarden and then played for AIK. From 1973 to 1977, Nilsson, or "Kenta," as the fans nicknamed him, played 112 games for the two teams, scoring 79 goals and getting 62 assists, only hinting at what was to come.

In the 1977–78 season, he made his debut with the WHA's Winnipeg Jets and earned 107 points—42 goals and 65 assists in 80 games. He earned the same total the next season—39 goals and 68 assists in 78 games.

Afterwards, Nilsson moved to the NHL, where he played with the Flames for six seasons. In 1980–81, he scored 49 goals and made 82 assists, earning 131 points and achieving third spot in the league after Wayne Gretzky and Marcel Dionne. In 1987, while Nilsson was with the Edmonton Oilers, the team won the Stanley Cup, marking the peak of his success.

In his later NHL years, Nilsson played for the Minnesota North Stars and the Edmonton Oilers, but his game wasn't as good as it had been, so he went to Europe, joining Bolzano in Italy. In the 1987–88 season, he scored 74 goals and made 86 assists. He went on to play for Lugano and Kloten in Switzerland, Austria's Graz and Norway's Valerengen.

After his remarkable hockey odyssey, Nilsson could claim some unprecedented achievements: He had been a WHA champion,

Nilsson, Kent
C, 6´1˝, 195 lbs, b: Nynashamn, Sweden, 8/31/1956

Season	Club, League	Regular Season					Playoffs				
		GP	G	A	Pts	PIM	GP	G	A	Pts	PIM
1974–75	Djurgarden, Sweden	28	13	12	25	14					
1975–76	Djurgarden, Sweden	36	28	26	54	10					
1976–77	AIK, Sweden	36	30	19	49	18					
1977–78	Winnipeg Jets, WHA	80	42	65	107	8	9	2	8	10	10
1978–79	Winnipeg Jets, WHA	78	39	68	107	8	10	3	11	14	4
1979–80	Atlanta Flames, NHL	80	40	53	93	10	4	0	0	0	2
1980–81	Calgary Flames, NHL	80	49	82	131	26	14	3	9	12	2
CCup–81	Sweden	5	0	2	2	4					
1981–82	Calgary Flames, NHL	41	26	29	55	8	3	0	3	3	2
1982–83	Calgary Flames, NHL	80	46	58	104	10	9	1	11	12	2
1983–84	Calgary Flames, NHL	67	31	49	80	22					
CCup–84	Sweden	8	3	8	11	4					
1984–85	Calgary Flames, NHL	77	37	62	99	14	3	0	1	1	0
WEC–85	Sweden	8	6	5	11	6					
1985–86	Minnesota North Stars, NHL	61	16	44	60	10	5	1	4	5	0
1986–87	Minnesota North Stars, NHL	44	13	33	46	12					
	Edmonton Oilers, NHL	17	5	12	17	4	21	6	13	19	6
CCup–87	Sweden	6	0	4	4	4					
1987–88	Bolzano, Italy	35	60	72	132	48	8	14	14	28	*
	Lugano, Switzerland	2	2	0	2	*					
1988–89	Djurgarden, Sweden	35	21	21	42	36	1	0	1	1	0
WEC–89	Sweden	10	3	11	14	0					
1989–90	Kloten, Switzerland	36	21	19	40	*	5	4	5	9	*
WEC–90	Sweden	10	10	2	12	6					
1990–91	Kloten, Switzerland	33	37	39	76	*	8	3	8	11	*
1991–92	Kloten, Switzerland	17	11	14	25	8	2	0	0	0	2
1992–93	Djurgarden, Sweden	40	11	20	31	20	6	2	3	5	0
1993–94	Graz, Austria	27	8	9	17	*					
1994–95	Valerengen, Norway	6	1	1	2	8					
	Edmonton Oilers, NHL	6	1	0	1	0					
	NHL Totals	553	264	422	686	116	59	11	41	52	14
	WHA Totals	158	81	133	214	16	19	5	19	24	14
	Sweden Totals	175	103	98	201	98	7	2	4	6	0
	WEC/CCup Totals	47	22	32	54	24					

Won Stanley Cup (1987)
Won Avco Cup (1978, 1979)
Sweden Champion (1989)
Italy Champion (1988)

Stanley Cup winner and champion of Switzerland and Italy. It seems he earned countless points during his career. In the NHL alone, he played 553 games and scored 264 goals. But Nilsson kept track of his personal statistics: He played 1,095 games, scored 621 goals, made 864 passes and had 236 penalty minutes.

These days, Nilsson is often seen in the crowd at Stockholm's Globe Arena. An alert and discriminating spectator, he watches the games intently as the Edmonton Oilers' European scout.

In 1980–81, Kent Nilsson scored 49 goals and made 82 assists, third in the league after Wayne Gretzky and Marcel Dionne.

Vasili Pervukhin

Among the players of the last "golden" generation of Soviet hockey, defenseman Vasili Pervukhin stands out as the one player least likely to make a mistake on the ice. His flawless play was really quite remarkable, whether in closing a breach in the defense line or winning a tussle with an opponent. And if Soviet hockey players had had wide-open access to the NHL two or three years earlier than 1989, when Pervukhin was still in quite good shape, the Soviets' most reliable defenseman and the world's leading hockey league would have made an excellent match. He wasn't very fond of slamming an opponent into the boards and seldom made a shot on goal, but an NHL club would have welcomed him with open arms for all his other considerable talents.

In unofficial ratings, the tandem of Vasili Pervukhin (center) and Zinatula Bilyaletdinov (left) was ranked as the second-best defense line on the Soviet national team.

"My shoulders are a little weak. I have trouble with the barbell, and I never could do chin-ups as they should be done," Pervukhin explained. "But knowledgeable coaches often used to tell me: 'Brain, not brawn. Accuracy rather than strength.'"

The easygoing Pervukhin would reach his stick out toward an oncoming forward entering the attack zone just like a sapper looking for a landmine. Pervukhin maneuvered himself as lightly as a butterfly to match the pace and rhythm of the attacker.

He was one of those rare and valuable players who needed no long explanations. During his 15 or so years of playing in the highest echelons of hockey—for the Soviet national team and Dynamo Moscow—there wasn't a single conflict nor a single instance of friction between Pervukhin and his coaches. For Pervukhin there were no slumps, nor opponents that he couldn't handle. But the most important thing was that Pervukhin showed up on the right team at the right time.

On the eve of Viktor Tikhonov's reign as coach, the leading Soviet players conducted themselves on the ice practically any way they wanted. The most memorable defense tandem in those years was the Valeri Vasiliev–Alexander Gusev pair. Coaches were particularly irked by Gusev's style of playing. He would dash forward into an attack and end up creating a situation in front of his own net just as dangerous as the one at the opponent's net. His partner, Vasiliev, began playing more cautiously in his more mature years, but Gusev continued to play in his impetuous fashion. Due to the rashness of these two, their goalie faced an unnecessary number of shots on goal, with many ending up in the net. But when Vasiliev and Gusev clicked, Vladimir Petrov's five-man squad that included these two defensemen could unleash such a flurry of activity in the zone of attack that the opposing team was left quite helpless.

Pervukhin had come from the provincial Penza club to Dynamo Moscow—a restrained, stringent but accurate club in which the hefty and daring Vasili soon stood out as a soloist rather than a cog in the team's well-oiled machine. In his very first season, Pervukhin won himself a spot in the nationals lineup when he took the place of the injured Gusev in tandem with Vasiliev.

Pervukhin recalls: "Of all the defensemen, I liked Vasiliev most even before we became partners. Perhaps subconsciously, I envied his openhearted nature, his ability to take out his opponent—all the more so, according to the rules—and his efficient way of joining the attack. But I decided once and for all to be cautious on the ice. That's what my inner voice told me."

Pervukhin really did choose his own particular style of play, staking his success on his own feeling for the game. He rationalized that someone else could play tough. If you played tough, there was a risk of getting carried away, and that kind of play could easily lead to failure.

Watching present-day hockey games, Pervukhin is rather amazed. "Look at those youngsters! It makes me feel sad. There the puck is, lying on the ice, and you can get hold of it practically without a struggle and mount an attack, but the player intentionally heads toward his opponent in order to nail him. So he gets his opponent with a bodycheck, but the puck is still lying there. Where's the logic?"

The voice of the usually taciturn Pervukhin mellows when the talk comes around to attacking the opponent's net. "A goal is practically the most joyful thing. For a forward, a goal scored is actually his job, but for a defenseman, a scored goal is a real treat. But I allowed myself to think about such treats only in very rare cases."

The power-play built around Pervukhin became a Soviet classic in those years. According to him, it was developed quite intensively in their training sessions, where five field players were set up against four. Of the five, the defense line consisted of Vasiliev on the right and Pervukhin on the left. Then there was Maltsev on the right wing. After the five players

Pervukhin, Vasili
D, 5′11″, 190 lbs, b: Penza, USSR, 1/1/1956

Season	Club, League	Regular Season					Playoffs				
		GP	G	A	Pts	PIM	GP	G	A	Pts	PIM
1974–76	Dizelist Penza, USSR	*	*	*	*	*					
1976–77	Dynamo Moscow, USSR	35	2	6	8	0					
WEC–77	USSR	10	1	1	2	0					
1977–78	Dynamo Moscow, USSR	36	4	7	11	4					
WEC–78	USSR	10	1	2	3	2					
1978–79	Dynamo Moscow, USSR	44	3	19	22	6					
WEC–79	USSR	7	0	3	3	0					
1979–80	Dynamo Moscow, USSR	44	5	9	14	4					
OWG–80	USSR	7	0	9	9	2					
1980–81	Dynamo Moscow, USSR	49	10	5	15	6					
WEC–81	USSR	8	1	3	4	2					
CCup–81	USSR	6	0	2	2	6					
1981–82	Dynamo Moscow, USSR	45	8	13	21	10					
WEC–82	USSR	10	0	1	1	0					
1982–83	Dynamo Moscow, USSR	42	6	12	18	8					
WEC–83	USSR	9	0	1	1	0					
1983–84	Dynamo Moscow, USSR	43	6	8	14	4					
OWG–84	USSR	7	0	2	2	0					
CCup–84	USSR	6	0	0	0	0					
1984–85	Dynamo Moscow, USSR	40	8	13	21	6					
WEC–85	USSR	10	0	1	1	0					
1985–86	Dynamo Moscow, USSR	40	7	8	15	8					
WEC–86	USSR	7	1	1	2	4					
1986–87	Dynamo Moscow, USSR	39	11	13	24	14					
WEC–87	USSR	7	0	1	1	0					
CCup–87	USSR	8	0	2	2	4					
1987–88	Dynamo Moscow, USSR	47	5	4	9	10					
1988–89	Dynamo Moscow, USSR	44	8	10	18	6					
1995–96	Krylja Sovetov, Russia	29	2	5	7	8					
1996–97	Krylja Sovetov, Russia	44	4	5	9	4					
1997–98	Molot-Prikamje, Russia	43	3	12	15	6	2	0	0	0	2
1998–99	Molot-Prikamje, Russia	35	0	10	10	4	0	0	0	0	0
	USSR/Russia Totals	699	92	159	251	100					
	OWG/WEC/CCup Totals	112	4	29	33	20					

Won OWG (1984)
Won WEC (1978, 1979, 1981, 1982, 1983, 1986)
Won CCup (1981)

took up their positions in the zone of attack, Maltsev would always pause. He controlled the puck so freely and with such ease that even the overly cautious Pervukhin would take the hint—now is the time to dash toward the net, open yourself up for a diagonal pass and tuck in a goal on the fly.

In the 1978 World Championship, the five-man Dynamo squad scored a goal exactly like the ones in training camp. And it was scored against not just anyone, but against the Czech national team that was defending two previous world titles on home ice. The lessons learned in training turned out to be quite valuable. They proved effective on about half of all power-plays. Occasionally, when facing opponents who lacked the ability to stop him, Pervukhin would steal up to the net and try his luck. "I finished off this play only because it was inconvenient for the right wing defenseman, Vasiliev," Pervukhin would say with modesty.

Vasili Pervukhin (left) didn't have slumps and could handle any and all opponents.

After Vasiliev, Pervukhin's partner—both in the national team lineup and in Dynamo—became Zinatula Bilyaletdinov for many long years. "With Bilyaletdinov," Pervukhin recalls, "we couldn't allow ourselves to resort to the solos we did together with Vasiliev. First and foremost, we tried to play a very disciplined game."

In unofficial ratings, the Pervukhin–Bilyaletdinov tandem ranked as the second-best defense line in the Soviet nationals. Thanks to Bilyaletdinov, they had no problem when it came to hard body-checking. And Pervukhin's initiating pass made mounting an attack relatively smooth.

It was only during CSKA–Dynamo games that Pervukhin and his teammates ran into trouble. In the games between Red Army and Dynamo, Viacheslav Fetisov and Alexei Kasatonov came on strong and often put the leading Dynamo defense line truly on the defensive. Bilyaletdinov and Pervukhin more often than not had to withdraw into their own zone, pressed back by their CSKA counterparts, Fetisov and Kasatonov. During Pervukhin's entire tenure with Dynamo, his team was never able to overtake the Red Army squad in the USSR championship.

In 1999, after a long career in hockey, playing until the age of 40, Pervukhin settled into a coaching job.

John Tonelli

John Tonelli was involved in one of the biggest legal battles in hockey.

John Tonelli's life in hockey began like any young man's growing up in the Toronto area in the 1970s. After playing midget, he joined the Toronto Marlboros to play junior hockey for the 1973–74 season. But very quickly he became part of one of the greatest legal battles hockey has ever known.

When the World Hockey Association began operations in 1972, it made no attempt to hide the fact that it wanted to draft and sign 18-year-old players, even though the NHL's limit was 20. Signing teenagers was a problem because any good 18-year-old was playing junior hockey in Canada, and every junior was under contract to that team for the duration of his career—that is, until he turned 20 and was drafted by an NHL team. However, the WHA argued that the junior contracts were null and void when a player turned 18, the legal age in Canada, and that any contract signed by a minor wasn't financially beneficial to him and therefore inapplicable in a court of law.

John Tonelli (left) established himself as a digger: a player who could go into the corners and come out with the puck.

Tonelli turned 18 near the end of the 1974–75 season with the Marlies, and he was advised by his agent, Gus Badali, to stop playing by his birthday. At the same time, he was being pursued by the Houston Aeros of the WHA, and all hell broke loose when Tonelli did in fact leave the Marlies and signed with the Aeros on his birthday. The Ontario Hockey Association sued him for breach of contract, and a bitter battle was fought in the courts over the summer. In the end, Tonelli was ruled an 18-year-old adult and free to do as he chose. Of the standard OHA player contract, Judge Blair ruled that: "It wasn't freely negotiated. It is really a set of standardized conditions prescribed by the major Junior A group and presented to the players on a 'take it or leave it' basis. From the child's standpoint, the obvious economic disadvantages of this contract can be measured in terms of both money and time."

That fall, Tonelli played pro in Houston with linemates Gordie and Marty Howe. "Gordie Howe was then 47 or 48 years old," Tonelli recalled, "and he was skating by everybody. He was the most phenomenal athlete I ever saw, and he was very helpful."

The Aeros, however, folded after three more years in Houston, and Tonelli was signed by the New York Islanders in the summer of 1978. He worked hard on his game every day and quickly established himself as a necessary piece of the Islanders' Stanley Cup puzzle. "He epitomizes what this game is all about," teammate Bob Nystrom said of him. "He is without doubt the hardest worker I have ever seen."

Tonelli established himself as a digger, someone who could go into the corners and come out with the puck. But as he gained confidence, he also became more aggressive in open ice and began to score more. Not coincidentally, the Islanders also started to win. Tonelli was part of the four Cup victories the team won from 1980 to 1983, but in some ways his career culminated in the fall of 1984 when he played for Canada in the Canada Cup, an invitation he almost turned down.

"When I first told Tonelli that Team Canada wanted him," general manager Bill Torrey said, "he told me I had to be joking. He didn't want to go because he felt he wasn't fast enough and there would be too many better players there for him to have a chance to make the tournament roster." Far from it. He not only made the team, he had nine points, including a key assist on Mike Bossy's goal in overtime of the semifinal. Canada won the championship and Tonelli

Tonelli, John
LW, 6'1", 200 lbs, b: Milton, Ont., 3/23/1957

Season	Club, League	Regular Season					Playoffs				
		GP	G	A	Pts	PIM	GP	G	A	Pts	PIM
1975–76	Houston Aeros, WHA	79	17	14	31	66	17	7	7	14	18
1976–77	Houston Aeros, WHA	80	24	31	55	109	11	3	4	7	12
1977–78	Houston Aeros, WHA	65	23	41	64	103	6	1	3	4	8
1978–79	New York Islanders, NHL	73	17	39	56	44	10	1	6	7	0
1979–80	New York Islanders, NHL	77	14	30	44	49	21	7	9	16	18
1980–81	New York Islanders, NHL	70	20	32	52	57	16	5	8	13	16
1981–82	New York Islanders, NHL	80	35	58	93	57	19	6	10	16	18
1982–83	New York Islanders, NHL	76	31	40	71	55	20	7	11	18	20
1983–84	New York Islanders, NHL	73	27	40	67	66	17	1	3	4	31
CCup–84	Canada	8	3	6	9	2					
1984–85	New York Islanders, NHL	80	42	58	100	95	10	1	8	9	10
1985–86	New York Islanders, NHL	65	20	41	61	50					
	Calgary Flames, NHL	9	3	4	7	10	22	7	9	16	49
1986–87	Calgary Flames, NHL	78	20	31	51	72	3	0	0	0	4
1987–88	Calgary Flames, NHL	74	17	41	58	84	6	2	5	7	8
1988–89	Los Angeles Kings, NHL	77	31	33	64	110	6	0	0	0	8
1989–90	Los Angeles Kings, NHL	73	31	37	68	62	10	1	2	3	6
1990–91	Los Angeles Kings, NHL	71	14	16	30	49	12	2	4	6	12
1991–92	Chicago Blackhawks, NHL	33	1	7	8	37					
	Quebec Nordiques, NHL	19	2	4	6	14					
	WHA Totals	224	64	86	150	278	34	11	14	25	38
	NHL Totals	1028	325	511	836	911	172	40	75	115	200
	CCup Totals	8	3	6	9	2					

NHL Second All-Star Team (1982,1985)
Won Stanley Cup (1980, 1981, 1982, 1983)
Won CCup (1984)

was named the tournament's best player. He then rejoined the Islanders and had his best season ever, scoring 42 goals and 100 points.

Midway through the 1985–86 season, he was traded to Calgary and two and a half years later he was in Los Angeles, far removed geographically and psychologically from the Cup-winning teams of New York. He finished his career in 1991–92, playing a handful of games with Chicago and Quebec, and then retired after having played 1,028 NHL games.

Peter Stastny

In November 1998 two former Quebec Nordiques players, Michel Goulet and Peter Stastny, became members of the prestigious Hall of Fame in Toronto. The Quebec Nordiques never made it farther in Stanley Cup playoffs than the semifinals. Nonetheless, they were a team who could even have won the Cup, given favorable circumstances. After Wayne Gretzky, Peter Stastny was the most successful hockey player in the NHL in the 1980s, and the terrific backup he had in Quebec included his brothers Anton and Marian. In fact, Peter Stastny often went out on the ice as forward on two different attack lines.

His excellent physical condition and careful diet gave him the strength to play like that. But though Stastny was a first-class star, he was always willing to talk to anybody. When journalists came to see him asking for a five-minute interview, the conversation often lasted for half an hour. Peter felt compelled to share his experiences on the ice.

After Wayne Gretzky, Peter Stastny was perhaps the most succesful player in the NHL in the 1980s.

Together with his brother Marian, Peter Stastny suddenly appeared on the international scene during the World Championship in Katowice in 1976. It was at this tournament that Poland surprised the Soviet Union with a 6–4 win and opened the door for Czechoslovakia to win the title. In live coverage during the intermission, a Polish TV commentator approached his Czech colleague and got straight to the point: "Where did Peter Stastny come from?" The Pole couldn't believe that Stastny was only 19.

But with the good times came the bad. After an embarrassing loss by the Czechs at the Lake Placid Olympic Games, newspapers were harsh in their criticism of the three Stastny brothers. It didn't matter that in six matches, Peter had scored seven goals and registered seven assists.

In the summer of 1980, Peter and Anton decided to go abroad, a move that stirred up a lot of emotion in their home country. The Czech newspapers reported the decision with just a few brief lines provided by the CTK press agency. The only difference from one report to another was the headline, ranging from the brief "CTK Report" and the emotional "Without Homeland" to the aggressive "Hockey Players Sell Out." This was also the final mention of one of the most promising threesomes in the history of Czech hockey. The eldest brother, Marian, did return home from Austria, but he was no longer wanted as a player by Slovan Bratislava. Even NHL charts, which sometimes appeared in Czech newspapers, had Peter Stastny's name missing, even though he was regularly among the top 10 scorers at the time, often right behind Wayne Gretzky. One event that the censors in the Czech communist regime couldn't keep out of the press, however, was the appearance of Peter Stastny in the jersey of the Canadian national team during the Canada Cup in 1984. The Czech media called his inclusion a provocation. They complained to the Canadian

In Quebec, Peter Stastny often went out as the center on two different lines.

coaches that there were plenty of good hockey players in Canada and that they had no need to use a player who wasn't Canadian. But the papers weren't quite correct. Peter Stastny had become a Canadian citizen and as such had a perfect right to line up for the game wearing the maple leaf.

Shortly after his 24th birthday, Peter Stastny joined the Quebec Nordiques. The greatest challenge at the time for hockey players coming to the NHL from behind the Iron Curtain was not, as a casual observer might think, the smaller ice surface and the tremendous workload of close to a 100 matches per season. It was quite simply old-fashioned culture shock. To add to the difficulty, the Stastny brothers started out in French-speaking Quebec. English was spoken in the locker room, but off the ice it was French and at home it was Slovak. Then there was the stress of leaving all their friends and family behind. Peter and Anton had no way of knowing if they would ever see them again.

In the first match they played together, Peter and Anton lined up against Calgary on October 9, 1980. Five days later, Anton scored his first goal, and 12 days later, Peter scored one into Tony Esposito's net in a game against Chicago. Peter and Anton became the hub of the team. They did whatever was necessary to get points. Over a two-day period in February, something happened that had probably never happened before in the NHL and will probably never happen again. On February 20, 1981, each of the brothers got a hat-trick to lead their team to a 9–3 win in Vancouver. And less than 48 hours later, that feat was improved upon. Peter scored four goals and Anton three and Quebec won the game 11–7. And a third hat-trick was scored in the game by the top scorer on the Nordiques team at the time, Jacques Richard, who scored 52 goals that season.

Peter Stastny got 39 goals in his first season in the NHL and registered 70 assists. This was a record among rookies until the arrival of another European, Finn Teemu Selanne. A year later, Stastny registered the most points overall on the team with 139. Peter Stastny, along with

Stastny, Peter
C, 6'1", 200 lbs, b: Bratislava, Czechoslovakia, 9/18/1956

Season	Club, League	Regular Season					Playoffs				
		GP	G	A	Pts	PIM	GP	G	A	Pts	PIM
1975–76	Slovan, Czechoslovakia	32	19	9	28	*					
WEC–76	Czechoslovakia	9	8	4	12	0					
CCup–76	Czechoslovakia	7	0	4	4	2					
1976–77	Slovan, Czechoslovakia	44	25	27	52	*					
WEC–77	Czechoslovakia	10	3	5	8	0					
1977–78	Slovan, Czechoslovakia	42	29	24	53	28					
WEC–78	Czechoslovakia	10	5	6	11	7					
1978–79	Slovan, Czechoslovakia	39	32	23	55	21					
WEC–79	Czechoslovakia	8	2	3	5	6					
1979–80	Slovan, Czechoslovakia	41	26	26	52	58					
OWG–80	Czechoslovakia	6	7	7	14	6					
1980–81	Quebec Nordiques, NHL	77	39	70	109	37	5	2	8	10	7
1981–82	Quebec Nordiques, NHL	80	46	93	139	91	12	7	11	18	10
1982–83	Quebec Nordiques, NHL	75	47	77	124	78	4	3	2	5	10
1983–84	Quebec Nordiques, NHL	80	46	73	119	73	9	2	7	9	31
CCup–84	Canada	8	1	2	3	0					
1984–85	Quebec Nordiques, NHL	75	32	68	100	95	18	4	19	23	24
1985–86	Quebec Nordiques, NHL	76	41	81	122	60	3	0	1	1	2
1986–87	Quebec Nordiques, NHL	64	24	53	77	43	13	6	9	15	12
1987–88	Quebec Nordiques, NHL	76	46	65	111	69					
1988–89	Quebec Nordiques, NHL	72	35	50	85	117					
1989–90	Quebec Nordiques, NHL	62	24	38	62	24					
	New Jersey Devils, NHL	12	5	6	11	16	6	3	2	5	2
1990–91	New Jersey Devils, NHL	77	18	42	60	53	7	3	4	7	2
1991–92	New Jersey Devils, NHL	66	24	38	62	42	7	3	7	10	19
1992–93	New Jersey Devils, NHL	62	17	23	40	22	5	0	2	2	0
1993–94	Slovan, Slovakia	4	0	4	4	0					
OWG–94	Slovakia	8	5	4	9	9					
1993–94	St. Louis Blues, NHL	17	5	11	16	4	4	0	0	0	2
1994–95	St. Louis Blues, NHL	6	1	1	2	0					
WC(B)–95	Slovakia	6	8	8	16	0					
	Czechoslovakia/Slovakia Totals	202	131	113	242	*					
	NHL Totals	977	450	789	1239	824	93	33	72	105	121
	OWG/WEC/WC/CCup Totals	72	39	43	82	30					

Won Calder Trophy (1981)
Won WEC (1976, 1977)
Won CCup (1984)

Michel Goulet, who topped the list in 1983–84 and again in 1986–87, took over the top scoring positions with Quebec at the time. But Peter clearly reigned as the best passer. In third place behind these two greats during this era was Peter Stastny's younger brother, Anton. Marian also played here for four seasons and, according to the Canadian point system, racked up 98 goals and 143 assists for a total of 241 points.

Their first year in the NHL was very successful for Peter and Anton. For the first time in history, Quebec made it to the Stanley Cup playoffs, but was eliminated at the hands of Philadelphia by a score of 3–2. The following year, the Nordiques eliminated their Quebec rivals, the Montreal Canadiens, after taking three of the first five games in the playoffs even though the goals were 16–11 for Montreal. Equally dramatic was another series with Boston. This series too was decided only in the last match. But in the semifinals they were met by the invincible New York Islanders, who trounced Quebec. On one more occasion—in 1985—the Nordiques made it to the Stanley Cup semifinals but were eliminated four games to two by Philadelphia. During his time in Quebec, Peter Stastny registered 24 goals and 57 assists in 64 Stanley Cup playoff games. His best memory, however, is of the goal scored in overtime in the seventh and deciding match against Montreal in the Forum on May 2, 1985. Quebec won the game with a 3—2 score and progressed to the next round. Upon their return to Quebec City at 3 in the morning, the players were welcomed by 11,000 excited fans.

Peter Stastny, representing the Quebec Nordiques, took part in six All-Star games. His brother Marian once played a game in this elite match as well. Near the end of his career, he played for the New Jersey Devils and then the St. Louis Blues, where he still works in management. It is probably to his credit that the great Slovak forward line of Demitra–Handzus–Bartecko is on the team.

Stastny was named general manager of the Slovakian entry in the 2002 Salt Lake City Olympics. Slovakia needed to qualify to advance to the main round of the tournament, but the team was forced to play its qualifying games without several key stars who hadn't been granted permission to leave their NHL teams. The team suffered a stunning loss at the hands of Germany and could muster no better than a tie against Latvia in the qualifying rounds, which eliminated it from advancing to the main draw at the Olympics. Stastny also enraged several NHL teams by using several players when he'd promised them he wouldn't.

In all likelihood, Peter Stastny holds yet another record. He must be the only player in the history of the game to have played for three national teams. In international competition over the years, he has represented Czechoslovakia, Canada and finally Slovakia, which earned a spot in the top ranks of world hockey with his help. Stastny was inducted into the Hockey Hall of Fame in 1998 and two years later into the International Ice Hockey Federation's Hall of Fame.

Peter Stastny played for three national teams: Czechoslovakia, Canada and Slovakia.

Bryan Trottier

Bryan Trottier was a modern-day player with old-fashioned attributes. At a time when specialists were beginning to take over from the all-round player, Trottier was a throwback. He was a defensively sound centerman with the vision and instincts of a pure scorer. Over an 18-year National Hockey League career, he led his teams to the Stanley Cup six times, including four consecutive

Bryan Trottier was a modern-day player with old-fashioned qualities.

titles with the New York Islanders in the early 1980s. And his achievements went beyond team success. He was the winner of the Calder Trophy as the league's top rookie, the Art Ross Trophy as top scorer and the Hart Trophy as the most valuable player. Trottier, at his retirement, was the league's sixth-highest all-time scorer.

His reputation as an oldtime player wasn't just for his play on the ice. Trottier was born and raised on a farm in Saskatchewan, and throughout his rise to the top of the hockey world, he stayed close to his prairie roots. The Trottier family struggled to make ends meet and Bryan, born in Val Marie in 1956, was forced to work from an early age to keep the farm alive. Even after he became a superstar, Trottier avoided the jet-setting lifestyle of so many of his peers. He didn't swear or smoke, and though he tried a rye and Coke once when he was an NHL rookie, he said he didn't like it. When his 1966 truck died midway through his second year in the league in 1977, he went out and bought another 1966 truck.

His heritage was a mix of French and Irish with Cree and Chippewa, and Trottier identified strongly with his Native background. He had some difficult early years in hockey, battling for respect in a sometimes less than tolerant atmosphere. He struggled in his first year of major junior hockey in 1972–73, collecting only 45 points in 67 games with the Swift Current Broncos of the western league. The next season he was better adapted and exploded for 112 points.

Normally, Trottier would have needed one or even two more years to develop his game before being considered for the professional circuits. In 1974, however, the NHL was reacting to the threat of the World Hockey Association. The elder league held a semi-secret draft with an emphasis on underaged players—teenagers who were 17 and 18 years old. Trottier was chosen 22nd overall in the second round, and he was the ninth underaged player taken that year. He was a promising forward, but hardly anyone pegged him as a dominating player. The New York Islanders, the team that selected him, even suggested he spend another year in junior, making him the only secret underaged player to wait to turn pro following that draft.

The Islanders offered to pay Trottier all the salary and bonuses he would have earned in the pro league—a strange arrangement for a young team in a rebuilding stage, but surely a vote of confidence that he appreciated and remembered. Still, that strategy would pay dividends for Trottier and the Islanders, not to mention Lethbridge, the WCJHL team he starred for in 1974—75. Trottier led that

Trottier, Bryan
C, 5′11″, 195 lbs, b: Val Marie, Sask., 7/17/1956

Season	Club, League	Regular Season					Playoffs				
		GP	G	A	Pts	PIM	GP	G	A	Pts	PIM
1975–76	New York Islanders, NHL	80	32	63	95	21	13	1	7	8	8
1976–77	New York Islanders, NHL	76	30	42	72	34	12	2	8	10	2
1977–78	New York Islanders, NHL	77	46	77	123	46	7	0	3	3	4
1978–79	New York Islanders, NHL	76	47	87	134	50	10	2	4	6	13
ChCup–79	NHL All-Stars	3	1	1	2	2					
1979–80	New York Islanders, NHL	78	42	62	104	68	21	12	17	29	16
1980–81	New York Islanders, NHL	73	31	72	103	74	18	11	18	29	34
CCup–81	Canada	7	3	8	11	6					
1981–82	New York Islanders, NHL	80	50	79	129	88	19	6	23	29	40
1982–83	New York Islanders, NHL	80	34	55	89	68	17	8	12	20	18
1983–84	New York Islanders, NHL	68	40	71	111	59	21	8	6	14	49
CCup–84	USA	6	2	3	5	8					
1984–85	New York Islanders, NHL	68	28	31	59	47	10	4	2	6	8
1985–86	New York Islanders, NHL	78	37	59	96	72	3	1	1	2	2
1986–87	New York Islanders, NHL	80	23	64	87	50	14	8	5	13	12
1987–88	New York Islanders, NHL	77	30	52	82	48	6	0	0	0	10
1988–89	New York Islanders, NHL	73	17	28	45	44					
1989–90	New York Islanders, NHL	59	13	11	24	29	4	1	0	1	4
1990–91	Pittsburgh Penguins, NHL	52	9	19	28	24	23	3	4	7	49
1991–92	Pittsburgh Penguins, NHL	63	11	18	29	54	21	4	3	7	8
1993–94	Pittsburgh Penguins, NHL	41	4	11	15	36	2	0	0	0	0
	NHL Totals	1279	524	901	1425	912	221	71	113	184	277
	ChalCup/CCup Totals	16	6	12	18	16					

NHL First All-Star Team (1978, 1979)
NHL Second All-Star Team (1982, 1984)
Won Hart Trophy (1979)
Won Art Ross Trophy (1979)
Won Conn Smythe Trophy (1980)
Won Calder Trophy (1976)
Won King Clancy Trophy (1989)
NHL Plus-Minus Leader (1979)
Won Bud Man of the Year Award (1988)
Won Stanley Cup (1980, 1981, 1982, 1983, 1991, 1992)

league with 98 assists and 144 points, earning most valuable player honors and confirming the wisdom of the decision to keep him in junior that extra year.

When the 1975–76 season began, Trottier was in the NHL, centering a line between Clark Gillies and Billy Harris. In his second game, he had a hat-trick and five points. After 11 games, he had 20 points and word began to spread, especially after his rugged defensive work shut down opposing stars. Trottier finished the year with league records for a rookie in assists and points, breaking Marcel Dionne's totals, and was an easy choice for the Calder Trophy as the top newcomer.

The rebuilding years for the Islanders were over in 1977–78, when Trottier and the team began to dominate the league. Trottier played most of the time with Mike Bossy on the right wing, a pure shooter who converted many of Trottier's pinpoint passes, and Gillies on the left wing, a grinder who provided the brawn and much of the corner work necessary for success. The line was the most dominant in the league since Phil Esposito had teamed with Ken Hodge and Wayne Cashman for the Bruins earlier in the decade—a troika that was successful for many of the same reasons as the Islanders' top guns.

Their years of rebuilding were over when Bryan Trottier (left) and the Islanders started to dominate the league in 1977–78.

Trottier was second to Guy Lafleur in the scoring race in 1978 and led the NHL with 77 assists. The next year he was unstoppable, using his playmaking skills to collect 87 assists and his tenaciousness around the net to record 47 goals. He was the league's top scorer and took home the Hart Trophy as the most valuable player. In 1980 the Islanders won the Stanley Cup and Trottier was the star of the show, leading all playoff scorers with 29 points and earning the Conn Smythe Trophy as the most outstanding post-season performer. With Wayne Gretzky's era still on the horizon, Trottier, the quiet guy from the Prairies, was the best center in pro hockey.

Trottier played for Team Canada in the 1981 Canada Cup and led his Islanders to three more Stanley Cup wins to begin the new decade. He scored 50 goals in 1981–82 and was again the top playoff scorer that season. In 1984, with another Canada Cup on the schedule, Trottier stunned the hockey world by declaring that he would play for the United States instead of Canada. He said that his Indian card, which gave him the right to work in either country and free border access, enabled him to don the red, white and blue of the U.S. He was living year-round on Long Island with his family—his wife and children were Americans—and Trottier, who still felt the sting of the discrimination he fought in the Canadian west, said he owed something to the country that had given him so much. He received his U.S. citizenship and a passport in the space of a few months and was soon on the ice at Montreal's Forum in an exhibition game against the Canadians. Trottier was booed relentlessly and fans cheered another recent citizen, Peter Stastny, the Czech-born star who had quickly been made a Canadian prior to the tournament.

"Funny, eh? The fans booed the Indian-Canadian who went American," Trottier said, "but they didn't boo the Czech who went Canadian, even when he tried to cut my head off." Stastny was continuing a long feud between the two players by taking a long swing with his stick at Trottier's head in the third period of the game in Montreal.

Trottier spent six more seasons in New York following the Canada Cup and saw his numbers steadily fall. He was still a dedicated and effective defensive player, however, and in 1990 the

Pittsburgh Penguins signed the veteran to bolster their playoff chances. Trottier was an important part of the Penguin team that won two straight titles after he joined the squad. Stars such as Mario Lemieux and Jaromir Jagr attributed much of the team's success to the aging star's leadership, his drive and desire. Trottier retired following the Penguins' second Cup victory and spent one year in the Islanders' front office.

But he was soon bored with his desk job and returned to the league as a player in 1993-94 at the age of 37. He played 41 games with the Penguins while acting as an assistant coach, a job he continued after finally hanging up his skates at the end of that season. Bryan Trottier was inducted into the Hockey Hall of Fame in 1997 and later became an assistant coach with Colorado, winning another Cup in the spring of 2001, his first as a coach.

Viacheslav Fetisov

Viacheslav Fetisov won all the major team titles in world hockey.

At the end of April 1978, Viacheslav Fetisov was voted the best defenseman at the World Championship in Prague. He had just turned 20 the week before. Twenty years later, the Detroit Red Wings won the Stanley Cup with the 40-year-old Fetisov for the second time in succession. And he said, "I feel as if I could still play about a dozen seasons in the NHL."

Detroit offered him a contract to play 30 games in the 1998–99 season. But, for him, that wasn't enough. He'd had invitations from other clubs in the league, but he couldn't find it in himself to come out on the ice against Detroit. He returned to the New Jersey Devils to try his luck—this time in the capacity of assistant coach.

For Fetisov, hockey sapped his energy and tried his nerves. The game continuously confronted him with one tribulation after another, though in many cases he brought them upon himself by always testing his own limits. As an eight-year-old, he'd been refused admission to the Dynamo club's hockey school. They told him it was a bit too early. Fetisov thought he had learned a lesson from that first bitter experience, so at the school run by the Central Red Army club, he added a year to his age. Although they told him he was a bit too late, they accepted him anyway.

At the age of 15, when playing hockey had gone completely to his head and both his emotions and his game were suffering from the strain, he almost quit. The coach of the Red Army's junior team, to which Fetisov had risen from the boys' squad, put it quite bluntly to his colleagues: "He's neither a defenseman nor a forward. He's weak when it comes to grabbing the puck, he's confused when it comes to positional playing, he's not much of a skater, and he's 'a floater' when it comes to tactics." Being a natural leader, he was trying to establish his own playing style as a "scoring defenseman," but this didn't sit well with the strategy espoused by the national team. Nonetheless, Fetisov persevered and his style, ironically, later became a trademark of the Russian school of hockey.

The 18-year-old Fetisov finally entered the grownup world of hockey by simply running right over Spartak player Alexander Yakushev—the heftiest forward at the time. Then he got into a fistfight with the biggest forward, Vyacheslav Starshinov, also from Spartak. Starshinov was twice as old as Fetisov and was quite surprised to see such a brazen challenge coming from this young upstart.

"I began coming out on the ice with the first line when I was about 17. I got accustomed to that—it couldn't be otherwise. Even when I was hooked up with Vladimir Petrov's forward line, I felt I could really open up—I could make mistakes, but still I found my place on the ice. I could say the same, only to an even greater degree, about playing in Igor Larionov's forward line. That I couldn't imagine myself playing outside crack forward lines wasn't conceit. Otherwise, I wouldn't have been able to play my game—I would've drooped. I simply would've turned into a good defenseman." Fetisov performed the primary duties of a defenseman quite conscientiously. Many opponents, at least in tournaments in the USSR, tried to avoid making direct contact with him. Defenseman Fetisov knew to make the first pass to his forwards—the kind of pass that set an attack in motion—from some of the most awkward positions. But Fetisov wasn't happy.

At the age of 20, Viacheslav Fetisov was voted the best defenseman at the World Championship in Prague, and 20 years later he won the Stanley Cup with the Red Wings for the second time in a row.

Players on the Central Red Army—the best hockey team in the USSR in the early 1980s—could without a moment's notice take up defensive positions or instantly switch to mounting an attack on the opposing team's goal. On the ice, Fetisov was the leader of that progressive model of hockey. The length and direction of his maneuvers were unpredictable and his playmaking initiatives verged on willfulness or caprice. But the kingpin of that forward line, Igor Larionov, knew that if Fetisov spurted forward, then at least he would go to the very end and finish off the attack.

When injuries put Fetisov out for quite a long period in the fall of 1984, his teammates admitted that his absence in the lineup was felt more than that of anyone else.

Speaking about Fetisov, Red Army coach Viktor Tikhonov said: "Quite an unusual player. It is rare to see a defenseman so tenacious, tough and competent on the defense line, and just as good in attacking. By his abilities, his energy and his craving for action, Fetisov seems to be able to solve all the problems that come up no matter where on the ice rink. I have probably never seen a hockey master like him, and I've seen practically all of our Soviet players."

In the 1987–88 season, the five-man unit showed what they could do. Three very tough final matches of the Canada Cup between Canada and the Soviet Union ended with an identical score of 6–5, twice in favor of the Canadians. And that is when, acting like a coach for the first time, Fetisov spoke out in an article he wrote for the press. He weighed the merits of the Soviet and Canadian players without giving preference to either side. "It is being pounded into our heads that we aren't inquisitive; that Canadian players 'live' on the bench; that some of our players are practically napping; that we trained for two months and the Canadians only one month. But at the end of the tournament, for some reason, they, the Canadians, looked fresher on the ice."

The great winner, however, was the fans and the game itself as both teams displayed a competitive ability rarely seen in sport.

"If any of the Soviet players demonstrated special talent, then it was Viacheslav Fetisov," declared Mike Keenan, the senior coach of the winning team, after the tournament. "As captain and leader, he was on the ice 30 minutes of pure time. And don't tell me they had six defensemen. Fetisov was in the game during the most difficult minutes."

In 1988 the Soviet national team, headed by its captain, won the Olympic hockey tournament in Calgary. Fetisov was at his best. The victory confirmed in Fetisov's own mind that he could compete at the NHL level.

During the flight home from Calgary after the Olympics, the leadership of the USSR Sports Committee told Fetisov that he'd be allowed to sign a contract with the New Jersey Devils. But despite that promise, the Soviets did nothing to help him get to the NHL in the ensuing months. The system prevented the individual from pursuing his own interests. In the winter of 1989, Fetisov opposed the system by announcing he would no longer play for the CSKA, but he in turn was told that he wasn't allowed to play. Officially, however, the media turned the dispute into a personal one between the player and his coach, Viktor Tikhonov. Fetisov, supported by a group of famous athletes, countered by hiring a lawyer to examine the Soviet constitution and to prove there was no law preventing a man from working or going to another country. In this way, and with great help from New Jersey Devils, Fetisov eventually made it to the NHL, overcoming a system that had always proved stronger than any individual in the past. In truth, he also realized the symbolic importance of his entry into the NHL and how it might pave the way for future Soviet stars to join the North American league without having to defect.

Fetisov's new lifestyle off the ice allowed him to relax somewhat. Working in the NHL gave him a higher standard of living, and he could afford to take time out of his schedule to enjoy life.

But the NHL had in store for him a burden that was much harder to carry than the whole year of red tape that led up to his departure from Moscow. First, he arrived in New Jersey worn out and emotionally exhausted. Second, he found himself playing on a team that had a different philosophy and style of play. Everything that Fetisov had become familiar with over the last 15 years had to be adapted to the North American game while playing for the New Jersey Devils. He was no longer team captain and on-ice leader, and he was no longer expected to be the top-scoring defenseman on the team. He was now one of 22 players on the team, not the superhero he had become in the Soviet Union.

Fetisov, Viacheslav
D, 6´1˝, 220 lbs, b: Moscow, USSR, 4/20/1958

Season	Club, League	Regular Season					Playoffs				
		GP	G	A	Pts	PIM	GP	G	A	Pts	PIM
1975–76	CSKA, USSR	1	0	0	0	0					
1976–77	CSKA, USSR	28	3	4	7	14					
WEC–77	USSR	5	3	3	6	2					
1977–78	CSKA, USSR	35	9	18	27	46					
WEC–78	USSR	10	4	6	10	11					
1978–79	CSKA, USSR	29	10	19	29	40					
1979–80	CSKA, USSR	37	10	14	24	46					
OWG–80	USSR	7	5	4	9	10					
1980–81	CSKA, USSR	48	13	16	29	44					
WEC–81	USSR	8	1	4	5	6					
CCup–81	USSR	7	1	7	8	10					
1981–82	CSKA, USSR	46	15	26	41	20					
WEC–82	USSR	10	4	3	7	6					
1982–83	CSKA, USSR	43	6	17	23	46					
WEC–83	USSR	10	3	7	10	8					
1983–84	CSKA, USSR	44	19	30	49	38					
OWG–84	USSR	7	3	8	11	8					
1984–85	CSKA, USSR	20	13	12	25	6					
WEC–85	USSR	10	6	7	13	15					
1985–86	CSKA, USSR	40	15	19	34	12					
WEC–86	USSR	10	6	9	15	10					
1986–87	CSKA, USSR	39	13	20	33	18					
RV'87	USSR	2	0	1	1	2					
WEC–87	USSR	10	2	8	10	2					
CCup–87	USSR	9	2	5	7	9					
1987–88	CSKA, USSR	46	18	17	35	26					
OWG–88	USSR	8	4	9	13	6					
1988–89	CSKA, USSR	23	9	8	17	18					
WEC–89	USSR	10	2	4	6	17					
1989–90	New Jersey Devils, NHL	72	8	34	42	52	6	0	2	2	10
WEC–90	USSR	8	2	8	10	8					
1990–91	New Jersey Devils, NHL	67	3	16	19	62	7	0	0	0	17
	Utica Devils, AHL	1	1	1	2	0					
WEC–91	USSR	10	3	1	4	4					
1991–92	New Jersey Devils, NHL	70	3	23	26	108	6	0	3	3	8
1992–93	New Jersey Devils, NHL	76	4	23	27	158	5	0	2	2	4
1993–94	New Jersey Devils, NHL	52	1	14	15	30	14	1	0	1	8
1994–95	Spartak Moscow, Russia	1	0	1	1	4					
	New Jersey Devils, NHL	4	0	1	1	0					
	Detroit Red Wings, NHL	14	3	11	14	2	18	0	8	8	14
1995–96	Detroit Red Wings, NHL	69	7	35	42	96	19	1	4	5	34
WCup–96	Russia	4	0	2	2	12					
1996–97	Detroit Red Wings, NHL	64	5	23	28	76	20	0	4	4	42
1997–98	Detroit Red Wings, NHL	58	2	12	14	72	21	0	3	3	10
	USSR/Russia Totals	480	153	221	374	378					
	NHL Totals	546	36	192	228	656	116	2	26	28	147
	OWG/WEC/CCup/RV'87/WCup Totals	145	51	96	147	146					

Named Best Defenseman at WEC (1978, 1982, 1985, 1986, 1989)
Won OWG (1984, 1988)
Won WEC (1978, 1981, 1982, 1983, 1986, 1989, 1990)
Won Stanley Cup (1997, 1998)
Won CCup (1981)
USSR Champion (1977, 1978, 1979, 1980, 1981, 1982, 1983, 1984, 1985, 1986, 1987, 1988, 1989)

Viacheslav Fetisov (front).

In 1996 he was invited to play for the Detroit Red Wings. Under the great coach Scotty Bowman, who was the first in the league to make a "Russian" five-men unit and brought European coaching into the North American game, Fetisov would get to play alongside his partner from the old days—Igor Larionov. Before he even had the chance to get comfortable with the Detroit Red Wings, his new Stanley Cup contender lost to none other than his former New Jersey Devils. At 38, his first real chance for the Stanley Cup had been lost. But, rather than give in to his age, he was defiant and promised himself that he would not retire until he had held the sacred trophy above his head. After eight years in the NHL, he had come to understand what was needed to win the most cherished trophy in all of sports.

Red Army coach Viktor Tikhonov (front row, left) said of Viacheslav Fetisov (front row, second from the left), "By his abilities, his energy and his craving for action, Fetisov seems to be able to solve all the problems that come up no matter where on the ice rink."

A year later, his dream came true. The Wings made it to the finals to face the Philadelphia Flyers, sweeping them in four straight games and winning the first Cup for the city since 1955. Just days later, Fetisov came close to losing his life. Together with Vladimir Konstantinov and masseur Sergei Mnatsakanov, he miraculously survived a terrible car accident. It was just one more example of Fetisov's tendency to live life on the edge.

But he kept up his busy schedule with the most diverse of undertakings. It was Fetisov who came up with the idea of sending Russian NHL players to Moscow every year to participate in the Spartak Cup tournament, a strategic idea that sent a clear message to those in political power that the new kind of Soviet player did not fear the government and valued his freedom and ability to travel without worry above all. It was Fetisov who took the risk of bringing the Stanley Cup to Moscow; and it was also Fetisov who stretched his nerves to the breaking point in an effort to organize a worthy Russian team to participate in the 1996 World Cup.

Fetisov retired at the end of 1997–98 season, then joined the New Jersey Devils as an assistant coach and helped the team to its second—and his third—Stanley Cup victory in 2000.

But the accolades didn't stop there. Fetisov was named the best European player of the 20th century by a panel of hockey experts in North America, and in August 2000 a special game was played in his honor at the Olympic Sports Complex in Moscow. Numerous dignitaries from Europe's hockey powers attended, along with the political leaders of Sweden, Finland, Latvia, Belarus, Russia and various European jurisdictions. After the game, Fetisov was awarded the prestigious Olympic Order for his lifetime achievements in international play and his number 2 sweater was retired by the Red Army club he'd so long been a part of.

In 2001, Fetisov reached two of his ultimate off-ice goals—perhaps the most prestigious and hardest-fought victories of his hockey career—when he was inducted into the Hockey Hall of Fame and later named general manager and head coach of the Russian entry for the 2002 Olympics. Russia defeated the defending Olympic champs from the Czech Republic in the playoff round at Salt Lake City, but lost to the United States for the right to play in the gold medal game. Russia then easily beat the Cinderella team from Belarus to take the bronze medal.

In April 2002, Fetisov was named to the prestigious position of Russia's Minister of Sports—a most fitting way to continue a stellar career and lifelong service to sports.

Mark Johnson

A fine offensive center, Mark Johnson was also admired in hockey circles for his tenacious work ethic. He came by his love of the game honestly, being the son of legendary coach Badger Bob Johnson. During the 16 years he played the game, Johnson excelled at the collegiate level—with the University of Wisconsin Badgers—and international levels, as well as in the NHL and European professional leagues.

The native of Madison, Wisconsin, was born to be a Badger. Under the guidance of his famous father, he enjoyed three outstanding years at the University of Wisconsin. He racked up 256 points over those years and was twice selected to the Western Collegiate Hockey Association All-Star Team after leading the conference in goals. His relative lack of size caused many teams to avoid drafting him, but the Pittsburgh Penguins selected him 66th overall at the 1977 Amateur Draft with the hope that he would mature in college and gain valuable international experience wearing the colors of the United States.

He played well for the U.S. at the 1978 and 1979 World Championships before committing to the national team as it prepared for the Lake Placid Olympics. Then Johnson proved to be one of the top players during Team USA's Miracle on Ice gold medal win in 1980. He scored 11 points in seven matches and was a respected figure in the dressing room. His two biggest goals came in the 4–3 upset over the USSR that paved the way to the gold medal.

After the Games, Johnson joined the Penguins for the last 17 regular-season games and first round of the playoffs. His acquisition brought the team some badly needed headlines in a city where the sports pages were dominated by the Steelers in football and the Pirates in baseball. He played solidly and proved he could stand the pace of the NHL game. As a rookie in 1980–81, he scored 33 points on a weak Pittsburgh squad and then represented the U.S. at the World Championship in the spring and the Canada Cup in the fall. Halfway through the 1981–82 season, he was traded to Minnesota. Following the North Stars' early exit from the playoffs at the hands of Chicago, Johnson again represented his country at the World Championship.

His career took a turn for the better when he was sent to Hartford in a deal consummated

Mark Johnson's two biggest goals came in the 4–3 upset over the USSR that became known as the Miracle on Ice at the Lake Placid Olympics in 1980.

Johnson, Mark
C, 5′9″, 170 lbs, b: Madison, WI, 9/22/1957

Season	Club, League	Regular Season					Playoffs				
		GP	G	A	Pts	PIM	GP	G	A	Pts	PIM
1976–77	University of Wisconsin, WCHA	43	36	44	80	16					
1977–70	University of Wisconsin, WCHA	42	48	38	86	24					
WEC–78	USA	10	0	2	2	0					
1978–79	University of Wisconsin, WCHA	40	41	49	90	34					
WEC–79	USA	2	0	0	0	0					
OWG–80	USA	7	5	6	11	6					
1979–80	Pittsburgh Penguins, NHL	17	3	5	8	4	5	2	2	4	0
1980–81	Pittsburgh Penguins, NHL	73	10	23	33	50	5	2	1	3	6
WEC–81	USA	5	0	2	2	2					
CCup–81	USA	6	1	3	4	2					
1981–82	Pittsburgh Penguins, NHL	46	10	11	21	30					
	Minnesota North Stars, NHL	10	2	2	4	10	4	2	0	2	0
WEC–82	USA	7	1	1	2	6					
1982–83	Hartford Whalers, NHL	73	31	38	69	28					
1983–84	Hartford Whalers, NHL	79	35	52	87	27					
CCup–84	USA	6	2	3	5	0					
1984–85	Hartford Whalers, NHL	49	19	28	47	21					
	St. Louis Blues, NHL	17	4	6	10	2	3	0	1	1	0
WEC–85	USA	10	4	1	5	6					
1985–86	New Jersey Devils, NHL	80	21	41	62	16					
WEC–86	USA	10	5	3	8	10					
1986–87	New Jersey Devils, NHL	68	25	26	51	22					
WEC–87	USA	10	3	6	9	8					
CCup–87	USA	5	0	1	1	0					
1987–88	New Jersey Devils, NHL	54	14	19	33	14	18	10	8	18	4
1988–89	New Jersey Devils, NHL	40	13	25	38	24					
1989–90	New Jersey Devils, NHL	63	16	29	45	12	2	0	0	0	0
WEC–90	USA	9	2	3	5	2					
1990–91	HC Milano, Italy	36	32	45	77	15	10	7	16	23	6
1991–92	HC Milano, Italy	2	1	3	4	0					
	Zell-am-Zee, Austria	33	23	49	72	*					
	NHL Totals	669	203	305	508	260	37	16	12	28	10
	OWG/WEC/CCup Totals	87	23	31	54	42					

Won OWG (1980)
Italy Champion (1991)

It took Mark Johnson (left) a few seasons to learn the little tricks that make a small man effective in the rough NHL.

at the NHL Entry Draft. The Whalers utilized his speed and offensive savvy in a way that allowed him to play his best hockey as a professional. He was often teamed with Sylvain Turgeon and Ray Neufeld and produced consecutive 30-goal seasons in 1982–83 and 1983–84. In 1984, after a 35-goal season, he was named the Whalers' most valuable player. As William Houston noted, "It took him a while to learn the little tricks needed to make a small man effective in the rough NHL—when to drive for the net, when to be aggressive and when to back off to save energy."

Johnson enjoyed his best Canada Cup performance in 1984 with five points in six matches. He was also enjoying a fine year in 1984–85 when the Whalers sent him to St. Louis in a package deal to acquire netminder Mike Liut. Part of Johnson's trouble in Connecticut stemmed from some constructive criticism he voiced toward coach Jack Evans. The Blues in turn sent him to New Jersey a few months later, on the eve of the 1985–86 season.

It was in New Jersey that Johnson found his niche as a solid two-way center. He played five years for the Devils and became one of the club's most popular skaters. For the first time in years, he stopped feeling as though he had to live up to the expectations created by Lake Placid. But he also continued to excel in international competition. He was one of the top players for the U.S. at the World Championships in 1985, 1986, 1987 and 1990 and the 1987 Canada Cup.

Following a solid effort at the 1987 World Championship, he was signed by the HC Milano club of the Italian first division. He proved to be one of the top players in Europe in 1990–91 with 77 points in 36 games. Early the next year he was acquired by the Zell-am-Zee club in Austria. Johnson starred with 72 points in 33 games to end his pro career on a high note. A popular player wherever he went, Johnson totaled 508 NHL points. He was often deployed on both the power-play and the penalty-killing units and was always highly regarded for his on-ice intelligence. And his performance at Lake Placid in 1980 made him one of the heroes of U.S. hockey to a whole generation of fans.

Randy Carlyle

Although Randy Carlyle never came close to winning a Stanley Cup, he was one of the most reliable defenseman of his generation.

Randy Carlyle's entrance into the NHL was controversial, if nothing else. After playing three years for the Sudbury Wolves in the OHA, the 20-year-old apparently signed a contract with the Cincinnati Stingers of the WHA prior to the NHL's Amateur Draft in the summer of 1976. However, the night before that draft, Toronto's general manager Jim Gregory got a phone call from a friend in Sudbury saying Carlyle hadn't signed a contract but merely a letter of intent, with a blank contract attached thereto. The next day, Gregory selected Carlyle 30th overall at the draft, surprising the NHL hockey world, which thought the defenseman was already spoken for.

"We know he has signed with Cincinnati, but we went after the best available player. You can never be content with what you've got," Gregory said, suggesting he'd be happy to wait for Carlyle to play out his Cincinnati contract before signing with the Leafs. In the ensuing days, however, the player and the general manager entered into contract negotiations, and Carlyle eventually signed a contract with the Leafs despite his apparent commitment elsewhere. "I just told the truth about what I'd signed," Carlyle explained, "that it was just a letter and not a contract."

The Stingers begged to differ and two weeks later took Carlyle to court for breach of contract. In the end, the matter was resolved out of court and he got to stay with the Leafs. While the Stingers had offered him $200,000 a year, the Leafs came in at $225,000 plus a kidney machine for Carlyle's sick father.

Paradoxically, while the Leafs were delighted with the coup, they showed little patience with the young defenseman. He split parts of two seasons with the NHL team and the Dallas minor-league affiliate, and then Toronto impatiently traded him to Pittsburgh with George Ferguson for Dave Burrows. After just 94 NHL games, they gave up on a 22-year-old defenseman with plenty of potential. Not surprisingly, Carlyle's career took off with the Penguins. He became an offensive presence, leader of the league's most potent power-play and key man on the emerging Pittsburgh blue line.

In 1980–81, he won the Norris Trophy as the league's best defenseman and that fall was invited to training camp for Team Canada at the 1981 Canada Cup. But that experience turned sour on Carlyle. "I reported out of shape, which was bad," Carlyle admitted before defending himself. "But I think Scotty Bowman, the coach, should have stuck with me. That club was thin on defense. I'd have helped." After Canada's embarrassing 7–1 loss to the Soviet Union in the finals, it was tough for his fans not to sympathize just a little bit with his comments.

Midway through the 1983–84 season, Carlyle hurt his knee and tried to come back too quickly. It proved to be a shortened season for him and one that saw him traded as a result to Winnipeg, where he spent the last 10 years of his lengthy career. His excellent season the next year, 1984–85, provided a measure of satisfaction. And he proved to be a leader in the Winnipeg dressing room. His career was back on track. "I looked at coming to Winnipeg as a fresh start. I wrote off the last two years in Pittsburgh as down years. I just wanted to come here and try to help as much as possible. The trade was good for me, for Pittsburgh and the Jets."

Carlyle's only other international experience was perhaps even worse than his first in the Canada Cup training camp. He was asked to play for Canada at the 1989 World Championship, and after a victory over West Germany, he was selected to take a urine test.

Randy Carlyle won the Norris Trophy as the league's best defenseman in 1980–81 and was invited to Canada's training camp for the 1981 Canada Cup.

Carlyle, Randy
D, 5´10˝, 200 lbs, b: Sudbury, Ont., 4/19/1956

Season	Club, League	Regular Season					Playoffs				
		GP	G	A	Pts	PIM	GP	G	A	Pts	PIM
1976–77	Toronto Maple Leafs, NHL	45	0	5	5	51	9	0	1	1	20
	Dallas Black Hawks, CHL	26	2	7	9	63					
1977–78	Toronto Maple Leafs, NHL	49	2	11	13	31	7	0	1	1	20
	Dallas Black Hawks, CHL	21	3	14	17	31					
1978–79	Pittsburgh Penguins, NHL	70	13	34	47	78	7	0	0	0	12
1979–80	Pittsburgh Penguins, NHL	67	8	28	36	45	5	1	0	1	4
1980–81	Pittsburgh Penguins, NHL	76	16	67	83	136	5	4	5	9	9
1981–82	Pittsburgh Penguins, NHL	73	11	64	75	131	5	1	3	4	16
1982–83	Pittsburgh Penguins, NHL	61	15	41	56	110					
1983–84	Pittsburgh Penguins, NHL	50	3	23	26	82					
	Winnipeg Jets, NHL	5	0	3	3	2	3	0	2	2	4
1984–85	Winnipeg Jets, NHL	71	13	38	51	98	8	1	5	6	13
1985–86	Winnipeg Jets, NHL	68	16	33	49	93					
1986–87	Winnipeg Jets, NHL	71	16	26	42	93	10	1	5	6	18
1987–88	Winnipeg Jets, NHL	78	15	44	59	210	5	0	2	2	10
1988–89	Winnipeg Jets, NHL	78	6	38	44	78					
WEC–89	Canada	9	1	4	5	4					
1989–90	Winnipeg Jets, NHL	53	3	15	18	50					
1990–91	Winnipeg Jets, NHL	52	9	19	28	44					
1991–92	Winnipeg Jets, NHL	66	1	9	10	54	5	1	0	1	6
1992–93	Winnipeg Jets, NHL	22	1	1	2	14					
	NHL Totals	1055	148	499	647	1400	69	9	24	33	132
	WEC Totals	9	1	4	5	4					

NHL First All-Star Team (1981)
Won James Norris Trophy (1981)

The IIHF announced he had failed the test, but Carlyle swore he had taken no banned substance of any sort. He was expelled from the competition, and the news, just months after the Ben Johnson scandal at the Seoul Olympics, made headlines worldwide. The next day, though, the IIHF announced that Carlyle's "B" sample was negative and that he was eligible to play again. No explanation was provided for the aberrant initial result and Carlyle's image had been tarnished.

After 17 years and 1,055 games, Carlyle retired after the 1992–93 season. Although he never came close to winning a Stanley Cup, he was one of the most reliable defensemen of his generation. It wasn't without irony that his last of 148 career goals came in his final career game—against Toronto.

Rod Langway

Rod Langway became a stalwart on the Montreal Canadiens' blue line from 1979 to 1982.

The quintessential defensive defenseman, Rod Langway took some of the attention away from the league's high-scoring rearguards. He began his 15-year NHL career with the Montreal Canadiens dynasty in the late 1970s before moving on to help establish the Washington Capitals as a competitive franchise in the 1980s. Langway's dogged consistency earned him awards and accolades throughout his NHL career and made him a valuable member of the United States national team when his services were required.

The son of a serviceman in the United States Air Force, Langway was born in Maag, Formosa (now Taiwan). He grew up in Randolph, Massachusetts, where he learned the game. He later starred for the University of New Hampshire and in 1976–77 caught the eye of Montreal Canadiens scouts, who selected him in the second round of the Amateur Draft that summer of 1977.

Unable to come to contractual terms with Montreal, Langway was signed by the Birmingham Bulls of the World Hockey Association. He split his first pro season between Alabama and the AHL's Hampton Gulls, then he rejoined the Habs organization prior to the 1978–79 NHL season.

Always confident in his abilities, Langway fit in well on Scotty Bowman's blue line, playing a strictly defensive role along with fellow American Bill Nyrop. The youngster was teamed with veteran Guy Lapointe and played well for a time before it was deemed necessary to give him a few more games with Nova Scotia in the AHL. Langway returned a short time later and, ironically, due to an injury suffered by his old partner Lapointe, he was given another chance to show his mettle. He dressed for eight playoff games later that year and played a useful role in Montreal's fourth straight Stanley Cup win. Many observers were impressed with the way the youngster, instead of being in awe of the stars surrounding him, went about his business efficiently and added depth to the Habs' powerhouse roster.

Between 1979–80 and 1981–82, Langway became a stalwart on the Hab's blue line as the "Big Three" of Lapointe, Robinson and Savard aged. Langway was also a vital cog on the United States squad in the 1981 Canada Cup and 1982 World Championship.

A tireless worker, Langway "removes his gloves, and it seems miraculous that his fingers haven't drowned inside," Bob Duffy of the *Boston Globe* noted. "The white bands of protective tape on his wrists appear welded into place. As he looks down to inspect the gloves, a waterfall pours from his curly blond hair."

Prior to the 1982–83 season, Rocket Rod and teammates Brian Engblom and Doug Jarvis were traded to the Washington Capitals for Ryan Walter and Rick Green. It was a controversial move and unquestionably benefited the Capitals immediately. Right away, Langway was named team captain and was the on-ice general of an improved Washington club that became competitive for the first time in its history. The squad improved from 65 to 94 points during his first year in the American capital. Doug Jarvis noted, "If Rod had stayed with the Canadiens, he always would have been in Robinson's shadow and never would have emerged as a team leader."

The three ex-Habs had one common trait—they were at their most proficient when they didn't have the puck. This was crucial to Washington's improvement in the standings during the 1980s. Between their inaugural season in 1974–75 and 1980–81, they were one of the worst defensive clubs in the history of the NHL. Their rise to competitive status was built around an emphatic commitment to defensive hockey, and for the Caps to play this style successfully, Langway's role was of paramount significance. Additionally, his exposure to winning with class in Montreal was a valuable addition to the uncompetitive Capitals.

Langway's greatest asset was playing to his strengths and drawing attention to the importance of having a stay-at-home defenseman on the roster. The lanky defender was in tremendous physical condition and was never intimidated on the ice. He rarely fought but tended to draw more penalties on the part of the opposition than he himself took. Langway himself commented: "You can call me whatever you want. I'm old-style. I know that. And I know my limitations."

Following both the 1982–83 and 1983–84 seasons, Langway won the Norris Trophy and was placed on the NHL First All-Star Team. He

Rod Langway (front) rarely fought and tended to draw more penalties from the opposition than he took himself.

Langway, Rod
D, 6'3", 218 lbs, b: Maag, Formosa, 5/3/1957

Season	Club, League	Regular Season					Playoffs				
		GP	G	A	Pts	PIM	GP	G	A	Pts	PIM
1976–77	University of New Hampshire, ECAC	34	10	43	53	52					
1977–78	Birmingham Bulls, WHA	52	3	18	21	52	4	0	0	0	9
	Hampton Gulls, AHL	30	6	16	22	50					
1978–79	Montreal Canadiens, NHL	45	3	4	7	30	8	0	0	0	16
	Nova Scotia Voyageurs, AHL	18	6	13	19	29					
1979–80	Montreal Canadiens, NHL	77	7	29	36	81	10	3	3	6	2
1980–81	Montreal Canadiens, NHL	80	11	34	45	120	3	0	0	0	6
CCup–81	USA	6	0	1	1	8					
1981–82	Montreal Canadiens, NHL	66	5	34	39	116	5	0	3	3	18
WEC–82	USA	6	0	2	2	4					
1982–83	Washington Capitals, NHL	80	3	29	32	75	4	0	0	0	0
1983–84	Washington Capitals, NHL	80	9	24	33	61	8	0	5	5	7
CCup–84	USA	6	1	1	2	8					
1984–85	Washington Capitals, NHL	79	4	22	26	54	5	0	1	1	6
1985–86	Washington Capitals, NHL	71	1	17	18	61	9	1	2	3	6
1986–87	Washington Capitals, NHL	78	2	25	27	53	7	0	1	1	2
RV'87	NHL All-Stars	2	0	0	0	0					
CCup–87	USA	5	0	1	1	6					
1987–88	Washington Capitals, NHL	63	3	13	16	28	6	0	0	0	8
1988–89	Washington Capitals, NHL	76	2	19	21	65	6	0	0	0	6
1989–90	Washington Capitals, NHL	58	0	8	8	39	15	1	4	5	12
1990–91	Washington Capitals, NHL	56	1	7	8	24	11	0	2	2	6
1991–92	Washington Capitals, NHL	64	0	13	13	22	7	0	1	1	2
1992–93	Washington Capitals, NHL	21	0	0	0	20					
1994–95	Richmond Renegades, ECHL	6	0	0	0	2	9	1	1	2	4
1995–96	San Francisco Spiders, IHL	46	1	5	6	38					
	NHL Totals	994	51	278	329	849	104	5	22	27	97
	WHA Totals	52	3	18	21	52	4	0	0	0	9
	WEC/CCup/RV'87 Totals	25	1	5	6	26					

NHL First All-Star Team (1983, 1984)
NHL Second All-Star Team (1985)
Won James Norris Trophy (1983, 1984)
Won Stanley Cup (1979)

became known throughout the NHL as the Caps' defensive leader. During the fall of 1984, he starred for Team USA in the Canada Cup and was placed on the tournament All-Star team. Under Langway's guidance, Washington topped the 100-point mark three straight years beginning in 1983–84.

Playing their defensive style to perfection and benefiting from timely scoring, the Capitals won 50 games in 1985–86. Former Philadelphia and New York Rangers coach Fred Shero once said, "The Oilers would survive without Coffey, but not the Caps without Langway." In 1988–89, Washington won its first Patrick Division title and the next year reached the semifinals for the first time in history. Langway remained captain until retiring early in 1992–93, at which time he was succeeded by Kevin Hatcher.

The veteran blueliner provided tutoring and served as a box office draw with the Richmond Renegades of the ECHL in 1994–95 and the IHL's San Francisco Spiders under Jean Perron the next year. In 1997–98, he played 10 games for the Providence Bruins of the AHL. One of the best Americans to ever play "Canada's game," Langway noted, "I enjoy going to Canada for the recognition and the fact that when you're there, hockey is back in your bones." In 1999 he was inducted into the U.S. Hockey Hall of Fame.

Alexei Kasatonov

Alexei Kasatonov was in the right place at the right time.

No one disputes the fact that the four most talented players from the USSR national team's greatest lineup were Viacheslav Fetisov, Sergei Makarov, Vladimir Krutov and Igor Larionov. Alexei Kasatonov, the fifth member of that outstanding lineup, was truly favored by fortune. His story is that of someone who managed to be in the right place at the right time.

He was born in Leningrad and for some unknown reason Leningrad hockey players rarely made it into the limelight. Only Nikolai Drozdetsky and Kasatonov went on to become world-class players. Says Kasatonov: "If I had stayed in Leningrad and not joined CSKA, I'm sure that I wouldn't have amounted to anything. I had too many personal shortcomings and I didn't have the personality for the sport."

Kasatonov was a big man but not aggressive, a kind of gentle giant. He was overwhelmed by the strenuous CSKA training exercises and always took time to relax and rest. Many wondered why Viktor Tikhonov would want a passive player like Kasatonov in the lineup. The coach claimed that he especially valued Kasatonov's ability to position himself on the ice. He provided a balancing force against the other more dynamic and aggressive players in the lineup, and Kasatonov was someone who would follow orders willingly.

Coach Igor Dmitriyev once remarked, "Kasatonov, an awkward and somewhat backward individual in everyday life, was indispensable to the line of five, completing it and bringing a perfect balance to the playing quality."

There is a theory about competence that says you tend to get smarter if you associate with smart people. For Kasatonov, the lineup's competence level was a gift. "I have no doubt," he said, "that what I have achieved is my absolute limit, the top of my potential. I know for sure I couldn't play any better under any circumstances."

In contrast to his teammates, Kasatonov never developed a trademark gesture meant to impress the audience. His contribution to the game was based on immaculate technique. His awkwardness eventually became a confident and elegant assurance that added to the collective teamwork on the ice. Besides being a reliable defenseman, he could shoot the puck from mid-distance and score a goal. He also managed to avoid injuries and was always in good shape.

He combined agility—he was once compared to a plane that has just taken off—with endurance. When he joined CSKA, he was told there were two rules: "Number one—the coach is always right. Number two—if you think you're right, refer to rule number one." Years later, Kasatonov confessed that if he hadn't learned that rule, he would have achieved nothing. Kasatonov's partners were the big stars and were more interested in how they were treated or how they were spoken to. But Kasatonov cared only about the game, and he silently obeyed the coach's instructions.

Tikhonov was instrumental in Kasatonov's career. And if Tikhonov was like a father to the player, then fellow teammate Fetisov was like a big brother. Unlike the other CSKA players, Fetisov took care of the gawky, uncomplicated Kasatonov and looked out for him. Kasatonov even lived with Fetisov's family. The impulsive Fetisov's concern for Kasatonov was genuine, not calculated to put Kasatonov in his debt. But when Fetisov fought with Tikhonov over the coach's objection to the pair's being transferred to the NHL, Fetisov couldn't forgive Kasatonov for taking a neutral position and sometimes even siding with the coach.

However, when Tikhonov invited Fetisov to join the national team for the 1989 World Championship, Fetisov was elected captain and Kasatonov backed him up. They appeared to be united by a common cause.

But things weren't as untroubled as they seemed. In a move not typical of the NHL, the New Jersey Devils had drafted both Fetisov and Kasatonov as a defense duo. When the pair joined the team, they were still smarting from their dispute with Tikhonov. In spite of their good fortune, the "brothers" couldn't bury the hatchet. They never spoke to one another again.

Kasatonov, Alexei
D, 6'1", 215 lbs, b: Leningrad, USSR, 10/14/1959

Season	Club, League	Regular Season					Playoffs				
		GP	G	A	Pts	PIM	GP	G	A	Pts	PIM
1976–77	SKA Leningrad, USSR	7	0	0	0	0					
1977–78	SKA Leningrad, USSR	35	4	7	11	15					
1978–79	CSKA, USSR	40	5	14	19	30					
1979–80	CSKA, USSR	37	5	8	13	26					
OWG–80	USSR	7	2	5	7	8					
1980–81	CSKA, USSR	47	10	12	22	38					
WEC–81	USSR	8	1	3	4	8					
CCup–81	USSR	7	1	10	11	8					
1981–82	CSKA, USSR	46	12	27	39	45					
WEC–82	USSR	10	0	3	3	6					
1982–83	CSKA, USSR	44	12	19	31	37					
WEC–83	USSR	10	1	10	11	14					
1983–84	CSKA, USSR	39	12	24	36	20					
OWG–84	USSR	7	3	3	6	0					
CCup–84	USSR	6	1	4	5	2					
1984–85	CSKA, USSR	40	18	18	36	26					
WEC–85	USSR	9	5	6	11	19					
1985–86	CSKA, USSR	40	6	17	23	27					
WEC–86	USSR	10	3	4	7	4					
1986–87	CSKA, USSR	40	13	17	30	16					
RV'87	USSR	2	1	0	1	2					
WEC–87	USSR	10	3	5	8	8					
CCup–87	USSR	9	1	4	5	4					
1987–88	CSKA, USSR	43	8	12	20	8					
OWG–88	USSR	7	2	6	8	0					
1988–89	CSKA, USSR	41	8	14	22	8					
WEC–89	USSR	10	2	0	2	2					
1989–90	CSKA, USSR	30	6	7	13	16					
	New Jersey Devils, NHL	39	6	15	21	16	6	0	3	3	14
	Utica Devils, AHL	3	0	2	2	7					
1990–91	New Jersey Devils, NHL	78	10	31	41	76	7	1	3	4	10
WEC–91	USSR	10	3	3	6	8					
CCup–91	USSR	5	0	1	1	6					
1991–92	New Jersey Devils, NHL	76	12	28	40	70	7	1	1	2	12
1992–93	New Jersey Devils, NHL	64	3	14	17	57	4	0	0	0	0
1993–94	Anaheim Mighty Ducks, NHL	55	4	18	22	43					
	St. Louis Blues, NHL	8	0	2	2	19	4	2	0	2	2
1994–95	CSKA, Russia	9	2	3	5	6					
	Boston Bruins, NHL	44	2	14	16	33	5	0	0	0	2
1995–96	Boston Bruins, NHL	19	1	0	1	12					
	Providence Bruins, AHL	16	3	6	9	10					
1996–97	CSKA, Russia	38	3	20	23	68	1	0	0	0	0
	USSR/Russia Totals	576	124	219	343	396	1	0	0	0	0
	NHL Totals	383	38	122	160	326	33	4	7	11	40
	OWG/WEC/CCup/RV'87 Totals	127	29	67	96	99					

Named Best Defenseman at WEC (1983)
Won OWG (1984, 1988)
Won WEC (1981, 1982, 1983, 1986, 1989)
Won CCup (1981)
USSR Champion (1979, 1980, 1981, 1983, 1983, 1984, 1985, 1986, 1987, 1988, 1989)

In an atypical move, the New Jersey Devils drafted both Alexei Kasatonov (front) and Viacheslav Fetisov as a defense duo.

Kasatonov played seven seasons in the NHL with New Jersey, Anaheim, St. Louis and Boston, his final season being 1995–96.

Kasatonov returned to Russia where he played one more year of hockey in 1996–97 under Viktor Tikhonov for CSKA Moscow in a show of support for his beleaguered mentor. Kasatonov was also the general manager of the Russian national team that won the silver medal in the 1998 Nagano Olympics. He is an Honoured Master of Sport, which is the Russian equivalent of the Hall of Fame, and remains an active high-ranking official within the Russian Hockey Federation.

Sergei Makarov

With Igor Larionov, Sergei Makarov made the San Jose Sharks a respectable club.

The Traktor Chelyabinsk hockey club that Sergei Makarov left to join the national squad of the USSR and CSKA earned a reputation as the fastest-skating team of all time in Russia. But inasmuch as high-speed skating is the hallmark of the Chelyabinsk team, it is also the team's weakness. The result is a lack of physical strength and endurance, which is a definite liability given the inevitable heavy bodychecks in high-level matches.

"In junior hockey," Makarov recalls, "I wasn't taken seriously. I was a fast little guy, but little, little, little…. For a long time, that word rang in my years as a verdict. I didn't believe in all those tall stories that one could gain height by performing all kinds of drills and exercises."

Sergei Makarov is probably the world champion at controlling the puck. Slightly crouched with his legs spread wide, he would slice through the length and breadth of the opponent's defense lines without bothering to pass the puck to the other players on his team. His teammates and the coaches accused him of hogging the puck, but in his own words, Makarov had "the demon in his soul." The coach even scratched him from the roster of the Chelyabinsk Juniors, but Sergei was already planning to give soccer a try.

After Canada played the USSR in the 1984 Canada Cup tournament, the famous Canadian defenseman Larry Robinson was asked to comment on an episode during the game in which Makarov slipped around him and scored a goal. A regular member of the All-Stars, Robinson shrugged his shoulders and said that he didn't think it was his error. He suggested that only nature could have endowed Makarov with the gift of breaking through to the goal with such virtuosity.

In reality, it was probably Makarov's coach, Anatoli Kostryukov, who drilled such efficiency into him. When he came to the helm of Traktor, Kostryukov immediately put Makarov on the senior squad roster, allowing him to bypass the junior team. In his first game of the USSR championship tournament, the 18-year-old Makarov slapped in a goal against Spartak on that team's home ice. In his first appearance in the World Championship, he caught the attention of a lot of fans by scoring a goal just moments after stepping off the bench and onto the ice. And when the five-man lineup with Igor Larionov began to click, Makarov started racking up goals like he was on a mission. For the next six years, he was the top scorer in the country.

Before joining Larionov's lineup, Makarov had the whole gamut of partners while with CSKA and the national squad. He was highly valued because he scored a lot and thrilled fans with his lone breakaways and stylish skating. Many nominations as most valuable player came his way in Europe and the USSR, and he headed the list of top scorers. Yet his style of play was always questioned. Did he hog the puck just to put on dazzling displays at the other end of the rink?

Once he made up his mind to finish an attack by scoring a goal, there was little that could stop him. But at times he would look around for an open partner, which of course would slow down the pace of the attack that he, Makarov, was spearheading. Eventually, the accusations that he was a lone operator were answered. When Viktor Tikhonov, the coach of the nationals and CSKA, selected Larionov to complete the Makarov–Krutov line, Makarov's virtuosity in stickhandling became the key element in endlessly changing the direction of attack. And that is when it became clear that Makarov, when playing with changing partners, intensely disliked waiting for a lucky break or setting up a flexible play when the intention was to score. Everything Makarov did on ice focused on planning for a sure thing.

As he was winding up his term with CSKA, Makarov almost accepted an offer to end his hockey career by going to France—to a cozy, comfortable and tranquil life. But he paused long enough to give it a second thought and wound up in Calgary, the home of the newest Stanley Cup winners. He even managed to make the NHL's rookie of the year. During the season, the two Calgary Flames coaches invited Soviet coach Vladimir Vasiliev to speak about their forward, Makarov.

They asked Vasiliev how they could persuade Makarov into finishing off an attack without his limiting himself to a pass. At that time, Makarov was playing on a forward line together with Joe Nieuwendyk and Gary Roberts. "Well,

Makarov, Sergei
RW, 5′8″, 185 lbs, b: Chelyabinsk, USSR, 6/19/1958

Season	Club, League	Regular Season					Playoffs				
		GP	G	A	Pts	PIM	GP	G	A	Pts	PIM
1976–77	Traktor, USSR	11	1	0	1	4					
1977–78	Traktor, USSR	36	18	13	31	10					
WEC–78	USSR	10	3	2	5	5					
1978–79	CSKA, USSR	44	18	21	39	12					
ChCup–79	USSR	3	1	2	3	0					
WEC–79	USSR	8	8	4	12	6					
1979–80	CSKA, USSR	44	29	39	68	16					
OWG–80	USSR	7	5	6	11	2					
1980–81	CSKA, USSR	49	42	37	79	22					
WEC–81	USSR	8	3	5	8	12					
CCup–81	USSR	7	3	6	9	0					
1981–82	CSKA, USSR	46	32	43	75	18					
WEC–82	USSR	10	6	7	13	8					
1982–83	CSKA, USSR	30	25	17	42	6					
WEC–83	USSR	10	9	9	18	4					
1983–84	CSKA, U3SR	44	36	37	73	28					
OWG–84	USSR	7	3	3	6	6					
CCup–84	USSR	6	6	1	7	4					
1984–85	CSKA, USSR	40	26	39	65	28					
WEC–85	USSR	10	9	5	14	8					
1985–86	CSKA, USSR	40	30	32	62	28					
WEC–86	USSR	10	4	14	18	12					
1986–87	CSKA, USSR	40	21	32	53	26					
RV '87	USSR	2	0	1	1	0					
WEC–87	USSR	10	4	10	14	8					
CCup–87	USSR	9	7	8	15	8					
1987–88	CSKA, USSR	51	23	45	68	50					
OWG–88	USSR	8	3	8	11	10					
1988–89	CSKA, USSR	44	21	33	54	42					
WEC–89	USSR	10	5	3	8	8					
1989–90	Calgary Flames, NHL	80	24	62	86	55	6	0	6	6	0
WEC–90	USSR	7	2	1	3	8					
1990–91	Calgary Flames, NHL	78	30	49	79	44	3	1	0	1	0
WEC–91	USSR	8	3	7	10	6					
1991–92	Calgary Flames, NHL	68	22	48	70	60					
1992–93	Calgary Flames, NHL	71	18	39	57	40					
1993–94	San Jose Sharks, NHL	80	30	38	68	78	14	8	2	10	4
1994–95	San Jose Sharks, NHL	43	10	14	24	40	11	3	3	6	4
1996–97	Dallas Stars, NHL	4	0	0	0	0					
	Fribourg, Switzerland	6	3	2	5	2	1	0	0	0	0
	USSR Totals	519	322	388	710	290					
	NHL Totals	424	134	250	384	317	34	12	11	23	8
	OWG/WEC/ChalCup/CCup/RV'87 Totals	150	84	102	186	115					

Named Best Forward at WEC (1979, 1985)
Won Calder Trophy (1990)
Won OWG (1984, 1988)
Won WEC (1978, 1979, 1981, 1982, 1983, 1986, 1989, 1990)
Won CCup (1981)
USSR Champion (1979, 1980, 1981, 1982, 1983, 1984, 1985, 1986, 1987, 1988, 1989)

Once Sergei Makarov (left) made up his mind to score, not much could stop him.

do they score when they get his pass?" Vasiliev inquired. "Yes, they do." Vasiliev: "That means Makarov is right." In the end, in the game against Vasiliev's Khimik club, Makarov came out on the ice in tandem with Theoren Fleury, a more diversified player, and each of them scored two goals. Meanwhile, Makarov's usual partners failed to score a single goal.

Makarov likes to recall the days in San Jose with Igor Larionov when they struggled to raise that team from the ashes into something respectable. He would say, "If you decide to march forward in life firmly and with confidence, then you have to go to the very end." At the age of 40, he moved on to Dallas, where he played four games.

Jiri Lala

Jiri Lala was considered one of the strongest and most elegant skaters of his time.

The setting was the World Championship in Prague in 1985. The teams representing Czechoslovakia and Canada were playing the final match for the gold. The host team was winning by a score of 4–3. In an effort to tie the game, the coach of the Canadian team, Bob Carpenter, recalled the goaltender, Pat Riggin, 97 seconds before the end. But the puck ended up on the stick of Jiri Lala. He aimed well and his long shot into the empty net left the final score at 5–3. After eight years, Czechoslovakia had once again won the title of world champion.

This right winger was once considered one of the best and most elegant skaters of his time. He was also thought to have excellent scoring technique and effective completions on plays. Most of his goals were scored with wrist shots from the blue line. In the Czech league alone he scored 297 goals and added 89 more while with the national team. But it was the final goal at the Prague championship that made him famous and it ranks as one of the most memorable moments in Czech hockey. "I have seen a lot in hockey. But even I would rank this goal as number one," he said in a comment on his part in the victory.

Lala comes from the small town of Sobeslav in southern Bohemia. There was no hospital maternity ward there, so he was born in Tabor, several kilometers away, on August 21, 1959. His father had been a talented soccer player with Spartak Sobeslav, and his son nearly stayed with that sport. Even as a junior soccer player, he was among the elite of Bohemia. However, in 1974 he decided to move to a more urban area and chose the city of Ceske Budejovice, which at the time was represented only in the hockey league. And that's how Lala chose hockey.

He spent almost 13 seasons in that city, 11 on the first team. He soon became one of the heroes of local hockey, and in his 1993–94 pro season he made a brief stopover there and played three games for his team. It was with Dukla Jihlava, however, where he did his military service from 1980 to 1982, that he matured in hockey. His success with that team came mainly as a scorer and he even won a title. In 1980–81, he scored 40 goals in 44 matches and became the top scorer in the league. "Playing next to me was Jindrich Kokrment. He came from Litvinov and was a center who could work out chances for the wings. I took many advantages from his passes," he recalled.

A terrific season in 1981 brought him a nomination to his first World Championship. After a disastrous fifth-place finish in the Lake Placid Olympics, Team Czechoslovakia underwent many changes. According to veterans such as Vladimir Martinec, who with this competition was bringing his career to a close, the up-and-coming generation of players that included Lala were just starting to learn hockey. But these players quickly matured, and four years later they won Czechoslovakia's sixth World Championship title.

After returning to Ceske Budejovice, Lala was unable to repeat the success of the season he had spent with Jihlava. Nonetheless, for a long time he ranked among the scoring elite and the established stars of the national team. With two 30-goal seasons in 1982–83 and 1987–88, he started involving his teammates more in the play and collected many assists. "My opponents started noticing me more, so I started passing more often so as not to attract attention," he said.

In addition to the gold medal, he won silver in the 1982 and 1983 championships and at the 1984 Sarajevo Olympics. He had also won a bronze after his debut in 1981. But there were also crushing defeats, such as at the 1986 World Championship in Moscow and at the 1988 Calgary Olympics. He said: "Both competitions brought great disenchantment. I even thought of quitting hockey. But fortunately better times came along and I banished such thoughts."

In 1982 he was drafted by the Quebec Nordiques as number 76 overall. He never did go overseas, though, for at that time the communist regime didn't allow players in their productive years to live and work abroad. Not until the 1989–90 season was he allowed to accept a contract in Germany. He lined up for Mannheim and Frankfurt, where he became the best scorer and the most productive player in 1990–91 with 47 goals and 106 points over 44 matches.

For a short time he also played in Switzerland and Great Britain. Finally he settled in Germany, proving in the lower ranks of hockey that a natural-born shooter still had his touch even after 40.

He said: "It is hard to say what brought me more joy—scoring by myself or having made a successful pass to someone else. It was just as nice to hear a word of thanks from the successful scoring player. Besides, it gave me the feeling that I wasn't just playing hockey for myself."

Lala, Jiri
RW, 5´10˝, 180 lbs, b: Tabor, Czechoslovakia, 8/21/1959

Season	Club, League	Regular Season					Playoffs				
		GP	G	A	Pts	PIM	GP	G	A	Pts	PIM
1976–80	Motor, Czechoslovakia	*	*	*	*	*					
1980–81	Dukla Jihlava, Czechoslovakia	44	40	*	*	*					
WEC–81	Czechoslovakia	8	7	3	10	2					
CCup–81	Czechoslovakia	6	4	2	6	0					
1981–82	Dukla Jihlava, Czechoslovakia	*	*	*	*	*					
WEC–82	Czechoslovakia	10	6	3	9	0					
1982–83	Motor, Czechoslovakia	*	*	*	*	*					
WEC–83	Czechoslovakia	10	9	5	14	4					
1983–84	Motor, Czechoslovakia	*	*	*	*	*					
OWG–84	Czechoslovakia	7	1	4	5	0					
CCup–84	Czechoslovakia	5	0	0	0	0					
1984–85	Motor, Czechoslovakia	*	*	*	*	*					
WEC–85	Czechoslovakia	10	8	5	13	6					
1985–86	Motor, Czechoslovakia	*	*	*	*	*					
WEC–86	Czechoslovakia	10	1	1	2	0					
1986–87	Motor, Czechoslovakia	*	*	*	*	*					
1987–88	Motor, Czechoslovakia	*	*	*	*	*					
OWG–88	Czechoslovakia	7	2	1	3	0					
1988–89	Motor, Czechoslovakia	*	*	*	*	*					
1989–90	Frankfurt, Germany	35	36	39	75	*					
1990–91	Frankfurt, Germany	44	47	59	106	*					
1991–92	Mannheim, Germany	36	32	34	66	28					
1993–94	Mannheim, Germany	41	21	29	50	18					
1994–95	Frankfurt, Germany	46	22	49	71	43					
1995–96	Frankfurt, Germany	50	36	49	85	18	3	0	3	3	0
1996–97	Ayr Scottish Eagles, Great Britain	40	24	20	44	10	7	11	4	15	0
1998–2000	ERC Selb, Switzerland	*	*	*	*	*					
	Czechoslovakia Totals	436	297	89	386	*					
	OWG/WEC/CCup/ Totals	73	38	24	62	12					

Named Best Forward at WEC (1983)
Won WEC (1985)
Czechoslovakia Champion (1982)

Thomas Steen

When Thomas Steen ended his career with the Jets in 1994, his number 25 jersey was retired and raised in Winnipeg's arena.

Steen, Thomas
C, 5'11", 190 lbs, b: Grums, Sweden, 6/8/1960

Season	Club, League	Regular Season					Playoffs				
		GP	G	A	Pts	Plm	GP	G	A	Pts	Plm
1976–77	Leksand, Sweden	2	1	1	2	2					
1977–78	Leksand, Sweden	35	5	6	11	30					
1978–79	Leksand, Sweden	23	13	4	17	35	2	0	0	0	0
1979–80	Leksand, Sweden	18	7	7	14	14	2	0	0	0	6
1980–81	Farjestad, Sweden	32	16	23	39	30	7	4	2	6	8
WEC–81	Sweden	8	1	3	4	6					
CCup–81	Sweden	3	0	0	0	2					
1981–82	Winnipeg Jets, NHL	73	15	29	44	42	4	0	4	4	2
1982–83	Winnipeg Jets, NHL	75	26	33	59	60	3	0	2	2	0
1983–84	Winnipeg Jets, NHL	78	20	45	65	69	3	0	1	1	9
CCup–84	Sweden	8	7	1	8	4					
1984–85	Winnipeg Jets, NHL	79	30	54	84	80	8	2	3	5	17
1985–86	Winnipeg Jets, NHL	78	17	47	64	76	3	1	1	2	4
WEC–86	Sweden	8	8	3	11	16					
1986–87	Winnipeg Jets, NHL	75	17	33	50	59	10	3	4	7	8
1987–88	Winnipeg Jets, NHL	76	16	38	54	53	5	1	5	6	2
1988–89	Winnipeg Jets, NHL	80	27	61	88	80					
WEC–89	Sweden	10	2	4	6	10					
1989–90	Winnipeg Jets, NHL	53	18	48	66	35	7	2	5	7	16
1990–91	Winnipeg Jets, NHL	58	19	48	67	49					
CCup–91	Sweden	6	0	3	3	11					
1991–92	Winnipeg Jets, NHL	38	13	25	38	29	7	2	4	6	2
1992–93	Winnipeg Jets, NHL	80	22	50	72	75	6	1	3	4	2
1993–94	Winnipeg Jets, NHL	76	19	32	51	32					
1994–95	Winnipeg Jets, NHL	31	5	10	15	14					
1995–96	Frankfurt, Germany	4	1	0	1	2	3	0	1	1	6
1996–97	Eisbaren Berlin, Germany	49	15	18	33	48	8	0	2	2	27
1997–98	Eisbaren Berlin, Germany	43	4	7	11	20	10	3	4	7	10
	Sweden Totals	110	42	41	83	111	11	4	2	6	14
	NHL Totals	950	264	553	817	753	56	12	32	44	62
	WEC/CCup Totals	43	18	14	32	49					

Sweden Champion (1981)

Young Alexander Steen of Gothenburg was recently voted the best forward of the popular junior ice hockey contest *TV-Pukken* (TV Puck), where he defended the colors of his native Gothenburg playing for Vastra Frolunda. But Alexander had received his primary hockey education in Canada, where his father, Thomas Steen, a great Swedish forward of the 1980s, played in the NHL. After he won the gold medal with Farjestad in the 1981 Swedish national championship, Thomas Steen was drafted by the Winnipeg Jets.

Thomas Steen was born on June 8, 1960, and he first played hockey with Grums IK. Later he joined one of Sweden's strongest clubs, Leksand, and then moved to Farjestad, where his partner in offense was Hakan Loob. Swedish coach Tommy Sandlin gave Steen high praise, calling him "a particularly intelligent and competent player."

Under Sweden's flag, Steen played in 75 official games and won two silver medals—at the 1981 World Championship in Gothenburg and at the 1986 World Championship in Moscow. He believes his most memorable contest was the 1984 Canada Cup, when his partners in offense were Kent Nilsson and Hakan Loob. Thanks mainly to their efforts, Sweden took second place in the contest. On Sweden's list of "Great Men," Steen is in 128th position.

Steen played with the NHL's Winnipeg Jets for 14 seasons and was also team captain. While in the NHL, Steen played in 950 games and scored 264 goals. When he ended his career with the Jets in 1994, his number 25 jersey was raised in Winnipeg's hockey arena. Only one other Jets player before him had been so honored—the legendary Bobby Hull.

At the end of his career in Canada, Steen returned to Europe, where in the 1996–97 season he played for Eisbaren in Berlin, Germany.

Steen got into coaching in his native Sweden, serving an assistant for Vastra Frolunda, where his son Alexander played for the junior team, carrying on a family tradition.

Sergei *Shepelev*

From a historical perspective, Sergei Shepelev is to Soviet hockey what Paul Henderson is to the Canadians. Henderson clinched Canada's victory over the USSR in the 1972 Summit Series; Shepelev's three goals drove the last nail into Canada's coffin at the 1981 Canada Cup tournament. For two years, 1981 and 1982, he was perhaps the greatest forward in the world.

Historically, Sergei Shepelev is to Soviet hockey what Paul Henderson is to the Canadian game.

But it would be a mistake to think that coach Viktor Tikhonov was waiting to present this player like a trump card at the right moment. Until he turned 24, Shepelev was an anonymous forward in an obscure club in Sverdlovsk and Moscow paid no attention to him.

At the 1981 Canada Cup tournament, everybody was watching Wayne Gretzky play cat and mouse with the opponent's defensemen. He would make a pass to either Guy Lafleur or Marcel Dionne or he'd score on his own.

During this series, Igor Larionov—a very good but unassuming player—was Tikhonov's big hope. Shepelev, on the other hand, was arrogant. He would dribble, fake and rush forward. He hoodwinked the opposing defensemen with a series of feints. When he was checked, he seemed to lose his balance but managed to evade sticks and bodychecks and resume his attack. In the final game, he was the first to fight his way behind the Canadian goal—and was reprimanded by Tikhonov for being too aggressive.

Before 1980, Shepelev was a winger. He was assigned to center by Spartak coach Boris Kulagin. In his new position, his two wing partners were Sergei Kapustin and Viktor Shalimov. The threesome turned out to be unbeatable in technique and joint action combined with an ability to score.

The Spartak trio was voted the best at the 1981 Canada Cup. They were better than the Larionov super-line, better than Gretzky–Lafleur–Dionne and the Islanders' Mike Bossy–Bryan Trottier–Clark Gillies lines. Shepelev scored three goals in the final and two in the semifinal against Czechoslovakia. Not even Gretzky could match that at the international level.

Shepelev would never be defined as an ideal center. He frequently fell behind in

Shepelev, Sergei
C, 5'11", 175 lbs, b: Sverdlovsk, USSR, 10/13/1955

Season	Club, League	Regular Season				
		GP	G	A	Pts	PIM
1977–78	Avtomobilist Sverdlovsk, USSR	36	20	*	*	*
1978–79	Avtomobilist Sverdlovsk, USSR	42	20	14	34	30
1979–80	Spartak Moscow, USSR	37	10	*	*	*
1980–81	Spartak Moscow, USSR	49	28	*	*	*
WEC–81	USSR	8	6	2	8	4
CCup–81	USSR	7	6	2	8	4
1981–82	Spartak Moscow, USSR	40	17	17	34	20
WEC–82	USSR	10	6	2	8	6
1982–83	Spartak Moscow, USSR	41	18	10	28	20
WEC–83	USSR	10	2	4	6	6
1983–84	Spartak Moscow, USSR	44	21	21	42	25
OWG–84	USSR	7	2	3	5	0
CCup–84	USSR	4	0	3	3	0
1984–85	Spartak Moscow, USSR	46	21	16	37	24
1985–86	Spartak Moscow, USSR	38	12	16	28	31
1986–87	Spartak Moscow, USSR	40	10	12	22	24
1987–88	Spartak Moscow, USSR	40	11	15	26	22
	USSR Totals	453	188	*	*	*
	OWG/WEC/CCup Totals	46	22	16	38	20

Won OWG (1984)
Won WEC (1981, 1982, 1983)
Won CCup (1981)

At the 1981 Canada Cup, Sergei Shepelev (right) scored two goals in the semifinal game against Czechoslovakia and a hat-trick in the final against Canada.

assisting his defensemen and he often failed to make a good pass. But Kulagin discovered that when he put the three wingers on one line, Shepelev, always a winger at heart, could work miracles on the ice.

The trio lasted only three years. Shepelev wasn't as successful without coach Kulagin and his partners Shalimov and Kapustin, who also fell by the wayside. They needed one another and they were lucky to have met at the right time and in the right place. To this day, no trio has been able to match their virtuosity and speed.

Mike **Bossy**

Mike Bossy vowed to score 50 goals for the Islanders in his rookie season—and he did.

The first training session of the season is normally a simple exercise in maneuverability, but for Mike Bossy it was a nightmare. Suffering an excruciating pain in the back, his first thought was that it was something new and he'd get over it. Bossy hated training camp, exhibition games and everything that preceded the opening of the season, and the pain reminded him of that.

Various doctors made different diagnoses, but treatment didn't produce any results. That 10th season was the worst in his entire NHL career. It was the first time he was unable to score 50 goals, managing only 38 instead. He refused to participate in the 1987 Rendez-Vous series when his affliction got the best of him. In fact, it was enough to put an end to the professional career of the Boss-, one of the top scorers in the entire history of the league—and the first player to speak out publicly against rough play on the ice.

Family legend has it that Bossy's father placed a plastic hockey stick in the hands of two-year-old Michael to see what would result. Ever since he was a kid, he had his sights set on the NHL. For him, it wasn't so much a dream as a plan and he realized full well the stages he would have to go through: the peewees, then juniors, followed by a draft and finally the NHL. Bossy's stats as a young player suggested he might indeed realize his goal. He had a season when he scored 170 goals. There was also a game in which he scored 23 times. The only reason he didn't have any assists in that game was that hardly anyone else but five-year-old Michael even touched the puck.

When the time came to choose a junior club, the family gave preference to the Laval Nationals, a very ordinary team that was based in a suburb of their native city of Montreal. The club even sponsored the entire family's move to a home near the stadium. That's how 14-year-old Mike Bossy joined the Quebec Major Junior Hockey League. And it was an experience that might make a player think about giving it all up.

The players had the habit of taking cheap shots at their opponents. In addition, the wild fans turned every game into a risky adventure. The coaches egged their boys on, and the boys readily followed instructions. Bossy had the misfortune of being on the wanted list. He had to pay for every goal he scored. During his junior career, he often heard sinister whispers from his opponents: "You'll

Mike Bossy

be lucky to make it to the end of this game," or "Watch your back." Bossy also doffed his gloves to protect himself but more often than not found himself lying on the ice. His father told him to keep his head up when fighting for the puck on the boards. His mother would leave the rink, unable to watch her son being beaten up. Friends attempted to comfort her: "Everybody goes through that. Things aren't so bad."

Young hockey players in North America do go through that, but Bossy learned from his own bitter experience that violence and bullying on the ice were unacceptable. The sad thing was that after finishing his junior career with a broken nose and missing teeth and 309 goals in four seasons, Bossy was considered a timid player by NHL scouts. In the Amateur Draft of 1977, 12 teams gave preference to other players. The New York Rangers and Toronto Maple Leafs did this twice. Only the New York Islanders made him their first choice, 15th overall.

Islanders general manager Bill Torrey called Bossy to break the good news. In the meeting to sign the contract, Bossy was asked what he was expecting from his first season. He replied, "If I play all the time, I'm going to score a pile of goals for the Islanders." Torrey asked him how many and Bossy told him 50. Torrey was somewhat surprised at such confidence. The record for a rookie in the NHL was 44 goals and this seemed insurmountable.

Bossy turned up at training camp with a desire to show what he could do. He bombarded the coach, Al Arbour, with questions. "How do you want me to play in such a situation? What should I do in a similar play?" Finally, Arbour lost his patience. "Play as you did in the juniors. If you make a mistake, you'll be the first to learn about it!" Arbour placed him on the same line as two other up-and-coming stars—Bryan Trottier and Clark Gillies. In their first exhibition game, the Islanders mounted a good attack. Bossy and Trottier raced the length of the ice, outmaneuvering their opponents and flipping passes back and forth. Bossy didn't score, but Arbour said after the game, "We picked the guy we needed!"

In his first season, Bossy proved that what he'd told Torrey wasn't empty words. He scored an all-time rookie record of 53 goals and chalked up a total of 91 points to win the Calder Trophy. No one doubted his talents as a sharpshooter, but questions surfaced about whether he would ever be able to play defense. In the junior league, Bossy hadn't ever tried to play defense well on a mediocre team that had needed a goal-scoring machine to remain afloat. It was in the NHL that he had to learn the ABCs of playing in his own end. It was very rare to come across press reports about how Wayne Gretzky or Mario Lemieux played in their own end zones, but journalists wrote a lot about Bossy's defensive skills.

During the first training camp, Bryan Trottier invited the rookie to have lunch at his home one day and an unusual friendship

---

Bossy, Mike
RW, 6´, 186 lbs, b: Montreal, Que., 1/22/1957

Season	Club, League	Regular Season					Playoffs				
		GP	G	A	Pts	PIM	GP	G	A	Pts	PIM
1977–78	New York Islanders, NHL	73	53	38	91	6	7	2	2	4	2
1978–79	New York Islanders, NHL	80	69	57	126	25	10	6	2	8	2
ChCup–79	NHL All-Stars	3	2	2	4	0					
1979–80	New York Islanders, NHL	75	51	41	92	12	16	10	13	23	8
1980–81	New York Islanders, NHL	79	68	51	119	32	18	17	18	35	4
CCup–81	Canada	7	8	3	11	2					
1981–82	New York Islanders, NHL	80	64	83	147	22	19	17	10	27	0
1982–83	New York Islanders, NHL	79	60	58	118	20	19	17	9	26	10
1983–84	New York Islanders, NHL	67	51	67	118	8	21	8	10	18	4
CCup–84	Canada	8	5	4	9	2					
1984–85	New York Islanders, NHL	76	58	59	117	38	10	5	6	11	4
1985–86	New York Islanders, NHL	80	61	62	123	14	3	1	2	3	4
1986–87	New York Islanders, NHL	63	38	37	75	33	6	2	3	5	0
	NHL Totals	752	573	553	1126	210	129	85	75	160	38
	ChalCup/CCup Totals	18	15	9	24	4					

NHL First All-Star Team (1981, 1982, 1983, 1984, 1986)
NHL Second All-Star Team (1978, 1979, 1985)
Won Conn Smythe Trophy (1982)
Won Calder Trophy (1978)
Won Lady Byng Trophy (1983, 1984, 1986)
Won Stanley Cup (1980, 1981, 1982, 1983)

---

between the two star players began. Fans nicknamed them "Bread and Butter." On the ice, Trottier would win the face-off, fight for the puck in front of the net and on the boards and follow up with a pass to his partner. Bossy would outplay his opponents, break out into the open and shoot from the most impossible angles.

Having scored over 50 goals in three successive seasons, Bossy needed a fresh impetus. So he invented it. The great forward for the Montreal Canadiens, Maurice "Rocket" Richard, scored 50 goals in 50 games in the 1944–45 season. Thirty-six years later, no one had ever been able to repeat that feat. Only a very few of his closest friends, including Trottier, knew about Bossy's plan. They liked the idea. But his partners couldn't imagine what it was going to cost them.

At first, everything went according to plan, even a little better as Bossy reached the mark of 25 goals in 23 games. The whole league began talking about Bossy. Players were assigned to personally guard Bossy. But the media hadn't caught on yet. It was only after 36 games in the regular season, when Bossy had six hat-tricks to his credit, that one journalist inquired whether the Islanders forward had his sights set on Phil Esposito's record—76 goals in 78 games. That was when Bossy admitted which record he was after. The news caused an uproar.

However, it wasn't until game 44 that he scored his next goal, and even that wasn't counted. There were only six games left and he had to score 10 goals. That was when Mike was called aside by Torrey, who warned him that someone had called the stadium threatening to kill Bossy. According to the police, the threat had come from a Montreal fan. Round-the-clock surveillance was set up.

Mike Bossy holds an NHL record for scoring more than 50 goals in nine consecutive seasons.

In the next game, Bossy scored again and another phone call came in with the same threat. During the following game, the Coliseum was packed with uniformed police and plainclothes men. Police warned that a sniper would probably shoot when the fans were jumping up to cheer a goal, so it would be better if the Islanders didn't score that evening. Especially Bossy. After the game, as he accompanied the player and his wife to their car to go home, a detective remarked with a smile, "I didn't seem to notice that you even tried to make life easier for us." Bossy had scored four goals.

Now the Islanders forward was under the close scrutiny of the mass media. Ignoring the threats, Bossy scored a hat-trick in the next game. To attain his objective, he still had to score two goals in three games. In the following two games, the opponents were more concerned about how to prevent Bossy from scoring than the actual outcome of the games. The Islanders scored twice but Bossy was shut down completely.

To add to the tension, Charlie Simmer, a forward with the Los Angeles Kings, had 46 goals in 49 games at the very same time. In Simmer's 50th game, which was played several hours earlier than the one at Long Island, Simmer got a hat-trick and was just one goal shy of the mark. It was up to Bossy.

After two periods in the game against the Quebec Nordiques, the scoreboard at the Coliseum showed 3–3, but Bossy hadn't scored any of those. Things just weren't clicking for him. All the tension in the crazy race for Richard's record was getting to him. During intermission, Bossy closeted himself in the washroom. Not wanting to hear the words of support from his partners, he smoked one cigarette after another, running his words for the post-game press conference through his head.

At the start of the third period, it was as if Bossy hadn't left the ice. Every time he touched the puck, the fans called out his name. With four minutes and 10 seconds left in the game, Mike scored a goal during a power-play. The fans went crazy. Over the noise in the stadium, the Islanders bench chanted: "Come on, Boss! We know you can do it!" Trottier said not a word.

With a minute and a half to go before the final whistle, Trottier made a beautiful pass to Bossy in the left face-off circle and Bossy dumped it in the net. He began jumping up and down on the ice and the fans went wild, throwing all kinds of objects onto the ice. In defiance of NHL rules, the Islanders also spilled onto the ice. A telegram of congratulations from Maurice Richard was waiting for Mike in the locker room.

During the draft, the scouts had tabbed Bossy as a timid player. He tried his best to lose this label during his professional career, but he also hated violence on the ice and considered fighting and roughing as beneath contempt. It seemed to him that that was why the fans in North America didn't treat hockey as seriously as they did baseball, basketball or football, but people in control of the game in North America believed the fans enjoyed watching the fights on the ice.

During his third season in the NHL, Bossy made it clear that he wouldn't resort to dirty play on the ice no matter how rough it might be. "Every time hockey bullies knock me down on the ice, I'm going to get up and score goals," he declared. After this statement, he received catcalls in Boston, Philadelphia and Detroit and all the toughs in the league went after him. But Bossy stuck to his word. He was the first to publicly denounce fighting on the ice and didn't hear many words of support, even though many agreed with him. The Islanders forward called for more severe penalties against the ruffians—first and foremost for poking a player in the back and second for high-sticking. He developed a complete system of penalties—including disqualification—for "dirty" players. If his suggestions had been implemented at the time, there wouldn't be any need for "cops" in the league today.

Bossy's goal was to become the best player of his era, but that title was always awarded to someone else: Guy Lafleur, Bryan Trottier, Wayne Gretzky. He was regarded more as a natural-born sniper than a great hockey player. Besides, Bossy was never the highest scorer in a season. Many of his individual records were eclipsed long ago. Gretzky scored 50 goals in 39 games. But in the record books, the most 50-or-more goal seasons list is headed by Mike Bossy (nine times). On top of that, Mike Bossy has four Stanley Cup rings to his credit. He was inducted into the Hockey Hall of Fame in 1991 and his number has been retired by the Islanders.

Anders Eldebrink

Anders Eldebrink wasn't a big man physically, but many considered him a giant among hockey players. His strength and powerful shooting ability contributed to many victories for his local team, Sodertalje, and Sweden's national team.

Although Eldebrink wasn't voted best defenseman at the 1987 World Championship in Vienna, at the farewell party at city hall in honor of Tre Kronor's first victory in 25 years, Russian player Viacheslav Fetisov told him he was, in his opinion, the tournament's best defenseman. That assessment meant more to Eldebrink than many of his other honors.

In Sweden, many still believe that Eldebrink was the country's top defenseman during the 1980s. In the 1987–88 season, he won Olympic bronze in Calgary, where he was the Swedish team's best scorer, and placed third in the Canada Cup. Then he played 27 games for Tre Kronor, scoring 10 goals plus 11 assists, an achievement as good as any forward's. In the 1988–89 season, he was the first Swedish player to be awarded the Golden Helmet prize established by *Hockey* magazine to honor the most valuable player of the Elite Series, Sweden's major league. He played his 100th game on the national team against the USSR on August 29 of that year in Calgary, where Sweden won 5–3.

In Sweden, many still believe that Anders Eldebrink (left) was his country's top defenseman in the 1980s.

Eldebrink was a defenseman with brilliant shooting technique combined with an instant readiness to back his forward on offense and to make an accurate and timely pass. He stands 123rd on the list of Swedish "Great Men" and remains loyal to his local team, Sodertalje. The team had been experiencing a slump and team managers asked Eldebrink to stay on a little longer. Eldebrink, who started playing hockey when he was 10 years old, continued to play until he turned 40 in the late 1990s. He was both a mentor and an inspiration to younger players.

Although considered a great player in Sweden, Eldebrink didn't meet with much success in the NHL. Between 1981 and 1983, he played with the Vancouver Canucks, the Quebec Nordiques and the Fredericton Express before returning to Sweden.

Eldebrink has won gold once and silver twice at the world level and one Olympic bronze. He placed both second and third in Canada Cup tournaments. In 1985, while playing for Sodertalje, he won the Swedish national championship. These statistics may not seem as impressive as others, but Eldebrink has earned his place among hockey greats by his long-standing commitment and loyalty to the game. Swedish coach Tommy Sandlin considered him the world's best defenseman and honored Eldebrink by including him on the national team many times.

Eldebrink, Anders
D, 5´11˝, 190 lbs, b: Kalix, Sweden, 12/11/1960

Season	Club, League	Regular Season					Playoffs				
		GP	G	A	Pts	PIM	GP	G	A	Pts	PIM
1976–77	Sodertalje, Sweden	2	0	0	0	2					
1977–78	Sodertalje, Sweden	27	4	2	6	14					
1978–80	Sodertalje, Sweden	*	*	*	*	*	*	*	*	*	*
1980–81	Sodertalje, Sweden	36	5	18	23	37					
WEC–81	Sweden	8	0	0	0	2					
1981–82	Vancouver Canucks, NHL	38	1	8	9	21	13	0	0	0	10
1982–83	Vancouver Canucks, NHL	5	1	1	2	0					
	Fredericton Express, AHL	47	7	26	33	14					
	Quebec Nordiques, NHL	12	1	2	3	8	1	0	0	0	0
1983–84	Sodertalje, Sweden	36	10	17	27	40	3	3	0	3	2
CCup–84	Sweden	8	0	4	4	6					
1984–85	Sodertalje, Sweden	34	10	12	22	20	8	2	6	8	14
WEC–85	Sweden	8	2	1	3	18					
1985–86	Sodertalje, Sweden	34	13	16	29	30	7	4	2	6	8
WEC–86	Sweden	7	1	0	1	6					
1986–87	Sodertalje, Sweden	31	11	15	26	40					
WEC–87	Sweden	10	3	2	5	4					
CCup–87	Sweden	6	1	2	3	4					
1987–88	Sodertalje, Sweden	40	12	18	30	54	2	0	0	0	0
OWG–88	Sweden	8	4	6	10	4					
1988–89	Sodertalje, Sweden	38	13	22	35	42	5	5	3	8	10
WEC–89	Sweden	9	5	3	8	2					
1989–90	Sodertalje, Sweden	39	10	20	30	32	2	0	1	1	8
WEC–90	Sweden	10	2	5	7	10					
1990–91	Kloten, Switzerland	34	15	23	38	*	10	1	6	7	*
1991–92	Kloten, Switzerland	38	16	17	33	22					
1992–93	Kloten, Switzerland	36	14	26	40	65	11	3	8	11	2
1993–94	Kloten, Switzerland	36	14	29	43	18	12	4	8	12	14
1994–95	Kloten, Switzerland	25	8	16	24	16	12	1	10	11	10
1995–96	Sodertalje, Sweden	32	9	11	20	28	4	2	3	5	4
1996–97	Kloten, Switzerland	39	10	13	23	22					
	NHL Totals	55	3	11	14	29	14	0	0	0	10
	OWG/WEC/CCup/ Totals	74	18	23	41	56					

Won WEC (1987)
Sweden Champion (1985)
Switzerland Champion (1993, 1994, 1995)

Vladimir **Krutov**

Anatoli Tarasov thought Vladimir Krutov was the most gifted player of his generation in the 1980s.

Anatoli Tarasov, who was fond of making eloquent statements, once spoke about the elements that went into a brilliant game of hockey. He concluded that a forward had to keep his eye on every move his partners made while not losing sight of the beautiful blonde sitting in the 10th row of the stands. And according to Tarasov, there were only two players who fit that bill—Valeri Kharlamov and Vladimir Krutov.

In general, Tarasov was fairly generous when it came to handing out compliments to Krutov. In his opinion, Krutov was the most gifted player among the generation of the 1980s. He called him the player of the future. Tarasov was dismayed and angered more than anyone else when Krutov was the only one of the all-time Soviet greats unable to make the grade in the NHL. "Who, I would like to know, advised Krutov to cross the Atlantic? Who forgot to warn him that in the locker room there would always be a crate of beer next to him?" Tarasov complained.

Krutov himself didn't place great importance on his poor performance in Vancouver—he didn't make it, so what? But judging by his brilliant craftsmanship and his high reputation in international hockey, it was a travesty. He was a player who attacked the goal head-on and scored even when the rest of the team, whether the USSR nationals or CSKA, had noticeably slowed their pace and given up the fight. In 1987 he scored two goals against the Swedes in the World Championship even as the USSR nationals, overtrained and nagged by the coach, were running on automatic pilot and looked quite helpless.

As the least egoistic among the outstanding Soviet forwards, Krutov dedicated himself totally to team play. On the ice, he always looked serious. Whenever he scored a goal—even if it was the winning goal—there was no joy on his face, not even a smile.

On Igor Larionov's forward line, Krutov, who was no less gifted than his partners and maybe even more so, did all the tough jobs the line needed done. He would scramble for the puck right on the goal crease, he would ram through the opposing team's defense line, and he would whisk his way along the boards without getting slammed up against them. The goals he scored weren't always pretty. Frequently they were slapshots from awkward positions taken on the rebound. His problem was that he played how he was told to play, not how he wanted to or was able to.

In December of 1982, with Larionov's forward line at its peak, Sergei Makarov was out for shoulder surgery. Formally, Makarov was replaced by various forwards, but

Krutov, Vladimir
LW, 5'9", 195 lbs, b: Moscow, USSR, 6/1/1960

Season	Club, League	Regular Season				
		GP	G	A	Pts	PIM
1977–78	CSKA, USSR	1	0	0	0	0
1978–79	CSKA, USSR	24	8	3	11	6
1979–80	CSKA, USSR	40	30	12	42	16
OWG–80	USSR	7	6	5	11	4
1980–81	CSKA, USSR	47	25	15	40	20
WEC–81	USSR	8	6	3	9	8
CCup–81	USSR	7	4	4	8	10
1981–82	CSKA, USSR	46	37	29	66	30
WEC–82	USSR	10	4	3	7	6
1982–83	CSKA, USSR	44	32	21	53	34
WEC–83	USSR	10	8	7	15	12
1983–84	CSKA, USSR	44	37	20	57	20
OWG–84	USSR	7	4	1	5	2
CCup–84	USSR	6	3	5	8	4
1984–85	CSKA, USSR	40	23	30	53	26
WEC–85	USSR	10	3	5	8	8
1985–86	CSKA, USSR	40	31	17	48	10
WEC–86	USSR	10	7	10	17	14
1986–87	CSKA, USSR	39	26	24	50	16
RV'87	USSR	2	2	0	2	2
WEC–87	USSR	10	11	3	14	8
CCup–87	USSR	9	7	7	14	4
1987–88	CSKA, USSR	38	19	23	42	20
OWG–88	USSR	8	6	9	15	0
1988–89	CSKA, USSR	35	20	21	41	12
WEC–89	USSR	10	4	2	6	12
1989–90	Vancouver Canucks, NHL	61	11	23	34	20
	USSR Totals	438	288	215	503	210
	NHL Totals	61	11	23	34	20
	OWG/WEC/CCup/RV'87 Totals	114	75	64	139	94

Named Best Forward at WEC (1986, 1987)
Won OWG (1984, 1988)
Won WEC (1981, 1982, 1983, 1986, 1989)
Won CCup (1981)
USSR Champion (1979, 1980, 1981, 1982, 1983, 1984, 1985, 1986, 1987, 1988, 1989)

when it came down to it, Krutov had taken over as the executioner on goal-scoring plays. Krutov was the workhorse. He would set out on prolonged and intricate stickhandling runs, cutting through the opposing defense lines to cheers from the fans, who gleefully discovered that Krutov was just like Kharlamov! After 12 successive games, Krutov came off the ice having failed to score in only two games. And in a matchup between the USSR nationals and the NHL's Minnesota North Stars, Krutov demonstrated the breadth as well as the depth of his talent. The agile, hard-driving Soviet hosts went all out to demonstrate their attacking skills and Krutov scored two goals. The whole audience applauded his first goal, when after evading the entire defense line with a number of intricate feints, Krutov drilled the puck right past the goalie and into the net. A while later he had the puck on his stick again and all he did was nudge it lightly a couple of times. He passed the first defenseman and then the second to score once again. The surprised goalie had been expecting him to fake at least one move.

Even a winning goal brought Vladimir Krutov (center) no joy.

The Makarov–Larionov–Krutov forward line was the most beautifully balanced in Soviet hockey. All three had equal skill and determination. Igor Larionov went on to earn fame and a handsome salary in the NHL. Sergei Makarov also made a name for himself across the Atlantic. But Krutov, who was able to control the play as well as himself on the ice—even when his partners seemed to be at a loss—didn't know exactly what he wanted to achieve in the NHL or how to go about it.

Miroslav Frycer

The arrival of Anton and Peter Stastny for the 1980–81 season marked a turning point for the Quebec Nordiques. The two rookies performed miracles in their first season and Peter racked up points every step of the way. He even set a rookie record that lasted over a decade until it was broken by Finn Teemu Selanne in the 1992–93 season. All the more was expected the following season when their older brother, Marian, also appeared with the team. Another rookie on the team, Miroslav Frycer, went completely unnoticed.

Miroslav Frycer scored a hat-trick in his second NHL game.

In October 1981 Frycer played his first match on home ice against Toronto. His performance was outstanding, and he even managed to overshadow the Stastny brothers when the Nordiques won by a score of 6–4. Frycer scored three of those goals and was named the game's star. The next day, a Toronto paper proclaimed in a one-inch headline, "Four Czechs are too much for Leafs." It was true, except for the fact that the Stastny brothers were Slovaks. The only Czech on the team was Miroslav Mirko Frycer, also known later as "Frigo" (the Czech nickname for comic Buster Keaton). His debut on home ice and his second NHL game made such an impression on the Maple Leafs management that next spring he left Quebec for Toronto, where he wore number 14 for the next few seasons.

In a game on March 17, 1981, Frycer faced his old team—and this time the results were reversed. The final score was 6–3 for Toronto and the architect of the victory was none other

Miroslav Frycer was part of the Czech colony playing for Toronto in the 1980s.

than Miroslav Frycer. Journalists flocked around the Toronto rookie in the dressing room, and John Anderson, who had a locker right next to him, joked: "Last year I couldn't get dressed because I had a locker next to Sittler. This year I have the same problem with Frycer."

One week later, on March 24, 1981, Frycer pulled another rabbit out of the hat. In a game that had them on the verge of being eliminated from Stanley Cup contention, the Leafs had to beat the St. Louis Blues. It was tied 3–3 and the clock was ticking away on the Leafs. Less than a minute remained in regulation play.

Fighting the odds, coach Mike Nykoluk took a gamble and pulled his goaltender, an unusual move in a tied situation. Miroslav Frycer appeared on the ice, and Toronto tensed up for the face-off in the Blues' zone. Winning control of the puck, Frycer skated with it almost to the far boards. When he got within shooting distance, he let go a shot and scored the winning goal—at least in that game. In the series, Toronto held on for a few more days but finally gave in to the stronger team.

Frycer's career in Toronto was only beginning, and in the summer of 1982 another countryman of sorts, Slovak Peter Ihnacak, joined him on the offense. Rounding out the trio was another talented technical player, Walt Poddubny. While Peter Ihnacak did a great job of feeding the puck to both wings, Frycer amazed everyone with his daring escapes and speed along the boards. Just as remarkable were his solo attacks when he got the goaltender in a prone position and scored from difficult angles right around the crease area.

In the 1982–83 season, another defenseman, Czech Vitezslav Duris, returned to the team, making a considerable Czech colony playing for Toronto in the 1980s. The oldest of the Stastny brothers, Marian, appeared on the team for one season, as did the Czech-speaking defenseman Rick Lanz, and later even Peter Ihnacak's brother Miroslav. The first Czech to wear a Toronto jersey, however, had been goaltender Jiri Crha, who joined the Maple Leafs in 1979.

Frycer can legitimately take his place as one of Toronto's best players. In 1985 he was the only Toronto player chosen to represent the Campbell Conference in the All-Star Game. In a game against Edmonton on January 8, 1986, that ended with an incredible score of 11–9, four of the Leafs goals were once again scored by Miroslav Frycer. After the game, even Wayne Gretzky referred to Frycer as a great hockey player.

His brazen attacks along the boards had negative consequences for him on more than

Frycer, Miroslav
RW, 6´, 200 lbs, b: Ostrava, Czechoslovakia, 9/27/1959

Season	Club, League	Regular Season					Playoffs				
		GP	G	A	Pts	Plm	GP	G	A	Pts	Plm
1977–78	Vitkovice, Czechoslovakia	34	12	10	22	24					
1978–79	Vitkovice, Czechoslovakia	44	22	12	34	*					
WEC–79	Czechoslovakia	1	0	0	0	2					
1979–80	Vitkovice, Czechoslovakia	44	31	15	46	*					
OWG–80	Czechoslovakia	6	1	2	3	7					
1980–81	Vitkovice, Czechoslovakia	34	33	24	57	*					
WEC–81	Czechoslovakia	8	1	2	3	0					
1981–82	Quebec Nordiques, NHL	49	20	17	37	47					
	Fredericton Express, AHL	11	9	5	14	16					
	Toronto Maple Leafs, NHL	10	4	6	10	31					
1982–83	Toronto Maple Leafs, NHL	67	25	30	55	90	4	2	5	7	0
1983–84	Toronto Maple Leafs, NHL	47	10	16	26	55					
1984–85	Toronto Maple Leafs, NHL	65	25	30	55	55					
1985–86	Toronto Maple Leafs, NHL	73	32	43	75	74	10	1	3	4	10
1986–87	Toronto Maple Leafs, NHL	29	7	8	15	28					
1987–88	Toronto Maple Leafs, NHL	38	12	20	32	41	3	0	0	0	6
1988–89	Detroit Red Wings, NHL	23	7	8	15	47					
	Edmonton Oilers, NHL	14	5	5	10	18					
1989–90	Freiburg, FRG	11	4	13	17	18					
1990–91	Freiburg, FRG	21	11	24	35	29					
	Czechoslovakia Totals	156	98	61	159	*					
	NHL Totals	415	147	183	330	486	17	3	8	11	16
	OWG/WEC Totals	15	2	4	6	9					

Czechoslovakia Champion (1981)

one occasion, however. Once, in the split second it took to jump through an opening between a defenseman and the boards, Frycer ended up with a serious knee injury. Another time it was an injured back. But Mirko never lost his sense of humor. When asked whether he would watch a hockey game on TV involving other teams, he replied that he wouldn't for the simple reason that it reminded him of work. Once he bought a painting from a Toronto artist and left a blank check. When he got a bonus for being player of the month, he declared that the money would be used to pay for a big party for the whole team. His team members gave him a round of applause.

It's no secret that the end of his tenure with the Toronto Maple Leafs came with the arrival of coach John Brophy. What started as a fairly good relationship quickly deteriorated. With his technical play, Frycer couldn't get along with Brophy at all and was even accused of leading a mutiny against him. Shortly after that he was traded to Detroit, where he got along fine with Jacques Demers. During his first great match against Toronto in a Detroit jersey, a big sign appeared on the wall in Maple Leaf Gardens welcoming Frycer back to Toronto and thanking him for all the wonderful moments he had brought his team. All the while, a disappointed coach Brophy sat on the bench. After the game, the press conference turned into a sideshow with Frigo as the comedian. He described life with Demers as a day full of sunshine whereas life with Brophy was a dreary, rainy autumn day.

Chronic injuries affected his game in Detroit and his days in the NHL were clearly numbered. But one last trade to Edmonton postponed the inevitable for a while. He retired from the NHL in 1989.

Doug Wilson

Although he was born in Ottawa, Doug Wilson lived in England from the age of three to six because his father was in the air force. Then the family returned to Canada, going first to Winnipeg and then back to Ottawa, and it was in the nation's capital that Wilson began his hockey playing in earnest. He was selected by the local 67s in the midget draft to play junior. He stayed in Ottawa for three years and became one of the finest players ever to skate for that storied Ottawa franchise.

Doug Wilson was drafted by Chicago in 1977 and made the Hawks' starting lineup after his first training camp as an 18-year-old.

He was drafted by Chicago in 1977 and made the Hawks' starting lineup in his first training camp as an 18-year-old. A fluid skater with one of the best shots in the league, he joined the blue line during Bobby Orr's brief final year in the NHL. "He was a big influence," Wilson admitted. "He kept telling me not to get down on myself and to play with confidence and not worry about making mistakes." Wilson was obviously a quick learner.

Like Orr, Wilson was also a scoring threat, though to a lesser degree, of course. In his fifth season in the league, he was the most dominant defenseman in the game. He scored an incredible 39 goals, was selected to the First All-Star Team and won the Norris Trophy to confirm what everyone already knew. He averaged nearly a point a game, was rock solid in his own end of the rink and was a natural leader on and off the ice. In the playoffs, the team made it as far as the semifinals before losing to Vancouver in five games.

After 14 years with Chicago, Doug Wilson (right) was traded to the expansion San Jose Sharks in 1991.

The reasons for his greatly improved game weren't restricted to skill and experience. He was hypoglycemic, but after he married in 1981 his wife began to ensure that he ate properly. "I'd had no energy at all," he said. "The problem can be controlled by diet, but I could never have managed it fixing my own meals. Once I started eating correctly, thanks to her, I became an effective player at last."

Early in the 1987–88 season, Wilson suffered a debilitating shoulder injury that required extensive surgery. At one point, doctors were so shocked by the accumulated damage to the muscle they wondered if he would ever play again. He missed the rest of that season and part of the next, but after months of rehabilitation he recovered fully and played his best hockey in years. Wilson was also one of the last bareheaded players in the league, but the following season he wore a helmet for the whole year on a trial basis. "In that one year," he said, "I had more cuts around the eyes than any two seasons combined." By the following training camp, he had ditched the headgear and played without protection until his retirement in 1993.

As he got to be a veteran in the league, he became more interested in the business of the game. After 1985 he was one of the vice-presidents of the NHL Players' Association, and when president Bryan Trottier joined the Islanders' executive in 1992, Wilson was named the NHLPA's new president at a critical time in league history. The collective bargaining agreement expired the next spring, and the fall of 1993 saw the owners lock the players out until a resolution of the contract had been reached. Meanwhile, Wayne Gretzky organized what became a hugely popular tour of NHL players throughout Europe called the Ninety-Nine All-Stars and Wilson joined the team as their coach. It was a symbolic gesture of support for all the players who weren't skating but biding their time until an agreement was reached.

After 14 years with Chicago, Wilson was traded to the expansion San Jose Sharks in 1991, a move he looked forward to as a time to teach young players and enjoy the game in a non-hockey market. After two part-time years on defense, he retired and moved into the front office with the Sharks. His number 7 was retired by the Ottawa 67s in 1998. During his 1,000-game NHL career, Wilson made it as far as the Stanley Cup semifinals on four occasions: 1982, 1985, 1989 and 1990. In 1985 the Hawks were hammered by the Oilers, who scored 44 goals in the six-game series; in 1989 they lost to Calgary in five games; and in 1990 Edmonton again eliminated Chicago in six, though the scores were much closer. The Sharks failed to qualify for the playoffs during Wilson's two seasons there.

Wilson, Doug
D, 6´1˝, 187 lbs, b: Ottawa, Ont., 7/5/1957

Season	Club, League	Regular Season					Playoffs				
		GP	G	A	Pts	PIM	GP	G	A	Pts	PIM
1977–78	Chicago Black Hawks, NHL	77	14	20	34	72	4	0	0	0	0
1978–79	Chicago Black Hawks, NHL	56	5	21	26	37					
1979–80	Chicago Black Hawks, NHL	73	12	49	61	70	7	2	8	10	6
1980–81	Chicago Black Hawks, NHL	76	12	39	51	80	3	0	3	3	2
1981–82	Chicago Black Hawks, NHL	76	39	46	85	54	15	3	10	13	32
1982–83	Chicago Black Hawks, NHL	74	18	51	69	58	13	4	11	15	12
1983–84	Chicago Black Hawks, NHL	66	13	45	58	64	5	0	3	3	2
CCup–84	Canada	7	2	1	3	4					
1984–85	Chicago Black Hawks, NHL	78	22	54	76	44	12	3	10	13	12
1985–86	Chicago Blackhawks, NHL	79	17	47	64	80	3	1	1	2	2
1986–87	Chicago Blackhawks, NHL	69	16	32	48	36	4	0	0	0	0
RV'87	NHL All-Stars	2	1	1	2	0					
1987–88	Chicago Blackhawks, NHL	27	8	24	32	28					
1988–89	Chicago Blackhawks, NHL	66	15	47	62	69	4	1	2	3	0
1989–90	Chicago Blackhawks, NHL	70	23	50	73	40	20	3	12	15	18
1990–91	Chicago Blackhawks, NHL	51	11	29	40	32	5	1	2	3	2
1991–92	San Jose Sharks, NHL	44	9	19	28	26					
1992–93	San Jose Sharks, NHL	42	3	17	20	40					
	NHL Totals	1024	237	590	827	830	95	19	61	80	88
	CCup/RV'87 Totals	9	3	2	5	4					

NHL First All-Star Team (1982)
NHL Second All-Star Team (1985, 1990)
Won James Norris Trophy (1982)
Won CCup (1984)

Dusan **Pasek**

Dusan Pasek was a high-energy, high-impact kind of hockey player. Although his greatest strength was scoring, he never won any league titles for it. Only in the 1986–87 season did he finally beat out the competition as the best passer but also as the bad guy of the league with his 81 penalty minutes in 38 matches.

He was born in Bratislava, Czechoslovakia, on September 7, 1960. Though he played hockey from a young age, his first passion was gymnastics. At the age of nine, he joined the BEZ Bratislava hockey club. From there he moved on to Slovan. From the time he was a boy, he played alongside Darius Rusnak and Ivan Dornic, who along with Pasek later ranked among the greatest players on the senior team. In 1979, with the weak Bratislava team being carried only by the Stastny brothers, Slovan won the national championship. The next generation of players, however, didn't repeat their success.

After only three years in the league, Pasek's debut on the national team came in 1982 during exhibition matches against Sweden. One year later he was on his way to the World Championship. As a forward playing alongside Jiri Lala and Jiri Sejba, he helped his team win a gold medal in Prague in 1985, and two years later, in Vienna, he came very close to another triumph. He was the captain of the national team in 1987–88 when he left for the NHL. He spent the 1988–89 season with the Minnesota North Stars, the next in Kalamazoo in the IHL. Then he returned to Slovan for a while. He later worked for the Italian clubs HC Asiago and Fassa Merlini and ended his career in 1992–93 with KalPa Kuopio in Finland. As a fitting end to his playing career, he returned to the place where it all began and where he had spent a big part of his life—Bratislava.

"I don't know what I will be when I finish with hockey. I would like to stay with hockey, but I don't know in what way," he said in an interview while still in the prime of his career. Although he had studied economics at college, Pasek never wanted to become an economist, and he didn't want to be a coach either. But after he retired from play, he proved over and over that the qualities he brought to the ice could serve him well as a manager or a hockey emissary.

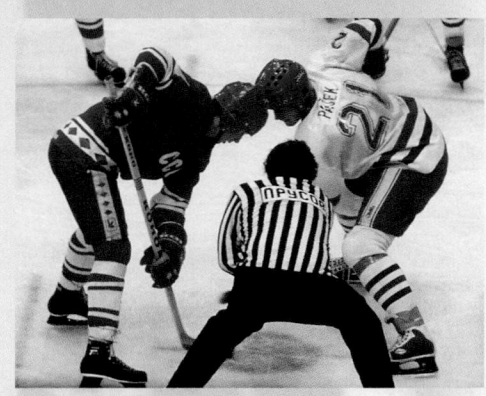

His greatest strength was scoring, but Dusan Pasek (number 21) never won league titles for it.

Pasek, Dusan
C, 6′1″, 200 lbs, b: Bratislava, Czechoslovakia, 9/7/1960, d: 3/15/1998

Season	Club, League	Regular Season					Playoffs				
		GP	G	A	Pts	PLM	GP	G	A	Pts	PLM
1977–78	Slovan, Czechoslovakia	5	0	1	1	0					
1978–79	Slovan, Czechoslovakia	36	9	12	21	18					
1979–80	Slovan, Czechoslovakia	40	18	1	19	22					
1980–81	Slovan, Czechoslovakia	*	*	*	*	*					
CCup–81	Czechoslovakia	6	0	2	2	2					
1981–82	Slovan, Czechoslovakia	*	*	*	*	*					
WEC–82	Czechoslovakia	10	1	2	3	4					
1982–83	Slovan, Czechoslovakia	*	*	*	*	*					
WEC–83	Czechoslovakia	10	3	2	5	6					
1983–84	Slovan, Czechoslovakia	*	*	*	*	*					
OWG–84	Czechoslovakia	7	0	4	4	2					
CCup–84	Czechoslovakia	5	0	0	0	4					
1984–85	Slovan, Czechoslovakia	40	23	14	37	60					
WEC–85	Czechoslovakia	10	3	3	6	6					
1985–86	Dukla Jihlava, Czechoslovakia	45	13	11	24	*					
WEC–86	Czechoslovakia	10	4	3	7	16					
1986–87	Slovan, Czechoslovakia	38	21	29	50	81					
WEC–87	Czechoslovakia	10	6	2	8	2					
CCup–87	Czechoslovakia	6	4	1	5	12					
1987–88	Slovan, Czechoslovakia	28	13	10	23	*					
OWG–88	Czechoslovakia	8	6	5	11	8					
1988–89	Minnesota North Stars, NHL	48	4	10	14	30	2	1	0	1	0
1989–90	Kalamazoo Wings, IHL	20	10	14	24	6					
1990–91	Slovan, Czechoslovakia	11	11	5	16	20					
	Asiago, Italy	34	35	41	76	22	3	5	1	6	0
1991–92	Fassa, Italy	25	22	33	55	22					
1992–93	KalPa, Finland	10	2	4	6	16					
	Czechoslovakia Totals	289	153	*	*	*					
	NHL Totals	48	4	10	14	30	2	1	0	1	0
	OWG/WEC/CCup Totals	82	27	24	51	62					

Won WEC (1985)
Czechoslovakia Champion (1979)

Pasek was ambitious and could be extraordinarily hard on himself, but his charming conduct off the ice earned him the endearing nickname "Ceco." He believed in modesty and integrity, and in his playing years, journalists often sought him out for his sensible, intelligent comments. If they criticized his performance, he didn't hold it against them. "I accept it as normal, as I would accept praise. Even criticism can open one's eyes and force one to think," he said.

There were only a few chapters in his career that he would rather have forgotten. At the top of the list would be the Czech national team's losses during the 1986 World Championship in Moscow, followed by a disastrous performance at the Calgary Olympics in 1988 and the unsuccessful 1985–86 season during his military service with Dukla Jihlava.

After Czechoslovakia split up, the Czech Republic was treated as the successor country. Slovakia's climb from the cellar back up to the elite ranks of professional hockey would be long and arduous and would come through a network of qualifying matches and C and B group championships. This was accomplished in three years, a remarkably short period of time. Much of the credit for this success goes to Dusan Pasek, who quickly got Slovan Bratislava back on a sound financial footing as president of the Slovakian Ice Hockey Association.

As manager of the national team, Pasek attended the Nagano Olympics. He was still the smiling, likeable man who didn't let the pressure get to him. So when news of his untimely death on March 15, 1998, made its way around the world, it shocked many people and a great deal of speculation has arisen as a result. According to the official line, he shot himself with one of several guns for which he had permits. It's possible that Pasek, who was spending a lot of money in the casino, had run up debts. Although six farewell letters were found in his briefcase, there were many mysterious circumstances surrounding his death, and suicide wasn't in keeping with his attitude to life and the game of hockey.

Mats Naslund

Canadiens fans nicknamed Mats Naslund "le Petit Viking."

At 5′7″ in his sock feet and tipping the scales at just over 160 pounds, Mats Naslund is an unlikely candidate for the title of Superman. But he was indeed a hockey superman—a nimble, cunning and swift player who could zip around the entire rink while keeping the puck on his stick and a fearless player who never shied away from a hefty defenseman. Born on October 31, 1959, Naslund became a formidable forward who was closely watched by the defense lines and goaltenders he played against.

The famous Soviet forward Vyacheslav Starshinov bestowed his blessing on this talented player long before his entry into big-league hockey. In 1967 the USSR national team and Tre Kronor were playing a game at Isstadion in Johanneshof. After the game, spectators were invited to watch a match between children's teams refereed by the Soviet nationals forward. After the game, Starshinov, impressed by the way a plucky little boy named Mats Naslund fought on the ice, picked up the seven-year-old and held him in his arms. The photograph appeared in Swedish newspapers across the country and the young Naslund became an instant celebrity.

First with Brynas, then with the Swedish national team and finally with the NHL's Montreal Canadiens, Naslund's primary claim to fame stemmed from his excellent playing style.

Naslund played for Timra before joining Brynas, who won the gold medal in 1980. He was always quick, skating with the speed of a sprinter. He scored his first goal for Tre Kronor 55 seconds after the face-off in a game against the USSR national team in the spring of 1979 and went on to score a second goal.

He had been in the Canadiens lineup for four seasons when they won the 1986 Stanley Cup. As the first European in the history of the team, it wasn't easy for him to win recognition and popu-

larity with Canadiens fans. Naslund had to work hard, but he finally managed it when admiring fans nicknamed him "le Petit Viking." He also played 34 games for the Boston Bruins and scored 251 NHL goals.

Another high point in his hockey career was the Olympic gold medal he won playing for Tre Kronor at the 1994 Winter Games in Lillehammer—15 years after he made his debut with the Swedish national team, for whom he played a total of 175 games, 173 of them official. Naslund became a unique award holder in Swedish hockey by winning gold medals at the World Championship, the Olympics and the European Championship, as well as winning the Stanley Cup. He also won the Swedish national championship three times, once while playing for Brynas and twice in the lineup for Malmo, where he played for three seasons after returning from the NHL.

Mats Naslund stands 109th on the Swedish list of "Great Men." A gifted player with superb technique, he played with great confidence in his strength and a sure understanding of hockey. Naslund continues to promote this understanding and vision of his favorite game as a TV sports commentator.

At 5′7″ in his sock feet and just over 160 pounds, Mats Naslund (in back) was a fearless player who never shied away from a hefty defenseman.

Naslund, Mats
LW, 5′7″, 160 lbs, b: Timra, Sweden, 10/31/1959

Season	Club, League	Regular Season					Playoffs				
		GP	G	A	Pts	PIM	GP	G	A	Pts	PIM
1977–78	Timra, Sweden	35	13	6	19	14					
1978–79	Brynas, Sweden	36	12	12	24	19					
WEC–79	Sweden	8	5	2	7	8					
1979–80	Brynas, Sweden	36	18	19	37	34	7	2	2	4	4
OWG–80	Sweden	7	3	7	10	6					
1980–81	Brynas, Sweden	36	17	25	42	34					
WEC–81	Sweden	8	0	3	3	6					
1981–82	Brynas, Sweden	36	24	18	42	16					
WEC–82	Sweden	10	2	4	6	6					
1982–83	Montreal Canadiens, NHL	74	26	45	71	10	3	1	0	1	0
WEC–83	Sweden	10	3	4	7	2					
1983–84	Montreal Canadiens, NHL	77	29	35	64	4	15	6	8	14	4
CCup–84	Sweden	8	2	3	5	6					
1984–85	Montreal Canadiens, NHL	80	42	37	79	14	12	7	4	11	6
1985–86	Montreal Canadiens, NHL	80	43	67	110	16	20	8	11	19	4
1986–87	Montreal Canadiens, NHL	79	25	55	80	16	17	7	15	22	11
CCup–87	Sweden	6	1	2	3	2					
1987–88	Montreal Canadiens, NHL	78	24	59	83	14	6	0	7	7	2
1988–89	Montreal Canadiens, NHL	77	33	51	84	14	21	4	11	15	6
1989–90	Montreal Canadiens, NHL	72	21	20	41	19	3	1	1	2	0
1990–91	Lugano, Switzerland	31	27	29	56	*	11	4	9	13	*
WEC–91	Sweden	10	3	5	8	0					
CCup–91	Sweden	6	1	3	4	0					
1991–92	Malmo, Sweden	39	15	24	39	10	10	3	2	5	*
OWG–92	Sweden	8	1	5	6	27					
1992–93	Malmo, Sweden	33	11	21	32	10	1	0	0	0	*
1993–94	Malmo, Sweden	40	14	30	44	8	11	2	4	6	4
OWG–94	Sweden	8	0	7	7	0					
1994–95	Boston Bruins, NHL	34	8	14	22	4	5	1	0	1	0
	Sweden Totals	291	124	155	279	145	29	7	8	15	8
	NHL Totals	651	251	383	634	111	102	35	57	92	33
	OWG/WEC/CCup Totals	89	21	45	66	63					

NHL Second All-Star Team (1986)
Won Lady Byng Trophy (1988)
Won OWG (1994)
Won WEC (1991)
Won Stanley Cup (1986)
Sweden Champion (1980, 1992, 1994)

A HISTORY OF WORLD HOCKEY

Dave **Christian**

Dave Christian was one of the NHL's most consistent right wingers in the 1980s. As a youth, he was inspired by his father, Bill, who played on the U.S. Olympic teams in 1960 and 1964. (His winning goal in a thrilling 3–2 win over the USSR paved the way for the Americans' gold medal triumph in 1960.) Two additional Olympic influences were Dave's uncles: Roger played in 1960 and 1964 and Gord won silver in 1956. Dave kept up the family tradition exactly 20 years later when he was a part of the U.S. Miracle on Ice team at the Lake Placid Olympics. And he followed this with an exemplary NHL career that saw him play over 1,000 regular-season games.

The native of Warroad, Minnesota, just south of the Manitoba border, was a versatile athlete in his youth. He earned recognition as an All-State high school hockey player while also lettering in football, baseball and track. His only regret was that his Warroad High School team never made it to the prestigious Minnesota state tournament.

Dave Christian kept up the family tradition as part of the Miracle on Ice team at the Lake Placid Olympics.

A standout with the University of North Dakota, Christian was drafted 40th overall by the Winnipeg Jets in 1979. Before joining the NHL, he spent several months with the U.S. national team as it prepared for the 1980 Olympic tournament. Christian scored 30 points in 59 exhibition games, then contributed eight assists in the seven memorable matches at Lake Placid. Although he worked as a center in college, Christian was used exclusively on the blue line by coach Herb Brooks.

Following the Olympics, he was given a rousing welcome and a key to the city of Warroad. Winnipeg Jets general manager John Ferguson was also on hand and presented Christian with his first multi-year NHL contract. Christian was still on cloud nine when he joined his new team and totaled 18 points in 15 games.

He registered 71 points in his first full NHL season, then starred with 11 points in eight games at the 1981 World Championship. A few months later, Christian experienced disappointment with only one goal in six games at the 1981 Canada Cup when the United States finished fourth in the round robin. Prior to the 1981–82 season, the Jets named him team captain. He averaged just under a point per game during his three years in Manitoba before he was traded to the Washington Capitals following a contract dispute with the Jets.

Christian was busy during his first year in Washington. He totaled 81 points and was a plus-26. In 1984 he played in his second Canada Cup and helped the U.S. reach the

Christian, Dave
RW, 5'11", 175 lbs, b: Warroad, MN, 5/12/1959

Season	Club, League	Regular Season					Playoffs				
		GP	G	A	Pts	PIM	GP	G	A	Pts	PIM
1977–78	University of North Dakota, WCHA	38	8	16	24	14					
1978–79	University of North Dakota, WCHA	40	22	24	46	22					
OWG–80	USA	7	0	8	8	6					
1979–80	Winnipeg Jets, NHL	15	8	10	18	2					
1980–81	Winnipeg Jets, NHL	80	28	43	71	22					
WEC–81	USA	8	8	3	11	6					
CCup–81	USA	6	1	0	1	4					
1981–82	Winnipeg Jets, NHL	80	25	51	76	28	4	0	1	1	2
1982–83	Winnipeg Jets, NHL	55	18	26	44	23	3	0	0	0	0
1983–84	Washington Capitals, NHL	80	29	52	81	28	8	5	4	9	5
CCup–84	USA	6	2	1	3	2					
1984–85	Washington Capitals, NHL	80	26	43	69	14	5	1	1	2	0
1985–86	Washington Capitals, NHL	80	41	42	83	15	9	4	4	8	0
1986–87	Washington Capitals, NHL	76	23	27	50	8	7	1	3	4	6
1987–88	Washington Capitals, NHL	80	37	21	58	26	14	5	6	11	6
1988–89	Washington Capitals, NHL	80	34	31	65	12	6	1	1	2	0
WEC–89	USA	6	4	3	7	2					
1989–90	Washington Capitals, NHL	28	3	8	11	4					
	Boston Bruins, NHL	50	12	17	29	8	21	4	1	5	4
1990–91	Boston Bruins, NHL	78	32	21	53	41	19	8	4	12	4
CCup–91	USA	7	1	1	2	0					
1991–92	St. Louis Blues, NHL	78	20	24	44	41	4	3	0	3	0
1992–93	Chicago Blackhawks, NHL	60	4	14	18	12	1	0	0	0	0
1993–94	Chicago Blackhawks, NHL	9	0	3	3	0	1	0	0	0	0
	Indianapolis Ice, IHL	40	8	18	26	6					
1994–95	Minneapolis Moose, IHL	81	38	42	80	16	3	0	1	1	0
1995–96	Minneapolis Moose, IHL	69	21	25	46	8					
	NHL Totals	1009	340	433	773	284	102	32	25	57	27
	OWG/WEC/CCup Totals	40	16	16	32	20					

Won OWG(1980)

semifinals. He recorded his finest year in 1985–86 with 41 goals and 83 points and was often paired with fellow speedsters Mike Gartner and Bengt Gustafsson on an effective and entertaining forward line.

In 1989 he enjoyed another strong showing at the World Championships with seven points in six games. Prior to the 1989–90 season, he traveled with the Capitals to the USSR on the NHL Friendship Tour. Later in the year, the Boston Bruins acquired Christian for his offense and experience. He enjoyed his longest spell in the playoffs by helping the Bruins reach the Stanley Cup finals against the eventual champion Edmonton Oilers.

Following the free-agent signing of Glen Featherstone and Dave Thomlinson, the St. Louis Blues received Christian as part of the compensation package. He recorded his 10th 20-goal season but was put on waivers at the start of the next year. The Chicago Blackhawks claimed him and he played his last 69 games in the Windy City. Christian left the NHL with 340 career goals before playing his last 190 pro games in the IHL.

Dave Christian (number 27) was one of the NHL's most consistent right wingers in the 1980s.

Reijo Ruotsalainen

At the very beginning, Reijo Ruotsalainen's lack of size forced him, to be a goalie. As a youngster, he couldn't afford skates, so he stood between the posts in felt boots while his feet turned to icicles. The next year, no suitable glove could be found for him so he left the net and joined the ranks of the skaters. In the long tradition of all great players, he practised harder than anybody else. And even when daylight faded, he would keep on playing under the glare of car headlights that somebody's father would turn on.

When Ruotsalainen was only 14, the coach of the Finnish men's team, Kari Makinen, was already interested in putting him on the team. Ruotsalainen remembers, "I was too young, and I didn't dare to make that move."

But he did end up there two years later. The club lost a defender just prior to the start of the season and Makinen convinced Ruotsalainen that it was the right time to make a move. He started the season as the number eight blueliner and by Christmas he was already number one on the team. It was quite a feat in his first year—and playing against men three to four years older.

"Rental Rexi," as the wags called him in the NHL, is perhaps the greatest skater ever to play Finnish hockey, but because he was a small defenseman, he has been underestimated, especially in pro circles. It all started with the NHL draft. Although Ruotsalainen was a star in the Finnish league, in the NHL he was rated lower than Timo Blomqvist, a blueliner with good size but not much potential. The scouts said he would never make it into the NHL and complained that he skated with his back to the puck, so how could he possibly know what was happening?

But Ruotsalainen proved all the doubters wrong. He eventually played 446 regular-season games plus 86 post-season ones, producing 344 and 47 points respectively. Lars-Erik Sjoberg—a famous

The scouts said Reijo Ruotsalainen would never get into the NHL, but he played 446 regular-season and 86 playoff games.

Herb Brooks, who coached Reijo Ruotsalainen (right) with the Rangers, claimed that the Finn was the best skater in the NHL at the time.

Swedish defenseman in his time and a pro for the Winnipeg Jets both in the WHA and after their transition to the NHL and later a scout for the New York Rangers—convinced the club that, in spite of everything, the fast young skater had promise beyond his reputation in pro circles. New York took a chance and picked him as the 119th player in the 1980 draft. It turned out to be a steal.

During his career, he played for the New York Rangers, the Edmonton Oilers and the New Jersey Devils and then returned to the Oilers to win the 1990 Stanley Cup with the team with which he had achieved post-season supremacy in 1987. On returning to Europe, he became a legend with SC Bern in Switzerland and was invited to return anytime he pleased to the team he effectively quarterbacked. In his role of controlling the action on the ice, he led the Bern team to two back-to-back titles in 1991 and 1992.

Ruotsalainen's main asset was his skating, and it was of such a caliber that from a young age he always played with older and bigger boys. Herb Brooks, who coached him with the Rangers, claimed that the Finn was the best skater in the NHL at the time. Ruotsalainen belongs to the generation of players from Karpat Oulu who put this northern city on the Finnish hockey map. He helped them become one of the top clubs in the league and eventually go on to win the national championship in 1981. During the regular season, Ruotsalainen was a sensational sixth in the scoring parade with 28 goals in 36 games. His total of 51 points left him trailing the club's top scorer—center Mikko Leinonen—by a single point.

In the Swedish playoffs, Ruotsalainen led his team to the title and along the way placed third overall in playoff scoring and was runner-up once again on the team. First place went to Kari Jalonen, a tall center also out to try his luck in the pro ranks.

Ruotsalainen still holds a joint record in the IIHF Junior World Championships for having performed in four tournaments. He sums himself up by saying, "If you are fast enough on skates, the opponent's size doesn't mean a lot as he will not catch you to make contact." In 1995-96, he played for KalPa Kuopio in the Finnish league.

Ruotsalainen, Reijo
D, 5′8″, 170 lbs, b: Oulu, Finland, 4/1/1960

Season	Club, League	Regular Season					Playoffs				
		GP	G	A	Pts	PIM	GP	G	A	Pts	PIM
1977–78	Karpat, Finland	30	9	14	23	4					
WEC–78	Finland	9	2	0	2	2					
1978–79	Karpat, Finland	36	14	8	22	47					
WEC–79	Finland	6	2	0	2	2					
1979–80	Karpat, Finland	30	15	13	28	31	6	5	2	7	0
1980–81	Karpat, Finland	36	28	23	51	28	12	7	4	11	6
WEC–81	Finland	8	3	4	7	4					
CCup–81	Finland	5	0	1	1	2					
1981–82	New York Rangers, NHL	78	18	38	56	27	10	4	5	9	2
1982–83	New York Rangers, NHL	77	16	53	69	22	9	4	2	6	6
1983–84	New York Rangers, NHL	74	20	39	59	26	5	1	1	2	2
1984–85	New York Rangers, NHL	80	28	45	73	32	3	2	0	2	6
WEC–85	Finland	10	0	4	4	6					
1985–86	New York Rangers, NHL	80	17	42	59	47	16	0	8	8	6
1986–87	Bern, Switzerland	36	26	28	54	*					
	Edmonton Oilers, NHL	16	5	8	13	6	21	2	5	7	10
CCup–87	Finland	4	0	0	0	2					
1987–88	HV 71, Sweden	40	10	22	32	26	2	0	1	1	2
OWG–88	Finland	8	4	2	6	0					
1988–89	Bern, Switzerland	36	17	30	47	*	9	4	8	12	*
WEC–89	Finland	10	2	4	6	6					
1989–90	New Jersey Devils, NHL	31	2	5	7	14					
	Edmonton Oilers, NHL	10	1	7	8	6	22	2	11	13	12
1990–91	Bern, Switzerland	36	13	25	38	*	10	5	9	14	*
1991–92	Bern, Switzerland	35	7	16	23	28	11	4	4	8	
1992–93	Bern, Switzerland	31	7	16	23	38	5	1	2	3	8
1993–94	Tappara, Finland	6	2	4	6	2	9	1	2	3	6
1994–95	Bern, Switzerland	19	3	7	10	28	6	1	5	6	4
1995–96	Zurcher, Switzerland	18	4	11	15	4					
	KalPa, Finland	16	3	5	8	4					
	Finland Totals	154	71	67	138	116	18	12	6	18	6
	OWG/WEC/CCup Totals	60	13	15	28	24					
	NHL Totals	446	107	237	344	180	86	15	32	47	44

Won Stanley Cup (1987, 1990)
Finland Champion (1981)
Switzerland Champion (1989, 1991, 1992)

Tomas Jonsson

Defenseman Tomas Jonsson is one of Sweden's "Great Three" who, along with forwards Mats Naslund and Hakan Loob, has won the national championship, the World Championship, Olympic gold and the Stanley Cup. The three played together on Sweden's national Tre Kronor and sometimes against each other in the NHL.

A skillful and experienced defenseman, Jonsson was distinguished by the brilliant skating technique and speed that enabled him to assist his teammates in scoring goals. Jonsson was born April 12, 1960, and began his career with the provincial Falun IK. At the age of 17, he moved to Ornskoldsvik to join MoDo, which was then supervised by Jonsson's favorite coach, Tommy Sandlin. While playing with MoDo, Jonsson won his first national championship gold medal and was drafted by the NHL's New York Islanders.

In 1981 the ambitious Jonsson left Sweden for the NHL, where he spent eight seasons playing for the Islanders and the Edmonton Oilers in a total of 632 games, scoring 96 goals. The Islanders won the Stanley Cup twice with Jonsson on the team.

During the period of the Islanders' supremacy in the late 1970s and early 1980s, Jonsson's teammates were his two countrymen Stefan Persson and Anders Kallur. Persson set a record among Swedish NHL players by winning the Stanley Cup four times while playing for the Islanders.

Tomas Jonsson returned to Sweden and continued playing for Leksand and the national team, adding to his many honors the "200" title, which is awarded to anyone who has played at least 200 games for Tre Kronor. And Jonsson might have done even better had his involvement in the NHL playoff series not kept him from playing for Sweden's national team.

Jonsson holds 110th place on Sweden's "Great Men" list. The 1998–99 season was the last he played for Leksand, where he remains as coach.

Defenseman Tomas Jonsson is one the "Great Three" who have won the Swedish national championship, the World Championship, Olympic gold and the Stanley Cup.

Jonsson, Tomas
D, 5′10″, 185 lbs, b: Falun, Sweden, 4/12/1960

Season	Club, League	Regular Season					Playoffs				
		GP	G	A	Pts	PIM	GP	G	A	Pts	PIM
1977–78	MoDo, Sweden	35	8	9	17	45	2	0	0	0	4
1978–79	MoDo, Sweden	34	11	9	20	77	5	1	2	3	13
WEC–79	Sweden	8	1	3	4	8					
1979–80	MoDo, Sweden	36	3	13	16	42					
WOG–80	Sweden	7	2	2	4	6					
1980–81	MoDo, Sweden	35	8	12	20	58					
WEC–81	Sweden	1	0	0	0	0					
CCup–81	Sweden	3	0	1	1	4					
1981–82	New York Islanders, NHL	70	9	25	34	51	10	0	2	2	21
1982–83	New York Islanders, NHL	72	13	35	48	50	20	2	10	12	18
1983–84	New York Islanders, NHL	72	11	36	47	54	21	3	5	8	22
1984–85	New York Islanders, NHL	69	16	34	50	58	7	1	2	3	10
1985–86	New York Islanders, NHL	77	14	30	44	62	3	0	1	1	4
WEC–86	Sweden	8	0	5	5	10					
1986–87	New York Islanders, NHL	47	6	25	31	36	10	1	4	5	6
CCup–87	Sweden	6	1	1	2	2					
1987–88	New York Islanders, NHL	72	6	41	47	115	5	2	2	4	10
1988–89	New York Islanders, NHL	53	9	23	32	34					
	Edmonton Oilers, NHL	20	1	10	11	22	4	2	0	2	6
1989–90	Leksand, Sweden	40	11	15	26	54	3	1	1	2	4
WEC–90	Sweden	8	0	1	1	8					
1990–91	Leksand, Sweden	22	7	7	14	16					
WEC–91	Sweden	10	0	4	4	8					
1991–92	Leksand, Sweden	22	6	7	13	26					
1992–93	Leksand, Sweden	38	8	15	23	90	2	1	1	2	4
1993–94	Leksand, Sweden	33	4	14	18	38	4	0	1	1	6
WOG–94	Sweden	8	1	3	4	10					
1994–95	Leksand, Sweden	37	8	17	25	38	4	1	3	4	27
WC–95	Sweden	8	0	2	2	12					
1995–96	Leksand, Sweden	34	5	17	22	24	5	0	4	4	2
1996–97	Leksand, Sweden	38	8	13	21	42	9	2	1	3	4
1997–98	Leksand, Sweden	38	7	10	17	34	4	0	0	0	12
	Sweden Totals	442	94	158	252	584	38	6	13	19	76
	NHL Totals	552	85	259	344	482	80	11	26	37	97
	WOG/WEC/CCup/WC Totals	67	5	22	27	68					

Won WOG (1994)
Won WEC (1991)
Won Stanley Cup (1982, 1983)
Sweden Champion (1979)

Bengt-Ake **Gustafsson**

Bengt-Ake Gustafsson is still considered one of the Washington Capitals' all-time best forwards.

Bengt-Ake Gustafsson was a sturdy and powerful forward with a broad chest and short legs that made him hard to knock down in a skirmish. He always skated upright, never losing sight of the puck and ignoring the opposition's hits and hooks.

Gustafsson was a natural leader and his teammates took their cues from him. Born in Karlskoga, Sweden, he made his debut with the local hockey club and then joined Farjestad. His commitment to hockey is evidenced by a successful 20-year playing career both at home and abroad. He remains one of Sweden's most renowned hockey players.

After the 1979 World Championship in Moscow, Gustafsson was invited to Canada to play for the Edmonton Oilers. He also appeared in a number of WHA playoff games with future star Wayne Gretzky.

In 1986, while he was playing for the Washington Capitals, an injured knee forced him to return to Sweden. He was 30 years old and not about to let the injury end his career. He started over again, joining the minor-league Bofors, Farjestad's farm club. There he re-established himself as a speedy forward but wasn't invited to join the national team. Tre Kronor's head coach at the time, Leif Bork, didn't think he was fit enough, but his replacement, veteran coach Tommy Sandlin, had a different opinion and recruited Gustafsson. It turned out to be a prophetic decision.

At the 1987 World Championship in Vienna, Tre Kronor captured the gold after a 25-year interruption. Gustafsson was one of the team's key players. The veteran's performance attracted the attention of Washington Capitals managers and Gustafsson returned to the NHL to play for two more seasons. The Swede is still considered one of the Capitals' all-time best forwards.

In the spring of 1989 Gustafsson again returned to Sweden, this time playing for Farjestad until 1993. He then signed a two-year contract with Austria's Feldkirch but stayed for

Gustafsson, Bengt-Ake
RW, 6´, 185 lbs, b: Karlskoga, Sweden, 3/23/1958

Season	Club, League	Regular Season					Playoffs				
		GP	G	A	Pts	PIM	GP	G	A	Pts	PIM
1977–78	Farjestad, Sweden	32	15	10	25	10	7	2	6	8	10
1978–79	Farjestad, Sweden	32	13	11	24	10	3	2	0	2	4
WEC–79	Sweden	8	4	2	6	0					
1978–79	Edmonton Oilers, WHA						2	1	2	3	0
1979–80	Washington Capitals, NHL	80	22	38	60	17					
1980–81	Washington Capitals, NHL	72	21	34	55	26					
WEC–81	Sweden	6	3	1	4	8					
1981–82	Washington Capitals, NHL	70	26	34	60	40					
1982–83	Washington Capitals, NHL	67	22	42	64	16	4	0	1	1	4
WEC–83	Sweden	10	2	7	9	6					
1983–84	Washington Capitals, NHL	69	32	43	75	16	5	2	3	5	0
CCup–84	Sweden	5	1	3	4	2					
1984–85	Washington Capitals, NHL	51	14	29	43	8	5	1	3	4	0
1985–86	Washington Capitals, NHL	70	23	52	75	26					
1986–87	Bofors, Sweden	28	16	26	42	22					
WEC–87	Sweden	10	3	8	11	4					
CCup–87	Sweden	6	3	0	3	4					
1987–88	Washington Capitals, NHL	78	18	36	54	29	14	4	9	13	6
1988–89	Washington Capitals, NHL	72	18	51	69	18	4	2	3	5	6
1989–90	Farjestad, Sweden	37	22	24	46	14	10	4	10	14	18
1990–91	Farjestad, Sweden	37	9	21	30	6	8	3	6	9	2
WEC–91	Sweden	10	0	5	5	6					
1991–92	Farjestad, Sweden	35	12	20	32	30	6	2	5	7	2
OWG–92	Sweden	8	0	1	1	0					
1992–93	Farjestad, Sweden	40	17	14	31	32	3	0	1	1	2
1993–94	Feldkirch, Austria	54	20	43	63	24					
1994–95	Feldkirch, Austria	41	21	42	63	22	13	9	13	22	2
1995–96	Feldkirch, Austria	36	20	46	66	12	4	1	5	6	2
1996–97	Feldkirch, Austria	52	24	54	78	10					
1997–98	Feldkirch, Austria	46	10	30	40	16					
	Sweden Totals	241	104	126	230	124	37	13	28	41	38
	WHA Totals						2	1	2	3	0
	NHL Totals	629	196	359	555	196	32	9	19	28	16
	OWG/WEC/CCup Totals	63	16	27	43	30					

Won WEC (1987, 1991)
Austria Champion (1994, 1995, 1996, 1997)

five seasons as a player and one as a coach. While with Feldkirch, he won five Austrian national championships and in 1998 became a Euroleague Cup winner. At 40, Gustafsson was voted one of the game's best players and he and his Farjestad teammate, Tomas Rundqvist, were the first Swedes to win the Euroleague Cup, a record that still holds.

Gustafsson is a double world champion. He played 117 games for Tre Kronor and is number 130 on Sweden's "Great Men" list. Today he works for a Swiss hockey club and hopes some day to coach a Swedish team.

Bengt-Ake Gustafsson (left) was one of Sweden's key players when his country won gold at the 1987 World Championship.

Jari Kurri

Symbolically, at least, Jari Kurri started his career with the Toronto Maple Leafs back in 1970 when he joined the Jokerit Helsinki junior development system, the Canada League. The league brought together over a thousand five- to 15-year-olds from the various suburbs of Helsinki under the banner of the Jokerit name. Each participating team had to adopt the name of an NHL club.

In order to qualify, coach Leo Virmanen required that each new boy skate around the ice with his son Matti, who was the best skater in the group. Jari did sufficiently well to be picked for the team, and so he began his fairytale story of association with title-winning teams. Three years later, with Kurri playing on the same line with Matti Virmanen—currently the GM for Jokerit—they won the national D-level junior championship. The victory was a first for the capital city area in junior hockey, which at the time was dominated by provincial teams, with Tampere as the hub.

In those days, the availability of ice time was limited but it was much easier to find outside the Finnish metropolis. Playing on indoor rinks was only a pipe dream for these boys. Three years later they won the Junior C title under mentor Pentti Katainen, Kurri's coach for many years at the junior level and today a scout for Atlanta. Kurri led the way with 65 goals in 58 games, the first of a long string of successes in his career. The team's success inspired a lot of people associated with it. Eleven of the boys from his first team still work in hockey, and Leo Virmanen still works with the juniors as general manager of the Jokerit Junior A team.

Jari Kurri became the first Finn to make the Hockey Hall of Fame on November 12, 2001.

Kurri's prowess on the club level quickly came to the attention of the junior national team. During the Christmas holidays in 1977, he played his first international game against Poland for the under-17 team. In the six-nation tournament, Finland placed second to Sweden, the only team to beat them. Kurri scored five goals in the five games. The following season the under-18 team was to play in the European Junior Championship on home ice in Helsinki. The Finnish Ice Hockey Association was employing a new strategy of using younger coaches, who they felt would fit better with the young team. They chose Alpo Suhonen, currently head coach with the Chicago Blackhawks, and Rauno Korpi, who led Tappara Tampere to a number of national titles.

Their opposition was the practically unbeatable Soviets, led that year by Igor Larionov and Vladimir Krutov. Going into the last game, both teams were undefeated. The Russians made an arrangement with the directors that, should the game be a tie after regulation time, rather than going into sudden death straight away, a full 20-minute overtime period would be played. They were counting on their traditionally superior physical condition to win the day if necessary. And they did.

The game ended in a 3–3 tie. With 90 seconds remaining in the fourth period, defender Yevgeny Popikhin (currently a coach in Switzerland) gave the Soviets a 5–4 lead with his second marker in a row. Finnish goalie Jari Paavola was pulled and the team, with 15 seconds remaining on the clock and an extra player, went on the attack. Center Jarmo Makitalo spotted defender Juha Huikari and fed him a perfect pass, which he converted into the tying goal. During the break, the coaches encouraged the players by saying the Russians were even more tired than they were. At the start of sudden-death overtime, the young Finnish players moved into the offensive zone and bombarded Russian goalie Dmitri Saprykin. Picking up a rebound, Kurri skated behind the net and fed the puck to Timo Blomqvist on the blue line and Blomqvist fired a hard shot that Saprykhin couldn't control. Kurri was first on the rebound again and put it in the net after only a minute and 42 seconds of play.

History was made, and Kurri had passed the first of many milestones he set in Finnish hockey. Until that moment, Finland had been a nation of individualists in sport. Now, for the first time in European or international competition, a team had won the title.

Two years later, in the under-20 World Championship, the Soviets got their revenge and Kurri and his teammates had to be satisfied with silver. Kurri won only two more medals with the national team, a silver medal in the 1994 World Championship in Italy and the classic bronze at the 1998 Olympics in Nagano. The medal game in Japan is still considered the greatest ever by Finland, as the team stole the win from a Canadian team that included all the best players from the NHL. In this game, Kurri opened the scoring early in the first period to set the stage for a 3–2 victory.

The next chapter in Kurri's life was the transition to the Edmonton Oilers and the NHL. When he joined the Oilers in the fall of 1980, he spoke very limited English. It was a stroke of luck that two of his teammates, Matti Hagman and Risto Siltanen, were from Finland and could make him feel comfortable and show him the ropes. Nineteen games into the season, he was placed on Wayne Gretzky's line

Kurri, Jari
RW, 6´1˝, 195 lbs, b: Helsinki, Finland, 5/18/1960

Season	Club, League	Regular Season					Playoffs				
		GP	G	A	Pts	PIM	GP	G	A	Pts	PIM
1977–78	Jokerit Helsinki, Finland	29	2	9	11	12					
1978–79	Jokerit Helsinki, Finland	33	16	14	30	12					
1979–80	Jokerit Helsinki, Finland	33	23	16	39	22	6	7	2	9	13
OWG–80	Finland	7	2	1	3	6					
1980–81	Edmonton Oilers, NHL	75	32	43	75	40	9	5	7	12	4
CCup–81	Finland	5	0	1	1	0					
1981–82	Edmonton Oilers, NHL	71	32	54	86	32	5	2	5	7	10
WEC–82	Finland	7	4	3	7	2					
1982–83	Edmonton Oilers, NHL	80	45	59	104	22	16	8	15	23	8
1983–84	Edmonton Oilers, NHL	64	52	61	113	14	19	14	14	28	13
1984–85	Edmonton Oilers, NHL	73	71	64	135	30	18	19	12	31	6
1985–86	Edmonton Oilers, NHL	78	68	63	131	22	10	2	10	12	4
1986–87	Edmonton Oilers, NHL	79	54	54	108	41	21	15	10	25	20
RV'87	NHL All-Stars	2	1	1	2	0					
CCup–87	Finland	5	1	1	2	4					
1987–88	Edmonton Oilers, NHL	80	43	53	96	30	19	14	17	31	12
1988–89	Edmonton Oilers, NHL	76	44	58	102	69	7	3	5	8	6
WEC–89	Finland	7	5	4	9	4					
1989–90	Edmonton Oilers, NHL	78	33	60	93	48	22	10	15	25	18
1990–91	Milano Devils, Italy	30	27	48	75	6	10	10	12	22	2
WEC–91	Finland	10	6	6	12	2					
CCup–91	Finland	6	2	0	2	7					
1991–92	Los Angeles Kings, NHL	73	23	37	60	24	4	1	2	3	4
1992–93	Los Angeles Kings, NHL	82	27	60	87	38	24	9	8	17	12
1993–94	Los Angeles Kings, NHL	81	31	46	77	48					
WC–94	Finland	8	4	6	10	2					
1994–95	Jokerit Helsinki, Finland	20	10	9	19	10					
	Los Angeles Kings, NHL	38	10	19	29	24					
1995–96	Los Angeles Kings, NHL	57	17	23	40	37					
	New York Rangers, NHL	14	1	4	5	2	11	3	5	8	2
WCup–96	Finland	4	1	0	1	0					
1996–97	Anaheim Mighty Ducks, NHL	82	13	22	35	12	11	1	2	3	4
1997–98	Colorado Avalanche, NHL	70	5	17	22	12	4	0	0	0	0
OWG–98	Finland	6	1	4	5	2					
	Finland Totals	115	51	48	99	56	6	7	2	9	13
	OWG/WEC/WC/CCup/RV'87/WCup	67	27	27	54	29					
	NHL Totals	1251	601	797	1398	545	200	106	127	233	123

NHL First All-Star Team (1985, 1987)
NHL Second All-Star Team (1984, 1986, 1989)
Won Lady Byng Trophy (1985)
Won Stanley Cup (1984, 1985, 1987, 1988, 1990)

and a very productive operation was born. But things didn't progress without a hitch, despite Kurri's starting off with a hat-trick, all assisted by number 99. Two games later, Kurri began a long streak of 17 games without a goal.

Four seasons later—in his own words—his "dream of dreams" came true when the Oilers won the Stanley Cup. Kurri was the first Finn ever to enjoy that honor, and to do it in style as the top goal scorer in the playoffs. Barry Frazer, who had a long association with the Oilers in many roles including scouting director, was responsible for picking Kurri in the draft on advice from his European scout, Matti Vaisanen. Vaisanen was of the opinion that Kurri's determination and professionalism opened up a lot of opportunities for Finns in the NHL.

In 1985 the Oilers won their second cup, their first back-to-back Stanley Cup, and two years after that, Kurri set another new milestone. Edmonton had won their third Cup in four years and Kurri made it into the history books by scoring the Cup-winning goal. It happened in the seventh and deciding game against the Philadelphia Flyers on May 31, 1987. Tikkanen won the puck in the corner and gave it to Gretzky, who passed it to Kurri as he was zeroing in from the blue line. Kurri put the puck between Peter Zezel's legs and into the lower right corner of goalie Ron Hextall's net at 14:59 of the second period. Less than two and a half minutes before the end of regulation play, Glenn Anderson established the 3–1 final score and the hometown Edmonton fans erupted.

Jari Kurri was the first Finn to win the Stanley Cup.

Jari Kurri was to enjoy Stanley Cup wins on two more occasions—the following season in 1988 and again in 1990. The last one was without Gretsky. Instead, it was Mark Messier and Kurri who lead the team to post-season success. The win also marked the end of an Edmonton Oilers dynasty for which eight other Finns had sported the drop of oil on their jersey. The most notable among them was Esa Tikkanen. The others were Risto Siltanen, Matti Hagman, Raimo Summanen, Reijo Ruotsalainen, Kari Makkonen, Risto Jalo and Kari Jalonen. Both Ruotsalainen and Jalonen were on the legendary 1978 European Junior Championship winning team.

Kurri's remaining years in the NHL were a lot less exciting for a player with two First Team and three Second Team All-Star selections, a Lady Byng Trophy and participation in eight NHL All-Star games as well as the 1987 Rendez-Vous series with the North Americans' archrivals, the Soviets. One achievement that he remembers fondly is being the league's top goal scorer in 1986 and ending a four-year domination of this category by Wayne Gretzky.

In 1990 he quit the NHL to play for Milan in the Italian league. He wanted to be traded to L.A. to play with Gretzky, but Edmonton wasn't prepared to release him to another rival in their own division. A year later, however, he was back in the NHL, and right where he wanted to be—playing for the Los Angeles Kings. The year caused him to give up his lead in overall points as the all-time top European to Peter Stastny, but he reclaimed the title a couple of seasons later. And the Kings didn't duplicate the success of Edmonton, but it wasn't for lack of trying. Kurri had three good seasons with the Kings and a decent fourth, though it was considerably shortened by the lockout, during which he returned to Finland and Jokerit.

The Finnish interlude produced yet another title as the powerhouse Jokerit qualified for the European Cup finals in Helsinki. With Kurri and Teemu Selanne in the lineup, Jokerit won the tournament and Kurri topped it off with the scoring crown, amassing nine points in four games. His

Jari Kurri had three good seasons with the Los Angeles Kings and a decent fourth, though it was considerably shortened by the 1994–95 lockout.

only title with Jokerit since his junior days, it brought back fond memories.

To round out what was claimed to be the most dynamic duo in the history of the NHL, L.A.'s problem was to find a left winger for the Gretzky–Kurri line. Many players had had a go at it in Edmonton, including Brett Callighen, Dave Semenko, Dave Lumley, Glenn Anderson, Czech player Jaroslav Pouzar, Dave Hunter, Raimo Summanen, Mike Krushelnyski and Esa Tikkanen.

Gretzky admits that it couldn't have been easy for those guys. When the understanding between him and Kurri was at its best, he would always prefer to give the puck to Kurri if he had the choice. On October 15, 1989, Gretzky overtook Gordie Howe as the all-time scoring leader with his 1,851st point. Kurri played a role in just over one-third of his linemate's scoring efforts, or 633 times, by scoring the goal on an assist from Gretzky, assisting on Gretzky's goals or getting joint assists.

Kurri is now working as a television color commentator for the Finnish league. Modest person that he is, he isn't making much of a fuss about the next milestone for him and hockey in Finland.

Kurri was inducted to the Hockey Hall of Fame on November 12, 2001, to become the first Finnish-born player so honored. Soon after, the head coach of Finland's national team, Hannu Aravirta, named Kurri as an assistant coach for the 2002 Olympics in Salt Lake City. Though there had been high hopes going into the Games of at least duplicating the bronze medal in Nagano in 1998, the Finns failed to win a medal in Salt Lake. Even so, on February 21, 2002, athletes participating in the Winter Games elected Kurri to the prestigious IOC Athletes' Commission, which has a mandate of four years.

Pelle Lindbergh

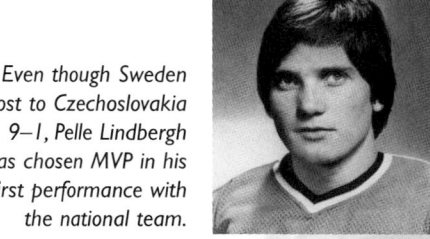

Even though Sweden lost to Czechoslovakia 9–1, Pelle Lindbergh was chosen MVP in his first performance with the national team.

Pelle Lindbergh was considered the most talented of Sweden's outstanding crop of goaltenders. As a seven-year-old boy, he announced to his skeptical elders, "I'm going to be a professional," and the determined youth resolutely improved his hockey skills until he realized his dream.

He began his hockey career with Stockholm's Hammarby, long known for sending able players to the best teams in Sweden, among them Djurgarden and AIK in Stockholm, where Lindbergh was born on May 24, 1959. In 1979, while still a junior, Lindbergh was spotted by Team Sweden's coach, Bengt Ohlsson, and made his debut with the national team against Czechoslovakia in Prague on May 6. The Swedes lost that game 9–1, but Lindbergh was chosen as the team's MVP.

The young goalie played well at the Olympic Games in Lake Placid in 1980. Hockey fans remember the exciting game on February 20 against Czechoslovakia. The Czechs fired 36 shots on goal and the Swedes returned with only 16 shots. The superiority of the Czech players was clear to anyone watching, but the Swedes won 4–2. Goaltender Lindbergh and forward Mats Naslund were outstanding that day.

That autumn, Lindbergh turned pro. It was a difficult beginning for the young Swede. He was sent to Portland, Maine, a farm club for the Philadelphia Flyers. Not all Swedish hockey players taken on by North American farm clubs could withstand the test, and many couldn't overcome the psychological barrier that existed for them. In the two years he spent in Portland, Lindbergh was voted best rookie in the AHL and the league's MVP.

The peak of Pelle Lindbergh's career came on June 13, 1985, when he became the first non-North American goaltender to receive the Vezina Trophy.

Lindbergh joined the Flyers in the 1981–82 season and played eight games. He was voted the best rookie goaltender in the NHL and was included on the NHL All-Rookie Team. The only Swede to accomplish this previously had been Borje Salming, a defenseman for the Toronto Maple Leafs.

The peak of Lindbergh's career came on June 13, 1985, when he was awarded the Vezina Trophy. He was the first foreign goaltender to receive the award, which is the highest honor bestowed on a goalie by the NHL. Long before Dominik Hasek appeared on the scene, Sweden's Pelle Lindbergh captivated North American hockey fans. Legendary Canadian goaltender Jacques Plante of the Montreal Canadiens once said of Lindbergh, "I've never seen a goalie with such fast legs."

Everything pointed to an outstanding career for Lindbergh. He signed a six-year contract with the Flyers and all doors were open to him. A month after receiving the Vezina Trophy, he bought himself the Porsche he had always wanted and was happier than he'd ever been. But, tragically, he hit a concrete wall while driving his car in New Jersey. Reports said there was alcohol in the 27-year-old goaltender's blood.

Lindbergh lay in a coma in the intensive care unit at the John F. Kennedy Hospital in Stratford until his parents made the difficult decision to ask doctors to disconnect the artificial life-support system that was keeping their son alive.

Lindbergh, Pelle
G, 5′9″, 165 lbs, b: Stockholm, Sweden, 5/24/1959, d: 11/10/1985

Season	Club, League	Regular Season				Playoffs			
		GP	Mins	GA	Avg	GP	Mins	GA	Avg
1978–79	AIK, Sweden	6	360	38	6.33				
WEC–79	Sweden	6	360	38	6.33				
1979–80	AIK, Sweden	32	1866	106	3.41				
OWG–80	Sweden	5	300	18	3.60				
1980–81	Maine Marines, AHL	51	3035	165	3.26	20	1120	66	3.54
CCup–81	Sweden	2	92	9	6.00				
1981–82	Philadelphia Flyers, NHL	8	480	35	4.38				
	Maine Marines, AHL	25	1505	83	3.31				
1982–83	Philadelphia Flyers, NHL	40	2333	116	2.98	3	180	18	6.00
WEC–83	Sweden	9	540	27	3.00				
1983–84	Springfield Indians, AHL	4	240	12	3.00				
	Philadelphia Flyers, NHL	36	1999	135	4.05	2	26	3	6.92
1984–85	Philadelphia Flyers, NHL	65	3858	194	3.02	18	1008	42	2.50
1985–86	Philadelphia Flyers, NHL	8	480	23	2.88				
	NHL Totals	157	9150	503	3.30	23	1214	63	3.11
	OWG/ WEC/CCup Totals	22	1292	92	4.27				

NHL First All-Star Team (1985)
Won Vezina Trophy (1985)

Michel Goulet

Michel Goulet was one of the most opportunistic scorers in NHL history.

One of the most opportunistic scorers in league history, Michel Goulet was an elite left winger during his 15-year career. He managed to score at least 20 goals in all but his last NHL year and once enjoyed a stretch of seven consecutive seasons with at least 40 goals. Although he wasn't considered a rough player, Goulet wasn't intimidated by aggressive play on the part of the opposition.

Goulet grew up on the family potato farm in Peribonka, Quebec, two hours north of Quebec City. There was no organized hockey in his area, so he only played a few planned matches each winter against nearby towns. When he was a midget player, he stole the key to the arena in neighboring Mistassini to skate in the wee hours of the morning. This was the only way he could improve, and as it turned out, he was never caught.

Goulet signed his first pro contract with the Birmingham Bulls of the World Hockey Association after a brilliant junior career with the Quebec Remparts of the QMJHL. In his last year as an amateur, he scored 73 goals and was placed on the league's Second All-Star Team. Goulet fared well as a rookie pro in Alabama's Deep South with 28 goals while taking a regular shift. Although he'd never heard English spoken in his youth, his transition was aided by rooming with fellow francophone Gaston Gingras. He worked well on a line with Rick Vaive and Rick Adduono. Vaive noted that, "Hockey is an international language and he spoke it superbly."

Following the NHL/WHA merger, Goulet was declared eligible for the 1979 Entry Draft. As one of the former WHA clubs, the Quebec Nordiques had to wait until the established NHL teams chose before they could make their first selection. Fortunately for them, Goulet was still available and they wasted no time in calling out his name.

The youngster put up excellent numbers as a rookie with 22 goals and held up well over the grind of an 80-game NHL schedule. Over the next three years, his goal-scoring increased to 32, 42 and a personal high of 57. His 13 points in 16 matches helped the Nordiques surprise many onlookers by reaching the Stanley Cup semifinals in 1982. On and off the ice, he was a quiet and understated personality. The press found him dull and some fans were perturbed when he didn't acknowledge their chants of "Gou, Gou, Gou!" But this was simply who he was, a gifted NHL star who let his performance do the talking for him. New York Islanders winger Bob Nystrom described his play as follows: "Michel's a deceptive sort of player. He's not the greatest skater in the world

Goulet, Michel
LW, 6´1″, 195 lbs, b: Peribonka, Que., 4/21/1960

Season	Club, League	Regular Season					Playoffs				
		GP	G	A	Pts	PIM	GP	G	A	Pts	PIM
1978–79	Birmingham Bulls, WHA	78	28	30	58	65					
1979–80	Quebec Nordiques, NHL	77	22	32	54	48					
1980–81	Quebec Nordiques, NHL	76	32	39	71	45	4	3	4	7	7
1981–82	Quebec Nordiques, NHL	80	42	42	84	48	16	8	5	13	6
1982–83	Quebec Nordiques, NHL	80	57	48	105	51	4	0	0	0	6
WEC–83	Canada	10	1	8	9	6					
1983–84	Quebec Nordiques, NHL	75	56	65	121	76	9	2	4	6	17
CCup–84	Canada	8	5	6	11	0					
1984–85	Quebec Nordiques, NHL	69	55	40	95	55	17	11	10	21	17
1985–86	Quebec Nordiques, NHL	75	53	51	104	64	3	1	2	3	10
1986–87	Quebec Nordiques, NHL	75	49	47	96	61	13	9	5	14	35
RV'87	NHL All-Stars	2	0	1	1	0					
CCup–87	Canada	8	2	3	5	0					
1987–88	Quebec Nordiques, NHL	80	48	58	106	56					
1988–89	Quebec Nordiques, NHL	69	26	38	64	67					
1989–90	Quebec Nordiques, NHL	57	16	29	45	42					
	Chicago Blackhawks, NHL	8	4	1	5	9	14	2	4	6	6
1990–91	Chicago Blackhawks, NHL	74	27	38	65	65					
1991–92	Chicago Blackhawks, NHL	75	22	41	62	69	9	3	4	7	6
1992–93	Chicago Blackhawks, NHL	63	23	21	44	43	3	0	1	1	0
1993–94	Chicago Blackhawks, NHL	56	16	14	30	26					
	WHA Totals	78	28	30	58	65					
	NHL Totals	1089	548	604	1152	825	92	39	39	78	110
	WEC/CCup/RV'87 Totals	28	8	18	26	6					

NHL First All-Star Team (1984, 1986, 1987)
NHL Second All-Star Team (1983, 1988)
Won CCup (1984, 1987)

and he doesn't go out of his way to bump you around, but he's a sneaky kind of guy who always seems to come out of nowhere at the right time."

Goulet's 57 goals in 1982–83 began a string of four consecutive 50-goal seasons. That spring he played on a line with Dennis Maruk and Mike Gartner while representing Canada at the World Championship, and the following year he was one of Canada's most reliable forwards at the 1984 Canada Cup tournament. This proved to be Goulet's longest pro season, as he didn't stop playing until the Nordiques were vanquished by the Philadelphia Flyers in the semifinals on May 16, 1985. The classy left winger was an almost insuperable force that post-season with 11 goals and 21 points in 17 games. All through this success, he remained in the background as the three Stastny brothers garnered most of the headlines in Quebec.

An unfortunate contract dispute delayed his return to the Nordiques at the start of the 1985–86 season. Goulet wanted his contract renegotiated, since a similar consideration had been made for Peter and Anton Stastny. The Nordiques refused at first and Goulet sat out training camp and the start of the regular season. It was a difficult period, as some of the fans began to turn against him, but all was forgotten when he returned two weeks into the schedule.

A boisterous home crowd at Le Colisee cheered Goulet when he repre-sented the NHL in the Rendez-Vous '87 exhibition series against the Soviet All-Stars. Held in place of the NHL All-Star Game, this two-game set finished dead-locked with each side gaining a victory. Later in the year he helped Canada defend its Canada Cup title in a memorable three-game finals against their archrivals from the USSR.

By the late 1980s, the Nordiques were in decline and many veterans were traded as part of a rebuilding and cost-cutting strategy. Just prior to the trading deadline in March 1990, Goulet was sent to the Chicago Blackhawks. He adjusted well to his first new team in a decade, but this change required his veteran poise; he was now playing on a tight-checking team that required him to play a defensive role while pro-viding timely scoring. Goulet thrived in this new environment, though in the summer of 1990 he was diagnosed with a condition that causes a rapid heartbeat. A complicated procedure saved his career.

Michel Goulet's 57 goals in 1982–83 began a string of four consecutive 50-goal seasons.

Goulet's 50-goal seasons on the free-skating Nordiques were a thing of the past, but he did manage three straight 20-goal seasons. On February 23, 1991, he notched a hat-trick against Minnesota to reach the 1,000-point mark. On February 16, 1992, he scored his 500th goal on a breakaway against the Calgary Flames in front of a thrilled audience at the old Chicago Stadium. And he played well when the Hawks reached the Stanley Cup finals in 1992, although they lost to the defending champion Pittsburgh Penguins.

Goulet was in the midst of another solid year in the Windy City when his life changed sud-denly. While playing the Canadiens at the Montreal Forum on March 16, 1994, he crashed into the end boards and struck his head. This resulted in a severe concussion that forced the veteran to retire and begin a difficult battle with the post-trauma symptoms. A year to the day after the acci-dent, Goulet's number was retired by the Nordiques before a cheering crowd at Le Colisee. The popular winger eventually recovered from his injury to lead a normal life and was thrilled when he was voted into the Hockey Hall of Fame along with former teammate Peter Stastny in 1998.

Glenn Anderson

"When I first started playing hockey, I hated it," Glenn Anderson said. "The first goal I ever scored was in my own net."

Glenn Anderson was one of the flying Oilers who dominated the game in the 1980s. He was a clutch performer in the playoffs, coming up with impressive numbers in important games to help his teams to six Stanley Cup titles. A speedy winger with incredible balance and a daredevil approach to crashing the net, Anderson also stands out as one of the more unusual men to play the game, skating to the tune of his own organist over 18 years of top-flight hockey.

Born in 1960, Anderson grew up in Burnaby, British Columbia, home of another future star who would one day grab headlines in Hollywood, actor Michael J. Fox. Although active as a child, Anderson didn't immediately warm to hockey. "When I first started playing hockey, I hated it. I hated getting up a 6 o'clock in the morning to go to the rink," he said. "I skated with my ankles turned in and everybody else skated the other way. The first goal I ever scored was in my own net."

When he was 12, he took up the sport again and worked hard at it. As a 17-year-old, he announced himself to the hockey world with a huge season in the British Columbia junior leagues, scoring 62 goals and totaling 131 points in just 64 games. He was outstanding the next year at the University of Denver, finishing the 1978-79 season with 55 points in 40 games as a freshman. He was selected 69th overall by the Edmonton Oilers at the 1979 Entry Draft. Anderson's objective, however, wasn't the NHL but the Olympics. He dreamed of gold medals, and he preferred to use his developing skills in the sport to see the world. He joined the Canadian national team and traveled with them throughout Europe and Asia to prepare for the 1980 Olympic Winter Games at Lake Placid, New York. Anderson earned four points in six games, but he and the Canadian team were forced to watch the American Miracle on Ice in the thrilling final game from the sidelines.

Unlike many national team members, Anderson didn't immediately rush to turn pro and play in the NHL. He returned to junior hoping the Canadian program would continue, allowing him both to travel and play the game. When it didn't, Anderson finally joined the Oilers for 58 games of the 1980–81 season. He scored 30 goals, an excellent season for a rookie, and made a much stronger impression the next season with 105 points to finish among the top 11 scorers in the league.

Anderson's Edmonton teammates called him "Mork," a reference to a character in the television series *Mork and Mindy* starring Robin Williams as a flaky alien. Anderson disliked the name, though his actions and personality most certainly set him apart from the crowd. On one trip to Europe, he brought all of his hockey equipment but decided that one set of clothes would be enough. On an exhibition trip to Houston, the Oilers were given a tour of NASA. "I can relate to outer space," Anderson told a reporter. "I've been there before. In fact, I think it would be closer to home."

A nickname that better suited his play on the ice was "Kamikaze." He launched himself at the net on off-wing rushes, using his balance to stay upright even while defenders were still hanging onto him. He was consistently near the top of the NHL in scoring and thrived in the playoffs, scoring overtime winners and game-clinching goals in each of the Oilers' five marches to the Stanley Cup in the 1980s and early 1990s. His temper and stickwork also earned him some names that were much nastier than "Mork." Even his own teammates agreed that Anderson was one of the dirtiest players in the game. Several times he was suspended by the league, including an eight-game benching for clipping Winnipeg's Dave Silk in the ear with his blade in 1986.

Off ice, tragedy struck Anderson in his own backyard in 1988. During a party at his home, his long-time friend George Varvis was found at the bottom of the backyard pool. He was revived and taken to the hospital, apparently recovering, but his condition worsened and he was put on life support. A few days later he died, and media attention focused on Anderson and the circumstances of the accident. No charges were laid, but Anderson was so unnerved by the coverage of the tragedy that he refused to speak to reporters for two years.

Anderson's play remained steady on the ice and he had 22 points in 22 playoff games when the Oilers won the Cup in 1990. Two years later he was involved in a blockbuster trade that saw some of the last pieces of the Oiler dynasty, himself and goalie Grant Fuhr, moved to the Toronto Maple Leafs. Anderson became one of the Leafs' top scorers and once again was a playoff leader as Toronto made it to within one game of the Cup finals in 1993. Ironically, in game six of the semifinals against Los Angeles, it was having Anderson in the penalty box for a vicious hit that helped former Oilers teammate Wayne Gretzky score the overtime winner to force a deciding seventh game.

In the middle of the 1993–94 season, Anderson asked the Maple Leafs organization for permission to play in the 1994 Lillehammer Olympics. He'd negotiated the option to play for Canada into his contract and the Leafs agreed to take his case to the NHL, for he'd have to clear waivers first. Anderson even received support from an 11-year-old girl, Tiffany Williams, who collected a petition with 5,000 signatures requesting that Anderson be allowed to play. Accompanied by a Toronto politician, she presented the petition to NHL commissioner Gary Bettman in New York. Anderson was turned down by the commissioner, who argued with the politician in front of television cameras after announcing his decision that no player could bypass the waiver rule.

Anderson was traded to the New York Rangers for Mike Gartner just before the 1994 playoffs and joined Mark Messier and other ex-Oilers in winning the Stanley Cup in those playoffs. Of his three goals, two were game winners. At the time, only Maurice Richard had more overtime playoff goals and only Messier, Gretzky and Jari Kurri had more playoff points.

Anderson's approach to the sport was ideologically different from that of many of his peers. More European in outlook, he never missed a chance to play in international competition, and later in his career he chose to play in such locales as Germany, Finland and

Anderson, Glenn
RW, 6´1˝, 190 lbs, b: Vancouver, B.C., 10/2/1960

Season	Club, League	Regular Season					Playoffs				
		GP	G	A	Pts	PIM	GP	G	A	Pts	PIM
1978–79	University of Denver, WCHA	40	26	29	55	58					
1979–80	Seattle Breakers, WHL	7	5	5	10	4	2	0	1	1	0
OWG–80	Canada	6	2	2	4	4					
1980–81	Edmonton Oilers, NHL	58	30	23	53	24	9	5	7	12	12
1981–82	Edmonton Oilers, NHL	80	38	67	105	71	5	2	5	7	8
1982–83	Edmonton Oilers, NHL	72	48	56	104	70	16	10	10	20	32
1983–84	Edmonton Oilers, NHL	80	54	45	99	65	19	6	11	17	35
CCup–84	Canada	8	1	4	5	16					
1984–85	Edmonton Oilers, NHL	80	42	39	81	69	18	10	16	26	38
1985–86	Edmonton Oilers, NHL	72	54	48	102	90	10	8	3	11	14
1986–87	Edmonton Oilers, NHL	80	35	38	73	65	21	14	13	27	59
RV'87	NHL All-Stars	2	1	0	1	2					
CCup–87	Canada	7	2	1	3	4					
1987–88	Edmonton Oilers, NHL	80	38	50	88	58	19	9	16	25	49
1988–89	Edmonton Oilers, NHL	79	16	48	64	93	7	1	2	3	8
WEC–89	Canada	6	2	2	4	4					
1989–90	Edmonton Oilers, NHL	73	34	38	72	107	22	10	12	22	20
1990–91	Edmonton Oilers, NHL	74	24	31	55	59	18	6	7	13	41
1991–92	Toronto Maple Leafs, NHL	72	24	33	57	100					
WC–92	Canada	6	2	1	3	16					
1992–93	Toronto Maple Leafs, NHL	76	22	43	65	117	21	7	11	18	31
1993–94	Toronto Maple Leafs, NHL	73	17	18	35	50					
	New York Rangers, NHL	12	4	2	6	12	23	3	3	6	42
1994–95	Augsburg, Germany	5	6	2	8	10					
	Lukko, Finland	4	1	1	2	0					
	St. Louis Blues, NHL	36	12	14	26	37	6	1	1	2	49
1995–96	Augsburg, Germany	9	5	3	8	48					
	Edmonton Oilers, NHL	17	4	6	10	27					
	St. Louis Blues, NHL	15	2	2	4	6	11	1	4	5	6
1996–97	Chaux-de-Fonds, Switzerland	23	14	15	29	103					
	OWG/WEC/WC/CCup/RV'87 Totals	35	10	10	20	46					
	NHL Totals	1129	498	601	1099	1120	225	93	121	214	442

Won Stanley Cup (1984, 1985, 1987, 1988, 1990, 1994)
Won CCup (1984, 1987)

Glenn Anderson (right) became one of the Leafs' top scorers and was once again a playoff leader as Toronto came within a game of the Cup finals in 1993.

Switzerland instead of the more lucrative NHL. From 1994 through 1996, he did suit up for more than 60 games over two years with the St. Louis Blues and Edmonton Oilers, but in each case left quickly. He retired in 1996.

"I see all of this as an opportunity to broaden my horizons. The more knowledge I can gain about the world, the better," Anderson said. "You can't put a price tag on that. Life is really short. You should experience it to its fullest."

Neal Broten

An outstanding playmaker, Neal Broten was one of the first players born and trained in America to star in the NHL.

An outstanding playmaking center, Neal Broten was one of the first American-born and -trained players to star in the NHL. He also excelled wearing the national uniform of the United States. Neal was the eldest of the three Broten brothers who skated in the league at the same time.

As an amateur, he played hockey with the University of Minnesota in 1978–79. After helping the Golden Gophers win the NCAA championship, the Minnesota North Stars chose him 42nd overall in the NHL Entry Draft. Many teams passed on him because he wasn't big and wasn't trained in the Canadian junior system.

Broten debuted on the international stage at the 1978 world junior tournament with his brother Aaron. He devoted the entire 1979–80 season to the U.S. national program, averaging a point a game in 55 matches. The high point of this experience took place at the 1980 Lake Placid Olympics, where he contributed to the Miracle on Ice gold medal victory. Broten's unselfish play and willingness to fill a checking role was a huge boost to the team's fortunes. He returned to college in 1980–81 and was named a First Team All-American and the recipient of the Hobey Baker Memorial Award as the top collegiate player in the country.

Following a late-season trial with the North Stars in 1980–81, he aided the club's drive to the Stanley Cup finals. During his first full season, in 1981–82, he scored 98 points playing on a line with Dino Ciccarelli and Tom McCarthy. The nifty playmaker made history in 1985–86 by becoming the first U.S.-born player to top the 100-point mark. During this time, his line with Ciccarelli and Scott Bjugstad was one of the most consistent in the league. Broten's 76 assists broke the team record and helped Bjugstad score a career high of 43 goals and Ciccarelli register a 44-goal season. The following year, Brian MacLellan joined the line in place of Bjugstad.

Broten developed a reputation as an elite playmaker who raised the performance level of his linemates. Rangers coach Ted Sator said: "Let's face it, Neal Broten is a world-class player. You have to give him full credit. Not only does he create a lot of scoring plays, but he also makes the kind of plays the fans might remember after the game and ask, 'Who made that play?'"

In 1991 the classy veteran helped the North Stars reach the Stanley Cup finals for the second time. During the final series loss to the Pittsburgh Penguins, Broten fired in three goals. His hard-working line with Stewart Gavin and Gaeten Duchesne checked the top players on the opposition throughout the team's unexpected playoff run.

He remained with the franchise when it relocated to Dallas in 1993. Early in the abbreviated 1994–95 schedule, he was traded to New Jersey. On April 28, 1995, when he suited up against the Florida Panthers, Broten became the first U.S.-born player to play in 1,000 regular-season games. That spring the rejuvenated veteran scored 19 points in 20 playoff contests to earn his first Stanley Cup ring. Observers noted a spark in Broten's skates that helped him play some of the finest hockey in his career. His speed and opportunistic scoring were a perfect fit with the Devils' style.

Broten ended his playing career in 1997 after a busy season in which he played in New Jersey, Los Angeles and Dallas. One of the most popular players in the history of the Minnesota/Dallas franchise, Broten retired as the career leader in games played, assists and points. Overall, he scored 923 regular-season points while serving as one of the leaders of the "American" invasion of the NHL in the 1980s.

On April 28, 1995, Neal Broten (number 9) became the first American-born player to play in 1,000 regular-season games, and later that spring he scored 19 points in 20 playoff games to earn his first Stanley Cup ring.

Broten, Neal
C, 5´9˝, 175 lbs, b: Roseau, MN, 11/29/1959

Season	Club, League	Regular Season					Playoffs				
		GP	G	A	Pts	PIM	GP	G	A	Pts	PIM
1978–79	University of Minnesota, WCHA	40	21	50	71	18					
OWG–80	USA	7	2	1	3	2					
1980–81	University of Minnesota, WCHA	36	17	54	71	56					
	Minnesota North Stars, NHL	3	2	0	2	12	19	1	7	8	9
CCup–81	USA	6	3	2	5	0					
1981–82	Minnesota North Stars, NHL	73	38	60	98	42	4	0	2	2	0
1982–83	Minnesota North Stars, NHL	79	32	45	77	43	9	1	6	7	10
1983–84	Minnesota North Stars, NHL	76	28	61	89	43	16	5	5	10	4
CCup–84	USA	6	3	1	4	4					
1984–85	Minnesota North Stars, NHL	80	19	37	56	39	9	2	5	7	10
1985–86	Minnesota North Stars, NHL	80	29	76	105	47	5	3	2	5	2
1986–87	Minnesota North Stars, NHL	46	18	35	53	33					
1987–88	Minnesota North Stars, NHL	54	9	30	39	32					
1988–89	Minnesota North Stars, NHL	68	18	38	56	57	5	2	2	4	4
1989–90	Minnesota North Stars, NHL	80	23	62	85	45	7	2	2	4	18
WEC–90	USA	8	1	5	6	4					
1990–91	Minnesota North Stars, NHL	79	13	56	69	26	23	9	13	22	6
1991–92	Preussen, Germany	8	3	5	8	2					
	Minnesota North Stars, NHL	76	8	26	34	16	7	1	5	6	2
1992–93	Minnesota North Stars, NHL	82	12	21	33	22					
1993–94	Dallas Stars, NHL	79	17	35	52	62	9	2	1	3	6
1994–95	Dallas Stars, NHL	17	0	4	4	4					
	New Jersey Devils, NHL	30	8	20	28	20	20	7	12	19	6
1995–96	New Jersey Devils, NHL	55	7	26	23	14					
1996–97	New Jersey Devils, NHL	3	0	1	1	0					
	Los Angeles Kings, NHL	19	0	4	4	0					
	Phoenix Roadrunners, IHL	11	3	3	6	4					
	Dallas Stars, NHL	20	8	7	15	12	2	0	1	1	0
	NHL Totals	1099	289	634	923	569	135	35	63	98	77
	OWG/WEC/CCup Totals	27	9	9	18	10					

Won Lester Patrick Trophy (1998)
Won OWG (1980)
Won Stanley Cup (1995)

A HISTORY OF WORLD HOCKEY

Wayne Gretzky

Born in Brantford, Ontario, on January 26, 1961, Wayne Gretzky lived perhaps the most famous childhood of any athlete. When he was six years old, his father, Walter, built a rink in the family's backyard, and it was there that Wayne skated for hours on end, every day, practising his skating, shooting and stickhandling and learning everything about the game from his dad. "It was for self-preservation," Walter admitted. "I got sick of taking him to the park and sitting there for hours freezing to death." From the time he was six, he played many leagues above his age. He scored only

Wayne Gretzky's (left) office.

one goal in his first year, when he was playing with 10-year-olds, but each season his skills increased dramatically and he soon set scoring records that seemed preposterous, notably a 378-goal season in his last year in peewee in Brantford. As he progressed, he earned the nickname "the White Tornado," because he wore white hockey gloves and because of his speed and skill. Each year he played at a higher level, and each year he maintained his superiority.

When he was 14, he decided that the pressure of playing in his small home town was too great and jealous players and parents made him unhappy. He decided to move to Toronto, and there he played for the Toronto Nats. When he was 15, he played three games with the Peterborough Petes in the Ontario Hockey Association as an emergency call-up, and even then the Great One impressed scouts with his abilities despite his small stature and youth. The next year, 1977–78, was his only full season in the OHA, and he finished second to Bobby Smith in the scoring race while playing for the Sault Ste. Marie Greyhounds. It was there that he first adopted the number 99 when his favorite number 9 was already taken by fourth-year player Brian Gualazzi. Gretzky also represented Canada internationally for the first time in January 1978 at the World Junior Championship in Quebec City. As a 16-year-old, he led the whole tournament in scoring and was named the top center. Ironically, the coaching staff invited him to the team's training camp only because he was leading the league in scoring; they thought he was otherwise too small to even make the team. After missing a month of league play with the juniors, he returned to the OHA—and he was still leading in scoring.

In the fall of 1978, Gretzky joined the Indianapolis Racers after signing a personal services contract with Nelson Skalbania, the team's owner. Gretzky had wanted to join the NHL, but the league's draft age was 20 and Gretzky didn't think it would help to play three years in the OHA until he was drafted. The Racers folded after only eight games, however, and Skalbania sold Gretzky to the Edmonton Oilers. In Edmonton, under coach Glen Sather, he became the most dominant player in the history of the game. He made records that are the stuff of legend, and his play was unlike anything the league had ever seen. He was surrounded by phenomenal talent in Mark Messier, Glenn Anderson, Jari Kurri, Paul Coffey, and Grant Fuhr in goal, and as a team they set virtually every scoring record that currently stands.

Wayne Gretzky (left).

When Gretzky first arrived in Edmonton, he stayed with coach Sather, who immediately promised him that he'd one day be captain of the team and win the Stanley Cup. Clearly, Sather knew how good Gretzky could be. In his first full NHL season, Gretzky tied Marcel Dionne for the scoring race but lost the Art Ross Trophy because Dionne had more goals. He couldn't win the Calder Trophy because the NHL had declared that players from the WHA weren't rookies, but he did win the Hart Trophy, the first time a first-year player was so honored. The next year, 1980–81, he won his first of seven straight scoring titles and broke Bobby Orr's assists record with 109. The year after, he shattered Phil Esposito's record of 76 goals (a record many thought was unbreakable) by scoring 92 times, a record that itself will surely stand the test of time. En route, he also scored an incredible 50 goals in the first 39 games of the season, including five in the historic 39th game. He also registered 212 points, the first of four times he'd score more than 200, and to this day he's the only player to have done so even once (Mario Lemieux came closest when he scored 199 in 1988–89).

His style was unique and almost impenetrable. The area behind the opposition goal was dubbed "Gretzky's office" because it was from there that he made so many perfect passes for goals. He was equally known for using the trailing man on rushes rather than a man skating ahead of him. Gretzky would come in over the blue line and then curl, waiting for a defenseman, often Coffey, to join the rush and create a great scoring chance. When on the ice to kill penalties, Gretzky wasn't looking to ice the puck in a defensive role; he was looking to take the other team by surprise, to take advantage of their defenselessness to score shorthanded. The result was goals and more goals—the Oilers scoring 400 a season as a matter of routine—and Gretzky won the scoring race virtually every year in the 1980s.

As Gretzky went, so went the Oilers. They went to the Stanley Cup finals in 1983, only to lose horribly to the Islanders in four straight games. But the loss was a learning experience. The next year they made their first of four Cup wins over the next five years by defeating those same Islanders in five games. That ended the dynastic run of four straight Cup wins for

Gretzky, Wayne
C, 6´, 185 lbs, b: Brantford, Ont., 1/26/1961

Season	Club, League	Regular Season					Playoffs				
		GP	G	A	Pts	PIM	GP	G	A	Pts	PIM
1978–79	Indianapolis Racers, WHA	8	3	3	6	0					
	Edmonton Oilers, WHA	72	43	61	104	19	13	10	10	20	2
1979–80	Edmonton Oilers, NHL	79	51	86	137	21	3	2	1	3	0
1980–81	Edmonton Oilers, NHL	80	55	109	164	28	9	7	14	21	4
CCup–81	Canada	7	5	7	12	2					
1981–82	Edmonton Oilers, NHL	80	92	120	212	26	5	5	7	12	8
WEC–82	Canada	10	6	8	14	0					
1982–83	Edmonton Oilers, NHL	80	71	125	196	59	16	12	26	38	4
1983–84	Edmonton Oilers, NHL	74	87	118	205	39	19	13	22	35	12
CCup–84	Canada	8	5	7	12	2					
1984–85	Edmonton Oilers, NHL	80	73	135	208	52	18	17	30	47	4
1985–86	Edmonton Oilers, NHL	80	52	163	215	46	10	8	11	19	2
1986–87	Edmonton Oilers, NHL	79	62	121	183	28	21	5	29	34	6
RV'87	NHL All-Stars	2	0	4	4	0					
CCup–87	Canada	9	3	18	21	2					
1987–88	Edmonton Oilers, NHL	64	40	109	149	24	19	12	31	43	16
1988–89	Los Angeles Kings, NHL	78	54	114	168	26	11	5	17	22	0
1989–90	Los Angeles Kings, NHL	73	40	102	142	42	7	3	7	10	0
1990–91	Los Angeles Kings, NHL	78	41	122	163	16	12	4	11	15	2
CCup–91	Canada	7	4	8	12	2					
1991–92	Los Angeles Kings, NHL	74	31	90	121	34	6	2	5	7	2
1992–93	Los Angeles Kings, NHL	45	16	49	65	6	24	15	25	40	4
1993–94	Los Angeles Kings, NHL	81	38	92	130	20					
1994–95	Los Angeles Kings, NHL	48	11	37	48	6					
1995–96	Los Angeles Kings, NHL	62	15	66	81	32					
	St. Louis Blues, NHL	18	8	13	21	2	13	2	14	16	0
WCup–96	Canada	8	3	4	7	2					
1996–97	New York Rangers, NHL	82	25	72	97	28	15	10	10	20	2
1997–98	New York Rangers, NHL	82	23	67	90	28					
OWG–98	Canada	6	0	4	4	2					
1998–99	New York Rangers, NHL	70	9	53	62	14					
	WHA Totals	80	46	64	110	19	13	10	10	20	2
	NHL Totals	1487	894	1963	2857	577	208	122	260	382	66
OWG/WEC/CCup/RV'87/WCup Totals		57	26	60	86	12					

NHL First All-Star Team (1981, 1982, 1983, 1984, 1985, 1986, 1987, 1991)
NHL Second All-Star Team (1980, 1988, 1989, 1990, 1994, 1997, 1998)
WHA Second All-Star Team (1979)
Won Hart Trophy (1980, 1981, 1982, 1983, 1984, 1985, 1986, 1987, 1989)
Won Art Ross Trophy (1981, 1982, 1983, 1984, 1985, 1986, 1987, 1990, 1991, 1994)
Won Conn Smythe Trophy (1985, 1988)
Won Lady Byng Trophy (1980, 1991, 1992, 1994, 1999)
Won Lester B. Pearson Award (1982, 1983, 1984, 1985, 1987)
Won Lester Patrick Trophy (1994)
Won Lou Kaplan Trophy – WHA Rookie of the Year (1979)
NHL Plus-Minus Leader (1982, 1984, 1985, 1987)
Won Stanley Cup (1984, 1985, 1987, 1988)
Won CCup (1984, 1987, 1991)

the Long Islanders. The playoffs became a mirror of the regular season, as Edmonton routinely scored seven goals a game, Gretzky led the playoffs in scoring and the team kept on winning and winning. The culmination of these years came in 1988, and after the Oilers won the Cup, Gretzky huddled the team at center ice for an on-ice group portrait, the first of what has since become a tradition for every winning team at every level.

That spring of 1988 was also Gretzky's last moment in an Oilers sweater. He married Janet Jones in July 16, and just days later he was traded to the Los Angeles Kings in one of the most stunning deals in NHL history. He, Mike Krushelnyski and Marty McSorley went to the Kings for Jimmy Carson, Martin Gelinas, first-round draft choices in 1989, 1991 and 1993 and $15 million. In the ensuing days, charges and countercharges flew in Edmonton because of the magnitude of the deal and because it came just after the Oilers' successful season-ticket drive had concluded. Fans felt betrayed, and many blamed Janet Jones for forcing the trade. Others blamed Gretzky for asking for a trade, and most people vilified owner Peter Pocklington for selling his most valuable asset simply for a large sum of cash. But in the end the result was the same—Gretzky was headed for the United States, never to wear a sweater of a Canadian team again in the NHL.

When Wayne Gretzky retired after the 1998–99 season, the NHL also retired number 99.

When the truth came out, Gretzky was exonerated. "The day after the Stanley Cup," Janet explained, "Pocklington told Wayne about an offer from Vancouver. Nelson Skalbania had called. Wayne replied to Pocklington, 'I can't believe you coming to me with this the day after we won the Cup.' Five days after the wedding, Wayne received the call from Kings owner Bruce McNall. McNall told Wayne that he had talked to Pocklington and was told, 'If you can swing him over, you've got him.' That's where it all happened. Wayne saw the writing right there. You're sold. You're out of here."

The league was never to be the same either. Gretzky brought to L.A. a truly winning attitude and ability and the Forum was sold out every game for the first time in franchise history. Gretzky's relationship with owner McNall was close, and with John Candy the three bought the Toronto Argonauts football club. Gretzky and McNall also bought valuable baseball cards and horses and were as close in business as they were in hockey. On ice, he won more Art Ross and Hart trophies, and in 1993 he took the Kings to the finals for the first time after eliminating the Maple Leafs in game seven of the semifinals in his favorite building, Maple Leaf Gardens. The deciding game in Toronto was a 5–4 win for L.A. in which he scored a hat-trick and which he called his finest NHL game ever. But in the finals the Kings were exhausted and the Great One's magic couldn't compensate. Montreal beat them in five games. After winning it four times with Edmonton, Gretzky was never again to get as close to the Cup.

Along the way in Los Angeles, Gretzky scored his 802nd goal to pass Gordie Howe as the all-time leading scorer, as well as his 1,851st point to pass Howe as all-time point-getter in the league. "The fact that the record was broken by someone who's such a great person takes away any sense of loss that I might have," Howe said. However, the otherwise dream-filled days in Los Angeles turned sour when Bruce McNall was found to have acquired his fortune through fraudulent means.

He was sent to jail after pleading guilty to fraud charges and was forced to sell the team. With Gretzky soon to be a free agent and his allegiance to Los Angeles no longer strong because of McNall's departure, he was traded to St. Louis to play with his friend Brett Hull and coach Mike Keenan, who had worked with Gretzky during Canada Cup competitions. He played only 18 games in St. Louis during the regular season, and after a disappointing showing in the playoffs, the Blues decided not to offer Gretzky a contract in the off-season. Instead, the Great One signed a three-year deal in the summer of 1996 to be with his oldest hockey friend, Mark Messier, and the New York Rangers. It seemed to be the perfect way to end a great career.

Wayne Gretzky (left) brought to Los Angeles a truly winning attitude and ability and the Great Western Forum was sold out every game for the first time in franchise history.

A year later, though, Messier became embroiled in a bitter contract negotiation with the Blueshirts and signed with the Vancouver Canucks. Gretzky was alone again—on Broadway, on a mediocre team, a situation he'd never wanted. He didn't want to be the center of attention or the one on whom all the expectations were focused. He continued to be the team's leading scorer, but his supporting cast grew weaker and the Rangers missed the playoffs in his last two years in the NHL. Time and again his perfect passes floated into open ice where no Ranger had anticipated the play or a pass would be badly missed on the awful Garden ice. Toward the end of the 1998–99 season, Gretzky announced his retirement, and his final two games, in Ottawa and New York, were emotionally difficult. When he retired after the season, the NHL retired his number 99 to ensure no one else would ever wear it. "In my heart, I know I made the right decision. My gut, my heart is telling me this is the right time. A year from now I could be in the exact same situation—everyone saying, 'Play just one more year.' I'm done. I haven't wavered at all and I will never play again."

Gretzky played in the NHL's All-Star Game every year he was in the league and was the first player to be named game MVP with three different teams. Internationally, his record is unparalleled among NHL players. After the World Juniors in 1978, he played in the World Championship in 1982, suiting up for his first game for Canada just 24 hours after the Oilers had been eliminated from the 1982 playoffs. The proudest of all Canadians ever to wear the national red and white sweater, he also played in each Canada Cup in 1981, 1984, 1987 and 1991. Each time he led the tournament in scoring, and only in his first year, 1981, did the team fail to claim the title of world champion. Gretzky also participated in the 1996 World Cup, the replacement tournament for the Canada Cup, where Canada placed second for the first time to the United States, and perhaps his greatest international honor came in late 1997, when he was selected to represent Canada at the 1998 Olympic Winter Games in Nagano, Japan. He was able to realize a boyhood dream, as the NHL shut down so that all the pros could represent their countries at those Olympics. Team Canada placed a disappointing fourth after losing in the semifinals on a shootout to Dominik Hasek and the Czech Republic, a result that was controversial for coach Marc Crawford since he didn't select Gretzky, the NHL's all-time leading scorer, to take one of the five penalty shots for Canada.

Naturally, Gretzky was inducted into the Hall of Fame as soon as he retired in 1999 and in century-end polls was consistently ranked the greatest hockey player of all time.

Although the 1999–2000 season marked Gretzky's first year of retirement, he was hardly inactive. The Edmonton Oilers retired his number 99 at the start of the season, and at the All-Star Game in Toronto in February 2000, his sweater was retired by the NHL in another special ceremony. Then, early in the summer, he became a minority owner of the Phoenix Coyotes, a move designed to help him get back in the game and one that also saved the franchise from moving because of ownership difficulties. He was also named general manager of Canada's entry for the Salt Lake Olympics in 2002.

During the Games at Salt Lake, Gretzky stunned many onlookers with a highly publicized tirade about how the rest of the world wanted to see Canada lose in hockey. Some viewed it as whining, while others saw it as a masterful and ingenious plan to deflect criticism away from Team Canada, which had been woefully underachieving till then. Some members of the media compared Gretzky's press conference rant to Phil Esposito's now famous emotional plea for Canadians to stand behind their team and their country when a shocking loss to the Russians in a game in Vancouver in the 1972 Summit Series had seen Team Canada loudly booed off the ice at the final buzzer. The fact that both teams turned their early bad fortunes into ultimate victory has made the comparison even more compelling and the verbal outbursts have been credited as the catalysts for the ultimate success on both occasions.

Ken Morrow

In the world of sports, the city of Flint, Michigan, is usually best known as the home of superstar basketball players. But in hockey it is also famous for producing Ken Morrow.

Morrow is one of the few hockey players to win the Stanley Cup and an Olympic gold medal in the same year. The magic year for him was 1980. Morrow was 23 years old and a member of the 1980 USA Miracle on Ice squad that won the gold in Lake Placid in February. He then finished the 1980–81 season with the New York Islanders, winning the Stanley Cup in May.

The modest Morrow was typically grateful for his good fortune. "I still can't believe it. I wake up and wonder if I was dreaming. I'm sure most players never get to play for a champion in their sports, a lot better players than I am, and for me to have played for two champions in a few months, well, it goes beyond anyone's wildest dreams. I was very lucky—I was in the right place at the right time." But U.S. Olympic coach Herb Brooks wouldn't let Morrow escape without the credit he deserved. "Ours was a team triumph, but I don't think we would have won without Kenny."

Morrow's father worked in an auto plant and died of cancer in 1976. His mother raised Morrow and two siblings on her own. "My dad worked hard all his life. I'm sorry he didn't get to see my success," said Ken. "There were times it was hard for me to get a buck or two to buy gas to get to a game," he admitted.

From 1975 to 1979, Morrow played college hockey on a scholarship for Bowling Green University in Ohio and was an NCAA West all-American there in 1978. His best collegiate year was in 1978–79, when he scored 15 goals and 37 assists in 45 games for Bowling Green. In 1979 Morrow was named Central Collegiate Hockey Association player of the year. He was drafted by the New York Islanders as their fourth choice, 68th overall, in the 1976 Amateur Draft, but he stayed in college until 1979.

Ken Morrow is one of the few players to win the Stanley Cup and an Olympic gold medal in the same year.

After Morrow started playing with the Islanders, he quickly proved he was an NHL-caliber player. The team's front office felt so confident with him in the lineup that they traded veterans Bill Harrison and Dave Lewis to the L.A. Kings for Butch Goring, the last player the Isles needed to put together a Cup-winning team. During the early part of Morrow's career, Islanders coach Al Arbour said: "Kenny knows what he can do and he doesn't try to do what he can't. He's surprisingly steady and dependable for a player so young and inexperienced."

Morrow was never a great goal scorer. In his best season with the Islanders, he accumulated only 19 points from one goal and 18 assists, but he made a significant contribution to the game in many other ways. In the 1983–84 playoffs, for example, he registered only three points, but two of them were crucial to the team's success. One was the winning goal in overtime that eliminated the New York Rangers in the first round of the playoffs; the other was an assist on the game-winning goal by Mike Bossy in the fourth game of the semifinals against Montreal.

The press was especially enthusiastic over Morrow's hard work on that assist. Well-known *Toronto Star* columnist Jim Proudfoot said that Morrow "did all the spadework" and "took the bull by the horns" with his assist. Proudfoot described the goal: "He dumped an aimless blooper into the Montreal zone and, acting totally out of character, elected to follow it in. As an offensive thrust, it had all the grace of a hippopotamus's charge. He piled into an enemy defender who was struggling for control of the situation, and they fell down in a heap of thrashing humanity. Spotting the puck nearby, unattended, Morrow reached over and hooked it back to the middle. Triggerman Bossy happened to be waiting there, hoping for just such a relay, and he wasted no time cashing in on the opportunity."

"I was able to get in there and take out a defenseman," Morrow remembered. "I was sure the Montreal goalie would make a play," he said of his dump-and-chase play. "But I took a look and, hey, it was as though nobody wanted it. I had no idea Bossy was out there, but I certainly thought there'd be a forward in the general vicinity." And he was right. Bossy was there to capitalize on Morrow's heads-up play.

In all, Morrow played 10 seasons in the NHL and was a member of the New York Islanders dynasty teams of 1980 to 1983 that won the Stanley Cup four straight times. Plagued by knee problems late in his career, Morrow was forced into early retirement. After his playing career, Morrow coached with Flint and Kansas City of the International Hockey League.

In 1991–92, Morrow returned to the Islanders as an assistant coach and then went on to serve as the team's director of pro scouting. Three years later he was inducted into the U.S. Hockey Hall of Fame and in 1996 got the Lester Patrick Award for his contribution to hockey in the United States.

Morrow, Ken
D, 6'4", 210 lbs, b: Flint, MI, 10/17/1956

Season	Club, League	Regular Season					Playoffs				
		GP	G	A	Pts	PIM	GP	G	A	Pts	PIM
1975–76	Bowling Green University, CCHA	31	4	15	19	34					
1976–77	Bowling Green University, CCHA	39	7	22	29	22					
1977–78	Bowling Green University, CCHA	39	8	18	26	26					
WEC–78	USA	6	0	0	0	0					
1978–79	Bowling Green University, CCHA	45	15	37	52	22					
1979–80	New York Islanders, NHL	18	0	3	3	4	20	1	2	3	12
OWG–80	USA	7	1	2	3	6					
1980–81	New York Islanders, NHL	80	2	11	13	20	18	3	4	7	8
CCup–81	USA	6	0	0	0	6					
1981–82	New York Islanders, NHL	75	1	18	19	56	19	0	4	4	8
1982–83	New York Islanders, NHL	79	5	11	16	44	19	5	7	12	18
1983–84	New York Islanders, NHL	63	3	11	14	45	20	1	2	3	20
1984–85	New York Islanders, NHL	15	1	7	8	14	10	0	0	0	17
1985–86	New York Islanders, NHL	69	0	12	12	22	2	0	0	0	4
1986–87	New York Islanders, NHL	64	3	8	11	32	13	1	3	4	2
1987–88	New York Islanders, NHL	53	1	4	5	40	6	0	0	0	8
1988–89	New York Islanders, NHL	34	1	3	4	32					
	NHL Totals	550	17	88	105	309	127	11	22	33	97
	OWG/WEC/CCup Totals	19	1	2	3	12					

Won Lester Patrick Trophy (1996)
Won OWG (1980)
Won Stanley Cup (1980, 1981, 1982, 1983)

Tim **Kerr**

He had soft hands and when parked in the slot was as immovable as the Rock of Gibraltar. Tim Kerr was one of the most productive goal-scoring machines in the 1980s. His immense size, quick release and willingness to absorb punishment in the offensive zone added a whole new dimension to the Philadelphia Flyers' game once he gained a place on their roster.

Kerr grew up in Tecumseh, a community near Windsor in south-western Ontario. He played junior with the Windsor Spitfires and the Kingston Canadians of the OHA, where he was a decent scorer even if he wasn't prolific. Had he not grown so much as a teenager, he would have put up bigger numbers. As it was, he soldiered on as his coordination slowly caught up with his size.

Tim Kerr was one of the most productive goal-scoring machines of the 1980s.

With 230 pounds on his 6′3″ frame, Kerr was known around the junior leagues as a slow skater who parked himself in the slot, collecting his share of "garbage" goals. He was never drafted by an NHL team but was signed by the Flyers after a 40-goal season in junior in 1979–80. He suited up immediately with their AHL affiliate in Portland, Maine, where he scored six points in seven games.

He played decently at Philadelphia's training camp in 1980 but didn't convince everyone that he could succeed in the NHL. In the end, he made the team because a broken leg suffered by Ken Linseman opened a spot on the roster. Kerr registered 22 and 21 goals in his first two seasons and established himself as an NHL regular. In 1982–83, he was on pace to top the 40-goal mark when a serious knee injury ruined his season.

Teamed with Brian Propp and Dave Poulin, Kerr took his game to another level in 1983–84. The tag "Sultan of Slot" became an apt description of his important role on the team. He recorded

his first of four consecutive 50-goal seasons and became one of the most feared and closely checked forwards in the league. Coach Mike Keenan commented, "They take him down inside the 10-yard line an awful lot." Regardless of how much physical abuse came his way, he stood his ground and used superior hand-eye coordination to pot goals almost at will. The NHL hadn't seen an individual dominate the slot since Phil Esposito was in his prime. More important, Kerr wasn't a streaky scorer. He never slumped and totaled over 50 goals for four years from 1983 to 1987.

The fortunes of the Flyers rose with Kerr's ascent to stardom. His presence on the ice could change the entire aspect of a game.

Kerr, Tim
C/RW, 6′3″, 230 lbs, b: Windsor, Ont., 1/5/1960

Season	Club, League	Regular Season					Playoffs				
		GP	G	A	Pts	PIM	GP	G	A	Pts	PIM
1979–80	Maine Mariners, AHL	7	2	4	6	2					
1980–81	Philadelphia Flyers, NHL	68	22	23	45	84	10	1	3	4	2
1981–82	Philadelphia Flyers, NHL	61	21	30	51	138	4	0	2	2	2
1982–83	Philadelphia Flyers, NHL	24	11	8	19	6	2	2	0	2	0
1983–84	Philadelphia Flyers, NHL	79	54	39	93	29	3	0	0	0	0
1984–85	Philadelphia Flyers, NHL	74	54	44	98	57	12	10	4	14	13
1985–86	Philadelphia Flyers, NHL	76	58	26	84	79	5	3	3	6	8
1986–87	Philadelphia Flyers, NHL	75	58	37	95	57	12	8	5	13	2
1987–88	Philadelphia Flyers, NHL	8	3	2	5	12	6	1	3	4	4
1988–89	Philadelphia Flyers, NHL	69	48	40	88	73	19	14	11	25	27
1989–90	Philadelphia Flyers, NHL	40	24	24	48	34					
1990–91	Philadelphia Flyers, NHL	27	10	14	24	8					
1991–92	New York Rangers, NHL	32	7	11	18	12	8	1	0	1	0
1992–93	Hartford Whalers, NHL	22	0	6	6	7					
	NHL Totals	655	370	304	674	596	81	40	31	71	58

NHL Second All-Star Team (1987)
Won Bill Masterton Trophy (1989)

*"The NHL is lucky that Tim Kerr is easygoing,"
Bryan Trottier said.
"If he was mean or a goon with his size and strength, we would all be in big trouble."*

Philadelphia reached the Stanley Cup finals in 1985 and won the first game against the favored Edmonton Oilers before succumbing in five games. Kerr notched 10 goals in 12 matches and drew accolades from his opponents. As usual, he attracted plenty of harsh attention from the Edmonton checkers, but Kerr was neither deterred nor drawn into taking penalties for retaliation. As Islanders forward Bryan Trottier said: "The NHL is lucky that Tim Kerr is easygoing. If he was mean or a goon with his size and strength, we would all be in big trouble."

During the 1985–86 season, he scored 58 goals, a personal high he equaled the following year. That first year he also set an NHL record with 34 power-play goals. This had an enormous impact on the strategy of opponents, who didn't dare get into penalty trouble against the Flyers' extra-man unit.

Philadelphia reached the finals against Edmonton for the second time in three years in 1987 and pushed the eventual victors to seven games before falling short. Unfortunately, Kerr suffered a shoulder injury that prevented him from playing in the finals. In addition to the individual sorrow it caused him, the team was heartbroken and felt he may have made a huge difference in such a close series. Following the season, Kerr was elected to the NHL Second All-Star Team.

A 48-goal season in 1988–89 was the last time Kerr made a huge impact in the NHL. His dedication was acknowledged when he was presented with the Bill Masterton Trophy that summer. The physical pounding by the opposition took its toll. More significantly, tragedy struck his family in October 1990 when his wife, Kathy, died of complications following the birth of their daughter. In the aftermath, he courageously tried to play, but the mental and physical agony became too much of a burden. On his return to the Spectrum, the crowd gave him an emotional standing ovation in one of the most memorable sights at that venue.

Kerr played parts of two seasons with the New York Rangers and Hartford before retiring in January 1993. He immediately accepted an assistant coach position with Springfield of the AHL, the Whalers' top farm club.

Glen Sather

Glen Sather (top) was the most successful hockey executive of the 1980s.

Glen Cameron Sather, "Slats" to most people, was the most successful hockey executive of the 1980s as Edmonton Oilers coach and general manager when the team won the Stanley Cup an unbelievable five times between 1984 and 1990.

Born in High River, Alberta, in 1943, Sather helped the Edmonton Oil Kings win the Memorial Cup for junior hockey in 1962–63. He also had a 10-year career as an NHL player. As a pro, he was known as an honest player, a hard worker, but not overly skilled or flashy. Sather was also much traveled in the hockey world. He played for the Boston Bruins, Pittsburgh Penguins, New York Rangers, St. Louis Blues, Montreal Canadiens and Minnesota North Stars in the NHL and the Edmonton Oilers in the World Hockey Association before it merged with the NHL. Sather once said: "I know what I am—I'm a journeyman hockey player. That means I make a lot of journeys." Looking back over all those trades during his playing days, Sather remarked: "I can't complain that I've been treated badly. I've been happy just to be playing hockey in the big leagues. There's not many things I like to do more."

In 1976–77, Sather resigned as a player and took over as coach of the Oilers, where he began to unveil his true talent. In his second year as WHA coach, Sather took the Oilers to the playoffs in 1977–78, where they lost to the New England Whalers. The next season, Sather helped purchase the contract of a 17-year-old player named Wayne Gretzky from the Indianapolis Racers. The Oilers had a fantastic 1978–79 campaign, finishing first in the league standings during the regular season though losing in WHA finals to the Winnipeg Jets. Later that summer, Edmonton became one of four teams to join the NHL along with Winnipeg (now Phoenix), Hartford (now Carolina) and Quebec (now Colorado).

During their first NHL season, the Oilers began to show promise and Wayne Gretzky was starting to show signs of being a superstar. Sather was made general manager of the team as well as coach in 1980, just before the NHL Entry Draft that year. In that draft, he picked future superstars Paul Coffey, Andy Moog and Jari Kurri. In the next year's draft, Sather selected goalie Grant Fuhr. Meanwhile, Mark Messier and Glenn Anderson, already on the team, started to emerge as superstars and the Oilers dynasty was underway.

By 1982–83, Edmonton had reached the Stanley Cup finals against the New York Islanders, who won the Cup for the fourth straight year. But the following season the Oilers became almost unbeatable. They won the Cup that year and three more times in the next five years between 1983 and 1988. Sather faced another big challenge in coaching the Oilers after Gretzky was traded to the Los Angeles Kings in 1988. He acquired goalie Bill Ranford from the Bruins and Mark Messier took over as team captain. With these important changes, the Oilers won the Cup again in 1990.

John Muckler, Sather's assistant coach with the Oilers during their prime, said of Sather's success: "I've never worked for a man who is so confident of himself. He's not afraid to hire people capable of doing their best jobs for him. He lets everybody do their own jobs and it takes a great deal of self-confidence to do that." Muckler later added: "Glen is like a father to these guys. Gretzky, Messier, Anderson, Coffey—the better players on our team were really creative, and that was a significant factor in molding the team. What Glen added to their creativity was an important part of his own personality—his aggressiveness. Glen's personality comes out in them. They love to win and they will win at any cost. And that's Glen."

Sather is famous for his trademark "smirk" behind the bench. While some have described his look as arrogance, consider that Sather has the best winning percentage in the playoffs of any coach in the history of the game. Internationally, he led Team Canada to the 1984 Canada Cup championship and was general manager of the Canadian team that won the World Championship in 1994, Canada's first since 1961. Commenting on his coaching and management philosophy, Sather said: "The first commitment I've always been interested in is competition. The reason I try to do this job is to win. I'm competitive. I enjoy winning. I hate losing."

Sather, Glen
LW, 5'11", 180 lbs, b: High River, Alta., 9/2/1943

Season	Club, League	Regular Season					Playoffs				
		GP	G	A	Pts	PIM	GP	G	A	Pts	PIM
1964–65	Memphis Wings, CHL	69	19	29	48	98					
1965–66	Oklahoma City Blazers, CHL	64	13	12	25	76	9	4	4	8	14
1966–67	Oklahoma City Blazers, CHL	57	14	19	33	147	11	2	6	8	24
	Boston Bruins, NHL	5	0	0	0	0					
1967–68	Boston Bruins, NHL	65	8	12	20	34	3	0	0	0	0
1968–69	Boston Bruins, NHL	76	4	11	15	67	10	0	0	0	18
1969–70	Pittsburgh Penguins, NHL	76	12	14	26	114	10	0	2	2	17
1970–71	Pittsburgh Penguins, NHL	46	8	3	11	96					
	New York Rangers, NHL	31	2	0	2	52	13	0	1	1	18
1971–72	New York Rangers, NHL	76	5	9	14	77	16	0	1	1	22
1972–73	New York Rangers, NHL	77	11	15	26	64	9	0	0	0	7
1973–74	New York Rangers, NHL	2	0	0	0	0					
	St. Louis Blues, NHL	69	15	29	44	82					
1974–75	Montreal Canadiens, NHL	63	6	10	16	44	11	1	1	2	4
1975–76	Minnesota North Stars, NHL	72	9	10	19	94					
1976–77	Edmonton Oilers, WHA	81	19	34	53	77	5	1	1	2	2
	NHL Totals	658	80	113	193	724	72	1	5	6	86
	WHA Totals	81	19	34	53	77	5	1	1	2	2

It was as GM during the late 1990s that Sather experienced problems contending with the big change in player salaries. "When we were winning the Stanley Cup, our entire budget was $6 million," he said. "Now you've got players asking for $6 million. When you look back at some of the things that have happened over the years, you can't blame the players. I blame the owners in the league. You can't blame the general managers, because they aren't the guys pulling the strings. It's the people who own these hockey teams that drive the salaries so far out of reality."

Slats knew that the new-style NHL would hamper his ability to wheel and deal on the league market as a general manager. "I want in some way to have an even keel in trying to negotiate with players around the league," he said. "And I know from a realistic point of view that it is virtually impossible if you live in Canada because of the small market and the exchange rate."

After tumultuous years under an ownership of some 37 men in Edmonton, Sather resigned from the Oilers shortly after the 1999–2000 season ended and signed as GM with the New York Rangers just a couple of weeks later. There, he immediately brought credibility to a team that had missed the playoffs for three years and he was eager to accept the great challenge that was Broadway. Though Sather and the Rangers missed the playoffs again in 2000–01, Ranger fans seemed willing to give him a year of grace to build the foundation for a new dynasty, and it appeared he was putting the pieces of the puzzle in place with the acquisition of Eric Lindros from the Philadelphia Flyers. When the Rangers still failed to reach the Stanley Cup playoffs, it posed the biggest dilemma of Glen Sather's 20-year career as an NHL general manager.

Sather, Glen
Head Coach, b: High River, Alta., 9/2/1943

Season	Club, League	Regular Season					Playoffs				
		GC	W	L	T	W%	GC	W	L	T	W%
1979–80	Edmonton Oillers, NHL	80	28	39	13	0.431	3	0	3	0	0.000
1980–81	Edmonton Oillers, NHL	62	25	26	11	0.492	9	5	4	0	0.556
1981–82	Edmonton Oillers, NHL	80	48	17	15	0.694	5	2	3	0	0.400
1982–83	Edmonton Oillers, NHL	80	47	21	12	0.663	16	11	5	0	0.688
1983–84	Edmonton Oillers, NHL	80	57	18	5	0.744	19	15	4	0	0.789
CCup–84	Canada	8	5	2	1	0.688					
1984–85	Edmonton Oillers, NHL	80	49	20	11	0.681	18	15	3	0	0.833
1985–86	Edmonton Oillers, NHL	80	56	17	7	0.744	10	6	4	0	0.600
1986–87	Edmonton Oillers, NHL	80	50	24	6	0.663	21	16	5	0	0.762
1987–88	Edmonton Oillers, NHL	80	44	25	11	0.619	19	16	2	1	0.868
1988–89	Edmonton Oillers, NHL	80	38	34	8	0.525	7	3	4	0	0.429
1993–94	Edmonton Oillers, NHL	60	22	27	11	0.458					
	NHL Totals	842	464	268	110	0.616	127	89	37	1	0.705

Won Jack Adams Award (1986)
Won Stanley Cup (1984, 1985, 1987, 1988, 1990)
Won CCup (1984)

Once asked the secret of his own success, Sather quipped, "I have a very understanding general manager." However, he has always refused to take any credit for his team's success. "It's not the coach that wins, it's the players," he said. "It has nothing to do specifically with one player. It's not a huge personal accomplishment. It's a team thing and it has always been a team thing."

Hakan Loob

Not very tall and slight of build, Hakan Loob, one of Sweden's best forwards during the 1980s, entered the spotlight at a young age. He defied the hockey pundits who doubted that a hockey player from Gotland could reach the level of the Elite Series, Sweden's highest league. Hockey played on the Swedish island of Gotland in the Baltic Sea wasn't considered to be of the highest standard.

As a youth, Loob played with the local Roma for a time before joining the popular Farjestad, in the city of Karlstad, with whom his career in sports would be forever connected.

KINGS OF THE ICE

In 1981, at the age of 21, he was playing for Farjestad when they won the Swedish Championship, but he really made his mark in the 1982-83 season. Farjestad was then at its zenith and the team's best five-man lineup consisted of Tommy Samuelsson and Peter Loob, Jan Ingman, Thomas Rundqvist and Hakan Loob. The quintet became the asset of the season and the agile Hakan Loob was its driving force.

The highest scoring record in the Elite Series was set by Loob that season and is still unbeaten. In 36 games he racked up 76 points: 42 goals plus 34 assists. This long-standing record remains unbeaten by Swedish championship players and foreign stars alike, in spite of the fact that the number of games in the Elite Series has been increased.

Farjestad lost the gold to Stockholm's Djurgarden in the 1982–83 season and Hakan Loob was seriously injured in one of the games. But that season became the turning point in his career. The talented forward caught the attention of the NHL Calgary Flames scouts. Once again the skeptics wondered whether this player who was slight of build could hold his own in the NHL, where tough bodychecking was the rule and rinks were smaller than those in Europe.

But Loob fooled them all. In the 1987–88 season, he became the first Swedish player to score 50 goals in the NHL regular season. Besides that, he had 56 assists to his credit, racking up a total of 106 points—an achievement that the present generation of Swedish players in the NHL can still be proud of. A year later, "Lucky Loob" was able to hold up the cherished Stanley Cup won by the Calgary Flames. Loob played 450 games for the NHL, scoring 193 goals.

For Loob and all Swedish hockey fans, 1987 was an especially memorable year. At the World Championship in Vienna, Tre Kronor won the gold after a hiatus of 25 years, largely thanks to the efforts of Hakan Loob.

The game between the Swedes and the USSR nationals in Vienna on May 1 was especially tense. With only 81 seconds to play before the final whistle, Swedish forward Tomas Sandstrom, on the receiving end of a brilliant pass from Loob, slammed a goal into the Soviet net to tie the score 2–2. In the next

The scoring record in Sweden's Elite Series was set by Hakan Loob in 1982–83 and is still unbeaten: 42 goals and 34 assists in 36 games.

Loob, Hakan
RW, 5′9″, 170 lbs, b: Karlstad, Sweden, 7/3/1960

Season	Club, League	Regular Season					Playoffs				
		GP	G	A	Pts	PIM	GP	G	A	Pts	PIM
1979–80	Farjestad, Sweden	36	15	4	19	20					
1980–81	Farjestad, Sweden	36	23	6	29	14	7	5	3	8	6
1981–82	Farjestad, Sweden	36	26	15	41	28	2	1	0	1	0
WEC–82	Sweden	8	3	1	4	6					
1982–83	Farjestad, Sweden	36	42	34	76	29	8	10	4	14	6
1983–84	Calgary Flames, NHL	77	30	25	55	22	11	2	3	5	2
CCup–84	Sweden	8	6	4	10	2					
1984–85	Calgary Flames, NHL	78	37	35	72	14	4	3	3	6	0
1985–86	Calgary Flames, NHL	68	31	36	67	36	22	4	10	14	6
1986–87	Calgary Flames, NHL	68	18	26	44	26	5	1	2	3	0
WEC–87	Sweden	8	5	4	9	4					
1987–88	Calgary Flames, NHL	80	50	56	106	47	9	8	1	9	4
1988–89	Calgary Flames, NHL	79	27	58	85	44	22	8	9	17	4
1989–90	Farjestad, Sweden	40	22	31	53	24	10	9	5	14	2
WEC–90	Sweden	10	4	7	11	10					
1990–91	Farjestad, Sweden	40	33	25	58	16	8	6	4	10	8
WEC–91	Sweden	10	2	7	9	6					
1991–92	Farjestad, Sweden	40	37	29	66	14	6	2	2	4	2
OWG–92	Sweden	8	4	4	8	0					
1992–93	Farjestad, Sweden	40	25	26	51	28	3	4	1	5	0
1993–94	Farjestad, Sweden	22	9	11	20	12					
OWG–94	Sweden	8	4	5	9	2					
1994–95	Farjestad, Sweden	39	13	25	38	58	4	2	0	2	2
1995–96	Farjestad, Sweden	40	17	31	48	37					
	Sweden Totals	405	262	237	499	280	48	39	19	58	26
	NHL Totals	450	193	236	429	189	73	26	28	54	16
	OWG/WEC/CCup Totals	60	28	32	60	30					

NHL First All-Star Team (1988)
Won OWG (1994)
Won WEC (1987, 1991)
Won Stanley Cup (1989)
Sweden Champion (1981)

In 1987–88, Hakan Loob (right) became the first Swedish player to score 50 goals in the NHL regular season.

game, the energized Swedes trounced the Canadians 9–0, Tre Kronor's greatest victory ever over Team Canada, and left the Soviet team facing the impossible. To win the World Championship title, the USSR nationals would have had to beat the Czech nationals in the final game by 10 goals.

The Swedish nationals, under the leadership of senior coach Tommy Sandlin, were a well-balanced and powerful team with an excellent lineup of players that year. Hakan Loob was a standout.

Returning to Farjestad in 1989, Loob continued to play the key role in the lineup of his native team, achieving one more gold medal at the 1991 World Championship as well as an Olympic gold medal at Lillehammer, Norway, in 1994. That gold medal became Loob's crowning achievement. He'd won practically every gold medal that a hockey player could dream of, including the championship of Sweden, the World Championship, the Winter Olympics and the Stanley Cup. Only two other Swedish hockey players have equaled such an achievement, defenseman Tomas Jonsson and forward Mats Naslund.

Loob quit playing in 1996 and was given a standing ovation as he left the ice. A jersey bearing the number 5 that he wore while playing for Farjestad was raised in the local hockey stadium in recognition of his exceptional role. Loob remained in hockey, becoming the sports training supervisor for Farjestad. In 1997 and 1998 the Karlstad team won the Swedish Championship.

Lars-Gunnar Pettersson

The Elite Series scoring record of 272 goals held by Lars-Gunnar Pettersson (left) is likely to remain unbroken for some time.

Every Swede knows that "L-G" is the nickname for outstanding forward Lars-Gunnar Pettersson—a player who gained fame in the 1980s as a great shooter. His Elite Series scoring record of 271 goals is still unbroken and is likely to remain that way for some time.

His best years were the late 1980s, when he won the world silver in Moscow in 1986, took Sweden's national championship playing for Bjorkloven of Umea the next year, and only weeks later won the World Championship in Vienna. Then came third place at the Canada Cup in 1987 and Olympic bronze at Calgary in 1988.

Pettersson was born on April 8, 1960, in Lulea, Sweden, just south of the Arctic Circle. Winter comes early there and the snow doesn't melt until mid-April. For hockey-loving children, it's paradise—the reason so many Swedish hockey stars come from Norrbotten, in the north of Sweden.

Pettersson began his career with Lulea, at that time a mediocre minor-league team but now one of the best. Then he joined Bjorkloven, which was then a leading team and has now fallen in the standings. Pettersson returned to Lulea but remained unsuccessful in the national championships.

He played for 14 seasons in the Elite Series and accumulated 453 points: 271 goals plus 182 assists in 495 games, averaging an outstanding one point per game.

Pettersson played 117 games for Tre Kronor as well as 28 games for Sweden's second national team, the Vikings, and 18 games for the national junior team. His first game with Tre Kronor was against Finland in 1984 and his most memorable goal was the one he scored against Canada in 1987 at the Canada Cup. "Back then, my partners on offense were Mikael Andersson and Tom Eklund," he recalls. "I scored a goal and Sweden was leading 2–1. In the end, though, we lost, but that was a first-rate game; to score a goal against Canada on Canadian ice was something special."

For his achievements, Pettersson stands 117th on Sweden's list of "Great Men." Still remembered by fans, he is cheered whenever he gets back on the ice for another veterans' hockey game.

Pettersson, Lars-Gunnar
LW, 6´, 176 lbs, b: Lulea, Sweden, 4/8/1960

Season	Club, League	Regular Season					Playoffs				
		GP	G	A	Pts	PIM	GP	G	A	Pts	PIM
1980–81	Bjorkloven, Sweden	33	7	10	17	12					
1981–82	Bjorkloven, Sweden	17	6	4	10	8	2	0	0	0	2
1982–83	Bjorkloven, Sweden	36	20	12	32	10	1	0	1	1	0
1983–84	Bjorkloven, Sweden	34	15	17	32	16	3	0	1	1	0
1984–85	Bjorkloven, Sweden	35	24	11	35	21	3	4	1	5	6
WEC-85	Sweden	10	3	3	6	4					
1985–86	Bjorkloven, Sweden	29	20	12	32	14					
WEC-86	Sweden	9	4	3	7	6					
1986–87	Bjorkloven, Sweden	36	28	13	41	16	6	3	3	6	4
WEC-87	Sweden	7	2	2	4	2					
CC-87	Sweden	5	2	0	2	0					
1987–88	Lulea, Sweden	40	11	16	27	18					
OWG-88	Sweden	8	3	4	7	2					
1988–89	Lulea, Sweden	40	29	24	53	14	3	1	1	2	0
1989–90	Lulea, Sweden	40	24	18	42	12	5	1	0	1	2
1990–91	Lulea, Sweden	40	30	16	46	6	5	2	1	3	0
1991–92	Lulea, Sweden	40	24	17	41	24	2	0	0	0	2
1992–93	Lulea, Sweden	39	19	6	25	6	11	2	2	4	0
1993–94	Lulea, Sweden	36	14	6	20	30					
	Sweden Totals	495	271	182	453	207	41	13	10	23	16
	OWG/WEC/CC Totals	39	14	12	26	14					

Won WEC (1987)
Sweden Champion (1987)

Thomas Rundqvist

No one can remember Thomas Rundqvist committing a foul or instigating a brawl in the rink, probably because it has never happened. Rundqvist was always a gentleman on the ice, focusing his mind on rapidly calculating his and his teammates' moves. His record of 267 games for Tre Kronor remained unbeaten until 1998, when his long-time colleague Jonas Bergqvist broke that record in Switzerland with 272 games.

Thomas Rundqvist was born on May 4, 1960, in Vimmerby, in southern Sweden. At age seven, the future hockey star stepped onto the ice to play for the local Vimmerbu. In 1977 he moved to Farjestad in Karlstad and stayed there for the rest of his Swedish career, except for a year-long break in 1984–85 when he played for the AHL's Sherbrooke Canadiens and two games for the Montreal Canadiens along-

Thomas Rundqvist (number 8) set a record of 267 games for Tre Kronor that remained unbeaten until 1998, when Jonas Bergqvist set a new high.

A HISTORY OF WORLD HOCKEY

No one can remember Thomas Rundqvist (left) committing a foul or instigating a brawl.

Rundqvist, Thomas
C, 6´3˝, 195 lbs, b: Vimmerby, Sweden, 5/4/1960

Season	Club, League	Regular Season					Playoffs				
		GP	G	A	Pts	PIM	GP	G	A	Pts	PIM
1978–79	Farjestad, Sweden	15	2	5	7	8	*	0	1	1	2
1979–80	Farjestad, Sweden	36	9	6	15	28					
1980–81	Farjestad, Sweden	36	15	19	34	22	7	1	2	3	0
1981–82	Farjestad, Sweden	36	14	13	27	30	2	0	1	1	2
WEC–82	Sweden	9	1	2	3	2					
1982–83	Farjestad, Sweden	36	22	21	43	28	8	3	8	11	6
WEC–83	Sweden	10	1	3	4	2					
1983–84	Farjestad, Sweden	36	13	22	35	38					
1984–85	Montreal Canadiens, NHL	2	0	1	1	0					
	Sherbrooke Canadiens, AHL	73	19	39	58	16	17	5	14	19	4
1985–86	Farjestad, Sweden	32	9	17	26	27	8	2	4	6	2
WEC–86	Sweden	10	2	3	5	8					
1986–87	Farjestad, Sweden	35	13	22	35	38	7	2	5	7	2
WEC–87	Sweden	10	1	2	3	4					
CCup–87	Sweden	6	0	2	2	10					
1987–88	Farjestad, Sweden	40	15	22	37	40	9	3	7	10	6
OWG–88	Sweden	8	0	3	3	0					
1988–89	Farjestad, Sweden	37	15	26	41	44	2	2	1	3	2
WEC–89	Sweden	9	1	2	3	6					
1989–90	Farjestad, Sweden	40	16	29	45	30	10	8	4	12	0
WEC–90	Sweden	10	3	8	11	6					
1990–91	Farjestad, Sweden	39	12	21	33	22	8	5	7	12	6
WEC–91	Sweden	10	6	4	10	4					
CCup–91	Sweden	6	2	2	4	2					
1991–92	Farjestad, Sweden	39	10	28	38	54	6	3	2	5	8
OWG–92	Sweden	8	3	4	7	8					
1992–93	Farjestad, Sweden	37	8	17	25	40	3	0	0	0	2
WC–93	Sweden	8	1	4	5	0					
1993–94	Feldkirch, Austria	53	20	37	57	18					
1994–95	Feldkirch, Austria	28	9	15	24	32	8	2	3	5	6
1995–96	Feldkirch, Austria	39	15	39	54	35					
1996–97	Feldkirch, Austria	52	11	34	45	61					
1997–98	Feldkirch, Austria	48	8	25	33	14					
	Sweden Totals	494	173	268	441	449	70	29	42	71	38
	OWG/WEC/WC/CCup Totals	104	21	39	60	52					
	NHL Totals	2	0	1	1	0					

Won WEC (1987, 1991)
Sweden Champion (1981, 1986, 1988)
Austria Champion (1994, 1995, 1996, 1997, 1998)

side fellow Swede Mats Naslund. Naslund did well in the NHL, but Rundqvist returned home without achieving fame in North America. His best games were played on the European scene in numerous international events.

Rundqvist made his debut with Tre Kronor in 1981 and the next year he played in his first World Championship. His partners on offense were Hakan Loob, a former teammate from Farjestad, and Mats Ulander of AIK.

One of the highlights of his career was Sweden's triumph at the Vienna World Championship in 1987 when Tre Kronor captured the gold thanks to the Soviets' 2–1 win over Czechoslovakia that put Sweden in first place. But in Rundqvist's opinion, Tre Kronor's success in Finland in 1991 was even more impressive. In Finland, Sweden won the gold without losing a single game.

Rundqvist's most memorable goal is the one he scored against Czechoslovakia in an overtime period at the 1993 World Championship in Germany. The goal put Sweden into the finals, where they were eventually beaten by Russia. Rundqvist scored many important goals playing for Austria's Feldkirch, where he moved with teammate Bengt-Ake Gustafsson in 1993. Significant among them were the ones that enabled the Austrians to defeat Dynamo Moscow in the Euroleague tournament.

Rundqvist is a double world champion, triple champion of Sweden and the winner of five national championships in Austria.

Recently, Rundqvist returned to Sweden, where he lives near Karlstad. He currently works for Farjestad, where he is responsible for training and marketing. His former teammate, Hakan Loob, is the team's sports director. Rundqvist is also involved in organizing the World Championship scheduled to be held in Sweden in 2002. Karlstad's rink will host the official games, giving Rundqvist plenty to do.

Brent Sutter

"If I had to be adopted, I'd want to be a Sutter," NHL coach Pat Burns once said. "Those guys have a special mixture." Indeed it's hard for anyone who has followed the game in the last 20 years not to feel just a little bit of envy when it comes to the Sutter family. In the 1980s, there were six Sutter brothers—Brian, Darryl, Duane, Brent, Ron and Rich—all playing in the NHL. The papers were filled with family photos of the six, all in NHL team sweaters or posing outside the family home.

"The Sutters know what it's all about," said ex-NHL coach Mike Keenan, now a TV commentator. "They woke up scared, not knowing if the crops were going to come in. You learn to respond." Born and raised on a farm in Viking, Alberta, the Sutter family not only raised pigs and cows and grew grain, but they raised their sons (seven in total) with the kind of spirit and determination that spelled success in the NHL. "Nothing was ever handed to us as a family—nothing," explained Brent Sutter. "We grew up seven boys in a two-bedroom house that didn't have running water. We'd use rainwater in the summer and melt the snow in winter. We learned early what hard work was all about."

"If I had to be adopted, I'd want to be a Sutter," NHL coach Pat Burns once said.

Brent Sutter was the second-last brother to remain in the NHL as a player, but two others—Darryl and Brian—have already gone on to careers in coaching. "Surprisingly, no one has really mentioned much about me being the last one left," he said. Perhaps that is because his impressive career speaks for itself. Brent spent 10 years with the New York Islanders and twice helped his team bring home the Stanley Cup. His best season was in 1984–85, when he had 42 goals and 102 total points. He was known around the league as a tough, hard-working player with a complete game, as adept at scoring goals as he was at mixing it up in the corners. Brent played the classic "Sutter" game, but he was likely the one who took the family business to the highest level.

Brent got his start in the NHL as a first-round pick of the Isles in the 1980 draft. When he was just 19, he got a chance to play on a Cup-winning team alongside his brother Duane. "It's really comforting to have a member of your family with you," he said. "Duane and I live together and we talk about a lot of things, not just hockey. I never felt better than on the day I found out that I'd been drafted by the same team as Duane."

Prior to making the Isles, Brent spent some time playing junior hockey with the Lethbridge Broncos, where he played on a line with twin brothers Ron and Rich. Early in the 1991–92

Sutter, Brent
C, 6′, 188 lbs, b: Viking, Alta., 6/10/1962

Season	Club, League	Regular Season					Playoffs				
		GP	G	A	Pts	PIM	GP	G	A	Pts	PIM
1980–81	New York Islanders, NHL	3	2	2	4	0					
1981–82	New York Islanders, NHL	43	21	22	43	114	19	2	6	8	36
1982–83	New York Islanders, NHL	80	21	19	40	128	20	10	11	21	26
1983–84	New York Islanders, NHL	69	34	15	49	69	20	4	10	14	18
CCup–84	Canada	8	2	2	4	10					
1984–85	New York Islanders, NHL	72	42	60	102	51	10	3	3	6	14
1985–86	New York Islanders, NHL	61	24	31	55	74	3	0	1	1	2
WEC–86	Canada	8	4	7	11	8					
1986–87	New York Islanders, NHL	69	27	36	63	73	5	1	0	1	4
CCup–87	Canada	9	1	3	4	6					
1987–88	New York Islanders, NHL	70	29	31	60	55	6	2	1	3	18
1988–89	New York Islanders, NHL	77	29	34	63	77					
1989–90	New York Islanders, NHL	67	33	35	68	65	5	2	3	5	2
1990–91	New York Islanders, NHL	75	21	32	53	49					
CCup–91	Canada	8	3	1	4	6					
1991–92	New York Islanders, NHL	8	4	6	10	6					
	Chicago Blackhawks, NHL	61	18	32	50	30	18	3	5	8	22
1992–93	Chicago Blackhawks, NHL	65	20	34	54	67	4	1	1	2	4
1993–94	Chicago Blackhawks, NHL	73	9	29	38	43	6	0	0	0	2
1994–95	Chicago Blackhawks, NHL	47	7	8	15	51	16	1	2	3	4
1995–96	Chicago Blackhawks, NHL	80	13	27	40	56	10	1	1	2	6
1996–97	Chicago Blackhawks, NHL	39	7	7	14	18	2	0	0	0	6
1997–98	Chicago Blackhawks, NHL	52	2	6	8	28					
	NHL Totals	1111	363	466	829	1054	144	30	44	74	164
	WEC/CCup Totals	33	10	13	23	30					

Won Stanley Cup (1982, 1983)
Won CCup (1984, 1987, 1991)

season, he was traded by the Islanders to Chicago with Brad Lauer for Adam Creighton and Steve Thomas. He spent the last seven years of his NHL life in the Windy City. During his time with the Hawks, Brent was coached by his older brother Darryl. Some observers felt that he got more playing time than he deserved. "In fact, the opposite was true," Brent responded. "He was probably harder on me than the other players. I think people tend to expect more from people in their family. He was the coach, I was the player—it was that cut and dried."

Brent also played for Team Canada as a member of the notorious Kamikaze Line along with Rick Tocchet. "I might not score as often as I once did," he said modestly later in his career, "but other areas of my game are better than when I was younger." Hawks coach Craig Hartsburg once described Brent's style of play: "He does all the little things that need to be done for a team to be successful." That sums up the Sutter family recipe for success on the farm—and on the ice.

Sutter has also followed in the footsteps of his older brothers Brian and Darryl by getting into the coaching ranks as the governor, general manager and head coach of the Western Hockey League's Red Deer Rebels. He was named the CHL's coach of the year in 2001 and led the Rebels to the Memorial Cup championship that spring. Under Sutter, the Rebels set team records for points (114) and most wins (54) in a season.

Grant Fuhr

Grant Fuhr's ability to handle the pressure made him one of the preeminent goaltenders of his time.

What are the key pieces in a Stanley Cup championship team? When you talk about the Edmonton Oilers dynasty, the potent offense of Wayne Gretkzy, Mark Messier and Jari Kurri come to mind, not to mention the constant threat of Paul Coffey pitching in from the blue line. In the days of "run and gun" offense, there were times when the door was open for opponents to come back at Grant Fuhr as if it were target practice. The ability to handle that kind of pressure made Grant Fuhr one of the dominating goaltenders of his time, though sometimes a forgotten component of a well-oiled machine that ruled the National Hockey League in the late 1980s.

After compiling an impressive 78–21–1 junior record for the Victoria Cougars of the WHL, this highly touted youngster was picked by Oilers general manager Glen Sather in the first round (eighth overall) in the 1981 Entry Draft. Fuhr was the runner-up for the Vezina Trophy that season, posting an impressive 28–5–14 record with a 3.31 goals-against average while sharing the duties with fellow backstop Andy Moog.

Over a 10-year period, the Spruce Grove, Alberta, native led the Oilers to five Stanley Cup championships from 1984 to 1990. But without a doubt, his best year was in 1987. Fuhr was a workhorse who accumulated a league-leading 4,304 minutes played and 40 wins. He earned his one and only Vezina Trophy as the league's best goaltender and was runner-up to teammate Wayne Gretzky for the Hart Trophy. Although his regular-season achievements weren't considered the best by some critics, Fuhr gained his reputation as the league's cream of the crop during the playoffs. His clutch play and cat-like reflexes frustrated adversaries who had the misfortune of playing against him and the Oilers juggernaut. Fuhr shares the single-season record for posting 16 playoff wins that season. During the 1983–1984 season, he gathered 14 points, which still stands as the single-season record for most points by a goaltender.

Earlier in 1987, the Canada Cup finals brought the best of Canada up against the Soviet Union's Red Army team. No hockey fan can forget Gretzky's drop pass to a young Mario Lemieux for the game-winning goal, and many will remember Grant Fuhr standing on his head to keep the Russians at bay. His clutch performance gave his team the confidence to open up against the high-powered offense of the Red Army. Fuhr's excellent play in the Canada Cup didn't only leave a lasting impression on Canadians. Internationally, he was praised as the best goaltender in the world.

As the 1980s made way for a new decade, Fuhr began falling on hard times. On September 27, 1990, the NHL suspended him for six months after he admitted to using drugs earlier in his career. The Oilers began to dismantle the team by trading Wayne Gretzky, the start of a fire sale. Then, on September 19, 1991, after playing only 13 games for the Oilers, the six-time All-Star was traded to the Toronto Maple Leafs in a seven-player blockbuster deal. His first season as a Leaf proved to be impressive and he showed a lot of promise. But, although Fuhr knew he was capable of being a number one goaltender, he began the next year spending more time on the bench backing up and helping out a hot rookie sensation by the name of Felix Potvin.

Grant Fuhr was traded to the Buffalo Sabres on February 2, 1993, where he came upon a highly acclaimed Dominik Hasek just as the Dominator was beginning to develop into a world-class goaltender. The year after, Fuhr joined Hasek in winning the William Jennings Trophy for the fewest goals scored against the goaltending duo. In the 1994–95 season, Fuhr was traded to the Los Angeles Kings, where he joined the Great One. But he played only 14 games for the franchise.

In 1995–96, just as many began to think that this once great goaltender was washed up, he signed as a free agent with the St. Louis Blues. Given another chance, the classy veteran didn't disappoint the team. Fuhr began playing with a rejuvenated love for the game and the energy to match any youngster in the league. He played an astonishing 79 games and appeared 76 consecutive times for the Blues that season. Both are still in the single-season record books. Grant's great play continued into the playoffs that year. He was once again in fine form and gave Blues fans high hopes for a Stanley Cup championship. Unfortunately, the playoff run ended prematurely when Maple Leafs forward Nick Kypreos crashed into Fuhr as he was attempting to cover the puck. His leg twisted awkwardly and he tore his knee ligaments.

Fuhr, Grant
G, 5′9″, 190 lbs, b: Spruce Grove, Alta., 9/28/1962

Season	Club, League	Regular Season				Playoffs			
		GP	Mins	GA	Avg	GP	Mins	GA	Avg
1981–82	Edmonton Oilers, NHL	48	2847	157	3.31	5	309	26	5.05
1982–83	Edmonton Oilers, NHL	32	1803	129	4.29	1	11	0	0.00
	Moncton Alpines, AHL	10	604	40	3.98				
1983–84	Edmonton Oilers, NHL	45	2625	171	3.91	16	883	44	2.99
CCup–84	Canada	2	120	6	3.00				
1984–85	Edmonton Oilers, NHL	46	2559	165	3.87	18	1064	55	3.10
1985–86	Edmonton Oilers, NHL	40	2184	143	3.93	9	541	28	3.11
1986–87	Edmonton Oilers, NHL	44	2388	137	3.44	19	1148	47	2.46
RV'87	NHL All-Stars	2	120	8	4.00				
CCup–87	Canada	9	575	32	3.00				
1987–88	Edmonton Oilers, NHL	75	4304	246	3.43	19	1136	55	2.90
1988–89	Edmonton Oilers, NHL	59	3341	213	3.83	7	417	24	3.45
WEC–89	Canada	5	298	18	3.62				
1989–90	Edmonton Oilers, NHL	21	1081	70	3.89				
	Cape Breton Oilers, AHL	2	120	6	3.01				
1990–91	Edmonton Oilers, NHL	13	778	39	3.01	17	1019	51	3.00
	Cape Breton Oilers, AHL	4	240	17	4.25				
1991–92	Toronto Maple Leafs, NHL	66	3774	230	3.66				
1992–93	Toronto Maple Leafs, NHL	29	1665	87	3.14				
	Buffalo Sabres, NHL	29	1694	98	3.47	8	474	27	3.42
1993–94	Buffalo Sabres, NHL	32	1726	106	3.68				
	Rochester Americans, AHL	5	310	10	1.94				
1994–95	Buffalo Sabres, NHL	3	180	12	4.00				
	Los Angeles Kings, NHL	14	698	47	4.04				
1995–96	St. Louis Blues, NHL	79	4365	209	2.87	2	69	1	0.87
1996–97	St. Louis Blues, NHL	73	4261	193	2.72	6	357	13	2.18
1997–98	St. Louis Blues, NHL	58	3274	138	2.53	10	616	28	2.73
1998–99	St. Louis Blues, NHL	39	2193	89	2.44	13	790	31	2.35
1999–2000	Calgary Flames, NHL	23	1205	77	3.83				
	NHL Totals	868	48945	2756	3.38	150	8834	430	2.92
	WEC/CCup/RV'87 Totals	18	1113	64	3.45				

NHL First All-Star Team (1988)
NHL Second All-Star Team (1982)
Won Vezina Trophy (1988)
Won William M. Jennings Trophy (1994)
Won Stanley Cup (1984, 1985, 1987, 1988, 1990)
Won CCup (1984, 1987)

Grant Fuhr appeared 76 consecutive times in 79 games for the St. Louis Blues in 1995–96.

Many people believed that Kypreos ran into him intentionally, but nevertheless, Fuhr's season was done.

In the 1996–97 season, he continued his fine play for the Blues, but he couldn't lead his team over the hump during the playoffs. Over the next two years, injuries became a problem. His knee never seemed to recover and time was catching up. The Blues began to look in another direction, picking up Roman Turek from the Dallas Stars to be their number one goaltender. That left the door open for Grant to be traded on September 4, 1999, to an old Oilers archrival, the Calgary Flames.

The Calgary Flames expected him to take the younger goaltenders under his wing and give some much-needed veteran leadership in the locker room. One of those youngsters between the pipes was Fred Brathwaite. In 1993 he'd been an up-and-comer in the Edmonton Oilers organization and was asked to wear number 31, which the great Grant Fuhr had worn in his Oilers heyday and throughout his career. The Oilers called Grant to ask his permission for Brathwaite to don his idol's number. He answered: "No problem. Go for it." Ironically, Grant and Fred would later became teammates on the Calgary Flames.

As a Flame, Grant joined an elite club of goaltenders. On October 22, 1999, he defeated the Florida Panthers, reaching his 400th career win—only the sixth goalie in NHL history to reach that milestone—and joining the likes of Terry Sawchuk, Jacques Plante, Tony Esposito, Glenn Hall and Patrick Roy. That is good company to be in, and it has undoubtedly reserved him a spot in the Hockey Hall of Fame. Fuhr announced his retirement before the 2000–01 season.

Tommy Sandlin

After Arne Stromberg, Tommy Sandlin became the most prominent among the new wave of Swedish coaches.

In Sweden, they call this calm man with a philosopher's face hockey's "Professor," and rightly so. After Arne Stromberg, Tommy Sandlin became the most outstanding of the new wave of Swedish coaches and affirmed his status by winning many victories in Sweden and in the international arena.

As the 30-year-old coach of Brynas, Sandlin had a hard time achieving success in international tournaments, such as the European Championship, because at the time the Soviet CSKA, headed by the legendary Anatoli Tarasov, sat solidly on the throne of European hockey. However, to Sandlin's credit, the internationally acclaimed Tarasov, known to be stingy with his compliments, noticed his young Swedish colleague and praised his talents.

Tommy Sandlin was born on March 31, 1944, in Gavle, a town famous for its hockey tradition. In 1957 he won the national championship playing for Gavle's Godtemplares IK. But he recognized that his potential as a player was limited and staked his future on a coaching career. His industriousness and ambition were boundless, but even at 30, when he helped Brynas win the national championship, many fans had to ask who the youngster was in the box beside the players.

A Chinese wise man once said, "Good is the leader who is hardly known to the people." Sandlin knew what he wanted and worked to become first a trainer, then a coach and finally a true leader. His achievement was due not only to his ambition but also to his innate ability and deeply felt commitment to the game of hockey.

He coined a number of phrases and invented several rules of conduct along the way. Most of all, he strove to create an atmosphere in which players were motivated to feel good about themselves and their ability to win, that made them feel committed and allowed them to feel confident of their part in the larger whole. He believed in preserving each individual's uniqueness, allowing them to develop self-reliance, endure failure and develop further.

This was Sandlin's philosophy and he applied it to both Tre Kronor and the local teams he worked with. Proof of his achievement are five gold medals won by Brynas and one gold medal won by Ornskoldsvik's MoDo.

When asked which event stands out in his memory, Sandlin recalls the 1987 Vienna Championship, when the Swedish team won the world gold for the first time in 25 years on the heels of its success at the Colorado Springs Olympics. Victory was all the sweeter because the team beat their toughest adversary, the Viktor Tikhonov-led USSR.

Sandlin also won the world bronze in 1979, two Olympic bronzes (Lake Placid in 1980 and Calgary in 1988) and the World Championship silver and European gold in 1990.

Tommy Sandlin, author of numerous books on hockey theory and practical wisdom, is Sweden's most celebrated and successful coach. He considers working with an obscure first division club, Mura, only the most recent in a long string of exciting challenges.

Sandlin, Tommy
Head Coach, b: Gavle, Sweden, 3/31/1944

Season	Club, League	Regular Season				
		GC	W	L	T	W%
1968–77	Brynas, Sweden	*	*	*	*	*
1977–82	MoDo, Sweden	*	*	*	*	*
1982–86	Bjorkloven	*	*	*	*	*
WEC–85	Sweden	10	4	6	0	0.400
WEC–86	Sweden	10	6	2	2	0.700
WEC–87	Sweden	10	5	3	2	0.600
CCup–87	Sweden	6	3	3	0	0.500
OWG–88	Sweden	8	4	1	3	0.687
WEC–89	Sweden	10	4	2	4	0.600
WEC–90	Sweden	10	7	2	1	0.750
	OWG/WEC/CCup Totals	64	33	19	12	0.609

Won WEC (1987)
Sweden Champion (1970, 1971, 1972, 1976, 1977, 1979)

Ron Hextall

One of the most colorful and controversial goalies of the modern game, Ron Hextall ruled the crease with an iron stick, brandishing it like Billy Smith when players interfered and using it like a forward when given the chance to handle the puck. His style was as intimidating as it was popular and for a while he was one of the best goalies of the modern era.

Hextall was the first NHL grandson to play in the league. His father and grandfather had also played. Bryan Hextall Sr. played 11 seasons with the New York Rangers and won the scoring title in 1941–42. His son, Ron's father, played nine less glamorous years before retiring in 1976. Ron's uncle Dennis also played in the league as a fourth-line player of limited talent. Ron, however, was the first Hextall to venture into the net. "My dad thought I was a little crazy at first," Ron admitted. "He wanted me to play up front for a while so I could learn to skate. In my first year, our goalie got sick and I took over. I've been in goal ever since."

Ron Hextall was the first NHL grandson to play in the league.

Ron Hextall was one of the most colorful and controversial goalies of the modern era.

The result of his time as a skater, though, was that Ron became perhaps the game's most mobile goalie of all time. It also gave him a desire to do something no goalie had ever done before—score. "I'm going to score a goal," he predicted when he first entered the NHL. "I've worked on my shot a lot. I can hit the net from our zone. I've even practised the bank shot. I'm just waiting for the right situation." Sure enough, the night of December 8, 1987, in a game against Chicago, the Flyers had a two-goal lead and the Hawks pulled their goalie in the last minute. Hextall got the puck near the side of his net and fired it in, the first time a goalie had ever shot a puck into the opposition goal. (Billy Smith of the Islanders was once credited with a goal for being the last player to touch the puck before the other team scored into its own goal.) Incredibly, Hextall replicated the feat in the playoffs. On April 11, 1989, he again fired the puck into the open net, against Washington, thus also becoming the first goalie to score in a playoff game.

Hextall's style was physical, aggressive and unheard-of. He would chase the puck anywhere in his own end, and his own players routinely shot the puck back to him when killing a penalty. Along with being a goal scorer, he also set every possible penalty-minutes record for a goalie, collecting more than 100 on two occasions—and no goalie had ever come anywhere near the 100 mark. The first time came in his rookie season, when he was assessed 104 minutes. The very next year he broke that mark. He was also the most willing fighter among pad-wearers the game had ever known and as a result was suspended on numerous occasions.

In that rookie season, 1986–87, he took the Flyers to the Stanley Cup finals against the dynasty of the Edmonton Oilers. He played heroically in defeat and earned the Conn Smythe Trophy for playoff excellence, but in game four of that series, he slashed Kent Nilsson viciously and was suspended for the first eight games of the 1987–88 season. In the 1989 playoffs, he committed a foul of equal violence. Late in the team's final game against the Montreal Canadiens, in which the Habs were clearly going to win and eliminate the Flyers, Hextall skated into the corner and attacked Montreal defenseman Chris Chelios, hitting the surprised player repeatedly with his blocker. For that Hextall received a 12-game suspension to start the 1989–90 season, and upon returning he suffered a series of small injuries that limited him to eight games for the year. In an exhibition game against Detroit to start the 1991–92 season, he slashed Jim Cummins and was given another six-game suspension.

Hextall, Ron
G, 6'3", 192 lbs, b: Brandon, Man., 5/3/1964

Season	Club, League	Regular Season				Playoffs			
		GP	Mins	GA	Avg	GP	Mins	GA	Avg
1984–85	Hershey Bears, AHL	11	555	34	3.68				
	Kalamazoo Wings, IHL	19	1103	80	4.35				
1985–86	Hershey Bears, AHL	53	3061	174	3.41	13	780	42	3.23
1986–87	Philadelphia Flyers, NHL	66	3799	190	3.00	26	1540	71	2.77
1987–88	Philadelphia Flyers, NHL	62	3561	208	3.50	7	379	30	4.75
1988–89	Philadelphia Flyers, NHL	64	3756	202	3.23	15	886	49	3.32
1989–90	Philadelphia Flyers, NHL	8	419	29	4.15				
	Hershey Bears, AHL	1	49	3	3.67				
1990–91	Philadelphia Flyers, NHL	36	2035	106	3.13				
1991–92	Philadelphia Flyers, NHL	45	2668	151	3.40				
WC–92	Canada	5	273	13	2.86				
1992–93	Quebec Nordiques, NHL	54	2988	172	3.45	6	372	18	2.90
1993–94	New York Islanders, NHL	65	3581	184	3.08	3	158	16	6.08
1994–95	Philadelphia Flyers, NHL	31	1824	88	2.89	15	897	42	2.81
1995–96	Philadelphia Flyers, NHL	53	3102	112	2.17	12	760	27	2.13
1996–97	Philadelphia Flyers, NHL	55	3094	132	2.56	8	444	22	2.97
1997–98	Philadelphia Flyers, NHL	46	2688	97	2.17	1	20	1	3.00
1998–99	Philadelphia Flyers, NHL	23	1235	52	2.53				
	NHL Totals	608	34750	1723	2.97	93	5456	276	3.04
	WC/RV'87/CCup Totals	5	273	13	2.86				

NHL First All-Star Team (1987)
Won Vezina Trophy (1987)
Won Conn Smythe Trophy (1987)
Won CCup (1987)

And his stickwork wasn't confined to the enemy. He was invited to Team Canada's camp for the 1987 Canada Cup and during practice he chopped Sylvain Turgeon's arm because he was apparently too close in front of Hextall's goal. Turgeon's forearm was fractured and he missed the tournament. Hextall didn't play in that Canada Cup, but he did play at the World Championship in 1992, his only international participation.

After being traded to the Nordiques and the Islanders, Hextall finished his career once again with the Flyers, taking the team to the 1997 finals before losing to the Detroit Red Wings, the closest he ever came to the Cup.

Igor Larionov

Wayne Gretzky and Igor Larionov made their debut in seniors world hockey practically on the same day in September 1981 as members of their national squads in the Canada Cup tournament. Canadian hockey fans were highly anticipating Gretzky's arrival, but there were nagging doubts as well, and a certain amount of public criticism. There were comments such as: "He gives the impression of being a player who isn't quite independent on ice. He needs someone else's help in order to make a play. He looks like someone else's kid brother." For Larionov, the criticism was even heavier.

Wayne Gretzky and Igor Larionov debuted as international players in the 1981 Canada Cup.

They said: "One partner isn't enough for him. For him to accomplish anything with his style of play, he needs a whole team. He looks like a holdover from collective-style Soviet hockey."

Larionov's style of play was clearly demonstrated in an episode that involved a rather unknown forward by the name of Konstantin Vinogradov. A capable player who always tried hard, Vinogradov found himself substituting in several matches on the first forward line of CSKA for the injured Vladimir Krutov. He would open himself up and then stop, waiting for a pass. But there was no pass. Again he would open himself up, but again no pass. He was shocked. "What a playmaker! Doesn't he see me when I'm in the open?" While sitting on the team bench, Larionov explained to him, "You manage to open yourself—great! But keep on going farther, because I see you. But I must feign my next move, and that is why I don't look in your direction."

According to Larionov, the essence of his game while playing for the USSR national team and CSKA was to feed his partners. "The players on both teams were real past masters, but all of them had their own styles. Makarov needed his own kind of pass, Krutov an altogether different kind. And if Viacheslav Fetisov joined the attack, I knew he would go right to the end. And he would by all means receive his pass on the dot."

"The day that I placed Larionov on the line together with Makarov and Krutov during training, I heaved a sigh of relief," Viktor Tikhonov recalled. "Igor fit the bill right away, and he immediately found a common language with the wingers."

Igor Larionov has been in hockey for 22 years. For eight years he played with CSKA and the USSR nationals—eight years that challenged every player on the team to the limit. And that was followed by 10 years in the NHL. Larionov's cool, calculating style of hockey and his long, smooth career are as much an accomplishment as the games and the awards he has won. He proved to be a companionable player in both the regimented Soviet system and in the individualistic NHL. It helped that he always had a good opinion of himself.

To quote Viktor Tikhonov once again: "He is an academician in ice hockey. A constructor—a playmaker. He sets up plays, and he can equally tone down or whip up the pace. On top of that, when he is on the ice, he is quite capable of defusing conflicting situations. And not only on the ice—he 'isolates' his partners from irritating external factors. Without giving in to the temptation of settling disputes by resorting to fisticuffs, he exerts a favorable influence on the players around him, especially Makarov and Krutov. Such a feature is especially valuable. I am an atheist, but I am ready to acknowledge that Igor Larionov is a 'divine' playmaker."

There are other parallels between Larionov and Gretzky. At first glance, both players seemed to be somewhat out of place in the ferocious game of hockey. On the outside, they appeared to be too gentle for the game, as if they ended up on the hockey rink by accident. Both players were quite good-looking and both were lucky enough to escape severe injuries.

Wayne's father and first coach taught his 16-year-old son how to do things on ice that the tough guys couldn't do. Essentially, the only way to beat the big guys was to outwit them by thinking faster and by acquiring superb stick-handling.

At about the same time, the experienced coach of the renowned Voskresensk hockey team, Nikolai Epshtein, was giving similar instructions to the youthful Larionov: "Take a look at Kharlamov, at his specifications—how much does he weigh? Not much. But look at the way he goes into battle. He is practically always the first one who gets control of the puck. And that's what you have to do—always be the first one to get hold of the puck."

At the age of 26, Larionov was able to explain in simple terms to the media how to avoid injury. "When you come up to the boards, you must not look your adversary in the eye as if to say, 'All right, let's fight it out!' Instead you must keep your eye on the puck and nail your opponent to the boards. And

---

Larionov, Igor
C, 5´9˝, 170 lbs, b: Voskresensk, USSR, 12/3/1960

Season	Club, League	Regular Season					Playoffs				
		GP	G	A	Pts	PIM	GP	G	A	Pts	PIM
1977–78	Khimik, USSR	6	3	0	3	4					
1978–79	Khimik, USSR	32	3	4	7	12					
1979–80	Khimik, USSR	42	11	7	18	24					
1980–81	Khimik, USSR	43	22	23	45	36					
CCup–81	USSR	7	4	1	5	8					
1981–82	CSKA, USSR	46	31	22	53	6					
WEC–82	USSR	10	4	6	10	2					
1982–83	CSKA, USSR	44	20	19	39	20					
WEC–83	USSR	9	5	7	12	4					
1983–84	CSKA, USSR	43	15	26	41	30					
OWG–84	USSR	6	1	4	5	6					
CCup–84	USSR	5	1	2	3	6					
1984–85	CSKA, USSR	40	18	28	46	20					
WEC–85	USSR	10	2	4	6	8					
1985–86	CSKA, USSR	40	21	31	52	33					
WEC–86	USSR	10	7	1	8	4					
1986–87	CSKA, USSR	39	20	26	46	34					
RV'87	USSR	2	0	2	2	0					
WEC–87	USSR	10	4	8	12	2					
CCup–87	USSR	9	1	2	3	6					
1987–88	CSKA, USSR	51	25	32	57	54					
OWG–88	USSR	8	4	9	13	4					
1988–89	CSKA, USSR	31	15	12	27	22					
WEC–89	USSR	8	3	0	3	11					
1989–90	Vancouver Canucks, NHL	74	17	27	44	20					
1990–91	Vancouver Canucks, NHL	64	13	21	34	14	6	1	0	1	6
1991–92	Vancouver Canucks, NHL	72	21	44	65	54	13	3	7	10	4
1992–93	Lugano, Switzerland	24	10	19	29	44					
1993–94	San Jose Sharks, NHL	60	18	38	56	40	14	5	13	18	10
1994–95	San Jose Sharks, NHL	33	4	20	24	14	11	1	8	9	2
1995–96	San Jose Sharks, NHL	4	1	1	2	0					
	Detroit Red Wings, NHL	69	21	50	71	34	19	6	7	13	6
WCup–96	Russia	5	0	4	4	2					
1996–97	Detroit Red Wings, NHL	64	12	42	54	26	20	4	8	12	8
1997–98	Detroit Red Wings, NHL	69	8	39	47	40	22	3	10	13	12
1998–99	Detroit Red Wings, NHL	75	14	49	63	48	7	0	2	2	0
1999–00	Detroit Red Wings, NHL	79	9	38	47	28	9	1	2	3	6
2000–01	Florida-Detroit, NHL	659	31	40	38	6	1	3	4	2	
2000–02	Detroit Red Wings, NHL	70	11	32	43	50					
OWG–02	Russia	6	0	3	3	4					
	USSR Totals	457	204	230	434	295					
	NHL Totals	798	158	432	590	406	127	25	60	85	56
OWG/WEC/CCup/RV'87/WCup Totals		105	36	53	89	67					

Won OWG (1984, 1988)
Won WEC (1982, 1983, 1986, 1989)
Won Stanley Cup (1997, 1998)
Won CCup (1981)
USSR Champion (1982, 1983, 1984, 1985, 1986, 1987, 1988, 1989)

since the other guy isn't expecting a bodycheck at this point in the tussle, you slip away with the puck. At the same time, you have to judge your opponent's capabilities. If he is heavier than you, then because of this you have to take a wider stance, with legs far apart in order to have a better center of gravity."

Larionov planned and followed a model diet during his years as a player (he preferred vegetables). His workloads at training sessions were always heavy. After receiving instructions from coach Tikhonov, Larionov's forward line would discuss general game strategy, and it often turned out that their tactics differed from those of the coach.

Igor Larionov proved to be a companionable player in both the regimented Soviet system and the individualistic NHL.

As one of the foremost representatives of the Soviet-style team collectivism, Larionov was the first to shatter the myth that Soviet achievements in the game of hockey came naturally. As the second 100% professional in the Soviet game after goalkeeper Vladislav Tretiak, Larionov made it known publicly that he was fed up with the year-round drilling at training camps, that he'd had his fill of the general dictatorship from coaches, that hockey in the USSR didn't belong to the players and that the players didn't even belong to themselves.

Fetisov went as far as complaining publicly about the coach. Tikhonov eventually forgave Fetisov and even put him on the roster of the national team for the World Championship. But not Larionov. He could forgive someone for an emotional outburst, but not a disagreement on principles—ever.

The conflict between Tikhonov and Larionov started to deepen even before Larionov appeared in the CSKA lineup. And Vladimir Krutov became an involuntary accomplice in this conflict. In the juniors, Krutov and Larionov were considered to be on a par. But Krutov, a "native" CSKA player who had grown up with the team, suddenly appeared with the senior national squad. Yet Tikhonov would not allow Larionov to join the nationals until he received his consent to switch from Voskresensk to CSKA. "That was probably the only time I was envious," declared Larionov. "But that was malicious envy."

About 10 years later, Larionov found himself shoulder to shoulder with Krutov in Vancouver. Not wanting to start his overseas career on the same footing, he very quickly distanced himself from his former buddy.

If anyone had told Larionov that he'd play in the NHL for more than 10 years, he wouldn't have believed it. None of his usual cool calculations or masterful planning would have helped. His mind was more troubled than ever as he was about to leave his homeland. "There is a whole season ahead," he deliberated with caution, "so who knows how things may turn out in such a meat grinder."

Viktor Tikhonov once said: "He is an academician in ice hockey. A constructor a playmaker.... I am an atheist, but I am ready to acknowledge that Igor Larionov [front] is a 'divine' playmaker."

A year later, Larionov reached his peak. "The coach constantly changes the lineup. And that suits me quite well. After playing for eight years in a five-man lineup in which practically nothing changed, I found myself in a position in which I had to find playing contact with new partners— both experienced and greenhorns, players who were able and those who weren't very able. This thing was new to me, and I liked it. In general, I was never admiring about my own style of playing. I take quite a restrained approach to myself. All the more so at the age of 30. But I think that each of the Canucks would like to play with me. I feed passes to all the wingers without exception."

Not everyone in North America placed such a high value on Larionov, however. For one whole season he ended up in Switzerland. He commented on that "break" in quite severe terms: "I upheld the right to play my own kind of hockey." But Larionov would later return to earn two Stanley Cup rings and to teach his fellow Voskresensk player, Detroit forward Vyacheslav Kozlov, not to lose heart.

Larionov signed with Florida as a free agent for the 2000–01 season, but his short stint there proved much less fulfilling than anticipated. The Panthers organization had hoped his arrival would help light a fire under star Pavel Bure, but the pairing didn't click. In fact, the Larionov experiment in Florida lasted just 26 games, during which he produced 11 points, before he was traded back to Detroit for Jan Golubovsky on December 28, 2000. At the age of 41, Larionov played in his third Olympics in 2002 and helped Russia bring home the bronze medal.

Mark Messier

Like Gordie Howe, Mark Messier is credited with being the most complete player of his generation.

Mark Messier's nickname, "the Moose," is a tribute to his size, strength and determination. A player renowned for his leadership abilities and one of the all-time leading NHL scorers, Messier emerged from the great Edmonton Oilers teams of the 1980s to become a hockey superstar. He was a powerful skater who combined playmaking skill and a goal-scoring touch with the toughness necessary to survive and thrive in the corners. Six times his teams sipped from the Stanley Cup and on two occasions Messier took home the Hart Trophy as the league's most valuable player.

Like Gordie Howe, Messier is credited with being the most complete player of his generation. He was a power forward, a two-way left winger and sometime center with talent and overwhelming power and size and an unpredictable mean streak. Messier acquired his multidimensional game during a childhood filled with hockey in his home town of Edmonton. At age four, he was attending his father's minor-league practices. At age 11, he was a stick boy for the Spruce Grove Mets in the Alberta junior leagues, the team he would star on just five years later.

Messier was a big kid, just 6′ and weighing close to 200 pounds, and his talent was so obvious that he skipped major junior and college hockey altogether. He was given a five-game tryout by the Indianapolis Racers of the World Hockey Association when he was a 17-year-old in 1978. Though he failed to register a point and was released by the Racers just before the franchise folded, he did celebrate his 18th birthday in the pro ranks after the Cincinnati Stingers, a competing WHA team, signed him as a free agent and he played 47 games for that team. In 1979 he was selected by the Edmonton Oilers as the team's second choice, 48th overall in the NHL's Entry Draft.

Messier began the 1979–80 season with the Oilers, but the poise and professionalism that would one day make him the game's premier leader were still being developed by the NHL rookie. He missed practices, showed up late for flights and finally earned a demotion to the Houston Apollos when he missed a team flight altogether early in the season. After four games with

Houston, Messier returned to the Oilers a changed man. His work rate increased and over the next two seasons he developed, along with his many talented but inexperienced teammates, into one of the league's best young players. He scored 50 goals in 1981–82, his third season, double his total of the year before, and was selected to the NHL's First All-Star Team.

When the Oilers won their first of four Stanley Cup championships in five years in 1984, Messier—on a team with such stars as Wayne Gretzky, Paul Coffey and Grant Fuhr—was the most valuable player in the playoffs, capturing the Conn Smythe Trophy for his 26 post-season points and his undeniable leadership. Gretzky was a dominant offensive player and Edmonton recorded new highs for team scoring. But the Oilers in their glory years were also a tight defensive group. Messier—fast, powerful and physical—was a perfect two-way player, able to excel at both ends of the ice.

Gretzky and Messier were very close during their years in Edmonton. When Gretzky was traded to the Los Angeles Kings in 1988, Messier was made the Edmonton captain, though many predicted the Oilers' run of success would leave with the Great One. In the 1989 playoffs, the Oilers were upset by Gretzky's Kings in a close first-round series and the skepticism surrounding the team seemed to be merited. One season later, however, in 1989–90, Messier had a career year, finishing second to Gretzky in the points race with 129. He also won the Hart Trophy over Boston's Ray Bourque as the league's most valuable player. In the playoffs, with the Oilers down 2–1 in games to the Chicago Blackhawks in the semifinals, Messier took over in the fourth game, scoring two goals and collecting two assists in Edmonton's 4–2 road win. His one-man display impressed everyone who watched, Chicago players, coaches and fans included, and his all-time performance spurred the Oilers. Edmonton swept the remaining games from Chicago and easily handled Bourque and the Bruins in the finals to give Messier his fifth Stanley Cup ring with Edmonton.

The small-market Oilers struggled following their 1990 victory, and Messier was traded to the New York Rangers prior to the 1991–92 season for Bernie Nichols, Steven Rice and Louie DeBrusk. The Rangers had last won the Stanley Cup in 1940 and it was believed all the

Messier, Mark
C, 6′1″, 205 lbs, b: Edmonton, Alta., 1/18/1961

Season	Club, League	Regular Season					Playoffs				
		GP	G	A	Pts	PIM	GP	G	A	Pts	PIM
1978–79	Indianapolis Racers, WHA	5	0	0	0	0					
	Cincinnati Stingers, WHA	47	1	10	11	58					
1979–80	Edmonton Oilers, NHL	75	12	21	33	120	3	1	2	3	2
	Houston Apollos, CHL	4	0	3	3	4					
1980–81	Edmonton Oilers, NHL	72	23	40	63	102	9	2	5	7	13
1981–82	Edmonton Oilers, NHL	78	50	38	88	119	5	1	2	3	8
1982–83	Edmonton Oilers, NHL	77	48	58	106	72	15	15	6	21	14
1983–84	Edmonton Oilers, NHL	73	37	64	101	165	19	8	18	26	19
CCup–84	Canada	8	2	4	6	8					
1984–85	Edmonton Oilers, NHL	55	23	31	54	57	18	12	13	25	12
1985–86	Edmonton Oilers, NHL	63	35	49	84	68	10	4	6	10	18
1986–87	Edmonton Oilers, NHL	77	37	70	107	73	21	12	16	28	16
RV'87	NHL All-Stars	2	1	0	1	0					
CCup–87	Canada	9	1	6	7	6					
1987–88	Edmonton Oilers, NHL	77	37	74	111	103	19	11	23	34	29
1988–89	Edmonton Oilers, NHL	72	33	61	94	130	7	1	11	12	8
WEC–89	Canada	6	3	3	6	8					
1989–90	Edmonton Oilers, NHL	79	45	84	129	79	22	9	22	31	20
1990–91	Edmonton Oilers, NHL	53	12	52	64	34	18	4	11	15	16
CCup–91	Canada	8	2	6	8	10					
1991–92	New York Rangers, NHL	79	35	72	107	76	11	7	7	14	6
1992–93	New York Rangers, NHL	75	25	66	91	72					
1993–94	New York Rangers, NHL	76	26	58	84	76	23	12	18	30	33
1994–95	New York Rangers, NHL	46	14	39	53	40	10	3	10	13	8
1995–96	New York Rangers, NHL	74	47	52	99	122	11	4	7	11	16
WCup–96	Canada	7	1	4	5	12					
1996–97	New York Rangers, NHL	71	36	48	84	88	15	3	9	12	6
1997–98	Vancouver Canucks, NHL	82	22	38	60	58					
1998–99	Vancouver Canucks, NHL	59	13	35	48	33					
1999–00	Vancouver Canucks, NHL	66	17	37	54	30					
2000–01	New York Rangers, NHL	82	24	43	67	89					
2001–02	New York Rangers, NHL	41	7	16	23	32					
	WHA Totals	52	1	10	11	58					
	NHL Totals	1602	658	1146	1804	1838					
	WEC/CCup/RV'87/WCup Totals	40	10	23	33	44					

NHL First All-Star Team (1982, 1983, 1990, 1992)
NHL Second All-Star Team (1984)
Won Hart Trophy (1990, 1992)
Won Conn Smythe Trophy (1984)
Won Lester B. Pearson Award (1990, 1992)
Won Stanley Cup (1984, 1985, 1987, 1988, 1990, 1994)
Won CCup (1984, 1987, 1991)

team required to tip the scales in its favor was a leader like Messier. His first season was an individual success—he had 107 points and was awarded the Hart Trophy for the second time in three years. But the Rangers failed to advance to the promised land in the playoffs.

A rift developed between Messier and Ranger coach Roger Neilson, a split which divided the team for much of the following season. Messier wanted a more open style of play and openly disagreed with the bench boss. Neilson was eventually replaced when the team failed to qualify for the 1993 playoffs and Mike Keenan took over as bench boss. Messier's offensive production declined in 1993–94, though he scored more than 20 goals for the 13th time in his career. In the playoffs, however, Messier was at his very best, engineering one of the great moments in New York sports history.

Mark Messier scored the Cup-winning goal for the Rangers in 1994 and became the first player to captain two different teams to Stanley Cup titles.

The Rangers were down 3–2 in games to New Jersey in the Eastern Conference finals. Messier publicly guaranteed a game six win. He followed up on his promise with a stellar performance, scoring a hat-trick in the third period to bring his team back from elimination and force a seventh game. Messier and the Rangers dispatched the Devils and then won the Cup in another thrilling series against Pavel Bure and the Vancouver Canucks. Messier scored the Cup-winning goal in the seventh game. With the victory, the franchise's first in 54 years, Messier became the first player to captain two different teams to Stanley Cup titles.

Messier continued to record big numbers with the Rangers, finishing with 99 points in 1995–96. In 1996–97, Wayne Gretzky joined him in New York. Both nearing 37 years of age, the long-time teammates and friends were also key members of Canada's second-place finish in the 1996 World Cup. Following the Rangers' early exit in the 1997 playoffs, Messier signed as a free agent with the Vancouver Canucks, but his time in Vancouver was filled with turmoil. Many long-time Canucks were traded or moved as the team struggled to find a winning formula. Trade rumors persisted around Messier for the next few seasons, especially with the playoffs nearing and teams around the league looking for veteran leadership.

Messier scored his 600th career goal in a win over Florida in October of 1998. He and two of his former Oilers teammates, Gretzky and Jari Kurri, were three of only 10 players to ever top that benchmark. Despite his accomplishments and his continuing high level of play, the coaches and general managers in charge of Canada's Olympic team decided against selecting him to the squad prior to the Nagano Olympics. A youth movement, led by Flyers and Team Canada captain Eric Lindros, left Messier on the outside looking in. When the team failed to win a medal, many fans and pundits pointed to the omission of Messier, a player whose leadership and determination ensure him of a place in the Hockey Hall of Fame when he retires—which has not happened yet.

In the summer of 2000, Messier signed on again with the New York Rangers as a free agent. Although the team missed the playoffs in his first year back, he scored 24 goals and shows no signs of letting up. Even the 2001–02 season began well for Messier and the Rangers, who had obtained Eric Lindros in a deal with the Philadelphia Flyers, though the team went into a mid-season slump that it couldn't come back from and the 41-year-old Messier was diagnosed with a serious shoulder problem at the beginning of March that sidelined him for the remainder of the regular season.

Vyacheslav Bykov

For a professional hockey player, Vyacheslav Bykov wasn't very big. Out on the ice he had to be particularly careful to avoid taking a beating. He survived and went on to become the captain of the championship Russian national team, following in the footsteps of such illustrious names as Boris Mikhailov, Valeri Vasiliev and Viacheslav Fetisov. As a player, he made a great impression not only on Soviet hockey fans but also on the fans in the usually staid Switzerland, where Bykov concluded his playing career to a standing ovation.

Vyacheslav Bykov made a big impression in his Soviet homeland, but even the normally staid Switzerland fans gave him a standing ovation as he concluded his career.

In the old Soviet days, a player was instructed to make logical choices at every step of the game—feint or pass, rush or pause, pass to the right or to the left. But hockey as played by Vyacheslav Bykov was a smooth, uninterrupted game. This style of play came after a break with the tradition of Soviet-style centers and only became fashionable at the height of Igor Larionov's career. It was Larionov whom Bykov replaced, and for almost 10 years he played in the uniforms of the USSR national squad, Russia and Central Red Army.

One has to wonder if Bykov's determination to excel in such an aggressive sport was his way of compensating for the shortcomings nature had bestowed upon him. As one of the last of the great hockey players of the Soviet Union, Bykov became a master of the game on his own initiative, just like the majority of the truly great players who came before him. Bykov discovered most of the basic techniques on his own, without any kind of prompting from instructors. Bykov hadn't planned on a career in hockey, having fooled around with a third-rate team when he wasn't busy with his studies at a college in Chelyabinsk. He wasn't invited to play for the youth or national junior squads because no one knew him. No one had seen him in action.

When the invitation to play finally did come—first for the Chelyabinsk Traktor hockey club and then for Central Red Army—he agreed. But he arrived pretty much ready-made as a player. He was an excellent skater, nimble-footed and superb at handling sudden changes in rhythm. He was also a talented sharpshooter. Based on the milestones he reached during his career, Bykov appears even more accomplished than the members of Larionov's five-man line.

Viktor Tikhonov didn't single-handedly discover the new kind of center—strategically flexible and highly mobile. The credit really goes to Larionov, who was the first to play the new style of game. It was only later that he caught the eye of Tikhonov, who took Larionov to fill the center slot in a top forward line he was putting together. On the secondary lines of the Red Army and the national team, Tikhonov stuck with centers of the traditional type—strong on defense and fearless of heavy bodychecking—such as Viktor Zhluktov and Sergei Nemichinov. But then Bykov suddenly appeared in Chelyabinsk the same way Larionov had come from nowhere a little earlier.

"Both at workouts and in games, he never allowed himself to play at half steam," Viacheslav Fetisov recalls. "For him, playing hockey, every instant of the game, was his life. Once, during a game for the European Championship Cup, he made a mistake in his own zone—from behind the net, he flicked a pass right on the tip of the stick of an opposing player who quite naturally slapped in a goal. You should have seen how hard Bykov took that—he was almost in tears. We of course tried to console him on the bench, 'Don't take it so badly, you'll get even with them.' But he kept on repeating: 'How could I? How could I?' It was a very long time before Bykov could erase that incident from his memory, and he never again allowed himself to make a similar mistake."

It took another year or so for the fastest and hardest-working Red Army line to change its style of playing under Bykov's command. In the beginning, there was so much confusion that it seemed to wear out the opponents. But then some kind of order to their intricate patterns on the ice was established. In 1986 the second-string Red Army line dazzled North American hockey fans in a series of games against NHL clubs.

When Valeri Kamensky came along, this forward line really began to work, becoming more physical and more solid all around. Bykov found himself in a position very similar to Larionov's—able to concentrate on plays rather than having to be the aggressor. And beginning that season, 1986–87, Bykov's line was regarded by hockey writers and fans as almost on a par with Larionov's.

The second line accepted the first line's favored status without resorting to scheming and backstabbing. But with the turmoil surrounding Fetisov's departure to America, the second line began to take up the slack when discord surfaced among the players on the first line. In the 1989 World Championship, even while the Larionov line was still intact, the Bykov line gave a demonstration of its true potential. In seven consecutive games, they didn't leave the ice without scoring a goal—a dazzling display of leadership. The combination of Bykov and Andrei Khomutov (who were approaching their 30th birthdays) with Kamensky produced not only the swiftest and most agile but also the most skillful forward line.

In 1990, as captain of the USSR national squad, Bykov introduced the world champions to the press for the first time. Among other things, he said: "At the last championship, Khomutov and Kamensky helped me to score a lot of goals. This time I considered it my duty to repay them with assists." And together with Khomutov, he immediately set out for Fribourg, Switzerland, where they would wrap up their hockey careers.

Why didn't they submit themselves to the ultimate challenge and join the NHL? Perhaps they wanted to, but in Viktor Tikhonov's

Bykov, Vyacheslav
C, 5'7", 155 lbs, b: Chelyabinsk, USSR, 6/24/1960

Season	Club, League	Regular Season					Playoffs				
		GP	G	A	Pts	PIM	GP	G	A	Pts	PIM
1979–80	Traktor, USSR	3	2	0	2	0					
1980–81	Traktor, USSR	48	26	16	42	4					
1981–82	Traktor, USSR	44	20	16	36	14					
1982–83	CSKA, USSR	44	22	22	44	10					
WEC–83	USSR	10	3	2	5	0					
1983–84	CSKA, USSR	44	22	11	33	12					
1984–85	CSKA, USSR	36	21	14	35	4					
WEC–85	USSR	10	7	2	9	2					
1985–86	CSKA, USSR	36	10	10	20	6					
WEC–86	USSR	10	6	6	12	2					
1986–87	CSKA, USSR	40	18	15	33	10					
WEC–87	USSR	10	5	6	11	0					
CCup–87	USSR	9	2	7	9	4					
1987–88	CSKA, USSR	47	17	30	47	26					
OWG–88	USSR	7	2	3	5	2					
1988–89	CSKA, USSR	40	16	20	36	10					
WEC–89	USSR	10	6	6	12	2					
1989–90	CSKA, USSR	48	21	16	37	12					
WEC–90	USSR	10	3	1	4	4					
1990–91	Fribourg, Switzerland	36	35	49	84	18	8	7	16	23	8
WEC–91	USSR	10	4	4	8	0					
1991–92	Fribourg, Switzerland	34	39	48	87	24	14	4	16	20	10
OWG–92	Russia	8	4	7	11	0					
1992–93	Fribourg, Switzerland	35	25	51	76	14	9	10	12	22	4
WC–93	Russia	8	4	3	7	6					
1993–94	Fribourg, Switzerland	36	30	43	73	2	11	11	21	32	2
1994–95	Fribourg, Switzerland	30	24	51	75	35	8	7	4	11	4
WC–95	Russia	6	2	2	4	4					
1995–96	Fribourg, Switzerland	28	10	25	35	8	4	2	1	3	0
1996–97	Fribourg, Switzerland	46	23	45	68	16	3	0	3	3	2
1997–98	Fribourg, Switzerland	18	14	18	32	4	12	2	6	8	6
1998–99	Lausanne, Switzerland	24	19	21	40	40	3	2	4	6	2
1999–2000	Lausanne, Switzerland	6	2	9	11	2					
	USSR/Russia Totals	430	195	170	365	108					
	Switzerland Totals	293	221	360	581	163	72	45	83	128	40
	OWG/WEC/WC/CCup Totals	108	48	49	97	26					

Won OWG (1988, 1992)
Won WEC/WC (1983, 1986, 1989, 1990, 1993)
USSR Champion (1983, 1984, 1985, 1986, 1987, 1988, 1989)

lineup, they'd had more than their fill of brutal, exhausting, high-speed games. Unlike the Larionov trio, whose pleasure came from putting on incredible performances working as a unit, Bykov and Khomutov, on looking back, derived satisfaction from the game itself rather than from realizing any particular ambitions. And they were still in demand.

In 1992 the CIS select team took gold at the Winter Olympics in Norway. And in 1993 they helped a "hopeless" Russian national team to its first gold medal at a World Championship. Bykov and Khomutov were the undisputed leaders on the team—an example even to the opposition of how a tournament had to be won.

Vyacheslav Bykov discovered most of the basic techniques on his own.

Paul Coffey

One of the swiftest skaters in hockey, Paul Coffey is near the top of the all-time NHL points list, a remarkable achievement for a defenseman. Only his former Edmonton Oilers teammate Wayne Gretzky has more assists. Coffey has often been compared to Bobby Orr for his ability to create offensive opportunities with his speed and puck-carrying ability. But, unlike Orr, Coffey has also had to contend with skeptics of his defensive abilities. Most often he contends by winning—games, the Stanley Cup and Norris Trophy awards as the game's best defender.

For a player with such impressive athletic ability, Coffey had a difficult transition into the professional game. He played two seasons of junior hockey in the Ontario Hockey Association, moving from the Sault Ste. Marie Greyhounds to the Kitchener Rangers in 1979. Following his season with the Rangers, immediately before the NHL Entry Draft in 1980, Coffey had an assessment meeting with Kitchener head coach Rod Seiling. Oblivious to his talents, Seiling told Coffey that he couldn't skate well enough to play pro hockey and that he didn't have the puckhandling or shooting skills necessary to play at the next level.

Only former Oilers teammate Wayne Gretzky has more assists than Paul Coffey.

The Edmonton Oilers obviously didn't agree. Looking for an offensive threat on the blue line, the Edmonton staff was impressed with Coffey's 102 points in his last junior season in the OHA and selected him sixth overall in the draft. Coffey joined the Oilers as a 19-year-old but struggled in his first season, losing confidence when he sat on the bench early in the season. Perhaps listening too closely to critics of his attacking style, he attempted to shore up his defensive play at the expense of carrying the puck and taking chances.

"I was coming in as a 'can't miss' player who should make the team—good puckhandler, good offensive skills, great skater—but 'can't play defensive hockey.' That was the knock against me," Coffey said. "Instead of doing what I should have done—stick to my game—I went to training camp with the attitude that, 'I'm going to show these guys, I'm going to play defensive hockey.' But that wasn't why Edmonton drafted me. They wanted me to lug the puck and get things going."

Oilers general manager and coach Glen Sather came close early that first season to trading Coffey to the Buffalo Sabres, whose general manager, Scotty Bowman, was interested in the young defenseman. Sather's patience would be rewarded the next season as Coffey and the Oilers blossomed as offensive standouts. With Wayne Gretzky weaving his magic, the Oilers scored 417 goals and Coffey led all defensemen with 89 points. He faltered periodically in the second half of the season, struggling still with his confidence and making errors due to anxiety. But after a solid third year, Coffey truly came into his own in 1983–84. His 126 points put him second only to Gretzky. The Oilers, scoring more goals than any team in the history of the league, went on to win the Stanley Cup.

Coffey didn't simply pass the puck to his superstar forwards and then watch them score, adding to his assist totals. He had breakaway speed that allowed him to make flashing end-to-end rushes. His shot, rated among the best in the league, was even harder when he was at full speed. If Coffey was caught out of position on one of these forays, he knew he had the ability to get back quickly to help his goalie.

His defensive reputation received a boost during the 1984 Canada Cup. In the semifinals against the Soviet Union, with the teams in overtime, Coffey was the lone defender as Vladimir Kovin and Mikhail Varnakov broke in on a two-on-one. Coffey coolly held his position, then dove to deflect Kovin's pass, regaining his feet in time to collect the puck and send it the other way. Canadian John Tonelli retrieved it and sent it to Coffey at the blue line. Coffey's shot was deflected by Mike Bossy for the winning goal and Canada went on to capture the tournament.

"Having a part in that goal was wonderful, an emotional high that's tough to describe," Coffey said. "But that defensive play was a bigger high. I think maybe a few people who figured I couldn't play defense changed their thinking after I broke up that rush."

After Edmonton again won the Stanley Cup in 1985, Coffey was awarded the Norris Trophy as the league's best defenseman. He would win the award again the next season for his best individual season to date—one of the best seasons ever for a defenseman. He finished with 138 points, one shy of Orr's record total, and scored 48 goals to better Orr's previous record of 46. And in a game in March of that year, Coffey scored two goals and had six assists to tie Tom Bladon's NHL record for points in a game by a defender.

Trouble was brewing, however, between the star defenseman and Glen Sather. A rift had developed since the last game of the 1985–86 season, when, with Coffey chasing Orr's

Coffey, Paul
D, 6´, 190 lbs, b: Weston, Ont., 6/1/1961

Season	Club, League	Regular Season					Playoffs				
		GP	G	A	Pts	PIM	GP	G	A	Pts	PIM
1980–81	Edmonton Oilers, NHL	74	9	23	32	130	9	4	3	7	22
1981–82	Edmonton Oilers, NHL	80	29	60	89	106	5	1	1	2	6
1982–83	Edmonton Oilers, NHL	80	29	67	96	87	16	7	7	14	14
1983–84	Edmonton Oilers, NHL	80	40	86	126	104	19	8	14	22	21
CCup–84	Canada	8	3	8	11	4					
1984–85	Edmonton Oilers, NHL	80	37	84	121	97	18	12	25	37	44
1985–86	Edmonton Oilers, NHL	79	48	90	138	120	10	1	9	10	30
1986–87	Edmonton Oilers, NHL	59	17	50	67	93	17	3	8	11	30
CCup–87	Canada	9	2	4	6	0					
1987–88	Pittsburgh Penguins, NHL	46	15	52	67	93					
1988–89	Pittsburgh Penguins, NHL	75	30	83	113	195	11	2	13	15	31
1989–90	Pittsburgh Penguins, NHL	80	29	74	103	95					
WEC–90	Canada	10	1	6	7	10					
1990–91	Pittsburgh Penguins, NHL	76	24	69	93	128	12	2	9	11	6
CCup–91	Canada	8	1	6	7	8					
1991–92	Pittsburgh Penguins, NHL	54	10	54	64	62					
	Los Angeles Kings, NHL	10	1	4	5	25	6	4	3	7	2
1992–93	Los Angeles Kings, NHL	50	8	49	57	50					
	Detroit Red Wings, NHL	30	4	26	30	27	7	2	9	11	2
1993–94	Detroit Red Wings, NHL	80	14	63	77	106	7	1	6	7	8
1994–95	Detroit Red Wings, NHL	45	14	44	58	72	18	6	12	18	10
1995–96	Detroit Red Wings, NHL	76	14	60	74	90	17	5	9	14	30
WCup–96	Canada	8	0	7	7	12					
1996–97	Hartford Whalers, NHL	20	3	5	8	18					
	Philadelphia Flyers, NHL	37	6	20	26	20	17	1	8	9	6
1997–98	Philadelphia Flyers, NHL	57	2	27	29	30					
1998–99	Carolina Hurricanes, NHL	44	2	8	10	28	5	0	1	1	2
1999–2000	Carolina Hurricanes, NHL	69	11	29	40	40					
2000–2001	Boston Bruins, NHL	18	0	4	4	30					
	NHL Totals	1399	396	1131	1527	1846	194	59	137	196	264
	WEC/CCup/WCup Totals	43	7	31	38	34					

NHL First All-Star Team (1985, 1986, 1989, 1995)
NHL Second All-Star Team (1982, 1983, 1984, 1990)
Won James Norris Trophy (1985, 1986, 1995)
Won Stanley Cup (1984, 1985, 1987, 1991)
Won CCup (1984, 1987, 1991)

KINGS OF THE ICE

Paul Coffey

record, Sather benched him for taking too many chances. In the summer of 1987 Coffey refused to report to training camp, demanding that his contract be renegotiated because of the raises given to others on the team and in the league. Edmonton offered an increase, but after two months of the season with no agreement and no Coffey in the lineup, management decided the only option was a trade. Pittsburgh made the best offer and Coffey was off to another offensive powerhouse in the making, leaving Gretzky and the Oilers and joining Mario Lemieux's Penguins.

Paul Coffey (front) became the first defender to lead the Red Wings in scoring and won his third Norris Trophy in 1994–95.

With the Penguins, Coffey continued his offensive feats, topping the 100-point mark in 1988-89 and again the next season. With Lemieux up front and Coffey in his prime, the Penguins won the Stanley Cup in 1990–91 for the first time. Less than a year later, however, Coffey was once again on the move, beginning a tumultuous trip through the 1990s. He landed first in Los Angeles for a short-lived reunion with Gretzky but left for Detroit before the end of the 1992–93 season. Detroit coach Scotty Bowman, who had coveted Coffey since the blueliner's first year in the league, finally had his man.

Coffey was injured for much of his first season with Detroit, missing all but 30 games with a bad knee. But in the 1994–95 season, which had been shortened due to a strike, he regained his form. He became the first Red Wing defender to lead the team in scoring and won his third Norris Trophy for his all-around effort.

Again, success seemed to breed dissension. In October, Bowman, in search of his 1,000th career victory, was intent on acquiring Hartford Whalers forward Brendan Shanahan for Coffey. When Coffey vetoed the trade, Bowman was incensed, forcing Coffey to return home early and to pay his own airfare. The trade eventually did go through, though Coffey played only 20 games with the Whalers before being sent to the Philadelphia Flyers. Having played with the Great One and the Magnificent One, it was only logical that Coffey team up with the Next One, Eric Lindros, which he did for two seasons until becoming a Chicago Blackhawk in 1998. He was then traded to Carolina and in the summer of 2000 signed as a free agent with the Boston Bruins. After an injury-riddled season that limited him to 18 games, he retired in the summer of 2001.

Al MacInnis

Known as one-dimensional early in his career—he had a huge shot that was famous for being the hardest in the history of hockey—Al MacInnis put all the pieces together as a professional. A perennial All-Star and always near the top of the defender scoring charts, MacInnis became a player coaches wanted on the ice in pressure situations both when they needed a goal and when they needed to prevent a goal.

Raised in Port Hood, a small town in Nova Scotia, MacInnis worked for hours on his shot, the only aspect of the game he could practise when there was no ice to skate on. "I used to practise against my dad's barn and every fall they'd have to reshingle it," he said of his early training regimen. After one year out west with the Regina Blues of the Saskatchewan Junior Hockey League, MacInnis moved to Ontario to play for the Kitchener Rangers in the Ontario Hockey League in

1980. He paced the team to the Memorial Cup in 1981 and was chosen by the Calgary Flames as the 15th overall pick in that summer's draft.

MacInnis first made his appearance in the National Hockey League playing two games in 1982 and 14 in 1983 while an All-Star in the OHL. He was already known for his booming shot, but many skeptics felt he didn't have the rest of the tools necessary to become a long-serving and dependable defenseman. Even the Calgary coaches, forced to bring up MacInnis earlier than they wanted because of injuries, used him only on the power-play. Under the guidance of Calgary assistant coach Bob Murdoch, MacInnis set to work to prove that he had more than a cannon in his arsenal. He stayed late in practice, putting in extra time on his skating, puckhandling, passing and positioning.

Al MacInnis has the hardest shot in the history of hockey.

"We educated him and he worked hard," Calgary head coach Bob Johnson said of MacInnis's improvement. "He is a player who made a complete commitment to his profession." In 1983–84, MacInnis saw more and more ice time. His power-play performance and his goal-scoring were impressive, as was expected, but his defensive game had come so far that he was soon being used on a regular shift. Johnson, thinking MacInnis's shot would be as effective at clearing the puck as it was at beating goaltenders, even started playing him in shorthand situations as well.

His reputation as a shooter didn't go away as his play became more well-rounded. And it was enhanced in a game against the St. Louis Blues in 1984, when MacInnis was asked to send a long shot in on Blues goalie Mike Liut to test him right away. MacInnis skated just over the blue line and then blasted a shot that caught Liut in the mask, knocking the goalie down. Just for good measure, the puck bobbled its way into the net past a dazed Liut, who, when he came to his senses, discovered that his mask had been split. He said later that he measured shots as "hard, and then there is MacInnis-hard." Even MacInnis didn't know the source of his power. "There are lots of bigger and stronger guys in the dressing room than me and they can't shoot as hard," MacInnis said. "I can only think it's timing. I don't know. I wish I had the answer. I'd pass it along to the other guys."

In 1986, after a solid regular season with 68 points, MacInnis led the league in playoff assists as the Flames came close to their first Stanley Cup championship, though they lost in the finals to the Montreal Canadiens. The next season, he scored 20 goals and 76 points and was selected to the league's Second All-Star Team.

MacInnis, Al
D, 6′2″, 196 lbs, b: Inverness, N.S., 7/11/1963

Season	Club, League	Regular Season					Playoffs				
		GP	G	A	Pts	PIM	GP	G	A	Pts	PIM
1981–82	Calgary Flames, NHL	2	0	0	0	0					
1982–83	Calgary Flames, NHL	14	1	3	4	9					
1983–84	Calgary Flames, NHL	51	11	34	45	42	11	2	12	14	13
	Colorado Flames, CHL	19	5	14	19	22					
1984–85	Calgary Flames, NHL	67	14	52	66	75	4	1	2	3	8
1985–86	Calgary Flames, NHL	77	11	57	68	76	21	4	15	19	30
1986–87	Calgary Flames, NHL	79	20	56	76	97	4	1	0	1	0
1987–88	Calgary Flames, NHL	80	25	58	83	114	7	3	6	9	18
1988–89	Calgary Flames, NHL	79	16	58	74	126	22	7	24	31	46
1989–90	Calgary Flames, NHL	79	28	62	90	82	6	2	3	5	8
WEC–90	Canada	9	1	3	4	10					
1990–91	Calgary Flames, NHL	78	28	75	103	90	7	2	3	5	8
CCup–91	Canada	8	2	4	6	23					
1991–92	Calgary Flames, NHL	72	20	57	77	83					
1992–93	Calgary Flames, NHL	50	11	43	54	61	6	1	6	7	10
1993–94	Calgary Flames, NHL	75	28	54	82	95	7	2	6	8	12
1994–95	St. Louis Blues, NHL	32	8	20	28	43	7	1	5	6	10
1995–96	St. Louis Blues, NHL	82	17	44	61	88	13	3	4	7	20
1996–97	St. Louis Blues, NHL	72	13	30	43	65	6	1	2	3	4
1997–98	St. Louis Blues, NHL	71	19	30	49	80	8	2	6	8	12
OWG–98	Canada	6	2	0	2	2					
1998–99	St. Louis Blues, NHL	82	20	42	62	70	13	4	8	12	20
1999–00	St. Louis Blues, NHL	61	11	28	39	34	7	1	3	4	14
2000–01	St. Louis Blues, NHL	59	12	42	54	52	15	2	8	10	18
2001–02	St. Louis Blues, NHL	71	11	35	46	52					
OWG–02	Canada	6	0	0	0	8					
	NHL Totals	1333	324	880	1204	1444					
	OWG/WEC/CCup Totals	29	5	7	12	43					

NHL First All-Star Team (1990, 1991, 1999)
NHL Second All-Star Team (1987, 1989, 1994)
Won James Norris Trophy (1999)
Won Conn Smythe Trophy (1989)
Won Stanley Cup (1989)
Won CCup (1991)
Won OWG(2002)

Between 1986 and 1994, Vernon was the Flames' undisputed first-string goalie. In 1987–88, he won 39 games and helped Calgary win the Presidents' Trophy for having the most points in the regular season. Unfortunately, the team's Stanley Cup express was derailed by the archrival Edmonton Oilers in the playoffs. The next year the team benefited from its experience and won the first Stanley Cup in franchise history. Although Al MacInnis won the Conn Smythe Trophy, it was Vernon's heroics that paved the way for Calgary's success by winning 16 games and recording three shutouts to lead all post-season goalies. Despite these numbers, he was best remembered for making an incredible save on Vancouver's Stan Smyl on a breakaway during overtime of the seventh and deciding game of the first round when the club was nearly upset by the upstart Canucks.

Mike Vernon played some of the best hockey of his career helping to win 16 games and leading Detroit to its first Stanley Cup in 42 years in 1997.

Through the early 1990s, the Flames remained one of the top clubs in the NHL but couldn't duplicate their playoff magic of 1989. Eventually the team began to rebuild and Vernon was traded in June 1994 to a Detroit Red Wings team in need of a proven goalie. Vernon downplayed his arrival in the Motor City: "It's not a savior-type thing. You can't put that much pressure on one individual. Everybody gets away from the philosophy that this is a team sport. It takes a good hockey club in front of a goaltender to have a good goals-against average." He shone when helping the Wings reach the 1995 Stanley Cup finals, where they were swept away by the New Jersey Devils. The following season he helped Detroit set an NHL record by winning 62 regular-season matches but was superceded by young netminder Chris Osgood once the playoffs began.

In 1996–97, Vernon was clearly the backup to Osgood during the regular season, but coach Scotty Bowman opted to turn to the veteran when the playoffs began. The Cup-winning netminder noted: "I thought for sure I'd be traded by the deadline. By the end of February, though, Scotty called me in and said, 'You're going to get some chances to play.' Maybe it was good for me not to play that much in the first half of the year and just let me boil inside for a while. I mean, I'm enjoying myself and having a lot of fun now and that's the bottom line." Vernon played some of the best hockey of his career by winning 16 games and leading Detroit to its first Stanley Cup title in 42 years. He was presented the Conn Smythe Trophy as the top player in the post-season, but this was the end of his career in Motown. The Wings banked on the talent and youth of Osgood and sent Vernon to the San Jose Sharks prior to the 1997–98 season.

The West Coast agreed with Vernon, as he recorded five shutouts and 30 wins while helping San Jose qualify for the playoffs. He did the same in 1998–99, but as in Detroit, the club decided to go with younger players and traded Vernon to the Florida Panthers, where the likable veteran provided solid goalkeeping and stability while helping the Panthers reach the post-season for the first time in three years in 1999–2000.

Vernon was claimed in the Expansion Draft in June 2000 and promptly traded to Calgary, where he seemed likely to end his career on the team where he'd had his greatest successes. Midway through the 2001–02 campaign, however, Flames general manager Craig Button sent Vernon down to the minors. The move came as a shock to many who were closely associated with the NHL and was viewed by some as a deliberate attempt to humiliate the 39-year-old player into retiring. Though Button said the decision was based solely on performance, it was hardly a storybook ending for a great NHL goaltender who at the pinnacle of his career had backstopped the Flames to their one and only Stanley Cup championship in 1989.

Esa Tikkanen

Esa Tikkanen has been the enfant terrible of Finnish hockey from early on. In the NHL, he added commentary during the action on the ice that made such an impact it has been given a name: "Tiki Talk."

Upon returning from overseas to play once again for Jokerit Helsinki in the 1999–2000 season, Tikkanen appeared to have mellowed. He was very pleased about his knees, which had been giving him a lot of trouble. "I really cannot remember when I have been feeling so good about my skating and my game," he reported. Tikkanen has five Stanley Cup rings, one for every finger on his hand. From the 1998 Olympics in Nagano, Japan, he has one of the most valuable bronze medals ever, snatched from a Canadian team that fielded their very best talent from the NHL. But the thing that he's missing is a gold medal in World Championship play, and that is his current aim.

Tikkanen is best known in Finland as a member of the HIFK Helsinki club, but he actually started out with Jokerit, their crosstown rivals. There is a now very famous photograph of Tikkanen as a five-year-old mascot skating down the ice in a Jokerit jersey before the start of a game. Jokerit has the biggest hockey budget in Finland, so it was no surprise that they snapped him up when he decided that the deal for his return to the club where he had his biggest success and his best memories—the Edmonton Oilers—wasn't attractive enough.

For his running commentary on what was happening on the ice, Esa Tikkanen was nicknamed "Tiki Talk."

During his career, Tikkanen has played all three forward positions, but he was predominantly a winger before his role-switching also made him a center. Tikkanen has amassed 630 points in his NHL career, many of them earned on the offense, where he wasn't supposed to be playing. This total places him third among the all-time best Finns in the league. In Edmonton, where he played in four Stanley Cup wins, he's been the most valuable Finn after Jari Kurri. Tikkanen was drafted by the Oilers in 1983 in the fourth round and he joined the team for the 1985 playoffs straight from the World Championship tournament in Prague, Czechoslovakia.

That kind of late-season move has since been outlawed, but for Tikkanen it was a real break walking right into a post-season title. He remembers that after watching one game on the sidelines, coach Glen Sather asked him if he was ready to play. Just like in a fairy tale, the next night, May 23, 1985, he was on the ice for the 3-1 victory over the Philadelphia Flyers. But even before that, the events seemed unreal to him.

Tikkanen had just returned from Prague when his father announced that Sather had been trying to reach him and would try again later. Tikkanen at first thought it was a joke. But Sather phoned again and asked him to jump on a plane to Chicago right away. Tikkanen asked if he should bring his equipment, but Sather said he was just inviting him to be part of the team and watch the games. The trip across the Atlantic wasn't completely trouble-free, since he had to stay in Zurich overnight to obtain a visa.

Esa Tikkanen

Two years later, when the Oilers were looking for a third man to round out the team's first line, he got the opportunity to play alongside Wayne Gretzky and Jari Kurri. The three seasons between 1986 and 1989, when he occupied left wing on the line with his famous teammates, were his most productive in the NHL, earning him 78, 74 and 78 points respectively. Kurri remembers that Tikkanen was just the type of young player they'd been looking for. "He had no trouble at all fitting in from the word go." Two of three seasons ended in Stanley Cup victories for the club, and Esa Tikkanen was without doubt one of the key players in the drive toward those titles.

With the departure of Gretzky from the Oilers, Tikkanen's role became even more important. In 1990, when the Alberta team captured the Cup a fourth time, their first without the illustrious number 99, Tikkanen had a truly great series with 24 points in 22 playoff games. That spring he was among the finalists nominated for the Frank Selke Trophy as the league's outstanding defensive forward. In fact, he was a Selke finalist on three separate occasions without ever winning the trophy. While he was with Edmonton, his considerable skills were recognized by the NHL selection committee when they put together the roster to face the feared Soviets in the Rendez-Vous series that replaced the All-Star Game in 1987.

The next stage of his NHL career was with the New York Rangers. It started out in a rather dramatic fashion, with Tikkanen playing against the Edmonton Oilers. His old club had traded him only four hours earlier on March 17, 1993, in a swap for American center Doug Weight. In the Big Apple, Tikkanen was again in the right place at the right time, helping the Rangers end their 54-year Stanley Cup drought. In Tikkanen's opinion, "If you score 40 or 50 goals, nobody will remember you 20 years later, but everybody remembers you when you win a championship title."

According to Tikkanen, who also claims to be the only Finn to have a key to the city, the celebrations that spring have never been matched anywhere. "It's a place where they never forget their champions." In the spring of 1994, an estimated two million people watched the Rangers' victory parade in Manhattan. It was a moment of glory for the players and an opportunity for fans to plant the faces of their heroes in their memories. And solid two-way performer Tikkanen—described by Rangers captain Mark Messier as "one of the top five all-around players in the league"—was certainly one of them.

Tikkanen, Esa
LW, 6′1″, 190 lbs, b: Helsinki, Finland, 1/25/1965

Season	Club, League	Regular Season					Playoffs				
		GP	G	A	Pts	PIM	GP	G	A	Pts	PIM
1982–83	HIFK, Finland						1	0	0	0	2
1983–84	HIFK, Finland	36	19	11	30	30	2	0	0	0	0
1984–85	HIFK, Finland	36	21	33	54	42					
WEC–85	Finland	10	4	5	9	12					
1984–85	Edmonton Oilers, NHL						3	0	0	0	2
1985–86	Edmonton Oilers, NHL	35	7	6	13	28	8	3	2	5	7
	Nova Scotia Oilers, AHL	15	4	8	12	17					
1986–87	Edmonton Oilers, NHL	76	34	44	78	120	21	7	2	9	22
RV'87	NHL All-Stars	2	0	1	1	2					
CCup–87	Finland	5	0	1	1	6					
1987–88	Edmonton Oilers, NHL	80	23	51	74	153	19	10	17	27	72
1988–89	Edmonton Oilers, NHL	67	31	47	78	92	7	1	3	4	12
WEC–89	Finland	8	4	4	8	14					
1989–90	Edmonton Oilers, NHL	79	30	33	63	161	22	13	11	24	26
1990–91	Edmonton Oilers, NHL	79	27	42	69	85	18	12	8	20	24
CCup–91	Finland	6	2	2	4	6					
1991–92	Edmonton Oilers, NHL	40	12	16	28	44	16	5	3	8	8
1992–93	Edmonton Oilers, NHL	66	14	19	33	76					
	New York Rangers, NHL	15	2	5	7	18					
WC–93	Finland	6	0	0	0	2					
1993–94	New York Rangers, NHL	83	22	32	54	114	23	4	4	8	34
1994–95	HIFK, Finland	19	2	11	13	16					
	St. Louis Blues, NHL	43	12	23	35	22	7	2	2	4	20
1995–96	St. Louis Blues, NHL	11	1	4	5	18					
	New Jersey Devils, NHL	9	0	2	2	4					
	Vancouver Canucks, NHL	38	13	24	37	14	6	3	2	5	2
WC–96	Finland	1	0	0	0	0					
1996–97	Vancouver Canucks, NHL	62	12	15	27	66					
	New York Rangers, NHL	14	1	2	3	6	15	9	3	12	26
1997–98	Florida Panthers, NHL	28	1	8	9	16					
OWG–98	Finland	6	1	1	2	0					
1997–98	Washington Capitals, NHL	20	2	10	12	2	21	3	3	6	20
1998–99	New York Rangers, NHL	32	0	3	3	38					
1999–2000	Jokerit, Finland	43	10	13	23	85	11	1	6	7	10
WC–2000	Finland	9	2	1	3	10					
	Finland Totals	134	52	68	120	173	14	1	6	7	12
	NHL Totals	877	244	386	630	1077	186	72	60	132	275
	OWG/WEC/WC/RV'87/CCup Totals	53	13	15	28	52					

Won Stanley Cup (1985, 1987, 1988, 1990, 1994)

In New York, Esa Tikkanen (right) was again in the right place at the right time when he helped the Rangers end their 54-year Stanley Cup drought.

After New York came the journeyman stage of his career when he moved from one NHL city to another. The first stop was St. Louis. The following season, 1995–96, he started out in St. Louis but was traded twice, first to the New Jersey Devils and then to the Vancouver Canucks. The next year, Vancouver sent him back to the Rangers, and then followed a season split between the Florida Panthers and the Washington Capitals. With the Capitals, he came close to yet another team victory when they won the conference title and went into the playoff finals with high hopes, only to be thwarted by the powerhouse Detroit Red Wings. For his last campaign in the NHL, he went back to the New York Rangers for a third stint, but trouble with his knees prevented him from giving his usual stellar performance.

Tikkanen embraced the new millennium in style. In the 1999–2000 season, he returned to his first love, Jokerit Helsinki, where he played well and took a key role in helping his old team rebuild. Very much against the odds, they managed to make the playoff finals, though it certainly helped that during the season, the club picked up another three veterans to bolster their drive to the playoffs. The Jokerit coaching duo of Erkka Westerlund and Raimo Summanen had led the other Helsinki club to a title in the two previous seasons, and in fact Summanen, who'd also seen action with the Edmonton Oilers while Tikkanen was there, was a key factor in Tikkanen's joining the club.

In 2000–01, the 36-year-old Tikkanen played one final season of pro hockey in Germany as a member of the Essen Mosquitoes, where he had 29 points in 46 games. But if his year with Jokerit is anything to judge by, Tikkanen—number 10 at all levels he's played in—still may have some hockey left in him.

Gary Suter

In 1984 Gary Suter had a job in a Madison, Wisconsin, beer plant lugging cases of beer. He'd been playing hockey for the University of Wisconsin Badgers when he learned that he'd just become the Calgary ninth pick—and the 180th selection overall—in the 1984 draft. When Suter made it to his first training camp, he wasn't phased at all. "Hockey's hockey," he said. "These guys all have two legs and arms, just like me."

Suter was quick to leave his mark in the league, making the All-Star Game his first year, and again wasn't daunted by the company he was in. "It's not really a big thrill to play with all those guys," he said. "To be selected to play in the game is, though." He also won the Calder Trophy in 1985–86. Everyone thought the Leafs' Wendel Clark would win, but not Suter. "I just felt I was getting stronger and stronger as the season went on."

In the 1987–1988 season, Suter led Calgary in assists with 70, a career high, and also set a career high of 91 points. He scored a point in each of 16 straight games and was a nominee for the Norris Trophy for best defenseman. For six consecutive years, Suter ranked fourth among

NHL defenders. Suter also competed for his native land, the U.S., in the World Championship in 1985.

"He's a very steady player," said Flames general manager Cliff Fletcher. "He moves the puck very well. He shoots the puck very well from the point. He's been an extremely valuable addition to our team." Suter helped the Flames to the Stanley Cup finals against Montreal in 1986, but victory eluded them. But he was a member of the 1989 Stanley Cup Champion Flames team.

In 1994 Suter was traded to Hartford by Calgary and the next day traded again to Chicago by Hartford. He played with Chicago for four years until he was signed as a free agent by San Jose on July 1, 1998.

Quick to make his mark, Gary Suter was chosen to play in the All-Star Game and won the Calder Trophy in his first year in the NHL.

The Sharks management and team members had been in a state of high anticipation for months over the prospects of having the mobile, hard-hitting defenseman dress in San Jose teal. Once the Blackhawks traded for Paul Coffey, the Sharks realized that the hockey decision-makers in the Windy City were getting ready to get rid of Suter. So at the Entry Draft on June 27th, San Jose cleverly and quietly traded a ninth-round pick to Chicago for the rights to negotiate with Suter a few days early.

It isn't difficult to imagine that the Sharks were excited about the possibility of acquiring him. In 918 career NHL games with the Flames and Blackhawks, he has amassed 744 points and 1,156 penalty minutes. He has played in four All-Star games and was part of the U.S. World Cup championship team of 1996. In 1995–96, Suter became the first Hawks defenseman to score 20 goals since former Blackhawk great and original Sharks captain Doug Wilson had accomplished the feat six seasons earlier.

Ironically, it was Wilson, the Sharks' new director of pro development, who played the key role in bringing Suter to San Jose. Wilson, himself one of the league's best defensemen for years, pointed out that adding Suter to the lineup meant the Sharks wouldn't have to rush their younger defenders into doing more than they were capable of. According to Wilson, Suter should do a good job of "mentoring" and leading by example. "Gary Suter is one of the best-conditioned players in the game," Wilson declared. "His commitment to training sends a strong message to other players."

GM Dean Lombardi was also impressed by

Suter, Gary
D, 6´, 205 lbs, b: Madison, WI, 6/24/1964

Season	Club, League	Regular Season					Playoffs				
		GP	G	A	Pts	PIM	GP	G	A	Pts	PIM
1983–84	University of Wisconsin, WCHA	35	4	18	22	32					
1984–85	University of Wisconsin, WCHA	39	12	39	51	110					
WEC–85	USA	10	1	2	3	22					
1985–86	Calgary Flames, NHL	80	18	50	68	141	10	2	8	10	8
1986–87	Calgary Flames, NHL	68	9	40	49	70	6	0	3	3	10
CCup–87	USA	5	0	3	3	9					
1987–88	Calgary Flames, NHL	75	21	70	91	124	9	1	9	10	6
1988–89	Calgary Flames, NHL	63	13	49	62	78	5	0	3	3	10
1989–90	Calgary Flames, NHL	76	16	60	76	97	6	0	1	1	14
1990–91	Calgary Flames, NHL	79	12	58	70	102	7	1	6	7	12
CCup–91	USA	8	1	3	4	4					
1991–92	Calgary Flames, NHL	70	12	43	55	128					
WC–92	USA	6	0	1	1	6					
1992–93	Calgary Flames, NHL	81	23	58	81	112	6	2	3	5	8
1993–94	Calgary Flames, NHL	25	4	9	13	20					
	Chicago Blackhawks, NHL	16	2	3	5	18	6	3	2	5	6
1994–95	Chicago Blackhawks, NHL	48	10	27	37	42	12	2	5	7	10
1995–96	Chicago Blackhawks, NHL	82	20	47	67	80	10	3	3	6	8
WCup–96	USA	6	0	2	2	6					
1996–97	Chicago Blackhawks, NHL	82	7	21	28	70	6	1	4	5	8
1997–98	Chicago Blackhawks, NHL	73	14	28	42	74					
OWG–98	USA	4	0	0	0	2					
1998–99	San Jose Sharks, NHL	1	0	0	0	0					
1999–00	San Jose Sharks, NHL	76	6	28	34	52	12	2	5	7	12
2000–01	San Jose Sharks, NHL	68	10	24	34	84	1	0	0	0	0
2001–02	San Jose Sharks, NHL	82	6	27	33	57					
OWG–02	USA	6	0	1	1	4					
	NHL Totals	1145	203	641	844	1349	96	17	52	69	112
	OWG/WEC/WC/CCup/WCup Totals	45	2	12	14	53					

NHL Second All-Star Team (1988)
Won Calder Trophy (1986)
Won Stanley Cup (1989)
Won WCup (1996)

In 1995–96, Gary Suter (number 12) became the first Hawks defenseman to score 20 goals since former Chicago great Doug Wilson.

the fact that Suter could excel at both ends of the ice. "He's not a one-dimensional player," Lombardi said. "He's very competitive. He's strong as an ox. He can play 25, 26 minutes." At 34, Suter believes he has several effective years ahead. "As far as physically skating and stuff, I don't know if I'm as fast as I was. But a lot of the game now is played with your head. I'm probably a smarter player."

But no matter what Suter does on the ice, it is going to be hard for him to make people forget a highly publicized and damaging hit he gave Paul Kariya. "That whole thing was a real unfortunate incident. I still feel bad about that," Suter says. "It was a bad hit and, as I've said a hundred times before, it wasn't intentional. I'm not that kind of player. Hopefully, I can put that in the past and move on here."

And the shot to Kariya wasn't the only time in his career that Suter has been at the center of this kind of controversy. In a 1987 Canada Cup game in Hamilton, Ontario, Suter slashed Soviet player Andrei Lomakin for 10 stitches in the USA's 5–1 loss to the USSR. Suter was retaliating for what he thought was a cheap shot from Lomakin. He took a two-handed swing at Lomakin and broke his stick over his face. Suter was given only a five-minute major for charging. A number of observers said it was the worst infraction they had ever seen. One coach said, "In the NHL, he would have gotten 20 games for that." Later in the series he cross-checked Wayne Gretzky into the boards, taking the Great One out for the rest of the games.

Suter was paired for much of the 2002 Winter Olympics alongside Chris Chelios as the United States claimed the silver medal in Salt Lake City. He also represented the U.S. at the 1998 Olympics in Nagano.

1991–1995

The NHL Expands Southward

ortunately for its growth and marketability, hockey is an extremely telegenic game. Thanks to slow-motion replays, a fan can see on TV what a spectator in the stands often can't. So it seems only logical that a significant increase in the number of televised NHL games would be matched by a growing number of fans in the U.S., and indeed that's what happened as the 20th century advanced and brought the world's fastest game into more and more homes. By now, nearly the whole world watches NHL hockey with the same fervor as its first fans in Canada and the National Hockey League itself has become international. In the 1990s, 15 countries were represented, and today fans in Russia or Sweden or Finland or the Czech Republic are often more interested in the turn of events in the NHL than in their own championships.

From the beginning of the 1990s, hockey clubs also began springing up in the southern states of America. The new fans had to have the rules of the game explained at first, but people in California, Texas and Florida had soon adopted and adapted to it. Of course, there was another side to this coin of expansion. In the homeland of hockey, the Quebec City Nordiques and Winnipeg Jets ran into financial problems and migrated southward to Denver and Phoenix. Even the legendary Oilers have repeatedly been on the verge of going under, though so far they have managed to hang on in Edmonton. But this apparently inexorable drift prompted Canada's Parliament to debate preserving the game in its homeland.

After Wayne Gretzky arrived in Los Angeles, the league was never to be the same.

In 1990–91, there were 21 clubs contending in the regular-season championship. Chicago was leading (in turn led by coach and GM Mike Keenan), followed in the overall standing by St. Louis and Los Angeles, two teams that were doing so well simply because their leaders scored goals. St. Louis forward Brett Hull scored 86 goals on assists from his partner, Adam Oates (with 90 assists), while Wayne Gretzky alone accumulated 163 points on 41 goals and 122 assists for Los Angeles. Even so, neither club made it to the semifinals. And for two other teams, the road to the Stanley Cup was barred by the Minnesota North Stars.

Minnesota had no upper-tier stars, but general manager Bobby Clarke and coach Bob Gainey placed their chips on intensifying the pace of the game in the playoffs. The Stars eclipsed their

---

A HISTORY OF WORLD HOCKEY

opponents in the number of shots on goal, finishing off attacks and an aggressiveness that had typified Philadelphia's play in Clarke's years as a Flyer.

In the Clarence Campbell Conference finals, Edmonton had retained a number of good forwards headed by Mark Messier and it seemed they would easily outplay Minnesota. However, the Calgary Flames and Los Angeles came to the accidental aid of the North Stars when the Flames

It isn't easy to be an expansion team.

wore Messier and his partners out in the first round of the playoffs, in which two of the seven games went into overtime. In the next round, with Gretzky's new team from Los Angeles, the Oilers had to play four out of six games in overtime. They won that series 4–2, but many of the Oilers veterans had nothing left for the finals and lost it 4–1 and the Stars made it to the Stanley Cup finals for the second time in the club's history. Furthermore, for the first time since 1934, two clubs that had never won the prize crossed sticks for the first time: Pittsburgh, which had placed seventh in the regular season, and 16th-place Minnesota.

The North Stars won games one and three of the series, but it wasn't so much those defeats as a back injury and the consequent absence of Mario Lemieux on the ice that sowed panic in the Penguins' dressing room. As it happened, the medics had Super Mario back on his feet by game four and the efforts of Lemieux and Paul Coffey put the Penguins in the lead 3–0 by the third minute of play. By the beginning of the third period, the Stars had reduced the gap to 4–3, but then they replaced goalie John Casey to put a sixth man on the ice and had another goal scored against them (5–3). After winning another home game 6–4, Pittsburgh went on to win by an even more impressive 8–0 in spite of the fact that the Stars surpassed their rivals in shots on goal (39–28) and the closely guarded Lemieux managed to score only once. In this sixth game that decided the Stanley Cup's fate, 11 Penguins collected points for goals scored and assists. And the MVP was rightly awarded to Lemieux, whose 44 points (on 16 and 28) were just shy of Wayne Gretzky's record of 47 in the 1985 Stanley Cup finals.

Learning to fly.

At the 1991 World Championship in Finland, the Soviet team appeared with the letters CCCP (USSR) on their sweaters for the last time. And as if to mark its own passing, Team USSR dropped only one point (in the game with Tre Kronor, which became runner-up) in the round-robin series among eight contenders. Two other participants in the quarterfinals had begun the tournament without a full lineup. Team Canada had 15 and the USA 18 players before their reinforcements from the NHL arrived for the finals that overturned everything that had gone before. In the decisive game between Sweden and the USSR, 20-year-old Mats Sundin (who had made his debut that season with Quebec) scored the winning goal for Sweden in a 2–1 game. The championship's MVP award went to a former NHLer from Calgary, the 30-year-old Swede Hakan Loob. And the Canadians, spearheaded by Theo Fleury and rising NHL star Joe Sakic, trounced the Americans 9–4 in the last round and squeezed the USSR into third place.

The 1991 Canada Cup tournament rapidly became a pale shadow of Canada Cup '87, first of all because the best hockey players had begun a mass exodus from the USSR after 1989 and the system of honing the Soviet national squad for international tournaments, which had taken decades to perfect, fell apart in a heartbeat. Several players who were approached by coach Viktor Tikhinov said "No!" Of the Pavel Bure–Alexander Mogilny–Sergei Fedorov line the coach had planned to replace the KLM Line, Tikhinov had to make do with Fedorov. The picture was approximately the same for the Czechs, and neither of these two teams that had so often created intriguing situations at Canada Cup tournaments made it to the semifinals this time. Without them, the playoffs between Canada and Sweden (4–0), the USA and Finland (7–3) and even the finals between Canada and the USA (4–1 and 4–2) didn't stimulate any particular interest in North American fans and the future of such contests was questioned.

In the 1990s, there was only one way to stop the Pittsburgh Penguins—neutralize Mario Lemieux (number 66).

The 1991–92 season saw Scotty Bowman take over in Pittsburgh as coach. Bowman's past credits as coach included five Stanley Cup victories for the Canadiens in the 1970s, after which he slipped into the shadows for almost 10 years. He worked with the Sabres without making much of a mark and headed up Pittsburgh's scouting arm, where he helped assemble the 1991 Cup-winning team. But this season didn't look promising. In February 1992, the Penguins' chances for reaching the playoffs didn't inspire hope. Towards the end of the season, however, the Pittsburgh stars had substantially upgraded their game and started to scramble for their second trophy.

The 1992 playoffs proved to be the most intense and unpredictable in two decades. In the first round, six duels, all cliffhangers, went the full seven games. Pittsburgh, Detroit and Vancouver all rebounded from 3–1 deficits. And the Penguins were saved by 20-year-old Jaromir Jagr when he scored winning goals in games five and seven in Washington. But Jaromir didn't stop there in Stanley Cup competition.

The Penguins faced off against the New York Rangers in the next round. With Roger Neilson in the coach's seat, the Rangers had won the Presidents' Trophy and become the only club to surpass 100 points. Moreover, with a psychological leader like Mark Messier now on his team, Neilson had no doubts about winning before the series with the Penguins: "For this, it will be enough to neutralize Mario Lemieux."

In game one the New Yorkers came close to fulfilling the task; Mario was able to record only two assists to his credit. But the Penguins still won it 4–2. Two days later the New Yorkers revenged themselves by the same score. More important, the Lemieux situation was resolved in the very first minutes of this second game with one slash from Adam Graves' stick that broke Mario's wrist. At the end of the game, Joe Mullen was also taken to the hospital and came back with his leg in a cast to his thigh. When they moved back to Madison Square Garden, the opponents were equal in games won (2–2) and it seemed that without Mario the Penguins were doomed.

How to check an opponent.

With 5:33 remaining in game five in New York, the score was tied at 2–2 when Jagr, picking up speed, zeroed directly in on Rangers defenseman Jeff Beukeboom. Almost directly in front of Beukeboom, Jagr shifted the puck sharply from the right to the left and put his opponent behind him. John Vanbiesbrouck tried to block the shot with his body, but the Czech outmaneuvered him and the goal was the clincher (3–2). Since the game that had brought the Penguins to the lead in the series, Mario Lemieux had watched from the stands and explained it all to the press: "Kevin

Stevens and I can outplay a defenseman one on one. But Jaromir can do that against three opponents." In the sixth and last game of the series, Mario was back in the press box, and again Jagr scored and then spearheaded plays that were finished off by Rick Tocchet and Ron Francis for a score of 5–1.

The Flyers bench.

Both sets of conference finals ended after four games, with the Penguins prevailing over the Bruins and Chicago over Edmonton. But the main subject throughout was the return of Lemieux to the lineup. Fortunately, even with his left wrist taped up, he could still use his right, so he played one-handed and put in four goals against Boston.

In the middle of the first game of the Stanley Cup finals at Civic Arena, the visitors from Chicago were ahead with more than an edge at 4–1. The last time anyone had managed to save a Stanley Cup game with such a wide spread had been when Montreal had crossed sticks with Chicago way back in 1944, but thanks to the determination of Tocchet, Lemieux and Jagr, the Penguins repeated the miracle. Just before tying the score, Jagr had to outplay three opponents. And a scant three seconds before the siren sounded, Mario Lemieux finished off an attack that had been started by Francis in a powerplay. That game ended 5–4, and after it there wasn't much resistance. Chicago wiped out and Pittsburgh took it in four—a clean sweep.

Before the playoff finals in the Patrick Division in the spring of 1993, the question of who would win in the series between the Penguins and the Islanders didn't even come up.

The team from the former USSR (now called Unified Team) was able to improve its reputation to some extent at the 1992 Winter Olympics in Albertville, France. The pace set by such seasoned players as Andrei Khomutov and Vyacheslav Bykov brought the team to the finals, where they faced Team Canada, led by the young Eric Lindros and Joe Juneau. This time, experience got the upper hand over youth and the Unified Team won the last game 3–1.

The 1992 World Championship in Czechoslovakia was full of surprises. Because of a 10-day strike in the NHL, the competition started late and the Canadian and American teams didn't have their full quota of pros. They reached the playoffs but dropped out after the quarterfinals. Moreover, the Canadians weren't eliminated by another favorite but suffered a sensational 4–3 loss to the Finns. The pairs in the semifinals were also unusual. For the first time in history, there were no players from Russia among the four contenders for medals, even though coach Viktor Tikhonov had retained all his Albertville Olympic champions with the exception of Bykov and Khomutov. Unfortunately for the Russians, one of the few NHLers who had made it to Czechoslovakia was Swede Mats Sundin. In the last minute of the first period in the game between Sweden and Russia, he put in a shot that left Team Russia out of the medals (2–0). Another former European grandee was also toppled in the semifinals when the hosting Czechs bowed out to the troubleshooters from Finland in a post-game shootout. The finals were capped by a victory for the more experienced Swedes (5–2).

The results of the 1992–93 regular-season championship confirmed the forecasts. The Penguins won the Presidents' Trophy, outpacing their closest pursuers from Boston by 10 points. Among the top scorers, Detroit edged out Pittsburgh by two goals with 369. And in their defensive performance, the Penguins had vaulted from 20th place in the previous season to third. Before the final playoffs in the Patrick Division, the question of who would win in the series between the Penguins and the Islanders (who stood 12th in the league) didn't even arise.

The first alarm bell rang in the third minute of game one in Pittsburgh when back spasms drove Mario Lemieux off the ice. He didn't come back till game five, by which time the series was tied at 2–2, a situation that still prevailed after the sixth. In the decisive game in Civic Arena, the Penguins unleashed a hurricane of shots on Glenn Healy's net (45 against 22). Even so, the Islanders were playing a strictly defensive game and leading 3–1 at the beginning of the third period. With a tremendous effort, the Penguins took the game into overtime. Six minutes later, Czech player David Volek intercepted a pass, broke away from his pursuers and outmaneuvered Tom Barrasso for a dramatic climax and unexpected Penguin defeat (4–3). The Islanders were done after that, though, and the Montreal Canadiens—who hadn't figured in any previous forecasts—and Wayne Gretzky's Los Angeles Kings played the 1993 Stanley Cup finals.

In the West, the Kings had overcome the Calgary Flames in six games in the first round of the playoffs without too much trouble (and in spite of predictions). Six games also sufficed for the Kings to outplay Vancouver. The Russian Pavel Bure had been the top scorer for the Canucks in the regular season, but now he was neutralized by his former teammate in the CSKA, Alexei Zhitnik, while the Great One seemed to forget his back pain and played against Vancouver with the kind of dash and intensity that had characterized his play in Edmonton in the 1980s.

In the decisive seventh game of the 1993 semifinals against Toronto, Wayne Gretzky (center) racked up a hat-trick, bringing Los Angeles to the Stanley Cup finals for the first time.

In the Clarence Campbell Conference finals against the Maple Leafs, Gretzky continued to demonstrate that he was always a player to be reckoned with. In game six—which evened out the score in the series—Wayne scored his 105th playoff goal, eclipsing one more Gordie Howe record of 869 goals in playoffs and regular-season championships. In the decisive seventh game, Wayne racked up another three and brought the Kings to the Stanley Cup finals for the first time.

There the Kings continued their winning streak by taking the first game 4–1 in Montreal's Forum. They were also leading 2–1 with a minute and 45 seconds before the end of the third period

Patrick Roy (right) used to talk to his goalpost—and won another Stanley Cup for the Montreal Canadiens as well as the Conn Smythe Trophy for his remarkable play in the spring of 1993.

in game two. Then Canadiens captain Guy Carbonneau asked the referees to measure the curve of the blade on 30-year-old veteran Marty McSorley's stick. The curve exceeded the permitted half inch and McSorley was sent to the penalty box. The Canadiens replaced goalie Patrick Roy with a sixth player, and 32 seconds later defenseman Eric Desjardins took the game into overtime with a slapshot from the blue line. This was the ninth overtime in 17 playoff games in the spring of 1993 for the Canadiens, and to this point they'd won seven of eight. They won this one too when Desjardins only took 51 seconds to score the winning goal and at the same time rack up his hat-trick.

In Los Angeles, game three went into overtime too. Luc Robitaille, Tony Granato and Gretzky covered a three-goal gap to make it 3–3, but Canadiens goalkeeper Roy played without

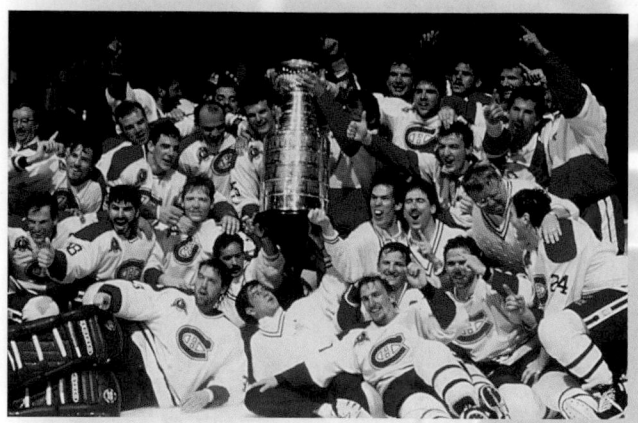

Montreal's 24th Stanley Cup victory in 1993 was the logical culmination of the Jubilee—the Cup's centennial—year.

a mistake. Finally, Canadiens sophomore John LeClair compelled Kings goalie Kelly Hrudy to error, giving the Canadiens their ninth overtime victory (4–3) and the leadership in the finals (2–1). The second game in Los Angeles was almost a carbon copy. Again Gretsky piled up his points and again the game went into overtime with a score of 2–2. And again LeClair took advantage of a hesitation by Hrudy and the Kings defense to score the winning goal. Mentally and physically broken, the Kings offered practically no resistance in game five and it ended 4–1.

The league proclaimed 1992–93 a Jubilee season as it marked a centennial of play for the Stanley Cup. And since the Canadiens held the record for winning the oldest prize in professional sports in North America, their 24th victory in the 1993 Stanley Cup tournament was a fitting climax to the Jubilee year.

At the 1993 World Championship in Munich, the Russian team won the gold medals with a new coach, Boris Mikhailov, but a rough start was the tournament's main claim to fame. Of the favorites, only Team Canada coach Mike Keenan brought a full roster to Germany. Both the Russians and Czechs were waiting for two or three NHLers to arrive from North America, while the Swedes and Finns started the group preliminaries with about three-quarters of their squads.

The Sharks were in the lead after five games in the 1994 Western Conference semifinals against the Maple Leafs but they didn't have enough steam for one more miracle.

Both Scandinavian teams made it to the playoffs, but the absolutely best team after the preliminaries was Canada, with a perfect performance led by top scorer Eric Lindros. In the semifinal game between Russia and Canada, the game's founders were leading 3–1 at the beginning of the second period when Mikhailov rearranged his attack. Thanks to fast skating and pinpoint passing, his three restructured forward lines not only tied the score but routed the Canadians 7–4. The Swedes also made it to the finals when they edged out the Czech team 4–3 in overtime in the semifinals. In previous games, the Swedes had been able to create scoring situations but not to capitalize on them with goals, and the same pattern held in the final game against Russia. Goalie Andrei Trefilov (who had already played a season with the Calgary farm club) was impenetrable and the Russians won it 3–1 to become that year's champions.

In contrast to the previous season, there were practically no surprises in the first round of the 1994 playoffs. Even a Pittsburgh defeat (4–2) in the series with Washington was predictable; Super Mario was ineffective because of illness and injuries. In the West, however, and contrary to all expectations, the favorites from Detroit bowed out to the rapidly advancing Sharks in seven games. The Sharks were also in the lead after five games in the Western Conference semifinals against Toronto, but they didn't have quite enough steam for another miraculous upset. In turn, the worn-out Maple Leafs lost in five games to the low-rated Canucks in the conference finals. Pavel Bure, who had racked up 60 goals for two seasons in a row, had been the outstanding solo star for coach and GM Pat Quinn's Canucks. But Vancouver's main weapon was that each of its three forward lines could tip the scales in a game; the harvest of goals by 14 Canucks in the regular season was a two-digit figure.

On their way to the Stanley Cup finals, the New York Rangers only had trouble with the New Jersey Devils in the Eastern Conference finals. In that series, three out of seven games including the last one required not one but two overtimes. Still, the Rangers prevailed in the last one and made it 2–1.

The Rangers and the Canucks crossed sticks in the 1994 Stanley Cup finals—which became the longest and toughest of the decade.

Thus it was that the Rangers and Canucks crossed sticks in a Stanley Cup series that proved to be the longest and toughest in the 1990s. After dropping the first one in Madison Square Garden, the Rangers swept three games straight. The duo of Pavel Bure and Trevor Linden helped the Canucks reduce the gap by two games when the series went back to the Garden, then two veterans, forward Geoff Courtnall and defenseman Jeff Brown, scored two goals each in Vancouver to take the contest back to New York.

Brian Leetch opened the scoring in the deciding game, but all the rest of the goals were scored when a team had an advantage. In the first period, young Russian defenseman Sergei Zubov once again demonstrated how dangerous he could be in a power-play when he started a move that was finished off by Adam Graves for a score of 2–0. Trevor Linden narrowed it by one with a man short, but another Canucks penalty allowed Mark Messier to bring the score to 3–1. In the last period, Linden once again capitalized on a one-man advantage and made it 3–2. After that, Rangers goalie Mike Richter weathered the ferocious blizzard generated by the Canucks and the Rangers brought the Stanley Cup back to New York for the first time in 54 years.

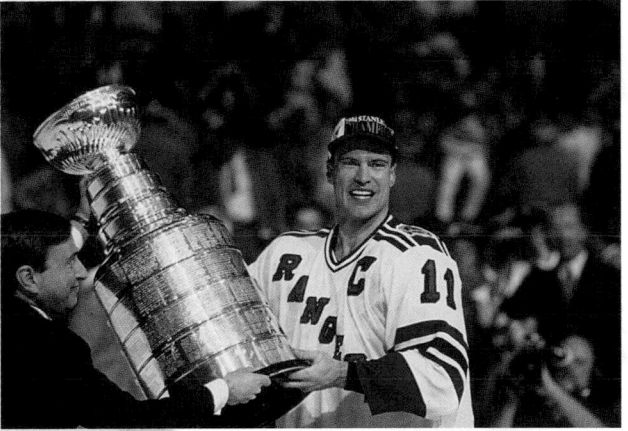

In the 1993–94 playoffs, Mark Messier (right) was at his very best, engineering one of the great moments in New York Rangers history.

When he took over as coach of the Swedish Olympic team, Curt Lundmark invited three 34- and 35-year-old players who had already had outstanding careers in the NHL to play for Tre Kronor. Defenseman Tomas Jonsson and forwards Mats Naslund and Hakan Loob had played the 1993–94 season in Swedish clubs and all three accepted Lundmark's invitation. Loob even promised that he would rack up 10 points in the 1994 Olympic tournament and was practically true to his word with nine (four goals and five assists).

With the all but total absence of active NHLers at the Olympic tournaments in the 1990s, the Swedish trio of ex-NHLers enabled Tre Kronor to surmount all obstacles in Lillehammer, though of course it wasn't all smooth sailing in the group competition of six national squads. The Swedes lost 3–2 to the Canadians and dropped a point in a 4–4 game with the Slovaks, who were

A solid contact.

making their debut and weren't highly regarded until they beat both North American teams and emerged at the top in their group. Furthermore, with 26 goals in five games, Team Slovakia was the best among all 12 participants in its scoring performance. The player responsible for this spectacular upset was 37-year-old Peter Stastny, while the young Zigmund Palffy and Miroslav Satan were able to turn in sparkling performances playing alongside this veteran who had 13 NHL seasons behind him.

Near miracles also occurred among the other six teams. Headed by Swedish coach Curt Lindstrom, the Finns whipped all their rivals, including the Czechs (3–1) and the Russians (5–0). After the first round, the semifinal pairs and results became more predictable with Sweden versus Russia (4–3) and Canada versus Finland (5–3). But in the game for third place, Suomi trounced Russia again (4–0) and won bronze.

In the finals, the Swedes took the lead and seemed to solve all their problems in the second period, even though both the young Peter Forsberg and the veteran Hakan Loob missed three or four chances to outplay Corey Hirsch in Canada's goal in their attempts not only to score but score beautifully. At the beginning of the third period, Paul Kariya tied the score, and by the 59th minute it was the Canadians who were leading 2–1. Then Tre Kronor defenseman Magnus Svensson saved the day, scoring from the blue line on a pass from Forsberg. After a scoreless 10-minute overtime, the fate of the medals had to be decided by a series of shootouts. After the first

A perfect landing.

series, the score was still 2–2. In the second series, Forsberg outwitted Hirsch with an elegant feint and made it 3–2 and future New York Islanders goalie Tommy Salo finished the job when he deftly and almost incredibly parried a shot aimed by Kariya at the top corner of the net.

At the 1994 World Championship two months after the Olympics, the winners were the same national teams, but they changed places on the pedestal.

A couple of Canadian players got lucky. Edmonton and Los Angeles didn't make it to the Stanley Cup playoffs, so seasoned goalie Bill Ranford and forward Luc Robitaille appeared on the roster in Italy. Meanwhile, the Americans once again compelled their followers to remember Lake Placid. In the quarterfinals, they outplayed the Russians 3–1. After a defeat at the hands of the Finns in the semifinals (8–0) and a loss to the Swedes in the game for third place (7–2), the optimism had vanished, however.

The Finns had already emerged in the leading roles in Europe and were thirsting to win the first World Championship in Team Suomi's history. Having retained their Olympic bronze-winning lineup, they indeed came very close and were leading shortly before the end of the deciding game against the Canadians. But Robitaille took the game into overtime when he slammed a goal into Jarmo Myllys's net, after which it had to be decided in a shootout, just as it had been in

Lillehammer. Here too Robitaille was up to the mark. Two of his goals—plus a number of spectacular saves by Ranford in goal—made the Canadians world champions after a 33-year hiatus.

For the first time in history, a strike by the NHL Players' Association shortened the 1994–95 season. The regular-season championship began at the end of January and the clubs played only 48 games each. Another historic first was recorded when the Red Wings won the Presidents' Trophy. Yet a third occurred when the Quebec Nordiques—in which Peter Forsberg was making his debut—took the lead in the Eastern Conference, only to bow out to the Rangers in the first round when rumors indicating the imminent financial collapse of the club swirled all around it that spring and wreaked havoc with a winning attitude. And the rumors turned out to be true. The Nordiques moved to Denver that summer and became the Colorado Avalanche. As a result, the New Jersey Devils made it to the 1995 Stanley Cup finals from the Eastern Conference without too much trouble, toppling Boston (4–1), Pittsburgh (4–1) and Philadelphia (4–2) along the way.

When the Devils had been defeated by the Cup-winning New York Rangers in the seventh game of the Eastern Conference finals in 1994, coach Jacques Lemaire had had only one top star on his team, goalie Martin Brodeur. Nothing had changed in the Devils lineup by the spring of 1995, so in the finals against the Detroit Red Wings, Lemaire bet on defense and team spirit. The result was astounding. In four games, the Devils outplayed the star-studded Detroit Red Wings and won the Stanley Cup for the

In the 1994–95 finals, the Devils outplayed the star-studded Red Wings in four games and won the Stanley Cup for the first time.

first time. Martin Brodeur played fantastically, while Claude Lemieux turned in a brilliant performance against the Red Wings. His winning goal in game one in Detroit psychologically bent his opponents. Lemaire's players used the middle zone trap and deployed four approximately equal forward lines to catch the opposition off guard. Nonetheless, the main component of the Devils' well-deserved victory was team spirit.

Due to the almost five-month strike by the NHL Players' Association, not one NHLer was able to participate in the 1995 World Championship. As usual, the Americans formed their team mainly from students and livened up the dull atmosphere that prevailed in Stockholm before the playoffs. For the first time in years, the Americans went through the preliminaries without losing a single point before the Canadians cut them short in the quarterfinals. The Canadians also lost the semifinals but won a duel against the Czechs for the bronze.

In addition to their long-standing rivalry with the Finns, there was another psychological barrier for the Swedes in the finals: The Tre Kronor players had never won a World Championship at home. Nor did they overcome this time. The Swedes were deprived of gold medals by Ville Peltonen, who scored three goals in the second half of the game between Sweden and Finland. The Suomi team won the finals 4–1 and became world champions for the first time. In Helsinki, 150,000 people turned out to meet the winners as they came back from Stockholm and hockey pushed everything else to the back pages of newspapers all over Finland.

A HISTORY OF WORLD HOCKEY

Joe **Mullen**

At 5´9˝, Joe Mullen wasn't big by league standards, but his will to compete and battle through injuries was formidable.

One of the deans of American-born NHL players, Joe Mullen was respected wherever he laced up his skates. Standing 5´9˝, he wasn't big by league standards, but his will to compete and battle through injuries was formidable. He was a reliable scorer who combined patience, anticipation and a quick release to top the 40-goal mark six times in his career. Mullen earned a permanent place in hockey history by becoming the first American player to score 500 goals and 1,000 points in the NHL.

A native of New York City's notorious "Hell's Kitchen," Joe and younger brother Brian learned the game playing on roller skates and using a roll of electrical tape for a puck. He starred in the local amateur league with the 14th precinct and the Westsiders. In 1974–75, he dominated the New York metro junior league with 182 points in a mere 40 games. He was immediately offered a partial scholarship to Boston College, which became a full scholarship in his second year. That first year Mullen had to pay $700 out of his own pocket to attend, but since he was on his way to four outstanding years as an amateur and a stellar pro career, it proved to be a worthwhile investment. During his last two years with the Eagles, Mullen was placed on the Eastern Collegiate Athletic Conference First All-Star Team and the NCAA East First All-American Team.

Following his senior year of college, Mullen represented the United States at the 1979 World Championship, where he averaged a point per game. Just prior to the 1979–80 season, the St. Louis Blues signed him as a free agent. Mullen adjusted to the pro game with ease and was named the Central Hockey League's top rookie in 1979–80 and led the circuit in scoring with 117 points in 1980-81.

Mullen was called up to the Blues in 1981–82 and, with 59 points in only 45 games, quickly became a fan favorite. Blues general manager Emile Francis observed, "Along the boards, he's not the biggest guy in the world, but he's strong and he's got great balance." Mullen was slowed by injuries the next year but still averaged nearly a point per game. In 1983–84, Mullen broke through with 41 goals and started gaining league-wide recognition as a bona fide scorer. Teammate Bernie Federko said: "There are only four or five like him in the league. He may go with the flow off the ice, but on it, that's a different matter. He takes charge out there." Later that year he registered four points in six games while helping the U.S. reach the 1984 Canada Cup semifinals. He scored a personal high of 92 points in 1984–85, but during this period the Blues failed to make any significant headway in the playoffs.

St. Louis traded Mullen to the Calgary Flames during the 1985–86 season, much to the chagrin of many Blues fans. He adjusted quickly to his new surroundings in Alberta, helping the team reach the Stanley Cup finals for the first time in franchise history, where they lost in five games to the Montreal Canadiens in the spring of 1986. Mullen observed: "This team lets me go out in the last couple of minutes in a close game. They showed that kind of faith in me. In St. Louis, I was a goal scorer. That was it. When I came up to the Blues, they said, 'Work on your defense.' When they sent me back down to Salt Lake City, it was, 'Too bad you didn't score more goals.' I couldn't figure it out."

Following the 1986–87 season, the respected Mullen was presented the Lady Byng Trophy. The classy forward stated: "When you continue to play, year in and out, and accomplish some of the things you set out to, it's nice to be rewarded with recognition of some kind. This isn't an award for being the top scorer or the best forward or the number one defenseman. It's an award that recognizes ability as well as sportsmanship–the way I think the game should be played."

The popular forward helped the Flames finish with the most points in the NHL in 1987–88, and the following season he registered his first 50-goal year. Mullen led all NHLers in the 1989 playoffs with 16 goals and helped Calgary to its first Stanley Cup victory at the expense of the Canadiens. He spent one more year in Alberta before he was traded to the Pittsburgh Penguins to contribute experience to a young and improving squad led by Mario Lemieux.

During Mullen's first year with the Penguins, he helped the team win the Stanley Cup for the first time in its history. He contributed 17 post-season points and his veteran savvy as the Pens outlasted the 1967 expansion Minnesota team in a six-game final series. Teammate Mark Recchi commented: "He's a great player. He's been to the Stanley Cup and won. We need players like that for the younger players. We can learn from guys like that."

Mullen started the next year by helping the United States reach the 1991 Canada Cup final. He then scored 42 goals and helped Pittsburgh repeat as Stanley Cup winners. Mullen remained a reliable scorer with 33- and 38-goal totals in 1992–93 and 1993–94. On February 7, 1995, he delighted the home crowd at the Civic Arena by becoming the first American to register 1,000 NHL points. Linemate John Cullen noted: "He's 37, almost 38, but he can still play. He's a freak of nature, like Nolan Ryan. He's getting up there in age, but he can play the game. He's still got a lot of life in his legs. He can probably play for five more years."

The popular veteran spent the 1995–96 season with the Boston Bruins before returning to play his final NHL season in Pittsburgh. Just a few weeks before retiring, Mullen scored on Patrick Roy of the Colorado Avalanche to

Joe Mullen (right) was the first American player to score 500 goals and 1,000 points in the NHL.

Mullen, Joe
RW, 5´9˝, 180 lbs, b: New York, NY, 2/26/1957

Season	Club, League	Regular Season					Playoffs				
		GP	G	A	Pts	PIM	GP	G	A	Pts	PIM
1975–76	Boston College, ECAC	24	16	18	34	4					
1976–77	Boston College, ECAC	28	28	26	54	8					
1977–78	Boston College, ECAC	34	34	34	68	12					
1978–79	Boston College, ECAC	25	32	24	56	8					
WEC–79	USA	8	7	1	8	2					
1979–80	Salt Lake Golden Eagles, CHL	75	40	32	72	21	13	9	11	20	0
	St. Louis Blues, NHL						1	0	0	0	0
1980–81	Salt Lake Golden Eagles, CHL	80	59	58	117	8	17	11	9	20	0
1981–82	St. Louis Blues, NHL	45	25	34	59	4	10	7	11	18	4
	Salt Lake Golden Eagles, CHL	27	21	27	48	12					
1982–83	St. Louis Blues, NHL	49	17	30	47	6					
1983–84	St. Louis Blues, NHL	80	41	44	85	19	6	2	0	2	0
CCup–84	USA	6	1	3	4	2					
1984–85	St. Louis Blues, NHL	79	40	52	92	6	3	0	0	0	0
1985–86	St. Louis Blues, NHL	48	28	24	52	10					
	Calgary Flames, NHL	29	16	22	38	11	21	12	7	19	4
1986–87	Calgary Flames, NHL	79	47	40	87	14	6	2	1	3	0
CCup–87	USA	4	3	0	3	0					
1987–88	Calgary Flames, NHL	80	40	44	84	30	7	2	4	6	10
1988–89	Calgary Flames, NHL	79	51	59	110	16	21	16	8	24	4
1989–90	Calgary Flames, NHL	78	36	33	69	24	6	3	0	3	0
1990–91	Pittsburgh Penguins, NHL	47	17	22	39	6	22	8	9	17	4
CCup–91	USA	8	2	3	5	0					
1991–92	Pittsburgh Penguins, NHL	77	42	45	87	30	9	3	1	4	4
1992–93	Pittsburgh Penguins, NHL	72	33	37	70	14	12	4	2	6	6
1993–94	Pittsburgh Penguins, NHL	84	38	32	70	41	6	1	0	1	2
1994–95	Pittsburgh Penguins, NHL	45	16	21	37	6	12	0	3	3	4
1995–96	Boston Bruins, NHL	37	8	7	15	0					
1996–97	Pittsburgh Penguins, NHL	54	7	15	22	4	1	0	0	0	0
	NHL Totals	1062	502	561	1063	241	143	60	46	106	42
	WEC/CCup Totals	26	13	7	20	4					

NHL First All-Star Team (1989)
Won Lady Byng Trophy (1987, 1989)
Won Lester Patrick Trophy (1995)
NHL Plus-Minus Leader (1989)
Won Stanley Cup (1989, 1991, 1992)

become the first American to score 500 goals. When he stepped away from the game after the 1996–97 season, Mullen stood as the top scoring American of all time. But he still had one more hockey challenge left. After a disastrous showing at the 1998 World Championship, the U.S. had to qualify for the 1999 Worlds during a tournament held in the middle of the NHL season. At 42, Mullen came out of retirement to help his country regain admittance to the most important annual international hockey tournament. With more than 500 career goals and 1,000 career points, Mullen was named the Hockey Hall of Fame's newest inductee in 2000.

Jiri Hrdina

Joining the NHL at the age of 30, Jiri Hrdina could hardly expect to become a star, but he hoisted the Stanley Cup over his head three times.

Joining the NHL at the age of 30, Jiri Hrdina could hardly expect to become a star. The best he could do was to play in such a way as to please himself and his club.

He came to the Calgary Flames in the middle of the 1987–88 season after the Winter Olympics, which had taken place in the team's home city. In the spring of 1989, he was one of the fortunate few to have picked the right club and he got to raise the Stanley Cup over his head for the first time. "How many more will you win?" he was asked upon his return home. "I don't know—the more the better," he replied. People shook their heads in amazement, but Jiri Hrdina had already been incredibly lucky several times in his life.

He was born in Mlada Boleslav, a town some 40 miles east of Prague. Although there were no Czech league games played in his town, he was noticed by talent scouts from Sparta Prague, and when he was 19 he left for the capital. After doing his military service with Dukla Trencin from 1981 until 1983, he played with Sparta and got to play overseas. Gradually he worked his way up to become one of the team's main supports. But in 1985 his place in the lineup for the Prague championship was suddenly in doubt. He was squeezed in only at the last minute after a terrific performance during a tournament of national B teams in St. Petersburg. He and Vladimir Ruzicka and Pavel Reichter created the most powerful lineup on the Czech team and walked away with the gold medal.

His nickname, "Geroy," was the Russian translation of his surname, which means "hero." But it also matched his game. He was physically one of the most prepared players and could play on the wing as well as center. He said: "In the beginning at Sparta they lined me up on the right whereas on the national team it was to the left side, which in our system of play with the defensive wing could almost be considered a defense post. For this reason also I didn't score very often in the beginning in international games."

In time, however, he was put in the center and could devote himself to playing forward. He asserted himself as a shooter and grew as a personality, too. In the 1986–87 season with Sparta, he made up an excellent attack line with the ambitious right winger Jiri Dolezal. They were a great success, and thanks to them, a complete line from one team went to play for Czechoslovakia in the World Championship in Vienna.

"Hrdina was a great hockey player. He wasn't endowed with an overly great talent, but he accepted good advice and worked hard to improve. Gradually hockey got into his system," Czech coach Stanislav Nevesely said of him. Everything that he achieved was through his own hard work. All that work, often tedious and tiring, paid off.

"In the NHL you learn quickly that if you let up, soon you have another 40 people pushing behind you, trying to take your place. You have to make a proportionate effort or it's over," he said once. In Calgary, and later in Pittsburgh, he wasn't among the key figures on the team. He was biding his time as an underrated defensive forward. But he did work successfully with some of the young Czech players who needed guidance. In the summer of 1990, the Penguins drafted a young man by the name of Jaromir Jagr in the first round. Jagr was 18 and felt quite lost in his new environment. Hrdina the experienced compatriot stuck by him to get him through the worst of it.

In 1991 and 1992, when the Pittsburgh Penguins won the Stanley Cup twice, the team was being pulled along by Mario Lemieux. But Jiri Hrdina was once again an integral part of the lineup. For a while it seemed that any NHL team who hired him was assured of a Stanley Cup victory. Nevertheless, Hrdina decided to quit in the summer of 1992.

He didn't return to Sparta, as he had been hinting, but threw himself into the job of talent scout. At first he worked for the Calgary Flames and from the summer of 1999 for the Dallas Stars. Occasionally he has worked with television stations as a color commentator and spent time playing his beloved golf. He sums up his hockey career this way: "I have lived through a lot of wonderful moments in my life. I am grateful that fate brought me onto the wonderful path of hockey back then in Mlada Boleslav. Today, I cannot imagine my life without hockey."

Together with Vladimir Ruzicka and Pavel Reichter, Jiri Hrdina (left) created the most powerful line on the Czech team in 1985 and won the gold medal at the World Championship at Prague.

Hrdina, Jiri
C, 6′, 195 lbs, b: Prague, Czechoslovakia, 1/5/1958

Season	Club, League	Regular Season					Playoffs				
		GP	G	A	Pts	PIM	GP	G	A	Pts	PIM
1977–78	Sparta Prague, Czechoslovakia	35	6	8	14	20					
1978–79	Sparta Prague, Czechoslovakia	31	7	8	15	18					
1979–80	Sparta Prague, Czechoslovakia	44	7	7	14	24					
1980–81	Sparta Prague, Czechoslovakia	42	14	20	34	54					
1981–82	Dukla Trencin, Czechoslovakia	44	11	27	38	36					
WEC–82	Czechoslovakia	9	1	0	1	4					
1982–83	Dukla Trencin, Czechoslovakia	36	40	24	64	4					
WEC–83	Czechoslovakia	9	1	0	1	4					
1983–84	Sparta Prague, Czechoslovakia	44	16	33	49	28					
OWG–84	Czechoslovakia	7	4	6	10	10					
CCup–84	Czechoslovakia	5	0	1	1	4					
1984–85	Sparta Prague, Czechoslovakia	44	18	14	37	30					
WEC–85	Czechoslovakia	10	2	2	4	4					
1985–86	Sparta Prague, Czechoslovakia	34	26	19	45	30	6	2	2	4	
WEC–86	Czechoslovakia	10	7	5	12	14					
1986–87	Sparta Prague, Czechoslovakia	31	18	18	36	50	6	2	5	7	
WEC–87	Czechoslovakia	10	3	3	6	6					
CCup–87	Czechoslovakia	6	1	2	3	0					
1978–88	Sparta Prague, Czechoslovakia	22	7	15	22	30					
OWG–88	Czechoslovakia	8	2	5	7	4					
1987–88	Calgary Flames, NHL	9	2	5	7	2	1	0	0	0	0
1988–89	Calgary Flames, NHL	70	22	32	54	26	4	0	0	0	0
1989–90	Calgary Flames, NHL	64	12	18	30	31	6	0	1	1	2
WEC–90	Czechoslovakia	9	1	5	6	8					
1990–91	Calgary Flames, NHL	14	0	3	3	4					
	Pittsburgh Penguins, NHL	37	6	14	20	13	14	2	2	4	6
1991–92	Pittsburgh Penguins, NHL	56	3	13	16	16	21	0	2	2	16
	Czechoslovakia Totals	412	170	194	369	328	12	4	7	11	0
	NHL Totals	250	45	85	130	92	46	2	5	7	24
	OWG/WEC/CCup Totals	83	22	29	51	58					

Won WEC (1985)
Won Stanley Cup (1989, 1991, 1992)

Mike Gartner

Right winger Mike Gartner was one of the fastest skaters and highest scorers in league history.

In his 19 years of NHL service, right winger Mike Gartner was one of the fastest skaters and most prolific scorers in league history. He was articulate and respected by fans and his peers, especially when he became heavily involved in the NHL Players' Association. But many of his accomplishments went relatively unnoticed in the era of Wayne Gretzky and Mario Lemieux. His strength on skates, along with blinding speed, made Gartner difficult to stop for even the best positional defensemen in the NHL.

Born in Ottawa but raised in Barrie, Ontario, Gartner excelled with his hometown club as champions of the Wrigley Tournament in 1975. Blessed with natural speed, he built his strength and perfected his technique by attending power skating camps in the summer when other kids were at standard hockey schools. Gartner totaled 74 goals in two seasons with the Niagara Falls Flyers of the OHA. In 1977–78, he represented Canada at the World Junior Championship held in Canada. Gartner gained six points in as many games but the team disappointed the home audience with a bronze medal finish.

During the 1978–79 schedule, Gartner played with the Cincinnati Stingers of the WHA. He accumulated 52 points but remained eligible for the NHL Entry Draft in 1979 after the NHL/WHA merger. At one point, midway through the season, he was ranked at the top of the NHL Central Scouting list of players available in June. By becoming one of the youngsters who turned pro while eligible for junior hockey, Gartner helped force the NHL to draft players in advance of their 20th birthday.

The Washington Capitals couldn't believe their good fortune when Gartner lasted until their selection, fourth overall. He scored 36 goals as a rookie but was overshadowed by Gretzky's remarkable debut and the Calder Trophy performance of Ray Bourque. This also began Gartner's NHL record string of 15 consecutive 30-goal seasons.

Between 1981 and 1983, Gartner represented Canada at the World Championship each April. In those days, the Capitals either missed the playoffs or suffered an early exit. A major disappointment occurred in the fall of 1981 when Gartner was the last player cut from the Canadian roster prior to the Canada Cup tournament. He went on to record a 35-goal season but struggled somewhat with this emotional setback. He was in the lineup in both 1984 and 1987 when Canada defeated Sweden and the USSR respectively to win the Canada Cup twice in a row.

His offense and veteran leadership helped the Capitals develop into one of the NHL's best teams in the early 1980s. The arrival of Jean Pronovost in 1980–81 exposed Gartner to Christianity, which became a major component in his life. In 1984–85, he recorded his only 50-goal season while playing with Washington on a line with Bengt Gustafsson and Bobby Carpenter. During this time, his goal production might have been higher had he not played on a defense-oriented team under coach Bryan Murray. Rather than complain about this situation, the classy Gartner helped the coach by selling the concept to some of the other Washington players.

On February 13, 1983, he was hit in the face by an opponent's clearing pass. His left cheekbone was broken in two places. More important, the optic nerve was badly damaged. For a time there was concern that his vision would be permanently altered. The nerve eventually did heal and Gartner returned to action with a visor he wore during games for the rest of his career.

Prior to the trading deadline in 1989, he was stunned when the Caps sent him to Minnesota as the key figure used to acquire Dino Ciccarelli. Gartner didn't play a full season there and was eventually sent to the New York Rangers almost 12 months to the day after he was packaged by Washington. He was a hit on Broadway, scoring 49 goals in his first complete year with the team in 1990–91. The following season he helped the Blueshirts finish at the top of the NHL regular-season standings. Late in 1991–92, he was at the center of a major labor dispute between the NHLPA and the league that shut down the NHL for several days.

After the 1992-93 edition of the Rangers inexplicably missed the playoffs, Gartner played inspired hockey for Canada at the World Championship with seven points in the same number of games. Another transaction sent him to the Toronto Maple Leafs late in the 1993–94 season. He aided the club's drive to the semifinals, notably when he scored a key overtime goal as the Leafs faced elimination in the sixth game of the Western Conference semifinal versus San Jose. Unfortunately for Gartner, just a few weeks after he was traded, the Rangers went on to win the Stanley Cup for the first time since 1940.

In 1993–94, Mike Gartner (center) aided Toronto's drive to the semifinals, notably scoring a key overtime goal as the Leafs faced elimination in the sixth game in the series against San Jose.

One of the most taxing years of Gartner's life was the 1994–95 season. As president of the NHLPA, he was constantly negotiating or defending the players' position to the media during the unprecedented owners' lockout. As one of the negotiators for the players, he worked long hours to help attain a resolution. Ironically, the condensed 48-game schedule after the resolution of the conflict made it virtually impossible for him to keep his 30 goals per season streak going. Gartner's last two seasons came in the uniform of the Phoenix Coyotes. In 1996–97, he reached the 30 mark for the 17th time in his career and on December 14, 1997, he became only the fifth player in NHL history to reach the 700-goal plateau.

As impressive as his goal-scoring prowess was, there was more to Gartner than just hockey. He was a generous person dedicated to charitable causes wherever he played. Supporting children's hospitals was a favorite activity. In Washington, he started to donate money every time he scored. Soon teammates and citizens in the community were doing the same. In this way, over $100,000 was raised every year.

Mike Gartner was inducted into the Hockey Hall of Fame in 2001 and continues to make headlines as an executive with the NHL Players' Association.

Gartner, Mike
RW, 6´, 187 lbs, b: Ottawa, Ont., 10/29/1959

Season	Club, League	Regular Season					Playoffs				
		GP	G	A	Pts	PIM	GP	G	A	Pts	PIM
1978–79	Cincinnati Stingers, WHA	78	27	25	52	123	3	0	2	2	2
1979–80	Washington Capitals, NHL	77	36	32	68	66					
1980–81	Washington Capitals, NHL	80	48	46	94	100					
WEC–81	Canada	8	4	0	4	8					
1981–82	Washington Capitals, NHL	80	35	45	80	121					
WEC–82	Canada	10	3	2	5	6					
1982–83	Washington Capitals, NHL	73	38	38	76	54	4	0	0	0	4
WEC–83	Canada	10	4	1	5	12					
1983–84	Washington Capitals, NHL	80	40	45	85	90	8	3	7	10	16
CCup–84	Canada	8	3	2	5	10					
1984–85	Washington Capitals, NHL	80	50	52	102	71	5	4	3	7	9
1985–86	Washington Capitals, NHL	74	35	40	75	63	9	2	10	12	4
1986–87	Washington Capitals, NHL	78	41	32	73	61	7	4	3	7	14
CCup–87	Canada	9	2	2	4	6					
1987–88	Washington Capitals, NHL	80	48	33	81	73	14	3	4	7	14
1988–89	Washington Capitals, NHL	56	26	29	55	71					
	Minnesota North Stars, NHL	13	7	7	14	2	5	0	0	0	6
1989–90	Minnesota North Stars, NHL	67	34	36	70	32					
	New York Rangers, NHL	12	11	5	16	6	10	5	3	8	12
1990–91	New York Rangers, NHL	79	49	20	69	53	6	1	1	2	0
1991–92	New York Rangers, NHL	76	40	41	81	55	13	8	8	16	4
1992–93	New York Rangers, NHL	84	45	23	68	59					
WC–93	Canada	7	3	4	7	12					
1993–94	New York Rangers, NHL	71	28	24	52	58					
	Toronto Maple Leafs, NHL	10	6	6	12	4	18	5	6	11	14
1994–95	Toronto Maple Leafs, NHL	38	12	8	20	6	5	2	2	4	2
1995–96	Toronto Maple Leafs, NHL	82	35	19	54	52	6	4	1	5	4
1996–97	Phoenix Coyotes, NHL	82	32	31	63	38	7	1	2	3	4
1997–98	Phoenix Coyotes, NHL	60	12	15	27	24	5	1	0	1	18
	WHA Totals	78	27	25	52	123	3	0	2	2	2
	NHL Totals	1432	708	627	1335	1159	122	43	50	93	125
	WEC/WC/CCup Totals	52	52	19	11	30	54				

Won CCup (1984, 1987)

Anders Carlsson

Anders Carlsson (center) has played in the Swedish Elite League in four decades: in the 1970s, 1980s, 1990s and the year 2000.

Leksand forward Anders Carlsson's two most memorable goals both happened during the 1986 World Championship in Moscow when Tre Kronor played Finland in the semifinals. With 40 seconds to go, the Finns were leading 4–2. In what looked like a hopeless situation, Carlsson scored two goals, knocking Finland out. The Russian crowd went wild over Carlsson's cool precision. "Even today," he says, "people in the street come up to me again and again and ask me to tell the story."

Carlsson was born in Gavle, Sweden, and made his debut with the local team, Gavle Godtemplare. Then he joined Brynas, one of the strongest teams in Sweden and a much-sought-after destination for every young hockey player in Gavle. He first appeared with Brynas in 1978 in only one game, but was lucky enough to play with two Swedish hockey legends, Tord Lundstrom and Lars-Goran Nilsson, who were playing their last game for Brynas.

Carlsson won the Swedish Championship three times—once with Sodertalje and twice with Brynas. He was a double world champion and made his debut with Tre Kronor playing alongside Jonas Bergqvist and Hakan Soderstrom. He also played for the NHL's New Jersey Devils for three seasons.

Back in Sweden, Carlsson, who turned 40 on November 25, 2000, has become one of Leksand's leading forwards. During the 1999–2000 season, he set three new records. On November 4, 1999, Leksand defeated HV 71 of Jonkoping 6–2, with Carlsson making two assists to break Hakan Loob's long-standing scoring record of 500 points with the Elite Series. By the end of the 1999–2000 season, Carlsson had 501 points—189 goals and 312 assists—accumulated in 614 games played with Sodertalje, Brynas, Vasteras and Leksand. Hakan Loob set his record in 406 Elite Series games.

Carlsson, Anders
C, 5′11″, 185 lbs, b: Gavle, Sweden, 11/25/1960

Season	Club, League	Regular Season					Playoffs				
		GP	G	A	Pts	PIM	GP	G	A	Pts	PIM
1978–79	Brynas, Sweden	1	0	0	0	2					
1979–80	Brynas, Sweden	17	0	1	1	6	1	0	0	0	0
1980–81	Brynas, Sweden	36	8	8	16	36					
1981–82	Brynas, Sweden	35	5	5	10	22					
1982–83	Brynas, Sweden	35	18	13	31	26					
1983–84	Brynas, Sweden	35	8	26	34	34					
1984–85	Sodertalje, Sweden	36	20	14	34	18	8	0	3	3	18
1985–86	Sodertalje, Sweden	36	12	26	38	20	7	2	4	6	0
WEC–86	Sweden	10	6	6	12	12					
1986–87	New Jersey Devils, NHL	48	2	18	20	14					
	Maine Mariners, AHL	6	0	6	6	2					
WEC–87	Sweden	10	4	3	7	6					
CCup–87	Sweden	6	1	0	1	0					
1987–88	New Jersey Devils, NHL	9	1	0	1	0	3	1	0	1	2
	Utica Devils, AHL	33	12	22	34	16					
1988–89	New Jersey Devils, NHL	47	4	8	12	20					
	Utica Devils, AHL	7	2	4	6	4					
WEC–89	Sweden	10	2	3	5	8					
1989–90	Brynas, Sweden	40	12	31	43	29	2	0	2	2	0
WEC–90	Sweden	8	1	0	1	2					
1990–91	Brynas, Sweden	34	11	24	35	22	2	1	1	2	2
WEC–91	Sweden	6	1	1	2	6					
1991–92	Brynas, Sweden	*	*	*	*	*					
1992–93	Brynas, Sweden	40	13	18	31	28	10	3	2	5	6
1993–94	Brynas, Sweden	36	6	11	17	47	7	2	2	4	4
1994–95	Vasteras, Sweden	39	16	22	38	40	4	1	3	4	4
1995–96	Leksand, Sweden	36	8	18	26	26	5	2	1	3	4
1996–97	Leksand, Sweden	50	12	27	39	52	9	1	8	9	12
WC–97	Sweden	11	1	1	2	6					
1997–98	Leksand, Sweden	41	11	20	31	28	2	0	0	0	0
1998–99	Leksand, Sweden	48	23	34	57	38	*	*	*	*	*
1999–2000	Leksand, Sweden	48	11	30	41	34					
	Sweden Totals	643	194	328	522	508	*	*	*	*	*
	NHL Totals	104	7	26	33	34	3	1	0	1	2
	WEC/WC/CCup Totals	61	16	14	30	40					

Won WEC (1987, 1991)
Sweden Champion (1980, 1985, 1993)

On November 23, 1999, Carlsson set another record. In a game against Karlstad's Farjestad, he scored one goal and made two assists, breaking the oldest assist record in the Elite Series—313 passes—set by Stefan Nilsson, forward for both Brynas and Sweden's national team.

Not ready to rest on his laurels, on February 1, 2000, in a game against Malmo, "Masken" (as he is known to Swedish fans) played his 633rd game for the Elite Series to break the record previously held by Jens Oling, forward for Djurgarden and Tre Kronor, of 632 Elite Series games.

Carlsson still believes that playing hockey is great fun, but he is determined that the 1999—2000 season was his last. However, the veteran player intends to stay with Leksand in an administrative capacity. He lives in the city with his wife, Kristina, and their three daughters.

This hockey legend left the game with four major records to his credit, the final one coming at the end of his last season. Carlsson had played with the Elite Series in four decades—the 1970s, 1980s, 1990s and the year 2000—an accomplishment worthy of note.

On November 4, 1999, Anders Carlsson (left) made two assists to break Hakan Loob's long-standing record of 500 points with the Elite League.

Raymond Bourque

Almost quietly, Ray Bourque became a superstar defenseman, considered one of the top two or three players at his position in modern hockey. He had all the offensive tools that propelled Denis Potvin, Paul Coffey and Bobby Orr, whose presence close by in Boston was always felt. Bourque had the ability to dominate consistently in his own end of the ice. He showed durability and longevity, leadership and character. Still, perhaps due partly to his quiet nature and partly to his timing with the Boston Bruins, his star never seemed to shine quite as brightly as his peers'.

Born in 1960, Bourque grew up in Montreal during the heyday of the Montreal Canadiens' domination of the league in the 1970s. He wasn't especially drawn to the darting style of Guy Lafleur. He preferred the solid defensive play of the "Big Three," Serge Savard, Larry Robinson and Guy Lapointe.

Bourque slipped on his first pair of skates at age five and progressed through Montreal's minor hockey system, playing one year at center before settling down on defense. He was a high scorer, but that wasn't his primary interest even as a youngster.

"Oh, I got points," he said of his minor playing days, "but only when I had the room. I worked very hard at defense. I'm very proud of my defense, then and now."

At the tender age of 16, Bourque made the jump to the junior hockey ranks, playing with the Sorel Eperviers in the Quebec Major Junior Hockey League in 1976–77. He moved with the Eperviers to Verdun to begin the next season. His offensive game increasingly began to show itself as he perfected the art of joining the rush, his preferred method of attack. He had 79 points in 72

Almost quietly, Ray Bourque became a superstar considered one of the top three defense players in modern hockey.

A HISTORY OF WORLD HOCKEY

games with Verdun, a total he improved greatly the next year when he notched 93 points in just 63 games, though he missed a few weeks near the end of the season with a kidney infection.

Although his talent was obvious, many teams had concerns when Bourque entered the 1979 Entry Draft as an underage player. Due to his illness, his play had declined at the end of the previous season. The teams picking early couldn't afford to gamble on a young player who might need another junior year to be truly ready for the NHL. The high-scoring QMJHL was also questioned by scouts and league executives, since more than a few players with inflated statistics had failed to measure up once they turned pro. Then there was the presence of Roderique Lemoyne, the outspoken owner of the Verdun team. He started talking up his defenseman as the next Bobby Orr and was threatening to ask for a wagonload of cash to let Bourque out of his junior contract. Seven teams went to the podium and picked before Bourque was selected by the Boston Bruins. Boston management privately expressed delight that their man was still around.

Boston avoided trouble with Lemoyne and signed Bourque to a contract to begin in the 1979–80 season. Bourque made an immediate impression in training camp, turning heads with his tricks and skills, not to mention his stifling defensive abilities. Word began to spread about the 18-year-old rookie defender. Boston forward Mike Milbury, who later became Bourque's coach with the Bruins, predicted the young player would win the Calder Trophy as the league's best rookie even before Bourque had played a game.

"When I came to my training camp I was 22 years old, and when I got the puck the first thing I wanted to do was pass it away," Milbury said. "But this kid is different. He holds it. He dekes and dives with it. He knows he can do something with it and he does."

Over the course of his first season, a lot of people began to agree with Milbury's assessment. For his part, Bourque worked hard but had some trouble adjusting. A quiet man in the first place, he arrived in Boston with a rudimentary grasp of English and struggled at times in groups of fast-talking strangers asking him if he was the next Bobby Orr—which they did often, even though the Bruins tried to avoid such comparisons.

Bourque did his talking on the ice. He scored the most points in history for a rookie defender and, as Milbury predicted, was an easy choice for the Calder Trophy. He was also placed on the league's First All-Star Team—the first non-goaltender to achieve that honor and win the Calder in the same year.

Bourque, Ray
D, 5′11″, 219 lbs, b: Montreal, Que., 12/28/1960

Season	Club, League	Regular Season					Playoffs				
		GP	G	A	Pts	PIM	GP	G	A	Pts	PIM
1979–80	Boston Bruins, NHL	80	17	48	65	73	10	2	9	11	27
1980–81	Boston Bruins, NHL	67	27	29	56	96	3	0	1	1	2
CCup–81	Canada	7	1	4	5	6					
1981–82	Boston Bruins, NHL	65	17	49	66	51	9	1	5	6	16
1982–83	Boston Bruins, NHL	65	22	51	73	20	17	8	15	23	10
1983–84	Boston Bruins, NHL	78	31	65	96	57	3	0	2	2	0
CCup–84	Canada	8	0	4	4	8					
1984–85	Boston Bruins, NHL	73	20	66	86	53	5	0	3	3	4
1985–86	Boston Bruins, NHL	74	19	58	77	68	3	0	0	0	0
1986–87	Boston Bruins, NHL	78	23	72	95	36	4	1	2	3	0
RV'87	NHL All-Stars	2	1	0	1	2					
CCup–87	Canada	9	2	6	8	10					
1987–88	Boston Bruins, NHL	78	17	64	81	72	23	3	18	21	26
1988–89	Boston Bruins, NHL	60	18	43	61	52	10	0	4	4	6
1989–90	Boston Bruins, NHL	76	19	65	84	50	17	5	12	17	16
1990–91	Boston Bruins, NHL	76	21	73	94	75	19	7	18	25	12
1991–92	Boston Bruins, NHL	80	21	60	81	56	12	3	6	9	12
1992–93	Boston Bruins, NHL	78	19	63	82	40	4	1	0	1	2
1993–94	Boston Bruins, NHL	72	20	71	91	58	13	2	8	10	0
1994–95	Boston Bruins, NHL	46	12	31	43	20	5	0	3	3	0
1995–96	Boston Bruins, NHL	82	20	62	82	58	5	1	6	7	2
1996–97	Boston Bruins, NHL	62	19	31	50	18					
1997–98	Boston Bruins, NHL	82	13	35	48	80	6	1	4	5	2
OWG–98	Canada	6	1	2	3	4					
1998–99	Boston Bruins, NHL	81	10	47	57	34	12	1	9	10	14
1999–2000	Boston Bruins, NHL	65	10	28	38	20					
	Colorado Avalanche, NHL	14	8	6	14	6	13	1	8	9	8
2000–2001	Colorado Avalanche, NHL	80	7	52	59	48	21	4	6	10	12
	NHL Totals	1612	410	1169	1579	1141	214	41	139	180	171
	OWG/CCup/RV'87 Totals	32	5	16	21	30					

NHL First All-Star Team (1980, 1982, 1984, 1985, 1987, 1988, 1990, 1991, 1992, 1993, 1994, 1996)
NHL Second All-Star Team (1981, 1983, 1986, 1989, 1995, 1999)
Won James Norris Trophy (1987, 1988, 1990, 1991, 1994)
Won Calder Trophy (1980)
Won King Clancy Trophy (1992)
Won CCup (1984, 1987)

Bourque wasn't known to trumpet his accomplishments, but he was acknowledged as a leader by example, a quiet player who showed his class on the ice, as he did on December 4, 1987.

It was Phil Esposito Night in Boston. Esposito had a history of problems with Boston management, but Bourque helped put that in the past. Bourque had worn Espo's old number 7 since he'd entered the league. Midway through the ceremonies, Bourque skated over to shake Esposito's hand. When he reached the retired star, he surprised just about everybody in the building by removing his number 7 sweater, which he handed to Espo, and revealing a new number, 77. Esposito was speechless.

Ray Bourque's total of five Norris Trophy awards is third in league history behind Doug Harvey with seven and Bobby Orr with eight.

Although he had seasons with impressive offensive statistics— 96 points in 1983–84—and a plus-minus rating that was always on the plus side, Bourque didn't win his first Norris Trophy until 1987. Almost as if he was making up for lost time, he won the award four out of the next seven years. His total of five Norris Trophy awards is third in league history next to Doug Harvey with seven and Bobby Orr, who won it for eight consecutive years.

Bourque was named the Bruins' captain in 1988–89 after being co-captain from 1985. Boston was a solid regular-season team but the Bruins struggled to find their feet in the playoffs. Bourque's teams reached two Stanley Cup finals—in 1988 and 1990—but the prize eluded him both years.

Bourque's offensive statistics rank him among the league's all-time leaders in points and assists. On March 27, 1997, he collected his 1,000th assist, putting him in an elite club with Gordie Howe, Marcel Dionne, Wayne Gretzky and Paul Coffey. He has been chosen as a league All-Star every year he has been in the NHL, and his selection to the North America team roster in the 1999–2000 All-Star Game tied him with Wayne Gretzky for most consecutive appearances at 18.

Despite his loyalty and longevity with the Bruins, Bourque never won a Cup title with the team. So when the opportunity to change teams presented itself at the trading deadline in March 2000, he accepted. After 20 years as a Bruin, he was on his way to Colorado. Although he strengthened the team's defense and power-play down the stretch drive, the Avs were eliminated in the conference finals by Dallas. In the summer of 2000, Bourque signed a two-year contract with Colorado and at age 40 continued to pursue his Stanley Cup dream, which was finally fulfilled in 2001. Bourque retired that summer.

Guy Carbonneau

In an exceptional career, center Guy Carbonneau began as an offensive spark plug and finished as a top-notch defensive forward and one of the most respected veterans in the game. Along the way, he contributed his share of goals and assists while becoming arguably the top shot-blocking forward in the NHL.

It was during his outstanding junior career with the Quebec Major Junior Hockey League's Chicoutimi Sagueneens that Carbonneau was chosen 44th overall by the Montreal Canadiens at

In an exceptional career, Guy Carbonneau began as a spark plug in offense and finished as a top-notch defensive forward.

the 1979 NHL Entry Draft. As an amateur, he was considered one of the elite playmakers in the country. In his last two years of junior alone, Carbonneau recorded 189 assists.

In the tradition of the Canadiens organization, Carbonneau wasn't rushed to the NHL. He spent two seasons with the Nova Scotia Voyageurs of the AHL, where he fine-tuned his defensive game while producing 88 and 94 points in his first and second seasons respectively. He made a brief appearance with the Habs in 1980–81 and, although he made a good impression, he was sent back to the minors.

Carbonneau gained a permanent slot in the Montreal lineup in 1982–83. He played a strong checking role with linemates Chris Nilan and veteran Bob Gainey but did manage to record a decent 47 points. The next year he hit the 20-goal mark for the first time. Although the team finished with a mediocre 75 points, Montreal upset Boston and Quebec to reach the semifinals. Carbonneau was one of the Habs' top players in this unlikely playoff drive, especially when they gave the defending champion New York Islanders a six-game scare in the "final four."

The sweet taste of a Stanley Cup victory came Carbonneau's way for the first time in 1986. In the post-season, he won face-offs, killed penalties and scored seven goals in 20 games in series wins over Boston, Hartford, the New York Rangers and Calgary. Had rookie goalie Patrick Roy not been so spectacular, Carbonneau would have been a strong candidate to win the Conn Smythe Trophy. His proficiency with the puck was recognized with Selke Trophy wins in 1988, 1989 and 1992. Carbonneau became the first player since Bob Gainey (the individual for whom the award was more or less instituted) to win this award in consecutive years. He also finished as the Selke runner-up to Dave Poulin in 1987 and Rick Meagher in 1990.

Under the guidance of first-year bench boss Pat Burns, Carbonneau scored a personal high of 26 goals and helped the club reach the 1989 finals versus eventual winner Calgary. Prior to the 1989–90 season, he and Chris Chelios were named co-captains. The next season, Carbonneau took over the captaincy after Chelios was traded to Chicago.

Over the years, Carbonneau became known as the Habs' "wise man" or "coach without portfolio." On November 25, 1992, he recorded his 500th point with an assist against the Hartford Whalers. His class and veteran leadership were never more evident than in the 1993 Stanley Cup finals versus the Los Angeles Kings. After his team dropped the first contest in front of a disappointed Forum crowd, the captain insisted on being assigned to check star forward Wayne Gretzky for the remainder of the series. This was the type of unselfish act for which Carbonneau was widely known. After the final buzzer sounded for Montreal's 23rd

Carbonneau, Guy
C, 5'11", 186 lbs, b: Sept-Iles, Que., 3/18/1960

Season	Club, League	Regular Season					Playoffs				
		GP	G	A	Pts	PIM	GP	G	A	Pts	PIM
1979–80	Nova Scotia Voyageurs, AHL						2	1	1	2	2
1980–81	Montreal Canadiens, NHL	2	0	1	1	0					
	Nova Scotia Voyageurs, AHL	78	35	53	88	87	6	1	3	4	9
1981–82	Nova Scotia Voyageurs, AHL	77	27	67	94	124	9	2	7	9	8
1982–83	Montreal Canadiens, NHL	77	18	29	47	68	3	0	0	0	2
1983–84	Montreal Canadiens, NHL	78	24	30	54	75	15	4	3	7	12
1984–85	Montreal Canadiens, NHL	79	23	34	57	43	12	4	3	7	8
1985–86	Montreal Canadiens, NHL	80	20	36	56	57	20	7	5	12	35
1986–87	Montreal Canadiens, NHL	79	18	27	45	68	17	3	8	11	20
1987–88	Montreal Canadiens, NHL	80	17	21	38	61	11	0	4	4	2
1988–89	Montreal Canadiens, NHL	79	26	30	56	44	21	4	5	9	10
1989–90	Montreal Canadiens, NHL	68	19	36	55	37	11	2	3	5	6
1990–91	Montreal Canadiens, NHL	78	20	24	44	63	13	1	5	6	10
1991–92	Montreal Canadiens, NHL	72	18	21	39	39	11	1	1	2	6
1992–93	Montreal Canadiens, NHL	61	4	13	17	20	20	3	3	6	10
1993–94	Montreal Canadiens, NHL	79	14	24	38	48	7	1	3	4	4
1994–95	St. Louis Blues, NHL	42	5	11	16	16	7	1	2	3	6
1995–96	Dallas Stars, NHL	71	8	15	23	38					
1996–97	Dallas Stars, NHL	73	5	16	21	36	7	0	1	1	6
1997–98	Dallas Stars, NHL	77	7	17	24	40	16	3	1	4	6
1998–99	Dallas Stars, NHL	74	4	12	16	31	17	2	4	6	6
1999–2000	Dallas Stars, NHL	69	10	6	16	36	23	2	4	6	12
	NHL Totals	1318	260	403	663	820	231	38	55	93	161

Won Frank J. Selke Trophy (1988, 1989, 1992)
Won Stanley Cup (1986, 1993, 1999)

Stanley Cup triumph, the classy veteran let inactive Denis Savard hoist the ultimate prize before anyone else. An admiring coach Jacques Demers noted: "Guy really showed me something. He really stepped forward to lead us."

A trade for promising center Jim Montgomery saw Carbonneau head to the St. Louis Blues' training camp in 1994. He summed up his feelings about the move by saying: "I didn't realize I was leaving the Canadiens until I walked into the dressing room and started cleaning out my locker. I had some of the greatest moments of my life here." His first year away from Montreal was disrupted by the unprecedented owners' lockout. On the eve of the following season, Dallas Stars general manager Bob Gainey seized the opportunity to trade for his former teammate. The Texas club was building a Cup contender but lacked veteran playoff experience.

Guy Carbonneau (number 21) was awarded the Selke Trophy in 1988, 1989 and 1992.

On February 6, 1996, Carbonneau played his 1,000th regular-season game in St. Louis. In perhaps the most emotional moment for Carbonneau that year, he was given a rousing ovation by the fans in attendance when the Stars played the last NHL game at the Montreal Forum. As a former captain of the team, he was invited to partake in the pre-game and post-game ceremonies. After the season, Carbonneau's dedication was recognized when he was chosen as a finalist for the Bill Masterton Trophy, which was won by Gary Roberts.

The next year the Dallas Stars jelled and recorded the first 100-point season in franchise history. Carbonneau played a solid checking role and passed on his Stanley Cup experience to the younger Dallas players. The team acquired valuable experience despite losing the 1998 Western Conference finals to the repeat champion Detroit Red Wings. But the following season, Carbonneau won his third Stanley Cup title when the Stars vanquished the Buffalo Sabres in a tight six-game series. After reaching the Stanley Cup finals again with the Stars in 2000, Carbonneau retired as the oldest player in the league. Not long after, Carbonneau returned to Montreal and was appointed supervisor of prospect development with the Canadiens on August 3, 2000.

Vladimir Ruzicka

On January 4, 2000, two sensational news items were circulating in the Czech hockey world. First, the Czechs had won the World Junior Championship for the first time ever, and second, Vladimir Ruzicka, who two years earlier was on the first Czech team to win an Olympic gold medal, announced that he was ending his hockey career.

The former captain of a team that won the most coveted victory in Czech hockey history, Ruzicka played his last match two months later, on March 4. Even that event was symbolic. Ruzicka lined up for Slavia Prague against Litvinov, where he had begun his magnificent career. A player was leaving the scene who meant as much to Czech hockey as Wayne Gretzky did to North Americans. After a groin injury and some back pain, he decided to quit.

With 39 goals and a total of 75 points for the Bruins, the 1991–92 season was the best in Vladimir Ruzicka's NHL career.

Because he had never liked grandiose spectacles and wasn't fond of long speeches, he regarded this final game as a normal league match. Slavia won 4–1, although Ruzicka didn't score.

Ruzicka started playing hockey at five years of age. At 16, he made his debut with Litvinov in high-level competition. In his first 10 minutes on the ice, he scored against goaltender Jiri Kralik. At 19, he made his first appearance on the national team. With the exception of two years spent with Trencin, he stayed in Litvinov until the end of 1989. Then he spent five years in the NHL playing for Edmonton, Boston and Ottawa. In his best season, 1991–92, he scored 39 goals for a total of 75 points.

After a brief stopover with Zug in Switzerland, he helped Slavia Prague graduate to the Czech elite in the 1994–95 season. Then he went on an extended scoring streak and garnered a lot of attention. On the charts of the Czech Club of League Scorers, where goals scored both in the league and on the national team are counted, he moved to second place behind Milan Novy. He retired with 543 goals.

He wasn't a particularly fast skater and coaches were at first upset that he wasn't interested in defense. But they were happy with his habit of scoring a goal a game. He had endless ways to complete a play and an excellent sense for passing. Ruzicka enjoyed outsmarting his opponents—luring the goaltender toward him, for example, and then getting the puck to a teammate who was perfectly positioned to score.

In the dressing room as well as on the ice, he tended to be somewhat impulsive and even volatile. He believed that nice guys finished last on the ice and referees sometimes had a hard time with him, as did players who weren't on his level or who misunderstand his intentions. "Personally I like to remember a whole lot of coaches. But I don't know if they'd say the same about me. I was a problem player," he admitted.

Five times he became the top scorer in Czech competition. Four times he was chosen the most productive player, the last time being in 1996. In 1986 and 1988 he won the Golden Stick Award as the most valuable player in the country. He has gold from the 1985 World Championship and from the 1998 Olympics. He was on the team when the Edmonton Oilers won the Stanley Cup in 1990, but because he hadn't played the necessary number of matches,

Ruzicka, Vladimir
C, 6´3˝, 215 lbs, b: Most, Czechoslovakia, 6/6/1963

Season	Club, League	Regular Season					Playoffs				
		GP	G	A	Pts	PIM	GP	G	A	Pts	PIM
1979–80	Litvinov, Czechoslovakia	9	1	1	2	0					
1980–81	Litvinov, Czechoslovakia	41	12	13	25	10					
1981–82	Litvinov, Czechoslovakia	44	27	22	49	50					
1982–83	Litvinov, Czechoslovakia	43	22	24	46	40					
WEC–83	Czechoslovakia	10	3	1	4	4					
1983–84	Litvinov, Czechoslovakia	44	31	23	54	50					
OWG–84	Czechoslovakia	7	4	6	10	0					
CCup–84	Czechoslovakia	5	0	0	0	2					
1984–85	Litvinov, Czechoslovakia	41	38	22	60	29					
WEC–85	Czechoslovakia	10	8	3	11	0					
1985–86	Litvinov, Czechoslovakia	43	41	32	73	*					
WEC–86	Czechoslovakia	10	4	11	15	6					
1986–87	Litvinov, Czechoslovakia	39	29	21	50	46					
WEC–87	Czechoslovakia	10	3	3	6	10					
CCup–87	Czechoslovakia	6	2	0	2	0					
1987–88	Dukla Trencin, Czechoslovakia	44	38	27	65	70					
OWG–88	Czechoslovakia	8	4	3	7	12					
1988–89	Dukla Trencin, Czechoslovakia	45	46	38	84	42					
WEC–89	Czechoslovakia	10	7	7	14	2					
1989–90	Litvinov, Czechoslovakia	32	12	23	44	*					
	Edmonton Oilers, NHL	25	11	6	17	10					
1990–91	Boston Bruins, NHL	29	8	8	16	19	17	2	11	13	0
1991–92	Boston Bruins, NHL	77	39	36	75	48	13	2	3	5	2
1992–93	Boston Bruins, NHL	60	19	22	41	38					
1993–94	Ottawa Senators, NHL	42	5	13	18	14					
1994–95	Slavia, Czech Republic	41	27	24	51	*	3	2	0	2	*
1995–96	Slavia, Czech Republic	37	21	44	65	*	5	2	1	3	*
1996–97	Slavia, Czech Republic	44	22	32	54	40					
1997–98	Slavia, Czech Republic	49	20	40	60	60	5	0	6	6	6
OWG–98	Czech Republic	6	3	0	3	0					
1998–99	Slavia, Czech Republic	50	22	29	51	61					
	Czechoslovakia/ Czech Republic Totals	646	409	415	833	*	13	4	7	11	*
	NHL Totals	233	82	85	167	129	30	4	14	18	2
	OWG/WEC/CCup Totals	82	38	34	72	36					

Won OWG (1998)
Won WEC (1985)

he didn't receive a gold ring. Similarly, he failed to win the Czech national title. It is ironic that he came closest in 1989, when he was with Trencin, where he played his shortest season of all. In the finals, his team lost to Pardubice, who had Dominik Hasek in the net.

Although many observers felt he was no longer a force in international hockey, the coach of the national team, Ivan Hlinka, decided to take him to Nagano as part of the country's 1998 Olympic team. He scored three goals in the competition, but above all he was treated as an experienced and valued player and role model for all, including Jaromir Jagr. His memorable speech after the first period of the quarterfinals against the Americans, when the Czechs were losing 1–0, made history. "Nothing special. I said that it just cannot go on like this. When we lost to Russia 2–1, my son cried at home. I simply added that I wouldn't want little Vladimir to cry again."

After the Czech team's great triumph, Ruzicka never again appeared on the national team, but he went on contributing his support to Slavia. At the same time, he started coaching the peewees. Because he knew he couldn't live without hockey, he became the club's sports manager. "I couldn't imagine myself sitting in an office. That's why I want to prepare myself together with the team. At least it won't feel as if hockey is over for me."

Vladimir Ruzicka (left) won gold at the 1985 World Championship and the 1988 Olympics, as well as the Golden Stick Award in 1986 and 1988.

Larry Murphy

Over his long National Hockey League career, Larry Murphy made the transformation from a dangerous offensive force in his youth to a savvy and solid defenseman in his late 30s. NHL teams valued him for his experience and for the success he often brought with him as a veteran—four times in the form of the Stanley Cup. Near the top of the league's all-time assists list, Murphy has played more games in the NHL than any other defenseman.

Murphy played his junior hockey with the Peterborough Petes. Under coach Gary Green, the team won the 1978–79 Memorial Cup and made the finals the next season with Mike Keenan behind the bench. Murphy acquired a firm foundation in the fundamentals from his two coaches, whose philosophies complemented his aggressive offensive style and his smooth skating. After the NHL introduced the "underage" draft in 1980, the 19-year-old Murphy was chosen fourth overall by the Los Angeles Kings. Murphy didn't feel confident when he first arrived in the league with the Kings as a rookie, and he was worried that he wouldn't be around to play in a single game, let alone a thousand.

"The toughest time was the first year in training camp," he admitted. "We were doing a three-on-two drill and I looked up to see Marcel Dionne, Dave Taylor and Charlie Simmer coming at me. I was shaking so bad, I was scared skinny."

He had another panic attack in his first game, in the Montreal Forum. "They started playing the national anthem and I felt my head get foggy and felt my knees buckling. I looked at our line, then over at the Canadiens and saw Guy Lafleur and the rest of them, and I really was worried about falling down. The first period I couldn't think straight. I might as well have spent the game on the

Larry Murphy made the transformation from a dangerous offensive force in his youth to a savvy and solid defenseman in his late 30s.

Leafs fans booed Larry Murphy (front) mercilessly, feeling he had failed to live up to expectations.

bench." Murphy held his composure, though, and went on to record the best offensive season by a rookie defenseman in league history. His 60 assists and 76 points easily surpassed Ray Bourque's total of 65 points the year before.

Murphy played three full seasons with the Kings before being traded to the Washington Capitals six games into the 1983–84 season. He had his best offensive season with the Caps in 1986–87, collecting 81 points and earning a place on the Canadian squad for the 1987 Canada Cup. Murphy played a role, albeit a secondary one, in the tournament-winning goal scored by Mario Lemieux against the Soviet Union. Wayne Gretzky carried the puck into the Soviet zone and Murphy jumped into the rush, waiting in front of the net for a pass that he and the Soviet goalie expected to come his way. Gretzky, of course, slid the puck instead to a trailing Lemieux, who calmly netted the winner. Murphy led the Canadian defense in the tourney in plus-minus, helping to quiet concerns about the blueliner's defensive abilities.

Murphy seemed to wear out his welcome with the Washington fans when the team struggled over the next few seasons. He was traded to the Pittsburgh Penguins in 1990 and became an important part—along with his Canada Cup teammate Lemieux—of the Penguins' two Stanley Cup wins in 1991 and 1992. Murphy spent several years with the Penguins after their championship seasons. He had a career year in 1992–93 with 85 points but moved to the Toronto Maple Leafs in a trade following the lockout-shortened 1994–95 season. After several years of respectable results and playoff efforts, the Maple Leafs stumbled in 1996–97. The fans booed Murphy mercilessly, feeling he had failed to live up to the expectations placed on him when he joined the team. Near the end of his stay with the Leafs, Murphy was scorned every time he touched the puck.

His former coach with the Penguins, Scotty Bowman, had moved to the Detroit Red Wings and rescued Murphy at the trading deadline. Bowman obtained him for no players and no money—the Leafs even paid part of his salary when he became a Red Wing. Though the defender had struggled without a solid team around him in Toronto, Bowman knew Murphy could help a playoff team such as Detroit. Murphy was paired with Nicklas Lidstrom, a

Murphy, Larry
D, 6'2", 210 lbs, b: Scarborough, Ont., 3/8/1961

Season	Club, League	Regular Season					Playoffs				
		GP	G	A	Pts	PIM	GP	G	A	Pts	PIM
1980–81	Los Angeles Kings, NHL	80	16	60	76	79	4	3	0	3	2
1981–82	Los Angeles Kings, NHL	79	22	44	66	95	10	2	8	10	12
1982–83	Los Angeles Kings, NHL	77	14	48	62	81					
1983–84	Los Angeles Kings, NHL	6	0	3	3	0					
	Washington Capitals, NHL	72	13	33	46	50	8	0	3	3	6
1984–85	Washington Capitals, NHL	79	13	42	55	51	5	2	3	5	0
WEC–85	Canada	8	2	6	8	4					
1985–86	Washington Capitals, NHL	78	21	44	65	50	9	1	5	6	6
1986–87	Washington Capitals, NHL	80	23	58	81	39	7	2	2	4	6
WEC–87	Canada	6	0	3	3	4					
CCup–87	Canada	8	1	6	7	4					
1987–88	Washington Capitals, NHL	79	8	53	61	72	13	4	4	8	33
1988–89	Washington Capitals, NHL	65	7	29	36	70					
	Minnesota North Stars, NHL	13	4	6	10	12	5	0	2	2	8
1989–90	Minnesota North Stars, NHL	77	10	58	68	44	7	1	2	3	31
1990–91	Minnesota North Stars, NHL	31	4	11	15	38					
	Pittsburgh Penguins, NHL	44	5	23	28	30	23	5	18	23	44
CCup–91	Canada	8	0	1	1	0					
1991–92	Pittsburgh Penguins, NHL	77	21	56	77	48	21	6	10	16	19
1992–93	Pittsburgh Penguins, NHL	83	22	63	85	73	12	2	11	13	10
1993–94	Pittsburgh Penguins, NHL	84	17	56	73	44	6	0	5	5	0
1994–95	Pittsburgh Penguins, NHL	48	13	25	38	18	12	2	13	15	0
1995–96	Toronto Maple Leafs, NHL	82	12	49	61	34	6	0	2	2	4
1996–97	Toronto Maple Leafs, NHL	69	7	32	39	20					
	Detroit Red Wings, NHL	12	2	4	6	2	20	2	9	11	8
1997–98	Detroit Red Wings, NHL	82	11	41	52	37	22	3	12	15	2
1998–99	Detroit Red Wings, NHL	80	10	42	52	42	10	0	2	2	8
1998–2000	Detroit Red Wings, NHL	81	10	30	40	45	9	2	3	5	2
WC–2000	Canada	3	0	0	0	0					
2000–2001	Detroit Red Wings, NHL	57	2	19	21	12	6	0	1	1	0
	NHL Totals	1615	287	929	1216	1086	215	37	115	152	201
	WEC/WC/CCup Totals	33	3	16	19	12					

NHL Second All-Star Team (1987, 1993, 1995)
Won Stanley Cup (1991, 1992, 1997, 1998)
Won CCup (1987, 1991)

young Swedish player just beginning to round into form as one of the league's best defensemen. There was instant chemistry between the two, and Murphy, who always looked a step slow in Toronto, was soon a fixture on the explosive Red Wing power-play. He was with the Wings when they won two consecutive Cup titles in 1997 and 1998.

Murphy's durability and reliability were nothing short of amazing. In his first 19 seasons in the NHL, he missed only 25 games, and never more than five in any one season. He played 1,558 games, second only to Gordie Howe. He surpassed Tim Horton to set the record for most games in the league by a defenseman on February 5, 1999, in Colorado. In the game against New Jersey in which he tied the record, Murphy sustained a concussion in a crushing collision. He sat out one game and then came back earlier than expected—in typical fashion—to pass Horton. By the end of the 2000–01 season, however, neither Detroit nor any other team wanted to sign him and Murphy retired after 1,615 regular-season games.

John Vanbiesbrouck

"The Beezer," as John Vanbiesbrouck is known, began playing hockey in his family basement with his brother and his friends using a taped, rolled-up sock as a puck. But by the time he was 15, he had yet to be claimed in the midget draft, so his father drove him to Sault Ste. Marie, Ontario, to a tryout with the Greyhounds of the Ontario Hockey League. Vanbiesbrouck made the team and for three years he was the number one goalie in the Soo. By the time he was eligible for the NHL Entry Draft, there was no doubt that he would be selected. The Rangers chose him 72nd overall in 1981 and just a few months later he made his professional debut with the Blueshirts as an emergency call-up.

John Vanbiesbrouck's ability to hold a game's score to 1–0 or 2–1 became legendary in Florida.

On December 5, 1981, he beat the now defunct Colorado Rockies 2–1, but at 18 years of age, he was returned to the Soo to develop. The next year, 1983–84, he played for the Tulsa Oilers, the famous CHL team that locked its doors one day and forced the team to play the remainder of its schedule on the road. "What I remember," Vanbiesbrouck said of that season, "was having to practise on a parking lot with tennis balls instead of pucks."

For two years he played goal for the United States at the World Junior Championships, and in the fall of 1984 he made the Rangers full-time. But the New Yorkers were eliminated quickly from the playoffs in the spring of 1985 and Vanbiesbrouck gladly accepted an invitation to represent the U.S. at the World Championship in Prague. "I gained a lot from that tournament," he acknowledged. "I beat three of the best teams in the world—Canada, Sweden, Czechoslovakia—which did a lot for my self-confidence, and a lot of people developed respect for me, more than they'd had previously."

Vanbiesbrouck's style of play was a hybrid of the old goalie and the new. He played the angles well and was very disciplined, but he also handled the puck and skated well. He used a butterfly rather than pads-together style and was excellent at flopping and regaining his feet quickly. He

John Vanbiesbrouck began playing hockey in his family's basement with his friends and his brother using a rolled-up, taped sock as a puck.

remained the Rangers' number one goalie until Mike Richter arrived on Broadway and established himself as an equal but younger talent. The two became the best duo in the game, but Beezer was left exposed in the Expansion Draft in 1993 by Vancouver after the Rangers had traded him to the Canucks for future considerations (Doug Lidster). The Panthers selected him first in that roster-building draft, and Vanbiesbrouck almost single-handedly legitimized a talent-thin team in Florida with his consistent brilliance. Right away, he gave the defensive-minded team a chance to win any night, and his ability to win 1–0 or 2–1 games became legendary in a state with little hockey history.

Mature and on his own again in the Florida net, Vanbiesbrouck established himself as one of the best goalies in the game. He was with the team for five years and led them to an improbable run to the Stanley Cup finals in the spring of 1996 before losing to Colorado in four games. In 1998 he found himself an unrestricted free agent for the first time in his career and auctioned his services to the highest bidder. That turned out to be Philadelphia, a Stanley Cup-contending team that had lost faith in its starter, Ron Hextall. Beezer signed a three-year contract for $11.25 million, but his first season with the new Flyers was disappointing. He failed to shine in the regular season and in the playoffs the Flyers were eliminated in the first round by the Toronto Maple Leafs. Still active—in the summer of 2000, he was traded to the New York Islanders—Vanbiesbrouck became the 15th goalie to win 300 NHL games, -and only the second American-born one, a month after the first, Tom Barrasso. Internationally, he played for the U.S. in the Canada Cup in 1987 and 1991, though he missed the inaugural World Cup because of shoulder surgery. He teamed again with Mike Richter at the Nagano Olympics in Japan in 1998 when the NHL shut down to allow all its pros to participate. However, the U.S. sixth-place finish was considered a disappointment.

In the summer of 2000, Vanbiesbrouck was traded to the New York Islanders and then New Jersey, and in the space of a year went from starter to backup as his career wound down. At 38, he was the backup for Martin Brodeur with the Devils in 2001–02.

Vanbiesbrouck, John
G, 5′8″, 176 lbs, b: Detroit, MI, 9/4/1963

Season	Club, League	Regular Season				Playoffs			
		GP	Mins	GA	Avg	GP	Mins	GA	Avg
1981–82	New York Rangers, NHL	1	60	1	1.00				
	Sault Ste. Marie Greyhounds, OHL	31	1686	102	3.62	7	276	20	4.35
1982–83	Sault Ste. Marie Greyhounds, OHL	62	3471	209	3.61	16	944	56	3.56
1983–84	New York Rangers, NHL	3	180	10	3.33	1	1	0	0.00
	Tulsa Oilers, CHL	37	2153	124	3.46	4	240	10	2.50
1984–85	New York Rangers, NHL	42	2358	166	4.22	1	20	0	0.00
WEC–85	USA	9	492	46	5.64				
1985–86	New York Rangers, NHL	61	3326	184	3.32	16	899	49	3.27
1986–87	New York Rangers, NHL	50	2656	161	3.64	4	195	11	3.38
WEC–87	USA	7	419	28	4.01				
CCup–87	USA	4	240	9	2.00				
1987–88	New York Rangers, NHL	56	3319	187	3.38				
1988–89	New York Rangers, NHL	56	3207	197	3.69	2	107	6	3.36
WEC–89	USA	5	*	20	4.53				
1989–90	New York Rangers, NHL	47	2734	154	3.38	6	298	15	3.02
1990–91	New York Rangers, NHL	40	2257	126	3.35	1	52	1	1.15
WEC–91	USA	10	526	41	4.67				
CCup–91	USA	1	60	3	3.00				
1991–92	New York Rangers, NHL	45	2526	120	2.85	7	368	23	3.75
1992–93	New York Rangers, NHL	48	2757	152	3.31				
1993–94	Florida Panthers, NHL	57	3440	145	2.53				
1994–95	Florida Panthers, NHL	37	2087	86	2.47				
1995–96	Florida Panthers, NHL	57	3178	142	2.68	22	1332	50	2.25
1996–97	Florida Panthers, NHL	57	3347	128	2.29	5	328	13	2.38
1997–98	Florida Panthers, NHL	60	3451	165	2.87				
OWG–98	USA	1	1	0	0.00				
1998–99	Philadelphia Flyers, NHL	62	3712	135	2.18	6	369	9	1.46
1998–00	Philadelphia Flyers, NHL	50	2950	108	2.20				
2000–01	NYI-New Jersey, NHL	48	2630	126	2.87				
2001–02	New Jersey Devils, NHL	5	300	10	2.00				
	NHL Totals	882	50480	2503	2.98				
	OWG/WEC/CCup Totals	37	1738	147	5.07				

NHL First All-Star Team (1986)
NHL Second All-Star Team (1994)
Won Vezina Trophy (1986)

Jonas Bergqvist

When Jonas Bergqvist was a teenager, he told his mother, "I'm going to be the best hockey player in Sweden." The 17-year-old Bergqvist played for Leksand and remained loyal to that team throughout his entire hockey career, except for occasional brief intervals when he played for the Calgary Flames in the NHL, for Germany's Mannheim and for Austria's Feldkirch, where he played the last season of his career in 1998–99.

Bergqvist made his debut with Tre Kronor in December 1984 in a game against the national team of Norway in which the Swedes trounced the Norwegians 11–2. He scored his first goal for Tre Kronor on December 14, 1984, in a game against the East German nationals on an open-air rink in Weisswasser.

In the spring of 1986, Bergqvist was awarded the Gold Puck as Sweden's best hockey player. This was a well-deserved award for a player who lived for hockey, always placing the interests of the team above his own. His devotion to the game made Bergqvist one of the most beloved hockey players in his country.

As an attacking forward, Bergqvist was also quite capable of playing defense, something not all forwards are willing to do. On the ice, he was a fierce competitor, ignoring bruises and black eyes. Bergqvist holds the record for playing 272 official games for Tre Kronor and eclipsed the record of his senior Swedish national teammate Thomas Rundqvist (267 games) at the 1998 World Championship in Zurich when, on May 10, Tre Kronor beat Team Canada by a score of 7–1. On that memorable day, his teammates presented Bergqvist with a jersey bearing the number 268, while Bergqvist himself marked the occasion by firing a third goal into the Canadian net.

Among his most memorable goals scored with the nationals, Bergqvist himself singles out the goal that he scored in the finals of the 1991 World Championship against the USSR, when he scored within seconds of coming onto the ice, giving Tre Kronor a 1–0 lead.

In the spring of 1986, Jonas Bergqvist (left) was awarded the Gold Puck as Sweden's best hockey player.

Bergqvist, Jonas
RW, 6´, 185 lbs, b: Hasselholm, Sweden, 9/26/1962

Season	Club, League	Regular Season					Playoffs				
		GP	G	A	Pts	PIM	GP	G	A	Pts	PIM
1981–82	Leksand, Sweden	33	6	7	13	10					
1982–83	Leksand, Sweden	35	8	11	19	20					
1983–84	Leksand, Sweden	29	11	11	22	16					
1984–85	Leksand, Sweden	35	11	11	22	26					
1905–06	Leksand, Sweden	06	16	21	37	16					
WEC–86	Sweden	10	4	3	7	12					
1986–87	Leksand, Sweden	36	9	11	20	26					
WEC–87	Sweden	9	1	3	4	4					
CCup–87	Sweden	6	2	0	2	4					
1987–88	Leksand, Sweden	37	19	12	31	32	3	0	0	0	0
OWG–88	Sweden	8	3	0	3	4					
1988–89	Leksand, Sweden	27	15	20	35	18	10	4	3	7	2
1989–90	Calgary Flames, NHL	22	2	5	7	10					
	Salt Lake Golden Eagles, IHL	13	6	10	16	4					
1990–91	Mannheim — Berlin, FRG	36	16	23	39	22					
WEC–91	Sweden	9	4	2	6	8					
CCup–91	Sweden	6	0	1	1	0					
1991–92	Leksand, Sweden	22	11	10	21	4					
1992–93	Leksand, Sweden	39	15	23	38	40	2	0	0	0	0
WC–93	Sweden	8	3	1	4	14					
1993–94	Leksand, Sweden	35	12	23	35	29					
OWG–94	Sweden	8	1	3	4	4					
WC–94	Sweden	8	3	5	8	4					
1994–95	Leksand, Sweden	33	17	12	29	16	4	0	0	0	4
WC–95	Sweden	5	1	0	1	0					
1995–96	Leksand, Sweden	37	16	14	30	30	5	2	1	3	0
WC–96	Sweden	6	4	0	4	0					
WCup–96	Sweden	4	1	0	1	2					
1996–97	Leksand, Sweden	38	13	16	29	22	9	4	2	6	12
1997–98	Leksand, Sweden	31	14	19	33	18	3	0	1	1	8
WC–98	Sweden	10	2	0	2	6					
1998–99	Feldkrich, Austria	46	22	26	48	28					
	Sweden Totals	503	193	221	414	323	36	10	7	17	26
	NHL Totals	22	2	5	7	10					
	OWG/WEC/WC/CCup/WCup Totals	97	29	18	47	62					

Won OWG (1994)
Won WEC/WC (1987, 1991, 1998)

Jonas Bergqvist played a record 272 official games for Tre Kronor.

Among his achievements, Bergqvist has an Olympic gold medal from the 1994 Lillehammer Games; he played in three Canada Cup tournaments; and he won three World Championship titles—the last in Switzerland in 1998. That victory put Bergqvist and Mats Sundin on a par with the famous Sven "Tumba" Johansson, who for decades was the only Swedish hockey player to become a three-time world champion. In the games he played for the Swedish national team, Bergqvist scored only 69 goals, but coaches were eager to have him play for Tre Kronor because of his competitiveness and his loyalty to team play.

Bergqvist ranks 137th on the list of "Great Men." His record of 272 official games for the national team will likely hold well into the 21st century—especially since the most talented Swedish hockey players are usually recruited by the best NHL teams and, for many of them, being in the Stanley Cup playoffs often precludes their participation in World Championships.

But records exist to be broken. Perhaps Bergqvist's will be overturned by someone from the new generation playing for Leksand—whose managing director during the 1999–2000 season happens to be Jonas Bergqvist, still loyal to his original team.

Chris Chelios

Chris Chelios's speed and exceptional lateral movement made him one of the toughest defensemen to beat one-on-one.

A mobile defenseman with a mean streak, Chris Chelios was one of the top American-born NHLers of his time. Blessed with a hard shot from the point and excellent offensive instincts, he was among the top-scoring defensemen in the league from the mid-1980s to late 1990s. Chelios was also a feared bodychecker who could be an intimidating presence in his own end. His speed and excellent lateral movement made him one of the toughest defensemen in the NHL to beat one-on-one.

The Chicago native grew up in San Diego and had a difficult time furthering his aspirations to develop into an NHL hockey player. As a teenager, he was twice cut by Junior B teams in Canada and hit a low point when he had to borrow money from strangers to get home to California one year. As Chelios said, "I wasn't any bigger or any better than the other guys, so they weren't going to take a kid from the States when they could have a local guy." He returned home and grew three inches and added 40 pounds. This gave him a second chance and he spent a useful season with the Moose Jaw Canucks of the Saskatchewan Junior Hockey League. He scored 87 points in 54 games while racking up 175 minutes in penalties. Now he was attracting the interest of many NHL scouts, including those of the Montreal Canadiens, who drafted him 40th overall that summer as an 18-year-old.

After being drafted, Chelios enjoyed two strong years at the University of Wisconsin. As one of the top collegiate players in the country, he was selected to play for the United States at the 1982 World Junior Championship. Following the 1982–83 season, he was named to the Western Collegiate Hockey Association Second All-Star Team and the National Collegiate Athletic Association Championship All-Tournament Team. Realizing a dream to play in the Olympics, Chelios postponed his NHL debut and committed to the U.S. national team program for most of

1983–84. The defending gold medalists from 1980 in Lake Placid disappointed with a seventh-place finish, but the robust blueliner was one of the few bright lights for his country.

Chelios arrived in Montreal in time to play the last 12 regular-season games of the 1983-84 season. In the regular season, the Habs finished well behind their first-round opponent, the Boston Bruins. Chelios's second-period goal in the 1–0 opening game victory paved the way for an upset. The squad reached the semifinals that year, where they gave the New York Islanders all they could handle. That fall the young Chelios was selected to play for the United States again, this time at the Canada Cup.

During his full rookie season the following year, Chelios racked up 55 assists and played in all situations for Montreal. He finished in the Calder Trophy voting as a runner-up to Mario Lemieux and his 100-point performance. Chelios's 64 points set a new Canadiens record for a first-year blueliner. In 1985–86, he missed nearly the half the season through injury, then played superbly in the Habs' run to the Stanley Cup.

Chelios added to his international experience by playing with the NHL All-Stars against their Soviet counterparts at Rendez-Vous '87 in Quebec City and by appearing in his second Canada Cup for the U.S. that same fall. In 1987–88, he hit the 20-goal mark for the first time while emerging as one of the elite NHL blueliners. His tenacity was summed up by ESPN analyst Bill Clement: "He is an incredible competitor. In one-on-one encounters when the battle is for the puck, Chris plays as if he is fighting for his life."

The 1988–89 season was rewarding in individual and team accomplishments. The Canadiens attained 115 points, their best performance since winning the Stanley Cup four straight times 10 years earlier. Chelios was singled out for his play by winning the Norris Trophy and being selected to the NHL First All-Star Team. The following year started well when he was named co-captain with Guy Carbonneau, the first American so honored in a Habs uniform. Unfortunately, he battled injuries and inconsistency all year and the team was knocked out by Boston in the Adams Division finals.

Montreal traded Chelios to Chicago to acquire local hero Denis Savard prior to the 1990–91 season. Chelios responded with 64 points while helping the Hawks finish at the

Chelios, Chris
D, 6'1", 190 lbs, b: Chicago, Il, 1/25/1962

Season	Club, League	Regular Season					Playoffs				
		GP	G	A	Pts	PIM	GP	G	A	Pts	PIM
1981–82	University of Wisconsin, WCHA	43	6	43	49	50					
1982–83	University of Wisconsin, WCHA	26	9	17	26	50					
OWG–84	USA	6	0	4	4	8					
1983–84	Montreal Canadiens, NHL	12	0	2	2	12	15	1	9	10	17
CCup–84	USA	6	0	2	2	2					
1984–85	Montreal Canadiens, NHL	74	9	55	64	87	9	2	8	10	17
1985–86	Montreal Canadiens, NHL	41	8	26	34	67	20	2	9	11	49
1986–87	Montreal Canadiens, NHL	71	11	33	44	124	17	4	9	13	38
RV'87	NHL All-Stars	2	0	0	0	0					
CCup–87	USA	5	0	2	2	2					
1987–88	Montreal Canadiens, NHL	71	20	41	61	172	11	3	1	4	29
1988–89	Montreal Canadiens, NHL	80	15	58	73	185	21	4	15	19	28
1989–90	Montreal Canadiens, NHL	53	9	22	31	136	5	0	1	1	8
1990–91	Chicago Blackhawks, NHL	77	12	52	64	192	6	1	7	8	46
CCup–91	USA	8	1	3	4	4					
1991–92	Chicago Blackhawks, NHL	80	9	47	56	245	18	6	15	21	37
1992–93	Chicago Blackhawks, NHL	84	15	58	73	282	4	0	2	2	14
1993–94	Chicago Blackhawks, NHL	76	16	44	60	212	6	1	1	2	8
WC–94	USA	0	0	0	0	0					
1994–95	Biel, Switzerland	3	0	3	3	4					
	Chicago Blackhawks, NHL	48	5	33	38	72	16	4	7	11	12
1995–96	Chicago Blackhawks, NHL	81	14	58	72	140	9	0	3	3	8
WCup–96	USA	7	0	4	4	10					
1996–97	Chicago Blackhawks, NHL	72	10	38	48	112	6	0	1	1	8
1997–98	Chicago Blackhawks, NHL	81	3	39	42	151					
OWG–98	USA	4	2	0	2	2					
1998–99	Chicago Blackhawks, NHL	65	8	26	34	89					
	Detroit Red Wings, NHL	10	1	1	2	4	10	0	4	4	14
1999–00	Detroit Red Wings, NHL	81	3	31	34	103	9	0	1	1	8
2000–01	Detroit Red Wings, NHL	23	0	3	3	45	5	1	0	1	2
2001–02	Detroit Red Wings, NHL	79	6	33	39	126					
OWG–02	USA	6	1	0	1	4					
	NHL Totals	1260	174	700	874	2556					
	OWG/WC/CCup/RV'87/WCup Totals	44	4	15	19	32					

NHL First All-Star Team (1989, 1993, 1995, 1996)
NHL Second All-Star Team (1991, 1997)
Won James Norris Trophy (1989, 1993, 1996)
Won Stanley Cup (1986)
Won WCup (1996)

During the Hawks' run in the 1992 playoffs, Chris Chelios (front) scored a personal high of 21 points in 18 games.

top of the NHL standings for the first time since 1967. Chelios and Steve Smith formed one of the toughest defense tandems in hockey and became crowd favorites. Unfortunately, the team faltered in a first-round upset at the hands of Minnesota. In the fall of 1991 Chelios played in his third Canada Cup and helped the Americans reach the final for the first time. He went on to enjoy a strong year and led Chicago to the Stanley Cup finals. During the team's 1992 playoff run, Chelios scored a personal high of 21 points in 18 games.

There were similarities between Chelios's performance in 1992–93 and his Norris Trophy-winning season, 1988–89. He registered identical statistics of 15 goals, 58 assists and 73 points and won his second Norris Trophy. The following season, he was on hand when Chicago played its last regular-season and playoff game at the historic Stadium. During the owners' lockout in 1994–95, Chelios's emotions got the better of him when he suggested to the media that NHL commissioner Gary Bettman's life might be increasingly in danger the longer the dispute lasted, but he wasn't suspended and the dispute was eventually resolved.

Prior to the 1995–96 season, Chelios was named captain of the Hawks. Inspired, he scored 72 points and won his third Norris Trophy. He formed one of the top power-play point duos in the league with Gary Suter. That fall he was a key veteran on the United States squad that captured the inaugural World Cup of Hockey in Montreal. In February 1998 he was part of the historic Nagano games that were fully open to professionals for the first time. Chelios was traded to defending Stanley Cup champion Detroit at the trading deadline in March 1999 and remained an important veteran on the Wings blue line as the club battled for first place in the NHL overall standings during the 1999–2000 season. The next season, his body was ravaged by injuries, but he returned healthy for 2001–02 and was named to the USA's team for the Salt Lake Olympics. And not only was Chelios picked for Team USA at the age of 40, he was named captain by head coach Herb Brooks. Chelios was a steady performer throughout the tournament in Salt Lake and helped the U.S. to a silver medal, losing 5–2 in the gold medal game to Canada. Chelios was humble in defeat, simply saying the better team won.

Ron Francis

Ron Francis was selected fourth overall in the 1981 Entry Draft although the Whalers had initially had no intention of selecting him.

Ron Francis played less than a year and a half of junior hockey before joining the Hartford Whalers in the NHL early in the 1981–82 season. He was selected fourth overall at the 1981 draft, although initially the Whalers had no intention of selecting him. They wanted Bobby Carpenter, but the team unwisely made their preference for the American-born player publicly known. The Washington Capitals, choosing third, beat Hartford to the punch and took Carpenter and the Whalers had to "settle" for Francis, who was just as happy. "Everybody in Hartford was talking about Bobby Carpenter and how he was going to lead them to the promised land. When they found out they couldn't get him, they wondered, 'Who's this guy?' and 'Where'd he come from?' Nobody ever heard of me and that took a lot of pressure off my shoulders because they didn't expect me to do anything."

Although just a 19-year-old rookie, Francis showed maturity well beyond his years when he first stepped onto NHL ice. He had 25 goals and 68 points his first season and instantly became a fan favorite both for his playing skill and his unfailing work in the community. He was blessed to be able to room with the great Dave Keon on road trips and the two became fast hockey friends. "Rooming with Dave has been a big help," he agreed. "He settles me down and gives me a lot of useful tips. He helps me with things like face-offs, coming out of our own end and forechecking."

While the Whalers were happy to have Francis, the team missed the playoffs the first four years he was with the team while it developed its young talent. Then it became a consistent playoff team but had an awful time winning even one round of the playoffs each spring, playing in the same division as Montreal, Boston and Quebec. However, since 1986 he has been in the playoffs for 14 consecutive seasons. Midway through the 1984–85 season, he was made team captain when incumbent Mark Johnson was traded to St. Louis. At 22, Francis became one of the youngest captains in NHL history, but he was able to live up to the expectations of wearing the "C" without it affecting his play. He routinely scored 25 goals and 80 points, but midway through the 1990–91 season, coach Rick Ley stripped him of the captaincy without an explanation. Francis took the demotion in stride, but just a few weeks later he was traded to one of the Stanley Cup favorites, the Pittsburgh Penguins.

In Pittsburgh, he played behind Mario Lemieux and a young Jaromir Jagr, but he took his game to another level. He became not only a goal scorer but one of the best passing centers and two-way players in the league. Pittsburgh won back-to-back Cup titles in 1991 and 1992 and Francis twice reached the 100-point plateau. He was equally consistent in the playoffs as in the regular season, and for 1994–95 he was named Penguins captain while Mario Lemieux recovered from injuries and missed the year. At the start of the next season, though, the captaincy was given back to Mario and Francis just kept on leading by example. And his sportsmanship paid off. When Lemieux retired in 1997, the "C" was once again sewn onto Francis's sweater.

Although he has played in four All-Star games and won the Selke Trophy (1995) and the Lady Byng Trophy (1995, 1998), Francis is perhaps the quietest superstar in the league. He is approaching 500 career goals, is one of only a few to record 1,000 career assists and is

In Pittsburgh, Ron Francis (number 10) played behind Mario Lemieux and a young Jaromir Jagr but managed to take his game to a new level.

Francis, Ron
C, 6´3˝, 200 lbs, b: Sault Ste. Marie, Ont., 3/1/1963

Season	Club, League	Regular Season					Playoffs				
		GP	G	A	Pts	PIM	GP	G	A	Pts	PIM
1981–82	Hartford Whalers, NHL	59	25	43	68	51					
1982–83	Hartford Whalers, NHL	79	31	59	90	60					
1983–84	Hartford Whalers, NHL	72	23	60	83	45					
1984–85	Hartford Whalers, NHL	80	24	57	81	66					
WEC–85	Canada	10	2	5	7	2					
1985–86	Hartford Whalers, NHL	53	24	53	77	24	10	1	2	3	4
1986–87	Hartford Whalers, NHL	75	30	63	93	45	6	2	2	4	6
1987–88	Hartford Whalers, NHL	80	25	50	75	87	6	2	5	7	2
1988–89	Hartford Whalers, NHL	69	29	48	77	36	4	0	2	2	0
1989–90	Hartford Whalers, NHL	80	32	69	101	73	7	3	3	6	8
1990–91	Hartford Whalers, NHL	67	21	55	76	51					
	Pittsburgh Penguins, NHL	14	2	9	11	21	24	7	10	17	24
1991–92	Pittsburgh Penguins, NHL	70	21	33	54	30	21	8	19	27	8
1992–93	Pittsburgh Penguins, NHL	84	24	76	100	68	12	6	11	17	19
1993–94	Pittsburgh Penguins, NHL	82	27	66	93	62	6	0	2	2	6
1994–95	Pittsburgh Penguins, NHL	44	11	48	59	18	12	6	13	19	4
1995–96	Pittsburgh Penguins, NHL	77	27	92	119	56	11	3	6	9	4
1996–97	Pittsburgh Penguins, NHL	81	27	63	90	20	5	1	2	3	2
1997–98	Pittsburgh Penguins, NHL	81	25	62	87	20	6	1	5	6	2
1998–99	Carolina Hurricanes, NHL	82	21	31	52	34	3	0	1	1	0
1999–00	Carolina Hurricanes, NHL	78	23	50	73	18					
1999–01	Carolina Hurricanes, NHL	82	15	50	65	32	3	0	0	0	0
1999–02	Carolina Hurricanes, NHL	80	27	50	77	18					
	NHL Totals	1569	514	1187	1701	935	136	40	83	127	87
	WEC Totals	10	2	5	7	2					

Won Frank J. Selke Trophy (1995)
Won Lady Byng Trophy (1995, 1998)
Won Alka-Seltzer Plus Award (1995)
Won Stanley Cup (1991,1992)

climbing into the top 10 of all-time scorers, yet few would put him in the same class as Lafleur, Dionne or Lemieux.

In the summer of 1998 he returned, sort of, whence he came. Pittsburgh felt Francis was getting on in years. He was 35 years old and an unrestricted free agent for the first time in his career and was in a position to negotiate one final contract for more money than he had ever made before. He signed with Carolina, which was where the Hartford Whalers had relocated the previous season, a three-year deal that will likely see him end his career as a Hurricane—and among the highest-scoring players of all time.

Francis played his fourth season with the Hurricanes in 2001–02—his 21st year in the NHL— and reached two milestones: 500 goals and 1,700 points.

Brian Bellows

Brian Bellows scored his 1,000th career point on January 2, 1999, and became the 54th NHL player to reach this milestone.

Tim Hunter, an assistant coach with the Washington Capitals, once said of Brian Bellows, "You have to know where he is every second, because if he gets the puck, it's in the net."

Bellows scored his 1,000th career point against Toronto on January 2, 1999, thus becoming the 54th player in the NHL to reach this career milestone. He scored a goal in the second period of that game to reach 999 and then assisted on a goal by Jeff Toms for the 1,000th point. "That one was a prime example of Bellows," said Hunter. "He was going to shoot, they were expecting it, he dished it off to Toms and he scores. Great instinct and a beautiful pass, too." Bellows took the 1,000-point mark in stride. "What it means to me is over the years you've been a player who's performed at a pretty high level."

Born in St. Catharines, Ontario, Bellows played junior hockey with the Kitchener Rangers and led them to a Memorial Cup championship. Leadership was a big component of his junior career and attracted the attention of a number of NHL teams. In 1982 Bellows entered the NHL after being drafted second overall by the Minnesota North Stars. Through his agent, Alan Eagelson, he signed a $1-million contract with the North Stars to go pro.

Bellows had a tough rookie year. Many fans compared him to Wayne Gretzky, but he simply wasn't as strong a player. Critics wondered what all the fuss was about a player just coming out of the junior ranks. Then, halfway through his first season, Bellows began to improve. "It takes a while to get adjusted to the NHL," he later explained. "The first part of the season was very tough for me. I knew it would eventually come. At least I hoped it would eventually come and it did. There was no one game in particular. Things just started to fall into place about midway through the season."

Things continued to improve for Bellows in his rookie season. North Stars coach Murray Oliver remarked, "He never loses his cool and panics. I've got veterans who panic more than Bellows does." In his second year, Bellows was named one of the North Stars' two captains (along with Craig Hartsburg), becoming one of the youngest players in league history to assume leadership duties. Unfortunately, he wasn't up to the task and many of his teammates didn't respect him. Regarding his difficulties in his role as captain, Bellows explained: "Age has nothing to do with it. The problem is, how does a guy who is 27 or 30 approach a second-year player about a communication problem with management? That was the toughest part of the job for me. No matter how hard they tried, it was difficult for someone that age to talk to me about their problems."

Bellows' communication problems didn't rest solely with his teammates. He also had trouble with his coach, Lorne Henning, who tried to get him traded and, Bellows claimed, embarrassed him in front of teammates. "It's tough to play well when your boss is trying to get rid of you," Bellows said.

However, when Minnesota appointed Herb Brooks as head coach in the fall of 1987, Bellows suddenly came alive. "Herb told me he expects a lot from me," said Bellows, "and has given me quite a bit of responsibility. After a couple of bad years, I just want to get up to the level I should be at." Brooks later admitted, "There have been times this season when Brian Bellows has carried this team on his back."

Following the 1987–88 season, after conferring with team owners George and Gordon Gund, Bellows signed a multi-year deal with Minnesota even though the team had finished last in the Norris Division that year. "The Gunds told me that they were committed to rebuilding the club and I decided that I wanted to make the same commitment." He added, "I think it will be more rewarding and satisfying to help build a winning team."

Bellows was well known and admired in Minnesota for his involvement in many charitable causes, ranging from Special Olympics and drug prevention to fundraising for multiple sclerosis, Easter Seals, the March of Dimes and MADD (Mothers Against Drunk Driving). He was especially recognized for placing special emphasis on drug education. "I work a lot with high schools, church groups and social groups. I work a lot with athletic groups. The toughest part," he added, "is in learning how to interact with the parents and kids and deal with the situations they are facing."

In all, Bellows played for Minnesota, Montreal, Tampa Bay, Anaheim and Washington during his NHL career. "He's not graceful, he's not a smooth stickhandler, there is nothing smooth about his game," said Ron Wilson, who played with Bellows in Minnesota and coached him in Anaheim. "He is still the original bull in a china shop. He's all legs driving to the net. He'd drive so hard he'd hurt you, even in practice."

Bellows joined the Canadiens in 1992 after scoring 342 goals in 10 seasons with Minnesota before he was traded for Russ Courtnall. His career high was 55 goals in one season, but he'd had other seasons of 40 goals or more.

Tim Hunter, an assistant coach with the Washington Capitals, once said of Brian Bellows, "You have to know where he is every second, because if he gets the puck, it's in the net."

Bellows, Brian
LW, 5′11″, 210 lbs, b: St. Catharines, Ont., 9/1/1964

Season	Club, League	Regular Season					Playoffs				
		GP	G	A	Pts	PIM	GP	G	A	Pts	PIM
1982–83	Minnesota North Stars, NHL	78	35	30	65	27	9	5	4	9	18
1983–84	Minnesota North Stars, NHL	78	41	42	83	66	16	2	12	14	6
CCup–84	Canada	5	0	1	1	0					
1984–85	Minnesota North Stars, NHL	78	26	36	62	72	9	2	4	6	9
1985–86	Minnesota North Stars, NHL	77	31	48	79	46	5	5	0	5	16
1986–87	Minnesota North Stars, NHL	65	26	27	53	34					
WEC–87	Canada	10	1	3	4	8					
1987–88	Minnesota North Stars, NHL	77	40	41	81	81					
1988–89	Minnesota North Stars, NHL	60	23	27	50	55	5	2	3	5	8
WEC–89	Canada	10	8	6	14	2					
1989–90	Minnesota North Stars, NHL	80	55	44	99	72	7	4	3	7	10
WEC–90	Canada	8	3	6	9	8					
1990–91	Minnesota North Stars, NHL	80	35	40	75	43	23	10	19	29	30
1991–92	Minnesota North Stars, NHL	80	30	45	75	41	7	4	4	8	14
1992–93	Montreal Canadiens, NHL	82	40	48	88	44	18	6	9	15	18
1993–94	Montreal Canadiens, NHL	77	33	38	71	36	6	1	2	3	2
1994–95	Montreal Canadiens, NHL	41	8	8	16	8					
1995–96	Tampa Bay Lightning, NHL	79	23	26	49	39	6	2	0	2	4
1996–97	Tampa Bay Lightning, NHL	7	1	2	3	0					
	Anaheim Mighty Ducks, NHL	62	15	13	28	22	11	2	4	6	2
1997–98	Berlin Capitals, Germany	31	15	17	32	18					
	Washington Capitals, NHL	11	6	3	9	6	21	6	7	13	6
1998–99	Washington Capitals, NHL	76	17	19	36	26					
	NHL Totals	1188	485	537	1022	718	143	51	71	122	143
	WEC/CCup Totals	33	12	16	28	18					

Named Best Forward at WEC (1989)
NHL Second All-Star Team (1990)
Won CCup (1984)

A HISTORY OF WORLD HOCKEY

When he joined the Canadiens, Bellows remarked: "I hope to score more than last year. I want to come in and prove I can still play to the levels expected. I was shocked about the trade but I'm excited about the new change. My idol was Ken Dryden. It's every kid's dream to play, for the Canadiens." That dream lasted three years before he was traded to Tampa Bay and then Anaheim. His final two years in the NHL were spent with the Washington Capitals. Bellows retired after the 1998–99 season with 485 goals and 1,022 points, and though he had talked about a possible comeback, nothing ever materialized. Still, his numbers should place him in the Hall of Fame before long.

Valeri **Kamensky**

Valeri Kamensky and Wayne Gretzky were voted the best players of the Rendez-Vous '87 tournament.

In the team-oriented Soviet style of hockey, there have been many self-centered players—Alexander Yakushev, Helmut Balderis, Sergei Kapustin and Nikolai Drozdetsky, among others. Valeri Kamensky, however, was the first to be obsessed with the opponent's net almost to the point of sacrificing the greater good of his team.

From 1986 to 1990, Kamensky's partners on offense were Vyacheslav Bykov and Andrei Khomutov. Theirs was the second-best line of forwards on the national team at the time. On the first line, Sergei Makarov, Igor Larionov and Vladimir Krutov were so much in sync that they could have played blindfolded. It didn't work that way on the second line, where Kamensky always seemed to stand aloof. He hadn't acquired the contemporary skills—the witty fakes or the swift change of pace and position on the ice. Bykov and Khomutov were leaders prone to skating with the puck and making passes en route to the opponent's goal. "We can make a pass without even looking at each other," Bykov recalled, "due to some intuitive understanding of the other guy's habits. Whereas Kamensky is a bulldozer, a torpedo, and nothing can stop him, not even the boards. I often imagined that the boards would yield before him when rushing forward—in order to let him sneak through. And his shots were smashing and accurate."

He was the only player from the Soviet era who joined the NHL as if he was coming home but retained the Soviet style of play—the elegance, the agility, the gentle handling of the puck. He was at his best when he had lots of space and tough resistance—space for the burst of speed, since he could cover the rink from one zone to the other in a few strides, and resistance to inspire him and wake up his killer instinct. Soviet defensemen almost always succumbed to a forward as aggressive as Kamensky. He would emerge from the chaos in front of the net and shoot from any position when even the more daring forwards preferred to find a clear patch of ice.

At the age of 19, when Pavel Bure and Alexander Mogilny were still only prospects for the future, Kamensky's career was about to take off. "He is a gift for us," admitted the scout who offered to promote him from the Voskresensk Khimik team to the CSKA hockey club. Tall and elegant, he had the ability to consistently put the puck in the opponent's net. With the CSKA style of play, there would be plenty of room for him in the center. At that point, Kamensky, a good stickhandler, had trouble skating through a crowd on the ice. It took him a year to get it right, but he developed a specialty with linemates Bykov and Khomutov. Weaving an intricate web with the puck, they would set their man up for the big goal.

Kamensky made his international debut in two games against the NHL All-Star Team at the Rendez-Vous '87 tournament. The Bykov trio scored three goals, with Kamensky getting two of them, and Gretzky and Kamensky were voted the best players of the series.

But Kamensky never established himself with the USSR national team. In the 1990 World Championship, Khomutov was the star of the Bykov trio. At the next world tournament, Kamensky was excellent in the beginning, when his only competition in the series was Sweden's Mats Sundin. But Sundin eventually outshone Kamensky and Pavel Bure and the great Swedish team overwhelmed the Soviet stars.

That was the beginning of the end of Kamensky's days with the national team. Without his partners Khomutov and Bykov, he played all over the rink, relying only on himself, and that hurt his performance. Before he left Moscow for the Quebec Nordiques, his agent, Paul Teophanos, said, "We are waiting for Valeri impatiently. Some say he will be one of the NHL's five superstars."

He didn't make the top five, but he wasn't a disappointment either. He played for four years with the Nordiques in Quebec and another four years when he moved with the team from Quebec City to Denver. His performance was always up to par, but it didn't match the output of the players from the next Russian draft— Alexander Mogilny, Bure and Sergei Fedorov.

Kamensky's North American style didn't differ from that of his Soviet days. He didn't lose his hawkish manner, but neither did he develop or refine it. He remained the expert in his field— engaging in plays based more on impulse than technique. "During the season," Kamensky said, "the Larionov lineup was in different shape.

Before Valeri Kamensky (right) left Moscow for the Quebec Nordiques, his agent, Paul Teophanos, said: "We are waiting for Valeri impatiently. Some say he will be one of the NHL's five superstars."

Kamensky, Valeri
LW, 6′2″, 198 lbs, b: Voskresensk, USSR, 4/18/1966

Season	Club, League	Regular Season					Playoffs				
		GP	G	A	Pts	PIM	GP	G	A	Pts	PIM
1982–83	Khimik, USSR	5	0	0	0	0					
1983–84	Khimik, USSR	20	2	2	4	6					
1984–85	Khimik, USSR	45	9	3	12	24					
1985–86	CSKA, USSR	40	15	9	24	8					
WEC–86	USSR	9	2	0	2	8					
1986–87	CSKA, USSR	37	13	8	21	16					
RV'87	USSR	2	2	1	3	2					
WEC–87	USSR	10	5	3	8	6					
CCup–87	USSR	9	6	1	7	6					
1987–88	CSKA, USSR	51	26	20	46	40					
OWG–88	USSR	8	4	2	6	4					
1988–89	CSKA, USSR	40	18	10	28	30					
WEC–89	USSR	10	4	4	8	8					
1989–90	CSKA, USSR	45	19	18	37	40					
WEC–90	USSR	10	7	2	9	10					
1990–91	CSKA, USSR	46	20	26	46	66					
WEC–91	USSR	10	6	5	11	10					
1991–92	Quebec Nordiques, NHL	23	7	14	21	14					
1992–93	Quebec Nordiques, NHL	32	15	22	37	14	6	0	1	1	6
1993–94	Quebec Nordiques, NHL	76	28	37	65	42					
WC–94	Russia	6	5	5	10	12					
1994–95	Ambri — Piotta, Switzerland	12	13	6	19	2					
	Quebec Nordiques, NHL	40	10	20	30	22	2	1	0	1	0
1995–96	Colorado Avalanche, NHL	81	38	47	85	85	22	10	12	22	28
1996–97	Colorado Avalanche, NHL	68	28	38	66	38	17	8	14	22	16
1997–98	Colorado Avalanche, NHL	75	26	40	66	60	7	2	3	5	18
OWG–98	Russia	6	1	2	3	0					
1998–99	Colorado Avalanche, NHL	65	14	30	44	28	10	4	5	9	4
1999–00	New York Rangers, NHL	58	13	19	32	24					
WC–2000	Russia	6	0	0	0	10					
2000-01	New York Rangers, NHL	65	14	20	34	36					
2001-02	Dallas-New Jersey, NHL	54	7	14	21	20					
	USSR/Russia Totals	329	122	96	218	230					
	NHL Totals	637	200	301	501	383					
	OWG/WEC/WC/RV'87/CCup Totals	86	42	25	67	86					

Named Best Forward at WEC (1991)
Won OWG (1988)
Won WEC (1986, 1989, 1990)
Won Stanley Cup (1996)
USSR Champion (1986, 1987, 1988, 1989)

Some played great, yet others somehow failed. But they could make up for these discrepancies with their technique and their intellect. As for me, I can make it great when I am inspired deep in my soul. If there are 100 games in a season, I may be inspired in 30."

In the end, Kamensky made his mark on the game. Over the space of his career, he played in the Soviet Union, Canada and the U.S. And he scored crazy goals from impossible angles following improvised attacks. He did what he could, given the painful adjustment that tended to follow Soviet players who were transplanted to the NHL. He didn't become a goal-scoring machine, but, together with Igor Larionov and Vyacheslav Kozlov, he helped an obscure provincial Voskresensk gain international acclaim as a pool for hockey talent. He made a name for himself as one of three players from Voskresensk who went on to become Stanley Cup winners.

In 1999–2000, he joined the New York Rangers, where he played for two years, but even with Kamensky and the likes of Theo Fleury on the team, the Rangers failed to reach the playoffs in either year. In 2001–02, he joined the Dallas Stars.

Raimo Helminen

Raimo Helminen participated in seven World Championships and five Olympics.

Raimo Helminen started out playing hockey with the Ilves junior team in his home town of Tampere, Finland, and, for the first time in four years, he's back with his first club. In 1999–2000, at the ripe old age of 36, he is still going strong. He participated in his seventh World Championship at the 2000 tournament held in St. Petersburg and has also performed in five Winter Olympics, including the only three in which Finland captured medals—one silver and two bronze. He has twice taken part in the Canada/World Cup. All in all, with 15 tournaments under his belt, he has done his fair share in representing his native country.

After the St. Petersburg event, he had to his credit a total of 190 points, with the lion's share coming in the form of 140 assists. In both these categories he is the all-time leader.

With 16 titles, more than any other team, the Ilves hockey club is Finland's answer to the Montreal Canadiens. The bulk of these titles were won before 1973, leaving Helminen with only one gold medal during his stint with the club. But in the World Championship, Finland has won one gold and four silvers, and of these, Helminen has missed only one silver. So Helminen's accomplishments on the ice quite closely match those of his country. They are achievements that will take years to surpass, and that may never happen, since with more and more jobs opening up in the NHL for the best Europeans, participation on the national team is automatically limited.

Helminen hit the limelight for the first time in his career during the World Junior Championship in 1984. He won the scoring race and established a new tournament record by a margin of four points. He was subsequently chosen to participate in the All-Star game and, more important, he caught the eye of the NHL scouts, who ranked him as the top forward in Europe in that summer's draft. It was eventually the New York Rangers who got him as their second pick, and the following autumn he joined the club. He had an outstanding rookie season with 40 points in 66 games.

Toward the end of the next season, he was traded to the Minnesota North Stars, with whom he played six games before spending the rest of the year in the minors. He returned to Finland for the 1987–88 season, then was back the next year in the New York area, but with the Islanders this time. However, he started to have back problems that at times caused him such pain that he couldn't walk. If it hadn't been for his determination, his career would likely have been at an end. It took him six years, but eventually, in the town of Kokkola in Finland, he found a physiotherapist, Leo Saario, who was able to fix his back. During those six years, he was playing for Malmo in the Swedish league.

His troubles almost finished his career with the national team in 1995. But Finland's coach, the Swede Curt Lindstrom, recalled how well he'd performed for Malmo and made him a late addition to the World Championship squad. It was an excellent choice for both coach and player, as the team went on to win its first-ever gold medal for Finland.

The other milestone in Finnish hockey, and another moment of pride for Helminen, was achieved in the 1988 Winter Olympics in Calgary. In the final game, the Finns managed to defeat the mighty Soviets, who had by that time already clinched the gold, but Helminen was sidelined in the final game with a knee problem.

During his time with Malmo, he led the club to two national titles and to first place in the European Championship. On his return to Finland in 1996–97, he led Ilves to a silver medal win and re-established himself, particularly in the 1998–99 season, as the top forward in the land.

Helminen's most outstanding trait has been his ambition, not only for himself but for his hockey clubs. One of his first Ilves coaches, Seppo Hiitela, said, "It is easy for a coach to lead a team that has a player with such dedication and leadership as Helminen."

After his second North American adventure, Raimo Helminen played seven seasons for the Red Hawks in Malmo, Sweden, and led the club to two national titles.

Helminen, Raimo
C, 6´, 185 lbs, b: Tampere, Finland, 3/11/1964

Season	Club, League	GP	G	A	Pts	PIM	GP	G	A	Pts	PIM
		Regular Season					Playoffs				
1982–83	Ilves, Finland	31	2	3	5	0	6	0	0	0	2
1983–84	Ilves, Finland	37	17	13	30	14	2	0	0	0	2
OWG–84	Finland	6	0	2	2	2					
1984–85	Ilves, Finland	36	21	36	57	20					
WEC–85	Finland	10	4	5	9	2					
1985–86	New York Rangers, NHL	66	10	30	40	10	2	0	0	0	0
1986–87	New York Rangers, NHL	21	2	4	6	2					
	New Haven Nighthawks, AHL	6	0	2	2	0					
	Minnesota North Stars, NHL	6	0	1	1	0					
CCup–87	Finland	5	0	3	3	0					
1987–88	Ilves, Finland	31	20	23	43	42					
OWG–88	Finland	7	2	8	10	4					
1988–89	New York Islanders, NHL	24	1	11	12	4					
	Springfield Indians, AHL	16	6	11	17	0					
1989–90	Malmo, Sweden	29	26	30	56	16					
WEC–90	Finland	4	0	0	0	0					
1990–91	Malmo, Sweden	33	12	18	30	14	2	0	1	1	4
1991–92	Malmo, Sweden	40	9	18	27	24	10	1	3	4	4
OWG–92	Finland	8	1	2	3	0					
1992–93	Malmo, Sweden	40	9	33	42	59	6	1	0	1	8
1993–94	Malmo, Sweden	38	20	34	54	26	11	1	7	8	8
OWG–94	Finland	8	1	5	6	8					
WC–94	Finland	8	1	5	6	0					
1994–95	Malmo, Sweden	35	10	19	29	55	7	3	2	5	4
WC–95	Finland	8	1	7	8	2					
1995–96	Malmo, Sweden	40	8	19	27	53	5	1	3	4	12
WC–96	Finland	6	0	4	4	0					
WCup–96	Finland	3	0	2	2	0					
1996–97	Ilves, Finland	49	11	39	50	8	8	1	5	6	2
WC–97	Finland	8	0	6	6	0					
1997–98	Ilves, Finland	46	12	36	48	42	9	3	5	8	10
OWG–98	Finland	6	2	0	2	2					
1998–99	Ilves, Finland	53	12	38	50	44	4	0	3	3	2
1999–2000	Ilves, Finland	51	7	38	45	68	3	1	0	1	12
WC–2000	Finland	9	2	2	4	0					
	Finland Totals	334	102	226	328	238	32	5	13	18	30
	NHL Totals	117	13	46	59	16	2	0	0	0	0
	OWG/WEC/WC/CCup/WCup Totals	96	14	51	65	20					

Won WC (1995)
Finland Champion (1985)
Sweden Champion (1992, 1994)

A HISTORY OF WORLD HOCKEY

Scott Stevens

If players could wear a "D" on their sweaters to signify defense, Scott Stevens would be one of the first in line for a fitting.

Team captains in the NHL wear a "C" on their sweaters to signify their team leadership. But if it were possible for players to sport a "D" to signify defense, Scott Stevens would be one of the first in line for a fitting.

The bruising defenseman grew up in Kitchener, Ontario, where he began playing the game when he was four years old. He and his brothers were bitten—and bitten hard—by the hockey bug. "All we did was play hockey," Stevens remembered. "We lived by a ski hill, and we never skied! All the time we were playing on the pond. We had an outdoor rink we made, and that's all we did. I started organized hockey in one of those leagues where they cut the ice in half and you had two games going on at the same time."

Growing up, Stevens loved the Toronto Maple Leafs. Perhaps it is no surprise that he has become such a defensive specialist—as a kid, his hero was the Leafs star Borje Salming. "I lived so close to Toronto, I saw Salming play a lot," Stevens explained. "The Leafs were on every Wednesday and Saturday and I used to sit by the TV all the time and watch them."

His size—6′2″ and 215 pounds—also helped Stevens decide on a career as a defense-first player. "I've always been one of the biggest guys on my team," he said. "I just tried to hit and take the body. That was my style when I was younger and I still try to play that way now. If I don't play that way, I am not really going to be effective." And Stevens didn't underplay the psychological benefits of good "D" either. "If you hit some guy good once," he explained, "he'll be thinking about that coming down the ice again!"

Stevens also gained a reputation as an NHL "iron man." He has played 18 seasons in the league and has often been among the leaders in games played. He is usually right near the top in penalty minutes as well. And even with all this emphasis on defense, Stevens is a complete enough player to hold the record for assists in a single season (60) with the New Jersey Devils.

Stevens was a first-round choice by Washington in the 1982 Entry Draft, the fifth pick overall. After several seasons with the Capitals, he signed a $5.145-million contract for four years

Stevens, Scott
D, 6′2″, 215 lbs, b: Kitchener, Ont., 4/1/1964

Season	Club, League	Regular Season					Playoffs				
		GP	G	A	Pts	PIM	GP	G	A	Pts	PIM
1982–83	Washington Capitals, NHL	77	9	16	25	195	4	1	0	1	26
WEC–83	Canada	10	0	2	2	8					
1983–84	Washington Capitals, NHL	78	13	32	45	201	8	1	8	9	21
1984–85	Washington Capitals, NHL	80	21	44	65	221	5	0	1	1	20
WEC–85	Canada	8	1	2	3	6					
1985–86	Washington Capitals, NHL	73	15	38	53	165	9	3	8	11	12
1986–87	Washington Capitals, NHL	77	10	51	61	283	7	0	5	5	19
WEC–87	Canada	2	0	1	1	2					
1987–88	Washington Capitals, NHL	80	12	60	72	184	13	1	11	12	46
1988–89	Washington Capitals, NHL	80	7	61	68	225	6	1	4	5	11
WEC–89	Canada	7	2	1	3	2					
1989–90	Washington Capitals, NHL	56	11	29	40	154	15	2	7	9	25
1990–91	St. Louis Blues, NHL	78	5	44	49	150	13	0	3	3	36
CCup–91	Canada	8	1	0	1	4					
1991–92	New Jersey Devils, NHL	68	17	42	59	124	7	2	1	3	29
1992–93	New Jersey Devils, NHL	81	12	45	57	120	5	2	2	4	10
1993–94	New Jersey Devils, NHL	83	18	60	78	112	20	2	9	11	42
1994–95	New Jersey Devils, NHL	48	2	20	22	56	20	1	7	8	24
1995–96	New Jersey Devils, NHL	82	5	23	28	100					
WCup–96	Canada	8	0	2	2	4					
1996–97	New Jersey Devils, NHL	79	5	19	24	70	10	0	4	4	2
1997–98	New Jersey Devils, NHL	80	4	22	26	80	6	1	0	1	8
OWG–98	Canada	6	0	0	0	2					
1998–99	New Jersey Devils, NHL	75	5	22	27	29	7	2	1	3	10
1999–00	New Jersey Devils, NHL	78	8	21	29	103	23	3	8	11	6
2000–01	New Jersey Devils, NHL	81	9	22	31	71	25	1	7	8	37
2001–02	New Jersey Devils, NHL	82	1	16	17	44					
	NHL Totals	1516	189	687	876	2722					
	OWG/WEC/CCup/WCup Totals	49	4	8	12	28					

NHL First All-Star Team (1988, 1994)
NHL Second All-Star Team (1992, 1997)
Won Conn Smythe Trophy (2000)
Won Alka-Seltzer Plus Award (1994)
Won Stanley Cup (1995, 2000)
Won CCup (1991)

with St. Louis in 1990–91. With Brett Hull on the wing and Curtis Joseph in net, the future looked good for Stevens both financially and with regard to team success.

Then, to his surprise, after only one season with the Blues, he was transferred to the Devils in 1991–92 in exchange for Brendan Shanahan in an arbitration case. In New Jersey, he was made team captain. With the "C" on his sweater, Stevens took on the role as inspirational leader for the Devils, who won the Stanley Cup in 1995 under his captaincy. The Devils players and fans were galvanized by Stevens' big hits on the Red Wings' Keith Primeau and Slava Kozlov, key psychological elements in the victory.

There have been a few disappointments for Stevens as well. Although he's had the satisfaction of hosting the NHL's greatest team trophy, he's never been able to win the top individual award for a defensive player, the Norris Trophy. He was second to Ray Bourque of Boston twice.

Near the beginning of his career, he was bitter at not being selected to the 1984 Canada Cup team by coach Glen Sather, who cited Stevens' inexperience at the time. "It was a difficult thing to take. It's been a long time since I was cut from a team," said Stevens after learning he'd gotten the axe. "I can't even remember the last time I was cut. I know I can play on that team. I'm just getting tired of people saying, 'You're too young.'" On the international level, Stevens was selected to the Canadian team for the 1998 Winter Olympics in Japan.

While Stevens has by now been a star in the NHL for years, the 2000 playoffs were his defining moment. His thunderous checks, notably on Eric Lindros in the semifinals, both inspired and dominated the post-season, and when his Devils won the Cup, there was no question that he would be chosen winner of the Conn Smythe Trophy. A year later, he was back in the finals, though his Devils lost to Colorado in game seven. But at the age of 37, Stevens was left off the roster for Team Canada at the 2002 Winter Olympics, which came as a surprise to many hockey fans.

As a defensive specialist, Stevens was fortunate to have served early in his career under two coaches who both stressed defensive hockey—Bryan Murray in Washington and Brian Sutter in St. Louis. And it has paid off. Even Wayne Gretzky rated Stevens as one of the best at what he does. "Scott Stevens is a very good player," said the Great One. "He's one of the quality defensemen in this league."

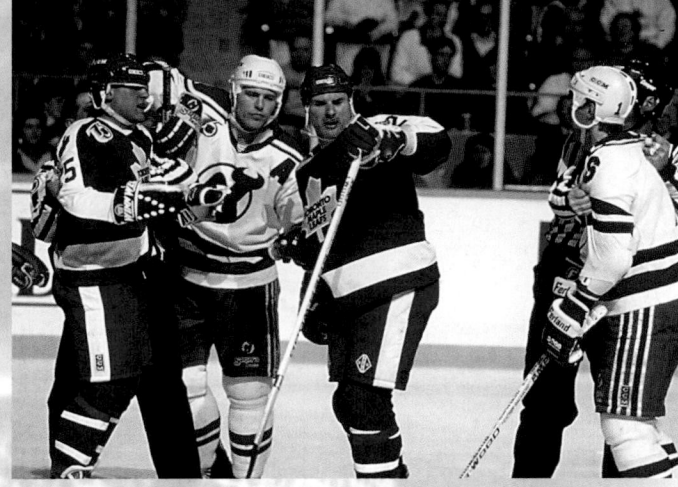

In New Jersey, Scott Stevens (center) was made team captain and he took on the role as inspirational leader for the Devils, who won the Stanley Cup in 1995 and 2000.

Uwe Krupp

Uwe Krupp's overtime goal—which earned the Colorado Avalanche a 1–0 win over the Florida Panthers and the 1996 Stanley Cup title—created more excitement in German hockey circles than any event since the West German national team won a bronze medal at the 1976 Olympics in Innsbruck.

Uwe Krupp's dogsled racing got him in big trouble with Detroit management.

The 6'6", 235-pound defenseman underwent ligament surgery in 1995 following a collision with Detroit's Martin Lapointe and missed most of the 1995–96 NHL season but returned in time to play outstanding hockey in the last few games of the regular season and the playoffs. He had played only six regular-season games for the Avalanche but had an excellent playoff series with four goals and 12 assists for 16 points in 22 games. Doctors had projected a recovery period of 10 to 12 months, but to attempt to shorten the time, Krupp started racing his dogsled team. He believes racing the dogs helped him get back on the ice months ahead of schedule, and he even finished second in a couple of two-day, 26-kilometer races in the Denver area.

But Krupp's dogsled racing got him in big trouble later in his career. He was suspended without pay by the Detroit Red Wings in August of 1999 for failing to turn over medical records concerning back problems that kept him sidelined for much of the 1998–99 season. Krupp finally agreed to release the records, but he remained suspended because the Red Wings found out he might have gone dogsledding without the team's permission while recovering from a herniated disc. He'd been complaining the persistent pain kept him from returning to the lineup. According to the standard player's contract, a player can't participate in any other organized sport without the written consent of his team. Krupp subsequently filed a grievance through the NHL Players' Association, claiming the Red Wings still owe him $12.3 million on his contract.

Krupp was a member of two German league championship teams with the Cologne Sharks in 1984 and 1986. He also played for his country at the World Championships of 1986 in Moscow and 1990 in Bern. Born in Cologne, he was selected by the Buffalo Sabres in the 13th round, 223rd overall in the 1983 draft, and improved rapidly to the point where he represented the Sabres in the 1991 All-Star Game.

He was traded to the New York Islanders in the fall of 1991, then to the Quebec Nordiques in the summer of 1994. The Nordiques became the Colorado Avalanche in 1995. The Nashville Predators claimed him from the Colorado roster in the 1998 Expansion Draft and he signed a multi-year contract with Detroit worth $16.4 million.

Despite his Stanley Cup success in the 1995–96 season, Krupp declined an invitation

Krupp, Uwe
D, 6'6", 235 lbs, b: Cologne, FRG, 6/24/1965

Season	Club, League	Regular Season					Playoffs				
		GP	G	A	Pts	PIM	GP	G	A	Pts	PIM
1982–83	Kolner, Cologne, FRG	11	0	0	0	0					
1983–84	Kolner, Cologne, FRG	26	0	4	4	22					
1984–85	Kolner, Cologne, FRG	31	7	7	14	36					
1985–86	Kolner, Cologne, FRG	35	6	18	24	83					
WEC–86	FRG	3	2	1	3	2					
1986–87	Buffalo Sabres, NHL	26	1	4	5	23					
	Rochester Americans, AHL	42	3	19	22	50	17	1	11	12	16
1987–88	Buffalo Sabres, NHL	75	2	9	11	151	6	0	0	0	15
1988–89	Buffalo Sabres, NHL	70	5	13	18	55	5	0	1	1	4
1989–90	Buffalo Sabres, NHL	74	3	20	23	85	6	0	0	0	4
WEC–90	FRG	2	0	0	0	2					
1990–91	Buffalo Sabres, NHL	74	12	32	44	66	6	1	1	2	6
1991–92	Buffalo Sabres, NHL	8	2	0	2	6					
	New York Islanders, NHL	59	6	29	35	43					
1992–93	New York Islanders, NHL	80	9	29	38	67	18	1	5	6	12
1993–94	New York Islanders, NHL	41	7	14	21	30	4	0	1	1	4
1994–95	Landshut, Germany	5	1	2	3	6					
	Quebec Nordiques, NHL	44	6	17	23	20	5	0	2	2	2
1995–96	Colorado Avalanche, NHL	6	0	3	3	4	22	4	12	16	33
1996–97	Colorado Avalanche, NHL	60	4	17	21	48					
1997–98	Colorado Avalanche, NHL	78	9	22	31	38	7	0	1	1	4
OWG–98	Germany	2	0	2	2	4					
1998–99	Detroit Red Wings, NHL	22	3	2	5	6	*	*	*	*	*
2001–02	Detroit Red Wings	8	0	0	1	8					
	FRG/Germany Totals	108	14	31	45	147					
	NHL Totals	725	69	212	281	650					
	OWG/WEC Totals	7	2	3	5	8					

Won Stanley Cup (1996)
FRG Champion (1984, 1986)

to play for Germany in the World Cup in the late summer of 1996, preferring to avoid further injury that would jeopardize him and the Avalanche in the 1996–97 season. He represented his country at the 1998 Olympics in Nagano, Japan, but arrived too late to help Germany make the medal round. Germany was forced to play in the preliminary round, and because the NHL schedule overlapped with that round, he couldn't make it to Japan before the Germans had been upset 8–2 by Belarus.

In a poll taken by the German publication *Eishockey News*, Krupp was selected the second-greatest defenseman in his country's history. Udo Kiessling, the only player to compete in five Olympic Games, was the only defenseman to collect more votes. Krupp has an excellent command of English, is very articulate and is considered a very good interview. During the 1995 Stanley Cup finals, he worked as the color man for German TV.

Krupp returned to the NHL for 2001–02, a relatively healthy defenseman intent on rejuvenating his career.

In a poll conducted by the German publication Eishockey News, Uwe Krupp was selected the second-greatest defenseman in his country's history.

Tomas Sandstrom

Few athletes are lucky enough to enjoy a moment of triumph while the whole world is watching. Forward Tomas Sandstrom experienced his moment in 1987 at the World Championship in Vienna.

There were 90 seconds left to go in the final game between Sweden and the USSR and the Soviets were leading 2–1. Tre Kronor began their final attack. Hakan Loob, to the left of the Soviet goal, grabbed the puck and immediately passed it to Sandstrom in front of the net, who scored. There were still 81 seconds left in the game. "After such a fine pass, even my grandmother would have scored a goal," the forward later joked.

Even though the decisive goal was made possible by the team's collective efforts, it was scored by Sandstrom, who became an instant legend in Sweden. The goal enabled the Swedes to eventually capture the World Championship. Spurred on by their tie with the USSR, Sweden crushed Canada 9–0 in the most stinging defeat the Canadians ever suffered at the hands of Tre Kronor, and in the end, Sweden won the gold medal 25 years after their triumph in Colorado Springs.

At the 1987 World Championship, Tomas Sandstrom's goal with 81 seconds left in the game against the Soviets helped Sweden win the gold medal.

Sandstrom grew up fast. Born on September 4, 1964, in Jakobstad, Sweden, he first played for Fagersta AIK, then moved to the famed Brynas. At 20, he won the Olympic bronze at Sarajevo and three years later the world gold in Vienna. He was also on the national team when it reached second place at the Canada Cup in 1984 and 4th place at the 1991 Canada Cup.

His record is impressive. Sandstrom spent 15 seasons with the NHL, nearly matching the

Tomas Sandstrom (right) spent 15 seasons with the NHL, nearly matching Borje Salming's record among Swedish players of 17 seasons.

Swedish record-holder, Borje Salming, with 17 seasons. Sandstrom played for the Los Angeles Kings, the Pittsburgh Penguins, the New York Rangers and the Detroit Red Wings. He played alongside the Wings' "Russian Five" when they won the Stanley Cup in 1997. He then spent two years with the Anaheim Mighty Ducks.

At 35, in the fall of 1999, Sandstrom returned to Sweden so his children could be educated there. But he didn't quit playing hockey. He joined Malmo, a team known for their tough and speedy style of play. At 6'2" and 205 pounds, Sandstrom had no trouble meeting the demands of Malmo's coach. He adapted in no time and by the end of the season he had scored 19 goals and made 15 assists.

The Tre Kronor coaches invited the veteran to play in the Swedish nationals again. Sandstrom had previously played 73 games on the national team and scored 20 goals. At the finals, which proved unsuccessful for Tre Kronor, he added four games and two goals to his personal scorecard.

During the finals, he was injured and left the rink before the end of the game. Sandstrom's numerous scars and injuries sustained while playing in the NHL were a result of his aggressive playing style. His opponents often complained loudly that he took too many risks and was usually the instigator in rough encounters.

Swedish coaches always wanted Sandstrom back because they desperately needed more ruthless players like him. During a recent season, Sandstrom still made many of his teammates seem small and tame by comparison.

He participated in the St. Petersburg World Championship and proved that his age isn't an obstacle to excellent performance on the ice. "I'm still happy playing hockey," he says, and remains committed to the game 13 years after his first triumph in Vienna. Tomas Sandstrom is 144th on Sweden's "Great Men" list.

Sandstrom, Tomas
RW, 6'2", 205 lbs, b: Jakobstad, Sweden, 9/4/1964

Season	Club, League	Regular Season					Playoffs				
		GP	G	A	Pts	PIM	GP	G	A	Pts	PIM
1982–83	Brynas, Sweden	36	23	14	37	50					
1983–84	Brynas, Sweden	34	19	10	29	81					
OWG–84	Sweden	7	2	1	3	6					
CCup–84	Sweden	8	1	1	2	2					
1984–85	New York Rangers, NHL	74	29	29	58	51	3	0	2	2	0
WEC–85	Sweden	10	3	6	9	18					
1985–86	New York Rangers, NHL	73	25	29	54	109	16	4	6	10	20
1986–87	New York Rangers, NHL	64	40	34	74	60	6	1	2	3	20
RV'87	NHL All-Stars	1	0	0	0	0					
WEC–87	Sweden	8	4	6	10	6					
1987–88	New York Rangers, NHL	69	28	40	68	95					
1988–89	New York Rangers, NHL	79	32	56	88	148	4	3	2	5	12
WEC–89	Sweden	10	4	3	7	14					
1989–90	New York Rangers, NHL	48	19	19	38	100					
	Los Angeles Kings, NHL	28	13	20	33	28	10	5	4	9	19
1990–91	Los Angeles Kings, NHL	68	45	44	89	106	10	4	4	8	14
CCup–91	Sweden	6	1	2	3	8					
1991–92	Los Angeles Kings, NHL	49	17	22	39	70	6	0	3	3	8
1992–93	Los Angeles Kings, NHL	39	25	27	52	57	24	8	17	25	12
1993–94	Los Angeles Kings, NHL	51	17	24	41	59					
	Pittsburgh Penguins, NHL	27	6	11	17	24	6	0	0	0	4
1994–95	Malmo, Sweden	12	10	5	15	14					
	Pittsburgh Penguins, NHL	47	21	23	44	42	12	3	3	6	16
1995–96	Pittsburgh Penguins, NHL	58	35	35	70	69	18	4	2	6	30
1996–97	Pittsburgh Penguins, NHL	40	9	15	24	33					
	Detroit Red Wings, NHL	34	9	9	18	36	20	0	4	4	24
1997–98	Anaheim Mighty Ducks, NHL	77	9	8	17	64					
OWG–98	Sweden	4	0	1	1	0					
1998–99	Anaheim Mighty Ducks, NHL	58	15	17	32	42	4	0	0	0	4
1999–2000	Malmo, Sweden	42	16	13	29	28	6	3	2	5	10
	Sweden Totals	124	68	42	110	173	6	3	2	5	10
	NHL Totals	983	394	462	856	1193	139	32	49	81	183
	OWG/WEC/CCup/RV'87 Totals	54	15	20	35	54					

Won WEC (1987)
Won Stanley Cup (1997)

Adam Oates

The name of Adam Oates is almost sure to come up when the conversation comes around to one-sided deals in the NHL. Near the beginning of his pro career, the hard-working center from Weston, Ontario, was at the heart of a trade that is often remembered as one of the biggest steals in league history. After the 1988—89 season, Oates and his Detroit Red Wings teammate Paul MacLean were traded to the St. Louis Blues for Bernie Federko and Tony McKegney.

Adam Oates' name always comes up when the conversation gets to one-sided deals in the NHL.

Within a year, Federko had retired and McKegney had been traded away again. In St. Louis, however, Oates' fortunes took a completely different turn. Playing on a line with Brett Hull, he quickly gained a reputation as one of the NHL's best passing centers and established himself as the number one setup man for his high-scoring teammate, Brett Hull. The two became friends, as well, rooming together on road trips and living close to one another in St. Louis. For Hull, it was a real pleasure to play alongside Oates, who he considered one of the best at what he did. "As far as I'm concerned, he's the second-best playmaking center behind Wayne Gretzky in hockey," said Hull. "He has the ability to look back at a play and know exactly how it unfolded and what made it work or not work. He is a tremendous student of the game."

Detroit's loss became the Blues' gain. Assessing the trade a few years later, Oates admitted that while he had no regrets about the way things worked out, he still couldn't figure out the trade. "I was really upset," he recalled. "I was just coming off my best year—I just didn't understand the trade. I guess the Red Wings wanted some veteran leadership."

Maybe it was the big hype that had surrounded Oates during his time with the Wings that made the eventual trade seem so odd. In 1985, just out of college—where he'd been a star with NCAA champion Rensselaer Polytechnic Institute—he'd been signed by Wings general manager Jim Devellano and team owner Mike Ilitch, who personally worked out the deal over the summer of 1985. Oates was 23 when he signed with the Wings, and despite his college success, he was still an unproven rookie. So the fact that he signed the richest rookie contract in league history at the time—$1 million over four years—didn't exactly endear him to his teammates and opponents. "It

Oates, Adam
C, 5′11″, 185 lbs, b: Weston, Ont., 8/27/1962

Season	Club, League	Regular Season					Playoffs				
		GP	G	A	Pts	PIM	GP	G	A	Pts	PIM
1982–83	RPI Engineers, ECAC	22	9	33	42	8					
1983–84	RPI Engineers, ECAC	38	26	57	83	15					
1984–85	RPI Engineers, ECAC	38	31	60	91	29					
1985–86	Detroit Red Wings, NHL	38	9	11	20	10					
	Adirondack Red Wings, AHL	34	18	28	46	4	17	7	14	21	4
1986–87	Detroit Red Wings, NHL	76	15	32	47	21	16	4	7	11	6
1987–88	Detroit Red Wings, NHL	63	14	40	54	20	16	8	12	20	6
1988–89	Detroit Red Wings, NHL	69	16	62	78	14	6	0	8	8	2
1989–90	St. Louis Blues, NHL	80	23	79	102	30	12	2	12	14	4
1990–91	St. Louis Blues, NHL	61	25	90	115	29	13	7	13	20	10
1991–92	St. Louis Blues, NHL	54	10	59	69	12					
	Boston Bruins, NHL	26	10	20	30	10	15	5	14	19	4
1992–93	Boston Bruins, NHL	84	45	97	142	32	4	0	9	9	4
1993–94	Boston Bruins, NHL	77	32	80	112	45	13	3	9	12	8
1994–95	Boston Bruins, NHL	48	12	41	53	8	5	1	0	1	2
1995–96	Boston Bruins, NHL	70	25	67	92	18	5	2	5	7	2
1996–97	Boston Bruins, NHL	63	18	52	70	10					
	Washington Capitals, NHL	17	4	8	12	4					
1997–98	Washington Capitals, NHL	82	18	58	76	36	21	6	11	17	8
1998–99	Washington Capitals, NHL	59	12	42	54	22					
1999–00	Washington Capitals, NHL	82	15	56	71	14	5	0	3	3	4
2000–01	Washington Capitals, NHL	81	13	69	82	28	6	0	0	0	0
2001–02	Wash-Philadelphia, NHL	80	14	64	78	28					
	NHL Totals	1210	330	1027	1357	391					

NHL Second All-Star Team (1991)

Coach Jacques Demers said of Adams Oates (center): "He's one of the nicest passers in the league. He's deceiving—you don't notice him for two of three shifts and then, boom, the puck is in the net."

was very difficult," said Oates later. "There was a lot of resentment—basically it was hard for everybody."

A hard worker without a lot of flash who was good on defense and at making plays, the young Oates—one of the few NHL stars never to have been chosen in the draft—was slotted into the Detroit lineup as a second-line center behind Steve Yzerman. "I just want to make the team," he said in his first year. "Every player has to adjust when he comes to the NHL. I'm sure no one expects me to come in and be the next Steve Yzerman. Who could? I'm sure they're prepared to let Adam Oates develop."

Oates split that rookie year between Detroit and Adirondack of the AHL, and in the majors he found it hard to get used to the style of play of new Wings coach Jacques Demers. "He's very defense-oriented. He came into a situation where the team was just awful," remembered Oates. "We discussed my role a couple of times and it wasn't until late in the season that I really started to understand it. I played defensively and that got me more ice time."

But Oates' Detroit tenure was short-lived, and it was only within the freer offensive system in place in St. Louis that he was able to come into his own as a playmaking center. After establishing his game there, Oates was traded again, this time to Boston in 1992. While there, he worked in the off-seasons for an accounting firm and acted as a spokesperson for the Massachusetts anti-drinking and driving campaign. Oates even admitted that, in some ways, he was a pretty strange choice of role model because he'd done his fair share of getting behind the wheel after parties as a kid. "Fortunately, I learned at a young age that it wasn't the right thing to do," he said. "In pro hockey, a lot of great players lose their careers, their families, even their lives because of too much drinking."

While a Bruin, Oates was extremely critical of the Bruins management and at one point was stripped of his team captaincy. So it was no big surprise to see the center on the move again in 1996. He was traded to the Washington Capitals in a highly publicized deal that saw Oates, winger Rick Tocchet and goalie Bill Ranford go to the Capitals for winger Jason Allison, center Anson Carter, goalie Jim Carey and a third-round draft pick. In the deal, Washington got veterans, Boston got youth. Oates again led the league in assists in 2000–01 with 69 and reached the mark of 1,000 assists midway through the next season, when the Philadelphia Flyers acquired Oates at the trade deadline as insurance heading into the playoffs when Jeremy Roenick went down with a serious injury. At 39, Oates was still the top playmaker in the NHL, leading the league in assists during the regular season.

Back when Oates was a newly minted NHL player in Detroit, coach Jacques Demers neatly summed up Adam's on-ice presence. "He's one of the nicest passers in the league," said Demers. "He's deceiving—you don't notice him for two or three shifts and then, boom, the puck is in the net. He has a chance to be a star in this league." For Demers—and for Adam Oates—the prediction was right on the money.

Petr Svoboda

It was the 49th minute of the game between the players of the Czech Republic and Russia in the 1998 Olympic hockey finals in Nagano. In the offensive zone, Pavel Patera won the face-off against Sergei Fedorov. From the left side of the rink, the puck got to Martin Prochazka. He sent it to the blue line, where Petr Svoboda was ready to fire. With barely a glance, Svoboda drilled it at the net and scored.

Cheers erupted from the fans of the Czech team who were lucky enough to get seats. No doubt the fans watching the game on television at home reacted the same way. That nerve-racking game of February 22, 1998, was also shown on the giant TV screen in Prague's Old Town Square.

With that goal, the Czechs won 1–0. In the clash of hockey titans, most people had favored the Russians over the Czechs. But the Czechs achieved a small miracle and won their first Olympic gold at that tournament. "I don't even know what went through my head in that moment. I was immensely happy. I have been playing hockey for some 25 years and have seen a lot. But I cannot remember anything as powerful and uplifting," confided Petr Svoboda after the game, talking about the magic goal.

He was the oldest on the team after its captain, Vladimir Ruzicka. Even then, he had over 900 NHL games under his belt. However, he arrived in Japan as a rookie on the national team. "Some time in the fall I got a call from coach Ivan Hlinka asking whether I wanted to line up. I was surprised that he remembered me. I have played hundreds of games, but the last time I was on the national team was in 1984 as a junior. I was very much looking forward to this tournament."

In the spring of 1984 he had taken part in the European Championship in the former West Germany with the elite of the under-18 category. After one match, he left the stadium, got on a bus and appeared on his aunt's doorstep in Munich.

Back then, NHL teams had to wait months, even years, to get the players they wanted who were behind the Iron Curtain. Petr Svoboda was one of the first to try to get a contract without going through the draft. The only thing he could tell his parents on the phone was that he had decided to stay. He just didn't want to wait the long months and years until officials in Czechoslovakia released him.

The list of youths suitable for the draft in the Montreal Forum was very long that year: Mario Lemieux, a clear number one, Kirk Muller, Ed

Petr Svoboda's shot won the Czech Republic's first gold at the 1998 Nagano Olympics.

Svoboda, Petr
D, 6'1", 195 lbs, b: Most, Czechoslovakia, 2/14/1966

Season	Club, League	Regular Season					Playoffs				
		GP	G	A	Pts	PIM	GP	G	A	Pts	PIM
1982–83	Litvinov, Czechoslovakia	4	0	0	0	2					
1983–84	Litvinov, Czechoslovakia	18	3	1	4	20					
1984–85	Montreal Canadiens, NHL	73	4	27	31	65	7	1	1	2	12
1985–86	Montreal Canadiens, NHL	73	1	18	19	93	8	0	0	0	21
1986–87	Montreal Canadiens, NHL	70	5	17	22	63	14	0	5	5	10
1987–88	Montreal Canadiens, NHL	69	7	22	29	149	10	0	5	5	12
1988–89	Montreal Canadiens, NHL	71	8	37	45	147	21	1	11	12	16
1989–90	Montreal Canadiens, NHL	60	5	31	36	98	10	0	5	5	7
1990–91	Montreal Canadiens, NHL	60	4	22	26	52	2	0	1	1	2
1991–92	Montreal Canadiens, NHL	58	5	16	21	94					
	Buffalo Sabres, NHL	13	1	6	7	52	7	1	4	5	6
1992–93	Buffalo Sabres, NHL	40	2	24	26	59					
1993–94	Buffalo Sabres, NHL	60	2	14	16	89	3	0	0	0	4
1994–95	Litvinov, Czech Republic	8	2	0	2	50					
	Buffalo Sabres, NHL	26	0	5	5	60					
	Philadelphia Flyers, NHL	11	0	3	3	10	14	0	4	4	8
1995–96	Philadelphia Flyers, NHL	73	1	28	29	105	12	0	6	6	22
1996–97	Philadelphia Flyers, NHL	67	2	12	14	94	16	1	2	3	16
1997–98	Philadelphia Flyers, NHL	56	3	15	18	83	3	0	1	1	4
OWG–98	Czech Republic	6	1	1	2	39					
1998–99	Philadelphia Flyers, NHL	25	4	2	6	28					
	Tampa Bay Lightning, NHL	34	1	16	17	53					
1999–00	Tampa Bay Lightning, NHL	70	2	23	25	170					
2000–01	Tampa Bay Lightning, NHL	19	1	3	4	41					
	Czechoslovakia Totals	30	5	1	6	72					
	NHL Totals	1028	58	341	399	1605					
	OWG Totals	6	1	1	2	39					

Won OWG (1998)
Won Stanley Cup (1986)

Petr Svoboda (front) was the first Czech hockey player to reach the mark of 1,000 NHL games.

Olczyk and Al Iafrate, to name a few. These four were picked before Svoboda. The fifth to choose were the Montreal Canadiens. When they announced his name, he went up on stage and shook hands with the general manager, Serge Savard.

A week before training camp, he injured his knee, preventing him from being ready for the season opener. Fourteen years later, as he flew to Nagano to represent the Czech Republic, members of that team had to bring him a passport from his native country. "That's life. I was born in Bohemia and still have a nice feeling for the country. I settled in Canada, but my views haven't changed. That's why I didn't refuse.... I longed for the gold medal."

After a long and successful period in Montreal during which the team won the Stanley Cup in 1986, Svoboda suffered a series of injuries. In the 1991–92 season, he was traded to the Buffalo Sabres, three years later to the Philadelphia Flyers and in 1998–99 to the Tampa Bay Lightning.

He always excelled with strong skating, brilliant puck control and hard shots, and he seldom made mistakes in defense. But his health problems somewhat hindered his further development. Still, in the end he was the first Czech hockey player to reach the 1,000 NHL games mark. During the lockout in the 1994–95 season, he was able to return to Litvinov in northern Bohemia, where he'd learned to play. In eight games, he scored two goals and collected 50 penalty minutes.

Dominik Hasek and Svoboda later became the greatest of the Czech Olympic heroes. "Even if I were to skate on the ice for 30 years, I would probably never succeed in doing it again," Svoboda said after the finals. He battled his way into the Stanley Cup finals three times. Once he even got to raise the Cup overhead. And now he could add the most coveted gold of all. "Before the tournament, I would have said that the winner's feelings are always the same. After two weeks at the Olympics, I must say that the medal won at Nagano absolutely means the most. In the NHL, you have time to think what will be and what lies ahead. At the Olympics, the games went one right after the other. Thank God, because otherwise it would have made me very nervous. Only when we won did I realize what had actually happened."

Svoboda finished his NHL career having played in 1,028 games, scoring 58 goals and 399 points in 17 years in the league.

Pat LaFontaine

An electrifying scorer everywhere he played, Pat LaFontaine was one of the NHL's brightest stars from 1984 to 1998. He combined speed, tenacity and a positive attitude with offensive gifts that nobody could have taught him. LaFontaine's big-league sojourn took him to three different New York State teams and won him a host of admirers throughout the hockey world. His ability to stay low to the ice while skating and his excellent balance helped him deal with the physical side of the game.

Although he was born in St. Louis, LaFontaine grew up in the Detroit suburb of Waterford and learned to play the game in the Motor City's minor hockey system. His statistics for Detroit

Compuware of the North American Junior Hockey League in 1981–82 were an incredible 175 goals and 324 points in 79 matches.

During a time when many young players opted for hockey scholarships at U.S. schools, LaFontaine decided to play in the Canadian junior system. In his only year in the league, he exploded for 104 goals and 234 points and helped his team reach the Memorial Cup finals. Two of the more prominent records he broke were Guy Lafleur's 40-game point-scoring streak and Mike Bossy's 70 goals by a rookie. He also outdueled future NHL icon Mario Lemieux in the scoring race. He was named the outstanding player of the Memorial Cup even though his team was eliminated in the round robin. After the season, LaFontaine was voted the Canadian Major Junior player of the year. He capped off an exhilarating year by being chosen third overall by the New York Islanders at the 1983 Entry Draft.

Pat LaFontaine wasn't healthy enough to play a full season but still scored 62 points in 67 games for the Rangers in 1997–98.

Rather than step directly into the NHL, LaFontaine opted to enrich his experience with the United States national squad, which was preparing to compete in the 1984 Sarajevo Olympics. He scored 111 points in 58 exhibition matches for the defending gold medal winners. And it was here he was first called "Franny," which was short for "the Franchise." LaFontaine was one of the team's best performers with eight points in six games, but the U.S. had a disappointing seventh-place finish.

Following the tournament, LaFontaine joined the Islanders for their drive for a fifth consecutive Stanley Cup championship. He adapted easily to the NHL and scored 13 goals in the last 15 regular-season games. Included in this run was a memorable four-goal performance before a national televi-

sion audience during an 11–4 romp over Toronto at Maple Leaf Gardens. He contributed nine points in 16 playoff games as the Isles fell short in the finals against Wayne Gretzky and the Edmonton Oilers. This was the closest LaFontaine would ever get to Stanley Cup glory.

Even though they lost some of their luster, the Islanders remained a superior team in the mid-1980s. LaFontaine was allowed to develop at his own pace but was also prevented from playing a major role on a team deep in veterans. He summed up his situation this way: "Being the leader of a team was something I always felt I could do, but the timing here didn't call for it, and since I'm not the kind of guy to speak up and complain, I waited for the slots to open and the opportunities to come." In 1986–87, he broke through with 38 goals and scored the memorable fourth overtime period winner against Washington in the seventh game of the Patrick Division semifinals. Later that year he represented the United States at the Canada Cup tournament.

LaFontaine, Pat
C, 5′10″, 182 lbs, b: St. Louis, MO, 2/22/1965

Season	Club, League	Regular Season					Playoffs				
		GP	G	A	Pts	PIM	GP	G	A	Pts	PIM
OWG–84	USA	6	5	3	8	0					
1983–84	New York Islanders, NHL	15	13	6	19	6	16	3	6	9	8
1984–85	New York Islanders, NHL	67	19	35	54	32	9	1	2	3	4
1985–86	New York Islanders, NHL	65	30	23	53	43	3	1	0	1	0
1986–87	New York Islanders, NHL	80	38	32	70	70	14	5	7	12	10
CCup–87	USA	5	3	0	3	0					
1987–88	New York Islanders, NHL	75	47	45	92	52	6	4	5	9	8
1988–89	New York Islanders, NHL	79	45	43	88	26					
WEC–89	USA	10	5	3	8	8					
1989–90	New York Islanders, NHL	74	54	51	105	38	2	0	1	1	0
1990–91	New York Islanders, NHL	75	41	44	85	42					
CCup–91	USA	6	3	1	4	2					
1991–92	Buffalo Sabres, NHL	57	46	47	93	98	7	8	3	11	4
1992–93	Buffalo Sabres, NHL	84	53	95	148	63	7	2	10	12	0
1993–94	Buffalo Sabres, NHL	16	5	13	18	2					
1994–95	Buffalo Sabres, NHL	22	12	15	27	4	5	2	2	4	2
1995–96	Buffalo Sabres, NHL	76	40	51	91	36					
WCup–96	USA	5	2	2	4	2					
1996–97	Buffalo Sabres, NHL	13	2	6	8	4					
1997–98	New York Rangers, NHL	67	23	39	62	36					
OWG–98	USA	4	1	1	2	0					
	NHL Totals	865	468	545	1013	552	69	26	36	62	36
	OWG/WEC/CCup/WCup Totals	36	19	10	29	12					

NHL Second All-Star Team (1993)
Won Bill Masterton Trophy (1995)
Won Lester Patrick Trophy (1997)
Won Dodge Performer of the Year Award (1990)
Won WCup (1996)

A HISTORY OF WORLD HOCKEY

Pat LaFontaine's excellent ballance helped him deal with the physical side of the game in the NHL.

In 1987–88, LaFontaine registered his first of six straight years of at least 40 goals. The following season he scored eight points in 10 games for the United States at the World Championships. During this period, his exploits went largely unnoticed as the Islanders fell to the lower echelons of the NHL standings. In 1989–90, he led a rejuvenated squad back into the playoffs with his first 50-goal season, but the team fell back out of the post-season picture the next year. In 1991 he was one of the veterans on the U.S. team that lost to Canada in the finals of the Canada Cup. Unable to resolve a contract dispute with New York, he was traded to Buffalo on October 25, 1991, for several players, including scoring star Pierre Turgeon. He exploded during his second season in western New York with a team-record 148 points.

LaFontaine was poised to become firmly entrenched as one of the NHL's superstars when a series of injuries began to wreak havoc with his career. He'd already missed 33 games in 1991–92, the result of a broken jaw caused by an opponent's slash. In the opening round of the 1993 playoffs against Boston, he banged up his right knee. He thought he was fully recovered for play in 1993–94 but lasted only 16 games. He underwent reconstructive surgery for a torn ligament, which cost him the remainder of the season and half of the abbreviated lockout schedule in 1995. His determination to play again earned him the Bill Masterton Trophy at the end of the season.

Early in the 1996 season, he suffered a concussion that took several months to recover from. In a cost-cutting measure, the Sabres traded him to the New York Rangers. He wasn't sufficiently healthy to play a full season but did score 62 points in 67 games for the Blueshirts. He also reached the 1,000-point mark on January 22, 1998, a month before he represented the U.S. at the Nagano Olympics. After suffering a second serious concussion, he retired at the end of the season with 468 goals and 1,013 points.

Doug Gilmour

Doug Gilmour entered the National Hockey League as a tenacious defensive forward, playing bigger than his small stature would seem to make possible and sacrificing his body to forge a successful career. But Gilmour was also a playmaker, a player who could camp out behind the opponent's net and find teammates in scoring positions on a regular basis. When he combined his defensive abilities and feistiness with his offensive savvy, he became one of the game's best two-way centers.

Born in hockey-mad Kingston, Ontario, Gilmour's hero as a boy was his older brother Dave. The elder Gilmour was signed by the NHL's Vancouver Canucks but never played a game for them and spent most of his disappointing hockey career in the minors. Dave was a good offensive player, some say better than Doug, but he once remarked, "When they said check, I thought they meant paycheck." His defensive liabilities prevented him from making the rise to the big leagues. Doug wasn't going to make the same mistake. He began playing with older kids when he was only six, scoring against and checking 10-year-olds who were much bigger. His father wanted him to have a healthy dose of defense in his early years and insisted Doug play on the blue line.

When Gilmour made the move to the Cornwall Royals in the Ontario Hockey League, he was a solid defensive forward who could also score, although his size was considered a major stumbling block in the eyes of most NHL scouts. In his first year with the Royals, 1980–81, Gilmour was 5´9˝ and 150 pounds. Though he'd gain a couple of inches in his three years in Cornwall, he didn't add many extra pounds. What did add up in the OHL were his offensive numbers. After an early injury curtailed his effectiveness in Cornwall's 1981 Memorial Cup championship, he returned to score 46 goals and 119 points in 1981–82. Gilmour, who'd been passed over in his first year of draft eligibility, was selected by St. Louis in the seventh round, 134th overall. He was returned to junior hockey by the Blues for the 1982–83 season and set the OHL on fire with 70 goals and 177 points. He set a record with a 55 consecutive games scoring streak and was named the league's most valuable player.

Doug Gilmour was traded to the Maple Leafs in a blockbuster deal involving 10 players, the largest trade in league history.

Still, Gilmour's size worried management in St. Louis and he almost began his pro career in Germany when he couldn't reach a deal with the Blues. St. Louis finally signed him and he joined the team two weeks before the 1983–84 season. Gilmour found himself near the bottom of the team's depth chart at center, but a depleted roster allowed him to play on the fourth line as a defensive specialist and he returned to his checking ways. The Blues' captain, Brian Sutter, nick-named Gilmour "Killer" for his intensity and for his vague resemblance to Charles Manson.

"I am two people, one when I'm on and one when I'm off the ice," said Gilmour. "You're going out there to hit people, to try to win. You can't be Mr. Nice Guy on the ice, you can't be carefree on the ice, because somebody's going to beat you, and you can't let that happen."

After three full seasons hovering around 50 points and concentrating on checking, Gilmour put on weight—in his words, he "ballooned" to 165 pounds—and he began to play a more open game. In the 1986 playoffs, he had 21 points in 19 games when the Blues came within a game of advancing to the Stanley Cup finals. The next season, 1986-87, he finished the regular schedule with a career-high 42 goals and 105 points and was selected to play for Team Canada in the Canada Cup. He scored two important goals in the series against the Soviet Union and was one of the team's most valuable players.

After another solid season in St. Louis, Gilmour was involved in a high-profile case off the ice that eventually led to a trade to the

Gilmour, Doug
C, 5´11˝, 172 lbs, b: Kingston, Ont., 6/25/1963

Season	Club, League	Regular Season					Playoffs				
		GP	G	A	Pts	PIM	GP	G	A	Pts	PIM
1983–84	St. Louis Blues, NHL	80	25	28	53	57	11	2	9	11	10
1984–85	St. Louis Blues, NHL	78	21	36	57	49	3	1	1	2	2
1985–86	St. Louis Blues, NHL	74	25	28	53	41	19	9	12	21	25
1986–87	St. Louis Blues, NHL	80	42	63	105	58	6	2	2	4	16
CCup–87	Canada	8	2	0	2	4					
1987–88	St. Louis Blues, NHL	72	36	50	86	59	10	3	14	17	18
1988–89	Calgary Flames, NHL	72	26	59	85	44	22	11	11	22	20
1989–90	Calgary Flames, NHL	78	24	67	91	54	6	3	1	4	8
WEC–90	Canada	9	1	4	5	18					
1990–91	Calgary Flames, NHL	78	20	61	81	144	7	1	1	2	0
1991–92	Calgary Flames, NHL	38	11	27	38	46					
	Toronto Maple Leafs, NHL	40	15	34	49	32					
1992–93	Toronto Maple Leafs, NHL	83	32	95	127	100	21	10	25	35	30
1993–94	Toronto Maple Leafs, NHL	83	27	84	111	105	18	6	22	28	42
1994–95	Rapperswil, Switzerland	9	2	13	15	16					
	Toronto Maple Leafs, NHL	44	10	23	33	26	7	0	6	6	6
1995–96	Toronto Maple Leafs, NHL	81	32	40	72	77	6	1	7	8	12
1996–97	Toronto Maple Leafs, NHL	61	15	45	60	46					
	New Jersey Devils, NHL	20	7	15	22	22	10	0	4	4	14
1997–98	New Jersey Devils, NHL	63	13	40	53	68	6	5	2	7	4
1998–99	Chicago Blackhawks, NHL	72	16	40	56	56					
1999–00	Chicago Blackhawks, NHL	63	22	34	56	51					
	Buffalo Sabres, NHL	11	3	14	17	12	5	0	1	1	0
2000–01	Buffalo Sabres, NHL	71	7	31	38	70	13	2	4	6	12
2001–02	Montreal Canadiens, NHL	70	10	31	41	48					
	NHL Totals	1412	439	945	1384	1265					
	WEC/CCup Totals	17	3	4	7	22					

Won Frank J. Selke Trophy (1993)
Won Stanley Cup (1989)
Won CCup (1987)

His father wanted Doug Gilmour (left) to have a healthy dose of defense in his early years and insisted his son play on the blue line.

Calgary Flames at the beginning of the 1988–89 campaign. The parents of Gilmour's babysitter went to the Blues asking for money, alleging the star player had assaulted their daughter. Lawsuits and countersuits were filed and then dropped and the allegations were never substantiated. But Gilmour's reputation in St. Louis had been irrevocably damaged.

In Calgary, Gilmour continued his strong play in the playoffs, adding 22 points in 22 games as the Flames won the Stanley Cup in 1989. Gilmour scored the series-winning goal in game six of the finals against Montreal. Halfway through the 1991–92 season, Gilmour became increasingly disenchanted with his pay from the Flames and an arbitrator's decision that saw his salary increase less than he expected. He decided to leave the team, but only a few hours later he was traded to the Toronto Maple Leafs in a blockbuster deal involving 10 players, the largest trade in league history.

Gilmour played his best hockey with the Leafs. He was a pesky defensive forward who seemed fearless in his checking. Offensively, he was the focal point of an improving team, setting a franchise record with 127 points in his first full season with Toronto in 1992–93. He became only the second Leaf after Darryl Sittler to register over a 100 points in a season and also led the team to within a game of the Stanley Cup finals, placing second in playoff scoring and leading the league with 25 assists. Gilmour placed second to Mario Lemieux in the race for the Hart Trophy as the league's most valuable player and won the Selke Trophy as the top defensive forward, a remarkable achievement for a player with such offensive numbers.

Gilmour had 111 points the next season, earning his second consecutive spot in the All-Star Game. He once again led the Leafs to the semifinals in the playoffs. Gilmour was named the team captain in 1994–95 before the lockout-shortened season and remained a popular player in Toronto even as the team began to struggle. When the Leafs went into rebuilding mode midway through the 1996–97 season, Gilmour was sent to the New Jersey Devils. He spent one full season with the defense-oriented Devils and was signed as a free agent by the Chicago Blackhawks in the summer of 1998. In the spring of 2000, he was traded to the Buffalo Sabres and a year later announced his retirement, though he reconsidered and signed a one-year contract with Montreal for the 2001–02 season. During that season, Gilmour was honored in absentia as one of the top 25 Toronto Maple Leafs of all time in a ceremony before a game at the Air Canada Centre.

Tom Barrasso

Tom Barrasso entered the NHL for the 1983–84 season as an 18-year-old, going straight from high school to the Buffalo Sabres. Observers around the league thought the native of Stowe, Massachusetts, would be a good professional goaltender. After all, he'd played well for the U.S. Olympic team and received some excellent coaching under Team USA's Eddie Johnson. But few people expected the impact the young goalie would have right out of the starting blocks as a teenager.

In his rookie season, Barrasso won the Vezina Trophy as the league's best netminder and the Calder Trophy as the top rookie. In Buffalo, he was the high-profile half of an amazing goaltending team with Bob Sauve, and the two shared the award for the NHL's best goals-against average in Barrasso's second year.

Barrasso gave a lot of credit for his early success to his coach on the Sabres. "I really owe a debt of gratitude to Scotty Bowman," he said after his dual award rookie year. "If he didn't take a chance on me, I wouldn't be here today." Through it all, he racked up huge phone bills with calls home to his closely knit family during his early time in Buffalo—a reminder that this was just a teenage kid holding his own in a game of grown men.

By 1984, some experts called Barrasso the best goalie in the world. At the Canada Cup that year, Team USA general manager and former NHLer Lou Nanne was one of them. "With Tretiak gone, no one is even close," said Nanne of the 19-year-old American. "I knew he was good, but the degree of his excellence just sort of shocks you. This is a guy who could dominate hockey for the next 10 years, and they just don't come along that often."

For his part, Barrasso wasn't paying much attention to the hype, preferring instead to concentrate on his performance between the pipes. "I've just got to let all that stuff blow by me," he said when he heard of Nanne's comments. "I can't afford to get caught up in all that." Looking back on his sensational early years with the U.S. team and in the pros, Barrasso remembered: "I didn't know how to play goal in those days. I was just getting by on raw talent."

Barrasso strapped on his first pair of goalie pads as a four-year-old. By the time he was in high school, he'd been recruited by just about every college in the U.S. He picked Providence College in Rhode Island as the place he wanted to play his collegiate hockey but went straight to the NHL instead after playing in the 1984 Canada Cup with Team USA. The move to the pros had initially surprised Barrasso. "It was going to be college or the U.S. Olympic team," he said during his rookie year, "because I had no idea that I would be offered a contract if I was drafted."

When he wasn't stopping pucks, though, controversy seemed to follow Barrasso

At the age of 18, Tom Barrasso won the Vezina Trophy as the league's best netminder and the Calder Trophy as the top rookie.

Barrasso, Tom
G, 6′3″, 211 lbs, b: Boston, MA, 3/31/1965

Season	Club, League	Regular Season				Playoffs			
		GP	Mins	GA	Avg	GP	Mins	GA	Avg
1983–84	Buffalo Sabres, NHL	42	2475	117	2.84	3	139	8	3.45
CCup–84	USA	5	252	13	3.00				
1984–85	Buffalo Sabres, NHL	54	3248	144	2.66	5	300	22	4.40
	Rochester Americans, AHL	5	267	6	1.35				
1985–86	Buffalo Sabres, NHL	60	3561	214	3.61				
WEC–86	USA	5	260	18	4.15				
1986–87	Buffalo Sabres, NHL	46	2501	152	3.65				
CCup–87	USA	1	60	5	5.00				
1987–88	Buffalo Sabres, NHL	54	3133	173	3.31	4	224	16	4.29
1988–89	Buffalo Sabres, NHL	10	545	45	4.95				
	Pittsburgh Penguins, NHL	44	2406	162	4.04	11	631	40	3.80
1989–90	Pittsburgh Penguins, NHL	24	1294	101	4.68				
1990–91	Pittsburgh Penguins, NHL	48	2754	165	3.59	20	1175	51	2.60
1991–92	Pittsburgh Penguins, NHL	57	3329	196	3.53	21	1233	58	2.82
1992–93	Pittsburgh Penguins, NHL	63	3702	186	3.01	12	722	35	2.91
1993–94	Pittsburgh Penguins, NHL	44	2482	139	3.36	6	356	17	2.87
1994–95	Pittsburgh Penguins, NHL	2	125	8	3.84	2	80	8	6.00
1995–96	Pittsburgh Penguins, NHL	49	2799	160	3.43	10	558	26	2.80
1996–97	Pittsburgh Penguins, NHL	5	270	26	5.78				
1997–98	Pittsburgh Penguins, NHL	63	3542	122	2.07	6	376	17	2.71
1998–99	Pittsburgh Penguins, NHL	43	2306	98	2.55	13	787	35	2.67
1999–00	Pittsburgh Penguins, NHL	18	869	46	3.18				
	Ottawa Senators, NHL	7	418	22	3.16	6	372	16	2.58
2001–02	Carolina-Toronto, NHL	38	2127	93	2.62				
OWG–02	USA	1	60	1	1.00				
	NHL Totals	771	43855	2369	3.24				
	OWG/WEC/CCup Totals	12	632	37	3.51				

NHL First All-Star Team (1984)
NHL Second All-Star Team (1985, 1993)
Won Vezina Trophy (1984)
Won Calder Trophy (1984)
Won William M. Jennings Trophy (1985)
Won Stanley Cup (1991, 1992)

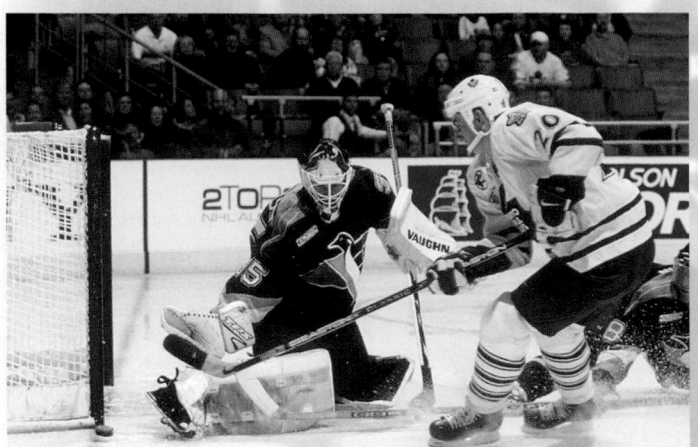

Tom Barrasso (left) became the first American-born goalie to win 300 career games in the NHL.

wherever he went. Before turning pro, he had pulled himself out of a Canada Cup game against Sweden when his U.S. team was down 4–0 (they eventually lost 9–2). Despite U.S. coach Johnson's urging that he would be called a quitter if he didn't return to the game, Barrasso wouldn't go back on the ice and a big argument with Johnson erupted under the stands.

What's more, the once happy relationship between Barrasso and Sabres coach Bowman was deteriorating fast. To teach his star netminder a lesson in humility, Bowman demoted Barrasso briefly to Rochester of the American Hockey League in 1984 and ordered the youngster not to talk to reporters while in the minors.

By 1987, things were getting worse. The Sabres were a struggling team, and their star goalie was shouldering a lot of the blame as well as the glory. "I'm looked on as a hero who can make his team win," he said. "That makes it easy for me to get ready to play, even if some nights we've been very disappointing."

Just after the start of the 1988–89 season, Barrasso was traded to the Pittsburgh Penguins, leaving in his wake rumors that he'd been responsible for Bowman's getting fired in Buffalo. "As my career progressed and Buffalo went south," he said after the trade, "I was the one who received the brunt of the attention and the brunt of the blame." Pittsburgh's powerful offense needed some defensive help and having Barrasso in the crease was a major piece of the championship puzzle for the Penguins. In 1991 and 1992 Pittsburgh won the Stanley Cup, due in large part to Barrasso's outstanding play in the net. Bryan Trottier, the New York Islanders center and a member of the Penguins during the twilight of his career, said during the 1992 playoffs: "Right now, Tom is the best money goalie in the game. As each game gets bigger, he gets better."

But after those great Cup-winning years, the controversy bug came back to bite Barrasso again. Injuries and family illnesses caused him to miss a number of games—in 1996–97 he played in only five—and to play inconsistently when he was on the ice. Home fans started to boo him and Pittsburgh sportswriters became highly critical. One of them called him the "biggest jerk in the NHL." Barrasso responded by refusing to talk to the media, preferring a terse "no comment" to questions before and after games.

Still, there were flashes of the old brilliance, especially in the 1996 playoffs and in particular in the Penguins' series against the Florida Panthers. "He is as good a goalie as has ever played this game, and right now he is in the zone," said Pittsburgh coach Eddie Johnson during the series. "The way he's stopping the puck now is the way he played when he won the two Cups." It also contributed to his becoming the first American-born goalie to win 300 career games in the league and has virtually assured him of a spot in the Hall of Fame after he retires.

After spending most of his career with Pittsburgh, the controversial Barrasso was traded to Ottawa during 1999–2000, only to lose to Toronto in the first round of the playoffs.

After sitting out the entire 2000-01 season Barrasso returned to the NHL in 2001–02, signing a free-agent contract with the Carolina Hurricanes, where he was the backup to Arturs Irbe. At the trade deadline, the Toronto Maple Leafs acquired Barrasso as insurance following an injury to starter Curtis Joseph. However, Barrasso himself suffered a pulled hamstring in just his third game with the Leafs while playing against the New Jersey Devils and was forced to miss the rest of the season.

Claude Lemieux

Claude Lemieux became the fourth player to win the Stanley Cup with three different teams, joining Al Arbour, Larry Hillman and Gord Pettinger.

Unless you were playing with him or cheering for his team, chances are you didn't like Claude Lemieux when he was at his pesky best—or worst—in the National Hockey League. Lemieux had all the obnoxious tricks that infuriated opposing players, often drawing them into needless penalties. His worst trick, if you were playing against him in the playoffs, was scoring a timely goal to win the game.

"If I watch tennis, I like John McEnroe," Lemieux said. "That's the way I wanted to be when I grew up. I liked Bobby Clarke. He was a little bit my style of player. He was aggressive and he liked to cause a lot of trouble. That's the way I always wanted to be and that's the way I am."

Born in 1965 in Buckingham, Quebec, Lemieux played junior hockey with the Verdun Junior Canadiens and was drafted by Montreal in 1983, the team's second pick and 26th overall. He had the perfect beginning to his NHL career, considering the style he would perfect later on. As an 18-year-old in Verdun, he was called up to his first pro game by Montreal. The problem was, all his equipment was locked up in the Verdun arena and it was a holiday. The security guard wouldn't let the rookie into the building. Lemieux, getting desperate about missing the plane to join the Canadiens, broke into the arena, gathered his things and then hightailed it for the airport. He got on the plane just as its doors were closing. In that first game he was in a particularly feisty mood, continually parking himself in front of Buffalo Sabres goalie Tom Barrasso. Barrasso didn't take kindly to such an infringement and gave Lemieux a slash that failed to deter him as he went on to score his first NHL goal.

At only eight games, his stay with the Canadiens wasn't a long one and he returned to play in the minors for the next several years, making the occasional trip with the Canadiens. He began to establish his reputation as a playoff performer in 1985, landing the Guy Lafleur Award as the most valuable player in the Quebec Major Junior Hockey League playoffs.

Lemieux, Claude
RW, 6′1″, 215 lbs, b: Buckingham, Que., 7/16/1965

Season	Club, League	Regular Season					Playoffs				
		GP	G	A	Pts	PIM	GP	G	A	Pts	PIM
1983–84	Montreal Canadiens, NHL	8	1	1	2	12					
	Nova Scotia Voyageurs, AHL						2	1	0	1	0
1984–85	Montreal Canadiens, NHL	1	0	1	1	7					
1985–86	Montreal Canadiens, NHL	10	1	2	3	22	20	10	6	16	68
	Sherbrooke Canadiens, AHL	58	21	32	53	145					
1986–87	Montreal Canadiens, NHL	76	27	26	53	156	17	4	9	13	41
RV'87	NHL All-Stars	2	0	0	0	4					
CCup–87	Canada	6	1	1	2	4					
1987–88	Montreal Canadiens, NHL	78	31	30	61	137	11	3	2	5	20
1988–89	Montreal Canadiens, NHL	69	29	22	51	136	18	4	3	7	58
1989–90	Montreal Canadiens, NHL	39	8	10	18	106	11	1	3	4	38
1990–91	New Jersey Devils, NHL	78	30	17	47	105	7	4	0	4	34
1991–92	New Jersey Devils, NHL	74	41	27	68	109	7	4	3	7	26
1992–93	New Jersey Devils, NHL	77	30	51	81	155	5	2	0	2	19
1993–94	New Jersey Devils, NHL	79	18	26	44	86	20	7	11	18	44
1994–95	New Jersey Devils, NHL	45	6	13	19	86	20	13	3	16	20
1995–96	Colorado Avalanche, NHL	79	39	32	71	117	19	5	7	12	55
WCup–96	Canada	8	1	1	2	19					
1996–97	Colorado Avalanche, NHL	45	11	17	28	43	17	13	10	23	32
1997–98	Colorado Avalanche, NHL	78	26	27	53	115	7	3	3	6	8
1998–99	Colorado Avalanche, NHL	82	27	24	51	102	19	3	11	14	26
1999–00	Colorado Avalanche, NHL	13	3	6	9	4					
	New Jersey Devils, NHL	70	17	21	38	86	23	4	6	10	28
2000–01	Phoenix Coyotes, NHL	46	10	16	26	58					
2001–02	Phoenix Coyotes, NHL	82	16	25	41	70					
	NHL Totals	1129	371	394	765	1712					
	RV'87/CCup/WCup Totals	16	2	2	4	27					

Won Conn Smythe Trophy (1995)
Won Stanley Cup (1986, 1995, 1996, 2000)
Won CCup (1987)

Claude Lemieux (center) had all the obnoxious tricks that could infuriate antagonists and often drew them into pointless penalties. His best—or worst— trick was scoring a timely goal to win the game.

The next season, after playing with Montreal for 10 games in the regular season, Lemieux helped the Canadiens land the Stanley Cup with his 10 playoff goals, including four game-winning goals—the equivalent of a series win.

He played his first full season with the Canadiens in 1986–87, scoring 27 goals and 53 points. For his clutch play, he was named to the Team Canada squad for the 1987 Canada Cup and to the NHL team in the Rendez-Vous matchup with the Soviet Union that replaced the All-Star Game.

Lemieux stayed with the Canadiens, scoring as many as 31 goals in a season (1987–88), until he was traded at the beginning of the 1990–91 season to the New Jersey Devils for Sylvain Turgeon. Lemieux had a breakout season offensively with New Jersey, scoring 41 goals in 1991–92, and the following season recorded a career-high 81 points. He saved his best for the playoffs, however. He had 18 points in 20 playoff games in 1994 when the Devils lost a close seven-game series to the eventual champion New York Rangers. Lemieux was the leading goal scorer in the 1995 playoffs with 13, including three more game-winning goals. After the Devils won the Stanley Cup, Lemieux was awarded the Conn Smythe Trophy as the most valuable player in the playoffs.

A month after winning the Smythe Trophy, he demanded a new contract and was eventually traded to the Quebec Nordiques in a three-team deal involving Wendel Clark and Steve Thomas. The next season, he became the fourth player to win a Stanley Cup with three different teams— joining Al Arbour, Larry Hillman and Gord Pettinger—when Quebec moved to Colorado and marched to the championship. It was only the fifth time a player had won the Cup two consecutive years with different teams.

Lemieux was selected to the Team Canada roster for the World Cup in 1996 and, with his chippy demeanor still intact, he picked up 19 penalty minutes in the eight games as Canada finished second. The next season, Lemieux starred again in the Stanley Cup playoffs, leading the league with 13 goals before Colorado was defeated by the Detroit Red Wings. Early in the 1999–2000 season, Lemieux returned once again to the Devils—a fitting name for the troublesome right winger's team—as New Jersey looked forward to the playoffs. His 21 game-winning goals in the playoffs puts him in third place on the NHL's all-time list behind Wayne Gretzky, who had 24, and one ahead of Maurice Richard. In the summer of 2000, he signed as a free agent with the Phoenix Coyotes, where he continues to play.

Steve Yzerman

Steve Yzerman had all the flashy adjectives applied to him when he entered the National Hockey League as a young, slick center. He could score the beautiful goal and his flair translated into some remarkable statistical seasons. But Yzerman's team, the Detroit Red Wings, had struggled before he arrived, and he didn't set the world on fire during his early years. Since then, though, Yzerman has become the longest-serving captain in league history and dedicated himself to an all-around game, finally leading the Wings to the Stanley Cup in 1997 after 42 years of futility.

Born in Cranbrook, British Columbia, in 1965, Yzerman moved with his family to Nepean, Ontario, when he was 10. He was an avid hockey player, spending hours playing ball hockey with neighbor Darren Pang, who would one day play in the NHL as a goalie. On Nepean's rep teams, Yzerman was a standout and led his squads to an undefeated streak that lasted more than two seasons and 143 games. "He was unbelievable; he never quit," Pang said of his young teammate. "Besides the fact that he was a highly skilled player, the thing that stood out in my mind was that he never quit. As a goalie on his team who stood and watched him, I thought he was fantastic. When we needed a goal, he got the puck and he didn't give it up until either he scored or he passed it to somebody else who scored."

Steve Yzerman became the longest-serving captain in league history.

At the age of 16, Yzerman made another move, this time to Peterborough to play with the Ontario Hockey League's Petes. He had 91 points in 56 games with Peterborough in his second year, but his numbers weren't the usual stratospheric kind registered by young phenomena in the OHL because of the team concept ingrained in the Petes by Dick Todd, the team's no-nonsense coach. Along with Pat LaFontaine and Sylvain Turgeon, Yzerman was still considered one of the top prospects as his draft year approached. He enriched that reputation with a strong performance on Canada's bronze medal team in the World Junior Championship in 1983.

The year before the 1983 NHL Entry Draft, the Detroit Red Wings were bought by Mike Ilitch, who entrusted general manager Jim Devellano with the job of rebuilding the failing franchise. The Red Wings had the fourth overall pick, and Devellano's first choice was LaFontaine, a hometown boy who would surely revive the interest of the Detroit fans. But LaFontaine was picked third and Devellano selected Yzerman to be the cornerstone of the new Wings.

"LaFontaine went on to have a good career. But over the years, Yzerman proved to be the better pick," Devellano said, adding that Peterborough's team-oriented system probably made Yzerman a less attractive choice to the three teams selecting ahead of Detroit. "He probably would've gone one, two or three if the Petes' coach had played his best players more."

Yzerman's father, Ron, was happy that Steve was chosen by Detroit, something he expressed to the Red Wings' new owner during a draft-day conversation. "I said I just hoped he'd be paid to play hockey," said Ron of his talk with Ilitch. "Geez, the price of sticks."

Still only 18, Yzerman immediately established himself as an impact player with the Red Wings. In his first year, 1983–84, he set Detroit records for goals by a rookie with 39 and for points with 87. He finished second behind goalie Tom Barrasso in the Calder Trophy voting and also made the NHL's All-Rookie Team. He played in the All-Star Game after half a season in the league, making him the youngest player ever to don an All-Star sweater. His success carried over into training camp for the 1984 Canada Cup. Yzerman played so well in the camp that he couldn't be left off the team. Ultimately, Denis Savard was sent home to make room for the young Red Wing. Canada won the tournament, though Yzerman missed most of the action due to recurring tonsillitis.

Detroit had missed the playoffs in 15 of the previous 17 seasons before Yzerman arrived and in his first season the Red Wings placed dead last in the league. "On many nights this young man carried the team on his shoulders. He couldn't accept that the team was the worst in hockey," one-time Red Wings coach Jacques Demers said. "I can't remember a night when he didn't come to play."

Although there were concerns about his size before he entered the league, Yzerman found his footing and his confidence early in his professional career. "I felt when I first came up last year that the pace was going to be that much quicker than I was used to in junior," Yzerman said in 1984. "But then I found out that I could hold onto the puck. You get to know when you've got to move it and when you can keep it. You sort of get a feel for it. It takes time, but it comes along with your confidence."

Yzerman continued to record impressive numbers. He had a knack for the pretty goal and began to draw fans back to the beleaguered team. He was named Red Wings captain as a 21-year-old in 1986, the youngest player ever to earn that honor.

"Being the captain has helped me to be a better player," Yzerman said. "I have no trouble with motivation now because I'm very conscious of the fact that I have to lead the way in the work ethic and play solid, consistent two-way hockey."

With Wayne Gretzky and Mario Lemieux carrying the superstar banner for the league over the next few seasons, Yzerman settled into his role as a highly talented member of the second tier of league stars. Between 1987 and 1993, he never failed to top 100 points, and five times he scored 50 goals or more. He set all-time marks for Detroit when he had 65 goals, 90 assists and 155 points in 1988–89, placing third in the league scoring race behind Gretzky and Lemieux, just as he would in voting for the Hart Trophy that season.

But respect as a winner and a two-way player didn't necessarily rest on statistics alone. Yzerman was left off the 1987 and 1991 Canada Cup squads by coach Mike Keenan. Yzerman began to work on his conditioning and added muscle with a weight program. He worked hard on his play in his own zone with and without the puck, not just to find openings to score timely goals but also to prevent them. Respect for Yzerman, loved in Detroit and nicknamed "Stevie Wonder," began to spread throughout the league. Detroit was consistently finishing near the top of the NHL standings instead of the bottom.

In 1994–95, the Wings ended the lockout-shortened season atop the standings, winning the Presidents' Trophy. The team coasted through the first three rounds of the playoffs undefeated on home ice. For the first time in his 11th year in the league, Yzerman was in the Stanley Cup finals. The joy didn't last long. New Jersey's stifling defense shut down Yzerman and the Wings and he had to watch Devils captain Scott Stevens hoist the Stanley Cup after a

Yzerman, Steve
C, 5´11˝, 185 lbs, b: Cranbrook, B.C., 5/9/1965

Season	Club, League	Regular Season					Playoffs				
		GP	G	A	Pts	PIM	GP	G	A	Pts	PIM
1983–84	Detroit Red Wings, NHL	80	39	48	87	33	4	3	3	6	0
CCup–84	Canada	4	0	0	0	0					
1984–85	Detroit Red Wings, NHL	80	30	59	89	58	3	2	1	3	2
WEC–85	Canada	10	3	4	7	6					
1985–86	Detroit Red Wings, NHL	51	14	28	42	16					
1986–87	Detroit Red Wings, NHL	80	31	59	90	43	16	5	13	18	8
1987–88	Detroit Red Wings, NHL	64	50	52	102	44	3	1	3	4	6
1988–89	Detroit Red Wings, NHL	80	65	90	155	61	6	5	5	10	2
WEC–89	Canada	8	5	7	12	2					
1989–90	Detroit Red Wings, NHL	79	62	65	127	79					
WEC–90	Canada	10	10	10	20	8					
1990–91	Detroit Red Wings, NHL	80	51	57	108	34	7	3	3	6	4
1991–92	Detroit Red Wings, NHL	79	45	58	103	64	11	3	5	8	12
1992–93	Detroit Red Wings, NHL	84	58	79	137	44	7	4	3	7	4
1993–94	Detroit Red Wings, NHL	58	24	58	82	36	3	1	3	4	0
1994–95	Detroit Red Wings, NHL	47	12	26	38	40	15	4	8	12	0
1995–96	Detroit Red Wings, NHL	80	36	59	95	64	18	8	12	20	4
WCup–96	Canada	6	2	1	3	0					
1996–97	Detroit Red Wings, NHL	81	22	63	85	78	20	7	6	13	4
1997–98	Detroit Red Wings, NHL	75	24	45	69	46	22	6	18	24	22
OWG–98	Canada	6	1	1	2	10					
1998–99	Detroit Red Wings, NHL	80	29	45	74	42	10	9	4	13	0
1999–00	Detroit Red Wings, NHL	78	35	44	79	34	8	0	4	4	0
2000–01	Detroit Red Wings, NHL	54	18	34	52	18	1	0	0	0	0
2001–02	Detroit Red Wings, NHL	52	13	35	48	18					
	NHL Totals	1362	658	1004	1662	852					
	OWG/WEC/CCup/WCup Totals	44	21	23	44	26					

Named Best Forward at WEC (1990)
NHL All-Star Team (1984, 1988, 1989, 1990, 1991, 1992, 1993, 1997, 2000)
Won Frank J. Selke Trophy (2000)
Won Conn Smythe Trophy (1998)
Won Lester B. Pearson Award (1989)
Won Stanley Cup (1997, 1998)
Won CCup (1984)

Steve Yzerman (left) and NHL commissioner Gary Bettman with the Stanley Cup.

Between 1987 and 1993, Steve Yzerman (left) never failed to top 100 points in a season and scored 50 or more goals five times.

four-game sweep. Still, after so many seasons of struggling even to make the playoffs, Yzerman was being talked about as the quiet but effective leader of a surging team.

Yzerman's high status was evident when his name began to surface in trade rumors in 1995. The Red Wings were a contending team, four games away from the Cup the previous season, an enviable position for which Yzerman had worked hard and sacrificed years of his career. Although it may have been unfair, many people said time had run out for him and general managers from around the league began circling the team like vultures. Red Wings fans, however, wanted to stick with their long-serving captain. When the rumors first became public, the Detroit building was filled with a long-lasting ovation before the Red Wings' next game with Edmonton. The Red Wings players responded, as well, whipping the Oilers 9–0. Yzerman stayed with the Wings.

"The ovation was a thrill for sure," Yzerman said. "That was definitely the most exciting moment I've ever experienced at Joe Louis Arena."

In the spring of 1996 the center exacted a measure of revenge on Mike Keenan, the coach who'd left him off those international teams. Yzerman scored a 60-foot goal to eliminate Keenan's St. Louis Blues from the playoffs. Although the Red Wings lost to the Colorado Avalanche in the next round, Yzerman had come into his own as a leader.

"He's one of those unsung leaders," said teammate Paul Coffey, a defenseman who'd played with Mark Messier, Lemieux and Gretzky before joining the Wings. "He's a great, great hockey player. He's right up there with the Gretzkys and the Messiers. He proved that with that goal."

Perhaps because the Keenan snubs had been exorcised, Yzerman was a standout player on Team Canada for the 1996 World Cup, scoring an important early-round goal against Slovakia to keep the Canadian team on track and notching another in overtime in the first game of the final series against the United States. When Canada fell in the final game, however, Yzerman was once again forced to watch another team celebrate.

In the 1997 playoffs, everything came together for the hard-working captain. He was a solid player at both ends of the ice as Detroit faced the Philadelphia Flyers for the Stanley Cup. In four consecutive games, the Wings were too much for the favored Flyers. At the end of the final game, Yzerman was the first to embrace goalie Mike Vernon. Moments later, in front of his home fans chanting "Stevie" over and over, Yzerman raised the Cup above his head, the first Red Wing to do so since 1955.

"It's been a long time for Detroit. It's been a long time for me in Detroit," Yzerman said. "It was the most rewarding and greatest moment of my career. As my career went on, the one thing I lacked in Detroit was a championship. I wanted desperately to have my name on the Stanley Cup with all the great players on it."

The next season, Yzerman's name was engraved on another award, this time the Conn Smythe Trophy, after the Red Wings repeated as Cup champions.

Yzerman was an effective checker and became a player Detroit coach Scotty Bowman could use in all situations. And he stands second only to Gordie Howe in all-time Red Wings scoring, entrenching himself as a throwback player who stayed and lived for one team through good times and bad for his entire career. "It certainly makes me very proud that the guy we took first to try and construct the franchise has really worked out well," former general manager Jim Devellano said. Later he added, "It's nice that he's been able to play his whole career in one city and win the fans' hearts. I don't know how much more often you're going to see that in sports."

Yzerman continues to captain the Wings into the 21st century, a sure Hall of Famer as soon as he becomes eligible to join the game's retired elite, and he added to his legacy at the 2002 Olympics, where he provided tremendous leadership along with the likes of Mario Lemieux and Joe Sakic. The three veteran players led Canada in the dressing room and on the scoreboard, with the climax coming in the gold medal-winning victory over the United States. Like Lemieux, Yzerman was in extreme pain for the entire tournament but fought through it in a true test of courage. Having undergone arthroscopic surgery a few weeks before, Yzerman's knee began acting up in the opening game of the tournament. The knee was swollen between games, but Yzerman iced it down and was in the lineup for all six of Canada's games.

Bill Ranford

When Bill Ranford was a child, he took figure skating lessons for two years in the hopes of perfecting that form of on-ice performance. But a friend of his father's was a hockey goalie and Ranford loved all the equipment associated with the position. He convinced his dad to take shots on him, and so his love for hockey and goaltending began and figure skating waned accordingly.

Ranford's father was in the armed forces and this meant a life of travel for Bill. Although born in Brandon, Manitoba, he moved to Germany for a while, traveling throughout Europe over the course of a few years. The family then returned to Canada: Portage La Prairie, Manitoba, then Prince Edward Island and finally Red Deer, Alberta. All the time Ranford, played hockey with local teams until finally he joined the New Westminster Bruins of the WHL.

A friend of his father's was a goalie and Bill Ranford loved all the equipment associated with the position.

During his time in junior, he once had the opportunity to practise with the Chicago Black Hawks. "One day I got to practise with Chicago when they came to Vancouver," he related. "Murray Bannerman had played all the games and they'd sent Darren Pang somewhere. Warren Skorodenski hadn't reported, so they needed a goalie. I practised with Doug Wilson and Denis Savard, and they paid me $50 at the end of it. It was the most money I'd seen."

It also turned out to be an impromptu tryout. That summer, 1985, Chicago wanted to draft him, but Boston, with the 52nd selection overall, beat the Hawks to it. Ranford's time with the Bruins was brief, in large part because of a coaching change that saw Terry O'Reilly replace Butch Goring as the head coach. "I don't think I would have played for the Bruins as long as Terry was there as coach," Ranford admitted. "He didn't like me as a goalie. We got along well when he was

In the 1989–90 season, Bill Ranford played in every game, after Grant Fuhr was injured, led the Oilers to the Stanley Cup and was awarded the Conn Smythe Trophy.

a teammate. We used to go to the movies together all the time. He used to stay on the ice after practices to shoot pucks at me."

But coach O'Reilly was happy to trade Ranford to Edmonton for another goalie, Andy Moog, during the 1987–88 season. With the Oilers, Ranford faced certain relegation to number two spot behind Grant Fuhr, but it also gave him the chance to apprentice with the best. "I learned a lot from Grant," he said. "Mostly on how to be more consistent. That's why Grant is so good. He doesn't have a lot of highs and lows in the games." But at the start of the 1989–90 season, Fuhr was rushed to hospital with appendicitis. He returned later in the season but hurt his shoulder. Ranford wound up playing most of that year, and playing spectacularly at that. "What happened to Grant was unfortunate, but it's something that I had to make the most of," he said. And he did.

The result was that come playoff time he had earned the starting job. He played in every game, led the team to the Stanley Cup and was named winner of the Conn Smythe Trophy. Younger than Fuhr by a few years, his play also meant that general manager Glen Sather could comfortably trade Fuhr and keep Ranford as the number one man.

At the start of the 1991–92 season, Ranford was perhaps the finest goalie in the world. He was named Canada's starter for the 1991 Canada Cup, and not only did he lead the team to victory, he was named the outstanding player of the tournament. His stand-up style was different from most young goalies, but for him it was effective. Midway through the 1995–96 season, he was traded back to Boston, and a series of trades and new teams that hurt his consistency began. After time in Washington, Tampa Bay and Detroit, Ranford signed in the summer of 1999 with the Oilers again as a free agent, hoping to reignite his career where it had seen its finest hour. Ranford played 16 games with the Oilers in 1999–2000 before retiring from the game at the age of 33.

Ranford, Bill
G, 5'11", 185 lbs, b: Brandon, Man., 12/14/1966

Season	Club, League	Regular Season				Playoffs			
		GP	Mins	GA	Avg	GP	Mins	GA	Avg
1983–84	New Westminster Bruins, WHL	27	1450	130	5.38	1	27	2	4.44
1984–85	New Westminster Bruins, WHL	38	2034	142	4.19	7	309	26	5.05
1985–86	Boston Bruins, NHL	4	240	10	2.50	2	120	7	3.50
	New Westminster Bruins, WHL	53	2791	225	4.84				
1986–87	Boston Bruins, NHL	41	2234	124	3.33	2	123	8	3.90
	Moncton Golden Flames, AHL	3	180	6	2.00				
1987–88	Maine Mariners, AHL	51	2856	165	3.47				
	Edmonton Oilers, NHL	6	325	16	2.95				
1988–89	Edmonton Oilers, NHL	29	1509	88	3.50				
1989–90	Edmonton Oilers, NHL	56	3107	165	3.19	22	1401	59	2.53
1990–91	Edmonton Oilers, NHL	60	3415	182	3.20	3	135	8	3.56
CCup–91	Canada	8	480	14	2.00				
1991–92	Edmonton Oilers, NHL	67	3822	228	3.58	16	909	51	3.37
1992–93	Edmonton Oilers, NHL	67	3753	240	3.84				
WC–93	Canada	6	354	11	1.86				
1993–94	Edmonton Oilers, NHL	71	4070	236	3.48				
WC–94	Canada	6	360	7	1.17				
1994–95	Edmonton Oilers, NHL	40	2203	133	3.62				
1995–96	Edmonton Oilers, NHL	37	2015	128	3.81				
	Boston Bruins, NHL	40	2307	109	2.83	4	239	16	4.02
WCup–96	Canada	0	0	0	0.00	0	0	0	0.00
1996–97	Boston Bruins, NHL	37	2147	125	3.49				
	Washington Capitals, NHL	18	1009	46	2.74				
1997–98	Washington Capitals, NHL	22	1183	55	2.79				
1998–99	Tampa Bay Lightning, NHL	32	1568	102	3.90				
	Detroit Red Wings, NHL	4	244	8	1.97	4	183	10	3.28
1999–2000	Edmonton Oilers, NHL	16	785	47	3.59				
	NHL Totals	647	35936	2042	3.41	53	3110	159	3.07
	WC/CCup/WCup Totals	20	1194	32	1.60				

Named Best Goaltender at WC (1994)
Won Conn Smythe Trophy (1990)
Won WC (1994)
Won Stanley Cup (1990)
Won CCup (1991)

Kevin Stevens

Born in Brockton, Massachusetts, Kevin Stevens had to make a tough choice between his two favorite sports, baseball and hockey. His first love was baseball. As a kid he played catcher, and while attending Boston College he was good enough behind the plate to win tryouts with the Toronto Blue Jays and the Philadelphia Phillies organizations. At 6′3″ and 217 pounds—and by his own admission not a great hitter—Stevens went for hockey. But he was a low draft pick, chosen 108th overall in the sixth round by Los Angeles. Soon after draft day, Stevens was traded to the Pittsburgh Penguins. Bouncing around to different teams and the minors would become one of the common elements of his career in hockey. All in all, he has been with Pittsburgh, Boston, the New York Rangers and Los Angeles in the NHL.

He also played for Team USA in the 1988 Olympics in Calgary. During that time, fans saw a big improvement in his performance under U.S. Olympic coach Herb Brooks' power skating program. Indeed, in his first game for Pittsburgh after the Games, Stevens scored his first career goal. During his first couple of seasons, Stevens alternated between Muskegon of the IHL and Pittsburgh, going up and down a total of four times in his second season. "I didn't have a very good training camp and I was sent to the minors. Being sent down really opened my eyes," admitted Stevens. "I worked hard right from the beginning and played well." While at Pittsburgh, he played on a line devised by coach Eddie Johnson that included John Cullen and Mark Recchi. "We all seem to complement each other's talents perfectly," said Stevens, who noted that the trio was dubbed the Option Line because all three were in the final or option year of their contracts.

Stevens' game really came together in Pittsburgh and the 1991–92 season was especially significant, as he finished the year behind only Mario Lemieux in scoring. Amazingly, Stevens never went more than three games without a point all season. That year—and the year after—the Penguins won the Stanley Cup. Stevens had four straight 40-goal seasons with the Pens and formed the core of a powerhouse team that included Jaromir Jagr and Ron Francis. With Lemieux off the ice for most of the 1993–94 season due to injuries and surgery, Stevens gained the spotlight.

The next year wasn't looking good for him. That season, the Penguins' new slogan was, "The three most feared words in hockey: Mario is back!" Some of the pundits added, "But nobody else will be." Stevens' reaction to the

Born in Brockton, Massachusetts, Kevin Stevens had to make a tough choice between baseball and hockey.

Stevens, Kevin
LW, 6′3″, 217 lbs, b: Brockton, MA, 4/15/1965

Season	Club, League	Regular Season					Playoffs				
		GP	G	A	Pts	PIM	GP	G	A	Pts	PIM
1983–84	Boston College, ECAC	37	6	14	20	36					
1984–85	Boston College, H.E.	40	13	23	36	36					
1985–86	Boston College, H.E.	42	17	27	44	56					
1986–87	Boston College, H.E.	39	35	35	70	54					
WEC–87	USA	8	1	1	2	10					
WOG–88	USA	5	1	3	4	2					
1987–88	Pittsburgh Penguins, NHL	16	5	2	7	8					
1988–89	Pittsburgh Penguins, NHL	24	12	3	15	19	11	3	7	10	16
	Muskegon Lumberjacks, IHL	45	24	41	65	113					
1989–90	Pittsburgh Penguins, NHL	76	29	41	70	171					
WEC–90	USA	10	5	2	7	18					
1990–91	Pittsburgh Penguins, NHL	80	40	46	86	133	24	17	16	33	53
1991–92	Pittsburgh Penguins, NHL	80	54	69	123	254	21	13	15	28	28
1992–93	Pittsburgh Penguins, NHL	72	55	56	111	177	12	5	11	16	22
1993–94	Pittsburgh Penguins, NHL	83	41	47	88	155	6	1	1	2	10
1994–95	Pittsburgh Penguins, NHL	27	15	12	27	51	12	4	7	11	21
1995–96	Boston Bruins, NHL	41	10	13	23	49					
	Los Angeles Kings, NHL	20	3	10	13	22					
WC–96	USA	8	4	3	7	12					
1996–97	Los Angeles Kings, NHL	69	14	20	34	96					
1997–98	New York Rangers, NHL	80	14	27	41	130					
1998–99	New York Rangers, NHL	81	23	20	43	64					
1999–00	New York Rangers, NHL	38	3	5	8	43					
2000–01	Philadelphia-Pittsburgh, NHL	55	10	22	32	73	17	3	3	6	20
2001–02	Pittsburgh Penguins, NHL	32	1	4	5	25					
	NHL Totals	874	329	397	726	1470					
	WOG/WEC/WC Totals	31	11	9	20	42					

NHL First All-Star Team (1992)
NHL Second All-Star Team (1991, 1993)
Won Stanley Cup (1991, 1992)

The 1991–92 season was an especially significant year for Kevin Stevens (right) as he finished second in scoring to Super Mario Lemiex.

upcoming year wasn't positive. "They have to cut their payroll with Mario coming back," he predicted. "His salary next year is astronomical. So I thought, 'I've got to get involved and make it clear what I want to do.'" What Stevens wanted was a trade to his home town, but he was worried he wouldn't get to Boston. "There are only two places I want to play—Pittsburgh and Boston. There is definitely the possibility of me not reporting to where I am traded." He added, "I am pretty bitter about the whole thing."

But in the end, things did work in his favor—for a little while, anyway. Stevens was traded to Boston for the 1995–96 season. However, he only stayed long enough to play 41 games in Beantown before he was traded once again, this time to Los Angeles. In 1997 Stevens was traded yet again, to the New York Rangers, where he remained for three years. He became one of the stars on the team after Wayne Gretzky retired in 1999.

After some off-ice problems Stevens signed with the Philadelphia Flyers in July 2000 as a free agent. However, the experiment in Philadelphia lasted just 23 games before he returned to the Penguins, where he played out the 2000–01 season in 32 games. Stevens returned for the start of the 2001–02 campaign, but it was clear he was merely a shadow of his former glory days and was dropped from the starting lineup midway through the season.

Mario Lemieux

Mario Lemieux was big and strong but rarely had to bully his way through defenders. Instead, he sent them flying with deft fakes and dekes.

Theorists in every sport love to play the "what if" game, trying to imagine the outcome of a game or a season or a career if not for an actual event that altered the perfect hypothesis. In the world of professional hockey, Mario Lemieux has inspired much reflection. "If it weren't for Gretzky," goes the argument, "Lemieux would be considered the greatest player of all time."

He was big and strong but rarely had to bully his way through defenders, sending them flying instead with deft fakes and dekes. In him, the attributes of the pure scorer and the playmaker were fused and his size, reach and balance made his end-to-end rushes seem effortless. In a few long strides, with a twist of those wide shoulders and quick change of direction, he found space on the ice where previously the way had been closed. Forced to choose between his accurate and heavy shot or his long arms reaching around them with a sweeping move, goalies were often left shaking their heads while they retrieved the puck from the net. Rarely has a sport's dominant player made the game look so easy and natural.

But if it is possible to call someone who was as great a player as Mario unlucky, Lemieux was just that in his NHL career. His battles with severe back injury and Hodgkin's disease may well have kept him from breaking many of the Great One's scoring records. Gretzky himself once acknowledged as much. "If he hadn't gone through all the back problems and cancer," said Wayne, "he might have been the guy who statistically could have shattered all my records. I mean all of them."

By the time he retired at age 31 in 1997, Lemieux was feared around the league by opposing goalies, some of whom made their apprehension at facing him a matter of public record. "I have no sympathy for goalies," he said when he heard of the complaints. "No sympathy at all. My job is to go out there and score goals, and their job is to try and stop me." After his retirement, the Hockey Hall of Fame waived the regular waiting period of three years and inducted him immediately. "What he could do, I couldn't do," said another Hall of Famer, Bobby Orr. "He could do more things than any other player I've ever seen." His number 66 was immediately retired by the Penguins.

"I have no sympathy for goalies," said Mario Lemieux (right). "My job is to go out there and score goals, and their job is to try and stop me."

A native of Montreal, Quebec, Lemieux (in French *le mieux* means "the best") was a sensational junior. He played for three seasons with the Laval Titans in the Quebec Major Junior Hockey League. In his final year he surpassed his childhood hero, Guy Lafleur, for the honor of being the top goal scorer in one QJMHL season. He set the record in his last game—in which Laval crushed Longueuil 16–4—by scoring six goals and adding six assists for good measure. He led the Titans to the Memorial Cup and was named the Canadian Major Junior player of the year for his 133 goals and 282 points, a total that easily topped Pierre Larouche's points record of 251. He set a Canadian record with a consecutive points streak that lasted 62 games.

Lemieux was the most talked about young player in the game and was picked first overall in the 1984 Entry Draft by the Pittsburgh Penguins, who were looking for a natural goal scorer to improve their fortunes. The Penguins had finished dead last in each of the previous two seasons and desperately needed to increase interest in a declining market. Lemieux responded to the challenge immediately. In his first shift in a regular-season game, he stole the puck from Boston's star defenseman Ray Bourque and moved in on goalie Pete Peeters. With a quick flick of his wrist, with his first shot on his first shift in his first game, he scored to announce himself to the league. In his home debut in Pittsburgh, he got an assist, again on his first shift, and won his first fight as well, using his amazing balance and reach to out-box Vancouver's Gary Lupul. He kept up the scoring pace that first year by becoming just the third rookie in league history to record 100 or more points. His 43 goals and 57 assists placed him behind only Dale Hawerchuk and Peter Statsny for all-time best rookie seasons. He was selected as the most valuable player in the All-Star Game, the perfect venue for his skills to shine, and Magnificent Mario easily won the Calder Trophy for top rookie in 1984–85. He ended his first professional year at the World Championships in Prague, leading Canada to a surprise victory over the Soviet Union en route to a silver medal.

Pittsburgh moved up 15 points in the standings, not enough to make the playoffs, but the excitement and increased attendance saved the franchise, something no other superstar had been looked upon to do so early in his career. "Without Lemieux, they pack up the team and move to another city," said Oilers general manager and president Glen Sather at the time of the young player's impact in his first season.

Lemieux had over 100 points in each of his next two seasons, but his first real claim to the status of the game's best player came in 1987. He played for the NHL in the Rendez-Vous series at the All-Star break, and then played a crucial role for the home team in the Canada Cup. He collected 18 points in nine games, none of them more timely or important than his series-winning goal against the Soviet Union in the final game. Lemieux tucked in behind Wayne Gretzky in the

Mario Lemieux (number 66) scores.

KINGS OF THE ICE

dying seconds, and when Gretzky slid a perfect pass back to him, he snapped a quick shot under the crossbar, starting off a wild celebration. In the following season, he outdistanced every scorer in the league—though Gretzky was injured—with 168 points to win the Art Ross and the Hart trophies as the league's top scorer and most valuable player.

Lemieux finished the 1988–89 season with 85 goals and 199 points to lead the league for the second consecutive season, this time beating a healthy Gretzky outright. His total points record that season was the only one ever to approach the 200-plus range inhabited by Gretzky earlier in his career on four occasions. Still, one of the criticisms leveled against Lemieux in these early years was that he'd need to win a Stanley Cup to be considered one of the all-time greats. Lemieux took that challenge in stride after a few difficult seasons with injuries. He first experienced trouble with his back during the 1989–90 season. The next year he missed most of the season before returning late to help a young Jaromir Jagr and some able veterans, including Larry Murphy and Paul Coffey, and in time for the playoffs. In one regular-season game against the New Jersey Devils, he put on what most people think was the greatest individual scoring performance in NHL history. He scored five goals in a game in five different ways: an even-strength goal, a power-play goal, a shorthanded goal, a penalty shot goal and an empty-net goal. No one had ever done that before and no one has yet done it since. With Lemieux picking up 44 points in 23 games to capture the Conn Smythe Trophy as the playoffs' top performer, Pittsburgh won its first Stanley Cup with a six-game victory over Minnesota. The next season, Lemieux repeated as the Smythe winner and Pittsburgh once again cheered a championship season, winning 11 games in a row to end the playoffs and claim the Stanley Cup.

Though now at the top of the game, Lemieux was known as a spectacular but enigmatic player with a reticent personality and a dislike for the spotlight that felt very uncomfortable for him. Serious back problems and his struggle with Hodgkin's disease combined to prevent him from ever playing a full season. His battle with this form of cancer included radiation treatments in 1992–93, when he missed a full month midway through the season before returning to lead the league again in scoring. He sat out 62 games in 1993–94 and the entire 1994–95 season because of health problems. In fact, Lemieux played in only 745 games throughout his entire career, which his fans point out was equivalent to only about nine and a half full seasons. The fact that he was able to do all he did in such a short period added weight to the "what if" arguments about his being the greatest of all time.

Other players who had missed games

Lemieux, Mario
C, 6′4″, 225 lbs, b: Montreal, Que., 10/5/1965

Season	Club, League	Regular Season					Playoffs				
		GP	G	A	Pts	PIM	GP	G	A	Pts	PIM
1984–85	Pittsburgh Penguins, NHL	73	43	57	100	54					
WEC–85	Canada	9	4	6	10	2					
1985–86	Pittsburgh Penguins, NHL	79	48	93	141	43					
1986–87	Pittsburgh Penguins, NHL	63	54	53	107	57					
RV'87	NHL All-Stars	2	0	3	3	0					
CCup–87	Canada	9	11	7	18	8					
1987–88	Pittsburgh Penguins, NHL	77	70	98	168	92					
1988–89	Pittsburgh Penguins, NHL	76	85	114	199	100	11	12	7	19	16
1989–90	Pittsburgh Penguins, NHL	59	45	78	123	78					
1990–91	Pittsburgh Penguins, NHL	26	19	26	45	30	23	16	28	44	16
1991–92	Pittsburgh Penguins, NHL	64	44	87	131	94	15	16	18	34	2
1992–93	Pittsburgh Penguins, NHL	60	69	91	160	38	11	8	10	18	10
1993–94	Pittsburgh Penguins, NHL	22	17	20	37	32	6	4	3	7	2
1995–96	Pittsburgh Penguins, NHL	70	69	92	161	54	18	11	16	27	33
1996–97	Pittsburgh Penguins, NHL	76	50	72	122	65	5	3	3	6	4
2000–01	Pittsburgh Penguins, NHL	43	35	41	76	18	18	6	11	17	4
2001–02	Pittsburgh Penguins, NHL	24	6	25	31	14					
OWG–02	Canada	5	2	4	6	0					
	NHL Totals	812	654	947	1601	769					
	OWG/WEC/RV'87/CCup Totals	25	17	20	37	10					

NHL First All-Star Team (1988, 1989, 1993, 1996, 1997)
NHL Second All-Star Team (1986, 1987, 1992)
Won Hart Trophy (1988, 1993, 1996)
Won Art Ross Trophy (1988, 1989, 1992, 1993, 1996, 1997)
Won Conn Smythe Trophy (1991, 1992)
Won Calder Trophy (1985)
Won Lester B. Pearson Award (1986, 1988, 1993, 1996)
Won Bill Masterton Trophy (1993)
Won Stanley Cup (1991, 1992)
Won OWG (2002)

through injury were incredulous that the 6′4″, 210-pound Lemieux could be away from the game for so long and then return to be the same dominating player as ever. He won the Hart and the Art Ross in 1995–96 after sitting out a full year. "That's what makes Mario the great player that he is," said Penguins veteran Bryan Trottier. "All I know is that having Mario on the ice at 50% is better than most players playing at 100%." Teammate Kevin Stevens agreed. "I don't know how he does it," said Stevens. "How do you keep your hands sharp? Your legs? If I miss a day or two of practice, it takes me a week or two just to get back. But Mario is scary out there. It's ridiculous how far ahead he is of everyone else."

His battles with severe back injuries and Hodgkin's disease may well have kept Mario Lemieux (number 66) from breaking many of Wayne Gretzky's scoring records.

Throughout his career, he was conscious of the fact that while Gretzky was viewed as a media darling, he was seen as an often sullen superstar without much if any of the Great One's public charm. Some felt that all the missed ice time was just an excuse, that he didn't work hard enough at the game, was too fond of parties and spent too much time at the golf course. Others faulted his reluctance to play in international competitions for Canada, including two World Junior Championships in the early 1980s, several World Championships when the Penguins finished out of the playoffs and two huge competitions near the end of his career, the 1996 World Cup and the 1998 Olympics in Nagano. Lemieux silenced many of those critics with his courageous return after battling cancer, surprising even himself by not retiring after the exhausting experience. Individually, Lemieux captured six Art Ross awards as the league's top scorer and won the Hart Trophy as the NHL's most valuable player three times. He won his final Art Ross Trophy in his last season.

For Pens fans and lovers of offensive hockey, the retirement of the Magnificent One in 1997 marked a sad time in the history of the game. About the only ones not shedding any tears, it seemed, were those fearful goalies. Lemieux did return to save the Penguin franchise again, though not with his offensive explosions on the ice. In the summer of 1999 the Pittsburgh team was mired in financial difficulty, facing bankruptcy and the possible transfer of the team. Lemieux, owed millions in deferred salary, stepped in as the head of an ownership group to buy the team and keep it in Pittsburgh, where he continued to live with his family. The cover of the 1999–2000 Penguins yearbook featured a uniformed Jagr—the heir to the scoring throne after his teammate's retirement—and a 33-year-old Lemieux in a suit and tie, looking very much the part of successful owner and chief executive officer of an NHL franchise.

Lemieux stunned the hockey world by returning to the game in December 2000, leading his team into the playoffs and accepting the role of captain for Canada's entry in the 2002 Salt Lake Olympics. He expressed his desire to play for at least three or four years, a decision welcomed by all hockey fans.

While Lemieux's notorious back problems seemed to be a thing of the past, the recurrence of hip problems began to be his number one health concern throughout the early part of the 2001–02 NHL season. The hip injury became so severe that Lemieux was forced to sit out the majority of Pittsburgh's games before Christmas and into 2002 and there were rumblings that he wouldn't be ready to play in Salt Lake City in February. He did play in the Olympics, however, albeit in tremendous pain. In the opening-game loss to Sweden, he was clearly not at his best, prompting a Swedish television announcer to say Lemieux "skated like an old tractor." He elevated his game for the all-important third game against the Czech Republic, turning in his best effort of the tournament and scoring a key goal in a 3–3 tie with the defending Olympic champs. Forced to sit out a game to rest his ailing hip, Lemieux still finished tied with Steve Yzerman for second in team scoring behind Joe Sakic. Although he estimates he was at no more than 50% capacity, it was enough to help Canada earn that elusive gold—and it was only after the Olympics were over that the public learned how bad Lemieux's hip had been. He took his doctor's advice and sat out the rest of the 2001–02 NHL season with the hope of returning healthy in 2002–03.

Patrick Roy

Patrick Roy was the first wave of the new breed of goalies that helped establish Quebec as the dominant training ground for that position. Confident and quirky, he developed a style that began with Tony Esposito and ended with Dominik Hasek, one that has seen him become the "winningest" goalie of all time.

Roy's career began with the Granby Bisons in Quebec junior, the worst team in a league that stressed offense. While this meant that his goals-against average and wins-to-losses ratio were awful, it meant equally that he was being peppered with 50 shots a game and developing greater skills than goalies on excellent teams who weren't getting a lot of work.

He was drafted 51st overall by the Montreal Canadiens, a team he had hated as a child growing up in a suburb of the home of the Habs' most dreaded foes, the Quebec Nordiques. In 1984–85, his final year with the Bisons, he was called up by the Canadiens, ostensibly to sit on the end of the bench for a few games and take in the action. But on February 23, 1985, he replaced starter Doug Soetaert, who was having a miserable game. The score was tied 4–4 to start the third period when Roy went in and the Habs won the game 6–4 to give him his first win in his first game after just 20 minutes of play.

After the game, Roy was sent to Sherbrooke to observe how the minor pro game was played. The junior Canadiens had two goalies and he didn't think he would play at all. But again fortune smiled on him and the one night he was the backup the starter had equipment troubles early in the game. He left, Patrick came in and played well and the starter never played another game the rest of the season. In the American Hockey League playoffs, he established what was to be his finest attribute—the ability to play under pressure. He led the team to Calder Cup victory, and the next fall he was at Montreal's training camp looking to join the famed Habs full-time.

In Sherbrooke, Roy met goalie coach Francois Allaire, who trained him to use the butterfly style of goaltending—knees together, feet apart—but to play a disciplined style so that when he went down, he was still covering the better part of the net. After all, Allaire reasoned, most goals are scored in the lower half of the net. To protect that half is to be a good goalie. "Nowadays, players don't have two or three seconds to shoot up top. That's why the bottom of the net is so important," Allaire argued.

In the 2000–2001 season, Patrick Roy passed Terry Sawchuk's total of 447 career wins and became the all-time shutout leader.

Patrick Roy (right) was drafted 51st overall by the Montreal Canadiens, a team he had hated as he grew up in a suburb of Quebec City.

Roy learned from Allaire in leaps and bounds. He took these experiences with him to the Forum every night and quickly became the number one man. In his rookie season of 1985–86, he played 47 games and became the starter when the playoffs arrived. By that point in the season, he couldn't be beaten. Montreal won an improbable Stanley Cup and Roy was named winner of the Conn Smythe Trophy for his outstanding play. "The more pressure there is, the more I like it," he said of his performance.

Roy's on-ice habits were both amusing and unusual. "I talk to my goalposts," he admitted. "It's a superstition. The forwards talk to each other. The defense is always close, but a goaltender is alone." Before each period, Roy would skate out to his blue line and look at the net, talk to the posts and get himself prepared for the game.

Roy's heroics in the 1986 playoffs were celebrated all over Montreal. He was dubbed "Saint Patrick" for his play, but now he was expected to keep up this high quality even though the team around him wasn't that good. In ensuing years he won 30 games with consistency, but it wasn't until 1993 that he was able to win another Cup for Montreal, with a team equally inferior to the one that won in 1986. And he won the Conn Smythe for his remarkable play on a team that finished with a regular-season record of 40–33–7.

Roy's life changed on December 2, 1995. At home to face the Red Wings, Montreal played the worst home game in franchise history, losing 12–1. Roy was kept in goal by coach Mario Tremblay for the first nine goals, and when he was finally pulled midway through the second period, he told team president Ronald Corey that he'd played his last game for the Habs. Corey was forced to trade him to Colorado and a new era in the Roy history book was underway. He was joining a top-flight team and within weeks he was holding the Stanley Cup in his new Avalanche colors.

At the end of 1999–2000, Roy played in his eighth All-Star Game. He has won the Vezina Trophy three times, in the 2000 playoffs he recorded three shutouts to become the all-time leader in that category, and early in the 2000–01 season he passed Terry Sawchuk in total career wins of 447, a number most fans thought was untouchable when Ukey retired. Early in 2001–02, he recorded his 200th win with the Avs and became the only goalie to

Roy, Patrick
G, 6´, 192 lbs, b: Quebec City, Que., 10/5/1965

Season	Club, League	Regular Season				Playoffs			
		GP	Mins	GA	Avg	GP	Mins	GA	Avg
1984–85	Montreal Canadiens, NHL	1	20	0	0.00				
	Sherbrooke Canadiens, AHL	1	60	4	4.00	13	769	37	2.89
1985–86	Montreal Canadiens, NHL	47	2651	148	3.35	20	1218	39	1.92
1986–87	Montreal Canadiens, NHL	46	2686	131	2.93	6	330	22	4.00
1987–88	Montreal Canadiens, NHL	45	2586	125	2.90	8	430	24	3.35
1988–89	Montreal Canadiens, NHL	48	2744	113	2.47	19	1206	42	2.09
1989–90	Montreal Canadiens, NHL	54	3173	134	2.53	11	641	26	2.43
1990–91	Montreal Canadiens, NHL	48	2835	128	2.71	13	785	40	3.06
1991–92	Montreal Canadiens, NHL	67	3935	155	2.36	11	686	30	2.62
1992–93	Montreal Canadiens, NHL	62	3595	192	3.20	20	1293	46	2.13
1993–94	Montreal Canadiens, NHL	68	3867	161	2.50	6	375	16	2.56
1994–95	Montreal Canadiens, NHL	43	2566	127	2.97				
1995–96	Montreal Canadiens, NHL	22	1260	62	2.95				
	Colorado Avalanche, NHL	39	2305	103	2.68	22	1454	51	2.10
1996–97	Colorado Avalanche, NHL	62	3698	143	2.32	17	1034	38	2.21
1997–98	Colorado Avalanche, NHL	65	3835	153	2.39	7	430	18	2.51
OWG–98	Canada	6	369	9	1.46				
1998–99	Colorado Avalanche, NHL	61	3648	139	2.29	19	1173	52	2.66
1999–00	Colorado Avalanche, NHL	63	3704	141	2.28	17	1039	31	1.79
2000–01	Colorado Avalanche, NHL	62	3585	132	2.21	23	1451	41	1.70
2001–02	Colorado Avalanche, NHL	63	3773	122	1.94				
	NHL Totals	966	56485	2409	2.56				
	OWG Totals	6	369	9	1.46				

NHL First All-Star Team (1989, 1990, 1992)
NHL Second All-Star Team (1988, 1991)
Won Vezina Trophy (1989, 1990, 1992)
Won Conn Smythe Trophy (1986, 1993)
Won William M. Jennings Trophy (1987, 1988, 1989, 1992)
Won Stanley Cup (1986, 1993, 1996)

have 200 with two different teams. And in the 2001 playoffs, Roy was spectacular, leading the Avs to their second Stanley Cup championship in five years and defeating the defending champion New Jersey Devils in a tough seven-game battle. It had been widely anticipated Roy would be named as the starting goaltender for Team Canada at the 2002 Winter Olympics, as he had been for the Nagano Games in 1998, but when Canadian hockey executives selected their initial eight members to the team, Roy wasn't among them.

A sure Hall of Famer, Roy's numbers are unmatched by any goalie in the history of the game.

Brett *Hull*

When Brett Hull of the Dallas Stars became the 53rd player in the NHL to score 1,000 points on November 14, 1998, it was something of an anticlimax. The milestone came on an assist into an empty net. Hull's 999th point the night before, though, was more typical of his superb style and skill. Hull broke in alone on Bruins goalie Byron Dafoe, waited until Dafoe went down and then rolled the puck in from the goal line. "I had a solid foot to go," said Hull with a laugh when he described the short shot.

Bobby and Brett Hull (front) became the only father and son combo in NHL history to score 1,000 points each.

As the son of "the Golden Jet," Bobby Hull, Brett came into the game with the disadvantage of the pressure a famous name can bring, a pressure he has shrugged off easily. After his 1,000th point, Brett and Bobby became the only father and son combo in NHL history to each score 1,000 points. The younger Hull was quick to point out that things had changed plenty since his dad's playing days. "I told him that if I played when he did, I would have done this three years earlier," Brett quipped. But he was equally adamant about the respect he had for his father's abilities. "Maybe one day I will be equal to my dad, but never better," he said. "I will always be Bobby's son."

Brett Hull would be the first to admit that he could never fill his father's shoes—or skates. "If you are going to be compared with someone, it is nice it's to one of the greatest players to play the game," Hull said. "If you are going to be in someone's shadow, that's not a bad one to have. I'm proud of who I am, of who my father is. But at the same time, yes, it would be nice if people recognized me for what I did." Even if his 1,000 mark wasn't a unique feat in the Hull family, it did bring the son up to the same level of recognition.

But this wasn't the first time the younger Hull hit a scoring milestone. Playing with the St. Louis Blues nine years earlier, he scored 50 goals in 49 games. He became just the fifth player in NHL history to do the 50/50-in a tie as the third-fastest ever-an achievement that put Hull in an elite group of superstar players alongside Wayne Gretzky, Maurice Richard, Mike Bossy and Mario Lemieux.

Despite his father's impressive career, Brett wasn't always seen as someone destined for hockey stardom. He himself admitted he was a bit lazy. "I'll take a couch and a television any day," he once said. After his parents' bitter divorce in 1979, Hull lived with his mother and four siblings. He began playing junior hockey in Penticton in the British Columbia Junior Hockey League. This was only a tier two junior team, one level below major junior hockey. In those days, Hull weighed 220 pounds and was nicknamed "Pickle." "I can't think of one food I don't like," he confessed. "Not a one!" Despite his size, he scored 105 goals in 56 games and won a scholarship to the University of

Goalie Ron Hextall once summed up the opposition's take on Brett Hull: "When he comes in on the wing, he's got an awful lot of speed. If you give him a hole, Hull hits it."

Minnesota at Duluth. As Brett once admitted, "I am the epitome of a late bloomer."

In 1984 the Calgary Flames drafted Hull 117th overall after just two years in college and he spent the next couple of seasons splitting his playing time between Calgary and their minor-league team in Moncton. On his first shift in his first game with the Flames, Hull took a pass in front of the net and slammed a shot off the goal post: "He may not skate like Bobby," said Flames general manager Cliff Fletcher, "but he sure shoots like him."

In 1988 the Flames traded him to St. Louis. "For us, it was the best thing that ever happened," said Blues general manager Ron Caron. With the way his game suddenly picked up, it was a positive career move for Hull, too. "In Calgary I didn't feel like part of the team, even when I was playing," said Brett, who'd sat out more than a dozen games in his last year with the Flames. In his first season with St Louis, he scored 41 goals. His explanation of how he did it was typical Brett: "I take myself out of the play to get open," he explains. "Sometimes when we are going into the other team's zone, I'm going out of their zone." And Hull praised his coach, former NHL star Brian Sutter, for motivating him to improve his performance. "He told me I could be better than a 40-goal scorer. He changed my work ethic, showed a lot of confidence in me."

In 1990–91, Hull scored more than 70 goals for the second consecutive season. It was another career milestone as he joined the ranks of Lemieux and Gretzky and became only the third player in the history of the NHL to achieve this feat. The following season, Hull returned for a 70-goal season and was offered a four-year, $1.7-million contract with St Louis. "I don't know if it was pressure," he said, "but I felt compelled to prove people wrong, those who said the Blues made a mistake giving a player that much money."

In 1998 Hull signed with the Dallas Stars. He had said he wanted to play for the Chicago Blackhawks, his father's team, but the Stars offered him a three-year, $17-million dollar contract—an offer he just couldn't refuse. Despite the big money, the move to the Stars took some pressure off Hull. "It's a little different for him here. He's more of a support player now," said Dallas coach Ken Hitchcock. "He is going to support the captain and that is a different role than he has had in the past." And

Hull, Brett
RW, 5′10″, 201 lbs, b: Belleville, Ont., 8/9/1964

Season	Club, League	Regular Season					Playoffs				
		GP	G	A	Pts	PIM	GP	G	A	Pts	PIM
1984–85	University of Minnesota–Duluth, WCHA	48	32	28	60	24					
1985–86	University of Minnesota–Duluth, WCHA	42	52	32	84	46					
WEC–86	USA	10	7	4	11	18					
1985–86	Calgary Flames, NHL						2	0	0	0	0
1986–87	Calgary Flames, NHL	5	1	0	1	0	4	2	1	3	0
	Moncton Golden Flames, AHL	67	50	42	92	16	3	2	2	4	2
1987–88	Calgary Flames, NHL	52	26	24	50	12					
	St. Louis Blues, NHL	13	6	8	14	4	10	7	2	9	4
1988–89	St. Louis Blues, NHL	78	41	43	84	33	10	5	5	10	6
1989–90	St. Louis Blues, NHL	80	72	41	113	24	12	13	8	21	17
1990–91	St. Louis Blues, NHL	78	86	45	131	22	13	11	8	19	4
CCup–91	USA	8	2	7	9	0					
1991–92	St. Louis Blues, NHL	73	70	39	109	48	6	4	4	8	4
1992–93	St. Louis Blues, NHL	80	54	47	101	41	11	8	5	13	2
1993–94	St. Louis Blues, NHL	81	57	40	97	38	4	2	1	3	0
1994–95	St. Louis Blues, NHL	48	29	21	50	10	7	6	2	8	0
1995–96	St. Louis Blues, NHL	70	43	40	83	30	13	6	5	11	10
WCup–96	USA	7	7	4	11	4					
1996–97	St. Louis Blues, NHL	77	42	40	82	10	6	2	7	9	2
1997–98	St. Louis Blues, NHL	66	27	45	72	26	10	3	3	6	2
OWG–98	USA	4	2	1	3	0					
1998–99	Dallas Stars, NHL	60	32	26	58	30	*	*	*	*	*
1999–00	Dallas Stars, NHL	79	24	35	59	43	23	11	13	24	4
2000–01	Dallas Stars, NHL	79	39	40	79	18	10	2	5	7	6
2000–02	Detroit Red Wings, NHL	82	30	33	63	35					
OWG–02	USA	6	3	5	8	6					
	NHL Totals	1101	679	567	1246	424					
	OWG/WEC/CCup/WCup Totals	35	21	21	42	28					

NHL First All-Star Team (1990, 1991, 1992)
Won Hart Trophy (1991)
Won Lady Byng Trophy (1990)
Won Lester B. Pearson Award (1991)
Won Stanley Cup (1999)
Won WCup (1996)

the trade worked out in favor of Dallas as well. A perennially strong team, the Stars had never played quite as well on the ice as their name suggested. When Hull joined their ranks, they went on to win the Stanley Cup in 1998–99.

Early in the 1999–2000 season, Hull scored his 600th goal, making himself and his dad the first and only father and son combination to reach that remarkable plateau, and in the summer of 2001, he signed as a free agent with Detroit on a team loaded with veterans. In February 2002, Hull joined the U.S. Olympic team and was a key performer throughout the Salt Lake City Games, helping his adopted homeland to a silver medal and losing only to Canada, where he had been born.

Long-time Flyers goalie Ron Hextall once summed up the opposition's take on Hull: "When he comes in on the wing, he's got an awful lot of speed. If you give him a hole, he hits it." And for his part, Hull has always had a pretty clear idea of what he's been paid to do. Possessed of a mean slap-shot and a solid frame, Hull has had a decided knack for finding the back of the net throughout his career. "I always feel like I have to score goals," Hull explains. "That is what keeps me going."

Jyrki Lumme

Jyrki Lumme is a rugged defenseman who is tough enough to take the hits without retaliating to protect the puck and carry it into the attack—his forte. His NHL career of 788 games and counting has been uprooted by two trades. After a couple of seasons with the Montreal Canadiens, who drafted him in 1986, he was let go to the Vancouver Canucks for as little as a second-round draft choice. In Vancouver, he became a key member of the defense corps over the next nine years and he left as the clubs all-time leading goal scorer among defensemen. Lumme's third stop in the NHL was with the Phoenix Coyotes in the summer of 1998 as a free agent.

While playing for Finland internationally, Lumme captured the nation's first-ever hockey medal, the 1988 Olympic silver at Calgary.

Lumme hails from Tampere in Finland and the nation's dominant club, Ilves, which has more championship titles than any other club in the country. When Lumme joined the corresponding club in North America in 1988, it was a historical move in several ways, for he was the first-ever Finn to don the legendary jersey of the Flying Frenchmen. The club's previous connection with Finland had been via six-time Stanley Cup winner Ralph Backstrom, who had ethnic origins in Vaasa in Finland but was born in Kirkland Lake, Ontario.

The unassuming Lumme was more than surprised in 1986 when he was informed in a telephone call that Montreal had drafted him. He couldn't imagine what for. Some athletes shine from childhood onwards and everybody knows that the kid is a future star. Others have to go a longer way via hard work and determination. The latter scenario was the early history of Lumme.

The measure of players in Finland is when they come to the attention of junior national team selectors at the age of 15 to be part of the under-16 team the following season. And then, if they have they right attitude, the necessary skills and perseverance, they go through the intermediate teams up to the under-20 team and the World Junior Championships. Lumme gradually made the grade, and following the 1986 World Junior Championships in Hamilton, Ontario, he was the only player on the Finnish team to become a full-fledged professional in the NHL.

In Finland, Lumme's career started as a nine-year-old in the Viinikka suburban team in the Ilves

In nine years in Vancouver, Jyrki Lumme (center) became the clubs all-time leading goal scorer among defensemen but signed with the Phoenix Coyotes in the summer of 1998 as a free agent.

system. His ice time reached respectability only when he joined crosstown Junior B team KooVee Tampere. He went on to play two seasons for the club, and since KooVee had an agreement with Ilves, he was called to the latter team's training camp in the fall of 1986. He made the team but saw little or no action during this first campaign in the SM-Liiga. On his first shift, after only a few seconds, the red light went on in the Ilves end, setting the pace for much of that year.

Lumme is a very balanced person on the ice as well as off and that helped him overcome adversity. Over the next two seasons, he gradually established himself as the top offensive defenseman with the Ilves club. The second of those two years was a roller coaster ride for him as well as for Ilves. The team captured the regular-season crown, only to be ousted by Lukko Rauma in the semifinals in three straight games. Lumme, who saw a lot of action in the series, was on the ice for nine goals out of 14, which didn't make for a great farewell as these were to be his last games in Finland until the NHL lockout. Primed by a couple of other Ilves players with knowledge of the pros—Risto Siltanen and Raimo Helminen—he set off on his Canadian adventure as a 22-year-old.

Again he had a slow start. A day before the start of the season, he was the last blueliner dropped and sent to Sherbrooke in the American Hockey League. But the Canadiens recalled him in November and his career took off, though it wasn't easy at the beginning. The smaller NHL rink and Montreal's style of play, which was much more defensive than at Ilves, caused some problems before he managed to adjust.

While playing for Finland internationally, Lumme captured the nation's first-ever hockey medal, the 1988 Olympic silver at Calgary. His best memories with the national team came 10 years later at the 1998 Olympics at Nagano as he and his team stole the bronze medal from the Canadians. At St. Petersburg, Russia, in 2000, he again stymied the Canadians in a battle for the bronze medal. That was his third but only medal from five World Championship tournaments. He also has appearances in a Canada Cup and a World Cup on his merit list.

While the NHL has provided him with many thrilling moments over the years, his

Lumme, Jyrki
D, 6'1", 205 lbs, b: Tampere, Finland, 7/16/1966

Season	Club, League	Regular Season					Playoffs				
		GP	G	A	Pts	PIM	GP	G	A	Pts	PIM
1984–85	KooVee, Finland	30	6	4	10	44					
1985–86	Ilves, Finland	31	1	4	5	4					
1986–87	Ilves, Finland	43	12	12	24	52	4	0	1	1	2
1987–88	Ilves, Finland	43	8	22	30	75					
OWG–88	Finland	6	0	1	1	2					
1988–89	Montreal Canadiens, NHL	21	1	3	4	10					
	Sherbrooke Canadiens, AHL	26	4	11	15	10	6	1	3	4	4
1989–90	Montreal Canadiens, NHL	54	1	19	20	41					
	Vancouver Canucks, NHL	11	3	7	10	8					
WEC–90	Finland	10	3	4	7	6					
1990–91	Vancouver Canucks, NHL	80	5	27	32	59	6	2	3	5	0
WEC–91	Finland	10	0	7	7	12					
CCup–91	Finland	6	0	2	2	8					
1991–92	Vancouver Canucks, NHL	75	12	32	44	65	13	2	3	5	4
1992–93	Vancouver Canucks, NHL	74	8	36	44	55	12	0	5	5	6
1993–94	Vancouver Canucks, NHL	83	13	42	55	50	24	2	11	13	16
1994–95	Ilves, Finland	12	4	4	8	24					
	Vancouver Canucks, NHL	36	5	12	17	26	11	2	6	8	8
1995–96	Vancouver Canucks, NHL	80	17	37	54	50	6	1	3	4	2
WC–96	Finland	1	0	0	0	0					
WCup–96	Finland	4	2	1	3	4					
1996–97	Vancouver Canucks, NHL	66	11	24	35	32					
WC–97	Finland	8	0	3	3	4					
997–98	Vancouver Canucks, NHL	74	9	21	30	34					
OWG–98	Finland	6	1	0	1	16					
1998–99	Phoenix Coyotes, NHL	60	7	21	28	34	7	0	1	1	6
1999–00	Phoenix Coyotes, NHL	74	8	32	40	44	5	0	1	1	2
WC–00	Finland	9	2	3	5	4					
1999–01	Phoenix Coyotes, NHL	58	4	21	25	44					
2001–02	Dallas-Toronto, NHL	66	4	9	13	44					
OWG–02	Finland	4	0	1	1	0					
	Finland Totals	159	31	46	77	199	4	0	1	1	2
	NHL Totals	912	108	343	451	574					
	OWG/WEC/WC/CCup/WCup Totals	64	8	22	30	56					

success has been limited to Vancouver's Western Conference win in 1994 and the subsequent playoff finals against the New York Rangers, when the Canucks were defeated in the seventh game.

Despite his ruggedness, he still carries the nickname "Sonja"—a famous pop singer with the same surname, no relation to Jyrki—his teammates gave him as a joke. Like so many others, it stuck.

Lumme was a member of the Phoenix Coyotes for three years, from 1999 to 2001, before joining the Dallas Stars in 2001–02. Early in the season he was released by the Stars and picked up on waivers by the Toronto Maple Leafs general manager Pat Quinn, who had held Lumme in high regard since Lumme had played for him in Vancouver in the early to mid-1990s. The Maple Leafs defensive system under Quinn was far more to Lumme's liking, and he once again began to perform like he had during his glory days with the Canucks.

Dmitri Mironov

In the summer of 1998, Dmitri Mironov brought the Stanley Cup to Toronto and invited his friends. The small street he lived on was packed with cars. One of the latecomers was confronted by a police officer who was writing out parking tickets. The friend explained the situation and pointed to Dmitri's house. The officer was invited into Dmitri's home, where he had his picture taken standing beside the Cup and the host. And that is the magic of the Stanley Cup, especially for a young man who gave his whole life to hockey and suddenly found himself holding the coveted trophy over his head for the first time.

Dmitri Mironov made his contribution to NHL history with his hard shot.

Mironov's preschool childhood was spent in the swimming pool of a communal apartment. He could have become a professional swimmer, but one day his father received a notice from his place of work that they were entitled to a new apartment all their own. Unfortunately, there was no pool in the new housing district and it would have been a long trek across the entire city several times a week. His father came across an ad announcing enrollment for the Central Red Army club hockey school. It was also far away, but training sessions were only once or twice a week. Selection was strict. Out of 100 applicants, only 30 were selected. But they included Dmitri, and that was the beginning of Mironov's hockey career. He was seven years old.

Dmitri liked to practise. Every boy dreamed of putting on a jersey of the famous CSKA club. And he had a good coach. They had to train outdoors with temperatures often well below freezing, but four years later they made up a team. Some boys became forwards, but Dmitri played defense. He didn't stand out among his teammates, as some of the boys were better on skates. But Mironov was the only one on that team destined to play in the NHL.

At the age of 14, Dmitri found he was distracted and he began to skip workouts. The club stopped sending him out on the ice, but he didn't want to play anyway and even considered forgetting all about hockey. But his father and, oddly enough, his younger brother set him straight. His father would go out looking for him and take him out of the company of his friends while his brother, Boris, who was enrolled with the CSKA club, would take him to the stadium. The training sessions were at different times, so at first Boris would watch Dmitri's workout and later his father would take over. In such a situation, Dmitri had to set a good example. Although they play on different teams in the NHL and at times against each other, the brothers are still close.

After finishing secondary school, Dmitri was drafted into the army. He found himself in the CSKA farm club with SKA MVO, which at that time was in the second league. Dmitri then realized that the Army club had actually taught him something about hockey. He ended his first season as the best defenseman on his team and moved up to the first league with the team, which was very young but talented and was able to outplay seasoned opponents by a wide scoring margin. At 18, Mironov proudly received his first paycheck of 180 rubles, which he gave to his parents.

The following year SKA MVO repeated their success in the first league and Mironov was once again out on top in his club. But right after the New Year he was called up by Central Red Army. Mironov was astounded and somewhat afraid. The Army squad was practically the national team. They had the best eight defensemen in their lineup and another two were on their way. It turned out that Dmitri was the 11th defenseman. He phoned his father to share the news and in reply he heard: "Well, come on. We'll go to meet Viktor Tikhonov."

In the beginning, Mironov spent most of his time on the bench. It later became known that Viktor Tikhonov considered Mironov a pretty good defenseman but wanted to find a stronger player for CSKA. Krylja Sovetov (Soviet Wings) needed experienced players and Dmitri agreed to the transfer, knowing he would get a lot more playing time. Everything fell into place and he ended the season as one of the top defensemen. Moreover, he was invited to return to the Army club. There were also invitations to join the national team. Mironov made his debut at the Izvestia Cup tournament in 1991. That was followed by the World Championships in Finland, where he made the second All-Star team. It was at that championship that Mironov was spotted by scouts and put on the draft list of the Toronto Maple Leafs.

In 1992 the Russians sent a very young team to the Olympics in France. At 25, Mironov was the most experienced defenseman. The press wrote—not without irony—that, "The Russians have brought some kind of kindergarten to the Olympics!" But they won the ice hockey tournament, beating the Eric Lindros-led Team Canada in the final. Two-thirds of the players from that Russian team are now in the NHL.

Back in Moscow, after a game against Spartak Moscow in which he scored a hat-trick, he was approached by a scout from the Leafs. The scout patted him on the shoulder and said: "It's been a long time since I've seen a defenseman score three goals in one game. We need defensemen like that." Then he gave Mironov a ticket to Toronto.

The NHL season was coming to an end and

Mironov, Dmitri
D, 6´3˝, 215 lbs, b: Moscow, USSR, 12/25/1965

Season	Club, League	Regular Season					Playoffs				
		GP	G	A	Pts	PIM	GP	G	A	Pts	PIM
1985–86	CSKA, USSR	9	0	1	1	8					
1986–87	CSKA, USSR	20	1	3	4	10					
1987–88	Krylja Sovetov, USSR	44	12	6	18	14					
1988–89	Krylja Sovetov, USSR	44	5	6	11	44					
1989–90	Krylja Sovetov, USSR	45	4	11	15	34					
1990–91	Krylja Sovetov, USSR	45	16	12	28	22					
WEC–91	USSR	10	4	2	6	6					
CCup–91	USSR	5	0	1	1	4					
1991–92	Krylja Sovetov, USSR	35	15	16	31	62					
OWG–92	Russia	8	3	1	4	6					
WC–92	Russia	6	1	1	2	2					
1991–92	Toronto Maple Leafs, NHL	7	1	0	1	0					
1992–93	Toronto Maple Leafs, NHL	59	7	24	31	40	14	1	2	3	2
1993–94	Toronto Maple Leafs, NHL	76	9	27	36	78	18	6	9	15	6
1994–95	Toronto Maple Leafs, NHL	33	5	12	17	28	6	2	1	3	2
1995–96	Pittsburgh Penguins, NHL	72	3	31	34	88	15	0	1	1	10
1996–97	Pittsburgh Penguins, NHL	15	1	5	6	24					
	Anaheim Mighty Ducks, NHL	62	12	34	46	77	11	1	10	11	10
1997–98	Anaheim Mighty Ducks, NHL	66	6	30	36	115					
OWG–98	Russia	6	0	3	3	0					
1997–98	Detroit Red Wings, NHL	11	2	5	7	4	7	0	3	3	14
1998–99	Washington Capitals, NHL	46	2	14	16	80					
1999–00	Washington Capitals, NHL	73	3	19	22	28	4	0	0	0	4
WC–00	Russia	6	0	0	0	4					
2000–01	Washington Capitals, NHL	36	3	5	8	6					
	USSR/Russia Totals	242	53	55	108	194					
	NHL Totals	556	54	206	260	568					
	OWG/WEC/WC/CCup Totals	41	8	8	16	22					

Won OWG (1992)
Won Stanley Cup (1998)
USSR Champion (1987)

the trip to Toronto was more to get acquainted. He played seven games, scored one goal and got a broken nose. His real debut came the next year. He had to get used to the tight game schedule, a completely new style of playing and constant changes of partners. Toronto head coach Pat Burns even tried Mironov out as a forward. It was the best season for the Maple Leafs in the 1990s.

After two poor conference finals in a row, the Leafs began a string of trades. Mironov was sent to the Pittsburgh Penguins in exchange for defenseman Larry Murphy. In Pittsburgh, Mironov's game didn't click, so Dmitri was careful in his next trade. The Anaheim Mighty Ducks were a very young team, only three years into their franchise. Before the season started, bookmakers were giving them 150–1 odds. But Mironov came to the team with one of the best young coaches in the NHL, Ron Wilson, and upcoming stars Paul Kariya and Teemu Selanne. It could be said that the years with Anaheim were the best in Mironov's NHL career. And the power-play unit led by Mironov, Kariya and Selanne was considered one of the best in the league. Dmitri also took part in the silver medal win by Russia at the Olympic tournament in Nagano. Then came his most surprising trade of all.

In 1997–98, Dmitri Mironov (left) came to the Detroit Red Wings near the end of the regular season, played three months with them and won the Stanley Cup.

He came to the Detroit Red Wings near the end of the regular season, played only three months for the team and won the Stanley Cup. And he was playing again with his former teammates—Viacheslav Fetisov, Igor Larionov and Sergei Fedorov. The parade of champions was held in Detroit, but Mironov's contract expired and for some reason the new Red Wings management was in no hurry to renew it. He began to search for a new club and settled on the Washington Capitals, whose coach, Ron Wilson, wanted Mironov back in his lineup.

Mironov's statistics prove that he is a classy attacking defenseman. He has played with many superstars in the league—Doug Gilmour, Mario Lemieux, Jaromir Jagr, Paul Kariya, Teemu Selanne, Steve Yzerman and Peter Bondra. He has learned something from each one of them, but he has also made his own contribution to the history of the NHL. He scored six goals for the Leafs in the playoffs and had five assists in a game while with Anaheim—records that had never been achieved by a defenseman in the history of the two clubs.

Mironov's NHL career ended as a member of the Washington Capitals following the 2000–01 season. He played 10 NHL seasons with five teams, dressing for 556 regular-season games and scoring 54 goals and 260 points.

Teppo Numminen

Finnish Phoenix Coyotes defenseman and assistant captain Teppo Numminen has gained a well-earned reputation as the "iron man" of the NHL. When Philadelphia center Rod Brind'Amour missed his team's home opener of the 1999–2000 season, Numminen became the league's new leader in consecutive games played, not having missed once since December 15, 1995. He'd compiled three consecutive seasons without missing a game and 1998–99 was the fifth time in his NHL career that he'd gone all season without missing one.

Finnish defenseman Teppo Numminen has a well-earned reputation as the "iron man" of the NHL.

But the "iron man" streak is only one aspect of Numminen's game. He also played in the 1999 All-Star Game, starting on the World Team, and led the entire Phoenix defensive corps in goals, assists and points. Numminen, who has spent his entire NHL career with the Winnipeg/Phoenix franchise, entered the league in 1988 after spending several seasons with the Finnish league team Tappara. The Jets selected him in the second round and 29th overall in the 1986 NHL Entry Draft and he eventually broke the team record for career points by a defenseman.

The typically modest Finn has been quick to deflect the attention away from himself after becoming the league's "iron man," though, preferring instead to give the credit to something more ephemeral—fate. "I've been lucky," he said. When pressed for an explanation for his longevity beyond simple good fortune, Numminen stuck to his guns. "No, I think it's just luck," he insisted. "You know, injuries are such a big part of the game. It's a physical game and anything can happen any night, so I look at it as I've been lucky. I've been so fortunate to be healthy this long time, so it's been good."

As well as establishing marks for consecutive games played, Numminen is a perennial leader on the Coyotes in the average minutes per game category. In other words, he not only plays in all of his team's games, he gets plenty of ice time as well. "You get used to it, so it's fun. You get to get into the game, and there are so many challenges for every game," he said. "You play so much and you don't want to let your team down, so it's a big challenge. Every game is an opportunity to play well and help your team."

As a kid growing up in Tampere, Numminen followed the exploits of his hometown team while casting an eye overseas to his NHL idol, Bobby Orr. But he never really entertained thoughts of a career in North America. "I think back then there weren't many Europeans [in the NHL], and so my career goal was just to play on the local team [Tappara] back in Finland," he recalled. "After that more players came, and when I was playing in the Finnish league, the [NHL] scouts came to talk to me, so I was thinking maybe I'll take a chance, see how it is."

The chance paid off, especially for Winnipeg/Phoenix, which has kept Numminen for his entire NHL career. As a long-time member of the franchise, Numminen has been able to compare life in two disparate cities,

Numminen, Teppo
D, 6´1˝, 190 lbs, b: Tampere, Finland, 7/3/1968

Season	Club, League	Regular Season					Playoffs				
		GP	G	A	Pts	PIM	GP	G	A	Pts	PIM
1985–86	Tappara, Finland	31	2	4	6	6	8	0	0	0	0
1986–87	Tappara, Finland	44	9	9	18	16	9	4	1	5	4
WEC–87	Finland	10	5	0	5	4					
CCup–87	Finland	4	1	0	1	2					
1987–88	Tappara, Finland	40	10	10	20	29	10	6	6	12	6
OWG–88	Finland	6	1	4	5	0					
1988–89	Winnipeg Jets, NHL	69	1	14	15	36					
1989–90	Winnipeg Jets, NHL	79	11	32	43	20	7	1	2	3	10
1990–91	Winnipeg Jets, NHL	80	8	25	33	28					
WEC–91	Finland	10	1	3	4	10					
CCup–91	Finland	6	1	1	2	2					
1991–92	Winnipeg Jets, NHL	80	5	34	39	32	7	0	0	0	0
1992–93	Winnipeg Jets, NHL	66	7	30	37	33	6	1	1	2	2
1993–94	Winnipeg Jets, NHL	57	5	18	23	28					
1994–95	TuTo, Finland	12	3	8	11	4					
	Winnipeg Jets, NHL	42	5	16	21	16					
1995–96	Winnipeg Jets, NHL	74	11	43	54	22	6	0	0	0	2
WC–96	Finland	1	0	1	1	0					
WCup–96	Finland	2	0	0	0	0					
1996–97	Phoenix Coyotes, NHL	82	2	25	27	28	7	3	3	6	0
WC–97	Finland	5	2	2	4	6					
1997–98	Phoenix Coyotes, NHL	82	11	40	51	30	1	0	0	0	0
OWG–98	Finland	6	1	1	2	2					
1998–99	Phoenix Coyotes, NHL	82	10	30	40	30	7	2	1	3	4
1999–00	Phoenix Coyotes, NHL	79	8	34	42	16	5	1	1	2	0
2000–01	Phoenix Coyotes, NHL	72	5	26	31	36					
2001–02	Phoenix Coyotes, NHL	76	13	35	48	20					
OWG–02	Finland	4	0	1	1	0					
	Finland Totals	127	24	31	55	55	27	10	7	17	10
	NHL Totals	1020	102	402	504	375					
	OWG/WEC/WC/CCup/WCup Totals	54	12	13	25	26					

Finland Champion (1986, 1987, 1988)

especially given their varied climate and geographical location. "Weather-wise it's a huge difference," he admitted. "Summer is here all the time and it's just perfect all year round, so weather-wise it's a good place." But when asked if he ever missed the snow—especially since he grew up in a northern clime as well as having lived in Winnipeg for the better part of eight years—Numminen admitted he did. "Yeah, especially around Christmastime. It's tough to get that Christmas spirit when you're used to having snow and that's the way you feel at Christmas," he answered. "It's different."

Teppo Numminen (right) hadn't missed a game in three consecutive NHL seasons and 1998–99 was the fifth time he went through the whole season without missing a game.

But as well as having played for the Jets/Coyotes in North America, Numminen also represented Finland in the 1988 Olympics. "Hockey is the biggest sport in Finland, so everybody follows it," he says. "It's a great honor to play for your national team. The Olympics was a great time, a great experience. I am really proud that I had a chance to play for the national team in Finland."

Numminen has also been active in hockey off the ice. In the mid-1990s, he and his brother and a friend bought a hockey stick company in Montreal. "It's something I was looking to get into, some kind of business," he explained. "I've been using this stick all my life, and the company was so close to me all my life, so when they wanted to sell it, me and my brother and our friend bought the company together. It's been a great experience learning the business side of hockey."

The 2002 Winter Olympics were the third Games for Numminen, who also participated in 1988 and 1998 for his native Finland. The country had high hopes of at least duplicating its bronze medal achievement attained in Nagano, but a loss to Canada in the playoff round in Salt Lake City ended any hopes of bringing home a medal.

Shayne Corson

A combination of scorer and enforcer, Shayne Corson often had positive adjectives such as "tough," "tenacious" and "talented" attached to his name during his career. However, as a victim of high expectations and problems off the ice, the power forward also had some troubled seasons in the National Hockey League. Still, Corson usually landed on his feet after adversity, acting as a leader for his teams in the NHL and on the international stage.

With his speed and playmaking ability, Shayne Corson could play all three forward postitions.

Corson was born in 1966 in Barrie, Ontario, where his father, Paul, owned a restaurant/bar called "Mom's Pantry." Like his son Shayne, Mr. Corson was known as a tough but friendly individual. Shayne, a standout player with Brantford in the Ontario Hockey League, spent some of his time off the ice helping his father clear the bar of burly troublemakers. "I always like to say, if there was trouble brewing and I needed help, I'd bring Paul and Shayne Corson," said Rick Curran, a close friend of the family and Shayne's agent. "You can bring whoever you want and however many you want."

The Montreal Canadiens selected Corson in the first round, eighth overall in the 1984 Entry Draft. He had 90 points in 54 games in 1984–85 with Hamilton in the OHL and won a gold medal with the Canadian team at the World Junior Championship. The next season he improved his offensive numbers, collecting 98 points, and maintained a physical style of play that saw him rack

Shayne Corson was a regular in the penalty box and often led Montreal in penalty minutes in his first few seasons.

up nearly four minutes of penalty time per game. At the World Junior Championship, he was named to the All-Star team and tied Joe Murphy for the tournament scoring title with 14 points in seven games.

Corson was big—6´1″ and just under 200 pounds—and with his speed and playmaking ability, he could play all three forward positions. He made his first appearance with Montreal in 1985–86 in three games and then joined the Habs as a regular the next season. He was a regular in the penalty box, too, often leading Montreal in penalty minutes over his first few seasons. At the same time, he also found his name more and more often on the scoresheet. By 1989–90, he was representing Montreal at the All-Star Game and leading the squad with 44 assists.

"On his best nights, Corson can be one of those guys who can be extremely valuable even when he doesn't pick up a goal or an assist," Montreal head coach Pat Burns said of his tough left winger. "I guess the best way to sum it up is that a right winger on another club wouldn't look forward to going out on the ice and skating opposite Corson. He'd know he was in for a tough night."

Though he was hard on opposing players, Corson nearly found himself on his way to Toronto in the middle of the 1990–91 season. Rumor had it that a trade for Leafs left wing Wendel Clark—which also involved Montreal's Claude Lemieux heading east—was scrubbed at the last minute over concerns about Clark's problem with injuries. Corson responded to the whispers with a strong playoff showing, leading the Canadiens in post-season scoring. However, there were more clouds on the horizon. His father, described by many as his best friend, was diagnosed with cancer and underwent surgery on his esophagus in February of 1992. A week before, Shayne had been involved in an incident at a Montreal bar—his second such altercation—when he stepped in to rescue two Habs rookies, Paul DiPietro and John LeClair. Corson was suspended for one game, though it would have been more if DiPietro and LeClair hadn't appealed the decision to Montreal management, stating that Corson had come to their defense. Corson's on-ice slump didn't escape notice, and in a poll of fans he was said to be overrated.

His days as a Canadien seemed to be numbered. Serge Savard, the team's general manager, warned the troubled winger that he wouldn't get another chance if his off-ice behavior didn't improve. That summer, with his father recovering, Corson was traded to Edmonton for Vincent Damphousse, who thus headed back to his home province of Quebec.

Corson was among the top scorers for the Oilers, but the team struggled during his three-season stay, finishing out of the playoffs for three consecutive years. Edmonton's poor showing gave Corson an opportunity to return to the international stage at the World

Season	Club, League	Regular Season					Playoffs				
		GP	G	A	Pts	Plm	GP	G	A	Pts	Plm
1985–86	Montreal Canadiens, NHL	3	0	0	0	2					
1986–87	Montreal Canadiens, NHL	55	12	11	23	144	17	6	5	11	30
1987–88	Montreal Canadiens, NHL	71	12	27	39	152	3	1	0	1	12
1988–89	Montreal Canadiens, NHL	80	26	24	50	193	21	4	5	9	65
1989–90	Montreal Canadiens, NHL	76	31	44	75	144	11	2	8	10	20
1990–91	Montreal Canadiens, NHL	71	23	24	47	138	13	9	6	15	36
CCup–91	Canada	8	0	5	5	12					
1991–92	Montreal Canadiens, NHL	64	17	36	53	118	10	2	5	7	15
1992–93	Edmonton Oilers, NHL	80	16	31	47	209					
WC–93	Canada	8	3	7	10	6					
1993–94	Edmonton Oilers, NHL	64	25	29	54	118					
WC–94	Canada	7	3	0	3	4					
1994–95	Edmonton Oilers, NHL	48	12	24	36	86					
1995–96	St. Louis Blues, NHL	77	18	28	46	192	13	8	6	14	22
1996–97	St. Louis Blues, NHL	11	2	1	3	24					
	Montreal Canadiens, NHL	47	6	15	21	80	5	1	0	1	4
1997–98	Montreal Canadiens, NHL	62	21	34	55	108	10	3	6	9	26
OWG–98	Canada	6	1	1	2	2					
1998–99	Montreal Canadiens, NHL	63	12	20	32	147					
1999–00	Montreal Canadiens, NHL	70	8	20	28	115					
2000–01	Toronto Maple Leafs, NHL	77	8	18	26	189	11	1	1	2	14
2001–02	Toronto Maple Leafs, NHL	74	12	21	33	120					
	NHL Totals	1093	261	407	668	2279	114	37	42	79	244
	OWG/WC/CCup Totals	29	7	13	20	24					

Corson, Shayne
LW, 6´1″, 200 lbs, b: Barrie, Ont., 8/13/1966

Won WC (1994)
Won CCup (1991)

Championships in 1993 and again in 1994—the year Canada won its first gold at the tournament since 1961. Corson was made captain of the Oilers in 1994 but clashed publicly with head coach George Burnett over the direction the squad was taking. Burnett was later fired because of the controversy and Corson was stripped of the captaincy. "I like Shayne, but he and Burnett were both wrong in what happened," said Oilers general manager Glen Sather. "It had to be fixed, so I fixed it."

When the St. Louis Blues offered a huge five-year deal to the tenacious winger in the summer of 1995, Sather wouldn't match it. The Oilers received two first-round picks but sent them back to the Blues in exchange for disgruntled goalie Curtis Joseph and tough winger Mike Grier. Mike Keenan, the St. Louis general manager, had long coveted Corson for his rugged two-way play. "I played for Mike before in the Canada Cup and I enjoyed it," Corson said. "I consider him one of the better coaches in the league. He's demanding, but if you go out and play the way he wants you to play, you'll play a lot." Corson was made the Blues' captain on October 23, 1995, but his stay in that role would once again be short-lived.

After only one year with the team—during which he led the Blues in penalty minutes—and 11 games into the 1996–97 season, Corson was on his way back to Montreal in a trade for Canadiens captain Pierre Turgeon. In 1997–98, Corson had one of his best overall seasons and was selected to the team that represented Canada at the 1998 Nagano Olympics. He was a role player on the team and earned praise for his all-out effort.

Corson and the Canadiens struggled in 1999–2000. Decimated by injuries, the Habs just missed the playoffs and once again trade rumors began to float around the veteran. Toronto, where Corson's brother-in-law, Darcy Tucker, was plying his trade, was continually mentioned as a possible destination. For his part, Corson, whose contract was for $4 million for the 2000–2001 season, offered to take a reduced salary to stay with the payroll-cutting Canadiens, the team that had shown renewed faith in him after cutting him loose during the tense early years of his career. Instead, he became a free agent and signed with the Toronto Maple Leafs in July 2000.

Since joining the Leafs, Corson has without a doubt been one of the team's clubhouse leaders and his willingness to defend the smaller players on the team has made everyone play with more confidence. In fact, since joining the Leafs, it's been most often Corson who has answered the call when a tussle with an opposing team's heavyweight became a necessity. In 2001 he went public with his long-standing battles with panic attacks in the hopes that his breaking the silence would help others with the same problem.

Philippe Bozon

As the first player trained in France to play in the NHL, Philippe Bozon had a tough road ahead. And having the demanding Mike Keenan as his coach didn't make life any easier. He played 144 NHL games with the St. Louis Blues between 1992 and 1994 and scored 16 goals before falling out of favor with Keenan in 1995 and returning to Europe to play for la Chaux-de-Fonds in Switzerland.

Bozon's father, Alain, who had been captain of France's national team, taught his son to play hockey, and at the age of 16, Philippe became the youngest player ever to wear the French tricolor.

At the age of 16, Philippe Bozon became the youngest player ever to wear the French tricolor.

Both Philippe and his father learned a lot from Paulin Bordeleau, a native of Noranda, Quebec, who had gone to France to play after spending three seasons in the NHL with the Vancouver Canucks. Philippe Bozon attended the training camp of the St. Jean Castors junior club in Quebec in the fall of the 1983–84 season, but didn't feel he was quite ready for major junior hockey in Canada and returned to France after three weeks. Jacques Tremblay, a Canadian coaching in France, had recommended him to Castors coach Yvan Gingras, who had traveled to France to see him play and invited him to camp.

Bozon was more than ready the following year, though, producing 32 goals and 82 points in 67 Quebec Major Junior Hockey League games. And in his second season with the Castors, he shot the lights out in the QMJHL with 59 goals and 111 points in only 65 games, earning himself a spot on the league's Second All-Star Team. The Blues invited him to their training camp the following year and signed him as a free agent after an exhibition game against Edmonton in the fall of 1985. He played some games with the Peoria Rivermen, a Blues farm club in the International Hockey League, but then returned to play in the French league until late in the 1991–92 season.

A native of Chamonix, France, site of the 1924 Olympics, the 5'11", 185-pound right wing has played in three Olympics—1988 in Canada, 1992 in France and 1998 in Japan. He missed the 1994 Games in Norway because he was playing with the Blues at the time, often on a line with superstar Brett Hull. Bozon produced three goals and five points in six games at his first Olympics in Calgary and played in the first Olympics game ever to have a shootout. France defeated Norway 8–6 in the battle for 11th place at the Father David Bauer Arena in Calgary.

Then, when the 1992 Olympics tournament was held in Meribel, France, just around the corner from his birthplace, he played a big role in getting his country through to the playoff round before losing to the United States. French fans cheered his every move.

Bozon, Philippe
LW, 5'10", 185 lbs, b: Chamonix, France, 11/30/1966

Season	Club, League	Regular Season					Playoffs				
		GP	G	A	Pts	PIM	GP	G	A	Pts	PIM
1985–86	Peoria Rivermen, IHL						5	1	0	1	0
1986–87	Peoria Rivermen, IHL	28	4	11	15	17					
1987–88	Mont-Blanc, France	18	11	15	26	34	10	15	6	21	6
OWG–88	France	6	3	2	5	0					
1988–89	Mont-Blanc, France	18	11	18	29	18	11	11	17	28	38
WEC–89 (B)	France	7	8	3	11	10					
1989–90	Grenoble, France	36	45	38	83	34	6	4	3	7	2
WEC–90 (B)	France	7	4	2	6	4					
1990–91	Grenoble, France	26	22	16	38	16	10	7	8	15	8
WEC–91 (B)	France	7	5	5	10	0					
1991–92	Chamonix, France	10	12	8	20	20					
OWG–92	France	7	3	2	5	4					
WC–92	France	3	1	1	2	4					
1991–92	St. Louis Blues, NHL	9	1	3	4	4	6	1	0	1	27
1992–93	St. Louis Blues, NHL	54	6	6	12	55	9	1	0	1	0
	Peoria Rivermen, IHL	4	3	2	5	2					
1993–94	St. Louis Blues, NHL	80	9	16	25	42	4	0	0	0	4
WC–94	France	3	0	0	0	2					
1994–95	Grenoble, France	21	8	20	28	38					
WC–95	France	6	2	3	5	0					
1994–95	St. Louis Blues, NHL	1	0	0	0	0					
1995–96	Chaux-de-Fonds, Switzerland	29	31	28	59	48	7	8	5	13	6
WC–96	France	7	4	2	6	4					
1996–97	Mannheim, Germany	22	11	7	18	6	9	6	9	15	2
WC–97	France	8	2	4	6	27					
1997–98	Mannheim, Germany	41	20	17	37	36	10	5	5	10	16
OWG–98	France	4	5	2	7	4					
WC–98	France	3	2	1	3	2					
1998–99	Mannheim, Germany	63	21	35	56	96					
WC–99	France	3	1	0	1	4					
1999–2000	Lugano, Switzerland	56	21	38	59	145	*	*	*	*	*
WC–2000	France	6	1	2	3	6					
	France Totals	129	109	115	224	160	37	37	34	71	54
	NHL Totals	144	16	25	41	101	19	2	0	2	31
	OWG/WC/WEC(B) Totals	77	41	29	70	71					

Named Best Forward at WEC-B (1991)
France Champion (1988, 1991)
Germany Champion (1997, 1998, 1999)

With the coaching of American Herb Brooks, architect of the American Miracle On Ice at Lake Placid in 1980, Bozon scored a natural hat-trick as France scored four goals in the third period and defeated Italy 5–1 in the 11th-place game at the 1998 Olympics in Nagano, Japan. He finished the Olympic tournament with five goals and seven points in just four matches. Only four players had more points, and three of those four were NHL stars Teemu Selanne and Saku Koivu (Finland) and Pavel Bure (Russia).

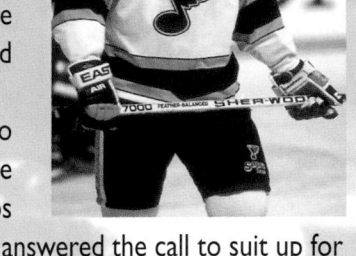

Philippe Bozon played 144 games with the St. Louis Blues between 1992 and 1994 before falling out of Mike Keenan's favor.

In recent years he teamed with countryman Christian Pouget to form the backbone of the Mannheim Eagles in Germany. The Mannheim club won three consecutive German championships between 1997 and 1999. Despite playing abroad, Bozon has always answered the call to suit up for France in international competitions, playing in seven World Pool A and three World Pool B Championships.

Bozon played his final year of professional hockey in 2000-01 as a member of Lugano in the Swiss League, retiring at season's end at the age of 34.

Mike Richter

Mike Richter is a clutch goalie, a winner who shines when games and championships are on the line. He has had success at the international level and in the NHL, winning the Stanley Cup with the New York Rangers in 1994 and almost single-handedly earning a World Cup for the United States two years later. He has been described as a wall, unflappable under pressure, and also as one of the classiest individuals in the game. When the U.S. chose its All-Time USA Hockey Team, Richter was the natural selection as the goaltender.

Mike Richter is a clutch goalie, a winner who shines when games and championships are on the line.

Richter had played his minor hockey in suburban Philadelphia, an area that had never produced an NHL player. He had good foot speed and quick hands, but what set Richter apart throughout his development and later in his professional career was his intelligence and work ethic. He kept notebooks on each performance and continually practised the fundamentals of his demanding position. Richter's involvement with the United States national program began when he played in the World Junior Championship in 1985. He was chosen for his standout play at Northland prep high school, a Lake Placid school known for its hockey teams.

Two weeks after his high school graduation, the New York Rangers chose Richter in the second round of the NHL amateur draft. He had decided to attend the University of Wisconsin instead of Harvard, partly because the athletic scholarship Wisconsin offered would ease the burden on his large family of four sisters and two brothers and his father, who had been ill. A few weeks into his first season at Wisconsin in 1985-86, Mike's father died. Richter attended the funeral but then redoubled his efforts on the rink on his return to school, finding in hockey a way to deal with his grief—and he was selected as the Western Collegiate Hockey Association's freshman of the year. He made the league's Second All-Star Team the following year and then left school to join the United States national team in preparation for the 1988 Olympics. He played for the team for a year and a half, including the 1987 World Championship, and was the starting goalie in four games for the U.S. at the Calgary Winter Olympics in February 1988.

Richter made his first appearance for the Rangers in the 1989 playoffs, but only after playing a full season with the Colorado Rangers in the International Hockey League and despite winning an award as the most outstanding player at the New York training camp in 1988–89. His one playoff game was followed in 1989–90 by a season split between the Flint Spirits of the IHL and the Rangers. Richter joined New York full-time in 1990–91 and shared the netminding duties with John Vanbiesbrouck. The two goalies made a formidable pair and neither was considered the default number one choice. In his second full year in the league, Richter was a finalist for the Vezina Trophy as the league's top goalie, and he posted his third consecutive winning season in 1991–92.

In 1992–93, Richter struggled, slumping to a 4.21 goals-against average in his first 22 games. He was sent to the Binghamton farm team in the American Hockey League to regain his form and conditioning. At the end of the season, for the first time in his NHL career, he had a losing record. He played four games for the United States at the World Championships, but his roller coaster year was far from over. When Vanbiesbrouck was traded to the Florida Panthers that summer, the focus of number one goalie shifted to Richter. He responded with some of the best play of his life. By early 1993–94, it became apparent that he was a different kind of goaltender and the Rangers were a different kind of team. He won 22 games over the first part of the year and New York was transformed from a squad that had missed the playoffs the year before to first place overall.

His standout performance in the first half of the season earned Richter a chance to play in the 1994 All-Star Game, a high-scoring contest held at his home rink of Madison Square Garden. Richter made some incredible saves, including five from Pavel Bure, and wasn't beaten until just over seven minutes remained in his second-period appearance. His Eastern squad went on to win the game 9–8, and due to his acrobatic performance in front of the home crowd, Richter was selected as the most valuable player, the first goalie to garner that honor since Grant Fuhr in 1986. "An unbelievable experience," Richter said. "Normally in a game you watch four or five shooters. But you don't know who to pick in a game like this." Richter was awarded a shiny new pickup truck, a prize his teammates in New York thought was long overdue. He had been driving a road-weary Honda for a decade and many refused to ride with him into Manhattan. "He should be forced to drive a lot more than he has in the past," Ranger defenseman Brian Leetch said.

Richter, Mike
G, 5′11″, 187 lbs, b: Abington, PA, 9/22/1966

Season	Club, League	Regular Season				Playoffs			
		GP	Mins	GA	Avg	GP	Mins	GA	Avg
1985–86	University of Wisconsin, WCHA	24	1394	92	3.96				
WEC–86	USA	1	53	5	5.66				
1986–87	University of Wisconsin, WCHA	36	2136	126	3.54				
WEC–87	USA	2	80	8	6.00				
1987–88	Colorado Rangers, IHL	22	1298	68	3.14	10	536	35	3.92
OWG–88	USA	4	230	15	3.91				
1988–89	Denver Rangers, IHL	57	3031	217	4.30	4	210	21	6.00
	New York Rangers, NHL					1	58	4	4.14
1989–90	New York Rangers, NHL	23	1320	66	3.00	6	330	19	3.45
	Flint Spirits, IHL	13	782	49	3.76				
1990–91	New York Rangers, NHL	45	2596	135	3.12	6	313	14	2.68
CCup–91	USA	7	420	22	3.00				
1991–92	New York Rangers, NHL	41	2298	119	3.11	7	412	24	3.50
1992–93	New York Rangers, NHL	38	2105	134	3.82				
	Binghamton Rangers, AHL	5	305	6	1.18				
WC–93	USA	4	237	13	3.29				
1993–94	New York Rangers, NHL	68	3710	159	2.57	23	1417	49	2.07
1994–95	New York Rangers, NHL	35	1993	97	2.92	7	384	23	3.59
1995–96	New York Rangers, NHL	41	2396	107	2.68	11	661	36	3.27
WCup–96	USA	6	370	15	2.00				
1996–97	New York Rangers, NHL	61	3598	161	2.68	15	939	33	2.11
1997–98	New York Rangers, NHL	72	4143	184	2.66				
OWG–98	USA	4	237	14	3.55				
1998–99	New York Rangers, NHL	68	3878	170	2.63				
1999–00	New York Rangers, NHL	61	3622	173	2.87				
2000–01	New York Rangers, NHL	45	2635	144	3.28				
2001–02	New York Rangers, NHL	55	3195	157	2.95				
OWG–02	USA	4	240	9	2.25				
	NHL Totals	653	37489	1806	2.89				
	OWG/WEC/WC/CCup/WCup Totals	32	1867	101	3.25				

Won Stanley Cup (1994)
Won WCup (1996)

Richter and the Rangers maintained their torrid pace in the second half of the season. With his career-high fifth shutout in a 3–0 win over the New Jersey Devils, Richter surpassed Eddie Giacomin's Ranger record for most wins in a season with 38. Richter finished the season with 42 wins and the Rangers won the Presidents' Trophy as the top regular-season team. Richter's winning hand continued into the playoffs. He had four more shutouts and won all 16 games as New York won its first Stanley Cup since 1940.

In 1996 Richter was once again a primary reason for his team's championship run, this time representing the United States at the World Cup. In the final game of the tournament, an incredible contest against goalie Curtis Joseph and the Canadians in Montreal, Richter faced a barrage of shots and kept his team alive. When the U.S. rallied in the third period to win the game and the title, Richter was selected as the World Cup's most valuable player. "It was like there was a brick wall out there," American coach Ron Wilson said. "I said right at the start our strength was in goal. The United States has always had great goaltending and Mike has done it before."

In the 1994 All-Star Game, Mike Richter (number 35) made some incredible saves and his athletic performance secured his selection as MVP, the first goalie to garner the honor since Grant Fuhr in 1986.

In the summer of 1998, Richter was selected by the Nashville Predators in the Expansion Draft, but it was a temporary move. He was re-signed by New York less than a month later and returned to the team as its top goaltender. Though Richter has remained a workhorse for the New York Rangers, his efforts have largely gone to waste, with the high-salaried club failing to advance to the post-season for the fourth year in a row in 2001–02. On the upside, he was the starting goaltender for Team USA in both the 1998 and 2002 Olympics. Richter played in all but two of the U.S. games in Salt Lake City and was very strong in a semifinal win over Russia and also the 5–2 loss to Canada in the gold medal game.

Throughout his career, Richter has given his time freely to charitable organizations. He has won the Thurman Munson Award for his charity efforts and the Sloan Kettering Award of Courage for his work with hospitals in the New York area.

Brian *Leetch*

In 1997 the New York Rangers named Brian Leetch their captain upon the departure of Mark Messier, putting him on center stage in the high-pressure media capital of the world. The cagey, fast-skating defenseman must have figured he'd come a long way from being a kid razzed on the ice by other young players because of his red hair and freckles.

Brian was born in Corpus Christi, Texas, an unlikely breeding ground for a future NHL superstar. Perhaps more fitting of a Texan, he was a star baseball pitcher in high school with a fastball that was timed at 90 miles an hour. Nevertheless, his idol growing up was Boston's star defenseman, Ray Bourque.

Leetch attended two years of prep school in New England and it was there that he came into his own. In 1986 he was picked ninth overall by the Rangers in the Entry Draft right from high school, but he didn't enter the NHL right away, joining the 1988 U.S. Olympic team instead. He also

Brian Leetch (front) recorded 23 goals and 48 assists to win the Calder Trophy as the league's outstanding rookie.

played a year for Boston College, following in the footsteps of his father, Jack, who had also played on the Eagles hockey team. "I thought I could improve and help the Rangers more and help myself more if I played in the Olympics," he said, noting that he, along with many young American players, needed opportunities to compete often on a high level to get the experience they would need for the NHL. "I think the Canadian system is more geared to playing in the NHL," he said. "They make it to the NHL a lot earlier than most Americans. For a lot of Americans, the real goal is to make it to the Olympics, and then the pros, if they can, after that." His loyalty to Team USA was rewarded in 1997, as he was one of 12 players voted to the All-Time USA Hockey Team.

When the Calgary Olympics ended, Leetch did enter the big leagues with New York. His arrival there was much anticipated by the team's front office. Jack Ferreira, the Rangers' director of player development, was one of the New York officials who couldn't wait to get the youngster into the blue, red and white uniform of the Broadway Blueshirts. "Every year there are three or four guys who don't go as number one in the draft," he said, "but have the ability to be the best player from the draft in three or four years. Brian was one of those guys."

Leetch didn't disappoint people, making a big impression right away. He scored 23 goals and recorded 48 assists in his initial season, winning the Calder Trophy as the league's outstanding rookie ahead of Trevor Linden of Vancouver. The rest of the league was beginning to notice the young Texan. "He's the hidden surprise of the Patrick Division," said Rangers assistant coach Colin Campbell. "He is similar to Wayne Gretzky in that he doesn't look dazzling but the puck seems to follow him."

He went through a bit of a sophomore slump the next year, and a fractured ankle at the end of that second season didn't help matters much either, forcing him out of playoff action. Two years later, in 1991–92, Leetch had his best single season, scoring 102 points and netting 22 goals (his 80 assists were a team record as well) to bag the Norris Trophy as the NHL's best defenseman.

That summer, Leetch signed a huge contract with the Rangers, for seven years and a reported $18 million. "He is only 24 years old. He'll be the foundation of this franchise for the next decade," said Rangers general manager Neil Smith. "There has never been any question that we'd find a way to keep him."

The next season, Leetch was on the wrong end of a scary incident on the ice. During a

---

Leetch, Brian
D, 5'11", 190 lbs, b: Corpus Christi, TX, 3/3/1968

Season	Club, League	Regular Season					Playoffs				
		GP	G	A	Pts	PIM	GP	G	A	Pts	PIM
1986–87	Boston College, H.E.	37	9	38	47	10					
WEC–87	USA	10	4	5	9	4					
1987–88	New York Rangers, NHL	17	2	12	14	0					
OWG–88	USA	6	1	5	6	4					
1988–89	New York Rangers, NHL	68	23	48	71	50	4	3	2	5	2
WEC–89	USA	10	3	4	7	4					
1989–90	New York Rangers, NHL	72	11	45	56	26					
1990–91	New York Rangers, NHL	80	16	72	88	42	6	1	3	4	0
CCup–91	USA	7	1	3	4	2					
1991–92	New York Rangers, NHL	80	22	80	102	26	13	4	11	15	4
1992–93	New York Rangers, NHL	36	6	30	36	26					
1993–94	New York Rangers, NHL	84	23	56	79	67	23	11	23	34	6
1994–95	New York Rangers, NHL	48	9	32	41	18	10	6	8	14	8
1995–96	New York Rangers, NHL	82	15	70	85	30	11	1	6	7	4
WCup–96	USA	7	0	7	7	4					
1996–97	New York Rangers, NHL	82	20	58	78	40	15	2	8	10	6
1997–98	New York Rangers, NHL	76	17	33	50	32					
OWG–98	USA	4	1	1	2	0					
1998–99	New York Rangers, NHL	82	13	42	55	42					
1999–00	New York Rangers, NHL	50	7	19	26	20					
2000–01	New York Rangers, NHL	82	21	58	79	34					
2001–02	New York Rangers, NHL	82	10	45	55	28					
OWG–98	USA	6	0	5	5	0					
	NHL Totals	1021	215	700	915	481					
	OWG/WEC/CCup/WCup Totals	50	10	30	40	18					

NHL First All-Star Team (1992, 1997)
NHL Second All-Star Team (1991, 1994, 1996)
Won James Norris Trophy (1992, 1997)
Won Conn Smythe Trophy (1994)
Won Calder Trophy (1989)
Won Stanley Cup (1994)
Won WCup (1996)

game against St. Louis, he skated in with the intention of hitting the Blues' Phillipe Bozon into the boards. But he missed the check and spent the next several minutes on the ice with a concussion. The result was an injury to his left shoulder—and a bad headache—but he had come close to a career-ending injury.

Leetch made up for all this lost time in 1993–94 as the Rangers won their first Stanley Cup in more than 50 years. He led the way as the top scorer in the post-season and was the Conn Smythe Trophy winner as the most valuable player of the playoffs. In the summer of 1999, the Rangers signed him to a reported $35-million contract. After an off year in 1999–2000, Leetch returned to form in 2000–01 and proved himself ready for the Salt Lake Olympics, where he turned in a strong performance in helping Team USA to advance to the gold medal game, though they came up on the short end of a 5–2 score to Canada. The silver medal in 2002 was the highlight of Leetch's season; the downside was the Rangers' failure to advance to the Stanley Cup playoffs for the fourth year in a row.

Leetchie has often been compared to Bobby Orr because of his abilities as a scoring defenseman, a comparison that Leetch has shied away from because of Orr's supreme reputation. But Ranger assistant coach Ron Smith once said that no less an authority than Orr's old teammate Wayne Cashman was also prepared to make the link. "Cash says Leetch is the closest thing he's ever seen to Bobby Orr, and he should know," said Smith.

Leetch works tirelessly for the leukemia society and Ronald McDonald House in New York and is instrumental in the latter organization's Skate with the Greats event that has raised more than $1.6 million dollars in five years. He has appeared on the *Late Show with David Letterman*, the *Today Show*, *Late Night with Conan O'Brien* and the *Howard Stern Show*.

Brian Leetch has often been compared to Bobby Orr because of his abilities as a scoring defenseman, but it's a comparison Leetch has shied away from because of Orr's supreme reputation.

Arturs Irbe

Arturs Irbe was among the first wave of players from communist countries who were finally allowed to leave their homeland to play in the NHL. He was drafted a lowly 196th overall by Minnesota in 1989, testament to the team's belief that he might never see North America. Indeed, it wasn't until two years later that he left Dynamo Riga to play for San Jose, which had selected him in the Dispersal Draft of 1991. He'd been with Riga for five years—from rookie of the year to number one goalie—but when the 24-year-old reached the NHL, he knew he'd made the big time.

The Sharks were an expansion team and Irbe spent most of his first year with Kansas City in the IHL, coached by eventual San Jose coach Kevin Constantine. By 1993–94, Irbe was the number one goalie with the NHL team and his impact on the team was unquestionable. He played a then record 74 games and 4,412 minutes and led the team to an improbable run in the playoffs. They eliminated the Cup-contending Detroit Red Wings in game seven right at Joe Louis Arena and in the next round took Toronto to seven games before losing in overtime at Maple Leaf Gardens.

Arturs Irbe was among the first wave of Soviet players who were finally allowed to leave their homeland to play in the NHL.

The summer of 1994 saw near tragedy visit Irbe. Back home in Riga, he was doing sit-ups one day next to his sleeping dog. At one point he nudged the animal, which woke up and went berserk, tearing and ravaging Irbe's hands and forcing him to go to the hospital. He suffered extensive damage to

Arturs Irbe had an impressive season in 1998–99 and led Carolina to a division title before the team lost to Boston in the first round of the playoffs.

the tendons and nerves in his hands and his career was threatened. "That dog was like a member of our family," he said mournfully, "and we had to put the dog to sleep. I was really worried. It was serious damage. I thought I might not play again." The lockout gave him a better opportunity to recover, but even six months later he still had trouble gripping his stick. His confidence began to wane and of course his play suffered as a result. The playoff performances against Detroit and Toronto in 1994 were to be the best Irbe would do with San Jose. The team faded in the next two years, and his weaknesses were beginning to overshadow his strengths. He was a small goalie who relied on quickness and agility, and these were qualities all his coaches recognized. However, he was without question the worst stickhandling goalie in the league, and he occasionally would have a lapse in concentration that would see a long shot go past him at a critical time. He was also pretty quirky, as were most goalies. He prepared for games by working on jigsaw puzzles, and during intermissions he would leave his mask and gloves on the players' bench, as he had always done in Riga.

A free agent, he signed with the Dallas Stars for 1996–97, but when the Stars pursued Ed Belfour, he was let go. After another middling year with Vancouver playing behind Garth Snow, he signed with Carolina and his career underwent an impressive resurgence. He regained his confidence as he realized Carolina might be his last chance to play in the NHL. He had an impressive 27-20-12 record in 1998–99 and led the team to a division championship before losing to Boston in the first round of the playoffs. He handled the puck less frequently, stayed positioned and remained disciplined in his goal and relied on his reflexes to make the majority of saves, just like the old days when he was at his best.

Internationally, Irbe was one of the main reasons Latvia earned a promotion from Pool B of the World Championships in 1996 to Pool A for 1997 and 1998. He played in all three tournaments as the number one goalie and provided a measure of stability to an otherwise changing and developing program that lacked funds and quality players.

In 1999–2000 and 2000–01, Irbe was one of the busiest goaltenders in the NHL, playing in 75 and 77 games respectively. In 2001–02, he completed his fourth season as the team's number one goalie by leading the Hurricanes into the playoffs.

Irbe, Arturs
G, 5'8", 175 lbs, b: Riga, Latvia, 2/2/1967

Season	Club, League	Regular Season				Playoffs			
		GP	Mins	GA	Avg	GP	Mins	GA	Avg
1986–87	Dynamo Riga, USSR	2	27	1	2.22				
1987–88	Dynamo Riga, USSR	34	1870	86	2.69				
1988–89	Dynamo Riga, USSR	40	2460	116	2.85				
1989–90	Dynamo Riga, USSR	48	2880	115	2.42				
WEC–90	USSR	6	315	5	0.95				
1990–91	Dynamo Riga, USSR	46	2713	133	2.94				
1991–92	San Jose Sharks, NHL	13	645	48	4.47				
	Kansas City Blades, IHL	32	1955	80	2.46	15	914	44	2.89
1992–93	San Jose Sharks, NHL	36	2074	142	4.11				
	Kansas City Blades, IHL	6	364	20	3.30				
1993–94	San Jose Sharks, NHL	74	4412	209	2.84	14	806	50	3.72
1994–95	San Jose Sharks, NHL	38	2043	111	3.26	6	316	27	5.13
1995–96	San Jose Sharks, NHL	22	1112	85	4.59				
	Kansas City Blades, IHL	4	226	16	4.24				
WC(B)–96	Latvia	4	300	7	1.75				
1996–97	Dallas Stars, NHL	35	1965	88	2.69	1	13	0	0.00
WC–97	Latvia	5	300	10	2.00				
1997–98	Vancouver Canucks, NHL	41	1999	91	2.73				
WC–98	Latvia	6	358	17	2.85				
1998–99	Carolina Hurricanes, NHL	62	3643	135	2.22	6	408	15	2.21
WC–99	Latvia	4	238	12	3.03				
1999–2000	Carolina Hurricanes, NHL	75	4345	175	2.42				
WC–2000	Latvia	7	420	17	2.43				
2000–01	Carolina Hurricanes, NHL	77	4406	180	2.45				
2001–02	Carolina Hurricanes, NHL	51	2974	126	2.54				
OWG–02	Latvia	1	60	4	4.00				
	USSR Totals	170	9950	451	2.72				
	NHL Totals	524	29618	1390	2.82				
	WEC/WC/WC(B) Totals	32	1931	68	2.11				

Named Best Goaltender at WEC (1990)
Won WEC (1990)

Luc Robitaille

Luc Robitaille couldn't skate well enough to play in the NHL—that's what the scouts and coaches and reporters said when he was still a youngster in the juniors. Possessed of great hands and a goal scorer's knack for finding the openings, Robitaille didn't seem to have the legs to survive in a league that was getting faster every year. But Robitaille worked hard at his skating. He became a reliable goal scorer and a regular First Team All-Star. Though he acquired the nickname "Lucky," luck had little to do with his long-lasting success.

Robitaille was born in Montreal, Quebec, in 1966. He played his junior hockey with the Hull Olympiques in the Quebec Major Junior Hockey League and had 85 points in 70 games in his rookie season. In the 1984 NHL Entry Draft, the big story wasn't Robitaille but another Quebec kid, Mario Lemieux, who was the top pick overall. Los Angeles selected Robitaille after 170 other players, the ninth player the Kings chose that year. Even a baseball player, Atlanta Braves ace pitcher Tom Glavine, was chosen ahead of Robitaille.

Luc Robitaille acquired the nickname "Lucky," but luck had little to do with his long-lasting success.

"One man believed in me and that was [Kings scout] Alex Smart," Robitaille said. "He's the only guy that ever looked at or talked to me. I think he saw how much I loved to play hockey." The word on Robitaille was that his skating was lacking. He had enough hockey sense to be in the right place at the right time, and with his good size and nifty set of hands there was no question he could score the odd goal. Still, expectations for Luc on entering his second year with the Olympiques centered on having a good junior career and then thinking about other employment.

Robitaille began to prove the experts wrong with his play in Hull. He worked on his skating and made the QJHML Second All-Star Team after posting 149 points in 64 games. The next season he was the best junior in Canadian hockey. He had 191 points, was bumped up to the Quebec league's First All-Star Team and was a standout for the Canadian team at the World Junior Championship. He was named the Canadian Major Junior player of the year.

Even after his incredible year, few people believed Robitaille could continue his prolific output in the bigger, stronger and faster NHL. Los Angeles gave him the chance in 1986–87. Robitaille said at the time that his personal goal was to make the team. He did that and then went a couple of giant steps further. After he impressed Kings coach Pat Quinn with his hard work and goal-scoring, Robitaille was given more and more playing time and was soon on the Los Angeles power-play. He went on to score 45 goals and record 84 points that first season. He won the Calder Trophy as the league's top rookie, outpacing Philadelphia goalie Ron Hextall, and not only earned a spot on the league's All-Rookie Team but also on the NHL's Second All-Star Team.

After his initial success, Robitaille continued to work hard. He spoke often of what a privilege it was to even be in the league and committed himself to staying there. The next season he scored 53 goals and collected 111 points and secured a berth on the NHL First All-Star Team, where he would stay for four years.

Wayne Gretzky joined the team in Robitaille's third year, 1989–90. Robitaille continued to score, finishing the season two shy of 100 points and 46 goals. Gretzky missed the first half of the 1992–93 season with an injury and Robitaille ably filled in the offensive gap, as well as serving as

The 1993–94 season was the eighth in a row in which Luc Robitaille (center) topped 40 goals, the third-longest streak in NHL history.

the team's captain. His 62 goals and 125 points established league records for a left wing. During the Kings' run to the Stanley Cup finals, which they lost to the Montreal Canadiens, Robitaille had 22 points in 24 games.

The Kings sagged a bit the next year, although Robitaille once again scored over 40 goals. It was the eighth consecutive season he had topped 40, the third-longest streak in NHL history behind his teammate Gretzky, who had 12 in a row, and Mike Bossy's nine. When Los Angeles missed the playoffs that year, Robitaille joined the Canadian team at the 1994 World Championship in Italy and scored the championship-winning goal in a shootout to give Canada its first gold medal in 33 years.

Robitaille was traded to the Pittsburgh Penguins prior to the lockout-shortened 1994–95 season. He had a solid year, collecting 23 goals in 46 games, but was sent to the New York Rangers in the summer of 1995. Aside from 1994–95, the fewest number of games he played in a season was 76, but for the first time in his career, Robitaille began to miss games because of injuries and struggled with his scoring. He scored 47 goals over two seasons with the Rangers, enjoying a brief turnaround when he was reunited with Gretzky in 1996. He returned to Los Angeles in 1997 but had an injury-riddled year, playing only 57 games and scoring just 16 goals.

At the beginning of the 1998–99 season, he recommitted himself to the game, spending hours strengthening his legs and his skating. Robitaille once again found his scoring magic and he reached the 500-goal milestone in a game against the Buffalo Sabres on January 7, 1999. Only the sixth left wing in league history to reach the mark, Robitaille scored the goal in his 928th NHL game, making him the 12th fastest ever to accomplish the feat. And all 11 of the players ahead of him are or will be in the Hockey Hall of Fame.

Early in the 2001–02 season, Robitaille scored his 600th career goal, and later notched his 1,300th career point. But perhaps the most intriguing aspect of reaching the 600-goal mark was that Robitaille became one of three active Red Wings on the 2001–02 roster to reach the plateau, joining future Hall of Famers Steve Yzerman and Brett Hull.

Robitaille, Luc
LW, 6´1˝, 195 lbs, b: Montreal, Que., 2/17/1966

Season	Club, League	Regular Season					Playoffs				
		GP	G	A	Pts	PIM	GP	G	A	Pts	PIM
1986–87	Los Angeles Kings, NHL	79	45	39	84	28	5	1	4	5	2
1987–88	Los Angeles Kings, NHL	80	53	58	111	82	5	2	5	7	18
1988–89	Los Angeles Kings, NHL	78	46	52	98	65	11	2	6	8	10
1989–90	Los Angeles Kings, NHL	80	52	49	101	38	10	5	5	10	10
1990–91	Los Angeles Kings, NHL	76	45	46	91	68	12	12	4	16	22
CCup–91	Canada	8	1	2	3	10					
1991–92	Los Angeles Kings, NHL	80	44	63	107	95	6	3	4	7	12
1992–93	Los Angeles Kings, NHL	84	63	62	125	100	24	9	13	22	28
1993–94	Los Angeles Kings, NHL	83	44	42	86	86					
WC–94	Canada	8	4	4	8	2					
1994–95	Pittsburgh Penguins, NHL	46	23	19	42	37	12	7	4	11	26
1995–96	New York Rangers, NHL	77	23	46	69	80	11	1	5	6	8
1996–97	New York Rangers, NHL	69	24	24	48	48	15	4	7	11	4
1997–98	Los Angeles Kings, NHL	57	16	24	40	66	4	1	2	3	6
1998–99	Los Angeles Kings, NHL	82	39	35	74	54					
1999–00	Los Angeles Kings, NHL	71	36	38	74	68	4	2	2	4	6
2000–01	Los Angeles Kings, NHL	82	37	51	88	66	13	4	3	7	10
2001–02	Detroit Red Wings, NHL	81	30	20	50	38					
2001–02	Detroit Red Wings, NHL	81	30	20	50	38					
	NHL Totals	1205	620	668	1288	1019					
	WC/CCup Totals	16	5	6	11	12					

NHL First All-Star Team (1988, 1989, 1990, 1991, 1993)
NHL Second All-Star Team (1987, 1992)
Won Calder Trophy (1987)
Won WC (1994)
Won CCup (1991)

Adam Graves

A top power forward in junior hockey, Adam Graves took a few years of development to step into the same role in the NHL after entering the league in 1987. After a slow start as a pro, he won a Stanley Cup with the Edmonton Oilers in 1989–90 and later helped the New York Rangers do the same in 1993–94. Graves earned respect throughout the league for his goal-scoring ability, his tough work in the corners and the slot and his tireless work off the ice for charity.

During his first year as the prospect for an NHL team, Graves scored 100 points and led the powerhouse Spitfires to the Memorial Cup tournament. Throughout the 1986–87 season, Windsor was the top-rated junior team in Canada, but the Spitfires were upset by the Medicine Hat Tigers in the Memorial Cup final. Graves returned for one last year of junior in 1987–88 but also played nine big-league games for Detroit.

Graves spent most of the 1988–89 season with the Wings in a support role. It seemed like more of the same through the first 13 games of 1989–90 before he was traded to the Edmonton Oilers as part of the package assembled to bring Jimmy Carson home to Detroit. This was Graves' first big break in the NHL. He compiled 21 points in 63 games while teaming with Martin Gelinas and former Wings teammate Joe Murphy on the Oilers' Kid Line. The inexperienced trio continued to excel in the playoffs and helped Edmonton win its fifth Stanley Cup in seven seasons. Coach John Muckler explained that he wasn't surprised by the trio's contribution to the team's success: "They play with a lot of enthusiasm. I'll use them a lot of times when things aren't going well. They bring the speed back up and they all play aggressively."

Comparisons were often made between the young forward and Oilers star Mark Messier. Veteran Edmonton defenseman Kevin Lowe commented: "Mess is Mess, but the way Graves bowls people over, absolutely there are similarities. And his disposition on the ice is similar."

During the 1990–91 season, Graves continued to fill a checking role but was unsatisfied. On the eve of the 1991–92 season, he was signed by the New York Rangers as a free agent and was asked to play the role of two-way power forward for the first time since junior. Coach Roger Neilson noted a few months later: "We've added some guys this season who have helped us to become a more close-knit team. Adam is exactly that type of player. He is a great team player. He kills penalties. He's on the power-play. He is a great leader who does everything well."

He responded to the challenge with 26- and 36-goal performances his first two seasons in

A top power forward in junior hockey, it took Adam Graves a few years to develop into the same role in the NHL.

Graves, Adam
C, 6´, 210 lbs, b: Toronto, Ont., 4/12/1968

Season	Club, League	Regular Season					Playoffs				
		GP	G	A	Pts	Plm	GP	G	A	Pts	Plm
1986–87	Adirondack Red Wings, AHL						5	0	1	1	0
1987–88	Detroit Red Wings, NHL	9	0	1	1	8					
1988–89	Detroit Red Wings, NHL	56	7	5	12	60	5	0	0	0	4
	Adirondack Red Wings, AHL	14	10	11	21	28	14	11	7	18	17
1989–90	Detroit Red Wings, NHL	13	0	1	1	13					
	Edmonton Oilers, NHL	63	9	12	21	123	22	5	6	11	17
1990–91	Edmonton Oilers, NHL	76	7	18	25	127	18	2	4	6	22
1991–92	New York Rangers, NHL	80	26	33	59	139	10	5	3	8	22
1992–93	New York Rangers, NHL	84	36	29	65	148					
WC–93	Canada	8	3	3	6	8					
1993–94	New York Rangers, NHL	84	52	27	79	127	23	10	7	17	24
1994–95	New York Rangers, NHL	47	17	14	31	51	10	4	4	8	8
1995–96	New York Rangers, NHL	82	22	36	58	100	10	7	1	8	4
WCup–96	Canada	7	0	1	1	2					
1996–97	New York Rangers, NHL	82	33	28	61	66	15	2	1	3	12
1997–98	New York Rangers, NHL	72	23	12	35	41					
1998–99	New York Rangers, NHL	82	38	15	53	47					
WC–99	Canada	10	5	2	7	8					
1999–00	New York Rangers, NHL	77	23	17	40	14					
2000–01	New York Rangers, NHL	82	10	16	26	77					
2001–02	San Jose Sharks, NHL	81	17	14	31	51					
	NHL Totals	1070	320	278	598	1192					
	WC/WCup Totals	25	8	6	14	18					

NHL Second All-Star Team (1994)
Won King Clancy Trophy (1994)
Won Stanley Cup (1990, 1994)

Adam Graves (left) broke through with a spectacular 52-goal season and helped the Rangers win the Stanley Cup in 1993–94.

Manhattan. During the first of these, he helped the Rangers win the Presidents' Trophy after amassing a league-high 105 points. Even though Graves improved in 1992–93, the team fell to sixth place in the Patrick Division and finished out of the playoffs. Another low point was the outpouring of abuse from the Pittsburgh Penguins fans and media after he accidentally broke Mario Lemieux's hand. A frustrated Graves stated: "People are questioning my character. It's the worst I've ever felt in my whole life. People I don't know think I'm a bad guy. People in Toronto who knew me all my life read stories about me and say, 'They mean Adam?' And they ask my friends and family."

Graves broke through with a spectacular 52-goal season and helped the Rangers lead the NHL with 112 points in 1993–94. In the process, he entered the record books as the first ex-Edmonton Oiler to record a 50-goal season. Former teammate Craig MacTavish observed: "What's happened since Adam Graves left here was he put on some extra weight and he's more physically dominating in front of the net. He's also playing with Mark [Messier], who's a great passer, and he's got Brian Leetch and Sergei Zubov moving the puck up the ice. It's pretty tough to get 50 on your own." That spring, Graves' 10 post-season goals helped the Blueshirts win their first Stanley Cup since 1940. Graves was placed on the NHL Second All-Star Team at left wing and was the recipient of the King Clancy Memorial Trophy in recognition of his continuing work with charitable causes.

Reflecting on why he'd originally signed with New York, Graves commented: "When you're a little younger, you just want to play in the NHL. And it doesn't matter for whom. As you get older, you want to play for winners. Even though I had won a Stanley Cup in Edmonton, I felt my chances for winning another one would be enhanced if I were in New York. I really liked the positive direction they were heading for in New York."

Through the remainder of the decade, the Rangers failed to make a significant impact in the playoffs, but Graves continued to be a reliable scorer. He topped the 30-goal mark twice while supplying leadership and grit for New York. Graves concluded the 1999–2000 season just seven goals shy of 300 for his career.

With the Rangers in need of rebuilding, they traded Graves to the San Jose Sharks on June 24, 2001, and his veteran leadership was a key factor in their regular-season success in 2001–02. Despite taking on much more of a defensive role with the Sharks, it was also the 10th time in 14 full NHL seasons that Graves managed to reach the 15-goal plateau.

Jarmo Myllys

Jarmo Myllys has had three lives as a top goaltender, the first in Finland, the second as a professional in North America and more recently as a hero in Lulea in Sweden. When adding up the merits and determining the ranking of the all-time greatest goalies in Finland, it is hard to overlook Jarmo Myllys, who brought home four of the first five medals his nation ever captured in international play. And in 1992 he missed a medal series because he was playing in the NHL with the San Jose Sharks.

Myllys was born in Savonlinna, a town famous for one of the most prestigious opera festivals in Europe, but moved to the hockey capitol of Finland—Tampere—and the Ilves ("Lynx") club as an 18-year-old. At Ilves, where he stayed for three years, he was unfortunate to share his goaltending duties with Jukka Tammi, the goalie who still holds the career record for most appearances in the Finnish league. Despite being considered the best goalie on the club by some observers, he had to be satisfied with the backup role. In 1985, when Ilves won the national league gold medal, Myllys saw action in only nine regular-season and two playoff games, all with superb statistics. In the playoff finals, Jukka Tammi lost the opening two games against TPS Turku. Myllys started in game three and turned the tide—bringing his team the gold medal.

From Ilves he moved to Lukko Rauma and the number one job. In the two seasons before his move to North America, he played all but one game for Lukko. After his spell in North America, Myllys made his decision to return to Finland too late in the year. All the goalie spots in the league were taken, so he had to spend the 1992–93 season in Division 1 with KooKoo Kouvola before returning to Lukko and leading them to another bronze medal.

Myllys made an early impact on the scouts while playing on the Finnish medal-winning team at the World Junior Championship. At Oslo, Norway, in 1983 he achieved his first international success by leading his team to a silver medal behind the powerhouse Soviets in the under-18 European Junior Championships. He also won twin awards as best goalie and a place on the media's first All-Star team. The following year the silver streak continued in Sweden with the under-20 team again finishing behind the Soviets in the World Junior Championship. This limelight performance made him the Minnesota North Stars' draft pick in 1987 and a year later he joined the club.

Since Minnesota already had a Finnish goalie in Kari Takko, Myllys—who also had trouble settling in to the North American style of play—spent most of the time in Kalamazoo with the IHL Wings. There he relearned his craft and was twice selected to the IHL All-Star Team. In the NHL, he played with the San Jose Sharks and saw action in 27 games without impressing coach George Kingston, who gave him every opportunity. The Sharks traded his rights to the Maple Leafs, but Jarmo decided to return to Finland.

In the summer of 1994, after two years at home, Lulea HF talked him into moving to Sweden. He has been there ever since, becoming a legend in that country too as the all-time

Jarmo Myllys has had three lives as a top goaltender: in Finland, in North America and in Sweden.

Myllys, Jarmo
G, 5′8″, 160 lbs, b: Savonlinna, Finland, 5/29/1965

Season	Club, League	Regular Season				Playoffs			
		GP	Mins	GA	Avg	GP	Mins	GA	Avg
1986–87	Lukko, Finland	43	2542	160	3.78				
WEC–87	Finland	8	464	27	3.49				
CCup–87	Finland	1	20	1	3.00				
1987–88	Lukko, Finland	43	2468	160	3.72	8	480	*	*
OWG–88	Finland	6	360	11	1.83				
1988–89	Minnesota North Stars, NHL	6	238	22	5.55				
	Kalamazoo Wings, IHL	28	1523	93	3.66	6	419	22	3.15
1989–90	Minnesota North Stars, NHL	4	156	16	6.15				
	Kalamazoo Wings, IHL	49	2715	159	3.51	7	356	22	3.71
1990–91	Minnesota North Stars, NHL	2	78	8	6.15				
	Kalamazoo Wings, IHL	38	2278	144	3.79	10	600	26	2.60
1991–92	San Jose Sharks, NHL	27	1374	115	5.02				
	Kansas City Blades, IHL	5	307	15	2.93				
1992–93	KooKoo (2), Finland	39	2310	120	3.11	6	359	24	4.01
1993–94	Lukko, Finland	46	2762	131	2.05				
OWG–94	Finland	5	300	3	0.60				
WC–94	Finland	7	40	10	1.35				
1994–95	Lulea, Sweden	37	2220	106	2.86	9	540	28	3.11
WC–95	Finland	7	420	12	1.71				
1995–96	Lulea, Sweden	39	2340	104	2.67	7	780	29	2.23
WC–96	Finland	4	238	12	3.02				
WCup–96	Finland	2	120	8	4.00				
1996–97	Lulea, Sweden	37	2158	80	2.22	10	612	25	2.45
WC–97	Finland	6	357	10	1.68				
1997–98	Lulea, Sweden	43	2534	111	2.63	3	180	10	3.33
OWG–98	Finland	4	237	14	3.54				
WC–98	Finland	2	119	4	2.02				
1998–99	Lulea, Sweden	47	*	129	2.73	3	*	10	3.33
1999–2000	Lulea, Sweden	40	2422	105	2.60				
	Finland Totals	132	7772	451	3.48	8	480	*	*
	NHL Totals	39	1846	161	5.23				
	OWG/WEC/WC/CCup/WCup Totals	52	2675	112	2.51				

Named Best Goaltender at WC (1995)
Won WC (1995)
Sweden Champion (1996)

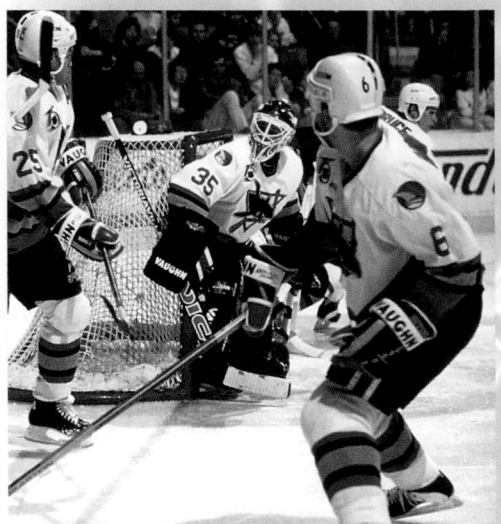

Jarmo Myllys (center) brought home four of the first five medals his nation ever won in international play.

shutout king with 29 zero-goals-against games and counting. He also became the first goalie in the Swedish league to score a goal. His 29 shutouts put him 12 ahead of Ake Liljebjorn, who needed 15 years to achieve his total. Getting a goal was a long-time ambition for Myllys, and on January 16, 1999, his dream came true when, late in a game against Leksand IF, his stickhandling skills were rewarded by an empty-net marker in a game Lulea won 4–2. Myllys claims it was a perfect effort—the puck sailed through the air and went into the net without anybody touching it.

After his initial season in Sweden, he was offered a contract by the Ottawa Senators but decided to stay put. It turned out to be a good choice. Led by Myllys, Lulea dominated the league. His impressive goals-against average helped the club capture the national title, but it did even better in the playoffs by going all the way to the its first and only gold in national championship play.

Having tasted international success at the junior level, it was logical that his generation would break some of the hitherto elusive barriers for Finnish hockey internationally. Finland has three major achievements in international hockey to date: the first medal ever, which was the Olympic silver at Calgary in 1988; its first world title, which was won in 1995 in Stockholm; and the victory over the best of Canada in the 1998 bronze medal game at the Nagano Olympics. Myllys was part of all three and in 1995 was awarded the trophy as the tournament's best goalie. In addition, he is one of the rare athletes to have won medals in three Olympic tournaments, with a bronze also from the 1994 event in Lillehammer, Norway. In addition to the 1995 gold, he has two silvers from the IIHF World Championships in 1994 at Milan and 1998 at Bern, Switzerland.

Myllys is still in his best years for a goalie and could come up with more league heroics. However, the spring of 2000 may have marked his end with the Finnish national team following two more wins—against Norway and then Latvia. His stats are as follows: 173 selections, 104 games played, 56 wins, 12 ties and 33 losses, a saves percentage of .906 and a goals-allowed average per game of 2.33.

Robert **Reichel**

Robert Reichel has demonstrated his great leadership qualities many times, whether as captain of the winning team during the 1996 Vienna World Championship or at the Nagano Winter Olympics two years later, where Czech hockey players won the coveted gold.

Reichel always knew that the road to victory wasn't easy, but his incredibly strong will and his toughness always carried him through. He became a natural authority, a leader recognized by players older than he. Even his mere presence inspired others. By rousing the players, he could affect the outcome of a game. It wasn't only what he demonstrated on the ice that made him a star, but also his willingness to sacrifice for the team and his work ethic during training and in the dressing room.

He started playing at the highest level as young as 16. Nobody could imagine a junior national selection that excluded him. He became the only player in history to win the points race before the age of 18 in the European Championship as well as the World Junior Championship. Only in 1993 were his records beaten by Swede Peter Forsberg.

In the 1989–90 season, with Litvinov, he came of age and scored 43 goals in 44 league matches and collected 71 points and became the best shooter and most productive player. He was immediately invited to the World Senior Championship.

The national team's young offense—Jaromir Jagr, Robert Reichel and Robert Holik—went into the tournament full of confidence. When leaving for the NHL at the end of the season, Reichel was considered the greatest talent in the country. According to many people, he was the one with all the prerequisites to have a great career and achieve stardom—even more than Jagr.

But he never rose to the heights that Jagr did in the NHL. Maybe he didn't play for the right team, or they didn't bet on him as much as Pittsburg did on Jagr. "Some have it easier, some have it more difficult. If I were to succumb to this, I certainly wouldn't be where I am today. I could have been further along, but I too have had a good career. Besides, all that I have gone through shaped and molded me and helped me to see that I have to work on myself as fully as before."

When he arrived in the summer of 1990, he brought the Calgary Flames an explosive style and scored many goals. In his first two seasons he scored close to 20 goals and in the next two years he doubled his output. In the 1993–94 season, he led the team with 93 points, ahead of Theo Fleury. Even during the next season, which began late because of the lockout, Reichel played for a German team, the Frankfurt Lions, and maintained his high points tally per game.

However, a dispute over a new contract hindered his further progress. The matter had to go to arbitration. When the court failed to comply with Reichel's demands, he returned to Frankfurt and racked up a remarkable 101 points in 46 games to become the most productive player in the German league. There he

When he left for the NHL in the 1990–91 season, Robert Reichel was considered his country's most talented player.

Reichel, Robert
C, 5′10″, 185 lbs, b: Litvinov, Czechoslovakia, 6/25/1971

Season	Club, League	Regular Season					Playoffs				
		GP	G	A	Pts	PIM	GP	G	A	Pts	PIM
1987–88	Litvinov, Czechoslovakia	36	17	10	27	8					
1988–89	Litvinov, Czechoslovakia	44	23	25	48	32					
1989–90	Litvinov, Czechoslovakia	44	43	28	71	*	8	6	6	12	
WEC–90	Czechoslovakia	10	5	6	11	4					
1990–91	Calgary Flames, NHL	66	19	22	41	22	6	1	1	2	0
WEC–91	Czechoslovakia	8	2	4	6	10					
CCup–91	Czechoslovakia	5	1	2	3	6					
1991–92	Calgary Flames, NHL	77	20	34	54	32					
WC–92	Czechoslovakia	8	1	3	4	2					
1992–93	Calgary Flames, NHL	80	40	48	88	54	6	2	4	6	2
1993–94	Calgary Flames, NHL	84	40	53	93	58	7	0	5	5	0
1994–95	Frankfurt, Germany	21	19	24	43	41					
	Calgary Flames, NHL	48	18	17	35	28	7	2	4	6	4
1995–96	Frankfurt, Germany	46	47	54	101	84	3	1	3	4	0
WC–96	Czech Republic	8	4	4	8	0					
WCup–96	Czech Republic	3	1	0	1	0					
1996–97	Calgary Flames, NHL	70	16	27	43	22					
	New York Islanders, NHL	12	5	14	19	4					
WC–97	Czech Republic	9	1	4	5	4					
1997–98	New York Islanders, NHL	82	25	40	65	32					
OWG–98	Czech Republic	6	3	0	3	0					
WC–98	Czech Republic	8	0	4	4	0					
1998–99	New York Islanders, NHL	70	19	37	56	50					
	Phoenix Coyotes, NHL	13	7	6	13	4	7	1	3	4	2
1999–2000	Litvinov, Czech Republic	45	25	32	57	24	7	3	4	7	2
WC–2000	Czech Republic	9	2	3	5	4					
2001–02	Toronto Maple Leafs, NHL	78	20	31	51	26					
OWG–02	Czech Republic	4	1	0	1	2					
	Czechoslovakia/ Czech Republic Totals	169	108	95	203	*					
	NHL Totals	680	229	329	558	332					
	OWG/WEC/WC/CCup/WCup Totals	78	21	30	51	32					

Won OWG (1998)
Won WC (1996, 2000)

Robert Reichel (front) was the only player in history to win the European Championship points race before the age of 18.

also encountered his younger brother Martin, who with his German ancestry was able to apply for German citizenship after 1990. In the quarterfinals of the World Championship in Vienna in 1996, they played on opposing teams, Robert for the Czechs and Martin for the Germans.

He was one of the workhorses on the national team—which in 1996 won its first World Championship title in 11 years—yet in the NHL Reichel never progressed in the playoffs beyond the first round, neither with Calgary, where he returned for the 1996–97 season; nor with the New York Islanders, to whom he was traded; nor with the Phoenix Coyotes, who he joined at the end of the 1998–99 season.

Perhaps the most glorious moment in his career came during what the Czechs consider the greatest tournament of the century—the 1998 Winter Olympics in Nagano, Japan. It was Reichel who beat Patrick Roy in a shootout during the semifinals with Canada. Dominik Hasek didn't let one goal through and the Czechs advanced a step further in the competition for a gold medal.

Although the Coyotes were eliminated in the first round, Reichel wasn't picked to go to the World Championship in Norway in 1999 and another title escaped him. "If I didn't already have one gold medal, I would probably be sadder about it." He was more troubled by disagreements with the team management. Ultimately, he did prolong his contract with Phoenix. He had offers from the Florida Panthers and the New York Rangers, but his advancement within the NHL didn't come to be. Reichel chose to play for Litvinov. "I wouldn't go anywhere else. That's where I grew up. It is my home and I have done enough traveling."

He improved the team's play tremendously. Before his arrival, the team was hovering somewhere in the lower half of the standings. However, from time to time he had to quit playing because of injuries. From the very start, he made no secret of the fact that he had another goal in mind—to help Litvinov win its first home title. "I would like to see the day before the end of my career. But if it doesn't happen, the world won't come to an end." In any event, he broke through another barrier in the 1998–99 season. For the first time in his career, he and his team got past round one.

After two years of playing back home in the Czech Republic, Reichel's rights were acquired by Toronto and he joined the Leafs for 2001–02, but in February Reichel represented the Czech Republic at the 2002 Olympics in defense of its 1998 triumph. The team came up short in the playoff round, losing a thrilling 1–0 contest to Russia and going home without a medal.

John LeClair

With his size and grit, left winger John LeClair was made for the modern NHL game. He had the ability to win the battles in the corners and the speed to be dangerous on the rush. Though a slow starter in terms of goal-scoring, LeClair made up ground fast, becoming the first American-born player in the history of the league to score more than 50 goals in a season three times.

Born in St. Albans, Vermont, in 1969, LeClair began receiving daily calls from U.S. college coaches while he was a star with the Bellows Free Academy.

"From the time we had the first person call us until after he committed to UVM [the University of Vermont], there wasn't a single evening that he didn't get a call from someone, sometimes several calls," his mother, Bev, recalled.

One call, the night of the NHL draft in 1987, was from a woman with a French accent. LeClair, the caller announced, had been chosen in the second round by the Montreal Canadiens, making him the 33rd player taken overall.

LeClair played for four seasons with UVM, leading the team in goals, points and penalty minutes in his senior season in 1990–91. After his last game in the college ranks, he was immediately called up to the Canadiens. He scored a goal in his first game in the NHL, against the Vancouver Canucks at the Montreal Forum on March 9th.

When he joined the Canadiens on a regular basis in 1993, LeClair earned comparisons to another much talked about youngster, Eric Lindros, and to the Pittsburgh Penguins' hot-scoring Kevin Stevens. LeClair had the size and the mobility to wreak havoc in the corners and in front of the net. But he didn't consider himself a scorer, finishing the season with just 19 goals after concentrating on the defensive part of his game. "I think of myself as a third-line checking forward who goes up and down the wing, not hurting the team and maybe chipping in with a goal once in a while," he said of his role with the Canadiens.

That began to change in the 1993 Stanley Cup playoffs. LeClair made scoring goals—namely overtime goals—his specialty, as did Montreal. The team won 10 consecutive overtime games. In the Stanley Cup finals against Wayne Gretzky's Los Angeles Kings, LeClair scored the overtime winner in two consecutive games, the first time any player had done that in the history of the playoffs. His second, which gave the Canadiens a commanding 3–1 lead in the series, showed just what kind of a roll he was on. In a two-on-one rush against Kings defenseman Darryl Sydor, LeClair ended up with the puck behind the net. His pass out front bounced off a sliding Sydor and past goalie Kelly Hrudey to give the Habs the win.

Montreal went all the way that year. LeClair toured through his St. Albans home town with the Stanley Cup, visiting nearby Camp Ta-Kum-Ta, a summer retreat for kids with cancer and one of his favorite charity projects. The next season, 1993–94, LeClair,

With his size and grit, left winger John LeClair was made for the modern NHL game.

LeClair, John
LW, 6′3″, 225 lbs, b: St. Albans, VT, 7/5/1969

Season	Club, League	Regular Season					Playoffs				
		GP	G	A	Pts	PIM	GP	G	A	Pts	PIM
1987–88	University of Vermont, ECAC	31	12	22	34	62					
1988–89	University of Vermont, ECAC	18	9	12	21	40					
1989–90	University of Vermont, ECAC	10	10	6	16	38					
1990–91	University of Vermont, ECAC	33	25	20	45	58					
	Montreal Canadiens, NHL	10	2	5	7	2	3	0	0	0	0
1991–92	Montreal Canadiens, NHL	59	8	11	19	14	8	1	1	2	4
	Fredericton Canadiens, AHL	8	7	7	14	10	2	0	0	0	4
1992–93	Montreal Canadiens, NHL	72	19	25	44	33	20	4	6	10	14
1993–94	Montreal Canadiens, NHL	74	19	24	43	32	7	2	1	3	8
1994–95	Montreal Canadiens, NHL	9	1	4	5	10					
	Philadelphia Flyers, NHL	37	25	24	49	20	15	5	7	12	4
1995–96	Philadelphia Flyers, NHL	82	51	46	97	64	11	6	5	11	6
WCup–96	USA	7	6	4	10	6					
1996–97	Philadelphia Flyers, NHL	82	50	47	97	58	19	9	12	21	10
1997–98	Philadelphia Flyers, NHL	82	51	36	87	32	5	1	1	2	8
OWG–98	USA	4	0	1	1	0					
1998–99	Philadelphia Flyers, NHL	76	43	47	90	30	6	3	0	3	12
1999–00	Philadelphia Flyers, NHL	82	40	37	77	36	18	6	7	13	6
2000–01	Philadelphia Flyers, NHL	16	7	5	12	0	6	1	2	3	2
2001–02	Philadelphia Flyers, NHL	82	25	26	51	30					
OWG–02	USA	6	6	1	7	2					
	NHL Totals	763	341	337	678	361					
	OWG/WCup Totals	17	12	6	18	8					

NHL First All-Star Team (1995, 1998)
NHL Second All-Star Team (1996, 1997, 1999)
Won Bud Light Plus-Minus Award (1997, 1999)
Won Stanley Cup (1993)
Won WCup (1996)

though buoyed by his performance in the playoff run, returned to his more defensive game and once again had 19 goals.

LeClair's overtime heroics didn't go unnoticed in Philadelphia. The Flyers were building their team around size, toughness and skill, as they had so often done in the past, and general manager Bobby Clarke believed he had a spot for the 6´3″, 225-pound LeClair. On February 9, 1995, nine games into the strike-shortened season, the Flyers acquired LeClair, Gilbert Dionne and Eric

John LeClair (left) became the first American-born player in the history of the league to score more than 50 goals in a season three times.

Desjardins from the Canadiens for Mark Recchi and a third-round draft pick. Placed on a line with Eric Lindros and Mikael Renberg, LeClair paid dividends for his new bosses immediately. In his first 13 games after the trade, he had 12 goals and 11 assists, a considerable improvement over his five points in nine games with Montreal.

LeClair's line was a powerful physical presence. With Lindros at 6´4″ and Renberg a muscular 6´2″, the threesome earned the nickname "the Legion of Doom" for its bruising and effective style. After picking up 25 goals in 37 games with the Flyers that first year, LeClair exploded for 51 in 1995–96.

"Never in my wildest dreams did I think I'd become a 50-goal scorer," he said. "If you look back on it, it's not like I played great hockey every single night. A lot of those 50 goals have to be attributed to my teammates."

LeClair proved it wasn't completely his teammates after his offensive awakening led to a spot on the U.S. team at the World Cup of Hockey in 1996. He was one of the leaders on that championship team, placing second in goals and points in the tournament and earning a selection to the All-Tournament Team.

LeClair's first full season with the Flyers began a streak of three consecutive 50-goal seasons, making him the second Flyer to accomplish such a feat after Tim Kerr. He was a member of the U.S. team at the 1998 Olympics, a disappointing sixth place showing for the team and LeClair. When he returned to the NHL, his pace slowed—but only marginally—as he scored 43 goals in 1998–99, playing with new linemate Keith Jones, who replaced the traded Renberg. The return of Renberg, who'd been sent to Tampa Bay for the season and then reacquired in 1999, set up a possible reunion of the Legion of the Doom just in time for a new millennium of rugged play.

LeClair missed all but 16 games in 2000–01 after suffering a career-threatening back injury, but proved himself ready to go for 2001–02 after a summer of rehab. LeClair returned to top form with the Flyers and teamed up with Mike Modano and Brett Hull on Team USA to form one of the top offensive lines at the 2002 Olympics. LeClair and his teammates advanced to the Olympic gold medal game but had to settle for silver, losing in the final against Canada by a score of 5–2.

Rob **Blake**

In the late 1980s, as a means of developing their skills, an ever-increasing number of Canadians were choosing American college hockey over junior hockey. Rob Blake was no different. A native of Simcoe, Ontario, he opted to attend Bowling Green University, and in 1987–88, following his second year, he was selected 70th overall by Los Angeles in the NHL's Entry Draft. Ironically, he also considered leaving the school at the time because he didn't feel he was making enough progress in his game. "Dave Ellett left us after two years and went on to the NHL," Bowling Green coach Jerry York said about another successful alumnus of the school's hockey program. "But Rob wasn't as mature as Dave. He needed to develop physically and mentally."

As it turned out, York was correct in his assessment. Blake stayed on for a third year, making the M division's First All-Star Team, being named a Hobey Baker Award finalist and getting called up to the Kings for the last four games of the regular season to experience a taste of NHL life. The following season he made the team with an outstanding performance in training camp and has been its number one defenseman ever since.

Blake was thrilled to be joining an L.A. team that featured Wayne Gretzky. An offensive defenseman who was equally adept in his own end, Blake cherished the opportunity to join the rush when Gretzky had the puck, and in his first year he had 12 goals and 46 points from the blue line. Gretzky took to Blake immediately and likened him to a young Paul Coffey due to his offensive talent and his superb shot, which became an integral part of the Los Angeles power-play that Gretzky orchestrated. On road trips, Blake roomed with Dave Taylor, an alumnus of Clarkson College, where Bowling Green's Jerry York had previously coached. It was York's idea to phone Taylor, then an experienced veteran with the Kings, and suggest he watch out for the talented but innocent, small-city Blake in a big new city.

In every full season Blake played, his numbers increased, but at the same time injuries were forever taking up a large part of his season. In 1994–95, he missed 24 games with a pulled groin and the next year he tore an anterior cruciate ligament (ACL) just six games into the season and missed the remainder of the year. He has also broken his hand and his foot, resulting in further long stretches away from the ice.

The highlight of Blake's career to date was the 1993 playoffs, when the team, led by Gretzky, made it to the Stanley Cup finals. Along the way, they beat Calgary and Vancouver and then eliminated Toronto in game seven at Maple Leaf Gardens. But in the

Rob Blake was thrilled to be joining the Los Angeles team that featured Wayne Gretzky.

Blake, Rob
D, 6´3˝, 215 lbs, b: Simcoe, Ont., 12/10/1969

Season	Club, League	Regular Season					Playoffs				
		GP	G	A	Pts	PIM	GP	G	A	Pts	PIM
1987–88	Bowling Green University, CCHA	43	5	8	13	88					
1988–89	Bowling Green University, CCHA	46	11	21	32	140					
1989–90	Bowling Green University, CCHA	42	23	36	59	140					
	Los Angeles Kings, NHL	4	0	0	0	4	8	1	3	4	4
1990–91	Los Angeles Kings, NHL	75	12	34	46	125	12	2	4	5	26
WEC–91	Canada	2	0	2	2	0					
1991–92	Los Angeles Kings, NHL	57	7	13	20	102	6	2	1	3	12
1992–93	Los Angeles Kings, NHL	76	16	43	59	152	23	4	6	10	46
1993–94	Los Angeles Kings, NHL	84	20	48	68	137					
WC–94	Canada	8	0	2	2	6					
1994–95	Los Angeles Kings, NHL	24	4	7	11	38					
1995–96	Los Angeles Kings, NHL	6	1	2	3	8					
WCup–96	Canada	4	0	1	1	0					
1996–97	Los Angeles Kings, NHL	62	8	23	31	82					
WC–97	Canada	11	2	2	4	22					
1997–98	Los Angeles Kings, NHL	81	23	27	50	94	4	0	0	0	6
OWG–98	Canada	6	1	1	2	2					
WC–98	Canada	5	1	0	1	6					
1998–99	Los Angeles Kings, NHL	62	12	23	35	128					
WC–99	Canada	10	2	5	7	12					
1999–00	Los Angeles Kings, NHL	77	18	39	57	112	4	0	2	2	4
2000–01	Los Angeles Kings, NHL	54	17	32	49	69					
	Colorado Avalanche, NHL	13	2	8	10	8	23	6	13	19	16
2001–02	Colorado Avalanche, NHL	75	16	40	56	58					
OWG–02	Canada	6	1	2	3	2					
	NHL Totals	750	156	339	495	1117					
	OWG/WEC/WC/WCup Totals	52	7	15	22	50					

Named Best Defenseman at WEC (1997)
NHL First All-Star Team (1998)
NHL Second All-Star Team (2000)
Won James Norris Trophy (1998)
Won WC (1994, 1997)
Won OWG (2002)

A HISTORY OF WORLD HOCKEY

Rob Blake (front) is one of the few defensemen in league history to take a penalty shot. On April 13, 1998, he was stopped by Dwayne Roloson of Calgary.

finals, Blake and the Kings faced a Montreal team that had won 10 overtime games in these playoffs and the Kings lost in six games. Blake had 10 points that spring and anchored a defense that was virtually impenetrable until that Habs series.

The Kings performed well on a regular basis during most of the 1990s but never fared well in the playoffs beyond 1993. The result was that Blake had a chance to successfully represent Canada internationally on many occasions, each time happily taking advantage of the honor and experience. He played at the World Championships in 1991, 1994, 1997 and 1998, winning a gold medal on the 1994 and 1997 teams and a silver in 1991. He also played in the World Cup in 1996 and was key to Canada's defense at the Nagano Olympics in 1998, where he was named the best defenseman in the tournament.

It is also interesting to note that Blake is one of the few defensemen in NHL history to take a penalty shot. On April 13, 1998, he was stopped by Dwayne Roloson of Calgary in a 4–2 win at home.

Prior to the 2001 trade deadline, Blake was sent to Colorado, where he helped the Avalanche win the Stanley Cup—his first championship. And at the 2002 Salt Lake City Olympics, Blake was Canada's top defenseman throughout the tournament and a main reason why Canada won its first Olympic gold in men's hockey in 50 years. He finished with a goal and two assists.

Pierre Turgeon

An immensely talented offensive center, Pierre Turgeon has elicited a range of opinions from observers of the game. Justified or not, many have questioned his fighting spirit, but there has been no denial of his pure talent. Since entering the NHL in 1987–88, he has been one of the most skilled and feared players in the NHL. In defiance of his detractors, Turgeon reached both the 400-goal and the 1,000-point milestones during the 1999–2000 season.

The gifted native of Rouyn, Quebec, appeared destined for stardom at a very young age. As a 15-year-old, he averaged over two points per game for the Bourassa squad in the Quebec Amateur Athletic Association. Around this time, he was also demonstrating a proficiency on the baseball diamond in a number of positions, including pitcher. His next step on the ice was the Quebec Major Junior Hockey League in the uniform of the Granby Bisons. As a rookie in 1985–86, he racked up 114 points in 69 games and gained valuable experience with an 11-game stint with the Canadian national team. Granby coach Real Paiement noted partway through Turgeon's first season: "He studies the player who's covering him and adjusts. Watch him now that he's gone twice around the league. He knows what the other guys are going to do and he's ready to roll."

Turgeon entered the 1986–87 season as the top-rated Canadian amateur prospect and he didn't wilt under the immense expectations this ranking sometimes induces in less mature players. He accumulated 154 points in only 58 games and represented Canada at the World Junior Championship. Still, a few scouts were wary of his rating and one commented: "Turgeon's a player who will either be great or a big disappointment. There doesn't seem to be an in-between."

The Buffalo Sabres didn't hesitate to call Turgeon's name as the first player to be chosen in the 1987 NHL Entry Draft. Buffalo general manager Gerry Meehan compared Turgeon's importance to former star Gilbert Perreault: "A great French-Canadian led the rise of the Buffalo Sabres, who bottomed out with his retirement. I like to think another French-Canadian will lead the Sabres back up again."

In 1991–92, Pierre Turgeon was the key player in the package that was sent to the Islanders by the Sabres to acquire Pat LaFontaine.

As a rookie, he scored a respectable 42 points on an improved Sabres squad that made the playoffs for the first time in three seasons. Buffalo coach Ted Sator noted: "The talent just jumps out at you. Players that dominate the junior ranks, they don't do that because they're lucky." For his part, the young rookie commented on the adjustment to the fast pace of the NHL: "It's so hard because you have to think a little bit faster and make your play a little bit faster. Sometimes you don't have enough time because they go right to you. Every player develops improvisation, and here they improvise before you make your play, so you have to be careful. The defense sometimes will see if you pass to the left wing on a regular basis, and before you even pass, the defenseman will forecheck the wing."

Turgeon broke through as a bona fide NHL star with 88 points as a sophomore and 106 points in 1989–90. Soon thereafter he was blamed for Buffalo's lack of playoff success as regular-season promise led to first-round losses each year. Turgeon's frustration showed in his play as he dropped to 79 points in 1990–91.

Early in 1991–92, Turgeon was the key to the package sent by the Sabres to the New York Islanders to acquire Pat LaFontaine. "Lucky Pierre" gained a new lease on life with 87 points in 67 games for his new team. The following season, Turgeon experienced the highs and lows of his career. During the regular season he established personal standards with 58 goals and 132 points. Turgeon continued to excel in the postseason and led the Islanders to a first-round upset over the Washington Capitals. Unfortunately, the young star suffered a shoulder injury late in the series-clinching game against Washington as a result of a dirty hit by Dale Hunter. Even though New York went all the way to the semifinals, Turgeon was clearly hampered by this injury when he returned to the lineup.

Turgeon continued to produce for the Islanders, but the team never built on its success of 1992–93. In 1994–95, he lived out a childhood fantasy when a trade brought him to

Turgeon, Pierre
C, 6′1″, 195 lbs, b: Rouyn, Que., 8/28/1969

Season	Club, League	Regular Season					Playoffs				
		GP	G	A	Pts	Plm	GP	G	A	Pts	Plm
1987–88	Buffalo Sabres, NHL	76	14	28	42	34	6	4	3	7	4
1988–89	Buffalo Sabres, NHL	80	34	54	88	26	5	3	5	8	2
1989–90	Buffalo Sabres, NHL	80	40	66	106	29	6	2	4	6	2
1990–91	Buffalo Sabres, NHL	78	32	47	79	26	6	3	1	4	6
1991–92	Buffalo Sabres, NHL	8	2	6	8	4					
	New York Islanders, NHL	69	38	49	87	16					
1992–93	New York Islanders, NHL	83	58	74	132	26	11	6	7	13	0
1993–94	New York Islanders, NHL	69	38	56	94	18	4	0	1	1	0
1994–95	New York Islanders, NHL	34	13	14	27	10					
	Montreal Canadiens, NHL	15	11	9	20	4					
1995–96	Montreal Canadiens, NHL	80	38	58	96	44	6	2	4	6	2
1996–97	Montreal Canadiens, NHL	9	1	10	11	2					
	St. Louis Blues, NHL	69	25	49	74	12	5	1	1	2	2
1997–98	St. Louis Blues, NHL	60	22	46	68	24	10	4	4	8	2
1998–99	St. Louis Blues, NHL	67	31	34	65	36	13	4	9	13	6
1999–00	St. Louis Blues, NHL	52	26	40	66	8	7	0	7	7	0
2000–01	St. Louis Blues, NHL	79	30	52	82	37	15	5	10	15	2
2001–02	Dallas Stars, NHL	66	15	32	47	16					
	NHL Totals	1074	468	724	1192	372	94	34	56	90	28

Won Lady Byng Trophy (1993)

Pierre Turgeon (left) reached both the 400-goal and the 1,000-point milestones during the 1999–2000 season.

the Montreal Canadiens. The highlight of his time with the Habs came in 1995–96 when he recorded 96 points and was the team's captain for the last game at the Montreal Forum.

Early in the 1996–97 season, Turgeon was traded again, this time to St. Louis, where he maintained a solid points per game average. The talented forward had requested a move away from the vaunted Habs and commented: "I never had a problem with Mario [Tremblay, Montreal's coach] or Rejean [general manager] personally. I respect them. It's strictly a professional matter. We had our differences as far as hockey was concerned. It's tough for me to be on the third line playing 17 minutes a game. If I was 32 or 35, maybe I could adjust to that, but I'm 27 and I feel I have a few good years left."

In 1999–2000, Turgeon began playing his most inspired hockey since the shoulder injury in the 1993 playoffs. Through most of the regular season, he was among the NHL's leading scorers before he was felled by injuries. In the end, he scored 66 points in 52 games and helped the Blues set a franchise record with 115 points and earn the Presidents' Trophy for finishing at the top of the NHL standings.

After five years in St. Louis, Turgeon joined the Dallas Stars for the 2001–02 season, inking a five-year, $32-million deal.

Tommy Soderstrom

Tommy Soderstrom had a weak heart and had four operations to cure it. And then he was back on the ice.

At 21, when he received the Elite Series rookie of the year award for the 1990–91 season, Djurgarden's young goalie Tommy Soderstrom said that if a position hadn't opened at the famous club, he would have quit hockey and turned to roulette. Thanks to his new status, Alta, the team where Soderstrom made his first appearance on the ice, was awarded 35,000 kronor for the development of juvenile and junior hockey.

That season the young goaltender made his successful debut in the big leagues. After 17 games, Djurgarden's sports director told everybody that the team had found a new Pelle Lindberg. Soderstrom had good reaction and was always calm, cool and collected. "Tommy is remarkably well adjusted," goaltender coach Thomas Magnusson said of him. "Despite his youth, he is extremely together and reads the game perfectly. Even before the season began, I was predicting great things would happen."

Djurgarden won the national title with the young goalie and, for the first time in the history of Swedish hockey, the European Cup. That same season, Tre Kronor chief coach Conny Evensson invited Soderstrom to join the national team. Evensson was one of the judges who had named him rookie of the year. Besides Soderstrom, the other candidates were Lulea forward Robert

Nordberg, Malmo forward Hakan Alund and 17-year-old MoDo whiz kid Peter Forsberg, who has become a star in the NHL.

Soderstrom was unanimously voted top honors with the following assessment: "Tommy Soderstrom, 21, Djurgarden's goaltender, voted the year's best rookie. In his first season playing for his team in the Elite Series, he won the Swedish national championship and the European Championship and was included on Tre Kronor to play at the World Championship. During this season, he appeared in 39 out of 40 regular-season games, as well as in all seven playoff games. In two games, including the decisive final game, he didn't let the opposition score a single goal."

In 1991 and 1992 Soderstrom won the world gold and in 1992 was voted the World Championship's best goaltender. In 1993 he won the silver when Sweden lost the final game to Russia. With Djurgarden, he was a two-time Swedish champion.

It's no wonder that the goaltender Swedes call "a living wall" attracted the attention of NHL scouts. Overseas he played for the Philadelphia Flyers, the AHL's Hershey, again for the Flyers, and ended his career with the New York Islanders.

Today, one thing about Soderstrom that is rarely remembered perhaps best illustrates his courage and his character as a player. Soderstrom was discovered to have a weak heart, a condition involving a nerve of the heart muscle, and he underwent surgery four times to cure the ailment. After the fourth operation, on January 26, 1993, he was soon back on the ice. In October of that same year, he left the ice because of chronic pain and endured a fifth surgical procedure. And again, after three weeks, he returned to the net.

Tommy Soderstrom is a very ambitious goaltender and likes to be number one. Back in Sweden, he returned to Djurgarden and, although he did his best, the team failed to win a championship. When Tre Kronor's general manager invited him to join the national team again, he turned down the offer, knowing coaches favored Tommy Salo, as at the Winter Olympics in Nagano, Japan.

In the 1999–2000 season, Djurgarden's young goalie Mikael Tellqvist was often substituted for Soderstrom, spawning a rumor that Soderstrom was ready to join the capital city's AIK, Djurgarden's long-time adversary. True to form, Soderstrom would rather be number one.

Tommy Soderstrom won World Championship gold in 1991 and 1992 and in the latter year was also voted the tournament's best goaltender—and attracted the attention of NHL scouts.

Soderstrom, Tommy
G, 5'7", 157 lbs, b: Stockholm, Sweden, 7/17/1969

Season	Club, League	Regular Season				Playoffs			
		GP	Mins	GA	Avg	GP	Mins	GA	Avg
1989–90	Djurgarden, Sweden	4	240	14	3.50				
1990–91	Djurgarden, Sweden	39	2340	104	2.67	7	423	10	1.42
WEC–91	Sweden	1	60	3	3.00				
CCup–91	Sweden	4	240	12	3.00				
1991–92	Djurgarden, Sweden	39	2340	109	2.79	10	635	28	2.65
OWG–92	Sweden	5	298	13	2.62				
WC–92	Sweden	5	299	7	1.40				
1992–93	Philadelphia Flyers, NHL	44	2512	143	3.42				
	Hershey Bears, AHL	7	373	15	2.41				
WC–93	Sweden	7	386	20	3.10				
1993–94	Philadelphia Flyers, NHL	34	1736	116	4.01				
	Hershey Bears, AHL	9	461	37	4.81				
1994–95	New York Islanders, NHL	26	1350	70	3.11				
1995–96	New York Islanders, NHL	51	2590	167	3.87				
WCup–96	Sweden	2	120	2	1.00				
1996–97	New York Islanders, NHL	1	1	0	0.00				
	Rochester Americans, AHL	2	120	8	4.00				
	Utah Grizzlies, IHL	26	1463	76	3.12				
1997–98	Djurgarden, Sweden	46	2760	103	2.24	15	936	34	2.18
1998–99	Djurgarden, Sweden	48	2918	134	2.76	4	240	11	2.75
1999–2000	Djurgarden, Sweden	21	1247	59	2.84				
	Sweden Totals	197	11845	523	2.65	36	2234	83	2.23
	NHL Totals	156	8189	496	3.63				
	OWG/WEC/WC/CCup/WCup Totals	24	1403	57	2.44				

Named Best Goaltender at WC (1992)
Won WEC (1991)
Won WC (1992)
Sweden Champion (1990, 1991)

Espen Knutsen

In 1997–98, Espen Knutsen played on an all-European line with Finn Teemu Selanne and Swede Tomas Sandstrom.

Espen Knutsen was aiming to be a role model for young hockey players in his native Norway when he joined the Anaheim Mighty Ducks of the NHL for the 1997–98 season at the age of 25.

Before he left Oslo for the Ducks' training camp in California, he even had his father get out the scissors and cut off the famous long blond locks that had been his trademark as a player in the Norwegian and Swedish leagues.

But Knutsen was also feeling the pressure from a nation of 4.5 million people who were willing him to succeed. Playing for the Djurgarden club in Stockholm, he'd finished second in scoring in the Swedish Elite League the previous season despite missing 11 games. Knutsen had been selected by Hartford in the 10th round of the 1990 Entry Draft, but his rights were traded to Anaheim in 1996 for Kevin Brown. Early in the 1997–98 campaign, he played on an all-European line with Finn Teemu Selanne and Swede Tomas Sandstrom, but he didn't adjust well to the more physical play of the NHL and was dropped to the fourth line. Finally, after scoring just three goals in 19 NHL games, he was demoted to the Mighty Ducks' American Hockey League farm club in Cincinnati, Ohio. With only a one-year contract, he became a Group II restricted free agent at the end of the season and chose to re-sign with Djurgarden in Sweden.

Knutsen was the third Norwegian-trained player to play in the NHL. Bjorn Skaare had played one game for the Detroit Red Wings in the 1978–79 season and defenseman Anders Myrvold had played a total of 13 games for the Colorado Avalanche and Boston Bruins in the previous two seasons.

A native of Oslo, Knutsen grew up just a few blocks from the rink of the Valerengen club, where his father had been a dynamic scorer. His father, a part-time hairdresser, was so slippery as a player he was given the nickname "Soap"—which is why Espen, who is even more evasive, is called "Shampoo." The joke in Norway was that Espen's son would be named "Balsam." The slick playmaking center started to play the game at the age of six and later became a huge fan of Wayne Gretzky and the Edmonton Oilers. Eventually he became too good for Norway after scoring 30 goals in 31 games for league champion Valerengen in the 1992–93 season at the age of 21. He became the glamour boy of Norwegian hockey after being named player of the year in 1994.

Canadian George Kingston, who was head of hockey in Norway, said that at junior tournaments people would ask if Knutsen was truly a Norwegian player. He wasn't a great skater but understood the game very well and had magnetism with the puck.

He recorded nine points at the 1990 World

Season	Club, League	Regular Season					Playoffs				
		GP	G	A	Pts	PIM	GP	G	A	Pts	PIM
1989–90	Valerengen, Norway	34	22	26	48	44					
1990–91	Valerengen, Norway	31	30	24	54	42	5	3	4	7	*
1991–92	Valerengen, Norway	30	28	26	54	37	8	7	8	15	*
1992–93	Valerengen, Norway	13	11	13	24	4					
1993–94	Valerengen, Norway	38	32	26	58	20					
OWG–94	Norway	7	1	3	4	2					
WC–94	Norway	6	3	2	5	0					
1994–95	Djurgarden, Sweden	30	6	14	20	18	3	0	1	1	0
WC–95	Norway	5	2	1	3	0					
1995–96	Djurgarden, Sweden	32	10	23	33	50	4	1	0	1	2
WC–96	Norway	5	3	0	3	0					
1996–97	Djurgarden, Sweden	39	16	33	49	20	4	2	4	6	6
WC–97	Norway	8	0	5	5	4					
1997–98	Anaheim Mighty Ducks, NHL	19	3	0	3	6					
	Cincinnati Mighty Ducks, AHL	41	4	13	17	18					
1998–99	Djurgarden, Sweden	39	18	24	42	32	4	0	1	1	2
1999–00	Djurgarden, Sweden	48	18	35	53	65	13	5	16	21	2
2000–01	Columbus Blue Jackets, NHL	66	11	42	53	30					
2001–02	Columbus Blue Jackets, NHL	77	11	31	42	47					
	Norway Totals	146	123	115	238	147	13	10	12	22	*
	NHL Totals	162	25	73	98	83					
	OWG/WC Totals	31	9	11	20	6					

Knutsen, Espen
C, 5'11", 168 lbs, b: Oslo, Norway, 1/12/1972

Norway Champion (1991, 1992, 1993)

Junior Championship and was named his team's best player in five of seven games at the 1991 world juniors despite having a horrible minus-20 mark.

His refusal to play in the 1992 World Junior Championship cost him a spot on the Norwegian Olympic team at Meribel, France, in 1992. Then an injury prevented him from playing in the 1993 World Championship. Because of his size—5′11″ and just 168 pounds—he was susceptible to being hit hard in the corners.

Knutsen signed with Djurgarden for the 1994–95 campaign while continuing to play for Norway at the World Championship tournaments at the end of the season. The 1994 Olympics were a minor disappointment for Knutsen. The Norwegian national team, playing in its own back-yard in the town of Lillehammer, managed only one win in the Olympic tournament and finished second last.

In the 1999–2000 season, he became the first Norwegian ever to lead the Swedish Elite League in scoring during the regular season. Then he signed with the NHL expansion Columbus team for the 2000–01 season. In 66 games, he scored 11 goals and 53 points to finish second in team scoring behind Geoff Sanderson's 56. In 2001–02, the 30-year-old Knutsen completed his third season in the NHL and second with the Blue Jackets.

Curt Lundmark

When goalie Tommy Salo deflected a shot by Canadian forward Paul Kariya during a series of shootouts between Sweden and Canada in the final game of the 1994 Olympics, making it clear that Tre Kronor was going to win the gold, a tall, graying man on the Swedish bench raised his hands in triumph. It was Sweden's head coach, Curt Lundmark. The victory at the 1994 Olympics in Lillehammer was the peak of his career. It was also Sweden's first-ever Olympic gold in hockey.

Lundmark was born on September 9, 1944, in the northern Swedish town of Skelleftea, which is well known for its hockey tradition. He debuted as a defenseman on the town's team and once won the national championship bronze. When he was drafted into the army, Lundmark found him-self even farther north, beyond the Arctic Circle in Kiruna, the birthplace of many Swedish hockey stars. He spent six seasons in the then second division's Kiruna IF. From 1968 to 1974, Lundmark played for Vasteras and was later appointed the team's coach.

In 1985 he joined Jonkoping's HV 71, which at the time was playing in Sweden's Elite Series, and helped the team win national bronze. It was Lundmark's first medal as a coach. In 1989–90, he coached Sweden's junior team and in 1990 joined Tre Kronor, where he worked with one of Sweden's best coaches, Conny Evensson. This duo helped Tre Kronor win the World Championship in 1991 and 1992.

The victory at the 1994 Olympics in Lillehammer was the peak of Curt Lundmark's career.

Then Lundmark was promoted to head coach of the national team. In 1993 they got to the world tournament finals but lost to Russia. After that came Lillehammer, the gold medal and the celebration that took Sweden by storm, with hockey fans converging on Stockholm's Sergelstorg Square. That same year, Tre Kronor won the world bronze in Italy. The next year, at the Globe Arena in Stockholm, Sweden lost the final World Championship game to Finland.

Lundmark, Curt
Coach/Head Coach, b: Skelleftea, Sweden, 9/9/1944

Season	Club, League	Regular Season					Playoffs
		GC	W	L	T	W%	
		*	*	*	*	*	
1985–89	HV-71 Jonkoping, Sweden	*	*	*	*	*	
WEC–91	Sweden	10	5	0	5	0.750	
CCup–91	Sweden	6	2	4	0	0.333	
OWG–92	Sweden	8	5	1	2	0.750	
WC–92	Sweden	8	4	2	2	0.625	
WC–93	Sweden	8	5	3	0	0.625	
OWG–94	Sweden	8	6	1	1	0.813	
WC–94	Sweden	8	5	2	1	0.687	
WC–95	Sweden	8	5	2	1	0.687	
1995–96	Preussen Berlin	50	35	8	7	0.770	
1996–97	Jokerit, Finland	50	35	11	4	0.740	
	OWG/WEC/WC /CCup Totals	64	37	15	12	0.672	

Won OWG (1994)
Won WEC/WC (1991, 1992)
Finland Champion (1997)

After his contract with Sweden's national team expired, Lundmark was invited to coach Berlin's Preussen (now Berlin Capitals). The next season he coached Helsinki's famous Jokerit, and under Lundmark's leadership they won the national championship.

In February 1998, while Lundmark was in Kiruna celebrating his wife's 50th birthday, he got a phone call from Finland's assistant coach telling him he was no longer needed. It seems that while his back was turned, the man who helped the team become national champion was ousted without explanation.

Even today, the amiable Lundmark is saddened by the fact that he has no idea why the Finnish hockey bosses made their decision. But life goes on and Lundmark was welcomed back by his former Vasteras team, where he now works as director.

According to a poll taken by the Swedish newspaper *Svenska Dagbladet*, Lundmark is considered Sweden's best coach of the last two decades of the 20th century. Despite this, Lundmark believes there were coaches better than he was. "I am a happy man," he says. "I was lucky to work with such great hockey players and great guys as Tommy Salo, Mats Sundin, Peter Forsberg, Tomas Jonsson, Fredrik Stillman and Thomas Rundqvist. It was great to be in the game with them all—and to win."

Martin Brodeur

Although Martin Brodeur hasn't yet reached his prime, he has the lowest career goals-against average in NHL history.

Although he hasn't even reached the prime years of his career, Martin Brodeur has the lowest career goals-against average in NHL history. He reached 100 wins faster than any other goalie and won a Stanley Cup during the lockout-shortened 1994–95 season with the New Jersey Devils—a team no one would have thought of as a contender for the hallowed trophy.

Brodeur's success began with his father, Denis, who was himself a goaltender on Canada's 1956 Olympic team that won a bronze medal at the Cortina Olympics in Italy. When Martin was small, he played as a forward, but at one tournament he was asked to be the team's backup goalie. "The next season," Martin explained, "my coach came up to me and said, 'Do you want to be a goalie or forward this year?' It was the biggest decision of my life, and I was seven years old. I don't know why I decided, but I thought it would be fun to play goal."

Martin was doubly blessed by his father, for not only had Denis been a goalie, he was also the long-time photographer of the Montreal Canadiens. For more than 20 years, Denis had been going to all Montreal games and practices, and of course, when Martin was old enough, he got to come along. Martin dreamed of playing for the Habs, but just as important, he idolized Patrick Roy. "He was a young guy from Montreal, like me." Brodeur explained. "I idolized him because he came in [to the NHL] so young and he showed he could do the job. He made me see the possibility of doing it myself."

Although there were some bumps along the way, Brodeur made it to the Quebec juniors to play for St. Hyacinthe for three years in the same league that produced Roy, Felix Potvin and an ever-increasing number of the world's best goalies. At the 1990 Entry Draft, Martin became one of the few goalies to be selected in the first round when the Devils selected him 20th overall, and after a year with Utica in the American Hockey League, he became New Jersey's starting goalie. His first game was against Boston, a night indelibly stamped in his memory. "I was 19, and I couldn't stop a puck in warmup. The coaches came up to me and said, 'Don't worry, kid, just go out there and have fun.' So I did. The first shot I stopped was a long one by Don Sweeney. We won the game 4–2."

Brodeur brought tremendous stability to the Devils. He played a stand-up style, challenged shooters and had fantastic mobility from side to side and a high crease-to-goal line. With positioning, he was so strong that he didn't need to flop—he relied on being in the right place at the right time. Because of his early years as a forward, he was also among the very best skaters and stickhandlers in the league, and he had one personal dream above all others when he knew he could play in the NHL. "I need to score a goal now," he said, sounding like a young Ron Hextall. "I'm looking for the chance all the time. If I get it, and it doesn't jeopardize my team, I'm going for it. I want a goal, there's no doubt about that."

That chance came during the 1997 playoffs against Montreal. With his team up by two goals late in the game of April 17, 1997, he fired the puck the length of the ice and into the net to ensure a 5–2 win in the opening game of the series. The aforementioned Hextall had been the only goalie to score a playoff goal previously.

The NHL's 1994–95 season was in jeopardy for a long time. The owners had locked the players out during heated contract negotiations and it wasn't certain there would be a season at all. Eventually a 48-game schedule was drawn up to begin in January and the short season was underway. New Jersey finished with a very average .500 record, but in the playoffs they got stronger and stronger and Brodeur took his playing to another level. In the finals against Detroit, he allowed just seven goals in four games and the Devils won the Stanley Cup in a clean sweep. Although he didn't win the Conn Smythe Trophy, it was Brodeur's play that allowed the team to win.

Since then, Brodeur has won his 200th career game in near-record speed. He's also won 30 or more games for three successive

"I'm looking for the chance [to score] all the time," says Martin Brodeur. "I want a goal, there's no doubt about that."

Brodeur, Martin
G, 6'1", 205 lbs, b: Montreal, Que., 5/6/1972

Season	Club, League	Regular Season				Playoffs			
		GP	Mins	GA	Avg	GP	Mins	GA	Avg
1991–92	New Jersey Devils, NHL	4	179	10	3.35	1	32	3	5.63
1992–93	Utica Devils, AHL	32	1952	131	4.03	4	258	18	4.19
1993–94	New Jersey Devils, NHL	47	2625	105	2.40	17	1171	38	1.95
1994–95	New Jersey Devils, NHL	40	2184	89	2.45	20	1222	34	1.67
1995–96	New Jersey Devils, NHL	77	4433	173	2.34				
WCup–96	Canada	2	60	4	4.00				
1996–97	New Jersey Devils, NHL	67	3838	120	1.88	10	659	19	1.73
1997–98	New Jersey Devils, NHL	70	4128	130	1.89	6	366	12	1.97
OWG–98	Canada	0	0	0	0.00	0	0	0	0.00
1998–99	New Jersey Devils, NHL	70	4239	162	2.29	7	425	20	2.82
1999–00	New Jersey Devils, NHL	72	4312	161	2.24	23	1450	39	1.61
2000–01	New Jersey Devils, NHL	72	4297	166	2.32	25	1505	52	2.07
2001–02	New Jersey Devils, NHL	73	4347	156	2.15				
OWG–02	Canada	5	300	9	1.80				
	NHL Totals	592	34583	1272	2.21				
	OWG/WCup Totals	7	360	13	2.17				

NHL Second All-Star Team (1997, 1998)
Won Calder Trophy (1994)
Won William M. Jennings Trophy (1997, 1998)
Won Stanley Cup (1995, 2000)
Won OWG (2002)

seasons—one of only seven goalies ever to do so—and added another 40-plus season to his portfolio in 1999–2000, followed with his second Stanley Cup win. The Devils and Brodeur returned to the Stanley Cup finals in the spring of 2001, looking to defend their championship, but were turned back in a thrilling seven-game series by the Colorado Avalanche.

Brodeur was selected as one of three goaltenders for the Canadian Olympic Team in Salt Lake City along with Curtis Joseph and Ed Belfour. In 1998 he'd been the designated number two goalie behind Patrick Roy and hadn't seen any playing time, but this time Brodeur and Canada went on to beat the United States in the championship, earning Canada's first Olympic men's hockey gold medal in 50 years. Ironically, his father, Denis, had tended goal for Canada's bronze medal-winning men's hockey team in the 1956 Winter Olympics.

Brodeur's consistent brilliance, helped by a remarkable Devils defense, might well threaten Patrick Roy's records in just a few years, since he's still fairly young. He wears the names of his children on the back of his mask, and if he stays healthy, it won't be luck that will make him one of the greatest goalies of all time.

Pat Quinn

After four seasons with Toronto and Vancouver, Pat Quinn (center) went in 1972–73 to the Atlanta Flames where he was considered a cornerstone of the team's defense.

As head coach of the Toronto Maple Leafs, Pat Quinn is best known among hockey fans today as one of the people responsible for bringing the team out of the doldrums and into NHL prominence in the late 1990s. But after several sometimes controversial stops as a coach around the league, the much-traveled Quinn is also a veteran of the big-league wars.

The son of a fire chief in Hamilton, Ontario, Quinn entered a seminary at the age of 14, thinking of becoming a priest. "It was one of those things that every good Catholic boy figures—that the next logical step is to become a priest," Quinn remembers. "But it just wasn't for me. I just wanted to play ball and hockey. I just wanted to be a kid, I guess."

In pursuit of those childhood hockey dreams, Quinn played for the OHA's Hamilton Tiger Cubs for two years and established an early reputation as a tough defenseman who wasn't afraid of a good fight. After that, he took a hockey scholarship at Michigan Tech but had to give it up after the NCAA banned players who had signed pro contracts from playing U.S. collegiate hockey. Quinn had signed his rights to the Detroit Red Wings, which made him ineligible. Instead, Quinn traveled to Alberta to play for the Edmonton Oil Kings, helping the team to a Memorial Cup.

At the end of his junior career, Quinn signed on with the Knoxville (Tennessee) Knights of the Eastern Hockey League. It was with the Knights that Quinn made an important decision about hockey—and life. "When I looked at some of the guys on that team, my eyes were opened," he said. "There were a couple of players in their mid-30s, struggling to hang on in the lowest league. They weren't prepared to do anything else, and when hockey was over for them, they'd be forced to take menial jobs. I decided then that I wasn't going to be that way when I was 35 and that maybe I wouldn't be good enough to make the NHL."

Beginning in 1963, Quinn started to study for his bachelor of arts degree. As he moved around in the minor leagues, Quinn attended classes at the University of Tennessee, the University of Tulsa, Memphis State and others, finally earning a degree from York University in 1972 after studying at six different schools.

But Quinn need not have worried about not being good enough to play in the NHL. In 1968 the long-time minor leaguer was called up by Toronto, where he played for two seasons. One of Quinn's best-known moments as a player was his crunching check of Bobby Orr as the Bruins were eliminating the Leafs in a four-game sweep in the 1969 playoffs. The two had engaged in a punch-up during the regular season, and many thought Quinn's controversial slam on Orr was payback for the earlier fracas. Although the Leafs said it was a clean hit, many in Boston wanted Quinn suspended for it—and, to this day, die-hard Bruins fans contend that it was the Quinn "elbow" that contributed to Orr's decline and ultimate retirement.

After his time in Toronto, Quinn was claimed by Vancouver in the 1970 Expansion Draft. He played for the Canucks for two more seasons and in 1972–73 he went to the Atlanta Flames, where he was considered a cornerstone on the team's defensive corps until his retirement in 1977. As a player, Quinn's forte was never offense—he scored only 18 goals and got 113 assists in a total of 606 games—but he nevertheless made an important contribution to the three teams he played for. "His experience is a valuable asset to us," said Flames general manager Cliff Fletcher. "He never places himself in a position where his lack of speed hurts him."

Fletcher wasn't the only one around the league who considered Quinn's experience a plus. In 1977 he joined the Philadelphia Flyers

Quinn, Pat
D, 6′3″, 205 lbs, b: Hamilton, Ont., 1/29/1943

Season	Club, League	Regular Season					Playoffs				
		GP	G	A	Pts	PIM	GP	G	A	Prs	PIM
1962–63	Edmonton Oil Kings, ASHL	*	*	*	*	*	*	*	*	*	*
1963–64	Knoxville Knights, EHL	72	6	31	37	217	8	1	3	4	34
1964–65	Tulsa Oilers, CHL	70	3	32	35	202	3	0	0	0	0
1965–66	Memphis Wings, CHL	67	2	16	18	135					
1966–67	Houston Apollos, CHL	15	0	3	3	66					
	Seattle Totems, WHL	35	1	3	4	49	5	0	0	0	2
1967–68	Tulsa Oilers, CHL	51	3	15	18	178	11	1	4	5	10
1968–69	Toronto Maple Leafs, NHL	40	2	7	9	95	4	0	0	0	13
	Tulsa Oilers, CHL	17	0	6	6	25					
1969–70	Toronto Maple Leafs, NHL	59	0	5	5	88					
	Tulsa Oilers, CHL	2	0	1	1	6					
1970–71	Vancouver Canucks, NHL	76	2	11	13	149					
1971–72	Vancouver Canucks, NHL	57	2	3	5	63					
1972–73	Atlanta Flames, NHL	78	2	18	20	113					
1973–74	Atlanta Flames, NHL	77	5	27	32	94	4	0	0	0	6
1974–75	Atlanta Flames, NHL	80	2	19	21	156					
1975–76	Atlanta Flames, NHL	80	2	11	13	134	2	0	1	1	2
1976–77	Atlanta Flames, NHL	59	1	12	13	58	1	0	0	0	0
	NHL Totals	606	18	113	131	950	11	0	1	1	21

as an assistant coach under Fred Shero, then coached the Maine Mariners of the American Hockey League for half a season before coming back to the Flyers as head coach and leading the team to two successful seasons in first and second place in the Campbell Conference. The Flyers recorded an NHL record 35-game winning streak under Quinn, who went on to sign a five-year contract with the team in 1981. But to the amazement of most Flyers fans, he was fired in just the second year of the deal. Quinn responded by enrolling in law school, continuing to draw his Flyers paycheck and keeping abreast of NHL activity by watching games on TV.

After being let go from the Flyers, Quinn wasn't finished with controversy in the coaching department. In 1987, back in the coaching game with the Los Angeles Kings, Quinn was suspended from the NHL for several months because he had accepted a $100,000 signing bonus to become president and general manager of the Vancouver Canucks while still under contract with L.A. The Canucks were also fined by league president John Ziegler for paying Quinn the bonus, as were the Kings for not reporting the deal promptly.

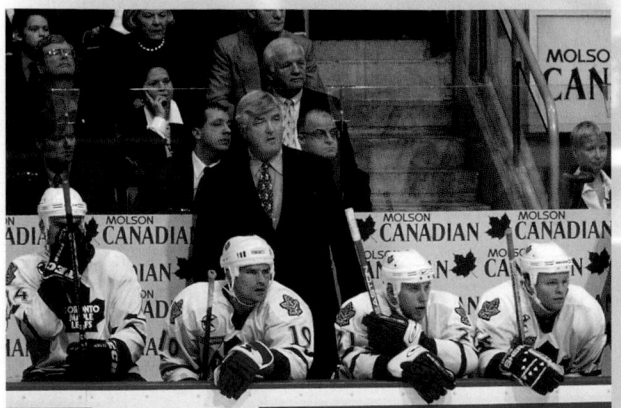

As head coach of the Toronto Maple Leafs, Pat Quinn (standing) is responsible for bringing the team out of the doldrums and back into prominence in the late 1990s.

Nevertheless, Quinn coached 11 seasons in Vancouver, leading the team to a narrow loss to the New York Rangers in a seven-game Stanley Cup finals in 1994 before coming back to the Maple Leafs for the 1998–99 season. He quickly made his presence felt, telling fans and reporters he had definite plans for his new team, one that had been a little flat in the goal-scoring department in past years. "I don't want to open up the offense at the expense of solid defense," he said. "That's the most important thing. When we do get the puck, I want us to do something assertive with it. Whether that breaks down to scoring more goals, we'll see."

Quinn certainly became a big hit in his early days with the team he once played with, leading them to their first playoff appearance since 1996 and their third trip to the conference finals in the 1990s. Quinn also led the team to a club-record 45 wins. He finished the season as runner-up for the Jack Adams Award as the NHL's coach of the year and during the off-season was named general manager of the Leafs as well.

As always, Quinn's uncompromising attitude to the game shone through. "You can set the bar wherever you want," he said. "But if we aren't capable of reaching it, then you're creating a falseness among your team, because we'll never get there."

Perhaps the defining moment and ultimate validation of Quinn's coaching credentials came at the Salt Lake City Olympics, where he led Team Canada to its first gold medal in 50 years. As Quinn is known to do in the NHL, he used the round robin as sort of a workshop, tinkering with lines and seeing which combinations worked best. Quinn seemed unflappable, even after a horrible opening-game loss to Sweden and a lackluster win over Germany, insisting the team was learning by its mistakes as it moved along. By the third game, against the Czechs, Team Canada was playing much better as a cohesive unit on the bigger ice surface. As further proof that he was going to win his way rather than worrying about offending others, Quinn took the bold step of benching Eric Lindros for much of the playoff-round game against Finland. Lindros responded in the next game with the best performance of the tournament in a game against Belarus, dishing out numerous bodychecks, backchecking and contributing a goal in the 7–1 win. But despite Quinn's strong presence behind the scenes, he never became the story. On the exterior, he guided his ship quietly along to the gold medal game where Canada ended its long Olympic frustration, defeating the United States on their own ground 5–2.

Quinn, Pat
Coach, b: Hamilton, Ont., 1/29/1943

Season	Club, League	\	Regul	ar Sea	son	\	\	Play	offs	\	\
		GC	W	L	T	W%	GC	W	L	T	W%
1978–79	Philadelphia Flyers, NHL	30	18	8	4	0.667	8	3	5	0	0.375
1979–80	Philadelphia Flyers, NHL	80	48	12	20	0.725	19	13	6	0	0.684
1980–81	Philadelphia Flyers, NHL	80	41	24	15	0.606	12	6	6	0	0.500
1981–82	Philadelphia Flyers, NHL	72	34	29	9	0.535					
1984–85	Los Angeles Kings, NHL	80	34	32	14	0.513	3	0	3	0	0
1985–86	Los Angeles Kings, NHL	80	23	49	8	0.338					
1986–87	Los Angeles Kings, NHL	42	18	20	4	0.476					
1990–91	Vancouver Canucks, NHL	26	9	13	4	0.423	6	2	4	0	0.333
1991–92	Vancouver Canucks, NHL	80	42	26	12	0.600	13	6	7	0	0.462
1992–93	Vancouver Canucks, NHL	84	46	29	9	0.601	12	6	6	0	0.500
1993–94	Vancouver Canucks, NHL	84	41	40	3	0.506	24	15	9	0	0.625
1995–96	Vancouver Canucks, NHL	6	3	3	0	0.500	6	2	4	0	0.333
1998–99	Toronto Maple Leafs, NHL	82	45	30	7	0.591	17	9	8	0	0.592
1999–00	Toronto Maple Leafs, NHL	82	45	30	7	0.591	12	6	6	0	0.500
2000–01	Toronto Maple Leafs, NHL	82	37	29	11	5	11	7	4	0	0
2001–02	Toronto Maple Leafs, NHL	82	43	25	10	4					
OWG–02	Canada	6	4	1	0	0					
	NHL Totals	1072	527	399	137	9					
	OWG Totals	6	4	1	0	0					

Won Jack Adams Award (1980, 1992)
Won OWG (2002)

Magnus Svensson

With only one minute and 49 seconds left in the final game between Sweden and Canada at the 1994 Olympics in Lillehammer, the Canadians were leading 2–1. Everyone watching the game in the stadium and on television was sure the Canadians would win—everyone except defenseman Magnus Svensson, wearing the yellow and blue jersey of Sweden, who tied the score with a powerful shot from the blue line and added his name to the list of Olympic gold medalists who played hockey for Sweden.

With only one minute and 49 seconds left in the final game between Sweden and Canada at the 1994 Olympics, Magnus Svensson (number 8) scored with a powerful shot from the blue line and added his name to the list of Olympic gold medalists.

Sweden was even luckier in the shootout that followed, with Svensson scoring on a penalty shot.

Svensson played at the top of his game during his entire hockey career—a fearless, tough performer who played by the rules. A defenseman who loved the feel of scoring a goal, the 19-year-old rookie began his career as a forward with Leksand in 1982. In a game against Bjorkloven on October 3, 1983, he scored his first goal in Sweden's national Elite Series. A year later, on December 11, 1984, in an exhibition game against Norway in Oslo, Svensson made his debut with Sweden and scored his first goal at the international level. However, he had to wait another three years to make his first appearance in a World Championship, in Vienna in 1987. He played only two games but shared the gold won by Sweden after a 25-year hiatus.

The 1990 World Championship in Switzerland was memorable for "Sigge," as he was nicknamed by fans. The defenseman scored his first goal in a World Championship in the game against Norway on April 17 in Fribourg and played out the tournament as a forward, a position he hadn't filled in some time. Sweden came in second, and Svensson was invited to play for Switzerland's Lugano, where he spent a year before returning to Leksand. Then came the 1994 Olympic Games in Lillehammer and Svensson's famous goal. Lady Luck smiled on Svensson once again in 1994. At the World Championship in Italy, Sweden won the bronze and, with eight goals to his credit, Svensson was named best defenseman of the tournament.

Svensson, Magnus
D, 5′11″, 180 lbs, b: Tranas, Sweden, 3/1/1963

Season	Club, League	Regular Season					Playoffs				
		GP	G	A	Pts	PIM	GP	G	A	Pts	PIM
1983–84	Leksand, Sweden	35	3	8	11	20					
1984–85	Leksand, Sweden	35	8	7	15	22					
1985–86	Leksand, Sweden	36	6	9	15	62					
1986–87	Leksand, Sweden	33	8	16	24	42					
WEC–87	Sweden	2	0	0	0	4					
1987–88	Leksand, Sweden	40	12	11	23	20	3	0	0	0	8
1988–89	Leksand, Sweden	39	15	22	37	40	9	3	5	8	8
1989–90	Leksand, Sweden	26	11	12	23	60	1	0	0	0	0
WEC–90	Sweden	10	2	1	3	8					
1990–91	Lugano, Switzerland	33	16	20	36	*	11	3	2	5	*
1991–92	Leksand, Sweden	22	4	10	14	32					
1992–93	Leksand, Sweden	37	10	17	27	36	2	0	2	2	0
1993–94	Leksand, Sweden	39	13	16	29	22	4	3	1	4	0
OWG–94	Sweden	7	4	1	5	6					
WC–94	Sweden	8	8	1	9	8					
1994–95	Davos, Switzerland.	35	8	25	33	46	5	2	2	4	8
	Florida Panthers, NHL	19	2	5	7	10					
1995–96	Florida Panthers, NHL	27	2	9	11	21					
1996–97	Leksand, Sweden	45	8	17	25	62	9	1	2	3	35
WC–97	Sweden	10	0	6	6	16					
1997–98	HV-71, Sweden	16	0	2	2	2					
	Leksand, Sweden	42	2	23	25	52	4	0	1	1	6
1998–99	Leksand, Sweden	48	11	24	35	70	4	1	1	2	2
1999–2000	Rapprswil-Jona, Sweden	42	7	25	32	44					
	Sweden Totals	535	118	219	337	586	*	*	*	*	*
	NHL Totals	46	4	14	18	31					
	OWG/WEC/WC Totals	37	14	9	23	42					

Named Best Defenseman at WC (1994)
Won OWG (1994)
Won WEC (1987)

1996–1999

———

The New Elite

*T*he regular season didn't yield many surprises in 1995–96. The Red Wings finished 27 points in front of their closest pursuers from Colorado in the overall standings and these two went into the playoffs as the favorites along with Philadelphia, led by Eric Lindros, and Pittsburgh, which had Mario Lemieux back in the lineup after a one-year hiatus. However, the championship had barely begun before the pundits were airing their views on the subject of the Florida Panthers— a club that had only been in the league for three seasons.

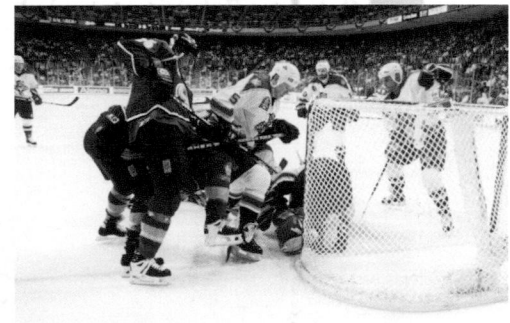

The four favorites would get ahead on wins in the end, but indeed the Panthers made a place for themselves in the playoffs for the first time in their very brief history. And they didn't stop there. They knocked Boston out 4–1 in the first round and then forced out Lindros and Co. Furthermore, the finals in the Eastern Conference were a thriller that went the full seven games when the Panthers' troubleshoot-ers managed to neutralize Pittsburgh's most illustrious forwards, Mario Lemieux and Jaromir Jagr, with considerable help from netminder John Vanbiesbrouck's inspired—and inspiring—performance.

In the West, the season developed uneventfully. Halfway through it, the Colorado Avalanche received a badly needed star goalkeeper, Patrick Roy, who had clashed with new Canadiens coach Mario Tremblay. Roy went on to win in six games against Vancouver, Chicago and Detroit with no special problems. Even the octopuses Detroit fans tossed on home ice at Joe Louis Arena as a token of admiration or indignation didn't hinder (or help). After long pauses for clearing the ice, the Avalanche came thundering down just as powerfully. And the NHL leadership would soon find such pauses couldn't be permitted. Starting with the following season, it was forbidden to throw out onto the ice—or even to bring into the arena—such objects as real octopuses or the toy rats that had become popular with Florida fans.

The 1996 Stanley Cup finals repeated the previous year's in that they were as brief as they could be and lacking in mystery. The Panthers retained their ability to cover the two Pittsburgh

In the 1995–96 season, the Panthers clinched a playoff spot for the first time in team history. And they didn't stop there and made it all the way to the finals. But in the end, even the good-luck rats couldn't save Florida.

A HISTORY OF WORLD HOCKEY

After three defeats in the 1995–96 Stanley Cup finals, Florida had managed to drag out game four through two overtimes when a long slapshot by Uwe Krupp brought down the final curtain at 4:31 of the third overtime period.

superstars and no one was able to neutralize the two fleet Colorado forward lines that excelled in a combination style of play. In the end, even the good-luck rats couldn't save the Panthers, however. After two defeats in Denver and one at home in Miami Arena, they managed to drag out game four through two overtimes until a long slapshot by Colorado defenseman Uwe Krupp brought down the final curtain at 4:31 of the third overtime period for a 1–0 loss.

As Team Finland's Swedish coach Curt Lindstrom was accepting congratulations after "the golden triumph" in Stockholm in 1995, he already knew it was going to be difficult to repeat the performance. In the fall of 1995, four of the five men on his strongest line went over to the NHL, Saku Koivu and Marko Kiprusoff to Montreal, Jere Lehtinen to Dallas and Ville Peltonen to San Jose. Peltonen's NHL career came to an end after two seasons with Nashville, but he was the only one who could come to Vienna for the World Championship in 1996 and the Finns were rolled back to fifth place.

Meanwhile, Team Russia's lineup was augmented with 12 NHLers headed by Alexei Yashin from Ottawa and six European league players led by Sergei Berezin. The efforts of Yashin and Berezin helped bring their countrymen to the semifinals, but their next attempt at a medal was foiled by Team Canada in a post-game shootout.

The Czech Republic met the United States in the other semifinals. Ron Wilson was coaching the American team on the eve of World Cup 1996, but he was limited in his choice of players. Kevin Stevens was the only certified star he was able to get, though he supplemented his lines with such hard-driving forwards as Chris Tangilla, Brian Rolston and Joe Sacco. Around these four players, Wilson was able to shape a team that lost to the Czechs but still managed to capture World Championship medals for the first time since 1962. In the game for third place, the Americans were three goals behind the Russians but tied it before time ran out and then Rolston scored the winning goal.

A perfect check.

Meanwhile, the man who led the Czech team to the finals was guided by principles diametrically opposed to what other European coaches were practising in the years he was building his lineup. Ludek Bukac invited 14 players from the Czech Republic to the World Championship, and indeed Pavel Patera, Otakar Vejvoda and Martin Prochazka—who were only dreaming of a career overseas—returned the title to Czech hockey after an 11-year interval. Prochazka became the main man of the series when he slapped in the winning goal in the finals against Canada with 19 seconds left on the clock.

The eight participants in the 1996 World Cup were broken into two groups of four, one playing in Europe (Sweden, Finland, Germany and the Czech Republic) and the other in North America (Canada, USA, Russia and Slovakia). The winners in each of the groups would go directly to the semifinals, the top three teams in each group would go to the playoffs, and the finals would consist of a three-game series.

The first and only upset occurred in the group that was playing in Europe. The Czech coaches

A double team.

were unable to find a common language with their NHLers and the team was trounced by both the Finns (7–3) and the Germans (7–1) and eliminated. In the second group, coach Ron Wilson's Americans beat the Canadians (5–3), the Russians (5–2) and the Slovaks (3–2) to rank first while Canadian victories over Russia (5–3) and Slovakia (3–2) put them second. The Slovaks lost to the Russians (7–4) and were out of the playoffs. The quarter- and semifinals that resulted conformed to both the forecasts and the new balance of forces in world hockey. First Canada took Germany 4–1 and Russia took Finland 5–0. Then Team USA whipped Russia 5–2 without any trouble. The Canadians had to work a bit harder, but they finally defeated the Swedes in the second overtime on a shot by Theo Fleury.

Before the final series, specialists seemed to agree that Ron Wilson's team had a more reliable defense line in Bryan Leetch, Chris Chelios and goalie Mike Richter. But the Canadians had a more powerful attacking line with Wayne Gretzky, Mark Messier, Eric Lindros, Steve Yzerman and Joe Sakic. In the event, Team Canada wasn't able to capitalize on its attacking potential until the overtime of the first game (which ended 4–3), but in the next games the Americans compelled everyone to recall the USA–USSR match in Lake Placid. The second and third games in the finals ended with identical scores of 5–2 in favor of the Americans. Brett Hull and John LeClair outpaced all the Canadian sharpshooters, in the decisive games Tony Amonte repeated the miracles wrought by Paul Henderson in the 1972 Summit Series, and behind it all Mike Richter repeatedly saved his team in seemingly hopeless situations and was named MVP.

In the spring of 1997, the Detroit Red Wings were too much for the favored Philadelphia Flyers and won the Stanley Cup, their first since 1955.

The majority of forecasts for the 1996–97 season seemed to agree on one point: Detroit and Colorado would make it to the finals in the Western Conference. Having suffered two setbacks in his attempt to take home the Cup, coach Scotty Bowman radically restructured the Detroit lineup and acquired the brilliant, hard-hitting forward Brendan Shanahan and the experienced defenseman Larry Murphy. Beyond that, Bowman didn't try to force events in the regular season; he was saving his men for the playoffs.

Colorado played like champions again and won the Presidents' Trophy although practically none of coach Marc Crawford's leading players was able to avoid injuries. Uwe Krupp was hurt during the season, and during the playoffs he was joined by forwards Keith Jones and Stephane Yelle and then Peter Forsberg. No one is exempt from getting injured in hockey, but losses in proportions like these substantially narrow the chances of winning a series. Colorado took the first game of the division finals in Denver, lost three in a row and finally managed a miracle with a home game of 6–0. And after that they were spent. The Red Wings played the decisive game of this spectacular series practically flawlessly and won it 3–1 to go on to the Stanley Cup finals for the first time since 1995.

In the first round of the 1996-1997 playoffs, having won that one 6–3 and the series 4–1, Philadelphia left the Penguins out in the cold.

In the conference finals, Lindros and Co. disappointed the Great One, who had rejoined former Edmonton teammates Mark Messier and Esa Tikkanen in the Rangers. It was getting close

A HISTORY OF WORLD HOCKEY

In 1997–98, the Washington Capitals surprised many as they went all way to the finals.

to Gretzy's last chance for one more sip from the Cup, too, and it was a chance that was missed when the Flyers won the series in five games.

The finals that pitted Detroit against Philadelphia reaffirmed the long-standing axiom that it was practically impossible to win in the playoffs without a stable star goalie. In the previous two seasons, Scotty Bowman had given preference to 25-year-old Chris Osgood. This time he placed his bet on the more experienced, 34-year-old Mike Vernon—who had already won the Stanley Cup when he was playing with Calgary—and it was a good call. Vernon halted the Legion of Doom, allowing an average of 1.5 goals against per game in the finals, for which he was awarded the Conn Smythe Trophy. (By way of comparison, the performance of Philadelphia goalies Ron Hextall and Garth Snow was half as good at 4.0.) As a result, the Stanley Cup finals were limited to four games for the third straight year. And this time they ended with a victory for the Red Wings for the first time in 42 years. Having molded a team that was nearly invulnerable, Bowman himself had been leading the Wings to this end for four years.

Unfortunately, the festivities in Detroit were marred by a tragedy. On June 13, Vladimir Konstantinov, Viacheslav Fetisov and Red Wings masseur Sergei Mnatsakanov were involved in a car accident. Fate was kindest to Fetisov; unlike his friends, he got away with minor injuries. But an injury to Konstantinov's skull put an end to his hockey career. He is still always greeted with a standing ovation on his frequent visits to Joe Louis Arena—but he's brought in a wheelchair.

At this point, the Stanley Cup had begun to visit cities beyond North America and to go through Europe as well. It had been in the small Swedish town of Ornskoldsvik, 1996 Cup winner Peter Forsberg's home town. And in the summer of 1997, the trophy was in Moscow's Red Square.

The 1998 Stanley Cup finals ended in a four-game win for the Detroit Red Wings that was typical of the second half of the 1990s.

The resounding sensation at the 1997 World Championship in Finland was another setback for Team Suomi, which was buried by its own walls, so to speak. The fans and the media demanded nothing less than a victory from the hosting national team, but the Finns ended up in fifth place and were eliminated when another change in the regulations meant that only four teams would make it to the final round of the tournament. The Czech Republic won 4–3 against Russia to win the bronze medal, while the finals were played in a best-of-three format for the first time. Sweden's coach, Kent Forsberg—with only defensemen Tommy Albelin and Mattias Norstrom and goalkeeper Tommy Salo as reinforcements from the NHL—had practically no one in his forward lines to put up against the aggressive Canadians, which included Travis Green (New York Islanders), Owen Nolan (San Jose), Jeff Friesen (San Jose), Anson Carter (Boston), Rob Zamuner (Tampa), Mark Recchi (Montreal), Keith Primeau (Hartford), Geoff Sanderson (Hartford) and Jarome Iginla (Calgary). And indeed the Canadians were the strongest for the second time in four years with scores of 2–3, 3–1 and 2–1.

The Dallas Stars continued their upward climb in the 1997–98 season. The addition of goalie extraordinaire Ed Belfour beefed up a strong defense line and Dallas soon occupied the top slot in both the Central Division and the league overall. Meanwhile, the Washington Capitals were *making the most obvious progress before truly astounding events unfolded in the first round of the Eastern Conference playoffs.*

The strongest teams in the division lost: the favorite, Philadelphia, to Buffalo (4–1), Pittsburgh to Montreal (4–2) and New Jersey to Ottawa (4–2). Only the Capitals played according to their rating when they overcame Boston 4–2. But then the expected tense struggle between Washington and Ottawa in the second round didn't materialize. Five games were enough for the Capitals to emerge in the finals, while four games sufficed for the Sabres.

In 1997–98, Steve Yzerman (shooting) saw his name engraved on the Conn Smythe Trophy after the Red Wings repeated as Stanley Cup champions.

The outcome of a contest between two clubs that both preached the gospel of defensive hockey was predetermined by the rich experience of Washington's defensemen and the brilliant performance of German-born goalie Olaf Kolzig. With a 1.83 goals-against average in the conference finals, Kolzig outplayed even Dominik Hasek (2.16) and the Capitals made it to the 1998 Stanley Cup finals when they won three games in overtime and six overall.

In the West, no one doubted that Dallas, Detroit and Colorado would emerge in the conference semifinals and one of them would become the chief contender for the Cup. One player alone dashed the Colorado team's hopes of repeating their triumph of 1996. After the first round of the playoffs, 31-year-old Edmonton goalie Curtis Joseph compelled virtually everyone to believe he had been underrated. In the three final games of the series, practically the highest-rated company of forwards in the NHL—Colorado's sharpshooters, led by Forsberg and Sakic—were able to score but a single goal against Joseph and the Oilers won the series 4–3. Meanwhile, Dallas and Detroit easily sailed to the Western Conference finals, where the holders of the Presidents' Trophy—in this case the Stars—were doomed to drop out. This unfortunate coincidence had all but turned into fate in the 1990s, and that's exactly what happened. The Red Wings won in six games.

The Stanley Cup finals ended in a four-game win for Detroit (2–1, 5–4, 2–1 and 4–1) that was typical of the second half of the 1990s. Only in game two had the Capitals had a chance of tipping the scales. The Capitals were ahead 4–2 at the 13-minute mark in the final period in Joe Louis Arena when 33-year-old Washington forward Esa Tikkanen had what appeared to be a 100% chance to take the score to 5–2. When the wily and well-seasoned Tikkanen outplayed two Red Wings defensemen and zeroed in on Chris Osgood's net, a goal seemed inevitable. The outcome of the game would be sealed and the series even.

Crawling to victory.

This is how it was played: Esa feinted, fooled Osgood into coming out of his crease, skated down on the now empty net and fired the puck from a distance of three meters—right past the far goal post. The Capitals were still trying to regain their senses after the Finn's fatal error as Martin Lapointe and Doug Brown took the game into overtime, the 16th minute of which became the moment of glory for Kris Draper when his only goal in the 1998 playoffs became the one that won it 5–4.

The 1998–99 season saw the appearance of the 27th team in the league, the Nashville Predators. The structure of the NHL also changed as the clubs were spread out among three divisions in each conference, the Atlantic, Northeast and Southeast in the East and the Central, Northwest and Pacific in the West. Teemu Selanne won the Maurice Richard Trophy with 47 goals in this, the first year that it was awarded.

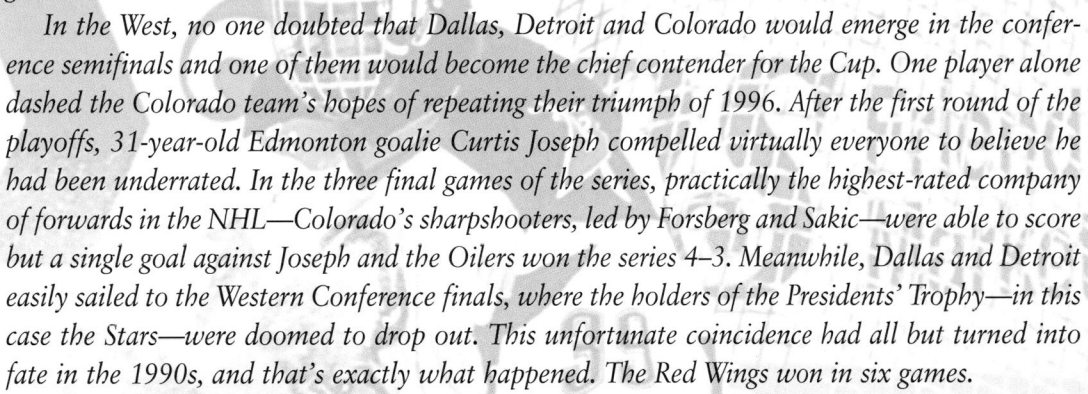

A HISTORY OF WORLD HOCKEY

In the 1998–99 season, the league made some rule changes in an attempt to protect the goalkeepers.

But the season was mainly distinguished by the 1998 Olympic Games in Nagano. For the first time in its history, the NHL agreed to take a two-week break so the best hockey players in the world could participate in the Olympiad. Furthermore, it was decided that the chief referees from the NHL would officiate in the final round and the playoffs to avoid any problems that might stem from different interpretations of the rules in North America and Europe. The conditions for forming Olympic teams also changed and the leading hockey countries had a unique opportunity to put all their best players on their national squads.

Not surprisingly, most of the coaches gave preference to NHLers as they drew up their rosters. The Canadian and U.S. teams were entirely made up of pros (and the Americans almost completely repeated the lineup that had won the World Cup in 1996). Only goalie Oleg Shevtsov played for a Soviet team, but a host of NHLers appeared in the national squads of Sweden (18) and Finland (14), while Czech coaches Ivan Hlinka and Stanislav Lerner gave half the berths on their national team to pros, along with seven who played in the Czech Republic itself and three from clubs in Sweden and Finland.

In a series of preliminary rounds, Germany and Slovakia, Kazakhstan and Belarus won the right to continue against the six strongest teams. In the end, the national teams from the former republics of the USSR lost all their games and were relegated to the level of stand-ins in the final round, but in much of the rest of the finals the turn of events was even more unexpected.

But it didn't work out.

In the first two periods of a game against Sweden, for example, Team USA had made double the shots on goal at 22–11 but was still losing with a score of 3–2. Ironically, it was the Swedish (and Leafs) player Mats Sundin who sealed the fate of the Americans in the 58th minute when he made it 4–2. A similar picture unfolded in the final game between Canada and the USA, where the score was 4–1 but the shots on goal 15–32, and the quarterfinal game between the Czechs and the Americans, where it was 4–1 and 20–39.

The American winners of the 1996 World Cup distinguished themselves by their undisciplined behavior on and off the ice in Nagano. In the opinion of Hockey News, only three of their players (defenseman Chris Chelios and forwards Brett Hull and Bill Guerin) played "above average." Canada turned in a more dignified performance, even if only two players sparkled like stars, defenseman Rob Blake and center Joe Nieuwendyk. Bursts of Canadian action in the second period took the score to 3–0 when Blake and Al MacInnis scored on passes from Nieuwendyk—who put in the third in a solo performance—and that squeezed out the Swedes even though they scored twice in the last period. In the semifinals against the Czechs, Trevor Linden took the game into overtime by tying it 1–1 just 63 seconds before the end of the third period, but neither Theo Fleury nor Ray Bourque nor Nieuwendyk nor Lindros nor Shanahan were able to outplay goalkeeper Dominik Hasek in the shootout. When Patrick Roy lost a duel with the Czech (and New York Islanders') Robert Reichel, Canada was out of the fight for the gold.

In the first game in Group B, the Czechs faced the Finns, who had brought to Nagano a whole constellation of stellar forwards: Jari Kurri, Teemu Selanne, Esa Tikkanen, Saku Koivu and Jere

Lehtinen. But with forwards including Jaromir Jagr actively helping, the Czech defense seemed impenetrable, and as a last resort there was always Hasek in goal to rectify rare mistakes. The Finns just couldn't score and it ended 3–0. Then the Czechs were ahead 1–0 in the game against the Russians when a 10-second mixup in the 44th minute cost the Czech team two goals, by Valeri Bure and Alexei Zhamnov. In the quarterfinal playoff, the Czechs outplayed the Americans 4–1, and once again this was executed in a style typical of Czechoslovakia's national squad in the Golden Era of the 1970s: reliable defense and instantaneous counterattacks.

For the first time in its history, the NHL agreed to take a two-week break so the best hockey players in the world could participate in the 1998 Olympics.

The Russian squad made its first bid for victory in the round-robin game against the Finns, who were leading 2–0 and 3–1 in the first half of the game before Russian coach Vladimir Yurzinov finally found the right words to fire up his team to tie it and then wrench out a victory. After that, they almost effortlessly outplayed the Belarus squad 4–1 in the quarterfinals.

The results were quite different in the playoffs. The Czechs hurdled the American and Canadian barriers on the way to the finals, but the Russians had to cross sticks again with the Finns. The game was virtually a solo performance by Russian forward Pavel Bure of the Vancouver Canucks, who put in five goals. Moreover, the Finns lost not only the game but star player Teemu Selanne, who was injured before the match against Canada for the bronze.

The Canadians seemed to have made up their minds not to leave Nagano without some kind of medal, but Finnish coach Hannu Aravirta risked entrusting the net to Ari Sulander—and guessed right. The substitute goalie was unable to stop the only two Canadian shots, but Finnish forwards Jari Kurri, Jere Lehtinen and Ville Peltonen each sent a puck in past Roy. With that game at 3–2, Finland ranked third and squeezed hockey's proud founders to fourth.

The final game between the Czech Republic and Russia didn't seem all that gripping. Pavel Bure and Alexei Yashin couldn't open up in the closed type of hockey the Czechs played and the game was decided in the last period by Czech defenseman Petr Svoboda when he sent the puck into the net past goalkeeper Mikhail Shtalenkov, who couldn't see anything over all the players' backs. When it ended with a score of 1–0, the team from the Czech Republic became Olympic champions for the first time—in a tournament that was without precedent in the history of world hockey in the level of players.

In 1999, Joe Nieuwendyk (number 25) scored six game-winning goals in the playoffs to help the Dallas Stars beat the Buffalo Sabres in the Stanley Cup finals.

The first round of the 1999 Stanley Cup playoffs began with a number of surprises. Toronto coach Pat Quinn and his international forward lines proved stronger than Philadelphia, which traditionally gave preference to power hockey, and the Leafs won 4–2. By now without Mario Lemieux, Pittsburgh surprised many and defeated the leading team in the Eastern Conference, the New Jersey Devils, in seven games. Having lost Jaromir Jagr, and then Alexei Kovalev in the second game of the series against the Leafs, Pittsburgh did allow Toronto into the finals of the conference, however. Meanwhile, the Buffalo Sabres had outplayed the Senators in four games and then Boston 4–2. Alas, the hopes of many North American fans that the home of attack

A HISTORY OF WORLD HOCKEY

hockey would reach the 1999 Stanley Cup finals and excite them as much as in years now long past weren't destined to materialize. Inspired by goalie Dominik Hasek, Buffalo's defense proved impassible. The Leafs won one game to the Sabres' four and Toronto was out of the finals.

In the Western Conference, Detroit wasn't only the favorite but had been bolstered by adding four strong, seasoned players in the course of the season: defensemen Chris Chelios and Ulf Samuelsson, forward Wendel Clark and goalie Bill Ranford. Alas, the dreams of Red Wings fans that the Stanley Cup would come to Detroit for the third year in a row weren't destined to materialize either. In the semifinals against Colorado, Detroit picked up the first two games but then dropped the next four in a row when their goalkeeping slipped below par.

In the goal-poor six-game finals with Buffalo, Dallas went on to win the first Stanley Cup in the club's history in 1999.

Nor was the Dallas Stars' road to the finals of the Western Conference an easy one. Led by Derian Hatcher and Sergei Zubov, the team's six defensemen were thought to be the most reliable in the league. They continued to play practically flawlessly and were further supported by most of the forwards, including Brett Hull, a pure sniper, who actively participated in the defense in accordance with the views of coach Ken Hitchcock. But the Stars scored with some difficulty. In four games with Edmonton, Dallas didn't once manage to score more than three goals, while in six games with St. Louis, four of which went into overtime, they only once eclipsed what now seemed like their limit. And after five games between Dallas and Colorado, the Avalanche was ahead 3–2 when the Stars were rescued by the player who would win the Conn Smythe Trophy, center Joe Nieuwendyk, whose combinations—twice finished off by Jamie Langenbrunner—allowed Dallas to take game six in Denver 4–1, which tied the score in the series.

In the decisive game, quite an important role was played by a circumstance that was considered negative for the Stars. At 29.8 years, its players were well above the average age in the NHL and a dozen main forwards were older than 30. However, this factor could be interpreted as a colossal psychological doping. The league's oldtimers realized that for them the 1999 playoffs was their last chance for the Cup, and it was precisely Mike Keane—with the support of Pat Verbeek and Guy Carbonneau—who helped bring the score to 3–0 with two shots. Having won the series 4–1, Dallas went to the finals for the first time.

Then, in a goal-poor six-game series with Buffalo, the Stars went on to win the first Stanley Cup in the club's history. Hasek and the Sabres defense managed to neutralize the Nieuwendyk line, but they were unable to stop Jere Lehtinen, Mike Modano and Brett Hull. Hull's winning shot at 14:51 in the third overtime of the sixth game drew the line under that year's Stanley Cup finals.

After the 1998 Winter Olympics, the finals of the 1998 World Championship were an anticlimax. In Switzerland, Sweden (with Peter Forsberg and Mats Sundin) managed to edge out Finland by minimal scores in two games that capped the playoffs while the Czech Republic (without Dominik Hasek and Jaromir Jagr) took third.

Scotty Bowman

In his acclaimed book *The Game*, Ken Dryden summed up his former coach better than anyone could: "Scotty Bowman isn't someone who is easy to like. He has no coach's con about him. He doesn't slap backs, punch arms or grab elbows. He doesn't search eyes, spew out ingratiating blarney or disarm with faint, enervating praise. He is shy and not very friendly…. Abrupt, straightforward without flair or charm, he seems cold or abrasive, sometimes obnoxious, controversial, but never colorful…. He is complex, confusing, misunderstood, unclear in every way but one: He is a brilliant coach, the best of his time."

In 27 years behind the bench, Scotty Bowman never lost when he was at the helm for a full season.

The high standards to which William Scott Bowman held himself and his players contributed to a landmark coaching career. A master of motivation and mind games, he knew how to get the most out of every player he handled. During his 27 years as a coach, he never experienced a losing record in any full season in which he was behind the bench. His eight Stanley Cup coaching wins as of 2001 left him tied with the legendary Toe Blake for the most ever.

A head injury ended Bowman's playing career while he was still a junior. He moved into coaching in the Canadiens' minor-league system and broke into the NHL with the expansion St. Louis Blues in 1967–68, leading that team to the Stanley Cup finals in each of its first three terms.

In 1971 the Montreal Canadiens hired Bowman to replace Al MacNeil, who had coached the team to a Stanley Cup just the year before but had lost the respect of players such as Henri Richard. The Canadiens won at least 45 games in each of Bowman's eight seasons at the helm, and they won the Stanley Cup five times. Those achievements speak volumes about Bowman's ability to prevent such an overpowering squad from growing complacent.

After the Habs' 1979 Cup championship— their fourth in a row—Bowman announced that he was stepping down from one of the most prestigious yet demanding jobs in hockey. A new challenge awaited him in Buffalo, where he was hired as the Sabres' coach and general manager prior to the 1979–80 season. The Sabres were a good team that failed to duplicate their playoff success of 1975, when they reached the finals only to lose to Philadelphia. Although he engineered a number of shrewd

Bowman, Scotty
Head Coach, b: Montreal, Que., 9/18/1933

Season	Club, League	Regular Season					Playoffs				
		GC	W	L	T	W%	GC	W	L	T	W%
1967–68	St. Louis Blues, NHL	58	23	21	14	0.517	18	8	10	0	0.444
1968–69	St. Louis Blues, NHL	76	37	25	14	0.579	12	8	4	0	0.667
1969–70	St. Louis Blues, NHL	76	37	27	12	0.566	16	8	8	0	0.500
1970–71	St. Louis Blues, NHL	28	13	10	5	0.554	6	2	4	0	0.333
1971–72	Montreal Canadiens, NHL	78	46	16	16	0.692	6	2	4	0	0.333
1972–73	Montreal Canadiens, NHL	78	52	10	16	0.769	17	12	5	0	0.706
1973–74	Montreal Canadiens, NHL	78	45	24	9	0.635	6	2	4	0	0.333
1974–75	Montreal Canadiens, NHL	80	47	14	19	0.706	11	6	5	0	0.545
1975–76	Montreal Canadiens, NHL	80	58	11	11	0.794	13	12	1	0	0.923
CCup–76	Canada	7	6	1	0	0.857					
1976–77	Montreal Canadiens, NHL	80	60	8	12	0.825	14	12	2	0	0.857
1977–78	Montreal Canadiens, NHL	80	59	10	11	0.806	15	12	3	0	0.800
1978–79	Montreal Canadiens, NHL	80	52	17	11	0.719	16	12	4	0	0.750
1979–80	Buffalo Sabres, NHL	80	47	17	16	0.688	14	9	5	0	0.643
CCup–81	Canada	7	5	1	1	0.786					
1981–82	Buffalo Sabres, NHL	35	18	10	7	0.614	4	1	3	0	0.250
1982–83	Buffalo Sabres, NHL	80	38	29	13	0.556	10	6	4	0	0.600
1983–84	Buffalo Sabres, NHL	80	48	25	7	0.644	3	0	3	0	0.000
1984–85	Buffalo Sabres, NHL	80	38	28	14	0.563	5	2	3	0	0.400
1985–86	Buffalo Sabres, NHL	37	18	18	1	0.500					
1986–87	Buffalo Sabres, NHL	12	3	7	2	0.333					
1991–92	Pittsburgh Penguins, NHL	80	39	32	9	0.544	21	16	5	0	0.762
1992–93	Pittsburgh Penguins, NHL	84	56	21	7	0.708	12	7	5	0	0.583
1993–94	Detroit Red Wings, NHL	84	46	30	8	0.595	7	3	4	0	0.429
1994–95	Detroit Red Wings, NHL	48	33	11	4	0.729	18	12	6	0	0.667
1995–96	Detroit Red Wings, NHL	82	62	13	7	0.799	19	10	9	0	0.526
1996–97	Detroit Red Wings, NHL	82	38	26	18	0.573	20	16	4	0	0.800
1997–98	Detroit Red Wings, NHL	82	44	23	15	0.628	22	16	6	0	0.727
1998–99	Detroit Red Wings, NHL	77	43	32	7	0.545	10	6	4	0	0.600
1999–00	Detroit Red Wings, NHL	82	48	24	10	0.659	9	5	4	0	0.556
2000–01	Detroit Red Wings, NHL	82	49	20	9	0.652	6	2	4	0	0.333
2001-02	Detroit Red Wings	82	51	17	10	0.682					
	NHL Totals	2141	1248	576	314	0.656					

Won Jack Adams Award (1977, 1996)
Won Stanley Cup (1973, 1976, 1977, 1978, 1979, 1992, 1997, 1998)
Won CCup (1976)

draft-day deals, Bowman was never able to fill the Buffalo roster with the same numbers of extraordinary role players he'd had at his disposal in Montreal.

Bowman temporarily quit coaching in 1987 to work as an analyst on the CBC's *Hockey Night in Canada* telecasts. His next stop was Pittsburgh, where he was hired as the Penguins' director of player development. During the summer of 1991, he was inducted into the Hockey Hall of Fame as a Builder. He returned to bench duty with the Penguins that autumn after Bob Johnson, a popular figure who had led the team to its first-ever Stanley Cup victory in 1991, succumbed to cancer during the off-season. Bowman molded the multi-talented club into a well-rounded squad that could control play at both ends of the ice. Their repeat championship in 1992 was attributable in no small measure to Bowman's leadership.

In 1992–93, Bowman's Penguins led the league with 56 wins and 119 points—both franchise highs—but were upset by the New York Islanders in the Patrick Division finals. Bowman moved on to Detroit, where he coached the Red Wings to 46 wins and 100 points. A stunning first-round defeat at the hands of the San Jose Sharks proved to be a short-term setback, as the Wings reached the Stanley Cup finals in 1995—their first appearance in 29 years. Although they were swept by the New Jersey Devils, Detroit appeared to be headed for long-term success.

In 1997, Scotty Bowman (left) earned a permanent place in the hearts of Red Wings supporters by leading the team to its first Stanley Cup in 42 years.

In 1995–96, the Red Wings won an NHL-record 62 games—eclipsing the previous standard of 60, which Bowman had set with Montreal in 1976–77—but they fell short against the eventual Cup winners, the Colorado Avalanche, in the Western Conference finals. On December 5, 1995, Bowman made history when he coached in his 1,607th game—another NHL record.

Bowman earned a permanent place in the hearts of Red Wings supporters in 1997 by leading the team to its first Stanley Cup win in 42 years. The following year his experience at keeping a dominant team hungry came in handy as he guided Detroit to a repeat championship. Along the way he reached another individual milestone on February 8, 1997, when the Wings beat Pittsburgh to give Bowman his 1,000th career regular-season victory. In 1999 the Wings fell short of a "three-peat" when they were upset by Colorado in the Western Conference semifinals, but Bowman has remained behind the bench to lead Detroit into the new millennium. Although the Wings were eliminated in the second round of the 2000 playoffs, again by Colorado, the legendary coach—whose career has spanned five decades—decided to stay in Detroit for 2000–01.

In 2001–02, Wings management made changes that seemed to indicate one last big push toward Lord Stanley's Cup with the core of star players who were mostly nearing the end of their fabulous careers. With such veterans as Yzerman, Chelios, Larionov, Shanahan and Hasek up for the challenge, the Wings bolstered their chances for another championship by acquiring Luc Robitaille and Brett Hull. Even with this wealth of talent, however, only Shanahan was under 35 (at 33) and Chelios and Larionov had already seen their 40th birthdays come and go. It was a team made up of the players Bowman was most successful with—an older veteran squad—but though many critics expected the long regular season to take its toll on the aging Red Wings, they would prove to be the class of the league throughout the 82-game regular season.

Dominik Hasek

The man they call "the Dominator" was the most influential—if not the most outstanding–goalie of the late 1990s. If the hallmark of a great player is his influence on the game, Hasek certainly qualifies. In much the same way that Wayne Gretzky single-handedly shifted the NHL game's emphasis to playmaking and touch after decades of bullying play, Hasek developed an idiosyncratic style of goalkeeping that skaters tried to beat and goalies tried to emulate. His acrobatic, body-contorting saves took away the lower part of the net, forcing shooters under pressure to find a small opening before he closed the door.

Dominik Hasek developed an idiosyncratic style that skaters tried to beat and other goalies to copy.

Hasek's career began in 1981 in Pardubice, Czechoslovakia, where he was born in 1965. It was a place where the idea of playing in the NHL seemed an unattainable fantasy. Dominik's mother loved tennis, and one of his early heroes was Bjorn Borg. His father was an avid soccer player, and Dominik first played goal in soccer, acquiring the fleetness of foot that would serve him so well later in his hockey career. He also loved watching the local hockey team when he was a youngster, and he was known to cry uncontrollably when they lost.

As soon as he began playing hockey, he ended up between the pipes. While still a teenager, he gained a reputation as one of the best young goalies in his city, then his region and finally his country. His Pardubice teams began to win regularly, and during one particular season, they lost only one game. Dominik also still enjoyed tennis, winning several regional tournaments as a youngster. And he played soccer with his brother Martin, who would play professionally with Sparta Prague.

At the age of 16, Dominik made the move to the top level of Czech hockey, playing for his home team in the Czech league's first division. At the 1983 NHL Entry Draft, the 18-year-old Hasek was drafted 207th overall by Chicago. Part of the reason he was selected so late was that Czechoslovakia was still a communist country and NHL teams had little hope of luring players from behind the Iron Curtain. Hasek didn't even find out he'd been drafted for several months and, when he did, the news didn't thrill him as it would have thousands of young North American players.

Hasek appeared in North America in 1984 and 1987 playing for Czechoslovakia at the Canada Cup tournament and he played in Calgary, Alberta, at the 1988 Winter Olympic Games. His international profile was also enhanced by his play at the World Championships each year. "He's the new Tretiak of Europe," said Canadian defenseman James Patrick before the Olympics. "He sets up way back in his net like Tretiak used to. Sometimes he's so far back that he's right under the crossbar, but his reactions are very quick. He's got great feet when he drops down to block a shot."

In Buffalo, Dominik Hasek (left) established himself as a winner and the most unorthodox goalie the NHL had ever seen.

When Hasek met with Chicago general manager Bob Pulford in 1987, he turned down the Blackhawks' offer to make him the third-highest-paid player on the team if he left his native country. The 22-year-old was happy in university and was enjoying the perks that came with being the top goalie in a hockey-mad country. Finally, nearly seven years after he was drafted, Hasek decided to join the Hawks. "By 1989, I had my degree and was married," Hasek said. "I thought more about the NHL and decided to try it. It was a tough transition, because in Czechoslovakia I was a pretty big star."

Hasek appeared in only 25 games over two seasons with the Hawks—1990–91 and 1991–92—as he was unable to wrest the starting job from young Canadian superstar Ed Belfour. In what would turn out to be one of the more lopsided trades of the decade, Chicago traded Hasek to the Buffalo Sabres for goalie Stephane Beauregard and a fourth-round draft choice with which the Hawks selected Eric Daze.

In Buffalo, Hasek was given the chance to be number one and he wasted no time in proving his worth. He established himself not only as a winner but also as the most unorthodox goalie the NHL had ever known. He was the furthest thing from a stand-up goalie—he went down on every shot, sometimes contorting his body and throwing out his arms or kicking up his legs to keep the puck out of the net. He was incredibly flexible, able to bend his legs any which way. From the waist on down, he was a padded snake. "How would I describe Dominik Hasek?" coach Ted Nolan was once asked. "Totally, and I mean totally, unpredictable."

Hasek was also unpredictable in his relationships with his teammates and others off the ice. In Buffalo, his nickname was "Kramer," a reference to the eccentric, unreliable character on the TV sitcom *Seinfeld* who launches himself through doors. Hasek resembled the character both in looks and in actions, often stumbling into team meetings at the last possible second. He once forgot his pads on his way to a game in the Czech Republic and didn't realize his error until a few minutes before the opening face-off. Using borrowed pads, he won the game for his team—and first-star honors as well. Some of his quirks ended up causing conflicts with Nolan, who eventually left the Sabres in part because of his poor relationship with the team's superstar goalie.

Part of Hasek's unique on-ice style involved scrambling around his crease on his knees and dropping his stick whenever he was in trouble. While most goalies cling to their stick the way a tightrope walker does to a pole, Hasek felt it was often an encumbrance. He also got a reputation for quirkiness for wanting to stop shots with his helmet, soccer-style, during practice and even sometimes during games. Because of his tendency to use his head—all parts of it—he continued to use a helmet and mask combination long after nearly all the goalies in the league had switched to molded facemasks.

Hasek, Dominik
G, 5'11", 168 lbs, b: Pardubice, Czechoslovakia, 1/29/1965

Season	Club, League	Regular Season				Playoffs			
		GP	Mins	GA	Avg	GP	Mins	GA	Avg
1981–82	Pardubice, Czechoslovakia	12	661	34	3.09				
1982–83	Pardubice, Czechoslovakia	42	2358	105	2.67				
WEC–83	Czechoslovakia	2	120	5	2.50				
1983–84	Pardubice, Czechoslovakia	40	2304	108	2.81				
CCup–84	Czechoslovakia	4	188	12	4.00				
1984–85	Pardubice, Czechoslovakia	42	2419	131	3.25				
1985–86	Pardubice, Czechoslovakia	45	2689	138	3.08				
WEC–86	Czechoslovakia	9	538	19	2.12				
1986–87	Pardubice, Czechoslovakia	43	2515	103	2.46				
WEC–87	Czechoslovakia	9	520	19	2.19				
CCup–87	Czechoslovakia	6	360	20	3.00				
1987–88	Pardubice, Czechoslovakia	31	1862	93	3.00				
OWG–88	Czechoslovakia	5	217	18	4.98				
1988–89	Pardubice, Czechoslovakia	42	2507	114	2.73				
WEC–89	Czechoslovakia	10	600	21	2.10				
1989–90	Dukla Jihlava, Czechoslovakia	40	2251	80	2.13				
WEC–90	Czechoslovakia	8	480	20	2.50				
1990–91	Chicago Blackhawks, NHL	5	195	8	2.46	3	69	3	2.61
	Indianapolis Ice, IHL	33	1903	80	2.52	1	60	3	3.00
CCup–91	Czechoslovakia	5	300	18	4.00				
1991–92	Chicago Blackhawks, NHL	20	1014	44	2.60	3	158	8	3.04
	Indianapolis Ice, IHL	20	1162	69	3.56				
1992–93	Buffalo Sabres, NHL	28	1429	75	3.15	1	45	1	1.33
1993–94	Buffalo Sabres, NHL	58	3358	109	1.95	7	484	13	1.61
1994–95	Pardubice, Czech Republic	2	124	6	2.90				
	Buffalo Sabres, NHL	41	2416	85	2.11	5	309	18	3.50
1995–96	Buffalo Sabres, NHL	59	3417	161	2.83				
1996–97	Buffalo Sabres, NHL	67	4037	153	2.27	3	153	5	1.96
1997–98	Buffalo Sabres, NHL	72	4220	147	2.09	15	948	32	2.03
OWG–98	Czech Republic	6	369	6	0.97				
1998–99	Buffalo Sabres, NHL	64	3817	119	1.87	19	1217	36	1.77
1999–00	Buffalo Sabres, NHL	35	2066	76	2.21	5	301	12	2.39
2000–01	Buffalo Sabres, NHL	67	3904	137	2.11	13	833	29	2.09
2001–02	Detroit Red Wings, NHL	65	3872	140	2.17				
OWG–02	Czech Republic	4	239	8	2.01				
	Czechoslovakia/								
	Czech Republic Totals	339	19690	912	2.78				
	NHL Totals	581	33744	1254	2.23				
	OWG/WEC/CCup Totals	68	3931	298	4.55				

Named Best Goaltender at WEC (1987, 1989)
NHL First All-Star Team (1994, 1995, 1997, 1998, 1999)
Won Hart Trophy (1997, 1998)
Won Vezina Trophy (1994, 1995, 1997, 1998, 1999)
Won William M. Jennings Trophy (1994)
Won Lester B. Pearson Award (1997, 1998)
Won OWG (1998)

Dominik Hasek

Hasek revolutionized the way a goalie approached making a save and his successful style has influenced many goalies to some degree. Shooters were completely baffled by his style, and this in turn became a form of intimidation. But while his flopping didn't allow players to shoot for particular corners, it sometimes meant Hasek gambled and lost. And while he regularly won games for his team, his playoff performance was less than perfect. Opponents realized his weakness wasn't in the body but the mind: He could be thrown off his game if he were nudged or screened in the crease, so they used this tactic when the Stanley Cup was on the line.

Hasek, especially after his conflicts with Nolan in 1997, became more erratic emotionally. He threw his blocker at a player he felt should have been penalized but hadn't been; he attacked a reporter who questioned whether his knee was really injured during the Ottawa–Buffalo playoff series of 1997; and he lost his composure when he was interfered with during the Sabres' 1999 run to the Cup finals. Hasek's value to his team was undeniable, however, and in 1997 and 1998 he won the Hart Trophy—making him the first goalie to receive the honor since Jacques Plante in 1962 and the first goalie ever to win the NHL's highest individual accolade in consecutive years.

Dominik Hasek won the Hart Trophy in 1997 and 1998—the first goalie ever to win the NHL's highest honor two years in a row.

The highlight of Hasek's career came during the 1998 Winter Olympics in Nagano, when the NHL shut down for three weeks to allow its players to participate. Hasek was the foundation of a solid Czech team that also included the high-scoring Jaromir Jagr. The Czechs lost once in the early rounds (2–1, to Russia) and were heavy underdogs in their semifinal match with Canada, a team that was undefeated. Hasek truly lived up to his "Dominator" nickname by shutting out the Canadians until late in the third period, when Trevor Linden found the net after a frantic scramble to tie the game. Hasek then shut down the Canadians in the 10-minute overtime period—a remarkable contribution since his team only managed one shot on net in the extra frame.

When the time came for a sudden-death shootout, the Czechs were confident. Hasek was at the top of his game, holding an almost hypnotic power over the Canadian skaters, who seemed to lose all confidence when they approached him one-on-one. Hasek stopped all five of Canada's shots, single-handedly sending his team into the Olympic finals against the Russians. With so much history between the two nations—Hasek's countrymen had only become independent five years before—the game was watched closely back home. When Hasek shut out the Russians to secure the gold medal, pandemonium broke out in the Czech Republic.

After the win, the entire team was honored with a parade in Prague, and hundreds of thousands of fans crowded the streets in celebration of their Cinderella team. Signs reading "Hasek is God" were to be seen everywhere and he was given a huge ovation before he made a speech. "It's absolutely wonderful what you have done for me," he said. "I can't explain the way I feel. I'm very happy we could win the gold medal for our country. It was the best moment in my hockey life."

Hasek's 1998–99 season was shortened by a nagging groin injury. Despite the pain, he was brilliant in the playoffs. Unfortunately, a controversial goal in the final game cost Hasek and the Sabres a chance to win the Stanley Cup. During the summer, Hasek announced that the coming season would be his last, but when he missed half of the 1999–2000 season with yet another serious groin injury, he postponed his plans to provide Buffalo's fans with one more year of the Dominator's unmistakable style of play. Unfortunately, his plans were derailed by his salary, which became too big a burden for the Sabres to bear. In the summer of 2001, Hasek was traded to Detroit—a team he hoped would give him his fifth career Stanley Cup.

In February 2002 Hasek joined his Czech countrymen in Salt Lake City to defend the gold medal the 37-year-old goaltender had provided them with four years before. In Salt Lake, Hasek was still at the top of his game and again allowed only one goal in the quarterfinals against Russia. However, his counterpart in the Russian net, Nikolai Khabibulin, upstaged Hasek and kept the Czechs off the scoreboard, thus dispatching the defending champs without a medal.

Vladimir Konstantinov

By the time he joined the NHL's Detroit Red Wings in 1991, Vladimir Konstantinov was already a standout defenseman with the Central Red Army team in Moscow and captain of the Soviet national team. Known for his hitting ability and solid defensive play, he helped the Wings end a 42-year drought to win the Stanley Cup in 1997. Tragedy struck shortly after that victory, however, ending his playing career and almost costing him his life.

Konstantinov was born in 1967 in Murmansk, a town above the Arctic Circle that receives only two hours of sunlight a day in winter. He dedicated himself to hockey in order to work his way out of there and by the age of 17 he was able to move to Moscow, joining the Red Army team. Although he was the youngest member of the squad, he looked and played with a maturity that belied his age and teammates called him "Dyadya," which is Russian for "Uncle." When Viacheslav Fetisov—the Red Army's long-time captain and top blueliner—left the team in 1989, Konstantinov was made captain, a role he also ably filled for the Soviet national team. "He played with my brother in junior hockey," Fetisov said of his young successor. "He's always had a big heart and has been a hard worker."

Vladimir Konstantinov captained the Soviet national team before joining the Red Wings in 1991.

Within a couple of years, Konstantinov grew interested in applying his talents to the North American game, so he made the necessary arrangements with Detroit, the team that had drafted him 221st overall in 1989. Konstantinov announced that he had a rare form of cancer that could only be treated in the United States, a falsehood that was corroborated by both the Wings' doctors and Russian state officials. Konstantinov received the documents he needed to leave Russia but was soon horrified to find they'd been stolen from his car. Fortunately for Vladimir, the thief later returned them in exchange for some hockey memorabilia.

In 1991 Konstantinov made the move to Detroit, and he made an immediate impact. An aggressive, crafty player who relished the physical nature of the North American game, he was selected

When the Wings won their second consecutive Stanley Cup in 1998, Vladimir Konstantinov (front) was at Joe Louis Arena in a wheelchair and captain Steve Yzerman presented him with the Cup as fans cheered.

to the league's All-Rookie Team in 1992. Over the next few years, he became one of the better defenders in the league. He became known for his hard hits, both on open ice and along the boards, and his liberal use of his stick earned him some nasty nicknames, including "Vladimir the Terrible," "Bad Vlad" and "Vlad the Impaler." He was an expert at forcing opponents to take penalties, hitting them legally—or otherwise—and then waiting for the referee to catch his adversary in the act of retaliating. Before home games, the Red Wings showed a video on their scoreboard that featured Konstantinov delivering a variety of bone-rattling hits. The film ended with the popular defenseman's signature saying—"Hasta la vista, baby!"— and never failed to draw cheers from the crowds at Joe Louis Arena.

In 1996 Konstantinov's defensive toughness earned him a plus-minus rating of plus-60—tops in the NHL—and he was selected to the Second All-Star Team that year. "An opposing player once told me that Vladi is the hardest-playing Russian he ever saw," longtime Wings teammate Bob Rouse said. "No one likes playing against him, but he has the respect of everyone in the league."

In 1996–97, Konstantinov had an outstanding season. He was nominated for the Norris Trophy as the league's best defenseman and the Wings team he toiled for was one of the best in the NHL. The team hadn't won the Stanley Cup since 1955, but with Konstantinov, Fetisov, Sergei Fedorov and Igor Larionov leading the way, the Red Wings easily dispatched the favored Philadelphia Flyers in the 1997 finals to win the Stanley Cup. Konstantinov was ecstatic after the victory, holding the Cup aloft and skating around the ice. "This Cup is for you, for Detroit, for Michigan," he yelled to the crowd. Three days later, he and his teammates were guests of honor at a rally in downtown Detroit that was attended by over a million fans.

On Friday, June 13, 1997, six days after their sweep of the Flyers, the Red Wings held a golf tournament and dinner for 17 players and staff. After the dinner, Konstantinov, Fetisov and Sergei Mnatsakanov, a masseur with the team, headed home in a limousine. The driver, Richard Gnida, who'd had his license revoked prior to the incident, fell asleep at the wheel. The three men in the back screamed for him to wake up, but he had already lost control of the vehicle. The car crossed three lanes of traffic, jumped a curb and struck a tree. Although Gnida was wearing a seatbelt, the three passengers were not. Fetisov suffered chest and lung injuries but wasn't at serious risk. Konstantinov and

Konstantinov, Vladimir
D, 5´11˝, 190 lbs, b: Murmansk, USSR, 3/19/1967

Season	Club, League		Regular Season					Playoffs			
		GP	G	A	Pts	PIM	GP	G	A	Pts	PIM
1984–85	CSKA, USSR	40	1	4	5	10					
1985–86	CSKA, USSR	26	4	3	7	12					
WEC–86	USSR	10	1	1	2	8					
1986–87	CSKA, USSR	35	2	2	4	19					
1987–88	CSKA, USSR	50	3	6	9	32					
1988–89	CSKA, USSR	37	7	8	15	20					
WEC–89	USSR	8	2	1	3	2					
1989–90	CSKA, USSR	47	14	14	28	44					
WEC–90	USSR	10	2	2	4	12					
1990–91	CSKA, USSR	45	5	12	17	42					
1991–92	Detroit Red Wings, NHL	79	8	26	34	172	11	0	1	1	16
1992–93	Detroit Red Wings, NHL	82	5	17	22	137	7	0	1	1	8
1993–94	Detroit Red Wings, NHL	80	12	21	33	138	7	0	2	2	4
1994–95	Wedemark, Germany	15	13	17	30	51					
	Detroit Red Wings, NHL	47	3	11	14	101	18	1	1	2	22
1995–96	Detroit Red Wings, NHL	81	14	20	34	139	19	4	5	9	28
1996–97	Detroit Red Wings, NHL	77	5	33	38	151	20	0	4	4	29
	USSR Totals	280	36	49	85	179					
	NHL Totals	446	47	128	175	838	82	5	14	19	107
	WEC Totals	28	5	4	9	22					

NHL Second All-Star Team (1996)
Won Alka-Seltzer Plus Award (1996)
Won WEC (1986, 1989, 1990)
Won Stanley Cup (1997)
USSR Champion (1985, 1986, 1987, 1988, 1989)

Mnatsakanov, however, were badly hurt with serious head injuries. Both men were hooked up to ventilators and both lapsed into comas.

"Vladi, he is a little brother to me. Sergei, everybody, loves him," Fetisov said. "That first night in the hospital, I kept asking, 'How are my friends?' I still don't like the answer. The whole thing is a terrible memory."

Konstantinov's teammates gathered around his hospital bed, talking to him and playing songs such as Queen's "We Are The Champions"—music he had been listening to in the days prior to the accident. Larionov spoke to Konstantinov daily in Russian. "You're a strong man," Larionov said. "You've fought through tough times in life and hockey. I know this is the toughest, but you can do it. We're waiting for you. We miss you. We want you back."

It would be five weeks before Konstantinov came out of the coma—a week after Mnatsakanov regained consciousness. Konstantinov recovered slowly, at first barely aware of what was going on around him. Teammates brought him the Stanley Cup, which brought a glimmer of recognition. Over the next year, he had to relearn basic skills such as recognizing friends and family, eating for himself and operating a wheelchair. His heroic fight to recover inspired his teammates. When the Wings won their second consecutive Stanley Cup in 1997–98, Konstantinov was present at Joe Louis Arena, in a wheelchair, and captain Steve Yzerman presented him with the Cup to the cheers of the crowd.

Joe Nieuwendyk

Born in Oshawa, Ontario, Joe Nieuwendyk played college hockey at Cornell University in New York State. He spent three years on the Ivy League school's team and was twice named to the East Coast Athletic Conference's First All-Star Team, in 1986 and 1987. He was also selected as an all-American in both years.

In 1985, after his freshman year, the Calgary Flames were sufficiently impressed to draft him in the second round-27th overall. Calgary scouting coordinator Ian McKenzie put it succinctly: "He is the superstar this franchise is looking for." McKenzie was right. In his first full season as a Flame, 1987–88, the young center scored 51 goals and 92 points, becoming only the second NHL player—after Mike Bossy—to score 50 goals in his

Joe Nieuwendyk was drafted in the second round but became a superstar in his first real campaign with Calgary.

rookie season. His totals also included an eye-popping 31 power-play goals and eight game winners, and he was rewarded with the Calder Trophy as rookie of the year. The one disappointment Nieuwendyk felt was that he'd fallen just short of breaking Mike Bossy's record of 53 rookie goals. "I put too much pressure on myself," he admitted, "but I gave it my best crack."

Fatigue probably played a big part, too. By the midpoint of his first season with Calgary, Nieuwendyk had already played more games than he was used to in a whole season at Cornell. "Now, if I begin to feel fatigued," he said after gaining a few years worth of pro experience, "I get off the ice right away. And I know that I have to take care of myself off the ice as well. It's not like college where you can have parties that go until 4 in the morning."

Joe Nieuwendyk (center) scored six game-winning goals in the playoffs as his new team, the Dallas Stars, won the Stanley Cup in 1999.

Nieuwendyk's second season with the Flames was just as impressive as his first. He was the leader of a team that won the Stanley Cup, again scoring 51 goals. In 1991 he was named captain of the Flames. But by 1995, his relationship with the Flames had soured and the two parties couldn't agree on a contract. They went to arbitration and Calgary was ordered to pay Nieuwendyk $3.5 million. When knee problems prevented him from playing early in the 1995–96 season, the Flames found few takers on the trade market. Finally, in December 1995, the Dallas Stars acquired Nieuwendyk for Corey Millen and Jarome Iginla.

Hockey seems to come naturally to the Nieuwendyk family. Joe's uncle, Ed Kea, played for Atlanta and St. Louis and his cousins are NHLers John and Jeff Beukeboom. Besides being an exceptional hockey player, Nieuwendyk was also considered to be the best lacrosse player in Canada and at one point he even played on a team that won the Minto Cup, the country's top award in that sport.

Known as an aggressive player in front of the net as well as a good passer, Nieuwendyk's style of play has caused a number of health problems—he missed most of the 1998 playoffs due to a knee injury after a vicious check by Bryan Marchment. However, in 1999 his health and luck returned as Nieuwendyk scored six game-winning goals in the playoffs to lead the Stars to victory over Buffalo in the Stanley Cup finals. He missed a good portion of 1999–2000 with another knee injury, but a healthy Nieuwendyk scored 29 goals in the 2000–2001 season to get his career back on track. Nieuwendyk was something of a surprise selection to Team Canada for the 2002 Olympics, but he proved the coaching staff made the right decision when he turned in an excellent performance throughout the tournament. Then, right at the deadline, the Dallas Stars and New Jersey Devils pulled off a major trade that saw Joe Nieuwendyk and Jamie Langenbrunner head north in exchange for Jason Arnott and Randy McKay. The move clearly helped the Devils, who had been sputtering along for most of the season, much as the Stars had been, too.

Nieuwendyk, Joe
C, 6′1″, 195 lbs, b: Oshawa, Ont., 9/10/1966

Season	Club, League	Regular Season					Playoffs				
		GP	G	A	Pts	PIM	GP	G	A	Pts	PIM
1984–85	Cornell University, ECAC	29	21	24	45	30					
1985–86	Cornell University, ECAC	29	26	28	54	67					
1986–87	Cornell University, ECAC	23	26	26	52	26					
	Calgary Flames, NHL	9	5	1	6	0	6	2	2	4	0
1987–88	Calgary Flames, NHL	75	51	41	92	23	8	3	4	7	2
1988–89	Calgary Flames, NHL	77	51	31	82	40	22	10	4	14	10
1989–90	Calgary Flames, NHL	79	45	50	95	40	6	4	6	10	4
WEC–90	Canada	1	0	0	0	0					
1990–91	Calgary Flames, NHL	79	45	40	85	36	7	4	1	5	10
1991–92	Calgary Flames, NHL	69	22	34	56	55					
1992–93	Calgary Flames, NHL	79	38	37	75	52	6	3	6	9	10
1993–94	Calgary Flames, NHL	64	36	39	75	51	6	2	2	4	0
1994–95	Calgary Flames, NHL	46	21	29	50	33	5	4	3	7	0
1995–96	Dallas Stars, NHL	52	14	18	32	41					
1996–97	Dallas Stars, NHL	66	30	21	51	32	7	2	2	4	6
1997–98	Dallas Stars, NHL	73	39	30	69	30	1	1	0	1	0
1998–99	Dallas Stars, NHL	67	28	27	55	34	23	11	10	21	19
1999–00	Dallas Stars, NHL	48	15	19	34	26	23	7	3	10	18
2000–01	Dallas Stars, NHL	69	29	23	52	30	7	4	0	4	4
2001–02	Dallas-New Jersey, NHL	81	25	33	58	22					
OWG–02	Canada	6	1	1	2	0					
	NHL Totals	1033	494	473	967	545					
	OWG/WEC Totals	7	1	1	2	0					

Won Conn Smythe Trophy (1999)
Won Calder Trophy (1988)
Won King Clancy Trophy (1995)
Won Dodge Ram Tough Award (1988)
Won Stanley Cup (1989, 1999)
Won OWG (2002)

Sergei Fedorov

If sports experts were to choose the best hockey players in the world for a specific decade, Sergei Fedorov would have a claim on the title of most versatile player of the 1990s. Equally superb at center or on the wing and a high scorer with outstanding defensive ability, Fedorov is a pure player who has mastered all facets of the game from A to Z. A gifted stickhandler, he can take on two or three opponents at a time. But if he spots a teammate in a better position, he will pass the puck, whether it's a few feet or halfway down the ice.

He has a powerful shot and a casual style of skating that resembles a figure skater's. One day, in Detroit, Fedorov and his teammate Nicklas Lidstrom were racing down the street on in-line skates. Sergei was a few yards ahead of Nicklas when a bicyclist suddenly darted out of a side alley. It seemed certain that Fedorov was headed for a collision, but he leapt over the bike's hind wheel and resumed skating. He shows just as much finesse on the ice as he does on asphalt, to the delight of his fans.

Sergei Fedorov may have been the most versatile player of the 1990s.

Fedorov is one of those players who can single-handedly turn the tide in his club's favor, and he frequently sets an example that motivates his teammates when they're in a slump. He has been a consistent performer in the Stanley Cup playoffs, the Winter Olympics in Nagano and the Spartak Cup tournaments that involve Russian stars of the NHL.

Fedorov is creative on the ice, and he tries to live like an artist off the ice as well. He makes every attempt to stand out from the crowd. One hot day, the Red Wings were set to fly across the country for a game. Sergei showed up dressed all in white, as if he were going on vacation. From the first moment he set foot in the United States, Fedorov set out to convince everyone that he had good taste. Journalists and fans noticed it in 1991, after the Canada Cup tournament, when he appeared at one of the various get-togethers with his friends from the Soviet team. A handsome man with light brown hair, dressed in a tailored beige suit and smiling at everyone around him, Fedorov's appearance and refined manners stood out from those of his compatriots. In Moscow, he could have passed as an opera singer or a violinist.

Journalists were also surprised to hear Fedorov praise coach Viktor Tikhonov, the same man whose team he had left illegally. For

Fedorov, Sergei
C, 6´1˝, 200 lbs, b: Pskov, USSR, 12/13/1969

Season	Club, League	Regular Season					Playoffs				
		GP	G	A	Pts	PIM	GP	G	A	Pts	PIM
1986–87	CSKA, USSR	29	6	6	12	12					
1987–88	CSKA, USSR	48	7	9	16	20					
1988–89	CSKA, USSR	44	9	8	17	35					
WEC–89	USSR	10	6	3	9	10					
1989–90	CSKA, USSR	48	19	10	29	22					
WEC–90	USSR	10	4	2	6	10					
1990–91	Detroit Red Wings, NHL	77	31	48	79	66	7	1	5	6	4
CCup–91	USSR	5	2	2	4	6					
1991–92	Detroit Red Wings, NHL	80	32	54	86	72	11	5	5	10	8
1992–93	Detroit Red Wings, NHL	73	34	53	87	72	7	3	6	9	23
1993–94	Detroit Red Wings, NHL	82	56	64	120	34	7	1	7	8	6
1994–95	Detroit Red Wings, NHL	42	20	30	50	24	17	7	17	24	6
1995–96	Detroit Red Wings, NHL	78	39	68	107	48	19	2	18	20	10
WCup–96	Russia	5	3	3	6	2					
1996–97	Detroit Red Wings, NHL	74	30	33	63	30	20	8	12	20	12
1997–98	Detroit Red Wings, NHL	21	6	11	17	25	22	10	10	20	12
OWG–98	Russia	6	1	5	6	8					
1998–99	Detroit Red Wings, NHL	77	26	37	63	66	10	1	8	9	8
1999–00	Detroit Red Wings, NHL	68	27	35	62	22	9	4	4	8	4
2000–01	Detroit Red Wings, NHL	75	32	37	69	40	6	2	5	7	0
2001–02	Detroit Red Wings, NHL	81	31	37	68	36					
OWG–02	Russia	6	2	2	4	4					
	USSR Totals	169	41	33	74	89					
	NHL Totals	828	364	507	871	535					
	OWG/WEC/CCup/WCup Totals	42	18	17	35	40					

NHL First All-Star Team (1994)
Won Hart Trophy (1994)
Won Frank J. Selke Trophy (1994, 1996)
Won Lester B. Pearson Award (1994)
Won WEC (1989, 1990)
Won Stanley Cup (1997, 1998)
USSR Champion (1987, 1988, 1989)

Sergei Fedorov became the real leader of the Red Wings in the 1993–94 season. Hockey News named him player of the year and other pundits tagged him the most valuable player in the NHL.

many years, Viktor Tikhonov, coach of the Soviet national team and the Central Red Army club, had wanted to create a super-line of Alexander Mogilny, Fedorov and Pavel Bure to replace the famous KLM Line of Vladimir Krutov, Igor Larionov and Sergei Makarov. But this dream never materialized. In 1989, Mogilny was the first to defect, and he was followed a year later by Fedorov. Bure entered the NHL in 1991.

Mogilny was a friend and roommate of Fedorov's when the two went to Sweden with a Soviet team that won the 1989 World Championships. After the tournament, Mogilny disappeared from the hotel—and turned up in the United States a short time later. The two players shared the same room, so each probably knew the other's intentions, but Fedorov nurtured the hope that he'd get to the United States the legal way.

Sergei's military service ended in 1990, and Tikhonov didn't want to lose the gifted player he had pegged as the leader of the Red Army and national teams. Tikhonov applied pressure on Fedorov to file an application to become a commanding officer in the army. He offered Fedorov an apartment in Moscow and told him that, if he refused, he'd never play for the national team. Tikhonov's aides also worked to stoke the young player's fears.

Fedorov felt he had no choice but to defect, and he soon got the opportunity when he accompanied the Soviet team to Seattle for the 1990 Goodwill Games. And he didn't wait long after defecting to sign with the Detroit Red Wings. Whereas Mogilny was a sensitive homebody who missed friends and family and didn't break through in the NHL until his third season with the Buffalo Sabres, the more self-reliant Fedorov felt quite at home in the NHL, scoring 31 goals and making the All-Rookie Team in 1990–91. The third young Russian star, Bure, was fortunate to have Igor Larionov as a teammate and mentor in his rookie season with the Vancouver Canucks. A year later, Larionov had left to play in Switzerland, but Anatoli Semenov became Bure's tutor and he turned in the first of two 60-goal seasons.

About half a dozen games into his NHL career, Fedorov was already second on the team in goals scored and ice time after Steve Yzerman. Although both were natural centers, the two often played on the same line, so seamlessly that a casual observer might assume that the two had been playing together all their lives.

Fedorov became a true leader of the Red Wings in 1993–94 when injuries forced Yzerman to miss the second half of the season. Sensing that he was expected to rally his teammates, Fedorov turned on the jets, scoring 56 goals and 120 points. The NHL named him to the First All-Star Team and awarded him the Hart Trophy as the league's most valuable player. The most prestigious hockey publication in North America, *The Hockey News*, named him player of the year, while his peers throughout the league also recognized him as the most outstanding player, presenting him with the Lester B. Pearson Award. He was also rewarded for his defensive efforts with the Frank J. Selke Trophy.

The NHL lockout delayed the start of the 1994–95 season, so Fedorov accepted an invitation from Viacheslav Fetisov to play a number of charity games in Russia in which he appeared on the same line as his friends Mogilny and Bure. The fans and other players welcomed the star trio with open arms and truly enjoyed watching them work together. Each was great in his own way, but

Fedorov definitely stood out, perhaps because he fulfilled two functions at the same time—first as playmaker, holding all the cards in his hand, and second as leader of the three-man unit. When the NHL season finally got underway, Fedorov's Red Wings went as far as the Stanley Cup finals, where they lost to New Jersey. Sergei led all scorers in the playoffs with 24 points.

Red Wings coach Scotty Bowman also had a say in player signings and trades and he used that muscle to acquire Viacheslav Fetisov in April 1995 and Larionov in October of the same year. When Bowman told Fedorov of the Fetisov trade during an airline flight, he was so happy that he jumped out of his seat and nearly broke the paneling with his head. Bowman put together an all-Russian power-play that featured Fetisov—who got his second wind with Detroit—and Konstantinov on defense, with Vyacheslav Kozlov, Larionov and Fedorov on the forward line. Although Fedorov had to move over to right wing to accommodate Larionov, he lost none of his effectiveness. The "Russian Five" played no small role in the team's Stanley Cup championship of 1997.

Since his contract problems, Fedorov has registered three successive years with 26 goals or more and continues to be a leader on the oldest team in the NHL. In 2001–02, Fedorov was a key figure in Detroit's splendid regular-season performance on the power-play and penalty-killing units, as well as taking his regular shifts. He was also one of the eight players initially selected to play for Russia at the 2002 Olympics, where he won a bronze medal to go with his silver one as part of the 1998 team in Nagano.

Today, Fedorov sometimes returns to Moscow on vacation, but he admits that he feels somewhat out of place. He feels more at home in the United States. "When I return to Detroit after road games," says Fedorov, "I'm always happy. I've finally come home!"

Peter Bondra

Defense, defense and more defense—that's the word that embodied the NHL in the 1990s. Yet in spite of the demand for ever-tighter defensive play, there were a few players who were able to score goals and to maintain a healthy offensive output over a number of years. Players such as John LeClair, Jaromir Jagr, Brett Hull and Teemu Selanne come to mind.

Perhaps the most anonymous of these offensive standouts would be Peter Bondra, who led the league in goals in 1994–95 and tied for the lead with Teemu Selanne in 1997–98. Hockey fans will recognize the name but might be hard-pressed to pick him out of a crowd. His anonymity may stem from the philosophy of his team, the Washington Capitals, where the greatest stars aren't usually glorified. Another reason may have been his own personality. "I am not timid, no, I wouldn't say that. But I cannot approach a stranger just like that and say, 'Hi, I'm Peter Bondra.'"

Bondra's path to the NHL was a straightforward one, without any particularly large setbacks or obstacles to overcome. He was born in Lutsk, Ukraine, in 1968, but his family soon moved to Poprad, Slovakia, where there's hardly a boy who isn't passionate about hockey. He played one season for Poprad in the lower ranks of competition and transferred to the VSZ Kosice team in the first division at the age of 18. His older brother Juraj also played there on defense.

Bondra has always been willful, a fighter who doesn't shy away from rough play but won't tolerate cheap shots. But he is best known as a skilled sharpshooter who can pick off a corner of the

Peter Bondra scores most consistently when he breaks away with the puck and leaves his opponents behind in a burst of a speed.

net from almost any distance. As early as his second season with Kosice, he was considered one of the top shooters in the Czech league. He even helped Kosice win a championship in 1988.

Kosice supporters were upset by Bondra's sudden departure for the Washington Capitals in 1990, but he was eager to show the NHL team—which had drafted him 156th overall in that year's draft—what he was worth. In his third season, 1992–93, he led Washington with 37 goals and 85 points. He enjoyed great support both on and off the ice from Czech center Michal Pivonka, who had been with the Capitals since 1986. Pivonka helped Bondra and his family get used to a new way of life. The two would also become holdouts in the fall of 1995 when neither player could agree to contract terms with the Caps; during their absence they played together briefly for the Detroit Vipers of the International league.

During the NHL lockout of 1994–95, Bondra made a temporary return to Kosice. When play resumed in North America, the right wing had a breakthrough year with a league-leading 34 goals in only 47 games. In 1995 Bondra became a Slovakian citizen, and during his standoff with the Capitals he played for the national team in an Olympic qualifying round as well as at a four-country tournament for the Pragobanka Cup, held in Zlin, Czech Republic. After re-signing with Washington, he appeared in only 67 games but still managed to score 52 goals.

Bondra took part in the 1996 World Cup of Hockey, where he played for Slovakia and scored three goals in three games. He was also a member of the national squad that hoped to qualify for the 1998 Winter Olympics in Nagano, Japan. "Some people may not even know where Slovakia is," he said. "We are a small country. Because of that, the great tournament means that much more to me." Bondra—and Florida Panthers defenseman Robert Svehla—took part in the third game of a three-game preliminary round. However, Slovakia didn't play as well in the preliminaries as the surprising team from Kazakhstan and so was denied the chance to proceed to the final round.

When the NHL season resumed after a three-week break for the Olympics, Bondra picked up where he'd left off, scoring a league-high 52 goals. If that weren't enough, the Washington Capitals fought their way to the club's first-ever appearance in the Stanley Cup finals. Bondra was truly a workhorse for the team, which even managed to eliminate the Buffalo Sabres—who were led by the phenomenal netminding of Dominik Hasek—in the Eastern Conference finals. After that victory, however, Washington was swept in four games by the powerful Detroit Red Wings. "It was extremely exciting," Bondra said afterward. "I

Bondra, Peter											
RW, 6′1″, 200 lbs, b: Lutsk, USSR, 2/7/1968											
Season	Club, League	Regular Season					Playoffs				
		GP	G	A	Pts	PIM	GP	G	A	Pts	PIM
1986–87	Kosice, Czechoslovakia	32	4	5	9	24					
1987–88	Kosice, Czechoslovakia	45	27	11	38	20					
1988–89	Kosice, Czechoslovakia	40	30	10	40	20					
1989–90	Kosice, Czechoslovakia	44	29	17	46	24	5	7	2	9	
1990–91	Washington Capitals, NHL	54	12	16	28	47	4	0	1	1	2
1991–92	Washington Capitals, NHL	71	28	28	56	42	7	6	2	8	4
1992–93	Washington Capitals, NHL	83	37	48	85	70	6	0	6	6	0
1993–94	Washington Capitals, NHL	69	24	19	43	40	9	2	4	6	4
1994–95	Kosice, Slovakia	2	1	0	1	0					
	Washington Capitals, NHL	47	34	9	43	24	7	5	3	8	10
1995–96	Detroit Vipers, IHL	7	8	1	9	0					
	Washington Capitals, NHL	67	52	28	80	40	6	3	2	5	8
WCup–96	Slovakia	3	3	0	3	2					
1996–97	Washington Capitals, NHL	77	46	31	77	72					
1997–98	Washington Capitals, NHL	76	52	26	78	44	17	7	5	12	12
1998–99	Washington Capitals, NHL	66	31	24	55	56					
1999–00	Washington Capitals, NHL	62	21	17	38	30	5	1	1	2	4
2000–01	Washington Capitals, NHL	82	45	36	81	60	6	2	0	2	2
2001–02	Washington Capitals, NHL	77	39	31	70	80					
OWG–02	Slovakia	0	0	0	0	0					
	Czechoslovakia/Slovakia Totals	163	91	43	134	88	5	7	2	9	
	NHL Totals	831	421	313	734	605					
	OWG/WCup Totals	3	3	0	3	2					

never made it this far before. I hope that I have the opportunity to experience this at least once more, and that we will bring our efforts to the very end."

After a sub-par 1999–2000 season, Bondra rebounded with 45 goals in 2000–01 and scored his 400th career goal in the next year.

The 2001–02 season looked promising. The acquisition of Jaromir Jagr seemed to bode well for the Capitals, who had been Stanley Cup finalists just four years before, but Washington sputtered through most of the season. Jagr didn't adjust well to his new surroundings and played well below expectations in the early going. By the time he finally caught fire, the season seemed all but lost, so the Capitals traded Adam Oates at the deadline. Although Bondra surpassed the 35-goal plateau for the seventh time in his 12 NHL seasons, 2001–02 was a year he'd prefer to forget from a personal standpoint. Capping a dismal year was the fact that Bondra's home country of Slovakia failed to advance to the main draw at the Salt Lake City Olympics after a stunning upset loss to Germany in the qualifying round.

In 1996–97, Peter Bondra (top) scored 52 goals, won the scoring crown and helped the Capitals reach the Stanley Cup finals.

Alexander Mogilny

Many of Alexander Mogilny's accomplishments in life were firsts: He was the first Soviet player to defect to the West; the first Russian to be included on the NHL All-Star Team; the first European-born player to score 76 goals in an NHL season; and the first Russian to become captain of an NHL team.

But before the good times started to roll, the outstanding forward endured plenty of bad times. Born in the city of Khabarovsk, in Far Eastern Russia, Mogilny was discovered by a scout from the Central Red Army club and invited to try out for the famous team when he was only 13. A year later, Mogilny began training with the big-name players and acquitted himself well with his excellent style, his tactics and feel for scoring, his wonderful speed and handling of the puck, and even with his unusual—to the veterans at least—lifestyle.

Whenever Mogilny had time off from the training camp in Archangel—where Red Army players spent 300 days of the year—Mogilny would hang out with people his age from morning till night at the nearest subway station, talking about nothing in particular but mostly listening. He had no life in Moscow and his circle of friends was very small. The majority of players on the team were old enough to be his father, and until Sergei Fedorov joined the team, there was no one he could relate to comfortably.

Alexander Mogilny was the first Soviet player to defect to the West.

Mogilny considered the five years he spent in a barracks-like residence to be the most dreadful of his life. He couldn't even welcome his mother when she came to visit—she wasn't allowed into the camp, which was guarded like a military base. The same thing happened when she flew to Kiev for the European Junior Championships—the tournament at which Mogilny established an international reputation as one of the best forwards in the game.

At that time, Mogilny played a very tough game. If anyone tried to catch him off guard when he wasn't carrying the puck, he'd retaliate, unleashing whatever emotional storm was brewing inside him and taking it out on his opponent. By 1989, Mogilny had had enough and set his sights on

A HISTORY OF WORLD HOCKEY

defecting to the West. His opportunity came immediately after the Soviet Union won the gold medal at the World Championships held in Sweden that year. He secretly flew to Buffalo, New York, where the Sabres, who had drafted him in 1988, held his rights.

Predictably, Mogilny's defection unleashed a firestorm of criticism in the Soviet Union, and the sensitive 20-year-old took it to heart. He also feared for the lives of his parents—as well as his own—and he looked quite pale and shaken during his first few NHL games.

"When Mogilny appeared in Buffalo, he looked like a caged wolf," remarked American journalist Mark Brender. "He didn't make contact with anyone and was completely inside himself." Brender added that Mogilny had seen footage of some airline disasters on television so he refused to fly, choosing instead to travel exclusively by car. That caused him to miss some road games. His on-ice performance was erratic—he would play superbly one night, then look completely out of his depth in the next.

But as time went on, Mogilny's confidence grew. After scoring only 15 goals in his rookie season, he registered 30 and 39 in the next two years. As Buffalo added more Russian players, such as Yuri Khmylev and Alexei Zhitnik, Mogilny was the one to help them overcome the barriers he had encountered. Having gained a fair command of English, he also began to ease himself into the American way of life. Among his favorite pastimes was golf and, with his help, it played an important role in the life of his Russian teammates.

"Mogilny is a creator," said Buffalo coach John Muckler, who was a tremendous help in developing Mogilny's skills. "He has super talent. He can…change the course of the game all by himself. By nature he is an individualist—even more so than many Americans—but Alex is an excellent pupil. Having accepted my concept of the game, he is doing a lot of passing, creating good scoring opportunities for his partners…. He can be placed on the same plane with Mario Lemieux, Mark Messier and Jari Kurri. He has everything he needs to become one of the best right wingers in NHL history."

When Buffalo acquired Pat LaFontaine, Mogilny's game took a quantum leap forward. Here was a player who performed at his level, and Alexander had no desire to play second fiddle. Instead, he was inspired and challenged. When the two were on the ice at the same time, it seemed as if they could take on the opposition without any help. In Winnipeg, on February 10, 1993, Mogilny single-handedly defeated the Jets team with four goals. Two weeks later, at home against Detroit, he scored another four. In 1992—93, LaFontaine led the team with 148 points, but Mogilny was close

Mogilny, Alexander
RW, 5´11˝, 187 lbs, b: Khabarovsk, USSR, 2/18/1969

Season	Club, League	Regular Season					Playoffs				
		GP	G	A	Pts	PIM	GP	G	A	Pts	PIM
1986–87	CSKA, USSR	28	15	1	16	4					
1987–88	CSKA, USSR	39	12	8	20	14					
OWG–88	USSR	6	3	2	5	2					
1988–89	CSKA, USSR	31	11	11	22	24					
WEC–89	USSR	10	0	3	3	2					
1989–90	Buffalo Sabres, NHL	65	15	28	43	16	4	0	1	1	2
1990–91	Buffalo Sabres, NHL	62	30	34	64	16	6	0	6	6	2
1991–92	Buffalo Sabres, NHL	67	39	45	84	73	2	0	2	2	0
1992–93	Buffalo Sabres, NHL	77	76	51	127	40	7	7	3	10	6
1993–94	Buffalo Sabres, NHL	66	32	47	79	22	7	4	2	6	6
1994–95	Spartak Moscow, Russia	1	0	1	1	0					
	Buffalo Sabres, NHL	44	19	28	47	36	5	3	2	5	2
1995–96	Vancouver Canucks, NHL	79	55	52	107	16	6	1	8	9	8
WCup–96	Russia	5	2	4	6	0					
1996–97	Vancouver Canucks, NHL	76	31	42	73	18					
1997–98	Vancouver Canucks, NHL	51	18	27	45	36					
1998–99	Vancouver Canucks, NHL	59	14	31	45	58					
1999–00	Vancouver Canucks, NHL	47	21	17	38	16					
	New Jersey Devils, NHL	12	3	3	6	4	23	4	3	7	4
2000–01	New Jersey Devils, NHL	75	43	40	83	43	25	5	11	16	8
2001–02	Toronto Maple Leafs, NHL	66	24	33	57	8					
	USSR/Russia Totals	99	38	21	59	42					
	NHL Totals	846	420	478	898	402					
	OWG/WEC/WCup Totals	21	5	9	14	4					

NHL Second All-Star Team (1993, 1996)
Won OWG (1988)
Won WEC (1989)
Won Stanley Cup (2000)
USSR Champion (1987, 1988, 1989)

behind with 127, including a league-leading 76 goals in 77 games.

Injuries limited LaFontaine to 16 and 22 games over the next two years and his absence naturally caused Mogilny's output to tail off. The burden of team leadership also fell to the Russian winger, who was named interim team captain, and he rose to the challenge, giving his all in practice and expecting the same from his teammates. Coach Muckler was surprised and delighted. "The transformation of Mogilny was astonishing," he declared. "A man of few words, as Alex seemed to me, showed he could explode in no time at all and work his teammates into a state of frenzy. I couldn't even dream of a better captain."

A 1995 trade to Vancouver proved to be a tonic for Mogilny, who led the team with 55 goals and 107 points in his first year as a Canuck. After "the Russian Rocket," Pavel Bure, left Vancouver, Mogilny became a fan favorite. But there were no Canucks—not even Mark Messier—who could take the place of Fedorov or LaFontaine, the sort of player who understood Mogilny instinctively. During the 1999–2000 season, Mogilny demanded to be traded and the Canucks obliged by sending him to the New Jersey Devils. He arrived just in time to help the team win the Stanley Cup in 2000 but became a free agent after the following season (which saw him score 43 goals). He signed a lucrative deal with Toronto after New Jersey refused to get into a bidding war and started a new era of his career in Canada's hockey capital.

"Mogilny is a creator," said Buffalo coach John Muckler. "He has super talent. He can transform any half scoring opportunity into a real one and change the course of the game all by himself."

Despite missing close to 20 games with the Leafs in 2001–02 due to injury, Mogilny reached the 20-goal plateau for the ninth time in his 13-year NHL career and Russian national coach Viacheslav Fetisov pleaded with Mogilny to represent his country at the 2002 Olympics. The 33-year-old forward adamantly declined. The resentment and bitterness toward his native country stem from the host of problems that hounded him after his 1989 defection, but they remain as strong as ever.

Ed Belfour

Ed "the Eagle" Belfour was one of the busiest and most successful NHL goalies in the 1990s. In that decade he appeared in at least 60 regular-season games five times and had eight 20-win seasons. Although his goaltending style—which relied on athletic ability rather than technique—wasn't admired by purists, few would question his ability to dominate a game and his fiery, competitive nature. Belfour can make saves while on his back, stomach, side or any other seemingly hopeless position. He also wanders from his net to handle the puck or interfere with the opposition.

After a successful year with Winkler of the Manitoba Junior Hockey League, Belfour attended the University of North Dakota. In his only season of college hockey, 1986-87, he posted a record of 29 wins and four losses, was named to the Western Collegiate Hockey Association's First All-Star Team and was voted onto the NCAA Championship All-Tournament Team. A few months later, he signed as a free agent with the Chicago Blackhawks and was assigned to Saginaw of the International Hockey League. In 1987–88, he led the league in minutes played and shared IHL top rookie honors with John Cullen. He spent the bulk of the following season with Saginaw but did appear in 23 games with Chicago.

Belfour spent 1989–90 with the Canadian national team but was recalled to Chicago for the Stanley Cup playoffs. He put himself in the good graces of team management by outplaying veterans Greg Millen and Jacques Cloutier in the post-season, and it was at this time that the Chicago Stadium crowds began chanting "Eddie! Eddie!" in honor of his netminding heroics.

The 25-year-old Belfour was still technically a rookie in 1990–91 when he finally had his breakout year. He led all goaltenders with 74 games played, 43 wins and a 2.47 goals-against average. Belfour won the Vezina, Calder and Jennings trophies and was placed on the NHL First All-Star Team. Although the Hawks finished at the top of the NHL standings for the first time since 1967, they lost in a shocking first-round upset to the Minnesota North Stars, who'd trailed them in the standings by 38 points.

Ed Belfour was one of the busiest and most successful NHL goalies in the 1990s.

The next year he led the NHL with five shutouts and backstopped Chicago all the way to the Stanley Cup finals. He also led the league in shutouts in each of the next three seasons, aided by the formidable blue line corps led by Chris Chelios, Steve Smith and Bryan Marchment. Belfour's wandering, aggressive style of play mirrored that of his defensemen; he frequently showed he wasn't afraid to lash out at any opponent who took liberties with him in the crease or who parked himself too comfortably in the slot. He usually registered an above-average number of penalties for a goalie. His short temper made him the target of opposition forwards as well as fans in enemy rinks.

Eddie "the Eagle" continued to perform well through the mid-1990s. He won his second Vezina Trophy in 1993 and was runner-up in 1995. There were also two more All-Star selections, one each to the First and Second teams. But a string of early Chicago departures from the playoffs left Belfour with a reputation for being less effective during the postseason than in the regular schedule. Many observers criticized his butterfly style and his tendency to drop to his knees to play shots close-in. They hinted that the credit for his shutouts and low goals-against averages really belonged to the stingy defense playing in front of him. Other detractors pointed to his quicksilver temper as a sign that he wasn't a fully mature NHLer. Late in 1996–97, Belfour was traded to San Jose, where his performance seemed to prove the critics were right. In 13 games, he posted a 3–9 record and an uncharacteristically high 3.41 goals-against average.

During the off-season, Belfour signed as a free agent with the Dallas Stars, who were

Belfour, Ed
G, 5′11″, 182 lbs, b: Carman, Man., 4/21/1965

Season	Club, League	Regular Season				Playoffs			
		GP	Mins	GA	Avg	GP	Mins	GA	Avg
1986–87	University of North Dakota, WCHA	34	2049	81	2.43				
1987–88	Saginaw Hawks, IHL	61	3446	183	3.19	9	561	33	3.53
1988–89	Chicago Blackhawks, NHL	23	1148	74	3.87				
	Saginaw Hawks, IHL	29	1760	92	3.10	5	298	14	2.82
1989–90	Chicago Blackhawks, NHL					9	409	17	2.49
1990–91	Chicago Blackhawks, NHL	74	4127	170	2.47	6	295	20	4.07
CCup–91	Canada	0	0	0	0.00	0	0	0	0.00
1991–92	Chicago Blackhawks, NHL	52	2928	132	2.70	18	949	39	2.47
1992–93	Chicago Blackhawks, NHL	71	4106	177	2.59	4	249	13	3.13
1993–94	Chicago Blackhawks, NHL	70	3998	178	2.67	6	360	15	2.50
1994–95	Chicago Blackhawks, NHL	42	2450	93	2.28	16	1014	37	2.19
1995–96	Chicago Blackhawks, NHL	50	2956	135	2.74	9	666	23	2.07
1996–97	Chicago Blackhawks, NHL	33	1966	88	2.69				
	San Jose Sharks, NHL	13	757	43	3.41				
1997–98	Dallas Stars, NHL	61	3581	112	1.88	17	1039	31	1.79
1998–99	Dallas Stars, NHL	61	3536	117	1.99	23	1544	43	1.67
1999–00	Dallas Stars, NHL	62	3620	127	210	23	1442	45	1.87
2000–01	Dallas Stars, NHL	63	3687	144	2.34	10	671	25	2.24
2001–02	Dallas Stars, NHL	60	3467	153	2.65				
OWG–02	Canada	0	0	0	0.00				
	NHL Totals	735	42329	1743	2.47				
	CCup Totals	0	0	0	0.00	0	0	0	0.00

NHL First All-Star Team (1991, 1993)
NHL Second All-Star Team (1995)
Won Vezina Trophy (1991, 1993)
Won Calder Trophy (1991)
Won William M. Jennings Trophy (1991, 1993, 1995, 1999)
Won Stanley Cup (1999)
Won CCup (1991)
Won OWG (2002)

showing signs of becoming a Stanley Cup contender. In his first season with Dallas, Belfour led the NHL with a career-best 1.88 goals-against average, but the team fell short in the Western Conference finals against the defending champion Detroit Red Wings. In 1998-99, he guided the Stars to their first Stanley Cup win with three shutouts and a 1.67 average in the playoffs. This triumph silenced the critics at last, as Belfour demonstrated that he could win in big games and control his emotions. And as if to put to rest any doubts about the Cup victory, Belfour was again one of the top goalies in the league in 1999–2000, leading the Stars to a second straight appearance in the finals and proving himself one of the best "money goalies" currently playing.

In 2000–01, he won 35 games—his fourth straight season of 30 or more wins—though the Stars were eliminated in the second round of the playoffs. But 2001–02 was a season of contrasts for the veteran netminder. On the one hand, Belfour was ecstatic at being selected to play for Team Canada at the 2002 Winter Olympics. On the other, he found himself in a prolonged battle with Marty Turco for the starting position in Dallas. Although Belfour didn't see any playing time in Salt Lake City, he did dress as the backup goalie for Canada's 3–2 win over Germany because the rules stipulate that a player must be in the lineup for at least one Olympic game to be eligible for a medal.

The breakout season for Ed Belfour (right) was 1990–1991, when he led the league with 43 wins and a 2.47 goals-against average, won the Vezina, Calder and Jennings awards and was chosen for the First All-Star Team.

Vladimir Malakhov

Thirty-three-year-old Russian defenseman Vladimir Malakhov has had a puzzling career pattern in North America. He is one of the NHL's best skaters, and at times he has all the makings of a Norris Trophy winner. Yet he seems unable to sustain his excellent performance for the duration of an NHL season. In the summer of 2000, Malakhov made the fourth move of his NHL career, joining the New York Rangers, and it remains to be seen if his pattern will change.

Malakhov's father was a hockey coach in the 1970s for Red Army Sverdlovsk. Later, Malakhov Sr. turned to bandy and was invited to supervise the local team in the coal-mining city of Kemerovo. His son was then 15 and good at ice hockey, but in Kemerovo, Vladimir was obliged to switch sports. He now believes his two-year flirtation with bandy helped his game.

Malakhov never played for a junior team, instead choosing to go to Moscow and enroll in the Physical Culture Institute. After passing the entrance exam, he was admitted to the hockey department. He played for the institute's team, where he met players from the Spartak junior team. At that time, many Spartak players were being drafted into the army and Malakhov was invited to replace one of the conscripts.

Malakhov proved his skill on the ice and Spartak head coach Boris Mikhailov offered him a contract. Two years later, Viktor Tikhonov persuaded Malakhov to join his Central Red Army team, for whom he would play for the next four years. Malakhov was also a member of the Soviet national team that won a World Championship in 1990 and the Olympic gold medal in 1992.

One of the league's best skaters, Vladimir Malakhov has had a puzzling career in the NHL.

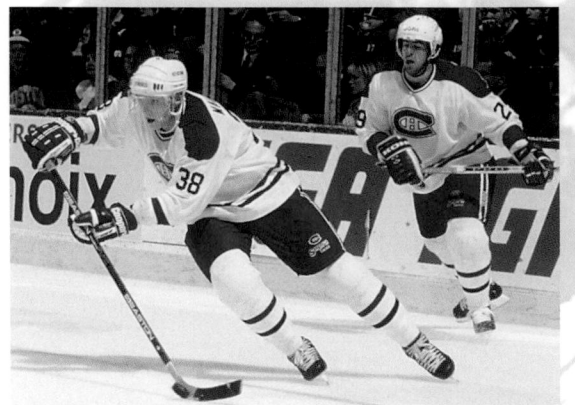

Vladimir Malakhov (left) was a leading defenseman for the Montreal Canadiens for five years.

After the Winter Olympics in Albertville, France, a number of Russian players thought about conditions in their home country, which was suffering a number of economic and political crises, and decided their futures lay in the NHL. Malakhov was among them, making his debut with the New York Islanders and scoring 52 points in 64 regular-season games. Malakhov's efforts helped the Islanders reach the Wales Conference finals and earned him a nomination to the NHL's All-Rookie Team. The next year Malakhov racked up 57 points and a plus-minus rating of plus-29, leading many to predict a bright future for the big 6´3˝, 220-pound defender.

The lockout-shortened 1994–95 season saw the Islanders fall into a tailspin and management decided to overhaul the lineup. About two-thirds of the way into the season, Malakhov was traded along with Pierre Turgeon to the Montreal Canadiens for Mathieu Schneider and Kirk Muller. In Montreal, Malakhov didn't get along with head coach Mario Tremblay. "He treated French-speakers in a different manner than the rest of us, and that attitude tore the team apart," Malakhov claims. "Once I went to a meeting of defensemen where there were French-Canadians, and the assistant coach spoke French the whole time. All I could do was say, 'Hey, I'm here too!' and he finally said 'Oh, excuse me,' and continued his lecture in English. I have never had any problem with the guys. I don't care who he is, English- or French-speaking. But I hated the feeling that this language factor just made you a second-rate member of the team."

During the 1999–2000 season, Malakhov was maligned for going skiing while he was supposed to be recuperating from a serious knee injury. It was the last straw for the Canadiens, who traded him to New Jersey during the regular season. He was a steady presence during the Devils' successful run for the Stanley Cup in 2000, but during the off-season he signed as a free agent with the New York Rangers, who no doubt hoped he would match the form he displayed in his first two NHL seasons.

In his first full season with the Rangers, Malakhov was a steady force on the defense, but the team missed the playoffs for the fourth year in a row. The highlight of his season was representing Russia at the Olympics and earning a bronze medal.

Malakhov, Vladimir
D, 6´3˝, 220 lbs, b: Sverdlovsk, USSR, 8/30/1968

Season	Club, League	Regular Season					Playoffs				
		GP	G	A	Pts	PIM	GP	G	A	Pts	PIM
1986–87	Spartak Moscow, USSR	22	0	1	1	12					
1987–88	Spartak Moscow, USSR	28	2	2	4	26					
1988–89	CSKA, USSR	34	6	2	8	16					
1989–90	CSKA, USSR	48	2	10	12	34					
WEC–90	USSR	10	0	1	1	10					
1990–91	CSKA, USSR	46	5	13	18	22					
WEC–91	USSR	10	0	0	0	4					
CCup–91	USSR	5	0	0	0	4					
1991–92	CSKA, Russia	40	1	9	10	12					
OWG–92	Russia	8	3	0	3	4					
WC–92	Russia	6	2	1	3	4					
1992–93	New York Islanders, NHL	64	14	38	52	59	17	3	6	9	12
	Capital District Islanders, AHL	3	2	1	3	11					
1993–94	New York Islanders, NHL	76	10	47	57	80	4	0	0	0	6
1994–95	New York Islanders, NHL	26	3	13	16	32					
	Montreal Canadiens, NHL	14	1	4	5	14					
1995–96	Montreal Canadiens, NHL	61	5	23	28	79					
WCup–96	Russia	4	1	0	1	8					
1996–97	Montreal Canadiens, NHL	65	10	20	30	43	5	0	0	0	6
1997–98	Montreal Canadiens, NHL	74	13	31	44	70	9	3	4	7	10
1998–99	Montreal Canadiens, NHL	62	13	21	34	77					
1999–00	Montreal Canadiens, NHL	7	0	0	0	4					
	New Jersey Devils, NHL	17	1	4	5	19	23	1	4	5	18
2000–01	New York Rangers, NHL	3	0	2	2	4					
2001–02	New York Rangers, NHL	81	6	22	28	83					
OWG–02	Russia	6	1	3	4	4					
	USSR/Russia Totals	218	16	37	53	122					
	NHL Totals	550	76	225	301	564					
	OWG/WEC/WC/CCup/WCup Totals	48	8	4	11	38					

Won OWG (1992)
Won WEC (1990)
Won Stanley Cup (2000)
USSR Champion (1989)

Brendan Shanahan

At 6′3″ and 218 pounds, Detroit Red Wings left winger Brendan Shanahan is a big presence on the ice. Away from the rink, he has a quick sense of humor that has earned him the nickname "Shenanigans." He was once quoted in a team media guide as saying that he'd been a ball boy in the U.S. Open tennis tournament, a professional soccer player and an extra in the movie *Forrest Gump*. None of these claims was true.

Shanahan, who was born in Mimico, Ontario, played his junior hockey with the London Knights of the Ontario Hockey League, and it was there that he made his reputation as a team leader by frequently running practices if the coach was away. He would be revered for his leadership throughout his pro career.

Brendan Shanahan was a key player in the Detroit dynasty of the 1990s.

In 1987, at 18, Shanahan was drafted second overall by the New Jersey Devils. His reputation was such that many people pegged him as a cornerstone player for the Devils franchise before he'd even played his first NHL game. But Shanahan was careful to downplay such lofty predictions. "I know I'm not ready for everything that is going to challenge me in the NHL," he said before his first game. "I have to work on my overall quickness and I have to work on my upper-body strength. But this is the team that I want to play for."

A severely sprained ankle suffered in his rookie year set him back temporarily, but Shanahan was able to take something positive from it. "It probably helped me out a bit because I could sit back and gain some composure," he said. "I was sitting back watching the habits of guys I would have been playing against. I was scouting."

After his fourth season with New Jersey, Shanahan was signed as a free agent by the St. Louis Blues. Under league rules, St. Louis had to compensate the Devils and an arbitrator ruled that the winger was worth no less than Blues captain and defensive star Scott Stevens. In his second year with St. Louis, Shanahan scored 51 goals. In addition to the offense he generated, Shanny had proved that he wasn't afraid to fight if he felt the situation called for it. His statistics in 1993–94 epitomized his style as he scored 52 goals and logged 211 minutes in the penalty box.

In 1995 Shanahan got the shock of his career when he was traded to the Hartford Whalers. He was so popular in St. Louis that local TV stations interrupted regular programming to announce the news on the day of the trade. The Whalers, meanwhile, were ecstatic to be getting a player of Brendan's caliber. Coach Paul Holmgren said: "I call it instant credibility. This is a guy who fills a vital role on the team, a guy who takes the pressure off the guys around him and makes everybody else around him better." Holmgren and Jim Rutherford were ready to name Shanahan captain of the team before the season even started, but the winger was cool to the idea at first. "I'd love the opportunity to wear the 'C' and I really want the pressure that comes with it," he said. "But I wanted the guys to see me first. I wanted to talk to several of the players about it." After training camp, he accepted the role.

Brendan Shanahan (right) was so popular in St. Louis that local TV stations interrupted their programming when he was traded to Hartford.

Shanahan didn't take long to get over his disappointment with the trade and got ready to play the kind of hockey that would put fans in the seats—no small task in Hartford. "I really think they are ready to embrace hockey again," he said of his plans to wow the Whalers' faithful. But even though he had a good 1995–96 season statistically, scoring 44 goals, the team continued to struggle on the ice and at the box office and Shanahan asked to be traded. He wanted to play for a contending team whose fans were passionate about the game. "I felt that pressure-packed hockey in an environment where people love the game was something that I really missed," he admitted.

The Red Wings, who had been improving themselves through some smart trades and prescient drafting, were ready for just such a player to come along. Scotty Bowman had signed on as coach in 1994 and was looking for the final element he needed to make the Wings a Cup winner after they lost in the 1995 finals to New Jersey and the 1996 Western Conference finals to Colorado. Detroit paid a steep price—trading forward Keith Primeau, defenseman Paul Coffey and a first—round draft pick-to land Shanahan.

"We have the best leader in the game in Steve Yzerman, and if we all play his game offensively and defensively, we are going to be tough to beat," he said upon arriving in the Motor City. As if on cue, Detroit captured the Stanley Cup in 1997—the team's first championship in more than 40 years—by sweeping the Philadelphia Flyers, and then duplicated the feat in 1998 against the Washington Capitals.

Shanahan scored 41 and 31 goals respectively in 1999–2000 and 2000–01, and his red-hot start to the next season ensured he'd be considered for Canada's team in Salt Lake. And indeed Shanahan did earn a spot on Team Canada's roster and played well throughout the six-game tournament, but he'd be the first to admit he didn't have the golden touch when it came to goal-scoring during the tournament. Still, the 2001–02 season was a prosperous one for Shanahan, who helped the Red Wings to the Presidents' Trophy, awarded to the team with the most points during the regular season. He also reached two personal milestones when he surpassed the 500-goal and 1,000-point marks.

Shanahan, Brendan
LW, 6´3˝, 218 lbs, b: Mimico, Ont., 1/23/1969

Season	Club, League	Regular Season					Playoffs				
		GP	G	A	Pts	PIM	GP	G	A	Pts	PIM
1987–88	New Jersey Devils, NHL	65	7	19	26	131	12	2	1	3	44
1988–89	New Jersey Devils, NHL	68	22	28	50	115					
1989–90	New Jersey Devils, NHL	73	30	42	72	137	6	3	3	6	20
1990–91	New Jersey Devils, NHL	75	29	37	66	141	7	3	5	8	12
CCup–91	Canada	8	2	0	2	6					
1991–92	St. Louis Blues, NHL	80	33	36	69	171	6	2	3	5	14
1992–93	St. Louis Blues, NHL	71	51	43	94	174	11	4	3	7	18
1993–94	St. Louis Blues, NHL	81	52	50	102	211	4	2	5	7	4
WC–94	Canada	6	4	3	7	6					
1994–95	Dusseldorf, Germany	3	5	3	8	4					
	St. Louis Blues, NHL	45	20	21	41	136	5	4	5	9	14
1995–96	Hartford Whalers, NHL	74	44	34	78	125					
WCup–96	Canada	7	3	3	6	8					
1996–97	Hartford Whalers, NHL	2	1	0	1	0					
	Detroit Red Wings, NHL	79	46	41	87	131	20	9	8	17	43
1997–98	Detroit Red Wings, NHL	75	28	29	57	154	20	5	4	9	22
OWG–98	Canada	6	2	0	2	0					
1998–99	Detroit Red Wings, NHL	81	31	27	58	123	10	3	7	10	6
1999–00	Detroit Red Wings, NHL	78	41	37	78	105	9	3	2	5	10
2000–01	Detroit Red Wings, NHL	81	31	45	76	81	2	2	2	4	0
2001–02	Detroit Red Wings, NHL	80	37	38	75	118					
OWG–02	Canada	6	0	1	1	0					
	NHL Totals	1108	503	527	1030	2053					
	OWG/WC/CCup/WCup Totals	33	11	7	18	20					

NHL First All-Star Team (1994, 2000)
Won WC (1994)
Won Stanley Cup (1997, 1998)
Won CCup (1991)
Won OWG (2002)

Bobby Holik

Bobby Holik comes from a true hockey family. His father, Jaroslav, and uncle Jiri both ranked among the best Czechoslovakian players of all time. His sister Andrea became a world-class tennis player who later married defenseman Frantisek Musil. From the time he was a child, Robert never doubted he would one day be a hockey player.

Hockey may have been in Holik's blood, but he worked hard every step of the way to becoming one of the greatest talents his country had ever known. His father, who couldn't stand sloppy habits or laziness, was sometimes very tough with him. Whenever young Robert slackened in his duties, his father would take him to a factory gate early in the morning. "If you don't work hard, you'll end up in here," he said. "It is better to make a living doing something you enjoy." That always helped Robert regain his focus.

The senior Holik also taught him not to be afraid. He would say: "If someone slugs you, return it. You will gain respect and feel good. Don't let yourself be intimidated. This will come in handy in hockey and in life." About this piece of advice, Bobby would later say, "Dad was always right."

Holik gained a reputation for his hard shot and physical style of play. He was also a headstrong player who stopped for no one. Just as Andrea Holik ruled the world's tennis courts in the late 1980s, so the offensive trio of Jaromir Jagr, Robert Reichel and Robert Holik reigned over junior hockey, playing together in the 1990 World Junior Championships. After that tournament, all three entered the NHL, but each headed to a different city, Reichel to Calgary, Jagr to Pittsburgh and Holik to Hartford. Along the way, Robert Holik became Bobby. "I always wanted to play in the NHL," he said. "The rest wasn't as important."

Bobby scored 21 goals in each of his first two seasons. In 1992 he was traded to the New Jersey Devils, where he didn't ease up one bit. "Whenever something unpleasant happened to me, I told myself it was only a matter of time before it got better. In New Jersey, it took a while for me to get used to things, but a terrific gang of players was formed. The result was a Stanley Cup victory, followed by the most beautiful feelings I ever had in my sports career. The enormous hard work had turned into excitement and joy."

After the Stanley Cup win in 1995, Bobby Holik took a drink of alcohol for the first time in his life. "They poured champagne in our glasses. I took a sip but didn't like it much," he said. "I will stick to my tried and tested beverages. I will touch alcohol only in the event of another Stanley Cup win. And I will drink it only from the Cup."

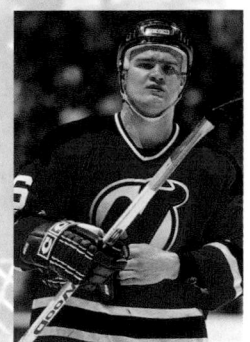

Bobby Holik never doubted for a minute that he would be a hockey player.

Holik, Bobby
LW, 6´3˝, 220 lbs, b: Jihlava, Czechoslovakia, 1/1/1971

Season	Club, League	Regular Season					Playoffs				
		GP	G	A	Pts	PLM	GP	G	A	Pts	PLM
1987–88	Dukla Jihlava, Czechoslovakia	31	5	9	14	16					
1988–89	Dukla Jihlava, Czechoslovakia	24	7	10	17	32					
1989–90	Dukla Jihlava, Czechoslovakia	42	15	26	41	58					
WJC–90	Czechoslovakia	7	6	5	11	12					
1990–91	Hartford Whalers, NHL	78	21	22	43	113	6	0	0	0	7
1991–92	Hartford Whalers, NHL	76	21	24	45	44	7	0	1	1	6
1992–93	New Jersey Devils, NHL	61	20	19	39	76	5	1	1	2	6
	Utica Devils, AHL	1	0	0	0	2					
1993–94	New Jersey Devils, NHL	70	13	20	33	72	20	0	3	3	6
1994–95	New Jersey Devils, NHL	48	10	10	20	18	20	4	4	8	22
1995–96	New Jersey Devils, NHL	63	13	17	30	58					
WCup–96	Czech Republic	3	0	0	0	0					
1996–97	New Jersey Devils, NHL	82	23	39	62	54	10	2	3	5	4
1997–98	New Jersey Devils, NHL	82	29	36	65	100	5	0	0	0	8
1998–99	New Jersey Devils, NHL	78	27	37	64	119	7	0	7	7	6
1999–00	New Jersey Devils, NHL	79	23	23	46	106	23	3	7	10	14
2000–01	New Jersey Devils, NHL	80	15	35	50	97	25	6	10	16	37
2001–02	New Jersey Devils, NHL	81	2	5	29	54	97				
	Czechoslovakia/										
	Czech Republic Totals	97	27	45	72	106					
	NHL Totals	878	240	311	551	954					
	WCup Totals	3	0	0	0	0					

Won Stanley Cup (1995, 2000)

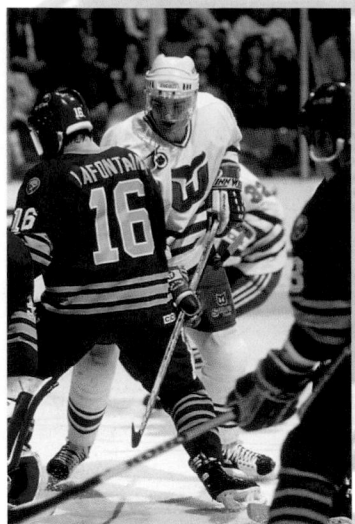

In North America, Robert became Bobby Holik (center): "I always wanted to play in the NHL. The rest wasn't as important."

However harsh he may sometimes appear on the ice, away from the rink he is the quiet, studious type, often reading up on history and the arts. On road trips he prefers visiting museums and galleries over lying in his hotel room and watching television. A short TV profile of him was filmed at the Thomas Alva Edison museum. In Dallas, on the 30th anniversary of the death of John F. Kennedy, he toured the spot where the president was shot. He also likes fishing and outdoor excursions.

During the lockout in 1994, Holik studied the history of communism at a university in Pennsylvania. "I wanted to compare my own experience with the views of American professors," he said.

In 1991 Holik had lined up for Czechoslovakia in the World Championships in Finland, but his next international experience didn't come until the World Cup of Hockey in 1996. It would be the first and only time he appeared in the uniform of the Czech Republic, as he became a U.S. citizen shortly after the tournament, giving up his Czech citizenship. He was quick to point out: "That doesn't mean that I will forget my native land, Bohemia, and the people who are rooting for me. But I have simply settled elsewhere. I did so voluntarily. I came to America when I was young. I married here and started a family. It is here that I got to know a decent life. When my parents come to visit, after two weeks they look forward to going back home. I cannot say the same. But of course I will always feel my roots."

In 1996–97 and 1997–98, Holik led his team in scoring, netting a career-high 29 goals in the latter season. In 2000 his checking ability was central to New Jersey's success in the Stanley Cup finals as New Jersey won its second championship, and the next year the ornery checker took his team back to the finals before losing to Colorado in seven games.

Pavel **Bure**

Pavel Bure, "the Russian Rocket," developed quickly as a youngster in the Soviet Union, and when he arrived in the National Hockey League, he proved to be that rare and thrilling player—a pure goal scorer. Maurice Richard, the original "Rocket," was capable of timely bursts of speed that came just as an opening appeared in a wall of defenders with the game on the line. Bure had that same ability, and, like Richard, his effort between daring attacks was often questioned. At times he seemed bored or indifferent, like a cat toying with a mouse, and these spells stood in stark contrast to the amazing feats he could perform when he was at his best.

When the Soviet Union began to lose its control over the careers of its best players, North American fans were able to see Pavel and his generation perform and flourish in NHL rinks on a full-time basis after years of getting only glimpses during World Championships and exhibition tours. Though diminutive, Bure's blazing speed, creativity and conditioning made him unstoppable, and his offensive pyrotechnics filled arenas wherever he played.

Bure grew up in Moscow and attended the Red Army sports school. As a six-year old, he tried out for the school's hockey team, wearing figure skates and hardly able to stand. He had only started skating earlier that year and, not surprisingly, he didn't come close to making the cut.

This didn't overly disappoint his father, Vladimir, a world-class swimmer who had participated in three Summer Olympics. The elder Bure had won a bronze medal in the relay in Mexico City in 1968 and three more medals at the Munich Games of 1972, including a bronze in one of Mark Spitz's seven victories that year. Vladimir was hopeful that his eldest son would paddle in his wake, but Pavel quickly grew bored with the endless repetition of swimming lap after lap.

When Pavel was seven, his father gave him a couple of months to prove he could be a hockey player. It was a tight deadline, especially since the youngster had had a late start on skates. But the youngster turned out to have a natural balance on the blades and he was soon skating circles around kids his own age. His hero was Valeri Kharlamov, one of the standouts of the 1972 Summit Series. In his teenage years, Bure came to the attention of the Soviet hockey machine and was given a roster spot on Viktor Tikhonov's Central Red Army team.

His blazing speed and creativity made Pavel Bure (top) unstoppable and his pyrotechnics packed them in wherever he played.

The 1989 World Junior Championships was a coming-out party for the players who'd been touted as the future of the game in the Soviet Union. In particular the line of Alexander Mogilny at left wing, Sergei Fedorov at center and Bure at right wing was expected to pick up where the famous KLM Line of Vladimir Krutov, Igor Larionov and Sergei Makarov had left off. But by 1991 all three young stars were making waves in the National Hockey League. Bure, who had been selected as the top forward in that World Junior tournament, was the last of the three to defect to North America.

By 1990 Pavel, who at 19 had already fulfilled his mandatory two years of military service, refused to re-sign with the Red Army club. The decision cost him a place on the 1991 Canada Cup squad. With his father and brother—Valeri would also star in the NHL with the Montreal Canadiens and Calgary Flames—he made his way to California. At the time, he and Eric Lindros were considered to be the two best unsigned players in the world.

Pavel's arrival in the NHL was preceded by some controversy over his playing rights. The Vancouver Canucks had drafted him in the fourth round in 1989, 113th overall, but a year later NHL president John Ziegler ruled the Canucks' claim invalid. The problem was an NHL rule that prohibited teams from drafting 18-year-old players later than the third round unless they'd played at least 10 games in a major league, and most sources said Bure had played only five. But Vancouver's head of scouting, Mike Penny, had done his research and turned up evidence that Bure met the requirement. Ziegler reversed his decision soon afterward.

The line of Pavel Bure (left), Sergei Fedorov (center) and Alexander Mogilny (right) was supposed to be the next great troika of Soviet hockey.

Bure made his National Hockey League debut with the Canucks in 1991–92, and his 34 goals and 60 points made him an easy choice as winner of the Calder Trophy as the league's top rookie.

In 1992–93, Bure cemented his reputation as a world-class scorer, gathering 60 goals and 110 points. He scored another 60 the next season, leading the league in that department and earning First Team All-Star honors. Only Mike Bossy and Wayne Gretzky had scored more goals in their first three NHL seasons.

As impressive as he was in the 1993–94 regular season, Bure saved his best for the post-season. His Canucks entered the Western Conference playoffs as the seventh seed out of eight teams.

A HISTORY OF WORLD HOCKEY

In the first round, they spotted Calgary to a lead of three games to one but came back to win three consecutive games in overtime and eliminated the Flames. Bure scored the series-winning goal in the second overtime period of game seven.

Vancouver disposed of Dallas in the next round and Bure was at his best, scoring six goals in the five games. After knocking off a tired Toronto team, the Canucks found themselves in the Stanley Cup finals, their first such appearance since 1982. Bure was matched against the New York Rangers and their captain, Mark Messier. Even though his Canucks lost to the Rangers in a thrilling seven-game series, Bure seemed on the cusp of superstardom after leading the league with 16 playoff goals.

Over the next few seasons, Bure's development was slowed by injuries and the owners lockout of 1994. Torn ligaments limited him to only 15 games in 1995–96. He was tentative and still far from his best during the next season, ending up with 23 goals and 55 points in 63 games. He regained much of his form in 1997–98, again breaking the 50-goal plateau and exciting crowds with his darting end-to-end rushes. It seemed at the time that Bure would once again lead Vancouver to respectability.

Bure played for Russia at the 1998 Winter Olympics in Nagano, Japan, and the team won a silver medal after being narrowly edged out 1–0 by Dominik Hasek and the Czech Republic in the final game. Pavel was selected as the tournament's top forward after his nine-goal performance led the field at the star-studded Games.

Before the 1998–99 season got underway, Bure announced he would never again play for the Canucks and demanded a trade. He refused to discuss his reasons for wanting to leave, but his salary—at around $8.5 million—could hardly have been the source of his unrest. He later allowed that he was angry with Pat Quinn, the team's former general manager and coach, as well as other Canucks brass. He also said he was no longer able to handle the high profile that hockey players had in Vancouver, comparing the experience to living in a fish bowl. "I'm losing lots of money, but…it's a sacrifice I'm willing to make," Bure said of his decision to hold out. "Money is important in our lives, but it's not everything to me. I have my principles. Hockey is number one for me. Money is number two, three or four—I haven't decided which."

Bure went home to Russia and kept in shape with the Red Army team, though the country's economic situation at the time made it difficult. (The team had been evicted from its home rink and players hadn't been paid for

Bure, Pavel
RW, 5′10″, 189 lbs, b: Moscow, USSR, 3/31/1971

Season	Club, League	Regular Season					Playoffs				
		GP	G	A	Pts	PIM	GP	G	A	Pts	PIM
1987–88	CSKA, USSR	5	1	1	2	0					
1988–89	CSKA, USSR	32	17	9	26	8					
1989–90	CSKA, USSR	46	14	10	24	20					
WEC–90	USSR	10	2	4	6	10					
1990–91	CSKA, USSR	44	35	11	46	24					
WEC–91	USSR	10	3	8	11	2					
1991–92	Vancouver Canucks, NHL	65	34	26	60	30	13	6	4	0	14
1992–93	Vancouver Canucks, NHL	83	60	50	110	69	12	5	7	12	8
1993–94	Vancouver Canucks, NHL	76	60	47	107	86	24	16	15	31	40
1994–95	Landshut, Germany	1	3	0	3	2					
	Spartak Moscow, Russia	1	2	0	2	2					
	Vancouver Canucks, NHL	44	20	23	43	47	11	7	6	13	10
1995–96	Vancouver Canucks, NHL	15	6	7	13	8					
1996–97	Vancouver Canucks, NHL	63	23	32	55	40					
1997–98	Vancouver Canucks, NHL	82	51	39	90	48					
OWG–98	Russia	6	9	0	9	2					
1998–99	Florida Panthers, NHL	11	13	3	16	4					
1999–00	Florida Panthers, NHL	74	58	36	94	16	4	1	3	4	2
WC–2000	Russia	6	4	1	5	10					
2000–01	Florida Panthers, NHL	82	59	33	92	58					
2001–02	Florida-NY Rangers, NHL	68	34	35	69	62					
OWG–02	Russia	6	2	1	3	8					
	USSR/Russia Totals	128	69	31	100	54					
	NHL Totals	663	418	331	749	468					
	OWG/WEC/WC Totals	38	20	14	34	32					

NHL First All-Star Team (1994)
NHL Second All-Star Team (2000)
Won Calder Trophy (1992)
Won Maurice Richard Trophy (2000)
Won WEC (1990)
USSR Champion (1989)

Pavel Bure

months on end.) The holdout extended midway through the season, leaving Canucks general manager Brian Burke no choice but to arrange a trade. On January 17, 1999, he sent Bure and two young defensemen, Brad Ference and Bret Hedican, to the Florida Panthers for defenseman Ed Jovanovski—a former first overall draft choice—forward Dave Gagner, goalie Kevin Weekes, junior prospect Mike Brown and a first-round draft pick.

Four Russian players at the 1994 All-Star weekend: Arturs Irbe (number 32), Alexei Kasatonov (number 7), Sergei Fedorov (number 91) and Pavel Bure (number 10).

The relative anonymity enjoyed by hockey players in Miami suited Bure, who set out to right the Panthers' ship and had an immediate impact. He scored two goals in his first game and added a hat-trick less than a week later. In his first six games, he had eight goals, but he strained a muscle in his right knee two weeks after joining the team and was sidelined for eight games. In his fourth game back in the lineup, he scored a natural hat–trick—three consecutive goals—in the first two periods of a game against Colorado before he felt something give out again in his knee. He had reinjured the ligament that had forced him to miss much of the 1995–96 season and underwent arthroscopic surgery on March 5 and more extensive work three weeks later to repair it. His season was over after only 11 games, in which he'd scored 13 goals.

During the summer of 1999, Bure dedicated himself to strengthening the knee muscles that were so important to his high-flying game. In his first full season with Florida, he led the NHL with 58 goals and became the second man to win the Maurice Richard Trophy. He and Valeri combined to set a league record for goals in one season by a pair of brothers with 93, surpassing the old mark set by Bobby and Dennis Hull. His hat-trick at the 2000 All-Star Game in Toronto earned him the game's MVP award. When the season resumed, his efforts were a key to the Panthers' improving from 78 to 98 points and returning to the playoffs after a two-year absence. Bure won another Rocket Richard award in 2000–01 with a league-leading 59 goals and in 2001–02 added another milestone to a string of accomplishments with his 400th career goal.

Bure was one of the eight players initially selected for Russia at the 2002 Olympics but failed to find the scoring touch he'd possessed at the 1998 Games in Nagano—where he'd scored five goals in a single game—although he played well throughout the whole tournament. At Salt Lake, the Russians defeated the Czechs 1–0 in a hard-fought quarterfinals to avenge their loss in the gold medal game four years before. Then Russia came up on the short end of a 3–2 score against the strong U.S. squad in the semifinals and had to settle for playing the bronze medal game against Belarus, which they handily dispatched 7–1.

Back in the NHL, the Panthers put Bure on the trade market when it became apparent they would miss the Stanley Cup playoffs again in 2001–02. The Panthers were hoping to free up some space on the payroll for the following season, while Glen Sather and the New York Rangers had spent three consecutive years of watching the post-season from the outside and become desperate enough to pick up Bure and his $10-million salary at the trade deadline. Unfortunately, it proved to be too little too late. Even Bure couldn't elevate the Rangers into a playoff position and critics were soon calling for another complete overhaul of the team.

Theo Fleury

At 5´6″ and 160 pounds, Theo Fleury is one of the smallest players in hockey and he had to dis-prove many doubters and skeptics to become a bona fide NHL star. Intense and fearless, Fleury made a name for himself for more than his stature—he could score, play defensively and lead teams to championships in junior hockey, in the NHL and on the international stage.

Born in Oxbow, Saskatchewan in 1968, Theo was so tiny as a baby that his mother named him after the smallest character in one of her favorite movies, *Old Yeller*. The Fleurys made a move to nearby Russell, Manitoba, but didn't have much money. Theo had to rely on others to pay his way when his teams traveled to tournaments and he wore borrowed skates right up until he reached the junior ranks, when he could finally buy himself a pair.

When he played shinny as a boy in Russell, Fleury learned that if he passed the puck to the big-ger, older kids, he'd never get it back. So he learned to skate with the puck and developed an arse-nal of tricks to maintain possession, along with a certain feistiness. These skills would form the basis of his game. An injury in his bantam year almost prevented Fleury from advancing to junior. A skate blade badly sliced his right arm, forcing him to miss a full year of hockey. He also perma-nently lost feeling in parts of his right hand for the rest of his career.

In 1984, as a 16-year-old, he did make the move up the ranks, joining the Moose Jaw Warriors of the Western Hockey League. In his second year he emerged as the team leader, and in his third and fourth years he became a star for his offensive achievements and for his enter-taining, all-out style of play. In 1986 he was invited to the training camp for the team that would represent Canada at the World Junior Championships in Czechoslovakia. Scouts were already voicing the opinion that Fleury would be too small to play in the NHL, giving Fleury that much more to prove as a member of Team Canada. "They had 12 first-round draft picks on that team," he recalled later. "It opened a lot of eyes of people who'd doubted me. If I could be one of the best juniors in the country, I figured I at least deserved to be drafted."

Fleury brought his typical pesky game to the championships but was involved in an infamous brawl that cost Canada a chance at the gold medal. Seeing a teammate in a fight, Fleury jumped on the Russian player's back. In no time, both benches were empty and the teams fought for 20 minutes, stopping only after tournament

At 5´6″ and 160 pounds, Theo Fleury overcame doubters and skeptics to become a bona fide star in the NHL.

Fleury, Theo
RW, 5´6″, 160 lbs, b: Oxbow, Sask., 6/29/1968

Season	Club, League	Regular Season					Playoffs				
		GP	G	A	Pts	PIM	GP	G	A	Pts	PIM
1987–88	Salt Lake Golden Eagles, IHL	2	3	4	7	7	8	11	5	16	16
1988–89	Calgary Flames, NHL	36	14	20	34	46	22	5	6	11	24
	Salt Lake Golden Eagles, IHL	40	37	37	74	81					
1989–90	Calgary Flames, NHL	80	31	35	66	157	6	2	3	5	10
WEC–90	Canada	9	4	7	11	10					
1990–91	Calgary Flames, NHL	79	51	53	104	136	7	2	5	7	14
WEC–91	Canada	8	5	5	10	8					
CCup–91	Canada	7	1	4	5	12					
1991–92	Calgary Flames, NHL	80	33	40	73	133					
1992–93	Calgary Flames, NHL	83	34	66	100	88	6	5	7	12	27
1993–94	Calgary Flames, NHL	83	40	45	85	186	7	6	4	10	5
1994–95	Tappara, Finland	10	8	9	17	22					
	Calgary Flames, NHL	47	29	29	58	112	7	7	7	14	2
1995–96	Calgary Flames, NHL	80	46	50	96	112	4	2	1	3	14
WCup–96	Canada	8	4	2	6	8					
1996–97	Calgary Flames, NHL	81	29	38	67	104					
1997–98	Calgary Flames, NHL	82	27	51	78	197					
OWG–98	Canada	6	1	3	4	2					
1998–99	Calgary Flames, NHL	60	30	39	69	68					
	Colorado Avalanche, NHL	15	10	14	24	18	18	5	12	17	20
1999–00	New York Rangers, NHL	80	15	49	64	68					
2000–01	New York Rangers, NHL	62	30	44	74	122					
2001–02	New York Rangers, NHL	82	24	39	63	216					
OWG–02	Canada	6	0	2	2	6					
	NHL Totals	1030	443	612	1055	1763					
	OWG/WEC/CCup/WCup Totals	44	15	23	38	46					

NHL Second All-Star Team (1995)
Won Alka-Seltzer Plus Award (1991)
Won Stanley Cup (1989)
Won CCup (1991)
Won OWG (2002)

"If a little guy like me is to succeed in the big leagues, I have to show all those guys, big or small, that I'll stand up for my rights," Theo Fleury (right) said. "I don't care if it's Jeff Beukeboom or Mario Lemieux that I hit."

organizers turned off the lights in the arena. The Canadian and Soviet teams were disqualified.

Fleury was selected in the 1987 NHL Entry Draft, but not until 165 players were chosen ahead of him. The Calgary Flames chose him with their ninth-round pick, projecting him as a potentially entertaining addition to their minor-league club in Salt Lake City. Fleury played a final season in Moose Jaw in 1987–88 and tied Swift Current's Joe Sakic for the league scoring title. He also racked up 235 minutes in penalties as he stepped up his aggressive play to combat the criticism of his size. He once again played in the World Junior Championships, this time as team captain in an uneventful affair in which Canada won the gold medal. Fleury was named to the tournament's All-Star team.

Though Fleury was confident in his abilities, the Flames seemed less than sure. They signed him to a pro contract late in the 1987–88 season, just in time for him to join Salt Lake for the International Hockey League playoffs. He seized the opportunity, scoring 11 goals in eight games and leading the Golden Eagles to the championship. He began the next season in Salt Lake, but an outburst of 37 goals and 74 points in only 40 games finally convinced the Flames that he deserved a chance to play in the NHL. He turned in a solid half-season in Calgary, impressing his head coach, Terry Crisp, who had also been a hard worker during his playing days. "He reminds me of Ken Linseman, and there's a little Bobby Clarke in him too," Crisp said after seeing Fleury play in the NHL. "And he also reminds me of Henri Richard, the way he bounces off hits to get up and score."

Used at center and at right wing, Fleury helped the Flames capture the Stanley Cup in 1989, and in his first full season he scored 31 goals. In 1990–91, he netted 51 goals and 104 points and made his first appearance at the NHL All-Star Game. Prior to the next season he played in the Canada Cup tournament, and he went on to score 30 goals in each of his next three seasons. He was also among the league leaders with 29 during the lockout-shortened 1994-95 season.

Though outspoken and often brash, aggravating teammates and opponents alike, Fleury matured in time, becoming team captain in 1995. He continued to pick up honors for his hard work, including a berth on the league's Second All-Star Team in 1995 and spots on Team Canada's roster at the 1996 World Cup of Hockey and the 1998 Nagano Olympics.

A speedy and feisty forward, Fleury continued to play with the same determination that helped him break into a league that didn't believe he could succeed. "If a little guy like me is to succeed in the big leagues, I have to show all those guys, big or small, that I'll stand up for my rights," he said after his arrival in Calgary. "I don't care if it's Jeff Beukeboom or Mario Lemieux that I hit."

On November 29, 1997, Fleury scored his 315th career goal, passing Joe Nieuwendyk for first place on the Flames' all-time list. In February 1999 the Flames felt they wouldn't be able to re-sign Fleury when his contract expired that summer and traded him to the Colorado Avalanche, where he ended up with a season total of 40 goals before he signed as a free agent with the New York Rangers during the off-season. Fleury wasn't a hit in his first season on Broadway, scoring only 15 goals, but the year after that, he was leading the league in scoring until he checked himself into a rehab program. He got himself ready for 2001–02 and resumed his place as one of the leaders on the team.

In the face of some criticism of executive director Wayne Gretzky's insistence that Fleury be chosen for Team Canada for the 2002 Winter Olympics, the coaches and other executives agreed he should be on the team if he had his personal problems under control. Fleury was able to convince them he was in control and played very well for Canada throughout the six-game tournament.

As joyous as winning Olympic gold was for Fleury, he was soon brought back to the harsh reality of the NHL. His New York Rangers struggled for a fourth consecutive season and failed to make the playoffs, while the late-season acquisition of Pavel Bure from the Florida Panthers underlined the fact that the team wasn't likely to exercise its option to keep Fleury in 2002–03.

Nicklas Lidstrom

Niklas Lidstrom is rated by many as the NHL's best defenseman of the past few years.

The date was Saturday, June 7, 1997, the night of the fourth game of the Stanley Cup finals between the Philadelphia Flyers and the Detroit Red Wings. Detroit held a 3–0 lead in the series, and it was Swedish-born defenseman Nicklas Lidstrom who opened the scoring in what would be a 2–1 win, giving the Wings their first Stanley Cup in 42 years.

With the goal, the fair-haired, blue-eyed Swede finally exacted a measure of revenge against the Flyers' star center, Eric Lindros. The two had met for the first time at the 1990 World Junior Championships in Finland, where the Big E's Canadian squad won the gold medal. Now, seven years later, it would be Lidstrom's turn to claim the laurels. In 1998 the Red Wings again won the Cup and Lidstrom joined his countrymen, former New York Islanders defensemen Stefan Persson and Tomas Jonsson, as the only Swedish-born defensemen to win two Stanley Cup championships (Persson set a record for Swedes with four Stanley Cups).

Lidstrom's greatest achievements occurred while he was with the Wings, but he was no stranger to winning. At 21, he had been a member of the Swedish national team that won the World Championships in Finland in 1991. A key to Tre Kronor's title was a 2–1 win over a Soviet squad that included Lidstrom's future NHL teammates Viacheslav Fetisov and Igor Larionov. He also played for Sweden in the Canada Cup that year.

Lidstrom's 1991 debut season in the NHL was a remarkable one. He accumulated 60 points (11 goals and 49 assists) and was second to Pavel Bure in Calder Trophy voting. When coach Scotty Bowman took over the Red Wings, he added a handful of Russian players to the lineup, enhancing the European flavor of this North American team. The skillful and sophisticated Lidstrom found it easy to become an important part of the Wings' new European-influenced style. He had acquired his elementary hockey education with Sweden's Vasteras club, but he didn't hesitate to point out that he learned even more from his Russian-born teammates, Viacheslav Fetisov and Vladimir Konstantinov. Lidstrom would also be used on the team's power-play with his defense partner, Paul Coffey.

Niklas Lidstrom (number 5) is a reliable defenseman and brilliant rusher who can score as well as back up his forwards.

Lidstrom was a reliable defenseman and a brilliant rusher, and his powerful shots from the blue line often took goalies by surprise. When the NHL suspended play during the 1997–98 season for the Nagano Winter Olympics, Lidstrom was the NHL's third-best-scoring Swede with 14 goals and 41 points to his credit in 57 games. Only forwards Peter Forsberg and Mats Sundin had outperformed him.

Many observers consider Lidstrom to be the NHL's best defenseman over the past few years. In 1998 he was named to the NHL's First All-Star Team, and in a poll conducted by the *Toronto Sun* in 1997, a panel of experts voted him the year's best defenseman. One columnist wrote: "He is a perfect skater; he is a powerful and steady player. He reads the play better than many defensemen and doesn't ignore a chance to make a good pass to his forward. His powerful, accurate slapshot from the blue line often results in a goal."

Lidstrom was overjoyed to be named captain of the World Team for the 2000 All-Star Game. "I've never been a captain in my life," he said, "not even on a kid's team." His coach, Scotty Bowman, was behind the bench for the team and said in an interview with the newspaper *Dagens Nyheter*, "If we didn't have Steve Yzerman, Lidstrom would be the Wings captain." High praise indeed.

In 2000–01, Lidstrom marked another major accomplishment when he became the first European to win the James Norris Trophy as the league's best defenseman—an honor he very much deserved, given that he had been runner-up in the previous three seasons.

Lidstrom anchored the Swedish defense during the 2002 Olympics and was one of the most dejected players after the stunning 4–3 loss to Belarus that eliminated Sweden from medal contention. That year's NHL season was much better for Lidstrom, who helped the Red Wings to the Presidents' Trophy for the most points during the regular season and also surpassed the 600-point plateau in his 11th year in the league, all with Detroit.

Recently, Lidstrom has been considering a return to Sweden so that his two sons, Kevin and Erik, can be educated there. If that happens, the 30-year-old defenseman will likely be welcomed by both Vasteras and Tre Kronor. At a time when so many of the best Swedish players go overseas, leaving few at home to play for the national team, someone of Lidstrom's caliber would be a real asset. Lidstrom himself played only 59 games for the national team before joining the NHL.

But for the time being, Lidstrom is still playing for the Detroit Red Wings and is very popular in North America.

Lidstrom, Nicklas
D, 6'2″, 185 lbs, b: Vasteras, Sweden, 4/28/1970

Season	Club, League	Regular Season					Playoffs				
		GP	G	A	Pts	PIM	GP	G	A	Pts	PIM
1987–88	Vasteras, Sweden	3	0	0	0	0					
1988–89	Vasteras, Sweden	19	0	2	2	4					
1989–90	Vasteras, Sweden	39	8	8	16	14	2	0	1	1	2
1990–91	Vasteras, Sweden	38	4	19	23	2	4	0	0	0	4
WEC–91	Sweden	10	3	3	6	4					
CCup–91	Sweden	6	1	1	2	4					
1991–92	Detroit Red Wings, NHL	80	11	49	60	22	11	1	2	3	0
1992–93	Detroit Red Wings, NHL	84	7	34	41	28	7	1	0	1	0
1993–94	Detroit Red Wings, NHL	84	10	46	56	26	7	3	2	5	0
WC–94	Sweden	4	1	0	1	2					
1994–95	Vasteras, Sweden	13	2	10	12	4					
	Detroit Red Wings, NHL	43	10	16	26	6	18	4	12	16	8
1995–96	Detroit Red Wings, NHL	81	17	50	67	20	19	5	9	14	10
WCup–96	Sweden	4	2	1	3	0					
1996–97	Detroit Red Wings, NHL	79	15	42	57	30	20	2	6	8	2
1997–98	Detroit Red Wings, NHL	80	17	42	59	18	22	6	13	19	8
1998–99	Detroit Red Wings, NHL	81	14	43	57	14	10	2	9	11	4
1999–00	Detroit Red Wings, NHL	81	20	53	73	18	9	2	4	6	4
2000–01	Detroit Red Wings, NHL	82	15	56	71	18	6	1	7	8	0
2001–02	Detroit Red Wings, NHL	78	9	50	59	20					
OWG–02	Sweden	4	1	5	6	0					
	Sweden Totals	112	14	39	53	24	6	0	1	1	6
	NHL Totals	853	145	481	626	220					
	OWG/WEC/WC/CCup/WCup Totals	28	8	10	18	10					

NHL First All-Star Team (1998, 1999, 2000)
Won WEC (1991)
Won Stanley Cup (1997, 1998)

Olaf Kolzig

A native of Johannesburg, South Africa, Olaf Kolzig was raised in Canada, but the fact that he has never applied for Canadian citizenship works to his advantage. Instead, the 6´3″, 225-pound goalie holds a German passport—both his parents are German—which qualifies him to play for that country's national team in international competition. Kolzig also says the German passport will make it easier for him to play in Europe when his NHL career is over.

Kolzig's family moved to Canada when he was three years old and lived in Halifax and Toronto before settling in Union Bay, Nova Scotia. He played junior hockey for the New Westminster Bruins and Tri-City Americans—with whom he became the first goalie in western league history to score a goal, in a game on November 29, 1989. He led that high-scoring circuit with a 3.48 goals-against average in 1988–89, prompting the Washington Capitals to draft him in the first round, 19th overall.

In September 1989, the Capitals played a series of exhibition games in the Soviet Union, winning both games in which the 19-year-old Kolzig played, against Spartak Moscow and Dynamo Riga. He turned pro in 1990, splitting the next couple of seasons between the minor-league Baltimore Skipjacks and Hampton Roads Admirals. In 1994 he was named most valuable player in the AHL playoffs after his Portland Pirates won the Calder Cup championship. His exploits earned him a permanent spot on the Washington roster, at first as backup to Jim Carey for three years.

During the first round of the 1996 Stanley Cup playoffs, the Vezina Trophy-winning Carey began to play poorly and Kolzig took over admirably, posting a 1.94 goals-against average and .934 save percentage in five appearances against the Pittsburgh Penguins. In one game, which lasted into a fourth overtime period, Kolzig played all 139 minutes and 15 seconds, saving 62 of 65 Pittsburgh shots. Petr Nedved finally scored on him to give the Penguins a 3–2 victory. The Penguins won the series, but Kolzig had won the affection of the Washington fans, who nicknamed him "Olie the Goalie."

Prior to the 1996–97 season, the World Cup of Hockey was held, and although he had never played a single minute for the German national team, the 26-year-old Kolzig was named to its roster. He played superbly in the Germans' first game, a 6–1 loss to Sweden in which his team was outshot 40–9 over the first two periods.

Olaf Kolzig tied an NHL record with four shutouts in the playoffs and the Capitals made it to the Stanley Cup finals in 1997–98.

Kolzig, Olaf
G, 6´3″, 225 lbs, b: Johannesburg, South Africa, 4/9/1970

Season	Club, League	Regular Season				Playoffs			
		GP	Mins	GA	Avg	GP	Mins	GA	Avg
1987–88	New Westminster Bruins, WHL	15	650	48	4.43	3	149	11	4.43
1988–89	Tri-City Americans, WHL	30	1671	97	3.48				
1989–90	Washington Capitals, NHL	2	120	12	6.00				
	Tri-City Americans, WHL	48	2504	250	4.38	6	318	27	5.09
1990–91	Baltimore Skipjacks, AHL	26	1367	72	3.16				
	Hampton Roads Admirals, ECHL	21	1248	71	3.41	3	180	14	4.66
1991–92	Baltimore Skipjacks, AHL	28	1503	105	4.19				
	Hampton Roads Admirals, ECHL	14	847	41	2.90				
1992–93	Washington Capitals, NHL	1	20	2	6.00				
	Rochester Americans, AHL	49	2737	168	3.68	17	1040	61	3.52
1993–94	Washington Capitals, NHL	7	224	20	5.36				
	Portland Pirates, AHL	29	1725	88	3.06	17	1035	44	2.55
1994–95	Washington Capitals, NHL	14	724	30	2.49	2	44	1	1.36
	Portland Pirates, AHL	2	125	3	1.44				
1995–96	Washington Capitals, NHL	18	897	46	3.08	5	341	11	1.94
	Portland Pirates, AHL	5	300	7	1.40				
WCup–96	Germany	1	45	5	6.67				
1996–97	Washington Capitals, NHL	29	1645	71	2.59				
WC–97	Germany	4	199	13	3.92				
1997–98	Washington Capitals, NHL	64	3788	139	2.20	21	1351	44	1.95
OWG–98	Germany	2	120	2	1.00				
1998–99	Washington Capitals, NHL	64	3586	154	2.58				
1999–00	Washington Capitals, NHL	73	4371	163	2.24	5	284	16	3.38
2000–01	Washington Capitals, NHL	72	4279	177	2.48	6	375	14	2.24
2001–02	Washington Capitals, NHL	71	4131	192	2.79				
OWG–02	Germany	0	0	0	0.00				
	NHL Totals	415	23784	1006	2.54				
	OWG/WC/WCup Totals	7	364	20	3.30				

NHL First All-Star Team (2000)
Won Vezina Trophy (2000)

Olaf Kolzig played all 139 minutes and 15 seconds of four overtimes against Pittsburgh in the 1995–96 playoffs and made 62 saves on 65 shots.

In 1997, after a disappointing season in which the Capitals missed the playoffs for the first time since 1982, Carey was traded to Boston and Kolzig earned the number one job. He won 33 games, played in his first NHL All-Star Game—stopping 14 of 17 shots in his one period of action—and was the key to Washington's excellent performance in the 1998 playoffs. He tied an NHL record with four shutouts and the Caps made it all the way to the Stanley Cup finals before losing to the defending champions, the Detroit Red Wings.

In November 1998, Kolzig was rewarded with a four-year, $12-million contract. He played for Germany at the 1998 Olympics in Nagano, Japan, but the NHL schedule overlapped the Olympic preliminary round, so Kolzig arrived too late to help his team make it to the final round. Nevertheless, he won two games in which Germany's final ranking in the tournament would be decided. With less than five minutes to go in the ninth-place game against Slovakia, Erich Goldmann, a German-born member of the AHL's Worcester Icecats, cross-checked Kolzig's Washington teammate Peter Bondra. Kolzig intervened and helped to defuse the ensuing altercation, leaving spectators to wonder which player he was trying harder to protect.

Bondra and Goldmann were both given game misconducts and ejected from the game. Germany won the game 4–2, earning ninth-place honors in the tournament—best among the teams that missed out on the medal round. Slovakia, which had been expected to qualify for the eight-team final round–but saw that berth go to the surprising team from Kazakhstan—finished 10th.

Kolzig has continued to be the Capitals' workhorse between the pipes, playing 73 games and a league-leading 4,371 minutes in 1999–2000, and was awarded the Vezina Trophy as the league's top goaltender for that season. Off the ice, Kolzig has taken a strong interest in the plight of the less fortunate. During the 1999–2000 season, he launched Olie's All-Stars, a children's program through which he purchases 10 sets of season tickets and donates the seats to local children's charities. And he had another superb year in 2000–01, winning 37 games in a remarkable 72 appearances, though his Caps were knocked out of the first round of the playoffs.

Kolzig had hoped to play for his native Germany at the Salt Lake City Olympics and did join the team when the NHL shut down for two weeks. At that point, Germany had already played three qualifying games and advanced to the main draw, but Kolzig was nursing an injury and watched the rest of the tournament from the stands, including the 5–0 loss to the U.S. hosts that took Germany out of the tournament in the quarterfinals.

Jiri Slegr

One of the shining stars on Czechoslovakian ice rinks during the 1970s was a defenseman by the name of Jiri Bubla. He was hard and uncompromising and had a great shot. In the Czech league, during a career spent mostly with CHZ Litvinov, he scored 93 goals in 470 games, adding another 37 in 230 games with the national team. In 1971, while he was playing for Dukla Jihlava and completing his two-year military stint, his son, also named Jiri, was born.

Jiri Jr. no longer goes by the surname Bubla, however. From the age of three he's been known as Jiri Slegr, taking on his stepfather's name. But he bears an unmistakable resemblance—both physically and on the hockey rink—to his biological father. He plays a very offensive-minded game, is a strong skater and passer and has a bodybuilder's physique. He also followed in the footsteps of his father by making the Vancouver Canucks his first NHL team. (Bubla played for them from 1981 until 1986.)

After five seasons with Litvinov of the Czech league, the 21-year-old Slegr joined the Canucks in 1992–93. He'd already had considerable seasoning on the international stage, having played for his country at the World Junior Championships in 1990 and 1991—winning bronze medals each time. He was named best defenseman at the 1991 tournament. He also took part in the senior World Championships in 1991 and brought home another bronze medal from the 1992 Winter Olympics in Albertville, France.

Slegr's NHL career hasn't been quite so glorious. He spent part of his rookie season with the Canucks' American league farm club in Hamilton, then played the entire 1993–94 season with Vancouver, posting 38 points in 78 games. But although he was the club's third-highest-scoring defenseman, he didn't suit up in a single playoff game during the Canucks' run to the 1994 Stanley Cup finals. "At first I was upset. But the coach had made a decision. In the end, I lived through the game even more than if I were fighting on the ice."

In April 1995 he was traded to the Edmonton Oilers, and by 1996–97 he was back in Europe, suiting up primarily with the Swedish club Sodertalje. He played in the 1996 World Cup of Hockey—in which the Czech Republic placed a disappointing eighth out of eight teams—and at the 1997 World Championships, where he helped his team win bronze. In 1997 he returned to the NHL after his rights were traded to the Pittsburgh Penguins.

The Penguins had once been an offensive powerhouse, but they were now emphasizing defense, a shift that had a profound influence over Slegr's style of play. His own experiences had also forced him to change his approach to the game. "Over the years, I understood that if I kept on flying forward mindlessly, mistakes could occur. Therefore I tried to be more responsible on the defense and sometimes help with the offense."

His new style also paid off at the 1998 Winter Olympics in Nagano, Japan, where the Czech team surprised everyone with its excellent defense. Slegr was paired off with a

Jiri Slegr is equally strong in skating and passing and has the physique of a bodybuilder.

Slegr, Jiri
D, 6´, 207 lbs, b: Jihlava, Czechoslovakia, 5/30/1971

Season	Club, League	Regular Season					Playoffs				
		GP	G	A	Pts	PLM	GP	G	A	Pts	PLM
1987–88	Litvinov, Czechoslovakia	4	1	1	2	0					
1988–89	Litvinov, Czechoslovakia	8	0	0	0	4					
1989–90	Litvinov, Czechoslovakia	51	4	15	19	*					
1990–91	Litvinov, Czechoslovakia	47	11	36	47	26					
WEC–91	Czechoslovakia	9	2	1	3	32					
CCup–91	Czechoslovakia	5	0	1	1	25					
1991–92	Litvinov, Czechoslovakia	42	9	23	32	38					
OWG–92	Czechoslovakia	8	1	1	2	14					
1992–93	Vancouver Canucks, NHL	41	4	22	26	109	5	0	3	3	4
	Hamilton Canucks, AHL	21	4	14	18	42					
1993–94	Vancouver Canucks, NHL	78	4	33	38	86					
1994–95	Litvinov, Czech Republic	11	3	10	13	80					
	Vancouver Canucks, NHL	19	1	5	6	32					
	Edmonton Oilers, NHL	12	1	5	6	14					
1995–96	Edmonton Oilers, NHL	57	4	13	17	74					
	Cape Breton Oilers, AHL	4	1	2	3	4					
WCup–96	Czech Republic	3	0	0	0	6					
1996–97	Litvinov, Czech Republic	1	0	0	0	0					
	Sodertalje, Sweden	30	4	14	18	62					
WC–97	Czech Republic	8	1	1	2	35					
1997–98	Pittsburgh Penguins, NHL	73	5	12	17	109	6	0	4	4	2
OWG–98	Czech Republic	6	1	0	1	8					
WC–98	Czech Republic	6	0	1	1	20					
1998–99	Pittsburgh Penguins, NHL	63	3	20	23	86	13	1	3	4	12
1999–00	Pittsburgh Penguins, NHL	74	11	20	31	82	10	2	3	5	19
2000–01	Pittsburgh-Atlanta, NHL	75	8	26	34	96					
2001–02	Atlanta-Detroit, NHL	46	3	6	9	59					
	Czechoslovakia/										
	Czech Republic Totals	164	28	85	113	*					
	NHL Totals	538	45	162	207	747					
	OWG/WEC/WC/CCup/WCup Totals	45	5	5	10	140					

Won OWG (1998)

In the summer of 1997, Jiri Slegr took another crack at the NHL with the Pittsburgh Penguins.

dependable hard worker, Richard Smehlik of the Buffalo Sabres, which gave him room to go out and take some chances. In the semifinals, he scored the goal of a lifetime from the blue line and the Czech Republic took a 1–0 lead. But Canada's Trevor Linden responded with a goal just before the end of regulation play to tie the game and rob Slegr of his glory. "I would hardly have been able to build my entire career on one successful shot. In any event, I was displeased that one minute before the end we had to get one and in overtime had to rely on Dominik Hasek to make our way along to the finals. But that actually made it all even more beautiful."

When Ivan Hlinka, assistant coach of the national team, was a coach back in Litvinov, he hadn't been afraid to give young hockey players such as Slegr, Martin Rucinsky, Robert Reichel, Josef Beranek and Robert Lang a chance to prove themselves. It often paid dividends. Those upstarts were all reunited at Nagano to help the Czech Republic win its first Olympic gold medal. The player who scored the winning goal in the final game against Russia, Petr Svoboda, also came from Litvinov, as did forward Jan Caloun. What makes this town's domination of the Czech national roster all the more impressive is the fact that Litvinov's population is only around 29,000.

Slegr has continued to be a dependable blueliner for the Penguins, scoring a career-high 11 goals in 1999–2000 while posting his best plus-minus rating to date, plus-20. And, in 2000–01, his new boss behind the Pittsburgh bench was to be none other than Ivan Hlinka, but Slegr was dealt to the Atlanta Thrashers during the season. On March 19, 2002 he was dealt to the Detroit Red Wings for center Yuri Butsayev and a 2002 third-round draft pick.

Slegr competed in his third Olympics in Salt Lake City, but the defending champion Czech Republic was knocked out of medal contention with a 1–0 loss to Russia in the quarterfinals.

Curtis Joseph

One of the true "money goalies" of the 1990s, Curtis Joseph developed into an NHL star while guarding the net of the St. Louis Blues, then blossomed as a member of the Edmonton Oilers and the Toronto Maple Leafs. Although he was usually excellent in the regular season, Cujo became the most feared of playoff opponents due to his tendency to step up his play in the post-season. His cat-like reflexes and indomitable competitive spirit made Joseph one of the toughest goalies in recent years.

A native of Keswick, Ontario, less than an hour north of Toronto, the shy Joseph noted that "sports was my outlet, my way to portray a personality." He initially struggled to make an impression as a hockey goalie at the amateur level and almost gave up altogether before venturing to Wilcox, Saskatchewan, to play for the Notre Dame Hounds, one of the most respected organizations in the world. His goal was to earn a hockey scholarship at a U.S. college, and he was eventually offered one by the University of Wisconsin, which was trying to find a replacement for the recently departed Mike Richter. Joseph later reflected on those days of uncertainty: "If I could get my schooling, get my college education paid for—geez, that was the world to me. I couldn't afford to pay for school and I thought, 'If I could just get that scholarship, I could get an education and really be something.'"

Joseph excelled for the Badgers during his one season of college hockey in 1988–89. He won 21 games and was voted to the Western Collegiate Hockey Association's First All-Star Team. A few weeks after that season, the St. Louis Blues drafted Cujo as a free agent. He turned pro a year later with the Peoria Rivermen of the International Hockey League but was called up to the Blues at mid-season after they traded goalie Greg Millen to the Quebec Nordiques. He played in 15 regular-season and six playoff games, backing up Vincent Riendeau, and in 1990–91 the duo backstopped the Blues to a 105-point season, the club's second-best performance to that date.

Joseph became the Blues' first-string goalie in 1991–92 and won 27 games in 60 appearances. He racked up another 29 wins in 1992–93 and earned league-wide attention for his brilliant efforts in the playoffs. Even though the club lost to Toronto in the Norris Division finals, Joseph emerged as a hero after stopping 119 of 122 shots in games one and two of the series—both of which went to double overtime. As one reporter commented, "You take Curtis Joseph away from the Blues and they fall off the face of the earth."

Prior to the 1995–96 season, the cost-cutting Blues shipped the popular Joseph to Edmonton. He played well, but the Oilers were in the early stages of a rebuilding process. In April 1996 he excelled for Canada at the World Championships but gave up the gold medal-winning goal to Martin Prochazka of the Czech Republic with only 19 seconds to go in the game. Later that year he again represented his country in the inaugural World Cup of Hockey, which saw Canada lose a three-game final to the United States.

In 1996–97 and 1997–98, Joseph helped the young Oilers reach the playoffs, where his brilliance guided the team to the second round both years. Oilers vice-president Bill Tuele noted, "Curtis obviously didn't have the attention Wayne [Gretzky] did, but in terms of impact on this city, he was every bit Wayne's equal." In the first of these post-seasons with Edmonton, Joseph's stellar play was a major reason behind the team's stunning first-round upset of the Dallas Stars. Fellow netminder Dominik Hasek once said: "I don't know any of his weaknesses. He's one of the best NHL goalies."

Joseph shocked the hockey world in July 1998 when he left the Oilers to sign as a free agent with the Toronto Maple Leafs. Although he had never dominated the NHL's goaltending statistics, Cujo was looked upon as one of the league's top netminders, one whose play only improved during the post-season. Joseph himself concurred: "I don't put that much stock in the statistics. Last season [in Edmonton] we had a young, offensive team that took a lot of chances and we had a lot

As the Maple Leafs closed out the 20th century, Curtis Joseph's netminding was a key reason the club came close to first place in the Eastern Conference.

Joseph, Curtis
G, 5′10″, 185 lbs, b: Keswick, Ont., 4/29/1967

Season	Club, League	Regular Season				Playoffs			
		GP	Mins	GA	Avg	GP	Mins	GA	Avg
1988–89	University of Wisconsin, WCHA	38	2267	94	2.49				
1989–90	St. Louis Blues, NHL	15	852	48	3.38	6	327	18	3.30
	Peoria Rivermen, IHL	23	1241	80	3.87				
1990–91	St. Louis Blues, NHL	30	1710	89	3.12				
1991–92	St. Louis Blues, NHL	60	3494	175	3.01	6	379	23	3.64
1992–93	St. Louis Blues, NHL	68	3890	196	3.02	11	715	27	2.27
1993–94	St. Louis Blues, NHL	71	4127	213	3.10	4	246	15	3.66
1994–95	St. Louis Blues, NHL	36	1914	89	2.79	7	392	24	3.67
1995–96	Las Vegas Thunder, IHL	15	874	29	1.99				
	Edmonton Oilers, NHL	34	1936	111	3.44				
WC–96	Canada	8	409	12	1.94				
WCup–96	Canada	7	468	18	2.00				
1996–97	Edmonton Oilers, NHL	72	4100	200	2.93	12	767	36	2.82
1997–98	Edmonton Oilers, NHL	71	4132	181	2.63	12	716	23	1.93
OWG–98	Canada	0	0	0	0.00				
1998–99	Toronto Maple Leafs, NHL	67	4001	171	2.56	17	1011	41	2.43
1999–00	Toronto Maple Leafs, NHL	63	3801	158	2.49	12	729	25	2.06
2000–01	Toronto Maple Leafs, NHL	68	4100	163	2.39	11	685	24	2.10
2000–02	Toronto Maple Leafs, NHL	51	3065	114	2.23				
OWG–02	Canada	1	60	5	5.00				
	NHL Totals	706	41122	1908	2.78				
	OWG/WC/WCup Totals	16	937	35	2.24				

Won King Clancy Trophy (2000)
Won OWG (2002)

His cat-like reflexes and competitive spirit made Curtis Joseph one of the toughest goalies to get past.

of offensive players when I played in St. Louis. What I have done, I think, is make a difference."

His impact on his new club was immediate. His excellent goaltending helped the Leafs register 99 points and reach the Stanley Cup semifinals in the spring of 1999. His coolness under fire impressed backup netminder Glenn Healy, who observed: "He's like the Rock of Gibraltar, no panic. If some other goalies were on the *Titanic*, they would be the ones in the lifeboats ahead of the women and children." Joseph won 35 games in the regular season and nine in the playoffs and was runner-up to Dominik Hasek in the voting for the Vezina Trophy.

In 1999–2000, the Leafs finished at the top of the Northeast Division standings—their first regular-season title since 1962–63—and were considered a legitimate contender for the Stanley Cup. Joseph's popularity reached epic proportions in hockey-mad Hogtown and the hero between the pipes noted: "I don't thrive on the attention. But I knew it would be this way. That's what you wish for, so how can you be upset about it?" The next year he led his team to game seven of the conference semifinals before losing a heart-breaking series to New Jersey. But Cujo had confirmed his place as one of the league's most dynamic goalies.

Heading into the 2001–02 season, Toronto fans had lots to be optimistic about, with several key off-season signings and of course Joseph's steady goaltending. And when Colorado's Patrick Roy announced he would skip the 2002 Salt Lake City Olympics, it was soon speculated that Joseph would be Canada's number one goaltender. Team Canada coach Pat Quinn said he planned to use Joseph for the opening game and New Jersey's Martin Brodeur in the second. From there, it was expected the coaching staff would go with the hot hand. Unfortunately for Joseph, he and the rest of Team Canada came out flat in their opener against Sweden, dropping a 5–2 decision. Brodeur won his game and didn't relinquish another playing minute for the remainder of the tournament.

Soon after returning to the Leafs, Joseph suffered a fractured hand when he was hit with a shot and was forced to sit out for a prolonged period. He returned to the Leafs completely recovered in the final week of the regular season.

Tony Amonte

Tony Amonte of the Chicago Blackhawks is one of an increasing number of players to reach the NHL via the U.S. collegiate system. After a stellar high school career at Thayer Academy, where he played alongside his good friend—and future NHL star—Jeremy Roenick, Amonte went on to become a standout for the Boston University Terriers from 1989 to 1991.

"I think college these days is a great way to go to the pros," Amonte said of his experience. "You get your education and some of the best hockey without being a professional. Juniors used to be the way to go, with the 80 games, fighting and no face masks. But college is better now, even though the kids are older now in college."

Although his collegiate career was an impressive one, the native of Hingham, Massachusetts, will always remember his final game for Boston University, a triple-overtime loss to Northern Michigan University in the 1991 NCAA Championships. Two days after the heartbreaking loss, Amonte signed an NHL contract with the New York Rangers. He scored his first NHL goal in his first regular-season game and his 35-goal debut season made him *The Sporting News'* selection as rookie of the year and earned him a berth on the NHL's All-Rookie Team.

Playing on a line with Mark Messier was particularly satisfying for Amonte. He says that when he was a kid, Messier was his favorite player. "In college, I was fortunate enough to see him raise the Cup over his head in the Boston Garden. Two years later, I was on his right wing."

Tony Amonte is one of a rare group of NHLers who have scored 30 or more goals in five seasons.

His best season as a Ranger came in 1992–93, when he recorded 33 goals and a career-best 43 assists. Toward the end of his third full season, 1993–94, he was traded to the Chicago Blackhawks for Stephane Matteau and Brian Noonan. Although he missed out on the Rangers' Stanley Cup victory that spring, he benefited from the trade, becoming one of the top scorers in the NHL during his years in the Windy City. He is one of a rare group of NHLers who have scored 30 or more goals in five seasons, and one of his career playoff highlights was scoring four goals against Toronto in the 1994 playoffs.

Leaving New York for Chicago was hard for Amonte. When asked if he missed living there, he answered: "All the time. I look forward to someday being back in the Big Apple. I'll always have a sweet spot in my heart since it was the first city I ever played an NHL game in." Still, he said he was happy to be in Chicago, even though the media there are sometimes highly critical of his team's play. "They were tough on us, but they have to be when you have a championship basketball team like the Bulls," he said of Michael Jordan's NBA team. "They're on top of the world. Before the Jordan era, it was the Hawks on top. A few years from now, it will be the Hawks on top again."

As an American, Amonte has also done an outstanding job of representing his country in international competition. As a junior, he played for the U.S. squad at the 1989 World Junior Championships in Alaska and the 1990

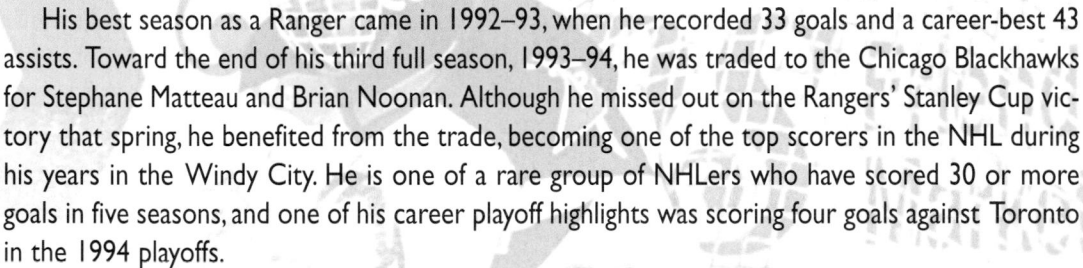

Amonte, Tony
RW, 6´, 195 lbs, b: Hingham, MA, 8/2/1970

Season	Club, League	Regular Season					Playoffs				
		GP	G	A	Pts	PIM	GP	G	A	Pts	PIM
1989–90	Boston University, H.E.	41	25	33	58	52					
1990–91	Boston University, H.E.	38	31	37	68	82					
WEC–91	USA	10	2	5	7	4					
1990–91	New York Rangers, NHL						2	0	2	2	2
1991–92	New York Rangers, NHL	79	35	34	69	55	13	3	6	9	2
1992–93	New York Rangers, NHL	83	33	43	76	57					
WC–93	USA	6	1	2	3	8					
1993–94	New York Rangers, NHL	72	16	22	38	31					
	Chicago Blackhawks, NHL	7	1	3	4	6	6	4	2	6	4
1994–95	Fassa, Italy	14	22	16	38	10					
	Chicago Blackhawks, NHL	48	15	20	35	41	16	3	3	6	10
1995–96	Chicago Blackhawks, NHL	81	31	32	63	62	7	2	4	6	6
WCup–96	USA	7	2	4	6	6					
1996–97	Chicago Blackhawks, NHL	81	41	36	77	64	6	4	2	6	8
1997–98	Chicago Blackhawks, NHL	82	31	42	73	66					
OWG–98	USA	4	0	1	1	4					
1998–99	Chicago Blackhawks, NHL	82	44	31	75	60					
1999–00	Chicago Blackhawks, NHL	82	43	41	84	48					
2000–01	Chicago Blackhawks, NHL	82	35	29	64	54					
2001–02	Chicago Blackhawks, NHL	82	27	39	66	67					
OWG–02	USA	6	2	2	4	0					
	NHL Totals	861	352	372	724	603					
	OWG/WEC/WC/WCup Totals	33	7	14	31	22					

Won WCup (1996)

Chicago's media "were tough on us, but they have to be when you have a championship basketball team like the Bulls," Tony Amonte (right) says. "Before the Jordan era, it was the Hawks on top. A few years from now, it will be the Hawks on top again."

tournament in Finland. He was one of only six collegians on Team USA in the 1990 Goodwill Games in Seattle, helping his team win a silver medal. He also played at the World Championships in 1991 and 1993 and was a member of the U.S. team at the World Cup of Hockey in 1996. In that tournament he scored the game-winning goal against Canada in the third and final game of the championship series and the USA won the gold medal. Today, he says that his top career highlight was "that World Cup-winning goal, without a doubt."

Amonte also credited his 1996 international experience with helping him get ready for NHL play. "It gave me more confidence for the start of the season. I couldn't wait to get going—I would be in more big situations." He followed through with a 41-goal season in 1996–97 and would again break the 40-goal barrier in 1998–99 (44) and 1999–2000 (43). Amonte also represented his country at the 1998 Winter Olympic Games in Nagano, Japan, although the team placed a disappointing sixth.

Among NHL fans, Amonte has been known for his trademark long hair, which he lets grow during winning streaks. Sports run in the Amonte blood—his sister played on the U.S. lacrosse team that won the World Championship in 1997.

Amonte finished his eighth full season with the Blackhawks in 2001–02, and thanks to many on-ice personnel changes made by general manager Mike Smith was able to see a renaissance of success for the club, which had sputtered badly in the previous several years. He was also a key member of the silver medal-winning U.S. squad at the 2002 Olympics.

Sergei Zubov

Sergei Zubov spent four seasons with CSKA Moscow before he joined the NHL.

In the late 1990s, the Dallas Stars emerged as one of the dominant franchises in the NHL, winning the Stanley Cup in 1999 and returning to the finals in 2000. Night in and night out, coach Ken Hitchcock sent out an incredible lineup that boasted goalie Ed Belfour and skaters Brett Hull, Mike Modano and Joe Nieuwendyk, to name just a few. But it might truly be said that no other player has been as crucial to the team's success as its Russian defenseman, Sergei Zubov.

An offensive-minded rearguard, the 6′1″, 200-pound Zubov adds tremendous scoring as well as consistent leadership on the power-play. "He brings his great skill with him, and his performance has been so consistent," says Stars general manager Bob Gainey.

Zubov played four seasons with Moscow's Central Red Army team between 1988 and 1992. He represented the Soviet Union at the World Junior Championships in 1989 and 1990, when his teams won the gold and silver medal respectively. He was also a gold medal winner as a member of the Unified Team at the 1992 Winter Olympics in Albertville, France. He played for Russia at the 1992 World Championships—a fifth-place finish—and at the 1996 World Cup of Hockey, where his team placed fourth.

In 1990 the New York Rangers drafted Zubov in the fifth round with the 85th overall pick. They assigned him to their farm team in Binghamton, New York, in 1992, and after 30 games he'd registered 36 points and earned a promotion. In his first 49 NHL games he generated a promising eight goals and 31 points. In his second season, 1993–94, Zubie reached his offensive zenith, scoring 77 assists and 89 points. He added five goals and 19 points during the playoffs to help the Rangers win their first Stanley Cup since 1940.

There were rumors that Zubov hadn't endeared himself to Rangers captain Mark Messier, and in 1995 he was traded—along with center Petr Nedved—to the Pittsburgh Penguins for Luc Robitaille and Ulf Samuelsson. After only one year in Penguin black and gold, he was dealt to the Dallas Stars for Kevin Hatcher. He quickly became a favorite of the Texas fans, wowing them with his strong skating and superb stickhandling—both traits that were at a premium in coach Hitchcock's defensive system.

Although Zubov has traditionally taken few penalties, he isn't afraid of physical play. He also specializes in quick rushes out of the defensive zone and is an expert at making short, hard passes to set up a forward. In 1996–97, his first season in Dallas, he was tops among all NHL defenders with 30 assists.

Bad publicity dogged Zubov in June 1998 when he was arrested for allegedly assaulting his wife, Irina, and threatening her with a knife just a few days after his Stars were eliminated from the Western Conference finals. A Dallas grand jury declined to indict him after Irina said that she didn't want to press charges.

Toward the end of the 1998–99 regular season, Hitchcock complained that he had expected more from the Russian star—especially on the power-play, which he was expected to anchor. When reporters asked if he was satisfied with Zubov's play, Hitchcock said: "No. He has to be a better player for us. He hasn't been effective on the power-play. He's just been okay." Zubov rose to the challenge and helped the Stars power through the Western Conference playoffs and a victory over the upstart Buffalo Sabres in the Stanley Cup finals.

In 2000 the Stars rewarded Zubov for his stellar play with a lucrative contract extension

An offense-minded Sergei Zubov (right) adds tremendous scoring potential to the Stars defense as well as consistent leadership on the power-play.

Zubov, Sergei
D, 6´1˝, 200 lbs, b: Moscow, USSR, 7/22/1970

Season	Club, League	Regular Season					Playoffs				
		GP	G	A	Pts	PIM	GP	G	A	Pts	PIM
1988–89	CSKA, USSR	29	1	4	5	10					
1989–90	CSKA, USSR	48	6	2	8	16					
1990–91	CSKA, USSR	41	6	5	11	12					
1991–92	CSKA, Russia	44	4	7	11	8					
OWG–92	Russia	8	0	1	1	0					
WC–92	Russia	6	2	2	4	10					
1992–93	CSKA, Russia	1	0	1	1	0					
	New York Rangers, NHL	49	8	23	31	4					
	Binghamton Rangers, AHL	30	7	29	36	14	11	5	5	10	2
1993–94	New York Rangers, NHL	78	12	77	89	39	22	5	14	19	0
	Binghamton Rangers, AHL	2	1	2	3	0					
1994–95	New York Rangers, NHL	38	10	26	36	18	10	3	8	11	2
1995–96	Pittsburgh Penguins, NHL	64	11	55	66	22	18	1	14	15	26
WCup–96	Russia	4	1	1	2	0					
1996–97	Dallas Stars, NHL	78	13	30	43	24	7	0	3	3	2
1997–98	Dallas Stars, NHL	73	10	47	57	16	17	4	5	9	2
1998–99	Dallas Stars, NHL	81	10	41	51	20	23	1	12	13	4
1999–00	Dallas Stars, NHL	77	9	33	42	18	18	2	7	9	6
2000–01	Dallas Stars, NHL	79	10	41	51	24	10	1	5	6	4
2001–02	Dallas Stars, NHL	80	12	32	44	22					
	USSR/Russia Totals	163	17	19	36	46					
	NHL Totals	697	105	405	510	207					
	OWG/WC/WCup Totals	18	3	4	7	10					

Won OWG (1992)
Won Stanley Cup (1994, 1999)
USSR Champion (1989)

that would last through the 2004–05 season. "His performance for our hockey club over the past four years has been exemplary," Gainey said. For his part, Zubov was happy to be staying in Dallas. "It's really exciting for myself and my family," he said. "We've spent four years over here; so far, it's just a great time with the team. I've been concentrating more on just playing hockey, but it's great to get back with one of the best teams again."

Almost immediately after the big signing, Zubov suffered a serious knee injury when he collided with Florida Panthers defenseman Bret Hedican and was forced out of the lineup for several weeks. Oddly, it was a game where the Stars clinched their fourth consecutive Pacific Division title. Zubov returned to active duty in time to help his Stars to a convincing march through the Western Conference playoffs, however, and they returned to the Stanley Cup finals, this time against the eventual Cup-winning New Jersey Devils. For the Stars, the premium blend of offense and defense that Sergei Zubov brings to the ice goes a long way toward winning games.

Without as much fanfare as other big-name players, "silent Star" Sergei Zubov has been holding fourth place on the NHL's top-scoring defensemen list for the last five seasons. He surpassed the 100-goal and 500-point levels in the NHL in 2001–02 and also played in his second Olympic Games in Salt Lake City.

Jaromir Jagr

Even when he was an up-and-coming junior, the puck seemed magnetically drawn to Jaromir Jagr's stick. His size—6'2″ and 216 pounds—makes the right winger tough to knock around, while his incredible touch, speed and creativity combine brilliantly to make him an almost unstoppable offensive force. His skills have propelled his teams, whether in the NHL or international play, to titles and championships.

Jagr grew up in Kladno, Czechoslovakia, where he played for his hometown team and his size and skill began to garner the attention of scouts. After scoring 60 points in 51 games in 1989–90, he was chosen to play for the Czechoslovakian team at the 1990 World Junior Championships in Finland. He was the star of the tournament, netting 18 points in only seven games as Czechoslovakia skated to the bronze medal. He also played for the Czech team at the World Championships that same year, winning another bronze medal.

"The one thing that intrigued me the most was that he was so strong with the puck," said Pittsburgh Penguins scout Greg Malone of Jagr's play in the junior championships. "Even though he was a young kid, when he got the puck and went wide with it, or came out of the corners, no one could take the puck away from him. He was doing that at the age of 18…and you don't see a lot of 18-year-olds play at that skill level."

NHL scouts were intrigued, but many teams were hesitant to use a high draft pick to select Jagr. Unlike other highly rated standouts from his homeland—such as Petr Nedved—Jagr was still in Czechoslovakia. He still had a year remaining on his contract with Kladno, after which he would have to perform two to three years of military service before he'd be available to sign with a North American team—assuming that Kladno didn't then hold him for a king's ransom. Unlike others before him, Jagr wasn't the type to defect. Although he held a high regard for the kind of personal freedom the West offered—as a schoolboy, he even carried around a picture of Ronald Reagan in his lunch box—he was proud of his country and unlikely to leave without going through the proper channels.

In the 1990 draft, the Penguins—who already had an established franchise player in Mario Lemieux—could afford to take a gamble and they chose Jagr fifth overall. It was an astute move, as the Penguins got their man much sooner than expected. The Eastern bloc dissolved that summer and Jagr, suddenly free to move once Kladno released him, arrived in the United States as an 18-year-old rookie. As a symbol of his pride in his country, Jagr chose to wear number 68 to represent the Prague Spring, a short-lived surge of social reform in 1968 that was cut short when Soviet tanks rolled into Wenceslas Square.

As a symbol of his pride in his country, Jaromir Jagr chose number 68 to represent the Prague Spring.

Jagr didn't immediately set the NHL on fire with his offensive skills. Over a four week span early in 1990–91, he managed only one point and 12 shots on goal in 15 games. He was homesick, and his sense of isolation was compounded by his shaky grasp of English. With no one to talk to, his depression soon affected his game—Jagr, usually an outgoing and energetic player on the ice, became despondent and quiet. The Penguins remedied the problem by making a trade with the Calgary Flames for 32-year-old Czech centerman Jiri Hrdina. Jagr's mood and his game were both elevated; he scored six goals and nine assists in the month after Hrdina arrived and he finished fourth in rookie scoring with 57 points. His performance earned him a berth on the NHL All-Rookie Team.

His play continued to improve as the Penguins entered the playoffs. He scored an incredible overtime goal to defeat the New Jersey Devils in the first round, fending off a defender with one hand while flipping the puck over Devils netminder Chris Terreri with the other. The Penguins won the Stanley Cup and Jagr contributed 13 points in a supporting role to the dominant Lemieux, who won the Conn Smythe Trophy.

In his second NHL season, Jagr's point total improved—as it would again in his third and fourth years. Seventeen of Jagr's 32 regular-season goals had come during the third period, earning him a well-deserved reputation as a man who could deliver a goal when his team needed it most. During the second game of the Patrick Division finals against the New York Rangers, Adam Graves delivered a vicious slash that broke Mario Lemieux's hand. The 20-year-old Jagr was suddenly thrust into the spotlight.

Jagr accepted the challenge gratefully. In game five he scored the game-winning goal on a penalty shot. The Penguins rallied to eliminate the Rangers, who had been the NHL's top team during the regular season. Lemieux returned for part of the Eastern Conference finals against the Boston Bruins and Pittsburgh set them down as well.

The Penguins' opponents in the 1992 Stanley Cup finals would be the Chicago Blackhawks. The series pitted the Penguins' offensive firepower against the Hawks' tight defensive style. In game one, Pittsburgh twice fell behind by three goals before storming back. Jagr scored the tying goal with a brilliant individual effort, slicing through defenders with a bob of his head and a change of direction before beating Ed Belfour with two minutes left in regulation time. Lemieux scored a minute later to win the game.

Over the course of the Stanley Cup playoffs, Jagr scored four game-winning goals and placed fourth in playoff scoring with 24 points. Best of all, the Penguins won their second consecutive Cup championship.

The best seemed yet to come. As the 1992–93 schedule wound down, Pittsburgh was unbeatable, winning 17 consecutive games before tying their last game of the year. With a franchise-record 119 points, the Penguins won the Presidents' Trophy, awarded to the team with the best regular-season record. But their 14-game playoff winning streak was halted in the second round by the Islanders, who eventually won the series and eliminated the Penguins.

Early in his career, Jagr was understandably overshadowed by his superstar teammate, Lemieux. One writer rearranged the letters in "Jaromir" to spell "Mario Jr."—and that was the impression most people had of the skilled winger, who shared many physical attributes with his captain: the long, dark hair spilling out beneath the helmet; a strong yet nimble body; and an offensive explosiveness. Even their jersey numbers—66 and 68—were similar.

Still, Jagr was becoming a star in his own right and his peers recognized his potential. "He's smart, he's a good skater and—most important, in my opinion—he has great size and he knows how to use it," said Wayne Gretzky. "He's the kind of guy who only comes along once in a while."

Injuries and health problems sidelined Lemieux for much of the mid-1990s and the Penguins looked to Jagr to become the team's primary scorer. Jagr thrived under the pressure, fully realizing his tremendous potential during the lockout-shortened 1994–95 season. His 70 points in 48 games tied Philadelphia's Eric Lindros for the league lead, but Jagr scored more goals—32 to Lindros's 29—and became the first European-born and -trained player to win the Art Ross Trophy. Jagr was also named to the First All-Star Team and was runner-up for the Hart Trophy, awarded to the league's most valuable player—the winner was none other than Lindros.

In 1995–96, Jagr had a career year, setting records for points (149) and assists (87) by a right winger, breaking marks set by Mike Bossy. He was again named to the First All-Star Team. After Lemieux retired in 1997, Jagr led the league in scoring for three consecutive seasons beginning in 1997–98. At the 1998 Winter Olympics in Nagano, he was partly responsible for once again filling Wenceslas Square in Prague with people—this time to watch Jagr and the rest of the Czech team defeat the Russians 1–0 for the Olympic gold medal.

Prior to the 1998–99 season, Jagr surprised many observers when he announced that he'd like to be team captain, replacing Ron Francis, who had left the Penguins as a free agent. Where he had once appeared nervous and shy, Jagr was now gregarious and fun-loving. But he

Jagr, Jaromir
RW, 6′2″, 216 lbs, b: Kladno, Czechoslovakia, 2/15/1972

Season	Club, League	Regular Season					Playoffs				
		GP	G	A	Pts	PIM	GP	G	A	Pts	PIM
1988–89	Kladno, Czechoslovakia	29	3	6	6	4	10	5	7	12	0
1989–90	Kladno, Czechoslovakia	42	22	28	50	10	9	8	2	10	
WEC–90	Czechoslovakia	10	3	2	5	2					
1990–91	Pittsburgh Penguins, NHL	80	27	30	57	42	24	3	10	13	6
CCup–91	Czechoslovakia	5	1	0	1	0					
1991–92	Pittsburgh Penguins, NHL	70	32	37	69	34	21	11	13	24	6
1992–93	Pittsburgh Penguins, NHL	81	34	60	94	61	12	5	4	9	23
1993–94	Pittsburgh Penguins, NHL	80	32	67	99	61	6	2	4	6	16
WC–94	Czech Republic	3	0	2	2	2					
1994–95	Kladno, Czech Republic	11	8	14	22	10					
	Bolzano, Italy	1	0	0	0	0					
	Schalke(2), Germany	1	1	10	11	0					
	Pittsburgh Penguins, NHL	48	32	38	70	37	12	10	5	15	6
1995–96	Pittsburgh Penguins, NHL	82	62	87	149	96	18	11	12	23	18
WCup–96	Czech Republic	3	1	0	1	2					
1996–97	Pittsburgh Penguins, NHL	63	47	48	95	40	5	4	4	8	4
1997–98	Pittsburgh Penguins, NHL	77	35	67	102	64	6	4	5	9	2
OWG–98	Czech Republic	6	1	4	5	2					
1998–99	Pittsburgh Penguins, NHL	81	44	83	127	66	9	5	7	12	16
1999–00	Pittsburgh Penguins, NHL	63	42	54	96	50	11	8	8	16	6
2000–01	Pittsburgh Penguins, NHL	81	52	69	121	42	16	2	10	12	18
2001–02	Pittsburgh-Washington, NHL	69	31	48	79	30					
OWG–02	Czech Republic	4	2	3	5	4					
	Czechoslovakia/ Czech Republic Totals	82	33	48	78	24					
	NHL Totals	875	470	688	1158	623					
	OWG/WEC/WC/CCup/WCup Totals	31	8	11	19	12					

NHL First All-Star Team (1995, 1996, 1998, 1999, 2000)
NHL Second All-Star Team (1997)
Won Hart Trophy (1999)
Won Art Ross Trophy (1995, 1998, 1999, 2000)
Won Lester B. Pearson Trophy (1999, 2000)
Won OWG (1998)
Won Stanley Cup (1991, 1992)

Jaromir Jagr

wasn't kidding about taking on added responsibilities. This included talking to the press, a group he once went out of his way to avoid. "He's definitely taken charge," said teammate Stu Barnes after the players voted unanimously to put the "C" on Jagr's jersey. "The talk all summer was about the loss of Ron Francis and what we would do. Jagr has taken that on himself. He's become more of a leader. He's our captain, and I think that's going to make him a better player."

Jagr became more of a playmaker on the ice, taking his time and holding the puck until he found an open teammate. Always dangerous on individual rushes, he became almost impossible to contain once he dedicated himself to the team game. Calgary coach Brian Sutter was asked what he could have done to keep Jagr off the score sheet after he single-handedly beat the Flames with three key assists and he replied, "Probably the only way we could have done that was if we'd shot him before the game." Jagr's all-around effort won him the Hart Trophy in 1999, proving that he was indeed the best choice as captain.

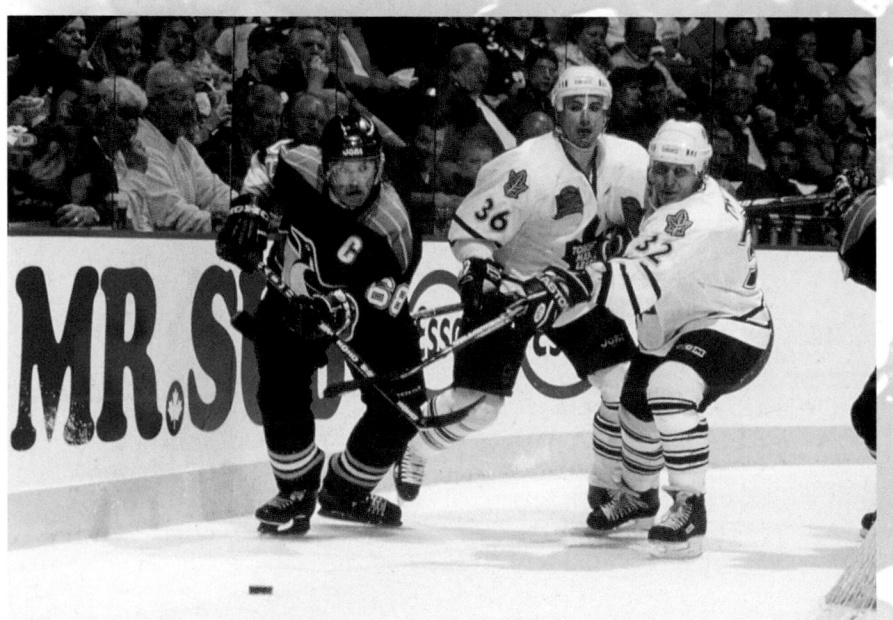

His great hands and size made it hard to knock Jaromir Jagr (left) around when he got possession and perfectly complemented his speed and creativity.

Although his flowing locks of hair were recognized around the world, Jagr changed his image at the beginning of the new century. His new haircut—shorter, though still curly—got almost as much attention as his continuing dominance of the scoring race in 1999–2000, mostly because observers had become accustomed to seeing his name at the top of the charts and needed something new to talk about. But Jagr continued in the limelight night after night mostly because of his flashy, daring goals. Opposing teams sent their best defensive players out after him on every shift, but Jagr beat them with his uncanny ability to keep the puck on his stick and find the openings. Jagr's signature gesture after scoring a goal—the military-style salute—was now accompanied by a huge smile. Jagr still loved to play, and loved nothing better than to score that perfect goal, the kind that silenced and awed even hostile fans.

"I want all the goals to be beautiful goals. That's what you want to do, score good-looking goals and build up confidence for the next one you score," said Jagr early in his career. "For me, the game is just a fun game. Being the MVP isn't my goal. I just want to show some moves, have some fun. That's what it's about."

After winning his fifth scoring race in 2000–01, he was traded to Washington in a deal motivated largely by his high salary. Jagr got off to a slow start with his new team but eventually rounded into form and also captained the Czech Republic at the 2002 Olympics, though he and his teammates left Salt Lake City unfulfilled. Not only did they fail in their attempt to duplicate the 1998 gold medal, but the team went home empty-handed after being eliminated 1–0 by Russia in the quarterfinals.

Alexei Zhamnov

There aren't many players in the history of the NHL who can claim to have scored five goals in a single game, but veteran Chicago Blackhawks center Alexei Zhamnov is one of them. Playing for the Winnipeg Jets on April 1, 1995, he scored five in a 7–7 tie against Wayne Gretzky's Los Angeles Kings. The Jets are now the Phoenix Coyotes, but Zhamnov's five-goal outing still stands as the club record for goals in a single game.

Zhamnov got the nickname "Archie" because his red hair makes him look like the classic comic book character. A native of Moscow, he embarked on the road to hockey stardom in 1988, joining Dynamo Moscow. His teammates included such future NHL stars as Darius Kasparaitis, Alexei Kovalev and Alexei Yashin. He played for the silver medal-winning Soviet team at the 1990 World Junior Championships and contributed to a bronze medal finish at the senior World Championships in 1991. He won gold with the Unified Team at the 1992 Winter Olympics in Albertville, France, and was with Russia when they won the silver medal at the 1998 Olympics in Nagano, Japan. He also played in the 1996 World Championships and at the World Cup of Hockey later that year.

Zhamnov's favorite player when he was growing up was Igor Larionov, who went on to play for the Detroit Red Wings. Like Larionov, young Alexei was also a center. "I'd go to the hockey games all the time and watch him. I'd try to learn," says Zhamnov. "He's still in the league and I'm still learning from him. He's a smart hockey player and a nice guy, on and off the ice."

Alexei also has a close connection with another Russian hockey star—he is married to the daughter of former Dynamo and Russian national team defenseman Valeri Vasiliev. And his career has been influenced by yet another legend from his homeland, netminder Vladislav Tretiak, who visits Chicago periodically to coach the Hawks goalies. "When Vladi's in Chicago, I score goals every time," laughs Zhamnov. "I don't know, maybe he's luck for me!"

After Albertville, Zhamnov joined the Winnipeg Jets, with whom he played for four NHL seasons. He had been the Jets' fifth pick—77th overall—in the 1990 draft. The lockout-shortened 1994–95 season was Zhamnov's best in the NHL so far. He finished with 30 goals and 65 points in 48 games, good enough for third in the league scoring race

Alexei Zhamnov (center) represented Russia seven times and won four medals at World Championships and Olympics.

Zhamnov, Alexei
C, 6´1˝, 195 lbs, b: Moscow, USSR, 10/1/1970

Season	Club, League	Regular Season					Playoffs				
		GP	G	A	Pts	PIM	GP	G	A	Pts	PIM
1988–89	Dynamo Moscow, USSR	4	0	0	0	0					
1989–90	Dynamo Moscow, USSR	43	11	6	17	21					
1990–91	Dynamo Moscow, USSR	46	16	12	28	24					
WEC–91	USSR	10	4	5	9	12					
CCup–91	USSR	5	3	0	3	2					
1991–92	Dynamo Moscow, Russia	39	15	21	36	28					
OWG–92	Russia	8	0	3	3	8					
WC–92	Russia	6	0	0	0	29					
1992–93	Winnipeg Jets, NHL	68	25	47	72	58	6	0	2	2	2
1993–94	Winnipeg Jets, NHL	61	26	45	71	62					
1994–95	Winnipeg Jets, NHL	48	30	35	65	20					
1995–96	Winnipeg Jets, NHL	58	22	37	59	65	6	2	1	3	8
WCup–96	Russia	4	0	2	2	6					
1996–97	Chicago Blackhawks, NHL	74	20	42	62	56					
1997–98	Chicago Blackhawks, NHL	70	21	28	49	61					
OWG–98	Russia	6	2	1	3	2					
1998–99	Chicago Blackhawks, NHL	76	20	41	61	50					
1999–00	Chicago Blackhawks, NHL	71	23	37	60	61					
WC–2000	Russia	5	0	1	1	0					
2000-01	Chicago Blackhawks, NHL	63	13	36	49	40					
2001-02	Chicago Blackhawks, NHL	77	22	45	67	67					
OWG–02	Russia	6	1	0	1	4					
	USSR/Russia Totals	132	42	39	81	73					
	NHL Totals	666	222	393	615	540					
	OWG/WEC/WC/CCup/WCup Totals	50	10	12	22	63					

NHL Second All-Star Team (1995)
Won OWG (1992)
USSR/Russia Champion (1990,1991,1992)

Alexei Zhamnov was the only player to score five goals in a single game in the whole 1994–95 season when he netted that many for the Winnipeg Jets on April 1, 1995.

behind Jaromir Jagr and Eric Lindros. During the summer of 1996, the Jets relocated to Phoenix, where they became the Coyotes. In August the club sent Zhamnov to Chicago along with minor-leaguer Craig Mills and a first-round draft pick for high-scoring center Jeremy Roenick.

Once he was traded to Chicago, Zhamnov proceeded to hold out for a more lucrative contract than the one Chicago was offering. Chicago general manager Bob Pulford would claim that Zhamnov wanted $4.5 million per season, compared with the $2.6 million the Hawks wanted to pay. In the end, Zhamnov signed a five-year contract worth $15 million. "I just want to play hockey," he said. "This negotiation is now behind me."

In his first three years with the Hawks, Zhamnov was consistently the team's number two scoring threat behind only Tony Amonte. But the many fans and hockey writers who expected him to save the franchise single-handedly have complained that Zhamnov hasn't met the high expectations set by his 1994–95 performance. "I don't have too many points," the quiet Russian said partway through the 1998–99 season. "I hope I can score more. But I can't get frustrated. I just want to help this team. Someday the puck will start going in."

Part of the problem, he said, was that the Russian style of play in which Zhamnov was drilled as a youth dictates that players pass the puck before shooting. "There, if you see that your partner has a better spot, you give him the puck right away," he said. "It's a different mentality." In Winnipeg, his coaches always exhorted Zhamnov to shoot more, but he'd never been able to completely lose the habit of passing first.

Blackhawks coach Dirk Graham was still confident that Zhamnov could help his team and stressed that his contributions didn't always show up in the scoring summaries. "Alex's speed is the key to his game," Graham said. "When he's really skating and competing, that's when he's at his best. He's a world-class talent."

The addition of Steve Sullivan and Michael Nylander during the 1999–2000 season provided additional scoring punch, which may take some of the pressure off Zhamnov in future seasons. In 2000–01, the Hawks will be coached by Alpo Suhonen, who came from a Toronto Maple Leafs club that favored a wide-open style of play. All signs point to Zhamnov becoming a more productive part of the Chicago offense.

He was a member of the 2002 Russian Olympic team that won bronze.

Rod Brind'Amour

A versatile player who can handle every position except goal, Rod Brind'Amour has established a reputation as an NHL coach's dream—the offensively talented, two-way team player. Though his primary task was often to check opposing superstars, Brind'Amour managed consistently to find his way onto the score sheet.

Born in Ottawa but raised in Campbell River, British Columbia, Brind'Amour began playing at a very young age, waddling around on double-bladed skates and a stick. His father, who worked nights, would find ice time during the day for his son to skate around and shoot a puck. When he first entered the youth hockey system, he became a little like Carl Brewer, the star defenseman of the 1960s who retired every few years. Brind'Amour twice gave up the game, at age six and then again at seven, but each time—after a few months of watching *Hockey Night in Canada* on Saturday nights—he'd be back at it by Christmas.

Rod played defense at first, often against players who were older than him, and scouts from junior teams took notice—even though he struggled for a year and a half in skates that were almost two sizes too large. (His father had bought him a used pair, expecting that Rod would grow into them, but he never did.) At the tender age of 13, Brind'Amour was drafted by a junior team, the New Westminster Bruins.

His parents weren't thrilled with the idea of their teenaged son playing major junior hockey. They wanted Rod to stay in school, so they gave him a choice: He could continue to play in his home town or he could go to Notre Dame College—the high school hockey factory in Wilcox, Saskatchewan, whose Hounds junior team had turned out such NHL notables as Russ Courtnall and Wendel Clark.

Brind'Amour chose Notre Dame, where the coaches moved him up to center to take advantage of his offensive skills. They even gave him a new pair of skates. Both changes helped Brind'Amour's game tremendously, and once he conquered his homesickness, he led the Hounds to the AAA midget title in 1986–87 and the Saskatchewan junior championship the next season. Prior to the 1988 draft, the NHL's scouting bureau ranked Brind'Amour as roughly the 20th-best prospect, but the St. Louis Blues were impressed by the forward's versatility and penchant for hard work and they made him the ninth overall choice.

Brind'Amour felt he wasn't yet ready for the NHL game and he opted to attend Michigan State University, a school that, like Notre Dame College, was known for the quality of its student athletes. He played one season, 1988–89, in the Central Collegiate Hockey Association, earning rookie of the year honors with 59 points in 42 games. That spring the 19-year-old joined the Blues in time for their second-round playoff series against the Chicago Blackhawks, scoring a goal on his first shot in his first NHL game.

Rod Brind'Amour has established himself in the NHL as a coach's dream—a team player with offensive talent.

Brind'Amour, Rod
C, 6´1˝, 202 lbs, b: Ottawa, Ont., 8/9/1970

Season	Club, League	Regular Season					Playoffs				
		GP	G	A	Pts	PIM	GP	G	A	Pts	PIM
1988–89	St. Louis Blues, NHL						5	2	0	2	4
1989–90	St. Louis Blues, NHL	79	26	35	61	46	12	5	8	13	6
1990–91	St. Louis Blues, NHL	78	17	32	49	93	13	2	5	7	10
1991–92	Philadelphia Flyers, NHL	80	33	44	77	100					
WC–92	Canada	6	1	1	2	4					
1992–93	Philadelphia Flyers, NHL	81	37	49	86	89					
WC–93	Canada	8	3	1	4	6					
1993–94	Philadelphia Flyers, NHL	84	35	62	97	85					
WC–94	Canada	8	4	2	6	2					
1994–95	Philadelphia Flyers, NHL	48	12	27	39	33	15	6	9	15	8
1995–96	Philadelphia Flyers, NHL	82	26	61	87	110	12	2	5	7	6
WCup–96	Canada	7	1	2	3	0					
1996–97	Philadelphia Flyers, NHL	82	27	32	59	41	19	13	8	21	10
1997–98	Philadelphia Flyers, NHL	82	36	38	74	54	5	2	2	4	7
OWG–98	Canada	6	1	2	3	0					
1998–99	Philadelphia Flyers, NHL	82	24	50	74	47	6	1	3	4	0
1999–00	Philadelphia Flyers, NHL	12	5	3	8	4					
	Carolina Hurricanes, NHL	33	4	10	14	22					
2000-01	Carolina Hurricanes, NHL	79	20	36	56	47	6	1	3	4	6
2001-02	Carolina Hurricanes, NHL	81	23	32	55	40					
	NHL Totals	983	325	511	836	811	93	34	43	77	57
	OWG/WC/WCup Totals	35	10	8	18	12					

Won WC (1994)

Rod Brind'Amour (number 17) retired twice, once at the age of six and again at seven, but after a few months of watching Saturday night NHL games, he'd be back at it by Christmas.

The Blues lost the series, but management was impressed with Brind'Amour's play and made plans to use him the next season on a line with Brett Hull and Adam Oates.

Although Brind'Amour's days in college hockey were over, he continued to attend Michigan State for several summers, studying business administration and marketing. His first full NHL season was a solid one, as he racked up 26 goals and 61 points and a plus-minus rating of plus 23. He collected 13 points in 12 playoff games—the Blues again lost to Chicago in the second round—and was named to the All-Rookie Team.

A 1991 trade sent Brind'Amour to the Philadelphia Flyers. The Flyers had made inquiries about him before and were told he was untouchable. But times had changed: While the Blues had always admired Brind'Amour's work ethic, they were now of the opinion he might be pushing himself too hard. The Flyers offered Ron Sutter in return, and the chance to reunite him with his twin brother, Rich, and older brother Brian—the Blues coach—was too tempting to pass up.

The trade would ultimately help Brind'Amour. Within the Flyers system, he discovered he could take more chances, have more fun and display all parts of his multifaceted game. He played center and wing and killed penalties and ran the power- play—from the point or from deep in the corner.

Brind'Amour scored more than 30 goals in each of his first three seasons with the Flyers, recording a career-high 37 goals in 1992–93 and a personal-best 97 points in the next season. The Flyers missed the playoffs in all three years, so Brind'Amour played for Canada at the World Championships and was a member of the 1994 team that won Canada's first gold medal since 1961. He would also don the red and white jersey for Canada in the 1996 World Cup of Hockey and the 1998 Winter Olympics.

In April 1997 the Flyers met the Pittsburgh Penguins in the first round of the playoffs and took a 3–1 lead in games. In game five—which would be the final match of Mario Lemieux's career — Brind'Amour stole the show early, scoring two shorthand goals in the first period to tie league records for most shorthand goals in a game and in a period. After they eliminated the Penguins, the Flyers made a run to the Stanley Cup finals, where they were beaten by the Detroit Red Wings. Brind'Amour's 13 playoff goals tied him for the league lead with Colorado's Claude Lemieux and further entrenched his reputation as a big-game performer.

Brind'Amour was a durable player. He suited up for the Flyers in 484 consecutive games in the late 1990s, a franchise record. The streak came to an end on September 25, 1999, in a pre-season game against the New Jersey Devils. True to form, he was blocking a shot when the puck hit his skate and one of the bones near the top of his foot was fractured. He missed 34 games, returning just before New Year's Day, much to the relief of the Philadelphia team and fans.

"Rod's the ultimate player because you can use him in all situations," said Flyers assistant coach Wayne Cashman, who knows. "He's got a work ethic that's incomparable. He's a guy you have to order off the ice sometimes because he loves to play. Rod's a legitimate offensive star while still being capable of being your top defensive player."

On January 23, 2000, Flyer fans were shocked when the popular Brind'Amour was traded to the Carolina Hurricanes along with goaltending prospect Jean-Marc Pelletier for forward Keith Primeau. Brind'Amour had trouble adjusting to his new team at first; his defense and skill at winning face-offs were as good as ever, but he went into an offensive slump. His future became uncertain toward the end of the season when in a game against Pittsburgh he was checked into the boards by Penguin defenseman Bob Boughner and suffered a concussion.

The Hurricanes are depending on Brind'Amour to make a full return to both his health and his old playing form. The departures of power winger Gary Roberts and defenseman Paul Coffey have left a fair amount of slack to be taken up in the goal-scoring department. And indeed Brind'Amour put up decent offensive numbers in 2001-02 as the Hurricanes won the Southeast Division.

Darius Kasparaitis

Unlike many countries in eastern Europe—such as Latvia, Ukraine or the Czech Republic—Lithuania isn't known as a hockey power. Instead, it has developed a reputation for turning out top basketball players. For over three decades, there wasn't a single Lithuanian on any team in the Soviet major league. That changed in 1988, when the 16-year-old Darius Kasparaitis made his debut with Dynamo Moscow, becoming the first Lithuanian to break into the league.

Kasparaitis had played hockey as a boy in his home town of Elektrenai, where he was noticed by Dynamo scouts who invited him to the Soviet capital. After two years at the Dynamo school, he was put on the team. His nickname during this period was "Hans" because his Lithuanian accent sounded like German to his Russian peers. But the cheerful and friendly Kasparaitis never took offense.

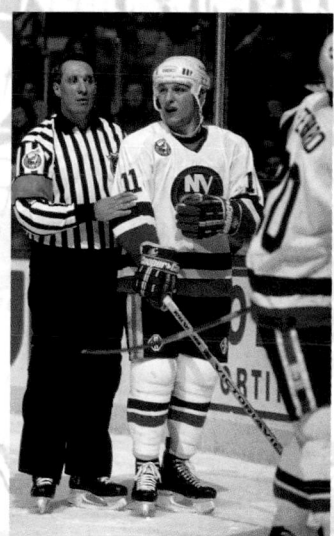

Darius Kasparaitis (center) is the first Lithuanian player in the NHL.

Kasparaitis spent four seasons with Dynamo, and his Soviet—now Russian—career culminated in a place on the Unified Team that won the gold medal at the 1992 Winter Olympics in Albertville, France. He was also named best defenseman at the World Junior Championships that year, which was enough to convince the New York Islanders to select him fifth overall in the 1992 draft. The 5′10″, 210-pound rearguard immediately became a full-time member of the Islanders, playing 79 games in his rookie season, and he quickly became a fan favorite.

In the second round of the 1993 playoffs, the Islanders faced the Pittsburgh Penguins, who were the league's best team during the regular season and the defending Stanley Cup champions. The 20-year-old Kasparaitis was an important part of an Islander blue line corps that neutralized the league's

Darius Kasparaitis (center) belongs in the special category of players who inspire great loyalty among hometown fans and equal animosity among those who support the opposition.

top scorer, Mario Lemieux. Early in the 1996–97 season, Lemieux would remember Kasparaitis's play and recommend to the Penguins brass that they acquire him to bolster their sagging fortunes.

During his career, the hard-hitting Kasparaitis has suffered at least as much pain as he has inflicted on others. Knee injuries limited him to only 13 games in 1994–95 and 46 games in 1995–96. He also suffered a personal loss during this period: After his first knee surgery—and right before Christmas—his wife, Irma, gave birth prematurely to triplets. They were stillborn. The couple recovered from the tragedy and they now have a three-year-old daughter, Elisabeth-Maria.

It is well known that Kasparaitis doesn't let off-ice distractions affect his play or vice versa. "Ice is ice," he says, "and life is life, and it's a big mistake to mix up the two. I feel sorry for those who think otherwise."

When the Islanders traded Kasparaitis to Pittsburgh for forward Bryan Smolinski, Islander fans were outraged. When he returned to Long Island as a member of the Penguins, he was greeted with a roaring ovation. Kasparaitis has always inspired great loyalty from hometown fans, but he has managed to generate just as much animosity from crowds in enemy rinks. That suits him just fine. "My coaches taught me since childhood that there can be no friends among your opposition during a game," Kasparaitis says.

Philadelphia fans are especially loud in their attacks, because Kasparaitis is one of the few NHLers brave enough to tackle Flyers star Eric Lindros. In one game during the 1996 World Cup of Hockey, the ruthless Lithuanian threw the Big E over the boards.

But Kasparaitis just shrugs off the jeers. "Hockey is a game," he says. "Today, I'm playing against their leading player and they hate me, but tomorrow I could be traded onto their team—and they'll start idolizing me. It was like that in Pittsburgh. They didn't love me there because of the way I handled Mario Lemieux. But you should have seen them after the trade. There's nothing personal in the fans' attitudes and it would be silly to get offended. Actually, I love to play in the cities where the audience hates me."

Kasparaitis was a member of the bronze medal-winning Russian entry at the 2002 Olympics. At the NHL trade deadline, the Colorado Avalanche bolstered their lineup heading into the playoffs when they acquired Kasparaitis from the Pittsburgh Penguins for defenseman Rick Berry and left wing Ville Nieminen.

Kasparaitis, Darius
D, 5´10˝, 210 lbs, b: Elektrenai, USSR, 10/16/1972

Season	Club, League	Regular Season					Playoffs				
		GP	G	A	Pts	PIM	GP	G	A	Pts	PIM
1988–89	Dynamo Moscow, USSR	3	0	0	0	0					
1989–90	Dynamo Moscow, USSR	1	0	0	0	0					
1990–91	Dynamo Moscow, USSR	17	0	1	1	10					
1991–92	Dynamo Moscow, Russia	31	2	10	12	14					
OWG–92	Russia	8	0	2	2	2					
WC–92	Russia	6	2	1	3	4					
1992–93	Dynamo Moscow, Russia	7	1	3	4	8					
	New York Islanders, NHL	79	4	17	21	166	18	0	5	5	31
1993–94	New York Islanders, NHL	76	1	10	11	142	4	0	0	0	8
1994–95	New York Islanders, NHL	13	0	1	1	22					
1995–96	New York Islanders, NHL	46	1	7	8	93					
WC–96	Russia	8	0	2	2	2					
WCup–96	Russia	5	0	2	2	14					
1996–97	New York Islanders, NHL	18	0	5	5	16					
	Pittsburgh Penguins, NHL	57	2	16	18	84	5	0	0	0	6
1997–98	Pittsburgh Penguins, NHL	81	4	8	12	127	5	0	0	0	8
OWG–98	Russia	6	0	2	2	6					
1998–99	Pittsburgh Penguins, NHL	48	1	4	5	70					
1999–00	Pittsburgh Penguins, NHL	73	3	12	15	146	11	1	1	2	10
2000–01	Pittsburgh Penguins, NHL	77	3	16	19	111	17	1	1	2	26
2001–02	Pittsburgh-Colorado, NHL	80	2	12	14	142					
OWG–02	Russia	6	1	0	1	4					
	USSR/Russia Totals	59	3	14	17	32					
	NHL Totals	648	21	108	129	1119	60	2	7	9	89
	OWG/WC/WCup Totals	39	3	9	12	32					

Won OWG (1992)

Mike Modano

Mike Modano's imposing blend of size, strength and sportsmanship made him one of the most exciting NHL stars of the 1990s and one of the most successful American-born players in league history. He is a consistent scorer whose point totals would likely be higher were it not for his team's defensive style. He has played his entire career for the Stars, in Minnesota and in Dallas, and he has been a vital part of the team's trip to the Stanley Cup finals in 1991 and its Cup championship in 1999.

Born in a suburb of Detroit in 1970, Modano was a local star who chose Canadian junior hockey over scholarship offers from U.S. colleges. He enjoyed three outstanding seasons with the Prince Albert Raiders of the Western Hockey League and was a standout for the U.S. team at the 1988 and 1989 World Junior Championships. One scout noted: "If you look at talent and talent alone, no one is close to him. He has all the offensive skills—great skating, puckhandling, hockey sense, shot—to be a dominant offensive player in the NHL. He's the kid most capable of breaking out and doing something mind-boggling with the puck."

After a 127-point season with Prince Albert in 1987–88, Modano was the first player chosen by the Minnesota North Stars at the NHL Entry Draft. The thrilled youngster exclaimed, "I wanted to play in Minnesota because it's close to my home in Detroit. It's an honor to be the number one pick, too. I think I can step in and help the North Stars next season." Instead, he was returned to the Raiders in 1988–89 and enjoyed another strong season, registering 105 points in only 41 games and earning a spot on the WHL East All-Star Team.

A member of the Stars franchise for his entire career, Mike Modano has become one of the most successful American players in NHL history.

Modano broke into the NHL in 1989 and immediately proved he was ready, totaling 75 points. He was at the center of controversy when he placed second to Calgary's Sergei Makarov in the Calder Trophy voting. Many observers complained that the selection of the 31-year-old Makarov was unfair and pointed out that he was a veteran of 14 seasons of elite Soviet and international hockey. However, the 19-year-old Modano did receive a small consolation, as he was selected to the NHL All-Rookie Team.

North Stars coach Pierre Page was exuberant about his young star: "What I really like about the kid is that he's a team player. You don't always find that in a young guy. He's very likable, very coachable. He's also got tremendous hockey sense and is very confident in his abilities." For his part, Modano said, "The North Stars have taken a lot of pressure off me by just telling me to try to play my game and not to do more than I'm capable of doing."

During his sophomore season in 1990–91, he scored 64 points. He saved his best hockey, however, for the playoffs. The North Stars—whose regular-season record was an unremarkable 27-39-14—upset the Presidents' Trophy-winning Chicago Blackhawks in the first round to launch a surprising drive to the Stanley Cup finals, where they were finally defeated in six games by Mario Lemieux's Pittsburgh Penguins. Modano scored 20 points in 23 games in the second season. His ability to play with finesse was also a surprise, considering his powerful build—6′3″ and 200 pounds.

Modano's climb to the upper echelon of NHL stars made him an important player for the United States on the international stage. He represented his country at the World Championships in 1990 and 1993 as well as at the 1998 Winter Olympics, where he was arguably the

Mike Modano (right) was a consistent scorer for the Stars and helped the team reach the 100-point mark for four straight seasons from 1996 to 2000.

most consistent American forward in a disappointing sixth-place finish. In 1991 he helped the U.S. finish second to Canada in the Canada Cup tournament, and five years later he scored six points in seven games as the Americans won the inaugural World Cup of Hockey.

Modano has continued to be a consistent scorer for the Stars. When the team moved to Dallas in 1993, he responded with his first 50-goal season. He later helped the team reach the 100-point mark in the standings for four years running from 1996 to 2000. Modano's excellence and flair on the ice was a key selling point as the club tried to develop a solid fan base in their new city.

On March 20, 1996, Modano recorded his 500th NHL point with a goal against the St. Louis Blues. In June 1998 he was named the Dallas professional athlete of the year by the Dallas All-Sports Association—no small feat in a city where the top headlines generally go to football's Dallas Cowboys or baseball's Texas Rangers.

Modano summed up the Stars's strength: "I think a lot has to do with the personnel that Ken Hitchcock has to coach. I think we have many players with a lot of ability, a lot of skill and talent and a lot of speed. So I think he wraps up all that in his system and we are able to go out there every night and play at a high level of intensity. He expects us to work hard in practice and in games and to put everything towards defensive thinking. I think we have always striven to check first, then feed off other team's mistakes, turnovers, and we have been able to capitalize on that."

In 1998–99, Modo led all playoff performers with 18 assists as the Stars won their first Stanley Cup in a hard-fought, six-game series against the Buffalo Sabres. During the 1999–2000 season, he led the Stars with 81 points in 77 games as they finished first in the Pacific Division and reached the Stanley Cup finals for the second year in a row.

Although Modano had another outstanding year in 2000–01 with 33 goals and 84 points, his Stars didn't last long in the playoffs and he had to prepare for his 14th NHL season. When the player and his team continued to struggle through the first segment of 2001–02, head coach Ken Hitchcock was fired, a move many attributed to the loss of his star center's support. The Stars had a difficult season by their lofty standards but did manage to regain their composure and qualify for the Stanley Cup playoffs. For the ninth time in 13 years, Modano managed to reach 30 goals and also

Modano, Mike
C, 6´3˝, 200 lbs, b: Livonia, MI, 6/7/1970

Season	Club, League	Regular Season					Playoffs				
		GP	G	A	Pts	PIM	GP	G	A	Pts	PIM
1988–89	Minnesota North Stars, NHL						2	0	0	0	0
1989–90	Minnesota North Stars, NHL	80	29	46	75	63	7	1	1	2	12
WEC–90	USA	8	3	3	6	2					
1990–91	Minnesota North Stars, NHL	79	28	36	64	65	23	8	12	20	16
CCup–91	USA	8	2	7	9	2					
1991–92	Minnesota North Stars, NHL	76	33	44	77	46	7	3	2	5	4
1992–93	Minnesota North Stars, NHL	82	33	60	93	83					
WC–93	USA	6	0	0	0	2					
1993–94	Dallas Stars, NHL	76	50	43	93	54	9	7	3	10	16
1994–95	Dallas Stars, NHL	30	12	17	29	8					
1995–96	Dallas Stars, NHL	78	36	45	81	63					
WCup–96	USA	7	2	4	6	4					
1996–97	Dallas Stars, NHL	80	35	48	83	42	7	4	1	5	0
1997–98	Dallas Stars, NHL	52	21	38	59	32	17	4	10	14	12
OWG–98	USA	4	2	0	2	0					
1998–99	Dallas Stars, NHL	77	34	47	81	44	23	5	18	23	16
1999–00	Dallas Stars, NHL	77	38	43	81	48	23	10	13	23	10
2000–01	Dallas Stars, NHL	81	33	51	84	52	9	3	4	7	0
2001–02	Dallas Stars, NHL	78	34	43	77	38					
OWG–02	USA	6	0	6	6	4					
	NHL Totals	946	416	561	977	634					
	OWG/WEC/WC/CCup/WCup Totals	39	9	20	29	14					

NHL Second All-Star Team (2000)
Won Stanley Cup (1999)
Won WCup (1996)

achieved the 70-point plateau for the 10th time. And at the 2002 Olympics, Modano centered the most potent offensive unit in the tournament with John LeClair and Brett Hull flanking him on the wings. The trio lit up the scoreboard in the first five games of the tournament. Only Canada managed to satisfactorily contain the explosive line in the gold medal game—and that may have been the ultimate difference between gold and silver.

Boris Mironov

Since Russians first began to play in the NHL, three pairs of brothers have appeared: Pavel and Valeri Bure, Viacheslav and Yuri Butsayev and Dmitri and Boris Mironov. The Mironov defensemen have played 16 seasons in the NHL, and neither 35-year-old Dmitri nor 28-year-old Boris is ready to hang up his skates.

Their father was a bicycle racer, even participating in national championships. He wanted his sons to become sportsmen, too. At the age of five, Dmitri began in the swimming pool at Moscow's famous Sokolniki Park. After the family moved, there was no swimming pool near their new home. Their father found out by accident that the CSKA hockey school was inviting gifted boys to join, and after a tough audition, Dmitri Mironov was admitted. Several years later, his younger brother followed in his footsteps. The seven-year-old Dmitri missed his first training session after getting lost in the subway. Their parents didn't have time to walk them to the arena, so the boys had to make it on their own.

Younger brother Boris doesn't want his own son to follow his example. "If we lived in Russia, I would send him to a hockey school—to save him from the mean streets. But I have no fears about his future here in America. I sacrificed much for my career's sake. As a kid, I would take my rucksack, ride a subway all the way across Moscow. It took me an hour and a half to get to the hockey school. I did my training exercises and got back home dog-tired. I sat down to do my homework and then fell asleep like a log. I missed my childhood. It was a hard life indeed. But now I have an opportunity to do what I like and make big money. So my sacrifice paid off."

The brothers are very close and always vacation together. They regularly bet on who will score more points the next season. The loser pays for dinner at a fancy restaurant, and so far Dmitri has been the winner. They never played on the same team, in Russia or in the NHL. It happened only once—at the 1998 Olympics in Nagano, Japan.

A bit hastily, sports reporters in Edmonton nicknamed Boris Mironov "Norris."

Mironov, Boris
D, 6´3˝, 220 lbs, b: Moscow, USSR, 3/21/1972

Season	Club, League	Regular Season					Playoffs				
		GP	G	A	Pts	PIM	GP	G	A	Pts	PIM
1988–89	CSKA, USSR	1	0	0	0	0					
1989–90	CSKA, USSR	7	0	0	0	0					
1990–91	CSKA, USSR	36	1	5	6	16					
1991–92	CSKA, Russia	36	2	1	3	22					
1992–93	CSKA, Russia	19	0	5	5	20					
1993–94	Winnipeg Jets, NHL	65	7	22	29	96					
	Edmonton Oilers, NHL	14	0	2	2	14					
1994–95	Edmonton Oilers, NHL	29	1	7	8	40					
	Cape Breton Oilers, AHL	4	2	5	7	23					
1995–96	Edmonton Oilers, NHL	78	8	24	32	101					
WC–96	Russia	8	0	3	3	12					
1996–97	Edmonton Oilers, NHL	55	6	26	32	85	12	2	8	10	16
1997–98	Edmonton Oilers, NHL	81	16	30	46	100	12	3	3	6	27
OWG–98	Russia	6	0	2	2	2					
1998–99	Edmonton Oilers, NHL	63	11	29	40	104					
	Chicago Blackhawks, NHL	12	0	9	9	27					
1999–00	Edmonton Oilers, NHL	58	9	27	36	72					
2000–01	Chicago Blackhawks, NHL	66	5	17	22	42					
2001–02	Chicago Blackhawks, NHL	64	4	14	18	68					
OWG–02	Russia	6	1	0	1	2					
	USSR/Russia Totals	99	3	11	14	58					
	NHL Totals	585	67	208	275	749					
	OWG/WC Totals	20	1	5	6	16					

Since Russians first began to play in the NHL, three pairs of brothers have appeared: Pavel and Valeri Bure, Viacheslav and Yuri Butsayev and Dmitri and Boris (right) Mironov.

After five years with Moscow's CSKA, Boris played for Winnipeg, who drafted him in the second round in 1993. At the time, the Winnipeg Jets were the first team with a contingent of Russian players: Alexei Zhamnov, Igor Korolev, Nikolai Khabibulin, Igor Ulanov and Sergei Bautin. However, the NHL wasn't quite ready to absorb the Russians and coaches started to get rid of Europeans. Although Mironov racked up 29 points in his first season with the Jets and captured 10th position among rookies, he was swapped in March 1994 together with Swede Mats Lindgren for Dave Manson of the Edmonton Oilers.

Boris soon took a leading role on his new team. A bit hastily, sports reporters in Edmonton even nicknamed him "Norris." His rapid progress led to Mironov's being traded to Chicago in the spring of 1999. "With Edmonton, I used to spend a lot of time on the ice and was happy," Boris recalled later. "Our manager, Glenn Sather, knew full well that he was unable to pay me as much money as I was really worth. That's why, after I came to a far wealthier club, I decided to fight for what I could."

The fight was to continue for three months. During the summer and fall of 1999, Blackhawks general manager Bob Murray repeatedly declined Mironov's demands. But after Chicago's poor performance at the start of the new season, Murray acquiesced and signed Mironov to a new three-year contract worth $9.6 million.

Mironov was a member of the bronze medal-winning Russian team in Salt Lake City, while his excellent defensive play with the Blackhawks in 2001–02 helped propel them in to the playoffs.

Andrei Kovalenko

In his days with Quebec, Andrei Kovalenko was nicknamed "the Russian Tank" by the North American media and it stuck.

In his days with the Quebec Nordiques, Andrei Kovalenko was nicknamed "the Russian Tank" by the North American media and it stuck. When he played for Moscow's CSKA as a teenager, his partners called him "Rambo." Monikers such as these point to a style that is somewhat unique for a Russian hockey player. The heftiest of Russian NHLers—his former partner with the Edmonton Oilers, Doug Weight, thought he had the biggest ankles he had ever seen—has a tendency to battle along the boards to the opposition zone and then charge to the net. In eight years in the NHL, the 30-year-old forward has played for five clubs.

Many Russian players came from poor families. Their less than promising prospects encouraged many of those boys to make something of themselves in the world of sports. Kovalenko is an exception. He was born in the small town of Balakovo on the Volga River, and his family, by Russian standards, was fairly well-to-do. At the age of nine, the future Russian Tank swore he would follow the example set by his elder brother and serve in the army. At the same time, however, he was showing potential on the hockey rink, and when he was 14, his coach offered to send him to a special sports school. Andrei promised his parents, "I'll be both an officer and a hockey player." By joining the CSKA club, he kept his promise.

Kovalenko never forgets his family. While in Edmonton, his father would come to watch every game and every Oilers workout. The coaches laughed and told Kovie they'd have to find a job with the club for his father.

Kovalenko has never forgotten his roots. He was grateful for the opportunity to play for his national team in the 1991 Canada Cup, the 1996 World Cup of Hockey and the 1998 Olympics. After a dismal season in Canada—he scored only six goals in the regular season—Kovalenko's performance in Nagano, Japan, was excellent. In six games, he scored four goals.

During his first three years in the NHL, Kovalenko's output was moderate. Then his team moved from Quebec City to Denver, Colorado. The Colorado Avalanche were headed for the Stanley Cup and wanted to get their hands on Montreal's Patrick Roy, who was in a dispute with Canadiens coach Mario Tremblay at the time. In order to get Roy, the Avalanche decided to sacrifice their young forwards Kovalenko and Martin Rucinsky. Kovalenko's nine goals in the previous 10 games with Colorado didn't encourage his team to keep him.

Former Edmonton partner Doug Weight thought Andrei Kovalenko (front) had the biggest ankles in the league.

Kovalenko stayed with Montreal for less than a season. His performance was good during the regular season but fell short in the playoffs. That was all the excuse the club's administration needed to trade him to Edmonton. In the regular season he scored 32 goals, but after a year with the Oilers, Kovalenko finally came through in the playoffs, scoring four important goals in the series. However, the next year scored only half a dozen goals and appeared on the ice in only one playoff game. Kovalenko asked general manager Glen Sather to trade him. Six months later, at the start of the 1998–99 season, his wish was granted.

His term with Philadelphia lasted less than two months. He saw little ice time and in 13 games he earned only one point. Kovalenko thought the Flyers only wanted him so they could get rid of the costly Alexandre Daigle, who wasn't on good terms with Bobby Clarke. Still, Philadelphia was actively seeking an experienced defenseman, and once they set their sights on Adam Burt of Carolina, Kovalenko was swapped. Philly coach Roger Neilson told him, "Don't blame it on yourself, you were just missing your chance."

After March of 1999, the Russian Tank played for the Carolina Hurricanes, who took advantage of his ability as a shooter. Coach Paul Morris and veteran players Ron Francis and Gary Roberts were firm in their opinion that Kovalenko had become an integral part of the team.

After playing the entire 1999–2000 season in Carolina, Kovalenko played for the Boston Bruins in 2000–01 but did not return to play in the NHL in 2001–02.

Kovalenko, Andrei
RW, 5'10", 215 lbs, b: Balakovo, USSR, 6/7/1970

Season	Club, League	Regular Season					Playoffs				
		GP	G	A	Pts	PIM	GP	G	A	Pts	PIM
1988–89	CSKA, USSR	10	1	0	1	0					
1989–90	CSKA, USSR	48	8	5	13	20					
1990–91	CSKA, USSR	45	13	8	21	26					
CCup–91	USSR	5	1	2	3	10					
1991–92	CSKA, Russia	44	19	13	32	32					
OWG–92	Russia	8	1	1	2	2					
WC–92	Russia	6	3	1	4	2					
1992–93	CSKA, Russia	3	1	1	4	4					
	Quebec Nordiques, NHL	81	27	41	68	57	4	1	0	1	2
1993–94	Quebec Nordiques, NHL	58	16	17	33	46					
WC–94	Russia	6	5	4	9	2					
1994–95	Lada Togliatti, Russia	11	9	2	11	14					
	Quebec Nordiques, NHL	45	14	10	24	31	6	0	1	1	2
1995–96	Colorado Avalanche, NHL	26	11	11	22	16					
	Montreal Canadiens, NHL	51	17	17	34	33	6	0	0	0	6
WCup–96	Russia	5	2	0	2	4					
1996–97	Edmonton Oilers, NHL	74	32	27	59	81	12	4	3	7	6
1997–98	Edmonton Oilers, NHL	59	6	17	23	28	1	0	0	0	2
OWG–98	Russia	6	4	1	5	14					
1998–99	Edmonton Oilers, NHL	43	13	14	27	30					
	Philadelphia Flyers, NHL	13	0	1	1	2					
	Carolina Hurricanes, NHL	18	6	6	12	0	4	0	2	2	2
1999–00	Carolina Hurricanes, NHL	76	15	24	39	38					
WC–2000	Russia	6	0	0	0	0					
2000–01	Boston Bruins, NHL	76	16	21	37	27					
	USSR/Russia Totals	161	53	29	82	96					
	NHL Totals	620	173	206	379	389					
	OWG/WC/CCup/WCup Totals	42	16	9	25	34					

Won OWG (1992)
USSR Champion (1989)

Joe **Sakic**

Like many of the great players, Joe Sakic had all the physical skills required to be a standout in professional hockey and also that little bit extra, the ability to see plays developing in advance and the patience to hold on to the puck for that extra second to find an opening. With speed to burn and an imaginative style, Sakic emerged as a quiet leader who lifted ordinary teams to respectability and made good teams into championship contenders.

Sakic was instilled with a healthy work ethic by his father, Marijan, who came to Canada from Croatia at 17. Joe worked hard at his game in Burnaby, British Columbia, where he grew up. He then went through an early traumatic experience before becoming a celebrated junior player in the Western Hockey League with the Swift Current Broncos. He joined the club as a shy 17-year-old in 1986. On December 30 of that year he was riding with the team when the bus crashed just outside of Swift Current. Four teammates were killed. Sakic reacted to the tragedy by focusing on the game, lifting the spirits of his teammates in the process. He would finish the year with 133 points and lead the Broncos into the playoffs.

In 1995–96, Joe Sakic produced the second-largest tally of playoff goals in history with 18.

In the summer of 1987, Sakic was selected 15th overall in the NHL Entry Draft by the Quebec Nordiques after the team chose Brian Fogarty ninth overall with its other pick in the first round. Just days into his first training camp with the Nordiques, Sakic told Quebec management he would rather spend another year in junior to prepare for the NHL. In 1987–88, Sakic won the WHL scoring title and the league's most valuable player honors, collecting 78 goals and 160 points in only 64 games. He entered the last game of the season four points behind Moose Jaw star Theoren Fleury. After his nervous teammates missed several easy chances created by Sakic, he took the task into his own hands by scoring four goals in the final 30 minutes to win the scoring crown. He finished the year by becoming a key member on the Canadian team that won the World Junior Championships and was named Canadian major junior player of the year.

In 1988–89, Sakic had a good rookie season with Quebec, though an injury cost him 10 games and maybe a chance at the Calder Trophy. The Nordiques as a team, however, were miserable, finishing tied for last at the bottom of the NHL pack. The next year, Sakic would truly come into his own as a professional scorer and playmaker, entering the top 10 on the year-end scoring list with 102 points and earning a spot in the All-Star Game. The Nordiques, aside from Sakic's play, were awful, finishing well below the second-last team in the final standings. Sakic bettered his scoring total in 1990–91, finishing the

Sakic, Joe
C, 5′11″, 185 lbs, b: Burnaby, B. C., 7/7/1969

Season	Club, League	Regular Season					Playoffs				
		GP	G	A	Pts	PIM	GP	G	A	Pts	PIM
1988–89	Quebec Nordiques, NHL	70	23	39	62	24					
1989–90	Quebec Nordiques, NHL	80	39	63	102	27					
1990–91	Quebec Nordiques, NHL	80	48	61	109	24					
WEC–91	Canada	10	6	5	11	0					
1991–92	Quebec Nordiques, NHL	69	29	65	94	20					
1992–93	Quebec Nordiques, NHL	78	48	57	105	40	6	3	3	6	2
1993–94	Quebec Nordiques, NHL	84	28	64	92	18					
WC–94	Canada	8	4	3	7	0					
1994–95	Quebec Nordiques, NHL	47	19	43	62	30	6	4	1	5	0
1995–96	Colorado Avalanche, NHL	82	51	69	120	44	22	18	16	34	14
WCup–96	Canada	8	2	2	4	6					
1996–97	Colorado Avalanche, NHL	65	22	52	74	34	17	8	17	25	14
1997–98	Colorado Avalanche, NHL	64	27	36	63	50	6	2	3	5	6
OWG–98	Canada	4	1	2	3	4					
1998–99	Colorado Avalanche, NHL	73	41	55	96	29	19	6	13	19	8
1999–00	Colorado Avalanche, NHL	60	28	53	81	28	17	2	7	9	8
2000–01	Colorado Avalanche, NHL	82	54	64	118	30	21	13	13	26	6
2001–02	Colorado Avalanche, NHL	82	26	53	79	18					
OWG–02	Canada	6	4	3	7	0					
	NHL Totals	1016	483	774	1257	416					
	OWG/WEC/WC/WCup Totals	36	17	15	32	10					

Won Conn Smythe Trophy (1996)
Won WC (1994)
Won Stanley Cup (1996)
Won OWG (2002)

season sixth in the league with 109 points. The Nordiques improved as a team but still missed the playoffs, finishing dead last in the league.

"Everybody hates to lose, but you can make that a positive, too," Sakic said after his third losing season. "It's like joy and sorrow. They say you can't experience joy to the fullest unless you have sorrow to measure it against. Every time we lose, I think how good it's going to feel when we start to win. Then I try even harder."

As the team struggled, Sakic continued to improve. He used his experience in international play to his advantage in 1991. During the World Championships in Finland, Sakic wasn't happy when he compared his skating ability to the Europeans on the bigger ice surface. Next fall he was the first player cut from the Canada Cup team at the Canadian training camp. A trainer there told him that he didn't have sufficient leg strength. Sakic resolved to improve his skating and strength and went on a weightlifting program for the next year.

"Every time we lose, I think how good it's going to feel when we start to win," said Joe Sakic (left) after a bad season with the Nordiques. "Then I try even harder."

In 1992–93, Sakic signed a new deal with Quebec, promised to improve his French—a sticking point with many francophone fans in the area—and was selected captain of the Nordiques. Sakic scored 48 goals and collected 105 points in the regular season and Quebec made the playoffs for the first time in six years, though it was a short stay in the promised land as they were cut down quickly by their provincial rivals from Montreal. Sakic played once again on the Canadian team at the World Championships and finally got a taste of a title, pacing Canada to only its second gold medal since 1961.

With the Eric Lindros saga over and a core of talented newcomers and draft picks rounding into form, the Nordiques blossomed over the course of the lockout-shortened 1994–95 season, ending up with the best record in the Eastern Conference. Though Quebec was upset in the first round by the defending champion New York Rangers, the stage was set for Sakic and the team—which moved to Colorado for the beginning of the next season–to challenge for the Stanley Cup.

Sakic had his best offensive year with the new Colorado Avalanche with 120 points and also gained respect for his improved all-around game. In the playoffs, he was dominating. He led the league in playoff scoring with 34 points, produced the second-largest tally of playoff goals in history with 18—six of them game winners to set an NHL record—and scored twice in overtime to be the hero as the Avalanche stormed through the playoffs to capture the 1996 Stanley Cup. Sakic was an easy choice for the Conn Smythe Trophy.

"Early on, it didn't look like we were ever going to get there. Now, just to get my name on the Cup is something special," Sakic said after the victory. "A lot of great players in this league have never won it. To be one who has, that is so special."

In January 1997 Sakic suffered a serious cut to his leg in a game against the Philadelphia Flyers. The calf injury required surgery, forcing Sakic to miss the All-Star Game and four weeks of the season. That summer he became a highly rated free agent. He signed an offer sheet for an estimated $21 million over three years with the New York Rangers, who had recently lost out on the battle to sign Mark Messier. Colorado had one week to match the offer, which they did, to keep their captain and leader. Sakic played for Canada in the 1998 Nagano Olympics, although he missed part of the action with a knee injury. He passed Hall of Famer Peter Stastny on the Quebec/Colorado franchise career scoring list during the 1999–2000 season and 2000–01 was a career year for him. He finished second in goals with 54 and second in points with 118, played in the All-Star Game and won three individual awards: the Hart, the Lady Byng and the Lester B. Pearson. He also led the league with 26 playoff points and won a second Stanley Cup.

Although Sakic's goal and point totals were down considerably in 2001–02, he still led the team to a strong regular-season finish. But his star shone brightest at the Salt Lake City Olympics, where he led Canada in scoring with six points in as many games. His inspired play—especially in the gold medal final against the U.S., where he tallied a goal and two assists—was by far the single biggest reason why Canada was able to end its 50-year Olympic drought. He was rewarded by being named the tournament MVP.

Dimitri Yushkevich

His idol was Vladislav Tretiak, so a young Dimitri Yushkevich dreamed of becoming a goalie.

Dimitri Yushkevich got acquainted with hockey like any other young hopeful in the former USSR: Kids would erect goals made of snow in the yard and play without skates. His idol was Vladislav Tretiak, so the young Yushkevich dreamed of becoming a goalie. At 11, he gained entry to the only hockey school in his home town of Cherepovets and duly attended the practices, hoping to be granted the gear of a goalie. Eventually the coach divided the students into teams of five and they competed against one another. Yushkevich was assigned to defense and angered opponents when he stopped them from scoring.

A year passed, but no gear was forthcoming. Disappointed, the young player started skipping the practices. One day he came to the rink and his teammates were sporting new jerseys—all except him. A boy who was leaving the school gave Dimitri his jersey, but by then he had lost his incentive and almost decided that he would quit, too. He was absent for almost a month. Finally his coach visited him at home and suggested that he should come back—or send the jersey instead. After that, Dimitri didn't miss a practice unless he could explain.

Before long, the young player's career truly started. In 1989 Yushkevich was invited to play at the World Junior Championships in Anchorage, Alaska, with the USSR junior team. He and Pavel Bure were the youngest at the training camp. Dimitri didn't believe he had a chance of making the team, but he was added to the first line—which included Pavel Bure, Sergei Fedorov and Alexander Mogilny—and won his first gold medal. He subsequently appeared at two more junior champi-onships, but his memories of these weren't as sweet. In the most important games in 1990 and 1991, the Soviet team lost to Sweden and Finland when the opposition scored last-minute goals.

In 1991 Yushkevich switched to Dynamo Moscow, then headed by Vladimir Yurzinov. The experienced Yurzinov favoured an NHL style of practice—tough play and swift passes—and pre-pared his boys both to win Russian championships and to migrate to the NHL. Thanks to this training, it wasn't hard for Yushkevich to play North American hockey when he came to the Philadelphia Flyers. By then, Dimitri was also an Olympic champion. To many experts' surprise, the young and ambitious Unified Team of the former USSR had won the gold in Albertville, France, and it was there that Yushkevich met his future partner in Philly, Eric Lindros.

Yushkevich made a successful debut on the Philadelphia team in 1992. In his opinion, hockey was different back then: "Philly, then not the league's strongest team, scored 300 goals, yet it missed as many. Playing at that time was easy, as there were no traps and other defensive systems in vogue. Goalies were weaker than nowadays, and there was more fun in the hockey. Today, hockey is hard work and big money. There are a number of stars who still have fun. Others just work hard."

After that first year at school, Yushkevich had never had problems with coaches. And for him, hockey was always both fun and hard work. But even he had to pay for a career that may have been going too smoothly. In 1995 he joined the Toronto Maple Leafs, where his first three years proved an ordeal and a test of his durability. When coaches wouldn't let him play much, Dimitri tried to show he was good—but more often than not it was bad. Every year, he requested a trade.

Everything changed after Pat Quinn arrived in 1998. Quinn says Dimitri has a defenseman's most significant trait—"Yushkevich always makes right decisions"—and he soon became the team's leading defenseman under the new coach. When you consider his smashing shots and ability to give a tough bodycheck without committing infractions, it is clear why Yushkevich came to be a fan favorite as well.

In the 1999 playoff series, the Toronto Maple Leafs eliminated the Pittsburgh Penguins, mostly because Yushkevich was so effective at hindering the Penguin's Jaromir Jagr. The great Czech player didn't succeed in getting rid of his antagonist for the whole series. In the end, he lost his temper and hit the defenseman on his back. It reminded Dimitri of the good old days at his hockey school when his young opponents got mad when he wouldn't permit them to score.

The 1999–2000 season validated Yushkevich's stature as one of the league's leading defensemen and an invitation to the All-Star Game confirmed it.

After another strong season in 2000–01, Yushkevich continued his consistent play on the Maple Leafs' blue line until an injury sidelined him 55 games into the season. The result was a blood clot in the leg, which for some time was not only deemed to be career-threatening, but had the potential to be life threatening if not properly treated. The injury also forced him to miss the 2002 Olympics.

His smashing shots and ability to throw a tough bodycheck without committing an infraction made Dimitri Yushkevich (right) a favorite in Toronto.

Yushkevich, Dimitri
D, 5′11″, 208 lbs, b: Cherepovets, USSR, 11/19/1971

Season	Club, League	Regular Season					Playoffs				
		GP	G	A	Pts	PIM	GP	G	A	Pts	PIM
1988–89	Torpedo Yaroslavl, USSR	23	2	1	3	8					
1989–90	Torpedo Yaroslavl, USSR	41	2	3	5	39					
1990–91	Torpedo Yaroslavl, USSR	41	10	4	14	22					
1991–92	Dynamo Moscow, Russia	35	5	7	12	14					
OWG–92	Russia	8	1	2	3	4					
WC–92	Russia	6	1	1	2	4					
1992–93	Philadelphia Flyers, NHL	82	5	27	32	71					
WC–93	Russia	7	1	4	5	10					
1993–94	Philadelphia Flyers, NHL	75	5	25	30	86					
WC–94	Russia	6	1	2	3	12					
1994–95	Torpedo Yaroslavl, Russia	10	3	4	7	8					
	Philadelphia Flyers, NHL	40	5	9	14	47	15	1	5	6	12
1995–96	Toronto Maple Leafs, NHL	69	1	10	11	54	4	0	0	0	0
WCup–96	Russia	5	1	1	2	2					
1996–97	Toronto Maple Leafs, NHL	74	4	10	14	56					
1997–98	Toronto Maple Leafs, NHL	72	0	12	12	78					
1998–99	Toronto Maple Leafs, NHL	78	6	22	28	88	17	1	5	6	22
1999–00	Toronto Maple Leafs, NHL	77	3	24	27	55	12	1	1	2	4
2000–01	Toronto Maple Leafs, NHL	81	5	19	24	52					
2001–02	Toronto Maple Leafs, NHL	55	6	13	19	26					
	USSR/Russia Totals	150	22	19	41	91					
	NHL Totals	703	40	171	211	613					
	OWG/WC/WCup Totals	32	5	10	15	32					

Named Best Defenseman at WC (1993)
Won OWG (1992)
Won WC (1993)
Russia Champion (1992)

A HISTORY OF WORLD HOCKEY

Petr *Nedved*

One day in January 1988, Petr Nedved walked away from a group of Litvinov juniors in Calgary. He was only 17 and couldn't speak a world of English. The last night before his planned return home he called a friend. Then he tried to convey his decision to his parents over the phone and his father urged him to return home. But he had made his decision.

He didn't have a contract with a team, nor had he taken care of the formalities for an extended stay. He simply decided that he wanted to play in the NHL one day. If he stayed in his homeland, the authorities would have let him go abroad only after he was 30. And he didn't want that. While he was weighing the advantages and the disadvantages in his head right there in Calgary, he attended a Calgary Flames match and that sealed it.

Eighteen months later he went up to the podium at B.C. Place in Vancouver as number two in the NHL draft after Owen Nolan. He had an excellent season with the Seattle Thunderbirds in the WHL behind him. Keith Primeau, Mike Ricci and Jaromir Jagr were selected after him. For all of them, the doors to top professional hockey were opening. For Nedved, it was the beginning of a career full of plenty of shining moments but some ups and downs as well.

He was born on December 9, 1971, in Liberec, but his hockey development took place in Litvinov, where his father, Jaroslav, had played in the league for eight years. This town of only 30,000 inhabitants raised the most Czech players ever to go on and succeed in the NHL. Ivan Hlinka, Jiri Bubla, Petr Svoboda, Petr Klima, Vladimir Ruzicka, Robert Reichel, Jiri Slegr and others, including Petr Nedved, grew up there. Nedved, however, was the only one not to play for the local senior team.

When his dispute over a new contract with the Vancouver Canucks was being negotiated in the fall of 1993, he already had three NHL seasons behind him. At the same time, he got his Canadian citizenship and decided to play on the national team.

At the 1994 Olympics in Lillehammer, he and Paul Kariya were the bedrock of the team and they won a silver medal, which was more than any of his Czech contemporaries could boast at the time. "It was terrific, although we had been greatly disappointed by the defeat by the Swedes in the finals. When I heard the Canadian national anthem and knew that all the people back home were watching me, it felt a little strange. But I was proud that I could play for Canada. In the Czech Republic, no one knew much about me. This presented a great chance."

He finished the season in St. Louis and missed the Stanley Cup finals in 1994 while Vancouver was moving on. He then headed for the New York Rangers. However, he had problems with coach Colin Campbell, captain Mark Messier and his own expectations, and after one year he was traded to Pittsburgh.

In January 1988, Petr Nedved walked away from a group of Litvinov juniors in Calgary. He was only 17 and couldn't speak a word of English.

Nedved, Petr
C, 6´3˝, 195 lbs, b: Liberec, Czechoslovakia, 12/9/1971

Season	Club, League	Regular Season					Playoffs				
		GP	G	A	Pts	PLM	GP	G	A	Pts	PLM
1989–90	Seattle Thunderbirds, WHL	71	65	80	145	80	11	4	9	13	2
1990–91	Vancouver Canucks, NHL	61	10	6	16	20	6	0	1	1	0
1991–92	Vancouver Canucks, NHL	77	15	22	37	36	10	1	4	5	16
1992–93	Vancouver Canucks, NHL	84	38	33	71	96	12	2	3	5	2
1993–94	St. Louis Blues, NHL	19	6	14	20	8	4	0	1	1	4
OWG–94	Canada	8	5	1	6	6					
1994–95	New York Rangers, NHL	46	11	12	23	26	10	3	2	5	6
1995–96	Pittsburgh Penguins, NHL	80	45	54	99	68	18	10	10	20	16
WCup–96	Czech Republic	3	0	1	1	8					
1996–97	Pittsburgh Penguins, NHL	74	33	38	71	66	5	1	2	3	12
1997–98	Sparta, Czech Republic	5	2	3	5	8	6	0	2	2	52
	Las Vegas Thunder, IHL	3	3	3	6	4					
1998–99	Las Vegas Thunder, IHL	13	8	10	18	32					
	New York Rangers, NHL	56	20	27	47	50					
1999–00	New York Rangers, NHL	76	24	44	68	40					
2000–01	New York Rangers, NHL	79	32	46	78	54					
2001–02	New York Rangers, NHL	78	21	25	46	36					
	Czech Republic Totals	5	2	3	5	8	6	0	2	2	52
	NHL Totals	730	255	321	576	500					
	OWG/WCup Totals	11	5	2	7	14					

Offensive hockey always suited him because he could make use of his strong skating ability and his broad perspective of the game, talents very much suited to the Penguins. The greater freedom was good for Nedved. He spent a great season, 1995–96, with the Penguins, scoring 45 goals and collecting 99 points. In the 80th minute of overtime in a conference quarterfinals game against Washington, he settled the outcome of one of the longest games in NHL history.

As a foreigner, he wasn't allowed to play for the Czech Republic in any of the competitions organized by the International Ice Hockey Federation. But this didn't apply to the World Cup of Hockey, which fell under the rule of the NHL. The Czechs failed miserably. They didn't even progress beyond their group. Much was said about the negative influence of stars such as Nedved, as neither the coach, Ludek Bukac, nor some of the other players got along with him. "It wasn't true that there was conflict. We just didn't play well, at least if I may speak for myself."

Due to another contract dispute, this time with Pittsburg, Nedved didn't play in the NHL for over a year. He opened his 1997–98 season with Sparta Prague, where he also met his older brother, defenseman Jaroslav Nedved. His stay in the Czech Extraleague, however, was limited to four games. When the NHL started its season, the rules didn't allow him to play in other high-level competition. He watched the Nagano "tournament of the century"—where the Czechs won the gold—purely as a spectator. "It bugged me that I couldn't play, but what could I do? I was happy for the guys and their great success."

Offensive hockey always suited Petr Nedved (left) because he could use his strong skating and broad perspective of the game.

In the 1993 playoffs, Vancouver encountered the Los Angeles Kings, who at the time were led by Wayne Gretzky. After being eliminated, Nedved approached his greatest idol to get a hockey stick and the media turned it into big news. At the time, however, the lanky center had no way of knowing that he would eventually be on the same team with number 99 during his last season. Once again the New York Rangers lent a helping hand.

Nedved returned to Manhattan at the end of November 1998. In spite of the long layoff, he did well, maybe because coach John Muckler placed him at the center of the team's offense, which suited Nedved the best. The next year, Muckler created a Czech lineup featuring Nedved, Jan Hlavac and Radek Dvorak, who had come from Florida. "It was a very good move. Each of us is different, but we can think and foresee equally well. When we do well, we can at least repay the Rangers for the trust they placed in us."

Unfortunately for Nedved and the Rangers, they have missed the playoffs in each of his four years with the club through the 2001–02 season. A concern for the Rangers was Nedved's more than 30-point dropoff from the year before.

Alexei Kovalev

In the theatrical arts, there is a term for an "actor's magic." This magic is difficult to develop. You either have it or you don't. If you manage to capture the audience's attention and hold it until the end of the play in your first appearance on the stage, you possess this gift. A charming fellow, Alexei Kovalev is one of the few hockey players with actor's magic. His superb technique on the ice, his

masterful stickhandling and feinting and his excellent skating have helped Kovalev become a favorite with fans from the day he stepped on the ice. And these talents served him in New York and Pittsburgh just as well as in Moscow and Togliatti.

It was two decades ago, in the small city of Togliatti—which grew up around an auto plant—that Alexei embarked on a career in sports. But oddly enough, the Togliatti fans had to wait until the NHL lockout in 1994 to catch a glimpse of the unusual talents of their fellow townsman. As a forward under contract with the New York Rangers, Kovalev played for Lada—one of the leading Russian teams at the time—in several games against teams in the European International Hockey League. Interestingly, Kovalev's father was one of the Lada managers.

In 1989, at the age of 16, Kovalev was included on the first string of a top-rated Soviet club, Dynamo Moscow. In that year, the mass exodus of Soviet hockey players hadn't yet begun. Even though he stood out among his teammates for his superb skating and original stickhandling technique, Kovalev didn't call the shots. "I immediately recognized that he was a talented player," declared Dynamo coach Vladimir Yurzinov several years later. "Proud and purposeful of mind, Kovalev was really avid for workouts and games."

In the Dynamo Moscow lineup, Kovalev flew across the Atlantic to participate in a number of exhibition games a year later. As Yurzinov admitted later, he took Kovalev on that tour in order to give him a chance to see the best of modern hockey with his own eyes and to size up his future opponents. But Kovalev wanted to play and became offended if the coach failed to include him on the playing list for a game.

At first, the eminent coach Mike Keenan—followed by his pupil and successor in the post of New York Rangers head coach, Colin Campbell—tried to restrain Kovalev's individualistic impulses while on the ice and get the young player to play strictly according to his position. But sticking to his guns and remaining true to his style of play was nothing new to Kovalev. Even as a 14-year-old, Kovalev had precipitated a conflict with the coach of the Lada junior team in his home town of Togliatti, who also attempted to convince him to stick to prescribed form on the ice. Because of that, Kovalev decided to quit the team, and set out for Moscow in search of "hockey truth."

Kovalev was grateful to Yurzinov for his lessons in game strategy and for the limited amount of freedom the coach did allow him within the constraints of the play. To his credit, Kovalev withstood the pressure from his coaches and didn't change his style. Just over a year later, he was playing such a stylish game of hockey that he attracted attention and was offered his first serious position. Keenan actually placed Kovalev on

In 1989, at the age of 16, Alexei Kovalev was put on the first string of a top-rated Soviet club, Dynamo Moscow.

Kovalev, Alexei
RW, 6´, 210 lbs, b: Togliatti, USSR, 2/24/1973

Season	Club, League	Regular Season					Playoffs				
		GP	G	A	Pts	PIM	GP	G	A	Pts	PIM
1989–90	Dynamo Moscow, USSR	1	0	0	0	0					
1990–91	Dynamo Moscow, USSR	18	1	2	3	4					
1991–92	Dynamo Moscow, Russia	33	16	9	25	20					
OWG–92	Russia	8	1	2	3	14					
WC–92	Russia	6	0	1	1	0					
1992–93	New York Rangers, NHL	65	20	18	38	17					
	Binghamton Rangers, AHL	13	13	11	24	35	9	3	5	8	14
1993–94	New York Rangers, NHL	76	23	33	56	154	23	9	12	21	18
1994–95	Lada Togliatti, Russia	12	8	8	16	49					
	New York Rangers, NHL	48	13	15	28	30	10	4	7	11	10
1995–96	New York Rangers, NHL	81	24	34	58	98	11	3	4	7	14
WCup–96	Russia	5	2	1	3	8					
1996–97	New York Rangers, NHL	45	13	22	35	42					
1997–98	New York Rangers, NHL	73	23	30	53	44					
OWG–98	Russia	6	5	2	7	14					
1998–99	New York Rangers, NHL	14	3	4	7	12					
	Pittsburgh Penguins, NHL	63	20	26	46	37	10	5	7	12	14
1999–00	Pittsburgh Penguins, NHL	82	26	40	66	94	11	1	5	6	10
2000–01	Pittsburgh Penguins, NHL	79	44	51	95	96					
2001–02	Pittsburgh Penguins, NHL	67	32	44	76	80					
OWG–02	Russia	6	3	1	4	4					
	USSR/Russia Totals	64	25	19	44	73					
	NHL Totals	693	241	317	558	766					
	OWG/WC/WCup Totals	31	11	7	18	40					

Won OWG (1992)
Won Stanley Cup (1994)
USSR/Russia Champion (1990, 1991, 1992)

the first forward line with the team's top offensive talent. The Kovalev–Mark Messier–Adam Graves line determined the outcome of the battle for the Stanley Cup in the spring of 1994. To top it off, Messier became a top scorer in the league during the playoffs.

"I would place this player in the same row with Lemieux and Gretzky," declared the Rangers' captain and acknowledged leader of the team, Mark Messier, of Kovalev. "He is an unusually talented player. If Kovalev adds to his ability, he will have no equals in the world."

With Keenan, one of the toughest coaches in the NHL, Kovalev was able to accomplish that. Many Europeans in the NHL had trouble adjusting to the different style of play after being pressured to give up their own style. Just a little over 20, Kovalev, with his fighting spirit and winning style, had conquered New York. With his peculiar stickhandling and masterly skating, his ability to set up his partners in scoring positions and his powerful shots on goal, he garnered a lot of attention in his new homeland. Over the years, fans began showing up for games in Madison Square Garden wearing hockey jerseys with the number 27 and Kovalev's name stamped on the back.

With the Pittsburgh Penguins, which he joined in 1998, Kovalev was allowed to continue his own style of play and immediately became one of the leaders of the team.

In 2000–01, he produced his finest offensive season, scoring 44 goals and 95 points in 79 games, but in 2001–02, the injury bug hit Kovalev and many of his Penguin teammates, including Mario Lemieux, who missed most of the season with a hip injury. The disjointed season resulted in the Pens missing the Stanley Cup playoffs. In February, Kovalev earned a bronze medal with Russia at the 2002 Salt Lake City Olympics.

"I would place Alexei Kovalev (front) in the same row with Lemieux and Gretzky," declared Mark Messier. "He is an unusually talented player."

Janne Laukkanen

Janne Laukkanen was born and raised in Lahti, Finland, where the number one sport is Nordic skiing in all its various forms, from jumping to gliding cross-country through the forest. It wasn't until he left Lahti and the Reipas hockey club behind him that he started to make an impact in Finland.

At the junior level, he was already established as a star and as such played on the various national teams. In his first major tournament, the under-18 European Championship in 1988, he won a silver medal. But the beginning of bigger and better things came in the summer of 1991, when Laukkanen was snapped up by the HPK Hameenlinna club. The Hockey Playing Knights, known as HPK on their crest, changed their strategy during the summer. Instead of going for established players, they picked three up-and-coming stars in Laukkanen, Juha Ylonen—also in the NHL now with the Phoenix Coyotes—and Jarkko Varvio, who tried a couple of seasons with the Dallas Stars before returning to Europe.

It was his first hockey club's financial troubles that led Laukkanen to leave his home town in search of greener pastures. The coach in Lahti, Matti Hagman, put his friend and players' representative Matti Vaisanen to work on the project, and he came up with HPK Hameenlinna. During his three seasons with HPK, the young blueliner was given a lot of responsibility and more ice time than ever. Laukkanen is still very pleased with the move to HPK. He says: "It was easy to go there, and I was very well received by both the management and the players, and it also helped that many of the players were in my age group. At one stage I was even allowed to be the team captain."

Janne Laukkanen (right) won a silver medal in his first major tournament, the under-18 European Junior Championship, in 1988.

Janne Laukkanen (right) began to establish himself as a bona fide NHLer with Ottawa in his third season and hasn't looked back.

Laukkanen is always looking for plenty of ice time. He feels that it is the best way to develop and he admits that the years in Hameenlinna were his springboard into the NHL. As springboards and stepping stones go, an even bigger opportunity came along when national team coach Pentti Matikainen added him to the Finland roster for the 1991 Canada Cup tournament. He was more than surprised by this honor, and the event left him with lasting memories. "Our confidence got a real boost from tying Canada 2–2 in the opening game on our way to claiming third place in this prestigious event."

In the spring of 1992 he played twice for Finland, first in the Winter Olympics in Albertville, France, and then in the World Championship in the former Czechoslovakia. In an era in Finnish hockey known for reaching milestones, a new one was passed in the finals at Prague. Finland had played an excellent tournament leading up to the semifinals, where they went all the way to penalty shots and managed to defeat the Czechs. With a historic first-ever medal at the World Championship level already in the bag, they advanced to the finals. There the price of gold was too high and the Swedes too good. Sweden had no trouble overcoming Finland with a 5–2 victory.

In their next World Championship, the Finns and Laukkanen made the finals once again with an even more impressive showing. At the end of regulation time, the score was 1–1 on an assist by Laukkanen. But when it came down to the crunch, Canada picked the longest straw and the game was decided once again with penalty shots. The current coach of the Finnish national team thought enough of Laukkanen to add him to the roster for the final game of the 1998 World Championship, where he helped Finland pick up a silver medal.

Even in the summer of 1991, as Laukkanen was about to join HPK, he was a Quebec Nordiques eighth-round draft pick. In the fall of 1994 he finally joined the Nords but played the bulk of his games with Cornwall in the AHL. In his second season, he moved with the team to Colorado and then the Ottawa Senators, but again most of the season was spent in Cornwall. In his third season, in Ottawa, he began to establish himself as a bona fide NHLer and he hasn't looked back. Towards the end of the 1999–2000 season, he moved to his fourth NHL club, the Pittsburgh Penguins. Joining Jaromir Jagr and Co. may prove to be his best move yet.

Laukkanen was a member of Team Finland at the 2002 Olympics, but the team failed to win a medal, being eliminated in the quarterfinals by Canada.

Laukkanen, Janne
D, 6´, 180 lbs, b: Lahti, Finland, 3/19/1970

Season	Club, League	Regular Season					Playoffs				
		GP	G	A	Pts	PIM	GP	G	A	Pts	PIM
1989–90	Ilves, Finland	39	5	6	11	10					
1990–91	Reipas, Finland	44	8	14	22	56					
CCup–91	Finland	6	1	2	3	2					
1991–92	HPK, Finland	43	5	14	19	62					
OWG–92	Finland	8	0	1	1	6					
WC–92	Finland	8	2	2	4	12					
1992–93	HPK, Finland	47	8	21	29	76	12	1	4	5	10
WC–93	Finland	6	1	0	1	10					
1993–94	HPK, Finland	48	5	24	29	46					
OWG–94	Finland	8	0	2	2	12					
WC–94	Finland	8	0	3	3	6					
1994–95	Cornwall Aces, AHL	55	8	26	34	41					
	Quebec Nordiques, NHL	11	0	3	3	4	6	1	0	1	2
1995–96	Colorado Avalanche, NHL	3	1	0	1	0					
	Cornwall Aces, AHL	35	7	20	27	60					
	Ottawa Senators, NHL	20	0	2	2	14					
WCup–96	Finland	4	0	0	0	4					
1996–97	Ottawa Senators, NHL	76	3	18	21	76	7	0	1	1	6
1997–98	Ottawa Senators, NHL	60	4	17	21	64	11	2	2	4	8
OWG–98	Finland	6	0	0	0	4					
1998–99	Ottawa Senators, NHL	50	1	11	12	40	4	0	0	0	4
1999–00	Ottawa Senators, NHL	60	1	11	12	55					
	Pittsburgh Penguins, NHL	11	1	7	8	12	11	2	4	6	10
2000–01	Pittsburgh Penguins, NHL	50	3	17	20	34	18	2	2	4	14
2001–02	Pittsburgh Penguins, NHL	47	6	7	13	28					
	Finland Totals	221	31	79	110	250	12	1	4	5	10
	NHL Totals	388	20	93	113	327	57	7	9	16	44
	OWG/WC/CCup/WCup Totals	54	4	10	14	56					

Robert Svehla

In establishing a career as a hockey player, Robert Svehla is the classic self-made man. He became a star almost overnight, even though for quite some time his potential was overlooked. His fate inspired many followers, such as Czech defenseman and later teammate Jaroslav Spacek, who made it into the NHL in a similar manner after Svehla.

For Svehla, the decisive break came in the 1991–92 season. It was his first time to play on Czechoslovakia's national team. With them he won the bronze at the Albertville Olympics and later at the World Championship, where he was named best defenseman. With the Dukla Trencin club he took the championship title, and at the end of the season he won the Golden Stick Award as the top player in the country. From there his career took off.

He wasn't necessarily unknown before, and after leaving his native town of Martin, Slovakia, his road to the top wasn't all smooth. It was just that his success came all at once. Back in 1987, he'd won silver in the European Junior Championship. However, as soon as he arrived in nearby Trencin, he immediately became a fixture on the back lines of his team. Only in his third season, playing next to Milos Holan and with the highly productive offense of Zigmund Palffy, Robert Petrovicky and Branislav Janos, did he draw attention to himself with some pretty high numbers. During 51 games in 1991–92, Svehla scored 23 goals and ended up with 51 points for the season. Trencin had a successful season mainly due to its hard-hitting offense, but it was too early to celebrate. The game of hockey was played in a very different style on international ice. To coaches of the day, Svehla seemed to be the most versatile player. With time, he could mature into a Milos Holan or a Zigmund Palffy.

In the summer of 1992, Svehla was drafted by the Calgary Flames. However, he didn't get the contract he desired, so he decided to stay in Europe, where he could already pick and choose from offers that others could only dream of. The freshly crowned Swedish champions, the Malmo IF club, won him over. "They played a more defensive hockey than we did back at home. At least I learned to be better at defense."

Svehla stayed in Malmo for three years. He was one of their most productive defensemen and at the same time had an average of 99 penalty minutes per season, with 127 in 1993–94. Although he hadn't played a single match in the NHL, the Calgary Flames in the meantime traded him to Florida together with Swede Magnus Svensson. Toward the end of the 1994–95 season, he managed to play five

Robert Svehla became a star almost overnight.

Svehla, Robert										
D, 6´1″, 190 lbs, b: Martin, Czechoslovakia, 1/2/1969										
Season	Club, League	Regular Season					Playoffs			
		GP	G	A	Pts	PIM	GP	G	A	Pts	PIM
1989–90	Dukla Trencin, Czechoslovakia	29	4	3	7	42				
1990–91	Dukla Trencin, Czechoslovakia	52	16	9	25	62				
1991–92	Dukla Trencin, Czechoslovakia	51	23	28	51	74				
OWG–92	Czechoslovakia	8	2	1	3	8				
WC–92	Czechoslovakia	8	4	4	8	14				
1992–93	Malmo, Sweden	40	19	10	29	86	6	0	1	1	14
1993–94	Malmo, Sweden	37	14	25	39	127	10	5	1	6	23
OWG–94	Slovakia	8	2	4	6	26				
1994–95	Malmo, Sweden	32	11	13	24	83	9	2	3	5	6
	Florida Panthers, NHL	5	1	1	2	0				
WC(B)–95	Slovakia	4	0	6	6	10				
1995–96	Florida Panthers, NHL	81	8	49	57	94	22	0	6	6	32
WCup–96	Slovakia	3	0	3	3	4				
1996–97	Florida Panthers, NHL	82	13	32	45	86	5	1	4	5	4
1997–98	Florida Panthers, NHL	79	9	34	43	113				
OWG–98	Slovakia	2	0	1	1	0				
WC–98	Slovakia	6	1	1	2	14				
1998–99	Florida Panthers, NHL	80	8	29	37	83				
1999–00	Florida Panthers, NHL	82	9	40	49	64	4	0	1	1	4
2000–01	Florida Panthers, NHL	82	6	22	28	76				
2001–02	Florida Panthers, NHL	82	7	22	29	87				
	Czechoslovakia/Slovakia Totals	132	43	40	83	178				
	NHL Totals	573	61	229	290	603				
	OWG/WC/WCup Totals	39	9	20	29	76				

Named Best Defenseman at WC (1992)
Czechoslovakia Champion (1991, 1992)

Former Florida coach Doug MacLean called Robert Svehla the toughest player to come through his hands in Svehla's three years with the Panthers.

games for the Panthers. No one could have imagined how quickly he would become their leading defenseman.

At the age of 25, he was still considered a rookie, but on the ice he didn't look at all like the typical nervous greenhorn. Instead, he became one of the team's workhorses. Former coach Doug MacLean called him the toughest player to come into his hands during his three years with the Panthers. Svehla could get respect in front of the net. As an experienced skater, he cleared space at the net and attacked near the boards just as strongly. But he wasn't getting about 30 minutes of ice time per game for those reasons alone. He brought the Panthers perspective and a talent for clever passing and hard shooting. "Even in the NHL, I try to play a typically European game," says Svehla. "That is—pass often, create. As soon as I get the puck, the first thing I try to do is find a free teammate."

In the spring of 1996 the Panthers quite unexpectedly progressed to the Stanley Cup finals. With 57 points, Svehla had an excellent season behind him. He also did quite well in the playoffs, where he and Terry Carkner allowed Mario Lemieux and Jaromir Jagr only two goals in the best-of-seven finals of the Eastern Conference against Pittsburgh.

Next season, Svehla scored a career-high 13 goals, collected 45 points and lined up for the NHL All-Star Game. But the Florida Panthers dropped out of the playoffs early and it became apparent that long breaks weren't good for Svehla. "Three months off is too much. When we lined up for the finals, it was no problem to get back into the game after a month. This time it took a while for me to find my usual frame of mind."

In the 1998–99 season, Svehla went through a crisis. His performance was up and down and he was struggling with his weight, but his entire team was going through a similar crisis. Gradually, however, his confidence returned and he was his former self again. "You constantly have to prove that you deserve your place on the team. Sometimes things go well, at other times they don't. Because I never got anything for free, I have learned to overcome difficult periods and prove that my spot belongs to me."

At 33, Svehla was selected to play for Slovakia at the Salt Lake City Olympics, but the team failed to advance to the main draw after a stunning loss to Germany in the qualifying round. Throughout the latter part of the 2001–02 season he made it known that he was losing interest in playing hockey in North America and would consider retiring in the off-season.

Alexei Zhitnik

At the end of the 1997–98 season, Alexei Zhitnik of the Buffalo Sabres won the team's Tim Horton Memorial Award for the "player whose performance is far superior to public recognition." It was a fitting tribute to a player who has developed a reputation as an anchor on the Sabres squad for solid, hard-working defense, a man who has matured quickly during his years in the NHL.

"He's been a workhorse for us," said Buffalo coach Lindy Ruff following a 3–1 Buffalo victory in 1997–98, one the team achieved despite playing with an injury-depleted roster. "We were down to five defenseman early in the game with an injury to Bob Boughner, and I knew I could play Alex every second shift. He's been great in both ends for us."

The Ukranian-born Zhitnik played for the Sokol club in his home town of Kiev in the Soviet league before joining the CSKA Moscow team in 1991–92. That season, he was a fourth-round pick (81st overall) of the Los Angeles Kings in the 1991 NHL Entry Draft, and he played for the gold medal-winning Unified Team at the Olympics in Albertville, France, in 1992.

Zhitnik played for L.A. for two full seasons before being traded partway through 1994–95 to Buffalo in a multi-player deal that saw him, Robb Stauber, Charlie Huddy and a fifth-round pick go to the Kings for Grant Fuhr, Philippe Boucher and Denis Tsygurov. Once in Buffalo, Zhitnik established himself as a defensive stalwart. But after playing there for two seasons, he started to pick up the pace on the offensive side of the ice as well. Overall, he developed into the kind of player the Sabres could count on to contribute wherever he was needed. "I try to keep things simple," said Zhitnik after the Sabres' undermanned win. "In the last couple of weeks, we've had some injuries and it's been important for me to play more defensively, play it safely. If I have an opportunity to jump up in the play and help the forwards, I will. But I've been trying to stay back more and protect our own end."

Alexei Zhitnik anchors the Sabres squad with solid, hard-working defense.

Although Buffalo has developed into a playoff contender of late, making it all the way to the Cup finals against Dallas in 1998–99, this hasn't been a club that has overpowered opponents with offense, relying instead on heroics between the pipes by all-World goalie Dominik Hasek. And that's why coach Ruff has come increasingly to value the offensive contributions of players like Zhitnik. "We'll take goals any way we can get them," Ruff says of his forwards. "It's not just our club; there are many teams in this league that have struggled scoring goals. In our case, we've had success with our defensemen joining the rush, and doing it on a consistent basis. It's added a great deal to our attack. Alex has really responded well for us. I think when you put a player in important situations all the time, you find out whether the guy can play in that situation, and he's proven that he can."

As a result, the Sabres went on a 13-game unbeaten streak (7–0–6) in early 1998, with Zhitnik a big part of the team's consistent success. Still, he was careful to put the streak in perspective. "It was really nice," he commented. "It was a pretty long unbeaten streak for everybody, but I think there was a little bit of pressure on everybody—win, win, win—we didn't want to lose. A couple of games before we finally lost to the Islanders, we weren't playing to win. We were playing not to lose. When you

Zhitnik, Alexei
D, 5'11", 204 lbs, b: Kiev, USSR, 10/10/1972

Season	Club, League	Regular Season					Playoffs				
		GP	G	A	Pts	PIM	GP	G	A	Pts	PIM
1989–90	Sokol, USSR	31	3	4	7	16					
1990–91	Sokol, USSR	46	1	4	5	46					
CCup–91	USSR	5	0	0	0	4					
1991–92	CSKA, Russia	44	2	7	9	52					
OWG–92	Russia	8	1	0	1	0					
WC–92	Russia	6	0	2	2	6					
1992–93	Los Angeles Kings, NHL	78	12	36	48	80	24	3	9	12	26
1993–94	Los Angeles Kings, NHL	81	12	40	52	101					
WC–94	Russia	6	1	0	1	8					
1994–95	Los Angeles Kings, NHL	11	2	5	7	27					
	Buffalo Sabres, NHL	21	2	5	7	34	5	0	1	1	14
1995–96	Buffalo Sabres, NHL	80	6	30	36	58					
WC–96	Russia	8	1	1	2	6					
WCup–96	Russia	3	0	1	1	2					
1996–97	Buffalo Sabres, NHL	80	7	28	35	95	12	1	0	1	16
1997–98	Buffalo Sabres, NHL	78	15	30	45	102	15	0	3	3	36
OWG–98	Russia	6	0	2	2	2					
1998–99	Buffalo Sabres, NHL	81	7	26	33	96	21	4	11	15	52
1999–00	Buffalo Sabres, NHL	74	2	11	13	95	4	0	0	0	8
WC–2000	Russia	6	0	1	1	2					
2000–01	Buffalo Sabres, NHL	78	8	29	37	75	13	1	6	7	12
2001–02	Buffalo Sabres, NHL	82	1	33	34	80					
	USSR/Russia Totals	121	6	15	21	114					
	NHL Totals	744	74	273	347	843	94	9	30	39	164
	OWG/WC/CCup/WCup Totals	48	3	7	10	30					

Named Best Defenseman at WC (1996)
Won OWG (1992)

Alexei Zhitnik (left) developed into the kind of player Buffalo could count on to contribute wherever he was needed.

play not to lose, it makes it pretty tough. Now we just try to play the hockey we know we can play and good things happen."

He added that he'd had some experience on teams trying to do more than just recording the "W" night after night. "When I played in L.A. we went through it," said Zhitnik. "Wayne Gretzky was trying to set a goal-scoring record, and he didn't score for 20 games. Something like that, there's a lot of pressure on everyone. I prefer just to play hockey and have fun. I'm playing a lot. I'm getting a lot of ice time, I feel good. I try to make good plays and help the team. Sometimes I don't need to skate 100 or 200 feet to help the team, I just try to play smart hockey."

But for all his hard work and determination, Zhitnik almost never made it onto the ice that season—at least not in a Sabres uniform. He was embroiled in a highly publicized contract dispute over the summer and fall of 1997 and missed the first four games of 1997–98 because of the tense negotiations. But he eventually signed a one-year, $1.5-million contract at the start of the season. In the off-season before 1998–99, he was in another war with the Sabres top brass, missing all of training camp before signing a $2.5-million deal for two years, plus bonuses that had the potential to add considerably more.

"It feels good to be back playing." Zhitnik said when the 1997 holdout was finished, after a long time away from serious hockey. "I just want a chance to do my best to help the team. It's been a long time since I played—I hadn't played hockey in five months, it's a long time. Now the pressure with the contract is off. I've played with most of these guys for two years and I'm glad to be back. It feels great."

And he contributed immediately, leading the team, especially on the power-play. "I knew Alexei would make a difference," said coach Ruff, "but I honestly didn't think it would be such a big difference so quickly. Obviously Alexei helps us by giving us a lot of speed coming out of our end. When you have the type of skating skills that Alex has, you can make an immediate impact. He may not be in full game shape, but that transition to game action is easier for a player of his caliber."

Still, the modest Zhitnik was quick to put a lot of the credit on his teammates. "It takes all five guys," he said. "It takes everyone working hard and playing their positions for a power-play to work."

The 2001–02 season marked the seventh full season Zhitnik spent in Buffalo and it was not an easy one. The loss of Michael Peca and Dominik Hasek proved too great for the Sabres, who failed to make the Stanley Cup playoffs just three short years after advancing to the finals.

Zhitnik was also on the bronze medal–winning Russian team at the 2002 Olympics.

Teemu Selanne

Teemu Selanne is both a hockey player and a celebrity in his home country of Finland. Outside the world of hockey, he does double duty in early childhood education, which has led to his becoming a figurehead for a children's hospital charity. Selanne initiated a trend in Finland. Many celebrities in the country now associate themselves with one charity or another, of which the children's hospital is still the biggest.

Selanne doesn't come from a family of athletes—his achievements in hockey are all his own doing. His father, Ilmar, hails from Savonlinna and Teemu was born when the family moved to Helsinki. When they moved to Rauma, Teemu played hockey for the local Lukko club. Eventually the family got a better apartment in Espoo, where from the age of 10 Selanne was considered a special talent mainly because of the determination he displayed in the three team sports he took up. He played hockey for EJK Espoo, later known as EPS Espoo, bandy for Botnia Helsinki and soccer for Honka Espoo.

Early on, he was overlooked due to his small stature and missed out on invitations to camp with the national junior

When Teemu Selanne (right) scored a record of 76 goals as a rookie—and eclipsed Mike Bossy's old mark by 23—he set a new plateau in this category.

soccer team despite being his team's most prolific goal scorer. All the same, his small size helped him become more competitive and hone his skills, which in the end made him a star. He was 16 years old before he finally began to fill out. But when he was 14, his parents took a gamble that paid off. His twin brother, Paavo, a field hockey star and national team goalie, choose to continue his education. Teemu, on the other hand, was given free rein to follow a career in sports at the expense of his schooling, which was what he wanted. His next move was joining Jokerit Helsinki as a Junior C player.

In Finland, Selanne has become synonymous with Jokerit. His crowning effort for the club as a junior was leading his team to the national title during the 1987–88 season. That year he was the top overall scorer in both the regular season and the playoffs. The pro level of the team was less fortunate and was relegated to Division 1. The next season, as an 18-year-old, was one of his hardest. He completed his military service and at the same time played in 111 games, amassing 131 points that included 73 goals while representing the Jokerit Junior A team, the Army Junior As, the under-20 national team, the senior national team and, to boot, helping Jokerit regain their place in the SM-Liiga. Jokerit defeated Karpat Oulu in the qualifying round, with Selanne as the top scorer. That season was a portent of things to come in the NHL, where a similar number of games are played, and Selanne passed with flying colors. However, his first season in the top league lasted only 11 games.

On October 19, a game against JyP HT Jyvaskyla ended in a tie. Fifty-six seconds into overtime, a harmless looking brush with another player resulted in a serious injury. Selanne was taken to hospital in an ambulance. The diagnosis wasn't good—his shank and calf bones were broken. On top of that, the season was his last to qualify for the World Junior Championships. With the tournament due to be staged in Finland and Selanne appearing on posters and on the cover of the media guide, big things were expected of him and his team.

In the end, without its leader, Finland finished sixth. Two years later, things were on course again as Jokerit won its third national championship with Selanne as the motivating force and the top scorer in the playoffs. That season also marked the end for Selanne in the Finnish league when the Winnipeg Jets of the NHL signed him up, though he did return for one more triumph with Jokerit during the NHL lockout. He and Jari Kurri led the Helsinki club to the coveted European Championship and Selanne helped Jokerit end the season in second place.

The Winnipeg Jets drafted him in the first round in 1988 and he joined the club four years later. He played for the Jets for three and a half seasons until they traded him to the Mighty Ducks of Anaheim for Russian defender Oleg Tverdovsky. In 1992-93, "the Finnish Flash" had an incredible rookie season. He won the Calder Trophy as rookie of the year hands down—leading all other rookies in goals, in power-play goals, in game-winning goals and in total points. His record 76 goals set a new plateau in this category for rookies, eclipsing the old mark set by Mike Bossy by 23 goals. The runner-up in goals among rookies with 41 was Eric Lindros, aptly named "the Next One," but he was completely overshadowed in what was supposed to be his year. Selanne also set a new record for points in a rookie season with 132, passing Peter Stastny and his 109 total to make hockey history. *The Hockey News* and *The Sporting News* also named him rookie of the year. Maybe his greatest achievement was his selection in his very first season to the league's First All-Star Team. In his sophomore season, however, he severed his Achilles tendon and missed the remainder of the season after January 6.

The third season was decimated by the lockout and Selanne placed 19th in the scoring race. He again surpassed the 100-point mark in the next two years, but in the two after that he was for the second and third time the top goal scorer in the league. The last of these also saw a new trophy named after Maurice "Rocket" Richard established for the goal-scoring leader and Selanne became its first recipient. He has played in the All-Star Game seven times—every season he spent in the NHL except for 1995, when there was no All-Star Game. He has 12 awards to date in the Finnish league. His first two full seasons in the SM-Liiga were bumper years as well, with a total of seven awards.

Teemu loves fast cars. He has quite a collection of them on both sides of the Atlantic. One of his cars in Anaheim is a 1968 Corvette. While in Finland during the summers, he competes in car rallies. His hockey club pretends to look the other way in order to keep their star happy. However, a mishap during the summer of 1999 may have spelled an end to his sideline. While practising for the Finnish rally, he met some friends—the president of the Finnish federation, Kalervo Kummola, and ex-NHL player Raimo Helminen—during a break in the session. As his friends were leaving, Selanne set off again at full speed. He turned back over the same stretch and momentarily forgot that they were coming the other way. By the time he spotted Kummola's car, it was too late to avoid a collision. Helminen, who was in the back seat, suffered minor injuries, but Kummola broke his ankle. The airbag prevented more extensive

Selanne, Teemu
RW, 6´, 200 lbs, b: Helsinki, Finland, 7/3/1970

Season	Club, League	Regular Season					Playoffs				
		GP	G	A	Pts	PIM	GP	G	A	Pts	PIM
1989–90	Jokerit, Finland	11	4	8	12	0					
1990–91	Jokerit, Finland	42	33	25	58	12					
WEC–91	Finland	10	6	5	11	2					
CCup–91	Finland	6	1	1	2	2					
1991–92	Jokerit, Finland	44	39	23	62	20	10	10	7	17	18
OWG–92	Finland	8	7	4	11	6					
1992–93	Winnipeg Jets, NHL	84	76	56	132	45	6	4	2	6	2
1993–94	Winnipeg Jets, NHL	51	25	29	54	22					
1994–95	Jokerit, Finland	20	7	12	19	6					
	Winnipeg Jets, NHL	45	22	26	48	2					
1995–96	Winnipeg Jets, NHL	51	24	48	72	18					
	Anaheim Mighty Ducks, NHL	28	16	20	36	4					
WC–96	Finland	6	5	3	8	0					
WCup–96	Finland	4	3	2	5	0					
1996–97	Anaheim Mighty Ducks, NHL	78	51	58	109	34	11	7	3	10	4
1997–98	Anaheim Mighty Ducks, NHL	73	52	34	86	30					
OWG–98	Finland	5	4	6	10	8					
1998–99	Anaheim Mighty Ducks, NHL	75	47	60	107	30	4	2	2	4	2
WC–99	Finland	11	3	8	11	2					
1999–00	Anaheim Mighty Ducks, NHL	79	33	52	85	12					
2000–01	Anaheim Mighty Ducks, NHL	61	26	33	59	36					
	San Jose Sharks, NHL	12	7	6	13	0	6	0	2	2	2
2001–02	San Jose Sharks, NHL	82	29	25	54	40					
OWG–02	Finland	4	3	0	3	4					
	Finland Totals	117	83	68	151	38	10	10	7	17	18
	NHL Totals	719	408	447	855	273					
	OWG/WEC/WC/CCup/WCup Totals	54	32	29	61	58					

NHL First All-Star Team (1993, 1997)
NHL Second All-Star Team (1998, 1999)
Won Calder Trophy (1993)
Won Maurice Richard Trophy (1999)
Finland Champion (1992)

*Teemu Selänne
(front).*

A HISTORY OF WORLD HOCKEY

In 1998–99, Teemu Selanne (number 8) became the first recipient of a new trophy named after Maurice "Rocket" Richard for the top regular-season goal scorer.

damage. Kummola didn't sue his friend, but six months later the local prosecutor decided to charge Selanne with dangerous driving. The trial is still in process. If the charges are upheld, it could cost Selanne—who already has several speeding offenses on record—well over $200,000.

Internationally, Selanne is still without a title. In his first time out with the under-18 team, he got a silver medal. At the senior level, he went home empty-handed from his first five tournaments. In the 1998 Olympics at Nagano, Japan, he was on the now famous team that defeated Canada in the bronze medal game. At the World Championship in 1998, he earned a silver medal. That year saw both of Finland's biggest stars—Selanne and Saku Koivu—on the roster. In the two-game final series versus the Czech Republic, Selanne gave everything he had. He assisted on Juha Lind's goal in a 3–1 win in the first game. He also had an assist in the second game, which Finland lost 4–1. The series was decided at 16:32 in overtime, when Jan Hlavac scored for the Czechs. Selanne, whose speed and explosive acceleration hadn't carried the day, was extremely disappointed. It was no consolation that in the post-game ceremonies he was named the tournament MVP and selected by the media to the All-Star team.

In 2000–01, the Ducks traded Selanne to San Jose. He finished the year with 13 points in 12 games with the Sharks and promised more significant achievements with the young and talented team in the coming season. In his first full season with the Sharks, Selanne teamed up with the likes of Owen Nolan and Mike Ricci to provide the offensive firepower for the team. The 31-year-old veteran also surpassed the 400-goal plateau late in the year. In adddition, Selanne and his Finnish teammates had high hopes of finishing in medal contention at the Olympics in Salt Lake City, but a loss to Canada in the quarterfinals put an end to those dreams.

Selanne is very popular in Finland and his advertising value is first rate. For that reason, he is the only athlete to publish a newsletter several times a year. His publication is entitled *Flash Mail* and serves among other things to promote his hockey school, where all the instructors are past or present Jokerit players.

Mats Sundin

There actually is a Canadian-based Web site dedicated to "the Nordic god of hockey" and there is also "the Mats Sundin worship page." Maybe that says something about Mats Sundin's greatness in Toronto, a city where "hockey crazed" is an understatement for dedication to a way of life.

Mats Sundin has gone on to become an ambassador for Swedish sport, unarguably one of the most popular Swedish sportsmen ever. But there was a time when Mats Sundin was banned from Swedish hockey. There was even a time when controversial Swedish Ice Hockey Association boss Rickard Fagerlund promised he'd see to it that Mats Sundin never again played in a blue and yellow jersey.

That was a decade and three World Championships ago. In 1991 in Helsinki, in 1992 in Prague and in 1998 in Zurich, Sundin led the proud Tre Kronor to gold medals in competition with the best the world could offer.

After winning the Swedish title with Djurgarden and competing successfully with Tre Kronor in the Bern World Championship, Sundin left for North America without further notice in the summer of 1990. At that point, he had become one of the all-time greats in Swedish hockey. Only two players besides Sundin have won three World Championships, Jonas Bergqvist of Leksand and the legendary Sven Tumba, a 1950s and 1960s star with Sundin's Djurgarden.

It was with Djurgarden that Sundin developed as a hockey player and recorded his first achievements. Born on February 13, 1971, in Bromma, outside Stockholm, the 15-year-old super-talent in 1986 led his Stockholm team to the national youth trophy on *TV-Pukken*, the first in a long series of trophies in a cabinet that has not yet seen the Stanley Cup.

The Nordic god of hockey, Mats Sundin.

"I was an all-around sportsman up until the age of 15," Sundin says. "I think it's good, developing with different sports before deciding to go in for one, as I did with hockey."

Mats Sundin and countryman Peter Forsberg are currently two of the dominant players on the world hockey stage. Since a very quick decision made when Sweden needed reinforcements for the 1991 championship team, Fagerlund has had no reason to regret his decision to let Sundin back into Swedish hockey. It was only a year earlier that the 19-year-old Sundin had "defected" from Djurgarden to try his luck with the Quebec Nordiques, the team that in 1989 chose Sundin as their first pick. Sundin became the first European ever to be chosen first overall in a draft.

Sundin left Sweden under a barrage of fire and slander from various hockey personalities. His decision was hard to fathom. But passions cooled and Mats Sundin was invited to return home in time to play with the national team in Ebo and Helsinki. Sundin was an instant smash hit when he single-handedly won the trophy for Sweden by scoring the most important goals of the tournament. He scored three goals in the game against archrival Finland (4–4) and then the decisive goal against Russia (2–1) in the finals. In all, he registered seven goals in the tournament.

He put in the same kind of performance in Prague in 1992. Accompanied by a team with 17 rookies—among them Peter Forsberg, then a 17-year-old hockey wunderkind from MoDo—Sundin played at his best. He scored a very important goal in the 2–0 game against Russia that propelled Sweden into the final game against Finland. Sweden won 5–2, securing its second World Championship trophy in two years.

Sundin, Mats
C/RW, 6′4″, 215 lbs, b: Bromma, Sweden, 2/13/1971

Season	Club, League	Regular Season					Playoffs				
		GP	G	A	Pts	PIM	GP	G	A	Pts	PIM
1989–90	Djurgarden, Sweden	34	10	8	18	16	8	7	0	7	4
WEC–90	Sweden	4	0	0	0	0					
1990–91	Quebec Nordiques, NHL	80	23	36	59	58					
WEC–91	Sweden	10	7	5	12	12					
CCup–91	Sweden	6	2	4	6	16					
1991–92	Quebec Nordiques, NHL	80	33	43	76	103					
WC–92	Sweden	8	2	6	8	8					
1992–93	Quebec Nordiques, NHL	80	47	67	114	96	6	3	1	4	6
1993–94	Quebec Nordiques, NHL	84	32	53	85	60					
WC–94	Sweden	8	5	9	14	4					
1994–95	Djurgarden, Sweden	12	7	2	9	14					
	Toronto Maple Leafs, NHL	47	23	24	47	14	7	5	4	9	4
1995–96	Toronto Maple Leafs, NHL	76	33	50	83	46	6	3	1	4	4
WCup–96	Sweden	4	4	3	7	4					
1996–97	Toronto Maple Leafs, NHL	82	41	53	94	59					
1997–98	Toronto Maple Leafs, NHL	82	33	41	74	49					
OWG–98	Sweden	4	3	0	3	4					
WC–98	Sweden	10	5	6	11	6					
1998–99	Toronto Maple Leafs, NHL	82	31	52	83	58	17	8	8	16	16
1999–00	Toronto Maple Leafs, NHL	73	32	41	73	46	12	3	5	8	10
2000–01	Toronto Maple Leafs, NHL	82	28	46	74	76	11	6	7	13	14
2001–02	Toronto Maple Leafs, NHL	82	41	39	80	94					
OWG–02	Sweden	4	5	4	9	10					
	Sweden Totals	46	17	10	27	30	8	7	0	7	4
	NHL Totals	930	397	545	942	759					
	OWG/WEC/WC/CCup/WCup Totals	58	33	37	70	64					

Named Best Forward at WEC (1992)
Won WEC/WC (1991, 1992, 1998)
Sweden Champion (1990)

Mats Sundin (right).

And in Zurich in 1998 came the third trophy for Sundin, who was once again one of the most valuable players on the team.

After being traded to the Toronto Maple Leafs in 1994—and experiencing the pleasure of seeing the Leafs give up local hero Wendel Clark to obtain his services—the young Swede became a smashing success. In just one year he rose to stardom in a city well known for its taste for fine hockey and fighting spirit. He won the honor of being named the team's captain, the first foreign captain in the history of the Maple Leafs. "It's an honor, but also a chance and a possibility to take a more active part in the whereabouts of the team," says Sundin.

Mats Sundin (right) has become one of the most popular Swedish athletes ever and an ambassador for his country's sportsmanship.

The 1998–99 season ended with the Stanley Cup semifinals, his highest level of achievement in the NHL to that point, but for Sundin, that was just the beginning. His play against Ottawa and New Jersey in the 2001 playoffs assured his place in Toronto for years to come. The captain signed a multi-year contract in the summer and promised to be the team's leader well into the 21st century.

Sundin was named captain of Team Sweden at the 2002 Olympics, and most would agree that he was the best performer during the three-game preliminary round, which included an impressive 5–2 win over Canada. However, the hockey world was turned on its ear when the heavily favored Swedes were upset in the medal round 4–2 by Belarus, eliminating them from further action.

Sundin returned to the Leafs and continued the fine play he had exhibited at Salt Lake, which resulted in leading the team into the Stanley Cup playoffs.

Keith Tkachuk

For Keith Tkachuk, even the seemingly simple act of putting on the "C" sweater as captain of the Phoenix Coyotes had a few ups and downs. But upon reflection, his is a story that's somehow strangely appropriate for a player who's been in the middle of many controversial events during his career.

In 1995 Tkachuk was the captain of the Winnipeg Jets, the Coyotes' precursor before the team moved to Arizona. But he was also a free agent, and at what looked like the end of his contract negotiations, he signed an offer sheet with the Chicago Blackhawks. The Jets, though, decided that they absolutely needed him. They matched Chicago's offer and signed Tkachuk to a $6-million-per-year contract—the third highest in the NHL at the time behind only Wayne Gretzky and Mark Messier.

For Keith Tkachuk, even the apparently simple act of putting on the sweater that marked him as captain had a few ups and downs.

After the Jets and Tkachuk came to terms, he took a 6 a.m. flight from his home in Boston to Winnipeg. But when he arrived, he was surprised by coach Terry Simpson and general manager John Paddock, who told him that he was no longer the team's captain and that Kris King was being given the honor instead. "Obviously, I was upset when I got stripped of the 'C'," said Tkachuk just after getting the news. "But there is nothing I can do about it. I know I am the leader and I know a lot of the guys know that." Eventually, when the team made its much-debated move to Phoenix in 1996, Tkachuk was renamed captain.

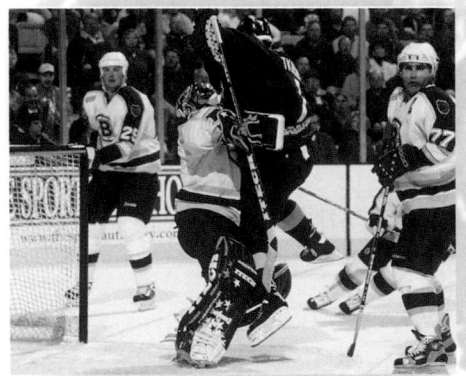

Keith Tkachuk (third from the left) is best known around the league as a power forward and he's never had fewer than 140 penalty minutes a season in his pro career.

His contract dispute in Winnipeg and his refusal to speak to the media during it—combined with his reputation as something of a "partier"—didn't exactly make Tkachuk the most popular player in Manitoba. Following his multi-million-dollar deal with the team, Tkachuk started the season very slowly with only two goals in the first 11 games. Fans booed him, and a groin injury kept him out of three of the next five games.

Soon he hit his stride and was tied for the league lead in goals. "I didn't think I would be tied for the lead after that start. Any time you get behind the eight ball like that, it's tough to get back," he said. "I obviously wasn't playing that well in the beginning. But that was then. I've adjusted my game a little bit and now I have to keep going. Things are toning down a bit. I haven't had much grief lately. I got my money, and I am happy to be back in Winnipeg. I just want to do well on the ice and show people I can play the game."

Tkachuk, one of many U.S. players in the NHL from the Boston area, is best known around league arenas as a power forward and it's no surprise that his hero as a kid was the Bruins' Cam Neely. He attended Boston University for just one year after becoming the first pick of the Jets in the 1990 Entry Draft out of high school. He joined the U.S. Olympic team in 1991 and 1992 and his first full season with the Jets was 1992–93. By his 4th NHL season, Tkachuk was a 50-goal scorer. The left wing (and sometimes center) was also developing into a very physical player. In fact, in his pro career he never had fewer than 140 penalty minutes in a season until 1999–2000, when he played only 50 games.

As the member of a franchise that relocated from Canada to a U.S. city—and as a U.S. citizen himself—Tkachuk was well qualified to comment on the trend of financial woes on Canadian pro hockey teams. "A lot of Canadian teams are going to lose out," he says. "Canadian teams other than Toronto or Montreal aren't going to get the players. I miss Winnipeg. But personally, I'm happy where we are."

This happiness didn't stop Tkachuk from making the headlines again in Phoenix. As his cousin Tom Fitzgerald of the Florida Panthers said, "Keith just kind of gets overworked—he's a little high-spirited." He was booed again in Phoenix after more contract negotiations before the 1998–99 season and made himself pretty unpopular for calling his experiences with the 1998 U.S. Olympic team in Nagano a "waste of time" because the team didn't win a gold medal. His name was also mentioned in conjunction with a well-publicized hotel room-trashing incident in Japan that allegedly involved several American players. And he has been outspoken in his dissatisfaction with the direction the Coyotes have been taking. "I'm sick of

Tkachuk, Keith
LW, 6´2˝, 210 lbs, b: Melrose, MA, 3/28/1972

Season	Club, League	Regular Season					Playoffs				
		GP	G	A	Pts	PIM	GP	G	A	Pts	PIM
1990–91	Boston University, H.E.	36	17	23	40	70					
OWG–92	USA	8	1	1	2	12					
1991–92	Winnipeg Jets, NHL	17	3	5	8	28	7	3	0	3	30
1992–93	Winnipeg Jets, NHL	83	28	23	51	201	6	4	0	4	14
1993–94	Winnipeg Jets, NHL	84	41	40	81	255					
1994–95	Winnipeg Jets, NHL	48	22	29	51	152					
1995–96	Winnipeg Jets, NHL	76	50	48	98	156	6	1	2	3	22
WCup–96	USA	7	5	1	6	44					
1996–97	Phoenix Coyotes, NHL	81	52	34	86	228	7	6	0	6	7
1997–98	Phoenix Coyotes, NHL	69	40	26	66	147	6	3	3	6	10
OWG–98	USA	4	0	2	2	6					
1998–99	Phoenix Coyotes, NHL	68	36	32	68	151	7	1	3	4	13
1999–00	Phoenix Coyotes, NHL	50	22	21	43	82	5	1	1	2	4
2000–01	Phoenix Coyotes, NHL	64	29	42	71	108					
	St. Louis Blues, NHL	12	6	2	8	14	15	2	7	9	20
2001–02	St. Louis Blues, NHL	73	38	37	75	117					
OWG–02	USA	5	2	0	2	2					
	NHL Totals	725	367	339	706	1639					
	OWG/WCup Totals	24	8	4	12	64					

NHL Second All-Star Team (1995, 1998)
Won WCup (1996)

being the captain of this team and everything reflecting on me and we're losing," he said. "It isn't a good feeling. I want to be a winner. Everybody wants to carry the Cup and one day I want to have that feeling." Perhaps his trade on March 13, 2001, will help that cause. Although the Blues lost in the semifinals that spring, the team remains a legitimate Cup threat.

Tkachuk was selected to play for the United States at the 2002 Olympics and was playing well for the team before injuring his leg in a collision during a preliminary game. The injury forced him to miss two games, but he did return to play in the gold medal game against Canada. The deep thigh bruise was more serious than originally suspected, however, as evidenced by his missing games with the Blues after the Olympics. Nonetheless, Tkachuk surpassed the 30-goal barrier for the seventh time in nine complete NHL seasons, excluding the shortened 1994–95 campaign.

Despite the controversies involving him, opposing coaches and players have come to respect Tkachuk for developing his all-around game. "Keith has worked himself into a player because of his dedication and determination," said Jets director of scouting Bill Lesuk as Tkachuk was honing his craft in Winnipeg, noting that Tkachuk's low-scoring, high-penalty-minutes rookie year didn't prepare anyone for his later success on the ice. "What it does is remind us how little we really know."

Sandis Ozolinsh

When the Colorado Avalanche's Latvian star Sandis Ozolinsh was growing up, his idol was Helmuts Balderis, "the Riga Express" on the great Soviet teams of the 1970s and early 1980s. Today, Ozolinsh himself fills that role for many young Latvian hockey fans. He co-founded the Arturs Irbe and Sandis Ozolinsh Youth Hockey Fund in Riga in 1997 along with his countryman and fellow NHLer. A popular biography of "Ozo" is available in Riga bookstores. And during the summers, Ozolinsh returns home to the Baltic country with his wife and two sons.

Sandis Ozolinsh trained as a figure skater and NHL fans were soon seeing the results.

But Latvians aren't the only ones who have been following Ozolinsh's career with great interest. In 1992 he earned the notice of the world hockey community as a member of the gold medal-winning Russian team at the World Junior Championships on a squad that included fellow NHL players Alexei Yashin, Darius Kasparaitis, Alexei Zhitnik and Alexei Kovalev.

Before the World Juniors, he had been the San Jose Sharks' third choice in the 1991 NHL Entry Draft and the 30th pick overall while a member of Dynamo Riga in the Soviet league. After a stint with Kansas City in the IHL, he started with the Sharks in 1992–93. The 6´3″ and 205-pound player had trained as a figure skater during his youth, and fans around the NHL were soon seeing the results of this early preparation—the young defenseman's blazing speed and stellar moves with the puck. Quickly gaining a reputation as one of the league's best rushing defensemen, Ozo also won the respect of his fellow players. "There are games when he plays 25 minutes," said Sharks teammate Jeff Friesen, "and it seems like he's had the puck for 20 of those minutes."

But while Ozolinsh was a master at scoring and setting up goals as a result of his spectacular end-to-end rushes, he was also aware that he needed to develop a more complete game. The NHL opposition, after all, was quick to figure out a player's particular habits and patterns on the ice and

A HISTORY OF WORLD HOCKEY

"There are times when he [Sandis Ozolinsh (left)] takes off and you go, 'No, no. No!'" confesses Sharks coach Kevin Constantine. "And then at the end of the rush you just say, 'Yes!'"

could capitalize on an attacking defender's absence from the front of his own goal. To that end, the Sharks coaching staff quickly got on Ozolinsh's case for what they thought was excessive offensive-mindedness. "I got tired of the coach always yelling at me," he said of Sharks coach Kevin Constantine's constant reminders to play more defensively. Still, Constantine, who tracked all his players' on-ice patterns with a complex videotape and computer program system, couldn't fail to be impressed with some of the Latvian star's offensive heroics. "There are times when he takes off and you go, 'No, no. No!'" confessed Constantine. "And then at the end of the rush you just say, 'Yes!'"

For all the reputation Ozolinsh was building as an offensive player, it was the one goal he didn't score that gained him considerable press—and represented for him the low point of his career. In a playoff game against the Toronto Maple Leafs, he found himself wide open in front of the net with only goalie Felix Potvin to beat. A goal would have put the Sharks into the Stanley Cup semifinals, but instead of blasting away, Ozo chose instead to pass off to Igor Larianov in the corner.

The gaffe led to what sportswriters began to call "the question" and Ozolinsh was pestered with "Why didn't you shoot?" wherever he went. When Potvin later confessed that he couldn't even remember the play, Ozo said the opposite was true for him. "I can't forget it," he admitted, trying to explain the shot that wasn't. "You know, there is a chance that he would have stopped my shot or I would have hit the post."

The incomplete-game knock against Ozolinsh stuck in San Jose, and he was even sent to the IHL's San Francisco Spiders for two games during a contract dispute midway through the 1994–95 season. Then, in October 1995, San Jose management traded Ozolinsh to Colorado for high-scor-ing winger Owen Nolan, a move that was met with great glee by Avalanche players and staff alike. Pierre Lacroix, the team's general manager, had big plans for the Latvian. "He will bring a new dimension to our team," said Lacroix, "and will fill a very important role on our power-play unit."

Colorado head coach Marc Crawford was equally expectant. "Sandis is a true asset as a pure offensive defenseman, something we have so desperately searched for," he explained. "There are so few defensemen like Ozolinsh in the league that we were willing to pay such a price to add this dimension to our game."

The trade paid big dividends for the Avs, who won the 1996 Stanley Cup with Ozolinsh firmly established as the team's power-play star and scoring defenseman. He was voted to the NHL First All-Star Team in 1997 but was traded

Ozolinsh, Sandis
D, 6´3˝, 205 lbs, b: Riga, USSR, 8/3/1972

Season	Club, League	Regular Season					Playoffs				
		GP	G	A	Pts	PIM	GP	G	A	Pts	PIM
1990–91	Dynamo Riga, USSR	44	0	3	3	51					
1991–92	Dynamo Riga, Latvia	30	6	0	6	42					
	Kansas City Blades, IHL	34	6	9	15	20	15	2	5	7	22
1992–93	San Jose Sharks, NHL	37	7	16	23	40					
1993–94	San Jose Sharks, NHL	81	26	38	64	24	14	0	10	10	8
1994–95	San Jose Sharks, NHL	48	9	16	25	30	11	3	2	5	6
1995–96	San Francisco Spiders, IHL	2	1	0	1	0					
	San Jose Sharks, NHL	7	1	3	4	4					
	Colorado Avalanche, NHL	66	13	37	50	50	22	5	14	19	16
1996–97	Colorado Avalanche, NHL	80	23	45	68	88	17	4	13	17	24
1997–98	Colorado Avalanche, NHL	66	13	38	51	65	7	0	7	7	14
WC–98	Latvia	4	0	2	2	0					
1998–99	Colorado Avalanche, NHL	39	7	25	32	22	19	4	8	12	22
1999–00	Colorado Avalanche, NHL	82	16	36	52	46	17	5	5	10	20
2000–01	Carolina Hurricanes, NHL	72	12	32	44	71	6	0	2	2	5
2001–02	Carolina-Florida, NHL	83	14	38	52	58					
	USSR/Latvia Totals	74	6	3	9	93					
	NHL Totals	661	141	324	465	498					
	WC Totals	4	0	2	2	0					

NHL First All-Star Team (1997)
Won Stanley Cup (1996)

on the day of the 2000 NHL Entry Draft to the Carolina Hurricanes. He fell short of fans' expectations during his first season with Carolina—a team that was eliminated in the first round of the playoffs by New Jersey—and on January 16, 2002, Ozolinsh and Byron Ritchie were traded to the Florida Panthers for Bret Hedican, Tomas Malec, Kevyn Adams and a conditional draft pick in 2003.

Peter Forsberg

When Tre Kronor won the gold medal at the 1998 World Championship in Switzerland, the senior coach was Kent Forsberg and the MVP was his son Peter. In spite of his young age, Peter already had to his credit the title of 1996 Stanley Cup winner while playing for the Colorado Avalanche, the 1992 World Championship gold medal and the Olympic title Tre Kronor had won in 1994 in Lillehammer, Norway. It was in that small Norwegian town that Peter Forsberg's star began to shine, and it has been bright ever since.

Born on July 20, 1973, in Ornskoldsvik, a town in the north of Sweden that gave Swedish hockey quite a number of illustrious players, Peter played for the local MoDo club, the coveted goal of every local boy. Before the 1994 Olympic season, Forsberg was offered a good contract to play for the Quebec Nordiques, but he displayed genuine firmness and maturity of character by refusing to play until after the Olympiad. And that proved to be a truly prophetic decision.

Peter Forsberg made a name for himself in the final game between Sweden and Canada at the Lillehammer Olympics.

He went on to make a name for himself during the final game of the Olympic ice hockey tournament in Lillehammer on February 27, 1994, between the national squads of Sweden and Canada. Both the spectators and the players were tense as the puck was picked up by Forsberg, number 21, who carried it, cool and composed, down the middle toward the opposing goal. Instead of shooting, he swerved to the left and almost ended up behind the goal line. Canadian goaltender Corey Hersch deflected the puck. At the very last second, the Swede regained control and, from his position almost behind the net, tipped it in. Called a "proprietary" play, it was first employed successfully by the famous forward Kent Nilsson and today the play bears his name in Sweden. That goal scored by Forsberg proved to be the game winner and the Tre Kronor players, headed by senior coach Curt Lundmark, spilled over the boards in celebration.

And so Peter Forsberg burst onto the

Forsberg, Peter
C, 6′, 190 lbs, b: Ornskoldsvik, Sweden, 7/20/1973

Season	Club, League	Regular Season					Playoffs				
		GP	G	A	Pts	PIM	GP	G	A	Pts	PIM
1990–91	MoDo, Sweden	23	7	10	17	22					
1991–92	MoDo, Sweden	39	9	18	27	78					
WC–92	Sweden	8	4	2	6	6					
1992–93	MoDo, Sweden	39	23	24	47	92	3	4	1	5	0
WC–93	Sweden	8	1	1	2	12					
1993–94	MoDo, Sweden	39	18	26	44	82	11	9	7	16	14
OWG–94	Sweden	8	2	6	8	6					
1994–95	MoDo, Sweden	11	5	9	14	20					
	Quebec Nordiques, NHL	47	15	35	50	16	6	2	4	6	4
1995–96	Colorado Avalanche, NHL	82	30	86	116	47	22	10	11	21	18
WCup–96	Sweden	4	1	4	5	6					
1996–97	Colorado Avalanche, NHL	65	28	58	86	73	14	5	12	17	10
1997–98	Colorado Avalanche, NHL	72	25	66	91	94	7	6	5	11	12
OWG–98	Sweden	4	1	4	5	6					
WC–98	Sweden	7	6	5	11	0					
1998–99	Colorado Avalanche, NHL	78	30	67	97	108	19	8	16	24	31
1999–00	Colorado Avalanche, NHL	49	14	37	51	52	16	7	8	15	12
2000–01	Colorado Avalanche, NHL	73	27	62	89	54	11	4	10	14	6
OWG–02	Sweden	0	0	0	0	0					
	Sweden Totals	151	62	87	149	294	14	13	8	21	14
	NHL Totals	466	169	411	580	444	95	42	66	108	93
	OWG/WC/WCup Totals	39	15	22	37	36					

Named Best Forward at WC (1998)
NHL First All-Star Team (1998,1999)
Won Calder Trophy (1995)
Won OWG (1994)
Won WC (1992, 1998)
Won Stanley Cup (1996)

A HISTORY OF WORLD HOCKEY

At the age of 23, Peter Forsberg (number 21) was already a Stanley Cup, Olympic and world champion.

international hockey scene at a young age. Ahead of him was an excellent career in the NHL, the Stanley Cup playoffs and the upcoming Olympiad in Nagano—already dubbed the tournament of tournaments by the media. In anticipation of the Nagano games, Swedish papers were plastered with praise and advice for the national squad and singled out three players: forwards Peter Forsberg and Mats Sundin from the *Toronto Maple* Leafs and Detroit Red Wings defenseman Niklas Lidstrom. Peter Forsberg had just been recognized as the NHL MVP for 1997 in a poll conducted by the Toronto Sun newspaper just before Christmas of that year. People were raving about his intelligent and rational way of handling the puck, his ability to play effectively deep in his own zone and his snappy transition in performing his main duty-scoring goals. Swedish newspapers nicknamed him "Peter the Great," comparing him to the former Russian czar. In the end, the Swedish hockey fans weren't disappointed.

Tre Kronor and its players weathered a storm of criticism from the media and the Swedish hockey union when the team was unable to get past the quarterfinals in Nagano, bowing out to their eternal rivals, the national squad of Finland, by a score of 2–1. It was a terrific blow, especially to Peter, who was also upset for his father.

The Swedes had enough sense not to ditch senior coach Kent Forsberg, under whose leadership the Swedish national squad won the World Championship in May of 1998. Rehabilitating them after the setback in Nagano, Swedish newspapers headlined father and son holding the World Cup and basking in the attention of the Swedish fans. Peter was especially happy to be able to return his debt as a son to his father.

The Swedes had the right to include in their lineup both domestic players and those playing overseas, and on numerous occasions Peter Forsberg shone on the symbolic All-Star team of Sweden. He became a holder of Stanley Cup, Olympic and World Championship titles.

Forsberg suffered a serious shoulder injury and underwent surgery in the summer of 1999. Though he would return to help the team win the 2001 Stanley Cup, by then he'd been injured again and his spleen was removed. He was wearing a suit on the night his team won. That summer, he shocked the hockey world by announcing he was taking a year off to recover his emotional desire to play a game that had caused him so many injuries. There were rumors that Forsberg was trying to fast- track his recovery so he would be able to play in the 2002 Olympics in February, but after consulting with family and medical staff, he decided it was too soon to come back. Forsberg began skating with the Avalanche in late March 2002 in anticipation of joining the team for that year's Cup playoffs.

Jere Lehtinen

Dallas Stars wing Jere Lehtinen has played in the NHL only since 1995, but he has already made his mark as one of the league's best. On a team replete with superstars, Lehtinen might not be the top goal scorer or the hardest hitter or flashiest player, but he is widely acknowledged by teammates and Stars coach Ken Hitchcock as the "glue" that holds the team's top line of him, Brett Hull and Mike Modano together.

"It's so great to play with these guys," says Lehtinen, a native of the town of Espoo, Finland. "It's still hard to believe sometimes that I'm playing on the same line with Brett Hull and Mike Modano. It's been great. It gives you so much energy playing on a line like this every night. I think we've really found a connection with each other. Brett is a great scorer, and he can pass really well also. Mike is an all-around player. He can do everything on the ice. I think I also bring some quickness to the line. I think it's a really good mix. The best thing about it is that I really like playing with them."

With Hull's arrival on the Stars, there was some initial confusion about where Lehtinen would play on the line with him and Modano, since prior to that, Lehtinen had been a right winger. The presence of two right-handers on the team's top line made a switch necessary for coach Hitchcock. Luckily, Lehtinen agreed to switch to the left to accommodate Hull. "Of course it isn't easy," he said. "But I also played left in the Olympics and that was fine. It's best when I just play my game and let things happen."

"I've been on the same line with Jere for three years now," says Mike Modano. "Ever since he was part of this club, it has been great playing with him, and very easy. He's got great speed, great feet, vision, and he knows the game really well." Hull agrees. "Jere has a great mind, he knows the game. I like that and have been impressed with his skills. Sometimes we're toying out there, we sometimes out-think ourselves—we've got to shoot. Really, it's a joke to have me on the same line with Mike and Jere. They are so smart! They both know the game mentally, and to me that is the most important thing. You don't have to be able to shoot the puck 100 miles per hour, or skate like the wind."

The Stars players and coaches aren't the only ones who recognize Lehtinen's contributions, though. In 1999 he won the Selke Trophy as the NHL's best defensive forward for the second time in a row, a feat accomplished by only two other players, Bob Gainey and Guy Carbonneau.

But even as a defensively-minded forward, he's been asked more and more to contribute some scoring and playmaking as well. "It's great to get the offensive opportunities," says Lehtinen. "But I know that the main thing I need to do on this line is focus on defensive play. Of course I know that in each game I will get offensive chances and that's good. I feel like whatever is best for the team is what I will do. I want to help the team win, that's the most important thing. When you help the team and it's winning, it gives you a sense of accomplishment. Point totals are really secondary. Scoring is nice, but I just want to do what the coaches ask of me and help the team win."

On a team replete with superstars, Jere Lehtinen is widely acknowledged as the glue that holds together the top line he forms with Brett Hull and Mike Modano.

Lehtinen, Jere
RW, 6´, 192 lbs, b: Espoo, Finland, 6/24/1973

Season	Club, League	Regular Season					Playoffs				
		GP	G	A	Pts	PIM	GP	G	A	Pts	PIM
1990–91	Espoo(2), Finland	32	15	9	24	12					
1991–92	Espoo(2), Finland	43	32	17	49	6					
WC–92	Finland	7	1	1	2	0					
1992–93	Kiekko-Espoo, Finland	45	13	14	27	6					
1993–94	TPS, Finland	42	19	20	39	6	11	11	2	13	2
OWG–94	Finland	8	3	0	3	0					
WC–94	Finland	8	3	5	8	4					
1994–95	TPS, Finland	39	19	23	42	33	13	8	6	14	4
WC–95	Finland	8	2	5	7	4					
1995–96	Dallas Stars, NHL	57	6	22	28	16					
	Michigan K-Wings, IHL	1	1	0	1	0					
WCup–96	Finland	4	2	2	4	0					
1996–97	Dallas Stars, NHL	63	16	27	43	2	7	2	2	4	0
1997–98	Dallas Stars, NHL	72	23	19	42	20	12	3	5	8	2
OWG–98	Finland	6	4	2	6	2					
1998–99	Dallas Stars, NHL	74	20	32	52	18	23	10	3	13	2
1999–00	Dallas Stars, NHL	17	3	5	8	0	13	1	5	6	2
2000–01	Dallas Stars, NHL	74	20	25	45	24	10	1	0	1	2
2001–02	Dallas Stars, NHL	73	25	24	49	14					
OWG–02	Finland	4	1	2	3	2					
	Finland Totals	201	98	83	181	63	24	19	8	27	6
	NHL Totals	430		113	154	267	94				
	OWG/WC/WCup Totals	45	16	17	33	12					

Won Frank J. Selke Trophy (1998, 1999)
Won WC (1995)
Won Stanley Cup (1999)
Finland Champion (1995)

Jere Lehtinen won the Selke Trophy as the NHL's best defensive forward for the second year a row in 1999.

Internationally, Lehtinen—who was originally the Minnesota North Stars' third pick in the 1992 Entry Draft, 88th overall—represented Finland at the 1993 World Juniors and was his country's top scorer in that event. He played on the Finnish Olympic team in 1994 and in 1998 and was a big part of the team's bronze medal-winning performance in Nagano, tying in scoring for seventh overall and third on his team in that NHL-led tournament. Lehtinen has also competed in two World Championships, in 1994 and 1995, and led the Finns to their first world victory in 1995. "I think he's European in style, in the element of defense," coach Hitchcock says. "And I think he is North American in his tenacity on the puck."

One of the reasons Dallas made it through to two consecutive Stanley Cup finals, in 1999 and 2000, is that Lehtinen thrives on playoff hockey. "I really like to play in playoff games," he admits. "They are such tight games defensively. There are a lot of one-on-one battles. You have to be more aware of the defensive side of your play. You can't make a lot of mistakes in the playoffs. Every game is so key. You have to always be aware of where the puck is and you have to be careful not to get caught on a change or on the wrong side of the ice."

In 2000–01 and 2001–02, Lehtinen again scored 20 goals and his superior two-way play continued to be key to any success the Stars had as a team. He also played for Finland at the 2002 Olympics, where they were eliminated from medal contention in the quarterfinals when they lost to Canada.

Alexei *Yashin*

After Alexei Yashin left Dynamo Moscow, he visited coach Vladimir Yurzinov every summer, first in Finland and then in Switzerland.

At 27, Alexei Yashin has already made history as the first Russian to be the full-time captain of an NHL team. His predecessor, Alexander Mogilny, wore the letter "C" on his jersey only when Pat LaFontaine had to miss a game because of injury. Yashin had been a part-time captain with the Ottawa Senators in the 1997–98 season when Randy Cunneyworth was absent. After Cunneyworth moved to Buffalo, Senators head coach Jacques Martin appointed the Russian center captain.

Yashin, then 25, was one of the league's youngest captains, but in the 1998–99 season he proved that Martin had made the right choice. The Senators reached second place in the Eastern Conference and Yashin had been among the regular season's six best scorers. Unfortunately, Yashin was captain for only one year when he ran into problems with management over his contract.

Yashin was born into a sports family. His father, Valeri, was a handball player, and his mother, Tatyana, played volleyball. His parents never pressured Yashin to become a champion but strove instead to ensure he received a good education. Since Yashin's first day in the NHL, his parents have been by his side creating a home-like atmosphere for him, which, he says, is one of the reasons he has been so successful.

Yashin's Dynamo Moscow coach Vladimir Yurzinov has also influenced his career. After he left Dynamo, Yashin visited Yurzinov every summer, first in Finland and then in Switzerland. According to Yashin, this was the best way to prepare for his next season. "He excels at knowing how to improve a shortcoming," Yashin says of Yurzinov. "He sees my weaknesses better than me and advises me about things I wouldn't even think of. Yurzinov always instructs me on how to improve my wrist shot, my slapshot and other techniques. I will continue to improve until the last day of my career."

During the 1999–2000 season, when Yashin refused to play for the Senators because of a financial dispute, he went to see Yurzinov in Switzerland and ended up spending the entire season there.

No Russian hockey player has ever been selected as the NHL's first draft pick. Yashin, along with Oleg Tverdovsky and Andrei Zyuzin, was a second-round draft pick. So far, he's surpassed them both. Few rookies are lucky enough to be invited to appear in the All-Star Game after their first season.

Despite the fact that the Senators were then a losing team, Yashin made good progress and soon became the team's leading player. At 25, he had scored over 30 goals in four not successive seasons, winning the respect of his teammates and earning the title of captain.

It is unfortunate that Yashin's career has been repeatedly interrupted by contract disputes. In 1995, after a conflict with the Senators administration, Yashin returned to Russia and even played four games for CSKA. Meanwhile, the Senators' losing streak continued. Four months later, the general manager and chief coach were ousted and Yashin signed a new five-year contract.

However, a second conflict with the team's management wasn't so easily resolved. A year before his five-year contract expired, Yashin and his agent demanded the terms be renegotiated. After his claim was turned down, Yashin went on strike over the existing contract. Yashin missed the entire 1999–2000 season in a contract dispute with the Senators that became more controversial as time went on. The Sens refused to trade him or renegotiate his contract, and at year's end he played in the World Championships during Russia's worst performance at the tournament. Yashin's situation got worse when a judge ruled he had to honor his contract with Ottawa, thus rendering his lost year meaningless.

He played 2000–01 with the Senators, scoring 40 goals and 88 points, and was dealt in the off-season to the Islanders, where GM Mike Milbury hoped the Soviet star could help resurrect the floundering franchise. Indeed, the addition of players such as Yashin, Michael Peca and Chris Osgoode in goal catapulted the Islanders into an immediate playoff contender, an enviable position that had been foreign to fans on Long Island for some time. Offensively, Yashin eclipsed the 30-goal level for the fifth year in a row. And at the 2002 Olympics, Yashin helped Russia to a bronze medal victory to go along with the silver he and the team had won in 1998.

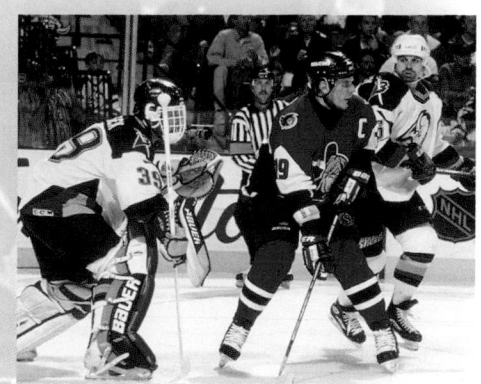

At 25, Alexei Yashin (center) had scored over 30 goals in four seasons, winning the respect of his teammates and the title of Ottawa's captain.

Yashin, Alexei
C, 6'3", 215 lbs, b: Sverdlovsk, USSR, 11/5/1973

Season	Club, League	Regular Season					Playoffs				
		GP	G	A	Pts	PIM	GP	G	A	Pts	PIM
1990–91	Avtomobilist Sverdlovsk, USSR	26	2	1	3	10					
1991–92	Dynamo Moscow, Russia	35	7	5	12	19					
1992–93	Dynamo Moscow, Russia	27	10	12	22	18	10	7	3	10	18
WC–93	Russia	8	2	1	3	5					
1993–94	Ottawa Senators, NHL	83	30	49	79	22					
WC–94	Russia	5	1	2	3	8					
1994–95	Las Vegas Thunder, IHL	24	15	20	35	32					
	Ottawa Senators, NHL	47	21	23	44	20					
1995–96	CSKA, Russia	4	2	2	4	4					
	Ottawa Senators, NHL	46	15	24	39	28					
WC–96	Russia	8	4	5	9	4					
WCup–96	Russia	5	0	2	2	6					
1996–97	Ottawa Senators, NHL	82	35	40	75	44	7	1	5	6	2
WC–97	Russia	5	3	0	3	12					
1997–98	Ottawa Senators, NHL	82	33	39	72	24	11	5	3	8	8
OWG–98	Russia	6	3	3	6	0					
1998–99	Ottawa Senators, NHL	82	44	50	94	54	4	0	0	0	10
WC–99	Russia	6	8	1	9	6					
WC–2000	Russia	5	1	1	2	8					
2000–01	Ottawa Senators, NHL	82	40	48	88	30	4	0	1	1	0
2001–02	New York Islanders, NHL	78	32	43	75	25					
OWG–02	Russia	6	1	1	2	0					
	USSR/Russia Totals	92	21	20	41	51	10	7	3	10	18
	NHL Totals	582	250	316	566	247					
	OWG/WC/WCup Totals	54	23	16	39	49					

NHL Second All-Star Team (1999)
Won WC (1993)
Russia Champion (1992, 1993)

Zigmund **Palffy**

"I don't want to be a star," said Ziggy Palffy.

Zigmund Palffy has brought every team for which he has played offensive strength as well as flair on the ice. He skates with the speed of lightning and attracts the puck like a magnet. He has the right hunger for scoring, uses his opportunities and is a very skilled creator in a game.

Although his name is known throughout the hockey world, that acclaim doesn't match up to his contribution to the game. Maybe his personal dislike for fanfare is to blame. He has always been his own man and still doesn't like life in the limelight. "I don't want to be a star," said the native of Skalica, Slovakia. "I want to play well for my team and be useful to my teammates. The rest doesn't interest me too much. What one demonstrates on the ice is what counts."

Palffy is slightly built but fast and cunning. He can change direction quickly, has an ability to formulate plays, stickhandles admirably and can shoot from every angle and in the tightest spots. He scores a lot of goals on lone breakaways and is quick to take advantage of mistakes by the opponent's defense and mount an attack.

Palffy entered big-league hockey with AC Nitra, which at the time was the weakest team in the joint Czech-Slovak league. As a 19-year-old youth, he scored 34 goals. It was also where he played for the first time on right wing next to Josef Stumpel. He also played with Stumpel for the junior national team.

Palffy then left for Dukla Trencin and together with Robert Petrovicky and Branislav Janos created the most feared offense in top-level competition. In the 1991–92 season, he became the best shooter and most productive player with 41 goals and 74 points in 45 matches. At the same time, he helped Trencin win the country's title. He had a knack for scoring goals when his team needed them the most. "He was dropped before a decisive match and tried to persuade the coach to leave him in," defenseman Milos Holan remembers. "He replied, 'Very well, but tomorrow you have to score three times.' He really did score those three goals."

In 1991 he took part in the World Junior Championship and he made his debut with the Czech senior team in the Canada Cup. However, a shoulder injury prevented him from taking part in the 1992 Olympics. The New

Palffy, Zigmund
LW, 5′10″, 183 lbs, b: Skalica, Czechoslovakia, 5/5/1972

Season	Club, League	Regular Season					Playoffs				
		GP	G	A	Pts	PIM	GP	G	A	Pts	PIM
1990–91	Nitra, Czechoslovakia	50	34	16	50	18					
CCup–91	Czechoslovakia	5	1	0	1	2					
1991–92	Dukla Trencin, Czechoslovakia	45	41	33	74	36					
1992–93	Dukla Trencin, Czechoslovakia	43	38	41	79	40					
1993–94	New York Islanders, NHL	5	0	0	0	0					
	Salt Lake Golden Eagles, IHL	57	25	32	57	83					
OWG–94	Slovakia	8	3	7	10	8					
1994–95	Denver Grizzlies, IHL	33	20	23	43	40					
	New York Islanders, NHL	33	10	7	17	6					
1995–96	New York Islanders, NHL	81	43	44	87	56					
WC–96	Slovakia	5	2	0	2	10					
WCup–96	Slovakia	3	1	2	3	2					
1996–97	Dukla Trencin, Slovakia	1	0	0	0	0					
	New York Islanders, NHL	80	48	42	90	43					
1997–98	New York Islanders, NHL	82	45	42	87	34					
1998–99	New York Islanders, NHL	50	22	28	50	34					
1999–00	Los Angeles Kings, NHL	64	27	39	66	32	4	2	0	2	0
2000–01	Los Angeles Kings, NHL	73	38	51	89	20	13	3	5	8	8
2001–02	Los Angeles Kings, NHL	63	32	27	59	26					
OWG–02	Slovakia	1	0	0	0	0					
	Czechoslovakia/Slovakia Totals	139	113	90	203	94					
	NHL Totals	531	265	280	545	251					
	OWG/WC/CCup/WCup Totals	22	7	9	16	22					

Czechoslovakia Champion (1992, 1993)

York Islanders drafted him in the summer of 1991 in the second round. "I was lucky that it was they who chose me." He said. "They are trying to build a young team. That is a good thing for me and for other young players." In the 1992–93 season, his last in competition in his home country, he collected 79 points in 43 matches and once again ascended the throne as the most successful points collector.

After his arrival on Long Island, he took number 68—made famous by Jaromir Jagr. But when he started his professional career in 1993, he didn't become a top-notch player right away. He couldn't speak a word of English and was getting used to a new lifestyle and a new style of playing hockey. The better part of the following two seasons were spent with the Salt Lake City Golden Eagles and the Denver Grizzlies of the IHL. He even got the chance to play for Slovakia when the country made its first independent appearance in elite competition during the 1994 Lillehammer Olympics.

Ziggy Palffy skates like lightning and attracts the puck like a magnet.

His game took off after that. Palffy had three seasons with the Islanders during which he scored over 40 goals and took his place among respected sharpshooters in the league. While back in Slovakia he used to be called "Zigo" or "Baron" because he had the same last name as a famous Slovak aristocratic family, in North America the self-made hockey man became "Ziggy," alluding to the main character in the famous David Bowie album *Ziggy Stardust*.

In the 1998–99 season, he got a late start because he and the Islanders couldn't agree on a new contract. Before the dispute was settled, he played at home in Skalica and in nine games gave his home team 11 goals and 19 points. After his return to Long Island, he kept earning a point a game. However, his teammates were leaving the team one by one. In the summer it was Palffy's turn.

In the summer of 1999, the Los Angeles Kings acquired Bryan Smolinski and Palffy for a pretty high price—young players Olli Jokinen, Josh Green, Mathieu Biron and the first choice in the next draft. On the new team, he once again met with his old acquaintance Josef Stumpel and together with Luc Robitaille they created a powerful new line.

The highly productive offensive line led the points race for the team, at least when none of them suffered from some injury or other. "No matter that Palffy plays the way he wants. It doesn't mean that he isn't working for the team. Being next to Stumpel and Robitaille works well for him. This Slovak trio—yes, I even consider Luc a Slovak—fulfills all tasks," claims coach Andy Murray.

On the new team, Palffy goes for the corners and tries to dig the puck out." You cannot just stand in front of the net and wait for passes. It isn't even so important how many goals I score. The most important thing is for the team to keep on winning." In 2000–01, Palffy had 38 goals and 89 points and the Kings were the early darlings of the playoffs, knocking off Detroit in the final round before losing to Cup champs Colorado in seven games in round two. Palffy had indeed found a new home.

In his eighth full season in the league, Palffy surpassed the 500-point plateau and was one of the Kings' key offensive threats along with Jason Allison and Adam Deadmarsh, then found himself something of an innocent victim in a controversy that arose during the Olympics. Slovakian general manager Peter Stastny had promised the Kings he wouldn't use Palffy in any qualifying games for the Salt Lake City Olympics, but reneged on the alleged agreement following a stunning loss to Germany. Even so, playing Palffy and some of the other Slovakian stars still wasn't enough, as they failed to advance to the main draw of the tournament.

Eric Lindros

Since he was a teenager—a big, man-sized teenager with quick feet and hands—Eric Lindros has been making hockey headlines. He was called "the Next One" as a youngster, when expectations for the burly center matched those of his superstar predecessors, Wayne "the Great One" Gretzky and Mario "the Magnificent One" Lemieux. A touch nasty and intent on getting his own way when it came to contracts and where he would play, Lindros showed flashes of the legend he was built up to be early in his NHL career after a tumultuous entry onto hockey's main stage.

"He [Eric Lindros (center)] is so much stronger than everyone else it's a joke," said Theo Fleury. "When he hits you, he can hurt you. No, check that— he can kill you."

Lindros was born and raised in London, Ontario. His father, Carl, was a towering man who was a star football and hockey player in his youth and had played in the Chicago Blackhawks system. He quit to pursue football when he realized he was only being used as a fighter.

Eric was first on skates when he was just over a year old and began to play organized hockey at five. "I was a real hyper and energetic kid, and I think my mom threw me in hockey just to keep me out of the house," Lindros said. Hockey didn't take over his life right away, as it does for so many promising young players. Lindros continued with activities outside of the game, playing the trumpet in the school band and cultivating friendships with kids away from the rink. When he was 10, the family moved to Toronto. Eric began playing with some of the best players in the country and a few years later, at age 13, he was practising with the older members of the St. Michael's College team. By the time he was in grade eight, he and his family knew he would make a career out of hockey.

At the age of 15, Lindros was playing for the St. Mike's Junior B team. He had 67 points in 37 games and made a habit of walloping players who were sometimes six years older, picking up 193 minutes in penalties along the way. Though he was huge and talented, Lindros lacked confidence off the ice. When he was eligible for the junior draft as a 16-year-old, his mother and father asked the Sault Ste. Marie Greyhounds not to choose their son since the team was situated too far away. The Greyhounds drafted him anyway, as they had Wayne Gretzky in 1977, but, unlike Gretzky, Lindros refused to report. He played instead with a Detroit junior team, Compuware. He went to school in Detroit and billeted with a family but remained nervous, sleeping with a knife under his mattress. He was pleased when the Greyhounds traded his rights to the Oshawa Generals, a team just outside Toronto, for three players, two future draft picks and $80,000. With the Generals, he averaged two points a game and led the team to the Memorial Cup in 1989–90. He was named Canadian Major Junior player of the year the next season after leading the OHL with 149 points and earning Canada another gold medal at the World Junior Championships in Saskatchewan, topping the team with 10 points in the seven games. Fans back in Sault Ste. Marie, insulted by the snub, exacted some measure of revenge later in the year in the league playoffs when the Greyhounds surprised the Generals to advance to the Memorial Cup finals.

The junior draft debacle was repeated at the 1991 NHL Entry Draft. Thousands of young players look forward to their draft day. Lindros described it as his least favorite day in hockey. "I've hated it since I was 14," he said at the time. "I hated it that people told me what to do that shouldn't have been in a position to run my life." He was the best player available and the Quebec Nordiques had the first overall pick. Once again Lindros's parents informed Quebec management that Eric wasn't interested in playing for the Nordiques. "There isn't a good fit between Eric and the Nordiques for a variety of reasons, including economically and in terms of lifestyle," Eric's father said. "We warned Quebec of that before the draft in order to save them any embarrassment over trying to sign Eric."

And once again the team ignored the complaints and chose Lindros. He refused to report, beginning a long and dramatic year for the promising player and the Nordiques. "The people that come out of high school with the best grades go to the best universities. The people with the lower grades have fewer choices," Lindros told *Maclean's* magazine in one of the many profiles published during the media frenzy that his holdout became. "Why should a player who comes out of junior hockey with top marks go to a city that isn't his choice? I'm thinking about my family and what the pressure's going to be like on them."

Eric Lindros (center)—"the Next One"—has been making hockey headlines since he was a teenager.

Even though Lindros had never played in the NHL, he was invited to the Team Canada training camp for the 1991 Canada Cup. He silenced many critics who said he'd never played against the game's elite with his physical play and scoring ability, often dominating many of the best pro players in the game on his way to making the team and playing in the tournament. Although he was 6´4˝ and 225 pounds, not all of the effects of his bruising play were felt by his opponents. In a practice, he collided with Brent Sutter, then with the New York Islanders, and suffered a minor concussion. He recovered in time to play in his first exhibition game in Montreal two nights later when Team Canada played the United States. The fans at the Forum were merciless at first, booing him every time he stepped on the ice in support of their French-Canadian brethren in Quebec City. The jeering didn't seem to bother Lindros, who scored two goals in the second period to earn player of the game honors. He further announced himself to the pro world when the tournament began, delivering a huge hit on Sweden's Ulf Samuelsson that separated the defenseman's shoulder. He became a solid part of the Canadian team that went unbeaten and took the title.

Theoren Fleury, who played with Lindros in the 1991 Canada Cup, said Eric had two things above all others in hockey at the time: "Size and strength. He is so much stronger than everyone else it's a joke," Fleury said. "When he hits you, he can hurt you. No, check that—he can kill you."

Lindros stayed in the Canadian national team program for the 1991–92 season, winning a silver medal at the Albertville Olympics in 1992, rather than joining Quebec in the NHL. In June 1992 a trade was finally arranged by the Nordiques at the draft. There was initially some confusion about which of two teams actually made a trade for Lindros first. The New York Rangers and the Philadelphia Flyers both felt they'd obtained the phenomenon. It was decided that the Flyers had indeed consummated a trade, sending six players (including Peter Forsberg, Mike Ricci, Ron Hextall and Steve Duchesne), two first-round draft choices and $15 million to the Nordiques for Lindros. The players who went to the Nordiques established Quebec, and later Colorado when the franchise moved, as a championship contender and then Stanley Cup winner in Denver.

Life wouldn't be as easy in Philly for Lindros, who, despite a huge contract that paid him approximately what his boyhood idol Mark Messier earned, still hadn't played a game in the league. In his first season, in 1992–93, he was met with an outpouring of anger when he visited Quebec. But he set a Flyers record in his first season with 41 goals and improved his offensive totals over the next two seasons while maintaining a combative edge to his play. In 1994–95, the lockout-shortened season, Lindros tied with Jaromir Jagr for the scoring lead, and though he lost the Art Ross Trophy because he scored fewer goals, he won the Hart Trophy as the league's most valuable player.

The Flyers began to round into form with Lindros as its captain in 1995–96. His line with John LeClair and Mikael Renberg came to be known as "the Legion of Doom" and beat up opposing defense to help Lindros score 115 points. Lindros added to his impressive international resume at the 1996 World Cup, though Team Canada fell short of expected victory. The next season in the NHL, he returned from a nagging knee injury as Philadelphia marched all the way to the Stanley Cup finals, leading all playoff scorers with 26 points en route to a heart-breaking loss to Detroit.

Lindros was a unique star in the league. He was perhaps the first superstar who was also an enforcer. Other large players, such as Bobby Hull and Jean Beliveau, were more gentlemanly and reserved, much like the reticent Lemieux. Gordie Howe had been tough and even dirty sometimes, using his strength all over the ice, but he couldn't have been categorized as an enforcer. Fans who filled rinks to see Lindros were expecting the odd flashy deke or highlight-reel goal, but there was also the anticipation of seeing the big man roll over a defender or even drop his gloves to fight with the league's toughest men. It was almost as if two-thirds of Boston's best line in the 1970s, the tough corner expert Wayne Cashman and the large-framed but skilled Phil Esposito, had been combined into one dangerous package. For his part, Lindros described himself as a blue-collar player, somebody who rolled up his sleeves and went into the corners, never shying away from a fight. "I'm not going to scare you with spectacular moves day in and day out," he said. "I just put my boots on and go to work."

Lindros's ascension to the top ranks of the game became complete when he was made Team Canada's captain for the 1998 Nagano Olympics. The man who put the team together, Lindros's boss in Philadelphia, Bobby Clarke, made an important statement about the future of the game by bypassing veterans like Wayne Gretzky for the honor. Lindros's childhood hero, Mark Messier, was even left off the team in favor of younger legs. Lindros, perhaps still slowed by his ongoing knee problems, didn't

---

Lindros, Eric
C, 6´4˝, 236 lbs, b: London, Ont., 2/28/1973

Season	Club, League	Regular Season					Playoffs				
		GP	G	A	Pts	PIM	GP	G	A	Pts	PIM
CCup–91	Canada	8	3	2	5	8					
OWG–92	Canada	8	5	6	11	5					
1992–93	Philadelphia Flyers, NHL	61	41	34	75	147					
WC–93	Canada	8	11	6	17	10					
1993–94	Philadelphia Flyers, NHL	65	44	53	97	103					
1994–95	Philadelphia Flyers, NHL	46	29	41	70	60	12	4	11	15	18
1995–96	Philadelphia Flyers, NHL	73	47	68	115	163	12	6	6	12	43
WCup–96	Canada	8	3	3	6	10					
1996–97	Philadelphia Flyers, NHL	52	32	47	79	136	19	12	14	26	40
1997–98	Philadelphia Flyers, NHL	63	30	41	71	134	5	1	2	3	17
OWG–98	Canada	6	2	3	5	2					
1998–99	Philadelphia Flyers, NHL	71	40	53	93	120					
1999–00	Philadelphia Flyers, NHL	55	27	32	59	83	2	1	0	1	0
2001–02	New York Rangers, NHL	72	37	36	73	138					
OWG–02	Canada	6	1	0	1	8					
	NHL Totals	558	327	405	732	1084					
	OWG/WC/CCup/WCup Totals	44	25	20	45	43					

Named Best Forward at WC (1993)
NHL First All-Star Team (1995)
NHL Second All-Star Team (1996)
Won Hart Trophy (1995)
Won Lester B. Pearson Award (1995)
Won CCup (1991)
Won OWG (2002)

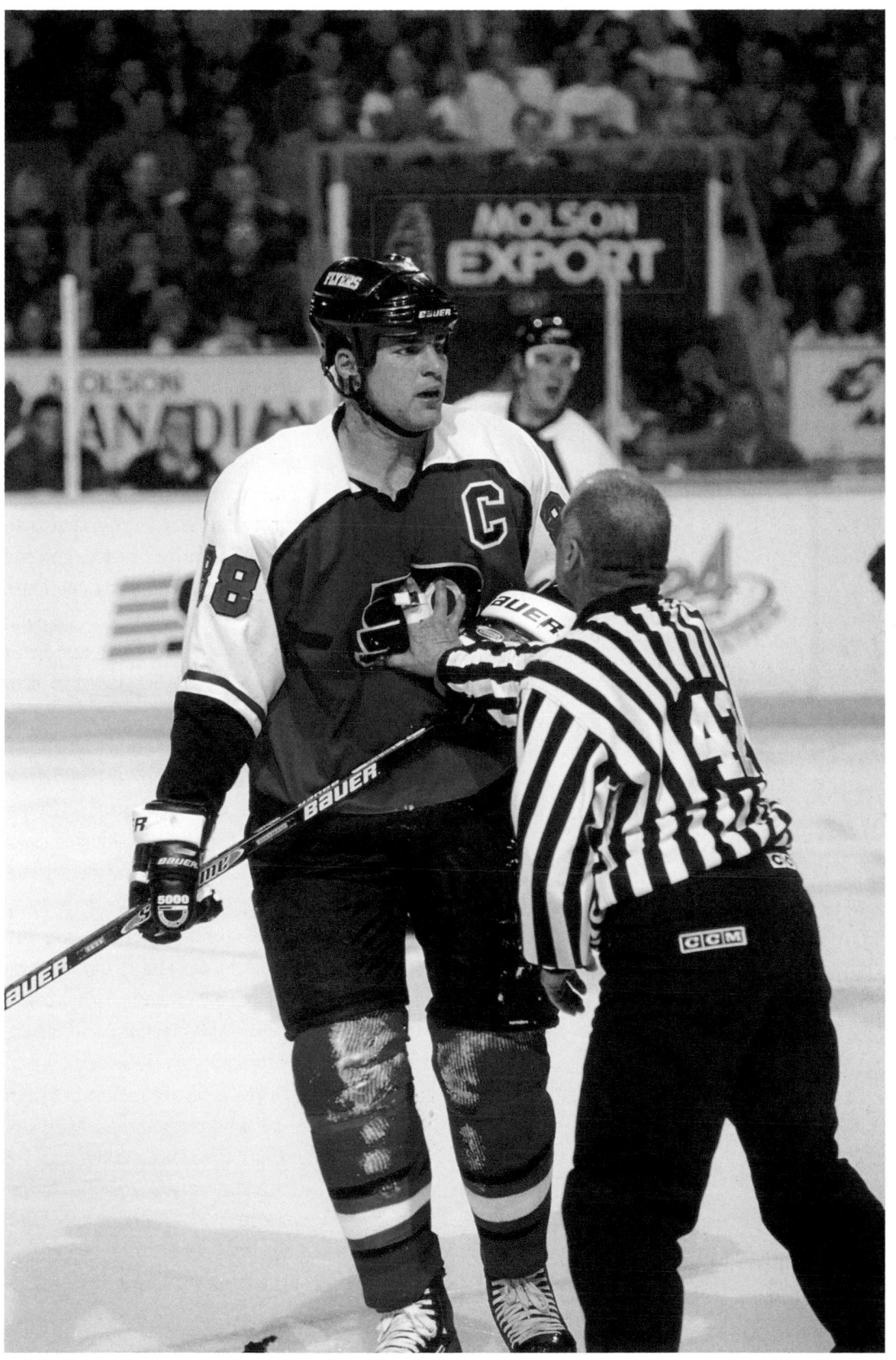

Eric Lindros (left).

shine during the tournament, which saw the Canadians lose in the semifinals to the Czech Republic and then disappoint during the bronze medal game against Finland to finish fourth.

Injuries continued to haunt him near the turn of the century, taking different forms as his aggressive ways took a toll on his huge body. His younger brother, Brett, was forced out of the league after receiving one too many concussions in 1996 and Eric missed the 1999 playoffs with a collapsed lung that forced him to watch the Flyers from the sidelines as they lost their series with the Toronto Maple Leafs.

Lindros's 1999–2000 season was a shambles. He suffered four concussions—the last the result of a devastating hit from New Jersey's Scott Stevens in the Stanley Cup semifinals—that left his career in doubt. His captaincy taken from him, his rapport with GM Bobby Clarke tarnished and his career in jeopardy, the season couldn't have ended quickly enough for Lindros. He demanded a trade to Toronto, but after a full year of negotiating, Clarke and Leafs GM Pat Quinn could not make a deal. In the summer of 2001, Lindros accepted a deal to the Rangers and it was on Broadway that he resumed his career, healthy for the first time in nearly two years. Just before Christmas, Lindros sat out several games and it was later revealed that he had indeed suffered another concussion, but the time out was considered more of a precautionary move on the part of the Rangers. For a good part of the season, Lindros and linemate Theo Fleury seemed to work well together, but a mid-season slump by the entire team took them out of playoff contention for the fourth straight year. At the 2002 Olympics, Lindros played decently but was certainly not the dominant force he had been in past international competitions.

Tommy Salo

Some Swedish hockey pundits believe Tommy Salo might surpass Pelle Lindbergh, the first European to be recognized as the top goalkeeper in the NHL.

Tommy Salo will always be known as the goalkeeper who won the gold medal for Sweden at the Lillehammer Olympics in 1994. Although the entire Swedish team played a winning game that day in Norway, the decisive contribution in the final game against Team Canada was made by three players: defenseman Magnus Svensson, who tied the game with less than two minutes left in regular time; forward Peter Forsberg, who scored in the second shootout against Corey Hirsch; and goalie Tommy Salo, who deflected a powerful shot by Canadian forward Paul Kariya. At that point, the Swedes cleared the bench and rushed onto the ice to salute their goaltender.

Salo was born in the industrial town of Sjurhammer on February 1, 1971, and made his debut in the international arena at the 1991 World Junior Championship. From the beginning, Salo was noticed not only for his physical strength and quick reaction time but also for his tremendous stamina. This caught the attention of Vasteras coaches, where he started his career in pro hockey. Playing for Vasteras, Salo had a league-best 2.47 goals-against average in the 1992–93 season. But it was the Lillehammer Olympic tournament that opened the doors to the NHL for him.

As the best rookie in the International Hockey League, Salo joined the New York Islanders in the 1994–95 season, beating out his compatriot Tommy Soderstrom and Canadian Eric Fichaud for the top spot. Islanders coach Mike Milbury pinned his hopes on the quiet Salo, and he wasn't disappointed.

Salo successfully defended the Islanders' net and played for Sweden in the World Championship whenever the Islanders didn't make it to the Stanley Cup playoffs. Salo got to go to Nagano in 1998 for the "tournament of the century," but, despite the fact that he played a good game, Sweden lost in the quarterfinals to their long-time rival, Finland.

Tommy Salo will be remembered as the goalie who won gold for Sweden at the Lillehammer Olympics in 1994.

Another goalkeeper might have lost heart and given up, but not Salo. He proved it that very same season at the 1998 World Championship in Switzerland, helping Sweden win the gold. To this he added the bronze at the 1999 World Championship in Norway, showing once again that he was a superior goaltender.

Salo now plays for the Edmonton Oilers and was voted that team's MVP in 1999–2000, while a poll among journalists has included him on Sweden's All-Star team for the third year running. In 2000–01, he rounded up by playing an amazing 73 games and posting a career-high 36 wins and eight shutouts. But the hero who had stopped Canada in the overtime shootout in the 1994 Swedish Olympic triumph was quickly cast as the villain in what the Swedish media called the biggest upset and largest international hockey humiliation in the country's history. In the quarterfinals at Salt Lake City, the undefeated Swedes were expected to handily dispatch the lightly regarded team from Belarus. But the Belarussians kept pace throughout the game and, with the game tied at 3–3, managed to score what can only be described as a one in a million fluke goal when Salo was handcuffed by a rising shot from near center ice that deflected off his mask, rolled up over his head and into the net.

The distinctive quality of Salo's career has been the consistency of his playing. Some Swedish hockey pundits believe that Salo might surpass Pelle Lindbergh, the first European to be recognized as the best goalkeeper in the NHL. And anything is possible. Even by hockey standards, Salo is still a very young man and his career bears watching.

Salo, Tommy
G, 5'11", 173 lbs, b. Surahammar, Sweden, 2/1/1971

Season	Club, League	Regular Season				Playoffs			
		GP	Mins	GA	Avg	GP	Mins	GA	Avg
1990–91	Vasteras IK, Sweden	2	100	11	6.60				
1992–93	Vasteras IK, Sweden	24	1431	59	2.47	2	120	6	3.00
1993–94	Vasteras IK, Sweden	32	1896	106	3.35				
OWG–94	Sweden	6	370	13	2.11				
WC–94	Sweden	3	180	10	3.33				
1994–95	Denver Grizzlies, IHL	65	3810	165	2.60	8	390	20	3.07
	New York Islanders, NHL	6	358	18	3.02				
1995–96	New York Islanders, NHL	10	523	35	4.02				
	Utah Grizzlies, IHL	45	2695	119	2.65	22	1342	51	2.28
WCup–96	Sweden	2	160	4	2.00				
1996–97	New York Islanders, NHL	58	3208	151	2.82				
WC–97	Sweden	10	597	20	2.01				
1997–98	New York Islanders, NHL	62	3461	152	2.64				
OWG–98	Sweden	4	238	9	2.27				
WC–98	Sweden	9	540	7	0.78				
1998–99	New York Islanders, NHL	51	3018	132	2.62				
	Edmonton Oilers, NHL	13	700	27	2.31	4	296	11	2.23
WC–99	Sweden	8	423	13	1.84				
1999–00	Edmonton Oilers, NHL	70	4164	162	2.33	5	297	14	2.83
WCup–2000	Sweden	6	359	10	1.68				
2000–01	Edmonton Oilers, NHL	73	4364	179	2.46	6	406	15	2.22
2001–02	Edmonton Oilers, NHL	69	4035	149	2.22				
OWG–02	Sweden	3	179	7	2.35				
	Sweden Totals	58	3427	176	3.08	2	120	6	3.00
	NHL Totals	412	23830	1005	2.53				
	OWG/WC/WCup Totals	51	3046	93	1.83				

Named Best Goaltender at WC (1997, 1999)
Won OWG (1994)
Won WC (1998)

Scott Niedermayer

One of the high points of Scott Niedermayer's career was his game-tying goal in the 1995 finals against Detroit.

Scott Niedermayer was known around the league as one of the brightest players in hockey. He was a strong defenseman and an excellent passer, a swift skater who loved to handle the puck and used speed to get back on defense after starting an offensive rush. So what was the secret? He took figure and power skating lessons to help him improve his on-ice ability.

Born in Edmonton, Alberta, Niedermayer grew up in Cranbrook, British Columbia, where his father was a general practitioner at the Cranbrook hospital. As a teen, his idol was Paul Coffey. Niedermayer played his junior hockey with the Kamloops Blazers of the WHL. More recently, Niedermayer played for the New Jersey Devils, with whom he realized an NHL player's ultimate dream by winning a Stanley Cup in 1995.

Niedermayer was the third overall draft pick in 1991 at the tender age of 18, a selection the Devils had acquired from Toronto for Tom Kurvers. In his first two years, he worked hard to refine his style under coach Jacques Lemaire. "I'm not against a defenseman carrying the puck," Lemaire said. "But I am against a defenseman losing the puck." Niedermayer's response was to respect Lemaire's experience. "Jacques doesn't say much, so when he speaks, you listen." And Niedermayer knew that there was room for improvement in his game. "I definitely lost confidence," he said of his having to learn to change his style. "I would find myself giving the puck up way too soon or making a bad pass. I wasn't confident I could make a better play."

The adjustment was difficult for Niedermayer as he tried to fit in on a team that had a reputation as one that emphasized physical play over finesse, with bruising stalwarts like Claude Lemieux and Scott Stevens leading the way under Lemaire's tutelage. Niedermayer began to wonder if his talent was eroding as he was changing his way of playing. "At one time I would just see the puck lying beside our net and I would grab it and skate with it," he said. "Now I always have to think about it. I don't think the creativeness is gone. But sometimes I do look around at other teams that play a different style and wonder if it could be different."

For his part, Lemaire was patient. "I want Scott to understand defense very well," said the coach, "and then use his talent offensively." Eventually, as the Devils started to improve, Niedermayer's game started to become more complete as well.

Perhaps one of the high points of Niedermayer's career was his game-tying goal in the 1995 finals against Detroit. Amazingly, he broke through the entire Red Wings team, pushed his first shot wide and then picked the puck up from the boards and put it past surprised goalie Mike Vernon. *The Hockey News* told readers that Niedermayer had conducted the whole play at "Warp 9 speed." Teammate

Niedermayer, Scott
D, 6´, 200 lbs, b: Edmonton, Alta., 8/31/1973

Season	Club, League	Regular Season					Playoffs				
		GP	G	A	Pts	PIM	GP	G	A	Pts	PIM
1991–92	New Jersey Devils, NHL	4	0	1	1	2					
1992–93	New Jersey Devils, NHL	80	11	29	40	47	5	0	3	3	2
1993–94	New Jersey Devils, NHL	81	10	36	46	42	20	2	2	4	8
1994–95	New Jersey Devils, NHL	48	4	15	19	18	20	4	7	11	10
1995–96	New Jersey Devils, NHL	79	8	25	33	46					
WCup–96	Canada	8	1	3	4	6					
1996–97	New Jersey Devils, NHL	81	5	30	35	64	10	2	4	6	6
1997–98	New Jersey Devils, NHL	81	14	43	57	27	6	0	2	2	4
1998–99	New Jersey Devils, NHL	72	11	35	46	26	7	1	3	4	18
1999–00	New Jersey Devils, NHL	71	7	31	38	48	22	5	2	7	10
2000–01	New Jersey Devils, NHL	57	6	29	35	22	21	0	6	6	14
2001–02	New Jersey Devils, NHL	76	11	22	33	30					
OWG–02	Canada	6	1	1	2	4					
	NHL Totals	730	87	296	383	372	111	14	29	43	72
	OWG/WCup Totals	14	2	4	6	10					

NHL Second All-Star Team (1998)
Won Stanley Cup (1995, 2000)
Won OWG (2002)

Claude Lemieux said the end-to-end rush belonged on the "all-time highlight reel." And proving he had gained some maturity and learned something about hockey in his own end of the rink, Niedermayer played patient defense for the rest of night. "That's the way it should be," he said. "I think now I feel comfortable playing defensively. I know what I'm doing."

Because of his speed and offensive instincts, Niedermayer was one the team's recognized leaders on the power-play. Internationally, he represented Canada at the 1991 and 1992 World Junior Championships. His brother, Rob, is a center for the Florida Panthers, and although they have yet to play together in the NHL, their influence on their respective teams is undoubted.

In 2000 Niedermayer again reached the pinnacle of NHL success as a member of the Devils' Stanley Cup-winning team. And Niedermayer was named as one of Team Canada's initial eight picks for the 2002 Olympics, which ultimately resulted in gold at Salt Lake City.

The adjustment to Jacques Lemaire's style was difficult for Scott Niedermayer as he tried to fit in on a team that emphasized physical play over finesse.

1999–2002

Stars of the 21st Century

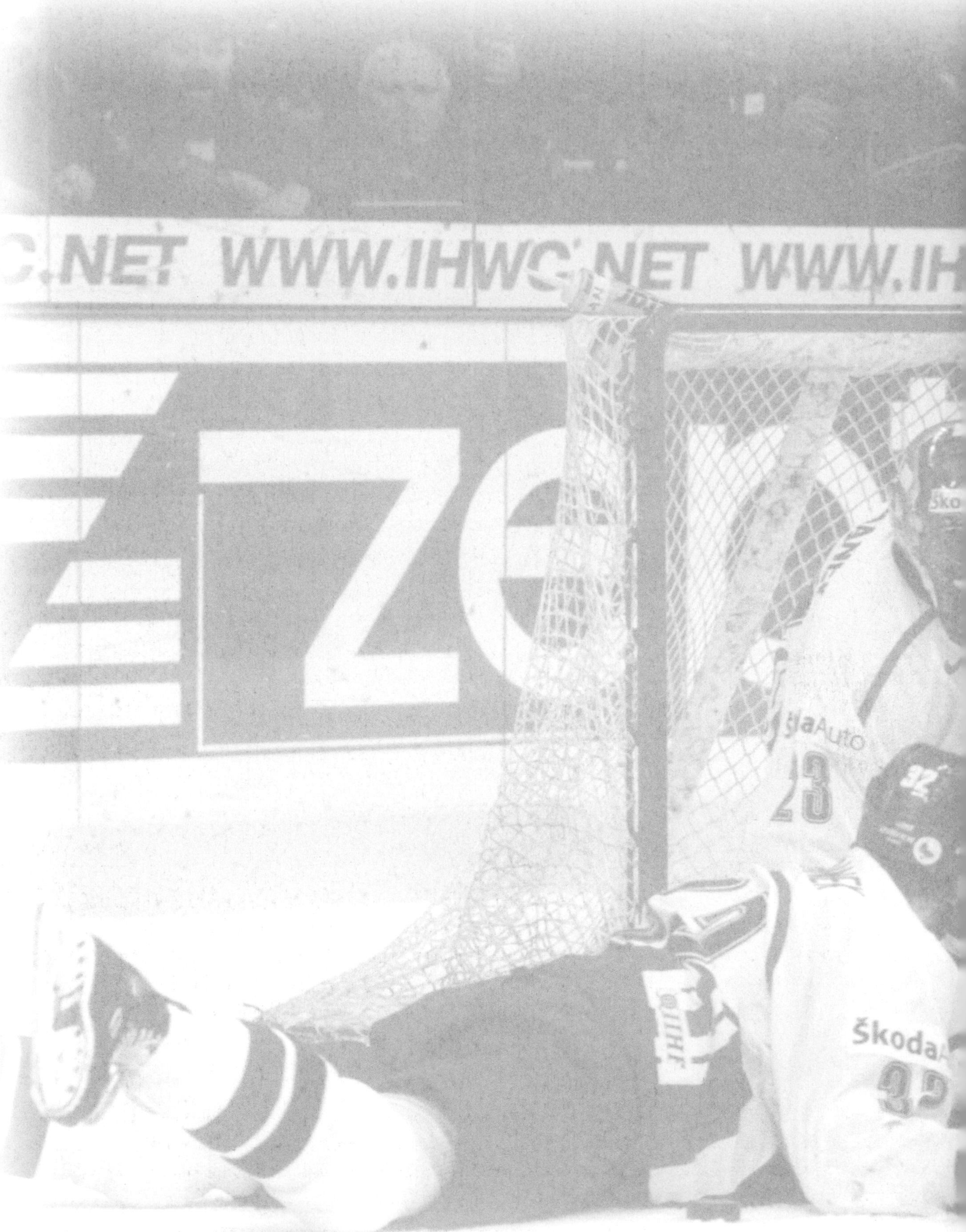
WWW.IHWC.NET

*T*he 20th century's last season was rich in events—the regular-season championship and the Stanley Cup finals in the NHL and the World Championship as well as a host of other national and international competitions—but one was in a class by itself.

In December, veteran players from Russia and Canada played a series in Russia. Quite a few of them had played in the 1972 Canada–USSR Summit and the 1974 series between the WHA and USSR. The games that were played a quarter of a century after those epochal events stirred fond memories in the hearts of an older generation of fans on both sides of the ocean and demonstrated to younger fans how this beautiful game could be played—even by yesterday's stars, some of whom were by then in their 50s and 60s. When the Canadian line of Marcel Dionne, Guy Lafleur and Steve Shutt or the tandem of Gilbert Perreault and Frank Mahovlich appeared on the ice, it seemed time had no power. Their fast breakaways and virtuoso plays astounded not only the spectators but also such seasoned Russian defensemen as Gennady Tsygankov and Vladimir Lutchenko. Even the great Canadian defenseman Brad Park had to recall the Summit Series, when his Russian rivals (forwards Alexander Yakushev, Alexander Maltsev, Vladimir Petrov and Vladimir Shadrin) more than once compelled him to play at the limit of what he could do. The Canadians won, as they had at the Summit, but it was perhaps more important that young fans in Russia and elsewhere saw with their own eyes what had opened a new era in hockey in 1972.

In December 1999, heroes of the 1972 Canada–USSR Summit and the 1974 series between the WHA and USSR met again.

The World Championship was held in St. Petersburg, Russia, in 2000 and will likely be remembered by fans for the Czech Republic's second consecutive title and the Slovaks winning the silver when they defeated such favorites as Canada, Russia, Sweden, Finland and the U.S. The disastrous performance of the hosts will no doubt be remembered as well.

A HISTORY OF WORLD HOCKEY

Tre Kronor working hard on defending its own net.

The games in St. Petersburg demonstrated that a number of European national teams that hadn't been serious contenders previously had sharply upgraded their play and were ready to take on all rivals. This championship also put paid to the axiom that the more NHLers, the greater the chances for medals. In what was thought to be—to date had been—a formula for success, Team Canada was made up entirely of young NHLers (but didn't have outstanding stars except veteran Larry Murphy). Headed by Pavel Bure and Alexei Yashin, the 14 NHLers on Team Russia got their team all the way to 11th place. And the Americans didn't proceed past the quarterfinals with 12 pros on their roster.

A preliminary round qualified 12 of 16 national squads. In Group A, Sweden, Latvia, Belarus and Ukraine had qualified in that order in the first stage and it all went according to forecasts when the Ukrainians dropped out of the running. In Group B (Slovakia, Finland, Italy and Austria), the Finns confounded expectations when they tripped up in the game with the Austrians (which ended 3–3) and stayed in second place. In Group C (the Czech Republic, Norway, Canada and Japan), the Canadian favorites found themselves in third place when they lost to the Czechs 2–1 and then to Norway, for the first time in history, 4–3. Yet another favorite, Russia, was also in third place after starting well in the preliminary round of Group D (USA, Switzerland, Russia and France) by trouncing the French squad 8–1. Russia's next two opponents, the U.S. and Switzerland, bet on defense and sudden counterattacks for success and easily outplayed the tournament's hosts; the 3–0 and 3–2 results weren't in favor of

Finnish fans had more to cheer about than Canadians in St. Petersburg in 2000.

Russia. In the second round, the Latvians took their cue from the Americans and Swiss. Like most hosts, Russia played a super-aggressive game and took 39 shots on goal, only to be foiled by the superb performance of the Carolina Hurricanes goalie, Arturs Irbe. A 3–2 defeat at the hands of the Latvians left Russia out of the playoffs, which became the most resounding sensation of the World Championship that year in St. Petersburg.

In Group E, the other favorites from the U.S. and Sweden made it to the playoffs along with Switzerland and Latvia, while in Group F (the Czech Republic, Finland, Canada, Slovakia, Norway and Italy) the Canadians won against the Finns 5–1, the Italians 6–0 and the Slovaks 4–3 and finally edged Norway out of the playoffs. As a result, the U.S. and Slovakia, Switzerland and Canada, Sweden and Finland and Latvia and the Czech Republic met in the quarterfinals. The bookmakers predicted the winners in three out of four—the Canadians (5–3), Finns (2–1) and Czechs (3–1)—but the as yet undefeated Americans bowed out to the Slovaks 4–1 and confounded all forecasts.

To a certain extent, it was sheer chance that brought the Czechs to the finals. Just before the curtain came down in the game against Canada with the score at 1–1, Canadian goalkeeper Jose Theodore—who had played the whole tournament practically flawlessly—allowed a fluke goal. Thus it was that the Czechs got their chance to take the title for the second time in a row in the last World Championship of the 20th century.

Unlike the coaches of the other leading European national squads, Ivan Hlinka had been betting for years on players who had been with Czech clubs. They'd had the advantage of honing their play through the entire season in Eurotour matches. The approach had already justified itself insofar as the Czechs had been Olympic champions in 1998 and world champions the year after that. Two months before the St. Petersburg tournament, Hlinka himself joined the Pittsburgh Penguins, but the new coaching staff (Josef Augusta and Vladimir Martinec, star forwards of the 1970s) didn't alter his principles. Furthermore, they achieved an ideal combination of youth and experience. Brilliant 28-year-old playmaker Robert Reichel, who had come back to the Czech Republic after eight seasons in the NHL, and 32-year-old Jiri Dopita, who could both mount and finish off an attack, enabled the coaches to mold two striking lines while defenseman Frantisek Kucera, who had played in the NHL for six years, and goalie Roman Cechmanek formed the backbone of the Czech defense. The game between the Czech Republic and Slovakia proved to be one of the most intriguing final championship games in years. The rivalry between the Slovaks and Czechs had always been as irreconcilable as the one between the Americans and Canadians or the Finns and Swedes, and the Czechs plunged the Slovak fans into the doldrums when they took the lead 3–0. Then the Slovaks reduced the gap to 3–2. In the third period, the teams exchanged goals and it was 4–3. Trying desperately to take the game into overtime, the Slovaks mounted a final charge that was interrupted by a beautiful counterattack. The game ended 5–3 with the Czechs the world champions once more.

The game between the Czech Republic and Slovakia proved to be one of the most intriguing final championship games in years.

Meanwhile, the first regular-season NHL championship in the 21st century had already started with 28 clubs. In the East, the Atlanta Thrashers appeared for the first time in the Southeast Division and the Presidents' Trophy was captured for the first time by the St. Louis Blues when coach Joel Quenneville managed to achieve what none of his predecessors, including the hugely successful Mike Keenan, had done. Quenneville whipped into shape a team that in many respects resembled the Dallas Stars. A brilliantly organized defense guaranteed stability—165 goals against was the best in the league— while at least three lines of fast forwards were available for attacks. It was this

Matrix 2000.

kind of offense that made up for the lack of real stars after Brett Hull departed, and it brought the St. Louis club to third place in the league by goals scored (248) after Detroit (278) and New Jersey (251). The Blues eclipsed all the other teams in individual prizes as well. Quenneville was named coach of the year; Chris Pronger was awarded both the Norris Trophy for outstanding defense and the Hart Trophy as the MVP of the season; Czech goalie Roman Turek won the Jennings Trophy for the fewest goals against; and another Czech player, Pavol Demitra, took home the Lady Byng Trophy for being the gentleman that he truly is.

The first round of the 2000 playoffs brought one more sensation with a St. Louis connection. Throughout the 1990s, winning the Presidents' Trophy practically doomed a team in the struggle for the Stanley Cup. The Blues brought that unfortunate tendency into the new millennium when they bowed out to San Jose in a seven-game series. In the rest of the first round, the favorites were predictable winners: Detroit beat Los Angeles 4–0, Colorado beat Phoenix 4–1,

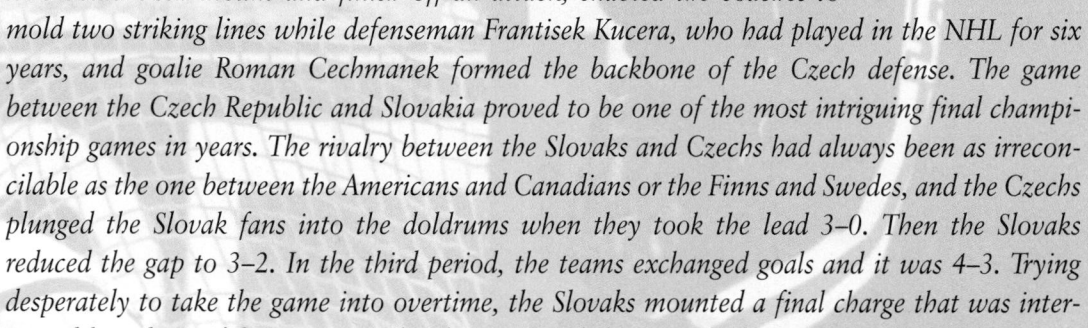

A HISTORY OF WORLD HOCKEY

What happens when you hit Dominik Hasek?

Dallas beat Edmonton 4–1, New Jersey beat Florida 4–0, Pittsburgh beat Washington 4–1, Philadelphia beat Buffalo 4-1 and Toronto beat Ottawa 4–2.

In the second round, only two of the Original Six were left in the elite at the end of the century. Toronto and Detroit both tried hard in a series of clashes that corresponded with one between New Jersey and Colorado. Attempting to revive their old barn-burning style, the Maple Leafs still had a chance to make it to the finals of the Eastern Conference after four games (it was tied at 2–2). Then defense problems dashed all such hopes and they lost 4–2 in the series. Meanwhile, the Red Wings closed a very big gap after two games in Denver, only to have second-year Colorado player Chris Drury seal the outcome of the series in the overtime of the fourth game. On home ice, the Avalanche didn't miss its chance and the Wings were snowed under 4–1, while the series between Dallas and San Jose also ended 4–1 in the stars' favor.

In Philadelphia, the Flyers were playing without Eric Lindros and couldn't seem to do anything about Jaromir Jagr (current holder of the Art Ross Trophy) in the first two games on home ice. They wrenched out their first victory in overtime in the third, but the next game in Pittsburgh turned into one of the longest in recent playoffs. The teams had been on the ice for 152 minutes and one second when Keith Primeau scored the winning goal for the Flyers and the series was tied at 2-2. After that, Pittsburgh's exhausted Czech line of Jaromir Jagr, Martin Straka and Jan Hrdina could no longer stand up to the three lines of star Flyers forwards. Mark Recchi, John LeClair, Keith Primeau, Rick Tocchet and Daymond Langkow were backed up by one of the leading attacking defensemen in Eric Desjardins, and the Flyers won both the fifth and sixth games and the series.

Thanks to the same players—and young goalie Brian Boucher—the Flyers seemed to have ensured themselves a trip to the Stanley Cup finals after the first four games with New Jersey in the Eastern Conference finals. They were leading 3–1, but there was someone who could make a miracle in the Devils' camp.

In his playing days, Larry Robinson had defended Montreal's colors and won the Stanley Cup six times. As a coach, he had assisted Jacques Lemaire with the Devils from 1993 and led Los Angeles for four seasons after 1995.

In 1999–2000 the Maple Leafs reached the 100-point mark in regular-season standings for the first time in club history.

He had taken the Kings to the playoffs only once, in 1998, but earned a solid reputation as a specialist. He'd come back to New Jersey for the final eight games in the regular season. Now his sound advice and ability to motivate players helped his boys turn the tide.

Robinson's team played game five as Devils should and it finished 4–1. But after the Devils scored two goals in game six, the newly returned Lindros reduced the gap to 2–1. And in the decisive game—at the beginning of which Lindros suffered another concussion after ramming into New Jersey defenseman Scott Stevens—the coup de grace was executed not by the seasoned Flyers but by a young Devil, forward Patrik Elias, and it ended 2–1.

The finals in the Western Conference between Colorado and Dallas also turned out to be breathtaking. It was decided in the seventh game by a fluke when Patrick Roy was unable to stop an aimless shot in the direction of the Colorado net, which made it 3–2 in the game and 4–3 in the series for Dallas.

The first finals in the 21st century promised to be lean on goals in that two teams who were strong on defense were about to lock sticks. The very first game brought an end to such doubts with 10 goals—more than enough to simply satisfy fans—when it went to 7–3 for the Devils. Interestingly enough, three of the goals were scored by three of the nine remaining Devils who had sipped champagne from the Cup in 1995, defensemen Scott Stevens and Ken Daneyko and forward Sergei Brylin, while the other four were registered by the combination of Petr Sykora (two goals), Jason Arnott (two goals) and Patrik Elias that had become the main line for New Jersey that season.

The Devils bench celebrates.

In the second game in East Rutherford, the veteran Stars were able to neutralize Arnott and Co. while Stars aces Mike Modano and Brett Hull—who twice finished off attacks—determined the final 2–1 outcome. Arnott and Sykora accepted the challenge again in the next game in Dallas by scoring one goal apiece, bringing New Jersey once more to the lead. When the strongest Devils lines were again neutralized in game four, however, it turned out that on Robinson's team, everyone knew how to score—even checkers. With the score at 1–0, Brylin evened it up. And then, in the course of three minutes, newcomers to the club—forward John Madden, on a power-play, and defenseman Brian Rafalski—scored two goals and the score was 3–1 at the end.

Game five lasted 106 minutes and 21 seconds of playing time. For the spectators, it dragged on for almost five hours—and for all of that time, the fans who had packed the Continental Airlines Arena were expecting their favored Devils were on the brink of ending the Stanley Cup battle in triumph. Had it not been for the brilliant performance of Dallas goalie Ed Belfour, the game would have ended in regulation time. And it would be hard to name a Devils forward who didn't have a good chance to score. Alexander Mogilny (who was with New Jersey between shifts in Vancouver); rookie of the year Scott Gomez; Elias (twice); Bobby Holik; Brylin—all were in situations where a goal seemed inevitable. And every time, there was Belfour, firmly planted right in the puck's path. Finally, in the third overtime, Brett Hull made a pass to Martin Brodeur's goal crease and Modano—who had been double-shifted for most of the game and had been on the ice now for more than an hour—beat Devils defenseman Vladimir Malakhov and redirected the puck into the net for the game's only goal.

Scott Stevens' thunderous checks inspired and dominated the post-season and there was no question he would win the Conn Smythe Trophy when New Jersey won the Cup.

Dallas, Reunion Arena, June 10, 2000: Not an empty seat in the 16,928 capacity (which isn't surprising; for two seasons and more than 100 games, the arena has been packed to the rafters). By the fifth minute of play, the Stars have already lost one of their outstanding defensemen. After a fall that injures his knee, Darryl Sydor becomes a spectator. Soon the visitors have suffered an even more serious loss. After a heavy bodycheck by Derian Hatcher, forward Petr Sykora is out of the Devils' strongest forward line and on his way to the hospital. Now both teams are playing tough hockey, and in the 14th minute the Devils are outnumbered. Even playing with a man extra doesn't click for the Stars in the duel with New Jersey, however. More than that, in the 26th minute, after a swift counterattack, Devils defenseman Scott Niedermayer escapes his pursuers, lures Belfour out of the net with a feint and opens the scoring. A scant 69 seconds later, veteran

Dallas Star Mike Keane takes a shot from the right face-off circle and puts it in the upper corner to light the red light behind Brodeur. It's tied.

In the next two periods of regulation time and the first overtime, both sides created a number of situations that might have seen goals. The Stars made prolonged positional attacks in which Nieuwendyk stood out; the Devils mounted swift counterattacks from Elias, Arnott and Holik. But the goalies remained in control.

In the ninth minute of the second overtime period, Elias received a pass in the corner at the Stars' end. Everything indicated he was going to pass back to his defenseman. Modano took this at face value and left Elias alone. Belfour couldn't stop a shot that came off Arnott's stick and the game was over, 2–1. And so it was that after five years the Devils won the Stanley Cup for a second time in spite of all forecasts in a series that was not rich in goals but whose hair-raising twists and turns will ensure it an honorable mention in the annals of hockey.

The 2000–01 season saw few changes from the previous year. The Czechs again won the World Championships and New Jersey again made it through to the finals. But this time, facing the powerful Colorado Avalanche, the Devils lost a tough seven-game finals that featured spectacular goaltending from Patrick Roy (who won the Conn Smythe Trophy) and inspirational play from the entire team whose "Mission 16W" was taken from the baseball cap worn by Ray Bourque. The campaign was dedicated to winning a Stanley Cup for the defenseman—his first in 22 years of NHL hockey—and just weeks after the victory, Bourque announced his retirement. (Early in the 2001–02 season, both the Bruins and Avs retired his number 77 sweater.) In the finals for the third time in the past seven years, New Jersey faced elimination in their series against Toronto, but won game six in Toronto and game seven at home to advance to the conference finals. Colorado was never as seriously threatened, and in the off-season signed Rob Blake, their newest star acquisition, to a long-term contract along with star and captain Joe Sakic and Roy.

Fresh off their spring playoffs victory, the Avalanche went into the 2001–02 campaign favored to repeat as Cup champs but were dealt a serious blow when star centre Peter Forsberg announced he would miss the entire season recovering from a spleenectomy. Amazingly, Forsberg was given medical clearance for the playoffs, putting him in the unprecedented position of being the only player in NHL history to miss an entire season and then perform in the Stanley Cup playoffs. At the trade deadline in March, Colorado had also bolstered its post-season chances by acquiring a top-ranked defenseman for the third year in a row, picking up noted agitator and defensive stalwart Darius Kasparaitis from the Pittsburgh Penguins. The Avs finished the regular season second in the Western Conference, second only to the Detroit Red Wings, their perennial rivals, who won the Presidents' Trophy for most points in the 82-game season with 116. The Wings also demonstrated a strong desire to take another serious run at the Stanley Cup when they loaded up with high-priced free-agent talent in the form of goaltender Dominik Hasek and sharpshooters Brett Hull and Luc Robitaille, each of whom received lucrative multi-year contracts.

Perhaps the biggest disappointment of the year was the fast decline of the Dallas Stars, who failed to make the post-season. With the club in turmoil midway through the year, general manager Bob Gainey fired head coach Ken Hitchcock and replaced him with Rick Wilson and removed himself from everyday duties as general manager. But the changes did little to help the team on the ice. Even a drastic late-season trade that sent Joe Nieuwendyk and Jamie

Langenbrunner to New Jersey in exchange for Jason Arnott and Randy McKay wasn't enough to kick-start a lost season. Another disappointment was Jaromir Jagr, who was traded early in the season after telling the Pittsburgh Penguins he was no longer interested in playing for them. A trade to Washington was looked upon as a new start for Jagr, but he failed to bolster the level of his game and the Capitals missed the playoffs despite a late-season surge.

The 2001–02 campaign also unveiled Calgary's Jarome Iginla as a bona fide star when the 24-year-old right winger won the Art Ross Trophy as the NHL's leading point-getter with 52 goals and 96 points. Although Iginla couldn't lead the Flames into the post-season, his strong individual effort earned him a spot on Team Canada's Olympic roster. And then there was the fantastic play of goaltender Jose Theodore, who almost single-handedly earned a playoff berth for the Montreal Canadiens with his excellent regular-season performance. The New York Islanders' acquisition of star forwards Michael Peca and Alexei Yashin and goaltender Chris Osgood also spearheaded a rebirth of sorts on Long Island, resulting in a post-season spot for the long-suffering franchise and its dedicated fans.

In February, the NHL shut down for two weeks while the league's elite represented their respective countries at the Salt Lake City Games. Although just about every country had its best players in the lineup, there were several big names missing. Sweden's Peter Forsberg was out and Alexander Mogilny refused an invitation for play for Russia despite exhaustive pleas from head coach Viacheslav Fetisov and fellow player and countryman Igor Larionov, among others. Canada was without goaltender Patrick Roy, whose official explanation was that he wanted the summer off to spend time with his family. (There had been rumors Roy was infuriated at not having been named as one of Canada's original eight players and refused to play, but Roy maintained that there was no truth to such scuttlebutt.)

Despite opening the tournament with a loss to Sweden, Canada regrouped and, led by such veterans as Mario Lemieux, Joe Sakic and Steve Yzerman, went on to capture the gold medal, defeating the United States 5–2 in the championship final for Canada's first Olympic triumph in 50 years. For the Americans, who settled for the silver, it marked just the second time they had ever lost a final Olympic game on home soil. Ironically, the other had also come at the hands of the Canadians, in the 1932 game at Lake Placid Games that decided the gold and the silver. In Salt Lake, Russia won bronze by defeating the Cinderella team from Belarus, while the defending champions from the Czech Republic left the 2002 Games without a medal, having been ousted by the Russians in the quarterfinals.

Doug Weight

By 1995–96, Doug Weight had become a top offensive performer and he recorded his first 100-point season that year.

A crafty offensive forward, Doug Weight has received numerous accolades for his grit and leadership. After a solid beginning with the New York Rangers, his career blossomed in Edmonton, where he became a key component in the resurgence of that club's fortunes.

The native of Warren, Michigan, grew up with hockey much like most Canadian children. He noted: "I was on skates when I was two and a half years old and, being so close to Canada, we got CBC and *Hockey Night in Canada*. Every Saturday I was on the couch watching with my dad. My family was always very hockey-oriented, so that was definitely my focus from a very young age."

Weight first made a name for himself while starring for the Bloomfield Jets in the North American Junior Hockey League. He then accepted a scholarship offer from Lake Superior State University, where he scored 144 points in two seasons, earned all-American honors and finished as one of the all-time leading scorers in school history.

After a strong freshman season at Lake Superior, Weight was chosen by the New York Rangers 34th overall in the 1990 NHL Entry Draft. Following his 75-point effort in 1990–91 at university, the slick playmaker was placed on the Central Collegiate Hockey Association First All-Star Team and the NCAA West Second All-American Team. That year he also represented the United States at the World Junior Championship in Saskatoon. He finished as the leading scorer in the tournament, two points ahead of Canada's Eric Lindros. In one game, Weight was particularly dominant, scoring seven points in the team's 19–1 shellacking of Norway on New Year's Day of 1991.

Weight played well as an NHL rookie in 1991–92, scoring 30 points in 53 games, though his fine adjustment to the pro game was overshadowed by the 35-goal performance of teammate and fellow rookie Tony Amonte. Both players injected life into the Rangers lineup and helped the club finish at the top of the NHL standings with 105 points.

In 1992–93, Weight was enjoying a more productive season, but the Rangers were fading in the standings. In an attempt to shake up the team, the promising Weight was dealt to Edmonton in return for veteran Esa Tikkanen. He noted a few months later: "At first I was upset. I liked New York and I had a lot of friends there. But I was traded for Tikkanen and that Sather and the Oilers had been after

Weight, Doug
C, 5′11″, 200 lbs, b: Warren, MI, 1/21/1971

Season	Club, League	Regular Season					Playoffs				
		GP	G	A	Pts	Plm	GP	G	A	Pts	Plm
1990–91	New York Rangers, NHL						1	0	0	0	0
1991–92	New York Rangers, NHL	53	8	22	30	23	7	2	2	4	0
	Binghamton Rangers, AHL	9	3	14	17	2	4	1	4	5	6
1992–93	New York Rangers, NHL	65	15	25	40	55					
	Edmonton Oilers, NHL	13	2	6	8	10					
WC–93	USA	6	0	6	6	12					
1993–94	Edmonton Oilers, NHL	84	24	50	74	47					
WC–94	USA	8	0	4	4	16					
1994–95	Rosenheim, Germany	8	2	3	5	18					
	Edmonton Oilers, NHL	48	7	33	40	69					
1995–96	Edmonton Oilers, NHL	82	25	79	104	95					
WCup–96	USA	7	3	4	7	12					
1996–97	Edmonton Oilers, NHL	80	21	61	82	80	12	3	8	11	8
1997–98	Edmonton Oilers, NHL	79	26	44	70	69	12	2	7	9	14
OWG–98	USA	4	0	2	2	2					
1998–99	Edmonton Oilers, NHL	43	6	31	37	12	4	1	1	2	15
1999–00	Edmonton Oilers, NHL	77	21	51	72	54	5	3	2	5	4
2000–01	Edmonton Oilers, NHL	82	25	65	90	91	6	1	5	6	17
2001–02	St. Louis Blues	61	15	34	49	40					
OWG–02	USA	6	0	3	3	4					
	NHL Totals	767	195	501	696	645					
	OWG/WC/WCup Totals	31	3	19	22	46					
	Won WCup (1996)										

me for two years. It's a good feeling to be wanted. When I came here for a player like Tikkanen, I knew they were pumped to get me. That makes it exciting for me."

In 1993–94, Tikkanen helped the Rangers win the Stanley Cup, but Weight pleased the Oilers officials by scoring 74 points and becoming an enthusiastic leader on an improving team. He summed up his success as follows: "The difference is that I'm playing more here and I'm part of a young team, whereas the Rangers are a veteran team. I'm glad to be a part of this team. There are a lot of great young guys and we're gelling together as time goes on. Hopefully, as we mature together, we can become more of a family here."

Doug Weight (left) likes to play physically, even if he has to wrap himself up.

By 1995–96, Weight was a top offensive performer and recorded his first 100-point season. He and captain Kelly Buchberger were key reasons behind the Oilers' return to the playoffs in 1996–97. They upset the heavily favored Dallas Stars in the first round before bowing to the Colorado Avalanche in five games in the conference semifinals.

The talented forward's grit and determination rubbed off on his Edmonton teammates. Weight observed: "I was born a pretty rugged competitor. I want to win in anything I do. That's sometimes a negative, especially with certain things like playing board games with your family. But on the ice it's a great asset to have because I hate to lose. Off ice I work very hard to get into shape to get myself to be a better player…every year I strive to become better and better and better. I'm still learning and I'm still working hard. I want to be better next year than I am this year. I'm persistent."

The next year, Weight scored 70 points in 79 games and was part of the United States contingent at the 1998 Nagano Olympics. The Oilers got revenge on Colorado and knocked the Avs out in the opening round of the playoffs before Dallas gained retribution of its own in five games over Edmonton in the next round. By this time, Weight was entrenched as a crowd favorite in Edmonton because he played hard and he came to the rink every night to give his all. He later noted: "I play the game physically, I get involved in the physical play. Being 5′11″, I feel I take my share of beatings and I play my share of games where I'm awfully sore, like everyone does…. I like to play every game, even if I have to wrap myself up in order to play."

Early in the 1998–99 season, the gritty forward suffered a serious knee injury that limited him to only 43 games. The veteran forward observed: "Adversity makes you stronger, and this is the worst injury I've ever had. I'm going to have to deal with it. You know, I'm pretty scared. It is an eye-opener. You consider yourself tough, but sitting back and thinking about it you get scared of the process of surgery and rehabilitation." Weight also reflected on the personal side of a serious injury. "The team is family. I love my wife to death, but I know she'll hate me in a while if I sit around and do nothing at home."

Weight was named the 10th captain in Oilers history prior to the 1999–2000 season. He scored 72 points in 77 games and helped the team reach the playoffs for the fourth straight year, but salary concerns forced the Oilers to trade him to St. Louis after another outstanding year in 2000–01.

Valeri **Bure**

By 1999–2000, Valeri Bure had become Calgary's leading scorer.

It is a hard lot in life to be a superstar's younger brother in the same sport. The pressure of expectations can be unbearable, and few can take it. For a long time, it seemed Valeri Bure, Pavel Bure's younger brother, wouldn't make it as an NHL star despite his talent. The Montreal Canadiens didn't believe in him and consequently didn't give him much time on the ice. His brother, though, had complete confidence in Valeri's eventual success. "Very few players, especially among Europeans, can flourish on the NHL at the age of 20. Valeri has been plagued by injuries, but I remember well that at kids' and junior tournaments, he wasn't worse than I was, and sometimes even better. His joining the All-Star Team is just a matter of time."

Time has proven that "the Russian Rocket" didn't simply endorse his junior brother—who came to be known as "the Pocket Rocket"—but made a portentous assessment of his potential. Three years later he was the Calgary Flames' leading scorer and one of the NHL's top goal-getters. And the opportunity of a lifetime came along when Valeri and Pavel played side by side in the 50th All-Star Game in Toronto and became the heroes of their team. Of all the brother duos that have ever participated in the All-Star games, the Bures obtained the most points.

At 16, Valeri, a gifted junior player who had played just three games with CSKA, left for North America with his brother. The would-be Pocket Rocket joined the WHL's Spokane Chiefs. At first Bure was disappointed and even thought of going back to Russia. His head coach was a former tough guy whose strategies made little sense to a graduate of the Russian hockey school. Yet in the end they made a pact, and in his second year in the WHL, with his 68 goals in 66 games, Bure was included on the league's All-Star Team. He was subsequently chosen by the Montreal Canadiens in the NHL draft, where he was expected to follow in Pavel's footsteps and shine immediately, but it simply didn't happen.

The Pocket Rocket later explained why his road in the NHL was so long and winding. "The Canadiens are a team that never admit juniors all at once." In the first two years the team sent him back to Spokane and in the third year they moved him to the Fredericton farm club. Bure was desperate for a swap, but his pleas were ignored. Canadiens coach Mario Tremblay didn't trust him.

Bure suffered numerous injuries. During the 1996–97 season, he had two concussions and his kidneys were damaged. He didn't feel at home in Montreal, where very demanding sports reporters pressured juniors. In the eyes of many hockey experts, there was serious doubt about Bure's future. In the summer of 1997, as a limited free agent, he managed to win a new contract with the Montreal Canadiens but on the least advantageous of terms that included only a 10% increase in his salary.

Bure, Valeri
RW, 5´10˝, 168 lbs, b: Moscow, USSR, 6/13/1974

Season	Club, League	Regular Season					Playoffs				
		GP	G	A	Pts	PIM	GP	G	A	Pts	PIM
1990–91	CSKA, USSR	3	0	0	0	0					
WC–94	Russia	6	3	0	3	2					
1994–95	Montreal Canadiens, NHL	24	3	1	4	6					
	Fredericton Canadiens, AHL	45	23	25	48	32					
1995–96	Montreal Canadiens, NHL	77	22	20	42	28	6	0	1	1	6
WCup–96	Russia	1	0	0	0	2					
1996–97	Montreal Canadiens, NHL	64	14	21	35	6	5	0	1	1	2
1997–98	Montreal Canadiens, NHL	50	7	22	29	33					
	Calgary Flames, NHL	16	5	4	9	2					
OWG–98	Russia	6	1	0	1	0					
1998–99	Calgary Flames, NHL	80	26	27	53	22					
1999–00	Calgary Flames, NHL	82	35	40	75	50					
2000–01	Calgary Flames	78	27	28	55	26					
2001–02	Florida Panthers	31	8	10	18	12					
OWG–02	Russia	6	1	0	1	2					
	USSR Totals	3	0	0	0	0					
	NHL Totals	502	147	173	320	185					
	OWG/WC/WCup Totals	19	5	0	5	6					

In his next season with Montreal, under new coach Alain Vigneault, Bure fared much better. And early 1998, when he was traded to the Calgary Flames, marked the turning point in his career. Perhaps he just needed a change of atmosphere. In one of his first outings with the Flames, he scored a hat-trick. He even made it to Nagano, Japan, to play for Russia at the Olympics. There he made an important contribution to Russia's capturing the silver medal. At the Olympic tournament, he scored his most memorable goal in a game against the Czech Republic and Dominik Hasek.

Always known as Pavel's brother, Valeri became a force all his own in Calgary during 1999–2000. He had 35 goals and 75 points, leading the team in both categories, and provided leadership that suggested he might be a late bloomer and someone the Flames can count on for years to come.

After recording 55 points in 78 games for the Flames in 2000–01, Bure joined his brother Pavel as a member of the Florida Panthers for the 2001–02 season. The union lasted less than a season, though, when management dealt Pavel to the New York Rangers at the trade deadline. The year was also a forgettable one for Valeri, who missed more than half the season with an injury.

Being an NHL superstar's little brother isn't easy. Valeri Bure (left).

Sami Kapanen

Sami Kapanen comes from one of Finland's finest hockey families. Father Hannu and his younger brother Jari were stars in the Finnish league in their time, playing 320 and 475 games respectively. In national team selections, Sami, with 94 already, has exactly twice as many games as his father (Uncle Jari only reached the B team internationally). Sami's own brother, Kimmo, is a Finnish league and national team goalie who is currently with HPK Hameenlinna. Father Hannu is also a famous coach and was behind Finland's surprise gold medal in the 1998 World Junior Championships.

Kapanen was born in Vantaa, one of the tri-cities making up the capital area, while his father played in Helsinki. His first club was EVU Vantaa, but the bulk of his junior eligibility was spent with JoKP Joensuu and KalPa Kuopio while his dad had coaching assignments. KalPa gave him his first chance in the top league as an 18-year-old, and Kapanen and his winning ways led to a fairytale career. His first season, 1990–91, coincided with the club's finest year ever when they won a silver medal. During the same spring season, he also played for Finland's bronze medal team in the under-18 European Junior Championship.

Sami Kapanen comes from one of Finland's finest hockey families.

It wasn't his skills but his stature that caused a reluctance among NHL observers to consider him for the draft. Four years later, he couldn't be overlooked and the Hartford Whalers—now the Carolina Hurricanes—picked him in the fourth round of the 1995 draft. He immediately joined the club in the fall. At the time of the draft he was on his honeymoon with his wife, Petra, and he only found out about the selection when he returned home and went through his telephone messages.

By his third season, Sami Kapanen (left) had established himself as a solid performer in the NHL.

He played his final season in the Finnish league for HIFK Helsinki with his father as coach and his brother as one of the goalies. The Helsinki club had secured the whole trio in the off-season. In 1994, his final year in Kuopio, he was selected to the First All-Star Team.

Unfortunately, his career almost came to an end even before it started. In his first training camp, he had a bad collision with defenseman Gerald Diduck. He lost his balance and while falling was hit by a knee. The result was a severe concussion and a lower-back injury. Recuperating, his first season was split between the Springfield Falcons and Hartford. He played his first game two months after the incident. Scoring the tying goal late in the game for the Falcons while making his debut in the AHL boosted his confidence. On December 13, 1995, Kapanen played in his first NHL game for the Whalers. A week later he got his first point, but it took until January 6th for him to get his first goal. On that day he put the puck into the Boston Bruins' net behind Craig Billington. His second season was a step forward—if not offensively, then at least in terms of adjusting to his new life and a new brand of hockey. The season also brought him the top plus-minus rating and the best scoring percentage on the team. In the third season he established himself as a bona fide NHL performer and has never looked back.

A lasting memory for Kapanen came during the last game in the Hartford Civic Center Veterans Memorial Coliseum. "I will always remember the atmosphere and the noise. Grown men were crying openly after the game." From his time with the Hurricanes, he was surprised that people in the shopping malls in Raleigh were starting to recognize him. But the good years in the new city were marred by the untimely demise of teammate Steve Chiasson in a tragic car accident.

While Kapanen plays wing in the NHL, on the Finnish national team he plays center and is very often the driving force on his line. He has five medals from international tournaments. The most prestigious is the nation's first-ever IIHF World Championship gold medal in Sweden in 1995. The bronze from the Nagano Olympics in 1998, when Finland defeated the Canadian "Dream Team" in the medal round, is a close second. He has another Olympic bronze from Lillehammer, Norway, in 1994 and silvers from the 1994 World Championship in Italy and the 1998 Worlds in Switzerland. The latter is his last World Championship to date, as he twisted his knee before the 1999 tournament and decided to pass on the 2000 event. He had given his all for the Hurricanes and was completely exhausted.

Kapanen, Sami
LW, 5′10″, 170 lbs, b: Vantaa, Finland, 6/14/1973

Season	Club, League	Regular Season					Playoffs				
		GP	G	A	Pts	PIM	GP	G	A	Pts	PIM
1990–91	KalPa, Finland	14	1	2	3	2	8	2	1	3	2
1991–92	KalPa, Finland	42	15	10	25	8					
1992–93	KalPa, Finland	37	4	17	21	12					
1993–94	KalPa, Finland	48	23	32	55	16					
OWG–94	Finland	8	1	0	1	2					
WC–94	Finland	8	4	2	6	0					
1994–95	HIFK, Finland	49	14	28	42	42	3	0	0	0	0
WC–95	Finland	8	2	2	4	6					
1995–96	Hartford Whalers, NHL	35	5	4	9	6					
	Springfield Falcons, AHL	28	14	17	31	4	3	1	2	3	0
WC–96	Finland	6	2	3	5	2					
WCup–96	Finland	3	0	0	0	4					
1996–97	Hartford Whalers, NHL	45	13	12	25	2					
1997–98	Carolina Hurricanes, NHL	81	26	37	63	16					
OWG–98	Finland	6	0	1	1	0					
WC–98	Finland	10	4	3	7	2					
1998–99	Carolina Hurricanes, NHL	81	24	35	59	10	5	1	1	2	0
1999–00	Carolina Hurricanes, NHL	76	24	24	48	12					
2000–01	Carolina Hurricanes, NHL	82	20	37	57	24	6	2	3	5	0
2001–02	Carolina Hurricanes, NHL	77	27	42	69	23	6	2	3	5	0
OWG–02	Finland	4	1	2	3	4					
	Finland Totals	190	57	89	146	80	11	2	1	3	2
	NHL Totals	477	139	191	330	93	11	3	4	7	0
OWG/WC/WCup Totals		53	14	13	27	20					

Won WC (1995)

In 2000–01, he played all 82 games and registered his sixth consecutive 20-goal season, though the 'Canes were eliminated in the first round of the playoffs.

Along with the likes of Teemu Selanne and Jere Lehtinen, Kapanen was again a central figure for the Finns at the 2002 Olympics, though the Games ended on a disappointing note when Canada eliminated Finland 2–1 in the quarterfinals. But then the strong play and balanced scoring attack of Kapanen, team captain Ron Francis, Jeff O'Neill and Rod Brind'Amour provided the catalyst for the Hurricanes to advance to the Stanley Cup playoffs later that year.

Sergei Berezin

From time to time, a boisterous body of fans wearing number 94 Maple Leafs sweaters invade the Air Canada Centre. And indeed they're from some other place (if not planet); these are members of the Sergei Berezin Fan Club based in Cologne, Germany. In fact, there are two Berezin fan clubs in Cologne. One is a modest affair, but the other is a well-organized institution with a charter, membership fees and a satellite TV to watch overseas games. And quite a few members are also proud owners of number 94 jerseys. You can buy the "personal" jerseys of Mats Sundin, Curtis Joseph and Tie Domi in Toronto quite easily, but others are hard to find even at specialized shops. Not to be deterred, the Cologne fan club has retained its own garment factory, and once a year German fans visit North America to noisily back up their idol.

Sergei Berezin is still more popular in Cologne than he is in Toronto.

Berezin played in Germany for only two years. True, he scored 117 goals in 120 games and was a bright star of the German national championships while he was on Cologne's team. Almost four years later, the loyalty among his admirers can be partly explained by the rich hockey traditions of the city he lived and played in (arguably, Cologne is to Germany what Toronto is to Canada). And true lovers of hockey naturally appreciated his fantastic velocity, his skating skills, his powerful shooting and his steadfast desire to score whenever he can. Now few NHL stars can boast such a following.

Nevertheless, Berezin's career in the league has had its grim moments. He made his debut with the Leafs immediately after the 1996 World Cup tournament. At first he played with Doug Gilmour—and easily scored 25

Berezin, Sergei
RW, 5'10", 187 lbs, b: Voskresensk, USSR, 11/5/1971

Season	Club, League	Regular Season					Playoffs				
		GP	G	A	Pts	PIM	GP	G	A	Pts	PIM
1990–91	Khimik, USSR	30	6	2	8	4					
1991–92	Khimik, Russia	36	7	5	12	10					
1992–93	Khimik, Russia	38	9	3	12	12	2	1	0	1	0
1993–94	Khimik, Russia	40	31	10	41	16	3	2	0	2	2
OWG–94	Russia	8	3	2	5	2					
WC–94	Russia	6	2	1	3	2					
1994–95	Kolner, Cologne, Germany	43	38	19	57	8	18	17	8	25	14
WC–95	Russia	6	7	1	8	4					
1995–96	Kolner, Cologne, Germany	45	49	31	80	8	14	13	9	22	10
WC–96	Russia	8	4	5	9	2					
WCup–96	Russia	2	1	0	1	0					
1996–97	Toronto Maple Leafs, NHL	73	25	16	41	2					
1997–98	Toronto Maple Leafs, NHL	68	16	15	31	10					
WC–98	Russia	6	6	2	8	2					
1998–99	Toronto Maple Leafs, NHL	76	37	22	59	12	17	6	6	12	4
1999–00	Toronto Maple Leafs, NHL	61	26	13	39	2	12	4	4	8	0
2000–01	Toronto Maple Leafs	79	22	28	50	8	11	2	5	7	2
2001–02	Phoenix-Montreal	70	11	15	26	8					
	USSR/Russia Totals	144	53	20	73	42	5	3	0	3	2
	NHL Totals	427	137	109	246	22	40	12	15	27	6
	OWG/WC/WCup Totals	36	23	11	34	12					

Germany Champion (1995)

His skating skills, powerful shooting and steadfast desire to score have endeared Sergei Berezin (left) to true lovers of hockey.

goals in the regular season and made the NHL All-Rookie Team. But the Toronto team was in a state of internal crisis at this time. Coaches and players and tactics revolved almost constantly and it all had a negative impact on the young Russian forward, who hadn't yet adapted to the new milieu. Berezin himself says the 1997–98 season was a waste of time. The coaches didn't yet trust him, so he was restricted to power-play units and his performance deteriorated. He was only able to restore his self-confidence at the 1998 World Championship, where he scored six goals in six games. Then Pat Quinn came to coach in Toronto and was mainly responsible for Berezin's smashing success the next season.

Having acquainted himself with his team's roster, the seasoned Quinn placed his bet on aggressive offense. In the course of a year, the once outsider club was transformed. The Leafs were the top-scoring team in the league in the regular season, and had it not been for injuries, Berezin could have claimed the Maurice Richard Trophy. In his first playoff series in the NHL, he did even better as he helped Toronto defeat Philadelphia and remained as aggressive and active in the play against Pittsburgh.

Berezin began his fourth season in the NHL in full command of the ice and led the league in shots on goal for quite a long stretch, only to have the year spoiled by consecutive injuries. In fact, he wasn't in good shape until the season drew to a close, when he had recovered enough to rank among Toronto's most aggressive forwards in the playoffs, though he couldn't save his team from losing to the New Jersey Devils in the second round.

Berezin is often accused of trying to shoot from any position and ignoring his partners. But Sergei thinks this is his job. As a forward, he must shoot at the goal. In the last two seasons, however, Berezin has proved more than once that he can make a timely pass and assist in scoring spectacular goals. And Pat Quinn's experiment in using him against power-play units has succeeded brilliantly, too. After four years in the NHL, it is clear that shooter Sergei Berezin has turned into an all-purpose player.

Following a 50-point season with the Maple Leafs in 2000–01, Berezin was dealt to the Phoenix Coyotes along with Danny Markov for Robert Reichel and Travis Green. His tenure in Arizona was short-lived, however, as he was again traded to the Montreal Canadiens on January 25, 2002, for Brian Savage, a third-round draft pick and future considerations.

Roman Turek

Goalie Roman Turek is known by his St. Louis Blues teammates as "Large." He lists his number one hobby as sleep. But for this Czech netminder, coming up big is something he does regularly and dozing between the pipes is something that almost never happens. "This Czech superstar is a netminder of the future," one reporter offers succinctly.

Born in 1970 in the Czech town of Strakonice, near Pisek, the 6′3″ and 215-pound dynamo started his big-league career as a mainstay on the Czech junior teams that competed in the European and World Junior Championships in the late 1980s. He went on to join the Budejovice club in the Czech league and was chosen MVP for Budejovice in the 1993–94 season. He also played on the Czech national team at the 1993 and 1994 World Championships and the 1994 Winter Olympics. In 1996 Turek starred for the Czechs in the World Championship, recording an impressive 7–0–1 result and leading his squad to the gold medal.

After a short and relatively unspectacular stint with Nurnberg in the German league, he made his debut with the Dallas Stars in the NHL in 1996–97 and split his time between the Texas club and Michigan of the International Hockey League for the next two seasons. He had been the Stars' (then the Minnesota North Stars) sixth pick, 113th overall, in the 1990 NHL Entry Draft. Turek consistently played well for Dallas in his first two seasons with the NHL club, recording goals-against averages of 2.05 and 2.22 respectively. He also battled injuries; a strained groin and an injured knee caused him to miss a total of 22 games over the two seasons.

In 1998–99, Turek played a role in the Stars' Stanley Cup victory, posting a 2.08 goals-against average and a .915 saves percentage while sharing goaltending duties with Ed Belfour. The impressive duo won the William M. Jennings Trophy for the team with the lowest goals scored against it, but more importantly brought the franchise its first-ever Cup.

The Dallas defense—with Belfour and Turek as its anchor—was notorious among opponents for its effectiveness. Turek summed up his relationship with the Dallas defensemen. "Sometimes the defense really helps you. They block the shots," he said. "But sometimes you don't see the puck and when it comes through you don't have a chance. I tell my defensemen, 'When you block shots, you have to block them 100%, because when you miss, I don't see the puck.'"

This Turek–Belfour goaltending partnership was working just fine as far as Turek was concerned, so long as his team was winning, a fact that was borne out by the Stars' Cup win in 1999. "It's nice when I read the newspaper and see all the stuff about how Belfour and Turek lead NHL goaltenders," he said. "But for me it's more important how the team plays and how I play for the team. When we win a game 5–3, it's better for me than when we lose 2–1. Of course it's nice to get a shutout, but mostly I like the victory."

Top 1999–2000 goalie Roman Turek lists his number one hobby as sleep.

Turek, Roman
G, 6′3″, 215 lbs, b: Pisek, Czechoslovakia, 5/21/1970

Season	Club, League	Regular Season				Playoffs			
		GP	Mins	GA	Avg	GP	Mins	GA	Avg
1990–91	Ceske Budejovice, Czechoslovakia	26	1244	98	4.70				
1992–93	Ceske Budejovice, Czech Republic	43	2555	121	2.84				
WC–93	Czech Republic	0	0	0	0.00	0	0	0	0.00
1993–94	Ceske Budejovice, Czech Republic	44	2584	111	2.51	3	180	12	4.00
OWG–94	Czech Republic	2	120	3	1.50				
WC–94	Czech Republic	2	120	4	2.00				
1994–95	Ceske Budejovice, Czech Republic	44	2587	119	2.76	9	498	25	3.01
WC–95	Czech Republic	6	359	9	1.50				
1995–96	Nurnberg, Germany	48	2787	154	3.31	5	338	14	2.48
WC–96	Czech Republic	8	480	15	1.88				
WCup–96	Czech Republic	3	82	10	7.00				
1996–97	Dallas Stars, NHL	6	263	9	2.05				
	Michigan K-Wings, IHL	29	1555	77	2.97				
1997–98	Dallas Stars, NHL	23	1324	49	2.22				
	Michigan K-Wings, IHL	2	119	5	2.51				
1998–99	Dallas Stars, NHL	26	1382	48	2.08				
1999–00	St. Louis Blues, NHL	67	3960	129	1.95	7	415	19	2.75
2000–01	St. Louis Blues, NHL	54	3232	123	2.28	14	908	31	2.05
2001–02	Czechoslovakia/ Calgary Flames	69	4081	172	2.53				
	Czech Republic Totals	157	8970	449	3.00	12	678	37	2.85
	NHL Totals	245	14242	530	2.23				
	OWG/WC/WCup Totals	21	1161	41	2.12				

Named Best Goaltender at WC (1996)
NHL Second All-Star Team (2000)
Won William M. Jennings Trophy (1999, 2000)
Won WC (1996)
Won Stanley Cup (1999)

In August 1999 Roman Turek signed as a free agent with St. Louis and became the anchor of the Blues defense.

Despite their success with their two top-notch netminders, things were getting a little crowded in the Stars' net with two of the game's top goalies struggling for playing time on a powerhouse team. Turek managed to stay sharp by practising more than he had been used to when he was a first-string goalie, often riding an exercise bike and jogging after practice. "In Europe I played lots of games and stayed after practice only sometimes," he said. "Not like here."

Reporters asked Turek whether he was getting frustrated in his role as backup to Belfour. "No, not really. Of course I want to play more games," he answered. "Every player, not just the goalie, is like that. When a skater plays two shifts a period, he's cold. Nobody feels good when they don't play a lot of games. Sometime I want to be the number one goalie on a team. I want to play. This is why I came here."

On June 20, 1999, Turek was traded to St. Louis Blues for a second-round draft choice. His multi-year contract freed him from the burden of having to play backup and he became the anchor of the Blues' defense. He was voted onto the NHL Second All-Star Team and his steady play was a big part of the St. Louis drive to the playoffs with a record-setting 1999–2000 regular season. Unfortunately, his play in the 2001 post-season persuaded St. Louis management to trade him to Calgary. With the Flames, Turek has proved invaluable, giving the team a chance to win every night he straps on the pads.

Viktor Kozlov

When Viktor Kozlov's father walked his six-year-old son to the local hockey school in Togliatti, he never imagined that 19 years later his son would be a star with the Florida Panthers, playing in the NHL's All-Star Game and making millions of dollars.

Kozlov's hockey talent was apparent to everyone by the time he was 15. ESPN's Barry Melrose tells of first seeing the 16-year-old Kozlov when he was in Canada with the Russian junior team. Even then, Kozlov was outstanding among his peers. At home in Russia, Moscow's leading teams fought to acquire him. When he was 17, the managers of CSKA and Dynamo wooed him while the young player tried to make up his mind. Finally he chose Dynamo at his father's request. The story goes that when Kozlov left for Moscow, a CSKA official was waiting for him at the railroad station in Moscow. But he never saw him because the Dynamo manager had already taken Kozlov off the train at a small station in the Moscow suburbs.

Then something happened that Kozlov would remember for the rest of his life. His agent, Paul Theophanos, took him and another young Russian player, Alexander Kharlamov, son of hockey great Valeri Kharlamov, to the 1992 NHL draft. He wanted to give them a preview of what to expect the following year. After the draft, a number of young, talented players with Theophanos' IMG agency went to Montreal to Wayne Gretzky's summer hockey school, where they were introduced to the Great One and allowed to train with the Canadian juniors for two days. Kozlov's mother still has the pictures showing her 17-year-old son with Gretzky.

At that time, Kozlov was considered a potential number one NHL draftee for 1993. His arms were compared to Mario Lemieux's and his height was good. But in the end, he was selected by the San Jose Sharks as number six. Kozlov claims it was because his performance at the World Junior Championships wasn't good enough. Now with the Florida Panthers, Kozlov is still grateful to the Sharks for selecting him in the first round and giving his career a big boost.

Kozlov's early North American career seemed to be plagued by bad luck. After he was drafted, Kozlov was doing well at his first training camp and was the team's best pre-season scorer (four goals and seven assists). He was anxious for the regular season to begin, but an NHL lockout was declared. It was a big shock for the non-English-speaking player to be asked to leave the hotel he was staying at. Fortunately, San Jose goalie Arturs Irbe invited Kozlov to stay at his home.

Kozlov was responsible for keeping himself in good shape during the lockout, since players with unilateral contracts aren't allowed to play for the farm team. So Kozlov returned to Dynamo Moscow, but during his third game he broke his leg. He returned to San Jose for medical treatment and after surgery convalesced at Irbe's home. "I can't find words to express my gratitude to him," Kozlov said at the time.

His first season in the NHL was difficult for Kozlov. Back on the ice, he felt awkward and unsure of himself. As well, his coaches and the media started to pressure him. The players who'd been selected with him in the first-round draft—Paul Kariya, Jason Arnott, Rob Niedermayer—were performing so much better than Kozlov that many were questioning his ability. All this was making him very nervous and he stopped reading the sports pages altogether.

In the NHL, not many young European players are successful right away. In Kozlov's case, observers were quick to draw unflattering conclusions about him. Perhaps his manner of playing was to blame. A big and powerful man, Kozlov doesn't like to get involved in fierce bodychecking. Darryl Sutter, the tough coach of the Sharks, especially disliked his understated style of play. And Kozlov's two goals and his record-setting 10 shots on goal in his first 1997–98 regular-season game didn't help. In the second game, he was moved to the fourth lineup. By the end of November, in the first round of the next year's draft, he was traded to the Florida Panthers. Sharks officials didn't even say goodbye. In his hotel room, after a game in Los Angeles, Kozlov found his equipment and a note saying, "You've been traded to the Florida Panthers. Your plane leaves tomorrow at 7.30 a.m."

In Miami, Kozlov's luck didn't improve. He was to be included on the Russian team going

Viktor Kozlov (right) was considered a potential number one NHL draftee in 1993.

Kozlov, Viktor
C/LW, 6'5", 232 lbs, b: Togliatti, USSR, 2/14/1975

Season	Club, League	Regular Season					Playoffs				
		GP	G	A	Pts	PLM	GP	G	A	Pts	PLM
1990–91	Lada, USSR(2)	2	2	0	2	0					
1991–92	Lada, Russia	3	0	0	0	0					
1992–93	Dynamo Moscow, Russia	30	6	5	11	4	10	3	0	3	0
1993–94	Dynamo Moscow, Russia	42	16	9	25	14	7	3	2	5	0
1994–95	Dynamo Moscow, Russia	3	1	1	2	2					
	San Jose Sharks, NHL	16	2	0	2	2					
	Kansas City, IHL	4	1	1	2	0	13	4	5	9	12
995–96	San Jose Sharks, NHL	62	6	13	19	6					
	Kansas City, IHL	15	4	7	11	12					
WC–96	Russia	8	0	3	3	0					
1996–97	San Jose Sharks, NHL	78	16	25	41	40					
1997–98	San Jose Sharks, NHL	18	5	2	7	2					
	Florida Panthers, NHL	46	12	11	23	14					
WC–98	Russia	6	4	5	9	0					
1998–99	Florida Panthers, NHL	65	16	35	51	24					
1999–00	Florida Panthers, NHL	80	17	52	69	16	4	0	1	1	0
WC–2000	Russia	6	1	3	4	2					
2000–01	Florida Panthers, NHL	51	14	23	37	10					
2001–02	Florida Panthers	50	9	18	27	20					
	Russia Totals	78	23	15	38	20	17	6	2	8	0
	NHL Totals	466	97	180	277	134					
	WC Totals	20	5	11	16	2					

Russia Champion (1993)

Viktor Kozlov found his equipment and a note—"You've been traded to the Florida Panthers. Your plane leaves tomorrow at 7:30 a.m."—in his hotel room.

to the Olympics in Nagano, Japan, but three days before the departure date he injured his shoulder. The following year he was invited for the first time to play in the All-Star Game, but he injured the same shoulder in the last game of the regular season. He was playing better than with the Sharks, but his coaches expected much more of him.

But all that changed when Pavel Bure arrived in Florida. Panthers general manager Bryan Murray said later, "We thought we were acquiring one star but it turned out we got two." Kozlov's performance was dazzling after he became a center in the Russian Rocket's trio in the 1999–2000 season. Kozlov says of Bure: "He never instructs you how to play. He just shows up at the right moment in the right place and you just have to make a pass to him. I play my game and don't even have to coordinate my moves with his. The puck just gets to him when he needs it." Finally, at 25, Kozlov had started to fulfill the promise he showed at 17. In the first half of the 1999–2000 season, he had beaten his personal points record and was among the top five scorers in the league. At his first All-Star Game, he tied Boston's Ray Bourque for first place in accurate shooting, hitting four out of five targets.

Back in Russia, when they started talking about the national team's superstar lineup for the 2002 Olympics in Salt Lake City—Pavel Bure, Viktor Kozlov and Valeri Bure—they noted that this was the same trio that had performed so well at the All-Star Game in Toronto. Kozlov was very excited about playing in the Olympics, though perhaps the bronze medal wasn't all he had hoped for.

The past two seasons in Florida have been somewhat frustrating for Kozlov, who hasn't emerged as the scoring star some scouts had said he was bound to become. When the team failed to even come close to making the playoffs again in 2001–02, management unloaded several large salaries at the trade deadline, including Pavel Bure's.

Nikolai Khabibulin

It's an unusual child who wants to be a goaltender. But at the age of seven, Nikolai Khabibulin loved to defend the net. His idol was Vladislav Tretiak and a poster of the great Russian goalie dominated one wall of his room.

In his first two months at sports school, Khabibulin played defense because there wasn't an extra set of goalie equipment. But he still dreamed of being a goaltender. At 15, Khabibulin was included on Sverdlovsk's Avtomobilist team. He spent most of his time on the bench, but when he was 17, CSKA Moscow invited him to play for them. In his first season with CSKA, head coach Viktor Tikhonov didn't let him play as first goaltender, but at the World Junior Championship, Khabibulin was the Soviets' first goalie.

Tikhonov took him as third goalie to the 1992 Olympics in Albertville, France, where Khabibulin didn't get a chance to play and contribute to the Russian victory; the more experienced goalies—Mikhail Shtalenkov and Andrei Trefilov—were doing just fine. An incident at the awards ceremony stayed in his mind forever. "There were 23 medals for 23 players," Khabibulin recalled, "and no medals for coaches. In the end, the 22 participants in the final game got their medals and the 23rd was awarded to Viktor Tikhonov."

Later, Khabibulin would say he wasn't upset over the loss of the medal since he had done nothing to secure the victory. But perhaps he was being less than honest. After his refusal to go to the 1998 Olympics in Nagano, his partner on the Phoenix Coyotes, Keith Tkachuk, remarked, "The Russians deprived him of a gold medal in Albertville, and now he's getting his revenge for that." Khabibulin argued it had nothing to do with his forfeited gold medal in Albertville, blaming his decision on tensions between players and the Russian Hockey Federation during the 1996 World Cup.

Since Khabibulin's refusal to play at the Olympics, the goaltender has been treated less warmly in his home country—not because of his stand (other Russian NHL players declined the offer to join the Russian team), but because he refused to meet with Russian head coach Vladimir Yurzinov and his assistants, Alexei Kasatonov and Vladislav Tretiak, when they came to America hoping to persuade him to play for them at the Olympics. When he was told about the visitors, Khabibulin left the room and disappeared. The incident launched a wave of indignation in Russia.

A talent for goaltending is uncommon, and to be successful in the NHL, a goalie needs outstanding skills and a lot of luck. Khabibulin has both. In 1994, after three seasons with CSKA, he joined the Winnipeg Jets, who had drafted him in the eighth round two years earlier. A lockout at the time prevented the young goalie from playing, but he had a two-way contract, giving him the opportunity to work on his technique in Springfield with the Jets' farm team. When the short 1994–95 season began, the Russian goalie was doing as well as the Jets' main goaltender, Tim Cheveldae.

At the beginning of the next season, Jets coaches told Khabibulin there would be no distinction between primary and secondary goaltenders—either would be allowed to defend the net equally until the first major error. Cheveldae's performance was uneven, but Khabibulin didn't make an error in 15 consecutive games. Then he sustained a knee injury and was forced to leave the ice. Without him, the Jets gained only 13 points in 20 games. When he returned, Khabibulin was able to regain his position as the number one goalie and didn't yield it again.

In his third season in the NHL, Khabibulin's team moved from Winnipeg to Arizona and was given a new name, the Phoenix Coyotes. In Phoenix, Khabibulin continued to be the leading goalie. By mid-season, he was in excellent form, with seven shutouts in 27 games. He didn't allow a single goal in three consecutive games against the Panthers, the Lightning and the Blackhawks. He set the team's all-time record and was named NHL player of the week. The next two seasons were equally successful for Khabibulin; he set a team record with a total of 126 wins. Unfortunately, the Coyotes have so far not made it beyond the first round in the Stanley Cup playoffs—but many believed this was mainly because of the goalie's youth.

Nikolai Khabibulin always dreamed of becoming a goaltender.

Khabibulin, Nikolai
G, 6´1˝, 176 lbs, b: Sverdlovsk, USSR, 1/13/1973

Season	Club, League	Regular Season				Playoffs			
		GP	Mins	GA	Avg	GP	Mins	GA	Avg
1991–92	CSKA, Russia	2	34	2	3.52				
OWG–92	Russia	0	0	0	0				
1992–93	CSKA, Russia	13	491	27	3.29				
1993–94	CSKA, Russia	46	2625	116	2.65	3	193	11	3.42
	Russian Penguins, IHL	12	639	47	4.41				
1994–95	Springfield Falcons, AHL	23	1240	80	3.87				
	Winnipeg Jets, NHL	26	1339	76	3.41				
1995–96	Winnipeg Jets, NHL	53	2914	152	3.13	3	359	19	3.18
WCup–96	Russia	2	100	10	6.00				
1996–97	Phoenix Coyotes, NHL	72	4091	193	2.83	7	426	15	2.11
1997–98	Phoenix Coyotes, NHL	70	4026	184	2.74	4	185	13	4.22
1998–99	Phoenix Coyotes, NHL	63	3657	130	2.13	7	449	18	2.41
2000–01	Tampa Bay Lightning, NHL	2	123	6	2.93				
2001–02	Tampa Bay Lightning	70	3896	153	2.36				
OWG–02	Russia	6	359	14	2.34				
	Russia Totals	61	3150	145	2.76	3	193	11	3.42
	NHL Totals	356	20046	894	2.68				
	OWG/WCup Totals	8	459	24	3.14				

Won OWG (1992)

A HISTORY OF WORLD HOCKEY

In his third season in the NHL, Nikolai Khabibulin set an all-time record for the Phoenix Coyotes with three shutouts in a row.

In the 1999–2000 season, the impressive pace of Khabibulin's career slowed down. A strike over a contract dispute proved to be a serious setback. Reluctant to compromise with the Coyotes administration, he declared he would never wear the team jersey again and signed a contract with the International Hockey League's Long Beach Ice Dogs. His outstanding performance led to the hope that before the trade deadline, an NHL club would agree to a trade from Phoenix, and there were rumors that the Red Wings and the Flyers were interested, but nothing came of them. Then Tampa Bay acquired his rights in a multi-player deal, and all of a sudden, with the Berlin Wall in the goal, it seemed the Lightning had a team that could win anytime.

But even Khabibulin's fantastic netminding couldn't vault the hapless Lightning into the 2001–02 playoffs when a lack of scoring prowess and the continued decline of Vincent Lecavalier's performance sealed the team's fate. So the highlight of Khabibulin's season came in Salt Lake City, where he helped Russia to the bronze medal. His best performance came in a head-to-head showdown with Czech goaltender Dominik Hasek. Although Hasek was excellent, stopping all but one shot, Khabibulin managed to top that, shutting out the defending Olympic champs and sending them home without the chance of winning a medal.

Sergei Gonchar

President Clinton is a Sergei Gonchar fan.

Sergei Gonchar was seven years old when he told his parents he wanted to play soccer. But his father gave him some unhappy news. He told the youngster he wouldn't make a good soccer player because he was too slow. Instead, he took his son to the skating rink.

As a boy, Gonchar was both sports-minded and a book-lover. His parents were avid readers, and he was never without a book of fiction. Later he started reading history and philosophy. "At 16, I began playing for junior teams," Gonchar recalled. "I traveled abroad and came to believe that if you have an opportunity to see and get to know the world, it's stupid to waste your time doing nothing."

After a season with Traktor in Chelyabinsk, Gonchar moved to Dynamo Moscow. In those days, the amiable scoring defenseman was often involved in fistfighting on the ice. Most often his opponent was Alexander Selivanov of Spartak Moscow, who now plays for the Columbus Blue Jackets. Gonchar almost never joined in the team's offensive rushes. "Now I see that I was doing wrong," he says. "I had learned only defensive skills and what was most natural for me wasn't being developed. I made up for lost time in the NHL. In America I stopped fighting for good—especially after I watched Washington tough guy Craig Berube using his fists. Then I knew I could quietly stay back."

Watching Gonchar play, the first thing you notice is his powerful wrist shot. Often you don't even see the puck flying through the air; you only spot it when it's already in the net. He didn't have such a powerful shot playing back in Russia. "While in the NHL, I began shooting more often," says Gonchar, "not only during the games, but also during workouts. It gets to be a habit because of the small rinks. At first it was hard to relearn my skills and abandon the typical Russian enthusiasm for passing. But after a number of years in the NHL, this appetite for shooting has become a habit."

In the 1998–99 season, Gonchar (front) became the first Russian defenseman to score over 20 goals in the regular season.

Gonchar transferred smoothly to the North American style of hockey. In a way, he was lucky that his first season was during the 1994 NHL lockout. Gonchar had a two-way contract with the Capitals, so he was able to spend the lockout months with Portland of the AHL, the Capitals' farm team. He perfected his English and started learning the North American playing style. And Portland's 16-game winning streak boosted his confidence.

In the second half of the season, Gonchar was called up to the regular team but was slow to get accustomed to his new milieu. At first he communicated only in Russian with Dmitri Khristich and Peter Bondra (a Slovak who spent the first 14 years of his life in the Ukrainian city of Lutsk and speaks perfect Russian). Eventually, though, he widened his circle.

One of his new friends in Washington was a White House guard. One evening before Christmas he invited Gonchar and his parents on a tour of the White House. All of a sudden President Clinton came out a door without his bodyguards and wearing jeans. He spoke briefly with Gonchar without knowing who he was. Then his bodyguards appeared and the President left. Later, however, Gonchar received a picture of the President with the inscription "To Sergei Gonchar—with all the best wishes."

New Capitals coach Ron Wilson has had an influence on Gonchar's career. Within six months they had gotten to know each other better, and Wilson soon considered Gonchar indispensable to the team. Gonchar's trip to Nagano, Japan, with the Russian Olympic team helped raise his profile. In Nagano he performed well, and back in Washington his star began to shine.

In the 1998–99 season, Gonchar became the first Russian defenseman to score over 20 goals in regular-season play. In January 2000 he got his first hat-trick, in a game against the Montreal Canadiens (only the second hat-trick among Russian defensemen after Vladimir Malakhov). The 25-year-old player's career is on the rise and he is considered a possible candidate for the Norris Trophy.

Gonchar, Sergei
D, 6´2˝, 212 lbs, b: Chelyabinsk, USSR, 4/13/1974

Season	Club, League	Regular Season					Playoffs				
		GP	G	A	Pts	PIM	GP	G	A	Pts	PIM
1991–92	Traktor, Russia	31	1	0	1	6					
1992–93	Dynamo Moscow, Russia	31	1	3	4	70	10	0	0	0	12
1993–94	Dynamo Moscow, Russia	44	4	5	9	36	10	0	3	3	14
	Portland Pirates, AHL						2	0	0	0	0
1994–95	Portland Pirates, AHL	61	10	32	42	67					
	Washington Capitals, NHL	31	2	5	7	22	7	2	2	4	2
1995–96	Washington Capitals, NHL	78	15	26	41	60	6	2	4	6	4
WCup–96	Russia	4	2	2	4	2					
1996–97	Washington Capitals, NHL	57	13	17	30	36					
1997–98	Lada, Russia	7	3	2	5	4					
	Washington Capitals, NHL	72	5	16	21	66	21	7	4	11	30
OWG–98	Russia	6	0	2	2	0					
1998–99	Washington Capitals, NHL	53	21	10	31	57					
1999–2000	Washington Capitals, NHL	73	18	36	54	52	5	1	0	1	6
WC–2000	Russia	6	1	0	1	2					
2000–01	Washington Capitals	76	19	38	57	70	6	1	3	4	2
2001–02	Washington Capitals	76	26	33	59	58					
OWG–02	Russia	6	0	0	0	0					
	Russia Totals	113	9	10	19	116	20	0	3	3	26
	NHL Totals	516	119	181	300	421					
	OWG/WCup Totals	22	3	4	7	6					

Russia Champion (1993)

In 2001–02 Gonchar played in his eighth NHL season, all with the Capitals, and marked the second time he reached at least 20 goals in a season. He was also a member of the bronze medal-winning Russian team at the 2002 Olympics.

Daniel **Alfredsson**

Daniel Alfredsson appeared in all 82 regular-season games in his rookie year.

Daniel Alfredsson had never played for Sweden's national junior team, and the Ottawa Senators got a real bargain when they selected the 5´11″, 187-pound right winger in the fifth round, 133rd overall, of the 1994 Entry Draft and then signed him for $250,000 in 1995. For their modest investment, the Senators got a Calder Trophy winner who was also named to the NHL's All-Rookie Team and was the only rookie in the league named to play in the All-Star Game. Alfredsson, 23 at the time, edged out Chicago Blackhawks winger Eric Daze, a star with Canada's gold medal-winning national junior team in 1995, and talented Florida Panthers defenseman Ed Jovanovski in the voting to honor the league's best first-year player. The Swede led all rookies in scoring with 26 goals and 61 points while appearing in all 82 regular-season games (Czech-born defenseman Stanislav Neckar was the only other Ottawa player who didn't miss a regular-season game). It took Alfredsson less than a month to score his first hat-trick, which came against the Hartford Whalers on November 2.

In his first NHL playoff series, in 1997, he led the Senators in scoring and scored two game-winning goals, though the Senators bowed to the Buffalo Sabres in seven games. Then, to prove that was no fluke, he scored seven goals in 11 playoff games in 1998, including three first-period goals in a span of 12 minutes as the Senators defeated the Washington Capitals 4–3.

Although he made an immediate impact in Ottawa, the total salaries of the players participating in the 1997 NHL All-Star Game in San Jose amounted to $108 million and Alfredsson was the lowest-paid player on the ice. He was one of only eight players in uniform earning less than $1 million a season. After sitting out the entire pre-season and the first six games of the 1997–98 season, he signed a lofty four-year contract reportedly worth $10 million.

Alfredsson played his first game in the Swedish Elite League with Vastra Frolunda in the city of Goteborg (where he'd been born) at the age of 19.

His most memorable international match came in the semifinals of the 1995 World Championship in Stockholm. He scored two goals, including the winner in overtime, as Sweden edged Canada 3–2. He also represented his country at the 1996 World

Alfredsson, Daniel
RW, 5´11″, 200 lbs, b: Goteborg, Sweden, 12/11/1972

Season	Club, League	Regular Season					Playoffs				
		GC	W	L	T	PLM	GC	W	L	T	PLM
1992–93	Vastra Frolunda, Sweden	20	1	5	6	8					
1993–94	Vastra Frolunda, Sweden	39	20	10	30	18	4	1	1	2	*
1994–95	Vastra Frolunda, Sweden	22	7	11	18	22					
WC–95	Sweden	8	3	1	4	4					
1995–96	Ottawa Senators, NHL	82	26	35	61	28					
WC–96	Sweden	6	1	2	3	4					
WCup–96	Sweden	4	0	0	0	2					
1996–97	Ottawa Senators, NHL	76	24	47	71	30	7	5	2	7	6
1997–98	Ottawa Senators, NHL	55	17	28	45	18	11	7	2	9	20
OWG–98	Sweden	4	2	3	5	2					
1998–99	Ottawa Senators, NHL	58	11	22	33	14	4	1	2	3	4
WC–99	Sweden	10	4	5	9	8					
1999–00	Ottawa Senators, NHL	57	21	38	59	28	6	1	3	4	2
2000–01	Ottawa Senators, NHL	68	24	46	70	30	4	1	0	1	2
2001–02	Ottawa Senators	78	37	34	71	45					
OWG–02	Sweden	4	1	4	5	2					
	Sweden Totals	81	28	26	54	48	4	1	1	2	*
	NHL Totals	474	160	250	410	193					
	OWG/WC/WCup Totals	36	11	15	26	22					

Won Calder Trophy (1996)

Championship tournament in Vienna but declined to join the Swedish national team in Finland in the spring of 1997—after Ottawa had been eliminated—because his contract had expired. A disappointed Kent Forsberg, Sweden's coach, told reporters that he had spoken with Alfredsson during the playoffs and Alfredsson had told him he was anxious to play in the World Championship. Sweden lost to Canada in a best-of-three series for the gold medal.

And, although Sweden failed to win a medal at the 1998 Olympics in Nagano, Japan, Alfredsson was one of the team's better performers, producing two goals and five points in four games.

It took Daniel Alfredsson (right) less than a month to score his first hat-trick in the NHL.

While Swedish players were easily intimidated in the early years of the European migration, Alfredsson is capable of playing tough hockey and is a good team player. In the fall of 1998, Daniel was reunited in Ottawa with his 19-year-old brother, Henric, who came to Canada to play for the Ottawa 67s junior club of the Ontario Hockey League. Although there is six years' difference in their ages, they wear the same number on their jerseys, are the same height and almost the same weight and play the same position in the same city. And the Senators showed their respect for Alfredsson when they named him captain of the team for the 1999–2000 season after Alexei Yashin, who had worn the "C" the year before, decided to sit it out when the club refused to renegotiate his contract.

After solid regular seasons in 1999–2000 and 2000–01, the Senators had their campaigns come to a quick end in the playoffs, losing to the Maple Leafs both times. Alfredsson also represented Sweden at the 2002 Winter Olympics and was part of the shocking loss to Belarus that eliminated them from medal contention in the quarterfinals.

Paul Kariya

When the superstars of the previous hockey generation went into retirement, Wayne Gretzky and Mario Lemieux chief among them, a great deal of attention was focused on Paul Kariya. He seemed to have all the necessary skills, as well as a relentless desire to better his game. A creative forward with great ability to anticipate plays, the speedy Kariya seemed poised to lead the game into the next century.

Kariya was a hockey perfectionist. He would mark a small "x" on the boards during practice and then stay on the ice when the rest of the team had left for the showers, snapping wrist shots, snapshots and slapshots at his tiny target.

Fast and creative, Paul Kariya seems poised to lead the game into the 21st century.

Kariya's development into a top-tier player came from his devotion to the game and the support of his sporting family. Of Japanese descent, Paul was born and raised in North Vancouver, British Columbia. His father, Tetsuhiko, toured for several years with the Canadian national rugby team. Paul took to the ice early, beginning at age three as a figure skater and then as a hockey player a year later. He had an instinctual balance on skates and excelled as a youngster, moving easily around the ice while the other kids struggled to stay upright. He moved up quickly and began playing with older players, listening to his father, who coached him as an underage Atom. As a youth,

Paul Kariya

Paul could score goals but preferred to make the pretty pass. When he wasn't on the ice, he was watching games on tape, concentrating on players such as Bobby Orr, Mario Lemieux and especially his favorite, Wayne Gretzky. He began to skate like the Great One, tucked his shirt in just like the Oiler star and camped out behind the opponent's net to find an open teammate.

"I watch Gretzky in my spare time because we're about the same size," Kariya said. "The way he uses his teammates and finds open people—the game seems to slow down when he has the puck. He does things with style, with class. I want to do things in a similar way. I've just tried to take the best things I've seen of Gretzky from the tapes."

Though a diminutive player, Kariya was head and shoulders above the competition as a 15-year-old. He made the trek north to Penticton, a hockey factory that had produced such stars as Andy Moog and Brett Hull, and with the Panthers he was able to attend a high-quality school, which his parents always stressed. Kariya was the youngest of the 170 teenagers trying out for the Penticton Panthers, a new team in the British Columbia Junior Hockey League. Not only did he make the team, but he was voted its captain. The Panthers struggled, but Kariya averaged more than two points a game on his way to winning junior player of the year honors in the province.

Halfway through the next season, Kariya was selected to play for Canada in the World Junior Championships in Germany, joining another much talked about junior, Eric Lindros. The two became friends during the tournament and Lindros, seeing that the smaller player was exhausted and sick after so many games, suggested Kariya take a break when he returned. Kariya didn't heed the advice and got sicker. He collapsed just before an all-star game and was diagnosed with mononucleosis. He returned after missing 12 games and led the Panthers to respectability. Kariya finished his final junior season with 132 points and was chosen the top junior player in Canada.

Kariya received scholarship offers from all over the United States, as well as a lucrative deal to play in the Western Hockey League with the Tri-City Americans. He decided to further his education and play for the University of Maine Black Bears in the U.S. collegiate ranks. In his first season, 1992–93, Maine was chosen the pre-season favorite to win the national championship. Fans filled the arena for practices and the Black Bears didn't disappoint, losing only one game in the regular season. Kariya had 100 points and won the Hobey Baker Award as the nation's top college player, the first freshman to win that honor. The day after winning the award, he led a third-period comeback against Lake Superior State to secure the national title for Maine.

That summer, Kariya was eligible for the NHL Entry Draft, but, surprisingly, he was worried he wouldn't be drafted. This draft was widely regarded as one of the finest in history and only one team, the Hartford Whalers, had

Kariya, Paul
LW, 5′11″, 175 lbs, b: Vancouver, B.C., 10/16/1974

Season	Club, League	Regular Season					Playoffs				
		GP	G	A	Pts	PIM	GP	G	A	Pts	PIM
1992–93	University of Maine, H.E.	36	25	75	100	12					
WC–93	Canada	8	2	7	9	0					
1993–94	University of Maine, H.E.	12	8	16	24	4					
OWG–94	Canada	8	3	4	7	2					
WC–94	Canada	8	5	7	12	2					
1994–95	Anaheim Mighty Ducks, NHL	47	18	21	39	4					
1995–96	Anaheim Mighty Ducks, NHL	82	50	58	108	20					
WC–96	Canada	8	4	3	7	2					
1996–97	Anaheim Mighty Ducks, NHL	69	44	55	99	6	11	7	6	13	4
1997–98	Anaheim Mighty Ducks, NHL	22	17	14	31	23					
1998–99	Anaheim Mighty Ducks, NHL	82	39	62	101	40	3	1	3	4	0
1999–00	Anaheim Mighty Ducks, NHL	74	42	44	86	24					
2000–01	Anaheim Mighty Ducks, NHL	66	33	34	67	20					
2001–02	Anaheim Mighty Ducks	82	32	25	57	28					
OWG–02	Canada	6	3	1	4	0					
	NHL Totals	524	275	313	588	165					
	OWG/WC Totals	38	17	22	39	6					

Named Best Forward at WC (1994, 1996)
NHL First All-Star Team (1996, 1997, 1999)
NHL Second All-Star Team (2000)
Won Lady Byng Trophy (1996, 1997)
Won WC (1994)
Won OWG (2002)

interviewed him. Kariya knew other top prospects had met with as many as 16 teams in the days leading up to the draft. The Mighty Ducks of Anaheim, owned by the Disney corporation, didn't want anyone to know how interested they were in Kariya—not even the player himself. Disney's chief executive, Michael Eisner, couldn't help himself after the top three picks were made without Kariya's name being announced. Just before the Mighty Ducks selected him with the fourth pick overall, Eisner conspicuously winked in the direction of Kariya and his family. Anaheim was convinced they could build their new franchise around the mature young man.

One of Kariya's dreams was to play for Canada in the Olympics, an assignment the Mighty Ducks management agreed might help the winger ready himself for the pro game. He began his season with Maine and then joined the Canadian Olympic team as it readied itself for the 1994 Games in Lillehammer, Norway. After a strong exhibition schedule, Kariya was Team Canada's top scorer in the tournament with four assists and three goals, including an overtime winner against the Czech Republic in the quarterfinals. In the gold medal game, the final event of the Olympics, Canada and Sweden had to go to a sudden-death shootout to decide the winner. After five shooters for both teams, including Kariya (who scored one of Canada's two goals), the teams were still deadlocked. In the sudden-death encore, Kariya had to score to keep Canada's chances alive after Peter Forsberg scored on a nifty deke. However, Swedish goalkeeper Tommy Salo made an acrobatic save on Kariya's close-in shot to win the game and the gold for Sweden.

After a nasty incident involving Gary Suter, Paul Kariya changed his approach to the game: "I don't think winning the Lady Byng is going to help me anymore."

Despite the disappointment, watched by millions of Canadians, Kariya rebounded to give everyone a taste of what was to come in 47 games with the Mighty Ducks and as a member of Canada's entry in the World Cup. The next season, 1995–96, he exploded for 108 points in his first full year in the NHL. It was a pace he would continue over the following three seasons, collecting 231 points in 173 games.

In February 1996 Kariya was named a starter for the All-Star Game. He was still in awe of his fellow stars, making comments to that effect to the man he stood next to during the introductions, Winnipeg's high-scoring Teemu Selanne. Three weeks later, Kariya became more familiar with the talented Finn when the Mighty Ducks made a trade with Winnipeg to bring Selanne to Anaheim. Selanne had the speed and goal-scoring touch to take advantage of Kariya's innate ability to find the open man. The twosome formed a dangerous and fast combination, often teaming with center Steve Rucchin, who, like Kariya, was a product of the post-secondary hockey system, joining the team after starring at the University of Western Ontario.

Anaheim was improving but still hadn't made the playoffs during Kariya's stay when the 1996–97 season began. Kariya was named the team's captain but missed the first 11 games of the season due to injury. And his importance to the Mighty Ducks became apparent. The team won only one game during his absence. When he returned, Anaheim began to climb in the standings, earning a playoff spot by the end of the season. Kariya scored an overtime goal to keep the team alive in the first round against the Phoenix Coyotes as the Ducks rallied to advance to the next round in seven games. The Detroit Red Wings—the eventual Stanley Cup champions—had too much depth for Anaheim in the conference semifinals, sending the upstarts from the West home in four games. But Anaheim's success and Kariya's 99 points in his shortened season had ensured his name was among the final three considered for the Hart Trophy as the league's most valuable player.

Just before he was to play in the 1998 All-Star Game, Kariya sustained his fourth career concussion in a nasty incident involving Chicago's Gary Suter. After scoring a goal, Kariya relaxed and was beginning to raise his arms in celebration when Suter cross-checked him to the head. Kariya never lost consciousness and could remember the details of the game. Only later did he feel the effects of the hit—the headaches and memory loss. He missed the rest of the season and the Nagano Olympics because of post-concussion syndrome. Suter received a four-game suspension for the hit, a punishment which many observers believed was too light given the severity of Kariya's injury and the length of his absence.

When Kariya did return, he took safety precautions such as wearing a padded helmet, tightening his chinstrap and wearing a mouth guard. The Mighty Ducks stocked up on muscle to protect their franchise player, acquiring Stu "the Grim Reaper" Grimson and Jim McKenzie. Kariya also changed his usually peaceful approach to the game. "I don't think winning the Lady Byng is going to help me anymore," Kariya said of the award for the league's most gentlemanly player, which he won in 1996 and 1997. "Maybe I've got to get my stick up and rack up some more penalty minutes."

Kariya didn't take so many penalties that his scoring decreased. Terrorizing defenders and goalies with Selanne, Kariya finished third in overall scoring in 1998–99 and—still only 25 years old entering the new century—appeared ready once again to take up the reins of superstardom. He continued to concentrate almost solely on hockey, declining many endorsement deals and maintaining his close family ties. He took advantage of his sister Michiko's organizational abilities to take care of his charitable and business affairs, while his younger brother Steve made a stir with the Vancouver Canucks at the beginning of the 1999–2000 season, showing some of the speed and poise with the puck that has established Paul at the top of the scoring charts.

Kariya missed part of 2000–01, again with a broken foot, and his play suffered as a result of the Selanne trade. Kariya was now the only bona fide superstar on the Ducks, and when opponents shut him down, they stood a much better chance of winning.

Kariya was one of the initial eight players selected by Team Canada brass to participate in the 2002 Olympics, where the bigger ice surface was much to Kariya's liking and he excelled. Fast breakouts out of his own end set up a number of scoring plays in the opposition's zone and Kariya took home a gold medal.

Patrik Elias

New Jersey winger Patrik Elias is a key cog in the Devils' well-oiled machine—one that won the 1999–2000 Stanley Cup even though they weren't considered one of the favorites. Elias's timely scoring throughout the regular season and into the playoffs was a big reason for the team's success, and especially its ability to climb back from a 3–1 deficit to overcome the Philadelphia Flyers in the Eastern Conference finals and make it to the Cup finals against Dallas.

Patrik Elias's late arrival as a goal-scoring threat is something of an anomaly.

But success in the NHL hasn't always been a given for Elias, one of the many outstanding Czech players to have made a mark in the NHL. In fact, in a league where almost a quarter of the players are from countries other than Canada and the U.S. and foreign superstars are expected to make an impression right away, Elias's delayed emergence as a goal-scoring threat is something of an anomaly.

He grew up in the Czech city of Trebic. His incredible quickness, solid checking and intelligence on the ice were all noticed by NHL scouts while he was still a member of the Czech junior national team and during his time in the Czech league with the Kladno team—the squad that also produced his hero, Jaromir Jagr. Elias says that one of his greatest thrills in hockey came when Jagr returned home to play 11 games with Kladno during the NHL lockout of 1994–95.

Elias was picked by New Jersey 51st overall in the second round of the 1994 NHL Entry Draft but decided to stay in the Czech Republic with Kladno for one more year before going to the NHL. At only 19 years of age, Elias refused the chance to play junior hockey with the Ontario Hockey League's Sarnia Sting, who had picked him third overall in the 1994 Import Draft. Instead, he immediately joined a powerful Devils team that had won the Stanley Cup in 1995. In 1995–96 Elias appeared in just one New Jersey game and spent most of the season playing for the Albany River Rats in the American Hockey League.

He bounced around between the River Rats and the Devils for the next two seasons, making the 1996–97 AHL All-Star game and registering 51 goals and 79 assists for 130 points in 131 total games in Albany in the process.

Impressed by his stats and his hard work on the farm club, management moved Elias up to the NHL for the 1997 playoffs and he produced immediately, scoring five points in eight post-season games. The following season, New Jersey called him up to the NHL again and he immediately met the challenge of big-league play, scoring 18 goals and registering 19 assists that year and finishing third in the balloting for the Calder Trophy as the NHL's best rookie. Close observers of the game noted that only Calder winner Sergei Samsonov of Boston scored more goals than Elias, and only Samsonov and Toronto's Mike Johnson had more points. The high point of Elias's rookie season was when he was named NHL player of the week after scoring five goals in three games in November of his first year.

The one significant downside to Elias's career in the NHL since making the move to the big time came in 1998 when he failed to make the powerful Czech Olympic team that ended up winning top honors at the Winter Games in Nagano, Japan. Off the ice, Elias had another rough go of it in 1999 as he and Devils management tried to come to an agreement over his contract. But Patrik's story ended happily, and

Elias, Patrik
LW, 6′1″, 200 lbs, b: Trebic, Czechoslovakia, 4/13/1976

Season	Club, League	Regular Season					Playoffs				
		GP	G	A	Pts	Plm	GP	G	A	Pts	Plm
1992–93	Poldi Kladno, Czechoslovakia	2	0	0	0	2					
1993–94	Poldi Kladno, Czech Republic	15	1	2	3	20	11	2	2	4	10
1994–95	Poldi Kladno, Czech Republic	28	4	3	7	37	7	1	2	3	12
1995–96	New Jersey Devils, NHL	1	0	0	0	0					
	Albany River Rats, AHL	74	27	36	63	83	4	1	1	2	2
1996–97	New Jersey Devils, NHL	17	2	3	5	2	8	2	3	5	4
	Albany River Rats, AHL	57	24	43	67	76	6	1	2	3	8
1997–98	New Jersey Devils, NHL	74	18	19	37	28	4	0	1	1	0
	Albany River Rats, AHL	3	3	0	3	2					
WC–98	Czech Republic	3	1	0	1	0					
1998–99	New Jersey Devils, NHL	74	17	33	50	34	7	0	5	5	6
1999–00	New Jersey Devils, NHL	72	35	37	72	58	23	7	13	20	9
	Czechoslovakia/										
2000–01	New Jersey Devils	82	40	56	96	51					
2001–02	New Jersey Devils	75	29	32	61	36	25	9	14	23	10
OWG–02	Czech Republic	4	1	1	2	0					
	Czech Republic Totals	45	5	5	10	59	18	3	4	7	22
	NHL Totals	395	141	180	321	209					
	OWG/WC Totals	7	2	1	3	0					

Won Stanley Cup (2000)

with 35 goals and 72 points in the regular season, Elias led the Devils in scoring in the 1999–2000 regular season and again with 13 playoff assists en route to their Stanley Cup victory, testament to his development as an on-ice leader.

Elias had his best offensive season in the NHL in 2000–01, scoring 40 goals and 96 points while appearing in all 82 games for the Devils. The team returned to the Cup finals in the spring looking to defend their title, where Elias again provided the team with an offensive spark, scoring 23 points in 25 games. Elias played in his first Olympics in 2002, but the defending champs from the Czech Republic returned home without a medal, losing in the quarterfinals 1–0 to Russia. Back in the NHL, the 96-point season of a year earlier certainly drew added attention from the opposition, which took to checking Elias much closer, and his production noticeably declined in 2001–02.

Patrik Elias (center) led the Devils in scoring in 1999–2000 and added 13 assists in the playoffs that led to their Stanley Cup victory.

Saku Koivu

Saku Koivu is a compact player with a big heart and a lot of determination. But the best elements of his game can also be his worst ones. The reckless abandon with which he flies headlong into each situation on the ice has led to many injuries and prevented the current captain of the Flying Frenchmen from playing to the full extent of his talents.

In another lifetime, he could have been blessed with a bigger frame, since his father—who coached him at the junior and senior levels—is quite tall. Size has never held him back, though. He has built up his strength to the point that, nine times out of 10, he's the guy who comes out of the corner with the puck. He applies a technique used by the old Soviet players against their bigger opponents from the NHL, namely, checking them before they have time to recover with the puck.

It could have been something he picked up while playing three seasons in Finland under the tutelage of legendary Russian mentor Vladimir Yurzinov, but he used similar survival tactics long before that. Perhaps they came from Yurzinov's second-in-command during this time—Koivu's father.

Saku Koivu is a compact player with a big heart and plenty of determination.

Koivu plays no favorites and is aggressive with all his opponents. Thus his Montreal teammate Brian Savage was surprised to see how he handled his own countrymen from Finland. According to Savage, Koivu appears to be on a mission to become the best Finn on the ice.

Hailed as a savior by the once mighty Montreal Canadiens, he rose to the position of captain of the club in only his fifth season with them. It has been his bad luck that the club spent his whole rookie year at the bottom of the standings. Nevertheless, he scored 20 goals and 45 points in 82 games. And a third member of his family, his 6′2″ brother Mikko, is following in his footsteps. In the spring of 2000, the underage Mikko had already become a world champion when the Finnish

Teammate Brian Savage believes Saku Koivu (right) is on a mission to become the best Finn on the ice.

Juniors won the under-18 crown in Kloten, Switzerlend. His age means he won't be drafted until 2001, when he has a good chance of being a first-round pick of the Canadiens, as Saku was in 1993—a rare family affair.

With the club's success curve pointing the wrong way, a healthy Koivu is a must. And one could argue that he shouldn't really be playing in Montreal, he should be playing for the Disney team in Anaheim because of the impact he and his linemates Jere Lehtinen (now with the Dallas Stars) and Ville Peltonen (now with the Nashville Predators) created when they led Finland to gold in the 1995 World Championship. The media christened them the Huey, Duey and Louie Line after Donald Duck's nephews, but these ugly ducklings turned into swans as they carried the brunt of the offense in the tournament final versus Sweden, with Ville Peltonen scoring a hat-trick and Koivu feeding the puck to him for the gold medal goal.

Internationally, Koivu has played on several high-impact teams for Finland, collecting two more World Championship silvers and, perhaps more significantly, a bronze medal from the last two Olympic ice hockey tournaments, at Lillehammmer and Nagano. In the 1999 World Cup event, he outshone Teemu Selanne in amassing 16 points in nine games, the kind of output generated by the Soviet stars of the past.

Born in Turku, Koivu went all the way through the system with the TPS hockey club. He still has some good memories from the domestic hockey scene. His good fortune started with a junior league gold medal in 1992. From his three years in the Finnish national league (SM-Liiga), he has a full complement of medals, with two golds and a silver in between. He also earned a bronze with TPS in a European Championship effort.

In Montreal, Koivu had taken his place as a king waiting to be crowned, but his brilliant career came to an abrupt halt before training camp in September 2001 when he was diagnosed with a form of cancer that threatened his life. Because of his exceptional physical strength, doctors remain hopeful he will make a recovery. And indeed, with his cancer in remission, Koivu shocked everyone when he announced he was ready to resume skating with the Canadiens at the beginning of April and returned in time for the playoffs in 2002. Koivu has vowed to play in the NHL again—and that's still a promise the whole hockey world hopes he will keep.

Koivu, Saku
C, 5′9″, 175 lbs, b: Turku, Finland, 11/23/1974

Season	Club, League	Regular Season					Playoffs				
		GP	G	A	Pts	PIM	GP	G	A	Pts	PIM
1992–93	TPS Turku, Finland	46	3	7	10	28	11	3	2	5	2
WC–93	Finland	6	0	1	1	2					
1993–94	TPS Turku, Finland	47	23	30	53	42	11	4	8	12	16
OWG–94	Finland	8	4	3	7	12					
WC–94	Finland	8	5	6	11	4					
1994–95	TPS Turku, Finland	45	27	47	74	73	13	7	10	17	16
WC–95	Finland	8	5	5	10	18					
1995–96	Montreal Canadiens, NHL	82	20	25	45	40	6	3	1	4	8
WCup–96	Finland	4	1	3	4	4					
1996–97	Montreal Canadiens, NHL	50	17	39	56	38	5	1	3	4	10
WC–97	Finland	6	2	2	4	2					
1997–98	Montreal Canadiens, NHL	69	14	43	57	48	6	2	3	5	2
OWG–98	Finland	6	2	8	10	4					
1998–99	Montreal Canadiens, NHL	65	14	30	44	38					
WC–99	Finland	10	4	12	16	4					
1999–00	Montreal Canadiens, NHL	24	3	18	21	14					
2000–01	Montreal Canadiens, NHL	54	17	30	47	40					
2001–02	Montreal Canadiens	3	0	2	2	0					
	Finland Totals	138	53	84	137	143	35	14	20	34	34
	NHL Totals	347	85	187	272	218					
	OWG/WC/WCup Totals	56	23	40	63	50					

Named Best Forward at WC (1995, 1999)
Won WC(1995)
Finland Champion (1993, 1995)

Miroslav Satan

It would appear at first glance that Miroslav Satan—his name has diacritical marks and a different pronunciation in Czech—does have something to do with the devil. Of course there have been comments, innuendoes and witticisms in plenty about his name. And, although he isn't a sympathizer with the horned beast, he is a devilishly good shooter who can raise hell in front of the opponent's net.

Satan comes from the tiny village of Jacovice. At 17, he was already lining up for nine matches in the second Slovak league for the VTJ Topolcany hockey club. His admission into top-level hockey came with Dukla Trencin, one of the best Slovak clubs, in the last year of the old joint Czech-Slovak league. One month before his 18th birthday, he scored his first goal with them. By the end of the season, the tally was 11.

As one of the eight Trencin hockey players who lined up for the now independent Slovakia's national team, he made the trip to the Winter Olympics in Lillehammer in February 1994. Also on the team was veteran Peter Stastny, a future member of the Hockey Hall of Fame, and Zigmund Palffy, who had chosen Trencin over a New York Islanders farm club and who was developing a reputation with his dangerous shooting.

Almost no one knew about the up-and-coming Satan. The Edmonton Oilers had drafted him one year before, but they showed about as much interest in their 111th-picked player as would the public. Yet in the Olympics, "Mr. Nobody" scored nine goals in eight games, thanks to two hat-tricks, and quite unexpectedly became the best shooter of the tournament. However, after Czechoslovakia split up into the Czech Republic and Slovakia, the latter wasn't considered the successor state and had to fight to regain its clout in international competition.

In the spring of 1994, during World Championship play within the C group, Satan was the best shooter on his team with seven goals in six matches. The team progressed and a year later played in the B group. Satan again scored seven goals and took over top spot on the Slovak scoring charts. In 1996 he helped Slovakia to premiere among the elite in the competition, but the team came up empty-handed.

At the Winter Olympics in Nagano, his team competed in qualifying games and stood on the brink of elimination. Satan didn't line up to play at all because there was room for only two players—defenseman Robert Svehla and another shooter, Peter Bondra.

There wasn't much faith in him overseas. He played 14 matches in the IHL for independent teams from Detroit and San Diego, scoring

Miroslav Satan became the top scorer in the 1994 Olympics with nine goals in eight games.

Satan, Miroslav
C, 6´1″, 195 lbs, b: Topolcany, Czechoslovakia, 22/10/1974

Season	Club, League	Regular Season					Playoffs				
		GP	G	A	Pts	PIM	GP	G	A	Pts	PIM
1992–93	Dukla Trencin, Czechoslovakia	38	11	6	17	*					
1993–94	Dukla Trencin, Slovakia	30	32	16	48	16					
OWG–94	Slovakia	8	9	0	9	0					
WC–94 (C–1)	Slovakia	6	7	1	8	18					
1994–95	Cape Breton Oilers, AHL	25	24	16	40	15					
	Detroit Wipers, IHL	8	1	3	4	4					
	San Diego Gulls, IHL	6	0	2	2	6					
WC–95 (B)	Slovakia	7	7	6	13	4					
1995–96	Edmonton Oilers, NHL	62	18	17	35	22					
WC–96	Slovakia	5	0	3	3	6					
WCup–96	Slovakia	3	0	0	0	2					
1996–97	Edmonton Oilers, NHL	64	17	11	28	22					
	Buffalo Sabres, NHL	12	8	2	10	4	7	0	0	0	0
1997–98	Buffalo Sabres, NHL	79	22	24	46	34	14	5	4	9	4
1998–99	Buffalo Sabres, NHL	81	40	26	66	44	12	3	5	8	2
1999–00	Buffalo Sabres, NHL	81	33	34	67	32	5	3	2	5	0
WC–2000	Slovakia	9	10	2	12	14					
2000–01	Buffalo Sabres	82	29	33	62	36	13	3	10	13	8
2000–02	Buffalo Sabres	82	37	36	73	33					
OWG–02	Slovakia	2	0	1	1	0					
	Czechoslovakia/Slovakia Totals	68	43	22	65	*					
	NHL Totals	543	204	183	387	227	51	14	21	35	14
	OWG/WC/WCup Totals	40	33	13	46	44					

A HISTORY OF WORLD HOCKEY

Miroslav Satan (left) is a devilishly good shooter who can raise hell in front of the net.

only one goal. However, during the 1994–95 season, he scored 24 goals in 25 games for Edmonton's Cape Breton farm team, helping him push his way into the Edmonton lineup during training camp in the summer. Injuries and illness, however, hindered his play. In October he was removed from the Oilers lineup after his lung failed and in January he sprained his shoulder.

Although he managed to get over the worst period, he didn't fulfill what was expected of him in Edmonton—helping the team get into the playoffs. He wasn't an outright disappointment, but his performance was uneven. In a string of 11 games between February 28 and March 23, 1996, he established a record for the club and for rookies. But there were weeks when he just couldn't score no matter what.

In March 1997 he went to the Buffalo Sabres in an unflattering exchange for Barrie Moore and Craig Millar. Had the Oilers suspected what a treasure they were dumping, they wouldn't have given him up so cheaply.

In addition to a good nose for goals, his assets always included excellent physical conditioning and brilliant skating. In the Sabres jersey, his productivity increased. In the 1998–99 season, he reached the 40-goal mark and was the team's best scorer. In an early playoff round against Ottawa, however, one of his own defenseman, Alexei Zhitnik, struck him on the ankle, causing him to miss nine matches. But he returned in the series against Toronto and together with Curtis Brown and Geoff Sanderson made Buffalo's offense more dangerous than ever. For the second time in history, the Sabres progressed to the Stanley Cup finals, with credit due to the most productive line that included Satan.

But Satan's one-sidedness manifested itself. He was as evasive as ever around the opponent's net but wasn't asserting himself as a scorer. Subsequent negotiations of his contract went on somewhat longer, partly for this reason, and Satan returned to Trencin and played in the Slovak league. In one particular match, he fed passes to rising 18-year-old star Martin Gaborik, who scored five goals. Soon after that, Satan returned to Buffalo. In an age of well-thought-out defense and superhuman goaltenders, there are never enough real shooters.

Satan had hoped to be a part of a medal-winning team for his native Slovakia at the Salt Lake Olympics, but the team was eliminated during the qualifying rounds.

Satan completed his seventh season in the NHL in 2001–02, of which five and a half years have been spent in Buffalo with the Sabres.

Chris Pronger

When Chris Pronger first entered the National Hockey League, he was considered the next generation in a long line of big, strong defenders who specialized in taking up space and preventing goals yet still had the skating speed to join the odd rush and create scoring opportunities. After a few years of growing pains under those high expectations, Pronger matured into a leader both on his team and in the league.

Pronger grew up in Dryden, Ontario, and began playing hockey in his parent's basement with his brother Sean. They would use plastic hockey sticks and a couch cushion as the goal. Chris played defense while Sean, who is two years older, liked to play forward. Sean grew up to become a center with the Pittsburgh Penguins in the NHL. For quite a while, Chris just grew, reaching 6'5" and 210 pounds. He made the move to junior hockey at 17 with the Peterborough Petes of the Ontario Hockey League. He quickly established himself as an impact player, especially to the unfortunate players who ran into him, but also on the score sheet. He was the top-scoring defenseman in the OHL that first season.

At 18, Chris Pronger was selected the best defenseman in major junior hockey in Canada.

The following year, 1992–93, he was even better, picking up honors across the country as he learned to dominate in the defensive zone with his size. He led the Petes to the Memorial Cup finals and was a stalwart defender on the Canadian team that won the gold medal at the World Junior Championships. He was selected as the best defenseman in Canadian major junior hockey—pretty good for an 18-year-old kid who was still growing. At the 1993 NHL Entry Draft, the Hartford Whalers chose him second overall behind Alexandre Daigle.

Pronger began his career with the Whalers as a young player with plenty of hype riding on his wide shoulders. Whaler general manager Brian Burke had made two trades on the draft floor to secure his rights and the team was relying on Pronger not just to have a good first season but potentially to save the team, which was struggling and losing money. Pronger steadily improved over the year and was named the Whalers' best defender. He also earned a place on the NHL's All-Rookie Team. The Whalers missed the playoffs for the second consecutive year, however, and the patience needed for a young player to develop into a star, let alone a franchise player, began to dissipate in Hartford.

In his second year, the lockout-shortened 1994–95 season, Pronger began to be booed during home games. After Hartford missed the playoffs again, the team decided to trade Pronger for a more established star, somebody to get the turnstiles spinning right away. At the same time, the St. Louis Blues were attempting to cut down on their sizable payroll, mainly in the form of their star winger, Brendan Shanahan. The trade was completed in July 1995, but the pressure didn't subside for Pronger. Now, instead of holding up a franchise, he was replacing a fan favorite and a 50-goal scorer.

The Blues showed a great deal of confidence in the young defender. He was given a contract extension soon after his arrival, but the fans were slow to come around to his side. His first year in St. Louis was branded a disappointment. He finished the season with 25 points, below his career high of 30 in his first year, and struggled with a minus-18 rating.

Pronger was still only 22 years old entering his fourth pro season, but he began to play like

Pronger, Chris
D, 6'5", 220 lbs, b: Dryden, Ont., 10/10/1974

Season	Club, League	Regular Season					Playoffs				
		GP	G	A	Pts	PIM	GP	G	A	Pts	PIM
1993–94	Hartford Whalers, NHL	81	5	25	30	113					
1994–95	Hartford Whalers, NHL	43	5	9	14	54					
1995–96	St. Louis Blues, NHL	78	7	18	25	110	13	1	5	6	16
1996–97	St. Louis Blues, NHL	79	11	24	35	143	6	1	1	2	22
WC–97	Canada	9	0	2	2	12					
1997–98	St. Louis Blues, NHL	81	9	27	36	180	10	1	9	10	26
OWG–98	Canada	6	0	0	0	4					
1998–99	St. Louis Blues, NHL	67	13	33	46	113	13	1	4	5	28
1999–00	St. Louis Blues, NHL	79	14	48	62	92	7	3	4	7	32
2000–01	St. Louis Blues, NHL	51	8	39	47	75	15	1	7	8	32
2001–02	St Louis Blues	78	7	40	47	120					
OWG–02	Canada	6	0	1	1	2					
	NHL Totals	637	79	263	342	1000					
	OWG/WC Totals	21	0	3	3	18					

NHL First All-Star Team (2000)
NHL Second All-Star Team (1998)
Won Hart Trophy (2000)
Won James Norris Trophy (2000)
Won Bud Light Plus-Minus Award (1998)
Won WC (1997)
Won OWG (2002)

In 1999–2000, Chris Pronger (left) was the first defenseman since Bobby Orr to win both the Norris and Hart awards.

a veteran. He showed remarkable improvement and had 35 points as well as a plus-15 rating to lead the team. In 1997 he was named Blues captain and with the added confidence became a dominating presence for the team. He used his size to shut down opponents and earned his first nomination for the Norris Trophy as the league's top defenseman after leading the league with a plus-47.

When the Team Canada roster was announced for the 1998 Nagano Olympics, Pronger's name was on it. He was the team's youngest member. In two seasons he had moved from a disappointment to a widely respected star.

"Chris was really under a microscope," St. Louis teammate Al MacInnis said in 1998. "It could have gone either way with him. It could have crushed him or it could have gone the way it has. He's developed into a strong defenseman the last two years."

Pronger had a strong offensive season in 1998–99, finishing with 46 points and playing in the All-Star Game for the North America Team. His defensive play placed him near the top in voting for the Norris Trophy again, a good position for a young player who honed his skills guarding a cushion in the basement.

Pronger's 1999–2000 season was the most dominating in years. He had a career-high 62 points and a plus-52 and led the Blues to their best season ever. Although the team was upset in the first round of the playoffs, Pronger won both the Norris and Hart trophies at the NHL awards ceremony—the first defenseman to accomplish this since Bobby Orr. His points were down in 2000–01, but the team went deeper into the playoffs, and with the huge defenseman anchoring the blue line, St. Louis remains a Stanley Cup threat.

Pronger was one of the original eight players selected for Team Canada for the 2002 Olympics, and he and his defensive partner in St. Louis, Al MacInnis, performed very well as they helped Canada take gold, even though Pronger got a nasty gash on the forehead when he was checked hard into the boards by Finland's Teemu Selanne. A gap in the glass partition behind the goal snapped shut after absorbing the collision between the two players and sliced Pronger's face badly, but he was stitched up and ready to play in the semifinal game against Belarus and the gold medal game against the U.S.

Milan Hejduk

When coaches Ivan Hlinka and Slavomir Lener invited Milan Hejduk onto the Czech national team for the Nagano Olympics, many people were surprised. At the time, he was barely old enough to play professional hockey, let alone represent his country in cutthroat international competition. In the end, he became an Olympic sensation.

"I remember saying in a newspaper interview at the start of the season that I was looking forward to relaxing in front of the TV and watching the games. We were told that each of us had a chance to push his way onto the team, but I didn't really believe it," he said some time later.

Nevertheless, he had made it into the lineup. Originally his role was to be that of a substitute—13th forward. However, Jan Caloun, who was to play on the right wing next to Pavel Patera and Martin Prochazka, wasn't doing all that well and the coaches opted for a change. From the quarterfinals on, Hejduk appeared next to Patera and Prochazka and stayed for good.

Hejduk made an impression on people on quite a few occasions, but the most widely renowed was the one where he isolated an opponent in front of the net and helped Petr Svoboda score the winning goal in the finals against Russia. "In the first few moments, I didn't realize what we had achieved. We won a beautiful tournament and nothing more, I kept telling myself. But when we returned home and saw the endless celebrations and congratulations, I realized that we had achieved tremendous results."

He was born in Usti nad Labem on February 14, 1976, and put on a pair of skates for the first time at the age of four. His father had also played hockey, including three years for Pardubice. Milan was in the midgets and was a guest player in Teplice for a year, then he too headed for Pardubice, where he worked his way up to the first team.

In the 1993–94 season, he was named top rookie in the Czech league and in the summer he was drafted by the Quebec Nordiques (later the Colorado Avalanche). He only made the sixth round—which may also have been because he'd torn his shoulder ligaments in the playoffs helping Pardubice progress to the finals. He then had to sit out the European Championship for under-18s. "But I was lucky in my bad luck. Had my injury happened in the fall, I would have lost much more."

He had more bad luck after making it onto the World Championship team. The tournament, held in Switzerland, ended quickly for him when he suffered a broken jaw in the opening match against Japan.

The injury came at a bad time. For a long time, Colorado had hesitated to lay claim to Hejduk. However, after the Nagano triumph, they expressed a more serious interest in him and he made the training camp. He also made his way onto the All-Rookie Team and with his 48 points became the most productive first-year pro, though his teammate Chris Drury walked away with the Calder Trophy in the end. There was speculation that Hejduk didn't win because the year before, Russian Sergei Samsonov had done so. But after the 1998–99 season, a number of prizes had been taken by Europeans, led by Jaromir Jagr and Dominik Hasek.

Hejduk wasn't disappointed. In fact, what bothered him more was another health problem he encountered during the playoffs. During the fourth match in the finals of the Western Conference against Dallas, he chipped his collarbone after a run-in with Richard Matvichuk. Colorado was leading the series 3–2 in games

Milan Hejduk (front) was the most productive rookie in the NHL in 1998–1999.

Hejduk, Milan
RW, 5′11″, 165 lbs, b: Usti nad Labem, Czechoslovakia, 2/14/1976

Season	Club, League	Regular Season					Playoffs				
		GP	G	A	Pts	PLM	GP	G	A	Pts	PLM
1993–94	Pardubice, Czech Republic	22	6	3	9	*	10	5	1	6	*
1994–95	Pardubice, Czech Republic	43	11	13	24	6	6	3	1	4	0
1995–96	Pardubice, Czech Republic	37	13	7	20	*					
1996–97	Pardubice, Czech Republic	51	27	11	38	10	10	6	0	6	27
1997–98	Pardubice, Czech Republic	48	26	19	45	20	3	0	0	0	2
OWG–98	Czech Republic	4	0	0	0	2					
1998–99	Colorado Avalanche, NHL	82	14	34	48	26	16	6	6	12	4
1999–00	Colorado Avalanche, NHL	82	36	36	72	16	17	5	4	9	6
2000–01	Colorado Avalanche, NHL	80	41	38	79	36	23	7	16	23	6
2001–02	Colorado Avalanche, NHL	62	21	23	44	24					
OWG–02	Czech Republic	4	1	0	1	0					
	Czech Republic Totals	201	83	53	136	*	29	14	2	16	*
	NHL Totals	306	112	131	243	102					
	OWG Totals	8	1	0	1	2					

Won OWG (1998)

In 1999–2000, Milan Hejduk (center) and Chris Drury did an excellent job of substituing for injured Avalanche stars Joe Sakic and Peter Forsberg.

but ultimately didn't progress to the Stanley Cup finals. "What a shame. I am convinced that we would have beaten Buffalo."

A winger with clever evasive skills and an accurate shot, Hejduk isn't especially tall or broad. He never played too hard, but he entered the NHL like a whirlwind. He could assert himself mainly through his agility and his clever play. In his second NHL season, Colorado was without its greatest offensive pillars, Peter Forsberg and Joe Sakic, who were injured. But young players such as Hejduk and Drury did an excellent job of substituting for them. Over a period of two years, they made immense progress and took their places among the team's stalwarts. But it wasn't only due to their talent. The two were also completely devoted to hockey. "Often I had to actually kick them off the ice after practice," said coach Bob Hartley. "I am pleased that they are willing to do so much in order to keep on improving. "

And improve he did. In 2000–01, Hejduk had a phenomenal 41 goals and led the league in the playoffs with 16 assists as his Avs won the Cup in a thrilling seven-game series with New Jersey. Then, at 25, Hejduk was looking to obtain his second gold medal with the Czech Republic at the 2002 Olympics, but in a rematch of the 1998 gold medal game, Russia exacted a form of revenge, defeating the Czechs 1–0 and eliminating them from medal contention.

Jason Allison

Jason Allison entered the 21st century as a cornerstone of the remodeled Bruins franchise.

Center Jason Allison was a junior standout whose immense potential was finally realized a few years into his NHL career. An impressive combination of size and skill, Allison had the pro scouts drooling while he starred in junior, but his development as a pro was slower than anticipated. His fortunes rose after a trade sent him to Boston late in the 1996–97 season. Alley entered the 21st century as one of the cornerstones of the Bruins' remodeled franchise.

The native of suburban Toronto was one of the top amateur players in Canada during his three years with the London Knights of the OHL. The Washington Capitals drafted him 17th overall after he scored 118 points in 1992–93. He was returned the next year to the amateur ranks, where he exploded with a league-high 142 points and scored nine points in seven games for the gold medal-winning Canadian team at the World Junior Championship. Allison was at his best with three assists in a 6–4 win over the Czech Republic. He also showed maturity by only drawing one minor penalty in his first world junior tourney. Following the 1993-94 season, he was placed on the OHL and Canadian Junior First All-Star teams and was named the top junior player in the country.

Much was expected of Allison in 1994–95, but the combination of the NHL owners' lockout and his questionable rate of development saw him return to junior back in London. He averaged more than two points per game for the Knights, then scored 15 points in seven games while helping Canada repeat as world junior champions in Red Deer, Alberta. An offensive force and team leader as an alternate captain, Allison was rewarded with a place on the tournament All-Star team. He was a dominant force in Canada's 7–5 win over the Czech Republic and 8–5 triumph over Russia. He also set up Eric Daze for the winning goal in the 4–3 win over Sweden that clinched the gold medal.

When the owners' lockout ended, Allison played a few games in Washington, as well as with the club's top farm club in Portland of the American Hockey League. He began his pro career by scoring in each of his first two games with the Capitals in January 1995, but it was evident that his development at this stage was better served in the American Hockey League.

Center Jason Allison (second from the right) was a junior hockey star who finally realized his tremendous potential a few years into his career in the NHL.

Allison had proved successful in the more offensive-oriented Ontario Hockey League and on the large ice surfaces at the World Junior Championships. However, the tight checking and physical rigor of the NHL was very different. He spent the bulk of 1995–96 in the AHL, continuing to have difficulty earning a place on the Capitals roster.

The next year Allison started quickly by leading the Capitals in scoring during the pre-season. The young forward noted with pride: "I have better vibes toward this year. I feel a little more confident and positive of the situation, myself and my scoring and working around the net. It means so much to me to be confident, especially getting ready for a game. This year I think I can put some numbers up."

He eventually saw more ice time and scored 22 points in 53 games before a trade sent him to the Boston Bruins. Big-name players Bill Ranford, Rick Tocchet and Adam Oates were sent to Washington while the centerpiece for the Bruins was Vezina Trophy-winning goalie Jim Carey. As it turned out, Allison was a gem for Boston and Carey a tremendous disappointment. The burly forward scored 12 points in the last 19 games of the 1996–97 regular season with Boston, but the Bruins finished at the bottom of the NHL standings. The youngster reflected: "I haven't scored consistently at this level, but I haven't played a lot at this level either. I haven't had a lot of ice time, so I haven't had a lot of production."

The following season, Allison blossomed with 33 goals and the Beantowners returned to the playoffs. On January 8, 1998, Alley victimized the Phoenix Coyotes for his first NHL hat-trick. His 83 points at the end of the regular season landed him ninth place in the NHL scoring race. In 1998–99, he proved that the previous year wasn't an aberration by recording 76 points. Allison also contributed 11 points in 12 playoff games as Boston reached the second round of the post-season for the first time in five years. On November 7, 1998, he appeared in his 200th NHL game in Pittsburgh. This was a momentous occasion for the young forward who earlier in his career had seemed destined to remain in the minors.

Allison, Jason
C, 6′3″, 205 lbs, b: North York, Ont., 5/29/1975

Season	Club, League	Regular Season					Playoffs				
		GP	G	A	Pts	Plm	GP	G	A	Pts	Plm
1993–94	Washington Capitals, NHL	2	0	1	1	0					
	Portland Pirates, AHL						6	2	1	3	0
1994–95	Washington Capitals, NHL	12	2	1	3	6					
	Portland Pirates, AHL	8	5	4	9	2	7	3	8	11	2
1995–96	Washington Capitals, NHL	19	0	3	3	2					
	Portland Pirates, AHL	57	28	41	69	42	6	1	6	7	9
1996–97	Washington Capitals, NHL	53	5	17	22	25					
	Boston Bruins, NHL	19	3	9	12	9					
1997–98	Boston Bruins, NHL	81	33	50	83	60	6	2	6	8	4
1998–99	Boston Bruins, NHL	82	23	53	76	68	12	2	9	11	6
1999–00	Boston Bruins, NHL	37	10	18	28	20					
2000–01	Boston Bruins, NHL	82	36	59	95	85					
2001-02	Los Angeles Kings	73	19	55	74	68					
	NHL Totals	460	131	266	397	343					

The 1999–2000 season proved frustrating for Allison, as he was hampered by a serious wrist injury. He tried to play through the pain and reduced strength and contributed 28 points in 37 games before shutting down his season altogether to undergo surgery. Allison's importance to the club was underscored when he finished fifth in team scoring even though he played less than half of the season, and he had a superb 95-point season in 2000–01, but his contract demands forced the Bruins to trade him to Los Angeles early in the following season.

Sergei Samsonov

No recent Russian player has had such an impressive beginning in the NHL as Sergei Samsonov.

No Russian player in recent years has had as impressive beginning with the NHL as Sergei Samsonov. Only Pavel Bure created as much excitement with the media and the public in his first season. Both former CSKA players captured the Calder Trophy, awarded to the league's best rookie. But "the Russian Rocket" was 20 and Samsonov made his spectacular debut in the NHL at 18.

His road to success began at the CSKA hockey school. It took Samsonov two hours to get there every day by bus from the town of Zelenograd, near Moscow. It was quite an ordeal for a boy, and Samsonov's father sacrificed his career for his son's sake, changing his job and working the night shift so he could drive his son to his training sessions. After Samsonov left for North America, his parents spent the first season with him in Boston. At the ceremony where he received his first NHL award, for the 1997–98 season, Samsonov ended his speech by saying, "Dad, this is your Calder Trophy."

Samsonov's idol was legendary CSKA forward Sergei Makarov, who was the best shooter in the Soviet Union for nine seasons during the 1980s. Samsonov bears a physical resemblance to Makarov, as well as emulating his manner of playing. Makarov made his debut with the NHL at the age of 31 and received the Calder Trophy—after which the league's authorities decided to reduce the age limit—and Samsonov again followed in his hero's footsteps.

In the fall of 1994, when he was just 16, Samsonov became a name in Russia. He appeared in a friendly game between CSKA and the Russian all-star team that toured Russia during the NHL lockout. In the final game of the tour, the young forward scored his first goal.

Soon Samsonov's picture was on the cover of *The Hockey News*, a popular weekly. The junior player was given a lot of advance publicity. Coach Viktor Tikhonov didn't hide his fondness for Samsonov and his desire to help the player perfect his skills. "My assistants and I sometimes have to order him off the ice. I'll take him by the hand and walk him out of the arena. Samsonov is better than his peers thanks to a rare talent for hard work."

Few could have imagined what the Russian hockey whiz kid's fate would be. In the summer

Samsonov, Sergei
LW, 5′8″, 184 lbs, b: Moscow, USSR, 10/27/1978

Season	Club, League	Regular Season					Playoffs				
		GP	G	A	Pts	PIM	GP	G	A	Pts	PIM
1994–95	CSKA, Russia	13	2	2	4	14	2	0	0	0	0
1995–96	CSKA, Russia	51	21	17	38	12	3	1	1	2	4
1996–97	Detroit Vipers, IHL	73	29	35	64	18	19	8	4	12	12
1997–98	Boston Bruins, NHL	81	22	25	47	8	6	2	5	7	0
1998–99	Boston Bruins, NHL	79	25	26	51	18	11	3	1	4	0
1999–00	Boston Bruins, NHL	77	19	26	45	4					
2000–01	Boston Bruins, NHL	82	29	46	75	18					
2001–02	Boston Bruins	74	29	41	70	27					
OWG–02	Russia	6	1	2	3	4					
	Russia Totals	64	23	19	42	26	5	1	1	2	4
	NHL Totals	393	124	164	288	75					
	OWG Totals	6	1	2	3	4					

Won Calder Trophy (1998)

of 1996, CSKA split into two teams because of an internal feud. Viktor Tikhonov's team continued to belong to the higher division but was transformed from an army team into a privately owned one. The other team, headed by Alexander Volchkov, was forced to play in the second division and still belonged to the army. All the 18-year-old boys, including Samsonov, chose to join Volchkov's team to avoid being drafted into the armed forces.

Sergei Samsonov (center) was lucky to be supervised by Ray Bourque in Boston.

However, Samsonov didn't play a single game for Red Army. One day in August 1996, without even saying goodbye to his buddies, he deserted CSKA and was soon seen playing for the IHL's Detroit Vipers. Later he said: "The split-up of CSKA was the main reason for my hurried departure to America. If the team hadn't split, I would possibly still be playing in Russia. I felt I had to leave. Playing in the second division wasn't going to do me any good."

One season with the Vipers did do him a lot of good. In the first game of the final series against the Long Beach Ice Dogs, Samsonov scored four goals. The team captured the Turner Cup and he was voted the IHL's rookie of the year.

His success in his first year with the Boston Bruins was hardly a matter of luck. Given eighth position in the draft because of his short stature, Samsonov performed far better in his first season than the 1997 number one draft pick, his partner, Joe Thornton.

In Boston, Samsonov was lucky to play under the supervision of Ray Bourque. Samsonov met Bourque at the beginning of his first training camp. As it turned out, Samsonov had rented a house close to Bourque's, and the next morning Bourque gave the junior a ride to show him the way. His friendship with the experienced star helped build Samsonov's self-confidence.

Samsonov did well in his second season in the NHL—which is often much harder than the first—and scored 25 goals. The third season began badly for Samsonov when one of his partners, Dmitri Khristich, moved to Toronto, and another, Jason Allison, was seriously injured. Eventually, however, Samsonov was able to improve his performance and score 19 goals. The next year, he set career highs with 29 goals, 46 assists and 75 points. Samsonov was one of six Bruins players to have more than 50 points and one of five players to surpass the 20-goal mark in 2001–02, giving the team a solid, balanced attack throughout the season, and he also earned a bronze medal playing for his native Russia at the 2002 Winter Olympics.

And his superiors expect a lot more of Samsonov, hoping he will become the second Pavel Bure. With such a brilliant start, it's no wonder expectations are high.

Joe Thornton

Joe Thornton was touted as one of the next superstars of the game while still in junior. Like Eric Lindros and Mario Lemieux, Thornton was a big, skilled man, a power forward with good hands and speed. He progressed through the hockey ranks quickly and cut his teeth in the National Hockey League while still a teenager. He struggled in his first year in professional hockey with the Boston

Bruins, perhaps the victim of oversized expectations, but after three seasons of steady progression, Thornton, still in his early 20s, is poised to grow into his reputation as one of the sport's best.

Thornton was born in London, Ontario, in 1979 and grew up in nearby St. Thomas. He played Junior B hockey with the St. Thomas team, following in the footsteps of his older cousin Scott, who broke into the NHL with the Toronto Maple Leafs when Joe was 10. Joe was consistently at the top of his age division. He finished the 1994–95 season with 104 points in 50 midget games.

Still just 15, he was drafted into the Ontario Hockey League by the Sault St. Marie Greyhounds with the team's first pick, second overall. In his first season, 1995–96, Thornton was the talk of the hockey world. He won the OHL rookie of the year award for his 76 points in 66 games. He was also named the Canadian major junior rookie of the year. He was tall and wiry at 6´4˝ and 180 pounds and was known more for his quick shot and playmaking skills than his physical play.

Many hockey scouts predicted that the draft class of 1997 would be one of the deepest on record and Thornton headed the list of a dozen young players from around the world who appeared to be on the track to bona fide stardom at the professional level. He began to get more and more attention—from the press, fans and, of course, opposing players. "Joe's a pretty level-headed kid," said Dave Mayville, director of hockey operations for the Greyhounds. "Yes, there have been quite a few scouts, and I think the fact that so many of them have come all the way up to the north country to see him says a lot about his potential."

In his second OHL season, Thornton exploded for 122 points in 59 games. He added 19 points in 11 playoff games and cemented his place at the top of his class. He also won a gold medal with Canada at the 1997 World Junior Championships as the youngest player on the Canadian team. Boston made him the first pick in the 1997 draft, surprising no one, and added another budding star, Sergei Samsonov, with the eighth overall pick.

Once one of the powerhouses of the league and a perennial challenger for the Stanley Cup, Boston had suffered its worst season ever in 1996–97 and missed the playoffs for the first time in 30 years. But with the two finest young players in the world, the Bruins looked ready to challenge again soon.

Much of the attention paid to Thornton in his first foray into the NHL was focused on his contract and salary. The league had made some fundamental changes following the 1994 lockout. One of the factors that had prompted the work stoppage was the enormous salary—$12.25 million over five years—handed to rookie Alexandre Daigle the year before the lockout. The new rules meant that Thornton would have to earn the bulk of his pay from bonuses attached to his performance.

The Bruins' general manager, Harry Sinden, wasn't pleased with the first offer Thornton and his agent submitted. "I brought it home to read, and I'm not sure if I'm going to digest it or throw it up," Sinden said on July 2, coincidentally Thornton's 18th birthday. The two sides ultimately did close the gap and Thornton signed the contract, described as the best entry-level deal since the salary cap had been put in place.

With the business side of his rookie season complete for the foreseeable future, Thornton's priority became making the team better. "I can't wait to get in the Fleet Center

Joe Thornton was being touted as one of the game's next superstars while he was still a junior.

Thornton, Joe
C, 6´4˝, 215 lbs, b: London, Ont., 7/2/1979

Season	Club, League	Regular Season					Playoffs				
		GP	G	A	Pts	Plm	GP	G	A	Pts	Plm
1997–98	Boston Bruins, NHL	55	3	4	7	19	6	0	0	0	9
1998–99	Boston Bruins, NHL	81	16	25	41	69	11	3	6	9	4
1999–00	Boston Bruins, NHL	81	23	37	60	82					
2000–01	Boston Bruins, NHL	72	37	34	71	107					
2001–02	Boston Bruins	66	22	46	68	127					
	NHL Totals	355	101	146	247	40					

and finally do up my skates there and go on the ice," Thornton said following the negotiations. "It's finally happened. I'm really thrilled right now."

That euphoria didn't last long. Thornton's bid to improve the team was cut short when he was injured in an exhibition game in September. A broken forearm kept him out of the young Boston lineup for the first three games of the season. Later in the year he missed 10 games with cellulitis in his ankle and another six games with a viral infection. Every time he seemed ready to establish himself on the team and in the league, an injury would slow his progress.

Boston coach Pat Burns also insisted on bringing Thornton along slowly. The young center with the curly blond hair acquired plenty of fans but had little impact on the scoresheet, finishing the season with only seven points in 55 games. "I never had a year like that, especially for weird things," Thornton said of his many setbacks and injuries. "It was kind of unbelievable at times."

In 1999–2000, Joe Thornton (left) played a more physical game and led the Bruins in penalty minutes while he continued to improve his offensive numbers.

Thornton dedicated himself in the off-season to preparing himself physically for the long grind of his second NHL season. He hit the gym and put on weight, going from just under 200 pounds to 215. "My biggest surprise was the speed of the game and the size of the players in the league," Thornton said of his first season, during which he averaged only eight minutes of ice time per game while Samsonov had a regular shift and finished with 47 points to win the Calder Trophy as the league's top rookie. "I want to use my speed and body more this season. I'm going to come into camp in shape."

Thornton's second season was considerably better. He played more, suiting up for 81 games and earning a regular place in coach Burns' lineup. Thornton and the Bruins reached the second round of the playoffs for the first time in his young career, and if his numbers, 16 goals and 41 points, were still behind expectations—and Samsonov's impressive totals—he was still considered a work in progress. He had years to go before reaching his prime and each season he was getting better.

The same couldn't be said for the Bruins in 1999–2000, Thornton's third year in the league. Near the end of the season, with Boston's playoff hopes dashed, the team traded the cornerstone of the franchise for almost two decades, All-Star defenseman Ray Bourque, to the Colorado Avalanche. For his part, Thornton played a more physical game, leading the team in penalty minutes, and continued to improve on his offensive numbers. In the final game of the season, a 3–1 win over Pittsburgh, Thornton collected a goal and an assist to bring his point total to 60. Because of his unique contract, those two points and his team-high total enabled the youngster to earn a $2.4-million bonus. He continued to improve in 2000–01 as he registered 37 goals and 71 points to go along with 107 penalty minutes, a sure sign this power forward will remain a force for the Bruins for years to come.

In fact, Thornton was acknowledged as one of the top players in the NHL in the first couple of months of the 2001–02 season and was the focus of a good deal of controversy when he was overlooked by the selection committee for Team Canada's roster for the 2002 Olympics. It was evident the executives of Team Canada realized the mistake in not giving Thornton a spot on the team and held the door open to the possibility of adding him at a later date if one of the other players was injured.

Tomas **Kaberle**

Tomas Kaberle is a rising star with the Maple Leafs.

On March 18, 2000, a one of a kind encounter took place at the Air Canada Centre in Toronto. In a game between the Toronto Maple Leafs and Atlanta Thrashers, two brothers, Tomas and Frantisek Kaberle, faced each other from opposing sides. It wasn't the first time in NHL history that brothers had played against one another, but this situation was unique. These two brothers were defensemen and ranked among the players with the most ice time.

The first-ever duel between the two defensemen was originally to take place on January 29 in a game between Toronto and the Los Angeles Kings. But shortly before the game, Frantisek was sent back to L.A.'s farm team and it looked as if their followers would have to wait another year. But a last-minute trade brought the hopes of fans back to life.

The road to the NHL was more complicated for the older Kaberle. He made it to the NHL from the Czech league via the Swedish league and thanks to his splendid performance on the Czech national team. But Frantisek still plays in the shadow of the younger Tomas.

Tomas was only 18 years old when he was drafted as number 204 in 1996 by the Toronto Maple Leafs. His father had been a Czech hockey representative and it was he who taught his sons the game of hockey. Tomas grew up in Kladno, 20 kilometers west of Prague. In the 1950s and 1960s, this town was known as a breeding ground for both soccer and hockey talent. In 1959 it created a sensation by winning the league hockey championship, gaining many of the players a spot on the national team for the World Championship. That team ended up in third place after a historic match in which the Czechs beat Canada 5–3. Kladno's most famous hockey talent is none other than Jaromir Jagr.

Tomas Kaberle appeared in an NHL training camp for the first time in 1997. He tested Canadian ice during two games with a farm team in St. John's, Newfoundland, but returned to the Czech Republic at the age of 19 to play 47 games for his old team, Poldi Kladno, registering four goals and 19 assists.

In September 1998 he was back in Toronto. This time he garnered the attention of coach Pat Quinn, who put him through the hoops. His verdict actually came as a surprise to Tomas. He was to stay with the team on a trial basis. He couldn't believe the news. And Pat Quinn didn't leave him on the bench but sent him out onto the ice at every opportunity. It was a chance for Tomas to refine his game. Tomas played well, and with time he got more daring.

But the first season wasn't easy. He went through a crisis and suffered from fatigue. While he was taking a rest from the game, it

Kaberle, Tomas
D, 6´2˝, 200 lbs, b: Rakovnik, Czechoslovakia, 3/2/1978

Season	Club, League	Regular Season					Playoffs				
		GP	G	A	Pts	PLM	GP	G	A	Pts	PLM
1995–96	Poldi, Czech Republic	23	0	1	1	2	2	0	0	0	0
1996–97	Poldi, Czech Republic	49	0	5	5	26	3	0	0	0	0
1997–98	Poldi, Czech Republic	47	4	19	23	12					
	St. John's Maple Leafs, AHL	2	0	0	0	0					
1998–99	Toronto Maple Leafs, NHL	57	4	18	22	12	14	0	3	3	2
1999–00	Toronto Maple Leafs, NHL	82	7	33	40	24	12	1	4	5	0
2000–01	Toronto Maple Leafs, NHL	82	6	39	45	24	11	1	3	4	0
2001–02	Toronto Maple Leafs	69	10	29	39	2					
OWG–02	Czech Republic	4	0	1	1	2					
	Czech Republic Totals	119	4	25	29	40	5	0	0	0	0
	NHL Totals	290	27	119	146	62					
	OWG Totals	4	0	1	1	2					

began to look as if he might never see Stanley Cup play. Ultimately, however, this move proved to be the right one. Tomas, rested up and anxious to get back in the game, appeared in the Stanley Cup after all and played brilliantly. The Toronto Maple Leafs fought their way to the semifinals, where they were eliminated by a magnificent Buffalo team.

From the start of the 1999–2000 season, Kaberle provided constant support for his team. He had acquired a healthy self-confidence and started collecting points. Though, like most defenseman, he earned his points mainly from passes, he even started scoring. Shooting at the least expected moment and from difficult angles, he has a tendency to surprise goalies, as he did in the season opener in Montreal. With the score at 2–1, he skated into the offensive zone and, rather than shooting from the blue line, carried the puck almost all the way to the boards and let his shot go from there, putting him one up on goalie Jeff Hackett. It was an auspicious start to Kaberle's second season in the NHL, when his play became bolder and he took more risks, gaining him an early place among the league's best defensemen.

Tomas Kaberle (right) provided constant support for his team from the very beginning of the 1999–2000 season.

Following the 2000–01 season, Kaberle and the Leafs couldn't come to terms on a new contract and he missed the first part of the season. With an agreement in place, he returned to Toronto in November 2001 and was again one of the team's best players.

Marian Hossa

The Hossa hockey dynasty is well known, especially in Slovakia. A star in his own right, father Frantisek was a fixture on the defense of Dukla Trencin for many years, playing 358 league matches. His older son Marian prefers a forward slot and scoring goals rather than preventing them. And Marian and his younger brother Marcel have gone in completely different directions.

Marian Hossa spent only one season with the seniors of Trencin. In 1996–97, he was 17 and within a period of one year, he managed to line up for three championships. At the start of the year he played in the World Junior Championship, then the European Championship for players 18 and over. Immediately after that, he traveled to the senior tournament in Finland. In the summer he was drafted by the Ottawa Senators as number 12 overall.

The Hossa dynasty is well known in Slovakia.

"You will hear a lot about this young man," claimed Julius Supler, who coached Trencin with Marian's father for three years. A native of the small village of Stara Lubovna, Hossa went to the Portland Winter Hawks in the WHL before the 1997–98 season and felt right at home. Coach Brent Peterson's assistant was none other than Supler. And forward Andrei Podkonicky, who knew Marian from the Slovak junior nationals, joined him on the team. Together they helped Portland to a Memorial Cup triumph. Until then, Hossa had had a reputation as a scorer. In Portland, he turned into a dominant power.

His solid performance in 1998–99 earned Marian Hossa (number 18) a selection to the NHL All-Rookie Team.

In the same season he appeared briefly with the Senators, but his next season was delayed by a serious knee injury. In the end, he played 60 matches and spent most of his time doing defensive work on the checking line. But when he began scoring goals and collecting points, he seemed to be making up for lost time. He played only two-thirds of the season, but in the voting for the Calder Trophy he came in second after Chris Drury. His solid performance also earned him selection on the NHL All-Rookie Team.

"It was a good start," he said. "I hope that I will go on being successful." The next season he started appearing on the right wing with forward Radek Bonk and doubled his previous output.

Many other players were drafted before him, such as Joe Thornton, Patrick Marleau, Olli Jokinen or Sergei Samsonov. None of them would necessarily have made a bigger contribution than Hossa. Nonetheless, the Senators proved best at assessing his hidden talents, and that is ultimately the key to the draft.

"So far, everything has gone well for me." Hossa said when he appeared in Norway in the spring of 1999 to represent Slovakia in another World Championship. "I don't think of myself as being the best, but I do want to be the best."

Hossa gave the game everything he had. It was becoming clear that Ottawa was offering him the opportunity to be a major player on their team. They started comparing him with Jaromir Jagr, who at the same age conducted himself in a similar manner. But as much as people plan—and always for the best—fate intervenes. In an unfortunate accident on the ice, Toronto defenseman Bryan Berard suffered a serious eye injury as a result of being hit by Hossa's stick.

"I keep thinking about it all the time and cannot get rid of it." Hossa says, crushed. "I have trouble falling asleep and I see the event before my eyes all the time. After this unfortunate accident, I wish that all players would start wearing protective visors."

It took 90 years for goaltenders to start using masks. It took 100 years for players to don helmets. Only the tragic death of Bill Masterton in 1968 moved them to take action. In the case of eye protection, players to this day are betting on pure luck. And the victim here isn't only Bryan Berard, but also a young Slovak player who has found himself under tremendous pressure and carries the burden of guilt and regret every day of his life.

In 2001–02, Hossa surpassed the 100-goal plateau in his fourth full season with the Senators.

Hossa, Marian
LW, 6'1", 185 lbs, b: Stara Lubovna, Czechoslovakia, 1/12/1979

Season	Club, League	Regular Season					Playoffs				
		GP	G	A	Pts	Plm	GP	G	A	Pts	PLM
1996–97	Dukla Trencin, Slovakia	46	25	19	44	33	7	5	5	10	*
WC–97	Slovakia	8	0	2	2	0					
1997–98	Portland Winter Hawks, WHL	53	45	40	85	50	16	13	6	19	6
	Ottawa Senators, NHL	7	0	1	1	0					
1998–99	Ottawa Senators, NHL	60	15	15	30	37	4	0	2	2	4
WC–99	Slovakia	6	5	2	7	8					
1999–00	Ottawa Senators, NHL	78	29	27	56	32	6	0	0	0	2
2000–01	Ottawa Senators, NHL	81	32	43	75	44	4	1	1	2	4
2001–02	Ottawa Senators, NHL	80	31	35	66	50					
OWG–02	Slovakia	2	4	2	6	0					
	Slovakia Totals	46	25	19	44	33	7	5	5	10	*
	NHL Totals	306	107	121	228	163	14	1	3	4	10
	OWG/WC Totals	16	9	6	15	8					

Slovakia Champion (1997)

Vincent **Lecavalier**

Tampa Bay Lightning center Vincent Lecavalier wears number 4 on his sweater as a tribute to another great player from Quebec—his idol, Jean Beliveau. That number is a rarity among players other than defensemen, but it is only fitting that it should be worn by a young man who many people think could be one of the next great players in the NHL.

Lecavalier was the first overall draft pick in 1998 after a stellar junior season with Rimouski of the Quebec Major Junior Hockey League. In his final two seasons he scored 86 goals and had 132 assists for an astounding 218 points in 122 regular-season games. He joined some exalted company coming out of the QJML, becoming only the fifth player from that league to be the first overall pick in the NHL. (The others were Guy Lafleur, Mario Lemieux, Pierre Turgeon and Alexandre Daigle.) He is also recognized in Quebec for accomplishments that go beyond the hockey rink. In 1998 Lecavalier was named the province's male amateur athlete of the year.

Prior to being drafted by Tampa Bay, Lecavalier combined his Quebec junior experience with some international competition. In 1997 he was a member of the gold medal-winning Canadian team at the under-18 Three Nations Tournament in the Czech Republic, and he also represented Canada at the 1998 World Junior Championship in Finland, scoring one goal and adding an assist in seven games in that competition.

Lecavalier found himself the center of attention as he began the 1998–99 NHL season with the Lightning. With his excellent combination of stickhandling ability, speed, size—6′4″ and 180 pounds as a junior—plus his pro-level on-ice judgement and foresight, observers of his game in the junior ranks noted that he had the potential to become an NHL great. But scouts also observed that, despite his amazing talents, he occasionally appeared unmotivated on the ice, a factor that sometimes led to inconsistent play.

In his rookie season, his much-touted scoring prowess didn't come to the fore as prominently as it had when he was a junior, however. He scored only 13 goals and added just 15 assists that first NHL year. These totals ranked him ninth among rookies in points, 12th in assists and eighth in goals.

Still, opposing defensemen checked him very closely, and he was playing without a tremendous supporting cast. On his team, Lecavalier was the second-highest goal scorer and fourth in total points. He won NHL honors as rookie of the month in February of his first year. During the off-season, Lecavalier concentrated on weight training in an attempt to bulk up in order to meet the rigors of NHL competition.

Lecavalier says that the biggest adjustment to the pro game for him was: "The speed and size of the players. It's a much tighter game up here. There isn't as much room, so you have to learn to get to where you want to be on the ice. By the end of the first season, I was pretty comfortable with things. I got a lot of help from some teammates with that type of stuff."

The young player was lucky that Tampa Bay had a number of veterans who were willing to

Vincent Lecavalier was named Quebec's male amateur athlete of the year in 1998.

Lecavalier, Vincent
C, 6′4″, 180 lbs, b: Ile Bizard, Que., 4/21/1980

Season	Club, League	Regular Season					Playoffs				
		GP	G	A	Pts	Pim	GP	G	A	Pts	Pim
1998–99	Tampa Bay Lightning, NHL	82	13	15	28	23					
1999–00	Tampa Bay Lightning, NHL	80	25	42	67	43					
2000–01	Tampa Bay Lightning, NHL	68	23	28	51	66					
2001–02	Tampa Bay Lightning	76	20	17	37	61					
	NHL Totals	306	81	102	183	193					

Vincent Lecavalier was the center of attention as he began the 1998–99 NHL season with the Lightning.

show him the ropes of the NHL game. "Stephane Richer helped a lot with teaching me how to do what I wanted to do," notes Lecavalier. "Also, Wendel Clark was great. He helped a lot with the way the league works—what to look for from opposing players and how life is up here. Michael Nylander was a big help, too."

Despite all the comparisons made between Lecavalier and other young superstars such as Gretzky and Lemieux, Lecavalier says that, because of his youth, he was just looking to improve to the point where he could be competitive in the big leagues. "I'm still only 19 and I have a lot to learn yet. I think I definitely have the talent, but it takes so much more than that," he observed in his first season with the pros. "I do feel that there won't be as many surprises since I've been around one time. To make an impact and contribute a lot, you have to get the ice time. Every player wants more ice time, but you have to earn it. I have to earn my ice time just like anybody else. I just have to keep working hard and do the things I need to do and everything else will come." But if youth and an absence of team talent provided excuses in the first three years of Lecavalier's career in Tampa, "disappointment" would have to be the word to describe his individual performance in 2001–02. At 21, Lecavalier looked very ordinary and was for a time demoted to the team's third line due to his lack of scoring.

Heatley Dany

Dany Heatly was the second pick overall in the 2000 NHL Entry Draft by Atlanta Thrashers

When the Atlanta Thrashers secured the second pick overall in the 2000 NHL Entry Draft, no one in the organization had any doubt about their selection. The New York Islanders had often publicly stated they would choose goaltender Rick DiPietro with the first pick overall—and that left the Thrashers with the golden opportunity of obtaining a young player named Dany Heatley.

In this day and age, drafting players is an in-depth and often complicated process for NHL clubs. Countless hours are spent analyzing each player's on-ice and off-ice credentials. The scouting reports listed Heatley as a good skater with very strong puckhandling and passing skills, an accurate release, good intensity and mental toughness. Strong character traits—and of course solid skills—are even more necessary when the young star will be heavily counted on to be one of the cornerstones in building a fledgling team like the Thrashers from the ground up. Only a select few can handle such a job, and Atlanta is betting that Heatley can respond to the challenge. Indeed, many believe he has all it takes to be one of the shining stars of the future.

Born in Freiburg, Germany, on January 21, 1981, to Murray and Karin Heatley, Dany was just a toddler when the family moved to Calgary, Alberta. He began playing hockey at the age of five and seemed a natural from the start. By the time he'd reached bantam in 1996–97, Heatley had clearly established himself as a premier scorer with a tally of 30 goals and 72 points in 25 games, which was merely a continuation of the many successes he'd enjoyed as a young star with the Southfour Minor Hockey Association. The following year, at the age of 16, he moved up to midget, where he once again displayed his incredible offensive talent, scoring 39 goals and 91 points in 36 games. Heatley capped a fantastic season by becoming the top scorer and MVP of the 1998 Air Canada Cup National Midget Hockey Championship.

In 1998–99, Heatley played Junior A with the Calgary Canucks and led the Alberta Junior Hockey League in scoring with 70 goals and 126 points in 60 games. His deft touch continued throughout the playoffs, where he once again led all scorers with 22 goals and 35 points in 13 games en route to the Doyle Cup Regional Junior Championship. The superb season was capped when Heatley was named the Canadian Junior A player of the year.

While it was obvious that Heatley had the talent to play major junior hockey—usually considered the quickest route to the NHL—he chose to follow in his father's footsteps and enrolled at the University of Wisconsin and played for the school hockey team. In his rookie season with the Badgers, 1999–2000, Heatley collected 28 goals and 28 assists in 38 games, was named the Western Collegiate Hockey Association rookie of the year and was selected to the NCAA West second All-Star team.

Many believe Dany Heatly has all it takes to be one of the shining stars of the future

Even with this impressive statistical background, Heatley had not represented Canada at an international competition until the 2000 World Junior Hockey Championships in Sweden, which resulted in a bronze medal. For the young star, the highlight of the tournament was being one of Canada's scorers in the overtime shootout against the United States that gave the victory to Canada. Heatley said afterwards he wasn't nervous about taking the penalty shot, but the same couldn't be said for his father, Murray. "I was kind of antsy, but the shootout is like a coin toss," said the elder Heatley. "His mother was going a little snaky." The tournament was a character-builder for Heatley, who went through a gamut of emotions during the championships, from feeling down about his early scoring slump to exuberance at having been able to contribute with big goals in the later games.

Heatley was selected in the NHL draft by the Thrashers that summer, but he wanted to stay in school and played one more year of NCAA hockey, where he had 57 points in 39 games. When he at last joined the Thrashers and the NHL a year later, in the fall of 2001, Heatley found the intense glare of the media spotlight normally associated with a high first-round draft pick had been dimmed considerably by the presence of 18-year-old Russian star Ilya Kovalchuk, the first pick overall by the Thrashers in 2001. Paired on a line from the start of training camp and part of an offensive unit throughout most of the year, Heatley and Kovalchuk were jointly tagged with the nickname "The Kids" and the pair have become good friends off the ice as well, though Heatley says the biggest obstacle was the fact Kovalchuk had limited ability in English when they were thrown together in camp. "It was a little rough at rookie camp," he said. "He's actually really good at it now. I have no problem communicating with him, on or off the ice."

In his first NHL game, against the Buffalo Sabres on October 4, 2001, Heatley picked up one assist. And, though the club predictably finished well out of a position for the 2002 Stanley Cup playoffs, Heatley gave the fans and the organization much optimism for the future with his spirited play. Down the stretch run of the regular season, he was easily the team's best performer.

Further evidence of the 21-year-old Heatley's character and maturity followed yet another mid-season loss. As the media hawks gathered for the post mortem dissection of the game with the players, most had already quickly undressed and scampered for the showers—a well-known ploy when athletes want to avoid tough media scrutiny. Heatley, on the other hand, simply sat at his locker, crammed a hat over his disheveled hair and waited for the verbal barrage. Asked why he was willing to answer for the misfortunes of the club, he simply said: "That's part of the job. I enjoy it a little bit more when we're winning, and I just have to deal with it when we're losing." He has also received high praise for his maturity and poise from his trainers and peers. He quickly earned the respect of Thrashers head coach Curt Fraser, who seems most impressed by Heatley's instinctive leadership qualities. "He is the kind of player that says, 'Hey, jump on my back and I'll take you there,'" Fraser was quoted as saying. And his style of play has drawn favorable comparisons to that of Joe Thornton of the Boston Bruins. "He's the complete package," said Ray Ferraro, an 18-year NHL veteran and captain of Atlanta before being moved to St. Louis at the trade deadline in March 2002. "Dany's a great kid. When he gains some weight, he'll be virtually unstoppable."

Kovalchuk Ilya

Kovalchuk became the first Russian ever to be selected number one overall in the NHL Entry Draft's history

As the 2001 NHL Entry Draft approached, who the Atlanta Thrashers would make their first overall pick was hotly debated. Jason Spezza of the Ontario Hockey League's Windsor Spitfires had gone into the season as the odds-on favorite, but the emergence of Russian star Ilya Kovalchuk changed those thoughts. By mid-season, the consensus had flagged Kovalchuk as the number one player and most talented prospect in the draft and the movement was underlined by the noticeable decline in Spezza's production. In spite of reports that Kovalchuk was headstrong, selfish with the puck and somewhat rebellious, the Thrashers went with the notion that you should always pick the best player available—which is how Kovalchuk became the first Russian ever to be selected number one overall in the NHL Entry Draft's history.

Kovalchuk began playing in his home town of Tver when his father registered him for a local hockey school. He was only five, but he immediately took to the sport and in no time at all was showing signs of an immense natural talent. He starred with the HC Tver minor-league team for a number of years before moving up to Moscow Spartak at the age of 16 and also played for the Spartak Juniors, where he totally dominated the league, scoring 70 goals in 1999—more than double his closest competitor. He first came to international prominence with his stellar performance for Russia at the 2000 Under-17 World Hockey Challenge in Timmins, Ontario, where he took home best forward honors after leading his country to the gold medal. In fact, his performance was so spectacular that the Hockey Hall of Fame made an unprecedented request to display one of his sticks in a public forum as a memento of his utter dominance throughout the tournament. He was also a key member of the under-18 Russian team that won silver at the World Championships, while in 2001 Kovalchuk was on the top forward line for Russia at the World Junior Championships in Moscow, finishing with four goals and six points in seven games.

Before he was picked first overall in the NHL draft, European scouts were saying he was the best young prospect to come out of Russia since Pavel Bure more than a decade before. Both players move with lightning speed and have amazing puckhandling and instinctive skills, but the one major advantage Kovalchuk has over Bure is size. At close to 6′2″ and 220 pounds, he plays a very aggressive physical style that has become a vital necessity in today's rough and tumble NHL game. And if NHL insiders had a general concern regarding Kovalchuk, it rested with his personality, not his talent. Just before the draft, some of Kovalchuk's brash confidence was seen in full swing when he was quoted as saying: "I simply do not know what fear is when I'm on the ice. Hockey should be played by real men. If you want to be safe, then don't step onto the ice. If you play this game, then be ready to fight."

At his first NHL training camp, he impressed the coaching staff with his strong work ethic and of course with his natural talent. He also led the NHL in scoring during the pre-season, which was something of a surprise. Still, the ego factor is an obvious concern for a player of Kovalchuk's caliber. Will the early success go to his head? "People say that I'm too young and it's easy to become conceited," counters Kovalchuk. "These things can happen, but they won't with me. My father and coach will never ease up on me. They will make me come down to earth and not lose my way."

Many NHL experts have labeled Kovalchuk a "can't miss" prospect

If his own self-assessment can be trusted, Kovalchuk appears to have a good head on his shoulders, but some notable detractors would indicate there's at least some small cause for concern. Fellow Russian and two-time Olympic champion Evgeny Zimin believes it will be a constant battle for Kovalchuk to keep on an even keel, even as he acknowledges the player has all the raw tools to become a bona fide NHL superstar. "He's got a few minuses, though, just like most junior players," Zimin diplomatically noted. "I'm sure Ilya knows how to pass the puck," he continued with a cutting tone of sarcasm. "But it seems to me that fame has gotten to him lately. His enormous desire to show his stuff results in him trying to beat the opponent one-on-one even when he has no chance to score the goal himself. That is a huge minus." Others in the Russian Hockey Federation have felt the same way, such as Kovalchuk's former coach with Moscow Spartak, Nikolai Solovyev. In fact, Solovyev went so far as to say the young star possesses a "selfish attitude" when it comes to passing the puck—and the blame—on to other teammates, but Solovyev attributes it to youth and inexperience and believes those character flaws will be corrected as he matures. And therein lies the single biggest question as to whether he will meet his enormous potential or not.

As much as Kovalchuk was generating a stir leading into his rookie NHL season with the Thrashers in the fall of 2001, he was also making headlines off the ice. On October 24, 2001, he signed his first major (and lucrative) deal to serve as an exclusive spokesperson for Pacific Trading Cards' "private stock" line of hockey cards for 2002—a deal that marked the first of what will no doubt be a long line of endorsements for Kovalchuk.

Many NHL experts have labeled Kovalchuk a "can't miss" prospect, and indeed he began his rookie season on a strong note. Along with fellow freshman and linemate Dany Heatley,

Kovaluchuk provided some of the most entertaining hockey of the year for the Thrashers. The pair seemed to work well together on the ice and soon developed a friendship off it that has become easier to sustain as Kovalchuk acquires a stronger command of the English language. In December, Kovalchuk and Heatley were named co-winners of the rookie of the month award, in January the young Russian phenom won it outright, and the season was progressing well until a shoulder injury sustained in a game against the New York Islanders on March 11 forced Kovalchuk to miss the remainder of the season. To that point, he had played in 65 games for the Thrashers, scoring 29 goals and 51 points. Even though he missed 17 games, Kovalchuk still finished second in team scoring behind Heatley.

Meanwhile, in February 2002, Kovalchuk represented his country at the Salt Lake City Olympics as the youngest member on the squad. (He'd been 10 months old when teammate Igor Larionov won his first Olympic medal at the 1984 Games in Sarajevo.) At Salt Lake, Kovalchuk contributed a goal and two assists to Russia's bronze medal.

With the Thrashers, Kovalchuk wears number 17 as a tribute to the late Russian star Valeri Kharlamov, who became known to Canadian fans during the unparalleled 1972 Summit Series, and the team and the whole hockey world hopes Kovalchuk will be remembered as well.

APPENDIXES

INDEX

A

M

L

LEAGUE AND INTERNATIONAL EVENTS ABBREVIATIONS

LEAGUES

AHA	American Hockey Association
AHL	American Hockey League
ASHL	Alberta Senior Hockey Leagues
Austria	Austrian Hockey League
Big 4	Alberta Big 4 Hockey League
CAHL	Canadian Amateur Hockey League
Cal-Pro	California Hockey League
Can-Am	Canadian-American Hockey League
Can-Pro	Canadian Professional Hockey League
CBSHL	Cape Breton Senior Hockey League
CCHA	Central Collegiate Hockey Association
CHA	Canadian Hockey Association
CHL	Central Hockey League, 1925 to 1941
CHL	Central Hockey League, 1992 to date
CHL	Central Professional Hockey League, 1963 to 1985
City Jr.	City and District Junior Hockey Leagues
City Sr.	City and District Senior Hockey Leagues
Czech Republic	Czech Extraleague
Czechoslovakia	Czechoslovakian Premier League
ECAC	Eastern College Athletic Conference
ECAHA	Eastern Canada Amateur Hockey Association
ECHA	Eastern Canada Hockey Association
ECHL	East Coast Hockey League
EHL	Eastern Hockey League
EOHL	Eastern Ontario Senior Hockey League
EPHL	Eastern Professional Hockey League
Finland	Finnish National League
France	French National Hockey Association
FRG\Germany	Bundesliga, Deutsche Eishockey Liga
Great Britain	British Ice Hockey League
H.E.	Hockey East
IAHL	International-American Hockey League
IHL	International Hockey League, 1945 to date

IHL	International Professional Hockey League, 1904 to 1907
IIHF	International Ice Hockey Federation
Italy	Italian National Hockey Association
Japan	Japanese League
Kootenay	British Columbia-Kootenay Hockey League
Latvia	Latvian Hockey League
MHL Sr.	Manitoba Senior Hockey Leagues
MIHL	Maritime Independent Hockey League
MMHL	Maritime Major Hockey League
MSHL	Maritime Senior Hockey League
Mtl-Sr.	Montreal and District Senior Hockey Leagues
NBSHL	New Brunswick Senior Hockey Leagues
NHA	National Hockey Association
NHL	National Hockey League
NOHA	Northern Ontario Hockey Association
Norway	Norwegian Eliteserien
NSSHL	Nova Scotia Senior Hockey League
NWHL	North West Hockey League
OHA Sr.	Ontario Hockey Association Senior A
OHA	Ontario Hockey Association Junior A
OHL	Ontario Hockey League
OPHL	Ontario Professional Hockey League
OSHL	Okanogan Senior Hockey League
Ott-Sr.	Ottawa and District Senior Hockey Leagues
PCHA	Pacific Coast Hockey Association
PCHL	Pacific Coast Hockey League
PEI Sr.	Prince Edward Island Senior Hockey Leagues
PHL	Pacific Hockey League
QHL	Quebec Hockey League
QPHL	Quebec Provincial Hockey League
QSHL	Quebec Senior Hockey League
RCHL	Regina City Senior Hockey League
Russia	Russian Pro Hockey League
Slovakia	Slovakian Extraleague
SSHL	Saskatchewan Senior Hockey League
Sweden	Swedish Elite Hockey League
Switzerland	Swiss National League
TBSHL	Thunder Bay Senior Hockey League
USAHA	United States Amateur Hockey Association
USHL	United States Hockey League
USSR	Soviet Premier League, 1946 to 1991

USSR	CIS National League, 1991–92
WCHA	Western Collegiate Hockey Association
WCHL	West Coast Hockey League, 1995 to date
WCHL	Western Canada Hockey League, 1921 to 1925
WCSHL	Western Canada Senior Hockey League
WHA	World Hockey Association
WHL	Western Canada Major Junior Hockey League, 1977 to date
WHL	Western Hockey League, 1925–26
WHL	Western Hockey League, 1951 to 1975
WIHL	Western International Hockey League

INTERNATIONAL EVENTS

CCup	Canada Cup, 1976, 1981, 1984, 1987, 1991
ChCup	NHL–Soviet Challenge Cup, 1979
RV'87	Rendez-vouz '87
SS	Canada–Soviet Summit Series, 1972
WC	IIHF World Championship, Pool A
WC-B	IIHF World Championship, Pool B
WCup	World Cup of Hockey, 1996
WEC	IIHF World and European Championship
OWG	Olympic Winter Games, 1920 to 2002

NOTES ON CONTRIBUTORS AND ACKNOWLEDGMENTS

CONTRIBUTORS

Ales Brezina is publisher of the newspaper *Satellite*. He has written about hockey since the 1970s, and has spent years as hockey reporter for the Czech section of *Voice of America*.

Andrew Podnieks is a hockey historian and photographer. He is the author of Canada's *Olympic Hockey Teams: The Complete History 1920-1998*, *Portraits of the Game*, *The Blue & White Book* and several other books about hockey.

Denis Gibbons specializes in international and Olympic hockey history. He has provided statistical work for CBS on network television coverage for the Nagano Olympic Games and has also worked for *The Hockey News*. He is a member of the Society for International Hockey Research.

Dmitri Ryzkov started writing about hockey in 1963 and went on to become editor of *Sovetskiy Sport*. He later wrote the screenplay for several movies about hockey and spent a decade as a commentator for NTV.

Igor Rabiner has been a hockey writer since 1990, notably as a special correspondent to the NHL for the Russian *Sport Express* since 1996, covering the Olympic Winter Games in Nagano in 1998.

Jan Bengtsson has been with Sweden's largest daily, *Svenska Dagbladet*, since 1982. In 1989, he became a hockey writer for the paper.

Jan Stark is former editor of the Swedish hockey annual èrets Ishockey. He has covered the game since 1973 and is one of the founding members of the Swedish Professional Icehockey Writers Association, as well as the Swedish Icehockey Historical and Statistical Society.

Nikolai Vukolov has represented ITAR TASS in Sweden since 1980, first as a reporter and later as its editor-in-chief.

Pavel Barta is a noted hockey journalist in the Czech Republic. For the last decade he has covered hockey for *Gol* magazine, the largest sports weekly in the Czech Republic.

Serge Chuev has spent 17 years covering hockey for *Hockey Week*, *Hockey*, and *Sovetskiy Sport* magazines.

Tom Ratschunas is a leading hockey statistician in Europe. He edited the IIHF International Hockey Guide during 1970s and 1980s and provides statistical services to many European hockey leagues and for IIHF tournaments.

Vlad Dimitrov has been a hockey writer and special correspondent to the NHL for *Sport Express* since 1994.

Yevgeny Bogatyrev has been a sports writer since 1977 and has written screenplays about famous hockey players for television and movies.

Yuri Lukashin was a member of the organizing committee for the Moscow Olympics of 1980, wrote for several newspapers, and put together a number of screenplays, some of which were about the NHL. He worked with other writers on *Hockey in the Winter Olympics*, and was a part of team that assembled *Hockey*, an encyclopedia of the game.

Yuri Tzybanev was a hockey writer for the weekly newspaper *Socker-Hockey* from 1976 until 1991 and subsequently for a variety of publications including *Nedelja*, *Sport Club*, and *Sovetskiy Sport*.

REFERENCES

Total Hockey, NHL Official Guide and Record Book, Hockey Encyclopedia.

PHOTO CREDITS

Photos from Hockey Hall of Fame archives on pages:
9, 11-17, 19, 20-30, 32, 33, 35-46, 48, 49, 50, 52, 55, 57-62, 64-71, 73-77, 79-81, 83, 85-91, 93, 94, 96, 97, 99, 100, 102, 104-107, 109113, 116-119, 121, 122, 124-129, 131, 132, 134-137, 139-151, 153, 155-162, 165, 169, 170, 172, 175, 178, 179, 181-183, 185, 187-189, 191-216, 218-225, 227-237, 239, 241-253, 255-257, 259, 261-263, 265, 266, 268-272, 274-277, 280-283, 289, 297, 298, 300-302, 312, 319, 320, 327, 329, 331, 336, 337, 343, 344, 346, 347, 358-363, 365, 366, 372-377, 392, 393, 398, 399, 403, 404, 407-414, 416, 421, 423-425, 429-435, 437, 439, 441-447, 449, 451, 452, 454, 455, 459, 461, 463, 465-474, 476-481, 484, 485, 492-498, 503, 504, 507, 509, 510, 522, 523, 529-531, 533, 536-539, 541, 546, 548-551, 553, 555, 557, 560, 561, 563, 568, 569, 572-575, 577-581, 583-586, 588-590, 592-602, 604, 605, 608-610, 611, 612, 614, 615, 617, 618, 620-622, 627-631, 633-641, 643-649, 651, 655-659, 662, 664, 666, 668, 669, 670, 675, 676, 677, 678, 680-683, 685-687, 689-699, 701-703, 705-708, 710, 713, 714, 716, 717, 718, 722, 724, 729-736, 738-740, 741, 743-757, 759, 761-768, 770, 772-775, 780-797, 799-806, 808-812, 814,815, 817-820, 823, 825-835, 837-844, 846-848, 850, 853, 855-865, 867, 868, 870-872, 874, 876-886, 889-903, 905, 907, 908, 910-925, 927-933, 935-951, 953-957, 963-965, 968-976, 978-984, 986, 988-990, 992-1007

NDE Publishing collection on pages:
279, 285, 287, 288, 290, 291, 293, 294, 296, 303, 305-309, 311, 314-319, 321, 322, 324-326, 328-330, 332-334, 339-342, 349, 351-353, 355, 357, 364, 369-371, 377-391, 393, 395-397, 400-402, 405, 406, 417-420, 422, 426-428, 448, 452, 453, 455-458, 464, 465, 473, 482, 483, 486, 487, 489-491, 499-503, 505, 506, 511-513, 515, 516, 518-521, 524, 525, 527, 528, 534-536, 543,544, 545, 547, 556, 558, 559, 564-567, 570, 571, 575, 576, 581, 582, 588, 603, 606, 607, 611, 612, 613, 615, 619, 623, 625, 631, 632, 641, 643, 650, 651-654, 660, 664, 667, 668, 673-675, 679, 684, 687, 710-712, 716, 719, 721, 725, 727, 755, 758-759, 763, 769, 770, 776-779, 813, 822, 827, 836, 845, 851, 861, 865, 869, 873, 877, 881, 887, 902, 906, 926, 946, 959, 961-963, 967, 971, 977, 980, 991, 1008, 1009

STATISTICAL CATEGORIES

Biographical Information - This field contains the player's/coach's name, nicknames, position (C - center, RW -right wing, LW - left wing, F - forward, D - defence), height in feet and inches, weight in pounds, date of birth (month/day/year), place of birth (city/town and province/state for North America, city/town and country for all others), and date of death. If the death date is not known, the date is represented by "Deceased." If any other biographical information is not known, the appropriate field is left blank.

Season - Hockey season starts in the fall and ends the following spring and is represented as, for example, 1998-99.

Club - This field gives information as to which team or teams the player/coach performed with during the season.

League - This field contains the league name or abbreviated league name or the national team name for each team line. A full list of the leagues found in *Kings of the Ice* and their abbreviations can be found on pages 1018-1020.

GP - Games Played

GC - Games Coached

G - Goals Scored

A - Assists

Pts - Points

PIM - Penalties In Minutes

Mins - Minutes played

GA - Goals Against

Avg - Goals-against Average

W - Wins

L - Losses

T - Ties

W% - Winning precentage

NHL/National Leagues/National Teams Totals - A total of a player's/coach's complete career.

Award and All-Star Notes - (located beneath a player's total lines) This field contains details of all-star selections and major trophies and awards won for the NHL, WHA, the minor leagues, and IIHF World Championship.